2758963

ALMANACS OF AMERICAN WARS

WORLD WAR II
ALMANAC

Keith D. Dickson

Facts On File
An imprint of Infobase Publishing

World War II Almanac

Copyright © 2008 Keith D. Dickson

Facts On File, Inc.
An imprint of Infobase Publishing
132 West 31st Street
New York NY 10001

Library of Congress Cataloging-in-Publication Data

Dickson, Keith D.
  World War II almanac / Keith D. Dickson.
    p. cm. — (Almanacs of American wars)
  Includes bibliographical references and index.
  ISBN 13: 978-0-8160-7913-1 (hc : alk. paper)
    1. World War, 1939–1945—Almanacs. 2. World War, 1939–1945—Chronology. 3. Almanacs, American. I. Title. II. Title: World War Two almanac. III. Title: World War 2 almanac.
  D731.D53 2008
  940.540973'03—dc22   2007011207

Text design by Erika K. Arroyo
Cover design by Pehrsson Design/Salvatore Luongo

Printed in the United States of America

VB Hermitage 10 9 8 7 6 5 4 3 2 1

This book is printed on acid-free paper and contains 30 percent postconsumer recycled content.

~ CONTENTS

DEDICATION

This book is dedicated to Captain Edward J. Irving, 77th Bomber Squadron, Tenth Air Force. During a diversionary bombing mission against Araito Island in the Kuriles on June 9, 1945, Irving's B-25 bomber came under attack from both Japanese fighter aircraft and Soviet antiaircraft fire and crashed near Cape Lopatka on the Kamchatka Peninsula in the Soviet Union. War is filled with tragic ironies that often make the losses bitterer still. Captain Irving and his crew were downed when they came under attack by a military unit of the Soviet Union—neutral in the Pacific war but an active partner in the war in Europe. The bomber was lost just a few days before Tenth Air Force halted all combat missions.

Captain Irving was an only child. He lies at rest next to his mother and father in his family cemetery in Appomattox County, Virginia, on the farm where he was raised. Captain Irving, like so many other young men who went to war and never came back, left behind an enormous number of unfulfilled hopes and promises; his parents, who spent the rest of their lives on the farm, undoubtedly often pondered what might have been.

I have the 1945 Esso Oil Company map of the Pacific his parents used to track their son's progress in the war and I used it as a reference while working on this project. Their wishes for his safe return undoubtedly pressed on their hearts every time they took out the map to follow the war news. Each time I took out the map to locate specific places, Captain Irving was on my mind as well.

May this American's sense of duty in serving his country inspire others to do the same, both today and in the years to come.

PREFACE

This is a time when we hear a great deal about the Greatest Generation, the Americans who came of age in the Great Depression and then went on to serve in the fields, the factories, and the Armed Forces to defeat a mortal threat. World War II is on everyone's mind through films, books, and a grand monument on the Mall in Washington, D.C. Part of this belated recognition and adulation is natural as the years pass. But there is a sense of urgency to honor this group of Americans, especially those who faced the enemy in combat. There is a feeling that when the World War II generation passes, something will also pass from America, because within these men and women exist certain qualities and ideals that have been bled from the consciousness of most Americans.

The victory achieved in World War II is one of America's proudest memories and a touchstone of national identity. This Almanac is an attempt to tell the story of arms and men in a different form. It is a chronicle of the daily events that represented the collective experience of tens of thousands of Americans in different parts of the world who participated in combat operations against the enemy. By examining these daily events, the reader can gain an appreciation for the scope and complexity of that experience. There are great battles included, to be sure—Midway, Wake, Guadalcanal, Tarawa, the Bulge, D-day, Okinawa, Savo Islands, Leyte and Luzon, Okinawa, Saipan, Leyte Gulf, and the Coral Sea. But in between the great battles there are the dangerous daily tasks that have to be done. Day after day, as this Almanac recounts, young men climbed into a tank, a fighter, or a bomber, or took watch on ship, or rolled upright from the protective ground with bodies that felt like lead to face another day of uncertainty.

In some portions of the chronology, there is a repetitive sameness about the missions, especially some air and naval missions. But in reality these missions were never routine. Danger was a constant companion, not just from the enemy, but from the weather, mechanical failure, fatigue, fear, and a host of other uncertainties that constantly weighed on the mind. Yet as the chronology shows, the same men, the same crews, and the same support organizations pursued the mission day after day. The entries in the chronology, then, represent men both collectively and individually facing fears, gathering their courage, and doing what was required of them. More often than not, they did the impossible.

Although struggling futilely and mightily to stay out of war, the United States, once involved, sought to win the war as quickly as possible and return to peacetime pursuits. All wartime decisions were made with this goal in mind. Americans were then, and remain today, impatient for results and insistent on a rapid resolution of the crisis. But Americans in 1941 were amateurs at warfare, lacking both expertise in large-scale operations and an appreciation for the complexities of combat fought simultaneously on land, air, and sea. Their tanks and weapons were inferior and their ships and aircraft outdated. What usually took a generation to accomplish, Americans accomplished in a matter of years, applying the country's vast human and material resources to produce the most modern and dominant military force ever created. But this capability was paid for through bitter experience. National guardsmen fought the Japanese on New Guinea while Old Breed marines battled for Guadalcanal. The navy, with little more than raw courage and instinct, fought outnumbered and challenged the enemy for supremacy of the seas in the South Pacific. The U.S. Coast Guard and the merchant marine faced the U-boat menace on the east coast of the United States with little more than prayers. The tiny regular army formed the nucleus of the troops that landed on the beaches of North Africa. The chronology reveals this period of weakness as the limited military resources of the nation are expended at a fearful rate between late 1941 and throughout 1942. But as time passes, the days show a growing capability as vast, air, naval, and ground forces are assembled and employed against the enemy's defenses in Europe and the Pacific starting in late 1943 and growing ever stronger every month after that.

The story of the United States at war from 1941 to 1945 is one of blood and bone and will pitted against a determined enemy—pure attrition warfare. The enemy, believing superior military skill would eventually win out over the application of mass numbers, is willing to fight a prolonged battle of attrition. But it is a battle that cannot be won; inexorably, American superiority in resources proves decisive. This is the American way of war that brought victory, but also the agony of the Hürtgen Forest, Okinawa, Metz, Cassino, Peleliu, and Anzio. But success was undeniable and the battlefields of World War II were the training ground for the generals who would lead new generations of soldiers onto new battlefields in Korea and Vietnam. They would seek the same approach to victory, but with far different results.

The war in the air in Europe and the Pacific followed a similar attritional approach. Air power advocates believed a nation could be brought to its knees through air bombardment alone. The United States was the only nation with the industrial capacity to put this theory into action. As a result, vast numbers of American bombers attacked the cities and industrial areas of Germany, Austria, and Japan. Despite this intense and continuous bombing, growing in intensity and effectiveness each year, Germany and Japan were unbowed. The bomber crews were subjected to fearful losses until American military production capacity and technology could develop fighter escorts capable of protecting the bombers throughout their entire mission. The role of air power was undeniable in establishing the air supremacy in 1944 that was essential for the ground war in Europe to succeed. Japanese garrisons were neutralized from the air and, after 1943, few Japanese aircraft ever threatened American ground forces. However, air power alone could not stop the major Japanese ground offensive in China in 1944, as the American commander of the Fourteenth Air Force had promised.

The emergence of the aircraft carrier as both the dominant combat ship and the most versatile operational platform is seen in the role carriers played in antisubmarine warfare in the Atlantic as well as their role in overcoming Japan's early advantage in deploying carrier aircraft against fleet forces. Carriers not only played a decisive role in eliminating enemy fleets but also were essential for supporting ground operations in later stages of the war in the Pacific.

Undersea warfare was also telling. U.S. unrestricted submarine warfare in the Pacific combined with the antisubmarine warfare in the Atlantic secured the means to victory. Without secure sea lines of communication in the Atlantic, the invasion of the continent of Europe was impossible; and without the destruction of Japan's sea lines of communication in the Pacific, no decisive advance into the inner defensive ring protecting the Japanese home islands was possible.

The role of the Marine Corps in the Pacific war was invaluable. Amphibious warfare techniques were perfected, but at a high cost. Nevertheless, marines fought with unsurpassed courage and tenacity in every battle against the Japanese. From the commanding general down to the marine rifleman, every man had a sense of responsibility for achieving victory. Well trained and superbly led, marines made the difference in numerous battles whose names are now spoken with a mixture of awe and reverence: Tarawa, Iwo Jima, Guadalcanal.

Airborne warfare also proved its worth, establishing a new capability of mobility and versatility in warfare. No soldiers were more aggressive or capable than the paratroopers who descended from the sky and, after landing, fought for days and often weeks with minimum support as infantrymen. Fighting on the rocky hills of Sicily, the bocage of Normandy, the frozen fields of Bastogne, in the jungles of Leyte, or amid the rubble of Corregidor, the American paratrooper proved to be an indomitable force, acting with initiative and courage in the most difficult situations. It is not surprising that the first American units to take on occupation duties were the 82nd Airborne Division in Germany and the 17th Airborne Division in Japan.

Army-Navy rivalry had a hand in crippling the war effort (the air force at the time was a part of the army). Neither service would accept working under the orders and overall direction of the other service. Therefore in the Pacific, an army theater of war existed under an army general (Southwest Pacific Area under General MacArthur) and a navy theater of war existed under a navy admiral (Pacific Ocean Areas under Admiral Nimitz). Although each commander had other service components under his direct command, the coordination between theaters was limited and far less effective than if the entire fore had been employed as a coherent whole. Only when the war was nearly over was a single commander (General MacArthur) appointed to control ground, air, and sea operations in the Pacific. The duplication of effort often led to the misapplication of forces and a lack of coordination as each theater pursued a different operational approach to achieve the same strategic goal.

The animosity between Great Britain and the United States over the strategic direction of the war and the employment of forces was also a problem. Acutely aware of their amateurism early in the war, Americans were stung by the British air of superiority and confidence. But as the preponderance of forces and capabilities shifted to the Americans after 1943, the mood changed and Americans came to dominate the partnership. The struggle over the direction of the main effort (whether British- or American-dominated) and the rivalry between British and American commanders created less and less cohesiveness and coordination. By 1945, the British and Americans were fighting two separate wars in Europe.

American general Joseph J. Stilwell's dislike of the British and his tumultuous relationship with Generalissimo Chiang Kai-shek of China hindered overall coordination of efforts in the China-India-Burma Theater. China demanded an ever larger share of resources from an already limited capability (supplies had to be flown by cargo aircraft over the Himalaya Mountains), and it was clear that British strategic goals in the theater were quite different from American goals for China. As in Europe, by 1945 the United States and Great Britain were fighting two separate wars in Burma and China.

At the strategic level, the partnership between American president Franklin D. Roosevelt and British prime minister Winston Churchill was essential for Allied victory. Churchill, undoubtedly the greatest man of the 20th century, had saved Britain from defeat in the dark days of 1940 when American neutrality appeared unassailable, but he needed American power to save the day and rescue Europe. The partnership that was born kept the alliance together even as their commanders argued over strategy. The Anglo-American partnership began to fray as the emerging power of the Soviet Union clearly indicated the eclipse of the old order in Europe. Even as President Roosevelt sought to find accord with the Soviet leader Joseph Stalin, Churchill never abandoned his role as the conscience of the free world, warning the Americans in 1945 that political objectives to forestall Soviet dominance in Europe were far more crucial than military objectives.

With Roosevelt's death in April 1945, the new president, Harry S. Truman, took a far more practical approach to international affairs and came to see Churchill's point of view. Events by that time had moved far too fast; Churchill was voted out of power in July and the Soviets had firm control of Eastern Europe. Truman was left to deal with the Soviets alone, recasting the relationship later in 1945 in terms of give and take, with the underlying power of the atomic bomb always in the forefront.

The American experience in World War II validated the faith Americans had placed in their ideals, exemplified in the Four Freedoms articulated by President Roosevelt (freedom of speech, freedom of worship, freedom from fear, freedom from want). American confidence, justification, and optimism were at their height. But the aftermath of the war created new dynamics within the United States and placed the world on a new plane of action. Trouble loomed on the horizon in devastated Europe and China. Ahead were new and unforeseen crises that would challenge America's satisfaction with the victory it had obtained at such cost.

How the Almanac Is Organized

The vast size and scope of military operations create a need to show several events happening at the same time in the same general geographic area but without combining them all under one general heading. Therefore, the following organizational system has been set up to assist the reader.

The entries entitled **Atlantic** and **Pacific** deal largely with strategic decisions, plans, and meetings, as well as actions of major units (deployments or redeployments of forces intended for a strategic purpose) or strategic activities related to the region (the bombing of Japan or the German U-boat campaign). After each strategic entry are the subordinate theaters, such as the **Aleutians, Southwest Pacific Area (SWPA), European Theater of Operations (ETO), Mediterranean, China-Burma-India (CBI).** These entries usually describe the activities of fleets, numbered air forces, and land forces at the corps, army, and army group level. Below each theater are subordinate geographic regions: **New Guinea, Southern Pacific, Central Pacific, Italy, North Africa.** These entries address deployments and operations conducted in the region, and focus on specific combat actions of ships, aircraft, divisions, regiments, battalions, and companies and occasionally will even reach down to the individual soldier, sailor, or marine.

The chronology can create an impression of detachment from the reality of warfare. The events become sterile and monotonous, giving the impression that nothing much was happening. For most combat actions, however mundane they may appear, there is a cost in killed and wounded. I have shown these costs throughout the text where appropriate. It is often a grim and sometimes shocking tally, but essential to appreciating the level of danger and sacrifice that these Americans were willing to bear every day. I have also, wherever appropriate, moved from the impersonal operational picture of fleets, divisions, and air forces to the personal and immediate—people facing great danger or impossible circumstances and taking extraordinary action. These stories are drawn from the citations awarding individuals the highest American medal for valor—the

Medal of Honor. These men, often at the cost of their lives, experienced both the devastation and the exhilaration of combat. These portraits of American heroes, it is hoped, will keep the reader aware of the human dimension of warfare and acquaint the reader with men who have gained a measure of immortality for their deeds.

KEEP THE FOLLOWING IN MIND

The inclusion of specific events or actions is based on an intent to provide a representative overview of land, sea, and air operations and provide a comprehensive overview of events as they unfold each day across the globe. The decisions made for including items or summarizing events is a subjective decision and have been mine alone. Therefore any mistakes, omissions, or inaccuracies are mine alone.

Dates for certain events can vary in a global war. What is happening in the Pacific is hours ahead of what is happening in the Atlantic. The dates correspond to daylight operations. To cover periods of darkness where events carry into the early hours of the next day, the earlier date on which the action or activity began is always used. To alert the reader that events are occurring past midnight of the date cited, a sentence prefaced by the phrase "during the night" is used.

All U.S. Army and Navy aircraft are identified by name and type throughout the text (B-25 Mitchell, P-51 Mustang, SBD Dauntless, A-26 Invader). There are several exceptions, however. The B-17 Flying Fortress, the main heavy American bomber of the war, is simply identified as the B-17, mostly because the bomber was and is universally known by its type and not its name. The P-40 Warhawk fighter also is identified only by its type in the text for the same reason. The B-29 Superfortress is best known by its type, but in the text the name and type are not always included together.

There are discrepancies in sources concerning numbers of aircraft involved in some missions, reports of numbers of enemy aircraft shot down, and level of destruction of targets. Wherever possible an accurate determination of numbers was verified, but this was not always possible. Aircrews and pilots often made claims on enemy aircraft destroyed that, when compared to actual combat loss numbers discovered after the war, are far removed from reality. This reflects the fear and excitement of combat and is certainly understandable. To indicate where sources have been used that do not verify the numbers of enemy aircraft shot down or level of destruction of targets attacked, the entry is prefaced with "pilots report" or "aircrews report." This reflects the immediacy of the events rather than the absolute, historically accurate account.

The names of locations used in the chronology are from the original reports and therefore may not correspond to modern transliterations. This is especially true of China and southern Europe.

 # HISTORY

THE UNITED STATES AND EUROPE, 1936–1941

The United States emerged from the Great War in 1918 as a major world power, but the results failed to bring about the idealistic goals that Americans had wished for when the nation intervened in Europe in 1917. Observing the peace conference at Versailles, Americans had become disillusioned by the vengeful treatment of Germany and the establishment of a new European order dominated by Britain and France. The League of Nations, established by the Versailles Treaty, was intended to be an international body dedicated to preserving peace and settling disputes between nations without war. But this plan to mitigate the problems arising from the postwar settlement was rendered almost immediately impotent when in March 1920 the U.S. Senate rejected the Versailles Treaty. Although desiring peace in the aftermath of the War to End All Wars, America showed no interest in supporting any international actions to preserve the peace through the League of Nations. As a compromise, American foreign policy in the 1920s sought to take a leading role in fostering collective security through diplomacy and treaties.

Unfortunately, conditions for an enduring peace did not exist. Europe itself was a patchwork of new states, all weak and suspicious of each other. The two dominant post-war powers, France and Britain, were uncertain and cautious. France was fearful of a resurgent Germany and looked to Britain for security guarantees. Britain was unwilling to make any commitments that would lead to fighting another war on the continent. Germany, although a fledgling democracy, had not abandoned either nationalism or its long-standing tradition of the military playing a substantial role in government policy. The new Soviet Union had isolated itself from Europe, but its proclaimed goal of fostering worldwide socialist revolution caused fear and added to the general political turmoil.

The 1920s were a period of peace and prosperity for the United States. The problems of Europe and Asia seemed far away beyond protective oceans. Defense issues were unimportant and a general public hostility to military expenditures led successive Republican administrations to gain security guarantees through diplomacy. During this decade, a flurry of U.S.-sponsored treaties to reduce international tensions and promote peaceful relations dominated the foreign policy agenda. In November 1921, at the invitation of the United States, eight nations met in Washington to hear an extraordinary proposal. The nations would initiate an immediate program of disarmament, starting with a 10-year pledge not to build any major combat ships (battleships and heavy cruisers) and a drive to scrap combat ships to a total of 1.9 million tons until the ratio of all types of warships maintained in the fleets of the United States, Britain, and Japan reached a balance of 5:5:3, respectively. This proposal was ratified in the Five Power Treaty in 1922, with France and Italy joining the original three and each pledging to disarm to a lower ratio of 1:75. The signatories agreed to a 10-year holiday during which no major combat ships would be built. The treaty was to remain in effect until 1936, when signatories could give a two-year notice before leaving the agreement. The Japanese agreed to the treaty, but asked for additional security guarantees to accommodate their inferior status in major warships. Both the United States and Britain agreed not to fortify their possessions in the Pacific. For the United States, this meant that, with the exception of the Hawaiian Islands, the islands of Wake, Guam, the Philippines, and the Aleutians would have no further defensive improvements.

The Four Power Treaty, signed in 1921 between Britain, France, the United States, and Japan, was essentially a small League of Nations for Asia, in which each nation pledged to respect each signatory's rights in Asia, and to hold a joint conference in case of a dispute. If an outside power threatened the status quo in Asia, then the four nations would consult to find a mutually agreeable response. This led to the Nine Power Treaty in 1922, which bound the participating nations to respect the territorial integrity, sovereignty, and independence of China. The United States gained what it had sought: Japanese recognition of America's commitment to China and a reaffirmation of its Open Door policy, ensuring equal access of all nations to the China market.

These treaties eased tensions, but did not guarantee security for the United States. Although the Five Power Treaty limited large warships, it put no limits on destroyers, submarines, or light cruisers, which Japan, France, and Britain began to build at rapid rates between 1922 and 1930. During this period, for example, the United States built 11 warships while the Japanese built 125. The Nine Power Treaty had no provisions for actually protecting China in case of a violation of the treaty, so it was nothing more than an empty promise. The Four Power Treaty simply acknowledged the status quo in Asia, again with only vague references to consultations and meetings in case of threat or dispute.

A conference in Geneva in 1927 to seek further limits on smaller warships failed to achieve any agreements, but another diplomatic breakthrough was in the making. France and the United States announced that they were willing to enter into a mutual agreement to outlaw war and invited other nations to join. The August 1928 Pact of Paris (or the Kellogg-Briand Pact), signed by the United States and France along with 15 other nations, pledged to outlaw war as an instrument of national policy. Defensive war was still allowed—and exactly what constituted defensive war was not defined. Other nations eagerly joined the pact over the next few months, leading to a feeling of great satisfaction among Americans.

A disarmament conference in London in 1929 led to a treaty the following year, signed by Britain, France, Japan, the United States, and Italy, that imposed limits on certain categories of smaller warships. It also scrapped a number of existing large warships, and maintained the balance of major warships that existed under the original Five Power Treaty. Although on paper the United States had maintained its credibility, the reality was that other nations were already eclipsing America's naval power. The pursuit of security through international agreements was faltering. The following year, the Japanese campaign in Manchuria illustrated how little the treaties of the 1920s meant. At the 1932 World Disarmament Conference in Geneva, President Herbert Hoover attempted to reduce land armaments by one-third and the destruction of all offensive weapons (although what marked an offensive weapon from a defensive weapon was never clarified). Hoover's noble gesture failed in the light of events in Europe and in China. While the conference was going on, Japan attacked Shanghai; its indiscriminate bombing of civilians in the city shocked the world. Given these events, disarmament lost its cachet. On December 29, 1934, Japan gave its two-year notice that it would no longer be bound by the limits of the 1922 Five Power Treaty. Another naval conference in 1935 accomplished nothing. When the United States refused to meet Japanese demands for absolute parity in warships, the Japanese delegation walked out of the meeting. This ominous warning was compounded by an unsettling economic downturn and a series of troubling events in Europe.

The worldwide depression that began to take hold in the first years of the 1930s only aggravated existing social and political problems in Europe. As the depression worsened and popular discontent grew, it appeared that democratic governments were particularly helpless. Desperate, angry people began to turn to communism and authoritarian models for solutions. In Germany, Adolf Hitler was attacking the Versailles Treaty and receiving an enthusiastic response from sullen Germans eager to hear his words. Hitler focused on the frustrations and fears of the nation and promised to return Germany to its destined greatness as the dominant power in Europe. His dreams for the future, though, were tinged with hatred for inferior peoples who would not exist in the new order. Germany's path to its destiny lay to the east, in Russia; the Jews and the Slavs, who blocked that path, would have to be destroyed.

In 1933 Hitler became chancellor of Germany and immediately embarked on a program to end the nation's subservient position in Europe, withdrawing from the League of Nations in October. On March 16, 1935, Hitler announced that Germany had an air force and that he would reinstate conscription and build an army of 550,000 men, both actions in direct violation of the Versailles Treaty restrictions. The League Council condemned Germany, but took no action. In effect, the league had given Germany the approval to become a major power in Europe again. Faced with problems at home and uncertain of Hitler's motives, France and Britain could not mount an effective counter. Neither France nor Britain had the means to use military force without significant political and economic cost, and neither nation was willing to consider war unless it suffered a direct attack. These conditions gave Hitler the opportunity to take greater and greater risks.

Fearing that war in Europe was an absolute certainty in the near future, Congress took the initiative to avoid American involvement and establish the rights of a neutral nation. The Neutrality Act of 1935 authorized the president to declare nations at war belligerents and thereby forbid the sale or transportation of armaments or munitions to them. The president could declare that American citizens traveling on belligerent ships did so at their own risk. These measures were intended to prevent the United States from becoming entangled in the conflict.

Benito Mussolini, the Fascist dictator of Italy since 1922, saw his opportunity to defy the league and pursue his ambitions to restore Italian imperial power in the Horn of Africa. A clash between Italian and Ethiopian troops on December 5, 1934, led to a full-scale invasion on October 3, 1935. The United States enacted the Neutrality Act provisions and awaited further action from the League of Nations. The league declared Italy an aggressor, but hesitated to impose sanctions on commodities, such as oil, that would truly affect Italian actions. The United States decided to impose a moral embargo on Italy and asked for U.S. oil companies to restrict shipments to Italy voluntarily. On February 29, 1936, President Roosevelt received another neutrality bill from Congress and signed it into law. The Neutrality Act of 1936 extended the provisions of the previous act and added a provision that prevented the president from authorizing loans to belligerents.

Meanwhile, on March 7, 1936, Hitler seized the French-occupied Rhineland area that bordered France and Belgium. Again the league met and condemned Germany for violating the Versailles Treaty but, outside of talk, nothing happened. Undeterred by the weak international response, Italy completed its conquest in May of 1936. Withdrawing from the league, Italy signed a pact with Germany in October 1936. Hitler had been willing to go to war over the Rhineland, but now, having taken the measure of his opponents, Hitler decided to press his demands even more stridently.

The United States believed that as long as neutrality was maintained and the nation avoided any political commitments, events in Europe would have no effect on its interests. This belief held when the Spanish civil war began on July 18, 1936. General Francisco Franco led a revolt against the republican government. Germany and Italy sent advisers and equipment to support Franco's pro-fascist forces. The USSR provided the bulk of the aid to the republican Loyalist forces. France and Britain declared an embargo on both sides, and the United States followed by initiating a moral embargo in August, followed by a formal embargo in January 1937. Isolated by the major democracies, which refused to embroil themselves in the conflict, the Loyalists were defeated by 1939.

Shaken by events in Europe and Asia, Congress again put new neutrality legislation on President Roosevelt's desk. On May 1, Roosevelt signed the Neutrality Act of 1937, which authorized him to declare embargoes on arms shipments to belligerents, a ban on loans to belligerents, and dictated that travel on belligerent ships was unlawful for U.S. citizens. The president was authorized to specify certain commodities that could be sold to belligerents for a period of two years, but only on a "cash and carry" basis. The buyer was required to come to the United States to purchase these goods and had to use its own ships to transport the goods to the home country. Although widely viewed as a major step in keeping the United States out of war, it also reflected the ambivalent attitude Americans had about neutrality. They wanted to avoid war, but still find a way to make a profit and, while desiring to declare neutral rights, did not want to assert those rights or take action to defend them.

In 1937, Adolf Hitler accelerated his timetable for war in Europe. He took personal control of both military policy and the German armed forces and then began to take control of events as he exploited opportunities presented to him. One such opportunity was Austria. Hitler's intent had been to bring Austria into the Greater Germany, and internal political conditions in Austria allowed him first to manipulate and then to overwhelm the opposition. German military forces moved into Austria without opposition on March 12, 1938. Europeans were angry at Germany's aggression, but desired peace more than anything. Hitler's conquest of Austria stood.

Hitler turned to his goal of wiping Czechoslovakia, with its multiethnic population (including about three million Germans), off the map. The German population must be returned to its native land or Germany would fight. He ordered his military staff to develop war plans to attack by October 1, 1938. Czechoslovakia, emboldened by an alliance with France and the USSR, decided to hold firm. President Roosevelt made direct appeals for peace to both Hitler and Mussolini. What effect Roosevelt had is unknown, but Italy and Germany decided to hold discussions with France and Britain in Munich between September 29 and 30. The USSR was not invited. The meeting pushed the Czechs to accept Hitler's demands and France decided not to honor the treaty of alliance. Czechoslovakia was at the mercy of Germany.

President Roosevelt sought to test U.S. public opinion in January 1939 by criticizing the aggressor governments that threatened the peace. On March 15, German forces occupied the remainder of Czechoslovakia. As Hitler rejoiced over another easy victory, the reality of the danger Hitler's Germany represented seemed to take hold in Europe. Britain and France offered security guarantees to both Romania and Poland if attacked by Germany. Roosevelt sought to make it clear that the United States would support the cause of democracy. He asked Congress to modify the 1937 Neutrality Act to allow the sale of war materiel to belligerents on a permanent cash and carry basis, to ensure that unfriendly nations would not be guaranteed an easy victory. Although the American people were willing to see a repeal of the Neutrality Act, Congress was not willing to listen.

Hitler shocked the world when, on August 23, 1939, Germany signed a pact with its sworn enemy, the Soviet Union. Each country pledged not to attack the other and would remain neutral if either country became involved in a war. A secret provision divided Poland between the two dictators. This cynical act put Poland in Hitler's sights. All that was needed was a suitable pretext to create the crisis necessary for war. Roosevelt's appeals for peace were fruitless. Hitler made his demands for the return of German territory now owned by Poland. Poland's steadfast refusal led to the invasion of Poland on September 1, 1939. With declarations of war by Britain and France, Europe was again at war.

Poland's rapid defeat and Americans' support for the democracies shaped American public opinion to favor changes in neutrality legislation to deal with the realities of war, even as Roosevelt dutifully invoked American neutrality.

Under current legislation, no belligerent could purchase arms. The cash and carry provisions had expired in May 1939. On September 21, the president addressed a special session of Congress to ask for repeal of the embargo on weapons to belligerents. He sought to return to the cash and carry provisions while keeping the strict ban on American ships or travelers entering a war zone. By November, Congress had responded to the president with a new Neutrality Act that allowed Americans to sell arms to belligerents but did not allow travel into declared war zones. The United States could still not provide loans to belligerents, nor could U.S. citizens travel on belligerent ships. The Western Hemisphere became a neutral zone in September with the Declaration of Panama. Nations of the Western Hemisphere below Canada established a neutral zone that stretched hundreds of miles into the ocean. This neutral zone was forbidden to belligerent warships. The zones would be patrolled by the navies of the signatories. Off the Atlantic coast of the United States, the zone stretched out for 300 miles and was patrolled by the U.S. Navy.

The illusion that America had solved its neutrality problem was shattered in April of 1940 when the German army struck north and westward. Denmark and Norway fell to the Germans, followed in rapid succession by Belgium, the Netherlands, and Luxembourg. By June 4, France had been decisively defeated and the British army had barely survived annihilation by an evacuation out of Dunkirk. The psychological effect of mechanized forces teamed with aircraft providing close support shattered armies expecting to fight another "Great War," in trenches year after dreary year. By June 22, France had signed an armistice, and Germany stood as the dominant power on the European continent. In the midst of Germany's lightning campaign in Europe, Congress appropriated $1.5 billion for defense; by September total defense appropriations reached $10.5 billion as the news from Europe became bleaker. Britain was fighting for its life—a German victory would put Hitler's full power against the United States, especially if the British fleet fell into German hands. The United States began to take action to assure Britain's survival.

Because Britain was dependent for its survival on ship convoys to sustain its war effort, protecting those convoys from German U-boats was essential. In June 1940 alone, nearly 300,000 tons of shipping had been lost to submarine attack. On September 3, Roosevelt responded to an earlier appeal from Prime Minister Winston Churchill for assistance in replacing destroyers lost in the war. By executive order he transferred 50 World War I–era destroyers in exchange for a 99-year lease on specific British bases stretching from Placentia Bay, Newfoundland to Georgetown, British Guiana. The destroyer deal, for all intents and purposes an act of war if the Germans had desired to see it so, ended any pretense of American neutrality. Germany was the enemy and Britain's survival was essential to America's survival.

In early December 1940, Churchill made Britain's position clear to Roosevelt. Britain was on the verge of economic collapse. Without U.S. loans or other means, Britain's future was bleak. Roosevelt created Lend-Lease, a means to support Britain without involving money. The United States, he proposed, would lend arms,

The USS *Black Hawk* tends destroyers at Chefoo, China, a few years before World War II. Destroyers such as these World War I–vintage ships were transferred to the British in the destroyers-for-bases program that preceded the Lend-Lease Act. *(National Archives and Records Administration)*

equipment, and matériel to Britain for a period of time until it was no longer needed, then it would be returned. After extensive debate, Congress passed the bill and the president signed it into law on March 11. Although sold as a measure to aid a democratic nation while keeping out of war, in essence the Lend-Lease bill committed the United States to a de facto alliance with Great Britain. In fact, while Congress was involved with the Lend-Lease bill, U.S. and British military staffs met in Washington, D.C., from January 29 to March 27 to discuss strategic options if the United States entered into the war against Germany at some future date. A general plan was developed called ABC-1, which served as the military basis of the Anglo-American alliance.

To stem the increasing number of ships lost to German submarines in the summer of 1941 and ensure that Lend-Lease supplies got through to Britain, and because as Germany extended its war zone farther west, allowing its submarines to operate more freely, the United States responded by extending its own neutral zone farther east and extending naval patrols. In April, Roosevelt signed an executive agreement with the Danish minister in exile to give the United States control of Greenland with the authorization to establish naval and air bases on the island. On May 21, 1941, the *Robin Moor,* a U.S. merchant ship, was torpedoed and sunk.

Although no lives were lost, the United States retaliated by freezing German and Italian assets and closing all consulates. A few days later Roosevelt publicly declared that supplying Britain was imperative and announced a state of "unlimited national emergency"; he was unwilling to take any further steps in the summer of 1941 than what he had already done.

Germany's June 22 attack on the Soviet Union created new challenges for the United States. Along with Great Britain, the United States pledged to support the Soviet Union in order to stop Nazi Germany. President Roosevelt announced that the Neutrality Act would not be invoked, allowing U.S. ships to carry war materiel to the USSR. Americans were uneasy supporting a communist government that only a short time ago had been a partner with the Germans in dismembering Poland, had invaded Finland, and occupied the Baltic States. But at the same time they saw the importance of making a common cause with any enemy of Hitler.

As German submarines continued to take a heavy toll on British merchant shipping in the Atlantic, Roosevelt moved the United States closer to co-belligerency with Great Britain when he announced on July 1, and with the agreement of Icelandic authorities, that U.S. Marines would be stationed in Iceland to protect the island and forestall any threat to the Western Hemisphere from Germany. Shortly thereafter, Roosevelt met with Churchill off the coast of Newfoundland to discuss a broad range of issues from aid to the USSR, to convoy security, to the situation in Asia, to postwar arrangements. Out of this meeting came the Atlantic Charter, a statement of common aims and principles. Churchill's assessment of the meeting was that the president intended to wage war without declaring it.

September 1941 saw a rise in British shipping losses to U-boats. Great Britain could not escort convoys across the Atlantic as well as escort convoys to the USSR without some assistance from the United States. The U.S. destroyer *Greer* had been attacked by a German submarine on September 4 in the North Atlantic. Even though the U.S. warship had been actively participating in antisubmarine operations with a British seaplane and had been justifiably attacked in self-defense, Roosevelt saw the incident as an opportunity to take aggressive action. He declared in a nationwide radio address on September 11 that U.S. warships could shoot Axis vessels on sight in the defensive zone and announced that U.S. warships would begin escorting multinational convoys from the shores of North America to Iceland. American support was immediate and enthusiastically in favor of the president's decision. By October, U.S. ships were attacking German submarines— but not without cost. Eleven sailors were killed when the destroyer USS *Kearney* was hit by a German torpedo. Over 100 sailors were killed when the destroyer USS *Ruben James* was torpedoed and sunk. The attack on the *Kearney* and *Ruben James* led to Congress modifying the Neutrality Act of 1939 in November to allow U.S. merchant ships to travel anywhere with any type of cargo; merchant ships were also allowed to be armed. Although Americans were still banned from travel on belligerent ships and no direct loans could be issued to belligerents (a restriction that Lend-Lease had made meaningless), the United States had abandoned neutrality in favor of active assistance to Great Britain and the USSR and was engaged in a quasi-war with Germany in the Atlantic. To get to this point, President Roosevelt had followed a cautious path, keeping one eye on Congress and one eye on public opinion as he made each decision. By late 1941, diplomacy had failed in Asia and Hitler was a clear threat to the United States. Roosevelt had committed the nation to a point-blank confrontation with the Axis. It was now only a question of when and where real war would start.

THE ROAD TO WAR IN THE PACIFIC, 1936–1941

The strategic interests of the United States and Japan had been at odds since the beginning of the 20th century. Japan's military prowess, demonstrated most effectively in the Russo-Japanese War of 1905, and its involvement in China during World War I led the United States to follow a policy of watchful concern. Japan had long viewed Manchuria and China proper as its rightful sphere of influence and had resented international actions that had made it back down from its territorial demands on China immediately after World War I. As a major power in Asia, the United States had built a sizable fleet. Its possessions in Hawaii, Guam, Wake, and the Philippines required protection and served as stepping stones to the Chinese market. The United States also championed the territorial integrity of China and equal access to trade for all foreign nations through its Open Door policy.

The postwar period marked an accommodation between Japan and the Western powers. Japan maintained its current position in Asia without major concessions. The 1921 Washington Naval Treaty reduced warships in the Pacific in an attempt to reduce the threat of war, but the Japanese were assigned a lower ratio of battleships than were maintained by either the United States or Great Britain. In exchange for Japanese acceptance of a smaller fleet of warships, the United States and Great Britain agreed not to fortify any of their Pacific island bases. Japan's participation in the Nine Power Treaty of 1922 committed the signatories (United States, Great Britain, Italy, China, Belgium, Japan, Portugal, France, and the Netherlands) to respect the sovereignty, independence, and territorial integrity of China. Although no enforcement provisions were contained in the treaty, the agreement seemed to solidify U.S. strategic goals in the Pacific. Americans, satisfied with their diplomatic efforts, turned their attention away from the Pacific. By the 1930s isolationism and the economic effects of the Great Depression combined to focus attention inward.

During this lull in tensions, Japan began fortifying and integrating economically its Pacific island mandates, the former German possessions transferred to Japan by the League of Nations. World economic conditions pressed the need for Japan to have both capital and raw materials for national survival. The Japanese believed that control of the natural resources in Manchuria and exporting its products abroad were the keys to their future. The Japanese had gained certain access rights in southern Manchuria and controlled the vital South Manchurian Railway.

But control was contested. Nationalist China had fought a short war with the USSR over control of northern Manchuria in 1929, and certainly desired to assert its control of southern Manchuria, despite Japanese claims.

In the 1930s, Japan had moved toward a strident patriotism based on worship of the emperor as a god. Military success bred a sense of invincibility and destiny that drove Japanese ambitions for the next decade. Whatever group claimed to speak and act for the emperor would immediately have the loyalty of the nation. Japanese politics moved in an increasingly authoritarian direction between 1928 and 1936. The voice of the military leadership, especially the army, began to have greater influence in politics. The Japanese government, under an increasingly powerful nationalist-militarist element, began efforts to expand Japanese control into China. In their view, Japan's survival relied upon access to critical raw materials in both Manchuria and the Southwest Pacific that would allow Japan's industrialized economy to be self-sufficient. Japan increasingly came to see the United States as an obstacle to its ambitions on the Asian mainland.

On September 18, 1931, using a bomb explosion on the tracks of the South Manchurian Railway as a pretext, Japanese forces in Korea attacked Chinese troops in Manchuria. From the speed and coordination of the attacks it was obvious that everything had been planned in advance and rehearsed. Although the military had acted without government approval, it soon became clear that Japan's government would no longer function without direct control by military officers. In January 1932, Japanese air and ground forces attacked Chinese forces defending Shanghai and caused thousands of civilian deaths before withdrawing in May. The world was horrified by the scenes of destruction and brutality that modern war visited upon the population. By February 1932, the Japanese had overrun Manchuria and established a puppet state called Manchukuo, declaring that it was no longer sovereign territory of China.

The United States's response to the aggression against Manchuria was to seek a way to support the international peace system, embodied in the League of Nations. Although the United States was not a member of the league, it was essential that the league demonstrate its ability to maintain order in this first great test of its authority. In an unprecedented move, a representative of the United States attended the meeting of the League Council. But the league, led by Britain and France, wanted no part of a possible war or sanctions that would hurt them economically. Although the league did send a commission to investigate the incident in Manchuria, its condemnation of Japan in February 1933 had no effect except to drive Japan out of the league. With neither President Herbert Hoover nor American public opinion willing to go further, the United States had to rely on moral force. Therefore, the United States announced on January 7, 1932 that it would refuse to recognize Japan's occupation of Manchuria because it violated the Nine Power Treaty. Although the United States gained some satisfaction when the league adopted the U.S. position in a formal resolution against Japan, the West had failed its first test to halt aggression.

Spurred by the success of the army's action in Manchuria, patriotic fever swept aside all moderation. The Japanese army continued to expand its control into northern China, annexing the province of Jehol. In November 1936, Japan joined

Nazi Germany in the Anti-Comintern Pact. Although touted as international resistance to communist influence, it was clearly intended to threaten the Soviet Union so that Japan could pursue its interests in China. By 1937, Japan was under military domination and certain that it had no need to accept an inferior position to the great powers of the West. In July 1937, Japanese troops clashed with Chinese soldiers near Peking (Beijing) at the Marco Polo Bridge. When the Nationalist Chinese refused to back down, Japan entered into an all-out war of conquest against China. Japan never declared war, choosing instead to refer to its invasion as the "China Incident." In August, Shanghai again was attacked, and by the end of the year, the Nationalist capital of Nanking had fallen and the population was subjected to savage violence. Japan had 700,000 troops engaged in combat operations. During this time the gunboat USS *Panay* was attacked and sunk. Although public opinion in the United States was aroused, Japan's quick apologies and reparation payment of over $2 million quieted things down quickly.

By 1938, Japanese troop strength in China had increased to one million. The capture of Hankow and Canton in late 1938 gave the Japanese control of China's richest and most populous areas. Nationalist leader Chiang Kai-shek moved his capital to Chungking. Although the Japanese were unsettled by the fierceness of Chinese resistance, the government announced it would establish a new order in Greater East Asia, a military-economic-cultural collaboration dominated by Japan. Thus, control of the Netherlands East Indies, French Indochina, Malaya, Borneo, Burma, and Thailand were important not only for oil, cotton, coal, rubber, and other natural resources, but also for achieving Japan's goal to replace European influence with Japanese influence and direction.

In 1939, Japan attempted to isolate China from outside assistance and force it into surrender. As China's seaports were closed one by one, there were only two routes of supply left. One was the railroad from Haiphong in French Indochina to Kunuwo in Chinese Yunnan. The other was the overland route from British Burma to Kunming. If China was to fall, it became clear that the Western colonial powers of France, Britain, the Netherlands, and the United States, which resisted Japanese ambitions, had to be dealt with. Of these, the United States was the most dangerous potential adversary. With 60 percent of Japan's oil, as well as billions of dollars in raw materials and machine tools coming from the United States, Japan sought to mollify its primary trading partner through a combination of negotiation and intimidation. Thus, while offering a variety of political and economic inducements for the United States to accept the fait accompli Japan had established in China, the Japanese government continued to declare that the "China Incident" would be resolved and peace would come to Asia as soon as third parties stopped interfering.

The United States was unmoved by the Japanese approach, and since 1939 had been slowly and cautiously pressuring Japan diplomatically. American opinion and the Congress saw no need to become involved in China. Believing the events in the Pacific were too far away for their concern and absorbed by a continuing economic crisis at home, Americans showed little interest. Japan had for all intents and purposes declared the Open Door invalid, and ignored the stream of official protests from the U.S. State Department, which refused to recognize territorial changes made by force, maintaining support of the Open Door policy, and protested Japanese treatment of American citizens and property. In 1938, the United States had enacted a moral embargo against Japan by refusing to sell aircraft. It supported loans to China, and in July 1939 the United States notified Japan that in six months it would terminate the 1911 trade treaty. This step was clearly intended to warn the Japanese government—loss of this lucrative and essential treaty marked a major threat to the Japanese economy. It meant that, once the treaty expired, the moral embargoes could be replaced with real economic embargoes.

Meanwhile, war had broken out in Europe and German victories in Europe between September 1939 and July 1940 created a new strategic situation for the United States. Neutrality was no longer a guarantee of security. With the fall of France, the focus of America was on Europe, not Asia. Britain was alone against the might of Hitler and under threat of invasion. If Britain fell, the entire continent of Europe would become an impregnable fortress of Nazism with dire consequences for the world. The Roosevelt administration began to move away from neutrality to open support of Britain. In the meantime, Japan had to be deterred from further expansion and China had to be supported. Roosevelt desired to maintain peace for as long as possible, but not on Japanese terms. The only weapon available to halt Japan was a powerful one—economic embargo. By cutting off Japan's access to oil and raw materials, the United States could at any time force Japan into economic ruin and cause the army and navy to grind to a halt. Such drastic action had dangers as well. Economic sanctions could actually bring on war rather than prevent it. There was no way to know what embargoes would deter and what would incite. On July 25, 1940, the president ordered export restrictions on petroleum products for use as aviation fuel, lubricants, and high-grade scrap metal, and less than a week later, he restricted the sale of all aviation fuel to the Western Hemisphere. The Japanese protested vigorously, and the United States responded that it was willing to continue to negotiate.

The Japanese continued their efforts to isolate China. In July, the Japanese pressured the British to close the Burma Road. Fearing for its colonial possessions and fighting for its very survival, Britain complied. The newly established French government in Vichy came under pressure to allow Japanese forces access to Indochina. In September, Japanese ground and air forces were operating in the country and the rail line into China was cut off. China was now isolated. Without China's resistance, Japan's ambitions to expand the "Greater East Asia Co-Prosperity Sphere" beyond French Indochina to the Netherlands East Indies, Thailand, Malaya, Burma, India, and the Philippines would be made a reality and Japan's power in Asia would be unchallengeable. American diplomatic protests were sharpened by the announcement that the United States would provide a $25 million loan to keep China in the war. On September 26, President Roosevelt declared an embargo on all iron and steel scrap sales outside of the Western Hemisphere (except for Great Britain). The next day, Japan announced that it had joined the Axis of Germany and Italy. The pact pledged mutual support if attacked by a power not currently involved in either the European or Asian war, a thinly veiled notice to the United States. Germany and

Italy also recognized Japan's leadership in establishing a new order in Asia. The Axis powers hoped the pact would deter the United States from threatening Japan. Nevertheless, Japan made it clear through diplomatic channels that a war between the United States and Germany would not obligate Japan to attack the United States. For its part, the American leadership viewed the Axis as an alliance aimed at world domination and a clear threat to democracy and freedom throughout the world. Attitudes toward Japan began to harden. The State Department warned American citizens to leave the Far East.

Negotiations between Japanese ambassador Nomura Kichisaburo and Secretary of State Cordell Hull opened in the spring of 1941. Nomura continued to stress that the United States accept the new status quo in Asia, while Hull laid out the U.S. position that Japanese aggression in Asia was immoral. Hull outlined the U.S. position: Japan must respect the territorial integrity of states in Asia and must not interfere with their internal affairs; accept equality of economic opportunity; and it must accept a return to the situation in the Far East that existed in the 1920s. As the days drifted by in negotiations, Japan's interpretation of the American position made it vital that the oil, rubber, and tin of the Netherlands East Indies had to come under Japanese control sooner rather than later. Thus, to secure its vital northern flank for a future thrust into the south, Japan signed a neutrality pact with the USSR on April 13. If either nation became engaged in a war, the other would remain neutral. Diplomatically, Japan would try to convince the United States and Britain that expansion was a matter of survival. It did not seek war, but if Japan had to fight, it would not be a two-front war.

By the summer of 1941, the United States was actively supporting China and the USSR, which had been attacked by Germany on June 22. Carefully gauging public opinion, Roosevelt was still seeking a way to bring the United States into a more direct role of supporting Britain without actually entering the war and at the same time keeping Japan at bay. Japan, however, had already made important strategic decisions that would affect the president's plans. On July 2, the Japanese government decided to commit itself to the realization of the Co-Prosperity Sphere by forcing Vichy France to allow Japanese forces to gain access to southern Indochina, building airfields, occupying harbors, and stationing troops. This decision would risk war with Britain and the United States, but the economic noose America had placed around Japan could not be drawn much tighter.

The Japanese decision was known in Washington almost as soon as it was made. Navy cryptologists had broken the Japanese diplomatic code. Known as "Magic," this code allowed the United States a number of options to counter Japanese moves in Indochina. After the Japanese invaded Indochina on July 24, Roosevelt took action. On July 25, the president ordered all Japanese assets in the United States frozen, which eliminated Japan's access to key technology, financial assets, and raw materials, most importantly, oil. The United States had also begun to build ground and air forces in a hasty effort to protect the Philippines and moved the bulk of its fleet to Pearl Harbor. Both the British and the Netherlands were supporting the American economic embargo and reinforcing bases in the Far East. Despite all these provocative actions, Roosevelt still believed that the Japanese could be held off long enough for the "show-down," as he called it, to be more advantageous to the United States. He presented this view to Prime Minister Churchill during their secret meeting off the coast of Newfoundland in August 1941. The British leader, doubtful of this approach, desired a much more decisive approach to Japan, but Roosevelt had faith in his approach of ambiguity and delay.

With its military forces consuming 12,000 tons of fuel per day, Japan had about an 18-month supply of oil without further imports. Faced with economic collapse or war, it became clear that the United States had to be forced to accept the Japanese new order in Asia. Japanese military leaders decided that war preparations would have to be initiated in October if the Netherlands East Indies were to be captured by the end of the year. Negotiations would continue with the United States, but if no progress was made, war was inevitable. A September proposal for a high-level conference between President Roosevelt and the Japanese premier failed to materialize, and a new government under General Tojo Hideki took power in October—a clear indication of Japan's intent to pursue its declared goals in Asia. On November 20, 1941, Japan presented its final terms: It would withdraw Japanese troops from southern Indochina to northern Indochina. In return, the United States would restore full trade to Japan, allowing oil and other strategic materials to flow freely, and allow Japan to settle the situation in China without interference. Once trade was restored, Japan would withdraw all troops from Indochina and make no further armed advances into Southeast Asia or the Pacific. Secretary of State Cordell Hull's response on November 26 was unequivocal: Japan must withdraw its forces from both China and Indochina and sign a nonaggression pact with the United States that pledged both countries to support the territorial sovereignty of the states of East Asia. In response, the United States would reopen trade and unfreeze Japanese assets. By November 25, the carrier force that would carry out the first strike had already left port, awaiting a recall message that never came. On December 1, the Japanese government rejected the American position and made the final decision for war.

Japanese military planners had formulated a bold offensive. A surprise attack on Pearl Harbor would cripple the U.S. fleet. Rapid and simultaneous attacks to seize the British possessions of Hong Kong and Singapore, the Netherlands East Indies, and the American possessions of the Philippines, Guam, and Wake would accomplish all of Japan's strategic goals. It would provide the Japanese economic self-sufficiency, a free hand to deal with China, and create a formidable defensive barrier that would force the Americans, Dutch, and British to face a long, exhausting struggle or make peace. As part of this strategy, the Japanese intended to draw the main strength of the U.S. Navy toward Japan so that it could be destroyed in a decisive battle. For Japan to succeed, hostilities had to end as early as possible. The main concern for the Japanese planners was this: After a swift early victory, could the nation sustain a protracted war?

As reports arrived that Japan was massing forces in Indochina, Roosevelt made a personal appeal to Emperor Hirohito for a withdrawal of these forces to prevent "further death and destruction in the world." The message was dispatched to Tokyo on December 6, 1941. Roosevelt's answer would come the next morning.

AMERICAN PREWAR STRATEGIC CHOICES: 1938–1941

Events in the world posed a unique problem for American military strategists in the last years of peace. Without a doubt, events pointed toward the worst-case scenario: The United States would fight a two-ocean war, either alone or as part of a coalition, opposed by the Axis powers, acting either separately or in concert. The strategic assessment, completed in April and May of 1939, concluded that the Western Hemisphere was safe from attack, but Germany and Italy could threaten the United States directly if Great Britain and France either remained neutral or were defeated in a European war. In the Far East, the assessment was that Japan would continue to expand into China and outlying areas of Asia peacefully, but would use force against Great Britain and the United States to achieve stated goals. The Axis was capable of acting together to support mutual interests, and would be willing to go to war if the United States or other nations opposed them.

For American military strategists, the problem of the two-ocean war required holding in the Pacific, while protecting vital areas such as the Panama Canal. Using the Caribbean as a strategic base of operations, the U.S. Fleet could operate on interior lines to block any direct threat to the homeland. The Atlantic had always been America's strategic lifeline and the approaches to the Western Hemisphere had to be secured as a priority.

In case of war with Germany and Italy, the United States would build combat strength sufficient to defeat unilaterally an Axis threat from the Atlantic. If Japan began a war in the Pacific first, then the United States, by still maintaining a defensive approach in the Pacific, would deter Germany and Italy from threatening the Western Hemisphere. A war in the Pacific would require U.S. forces to defeat Japan by a series of naval battles and amphibious assaults. The planners identified four major avenues of advance to the Japanese homeland originating from four bases: the Aleutians, Pearl Harbor, the Marshalls, and Samoa. The Aleutians offered a direct path to the Japanese islands. The Pearl Harbor avenue of advance included Midway Island and the main island of Luzon in the Philippines, then to Japan. The Marshalls avenue of advance led through the Carolines, the Marianas, and Yap and Peleliu to Japan. The final avenue of advance used Samoa as a base, then through New Guinea and thence to Mindanao in the Philippines. The planners believed that two avenues were necessary. The strategic approach had a common perspective—the Philippines could not be held. Reinforcing and protecting U.S. bases in Hawaii, Alaska, and Panama—but not the Philippines—were essential to the strategy.

By June 1939, American planners were examining five separate scenarios that the United States could face in the near future. Each of these was to have a plan associated with it. These came to be known as the Rainbow series of plans. Version 1 was a unilateral defense plan. The army and navy would act jointly to protect the homeland, U.S. possessions, and strategic lines of sea commerce. In the Pacific, the United States would hold Japan behind a line stretching from Alaska to Hawaii to Panama until strength could be built up for a counteroffensive. Version 2 was a multilateral defense plan involving Great Britain and France. With the Allies holding Germany and Italy at bay in Europe and the Atlantic, the United States could take the offensive to defeat Japan in the Pacific, supporting mutual interests and objectives in the region. Version 3 was a unilateral plan that assumed no threat to the homeland from Germany and Italy, allowing the United States to initiate offensive operations against Japan. Version 4 was also a unilateral plan that focused on reinforcing the Western Hemisphere's weak southern flank, while being prepared to conduct joint operations in the eastern Atlantic. This plan required that the United States remain on the defensive in the Pacific until victory was assured in the Atlantic, then forces would be moved to conduct offensive operations against Japan. Version 5 was a multilateral plan that included Great Britain and France as allies of the United States. The defense of the Western Hemisphere would be the U.S. priority, but joint and combined operations in the eastern Atlantic, Europe, and Africa were expected to defeat Germany and Italy. Again, the United States would hold in the Pacific until Germany and Italy were defeated, then forces would shift to the Pacific for a counteroffensive against Japan.

As Hitler's armies swept over Poland on September 1, 1939, American planners focused on Rainbow's version 2. As America maintained its neutrality, it took initial actions both diplomatically and militarily to protect the homeland. Hemispheric defense and military preparedness were the main efforts. By the spring and summer of 1940, American planners found themselves overwhelmed by events in Europe and the Pacific. By June, Germany had complete mastery of western Europe. France had collapsed and the British Expeditionary Force had been driven off the continent. Britain braced for invasion, and suddenly the prospect of a threat to the homeland from the European Axis powers appeared very possible. If the Axis took control of the British and French fleets, the U.S. Navy would be unable to stop an offensive aimed at the Western Hemisphere. In the Far East, the situation was not much better. The "China Incident," as the Japanese called their aggression, had put China close to collapse. Japan had not been swayed by diplomacy and appeared intent on creating its Greater East Asia Co-Prosperity Sphere at the expense of the Western powers. American planners now began to look at Version 4 of the Rainbow plans.

As Britain withstood the onslaught of German bombers, it became clear to President Roosevelt that America's survival depended on Britain remaining in the war. The fate of the British fleet was critical—it must not fall under Hitler's control. Thus, by necessity, British and American planners began a close cooperation. British and American strategies had to complement each other. The British had two strategic objectives: Secure the United Kingdom and the Empire from attack and control the water around the islands; maintain access to the Mediterranean and its lifeline through the Suez to British possessions in the Far East. Although Italy was a threat, Germany was the main enemy and had to be defeated first. Through a strategic bombing offensive combined with economic pressure, German morale and war-making capabilities would be weakened sufficiently to conduct an invasion of the continent by land forces. The offensive operations that followed would ensure the defeat of the Axis. In the Far East, the British had few resources to offer, and viewed the U.S. fleet as the main deterrent against Japan.

The growing belief that Britain's survival was a priority for America's own defense planning reinforced Rainbow versions 1 and 4, which put the United States on the defensive in the Pacific until the Atlantic was secure. This approach also supported the primary security concern for the United States, namely the security of the Western Hemisphere. The difficult task the United States had to pursue in the Far East was asserting American interests in the Pacific while avoiding a confrontation with Japan that would lead to war.

The initial British-American staff talks, known as the ABC meetings (American-British Conversations), were held in Washington from January 29 through March 29, 1941. The meetings were kept secret to avoid influencing American public opinion against the Lend-Lease bill, which was being debated in Congress. The British staff representatives intended to outline in broad terms a combined strategy in the event that the United States entered the war against the Axis powers. While the U.S. planners desired to focus on Europe and the Pacific, the British desired to broaden the discussion to include a combined strategy for the Mediterranean and the Middle East. This divergence of strategic perspective would haunt the British-American relationship for many months to come.

The final report was called ABC-1 and laid out several key decisions. The most important was that the priority of effort would be directed against the European theater. Germany and Italy would be defeated first, followed by Japan. The details of this strategy were include in the ABC-1 report, and later incorporated into the American strategic plan, called Rainbow 5. Both contained specific strategic tasks. These included the use of military, economic, and diplomatic measures to put pressure on Germany and Italy; a sustained regional air offensive to cripple German military strength; breaking the Axis by eliminating Italy early in the war; raids and small offensives aimed at weakening Axis strength; actively supporting resistance movements in occupied Europe; and building the necessary forces for an eventual decisive offensive against Germany.

Within this approach, the United States intended to protect the vital sea lanes of communications, as well as important outlying military bases or islands of strategic importance, and prevent any Axis incursions into the Western Hemisphere. At the same time, the primary effort of the United States would be directed toward building sufficient land, air, and naval power for decisive offensive operations against the Axis powers.

In the Far East, the army would defend the Philippines but would receive no reinforcements. The commander in chief, United States Asiatic Fleet, would support the U.S. Army, as well as the land and air forces of Britain, the Commonwealth, and other associated nations.

One of the problems for the United States in supporting this strategy was the weakness of the U.S. Army. It would take months before any trained force would be ready for combat operations. This left nearly all of the strategic tasks to the navy. In February German troops were fighting British and Commonwealth troops in North Africa; in April German forces overwhelmed the Balkans, supporting an ineffectual Italian offensive, and drove the British from Greece and Crete. As the summer of 1941 began, American planners were increasingly concerned about whether Great Britain could stand alone much longer. Britain's defeat would place the entire burden of the war on the United States. When Germany invaded the Soviet Union in June of 1941, it became clear that both Great Britain and the USSR had to be supported with military equipment and supplies until the United States had built its military capabilities sufficiently to enter the war. Britain desired to bring the United States into the war as soon as possible.

The August 9–12, 1941, Atlantic Conference between President Roosevelt and Prime Minister Churchill, on warships off the coast of Newfoundland, allowed the Anglo-American military staffs to update their earlier strategic discussions. Given the difficult situation the British were facing in the Mediterranean, the British proposed a combined operation against Axis forces by invading French North Africa and supporting operations in the Middle East. The rapid introduction of American forces into the Mediterranean would potentially reverse the current military situation.

The Americans rejected this proposal as far too optimistic. Outside of naval forces, the United States had neither land nor air forces capable of conducting such an operation. Thus, the United States believed it would be of greatest assistance to Great Britain and the USSR as a neutral rather than a belligerent. Although American planners believed that the time of entering the war would be at their choosing, events on the other side of the world would dictate a different timeline.

ALLIED STRATEGY 1941–1942: ARCADIA AND THE PACIFIC

At the Arcadia conference in Washington, held between December 24, 1941 and January 14, 1942, President Franklin Roosevelt, Prime Minister Winston Churchill, and the British and American chiefs of staff met to determine basic strategic goals for the war against the Axis. At this meeting, the Anglo-American Combined Chiefs of Staff was created to support the strategic conduct of the war. The agreement that Germany was the primary enemy and would be defeated first while holding Japan in Asia was an outgrowth of American prewar strategic planning. The ways to reach this strategic end reflected a decidedly British view that an indirect approach, attacking the periphery of the Axis-controlled areas of Europe, would form a ring that would be steadily squeezed as British-American military capability grew. The means decided upon were blockades, strategic bombing to weaken Axis war production capability, supporting resistance movements in Europe, and limited offensive operations against exposed Axis force concentrations. These efforts were intended to steadily weaken the Axis until a final decisive attack could be launched that would bring about its defeat. The buildup of the combat power necessary to conduct this decisive attack would be a concurrent effort to the peripheral approach.

But Japanese advances in the Far East forced the Allies to commit forces to protect and maintain the lines of communication and supply to Australia by securing a string of fortified island bases stretching from the New Hebrides to Hawaii.

In addition the Japanese threat to Australia itself, from New Guinea and the Solomons, had to be halted. By August 1942, the United States and Australia were involved in a brutal battle of survival to turn the Japanese tide. By February 1943, the Japanese had been halted, but not before consuming much of the initial land, air, and sea resources of U.S. forces. This first effort in the Pacific had an effect on the ABC-1 and Rainbow 5 planning that had focused on a Germany first strategy.

The Americans were impatient to undertake a decisive attack on Germany; uncomfortable with the peripheral strategy, they proposed a rapid buildup of British and American forces in Britain, followed by a cross-Channel invasion in 1943 to drive into Germany. The plan for the buildup of over one million men formed into 48 maneuver divisions was called Bolero; the invasion plan to include six divisions initially landing somewhere between Le Havre and Boulogne was called Roundup. An alternate plan was called Sledgehammer, intended as a contingency using just over three divisions, with two U.S. divisions making the initial assault. This invasion of Europe would be launched as a diversionary attack if the USSR was in danger of collapse, to draw German strength away from the eastern front. Or it could be conducted in the unlikely event of a rapid Axis collapse. These plans were completed and George C. Marshall visited London in April of 1942 to present them to the British. Although accepted in principle, the British soon began to back-track, especially about Sledgehammer, which they viewed as exceptionally perilous. The British had been pushed off the Continent in 1940; they were in no mood to return so quickly unless Germany had been sufficiently weakened to guarantee success. On April 3, 1942, the Combined Planning Staff estimated that predicted force strengths in September would be insufficient to conduct Sledgehammer. On April 9 General Marshall in London insisted on a decision on the timing of a cross-Channel invasion. The debate between the American and British chiefs of staff came close to ending any Anglo-American operations at all, with the Americans chiefs of staff recommending to the president in July 1942 that the United States abandon the Germany-first strategy altogether and apply all resources available to fighting the Japanese.

But President Roosevelt, as commander in chief, ordered Admiral King and General Marshall to London to find a compromise and insisted that U.S. forces be involved in combat in Europe as soon as possible. If Sledgehammer was not a feasible plan, then they had to find a compromise for operations in the Middle East or North Africa. On July 24, the plans for Sledgehammer were set aside and replaced with the basic outline of a British plan to invade North Africa, originally named Gymnast, but now retitled Torch. Torch met the president's requirements, but the commitment of resources would delay any cross-Channel attack for at least a year. Thus, the Americans found themselves supporting the peripheral strategy of the British, and to American strategists, following the British lead in the Mediterranean was folly; no decisive result could be obtained there, and the British were seen as pursuing their own imperial interests in securing the Mediterranean.

The Combined Chiefs issued a directive on August 13 for planning for Torch. General Dwight Eisenhower was designated as commander of Allied Force Headquarters responsible for the operation. Torch was the largest amphibious operation conducted up to that time, and the first Anglo-American operation. The North Africa landings and the subsequent campaign in Tunisia eventually did succeed in achieving the strategic objectives outlined by the Combined Chiefs of Staff. Axis forces were driven from North Africa, and the Mediterranean lines of communication were again opened from Gibraltar to Suez. The British and Americans learned many important lessons on cooperation. But the campaign ended all chances of launching Roundup in 1943. With an offensive in the Pacific underway and with U.S. and British forces occupying Tunisia, the question now was what would be the next step for the Allies?

In March of 1942, the Combined Chiefs of Staff agreed to give the strategic direction of the war in the Pacific to the U.S. Joint Chiefs of Staff (JCS). The strategy of winning in Europe while holding the Japanese, then winning in the Pacific, was reflected in the agreement that the buildup in Britain for a cross-Channel invasion would take priority, while the Japanese would be contained with the Allied forces available or allocated to the theater.

The Pacific Theater was divided on March 30 into the Southwest Pacific Area (SWPA), under Commander in Chief General Douglas MacArthur (CINCSWPA), which included the South China Sea, the Gulf of Siam, the Philippines, and the Netherlands East Indies minus Sumatra, the Solomons, Australia, and waters to the south. The Pacific Ocean Area (POA), under command of Admiral Chester Nimitz, included the land and water area outside of SWPA, from the west coast of North America to China and south to New Zealand. Nimitz as both commander in chief, U.S. Pacific Fleet (CINCPAC), and as commander in chief of the Pacific Ocean Area (CINCPOA), personally commanded two sub-regions, the North and Central Pacific, but had a subordinate commander for the South Pacific. Both MacArthur and Nimitz reported to the U.S. Joint Chiefs—MacArthur dealing with General George C. Marshall, army chief of staff, and Nimitz dealing with Admiral Ernest J. King, commander in chief, U.S. Fleet.

By the summer of 1942, the United States was facing a strategic dilemma. Its dedication to the priority of Germany as the main enemy was unchanged, and the U.S. Chiefs were sending air and ground forces to Britain in support of a buildup of forces for an eventual offensive against the European Axis powers. But Japanese advances in the Solomons and New Guinea threatened the vital lines of communication from the United States to Australia and New Zealand that had to be protected if the United States was ever to mount a counteroffensive against Japan in the future. Resources to support a two-front war and the win-hold-win strategy were stretched very thin, especially transportation assets and trained ground forces capable of functioning on the battlefield against tough, combat-experienced German and Japanese soldiers.

Nevertheless, the Japanese seaplane base at Tulagi and their new airfield under construction at Guadalcanal presented a threat against the Australia-Midway-Hawaii-U.S. line of communication in the Pacific. With the battles of the Coral Sea and Midway creating a short pause in the previously unstemmed Japanese advance across the Pacific, the U.S. Joint Chiefs of Staff issued a directive for a limited offensive in the Pacific on July 6, 1942—the ultimate objective being the Japanese base at Rabaul, via the Solomons, New Guinea, New Britain, and New Ireland. Ironically this directive came out just days before Japanese Imperial Headquarters cancelled its orders for an advance against New Caledonia, Samoa, and the Fiji Islands. It was a signal that the strategic initiative was shifting, but in which direction it would ultimately turn was completely unknown and would depend, as always, on a few courageous and resolute men.

ALLIED STRATEGY 1943: FROM CASABLANCA TO EUREKA

By the end of 1942, it was obvious that the Allies would need to clear Tunisia of Axis forces in order to achieve the strategic goal of acquiring complete control of North Africa, established by the Combined Chiefs of Staff in August of 1942. In the meantime, the British and American staffs had to agree on the next step after Torch.

Since Arcadia, Winston Churchill had maintained that the Mediterranean offered the best opportunities for the Allies. During his August 12–15 meeting with Stalin in Moscow, Churchill had stressed how Torch would expose "the underbelly of the Axis." He subsequently coordinated with Roosevelt in examining possibilities for offensive operations in the Mediterranean.

On December 10, 1942, Roosevelt discussed future actions with the JCS. General Marshall believed the Mediterranean approach was wasteful and that, once the objectives of Torch were accomplished, the main effort should return to the buildup of forces in Britain in preparation for a cross-Channel invasion of Europe (essentially the Roundup plan) in March or April of 1943. General Henry Arnold, chief of Army Air Forces, believed that employing an integrated air offensive from both Britain and North Africa could maintain the pressure on Germany regardless of where Allied forces were concentrated. He asserted that precision bombing raids against German targets would in six months cripple the enemy sufficiently so that a cross-Channel invasion would be possible.

American military planners understood the enormous logistical burdens that a cross-Channel invasion would impose. Attempting to land a minimum number of divisions capable of being supported with a limited supply line would have significant risks. With the failure of the Dieppe raid in August 1942 fresh in their minds, the planners were cautious about taking such risks without the sufficient logistical support needed to bring in as many divisions as possible in the initial landing force. Thus, Roundup appeared to be less of a possibility than some offensive action in the Mediterranean in 1943. While not the second front that Churchill and Roosevelt had promised to Stalin, the Mediterranean did offer the Soviets some relief. Italy was vulnerable, and U.S. and British forces were already concentrated at one location in North Africa, making logistics easier. Germany still would be under attack by British and American bombers the entire time.

Roosevelt decided to keep his options open, looking at a buildup in both North Africa and in Britain in order to take advantage of whatever strategic opportunities presented themselves, such as the participation of Turkey in the war or the further weakening of German air and land forces in France.

The Pacific was a different issue entirely. In October 1942, President Roosevelt pressed General Marshall to have General MacArthur secure the northeast coast of New Guinea quickly as a prelude to further land, air, and sea operations against the main Japanese base in Rabaul. On December 1, 1942, with the initiative at both Guadalcanal and New Guinea passing to American forces, General Marshall proposed to Admiral King what amounted to a continuation of the concept of operations laid out in the JCS July 2, 1942, directive. Offensive operations for 1943 would be directed at seizing and occupying the remainder of the Solomon Islands, northeast New Guinea, and the islands of New Britain and New Ireland with the objective of capturing Rabaul. General MacArthur, as the commander responsible for the Southwest Pacific Area, would provide the overall strategic direction of the campaign. Admiral Nimitz would provide the necessary task forces under the direct command of a naval officer, who would control all naval and amphibious operations. But Admiral King balked at the proposal, not wishing the Pacific Fleet to be divided between Nimitz and MacArthur, and nothing was resolved. By the time of the Casablanca Conference, the army and navy had reached no agreement on the details of the strategy and command arrangements for continuing operations against Rabaul.

From January 14 to 23, 1943, Roosevelt, Churchill, and the Combined Chiefs of Staff met in Casablanca to map out strategy for 1943. Because the U.S. Joint Chiefs of Staff had not defined a strategic plan by the time of Casablanca, the Americans found themselves tied to a British peripheral strategy that they had never liked, and they chafed at the British hesitation to commit to a definitive time for a cross-Channel invasion. Churchill and the Imperial General Staff had a well-prepared plan and simply outmatched the Americans during the debates over the strategic direction of the war in early 1943.

The major decisions were arrived at with limited debate. The Atlantic sea lanes had to be secured from the U-boat threat to ensure not only support to Allied efforts worldwide, but also supply convoys vital to sustaining the USSR war effort. Sicily would be the next target of the Allies. The goal was to secure the Mediterranean line of communications, provide a limited second front to draw German forces away from the USSR, and increase pressure on the weakest Axis power, Italy. A combined air offensive from Britain would strike at German submarine bases and key industrial production sites. The British chief of air staff would direct the offensive, but the American commander would maintain tactical control. This compromise allowed for the British to continue the night area attacks they preferred, while the Americans would conduct daylight precision bombing. The buildup for Bolero would continue, with a goal of 938,000 men and 15 divisions. Raids and support to resistance movements would also continue.

The decision that delayed a cross-Channel invasion until 1944 had been the major point of discussion. Despite American arguments for a cross-Channel invasion as the Allied priority, the British were not convinced that Germany had been sufficiently weakened to warrant an invasion in 1943. Essentially, the British idea that southern Europe, not northern France, offered the best approach to rapid victory won out. To the Americans, this hesitation to address a cross-Channel invasion appeared to be foot-dragging and a waste of resources directed against an ambiguous target.

Faced with a delay in launching the cross-Channel invasion, the United States stressed it would continue to pressure the Japanese as fully as possible, taking advantage of successes in the Pacific and moving over to the offensive. The United States would continue its offensive to capture the Japanese base at Rabaul, and advance toward Truk and Guam via the Marshalls and Carolines. An American proposal to launch an offensive into Burma to reopen the Burma Road lifeline to China was shelved. Although only about 15 percent of U.S. resources were committed to the Pacific at this time, the Casablanca decision to keep pressure on the Japanese gave the United States essentially a free hand to pursue the offensive and take advantage of opportunities.

In the aftermath of Casablanca, therefore, the United States moved deliberately toward a more balanced strategic approach of fighting a two-front war than the initial win-hold-win approach agreed upon at the Arcadia conference in 1941.

At the Trident conference, held in Washington, D.C., from May 12 to 25, 1943, the British continued to press for the peripheral strategy, advocating continuing offensives in the Mediterranean, especially concentrating on defeating Italy to avoid an operational pause that could have disastrous consequences for the USSR. It was best to continue the attack onto the Italian mainland, even if Bolero had to be delayed, the British planners argued. The Americans, seeking relief from what they believed to be an improper strategic focus, pressed for a cross-Channel invasion at the earliest possible date—or, if Bolero was delayed, the United States desired an increased emphasis on operations in the Pacific. The compromise was presented to Roosevelt and Churchill on May 25. The combined bomber offensive would attempt to cripple and demoralize the Germans sufficiently by April 1, 1944, so that a cross-Channel invasion was feasible. The target buildup was 29 divisions in Britain ready by the target date, which was set for May 1, 1944. A lodgement would be established with nine divisions, followed by a rapid buildup of three to five divisions per month, then a breakout and advance to the east supported by Allied air power. Meanwhile, support to the USSR and China would continue, as would the effort to eliminate the U-boat threat in the Atlantic. The Allies would continue the offensive in the Mediterranean to defeat Italy. As a trade-off for the agreement to continue operations in the Mediterranean, the Combined Chiefs of Staff approved "The Strategic Plan for the Defeat of Japan" on May 19. The main effort was designated in the Central Pacific. The objectives were the Philippines and the recapture of Hong Kong. Once bases in China were occupied, a strategic bombing campaign would be conducted against the Japanese home islands, followed by an amphibious offensive. No specific timelines were established, nor were additional forces allocated in the plan. Southwest and Central Pacific theaters were to work together, but operations would be sequential rather than simultaneous, due to limits on the availability of shipping and trained amphibious divisions.

Much of the discussion over feasibility of a cross-Channel invasion hung on the availability of heavy transports, the LST (Landing Ship Tank). There was enough landing craft of this size and capability in theater to carry only three divisions. The addition of two airborne divisions gave the Allies a five-division force, but it was considered to be the minimum force necessary to attack the fortified coast of Europe. To speed planning along, the Combined Chiefs established a headquarters on April 23, 1943, under General Sir Frederick Morgan to act as COSSAC—Chief of Staff of the Supreme Allied Commander. Morgan was to form the nucleus of an Anglo-American headquarters that would oversee the invasion and subsequent campaign to defeat Germany. His staff was ordered to begin planning for a cross-Channel invasion, scheduled for May 1, 1944. But the problem continued to be landing craft availability; although U.S. shipyards were producing 20 LSTs a month, nearly all of them were being sent to the Pacific, where Admiral King was overseeing a major campaign against the Japanese-held islands in the Central Pacific. It was not until the last three months of 1943 that LSTs were supplied to the ETO.

Even with all the LSTs produced and currently in theater, General Morgan found that there were not enough landing craft to support the invasion force. For the British, the invasion was their nation's last supreme effort; it had to succeed because there would be no second chance. Thus, Germany had to be sufficiently weakened and near collapse before an invasion should be launched. To the British the invasion marked the end of the war, so they continued to insist that the invasion be adequately resourced in terms of both combat divisions committed in the assault, and in the transport assets necessary to bring those divisions to the beaches of France. To the Americans, the invasion was only a first step in a long campaign. What was needed was a foothold from which a subsequent rapid buildup would allow for offensive operations designed to battle the Germans to ultimate defeat.

The Quadrant Conference was held in Quebec August 14—24, 1943. The Combined Chiefs of Staff accepted COSSAC's concept plan for Overlord and authorized detailed planning. The British advocated a major campaign in Italy to keep German forces occupied in order to support a cross-Channel invasion. An advance into northwest Italy would allow the Allies to establish airbases to support the strategic bomber offensive. The Americans were unwilling to commit too many resources to Italy, as their view was that Overlord was the priority effort. Quadrant reaffirmed a cross-Channel invasion for May of 1944, along with a simultaneous 10-division invasion of southern France. German U-boats had been sufficiently suppressed in the Atlantic and the U.S. war economy was fully mobilized, allowing for both the movement of forces across the Atlantic, and sufficient availability of support and sustainment for operations in Europe. In the Mediterranean, Rome and its surrounding air bases were designated as the objectives. After the fall of Rome, the Allies would advance as far as practicable.

The Sextant Conference in Cairo, held November 22–26 and December 3–7, 1943, gave the British an opportunity to question the invasion of southern France and push instead for support of an advance deeper into the Mediterranean with a goal of bringing Turkey into the war, moving into the Aegean to further stretch German defenses, and aiding partisans in Yugoslavia and Greece. If the resources necessary to conduct these operations delayed Overlord, the British saw no significant difficulties. To the Americans, Overlord was the most direct means to a rapid victory and the transfer of resources to the Pacific to finish Japan. Another delay would push the cross-Channel invasion into 1945. The situation was further complicated by a Roosevelt promise to Chiang Kai-shek and endorsed by Churchill to conduct an amphibious attack against the Japanese in the Bay of Bengal in 1944. The leaders' promise took American planners by surprise; there were not enough landing craft to conduct amphibious operations in the Mediterranean, the Bay of Bengal, and Europe. Something had to give.

At the Eureka Conference in Tehran (Teheran) November 28–30, 1943, the Combined Chiefs of Staff agreed to a compromise. Allied forces in Italy would advance as far north as the Pisa-Rimini Line and the partisans in Yugoslavia would receive additional aid. Turkey would be brought into the war, and Allied operations in the Aegean would support maintaining access to the Dardanelles. Overlord would be delayed to support the Bay of Bengal landing. On November 28, first day of the Eureka Conference, Roosevelt asked Stalin which operation would best support the Soviet war effort: the British offensive plan for the Mediterranean or the northwestern Europe invasion. Stalin promised to enter the war against Japan as soon as Germany was defeated. Barring Turkey entering the war, Stalin believed that a cross-Channel invasion by British and American forces in May of 1944 would best support the Soviet Union, still struggling to contain German counterattacks. The British continued to argue that operations in the Mediterranean would distract the Germans and prevent any reinforcements from the south being sent against the invasion force. On November 30, the Combined Chiefs of Staff agree to launch Overlord in May of 1944 in conjunction with an invasion of southern France. On December 5, the Bay of Bengal invasion would be limited in order that sufficient landing craft were available for Overlord and the landings in southern France, now called Anvil. Overlord and Anvil were designated as the priorities for 1944. The Italian campaign would continue, but the Bay of Bengal invasion would be cancelled. Overlord and Anvil finally gave the Americans free reign to do what they had wished since the beginning of the war—take the fight to the heart of Germany. The American strategic approach had finally won out, but only after the intervention of Stalin. The British, still clinging to an advance into Germany and Austria through Italy, were rebuffed at every turn, as more and more resources were diverted from the Mediterranean to the invasion of Europe.

OPERATIONS IN THE PACIFIC, 1943: THE SEARCH FOR A STRATEGY

A Pacific military conference was held in mid-March 1943 to determine the focus of operations. MacArthur proposed a single command for SWPA and South Pacific with efforts focused on Rabaul, using an indirect approach by seizing bases in New Georgia and New Guinea, followed by assaults on New Britain and Bougainville. The plan called for a total of nearly 13 divisions, 10 of which would be amphibious-capable.

Two carriers and several battleships would reinforce naval forces; air forces would include a total of 45 air groups and 14 independent squadrons. The JCS, faced with a buildup of air forces in Europe to support the strategic bombing campaign and hesitation from the navy in providing carriers to MacArthur to command, led to a modification of the strategy. MacArthur would be reinforced with two additional divisions and aircraft, but nothing near the proposed forces.

On March 28, 1943, a new strategic directive was issued to replace the July 1942 strategic plan. Rabaul would no longer be the objective of SWPA or SOPAC. Instead Rabaul would be isolated through Allied control of the Bismarck Sea with air and naval forces in New Guinea, Bougainville, and the Solomons. MacArthur was to command operations in the theater, with Admiral Halsey; SOPAC commander would operate quasi-independently, with MacArthur having general supervision. Commander POA, Admiral Nimitz, remained in control of naval and air assets in theater, but the JCS could direct naval assets to support operations. U.S. strategy in the Pacific, appearing as a mirror image of the 1941 Japanese strategy, would advance only as far as land-based aircraft could fly. The SWPA and SOPAC staffs coordinated on a plan called Cartwheel, which was completed on April 26, 1943. MacArthur's forces would move along the northwest coast of New Guinea, while Halsey's SOPAC forces moved into the Solomons. The campaign would end with landings on New Britain, Bougainville, and Buka Island, near Bougainville. A total of eight army and two marine divisions, plus a New Zealand and an Australian division, supported by a total of 686 fighters, 879 bombers, and 275 transport aircraft were involved. The operation began on June 30.

For the Central Pacific, the JCS planners submitted a concept of operations for an offensive against the Japanese in the Marshall Islands. Kusaire and Eniwetok were the targets of the combined amphibious invasion. These islands would be used as airbases for an attack on Truk, the key Japanese naval base. But Nimitz was hesitant to move into the Marshalls without having some support from airbases in the Gilbert Islands first. On July 10, the JCS planners revised their concept, focusing on Tarawa, Makin, and Nauru in the Gilbert Islands. To make this attack, significant support would have to come from the Southwest Pacific Theater, thus delaying any further operations there until 1944. Protests from MacArthur's staff led to modifications of Cartwheel. The coast of New Guinea would be cleared, and Manus Island would be seized. Subsequent operations would be directed to capture air bases at Wewak, New Guinea, followed by an invasion of New Ireland and the Admiralty Islands. Capturing these objectives would effectively neutralize Rabaul and consequently free additional land forces for the Central Pacific. An August 6 version of the plan saw MacArthur continuing west to capture the Vogelkop Peninsula in

U.S. carrier pilots get a pre-mission briefing below decks. *(National Archives and Records Administration)*

western New Guinea. The British would begin an attack into Burma to open the land supply routes into China. In the Central Pacific, Nimitz would seize objectives in the Gilberts and the Marshalls, aiming for the Japanese base at Truk in the Carolines. A follow-up offensive would capture bases in the Palau Islands. At the completion of Cartwheel, JCS planners envisioned an American ring stretching from New Guinea to the Palau Islands, all pointing to the Philippines and China.

MacArthur viewed the JCS plan as placing SWPA in a supporting role to the Central Pacific offensives. His staff devised an alternative concept of operations called Reno II, which had as its objective the Philippine Islands. Instead of attacks directed at the fringes of Japanese defenses, MacArthur looked at one combined attack directed to separate the Japanese home islands from their resources in the southeast, thereby crippling Japan's ability to continue the war. Mindanao would serve as the best airbase from which to launch air attacks against the Japanese sea lines of communication and supply. From Mindanao, U.S. forces would invade Luzon, which would put American air, land, and naval forces within striking distance of China, Indochina, and the home islands themselves. MacArthur viewed the capture of Rabaul as essential, along with seizure of the Vogelkop Peninsula, all supported by the Pacific fleet. But in the Central Pacific, MacArthur saw only the Palau Islands as significant, because they could serve as a base of operation for an attack on Mindanao. Nimitz argued that the Bismarck Sea was too constrictive for a large fleet, and the Central Pacific allowed for the U.S. fleet to be ready to engage the remainder of the Japanese fleet in open water. Also, an offensive in the Gilberts and Carolines would force the Japanese to divide their forces between the two theaters.

On August 24, 1943, the JCS issued instructions for offensive operations in the Pacific for 1943–44. Central Pacific Theater tasks were to seize the Gilbert Islands and to prepare to attack the Marshalls and the Carolines. Truk would be captured and used as an airbase. The Palau Island assault would follow, with a move to capture bases in the Mariana Islands. These islands would be used to support the strategic bomber offensive against the Japanese home islands. Southwest Pacific Theater objectives were New Guinea and the Admiralty Islands. Rabaul would be isolated, not captured. The Central Pacific Theater had the priority of effort primarily because capture of bases in the islands would support extended air operations, and most likely force the Japanese navy into a major battle to protect the home islands. Thus, the June initial plan was hardly changed.

The Combined Chiefs of Staff approved the American strategic concept for the defeat of Japan, essentially the same as laid out in the August 24 instructions. SWPA and Central Pacific Theater objectives would place U.S. forces in early 1945 in an area to support attacks against the Philippines, China, or Formosa. MacArthur submitted a plan for the recapture of the Philippines, called Reno III. Nimitz offered a Granite plan that would focus his offensive on the Palau Islands more quickly, bypassing Truk, in order to support MacArthur's advance toward the Philippines.

The division of the Pacific into two theaters of war caused significant problems for the U.S. Joint Chiefs of Staff planners throughout the war. Not only were commanders jealous of their prerogatives, but service biases also limited what each commander was willing to do in support of the other. Arguments over objectives reflected a lack of strategic clarity within the JCS concerning how the Japanese were to be defeated and what the appropriate sequence of events should be to bring about that result. As a result, commanders offered alternatives that arose from opportunities created through unexpected events of the campaigns in both theaters. Events in the two theaters, and not any JCS plan of operation, more often than not dictated the strategic direction of the war in the Pacific.

ALLIED STRATEGY 1944: FROM EUREKA THROUGH OCTAGON

By the end of 1943, the United States military planners had made important progress in planning future direction of the war against Germany and Japan. The battles of attrition in the Solomons, the Gilberts, and New Guinea, the brutal fighting in North Africa and Italy, the losses of men and aircraft in the skies over Europe, and the navy's hard-won triumphs in the North Atlantic and South Pacific had resulted in progress, but at a great cost. The danger for the Allies as they moved into 1944 was culmination and stalemate. Even though the Allies were superior in resources, the Germans and Japanese could through a skillful and stubborn defense, stretch the conflict out and progressively wear down the morale of the people of the United States and Great Britain. The Allied political and military leadership recognized that the tempo of operations must increase and the enemy must be pressed hard on all fronts if the war was to be brought to a satisfactory end. As the strategic initiative passed to the Allies in 1944, the most important problem to solve was how to take advantage of the opportunities presented.

STRATEGIC IMPERATIVES

The emphasis on timelines and schedules in strategic plans in late 1943 reflected an urgency to make identifiable progress. The declared goal for the rapid defeat of Germany in 1944 followed by the defeat of Japan one year later, as well as a desire to initiate an offensive to open the Burma Road and support China, reflected the views among American planners that enough time had already been wasted and decisive operations had to take place. The strategic direction of the European theater had finally been settled, but only by submitting the divergent British and American strategic options to Stalin for his resolution. Overlord, the cross-Channel invasion of Europe, would be the Allied supreme effort in the west. An amphibious landing in southern France, named Anvil, would support Overlord. The American strategy of a rapid and direct attack into the continent by a cross-Channel invasion in order to bring about the defeat of Germany in the shortest amount of time won out over the British desire to continue to wear the enemy down over time through limited operations in the Mediterranean. The agreement to limit operations in the Mediterranean, expand the Combined Bomber Offensive against Germany to include bases in the Mediterranean as well as in Britain, and commit the preponderance of resources to launch and support Overlord and Anvil initially brought a strategic clarity and unity of effort that had been lacking since 1942.

The basic planning for the cross-Channel invasion had been underway since March 5, 1943, with the creation of COSSAC (Chief of Staff to the Supreme Allied Commander). Logistics and transport were the critical factors that shaped planning. Because the Allies had put priority on the construction of antisubmarine assets, especially destroyers and escort carriers in 1943, landing craft and other transportation assets were not available in sufficient quantity to meet operational requirements in both the European and the Mediterranean theaters. Because there were not enough landing craft available to conduct both Overlord and Anvil, the Anvil operation was delayed until August 15.

THE BRITISH-AMERICAN STRATEGIC DEBATE IS RENEWED

Rapidly changing events in Europe by mid-1944 renewed the debates between British and American planners over the proper employment of forces in Europe and the Mediterranean to meet strategic goals. The British began to doubt the value of Anvil, especially after the fall of Rome just days before the Normandy landings. The British began to argue for keeping the Anvil forces in Italy to exploit success. But General Eisenhower, the Allied commander responsible for operations in Europe, was relying on an invasion of southern France. Anvil was to use the U.S. Seventh Army and General de Lattre de Tassigny's French First Army to secure two major ports and move north to join the rest of Allied forces in northern France in an advance into Germany.

While in agreement that the Italian campaign had kept German divisions out of France and the eastern front, American and British planners diverged on the value of any future operations in the Mediterranean theater. To the British, Italy offered additional strategic opportunities, especially in throwing the Germans off-balance in the Balkans. By landing forces in Trieste and advancing into the Ljubljana Gap, not only would additional German forces be occupied, but also there were political-strategic advantages in having British and American forces in Budapest and Vienna instead of Soviet forces. But the Americans were adamant that no diversion of forces from the main effort in France could be tolerated.

The United States grew suspicious of British motives, especially as military decisions took on postwar implications after the fall of 1944. To the Americans it appeared that the British were more interested in obtaining postwar strategic advantages in Europe than defeating Germany as quickly as possible. For the Americans, nothing mattered more than to end the war quickly and turn to the defeat of Japan. Any strategic maneuvering should come at the end of the war, when, after a short time of occupation, U.S. forces would leave Europe to its own devices.

The growing Soviet-American relationship became a driving factor in many decisions made in mid-1944. To the Americans, collaboration with the Soviets was essential not only for winning the war in Europe and Asia, but also for maintaining the peace and security of the world when the war ended. Without such cooperation, the Soviets would have to be confronted militarily and the United States was the only nation capable of doing so. A confrontation would most likely lead to yet another major war, but with U.S. power in Europe limited and the American people unwilling to make such a commitment, the only real recourse was cooperation. Therefore, the United States sought to build a strong relationship with the Soviet Union in order to create a sense of trust. This trust would be built largely by following through on promises made at the Eureka conference in Tehran in November 1943. Thus, long-term strategic interests for postwar Europe were subordinated to the immediate military requirement of defeating Germany as rapidly as possible once the cross-Channel attack had begun.

This rather narrow approach began to change, especially in the light of Soviet conduct in the fall of 1944. The Red Army's pause along the banks of the Vistula River in August while the Poles were battling the Germans in the city of Warsaw clearly indicated that Stalin was willing to let the Germans destroy any Polish armed resistance before Soviet forces advanced. Suspicions of Stalin's intent were confirmed when the Soviets refused to allow British or American aircraft to airdrop supplies to the Polish fighters. This event raised doubts about the optimistic American assessment of postwar conditions. Even as the Americans continued to cooperate in good faith with the Soviets, believing that the ground forces of the USSR were essential to victory both in Europe and the Pacific, concerns about the future grew ever larger in the months ahead.

ALLIED STRATEGY IN EUROPE

After gaining a secure beachhead in Normandy, the Allies planned to build sufficient combat power to defeat German forces in northern France, link up with Allied forces advancing from southern France along the way, and advance to the German border on a broad front. In the land campaign to defeat Germany, the Ruhr was the major objective. The Ruhr, located in the northwest part of Germany, was the industrial heart of the nation; to survive, Germany would have to commit significant ground and air forces to defend it.

Eisenhower envisioned an approach with two axes of advance, one following the northern route to the Ruhr through Belgium and Holland, and one following south of the Ardennes toward Metz, then turning northward to the Ruhr. The final advance through Germany would follow the destruction of German forces. The plan depended on opening enough port facilities to bring in supplies and reinforcements to sustain the advance. In July of 1944 Eisenhower had 18 Allied divisions in Normandy. On July 25, the Normandy breakout began at St-Lô, continued at Avranches, and culminated at the Falaise Gap on 19 August. In the aftermath of that series of battles, the German Fifth Panzer Army and Seventh Army had been destroyed. On August 25 Paris was liberated and, with the Germans in full retreat across northern France, the Allies were soon crossing the Seine River unopposed and months ahead of schedule. After the breakout from Normandy, which ended the Overlord plan, General Eisenhower directed strategy and took broad direction from the Combined Chiefs of Staff.

By September of 1944, logistics problems were crippling the speed of the Allied advance. Supplies of food, fuel, and ammunition could not be brought to the front line units in sufficient quantities from the beaches in Normandy and the port of Cherbourg. Other ports, particularly Antwerp, had not been captured. Motor transport was unavailable and the major road and rail routes in northern France had been destroyed in the bombing campaign prior to the landing. Faced with a difficult strategic decision, Eisenhower chose to give General Bernard Montgomery's 21st Army Group priority of support in order to cross the Rhine River, while General Omar Bradley's U.S. 12th Army Group made limited advances. Eisenhower would maintain both the broad front approach and the original strategic design of two simultaneous thrusts toward the Ruhr, but instead of an equal rate of advance, the priority of support would go to the 21st Army Group.

Montgomery's plan was to make an all-out rapid thrust by armored divisions deep into Germany, supported by a carpet of airborne forces securing key bridges in Holland on the line of advance, protected by overwhelming airpower. His plan, called Operation Market Garden, which began on September 17 with great confidence and collapsed in frustration and stalemate on September 26, ended any hope of outflanking the German armies and engaging in decisive operations by the fall of 1944. Between October and December of 1944, the Allies became involved in a battle of attrition against regrouped German forces defending the border along the Siegfried Line. It became very clear that there would be no victory in Europe in 1944.

General Eisenhower consolidated his forces in preparation for renewing the broad-front advance to the Rhine River in the spring. In December, the Germans launched a surprise offensive against the weakly held Allied line in the Ardennes forest with the intent to split the Allied armies and capture the port of Antwerp. The famous Battle of the Bulge was desperately fought, but the outcome was never in doubt. The preponderance of American land and airpower destroyed the last significant combat forces available to the German high command in the west. Although the Germans had been decisively defeated, the offensive was a deep shock to the Allies.

OPTIONS IN THE PACIFIC

As the fortunes of war shifted in Europe, strategic decisions in the Pacific were forced to shift as well. The United States was heartened by pledges from both Stalin and Churchill at the Eureka conference that they would participate in the final campaign to defeat Japan. Soviet manpower, the British and U.S. fleets, and U.S. strategic airpower appeared to be the keys to ending the war in the Pacific. The U.S. Joint Chiefs of Staff (JCS) had almost total control of the plan of operations for the Pacific, with the Combined Chiefs of Staff providing the British stamp of approval on the American plans. The desire was to press the Japanese throughout the Pacific and achieve significant results.

Despite this pressure to move forward, the goals for the Pacific theaters for most of 1944 remained purposely unclear. It was not yet decided how Japan was to be defeated. The divergence of views between the army and the navy over whether Formosa and China or the Philippines offered the best intermediate step toward the final assault on the Japanese home islands led to disruptions in the theaters of war as well as within the JCS planning staff as different options were submitted, modified, or rejected. With only broad direction, General Douglas MacArthur (Southwest Pacific Area—SWPA) and Admiral Chester Nimitz (Pacific Ocean Areas—POA) would have to pursue their campaign objectives in their theaters without a clear strategic focus to their operations. Meanwhile, in Southeast Asia Command (SEAC), General Stilwell, the American commander under Admiral Mountbatten, struggled to bring Chinese military power to bear in Burma against the Japanese.

During 1944, the two-pronged offensive plan remained the basis for offensive operations. But the JCS, with all the resources now being gathered for Overlord, had to decide how best to maintain the initiative and achieve the most advantageous results with the resources available. For General MacArthur, commanding the SWPA, this meant advancing through New Guinea to Mindanao and, later, Leyte in the Philippines. For Admiral Nimitz and the POA, it meant an advance in the Central Pacific through the Gilberts and the Marshalls to Formosa and ultimately to China. Pursuing a two-pronged offensive allowed for operational flexibility and prevented the Japanese from concentrating all of their strength at one point, but there was no clear direction or purpose to these operations, creating challenges for planners to decide who would do what, where, and for what purpose.

MacArthur's approach through New Guinea depended on speed of execution for success. Although not considered an objective by the JCS, MacArthur argued that the capture of the main island of Luzon in the Philippines was not only key to the defeat of Japan, but also a matter of national honor. Nimitz's approach was more deliberate, but offered the advantage of air and submarine bases in the Marshall and Mariana Islands that would allow the United States to strike the Japanese home islands quickly and would most likely lead to a decisive battle with the Japanese fleet. MacArthur pursued operations to isolate Rabaul and Kavieng and by August had advanced to the Vogelkop Peninsula in New Guinea, covering a distance of 1,000 miles and conducting 14 amphibious landings. Nimitz's forces cleared Kwajalein, Eniwetok, and isolated the Truk Atolls. In June, the battle for Saipan in the Marianas was underway and the Battle of the Philippine Sea ended Japanese naval airpower and crippled the Japanese carrier fleet. Guam and Tinian were captured in August. Meanwhile, the Japanese offensive in Burma had been halted at Imphal and Kohima and British forces were pursuing the remnants of the enemy. By June of 1944, SWPA had advanced along the northern coast of New Guinea as far as Biak Island. The Central Pacific offensive had begun in the Marianas. In the CBI, the Japanese offensive toward India had been stopped at Imphal. The reduction of the Japanese fleet and the growing weakness of Japanese air power gave the United States increasing freedom of action in the Pacific. It became clear to planners that Japan would not be subdued by a naval blockade or air attack. The Japanese home islands would have to be invaded.

General Stilwell's forces had reached Myitkyina in Burma, and the Japanese were pressing Chiang's armies in eastern China. It became apparent that China was not going to become a major contributor to the war. In the China-Burma-India theater, therefore, priority shifted toward keeping Chinese armies in the field and occupying Japanese forces so that those forces could not be shifted to the outer defense of other parts of the Pacific. China also could serve as a base for Allied aircraft to support other offensive operations.

DECISIONS ARE MADE

For months Formosa had been the key objective in preparation for the attack on the Japanese home islands. Luzon would be bypassed, but Leyte would be seized to serve as an airbase to support the attack on Formosa. The Palau Islands were to be captured to also provide sea and air bases. The reason for the decision to capture Formosa was related to the anticipated release of significant air and ground forces after Germany's defeat in late 1944. With these additional forces, attack on Formosa would be possible in 1944 and an attack on the Japanese home islands would be possible in early 1945.

But with the realization that Germany could not be defeated by the end of 1944, it became clear that an invasion of Formosa was unsupportable with the current resources available in theater. JCS planners then turned to Luzon as an alternative, because an invasion of Leyte and Luzon could be done with current forces and transportation available in theater. Both Nimitz and MacArthur were poised to converge their forces for a coordinated attack to capture the Philippines. MacArthur had played a key role in this decision, winning President Roosevelt to his side in a July Pacific strategy conference at Pearl Harbor by arguing passionately and eloquently for the liberation of the Philippines as a sacred American obligation.

As events in the Pacific took on a quicker tempo, the Allied planning staffs at the Octagon conference in Quebec in September established a schedule for the invasion of the Japanese home islands, starting with Kyushu in October 1945 (Operation Olympic) and the decisive assault on Honshu to capture Tokyo in December 1945 (Operation Coronet). The British would provide air and naval forces to support these operations once the war in Europe was over. Admiral Mountbatten was to recapture Burma as quickly as possible and an amphibious landing to capture Rangoon (Operation Dracula) was scheduled for March of 1945.

By October, the U.S. Navy had destroyed much of the Japanese air fleet on Formosa and marines were still fighting on Peleliu in the Palaus while MacArthur made preparations for an invasion of Leyte with 200,000 men of the Sixth Army under Lieutenant General Walter Krueger. The Battle of Leyte Gulf ended the Japanese navy as a threat, despite the near success of the Japanese plan. The successful landing at Leyte sealed the fate of Japan. Nevertheless, for the remainder of 1944, the Japanese and American forces would fight a series of pitiless battle on Leyte often in atrocious weather. By the end of the year, Krueger was preparing for the invasion of Luzon even as the fighting on Leyte continued. Increasingly desperate, the Japanese fought back, adding the suicide plane, the kamikaze, to their arsenal in the hope that these human-directed bombs would eliminate the American fleets. In the meantime, Marianas air bases had been established and the new B-29 Superfortress strategic bombers were arriving. On November 24, the B-29s flew their first bombing mission over Tokyo.

The Allies had been overly optimistic in early 1944 in both Europe and the Pacific. Both enemy resistance, which was much stronger than expected, and logistics constraints prevented the Allies from moving too far beyond plans developed in late 1943. In Europe, U.S. strategic interests continued to clash with British interests. While the Americans took a short-term view, concentrating on building trust with the Soviet Union and winning the war as quickly as possible, the British were far more concerned about the long-term consequences of Soviet power in Europe and believed military operations should be directed to broader political-strategic ends. The British viewpoint after late 1943 was increasingly discarded as American planners took control of the war.

In the Pacific, the desire to maintain the strategic initiative often made the objectives less clear as debate continued throughout most of 1944 over what the intermediate objectives were in preparation for an eventual invasion of Japan. High hopes for early and rapid advances were dashed, as were estimates that forces would be transferred from Europe to the Pacific with the rapid collapse of Germany. As the tempo of operations increased in the fall of 1944, strategic objectives became clearer and the Philippines became the intermediate objective while the strategic bombing of Japan continued.

THE ALLIES APPROACH VICTORY: 1945

The Allies were closing in on central Europe, but there was little movement when the new year began. The Italian front had stalled; reduced in manpower and faced with the formidable defenses of the Apennines, the Allies would make no major advances. The Battle of the Bulge still raged in the Ardennes as soldiers fought in temperatures colder than anyone alive in Europe could remember. The German surprise offensive had reached its limit, and the Bulge, 60 miles long and 40 miles wide and containing 24 German divisions, was slowly being pushed back.

German weapons such as the V-2 and the Me-262 jet fighter were significant additions to German capabilities, but came far too late in the war to have an effect. The Allied strategic bombing campaign reached its apogee. The German air force could no longer put up any significant resistance. The German fuel industry and transportation systems were attacked without pause for the last few months of the war, denying many German units both tactical and strategic mobility. Additional U.S. air force assets were diverted to supporting ground forces in order to isolate the Ruhr and deny Germany its economic base.

After the Battle of the Bulge, Eisenhower sought to employ his combat power to destroy as many German forces west of the Rhine River as possible. In keeping with his broad-front strategy, Eisenhower wanted a continuous and simultaneous effort from each army group so that the Allies all reached the Rhine at the same time. Stung by the German surprise attack in the Ardennes, he was more determined than ever to maintain a strong front to deal with any German counteroffensive. Once the Allies reached the Rhine River, Eisenhower believed it would serve as a strong line of defense from which the Allies could then concentrate forces and launch deep thrusts into the heart of Germany.

A German Me-262, photographed just before delivery to the Luftwaffe *(National Archives and Records Administration)*

The advance to the Rhine River, the last physical barrier into Germany, would occupy the Allies for most of the spring. The British disliked General Eisenhower's broad-front strategy, the approach that kept equal pressure on the German defenses throughout Germany. Instead, the British wanted to continue with a major offensive in northern Germany to gain access to the north German plain, seize the North Sea ports, and advance to Berlin.

In March 1945 the Allies crossed the Rhine in several places. Montgomery now hoped to lead his 21st Army Group in a thrust toward Berlin but was instead ordered to encircle the Ruhr while the American 12th Army Group advanced into central Germany and Austria and entered Czechoslovakia. Montgomery's forces advanced onto the north German plain and on May 4, at Luneberg Heath, he received the surrender of the German forces opposed to him. The official German surrender came on May 8, but the war had ended for all intents and purposes four days earlier. Instead of the United States and Britain occupying Berlin and most of central Europe, those spoils fell to the Soviets. The stage was set for the Cold War.

POLITICAL ISSUES DOMINATE

Throughout 1945, Great Britain was increasingly concerned about the encroaching Soviet power in eastern Europe, led by the advance of the Soviet armies. Churchill for years had sought both through military operations in the ETO and the Mediterranean theater and by direct political negotiations with Stalin to limit that advance.

For Roosevelt, America's larger political-strategic goals were simple: total military victory and the establishment of a lasting and secure peace in the shortest time possible with the fewest losses. To achieve these goals, cooperation with the Soviet Union was essential as long as the war against Germany continued. Roosevelt believed that he could deal with Stalin honestly and openly and the Soviet leader would respond in kind.

For both Great Britain and the USSR, Poland was the key issue. Great Britain had declared war in 1939 to defend Poland and had pledged to maintain a free and independent Poland. For the Soviets, half of Poland had been Soviet territory since 1939 (a result of the Nazi-Soviet nonaggression pact) and they had no intention of giving up this important buffer between the USSR and Germany. A pro-Soviet government in Poland was essential to Stalin's postwar security objectives. The United States was in the middle—largely uninterested in postwar arrangements and firm in the belief that all people, whether liberated by the Soviet, American, or British forces, had the right to free elections. Roosevelt had suspicions of Great Britain's true intentions, believing that Britain sought to reassert its prewar imperial dominance.

The strategic dilemma for the United States throughout the first half of 1945 was to maintain Stalin's cooperation and goodwill to ensure the USSR would contribute ground forces to the defeat of Japan even as the United States and the Soviet Union were growing further apart as each pursued separate postwar goals in Europe. The United States sought long-term peace and security in Europe through the promotion of liberty and democracy for the newly freed nations of Europe, while the Soviet Union increasingly displayed its interests to be the pursuit of long-term security through occupation and domination of the states of eastern Europe under the totalitarian control of pro-Soviet leaders. Great Britain, now the minor power, sought to keep the Soviets out of Europe as much as possible and to use the power and influence of the United States as leverage.

With the death of President Roosevelt in April of 1945 and the subsequent defeat and occupation of Germany, a new president and secretary of state now felt less sensitive to accommodating the Soviet Union. There were growing concerns within the military leadership that the Soviet Union intended to expand its influence and control at every opportunity in the postwar period. How much expansion should the United States accept became one of the most important military policy questions in mid-1945.

THE UNCERTAIN ROLE OF ALLIED FORCES IN THE PACIFIC

In the Pacific, the Allies still faced formidable Japanese land forces in China and Southeast Asia, even as the enemy was being worn down in the Philippines and Burma. The Japanese navy was powerless after the Battle of Leyte Gulf in October 1944 to change the strategic situation. For the Japanese, fighting decisive battles in China and the Philippines would grind down the Americans as they bought time to solidify the homeland defenses for a final battle of attrition that they believed they could win and from which they would still emerge victorious.

In January 1945 there were 27 U.S. combat divisions in the Pacific, six of those marine divisions. General MacArthur commanded 1.5 million men in the Allied air, land, and sea forces. Admiral Nimitz commanded the largest navy in the history of the world. The U.S. Navy in January 1945 consisted of 1,167 combat ships, nearly 55,000 landing craft and assault ships, and 37,000 aircraft.

For the Americans there were two strategic approaches to defeating Japan. One was the air bombardment and naval blockade of Japan to force the Japanese to surrender through starvation and massive destruction of their industrial base and cities. The other was the direct invasion of Japan and the direct conquest of the home islands. Like most of the major strategic issues for the Pacific during the war, no final decision was made until the press of events largely dictated the choice. The atomic bomb arrived almost as a deus ex machina, solving the immediate problem of direct invasion of the Japanese home islands.

By July 1945 the Joint Chiefs of Staff were against allowing any more concessions to the Soviet Union, especially in its demands for access to strategic waterways in northern and southern Europe. Only the need for Soviet manpower to deal with Japanese forces on the Asian mainland required the United States to maintain the spirit of cooperation that had marked the war years. With the successful detonation in the New Mexico desert of the first atomic weapon on July 16, the military leadership was even less willing to continue cooperating with the Soviets. They argued that the Red Army would not be necessary to end the war with Japan. However, the strategic goals of speeding the surrender of Japan and minimizing American casualties had always been the paramount reasons for keeping the Soviets in the planning for the Pacific. No one could be sure that the atomic bombs alone would have the decisive effect on Japan that would end the war. Therefore, the Soviets had to be involved as part of achieving the overall strategic purpose.

The surrender of Japan ended all pretenses for continuing good relations with the Soviet Union. Any hopes for a postwar cooperative effort with the USSR to maintain peace had been abandoned as the Soviets reneged on their pledges made at Yalta and Potsdam. The United States had realized too late its strategic interest in keeping Europe from being dominated by a hostile power. This concern now expanded to areas of the Pacific and Asia as well.

The atomic bomb opened a new chapter in strategy and deterrence, leaving a powerful and prosperous United States standing astride a shocked and uncertain world that struggled to adapt to the tumultuous new circumstances that had emerged from the most terrible war ever fought.

CHRONOLOGY OF
KEY EVENTS

1922

October 28
ITALY: The Italian Fascist Party under the leadership of Benito Mussolini conducts its famous "March on Rome." Mussolini is appointed premier two days later and will dissolve Parliament in 1926. He establishes an authoritarian dictatorship, gaining power through appeals to nationalism and by using a clever combination of bluff and intimidation.

1931

September 18
CHINA: Japan invades Manchuria.

1932

January 29
CHINA: Japanese land, air, and naval forces attack Shanghai.

February 18
CHINA: Japan establishes the puppet state of Manchukuo, formerly Manchuria.

1933

January 30
GERMANY: Adolf Hitler is appointed chancellor of Germany.

February 24
JAPAN: Japan withdraws from the League of Nations.

October 14
GERMANY: Germany withdraws from the League of Nations and initiates peacetime military conscription.

1935

October 3
ITALY: Italy invades Ethiopia without a declaration of war.

October 5
ATLANTIC: Under the Neutrality Act of 1935, the United States declares Italy and Ethiopia belligerents and embargoes arms to both countries. Americans are warned not to travel on ships of either belligerent. President Roosevelt issues a warning that Americans who engage in trade with ether Italy or Ethiopia do so at their own risk. This last warning is a diplomatic slap to Italy, since Ethiopia is a landlocked country anyway.

1936

October 25
GERMANY: Rome-Berlin Axis is formed

November 25
GERMANY: Japan signs an Anti-Comintern Pact with Germany.

1937

July 7
CHINA: Incident at the Marco Polo Bridge between Japanese and Chinese troops leads to full-scale war.

July 29
CHINA: Japanese forces occupy Beijing (Peking).

August 8
CHINA: Japanese naval forces land in Shanghai after two Japanese marines are killed by Chinese forces.

August 12
CHINA: The U.S. 4th Marines at Shanghai are reinforced by over 100 marines and sailors from the USS *Augusta*. Elements of the 4th Marines provide support to municipal police in accordance with an international agreement.

August 17
CHINA: Evacuations of American citizens from Shanghai begin.

September 19
CHINA: A brigade headquarters and the 6th Marines from San Diego arrive in Shanghai, bringing the entire marine detachment to over 2,500 men.

November 8
CHINA: Chinese forces are driven out of Shanghai.

November 9

ATLANTIC: The United States Joint Board directs its planners to examine how simultaneous threats from German and Italian aggression in Europe and from Japanese expansion in the Far East might threaten American security and interests.

December 11

ITALY: Italy withdraws from the League of Nations. Spanish civil war begins. Both Italy and Germany provide advisers and weapons to Spanish fascists.

December 12

CHINA: U.S. gunboat *Panay* on Yangtze River, assisting the evacuation of foreigners from the fighting near Nanking, is sunk by Japanese air attack. Three Americans are killed. Japan apologizes and pays a $2.2 million indemnity, while promising to control its forces around Nanking.

December 13

CHINA: Japanese forces occupy Nanking. More than 370,000 Chinese men, women, and children are brutally murdered in a series of atrocities that shocks the world.

1938

January 30

GERMANY: Germany announces it no longer is bound by the Versailles Treaty.

February 17

PACIFIC: The 6th Marines and the brigade headquarters redeploy to San Diego from Shanghai.

March 11

AUSTRIA: German troops cross the Austrian frontier.

March 12

AUSTRIA: Germany occupies Austria.

March 13

AUSTRIA: The Austro-German Union proclaimed at Vienna. Austria is part of the German Reich (empire).

April 16

BRITAIN: A British-Italian agreement signed. Great Britain recognizes the conquest of Ethiopia in exchange for a promise from Italy to withdraw all troops from Spain at the conclusion of the civil war.

April 27

BRITAIN: A three-day Anglo-French military conference begins in London. The British and French general staffs agree to collaborate more closely for mutual defense.

September 15
GERMANY: British prime minister Neville Chamberlain and Adolf Hitler hold talks in Berchtesgaden, Germany, over Hitler's demands to protect the German population in the Sudetenland of Czechoslovakia. Czechoslovakia is willing to go to war to defend itself against German aggression.

September 26
ATLANTIC: President Franklin Roosevelt appeals for peace directly to Hitler and President Eduard Beneš of Czechoslovakia.

September 29
GERMANY: Neville Chamberlain, Edouard Daladier, Adolf Hitler, and Benito Mussolini sign the Munich Pact. Germany wins control of the Sudetenland in Czechoslovakia.

September 30
GERMANY: Chamberlain and Hitler sign a declaration of peace.

October 1
GERMANY: German forces begin occupation of the Sudetenland.

November 9
ATLANTIC: The Joint Board begins reviewing U.S. national readiness for war. The board orders the Joint Planning Committee to "make exploratory studies and estimates" to examine the courses of action available to the United States in case of a violation of the Monroe Doctrine by Italy or Germany or an attack by Japan on the Philippines.

The Joint Board exists to coordinate on issues of mutual interest for the army and the navy and to make recommendations to the civilian service secretaries. The Joint Board is made up of the army chief of staff, his deputy, the head of the army's War Plans Division, the chief of naval operations, his assistant chief, and the director of naval war plans. It is not intended to be a higher staff or to provide unified direction of commanders in wartime.

November 13
PACIFIC: Japan closes the Yangtze River to all foreign ships.

December 6
GERMANY: A Franco-German peace declaration is signed.

1939

March 6
PACIFIC: Japan announces a full-scale naval building program to reach parity with United States and Great Britain.

March 15
CZECHOSLOVAKIA: Czechoslovakia is invaded and incorporated into Germany.

March 31
BRITAIN: Prime Minister Neville Chamberlain in the House of Commons announces that Great Britain and France pledge to come to the assistance of Poland in the event of any action that threatens Poland's independence.

April 1
SPAIN: General Francisco Franco declares the end of the civil war in Spain.

April 6
BRITAIN: Prime Minister Chamberlain announces in the House of Commons that Poland and Britain have joined with France in an alliance.

April 7
ITALY: Italy attacks Albania.

April 13
BRITAIN: Prime Minister Chamberlain announces in the House of Commons that Britain and France will guarantee the borders of Romania and Greece and will lend all support possible where there are clear threats to the independence of either Romania or Greece.

April 14
ATLANTIC: President Roosevelt appeals to both Hitler and Mussolini for a 10-year guaranty of peace.

April 28
GERMANY: The German government abrogates the 10-year nonaggression treaty with Poland signed in 1934 and demands the return of the free city Danzig and the Polish Corridor, taken from Germany in the Versailles Treaty after World War I to provide Poland access to the Baltic Sea.

May 22
ITALY: Italy signs a 10-year military pact with Germany, called the "Pact of Steel."

July 5
ATLANTIC: President Roosevelt orders that the Joint Board and other boards under control of the secretaries of the army and navy will now operate under the direction and supervision of the commander in chief. As world tensions mount, Roosevelt wants more direct approval authority for actions taken by the military departments.

July 26
PACIFIC: The United States informs Japan that it will not renew the 1911 trade agreement, leaving the United States free after six months to initiate economic sanctions against Japan.

August 1
ATLANTIC: Admiral Harold R. Stark becomes U.S. chief of naval operations. He presses for a coordinated effort by all representatives of government to address issues of national security.

August 23
Soviet Union: Germany and the Soviet Union sign a nonaggression pact.

August 24
Atlantic: President Roosevelt sends appeals for peace to European leaders.

August 25
Britain: Great Britain and Poland sign a formal treaty of mutual assistance.

September 1
Germany: Germany invades Poland, beginning the Second World War.
   General George C. Marshall becomes army chief of staff.

September 3
Britain: Britain and France declare war, honoring their pledge to protect Poland. Australia and New Zealand follow suit.

September 5
Atlantic: President Franklin D. Roosevelt declares America neutral. U.S. Navy begins offshore patrolling along the East Coast and in the Caribbean to monitor foreign warships.

September 8
Atlantic: Roosevelt declares a limited national emergency and orders the increase of the authorized strength of the navy and Marine Corps.

September 10
Atlantic: Canada declares war on Germany.

September 16
Atlantic: Soviet troops invade Poland.
   British begin convoy operations for merchant ships from Halifax to Great Britain to protect the vital flow of supplies from North America. German submarines begin attacks on convoys.

September 21
Atlantic: Roosevelt requests that the Neutrality Act of 1937 be changed to allow for sale of arms to belligerents.

September 27
Poland: Poland surrenders.

September 28
Soviet Union: German-Soviet border and friendship treaty is signed, resulting in the partition of Poland.

October 5
Pacific: Hawaiian Detachment, U.S. Fleet, led by the carrier USS *Enterprise* along with other warships and auxiliary vessels, moves to Pearl Harbor under command of Vice Admiral Adolphus Andrews.

October 15
TURKEY: The Anglo-French-Turkish 15-year mutual-assistance pact signed in Ankara.

November 4
ATLANTIC: Neutrality Act of 1939 allows for a policy of "cash and carry" for belligerents to replace a total arms embargo. The act prohibits U.S. ships from entering combat zones. Roosevelt declares the waters around Great Britain to be a combat zone.

November 30
SOVIET UNION: Soviet troops invade Finland.

1940

January 20
ATLANTIC: U.S. government issues an official protest to the British government concerning the boarding and inspection of neutral American ships in the Mediterranean.

March 8
PACIFIC: United States authorizes $20 million loan to China. Japan declares it an unfriendly act.

March 12
SOVIET UNION: Soviet-Finnish peace treaty and protocol is signed in Moscow.

April 2
PACIFIC: U.S. Fleet departs the West Coast for a major fleet exercise off Hawaii.

April 8
BRITAIN: Great Britain and France announce that three areas off the coast of Norway have been mined to prevent shipments of Scandinavian ore to Germany.

April 9
DENMARK: German troops invade Denmark. Germany attacks Norway.
ATLANTIC: U.S. planners begin to modify existing war plans to reflect a simultaneous threat in Europe and the Pacific.

April 10
ATLANTIC: Roosevelt extends the war zone in the waters northeast to the USSR.

April 17
ATLANTIC: Secretary of State Cordell Hull issues a formal statement declaring any change in status quo in the Pacific "would be prejudicial to the cause of stability, peace and security."

April 25
ATLANTIC: Roosevelt declares neutrality in war between Germany and Norway.

May 7
PACIFIC: Roosevelt orders the U.S. Fleet to remain in the Pacific as a deterrent to the Japanese.

May 9
ATLANTIC: British forces occupy Iceland.

May 10
WESTERN EUROPE: Germany invades Netherlands, Belgium, and Luxembourg. British prime minister Neville Chamberlain resigns. He is replaced by the first lord of the Admiralty, Winston S. Churchill.

May 11
ATLANTIC: Roosevelt declares America neutral in the conflict between Germany, Belgium, Luxembourg, and the Netherlands. The United States declares it will not allow any other nation to control the Netherlands (Dutch) East Indies, a pointed warning to Japan.

May 14
NETHERLANDS: Netherlands surrenders to Germany; German ground and air forces conduct a breakthrough of French defenses in the Ardennes area.

May 15
NETHERLANDS: The army of the Netherlands surrenders.

May 16
ATLANTIC: Roosevelt asks Congress to appropriate almost $900 million for defense and national security.

May 26
FRANCE: British and French troops begin evacuation at Dunkirk, crossing the English Channel to Britain and safety.

May 28
BELGIUM: Belgium surrenders to Germany.

June 9
NORWAY: The Norwegian high command orders the army to cease hostilities at midnight.

June 10
ITALY: Italy declares war on France and Great Britain. Norway surrenders to Germany.

June 11
ATLANTIC: Australia, New Zealand, and South Africa declare war on Italy. President Roosevelt declares the Mediterranean and the Red Sea a war zone.

June 14
ATLANTIC: President Roosevelt signs the Naval Expansion Act. The navy's carrier, cruiser, and submarine tonnage will expand to 167,000 tons. Auxiliary shipping will also increase by 75,000 tons. Naval aviation will grow by 4,500 aircraft.

June 14
FRANCE: German troops enter Paris.

June 15
ATLANTIC: Naval aviation strength increased to 10,000 aircraft.

June 15
SOVIET UNION: Soviet troops occupy Lithuania.

June 17
SOVIET UNION: The Soviet Union declares that Estonia and Latvia have agreed to the free passage of Soviet forces through their territory and will form new pro-Soviet governments.

June 19
ATLANTIC: President Roosevelt signs the Two Ocean Navy Act, expanding the size of the U.S. Fleet by 70 percent.

June 22
FRANCE: Armistice declared. France is divided into a German occupied area and a quasi-independent area with a government body led by Marshal Henri Pétain located in Vichy. A Free French government-in-exile is established in Britain under the nominal leadership of Charles de Gaulle.

June 24
FRANCE: Franco-Italian armistice signed.

June 26
PACIFIC: Roosevelt orders that no aviation gasoline, or steel, or iron scrap will be sold to Japan.

June 27
ROMANIA: Romania cedes Bessarabia to the Soviet Union.

June 28
BRITAIN: The British government recognizes General Charles de Gaulle as the leader of Frenchmen who continue to pledge resistance to the Nazis.

July 3
MEDITERRANEAN: The British sink or seize a major part of the French fleet in Oran, Algeria, to prevent combat ships from falling into German hands.

July 5
FRANCE: Vichy French government of Marshal Pétain breaks off diplomatic relations with Great Britain as result of British attack on the French fleet at Oran.

July 18
BRITAIN: Under pressure from the Japanese, Prime Minister Winston Churchill announces terms of a temporary agreement for stoppage of war supplies to China through Burma and Hong Kong.

August 10
PACIFIC: The Japanese extend their naval blockade of China southward.

August 17
ATLANTIC: Germany declares a total blockade of the British Isles. All ships in the area will be sunk without warning.

August 25
SOVIET UNION: Estonia, Latvia, and Lithuania are formally incorporated into the Soviet Union. The United States refuses to recognize the incorporation.

August 31
ATLANTIC: Roosevelt calls to active service 60,000 members of the National Guard.

September 1
PACIFIC: Fleet Marine Force establishes a detachment of nine officers and 168 enlisted men on Midway Island.

September 3
ATLANTIC: Roosevelt announces that the United States will provide Britain 50 World War I–era destroyers in exchange for use of air and naval bases in Newfoundland, Bermuda, Bahamas, Jamaica, St. Lucia, Trinidad, and British Guiana. Bases at these locations will be obtained by a 99-year lease.

September 4
ATLANTIC: Secretary of State Cordell Hull warns the Japanese not to attempt to change the status of French Indochina.

September 16
ATLANTIC: The Selective Training and Service Act is signed, creating the first peacetime draft in American history.

September 22
PACIFIC: Vichy France allows Japanese forces to access three airfields in French Indochina and maintain a 6,000-man garrison.

September 27
GERMANY: Germany, Italy, and Japan sign the Tripartite Pact. The Berlin-Rome-Tokyo Axis is formed.

October 5
PACIFIC: Japan offers recognition of U.S. dominance in the Western Hemisphere in return for U.S. recognition of Japanese dominance of East Asia.

October 28
ITALY: Italy attacks Greece prior to the expiration of its ultimatum.

November 5
ATLANTIC: Roosevelt wins his third consecutive term as president.

November 10

ATLANTIC: Marine Corps Reserve units are integrated into the regular Marine Corps.

November 12

ATLANTIC: Admiral Harold R. Stark, chief of naval operations, recommends that the U.S. Army and Navy begin secret talks with British, Canadian, and Dutch military leaders to reach agreements on cooperation in case the United States enters the war.

November 20

HUNGARY: Hungary signs a protocol of adherence to the Axis tripartite pact.

November 23

ROMANIA: Romania signs a protocol of adherence to the Axis tripartite pact.

November 24

SLOVAKIA: Slovakia signs a protocol of adherence to the Axis tripartite pact.

November 30

PACIFIC: U.S. loans $100 million to China for wartime needs.

December 6

PACIFIC: Japanese-Thai pact of amity is signed.

December 9

PACIFIC: Japan's foreign minister denies that its alliance with Germany is intended to threaten the United States. Japan pledges that it will not fight the United States unless the United States acts as an aggressor.

December 19

ATLANTIC: President Roosevelt approves $25 million in military aid to China. This will allow China to purchase 100 U.S. P-40 fighter planes.

December 20

ATLANTIC: President Roosevelt appoints William Knudsen to head a four-man defense board to plan for national defense and coordinating aid to Great Britain.

December 29

ATLANTIC: President Roosevelt, in a radio address to the nation, warns Americans of impending danger and appeals to citizens to support rearmament. "The people of Europe who are defending themselves do not ask where to do their fighting. They ask us for the implements of war, the planes, the tanks, the guns, the freighters which will enable them to fight for their liberty and for our security. Emphatically we must get these weapons to them, get them to them in sufficient volume and quickly enough so that we and our children will be saved the agony and suffering of war which others have had to endure. . . . We must be the great arsenal of democracy."

December 31
ATLANTIC: U-boats have sunk 2.6 million tons of Allied and neutral shipping, amounting to 55 percent of all shipping losses.

1941

January 6
ATLANTIC: In an address to Congress, President Roosevelt outlines a desire for a world not based on a "new order of tyranny" but on "four essential human freedoms." He describes these as freedom of speech and expression, freedom to worship God, freedom from want, and freedom from fear. "Freedom means the supremacy of human rights everywhere. Our support goes to those who struggle to gain those rights or keep them. Our strength is our unity of purpose. To that high concept there can be no end save victory."

January 9
PACIFIC: U.S. State Department advises American citizens to leave Japan.

January 29
ATLANTIC: Secret initial talks begin in Washington between U.S. and British planners to discuss options to determine the best way to defeat the Axis powers if the United States enters the war.

January 30
PACIFIC: French Indochina-Thailand armistice is signed in Saigon.

January 31
ATLANTIC: At the end of January, a total of 21 ships (over 126,000 tons) have been lost to U-boats in the Atlantic.

February 3
ATLANTIC: The Navy Department creates three independent fleets: U.S. Pacific Fleet, U.S. Atlantic Fleet, and U.S. Asiatic Fleet. Admiral Husband Kimmel is the commander in chief, Pacific Fleet, Admiral Ernest J. King is the commander in chief, Atlantic Fleet, and Admiral Thomas C. Hart is the commander in chief, Asiatic Fleet.

February 6
GERMANY: Hitler orders that all German sea and air assets be employed against Allied supply ships.

February 10
BRITAIN: Great Britain severs diplomatic relations with Romania.

February 28
ATLANTIC: At the end of February, a total of 39 ships (over 196,000 tons) have been lost to U-boats in the Atlantic.

March 1
BULGARIA: Bulgaria signs a protocol of adherence to the Axis tripartite pact.

March 5
BRITAIN: Great Britain severs diplomatic relations with Bulgaria.

March 11
ATLANTIC: Congress passes Lend-Lease Act. Aimed primarily at Great Britain, it allows the president to provide food aid, monetary loans, and war matériel to any country friendly to the United States as a means to keep out of the war in Europe and Asia.

March 12
SOVIET UNION: The Soviet Union establishes diplomatic relations with Thailand.

March 18
PACIFIC: The Marine 7th Defense Battalion arrives in Samoa.

March 24
TURKEY: Turkish-Soviet communiqué promises neutrality if either should be attacked.

March 25
YUGOSLAVIA: Yugoslavia signs a protocol of adherence to the Axis tripartite pact. The German war zone is extended beyond Iceland.

March 27
ATLANTIC: Military representatives of the United States, Canada, and Great Britain meet in Washington, D.C., to map out strategy in case of America entering the war against Germany. The U.S. Navy would support convoy operations to Britain, and the U.S. Pacific Fleet would be used offensively against Japanese economic power.

Anti-Axis coup d'etat is underway in Yugoslavia.

March 29
ATLANTIC: Meetings are completed and a report is produced known as ABC-1. The report addresses not only strategic policy but also command organization and strategic direction and planning. The emphasis is on collaboration in planning and execution of military operations, reflecting the unease of Americans in allowing the British to have too much influence on U.S. military affairs. The report sets the stage for a U.S.-Great Britain strategic partnership.

March 31
ATLANTIC: At the end of the month of March, a total of 41 ships (about 243,000 tons) have been lost to U-boats in the Atlantic. Five U-boats have been sunk.

April 3
IRAQ: Pro-Nazi coup d'etat is under way in Iraq.

April 5
YUGOSLAVIA: Yugoslav-Soviet treaty of friendship and nonaggression is signed.

April 6
YUGOSLAVIA: Germany invades Yugoslavia and Greece. Italy declares war on Yugoslavia.

April 7
BRITAIN: Great Britain severs diplomatic relations with Hungary.

April 9
ATLANTIC: The United States signs an agreement with Denmark, agreeing to defend Greenland against invasion in return for basing rights.

April 10
ATLANTIC: President Roosevelt under the provisions of Lend-Lease transfers Coast Guard cutters to Great Britain. Roosevelt issues a proclamation modifying the Red Sea combat zone.

April 12
ATLANTIC: Japanese ambassador to the United States Nomura presents Secretary of State Cordell Hull with a proposal for peace in the Pacific.

April 13
SOVIET UNION: Japan and the Soviet Union sign a five-year nonaggression pact with a joint declaration regarding the frontiers of the Japanese protectorate of Manchu-kuo. This agreement allows Japan to pursue the conquest of China without fear of Soviet interference.

April 17
YUGOSLAVIA: Yugoslavia surrenders to Germany.

April 18
PACIFIC: Admiral Husband E. Kimmel, commander in chief of the Pacific Fleet (CINCPAC), identifies Wake Island as a priority defense requirement to Admiral Harold R. Stark, chief of naval operations.

April 22
ATLANTIC: The regular army enlisted strength is authorized to increase to 232,000.

April 27
GREECE: German forces occupy Athens.

May 2
IRAQ: British begin fighting Iraqi troops in Iraq.

May 6
SOVIET UNION: Joseph Stalin is announced as Soviet premier.

May 6
PACIFIC: Japan and Vichy France sign an agreement for economic collaboration in French Indochina.

May 9
PACIFIC: A French Indochina-Thailand peace treaty is signed. Japan will guarantee the borders.

May 14

ATLANTIC: Germany declares a Red Sea danger zone.

The Joint Board approves the basic joint war plan and incorporates U.S. and British strategic and operational direction.

May 15

FRANCE: Marshal Pétain at Vichy announces the replacement of the armistice agreement with a new collaboration agreement.

May 16

SOVIET UNION: Iraq and the Soviet Union establish diplomatic relations.

May 21

ATLANTIC: Unarmed U.S. merchant ship *Robin Moor* is torpedoed and sunk off the coast of Africa by a German submarine. No American casualties.

May 27

ATLANTIC: Roosevelt announces the Atlantic neutrality patrols will be extended to prevent German warships from threatening the Western Hemisphere. He also announces that the United States will give all aid and support necessary to Great Britain and any other country resisting Hitler's Germany.

The American Liaison Committee, a group of military representatives, meets with British staff officers in London to receive information on current military operations and future plans.

May 31

IRAQ: British-Iraqi armistice is signed in Baghdad.

June 8

MIDDLE EAST: British and Free French troops enter French Syria and Lebanon.

June 18

TURKEY: German-Turkish 10-year friendship pact is signed in Ankara.

June 21

ATLANTIC: The War Department creates the Army Air Forces with its own general staff. General Arnold is the chief, on equal footing with Admiral King and General Marshall.

June 22

SOVIET UNION: Nazi Germany attacks the Soviet Union. Italy declares war on the Soviet Union. The Romanians occupy Bessarabia.

June 23

PACIFIC: Admiral Stark orders elements of the 1st Marine Defense Battalion to be established on Wake Island.

June 27

HUNGARY: Hungary declares war on the Soviet Union.

June 28
ATLANTIC: Albania declares war on the Soviet Union.

President Roosevelt creates the Office of Scientific Research. Dr. Vannevar Bush, the chairman of the new group, will coordinate war-related scientific research.

June 30
ATLANTIC: Vichy France severs diplomatic relations with the Soviet Union.

The active duty strength of the U.S. Marine Corps is 54,359.

July 1
ATLANTIC: Admiral King establishes task forces to escort convoys between the United States and Iceland.

July 2
ATLANTIC: The Joint Board approves the addition of two new members: Major General Henry H. Arnold, deputy chief of staff for air, and the chief of the Bureau of Aeronautics, Rear Admiral J. H. Towers.

July 3
CHINA: Army Chief of Staff General George C. Marshall establishes the American Military Mission to China (AMMISCA), and appoints Brigadier General John Magruder to lead the group, which will advise the Chinese on identifying military items needed to equip the Chinese military so that these can then be matched to U.S. defense production requirements.

July 7
ATLANTIC: Iceland authorizes U.S. forces to be stationed on the island. The 1st Marine Brigade lands at Reykjavik to prevent any possibility that German forces will occupy the island.

July 9
ATLANTIC: The British Joint Staff Mission is established in Washington, D.C. These officers arrive with the intention to act as counterparts to the U.S. Army chief of staff and the navy chief of naval operations.

July 12
ATLANTIC: A force of 5,000 marines relieves British troops at Reykjavik, Iceland, as the United States takes responsibility for the defense of Iceland.

British-Soviet mutual-assistance agreement is signed in Moscow.

July 25
PACIFIC: Japan announces a protectorate over French Indochina; United States freezes Japanese assets totaling $130 million and ends the export of oil to Japan; Canada freezes both Japanese and Chinese funds.

July 26
ATLANTIC: Great Britain freezes Japanese assets and announces its intention to end its commercial treaty. President Roosevelt orders the formation of the U.S. Army

Forces Far East (USAFFE) under the command of Lieutenant General Douglas MacArthur in the Philippines. The 150,000-man Philippine army is combined with U.S. Army forces.

July 27
PACIFIC: New Zealand freezes Japanese assets.

July 28
PACIFIC: Netherlands East Indies freezes Japanese assets and refuses to provide any further oil shipments to Japan. Australia freezes all Japanese assets.

July 30
ATLANTIC: The United States recognizes the Czechoslovak government-in-exile in London.

July 31
PACIFIC: Strength of the Philippine Division is reported at 10,473—over 2,000 are U.S. Army regulars, the rest are U.S.-led and trained Philippine Scouts. Total U.S. strength in the Philippines, including the Philippine Division, the air corps, harbor defenses, and service detachments, is 22,532.

August 1
ATLANTIC: President Roosevelt orders the end of shipment of oils and motor fuels to Japan. Japan and Thailand sign an economic trade agreement. Thailand will extend $3.6 million in credits. A naval air station is established on Midway Island.

August 9
ATLANTIC: President Roosevelt, on the cruiser USS *Augusta*, arrives in Placentia Bay off Newfoundland after a three-day secret trip and meets with Prime Minister Winston Churchill, who arrives on the battleship HMS *Prince of Wales.* The two leaders discuss strategy and war aims, producing the Atlantic Charter, a document outlining common democratic principles of free peoples. Roosevelt assures Churchill that America will fight against Germany first, and that the United States would protect British convoys from America to Britain.

August 12
ATLANTIC: The Roosevelt-Churchill meeting ends.

August 14
ATLANTIC: The Atlantic Charter is issued.

> The President and the Prime Minister have had several conferences. They have considered the dangers to world civilization arising from the policies of military domination by conquest upon which the Hitlerite government of Germany and other governments associated therewith have embarked, and have made clear the stress which their countries are respectively taking for their safety in the face of these dangers. . . . They have agreed upon the following joint declaration:
>
> Joint declaration of the President of the United States of America and the Prime Minister, Mr. Churchill, representing His Majesty's Government in the United Kingdom, being met together, deem it right to make known certain common principles

in the national policies of their respective countries on which they base their hopes for a better future for the world.

First, their countries seek no aggrandizement, territorial or other;

Second, they desire to see no territorial changes that do not accord with the freely expressed wishes of the peoples concerned;

Third, they respect the right of all peoples to choose the form of government under which they will live; and they wish to see sovereign rights and self-government restored to those who have been forcibly deprived of them;

Fourth, they will endeavor, with due respect for their existing obligations, to further the enjoyment by all States, great or small, victor or vanquished, of access, on equal terms, to the trade and to the raw materials of the world which are needed for their economic prosperity;

Fifth, they desire to bring about the fullest collaboration between all nations in the economic field with the objector securing, for all, improved labor standards, economic advancement and social security;

Sixth, after the final destruction of the Nazi tyranny, they hope to see established a peace which will afford to all nations the means of dwelling in safety within their own boundaries, and which will afford assurance that all the men in all the lands may live out their lives in freedom from fear and want;

Seventh, such a peace should enable all men to traverse the high seas and oceans without hindrance;

Eighth, they believe that all of the nations of the world, for realistic as well as spiritual reasons must come to the abandonment of the use of force. Since no future peace can be maintained if land, sea or air armaments continue to be employed by nations which threaten, or may threaten, aggression outside of their frontiers, they believe, pending the establishment of a wider and permanent system of general security, that the disarmament of such nations is essential. They will likewise aid and encourage all other practicable measures which will lighten for peace-loving peoples the crushing burden of armaments.

August 19
PACIFIC: Work begins on defenses at Wake Island.

September 1
ATLANTIC: U.S. Navy begins to escort convoys to Britain starting at Newfoundland and ending at Iceland. The Iceland-Greenland strait is patrolled by U.S. warships.

September 4
ATLANTIC: U.S. destroyer *Greer* is attacked by a German submarine southwest of Iceland; it responds with depth charges, damaging the sub.

September 8
ATLANTIC: President Roosevelt asks that recommendations of the Joint Board be presented to him by both the chief of naval operations and the army chief of staff. This increases the importance of these military leaders in providing advice directly to the president.

September 11
ATLANTIC: Roosevelt issues a "shoot on sight" order to the navy to protect both U.S.-flagged ships and those ships escorted by U.S. ships. Roosevelt warns that if

any German or Italian warship enters the American neutrality zone, it does so at its own risk.

September 14–28
ATLANTIC: Large-scale army maneuvers are conducted in Louisiana.

September 19
ATLANTIC: The Joint Board approves the addition of a Joint Intelligence Committee to provide daily intelligence summaries to the president and the leaders of the War Department as well as special intelligence studies, when requested by the Joint Board.

September 27
ATLANTIC: The first Liberty Ship (EC-2 type freighter), *Patrick Henry,* is launched at Baltimore, Maryland.

October 16
ATLANTIC: U.S. destroyers assist in fighting off German submarines from a British convoy, but the Germans succeed in sinking six merchant ships. The destroyer *Kearney* is attacked and damaged southwest of Iceland. Eleven crewmen are killed and 22 wounded. A British destroyer (a former U.S. destroyer given to Great Britain in the destroyer for bases deal) is also sunk.

October 18
PACIFIC: General Tojo Hideki takes control of Japanese cabinet as premier, war minister, and home minister.

October 31
ATLANTIC: U.S. destroyer *Reuben James* is torpedoed and sunk escorting a convoy off Iceland. It is the first American warship lost in action in World War II. There are 36 survivors; 115 sailors are killed.

November 2
PACIFIC: Total marine strength on Wake Island is increased to 15 officers and 373 enlisted men.

November 3
PACIFIC: Major General Lewis H. Brereton takes command of the new Far East Air Force (FEAF) in the Philippines. The chief of the Japanese Naval General Staff approves the draft plan for the attack on the U.S. Pacific Fleet at Pearl Harbor.

November 10
ATLANTIC: Prime Minister Winston Churchill, speaking in London about the situation in Asia, makes the following statement: "The United States' time-honored interests in the Far East are well known. They are doing their utmost to find a way of preserving peace in the Pacific. We do not know whether their efforts will be successful, but if they fail, I take this occasion to say—and it is my duty to say—that should the United States become involved in war with Japan the British declaration will follow within the hour."

November 10
PACIFIC: The commander of the Asiatic Fleet is given permission to withdraw marines and gunboats from China.

November 15–30
ATLANTIC: Army conducts a second set of large-scale maneuvers in North and South Carolina.

November 17
ATLANTIC: Congress authorizes arming of U.S. merchant ships and allows them to enter war zones.

November 20
PACIFIC: Japan submits its final proposal for peace in the Pacific. The United States must give Japan a free hand in China. Therefore, the United States must discontinue aid to the Chinese Nationalist government, recognize Manchukuo, recognize the Greater East Asia Co-Prosperity Sphere, restore the U.S.-Japanese trade treaties, and unfreeze Japanese assets.

November 26
ATLANTIC: Secretary of State Cordell Hull passes to the Japanese the final proposal of the United States for peace in the Pacific: Japan has to respect the territorial integrity of China, accept change in the Pacific through peaceful means, and respect open markets in China. Japan is to withdraw from the Axis and withdraw all military and police forces from Indochina and China before the United States will resume trade with Japan. A six-carrier task force departs Japan headed for Hawaii. If negotiations fail, the task force commander, Admiral Nagumo Chuichi, is to attack the U.S. Pacific Fleet at Pearl Harbor.

November 27
ATLANTIC: Admiral Harold R. Stark, chief of naval operations, and General George C. Marshall, army chief of staff both send out war warning messages to their respective commanders in Hawaii.

November 28
PACIFIC: Reports are received of transports sailing south toward Indochina carrying a sizable number of Japanese troops. A naval air station is established at Wake Island.

November 30
PACIFIC: The Japanese foreign minister rejects the U.S. final proposal. U.S. strength in the Philippines stands at 31,095. The arrival of the 200th Coast Artillery Regiment and the 192nd and 194th Tank Battalions from the National Guard, represent a part of a 40 percent increase in combat strength. The tank battalions bring 108 of the newest American tank, M3. The Far East Air Force (FEAF) has the largest concentration of air power outside of the continental United States, with 107 P-40 fighters and 35 B-17 Flying Fortress bombers. The Philippine army has mobilized 10

divisions for national defense, which have been integrated into MacArthur's defensive plan. The 4th Marines deploy from Shanghai to the Philippines.

December 4
PACIFIC: The carrier *Enterprise* takes on 12 Marine F4F-3 Wildcat fighters for transport to Wake Island.

December 5
PACIFIC: Dawn to dusk air patrols begin on Wake Island.

December 6
ATLANTIC: Great Britain declares war against Finland, Hungary, and Romania.

December 7
ATLANTIC: The U.S. Army as of this day has 1.6 million men available, including 29 infantry divisions, five armored divisions, two cavalry divisions, and an air corps of 270,000 men.

PACIFIC: Japanese naval task force launches air attack on Oahu at the U.S. naval base at Pearl Harbor with the intent to cripple the American Pacific Fleet. Coming in two waves, 353 Japanese carrier-based aircraft attack the fleet and the combat aircraft at Hickam and Wheeler airfields. The attack achieves near-total surprise and succeeds in sinking four battleships (USS *Oklahoma*, USS *West Virginia*, USS *Arizona*, and USS *California*), seriously crippling the battleship USS *Nevada*, and inflicting damage on 19 other ships. The Army Air Force loses all but 79 of its 239 aircraft. Almost half of the navy's 169 aircraft are destroyed. Nearly 3,400 Americans are killed or wounded. The Japanese lose less than 30 aircraft. A Japanese midget sub tries to enter Pearl Harbor before the morning attack, but is spotted and sunk by the destroyer USS *Ward* on channel entrance patrol. The captain's report of hostile contact appears to have no effect on the chain of command. During the attack, the destroyer USS *Monaghan* sinks another midget sub inside the harbor. Vice Admiral Nagumo Chuichi, commander of the task force, ends the attack without finding the American carriers. USS *Enterprise* and USS *Lexington* are deployed to support Wake and Midway Islands; *Saratoga* is in port in San Diego. Nagumo also misses the ship repair facilities, fuel storage tanks, and submarine base, all of which will prove invaluable to future operations. During the attack, Ensign Francis C. Flaherty is in a turret on the USS *Oklahoma*. The order is given to abandon ship when it becomes clear that the battleship is going to capsize. Ensign Flaherty orders the turret crew to escape, holding a flashlight so they can see their way out. Flaherty sacrifices his own life to save his men. For his gallantry, Ensign Flaherty will receive the Medal of Honor.

Hours after the attack, Chief of Naval Operations Admiral Harold R. Stark issues the following order: "Execute unrestricted air and submarine warfare against Japan."

December 8
PACIFIC: United States and Great Britain declare war on Japan. The Netherlands East Indies and Canada also declare war on Japan.

Japanese bombard Midway and Guam. At Guam, the Japanese sink a U.S. mine-sweeper and cause serious damage. Japanese bombers attack Wake Island, destroying seven of the eight fighter aircraft on the island. Japanese aircraft attack Clark and Iba airfields in the Philippines—half of the American aircraft are destroyed or heavily damaged. Rear Admiral William A. Glassford orders the Asiatic Fleet to seek safety in the waters off the Philippines. Japanese amphibious forces move into position to begin landings on Luzon, the main island of the Philippines. The marine garrison in Beijing (Peking) surrenders to the Japanese.

Thailand and Malaysia are invaded. Thailand surrenders.

December 9
PACIFIC: Australia, South Africa, and New Zealand declare war on Japan. China declares war on the Axis powers.

December 9
PACIFIC: Japanese forces invade the Gilbert Islands; Japanese bombers attack Nichols Field on Luzon, near Manila. China declares war on the Axis powers. Wake Island and Guam undergo another heavy air attack.

MacArthur intends to defend Luzon, dividing his command into four elements. The North Luzon Force is to defend against the most dangerous Japanese approach from the landing beaches at Lingayen Gulf. Major General Jonathan M. Wainwright commands the 26th Cavalry Regiment, Philippine Scouts, an infantry battalion of the Philippine Scouts, four Philippine army divisions, and three artillery batteries. The South Luzon Force, commanded by Brigadier General George M. Parker, Jr., protects the area south and east of Manila with two Philippine army divisions and two Philippine Scout artillery batteries. The Reserve Force under MacArthur's direct command has the FEAF and the U.S. Army Philippine Division of 10,233 officers and men located north and west of Manila. Major General George F. Moore commands the Harbor Defense Forces, which protect Manila Bay. The Visayan-Mindanao Force, commanded by Brigadier General William F. Sharp, has three Philippine infantry divisions and is responsible for the islands south of Luzon.

December 10
PACIFIC: About 6,000 Japanese troops capture an unfortified Guam from a garrison force of about 500 marines and sailors; Wake Island comes under air attack. A 4,000-man Japanese assault force makes two landings in north Luzon in the vicinity of Aparri and Vigan and begins to move inland to control major roads and seize a key airstrip. Japanese aircraft provide air cover for the initial invasion, attacking U.S. airfields. Cavite naval base and Nichols airfield are heavily damaged. Japanese gain air supremacy—the remaining U.S. aircraft of the Far East Air Force are able to fly only limited missions.

Captain Colin P. Kelly becomes the first hero of the war when it is reported that his B-17 bomber has crashed into the Japanese battleship *Haruna* and sunk it. In actuality, he has attacked the heavy cruiser *Ashigara,* but missed the target. Kelly ordered his crew to bail out over Luzon and tried to bring his badly damaged plane back to Clark airfield, but the intrepid pilot died in the crash. Awarded the

Distinguished Service Cross posthumously, the truth about Kelly's mission will not be revealed until later in the war.

Japanese landing forces seize Makin Atoll in the Gilberts. Tarawa is declared occupied.

December 11
ATLANTIC: Germany and Italy declare war on the United States. The United States in turn declares war on Germany and Italy.

December 11
PACIFIC: The Wake Island garrison, composed of 522 soldiers, marines, and sailors (assisted by a number of civilian contractors), repels the initial Japanese landing attempt, sinking two destroyers and damaging two other ships. Japanese casualties are estimated at between seven and eight hundred. A radio message from Wake is decoded in Hawaii and unwittingly reformed into the message "Send us more Japs." Although a great morale boost for Americans at home when publicized, the message itself is false and has nothing to do with the real attitude of the defenders.

December 12
PACIFIC: Task Force South Pacific is organized under Brigadier General Julian F. Barnes and heads for Australia, escorted by the cruiser USS *Pensacola*. A 2,500-man Japanese assault force from the Palau Islands lands in southern Luzon at Legaspi and captures the airfield. The initial Japanese landing force in northern Luzon continues to advance, supported by heavy air strikes on American airfields throughout Luzon. The 11th Division of the Philippine army offers little or no resistance.

December 12
BURMA: Japanese ground forces from Thailand enter Burma. General Sir Archibald Wavell is given responsibility for the defense of Burma and India. The American Volunteer Group (AVG) fighter aircraft from China arrive at Mingaladon to support the British.

December 13
ATLANTIC: Hungary and Bulgaria declare war with the United States and Great Britain.

Admiral Karl Dönitz initiates the U-boat campaign against American shipping on the Atlantic coast.

December 14
PACIFIC: Japanese air strikes virtually eliminate American airpower in Luzon; Major General Lewis H. Brereton, FEAF commander and General Douglas MacArthur's Air Corps commander, begins evacuating the remainder of his B-17s to Mindanao, then to Darwin, Australia. Admiral Thomas C. Hart, commander of U.S. Asiatic Fleet, withdraws naval air support as well. Encountering little opposition, the Japanese Luzon force moves toward Lingayen Gulf. Japanese air attacks on Wake Island leave the marines with only one operational aircraft.

December 15

PACIFIC: The Wake Island relief force, designated Task Force 14, leaves Hawaii under command of Rear Admiral Frank J. Fletcher. TF 14 has the carrier USS *Saratoga* with 117 aircraft, and grows to 13 destroyers, three cruisers, a seaplane tender, and an oiler.

December 17

PACIFIC: The fallout from the Pearl Harbor disaster leads to wholesale changes in American senior commanders. Admiral Chester W. Nimitz replaces Admiral Husband E. Kimmel as commander in chief, Pacific Fleet; Vice Admiral William S. Pye will be the acting commander until Nimitz arrives. The new commanding general of the Hawaiian Department is Lieutenant General D. C. Emmons, replacing Lieutenant General Walter C. Short. The Hawaiian Air Force Department's new commander is Major General Clarence L. Tinker, replacing Major General Frederick L. Martin. The U.S. Navy reinforces Midway with marine aircraft.

December 18

ATLANTIC: President Roosevelt issues an executive order that gives the commander in chief, United States Fleet (CominCh), command of operating fleets and coastal commands. The CominCh is immediately responsible to the president under the general direction of the secretary of the navy.

PHILIPPINES: The Japanese Legaspi landing force reaches Naga after pushing past Filipino defenders.

December 19

ATLANTIC: President Roosevelt signs an executive order establishing the Office of Censorship under Byron Price, a former Associated Press editor. Price is given absolute discretion to censor all international communications. Price seeks voluntary compliance by military and civilian supervisors to prevent information of potential benefit to the enemy from being published. By 1942, 10,000 federal employees in 18 censorship stations across the country will be examining mail going overseas.

PHILIPPINES: The Legaspi force advances toward Daet. A Japanese force of 5,000 troops from Palau lands at Davao on Mindanao, supported by heavy air attacks.

BURMA: The SS *Tulsa* issue quickly develops into an incident. The American Military Mission to China (AMMISCA) under Brigadier General John Magruder is authorized by the War Department to transfer Lend-Lease matériel awaiting transportation in the port of Rangoon from Chinese to British control, subject to Generalissimo Chiang Kai-shek's approval. An American officer in Rangoon requests that the government of Burma impound the Lend-Lease matériel, most of which is on board the SS *Tulsa* in Rangoon harbor and destined for China. The Chinese representative in Burma, objecting to the transfer of material to the British, suggests a committee be formed to determine the disposition of the supplies.

December 20

ATLANTIC: Admiral Ernest J. King is appointed commander in chief, United States Fleet (CominCh). Admiral Stark's position as chief of naval operations is reduced to mainly administrative duties within the Department of the Navy.

Pacific: Wake Island receives news of Task Force 14's approach from a navy PBY patrol plane.

Philippines: On Mindanao, the Japanese capture Davao and seize the nearby airfield. In Luzon, Japanese forces begin a movement from Vigan toward Lingayen Gulf. The 4th Marines are transferred to General MacArthur's operational control.

China: Colonel Claire Chennault's American Volunteer Croup (AVG), under control of the Chinese Air Force, attacks enemy aircraft headed to Kunming, reportedly downing nine bombers. The AVG, based at Kunming, is responsible for protecting the Burma Road and contesting Japanese air operations along the southwest border region. The popular press of China calls them *Fei Wing,* or flying tigers.

December 21

Pacific: Largest attack yet on Wake Island begins. Japanese send 49 aircraft, both dive bombers and fighters to hit American defenses. Task Force 14 is about 600 miles from Wake.

Philippines: The Japanese Fourteenth Army with 60,000 men under command of Lieutenant General Homma Masaharu arrives at Lingayen Gulf, supported by the Japanese Third Fleet. At Bacnotan, Philippine army units encounter the Japanese Vigan force as it advances.

December 22

Pacific: Wake Island loses the last of its F4F-3 Wildcats. Task Force 14 halts for refueling at sea, which consumes most of the day and evening.

Philippines: The Japanese land at Aringay, Agoo, and Bauang in Lingayen Gulf and advance inland, linking up with the Vigan force. The Philippine Scouts (26th Cavalry) and elements of the Philippine Army 71st Division offer resistance. U.S. submarines attack Japanese ships in the gulf, while a few American planes harass the enemy fleet. American B-17s from Darwin, Australia, bomb Japanese transports at Davao, land at Del Monte field, then proceed to attack Japanese forces in Lingayen Gulf.

China: Generalissimo Chiang Kai-shek releases the Chinese Fifth and Sixth armies to support the British defense of Burma. Wavell takes control of the Sixth Army's 93rd Division as it moves into Burma.

Southwest Pacific: U.S. Forces in Australia (USFIA) established in Brisbane under Brigadier General Julian F. Barnes.

December 23

Pacific: Task Force 14 is 425 miles from Wake, but has no information on the defenders' situation. Fletcher hesitates, then receives orders from Vice Admiral Pye, acting commander in chief of the Pacific Fleet, to move to Midway. The Japanese launch two attack waves of 1,000 men each to storm the beaches. Captain Henry T. Elrod, a Wildcat pilot from VMF-211 who sank a Japanese destroyer on December 11, is killed in furious fighting on the beach. Elrod defends his position with such tenacious courage that he will receive the Medal of Honor. After about 11 hours of resistance, the commander of Wake, Winfield S. Cunningham, orders American forces to surrender. About 1,600 Americans—both military and civilian—begin a long and brutal captivity.

PHILIPPINES: General Douglas MacArthur abandons Manila and orders a withdrawal of U.S. and Filipino forces to Bataan. USAAF B-17s attack Japanese ships in Lingayen Gulf and Davao; other American planes attack the Japanese landing force on Luzon.

SOUTHWEST PACIFIC: A convoy disembarks 4,600 soldiers of the U.S. Army Air Corps and artillery at Brisbane, Australia. The convoy has been diverted from its original destination, the Philippines.

December 24

ATLANTIC: The Arcadia Conference. The Anglo-American Arcadia conference begins in Washington, D.C. Prime Minister Winston Churchill, President Franklin Roosevelt, and the British and American chiefs of staff begin to determine a combined war strategy. Conference will end on January 14, 1942.

PACIFIC: Brigadier General Henry B. Claggett takes temporary command of the USFIA.

Midway receives reinforcements from the 4th Defense Battalion.

PHILIPPINES: A Japanese force of 7,000 men from the Ryukyu Islands lands at Lamon Bay, attacking Mauban and Siain, then moving in two directions with the intent of cutting off Manila to the north and linking with the Legaspi invasion force to the south. Major General Jonathan M. Wainwright, commanding the North Luzon Force, is unable to stop Homma's advance. With the Philippine Scouts conducting a brilliant defense, Wainwright falls back to the Agno River. The South Luzon Force, now under command of Brigadier General Albert M. Jones, begins a retreat past Manila and heading north to reach Bataan. The Bataan Defense Force, commanded by Brigadier General George M. Parker, Jr., begins preparations to establish two defensive lines for the arriving troops. The 4th Marines are ordered to Corregidor.

December 25

ATLANTIC: At the Arcadia conference, Chief of Staff of the Army General George C. Marshall suggests that all Allied forces in the Far East be placed under a single commander. This is the origin of the Australia-British-Dutch-American (ABDA) Command.

PACIFIC: Midway receives additional marine fighter aircraft, originally intended for Wake Island, from the carrier USS *Saratoga*.

PHILIPPINES: MacArthur establishes his headquarters on Corregidor, an island in the mouth of Manila Bay. Japanese breach Wainwright's Agno River line. The South Luzon Force continues to move north under heavy pressure from Japanese ground and air forces. Rear Admiral F. W. Rockwell takes command of all naval forces in the Philippines from Admiral Thomas C. Hart, who leaves by submarine for Java to establish a new Asiatic Fleet headquarters.

CHINA: Chiang Kai-shek announces through a military representative that he will recall Chinese troops from Burma after determining that the British seized the *Tulsa*'s Lend-Lease cargo with American assistance. He declares that the Chinese will no longer work with the British.

December 26

PACIFIC: Midway receives ground elements of the intended Wake Island relief force. Manila is declared an open city.

PHILIPPINES: The North Luzon Force retreats from the Agno River, defending from Santa Ignacia to San Jose. The Southern Luzon Force establishes a defensive line in the vicinity of Sariaya.

CHINA: Chiang is mollified over the *Tulsa* issue with promises of support from the U.S. representative of the American Military Mission to China. Although Chiang eventually will allow the transfer of the Lend-Lease shipment to Britain, it quickly becomes clear to the Americans that the Chinese leader will be a difficult ally.

December 27

PHILIPPINES: Wainwright withdraws to his final defensive position along the Tarlac-Cabanatuan line. Japanese forces, pressing the South Luzon Force, capture Candelaria.

December 28

ATLANTIC: U.S. Navy authorizes construction battalions (SEABEES).

PHILIPPINES: South Luzon Force is ordered to move to Bataan.

December 29

PHILIPPINES: Japanese aircraft begin bombardment of Corregidor. Japanese begin to crack the North Luzon defenses.

CHINA: The China theater established under command of Chiang Kai-shek, supported by an Allied staff. The theater boundaries include portions of China, Thailand, and Indochina not occupied by enemy forces.

December 30

PHILIPPINES: As the North Luzon Force's defense begins to crack under Japanese assaults, South Luzon Force rapidly moves to cross Calumpit Bridge over the Pampanga River to safety. Philippine president Manuel Quezon is inaugurated on Corregidor.

December 31

ATLANTIC: At the Arcadia conference, General Wavell is appointed commander of the Australian-British-Dutch-American Command (ABDA), with responsibility to coordinate Allied operations in the Far East.

PHILIPPINES: The North Luzon Force reaches its final defensive position along the Bamban-Arayat line. Commander of the South Luzon Force, Brigadier General Albert Jones conducts a desperate counterattack and North and South Luzon Forces are able to link at San Fernando. All forces east of the Pampanga River come under command of General Jones.

December 31

ATLANTIC: With 86 operational U-boats (36 in the Atlantic, 12 on the U.S. east coast) the German navy has sunk over 2.1 million tons of shipping in 1941, representing about 50 percent of all Allied and neutral shipping losses.

PACIFIC: Major General George H. Brett takes command of AFIA (American Forces in Australia). Admiral Chester W. Nimitz assumes duties as CINCPAC (commander in chief, Pacific).

CHINA: A Joint Military Council is established in Chungking.

1942

January 1

ATLANTIC: Declaration of the United Nations is signed in Washington, D.C.

PHILIPPINES: South Luzon Force disbanded and integrated into other units. Main defense line is established in southern Luzon between Porac and Guagua.

CHINA: Chinese request assistance from Lend-Lease to build an overland supply route from Ledo, India, through north Burma and on to Lungling, China.

January 2

PHILIPPINES: Japanese attack at Porac; Japanese forces cross Pampanga River and advance toward San Fernando, joining forces with Japanese troops advancing south. Manila is occupied and daily air attacks begin on Corregidor, but little damage results over the next week.

January 3

PACIFIC: General Archibald Wavell, as commander of all allied forces available in the Pacific under the title of ABDACOM (Australian-British-Dutch-American Command), is ordered by the CCS to hold Burma and Australia and defend as far forward as possible of the line stretching from Burma and the Malay Peninsula, through Sumatra and Java, across to the Philippines and Okinawa, North Australia, the Netherlands East Indies, New Guinea, to the Solomons, and as far south as New Zealand. Wavell is to maintain contact with all Allied forces in theater and block the Japanese advance by holding key areas. He is ordered to take the offensive at the earliest possible opportunity.

PHILIPPINES: The Japanese continue pressure on the Porac and Guagua defensive line in Luzon.

January 4

PHILIPPINES: Japanese outflank defenses at Guagua, forcing the defenders to retreat south and form another hasty line of defense between Lubao and Santa Cruz.

January 5

ATLANTIC: The U.S. government orders the rationing of tires to preserve limited rubber supplies for military vehicles.

PHILIPPINES: Troop rations for American and Philippine units are cut in half to save food. Brigadier General Richard J. Marshall establishes his headquarters in Bataan. Defenders establish a shorter defensive line at the base of the Bataan peninsula.

January 6

CHINA: As supreme Allied commander of the China theater, Chiang Kai-shek requests an American officer to serve as his chief of staff.

January 7

PHILIPPINES: The main Bataan defensive line stretching 20 miles from Mauban to Mabatang is established. Defenders are reorganized into I and II Philippine Corps. I Philippine Corps has 22,500 men and is responsible for the western half of the line. II Philippine Corps has 25,000 men and is responsible for the eastern half. A provisional unit is organized from navy, marine, and air force units to protect the main supply base at Mariveles.

January 8

ATLANTIC: The headquarters of U.S. Armed Forces in the British Isles is established to oversee the arrival of troops and supplies in Britain.

January 9

PHILIPPINES: Initial Japanese assault on Bataan advance defenses is repulsed. U.S. submarine *Pollack* sinks a Japanese merchant ship in the waters southwest of Inubo-zaki, Japan.

January 10

PHILIPPINES: General MacArthur inspects Bataan defenses.

January 11

ATLANTIC: Operation *Paukenschlag* ("roll of the kettledrums") begins. Five German submarines (*U-66, U-109, U-123, U-125,* and *U-130*) begin patrolling the east coast of the United States. Within the next month, over 26 Allied ships will be sunk by this group.

PHILIPPINES: Japanese attack Bataan's main defenses, achieve temporary success, but are driven back. Japanese forces pulled from Philippines land in Netherlands East Indies at Tarakan, Dutch Borneo, and Mendano on Celebes. Paratroops land near Mendano to support an attack to capture the main airfield.

PACIFIC: General Wavell, commander of ABDACOM, moves the U.S. 2nd Battalion, 131st Field Artillery to Surabaya in Java.

January 12

ATLANTIC: President Roosevelt establishes the War Labor Board by executive order. The 11-member board is to mediate and arbitrate labor and management disputes affecting war production.

PHILIPPINES: Japanese attacks on the Bataan defensive line continue.

January 14

ATLANTIC: Arcadia Conference Ends. The Allies decide to defeat Germany first and engage in discussions for possible offensive action. Prominently offered by the British is Gymnast, an invasion of North Africa. Japanese begin infiltration actions along the west coast of Bataan and through the center of the peninsula. The Combined chiefs of staff (CCS) is formed. The British Chiefs of Staff and their American counterparts will meet to make recommendations regarding U.S.-British strategic direction. In addition, the Combined Chiefs of Staff will provide recommendations on program requirements needed to support strategic decisions, submit general directives on policy for distribution of war matériel, and establish priorities for overseas military movements.

CHINA: Major General Joseph W. Stilwell is nominated to serve as Chiang Kai-shek's chief of staff.

January 15

ATLANTIC: U.S. government bans the production of new automobiles. Manufacturing plants will produce military vehicles.

PHILIPPINES: Japanese attacks threaten to split the Bataan defensive line in two at Mt. Natib. Reserves are committed to assist in holding the line. General Wavell establishes ABDA headquarters in Batavia, Java. Lieutenant General George H. Brett, USAAF, is the deputy commander and Admiral Thomas C. Hart U.S. Navy is the naval forces commander.

January 16

ATLANTIC: The War Production Board is established under Donald M. Nelson. Its function is to convert the civilian peacetime economy of the United States into full-scale war production. The War Production Board will take control of scarce resources and eliminate any manufacturing or production it deems nonessential to the war effort.

PHILIPPINES: When a gun position is knocked out of action during heavy fighting in the II Corps area on Bataan, Sgt. Jose Calugas, a mess sergeant of another battery, runs 1,000 yards to the gun position. Despite heavy enemy artillery fire, Calugas takes charge of a group of volunteers and puts the gun back in action. For his courage and daring, Sgt. Calugas later receives the Medal of Honor.

PACIFIC: Japanese forces from Thailand invade Burma.

January 17

PHILIPPINES: I Corps defenders pushed out of Morong on west flank of Bataan defensive line; reserves plugging gaps in center as Japanese exploit success. II Corps attempts to protect its open western flank.

PACIFIC: General Brereton is appointed commander of tactical forces in ABDA command.

January 18

ATLANTIC: Germany, Italy, and Japan renew the Axis Pact in Berlin. Japan will have complete freedom of action in all areas east of 70 degrees East Longitude.

A U.S. freighter is sunk by German submarine *U-552* off Newfoundland. Two U.S. tankers are attacked by submarines *U-66* and *U-123* off Cape Hatteras, North Carolina. One tanker sinks, the other is damaged.

January 19

ATLANTIC: A U.S. steamship is torpedoed and sunk off North Carolina by German submarine *U-123*.

January 20

PACIFIC: The 2nd Marine Brigade, commanded by Brigadier General Henry L. Larson, arrives at Samoa to support the protection of the U.S. line of communication to Australia. Two naval task forces, Task Force 8, formed around carrier USS *Enterprise* and commanded by Vice Admiral William F. Halsey, Jr., and Task Force 17, commanded by Rear Admiral Frank Jack Fletcher and formed around carrier USS *Yorktown*, escort the marines.

January 21

PACIFIC: Japanese air attacks on Rabaul (New Britain) and New Guinea near Lae and Salamaua.

CHINA: Chinese accept Stilwell as chief of staff and allow Stilwell to have executive authority over Allied forces.

January 22

ATLANTIC: A U.S. freighter is torpedoed and sunk by German submarine *U-123* south of Cape Hatteras, North Carolina.

PHILIPPINES: General MacArthur orders withdrawal to the second Bataan defensive line from Pilar to Bagac, just south of Orion on the east coast of the peninsula. A Japanese attempt to make an amphibious landing near Bagac is intercepted by U.S. PT boats and two enemy transports are sunk.

January 23

ATLANTIC: The Combined Chiefs of Staff conducts its first meeting in Washington, D.C. Admiral Harold R. Stark, chief of naval operations, Admiral Ernest J. King, commander in chief, United States Fleet, Lieutenant General Henry H. Arnold, chief of Army Air forces, and General George C. Marshall, army chief of staff, represent the United States. The first order of business is to attempt to deal with the disintegrating situation in the Far East.

A U.S. collier is sunk by German submarine *U-66* off Cape Hatteras, North Carolina.

PHILIPPINES: Bataan defenders begin a withdrawal to the second defensive line under pressure from Japanese attacks. An amphibious landing near Mariveles makes limited progress when scraped-together U.S. and Philippine troops counterattack.

PACIFIC: Japanese land troops at Rabaul and Kavieng, New Ireland, and land at Kieta, Bougainville, in the Solomons. U.S. submarine *Seadragon* damages a Japanese merchant ship off the northern coast of French Indochina.

January 24

PACIFIC: The Battle of Makassar Strait. A Japanese invasion force moving through the Makassar Strait to land at Balikpapan, Borneo, is intercepted by four U.S. destroyers. Three convoy ships, a cargo ship, and a patrol boat are sunk. A Japanese cruiser and two destroyers pursue, but the Americans escape. This is the first surface engagement of the war between American and Japanese ships. American P-40 fighters arrive in Java from Australia. Lae and Salamaua are evacuated in New Guinea.

January 25

ATLANTIC: A U.S. freighter is attacked and sunk by German submarine *U-125* off the North Carolina coast.

PACIFIC: Thailand declares war on the United States. Midway is shelled by Japanese submarine *I-73*.

January 26
ATLANTIC: German submarine *U-125* attacks and sinks a second U.S. freighter off the North Carolina coast.
PHILIPPINES: The second Bataan defensive line is established from Orion on the east to Bagac on the west. Heavy Japanese pressure continues all along the line. The Japanese continue to build a beachhead in the south in what is now called the Battle of the Points.

January 27
ATLANTIC: German submarines *U-66* and *U-130* sink a steamer, a freighter, and two tankers off the North Carolina coast.
PHILIPPINES: General Wainwright sends reinforcements south to try and dislodge enemy forces threatening the rear area, but the attacks are unsuccessful in dislodging the Japanese. Other Japanese attacks are made against the main defensive line.
PACIFIC: Near Borneo, U.S. B-17 bombers damage a Japanese seaplane carrier.

January 28
ATLANTIC: The Eighth Air Force is activated in Savannah, Georgia, commanded by Brigadier General Asa N. Duncan. The Eighth Air Force is initially designated the air component for Gymnast.

January 29
ATLANTIC: U.S. Coast Guard cutter *Alexander Hamilton* is torpedoed by German submarine *U-132* off Reykjavik, Iceland, and has to be scuttled.

January 30
ATLANTIC: A U.S. tanker is sunk by German submarine *U-106* off Chesapeake Bay.
PHILIPPINES: General MacArthur assumes command of all naval forces in the Philippines. The I Corps defensive line is broken, but the Japanese are contained in small pockets and are slowly eliminated in hard fighting.

February 1
PHILIPPINES: American fighter aircraft, PT boats, and artillery attack another Japanese amphibious movement near Quinauan Point on the west side of Bataan, but fail to prevent troops from landing. Philippine Scouts take heavy casualties attempting to control the beach.
PACIFIC: After departing from Samoa on 20 January, two American naval task forces conduct raids on Japanese bases. Halsey's Task Force 8, with the carrier USS *Enterprise,* attacks Kwajalein in the Marshal Islands, sinking a transport ship, a submarine chaser, and a gunboat, and damaging a cruiser, a submarine, and seven other auxiliary and support ships. Rear Admiral Yatsushiro Sukeyoshi is killed when his headquarters is bombed. Fletcher's Task Force 17, with the carrier USS *Yorktown,* attacks the Gilberts, but finds few targets. These are the first U.S. carrier strikes of the war.

February 2

ATLANTIC: An unarmed U.S. tanker is sunk by German submarine *U-103* near the mouth of the Delaware River.

Lieutenant General Joseph Stilwell is appointed to serve as Generalissimo Chiang Kai-shek's chief of staff and principal military adviser. His mission is to improve the combat capability of the Chinese army and maintain a supply line to keep China in the war. Stilwell and the Joint Chiefs of Staff agree that the overland route to China through Burma is the most important priority. Stilwell is to work toward improving the training of Chinese forces in India and overseeing the effort to equip the units properly for combat in Burma. Additional Chinese divisions will be trained and equipped in China to support future operations in Burma.

February 3

PHILIPPINES: First Lieutenant Willibald C. Bianchi of the 45th Infantry Regiment, Philippine Scouts, leads an attack on enemy machine gun positions. Wounded in the hand and unable to fire his rifle, he continues to lead, firing his pistol. Destroying one position with grenades, he is wounded again. Ignoring his injuries, Bianchi climbs on top of an American tank to fire its machine gun at the enemy until he is hit again and falls from the tank, unable to fight any longer. For his gallantry, Bianchi will receive the Medal of Honor.

February 4

ATLANTIC: An unarmed U.S. tanker is torpedoed and sunk by German submarine *U-103* off Cape May, New Jersey.

PACIFIC: A U.S.-Dutch ABDA naval force of four cruisers and 10 destroyers attempts to disrupt a Japanese landing on the coast of Borneo, but is driven off at Madoera Strait by enemy aircraft. Units of the Asiatic Fleet under Admiral Thomas C. Hart are reorganized into Naval Forces, Southwest Pacific Area, under Vice Admiral William A. Glassford.

February 5

ATLANTIC: Far East, Caribbean, Hawaiian, and Alaskan Air Forces are redesignated as Fifth, Sixth, Seventh, and Eleventh Air Forces, respectively.

February 6

ATLANTIC: The United States and Great Britain establish the Combined Chiefs of Staff in Washington to direct a combined war strategy.

February 7

ATLANTIC: President Roosevelt establishes the War Shipping Administration (WSA) by executive order. The WSA's mission is to provide overall control and operation of all U.S. merchant shipping. Rear Admiral Emory S. Land is appointed as director and reports directly to the president.

PHILIPPINES: I Corps conducts counterattack to eliminate Japanese pockets; enemy force trapped on Quinauan Point on the southwest coast of Bataan is eliminated; an attempt to rescue the trapped defenders is driven off by U.S. P-40 fighters and artillery.

February 8
PHILIPPINES: The Japanese commander, Lieutenant General Homma Masaharu, orders a withdrawal to rest and refit his weary units and receive reinforcements. Midway is shelled by Japanese submarine *I-69*.
PACIFIC: U.S. submarine *S-37* attacks a Japanese destroyer in the Makassar Strait.

February 9
ATLANTIC: The Joint Board meeting, now with Admiral King in attendance, shifts to the Joint Chiefs of Staff. A newly formed Joint Secretariat under Brigadier General Walter Bedell Smith serves both the JCS and the Joint Board. As time progresses, the JCS will subsume most of the activities of the Joint Board. The functions and duties of the JCS are never formally defined. Because the JCS evolves out of the Joint Board, the organization is able to adapt to meet the unprecedented requirements of a global war. Eventually Joint Staff Planners, a Joint Strategic Survey Committee, and a Joint Logistics Committee will be established to support JCS decisions.

The first formal meeting of the U.S. Joint Chiefs of Staff (JCS) is held in Washington. The JCS is composed of General George C. Marshall, army chief of staff, Lieutenant General Henry H. Arnold, chief of the Army Air Corps, Admiral Harold R. Stark, chief of naval operations, and Admiral Ernest J. King, COMINCH.
PACIFIC: U.S. submarine *Trout* sinks a Japanese gunboat off Formosa (Taiwan). A Japanese destroyer, torpedoed the previous day, sinks.

February 10
PACIFIC: While shelling Midway, Japanese submarine *I-69* is attacked and damaged by Marine F2A Buffalo fighters.

February 11
PACIFIC: Submarine USS *Shark* is sunk in the Celebes by a Japanese destroyer.

February 12
ATLANTIC: Tenth Air Force is activated at Patterson Field, Ohio, and assigned to General Stilwell for operations in China. In Bataan, I Corps continues to eliminate Japanese defenders trapped in pockets within the corps' main defensive line.

February 14
PACIFIC: Japanese paratroopers land on Sumatra near Palembang in the Netherlands East Indies to capture oil refineries. Vice Admiral Conrad E. L. Helfrich, Royal Navy, replaces Admiral Thomas C. Hart as Commander in Chief Allied Naval Forces in Southwest Pacific. U.S. submarine *Swordfish* sinks a Japanese transport off Davao in the Philippines.

February 15
PACIFIC: Singapore, the main bastion of British power in the Far East, with a garrison of 64,000 men, surrenders unconditionally to the Japanese.

February 18
ATLANTIC: Admiral Ernest J. King, commander in chief of the U.S. Fleet and chief of naval operations, proposes to Chief of Staff George C. Marshall that army troops

occupy islands in the south and southwest Pacific in preparation for using marine forces against the Japanese.

February 19

ATLANTIC: President Roosevelt signs an executive order authorizing the military to relocate and intern over 120,000 Japanese Americans living in California, Oregon, Washington, and Arizona. Within a month these people will move or be sent to internment camps throughout the United States.

A U.S. tanker is torpedoed and sunk by German submarine *U-128* off Cape Canaveral, Florida.

PACIFIC: As the Japanese begin landing forces on Bali, an ABDA naval force of Dutch and American ships launches an attack. Three Japanese destroyers are damaged, one Dutch destroyer is sunk, and an American destroyer is damaged. This night action is called the Battle of Badung Strait. Japanese carrier striking force under command of Vice Admiral Nagumo Chuichi attacks Darwin, Australia, sinking a U.S. destroyer, a transport ship, and a freighter. Airfields and depots are also damaged in the attack.

February 20

ATLANTIC: An unarmed U.S. freighter is torpedoed and sunk by German submarine *U-432* near Ocean City, Maryland.

PACIFIC: Japanese invade Timor Island in the Netherlands East Indies. A U.S. naval task force with the carrier USS *Lexington,* four heavy cruisers, and 10 destroyers under command of Vice Admiral Wilson Brown intends to conduct an air and surface attack on the Japanese base at Rabaul. Discovered by enemy patrol aircraft, a major air battle develops as Japanese bombers are sent to attack the carriers. Nine Japanese bombers are headed to attack the *Lexington* when Lieutenant Edward H. "Butch" O'Hare, piloting an F4F Wildcat, singlehandedly attacks the formation. Disregarding enemy fire, he fights alone until he runs out of ammunition. When he flies away six minutes later, he has downed five bombers and in all likelihood saved the *Lexington* from destruction. O'Hare becomes the first navy ace of the war and for his exceptional courage he will receive the Medal of Honor. The task force escapes damage and loses one pilot.

February 21

ATLANTIC: A U.S. freighter is attacked by German submarine *U-504* off the Florida coast.

PACIFIC: Fifth Air Force and U.S. troops are evacuated from Java.

February 22

ATLANTIC: A U.S. freighter is torpedoed and sunk by German submarine *U-504* and a U.S. tanker is sunk by German submarine *U-128* off the Florida coast. A U.S. freighter is sunk by German submarine *U-129* southeast of the island of Trinidad.

February 23

ATLANTIC: A U.S. freighter is torpedoed and later sinks after an attack by German submarine *U-161* near Martinique.

PACIFIC: B-17s attempt to bomb Rabaul with little success. General Brereton terminates Fifth Air Force Headquarters and leaves for India.

Japanese submarine *I-17* fires 13 shells at an oil refinery near Santa Barbara, California.

February 24
PACIFIC: Admiral William F. Halsey's *Enterprise* task force conducts air strikes on Wake Island.

February 25
ATLANTIC: U.S. Coast Guard assumes responsibility for coastal defense.
PACIFIC: ABDA command is dissolved.
BURMA: U.S. P-40s of the American Volunteer Group (AVG—also known as the Flying Tigers) and British Royal Air Force (RAF) fighters attack 40 Japanese fighters and 12 bombers over Burma. It is the AVG's best day in combat, recording 19 confirmed kills and eight probables.

February 26
ATLANTIC: A U.S. bulk carrier is torpedoed and sunk by German submarine *U-432* off the North Carolina coast; a U.S. tanker is torpedoed by German submarine *U-578* off Sea Girt, Delaware.

February 27
PACIFIC: The Battle of the Java Sea. A naval force of Dutch, American, British, and Australian cruisers and destroyers attempts to prevent a Japanese landing on Java. It encounters a 17-ship Japanese cruiser-destroyer force. In the ensuing fight lasting over seven hours, the ABDA force loses two cruisers and three destroyers; two Japanese destroyers are damaged. This Allied defeat allows the Japanese free access to the Java Sea from Malaya to Borneo. The U.S. Navy's first aircraft carrier, the USS *Langley,* now serving as an aircraft transport and carrying 32 P-40 fighters, is sunk by Japanese aircraft en route to Java.

February 28
ATLANTIC: U.S. destroyer *Jacob Jones* is sunk by a German submarine off the Delaware Capes.
PACIFIC: The Battle of Sunda Strait. A U.S. and a British cruiser, survivors of the Battle of the Java Sea, encounter a Japanese landing force at Banten Bay on the west end of Java in the Sunda Strait. The cruisers wreak havoc on the transports, sinking three and damaging three others, but they themselves are sunk by an overwhelming force of three cruisers and nine destroyers.

March 1
ATLANTIC: U.S. patrol aircraft sink the German submarine *U-565* off Newfoundland, marking the navy's first successful U-boat attack.
PACIFIC: Japanese air attacks sink the remainder of the ABDA Java Sea fleet. Two U.S. destroyers, one British destroyer, and a British cruiser are lost. Another U.S. destroyer and a gunboat are lost to enemy surface attack off Java. Of the origi-

nal combined naval force of five cruisers and 10 destroyers organized to defend the Netherlands East Indies, only four U.S. destroyers eventually escape to Australia. ABDA command is formally dissolved. Japanese units land on Java. They are opposed by an ad hoc ground force of two regiments and a brigade acting as a mobile reserve. This force contains one American army unit, the 2nd Battalion, 131st Artillery, a Texas National Guard unit.

March 3
ATLANTIC: President Roosevelt by executive order designates the Army Air Forces and the Army Ground Forces as the two major combat commands of the U.S. Army.

PACIFIC: U.S. submarine *Perch* is attacked by Japanese destroyers in the Java Sea. The boat is scuttled and the entire 59-man crew is taken prisoner.

The Java defenders, supported by the U.S. 2nd Battalion, 131st Artillery, hold the Japanese long enough for Allied forces to withdraw from Batavia.

The Western Pacific is reorganized. Responsibility for the area including Burma and all Southeast Asia west of Java and Sumatra is given to the British, commanded by Sir Archibald P. Wavell and under the strategic direction of the British Chiefs of Staff. The area eastward is controlled by the U.S. Joint Chiefs of Staff.

March 4
PACIFIC: Admiral Halsey's *Enterprise* task force aircraft attack Marcus Island, about 800 miles northwest of Wake Island. General MacArthur begins a reorganization of the command and control structure of the Philippine defense. Brigadier General William F. Sharp maintains command of forces on Mindanao, but the defense of Visayan is transferred to Brigadier General Bradford G. Chynoweth. MacArthur contemplates a Luzon-Bataan force under General Wainwright and harbor defenses under General Moore. His idea is to establish an indirect command headquarters at Corregidor under a deputy chief of staff of USAFFE, Colonel (on March 17, Brigadier General) Lewis C. Beebe, through which he can maintain command and control from Australia. MacArthur does not inform the War Department of his reorganization.

CHINA: At Chungking, Lieutenant General Stilwell establishes Headquarters, American Army Forces, China, Burma, and India (CBI). American Military Mission to China (AMMISCA) personnel are assigned to the new headquarters.

March 5
ATLANTIC: A U.S. freighter from convoy HX 178 (New York to Liverpool) is torpedoed and sunk by German submarine *U-404* off the coast of Nova Scotia.

March 7
PACIFIC: Major General Alexander M. Patch arrives in New Caledonia as the commander of the U.S. Army's New Caledonia task force.

March 8
ATLANTIC: The War Production Board regulates the production of clothing in the United States, specifying certain styles to conserve cloth.

March 8

ATLANTIC: U.S. Army forces relieve the 1st Marine Brigade on Iceland.
PACIFIC: Japanese forces land at Lae and Salamaua on New Guinea. Tenth Air Force begins movement from United States to India.

Allied forces on Java surrender to the Japanese. The men of the U.S. 2nd Battalion, 131st Artillery, essentially disappear once they fall into enemy hands. The prisoners endure a brutal captivity, eventually serving on railway labor gangs in Thailand. No news will be heard of the unit until the end of the war.

March 9

ATLANTIC: The Department of the Army is reorganized into three commands: Army Ground Forces, under Lieutenant General Lesley J. McNair; Army Air Forces (AAF), under Lieutenant General Henry H. "Hap" Arnold; and Services of Supply (later to become Army Service Forces), under Major General Brehon B. Somervell. This reorganization frees the chief of staff, General George C. Marshall, to focus on higher strategic issues dictated by his membership in the Joint Chiefs of Staff and the Combined Chiefs of Staff. The president, as commander in chief, exercises his duties directly through the army chief of staff.

Admiral Harold R. Stark is relieved as chief of naval operations and takes command of U.S. naval forces in Europe. Admiral Ernest J. King assumes his duties. The role of CNO and CominCh are thus combined. Admiral King is now the principal naval adviser to the president and responsible for the coordination and direction of the Navy Department. General Marshall and Admiral King are now the president's military advisers and provide the strategic direction for the war.

March 10

ATLANTIC: A U.S. tanker is torpedoed and sunk by submarine *U-588* near Barnegat, New Jersey.
PACIFIC: The Netherlands East Indies surrenders to the Japanese. Admiral Brown's Task Force 11 launches a 100-plane raid on New Guinea, attacking the Japanese invasion fleet of Rear Admiral Kajioka Sadamichi. Three enemy ships are sunk and several others, including a cruiser and five destroyers, are damaged. U.S. and Australian B-17 and Hudson bombers also strike targets on New Guinea but cause no damage. At Midway, marine fighters intercept a Japanese Kawanishi 97 flying boat, leading CINCPAC intelligence analysts to believe that the Japanese are planning an attack in the direction of Hawaii.

March 11

ATLANTIC: A U.S. freighter is torpedoed and sunk by German submarine *U-158* near Cape Lookout, North Carolina. German submarine *U-126* sinks a U.S. freighter in the waters off Cuba.
PACIFIC: Lieutenant General Douglas MacArthur, under direct orders of President Roosevelt, leaves Corregidor with his wife and son. Rear Admiral Francis W. Rockwell and selected staff officers accompany MacArthur. The group is on board four PT boats headed for Mindanao. Aircraft are waiting there to take them to Australia. General Jonathan M. Wainwright takes command of the forces in Luzon. General

Albert M. Jones takes command of I Corps. U.S. submarine *Pollack* sinks two Japanese cargo ships in the East China Sea.

BURMA: General Stilwell takes command of the Chinese Fifth and Sixth armies in Burma, a force of about 100,000 men. Stilwell's command is mostly ceremonial; Chiang Kai-shek retains primary control.

March 12

ATLANTIC: A U.S. tanker is damaged off the coast of North Carolina by German submarine *U-158*. German submarine *U-126* sinks a U.S. freighter and damages another off the coast of Cuba.

PACIFIC: Major General Alexander M. Patch's 17,500-man task force arrives in Nouméa, New Caledonia.

By executive order of the president, the duties of commander in chief U.S. Fleet and chief of naval operations are combined.

March 13

ATLANTIC: German submarine *U-332* sinks a U.S. schooner off the coast of Florida; a Chilean freighter is sunk by German submarine *U-404* off the New Jersey coast.

PACIFIC: U.S. submarine *Gar* sinks a Japanese cargo ship south of Tokyo Bay. Two U.S. prisoners of war who are on the ship are killed. The men were from an SBD Dauntless dive-bomber from USS *Enterprise,* shot down and captured on a 24 February raid on Wake Island.

American cryptanalysts break the Japanese navy's general-purpose code and identify the codeword for Midway Island. Two American naval intelligence centers are in operation in the Pacific providing communications intelligence on the Japanese navy. One is in Melbourne, Australia, and the other at Pearl Harbor, led by Commander Joseph J. Rochefort. The Navy Radio Intelligence Section in Hawaii, identified as OP-20-G, has the responsibility to intercept enemy radio communications, decode and translate the information, then pass it to the Pacific Fleet commander.

March 14

ATLANTIC: German submarine *U-404* torpedoes and sinks a U.S. collier off Atlantic City, New Jersey.

The U.S. Joint Chiefs of Staff commit to a buildup of U.S. forces in Great Britain to support the strategy of defeating Germany first.

PHILIPPINES: General MacArthur reaches Mindanao.

March 15

ATLANTIC: German submarine *U-158* sinks two U.S. tankers off Cape Lookout, North Carolina. A U.S. Navy PBO Hudson providing convoy security attacks and sinks German submarine *U-503* off the coast of Newfoundland. German submarine *U-161* sinks a U.S. Coast Guard lighthouse tender off Haiti.

March 16

ATLANTIC: German submarine *U-332* damages a U.S. tanker off the coast of North Carolina. The ship is later scuttled.

March 17

ATLANTIC: German submarine *U-124* off Diamond Shoals, North Carolina, damages two U.S. tankers in two days. One later sinks, the other is towed to Norfolk, Virginia. German submarine *U-332* sinks another tanker and a freighter in the same location.

PACIFIC: MacArthur arrives in Darwin, Australia, and is appointed supreme commander of the Southwest Pacific. Upon his arrival, MacArthur makes the following statement: "The President of the United States ordered me to break through the Japanese lines and proceed from Corregidor to Australia for the purpose, as I understand it, of organizing the American offensive against Japan, a primary objective of which is the relief of the Philippines. I came through and I shall return."

The United States agrees to accept responsibility for the defense of the Pacific Ocean.

U.S. submarine *Grayback* sinks a Japanese collier off the coast of Chichi Jima in the Bonin Islands.

March 19

PHILIPPINES: A message from President Roosevelt to General Wainwright pledges "every possible means and method" to assist the beleaguered defenders of Bataan and Corregidor and notifies him that he has been nominated for the rank of lieutenant general "because of the confidence I have in your leadership and in the superb gallantry of the devoted band of American and Filipino soldiers under your command."

March 20

ATLANTIC: Army Air Force (AAF) planners lay out a concept for a strategic bombing campaign against Germany launched from bases in Britain. The United States will emphasize precision daylight attacks against critical industrial targets, complementing the British emphasis on night area bombing.

March 21

ATLANTIC: German submarine *U-124* damages one U.S. tanker and sinks another off the North Carolina coast. Two U.S. tankers will be sunk by *U-124* the following day in the same area. Another U.S. tanker is sunk by *U-123*.

PHILIPPINES: Wainwright officially becomes a lieutenant general and moves to Corregidor to take command of U.S. forces in the Philippines. Major General Edward P. King takes command of the Luzon Force.

BURMA: General Stilwell's Chinese divisions support the British defenses, covering the area from Toungoo to Prome, defending along the Sittang and Salween Rivers. British and Indian forces under General William J. Slim will defend the area from the Irrawaddy River to Prome.

March 24

ATLANTIC: The Combined Chiefs of Staff designate the Pacific theater and assign to the United States primary responsibility for military operations.

March 25

ATLANTIC: Task Force 39, consisting of a battleship, two cruisers, the carrier USS *Wasp*, and a destroyer squadron, leaves for Britain to support the British Home Fleet.

March 26

ATLANTIC: The U.S. Navy is given operational control over U.S. Army Air Forces in conducting antisubmarine patrols. A U.S. Navy "Q ship," a warship disguised as a merchant vessel, is sunk by German submarine *U-123* in an engagement off the North Carolina coast. *U-123* is damaged in the fight, but the American crew is lost. A U.S. tanker is sunk by German submarine *U-71* off Diamond Shoals, North Carolina. *U-160* sinks a Panamanian freighter off the Virginia Capes.

PHILIPPINES: U.S. B-17s evacuate Philippine president Quezon and his family to Australia.

March 27

ATLANTIC: U.S. War Plans Division develops three options for Europe. Sledgehammer is the name for the contingency plan for a small-scale cross-Channel attack in 1942 as a raid or to establish a permanent foothold on the continent. It is intended as an emergency measure to divert German forces from the USSR if the USSR appears to be in danger of imminent collapse and defeat. The plan for the full-scale invasion of Europe in 1943 is called Roundup. The U.S.-British forces in the United Kingdom are considered to be the first phase of the buildup of additional U.S. forces for Roundup. This plan is called Bolero.

PACIFIC: U.S. submarine *Gudgeon* sinks a Japanese freighter off Kumun Island.

March 29

ATLANTIC: U.S. steamship is torpedoed and sunk by German submarine *U-160* off Cape Hatteras, North Carolina.

PACIFIC: The U.S. Marine 4th Defense Battalion and Fighter Squadron 212 arrive at Efate, New Hebrides, joining 500 army troops. Work begins on an airstrip.

March 30

ATLANTIC: A U.S. freighter, part of a convoy to Murmansk, USSR, is sunk by German submarine *U-435*.

PACIFIC: The Pacific theater is divided into two areas, each with its own commander. MacArthur has the Southwest Pacific area (Philippines, Australia, New Guinea, Solomons, Netherlands East Indies, and the Bismarck Archipelago). MacArthur is to protect lines of communication within his area and guard the approaches into his area, defend Australia, and support operations in the Pacific Ocean area. Admiral Nimitz has the Pacific Ocean area (North, Central, and South Pacific Ocean). His mission is to protect lines of communication in his area and support operations in the Southwest Pacific. Nimitz commands all naval forces in the Pacific, including those forces provided to MacArthur. Both commanders are ordered to prepare for offensive action. Nimitz's command has three subdivisions: North, South, and Central Pacific. Vice Admiral Robert L. Ghormley will command the South Pacific, while Nimitz has command of the North and Central Pacific. The Pacific War Council is established in Washington, D.C., to develop war policy. Nations represented are China, the Netherlands, Great Britain, Canada, New Zealand, Australia, and the United States. U.S. submarine *Tambor* damages a Japanese transport off Eniwetok Atoll. U.S. submarine *Sturgeon* sinks a Japanese transport off Makassar City in the Java Sea.

March 31

ATLANTIC: German submarine *U-754* attacks and sinks a tugboat and two barges at the mouth of Chesapeake Bay and will later sink a U.S. tanker in the same area. Italian submarine *Pietro Calvi* sinks a U.S. tanker in the Caribbean bound for Venezuela.
BURMA: Stilwell's Chinese division is driven out of Toungoo.

April 1

PACIFIC: Japanese forces begin landings on Dutch New Guinea.
   U.S. submarine *Seawolf* torpedoes a Japanese light cruiser off Christmas Island.

April 2

BURMA: General Brereton, commander of the Tenth Air Force, leads a bombing raid on Japanese shipping targets, claiming damage to a cruiser and a transport.

April 2

ATLANTIC: German submarine *U-123* torpedoes and damages a U.S. tanker off the North Carolina coast. *U-552* shells and sinks a U.S. freighter off the Eastern Shore of Virginia.

April 3

ATLANTIC: A U.S. freighter is torpedoed and sunk by German submarine *U-754* off Cape Henry, Virginia. A U.S. freighter is torpedoed and sunk off the west coast of Africa by German submarine *U-505*.
PACIFIC: Admiral Nimitz is named commander in chief Pacific Ocean area (CINCPOA) in addition to his position as commander in chief Pacific Fleet (CINCPAC).
PHILIPPINES: A five-hour air and artillery bombardment of the Bataan defensive line precedes a Japanese ground assault. Major General Albert Jones's I Corps holds, but the left flank of Major General George Parker's II Corps gives way and the 41st Division of the Philippine Army collapses. Attempts to block the Japanese advance with infantry and tanks from the reserve force are only partially successful.
BURMA: General Stilwell deploys the Chinese 96th Division in the Sittang Valley to support the withdrawal of the Chinese 22nd Division to Pyinmana.

April 4

ATLANTIC: A U.S. tanker is sunk off Puerto Rico by German submarine *U-552*.
PHILIPPINES: Japanese air and artillery bombardments open a second day of attacks to exploit the collapse of II Corp's left flank. Japanese tanks and infantry press remnants of the Philippine 41st and 21st Divisions back, opening a wide gap between I and II Corps.

April 5

ATLANTIC: A U.S. tanker is sunk by German submarine *U-154* off the shores of the Dominican Republic.

April 5

PHILIPPINES: Japanese forces seize Mount Samat, the key terrain feature in II Corps zone.

April 6
ATLANTIC: A U.S. tanker is damaged by a torpedo attack from German submarine *U-160* off Cape Lookout, North Carolina.

PACIFIC: Advance elements of the U.S. Army's 41st Infantry Division arrive in Melbourne, Australia.

PHILIPPINES: II Corps counterattacks to recapture Mount Samat, but poor coordination among units, including an inability of some units even to conduct an attack, combined with an effective Japanese defense supported by effective air and artillery support, cause the effort to fail. Two divisions and a regiment are lost and two other regiments are surrounded and cut off. Having committed its reserve to the counterattack, II Corps is forced into a small defensive line on the San Vicente River.

April 7
ATLANTIC: Eighth Air Force is ordered to Britain.

PHILIPPINES: The Japanese press their attack on II Corps, forcing the remnants to retreat to the Mamala River, but are unable to hold. Sensing victory, General Homma orders his forces to attack south to seize Cabcaben, on the southeast tip of the peninsula. Both the Luzon force reserve and I Corps reserve are committed, but fail to stop the Japanese advance.

April 8
ATLANTIC: Two U.S. tankers are sunk in shallow water by German submarine *U-123* off the Georgia coast. The two tankers are later salvaged and returned to service.

PHILIPPINES: A defensive line is established on the Alagan River, but the exhausted and starved men have become disorganized and command and control has broken down. Supported by artillery and air attacks, the Japanese easily locate gaps in the defenses and push south. "It is with deep regret," Wainwright reports to MacArthur, "that I am forced to report that the troops on Bataan are fast folding up." I Corps, untouched for the most part, is ordered to withdraw to the Binuangan River, and then receives an order originating from MacArthur to attack northward. Major General Jones, committed to a withdrawal, reports his troops are physically incapable of conducting an attack. Food stocks on Bataan are used up, and the rear area is in chaos.

U.S. submarine *Seadragon* arrives at Corregidor and takes off navy communications intercept and intelligence personnel.

April 9
ATLANTIC: German submarine *U-123* sinks a U.S. freighter off the coast of Georgia. German submarine *U-160* sinks a U.S. freighter and *U-552* sinks two U.S. tankers off Cape Hatteras, North Carolina. Italian submarine *Pietro Calvi* conducts a surface attack on a U.S. tanker off the coast of Brazil, forcing the crew to abandon ship.

PHILIPPINES: Despite direct orders from General Wainwright (which came from General MacArthur and President Roosevelt) to continue the fight and under no circumstances surrender, Major General Edward King, commander of Luzon Force, meets with Major General Nagano Kameichiro to arrange terms for surrender. Believing further resistance would lead only to the slaughter of his men, General King takes action without notifying Wainwright. About 2,000 American and Fili-

American prisoners on the Bataan Death March *(Library of Congress)*

pino troops escape to Corregidor. King unconditionally surrenders 78,000 soldiers to the Japanese. The Bataan Death March begins—a 65-mile march from Mariveles at the base of the Bataan peninsula to the railhead at San Fernando. Lacking food and water, and already exhausted and ill, the prisoners are treated with barbaric cruelty. An estimated 7,000 to 10,000 captives will die, including 2,330 Americans.

April 10
ATLANTIC: German submarine *U-123* conducts a surface attack on a U.S. tanker, which is silhouetted by the lights of Jacksonville, Florida.
PHILIPPINES: U.S. submarine *Snapper* evacuates personnel from Corregidor. Japanese forces land on Cebu Island at Cebu City. Philippine units on the island conduct a delaying action. The headquarters of the Visayan Force, under command of Brigadier General Bradford Chynoweth, is located on the island. U.S. submarine *Thresher* sinks a Japanese freighter near the mouth of Tokyo Bay.

April 11
ATLANTIC: A U.S. tanker is damaged by German submarine *U-203* south of Cape Lookout, North Carolina. A British steamship is sunk by *U-160* off the Virginia Capes.

PACIFIC: U.S. submarine *Trout* sinks a Japanese fleet tanker off the island of Honshu west of the air and naval base of Shiono Mikasi. Fifth Air Force aircraft attack Japanese cargo ships off Lae, New Guinea, damaging one ship.

April 12

ATLANTIC: A U.S. freighter is sunk by German submarine *U-123* off the coast of Florida. A Panamanian tanker is sunk off the North Carolina coast by German submarine *U-203*.

General Arnold, chief of Army Air Forces, provides General Marshall in London with the air plan for Bolero, calling for the establishment of the Eighth Air Force in Britain.

CARIBBEAN: A U.S. freighter is torpedoed and sunk near Haiti by German submarine *U-154*. A U.S. tanker is attacked by German submarine *U-130* near Puerto Rico.

PHILIPPINES: General Chynoweth retreats with elements of his force into the mountains of north Cebu to begin a guerrilla campaign. Fifth Air Force B-25 Mitchells from Australia bomb targets on Cebu, while B-17s from Mindanao also strike Cebu. Japanese artillery and aircraft from Bataan begin intensive attacks on Corregidor.

April 13

PACIFIC: Vice Admiral Robert L. Ghormley is designated as commander, South Pacific Area (COMSOPAC). Ghormley is responsible for all Allied base defense forces and local defense forces in the South Pacific, except New Zealand.

April 14

ATLANTIC: U.S. destroyer *Roper* sinks German submarine *U-58* off the Virginia Capes. A British freighter is sunk by German submarine *U-203* off Diamond Shoals, North Carolina.

The British accept the U.S. plan for Bolero, the buildup of Allied forces in Britain for a cross-Channel invasion.

Detachment 101 of the Office of Coordination of Information is activated. It is an American unit tasked with conducting guerrilla warfare, sabotage, and espionage in the Far East.

April 15

ATLANTIC: A U.S. freighter is torpedoed and sunk off the coast of Massachusetts by German submarine *U-575*.

Headquarters, U.S. Bomber Command, is established in England. Eighth Air Force is reassigned to Britain and no longer attached to Gymnast.

BURMA: British forces destroy the oilfields at Yenangyaung as General Slim begins to withdraw northward. The Chinese 38th Division fights well in covering the British retreat. With his flank exposed, Stilwell orders the Chinese to hold. One entire Chinese division deserts and disappears into the hills of Burma.

April 16

ATLANTIC: German submarine *U-123*, having used up all its torpedoes on this patrol, conducts a surface attack on a U.S. freighter. The submarine evades a ramming attempt and then allows the freighter's crew to abandon ship safely before destroying the ship with gunfire.

PACIFIC: U.S. submarine *Tambor* sinks a Japanese stores ship off Kavieng, New Ireland.

PHILIPPINES: Japanese forces land on Panay Island; Colonel Albert Christie's 7,000-man Panay Force retreats into the mountains to conduct guerrilla operations. General Wainwright designates Brigadier General William F. Sharp as the commander of the Visayan garrisons and orders him to organize his Visayan-Mindanao Force for a defense of Mindanao.

April 17

BURMA: General Stilwell, outflanked by rapidly advancing Japanese forces, abandons his plans to defend at Pyinmana. Stilwell continues to have trouble in getting the Chinese division commanders to respond to his orders. Chinese generals insist on getting guidance from Chiang Kai-shek. The Chinese 55th Division is destroyed south of Loikaw, leaving the road to Lashio and the Burma Road open.

April 18

ATLANTIC: A U.S. tanker is torpedoed off Cape Hatteras by German submarine *U-136,* but is able to make port in Norfolk, Virginia.

PACIFIC: The Doolittle Raid on Japan. Task Force 16 under command of Admiral William F. Halsey, with the carriers USS *Enterprise* and USS *Hornet,* approaches the coast of Japan. On board the *Hornet* are 16 B-25 Mitchell bombers of the Eighth Air Force's XVII Bomber Group. The pilots have been trained to take off from the carrier's small deck but are too large to land on the deck. The plan is a strike on the Jap homeland. The intent is to launch the bombers from the carrier, bomb targets, then fly to airfields in China. But on April 18, at 650 miles off, a Japanese patrol ship discovers the task force. Halsey decides to launch the B-25s, led by Lieutenant Colonel James H. Doolittle. Although launched at the maximum limit of their range, Doolittle's bombers still achieve surprise and hit targets in Tokyo, Yokohama, Kobe, Yakosuka, and Nagoya. After dropping their bombs, the planes head for China, but, unable to land at the planned airfields, the crews will either crash-land their planes or parachute out and attempt to escape to Chinese lines. One plane will land in Vladivostok and its crew will be interned by the Soviets. Of the 80 airmen who make the attack, 71 will survive. Doolittle and 62 others reach safety in China. Five are killed and eight others are captured.

Meanwhile, Halsey's carrier aircraft from USS *Enterprise* attack Japanese picket boats, damaging eight as well as an armed merchant cruiser. The cruiser USS *Nashville* sinks two picket boats with direct gunfire. Halsey's task force then withdraws safely. The attack will have little effect in terms of damage, but will be a deep psychological blow to the Japanese (one of Doolittle's bombers flies directly over the emperor's palace), demonstrating that the Japanese homeland is not secure. Most importantly, American morale receives a sorely needed boost. Doolittle will later receive the Medal of Honor for his daring act.

B-25 Mitchells are ready to take off from the deck of the USS *Hornet* to bomb Tokyo, April 18, 1942. Sixteen bombers were launched for this highly secret mission under the command of Lieutenant Colonel James H. Doolittle.

April 19
ATLANTIC: U.S. freighter is torpedoed and sunk by German submarine *U-136* west of Bermuda.

April 20
ATLANTIC: A U.S. freighter is torpedoed and sunk by German submarine *U-752* off Nantucket.

U.S. carrier *Wasp* is moved into the Mediterranean to deliver British fighter aircraft to Malta.

SOUTHWEST PACIFIC AREA: General George H. Brett assumes command of Allied Air Forces, subordinate to MacArthur's Southwest Pacific Area (SWPA) command. It includes the U.S. Fifth Air Force, as well as Australian and Dutch air forces. Also within SWPA, General Sir Thomas Blamey is appointed commander, Allied Land Forces, and Admiral Herbert F. Leary commands Allied Naval Forces.

April 21
ATLANTIC: U.S. freighter is torpedoed and sunk by German submarine *U-576* off the east coast. *U-201* sinks a U.S. freighter off the east coast.

April 23

ATLANTIC: A U.S. freighter is torpedoed and sunk by German submarine *U-125* off the east coast.

BURMA: Chinese Sixth Army retreats into China. Other units under Stilwell take up defensive positions in the Sittang Valley. The Chinese 200th Division moves to halt the Japanese advance near Loikaw.

April 24

PACIFIC: U.S. submarine *Trout* sinks Japanese merchant ship near Kii Strait.

April 25

PACIFIC: U.S. submarine *Spearfish* sinks Japanese military transport off Luzon.

April 26

ATLANTIC: U.S. freighter is torpedoed and sunk by German submarine *U-66* near the Netherlands West Indies.

PACIFIC: U.S. submarine *Pickerel* damages a Japanese hospital ship in Manipa Strait.

April 28

ATLANTIC: A joint U.S.-British naval task force sails from Scapa Flow to escort convoy PQ 15, heading for the USSR.

April 29

ATLANTIC: German submarine *U-108* torpedoes and sinks a U.S. tanker off the east coast; *U-507* torpedoes and sinks a U.S. tanker off Cuba.

PACIFIC: The Japanese Imperial General Staff Headquarters designates Port Moresby as a priority objective to assist in controlling New Guinea and the Solomons. The MO Plan is developed to establish a base in Tulagi while a major landing takes place at Port Moresby, New Guinea. The plan involves five elements, including a landing force element, a support group, a carrier striking force with the two fleet carriers, the *Shokaku* and *Zuikaku*, a patrol group, and a covering group, with the light carrier *Shoho*.

PHILIPPINES: Japanese forces begin offensive on Mindanao, landing nearly 5,000 men from Cebu on the island. Philippine army units are unable to halt the attackers and begin to withdraw.

The Japanese continue to intensify the bombardment of Corregidor. Rations and water are in short supply, and power to the Malinta tunnel, where the bulk of the garrison is located, is failing. Bombs and artillery shells have demolished most of the fixed defensive positions. A Japanese landing force occupies the abandoned Australian seaplane base at Tulagi in the Solomons.

BURMA: Japanese forces capture Lashio, cutting the Burma Road. British forces begin a retreat to India. Chinese Fifth Army retreats into China.

April 30

PACIFIC: Fifth Air Force aircraft attack Japanese bases on Lae and Salamaua in New Guinea. U.S. Navy PBY Catalinas take civilians and military personnel off

Corregidor. U.S. submarine *Greenling* sinks a Japanese ammunition ship in the Caroline Islands.

May 1
PACIFIC: U.S. submarine *Triton* sinks a Japanese cargo ship off Formosa.
BURMA: The Japanese capture Mandalay after the withdrawal of the Chinese 22nd Division from the city. Stilwell initiates plans for the withdrawal of his forces from Burma via Myitkyina.

May 2
ATLANTIC: General Carl A. Spaatz is designated commander of Eighth Air Force.
PACIFIC: Japanese force from Tulagi lands on Florida Island in the Solomons. U.S. submarine *Drum* sinks a Japanese seaplane carrier off the coast of Japan's Honshu Island; U.S. submarine *Trout* sinks a Japanese freighter off Honshu.

May 3
PHILIPPINES: A Japanese amphibious force from Panay lands on Mindanao; Corregidor faces steady air and artillery attacks. Japanese forces establish a seaplane base on Tulagi in the Solomon Islands. The U.S. submarine *Spearfish* arrives at Corregidor and takes 25 passengers along with vital records and mail to Australia.

May 4
ATLANTIC: Commander in Chief U.S. Fleet Admiral King orders the Coast Guard Auxiliary to use civilian small craft as coastal pickets in response to the German U-boat threat. U.S. freighter is sunk by German submarine *U-162* off the coast of British Guiana. Three U.S. tankers are sunk by *U-507* in the waters off Cuba. *U-564* torpedoes a U.S. freighter off the coast of Florida. *U-123* sinks a U.S. freighter in the southern Caribbean. The submarine rescues 34 survivors; the captain questions the group, then gives them directions to land and casts them off. The survivors will be picked up later by a steamship and brought to Cartagena, Colombia.

The War Production Board rations sugar to save scarce sources.
PACIFIC: Aircraft from Rear Admiral Frank Jack Fletcher's Task Force 17 with the carrier *Yorktown,* three cruisers, six destroyers, and the oiler USS *Neosho,* attack the Japanese at Tulagi, sinking a destroyer, a minesweeper, two auxiliary minesweepers, and damaging several other enemy ships. Japanese transports leave Rabaul for Port Moresby, New Guinea. The Japanese carrier striking force with the *Zuikaku* and *Shokaku* reaches San Cristobal Island at the southernmost end of the Solomon Island group to protect the Port Moresby invasion force coming from Rabaul. Meanwhile, Rear Admiral Aubrey Fitch with the carrier USS *Lexington,* five U.S. destroyers, and five Australian cruisers awaits a linkup at a predesignated area in the Coral Sea.

U.S. submarine *Trout* sinks a Japanese gunboat off the coast of Honshu, Japan. U.S. submarine *Greenling* sinks a Japanese gunboat near Truk.
PHILIPPINES: Philippine defenders on Mindanao establish a new defensive line. Corregidor undergoes greatest bombardment to date. A total of 16,000 artillery shells fall on the island in a 24-hour period. The garrison has suffered 600 casualties since

April 9 and the water supply is down to four days. Wainwright reports to General Marshall that "we have something less than even chance to beat off an assault."

May 5

ATLANTIC: U.S. freighter is torpedoed and sunk by German submarine *U-108* off Haiti. *U-133* torpedoes and damages a U.S. tanker off the coast of Florida.

PACIFIC: Japanese Imperial General Staff Headquarters sends orders to prepare for the invasion of Midway Island, called the MI Plan. A supporting operation to attack the Aleutians is named the AL Plan.

PHILIPPINES: The Japanese make a night landing on the north shore of Corregidor. Beach defenses have been thoroughly obliterated, and information can be sent only by messenger. Although American defenders cause heavy casualties to the initial landing force, the Japanese gain a foothold and advance rapidly using tanks and light artillery. American counterattacks are disrupted and the defenders begin to suffer heavy casualties. Between 600 and 800 men are killed and nearly 1,000 wounded by the middle of the day. Wainwright decides to surrender. In a message to President Roosevelt and General MacArthur notifying them of his decision, Wainwright writes: "Please say to the nation that my troops and I have accomplished all that is humanly possible and that we have upheld the best traditions of the United States. . . ."

May 6

ATLANTIC: German submarine *U-333* torpedoes and sinks a U.S. tanker off the coast of Florida. *U-507* and *U-125* each attack and sink a U.S. freighter in the Gulf of Mexico.

PACIFIC: U.S. submarine *Skipjack* torpedoes and sinks a Japanese cargo ship off Indochina. U.S. submarine *Triton* sinks two Japanese cargo ships off Formosa.

PHILIPPINES: Lieutenant General Jonathan Wainwright surrenders unconditionally to the Japanese. All U.S. and Filipino forces are ordered to end resistance throughout the Philippines. About 11,000 on Corregidor become prisoners. Japanese forces continue their attack on Mindanao, moving toward Dalirig, above the Del Monte airfields in northern Mindanao.

May 7

CBI: Japanese forces capture Myitkyina. Stilwell decides to walk to India with 80 handpicked staff members and a handful of other followers. The Chinese 22nd and 38th Divisions move in good order from upper Burma into India. Other Chinese units, including the 200th Division and part of the 55th Division, escape to China.

PACIFIC: The Battle of the Coral Sea. As the Japanese Port Moresby invasion force approaches New Guinea, Admiral Fletcher moves his united task force to intercept. The support group of the Port Moresby operation is attacked by 93 aircraft from the carriers USS *Lexington* and USS *Yorktown,* sinking the light carrier *Shoho.* Meanwhile, the U.S. destroyer *Sims* and the oiler *Neosho* are attacked by Japanese aircraft, which mistake them for a carrier and a cruiser. The *Sims* is sunk and the *Neosho* is heavily damaged and is later scuttled. Aircraft from the Japanese carrier striking force also attack three Australian cruisers and two destroyers sent by Fletcher to locate the Port Moresby landing force. Later, B-26 Marauders from Fifth Air Force mistakenly bomb the Allied ships. That night 27 planes are dispatched to locate the American carriers. Only six return, which will limit the strikes that the Japanese can later launch against the American carriers. Not knowing where the U.S. carriers are located, the Port Moresby landing is postponed for two days. The Japanese occupy Hollandia, New Guinea.

May 8

CBI: P-40s of the American Volunteer Group (Flying Tigers) attack Japanese forces on the banks of the Salween River in an attempt to prevent an advance to Kunming, China.

SOUTHWEST PACIFIC AREA: General Douglas MacArthur, commander of SWPA, offers to General George C. Marshall a plan to attack the Japanese base at Rabaul. He requests significant naval and air support, including aircraft carriers, along with additional army reinforcements.

U.S. submarine *Skipjack* torpedoes and sinks an army cargo ship off Indochina.

PACIFIC: The Battle of the Coral Sea. Aircraft from the USS *Lexington* locate the Japanese carrier striking force. Dive bombers and torpedo bombers from the carriers USS *Lexington* and USS *Yorktown* attack and damage the *Shokaku*. A 70-plane counterstrike from the Japanese carriers damages both the *Yorktown* and the *Lexington*. The *Lexington* is hit by two torpedoes and two bombs, lists badly and is unable to receive aircraft. A fuel explosion later in the day leaves the ship too badly damaged to survive, and she is sunk by a torpedo from an American destroyer. The Japanese lose 43 aircraft and American losses are 33 aircraft. Nimitz orders Fletcher to withdraw, while the Japanese, thinking both U.S. carriers are sunk, return to Truk. Although that order will be countermanded in Tokyo, the American fleet is gone.

Lieutenant John Powers on both May 7 and 8 plays a critical role in the outcome of the Battle of the Coral Sea. Leading a section of three Douglas SBD Dauntless dive-bombers, he ignores heavy antiaircraft fire to drop his bomb directly on the *Shoho* at an altitude that seems to guarantee his own destruction. The following day, Powers tells his fellow pilots, "Remember the folks back home are counting on us. I am going to get a hit if I have to lay it on their flight deck." Leading his section of dive-bombers to attack the *Shokaku* from an altitude of 18,000 feet, Powers again dives through antiaircraft fire and enemy fighter planes to drop his bomb on the deck of the carrier, scoring a direct hit. He disappears in smoke and flame attempting to recover from his harrowing dive. For his acts of skill and courage Lieutenant Powers will receive the Medal of Honor.

Lieutenant Milton E. Ricketts is in charge of a damage control party on the carrier USS *Yorktown* when a bomb explosion causes heavy casualties and a major fire. Although mortally wounded, Lieutenant Ricketts uses a fire hose to contain the blaze until his last breath. For his selfless sacrifice in saving his ship, Lieutenant Ricketts will receive the Medal of Honor.

The Battle of the Coral Sea is a tactical victory for the Japanese, but a strategic victory for the United States. It is the first naval battle in history where ships do not fire at each other; aircraft conduct all engagements; and carrier aircraft inflict all the damage on the ships. The Japanese for the first time have been stopped in naval combat. The Port Moresby landings are cancelled. More importantly, the damage to *Shokaku* prevents it from being added to the Midway MI Plan. The Japanese also lose irreplaceable skilled pilots.

U.S. submarine *Grenadier* sinks an army transport ship off the coast of Kyushu, Japan.

May 9
ATLANTIC: U.S. freighter is damaged by German submarine *U-588* off Nova Scotia; *U-564* sinks a U.S. freighter off Florida. U.S. Coast Guard cutter sinks German submarine *U-352* off the coast of North Carolina. U.S. carrier *Wasp* continues operations in the Mediterranean to deliver British aircraft to Malta.
PACIFIC: Japanese take Dalirig at Mindanao and pursue the scattered defenders.

May 10
ATLANTIC: U.S. freighter is torpedoed and sunk by German submarine *U-506* off the coast of Louisiana.
PHILIPPINES: General Sharp orders his Visayan-Mindanao force to surrender. Some units, still resisting, do so reluctantly.

U.S. submarine *Silversides* conducts a surface attack and damages a Japanese guardboat near Marcus Island.

May 11
PACIFIC: U.S. submarine *S-42* damages a Japanese minelaying ship in the Solomons. B-17 bombers attack Japanese ships in the northern Solomons.

May 12
CBI: Tenth Air Force B-17s attack Myitkyina in Burma to disrupt Japanese fighters from interfering with the aerial supply route to China.
ATLANTIC: U.S. tanker is sunk by German submarine *U-507* off the coast of Louisiana; *U-162* torpedoes and sinks a U.S. tanker off Barbados.
PACIFIC: U.S. submarine *S-44* sinks Japanese repair ship in the Solomons.

May 13
CARIBBEAN: A U.S. freighter is torpedoed and sunk by German submarine *U-169*.
SOUTHWEST PACIFIC AREA: B-17s and B-26 Marauders from Fifth Air Force bomb Rabaul.
PACIFIC: U.S. submarine *Drum* torpedoes and sinks a Japanese cargo ship off the coast of Honshu, Japan.

May 14
BURMA: Tenth Air Force B-17 bombers attack Myitkyina.
ATLANTIC: German submarine *U-213* lays mines off St. Johns, Newfoundland.

Congress enacts legislation establishing the Women's Army Auxiliary Corps (WAAC). These women, designated as neither military nor civilian, will provide support to the war effort through their knowledge, skills, and special training.

PACIFIC: Fifth Air Force B-17s and B-26 Marauders attack Rabaul and Lae.

May 15

ATLANTIC: U.S. freighter is torpedoed and sunk by German submarine *U-751* near the Bahamas. German aircraft attack the port of Murmansk in an attempt to damage U.S. cargo ships delivering supplies.

May 16

CBI: Tenth Air Force B-17 bombers attack Japanese positions at Myitkyina.

CARIBBEAN: *U-103* torpedoes and sinks a U.S. freighter.

ATLANTIC: Two U.S. tankers are damaged and one tanker is sunk by torpedoes from German submarine *U-506* off the coast of Louisiana.

SOUTHWEST PACIFIC AREA: Fifth Air Force B-25 Mitchells, B-17s, and B-26 Marauders attack Lae and Deboyne Island in New Guinea.

PACIFIC: U.S. submarine *Tautog* sinks Japanese tanker near Truk.

May 17

CARIBBEAN: U.S. freighter and a British tanker are torpedoed and sunk by German submarine *U-155*.

PACIFIC: U.S. submarine *Silversides* damages a Japanese transport off Honshu, Japan. U.S. submarine *Skipjack* sinks a Japanese army transport in the Gulf of Siam. U.S. submarine *Tautog* sinks Japanese submarine *I-28* near Rabaul. U.S. submarine *Triton* sinks Japanese submarine *I-64* off Kyushu, Japan.

May 18

ATLANTIC: German bombers attack the port of Murmansk, but cause little damage to American merchant ships. U.S. freighter is sunk by German submarine *U-156* in the Caribbean. *U-125* sinks two U.S. freighters in the Gulf of Mexico.

PACIFIC: The Japanese Imperial General Headquarters designates New Caledonia, Fiji, and Samoa as objectives for the Seventeenth Army and the Combined Fleet.

May 19

ATLANTIC: General Ira C. Eaker takes command of all U.S. Army air forces in Britain. U.S. freighter is torpedoed and sunk by German submarine *U-506* off the coast of Louisiana; *U-103* sinks a U.S. freighter off the coast of Mexico; *U-751* sinks a U.S. freighter off the coast of Haiti.

May 20

CBI: General Stilwell emerges from the jungles of Burma after a march of 150 miles through formidable terrain and reports to the British garrison at Imphal, India. No one in the group has been lost. Three days later, in Delhi for a strategy conference, Stilwell will face a group of reporters who are eager to label him a hero for his vaunted walkout of Burma. Stilwell will tell them plainly: "No military commander in history ever made a voluntary retreat. All retreats are ignominious as hell. I claim we got a hell of a beating. We got run out of Burma—and it is humiliating as hell. I think we ought to find out what caused it, go back, and retake it."

CARIBBEAN: A U.S. freighter is torpedoed and sunk by German submarine *U-752* off the coast of Mexico. German submarine *U-103* torpedoes and sinks two U.S. freighters off the coast of Cuba.

ATLANTIC: *U-506* torpedoes and sinks a U.S. tanker off the coast of Louisiana.

SOUTHWEST PACIFIC AREA: Fifth Air Force B-17s attack Japanese airfields on Timor Island.

PACIFIC: Rear Admiral John S. McCain takes command of naval air forces in the South Pacific.

May 21

ATLANTIC: A U.S. freighter is torpedoed and sunk by German submarine *U-588* off the East Coast.

SOUTHWEST PACIFIC AREA: Fifth Air Force B-17s bomb Lae in New Guinea.

May 22

ATLANTIC: A U.S. freighter is torpedoed and sunk by German submarine *U-588* off the East Coast.

SOUTHWEST PACIFIC AREA: Fifth Air Force B-17s attack shipping and airfields at Rabaul, while B-26 Marauders attack the harbor and airfields at Lae.

May 23

ALEUTIANS: U.S. fighter reinforcements arrive on Umnak Island in the Aleutians as part of the effort to counter the Japanese Midway attack plan.

CARIBBEAN: A U.S. tanker is torpedoed and sunk by German submarine *U-103* off the coast of Mexico.

SOUTHWEST PACIFIC AREA: Fifth Air Force B-25 Mitchells attack facilities at Lae.

May 24

CARIBBEAN: A U.S. freighter is torpedoed and sunk by German submarine *U-558* near Jamaica.

SOUTHWEST PACIFIC AREA: Fifth Air Force B-26 Marauders attacking Lae come under heavy attack by Japanese fighters. Several bombers are lost.

PACIFIC: U.S. submarine *Pompano* sinks a Japanese fishing boat off Formosa.

May 25

CBI: Tenth Air Force B-17s bomb Japanese logistics facilities at Rangoon, Burma.

CARIBBEAN: U.S. destroyer is torpedoed by German submarine *U-156* off the island of Martinique. U.S. freighter is sunk by German submarine *U-103* in the Gulf of Mexico.

SOUTHWEST PACIFIC AREA: Fifth Air Force B-17s bomb Rabaul.

U.S. submarine *Permit* damages a Japanese transport in the Makassar Strait.

PACIFIC: U.S. submarine *Tautog* sinks Japanese transport off the Caroline Islands; U.S. submarine *Pompano* sinks Japanese tanker off Okinawa; U.S. submarine *Drum* sinks a Japanese cargo ship off Honshu, Japan.

May 26

CARIBBEAN: German submarine *U-106* torpedoes and sinks one U.S. freighter and conducts an unsuccessful surface attack on another freighter in the Gulf of Mexico. The *U-106's* commander is reported to purposely kill survivors attempting to escape in a lifeboat.

ATLANTIC: U.S. and British air commanders meet to decide on allocation of assets against targets in Germany. Convoy PQ 16 on its way to Murmansk is attacked by German submarine *U-703*, which sinks a U.S. freighter.

PACIFIC: Reinforcements arrive at Midway, delivered by USS *Kittyhawk*. U.S. submarine *Salmon* sinks a Japanese repair ship off the coast of Indochina.

May 27

CARIBBEAN: A U.S. freighter is torpedoed and sunk by German submarine *U-502*.

ATLANTIC: German bombers attack convoy PQ 16 on its way to Murmansk, sinking three U.S. freighters and damaging one.

SOUTHWEST PACIFIC AREA: Fifth Air Force B-17s attack Rabaul.

PACIFIC: The Japanese carrier strike group leaves Japan for Midway. The Americal Division under General Alexander M. Patch is activated in New Caledonia. (Americal is an amalgamation of the words "America" and "Caledonia.") Under orders from Admiral Nimitz, Rear Admiral Robert A. Theobald organizes Task Force 8 to defend the Aleutians. It is composed of surface and air strike groups. Theobald believes Dutch Harbor is the Japanese objective, despite information from Nimitz's headquarters that the islands of Attu and Kiska are the targets of the Japanese invasion fleet.

May 28

CARIBBEAN: A U.S. tanker is torpedoed and sunk by German submarine *U-103*.

SOUTHWEST PACIFIC AREA: U.S. submarine *Salmon* sinks a Japanese freighter off the coast of Indochina; U.S. submarine *Seal* damages a Japanese cargo ship near Balbac Strait. Fifth Air Force B-26 Marauders attack Lae.

PACIFIC: The main body of the Japanese strike force leaves Japan for Midway. Rear Admiral Raymond A. Spruance's Task Force 16, with the carriers USS *Enterprise* and USS *Hornet*, leaves for Midway from Pearl Harbor. About 500 army soldiers are moved from Efate to occupy Espiritu Santo Island in the New Hebrides to build an airstrip large enough to accommodate bombers for future support of a planned offensive against the Solomons. Swampy ground and an outbreak of malaria delay construction. Admiral Nimitz, CinCPOA, rejects MacArthur's proposal to use his carriers to support an offensive against Rabaul. Instead, Nimitz offers to capture Tulagi with a marine Raider battalion.

May 29

ATLANTIC: Vyacheslav Molotov, Soviet commissar for foreign affairs, arrives in Washington, D.C., to meet with President Roosevelt. Molotov had been in London earlier arranging details of an Anglo-Soviet mutual support treaty. He is now in

Washington to push Roosevelt for a second front against the Germans in Europe in 1942.
SOUTHWEST PACIFIC AREA: U.S. submarine *Swordfish* sinks a Japanese cargo ship near Balbac Strait.

May 30

CBI: Tenth Air Force B-17s attack Myitkyina airfields, but find no activity there.
ATLANTIC: U.S. freighter is sunk by German submarine *U-404* off the East Coast. General Arnold, in a conference with British planners in London, announces that the USAAF will have 66 combat groups in the United Kingdom by March of 1943.
PACIFIC: Rear Admiral Frank Jack Fletcher's Task Force 17, with the carrier USS *Yorktown,* leaves Pearl Harbor for Midway. U.S. submarine *Pompano* sinks a Japanese transport off Okinawa.

May 31

SOUTHWEST PACIFIC AREA: Three Japanese midget submarines from submarines *I-22, I-24,* and *I-27* enter the harbor at Sidney, Australia, sinking one Australian naval vessel and severely damaging a Dutch submarine. The three midget submarines are destroyed.

   Fifth Air Force B-17s attack Lae and Salamaua in New Guinea.
PACIFIC: U.S. submarine *Pollack* sinks a Japanese submarine chaser off the southern coast of Japan.

June 1

CARIBBEAN: German submarines *U-106* and *U-158* each torpedo and sink a U.S. freighter off the coast of Mexico.
ATLANTIC: A U.S. freighter is torpedoed and sunk by German submarine *U-404* off the coast of North Carolina; a U.S. freighter is torpedoed and sunk by German submarine *U-172* off the East Coast.

June 2

CARIBBEAN: A U.S. freighter is torpedoed and sunk by German submarine *U-159* off Puerto Rico.
PACIFIC: Admiral Frank Jack Fletcher's Task Force 17 and Admiral Raymond Spruance's Task Force 16 rendezvous northeast of Midway. Fletcher is the senior officer. U.S. naval forces consist of three carriers, seven heavy cruisers, 16 destroyers, oilers, and a light cruiser. The U.S. task force is screened by 25 submarines surrounding Midway. Fifth Air Force bombers attack Rabaul.

June 3

ALEUTIANS: Japanese carriers from the second strike force make a surprise raid on Dutch Harbor in the Aleutians, killing 52 Americans. The base is moderately damaged in the attacks. A counterstrike by nine P-40s and six B-26 Marauders fails to locate the Japanese fleet. According to the Japanese plan, this attack is intended as a diversion to confuse the Americans about Japanese intentions and divert forces away from Midway.

ATLANTIC: A U.S. tanker is torpedoed and sunk by German submarine *U-502* off the Florida coast.

PACIFIC: The Battle of Midway. Unknown to the Japanese, American code breakers have provided Nimitz with the true Japanese operational objective—Midway. A Japanese occupation force of four heavy cruisers, two destroyers, and transport ships carrying 5,000 men is located 600 miles from Midway. B-17 bombers sent to attack the fleet cause no damage. The American task forces change course to approach the Japanese.

June 4

ALEUTIANS: A second Japanese raid on Dutch Harbor in the Aleutians is met by P-40 fighters. Two B-17s and eight B-26 Marauders attack the Japanese fleet, but miss their targets.

CARIBBEAN: A U.S. freighter is torpedoed and sunk by German submarine *U-158* off Mexico.

PACIFIC: The Battle of Midway. U.S. aircraft sink a Japanese tanker. The Japanese send 108 planes from their carrier strike group to attack Midway, causing extensive damage. Seventeen of 26 Marine F2A Brewster Buffalo and F4F Wildcat fighters are lost. A U.S. counterstrike of six Avengers and four B-26 Marauder bombers against the Japanese carriers fails; only one Avenger and two B-26s return to Midway. B-17 bombers are also employed, but cause no damage to the fleet. Carrier aircraft from USS *Enterprise* and USS *Hornet* take off to locate the Japanese carriers, followed shortly after by USS *Yorktown*'s aircraft. *Hornet*'s 15 TBD torpedo planes are all destroyed in making their attack; the *Enterprise*'s 14 TBD torpedo planes have no effect, and 10 are lost. At this time the *Yorktown* and *Enterprise*'s SBD Dauntless dive-bombers locate the Japanese carriers and conduct an attack, catching the Japanese by surprise. Two carriers, the *Kaga* and the *Akagi,* are hit. The *Kaga* later sinks. The third Japanese carrier, *Soryu,* is attacked by the *Yorktown*'s SBDs and TBD torpedo planes and is sunk. Meanwhile, Japanese planes from *Hiryu* locate the *Yorktown*. Hit with bombs and torpedoes, the ship is abandoned with the intention to tow it back to Pearl Harbor. Aircraft from the *Hornet* and *Enterprise* locate the *Hiryu*, and heavily damage it.

June 5

ALEUTIANS: Japanese forces occupy Attu Island in the Aleutians. Dutch Harbor is attacked by Japanese carrier aircraft.

CARIBBEAN: A U.S. tanker is torpedoed and sunk by German submarine *U-68.*

The Japanese carrier *Hiryu* attempts to avoid American air attack during the Battle of Midway, June 4, 1942. Antiaircraft bursts are visible at top left. The air attack fatally damages the carrier and on the following day she is abandoned and sunk.

TBD-1 Devastator torpedo bombers on the deck of USS *Enterprise* at the opening stages of the Battle of Midway. These planes will contribute to the destruction of four Japanese aircraft carriers and a cruiser. Most of the planes and their pilots will not return.

ATLANTIC: The U.S. Congress declares war on Bulgaria, Hungary, and Romania.
PACIFIC: The Battle of Midway. The carriers *Akagi* and *Hiryu*, now useless hulks, are sunk by Japanese destroyers. Two Japanese cruisers collide while trying to avoid the U.S. submarine *Tambor*.

June 6

PACIFIC: The Battle of Midway. The cruiser *Mikuma* is sunk by SBD Dauntless dive-bombers from USS *Enterprise* and USS *Hornet*. The carrier USS *Yorktown* and the destroyer USS *Hammann* are simultaneously torpedoed by Japanese submarine *I-168*. *Hammann* sinks, but the *Yorktown* stays afloat.

Midway will be the strategic turning point in the war in the Pacific. With the loss of four carriers and their 322 planes and pilots, the Japanese can no longer mount large-scale offensive operations. U.S. losses are 147 aircraft. The Japanese high command will continue its strategy of establishing a defensive perimeter by establishing control of New Guinea, using the southern Solomons as a base of support.

June 7

ALEUTIANS: Japanese forces land on Kiska Island.
CARIBBEAN: German submarines *U-159* and *U-107* each torpedo and sink a U.S. freighter.
PACIFIC: The carrier USS *Yorktown* sinks after efforts to save it fail.

June 8

CARIBBEAN: A U.S. tanker is torpedoed and sunk by German submarine *U-50*.

The crew of the carrier USS *Yorktown* fights to save their ship. She was hit by three bombs from Japanese aircraft of the carrier *Hiryu*. On June 4, 1942, the *Yorktown* was abandoned and later sank.

ATLANTIC: The European Theater of Operations, United States Army (ETOUSA), is established.

SOUTHWEST PACIFIC AREA: General MacArthur again argues with Army Chief of Staff George C. Marshall for an offensive, directed at New Britain and New Ireland. To support this offensive, he requires amphibious-capable forces and aircraft carriers to provide air support. The three divisions he has available, the Australian 7th Division and the 41st and 32nd U.S. Infantry Divisions are not trained to conduct the kind of amphibious assaults MacArthur has in mind.

June 9
CARIBBEAN: A U.S. freighter is torpedoed and sunk by German submarine *U-107* off the coast of Honduras.

June 10
CARIBBEAN: A U.S. tanker is torpedoed and sunk by German submarine *U-157* off the coast of Cuba.

June 11
ATLANTIC: German submarine *U-87* lays mines off Boston harbor; *U-373* lays mines at the mouth of Delaware Bay.

June 12
ALEUTIANS: Eleventh Air Force B-24 Liberators attack Kiska, damaging a Japanese destroyer.

CARIBBEAN: A U.S. tanker is sunk by German submarine *U-158* in the Gulf of Mexico; *U-159* sinks a U.S. steamship off the coast of Panama.

ATLANTIC: General Marshall meets with Admiral King to discuss options for a Pacific offensive. Marshall is inclined to support MacArthur's plan, presented on June 8, noting that the 1st Marine Division could be available in Australia in early July. The Australian and U.S. divisions available could be used as follow-on forces to clear the objectives once a beachhead is established. Nearly 150 heavy and light bombers will be available, as well as 371 fighter aircraft to provide air support. Lae and Salamaua in New Guinea are within range of these land-based aircraft, but attacking Rabaul with the land-based bombers would require aircraft carriers to provide the long-range air support.

German submarine *U-701* lays mines off Cape Henry, Virginia.

MIDDLE EAST: A detachment of 13 B-24 Liberators under command of Colonel Harry Halverson and en route to China, takes off from Fayid, Egypt, and attacks the oil fields at Ploeşti, Romania. The attack causes little damage, but it is the first American airstrike from the European-African-Middle East (EAME) Theater.

SOUTHWEST PACIFIC AREA: U.S. submarine *Swordfish* sinks Japanese freighter in the Gulf of Siam. Fifth Air Force B-17s attack Rabaul.

June 13
CARIBBEAN: A U.S. Coast Guard cutter sinks *U-157* off the coast of Cuba. *U-159* sinks U.S. freighter near the Panama Canal.

ATLANTIC: German submarine *U-584* puts four agents ashore at Amagansett, Long Island. A Coast Guard patrol spots the activity.

President Roosevelt signs an executive order creating the Office of War Information under Elmer Davis to deal with dissemination of information both within the United States and in all foreign countries. The Office of Coordinator of Information is redesignated as the Office of Strategic Services under the Joint Chiefs of Staff. The Office of Strategic Services has the following functions: collect and analyze strategic information and plan and operate special services. William J. Donovan is appointed director.

June 14
ALEUTIANS: Eleventh Air Force B-17s and B-24 Liberators hit two Japanese cruisers at Kiska.

CARIBBEAN: German submarines *U-172* and *U-161* each sink a U.S. merchant ship near the Canal Zone.

PACIFIC: The first elements of the 1st Marine Division arrive at Wellington, New Zealand.

June 15
CARIBBEAN: A U.S. freighter is torpedoed and sunk by German submarine *U-502* off Trinidad; *U-502* and *U-126* each sink a U.S. freighter.
ATLANTIC: Two U.S. tankers in convoy KN 109 (Key West to Norfolk) leaving the Chesapeake Bay strike mines laid by German submarine *U-701*. A U.S. tanker in convoy XB 25 (Halifax to Boston) hits a mine outside of Boston harbor laid by German submarine *U-87*.
PHILIPPINES: U.S. submarine *Seawolf* sinks Japanese gunboat off Corregidor.

June 16
CARIBBEAN: A U.S. freighter is torpedoed and sunk by German submarine *U-126* after it has completed rescuing survivors from a freighter sunk by *U-161* on June 14.

June 17
CARIBBEAN: A U.S. freighter is torpedoed and sunk by German submarine *U-129* near Cuba.
ATLANTIC: German submarine *U-202* puts four agents ashore at Ponte Vedra Beach, Florida, but the landing is compromised when American fisherman come upon them. A U.S. collier in convoy KS 511 (Norfolk to Key West) near the Chesapeake Bay hits a mine laid by *U-701*.

June 18
ALEUTIANS: Eleventh Air Force bombers attack Kiska, sinking a Japanese tanker.
ATLANTIC: British prime minister Winston Churchill arrives in Washington to meet with President Roosevelt to discuss assistance to China, war production, and a second front in Europe. In London, Lieutenant General Carl Spaatz takes command of the U.S. Eighth Air Force. A U.S. freighter is torpedoed and sunk by German submarine *U-124*.

June 19
ATLANTIC: A U.S. patrol vessel is torpedoed and sunk by German submarine *U-701* off Cape Hatteras, North Carolina.
MIDDLE EAST: Headquarters, U.S. Army Forces in the Middle East (USAFIME), is established in Cairo, Egypt. General Russel L. Maxwell assumes command.
PACIFIC: Vice Admiral Robert L. Ghormley takes command of the South Pacific Area and the South Pacific Force, with headquarters in Auckland, New Zealand.
   Fifth Air Force B-17s attack Rabaul.

June 20
CARIBBEAN: A U.S. freighter is torpedoed and sunk by German submarine *U-128* off Barbados.
ATLANTIC: Roosevelt and Churchill in private session agree upon a combined invasion of North Africa.
   General Marshall provides incoming commander of the European Theater of Operations (ETOUSA), Major General Dwight D. Eisenhower, with strategic guidance for the employment of Army Air Forces in the ETO. The objective is air superiority over the European continent in support of an eventual invasion.

Southwest Pacific Area: Fifth Air Force B-17s bomb airstrip at Lae in New Guinea.

Pacific: Major General William H. Hale takes command of the U.S. Seventh Air Force in Hawaii. The navy still maintains operational control of army assets.

June 21
Pacific: Japanese submarine *I-25* shells Fort Stevens, Oregon. U.S. submarine *S-44* sinks Japanese gunboat off the island of Gavutu in the Solomons.

June 22
CBI: Lieutenant General Joseph W. Stilwell's command is retitled American Forces in India, China, and Burma by order of the War Department. Stilwell is charged with accomplishing U.S. political and military goals in the theater. First he must maintain the cohesion of the Chinese army of about 3.8 million men, which is divided between support for Chiang Kai-shek and the Kuomintang, local warlords, and the Communists. The Communists are fighting a guerrilla war against not only the Japanese, but the Nationalist Kuomintang as well. Stilwell is troubled that Chiang keeps his most capable units focused on the Communists, not the Japanese.

Second, Stilwell must find a way to maintain logistical support to China so that the Nationalists can continue to fight the Japanese. If China's armies collapse, the Japanese could release tens of thousands of troops to other areas on their defensive perimeter. But the Germany-first strategy in Washington puts China near the bottom of the priority list. To build the 30-division army and 500 aircraft air force that has been promised to the Chinese, Stilwell will have to provide 7,500 tons of supplies a month. At best, only 3,500 tons a month can be delivered, based on priorities and airlift available. Stilwell has only 57 transport aircraft in theater.

Caribbean: A U.S. tanker is torpedoed and sunk by German submarine *U-67* off Louisiana.

Southwest Pacific Area: Major General Robert L. Eichelberger takes command of the U.S. I Corps.

June 23
Atlantic: Lieutenant General Carl Spaatz is informed that Roundup, the plan for a cross-Channel invasion of Europe, has been postponed in favor of Torch, the combined invasion of North Africa. He is ordered to prepare to divert Eighth Air Force assets to support the new plan.

Middle East: General Brereton deploys U.S. bombers from the CBI theater to the Middle East after the German army captures Tobruk and threatens the British defense of Egypt. B-17 bombers destined for Stilwell are diverted to Khartoum, Egypt. An Iran-Iraq Service Command is established in Basra, Iraq, under USAFIME command.

June 24
Atlantic: A U.S. freighter is torpedoed and sunk by German submarine *U-404.*

ETO: Major General Dwight D. Eisenhower arrives in London to assume command of the European Theater of Operation, USA (ETOUSA).

MIDDLE EAST: U.S. B-24 Liberators support British air attacks on German positions in Benghazi, Libya.

June 25

ATLANTIC: President Roosevelt and Prime Minister Churchill conclude their meeting in Washington. They agree to a joint effort to develop an atomic weapon.

Admiral King offers an alternate plan (discussed on June 12) to General Marshall's for the Pacific offensive. King argues that Admiral Nimitz should lead an operation beginning August 1, directed against New Guinea and New Britain, with intermediate objectives in the Solomon and Santa Cruz islands. King agrees that the 1st Marine Division and at least two carriers be included in the force list. The Southwest Pacific Theater would support with both ships and land-based aircraft to augment the navy and marine units. The islands captured would be occupied by MacArthur's infantry divisions. MacArthur would support the offensive with diversionary attacks against the island of Timor in the Netherlands East Indies. General Marshall argues that King's plans for an offensive in the Solomons, which lie in the Southwest Pacific, should be under General MacArthur's command as CinCSWPA. King, desiring an offensive to begin as quickly as possible, does not want to be troubled by arbitrary lines that divide up the geography. He asserts that Nimitz as CinCPac be designated commander for the operation.

A Norwegian freighter is damaged by a torpedo from German submarine *U-701* off Cape Hatteras, North Carolina.

PACIFIC: Admiral King, CominCh, orders CinCPac (Admiral Nimitz) and Com-SOPAC (Admiral Ghormley) to prepare for offensive operations in the southern Solomons. The initial objectives were to be Santa Cruz and Tulagi Islands. Marines are to be the ground forces involved, with army forces in Australia acting as follow-on forces. D-day for the operation is set for August 1. Nimitz notifies Admiral Ghormley, commander of the South Pacific Area to begin preparations.

U.S. submarine *Nautilus* sinks a Japanese destroyer off the coast of Japan near Yakosuka. U.S. submarine *Grouper* sinks Japanese oiler near the Ryukyus.

June 26

ATLANTIC: Germany announces unrestricted submarine warfare will be conducted along the Atlantic coast of the United States.

CBI: Brigadier General Earl L. Naiden takes command of the Tenth Air Force, replacing General Brereton who departs for the Middle East.

PACIFIC: Major General Alexander A. Vandegrift, commander of the 1st Marine Division, receives the warning order for the Solomons offensive from CinCPac.

June 27

ATLANTIC: German agents who landed at Long Island and in Florida are captured by the FBI before undertaking any operational activities. A total of eight are arrested; six are later tried and executed.

Two U.S. freighters are sunk by German submarines *U-128* and *U-153* off the Atlantic coast. Convoy PQ 17 leaves Iceland for Archangel, USSR with 33 ships, four cruisers, and six destroyers.

MIDDLE EAST: U.S. B-24 Liberators attack the harbor at Tobruk, Libya, to disrupt German resupply efforts.

PACIFIC: Plans for Operation TULSA I, the campaign against the Japanese-held areas on New Britain, New Ireland, and in the Admiralty Islands, are completed.

U.S. submarine *Nautilus* sinks Japanese minesweeper off the coast of Japan.

June 28

ATLANTIC: German submarines *U-332, U-203, U-505, U-701,* and *U-153* sink a total of four U.S. freighters and a tanker off the Atlantic coast.

MIDDLE EAST: Lieutenant General Brereton assumes command of U.S. Army Middle East Air Forces (USAMEAF) with headquarters in Cairo, Egypt. All U.S. military air assets in the theater are consolidated under his command.

PACIFIC: Navy PBY Catalinas bomb Tulagi. U.S. submarine *Stingray* sinks Japanese gunboat off Yap.

June 29

CBI: Generalissimo Chiang Kai-shek demands support from the United States in a meeting with General Stilwell. Chiang requires 500 combat aircraft, three U.S. divisions, and 5,000 tons of supplies per month delivered by air from India.

ATLANTIC: German submarine *U-505* torpedoes and sinks a U.S. freighter.

SOUTHWEST PACIFIC AREA: U.S. Army engineers arrive at Milne Bay to begin work to improve a base for Australian units defending Port Moresby, New Guinea.

PACIFIC: Questions arise over which service will have overall control of the planned Pacific offensive. Admiral King proposes to the Joint Chiefs that Admiral Ghormley command the lower Solomon Islands offensive, while General MacArthur deals with the New Guinea and New Britain offensive.

June 30

CBI: The inability of Allied forces to move supplies from India over the Himalaya Mountains (known as the Hump) air route to China begins to show. The Chinese are expecting 5,000 tons a month. Only 57 aircraft are available for the airlift and only 186 tons have been delivered over the past 60 days.

ATLANTIC: German submarine *U-158* is sunk by a Navy PBM Mariner patrol bomber off Cape Hatteras, North Carolina. *U-202* torpedoes and sinks a U.S. steamship off the North Carolina coast.

MIDDLE EAST: General Brereton moves his headquarters from Cairo to Palestine as a precaution against German advances in eastern Egypt. U.S. B-24 Liberators bomb the harbor at Tobruk.

SOUTHWEST PACIFIC AREA: Fifth Air Force B-24 Liberators and B-25 Mitchells attack Japanese positions near Lae in New Guinea.

PACIFIC: U.S. submarine *Plunger* sinks Japanese freighter off the coast of China near Shanghai.

A U.S. freighter is torpedoed and sunk by Japanese submarine *I-10* off the east coast of Africa.

July 1

CBI: Chinese Air Task Force (CATF) aircraft from Tenth Air Force based in Hengyang, attack Japanese positions near Hangkow.

CARIBBEAN: A U.S. freighter is torpedoed and sunk by German submarine *U-126* off Trinidad.

MIDDLE EAST: U.S. B-24 Liberators bomb the harbor at Tobruk.

SOUTHWEST PACIFIC AREA: U.S. submarine *Sturgeon* sinks a Japanese transport ship off Luzon. The ship was carrying U.S. prisoners of war to Hainan Island. More than 1,000 Americans are killed.

PACIFIC: Major General Millard F. Harmon takes control of all army forces in South Pacific, as a subordinate command to Admiral Ghormley, ComSOPAC.

July 2

CBI: Generalissimo Chiang Kai-shek names General Stilwell the commander of Chinese armies in India. The impressive title, though, carries little authority. Chiang still maintains direct control of the Chinese forces and they will answer only to his orders.

Chinese Air Task Force (CATF) bombers attack Hangkow and cause heavy damage.

U.S. submarine *Plunger* sinks Japanese cargo ship near the mouth of the Yangtze River.

ATLANTIC: The Joint Chiefs of Staff issues a Joint Directive for Offensive Operations in the Southwest Pacific Area (SWPA). This directive represents a compromise between King and Marshall. The directive lays out instructions for an offensive to seize New Britain-New Ireland-New Guinea. The first phase of the offensive, an attack on the Santa Cruz Islands, Tulagi, and nonspecified adjacent islands in the southern Solomons will be given to the navy under Admiral Nimitz. General MacArthur is to support this attack with air and naval forces from the Southwest Pacific Theater. The second phase involves the seizure of Lae, Salamaua, and the northwest coast of New Guinea and will be given to General MacArthur. The third phase is the capture of the Japanese base at Rabaul and the bases in New Britain and New Ireland. This phase will also be led by General MacArthur. The details of the attack on Rabaul and the offensive against New Britain and New Ireland will be determined later by the Joint Chiefs. For the initial phase of the campaign, named Operation Watchtower, all of General MacArthur's air, land, and naval forces will be employed in support, as well as two aircraft carriers, the South Pacific Amphibious Force, and South Pacific Army Forces. The boundary between SWPA and Pacific Ocean Areas (POA) is moved west ever so slightly to place Tulagi, Guadalcanal, and the Florida Islands within Admiral Nimitz's Pacific Ocean Areas theater of operations. Naval task force commanders will command all amphibious operations, and the Joint Chiefs will retain the authority to withdraw the carriers to employ them elsewhere as necessary. The staffs of Nimitz and Ghormley, hard-pressed for time and resources to make the plan work, begin calling Operation Watchtower "Operation Shoestring."

July 3

ALEUTIANS: Eleventh Air Force B-24 Liberators attack and damage Japanese seaplane carriers at Agattu Island.

ATLANTIC: German submarines *U-126, U-125, U-575,* and *U-215* sink a total of one U.S. tanker and three freighters. Convoy PQ 17 headed for Murmansk is attacked by German submarines and HE-111 torpedo bombers from Norway. Two U.S. freighters are sunk and one is damaged.

SOUTHWEST PACIFIC AREA: Fifth Air Force bombers strike Lae in New Guinea and Tulagi in the Solomons.

July 4

CBI: General Claire Chennault becomes the commander of China Air Task Force (CATF), replacing his previous command, the American Volunteer Group (AVG). Chennault's new command has a B-25 Mitchell bomber and a P-40 fighter squadron. Chennault will require 2,000 tons of supplies per month, further cutting into deliveries provided to China.

ETO: The U.S. Army Air Force conducts its first raid on Europe, participating in a Royal Air Force (RAF) raid on German airfields at Haanstead and Daltonburg in the Netherlands.

MIDDLE EAST: U.S. B-24 Liberators attack an enemy convoy in the Mediterranean, damaging one tanker.

SOUTHWEST PACIFIC AREA: Fifth Air Force bombers attack Lae and Salamaua in New Guinea.

PACIFIC: U.S. submarine *Triton* sinks Japanese destroyer off Agattu Island in the Aleutians.

July 5

ALEUTIANS: U.S. submarine *Growler* sinks a Japanese destroyer and damages two others off Kiska in the Aleutians.

ATLANTIC: German submarine and air attacks on convoy PQ 17 result in the loss of three freighters. Four other freighters are so heavily damaged that they are abandoned by their crews. London orders the convoy to break up and scatter, as reports of a possible attack by German surface ships come in. The reports will turn out to be false. Convoy QP 13 accidentally hits a British minefield in the Denmark Strait. One freighter is damaged, two freighters are sunk, and two others are abandoned.

SOUTHWEST PACIFIC AREA: U.S. submarine *Sturgeon* damages a Japanese oiler off Luzon.

July 6

CBI: General Stilwell establishes the command and control structure for the China-Burma-India theater. The main headquarters is at Chungking, with liaison headquarters at New Delhi, where U.S. and Chinese forces are located, and at Kunming, where the China Air Task Force is located.

ATLANTIC: Admiral William D. Leahy, former chief of naval operations and ambassador to Vichy France, is appointed as chief of staff to the president. General Marshall has argued for several months that the president needs a personal representative to chair JCS meetings, keep track of papers sent to the White House seeking approval from the president on JCS recommendations, and to arbitrate issues that arise between the army and the navy. Leahy, unlike Marshall and King, has no command authority. The command relationship of General Marshall and Admiral King to the president directly is not changed. Leahy's role is to pass on to the Joint Chiefs the general guidance of the president on war planning and strategy, and to represent the consensus of the Joint Chiefs to the president. This command arrangement, never before seen in American history, allows for a rapid exchange of information and decisions. Under Leahy's leadership, the Joint Chiefs of Staff will be responsible for U.S. strategy in the Pacific, China, Europe, and the Mediterranean.

Convoy PQ 17, headed for Murmansk, loses two more freighters to submarine and air attacks.

CARIBBEAN: German submarine *U-153* is damaged in an air attack by U.S. Sixth Air Force bombers from Panama.

July 7

ATLANTIC: A U.S. Army Air Force A-29 Hudson maritime patrol bomber sinks German submarine *U-701* off the coast of North Carolina. Convoy PQ 17 loses two freighters to submarine attacks.

CARIBBEAN: U.S. tanker is sunk by German submarine *U-67* off the coast of Louisiana.

PACIFIC: The Marine 1st Raider Battalion embarks from New Caledonia, headed for the Solomons.

July 8

ATLANTIC: A U.S. tanker is torpedoed and damaged off the coast of Florida by German submarine *U-571*.

MIDDLE EAST: U.S. B-17s attack Tobruk, while B-24 Liberators bomb Benghazi harbor.

PACIFIC: Admiral Nimitz issues orders for Admiral Ghormley to conduct an attack to seize Tulagi Island, Santa Cruz Island, and Guadalcanal. U.S. submarine *S-37* sinks Japanese transport off Rabaul.

July 9

CARIBBEAN: A U.S. tanker is torpedoed and sunk by German submarine *U-67* off the Louisiana coast.

PACIFIC: U.S. submarine *Sailfish* sinks Japanese cargo ship off the coast of Indochina. U.S. submarine *Thresher* sinks Japanese vessel at Kwajalein Atoll.

July 10

ALEUTIANS: A Japanese Mitsubishi A6M Type 0 carrier fighter known as the Zero, which had crash-landed on Akutan Island on June 3, is discovered by a U.S. reconnaissance aircraft. It will later be recovered, restored to flying condition, and studied carefully to design new U.S. aircraft to counter the Zero's capabilities.

ATLANTIC: The Joint Chiefs of Staff refuse requests from both General MacArthur and Admiral Ghormley to postpone the planned offensive in the Solomons until additional reinforcements arrive.

July 11

MIDDLE EAST: U.S. B-24 Liberators attack Benghazi, Libya.

PACIFIC: The loss at Midway leads Japanese Imperial Headquarters strategists to shelve plans for offensive operations against New Caledonia, Fiji, and Samoa. Tulagi in the southern Solomons with its excellent harbor will become a key base for defending Rabaul. The Solomons can serve as a new base for operations against Port Moresby. Japanese planes based at Rabaul and the Solomons can provide air cover for an invasion fleet. The capture of Port Moresby would assure Australia's isolation and allow the Japanese to control the Bismarck Sea and the approaches to Rabaul.

July 12
ATLANTIC: German submarines *U-84* and *U-129* each torpedo and sink a U.S. freighter.
PACIFIC: U.S. submarine *Seadragon* sinks Japanese freighter off the coast of Indochina.

July 13
ATLANTIC: President Roosevelt sends trusted adviser Harry Hopkins to London to obtain a final answer on offensive action in Europe in 1942. The president's instructions to Hopkins are clear: "Under any circumstances I wish Bolero and Roundup to remain an essential objective, even though it must be interrupted."
CARIBBEAN: German submarine *U-153* is sunk by a U.S. destroyer, supported by a subchaser and USAAF aircraft near Panama. *U-166* sinks a U.S. freighter off Cuba; *U-67* sinks a U.S. tanker off the Louisiana coast.
MIDDLE EAST: U.S. B-17s attack Tobruk, while B-24 Liberators attack Benghazi.
SOUTHWEST PACIFIC AREA: TULSA II, the plan by General Headquarters, Southwest Pacific Area, for operations directed at the capture of Rabaul, is completed. Major General George C. Kenney takes command of Fifth Air Force.
PACIFIC: U.S. submarine *Seadragon* sinks a Japanese auxiliary vessel off the coast of Indochina.

July 14
PACIFIC: Major General Millard F. Harmon assumes command of U.S. Army Forces in South Pacific (COMGENSOPAC). Japanese submarine *I-7* sinks a U.S. freighter off the Pacific coast of the United States. The submarine uses machine guns to sink the freighter's lifeboats.

July 15
ATLANTIC: German submarine *U-576* torpedoes three freighters off the coast of North Carolina. The submarine is attacked and sunk by a navy OS2U Kingfisher aircraft. *U-571* damages a U.S. tanker off Key West, Florida.

July 15
PACIFIC: Elements of the 4th Marine Defense Battalion move to Espiritu Santo Island from Efate and establish a heavy antiaircraft and automatic weapons battery.

July 16
CBI: CATF (China Air Task Force) bombers attack Hangkow.

CARIBBEAN: German submarine *U-166* torpedoes and sinks a U.S. fishing boat off Cuba.

ATLANTIC: German submarine *U-161* attacks convoy AS 4 headed for the Persian Gulf, sinking one U.S. steamship.

PACIFIC: Admiral Ghormley issues his operation plan for Watchtower. Task Force 61 commander, Vice Admiral Frank J. Fletcher, has the carriers USS *Saratoga, Wasp,* and USS *Enterprise* and the battleship USS *North Carolina,* along with six cruisers, 16 destroyers, and three oilers. Rear Admiral Richmond K. Turner commands amphibious shipping; Rear Admiral Leigh Noyes commands the air support force, and Task Force 63, under command of Rear Admiral John S. McCain, represents all the land-based air forces in the South Pacific.

U.S. submarine *Seadragon* sinks a Japanese freighter off the coast of Indochina.

July 17

ETO: Admiral King, General Marshall, and President Roosevelt's close adviser Harry Hopkins arrive in London to convince the British to support Sledgehammer, the cross-Channel invasion plan.

MIDDLE EAST: B-17s attack Tobruk and B-24 Liberators attack Benghazi, Libya, to disrupt German lines of supply.

July 18

PACIFIC: Rear Admiral Richmond Kelly Turner reports to Admiral Ghormley as commander of the amphibious force for Operation Watchtower. Ghormley has overall command of the operation, but Major General Alexander A. Vandegrift, Commander of the First Marine Division, is under Turner's command. Admiral Fletcher, although designated the joint expeditionary force commander, is in practice the naval force commander, largely providing air support to the marines.

July 19

CBI: General Stilwell proposes to Generalissimo Chiang Kai-shek that the most rapid way to bring sufficient aid to China is to retake Burma from the Japanese. U.S. B-25 Mitchells support a Chinese army attack on Linchwan, forcing Japanese forces out of the city.

ATLANTIC: As the result of improved U.S. convoy operations, Admiral Karl Dönitz orders German submarines *U-89, U-132, U-402, U-458,* and *U-754* away from the Atlantic coast to pursue more vulnerable targets.

PACIFIC: A Japanese force of 1,800 men leaves Rabaul for Buna, New Guinea.

July 20

CBI: B-25 Mitchells and P-40s attack Japanese supply lines on the Yangtze River.

ATLANTIC: Admiral William D. Leahy assumes his duties as chairman of the Joint Chiefs of Staff.

July 21

ATLANTIC: A U.S. freighter in convoy TAW (Trinidad to Aruba to Key West) is torpedoed by German submarine *U-84* in the Straits of Florida. The ship is recovered and later repaired.

ETO: Major General Eisenhower, CG ETOUSA, issues instructions to Eighth Air Force, requiring that the Allies have air domination over Europe no later than April 1, 1943.

SOUTHWEST PACIFIC AREA: Fifth Air Force B-26 Marauders attack Japanese convoy approaching Buna, New Guinea. Japanese forces land near Gona, New Guinea.

PACIFIC: B-17s attached to ComSOPAC arrive from Hawaii. U.S. freighter is sunk by Japanese submarine *I-11* in the South Pacific.

July 22

ATLANTIC: An unarmed U.S. freighter is torpedoed and sunk by German submarine *U-582* off the west coast of Africa.

ETO: British planners reject U.S. proposal for Sledgehammer.

July 22

NEW GUINEA: Because of the lack of sufficient air cover due to the loss of aircraft carriers after the Battle of Midway, the Japanese land ground forces at Buna in northeast New Guinea with the intention of conducting an overland campaign to capture Port Moresby.

MIDDLE EAST: U.S. Army Middle East Air Force (USAMEAF) B-17s and B-24s attack supply ships and bomb Tobruk.

SOUTHWEST PACIFIC AREA: Japanese forces expand their lodgment in New Guinea, reaching Buna, and advance past Giruwa, headed for Port Moresby. Fifth Air Force B-17s, B-25 Mitchells, and B-26 Marauders attack Japanese shipping off Buna, New Guinea, damaging a destroyer and sinking a cargo ship.

A U.S. freighter is torpedoed by Japanese submarine *I-24* off the coast of Australia.

PACIFIC: Task Force 61, with 1st Marine Division embarked, leaves Wellington, New Zealand.

July 23

CARIBBEAN: A U.S. freighter is torpedoed and sunk by German submarine *U-129* off Cuba.

MIDDLE EAST: U.S. Army Middle East Air Force (USAMEAF) is reinforced by 98th Bomb Group, deployed to Palestine.

SOUTHWEST PACIFIC AREA: Fifth Air Force fighters and bombers attack Japanese troops assembling near Buna and Gona. Salamaua harbor is also attacked.

July 24

ETO: U.S. Joint Chiefs redesignate certain bomber assets for Operation Torch and send orders deploying 15 combat groups from the ETO to the Pacific.

MIDDLE EAST: U.S. Army Middle East Air Force (USAMEAF) B-17s and B-24s attack Tobruk harbor and Benghazi harbor.

PACIFIC: U.S. submarine *Narwhal* sinks a Japanese guardboat and two cargo ships off the coast of Japan.

July 25

ATLANTIC: The Combined Chiefs of Staff establishes the command relationships for the U.S.-British invasion of North Africa. The operation, originally called Gymnast, is renamed Torch.

July 27

CARIBBEAN: German submarine *U-166* mines the waters off the Mississippi River delta.

ATLANTIC: A U.S. freighter is torpedoed and damaged by German submarine *U-582* off the west coast of Africa. The Germans use demolition charges to sink the ship after the crew escapes.

SOUTHWEST PACIFIC AREA: Fifth Air Force B-26 Marauders damage a Japanese transport off Buna, New Guinea.

PACIFIC: U.S. submarine *Spearfish* damages a Japanese submarine depot ship east of Cam Ranh Bay, Indochina.

July 28

ATLANTIC: A U.S. fishing trawler is shelled and sunk by German submarine *U-754* off Nova Scotia. Convoy PQ 17, arrives at the port of Molotovsk, USSR, with only 11 ships, losing 24 ships in transit—the greatest convoy disaster of the war.

Admiral William D. Leahy, as chairman of the U.S. Joint Chiefs of Staff, attends the meeting of the Combined Chiefs of Staff. The Joint Chiefs of Staff and the British Chiefs of Staff functioning as the Combined Chiefs of Staff also must plan Allied strategy in Europe, North Africa, and the Far East.

PACIFIC: Japanese Imperial General Headquarters orders that Port Moresby and Milne Bay be captured as part of the strategy to isolate Australia and threaten U.S. lines of supply in the Pacific. The airfield at Espiritu Santo on the New Hebrides becomes operational.

July 29

SOUTHWEST PACIFIC AREA: Japanese forces consolidate gains in New Guinea after pushing Australian defenders back from Kokoda. Fifth Air Force A-24 Banshees and P-39 Airacobras attack Japanese shipping off Gona.

July 30

CBI: Tenth Air Force P-40s defend CATF (China Air Task Force) airbase at Hengyang from heavy Japanese air attack. The Japanese lose 17 aircraft; three P-40s are lost in the day and night engagements.

ATLANTIC: German submarine *U-166* attacks convoy TAW 7 (Trinidad to Aruba to Key West) near the mouth of the Mississippi River, and sinks a U.S. passenger ship. A U.S. freighter is sunk by German submarine *U-155* near Barbados.

President Roosevelt signs a bill creating "Women Accepted for Volunteer Emergency Service" or WAVES. Lieutenant Commander Mildred H. McAfee is commissioned in the Naval Reserve, the first female line officer in navy history, as director of the WAVES. Within one year 27,000 women would be serving in a variety of maintenance, medical, support, intelligence, and communications positions.

July 31

ALEUTIANS: U.S. submarine *Grunion* torpedoes a Japanese transport off Kiska in the Aleutians, but the transport sinks *Grunion* with gunfire.

ATLANTIC: German submarine *U-751* lays mines off Charleston, South Carolina.

In the first seven months of 1942, 12 U-boats off the Atlantic coast of the United States have sunk 681 ships, nearly 3.5 million tons, representing 73 percent of all Allied and neutral shipping losses since January.

PACIFIC: U.S. submarine *Grenadier* torpedoes a Japanese tanker off Truk. B-17s of the 11th Bomb Group arrive at Espiritu Santo as part of SOPAC's air component.

SOUTH PACIFIC: 11th Bomb Group B-17s from SOPAC attack the airstrip at Guadalcanal and bomb Lunga Point. Rear Admiral John S. McCain's Task Force 63 departs from the Fiji islands, where it has been rehearsing for the Solomons landings.

August 1

CBI: Generalissimo Chiang Kai-shek approves General Stilwell's recommendation for an offensive against Burma, and modifies his previous support requirements from June 29. The offensive will require about 20 Chinese divisions, including two in India and 15 in Yunnan province. The divisions in India will be trained and led by Stilwell at the U.S. base in Ramgarh. Chiang, still unhappy that U.S. advisers and Lend-Lease supplies are slow in arriving, seeks greater concessions from the Americans. He demands a U.S. infantry division, 500 aircraft for the Chinese air force, and an additional 5,000 tons of supplies airlifted over the Hump. Chiang is reluctant to provide Chinese forces in Burma. An Allied victory in Burma would lead to the reestablishment of British colonial authority in the region. He hedges his pledge for an offensive by making impossible demands and siding with General Chennault, whose Tenth Air Force still needs 2,000 tons of supplies a month to keep flying. These demands will force Stilwell to split his resources and therefore delay any offensive in the near future.

For his part, Stilwell puts the majority of his effort toward preparing the Chinese divisions in India and trying to gain operational control of the Chinese divisions in Yunnan (known later as the Y Force).

CARIBBEAN: U.S. Coast Guard J4F bombs and sinks German submarine *U-166* in the Gulf of Mexico.

PACIFIC: U.S. submarine *Narwhal* sinks a Japanese cargo ship and an oiler off the coast of Honshu, Japan.

August 3

PACIFIC: U.S. submarine *Gudgeon* sinks a Japanese transport in the South Pacific.

August 4

CBI: U.S. P-40s attack Japanese headquarters at Linchwan, China.

MIDDLE EAST: USAMEAF B-24 Liberators bomb and damage two merchant ships in the Mediterranean.

PACIFIC: U.S. submarine *Narwhal* sinks a Japanese cargo ship off the coast of Japan.

August 5

MIDDLE EAST: General Brereton describes three major objectives for Allied air forces in the theater. The first objective is air support to ground forces fighting the Afrika

Korps. The second objective is securing the sea and air lines of communication throughout the Mediterranean. The third objective is to conduct an air offensive against Italy and the Ploeşti oil fields in Romania. If captured by German forces, Brereton designates oil fields in the Caucasus as part of the third objective.

PACIFIC: U.S. submarine *Greenling* sinks a Japanese transport and a passenger-cargo ship near Truk.

August 6

ATLANTIC: U.S. schooner is sunk by shellfire from German submarine *U-86* off Newfoundland.

PACIFIC: U.S. submarine *Tautog* sinks a Japanese army transport off Cam Ranh Bay, Indochina.

NEW GUINEA: New Guinea Force is designated, commanding all U.S. and Australian forces in Papua and northeast New Guinea. Major General Sydney F. Rowell, commanding the Australian I Corps, is designated the commander. Fifth Air Force B-24 Liberators and B-17s attack Japanese airfields at Lae and Salamaua.

August 7

ALEUTIANS: Kiska is attacked by a task force of U.S. surface ships.

PACIFIC: Operation Watchtower. Amphibious Force South Pacific (Rear Admiral Richmond K. Turner) lands task groups of the 1st Marine Division at Tulagi and Guadalcanal; the 5th Marine Regiment (without its 2nd Battalion) lands on Red Beach at Guadalcanal. Units push toward the Ilu River. Major General Alexander Vandegrift, commander of the marine landing force, orders that the airfield be captured and that a defensive line be established along the Lunga River. Marine 1st Raider Battalion and 2nd Battalion 5th Marines land on Tulagi. Marines land on Florida Island and Gavutu. Landings are supported by carrier-based aircraft (Rear Admiral Leigh Noyes) and shore-based aircraft (Rear Admiral John S. McCain). Fifth Air Force bombers attack a number of targets in support of the marine landing on Guadalcanal. U.S. submarine *Tambor* sinks a Japanese auxiliary vessel off Wotje, in the Marshall Islands.

August 8

ATLANTIC: German submarine *U-98* mines waters off Jacksonville, Florida. U.S. freighter in convoy SC 94 (Halifax Slow to United Kingdom) is torpedoed and sunk by shellfire of German submarine *U-379* in the Atlantic.

ETO: President Roosevelt and Prime Minister Churchill agree that Major General Dwight D. Eisenhower will command Operation Torch.

PACIFIC: U.S. submarine *Narwhal* sinks a Japanese crab boat off Honshu, Japan. Submarine *S-38* sinks a Japanese transport in the straits between New Britain and New Ireland. U.S. submarine *Silversides* attacks a convoy emerging from Kobe harbor, Japan, and sinks a cargo ship.

GUADALCANAL: General Vandegrift has 10,000 men on Guadalcanal and 6,075 on Tulagi. Japanese aircraft attack and sink a U.S. transport and damage a destroyer, and 21 F4F Wildcats from the carriers are lost in air combat protecting the fleet. Admiral Ghormley authorizes a request from Task Force 61's commander, Vice

Admiral Frank J. Fletcher, to withdraw until sufficient land-based air cover is available. Turner and Fletcher notify Vandegrift that the ships will leave Guadalcanal. The marines are left with 17 days' rations. Troops, supplies (including artillery), and everything else not already landed on the beaches is moved to Espiritu Santo Island. Marines cross Ilu and Lunga Rivers and encounter Japanese forces. The Guadalcanal airfield is captured and units occupy the east bank of the Lunga River.

The Battle of Savo Island. After midnight, a Japanese naval force of seven cruisers and one destroyer under Vice Admiral Mikawa Gunichi, slips past U.S. destroyers guarding the approach to the Amphibious Task Force and attacks Allied ships off Savo Island, sinking one Australian cruiser and three U.S. cruisers before returning to Rabaul. It is one of the greatest defeats in U.S. naval history.

August 9
CBI: CATF (China Air Task Force) bombers attack Haiphong harbor in French Indochina.

GUADALCANAL: Task Force 61 departs for Noumea. General Vandegrift's force is stranded without air or naval support. Tulagi Island and Tanambogo, near Tulagi, are secured by the marines. Gavutu Island is secured, along with several smaller surrounding islands. A U.S. destroyer, damaged the day before, is sunk by Japanese torpedo planes.

August 10
ALEUTIANS: Eleventh Air Force B-17s and B-24 Liberators attack Kiska; one B-24 is lost.

PACIFIC: U.S. submarine *S-44* sinks a Japanese heavy cruiser near Kavieng, New Ireland. This is the first major warship sunk by a U.S. submarine.

August 11
MIDDLE EAST: Persian Gulf Service Command (PGSC) is established, replacing the Iran-Iraq Service Command. PGSC is under command of U.S. Army Forces in the Middle East (USAFIME).

GUADALCANAL: Admiral Ghormley orders Task Force 63 to provide logistics support to the marines on Guadalcanal. U.S. logistics base is established at Port Moresby by U.S. Army Service of Supply (USASOS).

August 12
ETO: U.S. 31st Fighter Group is declared fully operational. The Royal Air Force (RAF) retains operational control of the unit.

August 13
ATLANTIC: U.S. tanker is torpedoed, shelled, and sunk by German submarine *U-171* off the Texas coast; *U-171* sinks a U.S. freighter later the same day. U.S. freighter in convoy TAW 12 (Trinidad to Aruba to Key West) is torpedoed and sunk by German submarine *U-600*.

PACIFIC: Japanese Imperial General Headquarters orders the Seventeenth Army to conduct offensive operations to defeat American forces on Guadalcanal.

NEW GUINEA: Japanese convoy with 3,000 reinforcements arrives near Gona.

August 14

ATLANTIC: A U.S. freighter is torpedoed, shelled, and sunk by Italian submarine *Reginaldo Giuliani.*

ETO: Lieutenant General Dwight D. Eisenhower, Commanding General, European Theater of Operations, is appointed Commander in Chief of Allied Expeditionary Forces for Operation Torch; the deputy commander is Major General Mark W. Clark. Admiral Sir Andrew B. Cunningham (RN) is appointed Allied naval commander. Brigadier General James Doolittle commands the American air forces, and Air Marshal Sir William Welsh will command the British air forces. The Combined Chiefs of Staff issues a directive to Eisenhower for Allied forces to establish lodgments in Oran-Algiers-Tunis with the intent of gaining control of French Morocco, Algeria, and Tunisia. Allied forces are to ensure the annihilation of Axis forces in order to conduct air and sea operations against Axis installations in the Mediterranean, open lines of communication, and facilitate further operations against the Axis on the continent of Europe.

Two U.S. fighters shoot down a German fighter off the coast of Iceland. This is the first aerial victory by U.S. pilots in the ETO.

August 15

ATLANTIC: U.S. freighter in convoy SC 95 (Halifax Slow to United Kingdom) is torpedoed and sunk by German submarine *U-705* southeast of Iceland.

August 17

CBI: Major General Clayton Bissell is designated as commander of Tenth Air Force.

CARIBBEAN: U.S. tanker is torpedoed and sunk by German submarine *U-108* off Dutch Guiana. Convoy TAW 13 (Trinidad to Aruba to Key West) comes under attack from German submarine *U-553.* A Swedish merchantman, a British freighter, and a U.S. freighter are torpedoed and sunk south of Cuba.

ETO: Eighth Air Force B-17s, escorted by British fighters, attack the marshaling yard at Rouen-Sotteville. A German fighter is downed by a B-17 gunner—the first aerial kill on a bombing run over Europe.

PACIFIC: Two companies of the Marine 2nd Raider Battalion, transported in submarines *Nautilus* and *Argonaut,* conduct a raid on Makin Atoll in the Gilbert Islands. The *Nautilus* provides gunfire support for the raid, intended to divert the Japanese from Guadalcanal and gather intelligence. The Japanese garrison of 83 men is eliminated in the attack. The Raiders suffer 30 casualties.

U.S. submarine *Gudgeon* damages two Japanese oilers near Truk.

August 18

CARIBBEAN: Convoy TAW (Trinidad to Aruba to Key West), with 15 ships escorted by a U.S. gunboat, a British corvette, two Coast Guard cutters, and four submarine chasers, is attacked by German submarine *U-162,* which torpedoes U.S. freighter off Grenada.

GUADALCANAL: Japanese destroyers land 900 reinforcements at Taivu Point on Guadalcanal. Colonel Ichiki Kiyanao commands this group, the advance element of 1,500 more soldiers from the 28th Regiment. The captured airfield at Guadalcanal is ready to receive aircraft. It is called Henderson Field in honor of Major Lofton Henderson, a marine pilot shot down while leading an attack on the Japanese carrier *Hiryu* during the Battle of Midway.

NEW GUINEA: Reinforcements bring Japanese forces to over 11,400 army and naval troops in New Guinea. The Japanese begin an advance along the Kokoda-Buna trail.

August 19

CARIBBEAN: German submarine *U-162* attacks the TAW convoy again, torpedoing a U.S. freighter and causing it to be abandoned. German submarine *U-564* later attacks the convoy, torpedoing and sinking a British tanker and a freighter.

ETO: A Canadian and British landing force conducts a raid on Dieppe. Eighth Air Force B-17s bomb Abbeville/Drucat airfield to create a diversion for the Allied raid on Dieppe. The raid itself is a disastrous failure. The first American soldier to die in occupied Europe is a member of the 50-man Ranger unit that accompanies the Allied force.

GUADALCANAL: Marines conduct company-sized patrols to clear coastal villages; one company of marines ambushes a 34-man detachment of recently landed Japanese soldiers near Taivu Point. A Japanese convoy with 1,500 reinforcements leaves Rabaul for Guadalcanal. Fifth Air Force B-17s, flying from Espiritu Santo, bomb Japanese destroyers off Guadalcanal, damaging one off Tulagi.

August 20

ATLANTIC: U.S. Navy PBY-5A sinks German submarine *U-464* in the North Atlantic. Twelfth Air Force is activated at Bolling Field.

ETO: Eighth Air Force bombers attack marshaling yard at Amiens.

GUADALCANAL: Henderson Field is home to 19 F4F-4 Wildcat fighters and 12 SBD-3 Dauntless dive-bombers of Marine Aircraft Group 23. Japanese forces prepare for an attack on Milne Bay in New Guinea.

August 21

ETO: Lieutenant General Carl Spaatz is designated as air officer for ETOUSA, ensuring that Eighth Air Force will be integrated into theater planning.

PACIFIC: U.S. submarine *Cuttlefish* damages a Japanese ammunition ship off the coast of Japan.

U.S. submarine *Tambor* sinks a Japanese collier off Ponape Island in the Carolines.

GUADALCANAL: The Battle of Tenaru. A Japanese attack across the Ilu River to capture Henderson Field is halted. Marine counteroffensive with troops and tanks surrounds the enemy force, leaving 800 killed and 15 men captured. Marine losses are 35 killed and 75 wounded. Colonel Ichiki and the survivors retreat. Taking the regimental flag, Ichiki burns it, then shoots himself.

NEW GUINEA: A Japanese convoy reaches New Guinea, unloading troops and supplies for an overland march to Port Moresby.

August 22
ATLANTIC: Brazil declares war on Germany and Italy.

August 22
CARIBBEAN: Sixth Air Force plane from the 45th Bombardment Squadron sinks German submarine *U-654* north of Panama.
PACIFIC: U.S. destroyer is torpedoed by Japanese destroyer off Guadalcanal and is scuttled; U.S. submarine *Haddock* torpedoes and sinks Japanese transport off the China coast, near Foochow.
GUADALCANAL: Five P-400 fighter aircraft from SOPAC arrive at Henderson Field on Guadalcanal. Fifth Air Force B-17s bomb Rabaul and Lae.
NEW GUINEA: P-400s arrive from the New Hebrides. Major General Cyril A. Clowes, Australian army, takes command of the combined U.S.-Australian force protecting Port Moresby. Of the nearly 9,500 men who make up the Milne force, there are nearly 1,400 Americans, most of them engineers and antiaircraft personnel.

August 23
ETO: U.S. heavy cruiser, escorted by two U.S. destroyers and a British destroyer, arrives at Murmansk, USSR, delivering men and equipment from two RAF Bomber Command squadrons transferred to the USSR.
SOUTHWEST PACIFIC AREA: U.S. submarine *Skipjack* damages a Japanese oiler southwest of Ambon, Netherlands East Indies.

August 24
ETO: Eighth Air Force bombers attack shipyards at Le Trait, France.
GUADALCANAL: The Battle of Eastern Solomons. U.S. Navy Task Force 61, under command of Vice Admiral Frank Jack Fletcher, with carriers *Enterprise* and *Saratoga*, engages a Japanese fleet east of Guadalcanal and bringing reinforcements to the island. Both carrier-based and land-based U.S. aircraft are employed. The *Enterprise* and a destroyer are damaged. The Japanese lose a carrier, a light cruiser, and a seaplane carrier before retiring to the north. Henderson Field is attacked by sea and air. Japanese aircraft attacking Henderson suffer heavy losses. The Japanese offensive in New Guinea begins. Troop transports from Rabaul move toward Milne Bay, while barges move Japanese troops from Buna along the coast.
SOUTHWEST PACIFIC AREA: U.S. submarine *Saury* torpedoes a Japanese army transport off Luzon in the Philippines.
PACIFIC: U.S. submarine *Guardfish* torpedoes and sinks a Japanese passenger-cargo ship off the coast of Honshu, Japan.
NEW GUINEA: The Japanese offensive in New Guinea begins. Troop transports from Rabaul move toward Milne Bay, while barges move Japanese troops from Buna along the coast.

August 25
SOUTHWEST PACIFIC AREA: The Japanese land 1,500 men near Milne Bay. U.S. P-40s from Milne Bay attack the Japanese barges coming from Buna, stranding the

Japanese force on two small islands. Japanese force from Rabaul lands near Rabi, New Guinea, and moves westward.

U.S. submarine *Seawolf* sinks a Japanese cargo ship off the northeast coast of Borneo.

PACIFIC: U.S. submarine *Growler* sinks a Japanese gunboat off Formosa.

GUADALCANAL: The Battle of Eastern Solomons. SOPAC B-17s from Espiritu Santo sink a Japanese destroyer off Santa Isabel, Solomons; aircraft from *Enterprise* sink a transport north of Guadalcanal. Marine SBD Dauntless dive-bombers from Henderson Field damage a light cruiser and destroyer off Guadalcanal.

August 26

CBI: Tenth Air Force B-25 Mitchells attack the rail center at Laisho, China.

PACIFIC: U.S. submarine *Haddock* sinks a Japanese merchant ship off Formosa.

SBD Dauntless dive-bombers from carrier USS *Wasp* damage Japanese submarine *I-17* in the Solomons.

NEW GUINEA: From Milne Bay and Port Moresby, Fifth Air Force B-17s, B-25 Mitchells, B-26 Marauders, and P-40s, along with Royal Australian Air Force (RAAF) Hudsons, attack beaches and transports and the Japanese landing force, damaging a transport and destroying supplies stockpiled on shore. Additional reinforcements arrive from New Ireland, and the Japanese advance against the Australian defenders. The U.S.-Australian Milne Force, consisting of three Australian infantry brigades, a U.S. engineer company, and a battery of U.S. antiaircraft artillery, defends two key airfields at Milne Bay against Japanese infantry assaults.

August 27

ALEUTIANS: Japanese begin withdrawal of units occupying Attu and redeploying them to Kiska Island.

ATLANTIC: German submarine *U-165* attacks convoy SG 6 (Sydney or St. Johns, Newfoundland to Greenland), torpedoing a U.S. oiler and a freighter. German submarine *U-517* attacks convoy SG 6F, torpedoing an army transport; 514 passengers and crew survive.

ETO: Eighth Air Force bombers attack the shipyards in Rotterdam, the Netherlands.

GUADALCANAL: Marines pursue Japanese toward Kokumbona; Henderson Field receives nine more P-400 fighters. Japanese continue advance toward Port Moresby.

August 28

CARIBBEAN: A U.S. Navy PBY Catalina and a Canadian corvette sink German submarine *U-94* in the Caribbean. German submarine *U-511* torpedoes and damages a U.S. tanker, and sinks a British and a Dutch tanker in convoy TAW 15 (Trinidad to Aruba to Key West) near Cuba.

ATLANTIC: U.S. freighter is torpedoed and sunk by German submarine *U-66.*

Eighth Air Force B-17s bomb an aircraft factory at Meaulte that repairs German fighters.

GUADALCANAL: Japanese submarine *I-123* is sunk near Guadalcanal. USMC and Navy SBD Dauntless dive-bombers bomb and sink a Japanese destroyer and damage three other destroyers bringing reinforcements to Guadalcanal, off Santa Isabel, Solomons. This nearly continuous effort to deliver men and supplies to Guadalcanal is termed "The Tokyo Express."

August 29

ETO: Eighth Air Force B-17s attack a German air base at Courtrai/Wevelghem.

NEW GUINEA: Japanese attempts to capture Airstrip No. 3 are halted by Milne Force. Fifth Air Force B-26 Marauders and P-400 Airacobras attack Buna; B-17s hit Rabaul; P-40s support ground forces at Milne Bay.

August 30

ALEUTIANS: Adak, chosen as the area for an advanced base to attack the Japanese-held island of Kiska, is occupied without opposition.

CARIBBEAN: U.S. freighter bound for Trinidad is torpedoed by German submarine *U-162* and abandoned. U.S. freighter is torpedoed and sunk by German submarine *U-66* off Trinidad.

ATLANTIC: U.S. tanker bound for Aruba fires on German submarine *U-705*; the tanker is torpedoed and sinks.

GUADALCANAL: A U.S. transport is sunk by Japanese aircraft near Guadalcanal. More than 6,000 Japanese troops land west of Lunga Point near Tasimboko.

NEW GUINEA: Japanese forces withdraw after another unsuccessful attack on Airstrip No. 3 in New Guinea.

August 31

ALEUTIANS: A U.S. destroyer and navy PBY Catalinas sink Japanese submarine *RO-61* off Atka Island.

MIDDLE EAST: USAMEAF B-24s attack Tobruk harbor; U.S. and RAF fighters provide ground support to British forces near El Alamein.

PACIFIC: U.S. submarine *Growler* sinks a Japanese merchant ship in Formosa Strait.

GUADALCANAL: U.S. carrier USS *Saratoga* is damaged by torpedo from Japanese submarine *I-26* west off Santa Cruz Islands. Marine Raider Battalion and the Marine 1st Parachute Battalion arrive from Tulagi to reinforce the Guadalcanal perimeter. Japanese destroyers put 1,000 troops ashore on Guadalcanal.

NEW GUINEA: The Australians take the offensive against Japanese in Milne Bay. U.S. P-40s support the Australians. Fifth Air Force B-26 Marauders and A-20 Havocs attack Lae airfield. B-17s bomb ammunition supplies at Buna.

September 1

ALEUTIANS: U.S. forces complete occupation of the airbase at Adak.

ATLANTIC: U.S. Navy PBY *Catalina* bombs and sinks German submarine *U-756*.

PACIFIC: Air Force, Pacific Fleet is established under command of Vice Admiral Aubrey W. Fitch.

GUADALCANAL: Guadalcanal receives 200 men from the 6th Naval Construction Battalion to improve Henderson Field. SOPAC B-17s bomb and damage a Japanese destroyer off Buka Island, Solomons. Adequately supplying the marines at Guadalcanal continues to be a problem.

September 2
PACIFIC: U.S. submarine *Guardfish* sinks Japanese cargo ship off Hokkaido, Japan.
MIDDLE EAST: USAMEAF B-24s attack Tobruk harbor; U.S. and RAF fighters provide ground support to British forces near Alam-el-Halfa.
NEW GUINEA: Japanese reinforcements from Rabaul land at Basabua.

September 3
ALEUTIANS: Two Eleventh Air Force P-38 Lightnings make a 1,260-mile round trip to attack Kiska harbor. It is the longest overwater attack flight in the war up to this time.
SOUTHWEST PACIFIC AREA: The Fifth Air Force is established in Brisbane, Australia, under the command of Lieutenant General George C. Kenney.

September 3
SOUTHWEST PACIFIC AREA: General Kenney, commander Fifth Air Force, releases the Royal Australian Air Force to defend Australian airspace.

U.S. submarine *Seal* damages Japanese merchant ship off the coast of French Indochina.

September 4
PACIFIC: U.S. submarine *Growler* sinks Japanese ammunition ship in Formosa Straits; U.S. submarine *Guardfish* sinks two merchant ships and a passenger cargo ship off Honshu; U.S. submarine *Pompano* sinks a guardboat off Honshu.
NEW GUINEA: Australian forces reach Goroni, forcing the Japanese to withdraw by transport. Japanese forces evacuate Milne Bay after taking over 600 casualties. Fifth Air Force P-40s support the Australian advance along Milne Bay toward Goroni.

September 5
ETO: After significant debate between U.S. and British planners, the Allies agree that the primary landing areas will be at Algiers and Oran in Algeria and at Casablanca in Morocco. Eighth Air Force B-17s attack the marshaling yard at Rouen-Sotteville in France.
PACIFIC: U.S. submarine *Seal* sinks a Japanese merchant ship off the coast of French Indochina.
GUADALCANAL: Two U.S. transports are sunk by Japanese destroyers off Lunga Point, Guadalcanal.
NEW GUINEA: General Eichelberger takes command of the 32nd and 41st Infantry Divisions as part of I Corps. Fifth Air Force P-400 Airacobras and A-20 Havocs attack Buna airfield. About 1,300 Japanese are evacuated from Milne Bay.

September 6
ETO: Eighth Air Force loses two B-17s in bombing raid on Meaulte aircraft plant.

September 7
PACIFIC: U.S. submarine *Growler* sinks a Japanese merchant ship near Formosa.

NEW GUINEA: Fifth Air Force A-20 Havocs and P-400 Airacobras support Australian forces defending along the Owen Stanley Range.

September 8
ETO: Lieutenant General Carl Spaatz and the RAF reach an agreement on fighter support for Eighth Air Force bombing operations. The RAF will support the U.S. daylight bombing raids, while the British will concentrate on night bombing. Spaatz orders priority of effort to be given to Torch, including the buildup of the Twelfth Air Force, which is to support Operation Torch in North Africa.

September 9
ATLANTIC: German submarine *U-755* torpedoes and sinks a U.S. Coast Guard weather ship in the Atlantic.
PACIFIC: A reconnaissance seaplane from Japanese submarine *I-25* drops incendiary bombs on a forest near Mount Emily, Oregon, in an attempt to start a forest fire. It is the first Japanese air attack on North America.

September 10
ATLANTIC: German submarine *U-69* lays mines at the mouth of Chesapeake Bay.

September 11
PACIFIC: U.S. submarine *Saury* sinks a Japanese aircraft transport in the Makassar Strait. Fifth Air Force B-17s and Royal Australian Air Force (RAAF) Hudsons sink a Japanese destroyer off Normanby Island in the D'Entrecasteaux Islands.
NEW GUINEA: Fifth Air Force A-20s and B-26 Marauders attack Japanese positions on the Owen Stanley Range.

September 12
ATLANTIC: U.S. Navy takes operational control of the Brazilian navy. A U.S. tanker fires on German submarine *U-512* but the submarine's accurate gunfire forces the crew to abandon the tanker.
ETO: Advance elements of the Twelfth Air Force arrive in Britain.
GUADALCANAL: Japanese light cruiser and three destroyers bombard Henderson Field; Japanese ground forces make a limited attack against Lieutenant Colonel Merritt A. Edson's 1st Marine Raider Battalion, defending the ridge that marks the main approach to Henderson Field from the south. It becomes known as Edson's, or more famously, Bloody Ridge.

September 13
ALEUTIANS: Eleventh Air Force B-24 Liberator bombers land at Adak.
ETO: German aerial and submarine attacks begin against convoy PQ 18, bound for Archangel, USSR; one U.S. freighter is torpedoed by German submarine *U-589* off the coast of Norway and abandoned, and two other freighters are abandoned after German torpedo planes attack.
GUADALCANAL: Colonel Merritt A. Edson's battalion, supported by the 2nd Battalion 5th Marines, defends the ridge that blocks the Japanese advance to Henderson Field. The Japanese turn back a marine counterattack on Bloody Ridge, and attack

the center and right of the marine defensive line. Major Kenneth D. Bailey, the commander of Company C, 1st Marine Raider Battalion, defends the right flank while covering the forced withdrawal of the main defensive line with protective fire. As the defensive line is reorganized, Major Bailey repeatedly leads his troops in brutal hand-to-hand combat with the enemy for nearly 10 hours. He continues fighting even though severely wounded. Although he will die of his wounds, his heroic actions allow the battalion to hold the ridge and will win him the Medal of Honor.

September 14

ALEUTIANS: Eleventh Air Force makes its first combined mission over Kiska. One B-17, 13 B-24 Liberators, 14 P-38 Lightnings, and 14 P-39 Airacobras bomb and strafe a number of targets. The Japanese lose five float planes, a flying boat, two minesweepers, and an ammunition ship. Several other vessels are damaged as well, including submarines *RO 63* and *RO 64.*

ETO: Eighth Air Force takes over the training and support for Twelfth Air Force units arriving in Britain. A U.S. freighter in a convoy bound for Archangel, USSR, is lost off the coast of Norway, and attacked by German torpedo bombers.

PACIFIC: SOPAC B-17s damage a Japanese heavy cruiser sailing from Truk to Guadalcanal.

GUADALCANAL: Marines hold Bloody Ridge against fierce Japanese assaults. The Japanese suffer over 1,200 casualties in the two-day fight. The 1st Marine Raider Battalion is no longer an effective fighting force. With over 200 casualties, only 89 men of the gallant unit are able to leave Bloody Ridge on their own two feet.

September 15

GUADALCANAL: Task Force 18, escorting 4,000 marines of the 7th Marine Regiment from Espiritu Santo to Guadalcanal, is attacked by Japanese submarine I-19. The carrier *Wasp,* the battleship *North Carolina,* and a destroyer are all damaged. The *Wasp* is later scuttled. Japanese battleships bombard U.S. positions at Guadalcanal.

NEW GUINEA: Fifth Air Force B-17s attack Rabaul. Elements of U.S. 32nd Infantry Division arrive at Port Moresby.

September 16

ALEUTIANS: Japanese complete withdrawal of forces from Attu to Kiska.

CARIBBEAN: A U.S. freighter is torpedoed and sunk by German submarine *U-558* off Trinidad.

ATLANTIC: U.S. B-24 Liberator from Ascension Island attacks three German submarines and one Italian submarine conducting rescue operations to save over a thousand Italian POWs aboard the British transport *Laconia,* torpedoed on September 12. The 3rd Marine Division is activated at Camp Elliott, California.

September 17

ATLANTIC: Chief of the Kriegsmarine Admiral Karl Dönitz issues the *Laconia* order, which no longer allows U-boats to rescue survivors of ships sunk in combat operations. A U.S. freighter is torpedoed and sunk by German submarine *U-515* north of British Guiana.

MIDDLE EAST: USAMEAF B-24s attack ports in Greece.

NEW GUINEA: Fifth Air Force P-400s, P-40s, and P-39s attack Japanese barges at Buna and Sanananda Point.

September 18

ATLANTIC: German submarine *U-455* lays mines off Charleston, South Carolina.

ETO: U.S. freighter in a convoy bound for Archangel, USSR, is lost off the coast of Norway when attacked by German torpedo bombers.

GUADALCANAL: The 7th Marine Regiment lands on Guadalcanal along with critically needed supplies.

September 19

CARIBBEAN: A U.S. freighter is torpedoed and sunk by German submarine *U-516* northeast of Barbados.

ETO: A U.S. freighter in convoy QP 14 is torpedoed and sunk by German submarine *U-225* north of Norway.

SOUTH PACIFIC: U.S. submarine *Amberjack* sinks a Japanese transport at northern entrance of Bougainville Strait.

September 20

ETO: The operational plan for Torch is finalized. It has simultaneous landings at Casablanca, Oran, and Algiers. The plan involves 370 merchant ships, 300 warships, over 400 fighters, and 107,000 troops. Three task forces are formed: a Western Task Force (35,000 men) will originate in the United States and land at Casablanca, Morocco, commanded by Major General George S. Patton, Jr. The naval commander will be Rear Admiral Henry K. Hewitt. The Central Task Force (39,000 men) from Great Britain will land at Oran, commanded by Major General Lloyd Fredendall. Admiral Sir Andrew Cunningham will be the naval force commander. The Eastern Task Force (33,000 men), with both British and American forces from Great Britain, will land at Algiers under the command of Lieutenant General Kenneth A. N. Anderson, with U.S. forces under command of Major General Charles W. Ryder. Vice Admiral Sir Harold Burrough will be the naval commander. Brigadier General James Doolittle will command the American air forces, and Air Marshal Sir William Welsh will command British air forces.

NEW GUINEA: Fifth Air Force A-20s provide air support to Australian forces defending on the Owen Stanley Range. P-40s attack Japanese positions on the Kokoda Trail.

September 21

PACIFIC: U.S. submarine *Grouper* sinks a Japanese cargo ship off Shanghai; U.S. submarine *Trout* sinks Japanese auxiliary vessel south of Truk.

GUADALCANAL: Marines from the 7th Marine Regiment, attempting to cross the Matanikau River, are stopped by strong Japanese defenses.

September 22

ATLANTIC: A U.S. tanker is torpedoed and sunk by German submarine *U-211* south of Cape Farewell, Greenland. U.S. freighter in convoy QP 14 is torpedoed and sunk by German submarine *U-435*.

MIDDLE EAST: USAMEAF B-24s attack Benghazi harbor.

INDIAN OCEAN: U.S. freighter is torpedoed and sunk by Japanese submarine *I-29* off the coast of India.

NEW GUINEA: P-40s attack Japanese positions at Buna and on the Kokoda Trail; B-26 Marauders attack Buna airfield; A-20 Havocs attack a number of areas occupied by Japanese forces. Fifth Air Force B-17s attack Rabaul.

September 23

ATLANTIC: A U.S. freighter is torpedoed and damaged by German submarine *U-515* off Georgetown, British Guiana. The submarine is chased off by gunfire from the freighter. The crew abandons, then reboards the ship, only to be torpedoed and sunk by *U-512* the following day.

U.S. freighter in convoy SC 100 (Halifax Slow to United Kingdom) is torpedoed and sunk by German submarine *U-432* near Iceland.

ETO: General Jimmy Doolittle takes command of Twelfth Air Force in Britain.

PACIFIC: SOPAC receives additional B-17s at Espiritu Santo from Seventh Air Force in Hawaii.

GUADALCANAL: Marines fail to cross the Matanikau River after encountering strong Japanese defenses. An attempt to make an amphibious assault west of Point Cruz fails.

NEW GUINEA: Fifth Air Force bombers and fighter aircraft attack the Buna airfield and Japanese positions along the Buna-Kokoda Trail.

September 24

ATLANTIC: U.S. freighter from convoy ON 131 (Liverpool to New York, fast) is torpedoed and sunk by German submarine *U-619* south of Iceland.

CARIBBEAN: U.S. freighter is torpedoed and sunk by German submarine *U-175* north of British Guiana.

INDIAN OCEAN: U.S. freighter is torpedoed and sunk by Japanese submarine *I-165* off the coast of India.

September 25

ALEUTIANS: The first U.S.-Canadian mission is flown over Kiska. Eleventh Air Force B-24 Liberators and B-17s, escorted by 15 P-39s, attack Kiska, damaging a radar station, a transport ship, Japanese submarine *RO-67,* and two float planes, as well as destroying several biplanes.

CBI: Tenth Air Force B-25 Mitchells escorted by P-40s attack Hanoi. The P-40s shoot down nine Japanese fighters.

PACIFIC: U.S. submarine *Sargo* sinks a Japanese merchant ship off the coast of French Indochina.

September 26

NEW GUINEA: Fifth Air Force B-17s attack Rabaul; A-20s provide air support to Australian forces counterattacking in Papua.

September 27

ATLANTIC: U.S. freighter with an armed guard fights a German auxiliary cruiser and supply ship in the central South Atlantic. The freighter is sunk, but only after damaging the German cruiser so badly that it also sinks.

GUADALCANAL: The attempt by Vandegrift's marines to drive the Japanese from the Matanikau River fails. A landing attempt west of Point Cruz runs into an ambush and is evacuated; two other separate attacks fail to cross the river. A total of 60 marines are killed and 100 are wounded. In the evacuation attempt, U.S. Coast Guard coxswain Douglas A. Munro brings his landing boat into shore, steering with one hand and firing at the Japanese with the other to draw fire so that marines can get on other boats. Munro is killed in the fight. For his extraordinary heroism, Munro will be awarded the Medal of Honor.

September 28

ALEUTIANS: Eleventh Air Force B-24 Liberators and B-17s attack Kiska. Five Japanese floatplanes are destroyed and one submarine is sunk.

CARIBBEAN: A U.S. freighter is torpedoed and sunk by German submarine *U-175* near the mouth of the Orinoco River.

PACIFIC: U.S. submarine *Nautilus* torpedoes and sinks a Japanese merchant ship east of Japan; U.S. submarine *Sculpin* torpedoes a Japanese seaplane carrier off Kokoda Island; U.S. submarine *Trout* torpedoes a Japanese escort carrier east of Truk.

NEW GUINEA: Fifth Air Force P-400 Airacobras and P-40s attack Wairopi bridge and targets along the Buna-Kokoda Trail. The U.S. 126th Infantry Regiment of the 32nd Infantry Division arrives at Port Moresby and is assigned to New Guinea Force to support the Australian advance on Wairopi.

September 29

PACIFIC: A reconnaissance seaplane from Japanese submarine *I-25* drops incendiary bombs on an Oregon forest in an attempt to ignite forest fires. This is the last Japanese attack on the U.S. mainland.

October 1

ATLANTIC: The Marine First Amphibious Corps is established at San Diego, California, under the command of Major General Clayton B. Vogel.

PACIFIC: U.S. submarine *Grouper* torpedoes and sinks a Japanese army transport in the East China Sea. U.S. submarine *Kingfish* torpedoes and sinks a Japanese merchant cargo ship off Japan. U.S. submarine *Nautilus* torpedoes and sinks a merchant cargo ship off Japan. U.S. submarine *Sturgeon* damages a Japanese aircraft transport off New Ireland.

NEW GUINEA: Fifth Air Force B-17s and P-400s bomb Menari, Kagi, Kokoda, and Wairopi bridge and the Buna-Wairopi Trail.

MacArthur's staff develops a plan for countering the Japanese advance in New Guinea. The Australian 7th Infantry Division, commanded by Major General George A. Vasey, is ordered to move from Port Moresby to Wairopi. The U.S. 2nd Battalion 126th Infantry Regiment is to move overland from Port Moresby to Jaure in support of the Australians. The 18th Australian Brigade is ordered to move along the northern coast to Wanigela and link up with the U.S. 128th Infantry Regiment, which will be moved by air from Port Moresby. After linkup the combined force will move to Embogo. The Japanese hold the Gona valley, Sanananda point, and Buna village. The intent is to force the Japanese to deal with multiple threats to their flanks and rear.

October 2

CARIBBEAN: German submarine *U-512* is sunk by U.S. aircraft off French Guiana. U.S. freighter is torpedoed and sunk by German submarine *U-201* near Trinidad.

ETO: Eighth Air Force B-17s, escorted by 400 Allied fighters, attack the Meaulte aircraft factory.

SOUTHWEST PACIFIC AREA: Fifth Air Force B-17s bomb Rabaul harbor, damaging a Japanese light cruiser.

October 3

ALEUTIANS: Japanese bombers attack Adak airfield but cause no damage.

CBI: The India Air Task Force is established and includes all AAF combat units in India. Its mission is to defend Assam province, attack Japanese lines of supply in southern Burma and shipping in the Andaman Sea, and raid Bangkok and Rangoon. The task force is composed of the 7th Bombardment Squadron (Heavy) with B-24 Liberators, the 51st Fighter Group with P-40s, and the 341st Bombardment Group (Medium) with B-25 Mitchells.

PACIFIC: U.S. submarine *Greenling* sinks a Japanese merchant cargo ship off the east coast of Japan.

GUADALCANAL: U.S. aircraft from Henderson Field attack a Japanese supply convoy headed for Guadalcanal.

October 4

ATLANTIC: A U.S. freighter is torpedoed and sunk by German submarine *U-175* off the mouth of the Orinoco River. A U.S. tanker in convoy HX 209 (New York to Liverpool) is torpedoed and sunk by German submarine *U-254* off Iceland.

PACIFIC: U.S. submarine *Greenling* sinks a Japanese merchant cargo ship off the coast of Japan. U.S. tanker is torpedoed by Japanese submarine *I-25* off the coast of Oregon and then abandoned.

NEW GUINEA: Fifth Air Force P-40s attack Japanese positions at Myola Lake, Kokoda, Wairopi, and Buna. A reconnaissance element from 126th Infantry Regiment 32nd Division locates and assesses the Kapa-Jauri trail as a possible approach for an attack on the Buna-Gona defenses.

October 5

CARIBBEAN: A U.S. freighter is torpedoed and sunk by German submarine *U-175* off the coast of Venezuela.

ATLANTIC: U.S. Navy PBY Catalina sinks German submarine *U-582* in the waters south of Iceland.

GUADALCANAL: Carrier aircraft from USS *Hornet* operate against Japanese targets in the Solomons. U.S. aircraft from Henderson Field attack a Japanese convoy and damage two destroyers. A navy PBY Catalina from COMAIRSOPAC sinks Japanese submarine *I-22* near Indispensable Strait in the Solomons.

NEW GUINEA: Fifth Air Force B-25 Mitchells attack a Japanese convoy off Buna; B-17s attack Buna airfield and Rabaul airfields; A-20 Havocs attack Sanananda Point.

October 6

ALEUTIANS: Eleventh Air Force B-24 Liberators, a B-17, and 10 P-38s attack Kiska. A transport ship and two other ships are badly damaged; several aircraft are damaged as well.

PACIFIC: A U.S. tanker is torpedoed by Japanese submarine *I-25* off the coast of Oregon and abandoned.

NEW GUINEA: Fifth Air Force supports airlift of Australian 18th Brigade to forward positions in preparation for the attack on Buna and Gona.

October 7

ATLANTIC: A U.S. freighter is torpedoed and sunk by German submarine *U-172* south of Cape Town, South Africa.

MIDDLE EAST: USAMEAF B-24s attack a tanker and fuel depot at Suda Bay, Crete. U.S. P-40s escort bombers providing ground support to British forces west of El Alamein.

PACIFIC: U.S. submarine *Amberjack* sinks a Japanese supply ship in the southern Carolines; U.S. submarine *Sculpin* sinks a Japanese army transport off Rabaul.

GUADALCANAL: Elements of the 5th Marines attempting to extend the defensive perimeter past the Matanikau River encounter a Japanese force attempting to move artillery closer to the marines' defensive lines. Heavy fighting ensues and continues through the next day, slowed only by a tropical downpour.

U.S. Navy Task Group 64.2, composed of two heavy cruisers, two light cruisers, and five destroyers under command of Rear Admiral Norman Scott, arrives near the Russell Islands in the Solomons with orders to intercept Japanese convoys headed to Guadalcanal.

October 8

ATLANTIC: A U.S. freighter is torpedoed, then shelled by German submarine *U-202* off the coast of Africa.

PACIFIC: U.S. submarine *Drum* sinks a Japanese merchant cargo ship off the east coast of Japan.

NEW GUINEA: Fifth Air Force A-20 Havocs attack Japanese positions on the Buna-Kokoda Trail.

October 9

ALEUTIANS: Eleventh Air Force B-17s and B-24 Liberators, escorted by P-38s and P-39s, attack Japanese ships in Kiska harbor.

CARIBBEAN: German submarine *U-505* is damaged by U.S. aircraft patrolling off Trinidad.

ATLANTIC: A U.S. freighter is torpedoed and sunk by German submarine *U-159* southwest of Cape Town, South Africa. Another U.S. freighter is sunk by German submarine *U-68* south of the Cape of Good Hope.

ETO: Eighth Air Force conducts bombing raid on the steel and locomotive works at Lille, France. A total of 69 B-24 Liberators and B-17s, escorted by U.S. and British fighters, attack these targets, part of a force of 100 bombers attacking a number of other targets in the area. Over 100 German planes are damaged or destroyed in the attack.

PACIFIC: Fifth Air Force B-17s attack Rabaul and Lae. The U.S. Army's 164th Infantry Regiment of the Americal Division departs from Nouméa, New Caledonia, for Guadalcanal. U.S. submarine *Drum* torpedoes and sinks a Japanese merchant cargo ship off the east coast of Japan.

GUADALCANAL: Elements of the 5th Marines, supported by a flanking attack by the 7th Marines, cross the Matanikau River and eliminate the Japanese defensive perimeter. Over 700 Japanese are killed. American casualties number nearly 200.

October 10

SOUTHWEST PACIFIC AREA: U.S. submarine *Amberjack* damages two Japanese vessels off Kavieng, New Ireland. U.S. submarine *Seadragon* torpedoes and sinks a Japanese transport off Borneo. U.S. submarine *Wahoo* sinks a Japanese collier off Bougainville, Solomons.

GUADALCANAL: A total of 12 P-39 Airacobras of the 67th Fighter Squadron arrive at Henderson Field.

October 11

GUADALCANAL: SOPAC B-17s spot Japanese cruisers and destroyers headed for Guadalcanal. Rear Admiral Scott is ordered to intercept a Japanese convoy arriving at midnight near Cape Esperance. In a confused battle, U.S. and Japanese ships fire at each other in the darkness. A U.S. heavy cruiser, a light cruiser, and a destroyer are damaged; one U.S. destroyer is sunk. A Japanese heavy cruiser and destroyer are sunk, and a heavy cruiser and destroyer are damaged.

October 12

CBI: General Stilwell requests assistance from the War Department to equip 30 more Chinese divisions.

PACIFIC: Navy SBD Dauntless dive-bombers sink a Japanese destroyer off Savo Island. A Japanese destroyer is scuttled off New Georgia Island after an air attack by navy and marine aircraft.

October 13

ATLANTIC: A U.S. freighter in convoy SC 104 (Halifax Slow to United Kingdom) is torpedoed and sunk by German submarine *U-221* in the waters west of Great Britain.

GUADALCANAL: The 164th Infantry Regiment of the Americal Division arrives at Guadalcanal. Japanese air strikes destroy fuel supplies at Henderson Field.

October 14

SOUTHWEST PACIFIC AREA: U.S. submarine *Sculpin* sinks Japanese cargo ship off Kavieng, New Ireland.

PACIFIC: U.S. submarine *Finback* sinks a Japanese army transport off Formosa. U.S. submarine *Greenling* torpedoes and sinks a Japanese cargo ship off the coast of Honshu, Japan. U.S. submarine *Skipjack* sinks a Japanese cargo ship near Truk.

GUADALCANAL: A Japanese surface force of two battleships, a light cruiser, and seven destroyers bombards Henderson Field, destroying 48 of 90 U.S. aircraft there, killing 40 Americans, and temporarily putting the airstrip out of action. Japanese destroyers prepare to land reinforcements at Tassafaronga.

New Guinea: Fifth Air Force airlifts the U.S. 128th Infantry Regiment and Australian units to Wanigela.

October 15

Guadalcanal: Japanese complete landing of nearly 4,000 reinforcements and supplies on Guadalcanal; marine and navy SBD Dauntless dive-bombers and F4F Wildcats from Henderson Field, along with SOPAC B-17s, P-39, and P-400 Airacobras, attack the transports and their escort ships. Two transports and a merchant cargo ship are sunk, and a destroyer is damaged. Japanese combat strength on Guadalcanal is about 20,000 men, roughly equal to U.S. force strength.

October 16

Aleutians: Eleventh Air Force B-26 Marauders and a B-17 attack Kiska and sink two Japanese destroyers. One B-26 is lost.

Pacific: USS *Thresher* conducts the first U.S. submarine mining operation of the war, laying mines off Bangkok, Thailand.

Guadalcanal: Twenty F4F Wildcats and 12 SBD Dauntless dive-bombers are added to Henderson Field, bringing the total number of aircraft to 66. SOPAC P-400s and P-39 Airacobras attack a Japanese landing force at Kokumbona, just a few miles from Henderson Field. Task Force 17, formed around carrier USS *Hornet,* conducts air strikes on Japanese troops. Japanese heavy cruisers, a light cruiser, and seven destroyers shell Henderson Field.

October 17

Atlantic: A U.S. freighter from convoy ON 137 (Liverpool to New York, fast) is torpedoed by German submarine *U-618* and later abandoned.

Torch convoys begin assembling in Great Britain.

Pacific: A U.S. submarine, *Trigger,* torpedoes and sinks a Japanese merchant ship off Kyushu.

October 18

Pacific: Admiral William F. Halsey replaces Admiral Ghormley as COMSOPAC at Nouméa, New Caledonia. U.S. submarine *Grampus* torpedoes a Japanese light cruiser near Truk, but the torpedo fails to explode. U.S. submarine *Greenling* sinks Japanese transport off the coast of Honshu, Japan.

New Guinea: The air movement of the 128th Infantry, 32nd Division to Wanigela, New Guinea, is completed.

October 19

CBI: U.S. War Department approves General Stilwell's request of equipment for 30 Chinese divisions.

Guadalcanal: Navy SBD Dauntless dive-bombers from Henderson Field attack three Japanese destroyers north of Guadalcanal, damaging one.

October 20

Middle East: Brigadier General Donald H. Connolly takes command of Persian Gulf Service Command (PGSC) in Basra, Iraq. The command includes 1,400 army and civilian workers

PACIFIC: A U.S. heavy cruiser is torpedoed by Japanese submarine *I-176* near San Cristobal, Solomons. U.S. submarine *Drum* torpedoes and sinks a Japanese merchant cargo ship off Honshu, Japan. U.S. submarine *Finback* attacks a Japanese convoy off Formosa and damages two cargo ships. U.S. submarine *Tautog* sinks a Japanese merchant trawler in the South China Sea.

GUADALCANAL: A Japanese attack across the Matanikau River, supported by tanks, is stopped by marine antitank and artillery fire. Admiral Halsey orders the 147th Infantry Regiment to reinforce Guadalcanal.

October 21

CBI: Air Transport Command is established to deliver supplies to China.

ATLANTIC: Admiral King informs Admiral Nimitz that the JCS has approved a request for additional air forces to be moved to the South Pacific before the beginning of 1943.

ETO: Eighth Air Force B-17s attack German submarine bases in an effort to prevent their interference with convoys headed for North Africa from Britain as part of Operation Torch. Three B-17s are lost.

NORTH AFRICA: Major General Mark W. Clark, the deputy commander of Allied forces for Operation Torch, Brigadier General Lyman M. Lemnitzer, two other army officers, and Captain Jerauld Wright (USN) are landed at Cherchel, French North Africa, from British submarine HMS *Seraph* to meet with a French military delegation and ascertain French attitudes toward impending Allied operations. Major General Charles Mast, a pro-Allied commander of the Algiers Division of Vichy French forces in North Africa, and U.S. Consul General Robert Murphy meet the officers. Mast states that with four days notice he can neutralize French resistance to the Allied landings. The meeting is twice interrupted by suspicious police, forcing Clark and others to hide in the wine cellar. The group returns to the submarine shortly before dawn.

PACIFIC: U.S. submarine *Guardfish* torpedoes and sinks a Japanese merchant ship off Formosa; U.S. submarine *Gudgeon* attacks a convoy in the Bismarck Sea and sinks a transport ship near Rabaul.

October 22

ETO: Twelfth Air Force headquarters begins deployment from Britain to North Africa.

MEDITERRANEAN: Major General Mark W. Clark and U.S. Consul Robert Murphy meet with French general Charles Mast, who supports U.S. plan to bring French forces in North Africa under Allied control, with the French accepting the command of General Henri Giraud.

Operation Torch convoy from Britain leaves for North Africa.

PACIFIC: At a conference at Nouméa, General Vandegrift informs Admiral Halsey, the new ComSOPAC, that to hold Guadalcanal he needs additional army and marine combat troops. Halsey tells Vandegrift: "You go back there.... I promise to get you everything I have."

October 23

MIDDLE EAST: British Eighth Army begins its El Alamein counteroffensive. USAMEAF fighters and bombers unable to hit targets because of bad weather.

SOUTHWEST PACIFIC AREA: Fifth Air Force B-17s damage two Japanese submarine chasers in a raid on Rabaul.

PACIFIC: U.S. submarine *Kingfish* sinks a Japanese gunboat off Honshu, Japan.

GUADALCANAL: An uncoordinated Japanese attack across the Matanikau River, supported by tanks, is stopped by marines supported by artillery. Over 650 Japanese are killed.

October 24

ATLANTIC: The Western Task Force for Operation Torch sets sail from Hampton Roads, Virginia, headed for Casablanca, Morocco.

President Roosevelt informs the JCS that Guadalcanal must be reinforced.

PACIFIC: U.S. submarine *Nautilus* torpedoes and sinks a Japanese merchant ship off northern Honshu, Japan. U.S. submarine *Trigger* damages a Japanese oiler off Kyushu, the southernmost of the Japanese home islands.

GUADALCANAL: Japanese forces launch a regimental-level attack in a driving rainstorm against the south flank of the Guadalcanal defensive perimeter, the full brunt falling on 1st Battalion, 7th Marines. Sergeant John Basilone's heavy machine-gun sections are the main target of Japanese grenade attacks and mortar fire. When his gun crews suffer heavy casualties, Sergeant Basilone rallies the survivors and personally repairs and fires one machine gun, holding the line under continuous enemy fire until reinforced. Throughout the night, in a pouring rain, Sergeant Basilone takes great personal risks to locate ammunition and bring it forward to keep his guns in action. For his extraordinary gallantry in the face of nearly impossible odds, Sergeant Basilone will receive the Medal of Honor. As Japanese attacks continue throughout the night, the army's 3rd Battalion, 164th Infantry Regiment, led by Lieutenant Colonel Robert K. Hall, joins the marines, led by Lieutenant Colonel Lewis B. "Chesty" Puller, and together they hold Bloody Ridge once more. At least 900 Japanese are killed in the failed attack.

October 25

CBI: CATF (China Air Task Force) B-25 Mitchells, with seven P-40s escorting, attack the docks at Hong Kong. One B-25 and one P-40 are lost. The Japanese lose nearly 21 fighters.

PACIFIC: U.S. submarine *Whale* lays mines off Honshu, Japan, at the entrance to Japan's Inland Sea.

GUADALCANAL: Japanese air and naval forces conduct heavy attacks on Henderson Field. A second Japanese assault is repulsed by 1st Battalion 7th Marines and the army's 3rd Battalion 164th Infantry Regiment. The Japanese assault on the Matanikau River is also stopped.

NEW GUINEA: The army's 2nd Battalion 126th Infantry Regiment reaches Jaure, but has suffered high casualties from disease, especially malaria, in its overland march. The 32nd Infantry Division commander, Major General Edwin F. Harding, requests that the remainder of his division be airlifted to required locations to maintain the combat effectiveness of his units.

October 26

CBI: Japanese aircraft attack airfields in India that are supporting the China air bridge over the Himalayas (the Hump). Numerous logistics storage areas are destroyed.

MIDDLE EAST: USAMEAF fighters and bombers provide air support to the Eighth Army's attack at El Alamein, destroying transportation and attacking Axis troop concentrations. B-17s and B-24 Liberators attack shipping off the coast of Libya.

SOLOMONS: The Battle of the Santa Cruz Islands. Task Force 16, centered around the carrier USS *Enterprise* under command of Rear Admiral Thomas C. Kinkaid, and Task Force 17, centered around the carrier USS *Hornet* under command of Rear Admiral George D. Murray, engage a numerically superior Japanese force with four carriers, four battleships, eight cruisers, and 30 destroyers. *Hornet* is severely damaged and is later sunk. The *Enterprise*, a light cruiser, and a battleship are both heavily damaged and a destroyer is scuttled. The Americans lose 74 aircraft. Two Japanese carriers are damaged, along with the loss of 100 aircraft; a heavy cruiser and a destroyer are also damaged.

GUADALCANAL: The naval victory at Santa Cruz Islands counts for little. The Japanese attack against the perimeter defended by the 1st Battalion of the 164th Infantry is stopped; Japanese forces make a short penetration in the lines defended by 2nd Battalion 7th Marines, but the enemy is repulsed in a counterattack led by Major Odell M. Conoley, the 2nd Battalion's executive officer. The 173rd Infantry Regiment of the 43rd Infantry Division arrives at Espiritu Santo Island.

The USS *Enterprise* receives slight damage from a bomb during an attack by 20 Japanese dive-bombers and torpedo planes during the Battle of the Santa Cruz Islands, October 26, 1942.

October 27

CBI: Generals Wavell and Stilwell map out a plan for an offensive in Burma. U.S. forces will advance into Hukwang Valley, seize Myitkyina, and link with Chinese forces in Yunnan. U.S. engineers will construct a road from Ledo to link with the Burma Road.

ATLANTIC: German submarines attack convoy HX 212 (New York to Liverpool); U.S. tanker is torpedoed by *U-436* and abandoned.

October 29

ALEUTIANS: Japanese forces reoccupy Attu Island.

ATLANTIC: President Roosevelt establishes a production objective of 107,000 aircraft for 1943.

German submarines attack convoy HX 212. A U.S. tanker is torpedoed and sunk by *U-624*; *U-224* torpedoes and sinks a Canadian tanker.

PACIFIC: U.S. submarine *Grenadier* lays mines off Haiphong, French Indochina. A U.S. Navy PBY Catalina sinks Japanese submarine *I-172* off San Cristobal Island, Solomons.

GUADALCANAL: Japanese forces on Guadalcanal begin a withdrawal to Koli Point and Kokumbona. Marines prepare to continue advance westward toward Point Cruz to pressure the Japanese.

October 30

GUADALCANAL: U.S. Task Group 64.2, commanded by Rear Admiral Norman Scott, with a light cruiser and four destroyers, bombards Japanese positions at Point Cruz, Guadalcanal, in support of an American ground advance west.

October 31

SOUTHWEST PACIFIC AREA: U.S. submarine *Grayback* damages a Japanese cargo ship off Rabaul.

November 1

GUADALCANAL: Marine and army units begin to expand the Guadalcanal perimeter out to the east and west to help protect Henderson Field from Japanese artillery fire. Marines begin an advance across the Matanikau River to isolate Point Cruz; Japanese land reinforcements to the east of the American defenses, near the Metapona River.

November 2

MIDDLE EAST: USAMEAF and RAF provide air support to Eighth Army's attack named Supercharge. U.S. B-25 Mitchells bomb targets in support of British 9th Armored Division; B-17s bomb Tobruk harbor; B-25s and P-40s attack Axis tanks and troops.

SOUTHWEST PACIFIC AREA: U.S. submarine *Seawolf* torpedoes and sinks a Japanese vessel off the island of Mindoro. U.S. submarines *Tambor* and *Tautog* lay mines in various sea lanes approaching French Indochina.

GUADALCANAL: Japanese land an additional 1,500 reinforcements and supplies near Koli Point on Guadalcanal.

NEW GUINEA: Fifth Air Force attacks Japanese shipping near Buna, sinking a cargo ship, and supports the Australian assault to seize Kokoda airfield on the Owen Stanley Range. The 7th Australian Infantry Division captures Kokoda airfield.

November 3

CBI: Generalissimo Chiang Kai-shek agrees to support U.S.-British offensive in Burma, and allows Stilwell to command Chinese forces in India. If backed by Allied air support, Chiang promises to supply the Y Force, the Yunnan divisions.

ATLANTIC: A U.S. tanker in convoy SC 107 (Halifax Slow to United Kingdom) is torpedoed and sunk by German submarine *U-521*; a U.S. freighter is sunk by German submarine *U-181* off the Cape of Good Hope.

SOUTHWEST PACIFIC AREA: U.S. submarine *Haddock* torpedoes and sinks a merchant ship in the East China Sea. U.S. submarine *Seawolf* sinks a Japanese transport off Davao, Philippines; U.S. submarine *Tambor* sinks a merchant ship in the Tonkin Gulf.

GUADALCANAL: Marine reconnaissance elements meet Japanese near Koli Point. They are reinforced by two tank companies, the army's 2nd Battalion 164th Infantry Regiment, and a marine battalion. These units, along with air strikes and artillery fire, force the Japanese to break contact.

November 4

ATLANTIC: A U.S. freighter headed to Murmansk, USSR, is torpedoed and sunk by German submarine *U-354* north of Iceland.

MIDDLE EAST: Lieutenant General Frank M. Andrews takes command of USAFIME.

MEDITERRANEAN: U.S. submarines *Shad, Gunnel, Herring, Barb,* and *Blackfish* conduct reconnaissance activities off the North African coast in support of Operation Torch, observing Rabat, Fedala, Casablanca, Safi, and Dakar.

GUADALCANAL: The 1st Battalion 164th Infantry supports the marines' western advance, while the 2nd and 3rd Battalions of the 164th support the advance to the east. Marine and army units reach Point Cruz and establish defensive positions.

November 5

CARIBBEAN: U.S. tanker in convoy TAG 18 (Trinidad to Aruba to Guantánamo) is sunk by German submarine *U-129*.

ATLANTIC: A U.S. Navy PBY Catalina sinks German submarine *U-408* off Iceland.

MEDITERRANEAN: Lieutenant General Eisenhower and his staff arrive in Gibraltar to oversee Operation Torch landings.

November 6

PACIFIC: U.S. submarine *Haddock* damages a Japanese cargo ship off the southeast coast of Japan.

NEW GUINEA: General MacArthur arrives at Port Moresby to direct offensive against Gona-Buna.

November 7

ALEUTIANS: The Japanese submarine base at Kiska is attacked by Eleventh Air Force B-24 Liberators and B-26 Marauders.

CARIBBEAN: U.S. freighter convoy TAG 19 (Trinidad to Aruba to Guantánamo) is sunk by German submarine *U-508*.

ATLANTIC: U.S. freighter is torpedoed and sunk by German submarine *U-159* off the Cape of Good Hope, South Africa; U.S. freighter is sunk by German submarine *U-161* off the coast of West Africa.

ETO: Eighth Air Force bombers attack U-boat facilities at Brest. Twelfth Air Force begins deployment from Britain to North Africa.

MEDITERRANEAN: General Henri Giraud arrives in Gibraltar after escaping from Lyons, France. Giraud, a hero of two wars, has been selected as the French commander most likely to command the loyalty of French officers in North Africa and rally them to the Allies. Giraud surprises Lieutenant General Eisenhower by demanding that he take charge of the operation and announces plans to divert some of the Allied landing forces to the southern coast of France.

U.S. transport is torpedoed by German submarine *U-205* in the western Mediterranean; USAMEAF aircraft sink Italian submarine *Antonio Sciesa* off the coast of Libya.

GUADALCANAL: U.S. aircraft from Henderson Field attack a Japanese convoy, damaging two destroyers. The 164th Infantry Regiment and 7th Marines advance east toward Matapona River.

November 8

ETO: Eighth Air Force bombers attack the Lille locomotive works and the Abbeville/Drucat airfield in France.

November 8

MEDITERRANEAN: Operation Torch. Allied forces invade Algeria and Morocco, landing at Casablanca, Oran, and Algiers. The Eastern Assault Force, led by Major General Charles W. Ryder, lands at Algiers. An attempt by two British destroyers to enter the port of Algiers with a battalion from a regimental combat team (RCT) of the U.S. 34th Division is met with heavy fire. Troops are landed but are withdrawn by 0900 hours. The 168th RCT from the 34th Division, the 39th RCT of the U.S. 9th Division, and a brigade from the British 78th Division advance toward Algiers without opposition. Key objectives of Blida and Maison Blanche airfields are captured. Algiers surrenders to Allied forces at 1900 hours.

The Center Assault Force, under command of Major General Lloyd R. Fredendall, lands at Oran. Arzew harbor is captured by U.S. rangers to support the landing of two RCTs of the 1st Infantry Division. One task force from Combat Command B of the 1st Armored Division captures Tafaraoui airfield Fighters from the 31st Fighter Group arrive at Tafaraoui to support operations. U.S. paratroopers of the 509th Parachute Infantry, intended to support the capture of La Senia and Tafaraoui airfields, are dropped far from their drop zones. Two British ships flying large American flags attempt to enter Oran harbor carrying a 400-man assault force of the 6th Armored Infantry Regiment, 1st Armored Division. Harbor defenses and the French sloop *La Surprise* fire on the ships, heavily damaging both as they disembark their landing force. Despite heavy casualties, those members of the assault force that make it ashore capture several objectives, but are later forced to surrender. A second task force from 1st Armored Division captures Lourmel airfield. The 26th RCT, 1st Infantry Division captures Bou Sfer and Aïn et Turk, but is unable to advance farther.

French resistance combined with confusion during the landing delays the Western Task Force, commanded by Major General George S. Patton, Jr. The French battleship *Jean Bart,* cruiser *Primaguet,* eight destroyers, and 13 submarines are at Casablanca harbor. The *Primaguet* and the destroyers leave the harbor and attempt to prevent the landings. The *Jean Bart,* in dry dock, supports with gunfire. U.S. naval gunfire and carrier aircraft knock out the cruiser and two of the destroyers and damage the *Jean Bart.* A beachhead is established at Fedala with the 3rd Infantry Division and a battalion of the 67th Armored regiment of the 2nd Armored Division. The French garrison at Fedala surrenders to American forces. The 60th RCT of 9th Infantry Division and a battalion of the 66th Armored Regiment of the 2nd Armored Division are attacked by French aircraft as they land at Port Lyautey. Port Lyautey and its airfield, key objectives of the task force, are strongly defended and the Americans are unable to advance beyond the beachhead. U.S. naval gunfire suppresses French coastal batteries at Safi harbor, and U.S. destroyers with two companies of infantry aboard enter the harbor and capture key objectives. The 47th RCT of the 9th Infantry Division along with two battalions of the 67th Armored Regiment of the 2nd Armored Division land at Safi and U.S. aircraft stop a French column of tanks and trucks attempting to counter the landings.

German aircraft bomb Allied ships near Algiers. Vichy France, led by Marshal Henri Pétain, breaks diplomatic relations with the United States.

PACIFIC: U.S. submarine *Seawolf* sinks a Japanese gunboat off Mindanao, Philippines. U.S. freighter is torpedoed by Japanese submarine *I-21* off Nouméa, New Caledonia.

GUADALCANAL: Admiral William F. Halsey, commander of SOPAC, visits Guadalcanal and meets with General Alexander A. Vandegrift. The meeting is interrupted by a Japanese air attack that forces both officers to seek shelter in a sandbagged dugout.

NEW GUINEA: The Fifth Air Force airlifts the 126th Infantry Regiment to Fasari and Pongani airfields in northern New Guinea and moves the remainder of the 128th Infantry Regiment, 32nd Infantry Division into Wanigela, as General MacArthur prepares for assault on the Buna-Gona defenses.

November 9

ALEUTIANS: One Eleventh Air Force B-17 and four P-38s attack Holtz Bay and Attu airfield, destroying eight Japanese floatplanes.

ETO: Eighth Air Force B-17s attempt to conduct low-level bombing runs (below 10,000 feet) on the U-boat base at St. Nazaire in France. Of the 31 aircraft participating in the attack, three are lost and 22 are damaged by antiaircraft fire. B-24 Liberator bombers attacking at 17–18,000 feet suffer minor damage from antiaircraft fire.

ALGERIA, OPERATION TORCH: General Henri Giraud's broadcasted appeals to French forces to join the Allies are ignored. La Senia airfield outside of Oran is captured. U.S. forces land supplies at Safi and on beaches near Casablanca. French troops continue to resist at Port Lyautey and the airfield. The British First Army is landed under command of General Kenneth A.N. Anderson at Algiers and prepares to advance along the coast road to Tunisia. German aircraft begin landing in Tunis.

A U.S. transport is sunk by German submarine *U-173* near Algiers.

British Spitfires of the Twelfth Air Force attack a French armored unit moving toward Tafaraoui, south of Oran.

NEW GUINEA: Fifth Air Force B-26 Marauders bomb Buna; airlift of the U.S. 126th Infantry Regiment to Pongani begins.

November 10

ATLANTIC: German submarine *U-608* lays mines off New York City.

MEDITERRANEAN, OPERATION TORCH: Major General Mark W. Clark meets with Admiral François Darlan, commander of all Vichy French military forces, seeking to end hostilities as quickly as possible. Darlan by pure chance has been in Algiers visiting his sick son when the Allies land. Deciding to act on Pétain's behalf, Darlan assumes full civil and military authority over French North Africa and orders a cease-fire. U.S. forces capture Oran after a coordinated armor assault against the defenses. Destroyer USS *Dallas* lands troops close to the Port Lyautey airfield, supported by two U.S. infantry battalions attacking from the beachhead. U.S. carrier *Chenango* launches 72 P-40s, which land at Port Lyautey airfield. Casablanca is still defended by French forces, which refuse to surrender. Patton prepares for an all-out assault on the city the next day.

A French submarine attacks U.S. carrier *Ranger* off the coast of French North Africa without effect; two French submarines attack the battleship *Massachusetts* and a U.S. heavy cruiser, but have no effect. Oran surrenders to U.S. forces. Allied forces sail from Algiers to occupy Bougie and Bône in preparation for an overland movement to Tunisia.

SOUTH PACIFIC: A U.S. minesweeper sinks Japanese submarine *I-15* off San Cristobal Island, Solomons.

November 11

CBI: P-40s from the Tenth Air Force attack Shinghbwiyang in Burma.

ALGIERS, OPERATION TORCH: Admiral François Darlan and General Alphonse Juin agree to an armistice, and all resistance ends. Casablanca surrenders to U.S. forces. British troops begin overland movement eastward toward Tunisia. Marshal Pétain rejects the cease-fire order. Darlan is put under house arrest by the Allies to prevent him from following Pétain's orders. Darlan also refuses to order the French fleet at Toulon to sail to Algiers to avoid capture by the Germans. German troops invade unoccupied France. Italian troops land on Corsica and move into France. The collapse of the Vichy government leaves Darlan as the default political head of North Africa. By agreement, Giraud is given command of all French forces, General Juin (previous commander in chief of all French forces in North Africa) is named commander of French land forces.

German submarine *U-173* torpedoes and sinks a U.S. transport and damages a destroyer and an oiler off the North African coast.

Twelfth Air Force fighters land at the Port Lyautey airfield after French end resistance. British 78th Infantry Division and a battalion of the 17th Lancers accompanied by light tanks from the U.S. 1st Armored Division land at Bougie, the first objective on the way to Tunis.

MEDITERRANEAN: USAMEAF B-24 Liberators attack Axis shipping near Benghazi.

PACIFIC: U.S. submarine *Haddock* torpedoes and sinks a Japanese cargo ship in the Yellow Sea.

GUADALCANAL: The 182nd Infantry Regiment of the army's Americal Division lands at Guadalcanal.

November 12

ALGERIA, OPERATION TORCH: The U.S. 509th Parachute Infantry is placed under operational control of the British to support the advance into Tunisia. Elements of the 509th are dropped at Duzerville airport near Bône.

Axis troops in Tunisia grow to 15,000; 581 tons of supplies are landed by air and sea at Tunis.

Three U.S. transports are sunk by German submarine *U-130* off French Morocco.

MIDDLE EAST: The U.S. Ninth Air Force, replacing USAMEAF, is established under General Brereton.

GUADALCANAL: Japanese torpedo planes escorted by Zero fighters attack Task Force 67, commanded by Rear Admiral Richmond K. Turner, while the 182nd Infantry Regiment is unloading at Guadalcanal. A heavy cruiser and a destroyer are damaged. A SOPAC B-17 on a reconnaissance mission spots a Japanese carrier and reports its position for two hours while driving off Japanese Zero fighters and downing six of them.

The Japanese have moved into the area three fleets with more than 60 ships, including two battleships, 11 cruisers, 39 destroyers, two aircraft carriers, and 11 transports, with 11,000 infantrymen and 3,000 naval infantry. While an escort of six cruisers and six destroyers supports the landing of troops at Tassafaronga, the battleships, cruisers, and destroyers will bombard Henderson Field; simultaneously, another fleet centered on the aircraft carriers will attack Henderson Field as well. The Japanese intend to win the Battle of Guadalcanal once and for all. Turner receives reports of a Japanese force headed toward Guadalcanal and sends Task Group 67.4, with two heavy cruisers, three light cruisers, and eight destroyers commanded by Rear Admiral Daniel J. Callaghan, to block the Japanese and protect Henderson Field.

NEW GUINEA: Units of the 126th Infantry Regiment, 32nd Infantry Division begin advance in New Guinea. The 3rd Battalion of the 126th is airlanded at Pongani.

November 13

ALGERIA, OPERATION TORCH: Lieutenant General Eisenhower arrives at Algiers to finalize the agreement with Admiral Darlan concerning the administration of North Africa.

November 13

SOUTH PACIFIC: The Naval Battle of Guadalcanal. Just after one o'clock in the morning, Naval Task Group 67.4 encounters 14 Japanese ships, including two battleships, preparing to bombard Henderson Field. Firing in the darkness at 3,000 yards, the Americans and Japanese fight a confused and brutal battle. Rear Admiral Callaghan and most of his officers are killed by a direct hit on his flagship. A cruiser is so badly damaged that it is later scuttled; another badly damaged cruiser, USS *Juneau,* is torpedoed and sunk by Japanese submarine *I-26* with a loss of 700 men; among the lost are the five Sullivan brothers. Four destroyers are sunk and three are damaged along with two cruisers sunk and the rest damaged. The Japanese lose two destroyers in the encounter. A Japanese battleship, badly damaged in the fight, will later be sunk by aircraft from both USS *Enterprise* and Henderson Field. Five Japanese destroyers are also damaged.

Boatswain's Mate First Class Reinhardt J. Keppler is aboard the heavy cruiser USS *San Francisco* when a Japanese torpedo plane crashes on the aft machine gun platform during an air attack. Keppler treats the injured sailors in the area. That night, as the *San Francisco* fights off Savo Island, Keppler mans a hose to fight a major onboard fire as Japanese gunfire rakes the ship. Mortally wounded, Keppler directs the fire fighting efforts and assists in treating wounded sailors until he collapses from loss of blood. For his great personal valor and dedication to his shipmates he will receive the Medal of Honor.

NEW GUINEA: The 7th Australian Infantry Division takes Wairopi.

November 14

ETO: Eighth Air Force B-17s attack U-boat pens at St. Nazaire.

GUADALCANAL: Henderson Field comes under heavy shellfire for 45 minutes from three Japanese cruisers and four destroyers, but they cause little lasting damage. Aircraft from the *Enterprise* and from Henderson Field attack the group, and Marine SBD Dauntless dive-bombers sink a heavy cruiser. Five other ships are damaged. This leaves the 11 transports headed to Guadalcanal virtually defenseless. Although the Japanese attempt to protect the convoy with air cover, it is insufficient. Carrier aircraft, marine and navy aircraft from Henderson Field, and SOPAC B-17s all participate in sinking six transports and damaging another. A cargo ship is sunk and another damaged. Just before midnight, Task Force 64, with two battleships and four destroyers commanded by Rear Admiral Willis A. Lee, Jr., intercepts another Japanese naval force with a battleship, a light cruiser, and six destroyers. In the narrow waters between Savo Island and Guadalcanal, where the major naval engagements have taken place—an area now known as Iron Bottom Sound—another Battle of Guadalcanal is fought. In this fight the Americans are able to get off the first shots, but the Japanese rapidly engage the Americans, sinking two destroyers and damaging another. One U.S. battleship is badly damaged, leaving the one remaining battleship, Lee's flagship USS *Washington,* to fight on alone. *Washington* cripples and sinks the Japanese battleship and a destroyer, and damages several cruisers so badly that the Japanese retreat.

November 15

ALGERIA, OPERATION TORCH: U.S. paratroopers of the 509th Parachute Infantry conduct assault on Youk-les-Bains near Tébessa in support of the British advance into Tunisia. Axis strength in Tunisia grows to 24,000; 213 tanks are now available.

GUADALCANAL: The four remaining Japanese transport ships are intentionally beached to allow troops to offload as quickly as possible. The ships are struck by

Destroyer Squadron 12 maneuvers off Savo Island during the Guadalcanal campaign.
(U.S. Navy)

artillery fire, air attack, and naval gunfire. About 2,000 men escape the attack to join their comrades in the jungle. The Japanese have attempted an all or nothing offensive intending to drive the Americans off Guadalcanal and regain the strategic initiative in the South Pacific. The U.S. Navy, in perhaps its finest hour, supported by the Marine Corps and the U.S. Army, succeeds in breaking the back of Japanese land and naval power. The turning point in the Pacific war has been reached and everyone seems to know it. In Washington, Secretary of the Navy Frank Knox tells reporters: "We can lick them. I don't qualify that. We'll defeat them." Admiral Halsey put it more directly: "We've got the bastards licked."

November 16

MEDITERRANEAN, OPERATION TORCH: U.S. paratroopers of the 509th Parachute Infantry conduct assault on Souk el Arba near Tabarka in support of the British advance into Tunisia. Allied troops make first contact with Axis forces in Tunisia.

U.S. destroyers sink German submarine *U-173* off Casablanca.

NEW GUINEA: The U.S. 32nd Infantry and the Australian 7th Division begin an attack on Japanese strongholds at Gona and on the Buna defenses. The Australians make some small gains against Gona, but are forced to retreat. Fifth Air Force A-20s attack targets around Gona, while B-25 Mitchells and B-26 Marauders attack Buna.

U.S. submarine *Haddock* torpedoes and sinks a Japanese cargo ship off the southern coast of Japan.

U.S. submarine *Seal* sinks a Japanese cargo ship in the Palau Islands.

November 17

ATLANTIC: President Roosevelt issues a statement that maintaining Admiral Darlan in his position as high commissioner is only a temporary expedient applying to local conditions. Roosevelt makes the statement in an attempt to diffuse criticism from American lawmakers in Congress over the appointment of a known anti-Semite and pro-fascist as leader of newly-liberated French North Africa.

ETO: B-17s from Eighth Air Force drop 102 tons of bombs on U-boat facilities at St. Nazaire, France.

NORTH AFRICA, OPERATION TORCH: The U.S. 509th Parachute Infantry occupies Gafsa airfield in Tunisia.

SOUTHWEST PACIFIC AREA: U.S. submarine *Salmon* attacks a convoy off the west coast of Luzon, sinking a Japanese ship.

PACIFIC: U.S. submarine *Searaven* torpedoes and sinks a Japanese transport off Christmas Island.

November 18

ATLANTIC: German submarines attack convoy ONS 144 (Liverpool to Halifax, slow). Two U.S. freighters are torpedoed by *U-624* in the North Atlantic past Iceland. One sinks, the other is abandoned by its crew. A U.S. tanker in convoy SC 109 (Halifax Slow to United Kingdom) is torpedoed and set afire by German submarine *U-43* in the mid-North Atlantic.

MEDITERRANEAN: Bombers from Ninth Air Force attack the railyard and port at Benghazi.

SOUTH PACIFIC: U.S. Fifth Air Force B-17s sink a Japanese cargo ship off Kahili airfield, Bougainville.

GUADALCANAL: U.S. Army 182nd and 164th Infantry Regiments, and the 8th Marine Regiment under command of Brigadier General Edmund B. Sebree, assistant commanding general of the Americal Division, advance to Point Cruz to find the Japanese. In a daylong battle, strong and determined Japanese attacks stop the Americans.

NEW GUINEA: Japanese aircraft attack the 32nd Infantry Division's supply boats carrying the division's food, ammunition, communications and medical equipment, and heavy weapons, sinking most of the boats. Major General Harding, who was traveling on one of the boats, narrowly escapes being killed.

November 19

ETO: Eighth Air Force adds the German U-boat yards at Kiel, Bremen, and Vegesack to its priority target list.

NEW GUINEA: The U.S. 128th Infantry Regiment attacks Buna. The 1st and 3rd Battalions, 128th Infantry, make contact with dug-in Japanese forces near the Duropa Plantation in heavy jungle. The inexperienced Americans are unable to locate the Japanese positions and their attack is stopped. General Harding requests tanks to support his attack against the extremely well camouflaged Japanese bunkers. Fifth Air Force B-26 Marauders conduct bombing and strafing runs on Japanese positions.

November 20

CBI: Tenth Air Force bombers attack Mandalay, Burma.

MEDITERRANEAN: Ninth Air Force P-40s support British forces capturing Benghazi.

NEW GUINEA: At Buna, without heavy weapons and with limited ammunition and little food, the 1st Battalion, 128th Infantry gains 200 yards; the 3rd Battalion makes no progress. The 1st Battalion, 126th Infantry arrives after completing an overland movement from Pongani.

November 21

ATLANTIC: A U.S. destroyer attacks the German blockade runner *Anneliese Essberger* in the South Atlantic, forcing the crew to scuttle the ship.

GUADALCANAL: The U.S. 182nd Infantry clears Japanese defenders from Point Cruz at Guadalcanal; well dug-in Japanese defenders halt advance of U.S. 164th Infantry. The Japanese begin surveying a runway at Munda, New Georgia Island. The new airfield, 150 miles northwest of Henderson Field at Guadalcanal, is intended to contest control of the air over the Solomons and establish a strongpoint against further American advances.

NEW GUINEA: The U.S. 126th Infantry Regiment is transferred to augment the 7th Australian Infantry Division's attack toward Sanananda. For the attack on Buna, General Harding designates the 1st and 3rd Battalions of the 128th Infantry Regiment, a detachment of 1st Battalion of the 126th Infantry Regiment, and an Australian infantry company as Warren Force. The 2nd Battalion 128th Infantry and the 2nd Battalion of the 126th Infantry Regiment are designated Urbana Force. Warren Force makes no progress, even with air and artillery support.

November 22

NORTH AFRICA, OPERATION TORCH: The final agreement is signed that commits the French to support the Allies against Axis forces in Tunisia and, later, France. French units are added to the Allied forces. Twelfth Air Force B-17s attack El Aouina airfield in Tunis. Algiers airfield is attacked by Axis aircraft, one B-17 is destroyed.

November 23

CBI: B-25 Mitchells with P-40 escorts of the China Air Task Force (CATF) bomb Haiphong harbor, sinking one freighter and damaging two others. Another B-25 mission attacks Tien Ho airfield, destroying as many as 40 Japanese aircraft.

ATLANTIC: A U.S. tanker is torpedoed and sunk by German submarine *U-518* in the mid-Atlantic on its way to Iceland.

The U.S. Coast Guard accepts women into service under the title SPARS (*Semper Paratus* Always Ready). Captain Dorothy Stratton is the commander.

November 24

TUNISIA, OPERATION TORCH: Allied attacks begin and are intended to capture Tunis-Bizerte. The British 78th Infantry Division attacks on three axes, each with one brigade, supported by tanks from the U.S. 13th and 1st Armored regiments, plus an artillery battalion and the 701st Tank Destroyer Battalion. Combat Command B of

U.S. 1st Armored Division begins movement into Tunisia. Twelfth Air Force fighters attack ground targets near Gabès.

PACIFIC: Japanese forces land at Munda Point on New Georgia Island in the Solomons.

Fifth Air Force B-17 bombers and Australian fighters sink a Japanese destroyer and damage torpedo boats off the northern New Guinea coast.

November 25

TUNISIA, OPERATION TORCH: Allied advance is stopped west of Mateur and at Djedeida and Medjez el Bab. The British 6th Armored Division and Combat Command B of the U.S. 1st Armored Division are stopped at Souk el Arba by Axis airpower and tanks.

GUADALCANAL: Japanese submarine *I-17* lands 11 tons of supplies for soldiers on Guadalcanal.

November 26

ALEUTIANS: Eleventh Air Force B-26 Marauders escorted by four P-38s damage Japanese cargo ship off Attu.

TUNISIA: The first U.S.-German tank battle of the war is fought at Chouigui Pass, near Teboura.

NEW GUINEA: Warren Force's attack is supported by air, artillery, and heavy machine gun fire. The 3rd Battalion, 128th Infantry Regiment, moving through swamps, encounters Japanese defenders in well concealed, heavily fortified positions and is unable to make any progress. Urbana Force halts several Japanese counterattacks. Fifth Air Force P-40s, A-20 Havocs, and B-25 Mitchells attack targets to suppress Japanese air defenses and win air superiority over Buna-Gona.

November 27

CBI: Hong Kong harbor is hit by 10 B-25 Mitchells and 20 P-40s of the Chinese Air Task Force of the Tenth Air Force in the largest raid to date.

November 28

TUNISIA: Effective Axis defenses and superior air power halt the Allied offensive. U.S. 2nd Battalion, 13th Armored Regiment of 1st Armored Division reaches Djedeida, about 15 miles west of Tunis. Twelfth Air Force B-26 Marauders attack facilities at Sfax.

November 29

SOUTH PACIFIC: Navy and marine aircraft from Henderson Field sink two Japanese cargo ships at New Georgia Island.

GUADALCANAL: The 1st Marine Division is relieved in place on Guadalcanal. Marine and army units land near Koli Point to construct an airfield.

NEW GUINEA: Fifth Air Force B-17s, P-40s, and A-20 Havocs attack Japanese positions at Gona.

Fifth Air Force B-17s damage two Japanese destroyers carrying reinforcements to Gona, New Guinea, near Vitiaz Strait; the other two destroyers depart without unloading troops.

November 30

GUADALCANAL: The Battle of Tassafaronga. Rear Admiral Carlton H. Wright, commander of Task Force 67, with four heavy cruisers, one light cruiser, and six destroyers, arrives at Iron Bottom Sound to intercept Japanese ships. Wright finds eight Japanese destroyers off Tassafaronga Point landing supplies to troops on Guadalcanal. The Japanese take aggressive action and torpedo four U.S. cruisers, damaging them all. One cruiser later sinks. One Japanese destroyer is hit by gunfire and later sinks. Although the resupply effort fails, the Japanese have a convincing victory.

NEW GUINEA: Elements of U.S. 126th Infantry Regiment near Sanananda are stopped by counterattacks. Urbana Force is unable to clear Japanese defenses to advance on Buna village; Warren Force encounters Japanese defenses at Duropa Plantation and is stopped.

December 1

ATLANTIC: Gas rationing begins in the United States to save wear on tires and conserve rubber.

TUNISIA: Axis counterattacks at Djedeida and Tebourba force the Allies to retreat. Twelfth Air Force B-17s bomb El Aouina airfield. P-38s attacks German forces at Djedeida. Lieutenant General Carl Spaatz arrives in Algeria to serve as Lieutenant General Eisenhower's air adviser. General Ira C. Eaker from VIII Bomber Command takes Spaatz's place as Eighth Air Force commander.

December 2

ATLANTIC: U.S. steamship is torpedoed and sunk by German submarine *U-604* off Bermuda.

At the University of Chicago scientists led by Enrico Fermi are able to initiate a self-sustaining nuclear chain reaction for the first time. The reaction is a critical step in the Manhattan Project, the secret plan to develop an atomic bomb.

NEW GUINEA: Both American and Australian forces are unable to break the Japanese defensive lines. The U.S. 126th Infantry continues to hold a roadblock before Sanananda against numerous Japanese attacks intended to eliminate it. Malaria, dengue fever, dysentery, and typhus have taken a serious toll on the Allied troops. Told by General MacArthur to take Buna or die in the attempt, Major General Robert L. Eichelberger, commander of I Corps, inspects the 32nd Division and finds that 66 percent of the men are too sick to fight at any given time. Major General Harding and several subordinates are relieved of command. Brigadier General Albert W. Waldron takes command in Harding's place.

December 3

GUADALCANAL: U.S. aircraft from Henderson Field attack a convoy attempting to resupply Japanese forces on Guadalcanal. A destroyer is damaged, and the resupply attempt is only marginally successful.

December 4

MEDITERRANEAN: Ninth Air Force B-24 Liberators conduct first American bombing raid on Italy. Attacking the port of Naples, the 20 bombers sink an Italian light cruiser and damage two other light cruisers as well as four destroyers.

TUNISIA: Twelfth Air Force B-17s attack Bizerte harbor; A-20 Havocs with P-38 escorts attack El Aouina airfield. Fighters attack Gabès.

December 5

ATLANTIC: President Roosevelt establishes the Office of Economic Stabilization to control wartime inflation and limit economic dislocation.

NORTH AFRICA: Lieutenant General Carl Spaatz is named deputy commander in chief for air operations.

TUNISIA: Twelfth Air Force B-17s attack Tunis; B-25 Mitchells and A-20 Havocs escorted by P-38 Lightnings attack Sidi Ahmed airfield.

PACIFIC: Army Air Force Units in SOPAC are notified that they will be designated as Thirteenth Air Force.

NEW GUINEA: Fifth Air Force B-25 Mitchells and A-20 Havocs support the ground attack on Buna. During Urbana Force's attack on Buna village, Lieutenant Robert H. Odell, the commander of F Company, 2nd Battalion 126th Infantry Regiment, finds himself taking orders directly from Major General Eichelberger, who is initially supervising the attack to assess the capabilities of the 32nd Division. The fighting becomes so heavy and confused that Eichelberger finds himself taking an active role. The general discovers firsthand the difficulty of the task for the infantrymen without additional artillery and tank support. Buna village is isolated. Warren Force attacks with Australian-supplied Bren gun carriers (small armored transports), but is unsuccessful. Brigadier General Waldron is wounded in the attack and Brigadier General Clovis E. Beyers takes command of the 32nd Infantry Division.

December 6

ETO: Eighth Air Force bombers attack Lille locomotive works and Abeville-Drucat airfield in France.

NEW GEORGIA: SOPAC aircraft locate construction equipment at Munda on New Georgia Island, indications that the Japanese are building at least one airfield there. This discovery initiates almost daily bombing of Munda by U.S. aircraft.

December 7

ATLANTIC: A U.S. freighter attempting to join convoy HX 217 (New York to Liverpool) is torpedoed and sunk by German submarine *U-600* east of Newfoundland.

TUNISIA: Twelfth Air Force B-17s attack Bizerte; A-20 Havocs attack German troops and tanks near Tebourba in support of the Allied defense.

PACIFIC: U.S. submarine *Kingfish* torpedoes and sinks a Japanese transport west of the Bonin Islands.

GUADALCANAL: U.S. aircraft from Henderson Field attack a 12-ship convoy with reinforcements and supplies bound for Guadalcanal. Two destroyers are damaged. A U.S. cargo ship is damaged by an attack from a Japanese midget submarine launched by submarine *I-24* off Lunga Point, Guadalcanal.

December 8

ATLANTIC: President Roosevelt receives the JCS plan for the offensive to recapture Burma. The assessment is that Stilwell requires additional resources to support the British, who have the primary responsibility for the campaign.

ETO: Eighth Air Force discovers that bombing of U-boat facilities in France is having no effect.

GUADALCANAL: The army's 132nd Infantry Regiment lands at Guadalcanal. Units on Guadalcanal include the American Division, the 147th and 132nd Infantry Regiments, two marine regiments, and four field artillery battalions.

Eight U.S. motor torpedo (*PT*) boats prevent eight Japanese destroyers from landing reinforcements at Guadalcanal. U.S. submarine *Gar* sinks a Japanese cargo ship off Borneo.

NEW GUINEA: Fifth Air Force B-17s and one B-24 Liberator damage two Japanese destroyers off Buna, New Guinea, attempting to land reinforcements.

December 9

SOUTH PACIFIC: Aircraft from Henderson Field attack the Japanese base at Munda, New Georgia.

GUADALCANAL: Major General Alexander A. Vandegrift and the 1st Marine Division depart Guadalcanal. Major General Alexander M. Patch, former commander of the army's American Division, takes over as commander of U.S. forces on Guadalcanal. It is estimated that one-third of all the marines who left with Vandegrift are unfit for duty due to illness. Vandegrift tells his soldiers, sailors, and marines that their "unbelievable achievements have made the name 'Guadalcanal' a synonym for death and disaster in the language of our enemy. . . ."

Motor torpedo boat *PT-59* sinks Japanese submarine *I-3* as it attempts to drop off supplies to Japanese troops on Guadalcanal.

NEW GUINEA: The Australian 7th Infantry Division captures Gona village. The 3rd Battalion of the 127th Infantry Regiment is airlifted to the vicinity of Buna. Fifth Air Force B-26 Marauders attack Buna; P-40s fly support missions for the 126th Infantry Regiment holding a blocking position near Sanananda.

December 10

ATLANTIC: A U.S. Navy PBY Catalina sinks German submarine *U-611* in the North Atlantic.

TUNISIA: Heavy rains prevent any air support missions for Allied forces.

PACIFIC: U.S. submarine *Halibut* torpedoes and sinks a Japanese merchant ship and damages a Japanese transport off Hokkaido.

SOUTH PACIFIC: U.S. submarine *Wahoo* sinks a Japanese collier and B-17s damage two Japanese oilers off Bougainville.

NEW GUINEA: At Buna, the 3rd Battalion, 127th Infantry relieves the 2nd Battalion, 126th Infantry Regiment, now reduced to about 150 men.

December 11

NORTH AFRICA: Twelfth Air Force establishes five area commands to support Allied operations throughout North Africa.

MEDITERRANEAN: Ninth Air Force B-24 Liberators bomb Naples harbor

SOUTH PACIFIC: U.S. submarine *Seadragon* torpedoes and damages a Japanese cargo ship in the eastern Solomons.

December 12
TUNISIA: Twelfth Air Force B-17s with P-38 escorts attack facilities at Tunis.
PACIFIC: U.S. submarine *Drum* torpedoes and damages Japanese aircraft carrier *Ryuho* in the northern Bonin Islands. U.S. submarine *Halibut* torpedoes and sinks a Japanese merchant cargo ship off the northeast coast of Honshu, Japan.
GUADALCANAL: Five U.S. motor torpedo boats attack 11 Japanese destroyers attempting a resupply mission off Cape Esperance, Guadalcanal. One motor torpedo boat and one destroyer are sunk in the engagement.

December 13
NEW GUINEA: Fifth Air Force B-17s and B-24 Liberators attack a convoy of five Japanese destroyers carrying more than 800 men off Madang, but do no damage. Buna village is heavily bombarded in preparation for an attack. The remaining Japanese defenders evacuate the village during the night.

December 14
PACIFIC: Fleet Air Command is established at Nouméa, New Caledonia, commanded by Rear Admiral Marc A. Mitscher. U.S. submarine *Sunfish* mines the entrance to Iseno Umi Bay, Japan.
NEW GUINEA: Buna village falls to Urbana Force. Fifth Air Force aircraft attack Japanese troops and supplies landed at Mambare River by the five destroyers previously attacked.

December 15
CBI: The all-black 45th Engineer General Service Regiment and the 823rd Engineer Aviation Battalion begin construction of the Ledo Road. Beginning at Ledo in India, the goal is to connect with the old Burma Road at Kunming, 271 miles away.
ATLANTIC: U.S. freighter is torpedoed and sunk by German submarine *U-174* en route from Trinidad to Brazil. U.S. Coast Guard cutter sinks German submarine *U-626* in the North Atlantic.
TUNISIA: Twelfth Air Force B-26s attack El Aouina airfield in Tunis, while B-17s attack the port. Other B-17s attack Bizerte. Ninth Air Force B-24 Liberators attack facilities at Sfax.
NEW GUINEA: As the 2nd Battalion, 128th Infantry Regiment attempts to clear Japanese defenders southeast of Buna village, three general officers are wounded in the day's fighting. General Eichelberger, the only U.S. general officer available, takes command of the battle.

December 16
PACIFIC: U.S. submarine *Halibut* torpedoes and sinks a Japanese merchant ship off Honshu, Japan.

December 17
CBI: CATF (China Air Task Force) bombers attack Laisho.
TUNISIA: Twelfth Air Force B-17s attack Bizerte and Tunis; A-20 Havocs attack Gabès.

PACIFIC: U.S. submarine *Drum* mines the Bungo Strait in the Japanese home islands.

SOUTH PACIFIC: U.S. submarine *Grouper* torpedoes and sinks a Japanese cargo ship in the Solomons.

GUADALCANAL: The U.S. 132nd Infantry of the Americal Division begins an attack on Mount Austen to protect Henderson Field and support offensive operations to the west. The attack is supported by the 1st Battalion, 2nd Marines, as well as by P-38s and marine SBD Dauntless dive-bombers providing air support. The Japanese are well entrenched and the attack fails.

The U.S. 35th Infantry Regiment, 25th Infantry Division arrives at Guadalcanal.

NEW GEORGIA: At Munda Point, New Georgia, the Japanese complete construction of a 4,700-foot-long airfield.

December 18

TUNISIA: Axis forces in Tunisia number 47,000, with 25,000 of them German combat veterans. Twelfth Air Force B-17s with P-38 Lightning escorts attack Bizerte; one bomber and three fighters are lost to enemy fighters. B-26 Marauders and P-38s attack Sousse; two bombers are lost. A-20 Havocs attack railyards in Mateur. Ninth Air Force B-17s attack Sousse.

PACIFIC: U.S. submarine *Sunfish* torpedoes and damages a Japanese transport west of the Bonin Islands.

NEW GUINEA: The Warren Force, directed by Australian brigadier general George F. Wootten and reinforced by two Australian infantry battalions and tanks, supports the 128th Infantry's attack on Buna.

Fifth Air Force B-17s attack Japanese convoy off Madang; B-24 Liberators bomb Lae airfield; other bombers and fighters provide air support to Allied ground attacks.

U.S. submarine *Albacore* torpedoes and sinks a Japanese light cruiser off Madang harbor in eastern New Guinea and torpedoes an armed merchant cruiser.

December 20

ALEUTIANS: Eleventh Air Force B-26 Marauders, B-24 Liberators, B-25 Mitchells, and nine P-38 Lightnings attack Kiska harbor, focusing on the submarine base and facilities. An ammunition dump is hit and a cargo ship is damaged by strafing P-38s.

ETO: The air depot at Romilly-sur-Seine is attacked by 72 Eighth Air Force B-17s. Six bombers are lost to enemy fighters.

PACIFIC: A Japanese merchant ship sinks off Honshu, Japan, after striking a mine laid moments earlier by U.S. submarine *Trigger*.

SOUTH PACIFIC: U.S. submarine *Seadragon* torpedoes and sinks Japanese submarine *I-4* in the waters between New Britain and New Ireland, as *I-4* attempts to resupply Japanese troops on Guadalcanal.

December 21

NEW GUINEA: Fifth Air Force B-17s attack Finschhafen harbor; B-24 Liberators attack Japanese supplies at the mouth of the Mambare River.

December 22

PACIFIC: U.S. submarine *Trigger* torpedoes and damages a Japanese merchant ship near the entrance of Tokyo Bay.

SOUTH PACIFIC: U.S. submarine *Greenling*, attacking a Japanese convoy, torpedoes and sinks a Japanese patrol boat near Bougainville.

December 23

TUNISIA: After relieving the British Coldstream Guards, the U.S. 18th RCT of the 1st Infantry Division is driven off Djebel el Ahmera, later known as Longstop Hill, by a German counterattack. Twelfth Air Force aircraft are completely grounded due to bad weather.

December 24

TUNISIA: The End of Operation Torch. Lieutenant General Eisenhower calls off further offensive action in order to regroup the Allied effort and resupply his exhausted units.

Admiral Darlan is assassinated by a young monarchist, leaving General Henri Giraud as the leader of French North Africa.

GUADALCANAL: The 132nd Infantry reaches the Japanese Gifu defensive lines on the west side of Mount Austen. Over 500 Japanese soldiers are in prepared positions.

NEW GEORGIA: U.S. SBD Dauntless dive-bombers, P-40s, and F4F Wildcats from Henderson Field attack and sink nine of 13 Japanese barges carrying reinforcements headed for Munda, New Georgia. SOPAC P-39 Airacobras assist in destroying 24 Japanese fighters at Munda.

NEW GUINEA: During an attack near Buna, First Sergeant Elmer J. Burr, of Company I, 127th Infantry Regiment, 32nd Infantry Division, sees a Japanese grenade land near his company commander. Without hesitation, he covers the grenade with his body and is killed instantly by the explosion. For his heroic act of self-sacrifice, First Sergeant Burr will receive the Medal of Honor.

December 25

SOUTH PACIFIC: U.S. submarine *Seadragon* torpedoes and damages a Japanese transport off New Britain.

NEW GUINEA: The Australians and Americans of Warren Force conduct an attack through heavily forested swamp against strong Japanese resistance. Colonel Clarence A. Martin climbs a tree to locate Japanese positions. Using his rifle, he kills several enemy soldiers. Working in coordination with tanks and artillery, the Allies begin to make progress.

U.S. submarine *Tautog* torpedoes and sinks a Japanese cargo ship off Timor; U.S. submarine *Thresher* torpedoes and sinks a Japanese army transport south of Borneo.

December 26

ALEUTIANS: Eleventh Air Force B-24 Liberators and P-38 Lightnings attack Sarana Bay and Attu. Japanese antiaircraft fire downs one P-38.

TUNISIA: Twelfth Air Force B-17s attack Bizerte and Sfax. Two bombers and two P-38s are lost; P-40s strafe barges off Sousse. C-47 transports drop a detachment of U.S. paratroopers near El Djem. Ninth Air Force B-24 Liberators attack Tunis, Sfax, and Sousse.

GUADALCANAL: Brigadier General Francis P. Mulcahy, commander of the 2nd Marine Aircraft Wing on Guadalcanal, relieves Brigadier General L. E. Woods as commander of air forces on Guadalcanal.

NEW GEORGIA: U.S. SBD Dauntless dive-bombers, F4F Wildcats, and P-38 Lightnings from Henderson Field sink three Japanese merchant cargo ships at Wickham Anchorage in New Georgia.

December 27

NEW GUINEA: Fifth Air Force B-17s attack Rabaul and B-26 Marauders support the attack on Gona.

December 28

TUNISIA: Twelfth Air Force B-17s bomb Sousse. P-38 and P-40 escort fighters down four enemy fighters. Ninth Air Force bombers attack Sousse.

PACIFIC: U.S. submarine *Kingfish* torpedoes and sinks a Japanese merchant ship off Formosa; U.S. submarine *Triton* torpedoes and sinks a Japanese merchant ship in the Central Pacific.

NEW GUINEA: The Warren Force meets the Urbana Force and begins to eliminate the final Japanese resistance in the Gona and Buna area.

December 29

CBI: Rangoon is attacked by 12 B-24 Liberators from Tenth Air Force.

December 30

ALEUTIANS: An initial attack by B-25 Mitchells with P-38 Lightning escorts at Kiska harbor is met by Japanese fighters, which shoot down two P-38s; a B-25 is also lost. A follow-on attack by B-24 Liberators, B-25 Mitchells, and B-26 Marauders targets two Japanese ships and three submarines in the harbor.

TUNISIA: An attack by Twelfth Air Force B-17s on Sfax continues with a second strike by B-25 Mitchells escorted by P-38s. German troop concentrations at Gabès are hit by B-17s. Gabès airfield is hit by P-40s and P-38 Lightnings. P-40s fly close air support missions near El Guettar.

PACIFIC: U.S. submarine *Greenling*, attacking a Japanese convoy in the central Pacific, torpedoes and sinks one cargo ship and damages another.

NEW GUINEA: U.S. submarine *Searaven* lands agents on the south coast of Ceram Island, Netherlands East Indies. U.S. submarine *Thresher* torpedoes and sinks a Japanese merchant ship off Borneo. Fifth Air Force B-17s attack Rabaul and sink a Japanese merchant ship in port.

December 31

ALEUTIANS: B-24 Liberators from Eleventh Air Force with nine P-38s as escort damage two Japanese merchant cargo ships off Kiska.

ATLANTIC: U-boats operating in the Atlantic have sunk a total of 1,160 ships (about 6.3 million tons) in 1942. U-boats have claimed nearly 70 percent of all Allied and neutral shipping losses (about 7.8 million tons). The German navy is winning the race, sinking one million more tons of shipping than has been built in 1942.

PACIFIC: Japanese Imperial Headquarters orders the evacuation of Guadalcanal. This is intended as a local withdrawal to consolidate severely stretched air, sea, and land forces. The Japanese cannot match the ability of the United States to supply and reinforce. Although giving up Guadalcanal, Japanese strategists intend to continue the campaign for New Guinea.

GUADALCANAL: The 2nd Battalion of the 132nd Infantry Regiment supports the attack on Mount Austen, but the Japanese defend tenaciously, forcing the American commander to call off the attack. B-26 Marauder bombers land at Guadalcanal.

1943

January 1

MEDITERRANEAN: German submarine *U-73* torpedoes and sinks U.S. freighter off Oran, Algeria.

In Tunisia, 15 Ninth Air Force B-24 Liberators attack Tunis harbor, along with Twelfth Air Force B-17s. B-26 Marauders from Twelfth Air Force hit the railyard at Tunis.

TUNISIA: Lieutenant General Eisenhower orders U.S. II Corps under command of Major General Lloyd R. Fredendall to concentrate in the Tebessa-Kasserine area in preparation for an attack on the Axis flank near the Tunisian-Libyan border.

SOUTHWEST PACIFIC AREA: Fifth Air Force B-24 Liberators and B-17s bomb Japanese ships and airfields at Rabaul.

PACIFIC: U.S. submarine *Porpoise* torpedoes and sinks a Japanese merchant cargo ship, and U.S. submarine *Trigger* damages a Japanese transport off the coast of Honshu, Japan.

NEW GUINEA: Urbana Force makes little progress in its attack toward Buna Mission; Warren Force surrounds Japanese defenders.

January 2

CBI: CATF (China Air Task Force) fighters attack a truck convoy on the Burma Road, destroying five trucks.

MEDITERRANEAN: B-25 Mitchells and B-24 Liberators of the Ninth Air Force attack airfields on Crete, destroying over 20 Axis aircraft. Twelfth Air Force B-17s bomb La Goulette harbor in Tunisia. Two escorting P-38 Lightnings are lost to German fighters. A-20 Havocs and Boston Mk IIIs, with fighter escorts, bomb Sousse harbor. B-26 Marauders with fighter escort bomb a bridge near El Djem.

PACIFIC: U.S. submarine *Argonaut* torpedoes and sinks a Japanese guardboat in the Bismarck Sea. U.S. submarine *Spearfish* damages a Japanese cargo ship off New Ireland.

GUADALCANAL: The army's American and 25th Infantry Divisions and units of the 2nd Marine Division are designated on Guadalcanal as XIV Corps with Major General Alexander M. Patch commanding. The 132nd Infantry Regiment overruns the Gifu defenses. The 25th Infantry Division and a portion of the 2nd Marine Division arrive on Guadalcanal. SBD Dauntless dive-bombers, F4F Wildcats, B-17s, B-26

Marauders, and P-38 Lightnings attack 10 Japanese destroyers carrying supplies to Guadalcanal. The SBDs damage a destroyer.

NEW GUINEA: Urbana Force captures Buna Mission; Warren Force completes clearing operations.

January 3

ETO: Eighth Air Force launches its heaviest attack on the St-Nazaire U-boat base. Although 85 B-17s and 13 B-24 Liberators begin the mission, only 60 B-17s and eight B-24s hit the target. Using formation precision bombing tactics for the first time, the bombers drop 171 tons of bombs, damaging the docks. The Germans lose approximately 14 aircraft; seven B-17s are lost, 51 B-17s and six B-24s are damaged. American casualties are 34 crewmen dead and wounded and 70 missing.

TUNISIA: An Axis tank and infantry attack breaks through French defenses at Fondouk. A-20 Havocs and Boston Mk IIIs of the Twelfth Air Force attack German tanks moving west from Fondouk, destroying several enemy vehicles.

American M3 Stuart tanks are employed against the Japanese Gifu stronghold on Guadalcanal.

January 4

CBI: Tenth Air Force bombers attack the railyard at Mandalay, causing heavy damage; a Japanese transport ship at the mouth of the Rangoon River is also damaged.

ATLANTIC: U.S. submarine *Shad* torpedoes and sinks a German minesweeper in Bay of Biscay.

GUADALCANAL: Japanese forces on Guadalcanal are ordered to move to New Georgia. The U.S. 132nd Infantry clears the Gifu area of resistance, suffering nearly 400 casualties in the dense jungle and hills. The Japanese reportedly have lost 500 men. The 161st RCT of the 25th Infantry Division arrives, as does the 6th Marine Regiment of the 2nd Marine Division.

January 5

MEDITERRANEAN: The U.S. Fifth Army is activated at Oujda, Morocco, under command of Lieutenant General Mark W. Clark. Lieutenant General Eisenhower creates Allied Air Force, under Lieutenant General Carl Spaatz. The command includes Twelfth Air Force, Eighth Air Force, and Eastern Air Command in the China-Burma-India Theater.

GUADALCANAL: Major General Patch orders the 25th Infantry Division, commanded by Major General J. Lawton Collins, to relieve the 132nd Infantry and attack west, supported on its right flank by the 2nd Marine Division.

NEW GEORGIA: Naval Task Group 67.2 under Rear Admiral Walden L. Ainsworth bombards Munda airfield on New Georgia Island.

January 6
ALEUTIANS: U.S. PBY Catalina sinks a Japanese cargo ship near Kiska; Eleventh Air Force B-24 Liberators sink a Japanese cargo ship off Holtz Bay.
ATLANTIC: A U.S. PBY-5A Catalina sinks German submarine *U-164* off Brazil.

January 7
NEW GUINEA: Fifth Air Force B-17s, B-24 Liberators, B-25 Mitchells, and B-26 Marauders, along with Australian and New Zealand air force aircraft, supported by U.S. P-38 Lightnings and P-40s, attack a Japanese convoy headed for Lae, New Guinea. One enemy cargo ship is·sunk, but the convoy arrives at Lae.

January 8
CBI: Chiang Kai-shek notifies President Roosevelt that the Chinese army will not undertake offensive operations in spring of 1943.
ATLANTIC: German submarine *U-124* attacks the 12-ship convoy TB 1 (Trinidad to Bahia), torpedoing a U.S. tanker and freighter.
TUNISIA: Twelfth Air Force B-17s bomb the naval base at Bizerte. B-26 Marauders bomb Kairouan airfield. A-20 Havocs with P-40 escorts attack Axis tanks near Gabès.
NEW GUINEA: Troops of the 127th Infantry Regiment, 32nd Infantry Division capture Tarakena; the 163rd Infantry Regiment, 41st Infantry Division begins the advance on Sanananda. Fifth Air Force B-17s, B-24 Liberators, B-25 Mitchells, and A-20 Havocs, supported by P-38 Lightnings, attack the Japanese ships unloading at Lae.

January 9
ATLANTIC: German submarine *U-384* attacks and sinks U.S. freighter in the North Atlantic after a prolonged fight by the freighter's crew. German submarine *U-124* attacks convoy TB 1 (Trinidad to Bahia) again, torpedoing and sinking two U.S. freighters off Dutch Guiana.
PACIFIC: U.S. submarine *Gar* torpedoes and damages a Japanese oiler in the Makassar Strait, Netherlands East Indies; U.S. submarine *Nautilus* torpedoes and sinks a Japanese transport ship near Bougainville; U.S. submarine *Searaven* torpedoes and damages a Japanese cargo ship off the far northwest corner of New Guinea; U.S. submarine *Tautog* torpedoes and damages a Japanese light cruiser northeast of Timor.

January 10
TUNISIA: Twelfth Air Force B-26 Marauders, with P-38 Lightnings escorting, attack the railyard and oil storage tanks at Gabès.
GUADALCANAL: The U.S. 25th Infantry Division, after gaining control of the Gifu-Mt. Austen area, crosses the Matanikau River and ties in with the U.S. 2nd Marine Division. The U.S. 182nd and 132nd Infantry Regiments of the Americal Division support the XIV Corps advance. Japanese forces defend a collection of hills called Galloping Horse, Sea Horse, and the Gifu Strongpoint, employing a system of interlocked, heavily fortified bunkers supported by heavy artillery. Two battalions of the 27th Infantry Regiment of the 25th Infantry Division

attack the hill complex, taking half of Galloping Horse, but are slowed by the steep terrain and Japanese defenses on Hill 53. Two battalions of the 35th Infantry Regiment of the 25th Infantry Division attack another hill mass called Sea Horse. Another battalion of the 35th continues to clear the Gifu area of enemy stragglers. The attacks are hampered by a lack of water resupply and formidable terrain. The 3rd Battalion, 35th Infantry attacks Sea Horse after calling for artillery fire. As K and L Companies moved forward to attack, K Company begins crossing a stream that is a branch of the Matanikau River. To protect the company's flank as it crosses the open area, two light machine guns from M Company are posted in an overwatch position along with a few riflemen. A sudden Japanese counterat-

A wounded soldier of the 25th Infantry Division receives first aid in the Guadalcanal jungle while litter bearers stand by, January 10, 1943.

tack hits the overwatch position, destroying one machine gun and killing and wounding the crew of the second machine gun. The riflemen are driven off, leaving the company exposed to a devastating attack when they are most vulnerable as they cross the river. Although ordered to withdraw, Sergeant William G. Fournier, the machine gun section leader, and Technical Sergeant/5 Lewis Hall of M Company charge up to the unmanned machine gun and begin firing on the Japanese, who are moving along the stream bed. Because the machine gun cannot be depressed low enough to fire on the enemy, Sergeant Fournier lifts it by its tripod while Hall fires the gun. Standing completely exposed to the enemy, Fournier and Hall continue to fire on the Japanese until both men are mortally wounded. The enemy withdraws and the company is saved. For their singular act of heroism Sergeant Fournier and Technical Sergeant/5 Hall will receive the Medal of Honor.

January 11

MEDITERRANEAN: Ninth Air Force B-24 Liberators bomb Naples harbor.
PACIFIC: U.S. submarine *Trigger* torpedoes and sinks a Japanese destroyer off Honshu. U.S. submarine *Trout* torpedoes and damages a Japanese oiler off Borneo.
GUADALCANAL: The Sea Horse area is under American control. Eight Japanese destroyers off Cape Esperance, Guadalcanal, are attacked by nine U.S. motor torpedo boats from Tulagi. A Japanese destroyer and a U.S. PT boat are damaged; one PT boat is sunk.

January 12

GUADALCANAL: Captain Charles W. Davis is the battalion executive officer of 2nd Battalion, 27th Infantry Regiment, 25th Infantry Division, facing Japanese defenders defending the ridge between Hills 52 and 53 on Guadalcanal. He volunteers to carry instructions to the battalion's forward companies now trapped in a crossfire from Japanese machine guns. He remains with the companies all day and throughout the night. The following day he leads an assault on the Japanese position. As he moves forward, his rifle jams, but he draws his .45 caliber automatic pistol and leads the men forward. Inspired by his heroic example, the soldiers seize the hill. For his decisive leadership and heroic example in the face of a determined enemy, Captain Davis will receive the Medal of Honor.

NEW GEORGIA: SOPAC B-26 Marauders, P-38 Lightnings, P-39 Airacobras, and P-40s attack Munda. Two B-26s are lost.

January 13

ATLANTIC: U.S. PBY-5A Catalinas sink German submarine *U-507* off Brazil.

ETO: Eighth Air Force sends 72 B-17s against industrial targets at Lille, France, dropping 125 tons of bombs and damaging the locomotive construction and repair works at the cost of three B-17s. At least three German aircraft are destroyed and five damaged in the raid.

SOUTH PACIFIC: Major General Millard F. Harmon, commander of U.S. Army forces in the South Pacific Area (COMGENSOPAC), establishes the Thirteenth Air Force, under the command of Brigadier General Nathan F. Twining, with headquarters at Espiritu Santo Island, New Hebrides. The Thirteenth Air Force takes operational control of all U.S. Army Air Forces in the Southern Pacific, except for Army Air Force units on Guadalcanal, which are under the operational control of the Marine Corps.

U.S. submarine *Whale* torpedoes and sinks a Japanese collier north of Kwajalein; U.S. submarine *Triton* damages a Japanese oiler north of New Ireland.

GUADALCANAL: Galloping Horse falls to the 25th Infantry Division, supported by massed artillery fire. The 2nd Marine Division begins its advance along the coast past Point Cruz, eliminating enemy positions with flamethrowers, and supported by naval gunfire, artillery, and tanks. The Gifu strongpoint still holds out. American infantrymen suffer from a lack of water in the thick jungle terrain.

NEW GUINEA: Fifth Air Force A-20 Havocs provide ground support to Allied forces near Sanananda. Bombers attack docks and airfields at both Lae and Salamaua.

January 14

MEDITERRANEAN: The Casablanca Conference. The Casablanca conference to outline Allied strategy for 1943 begins. This is the first great Allied wartime conference. President Franklin D. Roosevelt, Prime Minister Winston S. Churchill, the military chiefs of staff of both Britain and the United States, and the French leaders General Henri Giraud and Charles de Gaulle, leader of the French government-in-exile in Britain. Roosevelt arrives in secret and is the first American president to visit Africa while in office.

TUNISIA: Twelfth Air Force B-17s, with 17 P-38 Lightnings providing escort, bomb enemy shipping and the harbor facilities at Sfax.

PACIFIC: U.S. submarine *Searaven* attacks a Japanese convoy northwest of the Palaus, sinking the escort vessel and a cargo ship.

GUADALCANAL: Thirteenth Air Force P-39 Airacobras drop improvised gasoline bombs on the Japanese defenders near Mount Austen and defending at Kokumbona.

January 15

CBI: Tenth Air Force B-24 Liberators attack a Japanese convoy off the coast of Burma, sinking one cargo ship and damaging another. The cargo ship was moving Allied prisoners, and 500 men perish.

SOUTH PACIFIC: Navy SBD Dauntless dive-bombers, escorted by F4F Wildcats and P-39 Airocobras, attack a Japanese cargo ship off Munda, New Georgia. Seven enemy aircraft are shot down; one American fighter is lost. B-17s and PBY Catalinas bomb Kahili, Bougainville Island. B-24 Liberators bomb the airfield on Gasmata Island in the Bismarck Archipelago.

GUADALCANAL: The 2nd Marine Division makes little progress against Japanese defenses along the coast of Guadalcanal. SBD Dauntless dive-bombers from Henderson Field, with F4F Wildcats and P-39 Airacobras escorting, attack nine Japanese destroyers and pilots report four ships damaged. Eight enemy aircraft are shot down, but one SBD and five fighters are lost.

NEW GUINEA: Fifth Air Force A-20s provide support to the U.S. 163rd Infantry Regiment at Sanananda. B-25 Mitchells attack Japanese supply points at Lae.

January 16

CBI: Tenth Air Force China Air Task Force (CATF) P-40s intercept a Japanese attack on Yunnani. Pilots report that seven enemy aircraft are shot down.

SOUTH PACIFIC: Thirteenth Air Force B-17s bomb the Kahili airfield on Bougainville Island. U.S. submarine *Greenling* torpedoes and sinks a Japanese transport west of Kavieng, New Ireland; U.S. submarine *Growler* attacks a Japanese convoy, torpedoing a cargo ship north of Kavieng.

GUADALCANAL: Major General Alexander M. Patch, commander of XIV Corps, creates a composite unit, combining the 6th Marines, the 2nd Marine Division, and the 182nd and 147th Infantry Regiments, along with the Americal Division artillery, into an army-marine division known as CAM. This unit is to advance along the coast, while the 25th Infantry Division on CAM's flank attempts to clear Japanese defensive positions to the south and west, then drive north to encircle the enemy.

NEW GUINEA: The attack on Sanananda begins. The U.S. 163rd Infantry Regiment clears Japanese strongpoints in coordination with the Australian 18th Brigade. Fifth Air Force A-20 Havocs provide air support for the attack.

January 17

CBI: Tenth Air Force B-25 Mitchells bomb railroad targets in Burma.

MEDITERRANEAN: Ninth Air Force B-24 Liberators bomb Tripoli harbor in Libya. P-40s support the British Eighth Army's advance toward Tripoli.

PACIFIC: U.S. submarine *Finback* attacks and damages a Japanese cargo ship off southern Kyushu, Japan; U.S. submarine *Whale* damages a Japanese troopship near Truk. Fifth Air Force B-17s bomb Japanese airfields and shipping at Rabaul.

GUADALCANAL: Thirteenth Air Force P-39 Airacobras attack Japanese defenses near Mount Austen. B-17s from Henderson Field drop supplies, including much needed water, by parachute or by simply wrapping ammunition and food in burlap or canvas and dropping them out of the aircraft.

January 18
ALEUTIANS: Eleventh Air Force B-24 Liberators and B-26 Marauders, one B-25 Mitchell, and six P-38 Lightnings attempt a bombing run on Japanese ships reported at Kiska harbor. The attack scores no hits, but bad weather leads to six aircraft lost, including three B-24s. One B-24 crew will later be rescued.
SOUTHWEST PACIFIC AREA: A U.S. tanker is torpedoed and damaged by Japanese submarine *I-21* off the coast of southern Australia.
PACIFIC: U.S. submarine *Greenling* damages a Japanese ammunition ship north of Kavieng. U.S. submarine *Silversides* torpedoes and sinks a Japanese fleet tanker near Truk.
GUADALCANAL: The CAM Division advances 1,500 yards beyond Point Cruz.

January 19
CBI: Tenth Air Force P-40s and one B-25 Mitchell attack Japanese positions at Kamaing.
TUNISIA: Ninth Air Force B-24 Liberators bomb the harbor at Sousse; Twelfth Air Force B-17s, with P-38 Lightnings providing cover, bomb industrial targets south of Tunis. B-25 Mitchells attack Medenine. U.S. and British forces, including Combat Command B of the 1st Armored Division, move to reinforce French forces hard-pressed by an Axis attack in the Rebaa Valley.
SOUTHWEST PACIFIC AREA: U.S. submarine *Greenling* damages a Japanese cargo ship north of Rabaul.
PACIFIC: U.S. submarine *Swordfish* near Truk attacks a Japanese convoy headed for the Solomons and sinks a cargo ship. U.S. submarine *Haddock* attacks a Japanese convoy off southern Honshu, Japan, and damages a transport. U.S. submarine *Nautilus* damages a Japanese destroyer in the vicinity of Tulagi. U.S. submarine *Spearfish* is attacked and damaged by Japanese aircraft near the Gilberts while headed for Pearl Harbor.
NEW GEORGIA: Thirteenth Air Force B-17s with P-38 Lightnings and P-40s flying escort bomb the airfield at Munda, New Georgia.
NEW GUINEA: Japanese forces begin to withdraw from Sanananda. Pockets of resistance on the Soputa-Sanananda trail hold up the 163rd Infantry Regiment.

January 20
MEDITERRANEAN: Twelfth Air Force B-25 Mitchells, escorted by P-38 Lightnings, attack Axis ships in the Straits of Sicily and sink a tanker.
PACIFIC: U.S. submarine *Silversides* south of Truk attacks a Japanese convoy headed for the Solomons, torpedoing and sinking one transport ship and damaging another.

January 21
TUNISIA: Twelfth Air Force B-26 Marauders attack Axis shipping off Cape Bon, sinking a freighter and damaging another. Escorting P-38 Lightnings lose two aircraft while destroying five enemy aircraft. A-20s supporting Combat Command B of the U.S. 1st Armored Division attack enemy tanks and trucks near Ousseltia; P-38s attack Axis ground forces moving on the Gabès-Medenine-Ben Gardane road, destroying 65 vehicles and two enemy fighters.

SOUTHWEST PACIFIC AREA: Fifth Air Force B-17s bomb the airfield and shipping at Rabaul.

SOUTH PACIFIC: U.S. submarine *Gato* off Bougainville Island attacks a portion of the Japanese convoy headed for the Solomons, damaging a transport ship. Thirteenth Air Force transfers its headquarters from Nouméa, New Caledonia, to Espiritu Santo in the New Hebrides.

GUADALCANAL: Marine tanks support the army's 2nd Battalion, 35th Infantry Regiment in clearing Japanese positions at Gifu.

January 22

TUNISIA: Twelfth Air Force B-17s bomb El Aouina airfield, followed later by B-26 Marauders and B-25 Mitchells. P-39 Airacrobras and P-40s support the Allied attack in the Ousseltia Valley, which is stopped by strong enemy defenses. B-26s damage an Axis cargo ship in the Straits of Sicily.

GUADALCANAL: The CAM Division advances toward Kokumbona, making contact with U.S. 27th Infantry Regiment of the 25th Infantry Division coming from the south. U.S. freighter is torpedoed and damaged by Japanese submarine *I-21* off the southern coast of Australia, near Sidney.

NEW GUINEA: Sanananda, the final remaining position of the Japanese in Papua, is captured. The U.S. 163rd Infantry Regiment, 41st Infantry Division participates, with elements of the 32nd Infantry Division. The Japanese have been without food or ammunition for several weeks and can no longer mount serious resistance. The campaign has cost the Australians nearly 5,700 killed and wounded; the Americans suffered nearly 2,900 casualties. Over 27,000 cases of malaria have been reported. The 126th Infantry Regiment began the campaign with 131 officers and 3,040 enlisted men. When it is over, only 32 officers and 579 men can report for duty. Lacking training and experience, the U.S. Army has paid heavily in combat but gained important lessons that will bring success in the future.

January 23

ATLANTIC: German submarine *U-175* torpedoes and sinks a U.S. freighter off Liberia.

ETO: Eighth Air Force B-17s bomb the port of Lorient and the U-boat base at Brest, France. The attack on Lorient has 35 B-17s, which drop 86 tons of bombs on the target. Five of the bombers are lost. The U-boat base is raided by 19 B-17s; 45 tons of bombs are dropped on the target.

MEDITERRANEAN: The Casablanca conference is concluded. The U.S. Joint Staff planners find themselves outmaneuvered and outclassed in every way by their British staff counterparts, who have a clear political-military strategy. The Americans, plagued by a lack of consensus both within the military services and among the political leadership, find themselves following the British proposals for an overall strategic concept of the Allies in the prosecution of the war and specific tasks for the Allied forces against Axis forces in Europe and Asia. Major General Albert C. Wedemeyer, the chief army planner at the Casablanca meetings, will later say "We lost our shirts." He also wryly observed, "One might say we came, we listened and we were conquered." The Americans, angered and embarrassed by the lack of basic political-military coordination that is essential to any successful wartime activity, vow not to be caught short again. Overall, the British are able to implement their peripheral strategy focused on the Mediterranean and avoiding a commitment to a cross-Channel invasion. Giraud and de Gaulle refuse to cooperate with each other, but issue an empty statement, largely to placate the British and the Americans: "We have met. We have talked. We have registered our entire agreement on the end to be achieved, which is the liberation of France. . . . This end will be attained by a union in war of all Frenchmen."

The conference produces the following guidance:

The overall goal of the Allies is to force an unconditional surrender of the Axis powers in Europe while simultaneously maintaining pressure against Japan to reduce its military power and attain positions to force Japan's unconditional surrender at some time in the future.

In the Atlantic, the Allies are to secure the lines of communication by defeating the U-boat threat and other threats to sea communications. The Allies will conduct a full-scale assault from the United Kingdom against the European continent in the spring of 1944. Concurrently, the Allies will conduct a vigorous air offensive to reduce Germany's war potential and to make the cross-Channel attack feasible. The U.S. VIII Bomber Command and RAF Bomber Command are tasked to destroy submarine construction yards, aircraft production facilities, transportation centers, and oil production facilities. The appropriate forces to conduct the invasion will be built up in the United Kingdom.

In the Mediterranean, the Allies will accomplish Husky, the invasion of Sicily in June or July of 1943. After Husky, the Allies will conduct limited offensive operations intended to destroy Italian war potential by continuing air attacks from Mediterranean bases. The intent is to support the diversion of Axis forces and materials away from the USSR, while dispersing other Axis forces in France to facilitate a cross-Channel operation and maintain secure lines of communication in the Mediterranean. The strength of the forces to be employed in the Mediterranean will be limited so that priority of effort is directed to preparations for the cross-Channel invasion in 1944.

In the Pacific and Far East, the Allies will protect the lines of communication to Australia, maintain pressure on Japan, retain the initiative in preparation for a future full-scale offensive against Japan, and keep China in the war. Offensive operations in the Pacific and Far East in 1943–44 will have the following objectives: conduct air operations in and from China; gain control of Burma; drive the Japanese from the Aleutian Islands; seize the Marshall and Caroline Islands; seize the Solomons, the Bismarck Archipelago, and the Japanese-held areas of New Guinea. The Allies will also to the greatest extent possible, continue to sustain Soviet and Chinese forces, while also supporting the French forces in Northwest Africa.

General Joseph Stilwell's proposal for an offensive from India into Burma with three Chinese divisions, while 30 Chinese divisions attack from China westward, is favored by the U.S. Joint Chiefs of Staff; the British are not impressed. Political unrest in India and a lack of capability to conduct a sustained offensive in Burma lead to the plan collapsing later in the year. Instead, Major General Claire Chennault proposes airpower as the solution, offering a cheap and decisive effect on the Japanese in Burma and China. Both President Roosevelt and Generalissimo Chiang like the idea; although Stilwell thought it nonsense, the Tenth Air Force will be given the opportunity to prove itself.

Ninth Air Force B-24 Liberators bomb Palermo harbor in Sicily; P-40s fly support missions for British ground forces as the Eighth Army captures Tripoli.

TUNISIA: Twelfth Air Force B-17s bomb Bizerte naval base and are opposed by as many as 100 enemy fighters. The escorting P-38 Lightnings claim 20 enemy aircraft destroyed. The P-38s suffer six casualties. A-20 Havocs and P-40s support U.S. forces near Ousseltia.

SOUTHWEST PACIFIC AREA: U.S. submarine *Guardfish* torpedoes and sinks a Japanese destroyer near Kavieng, New Ireland.

GUADALCANAL: U.S. XIV Corps at Guadalcanal captures Kokumbona; after a Japanese night attack fails, U.S. forces eliminate the last defenders at Gifu.

January 24

CBI: Tenth Air Force B-24 Liberators attack the port facilities at Rangoon, Burma. P-40s attack Japanese ammunition storage base at Shaduzup, Burma.

TUNISIA: Ninth Air Force B-24 Liberators attack Medenine airfield. Twelfth Air Force B-25 Mitchells and B-26 Marauders also make sequential attacks on Medenine airfield. B-17s bomb ships in Sousse harbor. Combat Command B of U.S. 1st Armored Division, supported by infantry from the U.S. 1st Infantry Division, advances to clear enemy defenders from Ousseltia Valley.

SOUTHWEST PACIFIC AREA: Fifth Air Force B-17s bomb the airfield and harbor at Rabaul.

SOUTH PACIFIC: B-24 Liberators attack the airfield at Cape Gloucester, New Britain.

GUADALCANAL: The CAM Division reaches Kokumbona and begins movement to Cape Esperance.

NEW GUINEA: B-25 Mitchells hit supply areas at Lae. U.S. submarine *Wahoo* damages a Japanese destroyer in the waters off Wewak.

January 25

ATLANTIC: German submarine *U-575* torpedoes and sinks a U.S. freighter from convoy UGS 4 (United States to Mediterranean, Slow) south of the Azores.

GUADALCANAL: The U.S. XIV Corps begins to pursue retreating Japanese over the Poha River.

January 26

CBI: The first elements of Detachment 101 parachute behind Japanese lines in northern Burma to establish a guerrilla force of Kachins, the ethnic group that lives in the region and is hostile to Japanese occupation. Detachment 101 is commanded by Captain (later Colonel) William R. Peers.

SOUTHWEST PACIFIC AREA: U.S. submarine *Grayling* torpedoes and sinks a Japanese cargo ship near Mindoro, Philippines. U.S. submarine *Wahoo* attacks Japanese convoy off the northwestern coast of New Guinea, torpedoing and sinking two cargo ships. The submarine then surfaces and attacks other ships in the convoy.

PACIFIC: U.S. submarine *Flying Fish* damages a Japanese transport at Port Apra, Guam.

January 27

ATLANTIC: A U.S. freighter from Charleston, South Carolina, sailing to Sierra Leone, is torpedoed and sunk by German submarine *U-105* in the waters north of Puerto Rico. An armed U.S. freighter from convoy UGS 4 (United States to Mediterranean, Slow) is torpedoed by German submarine *U-514* southwest of the Azores, but fires on her attacker when the submarine surfaces nearby. The U-boat makes a hasty retreat from the accurate fire.

ETO: Eighth Air Force makes its first bombing raid on Germany. The Wilhelmshaven naval base is attacked by 53 B-17s dropping 137 tons of bombs on the target. Over 20 enemy aircraft are destroyed or damaged.

MEDITERRANEAN: Ninth Air Force B-24 Liberators bomb Naples and Messina. Twelfth Air Force B-25 Mitchells bomb two Axis warships off the coast of Algeria, damaging one destroyer.

NEW GUINEA: Fifth Air Force B-24 Liberators bomb Finschhafen.

January 28

CBI: General Stilwell reaches an agreement with the Chinese political and military leadership on the outlines of the program to train and equip 30 Chinese divisions.

ATLANTIC: German submarine *U-514* succeeds in sinking the freighter it has pursued. The survivors are questioned and released. German submarine *U-442* torpedoes and sinks another U.S. freighter from convoy UGS 4 south of the Azores.

TUNISIA: Twelfth Air Force B-17s, B-25 Mitchells, and B-26 Marauders, escorted by P-38 Lightnings, attack the harbor, shipping, and railyards at Sfax. P-40s fly missions against Axis defenders in the Ousseltia Valley.

NEW GUINEA: Fifth Air Force A-20 Havocs bomb Garrison Hill and B-17s bomb Wewak area. B-24 Liberators bomb Salamaua.

January 29

ATLANTIC: Mrs. Ruth Cheney Streeter is commissioned a major and designated as director of the Marine Corps Women's Reserve (MCWR).

TUNISIA: Twelfth Air Force B-17s attack the port facilities at Bizerte; B-26 Marauders bomb El Aouina airfield.

SOUTH PACIFIC: U.S. submarine *Gato* torpedoes and sinks a Japanese cargo ship off Bougainville, Solomons. Japanese aircraft attack U.S. cruisers and destroyers near Rennell Island, protecting a convoy headed for Guadalcanal. One heavy cruiser is damaged.

GUADALCANAL: U.S. XIV Corps at Guadalcanal continues drive toward Cape Esperance.

January 30

ATLANTIC: Grossadmiral Karl Dönitz is named Commander in Chief of the Kriegsmarine.

TUNISIA: German forces attack and seize Faid Pass. Units of the 1st Armored Division along with the 168th RCT of the 34th Infantry Division begin movement toward Maknasy.

Twelfth Air Force B-17s bomb the port facilities at Ferryville; B-25 Mitchells attack rail lines and storage facilities El Aouinet; A-20 Havocs support Allied ground forces near El Guettar.

SOUTH PACIFIC: Japanese continue the attack on the U.S. task group near Rennell Island, sinking the heavy cruiser damaged in the attack of the previous day, and damaging a destroyer. Japanese submarine *I-10* torpedoes and sinks U.S. freighter off New Caledonia.

GUADALCANAL: The U.S. 147th Infantry Regiment advances against Japanese troops attempting to cover the retreat to Cape Esperance.

NEW GEORGIA: Thirteenth Air Force B-17s and B-26 Marauders, escorted by P-39 Airacobras and P-40s, bomb Japanese antiaircraft defenses and the airfield at Munda, New Georgia.

January 31

CBI: C-46 Commando cargo aircraft prove unreliable for flying over the Hump, forcing many crewmen to abandon their aircraft and parachute into the jungle. Detachment 101 rescues more than 100 of them.

ATLANTIC: U-boats have sunk 37 ships (a total of 203,128 tons of shipping) in January. At present, 37 U-boats are near Greenland, 11 are northwest of the Azores, and 25 are south of the Azores and patrolling the west coast of Africa. Another 27 U-boats are in transit either to or from Atlantic patrol.

MEDITERRANEAN: Lieutenant General Lewis H. Brereton, commander of the Ninth Air Force, takes command of U.S. Army Forces in the Middle East (USAFIME) from Lieutenant General Frank M. Andrews. Lieutenant General Andrews will take command of U.S. forces in the ETO.

TUNISIA: Combat Command B of the U.S. 1st Armored Division attacks Faid Pass without success. Twelfth Air Force B-26 Marauders attack the Gabès airfield; B-17s bomb the port facilities at Bizerte.

NEW GEORGIA: Marine SBD Dauntless dive-bombers, F4F Wildcats, and Thirteenth Air Force P-39 Airacobras from Henderson Field sink a Japanese transport between the islands of Vella Lavella and Kolombangara in New Georgia. Off Kolombangara Island, First Lieutenant Jefferson DeBlanc is the leader of a section of six fighters escorting the dive-bombers and TBF Avenger torpedo bombers attacking the Japanese ships. When a large number of enemy fighters arrive to protect the ships, First Lieutenant DeBlanc engages the enemy aircraft and then quickly moves down to 1,000 feet to protect the dive-bombers and torpedo bombers under attack by enemy floatplanes. He provides cover so that the bombers can complete their runs on the targets. DeBlanc remains behind to continue fighting the enemy, scoring five kills, until, low on fuel and ammunition and his plane no longer airworthy, he bails out at tree-top level over Kolombangara. First Lieutenant DeBlanc's extraordinary skills and his courage and ferocity in combat will win him the Medal of Honor.

February 1

CBI: The Allies open a conference at New Delhi to develop a campaign plan for the reconquest of Burma and to open a land supply route to China. The operation, scheduled to begin in November of 1943, is code named Anakim.

TUNISIA: U.S. Combat Command A of 1st Armored Division attacks Faid, but fails to drive defenders from the town. Combat Command D of 1st Armored Division, supported by 1st Battalion 168th Infantry of the 34th Infantry Division, captures Sened Station. Twelfth Air Force B-17s bomb Tunis harbor. A-20 Havocs and P-40s bomb enemy troop concentrations.

SOUTHWEST PACIFIC AREA: Fifth Air Force B-17s bomb the airfield at Rabaul.

PACIFIC: U.S. submarine *Tarpon* torpedoes and sinks a Japanese cargo ship off the southern coast of Japan.

GUADALCANAL: Japanese destroyers take aboard 2,300 Japanese soldiers at Cape Esperance, evacuating the island secretly by night. The 2nd Battalion of the 132nd Infantry Regiment lands at Verahue in an attempt to cut off Japanese forces. One U.S. destroyer is sunk by Japanese air attack south of Savo Island.

February 2

ATLANTIC: German submarine *U-456* attacks convoy HX 224 (New York to Liverpool) in the North Atlantic and torpedoes a U.S. freighter, which is later abandoned and scuttled.

TUNISIA: Combat Command D of the U.S. 1st Armored Division stops an Axis counterattack east of Sened. Twelfth Air Force P-40s and P-39s fly missions to provide support to the ground forces. B-25 Mitchells and B-26 Marauders bomb an airfield at Sfax.

February 3

ATLANTIC: German submarine *U-223* attacks convoy SG 19 (Sydney or St. Johns, Newfoundland to Greenland) off Greenland, torpedoing and sinking one transport and damaging a Norwegian freighter. The transport sinks with 675 men on board. Among them are four army chaplains, representing four different faiths, who offer their life preservers to other soldiers, sacrificing their lives to save others.

German submarine *U-255* attacks a convoy northeast of Iceland, torpedoing and sinking a U.S. freighter.

PACIFIC: U.S. submarine *Tunny* torpedoes and damages a Japanese army transport ship in the South China Sea.

February 4

ALEUTIANS: Eleventh Air Force B-17s, B-24 Liberators, and B-25 Mitchells escorted by P-38 Lightnings and P-40s attack Japanese installations. Five Japanese bombers conduct a strike on Amchitka.

CBI: Tenth Air Force B-25 Mitchells and B-24 Liberators bomb the Myitnge bridge and railway facilities, located south of Mandalay. The bridge is not damaged.

ATLANTIC: German submarines attack convoy SC 118 (Halifax Slow to United Kingdom) in the North Atlantic, but are driven off. British destroyers sink German submarine *U-187.*

ETO: Eighth Air Force B-17s, diverted from the Hamm marshaling yard because of weather conditions, bomb the port and industrial sites at Emden, Germany. The bombers encounter German Ju-88 Junkers and Me-110 Messerschmitt twin-engine fighters for the first time. The fighters shoot down five of the 39 B-17s involved in the raid. Enemy losses are estimated at eight fighters destroyed.

MEDITERRANEAN: At Algiers, Lieutenant General Eisenhower takes command of the newly designated headquarters, North African Theater of Operations (NATOUSA). The boundary of NATOUSA includes Spain and Italy. Eisenhower is commander in chief, North Africa. The command of the European Theater of Operations (ETO) passes from Eisenhower to Lieutenant General Frank M. Andrews.

PACIFIC: U.S. submarine *Tunny* torpedoes and damages a Japanese transport in the South China Sea.

SOUTH PACIFIC: Thirteenth Air Force SBD Dauntless dive-bombers and TBF Avenger torpedo bombers damage four Japanese destroyers attempting to evacuate Japanese ground forces from Guadalcanal. U.S. losses are three F4F Wildcats, three SBDs, four TBFs, and one P-40.

February 5

CBI: Tenth Air Force B-25 Mitchells attack the Myitnge bridge, but fail to destroy it.

ATLANTIC: German submarine *U-413* torpedoes and sinks a U.S. freighter in the North Atlantic that is unable to keep up with convoy SC 118.

SOUTHWEST PACIFIC AREA: Fifth Air Force B-17s bomb Rabaul airfield; A-20 Havocs provide ground support to Allied forces in New Guinea.

February 6

ATLANTIC: A U.S. destroyer drives off three U-boats attempting to attack convoy SC 118.

February 7

ATLANTIC: A U.S. Coast Guard cutter escorting convoy SC 118 initially drives off German submarine *U-402*, but the U-boat later torpedoes and sinks a U.S. tanker and a U.S. passenger ship.

In the South Atlantic, German submarine *U-160* torpedoes and sinks a U.S. freighter headed to Brazil.

MEDITERRANEAN: Ninth Air Force B-24 Liberators bomb Naples harbor; Twelfth Air Force B-17s and B-26 Marauders bomb an airfield and a seaplane base in Sardinia.

SOUTHWEST PACIFIC AREA: U.S. submarine *Growler* rams a Japanese storeship northwest of Rabaul while making a night surface attack. *Growler*, with 18 feet of its bow bent sideways, comes under heavy Japanese fire. On the bridge, the submarine's commanding officer, Commander Howard W. Gilmore, makes an immediate decision. Although wounded, he orders the bridge cleared, and then gives the command, "Take her down!" He sacrifices himself to save his ship, and for this act of extraordinary gallantry, Commander Gilmore will receive the Medal of Honor.

GUADALCANAL: The last elements of the Japanese rear guard are evacuated from Guadalcanal. About 13,000 Japanese soldiers escape to fight another day.

February 8

ALEUTIANS: Eleventh Air Force B-24 Liberators and B-25 Mitchells bomb the Japanese base at Kiska.

CBI: Tenth Air Force B-24 Liberators of the India Air Task Force bomb the marshaling yard at Rangoon.

ATLANTIC: German submarine *U-608* makes an unsuccessful torpedo attack on a U.S. destroyer escorting convoy SC 118 (Halifax Slow to United Kingdom).

TUNISIA: Twelfth Air Force B-17s bomb the docks and shipping at the port of Sousse; B-26 Marauders and B-25 Mitchells bomb the airfield marshaling yard at Gabès. A-20 Havocs bomb enemy troops near Faid.

PACIFIC: U.S. submarine *Tunny* torpedoes and sinks a Japanese merchant ship southwest of Formosa.

February 9

ATLANTIC: After five days of running battle, convoy SC 118 (Halifax Slow to United Kingdom), with 63 ships, 10 escort ships, and land-based air cover, overcomes the constant attack of 20 U-boats. The losses are severe on both sides: three U-boats are sunk and two are damaged. The convoy suffers the loss of 13 ships.

PACIFIC: U.S. submarine *Tarpon* torpedoes and sinks a Japanese transport off the southeast coast of Japan.

GUADALCANAL: Guadalcanal is secured. The campaign has cost the United States nearly 1,600 killed and over 4,000 wounded. The Japanese have suffered approximately 25,000 men lost, including 600 aircraft. The epic land, air, and sea battle forces the Japanese to consolidate their gains while conceding the strategic initiative to the Americans. American losses in ships and planes can be rapidly replaced, but the Japanese cannot replace these critical combat assets.

February 10

ALEUTIANS: Eleventh Air Force B-17s, B-24 Liberators, and B-25 Mitchells, escorted by eight P-38 Lightnings, attack the airfield on Kiska Island.

ATLANTIC: B-24 Liberators of the 2nd Antisubmarine Squadron, attached to the 1st Antisubmarine Group (Provisional), sink German submarine *U-519* northwest of Spain.

SOUTHWEST PACIFIC AREA: Japanese submarine *I-21* torpedoes and damages U.S. freighter near Sidney, Australia. The freighter will sink while being towed to port.

PACIFIC: U.S. submarine *Pickerel* torpedoes and sinks a Japanese cargo ship off the western shore of Hokkaido, Japan.

February 11

SOUTHWEST PACIFIC AREA: U.S. submarine *Grayling* torpedoes and damages a Japanese army cargo ship off Corregidor.

SOUTH PACIFIC: U.S. destroyer sinks Japanese submarine *I-18* in the Coral Sea.

NEW GEORGIA: Thirteenth Air Force B-26 Marauders, P-38 Lightnings, and P-39 Airacobras bomb the Munda airfields on New Georgia Island and Vila airfield on Kolombangara Island, Solomons.

February 12

CBI: Tenth Air Force B-24 Liberators of the India Air Task Force use 2,000-pound blockbusters bombs in an attempt to destroy the Myitnge bridge. Twelve other B-24s bomb the marshaling yard at Rangoon.

ATLANTIC: The official statement of the Casablanca Conference (January 14–23) is issued. It says in part:

> In an attempt to ward off the inevitable disaster, the Axis propagandists are trying all of their old tricks in order to divide the United Nations. They seek to create the idea that if we win this war, Russia, England, China, and the United States are going to get into a cat-and-dog fight. This is their final effort to turn one nation against another, in the vain hope that they may settle with one or two at a time—that any of us may be so gullible and so forgetful as to be duped into making "deals" at the expense of our Allies.
>
> To these panicky attempts to escape the consequences of their crimes we say— all the United Nations say—that the only terms on which we shall deal with an Axis government or any Axis factions are the terms proclaimed at Casablanca: "Unconditional Surrender." In our uncompromising policy we mean no harm to the common people of the Axis nations. But we do mean to impose punishment and retribution in full upon their guilty, barbaric leaders . . .

SOUTHWEST PACIFIC AREA: SWPA headquarters drafts plans for an attack on New Britain and New Guinea, codenamed Elkton.

February 13

ALEUTIANS: Eleventh Air Force bombers, escorted by 10 P-38 Lightnings, attack facilities at Kiska.

TUNISIA: Twelfth Air Force B-26 Marauder bombers attack the airfield at El Aouina. Fighters escorting the B-26s strafe targets of opportunity around Sened Station and Faid.

February 14

TUNISIA: Axis offensive in the Faid-Sidi Bou Zid sector isolates the 168th RCT of the U.S. 34th Division. Combat Command A of the U.S. 1st Armored Division counter-attacks to attempt to restore the line. The 168th is almost eliminated as an effective unit.

SOUTHWEST PACIFIC AREA: U.S. submarine *Thresher* torpedoes and damages Japanese submarine *I-62* off the Lesser Sunda Islands. U.S. submarine *Trout* sinks a Japanese gunboat at south entrance to Makassar Strait after a surface gun battle, which wounds several U.S. sailors.

SOUTH PACIFIC: After the loss of eight P-38 Lightnings, three B-24 Liberators, two PB4Y Privateers (a B-24 variant), two P-40s, and two F4U Corsairs to Japanese defenses in the Bougainville area in the space of two days, Thirteenth Air Force calls off all daylight bombing missions in the northern Solomons until adequate fighter cover is available.

NEW BRITAIN: Fifth Air Force B-17s and B-24 Liberators bomb Japanese facilities at Rabaul.

U.S. submarine *Amberjack* is probably sunk by Japanese naval aircraft and surface vessels off New Britain.

February 15

ALEUTIANS: Six Japanese aircraft attack the runway on Amchitka Island.

ATLANTIC: German submarine *U-607* torpedoes and sinks a U.S. tanker separated from convoy ON 165 (Liverpool to New York, fast) in the North Atlantic.

ETO: Eighth Air Force B-24 Liberators bomb the port and shipping at Dunkirk, France. Two of 23 B-24s are lost.

MEDITERRANEAN: A portion of Ninth Air Force is designated the Desert Air Task Force (DATF). Commanded by Brigadier General Auby C. Strickland, the DATF's headquarters is established in Tripoli, Libya. Twelfth Air Force B-17s bomb the harbor and ships at Palermo, Sicily.

TUNISIA: Combat Command C of the U.S. 1st Armored Division with British armored infantry in support counterattacks at Sidi Bou Zid, suffering heavy tank losses. Axis forces capture the remnants of the 168th RCT. Twelfth Air Force B-25 Mitchells and B-26 Marauders bomb the airfield at Kairouan. Fighters provide ground support to Allied forces, and the air base at Sbeitla is evacuated as German forces advance.

PACIFIC: U.S. submarine *Pickerel* attacks a Japanese convoy off the east coast of Honshu, Japan, and sinks a cargo ship.

SOUTH PACIFIC: Thirteenth Air Force B-26 Marauders, P-39 Airacobras, and P-40s attack the airfield on Kolombangara Island. B-24 Liberators attack the airfields at Bougainville and Ballale Islands. Two B-24s are lost.

U.S. submarine *Gato* torpedoes and sinks a Japanese ship in Bougainville Strait.

February 16

ATLANTIC: A U.S. freighter is torpedoed by German submarine *U-607* off Port Elizabeth, South Africa, and later sinks.

ETO: Eighth Air Force B-17s and B-24 Liberators bomb the U-boat base at St-Nazaire, France. Six of 71 B-17s and two of 18 B-24 Liberators participating in the raid are lost; 28 B-17s and two B-24s are damaged. It is estimated that over 30 German aircraft are shot down.

TUNISIA: U.S. II Corps commander Major General Fredendall orders the 1st Armored Division to hold at Sbeitla for as long as possible to buy time for U.S. troops defending Kasserine Pass. U.S. tank losses mount under heavy enemy pressure. Germans advance past Gafsa and occupy Tozeur. A-20 Havocs bomb enemy positions west of Sidi bou Zid.

SOUTHWEST PACIFIC AREA: The U.S. Sixth Army is established in SWPA under command of Lieutenant General Walter Krueger. The U.S. I Corps, under General Eichelberger, the 2nd Engineer Special Brigade, the 503rd Parachute Infantry, and the attached 1st Marine Division make up Krueger's new organization.

PACIFIC: U.S. submarine *Flying Fish* torpedoes and sinks a Japanese ship off Pagan Island, in the Marianas.

SOUTH PACIFIC: Rear Admiral Charles P. Mason assumes command of Air Command Solomons (COMAIRSOLS), a composite force of U.S. Army, Navy, and

Marine Corps, and New Zealand aircraft. Mason has operational control of all U.S. Army, Navy, and Marine Corps, and Royal New Zealand Air Force (RNZAF) aircraft in the Solomon Islands.

February 17

MEDITERRANEAN: Air Chief Marshal Sir Arthur W. Tedder takes command of the newly designated Mediterranean Air Command (which absorbs Ninth Air Force, Twelfth Air Force, and British RAF). General Sir Harold Alexander is named deputy commander in chief of Allied forces and commands Allied ground forces under the Eighteenth Army Group, which includes the British First and Eighth armies, the U.S. II Corps, and the French XIX Corps. Admiral Sir Andrew Cunningham is commander in chief of all Allied naval forces in the Mediterranean.

TUNISIA: Elements of 1st Armored Division defend at Sbeitla, then move to defensive positions near Tebessa, while the U.S. 34th Infantry Division (minus the 168th RCT) takes up defensive positions at Sbiba to protect Kasserine Pass.

February 18

ALEUTIANS: A naval task group under command of Rear Admiral Charles H. McMorris, with one light and one heavy cruiser and four destroyers, fires on Japanese installations at Attu.

MEDITERRANEAN: The subordinate commands of Twelfth Air Force become the core of the North African Air Force (NAAF), subordinate to Mediterranean Air Command (MAC). Lieutenant General Carl Spaatz commands NAAF. Twelfth Air Force ceases to exist as an operational command.

TUNISIA: A battalion of the 39th Infantry Regiment, 9th Infantry Division reinforces engineers and elements of the 26th Infantry Regiment, 1st Infantry Division holding Kasserine Pass.

SOUTHWEST PACIFIC AREA: U.S. submarine *Grampus* torpedoes and damages a Japanese transport north of the Admiralty Islands.

NEW GEORGIA: Thirteenth Air Force B-24 Liberators attack the Munda airfield.

NEW GUINEA: B-17s attack Japanese shipping near Bougainville. Fifth Air Force B-24s bomb Finschhafen and Madang in New Guinea.

February 19

ALEUTIANS: A portion of Admiral McMorris's naval task group attacks a Japanese army cargo ship bound for Attu. The ship sinks the following day.

ATLANTIC: U.S. submarine *Blackfish* is damaged by depth charges after she torpedoes and sinks a German patrol boat in the Bay of Biscay.

TUNISIA: A mixed force of British, French, and American units holds at Sbiba Pass. German forces begin assault on Kasserine Pass.

SOUTHWEST PACIFIC AREA: Naval forces attached to SWPA are designated as Seventh Fleet.

U.S. submarine *Grampus* torpedoes and sinks a Japanese transport off New Ireland.

SOLOMONS: Fifth Air Force B-17s bomb Japanese shipping and facilities around Bougainville Island.

U.S. submarine *Gato* torpedoes a Japanese ammunition ship off Bougainville, causing it to run aground.

NEW GUINEA: U.S. Navy cryptanalysts provide information that the Japanese intend to reinforce Lae in early March.

February 20

ALEUTIANS: Eleventh Air Force B-24 Liberators, B-25 Mitchells, and P-38 Lightnings attack Japanese facilities on Kiska Island.

TUNISIA: German forces break through Kasserine Pass and attack Thala, defended by an ad hoc collection of British infantry, artillery, and armor. Bad weather limits Allied air power; a few P-39 Airacobras attack German forces as they move through Kasserine Pass.

SOUTHWEST PACIFIC AREA: U.S. submarine *Albacore* torpedoes and sinks a Japanese destroyer near the Admiralty Islands.

PACIFIC: U.S. submarine *Halibut* torpedoes and sinks a Japanese transport north of Ponape Island in the Carolines.

SOLOMONS: Thirteenth Air Force B-17s and navy PBY Catalinas bomb Bougainville Island. B-24 Liberators bomb Kolombangara Island. Fifth Air Force B-17s bomb targets near Kahili on Bougainville Island.

February 21

ATLANTIC: German submarines converge on Convoy ON 166 (Liverpool to New York, fast) in the mid-North Atlantic. *U-332* and *U-603* torpedo and sink a Norwegian ship. *U-92* torpedoes a British steamer, which is later scuttled. Two other German submarines, *U-454* and *U-753*, as well as *U-332*, are driven off by escorts. A U.S. Coast Guard cutter sinks German submarine *U-225*. A U.S. freighter in convoy ON 167 is torpedoed and sunk by German submarine *U-664*.

MEDITERRANEAN: Lieutenant General Carl Spaatz's North African Tactical Air Force (NATAF) gains operational control of the Western Desert Air Force, but Ninth Air Force maintains administrative control.

TUNISIA: Combat Command B of the 1st Armored Division, along with an infantry battalion from 1st Infantry Division, moves toward Kasserine to protect retreating U.S. troops moving to Tebessa and to halt the German advance. Weather continues to limit Allied air support to the ground forces.

SOUTHWEST PACIFIC AREA: U.S. submarine *Thresher* attacks a Japanese convoy in the Lesser Sunda Islands of the Netherlands East Indies, damaging a cargo ship.

PACIFIC: U.S. submarine *Sawfish* torpedoes and damages a Japanese oiler off Oagari Jima.

SOLOMONS: Operation Cleanslate begins. The Russell Islands are occupied to establish a forward airbase and logistics base for future operations in the Solomons. The Marine 3rd Raider Battalion lands on Pavuvu Island and two regiments of the 43rd Infantry Division land on Barrika Island. Both islands are unoccupied.

About 9,000 troops are involved, and no enemy forces are encountered. Four light cruisers and four destroyers of Task Force 68, under command of Rear Admiral Aaron S. Merrill, and Thirteenth Air Force fighters from Guadalcanal provide air support.

February 22

CBI: Tenth Air Force B-24 Liberators mine the Gulf of Martaban near Rangoon.

ATLANTIC: Continuing their attack on convoy ON 166, German submarines *U-92* and *U-753* torpedo and damage a Norwegian ship, which is later scuttled. German submarine *U-606* torpedoes and sinks a U.S. freighter and a British steamship, and damages another U.S. freighter (later torpedoed by *U-303*). A Canadian corvette and a Polish destroyer conduct a depth charge attack on *U-606*. When it is forced to surface, the U.S. Coast Guard cutter *Campbell* rams and sinks the U-boat.

TUNISIA: North African Air Force A-20 Havocs fly close air support missions for Allied ground forces. One A-20 is lost when it is attacked by three Bf-109 Messerschmitts. B-17s bomb the Kasserine Pass while P-38 Lightnings attack German forces retiring from Kasserine. B-25 Mitchells bomb the railyards at Gafsa.

February 23

CBI: Tenth Air Force P-40s destroy a railroad bridge west of Myitkyina. B-24 Liberators attack the bridge at Myitnge but fail to damage the bridge.

ATLANTIC: The attack on convoy ON 166 continues. German submarine *U-186* torpedoes and sinks a U.S. freighter and a British ship; *U-707* torpedoes and sinks a U.S. freighter lagging behind the convoy.

Convoy UC 1 (United Kingdom to New York) is attacked by German submarine *U-382*, which torpedoes a Dutch ship; *U-202* torpedoes two British tankers and a U.S. tanker.

TUNISIA: North African Air Force B-17s bomb the airfield at Kairouan. B-25 Mitchells, A-20 Havocs, and B-26 Marauders bomb retreating German forces near Kasserine.

February 24

ATLANTIC: German submarine *U-604* is damaged by depth charges from escort ships guarding convoy ON 166. *U-621* conducts an unsuccessful attack on a U.S. Coast Guard cutter.

February 25

ALEUTIANS: Eleventh Air Force P-40s, B-24 Liberators, and B-25 Mitchells attack Japanese facilities on Kiska Island.

CBI: Tenth Air Force fighters seriously damage a bridge west of Myitkyina. Over 40 Japanese aircraft attack Dinjan airfield in India. Defending P-40s shoot down at least 14 enemy fighters.

ATLANTIC: Before losing contact with convoy ON 166, German submarine *U-92* and *U-600* continue to attack the U.S. Coast Guard cutter, but are unsuccessful. German submarine *U-628*, however, is able to torpedo and sink a British steamship.

MEDITERRANEAN: Ninth Air Force B-24 Liberators bomb Naples harbor.

TUNISIA: Allies regain control of Kasserine Pass. North African Air Force B-17s bomb the airfield at El Aouina, while A-20 Havocs attack German forces around Kasserine and Sbeitla, and along the main road between Gafsa and Feriana.

February 26

ETO: Because of bad weather conditions over their primary target at Bremen, Germany, Eighth Air Force B-17s and B-24s bomb the docks at Wilhelmshaven, Germany. Over 30 enemy aircraft are assessed as destroyed or damaged, while five B-17s out of 59 and two B-24 Liberators out of six are lost.

February 27

CBI: Tenth Air Force B-24 Liberators sink a Japanese cargo ship off Rangoon, Burma.

ETO: Eighth Air Force B-17s and B-24 Liberators bomb the U-boat pens and port facilities at Brest, France. Of the 60 bombers that participate in the raid, only two B-24s are damaged.

PACIFIC: U.S. submarine *Plunger* torpedoes and damages a Japanese oiler west of Jaluit Atoll in the Marshall Islands.

NEW GUINEA: U.S. 162nd Infantry Regiment, 41st Infantry Division occupies Milne Bay.

February 28

CBI: U.S. engineers building the Ledo Road cross into Burma. Major General Lewis A. Pick, the chief engineer for the project, overcomes exceptionally difficult problems with terrain. The Ledo Road project is assisted by the efforts of a civilian-military team from the Office of Strategic Services (OSS) known as Detachment 101. Under the command of Major Carl Rifler, Detachment 101 conducts reconnaissance, trains native guerrillas, and rescues downed pilots. Stilwell orders an increase in the number of guerrillas trained and ready for operations by the end of the year.

ATLANTIC: In the month of February, German U-boats have sunk 63 ships, totaling over 359,000 tons.

March 1

ATLANTIC: A U.S. freighter straggling from convoy HX 227 is torpedoed and sunk by German submarine *U-405* in the White Sea. A U.S. freighter in convoy BT 6 (Bahia, Brazil to Trinidad) is torpedoed by German submarine *U-518* off the coast of Brazil and abandoned. The crew is rescued and the freighter later sinks.

MEDITERRANEAN: Lieutenant General Carl Spaatz takes command of Twelfth Air Force, now an administrative headquarters for the Northwest African Air Force.

March 2

ATLANTIC: German submarines *U-759* and *U-634* combine to attack and sink.a U.S. freighter straggling from convoy HX 227 (New York to Liverpool) southwest of Iceland.

MEDITERRANEAN: Northwest African Air Force B-17s bomb Palermo harbor. In Tunisia, B-26 Marauders attack bridges and enemy air defenses at La Hencha.

PACIFIC: U.S. submarine *Permit* torpedoes and damages a Japanese army cargo ship off the northeast coast of Honshu. U.S. submarine *Thresher* torpedoes and sinks a Japanese tanker in the southern Makassar Strait.

New Guinea: **Battle of the Bismarck Sea.** Fifth Air Force bombers attack a Japanese convoy escorted by eight destroyers and headed for Lae. One cargo ship is sunk by B-17s.

March 3

Atlantic: A U.S. freighter, headed to Rio de Janeiro from New York, is torpedoed and sunk by Italian submarine *Barbarigo* off the coast of Brazil.

Tunisia: Northwest African Air Force B-17s bomb the docks and shipping at Tunis harbor.

New Guinea: **Battle of the Bismarck Sea.** In Huon Gulf, off Finschhafen, New Guinea, a Japanese destroyer is sunk by Fifth Air Force B-25 Mitchells, one destroyer is sunk by B-17s, and two destroyers and a supply ship are sunk by other aircraft. Another cargo ship damaged by U.S. and Australian aircraft is sunk by U.S. motor torpedo boats *PT-143* and *PT-150*. U.S. and Australian aircraft sink four army cargo ships and a transport. In all, the Japanese lose eight transports and four destroyers. Only 1,000 of the approximately 7,000 soldiers of the Japanese 51st Division reach Lae.

March 4

ETO: Eighth Air Force launches its first attack against strategic industrial targets in the vital Ruhr area of Germany. With 14 B-24 Liberators flying a diversionary mission, 16 B-17s bomb the marshaling yard at Hamm. Enemy losses are estimated to be about 16 aircraft; four B-17s are lost and nine are damaged. In the same strike, 28 B-17s bomb the Rotterdam shipyards. One B-17 is lost and 15 are damaged.

March 5

Atlantic: Escort carrier USS *Bogue* begins escorting convoys to provide extended air cover during their transit of the North Atlantic.

New Georgia: A U.S. naval task force of destroyers and cruisers bombarding Japanese positions on Vila and Munda, New Georgia Island, uses radar and torpedoes to sink two Japanese destroyers in Kula Gulf.

New Guinea: Fifth Air Force A-20 Havocs bomb the airfield at Lae.

March 6

ETO: Eighth Air Force B-17s attack industrial targets at Lorient, France. Of the 65 B-17s involved, three are lost and eight others are damaged; enemy losses are estimated at around seven aircraft destroyed. A diversionary mission of 15 B-24 Liberators attacks the U-boat facilities at Brest, France. No bombers are lost and at least two enemy aircraft are downed.

Tunisia: Major General George S. Patton, Jr., takes command of U.S. II Corps, relieving Major General Fredendall. Major General Omar Bradley becomes Patton's deputy commander.

Southwest Pacific Area: U.S. submarine *Triton* sinks a Japanese cargo ship north of the Admiralties; after making its report, it will never be heard from again.

Pacific: U.S. submarine *Sawfish* torpedoes and damages a Japanese cargo ship off Toizaki, Japan.

March 7

ALEUTIANS: B-25 Mitchell bombers arrive at Amchitka Island, allowing Eleventh Air Force to increase attacks on Kiska. B-24 Liberators and P-38 Lightnings, along with B-25s, hit a number of Japanese installations on Kiska.

TUNISIA: Northwest African Air Force B-25 Mitchells bomb Axis supply ships traveling between Tunisia and Sicily. B-17s bomb an enemy convoy in the Gulf of Tunis and the marshaling yard at Sousse.

SOUTHWEST PACIFIC AREA: U.S. submarine *Tautog* lays mines off the southeast coast of Borneo.

SOUTH PACIFIC: Thirteenth Air Force B-24 Liberators bomb airfields on Kolombangara and Bougainville. Other B-24s attack Munda airfield on New Georgia.

March 8

CBI: Tenth Air Force B-25 Mitchells attempt to destroy the Myitnge bridge and eliminate enemy air defenses, but the 12 bombers sent against the target do little damage.

ATLANTIC: A navy PBY-5 Catalina sinks German submarine *U-156* in the West Indies. A U.S. freighter is torpedoed by German submarine *U-160* off the coast of South Africa and is later scuttled near Durban.

ETO: Eighth Air Force B-24 Liberators and B-17s attack industrial targets at Rouen, France. Two of the 13 B-24 Liberators are lost and four are damaged. Enemy losses are estimated at about 14 aircraft destroyed. Of the 54 B-17s that hit the target 30 minutes later, two are lost and 10 are damaged. The bombing attack is disrupted by waves of German fighters, the first of which draw off the fighter cover, allowing the second wave to attack the bombers directly.

PACIFIC: U.S. submarine *Permit* attacks a Japanese convoy off the northern tip of Honshu, Japan, and sinks a cargo ship.

March 9

ATLANTIC: German submarine *U-409* torpedoes U.S. freighter in convoy SC 121 (Halifax Slow to United Kingdom). The freighter is abandoned and later sinks. German submarine *U-510* attacks convoy BT 6 (Bahia to Trinidad) off the coast of French Guiana, torpedoing several U.S. freighters. A U.S. freighter from convoy RA 53 is torpedoed and sunk by German submarine *U-586* northeast of Iceland.

SOLOMONS: Thirteenth Air Force B-24 Liberators bomb airfields at Munda, New Georgia, and at Bougainville.

March 10

ALEUTIANS: Eleventh Air Force B-25 Mitchells and B-24 Liberators, escorted by 12 P-38 Lightnings and one F-5A (an unarmed P-38 variant: it carried cameras in the nose), attack facilities on Kiska.

CBI: The Fourteenth Air Force is created by special order of President Roosevelt under the command of Claire L. Chennault, who is promoted from brigadier to major general.

ATLANTIC: German submarine *U-185* attacks convoy KG 123 (Key West to Guantánamo), torpedoing a U.S. tanker and freighter.

German submarines *U-221* and *U-444* attack convoy HX 228 (New York to Liverpool), each torpedoing a U.S. freighter; *U-432* sinks a British destroyer escorting the convoy.

German submarine *U-255* torpedoes and damages a U.S. freighter straggling from convoy RA 53.

March 11

CBI: U.S. Fourteenth Air Force is organized under command of General Claire Chennault at Kunming and assigned to U.S. Army Forces in the China-Burma-India theater.

March 12

ATLANTIC: U.S. destroyers escorting convoy UGS 6 (United States to Mediterranean, Slow) sink German submarine *U-130*.

German submarine *U-68* attacks convoy GAT 49 (Guantánamo to Aruba to Trinidad) and torpedoes a U.S. tanker in the Caribbean. German submarine *U-172* torpedoes U.S. freighter straggling from convoy UGS 6 (United States to Mediterranean, Slow).

The Pacific Military Conference is held in Washington, D.C. Major General Richard K. Sutherland, MacArthur's chief of staff, represents SWPA interests. Admiral William F. Halsey represents SOPAC interests. The proposal is for a limited offensive against Japanese strongholds on the Huon Peninsula in New Guinea and the capture of Munda airfield on New Georgia Island, and the capture of Japanese airfields on New Britain and Bougainville, with the objective of isolating Rabaul and Kavieng in preparation for seizing both. To do this, MacArthur requests five infantry divisions and 45 air groups. Because all forces are now being directed to the European Theater of Operations, SWPA will have to conduct offensive operations with the ground and air units it currently commands.

TUNISIA: Northwest African Air Force B-17s bomb the docks and marshaling yards at Sousse. B-26 Marauders attack supply dumps and lines of supply. B-25 Mitchells bomb supply ships operating between Tunisia and Sicily.

SOUTHWEST PACIFIC AREA: Fifth Air Force B-17s bomb Rabaul airfield.

PACIFIC: U.S. submarine *Plunger* torpedoes and sinks a Japanese vessel in the Caroline Islands.

March 13

ETO: Eighth Air Force B-17s attack the rail marshaling yard and other targets at Amiens, France, while 16 B-24 Liberators fly a diversionary mission. Of the 71 B-17s involved in the attack, 11 are damaged and two enemy planes are reported destroyed.

SOUTHWEST PACIFIC AREA: U.S. submarine *Grayback* torpedoes and damages a Japanese transport northwest of Bismarck Archipelago.

PACIFIC: U.S. submarine *Sunfish* sinks a Japanese cargo ship in the Ryukyus.

NEW GUINEA: Fifth Air Force B-17s bomb Wewak airfield and Japanese shipping.

March 15

ALEUTIANS: Eighth Air Force B-25 Mitchells with P-38 Lightnings make two separate attacks on Kiska. One P-38 is shot down by enemy antiaircraft fire.

SOUTHWEST PACIFIC AREA: The U.S. Seventh Fleet is created to support SWPA under General Douglas MacArthur's operational control. Vice Admiral Arthur S. Carpenter is the commander. CINCUSFLEET maintains administrative control. The fleet consists of two Australian cruisers and a few U.S. and Australian destroyers. Suspicious of MacArthur, Admiral Ernest J. King, the COMINCH, keeps the majority of U.S. naval power in the area under Third Fleet, commanded by Admiral William F. Halsey, COMSOPAC.

U.S. submarine *Trigger* attacks Japanese convoy northwest of the Admiralty Islands, damaging one transport and sinking a cargo ship.

PACIFIC: Central Pacific Force is redesignated as U.S. Fifth Fleet.

NEW GEORGIA: Thirteenth Air Force B-17s bomb the airfield at Munda, New Georgia, and the airfield on Kolombangara Island.

March 16

CBI: Tenth Air Force B-25 Mitchells damage the Myitnge bridge but do not bring it down.

ATLANTIC: German submarine *U-563* spots convoy HX 229 (New York to Liverpool Fast). Although looking for convoy SC 122 (Halifax Slow to United Kingdom), bad weather has allowed this convoy to pass without being detected. Convoys HX 229 and SC 122 are soon intermingled in the rough seas. A pack of 44 U-boats attacks the convoys: German submarine *U-172* torpedoes and damages a U.S. freighter from convoy UGS 6. *U-758* and *U-435* each torpedo and damage a U.S. freighter.

TUNISIA: U.S. II Corps, made up of the 1st Armored, 1st Infantry, and 9th Infantry divisions, moves to capture Maknassy and divert German armor while General Bernard Montgomery's Eighth Army attacks north to break the Axis defenses at Mareth.

March 17

CBI: Tenth Air Force B-25 Mitchells unsuccessfully bomb the Myitnge bridge; P-40s attack support facilities and bridges at Kadrangyang and around Myitkyina.

ATLANTIC: German submarine *U-167* torpedoes and damages a U.S. freighter in convoy UGS 6. Later in the day *U-521* sinks the ship. German submarine *U-91* sinks three freighters damaged in the previous attack on convoy HX 229. *U-600* torpedoes and damages a U.S. freighter; *U-91* then sinks that ship.

TUNISIA: II Corps occupies Gafsa. Combat Command A of 1st Armored Division occupies Zannouch. Northwest African Air Force flies ground support missions against enemy defensive positions.

PACIFIC: U.S. submarine *Kingfish* torpedoes and damages a Japanese transport in the Formosa Strait.

March 18

CBI: Tenth Air Force B-24 Liberators damage the Pazundaung bridge, while B-25 Mitchells succeed in damaging both the Myitnge bridge and enemy antiaircraft positions defending it.

ATLANTIC: German submarine *U-221* torpedoes and sinks a U.S. freighter from convoy HX 229.

ETO: Nearly a hundred Eighth Air Force B-17 and B-24 Liberator bombers attack the submarine yards at Vegesack, Germany, using automatic flight control linked to bombsights. Two bombers are lost and 24 are damaged. Enemy aircraft losses are estimated at over 50 destroyed. Seven subs are reported damaged in the attack.

First Lieutenant Jack W. Mathis is the leading bombardier for his squadron on this mission. Just as his aircraft is starting its bomb run, Mathis is mortally wounded by enemy flak. Without any hesitation, and with his last breath, Mathis carefully lines up his target in the bombsight and releases his bombs. His squadron is able to follow his strike on the target and gain a maximum effect. First Lieutenant Mathis's act of bravery and dedication to the mission above and beyond the call of duty will win him the Medal of Honor.

TUNISIA: Northwest African Air Force fighters fly reconnaissance missions over Axis defensive lines.

March 19

CBI: Tenth Air Force B-25 Mitchells severely damage the Myitnge bridge with four direct hits.

ATLANTIC: German submarine *U-527* torpedoes and damages a U.S. freighter from convoy HX 229. It is later sunk by *U-523*. German submarine *U-533* torpedoes and sinks a Greek freighter from convoy SC 122. The attack on the convoys ends. In all, 12 ships from HX 229 and nine ships from SC 122 are sunk. No U-boats are lost.

PACIFIC: U.S. submarine *Kingfish* torpedoes and sinks a Japanese army hospital ship in the Formosa Strait. U.S. submarine *Sawfish* torpedoes and damages a Japanese guardboat southeast of Japan. U.S. submarine *Wahoo* torpedoes and sinks a Japanese cargo ship and damages another in the Yellow Sea.

March 20

PACIFIC: U.S. submarine *Scamp* torpedoes and damages a Japanese merchant ship off the east coast of Japan.

SOUTHWEST PACIFIC AREA: U.S. submarine *Trigger* fires a torpedo and hits a Japanese gunboat north of the Admiralty Islands, but the torpedo is a dud and damages only the gunboat.

SOUTH PACIFIC: Navy and marine aircraft of the Thirteenth Air Force lay mines off Bougainville near Buin-Tonolai area, while B-17s and B-24 Liberators conduct a diversionary raid on the airfield.

March 21

ATLANTIC: U.S. submarine *Herring* sinks German submarine *U-163* in the Bay of Biscay.

TUNISIA: U.S. 1st Armored Division captures Sened and advances to Maknassy, but further advances are halted by strong Axis defenses. U.S. 1st Ranger Battalion and the 26th Infantry Regiment of 1st Infantry Division capture 700 prisoners in the vicinity of El Guettar.

PACIFIC: U.S. submarine *Finback* torpedoes and damages a Japanese transport ship south of the Caroline Islands. U.S. submarine *Scamp* torpedoes and damages a Japanese transport ship off the east coast of Honshu, Japan. U.S. submarine *Wahoo* torpedoes and sinks two Japanese cargo ships in the Yellow Sea.

March 22

ATLANTIC: Northwest African Air Force heavy bombers of the 1st Antisubmarine Squadron sink German submarine *U-524* north of the Canary Islands.

ETO: Eighth Air Force B-17s and B-24 Liberators bomb the U-boat yards at Wilhelmshaven, Germany. Three bombers are lost, 22 are damaged. Enemy losses are reported to be nearly 40 aircraft lost or damaged. A German tanker is also sunk.

TUNISIA: Maknassy is occupied, but farther advance of the U.S. II Corps is stopped near Djebel Naemia. The 1st and 9th Infantry Divisions make unsuccessful attacks against enemy defenses past El Guettar. Northwest African Air Force fighters fly reconnaissance and ground support missions.

SOUTHWEST PACIFIC AREA: U.S. submarine *Gudgeon* attacks a Japanese convoy, torpedoing and sinking a cargo ship near Surabaya, Java. U.S. submarine *Tambor* torpedoes and damages a Japanese transport ship in the Sulu Sea.

March 23

PACIFIC: U.S. submarine *Whale* torpedoes and sinks a Japanese transport northwest of Saipan.

SOUTH PACIFIC: In response to the disaster in the Bismarck Sea, the Japanese plan to regain air superiority over Guadalcanal and Tulagi and over Papua. A total of 300 aircraft are to be employed in this effort. The Solomons are the target for the first half of April, to be followed by Papua in the second half of April. The Japanese stake inexperienced pilots against an increasingly confident and powerful U.S. air fleet.

March 24

ALEUTIANS: The plan for occupying Attu Island is approved by the JCS. Eleventh Air Force B-24 Liberators, B-25 Mitchells, and P-38 Lightnings conduct five attack missions over Kiska.

CBI: Tenth Air Force B-24 Liberators, along with two B-17s attacking from a height of 50 feet, are unable to damage the Myitnge Bridge.

MEDITERRANEAN: Ninth Air Force B-24 Liberators cause heavy damage to facilities at Messina.

TUNISIA: Major General Orlando Ward, commander of the U.S. 1st Armored Division, personally leads a night assault up Djebel Naemia after Patton orders that the objective be taken. Northwest African Air Force A-20 Havocs and B-25 Mitchells attack enemy troop concentrations.

PACIFIC: U.S. submarine *Wahoo* torpedoes and sinks three Japanese cargo ships in the Yellow Sea.

March 25

TUNISIA: Ward's attack on Djebel Naemia makes no progress; the 18th Infantry Regiment of the 1st Infantry Division is forced off Djebel Berda by an enemy attack. Northwest African Air Force B-17s bomb the docks and ships at Sousse.

The escort carrier USS *Bogue* on convoy duty in the Atlantic, camouflaged to break up her outline against the sea.

March 26

ALEUTIANS: Near the island of Komandorskiye Ostrova, Rear Admiral Charles H. McMorris's naval task group engages a Japanese force of two heavy cruisers, two light cruisers, and four destroyers escorting two transports with reinforcements for Kiska Island. The U.S. force, with one heavy cruiser, one light cruiser, and four destroyers drives the Japanese off. The U.S. heavy cruiser and two U.S. destroyers are damaged. One Japanese heavy cruiser is damaged. This engagement prevents the Japanese from reinforcing or supplying the Aleutians, except by submarine.

CBI: Tenth Air Force B-24 Liberators mine the Rangoon River while other B-24s conduct a diversionary raid on the city of Rangoon.

ATLANTIC: Escort carrier USS *Bogue* proves her worth to convoy SC 123 (Halifax Slow to United Kingdom) by launching aircraft and preventing German submarines *U-443* and *U-415* from approaching the convoy.

March 27

TUNISIA: The 135th and 168th Infantry Regiments of the U.S. 34th Infantry Division attempt to break through Fondouk Gap. The infantry moving on foot across open ground and through barbed wire and minefields make three separate attacks, but make no progress against heavy enemy fire.

NEW GUINEA: Fifth Air Force B-25 Mitchells bomb targets at Lae and Salamaua.

March 28

ETO: Eighth Air Force B-17s bomb the marshaling yard at Rouen-Sotteville, France. Of the 70 B-17s involved, one bomber is lost and nine are damaged. Enemy losses are estimated at 10 aircraft.

SOUTHWEST PACIFIC AREA: With approval of JCS, General MacArthur, COM-SWPA, issues orders that outline the objectives for an offensive plan code-named Cartwheel. The Elkton plan would implement Cartwheel. It is a campaign intended to envelop and isolate Rabaul in a series of coordinated alternating operations between SWPA and SOPAC. The objectives for SWPA are in northeast New Guinea and the Bismarck Archipelago. SOPAC's objectives are to advance from Guadalcanal to clear the Solomon Islands to Bougainville Island. MacArthur's forces will capture Woodlark and Kiriwina Islands to establish airbases in order to support future amphibious operations. Admiral William F. Halsey, COMSOPAC, then will take the offensive to capture New Georgia Island. SWPA will then move against northeast New Guinea at Lae, Salamaua, and Finschhafen. SOPAC will then move on the Shortland Islands and southern Bougainville Island, and SWPA on Madang and Cape Gloucester, clearing the Japanese from western New Britain. As outlined by the JCS, MacArthur will not have direct command of Admiral Halsey's forces, but will be able to provide general direction to COMSOPAC. This does not become a problem, as Halsey and MacArthur discover they work well together as a team.

PACIFIC: U.S. submarine *Tunny* torpedoes and damages a Japanese troopship off Wake Island, which subsequently runs aground on the island.

March 29
ATLANTIC: German submarine *U-160* torpedoes and sinks a U.S. freighter separated from convoy HX 230 (New York to Liverpool).

The War Production Board begins rationing fat (which is used for munitions) as well as meat and cheese.

SOUTHWEST PACIFIC AREA: A JCS directive designates the South Pacific Area as the water and land lying west of the 159th parallel to differentiate it from MacArthur's Southwest Pacific Area (SWPA).

U.S. submarine *Gudgeon* torpedoes and sinks a Japanese fleet tanker and damages another tanker in Makassar Strait.

PACIFIC: U.S. submarine *Wahoo* sinks a Japanese ship south of Kyushu.

March 30
ALEUTIANS: Eleventh Air Force B-24 Liberators, B-25 Mitchells, and P-38 Lightnings attack Kiska and Attu. One B-24 is lost to enemy antiaircraft fire.

TUNISIA: Northwest African Air Force A-20 Havocs bomb enemy forces and tanks in support of the 9th Infantry Division's attack on Djebel Berda.

SOUTHWEST PACIFIC AREA: U.S. submarine *Tuna* attacks a Japanese convoy north of Manus Island in the Admiralties and sinks a cargo ship.

NEW GUINEA: Fifth Air Force B-17s, B-25 Mitchells, B-24 Liberators, and A-20 Havocs attack Japanese ships and facilities at Finschhafen.

March 31
CBI: General Stilwell's 124 transport aircraft in theater can deliver only about 4,000 tons of supplies a month to China. General Chennault's Tenth Air Force uses 1,500 tons of these supplies. Chinese units are being trained at Kunming, but

at a far lower rate than Stilwell expects. Chennault claims that with more support, he will be able to attack the Japanese home islands by 1943. This outrageously optimistic proposal appeals to President Roosevelt, who raises the authorized supply tonnage to Chennault.

ETO: Eighth Air Force bombers attack the port facilities at Rotterdam, the Netherlands. Three B-17s and one B-24 are lost; eight bombers are damaged. Enemy losses are negligible.

TUNISIA: Ninth Air Force B-25 Mitchells bomb the airfield at Sfax, damaging several enemy aircraft; P-40s attack enemy transportation north of Gabès. Northwest African Air Force fighters and bombers attack enemy positions between the El Guettar-Gabès road in support of U.S. II Corps.

April 1

ALEUTIANS: Eleventh Air Force B-24 Liberators, B-25 Mitchells, and P-38 Lightnings attack Kiska. The Joint Chiefs of Staff approves the plan to retake Attu. Major General Albert E. Brown's 7th Infantry Division is identified as the land force to conduct Operation Sandcrab, scheduled to begin 7 May. Vice Admiral Thomas C. Kinkaid, Commander, North Pacific Force, will lead the operation.

ATLANTIC: U.S. submarine *Shad* torpedoes an Italian blockade runner in the Bay of Biscay.

TUNISIA: Northwest African Air Force A-20 Havocs bomb airfields while fighters continue to attack enemy motor transports and tanks.

SOLOMONS: Six U.S. fighters of 42 engaged are lost in a three-hour battle over the Russell Islands in the Solomons during a Japanese air attack on Guadalcanal, Tulagi, and the airfield under construction in the Russells. U.S. pilots claim 20 Japanese aircraft shot down.

April 2

PACIFIC: U.S. submarine *Tunny* torpedoes and sinks a Japanese transport west of Truk.

U.S. submarine *Haddock* torpedoes and sinks a Japanese tanker north of Palau; U.S. submarine *Pickerel* is sunk off northern Honshu, Japan.

April 3

ATLANTIC: German submarine *U-155* torpedoes and sinks a U.S. tanker off Key West, Florida.

TUNISIA: General Alexander alerts Patton's II Corps to be prepared to move north of the British First Army for the final offensive directed against Tunis.

April 4

ETO: Eighth Air Force B-17s attack the Renault armament and motor works in Paris against heavy German fighter attack. Of the 85 bombers involved, four B-17s are lost and 16 are damaged. German aircraft losses are estimated at over 50.

MEDITERRANEAN: Ninth Air Force B-24 Liberators bomb the docks at Naples; Northwest African Air Force B-17s bomb the airfield and the marshaling yards.

SOUTHWEST PACIFIC AREA: B-17s bomb the town and airfield at Kavieng, New Ireland.

SOUTH PACIFIC: Vice Admiral Marc A. Mitscher becomes Commander Air Solomons (COMAIRSOL), with operational control of all Royal New Zealand Air Force (RNZAF), U.S. Army, Navy, and Marine Corps aircraft in the South Pacific.

NEW GUINEA: Fifth Air Force B-25 Mitchells and A-20 Havocs attack Japanese positions near the Huon Gulf; B-17s bomb Salamaua.

April 5

ALEUTIANS: Eleventh Air Force B-24 Liberators and B-25 Mitchells bomb the airfields on Attu and Kiska, escorted by P-38 Lightnings and P-4Os.

CBI: Tenth Air Force B-25 Mitchells bomb rail targets at Mandalay.

ATLANTIC: German submarine *U-563* torpedoes and sinks a U.S. tanker separated from convoy HX 231 (New York to Liverpool).

ETO: Eighth Air Force B-17s bomb an aircraft factory and related industrial targets at Antwerp, Belgium. German fighters knock down four B-17s and damage 13 others out of the 82 bombers involved in the attack. At least 23 enemy aircraft are lost.

TUNISIA: Northwest African Air Force and Western Desert Air Force fighters and bombers concentrate on denying the enemy the ability to transport supplies and reinforcements to Tunisia. Pilots report over 60 enemy aircraft downed in air combat. Frustrated with what he believes to be Major General Orlando Ward's lack of action, Patton replaces Ward with Major General Ernest Harmon as commander of 1st Armored Division.

SOUTH PACIFIC: U.S. destroyer sinks Japanese submarine *RO-34* near Russell Island, Solomons.

April 6

CARIBBEAN: German submarine *U-185* torpedoes and sinks a U.S. freighter off Cuba.

MEDITERRANEAN: Ninth Air Force B-24 Liberators bomb Messina harbor in Sicily, while Northwest African Air Force B-17s bomb docks and shipping at Trapani, Sicily, and B-25 Mitchells and P-38 Lightinings attack enemy shipping in the Straits of Sicily.

TUNISIA: Axis forces abandon the key defensive positions in front of U.S. II Corps that had kept 1st Infantry Division and 9th Infantry Division units virtually frozen in place.

April 7

TUNISIA: U.S. II Corps patrols make contact with British Eighth Army patrols east of El Guettar. The 133rd and 135th Infantry Regiments of the U.S. 34th Infantry Division, along with tanks and infantry of the British IX Corps, attacks Fondouk Pass. Artillery and anti-tank fire cause the British-American advance to collapse.

Western Desert Air Force aircraft provide support to ground forces and attack enemy convoys between Sfax and Sousse.

MEDITERRANEAN: Ninth Air Force B-24 Liberators attack Palermo harbor in Sicily.

SOUTHWEST PACIFIC AREA: U.S. submarine *Trout* lays mines near Sarawak, Borneo.

PACIFIC: U.S. submarine *Tunny* torpedoes a Japanese ship northwest of Truk. The ship later sinks. U.S. submarine *Pickerel* torpedoes and sinks a Japanese cargo ship off Honshu, Japan.

GUADALCANAL: Nearly 400 Japanese bombers and fighters launched from carriers attack and sink a U.S. destroyer and a New Zealand corvette south of Guadalcanal. Two U.S. oilers are damaged. Thirteenth Air Force P-38 Lightnings and P-39 Airacobras, along with marine and navy F4F Wildcats and F4U Corsairs engage Japanese dive-bombers and fighters attempting to attack U.S. supply ships off Guadalcanal. Enemy losses are estimated at 39 aircraft; U.S. losses are seven fighters. Marine pilot Lieutenant James Swett, flying with four other Wildcats over Tulagi Harbor, spots about 20 enemy dive-bombers headed for the American ships. Swett is new to the theater and has never been in combat, yet he attacks the enemy formation with great skill, shooting down seven dive-bombers before receiving serious damage to his aircraft. Out of ammunition and with the engine dead, Lt. Swett ditches off Florida Island and is later rescued. For his exceptional skill and daring in taking on an entire enemy formation, Lieutenant Swett will receive the Medal of Honor.

April 8

CBI: Tenth Air Force B-25 Mitchells bomb the airfield at Meiktila. A Japanese storage depot at Ningam is attacked by P-40s and one B-25.

April 9

TUNISIA: The 133rd and 135th Infantry Regiments of the 34th Infantry Division attack to clear enemy positions above Fondouk Pass, while the British 6th Armored Division charges through the pass but fails to trap the retreating enemy. The performance of the demoralized 34th Division is so poor that the British 6th Armored Division commander recommends to General Eisenhower that the 34th be moved to the rear for retraining by British officers. This angers the Americans a great deal, especially since the British plan to attack the pass was seriously flawed.

During the battle at Fondouk, Private Robert D. Booker of the 34th Infantry Division advances alone over 200 yards of open ground with a light machine gun and a box of ammunition to a position where he can directly engage the enemy. Although under constant machine gun and mortar fire, Private Booker ignores a wound and puts his own machine gun into action, knocking out an enemy position. Shortly thereafter, Booker is mortally wounded but continues to fight, encouraging his squad and pointing out targets. For his courage and fortitude against great odds, Private Booker will receive the Medal of Honor.

The U.S. 1st Armored Division begins to move north to positions in anticipation of II Corps movement of 100,000 men 200 miles across Tunisia to take up attack positions on the northern coast. The mission is to attack toward Mateur in order to outflank Axis defenses in support of the British offensive to capture Bizerte.

SOUTHWEST PACIFIC AREA: U.S. submarine *Drum* attacks Japanese convoy, sinking a cargo ship north of Kavieng, New Ireland. U.S. submarine *Grayling* attacks a Japanese convoy, sinking a cargo ship off Mindoro in the Philippines. U.S. submarine

Tautog attacks a Japanese convoy south of Celebes Island, sinking a cargo ship and a destroyer.

April 10

TUNISIA: Tunisian offensive plan from General Alexander's headquarters, Operation Vulcan, is approved. While the British First Army makes the main attack to capture Tunis, the British Eighth Army is to maintain pressure on the Axis south flank. The corps mission is to attack toward Mateur in order to outflank Axis defenses in support of the British offensive.

NEW GUINEA: Fifth Air Force B-17s and B-24 Liberators bomb Wewak.

April 11

ALEUTIANS: Eleventh Air Force B-25 Mitchells, escorted by P-40s and P-38s, attack Kiska.

ATLANTIC: German submarine *U-615* torpedoes and sinks a U.S. freighter in convoy HX 232 (New York to Liverpool). German submarine *U-195* torpedoes and sinks a U.S. freighter in convoy UGS 7 (United States to Mediterranean).

MEDITERRANEAN: Ninth Air Force B-24 Liberators attack Naples harbor, losing one bomber to enemy fighters and antiaircraft fire.

TUNISIA: B-25 Mitchells bomb enemy locations near Sfax. Northwest African Air Force B-17s bomb Tunis harbor; P-38 Lightnings attack enemy fighter and transport aircraft; B-26 Marauders and B-25s bomb enemy-held airfields in northeast Tunisia.

April 12

CBI: Tenth Air Force B-25 Mitchells attack Magwe airfield. P-40s attack Japanese ammunition and supplies at Walawbum.

TUNISIA: Northwest African Air Force B-17s bomb Bizerte harbor. B-25 Mitchells and A-20 Havocs bomb enemy airfields in northeast Tunisia.

PACIFIC: U.S. submarine *Flying Fish* torpedoes and sinks a Japanese cargo ship off Honshu, Japan.

April 13

ALEUTIANS: Eleventh Air Force B-25 Mitchells and B-24 Liberators, escorted by 28 P-38 Lightnings and 20 P-40s, attack Kiska, dropping 43 tons of bombs on the runway and other targets. Enemy antiaircraft fire downs one P-38. A B-25 and another P-38 are damaged.

April 14

ALEUTIANS: Eleventh Air Force bombers and fighters attack Kiska, dropping 85 tons of bombs. One B-24 is shot down.

CBI: Tenth Air Force P-40s, carrying 1,000-pound bombs as an experiment, hit airfields at Myitkyina and Manywet and cause heavy damage.

PACIFIC: U.S. submarine *Pike* torpedoes and damages a Japanese cargo ship north of the Admiralty Islands.

NEW GUINEA: Fifth Air Force P-40s and P-38 Lightnings drive off an attack by the Japanese on Milne Bay, destroying 14 enemy aircraft. Fifth Air Force B-17s sink a Japanese cargo ship in Hansa Bay, New Guinea.

April 15
TUNISIA: Major General Omar N. Bradley takes command of U.S. II Corps, replacing Major General George S. Patton, Jr., who is now assigned to prepare the plan for the Allied attack on Sicily.

Northwest African Air Force A-20 Havoc and P-38 Lightning fighters fly ground support missions for Allied troops.

SOUTHWEST PACIFIC AREA: Fifth Air Force B-17s bomb Rabaul airfields and the airfield at Lae in New Guinea.

PACIFIC: U.S. submarine *Seawolf* torpedoes and sinks a Japanese transport south of Marcus Island.

SOUTH PACIFIC: Two new airfields to support future offensive operations in the Solomons are completed on Barrika Island in the Russell Islands.

April 16
CBI: Tenth Air Force P-40s bomb railroad bridges near Mogaung and Pinbaw. B-24 Liberators bomb the marshaling yard in Rangoon, and B-25 Mitchells bomb rail targets in Mandalay.

ETO: Eighth Air Force B-24 Liberators and B-17s raid U-boat bases at Brest and at Lorient in France. Enemy fighters and ground smoke limit the accuracy of the bombers. Enemy aircraft losses are estimated at over 14. U.S. losses are three B-24s out of 19 and one B-17 out of 59. A total of 18 other bombers are damaged.

MEDITERRANEAN: Ninth Air Force B-24 Liberators bomb Catania harbor in Sicily. Northwest African Air Force B-17s bomb docks at Palermo, Sicily.

NEW GUINEA: Fifth Air Force B-24 Liberators and B-17s bomb Wewak.

April 17
ALEUTIANS: Eleventh Air Force B-24 Liberators bomb and damage the runway at Attu. B-25 Mitchells, P-38 Lightnings, and P-40s attack Kiska.

CBI: Tenth Air Force bombers and P-40s attack bridges at Myitnge, Kamaing, Namti, and Pazundaung.

ATLANTIC: A U.S. Coast Guard cutter, escorting convoy HX 233 (New York to Liverpool), sinks German submarine *U-175* as it shadows the convoy.

ETO: Eighth Air Force B-17s attack an aircraft production facility at Bremen, Germany. Enemy fighters and antiaircraft defenses hit the 115-plane formation hard, destroying 16 and damaging 39 others. Over 60 enemy fighters are reported destroyed and 159 American crewmen are reported as missing.

MEDITERRANEAN: Ninth Air Force P-40Fs and 11 RAF Spitfires attack a massive German air formation of 65 transports with fighter escort, en route to Sicily. While the Spitfires fly cover, the P-40s attack the transports, destroying nearly all of them and shooting down 16 fighters as well.

PACIFIC: U.S. submarine *Flying Fish* torpedoes and sinks a Japanese cargo ship off Hokkaido, Japan.

April 18
TUNISIA: Allied aircraft are able to heavily damage the Axis aerial supply line, destroying nearly 70 transport aircraft and 16 escorts. U.S. losses are six P-40s.

The U.S. Coast Guard cutter *Spencer,* escorting convoy HX 233, attacks and sinks German submarine *U-175* on April 17, 1943.

Southwest Pacific Area: U.S. submarine *Drum* torpedoes and sinks a Japanese ammunition ship near the Bismarck Archipelago.

Pacific: Using information obtained from intercepted Japanese signals, 16 U.S. P-38 Lightnings locate and shoot down a plane transporting Commander in Chief of the Japanese Combined Fleet, Admiral Yamamoto Isoroku. Admiral Yamamoto was en route from Rabaul to the Solomons for an inspection.

April 19

Tunisia: The British attack on Axis defenses stretching along the general line of Enfidaville, Bou Arada, Medjez el Bab, and Sedjenane begins. U.S. II Corps is in place on the British First Army's north flank.

Pacific: U.S. submarine *Seawolf* torpedoes and sinks a Japanese cargo ship in the area of the Bonin Islands.

April 20

Pacific: U.S. submarine *Runner* mines approaches to Hong Kong. U.S. submarine *Scorpion* torpedoes and sinks a Japanese gunboat off Honshu, Japan.

Atlantic: German submarine *U-565* torpedoes and sinks a U.S. freighter in convoy UGS 7 (United States to Mediterranean, Slow) off the coast of North Africa.

April 21

ALEUTIANS: Eleventh Air Force commander, Brigadier General William O. Butler, takes operational control of all army and navy air units from Commander North Pacific Forces (NORPACFOR), which are designated as Task Group (TG) 16.1.

ATLANTIC: Italian submarine *Leonardo da Vinci* torpedoes and damages a U.S. freighter off the coast of South Africa. After the freighter is abandoned, the submarine sinks the ship with gunfire.

April 23

ATLANTIC: In the North Atlantic, German submarine *U-306* and *U-129* each torpedo and sink a U.S. freighter. *U-306*'s victim is in convoy HX 234 (New York to Liverpool); *U-129*'s victim was bound for Iraq.

ETO: Combined Chiefs of Staff designates Lieutenant General Sir Frederick E. Morgan as chief of staff to the Supreme Allied Commander responsible for an Allied planning organization tasked to prepare initial plans for a cross-Channel invasion. The new organization is referred to as COSSAC, after Morgan's title.

TUNISIA: U.S. II Corps makes its attack in zone to support the British advance. The 9th Infantry Division and 1st Infantry Division attack enemy defenses on key hills along the Tine River valley toward Mateur. Ninth Air Force B-25 Mitchells and P-40s provide support to the ground forces. The Northwest African Air Force B-25s, B-26 Marauders, and A-20 Havocs bomb enemy positions and vehicles.

CENTRAL PACIFIC: Seventh Air Force B-24 Liberators from Funafuti attack Japanese facilities on Tarawa Atoll.

April 24

ALEUTIANS: The U.S. 7th Infantry Division sails from San Francisco bound for Cold Harbor, Alaska.

TUNISIA: At Djebel Dardys near Sedjenane, Sergeant William L. Nelson, a heavy mortar section leader in the 60th Infantry Regiment, 9th Infantry Division, leads his men forward under heavy enemy fire. Placing himself in an exposed position forward of his gunners, he directs mortar fire on enemy soldiers attempting to form a counterattack. Although wounded, Sergeant Nelson crawls to a position only 50 yards from the enemy and continues to direct accurate fire on them. His skill and courage in employing his section against heavy odds and his devotion to duty at the cost of his life will win him the Medal of Honor.

PACIFIC: U.S. submarine *Flying Fish* torpedoes and sinks a Japanese cargo ship in Tsugaru Strait, Japan. U.S. submarine *Runner* torpedoes and damages a Japanese army hospital ship off Hong Kong.

April 25

ALEUTIANS: Eleventh Air Force bombers and fighters attack Kiska and Attu.

April 26

ALEUTIANS: Three light cruisers and six destroyers of Rear Admiral Charles H. McMorris's naval task group bombard Japanese installations at Attu.

April 26

TUNISIA: U.S. II Corps, with four divisions on the attack, attempts to break enemy first line defenses and prepares to send 1st Armored Division toward Mateur. The 34th Infantry Division attacks to seize a cluster of hills identified as Hill 609.

SOUTHWEST PACIFIC AREA: SWPA headquarters issues the Elkton III plan, which lays out the coordinated attack by SWPA and SOPAC forces on Rabaul. The entire operation against Rabaul is codenamed Cartwheel.

April 27

ATLANTIC: U.S. Navy PV-1 patrol bombers, providing coverage for convoy SC 128 (Halifax Slow to United Kingdom), sink German submarine *U-174*.

PACIFIC: Japanese submarine *I-178* torpedoes and sinks a U.S. freighter off Sydney, Australia. U.S. submarine *Scorpion* attacks a Japanese convoy and torpedoes and sinks a cargo ship off Honshu, Japan.

April 28

CBI: Japanese medium bombers and fighters attack Fourteenth Air Force airfields at Kunming, China, but the raid does little damage. P-40 pilots report shooting down 10 enemy aircraft.

ATLANTIC: Escort carrier USS *Bogue* and four destroyers protecting convoy HX 235 (New York to Liverpool) succeed in preventing attacks from five German submarines following the convoy.

MEDITERRANEAN: Ninth Air Force B-24s attack Naples harbor and Messina.

TUNISIA: Company A, 6th Armored Infantry Regiment, 1st Armored Division, encounters heavy enemy resistance as it begins an attack on German entrenchments near Medjez el Bab. A German machine gun position on the company's flank is especially dangerous, holding up the company's advance. Private Nicholas Minue, on his own and completely alone, charges the entrenched enemy position in the face of heavy fire. With only the bayonet on his M-1 rifle, Private Minue kills about 10 enemy soldiers in a trench. As soon as he has cleared this position, he moves forward, driving the enemy until he is mortally wounded. For his extraordinary act of courage and indomitable spirit, Private Minue will receive the Medal of Honor.

SOUTHWEST PACIFIC AREA: U.S. submarine *Gudgeon* torpedoes and sinks a Japanese ship off Panay Island, Philippines.

April 29

ATLANTIC: German submarine *U-258* torpedoes and damages a U.S. freighter in convoy ONS 5 (Liverpool to Halifax, slow). The crew abandons the freighter. Navy PBY Catalinas damage German submarine *U-528* as it attempts to attack the same convoy.

MEDITERRANEAN: At a planning conference in Algiers for Husky, the invasion of Sicily, Supreme Allied Commander General Dwight D. Eisenhower hears from General Bernard Montgomery's representative, who proposes a combined U.S.-British assault on the southeast corner of the island.

TUNISIA: A battalion of the 16th Infantry Regiment of the 1st Infantry Division captures Hill 523 and holds off determined enemy counterattacks during the day until overwhelmed and captured.

April 30
ATLANTIC: British and Canadian naval forces take responsibility for escorting the ONS (Halifax to Liverpool) convoys.

MEDITERRANEAN: Ninth Air Force P-40s attack Axis shipping, sinking one destroyer and damaging two others. Five enemy fighters and three P-40s are lost.

TUNISIA: The 135th Infantry Regiment of the 34th Infantry Division captures Hill 609, a key defensive position, and defends it against enemy counterattack. The U.S. 9th Infantry Division, with French units, advances on the Sedjenane Valley.

SOUTHWEST PACIFIC AREA: U.S. submarine *Gudgeon* lands men and equipment on Panay Island, Philippines.

PACIFIC: Japanese submarine *I-19* torpedoes and sinks a U.S. freighter south of the Fiji Islands. U.S. submarine *Snook* lays mines off Saddle Island, China.

May 1
ALEUTIANS: Eleventh Air Force B-24 Liberators and B-25 Mitchells with P-38 Lightnings and P-40s flying escort attack installations on Kiska. Installations at Holtz Bay and Chichagof Harbor on Attu are also attacked.

CBI: Fourteenth Air Force elements move into eastern China to allow U.S. aircraft to strike deeper into Japanese-occupied areas in China, Indochina, and Thailand.

ETO: Eighth Air Force B-17s attack the St-Nazaire, France, U-boat base and shipyard while a diversionary group of 24 B-24 Liberators flies along the coast of Brittany. Of the 29 B-17s that bomb the target, seven are lost and 22 are damaged. Enemy losses are estimated at about 20 fighters.

MEDITERRANEAN: Ninth Air Force B-24 Liberators bomb the harbor at Reggio di Calabria in Italy.

TUNISIA: The Tine Valley is open as the German defenders withdraw.

May 2
ALEUTIANS: Eleventh Air Force B-25 Mitchells, P-40s, and eight P-38 Lightnings attack antiaircraft positions and buildings on Kiska.

CBI: Fourteenth Air Force P-40s engage in air combat with about 30 Japanese fighters near Lingling and Changsha. Pilots claim seven enemy Zeroes downed with the loss of one P-40 out of the 17 involved.

MEDITERRANEAN: British Eighth Army commander, General Sir Bernard L. Montgomery, himself arrives in Algiers to press home his plan for Husky, even to the point of pursuing Eisenhower's Chief of Staff, General Walter Bedell Smith, into the men's latrine to win his point.

TUNISIA: Northwest African Air Force fighters fly reconnaissance missions and attack enemy tanks and troops near Massicault and Tebourba.

PACIFIC: Japanese submarine *I-19* torpedoes and sinks a U.S. freighter near the Fiji Islands.

New Georgia: Thirteenth Air Force B-17s along with P-38 Lightnings and P-39 Airacobras bomb Munda airfield in New Georgia.

May 3

Aleutians: Eleventh Air Force B-24 Liberators and B-25 Mitchells, with P-38 Lightnings and P-40s escorting, attack installations and the airfield on Kiska.

Mediterranean: General Dwight D. Eisenhower is the supreme allied commander for Husky, the invasion of Sicily; however, his deputy commander as well as all of his component commanders are British. General Sir Harold Alexander is both the deputy commander and the commander of the Fifteenth Army Group. The air commander is Air Chief Marshal Tedder, and the sea commander is Admiral Sir Andrew B. Cunningham. The Fifteenth Army Group consists of the British Eighth Army, commanded by General Sir Bernard L. Montgomery, and the Seventh Army, commanded by Lieutenant General George S. Patton, Jr.

The plan for Husky is very basic. The British will make the main attack and the Americans will support the British left flank as Montgomery's army marches on Messina. The U.S. forces are to land in the Gulf of Gela, stretching from Licatta eastward to the Pachino peninsula, which marks the boundary between the two armies. From the Pachino peninsula eastward, the British Eighth Army will land, capture Syracuse, advance on Catania and then to Messina. The Americans are given two limits of advance from the beachhead, the Yellow and Blue Lines. Control of this area will bring the U.S. forces to the high ground overlooking the beaches and provide a good defensive position to protect Montgomery's advance. After that, Alexander has no plan. He intends to sort things out once the armies have established themselves on the beach. The British also have the advantage of major ports, which, once captured, will supply their forces. The Allied amphibious landings will be preceded by a major airborne landing of U.S. paratroopers and British glider-borne infantry. The British 1st Airborne Division troops will land at Catania to seize key bridges along the British intended line of advance. The American 82nd Airborne Division will drop near Gela. The Americans will have no major port facility and will have to depend on ship-to-shore transport to maintain their supply lines. This transportation is in the form of the 2 ½-ton amphibious truck called the DUKW. The air attack on Sicily and Sardinia is intended to defeat Axis airpower. After the landings, there will be little coordination between air and ground forces. The intention is to allow the air forces the flexibility to attack targets they determine to be the priority. This plan, run by the British, for the British, leaves the Americans cold and puts further strain on a relationship which has not been all that amicable since the beginning of the Tunisian campaign.

Tunisia: 1st Armored Division captures Mateur. Northwest African Air Force B-17s bomb Bizerte and fighters conduct reconnaissance missions.

May 4

Aleutians: A planned strike on Kiska is cancelled due to bad weather. Eleventh Air Force B-24 Liberators and B-25 Mitchells, along with P-38 Lightnings and P-40s, attack Attu Island targets at Chichagof Harbor and antiaircraft positions at Holtz Bay.

CBI: From French Indochina Fourteenth Air Force B-24 Liberators bomb installations on Hainan Island; B-25 Mitchells and B-17s with P-40 escort bomb the docks at Haiphong and Hanoi.

ATLANTIC: German submarine *U-264* torpedoes and sinks a U.S. freighter in convoy ONS 5 (Halifax to Liverpool).

ETO: Eighth Air Force B-17s are dispatched against factories at Antwerp, Belgium, while a diversion flight of 20 B-17s and 13 B-24 Liberators heads toward France. The 65 bombers that hit the target are covered by 117 P-47C Thunderbolts for nearly 175 miles. Pilots report 10 enemy aircraft lost and 16 B-17s damaged.

TUNISIA: Northwest African Air Force A-20 Havocs attack enemy positions near Zaghouan.

SOUTHWEST PACIFIC AREA: U.S. submarine *Gudgeon* sinks a Japanese trawler west of Panay, Philippines.

PACIFIC: U.S. submarine *Seal,* attacking a Japanese convoy, torpedoes and sinks a fleet tanker southeast of the Palau Islands.

NEW GUINEA: Fifth Air Force B-24 Liberators bomb the harbor and shipping at Wewak.

May 5

ALEUTIANS: Eleventh Air Force B-24 Liberators and B-25 Mitchells, with P-38 Lightnings and P-40s escorting, attack installations on Attu and Kiska. Royal Canadian Air Force (RCAF) pilots support the attack on Kiska.

ATLANTIC: German submarine *U-707* torpedoes and sinks a U.S. freighter in convoy ONS 5.

TUNISIA: Northwest African Air Force B-17s and fighters attack docks and shipping in Tunis harbor.

PACIFIC: U.S. submarine *Permit* attacks and damages a Japanese transport ship in Apra Harbor, Guam. U.S. submarine *Sawfish* torpedoes and sinks a Japanese gunboat off Honshu, Japan. U.S. submarine *Snook* torpedoes and sinks a Japanese cargo ship in the Yellow Sea.

May 6

ALEUTIANS: Eleventh Air Force B-24 Liberators and B-25 Mitchells, with P-38 Lightnings and P-40s escorting, attack installations on Attu and Kiska, dropping over 52 tons of bombs.

ATLANTIC: German submarine *U-195* torpedoes and sinks a U.S. freighter in the South Atlantic.

MEDITERRANEAN: Northwest African Air Force B-17s bomb Marsala and Trapani in Sicily. B-25 Mitchells and B-26 Marauders bomb ships off Marettimo Island and the port of Favignana.

TUNISIA: Ninth Air Force B-25 Mitchells attack Massicault and surrounding areas, while P-40s attack shipping in the Gulf of Tunis. Fighters, A-20 Havocs, and bombers fly over 1,400 sorties, attacking airfields, enemy vehicles, and troops. B-25s and B-26 Marauders bomb ships and aircraft.

SOUTHWEST PACIFIC AREA: SWPA headquarters issues orders for the occupation of Kiriwina and Woodlark Islands by U.S. forces and the capture of the northern coast of New Guinea, including the Huon Peninsula, by Australian forces. Southern Bougainville and western New Britain are also to be occupied. Kiriwina and Woodlark Islands can support advance airfields to support future operations against Rabaul. The Allies will also be able to control the Vitaz Strait and have free access to the Bismarck Sea. The capture of Bougainville will give SOPAC forces a base of operations for strikes on Buka and Kavieng. Occupation of western New Britain will provide a base of operations to support SOPAC and threaten Rabaul.

U.S. submarine *Gar* torpedoes and sinks a Japanese cargo ship in Tarakan harbor, Borneo.

PACIFIC: U.S. submarine *Snook* torpedoes and sinks two Japanese cargo ships in the Yellow Sea. U.S. submarine *Wahoo* sinks Japanese cargo ship off Honshu, Japan.

NEW GEORGIA: U.S. ships lay mines in the western approaches to Kula Gulf, New Georgia Island.

May 7

TUNISIA: U.S. 9th Infantry Division enters Bizerte; Combat Command A of the 1st Armored Division reaches Ferryville.

May 8

CBI: Fourteenth Air Force B-24 Liberators and B-25 Mitchells bomb airfields and support facilities at Canton. The P-40s escorting the bombers destroy nearly 20 enemy aircraft.

ATLANTIC: JCS approves a planning estimate that projects 36 Allied divisions ready for a cross-Channel invasion by April 1944. German forces available in France to oppose the invasion are estimated at 32 divisions and 1,200 aircraft. Planners estimate that the Germans can reinforce these divisions in three weeks, increasing the total to 60 divisions and 1,700 aircraft. To succeed, the planners stress the need for a firm lodgment so that the Allied divisions can maintain a beachhead to support the flow of forces into France. To do this, ports are essential to build up sufficient supplies before an offensive can begin.

TUNISIA: Ninth Air Force P-40s attack shipping near Cap Bon and the Gulf of Tunis. P-40 fighter pilots claim five enemy fighters destroyed. Northwest African Air Force B-25 Mitchells bomb rail junctions and highways. P-40s and A-20 Havocs bomb shipping between Tunisia and Sicily as well as troop convoys and road networks around Tunis and Cap Bon.

SOUTHWEST PACIFIC AREA: Fifth Air Force B-17s bomb Rabaul airfield.

NEW GEORGIA: Thirteenth Air Force P-4O and P-38 Lightnings hit antiaircraft positions at Vila in New Georgia. Two Japanese destroyers hit the U.S. mines at Kula Gulf. One sinks, the other is damaged and later sunk in a U.S. air attack. U.S. aircraft attack two other destroyers, sinking one and damaging another off Rendova, New Georgia Islands.

May 9

MEDITERRANEAN: Ninth Air Force B-24 Liberators bomb the harbor facilities at Messina.

TUNISIA: Combat Command B of the U.S. 1st Armored Division cuts the Bizerte-Tunis Road and makes contact with elements of the British 7th Armored Division north of Tunis. P-40s fly reconnaissance, escort, and ground attack missions against enemy ships, troop concentrations, choke points, and gun positions in the vicinity of Cap Bon. The German commander meets with General Omar Bradley, commander of U.S. II Corps, and surrenders nearly 50,000 soldiers. General Bradley later passes the following message to his subordinates: "With their practical sense, their understanding of the enemy, their firsthand knowledge of the hardships and dangers of war, and above all else, their courage and loyalty, soldiers of the II Corps have played a major role in the winning of a great Allied victory."

SOUTHWEST PACIFIC AREA: U.S. submarine *Gar* torpedoes and sinks a Japanese gunboat off Mindanao, Philippines.

PACIFIC: U.S. submarines *Pogy* and *Wahoo*, both operating off Honshu, Japan, score hits in separate attacks. *Pogy* torpedoes and damages a Japanese transport. *Wahoo* torpedoes and sinks two cargo ships.

May 10

CBI: Fourteenth Air Force P-40s attack an enemy troop train and riverboats in the vicinity of Hanoi.

MEDITERRANEAN: Ninth Air Force B-25 Mitchells and P-40s bomb Pantelleria Island.

SOUTHWEST PACIFIC AREA: Fifth Air Force B-25 Mitchells bomb the Cape Gloucester airfield on New Britain Island in the Bismarck Archipelago.

PACIFIC: U.S. submarine *Plunger* attacks a Japanese convoy in the open ocean east of Saipan, sinking a cargo ship and damaging a transport.

NEW GEORGIA: Thirteenth Air Force P-38 Lightnings, along with navy and marine aircraft, attack Munda airfield in New Georgia.

May 11

ALEUTIANS: Operation Landgrab. The U.S. 7th Infantry Division begins landing on Attu Island. U.S. submarines *Nautilus* and *Narwhal* land scouts on the island. A provisional battalion lands and moves inland, while the 1st Battalion of the 17th Infantry Regiment lands at Holtz Bay, headed for Hill X, its initial objective and the linkup point with the advancing provisional battalion. Meanwhile, at Massacre Bay, delayed by heavy fog and threatening seas, the 2nd and 3rd Battalions of the 17th land and advance toward Jarmin Pass. Both the 1st and 3rd Battalions are stopped by enemy fire short of their objectives. Eleventh Air Force B-24 Liberators conduct several missions supporting the 7th Infantry Division on Attu. The bombers drop supplies, make bombing runs, and drop leaflets to convince the Japanese at Chichagof Harbor to surrender.

MEDITERRANEAN: Northwest African Air Force B-17s, B-26 Marauders, and B-25 Mitchells bomb Marsala in Sicily, targeting transportation and support sites.

SOUTHWEST PACIFIC AREA: Fifth Air Force B-17s and B-24 Liberators bomb Rabaul airfield. B-25 Mitchells bomb Penfoei and Dili in Timor.

U.S. submarine *Grayback* attacks a Japanese convoy northwest of Kavieng, New Ireland, and sinks a collier.

PACIFIC: Off Saipan, U.S. submarine *Plunger* sinks the damaged Japanese transport it had attacked previously.

May 12

ALEUTIANS: The 2nd Battalion, 32nd Infantry Regiment, attached to the 7th Infantry Division, lands at Massacre Bay. The 1st Battalion of the 17th Infantry Regiment takes the crest of Hill X, but fails to drive the Japanese off the hill. U.S. battleship *Pennsylvania* provides naval gunfire support to the Hill X attack. The battleship *Nevada* supports the landing at Massacre Bay with naval gunfire. Two Japanese submarines conduct torpedo attacks, but miss their intended targets. Shortly thereafter Japanese submarine *I-31* is detected and two U.S. destroyers sink the sub northeast of Chichagof Harbor. Eleventh Air Force B-24 Liberators, B-25 Mitchells, and P-38 Lightnings conduct ground support missions.

ATLANTIC: The Trident Conference begins. U.S. planners seek to obtain an agreement with the British that conforms to U.S. strategic interests. While supporting the British peripheral approach to defeating the Axis powers through offensive operations in the Mediterranean, these operations will be limited and subordinate to a cross-Channel invasion with a specific date in 1944. In addition, the United States will continue to pursue the strategic initiative gained in the Pacific during the summer of 1942. This includes keeping China in the war through offensive action in Burma, MacArthur's advance in the Southwest Pacific, as well as Nimitz's planned advance in the Central Pacific. Well coordinated among the army and navy, and the state Department, the American position is intended to overcome the lack of preparation that allowed British strategic priorities to dominate the Casablanca conference in January.

TUNISIA: The End of the Tunisian Campaign. Colonel General Jurgen von Armin formally surrenders to the British. About 275,000 Axis troops become prisoners of war. The Italian commander will surrender a day later, ending the campaign. The North African campaign has cost the United States 18,558 casualties. The inexperienced Americans have learned some brutal lessons about combat, yet have performed doggedly and, at times, exceptionally, and made significant contributions to the final phases of the campaign.

SOUTHWEST PACIFIC AREA: U.S. submarine *Gudgeon* torpedoes and sinks a Japanese cargo ship off southern Luzon, Philippines.

PACIFIC: U.S. submarine *Steelhead* conducts mine-laying activities off Japan.

May 13

ALEUTIANS: The Japanese continue to hold Jarmin Pass, despite the efforts of the 2nd Battalion 32nd Infantry and the 3rd Battalion of the 17th Infantry to capture the position. The 3rd Battalion of the 32nd Infantry Regiment lands at Holtz Bay to reinforce the attack on Hill X. The battleship USS *Idaho* and a destroyer support the landing with naval gunfire. The American troops, anticipating a quick victory against minimal enemy resistance, have no winter clothing. The extreme weather conditions on the island and lack of supplies will limit the effectiveness of the combat troops.

CARIBBEAN: German submarine *U-176* torpedoes and sinks two tankers off Hispaniola.

U.S. B-17s releasing bombs over a target in Germany *(National Archives and Records Administration)*

ETO: Eighth Air Force B-17s bomb the aircraft factory at Meaulte and the airfields at St. Omer, France. Of the 88 bombers that attack Meaulte, three B-17s are lost and 11 are damaged. Enemy losses are estimated at 11 aircraft destroyed. Of the 31 B-17s flown against the airfields, one bomber is lost and one damaged.

SOUTH PACIFIC: Thirteenth Air Force B-17s bomb Kahili airfields on Bougainville Island and on Ballale Island. Royal New Zealand Air Force (RNZAF) P-40s, U.S. P-38 Lightnings, P-39 Airacobras, and P-40s, along with navy and marine fighters, intercept and destroy 16 enemy aircraft over Russell Island and Tulagi.

NEW GEORGIA: Rear Admiral Walden L. Ainsworth's Naval Task Force 18 bombards Munda and Vila airfields in New Georgia. During the bombardment, minelayers cover the northwestern approaches to Kula Gulf.

NEW GUINEA: Fifth Air Force B-17s bomb the Rabaul airfields and targets at Wewak and Boram in New Guinea. A-20 Havocs attack the airfield at Cape Gloucester on New Britain Island.

May 14

ALEUTIANS: Eleventh Air Force B-24 Liberators and B-25 Mitchells conduct ground support bombing missions over Attu. One B-24 is lost dropping supplies for the infantry.

ATLANTIC: Navy PBY Catalinas sink German submarine *U-657* tracking convoy ONS 7 (Halifax to Liverpool, slow) in the North Atlantic.

ETO: Over 200 Eighth Air Force bombers fly missions against four targets in Europe. The submarine yards and naval base at Kiel, Germany, are attacked by 126 B-17s and 17 B-24 Liberators. Over 60 enemy aircraft are reportedly destroyed; eight U.S. bombers are lost and 37 are damaged. Over Antwerp, Belgium, 38 B-17s bomb industrial targets. One B-17 is lost in the attack and 15 others damaged; enemy aircraft losses are estimated at five destroyed. The B-17s are escorted by 118 P-47 Thunderbolts. At least four German fighters are downed, but three P-47s are lost and one is damaged. All three pilots are listed as missing. At Courtrai, France, 34 B-17s bomb the airfield. Two bombers are shot down and 10 others are damaged. Of the 11 B-26 Marauders that attack the Velsen power station at Ijmuiden, Netherlands, 10 are damaged. This is the first time that the B-26 is used in the strategic air offensive in Europe.

NEW BRITAIN: Fifth Air Force B-25 Mitchells bomb the airfield at Gasmata, New Britain; B-24 Liberators and B-17s bomb the airfield at Rabaul. B-25s bomb the Penfoei airfield and Dili in Timor.

NEW GUINEA: Two U.S. motor torpedo (PT) boats sink Japanese submarine *RO-102* in Vitiaz Strait, off Saidor.

May 15

ALEUTIANS: Eleventh Air Force P-38 Lightnings attack antiaircraft positions while B-24 Liberators bomb Holtz Bay and Chichagof Harbor. The Japanese fall back to Moore Ridge behind Hill X, continuing to delay the advance of the Americans, who are also hampered by a mistaken U.S. airstrike on their position. The provisional battalion finally links up with the 1st Battalion of the 17th Infantry.

CBI: Fourteenth Air Force P-40s intercept a Japanese raid on Kunming airfield. The bombers cause little damage and the P-40s claim 13 fighter and two bomber kills.

CARIBBEAN: U.S. OS2U Kingfisher observation scout aircraft and a Cuban submarine chaser sink German submarine *U-176* off Cuba.

ATLANTIC: The Trident Conference begins. President Franklin Roosevelt, Prime Minister Churchill, the Combined Chiefs of Staff, and Generals Wavell, Chennault, and Stilwell from the China-Burma-India (CBI) theater. U.S. strategists, taking a hard look at U.S. wartime objectives, assess that China's manpower and geographical position are the keys to victory in the war against Japan, just as the USSR's manpower and geography are the keys to victory over Germany in Europe. Unlike the British, the Americans want to press for a swift and decisive victory against Germany in order to put their full resources against what many U.S. military officers (especially in the navy) consider to be the main threat, Japan. Therefore, the centerpiece of this conference for the Americans is to get a commitment from the British on a firm date for the cross-Channel invasion.

Well coordinated among the Army, Navy, and State Departments, the American position is intended to overcome the lack of preparation that allowed British strategic priorities to dominate the Casablanca conference in January. The Americans obtain an agreement from the British for a cross-Channel invasion with a target date of May 1, 1944. While supporting the British peripheral approach to defeating the Axis powers through offensive operations in the Mediterranean, these operations will be limited and will be subordinate to a cross-Channel invasion. They agree to continue the Mediterranean offensive with the aim of knocking Italy out of the war.

The Allies reaffirm their commitment to a strategic air offensive as preparation for the invasion. But the Americans win support for an increased operational tempo in the Pacific. The United States will continue to pursue the strategic initiative gained in the Pacific during the summer of 1942. This includes keeping China in the war through offensive action in Burma, MacArthur's advance in the Southwest Pacific, as well as Nimitz's planned advance in the Central Pacific.

ETO: Eighth Air Force B-17s attack naval facilities and submarine construction at Helgoland Island and Wilhelmshaven, Germany. Over 30 enemy aircraft are declared destroyed; of the 76 B-17s, five are lost and 27 are damaged. Over Emden, Germany 59 B-17s attack the U-boat yard, marshaling yard, and airfield. One B-17 is lost and nine others are damaged. Enemy losses are estimated at 14 aircraft. The attack is preceded by a fighter sweep of 116 P-47 Thunderbolts over Amsterdam and Rotterdam. Two enemy aircraft are reported shot down, but one P-47 is lost and the pilot is reported as missing.

SOUTHWEST PACIFIC AREA: U.S. submarine *Gar* attacks a Japanese convoy, torpedoing and sinking two cargo ships between Mindoro and Marinduque Islands, in the Philippines.

CENTRAL PACIFIC: Seventh Air Force B-24 Liberators from Midway bomb Wake Island. They are attacked by 22 enemy fighters, which shoot down one B-24. Four enemy aircraft are claimed lost.

NEW GUINEA: Fifth Air Force B-25 Mitchells and A-20 Havocs bomb the Lae airfield on New Guinea.

May 16

ALEUTIANS: Admiral Kinkaid, dissatisfied with Major General Brown's performance, relieves him and puts Major General Eugene M. Landrum in command of the operation. Moore Ridge is captured. The Japanese withdraw to prepared defensive positions around Chichagof Harbor. Eleventh Air Force B-24 Liberators bomb Chichagof Harbor, while other B-24s drop supplies to ground forces. B-25 Mitchells and P-38 Lightnings fly ground support missions.

ATLANTIC: A U.S. destroyer sinks German submarine *U-182* west of Madeira Islands in the North Atlantic near the convoy routes to the Mediterranean.

SOUTHWEST PACIFIC AREA: U.S. submarine *Grayback* torpedoes and damages a Japanese destroyer northwest of Kavieng, New Ireland.

PACIFIC: Japanese submarine *I-19* torpedoes and sinks a U.S. freighter off the Fiji Islands. The submarine surfaces, fires on the survivors, then questions and releases the men.

May 17

ALEUTIANS: Jarmin Pass is captured after Japanese defenders abandon their positions.

ATLANTIC: A U.S. PBM Mariner patrol bomber damages German submarine *U-128* in the South Atlantic, and two U.S. destroyers then sink the U-boat.

SOUTHWEST PACIFIC AREA: U.S. submarine *Grayback* torpedoes and sinks a cargo ship northwest of the Saint Matthias Group Islands.

May 18

ALEUTIANS: The 1st Battalion of the 4th Infantry Division arrives to reinforce the 7th Infantry Division.

Eleventh Air Force B-24 Liberators bomb Kiska Island, while P-40s and a B-25 Mitchell conduct reconnaissance.

ATLANTIC: The Trident Conference. The CCS agrees to a two-phase approach to the cross-Channel invasion, specifically lodgment and buildup. Air superiority is identified as an essential factor in the success of the plan.

MEDITERRANEAN: Northwest African Air Force begins sustained air attacks on Pantelleria Island. The first attack against docks and airfields involves over 80 B-25 Mitchell and B-26 Marauder bombers escorted by P-38 Lightnings.

PACIFIC: U.S. submarine *Pollack* torpedoes and sinks a Japanese gunboat off Maloelap Atoll in the Marshall Islands. Japanese submarine *I-25* torpedoes then surfaces to finish off a U.S. tanker with gunfire off Villa Efate in the New Hebrides Islands.

May 19

ATLANTIC: The Trident Conference. The CCS accepts the JCS draft strategic plan for the defeat of Japan. The plan calls for a two-pronged offensive from the Southwest Pacific and from the Central Pacific, with the Central Pacific as the main effort. The objectives are to capture the Philippines, secure the coastal area of China, and retake Hong Kong. From air bases in China, U.S. bombers will initiate an attack on the Japanese home islands. If necessary, an amphibious invasion will be launched to conquer Japan. This planning outline has no specific timetable, and no additional resources are to be provided to accomplish these objectives.

The CCS also approves the general concept for the cross-Channel invasion. The initial assault will be made with nine divisions to establish the lodgment and be reinforced with three to five divisions per month to prepare for the breakout.

ETO: Eighth Air Force VIII Bomber Command conducts attacks on the U-boat yards at Kiel and the naval facilities at Flensburg, Germany. Of the 103 B-17s that attack Kiel, six are shot down and 28 others are damaged. Enemy aircraft losses are estimated to be over 50. Over Flensburg, 55 B-17s bomb the target and claim 12 enemy aircraft destroyed and have nine B-17s damaged.

MEDITERRANEAN: Northwest African Air Force B-25 Mitchells and B-26 Marauders bomb airfields in Sardinia. B-17s bomb Milo Airfield at Trapani in Sicily.

SOUTHWEST PACIFIC AREA: U.S. submarine *Gar* torpedoes and sinks a Japanese guardboat in the Makassar Strait.

NEW BRITAIN: Fifth Air Force B-24 Liberators bomb the airfield at Gasmata Island in the Bismarck Archipelago.

NEW GUINEA: Fifth Air Force B-25 Mitchells bomb Japanese positions around Salamaua.

May 20

ATLANTIC: Admiral Ernest J. King, COMINCH, establishes under his command the Tenth Fleet with headquarters in Washington, D.C. Tenth Fleet's responsibility is to oversee Atlantic antisubmarine operations.

MEDITERRANEAN: In Sardinia, Northwest African Air Force P-38 Lightnings bomb the docks at Gulfo Aranci and rail lines near Macomer. B-17s bomb the airfield at Grosseto in Italy.

PACIFIC: U.S. submarine *Pollack* torpedoes and sinks a Japanese armed merchant cruiser near Jaluit Atoll, Marshall Islands.

May 21

ALEUTIANS: Elements of the 32nd Infantry and 1st Battalion, 4th Infantry, clear the main passes that cover the approaches to Chichagof Harbor.

ATLANTIC: TBF Avenger torpedo bombers from the U.S. escort carrier USS *Bogue* damage German submarine *U-231* as it tracks convoy ON 184 (Liverpool to New York, fast). A U.S. and Canadian destroyer each drive off other U-boats threatening the convoy.

ETO: Eighth Air Force VIII Bomber Command attacks two targets over Germany, the U-boat yards at Wilhelmshaven and Emden. The 77 B-17s that attack Wilhelmshaven report over 50 enemy aircraft destroyed; seven B-17s are lost and 24 are damaged. The 46 B-17s attacking Emden lose five over the target and 11 other bombers are damaged. Over 30 enemy aircraft are claimed shot down. Over 100 P-47 Thunderbolts conduct a fighter sweep over Ostend and Ghent in Belgium. Three aircraft and pilots are lost.

MEDITERRANEAN: U.S. destroyer sinks Italian submarine *Gorgo* off Algeria as it attempts to make an attack on a U.S. convoy. Ninth Air Force B-24 Liberators attack San Giovanni and Reggio di Calabria in Italy. Crews report four enemy fighters shot down. Northwest African Air Force B-25 Mitchells and B-26 Marauders bomb Villacidro and Decimomannu airfields in Sardinia. B-17s bomb support facilities at Castelvetrano on Sicily.

SOUTHWEST PACIFIC AREA: Fifth Air Force B-17s bomb airfields around Rabaul and B-24 Liberators attack the airfield on Gasmata Island.

May 22

ATLANTIC: TBF Avengers from U.S. escort carrier USS *Bogue* protecting convoy ON 184 (Liverpool to New York, fast) sink German submarine *U-569* and damage *U-305*.

May 23

ALEUTIANS: Eleventh Air Force B-24 Liberators and 18 P-38 Lightnings flying air cover missions to Attu hear a report that 16 Japanese bombers are in the air. Five P-38s attack the bombers, shooting down five enemy planes and reporting seven others destroyed. Two P-38s are shot down in the battle over Attu.

MEDITERRANEAN: Northwest African Air Force P-40s attack gun positions as B-25 Mitchells and B-26 Marauders bomb the docks and airfield on Pantelleria Island.

SOUTH PACIFIC: Japanese submarine *I-17* torpedoes and sinks a U.S. tanker off Nouméa, New Caledonia.

NEW BRITAIN: Fifth Air Force B-24 Liberators and B-17s bomb Kavieng Harbor and the airfield. The bombers also attack Gasmata Island airfield off New Britain.

May 24

MEDITERRANEAN: Ninth Air Force B-24 Liberators bomb facilities supporting the ferry terminal at Villa San Giovanni. Northwest African Air Force P-40s, P-38 Lightnings,

B-25 Mitchells, B-26 Marauders, and B-17s bomb airfields, facilities, and transportation targets across Sardinia.

May 25
ALEUTIANS: Eleventh Air Force B-25 Mitchells and B-24 Liberators conduct ground support missions on Attu while P-38 Lightnings fly air cover. At Kiska and Little Kiska, 18 P-40s fly reconnaissance and attack missions.

ATLANTIC: The Trident Conference ends. The meetings between the British and the Americans are often stormy, as the Combined Chiefs of Staff hammer out a compromise that is decidedly slanted in favor of the American approach. The outcome is an agreed target date of May 1, 1944, for the cross-Channel invasion of Europe. Operation Husky, the invasion of Sicily, will be launched with the objective of knocking Italy out of the war. China will be supported through additional matériel and reinforcements to the U.S. Fourteenth Air Force. Japan's occupation force in the Aleutians will be eliminated; and as part of the U.S. strategic plan to defeat Japan, an attack through the Central Pacific will continue to pressure the Japanese. Offensive air operations will proceed in the ETO as a prelude to the invasion. In the Mediterranean, offensive air operations will be directed against the Ploeşti oil fields in Romania. General Stilwell's request for additional American ground forces for CBI is disapproved, although limited amphibious operations along the coast of Burma are considered possible.

U.S. PBY Catalina sinks German submarine *U-467* south of Iceland.

May 26
ALEUTIANS: U.S. forces are able to consolidate and conduct a coordinated effort to capture Fish Hook Ridge, on which Japanese defenders in deep entrenchments and hidden positions have halted the American advance for nearly a week. A reinforced battalion attempts to conduct a coordinated attack on this position. Private Joe P. Martinez, an automatic rifleman in K Company, 32nd Infantry Regiment, 7th Infantry Division, sets the example to press forward even in the face of heavy machine-gun, rifle, and mortar fire. Those who have dropped to the ground when the enemy began to fire are amazed that Private Martinez is still on his feet and gesturing to his comrades to follow. Martinez uses his Browning Automatic Rifle (BAR) and hand grenades to capture the first position. But the Japanese guarding the Chichagof Pass have a number of defensive positions along the ridges. Undaunted, Private Martinez pushes forward, leading by example and continuing to clear successive enemy trenches with his BAR until he is mortally wounded. The Japanese can no longer hold the key pass, and Martinez's exploits allow American forces to gain an important objective. For his courageous example and extraordinary dedication to duty, he will receive the Medal of Honor.

MEDITERRANEAN: Northwest African Air Force P-40s bomb Pantelleria Island.

SOUTHWEST PACIFIC AREA: U.S. submarine *Trout* lands advisers and supplies to support guerrilla operations on Basilan Island, Philippines.

PACIFIC: U.S. submarine *Whale* torpedoes and sinks a Japanese gunboat off Rota Island in the Marianas. U.S. submarine *Pogy* attacks a convoy off Honshu, Japan, and sinks a cargo ship. U.S. submarine *Saury* attacks a convoy south of Kyushu, Japan, and sinks a transport ship.

May 27

ATLANTIC: German submarine *U-154* attacks convoy BT 14 (Bahia, Brazil to Trinidad) off the coast of Brazil. The U-boat torpedoes and sinks two U.S. freighters and damages a tanker.

In Washington, D.C., Joint Staff planners begin examining forces and support necessary for offensive action against the Marshall Islands in the Pacific Operations Area.

MEDITERRANEAN: Northwest African Air Force P-40s attack targets on Pantelleria Island.

PACIFIC: U.S. submarine *Finback* torpedoes and sinks a Japanese cargo ship northwest of the Palau Islands. U.S. submarine *Runner* begins a patrol from Midway, but is never heard from again.

May 28

CBI: Fourteenth Air Force P-40s attack railroad facilities at Yoyang, China.

ATLANTIC: German submarine *U-177* torpedoes and sinks a U.S. freighter in the North Atlantic.

MEDITERRANEAN: Northwest African Air Force B-17s bomb the oil refinery, marshaling yard, harbor, and shipbuilding yards at Leghorn in Italy. P-40s and A-20 Havocs bomb Pantelleria Island.

SOUTHWEST PACIFIC AREA: Headquarters SWPA approves Alamo Force's plan for Kiriwina and Woodlark Islands assault. The plan is called Chronicle. The day for the assault is June 30.

PACIFIC: U.S. submarine *Saury* torpedoes and sinks a Japanese fleet tanker northwest of Okinawa.

May 29

ALEUTIANS: Nearly 1,000 Japanese soldiers make a night attack on U.S. positions in a desperate attempt to break out. Most of them are killed.

ETO: Eighth Air Force VIII Bomber Command attacks three targets in France. The submarine pens and locks at St-Nazaire are attacked by 147 B-17s. Eight bombers are lost and 59 are damaged. Enemy losses are six aircraft. Several armored versions of the B-17, the YB-40, accompany the bombers, but are unable to keep up with the formation and are largely ineffective. At the Rennes naval depot, 57 B-17s bomb the target, but six planes are lost and 31 are damaged. Enemy losses are estimated at over 20 aircraft. B-24 Liberators bomb the U-boat yards at La Pallice with no losses.

MEDITERRANEAN: Northwest African Air Force P-40s, P-38 Lightnings, and B-26 Marauders attack gun positions and a radar site on Pantelleria Island.

PACIFIC: U.S. submarine *Scamp* torpedoes and sinks a seaplane carrier north of Kavieng, New Ireland. U.S. submarine chaser sinks Japanese submarine *I-178* off Espiritu Santo Island in the New Hebrides. U.S. submarine *Tambor* torpedoes and sinks a cargo ship in the South China Sea. U.S. submarine *Gar* torpedoes and sinks a Japanese gunboat in the Sulu Sea.

May 30

ALEUTIANS: Eleventh Air Force P-40s conduct ground attack missions while B-24 Liberators and B-25 Mitchells conduct bombing missions over Kiska. B-24 Liberators and P-38 Lightnings fly air cover and patrol missions over Attu.

ATLANTIC: German submarine *U-126* torpedoes and sets afire a U.S. freighter off the coast of West Africa.

MEDITERRANEAN: Ninth Air Force B-24 Liberators bomb the airfield at Foggia, Italy, damaging facilities and aircraft, while B-25 Mitchells bomb Pantelleria Island. Northwest African Air Force P-38 Lightnings and B-17s bomb industrial and transportation targets in Sardinia.

PACIFIC: U.S. submarine *Saury* torpedoes and sinks two Japanese cargo ships off Shanghai, China. U.S. submarine *Steelhead* conducts mining operations off the coast of Japan.

May 31

ALEUTIANS: Operation Landgrab Ends. The U.S. 7th Infantry Division eliminates the last resistance on Attu. Of the estimated 2,500 defenders on the island, only 28 are alive as prisoners. The U.S. casualties are stunning: 549 killed, 1,148 wounded, and over 2,000 evacuated as nonbattle casualties, most due to exposure and trench foot. The capture of Attu will be one of the costliest campaigns in World War II for the United States.

CBI: Fourteenth Air Force B-24 Liberators, with U.S. and Chinese P-40s flying escort, bomb the airfield at Ichang, China. Enemy aircraft losses are reported at five shot down; one Chinese P-40 is lost.

MEDITERRANEAN: Northwest African Air Force B-17s bomb the airfield and marshaling yard at Foggia, Italy.

NEW GUINEA: Fifth Air Force B-24 Liberators bomb the airfield and other targets at Lae.

June 1

ALEUTIANS: Eleventh Air Force B-25 Mitchells, P-38 Lightnings, and P-40s attack facilities, radar sites, and gun positions on Kiska Island.

CBI: Fourteenth Air Force P-40s bomb warehouses and rail facilities at Changanyi, China.

ALEUTIANS: Planning begins for the invasion of Kiska. The Eleventh Air Force is directed to intensify air attacks on the island, and ground forces begin intensive training at Fort Ord, California.

MEDITERRANEAN: Northwest African Air Force P-38 Lightnings and B-17s bomb Pantelleria while P-40s attack gun positions. P-40s attack the seaplane base on Stagnone Island and P-38 Lightnings bomb the railroad near Balesrate in Sicily. In Sardinia, P-38 Lightnings, B-26 Marauders, and B-25 Mitchells bomb harbors.

PACIFIC: U.S. submarine *Trigger* torpedoes and sinks a Japanese collier off Honshu, Japan.

June 2

ATLANTIC: U.S. submarine chaser sinks German submarine *U-521* off the coast of Virginia.

SOUTHWEST PACIFIC AREA: Alamo Force plans the assaults on Kiriwina and Woodlark islands (Operation Chronicle). Two battalions of the 158th RCT, reinforced by the 46th Engineer Regiment, antiaircraft and support units, will capture Kiriwina. Colonel Prugh J. Herndon is to command the assault. Woodlark Island is the assignment of the 112th Cavalry Regiment, supported by the 12th Marine Defense Battalion, Seabees, and support units. Brigadier General Julian W. Cunningham, the commander of the 112th, will command the assault. One battalion of the 158th RCT will be the Alamo Force reserve.

PACIFIC: U.S. submarine *Tambor* torpedoes and sinks a Japanese cargo ship in the South China Sea.

June 3

INDIAN OCEAN: Japanese submarine *I-27* torpedoes and sinks a U.S. freighter off Oman.

SOUTH PACIFIC: Admiral Halsey (COMSOPAC) develops plans for Toenails, the attack on New Georgia Island, with the intent to seize Munda airfield. Halsey designates Major General John H. Hester, commander of the 43rd Infantry Division, as commander of ground forces for Toenails. Lieutenant General Millard F. Harmon, the commander of U.S. Army forces in the Southern Pacific (SOPAC), is concerned about the command arrangement for Hester and orders XIV Corps on Guadalcanal, under the command of Major General Oscar W. Griswold, to be prepared to take command of the New Georgia occupation force, so that neither Hester nor the 43rd Infantry Division staff is overburdened with commanding at two separate echelons. Marine forces designated for Toenails are the 1st and 4th Marine Raider Battalions.

BOUGAINVILLE: Thirteenth Air Force B-17s bomb the airfield at Kahili and other targets on Bougainville Island.

June 4

ATLANTIC: TBF Avenger torpedo bombers from the U.S. escort carrier USS *Bogue* damage German submarines *U-228, U-603,* and *U-641.*

NEW GUINEA: Fifth Air Force B-17s and B-24 Liberators bomb airfields in New Guinea, while B-25 Mitchells bomb targets on Timor.

June 5

ATLANTIC: TBF Avengers from USS *Bogue* sink German submarine *U-217.*

MEDITERRANEAN: Northwest African Air Force B-25 Mitchells and P-38 Lightnings attack gun positions on Pantelleria Island. B-17s bomb the harbor and shipping at La Spezia, Italy. B-26 Marauders bomb a port facility, while P-38s attack airfields in Sardinia.

June 6

MEDITERRANEAN: Ninth Air Force B-24 Liberators bomb the harbors at Villa San Giovanni and Reggio di Calabria in Italy; the ferry and railroad yards at Messina in Sicily are also attacked. Eight enemy fighters are reportedly destroyed. B-25 Mitchells bomb Pantelleria Island. Northwest African Air Force P-40s, P-38 Lightnings, B-26 Marauders, A-20 Havocs, A-36 Invaders (Apaches), and B-25 Mitchells bomb gun positions on Pantelleria, initiating the second phase of the air offensive against the tiny island.

June 6

SOUTHWEST PACIFIC AREA: U.S. submarine *Tautog* torpedoes and sinks a Japanese cargo ship in the Sulu Sea.

PACIFIC: U.S. submarine *S-30* torpedoes and sinks a Japanese cargo ship south of Kamchatka.

BOUGAINVILLE: Thirteenth Air Force P-38 Lightnings, P-40s, navy and marine F6F Hellcats, F4U Corsairs, TBF Avenger torpedo bombers, and SBD Dauntless dive-bombers attack Japanese shipping off Buin, on Bougainville Island, damaging a destroyer and two other vessels. A total of 15 enemy aircraft are reported shot down. P-38s and P-40s attack targets on Choiseul Island.

June 7

MEDITERRANEAN: Ninth Air Force B-25 Mitchells bomb gun positions and the airfield on Pantelleria Island.

GUADALCANAL: Thirteenth Air Force P-38 Lightnings and P-40s, navy and marine F6F Hellcats and F4U Corsairs, along with Royal New Zealand Air Force P-40s, intercept Japanese dive-bombers and fighters headed to attack shipping at Guadalcanal. Over 20 enemy aircraft are shot down. Although nine Allied fighters are lost, there are no pilot casualties.

June 8

ALEUTIANS: U.S. engineers complete the fighter airfield on Attu. An Eleventh Air Force C-47 is the first aircraft to land on the airfield.

June 8

CBI: Fourteenth Air Force B-24 Liberators and B-25 Mitchells, escorted by P-40s, bomb shipping, rail, and power facilities near Hanoi, French Indochina.

ATLANTIC: TBF Avenger torpedo bombers from the U.S. escort carrier USS *Bogue* damage German submarine *U-758*.

MEDITERRANEAN: Ninth Air Force B-25 Mitchells bomb Pantelleria Island. Northwest African Air Force aircraft, in addition to conducting bombing runs on the island, scatter surrender leaflets to further demoralize the defenders. P-38 Lightnings attack targets in Sardinia.

BOUGAINVILLE: Thirteenth Air Force B-24 Liberators bomb Kahili airfield on Bougainville Island. Fifth Air Force B-25 Mitchells bomb Koepang and areas near Dili in Timor. U.S. submarine *Finback* attacks a Japanese convoy about 100 miles north of Palau, sinking an auxiliary minelayer.

June 9

MEDITERRANEAN: Ninth Air Force B-24 Liberators bomb near Gerbini and Catania airfield in Sicily. B-25 Mitchells bomb Pantelleria Island. Northwest African Air Force P-40s, P-38 Lightnings, B-26 Marauders, A-20 Havocs, and B-25 Mitchells attack targets on Pantelleria as well.

PACIFIC: Thirteenth Air Force B-17s, P-40s, and P-38 Lightnings attack the airfields at Munda and Vila in New Georgia. U.S. submarine *Greenling* damages a Japanese oiler en route to Truk in the Marianas.

June 10

ALEUTIANS: Eleventh Air Force B-24 Liberators, B-25 Mitchells, and P-40 fighters conduct attacks on facilities at Kiska Island, while F-5As (unarmed P-38 variant) fly photo missions. A U.S. submarine chaser intentionally rams and sinks Japanese submarine *I-24* off Shemya Island.

CBI: Fourteenth Air Force P-40 fighters intercept about 25 Japanese bombers and fighters over Hengyang, China, destroying one bomber.

ATLANTIC: German submarine *U-66* torpedoes and sinks a U.S. tanker off the coast of Florida. Despite a raging fire that kills most of the crew and the armed guard aboard, the crewmen still serve the forward deck gun in an attempt to sink the U-boat.

President Roosevelt signs the tax withholding bill into law. It increases the number of U.S. taxpayers by 60 million and will bring a revenue increase of $43 billion by the end of the war.

ETO: The Combined Chiefs of Staff issues a directive to initiate the Combined Bomber Offensive against strategic targets in Germany. The Combined Operational Planning Committee is established to coordinate the offensive. The U.S. Army Air Force will use precision bombing to attack strategic targets during the day. The Royal Air Force will conduct bombing attacks against strategic city areas at night.

MEDITERRANEAN: Ninth Air Force B-25 Mitchells with P-40 escorts bomb Pantelleria Island. Northwest African Air Force P-40s, P-38 Lightnings, B-26 Marauders, A-20 Havocs, and B-25s conduct over 1,000 sorties against Pantelleria.

PACIFIC: U.S. submarine *Flying Fish* torpedoes but does not damage a Japanese cargo ship in the North Pacific. U.S. submarine *S-30* torpedoes and sinks a Japanese cargo ship in the northern Kurile Islands. U.S. submarine *Tinosa* damages an oiler off Kyushu, Japan. U.S. submarine *Trigger* damages the carrier *Hiyo* off eastern Honshu, Japan.

BOUGAINVILLE: Thirteenth Air Force B-17s and B-24 Liberators bomb the Kahili airfield on Bougainville Island.

NEW BRITAIN: Fifth Air Force B-17s and B-24 Liberators bomb the main airfields around Rabaul, New Britain.

June 11

ALEUTIANS: Eleventh Air Force B-24 Liberators, B-25 Mitchells, P-40s, and P-38 Lightnings conduct attacks on facilities at Kiska Island. Two F-5As (unarmed P-38 variant) conduct photo and reconnaissance missions.

ETO: Eighth Air Force VIII Bomber Command conducts an attack against two targets in Germany. A total of 218 B-17s, far beyond the range of fighter escort, attempt to bomb the U-boat yard at Wilhelmshaven and the port at Cuxhaven, Germany. Enemy fighters prevent an accurate bombing run and shoot down eight bombers and damage 62 others. At least 85 enemy aircraft are reported destroyed.

MEDITERRANEAN: Ninth Air Force B-25 Mitchells along with Northwest African Air Force B-26 Marauders and B-25s support the landing of the British 1st Division on Pantelleria Island. The landing is unopposed and the defenders surrender unconditionally.

PACIFIC: U.S. submarine *Finback* attacks a Japanese convoy in the Palau Islands, sinking a Japanese cargo ship just west of Babelthuap. U.S. submarine *Runner* torpedoes and sinks a Japanese cargo ship off northwest Honshu, Japan. U.S. submarine *S-30* torpedoes and sinks a cargo ship in the Kuriles; U.S. submarine *Silversides* attacks a Japanese convoy, sinking a transport north of New Ireland.

NEW GUINEA: Fifth Air Force B-25 Mitchells attack targets along the Huon Gulf coast of New Guinea. B-24 Liberators bomb the Rabaul airfields on New Britain. B-24s and B-25s bomb targets in Timor.

June 12

ATLANTIC: TBF Avenger torpedo bombers from the escort carrier USS *Bogue* sink German submarine *U-118*. U.S. submarine *R-12* sinks off Key West, Florida; cause is unknown.

MEDITERRANEAN: Ninth Air Force B-25 Mitchells and P-40s attack Lampedusa Island in preparation for a landing by British forces. The island garrison surrenders without a fight. Northwest African Air Force B-17s and B-26 Marauders bomb airfields at Castelvetrano, Boccadifalco, and Milo in Sicily.

PACIFIC: U.S. submarine *Trout* lands men and supplies on Mindanao in the Philippines.

GUADALCANAL: Thirteenth Air Force P-38 Lightnings and P-40s, navy and marine F6F Hellcats and F4U Corsairs, along with Royal New Zealand Air Force P-40s, intercept Japanese bombers and fighters headed to attack Guadalcanal. Over 30 aircraft are shot down and eight Allied aircraft are lost.

June 13

ALEUTIANS: U.S. destroyer sinks Japanese submarine *I-9* off Kiska Island.

CBI: In Burma, nine B-25 Mitchells from Tenth Air Force attack a railroad bridge on the Mandalay to Myitkyina railroad. Damage to the bridge is minor. Fourteenth Air Force B-25 Mitchells with 14 P-40 fighters as escorts attack Nanchang airfield in China.

ETO: Eighth Air Force VIII Bomber Command conducts two attacks on targets in Germany. The Bremen U-boat yards are hit by 122 B-17s; four bombers are lost and 31 are damaged. Only two enemy aircraft are reported destroyed. The U-boat yards at Kiel are attacked by 60 B-17s against the heaviest German fighter attack yet seen. The losses are serious—22 bombers are shot down and 24 are damaged, with nearly 240 crewmen killed, wounded, or missing. Enemy aircraft losses are reported to be over 40.

MEDITERRANEAN: Ninth Air Force B-24 Liberators and Royal Air Force heavy bombers conduct a combined attack on the airfields at Catania and Gerbini in Sicily. Five enemy fighters are reported destroyed and two B-24s are shot down.

PACIFIC: U.S. submarine *Guardfish* torpedoes and sinks a Japanese cargo ship off the southwest coast of New Ireland; U.S. submarine *Sargo* attacks a Japanese convoy in the Carolines and sinks an army transport ship.

BOUGAINVILLE: Thirteenth Air Force B-17s and B-24 Liberators bomb the airfield at Kahili on Bougainville Island.

New Britain: Fifth Air Force B-17s and B-24s bomb the airfields at Rabaul and on Gasmata Island. B-25 Mitchells bomb Dili and Koepang on Timor.

June 14

CBI: Fourteenth Air Force P-40s intercept eight Japanese bombers and 20 fighters near Nanchang, China, The eight P-40s report seven enemy fighters shot down.

New Georgia: Thirteenth Air Force B-25 Mitchells, escorted by F4U Corsairs, bomb the airfield at Vila in New Georgia. B-17s and B-24 Liberators bomb the airfield at Kahili on Bougainville Island.

June 15

CBI: Tenth Air Force B-25 Mitchells bomb the bridge at Myitnge in Burma and cause major damage. Fourteenth Air Force B-25s, escorted by P-40s, conduct ground support operations for Chinese ground forces at Owchihkow, China.

Mediterranean: Northwest African Air Force B-17s, B-25 Mitchells, B-26 Marauders, and P-38 Lightnings bomb airfields at Bo Rizzo, Milo, Sciacca, Castelvetrano, and Boccadifalco in Sicily. Radio stations near Marsala are also attacked.

Southwest Pacific Area: U.S. submarine *Trout* damages a Japanese oiler in the Celebes Sea.

Pacific: U.S. submarine *Gunnel* torpedoes and sinks a Japanese cargo ship in Tsushima Straits; U.S. submarine *Sailfish* torpedoes and sinks a cargo ship off Honshu, Japan.

New Britain: Fifth Air Force B-24 Liberators bomb the airfields at Rabaul, then rearm and refuel and bomb the airfield at Kendari in the Celebes later in the day.

June 16

Guadalcanal: Thirteenth Air Force P-38 Lightnings and P-40s, navy and marine F6F Hellcats and F4U Corsairs, along with Royal New Zealand Air Force P-40s, intercept about 120 Japanese aircraft attempting to attack Allied shipping off Tulagi and Guadalcanal. Over 100 Allied fighters are involved, as well as shipboard and ground-based antiaircraft fire. Although the Japanese hit an LST (Landing Ship Tank) and a cargo ship, they lose 79 aircraft to fighters and 17 other planes to antiaircraft fire. Only six Allied aircraft are lost in this lopsided victory.

Second Lieutenant Joseph R. Sarnoski volunteers to serve as the bombardier of a crew on an important photographic mapping mission covering Buka Island, near Bougainville. As the photoreconnaissance mission is ending, about 20 Japanese fighters swarm the aircraft. Second Lieutenant Sarnoski mans the nose guns and fights off the first attack, allowing the pilot to complete his track over the target area. The second attack wounds five of the crew and seriously damages the bomber. Sarnowski, also wounded, continues to fight, shooting down two enemy fighters. When a 20 millimeter explosive shell wounds him again and knocks him from the guns, he crawls back and continues to engage the enemy until he collapses and dies. Second Lieutenant Sarnoski's example of resolute courage under fire and dedication to the mission not only allows the bomber to return safely, but also will win him the Medal of Honor.

NEW GUINEA: Fifth Air Force B-25 Mitchells bomb Koepang and Oeikoesi on Timor. B-25s and A-20 Havocs attack barges and shore targets around New Guinea and New Britain.

June 17

ATLANTIC: JCS planners submit a concept of operations to support the strategic plan approved by the CCS on May 19. The planners propose an offensive against the Japanese in the Marshall Islands in December. Kusaire and Eniwetok are proposed as the targets of a combined amphibious invasion. These islands will then be used as airbases for an attack on Truk, the main base of the Japanese Combined Fleet. This approach is intended to attack directly into the center of the Japanese outer defensive perimeter without land-based air cover and will require resources from MacArthur's theater. MacArthur is already concerned that the limited resources he has available may not be sufficient to support the execution of Cartwheel, the campaign to capture Rabaul. Nimitz also has doubts about the concept. He is hesitant to move into the Marshalls without having some support from airbases in the Gilbert Islands first.

MEDITERRANEAN: Ninth Air Force B-24 Liberators attack airfields at Biscariy and Comiso in Sicily.

SOUTHWEST PACIFIC AREA: U.S. submarine *Drum* attacks a Japanese convoy north of Kavieng, New Ireland, and sinks a transport ship.

CENTRAL PACIFIC: Seventh Air Force B-24 Liberators take off from Funafuti Atoll in the Ellice Islands to conduct a diversionary raid on Tarawa Atoll in the Gilbert Islands. Of the four bombers dispatched, only two find their target. These two bombers are able to damage the runways, knock out an antiaircraft battery, and blow up an ammunition storage area. The diversion succeeds in allowing three B-24s to conduct a night photoreconnaissance mission over Mille Atoll in the Caroline Islands and areas near the Marshall Islands.

NEW GUINEA: Fifth Air Force B-25 Mitchells bomb targets around Madang and Salamaua. B-24 Liberators bomb Sorong, New Guinea, and Boela in the Molucca Islands.

June 18

MEDITERRANEAN: Northwest African Air Force B-17s bomb the ferry and railyards in Messina, Italy. P-38 Lightnings bomb the airfield at Milo in Sicily. B-26 Marauders and B-25 Mitchells escorted by P-38s bomb docks and shipping in Sardinia.

BOUGAINVILLE: Thirteenth Air Force B-24 Liberators bomb the airfield at Kahili on Bougainville Island.

NEW GUINEA: Fifth Air Force B-25 Mitchells bomb and strafe Japanese vessels off Cape Gloucester, New Britain, and at Finschhafen in New Guinea.

June 19

MEDITERRANEAN: Ninth Air Force B-24 Liberators bomb the ferry and railyards at Villa San Giovanni, ferries in the Straits of Messina, and the harbor of Reggio di Calabria in Italy.

June 19

SOUTHWEST PACIFIC AREA: U.S. submarine *Growler* attacks a Japanese convoy and sinks a cargo ship north of Mussau Island in the Saint Matthias Group north of New Ireland.

PACIFIC: U.S. submarine *Gunnel* torpedoes and damages a Japanese gunboat and sinks a cargo ship and a coastal minesweeper off southern Kyushu, Japan. U.S. submarine *Sculpin* torpedoes and sinks a Japanese guardboat and a cargo ship off eastern Honshu, Japan.

CENTRAL PACIFIC: Seventh Air Force B-24 Liberators take off from Funafuti Atoll in the Ellice Islands to conduct a night photoreconnaissance mission over Jaluit Atoll in the Marshall Islands.

NEW GUINEA: Fifth Air Force B-17s and B-24 Liberators attack the airfield at Vunakanau on New Britain. A-20 Havocs hit targets in New Guinea.

June 20

ATLANTIC: U.S. Navy PBY Catalinas sink German submarine *U-388* and damage submarine *U-420* in the North Atlantic. A U.S. freighter is damaged by a mine laid by German submarine *U-214* and is towed into port at Dakar, French West Africa.

MEDITERRANEAN: Northwest African Air Force B-26 Marauders bomb the airfields at Milo, Castelvetrano, and Bo Rizzo in Sicily.

PACIFIC: U.S. submarine *Seawolf* torpedoes and sinks a Japanese cargo ship in the South China Sea; U.S. submarine *Tautog* torpedoes and sinks a Japanese transport ship west of the Marianas.

CENTRAL PACIFIC: Seventh Air Force B-24 Liberators take off from Funafuti Atoll in the Ellice Islands to conduct a night photoreconnaissance mission over Jaluit Atoll in the Marshall Islands.

BOUGAINVILLE: B-24 Liberators bomb the airfield at Kahili and other targets on Bougainville Island.

NEW GEORGIA: Thirteenth Air Force P-40s, along with marine and navy F6F Hellcats and F4U Corsairs, attack the airfield at Vila in New Georgia, damaging the runway.

NEW GUINEA: General MacArthur redesignates U.S. Sixth Army as Alamo Force in order to have direct control of U.S. ground forces for upcoming operations. Alamo Force, under command of Lieutenant General Walter Krueger, establishes headquarters at Milne Bay. This subterfuge is intended to bypass Australian general Sir Thomas Blamey's authority as commander of all land forces in the Southwest Pacific Theater. Fifth Air Force B-24s bomb the airfields at Rapopo, Keravat, and Rabaul. In New Guinea, A-20 Havocs attack the airfield at Lae, and B-25 Mitchells and one A-20 attack Finschhafen and targets along the coast of New Britain.

June 21

CBI: Fourteenth Air Force B-25 Mitchells with an escort of eight P-40s, bomb Shihshow, China. Eight other B-25s, with P-40 escort, misidentify the village of Nanhsien as a different enemy-held village and bomb it, killing a number of Chinese civilians.

MEDITERRANEAN: Ninth Air Force B-24 Liberators bomb the ferry at Villa San Giovanni and the harbor facilities and railyards at Reggio di Calabria in Italy. Northwest African Air Force B-17s bomb the Naples railyards, the marshaling yard and trestle in Salerno, the marshaling yard in Battipaglia, and the airfield at Cancello Arnone.

PACIFIC: U.S. submarine *Harder* torpedoes and damages a Japanese oiler off eastern Honshu, Japan.

CENTRAL PACIFIC: A Seventh Air Force B-24 conducts armed photoreconnaissance over Nonouti Island, Beru Island, and Nukunau Island in the Gilberts.

NEW GEORGIA: Rear Admiral Richmond Kelly Turner, the commander of amphibious forces for Toenails, sends a detachment of the Marine 4th Raider Battalion to Segi Point on Vangunu Island, which is intended as a site for a future airfield.

NEW GUINEA: Fifth Air Force A-20 Havocs attack the airfields at Lae and Malahang, while B-25s bomb the airfield at Salamaua. B-25 Mitchells attack Koepang on Timor.

June 22

ALEUTIANS: U.S. destroyer damages Japanese submarine *I-7*, which runs aground 12 miles southwest of Kiska Island.

CBI: Tenth Air Force B-25 Mitchells bomb transportation targets in Ywataung and Monywa in Burma.

ETO: Eighth Air Force VIII Bomber Command conducts its first large-scale daylight raid on the heart of German industrial strength in the Ruhr. The targets are the chemical works and synthetic rubber plant at Huls. Of the 183 B-17s that hit the targets, 16 bombers are shot down and 75 others are damaged. Enemy aircraft losses are estimated at over 40 destroyed. The plants are heavily damaged. The mission had 11 YB-40s (an armored version of the B-17) dispatched to accompany the bombers, and one is lost. A second bombing raid involves the industrial plants at Antwerp, Belgium. Of the 39 B-17s that hit the target, four are lost and 18 are damaged. Only one enemy aircraft is reported destroyed. A diversion effort by 21 B-17s is apparently unsuccessful.

SOUTHWEST PACIFIC AREA: U.S. submarine *Grayling* torpedoes and damages a Japanese oiler in the Strait of Malacca.

CENTRAL PACIFIC: Three Seventh Air Force B-24 Liberators from Canton Island in the Phoenix Islands fly a photoreconnaissance mission over Beru Island, Nukunau Island, Tabiteuea Island, Onotoa Island, Tarawa Atoll, and Arorae Island in the Gilberts. While the bombers are conducting the mission, one bomber uses its guns on Arorae Island.

NEW GEORGIA: Two companies of the 103rd Infantry Regiment, 43rd Infantry Division, are landed to reinforce the marines. The combined force is to occupy Viru Harbor on D-day (June 30).

NEW GUINEA: An advance party of the U.S. 112th Cavalry makes an unopposed landing on Woodlark Island.

June 23

PACIFIC: U.S. submarine *Harder* torpedoes and damages a Japanese seaplane carrier off southern Honshu, Japan.

GUADALCANAL: Japanese submarine *RO-103* attacks a convoy off Guadalcanal and torpedoes and sinks one U.S. cargo ship and damages another. The second cargo ship is later scuttled.

NEW GUINEA: The 158th RCT lands on Kiriwini Island without opposition.

June 24

ATLANTIC: A U.S. Navy PBY Catalina sinks German submarine *U-200* in the North Atlantic southwest of Iceland.

SOUTHWEST PACIFIC AREA: Fifth Air Force B-24 Liberators bomb shipping, docks, and industrial targets at Makassar, Celebes Island. The 17 bombers cause extensive damage, including two light cruisers, which are also hit.

PACIFIC: U.S. submarine *Snook* torpedoes and damages a Japanese oiler in the East China Sea.

June 25

ALEUTIANS: Eleventh Air Force B-25 Mitchells, B-24 Liberators, and P-38 Lightnings attack facilities on Kiska Island. Two B-24s conduct photo and weather reconnaissance missions.

ATLANTIC: The Army Air Force Antisubmarine Command transfers the B-24 Liberators of the 19th Antisubmarine Squadron (Heavy), originally stationed in Newfoundland, to Britain. U.S. tanker en route to Bahia is torpedoed and damaged by German submarine *U-513* off Brazil. The armed guard defends the ship with gunfire to keep the U-boat submerged, allowing the ship to reach Rio de Janeiro for repairs.

ETO: Eighth Air Force bombers attempt to hit targets at Bremen and Hamburg, Germany, but cloud-cover cancels the mission. About 160 B-17s then make a number of attacks on various targets, with the loss of 18 bombers and over 60 others damaged. Seven YB-40 escort bombers (an armored version of the B-17) are included in the mission, but only four actually keep up with the bombers. Enemy losses are estimated at over 60 aircraft.

MEDITERRANEAN: Northwest African Air Force B-17s drop over 300 tons of bombs on storage areas, port facilities, and the marshaling yard in Messina, Sicily.

PACIFIC: U.S. submarine *Sailfish* attacks a Japanese convoy, sinking a collier off the northeast coast of Honshu, Japan.

BOUGAINVILLE: Thirteenth Air Force B-24 Liberators attack targets near Kahili on Bougainville Island and hit the airfield on Buka Island. B-25 Mitchells, escorted by P-40s, bomb the airfield at Vila in New Georgia.

June 26

ALEUTIANS: Eleventh Air Force bombers and P-38 Lightnings conduct weather and photo reconnaissance and attack missions to Kiska and Little Kiska Islands. Four P-38s are damaged by machine-gun fire.

ETO: Eighth Air Force B-17s attack several targets in France; five YB-40 escort bombers are unable to complete the mission. The Vilacoublay air depot is bombed by 12 B-17s; six bombers attack the airfield at Poissy, and another 39 bombers hit the airfield at Tricqueville. Five bombers are lost and 17 are damaged. Over 20 enemy aircraft are reported destroyed.

Air Marshal Trafford L. Leigh-Mallory is selected to oversee air support planning for the cross-Channel invasion.

PACIFIC: U.S. submarine *Jack* attacks a Japanese convoy, sinking two transports off southern Honshu, Japan. U.S. submarine *Runner* claims one Japanese cargo ship sunk off Matsuwa Island in the Kuriles.

NEW GUINEA: Fifth Air Force B-17s and B-24 Liberators bomb Rabaul and then attack Lae in New Guinea. B-25 Mitchells also bomb Lae and Salamaua and conduct an attack on Penfoei on Timor Island.

June 27

ATLANTIC: U.S. freighter en route from Mombasa, Kenya, to Bahia, Brazil, is torpedoed and sunk by German submarine *U-511* off the southern coast of Brazil.

MEDITERRANEAN: Ninth Air Force B-24 Liberators bomb airfields at Kalamaki and Eleusis in Greece. Aircrews report seven enemy fighters shot down.

June 27

BOUGAINVILLE: Thirteenth Air Force B-24 Liberators bomb the airfield at Kahili on Bougainville Island.

NEW GEORGIA: Marine Raiders reach positions to begin attack on Viru Harbor, the site of an intended PT boat base.

NEW GUINEA: Fifth Air Force B-25 Mitchells and A-20 Havocs attack a number of targets in New Guinea. B-24 Liberators bomb Taka, Saumlakki, and Malo Islands in the Moluccas and Boeroe Island in the Sunda Islands.

June 28

ALEUTIANS: Eleventh Air Force B-25 Mitchells bomb Gertrude Cove on Little Kiska Island.

ETO: Eighth Air Force B-17s attack two targets in France. The first target is the submarine pens at St-Nazaire and the second is the airfield at Beaumont-le-Roger. Of the 158 bombers that hit the target at St-Nazaire, eight bombers are lost to enemy fire and 57 are damaged. Nearly 30 enemy aircraft are reported destroyed. Against the Beaumont-le-Roger airfield, the 43 bombers that hit the target suffer only six aircraft damaged.

MEDITERRANEAN: Northwest African Air Force B-17s bomb support facilities in Leghorn, Italy. B-25 Mitchells bomb airfields in Sardinia and Sicily. B-26 Marauders attack airfield targets in Sardinia.

PACIFIC: U.S. submarine *Tunny* torpedoes and sinks a Japanese gunboat off Rota Island in the Marianas.

CENTRAL PACIFIC: Seventh Air Force B-24 Liberators on Funafuti Atoll in the Ellice Islands attempt a bombing mission against Nauru Island in the Gilberts; of the six bombers dispatched, only two attack the target. The others either abort the mission or are unable to locate the target.

June 29

ETO: Eighth Air Force B-17s attack three targets in France. The first is the air depot at Villacoublay, the second is the Tricqueville airfield, and the third is the aero engine works at Le Mans. Heavy cloud cover prevents the first two targets from being hit. Nevertheless, 14 B-17s are damaged and aircrews report three possible enemy aircraft shot down. Over Le Mans, 76 B-17s hit the target. Two YB-40 escort bombers fail to support the mission. The Eighth Air Force commander, Lieutenant General Ira C. Eaker, decides that if the escort bombers are to be useful at all, they must carry bomb loads and must be able to fly complete missions as expected of the other B-17s.

SOUTHWEST PACIFIC AREA: U.S. submarine *Gurnard* attacks a Japanese convoy in the south Philippine Sea but no ships are damaged.

BOUGAINVILLE: Four cruisers and four destroyers of Rear Admiral Aaron S. Merrill's Task Unit 36.2.1 bombard Vila on Kolombangara Island in New Georgia and Buin on Bougainville Island. A task unit, 36.2.2, of minelayers drop off mines near Shortland Harbor, Bougainville, between Alu and Munda Islands, and off New Georgia.

NEW GUINEA: Fifth Air Force B-25 Mitchells and A-20 Havocs attack Japanese positions on the Bitoi River and Nassau Bay in preparation for amphibious landings.

June 30

ETO: The Royal Air Force releases operational control of Eighth Air Force's VIII Fighter Command. U.S. fighter groups are now under control of the 4th Air Defense Wing.

MEDITERRANEAN: Over Sicily, Northwest African Air Force B-17s bomb the airfields at Palermo and Boccadifalco, while B-25 Mitchells hit the airfield at Sciacca and B-26 Marauders bomb the Bo Rizzo airfield.

The Germans have moved five divisions into Italy, and put two in Sicily.

PACIFIC: B-25s bomb Timor Island, while B-24 Liberators and B-17s bomb Rabaul. A Japanese cargo ship is hit off Cape Gloucester, New Britain.

NEW GEORGIA: A battalion of the 172nd Infantry Regiment of the 43rd Infantry Division lands on Rendova Island, encountering light resistance. Units also land on Kokorana Island to establish artillery and antiaircraft positions. The Japanese attempt to disrupt the landings with a heavy air attack of 49 bombers with fighter escort. Although 17 bombers are shot down by F4U Corsairs, F4F Wildcats, and antiaircraft fire, Admiral Turner's flagship, the attack transport *McCawley,* is hit and damaged by a torpedo. A U.S. PT boat accidentally torpedoes and sinks the ship later that night. Torrential rains begin, causing equipment and supplies to pile up on the beaches. Another attack early in the evening by about 30 aircraft is blunted by U.S. fighters. Later the pilots report 18 Japanese aircraft shot down. A B-24 Liberator attack on Kahili at Bougainville Island is aborted because of bad weather. At Munda airfield, 25 B-25 Mitchells with 18 SBD Dauntless and 18 TBF Avengers conduct bombing attacks. Another 16 Avenger torpedo bombers and 12 SBD Dauntless dive-bombers attack Vila airfield. A Japanese shore battery at Munda damages a U.S. destroyer.

Commander Aircraft Solomons (COMAIRSOLS), Rear Admiral Mark A. Mitscher, establishes ComAir New Georgia under Brigadier General Francis P. Mulcahy to provide coordination and control of all air missions flown over New Georgia.

Marine Raiders and a battalion of the 103rd Infantry Regiment, 43rd Infantry Division, land at Oliana Bay on Vangunu Island and move inland to assault Kaeruka.

NEW GUINEA: The remainder of the U.S. 112th Cavalry Regiment lands at Woodlark Island; the U.S. 158th Infantry Regiment lands at Kiriwina Island.

Air bases and supply bases are established for future amphibious operations. The 1st Battalion of the 162nd Infantry Regiment of the 41st Infantry Division lands at Nassau Bay. The assault unit is patched together, consisting of three PT boats, 29 LCVP landing craft, one LCV landing craft, mechanized, and two captured Japanese supply barges. Although heavy surf destroys 18 landing craft, the troops move off toward Salamaua. Fifth Air Force B-25 Mitchells conduct ground support missions for both the American troops landing and Australian troops attacking Japanese positions in support of the landing.

July 1

ATLANTIC: The Women's Army Auxiliary Corps (WAAC) is redesignated as the Women's Army Corps (WAC) under the direction of Colonel Oveta Culp Hobby. WACs receive basic military training and are sent to fill support jobs to free men to fight. WACs will serve in the Mediterranean theater, the ETO, the Southwest Pacific Area, and Southeast Asia Command.

CBI: Fourteenth Air Force commander General Claire Chennault designates port facilities and shipping as the primary targets for future air missions.

ETO: Brigadier General Frederick L Anderson, Jr., takes over VIII Bomber Command from Brigadier General Newton Longfellow.

SOUTHWEST PACIFIC AREA: U.S. submarine *Gar* lands commandos on south coast of Timor Island. U.S. submarine *Gurnard* unsuccessfully attacks a Japanese transport ship in the southern Philippine Sea; U.S. submarine *Thresher* attacks a Japanese convoy in the Straits of Makassar, damaging a destroyer and sinking a cargo ship. The destroyer is later salvaged in Sibaya harbor, Celebes.

NEW GEORGIA: Navy and marine Dauntless dive-bombers hit Japanese positions defending Viru Harbor. Marine Raiders capture Tombe and Tetemara villages, opening the port to U.S. supply ships. Japanese attempt to land supplies and reinforcements at Kaeruka, not knowing that U.S. forces already occupy the area. The enemy group is destroyed.

NEW GUINEA: The 1st Battalion of the 162nd Infantry Regiment is attacked by the Japanese at Nassau Bay. In a pouring rainstorm, in a fight that lasts most of the day, the Japanese finally retreat, leaving 50 dead. American losses are 18 killed and 27 wounded. The battalion pushes forward to threaten the Japanese holding Salamaua. Australian forces are simultaneously moving toward Lae from Wau.

Fifth Air Force A-20 Havocs support the advance of U.S. infantry and attack targets around Lae. B-25 Mitchells attack Kela Point and Logui. B-17s and B-24 Liberators bomb the Rabaul airfields.

July 2

ALEUTIANS: After several reconnaissance flights, Eleventh Air Force B-24 Liberators and B-25 Mitchells attack Kiska Island. Two of the five bombing missions against the facilities are radar-guided. Three bombers are damaged by antiaircraft fire.

ATLANTIC: Off the Carolina coast, German submarine *U-66* torpedoes and sinks a U.S. tanker en route from Houston, Texas, to New York City.

MEDITERRANEAN: In Italy, Ninth Air Force B-24 Liberators attack the airfields at Lecce, Grottaglie, and San Pancrazio Salentino. In Sicily, B-25 Mitchells, escorted by P-40 fighters, bomb the Sciacca airfield. One enemy fighter is shot down and one damaged, but two P-40s are shot down in the air battle. Northwest African Air Force B-25 Mitchells bomb Castelvetrano. The Tuskegee Airmen of the 99th Fighter Squadron escort the B-25s over Sicily.

SOUTHWEST PACIFIC AREA: U.S. submarine *Trout* torpedoes and sinks a Japanese cargo ship off the north coast of Marinduque Island, Philippines.

PACIFIC: U.S. submarine *Flying Fish* torpedoes and sinks a Japanese troopship in the Formosa Strait. U.S. submarine *S-35* torpedoes and sinks a Japanese cargo ship off the west coast of the Kamchatka Peninsula.

NEW GEORGIA: A five-ton dynamite storage area established by the 24th Naval Construction Battalion (Seabees) is blown up. Eighteen Japanese bombers with fighter escort attack Rendova Island, hitting fuel and explosives dumps and causing over 200 casualties. After the attack the area is called "Suicide Point." Later that night, a Japanese cruiser and nine destroyers bombard Rendova, but cause no damage. Thirteenth Air Force B-25 Mitchells and navy F4U Corsairs attack a Japanese auxiliary minelayer in the anchorage at Bairoko.

NEW GUINEA: Fifth Air Force B-25 Mitchells attack Japanese defenses around Kela Point. U.S. forces link up with Australian troops. B-24 Liberators and B-17s bomb the Rabaul airfields.

July 3

CBI: Tenth Air Force B-25 Mitchells bomb the bridge at Myitnge, Burma, and succeed in knocking one of the bridge spans out.

ATLANTIC: The B-24 Liberators of the 15th Antisubmarine Squadron (Heavy) under the Army Air Force Antisubmarine Command return to Jacksonville Municipal Airport, Florida, from their operating base at Langley Field, Virginia. German submarine *U-513* torpedoes and sinks a U.S. freighter off the coast of Brazil.

ETO: Lieutenant General Jacob L. Devers, Commanding General European Theater of Operations, U.S. Army (ETOUSA), notes in a report to General Henry H "Hap" Arnold, Commanding General USAAF, that while VIII Bomber Command bombardiers are well trained, high-altitude gunnery skills are less than satisfactory. Not only are bombers taking losses because of a lack of adequate fighter escort on strategic bombing missions, they are also less effective in defending themselves from fighter attack.

MEDITERRANEAN: Ninth Air Force B-25 Mitchells, with P-40s flying escort, bomb the Comiso airfield in Sicily. Northwest African Air Force B-17s, B-26 Marauders, and B-25 Mitchells bomb airfields in Sardinia, while fighters attack radar stations at Pula and Alghero. A-20 Havocs attack airfields at Sciaccay and Trapani in Sicily.

PACIFIC: U.S. submarine *Scorpion* attacks a Japanese convoy in the Yellow Sea and sinks two cargo ships.

NEW GEORGIA: Army and marine 155 mm artillery batteries begin firing on Munda airfield. The Southern Landing Group—composed of the 172nd and 169th Infantry Regiments of the 43rd Infantry Division, the 136th Field Artillery Battalion, and the 9th Marine Defense Battalion—lands at Zanana Beach. The landing group, commanded by Major General Leonard F. Wing, is to capture Munda. Meanwhile, Thirteenth Air Force B-25 Mitchells bomb the antiaircraft guns and the airfield at Munda.

NEW GUINEA: Fifth Air Force B-24 Liberators bomb the Rabaul airfields and the airfield at Kendari on Celebes Island. Two B-25 Mitchells bomb Koepang on Timor Island.

July 4

CBI: Tenth Air Force B-24 Liberators attack the Shweli bridge on the Burma Road.

ETO: Eighth Air Force B-17s strike the aircraft factories at Le Mans and Nanes and the submarine yards at La Pallice, France. The attack by 166 bombers over the aircraft factories is reported as very effective; over 50 enemy aircraft are reported destroyed. Seven bombers are lost and 54 others are damaged. The 71 B-17s that attack the submarine yards are also successful. One bomber is lost and another damaged. One enemy fighter is believed to have been killed.

MEDITERRANEAN: Ninth Air Force B-25 Mitchells, with P-40s flying escort, attack the Comiso airfield at Sicily. Fighters report three enemy aircraft shot down. American losses are four P-40s. Northwest African Air Force B-17s, B-25 Mitchells, and B-26 Marauders bomb the Catania and Gerbini airfields in Sicily. A-20 Havocs attack airfields in western Sicily. Bombers drop leaflets on Rome.

The 45th Infantry Division, fully loaded for combat, arrives in Oran from the United States and sails for Sicily.

PACIFIC: U.S. submarine *Jack* attacks a Japanese convoy off the southeast coast of Honshu, sinking a cargo ship. Off eastern Honshu, U.S. submarine *Pompano* torpedoes and sinks the seaplane carrier attacked by the U.S. submarine *Harder* on June 23. U.S. submarine *Snook* attacks a Formosa-bound Japanese convoy in the East China Sea, damaging a transport and sinking two cargo ships.

NEW GEORGIA: Sixteen Japanese bombers with fighter escort are hit by heavy marine antiaircraft fire. Marine gunners shoot down 12 bombers and one fighter using only 88 rounds of ammunition. Thirteenth Air Force B-17s bomb Bairoko.

July 5

CARIBBEAN: German submarine *U-759* torpedoes and sinks a U.S. freighter in convoy GTMO 134 (Guantánamo Bay, Cuba, to Ponce, Puerto Rico) south of Hispaniola.

ATLANTIC: The JCS receives the COSSAC Overlord concept of operations based on the planning guidelines provided by the CCS after the Trident Conference. In COSSAC's assessment, the Pas-de-Calais area of France, even though the shortest and most sustainable site for an invasion, is also the most heavily defended. The

Cotentin Peninsula has poor terrain for establishing and sustaining a lodgment, but the port of Cherbourg could provide the Allies with facilities to bring in supplies. Caen has a good port, is weakly defended, and has good surrounding terrain that can support airfields. It also has good defensive terrain to protect a beachhead. Based on this analysis, COSSAC recommends Caen as the site for the cross-Channel invasion. The staff notes that no matter what site is chosen, the destruction of the German air force is essential—not only the enemy's current fighter strength, but also fighter production facilities. The COSSAC planners have examined using airborne and amphibious forces to establish a beachhead at Caen (designated as D-day), followed by the seizure of Cherbourg 14 days after the initial landings (D+14). The Allies will have 18 divisions landed in France and 18 airfields operational by this time. By D+50, planners estimate 30 divisions in France. After this buildup, the Allies will attack to capture Paris and the Seine River ports, followed by an advance into Belgium and northern France.

MEDITERRANEAN: Over Sicily, Ninth Air Force B-24 Liberators attack harbor facilities, railyards, and oil storage areas at Messina. B-25 Mitchells bomb the Sciacca and Biscari airfields. Northwest African Air Force B-17s, B-25 Mitchells, and B-26 Marauders bomb the Gerbini airfields and the radar stations at Marsala and Licata. A-20 Havocs attack Sciacca and the Trapani, Comiso, and Biscari airfields. The 1st Infantry Division sails from Algiers for Sicily.

INDIAN OCEAN: Japanese submarine *I-27* torpedoes and damages a U.S. freighter off Oman. The freighter is in convoy PA 44, en route from Abadan, Iran, to Montevideo, Uruguay.

NEW GEORGIA: The Northern Landing Group, composed of the 1st Marine Raider Battalion and a battalion each of the 145th and 148th Infantry Regiments, 37th Infantry Division, under command of Marine Colonel Harry B. Liversedge, lands in a heavy rain at Rice Anchorage. The group's mission is to conduct a landing in northern New Georgia, attack Japanese positions at Enogai Inlet, and capture Bairoko Harbor to prevent Japanese reinforcements and supplies from reaching the defenders at Munda. Lightly armed and with three days' rations, the men struggle inland through dense jungle.

During a commander's meeting, Major General Millard Harmon requests Major General Oscar Griswold's XIV Corps headquarters be deployed to assist the overstretched 43rd Infantry Division staff, which is attempting to serve as both ground command for Admiral Kelly Turner and the command element for the New Georgia Occupation Force. Admiral Halsey gives his approval.

Thirteenth Air Force B-24 Liberators, unable to find their primary target at Buin, Bougainville Island, bomb Munda airfield.

During the night, while Rear Admiral Walden L. Ainsworth's Task Group 36.1 bombards Vila, Kolombangara, and Bairoko Harbor, a group of Japanese destroyers makes a torpedo attack on the U.S. ships in Kula Gulf, sinking one destroyer.

NEW GUINEA: Fifth Air Force B-25 Mitchells bomb and strafe the airfield and headquarters at Salamaua.

July 6

ALEUTIANS: Eleventh Air Force B-24 Liberators and P-40s conduct weather reconnaissance missions over Kiska and Segula Islands. Six B-24s bomb the main camp on Kiska. Three heavy cruisers, one light cruiser, and four destroyers of Task Group 16.7 under command of Rear Admiral Robert C. Giffen also bombard the island.

MEDITERRANEAN: Ninth Air Force B-24 Liberators and B-25 Mitchells, with P-40 escort, attack airfields at Gerbini and Biscari. Northwest African Air Force A-20 Havocs, B-25 Mitchells, and B-26 Marauders also bomb Biscari airfield and the airfields at Sciacca, Trapani, and Comiso. B-17s bomb Gerbini airfield.

PACIFIC: U.S. submarine *Permit* torpedoes and sinks a Japanese cargo ship in the Sea of Japan off Hokkaido, Japan.

SOLOMONS: Lieutenant Commander Bruce Van Voorhis, commander of Bombing Squadron 102, voluntarily takes a PB4Y-I Privateer (a B-24 variant) patrol bomber on a 700-mile flight without escort or support to attack a critical target on Greenwich Island. Arriving at the target after battling difficult winds and poor visibility, Lieutenant Commander Van Voorhis conducts six passes over the target even as antiaircraft fire bursts around his aircraft. Enemy aircraft also pursue him, but he manages to destroy one fighter plane in the air and three others on the water. Forced close to the ground by enemy fighters, Van Voorhis's plane is caught in an explosion created by the bomb he dropped over the target. Lieutenant Commander Van Voorhis's daring and selfless dedication to victory will win him the Medal of Honor.

BOUGAINVILLE: Thirteenth Air Force B-17s and B-24 Liberators attack the airfields at Kahili on Bougainville Island, on Ballale Island, and on Buka Island. B-25 Mitchells bomb a beached destroyer at Bamberi on New Georgia. Fifth Air Force B-25s attack the Penfoei airfield on Timor Island.

NEW GEORGIA: The task group of Rear Admiral Walden L. Ainsworth engages in a second encounter with the Japanese in Kula Gulf. Just before dawn, three light cruisers and four destroyers engage a Japanese reinforcement force of seven destroyers. Four of the enemy ships are carrying troops and supplies to Kolombangara. Japanese destroyers sink a light cruiser, and one Japanese destroyer is sunk and three destroyers are damaged by gunfire. One of the damaged troop-carrying destroyers is grounded and abandoned on the southeastern coast of Kolombangara. SBD Dauntless dive-bombers, TBF Avenger torpedo bombers, and F4F Wildcats will later bomb the grounded destroyer. This battle of Kula Gulf cuts off the Northern Landing Group from supply and naval gunfire support.

The 3rd Battalion of the 148th Infantry moves to block the Bairoko Trail while the rest of the group moves toward Enogai Inlet. The Southern Landing Group begins a cautious advance into the jungle from Zanana Beach.

July 7

CBI: Fourteenth Air Force B-25 Mitchells, with P-40 escort, attack shipping at Canton, China. The fighters claim two enemy aircraft shot down.

ATLANTIC: German submarine *U-185* attacks convoy BT 18 (Bahia to Trinidad) off the coast of Brazil, and torpedoes a U.S. freighter and a tanker. The freighter is abandoned and the tanker is scuttled. Later, *U-185* torpedoes and damages another tanker and freighter. The tanker is able to continue to Trinidad, but the freighter is later scuttled.

A B-24 Liberator of the 1st Antisubmarine Squadron (Heavy) sinks German submarine *U-951* off the coast of Portugal.

MEDITERRANEAN: Over Sicily, Ninth Air Force B-24 Liberators bomb rail lines and the airfields. B-25 Mitchells bomb airfields. In Italy, P-40s bomb and strafe Lucca airfield. As P-40s fly a diversionary sweep over the western portion of Sicily, Northwest African Air Force B-17s, B-25 Mitchells, and B-26 Marauders bomb airfields in Sicily. A-20 Havocs bomb Sciacca and airfields. The A-20s also attack the radar station at Marsala and other targets.

PACIFIC: U.S. submarine *Permit* torpedoes and sinks a Japanese cargo ship off Hokkaido, Japan. U.S. submarine *Peto* torpedoes and damages a Japanese oiler off eastern Honshu, Japan. U.S. submarine *Plunger* torpedoes and damages a Japanese cargo ship in the Sea of Japan.

SOLOMONS: Thirteenth Air Force B-25 Mitchells and P-38 Lightnings attack Vila airfield. B-24 Liberators bomb Kahili airfield on Bougainville Island.

NEW GUINEA: Fifth Air Force B-24 Liberators, B-25 Mitchells, and Royal Australian Air Force (RAAF) aircraft conduct ground support missions for Australian forces.

July 8
CBI: Fourteenth Air Force B-24 Liberators, escorted by P-40s, attack Haiphong harbor, bombing shipping, docks, and the cement works.

ATLANTIC: A B-24 Liberator sinks German submarine *U-232* off Portugal. German submarine *U-510* attacks convoy TJ 1 (Trinidad to Rio de Janeiro) northeast of Cayenne, French Guiana, and sinks a U.S. freighter.

German submarine *U-232* is sunk off the coast of Portugal by a B-24 Liberator of the 2nd Antisubmarine Squadron (Heavy).

ETO: Army Air Force Antisubmarine Command establishes the headquarters of the 479th Antisubmarine Group at St. Eval, England. The group is responsible for all antisubmarine squadron operations in England.

MEDITERRANEAN: Ninth Air Force B-24 Liberators attack transportation, industrial, and communication targets in Sicily. B-25 Mitchells and P-40s attack the airfields at Biscari and Comiso. Northwest African Air Force B-17s, B-25 Mitchells, and B-26 Marauders attack Gerbini airfield; P-38 Lightnings strafe radar installations in eastern Sicily, and A-20 Havocs bomb Sciacca airfield. B-26 Marauders bomb the airfields at Biscari and Comiso. A-36 Invaders (Apaches) attack targets throughout Sicily.

General d'Armata Alfredo Guzzoni, the commander of Axis forces in Sicily, orders the ports of Licata, Porto Empedocle, and Sciacca readied for demolition.

PACIFIC: Major General William H. Rupertus replaces Major General Alexander A. Vandegrift as commander of the 1st Marine Division.

NEW GUINEA: Fifth Air Force B-25 Mitchells fly ground support missions for Australian troops.

July 9

ALEUTIANS: U.S. destroyer bombards Japanese positions on Kiska Island.

CBI: Tenth Air Force B-25 Mitchells bomb the railroad bridge on the Mu River in Burma, causing moderate damage.

ATLANTIC: B-25 Mitchells of the 23rd Antisubmarine Squadron (Heavy), based at Drew Field, Tampa, Florida, begin operating from Langley Field, Virginia. PBY Catalina sinks German submarine *U-590* at the mouth of Amazon River, Brazil.

MEDITERRANEAN: In Sicily, General Guzzoni puts his forces on full alert. He has available on paper a sizable force of 200,000 Italian and 30,000 German troops, but only one Italian unit, the 4th Livorno Division located at Licata, is considered reliable. He commands two German divisions, the Hermann Göring Panzer Division (located near Gela) and the 15th Panzer Grenadier Division (located in western Sicily). His intent is to contain the Allied beachhead as quickly as possible, then counterattack to drive the invaders into the sea. The ports of Trapani and Marsala are rendered useless.

The Allies arrive off Sicily with 3,000 ships in two task forces, one under command of Admiral Henry K. Hewitt and the other commanded by Vice Admiral Sir Bertram H. Ramsey.

Over Sicily, Ninth Air Force B-24 Liberators bomb airfields at Comiso and Taormina, while B-25 Mitchells bomb Sciacca and Biscari airfield and P-40s escort bombers over Castelvetrano and Milo airfields. B-25s also bomb Maleme, Crete. Northwest African Air Force B-17s, B-25s, B-26 Marauders, and fighters attack Sciacca, Gerbini, Milo, and Biscari airfields, the Cape Passero Island radar stations, Sciacca, Porto Empedocle, key terrain northeast of Gela, and targets of opportunity. Northwest African Air Force Troop Carrier Command drops British and U.S. airborne units on Sicily in the first major airborne operation to be undertaken by the Allies in World War II.

That night, 266 C-47 transports pass over Sicily to drop 3,400 paratroopers of the 505th and 504th Parachute Infantry Regiments of the 82nd Airborne Division under command of Colonel James M. Gavin. They land in 35 MPH winds and are scattered from Nisconi to San Croce Camerina. Some are dropped over water and drown, some land in the British area. About 100 men land on Objective Y, the main target of the paratroopers. This road intersection north of Gela provides direct access to the beaches. They stop a column of Italian tanks, supported by naval gunfire and infantry from the 16th RCT. Paratroopers, working in small groups, take the initiative in ambushing enemy units, cutting communication lines, and generally slowing the Axis response to the landings.

PACIFIC: U.S. submarine *Thresher* lands men and supplies on Negros Island, Philippines. German submarine *U-511* torpedoes and sinks a U.S. freighter off Ceylon.

BOUGAINVILLE: Thirteenth Air Force B-24 Liberators bomb Kahili airfield and Buin on Bougainville Island, and Poporang Island. B-25s and several fighters strafe Buki and Ganongga Islands, and a destroyer beached on Kolombangara Island in New Georgia.

New Georgia: There is only one marine raider battalion on New Georgia. A marine Raider battalion attacks Japanese defenses at Enogai after an airstrike. The battle is halted by the onset of darkness.

After a heavy and continuous bombardment by naval gunfire, artillery, and aircraft, an intended major assault by the 172nd and 169th Infantry Regiments, 43rd Infantry Division, is delayed; when conducted, it advances only a few hundred yards along the Munda Trail before halting in a confused and frightened mass without having encountered the enemy in force.

New Guinea: Fifth Air Force B-25 Mitchells bomb airfields at Dili and Cape Chater on Timor Island.

July 10

Aleutians: Eleventh Air Force attacks the Japanese homeland. Using dead reckoning runs, eight B-25 Mitchells attack Paramushiru Island in the Kuriles; the B-25s stage through Attu Island and recover to Adak Island. A Japanese convoy off Attu Island is attacked by six B-24 Liberators and five B-25s. The bombers, conducting runs on the ships at deck level, reportedly sink two freighters.

CBI: Fourteenth Air Force B-24 Liberators bomb the dock area at Haiphong, French Indochina.

Atlantic: JCS planners revise their concept for the Central Pacific offensive, proposing that the Gilbert Islands be neutralized before the Marshalls. They propose a December 1 attack focusing on Tarawa, Makin, and Nauru. MacArthur will neutralize Rabaul and the Bismarcks to free marine forces under his command to support the offensive in the Gilberts.

German submarine *U-177* torpedoes and sinks a U.S. freighter off Durban, South Africa.

ETO: Eighth Air Force conducts three attacks on targets in France. The first target is the Caen/Carpiquet airfield. The second is the Abbevile/Drucat airfield. The third is Le Bourget airfield near Paris. Over Caen, 34 bombers hit the target; over Abbeville, 36 bombers hit the target. One B-17 is lost and 33 others are damaged. Enemy losses are estimated at over 17 aircraft. Over Le Bourget, cloud cover prevents the 101 bombers from hitting the target.

Mediterranean: Operation Husky. Operation Husky is the largest amphibious operation of World War II, in terms of both divisions landed and the size of the landing area. The Fifteenth Army Group consists of the British Eighth Army, commanded by General Sir Bernard Montgomery, and the Seventh Army, commanded by Lieutenant General George S. Patton, Jr. Montgomery commands six infantry divisions (one of these Canadian), one armored division, one airborne division, a tank brigade (Canadian), and an infantry brigade. Patton has under his command the 1st Infantry Division, the 3rd Infantry Division, the 45th Infantry Division, and the 9th Infantry Division; the 82nd Airborne Division, the 2nd Armored Division, and a Ranger battalion. The major maneuver element for the army is II Corps, under command of Major General Omar N. Bradley, which has the 45th Infantry Division, two regiments of the 1st Infantry Division, two Ranger battalions, a tank regiment from the 2nd Armored Division, and the 505th Parachute Regiment and the 504th Parachute Infantry Brigade, to link up with the main force from the beachhead. Afloat in reserve are the remaining Regimental Combat Team of the 1st Infantry Division and the remainder of the 2nd Armored Division. Awaiting movement from Africa if needed is the remainder of the 82nd Airborne and the 9th Infantry Division. The II Corps has 57 miles of beach to control. Naval gunfire hits Syracuse, Catania, Taorima, Augusta, and Trapani. Axis planes bomb the invasion fleet, sinking a destroyer, an LST (Landing Ship Tank), and a minesweeper.

The 45th Infantry Division will land on the eastern edge of the American landing area to link up with British forces near Comiso and Ragusa. The center sector at Gela is the responsibility of the 1st Infantry Division, commanded by Major General Terry de la Mesa Allen, and a battalion of Rangers. Elements of the 82nd Airborne Division will capture and hold the high ground above Gela to assist the 1st Infantry Division. The 3rd Infantry Division under command of Major General Lucian K. Truscott will land at Licata. The 1st and 45th Infantry Divisions will then advance to Route 124, the main east-west road and the approximate boundary of the Yellow Line. The landings go according to plan and there is little opposition. The beach landing sites are poor and rough seas have scattered the 180th Regiment of the 45th Infantry Division. At Gela, Rangers, engineers, and a mortar battalion supported by naval gunfire stop a poorly coordinated attack by two Italian infantry battalions supported by 13 tanks.

Ninth Air Force B-24 Liberators attack the marshaling yard at Catania and the Vibo Valentia airfield. B-25 Mitchells bomb Palazzolo, Sciacca, Catania, Agrigento, Floridia, Giarratana, Biscari, Syracuse, and Piazza Armerina while P-40 fighters cover the assault beaches. A-36 Invaders (Apaches) hit railroads, road junctions, trains, and vehicles while P-40s fly cover for amphibious landings. A-20 Havocs and B-26 Marauders bomb airfields at Sciacca, Canicatti, Ponte Olivo, and Trapani, as well as targets in Caltagirone and Palazzolo. B-17s and B-25s bomb Gerbini, Milo and Sciacca airfields, and targets in Palazzolo and Caltanissetta. P-38 Lightnings strafe radar installations. German submarine *U-371* attacks a convoy off the coast of Algiers, damaging a U.S. freighter and tanker. Both ships eventually are brought to port and salvaged.

PACIFIC: U.S. submarine *Pompano* damages a Japanese oiler off Honshu, Japan. U.S. submarine *Steelhead* damages a Japanese escort carrier north off the Carolines. U.S. submarine *Halibut* damages a Japanese transport near Guam.

BOUGAINVILLE: Thirteenth Air Force B-24s bomb Kahili airfield on Bougainville Island.

NEW GEORGIA: Enogai village is captured by marine Raiders but is exhausted by the effort and receives resupply by air. The Japanese coastal artillery battery at Enogai is also captured, allowing U.S. warships free access to Kula Gulf. The 3,300-foot-long Segi Point fighter airstrip is completed.

NEW GUINEA: Fifth Air Force B-25 Mitchells conduct ground support missions around Salamaua as Allied ground forces link up at Buigap Creek, cutting communications between Salamaua and Mubo.

July 11

ALEUTIANS: Eleventh Air Force B-24 Liberators attempt to conduct a second attack on Paramushiru Island, but are prevented by bad weather. B-25 Mitchells and B-24s attack facilities on Kiska Island. U.S. destroyer bombards Japanese positions at Gertrude Cove.

CBI: Tenth Air Force B-24 Liberators bomb the port of Haiphong, French Indochina.

Fourteenth Air Force B-24s also bomb Haiphong harbor, while other B-24s bomb shipping, enemy positions, and barracks in China. P-40s strafe enemy vehicles and an oil storage area near Lao Kay.

SICILY: The Axis forces begin their counterattack on U.S. forces. The Hermann Goering Division is to attack the 45th Infantry Division, commanded by Major General Troy Middleton, on the east flank, while the Livorno and 15th Panzer Grenadier Division attack the 3rd Infantry Division. The German advance is fiercely contested as enemy armor move within two kilometers of the beachhead before being stopped by U.S. naval gunfire in direct support of the infantry defending Gela. The Germans lose one-third of their tanks in the attack. At Biazzo Ridge, paratroopers and 45th Infantry Division troops stop a major German attack. The 45th Infantry Division captures Comiso and its airfield with 125 aircraft. The 3rd Infantry Division advances, moving beyond Licata, Naro, and Campobello. Off Gela, a U.S. freighter carrying ammunition is set afire by a bomb during a German air attack, is abandoned, and later explodes. Even after detailed coordination between Patton and Cunningham to prevent any mistakes, the 144 C-47 aircraft carrying over 2,000 reinforcements from the 1st and 2nd Battalions, 504th Parachute Infantry Regiment, the 307th Airborne Engineer Battalion, and the 376th Field Artillery Battalion, 82nd Airborne Division, to the landing zone in Gela are fired on by the naval task force. Twenty-three Northwest African Air Force Troop Carrier Command C-47s are shot out of the sky by friendly antiaircraft fire; 37 are damaged and 229 paratroopers are casualties of friendly fire. The survivors are added to the defenses at Gela. The airborne landing is intended to support the 1st Infantry Division in its advance to capture Ponte Olivo and Niscemi.

During the advance of the 15th Infantry Regiment, 3rd Infantry Division, Second Lieutenant Robert Craig volunteers to locate and destroy a machine-gun position at Favoratta that is preventing his company from moving forward. Craig locates the position, jumps up and runs 35 yards in the face of enemy fire and kills three soldiers in the position. Later in the day, as Craig's platoon advances down the exposed face of a ridge, it encounters 100 enemy soldiers. Craig orders his platoon to return to cover on the opposite side of the ridge while he stands alone to face the enemy. Charging forward until he is only 25 yards away, Second Lieutenant Craig kneels down and fires, killing five and wounding three others before he himself is killed. The platoon counterattacks and drive the enemy back, inflicting heavy casualties. Second Lieutenant Craig's singular act of courage will win him the Medal of Honor. Over Italy, Ninth Air Force B-24 Liberators bomb airfields at Vibo Valentia, Sicily, and Reggio di Calabria. Over Sicily, B-25 Mitchells, escorted by P-40s, bomb the airfields at Trapani, Milo, and Bo Rizzo, as well as areas between Sciacca and Enna. P-40s conduct ground support missions for invasion forces. Northwest African Air Force B-26 Marauders hit Milo, Sciacca, and Gerbini airfields as well as assembly areas, vehicle convoys, bridges, trains, and roads. B-17s bomb the Catania marshaling yard and B-25s and P-38 Lightnings hit Sciacca airfield and the town of Caltanissetta as well as truck convoys and gun positions.

PACIFIC: U.S. submarine *Flying Fish* torpedoes and sinks a Japanese guardboat near the Daito Islands. U.S. submarine *Gurnard* attacks a Japanese convoy, sinking a cargo ship northeast of Palau. PBY Catalinas sink one Japanese guardboat and damage another off Kamchatka.

CENTRAL PACIFIC: Seventh Air Force B-24s from Funafuti Island in the Ellice Islands fly a photoreconnaissance mission to Little Makin Island in the Gilbert Islands. Two of the three B-24s also bomb the island.

BOUGAINVILLE: Thirteenth Air Force B-24s and B-17s bomb Kahili airfield on Bougainville Island. Admiral Halsey, COMSOPAC, issues a directive for an attack on Bougainville. Lieutenant General Alexander A. Vandegrift, commander of the I Marine Amphibious Corps, is tasked to lead the invasion. Bougainville, with its six airbases and 45–65,000 Japanese troops, represents the outer Japanese defense barrier protecting Rabaul, only 250 miles distant. Capturing the island and its airbases opens Rabaul to sustained attack.

NEW GEORGIA: Major General Griswold, commander of XIV Corps, and his staff arrive on Rendova Island to size up the situation. The Americans have encountered the Japanese main line of resistance along hills and ridges; the center of the Japanese line is named Horseshoe Hill. A series of interconnected bunkers and pillboxes, 12 feet square and 10 feet deep, expertly camouflaged with rifle and machine-gun ports that provide interlocking lanes of fire, is supported by numerous spider holes and individual fighting positions for riflemen. Behind these positions are mortars that are targeted on selected areas intended to break up any organized attack. American supply lines are overstretched in the difficult jungle terrain. A battalion of the 169th Infantry becomes combat ineffective due to a large number of psychoneurosis casualties.

NEW GUINEA: Fifth Air Force A-20 Havocs and B-25 Mitchells conduct ground support missions around Salamaua. B-25s also bomb Penfoei on Timor Island, while B-17s and B-24 Liberators bomb the airfields at Rabaul.

July 12

CBI: Fourteenth Air Force B-24 Liberators attack docks, shipping, railroad yards, a power plant, and warehouses at various sites in French Indochina. Two cargo ships are sunk. P-40s attack trucks near Ha Giang.

ATLANTIC: A B-24 of the 1st Antisubmarine Squadron (Heavy) sinks German submarine *U-506* off Portugal. German submarine *U-172* torpedoes and sinks a U.S. freighter off the coast of Brazil. The entire crew of 56 safely abandons ship. Some of the men are questioned by the U-boat commander, who also gives the men directions to the nearest shoreline.

SICILY: Adolf Hitler decides to take personal command of the battle in Sicily and orders reinforcements shifted west. He intends to hold the island for as long as possible. In doing so, he cancels a scheduled major offensive on the eastern front. German paratroopers of the 1st Parachute Division land near Catania, while German tanks and infantry attack the 1st Infantry Division south of Nicosia. The division, supported by tanks from the 2nd Armored Division, stops the enemy, destroying 43 tanks and capturing 4,200 prisoners. The 1st Infantry Division captures

Ponte Olivo; the 45th Infantry Division captures Biscari; the 3rd Infantry Division advances to Canicatti.

Ninth Air Force B-24 Liberators attack the harbor, ferry slip, and marshaling yard at Reggio di Calabria, and the ferry slip and railroad yards at Villa San Giovanni in Italy. Over Sicily, B-25 Mitchells hit Bo Rizzo airfield while P-40s patrol over the Licata area. Northwest African Air Force B-17s bomb Messina railroad bridges, while B-26 Marauders and A-20 Havocs bomb Gerbini, Agrigento, Canicatti, and Milo airfields. P-40s attack Termini harbor, rail junctions, rail cars, vehicles, and communication targets throughout Sicily.

SOUTHWEST PACIFIC AREA: Fifth Air Force B-24 Liberators bomb the airfields at Rabaul. B-25 Mitchells bomb Lingat airfield and villages on Selaroe Island in the Moluccas.

PACIFIC: U.S. submarine *Mingo* attacks a Japanese convoy to the east of Sakhalin Island, but fails to cause any damage. U.S. submarine *Plunger* torpedoes and sinks a Japanese cargo ship in the Sea of Japan. U.S. submarine *Spearfish* torpedoes and damages a Japanese destroyer near Eniwetok Atoll.

NEW GEORGIA: Thirteenth Air Force B-25 Mitchells and B-24 Liberators attack Vila airfield; fighters join U.S. Navy SBD Dauntless dive-bombers to attack the Munda area. Four light cruisers and two destroyers of TG 36.9, under command of Rear Admiral Aaron S. Merrill, bombard Munda. U.S. destroyer sinks Japanese submarine *RO-107* east of Kolombangara Island.

July 13

CBI: In Burma, Tenth Air Force B-25 Mitchells lay mines in the Irrawaddy River.

ATLANTIC: TBF Avenger torpedo bombers from escort carrier *Core* sink German submarine *U-487* south of the Azores.

ETO: Eighth Air Force sends B-17s and five YB-40s (an armored version of the B-17) against three targets in France. Against the aircraft works at Villacoublay, 101 B-17s hit the target. Three bombers are lost and 67 are damaged. Enemy losses are reported at more than 15 aircraft destroyed. Another 53 B-17s bomb the Amiens/Glisy airfield. One bomber is lost, 37 are damaged. Enemy losses are nine aircraft. Of the 52 B-17s that bomb Le Bourget airfield in Paris, four are lost and 51 are damaged, and over 40 enemy aircraft are reported destroyed.

SICILY: Axis forces begin a withdrawal to the San Stefano defensive line and await the arrival of the Hermann Göring Panzer Division. General Montgomery, making no progress after capturing Syracuse and Augusta almost without a fight, convinces Alexander to shift the Eighth Army's boundary past Route 124 to allow him to maneuver westward using the main road to outflank the Axis defenses. With this shift in boundary come new orders from Alexander: the Americans will have a purely supporting role and have no other responsibility except to cover Montgomery's advance. However, General Alexander approves Patton's request for the 3rd Infantry Division to conduct a reconnaissance-in-force westward toward Agrigento and Porto Empedocle. The shift in boundary actually provides the Axis forces with an opportunity to consolidate their defenses as II Corps complies with Alexander's new order. Patton orders II Corps to advance northwest toward Caltanissetta in order to divide the island in two.

Ninth Air Force B-24 Liberators bomb the airfields at Crotone in Italy and at Vibo Valentia in Sicily. B-25 Mitchells bomb the Leonforte road and harbor at Termini in support of British forces. Northwest African Air Force B-17s, B-25s, B-26 Marauders, and fighters attack Enna and Milo airfields, Carcitella landing ground, and other targets. Fighters attack truck convoys, trains, railway stations, and troops throughout Sicily.

German air attacks cripple a U.S. freighter with British troops embarked. All but one of the soldiers are killed, as are most of the crew and the armed guard on board.

NEW GEORGIA: Elements of the 169th Infantry advance 500 yards, and take over 100 casualties to capture a Japanese strongpoint on a key ridge south of Munda Trail—now named Reincke Ridge after the regiment's 3rd Battalion commander.

General Griswold assesses that the mission against Munda is too big for the two understrength regiments of the 43rd Infantry Division alone. He recommends committing the 37th Infantry Division and bringing the 25th Infantry Division from Guadalcanal immediately.

During the night off Kolombangara Island, Rear Admiral Walden L. Ainsworth's three light cruisers and 10 destroyers of TG 36.1 engage a Japanese light cruiser and five destroyers escorting troop-carrying destroyers. Torpedoes damage two U.S. light cruisers. A New Zealand light cruiser and a U.S. destroyer are also damaged by a torpedo attack. The destroyer is later scuttled by gunfire. A Japanese light cruiser is sunk and a destroyer is damaged.

NEW GUINEA: Fifth Air Force B-17s and B-24 Liberators bomb the airfield and harbor at Lae. B-25 Mitchells bomb Salamaua area, hitting antiaircraft guns and enemy positions.

July 14

ALEUTIANS: U.S. destroyer bombards Japanese positions at Gertrude Cove, Kiska, but receives no return fire.

ATLANTIC: German submarine *U-178* torpedoes and sinks a U.S. freighter off Mozambique. The U-boat captain questions crew members before giving them directions to the nearest land.

TBF Avengers and F4F Wildcats from escort carrier *Santee* sink German submarine *U-160* south of the Azores.

MEDITERRANEAN: Benito Mussolini receives a report from General Vittorio Ambrosio of the *Commando Supremo* that Sicily's defenders cannot hold out for long. Mussolini is told Italy has no more resources to continue the war. He is urged to end the alliance with Hitler and end the war as soon as possible.

SICILY: The Axis leadership agrees to concentrate German-Italian defenses in the northeast part of Sicily. The 1st Infantry Division captures Niscemi and Mazzarivo. Ninth Air Force B-24 Liberators and Royal Air Force heavy bombers hit railroad, marshaling yard, harbor, and oil storage facilities at Messina. B-25 Mitchells bomb Enna and Palermo, while P-40s attack the Lentini area. Northwest African Air Force fighters attack supplies, trains, rail junctions, bridges, and convoys in Sicily. B-17s, B-26 Marauders, and B-25 Mitchells bomb Messina, Enna, Marsala, and Randazzo. U.S. light cruiser is damaged by mine off Licata.

NEW GEORGIA: In an attempt to break the stalemate along the main line of defense, a battalion of the 103rd Infantry Regiment lands at Laiana Beach, arriving from previous operations on Vangunu Island. Tanks from the 9th Marine Defense Battalion also land to support the infantry. Thirteenth Air Force B-25 Mitchells and P-40s strike barges and a small vessel off New Georgia Island. B-24 Liberators and B-17s bomb the Kahili airfield on Bougainville Island and the airfields on Ballale Island and Buka Island.

NEW GUINEA: Fifth Air Force B-24 Liberators bomb Koepang on Timor Island.

July 15

ALEUTIANS: Eleventh Air Force B-24 Liberators and B-25 Mitchells bomb the anti-aircraft positions on Kiska Island. One B-25 is damaged by enemy fire.

ATLANTIC: A U.S. PBY Catalina, a British destroyer, and two frigates sink German submarine *U-135* off the coast of Morocco. U.S. PBM Mariner patrol bomber sinks German submarine *U-159* in the central Caribbean. TBF Avengers and F4F Wildcats from escort carrier USS *Santee* sink German submarine *U-509* south of the Azores.

SICILY: Patton, gaining approval from Alexander to conduct reconnaissance forward allows the 3rd Infantry Division to capture Agrigento. Northwest African Air Force fighters attack trains, road junctions, radar installations, convoys, and railway stations.

SOUTHWEST PACIFIC AREA: SWPA GHQ circulates a plan for an attack on New Britain to control the western part of the island from Gasmata to Talasea. The plan outlines an attack by three separate elements to seize Cape Gloucester, neutralize Gasmata, and capture Talasea by a series of amphibious hops along the northern coastline. The Gasmata operation will take place seven days before the main attack on Cape Gloucester.

PACIFIC: U.S. submarine *Narwhal* shells the airfield on Matsuwa Island in the Kuriles. U.S. submarine *Tinosa* torpedoes and sinks a Japanese armed merchant cruiser north of Truk. A mine laid off Kavieng, New Ireland, by U.S. submarine *Silversides* on June 4 damages a Japanese light cruiser.

NEW GEORGIA: General Griswold takes command of the ground forces on New Georgia. Deputy SOPAC Commander Rear Admiral Theodore S. Wilkinson (who shows a great deal more willingness to cooperate with the army) replaces Rear Admiral Kelly Turner, who leaves to take command of Fifth Amphibious Corps. Griswold orders offensive operations suspended to rest, refit, and resupply the ground units. Admiral Halsey decides not to take on the strong Japanese defenses at Kolombangara Island, and shifts objectives to Vella Lavella. A force of about 27 Japanese bombers, with 40 to 50 fighters flying escort, is intercepted over Vella Lavella Island by Thirteenth Air Force and Allied fighters. Fifteen bombers and 30 fighters are shot down. Three Allied planes are lost.

July 16

ATLANTIC: TBF Avenger torpedo bombers from escort carrier USS *Core* sink German submarine *U-67* in the mid-Atlantic. German submarine *U-513* torpedoes and sinks a U.S. freighter off the coast of Brazil.

General George C. Marshall proposes an operation directed against Rome by seizing Naples and the airfields at Foggia. His proposal is code named Avalanche.

ETO: Eighth Air Force B-26B Marauders bomb the marshaling yard at Abbeville, France. Ten of the 14 are damaged. This is the first use of the B-26 in Europe. It will become one of the most reliable medium bombers in theater.

MEDITERRANEAN: In Italy, Ninth Air Force B-24 Liberators attack Bari airfield and lose three bombers to enemy fighters, but claim 11 fighters destroyed. Royal Air Force (RAF) heavy bombers bomb Reggio di Calabria airfield.

SICILY: The 3rd Infantry Division captures Agrigento and the Rangers capture Porto Empedocle. The British flanking maneuver is quickly halted as the Axis forces, reinforced by Hitler's order, hold along the defensive line from San Stefano through Adriana and on to Catania. Hitler orders German forces to take over the battle and delay the Allies as long as possible.

Over Sicily, B-25 Mitchells bomb Randazzo and Valguarnera. Northwest African Air Force fighters and light and medium bombers support ground operations.

BOUGAINVILLE: Thirteenth Air Force B-17s and B-24 Liberators attack Kahili airfield on Bougainville Island. Off Buin, seven B-24s along with over 70 navy SBD Dauntless dive-bombers and over 100 Allied fighters attack a Japanese convoy. Over 40 enemy aircraft are reported destroyed and seven vessels, including a destroyer, are reported sunk.

NEW GEORGIA: An airstrike of 84 navy-marine SBD Dauntless dive-bombers and TBF Avenger torpedo bombers attacks Lambetti plantation and Munda airfield. The 172nd Infantry attacks Japanese defenses north of Laiana, but is unable to advance because of poor coordination between the infantry and the marine tanks supporting them. The 3rd Battalion of the 169th Infantry captures Kelley Hill, named after Second Lieutenant John Kelley, killed after the hill was taken.

July 17

ATLANTIC: The B-18 Bolos of the 7th Antisubmarine Squadron (Heavy) cease conducting antisubmarine operations from their temporary base in Trinidad. The unit's home base is Jacksonville Municipal Airport, Florida.

ETO: While B-26s fly a diversion to Cayeux, France, Eighth Air Force B-17s attack two industrial targets in Germany, one at Hanover, the other at Hamburg. Bad weather prevents the main targets from being hit, and only 33 of the 205 B-17s and two YB-40s attack a target over Hannover. One B-17 is lost and 52 are damaged; enemy losses are reported at over 30 aircraft destroyed. The 125 B-17s sent against Hamburg find no targets, but 21 bombers attempt a bombing run on the cloud-shrouded Fokker plant at Amsterdam, Holland. The bombs miss their intended target and kill 150 civilians. This attack costs one B-17 lost and 42 others damaged. Aircrews report about 30 enemy aircraft destroyed.

MEDITERRANEAN: Patton meets Alexander in La Marsa, Tunisia, and requests permission to move on Palermo, the capital of Sicily. Alexander, however, decides to place significant restrictions on the advance to Palermo to ensure that Montgomery's flank and rear are protected. Patton's chief of staff, Brigadier General Hobart L. Gay, receives Alexander's revised order, but uses selective decoding, plus a request for retransmission to clarify the order. It is enough of a delay to allow Patton to continue with his original intent to capture Palermo without any limits on the use of his forces.

Based on events in Sicily, and the endorsement from General Marshall, Eisenhower begins examining opportunities for the invasion of the Italian mainland. Ironically and on the same day, Hitler comes to the conclusion that Sicily cannot be held.

Ninth Air Force B-24 Liberators bomb the marshaling yard in Naples, and Royal Air Force (RAF) heavy bombers hit Reggio di Calabria in Italy. One B-24 is shot down and enemy fighters damage several others. Aircrews report 23 enemy fighters destroyed. Over Sicily, B-25 Mitchells bomb Catania and the rail yards and roads at Paterno. P-40s fly escort to Gela and Comiso. Over 200 B-25 Mitchells, B-26 Marauders, and B-17s of the Northwest African Air Force bomb the marshaling yard at Naples, Italy.

SICILY: First Lieutenant David C. Waybur of the 3rd Reconnaissance Troop, 3rd Infantry Division, volunteers to lead a three-vehicle patrol to locate a Ranger unit. The patrol moves at night until it reaches a destroyed bridge near Agrigento. Lieutenant Waybur is in the lead vehicle, when suddenly four enemy tanks appear. Surprised and outmatched, the patrol opens fire with machine guns in a desperate attempt to break contact. The men in Waybur's vehicle are quickly out of action. Although he is seriously wounded, Waybur climbs out of his vehicle and stands directly in front of the first enemy tank with only a Thompson submachine gun. At 30 yards, his fire kills the tank crew and the tank itself tumbles off the damaged bridge. He organizes a hasty defense and sends for help, holding his position until help arrives the next morning. For his extraordinary courage and willingness to sacrifice himself for his comrades, First Lieutenant Wayburn will receive the Medal of Honor.

BOUGAINVILLE: Thirteenth Air Force B-24s and navy and Marine Corps SBD Dauntless dive-bombers and navy TBF Avenger torpedo bombers, escorted by over 100 Allied fighters (marine F4U Corsairs, P-39 Airacobras, U.S. and Royal New Zealand AF P-40s), attack Japanese shipping off Bougainville Island. The B-24s claim hits on two merchant cargo ships and the dive-bombers claim serious damage to two destroyers, an auxiliary minesweeper, a patrol ship, an oiler, and a merchant cargo ship. One Japanese destroyer is sunk. The Allied fighters claim over 40 enemy aircraft and four floatplanes shot down.

NEW GEORGIA: About 150 Japanese infantrymen attack Zanana Beach in an attempt to disrupt the flow of supplies to the front lines. The Japanese overrun a casualty clearing station, massacring the wounded. Marine antiaircraft gunners and army rear area personnel form a hasty defense under the command of an army lawyer and stop them. The 169th Infantry Regiment defends against Japanese attacks near Munda, but the 43rd Infantry Division has suffered over 700 combat casualties and has more than 1,000 men sick from malaria and dysentery. Psychoneurosis casualties average 150 men per day.

NEW GUINEA: Fifth Air Force B-25 Mitchells bomb Timor Island. B-24 Liberators bomb Adaoet Island in the Moluccas. B-25s attack the airfield, a headquarters compound, and various defensive positions around Salamaua.

July 18

ALEUTIANS: Eleventh Air Force B-24 Liberators and B-25 Mitchells bomb Kiska Island. Over the Kurile Islands, six B-24s attack cargo ships and the runway at Murakami Bay on Paramushiru Island.

CBI: Fourteenth Air Force B-24 Liberators bomb shipping at the harbors at Haiphong and Hongay in French Indochina.

ATLANTIC: U.S. Navy airship K-74 is shot down by German submarine *U-134* in the Florida Straits. This is the only airship lost to hostile fire in the war.

SICILY: The 1st Infantry Division captures Enna, a key position that allows the British to move freely eastward. The 45th Infantry Division moves toward the northern coast of the island. Ninth Air Force B-25 Mitchells attack targets near Randazzo and Catania. The Northwest African Air Force A-36 Invaders (Apaches) bomb targets at Santa Caterina, Adrano, Lercara, and Termini Imerese.

CENTRAL PACIFIC: Seventh Air Force B-24 Liberators from Funafuti in the Ellice Islands, bomb Japanese defensive works on Betio Island, Tarawa Atoll, Gilbert Islands.

GUADALCANAL: Japanese submarine *RO-106* torpedoes and sinks a U.S. LST (Landing Ship Tank) off Guadalcanal.

BOUGAINVILLE: Thirteenth Air Force B-24 Liberators, P-40s, and P-38 Lightnings, and over 140 navy and Marine Corps SBD Dauntless dive-bombers, TBF Avenger torpedo bombers and fighters attack Kahili airfield and shipping off Bougainville Island. The airfield is bombed by five B-24 Liberators, which suppress antiaircraft positions and crater the runways. Other U.S. aircraft attack shipping, claiming damage to two destroyers and one light vessel sunk. Enemy losses are estimated at 21 fighters. U.S. losses are nine navy aircraft.

NEW GEORGIA: The 4th Raider Battalion arrives to reinforce the Raiders at Enogai. The battalion of the 148th Infantry, having no effect on the Bairoko Trail, joins the marines.

NEW GUINEA: Fifth Air Force B-24 Liberators bomb the Makassar harbor area of Celebes Island. B-25 Mitchells, one B-24, and an A-20 Havoc bomb and strafe targets around Salamaua. Other B-25s attack shipping off New Britain Island.

July 19

ALEUTIANS: Eleventh Air Force receives three A-24-equipped dive-bomber squadrons from Tampa, Florida, which will fly from Amchitka Island. The A-24 Banshee is the SBD Dauntless dive-bomber without carrier landing equipment.

ATLANTIC: The B-24 Liberators of the 14th Antisubmarine Squadron (Heavy), 25th Antisubmarine Wing, relocate from Massachusetts and begin operations from Langley Field in Hampton, Virginia. US PBM Mariner patrol bomber sinks German submarine *U-513* off Santos, Brazil.

MEDITERRANEAN: Hitler meets with Mussolini at Feltre, Italy, and spends the entire meeting haranguing his gloomy and wavering partner on the need to stand firm. In Italy, over 100 Ninth Air Force B-24 Liberators attack the marshaling yards and airfield at Littoria and the rail lines at Anzio. The previous night, Northwest African Air Force bombers dropped over 800,000 leaflets on Rome.

Over Rome, 150 B-17s of the Northwest African Air Force bomb the railroad yards. B-25 Mitchells and B-26 Marauders attack Ciampino airfield outside of Rome. In Sicily, P-40s bomb rail facilities and A-36 Invaders (Apaches) attack trains and transports.

PACIFIC: U.S. submarine *Porpoise* torpedoes and sinks a Japanese transport south of Wake Island.

BOUGAINVILLE: Thirteenth Air Force B-17s bomb Kahili airfield at Bougainville Island. B-17s and B-25 Mitchells also bomb the airfield on Ballale Island. B-25s conduct ground support missions near Bairoko on New Georgia.

July 20

ALEUTIANS: Over Kiska Island, nine B-24 Liberators of the Eleventh Air Force bomb the airfield and facilities.

ATLANTIC: A B-24 Liberator of the 19th Antisubmarine Squadron (Heavy) sinks German submarine *U-588* in the Bay of Biscay.

PACIFIC: The Joint Chiefs of Staff issues orders to Admiral Chester W. Nimitz, Commander in Chief, Pacific Ocean Areas (CincPOA), to prepare to mount an offensive in the Gilberts in order to put pressure on the Japanese from another direction and to protect strategic lines of communications to the Solomons. The Gilberts will be the first islands to be captured, followed by Kwajalein, Eniwetok, Saipan, Guam, Iwo Jima, and Okinawa.

U.S. submarine *Pompano* torpedoes and damages a Japanese transport east of Kyushu, Japan.

BOUGAINVILLE: Over Bougainville, 18 B-24 Liberators from Thirteenth Air Force bomb airfields at Kahili and on Ballale Island. A Japanese surface force is spotted sailing between Vella Lavella and Choiseul Islands. TBF Avenger torpedo bombers from Henderson Field sink one destroyer and damage another. A heavy cruiser is also damaged. A later attack by B-25 Mitchells sinks a destroyer.

NEW GEORGIA: Marines attack Japanese defenses at Bairoko Harbor and are thrown back with 30 percent casualties. Marine colonel Harry B. Liversedge, commanding the Northern Landing Group, composed of the 1st Marine Raider Battalion and a battalion each of the 145th and 148th Infantry Regiments, 37th Infantry Division, decides to hold at Enogai. Japanese conduct an air attack on Rendova Island. Fighters strafe barges in Pakoi Bay.

NEW GUINEA: Fifth Air Force A-20 Havocs and B-25 Mitchells bomb Madang airfield and other Japanese defensive positions. On Timor Island, B-25s bomb airfields at Lautem, Dili, and Cape Chater.

July 21

ALEUTIANS: Two U.S. destroyers bombard suspected Japanese positions at Gertrude Cove, Kiska Island.

ATLANTIC: A navy PBY Catalina sinks German submarine *U-662* at the mouth of Amazon River, Brazil.

SICILY: Patton forms a Provisional Corps of the 3rd Infantry Division, the 82nd Airborne Division, an RCT of the 9th Infantry Division, along with elements of the 2nd Armored Division, and the 1st and 4th Ranger Battalions under command of

Major General Geoffrey Keyes, to move westward toward Palermo, the capital of Sicily. Allied forces have captured six airfields.

SOUTHWEST PACIFIC AREA: U.S. submarine *Haddock* torpedoes and sinks a Japanese army transport with 180 geishas on board in the Philippine Sea.

NEW GEORGIA: Major General J. Lawton Collins, commander of the 25th Infantry Division, arrives from Guadalcanal accompanied by the remainder of the 37th Infantry Division. Thirteenth Air Force B-25 Mitchells and over 170 navy dive-bombers supported by over 50 fighters attack Japanese defenses around Bairoko.

NEW GUINEA: Fifth Air Force B-25 Mitchells bomb Madang and other ground support targets, while B-26 Marauders bomb barges. The C-47-equipped 66th Troop Carrier Squadron arrives at Port Moresby from the United States.

July 22

ALEUTIANS: Eleventh Air Force B-25 Mitchells and B-24 Liberators, escorted by 13 P-40s and 20 P-38 fighters, attack a number of targets on Kiska Island. A B-25 is shot down by antiaircraft fire, and another 18 aircraft are damaged. One B-25 conducts a photoreconnaissance mission and a B-24 flies a radar reconnaissance mission over Kiska. Rear Admiral Robert C. Giffen's Task Group 16.21 and Rear Admiral Robert M. Griffin's TG 16.22, with two battleships, three heavy cruisers, one light cruiser, and nine destroyers, bombard the island.

ATLANTIC: German submarine *U-66* torpedoes and damages a U.S. tanker en route from New York to Aruba. When the U-boat surfaces to finish off the tanker with gunfire, the tanker's armed guard defends the ship with accurate fire from its deck gun and drives off the enemy. The tanker is able to reach port at San Juan, Puerto Rico, with no casualties.

ETO: A report issued by the British Joint Intelligence Committee claims the Combined Bomber Offensive is having an effect on Germany, noting German fighter strength is now directed mainly against Allied bombing missions in Europe, drawing assets away from other areas. The report claims strategic bombing is having an effect on strategic raw materials production, especially synthetic rubber, fuel, iron, and coal in the Ruhr industrial area of Germany.

MEDITERRANEAN: Over Italy, more than 100 B-17s of the Northwest African Air Force bomb the marshaling yard at Battipaglia and Foggia. B-26 Marauders attack a bridge and the marshaling yard at Salerno.

SICILY: The 45th Infantry Division reaches Termini Imerese on the northern coast. Patton's Provisional Corps is ready to assault the city of Palermo, but the attack is not necessary as city officials surrender to General Keyes.

PACIFIC: U.S. submarine *Sawfish* torpedoes and damages a Japanese ammunition ship in the East China Sea.

BOUGAINVILLE: Thirteenth Air Force B-17s and B-24 Liberators, along with more than 40 navy SBD Dauntless dive-bombers and over 100 Allied fighters attack Japanese shipping off Buin at Bougainville Island. A seaplane carrier is sunk and several other vessels are damaged.

NEW GEORGIA: Major General Griswold orders Major General Robert Beightler to take command of his 37th Infantry Division. The 161st Infantry Regiment from the

25th Infantry Division arrives and is placed under Beighter's command. Griswold issues orders for a coordinated attack on Munda to begin on July 25. The 37th Division takes the northern sector of the enemy line and the 43rd Division takes the southern sector. The 2nd Battalion of the 103rd Infantry Regiment from Vangunu Island reinforces the 43rd Division. The 169th Infantry is moved to the rear for rest and refitting.

A convoy with a Japanese seaplane tender and five destroyers with troops and supplies bound for New Georgia is attacked by 16 SBD Dauntless dive-bombers, 18 TBF Avenger torpedo bombers, and 16 heavy bombers.

NEW GUINEA: Fifth Air Force B-24 Liberators, B-25 Mitchells, and B-26 Marauders attack Japanese defensive positions and antiaircraft placements around Salamaua. B-24s bomb an oil refinery and transportation targets at Surabaya, Java. B-25s bomb targets on Selaroe Island in the Moluccas.

July 23

CBI: Japanese bombers and fighters begin a three-day attack on Kweilin, Hengyang, Lingling, Kanchow, and Suichan.

ATLANTIC: A U.S. destroyer sinks German submarine *U-613* south of Azores. TBF Avenger torpedo bombers from escort carrier USS *Bogue* attack German submarines *U-527* and *U-648* south of the Azores. The Avengers sink *U-527* and *U-648* escapes. Navy PB4Y Privateers sink German submarine *U-598* off Brazil.

The 23rd Antisubmarine Squadron (Heavy), which has operated B-25 Mitchells from Langley Field, Hampton, Virginia, returns to its base at Jacksonville, Florida.

MEDITERRANEAN: The CCS directs General Eisenhower to develop plans for an invasion of Italy, directed in the vicinity of Naples. In Italy, Northwest African Air Force B-17s, B-25 Mitchells, and B-26 Marauders bomb Leverano and Crotone.

SICILY: With Montgomery unable to make any progress, Alexander orders Patton to advance east with his army on the northern Route 113 and Route 120. The 82nd Airborne Division is in Trapani and moving toward Marsala. The 1st Infantry Division captures Enna with elements of the 1st Canadian Division, and prepares to advance on Petrali. The 45th Infantry Division attacks along the coastal road at Termini Imerese, but is halted by elements of the 29th Panzer Grenadier Division, one of the units ordered to Sicily by Hitler. Patton orders his reserve, the 9th Infantry Division, to be moved to Sicily. The II Corps is ordered to move along the coastal road and along Route 120, the main road in the center of the island, to capture Nicosia, Troina, and Randazzo. The 45th Infantry Division is ordered to advance along the coast, while the 1st Infantry Division advances west on Route 120. Northwest African Air Force light bombers support ground operations at Adrano, Paterno, and Troina.

NEW GUINEA: Fifth Air Force B-17s, B-26 Marauders, B-25 Mitchells, and B-24 Liberators bomb a number of targets along the northeast coast.

The airfield constructed on Woodlark Island is operational. The 67th Fighter Squadron, flying P-39 Airacobras, deploys to the island.

July 24

ALEUTIANS: Over Kiska and Little Kiska Islands, 62 U.S. P-40s, with two of the fighters piloted by men of the Royal Canadian Air Force, attack the airfield runway and antiaircraft positions. Although one battery is severely damaged, an Eleventh Air Force P-40 is lost to Japanese antiaircraft fire.

CBI: P-40 pilots report 25 enemy aircraft shot down defending the airspace over Fourteenth Air Force airfields.

ATLANTIC: TBF Avengers and F4F Wildcats from escort carrier *Santee* damage German submarine *U-373* west of the Madeira Islands. B-24 Liberators damage German submarine *U-466* off Cayenne, French Guiana.

ETO: Eighth Air Force conducts its first long-range attack on Norway. The three missions will involve a total distance of 1,900 miles to and from the targets. Against the nitrate works at Heroya, 167 B-17s and a YB-40 bomb the target and disrupt it sufficiently to halt production for at least three months. Enemy losses are reported at nine aircraft destroyed. U.S. losses are one B-17 destroyed and 53 damaged. The Trondheim port area is attacked by 41 B-17s. One B-17 is lost and nine others are damaged; enemy losses are estimated at nine aircraft. The Bergen port area is under cloud cover, and the 84 B-17s cancel the mission.

MEDITERRANEAN: The Fascist Grand Council meets at Mussolini's direction. After a debate over the direction of the war, 19 of 28 members vote against Mussolini remaining in power. The king of Italy, Victor Emmanuel III, orders Mussolini to resign in favor of Field Marshal Pietro Badoglio. Mussolini is put in an ambulance and moved to a secret location, where he is informed he is under arrest.

Northwest African Air Force B-17s and B-25 Mitchells bomb the Bologna railroad yards. B-26 Marauders bomb the Paola railroad yards.

SICILY: The 39th RCT occupies Marsala. Patton's Provisional Corps controls western Sicily. The engineers open Palermo for port operations. The Provisional Corps has captured 53,000 Italians and 400 vehicles.

PACIFIC: U.S. submarine *Tinosa* fires a total of 15 torpedoes at a Japanese oiler in the Carolines—13 are hits but only two explode. The oiler is damaged, but it is towed to Truk and salvaged. U.S. torpedo problems are common, forcing submariners to expend numerous torpedoes in order to get an explosion.

CENTRAL PACIFIC: Seventh Air Force B-24 Liberators from Midway Island attack Wake Island, bombing the oil storage area, barracks, and a gun emplacement. About 30 Japanese fighters attack the eight bombers over the target. One B-24 is lost in a collision with a falling Japanese fighter and nine enemy aircraft are reported destroyed.

NEW GEORGIA: U.S. Navy and marine SBD Dauntless dive-bombers along with 48 Thirteenth Air Force fighters support ground forces around Bairoko and at Bibilo Hill.

NEW GUINEA: Fifth Air Force B-25 Mitchells bomb the airfield and other targets at Lae. B-25s also bomb targets on Timor Island.

July 25

ALEUTIANS: Over Kiska and Little Kiska Islands, 40 U.S. P-40s, with two of the fighters piloted by men of the Royal Canadian Air Force, attack the airfield runway and antiaircraft positions.

CBI: Fourteenth Air Force B-25 Mitchells, escorted by P-40s and P-38 Lightnings, bomb the airfield at Hankow, China, in retaliation for Japanese air attacks on U.S. airfields.

ATLANTIC: The B-24 Liberators of the 15th Antisubmarine Squadron (Heavy) at Jacksonville, Florida, move operations to Battista Field in Cuba.

ETO: Eighth Air Force VIII Bomber Command attacks three targets in Germany. The first target is the diesel engine works at Hamburg, where during the previous night nearly 750 Royal Air Force heavy bombers damaged the city. Because of cloud cover during the day, 100 B-17s hit the shipyard as an alternate target. German fighters shoot down 15 bombers and damage 67 others. Enemy losses are estimated at over 40 aircraft destroyed. Against the shipyard at Kiel, 59 B-17s are unable to attack the target due to heavy cloud cover. Although 141 B-17s are sent against an aviation industrial target at Warnemunde, 118 bombers attack the shipyard at Kiel instead, losing four B-17s to enemy fighters. They return with 51 other bombers damaged and claim six German aircraft destroyed. Over Ghent, Belgium, 13 B-26B Marauders of the VIII Air Support Command bomb the coke ovens used for making steel. Six aircraft are damaged in the attack.

MEDITERRANEAN: Celebrations begin in Rome at the news of Mussolini's resignation. The king selects Pietro Badoglio, a former *Commando Supremo,* to lead the new government. The Italian Fascist Party is dissolved. Badoglio publicly announces that the war will continue, even though the king has instructed Badoglio to break the alliance with Germany and come to terms with the Allies. Badoglio's announcement is intended to keep the Germans from taking any precipitous action before he can carry out his instructions. Hitler, suspicious of Badoglio's motives, orders two divisions from southern France to move to the Italian border.

SICILY: Ninth Air Force B-25 Mitchells bomb docks and shipping at Milazzo. Nearly 100 P-40s strafe and bomb Catania harbor and targets at Milazzo and Taormina.

SOUTHWEST PACIFIC AREA: U.S. submarine *Pompon* torpedoes and sinks a Japanese cargo ship and damages a transport north of the Saint Matthias Group near the Bismarck Archipelago.

SOLOMONS: Lieutenant General Nathan F. Twining, USAAF, becomes Commander Air Solomons (COMAIRSOLS). Brigadier General Dean C. Strother becomes commander of Fighter Command Solomons (he remains the commander of XIII Fighter Command). Colonel William A. Matheny takes command of Bomber Command Solomons.

NEW GEORGIA: The general attack on Munda begins. Preceding the attack, 66 B-17s and B-24 Liberators bomb Lambetti plantation. Another strike of 84 aircraft hits Bibilo hill. The attack begins against Japanese positions on Shimuzu hill, supported by tanks and flamethrowers. The 43rd Infantry Division's two regiments, the 103rd and the 172nd, move along the coast, while three regiments of the 37th Infantry Division (the 148th, 161st, and the 145th) attack the Japanese strongpoint from the front and flank. Supported by marine tanks, the infantrymen fight yard by yard into the midst of the well camouflaged, heavily fortified positions.

The infantry attacks are supported by naval gunfire from seven destroyers. But within 30 minutes, over 170 B-17s, B-24 Liberators, B-25 Mitchells, SBD Dauntless dive-bombers, and TBF Avenger torpedo bombers, escorted by more than 70 fighters, drop 145 tons of bombs on enemy positions. Another 10 B-24s bomb Bibilo hill, while SBDs and TBFs hit Japanese gun positions. A Japanese air attack on U.S. forces on Rendova Island fails as Allied fighters shoot down at least eight fighters and disrupt the bombers so that they are unable to cause any damage.

July 26

ALEUTIANS: Eleventh Air Force B-24s, 38 P-40s, and 24 P-38s attack targets on Kiska Island and Little Kiska Island, dropping over 140 tons of bombs. One P-40 is shot down and three others are damaged by antiaircraft fire.

CBI: Fourteenth Air Force B-25 Mitchells escorted by 12 P-40s bomb the airfield at Hankow, China. An estimated 30 to 50 fighters intercept the attackers. The U.S. crews claim 14 enemy aircraft shot down and 17 probables. One P-40 is lost.

ATLANTIC: The CCS, responding to the news from Italy, decides to speed up the invasion of the mainland in order to bolster the new Italian government and forestall a German reaction.

PBM Mariner patrol bomber sinks German submarine *U-759* in the Caribbean.

ETO: Eighth Air Force VIII Bomber Command attacks two targets in Germany. Over Hannover, 96 B-17s and two YB-40s (an armored version of the B-17) hit rubber production factories. U.S. losses are 16 B-17s, while enemy aircraft losses are estimated to be nearly 50 destroyed. Another raid on Hannover by 61 B-17s turns into 49 bombers attacking targets of opportunity. Crews claim at least 15 enemy aircraft destroyed and six B-17s are lost to enemy fire. Another 54 of 121 B-17s sent against targets in Hannover, bomb the U-boat yards, losing two B-17s and destroying five enemy aircraft. A total of 89 B-17s are damaged on this mission. Over France, 15 B-26B Marauders of the VIII Air Support Command hit the Saint-Omer/Longuenesse airfield. Four bombers are damaged in the attack.

MEDITERRANEAN: In Italy, Northwest African Air Force B-26 Marauders bomb the marshaling yard at Marina di Paola. A German bomber damages a U.S. destroyer off Palermo, Sicily.

CENTRAL PACIFIC: Seventh Air Force B-24 Liberators flying from Midway Island attack Wake Island, hitting the oil storage area. The eight bombers are attacked by at least 20 fighters. The B-24 crews report 11 enemy fighters destroyed.

BOUGAINVILLE: Thirteenth Air Force B-24 Liberators, P-38 Lightnings, P-40s, and navy aircraft attack the airfield at Kahili on Bougainville Island. B-25 Mitchells, P-40s, and U.S. Navy fighters attack targets over Kolombangara Island in New Georgia.

NEW GEORGIA: Army infantry, with marine tanks, assault Lambetti plantation. Ilangana village falls to the 3rd Battalion of the 103rd Infantry, which advances 800 yards along a 600-yard frontage. Within this area the Americans have had to destroy 74 fortified defensive positions. The 161st Infantry Regiment meets heavy opposition on Bartley Ridge, named after Second Lieutenant Martin Bartley, killed during the attack.

NEW GUINEA: Fifth Air Force B-17s and B-24 Liberators bomb targets around Salamaua and Lae airfield. The 65th Troop Carrier Squadron, equipped with C-47s, arrives at Port Moresby from the United States.

July 27

CBI: Fourteenth Air Force B-24 Liberators attack shipping at Hainan Island, claiming two vessels severely damaged. The 10 bombers are attacked by between 25 and 30 fighters. Crews claim 13 enemy fighters shot down with no U.S. losses. Another six B-24s, supported by 14 fighters, attack targets of opportunity on Stonecutters Island near Hong Kong.

CBI: The Chinese-American Composite Wing (CACW) is activated. The wing has Chinese pilots and aircraft, led by Chinese and American officers. The wing consists of the 1st Bomber Group with B-25 Mitchells and the 3rd and 5th Fighter Groups with P-40s.

ETO: Eighth Air Force VIII Air Support Command B-26B Marauders bomb the Tricqueville airfield in France.

MEDITERRANEAN: In Italy, Northwest African Air Force B-17s bomb the Capua airfield and the rail lines at Lioni.

SICILY: The 1st Infantry Division captures Nicosia. The German forces begin a withdrawal in preparation for evacuation through Messina to the Italian mainland. Ninth Air Force P-40s attack both tactical targets on the island and shipping targets at Catania. Northwest African Air Force B-25 Mitchells and B-26 Marauders bomb the landing ground at Scalea.

PACIFIC: U.S. submarine *Sawfish* torpedoes and damages a Japanese minelayer off Kyushu, Japan. U.S. submarine *Scamp* torpedoes and sinks Japanese submarine *I-168* and damages an oiler near the Saint Matthias Group. U.S. submarine *Seadragon* off Wake Island adds damage to a crippled Japanese transport. Japanese cargo ship sinks off Hainan Island when it strikes a mine laid by U.S. submarine *Tambor* on November 2, 1942.

BOUGAINVILLE: Thirteenth Air Force B-17s bomb the Kahili airfields at Bougainville and Ballale islands. Brigadier General Ray L. Owens becomes the commanding general of Thirteenth Air Force.

NEW GEORGIA: P-38 Lightnings, along with navy and Marine Corps aircraft, attack Japanese positions on Bibilo hill, Gurasai, and Munda. Private First Class Frank J. Petrarca, a medic with the 145th Infantry Regiment, 37th Infantry Division, accompanies the infantry's attack on Japanese defenses near Horseshoe Hill. At 100 yards, the enemy opens fire on the Americans, causing several casualties. Petrarca locates the most seriously wounded soldiers, including one who is only 75 yards from the Japanese bunkers. Unable to move him from the direct line of fire, Petrarca provides first aid where the soldier fell, shielding the wounded man with his own body. He then moves to two other wounded soldiers. Petrarca will continue to perform extraordinary feats of heroism to save his comrades until he is killed on July 31 going to the aid of a wounded soldier only 20 yards from the enemy. His last conscious act will be to rise to his knees and shout his defiance to the Japanese. Private First Class Petrarca's numerous acts of selflessness and his indomitable will win him the Medal of Honor.

NEW GUINEA: The Salamaua area is hit by 35 B-25 Mitchells and 18 B-24 Liberators of the Fifth Air Force, representing one of the largest single-strike attacks to take place within the Southwest Pacific Area.

July 28

ALEUTIANS: In a masterstroke of deception and stealth, the Japanese bring in cruisers and destroyers to evacuate over 5,000 men from Kiska Island.

CBI: Fourteenth Air Force B-25 Mitchells, with an escort of nine P-40s, bomb the docks at Taikoo in Hong Kong.

ATLANTIC: A B-24 Liberator of the 4th Antisubmarine Squadron (Heavy) and a Royal Air Force B-24 sink German submarine *U-404* in the Bay of Biscay. A U.S. PBY Catalina sinks German submarine *U-359* in the West Indies. In a heavy fog, a U.S. freighter straggling from convoy BX 65 (Boston to Halifax) encounters a mine laid by German submarine *U-119*, but reaches port under tow.

ETO: Eighth Air Force VIII Bomber Command conducts the deepest U.S. bomber raid into Germany up to this time. For the first time, the bombers are escorted by 105 P-47 Thunderbolts, equipped with jettisonable belly tanks. Two aviation industry targets are selected; one is the Fieseler Works at Kassel and the other is the Focke-Wulf plant at Oschersleben. Weather over the targets limits the effectiveness of the strikes. Although 182 B-17s are launched against Kassel, only 58 hit the target; seven B-17s are shot down and 58 are damaged. Enemy aircraft losses are estimated at nearly 40 destroyed. Of the 120 B-17s intended for Oschersleben, only 37 hit the target; U.S. losses are 15 shot down and 65 damaged. Almost 80 enemy fighter kills are reported. P-47s meet the returning bombers and jump about 60 German fighters, destroying nine. The VIII Air Support Command conducts two strikes on targets in Belgium and France. The coke ovens at Zeebrugge, Belgium, are the target of 17 B-26B Marauders. Three B-26s are damaged in the attack. Another 18 B-26Bs head for Tricqueville airfield in France, but turn back when the fighter escort fails to meet them.

SICILY: Palermo receives supply ships for Patton's army. Lines of supply shift from the beaches to the road and rail lines in western Sicily. The 1st Infantry Division captures Nicosia and advances toward Cerami. Because of the mountainous terrain, the divisions of the II Corps will have to advance separately, unable to support each other. The German defenses have forced the Allies to fight on difficult terrain along narrow twisting roads, which limits maneuver and forces them to make frontal assaults on heavily fortified strongpoints. Destroyed bridges and minefields slow the advance even further. Ninth Air Force P-40s attack targets in Sicily. Over 100 aircraft are involved in the strikes. Northwest African Air Force A-36 Intruders (Apaches) and P-40s bomb enemy movements on the Troina-Randazzo road, attack the bridges and roads near Cesaro, and hit targets near Falcone and Randazzo.

SWPA: Fifth Air Force B-25 Mitchells attack the airfield at Cape Gloucester, New Britain Island, and sink two destroyers offshore. B-24 Liberators bomb targets in the Molucca Islands.

NEW GEORGIA: Two battalions of the 145th Infantry Regiment, 37th Infantry Division, attack to capture Horseshoe Hill.

NEW GUINEA: Fifth Air Force B-25s bomb the town of Lautem and the airfield at Cape Chater.

July 29

CBI: Fourteenth Air Force B-24 Liberators, with fighter escort, bomb shipping and dockyard installations at Hong Kong, Kowloon, and the docks at Taikoo. A force of 23 bombers and 30 fighters attacking Hengyang, China, is attacked by four P-40s. One Japanese fighter is shot down.

ETO: Eighth Air Force VIII Bomber Command attacks two targets in Germany: the Kiel shipyards and the Heinkel Aircraft Works at Warnemunde. Over Kiel, 91 B-17s hit the shipyard and 48 hit targets of opportunity, U.S. losses are six B-17s and 64 damaged. Enemy losses are estimated at over 50 aircraft destroyed. Over Warnemunde 54 B-17s hit the target, losing four B-17s and seven damaged. Enemy losses are light; only two are reported as probable kills. The VIII Air Support Command sends 18 B-26B Marauders against the Schipol airfield at Amsterdam, but a navigational error scrubs the mission. Over the Ft. Rouge airfield in France, 19 B-26Bs hit the target and eight bombers are damaged.

SICILY: Ninth Air Force sends over 200 P-40s against Axis targets on the northeast section of the island. Northwest African Air Force B-26 Marauders bomb the Aquino airfield.

NEW GEORGIA: Major General John Hester, commander of the 43rd Infantry Division, asks to be relieved due to illness. He is replaced by Major General John Hodge from the Americal Division. The 161st Infantry captures Bartley Ridge. The ridge contains 78 separate defensive positions, all of which have to be cleared individually. The Japanese begin a withdrawal to defensive positions around Munda airfield. The 148th Infantry Regiment stops a Japanese counterattack.

Lieutenant Robert S. Scott of the 172nd Infantry Regiment, 43d Infantry Division, advances with the leading platoon of his company to attack a Japanese position on a hilltop near Munda airfield. Although his battle-shaken and exhausted men retreat in the face of a sudden Japanese counterattack, Lieutenant Scott refuses to give up. Using grenades and his carbine, he single-handedly stops the attack. Scott's valiant act allows his men to move forward and capture the position. For his extraordinary courage, he will receive the Medal of Honor.

NEW GUINEA: Fifth Air Force B-17s, B-25 Mitchells, and B-24 Liberators bomb Salamaua. On New Britain Island, B-25s, B-26s, and a B-24 attack army HQ, barges, and villages. The bombers also attack shipping off Cape Gloucester.

July 30

ALEUTIANS: U.S. destroyers bombard the Gertrude Cove and main camp areas on Kiska Island. The Americans do not know that the Japanese have evacuated.

CBI: Fourteenth Air Force P-40s intercept 39 Japanese fighters and 24 bombers over Hengyang, China. The 15 P-40s destroy three bombers and two fighters and lose two of their own fighters.

ATLANTIC: Army Air Force Antisubmarine Command, which has been conducting antisubmarine patrols since January of 1942, ceases operations on the east and west coasts of the United States. These include the B-24 Liberators of the 3rd Antisubmarine Squadron (Heavy) at Fort Dix Army Air Base, New Jersey, the B-25 Mitchells of the 16th Antisubmarine Squadron (Heavy) at Charleston Army Air Field, South

Carolina, and the B-24s of the 27th, 30th, and 392nd Bombardment Squadrons (Heavy) at March Field, California. Only B-24s with the 8th Antisubmarine Squadron (Heavy) at Miami Army Air Field, Florida, will continue operation, but this unit will move to bases in the Caribbean. This marks the dominance of the Allies in the desperately fought Battle of the Atlantic.

German submarine *U-230* lays mines near the entrance to Chesapeake Bay. A PV-1 patrol bomber providing coverage for convoy TJ-2 (Trinidad to Rio de Janeiro) sinks German submarine *U-591* off the coast of Brazil. A PV-1 attacks German submarine *U-604* in the South Atlantic. Aircraft from escort carrier *Santee* sink German submarine *U-43* in the mid-Atlantic. *U-43*'s mission was to lay mines off Lagos, Nigeria. A U.S. submarine chaser sinks German submarine *U-375* off Tunisia.

ETO: Eighth Air Force VIII Bomber Command attacks two aviation-related industrial targets in the Kassel area, escorted by 107 P-47 Thunderbolts with auxiliary tanks. The Fieseler Works are bombed by 94 B-17s. Aircrews claim nearly 50 enemy aircraft destroyed; six B-17s are lost and 69 are damaged. Another 40 B-17s hit the Waldau Fieseler Works, losing six bombers and damaging 18. German aircraft losses are estimated at around 14. The P-47s are effective in countering the German fighters, who by now used to attacking bombers without fighter escort. Over Bocholt, Germany, the P-47s claim nearly 30 enemy aircraft destroyed. During the battle, seven P-47s are lost and one damaged. Six of the pilots are reported missing.

The VIII Air Support Command attacks airfields in the Netherlands and France. Over the Woensdrecht airfield, 11 B-26B Marauders hit the target. One B-26 is lost and six are damaged. The 24 B-26Bs sent against the Courtrai/Wevelghem airfield are recalled when fog prevents the fighter escort from joining the bombers. During the mission, however, the B-26 crews claim around 11 aircraft shot down.

SICILY: The 3rd Infantry Division replaces the 45th Infantry Division for the advance to Messina. The 39th RCT of the 9th Infantry Division is attached to the 1st Infantry Division. Ninth Air Force P-40s attack shipping at Milazzo, Messina, and Riposto. Over 100 P-40s are involved in ground support missions. Northwest African Air Force B-17s bomb Grottaglie airfield. B-25 Mitchells bomb the Pratica di Mare airfield. A-20 Havocs bomb Milazzo and attack Axis gun positions, while fighters hit shipping off Milazzo.

INDIAN OCEAN: U.S. freighter en route to Durban, South Africa, from Basra, Iraq, is torpedoed by German submarine *U-197,* but is able to reach its destination.

SOLOMONS: Thirteenth Air Force B-24 Liberators, with an escort of 16 P-38s and P-40s, along with more than 40 navy F4U Corsairs, attack the Ballale Island airfield.

NEW GUINEA: Fifth Air Force B-25 Mitchells hit barges off the Huon Peninsula and villages near Finschhafen. B-24s bomb Salamaua and Kela. A-20 Havocs destroy barges at Hanisch Harbor and Langemak Bay.

July 31

CBI: During the night, nine B-24 Liberators of the Tenth Air Force mine the Rangoon River in Burma.

ATLANTIC: A U.S. PBM Mariner patrol bomber and a Brazilian aircraft sink German submarine *U-199* off Rio de Janeiro, Brazil.

ETO: Eighth Air Force VIII Air Support Command launches raids on four targets in France. Against the airfield at Merville, 20 B-26B Marauders hit the target and two bombers are damaged. Against the airfield at Poix/Nord, 19 B-26Bs hit the target. One bomber is lost and five are damaged. Against the airfield at Abbeville/Drucat, 21 B-26Bs hit the target. Against the airfield at Tricqueville, 18 B-26Bs hit the target. One enemy fighter is believed destroyed and five bombers are damaged. Royal Air Force bombers strike Lille and Amiens in conjunction with the American attacks.

SICILY: The 1st Infantry Division, supported by the 39th Infantry Regiment of the 9th Infantry Division, begins the battle for Troina. Troina is a natural strongpoint and the key to the German defensive line. A 10-man detachment, with Sergeant Gerry H. Kisters and an officer, is sent forward to fill a large crater in the road so that the 1st Infantry Division can move its vehicles through Gagliano. Two hidden enemy machine guns fire on the group as they advance. Sergeant Kisters and the officer move forward and assault the first position, capturing the machine gun and four soldiers. Sergeant Kisters then begins crawling toward the other machine gun position. Although wounded five separate times, he kills three enemy soldiers, runs off the fourth, and captures the position. For his courage in the face of the enemy and willingness to sacrifice his life for his comrades, Sergeant Kisters will receive the Medal of Honor.

SOUTHWEST PACIFIC AREA: U.S. submarine *Finback* torpedoes and sinks a Japanese cargo ship south of Borneo. U.S. submarine *Grayling* lands supplies and equipment at Panay, Philippines. U.S. submarine *Saury* in the Philippine Sea is rammed by Japanese destroyer and damaged; *Saury* returns to base.

PACIFIC: U.S. submarine *Pogy* torpedoes and sinks a Japanese aircraft transport northwest of Truk.

BOUGAINVILLE: U.S. submarine *Guardfish* lands a survey party on the west coast of Bougainville Island.

NEW GEORGIA: Thirteenth Air Force P-40s and P-39 Airacobras, along with over 90 navy and Marine Corps aircraft, attack Japanese defensive positions on Bibilo hill. B-17s, B-25 Mitchells, P-40s, and navy aircraft attack the Vila airfield on Kolombangara Island. Private Rodger W. Young of the 148th Infantry Regiment, 37th Infantry Division, is a member of a platoon ordered to make a limited withdrawal in order to align the battalion's night defensive position. The platoon suddenly is pinned down by intense fire from a Japanese machine gun concealed on higher ground only 75 yards away. Private Young is wounded but can see the enemy position. As the platoon attempts to break contact, Young begins crawling toward the position. Another burst of fire wounds him again, but he continues to move forward, firing his rifle as he goes. He gets close enough to throw hand grenades, but is killed in the attempt. Private Young's great courage and heroic sacrifice will win him the Medal of Honor.

NEW GUINEA: Fifth Air Force B-25 Mitchells bomb the Finschhafen area and barges at Hanisch Harbor and Mange. At New Britain Island, B-25s and A-20 Havocs bomb barges near Cape Gloucester area and B-24 Liberators bomb Waingapoe on Sumba Island in the Sundas.

August 1

ALEUTIANS: Despite overcast skies, seven B-24 Liberators of the Eleventh Air Force bomb the Main Camp area on Kiska Island.

CBI: Tenth Air Force: B-25 Mitchells bomb the road bridge at Shweli, Burma, causing minor damage.

ATLANTIC: U.S. gunboat attacks German submarine *U-732*, diverting it away from convoy NG 376 (New York to Guantánamo).

ETO: The 392nd Bombardment Group (Heavy) arrives at Wendling, England, from the United States with B-24 Liberators.

MEDITERRANEAN: The Raid on Ploeşti. Brigadier General Uzal G. Ent, one of the primary planners for the attack on the oil refineries in Ploeşti, Romania, leads 179 B-24 Liberators carrying over 1,700 Americans and over 300 tons of bombs, on an 18-hour, 2,400-mile round-trip mission to destroy Nazi Germany's critical source of fuel. The plan, called TidalWave, has a large-scale attack with the bombers sweeping over Ploeşti low and fast—225 miles an hour at 30 to 100 feet above the ground—using delayed fuse bombs as well as other munitions intended to cause large fires and prevent the refinery from being used for months, even years. To get a sufficient number of aircraft for the mission, the 376th and 98th Bomb Groups of the Ninth Air Force are reinforced by the 93rd, 44th, and 389th Bomb Groups from Eighth Air Force. Launching from Benghazi, the groups maintain contact until three hours into the mission, when the lead aircraft carrying the primary navigator goes out of control and crashes. The plane carrying the second navigator goes down low to search for survivors and cannot return to the formation. Thus, the rest of the flight to the target will be done by dead reckoning. Over time, another 12 bombers abort due to mechanical trouble.

High cloud cover forces the formation to separate into two groups. The 58 B-24s of the 376th Bomber Group and the 93rd Bomber Group fly over the clouds, while Colonel John R. Kane's 98th Bomber Group, Colonel Leon W. Johnson's 44th Bomber Group, and the 389th Bomber Group fly through the clouds and are trailing the leaders by 15 minutes. The lead group becomes disoriented for a short period and arrives over the target from the south, where it is met by heavy antiaircraft fire. General Ent orders the bombers to move east, then approach from the north and attack whatever targets are available. As a result, the bombers of the first group begin to hit targets originally designated for the 44th and the 98th Bomber Groups. Within a short time, Colonel Kane's 98th, followed by Colonel Johnson's 44th and the 389th, fly in over Ploeşti at near-rooftop level as planned. The enemy is waiting and the antiaircraft fire begins to take a heavy toll on the formation. Even though it is clear that many of their assigned targets have already been bombed, Colonel Kane and Colonel Johnson decide to complete the mission, plunging through towering smoke and flames, not knowing what dangers lay on the other side.

Of the 179 B-24s planned for the mission, 165 actually attack Ploeşti. Antiaircraft fire destroys 33 bombers over the target and enemy fighters shoot down another 10. Casualties are heavy—532 airmen are lost. The rest of the bombers either return to Benghazi or are forced to land at other airfields. Nearly all of the aircraft that return from the mission are heavily damaged. Two targets attacked as planned are put out of commission for the rest of the war. The damage to the Ploeşti refineries ranges from total destruction of two targets to minor damage on other targets. Unfortunately for the Allies, the bomb damage does not seriously affect fuel production. The refinery was not operating at peak capacity before the raid, so idle capacity makes up quickly for the damaged areas.

The bombing raid on Ploeşti has required coolness, decisiveness, and, above all, courage. Five officers stand out in this action, the most highly decorated mission in American military history:

Major John L. Jerstad is the pilot of the lead aircraft in his group. Three miles from the target his airplane is badly damaged and begins to burn. Ignoring the damage, he continues toward the target as the flames spread through the aircraft. After dropping his bomb load over the target, Jerstad's B-24 crashes. Jerstad's heroic action to continue the mission regardless of cost and carry on beyond the call of duty will win him the Medal of Honor.

Second Lieutenant Lloyd H. Hughes is flying in the last bomber formation to attack the target. Approaching at the required low altitude, his bomber is seriously damaged by antiaircraft fire and leaking gasoline. The target area is already engulfed in flames, which means that Hughes would have to take his B-24 through the flames. Without hesitation, he flies into the inferno, holds his plane in formation at 30 feet, and drops his bomb load on target. The leaking gasoline from the wing catches fire and Hughes attempts to make an emergency landing, but the bomber is quickly engulfed and crashes. Second Lieutenant Hughes decided to complete the mission, even at the risk of his own life. His heroic sacrifice and dedication to duty will win him the Medal of Honor.

Lieutenant Colonel Addison E. Baker is approaching his target at Ploeşti when his B-24 is hit by antiaircraft fire. Although the aircraft has obviously suffered serious damage, Baker decides to continue to lead his formation. After dropping his bomb load early, Baker guides the bombers to their targets, even maneuvering between 50-foot smokestacks. Baker then leaves the formation and attempts to gain altitude, but the plane crashes soon afterward. Baker's sense of duty and dedication to the mission by exhibiting selfless leadership will win him the Medal of Honor.

Colonel John R. Kane leads the third element of B-24 Liberators over the target. Although separated from the formation to avoid cloud conditions over mountainous terrain, Kane continues the mission and arrives at Ploeşti to discover that another element has already bombed his assigned target. Kane's bombers fly through the heavy smoke of roiling oil fires and intense antiaircraft fire to hit the prescribed target. Kane's cool leadership, exceptional courage, and flying skill overcome an impossibly dangerous situation. Colonel Kane's exceptional devotion to duty wins him the Medal of Honor.

Colonel Leon W. Johnson leads the fourth element of the formation. Though the elements have become separated in the approach to the target and Johnson is lost, he joins the third element and continues to the target. Despite having discovered that his targets had already been hit by another element, Johnson decides to continue his attack in the face of heavy antiaircraft fire, enemy fighters, and the flames of the bombed refinery. Johnson's conspicuous gallantry in action, and intrepidity at the risk of his life above and beyond the call of duty wins him the Medal of Honor.

ITALY: Northwest African Air Force B-17s bomb Capodichino airfield.

SICILY: The remainder of the 9th Infantry Division arrives in Palermo. Northwest African Air Force B-25 Mitchells attack Milazzo.

SOUTHWEST PACIFIC AREA: U.S. submarine *Finback* torpedoes and damages a Japanese transport south of Borneo.

PACIFIC: U.S. submarine *Mingo* bombards Sorol Island in the Carolines. U.S. submarine *Steelhead* attacks the same Japanese convoy attacked by *Pogy* the previous day near Truk and damages an auxiliary vessel.

NEW GEORGIA: The 145th and 161st Infantry under command of the 37th Infantry Division capture Horseshoe Hill; the 169th and 103rd Infantry of the 43rd Infantry Division advance 800 yards without meeting opposition. The American ground attack is supported by 36 SBD Dauntless dive-bombers and TBF Avenger torpedo bombers. Thirteenth Air Force P-40s and U.S. Navy F4U Corsairs attack Munda, bombing anti-aircraft positions, ammunition storage dumps, and targets of opportunity. Kahili airfield on Bougainville Island is struck by 21 B-24 Liberators, 16 P-38 Lightnings, P-40s, and over 30 U.S. Navy aircraft. Japanese shipping off the island is attacked by P-40s and more than 80 navy aircraft. The 27th Infantry Regiment of the 25th Infantry Division arrives at Laiana.

August 2

ALEUTIANS: Eight Eleventh Air Force B-24 Liberators, nine B-25 Mitchells, and eight P-38 Lightnings hit Kiska and Little Kiska Islands in two separate attacks. Two naval task groups consisting of two battleships, two heavy cruisers, three light cruisers, and nine destroyers, bombard Kiska.

ATLANTIC: One B-24 of the 4th Antisubmarine Squadron (Heavy), 479th Antisubmarine Group, sinks German submarine *U-706* in the eastern Atlantic.

ETO: Eighth Air Force B-26 Marauders are sent against two airfields in France. Over Merville airfield, 31 B-26 Marauders hit the target; 16 bombers are damaged. Another 18 B-26s bomb the St. Omer/Ft. Rouge airfield; 13 aircraft are damaged.

MEDITERRANEAN: The 26th Infantry Regiment of the 1st Infantry Division assaults the key defensive position at Monte Basilio, holding it against powerful counterattacks for three days. Field Marshal Badoglio, through intermediaries in the Vatican, asks the Allies under what conditions can Rome be declared an open city.

General Eisenhower proposes a two-pronged invasion of Italy, using Montgomery's Eighth Army to cross the Straits of Messina, while U.S. forces land at Salerno.

Ninth Air Force P-40s attack shipping in the Straits of Messina. Northwest African Air Force P-40 fighters, B-25 Mitchells, and A-20 Havocs attack motor transport, storage areas, and roadways in northeast Sicily. Docks and shipping at Milazzo and Messina in Sicily are hit, as well as the area around Reggio di Calabria in Italy.

NEW GEORGIA: Thirteenth Air Force B-25 Mitchells, B-17s, P-40s, and U.S. Navy F4U Corsairs attack Bairoko harbor. Japanese supply points at Webster Cove are bombed by B-24 Liberators, B-25s, P-40s and U.S. Navy Corsairs. Motor torpedo boat *PT-109* is rammed and sunk by Japanese destroyer *Amagiri* in Blackett Strait; the commander, Lieutenant (j.g.) John F. Kennedy, and surviving crewmembers will be rescued.

NEW GUINEA: Fifth Air Force B-17s bomb supply dumps on the shore of Hansa Bay; A-20 Havocs attack Buiambun, and B-25 Mitchells bomb barges along the coast in the vicinity of Lae; B-24 Liberators bomb Lae harbor, Salamaua, and Voco Point. Fifteenth Air Force B-25s and P-38 Lightnings sink two Japanese motor torpedo boats off Lae.

August 3

ALEUTIANS: Eleventh Air Force B-24 Liberators, B-25 Mitchells, P-38 Lightnings, and P-40s attack a number of targets on Kiska Island.

ATLANTIC: PBM Mariner patrol bomber sinks German submarine *U-572* north of Dutch Guiana. TBF Avengers from escort carrier USS *Card* damage German submarine *U-66* near the Azores. PB4Ys (a B-24 variant) damage German submarine *U-60* in the South Atlantic.

ETO: Major General William E. Kepner becomes commanding general, VIII Fighter Command.

MEDITERRANEAN: Ninth Air Force B-25 Mitchells bomb the highway and town of Adrano; over 300 P-40s attack harbors and shipping at Milazzo and Messina. Northwest African Air Force A-20 Havocs conduct ground support missions; P-40s, A-20s, and B-25 Mitchells attack shipping in the Straits of Messina and Milazzo and attack enemy gun emplacements at Adrano and Biancavilla. U.S. destroyer sinks an Italian submarine off Tunisia. U.S. tanker in convoy KMS 20 (United Kingdom to Mediterranean) strikes a mine near Bizerte, Tunisia, and is heavily damaged.

SICILY: The 3rd Infantry Division attacks German defenses at San Fratello that control access to the coastal highway, but fail in an attempt to cross the Furiano River.

SOUTHWEST PACIFIC AREA: General MacArthur proposes his own outline of operations for an offensive in the Pacific. MacArthur proposes that the Philippines are the main objective of offensive operations. The capture of southern islands in the Philippines cuts the critical sea lines of supply to French Indochina and the Netherlands East Indies that the Japanese rely upon for raw materials. Capturing Mindanao and establishing airbases there will also allow a later attack on Luzon. Rabaul must be captured, not neutralized. The Admiralties also must be captured. MacArthur argues that no offensive will succeed without land-based airpower supporting ground and naval operations. The Vogelkop Peninsula and the Palau Islands need to be captured in order to protect the flanks of the main offensive thrust northward. MacArthur believes his forces can be invading Mindanao by early 1945.

NEW GEORGIA: Air and artillery attacks on Kokengolo Hill. A battalion from the 103rd and a battalion from the 169th Infantry sweep forward to Munda airfield. Japanese defenders on Bibilo hill stop the advance. Companies of the 145th Infantry gain the northern part of the hill, while the 2nd Battalion of the 148th Infantry cuts the Munda-Bairoko Trail.

August 4

ALEUTIANS: Over Kiska Island, three B-24 Liberators bomb through clouds, escorted by two P-40s. Two F-5As (photo reconnaissance P-38 Lightnings) take photos of

Main Camp and Little Kiska Island. This attack is followed by 48 B-25 Mitchells, 22 B-24s, 16 A-24 Dauntless dive-bombers, eight P-40s, and 40 P-38 Lightnings, which attack buildings and a gun battery. A radar-equipped PBY Catalina bombs the submarine base and main camp area on Kiska. A total of 153 tons of bombs are dropped on this day.

ETO: Eighth Air Force B-26 Marauders attack the shipyards at Le Trait, France; the 33 bombers hit the target without loss or casualties.

Mediterranean: Ninth Air Force P-40s attack shipping at Messina and conduct ground support missions. B-17s bomb the submarine base at Naples; B-26 Marauders and B-25 Mitchells bomb the railroad bridge at Catanzaro and railroad at Paola. In Sicily, P-40s, A-20s, and B-25s attack communication targets, gun positions, and logistics bases near Milazzo, Adrano, and Biancavilla and in the area near Bronte, Riposto, and Fiumefreddo. Other Northwest African Air Force aircraft hit rail sidings on the toe of Italy and attack shipping off the Straits of Messina. A U.S. destroyer is damaged by an Axis dive-bomber off Palermo, Sicily.

Sicily: The 9th Infantry Division, under command of Major General Manton S. Eddy, moves to Nicosia behind the 1st Infantry Division. The 3rd Infantry Division makes no progress against enemy defenses at San Fratello, suffering 103 casualties.

Southwest Pacific Area: U.S. submarine *Finback* torpedoes and sinks a Japanese army cargo ship south of Borneo.

Fifth Air Force B-25 Mitchells bomb and strafe the Itni River area on New Britain Island and hit several villages on Selaroe in the Tanimbar Islands.

Pacific: U.S. submarine *Seadragon* torpedoes and damages a Japanese transport near Ponape in the Carolines.

New Georgia: Thirteenth Air Force B-25 Mitchells and U.S. Navy Dauntless dive-bombers attack Gurasai-Kindu village area; P-38 Lightnings and P-40s claim 11 Japanese fighters downed in a series of dogfights over the central Solomons. U.S. motor torpedo boats engage Japanese guardboats off Kolombangara, sinking one and damaging another.

August 5

Atlantic: AAF Antisubmarine Command: The B-25 Mitchells of the 23rd Antisubmarine Squadron (Heavy), 26th Antisubmarine Wing, transfer from Drew Field, Tampa, Florida, to Edinburgh Field, Trinidad. German submarine *U-566* torpedoes and sinks a U.S. gunboat off Cape Henry, Virginia.

The Women Airforce Service Pilot (WASP) organization is formed under Jacqueline Cochran, director of women pilots. More than 1,000 women civil service volunteers are recruited and pass flight training to fly Army Air Force aircraft from factories to training bases.

ETO: The Eighth Air Force's 351st Fighter Squadron, 353rd Fighter Group, transfers from Goxhill to Metfield, England, with P-47 Thunderbolts.

Mediterranean: Ninth Air Force B-25 Mitchells bomb Francavilla and shipping in the Straits of Messina. Northwest African Air Force P-40s, A-20s, and B-25s attack troops, roads, motor transport, and gun positions at Adrano and Troina. They also sink or damage over 20 small vessels at Milazzo and in the Straits of Messina. B-17s bomb the docks and railroad yards at Messina. B-25s bomb a switching station in Sardinia, and P-40s, escorting the B-25s, attack and claim to have sunk a U-boat off Sardinia.

SICILY: The 3rd Infantry Division is stalemated at San Fratello, despite naval gunfire and artillery support. After conducting nearly 24 separate counterattacks against the 1st Infantry Division, German forces pull out of Troina at night. During one of these counterattacks, Private James W. Reese of the 26th Infantry Regiment is the acting squad leader of a 60 millimeter mortar squad. Reese maneuvers his squad forward to a position where he is able to direct fire on the enemy and break up the attack. Ordering the squad to take up a safer position, Private Reese moves forward with his mortar and uses his remaining three rounds to destroy an enemy machine gun position. Picking up his M-1 rifle, he then moves forward so that he can engage the enemy directly. He remains there, firing upon the enemy, until he is killed. His bravery, leadership, and complete determination to inflict the greatest damage upon his enemies win him the Medal of Honor.

PACIFIC: U.S. submarine *Pike* torpedoes and sinks a Japanese transport west of Marcus Island. U.S. submarine *Silversides* damages a Japanese minelayer off Rabaul.

NEW GEORGIA: Bibilo hill falls to American soldiers of the 145th Infantry Regiment. Munda is captured as the 3rd Battalion of the 172nd Infantry eliminates the last major Japanese defensive position.

NEW GUINEA: Fifth Air Force B-25 Mitchells attack barges near Madang and at Alexishafen, the Nuru River bridge, and towns of Bogadjim and Saidor.

August 6

CARIBBEAN: A PV-1 patrol bomber, PBM Mariner patrol bombers, and a B-18 Bolo medium bomber sink German submarine *U-615*.

ATLANTIC: JCS planners present an outline of operations in the Pacific from the present to the end of 1944. MacArthur's mission in the Southwest Pacific Area is to neutralize Rabaul and advance west along the north coast of New Guinea to the Vogelkop Peninsula. British forces will conduct an offensive in Burma to open the overland route to China. Forces in Nimitz's Central Pacific Area will attack to seize the Gilbert and Marshall Islands, and then advance to capture the Japanese naval base at Truk. An assault on the Palau Islands will follow. Airbases will be established in China to mount an air offensive against the Japanese home islands. The outline provides no direction for either SWPA or Central Pacific Area forces after accomplishing these objectives, nor are any details provided concerning how U.S. bombers will be supplied in China.

Operating as part of one B-25 Mitchell bomber of the 10th Bombardment Squadron (Medium), 25th Bombardment Group (Medium), and land-based navy aircraft sink German submarine *U-615* off Venezuela.

AAF Antisubmarine Command Headquarters of the 479th Antisubmarine Group and the B-24 Liberators of the 4th and 19th Antisubmarine Squadrons (Heavy) transfer from St. Eval to Dunkeswell, England.

ETO: Eighth Air Force's 352nd Fighter Squadron, 353rd Fighter Group, transfers from Goxhill to Raydon, England, with P-47 Thunderbolts.

MEDITERRANEAN: Hitler meets with Badoglio at Treviso, Italy. The meeting focuses on future plans and combined strategy. Secretly, neither trusts the other. In fact, Badoglio is awaiting word from the Allies in response to envoys he has sent to Lisbon and Tangiers to discuss surrender terms. Hitler has sent instructions to the German High Command to prepare plans for the capture of Rome, the seizure of the Italian fleet, and the occupation of northern Italy by German forces if the Italians surrender to the Allies or attempt to back out of the war.

SICILY: In Sicily, over 60 Ninth Air Force B-26 Marauders bomb Bronte, Catania, and Randazzo and the area near the Adrano-Biancavilla road; another 20 Marauders bomb road intersections in Adrano and Bronte. Over 100 P-40s attack shipping targets near Messina. Northwest African Air Force B-17s bomb coastal roads near Messina; B-26 Marauders and B-25 Mitchells attack road and rail transportation. A-20 Havocs and B-25 bombers hit transportation targets at Troina, Adrano, Biancavilla, Tortorici, Bronte, Piranino, and Randazzo. Other aircraft attack shipping in the Straits of Messina.

SOLOMONS: Over Santa Isabel Island, Thirteenth Air Force P-39 Airacobras and P-40s attack Tanagaba Harbor; 24 B-17s and B-24 Liberators, 24 B-25 Mitchells, and more than 50 U.S. Navy and Marine Corps F4U Corsairs, F4F Wildcats, and SBD Dauntless dive-bombers attack Japanese bivouac sites and supply points near Rekata Bay.

NEW GEORGIA: The Battle of Vella Gulf. Six U.S. destroyers of Task Group 36.2, commanded by Commander Frederick Moosbrugger, conduct a night attack on four Japanese destroyers attempting to bring troops and supplies to Kolombangara. Three enemy destroyers are sunk with no U.S. casualties.

U.S. submarine *Pike* torpedoes but fails to damage a Japanese aircraft carrier near Marcus Island.

NEW GUINEA: Fifth Air Force B-24 Liberators bomb Laha airfield on Amboina Island in the Celebes.

August 7

ATLANTIC: TBF Avengers from escort carrier USS *Card* sink German submarine *U-117* in the North Atlantic.

SICILY: Major General Lucian K. Truscott, commander of the 3rd Infantry Division, attempts to outflank the German defenses at San Fratello with an amphibious landing by the 2nd Battalion 30th Infantry, supported by tanks, artillery, and engineers, while the 3rd Battalion of the 15th Infantry and the 3rd Battalion of the 30th Infantry conduct a holding attack on the enemy's main defensive line. The Germans, withdrawing during the night, escape the threat to their rear. Ninth Air Force B-25 Mitchells attack Randazzo, while P-40s attack shipping at the Straits of Messina. Northwest African Air Force A-20 Havocs also attack Randazzo. P-40s and A-36 Intruders (Apaches) strafe and bomb small craft in the Straits of Messina, supply dumps on the toe of Italy, and vehicles and communication targets. In Italy, B-25 Mitchells and B-26 Marauders bomb railroad and highway bridges.

NEW GEORGIA: Thirteenth Air Force B-24 Liberators and B-25 Mitchells, plus nearly 30 navy aircraft, bomb the harbor and shore on Bairoko Island.

New Guinea: Fifth Air Force B-24 Liberators bomb Salamaua and Kela Village. B-25 Mitchells bomb Cape Chater airfield and Lautem on Timor Island.

August 8

Atlantic: TBF Avengers from escort carrier USS *Card* damage German submarine *U-262* in the North Atlantic, but *U-262* continues to attack, missing a U.S. destroyer, while *U-664* conducts an unsuccessful attack on the escort carrier.

Sicily: Ninth Air Force B-25 Mitchells bomb Randazzo area and P-40s attack shipping at Messina and provide ground support to Allied forces. Northwest African Air Force B-26 Marauders attack highway and rail bridges at Angitola, Italy, while P-38 Lightnings strafe trains.

Pacific: U.S. submarine *Salmon* torpedoes but fails to damage a Japanese vessel off the Kurile Islands. U.S. submarine *Whale* torpedoes and sinks a Japanese ammunition ship northwest of the Marianas.

New Georgia: Thirteenth Air Force B-25 Mitchells, with P-38 Lightnings, P-39 Airacobras, and U.S. Navy F4U Corsairs flying cover, bomb Vila and Buki harbors on Kolombangara Island.

August 9

Atlantic: TBF Avengers from escort carrier USS *Card* sink German submarine *U-664* west of the Azores.

ETO: Eighth Air Force VIII Air Support Command sends 72 B-26 Marauders to bomb the St. Omer/Ft. Rouge airfield in France. Because of heavy cloud cover, only one bomber hits the target. Nevertheless, 11 aircraft are damaged on the mission.

Sicily: Ninth Air Force P-40s attack shipping at Messina, Milazzo, and Palmi. Northwest African Air Force B-17s bomb a road intersection near Messina; P-40 fighters attack highways, rail transport, and gun positions. Over Italy, B-25 Mitchells attack the Catanzaro and Soverato River bridges, while B-26 Marauders bomb the bridges over the Angitola River. P-38 Lightnings attack targets of opportunity.

Pacific: U.S. submarine *Sculpin* torpedoes and sinks a Japanese merchant ship off Formosa.

New Georgia: An element of the 25th Infantry Division links up with Colonel Harry B. Liversedge's (USMC) Northern Landing Group (composed of the 1st Marine Raider Battalion and a battalion each of the 145th and 148th Infantry Regiments, 37th Infantry Division) at Enogai and assumes operational control of the marine-army force. Thirteenth Air Force B-25 Mitchells, followed by B-24 Liberators, bomb Vila on Kolombangara Island.

August 10

Aleutians: Eleventh Air Force P-38 Lightnings, P-40s, A-24 Dauntless dive-bombers, B-24 Liberators, and B-25 Mitchells bomb and strafe targets on Kiska Island.

Atlantic: Headquarters AAF redesignates Bombardment Groups and Squadrons (Dive) equipped with A-24s and A-36 Intruders (Apache) as Fighter-Bomber Groups and Squadrons, primarily because these type aircraft are not employed as dive-bombers.

The 14th Antisubmarine Squadron (Heavy), 25th Antisubmarine Wing, with B-24 Liberators, ceases operating from Langley Field, Virginia, and returns to Camp Edwards Army Airfield, Falmouth, Massachusetts.

MEDITERRANEAN: Ninth Air Force B-25 Mitchells bomb Randazzo, while P-40s attack shipping in the Straits of Messina. Northwest African Air Force P-38 Lightnings attack communication targets on the toe of Italy; other aircraft attack the straits, bomb Randazzo, and conduct ground support missions in Sicily.

PACIFIC: U.S. submarine *Salmon* torpedoes and sinks a Japanese merchant fishing boat near Sakhalin Island.

NEW GEORGIA: Thirteenth Air Force P-40s and P-39 Airacobras turn back about 40 Japanese fighters attacking engineers working on Munda airfield.

NEW GUINEA: Fifth Air Force B-24 Liberators bomb airfields in the Salamaua area. B-25 Mitchells hit Japanese barges near Lae. At New Britain, B-25s attack antiaircraft positions near Borgen Bay and A-20 Havocs attack barges and positions on Gasmata Island.

August 11

ALEUTIANS: Eleventh Air Force B-24 Liberators, B-25 Mitchells, A-24 Dauntless dive-bombers, and P-38 Lightnings attack Kiska Island. B-24s from Attu Island bomb an airfield on Paramushiru Island and a naval base on Shimushu Island in the Kuriles. The nine bombers report 40 enemy aircraft attacked them. They claim four confirmed kills, one probable, and four possibles.

ATLANTIC: TBF Avengers from escort carrier *Card* sink German submarine *U-525* near the Azores. German submarine *U-604*, previously damaged, is scuttled near Ascension Island.

MEDITERRANEAN: Northwest African Air Force B-17s bomb the marshaling yard at Terni; B-25 Mitchells bomb the Angitola River bridges, and B-26 Marauders and P-38 Lightnings attack a bridge at Catanzaro.

SICILY: German forces begin the evacuation of Sicily. On Patton's order, the 2nd Battalion, 30th Infantry, 3rd Infantry Division conducts another amphibious landing to cut off retreating German forces at Brolo. The landing force musters one LST (Landing Ship Tank), two LCI (Landing Craft Infantry), and six LCTs, supported by a battleship and six destroyers. There is no opposition, and the Americans advance to the dominant high ground of Monte Cipola and dig in. Although initially providing naval gunfire support, the ships move off once communications are lost. The battalion is quickly surrounded by German forces attempting to break through the defensive position that lies astride their line of retreat. Even though the Americans are supported with air and naval bombardment, the Germans are able to escape before the main body of the 3rd Infantry Division can link up. The battalion suffers 177 casualties. Ninth Air Force B-25 Mitchells bomb transportation targets near Randazzo. P-40s attack Messina, concentrating on shipping, transport, and troops. A-20 Havocs conduct ground attack missions in support of 3rd Infantry Division.

In the final stages of the Sicily campaign, Lieutenant General George S. Patton, Jr., commander of the U.S. Seventh Army, talks with a weary soldier of the 30th Infantry Regiment, 3rd Infantry Division, August 1943.

PACIFIC: U.S. submarine *Finback* torpedoes and sinks a Japanese auxiliary vessel bound for Singapore in the Flores Sea. Japanese submarine *I-11* torpedoes and damages a U.S. freighter near Espiritu Santo.

August 12

ALEUTIANS: Eleventh Air Force B-24 Liberators and B-25 Mitchells from Adak Island fly a number of sorties over Kiska Island. P-40s, P-38 Lightnings, B-24s, B-25s, and A-24 Dauntless dive-bombers fly from Amchitka Island to conduct bombing runs, while other B-24s, P-40s, and F-5As (photo reconnaissance variant of the P-38 Lightning) fly reconnaissance and photo missions over the island. A navy task unit consisting of two heavy cruisers, two light cruisers, and five destroyers bombards Kiska.

ETO: Eighth Air Force VIII Bomber Command targets manufacturing and synthetic oil production in the Ruhr. B-17s bomb synthetic oil production facilities at Bochum, Gelsenkirchen, and Recklinghausen. Of the 133 bombers that hit the targets, 23 B-17s are shot down and 105 suffer damage. German losses are reported to be about 30 aircraft destroyed. B-17s also bomb manufacturing plants at Bonn. Of the 110 bombers that hit the target, two are shot down and 70 are damaged. Enemy fighter losses are estimated at four confirmed kills. The raids are costly: Six crewmen are killed, 56 are wounded, and 253 are missing. Actor Clark Gable flies with the 351st Bomber Squadron on this mission. B-26 Marauders of the VIII Air Support Command bomb the Poix/Nord airfield in France. Nearly half of the 34 bombers that hit the target are damaged.

BOUGAINVILLE: Thirteenth Air Force B-24 Liberators, with P-40s and F4U Wildcats flying cover, attack Kahili airfield; they claim 11 enemy fighters shot down. U.S. losses are one P-40 and one Wildcat.

NEW BRITAIN: Fifth Air Force A-20 Havocs attack Gasmata Island and Japanese barges. A lone B-24 Liberator attacks Cape Gloucester airfield.

August 13

ALEUTIANS: B-25 Mitchells of the 406th Bombardment Squadron (Medium), 41st Bombardment Group (Medium), redeploy from Adak Island to Elmendorf Field, Anchorage, Alaska. The A-24 Douglas dive-bombers of the 515th and 516th Fighter-Bomber Squadrons, 407th Fighter-Bomber Group, will also redeploy from Amchitka Island to Drew Field, Tampa, Florida.

CBI: Fourteenth Air Force P-40s attack Japanese installations at Lungling, China.

MEDITERRANEAN: Ninth Air Force sends 61 B-24 Liberators on a 1,200-mile round trip to Austria to bomb the aircraft production facility at Wiener-Neustadt. This facility and the facility at Regensburg, Germany, account for nearly all the fighter aircraft produced for the German Luftwaffe. The same bombers had participated in the Ploești raid and are in poor condition; the bombing is largely ineffective. One bomber is shot down and one crash-lands in Switzerland on the return flight. German planes attack convoy off the coast of Algeria, damaging three U.S. freighters. The B-24 Liberators of the 67th Bombardment Squadron (Heavy), 44th Bombardment Group (Heavy), redeploy from Libya to England.

SICILY: Ninth Air Force B-25 Mitchells attack targets in Sicily and P-40s attack shipping at Messina. Northwest African Air Force P-40s, A-20 Havocs, and A-36 Intruders (Apache) attack shipping in the Straits of Messina. Despite the effort of the Allied air forces, the Germans move 15,000 troops, 1,300 vehicles, 21 tanks, and 22 assault guns to the mainland via ferries from Messina.

PACIFIC: Japanese Imperial Headquarters orders Japanese forces to withdraw from the central Solomons and consolidate forces for an anticipated attack from the Central Pacific area.

U.S. submarine *Paddle* torpedoes and damages a Japanese transport in the Sea of Japan. U.S. submarine *Sunfish* torpedoes and sinks a Japanese gunboat off Chichi Jima.

SOLOMONS: Japanese bomber and torpedo planes attack and sink a U.S. transport at Guadalcanal. Japanese submarine *I-19* torpedoes and damages a U.S. freighter near Espiritu Santo.

BOUGAINVILLE: Thirteenth Air Force B-24 Liberators bomb Kahili airfield on Bougainville Island.

NEW GEORGIA: Thirteenth Air Force P-40 fighters are the first to land on the reconstructed, U.S.-controlled airbase at Munda. After refueling, they conduct a sweep over Kolombangara Island.

NEW GUINEA: Fifth Air Force B-24 Liberators, B-17s, and B-26 Marauders bomb the Salamaua area, dropping 175 tons of bombs. On a night raid that covers 1,200 miles round-trip, nine B-24s bomb the oil production area at Balikpapan, Borneo.

August 14

ATLANTIC: Quadrant Conference. In Quebec, Canada, President Franklin D. Roosevelt, Prime Minister Winston S. Churchill, and their military chiefs of staff meet to discuss the primary operational objective of American strategy for 1944, the cross-Channel invasion of Europe, codenamed Overlord. The leaders approve the outline plan developed by the Combined Chiefs of Staff for use by the Supreme Allied Commander (COSSAC) staff and authorize preparations. Because the COSSAC planners are concerned about German fighter strength in western Europe interfering with the invasion, the combined bomber offensive against airfields and aircraft in France, Belgium, and the Netherlands is to continue with the "highest strategic priority." Although the Allies will continue offensive operations in Italy, they are clearly to be a low priority. An invasion of southern France as a companion to Overlord is to be planned, with the bulk of the forces for that operation coming out of Italy. The British agree to the U.S. timetable for offensive operations in the Central and South Pacific and recognize China's important role in American strategy; the Southeast Asia Command in the CBI theater will be formed. The idea of an Allied offensive into Burma is revisited. They agree that in early 1944, Chinese forces will advance from Yunnan into Burma, the British from India; the Americans with a Chinese-American force will attack from Shingbwiyang toward Myitkyina. The capture of Myitkyina will allow transport aircraft to fly the "Hump" route over the Himalayas easier and allow the Ledo Road to progress faster. With the overland route opened, 65,000 tons of supplies can be delivered to the Chinese. The plan to equip 30 Chinese divisions is quietly set aside. The program to establish airbases to put B-29s in China to attack the Japanese home islands will soon come to dominate all other support priorities in the CBI Theater.

In the Pacific, the Allies decide that Rabaul will be neutralized, not captured. The Japanese air and naval base at Rabaul is the centerpiece to MacArthur's Cartwheel campaign. This decision leaves the SWPA with what amounts to a holding mission while Nimitz's Central Pacific offensive takes priority.

The Allies agree that once Germany has surrendered, forces in Europe will be moved to the Pacific with the intent to defeat Japan within a year. With this conference, American strategic priorities and proposals now dominate Allied strategy.

MEDITERRANEAN: Ninth Air Force, using 61 B-24 Liberators from Eighth Air Force, bombs the aircraft production facility at Wiener-Neustadt, Austria.

The Italian government declares Rome an open city.

New Guinea: Fifth Air Force B-24 Liberators, B-17s, and B-25 Mitchells bomb the Salamaua area for a second day. A-20 Havocs strafe barges near Finschhafen. B-25 Mitchells bomb targets on New Britain Island.

August 15

Aleutians: Rear Admiral Thomas C. Kinkaid, Commander, North Pacific Force, launches Operation Cottage, the assault on Kiska Island. Major General Charles H. Corlett commands nearly 40,000 U.S. and Canadian troops, with full Arctic equipment, in the effort to capture the island from an estimated 10,000 Japanese defenders.

The 635th Bombardment Squadron (Dive), 407th Fighter-Bomber Group, operating from Amchitka Island, is disbanded and its A-24 Dauntless dive-bombers are transferred to other units.

Atlantic: The B-25 Mitchells of 17th Antisubmarine Squadron (Heavy), 26th Antisubmarine Wing, based at Miami, Florida, are reassigned from antisubmarine duty. The squadron will transfer to New Mexico and transition to B-24 Liberators. The squadron will be redesignated as the 855th Bombardment Squadron (Heavy) and assigned to the Eighth Air Force.

ETO: Eighth Air Force VIII Bomber Command attacks Vlissingen airfield in the Netherlands and the airfields at Amiens and Poix in France. The B-17s hit the targets, but 48 of the 147 bombers are damaged. Another 143 B-17s attack the airfields at Merville, Lille/Vendeville, and Vitry en Artois. Enemy losses are nine aircraft; U.S. losses are two bombers shot down and 11 damaged. The B-26 Marauders of the VIII Air Support Command also attack German airfields in France. Over St. Omer/Ft Rouge, 31 bombers hit the target and 18 are damaged. The marshaling yard at Abbeville is bombed by 19 B-26 Marauders and nine are damaged.

Italy: Northwest African Air Force B-25 Mitchells and B-26 Marauders bomb a railroad junction and marshaling yard. P-38 Lightnings attack rail lines, trains, and troops.

Pacific: U.S. submarine *Wahoo* torpedoes and damages a Japanese fleet tanker in the Sea of Japan.

New Georgia: The 35th Regimental Combat Team of the 25th Infantry Division lands on Vella Lavella Island under Brigadier General Robert B. McLure to establish a beachhead. The marine 4th Defense Battalion supporting the assault shoots down 42 Japanese planes. Fighters from Munda airfield are sent to cover the landings at Vella Lavella. The pilots claim that about 25 Japanese aircraft attempting to interfere with the landings are shot down. F4U Corsair pilots also claim 10 Japanese shot down over Kahili, Bougainville Island.

New Guinea: Japanese bombers with fighter escort attempting an attack are met by Fifth Air Force P-39 Airacobras, which claim 14 enemy aircraft destroyed. Three of the Airacobras are lost in the battle.

August 16

Atlantic: The 4th Marine Division, commanded by Major General Harry Schmidt, is activated at Camp Pendleton, California.

ETO: Eighth Air Force VIII Bomber Command attacks the Le Bourget air depot with 171 B-17s and one YB-40, escorted all the way to the target by P-47 Thunderbolts using drop tanks. U.S. losses are four bombers shot down and 46 damaged. Enemy losses are estimated at over 30 aircraft destroyed. The airfields at Poix and Abbeville are bombed by 66 B-17s. More than half of the aircraft are damaged. The VIII Air Support Command sends B-26 Marauders against the Bernay St. Martin airfield. Of the 31 bombers that hit the target, two are damaged. Another 29 B-26s attack Beaumont Le Roger airfield. Three bombers are damaged.

MEDITERRANEAN: Northwest African Air Force A-36 Intruders (Apache) and P-40s attack targets on the toe of Italy, concentrating on trains, trucks, railroad yards, and sidings. German torpedo bomber hits a U.S. freighter near Bône, Algeria, killing or wounding over 400 of the 1,800 Italian prisoners of war on board.

General Eisenhower issues a final plan for Operation Avalanche. He will use the Fifth Army, commanded by Lieutenant General Mark W. Clark, and the British Eighth Army, under Field Marshal Bernard L. Montgomery, to invade Italy. Montgomery will cross the Straits of Messina between September 1 and 4, advance up the toe of the Italian boot, capture Calabria and Taranto, and draw German forces south. As the Germans move to attack Montgomery, the Fifth Army will land at Salerno about September 9 to outflank the enemy. Salerno is chosen because it is closer to Montgomery's Eighth Army and it is within the limits of Allied air cover. From Salerno, the Fifth Army, composed of the British X Corps and the U.S. VI Corps, will capture Naples, the largest port in southern Italy and the large airfield at Capodichino in order to establish a base for further operations. Salerno's easy surf, 20-mile beach, and road network into the interior attract the planners' attention. The Salerno plain is dominated by mountains that resolute defenders can use to trap the invaders on the beach. The Calore and Sele rivers parallel each other, then join about four miles from the coast. This obstacle divides the plain into two sectors, limiting the support the X and VI Corps can provide each other. Capturing the Montecorvino airfield near the town of Salerno would support four Allied fighter squadrons.

SICILY: A regimental-size amphibious landing at Bivo Salica by the 3rd Infantry Division is useless, as the Germans have withdrawn and the remainder of the division is moving rapidly against light resistance. The 7th Infantry Regiment, 3rd Infantry Division, enters Messina. General Truscott meets the civilian leaders of the city, and General Patton formally accepts the surrender of the city. The Germans have evacuated 40,000 men, 9,600 vehicles, 94 guns, 47 tanks, nearly 2,000 tons of ammunition and fuel, and over 15,000 tons of other equipment. The Italians have evacuated about 75,000 men, 500 vehicles, and almost 100 artillery pieces with little or no interference from the Allies. U.S. casualties are 2,200 killed and 6,500 wounded. British casualties total 12,800. The Axis casualties are estimated at 29,000 and 147,000 prisoners. The Allies capture 70 tanks and over 280 artillery pieces. More importantly, over 100 aircraft are captured and 500 others are estimated destroyed on the ground. This is the first time the American forces fight as a separate army and they have proven themselves as a capable fighting force even in the face of British doubts about their abilities.

New Georgia: Thirteenth Air Force B-25 Mitchells, B-17s, and over 30 navy aircraft attack Vila airfield on Kolombangara Island.

New Guinea: Fifth Air Force B-24 Liberators bomb oil tanks at Balikpapan, Borneo. P-38 Lightnings and 32 P-47 Thunderbolts, operating for the first time in combat in the Pacific, intercept 25 Japanese fighters. Nearly half of the enemy aircraft are shot down.

August 17

CBI: Fourteenth Air Force B-24 Liberators bomb the barracks at Cau Lo, in French Indochina.

ETO: The Attack on Schweinfurt. Eighth Air Force launches a two-pronged attack into Germany. The 4th Bomb Wing with B-17Fs (a modified B-17 that can carry extra fuel for long-range missions) is to bomb the facilities at Regensburg where half of Germany's fighters are produced, then continue to North Africa. The standard approach for German fighters would be to attack the incoming bombers, then land to refuel and rearm in time to launch and attack the bombers on their expected return flight. The 1st Bomb Wing, following the 4th by 15 minutes, will pass over Schweinfurt to hit the four factories that produce more than half of the ball bearings for the German military. The plan is to catch the German fighters while they are on the ground preparing for the 4th Bomb Wing to make its return flight, leaving the 1st untouched over Schweinfurt.

At 1148, 127 B-17s begin bombing Regensburg at less than 20,000 feet. The 4th Bomb Wing loses eight bombers on the way in and another 14 on the raid itself. Over 50 bombers are damaged. Regensburg loses the equivalent of three weeks' production of fighter aircraft as a result of the accurate bombing. The bombers continue on to bases in North Africa. The 1st Bomb Wing arrives over Schweinfurt with 188 B-17s at 1459, more than five hours behind schedule. They find over 300 German fighters waiting for them after their fighter escorts drop off. German fighters shoot down 24 B-17s on the way to Schweinfurt. They approach from west to east over the target, the exact opposite track intended, which causes problems for the lead bombardier in locating the factories. In addition, the factories are protected by an artificial generator-produced fog. On the return trip, German fighters again assemble to harry the 1st Bomb Wing. The U.S. 56th Fighter Group with P-47 Thunderbolts comes to the heavy bombers' rescue over Belgium, shooting down 11 German aircraft in almost as many minutes. The wing loses 36 B-17s and over 120 are damaged. The damage to the ball bearing plants has no effect on production.

A total of 60 B-17s are lost in the fierce air battle; along with damaged aircraft, this represents 40 percent of the force dispatched. Crew losses are also heavy: Seven are killed, 21 are wounded, and 552 are missing. The bomber crews for the two missions together claim a total of 288 enemy aircraft shot down, 27 probable kills, and 99 possible kills. In reality, the Germans actually lose only 48 aircraft all together—36 shot down (mostly by fighters) and 12 damaged beyond repair. This is typical of the inflated reporting from gun crews on the bombers.

As a diversion for the Schweinfurt attack, VIII Air Support Command launches B-26 Marauders against two airfields in France. Over Bryas Sud airfield, 29 Marauders hit the target; two bombers are damaged. Over Poix/Nord airfield, 35 B-26s hit the target with 20 aircraft receiving damage.

During the night, the Royal Air Force begins Operation Crossbow, massive attacks on German V-weapon sites (from the German word *Vergeltungswaffen*—revenge weapons). The V-1 is a pilotless flying bomb launched from a ramp or by aircraft. It carries a 1,875-pound warhead, and uses a pulse jet engine guided by a gyroscope on automatic pilot. The entire missile weighs 4,800 pounds and travels at speeds near 400 miles per hour. At a predetermined time of flight, the fuel will be expended (usually between 10 and 125 miles) and the bomb will drop. Targeted at London, they are intended to cause terror

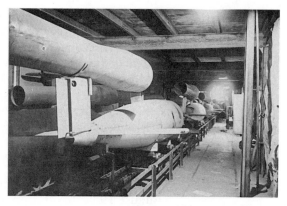

V-1s captured by the Allies *(Library of Congress)*

and weaken civilian morale. Once intelligence reveals that Peenemünde, Germany, is a main research and launching site, the British immediately launch 570 Lancaster bombers to drop 2,000 tons of bombs on the target, crippling activities there for more than a month, but 40 bombers are lost.

MEDITERRANEAN: Northwest African Air Force B-17s bomb Istres-Le-Tube airfield and Salon-de-Provence airfield in southern France. B-26 Marauders and B-25 Mitchells attack communication targets on the toe of Italy, while P-38 Lightnings escorting the bombers attack military vehicles.

NEW GUINEA: Fifth Air Force B-24 Liberators and B-17s make a predawn attack on Wewak and other smaller airfields and are followed by more than 30 B-25 Mitchells, with over 80 P-38 Lightnings providing cover. At Wewak, 100 Japanese aircraft are destroyed on the ground. The intent is to neutralize Japanese airfields in preparation for offensive operations against Lae. A-20 Havocs attack Japanese forces around the Salamaua area.

B-24 Liberators bomb the oil storage facilities at Balikpapan, Borneo.

August 18

ALEUTIANS: After three days of friendly fire casualties and evacuations for illness, the Allies find that there are no Japanese on the island. A U.S. destroyer strikes a mine offshore, causing over 100 casualties, including 70 dead.

The Eleventh Air Force since June 3, 1942, has destroyed 69 Japanese aircraft, sunk 21 ships, and damaged 29 others, with the loss of 29 aircraft.

ETO: B-26 Marauders bomb the Ypres/Vlamertinge airfield in Belgium. Every aircraft bombing the target is damaged, but there are no casualties. Over Woensdrecht airfield in the Netherlands, 32 B-26s hit the target; eight bombers are damaged and there are no casualties.

ITALY: Two U.S. light cruisers and four destroyers fire on the towns of Gioia Taura and Palmi.

PACIFIC: U.S. submarine *Plunger* torpedoes and damages a Japanese merchant ship in the Sea of Japan.

New Guinea: Fifth Air Force sends over 70 B-24 Liberators, B-25 Mitchells, and B-17s, with about 100 fighters flying cover, to attack Wewak and other smaller airfields. At least 28 more Japanese aircraft are destroyed. The Japanese have lost 75 percent of their air combat power in New Guinea in just 48 hours.

Near Wewak, New Guinea, Major Ralph Celi is leading his squadron in an attack on the Dagua airfield. Japanese fighters intercept the formation and concentrate on Celi's aircraft, which quickly bursts into flame. Disregarding the danger, Major Celi continues the attack, bringing his squadron down to make effective hits on the target. With the mission complete, Major Celi turns over command to his wingman before he is forced to crash into the sea. For his supreme act of courage and dedication to duty, major Celi is later awarded the Medal of Honor.

August 19
CBI: Brigadier General Howard C. Davidson takes command of Tenth Air Force.
Atlantic: Aircraft from escort carrier USS *Croatan* unsuccessfully attack German submarine *U-134* northwest of the Azores.
ETO: Eighth Air Force VIII Bomber Command attacks airfields in the Netherlands. With 175 P-47 Thunderbolts flying escort, 38 B-17s hit the Gilze-Rijen airfield; another 55 hit Flushing airfield. U.S. losses are four B-17s downed and 42 bombers damaged. The bomber crews claim about 30 German aircraft destroyed. The fighters report another nine German aircraft shot down. One P-47 is lost and the pilot is listed as missing. The VIII Air Support Command attacks two airfields in France: the Amiens/Glisy airfield and the Poix/Nord airfield. Against the former, 36 B-26 Marauders hit the target and have 10 bombers damaged and claim one enemy aircraft destroyed. Against the latter airfield, 35 Marauders hit the target with one bomber damaged and no casualties.
Italy: Ninth Air Force B-24 Liberators bomb the marshaling yard at Foggia, while P-40s fly coastal reconnaissance over the toe of Italy, bombing targets of opportunity. With P-38 Lightnings escorting the bombers, over 150 B-17s of the Northwest African Air Force also bomb the Foggia marshaling yard, while B-26 Marauders and B-25 Mitchells attack marshaling yards at Sapri and Salerno. Enemy losses are reported at 34 aircraft shot down. A-36 Intruders (Apache) attack the Catanzaro marshaling yard, while P-40s conduct sweeps over the toe of Italy to attack transportation targets.
Southwest Pacific Area: A U.S. Navy OS2N Kingfisher scout plane sinks Japanese submarine *I-17* off eastern Australia. U.S. submarine *Finback* torpedoes and sinks a Japanese auxiliary submarine chaser off the east coast of Celebes.
New Georgia: Thirteenth Air Force B-25 Mitchells, with fighter escort, attack barges off Vella Lavella Island. The Japanese continue to lose fighters to ground fire and air attack over New Georgia.

August 20
CBI: Army Air Forces, India-Burma Sector, China-Burma-India theater, is activated at New Delhi, India, under the command of Lieutenant General George E. Stratemeyer. The main component of this new command is Tenth Air Force. Fourteenth Air Force B-25 Mitchells bomb Tien Ho airfield at Canton. Fighters flying escort

report five enemy aircraft shot down over the target. Over Kweilin, 15 P-40s intercept 21 Japanese fighters. During the air battle, two P-40s and two Japanese fighters are shot down.

ETO: AAF Antisubmarine Command dispatches the B-24 Liberators of the 22nd Antisubmarine Squadron (Heavy), 479th Antisubmarine Group, to Dunkeswell, England.

ITALY: Northwest African Strategic Air Force B-26 Marauders bomb the marshaling yards at Capua and Aversa, while B-25 Mitchells bomb the Benevento marshaling yard.

SOUTHWEST PACIFIC AREA: U.S. submarine *Gar* torpedoes and sinks a Japanese transport in the Celebes Sea.

PACIFIC: Admiral Chester W. Nimitz, CINCPOA, submits an outline plan for an offensive against the Marshalls.

U.S. submarine *Pompano* departs Midway on her seventh war patrol and disappears. U.S. submarine *Plunger* torpedoes and sinks a Japanese cargo ship off the southwest coast of Hokkaido, Japan. U.S. submarine *Wahoo* torpedoes and sinks a Japanese merchant vessel near the Kurile Islands.

NEW BRITAIN: Fifth Air Force B-25 Mitchells strafe Japanese supply barges near Cape Gloucester on New Britain Island. Kiriwina Island airfield is operational. The Royal Australian Air Force takes control of the field.

NEW GUINEA: Fifth Air Force B-24 Liberators attack Boram airfield; the 46 P-38 Lightnings report 19 enemy fighters shot down. A-20 Havocs bomb Lae and the Salamaua area.

August 21

CBI: Fourteenth Air Force B-24 Liberators and B-25 Mitchells, escorted by 12 P-40s, bomb the docks and the airfield at Hankow. Over 50 Japanese fighters attack the formation. Two Liberators are shot down and 10 are damaged. Bomber aircrews and fighter pilots report 57 confirmed kills and 13 probables. In the Hengyang area, 19 P-40s encounter 33 enemy aircraft and shoot down five fighters. Near Changsha, nine P-38 Lightnings take on 12 enemy fighters and shoot down three of them.

ATLANTIC: Quadrant Conference Report to Stalin. President Roosevelt and Prime Minister Churchill send a summary message to Stalin advising him of the outcome of the Quadrant Conference.

> In our conference at Quebec, just concluded, we have arrived at the following decision as to military operations to be carried out during 1943 and 1944.
>
> The bomber offensive against Germany will be continued on a rapidly increased scale from bases in the United Kingdom and Italy. The objectives of this air attack will be to destroy the German air combat strength, to dislocate the German military, industrial, and economic system, and to prepare the way for a cross-Channel invasion.
>
> A large-scale buildup of American forces in the United Kingdom is now underway. It will provide an initial assault force of British and American divisions for cross-Channel operations. A bridgehead in the continent once secured will be reinforced steadily by additional American troops at the rate of from three to five

divisions per month. This operation will be the primary British and American ground and air effort against the Axis.

The war in the Mediterranean is to be pressed vigorously. Our objectives in that area will be the elimination of Italy from the Axis alliance, and the occupation of that country as well as Sardinia and Corsica as bases for operations against Germany.

Our operations in the Balkans will be limited to the supply of Balkan Guerrillas by air and sea transport, to minor raids by Commandos, and to the bombing of strategic objectives.

We shall accelerate our operations against Japan in the Pacific and in Southeast Asia. Our purposes are to exhaust Japanese air, naval, and shipping resources, to cut the Japanese communications and to secure bases from which to bomb Japan proper.

Roosevelt and Churchill reaffirm the unconditional surrender policy for the Axis powers. The Allies agree to reallocate seven divisions from Italy to Britain to prepare for the cross-Channel invasion.

ETO: AAF Antisubmarine Command dispatches the B-24 Liberators of the 6th Antisubmarine Squadron (Heavy), 479th Antisubmarine Group, from Gander Lake, Newfoundland, to Dunkeswell, England.

ITALY: Ninth Air Force B-24 Liberators attack a railroad station, marshaling yard, and air depot at Cancello Arnone. Northwest African Strategic Air Force B-26 Marauders and B-17s, escorted by P-38 Lightnings, bomb marshaling yards at Villa Literno and Aversa and report over 20 enemy fighters shot down.

SOUTHWEST PACIFIC AREA: SWPA planners identify a list of possible ground forces for an attack on New Britain. These include 1st Marine Division, the 32nd Infantry Division, and the 503rd Parachute Infantry Regiment.

August 22

CBI: Fourteenth Air Force P-40s bomb a supply depot, a unit headquarters, troops, and vehicles at Tengchung.

ETO: Eighth Air Force VIII Air Support Command B-26 Marauders bomb the Beaumont-le-Roger airfield in France. Of the 35 bombers that hit the target, one B-26 is lost and eight are damaged. Aircrews claim three enemy aircraft destroyed.

MEDITERRANEAN: All fighter and medium bomber groups of the Ninth Air Force are transferred to the Twelfth Air Force. This includes B-25 Mitchells of the 12th and 340th Bombardment Groups (Medium) in Sicily, the P-40s of the 57th Fighter and 79th Fighter Groups in Sicily, and the P-40s of the 324th Fighter Group in El Haouaria, Tunisia.

Northwest African Air Force B-26 Marauders, with A-36 Intruders (Apache) providing escort, bomb the Salerno marshaling yard. Aircrews claim 26 enemy fighters destroyed.

PACIFIC: U.S. submarine *Pike* torpedoes and damages a Japanese cargo ship near Yap. U.S. submarine *Plunger* torpedoes and sinks a Japanese merchant fishing ship in the Sea of Japan. U.S. submarine *Swordfish* torpedoes and sinks a Japanese cargo ship off Palau. U.S. submarine *Tullibee* torpedoes and sinks a Japanese transport west of Truk.

NEW GEORGIA: Thirteenth Air Force B-25 Mitchells and U.S. Navy SBD Dauntless dive-bombers attack supply barges on the coast of Vella Lavella Island.

August 23

CBI: Tenth Air Force B-25 Mitchells take out the center span of the Myitnge bridge in Burma using a low-level approach to the target.

MEDITERRANEAN: Ninth Air Force B-24 Liberators hit a marshaling yard at Bari, Italy.

Northwest African Air Force B-26 Marauders bomb the marshaling yard at Battipaglia, Italy. German submarine *U-380* torpedoes and damages a U.S. freighter en route from Sicily to Bizerte, Tunisia.

SOUTHWEST PACIFIC AREA: U.S. submarine *Grayling* delivers supplies to Filipino guerrilla forces on Panay.

PACIFIC: U.S. submarine *Paddle* torpedoes and sinks an Italian cargo ship off Hamamatsu, Japan.

NEW GUINEA: Fifth Air Force B-26 Marauders bomb Kela; B-25 Mitchells bomb Marawasa, Finschhafen, and Lillum Saun.

August 24

ALEUTIANS: Kiska Island is declared secured. About 140,000 troops will remain on the island for the next year, having absolutely no operational use.

CBI: Fourteenth Air Force B-24 Liberators and B-25 Mitchells, escorted by P-40s and P-38 Lightnings, bomb the airfields at Hankow and Wuchang. U.S. losses are four B-24s shot down and three damaged. Aircrews report 24 enemy fighters shot down.

ATLANTIC: Quadrant Conference ends. The Combined Chiefs of Staff accepts COSSAC's concept plan for Overlord and authorizes detailed planning. The British advocate a major campaign in Italy to keep German forces occupied in order to support a cross-Channel invasion, arguing that an advance into northwest Italy would allow the Allies to establish airbases to support the strategic bomber offensive. Unwilling to commit any additional resources to Italy and to ensure that Overlord is the priority of effort, Quadrant reaffirms a cross-Channel invasion for May of 1944, along with a simultaneous 10-division invasion of southern France. Objectives in Italy are designated as Rome and its surrounding air bases. After the fall of Rome, the Allies will advance as far as practicable.

President Roosevelt and Prime Minister Churchill issue a statement at the completion of the Quadrant Conference in Quebec. *"The whole field of world operations has been surveyed in the light of the many gratifying events which have taken place since the meeting of the President and the Prime Minister in Washington at the end of May, and the necessary decisions have been taken to provide for the forward action of the fleets, armies, and air forces of the two nations."* While the statement emphasizes Allied successes in recent months, it masks the British unease over the cross-Channel invasion and the American suspicion of British goals in the Mediterranean.

The CCS also approves a concept for offensive operations in the Pacific for 1944–45. In the Central Pacific, the intent is to seize the Gilbert Islands and then prepare to attack the Marshalls and the Carolines. Truk would be captured and used as an airbase. The Palaus would follow, with a move to capture bases in the Mariana Islands. These islands would be used to support the strategic bomber offensive against the Japanese home islands. The Central Pacific theater has the priority of effort primarily because capture of bases in the islands would support extended air operations, and most likely force the Japanese navy into a major battle to protect the home islands. Southwest Pacific Area objectives are New Guinea and the Admiralty Islands, to isolate Rabaul. Central Pacific theater has the priority of effort.

The Army Air Forces Antisubmarine Command is redesignated I Bomber Command and reassigned to the First Air Force as the Army Air Forces turn over responsibility for antisubmarine operations to the U.S. Navy. As a result, four antisubmarine squadrons (heavy) along the east coast are given new missions.

Aircraft from escort carrier *Core* sink German submarines *U-84* and *U-185* southwest of the Azores.

ETO: Eighth Air Force VIII Bomber Command attacks the Villacoublay air depot and airfields in France. The air depot is hit by 86 B-17s and 64 of them are damaged. One enemy fighter is claimed destroyed. Against the Conches and Evreux/Fauville airfields, 22 B-17s bomb the targets with the loss of one B-17 and 15 damaged. Two enemy fighters are reported as possible kills. The 85 B-17s of the 4th Bomb Wing, which had flown to North Africa after attacking Regensburg, Germany, on August 17, return to England by way of the Bordeaux/Merignac airfield. Three B-17s are lost over the target and two are damaged. Another nine bombers are forced to return to North Africa. The aircrews claim three enemy aircraft shot down. The VIII Air Support Command sends B-26 Marauders to fly two diversion missions for the VIII Bomber Command missions.

PACIFIC: U.S. submarine *Whale* torpedoes and damages a Japanese fleet tanker in the East China Sea.

NEW GEORGIA: The 3rd Battalion, 145th Infantry Regiment, 37th Infantry Division, captures Bairoko without a fight. The Japanese defenders evacuated the previous night to Arundel, Kolombangara, and Baanga. Thirteenth Air Force B-24 Liberators, with fighter escort, bomb Papatura Fa Island and attack the Ringa cove. P-39 Airacobras strafe barges off Choiseul Island.

NEW GUINEA: Fifth Air Force B-24 Liberators bomb Wewak and Salamaua, while B-25 Mitchells bomb Larat and barges near Wotap.

August 25

CBI: Fourteenth Air Force B-25 Mitchells, with fighter escort, bomb the Kowloon Docks at Hong Kong.

Admiral Louis F. Mountbatten is appointed Supreme Allied Commander, Southeast Asia Command (SEAC).

ETO: VIII Air Support Command attacks two targets in France. Against the power station at Rouen, 21 B-26 Marauders hit the target and have two bombers damaged. The Tricqueville airfield is hit by 31 B-26 Marauders. Two bombers are damaged and aircrews report one enemy aircraft destroyed.

ITALY: Ninth Air Force B-24 Liberators bomb the marshaling yard at Foggia, while 135 B-17s and 140 P-38 Lightnings of the Northwest African Air Force attack airfields around Foggia.

BOUGAINVILLE: Thirteenth Air Force B-24 Liberators with 24 fighters flying escort attack Kahili airfield.

NEW GEORGIA: Thirteenth Air Force B-25 Mitchells, along with more than 40 U.S. Navy SBD dive-bombers attack barge areas at Webster and Ringa Coves. Navy Task Group 34.4, covered by four destroyers, lays mines off Wilson Cove on western Kolombongara Island.

NEW GUINEA: Fifth Air Force sends nearly 100 B-24 Liberators, B-25 Mitchells, and B-17s to bomb the area around Hansa Bay. B-24s also attack Finschhafen. A-20 Havocs attack Gasmata Island off New Britain.

August 26

ALEUTIANS: Eleventh Air Force begins redeploying two heavy bomber squadrons (B-24 Liberators) and two medium bomber squadrons (B-25 Mitchells) to other duties in the continental United States.

CBI: Fourteenth Air Force B-24 Liberators, escorted by 17 fighters, bomb the Kowloon Docks at Hong Kong. A total of five enemy aircraft are reported downed. Over Tien Ho airfield in Canton, B-25 Mitchells, escorted by P-40s, take on enemy fighters. One P-40 is lost and five enemy aircraft are reported destroyed. The 449th Fighter Squadron, activated at Kunming, is established at Lingling and begins transition training with P-38 Lightnings. The squadron is under the 23rd Fighter Group.

ETO: VIII Air Support Command sends 36 B-26 Marauders against the Caen/Carpiquet airfield in France. One bomber crashes on the return landing.

MEDITERRANEAN: The C-47s of the 316th Troop Carrier Group, Ninth Air Force, are transferred to Twelfth Air Force. The USAAF and Royal Air Force units assigned to the Desert Air Force (DAF) are assigned to the Northwest African Air Force. B-17s and P-38 Lightnings of the Northwest African Air Force bomb Capua airfield. German submarine *U-410* attacks convoy UGS 14 (United States to Mediterranean, Slow) off the coast of Algeria, torpedoing two U.S. freighters, which later sink.

SOUTHWEST PACIFIC AREA: New Britain is the next target for offensive operations in SWPA. The objective is to seize the Cape Gloucester area and neutralize Gasmata, then establish control over the western half of New Britain to a point along a line from Gasmata to Talasea and from the Vitu Islands to Long Island.

PACIFIC: U.S. submarine *Tunny* unsuccessfully attacks a Japanese convoy off the Palau Islands.

BOUGAINVILLE: Fifteenth Air Force B-24 Liberators bomb Japanese destroyers near Buka Island, damaging one destroyer.

NEW GEORGIA: Thirteenth Air Force B-25 Mitchells and navy SBD Dauntless dive-bombers, escorted by fighters, attack enemy antiaircraft positions and barges at Ringa and Webster Coves. B-24 Liberators, escorted by fighters, bomb Kahili airfield on Bougainville Island.

August 27

CBI: Fourteenth Air Force P-40s attack a truck convoy between Sintsiang and Yoyang, destroying at least five vehicles. One P-40 is lost to ground fire. Another six P-40s attack targets of opportunity along the Japanese line of communication between Yoyang and Hankow.

ATLANTIC: TBF Avengers from escort carrier USS *Card* conduct an unsuccessful attack on German submarine *U-508*. Other aircraft sink *U-847* in the mid-Atlantic.

ETO: Eighth Air Force VIII Bomber Command Mission conducts its first raid on German V-weapons, in this case a launching site under construction at Watten, France. Escorted by 173 P-47 Thunderbolts, 187 bombers hit the target; four B-17s are lost and 99 are damaged. Aircrews claim seven enemy fighters destroyed. U.S. fighter pilots report eight probable kills with the loss of one P-47. The pilot is listed as missing. B-26 Marauders of the VIII Air Support Command bomb the Poix Nord airfield with no aircraft or personnel losses.

ITALY: Northwest African Air Force B-17s bomb marshaling yards at Sulmona and B-26 Marauders bomb the marshaling yards at Benevento and Caserta, escorted by about 150 P-38 Lightnings.

SOUTHWEST PACIFIC AREA: U.S. submarine *Drum* torpedoes and damages a Japanese transport north of the Admiralty Islands. U.S. submarine *Grayling* sinks a Japanese cargo ship off western Luzon Island in the Philippines.

PACIFIC: U.S. submarine *Pollock* torpedoes and sinks a Japanese cargo ship south of Kyushu, Japan.

NEW GEORGIA: The 172nd Infantry Regiment of the 43rd Infantry Division lands on Arundel Island, followed by the 169th Infantry Regiment from the 43rd and two battalions of the 27th Infantry Regiment of the 25th Infantry Division. Thirteenth Air Force P-39 Airacobras strafe barges and shore targets at Ringa Cove. Over Choiseul Island, 12 B-25 Mitchells, eight P-40s, and eight U.S. Navy F4U Corsairs strafe barges and shoreline targets at Kakasa.

NEW GUINEA: Fifth Air Force B-26 Marauders attack bridges in the Bogadjim area. A-20 Havocs attack barges and troops near Lae. B-25 Mitchells bomb the Dili and Cape Chater airfields on Timor Island.

August 28

ITALY: Northwest African Air Force B-17s bomb the marshaling yard at Terni. B-26 Marauders bomb the Aversa and Sparanise marshaling yards. B-25 Mitchells bomb the Cancello Arnone marshaling yard.

PACIFIC: U.S. submarine *Tarpon* torpedoes and damages a Japanese ship east of Shikoku, Japan.

SOLOMONS: Thirteenth Air Force B-25 Mitchells, P-40s, and U.S. Navy F4U Corsairs attack barges, personnel, and buildings on Sigolehe Island and Barora Ite Island.

NEW GUINEA: Fifth Air Force B-25 Mitchells bomb supplies and shipping in the Hansa Bay area. Several vessels are sunk in the attack. B-17s and A-20 Havocs bomb jetties at Lae and Voco Point and attack barges in Samoa harbor.

August 29

CBI: Fourteenth Air Force B-25 Mitchells, with fighter escort, bomb the airfield at Chingmen.

ETO: Major General William E. Kepner takes command of VIII Fighter Command.

ITALY: Northwest African Air Force B-17s bomb the marshaling yard at Orte.

NEW GUINEA: Fifth Air Force sends 35 B-24 Liberators, escorted by 44 P-38 Lightnings, to attack the airfields at Wewak and Boram. The Alexishafen and Bogadjim areas are attacked by 48 B-25 Mitchells and two B-17s. A-20 Havocs attack supply points on Gasmata Island off the coast of New Britain.

August 30

CBI: Fourteenth Air Force B-25 Mitchells bomb fuel storage sites at Owchihkow and Shihshow, while P-40s attack enemy gun positions. Four P-40s attack a ship convoy east of Hong Kong, damaging a freighter and two other vessels.

ETO: B-26 Marauders of the VIII Air Support Command bomb an ammunition dump near Saint-Omer, France. Of the 33 bombers that hit the target, 14 are damaged and three crewmen are wounded.

ITALY: Northwest African Air Force B-17s bomb Viterbo airfield. B-25 Mitchells bomb the marshaling yard at Civitavecchia, while B-26 Marauders bomb the Aversa marshaling yard. A-36 Intruders (Apache) bomb the marshaling yards at Sapri and Lamezia.

PACIFIC: U.S. submarine *Halibut* torpedoes and sinks a Japanese cargo ship in the Sea of Japan.

BOUGAINVILLE: Kahili airfield is attacked by 24 B-24 Liberators, along with 20 P-40s, P-39 Airacobras, and U.S. Navy F4U Corsairs. The Japanese reportedly lose 30 aircraft; six American planes are lost.

NEW BRITAIN: Thirteenth Air Force B-26 Marauders bomb Cape Gloucester airfield. B-25 Mitchells attack villages along the northwest coast of the island, bombing supply points and barges.

August 31

CBI: Fourteenth Air Force B-24 Liberators, with P-40s and P-38 Lightnings, attack Gia Lam airfield and a dike near Co Bi barracks in French Indochina. In China, B-25 Mitchells bomb Ichang airfield and P-38 Lightnings bomb the Yoyang railroad yards. Enemy ground fire shoots down one P-38.

ETO: Eighth Air Force VIII Bomber Command B-17s attack two air-related targets in France. The Amiens/Glisy airfield is hit by 105 bombers; three B-17s are lost and 36 are damaged. Enemy losses are reported to be five confirmed kills. Escorted by 160 P-47 Thunderbolts, 149 B-17s are sent against the aircraft plant at Meulan. Unable to see the target because of cloud cover, one bomber drops its bombs on a rail target near Rouen. The attack leaves 19 B-17s damaged with one crewman wounded. The U.S. fighters claim two confirmed kills on the enemy, but two P-47s are lost with both pilots reported as missing. VIII Air Support Command attacks three targets in France: the Rouen and Mazingarbe power stations; Poix/Nord and Lille/Nord airfields; and the fuel depot at Hesdin. Of the 104 B-26 Marauders that hit the target, one B-26 is lost and 13 are damaged.

ITALY: Ninth Air Force B-24 Liberators bomb the marshaling yard at Pescara and report nine enemy fighters destroyed. Northwest African Air Force sends 150 B-17s against the marshaling yard at Pisa, causing widespread damage to the target.

SOUTHWEST PACIFIC AREA: The 1st Marine Division in Australia is alerted to prepare to conduct operations on New Britain.

PACIFIC: U.S. submarine *Seawolf* torpedoes and damages a Japanese torpedo boat and sinks two cargo ships in the East China Sea.

Japanese submarine *I-20* torpedoes and damages a U.S. tanker near Espiritu Santo, New Hebrides.

CENTRAL PACIFIC: Task Force 15, commanded by Rear Admiral Charles A. Pownall, consisting of two carriers, one small carrier, one battleship, two light cruisers, 11 destroyers, and with the submarine *Snook* in support, bombs Marcus Island with TBF Avenger torpedo bombers, SBD Dauntless dive-bombers, and F6F Hellcats. TBF Avenger aircrews from the small carrier USS *Independence* report sinking three Japanese small craft.

NEW GEORGIA: Thirteenth Air Force P-40s intercept Japanese fighters over Vella Lavella Island, and claim five aircraft destroyed. P-40s also attack barges in Timbala Bay on Vella Lavella. Enemy gun positions and the radio station at Vila on Kolombangara Island are attacked by 22 B-25 Mitchells and 50 U.S. Navy aircraft.

September 1

CBI: Fourteenth Air Force B-25 Mitchells, supported by P-40s, attack a Japanese destroyer at Shihhweiyao, but cause no damage. Other P-40s attack vessels between Ocheng and Shihhweiyao, and troops at Ocheng on the Yangtze River. They also damage a small ship at Swatow harbor and strafe the nearby airfield. P-38 Lightnings and a P-40 attack a barracks and destroy locomotives at Yangsin, destroy a small steamer at Wuchang, a tug at Kutang, and attack a train and an antiaircraft position near Puchi.

ATLANTIC: The JCS allocates the 4th Marine Division and the 7th Infantry Division as ground forces for Nimitz's planned offensive in the Marshall Islands. The objectives of the offensive are initially designated as Wake, Eniwetok, and Kusaie.

The War Department begins recruiting for a specialized force of 3,000 American combat troops for operations in Burma.

MEDITERRANEAN: Twelfth Air Force takes administrative control of the Army Air Force elements of the Northwest African Air Force, which are transferred to the appropriate Twelfth Air Force organizations, although operational control remains with the Northwest African Air Force.

PACIFIC: U.S. destroyer sinks Japanese submarine *I-182* off Espiritu Santo, New Hebrides. U.S. submarine *Pompano* torpedoes and sinks a Japanese merchant vessel off Miyako.

NEW GUINEA: Fifth Air Force B-24 Liberators and B-25 Mitchells hit the Alexishafen-Madang area with its heaviest bombing attack to date—201 tons of bombs are dropped on the target. The C-47s of the 68th and 69th Troop Carrier Squadrons, 433rd Troop Carrier Group, arrive at Port Moresby, New Guinea.

September 2

CBI: Fourteenth Air Force sends 10 B-25 Mitchells, with five P-40s as escorts, to bomb shipping at Hong Kong.

ETO: Eighth Air Force VIII Bomber Command B-17s, escorted by 182 P-47 Thunderbolts, attack Mardyck and Denain/Prouvy airfields in France. Of the 34 bombers that hit the target, nine B-17s are damaged. Three P-47s are lost and five are damaged in a series of fighter sweeps. VIII Air Support Command launches 216 B-26 Marauders against five targets in France. Two are aborted due to weather, but 35 B-26s bomb the power station at Mazingarbe and 69 other bombers attack a fuel depot at Hesden. One B-26 is lost and 13 are damaged.

MEDITERRANEAN: First Air Force B-24 Liberators of the 1st Antisubmarine Squadron (Heavy), 480th Antisubmarine Group, based at Port Lyautey, French Morocco, begin operating from Protville, Tunisia.

ITALY: Twelfth Air Force XII Bomber Command sends almost 200 B-17s and B-25 Mitchells to bomb the marshaling yards at Bologna, Trento, Bolzano, and Cancello Arnone. Aircrews and escort fighters report 28 enemy aircraft destroyed.

SOUTHWEST PACIFIC AREA: U.S. submarine *Bowfin* delivers supplies and evacuates guerrillas from Binuni Point, Mindanao.

PACIFIC: U.S. submarine *Seawolf* torpedoes and sinks a Japanese cargo ship in the East China Sea. U.S. submarine *Snapper* torpedoes and sinks a Japanese escort vessel northwest of Truk.

NEW GEORGIA: Thirteenth Air Force B-25 Mitchells and U.S. Navy aircraft attack antiaircraft and artillery positions at Vila on Kolombangara Island. B-24 Liberators, P-40s, P-39 Airacobras, and navy aircraft attack the airfield and other targets surrounding the airfield at Kahili on Bougainville Island.

NEW GUINEA: Fifth Air Force B-25 Mitchells escorted by P-38 Lightnings attack shipping at Wewak harbor. Several ships are damaged and 10 enemy aircraft are reported destroyed. The ships are protected by barrage balloons, an unusual tactic by the Japanese.

September 3

CBI: Fourteenth Air Force P-40s and P-38 Lightnings attack the troop barracks at Pho Lu, in French Indochina.

ETO: Eighth Air Force VIII Bomber Command B-17s, with P-47 Thunderbolts escorting, attack German airfields, support installations, and industrial targets in France. The Romilly sur Seine air depot is hit by 100 B-17s; 28 hit the St. Andre de L'Eure airfield, and 12 bomb the Evreux/Fauvill airfield, a target of opportunity. German fighter losses are reported to be 11 confirmed kills; four B-17s are lost and 55 are damaged. Over Mureaux airfield, 38 B-17s hit the target and another 18 bombers hit a deception target made to look like an airfield near Dieppe. Two B-17s are damaged in the attack. The Caudron-Renault industrial area near Paris is bombed by 37 B-17s. Aircrews claim 15 confirmed kills on German fighters. Five B-17s are lost and 18 are damaged. P-47 pilots report four confirmed kills on enemy aircraft. Although one P-47 is lost and two are damaged, there are no casualties. VIII Air Support Command sends B-26 Marauders against the Beaumont le Roger, the Lille/Nord, and the Beauvais/Tille airfields.

MEDITERRANEAN: Italy signs an instrument of surrender, but the news is kept quiet; the Allies hope that it will give the Italians time to surrender and also forestall any German action to occupy Italy. Italy agrees to transfer its air and naval units to the Allies, withdraw ground forces from all battlefronts, and withdraw from any territory occupied by Axis forces. Eventually, nine Italian divisions will join the Allies.

The Germans will disarm another 43 divisions in France, the Balkans, and in Italy. The Italian navy, with six battleships 27 destroyers, 19 submarines, and eight cruisers, will join the Allies as well. The Germans sink one Italian battleship as it attempts leaves port. Another 10 destroyers and 10 cruisers, along with one partially completed battleship, fall into German hands.

ITALY: Ninth Air Force B-24 Liberators bomb the marshaling yard at Sulmona. Six bombers are shot down and aircrews report 11 German fighters destroyed. Twelfth Air Force A-20 Havocs, A-36 Intruder (Apache) fighters, and RAF light bombers bomb troops, airfields, gun positions, roads, and bridges throughout the toe of Italy in support of the British Eighth Army, which begins Operation Baytown with the crossing of the Straits of Messina. The British advance rapidly, facing little or no resistance.

PACIFIC: U.S. destroyer *Ellet* torpedoes and sinks Japanese submarine *I-25* northeast of Espiritu Santo. U.S. submarine *Pollack* torpedoes and sinks a Japanese transport off Mikura Jima. U.S. submarine *Pompano* torpedoes and sinks a Japanese cargo ship east of Hokkaido, Japan.

NEW GEORGIA: Thirteenth Air Force B-24 Liberators and U.S. Navy aircraft bomb Vila airfield on Kolombangara Island. P-40s strafe a wharf at Webster Cove. B-24 Liberators, P-40s, and navy aircraft attack Kahili airfield on Bougainville Island.

September 4

CBI: Fourteenth Air Force B-25 Mitchells and P-40s bomb the Tien Ho airfield at Canton. Aircrews report three enemy fighters shot down.

ETO: Eighth Air Force VIII Air Support Command attacks the marshaling yards at Courtrai Lille/Deliverance, St. Pol, and Hazebrouck in France with 144 B-26 Marauders.

PACIFIC: U.S. submarine *Albacore* torpedoes and sinks a Japanese gunboat southwest of Ponape in the Carolines. U.S. submarine *Pargo* torpedoes and damages a Japanese fleet tanker in the East China Sea. U.S. submarine *Sunfish* torpedoes and sinks a Japanese cargo ship southwest of Formosa. U.S. submarine *Tarpon* torpedoes and sinks a Japanese guardboat in the North Pacific.

NEW GEORGIA: Thirteenth Air Force B-25 Mitchells attack the area near Dulo Cove.

NEW BRITAIN: Fifth Air Force A-20 Havocs and Royal Australian Air Force aircraft bomb the airfield on Gasmata Island. P-38 Lightnings intercept enemy fighters and bombers and report 20 confirmed kills.

NEW GUINEA: Naval Task Force 76, commanded by Rear Admiral Daniel E. Barbey, lands 7,800 men of the Australian 9th Division in Operation Postern, about 18 miles east of the key Japanese base at Lae. Japanese aircraft sink one of the landing craft and damage a destroyer and two LSTs (Landing Ship Tank). Seaman First Class Johnnie D. Hutchins is serving on board an LST during the assault on Lae. The LST is hit by Japanese shore batteries and aerial attack as it approaches the beach. The LST's pilothouse is hit by a bomb, leaving the ship helpless. Hutchins, although mortally wounded in the attack, takes control of the wheel and uses the last of his strength to steer clear of an air-launched torpedo. He dies at the wheel, thinking only of saving his ship and shipmates. His courage and fortitude wins him the Medal of Honor.

Fifth Air Force B-24 Liberators and B-25 Mitchells support the Allied landings at Hopoi and at the mouth of the Buso River.

September 5
ETO: Eighth Air Force VIII Air Support Command attacks the marshaling yards at Ghent, Belgium, with 63 B-26 Marauders.

MEDITERRANEAN: The main body of the U.S. convoy for Operation Avalanche leaves Oran for Salerno.

ITALY: Twelfth Air Force XII Bomber Command sends over 130 B-17s to bomb the Viterbo airfield and Civitavecchia. B-25 Mitchells and B-26 Marauders bomb the landing grounds at Grazzanise.

PACIFIC: U.S. submarine *Albacore* attacks a Japanese transport south of the Carolines, launching two torpedoes that fail to explode. U.S. submarine *Swordfish* torpedoes and sinks a Japanese army transport north of New Guinea.

NEW GUINEA: Fifth Air Force B-24 Liberators and B-25 Mitchells bomb Nadzab and Lae airfields and A-20 Havocs spread a smokescreen over the target as C-47s of the 433rd Troop Carrier Group drop the U.S. 503rd Parachute Infantry Regiment at Nadzab near Lae to seize an airhead for the arrival of the 7th Australian Infantry Division. Japanese forces begin a retreat from Lae to Finschhafen, about 50 miles to the east. In the retreat, the jungle kills more Japanese troops than Allied firepower. Of the 8,000 that begin the overland trek to Finschhafen, 2,000 will die along the way.

September 6
ETO: Eighth Air Force VIII Bomber Command aims for industrial targets at Stuttgart, Germany. Cloud cover disperses the bomber formations, which then begin to attack targets of opportunity. The mission costs 45 B-17s lost and 116 others damaged. Aircrews report over 110 confirmed or probable kills on enemy aircraft. Casualties are two killed, 27 wounded, and 333 missing. Although 176 P-47 Thunderbolts fly escort for the B-17s, they are unable to stave off the German fighter attacks on the dispersed bombers. One P-47 is lost and pilots claim only one enemy fighter shot down. VIII Air Support Command attacks the marshaling yards at Amiens, Rouen, and Serqueux, France, with 192 B-26 Marauders. Six bombers are damaged over the targets.

ITALY: Twelfth Air Force XII Bomber Command sends B-17s against the airfield at Capodichino, the Villa Literno marshaling yard, the railroad facilities at Minturno, and the Gaeta harbor facilities. B-25 Mitchells and B-26 Marauders bomb Capua airfield and landing grounds at Grazzanise.

PACIFIC: U.S. submarine *Halibut* torpedoes and sinks a Japanese cargo ship east of Hokkaido, Japan, and torpedoes a heavy cruiser, but the warhead fails to explode.

U.S. submarine *Seahorse* is damaged by depth charges off the Palau Islands.

SOLOMONS: Thirteenth Air Force B-24 Liberators blast gun positions at Vila on Kolombangara Island. B-25 Mitchells and P-39 Airacobras attack enemy positions at Kakasa on Choiseul Island. P-39 Airacobras and U.S. Navy aircraft attack a radar site on Morgusaia Island and shoot down five enemy fighters; two P-39s are lost.

NEW GUINEA: Fifth Air Force B-24 Liberators and B-25 Mitchells attack Lae airfield and defenses in Malahang as Allied ground forces push toward Lae. Eight enemy aircraft are shot down over Lae. B-25 Mitchells fly a sweep against supply barges along the coast of New Britain.

September 7

ETO: Eighth Air Force VIII Bomber Command B-17s, escorted by 178 P-47 Thunderbolts, attack the Brussels/Evere airfield in Belgium and the V-weapon site at Watten, France. Of the 105 B-17s that hit the airfield, 11 bombers are damaged. Weather over the rocket site results in only 58 of the 147 B-17s dispatched hitting the target, and 39 B-17s are damaged. The fighter pilots report three enemy fighters as confirmed kills. One P-47 is lost and another is damaged. B-24 Liberators bomb the Bergen/Alkmaar airfield in the Netherlands. Only three bombers hit the assigned target; another 19 bombers attack a convoy off Texel Island. The VIII Air Support Command targets the Lille and St. Pol marshaling yards in France, but only St. Pol is hit due to confusion at the rendezvous point. The 81 B-26 Marauders that do bomb the target have two bombers damaged but suffer no casualties. Aircrews claim only one enemy fighter as a possible kill.

MEDITERRANEAN: Lieutenant General Lewis H. Brereton, commander of the Ninth Air Force, is directed to transfer his headquarters from Africa to Britain and reform his command in the European Theater of Operations by absorbing the VIII Air Support Command.

ITALY: Twelfth Air Force XII Bomber Command B-17s bomb outlying airfields at Foggia. B-25 Mitchells and B-26 Marauders attack road and rail bridges at Saptri and Trebisacce and roads at Lauria.

INDIAN OCEAN: Japanese submarine *I-27* torpedoes a U.S. freighter en route to Durban, South Africa, from Colombo, Ceylon, but its warhead fails to explode. The submarine surfaces and makes an ineffective attack with gunfire.

NEW GEORGIA: Thirteenth Air Force B-25 Mitchells bomb supplies and barges near Ringa Cove.

NEW GUINEA: Fifth Air Force B-24 Liberators and B-26 Marauders bomb the Lae area. B-25 Mitchells bomb and strafe targets on road to Markham. P-38 Lightnings flying air cover drive off Japanese bombers attacking Morobe. C-47s begin airlifting the Australian 7th Division to Nadzab. A-20 Havocs attack supply sites on Gasmata Island at New Britain.

September 8

CBI: Tenth Air Force B-24 Liberators mine the Rangoon River during the night.

ETO: The veterans of Ploești, the 44th and 93rd Bombardment Groups (Heavy), resume operations in-theater with the Eighth Air Force. VIII Air Support Command B-26 Marauders attack three targets in France. Over Lille/Nord airfield, 68 bombers hit the target and suffer no casualties, even though three B-26s are damaged. Another 68 bombers hit the Lille/Vendeville airfield and lose one B-26; 22 others are damaged. A coastal defense target at Boulogne is hit by 68 B-26 Marauders, with 26 of them returning with damage.

ITALY: General Eisenhower announces Italy's surrender just before Allied forces are to land on Salerno beach. "Hostilities between the United Nations and Italy have terminated effective at once." Due to a limit on landing craft, two divisions from the British X Corps, commanded by Lieutenant General Sir Richard L. McCreery, and one division from the U.S. VI Corps, commanded by Major General Ernest J. Dawley, will make the initial landing. Major General Fred L. Walker's 36th Infantry Division is chosen for the task. Three Ranger battalions, commanded by Lieutenant Colonel William O. Darby, and two British commando battalions are to guard the left flank of X Corps and seize the Nocera-Pagani pass. Two regimental combat teams from the 45th Infantry Division, commanded by Major General Troy Middleton, remain shipboard as reserve. The Allied force is 169,000 men and 20,000 vehicles.

Ninth Air Force B-24 Liberators bomb Foggia. About 130 B-17s of the Twelfth Air Force's XII Bomber Command hit Frascati. B-25 Mitchells and B-26 Marauders attack a highway at Lauria, and bridges at Trebisacce and Saptri. A convoy bound for Salerno to participate in Operation Avalanche is attacked by German dive-bombers.

NEW GEORGIA: Thirteenth Air Force B-25 Mitchells bomb the Vila airfield area on Kolombangara Island.

NEW GUINEA: In support of Australian ground forces, Fifth Air Force B-17s, B-24 Liberators, B-25 Mitchells, and B-26 Marauders bomb the area around Lae, while A-20 Havocs bomb Salamaua. U.S. destroyers bombard Lae. U.S. submarine *Drum* torpedoes and sinks a Japanese cargo ship off Hollandia.

September 9

CBI: During the night, Tenth Air Force B-24 Liberators mine the Rangoon River in Burma.

In China, Fourteenth Air Force B-25 Mitchells and P-40s bomb the airfield at Canton. P-38 Lightnings bomb the docks at Whampoa, and P-40s and P-38 Lightnings hit shipping on the Yangtze River and strafe targets of opportunity.

CARIBBEAN: German submarine *U-214* lays mines off Colon, near the Panama Canal Zone.

ETO: Eighth Air Force sends 330 B-17s and B-24 Liberators over France with an escort of 215 P-47 Thunderbolts in an attempt to bring German fighters into the skies so that they can be destroyed. The targets are German airfields. The Beaumont Suroise airfield is hit as a secondary target by 48 B-17s; two bombers are lost and 21 are damaged. Aircrews report 16 confirmed kills on enemy fighters. A total of 59 B-17s hit the Beauvais/Tille airfield; six B-17s suffer damage. The Lille/Nord airfield is hit by 37 B-17s; 10 are damaged and two crewmen are wounded. The Lille/Vendeville airfield is hit by 52 B-17s; seven bombers are damaged. The Vitry-en-Artois airfield is hit by 51 B-17s with no losses. The St. Omer/Ft. Rouge and St. Omer/Longuenesse airfields are hit by 28 B-24 Liberators; three bombers are damaged and one crewman is wounded. The Abbeville/Drucat airfield is hit by 35 B-24s with no losses; P-47 pilots report only one confirmed fighter kill. Two P-47s are shot down, with one pilot missing. VIII Air Support Command sends 217 B-26 Marauders to bomb coastal defense targets near Boulogne, France. Of the 202 bombers that hit the targets, three B-26s are lost and 26 are damaged. Aircrew casualties are 11 killed, eight wounded, and 19 missing.

ITALY: Operation Avalanche. The 141st and 142nd Regimental Combat Teams of the 36th Infantry Division land on the beach before Paestum and immediately take fire from German defenders. Reinforced by the 143rd Regimental Combat Team, the Americans fight through obstacles, mines, and sniper and machine-gun fire to advance to the foothills about five miles inland, forcing the defenders to withdraw. From these hills, the division controls the entire southern half of the Salerno plain.

A number of tanks from the 16th Panzer Division conduct counterattacks against the American beachhead but are driven off by close air support, artillery, naval gunfire, engineers, and antiaircraft guns, which are fired directly at the enemy. Infantrymen using grenades, rifles, and pistols stop several tanks. Elements of the U.S. 45th Division are sent ashore during the night to reinforce the 36th Division. The British X Corps, supported by naval gunfire, advances three miles against strong German resistance to the Montecorvino airfield just west of Highway 18 and has patrols in Battipaglia. The Rangers land unopposed at Maiori and the British commandos meet some opposition but overcome it and are moving into Salerno. The British and American landings, like the previous landing at Sicily, are essentially two independent operations. There is little coordination and a 10-mile gap lies between the two corps, marked by the Sele River. Nearly 130 miles away, General Montgomery orders a two-day halt for the Eighth Army, allowing German forces of the LXXVI Panzer Corps to move north to support the defense of the Salerno beaches. Ninth Air Force B-24 Liberators hit the airfield at Foggia; Twelfth Air Force XII Bomber Command sends over 100 B-17s to bomb bridges at Capua and Cancello Arnone. B-25 Mitchells and B-26 Marauders hit railroad bridges at Potenza and the landing ground at Scanzano. XII Air Support Command fighters maintain patrols over Salerno.

Sergeant James M. Logan of Company I, 3rd Battalion of the 141st Infantry Regiment, 36th Infantry Division, lands with the first wave at Salerno and advances about 800 yards inland when the Germans counterattack. The Germans have taken positions behind a rock wall and are firing on Logan's company. Sergeant Logan exposes himself to enemy fire to stop the initial advance, then runs 200 yards to reach the machine-gun position at the wall. He jumps the wall, kills the soldiers on the machine gun, then turns the weapon on the enemy until the ammunition is expended. He also succeeds in capturing an officer and private. Later in the morning, Sergeant Logan will singlehandedly clear a sniper from a house. Sergeant Logan's fearlessness and his inspiring actions will win him the Medal of Honor.

SOUTHWEST PACIFIC AREA: U.S. submarine *Grayling* is sunk in the South China Sea west of Luzon.

PACIFIC: U.S. submarine *Harder* torpedoes and sinks a Japanese cargo ship east of Honshu, Japan. U.S. submarine *Permit* torpedoes and damages a Japanese cargo vessel near Kwajalein Atoll. U.S. submarine *Pompano* torpedoes and damages a Japanese cargo ship east of Hokkaido, Japan.

NEW GEORGIA: Thirteenth Air Force B-25 Mitchells and U.S. Navy SBD Dauntless dive-bombers attack Vila airfield on Kolombangara Island. B-24 Liberators, with fighter escort, bomb Kahili airfield on Bougainville Island.

NEW GUINEA: Fifth Air Force B-25 Mitchells bomb and strafe coastal area from Alexishafen to Finschhafen and attack suspected supply points on New Britain Island.

September 10

CBI: Tenth Air Force B-25 Mitchells bomb the Gokteik viaduct in Burma. In China, Fourteenth Air Force sends 10 B-25 Mitchells and seven P-40s to attack warehouses near Wuchang and the docks at Hankow. P-40 pilots report nine Japanese aircraft destroyed. Nine P-38 Lightnings bomb the Whampoa docks.

ITALY: Salerno Beachhead. The Germans, with one division immediately available and two others arriving, are confident that the Allies can be driven into the sea. The expected arrival of the LXXVI Panzer Corps only reinforces that belief. The 179th RCT of the 45th Infantry Division lands and prepares for an advance toward Ponte Sele, near the area bound by the Sele and Calore Rivers. German aircraft conduct attacks on Allied ships in the Gulf of Salerno.

Ninth Air Force B-24 Liberators bomb an airfield at Foggia. Twelfth Air Force XII Bomber Command sends B-25 Mitchells, B-24 Liberators, and B-17s to bomb rail and road junctions and bridges to prevent the arrival of German reinforcements to Salerno. XII Air Support Command aircraft and RAF fighters of the Northwest African Air Force attack enemy road movement and cover the Salerno beachheads. B-25 Mitchells conduct a night bombing attack on communications centers at Corleto, Perticara, Auletta, and Saptri.

NEW BRITAIN: Fifth Air Force B-25 Mitchells bomb supply barges along the coast of the island.

September 11

ALEUTIANS: Eleventh Air Force sends 12 B-25 Mitchells and eight B-24 Liberators to attack Paramushiru Island in the Kuriles. Aircrews report one cargo ship and a transport are sunk, and a transport and two cargo ships are damaged. The bombers also attack structures and an antiaircraft position on Shimushu Island. Japanese defend the islands with 40 fighters. Aircrews report 13 enemy fighters are shot down and three more are probables. Two B-24 Liberators are forced to land in the Soviet Union, but seven B-25s and two B-24s are lost.

CBI: In China, Fourteenth Air Force sends 10 B-25 Mitchells and 11 P-40s to attack the docks at Hankow and the Wuchang cotton mills. A group of three P-38 Lightnings bomb supply depots at Tayeh and strafe warehouses and barracks at Yangsin.

ATLANTIC: German submarine *U-107* lays mines off Charleston, South Carolina.

ETO: Eighth Air Force VIII Air Support Command sends B-26 Marauders to attack the Rouen power station and the Beaumont le Roger airfield. Unable to attack the primary target at Rouen due to heavy clouds, 19 B-26s hit a secondary target, the shipyard at Le Trait. Fourteen bombers are damaged and one airman is wounded.

Over the Beaumont le Roger airfield, 32 B-26 Marauders hit the target. One bomber is damaged and four crewmen are reported killed.

ITALY: Salerno Beachhead. The 142nd RCT of the 36th Infantry Division advances toward the Altavilla hills, which dominate the Salerno plain. The 179th RCT of the 45th Infantry Division, with tanks and artillery, advances up Highway 18 to secure Ponte Sele and control the main corridor of advance into the U.S. beachhead. A German counterattack with tanks and infantry and supported by heavy artillery fire nearly surrounds the regiment and forces it into a defensive position. The 157th RCT is committed from the U.S. VI Corps reserve to attack and protect the 179th's vulnerable flank, but is stopped short by German troops near a cluster of five stone buildings known as the Tobacco Factory. A battalion from the 143rd RCT is shipped on landing craft to the British X Corps area near Maiori to stop a German attack.

Twelfth Air Force XII Bomber Command B-17s bomb the Benevento marshaling yard and bridge. B-25 Mitchells and B-26 Marauders attack lines of communication at Castelnuovo, Ariano, Mignano, and Isernia. U.S. and RAF aircraft of the Northwest African Air Force conduct ground support missions around Salerno. A U.S. destroyer is sunk by German motor torpedo boats and two light cruisers are damaged by radio-controlled bombs from German aircraft.

PACIFIC: U.S. submarine *Harder* torpedoes and sinks a Japanese transport south of Kyushu, Japan. U.S. submarine *Narwhal* torpedoes and sinks a Japanese transport northwest of Nauru Island. U.S. submarine *Spearfish* torpedoes and damages a Japanese army transport off Kyushu, Japan.

NEW GEORGIA: Thirteenth Air Force B-25 Mitchells bomb Japanese positions near Vila airfield on Kolombangara Island. B-24 Liberators also bomb the airfield. P-40s and P-39 Airacobras support SBD Dauntless dive-bombers in striking gun positions at Hamberi on New Georgia Island. Over Bougainville Island, 25 B-24 Liberators, with fighter escort, bomb Kahili airfield. Aircrews report seven Japanese fighters shot down.

NEW GUINEA: Fifth Air Force B-24 Liberators bomb Makassar.

September 12

CBI: In China, Fourteenth Air Force P-38 Lightnings bomb shipping near Hong Kong. Others attack Yangtze River traffic, and P-40s strafe a barracks and destroy a locomotive near Shihhweiyao.

MEDITERRANEAN: Ninth Air Force B-24 Liberators bomb Kalathos and Maritsa airfields on Rhodes.

ITALY: At Salerno, elements of two German divisions arrive to face the U.S. VI Corps. The 1st Battalion of the 142nd Infantry Regiment, occupying the key hills near Altavilla, takes heavy casualties and is driven off Hill 424. The 157th Infantry Regiment forces German defenders out of the Tobacco Factory. During the night the VI Corps commander, Major General Ernest J. Dawley, changes troop dispositions on his left flank to defend against a possible German counterattack from the British X Corps sector.

Twelfth Air Force XII Bomber Command B-17s bomb lines of communication at Mignano, Benevento, and Frosinone airfield. B-25 Mitchells attack roads and truck traffic at Ariano, Isernia, Castelnuovo, and Formia road junctions. U.S. and RAF aircraft of the Northwest African Air Force attack lines of communication around Potenza and Auletta, and fly ground support missions for the hard-pressed Fifth Army at Salerno.

German commandos led by Colonel Otto Skorzeny conduct a surprise glider assault on a mountaintop where Mussolini is being held at a ski lodge. The deposed Italian leader is whisked away to German-controlled territory and is eventually taken to Hitler's headquarters in East Prussia.

PACIFIC: U.S. submarine *Permit* torpedoes and damages a Japanese aircraft transport south of Kwajalein.

NEW GUINEA: Fifth Air Force B-17s and B-24 Liberators bomb Lae as the Australians advance. The Australian 5th Division captures Salamaua, while B-25 Mitchells strafe the area between Saidor and Langemak Bay.

American losses after landing at Nassau Bay in June in support of the Australian advance are 81 killed and 396 wounded, in a series of small-unit battles fought in the jungles where the enemy is usually within an arm's length. Disease and weather further weaken the troops.

B-25 Mitchells attack supply barges near Cape Gloucester on New Britain Island. A-20 Havocs bomb a radio station on Gasmata Island.

The neuropsychotic casualty rate for U.S. forces in the SWPA is 43.9 percent per 1,000 men.

September 13

ALEUTIANS: Major General William O. Butler gives up command of the Eleventh Air Force to Major General Davenport Johnson.

ETO: Eighth Air Force activates the 1st, 2nd, and 3rd Bombardment Divisions in England. They are commanded by Major General Robert B. Williams, Brigadier General James P. Hodges, and Major General Curtis E. LeMay, respectively. VIII Bomber Command's four bombardment wings are now redesignated as Combat Bombardment Wings (Heavy).

ITALY: At Salerno, General Dawley continues to reinforce his left flank with elements of the 36th Infantry Division, sending two battalions of the 141st Infantry Regiment and a battalion of the 143rd Infantry Regiment to defensive positions in support of the 157th and 179th Infantry Regiments of the 45th Infantry Division. The Americans are attacked by strong German combat formations with tanks and infantry. Two battalions of the 179th Infantry are driven back, opening a large gap in the lines. The 2nd Battalion 143rd Infantry Regiment is partially surrounded and suffers over 500 casualties. As the enemy advances south toward the beachhead, two artillery battalions, including the division artillery band, headquarters staff, and mechanics are turned into infantry to stop the advance. The two artillery battalions fire 3,600 rounds on the enemy and the attack is halted. The situation is so precarious toward the end of the day that Lieutenant General Clark orders the Fifth Army staff to begin planning to evacuate one of the two beachheads and consolidate British and American forces.

Two battalions of the 142nd Infantry attempt to retake Hill 424 supported by a battalion of the 143rd Infantry Regiment. The Germans are dug in and supported by artillery fire. Despite repeated attempts, Hill 424 remains in enemy hands.

Twelfth Air Force XII Bomber Command B-17s attack lines of communication at Torre del Greco, Sala, Consilina, and Atena Lucana. B-25 Mitchells bomb lines of communication around Pompeii, Castellammare di Stabia, and Torre Annunziata. XII Air Support Command A-36 Intruder (Apache) fighter-bombers destroy 25 to 30 vehicles near Potenza. U.S. and RAF A-20 Havocs and B-25 Mitchells of the Northwest African Air Force attack roads and vehicles around Auletta, Pompeii, Sala, Consilina, and San Severino Rota. More than 80 C-47s drop paratroopers of the U.S. 82nd Airborne Division south of the Sele River to protect the Salerno beachhead and reinforce the perimeter. A U.S. freighter is damaged by German air attack off Salerno.

At Altavilla, a company of the 36th Infantry Division attacks Hill 424. First Lieutenant Arnold L. Bjorklund, leading the first platoon around the right flank, encounters heavy machine-gun and rifle fire. As the platoon returns fire, Bjorklund crawls forward to within a few yards of a German machine-gun position. Using a hand grenade, he destroys the position. Taking fire from another machine-gun position, he moves forward and again, within a few yards of the enemy, throws a hand grenade and destroys the position. His platoon advances about 150 yards up the slope, but takes fire from a heavy mortar. Once more, First Lieutenant Bjorklund makes his way within 10 yards of the enemy and uses a hand grenade to knock out the mortar. Bjorklund's courage and dedication to his men will win him the Congressional Medal of Honor. During the same attack on Hill 424, the third platoon also encounters strong enemy resistance. Private William J. Crawford, without orders and on his own initiative, attacks an enemy machine-gun position, destroying it with a hand grenade. When the platoon's advance is stopped by two machine-gun positions, Private Crawford, faces intense fire to destroy both positions singlehandedly with grenades and rifle fire. His extraordinary courage and coolness under fire will win him the Medal of Honor.

PACIFIC: U.S. submarine *Permit* torpedoes and damages a Japanese fleet tanker south of Kwajalein. U.S. submarine *Snook* torpedoes and sinks Japanese army transport in the South China Sea, and narrowly avoids being sunk by an escorting destroyer.

NEW GUINEA: Fifth Air Force B-24 Liberators, with P-38 Lightnings flying escort, bomb airfields and ammunition dumps near Wewak. B-25 Mitchells bomb Lae.

September 14

CBI: Tenth Air Force receives A-36 Intruder (Apache) fighter-bombers from the United States to establish the 382nd Bombardment Squadron (Dive) at Nawadih, India.

Fourteenth Air Force B-24 Liberators bomb docks and shipping at Haiphong harbor in French Indochina. Three B-24s are lost and two are damaged. P-38 Lightnings severely damage two vessels on the Yangtze River at Chiuchiang, China.

ETO: Eighth Air Force VIII Air Support Command B-26 Marauders attempt to attack airfield targets in France and the Netherlands, but cloud cover over the targets aborts the mission. Of the 108 bombers involved, 18 B-26s are damaged. Three crewmen are wounded.

ITALY: At Salerno, the shattered 36th Infantry Division is retired from the front lines to reorganize, except for one company of the 143rd Infantry Regiment trapped on Hill 424, and two battalions of the 141st Infantry. A new defensive line is cobbled together from engineer units, tank destroyer units, and infantry units. The 45th Infantry Division holds the far left flank. German attacks on the 45th are stopped, and an enemy tank and infantry attack is stopped at the Calore River crossing by tank destroyers, naval gunfire, artillery, and infantry. The total artillery rounds expended during the day by the 45th and 36th divisions tops 10,000. The 180th Infantry Regiment of the 45th Infantry Division lands and becomes the VI Corps reserve. The British X Corps links with the 45th Infantry Division to close the gap between the two corps that has existed since the initial landings. About 2,000 men of the 505th RCT of the 82nd Airborne Division are dropped to strengthen the defenses. Another battalion of the 509th is dropped behind enemy lines in front of the British X Corps, but the troops are scattered away from their drop zones and have little effect. Of the 600 men who jump, 400 will return to friendly lines.

Ninth Air Force B-24 Liberators bomb the Pescara marshaling yard. Twelfth Air Force XII Bomber Command B-17s, B-25 Mitchells, and B-26 Marauders attack highways, road junctions, bridges, railroads, marshaling yards, and gun positions. Allied aircraft of the Northwest African Tactical Air Force conduct ground support missions.

A U.S. freighter is damaged by German air attack off Salerno.

SOLOMONS: Japanese aircraft attack U.S. airfields at Guadalcanal and at Barakoma and Munda on New Georgia Island. Thirteenth Air Force B-24 Liberators, escorted by army and navy fighters, bomb Kahili airfield on Bougainville Island. Aircrews report eight Japanese fighters downed. B-25 Mitchells and B-24 Liberators bomb Vila airfield and other targets on Kolombangara Island. P-39 Airacobras and U.S. Navy fighters and dive-bombers attack Ballale Island airfield.

NEW GUINEA: Fifth Air Force B-25 Mitchells attack Lae and barges in Hansa Bay.

September 15

CBI: In China, Fourteenth Air Force sends five B-24 Liberators to bomb a cement plant at Haiphong, French Indochina. The bombers are attacked by over 50 Japanese fighters, which shoot down four of the bombers. The aircrew of the surviving B-24 reports 10 enemy fighters destroyed. B-25 Mitchells, escorted by P-40s, attack a cotton mill near Wuchang, China.

ETO: Eighth Air Force VIII Bomber Command B-17s attack facilities in France. Over the Romilly-sur-Seine air depot, 87 B-17s hit the target and nine bombers are damaged. Over the Caudron-Renault industrial area in Paris, 40 B-17s hit the target; another 21 hit the Billancourt-Renault works, and 78 hit the Hispano-Suiza aircraft engine works in Paris. Aircrews report at least 12 enemy aircraft destroyed. U.S. losses are five B-17s lost and 33 damaged. B-24 Liberators bomb the airfield at Chartres. One B-24 is lost and three enemy aircraft are reported shot down. Five B-17s join the RAF on a night attack on the Dunlop factory at Montlucon, France. The VIII Air Support Command attacks the Merville airfield in France with 68 B-26 Marauders. All of the bombers return, but 27 are damaged and only two crewmen are wounded.

ITALY: General Bernard L. Montgomery's Eighth Army advance forces the Germans to begin a withdrawal that eases the pressure on U.S. forces at Salerno.

Ninth Air Force B-24 Liberators bomb the marshaling yard at Potenza. Twelfth Air Force XII Bomber Command B-17s bomb highways and rail lines. B-25 Mitchells and B-26 Marauders bomb highways and road junctions. XII Air Support Command and Northwest African Air Force fighters attack buildings, railroads, and highways in support of U.S. Fifth Army at Salerno.

PACIFIC: U.S. submarine *Haddock* torpedoes and sinks a Japanese collier north of Truk.

SOLOMONS: Thirteenth Air Force B-25 Mitchells bomb Vila airfield on Kolombangara Island and Kahili airfield on Bougainville Island. B-24 Liberators, with fighter escort, also bomb Kahili and Parapatu Point on New Georgia Island. The airfield facilities at Ballale Island are attacked by navy SBD Dauntless dive-bombers, supported by army, navy, and marine fighters. A U.S. destroyer and a PBY Catalina sink Japanese submarine *RO-101* near San Cristobal.

NEW GEORGIA: The 12,400 Japanese troops occupying Kolombangara Island are ordered to evacuate. A New Zealand brigade relieves U.S. Army forces on Vella Lavella, the initial transition to Allied forces occupying New Georgia.

NEW GUINEA: Fifth Air Force B-24 Liberators, with P-38 Lightnings escorting, bomb airfields near Wewak. Aircrews report 10 enemy aircraft destroyed on the ground and 14 others shot down. B-17s bomb the Lae area and B-25 Mitchells sink about 15 supply barges between Alexishafen and Finschhafen.

September 16

CBI: Fourteenth Air Force sends eight B-25 Mitchells with 12 P-40s flying escort against logistics targets at Liujenpa, China.

ETO: Eighth Air Force VIII Bomber Command attacks airfields and harbors in France. Escorted by 79 P-47 Thunderbolts, 79 B-17s hit the Nantes harbor and 52 B-17s hit the Nantes/Chateau-Bougon airfield. The bomber crews report over 22 enemy aircraft shot down, the fighter pilots report two confirmed kills and one possible kill. U.S. losses are severe: 7 B-17s lost and 48 damaged. La Pallice harbor, the La Rochelle/Laleau airfield, and the Cognac/Chateaubernard airfield are bombed by another 93 B-17s. Four bombers are lost and 22 are damaged. Aircrews report over 22 enemy fighters shot down. Five B-17s participate in a night attack with the RAF against the marshaling yard at Modane, France. VIII Air Support Command raids the Beaumont le Roger and the Tricoueville airfields with 67 B-26 Marauders. Two bombers are damaged.

ITALY: Lieutenant General Mark Clark and his staff establish Fifth Army headquarters ashore at Salerno, mostly in an effort to raise the morale of American troops. Two battalions of the 504th Parachute Infantry Regiment move to capture Altavilla and are held up by German infantry and artillery. Ninth Air Force B-24 Liberators bomb road junctions and a supply base at Potenza. Twelfth Air Force XII Bomber Command B-17s bomb bridges, rail lines, a marshaling yard, and trains around Benevento and Caserta. XII Air Support Command and Northwest African Tactical Air Force aircraft conduct ground support operations over Salerno.

SOLOMONS: Thirteenth Air Force P-40s and navy fighters support navy SBD Dauntless dive-bombers attacking the airfield on Ballale Island.

NEW GUINEA: Fifth Air Force B-17s, B-26 Marauders, B-25 Mitchells, and A-20 Havocs attack Japanese positions at Lae in support of the Australian attack. The Japanese later evacuate the area.

September 17
ITALY: Ninth Air Force B-24 Liberators bomb the marshaling yard and a road and rail junction at Pescara. Twelfth Air Force XII Bomber Command B-17s and B-26 Marauders bomb the Ciampino and Pratica di Mare airfields. B-25 Mitchells attack vessels at the mouth of the Tiber River. P-38 Lightnings conduct widespread dive-bombing missions against roads, rail lines, bridges, and targets of opportunity. XII Air Support Command and Northwest African Tactical Air Force aircraft bomb rail and road junctions, motor transport, and targets of opportunity.

September 18
CBI: Fourteenth Air Force sends four B-25 Mitchells and seven P-40s to attack rail and industrial targets at Shihhweiyao, China.

ATLANTIC: German submarine *U-260* torpedoes and damages a U.S. freighter in the mid-North Atlantic. The B-24 Liberators of the 12th Antisubmarine Squadron (Heavy), 25th Antisubmarine Wing, at Langley Field, Virginia, cease antisubmarine operations.

ETO: Eighth Air Force VIII Air Support Command B-26 Marauders bomb Beauvais/Tille airfield. Of the 25 B-26s that hit the target, 12 are damaged.

ITALY: At Salerno, the 45th Infantry Division encounters no enemy forces and advances to Persano. The 3rd Infantry Division commanded by Major General Lucian K. Truscott, begins landing at Salerno. Ninth Air Force B-24 Liberators bomb the marshaling yard at Pescara. Twelfth Air Force XII Bomber Command B-17s bomb the airfield at Viterbo. B-25 Mitchells and B-26 Marauders bomb the Ciampino and Pratica di Mare airfields. P-38 Lightnings strafe the airfields at Foggia and bomb roads, rail lines, and bridges.

PACIFIC: U.S. submarine *Spearfish* torpedoes but only damages a Japanese torpedo boat south of Kyushu, Japan, due to the premature explosion of two torpedoes. U.S. submarine *Trigger* torpedoes and sinks a Japanese cargo ship in the South China Sea.

CENTRAL PACIFIC: During the night, Seventh Air Force sends 24 B-24 Liberators from Funafuti Island and Canton Island to bomb Betio Island, Tarawa Atoll, and Maiana and Abemama Islands in the Gilberts. Navy Task Force 15, under command of Rear Admiral Charles A. Pownall, attacks the same targets with TBF Avengers, SBD Dauntless dive-bombers, and F6F Hellcats from fast carrier USS *Lexington* and small carriers *Princeton* and *Belleau Wood*. Thirteenth Air Force B-24 Liberators bomb the airfield and facilities on Nauru Island and Makin Atoll in the Gilberts.

NEW GUINEA: Fifth Air Force A-20 Havocs attack targets around Lae. B-26 Marauders strafe targets near Finschhafen. U.S. submarine *Scamp* attacks a Japanese convoy north of New Guinea, sinking a cargo ship. The C-47s of the 65th Troop Carrier Squadron, 54th Troop Carrier Wing move from Port Moresby to Tsili Tsili.

September 19

ETO: Eighth Air Force VIII Air Support Command targets the Lille/Nord airfield with 72 B-26 Marauders. Only 18 bombers hit the target and 10 B-26s are damaged. Four crewmen are wounded.

ITALY: Elements of the 504th Parachute Infantry Regiment, supported by tanks, capture Altavilla after the Germans withdraw.

PACIFIC: U.S. submarine *Harder* torpedoes and sinks a Japanese cargo ship off east Shikoku, Japan. U.S. submarine *Scamp* torpedoes and sinks a Japanese cargo ship north of the Admiralty Islands.

CENTRAL PACIFIC: From Funafuti Island and Canton Island, 20 Seventh Air Force B-24 Liberators bomb Tarawa Atoll and Abemama Island in the Gilberts and conduct photo reconnaissance of Betio Island and Tarawa Atoll. Japanese fighters shoot down one B-24.

NEW BRITAIN: Thirteenth Air Force B-25 Mitchells and navy SBD Dauntless dive-bombers, with fighter cover, bomb Vila airfield on Kolombangara Island and enemy positions on New Georgia Island.

NEW GUINEA: Fifth Air Force B-25 Mitchells and B-26 Marauders bomb Finschhafen as a preparation for Allied landings. B-17s and B-24 Liberators bomb the airfield and surrounding area at Cape Gloucester on New Britain Island.

September 20

CBI: The Fourteenth Air Force airfield at Kunming, China, is attacked by 27 Japanese bombers and 20 fighters. The attack causes little damage as 24 P-40s and three P-38 Lightnings intercept and attack the enemy formation, reporting 17 aircraft destroyed. One U.S. fighter is lost.

ATLANTIC: German submarine *U-238* attacks New York-bound convoy ON 202 (Liverpool to New York, Fast), torpedoing and sinking one U.S. freighter and forcing another to be abandoned in the mid-North Atlantic. *U-645* later finishes off the abandoned freighter.

ITALY: At Salerno, Lieutenant General Mark Clark, disappointed with Major General Dawley's performance during the crisis on the Salerno beaches, relieves him as VI Corps commander in favor of Major General John P. Lucas. The 36th Infantry Division is allowed to rest and refit as the corps reserve. The 3rd Infantry Division and the 45th Infantry Division enter the mountains in pursuit of the retreating Germans. The 3rd Division takes Highway 7, the 45th Division takes Highway 91. Ninth Air Force B-24 Liberators of the 98th and 376th Bombardment Groups (Heavy) are transferred to the Twelfth Air Force after raiding marshaling yards at Castelfranco Veneto and Pescara. Twelfth Air Force XII Bomber Command B-17s and B-26 Marauders bomb the Castelnuovo road junction, and roads and railroad near Sarno. XII Air Support Command A-36 Intruder (Apache) fighter-bombers attack enemy tank and troop concentrations forming near Nocera. Allied aircraft of the Northwest African Tactical Air Force attack enemy troop movements in the area around Naples and Benevento.

PACIFIC: U.S. submarine *Haddock* torpedoes and damages a Japanese fleet tanker east of the Palaus. U.S. submarine *S-28* torpedoes and sinks a Japanese gunboat off the Kuriles.

New Guinea: Fifth Air Force B-24 Liberators bomb Wewak and Boram airfields. B-25 Mitchells bomb Penfoei on Timor Island.

September 21

CBI: Fourteenth Air Force sends eight B-25 Mitchells and eight P-40s to attack railroad yards and warehouses at Chiuchiang, China.

ETO: Eighth Air Force VIII Air Support Command attacks the Beauvais/Tille airfield in France, but bad weather limits the effectiveness of the 44 B-26 Marauders that make it over the target. One enemy aircraft is reported destroyed and one B-26 is lost and 13 are damaged.

Mediterranean: Ninth Air Force IX Fighter Command headquarters at Tripoli, Libya, is inactivated. It will move to Middle Wallop, in England. German submarine *U-238* torpedoes and damages a U.S. freighter in a convoy bound for Salerno. The ship later sinks despite efforts to save her.

Italy: The 133rd Infantry Regiment of the 34th Infantry Division arrives at Salerno to reinforce VI Corps.

Twelfth Air Force XII Bomber Command B-17s bomb a bridge and the approaches to Benevento. B-25 Mitchells and B-26 Marauders bomb bridges at Cancello Arnone and Capua. B-24 Liberators on detached service from the Eighth Air Force bomb Leghorn and Bastia. B-25 Mitchells and A-36 Intruder (Apache) fighter-bombers of the Northwest African Air Force and XII Air Support Command attack enemy troop concentrations, trucks, tanks, and targets of opportunity near Solofra, Avellino, and Benevento.

Indian Ocean: German submarine *U-188* torpedoes a U.S. freighter off the Horn of Africa. The U-boat confidently surfaces to finish off the ship with gunfire, but encounters a crew fully armed and ready to fight. The accurate fire forces the U-boat to submerge and attack with torpedoes. The crew finally abandons ship.

Pacific: U.S. submarine *Haddock* torpedoes and sinks a Japanese collier northwest of Truk. U.S. submarine *Trigger* torpedoes and sinks two Japanese fleet oilers and damages another and sinks a cargo ship north of Formosa. U.S. submarine *Wahoo* torpedoes and sinks a Japanese merchant fishing vessel northeast of Hokkaido, Japan.

New Georgia: Thirteenth Air Force B-24 Liberators bomb the airfield on Buka Island. Two Japanese fighters are reported shot down in the attack.

New Guinea: Fifth Air Force A-20 Havocs, B-26 Marauders, and Australian aircraft attack Tami Island and bomb Finschhafen. B-25 Mitchells bomb and strafe the Bogadjim area and Langgoer. B-24 Liberators attack Cape Gloucester and a freighter near Talasea on New Britain and sink a transport southeast of the Admiralties. A-20 Havocs and Australian aircraft bomb Gasmata Island.

September 22

ETO: Eighth Air Force VIII Air Support Command attacks the Evreux/Fauville airfield with 70 B-26 Marauders. There are no losses or casualties. A fighter sweep over northeast France and Belgium by 240 P-47 Thunderbolts results in one fighter lost and another damaged; two enemy fighters are reported destroyed. Another 155 P-47 Thunderbolts sweep over northern Belgium and the coastal islands of the

Netherlands. VIII Bomber Command sends five B-17s with the RAF in a night raid on the city of Hannover, Germany.

MEDITERRANEAN: The Ninth Air Force IX Bomber Command B-24 Liberators are transferred to the Twelfth Air Force.

ITALY: The 30th Infantry Regiment of the 3rd Infantry Division captures Acerno after a strong defense by German infantry supported by self-propelled guns. The 180th Infantry Regiment of the 45th Infantry Division, with tank support, captures Oliveto. The 36th Engineer Regiment (Combat) follows the divisions, performing near-miracles in repairing bridges and roads destroyed by the retreating Germans.

Twelfth Air Force XII Bomber Command B-25 Mitchells and B-26 Marauders bomb roads, railroads, and bridges near Grottaminarda; XII Air Support Command aircraft attack troop concentrations, tanks, and trucks in the Foggia area, and the landing ground at Capua.

PACIFIC: U.S. submarine *Harder* torpedoes and sinks a Japanese merchant tanker and cargo ship east of Honshu, Japan. U.S. submarine *Hoe* torpedoes and sinks a Japanese fleet tanker east of Guam. U.S. submarine *Snook* torpedoes and sinks one Japanese cargo ship in the Yellow Sea and damages another. U.S. submarine *Trigger* torpedoes and damages a Japanese cargo ship in the East China Sea.

SOUTH PACIFIC: The planned landings on New Britain are postponed until December 26. Admiral William F. Halsey, COMSOPAC, requests a study on the possibility of landing at Empress Augusta Bay on Bougainville Island. Rear Admiral Theodore S. Wilkinson is named the commander of the planned offensive.

NEW GUINEA: Elements of the Australian 9th Division land at the mouth of the Song River north of Finschhafen. The Japanese occupy the Satelberg Ridge, which covers the approaches to Finschhafen. Fifth Air Force B-25 Mitchells bomb enemy defenses near Finschhafen. A-20 Havocs and B-25 Mitchells bomb the Lae area. The Japanese reportedly lose 38 aircraft to Allied fighters. B-24 Liberators and B-25 Mitchells bomb the airfield on Gasmata Island off New Britain. B-24 Liberators bomb Amboina Island in the Moluccas.

September 23

ALEUTIANS: Eleventh Air Force comes under the operational control of Commander Northern Pacific (COMNORPAC) Forces.

ATLANTIC: German submarine *U-952* torpedoes and sinks a U.S. freighter in convoy ONS 202 (Liverpool to Halifax, slow) off Newfoundland.

ETO: Eighth Air Force VIII Bomber Command B-17s attack the Nantes port area, the Vannes/Meucon airfield, and the Kerlin/Bastard airfield in France during the morning. Over Nantes, 43 of the 46 bombers that hit the target are damaged. Aircrews report at least 22 enemy aircraft destroyed. At Vannes/Meucon airfield, 55 bombers hit the target and seven B-17s are damaged. The 53 B-17s that hit the Kerlin/Bastard airfield lose one bomber and 10 others are damaged. Two enemy aircraft are reported destroyed. Later in the evening the Nantes port area is hit again by 61 B-17s and the Rennes/St. Jacques airfield is hit by 19 B-17s. Two B-17s are lost and 18 are damaged. Four of five B-17s accompany the RAF on a night raid on Mannheim, Germany. One B-17 is damaged in the attack.

ITALY: Twelfth Air Force XII Bomber Command B-26 Marauders bomb bridges near Capua. XII Air Support Command aircraft attack motor transport, roads, railroads, gun positions, and targets of opportunity in the mountains north and west of Salerno.

Corporal James D. Slaton, 157th Infantry Regiment, 45th Infantry Division, is the lead scout of an infantry squad with the mission of outflanking a German position, that has been holding the advance of two platoons near Oliveto. Moving ahead of his squad, Corporal Slaton approaches an enemy machine-gun position and uses his bayonet to kill the gunner. Unable to remove the bayonet from the body, he detaches it, then kills the other gunner with rifle fire. When he begins taking fire from another machine-gun position, Corporal Slaton attacks over open ground and destroys it with a hand grenade. When a third machine-gun position engages him, Corporal Slaton fires his rifle to kill the two gunners. Corporal Slaton stands alone until he is able to withdraw under the cover of friendly mortar fire. Slaton's tremendous courage and skills as a soldier win him the Medal of Honor.

SOUTHWEST PACIFIC AREA: Fifth Air Force P-40s bomb Gasmata Island off New Britain.

PACIFIC: U.S. submarine *Trout* torpedoes and sinks a Japanese transport and a cargo ship northwest of the Marianas. U.S. submarine *Tuna* torpedoes and attacks a Japanese cargo vessel east of Malaya.

SOLOMONS: The new commander of COMAIRSOLS is Brigadier General James T. Moore, relieving Brigadier General Francis Mulcahy. Moore takes command of 314 fighters and 317 bombers from the Royal New Zealand Air Force, Thirteenth Air Force bombers, and the 1st and 2nd Marine Air Wings. Most are located at Guadalcanal, but will redeploy to Munda and Vella Lavella airfields after New Georgia is secure.

BOUGAINVILLE: Thirteenth Air Force sends 23 B-24 Liberators, with 16 P-38 Lightnings and over 60 SBD Dauntless dive-bombers, to attack Kahili on Bougainville Island. It is reported that nine enemy fighters are shot down. Another 21 B-24 Liberators conduct a bombing raid on Kolombangara Island. U.S. submarine *Gato* lands a reconnaissance team off the northwest coast of the island to look for possible landing sites, while the *Guardfish* does the same for a team examining Empress Augusta Bay.

NEW GEORGIA: Barakoma airfield on Vella Lavella is operational.

September 24
ETO: Eighth Air Force VIII Air Support Command B-26 Marauders bomb the Evreux/Fauville airfield and the Beauvais/Tille airfield in France. Of the 71 B-26s that hit Evreux/Fauville airfield four bombers are damaged; aircrews claim one probable enemy fighter kill. Of the 66 B-26s that hit Beauvais/Tille airfield, 17 are damaged.

ITALY: Twelfth Air Force XII Bomber Command B-25 Mitchells and B-26 Marauders bomb roads, railways, and bridges, at Grottaminarda, Benevento, Avellino, and Capua.

INDIAN OCEAN: Japanese submarine *I-10* torpedoes and sinks a U.S. freighter southeast of Aden.

PACIFIC: U.S. submarine *Cabrilla* torpedoes and damages the Japanese carrier *Taiyo* northwest of Chichi Jima. The submarine fires six torpedoes at the carrier; three hit, but only one explodes. The *Taiyo* is towed by an escort carrier to Yokosuka.

September 25

ETO: Eighth Air Force VIII Air Support Command B-26 Marauders bomb the St. Omer/Longuenesse airfield. Four of the 68 bombers that hit the target are damaged.

ITALY: Twelfth Air Force XII Bomber Command B-17s bomb the Bologna marshaling yard and the railroad bridge at Bolzano. B-25 Mitchells and B-26 Marauders bomb airfields at Pisa, Lucca, and Bastia/Borgo, and road junctions, bridges, and rail lines. XII Air Support Command and RAF Desert Air Force aircraft attack roads near Serino, troops at Sarno, and supplies stored near Foggia. A U.S. minesweeper is sunk by German submarine *U-593* in the Gulf of Salerno.

PACIFIC: U.S. submarine *Bluefish* torpedoes and damages a Japanese cargo ship in the Flores Sea. U.S. submarines *Bowfin*, *Billfish*, and *Bonefish* attack a Japanese convoy. *Bowfin* sinks a tanker north of Nha Trang, French Indochina, in the South China Sea.

NEW GEORGIA: Thirteenth Air Force B-25 Mitchells with navy TBF Avengers and SBD Dauntless dive-bombers attack Japanese gun positions around Vila airfield on Kolombangara Island and at Disappointment Cove on New Georgia. Tank landing ship *LST-167* is damaged by a Japanese dive-bomber off Vella Lavella.

NEW GUINEA: Fifth Air Force B-17s, B-24 Liberators, and B-25 Mitchells bomb enemy installations and supply lines, while A-20 Havocs and Australian aircraft conduct ground support missions for the Australian 9th Division near Finschhafen. B-25s bomb and strafe antiaircraft positions on New Britain Island.

September 26

ETO: Eighth Air Force VIII Bomber Command B-17s attack the Reims/Champagne airfield and targets near Paris. One B-17 is lost and 31 are damaged in the two raids.

ITALY: The 45th Infantry Division captures Teora, controlling the key road junction of Highways 7 and 91. Twelfth Air Force XII Bomber Command cannot fly any missions due to weather. XII Air Support Command fighters conduct ground support missions in the Benevento area and at Foggia, and attack troops near Sarno.

BOUGAINVILLE: Thirteenth Air Force B-24 Liberators, escorted by 14 P-38 Lightnings, bomb troops near Kahili. P-40s, P-39 Airacobras, and 15 U.S. Navy F4U Corsairs supporting more than 50 navy SBD Dauntless dive-bombers attack the Kahili airfield as well as other targets on the island.

September 27

ATLANTIC: PBM Mariner patrol bombers sink German submarine *U-161* off Brazil.

ETO: An Eighth Air Force VIII Bomber Command attack on the port of Emden, Germany, is led by two H2S radar-equipped B-17s of the 482nd Bombardment

Group (Pathfinder). This squadron has been created to allow bombers to conduct missions over cloud-covered targets. Pathfinders lead the bombers over the target and when the Pathfinder releases its bombs, it is the signal for all the other bombers in the formation to release their bomb load.

The 246 B-17s that hit the Emden area are escorted by 262 P-47 Thunderbolts. A total of seven bombers are lost and 79 are damaged. Aircrews report at least 32 confirmed enemy kills. The fighter pilots report 21 confirmed kills and two probables. One P-47 is lost and two damaged. Four of five B-17s accompany the RAF on a night raid on Hannover, Germany. One B-17 is shot down and the 10 crewmen are reported missing. VIII Air Support Command B-26 Marauders bomb airfields in France. Over the Beauvais/Tille airfield, 65 B-26s hit the target and 24 bombers are damaged. Aircrews report at least four enemy aircraft destroyed. Over the Conches airfield, 68 B-26s hit the target. One bomber is lost and four are damaged. Six crewmen are listed as missing.

ITALY: Twelfth Air Force is nearly grounded by weather conditions. XII Air Support Command fighters attack Viterbo airfield and bomb a road junction at San Severo.

PACIFIC: U.S. submarine *Bluefish* torpedoes and sinks a Japanese torpedo boat south of the Flores Sea, Netherlands East Indies. In the South China Sea, U.S. submarine *Bonefish* torpedoes and sinks a Japanese army transport and damages a cargo ship south of Nha Trang, French Indochina.

Major General Charles D. Barrett takes command of I Marine Amphibious Corps from Lieutenant General Alexander A. Vandegrift. I Marine Amphibious Corps issues orders for 3rd Marine Division to land near Cape Torokina on Bougainville Island to "seize, occupy and defend" a beachhead, then be prepared to expand the beachhead with the arrival of the 37th Infantry Division.

BOUGAINVILLE: Thirteenth Air Force B-24 Liberators, P-40s, P-39 Airacobras, and navy fighters bomb the Kahili area. P-39 Airacobras over Choiseul Island strafe supply barges.

NEW GUINEA: Fifth Air Force sends 117 B-24 Liberators and B-25 Mitchells, escorted by 129 P-38 Lightnings and P-40s, to attack airfields and shipping near Wewak. Some 40 Japanese aircraft are destroyed on the ground and eight others are reported shot down. Bomber aircrews report extensive damage to 10 Japanese cargo ships.

September 28

ITALY: Bad weather allows only a few Twelfth Air Force fighter-bombers to attack motor transport in the area around Benevento and Caserta.

SOUTHWEST PACIFIC AREA: U.S. submarine *Cisco* is sunk off Panay Island. U.S. submarine *Grouper* lands men and supplies on south coast of New Britain.

PACIFIC: U.S. submarine *Gudgeon* torpedoes and sinks a Japanese merchant cargo ship near Guam.

CENTRAL PACIFIC: The 27th Infantry Division staff, which has been planning for an assault on Nauru in the Gilberts, is notified that its new objective will be Makin Atoll. Japanese troops on the atoll were estimated to be about 800, with antiaircraft guns and as many as 40 machine guns. Two battalions of the 165th RCT will make the initial landing as part of Task Force 54, under command of Rear Admiral Richmond Kelly Turner. The second battalion will initially be held in reserve, then conduct a second landing.

NEW GEORGIA: Japanese forces begin evacuating Kolombangara Island. The New Georgia campaign has been characterized by continuous, close combat in dreadful conditions and under extreme hardship. Lacking firepower and experience, and slowed by a lack of adequate supplies and disease, U.S. soldiers and marines have fought in the jungle against an invisible, disciplined enemy occupying defensive positions that could be taken only by direct assault. As the battles at Buna and Gona in New Guinea have proven earlier, infantry working with tanks and flamethrowers make the difference in overwhelming Japanese defenses. But the victory has taken a heavy toll. U.S. forces have suffered 5,100 casualties.

NEW GUINEA: Fifth Air Force sends 40 B-24 Liberators, escorted by 29 P-38 Lightnings, against Japanese defenses around Wewak. Enemy losses are estimated at eight fighters shot down. A-20 Havocs and Australian aircraft attack the Finschhafen and Lae area.

September 29

CBI: Fourteenth Air Force B-24 Liberators bomb Myitkyina and Sadon in Burma.

ITALY: The 3rd Infantry Division captures Avellino in a surprise night attack before German engineers can complete laying demolition charges.

Twelfth Air Force XII Bomber Command B-25 Mitchells, B-26 Marauders, and P-38 Lightnings bomb bridges at Piana, Castelvenere, Amorosi, and Cancello Amone, while U.S. and RAF aircraft attack San Giorgio del Sannio and roads near Benevento.

The 100th Infantry Battalion, a unit comprised of Japanese-American volunteers, is attached to Fifth Army and joins the 133rd Infantry Regiment, 34th Infantry Division.

PACIFIC: U.S. submarine *Bluefish* torpedoes and sinks a Japanese cargo ship in the Banda Sea. U.S. submarine *Gudgeon* torpedoes and damages a Japanese gunboat off Saipan.

SOLOMONS: Thirteenth Air Force P-40s, P-38 Lightnings, and P-39 Airacobras support navy fighters and SBD Dauntless dive-bombers in an attack on a barge depot at Kakasa on Choiseul Island.

September 30

ATLANTIC: The B-25 Mitchells of the 10th Antisubmarine Squadron (Heavy), 26th Antisubmarine Wing, cease antisubmarine operations from Galveston, Texas.

ITALY: Twelfth Air Force XII Bomber Command P-38 Lightnings, B-25 Mitchells, and B-26 Marauders bomb roads and bridges at Ausonia, Piana, Castelvenere, Amorosi, and Capua. B-25s bomb Benevento and road and rail networks. XII Air Support Command fighter-bombers conduct ground support missions outside of Naples.

SOUTHWEST PACIFIC AREA: U.S. submarine *Bowfin* delivers supplies and evacuates guerrillas from Siquijor Island in the Philippines. The submarine also torpedoes and sinks a cargo ship in the Celebes Sea.

PACIFIC: Japanese Imperial Headquarters issues an order to subordinate units to make every effort to hold the important southeastern area extending eastward from the eastern part of New Guinea to the Solomon Islands by repulsing all enemy attacks in the area. To accomplish this, Rabaul is considered as the center and every effort will be made for a protracted defense of important positions in the Bismarck Archipelago and on Bougainville. The Japanese realize that important positions in northern New Guinea area must be reinforced. Air and naval forces will be used to destroy the attacking enemy before landings are made. If landings are successful, the enemy must be destroyed as quickly as possible before any consolidation of the beachhead. Supply lines that can transport supplies to outposts rapidly, especially in New Guinea, must be maintained.

U.S. submarine *Harder* torpedoes and sinks a Japanese auxiliary submarine chaser in the North Pacific. U.S. submarine *Pogy* torpedoes and sinks a Japanese army transport near Palau.

BOUGAINVILLE: Thirteenth Air Force B-24 Liberators, escorted by P-38 Lightnings, P-40s, and navy F4U Corsairs, attack Kahili airfield and supply sites. Another six B-25s bomb Kakasa on Choiseul Island.

October 1

CBI: Fourteenth Air Force sends 21 B-24 Liberators and 24 fighters of the Chinese-American Composite Wing (CACW) against a power plant and port facilities at Haiphong, French Indochina. More than 65 Japanese fighters attack the formation, shooting down two aircraft. Aircrews report 30 enemy fighters destroyed. Three P-40s are lost and fighter pilots report two confirmed kills.

ATLANTIC: Navy PV-1 Ventura patrol planes attack German submarines *U-402* and *U-448* tracking convoy HX 258 (New York to Liverpool) in the North Atlantic.

ETO: Despite the Eighth Air Force's attempt to destroy the German Air Force in France as a precondition for the cross-Channel invasion, intelligence reports show that German fighter production has actually increased, as has the number of fighters available for combat in western Europe.

MEDITERRANEAN: Ninth Air Force and IX Bomber Command begin to redeploy from Egypt and Libya to England.

ITALY: Lieutenant General Sir Richard L. McCreery's X Corps captures Naples. Marshal Montgomery's Eighth Army captures the airfield at Foggia. Twelfth Air Force XII Bomber Command B-26 Marauders attack communication targets in the Capua, Grazzanise, Arce, and Mignano areas. B-24 Liberators bomb the aircraft factory at Wiener-Neustadt in Austria. XII Air Support Command aircraft attack Benevento, the bridge at Capua, and transportation targets near Isernia and Avezzano.

PACIFIC: U.S. submarine *Peto* torpedoes and sinks a Japanese transport and a cargo ship in the Carolines. U.S. submarine *Wahoo* torpedoes and sinks a Japanese cargo ship in the Sea of Japan.

SOLOMONS: Admiral William F. Halsey, COMSOPAC, informs General MacArthur of his intention to invade Bougainville on November 1.

NEW GEORGIA: Thirteenth Air Force B-24 Liberators bomb Japanese supply point and troops near Vila airfield on Kolombangara Island. B-25 Mitchells and P-38

Lightnings, along with navy SBD Dauntless dive-bombers, attack the barge depot at Kakasa on Choiseul Island.

NEW GUINEA: Fifth Air Force A-20 Havocs and Australian aircraft bomb and strafe the Finschhafen area in support of Australian ground forces.

October 2

CBI: Fourteenth Air Force P-40s attack Yangtze River shipping in the area near Chiuchiang, China.

The 51st Fighter Group receives the 25th and 26th Fighter Squadrons (with P-40s).

ETO: Eighth Air Force VIII Bomber Command attacks Emden, Germany, with 349 B-17s led by two B-17 Pathfinders with H2S radar and escorted by 227 P-47 Thunderbolts. Of the 339 bombers that hit the target, two B-17s are lost and 34 are damaged; aircrews claim at least 15 enemy fighters as confirmed kills. The P-47 pilots report one P-47 damaged and claim five enemy confirmed kills, two probable kills, and one possible. The VIII Air Support Command sends 72 B-26 Marauders against the St. Omer/Longuenesse airfield in France. Only six bombers hit the target due to cloud cover, but 12 B-26s are nevertheless damaged with one crewman killed and four wounded. Two B-17s join the Royal Air Force on a night raid against Munich, Germany.

ITALY: The 82nd Airborne Division enters Naples acting as the Allied security and occupation force. Despite bad weather, fighter-bombers of the XII Air Support Command attack targets and conduct reconnaissance missions in the Volturno Valley.

SOUTHWEST PACIFIC AREA: Fifth Air Force B-25 Mitchells strafe villages in the Talasea area and barges off Gasmata Island, while B-26 Marauders bomb Hoskins airfield. One B-24 bombs Cape Gloucester airfield.

U.S. submarine *Kingfish* lays mines off southern Celebes.

NEW GEORGIA: Thirteenth Air Force B-25 Mitchells and navy SBD Dauntless dive-bombers attack barges near Vila on Kolombangara Island.

October 3

CBI: In China, Fourteenth Air Force P-40s damage a vessel on the Yangtze River near Chiuchiang as four P-38 Lightnings bomb the docks at Chiuchiang. Off Hainan Island, six B-24 Liberators damage a freighter.

ETO: Eighth Air Force VIII Air Support Command B-26 Marauders attack the Amsterdam/Schiphol, Woensdrecht, and Haamstede airfields in the Netherlands. Of the 131 bombers that hit the targets, 47 B-26s are damaged. Another 63 B-26s bomb the Beauvais/Tille airfield in France. One bomber is lost and 27 are damaged. Only five crewmen are wounded in the raids.

ITALY: Twelfth Air Force XII Bomber Command B-26 Marauders, B-25 Mitchells, and P-38 Lightnings bomb rail and road bridges and a road junction at Capua, Castel Volturno, Piana, Arce, Mignano, and Isernia.

SOLOMONS: Thirteenth Air Force P-39 Airacobras strafe several barges west of Choiseul.

NEW BRITAIN: Fifth Air Force B-25 Mitchells attack supply barges along the west coast of the island.

NEW GUINEA: Japanese submarine *RO-108* torpedoes and sinks U.S. destroyer off eastern New Guinea.

October 4

CBI: The Fourteenth Air Force airfield at Kweilin is attacked by 17 Japanese bombers with 25 fighters providing escort. The bombers, avoiding U.S. fighters by flying above 20,000 feet, miss their target.

ATLANTIC: Aircraft from the carrier USS *Ranger* operating off the Norwegian coast attack a German-Norwegian convoy. TBF Avengers, SBD Dauntless dive-bombers, and F4F Wildcats sink four cargo ships and a German transport and damage a German tanker and three cargo ships. The Wildcats shoot down two German aircraft.

TBF Avengers from escort carrier USS *Card* with convoy UGS 19 (United States to Mediterranean, Slow) attack three German submarines north of the Azores, sinking *U-460* and *U-422*. *U-460* was in process of resupplying two other U-boats. In the North Atlantic, PV-1 patrol bombers overwatching convoy ONS 204 (Liverpool to Halifax, Slow) sink German submarine *U-336*.

ETO: Eighth Air Force VIII Bomber Command attacks industrial targets in Germany, escorted by 223 P-47 Thunderbolts. B-17s bomb Wiesbaden and Frankfurt. Five bombers are lost and 45 are damaged. Aircrews report 19 enemy aircraft destroyed. Another 37 B-17s bomb Frankfurt later in the morning, losing three bombers, and 35 others are damaged. Aircrews report 18 enemy fighters shot down. Over the Saarlautern industrial area and the St. Dizier/Robinson airfield, 105 bombers attack the targets, losing four B-17s while 23 others suffer damage. Aircrews report 37 enemy fighters destroyed. Over the Sarreguemnines and Saarbrucken marshaling yards, 47 B-17s hit their targets, with only two bombers damaged. A diversion flown by 38 B-24 Liberators results in four bombers lost and 19 damaged. Aircrews report that 13 enemy aircraft have been destroyed. The fighter pilots report 19 confirmed kills, one probable kill, and two possibles. U.S. losses are 16 P-47s damaged. Total casualties for these missions are four crewmen killed, 27 wounded, and 142 missing.

During the night four B-17s drop over 240,000 leaflets over Paris.

ITALY: Twelfth Air Force XII Bomber Command sends over 100 B-17s against the Pisa marshaling yard and Bolzano bridges. XII Air Support Command fighter-bombers attack trains, roads, rail lines, and vehicles near Isernia, Avezzano, Pescara, and Isolella.

MEDITERRANEAN: German bombers attack convoy UGS 18 (United States to Mediterranean, Slow) and damage a U.S. freighter off the coast of Algeria.

BOUGAINVILLE: Thirteenth Air Force B-24 Liberators, escorted by P-38 Lightnings and U.S. Navy F4U Corsairs, bomb Kahili airfield. About 30 Japanese fighters attempt to break up the attack and nine enemy aircraft are reported shot down. P-39 Airacobras and four Corsairs sink 18 supply barges located on the west coast of Choiseul Island.

October 5

MEDITERRANEAN: German bombers make another attack on convoy UGS 18 (United States to Mediterranean, Slow) and damage a second U.S. freighter off the coast of Algeria.

ITALY: Twelfth Air Force XII Bomber Command B-17s bomb the marshaling yard at Bologna. B-25 Mitchells and B-26 Marauders bomb the Formia road and Isernia. XII Air Support Command and RAF Desert Air Force aircraft bomb numerous targets around Isernia and Venafro.

PACIFIC: Navy Task Force 14, under command of Rear Admiral Alfred E. Montgomery and composed of six carriers, three heavy cruisers, four light cruisers, and 24 destroyers, bombards Wake Island. U.S. submarine *Wahoo* torpedoes and sinks a Japanese army transport in the Tsushima Straits.

CENTRAL PACIFIC: CINCPOA issues plans for a Central Pacific offensive. In the Gilbert Islands, Admiral Spruance is tasked to capture Makin, Tarawa, and Abemama. He is also to deny the Japanese the use of bases in the Marshall Islands and at Nauru. The offensive is to begin on November 19.

October 6

CBI: Fourteenth Air Force P-40s from Suichwan intercept 27 Japanese bombers and 21 fighters. The enemy loses one bomber and one fighter before turning back.

ITALY: The U.S. VI Corps establishes itself on the south bank of the Volturno River. Across the river valley are high hills where German forces are waiting. Since September 9, U.S. casualties have totaled nearly 4,900 men, with the 36th Infantry Division taking nearly 40 percent of these casualties. Some battalions of the 36th Infantry are down to less than 100 men.

Twelfth Air Force XII Bomber Command B-17s bomb the marshaling yard at Mestre. B-26 Marauders attack Isernia and the road junction at Formia. Northwest African Air Force aircraft hit targets at Teano, Alfedena, and Capua. XII Air Support Command P-40s and A-36 Intruder (Apache) fighter-bombers attack roads and vehicles in support of Fifth Army.

SOUTHWEST PACIFIC AREA: U.S. submarine *Kingfish* lands men and supplies on northeast coast of Borneo.

Fifth Air Force B-25 Mitchells bomb and strafe targets of opportunity on New Britain.

PACIFIC: U.S. submarine *Skate* is attacked and damaged by Japanese aircraft off Wake Island, but remains on patrol. U.S. submarine *Steelhead* torpedoes and damages a Japanese fast fleet tanker southwest of Guam. U.S. submarine *Tinosa* later finishes off the tanker northwest of Truk. U.S. submarine *Wahoo* torpedoes and sinks a Japanese army cargo ship in the Sea of Japan.

Navy Task Force 14 continues to bombard Wake Island. Fearing that the bombardment is a prelude to an amphibious landing, Rear Admiral Sakaibara Shigematsu orders the execution of 98 American civilian contractors, who have been kept on the island since its capture by the Japanese on December 23, 1941.

BOUGAINVILLE: Kahili airfield is attacked by 24 B-25 Mitchells and 14 P-38 Lightnings. Thirteenth Air Force P-39 Airacobras and U.S. Navy F4U Corsairs strafe barges off the west coast of Choiseul Island.

NEW GEORGIA: BATTLE OF VELLA LAVELLA As nine Japanese destroyers begin a nighttime evacuation of troops from Vella Lavella Island, three U.S. destroyers attack. All three U.S. destroyers are damaged by torpedoes and one destroyer is scuttled. U.S. torpedoes sink one Japanese destroyer.

October 7

CBI: Fourteenth Air Force B-25 Mitchells attack a freighter south of Amoy, China, causing heavy damage. B-24 Liberators bomb the cement plant at Haiphong, French Indochina.

ATLANTIC: German submarine *U-645* torpedoes and sinks a U.S. freighter in convoy SC 143 (Halifax Slow to United Kingdom) in the North Atlantic.

ETO: Four B-17s from Eighth Air Force drop 240,000 leaflets over Paris during the night. Ninth Air Force's 434th Troop Carrier Group with C-47s arrives at Fulbeck, England, from the United States.

PACIFIC: U.S. submarine *S-44* is sunk by Japanese escort destroyer east of the Kamchatka Peninsula.

October 8

CBI: Fourteenth Air Force B-24 Liberators, supported by P-40s, bomb Gia Lam airfield in French Indochina. B-24 Liberators bomb facilities and a headquarters at Tengchung, China.

ETO: Eighth Air Force VIII Bomber Command B-17s attack the Bremen shipyard and industrial facilities using airborne transmitters for the first time to jam German radar. The shipyard is hit by 105 B-17s. U.S. losses are nine bombers shot down and 61 damaged; aircrews report over 40 enemy aircraft destroyed. Another 53 B-17s hit the industrial area, losing four bombers and suffering damage to 44 others; aircrews report 24 enemy fighters destroyed. The U-boat yards at Vegesack are bombed by 43 B-24 Liberators. Three B-24s are lost and 21 are damaged; aircrews report 17 fighters destroyed. Later in the afternoon Bremen is again bombed by 156 B-17s. This time 14 bombers are shot down and 112 are damaged; aircrews report over 90 enemy fighters shot down. The raid over Bremen is escorted by 274 P-47 Thunderbolts. The pilots report 12 confirmed kills, two probables, and four possibles. Three P-47s are lost and five are damaged. Total casualties for this raid are four crewmen killed, 58 wounded, and 304 missing. VIII Air Support Command B-26 Marauders attack the Lille/Vendeville and Chievres airfields in France. Although the mission is aborted due to bad weather over the target, four B-26s are damaged. Two VIII Bomber Command B-17s drop 266,000 leaflets over Rennes during the night.

ITALY: The 30th Infantry Regiment of the 3rd Infantry Division drives the last German defenders over the Volturno River. General Lucian K. Truscott outlines a plan for the division to assault German positions on the hills across the Volturno River. The 7th and 15th Infantry Regiments will make the main attack while a battalion of the 15th Infantry conducts a diversion on the left flank.

MEDITERRANEAN: Twelfth Air Force XII Bomber Command B-24 Liberators bomb airfields in Athens and on Crete and Rhodes, in Greece. B-25 Mitchells also bomb an airfield in Athens.

SOUTHWEST PACIFIC AREA: U.S. submarine *Guardfish* torpedoes and sinks a Japanese cargo ship near the Admiralty Islands. U.S. submarine *Gurnard* torpedoes and sinks a Japanese cargo ship and a transport off northern Luzon, Philippines.

PACIFIC: Major General Charles D. Barrett, commander of I Marine Amphibious Corps, dies suddenly and Lieutenant General Alexander A. Vandegrift returns to temporary command.

U.S. submarine *Gato* torpedoes a Japanese cargo ship south of Truk, but the torpedo fails to explode. *Gato* escapes the attack of an escorting torpedo boat.

October 9
ALEUTIANS: Attu Island is bombed by 12 Japanese bombers based in the Kuriles.
CBI: Fourteenth Air Force B-25 Mitchells attack a tanker, other vessels, near Amoy and Quemoy islands off the coast of China. One B-25 is lost. P-40s bomb a fuel storage area and a barracks at Mangshih, China; one P-40 is shot down by ground fire.
ETO: Eighth Air Force VIII Bomber Command attacks targets in Germany and Poland to assist the advance of the Soviet army. Over Anklam, Germany, 106 B-17s hit the industrial area and lose 18 bombers and another 52 damaged; aircrews report at least 65 enemy fighters shot down. Over the Marienburg, Germany, industrial area, 96 B-17s hit the target with a loss of two bombers and damage to 13 others; aircrews report nine enemy fighters destroyed. The U-boat yards and the port area of Danzig (Gdańsk), Poland, are bombed by 41 B-24 Liberators; two bombers are lost and 20 others are damaged; aircrews report seven enemy fighters destroyed. Over 100 B-17s hit the port area at Gdynia, Poland. Enemy losses are estimated at over 40 aircraft, but six U.S. bombers are lost and 63 are damaged. VIII Air Support Command sends 72 B-26 Marauders to bomb the Woensdrecht airfield in the Neth-

A B-17 bomber of the Eighth Air Force hits an industrial target over Marienburg, Germany, on October 9, 1943.

erlands. Of the 66 bombers that hit the target, 26 are damaged. At the completion of this mission, the B-26s will be transferred from Eighth Air Force to Ninth Air Force. The total casualties for this mission are 35 wounded and 266 missing.

MEDITERRANEAN: Twelfth Air Force XII Bomber Command B-17s bomb airfields at Larissa, Athens, and Salonika in Greece. B-24 Liberators hit Kastelli/Pediada airfield on Crete.

ITALY: A U.S. destroyer is torpedoed and sunk by German submarine *U-616* in the Gulf of Salerno.

SOUTHWEST PACIFIC AREA: U.S. submarine *Kingfish* torpedoes and sinks a Japanese oiler in the Sulu Sea. U.S. submarine *Puffer* torpedoes and sinks a Japanese tanker in Makassar Strait but suffers damage from a depth charge attack and must terminate its patrol. U.S. submarine *Rasher* torpedoes and sinks a Japanese cargo ship in the Banda Sea.

PACIFIC: U.S. submarine *Wahoo* torpedoes and sinks a Japanese cargo ship in the Sea of Japan.

SOLOMONS: Thirteenth Air Force B-25 Mitchells and P-40s attack barges and troop concentrations on Choiseul Island. P-39 Airacobras and navy F4U Corsairs strafe buildings, a radar station, and gun positions at Poporang Island.

NEW GUINEA: Fifth Air Force A-20 Havocs and Australian aircraft bomb and strafe Japanese defensive positions near Finschhafen. B-24 Liberators bomb Makassar on Celebes Island.

October 10

CBI: Tenth Air Force sends seven B-24 Liberators against the Meza railroad bridge in Burma, causing serious damage. Fourteenth Air Force B-24 Liberators, with an escort of 18 P-40s, attack port facilities at Haiphong, French Indochina. In China, P-40s bomb ammunition supplies at Tengchung and a supply dump and targets of opportunity in the Lungling area.

ETO: Eighth Air Force VIII Bomber Command B-17s escorted by 216 P-47 Thunderbolts attack transportation targets near Munster, Germany. A total of 236 bombers hit the target as well as targets of opportunity at Coesfeld, Germany, and at the Enschede airfield in the Netherlands. Aircrews report over 180 enemy aircraft destroyed, but 30 B-17s are lost and 105 are damaged. Fighter pilots report 19 confirmed enemy kills; one P-47 is lost and three are damaged. Total U.S. losses for this mission are two crewmen killed, 18 wounded, and 307 missing.

ITALY: The 34th Infantry Division completes preparations for its attack across the Volturno River on the 3rd Infantry Division's right flank. The three regiments are to seize the hills behind the town of Squille. The 45th Infantry Division, approaching the Volturno River on VI Corps's right flank, continues to clear enemy delaying its advance.

MEDITERRANEAN: Twelfth Air Force B-17s bomb airfields at Athens, Greece. B-24 Liberators bomb the Maritsa airfield on Rhodes and the Calato and Heraklion airfields on Crete.

PACIFIC: U.S. submarine *Bonefish* torpedoes and sinks a Japanese cargo ship and a merchant transport off Cam Ranh Bay, French Indochina. U.S. submarine *Grayback* makes an unsuccessful attack on a Japanese troopship east of the Ryukyu Islands. U.S. submarine *Kingfish* lays mines in Makassar Strait.

BOUGAINVILLE: Thirteenth Air Force sends 24 B-24 Liberators, escorted by P-38 Lightnings, P-40s, P-39 Airacobras, and over 50 navy fighters and dive-bombers, to attack Kahili airfield and the supply areas. American pilots report 15 Japanese aircraft are shot down.

October 11

CBI: Fourteenth Air Force sends eight B-24 Liberators to bomb the area near Teng-chung, China, and Sadon and Myitkyina in Burma.

MEDITERRANEAN: Twelfth Air Force XII Bomber Command B-25 Mitchells bomb Garitsa airfield and P-38 Lightnings attack shipping in Corfu harbor.

PACIFIC: U.S. submarine *Skipjack* torpedoes and damages a Japanese transport off Kwajalein. U.S. submarine *Wahoo* is sunk by Japanese naval aircraft, submarine chasers, and a minesweeper in La Perouse Strait off northern Hokkaido, Japan.

GUADALCANAL: Japanese aircraft conduct a torpedo attack on U.S. shipping off Koli Point, damaging two cargo ships.

BOUGAINVILLE: Thirteenth Air Force sends 22 B-24 Liberators and more than 30 U.S. Navy SBD dauntless dive-bombers against Kahili airfield. Supply areas and the airfield are hit. Aircrews report that 12 Japanese airplanes are destroyed.

NEW BRITAIN: Photoreconnaissance over Rabaul reveals the Japanese building up air power. At least 128 bombers and 145 fighters are located on the three major airfields.

NEW GUINEA: Colonel Neel E. Kearby volunteers to lead a flight of four fighters to conduct an aerial reconnaissance of the Japanese airfield at Wewak. Kearby completes his mission and spots a Japanese fighter below him. Kearby dives down and destroys the fighter; shortly thereafter, Kearby's group spots 12 bombers accompanied by 36 fighters. Kearby gives the signal to attack and he quickly shoots down three fighters. Kearby then shoots down two fighters that are attacking one of his pilots. After breaking off the attack and assembling his flight, Kearby returns to base. For his great skill and daring in facing overwhelming odds, Colonel Kearby will be awarded the Medal of Honor.

October 12

CBI: Fourteenth Air Force sends five B-24 Liberators to bomb the warehouse area and railroad yards at Myitkyina, Burma.

ATLANTIC: TBF Avengers from escort carrier USS *Card* attack a German U-boat refueling operation north of the Azores. *U-731* is damaged in the attack.

PACIFIC: U.S. submarine *Cero* torpedoes and sinks a Japanese stores ship off Chichi Jima.

NEW BRITAIN: Fifth Air Force leads a major air offensive against the main Japanese naval and air base at Rabaul in order to isolate and neutralize it. Almost 350 B-24 Liberators, B-25 Mitchells, P-38 Lightnings, and Australian aircraft bomb Rabaul, the harbor, and the airfields. Aircrews report at least 50 enemy aircraft destroyed. Two transports are sunk, three destroyers and an oiler are damaged, and nine other vessels are hit. Ammunition storage areas are also heavily damaged.

October 13

CBI: Japanese fighters arrive over Sumprabum, Burma, to attack U.S. transports flying supplies to China over the Himalayas (the Hump). Three transports are shot down. To protect the Hump flights, P-40s attack the Japanese fighter base at Myitkyina.

ATLANTIC: TBF Avengers from escort carrier USS *Card* sink German submarine *U-402* in the North Atlantic.

MEDITERRANEAN: Italy declares war on Germany.

German submarine *U-371* torpedoes and sinks a U.S. destroyer off Bône, Algeria.

ITALY: The VI Corps attacks German defenses across the Volturno River. The 7th and 15th Infantry Regiments of the 3rd Infantry Division capture the heights dominating the river valley. The division is able to move all of its battalions across the river by the end of the day. Engineers begin bridging the river to bring tanks, artillery, and supplies to the forward lines. The 34th Infantry Division captures its objectives and moves to the junction of the Calore and Volturno Rivers. The 179th and 180th Infantry Regiments of the 45th Infantry Division clear the enemy from Monte Acero.

Twelfth Air Force XII Bomber Command B-25 Mitchells and B-26 Marauders bomb the town of Alife, a road junction at Sessa Aurunca, and the airfield at Tirana. XII Air Support Command, with RAF Desert Air Force fighters, supports the Fifth Army with attacks on enemy troops, transportation, and lines of communication, especially around Ortona, Giulianova, and Campobasso.

Captain Arlo L. Olson's company leads the advance of the 15th Infantry Regiment, 3rd Infantry Division as it crosses the Volturno River. As he wades into the chest-deep water, a German machine-gun opens fire on him. Upon reaching the opposite side, he knocks out the position with two hand grenades. Another enemy machine-gun position about 150 yards away begins firing at the company. With complete disregard for his own safety, Captain Olson approaches the enemy despite enemy bullets and hand grenades. Olson kills the five German soldiers in the position and continues to advance. The next position, defended by nine soldiers, also falls to Olson's fire. Over the next 13 days, Captain Olson continues to lead his men forward until he is killed on October 27, 1943. On that day, in two extraordinary acts of heroism he destroys an enemy defensive position singlehandedly with only his pistol, then leads a successful attack against German infantry defending the slopes of Monte San Nicola. Severely wounded in the aftermath of the battle, Captain Olson establishes a defensive perimeter and refuses medical aid until all of his men have been taken care of first. He dies as he is being evacuated. Olson's extraordinary dedication to duty and his selfless acts of courage will win him the Medal of Honor.

SOUTHWEST PACIFIC AREA: U.S. submarine *Rasher* attacks a Japanese convoy, sinking a cargo ship in the Banda Sea.

PACIFIC: U.S. submarine *Seadragon* conducts an unsuccessful attack on a Japanese ammunition ship and an auxiliary submarine chaser near Kwajalein. *Seadragon* avoids the response attack.

New Britain: Fifth Air Force sends over 100 B-24 Liberators and B-25 Mitchells against Rabaul, but bad weather aborts the mission. B-24 Liberators attack targets at Hoskins, Lindenhafen, Cape Gloucester, and Gasmata Island.

October 14

CBI: Fourteenth Air Force sends four B-25 Mitchells to attack shipping and the airfield near Amoy.

ETO: Eighth Air Force VIII Bomber Command B-17s return to Schweinfurt, Germany, to attack the ball bearing plants. Of the 229 B-17s that hit the target, 60 bombers are lost to especially strong enemy fighter attack and 145 are damaged. Aircrews report over 180 enemy fighters destroyed. The total casualties for this mission are five crewmen killed, 40 wounded, and 594 missing. U.S. bomber crew casualties have been so heavy over the past month that daylight bombing against strategic targets without fighter escort deep into Germany is suspended for a short period.

Italy: Lieutenant General Mark W. Clark changes the U.S. VI Corps to a two-division front, pulling the 45th Infantry Division back. The 3rd and 34th Infantry Divisions are to advance to take control of the upper Volturno valley. The valley is narrow and broken by deep ravines and steep brush-covered ridges. The weather continues to deteriorate, with rain and fog a constant condition.

Twelfth Air Force XII Bomber Command B-17s bomb the Terni marshaling yard. B-25 Mitchells attack the airfield at Argos, while B-17s and B-24 Liberators attack the Giulianova bridge. XII Air Support Command and RAF Desert Air Force aircraft attack transportation assets near the front lines at the Volturno River.

Southwest Pacific Area: SWPA headquarters issues an outline plan for the attack on New Britain. The 7th Marine Regiment, 1st Marine Division, will land between Cape Gloucester and Borgen Bay with two battalion landing teams (BLT) organized as Combat Team C. One separate BLT will land near Taual. Combat Team B will act as the reserve.

Pacific: Admiral Nimitz, CINCPOA, issues instructions for planners to focus on the capture of Kwajalein, Wotje, and Maloelap. The tentative planning date for the beginning of the Marshalls offensive is January 1, 1944. By use of carrier-based airpower to compensate for land-based aircraft, Nimitz believes the isolated islands can be captured quickly. The Central Pacific offensive has the advantage of being able to cut the Japanese off from oil supplies in the Netherlands East Indies and place American land-based airpower within range of the Japanese home islands. For Nimitz, the offensive also offers the possibility of a major open sea battle against the Japanese fleet, something both American and Japanese naval planners and strategists have been anticipating for years.

U.S. submarine *Grayback* torpedoes and sinks a Japanese fleet tanker in the East China Sea.

New Britain: Fifth Air Force sends over 60 B-25 Mitchells against the airfield and supply points at Cape Gloucester.

October 15

Atlantic: German submarine *U-371* torpedoes and damages a U.S. freighter in a convoy off the coast of Morocco. The ship is beached and later lost.

ETO: Lieutenant General Ira C. Eaker, Commanding General Eighth Air Force, also commands a new headquarters intended to provide a unified command and control structure for the Eighth and the Ninth Air Forces titled U.S. Army Air Forces in United Kingdom (USAAFUK).

MEDITERRANEAN: Twelfth Air Force XII Bomber Command sends B-25 Mitchells to attack airfields at Salonika and Megalo Mikra in Greece.

ITALY: The 7th Infantry Regiment of the 3rd Infantry Division captures Cisterna.

PACIFIC: U.S. submarine *Tullibee* attacks a Japanese convoy, sinking a transport in the Formosa Straits.

SOLOMONS: The I Marine Amphibious Corps issues an order for an amphibious assault on Bougainville at Empress Augusta Bay to seize Cape Torokina at the south end of the bay and establish a perimeter.

BOUGAINVILLE: Thirteenth Air Force sends 21 B-24 Liberators, with two P-38 Lightnings and 17 navy F4U Corsairs as escort, to bomb Kahili airfield and its supply base. Aircrews report six enemy fighters shot down.

NEW GUINEA: Fifth Air Force P-38 Lightnings and P-40s intercept about 100 Japanese aircraft intending to attack Allied shipping in Oro Bay. The fighter pilots claim 40 confirmed kills. Over Finschhafen, four P-40s report intercepting over 20 Japanese aircraft and shooting down five of them.

October 16

ETO: The Ninth Air Force is established at Sunninghill, England, as a tactical air force. The new commander is Lieutenant General Lewis H. Brereton.

ITALY: Twelfth Air Force XII Bomber Command B-25 Mitchells bomb the marshaling yard, rail lines, and industrial targets around Bologna.

PACIFIC: U.S. submarine *Mingo* makes an unsuccessful attack on the Japanese escort carrier *Chuyo* northwest of Truk and avoids a depth charge attack.

BOUGAINVILLE: Thirteenth Air Force sends eight B-24 Liberators to bomb Kara airfield. Later, six B-25 Mitchells bomb the airfield on Ballale Island.

NEW GUINEA: Fifth Air Force sends over 60 B-25 Mitchells to attack the Alexishafen area and bomb the Wewak airfield. A-20 Havocs bomb and strafe targets on Gasmata Island off New Britain.

October 17

CBI: Colonel Lewis A. Pick arrives in-theater to take charge of the construction of the Ledo Road. Beginning in Ledo, India, it is intended to link with the original Burma Road. Pick will follow as best as possible an old caravan route through northern Burma. The 849th and the 1883rd Aviation Engineer Battalions and the 382nd Construction Battalion will play a large role in the construction. These all-black units, along with the all-white 330th Engineer General Service Regiment and the 209th Engineer Battalion, will do a large share of this enormous undertaking. Black Americans make up about 60 percent of the 15,000 men assigned to this mission.

ITALY: Elements of the 168th Infantry of the 34th Infantry Division capture Alvignano.

Twelfth Air Force Allied aircraft of Northwest African Tactical Air Force attack targets near Teano and Alife and motor transport targets at Benedello, Penna, and

Pedesso. Enemy troops and vehicles are attacked at Vinchiaturo, Benedello, Teramo, and Sparanise.

PACIFIC: U.S. submarine *Tarpon* torpedoes and sinks a German auxiliary cruiser off Chichi Jima.

NEW GUINEA: Fifth Air Force B-25 Mitchells bomb Wewak and Boram airfields and report that 15 enemy aircraft have been destroyed on the ground and four others as confirmed kills in the air. Four P-39 Airacobras intercept 18 Japanese aircraft over Finschhafen and report six enemy aircraft shot down. Over Oro Bay, P-40s and P-38 Lightnings shoot down 24 Japanese aircraft.

Private Nathan Van Noy, Jr., is a member of Headquarters Company, Shore Battalion, Engineer Boat and Shore Regiment at Finschhafen, New Guinea. He is manning a machine-gun position about five yards from the shoreline when he is alerted that three Japanese troop barges are approaching the beach. As Van Noy peers over his sights in the early morning darkness, the barges appear. One barge is immediately hit by direct fire, but the other two land only ten yards from Van Noy's position. Although fully exposed, he engages the enemy troops until his ammunition is expended, killing at least 20 soldiers. During the course of the fight, he is wounded numerous times and, refusing to withdraw, dies at his post. His heroism and fighting spirit not only saved the lives of many of his comrades, but also will win him the Medal of Honor.

ETO: Major General Elwood R. "Pete" Quesada takes command of the IX Fighter Command.

ITALY: XII Air Support Command A-36 Intruder (Apache) fighter-bombers bomb the rail yards at Venafro. Fighters attack airfields around Rome and also hit Viterbo, Grosseto, the seaplane base at Bracciano, and attack trains connecting Rome and Orte and Rome and Naples. A-20 Havocs bomb the road and railway near Cassino and roads, bridges, and vehicles near Minturno and Chieti.

PACIFIC: U.S. submarine *Flying Fish* attacks Yokosuka-bound Japanese escort carrier *Chuyo* north of Guam, but fails to damage the carrier. U.S. submarine *Lapon* torpedoes and sinks a Japanese cargo ship off Shikoku, Japan, and fires two torpedoes at an auxiliary minesweeper, both of which fail to explode. U.S. submarine *Silversides* torpedoes and sinks a Japanese cargo ship north of the Marianas.

SOLOMONS: Thirteenth Air Force B-24 Liberators and SBD Dauntless dive-bombers, with over 50 fighters flying escort, bomb the airfield on Ballale Island. Over Choiseul Island 14 P-39 Airacobras and over 20 navy fighters conduct strafing attacks on Japanese positions.

NEW BRITAIN: Despite bad weather over the target, Fifth Air Force B-25 Mitchells bomb Rabaul from treetop and mast-height level. Aircrews report two vessels sunk and 70 enemy aircraft destroyed on the ground and in the air. B-24 Liberators diverted from Rabaul, bomb Cape Hoskins and Cape Gloucester.

October 19

ATLANTIC: THE MOSCOW CONFERENCE BEGINS U.S. secretary of state Cordell Hull, British foreign minister Anthony Eden, and Vyacheslav Molotov, the Soviet foreign minister, meet to discuss political conditions related to the end of the war in Europe.

ITALY: The 3rd and 34th Infantry Divisions begin to close on Dragoni to capture the important bridges over the Volturno River north of the town. The 168th Infantry Regiment of the 34th Infantry Division captures the town without a fight as the Germans withdraw. The 135th Infantry Regiment prepares to cross the Volturno to cut off the enemy and capture Alife.

XII Air Support Command, Northwest African Tactical Air Force, and RAF Desert Air Force aircraft attack enemy forces, supply bases, and transport near Boiano and Viterbo. Cassino and Anzio are also attacked as well as trains near Barisciano and troops near Mintumo.

BOUGAINVILLE: Thirteenth Air Force B-24 Liberators, PV-1 Ventura medium bombers, P-38 Lightnings, P-40s, and Navy fighters and Dauntless dive-bombers attack Kara and Kahili airfields.

October 20

CBI: Tenth Air Force B-25 Mitchells return to the bridge at Meza, Burma, to prevent further repairs on the bridge.

ATLANTIC: Aircraft from escort carrier *Core* with convoy UGS 20 (United States to Mediterranean, Slow) sink German submarine *U-378* north of the Azores.

At the Moscow Conference, the Soviets are briefed on Overlord (the overall plan for the invasion of Western Europe) but only the broadest details are provided.

ETO: Eighth Air Force VIII Bomber Command sends B-17s against industrial targets at Düren, Germany. Only 97 of the 170 B-17s sent hit the target, largely due to cloud cover and the failure of Oboe radar equipment, intended to allow accurate bombing despite cloud cover over a target. Pathfinder B-17s, guided by Oboe radar receivers on a curved course, will approach the target release point. At that point, the home station sends a second radar signal. The intersection of these two signals is the cue for the lead bombardier to release his bomb load. The other bombers will follow, releasing at the same point.

Another 42 bombers hit the Woensdrecht airfield in the Netherlands, but the target of opportunity costs the U.S. nine B-17s shot down and 11 damaged. Enemy losses are estimated to be at least four aircraft destroyed.

During the night, five B-17s drop over 876,000 leaflets over Rouen and Paris.

ITALY: Twelfth Air Force XII Bomber Command B-17s, B-26 Marauders, B-25 Mitchells, and P-38 Lightnings bomb airfields north and east of Rome. XII Air Support Command, Northwest African Air Force aircraft attack gun positions, trucks, and lines of communication near Cassino, where the Germans are preparing a new defensive line.

SOUTHWEST PACIFIC AREA: General MacArthur responds to the CCS offensive plan in the Pacific with an alternative schedule that proposes Rabaul be neutralized by February 1 by the capture of Hansa Bay, New Guinea, capture of the Admiralties, and the capture of Kavieng, New Ireland. By October, the Vogelkop Peninsula will be captured, along with Halmahera and Manado islands in the northeast Celebes in December. By February 1945 SWPA forces will be ready for an invasion of Mindanao in the Philippines.

PACIFIC: U.S. submarine *Gato* torpedoes and sinks a Japanese transport between Truk and Kavieng, New Ireland. U.S. submarine *Kingfish* torpedoes and sinks a Japanese cargo ship south of Nha Trang, French Indochina.

SOLOMONS: COMAIRSOLS headquarters moves to Munda airfield on New Georgia.
BOUGAINVILLE: Thirteenth Air Force P-40s and nearly fifty navy F4U Corsairs attack Kahili. Corsair pilots report three enemy fighters destroyed. Kakasa on Choiseul Island is attacked by PV-1 Venturas, P-40s, and navy fighters and SBD Dauntless dive-bombers.
NEW BRITAIN: A-20 Havocs attack Gasmata Island.

October 21

CBI: Fourteenth Air Force sends six B-24 Liberators to bomb Nawlang, Burma. Aircrews report destroying an enemy barracks.
ATLANTIC: Aircraft from escort carrier *Core* damage German submarine *U-271* north of the Azores.
ITALY: Twelfth Air Force XII Bomber Command B-17s bomb a railroad viaduct at Terni and rail and road bridges in Albania. B-24 Liberators attack the Orvieto railroad bridge. B-26 Marauders and B-25 Mitchells bomb the bridges and rail lines. P-38 Lightnings bomb a radar station at Pellegrino and the marshaling yard at Skopje, Yugoslavia. Allied aircraft attack troops and the railroad near Cassino.
PACIFIC: U.S. submarine *Steelhead* torpedoes and damages a Japanese aircraft transport east of Yap.
BOUGAINVILLE: Thirteenth Air Force sends 12 B-25 Mitchells with an escort of 36 fighters to attack Kara airfield
NEW GUINEA: Fifth Air Force sends over 50 B-24 Liberators and 19 B-25 Mitchells to bomb Japanese positions near Sattelberg. P-40s bomb Gasmata Island off New Britain and attack two Japanese light cruisers off New Ireland. One cruiser is reported damaged.

October 22

ATLANTIC: The Combined Chiefs of Staff approves the plan proposed by the U.S. Joint Chiefs of Staff to create a new, numbered air force in Italy from part of the Twelfth Air Force to be used to support the strategic bombing campaign in Germany and support Allied ground operations in Italy.
ETO: Ninth Air Force B-26 Marauders bomb Evreux/Fauville airfield in France, but most of the bombers abort due to bad weather.
ITALY: Twelfth Air Force XII Bomber Command B-26 Marauders bomb railroad bridges near Orvieto. B-25 Mitchells bomb a railroad bridge near Grosseto. The XII Air Support Command and Northwest African Air Force aircraft conduct ground support missions north of the Volturno River, attacking gun positions, strongpoints, and targets of opportunity.
PACIFIC: U.S. submarine *Grayback* torpedoes and sinks a Japanese transport in the East China Sea. U.S. submarine *Shad* makes an unsuccessful attack on two Japanese light cruisers in the East China Sea.
SOLOMONS: The I Marine Amphibious Corps develops plans for the 2nd Marine Parachute Battalion to raid Choiseul as a diversion prior to the landing on Bougainville.
BOUGAINVILLE: Thirteenth Air Force sends 22 B-24 Liberators, P-39 Airacobras, and P-40s, along with about 160 navy fighters and dive-bombers against Kahili and Kara airfields. Kahili airfield is rendered unserviceable after this raid. Choiseul Island is

bombed by B-24 Liberators and navy aircraft. One B-24 claims hits on a carrier off Buka Island.

NEW GUINEA: Fifth Air Force B-25 Mitchells bomb Wewak and sink two small cargo ships. The bombers also hit barges and parked aircraft. P-39 Airacobras and Australian air force aircraft strafe targets near Madang. Other P-40s attack Gasmata Island off New Britain.

October 23

CBI: Tenth Air Force B-25 Mitchells conduct a bombing raid on the Meza railroad bridge in Burma in an attempt to halt repairs.

ITALY: Twelfth Air Force XII Bomber Command B-26 Marauders bomb railroad and road bridges at Marsicano and Montalto di Castro. XII Air Support Command, RAF Desert Air Force, and Northwest African Air Force aircraft attack troops, vehicles, lines of communication, and gun positions from Gaeta to Isernia and from Vairano to Ancona. German aircraft attack U.S. shipping off Naples and hit a freighter carrying gasoline. The fire burns for 64 hours.

PACIFIC: U.S. submarine *Silversides* torpedoes and sinks a Japanese fleet tanker and two cargo ships north of the Admiralty Islands.

BOUGAINVILLE: Thirteenth Air Force sends 11 B-24 Liberators and 16 P-38 Lightnings to bomb Kahili airfield. Kara airfield is attacked by 36 P-40s and P-39 Airacobras, along with navy dive-bombers and fighters. Another combined strike by B-24 Liberators, army and navy fighters, and 42 navy SBD Dauntless dive-bombers hits both airfields later in the day. B-24s bomb Kakasa on Choiseul Island.

NEW BRITAIN: Fifth Air Force sends over 40 B-24 Liberators, escorted by P-38 Lightnings, to bomb the Rapopo airstrip. Aircrews report 20 enemy aircraft destroyed on the ground and another 20 fighters destroyed in the air.

October 24

CBI: Fourteenth Air Force B-24 Liberators, with 13 P-40s as escort, attack a barracks compound at Co Bi in French Indochina.

ETO: Ninth Air Force sends 200 B-26 Marauders against the Montdidier, Beauvais/Nivillers, and Saint-Andre-de-L'Eure airfields in France.

MEDITERRANEAN: Twelfth Air Force XII Bomber Command B-24 Liberators bomb the aircraft plant at Wiener-Neustadt in Austria.

ITALY: The 133rd Infantry Regiment of the 34th Infantry Division attacks north past San Angelo d'Alife, battling German tanks, artillery, infantry, and minefields to capture the hills above the town. The battalion suffers over 200 casualties in three days of fighting.

B-25 Mitchells attack the airfield at Tirana, a railroad bridge near Orvieto, and a viaduct at Terni. The XII Air Support Command, the Northwest African Air Force, and the RAF Desert Air Force bomb lines of communication and conduct ground support missions near Formia, Minturno, Sessa Aurunca, and Frosolone.

PACIFIC: Navy PBY Catalinas sink one Japanese destroyer and damage another near Truk.

BOUGAINVILLE: Thirteenth Air Force B-25 Mitchells, Royal New Zealand Air Force P-40s, and U.S. Navy F4U Corsairs attack Kahili airfield, followed shortly by another group of army and navy fighters accompanying over 70 navy SBD Dauntless dive-bombers, which also bomb the target.

NEW BRITAIN: Fifth Air Force B-25 Mitchells, escorted by over 50 P-38 Lightnings, report destroying 45 Japanese bombers on the ground at Vunakanau, Rapopo, and Tobera airstrips. Aircrews also report 40 enemy fighters destroyed in the air. Marine aircraft sink a Japanese destroyer southwest of Rabaul.

October 25

CBI: Fourteenth Air Force P-40s and B-25 Mitchells attack Haiphong and shipping in the Gulf of Tonkin. Boats, barges, a cargo ship, and a tanker are reported sunk or damaged.

ITALY: Twelfth Air Force XII Bomber Command P-39 Airacobras attack the landing ground at Podgorica. XII Air Support Command, Northwest African Air Force, and RAF Desert Air Force attack lines of communication, bridges, radio stations, and trains near Frosinone, Formia, Gaeta, and Cetraro.

PACIFIC: U.S. submarine *Tullibee* makes an unsuccessful attack on a Japanese transport in the East China Sea.

NEW BRITAIN: Fifth Air Force sends over 60 B-24 Liberators to bomb Rabaul. Aircrews report over 20 enemy aircraft destroyed on the ground and another 30 in the air. A-20 Havocs conduct ground support missions near Lae in New Guinea.

October 26

CBI: Fourteenth Air Force sends 13 B-24 Liberators and 15 P-40s to attack the railroad yards at Haiphong in French Indochina. B-25 Mitchells attack shipping at Kiungshan, China. Two B-25s are lost; aircrews report a tanker and a transport sunk.

B-24s begin flying the southern Hump route (the aerial resupply route to China flown over the Himalaya Mountains) to prevent Japanese fighters from taking such a heavy toll on unarmed transport aircraft. The heavily armed bombers lure the enemy fighters to make an attack, then blast them at close range with machine-gun fire. Using this tactic, bomber crews report 18 enemy fighters shot down.

MEDITERRANEAN: Twelfth Air Force XII Bomber Command B-25 Mitchells and P-38 Lightnings attack Salonika/Sedhes and Megalo Mikra airfields in Greece.

ITALY: The XII Air Support Command and RAF Desert Air Force aircraft attack gun emplacements and report destroying vehicles and parked aircraft in the Ancona area.

SOUTHWEST PACIFIC AREA: Fifth Air Force B-24 Liberators attack Pombelaa on Celebes Island. Japanese fighters shoot down two B-24 Liberators. Aircrews report 11 enemy fighters shot down.

PACIFIC: Navy PBY Catalina damages a Japanese destroyer off the eastern coast of New Ireland.

BOUGAINVILLE: Thirteenth Air Force B-24 Liberators, B-25 Mitchells, P-38 Lightnings, P-40s, P-39 Airacobras, and navy fighters and dive-bombers attack Kahili airfield. Navy fighters and SBD Dauntless dive-bombers, along with army P-39 Airacobras and P-40s, attack Kara airfield. The Buka Island airfield is attacked by B-25 Mitchells and P-38 Lightnings.

October 27

CBI: In China, Fourteenth Air Force sends six B-24 Liberators to bomb Tungting Lake area as 60,000 Japanese troops begin an offensive that will last into December. Aircrews report eight enemy fighters shot down.

ATLANTIC: General Marshall rejects MacArthur's October 20 proposed offensive plan in the Pacific, noting that it requires too many resources to undertake.

MEDITERRANEAN: Twelfth Air Force sends over 150 B-17s and B-24 Liberators to bomb the Wiener-Neustadt aircraft factory and rail lines and bridges at Friedberg and Ebenfurth in Austria.

ITALY: The 2nd Battalion of the 135th Infantry Regiment, reinforced by tanks, attempts to capture Hill 235, the dominant terrain that controls the valley near Raviscanna. The 135th makes no progress and the 2nd Battalion of the 168th moves to the attack. The entire 34th Division's advance is held up for 48 hours until the Germans give up Hill 235 on the 29th of October.

PACIFIC: U.S. submarine *Flying Fish* torpedoes and sinks a Japanese transport east of the Ryukyus. U.S. submarines *Shad* and *Grayback* torpedo and sink a Japanese cargo ship and damage another in the East China Sea. A transport is hit by a torpedo that fails to explode.

BOUGAINVILLE: Thirteenth Air Force B-24 Liberators attack Kahili and Kara airfields. P-40s providing cover over Kahili report three enemy fighters shot down. Navy cruisers and destroyers provide naval gunfire support for the Allied landing on Mono and Stirling Islands in the Treasury Island Group, south of Bougainville. Japanese aircraft damage a destroyer and mortar fire damages two LSTs.

NEW GUINEA: Fifth Air Force P-40s and P-39 Airacobras intercept Japanese bombers attempting to drop supply bundles near Sattelberg. The fighter pilots claim 12 aircraft shot down. A-20 Havocs hit the harbor and supply sites on Gasmata Island off New Britain.

October 28

ATLANTIC: Aircraft from escort carrier USS *Block Island* attack two German submarines east of Newfoundland. *U-220* is sunk and *U-256* escapes.

ITALY: XII Air Support Command A-36 Intruder (Apache) fighter-bombers attack roads, bridges, and gun positions near Vairano, and transportation targets near Rome.

SOUTHWEST PACIFIC AREA: U.S. submarine *Flying Fish* torpedoes and sinks a Japanese fleet oiler in the Philippine Sea.

SOLOMONS: A raiding force of 650 marines of the 2nd Marine Parachute Battalion lands on Choiseul Island as part of a deception plan to draw Japanese attention away from the assault on Bougainville. The battalion lands unopposed and advances inland.

BOUGAINVILLE: Thirteenth Air Force sends 19 B-24 Liberators, P-40s, and P-39 Airacobras, along with navy fighters and dive-bombers, to bomb Kara airfield. The airfield on Ballale Island is also attacked.

NEW BRITAIN: Fifth Air Force P-40s attack Gasmata Island off New Britain. P-47 Thunderbolts attack barges at Talasea.

October 29

CBI: Fourteenth Air Force sends 14 B-24 Liberators and 16 P-40s to attack the smelter area at Quang Yen in French Indochina. Nine P-40s attack transportation targets in the Chiuchiang area of China.

ITALY: Twelfth Air Force XII Bomber Command B-17s, escorted by P-38 Lightnings, bomb the marshaling yard and industrial targets in Genoa.

PACIFIC: U.S. submarine *Seawolf* torpedoes and sinks a Japanese cargo ship off Swatow, China.

SOLOMONS: Patrols from the 2nd Marine Parachute Battalion encounter Japanese on Choiseul as they move toward Sangigai.

BOUGAINVILLE: Thirteenth Air Force B-25 Mitchells, B-24 Liberators, and navy aircraft bomb the airfield on Buka Island and Bonis airfield on Bougainville.

NEW BRITAIN: Fifth Air Force sends 37 B-24 Liberators, escorted by 53 P-38 Lightnings, against Rabaul. Aircrews report 45 enemy aircraft destroyed on the ground and in the air. P-47 Thunderbolts strafe the Cape Gloucester area.

NEW GUINEA: Fifth Air Force B-25 Mitchells bomb Madang and P-47 Thunderbolts attack shipping in Hansa Bay, New Guinea.

October 30

CBI: Fourteenth Air Force sends seven B-25 Mitchells and 12 P-40s to attack support installations at Shayang, China.

ATLANTIC: The Moscow Conference Ends. The conference participants issue a declaration agreeing to continue the war until the Axis powers accept unconditional surrender. The Allies agree to participate in a postwar peace organization. The Allies pledge full cooperation and pledge to consult with each other "with a view to joint action on behalf of the community of nations." A commission will be established to address boundaries, occupation zones, and other questions regarding the status of the defeated nations. An advisory council will be established to deal with the return of Italy to democracy. Austria will be restored to independence, and war crimes will be tried and punished after the war.

The issue of a second front is a main topic at the conference. The USSR offers to join the war with Japan in return for opening a second front as soon as possible.

ETO: Ninth Air Force sends five B-26 Marauders to bomb the Cherbourg/Maupertus airfield in France.

ITALY: Twelfth Air Force XII Bomber Command B-24 Liberators bomb the Genoa marshaling yard and industrial targets. B-17s bomb Savona, Porto Maurizio, and Varazze. Northwest African Air Force B-25 Mitchells bomb Frosinone and XII Air Support Command aircraft attack bridges, roads, vehicles, and gun positions around Giulianova, Ancona, Ortona, Sessa Aurunca, Mignano, and Cassino.

SOLOMONS: Marines on Choiseul call in air strikes on Sangigai. TBF Avengers and 26 fighters bomb the village, but come close to killing a number of marines. The village is occupied after the Japanese withdraw. The enemy loses 72 men in counterattacks on the village. A number of important documents are captured in the village, providing information on Japanese intentions.

BOUGAINVILLE: Thirteenth Air Force sends 16 B-24s and more than 90 U.S. Navy SBD Dauntless dive-bombers against Kara airfield. Six B-25 Mitchells bomb Kieta, along with 12 P-39 Airacobras and navy fighters. P-40s and navy aircraft also attack Tonolai harbor.

NEW BRITAIN: Fifth Air Force B-25 Mitchells strafe supply barges in Rein Bay.

October 31

CBI: The 5307th Composite Unit (Provisional), known as Galahad, arrives in-the-ater. Galahad is the result of a blind call for volunteers for a hazardous mission. The collection of individuals ranges from highly experienced combat soldiers to misfits and dropouts. They are to be trained to become a deep penetration force along the model of the British Chindits. Stilwell is glad to see American combat troops, regardless of their reputation, and is eager to employ them in the upcoming offensive. Galahad becomes known by the last name of its new commander, Brigadier General Frank D. Merrill, a close associate of Stilwell's. Soon afterward the press is calling the unit Merrill's Marauders. The unit will be trained by British instructors of South East Asia Command (SEAC).

In Burma, Tenth Air Force P-40s, carrying 1,000-pound bombs, attack the Japanese airfield at Myitkyina with bomb runs and strafing attacks on antiaircraft positions. B-25 Mitchells attack the Meza railroad bridge. Air transports are delivering an average of over 8,000 tons of supplies in October. Chennault is getting at least half of this. As a result, Stilwell's plan to train and equip Chinese divisions in the Y Force for an offensive in Burma is far behind schedule. Another 30 Chinese divisions, called Zebra Force, is promised by Chiang, and Stilwell provides 2,200 Americans at Kweilin to serve as the cadre. Not enough supplies are provided by the airlift to do more than rudimentary support and training.

The Fourteenth Air Force reports that since February 2, 357 Japanese aircraft have been destroyed to 68 U.S. aircraft lost in combat.

ATLANTIC: TBF Avengers from escort carrier USS *Card* attack two German submarines, sinking *U-584* north of Flores Island, Azores. U.S. destroyer damages German submarine *U-256* north of the Azores.

ETO: Twelfth Air Force XII Bomber Command B-17s bomb the Antheor viaduct in France.

ITALY: Twelfth Air Force B-26 Marauders attack Anzio, while B-25 Mitchells attack docks and shipping at Civitavecchia.

General Mark Clark, commander of Fifth Army, takes operational control of the 1st Italian Motorized Group, a well-trained and eager, but inexperienced, unit that represents Italy's new status in the war.

SOUTHWEST PACIFIC AREA: U.S. submarine *Rasher* (SS-269) torpedoes and sinks a Japanese oiler in the Celebes Sea.

BOUGAINVILLE: Thirteenth Air Force sends over 20 B-25 Mitchells, with fighter support, to bomb Kara airfield.

November 1

CBI: Fourteenth Air Force B-25 Mitchells and P-40s bomb the railyards at Yoyang, China.

ATLANTIC: U.S. destroyer suffers damage in an encounter with German submarine *U-405* north of the Azores. The U-boat is rammed by the destroyer and sunk. The destroyer is scuttled the next day by TBF Avengers from the escort carrier *Card*.

ETO: The Allied Expeditionary Air Force (AEAF) is activated to provide a tactical air force for the Allied cross-Channel invasion of Europe. AEAF takes operational control of the Ninth Air Force to support this mission.

Mediterranean: Lieutenant General James H. Doolittle takes command of the Fifteenth Air Force, activated at Tunis, Tunisia. The B-17s and B-24 Liberators of the XII Bomber Command (Twelfth Air Force) are transferred to the Fifteenth Air Force.

Italy: The 34th Infantry Division advances along the Lete River, advancing on Capriati a Volturno. The 504th Parachute Infantry Regiment advances toward Gallo to protect the 34th Division's right flank. The 3rd Infantry Division, on the west side of the Volturno River, advances toward Mignano.

The XII Air Support Command (Twelfth Air Force) attacks bridges and road junctions near Pontecorvo.

Pacific: U.S. submarine *Haddock* makes an unsuccessful attack on two Japanese vessels north of Truk.

Bougainville: Amphibious Task Force 31, commanded by Rear Admiral Theodore S. Wilkinson, lands two regiments of the 3rd Marine Division and the 2nd Marine Raider Regiment of Lieutenant General Alexander A. Vandegrift's 1st Marine Amphibious Corps on Bougainville. Major General Allen H. Turnage commands the assault, which is preceded by minesweepers and two destroyers that provide close-in fire support and airstrikes by P-40s and P-39 Airacobras, P-38 Lightnings, F4U Corsairs, and SBD Dauntless dive-bombers. In a matter of minutes, nearly 8,000 men are on the beach. Marines on the northern beaches face heavy surf that damages 64 LCVPs and 27 LCMs, but encounter no enemy forces. The Raiders encounter a few bunkers and trenches, but rapidly overcome the enemy resistance. The 1st Battalion 3rd Marines landing along Cape Torokina encounters a major concentration of enemy defenses largely missed by preparatory fire. The beach defenses consist of pillboxes, trenches, and fighting positions dominated by a 75 millimeter gun in a well camouflaged and heavily fortified bunker, protected by two flanking bunkers. The gun hits several LCVPs as they approach the beach. Once on the beach, the marines fight their way through the defenses in what one observer described as the bloodiest fighting in the entire Solomons campaign. Sergeant Robert A. Owens, ordering his men to provide covering fire on the flanking bunkers, charges the 75 mm gun position; although wounded during the assault, he kills the crew and allows his fellow marines a better chance to land on the beach alive. Sergeant Owens's singular act of courage certainly contributes to the success of the landing and will win him the Medal of Honor. Over 150 Japanese troops are killed in this battle. As the marines move off the beach to establish the initial perimeter, they discover that just a few yards beyond the beach lies vast, swampy jungle. LSTs begin landing artillery and supplies as the first day's objectives are reached and a defensive perimeter is established.

TBF Avengers from a carrier task force (TF 38, commanded by Frederick C. Sherman) and naval gunfire support from four light cruisers and eight destroyers in Task Force 39 (Rear Admiral Aaron Merrill) support the landing, attacking airfields and installations in the area near Buka and Bonis and airfields on Shortland Island.

Marines of the 3rd Marine Division land in rough surf on Bougainville, November 1, 1943.

Two U.S. destroyers are damaged. Thirteenth Air Force B-24 Liberators bomb Kahili and Kara airfields. About 26 enemy fighters are reported shot down. B-25 Mitchells strafe barges at Faisi Island. An auxiliary submarine chaser is sunk west of Shortland Island.

NEW GUINEA: Fifth Air Force B-24 Liberators bomb Maniang Island in the Celebes.

November 2

CBI: Fourteenth Air Force B-25 Mitchells and P-40s attack the docks and warehouses at Shasi, China.

MEDITERRANEAN: Fifteenth Air Force B-17s and B-24 Liberators bomb the aircraft factory at Wiener-Neustadt in Austria. Aircrews report more than 50 fighters destroyed. In Italy, B-25 Mitchells bomb the marshaling yard at Ancona. B-26 Marauders bomb Civitavecchia harbor. P-38 Lightnings escort both missions.

BOUGAINVILLE: During the night, Naval Task Force 39, with four light cruisers and eight destroyers commanded by Rear Admiral Aaron S. Merrill, encounters a Japanese force of two heavy cruisers, two light cruisers, and six destroyers in Empress Augusta Bay. The Japanese intend to attack transports off Bougainville. Captain Arleigh Burke takes his destroyer squadron on an aggressive torpedo attack against a superior force. A U.S. light cruiser and two destroyers are lost to enemy gunfire and torpedoes. U.S. destroyers sink a Japanese destroyer and a light cruiser and damage two heavy cruisers. Three Japanese destroyers are damaged in collisions avoiding torpedoes. The Japanese retaliate with an air attack on the task force. The enemy loses 17 planes to shipboard antiaircraft fire, while AIRSOLS fighters claim another

16 aircraft. A U.S. cruiser is slightly damaged by Japanese aircraft. This battle establishes U.S. naval superiority in the Solomons.

TBF Avengers from Task Force 38, commanded by Rear Admiral Frederick C. Sherman, attacks enemy airfields around Buka. The task force has the fast carrier USS *Saratoga* and the light carrier USS *Princeton,* along with two light cruisers and nine destroyers. Thirteenth Air Force B-24 Liberators bomb Kahili airfield.

NEW BRITAIN: Fifth Air Force sends 75 B-25 Mitchells, escorted by 70 P-38 Lightnings, to attack Rabaul to support the marine landing on Bougainville. The bombers sink a stores ship and damage two heavy cruisers, a destroyer, another stores ship, and a minesweeper. Under intense antiaircraft fire, the B-25s and P-38s also report destroying 12 aircraft on the ground and 68 others destroyed in the air. The attack is costly—21 American aircraft are shot down.

Major Raymond H. Wilkins is leading the B-25 Mitchells of the 8th Bombardment Squadron, 3rd Bombardment Group, against Japanese shipping in Simpson Harbor at Rabaul, New Britain. Wilkins has flown 86 combat missions in the previous 22 months, a feat unequaled by any man in the Fifth Air Force. He already holds five Distinguished Flying Crosses for his courage in previous actions in New Guinea. Because previous air strikes have obscured the planned approach, Wilkins's squadron is forced to make a different approach, bringing them directly into heavy Japanese antiaircraft fire. Wilkins's B-25 is hit in the right wing but he continues as the lead aircraft, first strafing a group of small harbor vessels and then making a low-level bombing run on a destroyer, sinking it with a 1,000-pound bomb. Continuing the attack even as he fights for control of the B-25, he bombs a transport ship. Wilkins maneuvers to divert fire from a Japanese heavy cruiser to his own plane to allow the other aircraft of his squadron to escape. His bomber is subsequently downed by enemy fire. For his extreme courage and leadership in one of the most difficult bombing missions of the Pacific war, Major Wilkins will be awarded the Medal of Honor.

November 3

CBI: Fourteenth Air Force sends 21 B-24 Liberators with fighter escort to attack the Kowloon Docks at Hong Kong. Aircrews report four enemy fighters shot down.

ETO: Eighth Air Force VIII Bomber Command B-17s and B-24 Liberators, using both the British H2S and the new U.S. H2X radar, bomb the port at Wilhelmshaven, Germany. Of the 539 bombers that hit the target, seven B-17s are shot down and 49 are damaged. Aircrews report that the radar-assisted bombing improved accuracy and claim over 20 enemy fighters destroyed. The raid is supported by over 300 P-47 Thunderbolts. Another 45 P-38 Lightnings escort the bombers for most of the raid. The pilots report three confirmed kills, five probables, and five possibles. Overnight, two B-17s drop over 1.5 million leaflets on Antwerp and Rotterdam.

Ninth Air Force B-26 Marauders bomb the airfields at Saint-Andre-de-L'Eure and Triqueville in France. Other B-26s bomb the Schiphol airfield in the Netherlands.

ITALY: The 34th Infantry Division with a battalion of Rangers crosses the Volturno River to capture Venafro and cut Highway 6 northwest of Mignano. The 168th Infantry Regiment of the 34th Infantry Division crosses the Volturno River northeast of

Venafro. Twelfth Air Force aircraft conduct a number of ground support and bombing runs on German defenses, railyards, and the road network from Venafro to Cassino.

SOUTHWEST PACIFIC AREA: Thirteenth Air Force sends 19 B-24 Liberators to attack a convoy off Mussau Island, reporting three vessels damaged or sunk.

PACIFIC: The battleship USS *Oklahoma*, sunk on December 7, 1941, is refloated at Pearl Harbor. Navy PB4Ys (a B-24 variant) sink a Japanese stores ship off Ocean Island, near Tarawa in the Gilberts.

The Japanese Second Fleet dispatches seven heavy cruisers, a light cruiser, and four destroyers from Truk to attack the U.S. fleet at Bougainville.

SOLOMONS: The 2nd Marine Parachute Battalion is evacuated from Choiseul. U.S. casualties are six killed, 12 wounded, and one missing.

BOUGAINVILLE: Major General Turnage adjusts the positions of the 3rd and 9th Marines and moves units forward to occupy the Piva and Mission Trails. No Japanese are encountered.

NEW GUINEA: Fifth Air Force B-25 Mitchells attack supply barges around Alexishafen.

November 4

CBI: Fourteenth Air Force dispatches the Chinese-American Composite Wing against shipping and supply targets at Amoy and Swatow in China. The B-25s report four cargo ships damaged or sunk in the attack. One cargo ship sunk was carrying 100,000,000 yuan in Central Reserve Bank notes. B-24s damage a Japanese cargo vessel and destroyer north of New Ireland. U.S. submarine *Seawolf* torpedoes and sinks a Japanese cargo ship southwest of Hong Kong, China.

ITALY: Roca Pipirozzi falls to a battalion of the 180th Infantry Regiment of the 34th Infantry Division. The 2nd Battalion of the 168th Infantry Regiment, 34th Infantry Division, captures the town of Roccaravindola and S. Maria Oliveto. The 34th is able to consolidate its position, but units have suffered heavily from minefields in the hills. The 3rd Battalion of the 179th Infantry Regiment (45th Infantry Division) captures and consolidates its position at Venafro.

Fifteenth Air Force B-17s bomb rail lines between Montalto di Castro and Talamone, and between San Vincenzo and Cecina. P-38 Lightnings carrying bombs hit a tunnel near Terni. XII Air Support Command and RAF aircraft attack trucks and trains near Sora and Avezzano and attack the Furbara and Tarquinia airfields.

SOUTHWEST PACIFIC AREA: U.S. submarine *Silversides* lays mines off New Ireland, sinking a surveying ship and a transport and damaging a light cruiser and destroyer.

PACIFIC: U.S. submarine *Tautog* unsuccessfully attacks Japanese convoy in the Palau Islands.

SOLOMONS: Thirteenth Air Force B-24 Liberators bomb the Buka Island airfield.

The 21st Marine Regiment of the 3rd Marine Division, with 3,500 men and 5,000 tons of supplies, leaves Guadalcanal for Bougainville.

NEW BRITAIN: Thirteenth Air Force B-24 Liberators damage two tankers and damage a troop transport near Truk. Admiral Halsey orders Rear Admiral Frederick Sherman's Task Force 38 to intercept the Japanese naval force from Truk.

November 5

ATLANTIC: B-25 Mitchell bombers and U.S. Navy PB4Y Privateers on Ascension Island sink German submarine *U-848* off the coast of West Africa.

ETO: Eighth Air Force VIII Bomber Command B-17s, escorted by 47 P-38 Lightnings and 336 P-47 Thunderbolts, attack the marshaling yard and oil plants at Gelsenkirchen, Germany. Of the 323 bombers that hit the target, eight B-17s are shot down and 225 are damaged. Aircrews report at least 18 enemy fighters destroyed. Four P-47s are lost and one is damaged. Over Munster, Germany, 104 B-24 Liberators bomb the city's marshaling yard. Three B-24 Liberators are lost and 44 are damaged. Aircrews report over 20 enemy aircraft shot down. Later in the day five B-17s drop more than a million leaflets over Paris, Amiens, Rouen, and Caen.

ITALY: The 3rd Infantry Division attempts to overcome enemy defenses at the Mignano gap by making flanking attacks. A battalion of the 7th Infantry Regiment is stopped at Monte La Difensa, where impassible cliffs are defended by German positions blasted into the sides of the mountain and backed by artillery and mortar fire. A battalion-level attack of the 15th Infantry Regiment also fails to make any progress against enemy forces dug in at Monte Rotundo.

Fifteenth Air Force B-24 Liberators conduct a low-level bombing run on road and rail bridges between Falconara and Marittima. XII Air Support Command B-25 Mitchells, escorted by Fifteenth Air Force P-38 Lightnings, bomb the Berat-Kucove airfield in Albania. Other XII Air Support Command aircraft attack the road network around Isernia, Cassino, and Atena Lucana.

PACIFIC: U.S. submarine *Halibut* torpedoes and damages Japanese carrier *Junyo* east of Kyushu, Japan.

BOUGAINVILLE: Thirteenth Air Force B-25 Mitchells attack Japanese troops near Kieta and sink barges between Kieta and Banin Harbor. Navy fighter aircraft damage a Japanese cargo ship in Matchin Bay.

NEW BRITAIN: In order to prevent any Japanese counterattack while the landing on Bougainville takes place, Fifth Air Force sends more than 90 B-24 Liberators with fighter escort to attack Rabaul harbor. Naval Task Force 38 sends 16 TBF Avengers, 22 TBD Dauntless dive-bombers from *Saratoga* and seven Avengers from USS *Princeton,* covered by F6F Wildcats, to conduct an additional attack on Rabaul. Flying through intense antiaircraft fire, the navy planes damage five Japanese heavy cruisers, two light cruisers, and two destroyers. The combat air patrol for the task force's ships is provided by 52 F4F Hellcat fighters from Vella Lavella airfield. U.S. losses are five bombers and five fighters. Japanese aircraft losses are estimated at 14 probable kills. The Japanese naval force is ordered back to Truk.

NEW GUINEA: Fifth Air Force P-47 Thunderbolt pilots report shooting down more than 20 enemy aircraft over Wewak.

November 6

CBI: Tenth Air Force B-24 Liberators lay mines in the Rangoon River in Burma during the night.

ETO: Eighth Air Force VIII Bomber Command sends two B-17s to drop over 400,000 leaflets over Paris.

MEDITERRANEAN: German aircraft conduct a torpedo attack on a convoy off Tunisia and bound for Naples, sinking a U.S. destroyer and damaging a troop transport, which is later abandoned.

ITALY: Fifteenth Air Force B-17s bomb bridges over the Fiora River. P-38 Lightnings attack a bridge near Orvieto and Monte Molino. Fighters strafe the airfield at Tarquinia, rail traffic, and enemy vehicles. XII Air Support Command aircraft attack gun positions, bridges and roads, vehicles near Cassino, and rail traffic.

PACIFIC: U.S. submarine *Haddock* attacks a Japanese convoy sailing from Truk to Singapore, torpedoing and sinking a fleet tanker west of Truk. U.S. submarine *Scorpion* torpedoes another fleet tanker in the same vicinity. Although *Haddock* is attacked by an escorting destroyer, it escapes.

CENTRAL PACIFIC: Seventh Air Force's VII Air Force Service Command and VII Bomber Command establish advanced headquarters on Funafuti Atoll in the Ellice Islands. Baker, Nukufetau, and Nanumea Islands in the Ellice Islands will have airfields built on them to support the planned offensives against Tarawa Atoll and Makin in the Gilbert Islands, as well as Japanese strongholds in the Carolines and the Marshalls.

BOUGAINVILLE: The 21st Marine Regiment lands at Empress Augusta Bay. A hastily organized Japanese landing force of 800 men attacks the left flank of the perimeter defended by 3rd Battalion 9th marines near the Laruna River. In a daylong, confused fight both the marines and Japanese are surprised by what they encounter after U.S. Marine combat patrols beyond the perimeter stumble upon Japanese infantry in the swampy jungle. The Japanese establish a small defensive perimeter and hold off an attack by elements of 1st Battalion 3rd Marines.

Thirteenth Air Force sends 24 B-25 Mitchells with fighter escort to support an initial attack by navy SBD Dauntless dive-bombers and fighters on Kara airfield. In a follow-on attack, 17 B-24 Liberators bomb Bonis airfield. B-25 Mitchells attack Japanese shipping west of Buka, sinking a submarine chaser, an auxiliary submarine chaser, and a cargo vessel. Four other vessels are sunk in the same vicinity.

NEW BRITAIN: Fifth Air Force P-40s attack Gasmata Island.

NEW GUINEA: Japanese aircraft succeed in attacking Nadzab, Dumpu, and Finschhafen but cause little damage.

November 7

CBI: Fourteenth Air Force B-25 Mitchells bomb Amoy harbor in China, sinking two cargo ships and another vessel.

ETO: Eighth Air Force VIII Bomber Command attacks industrial targets in Wesel and Düren, Germany. Poor weather conditions limit the effectiveness of the attacks. Of the 53 B-17s that hit Wesel, four B-17s are damaged; one crewman is killed and two are wounded. Over Düren, only 37 B-17s hit the primary target because the two B-17 Pathfinders are unable to use the Oboe radar guidance system. Another 20 B-17s hit the secondary target at Randerath; two B-17s are damaged. The bombers are escorted by 283 P-47 Thunderbolts. Pilots report one confirmed enemy kill at a cost of six P-47s lost; the six pilots are reported as missing.

Ninth Air Force sends over 200 B-26 Marauders against the Montdidier and Meulan-Les Mureaux airfields in France, but the mission is aborted due to weather conditions over the target area. Nevertheless, two escorting P-38 Lightnings are lost.

MEDITERRANEAN: XII Air Support Command and Northwest African Air Force aircraft bomb the harbor and shipping at Split, Yugoslavia.

ITALY: XII Air Support Command and Northwest African Air Force aircraft attack bridges, road junctions, and transportation around Mignano-Cassino and Pontecorvo.

SOLOMONS: Task Force 53, the navy and marine element for the attack on Tarawa, departs in secrecy from the New Hebrides.

BOUGAINVILLE: The Japanese make attacks on the trail blocks established by the marines at the Piva and Numa Numa Trails. At the Koromokina River, Sergeant Herbert Joseph Thomas of the 3rd Marines, 3rd Marine Division, leads his squad against Japanese positions in the dense jungle. After successfully destroying two machine-gun positions, Sergeant Thomas prepares his men to assault a third position. Taking a hand grenade, Thomas throws it toward the enemy, but it strikes some vines and lands in the midst of the squad. Without hesitation, Sergeant Thomas covers the grenade with his body, saving the lives of his men. His selfless act of courage allows his men to capture the enemy position and wins him the Medal of Honor.

Thirteenth Air Force sends 21 B-24 Liberators to attack the Buka Island airfield.

NEW BRITAIN: Fifth Air Force sends 25 B-24 Liberators, escorted by over 60 P-38 Lightnings, to bomb Rapopo airfield. Japanese fighters intercept the formation and shoot down five P-38 Lightnings. Aircrews report more than 20 fighters destroyed in the air and several more destroyed on the ground.

NEW GUINEA: Fifth Air Force B-25 Mitchells bomb Wewak and Japanese aircraft attack Nadzab and Bena Bena, destroying or damaging about 16 U.S. planes. The raid costs the Japanese 14 aircraft shot down by U.S. fighters.

November 8

CBI: Tenth Air Force sends five B-24 Liberators to lay mines in the Rangoon River during the night.

ETO: Eighth Air Force sends two B-17s to drop leaflets over Paris.

MEDITERRANEAN: General Eisenhower, still in command of the Mediterranean theater, decides on a two-pronged attack on Rome. While Montgomery and Clark's armies attack the Winter Line, Clark's VI Corps will conduct an amphibious assault at Anzio, south of Rome and some 45 miles behind the Gustav Line. The Combined Chiefs of Staff approves Eisenhower's request to keep 68 LSTs (landing ship, tank) in the Mediterranean to support this assault but directs him to release them by the end of January 1944 so that they will be available for Overlord.

Fifteenth Army Group commander General Sir Harold Alexander orders Lieutenant General Mark Clark's Fifth Army to prepare plans for an amphibious attack using one division on the west coast of Italy to outflank the Gustav Line. Simultaneous attacks by the Eighth and Fifth Armies will leave the Germans unable to respond to an amphibious landing south of Rome. The initial target date of December 20 for the landing of one division has to be postponed due to a lack of progress against the Germans and a lack of landing craft.

Fifteenth Air Force attacks the Turin ball bearing factory and other nearby industrial targets with 81 B-17s. Northwest African Air Force bombers and RAF Desert Air Force fighters attack targets west of the Sangro River and trains at Civitanova and Pescara.

ITALY: A battalion of the 30th Infantry Regiment of the 3rd Infantry Division captures Monte Rotundo, while a battalion of the 15th Infantry Regiment captures Hill 253. Both hold against a number of strong German counterattacks. The 135th Infantry Regiment of the 34th Infantry Division along with an ad hoc task force of infantry, tanks, tank destroyers, and engineers captures Montaquila. The 45th Infantry Division advances past Pozzilli against strong resistance. The entire VI Corps suffers increasingly from the accumulated effects of rain, mud, and exposure as the infantrymen battle up hills so steep they often have to advance on their hands and knees. German troops are solidly protected in heavily fortified positions and are difficult to dislodge.

PACIFIC: U.S. submarine *Bluefish* torpedoes and sinks a Japanese army tanker in the South China Sea. U.S. submarine *Rasher* torpedoes and sinks a Japanese merchant tanker in the Makassar Straits, escaping from an auxiliary submarine chaser.

BOUGAINVILLE: A counterattack by 1st Battalion 21st Marines, preceded by a barrage from five artillery battalions, breaks the Japanese defensive positions. The transports carrying the 148th Regimental Combat Team of the 37th Infantry Division are attacked by Japanese aircraft as they enter Empress Augusta Bay. The attackers kill five soldiers and wound 20 more. The Japanese begin heavy attacks along the Piva Trail, but are repulsed by artillery, tanks, and mortar fire.

Thirteenth Air Force sends 22 B-24 Liberators to bomb Bonis airfield. B-25 Mitchells bomb targets at the month of the Laruma River and Kieta. Japanese dive-bombers attack U.S. ships off Cape Torokina, damaging a light cruiser.

The I Amphibious Corps takes control of the battle from 3rd Marine Division.

November 9

ITALY: Fifteenth Air Force B-24 Liberators attack the Turin ball bearing works, and B-17s bomb the Genoa-Ansaldo steel works. P-38 Lightnings provide escort for both raids. Northwest African Air Force aircraft attack Formia and Itri, while XII Air Support Command aircraft attack roads and bridges in the Mignano-Ceprano area and rail targets in the Rome-La Spezia area.

SOUTHWEST PACIFIC AREA: U.S. submarine *Rasher* makes an unsuccessful attack on a Japanese fleet oiler in the Celebes Sea. U.S. submarine *Sargo* torpedoes and sinks a Japanese cargo ship in the Philippine Sea.

PACIFIC: U.S. submarine *Seawolf* makes an unsuccessful attack on a Japanese cargo vessel in the South China Sea.

Major General Ray S. Geiger takes command of the I Marine Amphibious Corps from Lieutenant General Alexander A. Vandegrift, who leaves for Washington, D.C., to become commandant of the Marine Corps.

BOUGAINVILLE: Upon moving inland from the beach the marines discover that western Bougainville Island is covered by swamps. Any high ground is of important military value, as are trails that allow easy movement. Control of the trails becomes a key task for both the marines and the Japanese.

The Marine Raiders attack to clear Japanese away from Piva trail and run immediately into an advancing Japanese force preparing to attack. The Japanese attack is thrown back and the Raiders advance to the important junction of Numa Numa and Piva trails. In the first few minutes of the attack, Private First Class Henry Gurke and another Raider find themselves in the midst of a major fight. As Gurke's buddy is laying down suppressive fire with a Browning Automatic Rifle, a Japanese grenade drops into their foxhole. Gurke pushes his buddy aside and covers the grenade with his body. His act of devotion to a comrade by sacrificing his life will win him the Medal of Honor.

The 148th Infantry Regiment, 37th Infantry Division takes control of the left half of the perimeter.

Thirteenth Air Force B-25 Mitchells bomb Buka Island airfield. B-25s bomb Kieta and B-24 Liberators attack Kara and Kahili airfields. P-39 Airacobras along with navy aircraft also attack Kara airfield and the Ballale Island airfield.

NEW BRITAIN: B-25 Mitchells bomb fuel supplies and shipping in the Rein Bay area, while P-40s bomb supply dumps on Gasmata Island. B-24 Liberator aircrews report sinking a destroyer near Kavieng, New Ireland.

NEW GUINEA: Fifth Air Force B-25 Mitchells and A-20 Havocs, escorted by P-38 Lightnings and P-47 Thunderbolts, attack the airfield at Alexishafen, reporting at least 12 enemy airplanes destroyed on the ground. Another 10 to 15 Japanese fighters are reported destroyed in the air.

November 10

ATLANTIC: Navy PB4Y-1 Privateers and an RAF Wellington bomber sink German submarine *U-966* in the Bay of Biscay.

ETO: Eighth Air Force sends five B-17s to drop leaflets over Paris, Rennes, Le Mans, and Rouen, France.

Ninth Air Force B-26 Marauders bomb an airfield in Chievres, Belgium.

MEDITERRANEAN: Fifteenth Air Force B-24 Liberators bomb the Turin ball bearing works and B-17s bomb a bridge and the marshaling yards at Bolzano. P-38 Lightnings escort the B-24s completely through the mission and provide partial coverage to the B-17s.

Northwest African Air Force bombers attack shipping at Split, Yugoslavia, and Durazzo, Albania.

ITALY: The 3rd Infantry Division faces heavy counterattacks from the Germans. In one representative action north of Mignano, Lieutenant Maurice L. Britt and a small group of infantrymen stop an attack by over 100 enemy soldiers. Although repeatedly wounded by bullets and grenade fragments, Lieutenant Britt refuses treatment. Fighting valiantly against nearly impossible odds, he kills five enemy soldiers and knocks out a machine-gun crew, using every weapon he can lay his hands on. In the end, he holds his position and captures four prisoners. Lieutenant Britt's exemplary courage and determination stop the German counterattack and save his company. He will receive the Medal of Honor.

XII Air Support Command and RAF aircraft attack German positions at Rocca and Rome and attack truck and rail traffic in the Rome–La Spezia and Piombino-Leghorn areas.

SOUTHWEST PACIFIC AREA: U.S. submarine *Albacore* is damaged by a U.S. bomber off New Ireland, but continues on patrol.

PACIFIC: U.S. submarine *Barb* makes an attack on a Japanese convoy, damaging a cargo ship. *Barb* is forced to evade an auxiliary minesweeper escorting the convoy. U.S. submarine *Scamp* torpedoes and sinks a Japanese transport between Truk and New Ireland.

Task Force 52, the navy and army element for the attack on Makin atoll in the Gilberts, leaves Pearl Harbor. The task force consists of three escort carriers, four battleships, four heavy cruisers, and four destroyers. The 27th Infantry Division Task Force is composed of the 165th Regimental Combat Team, two companies of the 193rd Tank Battalion, the 152nd Engineer Battalion, and an antiaircraft battalion.

CENTRAL PACIFIC: B-24 Liberators of the 30th Bombardment Group (Heavy), Seventh Air Force, arrive from Hawaii to be stationed at Nanumea in the Ellice Islands and at Canton Island in the Phoenix Islands.

BOUGAINVILLE: Thirteenth Air Force B-25 Mitchells bomb the Kara airfield.

NEW BRITAIN: Fifth Air Force B-24 Liberators bomb Lakunai airfield and attack a new landing ground on Duke of York Island east of Rabaul.

NEW GUINEA: Fifth Air Force B-25 Mitchells attack the Alexishafen airfield.

November 11

CBI: Fourteenth Air Force sends six B-24 Liberators to bomb the Burma Road, causing heavy damage.

ETO: Eighth Air Force VIII Bomber Command attempts to attack two targets in Germany, the marshaling yard at Munster and industrial targets in Wesel. Weather limits the effectiveness of the raids. Only 57 of the 167 B-17s hit the target at Munster. Aircrews report 10 enemy fighters shot down while four B-17s are lost and 27 others damaged. The 180 B-17s sent to bomb Wesel, abort the mission over the English Channel. One B-17 is damaged and no casualties are reported. The two missions are escorted by 59 P-38 Lightnings and 342 P-47 Thunderbolts. The P-47 pilots report eight confirmed kills, one probable, and two possibles. Two P-47 Thunderbolts are lost and one is damaged. The two pilots are reported as missing. Ninth Air Force sends 157 B-26 Marauders to bomb targets near Cherbourg, France. Fifteenth Air Force sends 28 B-24 Liberators to bomb the ball bearing plant at Annecy, France. One Pathfinder B-17 flies an Oboe radar test over Emmerich, Germany.

ITALY: The 2nd Battalion 509th Parachute Infantry and the 1st Ranger Battalion capture Mount Santa Croce, after relieving a battalion of the 180th Infantry Regiment, 45th Infantry Division. The rest of the division makes only limited progress in trying to push the Germans from the hills guarding Acquafondata.

Twelfth Air Force A-20 Havocs and RAF aircraft attack troop concentrations and communication sites near Rocca and Palena. Northwest African Air Force aircraft bomb an explosive works near Popoli and the docks at Civitavecchia. Enemy strongpoints at Roccaraso and Atessa are attacked. Transportation targets between the Sangro and Pescara rivers are attacked.

In one of the attacks by the 3rd Infantry Division near Mignano, an infantry company is counterattacked by German infantry. Heavily outnumbered, Private First Class Floyd K. Lindstrom turns his machine gun on the attackers. Unable to get a clear shot at the enemy occupying the high ground, Lindstrom picks up his machine gun and carries it uphill until he is only 10 yards away from the enemy position. He begins firing again, even as bullets slam into the rocky ground all around him. Still unable to suppress the enemy, he abandons the machine gun and charges forward, drawing his pistol. He kills the two soldiers and takes their machine gun, employing it now against the enemy. As his men respond to his orders, Lindstrom retrieves two ammunition boxes from the enemy position, all the while ignoring the intense rifle fire directed his way. The heavy volume of fire from Lindstrom's guns stops the German counterattack. Lindstrom's initiative and aggressive action with total disregard for his own life in order to protect his comrades will win him the Medal of Honor.

SOUTHWEST PACIFIC AREA: U.S. submarine *Capelin* torpedoes and sinks a Japanese cargo ship northwest of Ambon, in the Banda Sea.

Japanese submarine *I-21* torpedoes a U.S. freighter with over 1,300 troops on board bound for Townsville, Australia. Over 200 men are killed or drowned.

PACIFIC: U.S. submarine *Drum* makes an unsuccessful attack on a Japanese convoy sailing from Truk to Rabaul. U.S. submarine *Sargo* torpedoes and sinks a Japanese transport in the Ryukyus.

CENTRAL PACIFIC: Japanese aircraft attack the airfield on Nanumea Island in the Ellice Islands, destroying a B-24 Liberator, even as more B-24s of the 11th Bombardment Group (Heavy) arrive from Hawaii to be stationed at Nukufetau Island and Funafuti Atoll in the Ellice Islands.

BOUGAINVILLE: Thirteenth Air Force B-25 Mitchells and Navy F4U Corsair fighters strafe barges and shore installations in Matchin Bay. Additional elements of the 21st Marines land at Empress Augusta Bay.

NEW BRITAIN: Fifth Air Force B-24 Liberators bomb Lakunai airfield near Rabaul. Thirteenth Air Force B-24s join Fifth Air Force aircraft and Royal Australian Air Force aircraft in a concentrated attack on Rabaul harbor. TBF Avengers and TBD Dauntless dive-bombers from Rear Admiral Frederick C. Sherman's Task Force 38 and Task Group 50.3 also participate. TG 50.3 has two new carriers, the USS *Essex* and USS *Bunker Hill,* and a light carrier USS *Independence.* This task group, under command of Rear Admiral Alfred Montgomery, was originally assigned to Admiral Spruance's Makin and Tarawa operation, but Admiral Halsey has requested additional carrier support, and Admiral Nimitz passes operational control to Halsey.) Fighter pilots report 17 Japanese fighters shot down; bomber aircrews report five enemy fighters destroyed. A destroyer is sunk and two light cruisers and three destroyers are damaged.

The new carriers from TG 50.3 employ 33 SB2C Helldiver dive-bombers for the first time in the Pacific. The task group is attacked by 199 Japanese aircraft, including 27 dive-bombers and 14 torpedo bombers. Air cover is provided by navy F4U

Corsairs and F4F Hellcats from Vella Lavella airfield on New Georgia. The fighters land on the carriers to refuel and rearm. Only three enemy bombers are able to release their ordnance near the carriers, causing only minor damage.

Although the Japanese attack reminds many Japanese of Midway in terms of the number of aircraft involved, this battle bears little resemblance to the original. These are not the superb airmen of the Imperial Japanese Navy of 1942. Instead, these are marginally trained pilots facing combat-experienced and highly trained American flyers. The Japanese pilots, for all their courage, have little chance of success. This devastating loss of pilots and aircraft marks the effective end of the ability of the Japanese to challenge American control of the air or sea. As a result of this attack, Rabaul is effectively neutralized, accomplishing the operational objective of the Cartwheel campaign. The Americans, however, will not realize this fact for several more weeks.

Small and elite, the U.S. Marines maintained their own aviation units, flying aircraft such as this F4U Corsair equipped with five-inch rockets, which prepares to take off from a carrier before dawn. (National Archives and Records Administration)

November 12

CBI: In Burma, Tenth Air Force sends two B-24 Liberators to mine the Rangoon River during the night.

In China, Fourteenth Air Force B-25 Mitchells and P-40s attack the railyard and warehouses at Yoyang. B-25s also bomb targets along the waterfront at Yangchi Kang and Puchi.

ATLANTIC: A U.S. Navy PB4Y-1 Privateer (a B-24 variant) patrol bomber sinks German submarine *U-508* in the Bay of Biscay.

ITALY: Fifteenth Air Force B-26 Marauders attack railroad bridges and rail lines near Montalto di Castro and Orbetello. Northwest African Air Force A-20 Havocs provide ground support near Palena and Atina, and attack targets along the road at Acquafondata. A-20s also bomb the Arezzo marshaling yard and Perugia airfield.

PACIFIC: U.S. submarine *Harder* torpedoes and sinks an auxiliary minesweeper and another vessel in a Japanese convoy in the northern Marianas. U.S. submarine *Scamp* torpedoes and sinks a Japanese light cruiser north of the Marianas, which had been damaged in the raid on Rabaul on November 11. U.S. submarine *Thresher* torpedoes and sinks a Japanese transport north of Truk, but is forced to terminate its patrol after sustaining damage from a depth charge attack.

CENTRAL PACIFIC: Seventh Air Force continues receiving B-24 Liberators from Hawaii from the 30th Bombardment Group (Heavy), stationing them on Nanumea Island in the Ellice Islands.

BOUGAINVILLE: The 129th and 145th Regimental Combat Teams of the 37th Infantry Division complete their landing, adding 10,277 men to the expanding perimeter.

Thirteenth Air Force attacks Tarlena with 18 B-25 Mitchells. B-25s also bomb the area near Matchin Bay. Eight P-38 Lightnings strafe Bonis airfield.

New Guinea: Fifth Air Force B-25 Mitchells and B-26 Marauders bomb Japanese positions between Finschhafen and Saidor. B-24 Liberators bomb targets on Java and on Amboina Island in the Moluccas.

November 13

ETO: Eighth Air Force VIII Bomber Command B-17s, B-24 Liberators, and three B-17 Pathfinder aircraft, escorted by 45 P-38 Lightnings and 345 P-47 Thunderbolts, attack the port of Bremen and targets in Kiel-Flensburg in Germany. Weather causes most of the bombers to abort the mission. Over Bremen, 79 B-17s and 61 B-24s hit the target. Three B-17s and 13 B-24s are lost; 15 B-17s and 13 B-24 Liberators are damaged. Aircrews report 20 enemy fighters shot down. Fighters report 10 confirmed enemy kills, three probables, and six possibles. U.S. losses are seven P-38 Lightnings and three P-47 Thunderbolts. A total of nine fighters are damaged. Nine pilots are reported missing.

Ninth Air Force's 354th Fighter Group in England receives P-51 Mustang fighters.

Italy: Northwest African Air Force A-20 Havocs bomb Palena, Atina, Civitavecchia harbor, and a road near Terracina. XII Air Support Command and RAF aircraft bomb Giulianova harbor and the landing grounds at Aquino, Frosinone, and Marcigliana. Transportation targets in the Pescara-Rieti area are also attacked.

Southwest Pacific Area: U.S. submarine *Narwhal* lands men and supplies at Paluan Bay, Mindoro, Philippines.

Pacific: U.S. submarine *Scorpion* torpedoes and damages a Japanese oiler northwest of the Marianas. U.S. submarine *Trigger* torpedoes and sinks a Japanese transport in the East China Sea, and receives slight damage from a depth charge attack.

Central Pacific: Seventh Air Force begins air operations in support of Operation Galvanic, with 18 B-24 Liberators flying from Funafuti Atoll in the Ellice Islands to bomb Tarawa atoll. One B-24 is lost in the raid.

Bougainville: The 2nd Battalion 21st Marines fights Japanese troops in what is called the Battle of Coconut Grove. The marines expand the northern and eastern perimeter, encountering Japanese defending a coconut grove, one of the few identifiable terrain features in the swampy jungle. The 37th Infantry Division takes control of its assigned sector. The division's commander, Major General Robert S. Beightler, arrives on the island.

Thirteenth Air Force attacks antiaircraft positions, dispersal areas, and the runway at Bonis airfield with 17 B-24 Liberators. Six B-25 Mitchells conduct low-level bombing runs on the Buka Island airfield. Japanese aircraft attack Naval Task Force 39 off Empress Augusta Bay and damage a U.S. light cruiser.

New Guinea: Fifth Air Force sends nearly 120 B-24 Liberators and B-25 Mitchells to bomb Alexishafen. P-40s conduct strafing attacks as well.

November 14

Mediterranean: Northwest African Air Force B-25 Mitchells, escorted by Fifteenth Air Force P-38 Lightnings, bomb the Sofia marshaling yard. Fighter pilots report shooting down five enemy aircraft.

Pacific: Just north of Truk U.S. submarine *Apogon* makes an unsuccessful attack on a Japanese convoy headed for the island.

CENTRAL PACIFIC: Seventh Air Force sends nine B-24 Liberators from Nukufetau Island in the Ellice Islands to bomb Tarawa Atoll. Another nine B-24s from Nanumea Island attack Mille Atoll in the Carolines.

BOUGAINVILLE: The 2nd Battalion 21st Marines, now reinforced, drives the Japanese defenders from the coconut grove and advances 1,500 yards. The attack is supported by 20 TBF Avengers flying ground support missions and a heavy pre-assault bombardment by artillery. The marines capture the key intersection of Numa Numa Trail and East-West Trail.

NEW GUINEA: Fifth Air Force B-25 Mitchells bomb Japanese supply and troop concentration near Sio.

November 15

CBI: Fourteenth Air Force B-24 Liberators bomb the docks in the Kowloon area of Hong Kong.

ATLANTIC: The JCS planners anticipate strikes on the Japanese homeland from the Marshall Islands by December 1944 with the B-29 Stratofortress, a strategic bomber capable of flying long distances.

MEDITERRANEAN: Fifteenth Air Force B-24 Liberators, with P-38 Lightnings flying escort, bomb Eleusis airfield. Twelfth Air Force XII Air Support Command B-25 Mitchells bomb Kalamaki airfield.

ITALY: Fifth Army commander Mark Clark orders an end to the offensives by X Corps and VI Corps. Weather, terrain, and exhaustion have forced the Allies to culminate as the divisions are unable to make any further progress. The Germans are able to reinforce with two divisions and assess that the Allies can be held south of Rome during the winter months. The Fifth Army begins a period of reorganizing and consolidating in preparation for a second offensive. Between October 7 and this day, VI Corps has taken nearly 9,700 casualties. The British X Corps suffers 2,800 casualties. Northwest African Air Force fighters attack road transports near Ancona.

SOUTHWEST PACIFIC AREA: U.S. submarine *Crevalle* torpedoes and sinks a Japanese cargo ship west of Luzon in the Philippines. U.S. submarine *Narwhal* lands supplies and evacuates fighters at Mindanao, Philippines.

PACIFIC: The V Amphibious Corps develops the operational plan for the invasion of the Marshalls. Major General Holland M. Smith commands the V Amphibious Corps. The 4th Maine Division, commanded by Major General Harry Schmidt, will seize Roi-Namur Islands. The army's 7th Infantry Division commanded by Major General Charles H. Corlett will seize Kwajalein. Eniwetok Atoll will be captured by an army-marine force led by marine brigadier general Thomas E. Watson. The small island of Majuro will be assigned to the V Amphibious Corps Reconnaissance Company and a battalion of the 106th Infantry Regiment of the 7th Infantry Division.

CENTRAL PACIFIC: Seventh Air Force B-24 Liberators from Canton Island and Nanumea Island bomb Jaluit Atoll in the Marshalls, Mille Atoll in the Carolines, and Makin Island in the Gilberts.

BOUGAINVILLE: Thirteenth Air Force B-24 Liberators bomb Kahili airfield. Fighters attack and destroy several barges along the coast and destroy two fuel supply points at Tonolai. The 419th Night Fighter Squadron, XIII Fighter Command, arrives on Guadalcanal Island from the United States with P-38 Lightnings and P-70 Havoc night fighters.

NEW GUINEA: Fifth Air Force sends over 30 B-24 Liberators against targets near Alexishafen. A group of 88 B-25 Mitchells with an escort of 16 P-40s heading for Wewak and Boram is intercepted by fighters escorting Japanese bombers headed for Gusap. The B-25s abort the mission and the P-40 pilots report 20 enemy aircraft destroyed with the loss of two fighters. P-47 Thunderbolt pilots report five enemy kills over Wewak.

November 16

CBI: Fourteenth Air Force sends 11 B-24 Liberators, two B-25 Mitchells, and four P-40s to attack the Kowloon docks at Hong Kong.

ETO: Eighth Air Force VIII Bomber Command attacks two targets in Norway, the industrial areas at Knaben and Rjukan, with B-17s. Over Knaben, 130 bombers hit the target. One B-17 is lost and seven others are damaged; aircrews report two enemy fighters shot down. Over Rjukan, 147 bombers hit the target; one B-17 is lost and one damaged. A later strike on Rjukan by 29 B-24 Liberators results in no losses or casualties.

Air Marshal Sir Trafford L. Leigh-Mallory, RAF, is named Air Commander in Chief, Allied Expeditionary Air Force (AEAF). Brigadier General William O. Butler, USAAF, is named deputy commanding general.

MEDITERRANEAN: Fifteenth Air Force B-17s bomb the airfield at Istres-Le-Tube, while B-26 Marauders, escorted by P-38 Lightnings, bomb the Salon-de-Provence airfield.

Northwest African Air Force and Twelfth Air Force B-25 Mitchells attack the Eleusis airfield in Greece. Fifteenth Air Force P-38 Lightnings provide cover for the raid.

ITALY: The U.S. 36th Infantry Division relieves the 3rd Infantry Division in the Mignano area.

PACIFIC: U.S. submarine *Corvina* is sunk by Japanese submarine *I-176,* south of Truk.

CENTRAL PACIFIC: Seventh Air Force B-24 Liberators from Nanumea and Nukufetau Islands bomb Jaluit and Maloelap Atolls in the Marshalls. Kwajalein Atoll in the Marshalls and Little Makin Island and Tarawa Atoll in the Gilberts are attacked by individual bombers.

BOUGAINVILLE: Thirteenth Air Force B-25 Mitchells and B-24 Liberators bomb the Buka Island airfield, while other B-25 Mitchells attack logistics targets along the coastline of Bougainville. P-40s and P-39 Airacobras also carry out attacks on gun positions along the coast and near Kieta and Tonolai Harbors.

NEW GUINEA: Fifth Air Force B-25 Mitchells bomb targets near Finschhafen. P-39 Airacobras, with P-40s providing cover, strafe barges from Saidor to Madang. P-38 Lightnings encounter a large force of Japanese fighters over Wewak. Pilots report six enemy aircraft shot down and two P-38s lost. PBY Catalinas attack Japanese shipping off New Guinea, sinking a Japanese cargo vessel.

November 17

CBI: Fourteenth Air Force sends eight P-40s to strafe the airfield and barracks at Kengtung, China. In French Indochina, four P-40s attack construction equipment at Dong Cuong airfield.

Mediterranean: Fifteenth Air Force B-17s, escorted by P-38 Lightnings, attack the Eleusis airfield, destroying several aircraft on the ground and damaging the runways and support buildings. Northwest African Air Force B-25 Mitchells attack the airfield at Kalamaki.

Pacific: U.S. submarine *Capelin* departs Darwin, Australia, and disappears without a trace. U.S. submarine *Drum* torpedoes and sinks a Japanese submarine depot ship northwest of New Ireland.

Central Pacific: Seventh Air Force sends more than 20 B-24 Liberators to bomb Mille atoll in the Carolines, Maloelap Atoll in the Marshalls, and Tarawa Atoll in the Gilberts.

Bougainville: Thirteenth Air Force B-24 Liberators bomb Buka and Bonis. B-25 Mitchells also bomb Kieta. Destroyers conduct naval gunfire missions against Buka airfield. Japanese aircraft attack convoy bringing reinforcements from the 21st Marine Regiment to the island. A high-speed transport is sunk.

November 18

CBI: Fourteenth Air Force P-40s strafe troops and sink a troop barge at Shihmen, China.

ETO: Eighth Air Force VIII Bomber Command sends B-24 Liberators against the Oslo/Kjeller airfield in Norway. Of the 82 bombers that hit the target, nine are lost and 13 are damaged; aircrews report 10 enemy aircraft destroyed. Over France, five B-17s drop 980,000 leaflets over Paris, Orleans, Chartres, Rennes, and Le Mans.

Ninth Air Force C-47s of the IX Troop Carrier Command conduct a rehearsal of the cross-Channel airborne operation with paratroopers of the U.S. 101st Airborne Division.

Mediterranean: Fifteenth Air Force B-17s, with P-38 escort, bomb Eleusis airfield.

Italy: Major General Geoffrey Keyes arrives from Sicily and takes command of the newly reorganized II Corps, made up of the 3rd and 36th Infantry Divisions. The Fifth Army is now made up of three corps: the British X Corps with two infantry divisions east of the Garigliano River Valley; the II Corps covering a five-mile front south of the town of Mignano and north of Route 6; and the VI Corps, commanded by Major General John P. Lucas, composed of the 45th and 34th Infantry Divisions, holding the area from Monte Sammucro north of Route 6 to the town of Pozzilli, then to the area north of the town of Coli, covering a front of about 15 miles.

Southwest Pacific Area: U.S. submarine *Bluefish* sinks a Japanese destroyer and damages an oiler *Ondo* in the Celebes Sea. U.S. submarine *Crevalle* unsuccessfully attacks a Japanese landing ship/aircraft transport in the Sulu Sea.

Central Pacific: Seventh Air Force sends 19 B-24 Liberators to bomb Mille Atoll, while two B-24s bomb Tarawa Atoll. Carrier Task Group 50.4, commanded by Rear Admiral Frederick C. Sherman, sends aircraft to attack Nauru.

Bougainville: The Battle of Piva Forks Continuing to expand the perimeter to clear an area believed to be suitable for an airfield, the 2nd and 3rd Battalions, 3rd Marines, attack along the east fork of the Piva River, a meandering stream that cuts through the swamp.

Thirteenth Air Force B-24 Liberators bomb the airfields at Kara and on Buka Island.

New Guinea: Fifth Air Force B-25 Mitchells and B-26 Marauders attack enemy positions near Sattelberg.

November 19

CBI: Fourteenth Air Force B-25 Mitchells attack Japanese shipping in the South China Sea, damaging a number of vessels and attacking warehouses and wharves at Swatow, China.

ETO: Eighth Air Force VIII Bomber Command sends 161 B-17s and three Pathfinder B-17s against targets near Gelsenkirchen, Germany. The bombers are unable to acquire the target due to a combination of weather and malfunctioning radar equipment and head to alternate targets. Over France, six B-17s drop over leaflets on Amiens and Reims, then head for the Netherlands and Belgium to drop leaflets over Amsterdam, The Hague, Brussels, and Ghent. Over two million leaflets are dropped on this mission.

Mediterranean: As the Fifth Army reorganizes, the British Eighth Army begins attacks against German defenses on the Adriatic coast of Italy. The Germans have established a forward line of defense called the Winter Line, anchored on the Garigliano River and stretching across the high hills guarding the Rapido River Valley and ending in the Apennines. The second line of defense is far more elaborate and is called the Gustav Line. It controls the dominating heights of the Rapido River Valley at the heights of Cassino, blocking Route 6, the main road to Rome. The plan is to draw German reinforcements away from the center, leaving weak defenses vulnerable to attack by the Fifth Army, which will push the enemy to the entrance of the Liri River Valley. The approach is marked by mountain peaks that stand like sentinels, providing clear observation and preventing any advance. The Germans have built log and earth fortifications on these peaks, and have carefully covered the approaches with mines and obstacles, all covered by machine guns, mortars, or artillery. There are three roads leading into Cassino, all of them covered by fire from the dominating hills above. No advance can be made until the mountain peaks are controlled by infantry.

Italy: Twelfth Air Force XII Air Support Command A-36 Intruder (Apache) fighter-bombers and P-40s bomb a bridge near Cassino and the bridge at Pontecorvo.

Bougainville: Thirteenth Air Force B-25 Mitchells bomb the Matchin Bay area and bomb the airfield on Ballale Island.

Pacific: U.S. submarine *Harder* attacks Japanese convoy and sinks two transports.

Captain John P. Cromwell, commanding a Submarine Coordinated Attack Group from USS *Sculpin*, possesses secret intelligence information concerning U.S. submarine and surface fleet operations, as well as future military plans. While establishing a line of submarines near Truk, the *Sculpin* is severely damaged by a

Japanese depth-charge attack. He orders the sub to surface and engage the enemy directly, buying time so the crew can abandon ship. Knowing his capture will provide the enemy with valuable intelligence information, Captain Cromwell decides to remain on board as the *Sculpin* sinks. By saving the crew and sacrificing himself in an unselfish act of gallantry Captain Cromwell will receive the Medal of Honor.

CENTRAL PACIFIC: Seventh Air Force sends 31 B-24 Liberators from Ellice Island bases to bomb Makin Island and Tarawa atoll.

BOUGAINVILLE: The Japanese roadblock on the Numa Numa Trail is captured by 3rd Battalion 3rd Marines, using light tanks. The 145th Infantry Regiment of the 37th Infantry Division arrives, along with the 135th, 136th, and 140th Artillery Battalions.

NEW GUINEA: Fifth Air Force B-25 Mitchells and B-26 Marauders bomb Japanese positions near Sattelberg and A-20 Havocs bomb enemy positions near Finschhafen.

November 20

ITALY: Northwest African Air Force B-25 Mitchells bomb the railway junction at Porto Civitanova, and attack targets around Pedaso, Giulianova, and Loreto.

SOUTHWEST PACIFIC AREA: Navy PBY Catalinas sink a Japanese cargo vessel north of New Ireland.

PACIFIC: U.S. submarine *Harder* torpedoes and sinks a Japanese transport northeast of the Marianas.

CENTRAL PACIFIC: Tarawa Operation Galvanic. The plan is for the V Amphibious Corps to capture three important objectives in the Carolines: Betio Island in Tarawa Atoll, which has an airstrip on it, Apamama atoll, which is suitable for an airfield, and Makin Atoll, which can be used as a base for future operations against the Marshalls. Marines of the 2nd Marine Division are assigned Betio Island, Tarawa Atoll, and Apamama. The 165th RCT of the 27th Infantry Division is to land on Makin Atoll. Vice Admiral Raymond A. Spruance, Commander of Central Pacific Forces, is the overall commander. The V Amphibious Corps is commanded by marine major general Holland "Howlin Mad" Smith. Rear Admiral Harry W. Hill commands Task Force 53, which has overall command and control of the amphibious landing on Tarawa. Major General Julian C. Smith is the 2nd Marine Division commander. Rear Admiral Richmond Kelly Turner commands Task Force 52, and has command and control of the amphibious assault on Makin. The army component is the 27th Infantry Division, commanded by Major General Ralph C. Smith. Admiral Chester W. Nimitz, concerned that the Japanese will attack the task forces with air and naval forces, has ordered the quick capture of the objectives. This has affected the support plan for the assaults.

Betio is about three miles long and 800 yards at its widest point and is surrounded completely by a coral reef that prevents landing craft from crossing and reaching shore. Sitting about 10 feet above sea level, it is one of the most heavily fortified positions in the world. There are nearly 500 pillboxes and reinforced bunkers, covered with obstacles, mines, and barbed wire, all covered by heavy caliber

Infantrymen from 2nd Battalion, 165th Infantry Regiment, approach Yellow beach on Makin Atoll, November 20, 1943.

guns and machine guns. Nearly 3,000 Japanese troops of the Special Naval Landing Force have been training and preparing for this attack for months.

The marine planners account for the limitations imposed by the coral reef by using LVT (Land Vehicle Tracked) amphibious tractors for the first wave. These tractors can swim from the ships and drive across the reef. The LVTs have no armor protection and no ramp, forcing troops to clamber over the sides. After a poorly coordinated air and naval bombardment, the initial assault makes the 10-mile approach to the island and lands three reinforced battalion landing teams on the northwest side of the island, centered on a lagoon, which has a long pier jutting into the ocean. Farthest west is Red Beach One, the target of 3rd Battalion 2nd Marines (3/2); in the center is Red Beach Two, the target of 2nd Battalion 2nd Marines (2/2); Red Beach Three is the responsibility of 2nd Battalion 8th Marines (2/8). Two destroyers enter the lagoon, preceded by minesweepers, but do not provide gunfire support until later. The LVTs are stopped at the seawall, and the marines jump over the sides of the Alligators into an intense volume of gunfire. About 1,500 Marines land in about 10 minutes, but are almost immediately pinned down on the narrow strip of sand against the seawall. Landing teams 3/2 and 2/2 take heavy casualties, but landing team 2/8 is able to land without serious casualties. Major Henry P. "Jim" Crowe commands on Red Beach Three; he wades in carrying a shotgun with a cigar clenched in his teeth. "Look," he calls to his men, "The sons of bitches can't hit me. Do you think they can hit you?" Get moving!" "Go!" Crowe's men are unable to join with 2/2. The initial assault bogs down as shocked and disorganized marines cluster in small groups. One group clusters on the western side of the island called Green Beach. Major Michael P. Ryan takes charge and organizes them to fight and moves about 500 yards eastward behind Red Beach One.

Colonel David M. Shoup, who had planned the entire operation, also commands the landing force and comes in with the first wave. Attempting to bring order out of chaos with only minimal communications to subordinates or to the division, Shoup orders reinforcements. The regimental reserve, landing team 1st Battalion 2nd Marines and the division reserve, 3rd Battalion 8th Marines in LCVP (Landing Craft Vehicle Personnel), cannot cross the reef, forcing the marines to wade in from 500 to 1,000 yards onto the beachhead. Japanese fire tears into the struggling ranks. Sherman tanks are landed, but only two of the 14, which make it to the shore, are operational at the end of the day. By the end of the day, five battalions are ashore, maybe 5,000 men—but at least 1,500 are casualties. General Julian Smith and Admiral Hill report to Spruance, "Issue in doubt." Yard by yard, individuals and small groups of marines advance into the teeth of enemy fire to take out Japanese positions close to the seawall.

Staff Sergeant William J. Bordelon is a member of the assault engineer platoon of the 1st Battalion, 18th Marines, attached to the 2nd Marine Division. Bordelon is one of only four survivors of his assault team who made it to the seawall. Staff Sergeant Bordelon begins improvising explosive charges and then scrambles from cover to attack and destroy two of the closest Japanese pillboxes. Painfully wounded when one of the demolition charges explodes in his hand, he continues to work, even after being wounded by enemy machine-gun fire as he tries to assault a third pillbox. Without explosives, he provides covering fire with his rifle to assist other marines as they scale the seawall. Disregarding his own wounds, Staff Sergeant Bordelon goes to the aid of one wounded marine demolition man and another marine wounded while trying to assist. He obtains additional explosives and sets out to attack a fourth Japanese machine-gun position when he is killed by enemy fire. Staff Sergeant Bordelon's exceptional heroism, his unselfish devotion to his fellow marines, and the skill he displayed in action against a determined and prepared enemy will win him the Medal of Honor.

First Lieutenant William Deane Hawkins, commanding a Scout Sniper Platoon, is among the first to land at Tarawa, taking on enemy defenders at the end of the Betio pier. As the situation becomes more desperate, First Lieutenant Hawkins leads his men in attacks on pillboxes and defensive positions using grenades and explosives. At dawn on 21 November, First Lieutenant Hawkins again leads an assault on a formidable position protected by five machine-guns. Ignoring the heavy fire directed against him, Hawkins returns fire, suppressing the enemy until he can destroy the position with hand grenades. Although wounded in the chest, he refuses to fall back, destroying three more pillboxes before he is fatally wounded. His extraordinary courage and relentless fighting spirit in the face of formidable opposition will win him the Congressional Medal of Honor.

Although suffering a serious and painful leg wound, Colonel Shoup rallies the broken elements that huddle along the sea wall and organizes the effort to advance against reinforced Japanese positions that have unrestricted fields of fire. Over the two days of major combat, Colonel Shoup has organized attacks against these exceptionally strong and fanatically defended positions. His personal leadership, indomitable will, and fearlessness in the face of enormous odds directly lead to the capture of the island, make him a legend in the Marine Corps, and he will win the Medal of Honor.

A turret fire on the battleship USS *Mississippi* kills 40 sailors and injures nine others.

CENTRAL PACIFIC: Makin Operation Galvanic. Preceded by closely coordinated naval gunfire and carrier air strikes, three battalion landing teams (designated as 1, 2, and 3 BLT) of the 165th Regimental Combat Team land on three beaches on Butaritari Island. The preparation includes 2,000-pound "daisy cutter" bombs on suspected Japanese positions in the center of the island. 1 BLT and 3 BLT land first on the far western side of the island and advance eastward encountering only light harassing fire from a few snipers. After another interval of naval and aerial bombardment, 2 BLT lands in the face of machine-gun fire on the northwestern side of the island in the lagoon and moves into the center of the Japanese defenses. The troops land with light and medium tanks and bring on communications equipment and immediately are able to emplace artillery. On order from Major General Holland Smith, V Amphibious Corps commander, 3 BLT goes into reserve in case it is needed on Tarawa. Some natives emerge from cover, shell-shocked but happy to see the Americans. They report that between 400 and 500 Japanese troops are on the island.

Encountering a formidable tank barrier, along with trenches, pillboxes, and gun emplacements, the infantrymen make a coordinated assault using tanks, engineers, and artillery to clear the eastern half of the island and consolidate their positions for the night. Major General Ralph C. Smith, the 27th Infantry Division commander, lands during the evening to take charge of the battle. Losses have been light, 25 killed and 62 wounded. One of the dead is Colonel J. G. Conroy, commander of the 165th RCT, killed while he was directing tanks against snipers.

BOUGAINVILLE: The Japanese counterattack the 3/3 Marines holding the Numa Numa roadblock. The enemy is thrown back after taking heavy losses.

Thirteenth Air Force attacks Bonis airfield with 45 B-25 Mitchells, Royal New Zealand Air Force Venturas, and P-38 Lightnings. B-25s also strafe coastal villages around Empress Augusta Bay.

NEW GUINEA: Fifth Air Force B-25 Mitchells and B-26 Marauders attack Japanese positions near the Sattelberg area and sink or damage transports in Hansa Bay. A-20 Havocs attack targets in the Lae area. B-24 Liberators bomb Gasmata Island off New Britain.

November 21

CBI: Fourteenth Air Force P-40s and four B-25 Mitchells attack the town of Tzeli, China. Four B-25s attack Japanese shipping on the South China Sea, damaging a cargo ship and buildings at Taiping-hsu airfield.

MEDITERRANEAN: Field Marshal Albert Kesselring takes command of Army Group C, the German command responsible for Italy. Army Group C consists of two armies, the Tenth Army, defending Rome and the southern area of Italy, and the Fourteenth Army, defending central and northern Italy. Kesselring intends to make the Allies fight for every mile gained, use the mountainous terrain to the best advantage, and wear them down with casualties.

ITALY: Fifteenth Air Force B-26 Marauders bomb the Civitavecchia harbor, a bridge at Fano, and the marshaling yard at Chiusi. Northwest African Air Force B-25 Mitchells bomb gun emplacements at Gaeta. Allied aircraft attack strongpoints in the Santa Maria Imbaro and Poggiofiorito areas.

PACIFIC: U.S. submarine *Trigger* sinks Japanese cargo ship in the Yellow Sea.

CENTRAL PACIFIC: Seventh Air Force B-24 Liberators from Funafuti Atoll and Nanumea Island in the Ellice Islands bomb Nauru Island in the Gilberts. U.S. submarine *Nautilus* lands a marine reconnaissance company on Abemama Island in the Gilberts.

TARAWA: Having gained some level of organization, Colonel Shoup orders each landing team to attack. Major Ryan is ordered to take all of Green Beach. 1st Battalion 8th Marines is to land on Red Beach Two near the pier. Unfortunately the marines of 1/8 begin to wade into the lagoon in the wrong direction and immediately are taken under fire from the Japanese positions. They suffer 300 casualties getting to the beachhead. Destroyers USS *Ringold* and USS *Dashiell* support with naval gunfire and are quite effective. Air support, however, is not. Ryan, making progress with his makeshift team, now supported by tanks, is reinforced with the 1st Battalion, 6th Marines. The 2nd Battalion 6th Marines lands on nearby Bairiki Island to secure the island for the landing of the artillery to land, which will fire support. Shoup sends a message to General Julian Smith: "Casualties many. Percentage dead: unknown. Combat efficiency: we are winning." On the night of November 21, Colonel Merritt A. "Red Mike" Edson, who won the Medal of Honor at Guadalcanal, takes command of the battle from Colonel Shoup.

The V Amphibious Corps Reconnaissance Unit, with a squad of army engineers supported by the submarine USS *Nautilus,* attacks Japanese defenders on Apamama Atoll. The *Nautilus* provides gunfire for the assault, but the Japanese are well prepared and the assault fails.

MAKIN: Supported by carrier air strikes, 1 BLT and 2 BLT clear enemy snipers and eliminate Japanese positions as they advance eastward into the heart of the Japanese defenses. The Japanese offer ineffective resistance, mostly due to the heavy volume of preparatory fire the day before. Again there is effective use of engineers, artillery, and tanks working with the infantry. Positions are consolidated and Japanese infiltrators are fought off during a long night. U.S. casualties are 18 killed, 26 wounded. Another two soldiers are killed and 13 wounded by a daisy cutter bomb from a navy aircraft that is mistakenly dropped on friendly lines.

SOLOMONS: Major General Ralph J. Mitchell (USMC) replaces Brigadier General Nathan F. Twining (USAAF) as Commander Air Solomons (COMAIRSOLS).

NEW GUINEA: Fifth Air Force A-20 Havocs attack the Finschhafen area. B-24 Liberators bomb Gasmata Island off New Britain.

November 22

CARIBBEAN: German submarine *U-516* torpedoes and sinks U.S. tanker off Panama.

MEDITERRANEAN: Sextant Conference. President Franklin D. Roosevelt, Prime Minister Winston S. Churchill, and Generalissimo Chiang Kai-shek confer in Cairo, Egypt. Talks are held concerning Operation Overlord (the overall plan for the invasion of western Europe) and the possibility of expanding operations in the Mediterranean Theater of Operations. Churchill desires an Allied operation to capture the Greek island of Rhodes (Operation Accolade), which could delay Overlord. The leaders also discuss future operations against Japan and plans for the China-Burma-India Theater (CBI). These included a plan for an amphibious landing and offensive in Burma (Operation Buccaneer and Champion) and basing the new long-range B-29 bombers in the CBI (Operation Twilight).

ITALY: Fifteenth Air Force B-26 Marauders, escorted by P-38 Lightnings, bomb the rail lines at Foligno and a bridge at Ciciana. Twelfth Air Force XII Air Support Command sends over 100 P-40s, B-25 Mitchells, and RAF aircraft against German positions in the Lanciano-Fossacesia area. P-40s also attack transportation targets at Fabriano, Viticuso, Vallerotonda, and Urbino. A-36 Intruder (Apache) fighter-bombers attack the chemical works, harbor, and railyards at Civitavecchia and bomb San Vittore del Lazio.

SOUTHWEST PACIFIC AREA: U.S. submarine *Drum* is damaged by depth charges north of New Guinea and ends its patrol.

PACIFIC: U.S. submarine *Seahorse* sinks a Japanese cargo ship in the East China Sea. U.S. submarine *Tinosa* sinks two Japanese cargo ships off Palau and receives minor damage in a depth charge attack.

CENTRAL PACIFIC: Seventh Air Force sends 11 B-24 Liberators to bomb Mille Atoll in the Carolines. Aircrews report two Japanese fighters shot down.

TARAWA: Colonel Edson orders 1/6, assembled on Green Beach and in good order, to attack eastward and make contact with marines on Red One. The 1/8 is to attack west to eliminate Japanese resistance facing the lagoon in front of Red One. The rest of the 8th Marines (2/8 and 3/8) are to attack east. The marines, better organized and receiving resupply, now launch coordinated attacks with engineers, tanks, and artillery. The 3rd Battalion 6th Marines lands on Green Beach.

On Red Beach Three, the 8th Marines are unable to advance against three heavily fortified strongpoints. A shore party led by First Lieutenant Alexander "Sandy" Bonnyman appears on the beach, and on his own initiative he organizes a team of 21 engineers with flamethrowers and demolition charges to make a coordinated assault on the positions. As the marine riflemen provide covering fire, Bonnyman leads his group into a maelstrom of fire, methodically taking down each position. As the Japanese begin to break, Bonnyman is killed in the firefight. Only 13 of his men survive the attack. Bonnyman's cool courage and leadership in turning the tide of battle for the 8th Marines will win him the Medal of Honor.

General Julian Smith links up with Colonel Edson after nearly being killed when he attempts to enter the lagoon. The exhausted marines are unable to sustain the

Marines of the 2nd Marine Division, working in teams, assault a Japanese defensive position on Tarawa about November 22, 1943.

momentum of their attacks. The 2/8 and 3/8 are rotated out of the battle line to Bairiki, while artillery is landed on Green Beach.

During the night, the Japanese attempt a furious coordinated counterattack on the marine positions. They are stopped by artillery, naval gunfire from destroyers (who use up every one of their five-inch gun shells during the night), and by determined marines, who often fight the enemy hand-to-hand.

U.S. destroyer rams Japanese submarine *I-35.*

MAKIN: General Holland Smith authorizes the release of 3 BLT to conduct the final attack on Butaritari Island. The fresh battalion makes a rapid advance, supported by tanks, artillery, and carrier air strikes. A water-borne flanking movement lands troops on the backside of the island to cut off the Japanese retreat and to clear Kuma Island of any enemy troops. The infantry stops about 5,000 yards short of the end of the island as night begins to fall. The advance results in six killed and 17 wounded. During the night, Japanese troops make several attacks on the American positions. It becomes quickly apparent to the men that many of the Japanese are drunk.

BOUGAINVILLE: Thirteenth Air Force P-40s encounter Japanese fighters over Empress Augusta Bay and report five enemy kills. P-38 Lightnings strafe barges and shore targets at Chabai.

NEW BRITAIN: Fifth Air Force sends over 100 B-25 Mitchells and B-24 Liberators to bomb Cape Gloucester and Gasmata Island.

November 23

CBI: Fourteenth Air Force sends 13 B-25 Mitchells, 24 P-40s, and seven P-51 Mustangs against the railroad yards and warehouse area of Yoyang, China.

ETO: Ninth Air Force B-26 Marauders bomb the Berck-sur-Mer and Saint-Omer/ Longuenesse airfields in France.

ITALY: The 1st Special Service Force, a group of Canadian and American commandos led by Colonel Robert T. Frederick, is attached to the U.S. 36th Infantry Division.

SOUTHWEST PACIFIC AREA: U.S. submarine *Blackfish* sinks a Japanese transport off northern New Guinea. U.S. submarine *Capelin* sinks a Japanese cargo ship in the Molucca Sea.

PACIFIC: U.S. submarine *Gudgeon* attacks a Japanese convoy, sinking an escort vessel and transport and damaging two fleet tankers in the East China Sea.

CENTRAL PACIFIC: Seventh Air Force sends six B-24 Liberators to bomb Emidj and Jabor islands in the Jaluit Atoll in the Marshalls.

TARAWA: Japanese resistance is shattered and 3/6 advances in a coordinated assault with tanks and engineers to the eastern tip of the island, killing 450 of the enemy and

Marines clear the final Japanese defensive positions on Tarawa with flamethrowers, November 23, 1943.

suffering 34 casualties. The last area to fall is the defenses in front of Red One, as both 1/8 and 3/2 attack to clear out the last few Japanese left alive. Many of the enemy kill themselves rather than be captured. By 1305, General Julian Smith notifies General Holland Smith that the island is secure. U.S. aircraft begin landing on the airstrip almost immediately. It is named Hawkins Field after Lieutenant Deane Hawkins, whose bravery on the first day of the battle as the scout-sniper platoon leader stood out among innumerable acts of bravery. The Americans capture 146 prisoners, but these are almost all Korean laborers. Only eight members of the Special Naval Landing Force are captured—the rest of the nearly 3,000 who defended the island are dead.

In the three-day assault on Tarawa, 18,088 marines and sailors landed and suffered 3,407 casualties. The marines lost 997 killed, 2,233 wounded, and 88 missing. Navy casualties are 30 killed and 59 wounded. The American public is shocked by the casualties and by the headlines of American newspapers, reporting that marines were slaughtered wholesale. Congress even talks of an investigation. But General Alexander Vandegrift, the new commandant of the Marine Corps, and Colonel Edson both provide full facts to the press and the shock is replaced by a resolve to face such terrible losses in the future.

The experience on Tarawa shapes the American approach to amphibious operations in the Central Pacific for the remainder of the war. Issues of fire support coordination for air and naval gunfire are resolved; the Japanese defenses are closely studied to make adjustments in the weapons and tactics employed against them. The LVT and the Sherman tank have proved their worth and will be incorporated in future amphibious assaults.

Most of all, Tarawa becomes one of those touchstones in American history, where the word is spoken reverently, like Gettysburg or Valley Forge, unforgettable places where American courage is enshrined forever.

Makin: The tip of Butaritari Island is reached by 3 BLT, as tanks and infantrymen kill isolated groups of Japanese. General Ralph Smith reports to General Holland Smith: "Makin Taken." Out of the 284 troops of the Japanese Special Naval Landing Force that occupied the island, three are captured. There are approximately 300 Korean laborers on the island as well, and 101 surrender. U.S. casualties are 66 killed and 150 wounded

Gilberts: The 2nd Battalion 6th Marines lands on Eita Island in pursuit of the last Japanese defenders on the Gilberts. Japanese sub *I-35* is sunk by two U.S. destroyers.

Bougainville: Chabai is attacked by 23 B-25 Mitchells, six Royal New Zealand Air Force Venturas, and 24 Navy F4U Corsairs. Two B-24 Liberators attack the target again, later in the day. Over Buka Island, 19 B-24 Liberators bomb Bonis and Buka airfields. Navy Task Force 39, the cruiser and destroyer force, bombards the area near Buka and Bonis.

New Guinea: Fifth Air Force B-25 Mitchells and A-20 Havocs bomb targets around Finschhafen.

November 24
CBI: Fourteenth Air Force B-25 Mitchells and 16 P-40s bomb Hanshow, China. B-25 Mitchells attack Amoy harbor and make two direct hits on a docked freighter.

CARIBBEAN: German submarine *U-516* torpedoes and sinks a U.S. freighter northwest of Cristobal, near the Panama Canal Zone.

ETO: Eighth Air Force sends seven B-17s to drop 2.4 million leaflets over Lille, France, and Brussels, Antwerp, Charleroi/Gosselies, and Ghent, Belgium.

MEDITERRANEAN: Fifth Army outlines its objectives for the December offensive, Operation Raincoat, the first assault on the German defenses known as the Winter Line. The offensive is aimed at capturing the three peaks that control the entrance to the Liri Valley. In Phase I, the British X Corps will assault the slopes of Monte Camino, while the II Corps attacks the lower hills of Monte la Difensa and Monte Maggiore. X Corps will then relieve II Corps in the area around Monte Maggiore. VI Corps will conduct simultaneous small diversionary attacks. Phase II is the capture of Monte Sammucro and the opening of the Colli-Atina Road. Phase III is an attack up the Liri Valley.

Twelfth Air Force Northwest African Air Force and Allied bombers support the British Eighth Army near Fossacesia. XII Air Support Command A-36 Intruder (Apache) fighter-bombers bomb Civitavecchia harbor.

Fifteenth Air Force B-17s, with P-38 escorts, attack the submarine base at Toulon.

PACIFIC: In successive separate attacks, USAAF B-24s and U.S. Navy PBY Catalinas damage a Japanese light cruiser transporting soldiers and supplies to Garove Island north of New Britain, forcing it to abandon the attempt.

CENTRAL PACIFIC: Seventh Air Force sends 20 B-24 Liberators to bomb Maloelap Atoll in the Marshalls. Aircrews report damage to the landing strip and hits on a cargo vessel. Japanese submarine *I-175* torpedoes and sinks an escort carrier, USS *Linscome Bay.* Over 600 men perish with the ship. *I-175* is damaged by depth charges from escort ships. The first attack in the Gilberts is costly for the navy; along with the loss of the *Linscome Bay,* nine aircraft are also lost in combat and the total casualties for the navy over a four-day period are 752 killed and 291 wounded.

MAKIN: The 165th RCT begins to re-embark, leaving behind an occupation force on Butaritari Island. For weeks afterward, individual Japanese soldiers will rush out from their hiding places to attack American troops.

BOUGAINVILLE: The 2nd and 3rd Battalions, 3rd Marines, advance on the East-West trail behind the heaviest artillery bombardment of the Pacific war. A 20-minute artillery preparation fires over 5,600 rounds on Japanese bunkers, foxholes, and trenches lying in the low swampy ground amidst heavy jungle. The advance is measured in yards. Even in the midst of battle, the frontline troops receive a real turkey dinner for Thanksgiving, an amazing logistical feat in itself. The men sit wherever convenient to eat their meal, completely ignoring the blood and carnage around them. The marines succeed in capturing the high ground beyond the trail but, during the course of the battle, suffer 115 casualties. Japanese losses are estimated at over 1,000.

Thirteenth Air Force sends B-25 Mitchells to hit the airfield at Kahili and a possible radio station at Mutupina Point. Fighters strafe Gazelle and Queen Carola harbors. Buka Island is bombed by 25 B-24 Liberators.

NEW GUINEA: Fifth Air Force B-25 Mitchells, B-26 Marauders, and A-20 Havocs bomb the village of Kalasa. Logistics sites near Finschhafen are bombed by 15 A-20

Havocs and B-25 Mitchells, escorted by P-38 Lightnings. B-24 Liberators, supported by P-38 Lightnings, bomb Gasmata Island.

November 25

CBI: Tenth Air Force B-25 Mitchells, escorted by P-51 Mustangs, bomb the Mingaladon airfield in Rangoon, Burma. Aircrews report two aircraft destroyed on the ground and two destroyed in the air. Two P-51 Mustangs are shot down. Fourteenth Air Force sends 14 B-25 Mitchells, with 16 P-38 Lightnings and P-51 Mustangs as escort, to attack the airfield at Shinchiku, China. Aircrews report damage to the airfield, hangars, and barracks. Enemy losses are estimated at 32 aircraft destroyed.

ATLANTIC: A U.S. Navy PB4Y Privateer (a B-24 variant) sinks German submarine *U-849* in the South Atlantic.

ETO: Eighth Air Force VIII Fighter Command employs P-47 Thunderbolts as bombers to attack the Saint-Omer airfield in France. P-38 Lightnings and P-47 Thunderbolts conduct offensive sweeps near Lille. The 401st Bombardment Group (Heavy) reaches operational status, giving the Eighth Air Force 22 operational heavy bomber groups. The Allied Expeditionary Air Force (AEAF) is activated. The RAF's Second Tactical Air Force and the U.S. Ninth Air Force are to be under the AEAF's operational control.

ITALY: Fifth Army's plan for an amphibious landing at Anzio (Operation Shingle) is approved. Twelfth Air Force XII Air Support Command aircraft bomb German gun positions and strongpoints near Lanciano and Fossacesia.

PACIFIC: U.S. destroyer sinks Japanese submarine *I-19* north of Gilberts. U.S. submarine *Albacore* sinks a Japanese cargo ship off northern New Guinea. U.S. submarine *Searaven* sinks a Japanese fleet tanker north of Ponape Island in the Carolines.

GILBERTS: The V Amphibious Corps Reconnaissance Unit, with a squad of army engineers supported by the submarine *Nautilus,* secures Apamama Atoll after discovering that the Japanese defenders have killed themselves. Work immediately begins on establishing an airfield capable of supporting Seventh Air Force bombers. The airfield will be named after the fighter ace, Lieutenant Commander Edward "Butch" O'Hare, killed in action on November 27. A destroyer sinks Japanese submarine *I-40* in the northern Gilberts.

BOUGAINVILLE: The 1st Battalion 9th Marines passes through the weary 3rd Marines to continue the advance. They encounter strongly entrenched Japanese defenders on a piece of high ground the marines later call Grenade Hill, because of the number of grenades the Japanese throw at the marines.

The Japanese send three destroyer transports with about 900 men and two destroyer escorts to reinforce Buka. Captain Arleigh A. Burke, commanding Destroyer Squadron 23, intercepts the force and in typical style makes an aggressive torpedo attack, sinking the two escort destroyers. The destroyer transports make a run for Rabaul, as Burke pursues.

NEW IRELAND: The Battle of Cape St. George. Destroyer Squadron 23, under command of Captain Arleigh A. Burke, attacks five Japanese destroyers. Three Japanese destroyers are sunk by torpedoes and gunfire and another destroyer is damaged. Burke's ships receive no damage.

November 26

CBI: Fourteenth Air Force B-25 Mitchells bomb Kiangling airfield in China. B-25s damage a freighter in Honghai Bay. Eight P-40s attack the Cam Duong railroad yards in French Indochina. B-25s sink a Japanese auxiliary minesweeper off Canton, China.

ATLANTIC: The Sextant Conference. The first part of the Sextant Conference concludes in Cairo. The CCS in preparation for the Eureka Conference in Teheran, lays out a plan for operations in Europe in 1944. In the Mediterranean, the Allies will advance to the Pisa-Rimini line. The partisans in Yugoslavia would be given aid. Turkey will be induced to enter the war. The Allies will capture the island of Rhodes to secure access to the Dardanelles. An amphibious operation will be conducted in the Bay of Bengal. Overlord, the cross-Channel invasion of Europe, will be delayed.

ETO: Eighth Air Force VIII Bomber Command attacks Bremen, Germany, and attempts to attack Paris, France. Over the port of Bremen, 350 B-17s and 77 B-24 Liberators are guided by 13 radar-equipped Pathfinder B-17s. U.S. losses are 22 B-17s and three B-24 Liberators. Another 142 B-17s, 17 Pathfinder B-17s, and 20 B-24s are damaged. Aircrews report at least 16 German fighters destroyed. Four B-17s are lost and 18 damaged in an attempt to attack Paris aborted due to heavy cloud cover. Aircrews report eight enemy aircraft destroyed. The 28 P-38 Lightnings and 353 P-47 Thunderbolts that escort these two missions report 36 enemy confirmed kills, three probables, and nine possibles. Four P-47s are shot down and the pilots are reported as missing. Another 10 fighters are damaged.

Ninth Air Force sends 140 B-26 Marauders to attack the Cambrai/Epinoy and Roye/Amy airfields in France. Military construction in Audinghen is also bombed.

ITALY: Fifteenth Air Force B-17s bomb the viaduct at Recco and the Rimini marshaling yard and bridge. B-26 Marauders bomb Cassino, and B-24 Liberators bomb bridges in the Fano, Cesano, Senigallia, and Falconara area. Twelfth Air Force B-25 Mitchells and A-20 Havocs attack the Ancona marshaling yard and harbor and German positions near Fossacesia, Lanciano, Castelfrentano, and troop concentrations near Palombaro and Casoli.

SOUTHWEST PACIFIC AREA: Vice Admiral Thomas C. Kinkaid takes command of the Seventh Fleet, replacing Vice Admiral Arthur S. Carpenter.

PACIFIC: U.S. submarine *Bowfin* sinks a Japanese army tanker and merchant cargo ship in the Andaman Sea. U.S. submarine *Raton* damages a Japanese ammunition ship northwest of the Saint Matthias Group. U.S. submarine *Ray* makes an unsuccessful attack on a Japanese cargo vessel between Truk and New Ireland, but sinks a Japanese transport southwest of Truk. U.S. submarine *Tinosa* sinks a Japanese cargo ship and damages another near the Palau Islands.

BOUGAINVILLE: The Japanese evacuate Grenade Hill, allowing the 1/9 Marines an easy victory.

Thirteenth Air Force B-24 Liberators, B-25 Mitchells, and fighter aircraft attack Buka and Bonis airfields.

NEW BRITAIN: Fifth Air Force B-24 Liberators bomb Gasmata Island and report hitting a Japanese cruiser off the coast.

NEW GUINEA: Australian forces clear the last Japanese defenders off Satelberg Ridge, opening the way to Finschhafen. The Japanese begin retreating westward to Saidor.

Fifth Air Force B-25 Mitchells attack barge locations near Sio. P-40s and P-47 Thunderbolts attack Japanese positions around Alexishafen, Madang, and Nubia. Over Finschhafen, P-39 Airacobras attack 40 Japanese fighters and bombers. Pilots report four aircraft shot down.

November 27
CBI: Tenth Air Force B-24 Liberators, escorted by P-38 Lightnings, and B-25 Mitchells, escorted by P-51 Mustangs, bomb Insein, Burma. Japanese fighters intercept the incoming strike and shoot down six fighters and three B-24s. Aircrews report 19 Japanese fighters shot down. B-24s sink Japanese army hospital ship in the Bismarck Sea. Fourteenth Air Force B-25 Mitchells bomb the docks and warehouses at Swatow, China, and attack a convoy of nine vessels heading toward Amoy in the Formosa Strait. Aircrews report one destroyer sunk and a destroyer and cargo ship damaged. In actuality, a transport is sunk and a torpedo boat damaged.
ITALY: Fifteenth Air Force B-17s, escorted by P-38 Lightnings, bomb the marshaling yard and bridges at Rimini and Grizzana and a bridge approach on the Reno River southwest of Bologna. Twelfth Air Force A-20 Havocs and B-25 Mitchells, with fighters and RAF aircraft of Northwest African Air Force, bomb enemy positions, gun emplacements, and transportation targets around Lanciano, Fossacesia, Castelfrentano, and Casoli. B-25s bomb Porto Civitanova.
PACIFIC: U.S. submarine *Bowfin* sinks a Vichy French cargo ship off the coast of French Indochina, near Binh Dinh. U.S. submarine *Seahorse* sinks a Japanese fleet tanker in the East China Sea.
CENTRAL PACIFIC: Seventh Air Force sends eight B-24 Liberators to bomb Mili Atoll in the Marshalls.
GILBERTS: The 2nd Battalion 6th Marines fights the Battle of Buariki on Eita Island in heavy jungle against determined Japanese of the Special Naval Landing Force. The combat is mostly close-in and brutal. Every one of the 175 Japanese is killed; 32 Americans are dead and 59 are wounded. This major combat action is eclipsed by the aftermath of the Battle of Tarawa.
BOUGAINVILLE: Thirteenth Air Force B-25 Mitchells bomb Queen Carola Harbor. B-24 Liberators bomb Bonis airfield. Other B-25 Mitchells and Royal New Zealand Venturas attack targets at the mouth of the Mobiai River and at Mutupina Point. The airfield on Buka Island is bombed by more than 20 B-24 Liberators.
NEW GUINEA: Fifth Air Force B-25 Mitchells and B-26 Marauders bomb the airfields at Boram and Finschhafen, and the town and harbor at Wewak. Aircrews report 15 enemy aircraft destroyed and 12 barges sunk.

November 28
CBI: Tenth Air Force B-24 Liberators bomb the Botataung docks at Rangoon. Aircrews report heavy damage to the docks and four enemy fighters shot down. B-25 Mitchells attack Sagaing. Fourteenth Air Force P-40s bomb and strafe Japanese barracks near Litsaoho, China. P-40s strafe the town area and airfield at Luang Prabang and attack the radio facilities and a barracks at Tran Ninh in French Indochina.

The "Big Three" at Tehran, Iran, during the Eureka conference, held from November 28 to December 1, 1943. Seated from left to right: Premier Joseph Stalin of the Soviet Union, President Franklin D. Roosevelt of the United States, and Prime Minister Winston S. Churchill of Great Britain. This is the first face-to-face meeting of the three war leaders.

MEDITERRANEAN: Twelfth Air Force B-25 Mitchells bomb warehouses, docks, marshaling yards, barracks, shipping, and other targets at Sibenik, Zara, and Dubrovnik.

Eureka Conference begins in Iran. President Franklin D. Roosevelt, Prime Minister Winston S. Churchill, and Marshall Joseph V. Stalin meet in Teheran, Iran, until November 30. Presented with the CCS proposals for operations in Europe in 1944, Stalin agrees with the American strategic approach for 1944 and endorses Overlord (the cross-Channel invasion of western Europe) and Anvil (the complementary plan for the invasion of southern France in support of Overlord), which are to be given priority over all other operations. Stalin promises to initiate an offensive timed with the cross-Channel invasion.

Concerning the Pacific, the United States will continue offensive operations in the Central and South Pacific drives, including seizure of the Marianas as a base for strategic bombing attacks on Japan. Much to the relief of the Americans, Stalin promises to enter the war against Japan once Germany has surrendered. The Allies discuss postwar plans, including a future United Nations organization and the settlement of boundaries for Poland.

SOUTHWEST PACIFIC AREA: U.S. submarine *Raton* sinks two Japanese cargo ships north of New Guinea.

PACIFIC: U.S. submarine *Bowfin* sinks two Japanese cargo ships off Binh Dinh, French Indochina, but is damaged by Japanese gunfire, ending its patrol. U.S. submarines *Pargo* and *Snook* attack a Japanese transport convoy northwest of the Marianas. *Snook* sinks one transport.

CENTRAL PACIFIC: Seventh Air Force sends 11 B-24 Liberators to bomb Nauru Island.

BOUGAINVILLE: Thirteenth Air Force B-25 Mitchells bomb and strafe the area near Mutupina Point. Fighters strafe Tinputs harbor and barges at Tonolai.

NEW GUINEA: Fifth Air Force B-24 Liberators bomb the airfields at Wewak and Boram. More than 40 B-25 Mitchells, B-26 Marauders, and A-20 Havocs attack villages on the Huon Peninsula and targets near Finschhafen.

November 29

CBI: Fourteenth Air Force B-25 Mitchells bomb the airfield and warehouses at Swatow and the power station at Amoy, China.

ATLANTIC: TBF Avengers from escort carrier USS *Bogue* accompanying convoy UGS (United States to Mediterranean, Slow) sink German submarine *U-86* east of the Azores. Two other U-boats are attacked, *U-238* and *U-764,* but escape without damage.

ETO: Eighth Air Force VIII Bomber Command sends 360 B-17s, escorted by 38 P-38 Lightnings and 314 P-47 Thunderbolts, against the port of Bremen, Germany. Only 154 bombers hit the target due to heavy clouds and malfunctioning radar equipment. Aircrews report 15 enemy fighters destroyed, but 13 B-17s are lost and 46 are damaged. The fighter pilots report 15 confirmed kills, four probables, and six possibles. U.S. fighter losses are seven P-38s and nine P-47s shot down; two P-47s are damaged. Over Paris, Reims, Chartres, Amiens, Le Mans, Orleans, and Rouen, France, eight B-17s drop more than a million-and-a-half leaflets.

Ninth Air Force sends 53 B-26 Marauders to bomb Chievres airfield in France.

MEDITERRANEAN: Twelfth Air Force B-25 Mitchells bomb Sarajevo, Yugoslavia.

ITALY: VI Corps makes diversionary attacks before Fifth Army's scheduled December 3 offensive, Operation Raincoat. Division and corps artillery fire on targets around San Pietro and San Vittore. The 3rd Ranger Battalion makes a diversionary reconnaissance in force toward San Pietro, an advance preceded by over 2,200 artillery rounds. Later in the day, after encountering strong German defenses, the battalion retreats, covered by an artillery barrage of 2,600 shells.

Other attacks are intended to capture limited objectives between Monte Corno and Monte Mare in order to draw German reserves north and away from the II Corps, where the main attack is to occur. The 45th Infantry Division is ordered to conduct attacks to seize favorable ground and open the Filignano-Sant' Elia road. The 179th Infantry Regiment attacks La Bandita and Monte La Posta to capture the village of Lagone. The 1st Battalion 179th Infantry attacks are stopped by heavy machine gun, mortar, and rifle fire from the hilltops. The 157th Infantry Regiment attacks to clear the road to Sant' Elia.

The 34th Infantry Division attacks to clear the Coli-Atina road and seize the hills north and south of Cerasuolo. The 1st Battalion 168th Infantry Regiment makes progress on Monte Pantano and stops several strong German counterattacks. The 133rd Infantry Regiment advances against German defenders on hills between Castelnuovo and Cerasuolo.

Seventy Fifteenth Air Force B-26 Marauders bomb the Grosseto airfield and marshaling yards. B-24 Liberators, with P-38 Lightnings flying escort, bomb near Furbara.

Near Cerasuolo, Staff Sergeant Allan M. Ohata, his squad leader, and three men, one of them Private Mikio Hasemoto, are ordered to protect the left flank of a platoon of Company B, 100th Infantry Battalion (Separate). When almost 40 enemy soldiers assault their position under the covering fire of two machine gunners, Private Hasemoto engages them with his Browning Automatic Rifle (BAR). When his weapon is damaged by enemy fire, he runs 10 yards to the rear, grabs another BAR and rejoins the fight. In the meantime, Staff Sergeant Ohata leaves his position and advances 15 yards through heavy fire to give Hasemoto covering fire, killing 10 of the enemy. When the second BAR jams, Hasemoto finds an M-1 rifle. Hasemoto and Ohata continue engaging the enemy until only three soldiers are left standing. The two men then charge forward to finish the fight. The following day Ohata and Hasemoto again defend their position against determined enemy attacks. Although Private Hasemoto is killed by enemy fire, his example of courage under fire and devotion to duty earns him the Medal of Honor. Staff Sergeant Ohata will also be awarded the Medal of Honor for his exemplary courage under fire.

During a flank attack on enemy-held high ground, Private Shizuya Hayashi of Company A charges an enemy machine-gun position singlehandedly, killing or driving off the defenders. Private Hayashi then engages an enemy antiaircraft gun, which opens fire on the company as it advances. Private Hayashi returns fire, killing nine enemy soldiers and capturing four others. Private Hayashi's extraordinary heroism in the face of enemy fire will win him the Medal of Honor.

SOUTHWEST PACIFIC AREA: U.S. submarine *Bonefish* sinks a Japanese cargo ship off Kangean Island, north of Bali. The ship is carrying 546 British prisoners of war.

PACIFIC: U.S. submarine *Paddle* attacks a Japanese fleet tanker near Eniwetok Atoll. U.S. submarines *Pargo* and *Snook* pursue the Japanese transport convoy northwest of the Marianas, each submarine sinking a transport and avoiding the escorts' counterattack. U.S. submarine *Snapper* sinks a Japanese transport off Hachijo Jima.

BOUGAINVILLE: The 1st Marine Parachute Battalion lands before dawn east of Cape Torokina at Koiari beach to attack a Japanese logistics base. Overrunning the site, they encounter heavy Japanese resistance. U.S. destroyer *Fullam* supported by F4U Corsairs provides close supporting fire to allow the marines to be evacuated.

Thirteenth Air Force sends 18 B-25 Mitchells against Tinputs Harbor. B-24 Liberators bomb Kieta, while P-39 Airacobras and navy SBD Dauntless dive-bombers attack warehouses at Mosigetta. Fighters attack Gazelle harbor and gun positions near Torokina Plantation. Navy Task Group 74.2, commanded by Captain Frank R. Walker, with two U.S. destroyers and two Australian destroyers, bombards enemy positions on Gasmata.

NEW BRITAIN: Fifth Air Force B-25 Mitchells and B-26 Marauders bomb Cape Gloucester.

November 30

CBI: Fourteenth Air Force P-40s bomb fuel and ammunition storage areas at Luchiangpa, China.

ATLANTIC: Eureka Conference statement

We the President of the United States, the Prime Minister of Great Britain, and the Premier of the Soviet Union, have met these four days past, in this, the Capital of our Ally, Iran, and have shaped and confirmed our common policy.

We express our determination that our nations shall work together in war and in the peace that will follow.

As to war—our military staffs have joined in our round table discussions, and we have concerted our plans for the destruction of the German forces. We have reached complete agreement as to the scope and timing of the operations to be undertaken from the east, west and south.

The common understanding which we have here reached guarantees that victory will be ours.

And as to peace—we are sure that our concord will win an enduring Peace. We recognize fully the supreme responsibility resting upon us and all the United Nations to make a peace which will command the goodwill of the overwhelming mass of the peoples of the world and banish the scourge and terror of war for many generations.

With our Diplomatic advisors we have surveyed the problems of the future. We shall seek the cooperation and active participation of all nations, large and small, whose peoples in heart and mind are dedicated, as are our own peoples, to the elimination of tyranny and slavery, oppression and intolerance. We will welcome them, as they may choose to come, into a world family of Democratic Nations.

No power on earth can prevent our destroying the German armies by land, their U Boats by sea, and their war plants from the air.

Our attack will be relentless and increasing.

Emerging from these cordial conferences we look with confidence to the day when all peoples of the world may live free lives, untouched by tyranny, and according to their varying desires and their own consciences.

We came here with hope and determination. We leave here, friends in fact, in spirit and in purpose.

Churchill, Stalin, and Roosevelt agree to support the Yugoslav partisans. They also agree to conduct Overlord in May of 1944, along with Anvil, the supporting attack in southern France. The Soviets will launch an offensive to contain as many German divisions as possible on the eastern front.

At the end of this conference, it is clear to Churchill that Britain has become the junior partner in the Alliance and that Britain's strategic objectives are growing irrelevant to the emerging partnership between Roosevelt and Stalin. Roosevelt leaves Teheran with a strong belief that a strong Soviet-American cooperation will both secure and maintain a peaceful postwar world.

TBF Avengers from escort carrier USS *Bogue* damage German submarine *U-238* east of the Azores.

ETO: Eighth Air Force VIII Bomber Command attacks the industrial area at Solingen, Germany, with B-17s, 29 B-24 Liberators, and three radar-equipped Pathfinder B-17s, escorted by 20 P-38 Lightnings and 327 P-47 Thunderbolts. Cloud cover limits the Liberators' effectiveness, and only 79 B-17s of 349 hit the target, led by one radar B-17. Three B-17s are shot down and 12 bombers are damaged. Aircrews report one enemy fighter destroyed. Fighter pilots report two probable kills and one possible kill. One P-38 is lost and one damaged, and five P-47s are lost and one damaged. The six pilots are listed as missing. Six B-17s drop over 1 million leaflets on Paris, Rouen, and Tours in France, then on Krefeld and Opladen in Germany.

ITALY: In the 45th Infantry Division sector, the 1st Battalion of the 179th continues its attack on La Bandita and attempts to take Langone. Both attacks are halted by enemy fire. In the 34th Division area, the 1st Battalion of the 168th Infantry Regiment holds positions on Monte Pantano against several German counterattacks. The 1st Battalion of the 133rd Infantry Regiment enters Castelnuovo; the 3rd Battalion moves to Monte la Rocca, and the 100th Battalion moves to Croce Hill. The regiment's progress is stopped by mortar and artillery fire.

Fifteenth Air Force B-26 Marauders bomb the Monte Molino railroad bridge, Montalto di Castro, Bastia, and Torgiano. B-24 Liberators, escorted by P-38 Lightnings, bomb Fiume. Twelfth Air Force A-20 Havocs attack German defenses around Lanciano, Fossacesia, Orsogna, Castelfrentano, and Guardiagrele. They also fly ground support missions for the 34th Infantry Division defending Monte Pantano.

SOUTHWEST PACIFIC AREA: Lieutenant General Walter Krueger, commander of Alamo Force, orders the 112th Cavalry Regimental Combat Team (in reality a 1,500-man detachment from the Texas National Guard, without horses) to be prepared to land on Arawe, New Britain, by December 15.

PACIFIC: U.S. submarine *Gato* sinks a Japanese army transport east of the Yap Islands, escaping counterattacks by an escorting submarine chaser. U.S. submarine *Skate* attacks Japanese carrier *Zuiho* with four torpedoes north of Truk. None of the torpedoes score a hit.

CENTRAL PACIFIC: Seventh Air Force B-24 Liberators bomb Maloelap Atoll in the Marshalls. A second strike of 20 additional B-24 Liberators on the atoll is aborted due to bad weather, but two bombers attack a cargo ship near the intended target.

BOUGAINVILLE: Thirteenth Air Force fighter aircraft with navy fighters attack barges and antiaircraft guns at Tonolai. Fighters are also active attacking targets around Numa Numa, Chabai, the Jakohina Mission area, Kangu, Malabita Hill, and Mosigetta.

NEW GUINEA: Fifth Air Force B-24 Liberators bomb Alexishafen and B-25 Mitchells and A-20 Havocs attack Kalasa and Japanese transports near Waroe.

December 1

CBI: Tenth Air Force B-24 Liberators, with P-38 Lightnings flying escort, bomb Insein in Burma. Over the target, they are attacked by Japanese fighters, and six B-24 Liberators are shot down and five others are damaged. B-25 Mitchells attack the newly-repaired Myitnge bridge and cause additional damage. Fourteenth Air Force sends 19 B-25 Mitchells, 24 P-40s, and 10 P-51 Mustangs against the Kowloon shipyards and the Taikoo docks in Hong Kong, China.

ETO: Eighth Air Force VIII Bomber Command attacks the industrial area at Solingen, Germany, with 206 B-17s, 69 B-24 Liberators, and five radar-equipped Pathfinder B-17s, escorted by 42 P-38 Lightnings and 374 P-47 Thunderbolts. U.S. losses are 19 B-17s and five B-24s shot down and 89 bombers damaged. Aircrew losses are 13 killed, 23 wounded, and 227 missing. They report that at least four enemy fighters are shot down. The P-47 pilots report 20 confirmed enemy kills, four probables, and seven possibles. Two P-38s are lost and one damaged; five P-47s are shot down and four are damaged. The seven pilots shot down are reported as missing. Ninth Air Force B-26 Marauders bomb the Chievres, Belgium, airfield and the airfields at Cambrai/Epinoy, Lille/Yendeville, and Cambrai/Niergnies in France.

ITALY: The 2nd Battalion 179th Infantry Regiment of the 45th Infantry Division attempts to take Hill 769, which overlooks Lagone from the south. German fire has been particularly effective in stopping the advance of the 179th. Patrols occupy the heights, but are pushed back by German counterattacks. In the 34th Infantry Division's area, the 168th Infantry Regiment battles to hold a series of small knobs on Monte Pantano. Minefields, steep terrain, and poor communications prevent any advance against the Germans defending in well-prepared positions.

Fifteenth Air Force sends over 100 B-17s against the ball bearing works and marshaling yard at Turin. B-26 Marauders, with fighter escort, attack bridges and railroad facilities at Aulla, Cecina, and Sestri Levante. Twelfth Air Force B-25 Mitchells bomb gun positions near Sant' Ambrogio. Other aircraft attack transportation and ground support targets around Casoli, Lanciano, Guardiagrele, Mignano, Minturno, and Chieti.

PACIFIC: U.S. submarine *Bonefish* sinks a Japanese transport in the Celebes Sea. U.S. submarine *Pargo* sinks a Japanese transport north of Ulithi Atoll near the Yap Islands. U.S. submarine *Peto* sinks a Japanese transport north of the Admiralty Islands, then escapes a counterattack from an escorting torpedo boat.

CENTRAL PACIFIC: Seventh Air Force sends four B-24 Liberators to bomb Mili Atoll in the Marshalls.

BOUGAINVILLE: Thirteenth Air Force B-25 Mitchells and P-38 Lightnings attack Malai. Over Empress Augusta Bay, P-39 Airacobras strafe Tonolai and support U.S. Navy SBD Dauntless dive-bombers attacking Japanese positions near the Jaba River and supply storage areas on Kara and Ballale Islands. Targets at Tenekow, Chabai, and Mutupina Point are also attacked.

NEW GUINEA: Fifth Air Force employs over 40 B-24 Liberators with P-47 escorts to bomb Wewak. About 50 Japanese fighters intercept them over the target. Aircrews report 11 enemy fighters shot down, but three B-24s are lost.

December 2

CBI: Fourteenth Air Force P-40s intercept 18 Japanese bombers and 30 fighters attacking Suichwan airfield in China. One enemy aircraft and two P-40s are shot down. Japanese positions near Changte, China, are attacked by 16 P-40s.

ETO: Four B-17s of Eighth Air Force VIII Bomber Command drop over two million leaflets on Bremen, Oldenburg, and Hamburg, Germany. One Pathfinder B-17 flies an Oboe test over Huls, Germany, dropping two 2,000-pound general purpose bombs and one photoflash bomb. The photoflash bomb is used for night photography and has a peak intensity of approximately 500,000,000 candlepower.

MEDITERRANEAN: Fifteenth Air Force B-17s bomb submarine pens at Marseilles.

ITALY: In the 34th Infantry Division area, the 3rd Battalion 168th Infantry Regiment attacks after a one-hour artillery bombardment and captures a small knob on Monte Pantano, but faces heavy counterattacks throughout the day and night.

Operation Raincoat begins in a steady rain with the heaviest artillery preparation yet seen in the campaign in Italy. A total of 22,500 rounds are fired in the II Corps sector. The 1st Special Service Force clears Monte la Difensa and moves to take Monte la Remetanea.

Fifteenth Air Force B-24 Liberators, with fighter escort, bomb the railroad bridge and marshaling yard at Bolzano. B-26 Marauders bomb the bridge near Orvieto and the marshaling yard at Arezzo. Twelfth Air Force B-25 Mitchells, A-20 Havocs, and RAF aircraft conduct ground support missions near Monte Trocchio and Sant' Ambrogio. B-25s attack the bridge and approaches near Chieti.

German aircraft bomb Allied shipping at Bari, Italy, sinking three cargo ships, two carrying ammunition, and one ship carrying mustard gas. The catastrophic explosions resulting from the German bomb hits on these ships damage five other cargo ships and a tanker. At least 130 merchant seamen and sailors are killed and more than 70 are wounded.

CAIRO: Allied Military Strategy Conference. The CCS outlines a plan for the defeat of Japan. MacArthur's forces in the Southwest Pacific Area will advance along the north coast of New Guinea to capture the Vogelkop Peninsula by August 1944. Nimitz's Central Pacific forces will capture islands in the Marianas for use as bomber bases for the strategic attack on the Japanese home islands. Guam, Saipan, and Tinian are specific targets and will be captured by October 1944, with bombing operations beginning in December of 1944. The British will move into upper Burma to open the overland supply route into China to improve logistics support for U.S. air operations in China.

PACIFIC: U.S. submarine *Narwhal* lands ammunition and stores, and evacuates guerrillas from Mindanao, Philippines.

BOUGAINVILLE: Thirteenth Air Force B-25 Mitchells attack Malai, the Porror River, and Rigu Mission at Kieta. B-24 Liberators bomb Korovo and fighters strafe Chabai.

NEW GUINEA: Fifth Air Force B-25 Mitchells bomb the Borgen Bay area. Japanese positions around Finschhafen are bombed by 20 B-25 Mitchells and B-26 Marauders. B-24 Liberators bomb the area near Sio.

December 3

CBI: Fourteenth Air Force sends eight P-40s to attack barracks at Wanling, China.

ATLANTIC: German submarine *U-193* torpedoes a U.S. tanker in the Gulf of Mexico. While the crew abandons ship, nine sailors and the commander of the armed guard stay on board to fire the aft 5-inch gun at the U-boat. Another torpedo from *U-193* sinks the tanker and only one of the courageous fighters survives.

CAIRO: Allied Strategy Conference. Second Cairo Conference (Sextant) begins, attended by President Roosevelt, Prime Minister Churchill, and Generalissimo Chiang Kai-shek, and lasts until December 7. The proposed amphibious operation in Burma is cancelled to focus priorities on the cross-Channel invasion. The Americans reject Churchill's requests for cancellation of Anvil in favor of offensive operations in Itay and Yugoslavia. Chiang is displeased and refuses to commit Chinese forces for an offensive in Burma. Chiang's stubbornness only reinforces the view that China is seen as less important to the Allied effort than the Soviet Union.

There is a discussion on the best option for securing air bases to force the unconditional surrender of Japan through strategic bombing. Suggested bases for the new B-29 strategic bomber include Tinian, Saipan, and Guam in the Marianas.

ITALY: In the II Corps area, the 142nd Infantry Regiment of the 36th Infantry Division captures Monte Maggiore. The 45th Infantry Division is still stalled before La Bandita and Hill 769. In the 34th Infantry Division area, the 3rd Battalion of the 168th Infantry Regiment relieves the 1st Battalion and continues the attack to capture a small knob on Monte Pantano, but is driven back with heavy casualties. The battalion has suffered over 400 casualties during the six-day fight to capture the position.

Fifteenth Air Force B-24 Liberators, with fighter escort, bomb the Casale airfield near Rome.

MEDITERRANEAN: Twelfth Air Force B-25 Mitchells bomb the harbor and marshaling yard at Sibenik.

PACIFIC: U.S. submarine *Guardfish* sinks a Japanese fleet tanker west of the Palau Islands.

BOUGAINVILLE: Thirteenth Air Force sends 23 B-25 Mitchells to bomb Kieta Harbor and logistics targets. B-24 Liberators bomb Bonis, while fighters, both USAAF and U.S. Navy, attack targets of opportunity.

NEW GUINEA: Fifth Air Force A-20 Havocs attack villages around Finschhafen. P-47 Thunderbolts shoot down several enemy aircraft over Wewak. Over Cape Gloucester on New Britain, more than 60 B-24 Liberators and B-25 Mitchells bomb the airfield.

December 4

CBI: Tenth Air Force B-24 Liberators mine the Rangoon River and the Salween River at Moulmein in Burma. In China, Fourteenth Air Force conducts ground support operations against advancing Japanese forces near Changte with B-25 Mitchells and P-40s.

Changte falls to Japanese forces.

ETO: Eighth Air Force B-17s drop 1.6 million leaflets over Tours, Rouen, Le Mans, Orleans, Laval, Lille, and Paris, France. Ninth Air Force initiates Operation Crossbow and directs IX Bomber Command to begin attacking German missile sites threatening Britain.

MEDITERRANEAN: During the Second Cairo Conference (Sextant), President Franklin D. Roosevelt, Prime Minister Winston S. Churchill, and President Ismet Inonu of

Turkey meet. Churchill discusses the possibility of Turkey entering the war; the plan for the amphibious assault in the Bay of Bengal is cancelled; a tentative timetable is set up for Pacific offensive; and a unified command is established in the Mediterranean effective December 10.

ITALY: On Monte Pantano in the 34th Infantry Division area, the 135th Infantry Regiment replaces the badly battered 168th Infantry Regiment.

In the II Corps area, the 1st Battalion of the 1st Special Service Force is pushed off Monte la Remetanea and returns to defenses established on Monte la Difensa. In the 36th Infantry Division area, the 142nd Infantry Regiment holds positions on Monte Maggiore, but can advance no farther. The divisions are having difficulty resupplying frontline troops on the mountainous terrain.

SOUTHWEST PACIFIC AREA: Brigadier General Julian W. Cunningham, commander of the 112th Cavalry, issues an operations order to his commanders for the assault on Arawe.

PACIFIC: U.S. submarine *Apogon* sinks a Japanese gunboat northeast of Ponape Island. U.S. submarine *Gunnel* sinks a Japanese transport northeast of Haha Jima and escapes an attack by an escorting destroyer. U.S. submarine *Sailfish* torpedoes and sinks Japanese escort carrier *Chuyo* southeast of Honshu. Perishing on the *Chuyo* are survivors from the submarine *Sculpin*, whose commander, Captain John P. Cromwell, had sacrificed himself to save his crew on November 19.

CENTRAL PACIFIC: Seventh Air Force sends 54 B-24 Liberators to bomb Mille atoll in the Carolines, but only 34 hit the target due to bad weather. Eight B-24s bomb Nauru atoll. Navy Task Force 50, commanded by Rear Admiral Charles A. Pownall, attacks Kwajalein and Wotje Atolls. Aircraft from the carrier USS *Lexington* and small carrier USS *Independence* sink a Japanese collier, a cargo ship, an auxiliary submarine chaser, and a guardboat. Two light cruisers are also damaged. Japanese torpedo dive-bombers damage the *Lexington.*

BOUGAINVILLE: Thirteenth Air Force B-24 Liberators and B-25 Mitchells bomb Chabai.

NEW GUINEA: Fifth Air Force A-20 Havocs attack villages and logistics in the Finschaffen area.

December 5

CBI: Tenth Air Force B-24 Liberators mine waters near Moulmein and in the Rangoon River in Burma. Fourteenth Air Force P-40s continue to attack Japanese forces around Changte. Japanese bombers and fighters attack Fourteenth Air Force airfields.

ATLANTIC: The CCS describes the intent for Anvil to support Overlord. The Mediterranean theater is notified to plan to commit two divisions to the landings in southern France.

ETO: Eighth Air Force VIII Bomber Command attacks the Cognac/Chateaubernard airfield in France with 96 B-24 Liberators. One bomber is lost and seven are damaged. Over the Bordeaux/Merignac air depot, only one of 236 B-17s sent hits the target. In this attack, eight bombers are lost and 19 are damaged. Aircrews report 12 German fighters shot down. The two missions are escorted by 34 P-38 Lightnings and 266 P-47 Thunderbolts, along with 36 Ninth Air Force P-51 Mustangs. One P-47 is lost. Total U.S. casualties for these missions are three killed, 14 wounded, and 51 missing. Ninth Air Force B-26 Marauders bomb Ligescourt, Campagne-les-Hesdin, and Saint-Josse, France.

MEDITERRANEAN: President Roosevelt and Prime Minster Churchill agree that General Dwight D. Eisenhower will be the Supreme Allied Commander for Operation Overlord, the cross-Channel invasion of Europe.

The Combined Chiefs of Staff (CCS) issues a directive creating the Mediterranean Allied Air Forces (MAAF), consolidating British and U.S. forces of the Mediterranean Air Command (MAC) and Northwest African Air Force (NAAF).

ITALY: In II Corps area, the 1st Special Service Force stops a German counterattack on Monte La Difensa, supported by concentrated artillery fire. Twelfth Air Force transfers its headquarters from Tunisia to Italy. B-25 Mitchells bomb a bridge at Pescara. Allied aircraft attack transportation targets near Aquino and bomb bridges near Mignano and Ladispoli. The airfields at Piombino and Aviano are also attacked.

SOUTHWEST PACIFIC AREA: U.S. submarine *Narwhal* sinks a Japanese cargo ship in the Sulu Sea.

BOUGAINVILLE: Thirteenth Air Force B-25 Mitchells and navy SBD Dauntless dive-bombers attack Monoitu, the Aitara mission, and Mosigetta.

NEW GUINEA: Fifth Air Force A-20 Havocs attack Japanese positions near Finschhafen. B-25 Mitchells, B-26 Marauders, and P-40s attack along the Bogadjim road. Over New Britain Island, 40 B-24 Liberators bomb Cape Gloucester and A-20s attack and destroy several small vessels.

December 6

CBI: In China, Fourteenth Air Force B-25 Mitchells attack Japanese forces at Changte, Chin and attack the railyard at Hsipaw.

ATLANTIC: The Combined Chiefs of Staff agrees to a general strategy in Europe for 1944. Overlord and Anvil are the supreme operations for the Allies. All resources necessary will be provided to ensure success. The Allies will attack in Italy to reach the Pisa-Rimini line. The amphibious assault in the Bay of Bengal is cancelled and all landing craft in Southeast Asia Command are to be transferred to the ETO for Overlord. In the Mediterranean Theater, 68 LSTs will remain until mid-January, when they will be transferred to support Anvil.

MEDITERRANEAN: Fifteenth Air Force sends 45 B-24 Liberators to bomb the Eleusis airfield and 56 B-17s to attack Kalamaki airfield. One B-24 is lost.

ITALY: In the 45th Division area, the 179th Infantry Regiment succeeds in pushing the Germans off Hill 769, but the enemy still controls the rear slope.

Twelfth Air Force P-40 and A-36 Intruder (Apache) fighter-bombers bomb bridges at Ceprano and Mignano.

BOUGAINVILLE: Thirteenth Air Force B-25 Mitchells bomb the Monoitu Mission area. Another 24 B-25s, with fighter support, bomb Tarlena village. P-40s strafe the Arawa Bay area near Kieta.

New Guinea: Fifth Air Force A-20 Havocs and B-25 Mitchells attack villages and logistics areas around Finschhafen. Over New Britain, nearly 100 B-24 Liberators and B-25 Mitchells bomb Cape Gloucester and Borgen Bay, while P-40s strafe Cape Hoskins.

December 7

CBI: Fourteenth Air Force sends 13 B-25 Mitchells to bomb Japanese positions at Changte, China. In Burma, eight P-40s strafe freight cars on the rail line between Mogaung and Myitkyina.

Atlantic: The Allied Leadership Statement. From both the Sextant and Eureka conferences comes a statement that expresses the goals and intent of Britain, the USSR and the United States in dealing with Japan.

> The several military missions have agreed upon future military operations against Japan. The Three Great Allies expressed their resolve to bring unrelenting pressure against their brutal enemies by sea, land, and air. This pressure is already mounting.
>
> The Three Great Allies are fighting this war to restrain and punish the aggression of Japan. They covet no gain for themselves and have no thought of territorial expansion.
>
> It is their purpose that Japan shall be stripped of all the islands in the Pacific which she has seized or occupied since the beginning of the first World War in 1914, and that all the territories Japan has stolen from the Chinese, such as Manchuria, Formosa, and the Pescadores, shall be restored to the Republic of China.
>
> Japan will also be expelled from all other territories which she has taken by violence and greed. The aforesaid three great powers, mindful of the enslavement of the people of Korea, are determined that in due course Korea shall become free and independent.
>
> With these objects in view the three Allies, in harmony with those of the United Nations at war with Japan, will continue to persevere in the serious and prolonged operations necessary to procure the unconditional surrender of Japan.

ETO: The Combined Chiefs of Staff directs that the U.S. Strategic Air Forces in Europe (USSAFE) will coordinate the operations of the Eighth and Fifteenth Air Forces for the air war against Germany.

Italy: As the last part of Phase I of Operation Raincoat is underway, Fifth Army initiates Phase II of the operation in the II Corps area to prevent the enemy from reorganizing or reinforcing its defenses. San Pietro is the key strongpoint, a village fortified by the Germans and protected by Monte Lungo and Monte Sammucro. German positions are primarily deep bunkers covered by logs and earth and protected by minefields and barbed wire. The approaches to these fortifications are covered by machine guns and by mortar and artillery fire. II Corps intends to capture Monte Lungo while simultaneously sweeping north of San Pietro to outflank it and seize the Monte Sammucro heights.

Two battalions of the 143rd Infantry Regiment of the 36th Infantry Division assemble at Cannavinelle Hill to prepare to attack San Pietro. A Company, 1st Battalion, of the 143rd Infantry Regiment moves toward Monte Sammucro, taking the position in a night attack, but takes heavy casualties when the Germans counterattack. Reinforced, the company holds the position.

The 3rd Ranger Battalion prepares to attack Hill 950 northeast of Monte Sammucro.

The Italian 1st Motorized Group, commanded by Division General Vincenzo Dapino, is attached to II Corps and is ordered to capture Monte Lungo. The Italians relieve the 1st Battalion, 141st Infantry Regiment.

Twelfth Air Force B-25 Mitchells and A-36 Intruder (Apache) fighter-bombers attack the harbor and town of Civitavecchia. B-25 Mitchells also attack rail and road networks near Pescara. A-36s, P-40s, and RAF fighters attack a German gun position near Orsogna and hit other targets near Viticuso, San Vittoria, and a bridge at Civitella Roveto.

PACIFIC: U.S. submarine *Pogy* sinks a Japanese collier north of Truk. U.S. submarine *Sailfish* is attacked by a Japanese aircraft off Kyushu, Japan, and suffers slight damage.

CENTRAL PACIFIC: Seventh Air Force sends 14 B-24 Liberators from Tarawa atoll on a night raid to hit targets on Maloelap and Wotje Atolls in the Marshalls. B-24s from Nukufetau Island also bomb Maloelap Atoll, initiating Operation Flintlock, the offensive against Kwajalein and Majuro Atolls in the Marshalls.

BOUGAINVILLE: Thirteenth Air Force sends 18 B-25 Mitchells to bomb Kahili and Kieta harbor.

NEW GUINEA: Fifth Air Force A-20 Havocs bomb troop encampments and supply areas near Finschhafen. P-40s strafe boats and barges near Madang. Over New Britain, B-24 Liberators and B-25 Mitchells attack Cape Gloucester and Borgen Bay.

December 8

CBI: Fourteenth Air Force B-25 Mitchells, escorted by 16 P-40s, bomb Japanese positions at Changte, China.

ETO: Lieutenant General Carl Spaatz, commanding the Twelfth Air Force, is named as the new commander of U.S. Strategic Air Forces in Europe (USSAFE).

MEDITERRANEAN: Fifteenth Air Force attacks the Tatoi and Eleusis airfields with over 120 B-24 Liberators and B-17s.

ITALY: The attack of the 1st Italian Motorized Group on Monte Lungo is preceded by a heavy artillery barrage. The Italians are stopped by the enemy. The 2nd and 3rd Battalions of the 143rd Infantry Regiment are stopped before San Pietro by strong defenses and mortar and artillery fire from Monte Lungo. The 1st Battalion of the 143rd holds off enemy counterattacks on Monte Sammucro. The 3rd Ranger Battalion attacks Hill 950 and is unable to push the German defenders off the hill despite repeated attempts.

In the VI Corps area, the 1st Special Service Force retakes Monte la Remetanea and is relieved by the 142nd Infantry Regiment, which has extended its position southward. The only way units are resupplied on Monte Maggiore is by men carrying everything on their backs up trails so slippery and steep that even mules cannot be used. Moving the wounded off the mountain takes about 12 hours.

The 34th Infantry Division is relieved by the 2nd Moroccan Infantry Division, commanded by Major General A. M. F. Dody.

Fifteenth Air Force B-26 Marauders bomb Spoleto viaduct, the marshaling yard at Orte, and Civitavecchia harbor. Twelfth Air Force B-25 Mitchells bomb transportation and industrial targets around Pescara, Ancona, and Aquila. A-20 Havocs and A-36 Intruder (Apache) fighter-bombers and Allied aircraft conduct ground support missions near Miplinnico and Orsogna and attack lines of communication at Avezzano, Frosinone, Viticuso, Gaeta, and Sant' Elia Fiumerapido.

PACIFIC: U.S. submarine *Sawfish* sinks a Japanese transport southwest of Chichi Jima.

CENTRAL PACIFIC: Seventh Air Force B-24 Liberators bomb Jaluit Atoll in the Marshalls and Mille Atoll in the Carolines. A naval task group of carriers, battleships, and destroyers under command of Rear Admiral Willis A. Lee bombards Nauru Island. A destroyer is damaged by shore battery fire.

BOUGAINVILLE: Marines advancing to expand the perimeter encounter Japanese defenders on a low ridge. The battle for what the Marines call Hellzapoppin Ridge begins.

Thirteenth Air Force fighters attack targets of opportunity near Kieta, Cape Torokina, and Baniu Plantation.

NEW GUINEA: B-25 Mitchells and B-26 Marauders bomb logistics bases on the Huon Peninsula near Finschhafen.

December 9

CBI: Fourteenth Air Force B-25 Mitchells bomb Japanese positions at Changte, Wuchang, and Hankow, China. These attacks allow Chinese forces to retake Changte.

ITALY: San Pietro holds against attacks by the two battalions of the 143rd Infantry Regiment, 36th Infantry Division. The Americans make progress measured in yards. They fall back to their starting positions in order for the artillery to destroy the enemy positions. The 1st Battalion 143rd Infantry Regiment holds against German counterattacks on Monte Sammucro, supported by accurate and deadly artillery fire from the 133rd Field Artillery Battalion.

In the VI Corps area, the 45th Infantry Division clears Hill 769, but is unable to push the Germans from La Bandita or Legone.

Twelfth Air Force B-25 Mitchells bomb lines of communication targets at Giulianova, Pescara, Teramo, and Terni. A-20 Havocs, A-36 Intruder (Apache) fighter-bombers, and P-40s attack Orsogna, the Avezzano marshaling yard, and German troops and gun positions at San Pietro, Infine, and Viticuso. Trains and trucks around Rome are also attacked.

CENTRAL PACIFIC: Seventh Air Force B-24 Liberators bomb Mille Atoll in the Carolines. Aircrews report five Japanese fighters destroyed.

NEW GUINEA: Fifth Air Force B-25 Mitchells and A-20 Havocs hit barges, coastal installations, and roads near Fortification Point, while over 60 P-39 Airacobras hit Bogadjim Road and barges and enemy positions along the northern coast of Huon

Peninsula and in the Ramu River valley. Over New Britain Island, 50 B-25 Mitchells bomb Japanese supply points along the coast from Borgen Bay to Rein Bay.

December 10

CBI: Fourteenth Air Force sends 12 B-25 Mitchells, escorted by 15 P-40s, to attack the marshaling yard at Hanoi, French Indochina. Aircrews report heavy damage to the warehouse area and railroad station. In China, Japanese aircraft bomb Hengyang airfield and are intercepted by eight P-40s, shooting down three, but two P-40s are shot down as well. One pilot is killed. Two B-25 Mitchells are damaged on the ground.

ATLANTIC: The Combined Chiefs of Staff orders establishment of the Mediterranean Theater of Operations to become effective.

ETO: Eighth Air Force B-17s drop 1.2 million leaflets over, Paris, Caen, Amiens, and Rouen, France, and Ghent, Belgium, during the night. The Germans strike Ninth Air Force airfields in Britain with 20 aircraft. Casualties are eight killed and over 20 wounded.

MIDDLE EAST: Persian Gulf Service Command is redesignated as Persian Gulf Command (PGC) and is responsible directly to the War Department. The commander, Brigadier General Donald H. Connolly, is responsible for coordinating U.S. activities in the region with Allied nations.

MEDITERRANEAN: Fifteenth Air Force B-24 Liberators, with fighter escort, bomb a marshaling yard at Sofia, Bulgaria.

ITALY: The 3rd Ranger Battalion captures Hill 950 after a pre-assault bombardment of 1,600 rounds of artillery are fired on the hill. The Rangers have suffered heavy loses in the two days of fighting.

Fifteenth Air Force B-26 Marauders attack the bridge approaches at Ventimiglia. Twelfth Air Force P-40s and A-36 Intruder (Apache) fighter-bombers attack oil tanks, warehouses, and railroads at Civitavecchia and Acquafondata.

BOUGAINVILLE: Thirteenth Air Force B-25 Mitchells bomb the logistics sites and the airfield at Kahili. P-39 Airacobras bomb logistics bases and antiaircraft positions at Tonolai and strafe barges in the harbor.

Torokina airfield is opened and a marine fighter squadron lands there to begin flying ground support missions the next day.

NEW GUINEA: Fifth Air Force B-25 Mitchells and B-26 Marauders bomb logistics sites and camps near the Bogadjim Road, while P-39 Airacobras strafe barges near Madang. Over New Britain Island, 27 B-24 Liberators bomb Cape Gloucester.

December 11

CBI: Fourteenth Air Force B-24 Liberators bomb the airfield at Hankow, China. An attack by 30 Japanese aircraft over Suichwan is intercepted by eight P-40s. The pilots report eight enemy kills.

ETO: Eighth Air Force VIII Bomber Command attacks industrial sites at Emden, Germany, with 437 B-17s and 86 B-24 Liberators, escorted by 31 P-38 Lightnings, 313 P-47 Thunderbolts, and 44 P-51 Mustangs from Ninth Air Force. Fifteen B-17s and two B-24s are lost and 121 B-17s and 18 B-24s are damaged. Aircrews report over 80 fighters downed. The fighter pilots report 21 confirmed kills and seven possibles. There are three P-47s and one P-51 lost, with four P-47s and one P-51 damaged. U.S. casualties are three killed, 20 wounded, and 189 missing. During the evening, four B-17s drop 800,000 leaflets over Nantes, Laval, Rennes, and Le Mans in France.

MEDITERRANEAN: German U-boats *U-223, U-593,* and *U-73* attack convoy KMS 34 (United Kingdom to Mediterranean, Slow).

ITALY: The Fifth Army shifts corps boundaries, giving the British X Corps the area between Monte la Difensa and Monte Maggiore, and narrowing the II Corps area, centering its line of advance along Route 6. The Fifth Army has met all its objectives for Phase I of Operation Raincoat. The German line has been weakened, but the approach to the Liri Valley is still controlled by the enemy.

The 1st Battalion 143rd Infantry Regiment holds against German counterattacks on Monte Sammucro, but the battalion has lost its commander and is down to 340 men. The 504th Parachute Infantry Regiment reinforces the defenses on Monte Sammucro and relieves the 3rd Ranger Battalion.

Twelfth Air Force P-40s and A-36 Intruder (Apache) fighter-bombers attack Anzio, Nettuno, Viticuso, San Vittore del Lazio, Pontecorvo, Acquafondata, and transportation targets at Arce, Ostia, and Lido di Roma.

SOUTHWEST PACIFIC AREA: U.S. submarine *Bonefish* damages a small Japanese cargo vessel in the Celebes Sea.

BOUGAINVILLE: Thirteenth Air Force B-25 Mitchells bomb Kahili and Arigua Plantation. B-24 Liberators bomb the village and wharf at Tsirogei. P-39 Airacobras bomb Tonolai and Allied night fighters attack Japanese camps along the Jaba River.

NEW GUINEA: Fifth Air Force B-25 Mitchells and B-26 Marauders hit Japanese camps near Fortification Point and Finschhafen. Over New Britain, B-25 Mitchells bomb and strafe the Borgen Bay area. B-24 Liberators bomb Makassar on Celebes Island and Balikpapan on Borneo.

December 12

CBI: Tenth Air Force strikes a major Japanese line of supply crossing the bridge at Myittha in Burma with 28 B-25 Mitchells and 13 B-24 Liberators. Damage is negligible. In China, Fourteenth Air Force P-40s and P-38 Lightnings intercept 11 Japanese bombers and 30 fighters attacking the U.S. airfield at Hengyang. Fighter pilots report five bombers and three fighters shot down. Two P-40s are lost. One pilot is killed, the other is wounded. Hankow airfield is bombed by nine B-24 Liberators.

ATLANTIC: TBF Avengers from escort carrier USS *Bogue* attack two German submarines southwest of the Canary Islands. *U-172* is damaged and *U-219* escapes.

ETO: Eighth Air Force sends four B-17s to drop 800,000 leaflets on Paris, Amiens, and Orleans, France.

ITALY: Twelfth Air Force B-25 Mitchells bomb lines of communication at Terracina. P-40 and A-36 Intruder (Apache) fighter-bombers attack trucks along roads between Chieti and Francavilla and bomb the town of Itri.

SOUTHWEST PACIFIC AREA: U.S. submarine *Tuna* (SS-203) sinks a Japanese naval transport north of Halmahera in the Molucca Sea.

CENTRAL PACIFIC: Seventh Air Force sends 25 B-24 Liberators to bomb Emidj Island in the Marshalls.

BOUGAINVILLE: Thirteenth Air Force B-25 Mitchells strafe Arigua Plantation and logistics at Bonis. B-24 Liberators bomb the Kahili area and Poporang. Fighters strafe Japanese forces between Kieta and the Aropa River and the harbor at Tonolai. Navy SBD Dauntless dive-bombers attack targets near the Ratsua-Porton-Chabai-Soraken areas and the Kieta Harbor-Tobera Bay area. B-24 Liberators bomb the Kahili area and Poporang.

NEW GUINEA: Fifth Air Force P-40s dive-bomb Bogadjim Road. B-24 Liberators bomb Ceram Island in the Moluccas.

December 13

CBI: A Japanese raid of 20 bombers, escorted by 25 fighters, attacks Tenth Air Force's Dinjan airfield in India, but causes little damage. Pilots report 12 bombers and five fighters shot down. Twelve Fourteenth Air Force B-25 Mitchells bomb Li-Chou, Kungan, and Wuchang airfield. P-40s strafe targets of opportunity near Changte, Linli, and Li-Chou.

ATLANTIC: German submarine *U-172* attacks a U.S. destroyer and damages it with gunfire southwest of the Canary Islands. The U-boat in turn is sunk by TBF Avengers from escort carrier USS *Bogue* and three destroyers.

ETO: Eighth Air Force VIII Bomber Command B-17s and B-24 Liberators, escorted by 31 P-38 Lightnings, 322 P-47 Thunderbolts, and 41 Ninth Air Force P-51 Mustangs, attack Bremen and Kiel, Germany. P-51s for the first time fly the limit of their escort range. Of the 171 B-17s that bomb the port of Bremen, 31 B-17s are damaged. Over Kiel, guided by Pathfinder B-17s and B-24 Liberators, 367 B-17s and 93 B-24 Liberators attempt to hit the target. The formation is disrupted and 78 B-17s move off to bomb targets of opportunity in Hamburg. Four B-17s and one B-24 are lost and 137 B-17s and five B-24 Liberators are damaged. Aircrews report seven enemy fighters shot down. Fighter pilots report one confirmed enemy kill and one possible. One P-47 and one P-51 are reported lost. One P-47 and two P-38s are damaged. During the night, five B-17s drop 1 million leaflets on Le Mans, Rennes, Tours, Nantes, and Chartres, France.

Ninth Air Force attacks Schiphol airfield in the Netherlands with nearly 200 B-26 Marauders.

MEDITERRANEAN: A U.S. destroyer and a British frigate sink German submarine *U-593* northeast of Algiers.

Twelfth Air Force B-25 Mitchells bomb an oil depot, harbor, warehouses, and railway yard at Sibenik and Split.

ITALY: In the VI Corps area, night attacks by the 157th Infantry Regiment, 45th Infantry Division, are stopped by strong German resistance on the hills overlooking the Sant' Elia road.

Twelfth Air Force P-40 and A-36 Intruder (Apache) fighter-bombers attack German positions near Miglionico and lines of communication at Terracina, Pontecorvo, Isolella, and near Atina and Acquafondsta.

SOUTHWEST PACIFIC AREA: U.S. submarine *Puffer* makes an unsuccessful attack on a Japanese transport west of Luzon, Philippines. A U.S. Navy PBY Catalina sinks a Japanese cargo vessel north of New Ireland.

PACIFIC: U.S. submarine *Pogy* damages a Japanese cargo ship off the Palau Islands; it is damaged in a depth charge attack and the submarine's patrol must be terminated. U.S. submarine *Pompon* lays mines off the southwest coast of French Indochina. U.S. submarine *Sailfish* sinks a Japanese cargo ship in the Ryukyus.

CENTRAL PACIFIC: Seventh Air Force sends 10 B-24 Liberators to bomb Wotje Atoll in the Marshalls.

BOUGAINVILLE: Thirteenth Air Force B-25 Mitchells bomb Porton and Numa Numa. Fighters strafe Tenekow. B-24 Liberators bomb Bonis.

NEW GUINEA: Fifth Air Force A-20 Havocs attack villages along Bogadjim Road and P-39 Airacobras strafe barges along the Huon Peninsula. Over 100 B-24 Liberators and B-25 Mitchells bomb Gasmata Island.

December 14

CBI: Fourteenth Air Force B-25 Mitchells, with fighter escort, bomb Shasi, China. P-40s strafe supply trucks near Tengchung. Over Gia Lam airfield and railroad yard in French Indochina, six P-40s conduct a low-level attack.

MEDITERRANEAN: Fifteenth Air Force B-17s and B-24 Liberators, with fighter escorts, bomb the Kalamaki, Eleusis, and Tatoi air depots at Athens. B-17s also bomb the docks and shipping at Piraeus. Aircrews report 10 German fighters destroyed.

ITALY: II Corps, in coordination with VI Corps, attacks, ordering the 36th Infantry Division to capture San Pietro and Monte Lungo. On Monte Sammucro, the 1st Battalion 143rd Infantry and the 2nd Battalion of the 504th Parachute Infantry will attack west to outflank San Pietro. The two battalions of the 143rd Infantry Regiment, reinforced by a company of tanks from the 753rd Tank Battalion, will assault San Pietro. Meanwhile, the 1st Italian Motorized Group, reinforced by the 142nd Infantry Regiment, will attack Monte Lungo from two directions.

In the VI Corps area, the 45th Infantry Division advances during the night to attack the village of Lagone, which has resisted numerous American assaults.

Twelfth Air Force B-25 Mitchells bomb the marshaling yard at Orte. A-20 Havocs attack lines of communication near Pontecorvo. P-40s and A-36 Intruder (Apache) fighter-bombers attack bridges near Roccasecca, Atina, Ceprano, and Sora. The docks and town of Civitavecchia are also attacked. The main roads to Sant' Elia and Attina are attacked to slow German reinforcements into the VI Corps area.

PACIFIC: Admiral Nimitz, CINCPOA, reschedules the attack on the Marshalls to January 17, 1944.

U.S. submarine *Herring* sinks a Japanese cargo ship in the East China Sea.

CENTRAL PACIFIC: Seventh Air Force sends 16 B-24 Liberators to bomb Maloelap Atoll in the Marshalls.

BOUGAINVILLE: Thirteenth Air Force fighters support navy SBD Dauntless dive-bombers attacking Japanese antiaircraft positions near Chabai.

NEW GUINEA: Fifth Air Force sends 228 B-24 Liberators, B-25 Mitchells, and A-20 Havocs to bomb Arawe. P-39 Airacobras strafe barges along the Huon Peninsula. B-24s bomb Saidor. B-26 Marauders and B-25s bomb Gasmata Island.

December 15

CBI: The Tenth Air Force and RAF Bengal Air Command are combined to form the Eastern Air Command (EAC), under Lieutenant General George E. Stratemeyer (USAAF). Air Vice Marshall Thomas M. Williams (RAF) is the assistant commander. The headquarters is located in New Delhi, India. This combined U.S.-British command is under the operational control of Southeast Asia Command (SEAC) in New Delhi, India, and is commanded by Admiral Lord Louis Mountbatten.

Fourteenth Air Force attacks the airfield at Pailochi, China, with 25 P-40s. Pilots report three enemy aircraft destroyed on the ground.

ATLANTIC: The Combined Chiefs of Staff estimates availability of forces in ETO by May 1, 1944, the date planned for the cross-Channel invasion (Operation Overlord). The Allies would have 31 2/3 divisions in Britain, 3,783 heavy bombers, 1,000 medium bombers, and 4,200 fighter aircraft. Four divisions per month would enter France. In the Mediterranean, the Allies had 31 divisions and would allocate 10 divisions to participate in Anvil, the landing in southern France supporting Overlord. The U.S. troop strength in the ETO by May 31, 1944, is estimated at 1.4 million.

ETO: In the ETO, the Allies have 3,783 heavy bombers, 1,000 medium bombers, and 4,200 fighter aircraft. The Ninth Air Force officially comes under operational control of the Allied Expeditionary Air Force (AEAF).

MEDITERRANEAN: Twelfth Air Force B-25 Mitchells bomb the airfield at Mostar, Yugoslavia. P-40s and A-36 Intruder (Apache) fighter-bombers attack targets near Mostar and the Zemonico landing ground.

ITALY: In the II Corps area, two battalions of the 142nd Infantry Regiment attack Monte Lungo after a long artillery bombardment. An American first sergeant, leading an infantry platoon, roots several Germans out of a cave and shakes out of one surprised and frightened prisoner information on the location of all the other German positions.

The 143rd Infantry Regiment, with two battalions supported by 16 medium tanks from A Company, 753rd Tank Battalion, renews its attack on San Pietro and meets heavy resistance, advancing about 300 yards. During the attack 12 tanks are lost due to mines and enemy fire.

An attack into the valley toward San Pietro by the 2nd Battalion 141st Infantry is stopped by German artillery fire and suffers heavy casualties. The Americans call the open area "Death Valley." They reorganize and continue the advance.

The 1st Battalion of the 143rd Infantry, reinforced by the 2nd Battalion 504th Parachute Infantry Regiment, moves to attack the hills beyond Monte Sammucro to outflank San Pietro. Both battalions are stopped with heavy losses. The 1st Battalion is down to 155 men and has expended all of its ammunition.

In the VI Corps area, the 1st and 3rd Battalions of the 179th Infantry Regiment of the 45th Infantry Division attack Lagone, while the 1st Battalion attacks to capture a key hill to the south of the village. The 1st and 3rd Battalions of the 157th Infantry Regiment, with a platoon of tanks from the 755th Tank Battalion, reach the top of Hill 470 and advance to La Rava Creek, but cannot advance farther.

Fifteenth Air Force B-17s, with P-38 Lightnings and P-47 Thunderbolts escorting, bomb the Bolzano marshaling yards. B-24 Liberators, with P-38 escort, attack the viaduct at Avisio. Twelfth Air Force B-25 Mitchells and A-20 Havocs bomb lines of communication near Pontecorvo and Frosinone.

SOUTHWEST PACIFIC AREA: Chief of Staff George C. Marshall arrives on Goodenough Island to meet with General MacArthur and Lieutenant General Walter Krueger. Marshall provides MacArthur with the outcomes of the recent Cairo-Teheran meetings and listens to MacArthur's plea for more aircraft and more ground troops. The Cartwheel campaign is moving slowly, and it seems to have no real purpose now, at the end of 1943. At the Sextant Conference at Cairo, Marshall was persuaded by the other members of the JCS that the Central Pacific offensive was the quickest way to win the war. MacArthur's SWPA can continue its offensive in New Guinea, but only as a holding action for the main effort by Nimitz.

MacArthur argues that Nimitz's timetable for an advance through the Marshalls is far too optimistic and will be costly. Cartwheel has been slow, he admits, but it has weakened the Japanese significantly and put the Americans in a position to approach the Philippines. The Philippines are essential to the Pacific campaign, not the Pacific islands and atolls in the Carolines and Marshalls. The Japanese lifeline from the Netherlands East Indies goes through the South China Sea, past the Philippines. The Philippine Islands are an ideal base from which to launch the attack on the Japanese home islands. Australia is a secure base of operations to support and sustain an offensive. The geography of Nimitz's Pacific operation areas lacks such a base, except for Pearl Harbor, which is too far away to be suitable. The Philippines will draw the Japanese navy to the final battle the American navy seeks; above all, a return to the Philippines would fulfill a sacred obligation that MacArthur had voiced in 1942—Americans would return.

MacArthur advocates a year-long campaign plan for Southwest Pacific Area just as Nimitz has for the Central Pacific. MacArthur's plan is to have all of New Guinea under Allied control in order to be ready for an attack on Mindanao in February 1945.

The meeting of these two towering figures of the Second World War is unique. No one called General Marshall by his first name, except the president of the United States, and even he rarely took advantage of the privilege. No one ever called General MacArthur by his first name—ever. Yet at this meeting, both men addressed each other using first names, a symbol of the power and prestige these two men held. It was clear to Marshall that CINCSWPA was determined not to be relegated to a strategic backwater by the navy. He listened sympathetically to MacArthur, but remained noncommittal.

CENTRAL PACIFIC: Seventh Air Force sends 30 B-24 Liberators to bomb Maloelap and Wotje Atolls in the Marshalls. One B-24 is lost over Maloelap. Aircrews report two Japanese fighters shot down.

BOUGAINVILLE: The XIV Corps, under command of Major General Oscar W. Griswold, arrives to take control of Bougainville from I Marine Amphibious Corps.

Thirteenth Air Force sends 23 B-25 Mitchells and 16 fighters to bomb Buka Island.

NEW BRITAIN: Operation Director. Navy Task Force 76, commanded by Rear Admiral Daniel E. Barbey, lands the 112th Cavalry Regiment on Arawe. The regiment is to "seize and defend a suitable location" for light naval facilities. The regiment, reinforced with artillery and engineers, conducts an amphibious assault; one troop attempts a diversionary attack using rubber boats to make a landing. The Japanese make short work of this attempt, but the LVTs that land the remainder of the regiment are unopposed. Fifth Air Force supports the landing on Arawe with B-25 Mitchells attacking villages in the area. Naval gunfire support from destroyers suppresses Japanese defenses to allow the troops to land and move to gain control of the Arawe peninsula and establish defensive positions. The regiment withstands attacks from over 100 Japanese aircraft, which return every day for over a week.

B-24 Liberators bomb Cape Gloucester and P-39 Airacobras strafe barges at Reiss Point. B-25 Mitchell aircrews report two cargo ships hit in an attack on Timor Island in the Sunda Islands.

December 16
CBI: Fourteenth Air Force B-25 Mitchells and 11 P-40s attack near Owchihkow, China. P-40s attack Pailochi airfield. P-38 Lightnings strafe a troop train near Changanyi and sampans on the Yangtze River.

Atlantic: German submarine *U-516* torpedoes and sinks a U.S. tanker en route from New York to Aruba (off Venezuela).

ETO: Eighth Air Force VIII Bomber Command attacks Bremen, Germany. Escorted by 31 P-38 Lightnings, 131 P-47 Thunderbolts and 39 P-51 Mustangs from the Ninth Air Force, 402 B-17s, 133 B-24 Liberators, and 10 Pathfinder aircraft hit the target. Ten B-17s are lost and a total of 159 bombers are damaged. Six crewmen are killed, eight wounded, and 104 are reported missing. Aircrews report more than 18 German fighters destroyed. The fighter pilots report two confirmed enemy kills. One P-47 is lost and two P-38s are damaged. One pilot is reported killed and another reported missing. Later that night, four B-17s drop nearly 2 million leaflets over Brussels, Belgium, Hannover, Germany, and Lille, France.

Mediterranean: German submarine *U-73* attacks a convoy off the Algerian coast, torpedoing and damaging a U.S. freighter. Three U.S. destroyers track and sink the U-boat northwest of Oran, Algeria.

Twelfth Air Force B-25 Mitchells, P-40s, and P-47 Thunderbolts bomb shipping at Zara, Yugoslavia.

Italy: In II Corps area, the 2nd Battalion 141st Infantry moves toward San Pietro and two companies enter the town, but the battalion suffers nearly 170 casualties, forcing it to retreat.

The 142nd Infantry Regiment clears Monte Lungo and the 1st Italian Motorized Group captures the smaller hills near the mountain.

The Germans counterattack from San Pietro to cover their withdrawal. The attack falls largely on the 3rd Battalion of the 143rd Infantry. One infantry company is so badly pressed by the enemy that a private first class is left to rally the men remaining. Artillery fire on the attacking German infantry ends the threat to the battalion.

The 1st Battalion 143rd Infantry and the 2nd Battalion of the 504th Parachute Infantry hold their positions on the western slope of Monte Sammucro against a heavy counterattack.

In VI Corps area, the 45th Infantry Division's 179th Infantry Regiment advances up La Bandita, occupies Lagone, and moves west toward Monte La Posta after the enemy withdraws. The 2nd Battalion of the 157th Infantry Regiment captures Fialla Hill just below the heights of Monte Cavallo and is forced back after an artillery bombardment and counterattack from German forces.

Fifteenth Air Force B-17s, escorted by P-38 Lightnings and P-47 Thunderbolts, bomb the marshaling yard at Padua. Aircrews report extensive damage to rail lines, rolling stock, and buildings. B-24 Liberators attack the rail lines between Dogna and Chiusaforte. Twelfth Air Force A-20 Havocs attack gun positions near Mignano, while P-40s and A-36 Intruder (Apache) fighter-bombers attack enemy positions near Hill 470, Chieti, Cassino, and Roccasecca. Civitavecchia's docks are also attacked.

BOUGAINVILLE: Thirteenth Air Force B-24 Liberators bomb Monoitu and dispersal areas at Bonis airfield. Fighters support navy SBD Dauntless dive-bomber strikes on gun positions at Bonis.

NEW BRITAIN: Fifth Air Force B-24 Liberators attack Cape Gloucester airfield.

NEW GUINEA: General MacArthur orders Lieutenant General Walter Krueger to organize a task force to capture Saidor, part of Operation Dexterity. Saidor will be used as a naval and air base and will pressure Japanese forces at Finschhafen. Brigadier General Clarence A. Martin, the deputy commander of the 32nd Infantry Division, will command the 126th RCT from his division.

December 17

CBI: Fourteenth Air Force sends six P-40s to bomb and strafe targets of opportunity in Hanoi, French Indochina.

ITALY: The Germans abandon San Pietro. The 1st Battalion 141st Infantry Regiment relieves the battered and depleted 1st Battalion 143rd Infantry on Monte Sammucro. The two battalions of the 143rd Infantry advance beyond San Pietro in pursuit of the Germans.

In VI Corps area, the 180th Infantry Regiment of the 45th Infantry Division captures Monte la Posta after moving forward through the positions occupied by the 179th Infantry Regiment and moves along the Sant' Elia road as far as Monte Molina and Monte Rotundo, the next obstacles to the American advance. The 157th Infantry Regiment discovers that the enemy had abandoned positions on Hill 640 and Fialla Hill. This marks a general withdrawal of German forces to reconsolidate.

Twelfth Air Force A-20 Havocs attack German artillery near Sant' Elia Fiumerapido. P-40s and A-36 Intruder (Apache) fighter-bombers attack enemy positions near Monte Trocchio, Cervaro, and Cardito. The Nettuno and Anzio marshaling yards, barracks, warehouses, and docks are also attacked.

SOUTHWEST PACIFIC AREA: Sixth Army receives orders to capture Saidor on the north coast of New Guinea to cut off retreating Japanese from Finschhafen.

BOUGAINVILLE: Thirteenth Air Force sends 18 B-25 Mitchells against Malai. Another six B-25s support navy SBD Dauntless dive-bombers in an attack on targets near Mutupina Point.

New Britain: The 112th Cavalry makes an amphibious movement to the Itini River to contain the Japanese retreat.

Fifth Air Force P-47 Thunderbolts intercept about 40 Japanese aircraft over the Arawe Peninsula and report shooting down at least 10. B-24 Liberators and B-25 Mitchells bomb Cape Gloucester and nearby shipping. The bombers drop 80 2,000-pound bombs on the airfield. The pilots of the Fifth Air Force begin to use the term "Gloucesterizing" to describe the thorough destruction of a target.

New Guinea: Sixth Army is to seize Saidor in support of the 9th Australian Division's advance past Finschhafen in order to cut off the Japanese retreat westward from the Huon Peninsula.

December 18

CBI: Generalissimo Chiang Kai-shek gives General Joseph Stilwell command of Chinese forces in India and those in the Hukawng Valley in Burma. This is a largely symbolic act, for Chinese commanders still secretly take orders from the Generalissimo. Thus, commanders often ignore or respond very slowly to Stilwell's orders.

Fourteenth Air Force B-25 Mitchells conducting a sea sweep report damaging a cargo ship and a tanker in the Hainan Straits. The Namsang airfield in China is attacked by 27 B-24 Liberators, supported by 28 P-40s. Japanese bombers and fighters attack the U.S. airfield at Kunming.

Mediterranean: Fifteenth Air Force B-26 Marauders bomb two Var River bridges; aircrews report destroying one and heavily damaging another.

Italy: The 2nd Battalion 504th Parachute Infantry is relieved by the 1st Battalion on Monte Sammucro. Patrols discover enemy forces holding the southern slope of Monte Sammucro, blocking any advance down Route 6.

Twelfth Air Force P-40s attack German positions in Tollo, Canosa Sannita, and Orsogna. A-36 Intruder (Apache) fighter-bombers attack German positions near Monte Trocchio, Cassino, and Viticuso and logistics sites near Tenacina.

Pacific: U.S. submarine *Aspro* attacks a Japanese convoy, damaging two fleet tankers east of Formosa and escapes from an escorting destroyer. U.S. submarine *Cabrilla* lays mines off Saracen Bay, Cambodia, French Indochina. U.S. submarine *Grayback* sinks a Japanese cargo ship northeast of Okinawa and escapes from an escorting destroyer.

Central Pacific: Seventh Air Force B-24 Liberators bomb Mille atoll in the Carolines. P-39 Airacobras of the 46th and 72nd Fighter Squadrons, 15th Fighter Group, transfer to Makin Island, joining the A-24s (the AAF version of the navy's SBD Dauntless) of the 531st Fighter-Bomber Squadron on Makin.

Bougainville: The 1st Battalion and 3rd Battalions of the 21st Marines conduct a double envelopment of Hellzapoppin Ridge behind the close support of TBF Avengers and TBD Dauntless dive-bombers. The marines lose 12 men killed and 23 wounded in capturing this important piece of key terrain.

Thirteenth Air Force sends 15 B-24 Liberators to bomb logistics bases at Kahili and Bonis. Another 19 bombers attack targets near Chabai-Porton. B-25 Mitchells carry out low-level strikes on troop concentrations at Poroporo and Korovo.

New Britain: Japanese forces land at Omoi to attack the 112th Cavalry's defensive positions at Arawe.

New Guinea: Fifth Air Force sends 33 A-20 Havocs to attack logistics areas near Finschhafen. On New Britain, over 70 B-24 Liberators, B-25 Mitchells, and B-26 Marauders bomb Cape Gloucester. B-25 Mitchells attack Borgen Bay and B-24s bomb Hoskins airfield.

December 19

CBI: Chiang Kai-shek rejects the request of the SEAC commander, Admiral Lord Louis Mountbatten, for Chinese forces to participate in the Burma offensive.

During the night, Tenth Air Force sends 20 B-24 Liberators against the new dock construction at Bangkok, Thailand. Aircrews report major destruction to the target.

In China, Japanese bombers and fighters attack Fourteenth Air Force's airfields at Hengyang and Yunnani. P-40s intercept the enemy and shoot down nine aircraft, but lose two fighters. Nanhsien and Ansiang are attacked by 12 B-25 Mitchells and eight P-40s.

ETO: Eighth Air Force sends five B-17s to drop one million leaflets on Paris, Amiens, and Chartres, France.

Mediterranean: Fifteenth Air Force B-17s attack the Messerschmitt plant at Augsburg and the marshaling yard at Innsbruck. A total of 150 B-24 Liberators and B-17s are involved in the attack, escorted by P-38 Lightnings and P-47 Thunderbolts. U.S. losses are nine bombers, to an estimated 37 German fighters shot down.

Italy: In II Corps area, the 15th Infantry regiment of the 3rd Infantry Division relieves the 142nd Infantry on Monte Lungo. German defenders retreat to a new defensive line at Cedro Hill, Monte Porchia, and the town of San Vittore, and still hold the lower slopes of Monte Sammucro, blocking any advance along Highway 6 or through the Mignano gap. The 143rd and 141st Infantry Regiments attack to clear the way, but are unable to capture the positions. The 143rd Infantry is down to 35 men per company.

In VI Corps area, elements of the 157th Infantry Regiment occupy Monte Cavallo.

Phase II of Operation Raincoat ends with the Fifth Army holding its gains while attempting to deal with increasingly bad winter weather, long supply lines, and units with almost as many non-battle casualties as combat casualties.

Fifteenth Air Force B-26 Marauders bomb the Perugia railroad installations and the marshaling yards at Castiglione della Valle and Foligno. P-47 Thunderbolts strafe Ancona airfield, truck convoys at Porto Civitanova, a train near Senigallia, and a vessel at Roseto degli Abruzzi. Twelfth Air Force B-25 Mitchells bomb the marshaling yards at Terni and Orte. A-20 Havocs attack Cassino, while P-40s bomb Orsogna and supplies near Arce. A-36 Intruder (Apache) fighter-bombers attack Civitavecchia.

Pacific: U.S. submarine *Grayback* sinks the destroyer that pursued it the previous day northeast of Okinawa. Fifteenth Air Force B-24 Liberators and navy PBY Catalinas sink a Japanese cargo ship southwest of Kavieng. A navy PBY damages a Japanese cargo vessel near Kwajalein.

CENTRAL PACIFIC: Seventh Air Force sends 29 B-24 Liberators to bomb barracks, hangars, and wharf areas on Mille and Maloelap Atolls. Aircrews report seven enemy fighters destroyed. P-39 Airacobras strafe Mille Atoll, reporting three enemy aircraft destroyed and an oil storage site set afire. Two P-39s are lost.

BOUGAINVILLE: Thirteenth Air Force sends 24 B-25 Mitchells to bomb logistics sites at Moisuru.

NEW BRITAIN: More than 140 Fifth Air Force B-24 Liberators, B-25 Mitchells, and B-26 Marauders bomb Cape Gloucester. Gasmata Island is bombed by 37 P-40s, and 20 A-20 Havocs attack Japanese positions near Arawe.

NEW GUINEA: Fifth Air Force B-25 Mitchells, A-20 Havocs, and P-39 Airacobras attack supply barges, troop sites, and gun positions near Finschhafen. B-25s and B-26 Marauders also bomb Madang. P-47 Thunderbolts sweep the northeast coastline.

December 20

CBI: Chiang Kai-shek has been pressing President Roosevelt for more money and supplies, but balks at Roosevelt's proposal to join in the Allied offensive against Burma as a means of obtaining additional aid. He tells Roosevelt that unless there is an amphibious operation against Rangoon, Moulmein, or the Andaman Islands, the Chinese divisions in Yunan (the "Y" Force) will not participate.

Fourteenth Air Force sends 11 B-25 Mitchells and six P-40s against the Yoyang railroad yards in China.

ATLANTIC: TBF Avengers from escort carrier USS *Bogue* sink German submarine *U-850* southwest of the Azores.

ETO: Eighth Air Force VIII Bomber Command attacks Bremen, Germany, with 357 B-17s and 103 B-24 Liberators, led by 12 Pathfinder aircraft and escorted by 26 P-38 Lightnings, 418 P-47 Thunderbolts, and 47 Ninth Air Force P-51 Mustangs. For the first time, some bombers deploy Window (today known as chaff), strips of metal foil intended to confuse radar detection equipment and mask the true location of the aircraft. The Germans employ rocket-firing fighters in an attempt to conduct standoff attacks, but these are more frightening than effective. Nevertheless, 27 bombers are lost. Another 216 B-17s and 34 B-24s are damaged. Aircrews report about 21 German fighters destroyed. The fighter pilots report 19 confirmed kills, three probables, and six possibles. Two P-47s and four P-51s are reported shot down and six P-47s are damaged. American casualties for this raid are nine killed, 42 wounded, and 275 missing. Later that night five B-17s drop one million leaflets on Lille and Lens in France and on Ghent and Brussels in Belgium.

Ninth Air Force sends more than 180 B-26 Marauders to attack German rocket bases in northern France. Only 35 actually hit any targets as bad weather forces the majority of the bombers to abort the mission.

Technical Sergeant Forrest T. Vosler is a radio operator-air gunner on the mission over Bremen. After bombing the target, antiaircraft fire severely damages his aircraft, forcing it out of formation. Enemy fighters savagely attack the lone bomber, firing their 20 millimeter cannon. Vosler is wounded and the tail gunner has also been seriously wounded. Without protection from the tail guns, the bomber cannot survive long. Vosler painfully makes his way to the rear and puts the tail guns into action. He is wounded again and loses most of his sight. Nevertheless, Vosler grimly hangs on, and continues to fight. When the pilot decides to make an emergency water landing, Vosler, primarily by touch, gets the radio set working and sends out a distress signal. After hitting the water, Vosler not only manages to find his way out of the aircraft, but also brings out the wounded tail gunner so his fellow crewmembers can load him into the survival raft. Technical Sergeant Vosler's extraordinary courage, dedication, and skill saves his aircraft and his comrades from certain destruction. He will receive the Medal of Honor.

MEDITERRANEAN: More than 100 Fifteenth Air Force B-17s bomb Eleusis airfield in Greece.

The Mediterranean Allied Air Force (MAAF) is established under command of Air Chief Marshall Sir Arthur Tedder of the Royal Air Force. The MAAF is a combined headquarters having operational control over all Allied air forces operating in the Mediterranean Theater of Operations. The reorganization disbands the Mediterranean Air Command and Northwest African Air Force (NAAF) and creates a subordinate component called U.S. Army Air Forces, North African Theater of Operations (USAAFNATO) under command of General Carl Spaatz, who has administrative control of the Twelfth and Fifteenth Air Forces.

ITALY: Twelfth Air Force P-40s attack Chieti, Orsogna, and bomb a fuel storage area near Manoppello. A-36 Intruder (Apache) fighter-bombers attack Terracina and transportation targets near Rome.

PACIFIC: U.S. submarine *Gato* sinks a Japanese transport in the East China Sea and is slightly damaged in a depth charge attack. U.S. submarine *Puffer* sinks a Japanese destroyer west of Manila and makes an unsuccessful attack on a cargo ship. Navy PBY Catalinas sink a Japanese transport off the northwest coast of New Britain.

CENTRAL PACIFIC: Seventh Air Force sends 16 B-24 Liberators to bomb Maloelap Atoll in the Marshalls. Aircrews report eight Japanese fighters shot down, but three B-24s are lost to enemy fire.

BOUGAINVILLE: The Americal Division, commanded by Major General John R. Hodge, relieves the 3rd Marine Division. XIV Corps commander, Major General Oscar W. Griswold, officially relieves Major General Ray S. Geiger and I Marine Amphibious Corps.

NEW BRITAIN: Fifth Air Force A-20 Havocs attack Arawe and P-38 Lightning pilots report downing 10 Japanese aircraft along the south coast of the island. B-24 Liberators bomb a cargo ship off Cape Pomas.

NEW GUINEA: Fifth Air Force B-26 Marauders and B-25 Mitchells attack Japanese camps near Finschhafen area and bomb Alexishafen.

December 21

ALEUTIANS: Navy PBY Catalinas from Attu Island bomb Shimushu and Paramushiru Strait in the Kuriles.

CBI: General Joseph Stilwell arrives in Ledo to take personal command of the upcoming Burma offensive.

Fourteenth Air Force sends 29 B-24 Liberators to bomb the railroad yards at Chiengmai, China. Aircrews report heavy damage to warehouses.

ETO: Ninth Air Force sends 84 B-26 Marauders against German rocket sites in France.

ITALY: Twelfth Air Force B-25 Mitchells and P-40s bomb Terracina. A munitions factory near Sant' Elia Fiumerapido is also attacked. A-36 Intruder (Apache) fighter-bombers attack a fuel storage site and a munitions factory near Cervaro. The A-36s also attack transportation targets around Rome and Civitavecchia.

PACIFIC: U.S. submarine *Grayback* sinks a Japanese auxiliary netlayer and merchant ship southwest of Kagoshima, Japan. U.S. submarine *Sailfish* sinks a Japanese transport south of Kyushu, Japan. U.S. submarine *Skate* sinks a Japanese fleet tanker northwest of Truk.

CENTRAL PACIFIC: Seventh Air Force sends eight B-24 Liberators, accompanied by four navy PB4Y Catalinas, on a photoreconnaissance mission over Kwajalein Atoll in the Marshalls. A-24 Banshees, along with U.S. Navy and Marine Corps aircraft, attack shipping and airfields at Emidj Island, while six P-39 Airacobras strafe fuel storage areas, shipping, and antiaircraft positions on Mille Atoll in the Carolines.

BOUGAINVILLE: Thirteenth Air Force B-25 Mitchells attack Monoitu Mission.

NEW GUINEA: Fifth Air Force A-20 Havocs hit camps near Finschhafen. B-25 Mitchells bomb Madang. P-40s attack Kaukenau. Fifteenth Air Force B-25 Mitchells sink a small Japanese cargo vessel at Wewak. Over New Britain, Cape Gloucester is bombed by over 100 B-24 Liberators, B-25 Mitchells, and A-20 Havocs. P-47 Thunderbolt pilots report 17 enemy fighters shot down over Arawe. P-40s and A-20 Havocs attack Hoskins airfield. P-39 Airacobras strafe targets around Borgen Bay and Rein Bay.

D-day for the Saidor landing is set for January 2, 1944.

December 22

CBI: Fourteenth Air Force's Kunming airfield in China is attacked by 65 Japanese bombers and fighters, destroying two U.S. aircraft on the ground. The attackers are challenged by 10 P-40s and a P-38 Lightning. The fighter pilots report 12 enemy aircraft shot down. Near Chengkung, seven P-40s intercept 58 Japanese aircraft heading toward the airfield and shoot down three. B-25 Mitchells, with fighter escort, bomb Hwajung.

ETO: Eighth Air Force VIII Bomber Command attacks the Osnabruck and Munster marshaling yards in Germany. Both heavy clouds and malfunctioning Pathfinder equipment result in many bombers missing their targets. Over Osnabruck, 147 B-17s and 87 B-24 Liberators led by two Pathfinder aircraft hit the target. Five B-17s and 12 B-24s are lost and 23 B-17s and 12 B-24s are damaged. Aircrews report 18 enemy fighters destroyed. Over Munster, 164 B-17s, 30 B-24 Liberators, and three Pathfinder aircraft hit the target. Three B-17s and two B-24s are lost; 30 B-17s are damaged. The bombers are escorted by 40 P-38 Lightnings, 448 P-47 Thunderbolts, and 28 P-51 Mustangs from Ninth Air Force. Pilots report 15 confirmed kills, one probable kill, and six possibles. Two P-38s and two P-47s are lost and one P-47 is damaged. U.S. total casualties on this raid are six killed, 14 wounded, and 214 missing. Later that night, six B-17s drop over one million leaflets on Paris, Amiens, Chartres, Orleans, and Rennes, France. One B-17 drops two 2,000-pound General Purpose (GP) bombs and one Photoflash (illumination) bomb on Cologne, Germany.

MEDITERRANEAN: General Carl Spaatz is ordered to take command of U.S. Strategic Air Forces in Europe. His replacement as commander of Air Forces Mediterranean Theater of Operation is Lieutenant General Ira C. Eaker.

ITALY: Twelfth Air Force P-40s attack transportation targets near Tortoreto and Benedello.

PACIFIC: U.S. submarine *Gurnard* damages a German cargo ship east of Shikoku, Japan.

CENTRAL PACIFIC: Seventh Air Force A-24 Banshees from Makin Island, escorted by 32 P-39 Airacobras along with navy F6F Hellcats and SBD Dauntless dive-bombers, attack cargo ships in Mille Atoll lagoon in the Marshalls. P-39s attack antiaircraft positions and fuel storage areas. A Japanese transport is sunk.

BOUGAINVILLE: Thirteenth Air Force B-25 Mitchells attack a logistics base at Kahili. B-24 Liberators attack targets near Bonis, Porton, and at Sohano Island.

NEW GUINEA: Fifth Air Force sends about 40 B-25 Mitchells, with P-38 escort, to bomb Wewak and Boram. Aircrews report more than 13 enemy aircraft shot down. B-25s and P-39 Airacobras bomb the airfield and supply barges at Madang and the town of Alexishafen, while A-20 Havocs and B-26 Marauders bomb Japanese positions near Finschhafen. Over New Britain, B-24 Liberators, B-25 Mitchells, and A-20 Havocs bomb Cape Gloucester.

December 23

CBI: The Chinese 38th Division begins operations in the Hukawng Valley in Burma.

Tenth Air Force B-24 Liberators bomb the railroad terminal at Bangkok, Thailand, during the night. Aircrews report heavy explosions and large fires. Fourteenth Air Force B-24 Liberators, escorted by seven P-51 Mustangs and 23 P-40s, bomb White Cloud airfield in China. Fighter pilots report 11 enemy aircraft destroyed. Huang Shan Kou is attacked by 14 P-38 Lightnings, and two B-25 Mitchells report a gunboat sunk in the Formosa Straits.

ATLANTIC: German submarine *U-415* makes an unsuccessful attack on escort carrier *Card* and a destroyer near the Azores, after escorting a convoy to the Mediterranean. German submarine *U-471* makes an unsuccessful attack on the battleship *Arkansas* screening troop convoy TU 5 (United Kingdom to United States) in the North Atlantic.

ETO: Eighth Air Force sends 92 P-47 Thunderbolts to attack the Gilze-Rijen airfield in the Netherlands.

ITALY: Fifteenth Air Force B-26 Marauders bomb the railroad bridge and marshaling yard at Imperia and rail lines at Ventimiglia.

CENTRAL PACIFIC: Seventh Air Force P-39 Airacobras conducting a night combat patrol intercept enemy bombers over Makin Island and shoot down two of them. One P-39 is lost in the battle. B-24 Liberators bomb Kwajalein, Wotje, and Maloelap Atolls. Mili Atoll is attacked by 10 A-24 banshees, escorted by 20 P-39 Airacobras.

NEW BRITAIN: Thirteenth Air Force sends 18 B-24 Liberators to bomb Taharai and Vunakanau airfields in Rabaul. Fighter pilots escorting the bombers report 30 enemy aircraft shot down. B-25 Mitchells bomb targets on Sohano Island and on Choiseul Island. Fifth Air Force sends 61 B-24 Liberators to bomb Cape Gloucester, followed by B-24 Liberators during the night. P-39 Airacobras attack supply barges between Borgen Bay and Rein Bay. P-40s bomb Gasmata Island and strafe Cape Hoskins.

NEW GUINEA: Fifth Air Force sends over 80 B-25 Mitchells, B-26 Marauders, and A-20 Havocs to attack coastal targets from Wewak to Hansa Bay, the Huon Peninsula, and the Alexishafen airfields.

December 24

CBI: Fourteenth Air Force sends 18 B-24 Liberators, escorted by 18 fighters, to bomb a satellite airfield at Tien Ho, China. Aircrews report 20 Japanese aircraft shot down. One B-24 is lost.

ATLANTIC: U.S. destroyer sinks German submarine *U-645* in the North Atlantic. German submarines *U-275* and *U-382* sink a U.S. destroyer northwest of Spain.

ETO: General Dwight D. Eisenhower is officially announced as Supreme Allied Commander, Allied Expeditionary Force. He has responsibility for planning Overlord, the invasion of Europe.

Eighth Air Force VIII Bomber Command attacks 23 German rocket sites around the Pas-de-Calais, France. It is the largest number of aircraft assembled against a target up to this time, a total of 478 B-17s and 192 B-24 Liberators hit the targets, escorted by 40 P-38 Lightnings, 459 P-47 Thunderbolts, and 42 Ninth Air Force P-51 Mustangs. Two P-38s and two P-51s are damaged. Ninth Air Force also sends over 60 B-26 Marauders against the same target set, but only half attack the targets, primarily due to bad weather.

MIDDLE EAST: Brigadier General Donald P. Booth takes command, relieving Brigadier General Donald H. Connolly as commander of Persian Gulf Command.

MEDITERRANEAN: General Sir Henry Maitland Wilson is named Supreme Allied Commander, Mediterranean Theater (SACMED).

ITALY: Fifteenth Air Force B-26 Marauders bomb the Cecina marshaling yard.

PACIFIC: U.S. destroyer escort sinks Japanese submarine *I-39* off Koli Point, Guadalcanal. U.S. submarine *Gurnard* sinks a Japanese transport and auxiliary minesweeper east of Shikoku, Japan. U.S. submarine *Raton* torpedoes a Japanese transport in Kaoe Bay, Halmahera Island. U.S. submarine *Skate* torpedoes Japanese battleship *Yamato* northeast of Truk.

CENTRAL PACIFIC: Seventh Air Force sends 18 B-24 Liberators to bomb Wotje Atoll. B-25 Mitchells of the 396th and 820th Bombardment Squadrons (Medium), of the 41st Bombardment Group (Medium), arrive at Tarawa Atoll.

BOUGAINVILLE: The Japanese abandon a small hill named 600A after a three-day fight. This is the final piece of key terrain that secures the American perimeter.

Navy Task Force 39 with three cruisers and four destroyers bombards the areas near Buka and Bonis.

NEW BRITAIN: Thirteenth Air Force sends B-24 Liberators to bomb Vunakanau airfield and Lakunai at Rabaul. Fighter pilots flying escort report 25 Japanese aircraft shot down. Seven fighters are lost. Fifth Air Force bombs Cape Gloucester with almost 190 B-24 Liberators, B-25 Mitchells, and A-20 Havocs. P-39 Airacobras attack a disabled destroyer offshore. Over Arawe, A-20 Havocs attack Japanese troops.

NEW IRELAND: Navy Task Group 50.2, commanded by Rear Admiral Frederick C. Sherman, attacks Japanese ships at Kavieng with aircraft from carrier USS *Bunker Hill* and small aircraft carrier USS *Monterey*. One transport is sunk and two minesweepers and a transport are damaged.

December 25

MEDITERRANEAN: At a meeting in Tunis, Allied planners draft a new plan for the amphibious assault south of Rome. Instead of one division as originally planned, two divisions, an airborne unit, and armored forces will land. The target date is set between January 20 and January 31, 1944. To support the landing, Fifth Army, reinforced by two divisions from Eighth Army, will cross the Garigliano and Rapido rivers and drive up the Liri Valley toward Rome. Eighth Army will attack to threaten Route 5, the alternate highway to Rome. Pressed on both fronts, the Germans will not be able to react to a landing near Anzio and Nettuno. After landing, the Allies will advance to capture the hills at Colli Laziali, 20 miles from the landing beaches and near Route 7. Once that key terrain is occupied, the German lines of supply will be threatened and both the Gustav Line and Rome will have to be abandoned. The landing force will then link up with the Fifth Army advancing up the Liri Valley. The amphibious assault plan is called Shingle and will be commanded by Major General John P. Lucas. General Sir Harold Alexander, commander of the Fifteenth Army Group (of which the Eighth and Fifth Armies are a part), notes that the Anzio landing will give the Allies an advantage and that to succeed "the two forces operating under the Commander, Fifth Army, join hands at the earliest possible moment."

ITALY: The 1st Regiment 1st Special Service Force captures Hill 730, the key enemy position on Monte Sammucro, but the unit takes heavy casualties. The 504th Parachute Infantry captures another German position and clears Monte Sammucro.

Fifteenth Air Force B-26 Marauders bomb the marshaling yards at Pisa and Porta Nuova. B-17s attack the Bolzano marshaling yard. B-24 Liberators bomb the Pordenone marshaling yard. Twelfth Air Force A-36 Intruder (Apache) fighter-bombers attack transportation targets at Pontecorvo.

CENTRAL PACIFIC: Seventh Air Force attacks the runway, ammunition storage, and an antiaircraft position on Mili Atoll in the Marshalls with 10 A-24 Banshees, supported by P-39 Airacobras.

BOUGAINVILLE: The Americal Division relieves the 3rd Marine Division.

NEW BRITAIN: The Japanese attack 112th Cavalry forward positions on Arawe. A-20 Havocs provide ground support as the cavalrymen fight back concentrated Japanese assaults. The 112th Cavalry suffers 25 killed and 71 wounded. The Japanese losses are estimated at 78 killed.

Fifth Air Force conducts sustained bombing of Cape Gloucester by over 180 B-24 Liberators, B-25 Mitchells, B-26 Marauders, and A-20 Havocs. Thirteenth Air Force B-24 Liberators bomb Lakunai airfield at Rabaul. Fighter pilots report shooting down 13 enemy fighters, but lose two escorting P-38 Lightnings.

NEW IRELAND: Navy Task Force 38 under command of Rear Admiral Frederick C. Sherman launches 86 aircraft against Kavieng harbor, but no shipping targets are located.

December 26

CARIBBEAN: German submarine *U-530* torpedoes and damages a U.S. tanker off the coast of Panama en route from Aruba to the Canal Zone.

ITALY: The 1st Battalion, 143rd Infantry, 36th Infantry Division captures Morello Hill.

Fifteenth Air Force B-26 Marauders bomb the marshaling yards at Prato, Empoli, and Pistoia.

Near Sommocolonia, Italy, Lieutenant John R. Fox from the 598th Field Artillery Battalion is serving as the forward observer with the 366th Infantry Regiment of the 92nd Division. Just before dawn, German infantry attack the town in strength, forcing the Americans to retreat. Lieutenant Fox and other members of the observer team stay in the town to direct artillery fire on the enemy. As the Germans continue the attack Lieutenant Fox continues to call in artillery shells closer and closer to his own position. Acknowledging the danger to himself, he orders a final adjustment to land on his own position just as the enemy is in his midst. Lieutenant Fox sacrifices himself to stop the German attack and allow his comrades to organize an effective counterattack. For this act of valor Lieutenant John Fox will receive the Medal of Honor.

CENTRAL PACIFIC: Seventh Air Force sends 16 B-24 Liberators to bomb Wotje Atoll, while P-39 Airacobras fly reconnaissance and strafing missions over Mili Atoll.

BOUGAINVILLE: Thirteenth Air Force sends seven B-25 Mitchells, with 34 fighters, to attack the Cape Saint George area. Another 25 B-25s attack camp and logistics at Kahili.

NEW BRITAIN: Operation Backhandler. Seventh Amphibious Force, commanded by Rear Admiral Daniel E. Barbey, lands the 1st Marine Division, commanded by Major General William H. Rupertus, at Cape Gloucester. Naval gunfire and LCIs with rocket launchers support the landing. Fifth Air Force supports the landing of the 1st Marine Division at Cape Gloucester with over 270 B-25 Mitchells, B-24 Liberators, and A-20 Havocs. A fuel dump is bombed, resulting in a large explosion and fire.

Three battalion landing teams (BLTs) of the 7th Marine Regiment, commanded by Colonel Julian N. Frisbie, land on a narrow beach to establish a beachhead perimeter. The marines find only a few Japanese and, moving inland toward Target Hill, quickly find themselves in a swamp forest, wading waist-deep in mud and water. The 1st Battalion 7th

The landing vehicle tracked (LVT) carried 6,500 to 8,000 pounds of cargo and was essential to the success of Marine landings from Tarawa to Peleliu. At Cape Gloucester, New Britain, in December 1944, the ground was so saturated and the mud so deep that only an LVT could bring supplies to the Marines pushing forward.

Marines occupies Target Hill protecting the left flank of the beachhead. Two battalions of the 1st Marine Regiment pass through the 3rd Battalion 7th Marines to move toward Gloucester airfield and encounter a Japanese roadblock. About 40 minutes after the initial landing, LSTs begin unloading supplies and tanks. Bulldozers begin cutting paths through the jungle, but as the units advance deeper into the swampy jungle, only LVT amphibious tractors can resupply them. The assistant commander of the 1st Marine Division, Brigadier General Lemuel Shepherd, Jr., takes control of the beachhead.

The Japanese respond to the landing with dive-bomber attacks, sinking one destroyer and damaging three others. One LST is also damaged. Major General William H. Rupertus, upon landing on the beach, requests the 5th Marines from the division reserve.

The 2nd Battalion 1st Marines, supported by 75-millimeter pack howitzers, lands on the western edge of New Britain near Tauali to cut the main coastal road and block any enemy movements to reinforce or retreat from Cape Gloucester. The marines are to locate and destroy any enemy forces in the area.

About 80 Japanese aircraft succeed in sinking a destroyer and damaging two others. P-38 Lightnings, P-40s, and P-47 Thunderbolts report shooting down over 60 enemy aircraft and report five U.S. aircraft as losses. Actual Japanese losses are 13 bombers and four aircraft lost. U.S. B-25 Mitchells, flying over the beach at the time of the enemy attack, are engaged by friendly antiaircraft fire and two are shot down. The bombers then accidentally drop bombs on marines at Silimati Point, killing one and wounding 14.

Engineers land on Long Island to establish a radar site.

The Japanese conduct a night attack on the 2nd Battalion 7th Marine sector in a rainstorm so severe that the marines have to leave their foxholes because they are filled with water. The Japanese attack fails, leaving 200 dead.

December 27

CBI: Brigadier General Lewis A. Pick opens the Ledo Road to Shingbwiyang in the Hakawng Valley.

The Japanese send 36 aircraft to attack Suichwan airfield in China, destroying a Fourteenth Air Force B-25 and fuel storage areas. Fighters intercepting the attackers report four enemy aircraft destroyed. One P-40 is lost.

INDIAN OCEAN: German submarine *U-178* torpedoes and sinks a U.S. freighter bound for Calcutta, India, west of the Maldives.

ETO: Eighth Air Force sends seven B-17s to drop over 1 million leaflets on Paris, Lille, Evreux, Rouen, and Caen in France.

ITALY: Fifteenth Air Force B-26 Marauders bomb the viaducts at Zoagli and Recco. Twelfth Air Force A-36 Intruder (Apache) fighter-bombers attack a factory and rail lines at Anagni and Civitavecchia, and a bridge at Pontecorvo.

SOUTHWEST PACIFIC AREA: U.S. submarine *Flying Fish* sinks a Japanese fleet tanker in the South China Sea north of Luzon, Philippines. U.S. submarine *Ray* sinks a Japanese fleet tanker west of the Celebes.

PACIFIC: U.S. submarine *Gurnard* damages a Japanese transport east of Shikoku, Japan. U.S. submarine *Tautog* damages a Japanese seaplane carrier off Shionomisaki, Japan.

BOUGAINVILLE: Thirteenth Air Force B-25 Mitchells bomb the seaplane anchorage at Buka, while P-38 Lightnings support over 70 navy SBD Dauntless dive-bombers in attacks on antiaircraft positions. B-25s attack logistics bases at Kahili and a camp at Kieta. Two cruisers and four destroyers of Task Force 39 bombard the Kieta area.

NEW BRITAIN: The 1st and 3rd Battalions of the 1st Marines, reinforced with tanks, move toward Cape Gloucester airfield with difficulty. The narrow trail and heavy jungle limits movement. The 1st Battalion 7th Marines consolidates positions on Target Hill, a small hilltop that is valuable as an observation point and controls any movement of troops along the shoreline.

Fifth Air Force A-20 Havocs attack positions on Cape Gloucester. B-25 Mitchells hit villages and roads from Rottock Bay to Riebeck Bay and strafe barges along the southern coast of the island. B-24 Liberators bomb the airfield at Hoskins.

In response to a request from General Cunningham, an infantry company from the 158th Infantry Regiment lands on Arawe to reinforce the 112th Cavalry.

Thirteenth Air Force and Allied fighters conduct a sweep of the Rabaul area and report destroying 17 enemy aircraft.

NEW GUINEA: Fifth Air Force B-24 Liberators bomb Alexishafen. B-25 Mitchells bomb Madang and targets along the Huon Peninsula.

December 28

CBI: The Chinese 38th Division clears Japanese strongpoints along the Tarung River in the Hukawng valley.

Fourteenth Air Force B-25 Mitchells and P-51 Mustangs attack Yangtze River shipping at Chihchow, China.

ATLANTIC: A U.S. PB4Y Privateer discovers five German destroyers and six torpedo boats in the Bay of Biscay. Six PB4Ys are able to conduct an attack, which is later supported by two British light cruisers. One German destroyer and two torpedo boats are sunk.

INDIAN OCEAN: Japanese submarine *I-26* torpedoes and damages a U.S. freighter en route to Mombasa, Kenya, off the Horn of Africa. The crew abandons ship, but the 27-man armed guard maintains a steady and accurate fire on the submarine, which breaks off its attack. The ship is dead in the water and is later towed to Suez, but it is unsalvageable.

ETO: VIII Bomber Command Mission sends one B-17 on an Oboe test, dropping two 2,000-pound bombs and a Photoflash bomb over Dusseldorf, Germany. Six B-17s drop two million leaflets over Osnabruck, Hannover, and Hildesheim, Germany, Amiens, France, and Zwolle in the Netherlands.

ITALY: Fifteenth Air Force sends over 100 B-26 Marauders against airfields and rail lines at Guidonia and Centocelle and railroad bridges near Orvieto. B-17s and B-24 Liberators bomb the marshaling yard at Rimini. Another 17 B-24s sent against the Vicenza marshaling yard without fighter escort are attacked by about 50 fighters.

German fighters claim 10 bombers, while aircrews report 18 fighters are shot down. Twelfth Air Force B-25 Mitchells, A-20 Havocs, and A-36 Intruder (Apache) fighter-bombers bomb the landing grounds at Ciampino, transportation targets at Frosinone, Roccasecca, and Civitavecchia. P-40s attack Anzio harbor and lines of communication in the Pontecorvo and Atina areas.

PACIFIC: U.S. submarine *Muskallunge* unsuccessfully attacks a Japanese convoy west of Truk.

CENTRAL PACIFIC: Seventh Air Force sends 15 B-24 Liberators to bomb Mille Atoll, Maloelap, and Majuro Atolls. Mille Atoll is also attacked by 18 A-24 Banshees escorted by 20 P-39 Airacobras, followed soon thereafter by nine B-25 Mitchells from Tarawa escorted by 12 P-39s.

BOUGAINVILLE: Thirteenth Air Force B-24 Liberators bomb logistics sites at Bonis and 22 B-25 Mitchells bomb the logistics base at Kahili. Over Rabaul, a fighter sweep reportedly nets over 20 enemy aircraft destroyed.

NEW BRITAIN: Advancing behind Fifth Air Force aircraft, two battalions of the 1st Marines battle a Japanese strongpoint in a heavy rainstorm. The marines lose eight killed and 16 wounded in clearing the enemy position. The 2nd Battalion 1st Marines near Tauali encounters Japanese patrols.

General Krueger releases the 5th Marines to reinforce the 1st Marine Division. The 112th Cavalry repels a Japanese counterattack on Arawe.

December 29

CBI: Fourteenth Air Force P-40s strafe the railroad station, railyards, and the town of Hsipaw, China

PACIFIC: Off Palau, U.S. submarine *Silversides* sinks a Japanese transport and two cargo ships and damages another cargo ship north of Yap.

ITALY: Troops from the 143rd Infantry enter San Vittore but are forced back.

The II Corps has reached all of its objectives for Phase II of Operation Raincoat. Fifteenth Air Force B-26 Marauders attack the marshaling yard at Certaldo and Poggibonsi. B-17s bomb the marshaling yards at Ferrara and Rimini. Twelfth Air Force A-36 Intruder (Apache) fighter-bombers attack the railway station at Ferentino, the harbor and railroad yard at Civitavecchia, and trucks near Aquino.

NEW BRITAIN: The Japanese abandon their defensive position, which the marines have named "Hell's Point." The 2nd Battalion of the 5th Marines lands to support the 1st Marines. The plan is to have the 5th Marines sweep around the left flank of the enemy while 1st Marines advances. The 1st Battalion 7th Marines holds Target Hill.

Fifth Air Force sends over 120 B-24 Liberators, B-25 Mitchells, and B-26 Marauders to attack Japanese positions at Cape Gloucester in support of the marine assault to capture the airfield.

The assistant commander of the 1st Marine Division, Brigadier General Lemuel Shepherd, Jr., takes two battalions of the 7th Marines to clear the Japanese from Borgen Bay. The marines are reinforced by artillery and a platoon of tanks from the 1st Tank Battalion.

NEW GUINEA: Fifth Air Force B-24 Liberators bomb camps and communication targets near Sio. B-25 Mitchells bomb Madang.

December 30

CBI: Tenth Air Force sends 20 B-24 Liberators to attack railway facilities at Monywa, Burma. Fourteenth Air Force's Suichuan airfield in China is attacked by eight Japanese fighters with 12 others providing cover. The attack destroys two aircraft on the ground, but eight P-40s intercept the enemy and shoot down three fighters.

Since April, Fourteenth Air Force has transported 2,592 tons of fuel to keep its aircraft flying, all of it brought over the treacherous Himalaya Mountains (the Hump). Since October 1, 39 vessels have been sunk and 19 damaged. At the end of the year the Fourteenth Air Force has 188 fighters, 51 B-24 Liberators, and 35 B-25 Mitchells

ETO: Eighth Air Force VIII Bomber Command targets the port area and oil refinery at Ludwigshafen, Germany. A force of 502 B-17s and 145 B-24 Liberators, led by 11 Pathfinder aircraft and escorted by 79 P-38 Lightnings, 463 P-47 Thunderbolts, and 41 Ninth Air Force P-51 Mustangs, hits the target. Fourteen B-17s and nine B-24s are lost and 110 B-17s and 12 B-24s are damaged. Aircrews report 12 German fighters destroyed. Fighter pilots report eight confirmed kills, three probables, and six possibles. Fighter losses are 11 P-47s and two P-51s. Five P-47s are damaged. Total American losses for this mission are 11 killed, 19 wounded, and 212 missing. Later in the evening, five B-17s drop one million leaflets on Cambrai, France, and on Antwerp, Ghent, and Lens in Belgium.

Ninth Air Force attacks the Saint-Omer airfield and German rocket sites on the northern coast of France with 100 B-26 Marauders.

ITALY: In II Corps area, the 36th Infantry Division is relieved in place by the 34th Infantry Division. The 142nd Infantry Regiment is placed under the 34th Division's operational control to maintain control of Monte Sammucro.

In VI Corps area, the 45th Infantry Division's 180th Infantry Regiment attempts to clear Monte Molino and Monte Rotondo, guarding the Sant' Elia road. Advancing behind a 15-minute artillery barrage, and supported by tanks from the 755th Tank Battalion, the Americans are able to occupy Monte Rotondo with a small force but are driven back everywhere else.

Fifteenth Air Force B-17s, escorted by P-38 Lightnings and P-47 Thunderbolts, bomb the marshaling yards at Rimini and Padua. Two bombers are lost and nine German fighters are reported destroyed. B-26 Marauders bomb the marshaling yard at Borgo San Lorenzo and Viareggio, and a road junction near Roccasecca. Twelfth Air Force A-20 Havocs attack Atina, while P-40s and A-36 Intruder (Apache) fighter-bombers attack enemy positions near Chieti and Miglianico. Gun positions near Arce and Minturno, Sant' Elia Fiumerapido, Ferentino, and Atina are also attacked.

SOUTHWEST PACIFIC AREA: U.S. submarine *Bluefish* sinks a Japanese oiler in the Java Sea.

CENTRAL PACIFIC: Seventh Air Force sends 17 B-24 Liberators to bomb Kwajalein Atoll. B-24s attack a Japanese cargo ship south of Kwajalein. B-25 Mitchells from Tarawa bomb Jabor on Jaluit Atoll in the Marshalls. A-24 Banshees, escorted by 24 P-39 Airacobras, dive-bomb gun positions on Mili Atoll, also in the Marshalls. Seventh Air Force's advanced headquarters moves from Funafuti Atoll to Tarawa.

BOUGAINVILLE: The newly constructed Piva airfield is operational. Thirteenth Air Force sends 16 B-24 Liberators and 35 B-25 Mitchells to bomb the logistics support areas at Kahili. Another six B-25s bomb the Korovo area.

NEW BRITAIN: The 7th Marines move out to expand their perimeter, clearing out Japanese defenses and capturing weapons and ammunition stores.

During the night, the 2nd Battalion 1st Marines fights the Battle of Coffin Corner. A Japanese assault in a heavy rainstorm, supported with mortar and machine-gun fire, temporarily breaks a company's defensive perimeter, but the marines counterattack with a platoon cobbled together by Lieutenant James R. Mallon and throw the enemy back. The Japanese lose 89 men and five prisoners are captured. The marines suffer six killed and 17 wounded.

Elements of the 1st and 5th Marines capture the Cape Gloucester airfield. Fifth Air Force A-20 Havocs hit positions in the Cape Gloucester area in support of the marines. The marines find that the airfield has been heavily damaged ("Gloucester-ized" in the air force terminology) by U.S. air attacks.

Thirteenth Air Force B-24 Liberators, with 25 fighters covering, attack shipping at Rabaul and also bomb Tobera airfield. The fighters report aggressive enemy fighter opposition with 12 aircraft shot down. Over the past month, the Thirteenth Air Force has flown 617 sorties and dropped 197 tons of bombs on Rabaul. U.S. losses have been 19 aircraft; Japanese aircraft losses are estimated at over 100.

NEW GUINEA: Fifth Air Force B-24 Liberators and B-25 Mitchells bomb Alexishafen, Sio, and Madang, and targets of opportunity along the coast of the Huon Peninsula. P-39 Airacobras strafe barges along the Huon Peninsula. P-47 Thunderbolts strafe the Madang area.

December 31

ALEUTIANS: Four PBY-5A Catalinas from Attu Island bomb Shimushu and Kashi-wabara in the Kuriles.

CBI: Fourteenth Air Force B-24 Liberators bomb the Lampang railroad yards. B-25 Mitchells attack shipping along the Yangtze River and attack a passenger vessel in the Hainan Straits. The Fourteenth Air Force is destroying an average of 50,000 tons of Japanese shipping per month, representing one-third of all enemy shipping losses and crippling the Japanese war effort.

ETO: Eighth Air Force VIII Bomber Command attacks airfields in France escorted by 74 P-38 Lightnings, 441 P-47 Thunderbolts, and 33 Ninth Air Force P-51 Mustangs. Over the Bordeaux-Merignac, Cognac-Chateaubernard, and Landes Bussac airfields 200 B-17s and 57 B-24 Liberators hit their targets. Eighteen B-17s and five B-24s are lost and 118 bombers are damaged. Aircrews report 17 German fighters destroyed. Four of 57 B-17s are damaged on a mission to find a blockade-running ship at Gironde. Over the St. Jean D'Angely airfield, 87 B-24 Liberators hit the target, losing one bomber and having eight damaged. Aircrews report nine enemy aircraft destroyed. Over the industrial areas at Paris-Ivry and Bois-Colombes, 120 B-17s hit the target, losing one B-17 and 50 others damaged. Fighter pilots report nine confirmed enemy kills, one probable kill, and one possible. Four fighters are lost and eight are damaged. Total U.S. casualties for this mission are 11 killed, 46 wounded, and 253 missing. For the month of December 1943, the Eighth Air Force has dropped over 13,000 tons of bombs.

Ninth Air Force sends about 200 B-26 Marauders to bomb German rocket sites on the coast of France.

ITALY: In II Corps area, the 6th Armored Infantry Regiment of the 1st Armored Division relieves the 15th Infantry, 3rd Infantry Division on Monte Lungo.

In VI Corps area, the 45th Infantry Division's 1st Battalion, 180th Infantry Regiment, in rain that later turns to snow, attempts to clear Monte Molino but is unable to advance under enemy fire. U.S. rifle companies in the two battalions are down to 65 men each. The Fifth Army has over 22,000 men being treated for illness and trench foot. Troops in the front lines must often be resupplied by mules. The VI Corps begins to be moved off the front lines, to be replaced by the French Expeditionary Corps, commanded by General Alphonse P. Juin. It is composed of the 2nd Moroccan Division and the 3rd Algerian Division.

Twelfth Air Force A-36 Intruder (Apache) fighter-bombers attack gun positions around Formia.

PACIFIC: U.S. submarine *Greenling* sinks a Japanese transport in the eastern Carolines and escapes the search of a submarine chaser. U.S. submarine *Herring* attacks a Japanese convoy east of Shikoku, Japan.

At the end of the year, U.S. submarines have sunk a total of 335 Japanese ships, totaling about 1.5 million tons. Using intercepted communications from Ultra, the submarine fleet is able to attack critical shipping targets and aims at first starving the outer defenses of the Japanese, while slowly strangling war production on the home islands.

NEW BRITAIN: Major General William H. Rupertus sends the following message to Lieutenant General Krueger: "Situation well in hand due to fighting spirit of troops, the usual Marine luck and the help of God." Fifth Air Force A-20 Havocs attack Japanese troops around Cape Gloucester. The 3/5 Marines complete their landing and relieve the 2/7 Marines, which now becomes the division reserve.

Japanese aircraft attempting to attack marines near Arawe are attacked by nearly 50 P-40s and P-47 Thunderbolts. The Japanese lose 12 aircraft to the American fighters.

Thirteenth Air Force attacks Rabaul with 15 B-24 Liberators, escorted by 48 F6F Hellcats and 25 P-38 Lightnings. They are met by heavy antiaircraft fire and are attacked by nearly 90 Japanese fighters. Three B-24s are lost and aircrews report 20 enemy fighters destroyed.

NEW GUINEA: Fifth Air Force B-24 Liberators and B-25 Mitchells bomb the areas around Madang, Alexishafen, and Bogadjim.

Allied casualties for the year in New Guinea total 24,000 men, 17,000 of those are Australian.

1944

January 1
CBI: The 5307th Composite Unit (Provisional) is activated. It is organized into three battalions, each with two combat teams of 100 men each. Along with infantry, each

combat team has a reconnaissance element, a medical detachment, a mortar and machine gun detachment, and engineer, communications, and command sections. All equipment for the unit is packed on mules or carried by individual soldiers. The unit will be resupplied by air. The 1st Provisional Tank Group under command of Colonel Rothwell H. Brown arrives at Ledo. It is composed of 90 M4A4 Sherman medium tanks armed with 76 millimeter main guns and M3A3 Stuart V light tanks armed with 37 millimeter main guns. The unit has a compliment of 29 officers and 222 enlisted men, both Chinese and Americans. Most of the Chinese soldiers, who range between the ages of 15 and 25, had never seen a machine until joining the unit a few weeks prior.

In Burma, Tenth Air Force B-25 Mitchells, along with 16 P-38 Lightnings, attack a bridge on the Mu River. Major Robert A. Erdin's maneuver to avoid a crash leads to the discovery of an effective bombing technique that puts bombs directly on target. The 490th Bombardment Squadron (Medium) of the 341st Bombardment Group (Medium) soon becomes known as the "Burma Bridge Busters."

A-36 Intruder (Apache) fighter-bombers and P-51 Mustangs attack the airfield at Myitkyina.

The 315th Troop Carrier Squadron with C-47s is activated at Dinjan, India, and assigned to Tenth Air Force.

ETO: The Allies have 11 combat divisions in Britain reserved for Overlord.

The 491st, 492nd, and 493rd Bombardment Groups (Heavy) arrive in England from the United States. These units will receive crews and be equipped with B-24 Liberators. The 492nd will fly its first mission on May 11; the 491st will follow on June 2; and the 493rd on June 6.

The U.S. Strategic Air Forces in Europe (USSAFE) is established to take operational control of the Eighth and Fifteenth Air Forces.

ITALY: The Twelfth Air Force's XII Bomber Command, commanded by Brigadier General Robert D. Knapp, is reorganized as a medium bomber command with three B-25 Mitchell groups and three B-26 Marauder groups.

Three B-26 Marauder groups from Fifteenth Air Force are transferred to Twelfth Air Force. The Fifteenth has six heavy bomber groups (four B-17 and two B-24) and four fighter groups (one P-47 and three P-38).

SOUTHWEST PACIFIC AREA: U.S. submarine *Puffer* torpedoes and sinks a cargo ship south of Negros Island in the Philippines.

PACIFIC: U.S. submarine *Herring* torpedoes and sinks an aircraft transport in the North Pacific, 220 miles southeast of the island of Honshu, Japan. The submarine evades an escorting destroyer.

U.S. submarine *Balao* torpedoes and damages a Japanese transport ship south of Truk.

CENTRAL PACIFIC: In the Marshalls, Seventh Air Force sends six P-39 Airacobras to attack Mille Atoll harbor and shipping.

The headquarters of VII Bomber Command is ordered to move from Funafuti Atoll in the Ellice Islands to Tarawa Atoll in the Gilbert Islands.

Four PB4Y-1 Privateers from Apamama Atoll, Gilbert Islands, mine the waters near Maloelap Atoll in the Marshalls. Three, PV-1 Patrol Bombers from Tarawa mine the waters off Jaluit Atoll in the Marshalls, and two PBY-5 Catalinas mine Jabor anchorage at Jaluit.

BOUGAINVILLE: Allied fighters and U.S. Navy SBD Dauntless dive-bombers provide air support to ground forces near Torokina. Thirteenth Air Force B-25 Mitchells and B-24 Liberators bomb Kahili, and four B-24s bomb Manob.

NEW BRITAIN: Thirteenth Air Force B-24 Liberators, escorted by over 70 P-38 Lightnings and navy F6F Hellcats, bomb Lakunai airfield. Antiaircraft fire is heavy over the target and about 90 Japanese fighters intercept the formation. About 20 enemy fighters are reported shot down. One B-24 is lost; two other Liberators are badly damaged and forced down near Torokina on Bougainville Island.

A-20 Havocs attack Japanese troop concentrations around Cape Gloucester; B-25 Mitchells bomb positions at Borgen Bay; and P-39 Airacobras attack barges on the northern coast.

NEW GUINEA: Fifth Air Force sends 60 B-24 Liberators, 48 B-25 Mitchells, and A-20 Havocs to the landing area at Saidor. The bombers drop 218 tons of bombs on the target. B-25 Mitchells bomb Madang and Alexishafen.

Navy Task Group 37.2, commanded by Rear Admiral Frederick C. Sherman, attacks a Japanese convoy escorted by cruisers and destroyers off Kavieng, New Ireland. Carrier pilots report one light cruiser damaged.

U.S. submarine *Ray* torpedoes and sinks a Japanese gunboat at the mouth of Ambon Bay, Netherlands East Indies.

Navy PBY Catalinas sink a Japanese cargo ship near Lorengau in the Admiralty Islands.

January 2

CBI: Major General Daniel L. Sultan arrives to serve as General Stilwell's deputy and handle most of the administrative matters that Stilwell had previously handled alone.

Tenth Air Force B-25 Mitchells escorted by 16 P-39 Airacobras attack industrial targets at Yenangyaung in Burma and damage an oilfield. B-24 Liberators also attack a refinery and a power station. Another 30 A-36 Intruder (Apache) fighter-bombers and P-51 Mustangs bomb the approaches to Loilaw bridge.

In China Fourteenth Air Force P-40s bomb and strafe Japanese barracks at Hopang.

Japanese submarine *I-26* torpedoes and sinks a U.S. freighter off the coast of Arabia.

ATLANTIC: A U.S. Navy PB4Y Privateer tracks a German blockade runner en route from Japan to Germany in the South Atlantic. A U.S. destroyer intercepts the vessel.

ITALY: Fifteenth Army Group directs the Fifth Army to use two infantry divisions to land at Anzio and cut the German lines of communication and supply behind the Gustav Line. The remainder of Fifth Army is to attack at Cassino, break the enemy lines, and link up with the Anzio force.

In the Fifteenth Air Force, B-24 Liberators of the 720th and 722nd Bombardment Squadrons (Heavy) of the 450th Bombardment Group (Heavy) arrive from the United States. The squadrons are scheduled to fly their first mission in early

January. The B-24 Liberators of the 724th, 725th, 726th, and 727th Bombardment Squadrons (Heavy) of the 451st Bombardment Group (Heavy) of the Fifteenth Air Force also arrive from the United States. The group will be ready for combat missions at the end of January.

XII Air Support Command conducts bombing missions on Monte la Chiaia in preparation for the II Corps attack. Twelfth Air Force B-25 Mitchells bomb the Terni marshaling yard, the iron works, and a military barracks.

PACIFIC: U.S. submarine *Finback* torpedoes and sinks a Japanese merchant tanker in the East China Sea.

CENTRAL PACIFIC: Seventh Air Force B-24 Liberators based at Tarawa bomb Maloelap Atoll in the Marshalls. B-25 Mitchells attack targets on Jaluit Atoll and P-39 Airacobras strafe Japanese shipping near Mille Atoll.

Five PV-1 Patrol Bombers from Tarawa and one PBY-5 Catalina conduct aerial mining in the Marshall Islands.

Japanese aircraft attack the airfield on Apamama Atoll, Gilbert Islands, destroying one PB4Y Privateer and damaging two others.

BOUGAINVILLE: Thirteenth Air Force B-25 Mitchells bomb a supply dump on Buka Island.

NEW BRITAIN: Brigadier General Lemuel C. Shepherd, the assistant division commander, leads an advance of the 2/7, 3/7, and 3/5 Marines toward Borgen Bay. As the 3/7 and 3/5 Marines advance to the southeast, the 2/7 Marines are to fall back as the reserve. Jungle movement becomes treacherous and slow. After marines hack their way about 300 yards, Japanese defenders along Suicide Creek stop the advance of the 3rd Battalion 7th Marines and 3rd Battalion 5th Marines. The creek's 12-foot-high banks are covered by interlocking fields of fire from cleverly hidden machine gun positions, making an attack suicidal—thus the name given to the creek by the marines.

Fifth Air Force P-40s strafe the airfield, antiaircraft positions, and supplies at Cape Hoskins.

NEW GUINEA: Task Force 76, commanded by Rear Admiral Daniel E. Barbey, lands the 126th Regimental Combat Team, 32nd Infantry Division (Reinforced), at Saidor. Six destroyers, six LSTs, nine APDs, and 16 LCIs support the landing. The 126th Regimental Combat Team, the 121st Field Artillery Battalion, two engineer battalions, and support troops land with 6,700 men, 300 vehicles, and 1,800 tons of supplies. The landing force is commanded by Major General Clarence A. Martin. B-24 Liberators and B-25 Mitchells, despite bad weather, succeed in dropping 100 tons of bombs on targets behind the beachhead. A-20 Havocs also provide ground support. The landing is intended to cut off the Japanese retreat from the Huon Peninsula before the advancing Australian 9th Division. P-40s attack Japanese bombers and fighters attacking the landing. One P-40 is lost and five Japanese aircraft are shot down. Although the intent is to trap the Japanese between the Americans and the Australians, torrential rains, heavy jungle, and mountainous terrain allow the Japanese to escape the trap. Japanese troops from Madang guard the trails leading west to allow their comrades to escape.

January 3

CBI: Tenth Air Force A-36 Intruder (Apache) fighter-bombers and P-51 Mustangs attack logistics storage sites at Sahmaw in Burma. Another attack by 19 B-25 Mitchells with 16 P-38 Lightnings flying escort bombs the oilfields at Yenangyaung; another 10 B-24 Liberators making a follow-on attack cause heavy damage to the target. Fourteenth Air Force B-24 Liberators bomb the railroad yards at Lampang, China.

ATLANTIC: The CCS temporarily allocates 87 LSTs to the Mediterranean theater to support Operation Shingle, the Anzio landings. General Eisenhower reports to the JCS that he believes the Shingle operation is very risky. The Germans can rapidly concentrate on the beachhead and quickly crush the two-division force. He is also concerned that there is insufficient means to resupply and sustain the landing force by sea. He believes that if the Anzio landing force and the rest of Fifth Army do not make the planned link-up within eight days of the first landing, then the operation must be considered a failure and the landing force must be withdrawn.

A U.S. destroyer sinks a German blockade runner in the South Atlantic, recovering 130 survivors.

ETO: The B-17s of the 728th, 729th, 730th, and 731st Bombardment Squadrons (Heavy) of the 452nd Bombardment Group (Heavy) arrive in England from the United States. The group's first mission is scheduled for early February.

MEDITERRANEAN: Lieutenant General Nathan F. Twining takes command of the Fifteenth Air Force.

B-17s with P-38 Lightnings and P-47 Thunderbolts flying escort bomb the Villarperosa ball bearing works, the marshaling yard at Lingotto, and the Fiat motor works near Turin.

The B-24 Liberators of the 719th Bombardment Squadron (Heavy) of the 449th Bombardment Group (Heavy) arrive from the United States. The B-24 Liberators of the 721st and 723rd Bombardment Squadrons (Heavy) of the 450th Bombardment Group (Heavy) also arrive from the United States. All three squadrons will fly their first mission early this month.

Brigadier General Edward M. Morris takes command of XII Fighter Command. Twelfth Air Force B-25 Mitchells bomb troops at Prijedor and hit other targets at Split and Sibenik in Yugoslavia.

ITALY: Twelfth Air Force P-40s and A-36 Intruder (Apache) fighter-bombers attack gun positions near Cassino, trains between Ceccano and Segni, and the harbor at Civitavecchia. Other P-40s attack vehicles near Avezzano and Sulmona.

SOUTHWEST PACIFIC AREA: U.S. submarine *Bluefish* lays mines off the eastern Malayan coast. U.S. submarine *Raton* torpedoes and sinks a Japanese fleet tanker east of Mindanao in the Philippines.

PACIFIC: U.S. submarine *Tautog* torpedoes and sinks a Japanese transport south of Honshu, Japan.

CENTRAL PACIFIC: Seventh Air Force A-24 Banshees, supported by P-39 Airacobras, attack Japanese antiaircraft positions, radar, radio facilities, oil storage facilities, and runways on Mille Atoll in the Marshalls.

Navy PB4Y-1 Privateers from Apemama Atoll in the Gilbert Islands conduct aerial mining in the Marshalls. Four PV-1 patrol bombers from Tarawa put down mines near Jaluit Atoll.

Japanese aircraft attack the airfield at Apamama, but cause little damage.

BOUGAINVILLE: Thirteenth Air Force B-25 Mitchells bomb a bivouac area near Kahili and 15 other B-25s attack supply storage areas near Buka Passage.

NEW BRITAIN: The 1st Battalion 7th Marines repulses a Japanese attack on Target Hill. Three Sherman medium tanks arrive on the banks of Suicide Creek on a corduroy road built with great difficulty and extraordinary effort by engineers. Engineers begin to rebuild Cape Gloucester airfield.

Thirteenth Air Force fighters attack Rabaul and report six enemy fighters destroyed.

Fifth Air Force B-24 Liberators bomb Kavieng on New Ireland. A-20 Havocs attack Japanese positions at Borgen Bay.

NEW GUINEA: Fifth Air Force B-24 Liberators and B-25 Mitchells bomb the Alexishafen area.

The 388th Bombardment Squadron (Light) of the 312th Bombardment Group (Light) will transition from P-40s to A-20 Havocs in February.

U.S. submarine *Kingfish* attacks a Japanese convoy, sinking two fleet tankers northwest of Borneo.

January 4

ATLANTIC: A U.S. light cruiser and a destroyer intercept and sink a German blockade runner with gunfire off the northeast coast of Brazil.

ETO: Eighth Air Force attacks two targets over Germany. Of the 371 B-17s and 115 B-24 Liberators that hit the port area at Kiel, 11 B-17s and six B-24s are lost; 113 B-17s and 19 B-24s are damaged. Aircrews report four enemy aircraft as confirmed kills, 12 as probable kills, and four as possibles. U.S. casualties are 22 killed, 53 wounded, and 170 missing. The bombers are escorted by 70 P-38 Lightnings and 42 P-51 Mustangs of the Ninth Air Force. The fighter pilots report one enemy fighter as a confirmed kill, one probable kill, and four possibles. One P-38 is shot down and one is damaged; a P-51 is also lost. Both pilots are reported missing.

Of the 68 B-17s that hit Munster, two B-17s are lost and 36 are damaged. One crewman is wounded and 20 others are missing. The 430 P-47 Thunderbolt pilots that escort the bombers report seven enemy fighters destroyed. Only one P-47 is damaged.

Ninth Air Force B-26 Marauders attack V-weapon sites in France.

Over France during the night, four B-17s drop 800,000 leaflets on Orleans, Lorient, Rouen, and Tours.

U.S. aircraft begin Operation Carpetbagger, airdropping supplies to underground resistance groups in western Europe.

The XIX Air Support Command is activated in England, commanded by Major General Elwood R "Pete" Quesada.

ITALY: The last phase of Operation Raincoat begins in the II Corps area. The intent is to drive the Germans back to Cassino at the opening to the Liri Valley and clear Route 6. Monte Majo and a chain of hills to the southwest, Monte la Chiaia, Monte

Porchia, and Cedro Hill guard the approach. Monte Trocchio, standing behind the chain of hills, is the last defensible terrain before Cassino. The 135th and 168th Infantry Regiments will outflank and clear Monte Chiaia. The 1st Special Service Force will capture Monte Majo, and the 6th Armored Infantry, 1st Armored Division, will capture Monte Porchia. The British X Corps is assigned the capture of Cedro Hill.

The 1st Special Service Force begins the offensive with an attack that captures the hills along the front slope of Monte Majo.

Fifteenth Air Force sends over 100 B-17s to bomb the Dupnica area of Bulgaria, but heavy cloud cover prevents all but 29 from bombing the target.

Twelfth Air Force B-25 Mitchells bomb the marshaling yard at Travnik in Yugoslavia.

SOUTHWEST PACIFIC AREA: U.S. submarines *Bluefish* and *Rasher* attack a Japanese convoy off the coast of French Indochina. *Bluefish* torpedoes and sinks a merchant tanker and *Rasher* damages a tanker and conducts mine-laying activities. U.S. submarine *Cabrilla* torpedoes and sinks a Japanese cargo ship off the coast of French Indochina.

PACIFIC: U.S. submarine *Tautog* torpedoes and sinks a Japanese cargo ship off southern Honshu, Japan.

CENTRAL PACIFIC: Two PV-1 patrol bombers and one PBY-5 Catalina from Tarawa, mine near Jaluit Atoll in the Marshalls.

BOUGAINVILLE: Thirteenth Air Force B-25 Mitchells attack gun positions at Tonolai and bomb Chabai.

NEW BRITAIN: After a 15-minute artillery preparation and with the help of engineers using bulldozers to plow over the steep banks of Suicide Creek, the 3rd Battalion 7th Marines and 3rd Battalion 5th Marines overwhelm the Japanese defenses. The 3/7 Marines tie in with the 1/7 Marines on the left flank, and 2/7 Marines moves to lengthen the line to the west, joining with 3/5 Marines.

Fifth Air Force B-25 Mitchells attack artillery positions in the Cape Gloucester area. More than 40 Allied fighters from Thirteenth Air Force attack the Rabaul area and report 10 Japanese aircraft shot down.

NEW GUINEA: Fifth Air Force sends over 100 B-24 Liberators and B-25 Mitchells to attack targets near Alexishafen, Madang, and Bogadjim and bomb Japanese troops and supplies located between Finschhafen and Saidor.

Fifth Air Force attacks Japanese shipping at Timor. Aircrews report one cargo ship sunk.

Navy aircraft from Task Group 37.2, commanded by Rear Admiral Frederick C. Sherman, attack Japanese shipping at Kavieng and damage two destroyers.

January 5
CBI: Tenth Air Force B-25s, supported by eight P-38 Lightnings, attack the Mu River bridge in Burma.

ATLANTIC: A Navy PBM-3S Mariner sights and tracks a German blockade runner while a U.S. light cruiser and destroyer sink the vessel with gunfire off the coast of Brazil.

ETO: Eighth Air Force attacks two targets over Germany and two over France. The first target is the shipyard and industrial area at Kiel. Of the 119 B-17s and 96 B-24 Liberators that hit the target, five B-17s and five B-24s are lost, 64 B-17s and 16 B-24s are damaged. Aircrews report 41 confirmed kills and 19 others unconfirmed. U.S. losses are 36 killed, five wounded and 100 missing. The mission is escorted by Ninth Air Force P-38 Lightnings and P-51 Mustangs. The fighter pilots report 22 enemy aircraft shot down and one probable kill. Seven P-38s are lost. The pilots are reported missing.

The second attack consists of targets of opportunity at Neuss, Geilenkirchen, Dusseldorf, and Wassenburg, Germany. Of the 73 B-17s that hit targets, two B-17s are lost and 23 are damaged. Aircrews report two confirmed enemy aircraft kills and five other probables. U.S. casualties are two wounded and 20 missing.

Over the Bordeaux/Merignac airfield in France 112 B-17s hit their target. Eleven bombers are lost and 51 are damaged. Aircrews report 50 enemy aircraft as confirmed kills and 10 others as probable kills; U.S. losses are 11 killed, 21 wounded, and 110 missing. The mission is escorted by 76 P-47 Thunderbolts. The pilots report two confirmed kills, but five P-47s are lost and two are damaged. The five fighter pilots are reported as missing.

Of the 78 B-17s that hit the Tours airfield in France, one B-17 is lost and 10 are damaged. Aircrews report two confirmed enemy aircraft shot down. The mission is escorted by 149 P-47 Thunderbolts and the pilots report three confirmed kills. Two P-47s are damaged.

ITALY: The 3rd Battalion, 168th Infantry, 34th Infantry Division attacks in very difficult terrain behind an artillery barrage, but makes slow progress. The 3rd Battalion of the 135th Infantry Regiment attacks and seizes half of the village of San Vittore, below Monte Chiaia. The 1st Battalion 135th Infantry calls in an artillery bombardment on German positions. American artillery batteries fire over 1,600 rounds. As the Americans advance, they are stopped by machine-gun fire from the village of Santa Giusta.

The 6th Armored Infantry advances against German positions on Monte Porchia.

Twelfth Air Force A-36 Intruder (Apache) fighter-bombers attack gun positions near Mignano and enemy positions on Monte Porchia.

SOUTHWEST PACIFIC AREA: U.S. submarine *Rasher* torpedoes and sinks a Japanese tanker in the South China Sea off Malaya.

PACIFIC: The V Amphibious Corps staff completes planning and preparation for an attack on the Marshall Islands. The force consists of 380 ships and 85,000 men.

CENTRAL PACIFIC: A U.S. Navy PBY-5 Catalina from Tarawa drops mines near Wotje Atoll.

U.S. submarine *Scorpion,* on her fourth war patrol, makes a scheduled rendezvous with USS *Herring,* but is never heard from again.

BOUGAINVILLE: Thirteenth Air Force B-24 Liberators attack Tonolai and a logistics base at Kahili.

NEW GEORGIA: Thirteenth Air Force B-25 Mitchells bomb troop concentrations near Choiseul Bay.

NEW BRITAIN: The 112th Cavalry at Arawe is reinforced by the 2nd Battalion, 158th Infantry. The Japanese have established themselves about 600 yards from the American perimeter and are able to fire machine guns and mortars into the U.S. lines. The Japanese have dug trenches and foxholes and covered them with vegetation, making them nearly impossible to locate.

NEW GUINEA: Fifth Air Force B-24 Liberators and B-25 Mitchells attack the Alexishafen, Madang, and Bogadjim areas. The bombers also hit supply and transport barges along the coast from Finschhafen to Saidor.

Infantrymen of the 158th Regimental Combat Team take cover from Japanese fire on Arawe, New Britain, January 1944.

January 6

CBI: Tenth Air Force P-51s and A-36 Intruder (Apache) fighter-bombers conduct ground support missions for the Chinese 38th Division at Sumprabum and Taihpa Ga in Burma. They also attack a Japanese cavalry unit and logistics storage areas at Kamaing.

Two Fourteenth Air Force B-25 Mitchells bomb a troop ship on the Yangtze River and report it as sunk.

ETO: Lieutenant General James H. Doolittle takes command of Eighth Air Force, replacing Lieutenant General Ira C. Eaker. Eaker will become commander of the Mediterranean Allied Air Force (MAAF).

General Carl Spaatz assumes command of U.S. Strategic Air Forces in Europe (USSAFE). Fifteenth Air Force's targets as part of the Combined Bomber Offensive will be assigned by Spaatz's headquarters.

The C-47s of 436th Troop Carrier Group and the 79th, 80th, 81st, and 82nd Troop Carrier Squadrons arrive in England from the United States.

During the night, five B-17s drop 984,000 leaflets on Amiens, Lille, Valenciennes, Cambrai, and Reims, France.

ITALY: The 100th and 3rd Battalions of the 34th Infantry Division are attached to 1st Special Service Force, forming Task Force B. Division artillery will be added and Task Force B's mission is to outflank Monte Trocchio. The 1st Battalion of the 168th Infantry, 34th Infantry Division attempts to move beyond German strongpoints, but makes no progress. Another attack by the 2nd Battalion captures the key position on Hill 396 and defends it against furious enemy counterattacks. The 1st Battalion 135th Infantry encounters strong resistance and is replaced by the 2nd Battalion, which makes a rapid advance. The 6th Armored Infantry, supported by tanks and artillery and by the 48th Engineer Combat Battalion, acting as infantry, captures the north end of Monte Porchia and holds off repeated German counterattacks. Combat casualties in one battalion of the 6th Armored Infantry have reduced its strength to 150 men.

The Fifteenth Air Force's 718th Bombardment Squadron (Heavy) of the 449th Bombardment Group (Heavy) arrives from the United States with B-24 Liberators. The squadron will fly its first mission early this month.

Twelfth Air Force B-26 Marauders bomb the marshaling yards at Pontedera and Lucca, the Piaggio aircraft factory, and the railway near Follonica. P-40s and A-36 fighter-bombers attack enemy positions at Monte la Chiaia and Monte Porchia, the Cervaro-Monte Trocchio area, and the town of Fondi.

CENTRAL PACIFIC: A navy PBY-5 Catalina from Tarawa drops mines near Wotje Atoll.

NEW BRITAIN: The 3/7 later moves back to act as the reserve. The 3rd Battalion 5th Marines captures Hill 150, but discovers the Japanese strongly entrenched at Aogiri ridge, located roughly in the center of the marine line of advance. Heavy jungle prevents any flanking maneuver.

Thirteenth Air Force P-38 Lightnings along with 32 F4U Corsairs and 26 F4F Wildcats head for Rabaul, but weather prevents all but 16 P-38 Lightnings and eight Corsairs from making the attack. They are intercepted by at least 40 Japanese aircraft, leading to a giant dogfight in which nine Japanese fighters and two P-38s are shot down.

NEW GUINEA: Fifth Air Force B-24 Liberators and B-25 Mitchells bomb the Alexishafen and Bogadjim areas. A-20 Havocs attack targets along the road from Bogadjim to Yaula. Other B-25s attack targets of opportunity on the Huon Peninsula and in the Borgen Bay area. P-39 Airacobras strafe barges at Borgen Bay and Rein Bay.

The 389th Bombardment Squadron (Light) of the 312th Bombardment Group (Light) will transition from P-40s to A-20 Havocs in February.

January 7

CBI: Tenth Air Force B-25 Mitchells and 15 P-38 Lightnings attack oil storage and production facilities near Lanywa in Burma. A-36 Intruder (Apache) fighter-bombers and P-51 Mustangs bomb supply points and troops at Nanyaseik.

Fourteenth Air Force B-25s and six P-40s report two large boats, a barge, and a small ore craft sunk on the Yangtze River. P-38 Lightnings report nearly 40 sampans destroyed along the river from Hankow to Chiuchiang, and two B-25s report sinking a passenger vessel off Hong Kong.

ETO: General Eisenhower's staff submits initial concept for Anvil to the CCS, proposing an initial assault with two divisions, followed by a buildup to 10 divisions (eight infantry and two armored). Objectives are the ports of Marseilles and Toulon, followed by an advance north to link up with Allied forces moving from northern France.

Eighth Air Force sends 382 B-17s and 120 B-24 Liberators against the I.G. Farben plant at Ludwigshafen, Germany. Of the 351 B-17s and 69 B-24s that hit the target, five B-17s and 17 B-24s are lost. Another 106 B-17s and 20 B-24s are damaged. Aircrews claim 30 enemy aircraft shot down and six others as probable kills. U.S. casualties are 14 killed, 13 wounded, and 121 missing. The mission is escorted by 71 P-38 Lightnings, 463 P-47 Thunderbolts, and 37 Ninth Air Force P-51 Mustangs. The fighter pilots report seven confirmed enemy kills and three possibles. One P-38 and five P-47s are lost and the pilots are reported as missing.

During the night, five B-17s drop over one million leaflets on Paris, Chartres, Caen, and Evreux, France.

ITALY: The 1st Special Service Force attacks to clear enemy positions on Monte Majo, supported by accurate artillery fire that breaks up enemy counterattacks. The 168th Infantry regiment expands its control of the hills and succeeds in breaking the entire German defensive line. The 135th Infantry Regiment captures Monte la Chiaia. The 3rd Battalion of the 135th Infantry moves from the village of San Vittore and clears the hills north of Route 6. The 6th Armored Infantry captures Monte Porchia, and stops another German counterattack.

Fifteenth Air Force B-17s, with P-38 Lightnings providing escort, bomb an aircraft factory at Maribor and a torpedo factory at Fiume. German fighters attack the formation over Maribor and the P-38s find themselves outnumbered. The air battle lasts over 30 minutes and three P-38s are shot down while U.S. fighter pilots claim four fighters as confirmed kills.

Twelfth Air Force B-25 Mitchells bomb Perugia airfield. B-26 Marauders hit the marshaling yards at Foligno and Arezzo. A-36 Intruder (Apache) fighter-bombers hit gun positions, trucks, and trains in the Cervaro-Aquino-Cassino area and bomb the railyards at Velletri. P-40s give close support to American ground troops in the Monte Maio, Monte Chiaia, Monte Porchia, and Cedro Hill areas. A-36 Intruder (Apache) fighter-bombers and P-40s disperse a German troop concentration near Monte Chiaia.

Sergeant Joe C. Specker's company of the 48th Engineer Combat Battalion advances up Monte Porchia. Sergeant Specker, acting as a scout, locates a German machine gun and riflemen barring the advance. Sergeant Specker then begins moving one of his own machine guns into a position to cover the engineers' advance. He is spotted by the enemy and wounded so badly that he is unable to walk. He drags himself into position and sets up the machine gun, then fires on the Germans so effectively that the engineers are able to capture their objective. During the attack Sergeant Specker dies of his wounds. For his act of courage and dedication to duty, Sergeant Specker will receive the Medal of Honor.

SOUTHWEST PACIFIC AREA: U.S. submarine *Kingfish* attacks a Japanese convoy southwest of Palawan Island and sinks a tanker.

PACIFIC: Major General Hubert R. Harmon takes command of Thirteenth Air Force.

NEW BRITAIN: Thirteenth Air Force B-24 Liberators bomb Vunakanau airfield.

Fifth Air Force B-24s bomb the Cape Gloucester area and A-20 Havocs hit Japanese forces near Arawe.

NEW GUINEA: Fifth Air Force B-24 Liberators and B-25 Mitchells, with P-39 Airacobras and P-47 Thunderbolts, bomb the Alexishafen-Madang area. They also attack targets near Erima and Bogadjim and along the Bogadjim Road. Huts and barges near Sidor are also attacked.

January 8

CBI: Tenth Air Force P-51s and A-36 Intruder (Apache) fighter-bombers damage a bridge near Hopin in Burma and damage rail stock at Tigyaingza.

Fourteenth Air Force moves the B-25 Mitchells of the 22nd Bombardment Squadron (Medium), 341st Bombardment Group (Medium), from Chakulia, India, to Yangkai, China.

The 5307th Composite Unit (Provisional) is released from South East Asia Command (SEAC) control and transferred to General Stilwell's Northern Combat Area Command. Stilwell appoints Brigadier General Frank D. Merrill as 5307th commander.

ETO: Eighth Air Force sends five B-17s to drop more than 2 million leaflets over Antwerp and Brussels in Belgium and over Rennes, Brest, and Nantes in France.

MEDITERRANEAN: The B-24 Liberators of the 449th and 450th Bombardment Groups (Heavy) of the Fifteenth Air Force are now operational, giving the Fifteenth a total of eight heavy bomber groups. Fifteenth Air Force B-24s bomb the airfield at Mostar, Yugoslavia, and Twelfth Air Force B-25 Mitchells bomb the harbor, warehouses, and railway at Metkovic.

ITALY: Fifteenth Air Force B-17s, with P-38 Lightnings and P-47 Thunderbolts flying escort, bomb the Reggio Emilia aircraft factory. Twelfth Air Force A-20 Havocs attack the Frosinone and Colleferro-Segni railway stations. B-26 Marauders bomb the Grosseto and Lucca marshaling yards. P-40s support the Fifth Army near Cassino. A-36 Intruder (Apache) fighter-bombers attack railway targets at Aquino, Frosinone, Palestrina, and Castelforte. P-40s attack Avezzano, and A-36s bomb transportation targets near Tarquinia.

SOUTH PACIFIC: Navy Task Force 38, commanded by Rear Admiral Walden L. Ainsworth, with two light cruisers and five destroyers, conducts a bombardment of Japanese shore installations on Faisi, Poporang, and Shortland Islands in the Solomons.

CENTRAL PACIFIC: Seventh Air Force B-24 Liberators and B-25 Mitchells operating from Tarawa bomb shipping, gun positions, and shore installations in the Marshalls.

Eight navy PB4Y-1 Privateers from Apemama Atoll in the Carolines, mine the waters off Wotje Atoll in the Marshalls and strafe facilities and shipping. Seven PBY-5 Catalinas from Tarawa also conduct aerial mining at Wotje.

BOUGAINVILLE: Thirteenth Air Force B-24 Liberators bomb Kahili.

NEW BRITAIN: The assault on Aogiri Ridge fails. Lieutenant Colonel Lewis W. Walt takes command of the 3/5 Marines after the commander and executive officer are wounded.

Fifth Air Force B-25 Mitchells and A-20 Havocs hit Japanese defensive positions near Arawe.

NEW GUINEA: Fifth Air Force B-24 Liberators and B-25 Mitchells bomb the Madang area, Uligan Harbor, Bogadjim, and the Bogadjim Road.

In the Celebes, B-24s bomb Kendari and other targets.

January 9

CBI: Tenth Air Force P-51 Mustangs and A-36 Intruder (Apache) fighter-bombers attack a bridge, barracks, and an ammunition storage area at Loilaw, Burma.

Fourteenth Air Force B-25 Mitchells bomb a cargo vessel near Swatow, China. Aircrews report the vessel sunk. In French Indochina, four B-25s bomb railroad yards and the Lao Kay railroad station.

MEDITERRANEAN: Fifteenth Air Force B-17s bomb the docks and shipping at Pola, Yugoslavia.

ITALY: Twelfth Air Force B-25 Mitchells attack the Ancona marshaling yard and docks. P-40s and A-36 Intruder (Apache) fighter-bombers attack German vehicles and defenses at Palena, Sulmona, and Cervaro.

BOUGAINVILLE: Thirteenth Air Force B-25 Mitchells attack the seaplane base on Buka Island and the supply depots at Kahili.

NEW BRITAIN: The heavy rains and excessive heat are taking a significant toll on the marines at Aogiri Ridge. Visibility in the terrain is less than 10 yards. The Japanese have placed machine guns in the roots of enormous trees that cover the ridge and have built stout log and earth bunkers interconnected with tunnels across the 200-yard front of the ridge. They are nearly invisible. Two companies from 3/7 arrive to support the renewed assault. The marines struggle forward, and occupy the lower slope of the western end of the ridge. In the face of heavy machine-gun fire, Lieutenant Colonel Lewis C. Walt organizes a volunteer crew to push a 37 millimeter gun up the muddy slopes of Aogiri Ridge to knock out enemy positions that have been holding up the assault. Walt and his marines are able to secure only the slightest toehold on the crest of the ridge.

Thirteenth Air Force B-24 Liberators attack Vunakanau airfield.

NEW GUINEA: Fifth Air Force fighters and bombers attack Alexishafen, Madang, Bogadjim, Uligan Harbor, and the area east of Saidor. The airfield outside of Saidor is repaired by engineers.

January 10

CBI: In Burma, Tenth Air Force A-36 Intruder (Apache) fighter-bombers and P-51 Mustangs attack a Japanese troop position at Nanyaseik. P-40s attack a bridge and rail lines at Namti.

B-24 Liberators bomb the marshaling yard and airfield in the Bangkok area and the main jetty at Akyab, Burma. Nine B-25 Mitchells mine the Mokpalin, Burma, ferry crossing over the Sittang River.

During the night, B-24s lay mines in the Menam River near Bangkok, Thailand, and in the Rangoon River.

In China, Fourteenth Air Force P-51 Mustangs bomb the approach to the Kienchang bridge and attack a troop train near Teian. B-25 Mitchells and P-40s sweep from Anking to Chiuchiang and report sinking a large motor launch, two barges, and a tug on the Yangtze River. B-25s and P-40s attack shipping near Wusueh, sinking a launch and damaging three tankers.

The B-25 Mitchells of the 491st Bombardment Squadron (Medium), 341st Bombardment Group (Medium), transfer from Chakulia, India, to Yangkai, China.

ETO: During the evening, Eighth Air Force sends five B-17s over France to drop nearly five million leaflets over Orleans, Chateauroux, Rouen, Le Mans, and Tours.

Ninth Air Force receives the Headquarters 366th Fighter Group and the 390th Fighter Squadron with P-47 Thunderbolts from the United States. The squadron will fly its first mission in early March.

MEDITERRANEAN: Fifteenth Air Force B-24 Liberators bomb the marshaling yard at Skoplje, Yugoslavia. B-17s escorted by P-38 Lightnings and P-47 Thunderbolts bomb the marshaling yards at Sofia, Bulgaria. They are attacked by about 60 enemy fighters, which shoot down two B-17s. Aircrews report 28 enemy aircraft destroyed.

A U.S. freighter is damaged by a German aerial torpedo during an air attack on convoy KMS 37 (United Kingdom to Mediterranean) en route to Augusta and Naples, Italy.

ITALY: The 168th Infantry Regiment of the 34th Infantry Division, advancing toward the village of Cervaro to flank Monte Trocchio, is forced to fight through German defenses reoccupied during the past few days.

PACIFIC: U.S. submarine *Seawolf* begins attacking a Japanese convoy off Okinawa and sinks two cargo ships. During a typhoon, U.S. submarine *Steelhead* attacks a Japanese convoy south of Honshu, Japan, sinking a repair ship.

CENTRAL PACIFIC: Two PBY-5 Catalinas from Tarawa lay mines at Wotje Atoll.

Japanese aircraft raid the airfield at Apamama. Only slight damage is reported.

BOUGAINVILLE: Thirteenth Air Force sends B-24s to bomb the logistics base at Kahili.

NEW BRITAIN: The Japanese counterattack from positions on the rear of the Aogiri ridge. Five times the Japanese attack the marines holding the crest of the ridge. Mortar and artillery fire hitting at times within 50 yards of the marines stops the attackers. The 37 millimeter gun Colonel Lewis C. Walt has brought forward fires canister shells against the enemy infantry. A Japanese officer leading one attack is killed just a few steps from Walt's position.

Thirteenth Air Force sends 10 B-24 Liberators against Vunakanau airfield, then initiates a night heavy bombing effort, sending 20 B-24s to attack Lakunai airfield.

Fifth Air Force P-39s strafe scattered villages and barges along the coast.

NEW GUINEA: Fifth Air Force bombers and fighters attack the Madang, Alexishafen, and Bogadjim areas and the coastline from Madang to Sio.

B-25 Mitchells bomb Koepang on Timor Island

January 11

CBI: The Fourteenth Air Force's airfield at Suichwan, China, is attacked by 14 Japanese bombers, followed by three medium bombers and 15 fighters. The second strike is intercepted by seven P-51 Mustangs and five P-40s. The fighter pilots report all three bombers shot down.

B-24 Liberators bomb the harbor, aluminum plant, and airfield at Takao, Formosa. Other B-24s mine harbors at Takao and at Hong Kong. One B-24 is lost during the mission.

ATLANTIC: President Roosevelt reports on the postwar world in his State of the Union Address:

> ... when I went to Cairo and Teheran in November, we knew that we were in agreement with our Allies in our common determination to fight and win this war. There were many vital questions concerning the future peace, and they were discussed in an atmosphere of complete candor and harmony. . . . The one supreme objective for the future, which we discussed for each nation individually, and for all the United Nations, can be summed up in one word: Security. . . .
>
> And that means not only physical security which provides safety from attacks by aggressors. It means also economic security, social security, moral security—in a family of nations. In the plain down-to-earth talks that I had with the Generalis-

simo [Chiang Kai-shek] and Marshal Stalin and Prime Minister Churchill, it was abundantly clear that they are all most deeply interested in the resumption of peaceful progress by their own peoples—progress toward a better life. All our Allies have learned by experience—bitter experience that real development will not be possible if they are to be diverted from their purpose by repeated wars—or even threats of war.

The best interests of each nation, large and small, demand that all freedom-loving nations shall join together in a just and durable system of peace. In the present world situation, evidenced by the actions of Germany, and Italy and Japan, unquestioned military control over the disturbers of the peace is as necessary among nations as it is among citizens in any community. And an equally basic essential to peace—permanent peace—is a decent standard of living for all individual men and women and children in all nations. Freedom from fear is eternally linked with freedom from want.

ETO: Eighth Air Force sends a total of 525 B-17s against three aircraft production facility targets in Germany. The Germans protect the target area with over 500 fighters. Against Oschersleben 177 B-17s are dispatched and 139 hit the primary target; 34 bombers are lost and 85 are damaged. Aircrews report destroying nearly 200 enemy aircraft. U.S. casualties are nine killed, 11 wounded, and 349 missing.

Over Halberstadt only 52 of the 114 B-17s dispatched hit the primary target. Eight bombers are lost and 43 damaged. Aircrews report 35 confirmed kills and 11 probable kills. U.S. casualties are one killed, 18 wounded, and 81 missing. The bombers are escorted by 177 P-47 Thunderbolts and 44 Ninth Air Force P-51 Mustangs. The fighter pilots report 29 confirmed kills and 11 probables. Two P-47s are lost, seven are damaged, and one P-51 is damaged. Two pilots are killed and two are missing.

Against Brunswick, 234 B-17s and 138 B-24s are dispatched and only 47 B-17s hit the primary target while the other bombers hit a variety of secondary targets. A total of 16 B-17s and two B-24s are lost. Aircrews report 19 confirmed kills and 16 probables. U.S. casualties are five wounded and 176 missing. The mission is escorted by 49 P-38 Lightnings and 322 P-47 Thunderbolts. The pilots report two confirmed kills and one probable. One P-38 and two P-47s are lost; one P-47 is damaged. One pilot is reported as missing. During this attack four B-24s serve as PFF (Pathfinder) aircraft for the first time.

MEDITERRANEAN: Fifteenth Air Force B-17s, with P-38 Lightnings as escort, bomb the harbor at Piraeus, Greece. Eight enemy fighters are shot down but six B-17s are lost in midair collisions due to heavy overcast conditions.

ITALY: Twelfth Air Force B-26 Marauders attack industrial targets at Piombino; B-25 Mitchells bomb rail targets at Falconara and Fabriano. P-40s and A-36 Intruder (Apache) fighter-bombers attack defenses and gun positions in Cervaro-Monte Trocchio, a gun position near Minturno, road traffic in the Macerata-Aquila-Popoli area, and railroad facilities at San Giorgio del Sannio.

PACIFIC: U.S. submarine *Seawolf* continues attacking the Japanese convoy off Okinawa, sinking a cargo ship. U.S. submarine *Sturgeon* attacks a Japanese convoy off Kyushu, Japan, and sinks a cargo ship. The submarine is undamaged after a depth charge attack by escort ships. U.S. submarine *Tautog* torpedoes and damages a Japanese ammunition ship off Honshu, Japan.

CENTRAL PACIFIC: Seventh Air Force B-25 Mitchells from Tarawa attack vessels and installations at Maloelap Atoll and Wotje, damaging a destroyer.

P-39 Airacobras from Makin Island attack runways on Mille Atoll.

Four navy PBY Catalinas from Tarawa conduct aerial minelaying operations at Wotje and Maloelap Atolls in the Marshalls.

BOUGAINVILLE: Thirteenth Air Force P-39s strafe targets of opportunity from Numa Numa to Koromira.

NEW BRITAIN: The 3rd Battalion 5th Marines captures Aogiri Ridge and discovers a hidden trail, well built and solid, that leads to Brogen Bay. It is the main Japanese supply route. The 1st Battalion 7th Marines, supported by tanks, clears out a Japanese strongpoint between Hill 150 and Aogiri Ridge. The strongpoint was protecting a major logistics base.

NEW GUINEA: The Saidor airfield receives C-47s bringing ammunition and other supplies. The 126th RCT encounters almost no enemy in the area.

Fifth Air Force B-25 Mitchells, P-39 Airacobras, and P-40s attack targets around Uligan Harbor, Bogadjim, Hansa Bay, and Alexishafen.

January 12

CBI: Tenth Air Force B-25 Mitchells and P-38 Lightnings attack the Letpadan marshaling yard in Burma.

The C-47s of the 27th Troop Carrier Squadron, Tenth Air Force (attached to Troop Carrier Command, Eastern Air Command), arrive at Sylhet, India, from the United States.

Fourteenth Air Force B-24 Liberators bomb the Bangsue marshaling yard at Bangkok, Thailand.

ETO: The 389th Fighter Squadron of the 366th Fighter Group, with P-47 Thunderbolts, arrives in England from the United States. The squadron's first mission will be in March.

MEDITERRANEAN: The naval air station at Port Lyautey, French Morocco, is operational.

ITALY: The 34th Infantry Division conducts several attacks. The 2nd Battalion 168th Infantry attacks to capture Cervaro, while the 1st and 3rd Battalions of the 168th attack north of the village to outflank the enemy positions on the hillsides overlooking Route 6. Tanks provide fire support. The 100th Battalion and the 1st Battalion 133rd Infantry Regiment capture Monte Caprono. The 2nd Battalion 135th Infantry pressures the Germans holding Point 189 southwest of Cervaro.

Twelfth Air Force A-20 Havocs attack San Donato; P-40s attack German positions at San Biagio Saracinesa, Sant' Elia Fiumerapido, Monte Trocchio, and Atina. A-36 Intruder (Apache) fighter-bombers attack the Avezzano and Cisterna di Latina railroad facilities and a village near Atina.

The final plan for Shingle (the Anzio landing) is approved. Fifth Army commander Mark Clark selects the VI Corps commander, Major General John P. Lucas, to lead the assault. The assault force will depart Naples and will consist of the U.S.

3rd Infantry Division, the 504th Parachute Infantry Regiment, the 751st Tank Battalion, and U.S. Army Rangers. The British will provide their 1st Division, the 46th Royal Tank Regiment, and Commandos. Each nation will provide support troops as well. This is the main landing force. A second landing force, to arrive within three days after the initial landing, consists of the U.S. 45th Infantry Division and two combat commands of the U.S. 1st Armored Division. The landing date (D-day) is set for January 22. Fifteenth Army Group expects Fifth Army to attack Cassino, crossing the Rapido River on January 20 to draw German reinforcements away from the Anzio area. Once the breakout has occurred, Allied forces will link up and drive German forces north past Rome.

PACIFIC: U.S. submarine *Hake* torpedoes and sinks a Japanese aircraft transport off Okinawa.

CENTRAL PACIFIC: Seventh Air Force A-24 Banshees from Makin Island dive-bomb antiaircraft positions and the storage area on Mille Atoll in the Marshalls. The Banshees are supported by 20 P-39 Airacobras, which strafe runways on the Atoll.

Navy PB4Y patrol bombers attack Japanese shipping in Kwajalein lagoon, sinking a gunboat. Five PBY-5 Catalinas from Tarawa conduct aerial minelaying operations at Maloelap Atoll in the Marshalls. One Catalina is hit by antiaircraft fire near Jaluit.

U.S. submarine *Albacore* torpedoes and sinks a Japanese gunboat off Truk and damages a gunboat being towed.

BOUGAINVILLE: Thirteenth Air Force P-39 Airacobras bomb and strafe Teop, Inus Point, Numa Numa, and Piano Mission.

NEW BRITAIN: Marine Company B, 1st Tank Battalion, arrives with M3A1 Stuart tanks to support the army on Arawe.

Thirteenth Air Force B-25 Mitchells bomb Vunakanau airfield in the morning, and 16 B-24 Liberators follow with a nighttime attack on Lakunai airfield.

NEW GUINEA: Fifth Air Force B-24 Liberators and B-25 Mitchells attack the Alexishafen area; A-20 Havocs attack Warai.

B-24s bomb Balikpapan, Borneo, as well as Makassar on Celebes Island and Dili on Timor Island.

January 13

CBI: In Burma, Tenth Air Force P-51 Mustangs attack Japanese troops at Lalawng Ga and bomb Maran Ga and Shaduzup. P-40s attack a communication center and supply points along the Kamaing-Mogaung Road. Another four P-51 Mustangs and a B-25 Mitchell bomb the airfield and supply area at Myitkyina.

Major General Kenneth B. Wolfe, commander of the Twentieth Air Force, arrives at New Delhi, India, with elements of the XX Bomber Command staff. The unit will direct Operation Matterhorn, the strategic bombing effort against Japan with the new B-29 Superfortress.

ETO: Ninth Air Force sends 193 B-26 Marauders against German V-weapon sites in France. The headquarters of the 368th Fighter Group, and 395th, 396th, and 397th Fighter Squadrons with P-47 Thunderbolts, arrive in England from the United States. The squadrons will fly their first mission in mid-March.

ITALY: Fifteenth Air Force B-17s, with P-38 Lightnings providing escort and P-47 Thunderbolts flying top cover, bomb Centocelle and Guidonia airfields.

Twelfth Air Force B-25 Mitchells and B-26 Marauders bomb Guidonia, Centocelle, and Ciampino airfields. A-20 Havocs bomb the town of Atina. A-36 Intruder (Apache) fighter-bombers attack the town and railway yards at Isola del Liri, a factory at Colleferro, docks at Formia, railroad yards at Valmontone, and a railway station near Frosinone. P-40s attack Sant' Elia Fiumerapido, San Biagio, Saracinesa, and a rail and road junction near Villa Latina.

PACIFIC: Admiral Nimitz outlines the tentative plan for a year-long campaign in the Central Pacific for 1944, called Granite. The focus of offensive operations is the Luzon-China-Formosa area, to be controlled by Allied forces by spring of 1945. Truk will be the target of carrier air raids to isolate the island, followed by an invasion of the Admiralty Islands and Kavieng, New Ireland. Eniwetok Atoll and Vjeland Island in the Marshalls will be captured, followed by the capture of Truk and Mortlock in the Carolines. Saipan, Tinian, and Guam will be captured at the end of the year. If Truk is bypassed as an option, then the Palau Islands can be attacked as early as August. This would allow Central Pacific and SWPA forces to link near the Philippines.

Southern Pacific forces are reorganized to support the emerging strategy in the Pacific. General MacArthur's SWPA will receive the army XIV Corps (25th, 37th, 40th, 43rd, and 93rd Infantry Divisions and the Americal Division) and will assume operational control of the Thirteenth Air Force. All combat support and service support units not required in the South Pacific Area will also be transferred to SWPA. All naval forces, except those assigned to Seventh Fleet under MacArthur's command, will be transferred to Admiral Nimitz in the Central Pacific Area. Nimitz will receive the 1st and 3rd Marine Divisions of the First Amphibious Corps as well.

The 4th Marine Division leaves San Diego, California, headed for the Marshalls.

U.S. submarine *Swordfish* is damaged by depth charges off Honshu, Japan, but remains on patrol.

CENTRAL PACIFIC: Seventh Air Force B-25 Mitchells from Tarawa attack shipping at Wotje Atoll. A-24 Banshees from Makin Island dive-bomb the dock, a barracks, and storage area on Mille Atoll. P-39 Airacobras escorting the bombers attack ground targets.

Thirteenth Air Force moves its headquarters from Espiritu Santo, New Hebrides Islands, to Guadalcanal, Solomon Islands.

NEW BRITAIN: Thirteenth Air Force B-25 Mitchells bomb a number of targets throughout the area in an early morning raid. Fifth Air Force B-24s bomb Gasmata Island.

The 3rd Battalion 7th Marines, after artillery and air strikes from Fifth Air Force aircraft, moves to take Hill 660, the last key position that can threaten the Marine beachhead. A boulder-strewn ravine cloaked in thick jungle vegetation marks the approach to the area. The Japanese have incorporated natural obstacles into their defenses. The first marine companies to make contact are immediately stopped by machine-gun fire.

The 2nd Battalion 1st Marines is transported from Tauali to Cape Gloucester airfield to rejoin the rest of the regiment.

NEW GUINEA: In Fifth Air Force, Major General Paul B. Wurtsmith becomes commanding general of the V Fighter Command.

Over 130 B-24 Liberators, B-25 Mitchells, and P-40s attack Alexishafen. B-24s and B-25s strike Kaukenau and Timoeka and damage a freighter off Tanimbar Island in the Molucca Islands. Fifth Air Force B-24 Liberators sink a Japanese transport north of the Admiralty Islands.

January 14

CBI: President Roosevelt sends a message to Generalissimo Chiang Kai-shek requesting the commitment of the Chinese Y Force to Burma, and hints broadly that Chiang's decision will affect his Lend-Lease supply shipments.

Fourteenth Air Force B-24 Liberators sink a cargo ship in the South China Sea off Hainan.

ATLANTIC: U.S. destroyers damage German submarine *U-382* off the coast of Spain.

ETO: COSSAC expands into Supreme Headquarters Allied Expeditionary Force (SHAEF) with the arrival of General Eisenhower as supreme Allied commander. He orders detailed planning to begin on Overlord. Air Marshall Sir Arthur Tedder is the deputy commander, Lieutenant General Omar N. Bradley is commander of the U.S. First Army, General Sir Bernard L. Montgomery is commander of the 21st Army Group, and Lieutenant General Carl Spaatz is commander of U.S. Strategic Air Forces Europe. Admiral Sir Bertram Ramsey is the Allied naval commander in chief, Air Marshall Sir Trafford Leigh-Mallory is the air commander in chief, and Lieutenant General Walter Bedell Smith is chief of staff for SHAEF.

Eighth Air Force sends 374 B-17s and 178 B-24 Liberators, escorted by 98 P-38 Lightnings, 504 P-47 Thunderbolts, and 43 Ninth Air Force P-51 Mustangs, against 21 V-weapon sites in France. Two B-17s and one B-24 are lost, 66 B-17s and 10 B-24s are damaged. Aircrews report eight enemy aircraft destroyed. U.S. casualties are one killed, 11 wounded, and 31 missing. The fighter pilots report 14 enemy aircraft as confirmed kills, one as a probable kill. U.S. aircraft losses are one P-38, one P-47, and one P-51 lost; 10 P-47s and one P-51 damaged. Three pilots are missing.

During the night four B-17s drop 840,000 leaflets over Amiens, Lille, Cambrai, and St. Omer in France. Two B-17s conduct an Oboe Mk II radar test over Wesel, Germany. One B-17 aborts while the other drops two tons of high-explosive bombs on the target.

MEDITERRANEAN: Fifteenth Air Force sends nearly 200 B-17s and B-24 Liberators against Mostar, Yugoslavia. P-38 Lightnings and P-47 Thunderbolts provide escort.

ITALY: Twelfth Air Force B-25 Mitchells bomb the bridge at Pontecorvo. A-20 Havocs attack German positions at Monte Trocchio; P-40s and A-36 Intruder (Apache) fighter-bombers attack defensive positions at San Giuseppe, Sant' Elia Fiumerapido, and Monte Trocchio. A-36s also attack enemy positions near Minturno, Isola, del Liri, and the harbor at Anzio.

PACIFIC: U.S. submarine *Seawolf* attacks a Japanese convoy near Okinawa and sinks a fleet tanker.

U.S. submarine *Swordfish* attacks a Japanese convoy and sinks a transport south of Honshu, Japan.

CENTRAL PACIFIC: Seventh Air Force B-24 Liberators staging through Tarawa bomb islands at Kwajalein Atoll. B-25s from Makin Island attack shipping at Wotje Atoll.

U.S. submarines *Scamp* and *Albacore* attack a Japanese convoy near the Palau Islands. *Scamp* sinks a fleet tanker and *Albacore* sinks a destroyer. Another submarine, *Guardfish*, attacks the same convoy later, sinking a fleet tanker.

The crew of the PBY-5 Catalina shot down near Jabor on January 12 is rescued.

BOUGAINVILLE: Thirteenth Air Force P-39 Airacobras together with navy SBD Dauntless dive-bombers attack Wakunai.

NEW BRITAIN: With tanks providing fire support, the 3rd Battalion 7th Marines captures Hill 660 in a heavy downpour.

Thirteenth Air Force B-24 Liberators conduct night bombing attacks on airfields and facilities. Over 50 SBD Dauntless dive-bombers attack Japanese shipping in Simpson harbor at Rabaul. Fifth Air Force B-24 Liberators, B-25 Mitchells, and A-20 Havocs attack targets along the northern and southern coasts.

NEW GUINEA: Fifth Air Force sends over 50 B-24 Liberators, B-25 Mitchells, and P-40s against targets in the Alexishafen and Erima areas.

Navy SBD Dauntless dive-bombers and TBF Avengers, supported by Allied fighters, bomb Japanese shipping in Simpson Harbor at Rabaul. Pilots report one destroyer and a fleet tanker damaged.

January 15

MEDITERRANEAN: Lieutenant General Ira C. Eaker takes command of the Mediterranean Allied Air Force (MAAF) and Army Air Forces Mediterranean Theater of Operations (AAFMTO). Eaker replaces Air Chief Marshall Sir Arthur Tedder, who becomes the deputy commander in chief for Overlord. The MAAF is a new organization that replaces Mediterranean Air Command.

The headquarters for the 455th Bombardment Group (Heavy), and the 740th, 741st, 742nd, and 743rd Bombardment Squadrons (Heavy) equipped with B-24 Liberators, arrive from the United States. The group's first mission is scheduled for mid-February.

ITALY: The Germans abandon their last defensive position on Monte Trocchio without a fight as units of the 34th and 36th Infantry Divisions prepare to attack. The Allies have broken the Winter Line. The Americans are now at the threshold of the Liri Valley, the most rapid avenue of advance to Rome. Between November 15 and this day, Fifth Army has combat losses of nearly 16,000 men. Of that total, 9,000 were Americans. Another 50,000 Americans in Fifth Army are nonbattle casualties.

Fifteenth Air Force B-24 Liberators bomb the marshaling yard and factories at Prato and hit the town of Pistoia. B-17s concentrate on transportation targets near Florence. Twelfth Air Force A-36 Intruder (Apache) fighter-bombers and P-40s attack enemy positions at Picinisco and Atina.

SOUTHWEST PACIFIC AREA: U.S. submarine *Crevalle* lays mines east of Saigon in French Indochina. U.S. submarine *Thresher* attacks a Japanese convoy and sinks a cargo ship and a tanker north of Luzon in the Philippines.

CENTRAL PACIFIC: Seventh Air Force B-25 Mitchells from Tarawa attack Japanese shipping and storage facilities on Maloelap Atoll in the Marshalls. The nine bombers make a low-level attack and one B-25 is downed by antiaircraft fire.

BOUGAINVILLE: Thirteenth Air Force sends 24 B-25 Mitchells, with 60 fighters flying escort, to attack East Cape. P-39 Airacobras attack Chabai.

NEW BRITAIN: Fifth Air Force B-25 Mitchells and P-39 Airacobras attack Japanese positions on the southern coast.

NEW GUINEA: An Australian patrol searching for the enemy near Soi discovers a trunk half submerged in a creek. In the trunk are the complete ciphers of the Japanese army's 20th Division. This allows MacArthur's cryptanalysts to break the Japanese army's cipher system; soon the Allies know the enemy's plans and intentions.

Fifth Air Force B-24 Liberators and B-25 Mitchells attack Uligan Harbor and B-25s with P-40s and P-47 Thunderbolts attack the Madang, Alexishafen, Erima, and Bogadjim areas.

January 16

ATLANTIC: TBF Avengers from escort carrier USS *Guadalcanal* sinks German submarine *U-544* in the mid-Atlantic.

A U.S. freighter straggling from the New York-bound convoy ON 219 (Liverpool to New York, fast) is torpedoed and sunk by German submarine *U-960* in the North Atlantic.

ETO: General Dwight D. Eisenhower assumes duties as Supreme Commander, Allied Expeditionary Force (AEF).

MEDITERRANEAN: Fifteenth Air Force B-17s escorted by P-38 Lightnings bomb the aircraft production facility at Klagenfurt, Austria, and the landing ground at Villaorba, Italy. The fighter pilots report nine enemy fighters shot down; U.S. losses are three P-38s lost.

ITALY: Twelfth Air Force B-25 Mitchells bomb the marshaling yard at Terni and B-26 Marauders attack the marshaling yard and bridge at Orte. A-20 Havocs bomb Atina; P-40s attack bridges near San Giorgio del Sannio and enemy positions near Cassino. A-36 Intruder (Apache) fighter-bombers hit the transportation targets at Cecina and Siena, and the town areas of Avezzano and Formia.

SOUTHWEST PACIFIC AREA: U.S. submarine *Redfin* torpedoes and damages a Japanese destroyer north of the Spratly Islands.

PACIFIC: U.S. submarine *Sturgeon* torpedoes and damages a Japanese destroyer south of Kyushu, Japan. U.S. submarine *Swordfish* torpedoes and sinks a Japanese gunboat off Honshu, Japan. U.S. submarine *Whale* attacks a Japanese convoy and sinks a cargo ship near Okinawa. U.S. submarine *Seawolf* also damages a transport, which USS *Whale* later sinks southeast of Okinawa.

CENTRAL PACIFIC: Seventh Air Force sends 25 A-24 Banshees, 16 P-39 Airacobras, and eight P-40s from Makin Island to attack Japanese barracks, antiaircraft positions,

A group of Marines, most likely from the 2nd Marine Raider Regiment, pause in January 1944 after nearly 60 days of combat on Bougainville Island.

and storage areas at Mille Atoll in the Marshalls. Three Japanese aircraft are reported destroyed and two P-39s are lost.

The B-24 Liberators of the 431st Bombardment Squadron (Heavy), 11th Bombardment Group (Heavy), arrive at Tarawa.

U.S. submarine *Blackfish* attacks a Japanese convoy and sinks a transport near Truk.

U.S. submarine *Seahorse* torpedoes and sinks a cargo ship southeast of the Marianas.

BOUGAINVILLE: The last elements of the 3rd Marine Division are replaced by the Americal Division, giving the army complete control of the defensive perimeter formed on the western side of the island. On the eastern side are still tens of thousands of Japanese soldiers, battered by American airpower, but still capable of offensive action.

NEW BRITAIN: Two companies of Japanese infantry attack to regain Hill 660, but are met with mortar and artillery fire. Over 110 Japanese are killed in the attack, and other infiltration-type attacks are also repulsed. The Japanese retreat toward Talasea and Hoskins Plantation. The marines have accomplished the near-impossible—attacking and defeating an enemy in prepared positions in some of the most challenging terrain in the world and in atrocious weather conditions.

Fifth Air Force B-24s and B-25s attack Japanese positions near Arawe. The 2nd Battalion 158th Infantry, supported by marine tanks, attacks the Japanese positions on Arawe. The tanks bog down in the soft ground as the infantry advances. The Japanese are forced to retreat and the 158th returns to its own lines. Two of the tanks have to be destroyed in place because they are so badly mired in the mud. American casualties in the attack are 20 killed and 40 wounded.

NEW GUINEA: Fifth Air Force B-25 Mitchells, A-20 Havocs, and P-40s attack targets around Madang, Erima, and Bogadjim.

Navy PBY Catalinas attack a Japanese convoy headed for Rabaul near the St. Matthias Group of islands, sinking two cargo ships and a transport. Japanese submarine *I-181* is damaged in the Vitiaz Strait.

January 17

CBI: In Burma, Tenth Air Force A-36 Intruder (Apache) fighter-bombers and P-51 Mustangs support ground forces around Taro and the Shaduzup-Ngamaw Ga area; supply dumps, warehouses, and rolling stock at Sahmaw are also attacked. P-40s attack Myitkyina airfield.

ITALY: The mission of the U.S. II Corps commanded by Major General Geoffrey T. Keyes is to draw German forces away from Anzio by attacking across the Rapido River. The rest of Fifth Army (the British X Corps and the French Expeditionary Corps) will attack along the high ground on both sides of the Liri Valley, opening the way to link up with the VI Corps at Anzio as it breaks out of the beachhead. The 36th Infantry Division commanded by Major General Frederick L. Walker has the mission of crossing the Rapido River. Melting snow makes the river between 25 and 50 feet wide and 10 to 15 feet deep. The French and British attack fails to capture the heights on the flanks of II Corps, leaving the intended river crossing area under direct enemy observation.

The Shingle force begins its final rehearsals for the Anzio landings on beaches near Salerno. The VI Corps is to make three simultaneous assaults. The entire 3rd Infantry Division, commanded by Major General Lucian K. Truscott, will land near Nettuno. Three battalions of Rangers, heavy mortars, and the 509th Parachute Infantry Battalion will land near Anzio harbor to capture the port and destroy any coastal defenses. The British 1st Division will land a brigade and Commandos northwest of Anzio to block routes into the beachhead and link up with American units at Anzio. The 504th Parachute Infantry will serve as Corps reserve and will land behind the 3rd Infantry Division. Airpower will limit any German advance toward the beachhead and destroy German aircraft. XII Air Support Command, led by Major General E. J. House, reinforced with two groups from the Desert Air Force, will provide direct support to the ground forces. Task Force 81 under the command of Rear Admiral F. J. Lowry will land the forces and ensure they are securely established on shore. Lowry has a British and American task force with a total of five cruisers, 16 destroyers, and 17 minesweepers. There will be no preliminary naval bombardment, to maximize surprise. Rocket-launching LCTs will provide the only covering fire approximately 10 minutes before the troops land on the beach. Most of the British 1st Division and the 46th Royal Tank Regiment will remain as a shipboard floating reserve.

Fifteenth Air Force B-17s bomb the marshaling yards at Prato and Pontassieve. B-24 Liberators escorted by P-38 Lightnings and P-47 Thunderbolts bomb the marshaling yard at Arezzo. Twelfth Air Force P-40s attack enemy positions at San Giuseppe and Formia, and the docks at Anzio. A-36 Intruder (Apache) fighter-bombers attack Anzio, Avezzano, and town and factory buildings at Tarquinia.

CENTRAL PACIFIC: Seventh Air Force sends nine B-25s from Abemama Island and four P-40s from Makin Island to attack supply storage area, antiaircraft positions, and the runway at Mille Atoll in the Marshalls.

NEW BRITAIN: Thirteenth Air Force fighters support a navy SBD dauntless dive-bomber attack on Japanese shipping at Rabaul. Pilots report 18 Japanese aircraft shot down. Ten Allied fighters are lost. During the night B-24 Liberators bomb the Rabaul area.

NEW GUINEA: Fifth Air Force sends 47 B-24 Liberators and B-25 Mitchells to bomb the Hansa Bay area. B-24s bomb Bandanaira in the Celebes Islands. Fifth Air Force B-24 Liberators sink two Japanese cargo ships off Manus in the Admiralty Islands.

Navy SBD Dauntless dive bombers and TBF Avengers, supported by fighter aircraft, bomb shipping at Rabaul, sinking a repair ship, a transport, and a cargo ship, and damaging an aircraft transport.

U.S. submarine *Bowfin* attacks a Japanese convoy in the Makassar Strait.

January 18

CBI: In Burma, Tenth Air Force B-24 Liberators and B-25 Mitchells bomb Japanese camps at Kyaukchaw. P-38 Lightnings attack the airfield at Meiktila. A-36 Intruder (Apache) fighter-bombers and P-51 Mustangs attack troops, supply dumps, and repair facilities at Sawnghka. P-40s attack troops and supplies at Shaduzup.

In French Indochina, two Fourteenth Air Force B-25 Mitchells bomb rail lines and the wharf at Campha and oil storage facilities at Mon Cay.

ITALY: The British X Corps attack with two divisions across the Garigliano River near Minturno causes two German Panzer Grenadier divisions to be moved away from Rome to the south, leaving the Anzio area completely unguarded.

Fifteenth Air Force B-17s, with P-38 Lightnings and P-47 Thunderbolts providing escort, attack marshaling yards, a bridge, and an airfield near Florence.

Twelfth Air Force B-25 Mitchells bomb the town and railway viaduct at Terni, and A-20 Havocs attack gun positions near Minturno. P-40s and A-36 Intruder (Apache) fighter-bombers attack troops, trucks, and gun positions in Minturno, Pontecorvo, and Atina.

PACIFIC: U.S. submarine *Flasher* torpedoes and sinks a Japanese oiler far off Marcus Island.

CENTRAL PACIFIC: Seventh Air Force sends 12 B-25 Mitchells from Abemama Island to attack Japanese facilities on Mille Atoll. Another mission sends 25 A-24 Banshees and eight P-40s from Makin to attack the oil storage area on Jabor Island in Jaluit Atoll. Aircrews report a tanker sunk.

NEW BRITAIN: The battered 7th Marines are relieved by the 2nd Battalion 1st Marines and the 2nd Battalion 5th Marines.

Thirteenth Air Force sends 34 B-25 Mitchells supported by more than 70 fighters to attack Tobera.

NEW GUINEA: Fifth Air Force sends 40 B-24 Liberators to attack the Hansa Bay area. More than 70 B-25 Mitchells attack the Madang and Bogadjim areas. Over Wewak, Japanese fighters engage 55 P-40s and P-38 Lightnings. Pilots report 12 Japanese fighters shot down. U.S. losses are three P-38s.

B-24s bomb Laha in the Celebes Islands.

U.S. submarine *Bowfin* torpedoes and sinks a Japanese tanker in the Makassar Strait.

January 19

CBI: Generalissimo Chiang Kai-shek threatens to discontinue providing housing and food to American forces in China unless he receives $1 billion in loans by March 1.

A-36 Intruder (Apache) fighter-bombers and P-51 Mustangs support the Chinese 38th Division in the Hukawng Valley in Burma. Tenth Air Force B-24 Liberators bomb the marshaling yard in Bangkok, Thailand.

In French Indochina, Fourteenth Air Force B-25 Mitchells and P-40s attack the barracks at Mon Cay.

MEDITERRANEAN: Fifteenth Army Group is redesignated as Headquarters, Allied Central Mediterranean Force (ACMF).

ITALY: The Anzio landing force completes its exercises on beaches near Salerno.

Twelfth Air Force A-36 Intruder (Apache) fighter-bombers attack transportation targets north of Rome. The A-36s and P-40s attack enemy positions in support of the British effort to expand the bridgehead on the Garigliano River. The British fail to gain ground, leaving the flank of the U.S. II Corps exposed as it prepares to cross the Rapido River the following day.

CENTRAL PACIFIC: Seventh Air Force sends 17 B-25s from Tarawa to attack Mille Atoll in the Marshalls. The bombers make a low-level run, hitting gun positions, fuel supplies, and the airfield. Japanese antiaircraft fire destroys two of the bombers.

U.S. submarine *Haddock* torpedoes and damage Japanese carrier *Unyo* near Guam.

Fifth Air Force B-24 Liberators sink a Japanese cargo ship at Manus in the Admiralty Islands.

NEW BRITAIN: Marines begin patrolling to locate the vanished enemy, setting ambushes and collecting information from the natives, following trails and looking for signs of the Japanese. There are a series of short, intense, company-sized firefights with Japanese elements delaying the approach of the marines.

Thirteenth Air Force launches 11 B-24 Liberators on a nighttime attack on Rabaul and Vunakanau.

NEW GUINEA: Two battalions of the 128th RCT land at Saidor.

Fifth Air Force B-24 Liberators bomb Amboina Island in the Molucca Islands and Halong in the Celebes Islands.

January 20

CBI: Tenth Air Force A-36 Intruder (Apache) fighter-bombers and P-51 Mustangs attack the railway near Mogaung and supplies at Mohnyin. P-38 Lightnings and B-25 Mitchells bomb rail lines and a bridge near Nattalin.

Fourteenth Air Force B-24 Liberators sink Japanese transports southeast of Swatow, China.

ETO: General Carl Spaatz, Commanding General USSAFE, assumes administrative control for all USAAF units in the United Kingdom.

Ninth Air Force receives headquarters, 437th Troop Carrier Group, and the 83rd, 84th, and 85th Troop Carrier Squadrons from the United States. The group is equipped with C-47s.

During the night, Eighth Air Force dispatches five B-17s to drop 960,000 leaflets on Lille, Brest, Caen, and Chartres in France.

ITALY: In the II Corps area, Major General Frederick L. Walker, commander of the 36th Infantry Division, is ordered to cross the Rapido River with two infantry regiments, one north and one south of Sant' Angelo. They are to capture the town of Sant' Angelo and open the way for Combat Command B of the 1st Armored Division to attack up the Liri Valley and link up with the VI Corps at Anzio.

Completely exposed to enemy fire, two battalions of the 141st Infantry Regiment attempt to cross the river north and about 100 men reach the other shore and dig in. The 143rd Infantry Regiment gets about one battalion across. After a futile effort to advance, the survivors are withdrawn back across the river. The attack fell apart almost immediately from a combination of poor preparation, mines, impassible mud, and poor coordination.

Twelfth Air Force B-26 Marauders bomb the marshaling yard at Viterbo and attack a bridge at Pontecorvo. B-25 Mitchells attack railroads near Carsoli area. A-20 Havocs attack enemy positions near Minturno. A-36 Intruder (Apache) fighter-bombers and P-40s fly nearly 200 sorties supporting the Fifth Army as the 36th Infantry Division attempts to cross the Rapido River. P-40s attack Sant' Angelo and 36 A-20 Havocs and 24 P-40s attack roads and gun positions around Cassino.

PACIFIC: U.S. submarine *Batfish* attacks a Japanese convoy off southern Honshu, sinking a transport.

CENTRAL PACIFIC: Seventh Air Force sends 13 B-24 Liberators, staging through Tarawa Atoll, to make a night raid on Wotje Atoll. P-40s from the Gilberts strafe ships at Jaluit Atoll. B-25 Mitchells sink a transport at Namu Atoll in the Marshalls.

B-24s of the 98th Bombardment Squadron (Heavy) and the Headquarters, 11th Bombardment Group (Heavy) arrive at Tarawa.

U.S. submarine *Gar* attacks a Japanese convoy coming from New Guinea and sinks a cargo ship off Palau. U.S. submarine *Seadragon* torpedoes and damages a stores ship northwest of Truk.

NEW BRITAIN: Thirteenth Air Force dispatches 18 B-25 Mitchells, escorted by about 70 fighters, to attack the airfield, fuel storage area, and gun positions at Vunakanau and Rabaul.

Fifth Air Force A-20s attack Japanese positions between Borgen Bay and Rein Bay and attack supply barges on Gasmata Island.

New Guinea: Fifth Air Force B-25 Mitchells and one B-24 bomb and strafe the Hansa Bay area.

U.S. submarine *Tinosa* lands men and equipment in northeast Borneo.

January 21

Aleutians: Navy PBY-5A Catalinas from Attu and PV-1 Patrol Bombers bomb and photograph Japanese installations on Paramushiru Island in the Kuriles.

ETO: At the supreme commander's conference in England the planning details for Overlord are briefed to the commanders. Overlord is a general plan for a cross-Channel invasion. Now that the exact location and date of the landing are identified in this detailed plan, the operation is called Neptune. General Sir Bernard L. Montgomery will be responsible for all ground forces in the cross-Channel invasion as commander of the 21st Army Group. This army group will be composed of the British Second Army and the U.S. First Army. After examining the plan, Montgomery believes a three-division initial landing is insufficient and the frontage for the attack is too narrow. He asks for five divisions in the first wave, extending from Caen to the Cotentin beaches, supported by an airborne landing in the rear of the enemy. More divisions in the initial assault will mean more landing craft and a certain postponement of the agreed upon landing date of May 1.

Eighth Air Force attacks 36 V-weapon sites in France escorted by 49 P-38 Lightnings, 531 P-47 Thunderbolts, and 48 Ninth Air Force P-51 Mustangs. Of the 302 B-17s and 68 B-24 Liberators that hit the targets, one B-17 and five B-24s are lost and 103 B-17s and 44 B-24s are damaged. Aircrews report five enemy aircraft as confirmed kills. U.S. casualties are two killed, 31 wounded, and 74 missing. The fighter pilots report six confirmed enemy kills in the air and four destroyed or damaged on the ground. One P-47 is lost with the pilot reported missing; two other P-47s are damaged. Ninth Air Force also sends 119 B-26 Marauders to bomb V-weapon sites.

During the night, five B-17s drop 1.2 million leaflets on Reims, Nantes, Le Mans, Tours, and Orleans, France.

Mediterranean: Fifteenth Air Force B-17s bomb airfields at Istres-Le-Tube and Salon-de-Provence in France.

The 738th and 739th Bombardment Squadrons (Heavy) of the 454th Bombardment Group (Heavy) arrive with B-24 Liberators from the United States. The group's first mission is scheduled for early March.

Italy: In the II Corps area, the Fifth Army commander, Lieutenant General Mark Clark, orders another attack despite concerns from subordinates; he is convinced that it is essential in drawing German forces away from Anzio. A battalion of the 143rd Infantry attempts another crossing behind heavy smoke and succeeds in reaching the opposite bank. The 141st Infantry crosses the river with two battalions. Accurate and heavy artillery fire limits any advance and prevents the engineers from bridging the river. The units are cut off and exposed to enemy fire all day. The 143rd Infantry withdraws under fire successfully, but the 141st is stranded.

Twelfth Air Force B-26 Marauders attack railroad bridges near Orvieto. B-25 Mitchells bomb the Pontecorvo bridge. P-40s attack German positions supporting the Garigliano and the Rapido River bridgeheads. A-36 Intruder (Apache) fighter-bombers attack targets around Veletri, Minturno, and Viterbo.

CENTRAL PACIFIC: Seventh Air Force sends 16 B-24 Liberators staging through Tarawa on a night raid against Kwajalein Atoll. B-25 Mitchells based at Tarawa attack Arno and Aur Atolls. B-25s from Abemama Island attack facilities and gun positions on Mille Atoll. A-24s and P-40s from Makin Island attack gun positions, storage facilities, and two small vessels at Jaluit Atoll.

NEW BRITAIN: Japanese forces on New Britain are ordered to retreat to Iboki and to prepare for holding the American advance at Talasea.

Fifth Air Force B-25 Mitchells and P-39 Airacobras strafe barges and attack other targets of opportunity along the northern coast of the island.

NEW GUINEA: Fifth Air Force B-25 Mitchells, A-20 Havocs, and P-39 Airacobras bomb the Madang Saidor areas.

U.S. submarine *Seahorse* attacks a Japanese convoy departing Palau for Hollandia and sinks an army transport and a cargo ship near Palau.

January 22

CBI: In Burma, Tenth Air Force A-36 Intruder (Apache) fighter-bombers, P-51 Mustangs, and one B-25 attack enemy supply dumps and communications between Kumnyen and Ngamaw Ga in support of Chinese forces.

In China, Fourteenth Air Force sends 11 P-40s and five P-51 Mustangs to attack the Nanchang airfield. P-38 Lightnings damage bridges at Shektan and Sheklung.

MEDITERRANEAN: Rear Admiral Frank J. Lowry commands the naval force for Operation Shingle. A minesweeper is sunk by mine and *LCI-20* is sunk by German aircraft.

ITALY: In the II Corps area, the Germans conduct a counterattack on the 141st Infantry Regiment holding the bridgehead across the Rapido River, and kill or capture the defenders. The 141st and 143rd Infantry Regiments lose 2,128 troops in their futile attempts to cross the Rapido River. General Mark Clark, Fifth Army commander, believes the sacrifice worthwhile, even if the attack is a failure.

At Anzio, the Allies achieve complete surprise and land with no opposition. The 3rd Infantry Division moves to its initial phase line. General Mark Clark lands a few hours later. The Rangers capture the port of Anzio and the 509th Parachute Infantry Battalion moves east to occupy Nettuno. By 1200, VI Corps has accomplished all of its D-day objectives. Allied aircraft fly over 1,200 sorties in support of the landings, attacking bridges and road junctions at Cisterna and Velletri. One minesweeper is lost to a mine and one LCI is bombed and sunk. By midnight 36,000 men and 3,200 vehicles have been landed. Casualties are 13 killed, 97 wounded, and 44 missing. The Allies have captured 227 German prisoners. The 30th Infantry Regiment has captured all the bridges over the Mussolini Canal, which controls any approaches to the right flank of the beachhead, but loses them during a night counterattack.

Twelfth Air Force supports the Anzio landings with A-20 Havocs and A-36 Intruder (Apache) fighter-bombers isolating the landing area by attacking the main road and rail routes into the bridgehead. Valetri, Valmontone, Colleferro, Ceprano, and Fondi are also targeted to prevent any opportunity for enemy forces to assemble. P-40s cover the airspace over the Anzio landing force, intercepting German fighter-bombers.

Fifteenth Air Force B-17s and B-24 Liberators bomb the marshaling yards at Terni, Arezzo, Pontedera and the bridge and town at Pontecorvo.

As F Company, 143rd Infantry, 36th Infantry Division, begins its night crossing of the Rapido River near San Angelo, the Germans begin dropping mortar and artillery rounds on the bridge while machine-gun fire seeks out the American troops as they reach the opposite bank. Staff Sergeant Thomas E. McCall commands a machine-gun section supporting the infantry. Exposing himself to enemy fire, McCall leads his men forward through a barbed wire obstacle to a firing position where his section can engage the enemy. When his soldiers are wounded by enemy fire, McCall again ignores enemy fire to render aid. When his entire machine-gun section is either killed or wounded, Staff Sergeant McCall charges forward alone, carrying the machine-gun in his arms and destroying two enemy positions; he is last seen attacking another position, firing his weapon from his hip. Staff Sergeant McCall's care for the men under his command, his exemplary leadership and supreme courage will win him the Medal of Honor.

SOUTH PACIFIC: Japanese submarine *RO-37* torpedoes an oiler off San Cristobal in the Solomons, but is sunk by the destroyer USS *Buchanan*.

CENTRAL PACIFIC: Seventh Air Force sends 18 B-24 Liberators from Tarawa against Kwajalein, Jaluit, and Mille Atolls. Nine B-25 Mitchells from Tarawa bomb shipping and targets on Wotje Atoll. Another 10 B-25s from Abemama Island attack Maloelap Atoll. Aircrews report 10 Japanese aircraft shot down and three B-25s lost.

NEW BRITAIN: Thirteenth Air Force attacks Lakunai airfield with 27 B-25 Mitchells, supported by more than 90 fighters. Aircrews report heavy damage to the airfield and 18 Japanese aircraft destroyed. One B-25 and four fighters are lost. Over Rabaul, six B-25s and more than 30 B-24 Liberators bomb facilities in the town.

Fifth Air Force A-20 Havocs and P-40s attack targets of opportunity on the island.

NEW GUINEA: Fifth Air Force B-25 Mitchells and P-38s attack Japanese shipping at Manus in the Admiralties. Pilots report an auxiliary submarine chaser is sunk and a cargo vessel is damaged.

U.S. submarine *Tinosa* attacks a Japanese convoy, sinking two tankers off Borneo.

January 23

ALEUTIANS: Navy PBY-5A Catalinas and PV-1 Patrol Bombers from Attu bomb Japanese installations on Paramushiru Island, Kuriles.

CBI: In Burma, Tenth Air Force B-24 Liberators attack shipping at Mergui harbor on the west coast of Malaysia. B-25 Mitchells and P-38 Lightnings destroy a bridge at Myittha and damage another at Samon. A-36 Intruder (Apache) fighter-bombers, P-51 Mustangs, and one B-25 damage enemy supply points at Kamaing and Mogaung. P-40s attack Myitkyina airfield.

In China, Fourteenth Air Force B-25 Mitchells and P-40s from Kweilin attack Kai Tek airfield in the Hong Kong-Kowloon area.

ETO: Allied planners outline the concept of operations for Neptune. The Americans have the responsibility for the western portion of the landing area closest to Cherbourg while the British have responsibility for the east closest to Caen. A total of 39 divisions are to be involved in the invasion: 20 American, 14 British, three Canadian, one French, and one Polish.

Allied planners evolve an elaborate deception to draw the attention of the Germans toward the Pas-de-Calais, the most obvious landing site, rather than the Cotentin Peninsula, the actual invasion site. A false army group is created near Dover, with giant campsites and inflated rubber tanks, landing craft, and vehicles all open to observation and counting. Naval maneuvers are held off the coast of the empty camps and German listening posts hear a constant stream of radio traffic reports directed to SHAEF headquarters from Lieutenant General George S. Patton, Jr., the well-known American combat leader and ostensible commander of the fictitious army group. The elaborate ruse works. The Germans over time will be convinced that the Pas-de-Calais is the Allied landing area and hold 19 divisions there even after the landings at Normandy.

Ninth Air Force sends almost 200 B-26 Marauders against V-weapon sites in France.

During the night, Eighth Air Force sends five B-17s to drop leaflets on Rennes, Le Mans, Chartres, Lille, and Orleans, France.

ITALY: At Anzio, the 30th Infantry Regiment of the 3rd Infantry Division, along with the 504th Parachute Infantry Regiment, recaptures the bridges over the Mussolini Canal. The 3rd Infantry Division, along with the paratroopers and Rangers, holds the right half of the beachhead, and a brigade of the British 1st Division holds the left half. German divisions are ordered to Anzio.

Fifteenth Air Force B-17s, escorted by P-47 Thunderbolts, bomb bridges at Pontecorvo and Ceprano.

Twelfth Air Force B-26 Marauders and B-25 Mitchells bomb near Avezzano. A-20 Havocs and A-36 Intruder (Apache) fighter-bombers attack Vallecorsa and road junctions at Fondi.

PACIFIC: U.S. submarine *Snook* torpedoes and sinks a Japanese gunboat near Chichi Jima.

Fourteenth Air Force B-25 Mitchells attack a Japanese convoy off Foochow, China, sinking a cargo ship.

CENTRAL PACIFIC: Seventh Air Force sends 21 B-25 Mitchells from Tarawa Atoll and Abemama Island against Taroa Island, Maloelap Atoll. Aircrews report three enemy fighters shot down. Another 23 B-24 Liberators from Makin and Abemama Islands bomb Wotje Atoll.

NEW BRITAIN: Thirteenth Air Force and marine fighters support over 60 navy SBD Dauntless dive-bombers attacking Lakunai airfield and Matupi Harbor. Fighter pilots report 30 Japanese aircraft shot down. Three Allied fighters are lost.

Fifth Air Force A-20 Havocs attack Japanese forces and antiaircraft positions near Cape Raoult and Gasmata Island.

NEW GUINEA: Fifth Air Force sends 35 B-24 Liberators with fighter escort to bomb Wewak. The Japanese intercept the Americans with 50 fighters. American pilots report 12 enemy fighters shot down. U.S. losses are five fighters. P-39 Airacobras attack barges and antiaircraft positions at Uligan Harbor.

U.S. submarine *Gar* attacks a Japanese convoy, sinking a transport near Palau.

January 24

CBI: Fourteenth Air Force B-25 Mitchells sink Japanese ship in Lishen Bay, China.

ATLANTIC: German submarines attack a convoy headed to Murmansk; a U.S. freighter is torpedoed and sunk by *U-278* off North Cape, Norway.

ETO: General Eisenhower informs the Combined Chiefs of Staff that five divisions are required for the initial assault for Neptune. One U.S. and one British division will be added. On D+2, another two divisions will be landed. This leads to a requirement to increase LSTs from 149 to 168. Eisenhower also requests that the Combined Bomber Offensive concentrate on eliminating the German fighter threat, to include fighter production facilities.

Eighth Air Force sends 857 B-17s and B-24 Liberators to attack transportation and industrial targets at Frankfurt-Heddernheim, Frankfurt/Main, and Russelsheim. Due to bad weather, the mission is recalled, but 58 B-17s do attack a power station near Eschweiler. Two bombers are shot down and seven are damaged. Aircrews report one enemy aircraft as a probable kill. Five crewmen are dead and 21 missing. Escorting P-38 Lightnings, P-47 Thunderbolts, and Ninth Air Force P-51 Mustangs report 19 confirmed kills and four probables. American losses are four P-38s, three P-47s, and two P-51 Mustangs; all the pilots are reported as missing. Six P-47s are damaged. The RAF and USAAF in the United Kingdom agree to assign all P-51s to Eighth Air Force to support long-range escort of the heavy bombers. The Ninth Air Force will be assigned all the P-38s and P-47s in theater.

Ninth Air Force sends over 175 B-26 Marauders against V-weapon sites in France.

MEDITERRANEAN: Fifteenth Air Force B-24s escorted by P-38 Lightnings bomb the airfield and town area at Skopje, Yugoslavia. B-17s escorted by P-47 Thunderbolts attack the marshaling yard at Vrattsa and the area near Dolno Tserovene in Bulgaria.

ITALY: General Mark W. Clark decides to attack the flanks of the Liri Valley using the British X Corps and French Expeditionary Corps, with the U.S. II Corps making an advance to the north of Cassino. Major General Charles W. Ryder's 34th Infantry Division will cross the Rapido River and seize three objectives: an Italian barracks area near Monte Villa, the town of Cassino, and Monte Castellone. Once these objectives are taken, the defenses at Monte Cassino can be outflanked and the Liri Valley will be open for the advance of Combat Command B of the 1st Armored Division. The 142nd Infantry of the 36th Infantry Division will conduct a diversionary attack toward Sant'Angelo after crossing the Rapido. The II Corps commander, Major General Geoffrey Keyes, passes Clark's instructions to his subordinates.

At Anzio, units of the 3rd Infantry Division conduct reconnaissance toward Cisterna, a key town on Route 7 that leads to Colli Laziali, the VI Corps objective. Meeting strong German resistance, they fall back to friendly lines. An LST hits a mine off Anzio and begins transferring troops to an LCI, when it, too, hits a mine. Nearly 300 men are killed or wounded.

At Anzio, German aircraft damage a destroyer and a minesweeper. An aerial torpedo damages a destroyer.

Twelfth Air Force A-36 Intruder (Apache) fighter-bombers attack Velletri and the road junction nearby.

PACIFIC: U.S. submarine *Sturgeon* attacks a Japanese convoy off Honshu, Japan, sinking a cargo ship.

CENTRAL PACIFIC: Seventh Air Force sends 24 A-24 Banshees from Makin Island, supported by 12 P-39 Airacobras and seven P-40s, to attack gun positions and storage facilities on Mille Atoll. B-25 Mitchells, staging through Makin Island, bomb the Wotje Atoll airfield. During the night, nine B-25s from Tarawa and 12 B-24s from the Ellice Islands, bomb targets on Maloelap Atoll.

Navy PB4Ys damage a cargo ship and submarine chaser off Kwajalein.

NEW BRITAIN: Thirteenth Air Force fighters, along with navy, marine, and RNZAF fighters, support navy and marine TBF Avengers attacking shipping in Simpson Harbor and Keravia Bay. Fighter pilots report more than 20 enemy aircraft shot down.

ADMIRALTIES: Fifth Air Force sends 38 B-25 Mitchells to attack shipping and harbor installations on Manus Island in the Admiralties.

NEW GUINEA: Fifth Air Force B-24 Liberators bomb airfields at Wewak and Boram, and B-25 Mitchells and P-47 Thunderbolts attack Madang in the Hansa Bay area.

Marine TBF Avengers, supported by navy, marine, New Zealand Air Force and U.S. Army Air Force fighters, attack Japanese shipping at Rabaul. Pilots report a water tanker, aircraft transport, and two cargo ships are sunk.

Japanese aircraft conduct a raid on American shipping in Dreger Bay, New Guinea, damaging a freighter.

Fifth Air Force B-25 Mitchells bomb Japanese shipping and harbor installations at Manus in the Admiralties. Aircrews report a transport and auxiliary minelayer sunk and another auxiliary minelayer damaged.

January 25

ETO: Eighth Air Force sends five B-17s to drop 1.2 million leaflets over Caen, Reims, Chartres, Chateauroux, and Brest in France.

ITALY: In the II Corps area, the 133rd Infantry Regiment of the 34th Infantry Division crosses the Rapido River and establishes a beachhead.

At Anzio, units of about eight German divisions establish a defensive line. An additional five divisions are on the way. German strength is about 40,000 men. The 3rd Infantry Division begins a two-battalion advance on Cisterna, supported by tanks and tank destroyers, but the advance is stopped by German strongpoints supported by tanks and self-propelled guns. A diversionary attack by the 504th Parachute Infantry Battalion across the canal on the right flank of the beachhead captures a few villages, but is driven back by German tanks. Off Anzio, a U.S. minesweeper is sunk by a mine, and a submarine chaser is damaged in a German air attack.

Twelfth Air Force B-25 Mitchells bomb Valmontone. B-26 Marauders bomb the Sezze and Rieti marshaling yard. A-20 Havocs attack Terelle and A-36 Intruder (Apache) fighter-bombers attack Civita Castellana, Itri, and Velletri. P-40s also attack Velletri and strafe trucks near Fondi.

CENTRAL PACIFIC: Seventh Air Force sends 24 A-24 Banshees from Makin Island, supported by 12 P-39 Airacobras, to attack gun positions on Mille Atoll. Eight B-25 Mitchells from Tarawa attack targets at Taroa Island, Maloelap Atoll. B-24s flying from the Gilbert Islands bomb Kwajalein Atoll.

NEW BRITAIN: Thirteenth Air Force conducts a night attack on Lakunai airfield with 19 B-24 Liberators preceded by three flare ships.

Fifth Air Force P-40s and A-20 Havocs attack targets on Gasmata Island.

NEW GUINEA: Fifth Air Force B-24 Liberators bomb the Hansa Bay area and B-25 Mitchells bomb Alexishafen and Madang.

January 26

CBI: President Roosevelt responds to Chiang Kai-shek's threat to reduce support to U.S. forces in China in a letter that states that on March 1 U.S. expenditures in China will be limited to $25 million per month.

In China, Fourteenth Air Force sends 18 P-40s from Kunming to attack the Kengtung airfield. General Claire Chennault proposes that the new B-29 strategic bombers be under his command as part of Fourteenth Air Force.

U.S. submarine *Crevalle* torpedoes and sinks a Japanese gunboat in the South China Sea near French Indochina.

German submarine *U-532* torpedoes and sinks a U.S. freighter south of Diego Garcia.

ATLANTIC: German submarine *U-716* torpedoes and sinks a U.S. freighter in a convoy headed for Murmansk.

ITALY: In the II Corps area, the 133rd Infantry Regiment attacks Hill 213, which must be captured before attacking Monte Castellone, the main objective. Mines and flooded terrain prevent any advance and the ground is too soft for tanks of the 756th Tank Battalion to cross over. Facing heavy enemy fire, the regiment falls back to the banks of the river. The 142nd Infantry Regiment of the 36th Infantry Division is attached to 34th Infantry Division.

At Anzio, the 3rd Infantry Division renews the attack toward Cisterna behind a heavy artillery barrage, but the attack stalls short of Route 7. An LCI (landing craft, infantry) is sunk and an LST is damaged by mines off Anzio. German air attacks damage a U.S. freighter. Another freighter is beached after a German fighter crashes into the ship. The ship is later repaired and returned to sea.

Twelfth Air Force A-20s attack Cisterna and A-36 Intruder (Apache) fighter-bombers and P-40s strafe roads and rail lines, trucks, and supply points.

CENTRAL PACIFIC: Seventh Air Force B-25 Mitchells from Makin Island attack the airfield on Maloelap Atoll and are met by about 20 Japanese fighters. As the bombers reach Aur Atoll, they are rescued by 12 P-40s, which drive off the enemy. Fighter pilots claim at least 10 confirmed kills and the bomber aircrews report five confirmed kills. B-25 Mitchells from Tarawa attack Aineman Island in Jaluit Atoll.

U.S. submarine *Skipjack* torpedoes and sinks a Japanese destroyer and a transport near Ponape in the Carolines.

NEW BRITAIN: Thirteenth Air Force fighters support U.S. Navy SBD Dauntless dive-bombers on Lakunai. More than 20 Japanese fighters are reported destroyed in the air. Three Allied fighters are lost.

ADMIRALTIES: Fifth Air Force sends 42 B-24 Liberators to bomb Momote on Los Negros Island and Lorengau on Manus Island.

NEW GUINEA: Fifth Air Force B-24 Liberators, A-20 Havocs, P-39 Airacobras, and P-40s attack targets in the Alexishafen-Madang area.

Navy Task Group 74.2, commanded by Rear Admiral Russell S. Berkey, with two light cruisers and three destroyers, bombards Japanese installations in Madang-Alexishafen area.

U.S. submarine *Hake* torpedoes and sinks a Japanese auxiliary netlayer off Ambon in the Netherlands East Indies.

January 27

ETO: Eighth Air Force sends five B-17s to drop nearly 1.5 million leaflets on Paris, Rennes, Le Mans, and Orleans in France.

Ninth Air Force receives the 572nd Bombardment Squadron (Medium) of the 391st Bombardment Group (Medium) from the United States. The squadron, equipped with B-26 Marauders, will fly its first mission in mid-February.

MEDITERRANEAN: Fifteenth Air Force B-17s bomb the Salon-de-Provence and Montpellier-Frejorgues airfields. B-24 Liberators bomb Istres-Le-Tube airfield. The bombers are escorted by P-38 Lightnings.

ITALY: In the II Corps area, the 168th Infantry Regiment of the 34th Infantry Division crosses the Rapido River and, with a few tanks from the 756th Tank Battalion, advances against German defensive positions on Hill 213 and Hill 56. The advance is negated by the panicked retreat of troops back across the river. Two companies reorganize and cross the river again, establishing defensive positions in front of Monte Cairo.

Twelfth Air Force B-25 Mitchells attack supply lines at Velletri, the railway at Colleferro, and the Orte marshaling yard. B-26 Marauders bomb bridges at Ceprano and the marshaling yard at Terni. A-20 Havocs provide close support near Terelle and A-36 Intruder (Apache) fighter-bombers attack rail and road traffic at Poggio Mirteto, Ceccano, and Ciampino. Over 70 P-40s attack German positions at Cisterna and Atina. Allied fighter pilots report 28 enemy aircraft shot down over Anzio. German aircraft damage a submarine chaser.

PACIFIC: Conference at Pearl Harbor. In a rejection of the Sextant agreement by the CCS that the Central Pacific should be the primary means for the attack on Japan, SWPA, POA, and SOPAC planners believe that New Guinea to the Philippines is the better choice. Two alternatives are discussed. The first is to capture Truk and concentrate on the Mariana and Palau Islands. The other option is to bypass Truk and attack the Palaus directly about one month earlier than planned. Nimitz, shaken by the cost of securing Tarawa, has less faith in his original plans outlined in Granite. The quickest approach to Japan may be through the Philippines and the coast of China. Truk could be bypassed, then an attack through the Marianas to the Palaus could be launched with the objective of supporting MacArthur's New Guinea offensive. The goal is the Philippines, with the main effort in SWPA under MacArthur's command. Admiral King, COMICH, sends Admiral Nimitz a note after the conference stating that "The idea of rolling up the Japanese along the New Guinea coast . . . and up through the Philippines to the exclusion of clearing our Central Pacific line of communications . . . is to me absurd. Further it is not in accordance with the decisions of the Joint Chiefs of Staff."

U.S. submarine *Swordfish* attacks a Japanese convoy sinking a gunboat off Honshu, Japan.

U.S. submarine *Thresher* attacks a Japanese convoy, sinking a transport and a cargo ship southwest of Formosa.

SOUTH PACIFIC: Major General Nathan F. Twining, Commanding General Thirteenth Air Force, and a crew of 14 are down at sea between Guadalcanal Island and Espiritu Santo Island. The entire group is rescued six days later. General Twining's raft has no radio, an item that Lieutenant General Millard F. Harmon, Commanding General U.S. Army Forces in the South Pacific, has been requesting for some time. This incident results in the rapid appearance of dinghy radio sets for aircrews.

CENTRAL PACIFIC: Seventh Air Force sends six B-25 Mitchells from Tarawa to attack Nauru Island. Nine B-25s, staging through Makin, attack Wotje Atoll in the Marshalls. Mille Atoll is attacked by 23 A-24 Banshees, supported by 10 P-39 Airacobras. Seven B-24 Liberators, staging through Makin Island, bomb Taroa Island in the Maloelap Atoll.

BOUGAINVILLE: Thirteenth Air Force P-39 Airacobras attack targets of opportunity.

NEW BRITAIN: Thirteenth Air Force B-25 Mitchells escorted by over 60 army and navy fighters, attack Lakunai airfield. Fighter pilots report more than 20 confirmed kills on Japanese aircraft. Six U.S. fighters are lost. B-24 Liberators bomb the Rabaul area.

ADMIRALTIES: Fifth Air Force sends 41 B-24 Liberators to bomb Lorengau on Manus Island.

NEW GUINEA: Fifth Air Force B-25 Mitchells, A-20 Havocs, and P-39 Airacobras attack targets around Madang and Bogia.

B-24 Liberators damage a cargo ship and bomb the town area at Dili on Timor Island.

January 28

ATLANTIC: A navy PB4Y-1 Privateer sinks German submarine *U-271* off Limerick, Ireland.

ETO: Eighth Air Force sends 54 B-24 Liberators escorted by 122 P-47 Thunderbolts against the Bonnieres V-weapon site in France. The attack is led by two radar-equipped bombers. The equipment malfunctions, targets are misidentified, and only 31 bombers hit the primary target. One bomber is damaged, but there are no casualties.

During the night five B-17s drop more than 1.36 million leaflets over Amiens, Rouen, Cambrai, Reims, and Caen in France.

ITALY: A motor torpedo boat carrying Lieutenant General Mark Clark is damaged by friendly fire from a minesweeper near Anzio. A U.S. submarine chaser is damaged in an air attack.

NEW IRELAND: Thirteenth Air Force B-24 Liberators, and navy PBY Catalinas sink a Japanese transport carrying a midget submarine off Kavieng, New Ireland.

NEW GUINEA: U.S. submarine *Bowfin* torpedoes and damages a Japanese oiler off Makassar on Celebes Island.

January 29

CBI: In Burma, Tenth Air Force B-24 Liberators, with 16 P-38s as escorts, bomb gasoline plants at Yenangyaung.

ETO: Eighth Air Force sends 675 B-17s and 188 B-24 Liberators, led by PFF aircraft and escorted by 89 P-38 Lightnings, 503 P-47 Thunderbolts, and 40 Ninth Air Force P-51 Mustangs against industrial targets at Frankfurt, Germany. Of the 590 B-17s and 170 B-24s that hit the primary target, 24 B-17s and five B-24s are lost and 118 B-17s and 22 B-24s are damaged. Aircrew casualties are 22 killed, 32 wounded, and 299 missing. Aircrews report 75 confirmed kills and 27 probables. The fighter pilots report 47 enemy confirmed kills and six probables. Five P-38s and 10 P-47s are lost; four P-38s are damaged along with one P-47 damaged. A total of 14 pilots are reported missing.

Ninth Air Force sends over 80 B-26 Marauders to bomb V-weapon sites in France.

During the night five B-17s drop 1.2 million leaflets over Lille, Tours, Lorient, Nantes, and Valenciennes in France.

ITALY: At Anzio, the U.S. 3rd Battalion 1st Armored Regiment supports the British advance on the Albano Road at Anzio, while Combat Command A and elements of a tank regiment and the 6th Armored Infantry attempt to support the attack, but the muddy ground with hills and gullies prevents any advance. An attack by over 100 German aircraft on the ships off Anzio sinks one cargo ship and a British cruiser.

Fifteenth Air Force B-17s bomb marshaling yards at Ancona, Fabriano, Rimini, and Bologna while P-47 Thunderbolts conduct sweeps over Rome and Florence.

Twelfth Air Force P-40s and A-36 Intruder (Apache) fighter-bombers attack German defenses at Anzio and attack road and rail communications in the area behind the beachhead.

PACIFIC: U.S. submarine *Tambor* attacks a Japanese convoy and sinks a cargo ship north of Okinawa.

CENTRAL PACIFIC: A pre-landing air and naval bombardment on Kwajalein expends 6,000 tons of ordnance on the island. Seventh Air Force B-24 Liberators operating from the Gilberts conduct nearly continuous attacks on Maloelap, Jaluit, Aur, Wotje, and Mille Atolls in the Marshalls. P-39 Airacobras conduct strafing attacks on Mille all day. B-25 Mitchells from Tarawa attack shipping and shore installations at Wotje. A-24 Banshees, supported by 12 P-40s, bomb Jaluit.

Aircraft from fast carrier force TF 58, commanded by Rear Admiral Marc A. Mitscher, conduct strikes against Japanese aircraft and shipping in the Marshall Islands.

NEW BRITAIN: Thirteenth Air Force fighters cover a strike by 40 navy SBD Dauntless dive-bombers on Tobera. B-24 Liberators, escorted by P-38 Lightnings and navy fighters, attack Lakunai airfield. Pilots report more than 20 Japanese aircraft shot down. Fifth Air Force sends 45 A-20 Havocs to attack Japanese positions at Cape Gloucester.

NEW GUINEA: Fifth Air Force B-25 Mitchells bomb landing fields at Bogia and Nubia.

U.S. submarine *Bowfin* lays mines off southeastern coast of Borneo.

January 30

ETO: Eighth Air Force attacks aircraft production facilities at Brunswick, Germany, with 623 B-17s and 154 B-24 Liberators, escorted by 635 fighters (P-38 Lightnings, P-47 Thunderbolts, and Ninth Air Force P-51 Mustangs). Cloud cover over the primary target leads 597 B-17s to bomb the city itself as a secondary target. The B-24 Liberators, finding the secondary target obscured, attack Hannover and other targets of opportunity. Aircraft losses are 18 B-17s lost and 107 damaged; two B-24s lost and 11 B-24s damaged. Aircrews report 51 confirmed kills and seven probables. U.S. casualties are four killed, 14 wounded, and 206 missing. The fighter pilots report 45 enemy confirmed kills and 15 probables. Fighter losses are two P-38s and two P-47 Thunderbolts; two P-38s, three P-47 Thunderbolts, and two P-51s are damaged. U.S. casualties are one wounded and four missing.

During the night, five B-17s drop 1.2 million leaflets over Chateauroux, Brest, Chartres, Le Mans, and Caen in France.

ITALY: In the II Corps area, the 168th Infantry Regiment captures Hill 213 and Hill 56 and stops several enemy counterattacks. Monte Castellone is now open to attack, which will support the French Expeditionary Corps.

At Anzio, the VI Corps commander, Major General John P. Lucas, orders an attack to break out of the beachhead. On the left, the British 1st Division, supported by the U.S. 1st Armored Division, will attack north, while the 3rd Infantry Division and the 504th Parachute Infantry Battalion and Rangers on the right will attack to cut Route 7 at Cisterna. Two battalions of Colonel William O. Darby's Rangers are to infiltrate enemy lines to assault Cisterna just before dawn. The 3rd Infantry Division would then launch the main attack, while the 504th Parachute Infantry Battalion makes a diversionary attack on the right. The Rangers are surprised and trapped within 800 yards of Cisterna; although a few make it into the outskirts of the town, the two battalions, nearly 700 men, are either killed or taken prisoner. The 15th Infantry Regiment makes little headway against boggy fields and strong German resistance. The 7th Infantry Regiment's attack advances about halfway to Cisterna before being halted by enemy fire.

Fifteenth Air Force adds its ninth heavy bomber Group with the addition of the B-24s of the 451st Bombardment Group. B-17s escorted by P-38 Lightnings bomb airfields at Villaorba, Maniago, and Lavariano. B-24s, also escorted by P-38s, bomb Udine airfield and Fier radar station. Aircrews report more than 60 aircraft destroyed in the air and more destroyed on the ground.

Twelfth Air Force B-25 Mitchells bomb road junctions at Valmontone and Genzano di Roma, and the town of Monte Compatri. A-20 Havocs attack targets near Cori.

Sergeant Truman O. Olson is a light machine gunner with B Company, 7th Infantry Regiment, 3rd Infantry Division. An attack on a German trench line near Cisterna di Littoria is slowed and stopped and most of the company are killed or wounded. Olson is one of the survivors who establish a small defensive perimeter and fight for their lives. Sergeant Olson and his crew operate the only machine gun left. For nearly 24 hours, Olson continues to break up enemy attacks. By daybreak, he is the only man left in his section and, though wounded, continues to engage the enemy. This time more than 200 troops attack his position, supported by mortar and machine-gun fire. Sergeant Olson refuses to be evacuated after being badly wounded again and succeeds in breaking up the attack. For his courage and dedication to duty in the face of overwhelming odds, Sergeant Olson will receive the Medal of Honor.

SOUTHWEST PACIFIC AREA: Navy SBD Dauntless dive-bombers and TBF Avengers, supported by Allied fighters, bomb Japanese shipping at Rabaul. Pilots report sinking a water supply ship and damaging an auxiliary vessel.

PACIFIC: During the night a navy PB2Y Coronado (a long-range maritime patrol bomber) from Midway bombs the airfield on Wake Island. Two motor torpedo boats are sunk.

CENTRAL PACIFIC: Seventh Air Force P-40s and P-39 Airacobras make continuous attacks on the Mille Atoll airfield. B-24 Liberators bomb Kwajalein Atoll throughout the night. During the preinvasion bombardment of Wotje Atoll, a destroyer is damaged by fire from a shore battery.

SBD Dauntless dive-bombers and F4F Hellcats from Naval Task Group 52.8, with the carriers USS *Enterprise, Yorktown,* and *Bunker Hill* and the small carrier USS *Belleau Wood,* sink a number of auxiliary submarine chasers at Kwajalein Atoll and Mille. Carrier aircraft also damage a cargo ship at Eniwetok, which is later sunk by a destroyer. Battleships USS *Washington, Indiana,* and *Massachusetts* and four destroyers bombard Japanese positions on Kwajalein. Battleship USS *North Carolina* sinks a transport off Roi. A destroyer sinks a transport and guardboat off Ujae Atoll.

U.S. submarine *Seahorse* attacks a Japanese convoy moving from Palau and sinks a cargo ship near Palau. U.S. submarine *Spearfish* attacks a Japanese convoy and sinks a transport off Saipan.

BOUGAINVILLE: Thirteenth Air Force sends 20 P-39 Airacobras to attack Kunrai.

Navy Task Group 31.8, with four destroyers, three high speed transports, and two motor torpedo boats, lands New Zealand troops and U.S. Navy personnel on the Green Islands, north of Bougainville, to conduct reconnaissance for suitable airfields and landing beaches.

Staff Sergeant Jesse R. Drowley of the Americal Division is a squad leader at Bougainville and has the mission during a platoon attack to establish a local perimeter defense and act as the platoon reserve. Seeing two men fall, he rushes forward in the face of heavy enemy fire to bring them back to safety. He locates a Japanese pillbox firing into the platoon and moves to an American tank supporting the attack. Climbing on the turret, he obtains a submachine gun and rides on top of the tank firing in the direction of the pillbox to mark the target for the tank crew. Fully exposed to enemy fire, Staff sergeant Drowley is hit in the chest. Ignoring his wound he continues to direct fire on the pillbox until, wounded again in the left eye, he falls off the tank. Pulling himself to his feet, Drowley stays alongside the tank until the pillbox has been eliminated and another behind it destroyed as well. Satisfied that the attack can progress, he walks to the rear for medical treatment. For his conspicuous bravery and extraordinary dedication to duty Staff Sergeant Drowley will receive the Medal of Honor.

NEW BRITAIN: Lieutenant Colonel Lewis B. "Chesty" Puller takes command of southern patrols to locate and clear Japanese forces from Borgen Bay to the Itni River as part of the effort to clear the enemy from western New Britain. Puller's force, consisting of 384 men, departs Agulupella. The force is resupplied periodically by air drops from small planes.

Thirteenth Air Force sends 26 B-25 Mitchells and fighters to bomb Lakunai airfield. B-24 Liberators and fighters bomb Vunakanau airfield. Fighters support a navy SBD Dauntless dive-bomber attack on Japanese shipping in the Rabaul area. Pilots report over 20 Japanese aircraft shot down.

Fifth Air Force A-20 Havocs attack barges along the northern coast and P-39 Airacobras strafe barges and fuel storage areas at Rein Bay.

NEW GUINEA: Fifth Air Force B-25 Mitchells bomb landing areas at Hansa Bay and Nubia.

January 31

ETO: Eighth Air Force attacks V-weapon construction at St-Pol/Siracourt, France. Of the 74 B-24 Liberators that hit the target, two bombers are damaged. P-47 Thunderbolts provide escort for the mission. Gilze-Rijen airfield in the Netherlands is attacked by 70 P-47 fighter-bombers, escorted by 47 P-38s and 87 P-47 Thunderbolts. Fighter pilots report that 13 enemy aircraft shot down and one probable kill. Six P-38s are lost, one P-38 is damaged, and two P-47s are damaged. Aircrew casualties are one wounded and six missing.

MEDITERRANEAN: Fifteenth Air Force B-17s with P-38 Lightnings escorting, bomb Klagenfurt airfield in Austria. Aircrews report 16 enemy aircraft shot down.

Twelfth Air Force A-20 Havocs bomb Artena. P-40s and A-36 Intruder (Apache) fighter-bombers attack German positions at Sezze, Fondi, and Priverno. P-47 Thunderbolts bomb San Benedetto de Marsi.

ITALY: At Anzio, the 7th and 15th Infantry Regiments of the 3rd Infantry Division renew the attack to cut off Route 7 at Cisterna. Supported by a heavy artillery bombardment and air attacks, the infantry advances with tanks in support but makes only a limited advance. On the left, the 6th Armored Infantry supported by tanks from the 1st Armored Regiment makes only a few hundred yards before being stopped by minefields and artillery. The units of the 1st Armored Division are ordered to VI Corps reserve that night.

Twelfth Air Force A-20 Havocs bomb Artena. P-40s and A-36 Intruder (Apache) fighter-bombers attack a road junction at Sezze, the town of Fondi, and Priverno; P-47 Thunderbolts bomb San Benedetto de Marsi.

SOUTHWEST PACIFIC AREA: Within the SWPA, General MacArthur has five army divisions: the 1st Cavalry, the 6th Infantry, the 24th Infantry, the 32nd Infantry, and the 41st Infantry. He also has three regimental combat teams, the 112th Cavalry, the 158th Infantry Regiment, and the 503rd Parachute Infantry Regiment. He can expect the arrival of three more divisions, the 31st Infantry, the 33rd Infantry, and the 43rd Infantry. The Fifth Air Force numbers about 1,000 aircraft, and Vice Admiral Thomas C. Kinkaid, commander of Seventh Fleet, has a greatly expanded amphibious and sea transport capability. In the month of January, 308 B-24, 107 B-25, and nine B-26 sorties have been carried out against Alexishafen and Madang, employing a total of 1,100 tons of bombs against the Japanese holding out against the Australians.

CENTRAL PACIFIC: Operation Flintlock, the campaign to seize the Marshall Islands, is commanded by Vice Admiral Raymond A. Spruance, Commander Central Pacific Force, designated as Task Force 50. It is composed of Southern Attack Force (Task Force 51), commanded by Rear Admiral Richmond K. Turner, the Northern Attack Force (Task Force 53), commanded by Rear Admiral Richard L. Conolly, and Reserve Force and Majuro Attack Group (Task Force 51.2), commanded by Rear Admiral Harry W. Hill. Aircraft from Task Force 58, commanded by Rear Admiral Marc A. Mitscher, and land-based aircraft from Task Force 57 (Rear Admiral John H. Hoover), have responsibility for covering the landings.

Aircraft from fast-carrier group Task Group 58.3 (Rear Admiral Frederick C. Sherman) bomb aircraft and the airfield facilities at Engebi Island, Eniwetok Atoll. TG 58.3 aircraft and a destroyer sink an auxiliary netlayer off Eniwetok.

The Majuro Island force, consisting of a marine reconnaissance company and the 2nd Battalion 106th Infantry Regiment, lands and find only one Japanese soldier serving as a caretaker. Marines land on small islands off Kwajalein to establish artillery firing positions to support the landings. The army's 145th Artillery Battalion occupies positions.

Seventh Air Force A-24 Banshees bomb the airfield on Mille Atoll, while P-39 Airacobras and P-40s provide continuous air cover to prevent any interference with the landings. P-40s attack Jaluit Atoll and during the night eight B-24 Liberators bomb Wotje Atoll.

U.S. submarine *Trigger* (SS-237) sinks a Japanese auxiliary submarine depot ship northwest of Truk and damages a destroyer. U.S. submarine *Tullibee* torpedoes and sinks an auxiliary netlayer off Saipan.

NEW BRITAIN: Over 1,300 bomber and 1,800 fighter sorties have been flown against Rabaul in January. American losses total 35 bombers and 65 fighters. Thirteenth Air Force fighters support Navy SBD Dauntless dive-bombers on Tobera. This is followed by an attack by 17 B-24 Liberators with fighter support on the same target. Aircrews report eight Japanese aircraft shot down.

NEW GUINEA: Fifth Air Force A-20 Havocs attack Uligan Harbor and P-39 Airacobras strafe a landing strip at Alexishafen. B-24 Liberators sink a Japanese guardboat off Celebes.

A lone Japanese aircraft makes a high-level bombing raid on American shipping in Langemak Bay, New Guinea. A freighter is damaged

February 1

CBI: In Burma, Tenth Air Force B-24 Liberators bomb Mingaladon Nyaungbinwun airfields. P-51 Mustangs and A-36 Intruder (Apache) fighter-bombers and a B-25

Mitchell bomb the Myitkyina airfield. Engineers begin construction of a permanent road in the Hukawng Valley.

ETO: The 21st Army Group issues its initial plan as part of the initial joint plan called Neptune. A landing beach is added part of the Cotentin Peninsula to bring Allied forces closer to the port of Cherbourg, a key objective in the operation. The U.S. First Army is assigned two beachheads between Vierville-sur-Mer and Colleville-sur-Mer. The VII Corps is to land at the beach named Utah to cut of the base of the Cotentin Peninsula and capture Cherbourg. Two airborne divisions are to land before the beach assault. The 101st Airborne Division is to capture the four western causeway exits that lead out from the beach over flooded ground. The 82nd Airborne Division is to land west of the Meredet River to capture Ste. Mère-Eglise and control the roads leading to the beachhead. The V Corps is to land at the beach named Omaha between Carentan and Bayeux and move south to St. Lô to cover the British and Canadian forces of the Second Army as it advances to Caen and Bayeaux. The LST requirement for the initial landings has increased from 149 to 168. Included in the plan is an effort to convince the enemy that Neptune is a diversion and Pas-de-Calais is the actual invasion site.

At the end of the first day (D-day), 8 2/3 divisions are to land. By D+1, 10 1/3 divisions are to be ashore; by D+12, 26–30 divisions are to be ashore. By D+30, these divisions will require 1,800 tons of fuel per day to support the approximately 92,000 vehicles estimated to be in France at that time and 42,000 tons of supplies per day to support nearly 500,000 men.

The Eighth Air Force receives the B-24 Liberators of the 752nd, 753rd, 754th, and 755th Bombardment Squadrons (Heavy) of the 458th Bombardment Group (Heavy), arrived in England from the United States. The group's first mission is scheduled for late February.

In the Ninth Air Force, the headquarters of the 416th Bombardment Group (Light) and 669th, 670th, and 671st Bombardment Squadrons (Light) with A-20 Havocs arrives from the United States. The group's first mission is scheduled for early march. The 30th Photographic Reconnaissance Squadron, III Reconnaissance Command, arrives with F-5 Lightnings.

Major General Elwood R. "Pete" Quesada assumes command of IX Air Support Command, which has operational control over all fighter and reconnaissance units of IX Fighter Command.

MEDITERRANEAN: German aircraft make a torpedo attack on convoy UGS 30 (United States to Mediterranean, Slow) in the western Mediterranean. One U.S. freighter is damaged and another is torpedoed and abandoned.

ITALY: In the II Corps area, the 133rd Infantry attacks the Italian barracks area at Monte Vella; the 135th Infantry attacks toward Monte Castellone. Both regiments belong to the 34th Infantry Division. The 142nd Infantry 36th Infantry Division attacks to support the French attack north of Monte Castellone.

At Anzio, the 3rd Infantry Division attacks toward Cisterna, but German tank and infantry counterattacks force Major General Truscott to order a consolidation of the line and prepare defensive positions.

General Sir Harold Alexander, commander of the Fifteenth Army Group, arrives at Anzio and meets with Major General John P. Lucas. After the meeting Lucas writes, "My head will probably fall in the basket but I have done my best. There were just too many Germans here for me to lick and they could build up faster than I could. As I told Clark yesterday, I was sent on a desperate mission, one where the odds were greatly against success, and I went without saying anything because I was given an order and my opinion was not asked."

The 45th Infantry Division and other units of the 1st Armored Division land at Anzio. German forces defending the area have now reached over 70,000 men. The Allies, even with additional reinforcements, have about 61,000 men ashore.

In the II Corps area the 135th Infantry Regiment of the 34th Infantry Division attacks toward Monte Castellone and captures its objectives, supported by fire from the 168th Infantry Regiment on Hill 213 and Hill 56.

Twelfth Air Force B-25 Mitchells bomb the Albano-Laziale road junction. P-40s bomb Cori, while A-36 Intruder (Apache) fighter-bombers hit Poggio Mieteto and P-47 Thunderbolts attack the station at San Valentino.

Private First Class Alton W. Knappenberger is a Browning Automatic Rifleman in the 3rd Infantry Division facing a German attack against his battalion near Cisterna di Littoria. Knappenberger crawls to an exposed knoll and begins a battle with an enemy machine gun 85 yards away. Rising to a kneeling position, Knappenberger knocks out the gun. When two Germans soldiers approach to throw grenades at him, Private First Class Knappenberger kills them both. As another German machine gun opens fire only 100 yards away, the American eliminates the crew with a burst of fire. Increasingly, Knappenberger finds himself the target of concentrated volumes of fire from a number of weapons. He fires on every target he can engage, then, out of ammunition, he crawls to find more ammunition and returns to the position, stopping the assault of a German platoon armed with automatic weapons. Only when his ammunition is exhausted does Knappenberger fall back to rejoin his unit. Private First Class Knappenberger's extraordinary feat of arms and his exceptional courage in the face of a determined enemy will win him the Medal of Honor.

PACIFIC: Amphibious Forces, Pacific Fleet, is established at Pearl Harbor. Vice Admiral Richmond K. Turner, Commander Fifth Amphibious Force, is selected to serve as the commander.

CENTRAL PACIFIC: Operation Flintlock. The 23rd Marine Regiment lands at Roi Island and the 24th Marine Regiment lands on Namur Island. Navajo code talkers are employed to transmit reports and instructions quickly and efficiently without having to take time to encrypt radio messages to prevent the Japanese from gaining any information.

The 32nd and 184th Infantry Regiments of the 7th Infantry Division land on Kwajalein Island and immediately encounter Japanese defenders in spider holes and camouflaged trenches. Clearing these initial defenses, the Americans face a number of counterattacks.

Seventh Air Force B-24 Liberators from Makin Island bomb beach defenses on Kwajalein. P-40s continue patrols over Mille Atoll.

Marines land on Roi and Namur and army troops land on Kwajalein under cover of heavy naval gunfire from battleships, cruisers, and destroyers. A cruiser is

Men of the 7th Infantry Division use a flamethrower on Japanese positions on Kwajalein Island, February 4, 1944.

damaged by an eight-inch shell ricochet and two destroyers and a minesweeper run aground. Two battleships are damaged in a collision.

U.S. submarine *Guardfish* attacks a Japanese convoy heading for Truk and sinks a destroyer. U.S. submarine *Seahorse* attacks a Japanese convoy moving from Palau to Rabaul and sinks a transport near Woleai Atoll.

First Lieutenant John V. Power, a platoon leader attached to the 4th Marine Division, is severely wounded in the stomach as he tosses a demolition charge against a Japanese bunker position. Without hesitation, he continues the attack, holding his wounded side with one hand while firing his carbine with his right hand. As he reloads he is killed. First Lieutenant Power's exceptional fighting spirit and courage in engaging the enemy will win him the Medal of Honor.

During the assault on Namur Island, Private Richard K. Sorenson and five other marines of the 4th Marine Division occupy a shell hole when a Japanese grenade lands among them. Private Sorenson falls on the grenade to save his comrades. He is severely wounded, but his act of selfless courage will win him the Medal of Honor.

On Roi Island, Private First Class Richard B. Anderson of the 4th Marine Division jumps into a shell crater with three other marines. Attempting to throw a grenade, Private First Class Anderson drops it and watches the live grenade roll toward his comrades. Anderson immediately jumps on the grenade and sacrifices himself to save the lives of his fellow marines. His sacrifice will earn him the Medal of Honor.

BOUGAINVILLE: Two U.S. destroyers sink Japanese submarine *I-171* near Buka Island.

NEW BRITAIN: Operation Appease begins. This is intended to capture Talasea and Hoskins Plantation, the last objectives of the campaign.

NEW GUINEA: The naval base at Finschhafen, New Guinea, is established.

U.S. submarine *Hake* torpedoes and sinks a Japanese cargo ship and transport off Halmahera.

B-24 Liberators damage a Japanese ship en route from Hollandia to Aitape.

February 2

ATLANTIC: Stalin agrees to provide six bases in the western USSR for American aircraft from the ETO.

ETO: Eighth Air Force attacks V-weapon construction at St.-Pol/Siracourt and Watten, France. Of the 95 B-24 Liberators that hit the target, two bombers are lost and three are damaged. The mission is escorted by 183 P-47 Thunderbolts. U.S. casualties are 10 killed and 19 missing.

Ninth Air Force sends 36 B-26 Marauders to attack the airfield at Triqueville, France. Eighth Air Force provides 34 P-38 Lightnings and 44 P-47 Thunderbolts as escort.

The 668th Bombardment Squadron (Light) of the 416th Bombardment Group (Light), with A-20 Havocs, arrives from the United States. The squadron's first mission is scheduled for early March.

MEDITERRANEAN: Fifteenth Air Force B-24 Liberators, with RAF Spitfire escort, bomb the radar station at Durazzo, Albania.

Twelfth Air Force B-25 Mitchells attack the Marino road junction and A-20 Havocs bomb Norma. A-36 Intruder (Apache) fighter-bombers and P-40s bomb transportation and supply targets and the road to Viterbo. P-40s attack Cisterna and Formia.

Major General Gordon P. Saville takes command of XII Air Support Command.

ITALY: In the II Corps area, the 133rd Infantry captures the Italian barracks at Monte Vella; the 135th Infantry seizes Monte Castellone.

At Anzio, the 2nd Battalion 7th Infantry Regiment of the 3rd Infantry Division stops an early morning battalion-size attack on its position, capturing 131 prisoners. Major General John P. Lucas receives orders from General Mark Clark to consolidate the beachhead and prepare for defensive operations. The 1st Special Service Force arrives to reinforce Lucas, guarding the right flank along the Mussolini Canal. German counterattacks west of Cisterna are stopped, largely by concentrated Allied artillery fire.

PACIFIC: U.S. submarine *Plunger* attacks a Japanese convoy south of Honshu, Japan, and sinks two cargo ships. Although depth-charged, the submarine escapes.

CENTRAL PACIFIC: Operation Flintlock. The 24th Marines secure Namur after repulsing a Japanese counterattack at dawn. Roi Island is secured later in the day. After a slow advance, units of the 184th and 32nd Infantry Regiments of the 7th Infantry Division report capturing nearly all of Kwajalein.

Seventh Air Force A-24 Banshees, P-39 Airacobras, and P-40s from Makin bomb Mille Atoll. B-24 Liberators from Tarawa bomb Rongelap Island.

Destroyer USS *Walker* sinks Japanese submarine *RO-39* off Wotje Atoll, Marshall Islands.

NEW GEORGIA: The B-24 Liberators of the 31st Bombardment Squadron (Heavy), 5th Bombardment Group (Heavy), Thirteenth Air Force, begin operating from Munda airfield.

NEW BRITAIN: Fifth Air Force B-25 Mitchells bomb targets along the coast from Cape Gauffre to Rein Bay.

NEW GUINEA: Fifth Air Force B-24 Liberators bomb Sorong and Alexishafen and A-20 Havocs attack installations near Madang.

February 3

CBI: In Burma, Tenth Air Force P-38 Lightnings attack bridges and camps along the Prome-Taungup road, destroying one bridge. P-51 Mustangs hit a Japanese camp at Sawnghka.

ETO: Eighth Air Force sends 671 B-17s and 193 B-24 Liberators against the port at Wilhelmshaven, Germany, escorted by 74 P-38 Lightnings, 508 P-47 Thunderbolts of the Eighth and Ninth Air Force, and 50 Ninth Air Force P-51 Mustangs. The B-24s abort the mission but 553 B-17s hit the main target. The B-17s also drop 1.8 million leaflets. Four bombers are lost and 48 bombers damaged. Aircrews report one probable kill. U.S. casualties are two killed, nine wounded, and 42 missing. The fighter pilots report eight confirmed kills on enemy aircraft. Eight P-47 Thunderbolts and one P-51 are lost; 16 P-47 Thunderbolts are damaged. U.S. casualties are nine pilots missing.

During the night, seven B-17s drop leaflets on Paris, Rouen, Amiens, Reims, Orleans, and Rennes.

ITALY: In the II Corps area, the 133rd Infantry Regiment of the 34th Infantry Division battles German defenders in the streets of Cassino, but cannot dislodge them. The New Zealand 2nd Divisions and the Indian 4th Division under command of Lieutenant General Sir Bernard C. Freyberg are redesignated as the New Zealand Corps and placed under command of Clark's Fifth Army.

A-36 Intruder (Apache) fighter-bombers hit roads and targets south of Rome and attack German positions near Sezze and Fondi.

Private First Class Leo J. Powers of the 133rd Infantry Regiment, 34th Infantry Division, attacks Hill 175 near Cassino. The Germans have machine guns and pillboxes on the hill and are supported by mortars. As his company begins to falter in the face of heavy enemy fire, Powers continues to advance, crawling close enough to attack one of the pillboxes with hand grenades. He stands in full view of the enemy to make an accurate throw and knocks out the position, killing and wounding the defenders. As the infantrymen begin to advance, a second machine gun in a pillbox begins firing on them. Private First Class Powers repeats his first amazing act of courage, approaching the pillbox, then standing in full view of the enemy to throw his grenades. He continues this same tactic against a third pillbox, destroying it, and takes the surrender of four German soldiers. This extraordinary act of courage will win PFC Powers the Medal of Honor.

PACIFIC: U.S. submarine *Tambor* attacks a Japanese convoy in the East China Sea, sinking a fleet tanker and a merchant fleet tanker off Shanghai. The submarine is damaged by depth charges, but remains on patrol.

CENTRAL PACIFIC: Operation Flintlock. The attack on Kwajalein continues as the 184th Infantry encircles one group of enemy defenders while the 32nd Infantry advances to clear the rest of the island.

Cruiser and destroyer gunfire support landings of army troops on Ebeye, Kwajalein Atoll, Marshalls.

NEW BRITAIN: Thirteenth Air Force P-40s and U.S. Navy fighters support a navy SBD Dauntless dive-bomber strike on Tobera. B-24 Liberators, with P-38 Lightning navy fighters escorting, bomb the Lakunai airfield. Aircrews report 13 Japanese aircraft shot down.

NEW IRELAND: Navy PBY Catalinas and Fifth Air Force B-25 Mitchells attack a Japanese convoy west of New Ireland and sink cargo ship.

ADMIRALTIES: Fifth Air Force P-39 Airacobras and B-25 Mitchells attack Momote and Hyane Harbor on Los Negros Island.

NEW GUINEA: Fifth Air Force sends nearly 100 B-24 Liberators and B-25 Mitchells, supported by P-38 Lightnings, P-40s, and P-47 Thunderbolts, to bomb airfields at Wewak. Aircrews report about 80 Japanese aircraft destroyed on the ground and in the air. A-20 Havocs attack targets near Alexishafen and Hansa Bay.

February 4

ETO: Eighth Air Force sends 589 B-17s and 159 B-24 Liberators to attack industrial targets and the railyards at Frankfurt am Main, Germany, escorted by 56 P-38 Lightnings, 537 Eighth and Ninth Air Force P-47 Thunderbolts, and 44 Ninth Air Force P-51 Mustangs. Weather and navigation problems result in only 346 B-17s and 27 B-24 Liberators hitting their target. The other bombers are scattered and hit Giessen, Wiesbaden, Trier, Arloff, Russelheim, Grafenhausen, Darmstadt, Koblenz, and some unidentified targets. Bomber losses are 18 B-17s and two B-24 Liberators; 362 bombers are damaged. Aircrews report four confirmed enemy aircraft kills. U.S. casualties are seven killed, 20 wounded, and 203 missing. Fighter pilots report eight confirmed kills. One P-38 is lost, five P-47 Thunderbolts and five P-38 Lightnings are damaged. One pilot is reported missing. During the night, seven B-17s drop 319 bundles of leaflets over Lorient, Tours, Nantes, Raismes, Lille, and Cambrai in France and over Antwerp, Belgium.

In the Ninth Air Force, Major General Otto P. Weyland takes command of XIX Air Support Command.

MEDITERRANEAN: The combined planning staffs meet to develop a detailed plan for Anvil, the invasion of southern France in support of Overlord. Seventh Army's mission is to make an amphibious and airborne assault on the south coast of France, secure a beachhead east of Toulon, and then capture the city. After Toulon is secured, Seventh Army will advance toward Lyon and join with Allied forces in northern France advancing from Normandy.

ITALY: In the II Corps area, an attack on the slopes of Monte Cassino by a battalion of the 135th Infantry fails. German infantry counterattacking with tanks drive the 133rd

Infantry out of the town of Cassino. The 34th Infantry Division has reached the limit of its capability and is unable to advance before Cassino and cannot reach Route 6.

The German Fourteenth Army, opposing Allied forces at Anzio, is reinforced and now totals five divisions. During the early morning hours, British defenders are driven from outside Campoleone. Both sides suffer heavy losses. One RCT of the 45th Infantry Division defends the left flank of the beachhead along the Moletta River. The 1st Special Service Force holds the right flank of the beachhead along the Mussolini Canal. The British 1st Division and the U.S. 3rd Infantry Division hold the center of the beachhead. The 3rd Infantry Division is responsible for the area from Carano to the Mussolini Canal. The remainder of the 45th Infantry Division and units of the 1st Armored Division are held in reserve to stop any penetrations of the defensive line. American units, depleted by combat losses, find replacements are slow in coming.

PACIFIC: Cruisers and destroyers of Navy Task Group 94.6, commanded by Rear Admiral Wilder D. Baker, bombard Japanese installations at Paramushiru in the Kurile Islands. One cargo ship is damaged.

CENTRAL PACIFIC: Operation Flintlock. Supported by naval gunfire, the 32nd Infantry Regiment of the 7th Infantry Division clears the last defenders of Kwajalein. Wotje, Mille, Maloelap, and Jaluit Islands are now isolated. The Japanese garrisons there will be subject to air attack and play no further role in the war.

Seventh Air Force B-24 Liberators from Tarawa and Makin Island bomb Wotje, Maloelap, and Mille Atolls. P-40s based on Makin bomb and strafe Mille Atoll. B-25 Mitchells from Tarawa and Abemama Island bomb Wotje and Maloelap Atolls.

A destroyer and destroyer escort sink Japanese submarine *I-175* north of Jaluit Atoll.

PV-1 Patrol Bombers sink a Japanese water tanker at Jaluit.

Marine PB4Y Privateers conduct an aerial reconnaissance of Truk.

BOUGAINVILLE: The P-38 Lightnings of the 68th Fighter Squadron, 347th Fighter Group, transfer from Fiji.

U.S. destroyers bombard Japanese positions on the northwest coast of Bougainville. A destroyer is damaged by fire from the shore battery.

NEW GEORGIA: Headquarters of the 5th Bombardment Group (Heavy) redeploys from Guadalcanal to Munda airfield.

NEW BRITAIN: Thirteenth Air Force sends 25 B-25 Mitchells escorted by over 40 fighters to attack the Tobera airfield. B-24 Liberators, escorted by P-38 Lightnings and navy fighters, attack Vunakanau airfield.

NEW GUINEA: Fifth Air Force sends over 170 B-24 Liberators, A-20 Havocs, and B-25 Mitchells to bomb airfields in the Marienberg, Madang, and Alexishafen areas. P-39 Airacobras attack targets of opportunity near Alexishafen.

February 5

ALEUTIANS: Eleventh Air Force B-24 Liberators and P-38 Lightnings provide air cover for light cruisers and destroyers after they bombard installations at the Kurabu Cape-Musashi Bay areas in the Kurile Islands. Eleventh Air Force and U.S. Navy aircraft also attack installations at Paramushiru and Shimushu.

CBI: In Burma, Tenth Air Force B-24 Liberators bomb the Heho and Aungban airfields. B-25 Mitchells also bomb the Heho, Sagaing, and Myittha airfields.

Fourteenth Air Force B-24 Liberators bomb Bangkok, Thailand. Two B-24s and two B-25 Mitchells attack a convoy near Hong Kong. Aircrews report sinking a gunboat and two cargo ships.

ETO: Eighth Air Force attacks the airfields at Chateauroux/Martinerie, Avord, Chateaudun, Orleans/Bricy, Villacoublay, and Romilly-sur-Seine in France with more than 300 B-17s. More than 100 B-24 Liberators are sent to bomb Meslay airfield. Two B-24s are lost and 34 are damaged. The B-24 crews report five confirmed kills. A total of 42 B-17s are damaged; U.S. casualties are one killed, 15 wounded, and 22 missing. The raids have 92 P-38 Lightnings, 496 Eighth and Ninth Air Force P-47 Thunderbolts, and 46 Ninth Air Force P-51 Mustangs escorting. Fighter pilots report six confirmed kills. Two P-47s are lost and two P-38s and two P-47s are damaged. Two pilots are missing.

During the night, five B-17s drop leaflets during a Carpetbagger mission (support to resistance groups in western Europe) on Ghent, Monceau-sur-Sambre, Antwerp, and Brussels, Belgium.

Ninth Air Force B-26 Marauders attack six V-weapon sites in France.

ITALY: The 2nd and 3rd Battalions, 30th Infantry Regiment, 3rd Infantry Division, repulse a German night attack near Ponte Rotto. Although the enemy captures Ponte Rotto, the Americans stabilize the line by a counterattack with tanks and infantry. The Germans begin bombarding the beachhead with 372 artillery pieces, including monster 170 millimeter guns at Colli Laziali and 210 and 240 millimeter railroad guns. A U.S. Navy cruiser and three destroyers return fire in an attempt to knock out some of the artillery.

Twelfth Air Force B-25 Mitchells bomb the Terni marshaling yard. A-20 Havocs attack the Lanuvio and Piedimonte areas. Twelfth Air Force P-40s and A-36 Intruder (Apache) fighter-bombers attack German positions at Cisterna, Vetralla, and Velletri and attack motor transport around Rome.

SOUTHWEST PACIFIC AREA: U.S. submarine *Flasher* torpedoes and sinks a Japanese cargo ship off Mindoro in the Philippines. U.S. submarine *Narwhal* delivers supplies and evacuates personnel from Panay.

CENTRAL PACIFIC: Seventh Air Force P-40s from Makin Island attack the oil storage area and radio facilities on Jaluit Atoll. P-39 Airacobras strafe the airfield on Mille Atoll.

NEW BRITAIN: The Japanese stubbornly resist the Americans on Arawe, but report they are running short on food and ammunition. Thirteenth Air Force P-40s support navy fighters in covering a strike by more than 60 SBD Dauntless dive-bombers on Lakunai. Soon after the first strike, 13 B-24 Liberators with P-38 and navy fighter escort follow up with another attack.

Fifth Air Force sends 48 B-24 Liberators to bomb Hoskins airfield and Gasmata Island.

NEW GUINEA: Fifth Air Force B-25 Mitchells and A-20 Havocs attack the Hansa Bay area.

February 6

CBI: Fourteenth Air Force sends six B-25 Mitchells to bomb bridges and trains at Anxuan, Tien An, Phong Loc, and Dong Hoi, French Indochina.

ATLANTIC: A U.S. Navy PB4Y-1 Privateer sinks German submarine *U-177* west of Ascension Island.

ETO: Eighth Air Force targets the Romilly-sur-Seine depot and the Nancy/Essay and Dijon/Longvic airfields, but most of the over 400 B-17s sent abort or attack other targets. Over 100 B-24 Liberators are dispatched to the St. Pol/Siracourt V-weapon site, but nearly all miss the target. Four B-17s are lost and 44 B-17s and eight B-24 Liberators are damaged. Aircrews report three confirmed kills. U.S. casualties are seven killed, three wounded, and 43 missing. The mission is supported by 85 P-38 Lightnings, 506 Eighth and Ninth Air Force P-47 Thunderbolts, and 47 Ninth Air Force P-51 Mustangs. Fighter pilots report 11 confirmed kills and two probables and report two additional aircraft destroyed on the ground. Three P-38 Lightnings and one P-47 are lost; two P-38s and three P-47s are damaged. Two pilots are wounded and four are missing.

Ninth Air Force sends over 100 B-26 Marauders to bomb V-weapon sites, airfields, and a factory in France.

During the night, in support of a Carpetbagger mission over Belgium, six B-17s drop leaflet bundles over Brussels, Antwerp, Ghent, Liege, and Monceau-sur-Sambre.

ITALY: The U.S. 88th Infantry Division arrives in Italy and begins combat training.

Twelfth Air Force P-40s bomb Cisterna, Santa Lucia (near Campoleone), Cori, and Atina. A-36 Intruder (Apache) fighter-bombers attack San Stefano al Mare, Cisterna, Frascati, and Albano Laziale, as well as vehicles, railroad cars, and targets of opportunity near Rome.

CENTRAL PACIFIC: Operation Flintlock. Marine aircraft begin landing on Roi Island airfield, named Dyess airfield, after a winner of the Medal of Honor. The Roi-Namur battle costs the 4th Marine Division 313 marines killed and 502 wounded. Japanese casualties are 3,563 dead, the majority killed during the opening air and naval bombardment.

Seventh Air Force B-24 Liberators from Tarawa bomb Maloelap and Wotje Atolls. A-24 Banshees and P-40s from Makin Island attack Mille Atoll, and P-39 Airacobras from Tarawa attack Jaluit Atoll.

NEW BRITAIN: Thirteenth Air Force sends 32 B-25 Mitchells escorted by army and navy fighters to bomb Lakunai airfield. Soon afterward another attack by 19 B-24 Liberators is conducted, escorted by nearly 50 Allied fighters. Fighter pilots report 16 Japanese aircraft shot down. Lakunai airfield has been rendered unserviceable.

NEW GUINEA: Fifth Air Force B-25 Mitchells and B-24 Liberators bomb Bunabun Harbor, Madang, and other targets. P-39 Airacobras attack and sink barges near Nubia. Fifth Air Force A-20 Havocs and P-40s sink two Japanese ships and damage another one off Wewak.

February 7

CBI: Fourteenth Air Force B-25 Mitchells damage the powerplant at Thanh Hoa, strafe nearby barracks, and attack the radio station at Vinh in French Indochina.

ITALY: At Anzio, German attacks push the British off Buonripso Ridge and head for Carroceto and the collection of buildings known as the Factory. The 3rd Battalion of the 504th Parachute Infantry moves to Carroceto and counterattacks to support the line. The 3rd Infantry Division conducts company-sized attacks near Ponte Rotto.

German aircraft bomb the Anzio beachhead day and night, targeting supplies, harbor facilities, shipping, and troop concentrations. The area near the evacuation hospital on the beachhead is bombed and shelled so often that the men at Anzio refer to it as "Hell's Half Acre." Allied antiaircraft fire accounts for seven enemy aircraft, while Allied fighters report 16 enemy aircraft destroyed.

Twelfth Air Force B-26 Marauders bomb the bridge approach near Manziana. B-25 Mitchells bomb the Viterbo marshaling yard and the town of Cisterna. A-20 Havocs attack Piedimonte and the road junction and railway station at Campoleone. A-36 Intruder (Apache) fighter-bombers attack Pontecorvo and artillery positions. P-40s attack an observation tower at Littoria, a railroad gun, the Sezze railyards, and German positions at Cisterna.

SOUTHWEST PACIFIC AREA: U.S. submarine *Narwhal* delivers supplies and evacuates personnel from Negros in the Philippines.

CENTRAL PACIFIC: Kwajalein Atoll is declared secured. U.S. casualties are nearly 1,000. About 500 Japanese are killed and 100 are taken prisoner. Operation Catchpole, the attack on Eniwetok, is moved up to mid-February.

Seventh Air Force B-25 Mitchells from Tarawa and Abemama Island bomb Wotje and Maloelap Atolls. P-40s from Makin Island attack storage area on Jaluit Atoll.

NEW BRITAIN: Thirteenth Air Force P-40s and navy fighters support an SBD Dauntless dive-bomber attack on Tobera. The airfield is reported unserviceable and several aircraft and gun positions are destroyed. Aircrews report 11 enemy aircraft shot down. B-24 Liberators, escorted by P-38 Lightnings and navy fighters, bomb Vunakanau airfield.

Fifth Air Force P-39 Airacobras fly strafing sweeps over the island.

February 8

CBI: General Headquarters in India reports that a major Japanese offensive is very probable. General Joseph Stilwell directs planning for a campaign to capture the key transportation hub at Myitkyina, an essential part of the Japanese defense of Burma. Myitkyina's capture is essential as part of the American goal of opening a land supply route to China. He intends to use two Chinese divisions, the 38th and the 22nd, and the U.S. 5307th Composite Unit (Provisional), also known as Merrill's Marauders, to attack through the Hukawng Valley. The Chinese divisions will fix Japanese forces with a frontal attack while the Marauders flank the enemy's defensive positions and force them to retreat to avoid being trapped. British unconventional war specialist general Orde Wingate's deep penetration raiding force, known as the Chindits, will operate south of Myitkyina and act as a diversion.

ETO: Eighth Air Force attacks V-weapon sites at Siracourt and Watten in France. Of the 127 B-24 Liberators that hit the targets, 41 are damaged and 10 crewmen are wounded. The bombers are escorted by 89 Eighth and Ninth Air Force P-47 Thunderbolts. Using blind-bombing techniques, only 88 of 236 B-17s hit their primary target, the marshaling yards at Frankfurt, Germany. Bomber losses are 13 B-17s and 110 damaged. Aircrews report one confirmed kill. U.S. casualties are 11 killed, four wounded, and 130 missing. The Frankfurt mission has 77 P-38 Lightnings, 435 Eighth and Ninth Air Force P-47 Thunderbolts, and 41 Ninth Air Force P-51 Mustangs flying escort. Fighter pilots report 16 confirmed kills and one probable. Aircraft losses are two P-38s, three P-47 Thunderbolts, and four P-51 Mustangs. Five P-47s are damaged. Nine pilots are reported missing.

Ninth Air Force attacks V-weapon sites in France with over 300 B-26 Marauders in a morning and afternoon attack.

The B-26 Marauders of the 494th Bombardment Squadron (Medium) of the 344th Bombardment Group (Medium) arrive from the United States. The squadron's first mission is scheduled for later in February.

Six Eighth Air Force B-17s drop leaflets in a Carpetbagger mission over Caen, Rouen, Paris, Rennes, and Amiens, France.

ITALY: In the II Corps area, the 133rd Infantry supported by a battalion of tanks, attacks the town of Cassino while the 135th and 168th Infantry of the 34th Infantry Division are stopped at the front slopes of Monte Cassino.

Naval gunfire, ground artillery fire, and dive-bombers all work together in an attempt to suppress enemy artillery fire aimed at the Anzio beachhead. A U.S. destroyer is damaged by shore battery fire off Anzio. Twelfth Air B-25 Mitchells bomb Cisterna and B-26 Marauders bomb the Siena marshaling yard. A-20 Havocs bomb Piedimonte and A-36 Intruder (Apache) fighter-bombers attack gun positions near Ausonia and fly strafing and bombing sweeps against motor transport and gun positions near Cisterna di Latina and Pontecorvo. P-40s attack targets near Roccasecca, Castello, Caprile, Piedimonte, and Aquino. P-47 Thunderbolts bomb Atina.

The 301st Fighter Squadron of the 332nd Fighter Group arrives in Italy from the United States. Equipped with P-39 Airacobras, the squadron will fly its first mission in mid-February.

Second Lieutenant Paul F. Riordan of the 34th Infantry Division leads a platoon against German strongpoints in Cassino, located in a jail house. Second Lieutenant Riordan is able to approach the building in spite of heavy enemy fire. Knowing that the rest of the platoon cannot advance any farther, Riordan attacks the building alone. As he enters the building, he kills two of the enemy before himself being killed. Second Lieutenant Riordan's courage and leadership will be worthy of receiving the Medal of Honor.

PACIFIC: U.S. submarine *Snook* attacks a Japanese convoy off the west coast of Kyushu, Japan, and sinks a transport and damages a cargo ship. *Snook* survives an enemy depth-charge attack.

CENTRAL PACIFIC: Seventh Air Force B-24 Liberators from Makin and Abemama Islands hit Maloelap and Mille Atolls.

NEW GUINEA: Fifth Air Force A-20 Havocs and B-25 Mitchells bomb areas near Alexishafen and Madang. P-39 Airacobras strafe targets of opportunity during sweeps over northeast New Guinea.

February 9

CBI: President Roosevelt requests that Generalissimo Chiang Kai-shek allow a U.S. observer mission to visit the Chinese Communist stronghold in Yenan to gather intelligence on Japanese forces and seek assistance in recovering downed American flyers. Chiang Kai-shek, suspicious of American motives, rejects the request. Chiang has perhaps 500,000 troops in Yenan, all watching the Communists as they conduct a guerrilla campaign against the Japanese. Chiang wants no U.S. contact with Mao Tse-tung (Mao Zedong), the leader of the Chinese Communists.

Tenth Air Force B-25 Mitchells, P-51 Mustangs, P-38 Lightnings, P-40s, and A-36 Intruder (Apache) fighter-bombers carry out 75 attack sorties against Japanese troops, supply points, and roads and bridges.

In China, Fourteenth Air Force P-40s strafe and bomb a barracks and oil storage area at Chefang and areas near Homun and Mangshih. In French Indochina two B-25 Mitchells destroy a radio station near Haiphong.

U.S. submarine *Bonefish* torpedoes and damages a Japanese merchant tanker off French Indochina.

ETO: Ninth Air Force sends 133 B-26 Marauders to bomb V-weapon sites and the marshaling yards at Tergnier in France.

ITALY: At Anzio, the 3rd Battalion, 504th Parachute Infantry counterattacks to support British units holding Carroceto against a strong German assault. The 1st Battalion of the U.S. 1st Armored Division attacks Buonripso Ridge in support of the British 1st Division, while the 3rd Battalion defends the Factory. The 180th Infantry Regiment of the 45th Infantry Division moves into the line to replace a depleted British brigade. After nearly 12 hours of combat, the Germans capture the Factory.

While protecting the right flank of the Anzio beachhead, one company of the 1st Special Service Force conducts an early morning raid on the village of Sessano, nearly wiping out the defenders and holding it for a short time before withdrawing.

Ground artillery, naval gunfire, and air attacks are coordinated against German artillery fire.

Twelfth Air Force B-25 Mitchells, A-20 Havocs, and B-26 Marauders bomb German transportation and troop concentrations near Campoleone. P-40s attack German positions at Cisterna. A-36 Intruder (Apache) fighter-bombers and P-40s attack German forces preparing for a counterattack at the Anzio area, at the villages of Piedimonte and Aquino, and at gun positions near Cassino and Ausonia.

CENTRAL PACIFIC: Seventh Air Force A-24 Banshees from Makin Island and P-40s bomb and strafe oil storage and gun positions on Jaluit Atoll. B-24 Liberators from Tarawa Atoll operate in a continuous cycle, bombing Wotje Atoll and Taroa Island in Maloelap Atoll.

NEW BRITAIN: Moving for 11 days, Lieutenant Colonel Puller's force reaches Gilnit village and occupies the Japanese supply base at Nigol, discovering 34 supply barges, along with weapons, ammunition, and food.

Thirteenth Air Force P-40s and navy fighters support an SBD Dauntless dive-bomber attack on Vunakanau airfield. This attack is followed by 24 B-24 Liberators escorted by navy fighters. B-24 Liberators, with P-38 Lightnings escorting, bomb Tobera airfield.

February 10

CBI: In Thailand, Tenth Air Force sends nine B-24 Liberators to bomb the Ban Mah arsenal at Bangkok and the Don Maung airfield. In Burma, B-24 Liberators bomb

Prome and Akyab. Nine B-25 Mitchells attack Chiradan and Godusara, and 16 P-51 Mustangs strafe a barracks and a road at Chishidu.

In China, Fourteenth Air Force P-40s bomb the supply base and training center at Wanling. Five B-24 Liberators mine the mouth of the Yangtze River. P-40s attack small boats along the river. B-25 Mitchells report two cargo ships sunk near Hainan Island. P-51 Mustangs and P-38 Lightnings strafe boats and aircraft near Chiuchiang.

ETO: Eighth Air Force sends 169 B-17s, escorted by 64 P-38 Lightnings, 357 Eighth and Ninth Air Force P-47 Thunderbolts, and 45 Ninth Air Force P-51 Mustangs, against industrial production at Brunswick, Germany. Of the 141 bombers that hit the target, 29 B-17s are lost and 53 are damaged. Aircrews report 42 confirmed kills and 30 probables. Two crewmen are killed and three are wounded, and 295 are reported as missing. Fighter pilots report 56 confirmed kills and one probable, with two possible aircraft destroyed on the ground. Aircraft losses are five P-38 Lightnings and four P-47 Thunderbolts and one P-38 and one P-51 and six P-47s damaged. One pilot is reported killed, one wounded and nine are missing.

Poor weather conditions limit the 81 B-24 Liberators sent against the Gilze-Rijen airfield in the Netherlands. Only 27 hit the target and four bombers are damaged. Aircrew casualties are 26 killed and 14 wounded. P-47 Thunderbolts escort the bombers and report no losses.

Eighth Air Force B-17s, supporting Carpetbagger missions to resistance groups, drop leaflets over Rennes, Caen, Rouen, and Amiens in France and over Antwerp, Belgium.

The headquarters of the 364th Fighter Group, and 383rd, 384th, and 385th Fighter Squadrons, arrives from the United States. They are equipped with P-38Js, a P-38 Lightning with a modified and improved powerplant. The first mission for the squadrons will be in early March.

Ninth Air Force attacks V-weapon sites, airfields at Poix and Beauvais/Tille, a bridge at Le Crotoy, and a coastal battery in France with 114 B-26 Marauders.

The B-26 Marauders of the 496th Bombardment Squadron (Medium), 344th Bombardment Group (Medium), arrive from the United States. The squadron's first mission is scheduled for late February.

ITALY: At Anzio, tank destroyers of B Company, 894th Tank Destroyer Battalion, and the 3rd Battalion 504th Parachute Infantry cover the withdrawal of British units near Carroceto. Allied artillery and air attacks stop the enemy advance. Most of the British 1st Division is relieved in place by the 180th and 179th Infantry Regiments of the 45th Infantry Division. The 3rd Battalion of the 504th Parachute Infantry along with British infantry units holds a shorter portion of the front line. The 36th Engineer Combat Regiment takes up defenses along the beachhead's left flank.

Fifteenth Air Force B-17s bomb Albano, Laziale, Cisterna, and Cecina while B-24 Liberators bomb Campoleone and Velletri. P-38 Lightnings bomb and strafe the Tivoli, Vicovaro, and Monterotondo areas.

Twelfth Air Force P-40s and A-36 Intruder (Apache) fighter-bombers support the withdrawal in the Carroceto area.

SOUTHWEST PACIFIC AREA: U.S. submarine *Pogy* torpedoes and sinks a Japanese destroyer and cargo ship near Formosa. U.S. submarine *Spearfish* torpedoes and damages a Japanese transport, also near Formosa.

CENTRAL PACIFIC: Aircraft from Navy Task Group 58.4, commanded by Rear Admiral Samuel P. Ginder, bomb Japanese installations on Eniwetok Atoll in preparation for Operation Catchpole.

BOUGAINVILLE: Thirteenth Air Force P-39 Airacobras attack facilities at Bonis and barges in Matchin Bay.

NEW BRITAIN: Thirteenth Air Force P-40s and navy fighters support an SBD Dauntless dive-bomber attack on Vunakanau airfield. A second attack is carried out by B-25 Mitchells. B-24 Liberators supported by P-38 Lightnings and navy fighters bomb Tobera. Aircrews report more than 30 Japanese aircraft shot down.

ADMIRALTIES: Fifth Air Force sends six B-25 Mitchells and a B-24 against Momote airfield on Los Negros Island and jetties at Manus Island.

NEW GUINEA: U.S. forces near Saidor link with the Australians advancing from the Huon Peninsula. This ends the campaign for control of western New Guinea after two years of long and often desperate fighting.

Fifth Air Force sends over 50 B-24 Liberators to bomb the airfield and harbor area at Wewak. A navy PBY Catalina sinks a Japanese fishing boat off Wewak.

U.S. submarine *Hake* attacks a Japanese mine and netlayer escorting a convoy to Manokwari; the Japanese ship is not damaged and drops depth charges.

February 11

CBI: In China, Fourteenth Air Force B-25 Mitchells, escorted by American and Chinese P-40s, bomb the storage area at Kai Tek airfield. The fighter pilots report five Japanese fighters shot down. Japanese aircraft bomb and strafe the Namyung airfield, preventing its use for several days.

U.S. submarine *Gudgeon* torpedoes and sinks a Japanese cargo ship damaged by air attack off Wenchow, China.

ETO: Eighth Air Force B-24 Liberators bomb the Siracourt V-weapon site in France. One bomber is lost and 18 are damaged. One crewman is killed, one wounded, and 10 are missing. The bombers are escorted by 85 Eighth and Ninth Air Force P-47s and 41 P-51 Mustangs. There are no losses to the fighters.

The marshaling yard at Frankfurt, Germany, is hit by 157 B-17s. Bomber losses are five B-17s and 127 damaged; they were escorted by 82 P-38 Lightnings, 486 Eighth and Ninth Air Force P-47 Thunderbolts, and 38 Ninth Air Force P-51 Mustangs. Aircrews report three confirmed kills. One crewman is killed, 26 wounded, and 51 are missing. Fighter pilots report 30 confirmed kills and two probables, with another seven destroyed on the ground. Aircraft losses are eight P-38 Lightnings, four P-47s, and two P-51s. Six P-47 Thunderbolts, two P-38s, and one P-51 are damaged. U.S. casualties are 14 pilots missing.

During the night five B-17s drop leaflets on Ghent, Brussels, and Antwerp in Belgium.

Ninth Air Force receives the B-26 Marauders of the 495th and 497th Bombardment Squadrons (Medium), 344th Bombardment Group (Medium), from the United States. The squadrons' first mission is scheduled for late February.

ITALY: At Anzio, the 1st Battalion, 179th Infantry Regiment of the 45th Infantry Division, supported by tanks from the 191st Tank Battalion, attempts to retake the Factory, the key position on the Albano Road and the main avenue of advance into the Anzio beachhead. Although reaching the outskirts, the infantrymen are unable to hold their gains and are driven back by German counterattacks.

Fifteenth Air Force receives Headquarters, 460th Bombardment Group (Heavy), and 760th, 761st, 762nd, and 763rd Bombardment Squadrons (Heavy) from the United States. Equipped with B-24 Liberators, the squadrons will fly their first mission in mid-March.

NEW BRITAIN: Thirteenth Air Force B-25 Mitchells, escorted by navy fighters, bomb Vunakanau airfield. B-24 Liberators with P-38 Lightnings and navy fighters bomb Tobera airfield.

NEW IRELAND: Fifth Air Force B-24 Liberators escorted by P-38 Lightnings bomb Kavieng airfield, hitting aircraft preparing to launch.

February 12

CBI: Tenth Air Force P-51 Mustangs and A-36 Intruder (Apache) fighter-bombers attack Japanese camps at Walawbum and Padaw and supply points near Chishidu. P-51 Mustangs and B-25 Mitchells attack camps between Tsumhpawng Ga and Walawbum, a supply area near Kamaing, and a convoy on the Myitkyina-Sumprabum road.

The 59th Fighter Squadron, 33rd Fighter Group, arrives at Karachi, India, after being redeployed from Italy. The squadron will receive P-47Ds, a modification of the Thunderbolt with improved cockpit armor, additional fuel capacity, and structural strengthening.

In French Indochina, Fourteenth Air Force P-40s attack a barracks at Vinh and the Dong Cuong airfield, railroad yards at Cam Duong, and sampans at Phu Tho. B-25 Mitchells report sinking two trawlers in the Gulf of Tonkin while attacking targets of opportunity near Haiphong.

In China, 24 American aircraft (P-38 Lightnings, P-51 Mustangs, and P-40s) intercept 25 Japanese fighters near Suichwan. In the resulting dogfight, six Japanese aircraft are reported shot down and six are reported as probable kills. Two P-38 Lightnings are lost. One pilot is killed and the other parachutes safely and is returned to friendly lines.

ATLANTIC: The CCS sends a directive to General Eisenhower, Supreme Commander Allied Expeditionary Force, with the mission statement for Overlord. *"You will enter the continent of Europe, and in conjunction with other United Nations, undertake operations aimed at the heart of Germany and the destruction of her armed forces."*

ETO: Ninth Air Force receives the headquarters of the 370th Fighter Group and the 401st, 402nd, and 485th Fighter Squadrons from the United States. The squadrons will transition to P-38 Lightnings and fly their first missions in May.

ITALY: At Anzio, the 1st Battalion, 179th Infantry Regiment of the 45th Infantry Division, supported by tanks from the 191st Tank Battalion, again attempts to retake the Factory. Storming into the collection of battered buildings, the battalion cannot hold what it has seized. German counterattacks force the Americans out. One company of the battalion has been reduced to three officers and 40 men. With control of Buonriposo Ridge, Carroceto, and the Factory, the Germans can threaten the entire Anzio beachhead. The German Fourteenth Army has nearly 120,000 troops available for an offensive.

Fifteenth Air Force B-17s and B-24 Liberators bomb German troop concentrations and highways near Cecina. Headquarters of the 459th Bombardment Group (Heavy) and 756th Bombardment Squadron (Heavy) arrive from the United States equipped with B-24 Liberators. The squadron's first mission will be in March.

Twelfth Air Force B-25 Mitchells attack gun positions at Campoleone and B-26 Marauders bomb Cecina. A-36 Intruder (Apache) fighter-bombers attack troops and gun positions near Roccasecca, and the towns of Fondi and Lanuvio. P-40s attack Sezze, Cori, and Atina.

PACIFIC: U.S. submarine *Tambor* torpedoes and sinks a Japanese merchant tanker in the East China Sea.

CENTRAL PACIFIC: Seventh Air Force B-25 Mitchells from Tarawa and Abemama Island bomb Wotje and Maloelap Atolls. A-24 Banshees and P-39 Airacobras from Makin Island bomb and strafe Mille Atoll.

Japanese flying boats bomb and destroy logistics storage areas on Roi Island and damage two LCTs (landing craft tank)

NEW BRITAIN: The 1st Marines dispatch a company to land on Rooke Island to locate and destroy Japanese forces. The island, off the western tip of New Britain, is unoccupied.

Thirteenth Air Force B-25 Mitchells, with navy fighters, bomb Tobera airfield. B-24 Liberators, escorted by P-39 Airacobras and navy fighters, attack Vunakanau airfield. P-40s and navy fighters support an SBD Dauntless dive-bomber attack on Lakunai.

NEW GUINEA: Fifth Air Force sends 50 A-20 Havocs to attack Japanese positions near Wewak.

February 13

CBI: Fourteenth Air Force B-25 Mitchells sink a Japanese cargo ship and damage another off Hainan Island.

ATLANTIC: The Combined Chiefs of Staff (CCS) directs changes to targets for the Combined Bomber Offensive (CBO) Plan. The number of targets is reduced and revised to account for relocation of vital industries. Destruction of major lines of communication and reducing the capability of the German Luftwaffe become high priorities in preparation for Overlord.

ETO: Eighth Air Force sends 277 B-17s and 192 B-24 Liberators against V-weapon sites in France. Of the 266 B-17s and 138 B-24s that hit the targets, four B-17s are lost and 75 damaged. The B-24s have 59 damaged. Aircrews report one probable kill. Aircrew losses are seven killed, 23 wounded, and 24 missing. The bombers are escorted by 189 P-47 Thunderbolts and 43 P-51 Mustangs. The pilots report six confirmed kills and one probable as well as four others possibly destroyed on the ground. One P-51 is lost and four P-47s are damaged. There are no casualties among the pilots.

Ninth Air Force sends 182 B-26 Marauders to attack V-weapon sites in France.
ITALY: Fifteenth Air Force receives the B-24 Liberators of the 757th and 758th Bombardment Squadrons (Heavy), of the 459th Bombardment Group (Heavy), from the United States. The squadrons will fly their first missions in March.

Twelfth Air Force B-25 Mitchells and A-20 Havocs support Allied forces at Anzio. P-40s and A-36 Intruder (Apache) fighter-bombers attack German troop concentrations, a railway tunnel, strongpoints, vehicles, supplies, and gun positions.
SOUTHWEST PACIFIC AREA: MacArthur's headquarters directs operations to control the Bismarck Archipelago, capturing Kavieng and the Admiralty Islands. Alamo Force is directed to seize the Seeadler harbor area on the Admiralties and establish naval and air facilities. D-day for Operation Brewer is set for April 1.

U.S. submarine *Robalo* attacks but fails to damage two cargo ships off Luzon in the Philippines.
CENTRAL PACIFIC: U.S. submarine *Permit* is damaged by depth charges far southwest of Truk, but remains on patrol.
NEW BRITAIN: Thirteenth Air Force B-25 Mitchells bomb Tobera airfield and 23 B-24 Liberators bomb Lakunai airfield. P-40s and U.S. Navy fighters escort navy SBD Dauntless and TBF Avenger torpedo-bombers attacking Vunakanau.
NEW IRELAND: Fifth Air Force sends 35 B-24 Liberators, with 32 P-38 Lightnings escorting, to bomb the Kavieng airfield. After the attack, the airfield is reported unserviceable.
ADMIRALTIES: Fifth Air Force B-25 Mitchells bomb Momote airfield on Los Negros Island.
NEW GUINEA: Fifth Air Force sends 24 A-20 Havocs to attack Japanese positions at Aitape. A-20s sink a Japanese cargo ship off Aitape.

February 14
CBI: Tenth Air Force P-51 Mustangs and A-36 Intruder (Apache) fighter-bombers carry out a number of attacks on Japanese targets in Burma, including logistics bases, transportation routes, convoys, and troop concentrations.
ETO: General Dwight D. Eisenhower establishes Supreme Headquarters Allied Expeditionary Force (SHAEF). Chief of Staff, Supreme Allied Commander (COSSAC) is now incorporated into SHAEF.
ITALY: The 133rd Infantry fails to capture the town of Cassino. The 34th Infantry Division is too weakened by casualties to make any further attacks. Lieutenant General Sir Bernard C. Freyberg's New Zealand Corps arrives at Cassino. Towering above the town is Monte Cassino and its Benedictine abbey founded in A.D. 524. General Clark authorizes Freyberg to fire on the ancient monastery if he believes it necessary, although Clark and the II Corps commander, Major General Geoffrey Keyes, both believe that bombing the monastery is unnecessary.

Fifteenth Air Force B-17s escorted by P-47 Thunderbolts attack the Modena, Brescia, and Verona marshaling yards and several targets of opportunity. Aircrews report 20 enemy fighters shot down. B-24 Liberators bomb the Mantua, Verona, Massa Lombarda, Fenara, and Arezzo marshaling yards and targets of opportunity. The B-24-equipped 759th Bombardment Squadron (Heavy), 459th Bombardment

Group (Heavy), arrives from the United States. The squadron will fly its first mission in early March.

Twelfth Air Force A-36 Intruder (Apache) fighter-bombers attack artillery in the Pontecorvo area, the railway yards at Civita Castellana and Frosinone, and motor transport. P-40s bomb and strafe troop concentrations at Anzio and attack tanks, motor transport, and guns near Cisterna, Cori, and Rocca di Papa. P-47 Thunderbolts attack Colleferro and Valmontone.

The Twelfth Air Force transfers the 12th Bombardment Group (Medium) and 33rd and 81st Fighter Groups to the China-Burma-India Theater and transfers the 52nd Troop Carrier Wing to the European Theater of Operations (ETO).

SOUTHWEST PACIFIC AREA: U.S. submarine *Flasher* torpedoes and sinks a Japanese cargo ship and a tanker off Luzon in the Philippines.

PACIFIC: U.S. submarine *Snook* torpedoes and sinks a Japanese cargo ship near Tsushima, Japan.

CENTRAL PACIFIC: Seventh Air Force sends over 40 B-24 Liberators based at Makin Island and Tarawa to attack Ponape Island in the Carolines.

BOUGAINVILLE: Thirteenth Air Force sends 19 B-25 Mitchells to attack Kara and Kahili, while P-39 Airacobras attack the bridges on the Puriata River.

A Japanese dive-bomber damages a U.S. light cruiser supporting the landing on Green Island.

NEW BRITAIN: Thirteenth Air Force B-25 Mitchells bomb Vunakanau airfield while 28 B-24 Liberators bomb Rapopo airfield. P-40s and navy fighters escort a navy SBD Dauntless dive-bomber attack on Tobera; four B-25 Mitchells later bomb the same target.

NEW IRELAND: Fifth Air Force B-24 Liberators bomb the Kavieng and Panapai airfields.

ADMIRALTIES: Fifth Air Force sends over 80 B-25 Mitchells to attack Momote airfield on Los Negros Island.

NEW GUINEA: Fifth Air Force A-20 Havocs, with P-40 support, bomb and strafe Dagua airfield. Pilots report destroying over 20 Japanese aircraft on the ground.

February 15

CBI: In Burma, Tenth Air Force P-40s, P-51 Mustangs, and A-36 Intruder (Apache) fighter-bombers attack targets of opportunity along the Hukawng-Walawbum road and supply points near Kamaing.

Fourteenth Air Force B-25 Mitchells attack targets in French Indochina, damaging a steamer at Haiphong harbor and attacking rail facilities.

Mines laid by Fourteenth Air Force B-24 Liberators on February 10 sink a Japanese cargo ship at the entrance to the Yangtze River.

ETO: Eighth Air Force sends 54 B-24 Liberators to bomb V-weapon sites in France. Although 29 bombers are damaged there are no casualties.

Ninth Air Force sends B-26 Marauders to bomb V-weapon sites in France in a morning and afternoon attack.

ITALY: At Anzio, the 45th Infantry Division takes control of the former British 1st Division area. Reinforcements arrive in the form of a British infantry brigade, artillery, and antiaircraft guns. Allied artillery is now firing an average of 20,000 rounds per day. An LCT (landing craft tank) carrying gasoline is destroyed in a German air attack. One cargo ship is damaged.

Fifteenth Air Force sends 100 B-17s to bomb the Benedictine abbey at Monte Cassino. Twelfth Air Force B-26 Marauders and B-25 Mitchells also bomb the abbey.

At Anzio, Twelfth Air Force A-20 Havocs attack motor transport and road networks near Albano and Valmontone. P-40s bomb enemy troop concentrations near Cisterna and logistics bases near Valmontone and Rocca di Papa. A-36 Intruder (Apache) fighter-bombers attack German troops north of Anzio. Offshore, a destroyer escort is damaged by a radio-controlled German bomb dropped from an aircraft, and an LCI (landing craft infantry) is damaged by mine. A freighter is destroyed by a bomb along with the LCT (landing craft tank) alongside.

SOUTHWEST PACIFIC AREA: U.S. submarine *Tinosa* attacks a Japanese convoy east of Mindanao and sinks a cargo ship.

PACIFIC: U.S. submarine *Snook* torpedoes and sinks a Japanese cargo ship off the south coast of Korea. U.S. submarine *Steelhead* torpedoes and damages a Japanese cargo ship off Chichi Jima.

CENTRAL PACIFIC: U.S. submarine *Aspro* torpedoes and sinks Japanese submarine *I-43* off Guam as it transports sailors to Truk.

BOUGAINVILLE: Navy Task Force 31, commanded by Rear Admiral Theodore S. Wilkinson, lands the New Zealand 3rd Division on Green Island. Task Force 38, commanded by Rear Admiral Walden C. Ainsworth, with two light cruisers and five destroyers, and Task Force 39, commanded by Rear Admiral Aaron S. Merrill, with two light cruisers and five destroyers, cover the landing.

NEW GEORGIA: The B-24 Liberators of the 424th Bombardment Squadron (Heavy), 307th Bombardment Group (Heavy), depart from Munda and return to Guadalcanal Island.

NEW BRITAIN: U.S. submarine *Gato* torpedoes and sinks a Japanese guardboat off Rabaul.

NEW IRELAND: Thirteenth Air Force sends 20 B-24 Liberators to attack Borpop airfield. Aircrews report heavy damage.

Fifth Air Force B-24 Liberators, A-20 Havocs, and B-25 Mitchells bomb Kavieng harbor, the town, shipping, and the Panapai airfield. Eight of the P-38 Lightnings escorting the bombers are shot down by antiaircraft fire. A navy PBY Catalina makes five separate take-offs and landings under heavy enemy fire to rescue downed pilots in the water.

February 16

CBI: Tenth Air Force A-36 Intruder (Apache) fighter-bombers and P-51 Mustangs hit supply dumps, troop concentrations, and camps near Myitkyina, Kamaing, Tonkin, and Walawbum. The 118th Tactical Reconnaissance Squadron arrives in India from the United States. The unit, equipped with P-51 Mustangs, is subordinate to Tenth Air Force.

ATLANTIC: The JCS issues an assessment of operations in the Pacific for 1945. U.S. forces in the Pacific have to be in position by early 1945 to support both an air and amphibious attack on Japan. A U.S. approach through the Philippines, as advocated by MacArthur, will not meet the timeline, nor make the best use of U.S. naval power. It appears that Nimitz's Central Pacific advance offers the fastest approach and best uses the U.S. advantage in naval and air power to allow for both strategic bombing and closing off the Japanese lines of supply in the South China Sea.

ITALY: The main German attack on the Anzio beachhead defensive line falls on the 45th Infantry Division, covering the critical left flank on the Albano Road. The 179th and 157th Infantry Regiments hold the road, repulsing the enemy attacks with heavy losses and supported by the fire of 144 guns massed by the 166th Field Artillery Battalion. German diversionary attacks on both flanks are disrupted by heavy and accurate artillery fire.

German artillery fire is also heavy and accurate. German aircraft bomb the beachhead. Allied aircraft support the 45th Infantry Division and heavy bombers attack the main routes into the battle area from Rome.

Twelfth Air Force P-40s attack Monte Cassino abbey and German positions and troops, and attack Fondi and Roccasecca.

A U.S. destroyer is damaged by a German air attack off Anzio.

SOUTHWEST PACIFIC AREA: U.S. submarine *Tinosa* continues to track a Japanese convoy and sinks a cargo ship off Sarangani Island, south of Mindanao Island in the Philippines.

CENTRAL PACIFIC: Seventh Air Force B-24 Liberators from Tarawa bomb Wotje Atoll and Taroa Island in Maloelap Atoll. P-40s from Makin Island attack Jaluit Atoll and A-24 Banshees bomb Mille Atoll.

Navy aircraft from Task Group 58.4, commanded by Rear Admiral Samuel P. Ginder, bomb Eniwetok.

A U.S. destroyer and a minesweeper sink Japanese submarine *RO-40* off Kwajalein. U.S. submarine *Skate* torpedoes and sinks a Japanese light cruiser north of Truk.

NEW BRITAIN: Lieutenant Colonel Puller's force begins to return to friendly lines after eight days of patrolling. His estimate is that the Japanese have not been in the Gilnit area in any size for at least two months.

Thirteenth Air Force B-24 Liberators, with P-38 Lightnings and navy F4U Corsairs flying escort, bomb Vunakanau airfield.

NEW IRELAND: Fifth Air Force B-25 Mitchells attack a Japanese convoy off New Hanover and Kavieng, New Ireland, sinking two submarine chasers and a transport.

February 17

CBI: In French Indochina, Fourteenth Air Force B-25 Mitchells damage a cargo ship in the Gulf of Tonkin and destroy rail targets.

ITALY: At Anzio, German tanks and infantry, supported by enemy aircraft, attack the 179th Infantry Regiment, 45th Infantry Division, in an attempt to break through the Albano Road and rupture the defensive line at Anzio. Desperate fighting takes place as American infantrymen and tanks fall back over two miles. Tanks from the 1st Armored Division, antiaircraft guns, naval gunfire, artillery, fighters, and bombers combine to halt the attack. Air support from 198 fighter-bombers, 176 medium bombers, and 288 heavy bombers is employed in support of the division.

The commander of the 45th Infantry Division, Major General William W. Eagles, orders two battered battalions of the 179th Infantry to make a night attack to regain lost ground. It is a disaster, as fresh German units already in prepared positions easily stop the attack and leave the men in a dangerously exposed position.

Casualties among British generals leads to General Lucian K. Truscott taking command as deputy commander of VI Corps. Brigadier General John W. O'Daniel takes over Truscott's position as commander of the 3rd Infantry Division.

In an effort to stop the German attack on the Allied beachhead at Anzio, Fifteenth Air Force B-17s and B-24 Liberators attack Campoleone and Grottaferrata and supply bases near Campoleone and Rocca di Papa. They also attack troop concentrations near Frascati and logistics bases near Grottaferrata. Twelfth Air Force B-25 Mitchells bomb the Campoleone and Lanuvio area. A-20 Havocs attack logistics sites and troop concentrations in the Anzio area. P-47 Thunderbolts bomb logistics sites near Valmontone, while A-36 Intruder (Apache) fighter-bombers attack Carroceto, a railroad underpass, and a factory north of Anzio. P-40s attack German transportation assets, guns, bridges, and assembly areas near Cisterna, and stations at Campoleone and Carroceto. A-36 Intruder (Apache) fighter-bombers bomb Monte Cassino Abbey.

Over 500 Allied aircraft drop 1,100 tons of bombs in support of VI Corps.

CENTRAL PACIFIC: Operation Hailstone. Navy Task Force 58, commanded by Vice Admiral Raymond A. Spruance and consisting of nine carriers and six battleships, attacks facilities and shipping at Truk. The carrier USS *Intrepid* is damaged during a Japanese air attack with an aerial torpedo. SB2C Helldivers and TBF Avengers sink a Japanese light cruiser, armed merchant cruiser, three cargo ships, a motor torpedo boat, two support vessels, 17 transports, four fleet tankers, an aircraft transport, and two destroyers. Two destroyers, two submarines, an ammunition ship, a seaplane tender, and several other smaller ships are also damaged. Naval gunfire sinks a destroyer and a submarine chaser.

A destroyer sinks Japanese submarine *I-11* near Wotje Atoll.

U.S. submarine *Cero* torpedoes and sinks a Japanese transport between Truk and New Ireland. U.S. submarine *Sargo* attacks a Japanese convoy about 150 miles northeast of Palau and sinks an ammunition ship and damages an oiler.

U.S. submarine *Tang* attacks a Japanese convoy and sinks a cargo ship and merchant tanker in the vicinity of Truk. *Tang* escapes a depth charge attack.

Operation Catchpole. The naval and air bombardment of Parry and Eniwetok Islands begins. Artillery is landed at Aitsu and Rujoru Islands to support the upcoming assaults.

Seventh Air Force B-24 Liberators from Tarawa and Abemama Island bomb Ponape and Kusaie Islands and attack Jaluit Atoll.

NEW BRITAIN: Thirteenth Air Force P-40s and navy fighters support 70 navy SBD Dauntless dive-bombers attacking shipping in Keravia Bay. Aircrews report eight Japanese aircraft shot down. Two navy fighters are shot down.

NEW GUINEA: Navy SBD Dauntless dive-bombers and TBF Avenger torpedo-bombers attack Japanese shipping in Keravia Bay, near Rabaul, sinking a minesweeper, a guardboat, and a cargo ship.

February 18

CBI: The 58th Fighter Squadron of the 33rd Fighter Group arrives at Karachi, India, from Italy. The squadron will be equipped with P-47D Thunderbolts.

Fourteenth Air Force B-25 Mitchells sink a Japanese transport south of Takhow Island, Wenchow, China.

ITALY: At Anzio, the German attack along the Albano Road all but annihilates two battalions of the 179th Infantry Regiment (45th Infantry Division). One company of the 2nd Battalion, 157th Infantry, defending the road is battered by artillery fire and suffers heavy casualties, but holds its position. The 2nd Battalion 180th Infantry is nearly surrounded. Although the Germans are able to advance about half a mile deeper toward the final line of defense at Anzio, small groups of American infantrymen hold their positions and prevent a breakthrough. The defense is aided by the timely concentration of Allied artillery, with over 200 guns massing fire on German troops. Colonel William O. Darby takes command of the 179th Infantry and organizes a last-ditch defense. Supported by 1st Armored Division tanks, the 180th and 179th hold their positions. After a full day of combat, the Germans finally withdraw at dark. The 2nd Battalion 6th Armored Infantry makes contact with isolated elements of the 157th Infantry. Rear echelon troops are brought up to the front line as infantry, and the 45th Infantry Division consolidates its defenses.

CENTRAL PACIFIC: Operation Catchpole. Rear Admiral Harry W. Hill's Navy Task Group 51.11 lands the 22nd Marine Regiment at Engebi Island near Eniwetok preceded by intense artillery fire, naval gunfire, air strikes, and several rocket-firing LCIs. Tanks land with the marines and the island is captured quickly, with over 1,000 Japanese defenders killed. Documents captured on the island indicate that Parry and Eniwetok islands are more strongly defended than originally estimated. Two battalions of the 106th Infantry Regiment, 7th Infantry Division, land at Eniwetok and are slowed by difficult terrain and formidable enemy defensive positions near the beach. The Japanese launch a counterattack with over 400 men, breaking the American line. The enemy attack is stopped after brutal close combat. The decision is made to support the 106th Infantry Regiment's attack on Eniwetok with tanks and the 3rd Battalion of the 22nd Marines. The army and marines fail to coordinate and the marines are left in an exposed position overnight to fight off numerous Japanese attacks alone.

Seventh Air Force P-40s from Makin Island bomb and strafe Jaluit and Mille Atolls.

Operation Hailstone. Vice Admiral Raymond A. Spruance's TF 58 continues to attack facilities and shipping at Truk. Carrier aircraft sink a Japanese destroyer, a motor torpedo boat, and a submarine chaser.

NEW BRITAIN: Lieutenant Colonel Puller's force returns to friendly lines; the 1/5 Marines is left to garrison Agulupella to protect a radar unit.

Thirteenth Air Force B-25 Mitchells and B-24 Liberators bomb Vunakanau airfield, while two B-25 Mitchells and four P-38 Lightnings attack Tobera airfield.

Destroyer Squadron 12 (Captain Rodger W. Simpson) bombards Rabaul, New Britain.

NEW IRELAND: Destroyer Squadron 23, commanded by Captain Arleigh A. Burke, bombards Japanese positions at Kavieng, New Ireland.

February 19

CBI: Tenth Air Force sends A-36 Intruder (Apache) fighter-bombers and P-51 Mustangs and B-25 Mitchells to attack supply and transportation targets in Burma.

Fourteenth Air Force B-24 Liberators, B-25 Mitchells, and P-40s fly sea sweeps over coastal areas from the Formosa Straits to French Indochina. Aircrews report sinking three ships and damaging rail lines and bridges.

ITALY: At Anzio, a weak German attack on the Albano Road is stopped by heavy concentrations of artillery fire, tanks, and the stubborn refusal of the men of the 45th Infantry Division to give up in the face of determined attacks by the enemy.

VI Corps prepares to counterattack as the enemy offensive wears down. Two battalions of the 6th Armored Infantry and a battalion of tanks, along with the 30th Infantry Regiment from the 3rd Infantry Division, attack west to force the advanced elements of the German forces to retreat. The tanks and infantry advance over a mile, capturing over 200 prisoners.

Twelfth Air Force B-25 Mitchells, A-36 Intruder (Apache) fighter-bombers, and P-40s provide continuous air cover, attacking troops, tanks, and transportation targets to stall the German offensive.

U.S. light cruiser USS *Philadelphia* arrives off Anzio to provide gunfire support.

PACIFIC: U.S. submarine *Grayback* torpedoes and sinks a Japanese cargo ship off Formosa, and sinks another cargo ship as it attempts to rescue survivors. U.S. submarine *Jack* attacks a Japanese convoy of six tankers in the South China Sea, sinking four of them.

CENTRAL PACIFIC: Seventh Air Force B-24 Liberators from Tarawa and Makin Island attack Ponape and Kusaie Islands, while B-25 Mitchells from Tarawa hit Wotje Atoll and P-40s from Makin attack Mille Atoll. The 3rd Battalion of the 22nd Marines lands to reinforce and begins advancing inland.

NEW BRITAIN: U.S. bomber aircraft have flown over 1,100 sorties and fighters have flown over 1,500 sorties since February 1. Shipping in the harbor is almost nonexistent and fighters are attacking more Japanese antiaircraft positions. Most of the Japanese aircraft remaining on Rabaul are relocated to Truk to counter the carrier attacks on the island.

Thirteenth Air Force P-40s and navy fighters escort navy SBD Dauntless dive-bombers attacking Lakunai airfield. Fighter pilots report 22 Japanese aircraft shot down. Soon after the navy strike, six B-24 Liberators bomb the airfield. Meanwhile 14 B-24 Liberators, with P-38 Lightnings and navy fighters escorting, attack Tobera airfield.

NEW IRELAND: Fifth Air Force B-25s, A-20 Havocs, and P-38 Lightnings destroy a Japanese convoy off Kavieng, sinking four ships.

NEW GUINEA: U.S. submarine *Cero* torpedoes a Japanese cargo ship headed for Palau off the northwest coast of New Guinea, but causes no damage.

February 20

CBI: Headquarters, 33rd Fighter Group and 60th Fighter Squadron arrives at Karachi, India, from Italy. The squadron will receive P-47D Thunderbolts.

ATLANTIC: The commander of Southeast Asia Command (SEAC), Admiral Lord Louis Mountbatten, offers an option for future offensive operations. SEAC forces will capture a port in China and move to Sumatra in the Netherlands East Indies once Germany has been defeated and additional forces are made available from the ETO. This offensive will begin no earlier than October of 1944. General Joseph Stilwell, the SEAC deputy commander, offers a different option. Discounting any offensive into the Netherlands East Indies, Stilwell advocates an offensive to capture a Chinese port with the resources at hand rather than waiting for support from another theater.

ETO: Big Week. This is the first day of Big Week, a series of missions directed against aircraft production facilities in German cities. Bombers are escorted to the target and back by fighters equipped with drop tanks, which increases their range and allows them to stay with the bombers for longer distances.

Eighth Air Force sends more than 1,000 bombers to attack the Leipzig/Mockau airfield, the Tutow airfield, and aircraft production facilities. Of the 417 B-17s sent against the airfield, 239 hit the primary target. Aircrews report 14 confirmed kills and five probables. Over Tutow airfield 105 of the 314 sent hit the primary target. Aircrews report 15 confirmed kills and 15 probables. Of the 272 B-24 Liberators sent against aircraft production facilities at Brunswick, Wilhelmtor, and Neupetritor, 76 hit the primary target. Aircrews report 36 confirmed kills and 13 probables. The B-17s and B-24s are escorted by 94 P-38 Lightnings, 668 Eighth and Ninth Air Force P-47 Thunderbolts, and 73 Eighth and Ninth Air Force P-51 Mustangs. Fighter pilots report 61 confirmed kills and seven probables. Fighter losses are one P-38, two P-47 Thunderbolts, and one P-51. Six P-47s are damaged. Four pilots are reported missing.

Bomber losses for the first day of Big Week are 21 bombers lost and 239 damaged. Aircrew losses are 20 killed, 27 wounded, and 209 missing.

Sergeant Archibald Mathies is a ball turret gunner in a B-17 of the 510th Bomber Squadron, 351st Bomber Group. When his bomber is attacked by German fighters, the pilot is wounded and the copilot is killed. Mathies and other members of the crew are able to bring the severely damaged bomber back to the airfield. Mathies and the navigator volunteer to land the bomber to save the life of the wounded pilot. As the other crewmen parachute from the aircraft, Sergeant Mathies and the navigator prepare to make a landing. After several attempts, the bomber crashes, killing the three men. Because Sergeant Mathies would not abandon a comrade and displayed exemplary courage in his willingness to risk his life, he will receive the Medal of Honor.

First Lieutenant William R. Lawley, Jr., 364th Bomber Squadron, 305th Bomber Group, is piloting a B-17 when about 20 German fighters attack his bomber. Severely damaged, with an engine on fire, eight crewmen wounded, and the copilot killed, the aircraft falls out of the protective formation. Lieutenant Lawley has suffered facial wounds but brings the bomber out of a steep dive and is able to fly with only his left hand. Blood has covered the instruments and windshield and, as fire spreads in the aircraft, Lawley gives the order for the crew to bail out before the fire reaches the bomb load the aircraft still carries. Lawley hears that two crewmen are badly wounded and unable to exit the aircraft, so he decides to keep the bomber in the air as long as possible and land safely. Lawley battles to keep the bomber aloft, fighting the damaged controls, evading enemy fighters, and putting out flames in a damaged engine. At one point Lawley passes out, but regains consciousness and guides the bomber back to England where he is able to make a successful crash landing at a fighter airfield. For his dedication to duty, his heroism and exceptional flying skill, First Lieutenant Lawley will be awarded the Medal of Honor.

Second Lieutenant Walter E. Truemper is a navigator on a B-17 of the 510th Bomber Squadron, 351st Bomber Group, on a mission over Europe when German fighters attack the bomber and cause severe damage. The copilot is killed, the pilot and radio operator wounded. Truemper and other members of the crew manage to bring the aircraft back to the airfield. The aircraft is too badly damaged to land and the crew is ordered to bail out. Truemper and an engineer reply that the pilot is too badly injured to bail out and that they will attempt to land the plane. The men make two unsuccessful attempts and crash the bomber into a field on the third attempt, killing all aboard. For his exceptional courage and self-sacrifice, Second Lieutenant Truemper will be awarded the Medal of Honor.

ITALY: The German offensive at Anzio stalls after five days of continuous attack to break the Allied defensive line at the Albano Road. The Germans suffer casualties estimated at over 5,300, with 600 prisoners. VI Corps casualties are nearly 4,500 men with 1,300 captured. Another 1,600 are non-battle casualties. The 45th Infantry Division's boundary is reduced to strengthen the line and account for the heavy losses sustained. The 3rd Battalion 180th Infantry of the 45th Infantry Division, supported by tanks of the 1st Armored Regiment, holds off a strong German attack.

Fifteenth Air Force B-24 Liberators attack German defenses. Twelfth Air Force B-25 Mitchells hit logistics sites and assembly areas and A-20 Havocs bomb troops and vehicles near Carroceto. A-36 Intruder (Apache) fighter-bombers and P-40s attack German troop vehicles, strongpoints, the factory, and tanks near Carroceto and bomb strongpoints at Fondi and targets of opportunity around Piedimonte.

German submarine *U-410* torpedoes and sinks *LST-348* (landing ship tank) south of Naples.

PACIFIC: U.S. submarine *Pogy* torpedoes and sinks a Japanese cable layer and a cargo ship off Formosa.

CENTRAL PACIFIC: Operation Catchpole. The 22nd Marines begin clearing the southwest corner of Eniwetok, while the 106th Infantry clears the east end.

Air and naval bombardment of Parry Island begins. Artillery is landed on Japten Island to support the assault on Parry.

Navy aircraft from Task Group 58.1 (Rear Admiral John W. Reeves, Jr.) bomb facilities on Jaluit Atoll.

BOUGAINVILLE: Thirteenth Air Force P-39 Airacobras attack barges off the Island. Pilots report 20 barges sunk.

New Britain: Thirteenth Air Force sends 35 B-25 Mitchells with fighter escort to attack Lakunai airfield

New Guinea: Fifth Air Force sends 38 B-24 Liberators to bomb the Alexishafen-Hansa Bay area. B-24s damage a Japanese cargo vessel northwest of Wewak.

February 21

CBI: Tenth Air Force P-51 Mustangs, A-36 Intruder (Apache) fighter-bombers, and B-25 Mitchells attack bridges, roads, camps, and logistics facilities in Burma.

ETO: Eighth Air Force attacks airfield targets in Germany. A total of 336 B-17s are sent against the Gutersioh, Lippstadt, and Werl airfields, but cloud cover leads 285 of the bombers to hit alternate airfields and marshaling yards. Aircrews report 12 confirmed kills and five probables. Of the 281 B-17s sent against Diepholz and Brunswick airfields, 175 hit the primary targets. Aircrews report two confirmed kills and five probables. Achmer and Handorf airfields are the target of 244 B-24 Liberators, but nearly all hit alternate airfield targets. Aircrews report five confirmed kills and six probables. The mission is escorted by 69 P-38 Lightnings, 542 Eighth and Ninth Air Force P-47 Thunderbolts, and 68 Eighth and Ninth Air Force P-51 Mustangs. The fighter pilots report 33 confirmed kills and five probables. Two P-47s and three P-51s are lost; six fighters are damaged. Five pilots are reported as missing. In the second day of Big Week, 16 bombers are lost and 111 are damaged. Aircrew losses are 24 killed, 20 wounded, and 163 missing.

Atlantic: President Roosevelt and the JCS agree that the British proposal to cancel Anvil, the invasion of southern France, and divert the forces to landings in the Adriatic is not within U.S. interests. The British propose that, instead of Anvil, a landing at Trieste will allow Allied forces to advance through the Ljubljana Gap and reach Budapest and Vienna before the Soviets did. The United States argues that such a plan is logistically unsupportable and that the use of French or American forces in the Balkans would have little effect on the outcome of the war. The Americans also fear that the British plan will antagonize the Soviets and put U.S. forces in the Balkans when the war ends.

Italy: Heavy German artillery fire followed by dive-bombers precedes an attack on the 180th Infantry at Anzio. The Americans are able to stop the enemy with tanks and concentrated artillery fire.

Twelfth Air Force A-20 Havocs attack German troops near Campoleone. P-40s and A-36 Intruder (Apache) fighter-bombers attack troops as well as a fuel storage area, tank and truck assembly areas, and gun positions. The A-36s also bomb and block the road between Itri and Gaeta.

Central Pacific: Operation Catchpole. The combined army-marine force succeeds in clearing Eniwetok Island of Japanese. U.S. losses since the beginning of the attack on the Marshalls are about 1,750 killed and wounded. Japanese casualties are estimated at 8,500 dead. The 3rd Battalion 22nd Marines reembarks in preparation for the attack on Parry.

Seventh Air Force B-24 Liberators from Tarawa and Abemama Island bomb Ponape and Kusaie Islands and Jaluit Atoll. B-25 Mitchells from Abemama bomb

Maloelap Atoll and P-40s from Makin Island attack Mille Atoll. As the campaign for the Marianas progresses, the Seventh Air Force's mission is to neutralize and isolate those islands in the Marianas that will not be occupied by ground forces.

BOUGAINVILLE: Thirteenth Air Force B-24 Liberators bomb Kara airfield while P-39 Airacobras attack buildings, barges, and targets of opportunity.

NEW BRITAIN: Thirteenth Air Force B-24 Liberators bomb Lakunai and Rapopo airfields. P-38 Lightnings and navy fighters support Navy SBD Dauntless dive-bomber strikes on gun positions at Lakunai. Navy SBD Dauntless dive-bombers and TBF Avengers bomb antiaircraft positions and facilities at Rabaul. Pilots report one guardboat sunk.

Fifth Air Force P-39 Airacobras attack Raiven Plantation.

NEW GUINEA: Fifth Air Force A-20 Havocs attack targets in the Madang and the Hansa Bay areas.

Fifth Air Force B-25 Mitchells attack a five-ship convoy headed to Palau off New Hanover in the Bismarck Archipelago, sinking four of the ships.

U.S. submarine *Cero* torpedoes and damages a Japanese cargo ship north of New Guinea.

February 22

CBI: Tenth Air Force sends over 70 aircraft (B-25 Mitchells, P-51 Mustangs, and P-40s) against logistics and transportation targets. A number of bridges are destroyed.

Fourteenth Air Force P-40s strafe the Kengtung airfield and a truck convoy.

U.S. submarine *Ray* lays mines off Saigon, French Indochina.

A Vichy French river gunboat is sunk by mines dropped by Fourteenth Air Force aircraft off the coast of French Indochina near Saigon.

ETO: Eighth Air Force attacks aircraft production facilities and airfields in Germany. A total of 289 B-17s are sent against facilities at Aschersleben, Bernburg, and Halberstadt. Less than 100 hit the primary targets while the others hit secondary targets. Aircrews report 32 confirmed kills and 18 possibles. A mission of 333 B-17s to Schweinfurt is aborted due to weather; 177 B-24 Liberators are recalled and the bombers drop on various towns in the Netherlands, including Arnhem and Nijmegen. Aircrews report two confirmed kills. The missions are escorted by 67 P-38 Lightnings, 535 Eighth and Ninth Air Force P-47 Thunderbolts, and 57 Eighth and Ninth Air Force P-51 Mustangs. The fighter pilots report 59 confirmed kills and seven probables. Eight P-38s and three P-51s are lost and 22 fighters are damaged. Eleven pilots are missing. In the third day of Big Week, 41 bombers are lost and 150 are damaged. Aircrew losses are 35 killed, 30 wounded, and 397 missing.

Ninth Air Force sends nearly 200 B-26 Marauders to bomb Gilze-Rijen airfield in the Netherlands. Only 66 hit the target after bad weather causes most of the bombers to abort the mission.

MEDITERRANEAN: In support of Eighth Air Force's attack, Fifteenth Air Force sends a total of 65 B-17s and 118 B-24 Liberators, escorted by 122 P-38 Lightnings and 63 P-47 Thunderbolts to attack aircraft production facilities at Regensburg, Germany. Over 120 German fighters attack the formations en route to and over the targets.

A total of 19 bombers are lost; one P-47 and one P-38 are lost. B-17s also bomb Zagreb, Yugoslavia, while B-24s bomb Sibenik and the harbor at Zara, also in Yugoslavia. Aircrews report 40 confirmed kills. U.S. losses are 13 bombers and crews.

German submarine *U-969* attacks convoy UGS 31 (United States to Mediterranean, Slow) off the coast of Algeria, damaging two U.S. freighters, which are later beached and salvaged.

ITALY: The New Zealand Corps completes the relief of the 34th Infantry Division at Cassino. General Sir Harold R. L. G. Alexander, Supreme Commander Allied Forces in Italy, decides to use the British Eighth Army to break through the Liri Valley and link with the Allies breaking out of the Anzio beachhead. Clark's Fifth Army will shift to the area bounded by the west coast of the Italian Peninsula and the Liri Valley, about 12 miles wide.

Twelfth Air Force A-20 Havocs attack Campoleone and P-47 Thunderbolts attack German troops, gun positions, and roads in the Carroceto-Roccasecca-Campoleone area. A-36 Intruder (Apache) fighter-bombers attack German guns around Carroceto and Formia. P-40s attack gun positions near Campoleone.

First Lieutenant Jack C. Montgomery commands a rifle company in the 45th Infantry near Padiglione, Italy. As German troops begin establishing a series of positions in front of his unit, First Lieutenant Montgomery attacks the closest position alone with only his M-1 rifle and hand grenades. He quickly overcomes the enemy position, killing eight and capturing four soldiers. After calling for artillery fire, Montgomery then attacks a second position, capturing machine guns and seven German soldiers. Montgomery then clears a house and in the face of enemy fire, moves 32 prisoners to the rear. His inspiring acts of courage and leadership will win him the Medal of Honor.

CENTRAL PACIFIC: Operation Catchpole. The 3rd Battalion 22nd Marines lands on Parry Island near Eniwetok after a naval and air bombardment. The enemy must be cleared out of a network of nearly invisible spider holes, trenches, and bunkers. Japanese soldiers attack marine positions with landmines attached to their legs and waists and are killed.

Seventh Air Force A-24 Banshees and P-40s from Makin Island bomb Mille Atoll. One of the P-40s uses wing-mounted rockets for the first time.

Carrier aircraft from five carriers and seven small carriers in Rear Admiral Marc A. Mitscher's TF 58 bomb Saipan, Tinian, Rota, and Guam, sinking two Japanese transports off Saipan.

U.S. submarine *Gato* torpedoes and sinks a Japanese repair ship off Truk.

U.S. submarine *Tang* attacks a Japanese convoy, sinking a gunboat near Saipan.

NEW BRITAIN: Fifth Air Force sends over 60 B-25 Mitchells and B-24 Liberators to bomb Iboki plantation in support of the marines.

Thirteenth Air Force sends more than 40 B-24 Liberators to bomb Lakunai and Keravat airfields. In another attack, 20 P-40s and navy fighters support over 70 navy SBD Dauntless dive-bombers in an attack on shipping in Keravia Bay.

The B-24 Liberators of the 370th Bombardment Squadron (Heavy), 307th Bombardment Group (Heavy), redeploy from Guadalcanal to Munda.

NEW IRELAND: Captain Arleigh A. Burke's TG 39.4 bombards airstrips, piers, and anchorages at Kavieng. A Japanese minelayer, two cargo ships, and two other vessels are sunk by gunfire off New Ireland. A Japanese auxiliary submarine chaser is sunk by a mine near Kavieng.

Navy SBD Dauntless dive-bombers and TBF Avengers attack shipping at Rabaul, sinking two guardboats, a merchant tanker, and a cargo ship.

NEW GUINEA: Fifth Air Force sends over 30 B-25 Mitchells and P-39 Airacobras to attack the Madang area.

U.S. submarine *Puffer* torpedoes and sinks a Japanese army transport off Borneo.

February 23

CBI: In Burma, Chinese forces capture Yawngbang Ga without meeting any opposition.

MEDITERRANEAN: Fifteenth Air Force sends 102 B-24 Liberators escorted by P-38 Lightnings to attack the Steyr ball bearing factory in Austria. Over 120 German fighters attack the formations and 17 bombers are lost. Aircrews and fighter pilots escorting the mission report at least 30 confirmed kills.

German submarine *U-510* torpedoes and sinks a U.S. tanker in the Gulf of Aden.

ITALY: At Anzio, Major General Lucas is relieved of command of VI Corps and replaced by his deputy commander, Major General Lucian Truscott. General Sir Harold Alexander, commander of the Fifteenth Army Group, is disappointed in Lucas and has General Clark remove him from command.

Twelfth Air Force P-40s attack a gun position near Campoleone and patrol the skies over Anzio.

SOUTHWEST PACIFIC AREA: Reconnaissance by B-25 Mitchells over the Admiralties shows no signs of activity on Los Negros Island or on Momote airfield. Given this information, MacArthur rejects the assessment of his intelligence chief (confirmed from Ultra intercepts) that the Japanese have over 4,000 men on the island and decides to launch an immediate attack. He terms this a reconnaissance in force. If successful, he intends to press the attack; if unsuccessful, he can recall his forces. MacArthur calls his plan "a gamble in which I have everything to win, little to lose."

PACIFIC: U.S. submarine *Plunger* attacks a Japanese convoy and sinks a transport near Chichi Jima. U.S. submarine *Pogy* attacks a Japanese convoy, sinking a cargo ship and damaging a merchant tanker near Okinawa. U.S. submarine *Snook* attacks a Japanese convoy, sinking a transport near Chichi Jima.

CENTRAL PACIFIC: Operation Catchpole. The 22nd Marines report Parry Island is secured. The 3rd Battalion of the 106th Infantry Regiment takes control of the island. American casualties for this operation are 1,096. Japanese losses are 1,000 killed. Brigadier General Thomas E. Watson (USMC), the amphibious commander for the Marshalls operation, is unimpressed by the army's performance, an opinion he is more than willing to share. The rapid and unexpected success of the attack on the Marshalls allows Admiral Nimitz to advance his planning timetable for the scheduled assault on the Mariana Islands by nearly 12 weeks. The formula for success for amphibious assaults has clearly been validated during the Marshalls operation: heavy volumes of concentrated firepower from artillery, air strikes, and naval gunfire followed by an amphibious assault that joins tanks, infantry, demolition, and flamethrower teams working together to destroy Japanese defensive positions and move rapidly inland.

Navy F4F Hellcats, TBF Avengers, and SBD Dauntless dive-bombers from TG 58.2 and TG 58.3 sink a cargo ship off Tinian and another off Saipan. A Japanese gunboat is also sunk. U.S. submarine *Sunfish* and aircraft from the carrier USS *Yorktown* sink a Japanese collier west of Saipan. U.S. submarine *Tang* torpedoes and sinks a Japanese repair ship west of Saipan.

NEW BRITAIN: Thirteenth Air Force B-25 Mitchells, with navy fighter support, bomb Vunakanau and Keravat airfields. P-38 Lightnings, freed from defending bombers against the threat of Japanese aircraft, attack Rabaul for the first time.

NEW GUINEA: Fifth Air Force sends B-24 Liberators and A-20 Havocs to attack the airfield, support facilities, and antiaircraft positions at Wewak.

U.S. submarine *Balao* attacks a Japanese convoy north of Biak and sinks a cargo ship. U.S. submarine *Cod* torpedoes and sinks a Japanese fleet tanker off Halmahera.

February 24

CBI: The U.S. 5307th Composite Unit (Provisional), known as Merrill's Marauders, begins moving from Ningbyen to establish the trail block at Walawbum and conduct raids on Japanese forces in the Hukawng Valley in cooperation with Chinese forces. The unit's total strength is 2,750 men.

In Burma, Tenth Air Force B-24 Liberators bomb the marshaling yard at Mandalay and targets of opportunity at Akyab, Monywa, and Pakokku. P-51 Mustangs, A-36 Intruder (Apache) fighter-bombers, and P-40s attack bridges, radio stations, supply points, and Japanese troops.

Fourteenth Air Force P-40s strafe the airfield at Myitkyina in Burma.

ETO: Eighth Air Force sends 81 B-24 Liberators against V-weapon sites in France. The B-24s are escorted 61 P-47 Thunderbolts and 49 hit the primary targets. Against another V-weapon site, 258 B-17s are sent and 109 hit the primary target. The B-17s are escorted by 81 P-38 Lightnings, 94 P-47 Thunderbolts, and 22 P-51 Mustangs. Pilots report one enemy aircraft destroyed on the ground. One P-38 is damaged. Seven B-17s are lost and 76 bombers are damaged. Aircrew losses are five wounded and 63 missing.

During the night, five B-17s drop leaflets over Amiens, Rennes, Paris, Rouen, and Le Mans.

Ninth Air Force sends 180 B-26 Marauders to attack V-weapon sites in France.

MEDITERRANEAN: The CCS instructs the commander in chief of the Mediterranean Theater to continue operations in Italy, while preparing operational plans to support Overlord with two divisions for an amphibious landing in southern France (Anvil).

Fifteenth Air Force sends 87 B-17s escorted by 87 P-38 Lightnings and 59 P-47 Thunderbolts to attack the aircraft component factory in Steyr, Austria. Over 120 German fighters, some firing rockets, attack the formations. A total of 16 bombers are lost and 18 damaged. Aircrews report nine confirmed kills and seven probables. Three P-38s are lost. Fighter pilots report 26 confirmed kills and five probables.

Navy PBY-5A Catalinas, employing Magnetic Anomaly Detection (MAD) equipment, a PV-1 Patrol Bomber, and a Royal Air Force Catalina bomb German submarine *U-761* in the Straits of Gibraltar. British destroyers rescue 51 survivors. This is the first U-boat detected and destroyed by MAD.

SOUTHWEST PACIFIC AREA: General MacArthur orders Alamo Force to plan for an immediate reconnaissance of Los Negros Island. The 2nd Squadron, 5th Cavalry Regiment, 1st Cavalry Division is tasked with the mission. Brigadier General William Chase is to command the operation, which consists of about a thousand men. MacArthur announces he will personally supervise the landings.

U.S. submarine *Grayback* torpedoes and sinks a Japanese oiler and damages a transport off Formosa.

CENTRAL PACIFIC: U.S. transport planes begin landing on the airfield at Kwajalein.

U.S. submarine *Tang* attacks a Japanese convoy west of Saipan and sinks a cargo ship.

NEW GEORGIA: The B-24 Liberators of the 394th Bombardment Squadron (Heavy), 5th Bombardment Group (Heavy), redeploy from Guadalcanal to Munda.

NEW BRITAIN: Amphibious elements leapfrogging along the northern coast land the 5th Marines near Iboki to locate the Japanese.

On Arawe, the Japanese withdraw, following the order for a general retreat toward Rabaul.

Thirteenth Air Force B-25 Mitchells, with fighter escort, bomb Rabaul. This attack is followed by 12 P-38 Lightnings with bombs, followed by a bombing run by 11 B-24 Liberators. Other B-24s bomb Rapopo.

The P-38 Lightnings of the 80th Fighter Squadron, 8th Fighter Group, redeploy from Dobodura, New Guinea, to Cape Gloucester.

NEW IRELAND: Two U.S. destroyers are damaged by a shore battery on New Ireland.

ADMIRALTIES: Fifth Air Force sends over 50 B-25 Mitchells and B-24 Liberators to bomb Momote airfield on Los Negros Island and Lorengau on Manus Island.

NEW GUINEA: Fifth Air Force B-24 Liberators and A-20 Havocs attack targets around Hansa Bay.

February 25

CBI: The 91st Fighter Squadron, 81st Fighter Group arrives at Karachi, India, from Italy. The squadron will be equipped with P-47D Thunderbolts.

ATLANTIC: President Roosevelt writes to Prime Minister Churchill recommending an all-out attack in upper Burma to build air strength in China that will provide support for the attack against either Formosa or Luzon.

ETO: End of Big Week. Eighth Air Force attacks aircraft production facilities and industrial targets in Germany. Over Augsburg and Stuttgart, 246 of 268 bombers hit the primary targets. Aircrews report eight confirmed kills and four probables. Over Regensburg, 267 of 290 B-17s hit the primary target. Aircrews report 13 confirmed kills and one probable. Over Furth, 172 of 196 B-24 Liberators hit the primary target. Aircrews report two confirmed kills and two probables. The missions are escorted by 73 P-38 Lightnings, 687 Eighth and Ninth Air Force P-47 Thunderbolts, and 139 Eighth and Ninth Air Force P-51 Mustangs. Fighter pilots report 26 confirmed kills and four probables. A P-47 and two P-51s are lost. Eight fighters are damaged. Three pilots are missing. For the final day of Big Week, 31 bombers are lost and 301 are damaged. Aircrew losses are four killed, 26 wounded, and 301 missing.

Ninth Air Force sends 191 B-26 Marauders to bomb Venlo, Saint-Trond, and Cambrai/Epinoy airfields in France as a diversion in support of Big Week bombing missions.

Together the Eighth and Fifteenth Air Force have dropped 10,000 tons of bombs on targets during Big Week. Big Week will have important effects on the preparation for the Normandy landing. First, German fighter squadrons will be forced to redeploy from France to Germany. Second, German fighters will be pulled from the eastern front to protect German cities. Finally, more and more inexperienced German pilots will be forced to fly missions they are not prepared for because of the heavy losses in experienced combat pilots.

The cost for the Americans is high. During the week Eighth Air Force has lost 109 bombers and over 800 are damaged. Crew losses are 83 killed, 103 wounded, and over a thousand missing. A total of 20 fighter pilots are also missing. It is a battle of attrition that the United States Army Air Force is capable of winning.

MEDITERRANEAN: Fifteenth Air Force sends 46 B-17s and 103 B-24 Liberators, escorted by 85 P-38 Lightnings and 40 P-37s, to attack aircraft production facilities at Regensburg, Germany. The Germans respond with over 200 fighters, shooting down 33 bombers and damaging 20 others. Aircrew casualties are three killed, seven wounded, and 110 missing. Aircrews and fighter pilots report 93 confirmed kills and 17 probables.

Other B-17s attack Klagenfurt, Austria, and the docks at Pola, Italy. B-24 Liberators attack Fiume, Italy, and the Graz airfield in Austria, as well as the port area at Zara, Yugoslavia. Over 30 aircraft are lost. Aircrews report 90 confirmed kills.

ITALY: Twelfth Air Force P-40s attack guns and troop concentrations near Campoleone and Carroceto. A-36 Intruder (Apache) fighter-bombers attack Terracina.

SOUTHWEST PACIFIC AREA: U.S. submarine *Hoe* attacks a Japanese convoy, sinking a fleet tanker and damaging another near Davao in the Philippines.

CENTRAL PACIFIC: U.S. submarine *Tang*, continuing its attack on the Japanese convoy engaged previously, sinks a fleet tanker west of Saipan.

NEW BRITAIN: Thirteenth Air Force B-25 Mitchells bomb Rapopo; this attack is followed by 21 B-24 Liberators and 17 P-38 Lightnings attacking the same target.

Destroyer Division 90 (Commander Edmund B. Taylor) bombards Rabaul.

NEW IRELAND: Destroyer Squadron 12 (Captain Rodger W. Simpson) encounters and sinks two cargo ships en route to bombard Kavieng. Two destroyers are damaged by shore batteries during the bombardment.

ADMIRALTIES: Fifth Air Force B-25 Mitchells bomb Lorengau on Manus Island

NEW GUINEA: Fifth Air Force B-25 Mitchells and A-20 Havocs attack targets in the Alexishafen-Madang area.

U.S. submarine *Rasher* torpedoes and sinks two Japanese cargo ships off Bali.

February 26

ALEUTIANS: Eleventh Air Force XI Bomber Command is directed to conduct day and night armed photographic reconnaissance missions in the Kurile Islands whenever weather permits.

CBI: Fourteenth Air Force B-25 Mitchells attack shipping in French Indochina, sinking a Vichy surveying vessel and dredging ship.

ITALY: In the II Corps area, elements of the 88th Infantry Division and French troops relieve units of the 36th Infantry Division at Monte Castellone.

PACIFIC: Japanese aircraft attack U.S. submarine *Grayback* in the East China Sea and cause some damage.

CENTRAL PACIFIC: Seventh Air Force B-25 Mitchells from Tarawa and Abemama Island attack Wotje and Jaluit Atolls. P-40s from Makin Island bomb and strafe targets on Mille Atoll.

The B-24 Liberators of the 27th and 38th Bombardment Squadrons (Heavy), 30th Bombardment Group (Heavy), redeploy from Nanumea Island in the Ellice Islands to Abemama and Makin Islands.

NEW BRITAIN: Thirteenth Air Force P-40s and navy fighters support a navy SBD Dauntless dive-bomber attack on logistics targets at Wunapope. Soon afterward, 22 B-25 Mitchells, with fighter support, attack the same target. This is followed by seven P-38 Lightnings making a follow-on attack.

ADMIRALTIES: Fifth Air Force B-24 Liberators bomb Momote on Los Negros Island.

NEW GUINEA: Fifth Air Force B-24 Liberators bomb Wewak. B-25 Mitchells, along with P-39 Airacobras, attack targets in the Madang-Alexishafen area.

U.S. submarine *Gato* attacks a Japanese convoy and sinks a cargo ship carrying troops northwest of Hollandia.

February 27

CBI: Tenth Air Force P-51 Mustangs and A-36 Intruder (Apache) fighter-bombers and two B-25 Mitchells attack ammunition dumps near the Kamaing-Walawbum road.

In China, Fourteenth Air Force P-40s bomb and heavily damage the railroad bridge at Puchi.

ITALY: The light cruiser USS *Philadelphia* provides naval gunfire support to Allied forces at Anzio.

SOUTHWEST PACIFIC AREA: The Alamo Scouts, an independent reconnaissance unit, land a six-man team on Los Negros to gain firsthand information on Mamote airfield and the status of Japanese forces on the island.

PACIFIC: U.S. submarine *Trout* torpedoes and sinks a Japanese cargo ship east of Formosa, and USS *Grayback* torpedoes and sinks a cargo ship in the East China Sea.

NEW BRITAIN: At Arawe, a company of the 112th Cavalry with two platoons of tanks advances north to locate the enemy and finds the area abandoned.

Thirteenth Air Force sends 21 B-24 Liberators and 24 B-25 Mitchells escorted by 14 P-38 Lightnings to bomb Wunapope. Navy SBD Dauntless dive-bombers, escorted by army P-40s and navy fighters, attack antiaircraft positions at Lakunai.

ADMIRALTIES: Fifth Air Force B-25 Mitchells attack Momote on Los Negros Island and Lorengau on Manus Island.

NEW GUINEA: Fifth Air Force B-24 Liberators escorted by P-40s bomb airfields at Wewak. B-25 Mitchells bomb targets in the Hansa Bay area, and over 30 A-20 Havocs attack Alexishafen.

U.S. submarine *Cod* torpedoes and sinks a Japanese cargo ship near Halmahera.

February 28

CBI: The Marauders arrive at Tanja Ga and are ordered to Walawbum at the southern end of the Hukwang valley to cut the Kamaing road south of Walawbum and threaten the headquarters of the Japanese 18th Army.

Tenth Air Force B-24 Liberators bomb the Mandalay marshaling yard.

Fourteenth Air Force P-40s strafe the Myitkyina airfield.

ETO: Eighth Air Force attacks V-weapon sites in France. Bad weather over the targets minimizes effectiveness. The first target is hit by 49 B-24 Liberators with 61 P-47 Thunderbolts providing escort. One B-24 is damaged. On another raid, B-17s are sent, escorted by 81 P-38 Lightnings, 94 P-47 Thunderbolts, and 22 P-51 Mustangs. Only 109 of the 258 dispatched hit the primary target. Fighter pilots report one probable enemy aircraft destroyed on the ground. Seven B-17s are lost and 75 damaged. Aircrew losses are five wounded and 63 missing.

Ninth Air Force sends 180 B-26 Marauders to attack V-weapon sites, but bad weather also limits the effectiveness of the attack.

PACIFIC: U.S. submarine *Sand Lance* torpedoes and sinks a Japanese transport east of Musashi Wan, off Paramushiru, Kuriles. The submarine later runs aground off Paramushiru.

CENTRAL PACIFIC: Seventh Air Force P-40s from Makin Island bomb the runway and radio installation on Mille Atoll. B-25 Mitchells from Tarawa bomb the airfield on Wotje Atoll.

NEW BRITAIN: Thirteenth Air Force B-25 Mitchells, with fighter escort, bomb Rabaul and P-38 Lightnings make a follow-on attack a few minutes later. Shortly thereafter, 11 B-24 Liberators continue the bombing. P-39 Airacobras attack Monoitu Mission. B-24s also bomb Rapopo, while army P-40s and navy fighters escort SBD Dauntless dive-bombers in an attack on Wunapope.

ADMIRALTIES: Fifth Air Force sends over 50 B-25 Mitchells and B-24 Liberators to bomb Momote airfield on Los Negros Island and Lorengau on Manus Island.

NEW GUINEA: Fifth Air Force B-24 Liberators and A-20 Havocs attacks targets in the Hansa Bay area.

U.S. submarine *Balao* attacks a Japanese convoy and sinks a cargo ship and transport northwest of Manokwari.

February 29

CBI: In China, Fourteenth Air Force sends 23 B-24 Liberators and B-25 Mitchells to attack Yoyang. B-24 aircrews report fires and secondary explosions from supply warehouses. B-25 aircrews report damage to the railroad yards. The bombers are escorted by 16 P-40s.

ETO: Eighth Air Force sends B-17s to attack aircraft production facilities and B-24 Liberators to attack V-weapon sites. Of the 218 B-17s that hit the primary target over Brunswick, Germany, one bomber is lost and 54 are damaged. Aircrew losses are four wounded and 10 missing. Escorting the bombers are 61 P-38 Lightnings, 346 Eighth and Ninth Air Force P-47 Thunderbolts, and 147 Eighth and Ninth Air

Force P-51 Mustangs. The fighter pilots claim only one confirmed kill. Four fighters are lost and two are damaged. The four pilots are reported missing. There are no losses for the 38 B-24 Liberators that hit the primary target. One P-47 from the 79 P-47s escorting the bombers is lost. The pilot is reported as missing.

During the night, five B-17s drop leaflets over Orleans, Lille, Reims, Cambrai, and Chateauroux, France.

Ninth Air Force B-26 Marauders bomb a coastal gun position and the Breck-sur-Mer airfield in France.

ITALY: German forces attack the 3rd Infantry Division's defenses at Anzio in an attempt to crush the center of the Allied line. At Carano, units of the 509th Parachute Infantry, the 30th Infantry, and the 7th Infantry, supported by tanks and artillery, hold the German attack. Allied artillery fires about 66,000 shells during the attack and 247 fighter bombers and 24 light bombers attack German troop and tank concentrations. The 504th Parachute Infantry, the 1st Special Service Force, and the Rangers turn back a diversionary attack on the right flank of the beachhead at the Mussolini Canal.

Twelfth Air Force B-26 Marauders bomb the airfields at Viterbo, while B-25 Mitchells bomb troops and gun positions near Cisterna. P-40s, A-36 Intruder (Apache) fighter-bombers, and A-20 Havocs attack German troop concentrations around the Anzio beachhead. P-40s attack targets at Littoria and a German tank assembly area near Cisterna.

A U.S. LST is damaged by German shore battery fire off Anzio.

PACIFIC: Navy PB4Y-1 Privateers from Apamama, and staging through Kwajalein and Roi, conduct out low-level bombing raid on Wake Island.

During the night U.S. submarine *Rock* makes a surface attack on a three-ship convoy and is damaged by surface gunfire southeast of Okinawa and is forced to terminate her patrol.

CENTRAL PACIFIC: U.S. submarine *Sargo* attacks a Japanese convoy and damages a cargo ship near Palau.

U.S. submarine *Trout* attacks a Japanese convoy headed for Guam, sinking a transport southeast of Okinawa and damaging another transport. USS *Trout* is sunk shortly after the attack.

NEW BRITAIN: Thirteenth Air Force B-25 Mitchells, with navy fighter escort, bomb targets around Rabaul. This attack is followed by P-38 Lightnings attacking the same targets.

Destroyer Division 44 (Commander James R. Pahl) bombards wharf areas and installations at Rabaul.

ADMIRALTIES, LOS NEGROS: Operation Brewer. Rear Admiral William M. Fechteler's Naval Task Group 76.1, with nine destroyers and three high-speed transports, lands the 2nd Squadron 5th Cavalry at Hayne Harbor on Los Negros in the midst of a heavy rainfall and after an air and naval bombardment. Two light cruisers and four destroyers of Task Force 74 bombard Japanese positions on Los Negros and Manus.

The first troops ashore rapidly advance and capture Momote airfield. MacArthur lands on shore, walks up to Lieutenant Marvin J. Henshaw, and pins the Distinguished

Service Cross on him. The Americans pull back off the airfield to a smaller and more defensible perimeter. Later that night the Japanese attack the American positions, threatening to overwhelm the small force.

Fifth Air Force B-24 Liberators and B-25 Mitchells make limited attacks on Japanese positions due to bad weather over the island.

NEW GUINEA: Fifth Air Force B-24 Liberators and A-20 Havocs bomb Wewak and Hollandia.

March 1

ALEUTIANS: Eleventh Air Force's XI Strategic Air Force (Provisional) is activated at Shemya Island. The command's subordinate units are the XI Bomber Command and XI Fighter Command, both located at Near Island.

CBI: One regiment of the Chinese 30th Division leaves Ledo for Shingbwiyang. The 93rd Fighter Squadron, 81st Fighter Group arrives at Karachi, India, from Italy. The squadron will be equipped with P-47D Thunderbolts and will fly its first mission in mid-August. Tenth Air Force P-40s attack the Myitkyina airfield.

In China, Fourteenth Air Force sends 14 B-25 Mitchells and 16 P-40s to attack targets around Nanchang.

ATLANTIC: In the North Atlantic, a U.S. destroyer escort sinks German submarine *U-603* and, in coordination with two destroyers, sinks *U-709* as well.

ETO: The Ninth Air Force's IX Troop Carrier Command establishes a Pathfinder school to provide pre-invasion training to paratroopers in all navigational aids for guiding planes to the drop zones.

The P-47 Thunderbolts of the 390th Fighter Squadron, 366th Fighter Group arrive from the United States. The squadron's first mission will be in mid-March.

ITALY: German attacks against the 7th and 15th Infantry of the 3rd Infantry Division defending the line south of Cisterna at Anzio fail to gain any ground.

Twelfth Air Force P-40s attack gun positions and vehicles.

CENTRAL PACIFIC: Seventh Air Force A-24s and P-40s from Makin Island attack Jaluit and Mille Atolls in the Marshalls. B-25 Mitchells bomb Maloelap Atoll.

BOUGAINVILLE: Thirteenth Air Force B-24 Liberators bomb Kahili and P-39 Airacobras bomb and strafe Monoitu Mission.

ADMIRALTIES, LOS NEGROS: Alamo Force commander Lieutenant General Walter Krueger, anticipating trouble, orders immediate reinforcements from the remainder of the 5th Cavalry to Los Negros.

Fifth Air Force B-24 Liberators and B-25 Mitchells bomb Los Negros Island and Lorengau on Manus Island.

NEW GUINEA: Over 100 army aircraft and Royal Australian Air Force aircraft participate in an attack on Hansa Bay, Madang, Alexishafen, and Wewak.

March 2

CBI: The Chinese 22nd and 38th Divisions attack Japanese forces near Maingkwan. The Marauders begin a flanking movement in an attempt to block the line of retreat at Walawbum. Japanese forces fail to drive the Americans off.

Tenth Air Force P-40s attack a fuel storage area at Myitkyina, artillery at Shingban, and trucks on a road near Walawbum.

ETO: Eighth Air Force sends 327 B-17s and 154 B-24 Liberators against the Frankfurt am Main marshaling yard. The PFF system fails and many of the bombers miss the primary target. A total of 136 bombers hit the primary target. Aircrews report two confirmed kills. Eight B-17s and one B-24 are lost. Aircrew losses are 17 killed, nine wounded, and 91 missing. Fighter escort is provided by 33 P-38 Lightnings, 445 Eighth and Ninth Air Force P-47 Thunderbolts, and 111 P-51 Mustangs. Fighter pilots report 17 confirmed kills and two probables. Three fighters are lost and 10 are damaged. Three pilots are reported as missing.

Over the air depot at Chartres, France, 84 of 106 B-17s hit the primary target, escorted by 89 P-38 Lightnings, 145 Eighth and Ninth Air Force P-47 Thunderbolts, and 47 Ninth Air Force P-51 Mustangs. One bomber is lost and 12 are damaged. Aircrew losses are one wounded and 10 missing. Fighter pilots report two enemy aircraft destroyed on the ground. One P-38 is shot down.

During the night, five B-17s drop leaflets over Caen, Amiens, Rouen, Chartres, and Rennes in France.

Ninth Air Force sends B-26 Marauders to attack V-weapon sites and airfields.

MEDITERRANEAN: Lieutenant General Alexander M. Patch is selected as commander of the Seventh Army, which will conduct Anvil/Dragoon, the invasion of southern France.

The 459th Bombardment Group (Heavy) with B-24 Liberators becomes operational, giving the Fifteenth Air Force 13 heavy bomber groups.

ITALY: Fifteenth Air Force sends 241 B-24 Liberators and 100 B-17s, with 113 P-38 Lightnings and 63 P-47 Thunderbolts, to attack German positions in front of the 3rd Infantry Division at Anzio. The bombing attacks limit the effectiveness of the enemy's attack against the 7th Infantry.

Twelfth Air Force B-26 Marauders attack an assembly area near Carroceto. B-26s and B-25 Mitchells bomb enemy positions near Cisterna. P-40s, A-36 Intruder (Apache) fighter-bombers, and A-20 Havocs attack German troops at Cisterna and Littoria.

SOUTHWEST PACIFIC AREA: U.S. submarine *Narwhal* delivers ammunition and supplies and evacuates personnel on Mindanao in the Philippines.

CENTRAL PACIFIC: Seventh Air Force B-25 Mitchells bomb Maloelap Atoll. B-24s from Makin and Abemama Islands bomb Ponape and Kusaie Islands in the Carolines.

U.S. submarine *Burrfish* attacks a Japanese cargo ship south of Truk, but fails to damage it; the USS *Picuda* follows with a torpedo attack that sinks the cargo ship.

BOUGAINVILLE: Thirteenth Air Force P-39 Airacobras attack Japanese positions at Piano and Monoitu Missions.

The 67th Fighter Squadron, 347th Fighter Group, based in the Russell Islands, redeploys to Bougainville Island. The squadron will transition from P-39 Airacobras to P-38 Lightnings.

NEW BRITAIN: Thirteenth Air Force B-25 Mitchells bomb Rabaul and Rapopo. B-24 Liberators conduct a follow-on attack on Rabaul. Minutes later, 14 P-38 Lightnings follow the bombers with another strike.

NEW IRELAND: Navy SBD Dauntless dive-bombers and TBF Avengers damage a small Japanese cargo vessel near Rabaul.

ADMIRALTIES, LOS NEGROS: The Momote airfield is occupied as 5th Cavalry troopers expand their perimeter. Japanese infiltrators attack during the night. The 40th Seabee Battalion fights as infantry to repel attacks. Additional artillery is also landed.

Fifth Air Force sends more than 60 B-25 Mitchells and A-20 Havocs to attack Japanese positions on the island. The bombers are escorted by P-47 Thunderbolts. The fighter pilots report seven Japanese fighters shot down.

NEW GUINEA: Fifth Air Force B-24 Liberators and P-40s attack targets near Hansa Bay area and around Madang and Alexishafen.

March 3

ALEUTIANS: Eleventh Air Force sends nine B-24 Liberators from Shemya Island to search for enemy shipping and six P-40s search between Shemya and halfway to Attu. Bad weather and dangerous flying conditions limit the missions. Headquarters XI Bomber Command moves from Adak Island to Shemya Island.

CBI: The Marauders block the road to Walawbum. A battalion of troops from the Chinese 65th Regiment attacks Japanese defenses at Maingkwan, supported by tanks of the 1st Provisional Tank Group. Lagang Ga is cleared for a landing strip.

Tenth Air Force P-40s, A-36 Intruder (Apache) fighter-bombers, P-51 Mustangs, and B-25 Mitchells attack logistics and transportation targets.

ATLANTIC: President Roosevelt announces that ships of the Italian fleet will be distributed among the United States, Great Britain, and the Soviet Union.

ETO: Eighth Air Force sends 555 B-17s and 193 B-24 Liberators against industrial targets and aircraft production facilities at Berlin, Erkner, and Oranienburg. Bad weather forces most of the bombers to abort the mission. Eleven bombers are lost. Aircrews report three confirmed kills and one probable. Aircrew losses are five killed, 11 wounded, and 103 missing. The mission is escorted by 89 P-38 Lightnings, 484 Eighth and Ninth Air Force P-47 Thunderbolts, and 130 Eighth and Ninth Air Force P-51 Mustangs. Seven fighters are lost and 15 are damaged. Pilots report eight confirmed kills and one probable. One pilot is wounded and six are reported as missing.

During the night, two B-24s are lost during a Carpetbagger mission.

Ninth Air Force sends 218 B-26 Marauders to bomb airfields and military installations in France.

ITALY: The 3rd Infantry Division begins local counterattacks from the Anzio beachhead. The Germans have lost 3,500 men and 30 tanks in five days of fighting. With its forces used up, the German Fourteenth Army goes on the defensive.

Fifteenth Air Force sends over 200 B-17s and B-24 Liberators with over 50 P-47 Thunderbolts as escort to bomb the marshaling yards at Rome, Littorio, and Tiburtina. B-24s also bomb air facilities at Canino, Viterbo and Fabrica di Roma.

At Anzio, Twelfth Air Force P-40s attack gun positions and A-36 Intruder (Apache) fighter-bombers attack targets between Magliano Romano and Rome.

SOUTHWEST PACIFIC AREA: U.S. submarine *Narwhal* torpedoes and damages a Japanese river gunboat in the Sulu Sea, as it searches for an American submarine.

PACIFIC: Navy Task Force 94, commanded by Rear Admiral Wilder D. Baker, with one light cruiser and eight destroyers, begins a two-day sweep of the Kuriles. Weather conditions force the mission to be cancelled. All TF 94 ships are damaged by heavy weather.

U.S. submarine *Sand Lance* attacks a Japanese convoy and sinks a transport west of Uruppu Island in the Kuriles. The *Sand Lance* later torpedoes and sinks a Soviet cargo ship *Belorussia*, believing it to be a Japanese ship.

CENTRAL PACIFIC: Seventh Air Force B-24 Liberators out of Makin Island bomb Ponape Island. B-25 Mitchells from Tarawa bomb Maloelap Atoll.

NEW BRITAIN: Thirteenth Air Force P-40s and navy fighters support an SBD Dauntless dive-bomber attack on Rabaul. This is followed by 24 B-25 Mitchells and 20 B-24 Liberators attacking the same target.

ADMIRALTIES, LOS NEGROS: The Japanese attack the American perimeter throughout the night. The destroyer U.S. *Mullany* provides point-blank fire support to the infantry. Over 750 Japanese are killed. U.S. casualties are 61 killed.

Fifth Air Force supports the ground forces with 14 A-20 Havocs and B-25 Mitchells attacking enemy positions.

NEW GUINEA: Fifth Air Force B-24 Liberators bomb targets near Hansa Bay and Alexishafen. P-39 Airacobras attack Madang.

U.S. submarine *Rasher* attacks a Japanese convoy in Celebes Sea, sinking an army transport off Halmahera.

March 4

CBI: In Burma, the 3rd and 2nd Battalions of the Marauders complete roadblocks on the Kamaing Road. The Japanese unsuccessfully attack the 3rd Battalion, now in established defensive positions.

In China, Fourteenth Air Force B-25 Mitchells and 23 P-40s (16 of them Chinese) attack Kiungshan airfield. Aircrews report heavy damage. Fighter pilots report 17 Japanese aircraft shot down. Japanese aircraft bomb the airfield at Suichwan and cause major damage. B-25 Mitchells and P-40s attack industrial and transportation targets in French Indochina.

ETO: Eighth Air Force sends over 500 B-17 bombers escorted by 86 P-38 Lightnings, 563 Eighth and Ninth Air Force P-47 Thunderbolts, and 121 Eighth and Ninth Air Force P-51 Mustangs against industrial targets in Berlin. Bad weather prevents about half from hitting the primary targets. Fifteen bombers are lost and 121 damaged. Aircrew losses are three killed, 11 wounded, and 141 missing. Fighter pilots report eight confirmed kills and three probables. U.S. losses are 24 fighters shot down and eight damaged. Two pilots are killed and 22 are missing.

Bad weather aborts a Ninth Air Force mission against airfields in France.

PACIFIC: In the South China Sea, U.S. submarine *Bluefish* attacks a Japanese convoy, sinking an oiler and escaping during a depth-charge attack.

CENTRAL PACIFIC: Seventh Air Force P-40s from Makin Island bomb and strafe runways at Mille Atoll. B-25 Mitchells from Tarawa bomb the airfield at Wotje Atoll.

NEW BRITAIN: Thirteenth Air Force P-40s and navy fighters and dive-bombers attack Rabaul.

ADMIRALTIES, LOS NEGROS: The 2nd Squadron 7th Cavalry arrives on the island after a preparatory bombardment. Fifth Air Force A-20 Havocs and B-25 Mitchells attack Japanese positions.

Navy Task Force 74, commanded by Rear Admiral Victor A. C. Crutchley (RN), with an Australian heavy cruiser, two U.S. light cruisers, and four U.S. destroyers, bombards Japanese shore batteries and positions in the Admiralty Islands.

Sergeant Troy A. McGill leads a squad in G Troop, 5th Cavalry Regiment, 1st Cavalry Division. His men are suddenly attacked near dawn by over 200 Japanese soldiers. McGill, with eight men, holds for only a short time until only one other trooper is still standing. Sergeant McGill orders the man to safety while he continues the fight, firing his rifle until it ceases to function. Without hesitation Sergeant McGill attacks the onrushing Japanese, using his rifle as a club and fighting with great ferocity until he is killed. More than 100 dead enemy soldiers lie around his squad's position. For his heroism and leadership Sergeant McGill will be awarded the Medal of Honor.

NEW GUINEA: Fifth Air Force B-24 Liberators bomb airfields at Wewak. Other B-24s bomb Hollandia and A-20 Havocs bomb targets in the Saidor area.

U.S. submarine *Peto* attacks a Japanese convoy, and sinks a cargo ship off Hollandia. The enemy depth-charge attack is ineffective.

March 5

CBI: The Japanese conduct several unsuccessful attacks on defensive positions of the 2nd Battalion of Merrill's Marauders. To avoid fighting an increasingly stronger enemy force, the 2nd Battalion withdraws to the 3rd Battalion location near the Numpyek River at Wesu Ga.

The Chinese force the Japanese out of Maingkwan, and guerrillas from Detachment 101 ambush Japanese forces as they retreat. Elements of the 1st Provisional Tank Group encounter the headquarters of the Japanese 18th Division.

During the night, Colonel Philip G. Cochran's Air Commando Unit flies Major General Orde C. Wingate's Chindits by glider into an area about 50 miles northeast of Indaw in central Burma to raid Japanese lines of communication. U.S. engineer troops land first to prepare the landing zone, code-named Broadway. Of the 67 gliders launched on the mission, 32 reach Broadway. These gliders land 539 men and nearly 66,000 pounds of supplies.

Tenth Air Force B-25 Mitchells, A-36 Intruder (Apache) fighter-bombers, P-51 Mustangs, and P-40s attack targets in Shingban and Myitkyina.

ETO: Eighth Air Force sends 219 B-24 Liberators, escorted by 34 P-38 Lightnings, 185 P-47 Thunderbolts, and 88 Eighth and Ninth Air Force P-51 Mustangs, to attack a number of airfields in France. Bad weather forces most of the bombers to abort the mission. Aircrews report 14 confirmed kills and two probables. Four B-24s are lost and 23 are damaged. Aircrew losses are one wounded and 35 missing. Fighter pilots report 14 confirmed kills. Five fighters are lost and five are damaged. Two pilots are killed, two are wounded, and five are missing.

During the night, five B-17s drop leaflets over Le Mans, Paris, Orleans, and Reims. A Carpetbagger mission in support of resistance fighters is also flown.

Ninth Air Force sends 217 B-26 Marauders to attack V-weapon sites in France.

ITALY: Twelfth Air Force P-40s attack Pontecorvo and A-36 Intruder (Apache) fighter-bombers attack Formia.

Southwest Pacific Area: U.S. submarine *Narwhal* delivers cargo and evacuates personnel from the Philippines.

U.S. submarine *Rasher,* continuing its pursuit of a Japanese convoy in the Celebes Sea, torpedoes and damages a cargo ship.

Central Pacific: Seventh Air Force P-40s from Makin Island attack the runways and airfield installations at Mille Atoll. B-25 Mitchells bomb Maloelap and Mille Atolls.

New Britain: Thirteenth Air Force sends 22 B-25 Mitchells with navy fighter escort to bomb Simpson Harbor. B-24 Liberators bomb Rabaul and the airfield at Tobera. P-38 Lightnings attack Borpop airfield.

Admiralties, Los Negros: Major General Innis P. Swift, the 1st Cavalry Division commander, lands on the island to lead the final phase of the operation.

Fifth Air Force sends 30 B-24 Liberators to bomb enemy positions on the island.

March 6

CBI: The Marauders meet elements of the Chinese 38th Division. Over the past three days the Marauders have lost eight killed and 36 wounded. Japanese casualties are estimated at 800 killed. The Japanese abandon Walawbum to defend Kamaing, the major logistics and support base for the Fourteenth Army now fighting at Kohima and Imphal. First Lieutenant James L. Tilly and his section of Kachin Rangers ambushes Japanese supply lines.

Tenth Air Force P-40s attack supply sites near Walawbum.

ETO: Eighth Air Force sends 504 B-17s and 226 B-24 Liberators, escorted by 86 P-38 Lightnings, 615 Eighth and Ninth Air Force P-47 Thunderbolts, and 100 Eighth and Ninth Air Force P-51 Mustangs, to attack industrial facilities in the suburbs of Berlin. The bombers hit mostly secondary targets or targets of opportunity. Bomber losses are the highest yet for a single day: 53 B-17s are lost and 298 damaged; 16 B-24s are lost and 55 damaged. Aircrew losses are 17 killed, 31 wounded, and 686 missing. Fighter pilots report 82 confirmed kills in the air, one on the ground, and eight probables. Eleven fighters are lost and nine damaged. Two pilots are wounded and 11 are missing.

During the night, five B-17s drop leaflets over Nantes, Cambrai, Lille, Chateauroux, and Lorient in France. A Carpetbagger mission in support of the resistance fighters is also flown.

Ninth Air Force sends 260 B-26 Marauders to bomb V-weapon sites and airfields in France.

The 93rd and 94th Troop Carrier Squadrons of the 439th Troop Carrier Group and the 510th and 511th Fighter-Bomber Squadrons, 405th Fighter-Bomber Group with P-47 Thunderbolts, arrive in England from the United States.

Mediterranean: Convoy UGS 33 (United States to Mediterranean, Slow) headed to Alexandria, Egypt, hits an Allied minefield off Tunis. One U.S. freighter is sunk and another freighter is heavily damaged.

Italy: Twelfth Air Force P-40s attack German gun positions north of the Anzio beachhead and near Littoria, and bomb Frosinone.

SOUTHWEST PACIFIC AREA: General MacArthur accepts Reno IV, a plan that proposes an offensive along western New Guinea, followed by a strike north to Mindanao in the Philippines. From Mindanao, U.S. forces will be in position to move into the China-Formosa area. A long-range bomber offensive against Japan can be launched from Luzon. With the Reno IV plan, MacArthur is determined not to take a secondary role to the navy and uses the recapture of the Philippines as the focus of the American strategic bombing campaign against Japan rather than the Mariana Islands. He also believes that the recapture of the Philippines is essential to the restoration of American honor.

CENTRAL PACIFIC: Seventh Air Force A-24 Banshees and P-40s from Makin Island attack the airfield on Mille Atoll. B-25 Mitchells from Tarawa bomb the airfield at Wotje Atoll.

U.S. submarine *Nautilus* attacks a Japanese convoy near Saipan and sinks a transport. A Japanese torpedo boat makes an unsuccessful attack on the *Nautilus.*

BOUGAINVILLE: Thirteenth Air Force P-39 Airacobras attack Monoitu Mission.

NEW BRITAIN: The 5th Marines land on the west coast of Willaumez Peninsula and locate a large Japanese force, which is consolidating after the retreat from western New Britain. The 1st and 2nd Battalions of the 5th Marines land and, supported by tanks, move inland. Two tanks are immediately disabled, one by mud and another by mines. Fifth Air Force P-39 Airacobras and P-38 Lightnings from Cape Gloucester airfield strafe and bomb the Cape Hoskins-Talasea area. Japanese mortar attacks on the beachhead kill nine marine artillerymen and wound 39 others.

Thirteenth Air Force B-25 Mitchells with fighter escort bomb Tobera.

NEW IRELAND: Thirteenth Air Force B-24 Liberators and P-38 Lightnings bomb Kavieng and Panapai airfield.

ADMIRALTIES, LOS NEGROS: The 2nd Squadron 7th Cavalry (2/7 Cavalry) attacks north to protect the flank of the 12th Cavalry Regiment, which attacks with artillery, tanks, and engineers attached to capture Salami Plantation and Salami beach. The 12th Cavalry has just landed that morning and is to assist the 2/7 Cavalry in opening Seeadler Harbor to prepare for additional landings.

Fifth Air Force B-25 Mitchells bomb Japanese positions.

A destroyer in TF 74 is damaged by Japanese guns at the mouth of Seeadler Bay.

NEW GUINEA: Fifth Air Force P-39 Airacobras attack Madang,

March 7

CBI: At Walawbum, the Chinese 22nd Division, reinforced by Marauders and supported by tanks from the 1st Provisional Tank Group, breaks the front lines of the Japanese 18th Division. They recapture jeeps, armored cars, and trucks that had been captured from the British at Rangoon in 1942. They also acquire the official seal of the 18th Division. About 2,500 Marauders are still fit for combat.

Tenth Air Force P-51 Mustangs and A-36 Intruder (Apache) fighter-bombers attack targets of opportunity from Walawbum to Shaduzup, and two B-25 Mitchells attack troop concentrations northwest of Shaduzup.

ETO: Ninth Air Force sends 112 B-26 Marauders and 18 A-20 Havocs to attack V-weapon sites, military installations, and targets of opportunity in France.

The headquarters of the 371st Fighter Group and the 404th, 405th, and 406th Fighter Squadrons arrive in England from the United States. The squadrons, equipped with P-47 Thunderbolts, will fly their first mission in mid-April. The headquarters of the 405th Fighter-Bomber Group and 509th Fighter-Bomber Squadron arrive with P-47 Thunderbolts. The squadron's first mission is in mid-April. The headquarters of the 409th Bombardment Group (Light) and the 640th, 641st, and 643rd Bombardment Squadrons (Light) arrive with A-20 Havocs and their first mission will be in mid-April. The Ninth Air Force receives the 422nd Night Fighter Squadron with P-61 Black Widow night fighters. Its first mission is scheduled for early July.

MEDITERRANEAN: Fifteenth Air Force sends B-17s to attack the submarine base at Toulon, France. B-24 Liberators bomb marshaling yards and air depots in Italy. P-47 Thunderbolts and P-38 Lightnings fly escort.

ITALY: Twelfth Air Force P-40s attack enemy positions at Anzio. A-36 Intruder (Apache) fighter-bombers hit transportation targets.

SOUTHWEST PACIFIC AREA: SWPA headquarters notifies Alamo Force to prepare plans to seize Aitape and Hollandia. Aitape is 90 miles west-northwest of Wewak and has an airfield. Hollandia is a major Japanese base located on the coast of north-central New Guinea. General MacArthur is reading the Japanese military codes provided by Ultra. He realizes that Hollandia has few defenses against amphibious attack and the Japanese are anticipating an attack on Madang. In defending against the expected attack on Madang, the Japanese are moving fighter aircraft into Hollandia and preparing to defend Hansa Bay and Wewak. MacArthur plans to bypass these defenses completely and attack the Japanese where they least expect it.

CENTRAL PACIFIC: Seventh Air Force B-24 Liberators from Abemama Island bomb Kusaie Island and Jaluit Atoll. P-40s bomb the airfield at Mille Atoll. B-25 Mitchells bomb antiaircraft positions, storage areas, and barracks on Taroa Island in the Maloelap Atoll.

NEW BRITAIN: The Japanese defend Volupai plantation, especially the trails leading out, as they are the main routes of escape to Rabaul for the Japanese. The 2nd battalion 5th Marines attacks and pushes the enemy back along the trails.

Thirteenth Air Force sends 24 B-25 Mitchells with navy fighters to attack the airfield at Tobera. P-40s bomb and strafe Rabaul.

Fifth Air Force P-38 Lightnings attack targets in the Talasea area.

ADMIRALTIES, LOS NEGROS: The 2nd Squadron 12th Cavalry conducts an amphibious assault from Salami plantation to Papitalai mission. The 5th Cavalry occupies Porlaka.

Fifth Air Force B-24 Liberators and B-25 Mitchells attack Japanese positions.

Task Force 74 continues bombardment of Japanese defensive positions and shore batteries in the Admiralties.

NEW GUINEA: Japanese shore battery sinks a U.S. motor torpedo boat in Hansa Bay, New Guinea.

March 8

CBI: The JCS issues instructions to General Stilwell and Admiral Mountbatten establishing command and control relationships for the B-29 strategic bombing offensive against Japan called Operation Matterhorn. The JCS will be responsible for the direction of the Tenth and Fourteenth Air Forces, determining targets for Matterhorn strikes. Stilwell remains responsible for the defense of the B-29 bases in China, and Admiral Mountbatten for bases in the SEAC area. The targets are Japanese urban industrial areas, shipping, and aircraft production facilities. The oil fields in Sumatra, Netherlands East Indies, are designated as secondary targets.

Tenth Air Force B-24 Liberators mine waters off Thailand in the Gulf of Siam. A cargo ship is sunk.

ETO: Eighth Air Force sends 414 B-17s and 209 B-24 Liberators, escorted by 104 P-38 Lightnings, 613 Eighth and Ninth Air Force P-47 Thunderbolts, and 174 Eighth and Ninth Air Force P-51 Mustangs, to attack a ball bearing plant at Erkner, a suburb of Berlin. Of the 320 B-17s and 150 B-24 Liberators that hit the primary target, 28 B-17s and nine B-24s are lost and one B-17 and two B-24s are damaged. Aircrews report 63 confirmed kills and 17 probables. Aircrew losses are four killed, 14 wounded, and 364 missing. Fighter pilots report 87 confirmed kills and 12 probables in the air as well as eight confirmed kills and four probables on the ground. Eighteen fighters are lost and 23 are damaged. Pilot losses are three killed, two wounded, and 18 missing.

The B-24s of the 786th Bombardment Squadron (Heavy), 466th Bombardment Group (Heavy) arrive in England from the United States. The squadron's first mission is late March.

Ninth Air Force sends over 225 B-26 Marauders to attack Volkel and Soesterberg airfields in the Netherlands. Headquarters 303rd Fighter Wing and the 95th, 97th, and 98th Troop Carrier Squadrons of the 440th Troop Carrier Group arrive in England from the United States. The squadrons are equipped with C-47s.

ITALY: Twelfth Air Force B-25 Mitchells and B-26 Marauders attack transportation targets. P-40 fighter-bombers, A-36 Intruder (Apache) fighter-bombers, and P-47 Thunderbolts attack targets around Rome.

SOUTHWEST PACIFIC AREA: MacArthur submits his Reno IV plan to the JCS. The plan focuses on an attack on Mindanao in November 1944, followed by an attack on Luzon in January 1945.

PACIFIC: In the South China Sea, U.S. submarine *Lapon* attacks a Japanese convoy southeast of Hong Kong and damages a cargo ship.

CENTRAL PACIFIC: Japanese aircraft bomb logistics storage areas on Engebi Island at Eniwetok.

BOUGAINVILLE: A Japanese force of about 19,000 soldiers converges from all over the island to attack the 23,000-yard perimeter of General Oscar W. Griswold's XIV Corps. About 27,000 infantrymen of the Americal Division, commanded by General John R. Hodge, and 37th Infantry Division, commanded by Major General Robert S. Beightler, have established strong defensive positions with mines, bunkers, trenches, and barbed wire. Artillery, air, and naval gunfire support is also available.

The XIV Corps defensive position is anchored on Hill 700 (defended by the 145th Infantry Regiment, 37th Infantry Division) in the center and Hill 260 (defended by the 182nd Infantry Regiment of the Americal Division) on the east side of the crescent-shaped perimeter. During the night the Japanese attack Hill 700, but are stopped.

NEW BRITAIN: As the 1st Battalion 5th Marines struggles forward through thick jungle and muddy ravines, the 2nd Battalion occupies Bitokara Mission after the Japanese abandon the position. The battalion pushes forward and occupies an abandoned airstrip. Patrols run into heavy resistance near Mount Schleuther.

Thirteenth Air Force B-24 Liberators and B-25 Mitchells, along with P-40s and P-39 Airacobras, attack Rabaul.

ADMIRALTIES, LOS NEGROS: The 2nd Squadron 7th Cavalry eliminates the last Japanese stronghold protecting Seeadler Harbor.

Fifth Air Force B-25 Mitchells conduct several low-level strikes supporting the capture of Lombrun plantation.

March 9

CBI: Tenth Air Force B-24 Liberators, P-51 Mustangs, and P-40s attack Japanese supply sites and the road bridge at Kamaing. P-51s, P-40s, and A-36 Intruder (Apache) fighter-bombers support Chinese ground forces at Walawbum and Shaduzup.

In China, Fourteenth Air Force B-25 Mitchells and 24 Chinese P-40s of the Chinese-American Composite Wing (CACW) attack industrial and transportation targets at Shihhweiyao.

ATLANTIC: German submarine *U-255* torpedoes destroyer escort *Leopold* 650 miles west of Scotland. The ship is badly damaged and later scuttled.

ETO: Eighth Air Force sends 361 B-17s and 165 B-24 Liberators against targets in Berlin, escorted by 83 P-38 Lightnings, 572 Eighth and Ninth Air Force P-47 Thunderbolts, and 153 Eighth and Ninth Air Force P-51 Mustangs. Of the 339 B-17s that hit the target, six are lost and one damaged. Of the 150 B-24s that hit secondary targets, two are lost and one damaged. Aircrew losses are 10 killed, 18 wounded, and 63 missing. One fighter is lost and three are damaged. One pilot is killed, one wounded, and one missing.

The B-24s of the 784th, 785th, and 787th Bombardment Squadrons (Heavy), 466th Bombardment Group (Heavy), arrive in England from the United States. The squadrons will fly their first mission in late March.

ITALY: Fifteenth Air Force receives Headquarters, 463rd Bombardment Group (Heavy), from the United States.

Twelfth Air Force B-25 Mitchells bomb a bridge at Montalto di Castro. A-20 Havocs attack a tank repair depot near Tivoli, and P-40s attack German gun positions near Campoleone.

German submarine *U-450* is sunk by a U.S. destroyer off Anzio.

PACIFIC: In the South China Sea, USS *Lapon* continues its attack on the Japanese convoy it encountered previously, sinking a cargo ship that is towing the cargo ship that *Lapon* damaged the previous day.

CENTRAL PACIFIC: Seventh Air Force B-25 Mitchells based on Abemama Island attack Taroa Island, Maloelap Atoll. B-24 Liberators from Tarawa attack Ponape and Kusaie Islands.

BOUGAINVILLE: The Japanese attack Hill 700 again, seizing a key position and making a small penetration in the defensive line. SBD Dauntless dive-bombers and TBF Avengers from the 1st Marine Air Wing support the defense. Despite heavy artillery fire and repeated counterattacks for two days, the Japanese hold the position.

Thirteenth Air Force B-25 Mitchells bomb Japanese installations on the hills beyond Empress Augusta Bay.

NEW BRITAIN: The 1/5 and 2/5 Marines, advancing to the attack, discover the enemy has abandoned Mount Schleuther.

Thirteenth Air Force sends 24 B-25 Mitchells along with over 40 P-39 Airacobras and P-40s to bomb the docks at Simpson Harbor at Rabaul, followed by 19 B-24 Liberators, which bomb Rabaul and the airfields.

ADMIRALTIES, LOS NEGROS: The 2nd Brigade (7th and 8th Cavalry Regiments), 1st Cavalry Division, commanded by Brigadier General Verne Mudge, arrives at Seeadler Harbor on Los Negros. The brigade is ordered to seize Manus Island.

Fifth Air Force B-25 Mitchells bomb Lorengau and other targets on Manus Island.

March 10

CBI: General Joseph Stilwell's Northern Combat Area Command headquarters approves General Merrill's plan to gain control of the Moguang Valley by making a flanking movement south to cut the Kamaing Road. The movement will be supported by two regiments of the Chinese 38th Division. The 1st Battalion of the Marauders and a Chinese regiment will move to Shaduzup; the 2nd and 3rd Battalions will move south of Shaduzup to Inkangahtawng, followed by another Chinese regiment. Meanwhile, the 22nd and 38th Chinese Divisions and elements of the 1st Provisional Tank Group will attack along the main road toward Kamaing.

Tenth Air Force B-24 Liberators and B-25 Mitchells bomb Kamaing. P-40s, P-51 Mustangs, and P-38 Lightnings hit Japanese near Walawbum.

In China, Fourteenth Air Force sends six B-24 Liberators to bomb the docks at Kowloon.

ETO: During the night five Eighth Air Force B-17s drop leaflets over Brussels, Antwerp, Ghent, and Monceau-sur-Sambre, Belgium.

Ninth Air Force receives the B-26 Marauders of the 585th Bombardment Squadron (Medium), 394th Bombardment Group (Medium), from the United States. The squadron's first mission will be in late March. The 96th Troop Carrier Squadron, 440th Troop Carrier Group, with C-47s arrives in England from the United States.

MEDITERRANEAN: German submarine *U-952* torpedoes and sinks a U.S. freighter off Palermo, Sicily. An Italian destroyer, acting as escort, makes no effort to respond to the attack.

ITALY: Twelfth Air Force B-26 Marauders and B-25 Mitchells bomb rail targets. P-40s and A-36 Intruder (Apache) fighter-bombers attack German positions near Littoria and guns and tanks at Cisterna.

CENTRAL PACIFIC: Seventh Air Force A-24s and P-40s from Makin Island and B-25 Mitchells from Tarawa attack airfields, antiaircraft positions, and radio installations at Mille and Wotje Atolls. B-25 Mitchells, operating out of Engebi Island in Eniwetok Atoll, bomb Kusaie Island.

BOUGAINVILLE: The Japanese make an early morning attack on Hill 260, a strongpoint outside of the American Division's main defensive line, occupied by 80 men and divided into two positions, North Knob and South Knob. South Knob is captured in the attack except for six Americans who hold out in a bunker and resist all attempts to finish them off. General Oscar W. Griswold, the XIV Corps commander, orders the 182nd Infantry Regiment,

A portion of Hill 260, where the American Division's 182nd Infantry Regiment fought for nine days against a Japanese attempt to take this position. Company E of the 182nd won a Distinguished Unit Citation for its heroic defense of this ground.

American Division, to hold Hill 260 at all costs. A counterattack fails to drive the Japanese off the hill.

Thirteenth Air Force B-25 Mitchells bomb Japanese positions and P-39 Airacobras attack targets at Kepiai Plantation.

NEW BRITAIN: Thirteenth Air Force B-24 Liberators bomb Rabaul.

ADMIRALTIES: Fifth Air Force sends 11 B-25 Mitchells to bomb Lorengau and targets of opportunity on Manus Island.

NEW GUINEA: U.S. submarine *Bowfin* attacks a Japanese convoy in the Ceram Sea and damages a cargo ship.

March 11

ETO: Eighth Air Force sends 124 B-17s, escorted by 90 P-47 Thunderbolts and 50 P-51 Mustangs, to attack the marshaling yard at Munster, Germany. Of the 120 bombers that hit the primary target, one is lost and 24 are damaged. Ten crewmen are reported missing. Two P-51s are lost and two P-47s are damaged. Two pilots are reported missing.

Another raid by 51 B-24 Liberators, escorted by 40 P-38 Lightnings and 213 P-47 Thunderbolts, on V-weapon sites in France results in 34 bombers hitting the primary target. One bomber is damaged, two P-47s are lost, and three damaged. One pilot is wounded and two are reported as missing.

Headquarters of the 467th Bombardment Group (Heavy) and the 789th, 790th, and 791st Bombardment Squadrons (Heavy) arrive in England from the United States. The B-24-equipped squadrons will fly their first mission in mid-April.

Ninth Air Force sends 61 B-26 Marauders to bomb V-weapon sites in France.

Headquarters for the 53rd Troop Carrier Wing and Headquarters of the 440th Troop Carrier Group arrive from the United States. Headquarters for the 394th Bombardment Group (Medium) and the 484th, 586th, and 587th Bombardment Squadrons (Medium) arrive in England from the United States. The B-26-equipped squadrons will conduct their first mission in late March.

Over 100 B-17s, escorted by P-47 Thunderbolts, bomb the marshaling yard at Padua. B-24 Liberators bomb the marshaling yards at Pontassieve and Prato and the Iesi airfield.

Fifteenth Air Force sends over 100 B-24 Liberators, escorted by P-38 Lightnings, to bomb the harbor at Toulon, France.

B-17s of the 772nd Bombardment Squadron (Heavy), 463rd Bombardment Group (Heavy), arrive in Italy. The squadron's first mission is scheduled for mid-March.

Allied aircraft sink German submarines *U-380* and *U-410* near Toulon, France.

ITALY: Twelfth Air Force P-40s, A-36 Intruder (Apache) fighter-bombers, and P-47 Thunderbolt fighter-bombers attack a logistics depot, industrial sites, supply trains, and railroad facilities.

CENTRAL PACIFIC: Seventh Air Force B-24 Liberators, operating from Kwajalein Atoll, bomb Wake Island.

BOUGAINVILLE: The 2nd Battalion 148th Infantry Regiment (37th Infantry Division) supported by artillery fire attacks to recapture Hill 700, but fails to gain ground.

The Japanese reinforce Hill 260 and press the American defenders to a perimeter around North Knob. A counterattack by the 182nd Infantry of the Americal Division with flamethrowers allows the six trapped Americans to escape but makes no further progress to capture South Knob on Hill 260.

During the night the Japanese attack the 129th Infantry Regiment of the 37th Infantry Division defending positions west of Hill 700. This position is strongly defended and the Japanese make no gains.

Thirteenth Air Force P-40s and B-24 Liberators bomb Japanese positions.

NEW BRITAIN: As the 3/5 Marines land on the Willaumez Peninsula beachhead, patrols seek to locate the retreating Japanese.

Thirteenth Air Force B-24 Liberators and B-25 Mitchells, supported by P-38 Lightnings, bomb Rabaul.

ADMIRALTIES: The 5th Cavalry attacks Hill 260 on Los Negros Island and fails to capture the position.

Fifth Air Force sends 12 B-25 Mitchells to bomb Lorengau on Manus Island.

NEW GUINEA: A-20 Havocs and P-39 Airacobras attack targets in the Madang area. P-47 Thunderbolts attack targets in the Hansa Bay area.

U.S. submarine *Bowfin* torpedoes and sinks a Japanese cargo ship west of Halmahera Island.

March 12

CBI: The 1st Battalion of the Marauders moves south to cut the main road near Shaduzup as the Chinese 22nd and 38th Divisions advance. The Marauders have the Chinese 113th Regiment attached to them. The 2nd Battalion and 3rd Battalion of the Marauders move toward Inkangahtawng. The rest of the 3rd Battalion moves to block Japanese troop movement over the Chindwin River.

Tenth Air Force P-40s, A-36 Intruder (Apache) fighter-bombers, and P-51 Mustangs attack troops and supply sites near Kamaing and bomb the town of Shaduzup.

ATLANTIC: The JCS issues a directive declaring Formosa-China-Luzon to be the operational objectives in the Pacific for 1944, ordering Admiral Nimitz's staff to begin planning for the invasion of Formosa (Operation Causeway), scheduled for the spring of 1945.

The JCS orders offensive operations against Kavieng, New Ireland, cancelled, but allows seizure of the Mussa Islands or Emirau, north of Kavieng, as a substitute. Offensive operations to seize Hollandia in New Guinea are approved as outlined in MacArthur's Reno IV plan. Truk will be bypassed and the Mariana Islands will be captured by June 15, with the Palau Islands following in September. General MacArthur is to prepare plans for an invasion of Mindanao scheduled for November 15. The JCS sets February 15, 1945 as the date for a decision on whether to continue with the conquest of the Philippines by capturing Luzon, or to conduct operations to capture Formosa. The JCS maintains its two-pronged offensive plan, which was first laid out in May 1943, but does not indicate whether the Philippines will be liberated as the main effort (MacArthur's plan) or bypassed in favor of a main effort directed against Formosa (Nimitz's plan).

ETO: Eighth Air Force sends 52 B-24 Liberators against a V-weapon site in France. Of the 46 bombers that hit the primary target, one is lost and 26 are damaged. Only one crewman is wounded.

Eighth Air Force receives the B-24s of the 788th Bombardment Squadron (Heavy), 467th Bombardment Group (Heavy), from the United States. The squadron will fly its first mission in mid-April.

Ninth Air Force receives Headquarters, 474th Fighter Group, and the 428th, 429th, and 430th Fighter Squadrons. The squadrons, equipped with P-38 Lightnings, will fly their first mission in late April.

ITALY: The light cruisers USS *Philadelphia* and USS *Brooklyn* provide gunfire support at Anzio.

PACIFIC: The JCS instructs Admiral Nimitz to plan for offensive operations to occupy the Palau Islands beginning September 8, 1944. The operation is called Stalemate.

U.S. submarine *Flying Fish* torpedoes and sinks a Japanese cargo ship southeast of the Ryukyu Islands.

BOUGAINVILLE: The 148th Infantry Regiment captures Hill 700 after methodically attacking the captured pillboxes on the hill one at a time with grenades, flamethrowers, and bazookas. Over 300 Japanese soldiers are found dead on the hill.

The 182nd Infantry Regiment supported by infantry companies from the 132nd Infantry attacks again to capture South Knob on Hill 260 but is unable to hold the gains made.

During the night the Japanese make another assault against the 129th Infantry Regiment's defensive line west of Hill 700. One small penetration is stopped and an infantry counterattack supported by tanks restores the original line.

NEW BRITAIN: Thirteenth Air Force sends 22 B-25 Mitchells, with navy fighters, to bomb Simpson harbor at Rabaul. This is followed by 18 B-24 Liberators, with navy fighter cover, attacking the Rabaul customs wharf area. This is followed by 64 P-40s, P-38 Lightnings, and P-39 Airacobras bombing the town of Rabaul.

ADMIRALTIES: The 2nd Squadron, 7th Cavalry, supported by naval gunfire and Australian Air Force P-40 aircraft, lands with one tank to clear Hauwei Island, to secure it as an artillery base in support of the attack on Lorengau on Manus Island.

Fifth Air Force sends 12 B-25 Mitchells to bomb Japanese positions and communication at Lorengau.

NEW GUINEA: Fifth Air Force B-24 Liberators, B-25 Mitchells, and A-20 Havocs bomb Wewak.

U.S. submarine *Gato* torpedoes and sinks a Japanese cargo ship north of Manokwari.

March 13

CBI: The 1st Battalion of the Marauders reaches Makuy Bum.

Tenth Air Force sends B-25 Mitchells, P-40s, A-36 Intruder (Apache) fighter-bombers, and P-51 Mustangs to attack targets of opportunity in the Shaduzup area.

Japanese submarine *I-26* torpedoes, then bombards a U.S. collier off the east coast of India.

ATLANTIC: In the North Atlantic west of Ireland, TBF Avengers from escort carrier USS *Bogue,* British B-17s working with a destroyer, a destroyer escort, and a Canadian armed merchant cruiser sink German submarine *U-575.*

ETO: Eighth Air Force sends 127 B-17s and 144 B-24 Liberators, escorted by 213 P-47 Thunderbolts, to bomb V-weapon sites in France, but the mission is cancelled because of poor weather conditions over the target. Two B-17s are lost and 61 damaged; 14 B-24s are damaged. Aircrew losses are six killed, one wounded, and 20 missing. One P-47 is damaged.

During the night, seven B-17s drop leaflets over Reims, Orleans, Paris, Amiens, Rouen, and Chartres.

Ninth Air Force sends 40 B-26 Marauders to attack a V-weapon site in France.

ITALY: Fifteenth Air Force receives the 775th Bombardment Squadron (Heavy), 463rd Bombardment Group (Heavy) from the United States. The B-17-equipped squadron will fly its first mission in mid-March.

Twelfth Air Force B-26 Marauders and B-25 Mitchells bomb marshaling yards and railroad bridges. P-40s attack logistics targets near Velletri and gun positions.

PACIFIC: U.S. submarine *Sand Lance* attacks a Japanese convoy off Honshu, Japan, sinking a light cruiser and a cargo ship. Japanese escort ships drop 105 depth charges, keeping *Sand Lance* at deep submergence for 18½ hours.

U.S. submarine *Tautog* torpedoes and sinks a Japanese cargo ship and a transport west of Rashuwa Island in the Kuriles.

CENTRAL PACIFIC: Seventh Air Force B-25 Mitchells from Engebi Island, Eniwetok Atoll, bomb Kusaie Island. The B-24 Liberators of the 38th Bombardment Squadron (Heavy), 30th Bombardment Group (Heavy), redeploy from Nanumea in the Ellice Islands to Kwajalein Atoll.

BOUGAINVILLE: The 129th Infantry of the 37th Infantry Division, supported by tanks, drives the Japanese back and regains its original positions. The Japanese abandon Hill 700 and the 1st Battalion of the 132nd Infantry fights the Japanese for control of the South Knob of Hill 260.

NEW GEORGIA: The B-24 Liberators of the 31st Bombardment Squadron (Heavy), 7th Bombardment Group (Heavy), Thirteenth Air Force, redeploy from Munda to Guadalcanal.

NEW BRITAIN: Thirteenth Air Force B-24 Liberators and B-25 Mitchells bomb the Rabaul area. P-39 Airacobras, P-40s, and P-38 Lightnings bomb logistics sites in the Wunapope area.

ADMIRALTIES: The 2nd Squadron of the 7th Cavalry, supported by tanks, clears the last enemy resistance on Hauwei Island. Artillery is landed to support the attack on Manus Island.

NEW GUINEA: Fifth Air Force sends over 160 aircraft (B-24 Liberators, B-25 Mitchells, A-20 Havocs, P-47 Thunderbolts, and P-40s) against the Japanese airbase at Wewak. Aircrews report eight Japanese aircraft shot down.

March 14

CBI: In China, 20 Japanese bombers attack Fourteenth Air Force airfields at Hengyang and Suichwan.

ITALY: Twelfth Air Force B-26 Marauders and B-25 Mitchells bomb marshaling yards. P-40s attack German positions at the Anzio beachhead and bomb logistics targets. A-36 Intruder (Apache) fighter-bombers and P-47 Thunderbolts attack rail targets at Ortia.

CENTRAL PACIFIC: Seventh Air Force B-25 Mitchells from Engebi Island, Eniwetok Atoll, bomb Kusaie Island. B-25 Mitchells from Tarawa bomb Wotje Atoll.

NEW BRITAIN: Thirteenth Air Force P-40s and P-39 Airacobras attack Wunapope. B-24 Liberators, with navy fighter cover, bomb Rabaul near Simpson Harbor while B-25 Mitchells, with navy fighter cover, bomb the town of Rabaul.

NEW IRELAND: The 4th Marine Regiment lands on Emirau Island, between Kavieng and the Admiralties. The island becomes a base for PT boats and aircraft.

ADMIRALTIES: On Los Negros Island, the 5th Cavalry captures Hill 260 with the support of the 12th Cavalry and artillery fire and air bombardment.

NEW GUINEA: Fifth Air Force B-24 Liberators, B-25 Mitchells, and A-20 Havocs, supported by Allied fighters, bomb the Japanese airbase at Wewak.

March 15

ETO: Eighth Air Force sends 187 B-17s and 157 B-24 Liberators, escorted by 121 P-38 Lightnings and 467 Eighth and Ninth Air Force P-47 Thunderbolts, against industrial targets at Brunswick, Germany. One B-17 and two B-24 Liberators are lost and 45 bombers are damaged. Aircrew losses are one killed, four wounded, and 30 missing. Fighter pilots report 39 confirmed kills and three probables. Five fighters are lost and six are damaged. Five pilots are missing.

During the night seven B-17s drop leaflets over Rennes, Lille, Reims, Le Mans, Paris, and Chartres.

Ninth Air Force sends 118 B-26 Marauders to attack marshaling yards and airfields in France.

ITALY: Major General Sir Bernard Freyberg gains the approval of the Mediterranean Theater commander in chief, General Sir Henry Maitland Wilson, to attack the monastery on Monte Cassino—against the recommendation of the Fifth Army commander, Lieutenant General Mark Clark. Freyberg plans to blast Monte Cassino and drive Combat Command B of the 1st Armored Division through on Route 6. Over Monte Cassino, Fifteenth Air Force and Twelfth Air Force bombers attack in waves every 15 minutes. In between the waves, artillery concentrations hit the mountain. A total of 72 B-25 Mitchells, 101 B-26 Marauders, and 262 B-17s and B-24 Liberators drop more than 2,000 bombs equal to nearly 1,200 tons of explosives on Monte Cassino. Nearly 750 Allied artillery pieces fire 200,000 rounds on the target as well. Tragically, a number of bombs and artillery shells land short of their intended target, killing or wounding 142 friendly troops. P-47 Thunderbolts, A-36s, P-40s, and A-20 Havocs follow up with low-level attacks on Cassino. Despite the incredible firepower, there is no appreciable damage to the enemy defenses.

The U.S. 85th Infantry Division, commanded by Major General John B. Coulter, arrives in Italy as part of Fifth Army. This is one of the first all-draftee divisions formed.

The Fifteenth Air Force receives the B-17s of the 773rd Bombardment Squadron (Heavy), 463rd Bombardment Group (Heavy). The squadron's first mission is scheduled for late March. The B-24 Liberators of the 780th Bombardment Squadron (Heavy), 465th Bombardment Group (Heavy) arrive from the United States. The squadron will fly its first mission in early May.

SOUTH PACIFIC: Major General Hubert R. Harmon, commander of Thirteenth Air Force, is designated Commander Air Solomons (COMAIRSOLS).

CENTRAL PACIFIC: Seventh Air Force B-24 Liberators from Kwajalein Atoll bomb Truk Atoll in the Carolines. B-25 Mitchells from Tarawa bomb Maloelap Atoll. The B-24 Liberators of the 27th Bombardment Squadron (Heavy), 30th Bombardment Group (Heavy), redeploy from Nanumea Island to Kwajalein Atoll.

BOUGAINVILLE: After two days of nearly continuous artillery barrages and company-size raids, the Japanese abandon South Knob on Hill 260, leaving behind over 560 dead. The Americal Division's casualties mount to over 700.

The Japanese assault the 129th Infantry Regiment's defensive line, again attacking toward Piva airfield, and break through and advance 100 yards before being turned back by tank and infantry counterattacks.

NEW BRITAIN: Thirteenth Air Force B-25 Mitchells, P-40s, P-39 Airacobras, P-38 Lightnings, and navy fighters attack logistics bases at Wunapope. B-25 Mitchells, with navy fighter cover, bomb Lakunai airfield. B-24 Liberators bomb Rapopo airfield.

ADMIRALTIES: The 2nd Brigade 1st Cavalry lands on Manus Island. The 8th Regiment moves toward Lorengau airfield, supported by the 7th Cavalry, which establishes a beachhead defensive perimeter. Over 200 bunkers are cleared during the advance. Fifth Air Force sends 36 B-25 Mitchells to bomb Tingo village and the Lugos Mission areas.

NEW GUINEA: Fifth Air Force sends over 200 aircraft (B-24 Liberators, B-25 Mitchells, A-20 Havocs, P-38 Lightnings, P-47 Thunderbolts, and P-40s) to attack facilities and the airbase at Wewak. Fighter pilots report 11 confirmed kills.

March 16

ETO: Eighth Air Force sends 501 B-17s and 213 B-24 Liberators, escorted by 125 P-38 Lightnings, 608 Eighth and Ninth Air Force P-47 Thunderbolts, and 135 Eighth and Ninth Air Force P-51 Mustangs, to bomb targets in Germany. Aircrews report 68 confirmed kills and 32 probables. A total of 23 bombers are lost and one B-24 is damaged. Aircrew losses are seven killed, 17 wounded, and 217 missing. Fighter pilots report 78 confirmed kills and seven probables, with one confirmed kill on the ground. Ten fighters are lost and 12 are damaged. Nine pilots are missing.

MEDITERRANEAN: Navy PBY-5A Catalinas, using magnetic anomaly detection (MAD) equipment, detect German submarine *U-392* as it transits the Straits of Gibraltar. The Catalinas bomb the U-boat, and a British frigate and destroyer conduct a depth charge attack, sinking the U-boat.

ITALY: Twelfth Air Force B-26 Marauders, A-20 Havocs, and A-36 Intruder (Apache) fighter-bombers attack German positions around Cassino-Piedimonte area and gun positions along the Anzio battlefront.

PACIFIC: U.S. submarine *Flying Fish* attacks a Japanese convoy in the Ryukyus, sinking a cargo ship but failing to damage a tanker.

U.S. submarine *Tautog* torpedoes and sinks a Japanese destroyer and cargo ship off Hokkaido, Japan. *Tautog* escapes a pursuit by two destroyers.

SOUTHWEST PACIFIC AREA: U.S. submarine *Lapon* attacks but fails to hit a Japanese seaplane tender west of Luzon in the South China Sea.

CENTRAL PACIFIC: Seventh Air Force B-25 Mitchells from Tarawa and Abemama Island bomb Wotje and Mille Atolls.

U.S. submarine *Silversides* attacks a Japanese convoy and sinks a cargo ship in the vicinity of Palau.

BOUGAINVILLE: Thirteenth Air Force B-24 Liberators bomb Monoitu Mission.

NEW BRITAIN: Thirteenth Air Force B-24 Liberators and B-25 Mitchells bomb the Vunakanau airfield and radar site. B-25 Mitchells, P-39 Airacobras, and P-40s attack Wunapope.

NEW GUINEA: Fifth Air Force B-24 Liberators, B-25 Mitchells, and A-20 Havocs attack antiaircraft positions, support facilities, and logistics sites at Wewak.

Navy PBY Catalinas attack a Japanese convoy north of Hollandia, damaging four ships

March 17

CBI: The SEAC commander, Admiral Lord Louis Mountbatten, sends a message to Prime Minister Churchill and President Roosevelt requesting that the two leaders appeal to Generalissimo Chiang Kai-shek to release another Chinese division to Burma.

Tenth Air Force B-25 Mitchells, P-51 Mustangs, and A-36 Intruder (Apache) fighter-bombers attack Japanese positions and supplies around Kamaing. P-40s attack Myitkyina airfield.

ATLANTIC: TBF Avengers from the escort carrier USS *Block Island,* along with a destroyer and destroyer escort, sink German submarine *U-801* west of the Cape Verdes.

ETO: Eighth Air Force sends 135 P-47 Thunderbolts on a low-level strafing run against airfields in France and the Netherlands. Fighter pilots report three confirmed kills and two probables, all on the ground. Two P-47s are lost and the pilots are reported as missing.

Ninth Air Force sends 70 B-26 Marauders to bomb the marshaling yard at Criel-sur-Mer, France.

The headquarters of the 441st Troop Carrier Group and the 99th, 100th, 301st, and 302nd Troop Carrier Squadrons arrive in England from the United States. The squadrons are equipped with C-47s.

MEDITERRANEAN: Fifteenth Air Force sends over 200 B-24 Liberators escorted by P-47 Thunderbolts and P-38 Lightnings to bomb Vienna, Austria. Half of the bombers abort due to bad weather.

German submarine *U-371* attacks a convoy headed for Naples off Bougie, Algeria, and torpedoes a U.S. freighter.

ITALY: Twelfth Air Force B-25 Mitchells bomb marshaling yards. A-20 Havocs attack German troops around Cassino.

CENTRAL PACIFIC: Seventh Air Force redeploys the B-24 Liberators of the 392nd Bombardment Squadron (Heavy), 30th Bombardment Group (Heavy), from Abemama Island to Kwajalein Atoll.

NEW BRITAIN: Thirteenth Air Force B-25 Mitchells bomb logistics sites at Wunapope.

ADMIRALTIES: The 1st Squadron 8th Cavalry Regiment captures Lorengau airfield after heavy air and naval bombardment.

NEW GUINEA: Fifth Air Force sends almost 100 aircraft (B-24 Liberators, B-25 Mitchells, and A-20 Havocs) to attack the Japanese base at Wewak.

March 18

CBI: General Joseph Stilwell orders Merrill's Marauders (the U.S. 5307th Composite Unit (Provisional)) to block the Tanai Valley from the south.

In China, Fourteenth Air Force P-40s attack transports on the Yangtze River. In French Indochina, P-40s damage a bridge north of Haiphong.

ATLANTIC: German submarine *U-311* torpedoes a U.S. tanker in convoy CU 17 (New York to United Kingdom) in the North Atlantic. The tanker is abandoned and scuttled.

ETO: Eighth Air Force sends over 500 B-17s and over 200 B-24 Liberators, escorted by 113 P-38 Lightnings, 598 Eighth and Ninth Air Force P-47 Thunderbolts, and 214 Eighth and Ninth Air Force P-51 Mustangs, against aircraft production facilities, airfields, and air depots in Germany. A total of 43 bombers are lost and 246 damaged. Aircrew losses are 10 killed, 22 wounded, and 436 missing. Fighter pilots report 39 confirmed kills and five probables in the air and three confirmed kills and two probables on the ground. Thirteen fighters are lost and 133 are damaged. Pilot losses are one wounded and 12 missing.

During the night six B-17s drop leaflets over Cambrai, Lille, Paris, Amiens, Rouen, and Caen.

ITALY: Fifteenth Air Force sends nearly 1,000 B-17s and B-24 Liberators to bomb aviation targets, including 406 B-17 and B-24 Liberators escorted by 186 P-38 Lightnings and P-47 Thunderbolts to attack German airfields in northern Italy. A total of 56 German aircraft are destroyed on the ground. Aircrews report 23 confirmed kills and seven probables. Fighter pilots report 33 confirmed kills and three probables. Seven bombers and four fighters are shot down.

The 774th Bombardment Squadron (Heavy), 463rd Bombardment Group (Heavy), brings B-17s to Italy. The squadron's first mission will be in late March.

Twelfth Air Force B-25 Mitchells, B-26 Marauders, and A-20 Havocs bomb marshaling yards and railroad bridges. P-40s, A-36 Intruder (Apache) fighter-bombers, and P-47 Thunderbolts attack gun positions in the Anzio beachhead area and motor transport and logistics support facilities around Cassino.

SOUTHWEST PACIFIC AREA: SWPA headquarters sets a date for the Hollandia invasion named Operation Reckless—April 22. The plan involves an amphibious assault to capture Aitape and the Tadji airfield, followed by two simultaneous amphibious landings at Humboldt Bay and Tanahmerah Bay to seize airfields at Hollandia.

PACIFIC: U.S. submarine *Lapon* attacks a Japanese convoy, sinking a transport near Hong Kong.

CENTRAL PACIFIC: Naval Task Group 50.10—formed around the carrier *Lexington* and battleships USS *Iowa* and *New Jersey,* with a seven-destroyer screen, under the command of Rear Admiral Willis A. Lee—attacks Japanese installations on Mille Island in the Marshalls. The *Iowa* is damaged by fire from a shore battery.

BOUGAINVILLE: Eighteen P-39 Airacobras of Thirteenth Air Force, along with several navy fighter-bombers, attack Japanese shipping.

ADMIRALTIES: Lorengau village is captured. The 7th Cavalry Regiment clears more enemy bunkers and moves to clear Rossum Road.

NEW GUINEA: Fifth Air Force sends B-24 Liberators, B-25 Mitchells, and A-20 Havocs against support facilities and antiaircraft positions at Wewak.

TG 74.5 (Captain Kenmore M. McManes) bombards Japanese installations at Wewak.

U.S. submarine *Rock* is damaged by depth charges off North Borneo but remains on patrol.

March 19

CBI: The 2nd Battalion and a portion of the 3rd Battalion of the Marauders, supported by the Kachin Rangers, establish a road block on the Kamaing Road. The remainder of the 3rd Battalion provides security against a Japanese surprise attack.

The B-25 Mitchells of the 82nd Bombardment Squadron (Medium), 12th Bombardment Group (Medium), arrive at Tezgaon, India, from Italy. The squadron's first mission is scheduled for late April.

In China, Fourteenth Air Force B-25 Mitchells, P-38 Lightnings, and P-51 Mustangs attack vessels on the Yangtze River.

German submarine *U-510* torpedoes and sinks a U.S. freighter off the west coast of India.

ATLANTIC: TBF Avengers from escort carrier USS *Block Island* sink German submarine *U-1059* near the Cape Verde Islands.

ETO: Nearly 200 B-17s of Eighth Air Force, escorted by 82 P-47 Thunderbolts, bomb V-weapon sites in France. One B-17 is lost and 88 are damaged. Two crewmen are wounded and 100 are missing. One P-47 is damaged and the pilot wounded. P-47 Thunderbolts with 500-pound bombs attack Gilze-Rijen airfield in the Netherlands, supported by 39 P-51 Mustangs.

During the night, six B-17s drop leaflets over The Hague, Rotterdam, Leeuwarden, Utrecht, and Amsterdam in the Netherlands.

Ninth Air Force sends 152 B-26 Marauders and 65 A-20 Havocs to bomb V-weapon sites in France.

MEDITERRANEAN: Fifteenth Air Force sends 234 B-17s and B-24 Liberators, escorted by over fighters, to bomb the Klagenfurt, Austria, air depot. B-24s also bomb the Graz air depot and the marshaling yards at Knin and Metkovic in Yugoslavia. Aircrews report 30 confirmed kills. U.S. aircraft losses are 17 bombers and one fighter.

Twelfth Air Force B-26 Marauders and B-25 Mitchells attack roads, bridges, ports, and logistics support facilities. P-40s attack German positions at Anzio.

ITALY: U.S. submarine chaser sinks a German E-boat near Anzio.

CENTRAL PACIFIC: Seventh Air Force B-24 Liberators from Kwajalein Atoll bomb Wake Island. B-25 Mitchells from Abemama Island and Tarawa bomb Maloelap, Jaluit, and Mille Atolls.

NEW BRITAIN: Thirteenth Air Force sends B-25 Mitchells to bomb Wunapope.

NEW GUINEA: Fifth Air Force B-24 Liberators, B-25 Mitchells, A-20 Havocs, and P-38 Lightnings bomb the area around Wewak and destroy a convoy northwest of Wewak, sinking two cargo ships and two escort vessels.

March 20

CBI: The Chinese 38th Division is ordered to trap Japanese forces near Kamaing.

The B-25 Mitchells of the 12th Bombardment Group (Medium) arrive at Tezgaon, India, from Italy. The squadron's first mission will be in mid-April.

ETO: Eighth Air Force sends nearly 500 B-17s and B-24 Liberators, escorted by 44 P-38 Lightnings, 345 P-47 Thunderbolts, and 205 Eighth and Ninth Air Force P-51 Mustangs, to attack targets in Germany, but bad weather causes over 300 bombers to abort the mission. Seven bombers are lost and 166 damaged. Aircrews report two confirmed kills. Aircrew losses are one killed, 11 wounded, and 61 missing. Fighter pilots report four confirmed kills with one additional confirmed kill on the ground. Eight fighters are lost and 13 are damaged. Pilot losses are eight missing.

The Ninth Air Force sends B-26 Marauders and A-20 Havocs to bomb V-weapon sites and airfields in France. The 67th Tactical Reconnaissance Group completes a mission begun on February 23 to photograph 160 miles of French coastline.

ITALY: Fifteenth Air Force receives the headquarters of 464th Bombardment Group (Heavy) and 778th Bombardment Squadron (Heavy) from the United States. The B-24 Liberator-equipped squadron will fly its first mission at the end of April.

Twelfth Air Force B-25 Mitchells bomb marshaling yards, railroad bridges, and ports. A-36 Intruder (Apache) fighter-bombers drop food bundles for ground forces near Cassino.

SOUTHWEST PACIFIC AREA: U.S. submarine *Angler* evacuates 58 people, including women and children, from Panay in the Philippines.

PACIFIC: U.S. submarine *Pollack* torpedoes and sinks a Japanese auxiliary netlayer off Torishima in the Nanpo Islands south of Honshu, Japan. *Pollack* avoids the submarine chaser.

CENTRAL PACIFIC: Headquarters, 30th Bombardment Group (Heavy) moves from Abemama Island to Kwajalein Atoll.

U.S. submarine *Picuda* (SS-382) torpedoes and sinks a Japanese stores ship near Yap in the Carolines.

BOUGAINVILLE: Thirteenth Air Force P-40s and P-39 Airacobras bomb Numa Numa and targets of opportunity along the coast.

NEW BRITAIN: Thirteenth Air Force B-24 Liberators bomb Vunakanau airfield and B-25 Mitchells bomb Lakunai. Fifth Air Force P-40s on armed reconnaissance attack villages and barges.

NEW IRELAND: Rear Admiral Robert M. Griffin's Task Force 37, with four battleships, two escort carriers, and destroyers, bombards Kavieng, New Ireland.

Navy Task Group 31.2 under command of Commodore Lawrence F. Reifsnider lands the 4th Marine Division on undefended Emirau Island, Bismarck Archipelago, completing the strategic encirclement of Rabaul.

ADMIRALTIES: The 868th Bombardment Squadron (Heavy) of the Thirteenth Air Force redeploys from Munda, New Georgia, to Los Negros Island with radar-equipped B-24 Liberators.

NEW GUINEA: Fifth Air Force B-24 Liberators bomb the Aitape airfield. P-39 Airacobras and A-20 Havocs attack a Japanese headquarters on the Bogadjim Road.

March 21

CBI: The 22nd and 38th Chinese Divisions and elements of the 1st Provisional Tank Group continue the attack toward Jambu Bum. A battalion and other elements of the Marauders advance toward Inkangahtawng.

Headquarters, 12th Bombardment Group (Medium), arrives at Tezgaon, India. The B-25 Mitchells of the 83rd and 434th Bombardment Squadrons (Medium) arrive at Kurmitola, India, from Italy. The squadrons will fly their first mission in late April.

ETO: Eighth Air Force sends 65 B-24 Liberators escorted by 48 P-47 Thunderbolts against V-weapon sites in France. Of the 56 bombers that hit the target, seven are damaged. After an attack on the Bordeaux area by 41 P-51 Mustangs, fighter pilots report 12 confirmed kills in the air and another nine confirmed kills on the ground. Seven P-51 Mustangs are lost and two are damaged. Pilot losses are one wounded and seven missing.

During the night, seven B-17s drop leaflets over The Hague, Amsterdam, Leeuwarden, Rotterdam, and Utrecht in the Netherlands.

ITALY: The 34th Infantry Division begins landing at Anzio to relieve the 3rd Infantry Division. The beachhead is far from quiet, even though no major combat has taken place since March 3. German artillery and aircraft attack the Allied troops almost daily. About 3,000 tons of supplies are landed at the beach every day. Raids and artillery fire cost the Allies about 100 casualties per day.

Twelfth Air Force B-26 Marauders attack railroad bridges and viaducts and P-47 Thunderbolts attack railroad bridges. P-40s attack German positions on the Anzio battleline and A-36 Intruder (Apache) fighter-bombers airdrop food to ground troops near Cassino.

CENTRAL PACIFIC: Seventh Air Force B-24 Liberators and B-25 Mitchells from Tarawa bomb Maloelap Atoll.

U.S. submarine *Bashaw* torpedoes and damages a Japanese vessel in the Palau Islands.

NEW BRITAIN: Thirteenth Air Force B-25 Mitchells bomb Lakunai airfield and B-24 Liberators bomb Vunakanau airfield. Fifth Air Force P-40s and A-20 Havocs on armed reconnaissance attack targets of opportunity.

March 22

CBI: The Japanese offensive against India makes significant gains, advancing 30 miles into India toward Imphal.

In French Indochina, Fourteenth Air Force sends four B-25 Mitchells to attack transportation targets. One bomber is lost.

ATLANTIC: In establishing priorities for the Allied air forces, the CCS decides Neptune has priority over Pointblank (attacks on German war production). General Eisenhower, as Supreme Commander, Allied Expeditionary Force, will direct the operations of Allied air forces to attack targets in support of the invasion and to limit the ability of German forces to reinforce Normandy. The road and rail networks of France are to become primary targets.

ETO: Eighth Air Force sends 474 B-17s and 214 B-24 Liberators, escorted by 125 P-38 Lightnings, 496 Eighth and Ninth Air Force P-47 Thunderbolts, and 196 Eighth and Ninth Air Force P-51 Mustangs, to bomb aviation industry plants at Oranienburg and Basdorf, Germany. Cloud cover forces the bombers to attack secondary targets near Berlin and targets of opportunity. The bombers also drop over six million leaflets. Bomber losses are 12 downed and 348 damaged. Aircrew losses are 20 wounded and 135 missing. Fighter pilots report only one confirmed kill on the ground. Twelve fighters are lost and 11 are damaged. Pilot losses are one wounded and 12 missing.

ITALY: Fifteenth Air Force B-17s bomb marshaling yards, supported by P-38 Lightnings and P-47 Thunderbolts. Twelfth Air Force B-26 Marauders and B-25 Mitchells attack railroad bridges. P-40s bomb German positions around Avezzano and Pico.

Pilots of P-40s, flying cover over Anzio and Cassino, report two German fighters shot down.

PACIFIC: U.S. submarine *Growler* makes an unsuccessful attack on a Japanese cargo vessel in the Ryukyus.

CENTRAL PACIFIC: U.S. submarine *Tunny* torpedoes and damages a Japanese tanker west of the Palaus,

BOUGAINVILLE: Thirteenth Air Force B-24 Liberators bomb targets around Buka, Monoitu, Kahili, and Kara.

NEW BRITAIN: Thirteenth Air Force B-25 Mitchells bomb Lakunai airfield and B-24 Liberators bomb Tobera.

NEW GUINEA: Fifth Air Force sends over 130 aircraft (B-24 Liberators, B-25 Mitchells, A-20 Havocs, and P-40s) to attack Wewak.

March 23

ALEUTIANS: Eleventh Air Force sends a detachment of P-40s and P-38 Lightnings of the 11th Fighter Squadron, 343rd Fighter Group, from its man base on Adak Island to Amchitka Island.

CBI: Two battalions of Merrill's Marauders arrive at Inkanghtawng intending to block the Kamaing Road, but the Japanese are in defensive positions.

Tenth Air Force P-40s bomb Japanese logistics sites at Kamaing and other P-40s fly armed reconnaissance over the Mogaung Valley.

In French Indochina, Fourteenth Air Force B-25 Mitchells attack railroad targets and rolling stock and attack bridges between Vinh and Thanh Hoa.

ETO: Eighth Air Force sends 524 B-17s and 244 B-24 Liberators, escorted by 119 P-38 Lightnings, 539 Eighth and Ninth Air Force P-47 Thunderbolts, and 183 Eighth and Ninth Air Force P-51 Mustangs, to bomb airfields and aircraft production facilities in Germany. Due to cloud cover, only 68 B-24 Liberators hit the primary target and 639 bombers hit secondary targets or targets of opportunity. A total of 28 bombers are lost and 323 are damaged. Aircrews report 33 confirmed kills and eight probables. Fighter pilots report 22 confirmed kills and one probable, and two confirmed kills on the ground. Four fighters are lost and three are damaged. Aircrew casualties are five killed, nine wounded, and 278 missing. Four fighter pilots are reported as missing.

During the night five B-17s drop leaflets over Grenoble, Vichy, Lyon, Toulouse, and Limoges in France.

Ninth Air Force sends 220 B-26 Marauders on a morning mission to bomb a marshaling yard and airfields in France. This is followed by an afternoon raid by 146 B-26s on a marshaling yard.

ITALY: Twelfth Air Force B-26 Marauders and B-25 Mitchells bomb marshaling yards and railroad bridges. P-40s and A-36 Intruder (Apache) fighter-bombers attack German positions in the Cassino area.

SOUTHWEST PACIFIC AREA: U.S. submarine *Bowfin* attacks a Japanese convoy off the south coast of Mindanao, sinking a transport and a cargo ship. *Bowfin* escapes a counterattack from an escort vessel.

CENTRAL PACIFIC: Seventh Air Force B-24 Liberators from Kwajalein Atoll bomb Wake Island. B-25 Mitchells from Eniwetok Atoll bomb Ponape Island. B-25s from Tarawa bomb Maloelap and Jaluit Atolls, using the navy's new airfield at Majuro Atoll to refuel and rearm for multiple strikes.

U.S. submarine *Tunny* torpedoes and sinks Japanese submarine *I-42* southwest of Angaur Island in the Palaus.

BOUGAINVILLE: Another Japanese assault begins on the 129th Infantry Regiment's lines. Seven battalions of artillery hit the attackers who still must be stopped by a series of tank and infantry counterattacks. An estimated 5,000 Japanese are killed. U.S. casualties are 263 killed.

NEW BRITAIN: Two destroyers bombard Japanese installations on the Mussau Islands of the St. Matthias Group, Bismarck Archipelago.

NEW GUINEA: The Reckless Task Force is assembled under the I Corps commander, Lieutenant General Robert L. Eichelberger. The Aitape landing force is composed of the 163rd RCT of the 41st Infantry Division. It is commanded by Brigadier General Jens A. Doe and has a combination of 7,000 combat troops and nearly 9,000 service and air force personnel in support. It is to seize the Tadji airfield and make it operational for Allied aircraft to support the Hollandia landings. The Hollandia Task Force is composed of the 24th Infantry Division and the 41st Infantry Division (less the 163rd). The 41st Division, commanded by Major General Horace A. Fuller, will land at Humboldt Bay; the 24th Division, commanded by Major General Frederick A. Irving, will land at Tanahmerah Bay. The divisions will move to capture the several airfields in the area and consolidate forces to defend the established perimeter. Task Force 77, under Rear Admiral Daniel E. Barbey, will support the landing along with Task Force 58 from Fifth Fleet, which will provide carrier air support. The total operation consists of 58,000 men, 13,000 of whom are engineers essential to opening roads through nearly impassable jungle and building the airfields necessary to support offensive operations.

Fifth Air Force B-24 Liberators, B-25 Mitchells, A-20 Havocs, and P-47 Thunderbolts attack numerous targets in Aitape, Wewak, Alexishafen, and Hansa Bay.

March 24

CBI: The Marauders of the 2nd Battalion discover Japanese forces are occupying Inkangahtawng in strength. In the skirmishes that follow, 200 Japanese troops are killed and the Marauders suffer 15 casualties.

ETO: Eighth Air Force sends 230 B-17s to attack Schweinfurt but most bomb the Frankfurt am Main marshaling yard. Three B-17s are lost and 71 damaged. Also, 206 B-24 Liberators are sent against the Metz and Nancy airfields in France. The primary target is cloud covered and most bomb secondary targets. There are no losses, but 24 bombers are damaged. Aircrew casualties for the two missions are 14 killed, four wounded, and 30 missing. The missions are escorted by 84 P-38 Lightnings, 301 Eighth and Ninth Air Force P-47 Thunderbolts, and 55 Eighth and Ninth Air Force P-51 Mustangs. Fighter pilots report one confirmed kill in the air and two on the ground. Five aircraft are lost and four pilots are reported missing.

During the night five B-17s drop leaflets over Tours and Lorient in France, and over Charleroi, Brussels, and Antwerp in Belgium.

ITALY: The Mediterranean Allied Tactical Air Force and Twelfth Air Force under Major General John K. Cannon begins Operation Strangle, large-scale air interdiction operations intended to prevent supplies and reinforcements from reaching southern Italy. The air campaign will last until May 11. Combat Command B of the 1st Armored Division is withdrawn from Cassino to move to Anzio.

Fifteenth Air Force sends over 100 B-24 Liberators to bomb marshaling yards and road bridges. Six bombers are lost and aircrews report 10 German fighters shot down.

Twelfth Air Force B-25 Mitchells attack logistics sites, harbor installations, bridges, and railroads. A-20 Havocs, P-40s, and A-36 Intruder (Apache) fighter-bombers bomb German positions near Cassino.

CENTRAL PACIFIC: Seventh Air Force B-25 Mitchells from Tarawa bomb Jaluit while B-25s flying from Eniwetok Atoll attack Ponape Island and Ant Island in the Carolines.

BOUGAINVILLE: The Japanese again attack the 129th Infantry Regiment, but are halted. This ends the Japanese attempt to break the defensive line of XIV Corps. They have lost over 8,000 casualties and begin to withdraw into the jungle.

NEW BRITAIN: B-25 Mitchells bomb Tobera airfield. P-38 Lightnings, P-39 Airacobras, and P-40s attack Wunapope.

ADMIRALTIES, LOS NEGROS: The 1st Squadron, 5th Cavalry and 2nd Squadron, 12th Cavalry make a coordinated attack and seize the crest of Hill 260. The capture of this position ends organized resistance on the island.

March 25

ALEUTIANS: Eleventh Air Force B-24 Liberators from Shemya Island bomb Kurabu Cape and part of Onnekotan Island.

CBI: The 1st Battalion of Marauders establishes a road block south of Shaduzup. The 2nd Battalion retreats toward Manpin.

Tenth Air Force P-40s bomb the Kamaing area. The Japanese send five medium bombers and 30 fighters to attack Allied airfields in Burma and India.

ETO: Ninth Air Force sends over 140 B-26 Marauders to attack the Hirson marshaling yard in France.

ITALY: Twelfth Air Force B-26 Marauders bomb the dockyard at Leghorn. P-40 fighter-bombers attack German positions along the Anzio battleline.

PACIFIC: JCS approves the reassignment of all SOPAC forces to MacArthur's Southwest Pacific Area command and to Admiral Nimitz's Pacific Oceans Area command. General MacArthur will take operational control of XIV Corps headquarters and the 37th, 25th, 43rd, 93rd, and 40th Infantry Divisions, as well as the Thirteenth Air Force and all navy and marine air units. Nimitz will take operational control of the I Marine Amphibious Corps and the 1st and 3rd Marine Divisions.

U.S. submarine *Pollack* attacks a Japanese convoy and sinks a submarine chaser in the Bonin Islands.

CENTRAL PACIFIC: Headquarters of VII Bomber Command moves from Tarawa to Kwajalein Atoll.

A destroyer escort and a submarine chaser sink Japanese submarine *I-32* south of Wotje Atoll in the Marshalls.

NEW BRITAIN: Fifth Air Force P-40s attack a Japanese headquarters at Cape Hoskins.

ADMIRALTIES: The 7th Cavalry, reinforced by the 8th Cavalry, along with artillery and air support, defeats the last remnant of Japanese defenders on Manus Island. At Los Negros, Seeadler Harbor becomes one of the largest naval bases in the Pacific. Los Negros airfield is established along with hospitals and supply depots. With the Admiralties under Allied control, the Japanese stronghold at Rabaul is isolated, allowing MacArthur's forces to concentrate on western New Guinea. The battle for these key islands has cost the Americans 330 killed and 1,189 wounded.

NEW GUINEA: Fifth Air Force B-24 Liberators, B-25 Mitchells, and A-20 Havocs bomb Wewak. The Japanese move their air headquarters from Wewak to Hollandia.

March 26

CBI: The 2nd Battalion of the Marauders moves to Nhpum Ga where it receives resupply by airdrop. The Marauders are supported by the 1st and 2nd Troop Carrier Squadrons and the 27th and 315th Troop Carrier Squadrons. The C-47s drop 376 tons of supplies to the Marauders during March. L-4 and L-5 light aircraft of the 71st Liaison Squadron provide rapid medical evacuation of casualties from small jungle clearings. The 3rd Battalion arrives and the Marauders establish a hasty defense awaiting an expected flank attack against Shaduzup.

ETO: Eighth Air Force sends over 400 B-17s and B-24 Liberators, escorted by 266 P-47 Thunderbolts, to attack V-weapon sites in France. Five bombers are lost and 117 are damaged. Aircrew losses are two killed, 15 wounded, and 50 missing. Fighter pilots report one confirmed kill and one probable. One fighter is lost and five damaged. One pilot is reported missing.

During the night, six B-17s drop leaflets over Caen, Rennes, Amiens, Paris, and Rouen.

Ninth Air Force sends 338 B-26 Marauders and 35 A-20 Havocs to attack the torpedo-boat pens at Ijmuiden in the Netherlands. Nearly 140 P-47 Thunderbolts and P-51 Mustangs attack the Creil marshaling yard and other military installations in France.

ITALY: Fifteenth Air Force B-17s and B-24 Liberators escorted by P-47 Thunderbolts and P-38 Lightnings attack docks, marshaling yards, and air depots.

Twelfth Air Force B-26 Marauders and B-25 Mitchells attack transportation targets. A-20 Havocs attack German troops near Velletri. P-47 Thunderbolts damage a railway bridge while P-40s attack German positions along the Anzio battleline.

Lieutenant General Willis D. Crittenberger arrives in Italy with his IV Corps headquarters.

CENTRAL PACIFIC: Admiral Nimitz sends a warning order to General William H. Rupertus, commander of the 1st Marine Division, to be prepared to invade Peleliu Island by September 15.

Seventh Air Force B-25 Mitchells fly from Eniwetok Atoll to bomb Ponape Island. B-25s from Tarawa bomb Jaluit Atoll, rearm at Majuro Atoll, and attack Jaluit again en route back to Tarawa.

U.S. submarine *Tullibee* is sunk by a circular run of its own torpedo, north of the Palaus.

NEW BRITAIN: Thirteenth Air Force B-25 Mitchells bomb Vunakanau airfield and make a night raid on Rabaul. Fifth Air Force P-39 Airacobras and P-40s attack Cape Hoskins and troops around Talasea.

BOUGAINVILLE: Thirteenth Air Force B-24 Liberators attack Japanese positions and targets of opportunity on islands at the mouth of the Tekessi River and near Monoitu. Fighters support ground forces who attack supply points and Japanese positions near the mouths of the Tekessi and Maririei Rivers.

NEW GUINEA: Fifth Air Force sends over 220 aircraft (B-24 Liberators, B-25 Mitchells, A-20 Havocs, and fighters) to attack Wewak, Aitape, and the Hansa Bay area.

March 27

CBI: The 2nd and 3rd Battalions of the U.S. 5307th Composite Unit (Provisional), known also as Merrill's Marauders, arrive at Auche.

Tenth Air Force B-24 Liberators hit logistics sites at Kamaing, while about 50 A-36 Intruder (Apache) fighter-bombers and two B-25 Mitchells attack Japanese forces near Myitkyina and support ground forces near Kamaing.

ETO: Eighth Air Force sends nearly 550 B-17s and 168 B-24 Liberators, escorted by 132 P-38 Lightnings, 706 Eighth and Ninth Air Force P-47 Thunderbolts, and 122 Eighth and Ninth Air Force P-51 Mustangs, against airfields in France. Six bombers are lost and 10 are damaged. Aircrew losses are 31 killed, four wounded, and 61 missing. Fighter pilots report eight confirmed kills in the air and 30 on the ground with one probable on the ground. Ten aircraft are lost and seven are damaged. One pilot is wounded and 10 are reported missing.

Ninth Air Force sends 18 B-26 Marauders to attack V-weapon sites in France.

The C-47s of the 303rd, 305th, and 306th Troop Carrier Squadrons, 442nd Troop Carrier Group, arrive from the United States.

ITALY: Twelfth Air Force B-26 Marauders and B-25 Mitchells bomb railroad bridges. P-47 Thunderbolts and P-40s maintain cover over the Cassino and Anzio battlelines.

The destroyer USS *Livermore* provides gunfire support at Anzio.

CENTRAL PACIFIC: Seventh Air Force B-25 Mitchells and B-24 Liberators from Tarawa attack Maloelap, Mille, and Wotje Atolls. B-25s from Eniwetok Atoll bomb Jaluit Atoll.

The 9th Troop Carrier Squadron with C-47s deploys from Hickam Field, Hawaii, to Abemama Island.

BOUGAINVILLE: Japanese forces begin withdrawing from the Empress Augusta Bay area.

NEW BRITAIN: Thirteenth Air Force B-25 Mitchells attack Wunapope with incendiaries, causing heavy damage.

New Guinea: Fifth Air Force sends over 200 aircraft (B-24 Liberators, B-25 Mitchells, A-20 Havocs, P-47 Thunderbolts, P-40s, and P-39 Airacobras) to attack logistics sites, shipping, bridges, and troop concentrations around Wewak, Hansa Bay, and Madang.

Saidor becomes the new base for the P-47 Thunderbolts of the 341st Fighter Squadron, 348th Fighter Group.

U.S. submarine *Hake* torpedoes and sinks a Japanese merchant tanker south of Borneo.

U.S. submarine *Rasher* attacks a Japanese convoy in the Java Sea, sinking a cargo ship.

March 28

Aleutians: Eleventh Air Force deploys the P-38 Lightnings of the 18th Fighter Squadron, 343rd Fighter Group, from Amchitka Island to Attu Island.

CBI: The Japanese make their first attack on the 2nd Battalion's defenses at Nhpum Ga.

The 3rd Battalion now at Hsamshingyang provides artillery support and protects the only available drop zone for resupply and evacuation of casualties in the area. The 1st Battalion, after driving Japanese defenders off, blocks the Kamaing Road below Shaduzup and is reinforced by Chinese forces. The Chinese 38th and 22nd Divisions are now pressuring Japanese forces from two directions.

Headquarters of XX Bomber Command arrives at Kharagpur, India, from the United States.

ETO: Eighth Air Force sends nearly 400 B-17s against airfields in France and 77 B-24 Liberators against the Ijmuiden E-boat pens in the Netherlands. The missions are escorted by 46 P-38 Lightnings, 284 P-47 Thunderbolts, and 123 P-51 Mustangs. The B-24 Liberators abort the mission due to weather conditions over the target. Two B-17s are lost and 120 damaged. Aircrew losses are three killed, two wounded, and 28 missing. Fighter pilots report 30 confirmed kills and one possible, all on the ground. Three fighters are lost and the pilots reported as missing.

Italy: Fifteenth Air Force sends almost 400 B-17s and B-24 Liberators escorted by P-38 Lightnings and P-40s to bomb marshaling yards. Fighter pilots report 12 German fighters shot down. Five U.S. fighters are lost.

The Fifteenth Air Force receives the B-24 Liberators of the 781st Bombardment Squadron (Heavy), 465th Bombardment Group (Heavy), from the United States.

Twelfth Air Force B-25 Mitchells bomb bridges, railway junctions, and marshaling yards. P-40s attack German gun positions on the Anzio battleline and targets of opportunity in the Cassino area.

Pacific: U.S. submarine *Barb* torpedoes and sinks a Japanese cargo ship off Rasa Island.

Central Pacific: Seventh Air Force B-25 Mitchells from Abemama Island and Tarawa bomb Jaluit, Mille, and Maloelap Atolls.

Bougainville: Elements of the 93rd Division arrive at Empress Augusta Bay. American infantrymen find the Japanese have abandoned Hill 260.

Thirteenth Air Force P-40s attack the Numa Numa logistics base.

New Britain: Thirteenth Air Force B-25 Mitchells bomb Tobera airfield.

New Ireland: Destroyers bombard Japanese positions on Kapingamarangi Atoll, north of New Ireland, destroying a radio and meteorological station.

New Guinea: U.S. submarine *Silversides* torpedoes and sinks a Japanese cargo ship off Manokwari.

March 29

CBI: General Stilwell makes a formal request to Generalissimo Chiang Kai-shek for additional Chinese forces to be sent to Burma. Chiang offers two divisions.

In Burma, General Merrill is evacuated and Colonel Charles N. Hunter takes command temporarily as the Japanese make their second attack on Nhpum Ga. Despite the 3rd Battalion's attempts to stall the Japanese with ambushes, the enemy begins surrounding the 2nd Battalion of the Marauders.

The headquarters of the 1st Air Commando Group is activated at Hailakandi, India. The group has a B-25 Mitchell bomber section, a P-51 Mustang fighter section, a light-plane section with L-1 Stinsons and L-5 Sentinels (short take-off and landing light aircraft), a C-47 transport section, a glider section with CG-4As and TG-5s, and a light-cargo section with UC-64s.

In China, Fourteenth Air Force P-40s and P-51 Mustangs attack the railroad station, airfield and bridge near Nanchang.

Japanese submarine *I-26* torpedoes a U.S. freighter of the coast of India. As the ship is abandoned, the *I-26* surfaces and shells the ship, setting it afire. The Japanese gun crew then turns to the lifeboats and rafts, killing one American. The submarine rams and sinks one of the lifeboats, takes four men prisoner, then departs.

ETO: Eighth Air Force sends 236 B-17s, escorted by 50 P-38 Lightnings, 242 P-47 Thunderbolts, and 136 Eighth and Ninth Air Force P-51 Mustangs, against industrial targets in Germany. Nine bombers are lost and 67 damaged. Aircrews report eight confirmed kills and three probables. Aircrew losses are two killed, five wounded, and 90 missing. Fighter pilots report 44 confirmed kills and four probables and another 13 confirmed kills and seven probables on the ground. Twelve fighters are lost and 18 are damaged. Pilot losses are two killed, three wounded, and 10 missing.

Another attack by 77 B-24 Liberators on V-weapon sites in France escorted by 37 P-47 Thunderbolts results in only 30 hitting the primary target due to radar guidance failures. Eight bombers are damaged. Aircrew losses are 18 killed and one wounded.

Ninth Air Force receives the P-47 Thunderbolts of the 48th Fighter Group and 492nd, 493rd, and 494th Fighter Squadrons. The first mission for the squadrons is scheduled for late April. The headquarters of the 442nd Troop Carrier Group and 304th Troop Carrier Squadron arrives from the United States with C-47s.

Mediterranean: Two U.S. destroyers, three submarine chasers, and four British destroyers conduct antisubmarine operations off Sicily and sink German submarine *U-223*.

Italy: Fifteenth Air Force sends nearly 400 B-17s and B-24 Liberators against ball bearing production, marshaling yards, and industrial production. The bombers are escorted by P-47 Thunderbolts and P-38 Lightnings. Aircrews report 13 aircraft destroyed. Six U.S. aircraft are lost.

Twelfth Air Force B-25 Mitchells attack Viterbo airfield. B-26 Marauders bomb Leghorn. P-40s attack logistics sites and tank repair facilities. A-36 Intruder (Apache) fighter-bombers attack Civitavecchia and targets of opportunity. Spitfires, P-40s, and P-47 Thunderbolts patrol the Anzio battlelines.

SOUTHWEST PACIFIC AREA: U.S. submarine *Haddo* torpedoes and damages a Japanese cargo ship in the South China Sea, northwest of Luzon Island.

CENTRAL PACIFIC: Thirteenth Air Force B-24 Liberators from Munda on New Georgia carry out the first daylight raid on Truk Atoll. En route, the bombers arm at Torokina on Bougainville, then fly to Nissan Island in the Solomons for refueling before moving on to Truk. Aircrews report 31 Japanese aircraft destroyed in the air and 50 aircraft on the ground. Two B-24s are lost.

U.S. submarine *Tunny* torpedoes and damages the Japanese battleship *Musashi* off Palau.

NEW GUINEA: Fifth Air Force B-24 Liberators bomb Hollandia; B-25 Mitchells and A-20 Havocs bomb Wewak.

March 30

ETO: Eighth Air Force sends 24 P-47 fighter-bombers escorted by 50 other P-47 Thunderbolts to dive-bomb Eindhoven and Sosterburg airfields in the Netherlands. P-47s strafe Venlo, Deelen, and Twente/Enschede airfields. One fighter is lost and three damaged. The pilot is reported missing. Two German aircraft are reported destroyed.

During the night, six B-17s drop leaflets over Rouen, Rennes, Reims, Paris, and Amiens.

MEDITERRANEAN: Nearly 350 Fifteenth Air Force B-17s and B-24 Liberators bomb marshaling yards at Sofia, Bulgaria, and industrial targets and airfield at Imotski, Yugoslavia. Four bombers are lost. Reports state 13 German fighters are shot down.

The Fifteenth Air Force receives the B-24 Liberators of the 777th Bombardment Squadron (Heavy), 464th Bombardment Group (Heavy), in Italy from the United States.

Twelfth Air Force B-25 Mitchells bomb the harbor at Leghorn. P-40s and A-36 Intruder (Apache) fighter-bombers attack an ammunition storage area near Roccasecca and trucks, bridges, and logistics sites.

ITALY: Destroyer USS *Eberle* provides gunfire support off Anzio.

CENTRAL PACIFIC: Seventh Air Force B-24 Liberators from Kwajalein and Eniwetok Atolls bomb Truk.

Task Force 58 under Admiral Raymond A. Spruance (Commander Fifth Fleet), with the fast carriers USS *Lexington,* USS *Bunker Hill,* and USS *Hornet,* begins attacking airfields, shipping, facilities, and installations at Palau, Yap, Ulithi, and Woleai in the Carolines. For the first time carrier aircraft lay minefields. Carrier aircraft also sink five fleet tankers, a destroyer, 12 smaller support ships, five transports, three tankers, two guardboats, six cargo ships, and a number of other smaller vessels.

While on lifeguard duty off the Palaus the USS *Tunny* is mistaken for a Japanese submarine and attacked by TBF Avengers. The damage forces *Tunny* to terminate her patrol.

U.S. submarine *Picuda* attacks a Japanese convoy and sinks a transport southwest of Guam. U.S. submarine *Stingray* attacks a Japanese convoy and sinks a transport near Saipan.

NEW BRITAIN: Thirteenth Air Force P-38 Lightnings attack Rabaul with incendiaries. B-25 Mitchells bomb Wunapope.

NEW GUINEA: Fifth Air Force sends 60 B-24 Liberators, escorted by 90 P-38 Lightnings and P-47 Thunderbolts, to attack Hollandia to eliminate Japanese air power. At least 199 Japanese aircraft are destroyed on the ground or shot down. B-25 Mitchells, A-20 Havocs, P-47 Thunderbolts, P-40s, and P-39 Airacobras attack Wewak and Madang.

U.S. submarine *Darter* torpedoes and sinks a Japanese cargo ship northwest of Manokwari.

March 31

ALEUTIANS: Eleventh Air Force inactivates the headquarters units of XI Bomber Command and XI Fighter Command.

CBI: The 2nd Battalion of the Marauders is surrounded at Nhpum Ga. The beleaguered troops are resupplied with water and ammunition by airdrops.

ITALY: The Allies complete the shift of forces across the Italian peninsula, giving Eighth Army the Liri valley and the potentially fastest way to Rome. Mark Clark's Fifth Army is to advance on a narrow front to turn the right flank of the German army while holding the southern edge of the Liri valley. The Eighth Army will then break through at Cassino and push up the Liri valley to Valmontone and trap the German Tenth Army with the help of VI Corps from Anzio. Clark has little interest in playing second fiddle to the British. He plans to use the French Expeditionary Corps and the U.S. II Corps to cut the Itri-Pico Road and be in a position to move faster than the Eighth Army on the road to Rome and capture the city first.

PACIFIC: Commander in Chief of the Japanese Combined Fleet, Admiral Koga Mineichi, is killed in a plane crash en route to Davao Island in the Philippines.

CENTRAL PACIFIC: Seventh Air Force B-24 Liberators from Eniwetok Atoll bomb Truk.

The B-24s of the 431st Bombardment Squadron (Heavy), 11th Bombardment Group (Heavy), redeploy from Tarawa to Kwajalein Atoll.

Carrier aircraft from Admiral Raymond A. Spruance's TF 58 sink a Japanese guardboat in the Palau Islands.

NEW BRITAIN: Thirteenth Air Force B-25 Mitchells bomb logistics sites, while P-40s attack Wunapope. P-39 Airacobras and P-38 Lightnings bomb Rabaul with incendiaries.

NEW GUINEA: Fifth Air Force sends 60 B-24 Liberators escorted by P-38 Lightnings to bomb Hollandia, damaging the three airfields and a large number of aircraft on the ground. Reporting shows 14 Japanese aircraft shot down. Over 120 A-20 Havocs and B-25 Mitchells bomb targets around Tadji, Wewak, and Hansa Bay.

April 1

CBI: A combat team of the 3rd Battalion of Marauders attempts to clear Japanese defenders from the trail to Nhpum Ga.

ATLANTIC: General Arnold is designated as the executive agent to the JCS for B-29 deployments, missions, and targets.

ETO: Eighth Air Force sends 245 B-17s and 195 B-24 Liberators, escorted by 280 P-47 Thunderbolts and 195 Eighth and Ninth Air Force P-51 Mustangs, to bomb the chemical production facilities at Ludwigshafen, Germany. The B-17s abort the mission and the B-24s disperse to attack targets of opportunity. Seven B-17s are damaged. Aircrews report one confirmed kill. Twelve B-24s are lost and 45 are damaged. Aircrew losses are nine killed, 12 wounded, and 113 missing. Fighter pilots report 13 confirmed kills on the ground and five in the air with two probables. Four aircraft are lost and 14 are damaged. Four pilots are reported missing.

MEDITERRANEAN: German aircraft using aerial torpedoes attack convoy UGS 36 (United States to Mediterranean, Slow) off Algiers, damaging a freighter. It is later beached and returned to service.

ITALY: Fifteenth Air Force receives the headquarters of the 49th Bombardment Wing (Heavy).

Twelfth Air Force B-25 Mitchells and B-26 Marauders attack bridges and railroads. A-20 Havocs attack ammunition storage area and P-40s attack fuel storage areas and bridges.

PACIFIC: U.S. submarine *Flying Fish* torpedoes and sinks a cargo ship in the Bonin Islands.

CENTRAL PACIFIC: Seventh Air Force B-24 Liberators from Makin Island, the Gilbert Islands, and Kwajalein Atoll, bomb Truk.

BOUGAINVILLE: Thirteenth Air Force P-38 Lightnings bomb the mission at Monoitu and P-40s attack logistics bases at Numa Numa.

NEW BRITAIN: Thirteenth Air Force P-39 Airacobras and P-40s attack the wharf area at Simpson Harbor. Three P-40s conduct a follow-on attack on oil and coal storage areas. During the night B-25 Mitchells bomb Rabaul.

NEW GUINEA: The Japanese effort to reinforce western New Guinea brings their total number of ground troops available to 50,000 men.

Fifth Air Force B-24 Liberators bomb Ceram Island in the Moluccas and B-25 Mitchells attack Penfoei on Timor Island.

April 2

CBI: The Marauders receive 75 millimeter pack howitzers via airdrop at Hsamshingyang. The 3rd Battalion can now provide artillery support to the 2nd Battalion surrounded at Nhpum Ga.

Tenth Air Force P-40s bomb Kamaing.

The first operational B-29 of the XX Bomber Command, piloted by Colonel Leonard F. Harman, lands at Chakulia, India. The headquarters of 40th Bombardment Group (Very Heavy) arrives at Chakulia from the United States.

MEDITERRANEAN: Fifteenth Air Force sends a total of 125 B-17s and over 150 B-24 Liberators against the Steyr, Austria, ball bearing factory and aircraft component production facility. Twenty bombers are lost and 30 damaged. Aircrews report 84 confirmed kills and fighter pilots report 32 confirmed kills. One P-38 is lost.

B17s bomb the marshaling yard at Brod, Yugoslavia. B-24s bomb an air depot at Mostar and a marshaling yard at Bihać in Yugoslavia. Nineteen bombers are lost to enemy fighters. Aircrews report over 150 enemy fighters shot down.

SOUTHWEST PACIFIC AREA: U.S. submarine *Hake* torpedoes and damages a tanker off Singapore.

CENTRAL PACIFIC: Seventh Air Force B-24 Liberators from Eniwetok bomb Truk and B-25 Mitchells bomb Jaluit and Maloelap Atolls. Thirteenth Air Force sends 31 B-24 Liberators on a raid on against Dublon Island, Truk Atoll. Warehouses and the docks are damaged. Aircrews report over 30 enemy fighters shot down. Four B-24s are lost.

U.S. submarine *Greenling* is conducting a month-long reconnaissance of islands in the Marianas. USS *Salmon* is conducting a similar reconnaissance mission in the Carolines, examining Ulithi, Yap, and Woleai Atoll.

NEW BRITAIN: Thirteenth Air Force sends 23 B-25 Mitchells to bomb Lakunai.

NEW GUINEA: Fifth Air Force sends over 120 bombers and fighters against Wewak, Hansa Bay, Madang, and Bogadjim. B-25 Mitchells bomb Dili and Penfoei on Timor Island.

April 3

CBI: President Roosevelt appeals to Generalissimo Chiang Kai-shek to move Y Force against the Japanese holding the Burma Road in Yunnan province. The request is backed up with a threat to divert all supplies to the Fourteenth Air Force. Chiang accepts and orders the Y Force of six armies (16 infantry divisions total) to joint the offensive.

General Stilwell meets with Admiral Louis Mountbatten, commander of SEAC, and General William Slim, British Fourteenth Army commander, to review campaign objectives for Burma. Stilwell is given the task of using the Chinese-American forces under his command to clear the Japanese from the Mogaung Valley to Myitkyina.

ETO: Ninth Air Force IX Bomber Command establishes a new operational leave policy to adjust to conditions that make it nearly impossible for any bomber crew to survive the 50-mission tour of duty limit. Aircrews can take one week leave between the 25th and 30th missions. Aircrews can take two weeks leave between their 40th and 50th missions.

MEDITERRANEAN: Fifteenth Air Force sends over 450 B-17s and B-24 Liberators to bomb targets in Hungary and Yugoslavia. B-17s attack hit an aircraft production facility in Budapest, Hungary, and a marshaling yard at Brod, Yugoslavia. B-24s miss the rendezvous with escorting fighters, but continue the mission against a marshaling yard at Budapest. The 137 fighters that escort the B-17s report 24 confirmed kills.

ITALY: Twelfth Air Force B-25 Mitchells and B-26 Marauders bomb railway bridges and ammunition storage sites. A-36 Intruder (Apache) fighter-bombers attack railroad targets and P-40s attack supply and transportation targets.

PACIFIC: U.S. submarine *Pollack* attack a Japanese convoy, sinking a cargo ship off Honshu, Japan.

CENTRAL PACIFIC: Seventh Air Force B-24 Liberators, staging through Eniwetok, bomb Truk. B-25 Mitchells from Abemama and Tarawa attack Maloelap and Jaluit Atolls.

B-24 Liberators of the 98th Bombardment Squadron (Heavy), 11th Bombardment Group (Heavy), redeploy from Tarawa to Eniwetok Atoll.

NEW BRITAIN: Thirteenth Air Force sends 23 B-25 Mitchells against Rabaul after six B-25 Mitchells bomb Rabaul during the night.

NEW GUINEA: Fifth Air Force sends over 300 B-24 Liberators, B-25 Mitchells, A-20 Havocs, and P-38 Lightnings to attack the airfields at Hollandia. Supported by Ultra intelligence, the Americans are able to destroy several hundred aircraft parked on the ground and 26 are reported to have been destroyed in the air. This attack completely eliminates the Japanese air force over central New Guinea and marks American air dominance for the remainder of the campaign.

P-40s, P-47 Thunderbolts, and P-39 Airacobras attack targets around Wewak, Hansa Bay, Bogia, and Madang.

April 4

CBI: Sergeant Ray Matsumoto, a Marauder with 2nd Battalion on Nhpum Ga, places himself close to the Japanese lines to overhear the officers briefing their soldiers on the next attack. He returns and warns the defenders, who fall back from their main line of defense and establish new positions. When the Japanese do attack, they find the defensive line abandoned. The Japanese are confused by this discovery, but then Matsumoto pretends to be a Japanese officer and begins giving orders to charge. The soldiers respond and move directly into the massed fire of the prepared Marauders. Matsumoto's initiative and resourcefulness by all accounts probably save the battalion from being overrun.

Tenth Air Force sends over 120 fighter-bombers and four B-25 Mitchells against supply sites around Mogaung and support ground forces near Kamaing and Myitkyina.

ATLANTIC: Headquarters of the Twentieth Air Force is activated in Washington, D.C.

ETO: Eighth Air Force receives the B-24 Liberators of the 836th, 837th, 838th, and 839th Bombardment Squadrons (Heavy), 487th Bombardment Group, and the headquarters of the 339th Fighter Group from the United States. The bomber squadrons will fly their first missions in early May.

Ninth Air Force receives the P-47 Thunderbolts of the 410th Fighter Squadron and headquarters of the 373rd Fighter Group. The squadron's first mission is scheduled for early May. Headquarters units of the 404th Fighter-Bomber Group, the 406th Fighter-Bomber Group, and the 410th Bombardment Group (Light) arrive. The A-20 Havocs of the 644th, 645th, 646th, and 647th Bombardment Squadrons (Light) will fly their first missions in early May. P-38 Lightnings of the 393rd and 394th Fighter Squadrons of the 367th Fighter Group will fly their first missions in early May.

MEDITERRANEAN: To assist the Soviet offensive, Fifteenth Air Force bombers attack rail transportation and rail facilities in Romania and Hungary to prevent resupply or reinforcement of German forces in the east. One mission involves 350 B-17s and B-24 Liberators escorted by 119 P-38 Lightnings targeting the marshaling yards at Bucharest, Romania. Only 28 B-24s hit the target as others turn back in heavy weather. The bombers without fighter escort are attacked by 50 German fighters, which shoot down seven bombers. Aircrews report 40 confirmed kills and 13 probables.

CENTRAL PACIFIC: Shore battery fire damages a U.S. destroyer off Wotje Atoll.

BOUGAINVILLE: Thirteenth Air Force P-40s attack barges in Gazelle Harbor. Ten B-25 Mitchells bomb Buka airfield and P-38 Lightnings conduct ground support missions along Empress Augusta Bay.

CENTRAL PACIFIC: Seventh Air Force B-25 Mitchells from Abemama Island and Tarawa attack Ponape Island, and Jaluit and Maloelap Atolls.

NEW GUINEA: Fifth Air Force B-24 Liberators bomb Wewak.

April 5

ETO: Eighth Air Force B-24 Liberators sent to bomb V-weapon sites in France abort the mission due to heavy clouds. An attack by 96 P-38 Lightnings, 236 P-47 Thunderbolts, and 124 P-51 Mustangs against German airfields is also limited by heavy cloud cover. Fighter pilots report 98 confirmed kills and four probables. Nine aircraft are lost and 11 are damaged. Pilot casualties are one killed and eight missing.

One of 17 B-24 Liberators sent to support a Carpetbagger mission is lost over Europe.

Eighth Air Force receives the headquarters of the 487th Bombardment Group (Heavy), the 503rd, 504th, and 505th Fighter-Bomber Squadrons, 339th Fighter-Bomber Group. The P-51 Mustang-equipped squadrons will fly their first missions in late April. The B-24 Liberators of the 832nd, 833rd, 834th, and 835th Bombardment Squadrons (Heavy) of the 486th Bombardment Group (Heavy) will fly their first missions in early May.

Ninth Air Force receives the headquarters, 36th Fighter Group, and the P-47 Thunderbolts of the 22nd Fighter Squadron. The squadron's first mission is scheduled for early May. The headquarters, 50th Fighter Group, and the P-47s of the 10th, 81st, and 313th Fighter Squadrons are scheduled for their first missions in early May. The P-38 Lightnings of the 392nd Fighter Squadron and headquarters, 367th Fighter Group, arrive. The squadron's first mission will be in early May. Headquarters, 397th Bombardment Group (Medium), and the B-26 Marauders of the 596th, 597th, 598th, and 599th Bombardment Squadrons (Medium) will fly their first missions in late April. The P-47s of the 411th and 412th Fighter Squadrons, 373rd Fighter Group, will fly their first missions in early May. The P-47s of the 506th, 507th, and 508th Fighter-Bomber Squadrons, 404th Fighter-Bomber Group, and the 513th Fighter-Bomber Squadron, 406th Fighter-Bomber Group, will also fly their first missions in early May.

MEDITERRANEAN: Fifteenth Air Force sends over 300 B-17s and B-24 Liberators against marshaling yards in Ploeşti, Romania and at Nis and Leskovac in Yugoslavia.

A total of 95 B-17s and 135 B-24 Liberators are sent to bomb the Ploeşti marshaling yards. Aircrews report 41 confirmed kills. Thirteen bombers are lost.

ITALY: Twelfth Air Force P-40s and A-36 Intruder (Apache) fighter-bombers attack transportation and logistics targets.

CENTRAL PACIFIC: Seventh Air Force B-25 Mitchells from Tarawa bomb Maloelap Atoll, then land at Majuro Atoll in the Marshall Islands to rearm and refuel, then bomb Jaluit Atoll en route back to Tarawa.

Headquarters of the 11th Bombardment Group (Heavy) moves from Tarawa to Kwajalein.

Navy PB4Y Privateer sinks a Japanese auxiliary submarine chaser off Moen Island at Truk.

Navy TBM Avengers and FM-2 Wildcat fighters damage Japanese submarine *I-45* operating northeast of the Marshalls.

BOUGAINVILLE: Thirteenth Air Force sends 12 B-25 Mitchells to bomb Kara.

NEW GUINEA: Fifth Air Force B-24 Liberators, B-25 Mitchells, A-20 Havocs, and P-38 Lightnings attack Hollandia and Humboldt Bay. P-47 Thunderbolts and P-40s attack targets around Hansa Bay-Bogia and Wewak. B-24 Liberators bomb Kaimana and Efman Island.

B-25 Mitchells bomb Koepang on Timor Island.

April 6

CBI: Elements of the 1st Provisional Tank Group support the Chinese 22nd Division at Shaduzup.

General Chennault, commander of Fourteenth Air Force, sends General Stilwell an assessment warning of a possible large-scale Japanese offensive in eastern China. To stop the Japanese attack and provide air support for Chinese forces, he requests an additional 8,000 to 10,000 tons of supplies a month be flown over the Hump. Stilwell, pressed to provide logistics support for the B-29 strategic bombing program, fly supplies to British forces, and support the Chinese-American offensive in Burma, is unable to provide any more assistance to Chennault.

ATLANTIC: General Henry H. "Hap" Arnold assumes command of the Twentieth Air Force at Washington, D.C.

ETO: Eighth Air Force Mission sends 12 B-24 Liberators with 27 P-47 Thunderbolts escorting to attack V-weapon sites in France.

Ninth Air Force receives the P-47 Thunderbolts of the 23rd Fighter Squadron, 36th Fighter Group, and the 512th Fighter-Bomber Squadron, 406th Fighter-Bomber Group. The squadrons' first missions are scheduled for early May.

MEDITERRANEAN: Fifteenth Air Force B-24 Liberators bomb the airfield at Zagreb, Yugoslavia. Six bombers are lost. Aircrews report 17 enemy fighters shot down.

ITALY: Twelfth Air Force B-25 Mitchells bomb the airfield at Perugia. B-26 Marauders bomb a bridge near Orvieto. A-36 Intruder (Apache) fighter-bombers attack rail lines and bridges.

CENTRAL PACIFIC: Seventh Air Force B-24 Liberators from Kwajalein bomb Wake Island. B-25 Mitchells from Abemama Island bomb Jaluit Atoll, rearm at Majuro Atoll, and hit Maloelap Atoll en route back to Abemama. Thirteenth Air Force sends 34 B-24 Liberators to attack Dublon Island at Truk.

New Britain: Thirteenth Air Force sends 22 B-25 Mitchells to bomb Lakunai airfield.

New Guinea: Fifth Air Force P-39 Airacobras, P-40s, and P-47 Thunderbolts attack targets around Wewak, Aitape, and Madang.

B-25 Mitchells bomb Koepang, Timor Island.

April 7

Aleutians: Eleventh Air Force sends eight B-24 Liberators to attack a Japanese convoy located near Matsuwa Island in the Kuriles, but they turn back due to a variety of engine, navigation, and weather problems.

Caribbean: Sixth Air Force VI Bomber Command redeploys the B-24 Liberators of the 74th and 397th Bombardment Squadrons (Heavy) from Guatemala City, Guatemala, and the Galapagos Islands to Rio Hato, Panama.

CBI: The 3rd Battalion of Marauders makes slow progress against Japanese strongpoints set up around Nhpum Ga. The 1st Battalion makes a forced march to join the rest of the unit at Nhpum Ga.

Tenth Air Force P-51 Mustangs and B-25 Mitchells attack Japanese positions throughout the Mogaung Valley.

In China, Fourteenth Air Force B-24 Liberator aircrews on a sweep from Hong Kong to Formosa report sinking a large riverboat and a small cargo ship and damaging two other cargo ships. One of the two B-24s sent on the mission is lost. In French Indochina, P-40s attack small vessels in Haiphong harbor and report sinking four.

The headquarters of the 462nd Bombardment Group (Very Heavy), XX Bomber Command, arrives at Piardoba, India, from the United States.

Atlantic: Destroyer USS *Champlin* rams German submarine *U-856* in mid-Atlantic. *Champlin* and a destroyer escort subsequently sink the U-boat.

Italy: Fifteenth Air Force sends over 400 B-17s and B-24 Liberators escorted by nearly 100 P-38 Lightnings to attack marshaling yards. Aircrews report 20 confirmed kills.

Twelfth Air Force A-36 Intruder (Apache) fighter-bombers attack gun emplacements and rail targets near Orvieto. P-40s and P-47 Thunderbolts attack logistics sites, bridges, and transportation targets around Rome.

Southwest Pacific Area: U.S. submarine *Scamp* is damaged by a bomb from a Japanese floatplane off Mindanao and terminates her patrol.

Central Pacific: Seventh Air Force B-25 Mitchells from Tarawa bomb Maloelap Atoll, rearm at Majuro Atoll, and bomb Jaluit Atoll en route back to Tarawa.

U.S. submarine *Pampanito* is damaged by depth charges off the Marianas but remains on patrol.

Bougainville: Thirteenth Air Force P-40s attack Japanese pillboxes near the Reini River and B-24 Liberators bomb Monoitu mission.

New Britain: Thirteenth Air Force B-25 Mitchells bomb Talili Bay and Vunakanau and Tobera airfields. Another six B-25s conduct a night bombing raid on Rabaul.

The headquarters of the 5th Bombardment Group (Heavy) moves from Munda, New Georgia, to Momote airfield, Los Negros Island, in the Admiralties.

U.S. destroyer *Saufley* sinks Japanese submarine *I-2* off New Hanover in the Bismarck Archipelago.

NEW GUINEA: Fifth Air Force B-24 Liberators bomb Wakde Island. B-25 Mitchells bomb the barracks at Penfoei, on Timor Island.

April 8

CBI: In French Indochina, Fourteenth Air Force sends 11 B-24 Liberators to bomb the railyards in Hanoi. In China, nine B-24 Liberators bomb the airfield on Samah Bay, Hainan Island, while four others lay mines in the bay.

ETO: Eighth Air Force sends 314 B-17s and 350 B-24 Liberators divided into three separate forces, escorted by 136 P-38 Lightnings, 438 Eighth and Ninth Air Force P-47 Thunderbolts, and 206 Eighth and Ninth Air Force P-51 Mustangs, to attack airfields in northwest Germany and aircraft production facilities near Brunswick. Aircrews report 58 confirmed kills and four probables. Thirty-four bombers are lost and 349 damaged. Aircrew casualties are nine killed, 31 wounded, and 340 missing. Fighter pilots report 88 confirmed kills in the air and 49 on the ground with nine probables. A total of 23 fighters are lost and 20 are damaged. All 23 pilots of the downed aircraft are reported missing.

During the night five B-17s drop one million leaflets over Liege, Brussels, Ghent, Antwerp, and Mont-sur-Sombre, Belgium.

Ninth Air Force sends 198 B-26 Marauders to attack the marshaling yard at Hasselt and bomb Coxyde airfield in Belgium. P-47 Thunderbolts bomb targets near Hasselt.

ITALY: Fifteenth Air Force receives the headquarters of the 484th Bombardment Group (Heavy) and the B-24 Liberators of the 824th and 827th Bombardment Squadrons (Heavy) from the United States. The squadrons' first missions will be in late April.

CENTRAL PACIFIC: Seventh Air Force B-24 Liberators flying out of Kwajalein bomb Truk. B-25 Mitchells from Abemama Island bomb Ponape Island and B-25s from Tarawa attack Maloelap Atoll, rearm at Majuro Atoll and bomb Jaluit Atoll en route to Tarawa.

U.S. submarine *Seahorse* attacks a Japanese convoy off Guam, hitting an ammunition ship, which explodes and damages a destroyer. A water tanker is also damaged in another attack. *Seahorse* avoids a depth charge attack.

U.S. submarine *Trigger* is damaged by depth charges off the Marianas but remains on patrol.

BOUGAINVILLE: Thirteenth Air Force B-24 Liberators bomb Monoitu mission.

NEW BRITAIN: Thirteenth Air Force B-25 Mitchells bomb Lakunai airfield.

NEW IRELAND: Thirteenth Air Force B-25 Mitchells bomb Kavieng airfield during the night.

NEW GUINEA: Fifth Air Force P-40s attack targets of opportunity in the Aitape-Wewak area.

April 9

CBI: Japanese abandon their attack on Nhpum Ga as the 3rd Battalion of the Marauders links up with the 2nd Battalion. The 2nd Battalion has held off Japanese forces for seven days. The Japanese withdraw toward Kamaing. U.S. losses are 59 killed, 314 wounded, and 379 evacuated for various diseases. About 400 Japanese are killed. The Marauders have about 1,400 men available to continue the campaign out of the 3,000 who began. The 1st and 3rd Battalions of the Marauders withdraw to Nawbum, while the 2nd Battalion rests and reorganizes at Senjo Ga. The 2nd Battalion is reduced by casualties and sickness to less than half-strength. The Marauders believe that after 90 days in the field they should be relieved, but General Stilwell needs them for the capture of Myitkyina.

Fourteenth Air Force B-25 Mitchells sink a merchant vessel off Hainan Island.

ATLANTIC: TBM Avengers and FM-2 Wildcat fighters from the escort carrier USS *Guadalcanal* together with four destroyer escorts sink German submarine *U-515* off Madeira Island.

ETO: Eighth Air Force sends 296 B-17s and 246 B-24 Liberators, escorted by 119 P-38 Lightnings, 387 Eighth and Ninth Air Force P-47 Thunderbolts, and 213 Eighth and Ninth Air Force P-51 Mustangs, against aircraft production facilities at Rahmel and Poznan in Poland and Marienburg and Warnemund in Germany. Aircrews report 45 confirmed kills and eight probables. A total of 32 bombers are lost and 117 damaged. Aircrew casualties are 25 killed, 21 wounded, and 320 missing. Fighter pilots report 20 confirmed kills and one probable in the air and 19 confirmed kills on the ground. Ten fighters are lost and 15 are damaged. Pilot losses are three killed, two wounded, and six missing.

During the night, five B-17s drop nearly three million leaflets over Rouen, Paris, Amiens, and Caen. A total of 23 B-24 Liberators support Carpetbagger operations.

ITALY: Fifteenth Air Force receives the B-17s of the 815th, 816th, and 840th Bombardment Squadrons (Heavy) of the 483rd Bombardment Group (Heavy). The squadrons' first mission is scheduled for mid-April.

Twelfth Air Force P-40 and A-36 fighter-bombers attack railroad targets, motor transport, and gun positions.

Destroyer USS *Hilary P. Jones* provides gunfire support at Anzio.

PACIFIC: U.S. submarine *Whale* torpedoes and sinks a Japanese cargo ship off the northwestern coast of Kyushu, Japan.

CENTRAL PACIFIC: Seventh Air Force B-25 Mitchells from Abemama Island bomb Jaluit Atoll, rearm at Majuro Atoll, and then attack Maloelap Atoll en route back to Abemama.

U.S. submarine *Seahorse* attacks a Japanese convoy and sinks a transport off Saipan.

U.S. submarine *Trigger* takes on more damage after a second depth charge attack near the Marianas but continues her patrol.

NEW BRITAIN: Thirteenth Air Force B-25 Mitchells bomb Lakunai. Other B-25s bomb Rabaul during the night.

NEW GUINEA: Fifth Air Force B-25 Mitchells bomb Aitape. B-24 Liberators and A-20 Havocs bomb Wewak and P-39 Airacobras attack targets in the Madang area.

April 10

CARIBBEAN: Sixth Air Force VI Bomber Command redeploys the B-24 Liberators of the 9th Bombardment Squadron (Heavy) from the Galapagos Islands to Howard Field, Panama Canal Zone.

CBI: In French Indochina, Fourteenth Air Force B-25 Mitchells damage bridges at Phu Dien Chau.

The JCS informally approves Operation Matterhorn, the plan for the strategic bombing of Japan, which had been approved in principle by President Roosevelt on November 10, 1943. The B-29 Superfortresses based in Calcutta, India, and staging through advanced airfields in the area of Chengtu, China, will be assigned to the 58th Bombardment Wing (Very Heavy) of the XX Bomber Command. The XX Bomber Command in turn will be assigned to the newly activated Twentieth Air Force, operating under General Henry H. "Hap" Arnold, who will serve as the executive agent for the JCS in determining missions and targets.

ATLANTIC: TBM Avengers and FM-2 Wildcat fighters from the escort carrier *Guadalcanal* sink German submarine *U-68* off Madeira Island.

ETO: Eighth Air Force sends 486 B-17s and 243 B-24 Liberators against aviation production targets and airfields in Belgium and France, escorted by 51 P-38 Lightnings, 295 P-47 Thunderbolts, and 150 Eighth and Ninth Air Force P-51 Mustangs. Aircrews report six confirmed kills and two probables. Three bombers are lost and 123 damaged. Aircrew losses are five wounded and 30 missing. Fighter pilots report 52 confirmed kills. Two aircraft are lost and five are damaged. Two pilots are reported missing.

P-38 Lightnings and P-47 Thunderbolts are sent against airfields in France. Three aircraft are lost and one damaged. Fighter pilots report two confirmed kills on the ground. Three pilots are reported missing.

During the night five B-17s drop two million leaflets over Lille, Le Mans, Chartres, Reims, and Orleans in France. A total of 23 B-24s fly in support of Carpetbagger operations.

Ninth Air Force sends 258 B-26 Marauders and 41 A-20 Havocs, including 12 aircraft dropping Window (aluminum chaff to eliminate radar tracking), to attack coastal batteries in France. Another 267 B-26 Marauders and A-20 Havocs are sent to bomb a marshaling yard, an airfield, coastal defenses, and V-weapon sites in Belgium. P-47 Thunderbolts attack the Evreux airfield in France.

ITALY: In the III Corps area the 85th Infantry Division begins moving into the Allied line near Minturo.

Fifteenth Air Force receives the B-24 Liberators of the 776th Bombardment Squadron (Heavy) of the 464th Bombardment Group (Heavy) from the United States. The squadron's first missions are scheduled for late April.

Twelfth Air Force B-25 Mitchells and B-26 Marauders attack transportation targets. A-20 Havocs bomb an ammunition storage area.

SOUTHWEST PACIFIC AREA: MacArthur approves Alamo Force's plan for Reckless, the assault on Hollandia. MacArthur's confidence is high. "It should win without question," he notes.

CENTRAL PACIFIC: Seventh Air Force B-24 Liberators, staging through Eniwetok, bomb Truk and B-25 Mitchells attack Ponape from Abemama Island.

NEW BRITAIN: Admiral Nimitz releases the 40th Infantry Division to Southwest Pacific Area command in order to get the 1st Marine Division back under his operational control for future operations in the Central Pacific. Major General Rapp Brush, commander of the 40th, begins preparations to occupy New Britain.

Thirteenth Air Force B-25 Mitchells bomb the Ratawul logistics base.

New Guinea: Fifth Air Force sends 60 B-24 Liberators to work with navy destroyers offshore in attacking antiaircraft positions near the airfields at Hansa Bay.

April 11

CBI: Tenth Air Force P-51 Mustangs, A-36 Intruder (Apache) fighter-bombers, and B-25 Mitchells fly ground support missions near Maungkan and attack Japanese positions in the Mogaung Valley.

The XX Bomber Command receives the headquarters, 444th Bombardment Group (Very Heavy), and 676th Bombardment Squadron (Very Heavy) at Charra, India, with B-29 Superfortresses. The 25th Bombardment Squadron (Very Heavy), 40th Bombardment Group (Very Heavy), arrives at Chakulia, India with B-29 Superfortresses. The squadrons' first missions are scheduled for early June.

ETO: Eighth Air Force sends 643 B-17s and 274 B-24 Liberators escorted by 124 P-38 Lightnings, 454 Eighth and Ninth Air Force P-47 Thunderbolts, and 241 Eighth and Ninth Air Force P-51 Mustangs against aircraft production facilities in northern Germany. The bombers also drop 2.4 million leaflets. Aircrews report 73 confirmed kills and 24 probables. A total of 64 bombers are lost and 411 damaged. Aircrew casualties are 19 killed, 31 wounded, and 652 missing. Fighter pilots report 51 confirmed kills and five probables in the air and 65 confirmed kills on the ground. A total of 16 fighters are lost and 29 are damaged. Pilot losses are 16 missing.

During the night, five B-17s drop two million leaflets over Paris, Rouen, Le Mans, Rennes, Vichy, Lyon, Limoges, and Toulouse.

Ninth Air Force sends 229 B-26 Marauders and 36 A-20 Havocs (including three dropping Window) to attack military installations in Belgium. P-47 Thunderbolts dive-bomb a military installation and an airfield in France.

First Lieutenant Edward S. Michael of the 364th Bomber Squadron, 305th Bomber Group, is piloting a B-17 over Germany when his group is attacked by a number of German fighters. Michael's B-17 receives heavy damage from antiaircraft fire and the fighters, forcing it to fall out of the protective air formation. It becomes the focus of enemy fighter attention. Although seriously wounded, and his copilot unconscious, Michael maintains control of the bomber. When notified that the load of incendiary bombs his plane carries is in danger of catching fire, he orders the crew to bail out. Michael continues to avoid enemy antiaircraft and fighters, seeking a place to land within friendly lines. His own heavily bleeding wounds cause him to lose consciousness even as the copilot takes the controls. Michael regains consciousness and flies the damaged bomber to an airfield on the coast of England, landing safely and saving the members of the crew who remained with the bomber. For his heroic skill and dedication to duty, First Lieutenant Michael will receive the Medal of Honor.

Mediterranean: German bombers and torpedo bombers attack Convoy UGS 37 (United States to Mediterranean, Slow) east of Algiers. One destroyer escort and one freighter are damaged.

German aircraft begin active aerial mining near Anzio.

Italy: Twelfth Air Force B-25 Mitchells and B-26 Marauders attack rail targets.

Southwest Pacific Area: General George C. Kenney, commanding general of Allied Air Force, SWPA, creates the Thirteenth Air Task Force (Provisional) from elements of the Thirteenth Air Force and other units.

U.S. submarine *Redfin* torpedoes and sinks a Japanese destroyer in the northern Celebes Sea.

Central Pacific: Seventh Air Force B-25 Mitchells from the Gilbert Islands bomb Ponape Island, rearm at Majuro Atoll, and bomb Jaluit and Maloelap Atolls on the return to the Carolines.

Bougainville: Thirteenth Air Force P-40s and P-39 Airacobras bomb Aitara and pilots report destroying a bridge near Mawareka.

New Britain: Thirteenth Air Force P-40s and P-39 Airacobras attack Rabaul and Talili Bay ammunition storage sites.

New Guinea: Fifth Air Force A-20 Havocs and B-25 Mitchells supported by 30 P-47 Thunderbolts and P-40s, attack antiaircraft positions, logistics bases, and personnel areas at Hollandia. B-24 Liberators and B-25s bomb barges and antiaircraft positions near Hansa Bay.

April 12

CBI: Tenth Air Force B-25 Mitchells, P-40s, A-36 Intruder (Apache) fighter-bombers, and P-51 Mustangs conduct a ground support mission in the Mogaung Valley and attack logistics sites and targets of opportunity in the Mogaung, Myitkyina, Kamaing, Taungni, and Shaduzup areas.

ETO: Eighth Air Force sends 455 B-17s and B-24 Liberators against industrial facilities in Germany, escorted by 124 P-38 Lightnings, 449 Eighth and Ninth Air Force P-47 Thunderbolts, and 193 Eighth and Ninth Air Force P-51 Mustangs. Aircrews report 10 confirmed kills and six probables. Six B-17s are lost and 28 bombers are damaged. Aircrew casualties are 12 killed, 16 wounded, and 56 missing. Fighter pilots report 18 confirmed kills and one probable, with another confirmed kill on the ground. Five fighters are lost and 23 damaged. Pilot losses are five missing.

Ninth Air Force sends 231 B-26 Marauders and 20 A-20 Havocs to attack railroad, shore batteries, radar installations, airfields, and V-weapon sites along the coast of Belgium and France. Over 70 P-47 Thunderbolts conduct dive-bombing attacks on military installations in northern France.

Mediterranean: Fifteenth Air Force sends over 400 B-17s and B-24 Liberators escorted by more than 200 P-38 Lightnings and P-47 Thunderbolts to attack production facilities in Austria and Yugoslavia. One B-17 and six B-24s are lost. Aircrews and fighter pilots report a total of 43 confirmed kills and 13 probables.

The Fifteenth Air Force receives the headquarters of the 465th Bombardment Group (Heavy) and the B-24s of the 783rd Bombardment Squadron (Heavy) from the United States. The squadron's first mission will be in early May.

Italy: Twelfth Air Force B-25 Mitchells and B-26 Marauders attack road and rail bridges. A-36 Intruder (Apache) fighter-bombers, P-40s, and P-47 Thunderbolts attack logistics sites, railroad bridges, and vehicles.

Pacific: U.S. submarine *Halibut* torpedoes and sinks a Japanese army passenger-cargo ship near the Ryukyus.

CENTRAL PACIFIC: Seventh Air Force B-25 Mitchells from Abemama Island, bomb Maloelap Atoll, rearm at Majuro Atoll, and bomb Jaluit Atoll en route back to Abemama.

BOUGAINVILLE: Thirteenth Air Force P-40s and P-39 Airacobras attack the Numa Numa trail and harbor area.

NEW BRITAIN: Thirteenth Air Force sends 23 B-25 Mitchells and 11 P-39 Airacobras to attack Rabaul and seven B-25 Mitchells attack the logistics base at Ratawul. P-40s and P-39 Airacobras attack Vunakanau airfield.

ADMIRALTIES: The headquarters of Thirteenth Air Force's 5th Bombardment Group (Heavy) is ordered to redeploy from Guadalcanal and New Georgia to Los Negros Island. This headquarters will become the core of the newly created Thirteenth Air Task Force.

NEW GUINEA: Fifth Air Force sends B-24 Liberators, B-25 Mitchells, and A-20 Havocs, with over 60 P-38 Lightnings, to bomb antiaircraft positions, airfields, logistics sites, and shipping construction. B-24 Liberators, B-25 Mitchells, A-20 Havocs, and P-39 Airacobras bomb and strafe targets around Wewak, Madang, and along Hansa Bay.

Fifth Air Force B-24 Liberators, B-25 Mitchells, B-26 Marauders, and P-38 Lightnings bomb Japanese installations in Hollandia, sinking a cargo ship and three fishing vessels. A-20 Havocs sink a cargo ship in Humboldt Bay, Hollandia.

April 13

ALEUTIANS: Eleventh Air Force sends three B-24 Liberators on an armed reconnaissance and bombing mission over the Matsuwa Island airfield and installations on Onnekotan Island.

CBI: Tenth Air Force B-25 Mitchells, P-40s, P-51 Mustangs, and A-36 Intruder (Apache) fighter-bombers fly ground support missions near Kamaing and attack Japanese positions in the Mogaung Valley.

B-29 Superfortresses of the XX Bomber Command arrive in India. The headquarters 468th Bombardment Group (Very Heavy) and the 792nd, 793rd, 794th, and 795th Bombardment Squadrons (Very Heavy) are located at Kharagpur. The 444th Bombardment Group (Very Heavy) and the 677th and 679th Bombardment Squadrons (Very Heavy) are located at Charra. The squadrons' first missions are scheduled for early June.

ETO: Eighth Air Force sends 415 B-17s and 211 B-24 Liberators against industrial production facilities in Germany, escorted by 134 P-38 Lightnings, 504 Eighth and Ninth Air Force P-47 Thunderbolts, and 233 Eighth and Ninth Air Force P-51 Mustangs. A total of 38 bombers are lost and 352 damaged. Aircrew casualties are 15 killed, 19 wounded, and 369 missing. Nine fighters are lost and 13 damaged. Two pilots are wounded and eight are missing.

During the night four B-17s drop leaflets over Amsterdam, The Hague, and Eindhoven in the Netherlands.

Ninth Air Force sends 121 B-26 Marauders and 37 A-20 Havocs to attack a marshaling yard, coastal batteries, airfields and V-weapon sites along the coast of

France and Belgium. Bad weather causes most of the aircraft to abort the mission. P-47 Thunderbolts conduct dive-bombing attacks on V-weapon sites.

MEDITERRANEAN: Fifteenth Air Force sends 535 B-17s and B-24 Liberators against aircraft production facilities in Hungary. Fourteen bombers are lost and aircrews report 40 enemy fighters shot down and over 120 aircraft destroyed on the ground.

The Fifteenth Air Force receives the B-24 Liberators of the 779th Bombardment Squadron (Heavy) of the 464th Bombardment Group (Heavy) from the United States. The squadron's first mission is scheduled for the end of April.

ITALY: Twelfth Air Force B-25 Mitchells and B-26 Marauders attack bridges and a marshaling yard. A-36 Intruder (Apache) fighter-bombers and P-40s attack bridges, rail lines, and vehicles.

CENTRAL PACIFIC: Seventh Air Force B-24 Liberators from Eniwetok bomb Truk. B-25s from Abemama Island bomb Ponape Island. B-25s from Tarawa bomb Jaluit Atoll, rearm at Majuro Atoll, and bomb Maloelap Atoll on their return to Tarawa.

Thirteenth Air Force B-24 Liberators bomb Truk.

U.S. submarine *Harder* torpedoes and sinks a Japanese destroyer near Guam.

NEW BRITAIN: Thirteenth Air Force sends 24 B-25 Mitchells to attack logistics bases at Talili Bay and Ratawul, while P-40s and P-39 Airacobras attack the Rabaul area.

ADMIRALTIES: The B-17s and B-24 Liberators of the 394th Bombardment Group (Heavy), 5th Bombardment Group (Heavy), Thirteenth Air Force redeploy from Guadalcanal to Momote airfield on Los Negros Island.

NEW GUINEA: Fifth Air Force B-24 Liberators and A-20 Havocs attack airfields on the north coast of New Guinea. A-20 Havocs attack Japanese facilities at Aitape. P-39 Airacobras, B-25 Mitchells, and B-24s attack targets around Hansa Bay and Wakde Island.

April 14

CBI: The Chinese agree to support an offensive in Burma with Y Force.

Tenth Air Force P-40s attack Japanese positions in the Mogaung Valley.

ETO: The air plan for Neptune is laid out, consisting of a preparation phase and an assault phase. Air Chief Marshall Trafford Leigh-Mallory is the commander of the tactical air forces. The British Second Tactical Air Force and the U.S. Ninth Air Force are to provide support to the ground forces landing on the beaches. The Second Tactical Air Force targets are rail lines, bridges, airfields, coastal batteries, and radar sites in order to restrict German reinforcements from reaching the beachhead.

General Eisenhower, commander of Supreme Headquarters Allied Expeditionary Forces (SHAEF), takes operational control of strategic air forces from the CCS to support the invasion of Europe. Eisenhower now can direct what targets are to be attacked within the ETO, subject to the approval of the CCS. As a primary mission, the strategic air forces will target industrial and economic targets in Germany and provide direct support to the ground forces as a secondary mission. Strategic forces will attack French and Belgian rail lines to restrict resupply and reinforcement of German forces in Normandy.

ITALY: Twelfth Air Force B-25 Mitchells and B-26 Marauders target rail facilities, viaducts, and bridges. A-36 Intruder (Apache) fighter-bombers and P-40s attack rail lines and bridges as well as logistics sites, gun positions, and production facilities.

CENTRAL PACIFIC: Seventh Air Force B-25s from Eniwetok bomb Ponape Island. B-25s from Abemama Island bomb Jaluit Atoll rearm at Majuro Atoll, and bomb Maloelap Atoll on the return to Tarawa. Thirteenth Air Force sends 19 B-24 Liberators to bomb Truk.

Japanese bombers attack Eniwetok Atoll but cause no significant damage.

BOUGAINVILLE: Thirteenth Air Force P-40s and P-39 Airacobras attack targets in the northeast section of the island.

NEW BRITAIN: Thirteenth Air Force sends 24 B-25 Mitchells and P-40s and P-39 Airacobras to attack the logistics base at Ratawul and hit targets at Wunapope.

April 15
ALEUTIANS: During the night three Eleventh Air Force B-24 Liberators on an armed reconnaissance mission over Matsuwa and Onnekotan Islands attack several targets, including Matsuwa airfield.

Vice Admiral Frank Jack Fletcher takes command of Alaskan Sea Frontier at Adak, Aleutian Islands.

ATLANTIC: The CCS authorizes an increase in naval forces to support the new assessment that increases the number of assault divisions for Neptune from three to five. The total naval force available includes six battleships, 22 cruisers, and 93 destroyers.

ETO: Eighth Air Force sends 132 P-38 Lightnings, 262 P-47 Thunderbolts, and 222 Eighth and Ninth Air Force P-51 Mustangs on a fighter sweep attacking airfields in central and western Germany. Fighter pilots report a total of 57 confirmed kills and one probable. U.S. aircraft losses are 33 downed and 36 damaged. Thirty pilots are reported missing.

MEDITERRANEAN: Fifteenth Air Force sends 448 B-17s and B-24 Liberators with fighter escort to attack marshaling yards in Romania and Yugoslavia.

Army Air Force personnel begin meetings with Josef Broz Tito, leader of the Yugoslav partisans, at his headquarters in Drvar, Yugoslavia. The objective is to enlist Tito's support in assisting downed U.S. air crewmen to escape capture and return to friendly lines.

ITALY: Twelfth Air Force B-25 Mitchells and B-26 Marauders attack the Leghorn marshaling yard. P-47 Thunderbolts, P-40s, and A-36 Intruder (Apache) fighter-bombers attack rail lines, vehicles, tanks, and gun positions.

SOUTHWEST PACIFIC AREA: U.S. submarine *Redfin* attacks a Japanese convoy southwest of Mindanao and damages a cargo ship.

PACIFIC: Japanese cargo ship is sunk off Honshu, Japan, probably by a mine laid by U.S. submarine *Steelhead*.

CENTRAL PACIFIC: Major General Robert W. Douglass, Jr., takes command of the Seventh Air Force.

B-25 Mitchells from Tarawa bomb Maloelap Atoll, rearm at Majuro Atoll, and bomb Mille and Jaluit Atolls on the return to Tarawa.

Abemama Naval Base in the Gilbert Islands is established.

NEW BRITAIN: Thirteenth Air Force sends 24 B-25 Mitchells to bomb an ammunition storage facility on Talili Bay, followed by 11 P-39 Airacobras hitting the same target. P-38 Lightnings attack the logistics base at Wunapope.

ADMIRALTIES: Thirteenth Air Force redeploys the B-24 Liberators of the 72nd Bombardment Squadron (Heavy), 5th Bombardment Group (Heavy), from Munda, New Georgia, to Momote airfield, Los Negros Island.

NEW GUINEA: Fifth Air Force sends over 180 B-24 Liberators, B-25 Mitchells, and A-20 Havocs to attack airfields and Japanese positions near Aitape and along the northern coast. P-39 Airacobras attack Japanese positions, logistics sites, and vehicles between Hansa Bay and the Alexishafen area.

April 16

CBI: Nine P-38 Lightnings from the Tenth Air Force shoot down three Japanese medium bombers at Zayatkwin, near Rangoon.

The XX Bomber Command receives the 768th Bombardment Squadron (Very Heavy), 462nd Bombardment Group (Very Heavy), at Piardoba, India. The B-29 Superfortresses will fly their first missions in early June.

ATLANTIC: The battleship USS *Wisconsin* is commissioned at Philadelphia, Pennsylvania. It is the last battleship built for the U.S. Navy.

German submarine *U-550* torpedoes a tanker in convoy CU 1 (New York to United Kingdom) off the New Jersey coast. The tanker is abandoned. Later, the destroyer escort USS *Gandy* rams *U-550* off Nantucket Shoals and, with other escort ships, sinks the U-boat.

MEDITERRANEAN: Fifteenth Air Force sends 432 B-17s and B-24 Liberators to attack industrial production facilities in Romania and Yugoslavia and marshaling yards in Romania.

The Fifteenth Air Force reports the 31st Fighter Group is operational. The P-51 Mustang-equipped unit had been transferred from Twelfth Air Force earlier in the month.

German submarine *U-407* attacks convoy UGS 37 (United States to Mediterranean, Slow) off Libya and torpedoes two U.S. freighters. One is sunk and the other is beached.

ITALY: Twelfth Air Force B-25 Mitchells bomb railway bridges. A-20 Havocs attack fuel storage areas. P-40s, P-47 Thunderbolts, and A-36 Intruder (Apache) fighter-bombers attack transportation targets, vehicles, and ammunition storage sites.

SOUTHWEST PACIFIC AREA: U.S. submarine *Redfin* makes a second attack on a Japanese convoy southwest of Mindanao, sinking a cargo ship.

CENTRAL PACIFIC: Seventh Air Force B-25 Mitchells, staging through Eniwetok, bomb Truk. B-25s from Abemama Island bomb Maloelap Atoll, rearm at Majuro Atoll, and bomb Mille Atoll en route back to Abemama.

NEW BRITAIN: Thirteenth Air Force sends 24 B-25 Mitchells to attack the logistics base at Ratawul. P-40s and P-39 Airacobras attack Rabaul.

ADMIRALTIES: Thirteenth Air Force redeploys the B-24 Liberators of the 23rd Bombardment Squadron (Heavy), 5th Bombardment Group (Heavy), from Munda, New Georgia, to Momote airfield, Los Negros Island.

NEW GUINEA: Fifth Air Force sends over 170 B-24 Liberators, B-25 Mitchells, and A-20 Havocs to bomb targets around Hollandia. P-38 Lightnings attack targets around Madang. B-24s attack Wakde Island.

B-25s bomb Koepang on Timor Island.

U.S. submarine *Paddle* attacks a Japanese convoy and sinks a transport and a cargo ship in the Ceram Sea.

April 17

CBI: The Japanese *Ichigo* Offensive in China. The Japanese attempt to forestall Allied efforts to establish B-29 bases in China and to secure for themselves an overland supply route stretching from Seoul, Korea, to Saigon, French Indochina. Because of the effectiveness of the U.S. submarine campaign on shipping, the Japanese armies in China require this overland supply route to sustain any offensive operations. The Japanese employ 820,000 men in this offensive, with the initial attack directed against Hunan province. The Chinese are completely unprepared and the Fourteenth Air Force has already warned Stilwell and Chiang Kai-shek that it will be unable to stem the advance. The Japanese forces cross the Yellow River and begin an advance toward the rail line at Hankow.

General Stilwell orders General Chennault to defend the B-29 airbases at Chengtu as the Japanese begin an offensive to open a north-south corridor from the Yellow River to Hangkow and south to Changsha and then to Hengyang. The intent is to link with Japanese forces in Indochina. Two Japanese divisions cross the Yellow River with tanks.

Tenth Air Force B-25 Mitchells and P-51 Mustangs support ground forces. P-51s are diverted to intercept Japanese aircraft over Imphal, India. Fighter pilots report three confirmed kills.

ATLANTIC: A minesweeper and submarine chaser sink German submarine *U-986* in the North Atlantic.

ETO: Eighth Air Force sends 15 B-24 Liberators escorted by 33 P-47 Thunderbolts to bomb the V-weapon site at Wizernes, France. During the night five B-17s drop one million leaflets over Rennes, Brest, Nantes, Lorient, and St-Nazaire France.

MEDITERRANEAN: Fifteenth Air Force sends 470 B-17s and B-24 Liberators to attack production facilities in Bulgaria and Yugoslavia; B-17s bomb industrial areas marshaling yards, and an air depot in Yugoslavia and Bulgaria. Over 20 fighters escort the bombers. Aircrews and fighters report 25 confirmed kills.

Two U.S. freighters are damaged when they hit Allied mines off the Isle of Capri.

ITALY: Twelfth Air Force B-25 Mitchells attack bridges and A-20 Havocs attack a fuel storage area. P-40s, P-47 Thunderbolts, and A-36 Intruder (Apache) fighter-bombers attack logistics sites, rail lines, and gun positions.

SOUTHWEST PACIFIC AREA: U.S. submarines *Barb* and *Steelhead* shell the phosphate works on Rasa Island in the southwest Philippines.

PACIFIC: U.S. submarine *Searaven* torpedoes and sinks a Japanese auxiliary mine-sweeper south of Haha Jima in the Bonin Islands.

CENTRAL PACIFIC: Seventh Air Force B-25 Mitchells based on Tarawa bomb Maloelap Atoll, rearm at Majuro Atoll, and bomb Mille Atoll on the return to Tarawa.

U.S. submarine *Harder* attacks a Japanese convoy and sinks a cargo ship near Woleai Atoll in the Carolines.

NEW BRITAIN: Thirteenth Air Force sends 24 B-25 Mitchells to attack Rapopo airfield. Over 40 P-39 Airacobras and P-40s attack Matupi with incendiaries.

NEW GUINEA: Fifth Air Force sends more than 20 B-24 Liberators to bomb logistics depots and troop concentrations in Kai Island in the Moluccas.

April 18

ALEUTIANS: U.S. freighter hits a mine and sinks off Sanak Island in the Aleutians.

CBI: Tenth Air Force sends 15 B-25 Mitchells and four P-51 Mustangs to bomb Kamaing and attack the Myitkyina-Bhamo road.

ETO: Eighth Air Force sends 501 B-17s and 275 B-24 Liberators, escorted by 119 P-38 Lightnings, 296 P-47 Thunderbolts, and 219 Eighth and Ninth Air Force P-51 Mustangs, against airfields and aircraft production facilities in Germany. Weather conditions force some aircraft to attack targets of opportunity around Berlin. Aircrews and fighter pilots report 33 confirmed kills and five probables. A total of 19 bombers are lost and 204 are damaged. Aircrew casualties are two killed, 17 wounded, and 188 missing. Fighter pilots report five aircraft lost and 31 damaged. Four pilots are reported missing.

B-24 Liberators, escorted by 36 P-47s attack a V-weapon site at Watten, France. One bomber is damaged.

During the night, five B-17s drop over two million leaflets over Stavanger, Oslo, Bergen, and Trondheim, Norway.

Eighth Air Force receives the headquarters of the 492nd Bombardment Group (Heavy) from the United States.

Ninth Air Force sends 277 B-26 Marauders (including 24 dropping Window, strips of aluminum intended to disrupt radar) and 37 A-20 Havocs to bomb gun positions and marshaling yards at Dunkirk, Calais, and Charleroi in France.

ITALY: Fifteenth Air Force P-38 Lightnings and P-47 Thunderbolts strafe airfields.

Twelfth Air Force P-40s and P-47s attack fuel storage areas and a railroad bridge.

PACIFIC: U.S. submarine *Gudgeon* is sunk off Iwo Jima.

U.S. submarine *Tambor* torpedoes and sinks a Japanese guardboat near Wake Island.

A Japanese convoy of four transports and escorts from Pusan, Korea, carrying elements of the 32nd and 35th Divisions to reinforce garrisons in the Halmaheras and in northwestern New Guinea, meets a second convoy from Shanghai.

CENTRAL PACIFIC: Seventh Air Force B-24 Liberators from Eniwetok escort navy PB4Y Privateers on a photographic reconnaissance mission of Saipan, Tinian, and Aguijan Islands. The B-24s bomb Saipan in the Marianas, and two bombers are lost. Other B-24s from Eniwetok attack Truk. B-25 Mitchells from Tarawa bomb Ponape

Island. B-24s from Kwajalein bomb Wake Island. B-25 Mitchells from Abemama Island bomb Jaluit Atoll, rearm at Majuro Atoll, and bomb Maloelap Atoll on the return flight to Abemama.

NEW BRITAIN: Thirteenth Air Force B-25 Mitchells, unable to bomb the primary target at Vunakanau, bomb Tobera airfield. P-39 Airacobras and P-40s attack the logistics base at Wunapope.

ADMIRALTIES: B-24 Liberators of Thirteenth Air Task Force launch from Momote Airfield, Los Negros Island, to bomb Woleai Atoll and Mariaon Island in the Carolines.

NEW GUINEA: Fifth Air Force takes operational control of the new Thirteenth Air Task Force (Provisional) commanded by Major General St. Clair Streett. The unit has elements of the Thirteenth Air Force, some Royal Australian Air Force (RAAF) squadrons, navy air units from Seventh Fleet, and Fifth Air Force units located in the Admiralties and New Britain.

April 19

ATLANTIC: TBF Avengers from escort carrier USS *Tripoli* attack German submarine *U-543* without success.

ETO: Eighth Air Force sends 246 B-17s and 249 B-24 Liberators, escorted by 127 P-38 Lightnings, 439 Eighth and Ninth Air Force P-47 Thunderbolts, and 131 Eighth and Ninth Air Force P-51 Mustangs against airfields in Germany. Aircrews report 17 confirmed enemy aircraft kills and one probable. Five bombers are lost and 33 are damaged. Aircrew casualties are three killed, 11 wounded, and 63 missing. Fighter pilots report 16 confirmed kills and one probable. Two fighters are lost and nine are damaged. Two pilots are reported missing.

Another attack by 27 B-24s escorted by 47 Ninth Air Force P-47 Thunderbolts against V-weapon sites at Watten, France, results in no losses.

Ninth Air Force sends over 350 B-26 Marauders and A-20 Havocs to bomb marshaling yards, city areas, and targets of opportunity in southern Germany.

MEDITERRANEAN: The CCS orders Mediterranean theater commander in chief, General Sir Henry Maitland Wilson, to initiate offensive operations in Italy to support Overlord.

ITALY: Twelfth Air Force B-26 Marauders and B-25 Mitchells bomb marshaling yards, and P-47 Thunderbolts attack rail lines, rail cars, and a marshaling yard.

SOUTHWEST PACIFIC AREA: U.S. submarine *Finback* torpedoes and sinks a Japanese sampan in the Strait of Malacca.

PACIFIC: Headquarters Twentieth Air Force takes operational control of XX Bomber Command. Twentieth Air Force receives the 769th and 770th Bombardment Squadrons (Very Heavy) of the 462nd Bombardment Group (Very Heavy) from the United States. Arriving at Piardoba, India, the B-29 Superfortresses will fly their first missions in early June.

CENTRAL PACIFIC: Seventh Air Force B-24 Liberators from Eniwetok bomb Truk. B-25 Mitchells from the Gilbert Islands bomb Ponape Island.

Thirteenth Air Force sends 21 B-24 Liberators to bomb the airfield on Satawan Atoll in the Carolines, located west of Truk.

NEW BRITAIN: P-39 Airacobras and P-40s attack logistics sites at Matupi and the airfield at Rapopo.

NEW GUINEA: An Allied naval force initiates Operation Cockpit. Admiral Sir James F. Somerville (RN), commander in chief of the British Eastern Fleet, commands a combined force of British and American ships (the carrier USS *Saratoga* and three destroyers) intended to attack Japanese defenses and shipping in the Netherlands East Indies. This is the first combined offensive operation in the Indian Ocean. Carrier aircraft from the *Saratoga* and HMS *Illustrious* sink a minelayer and two transports.

April 20

CBI: The Chinese 22nd Division finally advances after strong pressure from General Stilwell. Chiang Kai-shek's influence on the division commander has prevented Stilwell's orders from being carried out.

ETO: Eighth Air Force sends 630 B-17s and 212 B-24 Liberators, escorted by 89 P-38 Lightnings, 211 P-47 Thunderbolts, and 88 P-51 Mustangs, to attack 33 V-weapon sites in France. Nine bombers are lost and 348 are damaged. Aircrew casualties are 12 killed, 34 wounded, and 89 missing. Fighter pilots report four confirmed kills in the air and four on the ground. Two fighters are lost and one is damaged. Two pilots are reported missing.

Eighth Fighter Command sends 35 P-51 fighter-bombers and 56 P-38 fighter-bombers to attack airfields in France and Belgium. The P-38s abort the mission.

During the night, five B-17s drop nearly two million leaflets over Nantes, Orleans, Tours, and Paris.

Ninth Air Force sends nearly 400 B-26 Marauders and A-20 Havocs to attack gun positions, the airfield at Poix, and V-weapon sites. In addition, nearly 140 P-47 Thunderbolts bomb marshaling yards in France.

MEDITERRANEAN: German torpedo planes attack the 87-ship convoy UGS 38 (United States to Mediterranean, Slow) off the coast of French Morocco. Destroyer USS *Lansdale* is sunk as well as a U.S. freighter carrying ammunition. Another freighter is torpedoed and damaged, but makes it to Algiers.

ITALY: Fifteenth Air Force sends over 300 B-17s and B-24 Liberators escorted by over 250 fighters to attack marshaling yards and harbor installations.

Twelfth Air Force B-25s and B-26 Marauders bomb the marshaling yard and fuel storage areas at Leghorn. A-36 Intruder (Apache) fighter-bombers and P-40s attack rail lines, rail cars, and fuel storage areas. Around Cassino fighter-bombers attack gun positions, bridges, trucks, troops, and other targets.

CENTRAL PACIFIC: U.S. submarine *Seahorse* (SS-304) torpedoes and sinks Japanese submarine *RO-45* off the Marianas.

SOUTHERN PACIFIC: Major General Field Harris (USMC) becomes Commander Air Solomons (COMAIRSOLS).

CENTRAL PACIFIC: Seventh Air Force B-25 Mitchells from Tarawa bomb Maloelap, rearm at Majuro Atoll, and bomb Jaluit Atoll on the return to Tarawa. The B-25s of the 396th Bombardment Squadron (Medium), 41st Bombardment Group (Medium), redeploy from Tarawa to Makin Island.

New Britain: Thirteenth Air Force B-25 Mitchells attack the logistics base at Matupi and P-39 Airacobras and P-40s attack the Lakunai and Keravat airfields.

Admiralties: B-24 Liberators of the 31st Bombardment Squadron (Heavy), 5th Bombardment Group (Heavy) redeploy from Guadalcanal to Momote airfield, Los Negros Island.

New Guinea: Fifth Air Force B-24 Liberators bomb the airfields on Noemfoor Island.

B-24s of the Thirteenth Air Task Force of the Fifth Air Force bomb Woleai Atoll in the Carolines.

April 21

CBI: In Burma, Tenth Air Force B-25 Mitchells bomb logistics sites and camps at Kamaing. B-24 Liberators bomb fuel storage sites at Lashio. Fourteenth Air Force P-40s attack construction equipment and troops at Lashio.

ETO: Ninth Air Force sends 236 B-26 Marauders and 34 A-20 Havocs to attack gun positions, coastal defenses, and V-weapon sites in France. Four B-26s are lost. Over 175 P-47 Thunderbolts conduct dive-bombing attacks on marshaling yards in France.

Mediterranean: Fifteenth Air Force sends over 100 B-24 Liberators to bomb marshaling yards at Bucharest, Romania. Some bombers fail to receive the recall message and hit the primary target. About 40 P-38 Lightnings and P-51 Mustangs accompany the bombers to the target and fight off 30 German fighters. P-51 Mustangs report 17 confirmed kills and seven probables. This is the first combat action for P-51 Mustangs over deep targets. Other fighters returning to base encounter 40 German fighters. Aircrews and fighter pilots report 35 confirmed kills.

Italy: Twelfth Air Force A-20 Havocs attack an ammunition storage area. P-47 Thunderbolts, along with P-40s and A-36 Intruder (Apache) fighter-bombers, attack rail lines, vehicles, trains, a motor transport concentration, and several gun positions.

Central Pacific: Seventh Air Force B-24 Liberators from Kwajalein bomb Wotje Atoll. B-24 Liberators from Eniwetok stage through Kwajalein and bomb Truk. B-25 Mitchells from Engebi Island, Eniwetok Atoll, bomb Ponape Island. B-25 Mitchells on Abemama Island bomb Maloelap Atoll, rearm at Majuro Atoll, and bomb Jaluit Atoll on their return to Abemama.

U.S. submarine *Stingray* sinks after hitting an underwater obstacle west of the Marianas.

Bougainville: Thirteenth Air Force P-39 Airacobras, unable to attack Rabaul due to bad weather over the target, divert to attack targets around Tinputs Harbor.

New Britain: Thirteenth Air Force sends 24 B-25 Mitchells to attack the logistics base at Matupi.

Admiralties: Construction of a new airfield is completed at Mokerang on Manus Island.

Thirteenth Air Force orders Headquarters, 307th Bombardment Group (Heavy), to redeploy from New Georgia and Guadalcanal to the Admiralty Islands, where it will become part of the Thirteenth Air Task Force.

New Guinea: Fifth Air Force sends 21 B-24 Liberators to bomb the airfields on Noemfoor Island. Over 300 B-24 Liberators, B-25 Mitchells, and A-20 Havocs attack targets around Tadji, Wewak, and Madang.

Navy Task Force 58, with five carriers and seven small carriers, commanded by Vice Admiral Marc A. Mitscher, attacks Japanese airfields and defensive positions at Hollandia, Wakde, and Sawar, in preparation for Operations Persecution and Reckless. A Japanese cargo ship is sunk by aircraft off Sarmi and U.S. Navy aircraft sink several small Japanese cargo vessels.

April 22

CBI: Elements of the U.S. 1st Provisional Tank Group support Chinese infantry near Warazup.

In Burma, Tenth Air Force B-25 Mitchells bomb Kamaing. Fourteenth Air Force P-40s report destroying 10 boxcars and a truck near Lashio.

Fourteenth Air Force B-24 Liberators attack a Japanese convoy from Singapore anchored off the coast of French Indochina, near Saigon, and sink a transport, a fleet tanker, a cargo vessel, and a merchant tanker. Another tanker is damaged.

ETO: Eighth Air Force sends 526 B-17s and 277 B-24 Liberators, escorted by 132 P-38 Lightnings, 485 Eighth and Ninth Air Force P-47 Thunderbolts, and 242 Eighth and Ninth Air Force P-51 Mustangs against the marshaling yard at Hamm, Germany. Aircrews report 20 confirmed kills and six probables. A total of 15 bombers are lost and 212 are damaged. Aircrew casualties are seven wounded and 89 missing. Fighter pilots report 40 confirmed kills and two probables. A total of 13 fighters are lost and 23 are damaged. One pilot is wounded and 12 are reported missing.

During the night five B-17s drop more than 1 million leaflets over Orleans, Tours, Rouen, Nantes, Lille, Reims, Chartres, and Paris.

Eighth Air Force receives Headquarters, 398th Bombardment Group (Heavy), and the B-17s of the 600th, 601st, 602nd, and 603rd Bombardment Squadrons (Heavy). The squadrons' first missions are scheduled for early May. The B-24s of the 844th, 845th, 846th, and 847th Bombardment Squadrons (Heavy) of the 489th Bombardment Group (Heavy) arrive from the United States. The squadrons' first missions are scheduled for late May.

Ninth Air Force sends over 400 B-26 Marauders and nearly 90 A-20 Havocs against V-weapon sites in France. About 275 P-47 Thunderbolts and P-51 Mustangs conduct dive-bomb attacks on marshaling yards in Belgium.

Italy: Twelfth Air Force B-25 Mitchells and B-26 Marauders attack bridges and viaducts. A-20 Havocs attack the Valmontone ammunition storage area and P-47 Thunderbolts attack rail lines, trains, and a marshaling yard. P-40s attack gun positions north of the Anzio battle line and attack logistics storage areas and troop positions at Fondi, Terracina, and Formia.

Central Pacific: Seventh Air Force B-24 Liberators from Kwajalein bomb Wotje Atoll on a nighttime raid. B-24s from Kwajalein attack Wotje during the day. B-25 Mitchells from Tarawa bomb Maloelap and Mille Atolls, rearm at Majuro Atoll, and bomb Jaluit Atoll on return to Tarawa. Thirteenth Air Force sends 17 B-24 Liberators to bomb Dublon, Param, and Eten Islands in Truk Atoll.

A Navy PB4Y Privateer sights survivors of USAAF B-24 Liberators damaged over the Marianas and ditched on April 18; a PBY sent to rescue the aviators suffers damage in landing and is unable to take off (see April 23).

New Britain: The marines fight the final engagement with elements of Japanese forces in western New Britain. The campaign has cost the Americans 310 killed and 1,083 wounded and has been fought in some of the most forbidding conditions any combat unit will encounter in the Second World War. The Japanese have lost nearly three times the number of American casualties and are now clustered around Rabaul, virtual prisoners and no longer a factor in the war.

Thirteenth Air Force B-25 Mitchells bomb logistics bases at Ratawul and Talili Bay. P-39 Airacobras and P-40s attack Rapopo and Lakunai airfields.

New Guinea: Operation Reckless. Navy Task Force 77 under Rear Admiral Daniel E. Barbey lands troops at Aitape and Tanahmerah Bay in Operation Persecution, and at Humboldt Bay, Hollandia, in Operation Reckless. The landings take place 300 miles behind the main Japanese defensive perimeter. Rear Admiral Barbey also commands Naval Task Group 77.1, which lands the 163rd RCT, 41st Infantry Division (Brigadier General Doe), at Aitape. TG 77.2 under command of Rear Admiral Fechteler lands the 24th Infantry Division (Major General Irving) at Tanahmerah Bay. TG 77.3 (Captain Alfred G. Noble) lands the 41st Infantry Division (Major General Irving) at Humboldt Bay. TF 78 is the escort carrier force under Rear Admiral Ralph E. Davison, which provides air cover for the landings. TF 74 (Rear Admiral Victor A. C. Crutchley, Royal Navy) and TF 75 (Rear Admiral Russell S. Berkey) provide gunfire support. TF 58 with five carriers and seven small carriers under Vice Admiral Marc A. Mitscher also provides air support.

The 24th Infantry Division and 41st Infantry Division land on the beaches near Hollandia after a 45-minute naval and air bombardment and encounter no opposition. Lieutenant General Robert L. Eichelberger, commander of I Corps, along with Lieutenant General Walter Krueger, Alamo Force commander, Rear Admiral Daniel E. Barbey, and General MacArthur accompany the troops. At Tanahmerah Bay, the 19th and 21st RCTs of the 24th Infantry Division encounter a swamp that prevents inland movement. The beach at Humboldt Bay is shallow and supplies begin to pile up along the shore until engineers can open roads into the interior.

Two battalions of the 163rd RCT land at Aitape and encounter no enemy. They move inland and capture Tadji airfield.

Fifth Air Force sends over 20 B-24 Liberators to bomb airfields on Noemfoor Island. Over 80 B-24s and A-20 Havocs attack targets near Wewak. Over 100 B-24s and B-25 Mitchells attack Hansa Bay, Wewak, Bogia, and Madang.

April 23

Aleutians: Eleventh Air Force sends three B-24 Liberators to conduct photographic reconnaissance of Matsuwa Island and operate within 100 miles of the Kurile Islands.

CBI: In China, Fourteenth Air Force sends 14 P-40s to attack artillery at Sienning and cavalry forces at Kuan-Fou-Chiao.

ETO: Eighth Air Force sends 136 P-38s, 166 P-47 Thunderbolts, and 80 P-51 Mustangs to attack airfields and other targets in France, Belgium, and Germany. Fighter pilots report 11 confirmed kills on the ground. Seven aircraft are lost and 25 are damaged. Seven pilots are reported missing.

During the night five B-17s drop nearly two million leaflets over Rennes, Brest, Lorient, St-Nazaire, and Nantes, France. Nine B-24s support Carpetbagger operations.

The Eighth Air Force receives the B-24s of the 4th, 7th, 18th, and 391st Bombardment Squadrons (Heavy) of the 34th Bombardment Group (Heavy). The squadrons' first missions are scheduled for late May.

Ninth Air Force sends 307 B-26 Marauders and 57 A-20 Havocs to attack V-weapon sites, gun positions, and marshaling yards in France and Belgium. About 1,000 P-47 Thunderbolts and P-51 Mustangs conduct dive-bombing attacks on targets throughout France and the Netherlands.

MEDITERRANEAN: Fifteenth Air Force sends 583 B-24 Liberators and 171 B-17s to attack three aircraft production targets near Vienna, Austria. Over 100 German aircraft attack the formations and shoot down two B-17s and 11 B-24s along with three fighters. Aircrews and fighter pilots report a total of 51 confirmed kills and 16 probables.

ITALY: Twelfth Air Force B-25 Mitchells and B-26 Marauders attack bridges, a marshaling yard, and viaducts. P-47 Thunderbolts, A-36 Intruder (Apache) fighter-bombers, and P-40s attack rail lines and bridges.

SOUTHWEST PACIFIC AREA: A Japanese destroyer hits a mine dropped by Fourteenth Air Force aircraft in the Makassar Strait.

PACIFIC: U.S. submarine *Seadragon* attacks a Japanese convoy and sinks a cargo ship off Honshu, Japan.

CENTRAL PACIFIC: Plans for Operation Forager are completed. The naval force is composed of 14 battleships, seven fleet carriers, eight light carriers, and 14 escort carriers, supported by 136 destroyers. Land forces consist of two amphibious corps, composed of three marine and two army divisions and one marine brigade. On June 15, the first landings will begin on Saipan, followed by Tinian and Guam.

Seventh Air Force B-24 Liberators from Kwajalein bomb Truk and Wotje Atolls. B-25 Mitchells from Makin Island bomb Ponape Island and Jaluit and Maloelap Atolls.

In the Marianas, destroyer *Gansevoort* rescues B-24 Liberator crewmen and the crew of a Navy PBY Catalina initially sent to rescue the bomber crew, shot down on April 18.

NEW BRITAIN: Thirteenth Air Force P-39 Airacobras and P-40s attack Tobera and B-25 Mitchells bomb Matupi Island.

NEW GUINEA: Operation Reckless. Elements of the 24th Infantry Division struggle through exceptionally difficult terrain and advance 10 miles from their landing site at Tanahmerah Bay. At Humboldt Bay, a lone Japanese aircraft drops a single bomb that hits the supplies piled all along the beach. Ammunition, gasoline, vehicles, rations, and every other type of supplies are destroyed in a terrific inferno. The heroic efforts of the 2nd Engineer Special Brigade prevent a total disaster, but over 120 Americans are killed or wounded.

The 127th Infantry Regiment of the 32nd Infantry Division lands at Aitape to reinforce the 163rd RCT in case of a Japanese counterattack.

Fifth Air Force B-24 Liberators bomb the airfields on Noemfoor Island. Aircrews report 14 enemy aircraft shot down. B-24s bomb Wewak, Boram, and But airfields; B-24 Liberators, B-25 Mitchells, and A-20 Havocs attack airfields, antiaircraft positions, and troops at Hansa Bay. A-20 Havocs, P-47 Thunderbolts, P-38 Lightnings, and P-39 Airacobras also attack targets along Hansa Bay and around Wewak and also near Uligan harbor.

Thirteenth Air Task Force B-24 Liberators under Fifth Air Force bomb the airfield and logistics bases on Woleai Atoll.

April 24

ALEUTIANS: In the Kurile Islands, an Eleventh Air Force B-24 Liberator flies a photo reconnaissance and bombing run over Matsuwa Island. A second B-24 flies weather and bombing runs over Shasukotan, Yekaruma, Kharimkotan, and Onnekotan Islands.

CBI: Tenth Air Force P-40s, P-51 Mustangs, A-36 Intruder (Apache) fighter-bombers, and B-25 Mitchells bomb logistics storage areas, railroads, and Japanese positions near Kamaing and Myitkyina.

In Thailand, Fourteenth Air Force B-25 Mitchells damage bridges.

Two Twentieth Air Force B-29 Superfortresses are the first to fly the Hump route. They land at Kwanghan, China.

U.S. submarine *Robalo* is damaged by an air attack off the coast of French Indochina but remains on patrol.

ATLANTIC: The zones of occupation for postwar Germany are allocated. The United States will occupy southwest Germany. Berlin, although in the Soviet Zone, will be divided into occupation zones as well.

ETO: Eighth Air Force sends 524 B-17s and 230 B-24 Liberators, escorted by 131 P-38 Lightnings, 490 Eighth and Ninth Air Force P-47 Thunderbolts, and 246 Eighth and Ninth Air Force P-51 Mustangs, against aircraft production facilities, airfields, and targets of opportunity in Germany. A total of 40 bombers are lost and 257 damaged. Aircrew casualties are 11 killed, 27 wounded, and 371 missing. Fighter pilots report 70 confirmed enemy kills and six probables in the air and 57 confirmed kills on the ground. Seventeen fighters are lost and 31 damaged. Seventeen pilots are reported missing.

During the night five B-17s drop over one million leaflets on Amsterdam, Rotterdam, The Hague, and Utrecht in the Netherlands and over Lille and Reims in France. Eight B-24s support Carpetbagger missions.

Ninth Air Force sends 32 P-47 Thunderbolts against the Louvain marshaling yard in Belgium.

MEDITERRANEAN: Fifteenth Air Force sends over 520 B-17s and B-24 Liberators escorted by over 250 fighters against marshaling yards, aircraft production facilities, and rail lines in Romania, Yugoslavia, and Italy.

ITALY: Twelfth Air Force B-26 Marauders attack railroad bridges. A-20 Havocs attack the ammunition storage area at Valmontone. P-40s, P-47 Thunderbolts, and A-36 Intruder (Apache) fighter-bombers attack shipping off Leghorn, marshaling yards, rail lines, vehicles, and targets of opportunity.

Private First Class John C. Squires is the platoon messenger in A Company, 30th Infantry Regiment, 3rd Infantry Division, as it attacks German positions at Spaccasassi Creek near Padiglione. This is his first offensive action, and he reaches the leading platoon, makes a quick assessment of the situation, and makes a recommendation to the platoon leader for an alternate approach. On his own initiative, Private First Class Squires organizes a group of stragglers into an ad hoc squad and leads them forward. At Spaccasassi Creek Squires puts troops in position and brings up reinforcements as his platoon is reduced to only 14 men by enemy fire. On every trip to bring up reinforcements he has to cross a minefield under artillery fire. The Germans make three counterattacks on the platoon's position, and each time Private First Class Squires engages the enemy with a Browning automatic rifle and a captured German machine gun. He also engages 21 German soldiers in a close battle on the flank of the American position, firing a machine gun into their midst and capturing the entire attacking force. He employs additional captured machine guns, instructing the members of his platoon on their operation and function. He continues to hold the position against German attacks. For his dedication to duty and leadership Private First Class Squires will receive the Medal of Honor.

CENTRAL PACIFIC: Seventh Air Force B-25 Mitchells from Engebi Island bomb Ponape Island. B-25s from Makin Island bomb Jaluit and Wotje Atolls.

The headquarters of the 41st Bombardment Group (Medium) moves from Tarawa to Makin Island.

NEW BRITAIN: Thirteenth Air Force P-40s attack the airfield at Tobera.

NEW GUINEA: At Aitape, Tadji airfield is operational. Australian Air Force P-40s arrive to support the American infantry.

Fifth Air Force B-24 Liberators bomb the airfields on Noemfoor Island. B-24s also bomb airfields at Wewak area. B-25 Mitchells and A-20 Havocs attack targets around Hansa Bay, and Uligan harbor and support Allied forces at Madang.

April 25

CBI: Tenth Air Force B-25 Mitchells, P-51 Mustangs, and B-24 Liberators attack Japanese enemy positions, logistics sites, airfields, and headquarters elements.

ETO: Eighth Air Force sends 355 B-17s and 199 B-24 Liberators against marshaling yards and airfields in France and Germany, escorted by 177 P-38 Lightnings, 296 P-47 Thunderbolts, and 246 Eighth and Ninth Air Force P-51 Mustangs. A total of 36 bombers are lost and 59 damaged. Aircrew casualties are two killed, seven wounded, and 69 missing. Fighter pilots report 39 confirmed kills and seven probables in the air and 29 confirmed kills and seven probables on the ground. Two fighters are lost and eight are damaged. One pilot is killed and two are missing.

An attack by 28 B-24s escorted by 40 P-47s to bomb V-weapon sites in France results in no friendly losses.

During the night, six B-17s drop four million leaflets over northeastern France.

Ninth Air Force sends 240 B-26 Marauders and 69 A-20 Havocs to attack V-weapon sites and gun positions in France. Bad weather over the targets causes most of the bombers to abort the mission. Nearly 150 P-47 Thunderbolts conduct dive-bomb attacks on airfields in France and Belgium.

ITALY: Fifteenth Air Force B-24 Liberators bomb an aircraft production facility and marshaling yards in northern Italy.

Fifteenth Air Force receives the B-24s of the 782nd Bombardment Squadron (Heavy), 465th Bombardment Group (Heavy), from the United States. The squadron's first missions are scheduled for early May.

Twelfth Air Force A-20 Havocs, P-40s, and P-47 Thunderbolts attack lines of communication north of Rome, attacking fuel storage areas, marshaling yards, bridges, gun positions, and logistics support sites.

PACIFIC: U.S. submarine *Guavina* torpedoes and sinks a Japanese cargo ship northwest of Chichi Jima in the Bonin Islands.

CENTRAL PACIFIC: Seventh Air Force B-24 Liberators from Kwajalein stage through Eniwetok to conduct a night bombing attack on Guam and Truk. The bombers then fly on to Los Negros Island in the Admiralties. During the day the B-24s bomb Wotje and Maloelap Atolls. B-25 Mitchells from Engebi Island bomb Ponape Island. B-25s from Makin Island bomb Jaluit and Wotje Atolls.

Thirteenth Air Force sends 15 B-24s on a dawn raid on Truk.

BOUGAINVILLE: Thirteenth Air Force P-39 Airacobras cause heavy damage to a logistics base at Baitsi.

NEW BRITAIN: Thirteenth Air Force sends 23 B-25 Mitchells to attack Tobera airfield.

NEW GUINEA: Heavy rains wash out the Tadji airfield at Aitape. Despite several efforts to maintain it, the airfield is eventually abandoned.

Fifth Air Force B-25 Mitchells bomb Japanese troops near Hollandia and attack villages near Tanahmerah.

U.S. submarine *Crevalle* torpedoes and sinks a Japanese cargo ship north of Borneo.

April 26

ALEUTIANS: Destroyer escort USS *Gilmore* sinks Japanese submarine *I-180*, southwest of Cherikof Island, Aleutians.

CBI: Tenth Air Force A-36 Intruder (Apache) fighter-bombers, P-40s, and P-51 Mustangs together with three B-25 Mitchells attack Japanese positions, logistics storage areas, and targets of opportunity at Mogaung, Kamaing, and elsewhere in the Mogaung Valley.

Japanese fighters intercept Twentieth Air Force B-29 Superfortresses as they are flying over the Hump to China. No losses are reported.

ATLANTIC: Four U.S. destroyer escorts sink German submarine *U-488* in mid-Atlantic.

ETO: Eighth Air Force sends 357 B-17s and 238 B-24 Liberators, escorted by 90 P-38 Lightnings, 311 Eighth and Ninth Air Force P-47 Thunderbolts, and 153 Eighth and Ninth Air Force P-51 Mustangs, against industrial production facilities in Germany. No bombers are lost and 141 are damaged. Five fighters are lost and one damaged. LSTs carrying American infantry.

An attack by 33 P-38 Lightnings against Le Mans airfield and 24 P-51 Mustangs against Cormeilles-en-Vexin airfield results in no friendly losses.

During the night five B-17s drop leaflets over Ghent, Antwerp, Brussels, Liege, and Gosselies in Belgium.

Ninth Air Force publishes its tactical air plan to support Operation Neptune.

SOUTHWEST PACIFIC AREA: U.S. submarine *Bonefish* torpedoes and sinks a Japanese transport at the entrance to Davao Gulf in the Philippines.

U.S. submarine *Jack* spots a Japanese convoy carrying the 32nd and 35th Divisions to reinforce garrisons in the Halmaheras and in northwestern New Guinea off the west coast of Luzon. The submarine *Jack* sinks a transport and damages a cargo ship.

PACIFIC: U.S. submarine *Guavina* attacks a Japanese convoy in the Bonin Islands and sinks a transport, but a second attack on a cargo ship is unsuccessful.

U.S. submarine *Sargo* attacks a Japanese convoy and sinks a cargo ship off Honshu, Japan.

CENTRAL PACIFIC: Seventh Air Force B-25 Mitchells from Makin Island bomb Jaluit and Wotje Atolls. B-24 Liberators returning to Kwajalein from Los Negros Island bomb Ponape Island.

BOUGAINVILLE: Thirteenth Air Force P-40s attack Japanese positions near Tabut and Wariki.

NEW BRITAIN: Thirteenth Air Force sends 24 B-25 Mitchells to bomb the Lakunai airfield. P-38 Lightnings and P-39 Airacobras attack Tobera airfield.

NEW GUINEA: Operation Reckless. The 21st Infantry Regiment of the 24th Infantry Division occupies Hollandia airfield. The 186th Infantry Regiment of the 41st Infantry Division captures Cyclops and Sentari airfields.

Fifth Air Force B-25 Mitchells and A-20 Havocs attack airfields at Wewak. P-39 Airacobras and P-47 Thunderbolts attack bridges and targets of opportunity near Madang.

April 27

CBI: General Stilwell meets with Brigadier General Merrill (now recovered and returned to duty) to discuss the capture of Myitkyina, the next mission for the Marauders. Myitkyina is the key to achieving U.S. objectives in Burma. Myitkyina's airfield will allow Tenth Air Force fighters to escort air resupply missions flying the Hump route into China. Control of Myitkyina is an essential requirement allowing the construction of the Ledo Road to China.

To accomplish this mission, the Galahad Task Force is created by combining the battalions of Marauders with Chinese units and irregular forces. K Force is composed of the 3rd Battalion of the Marauders plus the 88th Regiment of the Chinese 30th Division. M Force is composed of 2nd Battalion of the Marauders plus 200–250 Kachin Rangers from Detachment 101. H Force is composed of 3rd Battalion of the Marauders plus the 150th Regiment of the Chinese 50th Division. The Chinese 22nd and 38th Divisions are to capture Kamaing and clear the Hukawng Valley while K Force, leading the way and followed by H Force, heads for Nawbum. The Marauders have to cross the Kumon mountain range, reaching heights of over 9,000 feet.

Tenth Air Force sends P-40s, P-51 Mustangs, A-36 Intruder (Apache) fighter-bombers, and B-25 Mitchells to attack fuel storage areas, gun positions, and troops in the Mogaung valley.

ETO: The Allies conduct the first full-scale rehearsal of the Neptune Plan, an exercise called Tiger near Plymouth, England. This rehearsal involves the Utah assault landing group under Rear Admiral D. P. Moon. German fast-attack boats torpedo eight LSTs (landing ship tank) conducting invasion rehearsals. One LST is sunk and two are heavily damaged. Over 600 soldiers and sailors die in the attack, but the losses are not reported, in order to protect operational security.

Eighth Air Force sends 596 B-17s and B-24 Liberators, with 47 P-38 Lightnings, 262 P-47 Thunderbolts, and 48 P-51 Mustangs flying as escort, to bomb V-weapon sites near Pas-de-Calais and Cherbourg in France. Of the 307 B-17s and 169 B-24s that hit the primary targets, four bombers are lost and 254 are damaged. Aircrew losses are three killed, 16 wounded, and 40 missing. Fighter pilots report two aircraft lost and two pilots missing.

Another attack by 288 B-17s and 198 B-24s, escorted by 106 P-38 Lightnings, 283 P-47 Thunderbolts, and 154 P-51 Mustangs against marshaling yards and airfields in France and Belgium, results in four bombers lost and 86 damaged. Fighter pilots report three confirmed kills in the air and four on the ground. Four aircraft are lost and three damaged.

During the night five B-17s drop five million leaflets over cities in northwestern France. One B-24 is lost out of 21 sent in support of Carpetbagger operations.

P-38 Lightnings, modified to carry a bombardier and a Norden bombsight in place of guns, are called Droopsnoots. The P-38H/Ls can carry a 4,000-pound bomb load (the same as a B-17) and, because of its speed, does not require fighter escort. These Droopsnoot P-38s attack Albert/Meaulte airfield in France. Six bombers are damaged. P-51s conduct a dive-bomb attack on Cormeilles-en-Vexin airfield in France without any friendly losses.

The Eighth Air Force receives the B-24s of the 849th and 850th Bombardment Squadrons (Heavy), of the 490th Bombardment Group (Heavy) from the United States. The squadrons' first missions are scheduled for late May.

Ninth Air Force sends B-26 Marauders and A-20 Havocs with over 275 P-47s and P-51 dive bombers to attack gun emplacements, marshaling yards, and airfields in France and Belgium.

SOUTHWEST PACIFIC AREA: The Japanese convoy carrying the 32nd and 35th Divisions to reinforce garrisons in the Halmaheras and in northwestern New Guinea arrives at Manila.

Pacific: U.S. submarine *Halibut* attacks a Japanese convoy and sinks a minelayer and a merchant transport near Okinawa.

U.S. submarine *Seadragon* torpedoes and damages a Japanese cargo ship off Shikoku, Japan.

Central Pacific: Seventh Air Force B-24 Liberators, staging through Eniwetok Atoll, bomb Truk in a night raid. B-25 Mitchells from Eniwetok attack Ponape Island. Other B-25s from Makin Island attack Jaluit, Wotje, and Mille Atolls.

Thirteenth Air Force sends 16 B-24 Liberators to bomb Truk.

The B-25s of the 820th Bombardment Squadron (Medium), 41st Bombardment Group (Medium), redeploy from Tarawa to Makin Island.

U.S. submarine *Bluegill* (SS-242) sinks a Japanese light cruiser west of the Sonsorol Islands.

U.S. submarine *Seahorse* attacks a Japanese convoy and sinks a transport near Saipan. *Seahorse* escapes a depth-charge attack.

U.S. submarine *Trigger* attacks a Japanese convoy north of Palau, and sinks a transport and damages an escort vessel and a cargo ship.

New Britain: Thirteenth Air Force B-25 Mitchells and P-39 Airacobras bomb the logistics base at Talili Bay.

New Guinea: Engineers begin construction of airfields at Hollandia.

April 28

CBI: In Burma, Galahad's K Force and H Force begin the overland movement to Myitkyina. The arduous trip takes a heavy toll on men and animals. Many of the men are infected with scrub typhus. Colonel Henry L. Kinnison, leader of K Force, dies of the disease on the march.

Tenth Air Force A-36 Intruder (Apache) fighter-bombers, P-40s, P-51 Mustangs, and one B-25 Mitchell attack targets in the Mogaung Valley.

In China, Fourteenth Air Force sends 26 B-24 Liberators, escorted by 10 P-51 Mustangs, to destroy two bridges over the Yellow River near Chengchow after the Japanese drive Chinese forces from the area. The Japanese continue to make progress, forcing the Chinese-American Composite Wing to guard the B-29 fields at Cheng-tu. The Fourteenth Air Force is to prevent Japanese forces from crossing the Yellow River and attack the rail lines providing supplies to the armies.

U.S. submarine *Flasher* damages a Vichy cargo ship in the South China Sea.

Atlantic: Secretary of the Navy Frank Knox dies in Washington, D.C.

Nine German motor torpedo boats attack a convoy of eight LSTs entering Lyme Bay, England, sinking two and damaging another.

ETO: Eighth Air Force sends 117 B-17s against airfields in France escorted by 118 P-47 Thunderbolts and 87 P-51 Mustangs. Two bombers are lost and 38 damaged. Fighter pilots report eight confirmed kills on the ground. Two fighters are lost and two are damaged. Casualties are 20 crewmen and two fighter pilots missing. Another attack on V-weapon sites in France by 106 B-17s escorted by 46 P-47 Thunderbolts results in two bombers lost and 47 damaged. Three air crewmen are wounded and 21 are missing.

Tours and Chateaudun airfields in France are attacked by Droopsnoot P-38 Lightnings. One bomber is lost and two are damaged. Later, 32 P-47 Thunderbolts, with four P-47 escorts, dive-bomb Chateaudun airfield and report one confirmed kill on the ground.

B-24s bomb V-weapon sites in France escorted by 50 P-47 Thunderbolts. Six bombers are damaged and nine crewmen are wounded.

During the night five B-17s drop leaflets over cities in France, Belgium, and the Netherlands. B-24s support Carpetbagger operations.

Eighth Air Force receives the B-24s of the 848th and 851st Bombardment Squadrons (Heavy), 490th Bombardment Group (Heavy), from the United States. The first mission of the 848th is scheduled for early June; the first mission of the 851st is scheduled for late May.

Ninth Air Force sends nearly 250 B-26 Marauders to bomb marshaling yards in France. The bombers are recalled due to bad weather, but 18 B-26s bomb an airfield as a secondary target.

ITALY: Fifteenth Air Force sends over 450 B-17s and B-24 Liberators escorted by P-51 Mustangs and P-47 Thunderbolts to attack port facilities. During the air attack on Toulon, German submarine *U-421* is sunk in the harbor.

Twelfth Air Force B-26s and B-25 Mitchells attack railway bridges and viaducts. A-20 Havocs, P-40s, and P-47 Thunderbolts attack fuel storage areas.

SOUTHWEST PACIFIC AREA: U.S. submarines *Bang, Parche,* and *Tinosa* attack a Japanese convoy off of Luzon. USS *Bang* sinks a cargo ship and damages another.

PACIFIC: U.S. submarine *Halibut* bombards Japanese installations on Kure Jima in the Bonin Islands. U.S. submarine *Pogy* torpedoes and sinks Japanese submarine *I-183* off Shikoku Island, Japan.

CENTRAL PACIFIC: Seventh Air Force B-25 Mitchells from Makin Island attack Jaluit and Mille Atolls, rearming at Majuro Atoll, and then return to Makin.

Vice Admiral Marc A. Mitscher's TF 58 with five carriers and seven small carriers begins a two-day attack on Japanese shipping, oil and ammunition storage sites, aircraft facilities, and other installations at Truk. TBF Avengers with two destroyers sink Japanese submarine *I-174* north of Truk.

BOUGAINVILLE: Thirteenth Air Force P-39 Airacobras attack gun positions near Mamagata and logistics sites in the area.

NEW BRITAIN: The 40th Infantry Division begins the relief of the 1st Marine Division.

Thirteenth Air Force B-25 Mitchells bomb the logistics base at Wunapope and bomb Rapopo airfield. P-40s and P-39 Airacobras attack Vunakanau airfield.

NEW GUINEA: Fifth Air Force B-24 Liberators and B-25 Mitchells bomb the airfields at Wakde and Biak. P-47 Thunderbolts, P-39 Airacobras, A-20 Havocs, and P-70s hit targets along the northern coast.

Thirteenth Air Task Force of the Fifth Air Force sends 21 B-24s to bomb the airfield on Woleai Atoll.

April 29

ETO: Eighth Air Force sends 446 B-17s and 233 B-24 Liberators against targets in Berlin, escorted by 117 P-38 Lightnings, 463 Eighth and Ninth Air Force P-47

Thunderbolts, and 234 Eighth and Ninth Air Force P-51 Mustangs. A total of 63 bombers are lost and 434 damaged. Aircrew casualties are 18 killed, 38 wounded, and 606 missing. Fighter pilots report 13 aircraft lost and 31 damaged. One pilot is wounded and 12 are missing.

During the night four B-17s drop one million leaflets over cities in northern France and the Netherlands. Fourteen B-24s support Carpetbagger operations.

Ninth Air Forces ends 217 B-26 Marauders to attack marshaling yards in France, but the mission is aborted due to heavy cloud cover over the targets.

MEDITERRANEAN: Fifteenth Air Force sends 573 B-17s and B-24 Liberators, with fighter escort, to attack the naval base at Toulon, France.

ITALY: Twelfth Air Force B-25 Mitchells and B-26 Marauders attack bridges, while A-20 Havocs attack a fuel storage area. P-40s and P-47 Thunderbolts attack rail lines, gun positions, vehicles, bridges, logistics sites, and a marshaling yard.

CENTRAL PACIFIC: Seventh Air Force B-24 Liberators, staging through Eniwetok from Kwajalein, bomb Truk and Jaluit Atolls. B-25 Mitchells from Makin Island also bomb Jaluit and Ponape Islands.

BOUGAINVILLE: Thirteenth Air Force P-39 Airacobras bomb and strafe targets on Buka Island and throughout Bougainville, including Kieta and Numa Numa. B-25 Mitchells bomb Kara and Buka airfields.

ADMIRALTIES: The headquarters of the 307th Bombardment Group (Heavy) moves from New Georgia Island to Los Negros Island.

NEW GUINEA: Fifth Air Force sends over 90 B-24 Liberators and B-25 Mitchells to bomb Japanese positions on Wakde Island.

April 30

CBI: Tenth Air Force B-25 Mitchells attack Japanese tanks, bridges, and logistics sites around Kalewa.

H Force, following K Force, begins the attack toward Myitkyina.

Fourteenth Air Force has about 400 operational aircraft out of a total of 500. General Chennault is receiving about 6,000 tons of supplies a month to keep his aircraft operational.

Chiang Kai-shek demands that the stockpile of supplies for the B-29 strategic bombers at Chengtu be diverted to Fourteenth Air Force to stop the Japanese offensive. Stilwell, backed by President Roosevelt, refuses.

ATLANTIC: German submarine *U-711* torpedoes and sinks a U.S. freighter south of Bear Island in the Norwegian Sea.

ETO: Eighth Air Force sends 240 B-17s and 55 B-24 Liberators, escorted by 128 P-38 Lightnings, 268 P-47 Thunderbolts, and 248 Eighth and Ninth Air Force P-51 Mustangs, to attack airfields and V-weapon sites in France. One bomber is lost and 21 are damaged. One crewman is wounded and 10 are missing. Fighter pilots report 20 probable kills. Four aircraft are lost and seven damaged. One pilot is wounded and three are missing.

P-38 Lightnings with Droopsnoot bomb Tours airfield in France. One P-38 is lost and one damaged. Another 22 P-38 Lightnings with Droopsnoot attack

Orleans/Bricy airfield. Two P-38s are damaged. P-47 Thunderbolts bomb the airfield and attack a V-weapon site. P-47 Thunderbolts conduct a dive-bomb attack on Romorantin airfield. The pilots report nine confirmed kills and one probable.

During the night four B-17s drop two million leaflets over cities and towns in Belgium, France, and the Netherlands. Twenty B-24s support Carpetbagger operations.

Ninth Air Force sends over 300 B-26 Marauders and A-20 Havocs to attack marshaling yards and V-weapon site construction in France.

ITALY: Fifteenth Air Force sends 500 B-17s and B-24 Liberators to attack industrial production facilities and marshaling yards. For this month, fighter pilots report 209 confirmed kills, 38 probable kills, and 104 possibles in air combat.

The Fifteenth Air Force receives the headquarters of 485th Bombardment Group (Heavy) and the B-24s of the 828th, 829th, 830th, and 831st Bombardment Squadrons (Heavy). The squadrons' first missions are scheduled for mid-May.

Twelfth Air Force B-25 Mitchells and B-26 Marauders attack railroad bridges. P-40s attack rail lines and P-47 Thunderbolts attack rail lines, rail cars, and other targets.

SOUTHWEST PACIFIC AREA: The Japanese convoy carrying the 32nd and 35th Divisions to reinforce garrisons at Manokwari and Halmahera departs Manila.

U.S. submarine *Bang* again attacks the convoy it had encountered previously, sinking a merchant tanker off the northwest coast of Luzon.

U.S. submarine *Flasher* torpedoes and sinks a French gunboat in the South China Sea.

CENTRAL PACIFIC: Seventh Air Force sends 41 B-24 Liberators from Kwajalein to bomb Wake Island. B-25 Mitchells from Makin Island bomb Jaluit Atoll. B-25s from Engebi Island bomb Ponape Island.

Navy TF 58 continues air attacks on targets in the Carolines and expands toward the Palau Islands as well. A transport and merchant vessel are sunk. A gunboat is damaged at Truk by carrier aircraft.

BOUGAINVILLE: Thirteenth Air Force P-39 Airacobras attack targets on Buka Island and Ivituri mission, the Kieta area, and the Mamagata logistics base at Bougainville.

NEW BRITAIN: Thirteenth Air Force P-40s and P-38 Lightnings bomb Vunakanau airfield and B-25 Mitchells bomb Vunakambi Plantation.

NEW GUINEA: Fifth Air Force P-39 Airacobras and P-47 Thunderbolts attack Japanese troops and logistics sites around Hansa Bay. A-20 Havocs and B-25 Mitchells bomb Wewak. B-24 Liberators bomb Noemfoor Island.

Thirteenth Air Task Force under Fifth Air Force sends 23 B-24s to bomb Woleai Atoll.

May 1

CBI: Tenth Air Force P-40s attack Kamaing; B-24 Liberators bomb Maymyo, the Mandalay marshaling yard, and oil facilities at Yenangyaung.

In China, Fourteenth Air Force P-40s attack the airfield at Yuncheng and B-25 Mitchells along with P-40s bomb Tangyang airfield.

Twentieth Air Force reports the four B-29 airfields in the Cheng-tu area are operational.

ETO: General Eisenhower receives instructions from the JCS to plan for U.S. forces to occupy the Netherlands and northwest Germany once hostilities end in Europe.

Eighth Air Force sends 531 B-17s and B-24 Liberator bombers with 209 fighters as escort to attack 23 V-weapon sites in France. Due to heavy cloud cover, only three of the primary targets are hit. A total of 37 bombers are damaged and five crewmen are killed.

A second attack by 135 B-17s and 151 B-24 Liberators, escorted by 120 P-38 Lightnings, 272 P-47 Thunderbolts, and 166 P-51 Mustangs, targets marshaling yards in France and Belgium. Three bombers are lost and 117 are damaged. Thirty crewmen are missing. Fighter pilots report six confirmed kills. Three fighters are lost and five are damaged.

During the night five B-17s drop one million leaflets over cities and towns in France and the Netherlands. A total of 25 B-24 Liberators support Carpetbagger operations.

Eighth Air Force receives the headquarters of the 489th Bombardment Group (Heavy) from the United States.

Ninth Air Force sends 450 B-26 Marauders and A-20 Havocs to attack marshaling yards and industrial production facilities in France and Belgium.

ITALY: At the planning conference for Operation Diadem, the breakout of the Liri Valley and the drive to Rome, Lieutenant General Mark Clark seeks to get the Fifteenth Army Group commander, General Sir Harold Alexander, to approve Clark's desire for the U.S. forces of the Fifth Army to capture Rome. Although his direct request is denied, Alexander gives enough vague guidance to Clark to allow him to shift forces as necessary. May 11 is set as D-day for the attack.

Twelfth Air Force B-26 Marauders and B-25 Mitchells attack bridges and viaducts and a marshaling yard. P-40s and P-47 Thunderbolts attack rail tracks, bridges, logistics bases, rail cars, and industrial targets.

SOUTHWEST PACIFIC AREA: U.S. submarine *Bluegill* torpedoes and sinks a Japanese cargo ship east of Mindanao in the Philippines.

CENTRAL PACIFIC: Shore-based Air Force Forward Area (Task Force 59) is activated under Major General Willis H. Hale to control all army, navy, and Marine Corps shore-based aircraft in the Central Pacific forward area.

Seventh Air Force B-25 Mitchells from Makin Island bomb Jaluit Atoll.

Naval Task Group 58.7, commanded by Vice Admiral Willis A. Lee, with seven battleships and 14 destroyers, bombards facilities on Ponape Island in the Carolines. Carrier aircraft provide cover.

BOUGAINVILLE: P-39 Airacobras attack a number of targets on the island.

NEW BRITAIN: Thirteenth Air Force B-24 Liberators bomb coastal guns, and P-39 Airacobras, P-40s, and 30 navy SBD Dauntless dive-bombers attack Vunakambi Plantation.

NEW GUINEA: Fifth Air Force sends over 180 B-25 Mitchells, A-20 Havocs, and P-40s to attack Wewak and the Hansa Bay area.

Fifth Air Force receives the headquarters of the 86th Fighter Wing at Finschhafen from the United States.

The Thirteenth Air Task Force under Fifth Air Force sends B-24s against the Woleai and Eauriprik Atolls in the Carolines.

A Navy PB4Y Privateer damages a Japanese cargo vessel off Biak.

May 2

CBI: Fourteenth Air Force B-24 Liberators report sinking two cargo ships in the Formosa Straits. The Japanese commit nearly 75,000 troops to accomplish their offensive objectives in China.

ATLANTIC: The JCS orders General Stilwell to shift his emphasis from supporting the British efforts in Burma and opening the Burma Road to developing air bases in China by February 1945 to support the planned attack on Formosa, the Philippines, the Ryukyus, or the coast of China.

ETO: Eighth Air Force sends 50 B-24 Liberators escorted by 50 P-47 Thunderbolts and 52 P-51 Mustangs to attack V-weapon sites in the Pas-de-Calais area of France.

Ninth Air Force sends over 250 B-26 Marauders and A-20 Havocs to bomb marshaling yards in France. A total of 400 P-47 Thunderbolts and P-51 Mustangs conduct dive-bomb attacks on airfields and marshaling yards in France and the Netherlands.

ITALY: Fifteenth Air Force sends over 250 B-17s and B-24 Liberators against a marshaling yard and railroad bridge. Most of the bombers abort the mission due to bad weather.

Twelfth Air Force B-25 Mitchells and B-26 Marauders attack bridges and marshaling yards. P-40s and P-47 Thunderbolts attack rail lines, gun positions near Anzio, a road bridge, vehicles, and logistics bases.

CENTRAL PACIFIC: During the night Seventh Air Force B-24 Liberators, staging through Eniwetok Atoll from Kwajalein, bomb Truk.

B-25 Mitchells from Makin Island attack Wotje Atoll, rearm at Majuro Atoll, and bomb Jaluit Atoll on the return to Makin. B-25 Mitchells from Engebi Island, Eniwetok, attack Ponape Island.

BOUGAINVILLE: Thirteenth Air Force P-39 Airacobras bomb a village near Kieta, the airfield at Koromira, and Rigu mission. P-40s also attack targets near Kieta.

NEW BRITAIN: P-38 Lightnings, P-39 Airacobras, and P-40s attack Rabaul and Vunakambi Plantation logistics sites, while B-25 Mitchells bomb the Talili area.

NEW GUINEA: Fifth Air Force A-20 Havocs, P-47 Thunderbolts, and P-40s attack Japanese positions and facilities from Wewak to Hansa Bay. B-25 Mitchells bomb airfields at Wewak and Boram and facilities on Wakde Island. B-24 Liberators bomb Biak Island.

May 3

CBI: Tenth Air Force B-25 Mitchells bomb Kohima.

In China, Fourteenth Air Force Chinese-American Composite Wing B-25 Mitchells bomb vehicles and troops. B-25 Mitchells and P-40s from the Chinese-American

Composite Wing (CACW) attack logistics sites at Tangyang airfield and damage a bridge over the Yellow River near Chenghsien, destroying several trucks with troops.

Fourteenth Air Force B-24 Liberators attack a Japanese convoy near Formosa, sinking a cargo ship.

ATLANTIC: German submarine *U-765* torpedoes and damages a destroyer escort near Cape Clear, Ireland.

ETO: Eighth Air Force sends 51 B-24 Liberators escorted by 48 P-47 Thunderbolts and 53 P-51 Mustangs to bomb the V-weapon site at Wizernes, France. Of the 47 bombers that hit the target, 33 are damaged and three airmen are wounded.

During the night, five B-17s drop leaflets on cities and towns in France, Belgium, and the Netherlands. One bomber is damaged. Nine B-24 Liberators support Carpetbagger operations.

MEDITERRANEAN: German submarine *U-371* stalks a convoy moving west toward the Straits of Gibraltar, damaging a destroyer escort off Bougie, Algeria. Although tracked by a group of U.S., French, and British destroyers, destroyer escorts, and a minesweeper *U-371* escapes.

ITALY: Twelfth Air Force B-25 Mitchells and B-26 Marauders attack railway bridges and marshaling yards. A-20 Havocs attack an ammunition storage site. P-40s and P-47 Thunderbolts attack rail lines, bridges, logistics sites, and an observation post near Cassino.

SOUTHWEST PACIFIC AREA: U.S. submarine *Flasher* torpedoes and sinks a Japanese cargo ship in the South China Sea.

U.S. submarine *Tinosa* torpedoes and sinks a Japanese cargo ship in the Luzon Strait.

PACIFIC: U.S. submarine *Tautog* torpedoes and sinks a Japanese cargo ship off Uruppu Island in the Kuriles.

CENTRAL PACIFIC: Seventh Air Force B-25 Mitchells from Kwajalein bomb Wotje Atoll. B-25s from Makin Island bomb Wotje Atoll, rearm at Majuro Atoll, and bomb Jaluit Atoll on the return to Makin.

U.S. submarine *Sand Lance* torpedoes and sinks a Japanese transport off Saipan.

BOUGAINVILLE: Thirteenth Air Force sends P-39 Airacobras to bomb targets of opportunity over the island. P-40s returning from the New Britain Island area bomb Pororan.

NEW BRITAIN: Thirteenth Air Force B-25 Mitchells bomb Kulon Plantation and troops nearby.

NEW GUINEA: Fifth Air Force B-24 Liberators, B-25 Mitchells, and A-20 Havocs attack Wewak and Boram airfields, causing heavy damage. Over 100 A-20 Havocs, B-25s, P-47 Thunderbolts, and P-40s also attack Wewak and Hansa Bay. The P-40s of the 7th and 8th Fighter Squadrons, 49th Fighter Group deploy to Hollandia; C-47s of the 65th Troop Carrier Squadron, 433rd Troop Carrier Group, begin operating from Tadji airfield.

May 4

CBI: In Burma, the Chinese 22nd Division captures Inkangahtawng.

Tenth Air Force sends 24 B-24 Liberators to bomb the marshaling yard and a Japanese barracks at Mandalay.

Chinese forces halt on the road to Kamaing after capturing Inkangahtawng.

Fourteenth Air Force P-40s attack Japanese gun positions in China.

ETO: Eighth Air Force sends 591 B-17s, escorted by 50 P-38 Lightnings, 179 P-47 Thunderbolts, and 287 Eighth and Ninth Air Force P-51 Mustangs, to attack targets in Berlin, Brunswick, and in central Germany. The mission is recalled, but 40 B-17s bomb an airfield in the Netherlands. Sixteen bombers are damaged. Two air crewmen are killed and one wounded. Fighter pilots report nine confirmed kills and two probables. Three aircraft are lost and 14 are damaged. Three pilots are missing and one is wounded.

Ninth Air Force sends over 170 B-26 Marauders and 36 A-20 Havocs to attack gun emplacements and other military targets in France.

MEDITERRANEAN: German submarine *U-371* torpedoes and damages a U.S. destroyer escort and a French destroyer escort off the Algerian coast near Constantine, but is heavily damaged by depth charges from two U.S. destroyer escorts, a French destroyer escort, and a British destroyer escort. Three of the crew are killed and 49 are captured after her crew scuttles the U-boat and abandons her. *U-371* is detected and sunk by air and naval assets using the swamp technique of blanketing an area where a U-boat is known or suspected to be located, forcing the submarine to stay submerged until it has to surface to recharge its batteries to survive. Once on the surface, ships and aircraft will converge and overwhelm (swamp) the submarine.

ITALY: Twelfth Air Force B-25 Mitchells and B-26 Marauders attack bridges, rail lines, and marshaling yards. P-40s and P-47 Thunderbolts attack rail lines, marshaling yards, motor transport, logistics sites, and trucks and personnel on the Fondi-Pico road.

SOUTHWEST PACIFIC AREA: U.S. submarines *Bang, Parche,* and *Tinosa* attack Japanese convoy ships in the Luzon Strait. USS *Bang* sinks a cargo ship, USS *Parche* and *Tinosa* both sink two cargo ships.

U.S. submarine *Pargo* torpedoes and sinks a Japanese auxiliary netlayer east of Mindanao in the Philippines.

PACIFIC: U.S. submarine *Tuna* torpedoes and sinks a Japanese guardboat near Wake Island.

CENTRAL PACIFIC: Seventh Air Force B-24 Liberators from Kwajalein and Eniwetok Atolls bomb Ponape Island. B-25s from Makin Island bomb Wotje Atoll, rearm at Majuro Atoll, and bomb Jaluit Atoll on the return to Makin.

BOUGAINVILLE: Thirteenth Air Force sends 38 P-39 Airacobras to attack buildings at Sovele, Tinputs, the Reboine Bay area, Monoitu, and the area near Taki. P-39s attack targets around Koromira.

NEW BRITAIN: The last elements of the 1st Marine Division leave New Britain.

Thirteenth Air Force sends 24 B-25 Mitchells to bomb the Talili Bay area.

NEW GUINEA: Major General William H. Gill, the 32nd Infantry Division commander, takes control of the Aitape Task Force, relieving the 163rd RCT for the Wakde-Biak operation.

Fifth Air Force send over 60 B-24 Liberators, B-25 Mitchells, A-20 Havocs, and P-47 Thunderbolts to attack airfields and other targets around Wewak. A-20 Havocs attack bridges over the Awar River and targets of opportunity in the Hansa Bay area.

Thirteenth Air Task Force under Fifth Air Force sends 26 B-24 Liberators to bomb Mokmer airfield at Biak Island.

May 5

CBI: Tenth Air Force sends over 80 P-40s, P-51 Mustangs, A-36 Intruder (Apache) fighter-bombers, and B-25 Mitchells to attack Japanese positions, logistics sites, vehicles, and targets of opportunity in the Mogaung Valley. B-24 Liberators lay mines in the harbor off Koh Si Chang Island in Thailand.

Fourteenth Air Force sends 11 B-24 Liberators to bomb docks and shipping at Haiphong, French Indochina. In China, the Chinese-American Composite Wing's B-25 Mitchells and P-40s attack a marshaling yard, a logistics site, and troops and vehicles on the road from Loyang to Juchou.

ETO: Eighth Air Force sends 46 B-24 Liberators escorted by 52 P-51 Mustangs to bomb the V-weapon site at Sottevast, France. Of the 33 that hit the target seven B-24s are damaged; four airmen are killed.

During the night, 21 B-24 Liberators support Carpetbagger operations and one bomber is lost.

MEDITERRANEAN: Fifteenth Air Force sends over 640 B-17s and B-24 Liberators to attack targets in Romania and Yugoslavia. The B-17s bomb marshaling yards at Ploeşti and Brasnov in Romania. The 485 B-24s attack the Ploeşti marshaling yard. Nineteen bombers are lost and 19 German fighters are destroyed over the target. Another 147 B-17s and 126 B-24 Liberators attack aircraft production facilities near Vienna, Austria. A total of 28 bombers are lost and three fighters. Aircrews and fighter pilots report a total of 50 confirmed kills and 22 probables.

Twelfth Air Force A-20 Havocs bomb a logistics base. A-36 Intruder (Apache) fighter-bombers, P-47 Thunderbolts, and P-40s attack rail lines around Rome and gun positions near the Anzio battleline.

German submarine *U-967* torpedoes and sinks a U.S. destroyer escort northwest of Oran, Algeria.

PACIFIC: U.S. submarine *Pogy* attacks a Japanese convoy, sinking a transport off Honshu, Japan.

CENTRAL PACIFIC: Seventh Air Force B-25 Mitchells from Eniwetok Atoll bomb Ponape Island. B-25s from Makin Island bomb Wotje Atoll, rearm at Majuro Atoll, and bomb Jaluit Atoll on the return to Makin. B-24 Liberators from Kwajalein Atoll staging through Eniwetok Atoll bomb Truk Atoll during the night.

BOUGAINVILLE: Thirteenth Air Force sends 24 B-25 Mitchells to bomb gun positions on Buka Island. P-39 Airacobras attack buildings and logistics sites. P-40s bomb buildings at Kieta and at nearby Rigu mission.

U.S. motor torpedo boats blockading the southeastern coast of Bougainville encounter several heavily armed barges. One PT boat is sunk.

New Guinea: Fifth Air Force B-24 Liberators bomb Mokmer airfield at Biak Island and B-25 Mitchells bomb logistics sites at Wakde Island. A-20 Havocs, P-47 Thunderbolts, and P-40s attack targets around Wewak and along the coast of Hansa Bay.

May 6

CBI: After marching 65 miles over a 6,000-foot-high mountain trail, the Marauders reach Ritpong, where patrols encounter Japanese forces.

Tenth Air Force P-40s, P-51 Mustangs, and B-25 Mitchells attack targets in the Mogaung Valley.

Fourteenth Air Force sends 61 P-40s and five B-25 Mitchells attack bridges, rail cars, and vehicles in southern China.

Atlantic: Destroyer escort USS *Buckley* rams German submarine *U-66*, which has been damaged by air attack in the mid-Atlantic. The sailors of the *Buckley* fight the German submarine crew at close quarters, using small arms, hand grenades, fists, and even coffee mugs before the stricken U-boat sinks.

ETO: Eighth Air Force sends 90 B-17s and 78 B-24 Liberators, escorted by 57 Ninth Air Force P-38 Lightnings, 47 P-47 Thunderbolts, and 81 P-51 Mustangs, against V-weapon targets in France. The B-17s abort the mission due to heavy cloud cover, but 70 B-24s attack the target. A total of 48 bombers are damaged. No losses are reported.

During the night five B-17s drop over three million leaflets on cities and towns in Belgium and France. One B-17 encounters a night fighter and is damaged in the attack, but the aircrew reports the enemy fighter as a probable kill. A total of 22 B-24s support Carpetbagger missions.

A Ninth Air Force mission to attack coastal defenses in France is aborted due to weather.

Mediterranean: Fifteenth Air Forces ends 300 B-17s and B-24 Liberators escorted by P-51 Mustangs and P-38 Lightnings against aircraft production facilities and marshaling yards in Romania.

Twelfth Air Force A-20 Havocs attack a logistics base at Itri. A-36 Intruder (Apache) fighter-bombers bomb rail lines. P-40s attack gun positions and rail lines. P-47 Thunderbolts attack a marshaling yard and lines of communication.

Southwest Pacific Area: U.S. submarine *Gurnard* spots a Japanese convoy from Manila carrying the 32nd and 35th Divisions to reinforce garrisons at Manokwari in the Celebes Sea and sinks three cargo ships.

Pacific: U.S. submarine *Spearfish* attacks a Japanese convoy in the East China Sea west of Kyushu, Japan, and sinks a cargo ship and damages a supply ship.

Central Pacific: Seventh Air Force B-25 Mitchells from Makin Island and Kwajalein bomb Wotje and Jaluit Atolls. B-24 Liberators, staging through Eniwetok Atoll, escort Navy aircraft on a photo reconnaissance of Guam and bomb the island's two airfields and proceed to Momote airfield at Los Negros Island, Admiralties. Aircrews report four enemy aircraft shot down.

BOUGAINVILLE: Thirteenth Air Force sends 37 P-39 Airacobras and 19 P-40s to attack targets around Porton.

NEW BRITAIN: Thirteenth Air Force sends 24 B-25 Mitchells and 12 P-39 Airacobras to attack targets around Talili Bay.

NEW GUINEA: The 41st Infantry Division is ordered to Wakde Island to support the attack on the Japanese base at Sarmi.

Fifth Air Force sends over 150 B-25 Mitchells, A-20 Havocs, P-47 Thunderbolts, and P-40s to attack targets from Wewak to Hansa Bay.

Thirteenth Air Task Force B-24 Liberators under Fifth Air Force bomb Woleai Atoll.

U.S. submarine *Crevalle* attacks a Japanese convoy off northern Borneo, sinking a fleet tanker.

May 7

CBI: Tenth Air Force B-24 Liberators lay mines in the Gulf of Siam off Sattahib, Thailand.

In China, Fourteenth Air Force B-25 Mitchells bomb Japanese vehicle concentrations and P-40s attack trucks, tanks, and other vehicles.

ETO: Eighth Air Force sends 600 B-17s and 322 B-24 Liberators, escorted by 153 P-38 Lightnings, 317 P-47 Thunderbolts, and 284 P-51 Mustangs, against targets in Berlin. Nine bombers are lost and 300 are damaged. Aircrew casualties are nine killed, 16 wounded, 89 missing. Fighter pilots report four aircraft lost and 10 damaged. Three pilots are reported missing.

During the night three B-17s drop leaflets over towns in central France. A total of 14 B-24s support Carpetbagger missions.

MEDITERRANEAN: Fifteenth Air Force sends over 400 B-17s and B-24 Liberators escorted by P-51 Mustangs and P-38 Lightnings to bomb marshaling yards in Romania and a railroad bridge in Yugoslavia.

Twelfth Air Force A-20 Havocs, A-36 Intruder (Apache) fighter-bombers, P-51 Mustangs, and P-40s attack logistics sites, motor transport, rail lines, gun positions, bridges, and marshaling yards.

SOUTHWEST PACIFIC AREA: U.S. submarines *Bonefish* and *Flasher* torpedo and damage a Japanese cargo ship in the Sulu Sea.

PACIFIC: U.S. submarine *Burrfish* torpedoes and sinks a German oiler bound for Balikpapan off Honshu, Japan.

CENTRAL PACIFIC: Seventh Air Force B-25 Mitchells from Engebi Island bomb Ponape Island. B-25s from Makin Island bomb Jaluit and Wotje Atolls. B-24 Liberators, staging through Eniwetok, bomb Truk during the night.

BOUGAINVILLE: Thirteenth Air Force P-39 Airacobras, P-38 Lightnings, and P-40s bomb logistics sites, bridges, and huts throughout Buka and Bougainville.

NEW GUINEA: The 163rd RCT is relieved from the Aitape operation to prepare for the attack on Wakde Island.

Fifth Air Force B-24 Liberators, B-25 Mitchells, and P-40s attack Biak Island and the coast from Wakde to Hollandia. A-20 Havocs, B-25 Mitchells, P-38 Lightnings, and P-47 Thunderbolts attack targets of opportunity from Wewak to the Hansa Bay area.

The A-20s of the 90th Bombardment Squadron (Light), 3rd Bombardment Group (Light), deploy to Hollandia.

May 8

CBI: The Chinese 38th Division begins its advance to Kamaing.

Tenth Air Force sends nine B-24 Liberators and nine B-25 Mitchells to bomb Moirang. Aircrews report heavy damage to a road bridge. P-38 Lightnings attack Kangaung airfield.

ETO: Eighth Air Force sends 500 B-17s and 307 B-24 Liberators, escorted by 152 P-38 Lightnings, 295 P-47 Thunderbolts, and 282 P-51 Mustangs, to attack Berlin and Brunswick. Aircrews report 76 confirmed kills and 16 probables. A total of 36 bombers are lost and 205 are damaged. Aircrew casualties are eight killed, 15 wounded, and 373 missing. Fighter pilots report 55 confirmed kills and four probables. Thirteen aircraft are lost and six are damaged. One pilot is wounded and 13 are missing.

A second attack with 101 B-17s and 63 B-24s escorted by 97 P-47 Thunderbolts is directed against V-weapon sites at Glacerie and Sottevast, France. Five bombers are lost and 59 are damaged. Two air crewmen are killed, two are wounded, and 47 are missing.

During the night three B-17s drop a million leaflets over cities and towns in France.

Ninth Air Force sends more than 400 B-26 Marauders and A-20 Havocs to bomb marshaling yards, coastal defenses, bridges, airfields, and V-weapon sites in France and Belgium.

MEDITERRANEAN: German submarine *U-230* torpedoes and sinks a U.S. submarine chaser near Palermo, Sicily.

ITALY: Twelfth Air Force A-20 Havocs and P-40s attack logistics sites, rail cars, and vehicles around Rome and Anzio.

SOUTHWEST PACIFIC AREA: U.S. submarine *Hoe* torpedoes and damages a Japanese escort vessel and a tanker in the South China Sea.

PACIFIC: U.S. submarine *Tautog* attacks a Japanese convoy in Tsugaru Strait, sinking a cargo ship.

CENTRAL PACIFIC: Seventh Air Force B-24 Liberators returning from Los Negros to Eniwetok Atoll bomb Ponape Island. B-25 Mitchells from Engebi Island also bomb Ponape.

B-25s from Makin Island bomb Wotje Atoll, rearm at Majuro Atoll, and bomb Jaluit Atoll on the return to Makin.

BOUGAINVILLE: Thirteenth Air Force P-39 Airacobras and P-40s attack a number of targets around Porton, Tsimba, Tarara, Kieta, and Numa Numa. B-25 Mitchells bomb the coast and the airfield area on Buka Island.

NEW BRITAIN: Thirteenth Air Force P-39 Airacobras and P-40s attack Tobera airfield.

New Guinea: Fifth Air Force B-24 Liberators and P-40s attack Mokmer airfield and shipping at Biak Island. A-20 Havocs, P-47 Thunderbolts, and P-40s attack targets of opportunity along the coast from Wewak to Hansa Bay.

The Japanese convoy carrying elements of the 32nd and 35th Divisions reaches Wasile Bay, Halmahera, with only five of its original nine ships.

May 9

CBI: Galahad's M Force and K Force, along with the Chinese 88th Regiment, clear Ritpong of Japanese forces.

Tenth Air Force B-25 Mitchells, A-36 Intruder (Apache) fighter-bombers, P-51 Mustangs, and P-40s attacks targets in the Mogaung Valley.

ETO: The Eighth Air Force participates with all Allied air components to initiate intensive bombing against airfields to prevent their use prior to D-day. The mission involves 462 B-17s and 361 B-24 Liberators, escorted by 144 P-38 Lightnings, 277 P-47 Thunderbolts, and 247 P-51 Mustangs, attack airfields in France, Luxembourg, and Belgium. Four bombers are lost and 117 are damaged. Aircrew casualties are three killed, two wounded, and 64 missing. Fighter pilots report three confirmed kills in the air and one on the ground. Seven aircraft are lost and two are damaged. Six pilots are missing.

During the night three B-17s drop over a million leaflets on the Netherlands and Belgium. A total of 13 B-24s fly in support of Carpetbagger operations.

Ninth Air Force sends over 40 B-26 Marauders to attack marshaling yards, coastal defense guns, bridges, and V-weapon sites in France.

Italy: Twelfth Air Force B-26 Marauders attack a railroad bridge and viaduct. A-20 Havocs attack fuel storage areas. P-47 Thunderbolts and P-40s attack lines of communication.

Southwest Pacific Area: A planning meeting is held at SWPA headquarters to address the need for additional airfields that can handle bombers. The Hollandia airfields are inadequate and planners look to Wakde, 110 miles west of Hollandia, as a solution.

Central Pacific: B-25s from Makin Island bomb Wotje Atoll, rearm at Majuro Atoll, and bomb Jaluit Atoll on the return to Makin. B-24 Liberators from Kwajalein Atoll staging through Eniwetok Atoll bomb Truk during the night.

Bougainville: Thirteenth Air Force P-39 Airacobras and P-38 Lightnings attack barges and an ammunition storage facility near Aitara Mission, while 10 other P-38 Lightnings and 12 B-25 Mitchells bomb Bonis airfield and targets of opportunity in Buka Passage.

New Britain: Thirteenth Air Force P-39 Airacobras and P-40s bomb the Lakunai airfield.

New Guinea: Fifth Air Force sends over 220 A-20 Havocs, P-47 Thunderbolts, and P-40s to attack targets of opportunity along the coast from Wewak to Hansa Bay.

Thirteenth Air Task Force B-24 Liberators under Fifth Air Force bomb Woleai Atoll.

May 10

CBI: The Chinese 198th Division Y Force, or the Chinese Expeditionary Force, under command of General Wei Li-huang and advised by Brigadier General Frank Dorn, crosses the Salween River to join the offensive to drive the Japanese out of north Burma and open the Burma Road.

Tenth Air Force B-25 Mitchells, A-36 Intruder (Apache) fighter-bombers, P-51 Mustangs, P-40s, and 10 B-24 Liberators attack Japanese barracks and logistics sites around Myitkyina and Mogaung as well as gun positions and bridges at Kamaing.

In China, Fourteenth Air Force P-40s attack Japanese convoys, river traffic, and bridges.

ETO: Ninth Air Force sends nearly 300 B-26 Marauders to attack marshaling yards, airfields, and V-weapon targets in France and Belgium.

Mediterranean: Fifteenth Air Force sends 400 B-17s and B-24 Liberators to attack aircraft production facilities at Wiener Neustadt, Austria. Most of the bombers abort the mission after encountering bad weather, but 147 B-17s and 126 B-24 Liberators hit the target. A total of 28 bombers are lost and three fighters. Aircrews and fighter pilots report a total of 50 confirmed kills and 22 probables. Twelfth Air Force B-25 Mitchells and B-26 Marauders attack bridges while A-36 fighter-bombers, P-51 Mustangs, and P-40s attack lines of communication north of Rome.

Italy: Destroyers USS *Charles F. Hughes* and USS *Hilary P. Jones* bombard German logistics storage areas near Anzio.

Southwest Pacific Area: MacArthur approves the Wakde operation and sets May 17 as the date for the attack. The status of Japanese forces in the area is uncertain. The Japanese army has changed its codes, preventing any Ultra intelligence for at least several weeks until the new codes can be broken. The 163rd RCT is given the mission to seize and secure a beachhead in the area of Toem-Arara and capture Wakde Island. Brigadier General Jens A. Doe of the 41st Infantry Division will command the landing force. The rest of the 41st Infantry Division is scheduled to land on Biak Island, 200 miles west of Wakde, on May 27.

U.S. submarine *Cod* attacks a Japanese convoy off the west coast of Luzon, sinking a destroyer and a transport.

Central Pacific: Seventh Air Force B-25 Mitchells from Engebi Island bomb Ponape Island. B-25s from Makin Island bomb Jaluit and Wotje Atolls. B-24 Liberators from Kwajalein Atoll staging through Eniwetok Atoll bomb Truk during the night.

A naval base is established at Eniwetok.

U.S. submarine *Silversides* attacks a Japanese convoy near Guam, sinking an auxiliary cable ship, a gunboat, and a collier. USS *Silversides* survives depth-charging from several escort vessels.

U.S. submarine *Tambor* encounters a Japanese convoy and torpedoes an aircraft transport near Saipan.

Bougainville: Thirteenth Air Force sends four B-25 Mitchells to bomb Majuai mission. P-39 Airacobras and P-40s attack barges, villages, enemy positions, a bridge, and the area around Porton Plantation.

New Britain: Thirteenth Air Force sends 41 P-39 Airacobras and P-40s to attack Tobera airfield.

New Guinea: Fifth Air Force B-24 Liberators, A-20 Havocs, P-47 Thunderbolts, and P-40s, along with Royal Australian Air Force aircraft continue to attack targets of opportunity along the coast from Wewak to the Hansa Bay area. B-24s bomb Mokmer airfield on Biak Island.

Thirteenth Air Task Force under Fifth Air Force sends 45 B-24s to bomb the airfield on Eten Island and logistics base at Dublon Island in Truk Atoll.

May 11

CBI: In Burma, Tenth Air Force B-25 Mitchells, A-36 Intruder (Apache) fighter-bombers, P-51 Mustangs, and P-40s attack Myitkyina, Kamaing, and targets of opportunity along the road from Inkangahtawng to Kamaing. The 24 P-51 Mustangs sent to attack the airfield at Meiktila, Anisakan, and Heho report 13 enemy aircraft shot down. B-25 Mitchells attack the railroad in the Shwebo-Sagaing area and other B-25s destroy bridges.

In China, Fourteenth Air Force P-40s destroy the main bridge north of Mangshih.

ETO: Eighth Air Force sends 364 B-24 Liberators escorted by 147 P-38 Lightnings, 188 P-47 Thunderbolts, and 201 P-51 Mustangs to bomb marshaling yards in France. Eight bombers are lost and 50 are damaged. Aircrew casualties are one killed, eight wounded, and 71 missing. Fighter pilots report eight confirmed kills on the ground, and three in the air. Five fighters are lost and 11 are damaged. Five pilots are missing.

Another attack by 609 B-17s, escorted by 99 P-38 Lightnings, 182 Eighth and Ninth Air Force P-47 Thunderbolts, and 190 Eighth and Ninth Air Force P-51 Mustangs, against marshaling yards in Belgium, France, Germany, and Luxembourg results in eight bombers lost and 173 damaged. Aircrew casualties are two killed, 23 wounded, and 83 missing. Fighter pilots report 11 confirmed kills. Four aircraft are lost and the pilots reported missing.

Four B-24s support Carpetbagger operations.

Ninth Air Force sends over 300 B-26 Marauders to attack airfields in France and Belgium.

Italy: Operation Diadem begins. The goal is to occupy German forces in Italy prior to Overlord and capture Rome by breaking the Gustav Line and then breaking out from the Anzio beachhead. Massed artillery fire precedes the infantry attack. Supported by naval gunfire, the French Expeditionary Corps and II Corps, with the 85th and 88th Infantry Divisions abreast, cross the Garigliano River along the western coastline and meet strong opposition. The two divisions are the first made up of all-draftees and this will be their first major combat action. The 85th Infantry Division is commanded by Major General John B. Coulter and the 88th Infantry Division is commanded by Major General John E. Sloan. The 351st Infantry Regiment of the 88th Division leads the II Corps attack. At the hills surrounding the town of Santa Maria Infante, they are stopped. The 350th Infantry Regiment captures Monte Damiano and holds it against a German counterattack. Lieutenant Colonel Raymond E. Kendall of the 2nd Battalion, 351st Infantry, personally leads an attack on a German strongpoint that is holding up his men and slowing the momentum of the attack. Kendall rushes the enemy position, firing a weapon until it runs out of ammunition, then picks up another weapon and fires it. He is killed as he succeeds in destroying a machine gun position. For his exceptional display of courage, Lieutenant Colonel Kendall will be awarded the Distinguished Service Cross.

Twelfth Air Force B-25 Mitchells and B-26 Marauders bomb bridges and rail lines. A-20 Havocs, P-40s, and P-47 Thunderbolts support Allied ground forces, attacking enemy positions along the Gustav Line.

SOUTHWEST PACIFIC AREA: U.S. submarine *Crevalle* evacuates 28 women and children from Negros Island in the Philippines.

PACIFIC: U.S. submarine *Sturgeon* attacks a Japanese convoy, sinking a cargo ship near Chichi Jima in the Bonin Islands.

CENTRAL PACIFIC: Seventh Air Force B-25 Mitchells from Engebi Island bomb Ponape Island and B-25s from Makin Island bomb Jaluit Atoll.

B-24 Liberators from Kwajalein Atoll staging through Eniwetok Atoll bomb Truk during the night.

U.S. submarine *Sand Lance* attacks a Japanese convoy, sinking a transport off Tinian.

BOUGAINVILLE: Thirteenth Air Force P-39 Airacobras, P-40s, and P-38 Lightnings attack piers at Chabai, Ratsua, and Porton, a bridge at Tokinotu, and the Buka Island airfield.

NEW BRITAIN: Thirteenth Air Force P-38 Lightnings bomb a logistics support area near Tobera. B-25 Mitchells, P-40s, and B-24 Liberators attack Vunakanau airfield.

NEW GUINEA: Fifth Air Force B-24 Liberators and B-25 Mitchells bomb gun emplacements and logistics bases on Wakde Island and Mokmer airfield on Biak Island. P-47 Thunderbolts, P-40s, and A-20 Havocs, along with B-24s and B-25s attack bridges and villages, fuel storage areas, and logistics sites along the coast from Hansa Bay to Wewak.

U.S. submarine *Rasher* attacks a Japanese convoy, sinking an auxiliary vessel in the Molucca Sea.

May 12

CBI: The Marauders' K Force meets strong Japanese resistance at Tingkrukawng. H Force moves toward Myitkyina, stopping at the Detachment 101 base at Arang to evacuate the sick and obtain resupply by air.

Tenth Air Force B-25 Mitchells and P-40s attack gun positions and logistics support sites at Myitkyina. P-51 Mustangs attack airfields, reporting eight Japanese aircraft destroyed.

In China, Fourteenth Air Force B-25 Mitchells and P-40s attack military installations, artillery positions, and tanks near Yoyang.

ETO: Eighth Air Force sends 326 B-17s and 265 B-24 Liberators to bomb oil production facilities in Germany. Another 295 B-17s are sent against targets in Czechoslovakia. Aircrews report seven crewmen killed, 21 wounded, and 430 missing. The mission is escorted by 153 P-38 Lightnings, 201 P-47 Thunderbolts, and 381 P-51 Mustangs. Fighter pilots report 61 confirmed kills in the air and another five on the ground. Seven aircraft are lost and 13 are damaged. Pilots report seven pilots missing.

Later that night, five B-17s drop over one million leaflets on Denmark. One bomber is damaged.

Ninth Air Force B-26 Marauders attack coastal defenses, airfields, bridges, railroads, gun positions, and V-weapon sites in France and Belgium. IX Troop Carrier Command runs Operation Eagle, a full-scale rehearsal of the airborne landing plan for Neptune.

ITALY: Fifteenth Air Force sends 730 B-17s and B-24 Liberators to attack command and control targets, airfields, marshaling yards, and railroad bridges. P-38 Lightnings strafe the airfield at Piacenza.

Twelfth Air Force A-20 Havocs attack command and control targets along the battle line, while B-16s and B-25 Mitchells bomb German defensive positions. P-47 Thunderbolts and P-40s attack command posts, gun positions, bridges, lines of communication, and German troops near Monte Cassino.

Second Lieutenant Charles W. Shea, of F Company, 350th Infantry Regiment, 88th Infantry Division, leads his platoon toward a German position on a hilltop near Monte Damiano. German machine guns fire on the company, inflicting a number of casualties and stopping the attack. Second Lieutenant Shea takes the initiative to eliminate the German machine guns. Despite heavy fire, he is able to crawl to one of the positions and throw hand grenades. The survivors surrender to Shea who then moves to the next position and forces them to surrender as well. As the third machine gun fires at him, Second Lieutenant Shea stands up and rushes the position, killing the enemy with rifle fire. For his great courage under fire and his determination to close with the enemy, Second Lieutenant Shea will receive the Medal of Honor.

PACIFIC: U.S. submarine *Tautog* attacks a Japanese convoy off northeast Honshu, Japan, sinking a collier.

CENTRAL PACIFIC: Seventh Air Force B-25 Mitchells from Makin Island bomb Nauru Island.

NEW BRITAIN: Thirteenth Air Force B-25 Mitchells, P-40s, and P-38 Lightnings attack troops and the airfield at Tobera. Army P-39 Airacobras and navy SBD Dauntless dive-bombers and TBF Avenger torpedo-bombers attack barges at Simpson Harbor and Keravia Bay near Rabaul.

NEW GUINEA: Fifth Air Force B-24 Liberators bomb Mokmer airfield on Biak Island. A-20 Havocs, B-25 Mitchells, and P-39 Airacobras and P-40s attack targets near Wewak and the Hansa Bay area. B-21s attack Ambon, Ceram, and Amboina Islands in the Moluccas as well as Timor Island.

May 13

CBI: Tenth Air Force sends almost 100 P-40s and P-51 Mustangs to attack troops, gun positions, and targets of opportunity in the Mogaung Valley. A-36 Intruder (Apache) fighter-bombers, B-25 Mitchells, and B-24 Liberators attack other targets.

In China, Fourteenth Air Force B-25 Mitchells and P-40s attack logistics sites, lines of communication, and convoys.

Twentieth Air Force receives the B-19 Superfortresses of the 771st Bombardment Squadron (Very Heavy), 462nd Bombardment Squadron (Very Heavy), at Piardoba, India, from the United States. The squadron's first mission is scheduled for early June.

ATLANTIC: In the North Atlantic, south of the Azores, destroyer escort *Francis M. Robinson* sinks Japanese submarine *RO-501*, previously German submarine *U-1224*, on its way to Japan.

ETO: Allied planners solidify the force build-up estimates for Neptune. On D-day, the plan calls for 8 2/3 divisions to be on the beachhead. Staff estimates of casualties on D-day are set at 12,000 killed and wounded. On D+1, 10 1/3 divisions will be available, on D+6, 15 1/3 divisions are to be landed, and on D+12, 26–30 divisions will have arrived. By D+40, planners estimate that sufficient forces will be available to separate the U.S. First Army from the 21st Army Group and create the U.S. 12th Army Group. At that time, the estimated troop strength in France is to be 450,000 men and 92,000 vehicles.

Between D+1 and D+10, planners estimate a logistics requirement of 19,500 long tons of supplies per day. By D+25 to D+40, that number is estimated to increase to 42,000 long tons per day. These planning figures do not include fuel, which is estimated at 1,800 tons a day just for the Americans. By D+330 (330 days after D-day), the Allies plan to reach the German border.

Eighth Air Force sends 289 B-17s to attack oil targets in Poland, 199 B-17s against the Osnabruck marshaling yard, and 261 B-24 Liberators against aircraft production facilities. The mission is escorted by 153 P-38 Lightnings, 238 P-47 Thunderbolts, and 346 P-51 Mustangs. Aircrews report 12 bombers lost and 144 damaged. Aircrew losses are one killed, four wounded, and 108 missing. Fighter pilots report 47 confirmed kills in the air and three probables. Five fighters are shot down and 13 are damaged. One pilot is wounded and five are reported missing.

Ninth Air Force sends over 300 B-26 Marauders and A-20 Havocs to attack airfields, coastal defenses, and V-weapon sites in France and Belgium. P-47 Thunderbolts conduct dive-bombing attacks.

ITALY: The French Expeditionary Corps captures Monte Majo and threatens the left wing of the German defensive line in the Liri Valley. II Corps renews its attack, with the 99th Infantry Division ordered to seize Santa Maria Infante and Spigno in order to control the road that links the Liri Valley with Route 7. The 85th Infantry Division is to support the attack. German aircraft attack the 85th Infantry Division near Minturno. Santa Maria Infante falls quickly.

Fifteenth Air Force sends over 670 B-17s and B-24 Liberators to bomb marshaling yards and rail lines to limit German reinforcements. Four AZON-equipped B-17s attack a viaduct near the Brenner Pass. Out of 21 bombs, four are direct hits. AZON (azimuth only) is a 1,000-pound bomb with a device to control the trajectory of the bomb after release. The bomb has radio-controlled fins and is balanced by a battery-powered gyroscope to stabilize the weapon as it falls. A smoke generator in the tail allows for visual tracking to the target.

Twelfth Air Force B-26 Marauders and B-25 Mitchells with A-20 Havocs and P-40s attack German lines of communication, command and control sites, and defensive positions all along the battlefront.

PACIFIC: U.S. submarine *Pogy* torpedoes and sinks a Japanese cargo ship off Honshu, Japan.

CENTRAL PACIFIC: Seventh Air Force B-24 Liberators attack Truk, staging through Eniwetok Atoll from Kwajalein. B-24s from Kwajalein bomb Maloelap and Jaluit Atolls. B-25 Mitchells from Engebi Island bomb Ponape Island.

Navy F4U Corsairs, F4F Hellcats, and SBD Dauntless dive-bombers, B-24 Liberators, and B-25 Mitchells bomb Japanese facilities on Jaluit Atoll.

BOUGAINVILLE: Thirteenth Air Force B-25 Mitchells, P-39 Airacobras, and P-40s attack piers, logistics sites, and villages.

NEW BRITAIN: Thirteenth Air Force B-25 Mitchells, P-39 Airacobras, P-40s, and P-38 Lightnings attack logistics sites at Talili Bay.

ADMIRALTIES: Thirteenth Air Force deploys the B-24 Liberators of the 370th, 371st, 372nd, and 424th Bombardment Squadrons (Heavy), of the 307th Bombardment Group (Heavy), from New Georgia to Momote airfield at Los Negros Island, Admiralties.

NEW GUINEA: Fifth Air Force B-24 Liberators and B-25 Mitchells bomb the Wakde and Arare airfields. P-39 Airacobras, P-40s, A-20 Havocs, and B-25s attack airfields, fuel storage areas, trucks, bridges, and other targets between Wewak and Hansa Bay.

May 14

CBI: Tenth Air Force P-38 Lightnings and P-40s attack lines of communication. B-25 Mitchells and P-51 Mustangs attack Japanese troops. Fighter pilots report four confirmed kills.

In China, Fourteenth Air Force P-40s and P-51 Mustangs attack road and rail traffic. Six Japanese bombers damage the airfield at Kienow.

ETO: Eighth Air Force receives the 435th Fighter Squadron, 479th Fighter Group, in England from the United States. The squadron, equipped with P-38Js (a variant of the P-38 Lightning with additional fuel tanks and an improved engine), is scheduled to fly its first mission in late May.

MEDITERRANEAN: German submarine *U-616* attacks a convoy off Morocco.

ITALY: The 88th Infantry Division reaches Spigno having suffered 2,000 casualties in three days of fighting.

Fifteenth Air Force sends 700 B-17s and B-24 Liberators to attack a marshaling yard and air depots.

Twelfth Air Force B-26 Marauders and B-25 Mitchells attack lines of communication; A-20 Havocs, P-47 Thunderbolts, and P-40s attack command and control sites, defensive positions, and lines of communication all along the battlefront.

First Lieutenant Robert T. Waugh is a platoon leader in the 339th Infantry Regiment, 85th Infantry Division, attacking six German bunker positions on a hill near

Tremensucli. After personally negotiating a minefield, he leads his platoon forward. Waugh orders the platoon to provide covering fire as he advances alone to engage the bunker positions. Throwing phosphorus grenades into the bunkers and firing on the defenders with his Thompson submachine gun, he clears each position. Several days later First Lieutenant Waugh performs the same heroic act, ordering his platoon to lay down a base of fire as he advances alone to destroy two pillboxes with grenades. As a result of his actions Waugh singlehandedly opens a breach in the Gustav Line, having killed 30 enemy soldiers and captured 25 others. For his gallantry in the face of the enemy beyond the call of duty, First Lieutenant Waugh will be receive the Medal of Honor.

CENTRAL PACIFIC: Seventh Air Force sends 53 B-24 Liberators from Kwajalein and 43 B-25 Mitchells from Makin Island to support navy aircraft in a raid on Jaluit Atoll.

U.S. submarines *Aspro* and *Bowfin* attack a Japanese convoy near Palau and sink a cargo ship.

U.S. submarine *Bonefish* attacks a Japanese convoy east of Borneo and sinks a destroyer.

U.S. submarine *Crevalle* is damaged by depth charges off northern Celebes Island.

U.S. submarine *Sand Lance* sinks a cargo ship near Guam. *Sand Lance* escapes after being depth-charged.

BOUGAINVILLE: Thirteenth Air Force P-39 Airacobras and P-40s bomb targets of opportunity.

NEW BRITAIN: Thirteenth Air Force sends 23 B-25 Mitchells to bomb the airfield at Tobera. P-39 Airacobras and P-40s attack logistics and troop areas at Vunakanau.

NEW GUINEA: Fifth Air Force B-24 Liberators and B-25 Mitchells attack the Wakde area. P-39 Airacobras and P-40s, A-20 Havocs, B-24s and B-25s attack targets between Wewak and Hansa Bay.

May 15

CBI: Tenth Air Force B-25 Mitchells, A-36 Intruder (Apache) fighter-bombers, and P-51 Mustangs attack Myitkyina airfield. B-24 Liberators also bomb Myitkyina, Kalewa, and Mandalay.

Fourteenth Air Force receives the 92nd Fighter Squadron, 81st Fighter Group, from Karachi, India, at Kwanghan, China. The squadron, equipped with P-47 Thunderbolts, is scheduled to fly its first mission in early June. The Japanese offensive opens a corridor along the rail line from the Yellow River to Hangkow.

ETO: The final plans for Neptune are briefed to senior commanders at General Montgomery's 21st Army Group Headquarters in London. Montgomery is the commander of all Allied ground forces for the operation. Prime Minister Churchill attends the briefings.

The 21st Army Group's Neptune plan calls for the British Second Army and the U.S. First Army to make the initial landings. On D-day, the United States will land 2 2/3 divisions and 6,800 vehicles on two beaches. The British and Canadians collectively will land three divisions and 8,900 vehicles on three beaches. The airborne forces will be moved by 1,300 transports and 2,000 gliders to their drop zones. The landings will be covered by 800 medium bombers and 2,500 fighter aircraft.

Eighth Air Force sends 166 B-17s and B-24 Liberators, escorted by 104 P-51 Mustangs, to attack V-weapon sites in France. A total of 13 bombers are damaged and one P-51 is lost.

During the night, three B-17s drop over one million leaflets on towns and cities in Belgium and France; five B-24s support Carpetbagger operations.

Eighth Air Force receives the headquarters, 479th Fighter Group, and the P-38J Lightnings of the 434th and 436th Fighter Squadrons from the United States. The squadrons' first missions will be in late May.

Ninth Air Force sends B-26 Marauders and A-20 Havocs to bomb airfields in France.

MEDITERRANEAN: Navy PBY-5 Catalinas and British escort vessels sink German submarine *U-731* in the western Mediterranean.

ITALY: In the II Corps area, the 337th Infantry Regiment of the 85th Infantry Division captures Castellonorato. The 338th Infantry captures Santa Croce, forcing the Germans to abandon other positions. The 351st Infantry of the 88th Infantry Division captures Spigno and pushes on to Itri to cut Route 82, the road link to the Liri Valley and the key to the German defensive line. The 85th Infantry Division is ordered to clear the coastal road to Monte Campese.

Twelfth Air Force B-25 Mitchells and B-26 Marauders attack lines of communication. A-20 Havocs, P-47 Thunderbolts, and P-40s attack German defensive positions, logistics bases, bridges, and motor transport throughout the battlefront.

CENTRAL PACIFIC: U.S. submarine *Aspro* attacks a Japanese convoy near Palau, sinking a transport.

BOUGAINVILLE: Thirteenth Air Force sends 24 B-25 Mitchells and P-40s, P-38 Lightnings, and P-39 Airacobras, along with Navy TBF Avenger torpedo-bombers and SBD Dauntless dive-bombers, to attack a number of targets throughout the island.

NEW GUINEA: Fifth Air Force B-24 Liberators, A-20 Havocs, P-47 Thunderbolts, and P-40s attack targets between Wewak and Hansa Bay. B-24s and B-25 Mitchells attack targets near Wakde and Sarmi and bomb Biak Island.

Thirteenth Air Task Force B-24s from Los Negros Island bomb troops, antiaircraft positions, and logistics sites on Woleai Atoll.

Hollandia airfields support redeployment for A-20 Havocs of the 89th Bombardment Squadron (Light), 3rd Bombardment Group (Light), and P-38 Lightnings of headquarters, 475th Fighter Group and 431st, 432nd, and 433rd Fighter Squadrons.

May 16

CBI: Tenth Air Force B-25 Mitchells, A-36 Intruder (Apache) fighter-bombers, and P-51 Mustangs attack Myitkyina.

ITALY: In the II Corps area the 338th Infantry Regiment of the 85th Infantry Division reaches Route 7. The 351st Infantry of the 88th Infantry Division continues toward Itri and reaches Monte Sant'Angelo. The Gustav Line is finally broken.

Twelfth Air Force B-25 Mitchells and B-26 Marauders attack railroad bridges and a tunnel. A-20 Havocs, P-47 Thunderbolts, and P-40s attack vehicles and major roads to cut off or delay the retreating German forces.

SOUTH PACIFIC: Two U.S. destroyers sink Japanese submarine *I-176*, off northern Choiseul in the Solomons.

CENTRAL PACIFIC: Seventh Air Force B-24 Liberators from Kwajalein bomb Wake Island. B-25 Mitchells from Makin Island bomb Nauru and Ponape Islands.
BOUGAINVILLE: Thirteenth Air Force P-38 Lightnings and P-40s attack Japanese positions.
NEW BRITAIN: Thirteenth Air Force P-39 Airacobras and P-40s attack targets in the Vunakanau area.
NEW GUINEA: Fifth Air Force B-24 Liberators, P-38 Lightnings, A-20 Havocs, and P-40s attack airfields and logistics sites on Wakde, Noemfoor, and Biak Islands.

The A-20 Havocs of the 8th Bombardment Squadron (Light), 3rd Bombardment Group (Light), and the P-47 Thunderbolts of the 9th Fighter Squadron, 49th Fighter Group, redeploy to Hollandia airfields.

May 17

CBI: The H Force of the Marauders conducts an attack on the Myitkyina airfield and captures it, allowing immediate reinforcement by the 679th Engineer Aviation Battalion, which flies in by glider. Chinese and British antiaircraft units also arrive by glider. The 1st Battalion captures the ferry at Pamati, taking advantage of a feint toward the north by 3rd Battalion. Chinese forces reach the outskirts of the city of Myitkyina.

General Stilwell orders two Chinese battalions to capture the town of Myitkyina. The troops end up shooting each other and disintegrate without ever encountering the enemy. The battalions are withdrawn. In the meantime, the Japanese rush reinforcements to Myitkyina. Only 1,310 Americans of the Galahad Task Force reach the objective. By June 1, the large majority of the remainder will be evacuated because of illness.

Tenth Air Force B-25 Mitchells, A-36 Intruder (Apache) fighter-bombers, and P-51 Mustangs attack targets in the Mogaung Valley, including a bridge at Kamaing and Japanese troops near Myitkyina.

In China, Fourteenth Air Force P-40s support Chinese ground forces.
ETO: General Eisenhower, commander of SHAEF, sets the date of the invasion of Europe for June 5 based on tidal and light conditions necessary for the landings. On this date the tides are low enough to expose beach obstacles and there is enough light for visual aerial and naval bombardment of German defenses.

The naval forces available to support Neptune under command of Sir Bertram H. Ramsay are divided into a Western Task Force and an Eastern Task Force. The Western Task Force, under Rear Admiral A. G. Kirk, is subdivided into assault forces U (Utah beach) and O (Omaha beach). The assault forces, preceded by minesweeping flotillas and naval gunfire, will make the initial landings at 0630 hours. The navy is to provide five artificial anchorages (codenamed Gooseberries), two of which will be developed into artificial harbors (codenamed Mulberries) after the beachheads have been established.

These small, versatile, 75 millimeter pack howitzers prove to be invaluable to Merrill's Marauders during the Burma campaign. Here they are providing fire support at Myitkyina during the siege, probably in late May 1944.

The Neptune ground plan calls for General Omar N. Bradley's First Army, composed of the VII Corps under Major General J. Lawton Collins and V Corps commanded by Major General Leonard T. Gerow, to make the landings to establish a beachhead. On D-day, the VII Corps (4th, 90th, and 9th Infantry Divisions) is to land on the beach codenamed Utah, supported by the landings of the 82nd and 101st Airborne Divisions behind the enemy's beach defenses. The VII Corps is expected to cut off the Cotentin Peninsula and capture the port city of Cherbourg in eight days (D+8). The V Corps (1st, 29th, and 2nd Infantry Divisions) is to land on the beach codenamed Omaha and capture the city of St-Lô in nine days (D+9). By D+20, the two corps will close the gap between the forces and drive forward to Avranches. Lieutenant General George S. Patton, Jr.'s Third Army will be landed and under the operational control of Bradley's First Army until D+30, when the Third Army will be dispatched to clear the Brittany peninsula and capture the coastal ports while the First Army attacks south and east toward the Loire River. By D+90, Allied forces are to be ready to capture Paris and then advance on a broad front, with the main effort in the north under General Bernard L. Montgomery's 21st Army Group.

To support Neptune, the navy will provide seven battleships, 32 cruisers, over 100 destroyers, and nearly 100 minesweepers. In total, the Allies will employ 1,213 warships of all types. The landings will employ 229 LSTs and 3,372 landing craft.

MEDITERRANEAN: Fifteenth Air Force sends nearly 500 B-17s and B-24 Liberators against lines of communication and transportation targets in Italy and Yugoslavia. P-38 Lightnings also attack airfields in Italy.

Eight U.S. destroyers, supported by Royal Air Force Wellington bombers, sink German submarine *U-616* in western Mediterranean. German submarine *U-960* attacks one of the destroyers, but its torpedo fails to hit.

ITALY: In the II Corps area the 338th Infantry Regiment of the 85th Infantry Division moves through Formia. The 337th Infantry is at Maranola, isolating Formia on the coastal road. The 351st Infantry Regiment of the 88th Infantry Division captures Monte Ruazzo, but is stopped by strong defenses near the Itri-Pico road.

Monte Cassino falls to the Polish Corps and British forces.

Twelfth Air Force B-26 Marauders and B-25 Mitchells bomb road bridges and airfields. A-20 Havocs attack a command and control target near Valmontone and drop supplies to French troops on Monte Revole. A-20 Havocs, P-47 Thunderbolts, and P-40s attack German defensive positions, lines of communication, and vehicles as the German defenders continue to regroup.

CENTRAL PACIFIC: Seventh Air Force B-24 Liberators from Kwajalein Atoll bomb Wake Island. B-25 Mitchells from Engebi Island bomb Ponape Island.

U.S. destroyers *Frazier* and *Meade* bombard Japanese defenses at Maloelap Atoll in the Marshalls.

U.S. submarines *Sand Lance* and *Tunny* attack a Japanese convoy carrying troops to reinforce Yap and Palau. USS *Sand Lance* sinks a transport near Saipan and USS *Tunny* sinks a cargo ship west of the Marianas. USS *Sand Lance* torpedoes a cargo ship picking up survivors. Both submarines are attacked with depth charges but escape without damage.

New Britain: Thirteenth Air Force sends 25 B-25 Mitchells to bomb the Tobera airfield. Army P-39 Airacobras, P-38 Lightnings, and P-40s support more than 40 U.S. Navy SBD Dauntless dive-bombers in an attack on targets near Vunakanau.

New Guinea: Operation Straightline. Naval Task Force 77, commanded by Rear Admiral William M. Fechteler and with two heavy cruisers, 10 destroyers, and six destroyer escorts, supports the 163rd RCT as it lands at Arara with an hour-long naval gunfire bombardment. Air strikes and rocket-firing LCIs also support the landing. No enemy forces are found in the area. After establishing a beachhead perimeter to serve as a support base for the attack on Wakde Island, elements of the 163rd move to secure Toem.

Fifth Air Force B-24 Liberators and B-25 Mitchells support the landing with early bombing runs. B-24s, with P-38 Lightnings as escort, bomb Sarmi and Mokmer, as well as Noemfoor Island. P-38 Lightnings, P-47 Thunderbolts, P-40s, A-20 Havocs, and medium bombers attack targets between Wewak and the Hansa Bay area.

British Admiral James F. Somerville's combined task force conducts Operation Transom to coincide with the landings at Wakde. Aircraft from the carrier USS *Saratoga* and the British carrier HMS *Illustrious* bomb Japanese shipping and harbor facilities at Surabaya, Java. A transport is sunk and two cargo ships, a tanker, and two submarine chasers are damaged.

May 18

Aleutians: Eleventh Air Force B-25 Mitchells sink two auxiliary vessels in the Kurile Islands.

CBI: Brigadier General Merrill suffers a heart attack and is relieved of command of the Marauders. Colonel John E. McCammon, Merrill's assistant, takes temporary command. The Myitkyina Task Force is formed and includes two regiments of the Chinese 30th Division, elements of the Chinese 50th Division, and the remainder of the Marauders under command of Colonel Charles N. Hunter.

P-40s from the 88th Fighter Squadron arrive at Myitkyina.

Tenth Air Force sends B-25 Mitchells, A-36 Intruder (Apache) fighter-bombers, and P-51 Mustangs to attack Japanese positions in the Mogaung Valley.

Mediterranean: Fifteenth Air Force sends over 400 B-17s and B-24 Liberators to attack industrial targets and marshaling yards in Romania and Yugoslavia. Bad weather over the targets causes most of the bombers to abort the mission. A total of 206 B-17s attack the Ploeşti oil refineries in Romania. The bombers are attacked by over 100 German fighters over the target. A total of 14 bombers are lost. Aircrews report 28 confirmed kills and 30 probables.

Italy: In the II Corps area, elements of the 85th Infantry Division advance along Route 7.

Twelfth Air Force B-25 Mitchells and B-26 Marauders attack road and rail communications. A-20 Havocs, P-47 Thunderbolts, and P-40s attack German troops, tanks, vehicles, roads, and logistics sites.

Central Pacific: Seventh Air Force B-25 Mitchells from Makin Island bomb Taroa Island on Maloelap Atoll. After rearming at Majuro Atoll the bombers attack Taroa again en route to Makin.

BOUGAINVILLE: Thirteenth Air Force P-39 Airacobras and P-38 Lightnings attack barges off the coast and a logistics base near Mupuai.

ADMIRALTIES: A naval base and naval air station, Manus Island, Admiralty Islands, are established.

NEW GUINEA: Four infantry companies of the 163rd RCT supported by tanks fight nearly 800 Japanese defending Wakde Island in caves, concrete pill boxes, and log bunkers. After a bloody struggle that lasts all day, in which nearly every foot of ground is contested, the Americans kill all but four of the defenders, suffering 40 killed and 107 wounded.

Fifth Air Force B-25 Mitchells, B-24 Liberators, and A-20 Havocs, along with P-38 Lightnings, P-40s, and P-47 Thunderbolts, attack targets between Wewak and Hansa Bay.

B-24s attack targets of opportunity on Halmahera Island in the Moluccas; B-25s bomb targets in the Celebes Islands and the Moluccas.

U.S. submarine *Puffer* attacks a Japanese convoy in the Java Sea, sinking a cargo ship.

May 19

CBI: The Marauders' K Force captures the Mogaung Road. Chinese units arrive by air to reinforce the Allied forces.

Tenth Air Force B-25 Mitchells, A-36 Intruder (Apache) fighter-bombers, P-40s, and P-51 Mustangs attack Japanese positions around Myitkyina.

In China, Fourteenth Air Force B-24 Liberators cause heavy damage to two cargo ships off Hong Kong. P-40s of the Chinese-American Composite Wing (CACW) attack Japanese vehicles, troops, and trucks.

ATLANTIC: James V. Forrestal, undersecretary of the navy since 1940, is appointed secretary of the navy.

ETO: Eighth Air Force sends 588 B-17s to Berlin and 300 B-24 Liberators to Brunswick, escorted by 155 P-38 Lightnings, 182 P-47 Thunderbolts, and 363 P-51 Mustangs. The primary targets are cloud covered, and bombers with H2X radar use it to guide them to the targets. A total of 28 bombers are lost and 355 are damaged. Aircrew casualties are four killed, 24 wounded, and 256 missing. Fighter pilots report 70 confirmed kills in the air and seven on the ground. Fighter losses are 19 aircraft with another 18 damaged. Seventeen pilots are reported missing.

Ninth Air Force sends nearly 300 B-26 Marauders and A-20 Havocs to bomb coastal defenses, ports, and V-weapon sites in France. Cloud cover prevents most bombers from reaching their targets. P-47 Thunderbolts conduct dive-bombing attacks on a number of targets.

MEDITERRANEAN: U.S. light cruiser *Brooklyn* shells German logistics sites along the Italian coast.

Two U.S. destroyers and British aircraft sink German submarine *U-960* in the western Mediterranean.

ITALY: In the II Corps area the 338th Infantry Regiment of the 85th Infantry Division captures Gaeta after the Germans abandon the city. The 351st Infantry captures

Itri and Monte Grande, opening the way for the II Corps to link up with the VI Corps at Anzio.

Fifteenth Air Force sends over 500 B-17s and B-24 Liberators to attack oil storage facilities, railroad bridges, and ports.

Twelfth Air Force B-25 Mitchells and B-26 Marauders attack road and rail communications. A-20 Havocs, P-47 Thunderbolts, and P-40s attack German troops, tanks, vehicles, roads, and logistics sites.

PACIFIC: U.S. submarine *Skate* torpedoes and sinks a Japanese guardboat in the Bonin Islands.

SOUTH PACIFIC: Guided by intercepted Japanese radio traffic, the destroyer escort USS *England* is able to pinpoint the location of Japanese submarines operating in the Solomons as they attempt a redeployment farther north. Japanese submarine *I-16* is the first kill, sunk off Choiseul Island. Over the next five days, USS *England* will sink another five Japanese submarines.

CENTRAL PACIFIC: Navy aircraft from TG 58.6 (Rear Admiral Alfred E. Montgomery) bomb Marcus Island.

NEW BRITAIN: Thirteenth Air Force sends 16 B-25 Mitchells to attack Japanese gun positions and a logistics base at Talili Bay.

NEW GUINEA: Fifth Air Force B-24 Liberators, A-20 Havocs, and P-38 Lightnings attack targets at Noemfoor Island. Other B-24s bomb Biak Island. Nearly 300 B-25 Mitchells, A-20 Havocs, P-47 Thunderbolts, and P-38 Lightnings attack targets from Wewak to Hansa Bay.

May 20

CBI: Tenth Air Force A-36 Intruder (Apache) fighter-bombers, P-40s, and P-51 Mustangs attack bridges, troop assembly areas, and targets of opportunity near Myitkyina and Kamaing.

In China, Fourteenth Air Force B-24 Liberators bomb a Japanese convoy in the South China Sea south of Hong Kong, sinking a cargo ship and damaging two others. Three bombers are lost. Other B-24s attack Japanese warships, damaging an auxiliary submarine chaser in the South China Sea.

P-40s attack Japanese trucks, tanks, and troops.

ETO: Eighth Air Force sends 190 B-17s to bomb the airfield at Orly and the air depot at Villacoublay in France and 177 B-24 Liberators to bomb the airfield and marshaling yard at Reims. Another 271 B-17s and B-24 Liberators are sent against the marshaling yards at Liege and Brussels in Belgium, but heavy cloud cover forces the bombers to abort. A total of two bombers are lost and 102 are damaged. Aircrew casualties are 37 killed, 22 wounded, and 17 missing. The missions are escorted by 146 P-38 Lightnings, 177 P-47 Thunderbolts, and 334 P-51 Mustangs. Fighter pilots report three confirmed kills. Four fighters are lost and five are damaged. The four pilots are reported missing.

Ninth Air Force sends B-26 Marauders to attack airfields, coastal defenses, and V-weapon sites in France. Bad weather causes most of the bombers to abort the mission. P-47 Thunderbolts conduct dive-bombing attacks on numerous targets.

ITALY: The 91st Reconnaissance Squadron reports Fondi is weakly defended. The 350th Infantry of the 88th Infantry Division captures the town and then advances 10 miles toward Monte Alto.

Twelfth Air Force A-20 Havocs, P-47 Thunderbolts, and P-40s attack targets around Vallecorsa and Terracina.

SOUTHWEST PACIFIC AREA: U.S. submarine *Angler* torpedoes and sinks a Japanese transport off eastern Malaysia. USS *Angler* escapes after surviving a depth-charging attack.

U.S. submarine *Picuda* is damaged by depth charges in the Luzon Strait but remains on patrol.

CENTRAL PACIFIC: Seventh Air Force B-25 Mitchells from Engebi Island bomb Ponape Island.

U.S. submarine *Silversides* torpedoes and sinks a Japanese gunboat off Saipan.

Aircraft from the small carrier *San Jacinto* sink a guardboat near Marcus Island.

BOUGAINVILLE: Thirteenth Air Force B-25 Mitchells, P-39 Airacobras, P-40s, and P-38 Lightnings support over 30 U.S. Navy and Marine Corps aircraft in attacking Japanese logistics bases, antiaircraft positions, and troop assembly areas. P-39 Airacobras attack barges in Matchin Bay and bridges at Kieta.

NEW GUINEA: Fifth Air Force B-24 Liberators, A-20 Havocs, and B-25 Mitchells attack targets at Noemfoor Island. Other B-24s bomb Biak Island. B25s, A-20 Havocs, P-47 Thunderbolts, and P-38 Lightnings attack targets from Wewak to Hansa Bay. P-38 Lightnings land on Wakde airfield.

U.S. submarine *Bluegill* torpedoes and sinks a Japanese cargo ship in the Morotai Strait.

May 21

CBI: A Japanese counterattack is stopped by the 3rd Battalion of the Marauders. The men are so weak from illness that many collapse in the middle of the fighting. About 75 to 100 men of the Marauders are being evacuated every day for sickness.

Tenth Air Force B-25 Mitchells, A-36 Intruder (Apache) fighter-bombers, P-40s, and P-51 Mustangs attack Japanese positions, bridges, and troops near Myitkyina.

ETO: Eighth Air Force sends 40 B-17s and 110 B-24 Liberators escorted by 48 P-47 Thunderbolts against V-weapon sites in France. A total of 14 bombers are damaged. Over 600 P-38 Lightnings, P-51 Mustangs, and P-47 Thunderbolts attack railroad bridges and locomotives in Germany. Fighter pilots report 18 confirmed kills in the air and another 17 confirmed kills on the ground. A total of 19 fighters are lost and four damaged. Eighteen pilots are reported missing.

Ninth Air Force sends 50 B-26 Marauders to bomb airfields in France.

ITALY: In the 88th Infantry Division area, the 349th and 351st Infantry move forward to protect the advance of the 350th Infantry toward Monte Alto. The 337th Infantry of the 85th Infantry Division moves toward Terracina.

Twelfth Air Force A-20 Havocs, P-47 Thunderbolts, and P-40s attack lines of communication and German troops.

SOUTHWEST PACIFIC AREA: U.S. submarine *Cero* attacks a Japanese convoy east of the Philippines and misses its target; *Cero* avoids a counterattack by several escort ships. USS *Narwhal* also unsuccessfully attacks a convoy off the east coast of Mindanao Island.

PACIFIC: A tremendous explosion occurs at West Loch, Pearl Harbor, while ammunition is being loaded on LSTs. The accident destroys seven LSTs, three LCTs (landing craft tank), 17 LVTs (landing vehicles tracked), and eight 155 millimeter guns. Two LSTs are damaged.

CENTRAL PACIFIC: Seventh Air Force sends 53 B-24 Liberators from Kwajalein to bomb Wotje Atoll. B-25 Mitchells from Makin Island conduct a follow-on attack. B-24s staging through Eniwetok Atoll bomb Rota Island in the Marianas, rearming at Momote airfield on Los Negros in the Admiralties.

Navy F4U Corsairs, PV-1 Patrol Bombers, B-24 Liberators, and B-25 Mitchells bomb Japanese positions on Wotje Atoll.

U.S. submarine *Billfish* torpedoes and damages a Japanese cargo ship west of the Marianas. The *Billfish* escapes a counterattack from an escort ship.

BOUGAINVILLE: Thirteenth Air Force P-39 Airacobras, P-38 Lightnings, and P-40s attack and destroy two bridges.

NEW BRITAIN: Thirteenth Air Force B-24 Liberators, P-39 Airacobras, and P-40s support Navy SBD Dauntless dive-bombers in an attack on Vunakanau airfield. P-38 Lightnings and navy aircraft bomb Lakunai airfield.

NEW GUINEA: The 158th RCT under Brigadier General Edwin D. Patrick arrives at Toem to expand American control to Sarmi and clear out any remaining Japanese forces in the area.

Fifth Air Force B-24 Liberators, A-20 Havocs, and P-38 Lightnings attack Noemfoor and Biak Islands. B-25 Mitchells, P-47 Thunderbolts, P-40s, and P-38 Lightnings attack targets from Wewak to Hansa Bay.

A-20 Havocs of the 13th Bombardment Squadron (Light), 3rd Bombardment Group (Light), redeploy to airfields in Hollandia.

Thirteenth Air Task Force B-24 Liberators bomb Truk.

May 22

ALEUTIANS: Eleventh Air Force B-25 Mitchells from Attu Island attack a Japanese picket boat near Paramushiru.

CBI: In China, Fourteenth Air Force B-25 Mitchells attack and damage a large cargo ship near Hong Kong. P-51 Mustangs and P-40s attack bridges and convoys.

U.S. submarine *Picuda* torpedoes and sinks a gunboat and the cargo ship it is towing in the South China Sea. The cargo ship was damaged by Fourteenth Air Force bombers on May 20.

ETO: Eighth Air Force sends 342 B-17s against the port at Kiel, Germany, and sends 94 B-24 Liberators to attack V-weapon sites in France. The missions are escorted by 145 P-38 Lightnings, 95 P-47 Thunderbolts, and 328 P-51 Mustangs. Over Kiel, five bombers are lost and 210 are damaged. Only one of the B-24s is damaged. Aircrew losses are four killed, three wounded, and 78 missing. Fighter pilots report 22 confirmed kills and four probables. Seven fighters are lost and seven are damaged. Six pilots are reported missing.

P-47 Thunderbolts conduct attacks on railroad bridges at Hasselt and Liege in Belgium. One P-47 is lost and one is damaged.

During the night, four B-17s drop 320,000 leaflets on The Hague, Haarlem, Rotterdam, and Utrecht in the Netherlands. A total of 12 B-24s fly in support of Carpetbagger operations.

Ninth Air Force sends over 600 B-26 Marauders, A-20 Havocs, P-47 Thunderbolts, and P-51 Mustangs to attack airfields and marshaling yards around Cherbourg, Calais, and Paris.

ITALY: In the II Corps area, the 337th Infantry Regiment attacks Terracina while the 338th Infantry Regiment (85th Infantry Division) moves to Leano to outflank the defenders.

The 36th Infantry Division lands at Anzio. The VI Corps now has seven divisions available for an attack.

Fifteenth Air Force sends over 500 B-17s and B-24 Liberators against marshaling yards and ports. Fifteenth Air Force receives the P-47 Thunderbolts of the 332nd Fighter Group from the Twelfth Air Force.

Twelfth Air Force A-20 Havocs, P-47 Thunderbolts, and P-40s fly ground support missions and attack roads and bridges throughout the battle area.

SOUTHWEST PACIFIC AREA: U.S. submarine *Ray* attacks the convoy attacked previously by USS *Cero*, sinking a cargo ship off the south coast of Mindanao.

PACIFIC: U.S. submarine *Pollack* attacks a Japanese convoy near the Bonin Islands and sinks a destroyer.

CENTRAL PACIFIC: Seventh Air Force sends eight B-25 Mitchells from Engebi Island to bomb Ponape Island.

U.S. destroyers *Bancroft* and *Edwards* bombard Japanese facilities at Wotje Atoll.

BOUGAINVILLE: Thirteenth Air Force P-39 Airacobras bomb logistics depots at Bonis and attack bridges near Kieta.

NEW BRITAIN: Thirteenth Air Force P-39 Airacobras, P-38 Lightnings, and P-40s attack targets of opportunity along the coast near Talili Bay.

NEW IRELAND: Destroyer escort USS *England* sinks Japanese submarine *RO-106* north of Kavieng, New Ireland.

NEW GUINEA: Fifth Air Force B-24 Liberators and B-25 Mitchells bomb Biak Island. P-40s attack Wakde Island. B-24s, B-25 Mitchells, P-38 Lightnings, P-47 Thunderbolts, and P-40s attack targets between Wewak and Hansa Bay.

Headquarters of the 348th Fighter Group and the P-47s of the 341st and 342nd Fighter Squadrons redeploy from Saidor to Wakde Island.

U.S. submarine *Bluegill* is damaged by an air attack off Halmahera but remains on patrol.

May 23

CBI: Tenth Air Force sends 23 P-40s and four A-36 Intruder (Apache) fighterbombers to attack Japanese positions and logistics storage areas near Myitkyina.

ETO: Eighth Air Force sends 580 B-17s and 465 B-24 Liberators against airfields and marshaling yards in France, escorted by 96 P-38 Lightnings, 142 P-47 Thunderbolts, and 324 P-51 Mustangs. Ninth Air Force supports the raid with 644 P-47 Thunderbolts and P-38 Lightnings. Three bombers are lost and 86 are damaged. Aircrew losses are 22 killed, four wounded, and 10 missing. Fighter pilots report no enemy aircraft kills and three aircraft damaged. Ninth Air Force pilots report two P-38s and two P-47s are lost.

P-51s conduct dive-bombing attacks on a railroad bridge in Belgium, losing one aircraft.

During the night, four B-17s drop over 900,000 leaflets on towns and cities in Belgium and the Netherlands. A total of seven B-24s fly in support of Carpetbagger operations.

Ninth Air Force B-26 Marauders bomb airfields and coastal batteries in France while P-38 Lightnings attack rail cars.

ITALY: In the II Corps area, the 337th Infantry Regiment of the 85th Infantry Division captures Terracina as the Germans withdraw.

A massive artillery bombardment at Cisterna precedes the Allied breakout from Anzio (called Operation Buffalo). The 1st Special Service Force gains control of Route 7 at Cisterna. The 1st Armored Division, supported by two battalions of the 135th Infantry Regiment of the 34th Infantry Division and two battalions of the 6th Armored Infantry Regiment, attacks toward Cisterna. Initially stopped by large minefields, the engineers use a device called a snake, a line of explosives that clears paths through minefields. Once clear of the mines, the tanks break through the German defenses. The objective is Valmontone along Route 6, to cut off the German forces in the Liri and Sacco valleys. The 3rd Infantry Division makes small gains as it attacks toward Cisterna, suffering heavy casualties. The 45th Infantry Division attacks on the left flank of the beachhead and makes good initial progress. The 1st Special Service Force is stopped by a German counterattack and one company is captured. The 133rd Infantry Regiment from the 34th Infantry Division relieves the 1st SSF on the line.

Fifteenth Air Force sends over 300 B-17s and B-24 Liberators to attack German troops and lines of communications at Avezzano and Valmontone.

Twelfth Air Force A-20 Havocs, P-47 Thunderbolts, and P-40s attack targets in the Liri Valley and German defenses at Anzio, in support of Operation Buffalo.

Light cruiser USS *Brooklyn* and destroyers USS *Kearny* and *Ericsson* shell German positions near Ardea, Italy.

In the midst of an attack against German positions near Carano, Italy, Second Lieutenant Thomas W. Fowler of the 1st Armored Division encounters two infantry platoons stopped before a minefield. Lieutenant Fowler makes his way through the minefield, clearing a path by lifting the mines out of the ground with his hands. He then leads the infantrymen through the minefield and deploys the men in position. He then guides tanks through the minefield to support the infantry. Moving out in front of the infantry, he scouts German positions and leads an attack that succeeds in capturing the positions. He organizes his troops for a counterattack and fights without regard for his personal safety, rescuing wounded tankers and infantrymen in the face of intense enemy fire. Second Lieutenant Fowler's initiative, selflessness, and leadership will win him the Medal of Honor.

Private First Class John W. Dutko of the 3rd Infantry Division takes cover in an abandoned enemy trench near Ponte Rotto, Italy, as German artillery shells rain down around him. Leaving cover, he makes a singlehanded attack on three German machine-gun positions and an 88 millimeter gun. Private First Class Dutko advances to within 30 yards of the first machine gun and knocks out the position with a hand grenade. Wounded by fire from the second machine-gun position, Dutko charges the 88 millimeter gun, firing his Browning automatic rifle (BAR) from the hip and kills the crew. He then turns on the machine-gun position that had wounded him and eliminates it. He is then hit and wounded again by another machine-gun crew. Running the next 20 yards he kills the last of the enemy with a burst of fire from his BAR, then collapses and dies. For his extraordinary gallantry and courage, Private First Class John W. Dutko will receive the Medal of Honor.

Technical Sergeant Van T. Barfoot of the 157th Infantry Regiment, 45th Infantry Division, is participating in an assault against German troops holding entrenchments on dominating terrain near Carano, Italy. As his platoon is halted by enemy fire, Technical Sergeant Barfoot moves off alone to locate the enemy's left flank. He crawls to within hand grenade range of a machine-gun position and eliminates it. Now outflanking the enemy, he moves parallel to the trench line, killing and capturing Germans. Firing his Thompson submachine gun as he goes, he accounts for the capture of 17 prisoners, then consolidates his platoon on the captured position, on which the Germans launch an infantry counterattack supported by three tanks. Taking a bazooka, Technical Sergeant Barfoot places himself directly in the path of the tanks and knocks the first one out with a well-aimed shot. Barfoot uses his submachine gun to kill the tank crew. Barfoot drives off the enemy and is able to destroy a German artillery piece. He then assists in moving two of his wounded soldiers to safety. For his extraordinary acts of heroism, Technical Sergeant Barfoot will receive the Medal of Honor.

Technical Sergeant Ernest H. Dervishian of the 135th Infantry Regiment, 34th Infantry Division, finds himself ahead of his company during an attack against German defenses near Cisterna, Italy. Dervishian, with four other soldiers, approaches a railroad embankment and comes upon German soldiers hiding in dugouts. He then begins moving among the dugouts, forcing the Germans to surrender, and gathers 25 prisoners. Technical Sergeant Dervishian then captures six more enemy soldiers as they attempt to retreat. When another four Americans join Dervishian's group, he sends them to occupy a large vineyard, but when the men come under machine-gun fire he leads an attack into the vineyard. Dervishian uses a hand grenade and his M-1 carbine to force four Germans to surrender. As another machine gun opens up on the Americans, Dervishian leaps into the abandoned enemy position and, taking their machine gun, engages the other position. As German soldiers attempt to flank him, Dervishian engages both threats simultaneously, using a captured machine pistol and the machine gun. Five enemy soldiers signal they want to surrender, and Dervishian moves past them to eliminate all resistance in the vineyard. Locating another machine-gun position, he fires on it and forces six more Germans to surrender to him. For his exemplary courage and combat skill, Technical Sergeant Dervishian will receive the Medal of Honor.

Central Pacific: Seventh Air Force B-25 Mitchells from Makin Island bomb Jaluit Atoll. B-24 Liberators staging from Los Negros Island bomb Ponape Island.

Bougainville: Thirteenth Air Force P-39 Airacobras and P-40s attack bridges and barges throughout the island.

New Britain: Thirteenth Air Force B-24 Liberators bomb Tobera. B-25 Mitchells, P-39 Airacobras, P-38 Lightnings, and P-40s attack Japanese positions around Rabaul.

New Ireland: Destroyer escort USS *England* sinks Japanese submarine *RO-104* north of Kavieng.

New Guinea: Fifth Air Force B-24 Liberators, A-20 Havocs, and P-38 Lightnings bomb Biak Island. P-40s attack Japanese positions on the Biri River and P-38 Lightnings fly ground support missions near Aitape. B-24s and B-25s, along with A-20 Havocs and P-39 Airacobras, attack targets between Wewak and Hansa Bay.

U.S. submarine *Cero* torpedoes and sinks a Japanese cargo ship. Working with USS *Ray,* an army tanker is successfully torpedoed and damaged off Halmahera Island.

U.S. submarine *Raton* torpedoes and sinks a Japanese merchant vessel west of Borneo.

May 24

CBI: General Joseph Stilwell reinforces Myitkyina with the 209th Engineer Combat Battalion, converting them to infantry.

Tenth Air Force sends over 20 P-40s to attack targets at Myitkyina. Pilots report destroying eight barracks buildings, a railroad bridge, and a defensive position.

ETO: Eighth Air Force sends 616 B-17s and 490 B-24 Liberators against airfields in France and targets near Berlin. The mission is escorted by 144 P-38 Lightnings, 178 P-47 Thunderbolts, and 280 P-51 Mustangs. A total of 33 bombers are lost and 257 are damaged. Aircrew casualties are four killed, 24 wounded, and 482 missing. Fighter pilots report 33 confirmed kills in the air and seven probables. Ten aircraft are lost and seven are damaged. One pilot is wounded and 10 are reported missing.

Nearly 200 P-47s and P-51s attack bridges and airfields in France. Pilots report three confirmed kills in the air and two on the ground. Three P-51s are lost and six are damaged.

During the night four B-17s drop two and one-half million leaflets on towns and cities in France and Belgium. Three B-24 Liberators fly in support of Carpetbagger.

Ninth Air Force sends over 450 B-26 Marauders to attack airfields, coastal defenses, and V-weapon sites in France. P-38 Lightnings and P-47s conduct dive-bombing attacks on airfields.

Mediterranean: Fifteenth Air Force sends over 600 B-17s and B-24 Liberators to bomb aircraft production facilities and airfields in Austria. Six B-24s are lost over Bad Voslau airfield.

Italy: In the II Corps area, elements of the 337th Infantry of the 85th Infantry Division capture Terracina, the II Corps objective. Combat Command B of 1st Armored Division advances beyond Route 7. Combat Command A advances and isolates

Cisterna. The 3rd Infantry Division begins an attack on Cisterna supported by artillery, but is slowed by enemy defenses. At Carano, the 180th Infantry Regiment of the 45th Infantry Division stops an enemy counterattack.

Twelfth Air Force B-25 Mitchells and B-26 Marauders bomb roads north of the battle area to block German forces. A-20 Havocs, P-47 Thunderbolts, and P-40s attack convoys and troop movements.

Private James H. Mills of F Company, 15th Infantry Regiment, 3rd Infantry Division, is in his first combat action near Cisterna di Littoria. Moving ahead of his platoon to reach a flanking position on a German strongpoint, Private Mills kills or captures several enemy soldiers. He then charges a German position while firing his rifle from his hip and forces the six soldiers to surrender. He continues to advance, and several more enemy soldiers are killed or captured. Realizing that the strongpoint is heavily defended, Mills volunteers to approach within 100 yards of the strongpoint and draw enemy fire while the rest of the platoon maneuvers. Mills crawls close to the strongpoint and stands up to deliver rifle fire into the position. The Germans react with a heavy volume of machine-gun and rifle fire. Untouched, he ducks into a small draw to reload and continues firing. He repeats this four times until his platoon is able to capture the position in a quick rush, taking 22 Germans prisoners and without American casualties. For his extraordinary courage and skill, Private Mills will receive the Medal of Honor.

Private First Class Henry Schauer, 3rd Infantry Division, is a member of a patrol operating near Cisterna di Littoria. Carrying a Browning automatic rifle, Private First Class Schauer demonstrated exceptional courage and coolness under fire the previous day, engaging enemy troops in several stand-up fights at close range, eliminating snipers and several German machine-gun positions. When a German tank and a machine-gun fire from positions only 100 yards away from the patrol, Private First Class Schauer crawls 20 yards toward the enemy and then stands up. Bringing the Browning automatic rifle to his shoulder as bullets and tank rounds strike all around him, Schauer eliminates the machine gun with a short, accurate burst of fire. For his exceptional courage and skill, Private First Class Schauer will receive the Medal of Honor.

Sergeant Sylvester Antolak of B Company, 15th Infantry Regiment, 3rd Infantry Division, leads his squad near Cisterna di Littoria. Encountering enemy fire from a position nearly 200 yards away, Sergeant Antolak moves forward to engage the Germans. As he advances he is hit several times. Each time he drops, but struggles to his feet and continues to move forward, firing his Thompson submachine gun. As he reaches the German position he kills two Germans and forces 10 others to surrender. Consolidating his squad on the objective, he refuses medical attention and orders his men to follow him on an assault of a second position 100 yards distant. As he advances to close with the enemy he is killed, but his squad continues forward and captures the position in close combat. His superb fighting courage and heroic leadership will win Sergeant Antolak the Medal of Honor.

SOUTHWEST PACIFIC AREA: U.S. submarine *Flying Fish* suffers some damage when one of her torpedoes explodes prematurely. The *Flying Fish* remains on patrol in the Philippine Sea.

U.S. submarine *Gurnard* attacks a Japanese convoy in the Celebes Sea and sinks a fleet tanker off the coast of Mindanao. U.S. submarine *Narwhal* lands men and supplies on Samar Island.

In the South China Sea U.S. submarine *Lapon* torpedoes and sinks two Japanese cargo ships.

U.S. submarine *Perch* attacks a Japanese convoy in the South China Sea, but misses its target.

U.S. submarine *Raton* attacks a Japanese convoy east of Singapore and sinks one escort vessel and damages another.

PACIFIC: Lieutenant General Robert C. Richardson, Jr., is assigned as the overall army commander in the Pacific Ocean Areas including responsibility for the Twentieth Air Force. Lieutenant General Millard F. Harmon is named air commander and deputy commander of the Twentieth Air Force. The assignments will be effective as of August 1.

CENTRAL PACIFIC: Seventh Air Force B-25 Mitchells from Makin Island bomb Wotje Atoll, rearm at Majuro Atoll, and bomb Jaluit Atoll on the return to Makin. B-25s from Engebi Island bomb Ponape Island.

BOUGAINVILLE: Thirteenth Air Force sends 51 P-39 Airacobras, P-40s, and P-38 Lightnings to attack the airfield on Buka Island and the radar station at Cape Lalahan.

NEW BRITAIN: Thirteenth Air Force B-25 Mitchells, P-38 Lightnings, and P-40s attack targets in and around Rabaul.

NEW IRELAND: Destroyer escort USS *England* sinks Japanese submarine *RO-116* north of Kavieng.

NEW GUINEA: Brigadier General Edwin D. Patrick takes command of the Wakde Task Force from Brigadier General Doe, who leaves for Biak. Elements of the 158th RCT cross the Tor River moving toward Sarmi and encounter heavy fire from Japanese in prepared defensive positions at the Tirfoam River.

Fifth Air Force B-25 Mitchells, A-20 Havocs, P-38 Lightnings, P-47 Thunderbolts, and P-39 Airacobras attack targets from Wewak to Hansa Bay.

Lieutenant General Walter Krueger, commander of Alamo Force, moves his headquarters to Hollandia.

May 25

ALEUTIANS: An Eleventh Air Force B-24 Liberator from Shemya Island flies a reconnaissance and bombing mission in the Kurile Islands.

CBI: A Chinese attack against the Japanese defenses at Myitkyina fails. The Marauders are losing 75 to 100 men a day to disease as the siege of Myitkyina continues.

U.S. infantry replacements arrive in India. They are minimally trained and completely unprepared for jungle warfare, but are sent to Myitkyina three days later. Chinese forces capture Kamaing and defeat Japanese counterattacks.

Tenth Air Force sends 28 P-38 Lightnings to attack targets near Mandalay. Pilots report destroying 10 railroad cars near Shwebo. The Chinese Y Force is near Lungling.

ETO: Eighth Air Force sends 600 B-17s and 428 B-24 Liberators against airfields, gun batteries, and marshaling yards in France and Belgium, escorted by 136 P-38 Lightnings, 181 P-47 Thunderbolts, and 287 P-51 Mustangs. Four bombers are lost and 152 are damaged. Aircrew casualties are one killed, six wounded, and 48 missing. Fighter pilots report 13 confirmed kills in the air and three on the ground as well as two probables. A total of 12 aircraft are lost and 15 are damaged. The 12 pilots are reported missing.

Ninth Air Force sends over 200 B-26 Marauders to attack bridges and airfields in Belgium and France. P-47s conduct dive-bombing attacks on a number of targets.

MEDITERRANEAN: Fifteenth Air Force sends B-17s and B-24 Liberators fly against targets in southern France. The B-17s attack the marshaling yard at Lyon, while B-24s attack marshaling yards at Amberieux, Toulon, and Givors.

ITALY: At Anzio, Cisterna falls to the 7th Infantry Regiment of the 3rd Infantry Division and 1,000 German soldiers are taken prisoner. The 1st Armored Division moves into the Velletri Gap, which leads to Valmontone and Route 6—the main highway to Rome. The 91st Reconnaissance Squadron of the II Corps meets engineers from VI Corps at Borgo Grappo.

Lieutenant General Mark Clark informs the VI Corps commander, Major General Lucian Truscott, of his intent to move the direction of the attack toward Rome. The 3rd Infantry Division and the 1st Special Service Force will hold Route 6.

Twelfth Air Force B-25 Mitchells and B-26 Marauders bomb roads north of the battle area to block German forces. A-20 Havocs, P-47 Thunderbolts, and P-40s attack German defensive positions, convoys, and troop movements.

U.S. destroyer *Kendrick* shells German positions in Ardea, Italy.

CENTRAL PACIFIC: Seventh Air Force B-25 Mitchells from Engebi Island bomb Ponape Island.

U.S. submarine *Flying Fish* attacks a Japanese convoy and sinks a guardboat and a cargo ship north of Palau.

BOUGAINVILLE: Thirteenth Air Force sends 15 B-25 Mitchells, with 32 P-39 Airacobras and P-40s, in support of 25 navy SBD Dauntless dive-bombers to attack logistics sites at Porton. P-40s attack Monoitu mission and P-39 Airacobras attack the Cape Lalahan radar station.

NEW BRITAIN: Thirteenth Air Force B-24 Liberators bomb Rabaul, Lakunai, and Rapopo and B-25 Mitchells bomb logistics depots near Talili Bay.

NEW GUINEA: A battalion of the 158th Infantry continues the attack against Japanese defenses, but is stopped before Lone Tree Hill. The hill is actually a number of hills covered by heavy jungle and has been converted into a formidable strongpoint.

The 162nd and 186th Infantry Regiments of the 41st Infantry Division depart Humboldt Bay for Biak Island. Major General Horace H. Fuller commands the division. Task Force 77 under Rear Admiral William M. Fechteler supports the attack with two heavy cruisers, three light cruisers, and 21 destroyers.

Fifth Air Force B-24 Liberators attack targets near Wakde. B-25s, and B-24s along with P-38 Lightnings, P-40s, P-47 Thunderbolts, and A-20 Havocs attack targets near Wewak.

May 26

CBI: Operational control of the 27th Troop Carrier Squadron is transferred from Tenth Air Force to Fourteenth Air Force to fly aerial resupply missions to the Chinese Y Force.

The Japanese begin another offensive in central China, advancing toward Tungling Lake with 70,000 troops.

ETO: Ninth Air Force sends over 400 B-26 Marauders and A-20 Havocs to attack airfields and bridges in France while over 100 P-47 Thunderbolts and P-51 Mustangs also attack other airfields. P-47s and P-38 Lightnings conduct dive-bombing attacks on various targets.

MEDITERRANEAN: Fifteenth Air Force sends nearly 700 bombers against targets in southern France and Yugoslavia. B-17s and B-24 Liberators bomb marshaling yards in France while other B-24s attack assembly areas at Bihać, Yugoslavia.

ITALY: At Anzio, General Clark shifts the attack from the east to the Albano Road. The 1st Armored Division supports the attack from the right while the 3rd Infantry Division continues its advance toward Velletri. The 34th and 45th Infantry Divisions are to drive toward Lanuvio and Campoleone respectively. Clark is unwilling to continue the attack toward Valmontone, although it will gain the most promising result and has the potential to cut off German forces. In that case, the British Eighth Army would have the main route to Rome and the glory of capturing the city. Clark, unwilling to give General Montgomery that opportunity, drives the bulk of his forces westward to the shorter and more direct route to Rome. This leaves the Germans an opening for a general retreat.

Twelfth Air Force B-26 Marauders and B-25 Mitchells attack railroad targets and bomb roads. A-20 Havocs, P-47 Thunderbolts, and P-40s attack convoys on the Rome-Bracciano road as the Germans attempt to reinforce defenses south of Rome.

First Lieutenant Beryl R. Newman leads a platoon of inexperienced infantrymen in the 133rd Infantry Regiment, 34th Infantry Division. Approaching German defenses near Cisterna, he and several scouts are fired upon by two German machine guns on a hill about 100 yards away. Ignoring the fire, First Lieutenant Newman remains standing to locate the enemy. He then gives orders for one squad to maneuver to flank the enemy position while another squad joins him. All the time Newman is returning fire on the German positions. As the maneuvering squad is stopped by enemy fire, First Lieutenant Newman attacks alone, firing his weapon as he advances, and captures the two positions. As he encounters other German soldiers, he kills them and then clears a nearby house and captures 11 heavily armed Germans inside. His leadership, determination, and extraordinary acts of courage in the face of the enemy will win him the Medal of Honor.

CENTRAL PACIFIC: Forty-five Seventh Air Force B-25 Mitchells from Makin Island attack Jaluit Atoll. B-25s from Engebi Island search for a downed B-25 crew around Ponape Island. The bombers locate the crew and a navy destroyer will later rescue them.

Destroyers bombard Japanese shore batteries and installations on Mille Atoll.

Destroyer escort USS *England* sinks Japanese submarine *RO-108* northeast of Manus.

U.S. submarine *Permit* torpedoes and damages Japanese submarine *I-44* near Truk.

U.S. submarine *Tambor* torpedoes and sinks a Japanese stores ship west of the Marianas.

NEW BRITAIN: Thirteenth Air Force P-39 Airacobras and P-40s attack targets around Rabaul. B-25 Mitchells attack logistics depots at Talili Bay.

NEW GUINEA: Naval gunfire and air strikes on Lone Tree Hill fail to cause any damage to the enemy; follow-on infantry attack falters in the deep undergrowth.

Fifth Air Force B-24 Liberators bomb Biak Island; B-25 Mitchells bomb Lone Tree Hill. B-25s, A-20 Havocs, P-38 Lightnings, P-40s, and P-47 Thunderbolts attack targets from Wewak to Hansa Bay.

The P-47s of the 340th Fighter Squadron, 348th Fighter Group, redeploy from Saidor to Wakde Island.

U.S. submarine *Cabrilla* torpedoes and sinks a Japanese transport off Celebes Island.

May 27

CBI: Fourteenth Air Force P-40s, using rockets, attack targets at Nanchang and Puchi.

ETO: Eighth Air Force sends 653 B-17s and 473 B-24 Liberators against airfields, marshaling yards, and gun positions in France and Germany, escorted by 170 P-38 Lightnings, 238 P-47 Thunderbolts, and 302 P-51 Mustangs. A total of 24 bombers are lost and 207 are damaged. Aircrew casualties are seven killed, 12 wounded, and 234 missing. Fighter pilots report 39 confirmed kills in the air, one probable, and nine confirmed kills on the ground. Seven fighters are lost and 10 are damaged. The seven pilots are reported missing.

During the night, three B-17s drop leaflets over towns and cities in Belgium and France.

Ninth Air Force sends nearly 600 B-26 Marauders against railroad bridges and marshaling yards in France.

MEDITERRANEAN: Fifteenth Air Force sends nearly 700 B-17s and B-24 Liberators against marshaling yards in southern France, escorted by P-38 Lightnings and P-51 Mustangs.

ITALY: The 6th Armored Infantry of the 1st Armored Division stops a German counterattack near Artena. The 15th Infantry of the 3rd Infantry Division later captures Artena. Elements of the 36th Infantry Division locate a gap in the German lines atop Monte Artemisio, which marks an undefended gap between two German corps. The three regiments of the division occupy the hill and bring up artillery to fire on German positions along Route 6. This makes the German defense of Valmontone no longer possible. The 34th and 45th Infantry Divisions make slow progress toward Lanuvio and Campoleone.

Twelfth Air Force B-26 Marauders and B-25 Mitchells attack lines of communication. A-20 Havocs, P-47 Thunderbolts, and P-40s attack a number of targets throughout the battle area, including bridges, rail lines, enemy defensive positions, and roads.

CENTRAL PACIFIC: Seventh Air Force sends 24 B-24 Liberators from Kwajalein and 52 B-25 Mitchells from Engebi Island to attack Ponape Island.

NEW BRITAIN: Thirteenth Air Force P-39 Airacobras, P-38 Lightnings, and P-40s along with navy and marine aircraft hit targets at Rabaul.

NEW GUINEA: At Sarmi, the 158th RCT attack on Lone Tree Hill makes little progress. The Americans are fighting well trained and disciplined Japanese troops who are experts at camouflage. The American attack collapses into a series of uncoordinated assaults. Two battalions of the 163rd Infantry depart for Biak, leaving one battalion at Toem.

At Aitape, a 5,000-foot runway to accommodate bombers is completed near the abandoned Tadji airfield.

Naval Task Force 77 (Rear Admiral William M. Fechteler) commands the landing on Biak (Operation Horlicks). Heavy and light cruisers and destroyers of TG 77.2 (Rear Admiral Victor A. C. Crutchley, RN) and TG 77.3 (Rear Admiral Russell S. Berkey) provide gunfire support. At Biak, a bombing run by 54 Fifth Air Force B-24 Liberators precedes the landing of the 186th and 162nd Infantry Regiments on the beachhead near Bosnek. On the first day, 12 tanks, 500 trucks, and 2,400 tons of supplies are landed. Japanese bombers attack the beachhead and all are shot down before causing any damage. The Americans meet no resistance as they expand the beachhead.

Fifth Air Force sends B-24s and B-25 Mitchells to attack targets on Biak after the initial bombardment. B-25s, A-20 Havocs, P-38 Lightnings, and P-40s bomb targets near Wewak.

May 28

CBI: The 236th Engineer Combat Battalion arrives at Myitkyina. The collection of American troops who arrive as replacements is integrated into the engineer-Marauder unit and eventually become known as New Galahad.

ATLANTIC: German submarine *U-549* torpedoes and sinks escort carrier USS *Block Island* and damages a destroyer escort northwest of Canary Islands. Two destroyer escorts sink *U-549*.

ETO: Eighth Air Force sends 865 B-17s and 417 B-24 Liberators against oil production facilities in Germany, escorted by 182 P-38 Lightnings, 208 P-47 Thunderbolts, and 307 P-51 Mustangs. Aircrews report 37 confirmed kills and 29 probables. A total of 33 bombers are lost and 211 damaged. Aircrew casualties are seven killed, 19 wounded, and 272 missing. Fighter pilots report 27 confirmed kills and one probable. Nine fighters are lost and 14 are damaged. Nine pilots are reported missing. Ninth Air Force supports the bombing mission with 527 fighters. Pilots report 33 confirmed kills in the air and five on the ground. Five U.S. fighters are lost.

During the night five B-17s drop leaflets over Belgium and Norway. A total of 22 B-24s fly in support of Carpetbagger operations. One bomber is lost.

Ninth Air Force sends over 600 B-26 Marauders and A-20 Havocs to attack marshaling yards, railway bridges, and V-weapon sites in France and Belgium. Eight aircraft are lost. P-47s conduct dive-bombing attacks on targets close by.

Mediterranean: Fifteenth Air Force B-24 Liberators bomb a marshaling yard and port facilities in Italy and troop assembly areas at Niksic in Yugoslavia.

U.S. motor torpedo boats sink a German corvette in the Ligurian Sea.

Italy: 1st Armored Division moves to support 45th Infantry Division. The 36th Infantry Division takes 1st Armored Division's place in the line to the right of the 34th Infantry Division. The 34th reaches Lanuvio. II Corps gives operational control of the 88th Infantry Division to IV Corps. General Truscott learns of the gap in the German lines at Monte Artemisio.

Twelfth Air Force B-26 Marauders and B-25 Mitchells attack lines of communication. A-20 Havocs, P-47 Thunderbolts, and P-40s attack a number of targets throughout the battle area, including bridges, rail lines, enemy defensive positions, and roads.

Central Pacific: Seventh Air Force sends 29 B-25 Mitchells staging from Eniwetok to bomb Jaluit Atoll. The bombers continue on and land at Makin Island. B-25s from Engebi Island bomb Mille Atoll in the Marshalls. B-24 Liberators from Eniwetok bomb Saipan and Guam Islands in the Marianas. The B-24s that hit Guam continue to Momote airfield at Los Negros Island to rearm. The B-24s targeting Saipan return to Eniwetok.

U.S. submarine *Silversides* torpedoes and sinks two Japanese transports north of Saipan and escapes counterattacks by aircraft and escorts.

New Britain: Thirteenth Air Force B-24 Liberators, B-25 Mitchells, and P-38 Lightnings attack the Lakunai airfield. P-39 Airacobras and P-40s support navy SBD Dauntless dive-bombers attacking Tobera airfield.

New Ireland: Destroyers from Destroyer Squadron 41 bombard Japanese installations on northern coast of New Ireland.

New Guinea: At Sarmi, a third attack on Lone Tree Hill fails to make any progress. The 158th RCT withdraws to the Tirfoam River.

At Biak, the 162nd Infantry Regiment advances toward three airfields, which are the objectives of the operation. These airfields are critical to both the Americans and the Japanese. Japanese control of the Biak airfields is essential to any type of air attack on Nimitz's fleet to the north and to providing air cover for the Japanese fleet. For the Americans, Biak's airfields are essential for further operations in western New Guinea and the Philippines. From Biak, MacArthur's air force can provide cover for Nimitz's upcoming operations in the Palau Islands. The Japanese have put 10,700 troops on Biak, and unlike other garrisons, they intend to reinforce the island.

The leading battalion of the 162nd is hit by a Japanese counterattack using tanks and infantry. Forced to retreat, Major General Fuller requests from Lieutenant General Krueger the 163rd Infantry to reinforce the division.

Fifth Air Force B-24 Liberators and B-25 Mitchells bomb Japanese defenses and gun positions on Biak Island and other targets on Noemfoor Island. B-25s, A-20 Havocs, and P-38 Lightnings attack targets near Wewak. A-20 Havocs conduct tree-top-level airstrikes on Japanese positions on Lone Tree Hill.

Thirteenth Air Task Force B-24s bomb the airfield on Woleai Atoll.

U.S. submarine *Rasher* attacks a Japanese convoy in the eastern Celebes Sea, damaging a gunboat off Halmahera.

Fire from a shore battery on Biak Island damages destroyer *Stockton*.

May 29

ALEUTIANS: Eleventh Air Force B-25 Mitchells bomb Shimushu and attack vessels off the island. Other B-25s escorted by four P-38 Lightnings sink a patrol boat in the Kurile Islands.

CBI: The 209th Engineers and the Marauders attack in an attempt to break the Japanese lines. Although they take their initial objectives, they are forced back after heavy Japanese counterattacks.

Tenth Air Force B-25 Mitchells and P-40s attack Japanese defensive positions at Bhamo and Mohnyin.

ETO: Eighth Air Force sends 50 B-17s and 443 B-24 Liberators, escorted by 184 P-38 Lightnings, 187 P-47 Thunderbolts, and 302 P-51 Mustangs, to attack aircraft and oil production facilities in Germany and Poland. Aircrews report 62 confirmed kills and 37 probables. A total of 34 bombers are lost and 330 are damaged. Aircrew casualties are two killed, 18 wounded, and 318 missing. Fighter pilots report 39 confirmed kills in the air, one probable, and 16 confirmed kills on the ground. Ten aircraft are lost and nine are damaged. Eight pilots are reported missing.

Ninth Air Force supports the mission with 592 fighters. The pilots report one confirmed kills and two U.S. aircraft lost. Ninth Air Force sends over 400 B-26 Marauders and A-20 Havocs to bomb airfields, marshaling yards, railroad bridges, coastal batteries, and V-weapon sites in France and Belgium. P-47 Thunderbolts bomb targets nearby.

MEDITERRANEAN: Fifteenth Air Force sends 829 B-17s and B-24 Liberators against aircraft production facilities in Austria and assembly areas in Yugoslavia. Over 530 B-24 Liberators attack aircraft production facilities near Vienna, Austria. More than 150 German fighters attack the formations and eight bombers are lost. Fighter pilots escorting this mission report 18 confirmed kills in the air and 12 on the ground. For all the targets, a total of 23 bombers are lost and fighter pilots report over 60 confirmed kills.

ITALY: At Anzio, the 45th Infantry Division, with 1st Armored Division in support, reaches Campoleone. The Americans make a two-mile penetration of German lines; strongpoints are bypassed by tanks and are reduced by infantry. The 168th Infantry Regiment of the 34th Infantry Division captures Lanuvio but fails to hold the high ground against German counterattacks. The 36th Infantry Division reaches Velletri, taking the place of the 1st Armored Division.

Twelfth Air Force B-25 Mitchells and B-26 Marauders bomb railroad bridges and transportation targets. A-20 Havocs attack assembly areas and logistics depots. A-20 Havocs, P-47 Thunderbolts, and P-40s attack enemy defensive positions and roads.

Captain William W. Galt, 168th Infantry Regiment, 34th Infantry Division, is a battalion operations officer who volunteers to lead an attack on German positions at Villa Crocetta. He commandeers the only operational tank destroyer and takes the lead, followed by a company of infantry. Captain Galt stands on the turret of the tank destroyer, designating targets with the vehicle's .30-caliber machine gun and tossing hand grenades into the German trenches. As the trench line is cleared, Captain Galt is killed when an anti-tank round hits the American tank destroyer. For his supreme act of courage and leadership, Captain Galt will receive the Medal of Honor.

PACIFIC: Admiral Nimitz's staff issues an order to prepare for an attack on the Palau Islands scheduled for September 8. Major General Geiger, commander of the III Amphibious Corps, is designated as commander of the ground forces, with four divisions divided into two corps. The 1st Marine Division and the army's 81st Infantry Division will make up III Amphibious Corps and will capture the islands of Peleliu and Angaur. XXIV Corps, made up of the 7th and 77th Infantry Divisions, will attack Babelthuap. The 27th Infantry Division in New Caledonia will be the reserve.

SOUTH PACIFIC: Major General James T. Moore (USMC) is appointed Commander, Air Solomons (COMAIRSOLS).

BOUGAINVILLE: Thirteenth Air Force sends 24 P-39 Airacobras and 16 P-40s to attack Japanese positions near Tinputs Harbor and Arigua Plantation.

NEW BRITAIN: Thirteenth Air Force B-25 Mitchells, P-38 Lightnings, P-39 Airacobras, and U.S. Navy aircraft attack antiaircraft positions and logistics sites in the Rabaul area.

NEW GUINEA: At Biak, the 163rd Infantry fights off three Japanese counterattacks at Mokmer village, one of which is led by tanks. The 162nd Infantry is forced to retreat to the beachhead.

B-24 Liberators bomb Japanese positions on Biak. A-20 Havocs, B-25 Mitchells, and P-47 Thunderbolts attack targets in the Wewak area. B-25s and P-40s attack Japanese positions near Sarmi. B-24s of the Thirteenth Air Task Force bomb Woleai Atoll and nearby islands in the Carolines.

May 30

ALEUTIANS: Eleventh Air Force B-25 Mitchells sink a Japanese guardboat northeast of Paramushiro, Kuriles, and damage a guardboat east of the Kuriles.

CBI: General Joseph Stilwell replaces Colonel John E. McCammon with General Haydon L. Boatner to take command of the Myitkyina Task Force.

Tenth Air Force B-25 Mitchells and P-40s attack railroad targets around Mogaung, Myitkyina, Hopin, and Loilaw.

In China, Fourteenth Air Force B-25 Mitchells and P-40s attack strongpoints, supply, and defensive positions at Loyang. Japanese aircraft bomb Hengyang and Liangshan airfields, causing extensive damage to the fuel storage areas and destroying four aircraft on the ground.

ETO: Eighth Air Force sends 518 B-17s and 460 B-24 Liberators, escorted by 186 P-38 Lightnings, 184 P-47 Thunderbolts, and 302 P-51 Mustangs, to attack aircraft production facilities in Germany, marshaling yards in France and Belgium, and V-weapon sites in France. Aircrews report eight confirmed kills and five probables. A total of 12 bombers are lost and 131 damaged. Aircrew losses are five killed, 12 wounded, and 114 missing. Fighter pilots report 50 confirmed kills in the air, three probables, and seven confirmed kills on the ground. Nine aircraft are lost and nine are damaged. Nine pilots are reported missing. Ninth Air Force supports the mission with 637 fighter aircraft. The pilots report eight confirmed kills in the air and three U.S. aircraft lost.

In another mission Eighth Air Force sends 100 P-47s to attack four railroad bridges in France. One Thunderbolt is lost.

Ninth Air Force sends over 300 B-26 Marauders against airfields and highway bridges while about 400 P-47s conduct dive-bombing attacks on targets in France.
MEDITERRANEAN: Fifteenth Air Force sends almost 500 B-17s and B-24 Liberators to bomb marshaling yard in Yugoslavia and aircraft production facilities in Austria. The bombers are escorted by P-38 Lightnings and P-51 Mustangs.
ITALY: The 3rd Infantry Division and the 1st Special Service Force link up with units from II Corps advancing from the west and come under the Corps' operational control for the attack into Valmontone. The 1st Armored Division and the 45th Infantry Division are unable to move beyond Campoleone on the Albano Road. Combat Command A is reinforced with a battalion from the 135th Infantry Regiment of the 34th Infantry Division. Combat Command B is reinforced with an armored infantry battalion of the 6th Armored Infantry Regiment. The tanks and infantry advance about a mile and are halted by enemy fire. The 1st Armored Division loses 23 tanks and the Americans suffer 200 casualties in the failed attack. The rest of the 34th Infantry Division again attacks Lanuvio and again is driven off by heavy fire. The 142nd and 143rd Infantry Regiments of the 36th Infantry Division climb Colli Laziali and are in position to overlook the entire rear of the enemy. The 141st Infantry Regiment of the 36th Infantry Division moves to outflank the German defenses at Velletri. The 85th Infantry Division reaches the Anzio beachhead.

Twelfth Air Force B-26 Marauders and B-25 Mitchells attack bridges and viaducts. A-20 Havocs attack assembly areas and logistics depots. P-47 Thunderbolts and P-40s attack enemy defensive positions and roads.
SOUTHWEST PACIFIC AREA: U.S. submarine *Guitarro* torpedoes and sinks a Japanese cargo ship southeast of Formosa.
PACIFIC: U.S. submarine *Pompon* torpedoes and sinks a Japanese passenger-cargo ship off Kyushu, Japan.
CENTRAL PACIFIC: Seventh Air Force B-24 Liberators from Kwajalein Atoll bomb Truk and Wake Island. B-25 Mitchells from Engebi Island bomb Ponape Island.
BOUGAINVILLE: Thirteenth Air Force P-39 Airacobras and P-40s bomb bridges, roads, the airfield at Buka Island, a barge anchorage, and logistics sites.
NEW BRITAIN: Thirteenth Air Force B-25 Mitchells bomb Tobera and P-38 Lightnings, P-40s, and P-39 Airacobras attack logistics sites.
NEW GUINEA: Fifth Air Force B-25 Mitchells bomb Japanese positions on Biak Island. B-25s bomb and strafe the coastline near Sarmi Point. B-24s, B-25s, and A-20 Havocs bomb Wewak.

U.S. submarine *Rasher* attacks the convoy it had attacked previously, sinking a gunboat in the eastern Celebes Sea.

Fifth Air Force B-25 Mitchells damage a Japanese cargo vessel west of Manokwari.

May 31

CBI: By the end of May at least 5,000 Japanese troops are in defensive positions around the town of Myitkyina as the monsoon rains begin. Even though Allied strength reaches 12,000, the Japanese continue to defend tenaciously. The siege of Myitkyina begins and will last until August.

Tenth Air Force B-25 Mitchells and P-40s attack Japanese positions, rail lines, and logistics sites near Myitkyina, Kamaing, and the Mogaung area. The airfield and town of Bhamo are also attacked.

In China, Fourteenth Air Force P-51 Mustangs and P-40s attack shipping on the Yangtze River. Pilots report five small ships are hit. B-25 Mitchells damage a bridge at Kengluang and B-24 Liberators bomb Lungling.

ETO: Twenty Allied combat divisions are in Britain to support Overlord. The total number of U.S. troops in Britain is 1.5 million, completing the target numbers established for the Bolero plan in early 1942.

Eighth Air Force sends 533 B-17s and 496 B-24 Liberators, escorted by 193 P-38 Lightnings, 180 P-47 Thunderbolts, and 309 P-51 Mustangs against marshaling yards, rail lines, and aircraft production facilities in France, Belgium, the Netherlands, and Germany. One bomber is lost and 111 are damaged. Aircrew casualties are two killed, four wounded, and 10 missing. Fighter pilots report four confirmed kills on the ground. Three fighters are lost and four are damaged. Three pilots are reported missing.

P-47s attack Gutersloh airfield and report five confirmed kills and one probable. One U.S. fighter is damaged. P-38 Lightnings with Droopsnoot attack Rehein/Hopsten airfield. Pilots report five confirmed kills on the ground.

A total of 22 B-24s fly in support of Carpetbagger operations.

Ninth Air Force sends nearly 200 B-26 Marauders to bomb canal locks and highway bridges in France.

MEDITERRANEAN: Fifteenth Air Force sends nearly 500 B-17s and B-24 Liberators to bomb oil refineries at Ploeşti, Romania. A total of 15 bombers are lost to antiaircraft fire or German fighters. U.S. fighter pilots report over 40 confirmed kills.

ITALY: At Anzio, II Corps has operational control of the 3rd Infantry Division, the 85th Infantry Division, the 88th Infantry Division, and the 1st Special Service Force. The 85th Infantry Division attacks at Lariano to protect the 36th Infantry Division's flank and prevent a German counterattack from the enemy position on the Alban Hills.

Twelfth Air Force B-26 Marauders and B-25 Mitchells attack assembly areas and roads. A-20 Havocs, P-47 Thunderbolts, and P-40s attack enemy defensive positions, bridges, roads, and logistics sites.

Private Furman L. Smith of the 135th Infantry Regiment, 34th Infantry Division, is among the lead elements advancing to capture a German strongpoint near Lanuvio. About 80 German soldiers mount a counterattack, inflicting many casualties and forcing the company to retreat. Private Smith refuses to leave his wounded comrades behind. Moving them to relative safety in nearby shell craters, Smith then defends the position, firing his rife on the enemy until killed. Private Smith's courage and dedication to duty at the cost of his own life will win him the Medal of Honor.

PACIFIC: U.S. submarines *Barb* and *Herring* rendezvous in the Sea of Okhotsk to coordinate operations against Japanese shipping. *Herring* attacks a convoy, sinking an escort vessel and a cargo ship west of Matsuwa Island. *Barb* sinks a cargo ship and a transport southwest of Paramushiru.

NEW BRITAIN: Thirteenth Air Force B-25 Mitchells, P-38 Lightnings, P-39 Airacobras, and P-40s bomb logistics depots, vehicle concentrations, and wharves around Rabaul.

NEW IRELAND: Destroyer escort USS *England*, assisted by destroyers USS *McCord* and *Hazelwood* and destroyer escorts USS *George, Raby,* and *Spangler*, sinks Japanese submarine *RO-105* north of Kavieng.

NEW GUINEA: At Biak, the 163rd Infantry Regiment lands at Bosnek, having been ordered to move from Wakde.

Fifth Air Force B-25 Mitchells and A-20 Havocs fly cover over the beachhead on Biak Island. B-25s and P-47 Thunderbolts attack Japanese positions near Sarmi. B-24 Liberators and P-39 Airacobras attack targets near Wewak.

June 1

ALEUTIANS: Eleventh Air Force sends two B-24 Liberators from Shemya Island in the Aleutians to photograph and bomb installations at Buroton Bay in the Kuriles.

CBI: The Japanese 18th Division is withdrawn from the Burma battlefront.

Tenth Air Force B-25 Mitchells bring ammunition into the Imphal area. P-40s attack Japanese positions near Myitkyina.

In China, Fourteenth Air Force redeploys the P-51 Mustangs of the 76th Fighter Squadron, 23rd Fighter Group, to Lingling from Suichwan. P-47 Thunderbolts of the 91st Fighter Squadron, 81st Fighter Group, move from Karachi, India, to Fungwanshan. The P-38 Lightnings of the 449th Fighter Squadron, 51st Fighter Group, will redeploy from Suichwan to Kweilin.

ETO: General Eisenhower and his staff begin meeting daily to work out last-minute details and receive weather updates. On this day in England sit 10 armored divisions and 48 infantry divisions, a total of 1.5 million men and 16 million tons of supplies. There are 4,200 tanks, 13,700 vehicles, and 3,500 artillery pieces assembled and waiting for the order that will send them off to participate in one of the greatest events in history.

Ninth Air Force sends nearly 100 B-26 Marauders to attack airfields and coastal defense batteries from the Belgian border to the Cherbourg Peninsula in France.

ITALY: In the II Corps area, the 85th and the 3rd Infantry Divisions attack to capture Route 6, but the attack is slowed by a German counterattack. The 338th Infantry Regiment of the 85th Infantry Division is stopped near Lariano, and the 337th Infantry Regiment advances toward Monte Castellaccio. The 1st Special Service Force reaches Colle Ferro south of Valmontone, capturing 200 prisoners and opening the way for the French Expeditionary Corps to advance on Route 6 from the east.

In the VI Corps area, the 179th and 180th Infantry Regiments of the 45th Infantry Division attack up the Alban Road, but make no progress. The 34th Infantry Division is stalled by German defenses at Lanuvio. The 36th Infantry Division captures Velletri after the Germans withdraw. American artillery units occupy Monte Artemisio and begin to fire directly on German positions.

Twelfth Air Force B-25 Mitchells and B-26 Marauders support the Fifth Army offensive, attacking German defensive positions, vehicles, and lines of communication. P-40s attack German positions along the east coast of Italy. Destroyers USS *Champlin* and *MacKenzie* shell German strongpoints and shore batteries.

SOUTHWEST PACIFIC AREA: U.S. submarine *Narwhal* lands men and supplies on Mindanao.

PACIFIC: U.S. submarine *Herring* continues attacks against Japanese shipping, sinking a transport and a cargo ship while at anchor near Matsuwa Island, Kuriles. Japanese shore batteries score two direct hits on the submarine's conning tower, and the *Herring* is lost with all hands.

U.S. submarine *Pintado* torpedoes and sinks a Japanese transport and damages another northwest of Saipan.

CENTRAL PACIFIC: Seventh Air Force B-25 Mitchells from Eniwetok bomb Ponape Island.

NEW BRITAIN: Thirteenth Air Force B-25 Mitchells bomb Rabaul and logistics depot near Tobera. P-38 Lightnings and P-40s attack barges and buildings.

ADMIRALTIES: The headquarters of Thirteenth Air Force's XIII Bomber Command redeploys from Guadalcanal to Los Negros Island.

NEW GUINEA: At Biak, the 186th Infantry Regiment advances north to cover the flank of the 162nd Infantry as it advances down the coastal road toward the airfields.

Fifth Air Force B-25 Mitchells and A-20 Havocs attack targets on Noemfoor and Biak Islands. B-25s, A-20 Havocs, and P-39 Airacobras attack targets along the coast from Wakde to Hollandia, and bomb Wewak.

B-24 Liberators bomb Amboina on Ambon Island, Kai Island in the Moluccas, and Boeroe Island in the Sunda Islands.

June 2

ALEUTIANS: Eleventh Air Force B-24 Liberators conduct a photoreconnaissance and bombing run on Matsuwa Island in the Kuriles.

CBI: An attack by Chinese and American forces at Myitkyina gains about 100 yards in the face of strong Japanese resistance.

Tenth Air Force B-25 Mitchells fly ammunition into the Imphal, India, area in support of British forces.

In China, Fourteenth Air Force sends over 80 P-40s and P-51 Mustangs to attack Japanese infantry and vehicles at Tungcheng and Chungyang.

ETO: For the next three days, the Eighth Air Force will attack transportation and airfields in France and attack coastal defenses in the Pas-de-Calais area, to provide a diversion that will focus German attention on the expected invasion area, rather than the actual invasion area in Normandy. An attack against V-weapon sites in the Pas-de-Calais area involves 633 B-17s and 293 B-24 Liberators. Another 242 B-17s bomb rail lines around Paris, while 77 B-24s attack the Bretigny airfield. Seven bombers are lost and 140 are damaged. Aircrew casualties are two killed, five wounded, and 69 missing.

During the evening, five B-17s drop leaflets on towns and cities in Belgium and France. A total of 18 B-24 Liberators fly in support of Carpetbagger operations.

Ninth Air Force sends over 300 B-26 Marauders and A-20 Havocs to bomb V-weapon sites and coastal defense batteries along the English Channel. P-38 Lightnings and P-47 Thunderbolts conduct dive-bombing attacks on V-weapon sites, fuel storage areas, railroad bridges, and rail lines.

MEDITERRANEAN: Under command of Lieutenant General Ira C. Eaker, the Fifteenth Air Force initiates the first Frantic shuttle-bombing mission. The intent of Frantic is to support the Soviet armies by flying bombing missions from the Mediterranean and Britain and landing at three bases opened to the western Allies: Poltava, Mirgorod, and Piryatin. A total of 130 B-17s, escorted by 70 P-51 Mustangs, bomb the marshaling yard at Debreczen, Hungary, and land in Soviet Ukraine at Poltava and Mirgorod. The P-51 Mustangs land at Piryatin. One B-17 is lost. A total of seven Frantic missions will be flown. Pathologically suspicious of the Americans, the Soviets demonstrate a reluctance to cooperate and impose strict controls on Allied aircrews, which limits the effectiveness of the mission.

Nearly 400 B-24 Liberators attack marshaling yards at Szeged, Miskolc, and Szolnok, Hungary, and Simeria in Romania. P-51s and P-38 Lightnings provide escort.

ITALY: Outflanked and pressured from two directions, German forces begin a general retreat toward Rome. In II Corps, the 30th Infantry Regiment of the 3rd Infantry Division captures Valmontone. The 8th Infantry Division cuts Route 6 and the 351st Infantry Regiment occupies San Cesareo. In the VI Corps, the 34th Infantry Division captures Villa Crocetta before Lanuvio. The 142nd and 143rd Infantry Regiments of the 36th Infantry Division advance toward the Alban Hills, while the 141st Infantry moves toward Nemi. Once the German command is aware that this is happening, their entire Fourteenth Army is ordered to retreat.

Twelfth Air Force B-26 Marauders and B-25 Mitchells attack assembly areas and roads. A-20 Havocs, P-47 Thunderbolts, and P-40s attack enemy defensive positions, bridges, roads, and logistics sites.

U.S. destroyer *MacKenzie* bombards German guns near Anzio.

Technical Sergeant Yeiki Kobashigawa's platoon runs into heavy fire from German machine gun positions in the vicinity of Lanuvio, Italy. Technical Sergeant Kobashigawa locates one of the positions and crawls forward with one of his men to throw a grenade. Kobashigawa then stands up and assaults the position, firing his Thompson submachine gun while the other soldier provides covering fire. During the fight one German soldier is killed and two surrender. Another German machine gun fires on Kobashigawa and his comrade. The two men again work together to attack the position, with Kobashigawa throwing grenades and providing covering fire as his fellow soldier charges in to capture four Germans. Technical Sergeant Kobashigawa continues to direct the efforts of his men in eliminating two more machine gun positions. For his extraordinary courage and skill in close combat with the enemy, Technical Sergeant Kobashigawa will receive the Medal of Honor.

Private Shinyei Nakamine of the 100th Infantry Battalion is halted by German fire as he participates in an attack on German defenses near La Torreto, Italy. German machine guns firing from a small knoll 200 yards to the front have forced the soldiers to seek cover. Private Nakamine begins crawling uphill toward the German positions. At about 25 yards, he charges forward and eliminates the position, firing his Thompson submachine gun, killing three enemy soldiers, and capturing two others. As his unit resumes its advance, Private Nakamine attacks another machine gun position and destroys it with hand grenades. Another machine gun position fires on him and, as he leads an automatic rifle team toward the enemy, he is killed. For his extraordinary heroism and devotion to duty Private Nakamine will receive the Medal of Honor.

SOUTHWEST PACIFIC AREA: U.S. submarine *Guitarro* torpedoes a Japanese escort vessel near Formosa.

U.S. submarine *Picuda* attacks a Japanese convoy headed to Singapore, sinking an escort vessel east of Formosa.

U.S. submarine *Shark* attacks a Japanese convoy, sinking a transport west of the Marianas.

CENTRAL PACIFIC: Seventh Air Force B-25 Mitchells from Makin Island bomb Nauru Island.

BOUGAINVILLE: Thirteenth Air Force P-39 Airacobras attack the airfield on Buka Island and bomb logistics depots in the Kara-Kahili area.

NEW BRITAIN: Thirteenth Air Force P-38 Lightnings, P-39 Airacobras, and P-40s attack targets near Vunakanau.

NEW GUINEA: At Biak, Japanese aircraft bomb the Bosnek beachhead. The Americans occupy nearby Owi Island and find it unoccupied.

Fifth Air Force B-24 Liberators bomb Japanese defensive positions above Mokmer airfield. B-24s, P-39 Airacobras, and Royal Australian Air Force (RAAF) fighters attack targets around Wewak.

Thirteenth Air Task Force B-24s bomb Truk Atoll.

June 3

CBI: The CCS instructs Admiral Lord Louis Mountbatten, SEAC commander, to concentrate his efforts on opening an overland route to China, employing all the resources he has currently available in theater.

Tenth Air Force B-25 Mitchells bomb Japanese troops near Imphal, India, while other B-25s fly ammunition resupply missions to British forces. P-40s attack the Mogaung area.

ETO: The weather forecast for June 5, the expected date of the invasion of Europe, is poor. Assault shipping begins moving out into the English Channel in anticipation of the execute order.

Eighth Air Force sends 238 B-17s and 124 B-24 Liberators, escorted by 91 P-38 Lightnings and 129 P-47 Thunderbolts, to attack 22 coastal defenses in the

Pas-de-Calais area. A total of 45 bombers are damaged, but aircrews report no casualties. A second strike on 16 of the original targets by 97 B-17s and 98 B-24 Liberators is escorted by 102 P-38 Lightnings, 34 P-47 Thunderbolts, and 83 P-51 Mustangs. Two B-17s are damaged. One P-51 is lost and one P-38 is damaged. One pilot is reported missing.

During the night 23 B-24 Liberators fly in support of Carpetbagger operations.

Ninth Air Force sends over 250 B-26 Marauders and A-20 Havocs against airfields, highway bridges, and coastal defense batteries in northern France. P-38 Lightnings and P-47s conduct dive-bombing attacks on widespread targets.

ITALY: In the VI Corps area, the 168th Infantry Regiment of the 34th Infantry Division captures Lanuvio as the rest of the division moves to block Route 7. The 45th Infantry Division prepares to move to Albano with the 1st Armored Division to follow and reach Route 7 in order to get to Rome as quickly as possible.

In the II Corps area, the 85th Infantry Division crosses the Alban Hills toward Frascato. The 88th Infantry Division advances on Route 6, occupying Colona after fighting small elements of retreating Germans.

Intercepts from Ultra confirm that the Germans will not fight for Rome.

Twelfth Air Force A-20 Havocs, P-47 Thunderbolts, and P-40s support II Corps south of Rome and attack bridges to cut off the German retreat.

Private Elden H. Johnson, 15th Infantry Regiment, 3rd Infantry Division, faces a German night ambush near Valmontone, Italy. As flares light the kill zone, Private Johnson stands up and signals his patrol leader to withdraw the other 12 men of the patrol. Johnson then advances toward the enemy, firing his Browning automatic rifle from the hip. After killing a machine gun crew, he reloads and continues his assault, firing on enemy soldiers nearest him. Critically wounded by a burst of machine gun fire, Private Johnson refuses to stop fighting as he pulls himself up to a kneeling position to fire a final burst. His extraordinary courage and willingness to sacrifice himself for his comrades will win him the Medal of Honor.

CENTRAL PACIFIC: Seventh Air Force B-24 Liberators staging through Eniwetok Atoll bomb Truk. B-25 Mitchells from Engebi Island bomb Nauru Island.

NEW GUINEA: At Biak, the 162nd Infantry fights Japanese defenders at a strongpoint identified as Parai defile, a large outcropping of coral covered with trees and brush.

Fifth Air Force B-24 Liberators, B-25 Mitchells, and A-20 Havocs attack Japanese positions above Mokmer airfield and attack the airfields themselves. P-38 Lightnings and P-47 Thunderbolts clear Japanese fighters over the island.

Thirteenth Air Task Force B-24s bomb Eten and Dublon Islands at Truk Atoll.

A Japanese dive-bomber hits U.S. destroyer *Reid* north of Biak.

A navy PBY Catalina damages a Japanese torpedo boat northwest of Manokwari. Fifth Air Force A-20 Havocs sink a fishing boat in the same area.

June 4
CBI: Tenth Air Force B-25 Mitchells fly ammunition resupply missions to British forces at Imphal, India. In Burma, P-40s attack Japanese positions near Myitkyina and Kamaing.

ATLANTIC: When Naval Task Group 22.3 (commanded by Captain Daniel V. Gallery and composed of escort carrier USS *Guadalcanal* and destroyer escorts USS *Pillsbury, Pope, Flaherty, Chatelain,* and *Jenks*) forces German submarine *U-505* to surface off the coast of French West Africa, Lieutenant (j.g.) Albert L. David of USS *Pillsbury* leads a boarding party onto the stricken submarine, knowing full well that at any moment scuttling charges can detonate and destroy the U-boat. Without hesitation, he climbs down the conning tower hatch and begins directing the efforts of his men to keep the U-boat seaworthy until additional salvage personnel can arrive and prepare it for movement to the United States. This is the U.S. Navy's first successful boarding and capture of an enemy warship on the high seas since 1815. For his exceptional courage and determination, Lieutenant (j.g.) David will receive the Medal of Honor.

ETO: Receiving current weather reports of heavy overcast and choppy seas, General Eisenhower decides to delay the landings by 24 hours as assault ships are recalled to ports.

Eighth Air Force sends 201 B-17s and 56 B-24 Liberators against seven targets in the Pas-de-Calais area, escorted by 130 P-47 Thunderbolts and 42 P-51 Mustangs. Ten B-17s are damaged and aircrews report no casualties. Fighter pilots report two P-51s lost but no casualties. A second strike sends 222 B-17s and 68 B-24s against eight coastal defense positions also in the Pas-de-Calais area. The bombers use radar Pathfinders to hit their targets. Only 19 bombers are damaged. Aircrews report one killed. A third strike with 263 B-17s and 185 B-24s attacking railroad bridges, airfields, and rail lines is escorted by 135 P-47 Thunderbolts and 277 P-51 Mustangs. A total of 65 bombers are damaged. Aircrews report 10 killed and four wounded. Fighter pilots report one confirmed kill. One P-51 is lost and two are damaged. No casualties are reported. Ninth Air Force sends over 300 B-26 Marauders and A-20 Havocs to attack roads, bridges, and coastal defense batteries. Nearly 200 P-47s and P-51s conduct dive-bomber attacks on rail lines, rail cars, and bridges.

ITALY: Rome Falls. The 3rd Infantry Division arrives at the Aniene River east of Rome and the 30th Infantry Regiment captures the bridges over the river. The first troops to arrive in the city are from the 88th Infantry Division's cavalry reconnaissance troop. Brigadier General Robert T. Frederick enters Rome with the 1st Regiment of the 1st Special Service Force linked up with 3rd Battalion, 13th Armored Regiment, and artillery. Elements of the 338th Infantry Regiment of the 85th Infantry Division enter Rome as the first unit of VI Corps. Elements of the 1st Armored Division and the 36th Infantry Division move in to occupy the city. Ecstatic Italians crowd around the tired troops. Since May 11, the Fifth Army has suffered 17, 931 casualties to reach the city.

Fifteenth Air Force sends more than 500 B-17s and B-24 Liberators against marshaling yards and railroad bridges.

Twelfth Air Force A-20 Havocs, P-47 Thunderbolts, and P-40s attack bridges and convoys.

PACIFIC: U.S. submarine *Flier* torpedoes and sinks a Japanese troopship off the Bonin Islands.

U.S. submarine *Golet* torpedoes and sinks a Japanese guardboat east of Japan.

CENTRAL PACIFIC: Seventh Air Force B-24 Liberators staging through Eniwetok Atoll, bomb Truk during the night. B-25 Mitchells from Engebi Island attack Ponape Island.

USS *Shark*, *Pilotfish*, and *Pintado* form a coordinated submarine attack group (TG 17.12) to seek out Japanese convoys. *Shark* torpedoes and sinks an army transport northwest of Saipan.

BOUGAINVILLE: Thirteenth Air Force P-39 Airacobras attack a vehicle park near Komai. P-38 Lightnings attack logistics sites and one B-25 bombs Kahili.

NEW GUINEA: Japanese bombers attack Rear Admiral Victor A. C. Crutchley's Allied cruiser and destroyer task forces (TF 74 and TF 75) off Biak. U.S. light cruisers *Nashville* and *Phoenix* are damaged.

Fifth Air Force A-20 Havocs bomb the town and harbor at Manokwari and shipping in Geelvink Bay.

Fifth Air Force B-24 Liberators sink a Japanese landing ship northeast of Morotai Island.

A-20 Havocs bomb Manokwari and Japanese shipping in Geelvink Bay. Pilots report four ships sunk.

June 5

CBI: General Stilwell arrives in Chungking from Burma to meet with Generalissimo Chiang Kai-shek and General Chennault on the situation in China. Although he is very doubtful that Chennault can stop the Japanese, Stilwell agrees to divert an additional 1,500 tons of supplies destined for the B-29s at Chengtu to the Fourteenth Air Force. Tenth Air Force B-25 Mitchells bomb Bhamo and other B-25s fly ammunition resupply missions to support British forces at Imphal. P-40s bomb the Myitkyina area and Mogaung.

The headquarters of the 3rd Combat Cargo Group is activated in India, along with the C-47-equipped 9th, 10th, 11th, and 12th Combat Cargo Squadrons. This will allow the 4th Troop Carrier Squadron, 62nd Troop Carrier Group, and the 16th, 17th, 18th, and 35th Troop Carrier Squadrons of the 64th Troop Carrier Group to return to Italy and Sicily. These units have been supporting the CBI theater since April.

ETO: Weather reports indicate poor weather in the English Channel, but the forecast for the next 24 hours shows improvement over the invasion area. High winds and rough seas are expected for the evening of June 6. At 0400, General Eisenhower makes the decision to go, authorizing the order for the invasion of Europe to proceed on June 6.

Eighth Air Force sends 464 B-17s and 206 B-24 Liberators escorted by 127 P-47 Thunderbolts and 245 P-51 Mustangs to attack coastal defenses in the Normandy area. Six bombers are lost and 77 are damaged. Aircrew casualties are one killed, 10 wounded, and 47 missing. Fighter pilots report one P-47 and one P-51 lost. One fighter is damaged. P-51s attack a truck convoy and the airfield near Lille.

A total of 11 B-24 Liberators fly in support of Carpetbagger operations. One bomber is lost over Belgium.

A U.S. minesweeper hits a mine off Normandy, France, and sinks. An LST is damaged when it also hits a mine nearby.

Ninth Air Force sends over 100 B-26 Marauders to attack coastal defense batteries, while over 100 P-47s conduct dive-bombing attacks against targets in the same area.

During the night 1,662 aircraft and 517 gliders of the IX Troop Carrier Command begin their flight to the Cotentin Peninsula to drop paratroopers of the 82nd and 101st Airborne Divisions and thus initiate the Allied invasion of Europe. The paratroopers are to be dropped near Ste-Mère Eglise and Carentan to capture bridges, road junctions, and beach exits that will allow VII Corps to move inland to capture Cherbourg.

Lieutenant Colonel Leon R. Vance, Jr., of the 489th Bomber Group is in a B-24 as part of an attack against German coastal defensive positions near Wimereaux, France. As the bomber approaches the target, antiaircraft fire causes serious damage to the engines and kills the pilot and wounds several crewmen, including Lieutenant Colonel Vance, whose right foot is nearly severed. Vance continues to lead the formation and releases bombs on target. After applying a tourniquet to his leg, Lieutenant Colonel Vance and the copilot attempt to bring the stricken bomber back to England on one engine. Bringing the bomber over land, the crew is able to bail out safely. When he hears that one of the crewmen is unable to bail out of the bomber, and that a 500-pound bomb is lodged in the bomb bay, Vance decides to ditch in the English Channel as the best means to give the crewman a chance for survival. Vance's nearly severed foot has become trapped behind the copilot's seat, forcing him to lie on the floor using only aileron and elevators for control while watching out from the side window of the cockpit as he brings the plane down to the water. On landing, Vance is trapped in the cockpit but is thrown clear by an explosion. Recovering from the blast, he begins a search to locate the remaining crewman until rescued. For his extraordinary acts of courage and skill in the face of a life-threatening injury Lieutenant Colonel Vance will receive the Medal of Honor.

ITALY: Lieutenant General Mark Clark and his commanders lead a victory parade through the streets of Rome to the city hall. Brigadier General Edgar E. Hume will become the Allied military governor of Rome.

VI Corps continues to move north to capture Civitavecchia, which has a 100,000-barrel oil terminal that is critical to sustainment of the Fifth Army. Another objective is the major airfields at Viterbo, which will provide a base for close air support missions as well as long-range bombing missions to Germany.

Fifteenth Air Force sends over 400 B-17s and B-24 Liberators escorted by P-38 Lightnings and P-51 Mustangs against railroad bridges and marshaling yards.

Twelfth Air Force B-25 Mitchells and B-26 Marauders attack road bridges north of Rome. A-20 Havocs, P-47 Thunderbolts, and P-40s attack convoys, bridges, rail lines, and roads.

SOUTHWEST PACIFIC AREA: U.S. submarine *Nautilus* lands supplies at Mindanao in the Philippines.

U.S. submarine *Puffer* attacks a Japanese convoy in the Sulu Sea and sinks an underway replenishment vessel and oiler and damages a tanker.

PACIFIC: Twentieth Air Force sends 98 B-29 Superfortresses from India on their first combat mission, the railroad shops at Bangkok. Of the 77 that hit the target, five bombers are lost, all due to events unrelated to combat.

CENTRAL PACIFIC: Seventh Air Force B-25 Mitchells from Makin Island bomb Nauru Island. B-25s from Engebi Island bomb Ponape Island. B-24 Liberators from Eniwetok Atoll attack Guam and proceed to Momote airfield on Los Negros Island.

The USS *Shark, Pilotfish,* and *Pintado* submarine attack group (of TG 17.12) pursue the convoy encountered the previous day west of the Marianas. USS *Shark* torpedoes and sinks two transports.

BOUGAINVILLE: Thirteenth Air Force P-39 Airacobras attack vehicles, logistics sites, and the Buka airfield.

NEW BRITAIN: Thirteenth Air Force sends 23 B-25 Mitchells to attack a vehicle park at Rabaul. P-39 Airacobras and P-38 Lightnings attack targets in the Rabaul area.

NEW GUINEA: Japanese aircraft attack Wakde airfield, damaging nearly 100 U.S. aircraft parked on the field.

MacArthur is troubled by the lack of progress on Biak and tells Lieutenant General Krueger to get the 41st Infantry Division moving. MacArthur asks, "Is the advance being pushed with sufficient determination?" This question will drive Krueger to pressure Major General Fuller to achieve decisive results fast.

The P-38 Lightnings of the 7th Fighter Squadron, 49th Fighter Group, move from Hollandia to Biak Island. P-39 Airacobras of the 110th Tactical Reconnaissance Squadron, 71st Tactical Reconnaissance Group, redeploy to Tadji.

June 6

CBI: Tenth Air Force B-25 Mitchells attack Japanese positions around Imphal, while other B-25s fly resupply missions to British forces. A-36 Intruder (Apache) fighter-bombers, P-51 Mustangs, and P-40s attack the areas near Myitkyina and Mogaung.

In China, Fourteenth Air Force B-25 Mitchells, P-40s, and P-51 Mustangs attack Japanese positions near Tayang Chiang. B-25s bomb Pailochi airfield.

U.S. submarine *Raton* attacks a Japanese convoy and sinks a coast defense vessel off the shores of French Indochina near Saigon. Although damaged by depth charges, *Raton* remains on patrol.

ETO: D-day: The Normandy Invasion. At 0115 hours, the 13,000 paratroopers of the 101st and 82nd Airborne Divisions, in 925 C-47s from IX Troop Carrier Command, begin dropping over the Cotentin Peninsula. The drops are scattered due to German antiaircraft fire and misidentified drop zones. About 1,500 of the 6,000 paratroopers from the 101st Airborne Division land outside of their designated drop zones. The 507th and 508th Parachute Infantry Regiments of the 82nd Airborne are dropped far from their intended drop zones. Many drown in flooded fields; others land directly on German positions. Nevertheless, small bands of paratroopers gather and seek a way to accomplish their assigned missions. The 500 gliders with 4,000 additional reinforcements, anti-tank guns, ammunition, medical supplies, and rations will not arrive for another four hours. At 0300 transports in the English Channel begin loading troops into landing craft.

This famous photo by Robert Capa illustrates the confusion and shock of combat. Here soldiers cluster around German landing obstacles at Normandy, June 6, 1944.

At 0430, the 4th and 24th Cavalry Squadrons capture the islands at St. Marcouf to secure them in preparation for the landings. Elements of the 3rd Battalion, 505th Infantry Regiment, 82nd Airborne Division, capture Ste-Mère Eglise, the first town in France to be liberated by Allied forces. The division is missing 4,000 men and more than half of its equipment is lost.

The invasion fleet of thousands of warships, merchantmen, and landing craft is under the command of Admiral Sir Bertram H. Ramsay (RN). Ramsay's command is divided into two task forces: a Western (American) Task Force and an Eastern (British) Task Force. The Western Task Force, commanded by Rear Admiral Alan G. Kirk, is composed of two assault forces—the O Force, under command of Rear Admiral John L. Hall, and the U Force, under command of Rear Admiral Donald P. Moon. O Force is responsible for the Omaha landing beach and U Force is responsible for Utah beach.

U.S. destroyer *Corry* is sunk by a mine off Utah beach as it attempts to avoid fire from German shore batteries.

At 0550 the naval bombardment begins, intending to destroy beach obstacles and German strongpoints, followed by 276 B-26 Marauders from Ninth Air Force.

At 0600, Eighth Air Force bombers begin dropping 2,746 tons of bombs on suspected German positions.

At 0630 on Utah beach, the 2nd Battalion, 8th Infantry Regiment, 4th Infantry Division, of the VII Corps under Major General J. Lawton Collins is the first ashore. The soldiers find themselves far south of their intended landing site as a result of high seas and strong currents. A group of 28 tanks also lands on the

beach. The assistant division commander of the
4th Infantry Division has landed with the first
wave. Brigadier General Theodore Roosevelt, Jr.,
makes a quick assessment and decides to assault
the beach exit from the division's current position. Moving under enemy fire, he directs troops
off the beach and moves them inland. The 22nd
and 12th Infantry Regiments clear beach exits 1,
3, and 4 and move off the beach, advancing six
miles inland. Casualties have been light: 20 men
killed and 200 wounded. Roosevelt's seasoned,
precise, calm, and unfaltering leadership is critical in making the beach assault a success. For his
courage and inspired leadership under fire, Roosevelt will receive the Medal of Honor. By the end
of the day, 20,000 men and 7,000 vehicles have
landed on Utah.

Soldiers crowded
into a landing craft
approach the beach
at Normandy, June
6, 1944.

At 0630 on Omaha beach, the 16th and 18th Regimental Combat Teams from
the 1st Infantry Division and the 115th and 116th Infantry Regiments of the 29th
Infantry Division land and are immediately brought under heavy fire from 12

On Utah beach, the 8th Infantry Regiment of the 4th Infantry Division begins moving
inland on the causeways to link up with paratroopers of the 101st Airborne Division.

German strongpoints manned by two regiments of combat-experienced soldiers. The initial wave is nearly annihilated as the troops struggle through three bands of untouched beach obstacles. Mines destroy many landing craft on approach, and heavy seas swamp landing craft and tanks attempting to reach the beach. In the first half-hour of the attack, casualties are approaching 30 percent. The rising tide has trapped landing craft on a sandbar, forcing disembarking troops to wade nearly 100 yards directly into German machine-gun fire. Obstacles and mines on the beach prevent any organized landing effort. Brigadier General Norman D. Cota, the assistant division commander of the 29th Infantry Division, walks along the beach pushing his men forward and ignoring the fire of the German machine guns. Slowly the American soldiers gain a bit of cohesion and begin making small advances through small gaps in the defenses.

About 100 men of the 2nd Ranger Battalion scale the cliffs at Pointe du Hoc, three miles west of Omaha, to destroy a coastal battery position but find it abandoned. The Rangers later locate the guns in the rear of the German lines and destroy them. The Rangers then form a defensive perimeter and must fight for their lives against German counterattacks.

First Lieutenant Jimmie W. Monteith, Jr., of the 16th Infantry Regiment, 1st Infantry Division, lands as part of the first assault wave on Omaha beach. Despite the heavy fire that sweeps the beach, First Lieutenant Monteith gathers the survivors and leads them to a place of relative safety near the cliffs. He returns to the beach to lead two tanks through a minefield to positions where they can begin providing supporting fire. He rejoins his men and leads them in an assault to capture a hill from which he can outflank enemy positions. Defending the position against a number of counterattacks, First Lieutenant Monteith risks his life often to reorganize the defense. Although soon surrounded, he continues to encourage his men until killed. In recognition of First Lieutenant Monteith's courage and determination to accomplish his mission in the face of all odds, he will receive the Medal of Honor.

On the assault on Omaha beach, Technician Fifth Grade John R. Pinder, Jr., of the 6th Infantry Regiment, 1st Infantry Division, finds himself 100 yards offshore under concentrated machine-gun and artillery fire. Carrying a radio, he is attempting to wade ashore when he is seriously wounded. Continuing to struggle ashore, Technician Fifth Grade Pinder ignores his wound and refuses medical assistance. Knowing how critical the communications equipment is to the success of the mission, Pinder makes several trips into the open, fire-swept beach to retrieve equipment. Wounded again, he returns to assemble a radio set and establish communications. Shortly thereafter he is killed by enemy fire. Technician Fifth Grade Pinder's dedication to duty and courage will win him the Medal of Honor.

At 0730 the situation on Omaha beach is critical. Only 16 of 48 tanks reach the beach and the engineer demolition teams are almost entirely eliminated. Those still alive are struggling to survive in the midst of heavy mortar and machine-gun fire. Nevertheless, the soldiers collect in small groups, and anonymous pockets of men begin pushing forward to make the critical 200 yards and reach the five exit corridors in the cliffs facing the beach.

Naval gunfire support for the VII Corps at Utah beach is under the command of Rear Admiral Morton L. Deyo. Admiral Carleton F. Bryant commands the bombardment group supporting the V Corps at Omaha. The groups are evenly balanced, although Bryant's group has received one additional battleship and two additional destroyers. At Omaha beach, American destroyers play a critical role in eliminating German defensive positions and allowing the infantrymen to advance inland. The USS *McCook* moves to within 1,300 yards of the beach, firing over 1,000 five-inch rounds into German positions. USS *Carmick* moves to within 900 yards, firing a total of 1,127 rounds. The USS *Frankford* hits targets on the beach located 400 yards away.

At Pointe-du-Hoc, two destroyers (USS *Satterlee* and HMS *Talybont*) come within 1,000 yards of the shore to put devastating fire on German positions and allow the Rangers to climb the cliffs.

At 0900, American troops are moving inland, encountering German forces defending the access to the roads at Vierville-sur-Mer, Colleville-sur-Mer, and St. Laurent. American casualties for the V Corps on Omaha are assessed at 2,400 killed, wounded, and missing. At the end of the day 13 gaps in the German defensive line have been made. The 116th RCT of the 29th Infantry Division has control of Vierville and St. Laurent and is advancing west to find VII Corps. The 16th RCT of the 1st Infantry Division controls Colleville and is establishing defensive positions to protect the southeastern portion of the beachhead.

At 1300, Lieutenant Colonel Robert G. Cole of the 101st Airborne Division meets elements of the 8th Infantry Regiment of the 4th Infantry Division coming off Utah beach. Elements of the 502nd Parachute Infantry Regiment capture Poppeville, securing the last of the four causeway exits off the beach. The 101st suffers 1,200 casualties during the first day of the invasion. The 82nd Airborne secures the western edge of the beachhead, but is unable to hold the key bridges over the Merderet River.

Eighth Air Force supports the invasion with a dawn attack by 882 B-17s and 543 B-24 Liberators on targets along the coast near the invasion beaches. Bad weather causes most of the bombers to miss their targets or not continue the mission. Most of the bombs are dropped up to three miles inland, leaving the main targets untouched. One B-24 is lost and 16 bombers are damaged. Aircrew casualties are 12 killed, two wounded, and 13 missing. A follow-on mission intended to help seal off the invasion area from German reinforcements also runs into bad weather and all but 37 B-24 Liberators of the 380 B-17s and B-24s sent bomb a secondary target at Argentan. Two B-24s are lost and one B-17 is damaged. Aircrews report no casualties. A third attack on the key city of Caen, which is the main route into the flat, open terrain essential for the Allied breakout, is conducted by 58 B-24s through low-hanging clouds. A fourth attack by over 400 B-17s and 300 B-24s hits key defensive areas that must be controlled by the Germans to keep the Allies contained within the beachhead. Of the 325 B-17s and 125 B-24s that hit the primary targets of St-Lô, Coutances, Falaise, Lisieux, Argentan, and Conde-sur-Noireau, one B-24 is lost and 17 bombers are damaged. Aircrew casualties are 10 killed.

P-47 Thunderbolts and P-51 Mustangs escort bombers and attack bridges, rail lines, marshaling yards, rail cars, and roads. Vehicles, communications sites, troops, buildings, artillery, and trains are attacked directly. Fighter pilots report 26 confirmed kills in the air and four on the ground. A total of 25 fighters are lost.

Ninth Air Force sends over 800 A-20 Havocs and B-26 Marauders against coastal defense positions, rail and road junctions, bridges, and marshaling yards. Over 2,000 P-51s and P-47s conduct close air support and dive-bombing missions.

By nightfall 34,000 troops are ashore on Omaha and 23,000 more are moving inland from Utah. Casualties for the American ground forces are 2,500 at Omaha, 197 on Utah, and another 2,500 among the paratroopers.

During the night, 12 B-17s drop leaflets on cities and towns in France and the Netherlands.

MEDITERRANEAN: The 104 B-17s and 42 P-51 Mustangs from Fifteenth Air Force participating in Frantic attack an airfield at Galati, Romania, and return to bases in the Soviet Ukraine. Fighter pilots report eight confirmed kills and two U.S. P-51s are lost. Lieutenant Cullen J. Hoffman is the first fighter pilot to shoot down a German aircraft during a Frantic combat mission when his P-51 happens upon a German dive-bomber over Poland. From Italy, Fifteenth Air Force sends over 500 B-17s and B-24s against a marshaling yard in Yugoslavia and the Ploeşti oil refineries in Romania.

ITALY: Twelfth Air Force B-26 Marauders and B-25 Mitchells attack lines of communication. A-20 Havocs, P-47 Thunderbolts, and P-40s attack roads and rail lines.

SOUTHWEST PACIFIC AREA: U.S. submarine *Harder* attacks a Japanese convoy in the Celebes Sea and sinks a Japanese destroyer off Borneo. Another Japanese destroyer makes an unsuccessful depth-charge attack on the *Harder*.

CENTRAL PACIFIC: Seventh Air Force B-24 Liberators bomb Ponape Island en route to Eniwetok Atoll from Los Negros Island.

USS *Shark, Pilotfish,* and *Pintado* of submarine attack group TG 17.12 continue to pursue the Japanese convoy previously engaged. USS *Pintado* torpedoes and sinks a cargo ship and army transport west of the Marianas.

BOUGAINVILLE: Thirteenth Air Force P-39 Airacobras and U.S. Navy aircraft attack a number of targets, including buildings and a pier near Kahili.

NEW BRITAIN: Thirteenth Air Force P-38 Lightnings bomb a logistics depot near Nordup.

NEW GUINEA: The Reckless operation is completed. The airfields at Hollandia, the target of the operation, are unsuitable for bombers. Nevertheless, Hollandia becomes an important base for future operations. The capture of Hollandia splits the Japanese defenses in half and forces thousands of Japanese into the forbidding interior of New Guinea in an attempt to reach Sarmi; thousands more are isolated from any supply or support. The Japanese losses are over 1,700 killed and 376 captured. American losses are 152 killed and 1,057 wounded.

The 6th Infantry Division begins landing at Toem in support of the 158th RCT facing the enemy at Lone Tree Hill.

Fifth Air Force A-20 Havocs and B-25 Mitchells hit Number airfield and Japanese tanks near Mokmer on Biak Island. P-39 Airacobras, A-20 Havocs, and Royal Australian Air Force (RAAF) aircraft attack targets between Wewak and Hansa Bay.

Thirteenth Air Task Force B-24 Liberators bomb Truk.

A-20 Havocs attack Japanese shipping off Manokwari. Three vessels are reported sunk.

June 7

CBI: In China, Fourteenth Air Force sends 10 B-25 Mitchells to bomb Lashio and attack targets of opportunity along the Salween River battle line.

ATLANTIC: The JCS, following President Roosevelt's guidance, instructs General Eisenhower that no U.S. forces will occupy southern or southeastern Europe or southwest Germany at the end of the war. Roosevelt seeks to avoid any potential postwar entanglements, especially in the volatile Balkan region.

ETO: The V Corps clears the exit roads for Omaha beach and reaches the line of the Bayeaux-Carentan Road.

Eighth Air Force bombs outlying areas to limit German reinforcements from threatening the beachhead. The first attack by 182 B-17s and 291 B-24 Liberators is supported by radar-equipped Pathfinder aircraft. A total of 18 bombers are damaged. Aircrew casualties are eight killed and three wounded. A second attack by 487 B-17s and 88 B-24 Liberators targets airfields and bridges. Heavy cloud cover prevents many from hitting assigned targets. Two bombers are lost and 182 are damaged. Aircrew casualties are 21 killed, 12 wounded, and 12 missing.

Over the beachhead, 526 P-38 Lightnings and 294 P-51 Mustangs provide aircover and escort bombers. Fighter pilots report two confirmed kills. Eight P-51 Mustangs are lost. One pilot is reported killed and the others are missing. A total of 505 P-47 Thunderbolts and 148 P-51s conduct strafing missions over German lines and pilots report 29 confirmed kills and one probable in the air and 25 confirmed kills on the ground. Fourteen fighters are lost and three damaged. One pilot is reported killed and the others are missing.

B-17s drop leaflets over France, the Netherlands, and Belgium. A total of 14 B-24 Liberators fly in support of Carpetbagger operations in France.

Ninth Air Force sends over 600 B-26 Marauders to attack transportation targets and lines of communication in France. More than 1,000 P-51s and P-47s conduct dive-bombing attacks against German positions; they also escort the B-26 Marauders. Fighters also escort the more than 400 C-47s, C-53s, and gliders that resupply the airborne divisions.

Construction of Mulberries, artificial harbors and sheltered anchorages, begins off Normandy. Mines sink a minesweeper, two LCTs, a motor torpedo boat, and a transport. A U.S. freighter in a convoy carrying troops headed toward Omaha beach hits a mine and suffers some damage but is able to unload the troops on the beach.

ITALY: The 168th Infantry Regiment of the 34th Infantry Division clears Civitavecchia. General Sir Harold R. L. G. Alexander, the Allied ground forces commander, instructs the Fifth Army to advance to the area defined by Pisa, Lucca, and Pistoia as quickly as possible, but logistics and the mountainous terrain limit the speed of the advance. The Fifth Army is about to give up VI Corps and the French Expeditionary Corps to Anvil. The 3rd Infantry Division remains to garrison Rome.

Fifteenth Air Force sends 340 B-17s and B-24 Liberators against harbor facilities, shipyards, and a marshaling yard. A-20 Havocs, P-47 Thunderbolts, and P-40s attack roads, bridges, rail lines, and vehicles.

PACIFIC: U.S. submarine *Whale* torpedoes and damages two Japanese transports north of the Bonin Islands.

CENTRAL PACIFIC: Seventh Air Force B-25 Mitchells from Makin Island bomb Ponape Island.

Remnants of the Japanese convoy attacked by USS *Shark, Pilotfish,* and *Pintado* of submarine attack group TG 17.12 reach Saipan, but only half of an infantry regiment's soldiers have survived the trip and most of the unit's equipment has been lost. This will have an important effect on the outcome of any future battle for Saipan.

BOUGAINVILLE: Thirteenth Air Force P-39 Airacobras and P-38 Lightnings attack Japanese positions near Monoitu.

NEW GUINEA: At Biak, the 186th Infantry Regiment of the 41st Infantry Division captures Mokmer airfield, but finds itself trapped by heavy Japanese fire coming from the high ridges overlooking the airfield. One battalion of the 162nd Infantry holds the Japanese at Parai defile, while the rest of the regiment joins the 186th at Mokmer airfield.

Fifth Air Force B-25 Mitchells bomb Japanese positions on Biak Island. A-20 Havocs attack shipping near Manokwari.

Thirteenth Air Task Force B-24 Liberators attack Truk.

Naval advanced base at Hollandia, New Guinea is established.

U.S. submarine *Harder* torpedoes and sinks a Japanese destroyer north of Celebes Island.

June 8

CBI: In Burma, Tenth Air Force B-25 Mitchells attack Japanese positions around Imphal, while others fly ammunition resupply missions. B-24 Liberators mine approaches to Bangkok. A-36 Intruder (Apache) fighter-bombers and P-51 Mustangs attack Japanese positions near Mogaung.

ETO: The 29th Infantry Division relieves the Rangers at Pointe du Hoc and advances to capture Grandcampe. V Corps establishes contact with the British 50th Division advancing from Gold beach. Eighth Air Force sends 640 B-17s and 538 B-24 Liberators escorted by 116 P-51 Mustangs to attack lines of communication and airfields outside of the invasion area. Three bombers are lost and 140 are damaged. Aircrew losses are 28 killed, four wounded, and 30 missing. Fighter pilots report three confirmed kills. Two fighters are lost and one is damaged. One pilot is reported killed and one missing.

Over the beachhead, 381 P-38 Lightnings, 24 P-47 Thunderbolts, and 89 P-51 Mustangs fly sweeps and patrols. Another 333 P-47s and 526 P-51s fly fighter-bomber missions against lines of communication. The fighter pilots report 28 confirmed kills in the air and two probables. Another 21 German aircraft are reported as confirmed kills on the ground. A total of 20 aircraft are lost and three are damaged. Twenty pilots are reported missing.

Ninth Air Force sends almost 400 B-26 Marauders to attack lines of communication, assembly areas, and logistics bases around Calais, France. Over 1,000 fighters escort the bombers.

General Carl Spaatz, commander of the U.S. Strategic Air Forces in Europe (USSTAF), directs that Germany's oil production capability will be the primary target for offensive bombing operations.

A U.S. destroyer escort and LST hit mines off the Normandy beaches and sink. Two destroyers are damaged by mines.

Technical Sergeant Frank D. Peregory of K Company, 3rd Battalion, 116th Infantry Regiment, 29th Infantry Division, encounters a German strongpoint overlooking the town of Grandcampe. When neither tank nor artillery fire is effective against the position, Technical Sergeant Peregory makes the decision to attack the enemy alone. Advancing up the hill in the face of heavy fire, he comes upon a trench that leads to the strongpoint. Entering the trench, he finds himself in the midst of a squad of Germans soldiers. Using hand grenades and his bayonet, he kills eight men and captures three others. Advancing through the trench, he captures 32 more Germans, including the machine gunners holding up his unit's advance. Technical Sergeant Peregory's extraordinary courage and determination will win him the Medal of Honor.

MEDITERRANEAN: Fifteenth Air Force sends 52 B-17s, with P-47 Thunderbolts providing escort, to bomb the navy yard and drydocks at Pola, Yugoslavia.

ITALY: An armored task force from Combat Command A of the 1st Armored Division captures Viterbo.

Twelfth Air Force A-20 Havocs, P-47 Thunderbolts, and P-40s attack convoys, bridges, rail lines, and roads.

SOUTHWEST PACIFIC AREA: U.S. submarine *Hake* torpedoes and sinks a Japanese destroyer at Davao Gulf, Mindanao.

U.S. submarine *Rasher* attacks a Japanese convoy in the Celebes Sea, sinking an underway replenishment vessel south of Davao.

PACIFIC: U.S. submarine *Whale* remains on patrol after being damaged by depth charges north of the Bonins.

CENTRAL PACIFIC: Seventh Air Force B-24 Liberators from Eniwetok Atoll conduct a night raid on Truk and Ponape Island. B-25 Mitchells from Makin Island bomb Nauru Island.

BOUGAINVILLE: Thirteenth Air Force sends 32 P-39 Airacobras and six P-38 Lightnings to attack logistics sites and Japanese positions.

NEW BRITAIN: Thirteenth Air Force sends 24 B-25 Mitchells to bomb logistics sites.

ADMIRALTIES: Thirteenth Air Task Force B-24 Liberators staging from the Admiralties bomb Truk.

NEW GUINEA: At Sarmi, Lieutenant General Walter Krueger orders Brigadier General Edwin D. Patrick to halt his attack on Lone Tree Hill and reform at Toem to be prepared to depart and support the planned attack on Noemfoor Island.

At Biak, the Japanese bring reinforcements by ship. During this operation, Task Force 74, commanded by Australian rear admiral Victor Alexander Charles Crutchley, with one heavy cruiser, three light cruisers, and 10 destroyers, engages five Japanese destroyers.

Fifth Air Force B-25 Mitchells, P-38 Lightnings, B-24 Liberators, and A-20 Havocs encounter Japanese fighters over Manokwari during a bombing run against shipping off the town. P-40s attack logistics sites near Sarmi. A-20 Havocs attack targets near Wewak.

Off Manokwari, Fifth Air Force B-25 Mitchells escorted by P-38 Lightnings attack a Japanese convoy of seven destroyers, each towing a large landing barge bringing reinforcements to Biak. Aircrews report two destroyers damaged and three barges sunk. As the convoy approaches Biak, the Allied combined surface forces, TF 74 and TF 75, attack the destroyers. The Japanese ships retreat.

U.S. submarine *Harder* evacuates coast-watchers from the northeast coast of Borneo.

June 9

CBI: American engineers, now a provisional regiment, are joined with the Marauders to form a brigade. The engineers attack Myitkyina and advance toward the town.

Tenth Air Force B-25 Mitchells attack Japanese positions around Imphal, while others fly ammunition resupply missions. A-36 Intruder (Apache) fighter-bombers, P-51 Mustangs, and P-40s attack Japanese positions near Myitkyina and Mogaung.

In China, Fourteenth Air Force B-25 Mitchells, P-40s, and P-51 Mustangs attack river shipping, Japanese troops, and the airfields at Hankow and Wuchang.

ETO: The VII Corps has reached most of its D-day objectives. The 4th Infantry Division is advancing toward Cherbourg but is halted before Varreville. The 82nd Airborne Division has established a bridgehead over the Merderet River beyond Ste-Mère Eglise and links with groups of paratroopers dropped west of the bridges. An eight-mile gap still exists between VII and V Corps on the beachhead. General Bradley orders VII Corps to capture Carentan and V Corps to capture Isigny in order to close the gap. V Corps attacks with three divisions. The 1st Infantry Division makes contact with British forces along the Bayeux Road; elements of the 29th Infantry Division capture Isigny.

V Corps is reinforced by the 2nd Infantry Division and advances south and west to link up with VII Corps. The 1st Infantry Division moves east to link with the British advancing from Gold beach. The 29th Infantry Division captures Isigny.

A U.S. destroyer damaged by a mine the previous day is sunk by German aircraft off the Normandy beaches. German fast torpedo boats attack a convoy in the English Channel, torpedoing and sinking one LST and damaging another. Fire from a German shore battery hits a U.S. freighter as it disembarks troops on the beach.

Private First Class Charles N. DeGlopper is a paratrooper in C Company, 325th Glider Infantry Regiment, 82nd Airborne Division, advancing to secure a bridgehead across the Merderet River at La Fiere, France. After clearing a few enemy positions, the platoon finds itself cut off and takes cover in a shallow roadside ditch. Private DeGlopper volunteers to hold the enemy off as the platoon attempts a withdrawal through a hedgerow. Picking up his Browning automatic rifle (BAR), DeGlopper emerges from the ditch and stands in the road to fire on German troops. Although immediately wounded, DeGlopper continues to fire. Hit again, he falls to his knees and continues to fire on the enemy until killed. His courageous act of sacrifice saves his fellow paratroopers and will win Private First Class DeGlopper the nation's highest award for valor, the Medal of Honor.

MEDITERRANEAN: Fifteenth Air Force sends nearly 500 B-17s and B-24 Liberators to attack production facilities and depots in Munich, Germany. B-24s also bomb oil storage sites at Porto Marghera in Italy. The bombers are escorted by P-47 Thunderbolts, P-38 Lightnings, and P-51 Mustangs. Fighter pilots report more than 30 confirmed kills.

ITALY: The 1st Armored Division and the 85th and 88th Infantry Divisions capture Viterbo. The IV Corps relieves VI Corps. The IV Corps is commanded by Major General Willis D. Crittenberger; it is made up of the 34th and 36th Infantry Divisions and the 1st Armored Division. Two other divisions, the 88th and 91st Infantry Divisions, will be added later in the campaign. The VI Corps is to prepare for Operation Anvil, the invasion of southern France. The 85th and 88th Infantry Divisions are replaced by the 6th South African Armored Division.

Twelfth Air Force B-25 Mitchells and B-26 Marauders attack road bridges north of Rome. A-20 Havocs, P-47 Thunderbolts, and P-40s attack convoys, bridges, rail lines, and roads.

SOUTHWEST PACIFIC AREA: U.S. submarine *Harder* torpedoes and sinks a Japanese destroyer south of Davao Island.

PACIFIC: U.S. submarine *Swordfish* attacks a Japanese convoy east of the Bonins, sinking a destroyer.

CENTRAL PACIFIC: Seventh Air Force B-24 Liberators conduct a night raid on Truk from Eniwetok Atoll.

Fifth Air Force B-24s bomb the airfield on Peleliu in the Palau Islands.

BOUGAINVILLE: Thirteenth Air Force P-39 Airacobras bomb Buka, logistics sites near the Buka airfield, and attack Japanese positions at Arigua Plantation.

NEW BRITAIN: Thirteenth Air Force sends 32 B-25 Mitchells, 20 P-39 Airacobras, and five P-38 Lightnings to attack logistics bases and gun positions around Talili Bay.

NEW IRELAND: U.S. destroyers bombard Japanese repair facilities on New Ireland.

NEW GUINEA: At Biak, engineers land near the Mokmer airfield to begin reconstruction. Elements of the 162nd and 186th Infantry Regiments assault the ridge overlooking the airfield. This begins a three-day battle in intense tropical heat and on nearly impassible ridges of coral.

Fifth Air Force A-20 Havocs bomb shipping in Manokwari harbor. B-24 Liberators, B-25 Mitchells, A-20 Havocs, and P-39 Airacobras, along with Royal Australian Air Force (RAAF) aircraft, bomb targets in Wewak area. The P-47s of the 39th Fighter Squadron, 35th Fighter Group, redeploy to Nadzab. Fifth Air Force A-20 Havocs attack Japanese shipping off Manokwari, sinking six cargo vessels.

Thirteenth Air Task Force B-24s bomb Alet airfield and other targets on Truk.

June 10

CBI: Tenth Air Force B-24 Liberators fly ammunition resupply missions to British forces at Imphal. A-36 Intruder (Apache) fighter-bombers, P-51 Mustangs, and P-40s attack Japanese positions near Myitkyina and Mogaung.

In China, Fourteenth Air Force redeploys P-51s of the 75th Fighter Squadron, 23rd Fighter Group, from Hengyang to Lingling.

ETO: In England, three members of the JCS, General Marshall, General Arnold, and Admiral King, meet informally with the British Chiefs of Staff to discuss future operations in the Mediterranean and the Pacific.

Four Allied corps are ashore at Normandy. The 4th Infantry Division of VII Corps begins to move north against Montebourg on its way to capture Cherbourg. The 90th Infantry Division passes through the 82nd Airborne Division to enlarge the bridgehead over the Merderet River and advances west to cut the Cotentin Peninsula.

Elements of the 101st Airborne Division make contact with the 29th Infantry Division near Carentan, making the initial link between V and VII Corps on the American portion of the Normandy battlefront and forming a cohesive and continuous front line. German forces retreat to the Elle River as V Corps advances. The 2nd Infantry Division of V Corps clears Trévières and Forêt de Cerisy.

Eighth Air Force sends 507 B-17s and 495 B-24 Liberators, escorted by 364 P-51 Mustangs and 405 P-38 Lightnings flying sweep and escort, to attack lines of communication and airfields outside of the invasion area. Cloud cover prevents many bombers from hitting their primary targets. One bomber is lost and 67 are damaged. Aircrew losses are six killed, four wounded, and 10 missing. Fighter pilots report five confirmed kills in the air and two probables, as well as one probable kill on the ground. Seven fighters are lost. The pilots are reported as missing.

Over the beachhead, 506 P-47 Thunderbolts and 213 P-51s fly fighter-bomber missions. The fighter pilots report eight confirmed kills in the air and one on the ground. A total of 17 aircraft are lost and three are damaged. One pilot is reported killed and the others are missing.

During the night 11 B-17s drop leaflets on Norway and France.

Ninth Air Force sends over 500 B-26 Marauders and A-20 Havocs against German assembly areas, bridges, artillery positions, and marshaling yards.

A German shore battery sinks a U.S. destroyer off Normandy. A freighter unloading on Utah beach is damaged by a bomb.

MEDITERRANEAN: Fifteenth Air Force sends 46 P-38 Lightnings all armed with a 1,000-pound bomb and escorted by 48 P-38s to conduct dive-bombing attacks on the oil refinery at Ploeşti, Romania. A total of 22 P-38s are lost and pilots report 20 German fighters shot down.

ITALY: Fifteenth Air Force sends over 500 B-17s and B-24 Liberators against marshaling yards, oil storage facilities, and an oil refinery.

Twelfth Air Force B-25 Mitchells and B-26 Marauders attack road bridges north of Rome. A-20 Havocs, P-47 Thunderbolts, and P-40s attack convoys, bridges, rail lines, and roads.

German aircraft attack U.S. ships off Anzio. A minesweeper, an LST, an LCI, and a cargo ship are damaged.

CENTRAL PACIFIC: Seventh Air Force B-24 Liberators from Eniwetok Atoll conduct a night raid on Truk and Ponape Island. B-25 Mitchells from Makin Island bomb Nauru Island.

Navy PB4Y Privateers cover the movement of Vice Admiral Marc A. Mitscher's Task Force to the Marianas to provide early warning and to intercept and destroy any Japanese aircraft. Sightings of the PB4Y Privateers are commonplace for the Japanese and will not arouse suspicion of a major American fleet movement, which would be the case if other aircraft were suddenly sighted in the area.

Destroyer escort *Bangust* sinks Japanese submarine *RO-42* northeast of Kwajalein.

BOUGAINVILLE: Thirteenth Air Force P-39 Airacobras and navy aircraft attack logistics sites on Buka Island and trucks near Tsirogei on Bougainville.

NEW BRITAIN: Thirteenth Air Force P-38 Lightnings use skip-bombing to hit supply tunnels at Keravia Bay. B-25 Mitchells attack antiaircraft positions, while P-39 Airacobras support navy SBD Dauntless dive-bombers in attacking other antiaircraft positions.

NEW IRELAND: Destroyer USS *Taylor* sinks Japanese submarine *RO-111* north of New Ireland.

NEW GUINEA: The Japanese assemble a task force consisting of two battleships, three heavy cruisers, two light cruisers, and seven destroyers to escort transports with over 800 soldiers to reinforce Biak. As the 41st Infantry Division continues to make little progress, Lieutenant General Krueger notifies Lieutenant General Robert L. Eichelberger of I Corps to be prepared to take control of the battle.

Fifth Air Force B-25 Mitchells, A-20 Havocs, and Royal Australian Air Force (RAAF) aircraft attack targets at Wewak. Fifth Air Force B-25 Mitchells bomb Japanese shipping off Manokwari, sinking one vessel.

The headquarters of the 312th Bombardment Group (Light) and the 387th Bombardment Squadron (Light) redeploy to Hollandia. The 389th Bombardment Squadron (Light) redeploys to Nadzab. Both squadrons are equipped with A-20 Havocs.

June 11

CBI: In Burma, Tenth Air Force sends 30 B-25 Mitchells to fly ammunition resupply missions to the Imphal area in support of British forces. A-36 Intruder (Apache) fighter-bombers, P-51 Mustangs, and P-40s attack targets at Myitkyina and Mogaung.

In China, Fourteenth Air Force P-40s, P-51 Mustangs, and P-38 Lightnings attack Japanese garrisons and river traffic. Aircrews on three B-25 Mitchells report sinking a cargo ship in the South China Sea.

ATLANTIC: Navy TBM Avengers and FM-2 Wildcat fighters from escort carrier USS *Croatan* and its destroyer escorts sink German submarine *U-490* in the North Atlantic west of the Azores.

ETO: Eighth Air Force sends 471 B-17s and 584 B-24 Liberators to attack airfield targets in France, escorted by 87 P-47 Thunderbolts and 144 P-51 Mustangs. Over 400 bombers abort the mission or fail to bomb due to clouds and limited Pathfinder support. Three bombers are lost and 26 bombers are damaged. Aircrew casualties are one killed, three wounded, and 24 missing. Over the beachhead 143 P-38 Lightnings support ground operations. Fighter pilots report two confirmed kills. Seventy-seven P-38 Lightnings, 195 P-47 Thunderbolts, and 268 P-51 Mustangs

The battleship USS *Nevada,* damaged at Pearl Harbor and refitted, fires her 14-inch and five-inch guns at German positions on the Normandy beachhead, June 6, 1944.

fly fighter-bomber missions against gun emplacements, rail and road traffic, and other communication targets in France. Fighter pilots report three confirmed kills and two probables. Eight aircraft are lost and seven of the eight pilots are reported missing.

During the night five B-17s drop leaflets on France and the Netherlands.

Ninth Air Force sends 129 B-26 Marauders and A-20 Havocs to attack rail and road bridges, rail lines, oil tanks, and artillery.

The battleships *Nevada, Texas,* and *Arkansas* provide naval gunfire support to ground forces 10 miles inland at Carentan.

German fast torpedo boats attack Allied shipping near Normandy, sinking an LST and damaging another. A U.S. destroyer is damaged. German aircraft sink an LCI.

Lieutenant Colonel Robert G. Cole commands the 3rd Battalion, 502nd Parachute Infantry Regiment, 101st Airborne Division. As the paratroopers approach the bridges that lead to Carentan, his unit comes under rifle, machine-gun, mortar, and artillery fire from strongpoints 150 yards to its front. Unable to move forward or backward and suffering casualties, Cole decides to take decisive action. He orders a bayonet charge on the enemy positions. He is the first to stand up and, carrying a pistol, he moves forward heedless of the fire directed at him. He picks up an

M-1 rifle with a bayonet and leads his men forward, capturing the strongpoint and securing the bridgehead across the Douve River. For his extraordinary act of courage and decisive leadership in the face of a determined enemy, Lieutenant Colonel Cole will receive the Medal of Honor.

MEDITERRANEAN: From the Soviet Ukraine 126 B-17s and 60 P-51 Mustangs from Fifteenth Air Force supporting Frantic fly back to Italy. En route, 121 B-17s bomb the Focsani airfield in Romania. One B-l7 is lost.

Fifteenth Air Force sends over 500 B-17s and B-24 Liberators against a marshaling yard in Yugoslavia and oil production and storage facilities in Constanta and Giurpiu in Romania. Fighter pilots and aircrews report over 60 confirmed kills.

ITALY: The Fifth Army occupies a position from Viterbo to Tusconia and north to Tarquinia. The IV Corps occupies a 30-mile front. The IV Corps relieves VI Corps and takes operational control of the 36th Infantry Division. The 36th Infantry Division is reinforced with tanks and the newly arrived 361st RCT of the 91st Infantry Division.

Twelfth Air Force A-20 Havocs, P-47 Thunderbolts, and P-40s attack convoys, bridges, and roads.

SOUTHWEST PACIFIC AREA: U.S. submarine *Redfin* torpedoes and sinks a Japanese tanker west of Davao.

PACIFIC: U.S. submarine *Barb* torpedoes and sinks two Japanese merchant fishing vessels in the Sea of Okhotsk.

CENTRAL PACIFIC: Operation Forager. The air and naval bombardment of Saipan in the Mariana Islands begins. Admiral Raymond A. Spruance is overall commander. Admiral Kelly Turner is the amphibious task force commander. Lieutenant General Holland M. Smith, commanding the V Amphibious Corps of two marine divisions and one army division, is the ground force commander. Major General Thomas E. Watson commands the 2nd Marine Division; Major General Harry Schmidt commands the 4th Marine Division; Major General Ralph C. Smith commands the 27th Infantry Division. The ground forces involved in the invasion of Saipan number over 71,000 men.

Task Force 58 sends F4F Hellcats, accompanied by TBF Avengers and SB2C Helldiver dive-bombers, to conduct attacks on airfields in the Marianas. These attacks are a complete surprise, allowing the Americans to gain air superiority. F4F Hellcats on combat air patrol intercept and shoot down Japanese aircraft venturing near TF-58's carriers.

Seventh Air Force B-24 Liberators from Eniwetok Atoll make a night bombing raid on Truk. B-25 Mitchells from Makin Island bomb Ponape Island.

BOUGAINVILLE: Thirteenth Air Force P-39 Airacobras attack Japanese troop positions and antiaircraft guns.

NEW BRITAIN: Thirteenth Air Force sends B-25 Mitchells, P-38 Lightnings, and P-39 Airacobras to support navy SBD dive-bombers attacking antiaircraft positions near Rapopo.

NEW GUINEA: Fifth Air Force B-25 Mitchells, A-20 Havocs, and P-47 Thunderbolts attack targets along the coast between Wewak and Hansa Bay.

Thirteenth Air Task Force B-24 Liberators bomb Dublon Island at Truk and the airfield on Peleliu Island.

A naval base is established at Biak Island.

June 12

ETO: On this day, the Allied beachhead is secured, approximately 2,500 prisoners have been captured, and 16 additional Allied divisions have landed. This translates into a total of 326,547 men, 54,186 vehicles, and 104,428 tons of supplies.

In the VII Corps area, Carentan is captured by Task Force F, composed of the 501st Parachute Infantry Regiment and the 327th Glider Infantry Regiment.

The V corps attacks with the 1st Infantry Division to capture Caumont. The 29th Infantry Division attacks toward St-Lô, the town that occupies a key road intersection that is the only way out of the *bocage* and marshes that hold the American advance to a costly crawl. The *bocage* is a maze of man-made hedgerows on dirt embankments that are often 12 to 14 feet high. Each one has been made into a fortress by German troops and allows a small number of soldiers to create an extensive and formidable defense-in-depth. The sunken roads and trails into the *bocage* have been turned into death traps. The Americans must fight exhausting battles for each and every field. Casualties in the V Corps infantry divisions are high, a total of 5,846 since D-day (1,225 of those are killed in action). The casualties among American divisions will be so high that an infantry unit's entire strength will be replaced about every 90 days.

Carentan is captured by elements of the 101st Airborne Division. German counterattacks fail to dislodge the Americans. In the VII Corps area, the 82nd Airborne and 9th Infantry Divisions advance toward the town of St-Sauveur-le-Victome to cut the base of the Carentan Peninsula. The 4th and 90th Infantry Divisions move north toward Cherbourg.

In the V Corps area, the 1st Infantry Division attacks toward Caumont in support of the British XXX Corps attack and captures the town.

Eighth Air Force sends 769 B-17s and 673 B-24 Liberators against 16 airfields and six railroad bridges in northwest France, escorted by 234 P-38 Lightnings, 80 P-47 Thunderbolts, and 201 P-51 Mustangs. Aircrews report one confirmed kill and one probable. Eight bombers are lost and 243 are damaged. Casualties reported are seven killed, 14 wounded, and 58 missing. Fighter pilots report 20 confirmed kills in the air and one on the ground. Seven aircraft are lost and one is damaged. Six pilots are reported missing.

A separate attack by 93 P-38 Lightnings and 183 P-47 Thunderbolts is conducted against railroad bridges. Pilots report five confirmed kills in the air and one on the ground. Nine fighters are lost and two are damaged. The nine pilots are reported missing.

During the night seven B-17s drop leaflets on France and Belgium. A total of 16 B-24 Liberators fly in support of Carpetbagger operations.

Ninth Air Force sends 509 B-26 Marauders and A-20 Havocs to attack marshaling yards, road and rail junctions, bridges, artillery positions, and troop assembly areas. The bombers are escorted by 45 P-38 Lightnings and 152 P-51 Mustangs of the Eighth Air Force.

Admiral King, General Marshall, and General Arnold visit the Normandy beachhead.

ITALY: The 141st Infantry Regiment of the 36th Infantry Division receives engineers, artillery, the 91st Reconnaissance Squadron, and a battalion of infantry from the 361st Infantry Regiment of the 91st Infantry Division, forming Task Force Ramey, named after its commander, Brigadier General Rufus S. Ramey. Task Force Ramey is ordered to capture Orbetello.

Twelfth Air Force B-25 Mitchells and B-26 Marauders attack bridges, rail lines, and roads.

CENTRAL PACIFIC: Navy F4F Hellcats, accompanied by TBF Avengers and SB2C Helldiver dive-bombers from the 15 fast carriers and escort carriers of Vice Admiral Marc A. Mitscher TF 58, attack airfields and coast defenses on Saipan, Tinian, Guam, Rota, and Pagan Islands in preparation for the landings on Saipan. Carrier aircraft attack a Japanese convoy northwest of Saipan, sinking seven transports, three cargo ships, and several other vessels. A number of minesweepers and auxiliary submarine chasers are damaged.

Destroyer USS *Melvin* sinks Japanese submarine *RO-36* east of Saipan.

Seventh Air Force B-24 Liberators from Eniwetok Atoll attack Truk during the night and follow up with a daylight bombing raid.

BOUGAINVILLE: Thirteenth Air Force sends 20 B-25 Mitchells to attack Malapau village. P-39 Airacobras attack the airfield on Buka Island and attack targets near Komai.

NEW BRITAIN: Thirteenth Air Force B-24 Liberators bomb the runways at Tobera and Rapopo. P-39 Airacobras and 10 P-38 Lightnings support navy aircraft in attacks on logistics depots.

NEW GUINEA: Major General Franklin C. Siebert, commander of the 6th Infantry Division, takes command at Wakde-Sarmi with orders to seize Lone Tree Hill.

Fifth Air Force P-47 Thunderbolts flying cover over the beachhead at Biak engage Japanese fighters. A-20 Havocs bomb troop concentrations and communications between Wewak and Hansa Bay.

Thirteenth Air Task Force B-24 Liberators bomb Truk Atoll and the airfield on Peleliu Island.

June 13

CBI: The American engineer attack on Myitkyina is stopped by a Japanese counterattack, isolating two companies.

In China, Fourteenth Air Force sends 18 B-25 Mitchells and 56 P-51 Mustangs to attack the marshaling yard at Wuchang. B-25 Mitchells and P-51s attack river shipping, troop assembly areas, and airfields in the Tungting Lake region. Changsha, Hankow, Hanyang, and Wuchang are major communication, transport, and logistics areas for the Japanese forces, connecting road, rail, and river traffic in south-central China.

ETO: A German counterattack to prevent V and VII Corps from linking together fails as Combat Command A of the 2nd Armored Division and elements of the 101st Airborne Division defeat the attack.

Eighth Air Force sends 251 B-17s and 408 B-24 Liberators, escorted by 12 P-38 Lightnings, 47 P-47 Thunderbolts, and 174 P-51 Mustangs, against airfields in France. Two bombers are lost and 32 are damaged. Aircrew losses are one killed and 19 missing.

Fighter pilots report four confirmed kills. One fighter is lost and the pilot is reported as missing. The continuous Allied air attacks have destroyed nearly all of the German fuel and ammunition stocks in the battle area. The German Fifteenth Army is still inactive at Pas-de-Calais, as the high command remains convinced that the Normandy landings are a diversion and the main attack is yet to come.

In separate attacks, 97 P-38 Lightnings and 199 P-47s report two confirmed kills and three U.S. aircraft lost and one damaged. The three pilots are reported missing.

During the night eight B-17s drop leaflets on France. Six B-24 Liberators fly in support of Carpetbagger operations in France.

Ninth Air Force sends 397 B-26 Marauders and A-20 Havocs against transportation targets, marshaling yards, and fuel storage sites. The bombers are escorted by 12 P-38 Lightnings and 35 P-47 Thunderbolts from Eighth Air Force.

The first V-1 rocket is launched from Pas-de-Calais against London, initiating a campaign in which over 2,400 V-1s will be launched against England during this month alone. The V-1 is about 17 feet long and carries a 1,875-pound warhead. It is powered by a pulse jet engine and guided by a gyroscope on automatic pilot; it is called a "buzz bomb" for the rapid, sputtering noise the engine makes. The V-1 is intended to change the course of the war by raining destruction on English cities. Although not especially effective, the cumulative impact on the people of London, the main target of the V-1 attacks, worries British leaders. The launch sites of the V-weapons have been priority targets for the British RAF since August 17, 1943, and for the U.S. Eighth Air Force since August 27.

The Germans will launch about 10,000 of these flying bombs at England between June 1944 and March of 1945. Another 10,000 will be launched at targets within Europe during the same period. Only about 3,500 actually hit England. Nearly 4,000 are intercepted and destroyed before reaching their targets and the others never complete the flight. The bombs that do hit cause a total of nearly 24,000 casualties.

MEDITERRANEAN: Fifteenth Air Force sends over 500 B-17s and B-24 Liberators against the aircraft component plants and marshaling yards near Munich, Germany. Aircrews and fighter pilots report more than 30 enemy aircraft shot down. Ten U.S. aircraft are lost and several others are reported missing.

ITALY: Twelfth Air Force B-25 Mitchells and B-26 Marauders attack rail and road traffic and bridges. A-20 Havocs, P-47 Thunderbolts, and P-40s attack convoys, bridges, and roads.

SOUTHWEST PACIFIC AREA: U.S. submarine *Flier* torpedoes and damages a Japanese merchant tanker west of Luzon.

PACIFIC: Cruisers and destroyers of Naval Task Force 94 (Rear Admiral Ernest G. Small) bombard Japanese position on Matsuwa Island in the Kuriles.

U.S. submarine *Barb* torpedoes and sinks a Japanese transport in the Sea of Okhotsk, and escapes a counterattack from a destroyer.

CENTRAL PACIFIC, SAIPAN: Vice Admiral Raymond A. Spruance commands the Fifth Fleet. Vice Admiral Richmond Kelly Turner commands the Joint Expeditionary Force and is responsible for the amphibious landings on Saipan, Tinian, and Guam. Turner also commands the Northern Attack Force responsible for operations at Saipan and Tinian. Rear Admiral Richard L. Conolly commands the Southern Attack Force responsible for operations at Guam. Vice Admiral Marc A. Mitscher's fast carrier task force and Vice Admiral Charles A. Lockwood's submarine force, Pacific Fleet, support the landings. Lieutenant General Holland M. Smith, as V Amphibious Corps commander, controls the ground forces. Smith also will command ground forces on Saipan. Major General Harry Schmidt will command forces on Tinian and Major General Roy S. Geiger will command ground forces on Guam. The ground units consist of three marine divisions (the 2nd, 3rd, and 4th) and two army divisions (27th and 77th Infantry), a separate marine brigade and the army's XXIV Corps Artillery. Lieutenant General Robert C. Richardson commands the army element.

Crewmen of the submarine USS *Barb* display their battle flag, showing Japanese shipping sunk. *(National Archives and Records Administration)*

Carrier aircraft from Task Force 58 continue to attack targets on Saipan. An aircraft transport and a convoy of five cargo vessels are sunk during the air strikes. Vice Admiral Willis A. Lee's TG 58.7 conducts a heavy bombardment of Japanese positions on Saipan and Tinian. Commander William I. Martin is shot down and parachutes into the sea off one of the intended landing beaches on Saipan. After being recovered from the water, he reports that the Japanese have carefully placed markers offshore to guide artillery spotters targeting the incoming American assault waves.

The appearance of Nimitz's naval task force off Saipan leads the Japanese navy to move away from New Guinea and speed northward to seek the climactic naval battle both sides have eagerly sought and planned for decades.

Seventh Air Force B-24 Liberators from Eniwetok Atoll conduct a night raid on Truk and Ponape Island.

NEW BRITAIN: B-25 Mitchells and B-24 Liberators bomb the airfield and antiaircraft positions at Tobera.

NEW GUINEA: U.S. submarine *Narwhal* shells oil tanks at Ceram Island.

Japanese aircraft hit U.S. destroyer *Kalk* off Biak.

June 14

ALEUTIANS: Eleventh Air Force sends four B-24 Liberators on a photoreconnaissance mission over the Kurile Islands. About 20 Japanese fighters intercept the bombers.

CBI: Fourteenth Air Force sends 43 P-40s to attack river shipping and troops near Tungting Lake, Changsha, and Linyang.

U.S. combat air strength in-theater reaches the highest level of the war.

ETO: VII Corps commanded by Major General J. Lawton Collins attacks west toward St-Sauveur-le-Victome with the 9th Infantry Division and the 82nd Airborne Division. The XIX Corps is operational under the command of Major General Charles H. Corlett.

Eighth Air Force sends 853 B-17s and 672 B-24 Liberators against airfields in France, Belgium, and the Netherlands. An oil refinery in Emmerich, Germany, is hit by 61 B-24s. The bombers are escorted by 103 P-47 Thunderbolts. A total of 14 bombers are lost and 605 are damaged. Aircrew casualties are 16 killed, 16 wounded, and 102 missing. Fighter pilots report five probable kills.

Other strikes by 176 P-47 Thunderbolts and 242 P-38 Lightnings attack a German Luftwaffe headquarters at Chantilly, France, and tank columns moving toward the beachhead. Over the beachhead, 200 P-38s and nearly 400 P-47s and P-51 Mustangs fly cover and conduct sweeps in front of the bombers.

During the night three B-17s drop leaflets in France. A total of 20 B-24 Liberators fly in support of Carpetbagger operations.

Ninth Air Force sends over 500 B-26 Marauders and A-20 Havocs to attack road and rail targets, including bridges, marshaling yards, gun positions, and strongpoints. P-47s and P-51s attack troops and vehicle movements around the Cherbourg Peninsula.

German submarine *U-621* torpedoes and sinks an LST off the Normandy beaches.

MEDITERRANEAN: Fifteenth Air Force sends nearly 700 B-17s and B-24 Liberators to attack oil production facilities in Czechoslovakia and Hungary. P-38 Lightnings, P-47 Thunderbolts, and P-51 Mustangs escort the bombers.

ITALY: The 142nd Infantry Regiment of the 36th Infantry Division encounters German forces at Magliano, captures the town, and is replaced by the 361st Infantry Regiment. The 143rd Infantry Regiment moves up the coastal road toward Grosseto.

Twelfth Air Force B-25 Mitchells and B-26 Marauders attack rail and road traffic, ports, and bridges. A-20 Havocs, P-47 Thunderbolts, and P-40s attack bridges and roads.

Staff Sergeant Homer L. Wise of L Company, 142nd Infantry Regiment, 36th Infantry Division, acts to support his platoon's attack at Magliano. After first risking his life to rescue a wounded soldier, Staff Sergeant Wise advances to kill three enemy soldiers with his Thompson submachine gun. Taking a Browning automatic rifle he advances in front of his platoon, destroying a German machine gun with his fire. As enemy fire comes from the flank, Wise approaches a tank and, fully exposed to enemy fire, employs the turret-mounted machine gun, disrupting the enemy and allowing the battalion to capture its objective. For his heroic actions beyond the call of duty, Staff Sergeant Wise will receive the Medal of Honor.

SOUTHWEST PACIFIC AREA: SWPA headquarters instructs Lieutenant General Krueger's Alamo Force to prepare plans for the capture of Noemfoor Island. The island has three airfields and controls the approaches to western New Guinea. More importantly, MacArthur is frustrated that his timetable has been upset by the delay in capturing the airfields at Biak. Unsure when those airfields will be available, he orders an attack to capture other airfields.

U.S. submarine *Rasher* attacks a Japanese convoy in the Celebes Sea, sinking a cargo ship.

PACIFIC: U.S. submarine *Golet* is sunk off northern Honshu, Japan.

CENTRAL PACIFIC: Rear Admiral Jesse B. Oldendorf's TG 52.17 and Rear Admiral Walden L. Ainsworth's TG 52.18 conduct bombardments of Japanese positions on Saipan and Tinian. Fire from a shore battery on Saipan damages the battleship USS *California*. The battleship USS *Tennessee*, heavy cruiser USS *Indianapolis*, a light cruiser, and two destroyers are damaged by enemy fire off Tinian. Destroyer USS *Wadleigh* provides close support for the withdrawal of an underwater demolition team (UDT) after completing a beach reconnaissance mission.

BOUGAINVILLE: Thirteenth Air Force P-39 Airacobras attack targets along the eastern coast of the island from Bonis to Kieta.

NEW BRITAIN: Thirteenth Air Force B-25 Mitchells, P-38 Lightnings, P-39 Airacobras, and U.S. Navy aircraft bomb logistics depots at Wunapope, Ralum, and Keravia Bay.

NEW GUINEA: At Sarmi, the 20th RCT of the 6th Infantry Division replaces the 158th RCT on the Tirfoam River.

At Biak, the 162nd and 186th Infantry Regiments of the 41st Infantry Division attempt a flank attack to drive the Japanese off the ridge overlooking Mokmer airfield. They encounter a position called the West Caves, a major strongpoint and the key to the Japanese defense. A Japanese counterattack with tanks and infantry drives the Americans from the position.

Fifth Air Force B-25 Mitchells, A-20 Havocs, and P-39 Airacobras attack the Wewak area and B-24 Liberators bomb Kamiri airfield on Noemfoor Island.

June 15

CBI: Tenth Air Force sends 30 B-25 Mitchells to fly ammunition resupply missions to British forces at Imphal. A-36 Intruder (Apache) fighter-bombers, P-51 Mustangs, and P-40s attack Mogaung and Myitkyina.

In China, Fourteenth Air Force sends 24 B-24 Liberators to bomb warehouses at Canton. Aircrews report heavy damage to the target.

Twentieth Air Force sends 47 B-29 Superfortresses from Chengtu, China, to bomb the Imperial Iron and Steel Works at Yawata, Japan. This is the first B-29 strike on the Japanese homeland. One B-29 is lost when Japanese fighters catch up with the bomber as it lands with engine trouble at Neihsiang airfield in China.

ATLANTIC: Navy TBF Avengers and FM-2 Wildcats from escort carrier USS *Solomons* sink German submarine *U-860* in the South Atlantic.

ETO: By this day (D+9) 500,000 Allied soldiers have landed on the Normandy beaches. In the VII Corps area, the 82nd Airborne and the 9th Infantry Division attack west of the Meredet River to prevent German forces from threatening the beachhead.

The VIII Corps becomes operational under the command of Major General Troy Middleton. The 101st and 82nd Airborne Divisions and the 90th Infantry Division make up the corps.

Eighth Air Force sends 747 B-17s and 614 B-24 Liberators, escorted by 96 P-38 Lightnings, 202 P-47 Thunderbolts, and 211 P-51 Mustangs, against airfields, V-weapon sites, railroad bridges, and marshaling yards in France and aircraft production facilities and an oil refinery in Germany. Two bombers are lost and 268 are damaged. Aircrew casualties are seven wounded and 18 missing. Fighter pilots report five confirmed kills. Three fighters are lost and the pilots are missing.

P-47s bomb Etaples, France, and one P-47 is lost; P-38 Lightnings fly a fighter sweep in front of the bomber forces.

Ninth Air Force sends over 500 B-26 Marauders and A-20 Havocs to attack fuel and ammunition storage areas, road and rail lines and an armored division headquarters near the Douve River. More than 1,400 P-47s and P-51s fly armed reconnaissance over the Cherbourg Peninsula.

ITALY: The 145th Infantry Regiment of the 36th Infantry Division captures Grosseto after the Germans abandon the town.

Twelfth Air Force B-25 Mitchells and B-26 Marauders attack rail and road traffic and bridges. A-20 Havocs, P-47 Thunderbolts, and P-40s attack convoys, bridges, and roads.

SOUTHWEST PACIFIC AREA: General MacArthur issues Reno V, a revision of earlier plans focused on offensive operations against the Japanese on New Guinea. Reno V lays out the details for an invasion of Mindanao for October 25 and an assault on Leyte in November. With airbases established on these two islands, American forces would have sufficient air cover to attack Luzon and other islands in the Philippines in preparation for an invasion of Formosa. MacArthur believes any operations against Formosa will require the capture of Luzon and the support of the Pacific Fleet. For his part, Admiral Nimitz supports the Leyte invasion, but continues to have doubts on the utility of landing on Luzon.

To support anticipated future operations against the Philippines, the Far Eastern Air Force (FEAF) is formed, combining the Fifth and Thirteenth Air Forces. General George C. Kenney is designated as FEAF commander, and FEAF headquarters is established in Brisbane, Australia. Lieutenant General Ennis C. Whitehead takes command of the Fifth Air Force with headquarters at Nadzab, New Guinea. Thirteenth Air Force headquarters moves from Guadalcanal to Los Negros Island, incorporating the Thirteenth Air Task Force headquarters already operating on the island. Major General St. Clair Streett is designated as the commander of Thirteenth Air Force. The position of Commander Air Solomons (COMAIRSOLS) is redesignated as Commander Air North Solomons (COMAIRNORSOLS). The B-25 Mitchells and fighters, together with other COMAIRSOLS aircraft, will continue to attack targets supporting the neutralization of Rabaul and limiting Japanese actions on Bougainville and Buka islands.

PACIFIC: Carrier-based aircraft from Task Group 58.1 (Rear Admiral Joseph J. Clark) and Task Group 58.4 (Rear Admiral William K. Harrill) attack Japanese positions on Iwo Jima, Chichi Jima, and Haha Jima.

U.S. destroyers sink a crippled Japanese transport damaged by carrier aircraft north of the Bonin Islands. U.S. submarine *Swordfish* attacks a Japanese convoy, sinking a cargo ship north of the Bonin Islands.

CENTRAL PACIFIC, SAIPAN: A false amphibious landing at Tanapag harbor to lure the Japanese away from the actual landing sites on Saipan is unsuccessful. Along with marine amtracs, marines are landed by the army's 708th, 773rd, and 715th Amphibian Tractor Battalions. During the actual landings, the 6th and 8th Marines of the 2nd Marine Division land too far north of the intended beachhead, creating a gap between them and the 23rd and 25th Marines of the 4th Marine Division. Despite a heavy bombardment, the Japanese are well prepared and drop artillery and mortar fire on the marines as they consolidate on the beachhead, causing many casualties. At Afetan Point, the 8th Marines run into strong Japanese resistance, while the 25th Marines begin advancing inland toward Mount Fina Susu. At Agingan Point, elements of the 25th Marines repel a Japanese counterattack. That night the 6th Marines face a Japanese counterattack of nearly 2,000 men supported by tanks. Navy ships fire starshells to illuminate the battlefield while the marines fight a desperate battle to hold their positions. A total of 24 tanks are destroyed. Privates First Class Herbert Dodge and Charlie Merritt, a bazooka team operating on their own, kill seven tanks. They will each be awarded the Navy Cross for gallantry.

Task Force 52, commanded by Vice Admiral Richmond K. Turner, lands marines on Saipan supported by naval gunfire and carrier-based aircraft. Battleship *Tennessee* is damaged by enemy fire.

Task Force 58 TBF Avengers and F4F Hellcat aircraft sink an auxiliary submarine chaser off Rota Island in the Marianas.

NEW BRITAIN: Thirteenth Air Force B-25 Mitchells, P-38 Lightnings, P-39 Airacobras, and P-40s attack Tobera airfield.

NEW GUINEA: At Biak, Lieutenant General Eichelberger arrives with members of his I Corps staff to supervise the battle. The 41st Infantry Division commander, Major General Horace Fuller, immediately submits his resignation to Lieutenant General Krueger, stating that the Sixth Army commander has given his unit too big a mission to be accomplished in such an impossibly short timeline. Eichelberger appoints Brigadier General Jens A. Doe as the new division commander.

FEAF B-24 Liberators, B-25 Mitchells, A-20 Havocs, and P-38 Lightnings attack barges near Manokwari.

June 16

CBI: After several unsuccessful attempts to reach the isolated engineer companies at Myitkyina, survivors are able to withdraw to friendly lines on their own.

Near Lung-ling on the Burma Road, the Y Force is pushed back by a Japanese counterattack.

Tenth Air Force sends 28 A-36 Intruder (Apache) fighter-bombers, P-51 Mustangs, and P-40s against targets near Myitkyina.

ETO: The 82nd Airborne clears St-Sauveur-le-Victome and captures the bridge over the Douve River. This allows for a rapid advance by infantry west toward the coast. The 9th Infantry Division establishes a bridgehead over the Douve River.

A total of 244 V-1 rockets are launched against London.

Eighth Air Force sends 146 B-17s and 224 B-24 Liberators, escorted by 165 P-38 Lightnings, 88 P-47 Thunderbolts, and 172 P-51 Mustangs, to attack airfields and V-weapon sites in France. One bomber is lost and 72 are damaged. Aircrew casualties are five killed, five wounded, and nine missing. Fighter pilots report one confirmed kill and no friendly losses.

70 P-51s performing a sweep against stalled trains drop their external fuel tanks near the rail cars then fire on the tanks to ignite them, setting the rail cars on fire. This improvised maneuver is highly successful. Flying over the front lines, 50 P-38 Lightnings and 75 P-47s attacks German troops, tanks, vehicles, trains, and transportation targets. Three P-38s are reported lost and one is damaged.

During the night 10 B-17s drop leaflets over France.

Ninth Air Force sends over 500 P-47s and P-51s to attack rail lines, bridges, and vehicles on the Cherbourg Peninsula.

MEDITERRANEAN: Fifteenth Air Force sends nearly 600 B-17s and B-24 Liberators to attack oil refineries around Vienna, Austria, and industrial production facilities in Czechoslovakia. The bombers are intercepted by about 250 fighters, which shoot down a total of 15 aircraft. Aircrews and fighter pilots report 70 confirmed kills.

ITALY: The 143rd Infantry Regiment and the 361st Infantry Regiment cross the Ombrone River east of Grosseto on a bridge erected by engineers. Task Force Ramey enters Triana. In less that a week, IV Corps has advanced 22 miles on a 20-mile front.

Twelfth Air Force B-26 Marauders and B-25 Mitchells attack rail and road bridges, viaducts, and other communication targets. A-20 Havocs bomb ammunition storage areas, while P-47 Thunderbolts and P-40s attack bridges, trucks, and rail lines across the front.

SOUTH PACIFIC: Major General Ralph J. Mitchell (USMC) is designated as Commander Air North Solomons (COMAIRNORSOLS).

CENTRAL PACIFIC: Seventh Air Force B-25 Mitchells form Makin Island bomb Ponape Island.

A task group commanded by Rear Admiral Walden L. Ainsworth with battleships, cruisers, and destroyers bombards Guam.

Two U.S. destroyers sink Japanese submarine *RO-114* west of Tinian.

A U.S. destroyer escort sinks Japanese submarine *RO-44* east of Eniwetok.

CENTRAL PACIFIC, SAIPAN: The 6th Marines advance toward Mount Tipo Pale, while the 2nd Marines move to Garapan. The 8th Marines struggle through swampy terrain, while the 25th Marines capture Agingan Point. The 165th and 105th Infantry Regiments and the 249th Field Artillery Battalion land on Saipan. The 165th Infantry Regiment is to attack south and west to seize Aslito airfield.

When Gunnery Sergeant Robert H. McCard's tank is hit and damaged by Japanese anti-tank fire and cut off from the rest of his platoon, McCard orders his crew out of the tank while he throws hand grenades to attract enemy fire. Although seriously wounded, McCard remounts his tank and uses a machine gun to engage the enemy. He dies at his position, having saved the lives of his tank crew and killed 16 Japanese soldiers. For his courage under fire and determined effort to continue the fight, Gunnery Sergeant McCard will receive the Medal of Honor.

NEW BRITAIN: FEAF B-24 Liberators bomb Vunakanau airfield at Rabaul. B-25 Mitchells, A-20 Havocs, P-39 Airacobras, and P-40s attack targets from Tobera airfield to Rabaul.

ADMIRALTIES: FEAF B-24 Liberators attack Truk Atoll and the Yap Islands in the Carolines.

NEW GUINEA: FEAF A-20 Havocs, P-39 Airacobras, and P-40s attack targets between Wewak and Hansa Bay.

U.S. submarine *Bluefish* attacks a Japanese convoy, sinking a cargo ship in the Celebes Sea. U.S. submarine *Bream* torpedoes and sinks a Japanese cargo ship and damages another off Halmahera Island.

June 17

ALEUTIANS: Eleventh Air Force supports a naval task force with 12 B-25 Mitchells flying cover for the ships after the task force bombards installations at Kurabu Cape on Paramushiru Island in the Kuriles.

CBI: The Marauders reach the Irrawaddy River north of Myitkyina to stop Japanese reinforcements from arriving.

Tenth Air Force sends 25 B-25 Mitchells to fly ammunition resupply missions to the Imphal area. Eight A-36 Intruder (Apache) fighter-bombers attack Japanese forces at Mogaung.

In China, Fourteenth Air Force B-25 Mitchells and P-51 Mustangs attack troop barges at Changsha. Changsha falls to Japanese forces.

ATLANTIC: Navy TBF Avengers and FM-2 Wildcats from escort carrier USS *Croatan* damage German submarine *U-853*.

ETO: The 9th Infantry Division of the VII Corps reaches the west coast of the Cotentin Peninsula, isolating the remnants of four German divisions.

A total of 174 B-17s and 470 B-24 Liberators attack airfields in France. The B-17s are escorted by 43 P-38 Lightnings, 39 P-47 Thunderbolts, and 90 P-51 Mustangs. Two bombers are lost and 22 are damaged. Aircrew casualties are 22 missing. A total of 470 B-24 Liberators are escorted by 209 P-47 Thunderbolts and 318 P-51s. One bomber is lost and 35 are damaged. Aircrew casualties are 10 missing. Fighter pilots report two confirmed kills in the air and three on the ground.

Nearly 100 P-38s make attacks on railroad bridges. Four P-38s are lost and the pilots are reported missing. A second attack against the same targets is done by 49 P-38s and 39 P-47s, escorted by 47 P-38s. Two additional P-38s are lost.

During the night nine B-17s drop leaflets over French towns and cities.

Ninth Air Force sends 265 B-26 Marauders to attack fuel storage areas, bridges, and rail lines. P-47s and P-51s escort the bombers and attack troop assembly areas, tanks, vehicles, bridges, and gun emplacements.

The 354th Fighter Group (353rd and 356th Fighter Squadrons), the 366th Fighter Group (389th and 391st Fighter Squadrons), and the 371st Fighter Group (405th and 406th Fighter Squadrons) redeploy from England to France. The squadrons all fly P-47s.

Mediterranean: An Allied naval task force commanded by Rear Admiral Thomas H. Troubridge (RN), including six U.S. destroyers, one destroyer escort, five mine-sweepers, and a number of other smaller ships and landing craft, puts French troops ashore on the island of Elba.

Southwest Pacific Area: FEAF B-24 Liberators bomb Truk. MacArthur receives intercepts from Ultra indicating that the Japanese have decided to reinforce the Philippines to stop the anticipated approach of American forces. The Japanese view maintaining the Philippines as essential to the security of their home islands.

U.S. submarine *Hake* attacks a Japanese convoy, sinking a transport southeast of Davao. U.S. submarine *Flounder* attacks the same convoy later in the day and sinks a torpedo recovery ship south of Mindanao. *Flounder* is depth-charged but is not damaged and escapes.

Central Pacific: Seventh Air Force B-24 Liberators from Kwajalein bomb Ponape Island. B-25 Mitchells from Makin Island bomb Nauru Island.

Escort carrier USS *Fanshaw Bay* is damaged east of Saipan by Japanese aircraft. A navy PB4Y-1 Privateer from Eniwetok sinks Japanese submarine *RO-117* north of Truk.

Central Pacific, Saipan: The 165th Infantry Regiment of the 27th Infantry Division lands. The 24th and 25th Marines advance toward Aslito airfield, a major objective.

Elements of the 27th Infantry Division arrive on Saipan about June 17, 1944, wading in from offshore LSTs (landing ship tanks).

Admiral Spruance takes his carriers to meet the Japanese fleet approaching Saipan.

NEW BRITAIN: FEAF B-24 Liberators bomb Lakunai airfield. B-25 Mitchells, A-20 Havocs, P-39 Airacobras, and P-38 Lightnings attack targets between Rapopo and Tobera.

NEW GUINEA: Fifth Air Force B-25 Mitchells supported by P-38 Lightnings attack Japanese ships in Sorong harbor on the Vogelkop Peninsula, sinking three cargo ships.

June 18

CBI: The New Galahad Force cuts the Mainga Ferry Road, the main supply route for the Japanese defending Myitkyina.

Tenth Air Force A-36 Intruder (Apache) fighter-bombers, P-51 Mustangs, and P-40s attack targets near Myitkyina and Mogaung.

In China, Japanese forces capture Changsha, at the hub of the major road and rail network. Fourteenth Air Force B-25 Mitchells and P-40s bomb Yoyang. P-40s and P-51 Mustangs attack supply boats at Tungting Lake and strafe cavalry units between Siangyin and Changsha.

ETO: Engineers have cleared the beachheads at Normandy of mines and obstacles and established roads to support the movement of supplies inland. Each infantry division now in Normandy requires about 700 tons of supplies a day to sustain itself in combat.

The 9th Infantry Division captures Barneville, opening a corridor across the Cotentin Peninsula. In the VII Corps area the 4th Infantry Division attacks toward Montebourg, while the 79th and 9th Infantry Divisions attack toward Valognes.

Eighth Air Force sends 890 B-17s against oil refinery targets around Hamburg, Germany. Nearly 500 B-24 Liberators attack V-weapon sites, airfields, and marshaling yards in France. Seven B-17s are lost and 286 damaged. Four B-24s are lost and 53 damaged. Aircrew casualties are one killed, 18 wounded, and 189 missing. The missions are escorted by 198 P-38 Lightnings, 172 P-47 Thunderbolts, and 215 P-51 Mustangs. Fighter pilots report only one P-38 damaged.

Over France, 98 P-38 Lightnings and 87 P-47 Thunderbolts attack railroad bridges; 47 P-51 Mustangs conduct fighter sweeps. Three P-51s are lost and the pilots are reported missing.

A total of nine B-24 Liberators fly in support of Carpetbagger operations in France. One bomber is lost.

Ninth Air Force sends nearly 130 B-26 Marauders and A-20 Havocs against fuel storage areas, marshaling yards, and V-weapon sites. P-47s escort the bombers and attack rail lines, troop assembly areas, and vehicles on the Cherbourg Peninsula.

The 48th Fighter Group (492nd and 493rd Fighter Squadrons) redeploys from England to France and the 354th Fighter Group's 355th Fighter Squadron joins the rest of the group in France. The squadrons all fly P-47s.

SOUTHWEST PACIFIC AREA: In response to a Combined Chiefs of Staff query on the possibility of bypassing the Philippines and the Palaus to attack Formosa or attack the Japanese home island of Kyushu directly, General MacArthur declares these options as unsupportable logistically. He states the Philippines are absolutely necessary as a base of operations for either Formosa or Kyushu. In addition, he repeats his contention on that America has a moral obligation to return to the Philippines.

CENTRAL PACIFIC: Seventh Air Force B-24 Liberators staging from Eniwetok bomb Truk. B-25 Mitchells from Makin Island bomb Nauru Island.

CENTRAL PACIFIC, SAIPAN: The 2nd Battalion of the 165th Infantry Regiment occupies Aslito airfield. The 27th Infantry Division becomes a separate command under Major General Ralph C. Smith.

The 105th Infantry Regiment joins the 165th Infantry Regiment, but has no equipment due to cargo mishandling. Aslito airfield is captured. The 23rd Marines struggle against Japanese defenses near Susupe and suffer heavy casualties. The 8th Marines begin an attack to capture Hill 240. The 24th and 25th Marines reach the east coast of the island on Magicienne Bay and begin the difficult and costly task of blasting Japanese defenders from defensive positions within caves. In the first three days of the attack on the island, the marines have suffered about 5,000 casualties and have not reached the central mountains where the main Japanese defenses are located.

Battleship USS *California* is damaged by friendly fire. Shore battery fire hits a destroyer. Two oilers are damaged by air attacks.

BOUGAINVILLE: FEAF P-39 Airacobras and P-38 Lightnings conduct sweeps over the coastal areas of the island.

NEW BRITAIN: FEAF B-24 Liberators, B-25 Mitchells, P-39 Airacobras, P-38 Lightnings, and P-40s conduct a heavy raid on Rabaul, dropping more than 18 tons of bombs.

NEW GUINEA: At Biak, the 34th Infantry Regiment of the 24th Infantry Division arrives to reinforce the 41st Infantry Division.

FEAF B-25 Mitchells, A-20 Havocs, P-38 Lightnings, P-40s, and P-47 Thunderbolts attack Japanese logistics bases and positions along the coast near Wewak.

June 19

ALEUTIANS: Eleventh Air Force sends two B-24 Liberators to fly an armed photoreconnaissance mission over Paramushiru Island. The bombers then bomb the Suribachi area.

CBI: In Burma, Tenth Air Force sends 30 B-25 Mitchells to fly ammunition resupply missions to Imphal. A-36 Intruder (Apache) fighter-bombers, P-51 Mustangs, and P-40s attack Myitkyina and Mogaung.

In China, Fourteenth Air Force B-25 Mitchells supported by nearly 150 P-40s and P-51 Mustangs attack shipping targets around Tungting Lake. P-40s attack trucks and buildings near the Salween River.

ETO: A storm in the English Channel blows up and lasts for three days. With winds blowing between 25 and 40 miles per hour and waves six-to-eight feet high, the storm is so strong that nearly 1,300 small craft are thrown upon the beaches. The gale wrecks Omaha beach, 300 ships, and the Mulberry dock. As a result, the beach's capacity to offload supplies is reduced by 40 percent. C-47 cargo planes are pressed to deliver supplies of ammunition to Bradley's First Army and VII Corps.

Major General Collins reorganizes units of VII Corps and advances north with the 4th, 79th, and 9th Infantry Divisions, capturing Montebourg in a surprise dawn attack. The 4th Infantry Division clears Montebourg, opening the main road to Cherbourg.

Eighth Air Force sends 464 B-17s to attack airfields in France escorted by 88 P-38 Lightnings and 261 P-51 Mustangs. Seven bombers are lost and 13 damaged. Aircrew casualties are three wounded and 59 missing. Ten fighters are lost and the pilots are reported as missing.

391 B-17s and 312 B-24 Liberators are sent against 35 V-weapon sites in the Pas-de-Calais area, escorted by 196 P-38s, 122 P-47s, and 48 P-51s. One B-24 is lost and 88 bombers are damaged. Aircrew casualties are two wounded and 10 missing. One fighter is damaged.

Ninth Air Force establishes the first operational U.S. airfield in France at Cardonville. Nearly 200 P-47s conduct armed reconnaissance and dive-bombing attacks on six V-weapon sites.

SOUTHWEST PACIFIC AREA: FEAF B-24 Liberators bomb Truk.

CENTRAL PACIFIC: Battle of the Philippine Sea. The Japanese deploy the First Mobile Fleet, commanded by Vice Admiral Jisaburo Ozawa, into three groups to draw the American fleet into a position where both land-based and carrier-based aircraft can converge to destroy the American carriers in a decisive battle. The Japanese fleet is divided into three groups. Vice Admiral Takeo Kurita commands the main battle fleet of four battleships and three light carriers, along with cruisers and destroyers. Vice Admiral Ozawa commands a group of three fleet carriers, supported by cruisers and destroyers. A third group is placed in reserve, consisting of two fleet carriers, one light carrier, a battleship, and cruisers. Admiral Raymond A. Spruance's ships of the Fifth Fleet, consisting of seven fast battleships, 21 cruisers, 69 destroyers, and Mitscher's Task Force 58 with one carrier and 956 aircraft have already been warned of the Japanese approach by U.S. submarines.

Japanese carrier aircraft attack, damaging the battleships USS *South Dakota* and USS *Indiana,* but the Japanese plan has already fallen apart. In the Mariana Islands there are no land-based aircraft left in any condition to assist Vice Admiral Ozawa in overwhelming the Americans. As the Japanese send wave after wave of aircraft to attack Admiral Mitscher's carriers, American fighters rise to meet them and eliminate them with little trouble. At the end of this day pilots and gun crews report 385 of 545 Japanese planes destroyed. One Japanese carrier and two oilers are sunk. Seventeen other Japanese aircraft are destroyed on Guam. U.S. losses are 26 aircraft and 64 crewmen.

In actuality, 330 out of 430 Japanese planes are shot down. Navy pilots call it "The Great Marianas Turkey Shoot."

U.S. submarine *Albacore* torpedoes and sinks the Japanese carrier *Taiho* north of Yap. U.S. submarine *Cavalla* torpedoes and sinks the Japanese carrier *Shokaku* a few miles farther north. Both submarines are heavily depth-charged, but escape unhurt.

Aircraft from escort carrier USS *Suwannee* sink Japanese submarine *I-184* south of Guam.

A Japanese aircraft is shot down in the "Marianas Turkey Shoot."

Seventh Air Force B-24 Liberators staging from Eniwetok bomb Truk. B-24s from Kwajalein and B-25 Mitchells from Makin Island bomb Ponape Island.

CENTRAL PACIFIC, SAIPAN: The 2nd and 4th Marine Divisions consolidate and begin a sweeping movement northward to establish a solid line oriented toward Mount Tapotchau, the dominant terrain feature on the island. The 27th Infantry Division moves to corps reserve and the 2nd Battalion 105th Infantry Regiment is to contain Japanese troops trapped at Nafutan Point on the southern tip of the island. As Lieutenant General Holland Smith reorients the marine divisions toward the north and east, the 105th and 165th Infantry Regiments of the 27th Infantry Division conduct low-level operations to clear the Nafutan Peninsula.

NEW GUINEA: At Sarmi, the 1st Infantry Regiment of the 6th Infantry Division crosses the Tor River in support of the 20th RCT, halted by enemy fire before Lone Tree Hill.

At Biak, the 186th Infantry captures the ridge overlooking Mokmer airfield.

FEAF A-20 Havocs, P-38 Lightnings, P-40s, and P-47 Thunderbolts attack targets along the coast near Wewak. A-20 Havocs bomb airfields at Manokwari on Noemfoor Island.

Fifth Air Force A-20 Havocs attack Manokwari, sinking two Japanese cargo vessels.

June 20

CBI: Vice President Henry Wallace arrives in Chungking, China, as President Roosevelt's personal emissary to assess the situation in China. General Stilwell is in

Burma and unable to meet with Wallace. Chiang Kai-shek and General Chennault, however, are available for meetings and are more than willing to paint the gloomiest possible picture of events. They also press for Stilwell's removal in the interest of preserving Allied unity.

In Burma, Tenth Air Force sends 13 B-25 Mitchells to fly ammunition resupply missions to Imphal. A-36 Intruder (Apache) fighter-bombers and P-40s attack Japanese positions at Myitkyina.

In China, Fourteenth Air Force attacks river shipping and logistics sites along the Yangtze River and at Tungting Lake area with over 100 B-25 Mitchells, P-40s, and P-51 Mustangs. Along the Salween River, B-25s bomb Lungling and P-40s attack Japanese positions.

ETO: The Germans are pushed back to the defenses around Cherbourg, as Major General Collins orders VII Corps (4th, 79th, and 9th Infantry Divisions) to attack toward the city.

Eighth Air Force sends 146 B-24 Liberators against V-weapon sites in the Pas-de-Calais area escorted by 44 P-47 Thunderbolts. Of the 126 that hit the targets, one bomber is lost and 84 are damaged. Aircrew casualties are four killed, eight wounded, and 24 missing. Fighter pilots report three confirmed kills. One P-47 is lost and the pilot is reported as missing.

A total of 341 B-17s and 191 B-24 Liberators are sent against targets in northern Germany. B-17 aircrews report two confirmed kills. Seven bombers are lost and 208 are damaged. Aircrew casualties are four killed, 17 wounded, and 69 missing. The B-24s are escorted by 98 P-38 Lightnings, 86 P-47 Thunderbolts, 38 P-51 Mustangs, and 81 Ninth Air Force P-51 Mustangs. Fighter pilots report 10 confirmed kills in the air and eight on the ground. Three aircraft are lost and two of the pilots are reported missing. Another attack by 512 B-17s against oil refineries in Hamburg, Germany, escorted by 96 P-38 Lightnings and 48 P-47 Thunderbolts, results in seven B-17s lost and 349 damaged. Aircrews report one killed, 13 wounded, and 63 missing. Fighter pilots report no losses.

More than 350 B-24 Liberators attack targets of opportunity in Germany escorted by 50 P-38 Lightnings and 221 P-51 Mustangs. Aircrews report 10 confirmed kills. A total of 34 B-24s are lost and 205 damaged. Aircrew casualties are three killed, six wounded, and 343 missing. Fighter pilots report 28 confirmed kills in the air and five on the ground. Three P-38s are lost and the pilots are reported missing. Over 400 B-17s and B-24s attack ten V-weapon sites in the Pas-de-Calais area, escorted by 72 P-47s and 40 P-51s. One B-24 is lost and 96 are damaged. Ten crewmen are reported missing.

During the night five B-17s drop leaflets over France. A total of 25 B-24 Liberators fly in support of Carpetbagger operations in France.

Ninth Air Force sends over 300 B-26 Marauders and A-20 Havocs to bomb nine V-weapon sites and a coastal defense battery. Over 1,000 P-47s and P-51s attack vehicles, lines of communication, and German troop locations on the Cherbourg Peninsula.

The P-47s of the 390th Fighter Squadron join the other two squadrons of the 366th Fighter Group in France.

ITALY: The Germans establish a defensive line across the rolling hills of the peninsula, called the Trasimeno Line. It protects the ports of Leghorn, Livorno, and Ancona. The IV Corps begins an attack to break the line by advancing up Route 1.

Twelfth Air Force B-25s and B-26 Marauders attack rail lines, while P-47 Thunderbolts and P-40s attack road and rail bridges.

SOUTHWEST PACIFIC AREA: FEAF B-24 Liberators bomb Woleai Atoll, in the Carolines, and Truk.

U.S. submarine *Hake* attacks a Japanese convoy off the south coast of Mindanao, sinking a cargo ship. U.S. submarines *Narwhal* and *Nautilus* land supplies and evacuate personnel from Negros and Panay Islands.

CENTRAL PACIFIC: The Battle of the Philippine Sea. Task Force 58 sends 216 F4F Hellcats, SB2C Helldivers, and TBF Avengers from fleet carriers USS *Hornet, Yorktown, Bunker Hill,* and *Lexington* and from light carriers (carriers built over the incomplete hulls of light cruisers by order of President Roosevelt in 1942) USS *Belleau Wood, Monterey,* and *San Jacinto* to attack the Japanese fleet when it is discovered late in the afternoon. TBF Avengers from USS *Belleau Wood* sink the Japanese carrier *Hiyo* northwest of Yap. The carrier *Zuikaku,* and two small carriers, a battleship, a heavy cruiser, and two destroyers are damaged along with tankers and an oiler. Because the U.S. aircraft were launched at maximum range, Vice Admiral Mitscher orders the ships of the task force to turn on lights to guide the aircraft through the dark night, despite the deadly threat posed by Japanese submarines.

The Battle of the Philippine Sea leaves the Japanese Fleet with only 35 carrier aircraft left. The last of Japan's skilled pilots have been lost and three fleet carriers have been sunk. Another 50 Japanese aircraft on Guam are destroyed, bringing Japanese aircraft losses to a total of 476. American losses are 130 aircraft and 76 pilots and crewmen. Ozawa's fleet retreats toward Okinawa, leaving the Mariana Islands and the sea routes to the Philippines undefended.

Seventh Air Force B-25 Mitchells from Makin Island bomb Ponape Island. B-24 Liberators from Kwajalein bomb Truk.

CENTRAL PACIFIC, SAIPAN: Aslito airfield is serviceable and can support tactical aircraft to support the marine attack northward.

A U.S. destroyer is damaged by a shore battery off Saipan.

NEW BRITAIN: FEAF P-38 Lightnings and some Royal New Zealand Air Force (RNZAF) aircraft attack antiaircraft positions near Rapopo.

NEW GUINEA: At Biak, the 34th RCT of the 24th Infantry Division captures Sorido and Borokoe airfields. The 163rd Infantry captures Hill 320, while the 186th and 162nd Infantry begin an assault on the West Caves, which quickly reveal themselves to be a vast underground complex of tunnels completely invulnerable to air or naval bombardment.

FEAF A-20 Havocs, P-39 Airacobras, and Royal Australian Air Force (RAAF) aircraft attack targets along the coast near Wewak. B-24 Liberators bomb Kamiri airfield on Noemfoor Island.

June 21

CBI: In Burma, Tenth Air Force sends 34 B-25 Mitchells to fly ammunition resupply missions to Imphal. A-36 Intruder (Apache) fighter-bombers and P-40s attack Japanese positions at Myitkyina and Mogaung.

ETO: The XIX and V Corps are ordered to hold positions because of a lack of ammunition availability due to storm damage at the beachhead.

Eighth Air Force sends 163 B-17s in the first Frantic shuttle-bombing mission from Britain. The bombers are escorted by 72 P-38 Lightnings, 38 P-47 Thunderbolts, and 57 P-51 Mustangs. En route to the USSR, 123 of the bombers hit the primary target, the synthetic oil plant at Ruhland, Germany. The 57 P-51s are replaced over Poland by 65 other P-51s. Nearly 30 German fighters attack the bomber formation. Fighter pilots report six enemy aircraft shot down and one P-51 lost. Of the 163 bombers sent on the mission, 144 land at Poltava and Mirgorod. One B-17 is lost. The P-51s land at Piryatin. Total casualties are one killed, five wounded, and 10 missing. During the night 75 German bombers attack the Poltava airfield. The Germans destroy 47 B-17s and heavily damage the rest as well as destroying fuel and ammunition.

A total of 496 B-17s fly on a mission over Berlin escorted by 99 P-38 Lightnings, 95 P-47 Thunderbolts, and 73 P-51 Mustangs. Aircrews report 16 confirmed kills and 20 probables. Sixteen B-17s are lost and 216 damaged. Aircrew casualties are one killed, 10 wounded, and 148 missing. Fighter pilots report four confirmed kills. One fighter is lost and the pilot is reported as missing. Over 360 B-24 Liberators attack targets around Berlin escorted by 148 P-38 Lightnings, 147 P-47 Thunderbolts, and 116 P-51 Mustangs. Aircrews report 13 confirmed kills and three probables. Nineteen B-24s are lost and 152 damaged. Aircrew casualties are 21 killed, 20 wounded, and 182 missing. Fighter pilots report 13 confirmed kills. One fighter is lost and one damaged. One pilot is reported as missing. Another 207 B-17s attack targets in and around Berlin escorted by 108 P-38 Lightnings, 81 P-47 Thunderbolts, and 91 P-51 Mustangs. Nine bombers are lost. Three fighters are lost and one damaged. The pilots are reported missing. Thirty-one B-24s escorted by 99 P-47 Thunderbolts bomb V-weapon sites in France. One B-24 is lost.

During the night five B-17s drop leaflets in France. A total of 21 B-24 Liberators fly in support of Carpetbagger operations in France. Ninth Air Force sends over 250 B-26 Marauders and A-20 Havocs against 13 V-weapon sites in the Pas-de-Calais area of France. P-47 Thunderbolts and P-51 Mustangs bomb bridges and attack lines of communication around Paris.

U.S. destroyer *Davis* is damaged by a mine off the Normandy beaches.

ITALY: Allied forces are presently 110 miles north of Rome. On the front line, Task Force Ramey is relieved by the 1st Armored Division.

Twelfth Air Force B-25 Mitchells and B-26 Marauders attack ships at Leghorn, rail and road traffic, and bridges. A-20 Havocs, P-47 Thunderbolts, and P-40s attack ammunition storage areas, bridges, and roads near the Gothic Line.

SOUTHWEST PACIFIC AREA: U.S. submarine *Bluefish* torpedoes and sinks a Japanese cargo ship near the southern end of the Makassar Strait.

CENTRAL PACIFIC: Seventh Air Force B-24 Liberators from Kwajalein bomb Truk.

U.S. destroyer *Newcomb* and a high-speed minesweeper sink Japanese submarine *I-185,* north of Saipan. TBF Avengers and F4F Wildcats from escort carrier USS *White Plains* sink a Japanese cargo ship off Saipan.

NEW GUINEA: At Biak, Mokmer airfield is open to Allied aircraft.

The Alamo Scouts conduct a reconnaissance of possible landing sites at Noemfoor Island. Lieutenant General Krueger designates the 158th RCT as the Noemfoor Task Force, commanded by Brigadier General Edwin D. Patrick. Over 13,500 men will be involved in the landing. D-day is set for July 2. Krueger designates the 503rd Parachute Infantry Regiment and the 34th Infantry Regiment as the task force reserve. Rear Admiral William M. Fechteler commands Task Force 77, with three cruisers, 23 destroyers, and three rocket-firing LCIs.

FEAF P-39 Airacobras and Royal Australian Air Force (RAAF) aircraft attack targets near Wewak. B-24 Liberators bomb Kamiri airfield on Noemfoor Island and attack shipping at both the Palau Islands and at Truk.

June 22

CBI: Tenth Air Force sends six B-24 Liberators to fly fuel to Kamaing and 40 B-25 Mitchells to supply British forces at Imphal, India, with ammunition. A-36 Intruder (Apache) fighter-bombers, P-51 Mustangs, and P-40s attack Japanese positions at Mogaung and Myitkyina.

In China, Fourteenth Air Force P-40 pilots report damaging a troopship on Tungting Lake. B-24 Liberators bomb dock facilities at Bakli harbor on Hainan Island. Aircrews report one cargo ship sunk.

ATLANTIC: President Roosevelt signs the GI Bill of Rights, authorizing a broad package of benefits for World War II veterans. The bill is intended to smooth demobilization for 16 million discharged American veterans. Veterans will be able to finance their education or purchase a home. It will become among the most important and far-reaching pieces of social legislation ever passed in America and will contribute to the postwar transformation of America.

ETO: The 9th and 79th Infantry Divisions of the VII Corps attack Cherbourg, the heavily defended port that is essential to the success of the Normandy operation. Over 1,000 bombers and fighters also attack the Cherbourg defenses.

As American forces struggle in the *bocage*, Sergeant Curtis G. Cullin, Jr., of the 102nd Cavalry Regiment is credited with discovering a way to turn the tide of battle. He welds scrap steel onto the front of a tank to form a fork-like contraption that allows the tank to bulldoze its way through the hedges, opening a path for the infantry into the open fields behind the hedgerows where they can drive the Germans from their positions.

The Frantic mission B-17s at Mirgorod and P-51 Mustangs at Piryatin are moved east temporarily and will thus avoid a German bomber attack on the two airfields during the night. The bombers and fighters will fly to Italy.

Eighth Air Force sends 108 B-17s and 194 B-24 Liberators escorted by 165 P-47 Thunderbolts and 97 P-51 Mustangs against 12 V-weapon sites near Pas-de-Calais area. One B-17 is lost and 123 bombers are damaged. Aircrew casualties are 10 missing. One P-51 is lost and two P-47s are damaged. One pilot is killed and the other reported missing. Another 216 B-17s are sent to attack the V-weapon site at Nucourt. Only 70 hit the primary target; the rest bomb airfields, bridges, rail lines, and marshaling yards. Four bombers are lost and 188 damaged. Aircrews report one confirmed kill. Aircrew casualties are two killed and 30 missing. One hundred

An infantry squad of the 60th Infantry Regiment, 5th Infantry Division moves into a
Belgian town on September 9, 1944, behind the cover of an M4 Sherman tank. The last
man in the squad carries a Browning Automatic Rifle; the others are armed with the
M-1 Garand rifle. Note that the Sherman tank has a steel rake mounted on its front,
used to break through the hedgerows of the Normandy countryside.

and thirteen B-24 Liberators are sent to attack the oil storage facilities near Paris,
escorted by P-51 Mustangs. Two bombers are lost and 40 damaged. Aircrew casualties are one killed, two wounded, and 23 missing. Three fighters are lost and the
pilots are reported missing.

Another 319 B-17s escorted by 108 P-47 Thunderbolts attack a marshaling yard,
an oil depot, airfields, and rail lines in France and Belgium. Three B-17s are lost and
82 are damaged. Aircrew casualties are two killed, five wounded, and 29 missing.
Fighter pilots report one confirmed kill. In addition, 149 B-24s escorted by over 200
P-38 Lightnings and P-47s bomb airfields in France. Aircrews report one confirmed
kill. A total of 67 B-24 Liberators are damaged. Aircrew losses are one killed and
three missing. Fighter pilots report one confirmed kill. Five P-38s are lost and one
damaged. The pilots are reported as missing.

During the night nine B-17s drop leaflets over cities and towns in France and
the Netherlands. A total of 10 B-24 Liberators fly in support of Carpetbagger operations over France.

Ninth Air Force sends nearly 600 B-26 Marauders and A-20 Havocs supported by more than 1,200 fighters against Cherbourg, supporting the VII Corps attack. B-26s and A-20s also support First Army to reduce several strongpoints. B-26s also attack marshaling yards, fuel supply depots, and a German headquarters. A total of 25 P-47 Thunderbolts are lost.

ITALY: Fifteenth Air Force sends over 600 B-17s and B-24 Liberators against marshaling yards and bridges.

Twelfth Air Force B-25 Mitchells and B-26 Marauders attack rail and road traffic and bridges. A-20 Havocs, P-47 Thunderbolts, and P-40s attack bridges and roads.

SOUTHWEST PACIFIC AREA: U.S. submarine *Flier* torpedoes and sinks a Japanese cargo ship west of Mindoro. U.S. submarine *Narwhal* torpedoes and damages a Japanese tanker in the Sulu Sea.

PACIFIC: U.S. submarine *Batfish* torpedoes and sinks a Japanese cargo ship off Honshu, Japan.

CENTRAL PACIFIC: Seventh Air Force B-24 Liberators from Kwajalein, staging through Eniwetok Atoll, bomb Truk.

CENTRAL PACIFIC, SAIPAN: The 2nd and 4th Marine Divisions begin the assault to seize Mount Tapotchau. The rugged terrain is expertly defended with positions that use every contour of the ground to best advantage. The marines are supported by 18 battalions of artillery, but are able to advance only 1,000 yards. Lieutenant General Holland Smith, bothered by what he believes to be a very slow and cautious movement into Naftuan Peninsula, withdraws the 165th Infantry Regiment and a battalion of the 106th Infantry Regiment of the 27th Infantry Division to support the marine attack.

P-47 Thunderbolts of the 19th Fighter Squadron land at Aslito airfield.

Battleship USS *Maryland* is damaged by an aerial torpedo off Saipan.

NEW GUINEA: The 20th RCT attacks Lone Tree Hill supported by artillery fire and airstrikes from FEAF P-47 Thunderbolts. Advancing up the hill, two battalions are trapped on the slopes and begin a fight for survival after becoming surrounded by Japanese infantry.

FEAF B-25 Mitchells, A-20 Havocs, and P-47 Thunderbolts attack airfields on Noemfoor Island and targets on Manokwari. B-24 Liberators bomb the Yap Islands, Sorol Atoll in the Carolines, and Woleai Atoll.

June 23

CBI: General Joseph Stilwell, concerned about low morale and lack of progress against the Japanese at Myitkyina, replaces Brigadier General Haydon L. Boatner with Brigadier General Theodore F. Wessels as commander of the Myitkyina Task Force.

Tenth Air Force sends 12 B-24 Liberators to fly gasoline to Kamaing and 29 B-25 Mitchells to fly ammunition resupply missions to Imphal, India. A-36 Intruder (Apache) fighter-bombers, P-51 Mustangs, and P-40s attack Japanese positions at Mogaung and Myitkyina.

In China, Fourteenth Air Force sends 20 B-24s to bomb the Hankow docks. Over the Tungting Lake area B-25s, P-40s, and P-51s attack river shipping, bomb a runway at Hengyang, and attack Japanese cavalry troops.

ETO: The 9th Infantry Division captures the German strongpoint at Mont Roc as the battle for Cherbourg continues.

General Eisenhower, SHAEF, responds to the Combined Chiefs of Staff on future operations in the Mediterranean. Eisenhower argues for Anvil, the invasion of southern France in support of Overlord, to go as planned. Overlord is the priority effort for the Allies. A diversion of forces away from France will deny the Allies a major port, which is essential for future operations against Germany, and will prevent a concentration of forces for the decisive battle in the Ruhr.

Eighth Air Force sends 134 B-17s and 106 B-24 Liberators escorted by 161 P-51 Mustangs to attack V-weapon sites. Six of the 12 primary targets are hit. Five bombers are damaged. Fighter pilots report destroying three locomotives, 100 rail cars, and 14 vehicles. One fighter is lost and the pilot is reported missing.

In a later attack, 109 B-17s and 219 B-24 Liberators escorted by 155 P-47 Thunderbolts and 83 P-51 Mustangs attack airfields in France. Most of the B-17s abort the mission due to heavy cloud cover. One B-17 is lost and two are damaged. Aircrew losses are one wounded and 10 missing. Six B-24s are lost and 83 are damaged. Aircrew losses are one killed, three wounded, and 58 missing. Fighter pilots report destroying vehicles, locomotives, and rail cars. P-38 Lightnings fly fighter-bomber missions in the Paris area. Two P-38s are lost and the pilots are reported missing.

A total of 21 B-24s fly in support of Carpetbagger operations.

Ninth Air Force sends nearly 200 A-20 and B-26 Marauders and more than 600 fighters against V-weapon sites in France. The fighters attack road and rail traffic.

The P-47s of the 404th Fighter Squadron, 371st Fighter Group, redeploy from England to France.

MEDITERRANEAN: Fifteenth Air Force sends over 400 B-17s and B-24 Liberators to attack oil facilities and storage depots at Ploeşti and Guirgiu in Romania. The mission, involving 139 B-24 Liberators with P-51 Mustangs as escort against the Ploeşti, Romania, oil refinery, results in six bombers lost. Aircrews and pilots report 24 German aircraft shot down.

Twelfth Air Force A-20 Havocs attack ammunition storage facilities and P-47 Thunderbolts attack rail lines.

Second Lieutenant David R. Kingsley, 97th Bombardment Group, 15th Air Force, is a bombardier of a B-17 approaching Ploeşti, Romania. The bomber takes several hits from antiaircraft fire and is badly damaged, but the pilot is able to bring the B-17 over the target for Kingsley to drop bombs. Losing altitude and straggling behind the formation on the return from Ploeşti, three German fighters attack the B-17. When the tail gunner is badly wounded, Second Lieutenant Kingsley goes to his aid. A few minutes later, the ball turret gunner is wounded and Kingsley treats him as well. When the pilot gives the order for the crew to bail out, Kingsley assists the two wounded crewmen, giving one his parachute. After helping the wounded men to exit the aircraft, he remains in the disintegrating bomber until it crashes. Second Lieutenant Kingsley's heroic and unselfish act saves the life of one of his crew and will win him the Medal of Honor.

PACIFIC: The U.S. submarine *Seawolf* arrives off Peleliu to photograph prospective landing beaches.

CENTRAL PACIFIC: Seventh Air Force B-24 Liberators from Eniwetok bomb Truk. B-25 Mitchells from Engebi Island and B-24s from Kwajalein bomb Ponape Island both day and night.

Aircraft from Rear Admiral Joseph J. Clark's carrier task group (Task Group 58.1) bomb Japanese air facilities and shipping in the Marianas.

CENTRAL PACIFIC, SAIPAN: The 27th Infantry Division is assigned a two-mile front in the center of the battle line. As the 106th and 165th advance to occupy the forward lines, the regiments get entangled and it takes several hours to sort out the confusion. Once the regiments do attack, they encounter heavy Japanese defenses. The 165th makes about 700 yards; the 106th Infantry Regiment about 100 yards. The infantrymen have run into one of the strongest defensive positions on the island. Certain terrain features gain names quickly: "Hell's Pocket," "Purple Heart Ridge," and "Death Valley." By the end of the day only the 2nd Battalion of the 105th Infantry Regiment has been left to guard the Nafutan Peninsula as other battalions are brought to the battle line. The Japanese conduct counterattacks with tanks and infantry on the army positions at night. The 106th Infantry Regiment retreats from its forward position during the night when an ammunition storage site is blown up.

Seventh Air Force P-47 Thunderbolts of the 73rd Fighter Squadron, 318th Fighter Group, are launched from USS *Manila Bay* and land on Saipan Island.

During the night Japanese aircraft conduct high-altitude bombing attacks on amphibious ships off Saipan.

NEW BRITAIN: FEAF B-24 Liberators bomb Tobera airfield and B-25 Mitchells and Allied aircraft attack antiaircraft positions.

NEW GUINEA: At Biak, the main resistance in the West Caves is overwhelmed using tanks, mortars, grenades, TNT charges, and barrels of gasoline. All the airfields on Biak are opened to aircraft. Parai defile also finally is captured, but Japanese infiltrators continue to fight.

FEAF A-20 Havocs, P-39 Airacobras, P-47 Thunderbolts, and Royal Australian Air Force (RAAF) aircraft bomb Wewak. A-20 Havocs and the new A-26 Invader light bomber, intended to replace the A-20s, attack targets off Manokwari. The P-38 Lightnings of the 8th Fighter Squadron, 49th Fighter Group, redeploy from Hollandia to Biak Island.

B-24 Liberators bomb the airfields at Yap and Woleai Atoll. Other B-24s bomb Truk and Peleliu in the Palaus. The A-26 is flown with the 3rd Bombardment Group and aircrews soon determine that the aircraft has insufficient visibility for jungle operations.

June 24

ALEUTIANS: Eleventh Air Force sends three B-24 Liberators on a dawn raid against the airfield at Kurabu Cape on Paramushiru Island.

CBI: Tenth Air Force sends 12 B-24 Liberators to fly gasoline to Kamaing and 29 B-25 Mitchells to fly ammunition resupply missions to Imphal, India. A-36 Intruder (Apache) fighter-bombers, P-51 Mustangs, and P-40s attack Japanese positions at Mogaung and Myitkyina.

In China, Fourteenth Air Force P-40s and P-38 Lightnings attack Japanese cavalry troops near Hengyang.

ATLANTIC: The JCS supports Anvil (the invasion of southern France) because it focuses Allied power on the rapid defeat of Germany. Southern France would provide major ports and allow French forces to assist in liberating their own country.

Navy TBM Avengers from escort carrier USS *Bogue* sink Japanese submarine *I-52* in the Atlantic west of the Azores.

ETO: The VII Corps continues its attack on the forts guarding Cherbourg. Naval gunfire and air bombardment support tanks and infantrymen with bazookas and demolitions.

Eighth Air Force sends 340 B-17s escorted by 185 P-38 Lightnings and 85 P-47 Thunderbolts to attack oil production facilities in Germany. One bomber is lost and 105 are damaged. Aircrew losses are two wounded, and nine missing. Fighter pilots report two confirmed kills on the ground.

In another mission, 407 B-24 Liberators escorted by 45 P-38 Lightnings and 36 P-47 Thunderbolts attack airfields in France. Two bombers are lost and 81 are damaged. Aircrew losses are 20 missing. Fighter pilots report one fighter lost and the pilot missing.

V-weapon sites are the target of 148 B-17s and 227 B-24s throughout the day. Three bombers are lost and 76 bombers are damaged. Aircrew casualties are 20 missing. Another 74 B-17s are sent to attack the Saumur bridge with P-51 Mustangs flying escort. Fighter pilots report four confirmed kills on the ground. More than 200 B-17s and B-24s escorted by 71 P-47s and 50 P-51s attack targets in France. Two bombers are lost. Fighter pilots report 25 confirmed kills on the ground.

During the night five B-17s drop leaflets over France.

Ninth Air Force sends over 400 A-20 and B-26 Marauders and over 400 P-47s against fuel depots, marshaling yards, and rail bridges in France.

The P-47s of the 313th Fighter Squadron, 50th Fighter Group, redeploy from England to France.

MEDITERRANEAN: Fifteenth Air Force sends over 300 B-17s and B-24 Liberators, escorted by P-51 Mustangs, P-47 Thunderbolts, and P-38 Lightnings, to attack rail targets and oil production facilities in Romania. Aircrews report over 20 confirmed kills. Ten U.S. aircraft are lost and others are reported missing.

ITALY: Twelfth Air Force P-47 Thunderbolts attack bridges, rail lines, and German gun positions.

SOUTHWEST PACIFIC AREA: U.S. submarine *Redfin* attacks a Japanese convoy off the southern coast of Leyte, sinking a cargo ship.

PACIFIC: U.S. submarine *Grouper* attacks a Japanese convoy and sinks a cargo ship and merchant tanker south of Yokohama, Honshu, Japan.

U.S. submarine *Tang* (SS-306) attacks a Japanese convoy, sinking three cargo ships and a merchant tanker outside Nagasaki harbor, Kyushu, Japan.

Rear Admiral Joseph J. Clark and Rear Admiral Alfred E. Montgomery's carrier aircraft bomb airfields and facilities on Iwo Jima and Pagan Island in the Marianas.

CENTRAL PACIFIC, SAIPAN: The 106th and 165th Infantry Regiments again make an attack, but it is not effective. The 2nd Marine Division likewise makes little progress. The 4th Marine Division approaches the Kagman Peninsula and encounters civilians and Japanese soldiers in caves. Heat and lack of water have taken a physical toll on the Americans and slow the overall advance.

Unsatisfied with the 27th Infantry Division's lack of progress, Lieutenant General Holland M. Smith, a marine, removes Major General Ralph C. Smith, an army officer, from command and replaces him with Major General Sanderford Jarman, the army officer slated to become the occupation force commander for Saipan. Holland Smith's action creates the greatest interservice furor of the war and is so potentially dangerous to the war effort that the Joint Chiefs of Staff addresses the incident at its meeting in Washington.

P-47 Thunderbolts on Saipan strafe Japanese defensive positions and attack Japanese defenses on Tinian Island.

During the night Japanese aircraft conduct high-altitude bombing attacks on amphibious ships off Saipan.

New Britain: FEAF B-24 Liberators, B-25 Mitchells, P-38 Lightnings, P-39 Airacobras, and P-40s supporting other Allied aircraft attack Tobera airfield and other targets.

New Guinea: The 20th RCT continues its fight for survival on Lone Tree Hill. An amphibious assault with an infantry company, the 6th Reconnaissance Troop, and tanks lands at Rocky Point in an attempt to outflank the defenders on the hill. The Japanese effectively prevent any further movement off the narrow beachhead.

FEAF A-20 Havocs, P-39 Airacobras, P-47 Thunderbolts, and Royal Australian Air Force (RAAF) aircraft bomb Wewak. B-25 Mitchells and A-20 Havocs attack Japanese positions within the caves on Biak and the Kamiri airfield on Noemfoor Island.

June 25

Aleutians: Eleventh Air Force sends two B-24 Liberators to bomb the airfield at Kurabu Cape, on Paramushiru Island.

CBI: Tenth Air Force sends 50 B-25 Mitchells to fly ammunition resupply missions to Imphal, India. A-36 Intruder (Apache) fighter-bombers, P-51 Mustangs, and P-40s attack Japanese positions at Mogaung and Myitkyina.

In China, the Fourteenth Air Force reports that its efforts to stall the Japanese ground offensive in the Tungling Lake area since June 17 has resulted in 1,600 Japanese casualties and 377 supply boats destroyed.

Seven B-25 Mitchells of the Chinese-American Composite Wing (CACW) bomb logistics sites near Shayang. B-25 Mitchells and P-40s bomb logistics sites and damage a bridge at Chenghsien. The P-40s of the 75th Fighter Squadron, 23rd Fighter Group, redeploy from Lingling to Kweilin.

ETO: The VII Corps attacks Cherbourg preceded by a heavy naval bombardment by three battleships, four cruisers, and 11 destroyers. The Americans fight their way into the city.

Eighth Air Force sends 263 B-17s, escorted by 46 P-38 Lightnings, 36 P-47 Thunderbolts, and 146 P-51 Mustangs, to attack airfields in France. Five bombers are lost and 115 are damaged. Aircrew losses are 10 killed, five wounded, and 45 missing. Fighter pilots report 10 confirmed kills. One P-51 is lost and the pilot is reported missing. A second mission sends 258 B-24 Liberators escorted by 68 P-47 Thunderbolts and 34 P-51 Mustangs against airfields in France. One bomber is lost and 27 are damaged. Aircrew losses are one killed and two wounded. Another 137 B-24 Liberators escorted by 102 P-38s and 44 P-47s attack airfields. One B-24 is lost and 10 air crewmen are missing. Fighter pilots report eight confirmed kills.

Airfields and bridges in France are attacked with 189 B-17s and 274 B-24 Liberators escorted by 127 P-38s, 35 P-47s, and 181 P-51s. Six bombers are lost and 126 are damaged. Aircrew losses are 11 killed, nine wounded, and 78 missing. Fighter pilots report four confirmed kills. One P-51 is lost and the pilot is reported missing.

A total of 24 B-24s fly in support of Carpetbagger operations.

Ninth Air Force sends over 400 A-20 and B-26 Marauders and over 500 P-47s against fuel storage depots, road, and rail lines in France.

The headquarters of the 50th Fighter Group and the P-47s of the 10th and 81st Fighter Squadrons redeploy from England to France.

Rear Admiral Morton L. Deyo employs gunfire from a battleship, a cruiser, and a destroyer to bombard German shore batteries and coastal defenses at Cherbourg, France. The battleship USS *Texas* and three destroyers are damaged by the gunfire.

First Lieutenant Carlos C. Ogden, commander of K Company, 314th Infantry Regiment, 79th Infantry Division, leads his unit in an attack near Fort de Roule, which guards the approaches to Cherbourg. When First Lieutenant Ogden's company is halted by German fire, Ogden takes an M-1 rifle and rifle grenades and advances toward the enemy alone. Although wounded, he continues to climb the hill and uses the rifle grenades to destroy an 88 millimeter gun position, then uses hand grenades to destroy a machine gun position. Wounded again, First Lieutenant Ogden orders his men forward to take the objective. For his exceptional display of courage and leadership, First Lieutenant Ogden will be awarded the Medal of Honor.

MEDITERRANEAN: In preparation for Anvil, Fifteenth Air Force sends over 600 B-17s and B-24 Liberators to attack marshaling yards, oil storage facilities, and industrial production facilities in southern France and the harbor at Toulon.

ITALY: The 36th Infantry Division is pulled out of the line to prepare for Anvil and is replaced by the 34th Infantry Division.

Twelfth Air Force A-20 Havocs attack ammunition storage facilities. P-40s and P-47 Thunderbolts attack rail lines and bridges.

SOUTHWEST PACIFIC AREA: U.S. submarine *Jack* attacks a Japanese convoy and sinks a merchant tanker off the northwest coast of Luzon.

CENTRAL PACIFIC: Seventh Air Force B-24 Liberators from Kwajalein bomb Truk and Wotje Atolls.

CENTRAL PACIFIC, SAIPAN: The 2nd Battalion of the 105th Infantry Regiment attacks Japanese defenses on the Nafutan Peninsula. Elements of the 8th and 29th Marines reach the heights of Mount Tapotchau. The 165th Infantry Regiment attacks along Purple Heart Ridge into the complex of caves, valleys, and sharp ridgelines. The 106th Infantry Regiment is stopped at Death Valley. Kagman Peninsula is cleared, but at a frightful cost to Japanese civilians, who either refuse to give up or are coerced to stay by Japanese soldiers.

P-47 Thunderbolts on Saipan conduct armed reconnaissance and strafing missions over Saipan and Tinian.

New Britain: FEAF B-25 Mitchells, P-38 Lightnings, P-39 Airacobras, and P-40s with Allied aircraft attack antiaircraft positions near Wunapope and plantations at Wide Bay.

New Guinea: The 20th RCT reaches the top of Lone Tree Hill; the tanks at Rocky Point are withdrawn. Although the Americans have gained one position, there are several other strongpoints that must be attacked.

FEAF A-20 Havocs, P-39 Airacobras, P-47 Thunderbolts, and Royal Australian Air Force (RAAF) aircraft bomb Wewak. P-40s and B-24 Liberators attack Kamiri airfield on Noemfoor. B-24s also bomb Yap and Sorol Atoll.

U.S. submarine *Bashaw* attacks a Japanese convoy and sinks a cargo ship northwest of Halmahera Island.

June 26

Aleutians: Eleventh Air Force sends 12 B-25 Mitchells to fly air cover missions for a naval task force after it bombards installations on Paramushiru Island.

CBI: Vice President Henry Wallace sends his report to President Roosevelt from Chungking shortly before departing China. Completely convinced that General Stilwell is the problem, after hours of conversation with Generalissimo Chiang Kai-shek, he recommends that General Stilwell be recalled. He offers General Albert Wedemeyer as a possible replacement.

The Chinese Y Force attacks Tengchung.

Tenth Air Force sends over 30 B-25 Mitchells to fly ammunition resupply missions to Imphal, India. A-36 Intruder (Apache) fighter-bombers, P-51 Mustangs, and P-40s bomb Myitkyina.

In China, Fourteenth Air Force sends 14 B-24 Liberators to attack Hankow. Aircrews report heavy damage. Over the Tungting Lake area more than 180 B-25s, P-51 Mustangs, and P-40s attack river shipping and villages.

Japanese bombers and fighters attack Lingling airfield, damaging the runway and destroying a P-51.

ETO: The 79th Infantry Division captures Fort du Roule, the main stronghold defending Cherbourg. The German garrison of 10,000 men surrenders shortly thereafter. The American victory is lessened by the discovery that the harbor, so critical to the sustainment of American forces in Normandy, is completely wrecked.

Omaha beach is operating at 122 percent above its planned capacity, having landed 268,718 men, 40,191 vehicles, and 125,812 tons of supplies since D-day.

Operation Frantic B-17s leave Poltava and Mirgorod in the Ukraine, USSR, rendezvous with 55 P-51 Mustangs from Piryatin, and proceed to bomb the oil refinery and marshaling yard at Drohobycz, Poland, en route to Italy. Fifteenth Air Force P-51s meet the 71 bombers and escort them to Foggia.

Ninth Air Force loses three P-47 Thunderbolts supporting the attack on Cherbourg. Pilots report three confirmed kills.

MEDITERRANEAN: Fifteenth Air Force sends over 650 B-17s and 36 B-24 Liberators against aircraft production facilities and oil refineries near Vienna, Austria. Nearly 30 bombers and fighters are lost. Aircrews report more than 60 confirmed kills. The 36 B-24 Liberators are attacked by 80 German fighters as they approach the oil refinery. Immediately, 60 more attack as the B-24s begin their bombing run. Ten bombers are lost and aircrews report 34 confirmed kills.

PACIFIC: Cruisers and destroyers, under command of Rear Admiral Ernest G. Small, bombard Japanese positions at Kurabu Zaki, Paramushiro, Kuriles.

CENTRAL PACIFIC: Seventh Air Force B-25 Mitchells from Makin bomb Ponape and Nauru Islands.

CENTRAL PACIFIC, SAIPAN: A force of about 500 Japanese soldiers conducts a breakout from Nafutan Point, slipping past the troops of the 105th Infantry and destroying one P-47 and damaging 20 others at Aslito airfield. As the group moves northward to cross into Japanese lines, they encounter the 25th Marines and are destroyed. Major General Sanderford Jarmin relieves the commander of the 106th Infantry Regiment in an attempt to spur the unit to capture Death Valley. The attack with a new commander is unsuccessful.

P-47 Thunderbolts continue ground support missions on Saipan and attack Japanese positions on Tinian Island. P-61 Black Widow night fighters carry out patrols over Saipan.

NEW BRITAIN: FEAF B-25 Mitchells, P-38 Lightnings, P-39 Airacobras, and P-40s with Allied aircraft attack airfields and antiaircraft positions near Rabaul.

NEW GUINEA: The 1st and 63rd Infantry Regiments of the 6th Infantry Division replace the 20th RCT of the division and launch an attack on the remaining strongpoints at Lone Tree Hill: Hill 225, Mount Saksin, and Hill 265. The two infantry companies isolated on the Rocky Point beachhead finally are able to make contact with the 1st Infantry.

FEAF A-20 Havocs, P-39 Airacobras, P-47 Thunderbolts, and Royal Australian Air Force (RAAF) aircraft bomb Wewak. P-38 Lightnings, P-47 Thunderbolts A-20 Havocs, B-24 Liberators, and B-25 Mitchells attack airfields, shipping, and roads at Noemfoor and Biak Islands and Manokwari, and Japanese defensive positions near Sarmi.

The P-38s of the 9th Fighter Squadron, 49th Fighter Group, redeploy from Hollandia to Biak Island. The 419th Night Fighter Squadron, 18th Fighter Group, Thirteenth Air Force, deploys a detachment of P-61 Black Widow night fighters from its base on Guadalcanal to Nadzab.

Fifth Air Force P-38 Lightnings sink a Japanese cargo ship east of Halmahera Island.

June 27

CBI: Chinese forces and Chindits capture Mogaung, isolating Myitkyina and opening a land route for the Allies to send supplies and reinforcements to Myitkyina.

Tenth Air Force sends eight B-24 Liberators to fly gasoline to Kamaing, Burma, and 52 B-25 Mitchells fly ammunition resupply missions to Imphal, India.

Fourteenth Air Force sends 160 B-25s, P-51 Mustangs, and P-40s over the Tungting Lake area to attack Japanese troop concentrations, logistics sites, and river transportation between Changsha and Hengyang. Aircrews from four B-25s sent against shipping targets in the Formosa Strait report two cargo ships sunk.

ATLANTIC: The JCS rejects the British arguments against Anvil and rejects any further major operations in Italy.

ETO: VII Corps takes the surrender of the last German defenders at Cherbourg. The Germans have destroyed the port so thoroughly that no supplies will be able to move through until July.

Eighth Air Force sends over 250 bombers against V-weapon sites and logistics depots in France, escorted by 149 P-51 Mustangs. Five bombers are lost and 114 are damaged. Aircrew losses are two killed, seven wounded, and 51 missing. Fighter pilots report six confirmed kills during attacks on marshaling yards, bridges, rail lines, and airfields. Two fighters are lost and one is damaged. The two pilots are reported missing.

VII Fighter Command sends 644 P-38 Lightnings, P-47 Thunderbolts, and P-51 Mustangs against airfields and transportation targets. Three P-38s are lost and three are damaged. Three pilots are reported missing and one pilot is wounded. The P-47 pilots report 10 confirmed kills and the P-51 pilots report one confirmed kill.

A total of 16 B-24s fly in support of Carpetbagger operations. During the night four B-17s drop leaflets over France.

Ninth Air Force sends over 700 P-47s against rail facilities, roads, troop concentrations, and artillery positions. The P-47s of the 365th Fighter Group (386th and 387th Fighter Squadrons) redeploy from England to France.

MEDITERRANEAN: Fifteenth Air Force sends nearly 300 B-17 bombers and B-24 Liberators to bomb marshaling yards in Budapest, Hungary, and Brod, Yugoslavia, and bomb oil production facilities in Drohobycz, Poland. About 90 German fighters attack the formations. Three bombers are lost and aircrews report over 30 confirmed kills. P-51s flying a sweep over Budapest report seven confirmed kills.

ITALY: The 34th Infantry Division is stopped by German defenses at the Cecina River, an indication that the Germans have formed a new defensive line.

Twelfth Air Force A-20 Havocs attack ammunition storage facilities. P-40s and P-47 Thunderbolts attack roads, rail lines, and bridges.

SOUTHWEST PACIFIC AREA: U.S. submarine *Seahorse* attacks a Japanese convoy and sinks a merchant tanker off Formosa.

CENTRAL PACIFIC: Seventh Air Force B-24 Liberators staging through Eniwetok bomb Truk.

Aircraft from TF 58 finish off a Japanese water tanker damaged irreparably by USS submarine *Seahorse* off Guam in early April.

CENTRAL PACIFIC, SAIPAN: The 2nd Battalion of the 105th Infantry Regiment clears the last Japanese defenders from Nafutan Peninsula. The 1st Battalion of the 106th Infantry Regiment fights the Japanese for Hell's Pocket and Death Valley. The rest of the 106th Infantry and the 165th Infantry Regiment attack Purple Heart Ridge.

Japanese planes bomb Aslito airfield and Charan Kanoa.

P-47 Thunderbolts strafe Japanese defensive positions and fire rockets on suspected strongpoints on Saipan and attack Japanese positions on Tinian. P-61 Black Widow night fighters fly defensive night patrols.

NEW BRITAIN: Thirteenth Air Force B-25 Mitchells with P-39 Airacobras, P-38 Lightnings, and P-40s attack antiaircraft positions and other targets around Rabaul.

ADMIRALTIES: Thirteenth Air Force's 419th Night Fighter Squadron, 18th Fighter Group, deploys a detachment of P-61 Black Widow night fighters from Guadalcanal to Los Negros Island.

NEW GUINEA: Major General Charles P. Hall, XI Corps commander, takes command of the Aitape Task Force as part of a buildup of forces to conduct a counteroffensive against a major Japanese attack. Ultra intercepts have given the Americans advance warning of enemy plans. The 112th Cavalry RCT reinforces the 32nd Infantry Division along the Driniumor River and supports the defense of the airfield.

FEAF A-20 Havocs, P-39 Airacobras, P-47 Thunderbolts, and Royal Australian Air Force (RAAF) aircraft bomb Wewak. B-24 Liberators, B-25 Mitchells, A-20 Havocs, P-40s, and P-47s attack airfields and gun positions at Manokwari, Biak, and Noemfoor Islands. B-24s bomb the Yap Islands and Sorol Atoll in the Caroline Islands.

June 28

CBI: In China, the Japanese begin offensive operations to capture Henyang, the main city along the axis of advance toward Indochina and the key to the success of the *Ichigo* offensive. About 40 poorly equipped and trained Chinese divisions defend the city. Fourteenth Air Force B-25 Mitchells, P-51 Mustangs, and P-40s conduct attacks on Japanese headquarters, cavalry troops, and lines of communication and supply in the Hengyang area as enemy forces threaten the Fourteenth Air Force's airfield. The B-25s of the 11th Bombardment Squadron (Medium), 341st Bombardment Group (Medium), move from Kweilin to Yang Tong.

Fourteenth Air Force B-24 Liberators attack Japanese convoy off Formosa, sinking a transport.

ATLANTIC: Prime Minister Winston Churchill writes to President Roosevelt with a direct appeal to cancel Anvil, the invasion of southern France in support of Overlord, and divert the resources toward Yugoslavia and northern Italy. Churchill points out that the smaller ports in Normandy are sufficient to supply the Overlord lodgment rather than trying to resupply them from ports in southern France. Instead of southern France, Churchill offers an advance north into the Hungarian plains through the Ljubljana Gap to tie down German divisions that could be used to reinforce the German defenses at Normandy. Finally, Churchill stresses the political-strategic benefits of having Allied forces in the Balkans before the Soviets.

ETO: Eighth Air Force sends 485 B-17s and 378 B-24 Liberators escorted by 188 P-38 Lightnings, 169 P-47 Thunderbolts, and 231 P-51 Mustangs to attack marshaling yards, airfields, bridges, and oil storage facilities in France. Two bombers are lost and 225 damaged. Ten crewmen are wounded and 19 are missing. Fighter pilots report one confirmed kill and three locomotives destroyed. Two fighters are lost and two are damaged. Both pilots are reported missing.

A total of 18 B-24s fly in support of Carpetbagger operations.

Ninth Air Force sends over 200 fighters, all based in France, against bridges, marshaling yards, troop areas, gun emplacements, and ammunition storage sites in France.

The headquarters of the 365th Fighter Group deploys from England to France.

MEDITERRANEAN: The Mediterranean Commander in Chief, General Sir Henry M. Wilson, approves the concept plans for Anvil.

Fifteenth Air Force sends over 200 B-24 Liberators to bomb the marshaling yards and oil refineries at Bucharest, Romania. Another 138 B-24s attack the Karlovo airfield in Bulgaria. Fighter pilots report over 20 confirmed kills over Bucharest.

SOUTHWEST PACIFIC AREA: U.S. submarine *Pargo* attacks a Japanese convoy in Moro Gulf, sinking a cargo ship and damages a smaller vessel about 35 miles east of Zamboanga on Davao Island, Philippines.

PACIFIC: U.S. submarine *Archerfish* sinks a Japanese coast defense vessel southwest of Iwo Jima.

U.S. submarine *Sealion* torpedoes and sinks a Japanese collier in Tsushima Strait.

CENTRAL PACIFIC, SAIPAN: Major General George W. Griner takes command of the 27th Infantry Division from Major General Sanderford Jarmin. Hell's Point is captured.

Seventh Air Force P-47 Thunderbolts attack Japanese defenses on Saipan and Tinian, and P-61 Black Widow night fighters carry out defensive night patrols.

NEW GUINEA: The XI Corps under Major General Charles P. Hall is organized at Aitape. It consists of the 32nd and 43rd Infantry Divisions, along with the 112th Cavalry RCT, corps artillery, and a tank destroyer battalion. Hall is waiting for the Japanese 18th Army, which has been ordered to move west and threaten the American advance and slow down MacArthur's offensive in New Guinea. The Japanese actually have little choice—it is either attack Aitape or die in the jungle.

FEAF A-20 Havocs, P-39 Airacobras, P-47 Thunderbolts, and Royal Australian Air Force (RAAF) aircraft bomb Wewak. B-24 Liberators, B-25 Mitchells, A-20 Havocs, P-40s, and P-47s attack airfields and fuel storage facilities on Noemfoor Island. B-24s bomb the airfield and town on Yap and communications on Sorol and Woleai Atolls.

June 29

CBI: Tenth Air Force sends 16 B-24 Liberators to fly gasoline to Kamaing and 45 B-25 Mitchells to fly ammunition resupply missions to Imphal, India. A-36 Intruder (Apache) fighter-bombers, P-51 Mustangs, and P-38 Lightnings attack Japanese positions at Myitkyina and the Myitnge bridge.

Fourteenth Air Force sends B-25 Mitchells, P-40s, and P-51 Mustangs against Japanese troops and logistics targets in the Tungting Lake area and at Hengyang. Three B-24 Liberators bomb Takao docks in Formosa. P-40s attack rail lines and bridges in French Indochina.

ATLANTIC: President Roosevelt informs Prime Minister Churchill that Anvil is vital to the success of the Normandy invasion. He reminds Churchill of the agreement at Tehran that France is to be the decisive theater in 1944. An advance north in Italy, as the prime minister proposes, followed by offensive operations into Yugoslavia and Hungary would be done in difficult terrain and with limited logistics support. Anvil's advance north in support of the Normandy forces would be slow, but not as slow as an advance through the Alps, which would contribute little or nothing to the Allied effort in France. For these reasons, Roosevelt stands by the decision that Anvil will go as planned. The president also makes it clear that no U.S. forces will be used in the Balkans and notes that there will be 21 divisions and 5,500 aircraft in the Mediterranean Theater available for offensive operations even after the Anvil forces have been removed. Roosevelt also reminds his fellow politician that the political costs of informing American voters that U.S. forces are being sent somewhere other than France would be catastrophic for him.

ETO: Eighth Air Force sends 179 B-17s to attack the synthetic oil production plant at Bohlen and an aircraft components production facility at Wittenberg. Four bombers are lost and 111 are damaged. Aircrew casualties are two killed, five wounded, and 30 missing. Another mission involves 380 B-17s that attack airfields around Leipzig. Two B-17s are lost and 77 are damaged. Aircrew casualties are two wounded and 21 missing. A separate mission sends 591 B-24 Liberators against airfields and marshaling yards. Nine B-24s are lost and 207 are damaged. Aircrew casualties are two killed, 12 wounded, and 92 missing. The missions are escorted by 203 P-38 Lightnings, 216 P-47 Thunderbolts, and 352 P-51 Mustangs of the Eighth and Ninth Air Forces. Fighter pilots report 34 confirmed kills in the air and 16 on the ground. Three P-51s are lost and the pilots are reported missing.

Ninth Air Force sends almost 200 B-26 Marauders and A-20 Havocs to bomb gun batteries, bridges, and rail lines in France. P-47 and P-38 fighters fly armed reconnaissance and attack enemy aircraft, road and rail junctions, bridges, artillery, and troop concentrations. The P-47s of the 509th and 511th Fighter Squadrons of the 405th Fighter Group redeploy from England to France.

German submarine *U-984* attacks a convoy headed for Omaha Beach, torpedoing and damaging three U.S. freighters.

ITALY: Twelfth Air Force B-25 Mitchells, B-26 Marauders, and A-20 Havocs attack rail and road traffic, ammunition storage sites, and bridges.

SOUTHWEST PACIFIC AREA: U.S. submarine *Bang* torpedoes and damages a Japanese fleet tanker and a merchant tanker west of Luzon.

U.S. submarine *Growler* torpedoes and sinks a Japanese transport in the Luzon Strait.

U.S. submarine *Flasher* attacks a Japanese convoy and sinks a cargo ship and damages an oiler southeast of Singapore.

PACIFIC: U.S. submarine *Sturgeon* attacks a Japanese convoy, sinking a cargo ship off Taira Jima.

CENTRAL PACIFIC: Seventh Air Force B-24 Liberators staging through Eniwetok bomb Truk. B-25 Mitchells from Makin Island bomb Ponape Island.

CENTRAL PACIFIC, SAIPAN: The 27th Infantry Division breaks Japanese resistance at Purple Heart Ridge and Death Valley. The 2nd Marine Division advances toward the town of Garapan. The 6th Marines captures Mount Tipo Pale. The 27th Infantry Division has suffered over 1,800 casualties since landing on Saipan. The 2nd Marine and 4th Marine Divisions have lost about 4,400 men each in 15 days of combat.

Seventh Air Force P-47 Thunderbolts from the airfield on Saipan carry out bombing and strafing missions and attack targets at Tinian.

NEW GUINEA: At Sarmi, the 158th RCT is designated as the Noemfoor Task Force. Elements of 6th Infantry Division reach Maffin airfield past Lone Tree Hill, even as the battle on Lone Tree Hill continues.

As the 34th Infantry attacks Japanese defenses north of the West Caves, Lieutenant General Eichelberger and the I Corps staff depart Biak for Hollandia. Biak, now securely in American hands, protects Hollandia and limits any Japanese movement from their base at Manokwari on the Vogelkop Peninsula in western New Guinea.

FEAF B-24 Liberators, A-20 Havocs, B-25 Mitchells, P-39 Airacobras, P-38 Lightnings, P-40s, and P-47 Thunderbolts attack Japanese positions near Aitape and on Noemfoor Island.

U.S. submarine *Darter* attacks a Japanese convoy off the northern tip of Halmahera Island and sinks a minelayer.

June 30

CBI: Air Transport Command is averaging 46,000 tons of supplies a month delivered to China over the Hump.

Tenth Air Force sends 17 B-24 Liberators to fly gasoline to Kamaing and 47 B-25 Mitchells to fly ammunition resupply missions to Imphal, India. P-38 Lightnings attack the Myitnge bridge.

In China, Fourteenth Air Force B-25 Mitchells P-47 Thunderbolts, and P-40s attack Japanese positions, troop concentrations, and road and river traffic near Tungting Lake.

A P-40 detachment of the 26th Fighter Squadron, 51st Fighter Group, operating from Kweilin returns to Kunming.

ATLANTIC: Guidance from the JCS to Admiral Nimitz maintains the intent for forces in the Pacific Ocean areas to invade Formosa (Operation Causeway), after General MacArthur's Southwest Pacific Area forces have gained control of the central and southern Philippines. The Pacific Ocean Area forces will follow the Formosa operations with operations against the Ryukyu and Bonin Islands in preparation for an assault on the Japanese home islands.

The U.S. Navy has 46,032 vessels of all types currently in active service. The navy has a current strength of 2,981,365. The Marine Corps stands at 472,582. The Coast Guard's personnel strength is 169,258.

ETO: Logisticians on the beachheads at Omaha and Utah achieve nearly impossible results during the last week of June, operating far above planning estimates. An average of 13,500 tons per day has moved across Omaha, and Utah has moved an average of 7,000 tons per day.

Eighth Air Force sends over 150 bombers escorted by more than 160 P-51 Mustangs to attack airfields in France. A total of 27 B-17s are damaged. P-38 Lightnings, P-47s, and P-51s attack bridges and marshaling yards in France. Fighter pilots report three confirmed kills and three probables in the air and one confirmed kill on the ground. One P-38 is lost and one P-47 is damaged. One pilot is reported missing; the other is reported killed.

Ninth Air Force sends over 100 A-20 and B-26 Marauders and more than 600 fighters against fuel storage areas and road junctions. The weather prevents most from making an effective attack. P-47s attack rail lines and marshaling yards.

The headquarters of the 405th Fighter Group and P-47s of the 510th Fighter Squadron redeploy from England to France.

MEDITERRANEAN: Fifteenth Air Force sends 188 B-17s and B-24 Liberators, escorted by 138 P-51 Mustangs and P-38 Lightnings, to bomb an airfield at Zagreb and at Banjaluka in Yugoslavia. The bombers also attack marshaling yards, bridges, and airfields around Budapest, Hungary.

During this month Fifteenth Air Force fighter pilots report a total of 299 confirmed kills, 30 probables, and 87 possibles in the air and 33 confirmed kills and 34 probables on the ground.

ITALY: The 1st Armored Division meets strong resistance on the Cecina River. The 135th and 133rd Infantry Regiments of the 34th Infantry Division in support of the tanks are unable to make a successful attack across the river.

Twelfth Air Force B-25 Mitchells attack the Pietrasanta railway bridge. A-20 Havocs, P-47 Thunderbolts, and P-40s attack convoys, bridges, rail lines, and roads.

SOUTHWEST PACIFIC AREA: SWPA headquarters orders Lieutenant General Krueger's Alamo Force to develop plans to seize, occupy, and defend Cape Sansapor to allow for the uninterrupted movement of Allied naval and air forces. The Vogelkop Peninsula in western New Guinea is the last Japanese stronghold on the island. Controlling Cape Sansapor would put U.S. forces between the Japanese bases of Sorong and Makwari. This achieves two objectives by isolating a large number of Japanese without having to fight them and allows SWPA forces to reach the Netherlands East Indies and the Philippines.

U.S. submarine *Jack* attacks a Japanese convoy west of Manila and sinks two cargo ships.

PACIFIC: U.S. submarine *Plaice* torpedoes and sinks a Japanese gunboat northwest of Chichi Jima.

U.S. submarine *Tang* torpedoes and sinks a Japanese cargo ship in the Yellow Sea off Korea.

CENTRAL PACIFIC, SAIPAN: The 2nd Battalion of the 165th Infantry Regiment captures the last Japanese position on Purple Heart Ridge.

NEW GUINEA: The airfield constructed on Owi Island off Biak is completed.

FEAF B-24 Liberators, A-20 Havocs, B-25 Mitchells, P-40s, and P-47 Thunderbolts attack Noemfoor Island airfields.

The A-20 Havocs of the 389th Bombardment Squadron (Light), 312th Bombardment Group (Light), redeploy from Nadzab to Hollandia.

July 1

ALEUTIANS: Eleventh Air Force sends four B-24 Liberators on a dawn raid on the Kurile Islands. The bombers use radar to bomb Shimushu Island and the Kurabu Cape airfield on Paramushiru Island, through heavy cloud cover.

CBI: General Marshall asks General Stilwell if anything can be done to improve the situation in China. Stilwell's reply is straightforward: He requests command of all Chinese forces. It will take the president to convince Chiang Kai-shek.

In Burma, Tenth Air Force P-40s fly ground support missions near Myitkyina.

In China, Fourteenth Air Force B-25 Mitchells, P-40s, and P-51 Mustangs attack river shipping at the Tungting Lake region. About 300 trucks are strafed and Heng-yang airfield is bombed.

The P-40s of the 76th Fighter Squadron, 23rd Fighter Group redeploy from Lingling to Liuchow.

The B-29 Superfortresses of Twentieth Air Force's 444th Bombardment Group (Very Heavy) and the 676th, 677th, 678th, and 679th Bombardment Squadrons (Very Heavy) redeploy from Charra to Dudhkundi, India.

ATLANTIC: Delegates from 44 countries begin meeting at Bretton Woods, New Hampshire, to deal with anticipated postwar economic disruptions. The International Monetary Fund and the International Bank for Reconstruction and Development (known today as the World Bank) will be established and ready to operate with $10 billion by December 1945. The agreement also provides for a gold exchange standard with only the United States required to convert its currency into gold at a fixed rate. Only central banks of other nations are allowed to redeem U.S. currency for gold.

ETO: The 9th Infantry Division of VII Corps clears final German resistance in the Cotentin Peninsula. U.S. forces have captured 39,000 prisoners. Only Brest remains in German hands. The Allies have landed one million men since D-day, along with 177,000 vehicles. The beachhead is about 70 miles long and 25 miles deep.

Eighth Air Force sends 245 B-24 Liberators and 78 B-17s to bomb V-weapon sites in France. Bad weather forces the recall of all but nine B-24 Liberators, which continue on to their targets. One bomber is lost and several are damaged. Aircrew casualties are one wounded and nine missing. Escorting the bombers are 124 P-51 Mustangs. Fighter pilots report five confirmed kills and one P-51 lost; the pilot is reported missing.

P-38 Lightnings, P-47 Thunderbolts, and P-51s attack rail and road targets in northern France. Pilots report three confirmed kills. One P-47 is lost and two are damaged. Two pilots are reported killed and two are missing.

A total of 18 B-24 Liberators fly in support of Carpetbagger operations over France.

Headquarters of XIX Tactical Air Command redeploys from England to France.

ITALY: In the IV Corps area, Cecina falls to the 34th Infantry Division. The Germans conduct a skilful delaying action, holding the line from Cecina to Ancona with counterattacks, then destroying the bridges as they retreat.

Twelfth Air Force B-25 Mitchells and B-26 Marauders attack docks, rail and road traffic, and bridges. A-20 Havocs, P-47 Thunderbolts, and P-40s attack gun positions, convoys, bridges, and roads.

PACIFIC: U.S. submarine *Tang* torpedoes and sinks a Japanese fleet tanker and a cargo ship off Korea.

Central Pacific: Seventh Air Force B-24 Liberators, staging through Eniwetok Atoll, bomb Truk during the night and follow up with another daylight raid. B-25 Mitchells from Makin Island bomb Ponape Island.

U.S. submarine *Batfish* torpedoes and sinks two Japanese guardboats northwest of the Marianas.

New Guinea: At Owi Island an epidemic of scrub typhus breaks out and spreads to Biak. Before it is stopped, over 1,000 Americans will be stricken and 12 will die of the disease.

FEAF B-24 Liberators, B-25 Mitchells, A-20 Havocs, P-39 Airacobras, P-40s, and P-38 Lightnings attack the airfield, antiaircraft positions, and defensive positions on Noemfoor Island, followed by an attack on the airfield at Manokwari.

B-24s bomb the airfield at Namlea and hit shipping throughout the Molucca Islands.

The C-47s of the 39th Troop Carrier Squadron, 317th Troop Carrier Group, redeploy from Finschhafen to Hollandia.

July 2

CBI: Tenth Air Force P-40s continue support of ground forces near Myitkyina.

In China, Fourteenth Air Force sends 11 B-25 Mitchells and P-40s, P-51 Mustangs, and P-47 Thunderbolts to attack river shipping, assembly areas, and logistics sites in the Tungting Lake region.

Japanese submarine *I-8* torpedoes and damages a U.S. freighter in the Maldives. The ship is abandoned and the submarine surfaces and bombards the ship until it is set afire. The submarine crew picks up survivors and questions them, killing one and beating a number of others. After destroying the lifeboats, the Japanese take three of the American crew below, then leave the rest of the captured Americans to drown. Some are able to return to the stricken freighter and obtain rafts.

Atlantic: The Combined Chiefs of Staff issues instructions for the Mediterranean theater commander in chief, General Sir Henry Maitland Wilson, to plan for Anvil, the invasion of southern France in support of Overlord. The execution date is August 15. Three divisions will land initially, with a buildup to a total of 10 divisions. French forces are to capture Toulon and Marseilles. After the cities are captured, Allied forces are to advance north up the Rhône Valley.

Navy TBM Avengers from escort carrier USS *Wake Island* sink German submarine *U-543* southeast of the Azores.

ETO: Eighth Air Force sends 78 B-17s and 272 B-24 Liberators, escorted by 171 P-51 Mustangs, to attack V-weapon sites in France. One B-24 is lost and 34 are damaged. Aircrew losses are four wounded, and nine missing.

In support of Frantic missions, 41 P-51 Mustangs in Italy while en route from the USSR to England join Fifteenth Air Force fighters in escorting Fifteenth bombers against targets in Budapest, Hungary. Fighter pilots report nine confirmed kills. Four fighters are lost and the pilots reported missing.

A total of 37 B-24s fly in support of Carpetbagger operations.

Mediterranean: Fifteenth Air Force sends over 600 B-17s and B-24 Liberators against oil refineries, rail bridges, airfields, and marshaling yards in Hungary and Yugoslavia.

P-38 Lightnings and P-51 Mustangs sweep over Budapest. Aircrews and fighter pilots report over 50 enemy fighters shot down. About 28 fighters and bombers are lost.

ITALY: Twelfth Air Force B-25 Mitchells and B-26 Marauders attack fuel storage areas, rail and road traffic, and bridges. A-20 Havocs, P-47 Thunderbolts, and P-40s attack bridges and roads.

CENTRAL PACIFIC, SAIPAN: The 2nd Marine Division captures Flame Tree Hill and attacks the town of Garapan.

Seventh Air Force P-47 Thunderbolts on Saipan conduct bombing and strafing attacks on Japanese positions on both Saipan and Tinian.

NEW GUINEA: At Aitape, the 124th Infantry Regiment of the 31st Infantry Division arrives to reinforce XI Corps. General Hall decides to divide his forces between Aitape airfield and the Driniumor River. Although the river appears to be an obstacle to an enemy advance, it is too shallow and too weakly defended to stop a strong attack.

Operation Tabletennis's (Noemfoor Island) Naval Task Force 77, commanded by Rear Admiral William M. Fechteler, lands the 158th Infantry Regiment. Task Force 74 under command of Commodore John A. Collins, Royal Australian Navy, and Task Force 75, commanded by Rear Admiral Russell S. Berkey, provide gunfire support with heavy cruisers, light cruisers, and destroyers. At Noemfoor Island, 33 B-24 Liberators, six B-25 Mitchells, and 15 A-20 Havocs provide air support for the landing. The 158th RCT lands without encountering any opposition near Kamiri airfield, a major objective. Navy demolition teams are forced to blast lanes in the coral reef to get follow-on supplies ashore. Major General Patrick has received information from a captured Japanese soldier that there are 3,000 to 5,000 troops defending the island. Patrick, expecting a tough fight after his experience at Lone Tree Hill, requests reinforcements from the 503rd Parachute Infantry.

Other FEAF B-25s attack barges near Manokwari.

July 3

CBI: Tenth Air Force A-36 Intruder (Apache) fighter-bombers support ground forces near Myitkyina.

In China, Fourteenth Air Force B-24 Liberators bomb Yoyang railroad yards in the Tungting Lake area. B-25 Mitchells drop ammunition to Chinese ground forces at Hengyang. In French Indochina, P-40s damage a bridge.

ITALY: The 135th and the 168th Infantry Regiments of the 34th Infantry Division and the 442nd RCT (a unit made up entirely of Japanese Americans) fight the enemy for control of Rosignato Marittimo and Castellino Marittimo.

ATLANTIC: Destroyer escorts *Frost* and *Inch* sink German submarine *U-154* off the Madeira Islands.

ETO: VII Corps (made up of the 4th, 83rd, 9th, and 30th Infantry Divisions) moves south to support First Army at Carentan. VIII Corps (79th and 90th Infantry Divisions and the 82nd Airborne Division) attacks toward La Haye du Puits, one of the strongest defensive positions in Normandy, with marshes and *bocage* protecting wooded hills that overlook the main roads into the town. The 90th Infantry Division advances toward Mont Castre, but gains only a mile. The 82nd Airborne is held up at La Poterie.

General Omar N. Bradley's 12th Army Group is organized and ready for further combat operations. Since June 6 (D+28), 1 million soldiers, 1 million tons of supplies, and 300,000 vehicles have landed at the Normandy beaches.

Eighth Air Force has 55 B-17s in Italy supporting Frantic operations, joining Fifteenth Air Force bombers in an attack on the marshaling yards at Arad, Romania. The B-17s are escorted by 38 P-51 Mustangs.

Ninth Air Force sends more than 250 P-47 Thunderbolts to attack strongpoints, gun positions, and a fuel storage area, as well as lines of communication in support of the First Army.

The Headquarters of the 358th Fighter Group and the 365th Fighter Squadron with P-47s redeploys from England to France. The P-51 Mustangs of the 382nd Fighter Squadron of the 363rd Fighter Group redeploy from England to France.

MEDITERRANEAN: Fifteenth Air Force sends over 600 B-17s and B-24 Liberators against oil storage facilities, an oil refinery, and a locomotive works at Bucharest, Romania, and transportation targets in Yugoslavia and an oil storage site at Belgrade.

ITALY: Twelfth Air Force B-26 Marauders and A-20 Havocs attack fuel storage sites, and B-25 Mitchells attack bridges, fuel storage tanks, tunnels, and viaducts. A-20 Havocs, P-47 Thunderbolts, and P-40s attack vehicles, ammunition storage areas, and bridges.

PACIFIC: U.S. submarine *Sturgeon* attacks a Japanese convoy, sinking a transport in the Ryukyu Islands. U.S. submarine *Tinosa* attacks a Japanese convoy in the East China Sea, sinking a cargo ship and tanker west of Kyushu, Japan.

CENTRAL PACIFIC: Seventh Air Force B-24 Liberators staging through Eniwetok bomb Truk.

U.S. submarine *Albacore* torpedoes and sinks a Japanese steamer west of Palau.

NEW GUINEA: At Noemfoor, a battalion of the 503rd Parachute Infantry Regiment jumps on the Kamiri airfield as the 158th Infantry extends its perimeter. The jump is poorly conducted and many paratroopers are injured. FEAF P-38 Lightnings and B-25 Mitchells attack Japanese positions and logistics sites near Kamiri and conduct ground support missions. FEAF B-24 Liberators, A-20 Havocs, P-39 Airacobras, P-38 Lightnings, P-40s, and P-47 Thunderbolts attack targets on Manokwari, Biak, and the area around Wewak. B-24s attack airfields, antiaircraft positions, and targets of opportunity on Yap, at Woleai Atoll, and at Peleliu Island.

The C-47s of the 70th Troop Carrier Squadron of the 433rd Troop Carrier Group redeploy from Nadzab to Hollandia.

July 4

CARIBBEAN: German submarine *U-539* torpedoes and damages a U.S. tanker near the Panama Canal Zone.

CBI: Tenth Air Force P-40s support ground forces near Myitkyina. P-47 Thunderbolts and P-51 Mustangs fly an offensive sweep over the Lashio area and patrol the Mogaung area.

In China, Fourteenth Air Force sends 38 B-25 Mitchells, P-40s, P-51 Mustangs, and P-38 Lightnings to attack roads, bridges, artillery, town areas, troop concentrations, and various targets of opportunity throughout the Tungting Lake-Yangtze River area. Hengyang airfield is bombed and supplies are dropped to Chinese troops in the area. Yellow River shipping and airfields and logistics sites and storage facilities in Canton are also attacked.

U.S. submarine *Seahorse* attacks a Japanese convoy in the South China Sea and sinks three cargo ships south of Hong Kong.

ATLANTIC: The Joint Chiefs of Staff presents an assessment of the China crisis to President Roosevelt. The report staunchly defends General Stilwell and questions General Chennault's belief that the Fourteenth Air Force can stem the Japanese offensive only if provided more supplies. The report notes that the diversion of thousands of tons of supplies to the Fourteenth Air Force has had no appreciable effect on the Japanese offensive but is having an effect on the support to Allied forces in the ETO. The JCS recommends a reorganization of the Chinese army and the placement of all forces in China under one commander—General Stilwell.

ETO: VII Corps attacks with two infantry regiments of the 83rd Infantry Division to capture Sainteny. The division is stopped by German positions in the hedgerows, minefields, and marshes, and takes heavy casualties.

Eighth Air Force sends 300 B-17s and 258 B-24 Liberators, escorted by 199 P-38 Lightnings, 189 P-47 Thunderbolts, and 244 P-51 Mustangs, to attack airfields in France. Bad weather over the targets forces most of the bombers to abort the mission. One B-17 is lost, 93 are damaged. Aircrew losses are three wounded, and nine missing. Fighter pilots attack marshaling yards and bridges and report 17 confirmed kills in the air and one on the ground. One P-38 is lost and one is damaged. The pilot is reported missing.

A total of 36 B-24s fly in support of Carpetbagger operations.

Ninth Air Force sends 95 A-20 and B-26 Marauders to bomb a rail bridge and German strongpoints. Over 900 P-47s attack troop concentrations, gun positions, rail lines, marshaling yards, bridges, highways, and a unit headquarters.

The P-47s of the 366th and 367th Fighter Squadrons of the 358th Fighter Group and the 494th Fighter Squadron, 48th Fighter Group, redeploy to France. The P-51s of the 381st Fighter Squadron of the 363rd Fighter Group also arrive in France.

MEDITERRANEAN: The headquarters of Seventh Army moves to Naples, Italy, and continues planning for Anvil. Seventh Army is composed of VI Corps commanded by Major General Lucian K. Truscott, and three divisions, the 3rd Infantry Division, commanded by Major General John W "Iron Mike" O'Daniel, the 36th Infantry Division, commanded by Major General John E. Dahlquist, and the 45th Infantry Division, commanded by Major General William W. Eagles. An airborne task force and two French corps under the command of General Jean de Lattre de Tassigny will be added to the invasion force.

Fifteenth Air Force sends over 250 B-17s and B-24 Liberators against an oil refinery, bridges, and railroad repair works in Romania. P-51 Mustangs and P-38 Lightnings escort the bombers and the pilots report 17 confirmed enemy aircraft kills.

ITALY: Combat Command A of the 1st Armored Division and the 361st Infantry Regiment break enemy defenses near Cecina. The 1st Armored Division is relieved on the line by the 88th Infantry Division.

Twelfth Air Force A-20 Havocs attack ammunition storage facilities and P-40s and P-47 Thunderbolts attack bridges, rail lines, roads, and guns.

PACIFIC: U.S. submarine *Tang* torpedoes and sinks two Japanese cargo ships in the Yellow Sea off the west coast of Korea.

U.S. submarine *S-28* is lost during training exercises off Oahu, Hawaii. No cause is determined.

CENTRAL PACIFIC: B-24 Liberators, staging through Eniwetok Atoll, bomb Truk.

Carrier aircraft and surface ships under Rear Admiral Joseph J. Clark and Rear Admiral Ralph E. Davison attack Japanese installations on Iwo Jima, Chichi Jima, and Haha Jima.

A submarine chaser, landing ships, and a number of other auxiliary vessels are sunk or damaged in the area.

Destroyer *David W. Taylor* and destroyer escort *Riddle* sink Japanese submarine *I-10* northeast of Saipan.

U.S. submarine *Guavina* torpedoes and sinks a Japanese transport near Palau.

NEW GUINEA: At Noemfoor, the 503rd Parachute Infantry Regiment drops another battalion on the Kamiri airfield. This jump is also poorly conducted. In two days the regiment has suffered 126 jump injuries—before encountering the enemy. Kornasoren airfield is captured.

FEAF A-20 Havocs fly ground support missions near Kamiri airfield. P-47 Thunderbolts strafe targets of opportunity on Biak Island.

B-24 Liberators bomb Yap, Woleai, and Sorol Atolls, and Peleliu Island.

The A-20 Havocs of the 388th Bombardment Squadron (Light), 312th Bombardment Group (Light), redeploy from Nadzab to Hollandia.

July 5

CBI: Tenth Air Force P-40s and A-36 Intruder (Apache) fighter-bombers attack targets around Myitkyina.

Fourteenth Air Force B-25 Mitchells with eight P-40s escorting the bombers attack Japanese forces north of Hengyang. Twelve Japanese aircraft intercept the formation; in the fight, three enemy aircraft are shot down and three are damaged. One P-40 is shot down and two are damaged. The downed pilot is captured and one pilot is wounded. P-51s and P-40s and B-25 Mitchells attack logistics sites, gun batteries, bridges, vehicles, ammunition dumps, town areas, and troops throughout the Tungting Lake area.

ATLANTIC: Destroyer escorts *Thomas* and *Baker* sink German minelayer submarine *U-233* off Halifax, Nova Scotia.

ETO: The 313th Infantry Regiment of the 79th Infantry Division, VIII Corps, cuts through *bocage* to attack the left flank of the German position at La Haye du Puits and gain a small foothold on Montgardon Ridge, the key to the German defensive line.

The headquarters element of Lieutenant General George S. Patton, Jr.'s Third Army lands in France to prepare to take command of the right flank of the American line.

Eighth Air Force sends 79 B-17s to attack airfields in the Netherlands and 221 B-24 Liberators against V-weapon sites in France, escorted by P-51 Mustangs. A total of 49 B-24s are damaged. Aircrew losses are one wounded. Fighter pilots report four confirmed kills in the air and one on the ground. Two fighters are lost and the pilots are reported missing. Another 70 B-17s attack the marshaling yard at Béziers escorted by 228 P-47 Thunderbolts and P-51s. Fighter pilots report 18 confirmed kills and one probable in the air and one confirmed kill on the ground. Three fighters are lost and the pilots are reported missing. A raid by 93 P-47s escorted by P-38 Lightnings on bridges and transportation targets in France results in pilots reporting three confirmed kills in the air and one on the ground. Two P-47s and two P-38s are lost. One P-38 is damaged.

A total of eight B-24s fly in support of Carpetbagger operations. During the night eight B-17s drop leaflets over France. One bomber is lost.

Eighth Air Force B-17s, as part of the Frantic operation, bomb a marshaling yard at Béziers, France with Fifteenth Air Force B-24 Liberators while en route to Britain from Italy. P-51 Mustangs escorting the bombers also return to Britain.

The P-51s of the 380th Fighter Squadron, 363rd Fighter Group, move from England to France.

Ninth Air Force sends 180 A-20 and B-26 Marauders and over 600 fighters against transportation targets along the battlefront.

German submarine *U-390* torpedoes and damages a U.S. freighter en route from Utah Beach to Southampton, England. It will be repaired and returned to service.

MEDITERRANEAN: Fifteenth Air Force sends nearly 500 B-17s and B-24 Liberators against the Montpellier and Béziers marshaling yards and the submarine pens and harbor installations at Toulon.

ITALY: Allied Forces Headquarters Mediterranean instructs General Sir Harold R. L. G. Alexander, Allied ground force commander, to give all priority to the preparations for Anvil, the invasion of the southern coast of France.

Twelfth Air Force B-25 Mitchells bomb marshaling yards, a railroad bridge, and fuel supply depots. A-20 Havocs attack logistics storage areas and rail lines. P-47 Thunderbolts and P-40s attack bridges and roads.

Twelfth Air Force B-17s and B-24 Liberators bomb marshaling yards, submarine pens, and harbor installations at Toulon. German submarines *U-586* and *U-642* are sunk in Toulon harbor.

PACIFIC: U.S. submarine *Plaice* sinks Japanese auxiliary netlayer in the Bonin Islands.

U.S. submarine *Sunfish* torpedoes and sinks a Japanese cargo ship off Paramushiru in the Kuriles.

NEW GUINEA: At Noemfoor, a Japanese counterattack against Kamiri airfield is driven back.

FEAF P-38 Lightnings, P-40s, and P-47 Thunderbolts fly ground support missions on Noemfoor Island and attack barges, airfields, and troop concentrations on Biak Island and at Moemi, Manokwari, and in the Wakde area. B-24 Liberators bomb airstrips and antiaircraft guns on Yap Island, Woleai and Sorol Atolls, and Peleliu Island.

Fifth Air Force B-24 Liberators sink a Japanese cargo vessel off western New Guinea.

July 6

CARIBBEAN: German submarine *U-516* torpedoes and sinks a U.S. tanker in the Caribbean north of Venezuela.

CBI: President Roosevelt contacts Generalissimo Chiang, proposing that Stilwell be promoted to full general and given command of all Chinese forces. "I feel that the case of China is so desperate that if radical and properly applied remedies are not immediately effected, our common cause will suffer a disastrous setback." Chiang Kai-shek makes a surprisingly positive response, but ultimately takes no action.

Tenth Air Force sends 12 P-40s to attack a bridge near Myitkyina.

In China, Fourteenth Air Force B-25 Mitchells, P-40s, and P-51 Mustangs attack river shipping, bridges, troop concentrations, and road traffic around Tungting Lake and the Yangtze River. B-25s airdrop supplies to Chinese ground forces on the Salween River front. During the night the bombers attack Tien Ho airfield at Canton.

Brigadier General LaVern G. Saunders becomes the commander of XX Bomber Command, Twentieth Air Force, with headquarters at Kharagpur, India.

CENTRAL PACIFIC: U.S. submarine *Sealion* attacks a Japanese convoy in the East China Sea and sinks a cargo ship off Ningpo, China.

B-24 Liberators staging through Eniwetok Atoll conduct a night raid on Truk and conduct a follow-on attack during the day. B-25 Mitchells from Makin Island bomb Nauru Island.

ETO: The 90th Infantry Division of VIII Corps captures Monte Castre, the main defensive position protecting the right flank of the German defenses at La Haye du Puits.

Major General Collins, the VII Corps commander, employs the 4th Infantry Division to support the 83rd Infantry Division's attempt to capture Sainteny. Entire infantry companies have to be committed to capture just one section of the *bocage*, expertly defended by German infantrymen and tanks.

Eighth Air Force sends 641 B-17s and 159 B-24 Liberators, escorted by 141 P-38 Lightnings and 83 P-51 Mustangs, to attack V-weapon sites in France. One B-17 is damaged. Aircrew losses are two killed and three wounded. Fighter pilots report four confirmed kills. One P-38 is lost. The pilot is reported missing. Another 262 B-24s bomb the dock area at Kiel, Germany, escorted by P-51 Mustangs. Three bombers are lost and 106 damaged. Aircrew losses are eight wounded and 22 missing. One P-51 is lost and the pilot is reported missing. In the late afternoon 73 B-17s and 148 B-24s attack six V-weapon sites, bridges, and an airfield in northern France, escorted by 443 P-38s, P-47s, and P-51s. One P-47 is lost. Over Paris, 212 P-38s and P-47s fly fighter-bomber missions against rail and road targets. Pilots report 11 confirmed kills and one probable. Two P-47s are lost and the pilots are reported missing.

A total of 20 B-24s fly in support of Carpetbagger operations. One bomber is lost.

During the night seven B-17s drop leaflets over Belgium and France.

Ninth Air Force sends 500 A-20 and B-26 Marauders and about 600 fighters against bridges, fuel depots, rail lines, and a V-weapon location in France. The fighters attack rail facilities, roads, troop concentrations, and artillery positions.

The headquarters of the 404th Fighter Group and the P-47s of the 506th, 507th, and 508th Fighter Squadrons redeploy from England to France. The P-47s of the 388th Fighter Squadron, 365th Fighter Group, also redeploy to France.

ITALY: Fifteenth Air Force sends over 500 B-17s and B-24 Liberators, escorted by P-51 Mustangs and P-38 Lightnings, against marshaling yards, railroad bridges, an oil refinery, and fuel storage areas.

Twelfth Air Force A-20 Havocs attack an ammunition ship at La Spezia and also attack fuel storage depots. A-20 Havocs, P-47 Thunderbolts, and P-40s attack rail lines and bridges.

PACIFIC: U.S. submarine *Cobia* torpedoes and sinks a Japanese guardboat east of the Bonin Islands.

U.S. submarine *Tang* torpedoes and sinks a Japanese cargo ship in Chosin Bay, Korea.

CENTRAL PACIFIC: Admiral Nimitz proposes to support General MacArthur's attack on the Philippines by attacking the Palaus, specifically Peleliu, Angaur, Yap, and Ulithi, to establish naval and air bases to support MacArthur's invasion.

Seventh Air Force P-47 Thunderbolts based on Saipan bomb and strafe Japanese positions on Saipan and Tinian.

Carrier aircraft bomb coastal defenses, antiaircraft guns, logistics storage sites, and airfields on Guam and Rota.

NEW GUINEA: At Sarmi, the 63rd Infantry Regiment of the 6th Infantry Division holds Hill 225 and Mount Saksin at Lone Tree Hill. Hill 265 is still in Japanese hands.

At Noemfoor, the 2nd Battalion 158th RCT conducts an amphibious landing at Romboi Bay to capture Namber airfield.

FEAF B-25 Mitchells, A-20 Havocs, P-39 Airacobras, P-38 Lightnings, P-40s, and P-47 Thunderbolts attack targets in the Wewak area. B-25s, P-39s, P-38s, P-40s, and P-47s attack along the coast of the Vogelkop Peninsula; the P-38s, P-40s, and P-47s attack targets in the Manokwari area. B-24 Liberators bomb the town and logistics storage areas on Yap and the airfield at Woleai Atoll.

U.S. submarine *Paddle* attacks a Japanese convoy and sinks a destroyer northwest of Halmahera.

July 7

CBI: In China, Fourteenth Air Force B-25 Mitchells and P-51 Mustangs and P-47 Thunderbolts attack bridges, river shipping, troop areas, gun emplacements, and ammunition storage sites in the Tungting Lake area. B-25s and P-51 Mustangs bomb Tien Ho and White Cloud airfields.

During the night Twentieth Air Force sends 14 B-29 Superfortresses from bases at Chengtu, China, to bomb Sasebo, Omura, and Tobata in Japan. Sasebo takes the heaviest hit, while three bombers attack secondary and last resort targets at Laoyao and around Hankow in China.

U.S. submarine *Flasher* torpedoes and sinks a transport off the coast of French Indochina.

ETO: The XIX Corps (the 35th and 29th Infantry Divisions) attacks across the Vire River. The 313th Infantry Regiment of the 79th Infantry Division, VIII Corps, captures Montgardon Ridge at La Haye du Puits and defends it against German tank and infantry counterattacks. The division has suffered 2,000 casualties in five days of combat.

The XIX Corps (30th Infantry Division and 29th Infantry Division) crosses the Vire River north of St-Lô. General Bradley adds the 3rd Armored Division to XIX Corps to use its tanks to exploit a possible breakthrough. The 3rd Armored Division passes one combat command through the bridgehead heading for St-Lô, but the result is chaos as the tanks of the 3rd Armored and the infantry of the 30th Infantry Division are hopelessly entangled. Meanwhile, the Germans reinforce St-Lô.

German tanks and vehicles were vulnerable to air attack by the Ninth Air Force throughout July and August of 1944. This group of vehicles was hit near Mortain, France.

Eighth Air Force sends 303 B-17s and 373 B-24 Liberators, escorted by 409 P-38 Lightnings, P-47 Thunderbolts, and P-51 Mustangs, to attack oil production facilities and refineries, aircraft production facilities, a marshaling yard, and airfields in Germany. Aircrews report 39 confirmed kills and five probables. Thirty bombers are lost and 239 are damaged. Aircrew losses are three killed, 17 wounded, and 294 missing. Fighter pilots report 55 confirmed kills in the air and three on the ground and one probable in the air. Six fighters are lost. The pilots are reported missing.

In another attack, 453 B-17s, escorted by 247 P-47s and P-51s, bomb oil production facilities, airfields, and ball bearing plants in Germany. Seven B-17s are lost and 154 are damaged. Aircrew casualties are 15 killed, five wounded, and 50 missing. Fighter pilots report 20 confirmed kills in the air and one on the ground. One P-51 is damaged and the pilot is wounded.

A total of 21 B-24s fly in support of Carpetbagger operations. During the night six B-17s drop leaflets over France and Belgium.

Ninth Air Force sends over 100 A-20 and B-26 Marauders and more than 500 fighters against bridges, railroads, gun emplacements, marshaling yards, ammunition storage sites, rail and road traffic, and also to conduct ground support missions in France.

The headquarters of the 36th Fighter Group redeploys from England to France. The P-47s of the 362nd Fighter Group (377th, 378th, 379th Fighter Squadrons) redeploy to France.

MEDITERRANEAN: Fifteenth Air Force sends over 500 B-17s and B-24 Liberators to attack synthetic oil plants in Germany and an airfield and marshaling yard in Zagreb, Yugoslavia.

Twelfth Air Force A-20 Havocs bomb La Spezia harbor, motor transport, and fuel storage areas. B-26 Marauders and B-25 Mitchells bomb railway bridges. A-20 Havocs, A-36 Intruder (Apache) fighter-bombers, P-51 Mustangs, and P-40s attack rail lines, bridges, ammunition storage areas, and roads.

ITALY: Twelfth Air Force's XII Tactical Air Command with fighters and fighter-bombers redeploys to Corsica to support Anvil/Dragoon.

SOUTHWEST PACIFIC AREA: U.S. submarine *Mingo* torpedoes and sinks a Japanese destroyer west of Mindoro Island.

PACIFIC: Admiral Nimitz redraws plans for the attack on the Palaus, changing the name of the operation from Stalemate to Stalemate II. The target date for the invasion is reset for September 15. Because the battles at Guam and Saipan have involved army and marine forces for far longer than originally planned, the III Amphibious Corps (1st Marine Division and 81st Infantry Division) are tasked with capturing Peleliu and Angaur. To prevent any Japanese interference with the Palau operation, Iwo Jima, Chichi Jima, and Yap are to be attacked to eliminate Japanese air forces.

U.S. submarine *Skate* attacks a Japanese convoy in the south of the Sea of Okhotsk, sinking a destroyer and damaging a cargo ship.

U.S. submarine *Sunfish* attacks a group of Japanese fishing boats in the Kuriles, sinking four of them.

CENTRAL PACIFIC, SAIPAN: The Japanese make a suicide attack against the 105th Infantry Regiment and break through its defenses, charging through an unnoticed gap between the two forward battalions. The 3rd Battalion, 10th Marine artillery fires its guns point-blank against the waves of attackers. Over 900 soldiers and marines are killed. The Japanese suffer 4,300 casualties. The 106th Infantry Regiment conducts a counterattack.

Seventh Air Force P-47 Thunderbolts on Saipan bomb and strafe Japanese positions on Saipan and Tinian. P-61 Black Widow night fighters carry out interceptor missions over Guam and Saipan.

Between late June and early July, Lieutenant Colonel William J. O'Brien, commander of the 1st Battalion, 105th Infantry Regiment, 27th Infantry Division, leads his unit through some of the most difficult terrain yet encountered in the Pacific, at Saipan. When Japanese fire stops the forward elements of the battalion, Lieutenant Colonel O'Brien mounts a tank and, fully exposed to enemy fire, directs the attack. He later leads a small detachment to maneuver around an enemy position to clear the area and regain the momentum of the attack, capturing machine guns and an artillery piece. On the seventh of July, O'Brien's battalion is one of the targets of the Japanese night counterattack. Faced with thousands of enemy soldiers overrunning his unit, Lieutenant Colonel O'Brien leads his men, carrying two .45-caliber automatic pistols and firing at the enemy. Seriously wounded and out of ammunition, O'Brien takes over a .50-caliber machine gun mounted on a jeep and continues to fight. He dies surrounded by Japanese bodies. For his unsurpassed courage under fire, his dramatic leadership, and his unconquerable spirit, Lieutenant Colonel O'Brien will be awarded the Congressional Medal of Honor.

During the Japanese night assault, Private First Class Harold C. Agerholm of the 4th Battalion, 10th Marines, 2nd Marine Division, volunteers to assist in evacuating the wounded. He drives a litter Jeep back and forth along the American lines in the midst of desperate fighting and personally brings in 45 wounded. He is killed by enemy fire as he attempts to rescue two wounded marines. For his unselfish acts of courage and dedication to duty, Private First Class Agerholm will receive the Medal of Honor.

NEW GUINEA: Hill 265, the last remaining Japanese stronghold on Lone Tree Hill, is attacked in a simultaneous assault from the 63rd and 1st RCTs, which assault the enemy with tanks, flamethrowers, artillery fire, and bazookas. It will take five days to complete the task.

FEAF A-20 Havocs, P-39 Airacobras, P-47 Thunderbolts, and Royal Australian Air Force (RAAF) aircraft bomb Wewak. B-24 Liberators bomb Yap Island, the Sorol Atoll radio station, and the airfield on Woleai Atoll.

U.S. submarine *Bonefish* torpedoes and sinks a Japanese guardboat off Borneo.

July 8

CBI: The Chinese Y Force surrounds Tengchung with eight divisions.

Tenth Air Force sends 12 B-25 Mitchells, A-36 Intruder (Apache) fighter-bombers, and P-40s to attack targets and a bridge at Myitkyina and fly ground support missions.

In China, Fourteenth Air Force sends B-25 Mitchells, P-40s, P-38 Lightnings, and P-47s against river shipping, trucks, bridges, logistics storage areas, troop concentrations, and command posts around Tungting Lake. Twenty Japanese aircraft bomb Kanchou and Suichwan airfields. At Suichwan they cause enough damage to make the airfield unusable for a few days. In French Indochina 10 P-40s attack coastal shipping and five B-25s destroy two bridges at Cam Lo.

ETO: The 82nd Airborne Division is relieved by the 8th Infantry Division in VIII Corps. The 82nd will return to England as a strategic reserve and prepare for another possible airborne landing.

Although over 1,000 bombers are sent against bridges, tunnels, rail lines, and V-weapon sites in France, bad weather allows only about 460 to hit their primary targets.

The bombers are escorted by 266 P-38 Lightnings and P-51 Mustangs and 36 P-47 Thunderbolts. Four bombers are lost and 92 are damaged. Aircrew losses are two killed, seven wounded, and 32 missing. Fighter pilots report 20 confirmed kills on the ground. One fighter is lost and the pilot is reported missing.

In another mission, 264 B-17s and 130 B-24 Liberators, escorted by 286 P-38s, P-47s, and P-51s, attack airfields and rail lines. Eight bombers are lost and 130 are damaged. Aircrew losses are four killed, 16 wounded, and 51 missing.

A total of 17 B-24s fly in support of Carpetbagger operations. During the night four B-17s drop leaflets over France.

Ninth Air Force sends nearly 300 A-20 and B-26 Marauders to bomb V-weapon sites, strongpoints, railroad bridges, ammunition storage areas, and troop assembly areas in France.

MEDITERRANEAN: Fifteenth Air Force sends over 500 bombers to attack oil refineries, oil storage areas, airfields, and a marshaling yard near Vienna, Austria. More than 100 German fighters attack the formations. Aircrews and fighter pilots report 50 confirmed kills. A total of 14 fighters and bombers are lost over the target.

ITALY: Volterra falls to the 350th Infantry Regiment of the 88th Infantry Division, opening a gap in the German lines and forcing a withdrawal. Major General Paul W. Kendall takes command of the division from Major General John E. Sloan.

Twelfth Air Force B-25 Mitchells and B-26 Marauders attack marshaling yards and rail lines. A-20 Havocs attack fuel storage areas. P-47 Thunderbolts and P-40s attack rail lines, bridges, and roads.

SOUTHWEST PACIFIC AREA: General MacArthur's headquarters submits the Reno V plan, outlining a series of offensive actions from the Vogelkop Peninsula and Morotai in western New Guinea to southern Mindanao in the Philippines for late October, an attack on Leyte in mid-November, and an attack on Luzon in April of 1945. To accomplish his plan, he requires six divisions, including one airborne and one armored division.

PACIFIC: U.S. submarine *Tautog* torpedoes and sinks a Japanese cargo ship off Honshu, Japan.

CENTRAL PACIFIC: During the night Seventh Air Force B-24 Liberators staging through Eniwetok Atoll bomb Truk and conduct a follow-on raid during the day.

Naval Task Group 53.18 under Rear Admiral C. Turner Joy bombards defenses on Guam.

Aircraft sink seven Japanese guardboats off Saipan.

CENTRAL PACIFIC, SAIPAN: The 6th Marines, supported by tanks from Company B, 2nd Tank Battalion, restore the shattered defensive line. Americans witness mass suicides as Japanese civilians jump from cliffs rather than accept defeat. Japanese soldiers commit suicide in large numbers as marines move to occupy Mount Marpi, the last significant defended terrain on the island.

Seventh Air Force P-47 Thunderbolts fly fighter-bomber missions against Japanese defensive positions on Saipan and Tinian.

Sergeant Grant F. Timmerman is a tank commander serving with the 2nd Battalion, 6th Marines. As his tank leads an infantry advance, Sergeant Timmerman maintains a steady fire from the turret-mounted machine gun. Encountering trenches and pillboxes Timmerman begins to fire on the enemy when a grenade lands on top of the turret. To keep it from falling into the open hatch where he stands, Timmerman shouts a warning and covers the grenade with his body. His exceptional valor and dedication to his crew in saving them at the cost of his own life will win him the Medal of Honor.

NEW GUINEA: FEAF B-24 Liberators, A-20 Havocs, P-39 Airacobras, P-47 Thunderbolts, and Royal Australian Air Force (RAAF) aircraft bomb Wewak.

July 9

CBI: Tenth Air Force A-36 Intruder (Apache) fighter-bombers, P-51 Mustangs, P-47 Thunderbolts, and P-40s attack a bridge near the Myitkyina area and strafe Japanese gun positions at Shwebo and targets along the Irrawaddy River.

Fourteenth Air Force B-25 Mitchells bomb a power plant and buildings at Tinh Soc in French Indochina.

ETO: Eighth Air Force sends 150 B-17s escorted by 155 P-47 Thunderbolts and P-51 Mustangs to bomb bridges and airfields in France. Heavy clouds force most to bomb secondary targets. One B-17 is lost and 10 are damaged. Aircrew casualties are nine missing. One P-47 and one P-51 are lost; one pilot is reported missing.

Another mission involves 104 B-24 Liberators and 77 B-17s escorted by 158 P-47s and P-51s attacking V-weapon sites in France. Bad weather conditions limit the bombers and secondary targets are hit. One B-24 is lost and 60 are damaged. Two crewmen are wounded. Fighter pilots report five confirmed kills.

A total of 37 B-24s fly in support of Carpetbagger operations. During the night five B-17s drop leaflets over France.

Ninth Air Force sends over 250 A-20 and B-26 Marauders along with fighters to bomb and strafe rail lines, gun batteries, bridges, fortifications, tanks, ammunition dumps, town areas, and strongpoints in the battle area.

MEDITERRANEAN: Fifteenth Air Force conducts its first Pathfinder-led mission. A total of 222 B-17s and B-24 Liberators, escorted by P-38 Lightnings and P-51 Mustangs, attack oil refineries at Ploeşti, Romania. Aircrews and pilots report 14 confirmed kills. Six fighters and bombers are lost.

First Lieutenant Donald D. Pucket of the 98th Bombardment Group is flying a B-24 Liberator over Ploeşti and has just dropped his bomb load when the aircraft is hit and seriously damaged by antiaircraft fire. With one crewman killed and six others badly wounded, First Lieutenant Pucket turns the controls over to the copilot and begins taking several steps to save the bomber and take care of the wounded. As the crippled bomber continues to lose altitude, First Lieutenant Pucket orders everyone to bail out. Three crewmen refuse to leave the bomber and Pucket decides to stay with the aircraft. As he fights to maintain altitude, the bomber crashes into a mountainside. For his courage, leadership, and dedication to his crew, First Lieutenant Pucket will receive the Medal of Honor.

ITALY: Twelfth Air Force A-20 Havocs attack rail lines and gun positions. P-40s and P-47 Thunderbolts attack rail lines and bridges.

SOUTHWEST PACIFIC AREA: U.S. submarine *Dace* attacks a Japanese cargo vessel in the Celebes Sea but fails to do any damage.

U.S. submarine *Nautilus* lands men and supplies on Pandan Island off the west coast of Mindoro Island.

PACIFIC: U.S. submarine *Sunfish* attacks a Japanese convoy in the Kuriles, sinking a cargo ship.

U.S. submarine *Tautog* torpedoes and sinks a Japanese fishing boat off Hokkaido, Japan.

CENTRAL PACIFIC: B-25 Mitchells from Makin Island bomb Jaluit Atoll.

CENTRAL PACIFIC, SAIPAN: Lieutenant General Holland M. Smith declares Saipan secured, calling it "the decisive battle of the Pacific offensive." Saipan will become an advance base for air attacks on the Japanese home islands. The Americans estimate that 23,811 Japanese soldiers have died on the island and 736 prisoners have been captured. U.S. losses are heavy: 3,225 killed, 13,061 wounded, 326 missing. Army losses are 3,674; marine losses are 10,437.

Just south of Saipan is the island of Tinian. Reconnaissance of beaches for potential landings begins.

Seventh Air Force P-47 Thunderbolts from Saipan attack Japanese forces on Saipan and Tinian. Saipan will become a B-29 Superfortress base for strategic attacks on the Japanese home islands.

New Guinea: FEAF A-20 Havocs and P-47 Thunderbolts attack targets both at Biak and along the coast of Geelvink Bay. B-25 Mitchells, P-39 Airacobras, P-38 Lightnings, and P-40s sink a cargo ship and several barges around Halmahera Island. B-24 Liberators bomb Namlea Airfield and attack Yap and Woleai Atolls.

Fifth Air Force B-25 Mitchells sink Japanese cargo ship near Halmahera Island.

July 10

CBI: Tenth Air Force P-40s and P-51 Mustangs support ground forces at Myitkyina. A-36 Intruder (Apache) fighter-bombers, P-51 Mustangs, P-47 Thunderbolts, and P-40s attack Mogaung.

ETO: First Army staff develops the concept for Operation Cobra, intended to use VII Corps to penetrate German defensive lines west of St-Lô, then exploit the gap with armored and motorized units to reach Coutances.

Six B-17s drop leaflets over France and the Netherlands during the night. A total of 12 B-24 Liberators fly Carpetbagger missions during the night.

Ninth Air Force P-47 Thunderbolts and P-38 Lightnings bomb and strafe gun positions, bridges, troop concentrations, and roads in France. The headquarters of the 71st Fighter Wing redeploys from England to France.

Rear Admiral John Wilkes takes command of U.S. Ports and Bases Command, France, with headquarters at Cherbourg, France.

Italy: Twelfth Air Force B-25 Mitchells and B-26 Marauders attack marshaling yards, railroad bridges, and viaducts. A-20 Havocs, P-47 Thunderbolts, and P-40s attack airfields, rail lines, and roads.

Southwest Pacific Area: USS *Thresher,* part of a U.S. submarine attack group (TG 17.16, commanded by Captain William V. O'Regan), in the South China Sea near Formosa locates and tracks a seven-ship convoy headed for the Philippines.

Pacific: U.S. submarine *Tinosa* torpedoes and sinks a Japanese merchant fishing boat in the East China Sea west of Kyushu.

U.S. submarine *Sealion* torpedoes and sinks two cargo ships in the Yellow Sea off the west coast of Korea.

Central Pacific: Seventh Air Force P-47 Thunderbolts attack Japanese gun positions on Tinian Island. During the night B-24 Liberators stage through Eniwetok Atoll, bomb Truk, and conduct another raid during the day.

New Guinea: Major General Hall orders a battalion of the 128th Infantry and a squadron of the 112th Cavalry to conduct a reconnaissance across the Driniumor River to locate Japanese forces. At the same time over 10,000 Japanese attack XI Corps positions at the river where only an infantry battalion and a cavalry squadron remain to defend the line. The enemy breaks through, isolating the reconnaissance force and other units of the 128th Infantry. Heavy artillery fire slows the Japanese attack.

Lieutenant General Krueger designates 6th Infantry Division as the Sansapor Task Force. Major General Franklin C. Sibert will command 20,500 men in this operation. The 20th RCT of the 6th Infantry Division will serve as the task force reserve at Wakde. D-day is set for July 30. Task Force 77, under Rear Admiral William M. Fechteler, will consist of 24 LSTs, 15 LCIs, five APDs, and 19 destroyers. Task

Force 78, under Rear Admiral Robert S. Berkey, will consist of one heavy cruiser, two light cruisers, and nine destroyers.

July 11

CBI: Tenth Air Force A-36 Intruder (Apache) fighter-bombers, P-51 Mustangs, P-47 Thunderbolts, and P-40s attack a barracks at Myitkyina, bridges at Namkwin and Mohnyin, and the airfield at Lashio.

In China, Fourteenth Air Force sends 28 B-24 Liberators to bomb a logistics storage base at Sinshih. P-40s attack river traffic and the town at Hengyang. B-25 Mitchells bomb the railyards at Sinyang. P-40s and P-47 Thunderbolts support Chinese ground forces between Tengchung and Lungling.

The P-47s of the 93rd Fighter Squadron 81st Fighter Group redeploy from Karachi, India, to Kwanghan.

ETO: A German tank counterattack is stopped by the 9th and 30th Infantry Divisions. The V Corps and the XIX Corps of Bradley's First Army move to capture the town of St-Lô, the key crossroads that leads to the open high ground suitable for large maneuvering forces. St-Lô's formidable defensive terrain is anchored on Hill 192 and Hill 122 and defended by some of the finest quality soldiers in the German Wehrmacht who have made the *bocage* and stone farmhouses into fortresses. Near St-Lô, the 2nd Infantry Division attacks Hill 192 as the 29th Infantry Division fights Germans in the hedgerow defenses and strongpoints. The 38th and 23rd Infantry Regiments of the 2nd Infantry Division attack in a low fog behind an artillery bombardment employing 20,000 artillery rounds with four tank companies. Hill 192 is captured at low cost and secures the flank for the attack of XIX Corps. The 116th and 115th Infantry Regiments of the 29th Infantry Division reach Martinville Ridge and attempt to advance to Hill 122, but are held up by German fire from Hill 122. The 35th Infantry Division of XIX Corps is stopped in the *bocage* after advancing only a mile-and-a-half.

Eighth Air Force sends over 700 B-17s against a marshaling yard and production facilities in Munich, Germany. Over 300 P-38 Lightnings, P-47 Thunderbolts, and P-51s escort the bombers. Four bombers are lost and 133 are damaged. Aircrew casualties are four killed, five wounded, and 40 missing.

Another attack by 435 B-24 Liberators escorted by 324 P-38 Lightnings, P-47 Thunderbolts, and P-51 Mustangs bombs airfields, bridges, and roads in Munich. Sixteen bombers are lost and two are damaged. Aircrew losses are eight killed, 14 wounded, and 149 missing. Fighter pilots report two confirmed kills. One P-47 and two P-51s are lost and one P-51 is damaged. Two pilots are reported missing.

During the night, six B-17s drop leaflets over France. A total of 29 B-24s fly in support of Carpetbagger missions during the night.

Ninth Air Force A-20 Havocs and B-26 Marauders attack fuel storage areas, V-weapon sites, and a rail bridge. P-47s escort the bombers and attack trains, gun positions, and ammunition storage areas.

MEDITERRANEAN: The 1st Airborne Task Force is organized under the command of Major General Robert T. Frederick. The task force is composed of the 2nd Independent British Parachute Brigade, the 509th Parachute Infantry Battalion, the 463rd

Parachute Field Artillery Battalion, the 517th Parachute Regimental Combat Team, the 550th Glider Infantry Battalion, and the 551st Parachute Infantry Brigade. The task force is assigned to Lieutenant General Patch's Seventh Army for Operation Anvil.

Fifteenth Air Force B-24 Liberators bomb the harbor and marshaling yard at Toulon, France.

Twelfth Air Force B-25 Mitchells and B-26 Marauders attack marshaling yards, railroad bridges, and viaducts. A-20 Havocs, A-36 Intruder (Apache) fighter-bombers, P-51 Mustangs, and P-40s attack airfields, fuel storage areas, rail lines, gun positions, and roads.

NEW GUINEA: FEAF B-25 Mitchells bomb airfields at Manokwari during the night. A-20 Havocs, B-25s, P-39 Airacobras, P-38 Lightnings, P-40s, and P-47 Thunderbolts attack Japanese forces in the Sarmi-Sawar area and bomb airfields, shipping, and various installations on Halmahera Island.

July 12

CBI: An attack against Japanese defenses at Myitkyina fails.

Tenth Air Force P-40s support ground forces and 13 B-25 Mitchells attack targets around Myitkyina. The fighters accidentally bomb friendly troops during the attack.

In China, Fourteenth Air Force P-40s attack river shipping at Hengyang.

ATLANTIC: Convoy UGS 46 (United States to Mediterranean, Slow) is attacked off Algiers at dawn by 30 German aircraft. The convoy suffers no damage.

ETO: Before St-Lô at Martinville Ridge, the 29th Infantry Division faces repeated German counterattacks and heavy German artillery fire. Hill 122 remains in German possession and the Americans suffer 2,000 casualties in two days of fighting. German strongpoints and interlocked defensive positions at Hill 101 stop the attack. The 115th Infantry Regiment is stopped at le Cauchais.

Eighth Air Force sends over 1,200 B-17s and B-24 Liberators, escorted by 717 P-38 Lightnings, P-47 Thunderbolts, and P-51 Mustangs, to attack Munich, Germany. A total of 24 bombers are lost and 301 are damaged. Aircrew losses are two killed, seven wounded, and 216 missing. One P-38 is damaged.

During the night six B-17s drop leaflets over France.

Ninth Air Force sends over 300 A-20 and B-26 Marauders to attack fuel storage sites and bridges in France. Escorting P-47s also attack fuel storage sites, rail lines, artillery positions, and troops.

MEDITERRANEAN: Fifteenth Air Force sends over 400 B-24 Liberators to attack marshaling yards, bridges, and rail lines in southern France. Aircrews report 14 confirmed kills. Seven U.S. aircraft are lost.

ITALY: The 362nd and 363rd Infantry Regiments of the 91st Infantry Division attack with elements of the 88th Infantry Division toward the Arno River to capture Pontedera.

Naval units begin mine-clearing operations near Leghorn and at the mouth of the Arno River, raising fears in the German high command that another amphibious landing is being conducted. All landing craft in the Mediterranean at this time is now marked for the Anvil operation. Operation Mallory Major begins as Twelfth Air Force B-26 Marauders and B-25 Mitchells attempt to destroy all the bridges over the Po River. A-20 Havocs attack ammunition storage sites and P-47 Thunderbolts and P-40s attack barges and small boats on the Arno River, as well as roads, vehicle traffic, ammunition storage areas, and gun positions.

SOUTHWEST PACIFIC AREA: Submarine attack group TG 17.16 attacks a Japanese convoy spotted the previous day off the north coast of Luzon. USS *Apogon* makes a torpedo run on a cargo ship, but is damaged by a collision with another cargo ship, forcing *Apogon* to terminate her patrol. USS *Piranha* torpedoes and sinks a cargo ship.

CENTRAL PACIFIC: Seventh Air Force P-47 Thunderbolts from Saipan attack Japanese gun positions on Tinian Island. During the night B-24 Liberators stage through Eniwetok Atoll, bomb Truk and conduct another raid during the day.

NEW GUINEA: A battalion of the 128th Infantry (32nd Infantry Division) stops a Japanese attack toward Aitape. Reconnaissance elements of the 112th Cavalry and the 128th Infantry withdraw westward.

FEAF B-24 Liberators bomb Manokwari airfield and other B-24s bomb Yap. A-20 Havocs, B-25 Mitchells, P-39 Airacobras, P-38 Lightnings, P-40s, and P-47 Thunderbolts attack targets at Wewak.

The A-20 Havocs of the 386th Bombardment Squadron (Light), 312th Bombardment Group (Light), redeploy from Nadzab to Hollandia. The P-38 Lightnings of the 475th Fighter Group redeploy from Hollandia to Biak Island.

July 13

CBI: Tenth Air Force P-40s and P-51 Mustangs conduct ground support missions near Myitkyina. A-36 Intruder (Apache) fighter-bombers, P-51 Mustangs, and P-47 Thunderbolts attack bridges.

Fourteenth Air Force P-40s attack trucks, river shipping, and troop concentrations around Hengyang.

ETO: XIX Corps presses German defenders from the north and east near St-Lô. V Corps (2nd and 5th Infantry Divisions with the 2nd Armored Division and 1st Infantry Division in reserve).

Eighth Air Force sends 677 B-17s escorted by 462 P-38 Lightnings, P-47 Thunderbolts, and P-51 Mustangs to attack rail and industrial facilities at Munich, Germany. Aircrews report 11 confirmed kills and four probables. Nine bombers are lost and 288 are damaged. Aircrew losses are eight killed, 16 wounded, and 86 missing. Fighter pilots report two confirmed kills and one probable. Three fighters are lost and one is damaged.

In another strike, 366 B-24 Liberators escorted by over 80 P-51s are sent against the marshaling yards at Saarbrücken, Germany. One B-24 is lost and 38 are damaged. Aircrew casualties are 23 killed, nine wounded, and 19 missing. One P-51 is lost and one is damaged.

A total of 28 B-24s fly in support of Carpetbagger operations.

Ninth Air Force P-47s and P-38s attack German armor, rail lines, marshaling yards, and bridges in France.

ITALY: Fifteenth Air Force sends 581 B-17s and B-24 Liberators to attack marshaling yards, railroad bridges, and an oil storage facility in northern Italy.

Twelfth Air Force B-25 Mitchells and B-26 Marauders bomb bridges along the Po River valley. A-20 Havocs bomb an ammunition production facility. P-47 Thunderbolts and P-40s attack rail targets.

PACIFIC: U.S. submarine *Cobia* attacks a Japanese convoy, sinking a cargo ship north of the Bonin Islands.

CENTRAL PACIFIC: Seventh Air Force P-47 Thunderbolts from Saipan bomb Japanese positions on Tinian Island. B-24 Liberators from Kwajalein bomb Truk and B-25 Mitchells from Makin Island bomb Nauru Island.

NEW GUINEA: The Americans mount a counterattack to recapture the Driniumor River line. Supported by artillery, the 124th Infantry Regiment (31st Infantry Division), the 112th Cavalry, and the 127th and 128th Infantry Regiments (32nd Infantry Division) advance against the enemy. Fifth Air Force supports the attack with air strikes and aerial resupply of troops in heavy jungle.

Fifth Air Force B-25 Mitchells sink one cargo ship and damage another off Halmahera.

At Noemfoor, the 503rd Parachute Infantry encounters the Japanese at Hill 670.

FEAF P-47 Thunderbolts and P-40s provide ground support along the Driniumor River line. B-24 Liberators bomb Yap and Sorol Atoll.

The B-25s of the 345th Bombardment Group (Medium) redeploy from Nadzab to Biak Island.

July 14

CBI: Tenth Air Force P-40s attack Japanese positions near Myitkyina and 38 P-51 Mustangs and P-47 Thunderbolts attack bridges.

In China, Fourteenth Air Force B-25 Mitchells, P-40s, P-51 Mustangs, and P-47 Thunderbolts attack a Japanese fighter airstrip near Changsha and road and river traffic around Hengyang.

ETO: The 137th Infantry Regiment of the 35th Infantry Division of XIX Corps, supported by tanks, breaks the German line northwest of St-Lô, captures a bridge over the Vire River, and threatens Hill 122, the main German position defending the city. VIII Corps has moved through the *bocage* for 12 straight days and has advanced only eight miles. The 90th Infantry Division has suffered 5,000 casualties.

Eighth Air Force sends 359 B-17s escorted by 465 P-47 Thunderbolts and P-51 Mustangs to drop supplies to French irregular forces in France. Fifteen bombers are damaged. Aircrews report five confirmed kills and two probables. Fighter pilots report four confirmed kills. In another mission, 131 B-24 Liberators escorted by 79 P-38 Lightnings and P-51 Mustangs are sent to attack airfields in France. Nine bombers and one P-38 are damaged. P-38 Lightnings fly fighter-bomber missions against rail targets near Paris. Pilots report two confirmed kills and one P-38 is lost. The pilot is reported missing.

The 55th Fighter Group makes the transition from P-38s to P-51s.

Ninth Air Force sends over 60 A-20 and B-26 Marauders using Oboe (see October 20, 1944 ETO) to bomb rail lines in France. Escorting P-47 Thunderbolts encounter 85 German fighters and report six confirmed kills. Five fighters and their pilots are reported missing. The P-47s attack German defenses along the U.S. First Army front lines and attack rail targets.

MEDITERRANEAN: Fifteenth Air Force sends over 400 B-17s and B-24 Liberators to attack oil refineries at Budapest and at Petfurdo in Hungary. The bombers also hit the marshaling yard at Mantua, Italy.

Twelfth Air Force B-25 Mitchells and B-26 Marauders bomb bridges along the Po River valley. A-20 Havocs bomb an ammunition production facility. P-47 Thunderbolts and P-40s attack gun positions and rail targets.

CENTRAL PACIFIC: Seventh Air Force P-47 Thunderbolts from Saipan attack Japanese defenses on Tinian Island.

Navy PB4Y Privateers bomb Iwo Jima.

Underwater Demolition Team 3 conducts beach reconnaissance at Asan, Guam.

Destroyer escort *William C. Miller* sinks Japanese submarine *RO-48* east of Saipan. Later, the *William C. Miller* will join with high-speed transport *Gilmer* to sink Japanese submarine *I-6* west of Tinian.

NEW GUINEA: FEAF P-47 Thunderbolts, P-38 Lightnings, and P-40s support ground forces along the Driniumor River and bomb Japanese troops near Afua.

P-61 Black Widow night fighters attack airfields on the Vogelkop Peninsula. B-24 Liberators attack Yap. A-20 Havocs attack oil production facilities at Boela on Ceram Island in the Celebes. B-24s and B-25 Mitchells attack barge facilities and gun positions on Timor Island.

The headquarters of the 475th Fighter Group and the P-38s of the 433rd Fighter Squadron move from Hollandia to Biak Island.

U.S. submarine *Sand Lance* attacks a Japanese convoy in the Banda Sea south of Celebes Island and sinks a gunboat.

July 15

CBI: Tenth Air Force P-40s conduct ground support missions against Japanese defenses at Myitkyina. P-47 Thunderbolts and P-51 Mustangs attack bridges. Twenty B-25 Mitchells bomb near Myitkyina area and attack bridges and a logistics site.

Fourteenth Air Force sends 26 P-40s to provide ground support to Chinese forces in the Salween River area. Twelve B-25s bomb Mangshih and Lungling.

ETO: The 134th Infantry Regiment, 35th Infantry Division, of XIX Corps attacks Hill 122 and clears Germans from positions blocking the Isigny–St-Lô road. The infantrymen are supported by 21 tanks, three tank destroyers, and engineers. They advance behind an artillery barrage and airstrikes from P-47 Thunderbolts. The 115th Infantry Regiment attacking toward St-Lô suffers heavy casualties. The 116th and the 175th Infantry of the 29th Infantry Division make advances measured in yards. The 2nd Battalion of the 116th Infantry conducts a night attack and successfully breaks the German defenses, reaching the La Madeleine crossroads on the outskirts of St-Lô. By morning the battalion is isolated from American lines.

Eighth Air Force sends 169 P-38 Lightnings and P-47 Thunderbolts to make fighter-bomber attacks on enemy transport near Paris. Fighter pilots report three fighters lost and 13 damaged. Four pilots are reported missing.

A total of 27 B-24s fly in support of Carpetbagger operations. During the night six B-17s drop leaflets over France.

Ninth Air Force sends P-47s and P-38s to bomb infantry and artillery positions, a marshaling yard, and a bridge in the St-Lô, Argentan, and Falaise areas.

MEDITERRANEAN: Fifteenth Air Force sends over 600 B-17s and B-24 Liberators escorted by P-51 Mustangs and P-38 Lightnings to bomb oil refineries at Ploeşti, Romania.

ITALY: Twelfth Air Force B-25 Mitchells and B-26 Marauders bomb bridges along the Po River valley. A-20 Havocs bomb an ammunition production facility. P-47 Thunderbolts and P-40s attack gun positions, roads, and rail targets.

PACIFIC: U.S. submarine *Skate* torpedoes and sinks a Japanese fishing vessel in the Kuriles.

CENTRAL PACIFIC: Seventh Air Force P-47 Thunderbolts from Saipan bomb and strafe Japanese positions on Tinian Island. B-24 Liberators staging through Eniwetok Atoll bomb Truk.

NEW GUINEA: The 43rd Infantry Division arrives at Aitape, commanded by Major General Leonard T. Wing. High surf and nearly continuous rain delay the landing.

The 34th Infantry Regiment of the 24th Infantry Division leaves Biak Island for Hollandia.

FEAF A-20 Havocs bomb gun emplacements on an island off Manokwari. B-25 Mitchells, P-39 Airacobras, P-38 Lightnings, P-40s, and P-47 Thunderbolts attack targets around Wewak. B-24s bomb the town area, radio station, and barracks buildings on Yap.

The P-38s of the 431st Fighter Squadron 475th Fighter Group redeploy from Hollandia to Biak Island.

July 16

CBI: The Myitkyina Task Force, led by the American combat engineers fighting as infantry, assaults Japanese positions.

Tenth Air Force P-40s conduct ground support missions against Japanese defenses at Myitkyina. P-47 Thunderbolts and P-51 Mustangs attack bridges. Twenty B-25 Mitchells bomb near the Myitkyina area and attack bridges and a logistics site.

In China, Fourteenth Air Force sends 23 B-24 Liberators along with 40 P-51 Mustangs and P-40s to bomb Changsha and targets of opportunity near Hengyang.

The P-38s of the 449th Fighter Squadron 51st Fighter Group redeploy from Kweilin to Chengkung.

ATLANTIC: General Marshall, the army chief of staff, instructs General Jacob L. Devers to form an army group command for Anvil. Devers will be subordinate to General Sir Henry Maitland Wilson until General Eisenhower is ready to take operational control. Devers will have the U.S. Seventh Army under Lieutenant General Alexander M. Patch and the First French Army as his major forces.

ETO: Although the port of Cherbourg has been opened, the Allies can move only about 2,000 tons of supplies a day through the port. Within a month, the tonnage will rise to 12,000 a day, but the amount will still be insufficient to support divisions now requiring a total of up to 26,000 tons of supplies per day.

The 134th Infantry Regiment of the 35th Infantry Division is forced to abandon Hill 122 after a German counterattack, but the infantrymen rally and recapture the hill. A German counterattack on Martinville also fails.

Eighth Air Force sends over 640 B-17s, escorted by 454 P-38 Lightnings, P-47 Thunderbolts, and P-51 Mustangs, to attack Munich and Stuttgart, Germany. Eleven bombers are lost and 160 are damaged. Aircrews report two confirmed kills and three probables. Aircrew losses are two killed, eight wounded, and 91 missing. Two fighters are lost and the pilots are reported missing. Another attack sends over 400 B-24 Liberators

A U.S. M-10 tank destroyer fires on German positions during the battle for St-Lô, France, in July 1944.

escorted by 169 P-38s and P-47s against the marshaling yards at Saarbrücken, Germany. A total of 47 bombers are damaged. Aircrew casualties are one killed, and three wounded. One P-38 is lost and one is damaged.

A total of 24 B-24s fly in support of Carpetbagger operations. During the night five B-17s drop leaflets over France.

Ninth Air Force sends 375 A-20 and B-26 Marauders with P-47s and P-38s to attack German strongpoints and defensive positions outside of St-Lô and bridges and fuel storage sites near Rennes.

MEDITERRANEAN: Major General Paul L. Williams, commander of IX Troop Carrier Command, arrives in Italy from England to activate the Provisional Troop Carrier Division to support Anvil.

Fifteenth Air Force sends over 300 bombers escorted by P-51 Mustangs and P-38 Lightnings against oil depots, aircraft production facilities, a marshaling yard, and airfields around Vienna, Austria. Over 100 German fighters attack the formations and shoot down 10 U.S. aircraft. Aircrews and fighter pilots report over 30 enemy fighters shot down.

ITALY: Twelfth Air Force B-25 Mitchells and B-26 Marauders bomb bridges along the Po River valley. A-20 Havocs bomb an ammunition production facility. P-47 Thunderbolts and P-40s attack gun positions, roads, and rail targets.

SOUTHWEST PACIFIC AREA: Submarine attack group TG 17.16 attacks a Japanese convoy off northern Luzon. USS *Piranha* torpedoes and sinks an army transport; USS *Guardfish* torpedoes and sinks a transport and a cargo ship; USS *Thresher* torpedoes and sinks a cargo ship and damages two other cargo ships.

U.S. submarine *Bonefish* torpedoes and sinks a Japanese cargo vessel south of Palawan.

U.S. submarine *Cabrilla* makes an unsuccessful attack on a Japanese convoy off the west coast of Mindanao.

PACIFIC: U.S. submarine *Skate* torpedoes and sinks a Japanese transport east of Sakhalin Island.

CENTRAL PACIFIC: Seventh Air Force P-47 Thunderbolts from Saipan bomb Japanese positions on Tinian Island.

Shore battery fire damages an infantry landing craft supporting the UDT 3 beach reconnaissance operation at Guam.

NEW GUINEA: At Wakde, the 31st Infantry Division under command of Major General John C. Pearsons begins the relief of the 6th Infantry Division. The battle for Wakde-Sarmi and Lone Tree Hill has cost the Americans 114 killed and 284 wounded. There are over 400 non-combat casualties, most of which are classified as neuropsychotic. Over 900 Japanese are dead. Wakde and Maffin Bay will become an important staging base for future operations.

FEAF B-24 Liberators bomb antiaircraft positions at Manokwari. B-24s bomb Yap and Atamboea airfield on Timor Island.

Second Lieutenant Dale E. Christensen of Troop E, 112th Cavalry Regiment, is leading his platoon during one of the many bitter firefights that have occurred on the Driniumor River. A Japanese machine gun is causing casualties among his men and Christensen orders his men to stay in place while he goes forward. Creeping to within range, he eliminates the position with hand grenades. During several subsequent encounter with the enemy, Second Lieutenant Christensen moves ahead alone to locate and destroy enemy positions and leads attacks to throw the Japanese off-balance. On August 4 near Afua, Christensen is killed leading his men in another attack. For his extraordinary and sustained courage and exceptional leadership in a desperate defense against a determined enemy, Second Lieutenant Dale Christensen will be awarded the Medal of Honor.

July 17

CBI: Tenth Air Force P-40s, P-47 Thunderbolts, and P-51 Mustangs attack Japanese positions at Myitkyina in support of Allied ground forces.

In China, Fourteenth Air Force sends 22 B-24 Liberators to bomb Changsha. B-25 Mitchells and P-40s attack the Kaifeng railyards. B-25s and 12 P-40s also attack Tengchung.

ETO: The commander of the 3rd Battalion 116th Infantry Regiment, Major Thomas D. Howie, is killed shortly after telling the division commander "I'll see you in St.-Lô!" The rifle companies in the 29th Infantry Division have been reduced to 30–40 men. Elements of the 116th and 115th Infantry Regiments break German lines using infiltration tactics instead of company formations and relieve the isolated 2nd Battalion of the 116th Infantry. German forces begin the evacuation of St-Lô. Although only a mile from St-Lô, neither battalion is able to advance.

Eighth Air Force sends 331 B-17s and 339 B-24 Liberators, escorted by 433 P-38 Lightnings, P-47 Thunderbolts, and P-51 Mustangs, to attack marshaling yards, roads, bridges, and fuel storage sites in France. One B-17 is lost and 122 are damaged. Aircrew losses are two killed, 10 wounded, and nine missing. Fighter pilots report 18 trucks and 55 rail cars destroyed in strafing attacks. One P-47 is lost and the pilot is reported missing.

During the evening 140 B-17s and B-24 Liberators escorted by over 200 P-51s attack 12 V-weapon sites in the Pas-de-Calais area. A total of 55 bombers are damaged. Aircrew casualties are one killed and five wounded. One P-51 is damaged.

A total of 16 B-24s fly in support of Carpetbagger operations. During the night five B-17s drop leaflets over France and the Netherlands.

Ninth Air Force sends 37 A-20 and 69 B-26 Marauders to attack marshaling yards and a fuel storage site in France. P-47s and P-38s escort the bombers and attack German positions at St-Lô in support of the 29th Infantry Division.

MEDITERRANEAN: Fifteenth Air Force sends 162 B-24 Liberators escorted by P-51 Mustangs and P-38 Lightnings to bomb a marshaling yard and railroad bridges in southern France.

ITALY: The 168th and 133rd Infantry Regiments of the 34th Infantry Division advance toward Leghorn. Major General Vernon E. Pritchard takes command of the 1st Armored Division from Major General Ernest Harmon.

Twelfth Air Force B-25 Mitchells and B-26 Marauders bomb bridges along the Po River valley. A-20 Havocs bomb an ammunition production facility. P-47 Thunderbolts and P-40s attack bridges and rail targets.

SOUTHWEST PACIFIC AREA: U.S. submarine *Cabrilla* again attacks the Japanese convoy, sinking an army transport and damaging another transport off the west coast of Mindanao.

U.S. submarine attack group TG 17.16 locates Japanese ships west of Luzon. USS *Guardfish* torpedoes and sinks a cargo ship; USS *Thresher* torpedoes and sinks a cargo ship near Luzon Strait.

PACIFIC: A cargo ship carrying ammunition explodes at the Port Chicago, California, ammunition depot, destroying a nearby freighter as well. About 5,000 tons of explosives were detonated. The casualties include 250 African-American sailors. Survivors refuse to return to work and 50 are later sent before a court-martial on charges of mutiny.

U.S. submarine *Gabilan* torpedoes and sinks a Japanese minesweeper south of Kyushu, Japan.

CENTRAL PACIFIC: Seventh Air Force P-47 Thunderbolts from Saipan attack Japanese positions at Tinian Island. B-25 Mitchells from Makin Island stage through Engebi Island on Eniwetok Atoll to bomb the airfield and antiaircraft positions on Ponape Island.

Frogmen of UDT 3 begin to use demolitions to clear obstacles off the landing beaches on Guam.

NEW GUINEA: At the Driniumor River, the 112th Cavalry attempts to close the gap to the north with the 124th Infantry Regiment (31st Infantry Division) and to establish a continuous defensive line, but is stopped by a Japanese counterattack.

FEAF B-25 Mitchells, A-20 Havocs, and P-39 Airacobras attack Japanese troops and logistics storage sites between Aitape and Wewak. B-25s bomb Timor Island.

July 18

CBI: Tenth Air Force P-40s and B-25 Mitchells attack Japanese positions at Myitkyina area. P-51 Mustangs support ground forces at Pyindaw.

Fourteenth Air Force P-40s attack river shipping in the Hengyang-Tungting Lake region and bomb the airfield and antiaircraft positions at Hengyang.

ETO: General Norman Cota of the 29th Infantry Division enters St-Lô with the 3rd Battalion of the 116th Infantry, preceded by the body of Major Howie. His soldiers place the body, lying underneath an American flag, in the ruins of St. Croix church;

he becomes known as the "Major of St-Lô." In about two weeks of fighting in the advance to St-Lô, American forces have suffered 40,000 casualties, most of them in infantry units. Since June 6, the fighting in the *bocage* has severely depleted the American infantry divisions. The high casualties have reduced rifle companies to 40 percent strength and only about 30 percent of the officers who landed on the beaches with their soldiers are still with their units. German losses have been estimated at 160,000, including 400 tanks.

The VII Corps reaches the Périers-St-Lô Road, gaining valuable territory in the open fields beyond the *bocage* and an opportunity for maneuver. The 9th and 30th Infantry Divisions from VII Corps cross the Vire River and occupy the high ground.

Bradley's task is to break through west of St-Lô and move to Coutances in order to isolate German forces and attack south to seize Avranches. General Montgomery approves General Bradley's plan for Operation Cobra. Bradley plans to employ over 2,200 aircraft to bomb German positions south of the St-Lô–Périers Road, followed by a 1,000-gun artillery barrage. VII Corps (the 4th, 9th, and 30th Infantry Divisions) will advance through the German lines, followed by an exploitation force of the 2nd and 3rd Armored Divisions and the 1st Infantry Division. Montgomery desires First Army to cut off German defenders in the Périers-Lessay area in the southern section of the Cotentin Peninsula while Lieutenant General Patton's Third Army attacks into Brittany. The Second British Army is to hold German forces in place.

Eighth Air Force sends 644 B-24 Liberators, in conjunction with Ninth Air Force and RAF Bomber Command, to bomb German positions in support of the British Second Army's attack on Caen. One B-24 is lost and 184 are damaged. More than 750 B-17s attack the Kiel port area and the Peenemünde experimental area, which is used for developing V-weapons. Three bombers are lost and 85 are damaged. The bombers are escorted by over 400 P-38 Lightnings and P-51 Mustangs. Over Peenemünde, fighter pilots report 21 confirmed kills. Three P-51s are lost and one damaged. Two pilots are reported missing.

A total of 25 B-24s fly in support of Carpetbagger operations. One bomber is lost.

Ninth Air Force sends over 400 B-26 Marauders and A-20 Havocs to attack German defensive positions in the Caen area.

MEDITERRANEAN: En route to Memminger airfield in Germany 200 B-24 Liberators and B-17s encounter 200 German fighters. In the ensuing air battle, 14 B-17s and 66 German fighters are lost. B-17 aircrews report 66 confirmed kills in the air and 35 aircraft destroyed on the ground. Twenty U.S. aircraft are shot down.

The C-47s of the 439th, 440th, 441st, and 442nd Troop Carrier Commands redeploy from England to Italy as part of the provisional troop carrier division supporting Anvil.

ITALY: The 442nd RCT along with the 133rd and 168th Infantry Regiments of the 34th Infantry Division enter the Arno River Valley to outflank German defenders at Leghorn.

A-20 Havocs and P-47 Thunderbolts make limited attacks on bridges, roads, and rail lines due to bad weather.

SOUTHWEST PACIFIC AREA: U.S. submarine attack group TG 17.3, commanded by Captain Warren D. Wilkin, attacks a Japanese convoy near Luzon Strait. USS *Tilefish* torpedoes a coastal patrol ship, while USS *Sawfish* torpedoes an oiler.

PACIFIC: Tojo Hideki is removed as Japanese premier and war minister, largely as a result of the loss of Saipan, considered an essential part of the outer defensive line protecting Japan.

U.S. submarine *Cobia* torpedoes and sinks a Japanese gunboat and a cargo ship near Chichi Jima.

U.S. submarine *Plaice* attacks a Japanese convoy, sinking a submarine chaser northwest of Chichi Jima.

CENTRAL PACIFIC: Seventh Air Force P-47 Thunderbolts from Saipan attack Japanese positions on Tinian Island. B-24 Liberators from Kwajalein bomb Wotje Atoll. B-24 Liberators staging through Eniwetok Atoll bomb Truk.

NEW GUINEA: American forces establish a continuous defensive line along the Driniumor River, having pushed the Japanese back with concentrated artillery fire and close combat.

FEAF A-20 Havocs and P-47 Thunderbolts attack barges, supply routes, and Japanese troops along the coast from Aitape to Wewak. B-24 Liberators bomb Yap.

U.S. submarine *Lapon* torpedoes and sinks a Japanese auxiliary submarine chaser off Palawan Island and survey ship and auxiliary submarine chaser northwest of Borneo in the Sulu Sea. U.S. submarine *Ray* torpedoes and sinks a Japanese merchant tanker in the Java Sea.

Fifth Air Force B-24 Liberators sink a Japanese transport northwest of Morotai Island.

July 19

CBI: Tenth Air Force B-25 Mitchells, P-40s, and P-51 Mustangs attack Japanese positions at the Myitkyina area and ground force support near Kamaing.

In China, Fourteenth Air Force sends more than 80 P-40s to attack shipping, logistics sites, and Japanese troops in the Tungting Lake area and around Hengyang. The fighters also bomb a radio station, logistics depots, and shipping at Changsha. P-40s also bomb the airfield at Siangtan.

ETO: Eighth Air Force sends over 1,200 B-17s and B-24 Liberators, escorted by over 700 P-38 Lightnings, P-47 Thunderbolts, and P-51 Mustangs, to attack industrial production and transportation targets in Germany. These targets are related to industrial production and transportation. Seventeen bombers and seven fighters are lost. Aircrews report six confirmed kills and four probables. Fighters escorting the bombers also strafe locomotives, rolling stock, and vehicles. Fighter pilots report 17 confirmed kills in the air and 38 on the ground.

A total of five B-24s fly in support of Carpetbagger operations. During the night five B-17s drop leaflets over France and Belgium.

Ninth Air Force sends 262 A-20 and B-26 Marauders against bridges and fuel storage facilities in France. P-47s escorting the bombers attack German positions.

The headquarters of the 373rd Fighter Group redeploys to France. The P-47s of the 513th Fighter Squadron 406th Fighter Group redeploy to France as well.

MEDITERRANEAN: Fifteenth Air Force sends over 400 B-17s and B-24 Liberators escorted by P-51 Mustangs and P-38 Lightnings to conduct follow-on bombing of an ordnance depot, an aircraft production facility, a motor works, and an airfield in the Munich area after Eighth Air Force bombers have hit the targets. A total of 16 U.S. aircraft are lost with others reported missing.

ITALY: Leghorn falls to the 135th and 363rd Infantry Regiments. The Germans have systematically destroyed the port and have sowed the entire city with mines and booby traps.

Twelfth Air Force B-25 Mitchells and B-26 Marauders attack bridges. A-20 Havocs and P-47 Thunderbolts attack rail lines.

SOUTHWEST PACIFIC AREA: U.S. submarine *Flasher* torpedoes and sinks a Japanese light cruiser in the South China Sea. U.S. submarine *Guardfish* attacks a Japanese cargo ship in the South China Sea southwest of Formosa.

PACIFIC: U.S. submarine *Tautog* torpedoes and sinks a Japanese guardboat in the Bonin Islands.

CENTRAL PACIFIC: Seventh Air Force P-47 Thunderbolts attack Japanese positions on Tinian Island.

Destroyer escort USS *Wyman* sinks Japanese submarine *I-5* east of Guam.

NEW GUINEA: FEAF-20 Havocs, P-47 Thunderbolts, P-38 Lightnings, and P-40s attack Japanese troops, logistics sites, gun positions, and targets of opportunity along the Driniumor River and support Allied ground forces around Sarmi and Sawar. B-24 Liberators bomb the airfield on Yap. Some of the bombers miss the primary target and bomb Ngulu and Sorol Atolls in the Carolines.

July 20

CBI: Tenth Air Force P-40s attack targets around Myitkyina.

Fourteenth Air Force B-24 Liberators bomb Changsha. Aircrews report heavy damage. Over 140 P-40s and P-51 Mustangs attack river shipping and road traffic in the Tungting Lake area and attack troop compounds and gun positions near Hengyang.

ATLANTIC: JCS planners reject MacArthur's Reno V plan, indicating that the plan requires more air support than is available in-theater and would require most of the Pacific Fleet. They assess that MacArthur's approach would delay the invasion of Japan by one year.

President Roosevelt is nominated for an unprecedented fourth term of office at the Democratic National Convention in Chicago.

ETO: First Army occupies a line stretching 40 miles from Lessey on the west coast of the Cotentin Peninsula, east along the Pèriers–St-Lô Road to Caumont. Ultra intercepts of German communications indicate that the defenders are nearly at the end of their resources.

The damage to the Normandy beaches from a four-day storm in the English Channel, June 19–22, is repaired. The artificial ports (called Mulberries) are now the main means of moving cargo from ships to shore. During this time the ports handle an average of 6,700 tons of supplies per day.

Eighth Air Force sends 417 B-17s escorted by 253 P-38 Lightnings, P-47 Thunderbolts, and P-51 Mustangs to attack airfields and industrial targets in Germany. Fifteen bombers are lost and 188 are damaged. Aircrew losses are one killed, 10 wounded, and 129 missing. Fighter pilots report five confirmed kills in the air and two on the ground. Four fighters are lost and one P-51 is damaged. Three pilots are reported missing and one pilot is wounded. Another 295 B-17s escorted by 178 P-38 Lightnings, P-47 Thunderbolts, and P-51 Mustangs attack German industrial targets. Two B-17s are lost and 153 are damaged. Aircrew casualties are two wounded and 21 missing. Aircrews report one confirmed kill and one probable in the air and one confirmed kill on the ground. Fighter pilots report one confirmed kill and one probable in the air and one confirmed kill on the ground. One P-51 is lost and one damaged; the pilot is reported missing.

Over 400 B-24 Liberators bomb industrial targets and airfields in Germany escorted by 45 P-47s. One bomber is lost and 31 are damaged. Aircrew casualties are two wounded and nine missing. Fighter pilots report six confirmed kills on the ground. One P-47 is lost. The pilot is reported missing.

A total of 12 B-24s fly in support of Carpetbagger operations.

Ninth Air Force sends 62 A-20 and B-26 Marauders to attack a marshaling yard, and P-47s conduct attacks on rail lines, German troop positions, and bridges.

The C-47 squadrons of the 435th, 436th, and 438th Troop Carrier Groups begin redeployment from England to Italy in preparation for the airborne operation supporting Anvil.

At his secret headquarters in East Prussia, Adolf Hitler survives an assassination attempt when a hidden bomb explodes under a table during a military briefing.

MEDITERRANEAN: Fifteenth Air Force sends over 400 B-17s and B-24 Liberators escorted by P-38 Lightnings and P-51 Mustangs against airfields and aircraft production facilities in Germany. Aircrews and fighter pilots report 19 German fighters shot down.

ITALY: Twelfth Air Force B-25 Mitchells and B-26 Marauders bomb bridges along the Po River valley. A-20 Havocs bomb an ammunition production facility. P-47 Thunderbolts attack rail targets.

PACIFIC: U.S. submarine *Cobia* attacks a three-ship Japanese convoy northwest of Chichi Jima, sinking two auxiliary submarine chasers and damaging a cargo ship. The *Cobia* is rammed during the attack, but the submarine sustains only minor damage.

CENTRAL PACIFIC: Vice Admiral Kelly Turner, commander of the amphibious force, sets a date for the landing on Tinian of July 24. The 2nd and 4th Marine Divisions will make the landings. The 4th Marine Division is commanded by Major General Clifton B. Cates. The previous commander, Major General Harry Schmidt, takes command of V Amphibious Corps, replacing Lieutenant General Holland M. Smith, who is appointed commander, Fleet Marine Forces Pacific.

Seventh Air Force P-47 Thunderbolts from Saipan bomb Tinian Island. B-25 Mitchells from Engebi Island bomb Ponape Island.

NEW GUINEA: At the Driniumor River, the 112th Cavalry and the 127th Infantry Regiments of the 32nd Infantry Division stop a Japanese attack to outflank the American defensive line.

FEAF B-24 Liberators attack the airfield and antiaircraft positions at Manokwari and B-25 Mitchells attack shipping. A-20 Havocs support the American defense at the Driniumor River.

B-24s bomb Yap and targets in the Molucca Islands. B-25 Mitchells attack shipping at Dili on Timor Island.

July 21

CBI: In China Fourteenth Air Force sends 41 P-40s to attack the town, airfield, trucks, river shipping, and troops at Changsha and vehicles, river transportation, and troop positions at Hengyang.

ATLANTIC: The Democratic National Convention in Chicago nominates Senator Harry S. Truman of Missouri to be vice president.

ETO: Eighth Air Force sends 581 B-17s and 529 B-24 Liberators, escorted by over 700 P-38 Lightnings, P-47 Thunderbolts, and P-51 Mustangs, to attack aircraft production facilities and airfields in southern Germany. A total of 31 bombers are lost and 365 are damaged. Aircrews report 10 confirmed kills and two probables. Aircrew casualties are four killed, 11 wounded, and 288 missing. Fighter pilots report six confirmed kills in the air and three on the ground. Eight fighters are lost.

During the night eight B-17s drop leaflets over France. One bomber is damaged.

Ninth Air Force redeploys the headquarters of the 323rd Bombardment Group (Medium) and the B-26 Marauders of the 453rd, 454th, 455th, and 456th Bombardment Squadrons from England to France.

MEDITERRANEAN: Fifteenth Air Force sends 362 B-17s and B-24 Liberators escorted by P-38 Lightnings and P-51 Mustangs to attack a synthetic oil refinery and a marshaling yard in Czechoslovakia. Many bombers are forced to abort the mission due to bad weather en route to the targets.

ITALY: Major General Charles Bolte replaces Major General Charles W. Ryder as commander of the 34th Infantry Division.

Twelfth Air Force A-20 Havocs and P-47 Thunderbolts attack convoys, bridges on the Po River, and roads.

SOUTHWEST PACIFIC AREA: SWPA headquarters orders Lieutenant General Krueger's Alamo Force to prepare plans to seize a section of Morotai Island and establish an airfield there. Morotai Island is 10 miles northeast of Halamahera Island. An airfield at Morotai would isolate the Japanese base at Halamahera Island, holding 30,000 troops. Aircraft from Morotai would also eliminate Japanese air attacks originating from the Netherlands East Indies and the Celebes. More importantly, U.S. aircraft from Morotai can reach Leyte and Mindanao, two key islands in the Philippines, and the ultimate goal of General Douglas MacArthur's efforts since the defeat at Corregidor in 1942.

CENTRAL PACIFIC, GUAM: Operation Stevedore. Landings begin at Guam. The Americans have returned for the first time since the Japanese invasion on December 10, 1941. Admiral Raymond A. Spruance is commander of Fifth Fleet; Naval Task Force 53 is commanded by Rear Admiral Richard L. Conolly. Conolly employs both naval gunfire and aircraft to support the landings. Air cover is provided by 85 fighters, 65 bombers, and 53 torpedo planes from the carrier USS *Wasp*.

The Stars and Stripes is planted on Guam minutes after marines land on the beach, July 20, 1944.

The ground force is the III Marine Amphibious Corps, commanded by Major General Roy S. Geiger. It is composed of the 3rd Marine Division, the 1st Provisional Marine Brigade, and the army's 77th Infantry Division. The 3rd and 21st Marine Regiments of the 3rd Marine Division land between Asan Point and Adelup Point. The 3rd Marines are stopped by heavy fire from steep cliffs facing the beachhead. The 21st Marines find a gap in the Japanese defenses and occupy the ridge above their beachhead. Captain Geary R. Bundschu, commanding A Company of the 1st Battalion 3rd Marines, holds a precarious position on the ridge and is unable to advance in the face of heavy fire. He is killed on the ridge and his marines rename the position Bundschu Ridge. The 22nd Marines take heavy casualties on the beach from artillery fire and mines and advance only about 2,000 yards in the face of enemy fire. The 4th and 22nd Marines make a night attack to seize key high ground and move off the beachhead.

The 1st Provisional Brigade lands between Apaga Point and Bangi Point in Agat Bay. The 77th Infantry Division, commanded by Major General Andrew D. Bruce, lands later in the day, and the 305th Infantry Regiment supports the marines in throwing back a Japanese counterattack that night. The 4th Marines captures Bangi Point and establishes a roadblock. There are 18,500 Japanese troops on the island.

Seventh Air Force P-47 Thunderbolts from Saipan attack Japanese defensive positions on Tinian Island. B-24 Liberators, staging through Eniwetok Atoll, bomb Truk.

Private First Class Luther Skaggs, Jr., becomes the squad leader of a mortar section in a rifle company of 3rd Battalion, 3rd Marines, 3rd Marine Division, after the section takes casualties landing on Asan-Adelup beachhead. Leading the men inland 200 yards he sets up his mortars to provide support for the infantry. During the night, the Japanese conduct several counterattacks. Although sustaining a severe leg wound from a grenade explosion, Private First Class Skaggs applies a tourniquet to his injured leg and, propping himself up in his foxhole, continues to fight. Only after the attack has been stopped by eight hours of continuous fighting does Private First Class Skaggs crawl back to the rear to get medical assistance. For his amazing feat of courage and determination Private First Class Skaggs will be awarded the Medal of Honor.

NEW GUINEA: FEAF B-24 Liberators bomb antiaircraft positions and the airfield at Manokwari. P-39 Airacobras bomb caves and barge locations on Biak Island and support ground forces. B-25 Mitchells attack shipping off the Vogelkop Peninsula. A-20 Havocs, P-39s, and P-47 Thunderbolts attack targets of opportunity.

B-24s attack the airfield at Yap. Aircrews report seven Japanese fighters shot down.

July 22

CBI: Tenth Air Force P-40s attack Japanese positions at Myitkyina.

In China, Fourteenth Air Force sends over 120 P-40s and P-51 Mustangs to attack the town, airfield, railroad yards, and shipping at Hengyang. Over 20 B-24 Liberators bomb Changsha. Aircrews report heavy damage. P-40s sink several large junks off the northeast coast of French Indochina.

ATLANTIC: President Roosevelt departs Washington, D.C., aboard the heavy cruiser USS *Baltimore* to travel to Hawaii and meet with Admiral Nimitz and General MacArthur to discuss the future direction of the Pacific campaign.

ETO: Eighth Air Force sends seven B-17s escorted by 27 P-51 Mustangs to drop leaflets on Bremen, Hamburg, and Kiel in Germany. One B-17 and two P-51s are damaged. One crewman is reported killed.

A total of 44 B-24s fly in support of Carpetbagger operations.

Ninth Air Force redeploys the headquarters of the 367th Fighter Group to France.

MEDITERRANEAN: Fifteenth Air Force sends 76 P-38 Lightnings and 58 P-51 Mustangs on a Frantic mission, attacking airfields at Zilistea and Buzau in Romania en route to airfields in the Soviet Ukraine. Fighter pilots report 56 German aircraft destroyed.

Another mission sends 458 B-17s and B-24 Liberators against the Ploeşti oil refinery in Romania and marshaling yards and a railroad bridge in Yugoslavia.

ITALY: The French Expeditionary Corps is moved out of the front line for the Anvil operation. The British Eighth Army extends its front to fill the gap and link with Fifth Army.

Twelfth Air Force B-25 Mitchells attack bridges. A-20 Havocs and P-47 Thunderbolts attack rail lines, bridges, gun positions, and vehicles.

CENTRAL PACIFIC: Seventh Air Force P-47 Thunderbolts from Saipan use napalm bombs on Japanese positions on Tinian. Napalm is jelled gasoline that creates heavy flames and smoke and is especially effective against Japanese defenses in the caves and deep crevasses that troops have turned into fortresses, often resistant to regular high-explosive bombs.

B-25 Mitchells from Makin Island bomb Ponape Island.

CENTRAL PACIFIC, GUAM: The 21st and 3rd Marine Regiments are held up at Bundschu Ridge by mortar fire and Japanese machine-gun positions placing an effective crossfire across the ridge. The 9th Marines make progress against minimal resistance and occupy Piti on Apra Harbor. That night, elements of the 21st Marines stop a weak Japanese counterattack.

Private First Class Leonard F. Mason of the 2nd Battalion, 3rd Marines, 3rd Marine Division finds himself in a narrow gully when his unit takes fire from two Japanese machine guns concealed only 15 yards away. Mason moves out of the gully to locate the rear of the enemy position and is almost immediately wounded by fire from another enemy position. Although mortally wounded, he destroys the machine guns threatening his platoon and rejoins his unit before being evacuated. Private First Class Mason's extraordinary courage and sacrifice will win him the Medal of Honor.

NEW GUINEA: During the battle along the Driniumor River, Private First Class Donald R. Lobaugh of the 127th Infantry Regiment 32nd Infantry Division finds himself in a precarious situation. He and his platoon have been cut off and surrounded by Japanese troops when his company attempted to withdraw the day before. The platoon has survived the night, but the Japanese have set up a blocking position supported by a machine gun that cuts off their escape route. PFC Lobaugh volunteers to attack the enemy position and leaves the safety of his fighting position to advance across 30 yards of open ground. In full view of the enemy, PFC Lobaugh throws a hand grenade and is wounded. Without pause, he charges the position, firing his weapon. Although hit several times, he continues to fight the enemy until finally killed. PFC Lobaugh's heroic act causes his fellow infantrymen to sweep the enemy position and allows the platoon to reach friendly lines. PFC Lobaugh's extraordinary determination in battle will win him the Medal of Honor.

At Biak, the 163rd Infantry eliminates the last Japanese defensive strongpoint, called the Ibdi pocket. Biak is won but at a cost of 400 dead and 2,000 wounded.

FEAF B-24 Liberators, B-25 Mitchells, A-20 Havocs, P-39 Airacobras, P-38 Lightnings, P-40s, and P-47 Thunderbolts attack shipping targets around the Vogelkop Peninsula and report sinking a Japanese submarine chaser. B-24s attack the airfield at Yap.

July 23

CBI: Under pressure by the Allied attack on Myitkyina, Japanese forces begin to withdraw.

Tenth Air Force B-25 Mitchells and over 100 P-51 Mustangs, A-36 Intruder (Apache) fighter-bombers, P-47 Thunderbolts, and P-40 fighter-bombers hit enemy positions in the Myitkyina area and bomb the Kamaing and Mogaung areas.

In China, Fourteenth Air Force P-40s attack warehouses, trucks, and troops near Changsha and Hengyang. B-25 Mitchells and P-40s attack warehouses and rail lines along the Yellow River. P-40s support Chinese forces along the Salween River. The 449th Fighter Squadron 51st Fighter Group at Chengkung redeploys a detachment of P-38 Lightnings to operate from Yunnani.

ATLANTIC: German submarine *U-861* torpedoes and sinks a U.S. freighter off the Brazilian coast near Rio de Janeiro.

ETO: The headquarters of the 12th Army Group arrives in France. It will become operational on August 1.

Eighth Air Force sends 82 B-17s and 198 B-24 Liberators escorted by 177 P-38 Lightnings and P-51 Mustangs to attack airfields in France. One B-17 is lost and six are damaged; aircrew losses are three killed and three wounded.

A total of 21 B-24s fly in support of Carpetbagger operations.

Ninth Air Force sends over 300 A-20 and B-26 Marauders to attack fuel storage areas and bridges. P-47 Thunderbolts escorting the bombers attack roads, bridges, artillery, strongpoints, troop concentrations, and various targets of opportunity.

MEDITERRANEAN: Fifteenth Air Force sends 42 B-24 Liberators escorted by 15 P-51 Mustangs to bomb the oil refinery at Berat, Albania.

ITALY: The 363rd Infantry Regiment of the 91st Infantry Division occupies Pisa, south of the Arno River. The Fifth Army is halted for rest and resupply.

Twelfth Air Force B-25 Mitchells and B-26 Marauders attack bridges along the Po River valley. A-20 Havocs and P-47 Thunderbolts attack rail lines and roads.

CENTRAL PACIFIC: Seventh Air Force P-47 Thunderbolts on Saipan Island bomb Japanese positions on Tinian Island. The B-25 Mitchells of the 48th Bombardment Squadron (Medium), 41st Bombardment Group (Medium), redeploy from Abemama Island in the Gilbert Islands to Saipan. B-25s from Makin Island attack Nauru Island. B-24 Liberators staging through Eniwetok Atoll, bomb Truk. Other B-24s from Kwajalein bomb Wotje Atoll.

CENTRAL PACIFIC, GUAM: The 3rd and 21st Marine Regiments battle to the top of Bundschu Ridge, but are unable to continue any farther against numerous enemy positions. The Japanese begin marshaling reinforcements near Mount Tenjo.

NEW GUINEA: FEAF B-24 Liberators, A-20 Havocs, B-25 Mitchells, P-39 Airacobras, P-38 Lightnings, P-40s, and P-47 Thunderbolts attack targets on the Vogelkop Peninsula. The headquarters of the 345th Bombardment Group (Medium) and the B-25s of the 500th and 501st Bombardment Squadrons (Medium) redeploy from Nadzab to Biak Island.

B-24s attack the airfield at Yap.

Sergeant Ray E. Eubanks of D Company, 503rd Parachute Infantry Regiment, is attempting to come to the aid of a platoon isolated by the Japanese on Noemfoor Island. When his company takes machine-gun, rifle, and mortar fire from a strong enemy position, Eubanks is ordered to take a squad and lay down a base of fire to suppress the Japanese so that the rest of the company can move forward.

Maneuvering to within 30 yards of the enemy, Sergeant Eubanks halts his men and orders them to continue firing while he moves closer to the enemy position. Taking a Browning Automatic Rifle (BAR) he braves heavy fire to reach a position about 15 yards from the enemy where he is able to deliver accurate fire on the Japanese. Sergeant Eubanks is quickly wounded and his weapon is damaged by a bullet. He nevertheless charges into the enemy position, and using the BAR as a club, eliminates the position before falling mortally wounded. For his great courage in the face of the enemy, Sergeant Eubanks will be awarded the Medal of Honor.

Second Lieutenant George W. G. Boyce, Jr., a platoon leader in the 112th Cavalry Regimental Combat Team, is ordered to attack with his platoon to overcome Japanese defenses near Afua, on the Driniumor River, and open the way for the troop to reach an isolated American unit. As Boyce's platoon moves forward, the Japanese immediately respond with rifle, machine-gun, and mortar fire. As he moves forward with a squad to establish a base of fire, the Japanese throw hand grenades into the midst of the Americans. Second Lieutenant Boyce throws himself on a grenade and saves the lives of several of his men. Boyce's sacrifice will win him the Medal of Honor.

July 24

CBI: Tenth Air Force P-51 Mustangs attack targets near Kamaing and Mogaung and P-40s attack Japanese positions at Myitkyina.

In China, Fourteenth Air Force B-25 Mitchells and P-40s bomb rail facilities at Sienning. P-40s attack Pailochi airfield. Fighter pilots report 30 Japanese aircraft destroyed. P-40s attack river and road transportation and Japanese troop concentrations at Changsha and Hengyang. P-51 Mustangs dive-bomb White Cloud airfield near Canton.

ATLANTIC: German submarine *U-861* attacks convoy JT 99 (Rio de Janeiro to Trinidad) and escapes as aircraft from escort carrier USS *Solomons* close in.

ETO: Operation Cobra. Eighth Air Force sends 909 B-17s and 677 B-24 Liberators, escorted by 478 P-38 Lightnings, P-47 Thunderbolts, and P-51 Mustangs, to attack German defensive positions in front of the U.S. First Army for Operation Cobra, but the mission is cancelled due to heavy cloud cover. One group of bombers, however, continues the mission and flies perpendicular to the intended target, not parallel, as Bradley had desired. The 452 bombers that continue the mission attack German positions and road and rail lines west of St-Lô, but drop 700 tons of bombs short of the intended target, causing 150 American casualties from the 30th Infantry Division.

Three bombers are lost and 144 are damaged. Aircrew casualties are two killed, two wounded, and 21 missing. Fighter pilots report one confirmed kill in the air and one on the ground. Three fighters are lost and two are damaged.

Over Germany 143 P-51 Mustangs fly a sweep over Lechfeld and Leipheim airfields. Pilots report three confirmed kills in the air and 12 on the ground. Two P-51s are lost and seven are damaged. The two pilots are reported missing.

During the night seven B-17s drop leaflets over France. A total of six B-24s fly in support of Carpetbagger operations.

Ninth Air Force sends A-20 and B-26 Marauders to attack bridges and fuel storage sites. P-47s and P-38s attack roads, bridges, and logistics storage sites.

The headquarters of the 370th Fighter Group redeploys to France. Ninth Air Force is now operating from 15 airfields in Normandy.

ITALY: Fifteenth Air Force sends 200 B-17s and B-24 Liberators against a tank repair facility, a ball-bearing production facility, harbor facilities, and airfields in Italy.

Twelfth Air Force B-25 Mitchells and B-26 Marauders attack bridges. A-20 Havocs attack ammunition storage facilities. P-47 Thunderbolts attack bridges, rail lines, and roads.

CENTRAL PACIFIC, TINIAN: Naval Task Force 52, commanded by Rear Admiral Harry W. Hill, lands the 4th Marine Division (Major General Harry Schmidt, USMC) on Tinian. Naval gunfire, carrier aircraft, and land-based aircraft from Saipan support the landing. The 2nd Marine Division conducts a feint off the shore in view of Tinian town, supported by air and naval bombardment and artillery fire from Saipan. The deception becomes a real fight when 6-inch Japanese guns fire on the ships supporting the marines. The battleship *Colorado* is hit 22 times, but is saved by the heroic act of the captain of the destroyer *Norman Scott*, who puts his ship in the line of fire and takes six hits as well. The deception costs 62 men killed and 322 wounded. The Japanese report that the American attempt to land on Tinian has been stopped.

Meanwhile, the 4th Marine Division lands on the northwest corner of the island with minimum resistance. The army's XXIV Corps Artillery supports the landings with fire from Saipan. The 25th Marine Regiment encounters mines, but the 24th Marines reach their objective line. After much confusion and delay, the 23rd Marines land. The 8th Marine Regiment of the 2nd Marine Division, now redeployed north after the deception operation, lands shortly afterward. Within a few hours, 15,600 men are on the island at a cost of 15 killed and 225 wounded. That night, the Japanese counterattack with infantry and tanks, but are driven back by the 24th and 23rd Marines.

Seventh Air Force P-47 Thunderbolts from Saipan attack Japanese positions.

CENTRAL PACIFIC, GUAM: The 77th Infantry Division has completed its landing on Guam and now has responsibility for the southern perimeter of the beachhead.

NEW GUINEA: FEAF B-25 Mitchells of the 499th Bombardment Squadron (Medium), 345th Bombardment Group (Medium), redeploy from Nadzab to Biak Island. The headquarters of the 85th Fighter Wing redeploys to Hollandia.

Fifth Air Force B-24 Liberators sink a Japanese transport in Kau Bay, Halmahera Island.

July 25

CBI: Tenth Air Force P-40s and P-51 Mustangs attack targets around Myitkyina, Kamaing, and Mogaung.

In China, Fourteenth Air Force sends 24 B-24 Liberators to bomb the railyards at Yoyang. P-40 pilots escorting the bombers report six Japanese fighters shot down. P-40s and P-51 Mustangs attack road and river traffic and cavalry units at Changsha and Hengyang. P-47 Thunderbolts and P-51 Mustangs support Chinese ground forces at the Salween River front.

Fourteenth Air Force B-25 Mitchells sink a Japanese salvage vessel east of Hong Kong.

ATLANTIC: German submarine *U-862* torpedoes and sinks a U.S. freighter in the central South Atlantic.

ETO: Operation Cobra. The 21st Army Group begins the breakout from Normandy. Bradley's concept for Cobra is to employ an overwhelming air attack against German positions along a narrow front. Before the enemy can recover, a massed artillery bombardment will follow. The infantry will attack with three divisions of VII Corps followed by three more divisions of VIII Corps to capture Coutances and Granville. The First Army will make the main effort. VII Corps of First Army is to attack on a narrow front along the Périers Road west of St-Lô after heavy air and artillery bombardment and break through the German lines. The 83rd and 9th Infantry Divisions will hold the west side of the breakthrough; the 4th and 30th Infantry Divisions will hold the east side. The 1st Infantry Division, reinforced by a combat command from 3rd Armored Division, will attack to exploit the gap in the German defenses and move toward Coutances. The 2nd Armored Division and the rest of 3rd Armored Division will move into the open country beyond. V Corps and XIX Corps will conduct holding attacks to limit the German response.

Eighth Air Force sends 917 B-17s and 664 B-24 Liberators, escorted by 483 P-38 Lightnings, P-47 Thunderbolts, and P-51 Mustangs, to attack German positions in an area 3,000 yards deep and 7,000 yards wide, saturating it by dropping 4,700 tons of bombs. During the approach to the target, 35 bombers drop their bomb loads early and the 9th and 30th Infantry Divisions are hit. The mistake kills 102 and wounds 380 infantrymen; among those killed is Lieutenant General Lesley J. McNair, the most senior officer in the U.S. Army. Ninth Air Force sends A-20 and B-26 Marauders and P-47 Thunderbolts to strafe and bomb German positions. Three divisions attack on a six-mile front. VII Corps advances two miles. Despite the massive devastation caused by the air attacks and artillery, the Germans are able to recover and mount a defense. The 330th Infantry Regiment of the 83rd Infantry Division makes no progress in the hedgerows. The 9th and the 4th Infantry Divisions stall, and the 30th Infantry Division advances about a mile. The VII Corps commander, Major General J. Lawton Collins, decides to send his exploitation force into the fight, believing that the Germans must not be allowed to recover and regain momentum in the attack.

VII Corps attacks with the 9th, 4th, and 30th Infantry Divisions and, despite the massive destruction of the aerial bombing, make a limited advance.

During Operation Cobra, five bombers are lost and 175 are damaged. Aircrew losses are nine wounded and 46 missing. Fighter pilots report 12 confirmed kills and one probable in the air and two confirmed kills on the ground. Two fighters are lost and five are damaged; two pilots are reported missing.

A total of 17 B-24s fly in support of Carpetbagger operations.

General Eisenhower orders that all American ground forces in France will be reorganized into two armies, designated as the First and the Third, under the 12th Army Group commanded by General Omar Bradley. General Montgomery has operational control over all Allied ground forces until the 12th Army Group is operational.

MEDITERRANEAN: The Anvil Dragoon invasion force begins loading equipment at Naples, Italy. The airborne assault plan is approved. The plan calls for the employment of an airborne division parachuting from 396 C-47s, followed by over 300 gliders. The day after the landings 112 cargo planes will be used for resupply.

Fifteenth Air Force sends 420 B-17s and B-24 Liberators to attack the Hermann Göring tank works in Linz, Austria. P-51 Mustangs and P-38 Lightnings provide escort and encounter nearly 200 German fighters. Aircrews and fighter pilots report over 60 fighters shot down. U.S. aircraft losses total 21.

Operating from airfields in Soviet Ukraine as part of the Frantic missions, 34 P-51s and 33 P-38s attack the airfield and vehicle convoys near Lwow, Poland, and return to the USSR. Pilots report 27 confirmed kills and three probable kills on German dive-bombers.

ITALY: II Corps takes operational control of the 85th, 88th, and 91st Infantry Divisions.

Twelfth Air Force B-25 Mitchells and B-26 Marauders attack bridges. A-20 Havocs attack ammunition storage facilities and rail lines. P-47 Thunderbolts attack bridges, rail lines, and roads.

CENTRAL PACIFIC: Seventh Air Force B-24 Liberators from Kwajalein bomb Truk. The B-24s of the 819th Bombardment Squadron (Heavy), 30th Bombardment Group (Heavy), arrives on Saipan from Hawaii.

Carrier aircraft from Vice Admiral Marc A. Mitscher's TF 58 attack Japanese positions and shipping at Yap, Ulithi, and Palau. F4F Hellcats damage a destroyer north of Babelthuap. Other F4F Hellcats sink a guardboat in the Palaus.

CENTRAL PACIFIC, GUAM: The 3rd and 21st Marine Regiments continue the attack to clear Japanese positions on the ridges. The 9th Marines reach the Sasa River. A Japanese counterattack on the 3rd Marine Division is disorganized, but many enemy attackers are able to reach the beachhead before being killed. The 77th Infantry Division controls the beachhead, allowing the 22nd and 4th Marine Regiments to focus their efforts on the Japanese defenses on the Orote Peninsula.

Captain Louis H. Wilson, Jr., commands a company in the 2nd Battalion, 9th Marines, 3rd Marine Division, and is ordered to attack Fonte Hill. Capturing the position, Captain Wilson organizes a defense and is wounded three times as the Japanese concentrate fire on the marines. He returns from the aid station and reassumes command to defend the position against numerous counterattacks through the night. During one action, he rescues a wounded marine in the face of heavy enemy fire. He battles the Japanese hand-to-hand several times as the marines repel the enemy. In the morning hours, Captain Wilson organizes a patrol to seize a critical position dominating his own position. Despite enemy fire that causes 13 casualties, Captain Wilson and the remaining marines succeed in occupying the position. Captain Wilson's extraordinary dedication to duty and his heroic actions in the face of a superior enemy force will win him the Medal of Honor.

NEW GUINEA: At Noemfoor, after engineers work around the clock for 11 straight days, the Kornasen airfield is made ready for FEAF P-38 Lightnings to land.

July 26

CBI: Tenth Air Force P-40s attack Japanese positions at Myitkyina. P-51 Mustangs attack targets near Mogaung and Kamaing.

In China, Fourteenth Air Force sends B-25 Mitchells and P-40s to attack the town of Tengchung. P-40s and P-38 Lightnings attack targets of opportunity near Tengchung, Lungling, and Mangshih. P-40s bomb Hengyang airfield.

ATLANTIC: President Roosevelt approves the plans for the seizure of Peleliu and the invasion of the Philippines. Both Admiral Nimitz and General MacArthur believe that Peleliu with its airfield must be captured to protect the right flank of MacArthur's Philippine invasion force. The plan for Peleliu is called Operation Stalemate.

ETO: VII Corps commander Major General Collins orders the advance of his armored divisions to exploit the weakened German lines. The 9th, 4th, and 30th Infantry Divisions make steady progress. The 2nd Armored Division advances past St. Gilles and reaches Cauisy. The 3rd Armored Division and the 1st Infantry Division capture Marigny. The V and XIX Corps advance three miles against strong resistance. B-26 Marauders and P-47 Thunderbolts destroy German tank formations attempting to stem the American breakthrough.

Eighth Air Force sends 192 P-47 Thunderbolts to bomb marshaling yards and a fuel storage area in France. One P-47 is lost and 10 are damaged; the pilot is reported missing. A total of nine B-24s fly in support of Carpetbagger operations. During the night seven B-17s drop leaflets over France.

Ninth Air Force sends A-20 Havocs and B-26 Marauders against a fuel storage site. P-47s attack German positions near St-Lô.

MEDITERRANEAN: Operating from airfields in Soviet Ukraine as part of the Frantic missions, 34 P-51s and 33 P-38 Lightnings attack German aircraft near Bucharest and Ploeşti and return to bases in Italy.

More than 300 B-17s and B-24 Liberators attack aircraft production facilities and airfields near Vienna, Austria, an airfield in Hungary, and an oil storage facility at Berat, Albania. Aircrews and fighter pilots report over 70 German fighters shot down.

ITALY: Twelfth Air Force B-25 Mitchells and B-26 Marauders attack bridges. A-20 Havocs bomb roads and vehicles. P-47 Thunderbolts attack gun positions and the airfield at Valence. Pilots report more than 20 aircraft destroyed on the ground.

SOUTHWEST PACIFIC AREA: U.S. submarines carry out a succession of attacks on a Japanese convoy in the South China Sea. USS *Angler* torpedoes and damages a transport; USS *Flasher* torpedoes and sinks a merchant tanker and supports USS *Crevalle* in sinking a cargo ship and transport.

U.S. submarine *Robalo* is sunk by a mine in the Balabac Strait.

U.S. submarine *Sawfish* torpedoes and sinks Japanese submarine *I-29* in Luzon Strait.

PACIFIC: President Roosevelt, aboard the heavy cruiser USS *Baltimore*, arrives at Pearl Harbor. The president and Admiral Leahy will meet with Admiral Nimitz and General MacArthur to discuss future Pacific operations.

CENTRAL PACIFIC: B-25 Mitchells from Engebi Island bomb Ponape Island.

Carrier aircraft from Vice Admiral Marc A. Mitscher's TF 58 attack ground targets and shipping in the western Carolines.

CENTRAL PACIFIC, TINIAN: Seventh Air Force P-47 Thunderbolts and B-25 Mitchells from Saipan attack Japanese positions on Tinian Island. On Tinian, the marines capture Mount Lasso.

CENTRAL PACIFIC, GUAM: A Japanese attack against the marines advancing into the Orote Peninsula is stopped by devastating artillery fire from the 77th Division artillery. Altogether about 26,000 artillery shells are fired. Nevertheless, the advance of the marines into the Orote defenses moves only about 1,500 yards.

NEW GUINEA: FEAF A-20 Havocs and B-25 Mitchells, along with RAAF fighter-bombers, attack Japanese troops, coastal shipping, and other targets of opportunity from Hollandia to Wewak.

B-24 Liberators bomb logistics sites on Woleai Atoll.

July 27

CBI: New Galahad forces capture the northern airfield at Myitkyina.

Tenth Air Force P-51 Mustangs, P-40s, and A-36 Intruder (Apache) fighter-bombers attack Japanese positions around Myitkyina and the area around Kamaing and Mogaung.

ETO: VII Corps captures Périers and Lessay. The 3rd Armored Division and 1st Infantry Division move west to threaten the flank of the German forces at Coutances. VIII Corps captures Avranches, which opens Brittany to American forces. XIX Corps is ordered to capture Vire, a key road junction southeast of St-Lô. The German Seventh Army begins a withdrawal.

Eighth Air Force sends 26 B-17s to bomb coastal batteries in France and Belgium. Another 120 B-24 Liberators attack a command center and industrial targets in Belgium. The bombers are escorted by 154 P-38 Lightnings, P-47 Thunderbolts, and P-51 Mustangs. One B-24 is lost and 32 are damaged. Fighter pilots report one confirmed kill. One P-51 is lost and the pilot is reported missing. Nearly 200 P-38 Lightnings, P-47 Thunderbolts, and P-51 Mustangs fly a fighter-bomber mission against railroad traffic in France. Three fighters are lost and two are damaged. The pilots are reported missing.

During the night seven B-17s drop leaflets over France and the Netherlands.

Ninth Air Force A-20 Havocs and B-26 Marauders bomb Loire and Seine River bridges. P-47s attack German positions near Coutances and St-Lô.

The P-38s of the 393rd and 394th Fighter Squadrons of the 367th Fighter Group and the P-47s of the 512th and 514th Fighter Squadrons of the 406th Fighter Group redeploy to France.

MEDITERRANEAN: Fifteenth Air Force sends 366 B-17s and B-24 Liberators escorted by P-38 Lightnings and P-51 Mustangs to attack an armament plant at Budapest, Hungary.

ITALY: Operation Mallory Major succeeds in cutting the German Fourteenth Army from its supply bases in northern Italy by bombing bridges and roads leading south. However, the benefits are negated because the Allied armies are standing down to rest and refit. Lack of action on the front lines allows the Germans to rebuild and restore their supply lines by August 6, in time for the next Allied offensive. In its advance to the Arno River, the Fifth Army has suffered 18,000 casualties and collected 16,000 German prisoners since the capture of Rome.

Twelfth Air Force A-20 Havocs attack vehicles moving along the Po River valley. B-35s, B-26 Marauders, and P-47 Thunderbolts attack bridges in the Po River valley and aircraft, guns, and rail lines in northwest Italy.

SOUTHWEST PACIFIC AREA: U.S. submarine *Dace* attacks a Japanese convoy and sinks a fleet tanker south of Zamboanga, Philippines.

PACIFIC: The Pearl Harbor Conference. President Roosevelt meets with the Southwest Pacific Area commander, General Douglas MacArthur, and Pacific Ocean Areas commander, Admiral Chester Nimitz, to discuss strategic options in the Pacific. Nimitz lays out his arguments for his Granite plan, directed at Formosa, but leaving open the possibility of capturing Luzon first. MacArthur argues for his Reno V plan, liberating the Philippines prior to invading Japan. He notes that Luzon is a better objective than Formosa. First, the Philippine people will cooperate with Americans, while the population on Formosa may not. The Japanese can also counterattack from China if U.S. forces land on Formosa. MacArthur stresses to Roosevelt the moral obligation of the United States to free the Philippines. In their presentations to the president, MacArthur and Nimitz are in agreement on the basic strategic approach to the defeat of Japan, but differ on the operational objectives that will best achieve this goal.

CENTRAL PACIFIC: Seventh Air Force B-24 Liberators from the Marshall Islands bomb Truk. B-25 Mitchells from Makin Island bomb Jaluit Atoll.

Carrier aircraft from Vice Admiral Marc A. Mitscher's TF 58 attack shipping and ground targets in the western Carolines.

CENTRAL PACIFIC, TINIAN: The 2nd and 4th Marine Divisions advance southward along flat, open terrain, strung out in a single line across the island. Seventh Air Force P-47 Thunderbolts and B-25 Mitchells from Saipan support the advance.

NEW GUINEA: FEAF P-39 Airacobras strafe Japanese troops and small vessels along the west coast of Geelvink Bay. A-20 Havocs, B-25 Mitchells, and P-40s attack Japanese troops, logistics, support facilities, barges, and gun positions along the coast from Aitape to Wewak.

B-25s bomb the airfield on Halmahera Island. B-24 Liberators bomb the airfield on Woleai Atoll and logistics sites on Mariaon and Tagaulap Islands in the Carolines. Other B-24s bomb Dili on Timor Island.

Fifth Air Force B-24 Liberators, B-25 Mitchells, and P-38 Lightnings attack Japanese shipping near Halmahera Island.

July 28

CBI: Tenth Air Force sends over 100 A-36 Intruder (Apache) fighter-bombers, P-40s, and P-51 Mustangs to attack Myitkyina, Kamaing, Mogaung, and Bhamo.

In China, Fourteenth Air Force P-40s and P-51 Mustangs attack Japanese troops, road and river transportation traffic, and targets of opportunity around Tungting Lake. B-25 Mitchells attack the Yoyang railroad yards, a bridge over the Yellow River, and the White Cloud, Tien Ho, and Hankow airfields.

ETO: The 4th Armored Division of VIII Corps establishes contact with the 1st Infantry Division of VII Corps at Coutances, capturing 4,500 prisoners. This is the objective of Operation Cobra. The 2nd and 3rd Armored Divisions attack toward

Granville and Avranches. The 4th Armored Division followed by the 6th Armored Division serves as the spearhead of VIII Corps as it attacks toward the Seine River. XIX Corps reaches Tessy-sur-Vire, while V Corps attacks at Forêt de Cerisy.

Eighth Air Force sends 291 B-24 Liberators escorted by nearly 300 P-47 Thunderbolts and P-51 Mustangs to attack fuel storage sites and V-weapon supply sites in Belgium and France, but the forces are recalled because of cloud cover over the targets. Nine bombers are lost and eight are damaged. Aircrew losses are ten killed. Three fighters are damaged. In another mission 766 B-17s escorted by 386 P-38 Lightnings and P-51 Mustangs attack the synthetic oil plant at Merseburg, Germany. Seven bombers are lost and 217 are damaged. Aircrew losses are one killed, seven wounded, and 67 missing. Fighter pilots report four confirmed kills and one probable. Two fighters are lost and three are damaged. Three pilots are reported missing.

During the night six B-17s drop leaflets over France.

Ninth Air Force sends A-20 Havocs and B-26 Marauders escorted by P-47 Thunderbolts against rail bridges, logistics sites, and ammunition storage areas in France. P-47s and P-38s also provide air cover for U.S. First Army units.

MEDITERRANEAN: Fifteenth Air Force sends 349 B-17s and B-24 Liberators with P-51 Mustangs as escort to attack the Ploeşti, Romania, oil refinery. A total of 20 bombers are lost.

ITALY: Twelfth Air Force A-20 Havocs attack vehicles moving along the Po River valley. B-35s and B-26 Marauders, A-20 Havocs, and P-47 Thunderbolts attack bridges in the Po River valley and aircraft, guns, and rail lines in northwest Italy and vehicles in the Rhône River valley of France.

SOUTHWEST PACIFIC AREA: U.S. submarine *Crevalle* attacks a Japanese convoy off northwestern Luzon, sinking a cargo ship.

CENTRAL PACIFIC, TINIAN: Ushi Point airfield, captured intact by the marines, receives P-47 Thunderbolt fighters. The marines also capture Gurguan airfield without encountering any Japanese.

Seventh Air Force B-25 Mitchells and P-47 Thunderbolts based on Saipan attack suspected Japanese positions.

U.S. Destroyer escorts *Wyman* and *Reynolds* sink Japanese submarine *I-55* east of Tinian.

CENTRAL PACIFIC, GUAM: Fonte Ridge is captured by the 3rd and 21st Marines after days of bitter fighting. The 1st Provisional Marine Brigade captures the Orote airfield after a 45-minute air and naval bombardment; the airfield had been part of the U.S. base on Guam. On December 10, 1941, a Japanese landing force captured the airfield as the marines defending this portion of Guam were forced to surrender.

NEW GUINEA: FEAF P-39 Airacobras strafe Japanese troops and small vessels along the west coast of Geelvink Bay. A-20 Havocs, B-25 Mitchells, and P-40s attack targets along the coast from Aitape to Wewak. B-24 Liberators bomb the airfield on Woleai Atoll. Other B-24s bomb Dili on Timor Island.

The headquarters of the 309th Bombardment Wing (Heavy) redeploys from Saidor to Noemfoor Island.

July 29

ALEUTIANS: Eleventh Air Force sends three B-24 Liberators to fly bombing and reconnaissance missions over Shimushu and Paramushiru Islands.

CBI: Tenth Air Force sends about 100 A-36 Intruder (Apache) fighter-bombers and P-40s to bomb targets at Myitkyina, Kamaing, and Mogaung.

In China, Fourteenth Air Force sends 26 B-24 Liberators to bomb a logistics storage area in Samah Bay on Hainan Island. B-25 Mitchells bomb Hankow airfield, the Kaifeng railroad yards, and the town of Tengchung. P-40s and P-51 Mustangs attack bridges, troops, and river, road, and rail traffic.

Twentieth Air Force sends over 70 B-29 Superfortresses from Chengtu airfield in China to bomb the Showa Steel Works at Anshan and the harbor at Taku. One B-29 is lost to Japanese fighters. It is the first Superfortress to be lost in combat. Another B-29 bombs Chinwangtao and then makes a forced landing at a friendly field near Ankang.

ATLANTIC: The JCS planners reject the idea of an invasion of Luzon as a preliminary operation to the seizure of Formosa, as outlined in MacArthur's Reno V plan. Leyte would serve as the base for the reduction of Japanese air power to prepare for the assault on Formosa. The capture of Formosa is seen as essential in the defeat of Japan, as it would provide air bases for strategic attack on the home islands. The Palau Islands are considered essential to sea and air forces supporting landing in the Philippines. The Bonin Islands will be attacked in April 1945, followed by an invasion of Kyushu in October and a final assault on Tokyo in December.

ETO: Coutances is captured. American air attacks destroy an estimated 137 tanks and 500 other vehicles. VIII and VII Corps attack toward Avranches as German resistance weakens. VIII Corps crosses the Seine River.

Eighth Air Force sends 657 B-17s escorted by 429 P-38 Lightnings, P-47 Thunderbolts, and P-51 Mustangs to attack oil production and storage facilities in Germany and airfields in France. Fifteen bombers are lost and 350 are damaged. Aircrews report 15 confirmed kills and eight probables. Aircrew losses are one killed, 17 wounded, and 138 missing. Fighter pilots report 21 confirmed kills and two probables and three confirmed kills on the ground. At least one of these is the new German Messerschmitt 262 (Me-262), the world's first jet fighter. Seven fighters are lost and seven are damaged; the seven pilots are reported missing.

Another 473 B-24 Liberators escorted by 106 P-51s attack an oil refinery near Bremen, Germany. Two bombers are lost and 96 are damaged. Aircrew losses are three killed, two wounded, and 15 missing. Airfields in France are attacked by 98 B-24s escorted by 142 P-51s. Two bombers are damaged. Aircrew losses are five killed and seven wounded.

A total of 44 B-24s fly in support of Carpetbagger operations. During the night six B-17s drop leaflets over France.

Ninth Air Force P-47 Thunderbolts and P-38 Lightnings provide cover in support of the U.S. First Army.

Eighth Air Force B-17s bomb U-boat facilities in Bremen, destroying German submarines *U-878* and *U-2323*.

Sergeant Hulon B. Whittington, a squad leader with the 41st Armored Infantry Regiment, 2nd Armored Division, faces a German tank and infantry counterattack during the night. Taking charge of the platoon, Whittington reorganizes the defense and takes action to stop a threat by leaping on top of an American tank and directing its fire against oncoming German tanks. In the face of intense fire, Sergeant Whittington then leads a bayonet assault on the stalled enemy column, completely disrupting the German attack. Whittington continues to lead and inspire his men, even providing first aid to the wounded. For his inspiring leadership, devotion to duty, and intrepid acts of courage, Sergeant Whittington will receive the Medal of Honor.

MEDITERRANEAN: The Seventh Army issues the final planning order for Dragoon. The Western Task Force composed of British, French, and American warships under Vice Admiral H. Kent Hewitt will support the landing with five battleships, 20 cruisers, 98 destroyers, and 283 other combat ships. A total of 1,300 landing craft will be employed for the invasion. The XII Tactical Air Force under Brigadier General Gordon P. Saville will have 1,100 aircraft available to fly air cover over the landing beaches. These include British, French, and U.S. squadrons operating from bases in Corsica. Additional air support will be provided by seven British and two U.S. escort carriers with 200 aircraft. VI Corps is to land at three different points on the coast of southern France between Cavalaire-sur-Mer (17 km from St. Tropez) and Saint Raphaël. The divisions of VI Corps are designated as Alpha Force (3rd Infantry Division), Delta Force (45th Infantry Division), and Camel Force (36th Infantry Division). Rear Admiral Spencer S. Lewis will land Camel Force, Rear Admiral Frank J. Lowry will land Delta Force, and Rear Admiral Bertram J. Rodgers will land Alpha Force. The 1st Special Service Force will attack coastal batteries prior to D-day. The 1st Airborne Task Force will land in the vicinity of Le Muy and Le Luc to block German reinforcements from reaching the beachhead. The French Army B, led by General of the Army Jean de Lattre de Tassigny, will follow the 3rd Infantry Division and capture Toulon and Marseilles. D-day is set for August 15.

Frantic operations involve 14 P-38 Lightnings, taking off from bases in Soviet Ukraine to attack targets in Hungary.

ITALY: Twelfth Air Force A-20 Havocs and P-47 Thunderbolts attack airfields, bridges, and rail lines.

SOUTHWEST PACIFIC AREA: U.S. submarine *Perch* torpedoes and sinks a Japanese guardboat in the Philippine Sea, east of Leyte Island.

PACIFIC: President Roosevelt departs Hawaii aboard heavy cruiser *Baltimore* for Adak, Aleutians.

CENTRAL PACIFIC: Seventh Air Force B-24 Liberators from Kwajalein bomb Truk and B-25 Mitchells from Engebi Island bomb Ponape Island.

U.S. submarine *Drum* torpedoes and sinks a Japanese sampan off Palau.

CENTRAL PACIFIC, TINIAN: The 2nd and 4th Marine Divisions continue advancing south and encounter several Japanese strongpoints and repulse weak counterattacks.

Seventh Air Force P-47 Thunderbolts provide ground support to the marines.

CENTRAL PACIFIC, GUAM: The Japanese defenders are driven into a pocket on the Orote Peninsula. The marine barracks is recaptured and the American flag is raised in an emotional ceremony. Major General Roy S. Geiger orders a consolidation to prepare his forces for the second phase of the operation to capture Guam.

NEW GUINEA: FEAF P-39 Airacobras strafe Japanese troops along the west coast of Geelvink Bay. A-20 Havocs, B-25 Mitchells, and P-40s attack Japanese troops, logistics support facilities, barges, and gun positions along the coast from Aitape to Wewak.

B-24 Liberators bomb the airfield on Woleai Atoll and logistics sites on Mariaon and Tagaulap Islands in the Carolines. Other B-24s bomb targets on Timor Island.

July 30

CBI: Tenth Air Force A-36 Intruder (Apache) fighter-bombers and P-40s attack Myitkyina and the Kamaing-Mogaung area.

In China, Fourteenth Air Force sends 11 B-24 Liberators to bomb Wuchang. P-40s and P-51 Mustangs attack bridges, railyards, logistics bases, and road, river, and rail traffic near Tungting Lake. In French Indochina more than 20 P-40s and P-38 Lightnings attack shipping and road traffic around Hanoi.

ETO: The 6th Armored Division captures Avranches. The seizure of Avranches breaks the German defensive line, allowing Third Army to drive across Brittany.

Commander of the Eighth Air Force, Lieutenant General James H. Doolittle, orders that the VIII Air Force Composite Command take operational control of all Carpetbagger, H2X (radar-supported bombing), night leaflet, and weather missions.

Eighth Air Force sends 237 P-47 Thunderbolts and P-51 Mustangs to attack fly fighter sweeps over France seeking German aircraft. Pilots report three confirmed kills in the air and nine on the ground. One fighter is lost and five are damaged. The pilot is reported as missing.

A total of 31 B-24s fly in support of Carpetbagger operations.

Ninth Air Force sends more than 450 A-20 Havocs and B-26 Marauders to attack German defenses in the Chaumont area in support of the U.S. First Army. P-47s escort the bombers and conduct armed reconnaissance in the Orleans-Paris area.

The P-47s of the 410th, 411th, and 412th Fighter Squadrons of the 373rd Fighter Group redeploy from England to France.

MEDITERRANEAN: Fifteenth Air Force sends over 300 B-17s and B-24 Liberators escorted by P-38 Lightnings and P-51 Mustangs to attack marshaling yards in Yugoslavia and an aircraft production facility in Budapest, Hungary.

ITALY: Twelfth Air Force A-20 Havocs and P-47 Thunderbolts attack shipping, rail lines, and bridges.

CENTRAL PACIFIC: Seventh Air Force B-25 Mitchells from Makin Island bomb Jaluit Atoll.

CENTRAL PACIFIC, TINIAN: The 24th Marines attack the town of Tinian supported by artillery and naval gunfire. Flamethrower tanks assist in clearing Japanese defensive positions located in caves. The 25th Marines capture Airfield Number 4. With the capture of the island's main town, the Japanese are squeezed into a four-square-mile area of rocky hills with numerous caves and covered in brush.

Seventh Air Force B-25 Mitchells and P-47 Thunderbolts from Saipan attack Japanese positions.

Private Joseph W. Ozbourn, a Browning Automatic Rifleman with the 1st Battalion, 23rd Marines, 4th Marine Division, is engaged in clearing Japanese troops from dugouts and pillboxes. As he and several other marines approach an enemy position, they are hit by an explosion near a dugout. Private Ozbourn was ready to throw a grenade when the explosion went off. Seeing the live grenade lying on the ground near his comrades, Ozbourn covers it with his body and is killed by the explosion. For his act of self-sacrifice, Private Ozbourn will receive the Medal of Honor.

NEW GUINEA: At the Driniumor River, the 112th Cavalry and the 127th Infantry are almost surrounded during a series of nearly continuous battles that have lasted several days. The Americans, fighting in heavy jungle, are resupplied by airdrops. Over 1,000 men are casualties.

The 6th Infantry Division with 7,300 men lands at Sansapor on Vogelkop, between two Japanese garrisons, one at Manokwari and the other at Sorong airfield. American engineers immediately begin laying out a new airfield.

Operation Globetrotter begins. Naval Task Force 77, commanded by Rear Admiral William M. Fechteler, lands two battalions of the 1st Infantry Regiment of the 6th Infantry Division (Major General Franklin C. Sibert) near Cape Opmari, at the Vogelkop Peninsula. A battalion of the 63rd Infantry lands to support, while other units of the 63rd occupy Middelburg and Amsterdam Islands. The Americans encounter no initial resistance. The engineers begin surveying the area for an airfield. The infantry skirmishes with some Japanese, but the area is secured with the loss of 14 men killed, 29 wounded, and two missing.

FEAF P-39 Airacobras support ground forces on Biak Island and support the landing on the Vogelkop Peninsula. A-20 Havocs, B-25 Mitchells, and P-40s attack Japanese troops, logistics support facilities, barges, and gun positions along the coast from Aitape to Wewak. B-24 Liberators and P-38 Lightnings attack the airfield and oil installations at Boela on Ceram Island in the Moluccas, and other B-24 Liberators hit Morotai Island in the Celebes Islands.

U.S. submarine *Bonefish* torpedoes and sinks a Japanese fleet tanker northeast of Borneo.

Fifth Air Force B-25 Mitchells attack Japanese installations and shipping at Tobele, Halmahera, sinking a small cargo vessel.

July 31

CBI: The Air Transport Command is averaging the delivery of 71,000 tons of supplies a month to China over the Hump.

Tenth Air Force A-36 Intruder (Apache) fighter-bombers and P-40s attack Japanese defenses at Myitkyina and others attack the Kamaing-Mogaung area.

In China, Fourteenth Air Force B-24 Liberators bomb the Wuchang railyards. B-25 Mitchells bomb Hengshan, Siangtan, and Hankow and attack the airfields at Tien Ho, White Cloud, Hengyang, and Wuchang. P-40s and P-51 Mustangs attack bridges, railyards, logistics bases, and road, river, and rail traffic near Changsha and Hengyang.

ETO: Avranches is captured by the 4th Armored Division; the 6th Armored Division advances on Granville. The German flank is completely open. General Eisenhower now attempts to encircle and destroy all German forces in France.

Eighth Air Force sends 705 B-17s escorted by 439 P-47 Thunderbolts and P-51 Mustangs to attack Munich industrial targets and airfields. Ten bombers are lost and 331 are damaged. Aircrew losses are two killed, six wounded, and 82 missing. Fighter pilots report 18 confirmed kills on the ground and one probable in the air. Three fighters are lost and eight are damaged. Three pilots are reported missing.

More than 400 B-24 Liberators escorted by 135 P-38 Lightnings bomb the chemical works at Ludwigshafen and the city of Mannheim. Six bombers are lost and 186 damaged. Aircrew losses are one killed, seven wounded, and 62 missing. One fighter is damaged. Another 104 B-24 Liberators escorted by 38 P-47s and P-51s bomb airfields in France. Four bombers are damaged.

A total of 13 B-24s fly in support of Carpetbagger operations.

Ninth Air Force sends nearly 500 A-20 Havocs and B-26 Marauders to attack bridges and a fuel storage site. P-47s conduct dive-bomb attacks on German positions in support of the U.S. First Army.

The headquarters of the 303rd Fighter Wing and the P-38s of the 392nd Fighter Squadron, 367th Fighter Group, redeploy from England to France.

MEDITERRANEAN: Fifteenth Air Force sends over 350 B-17s and B-24 Liberators to attack oil refineries in Ploeşti, Doicesti, and Targoviste, Romania. At the end of the month Fifteenth Air Force reports 142 German aircraft shot down.

ITALY: Twelfth Air Force A-20 Havocs and P-47 Thunderbolts attack airfields, rail lines, and bridges. Pilots report 50 rail cars destroyed.

SOUTHWEST PACIFIC AREA: The submarine attack group TG 17.15 (Commander Lewis S. Parks) attacks a Japanese convoy northeast of Luzon.

U.S. submarine *Dace* torpedoes and sinks a Japanese cargo vessel south of Davao.

U.S. submarine *Lapon* attacks a Japanese convoy, sinking a merchant tanker off the southern tip of Palawan Island.

Commander Lawson P. "Red" Ramage is commander of the submarine USS *Parche* and is in the Straits of Luzon with two other submarines, searching for convoys headed for Luzon to reinforce Japanese forces. Ramage makes a surface attack on a convoy after evading the protective destroyer screen and proceeds to torpedo a cargo ship and sink one tanker and damage another with successive torpedo hits. As the flaming tankers illuminate the area, Ramage torpedoes a transport ship and orders members of the crew below as he maneuvers to avoid a ramming attack by a fast transport ship. The *Parche* is now caught in a crossfire from Japanese escort ships on all sides and the transport dead ahead. He destroys the ship, firing three torpedoes, and is able to break contact without any harm to the boat. For his valiant fight and calm courage, Commander Ramage will win the Medal of Honor. USS *Steelhead*, supporting *Parche*, sinks one previously damaged cargo ship and sinks another.

CENTRAL PACIFIC: Seventh Air Force B-25 Mitchells from Makin Island bomb Nauru Island. B-24 Liberators from the Marshall Islands bomb Truk.

CENTRAL PACIFIC, TINIAN: The last Japanese defensive position on the island is subjected to an intense air, naval gunfire, and artillery bombardment in preparation for the attack of the 23rd and 24th Marines. The Japanese, in well-concealed positions, are able to survive and battle the marines as they advance. The enemy is overwhelmed and the 8th Marines reach the top of the plateau and defend it against several enemy counterattacks. Seventh Air Force B-25 Mitchells and P-47 Thunderbolts based on Saipan bomb the final defensive positions of the Japanese defenders of Tinian.

CENTRAL PACIFIC, GUAM: The 3rd Marine Division and the 77th Infantry Division attack north to eliminate Japanese defenses. The 1st Provisional Marine Brigade controls the southern half of Guam and the beachhead. The 3rd Marine Regiment captures Agana, the capital of the island. The 307th and 305th Infantry Regiments secure the critical Pago-Agana Road, which allows the forward forces to be resupplied.

NEW GUINEA: The 124th Infantry Regiment, 31st Infantry Division, and a battalion of the 169th Infantry, 43rd Infantry Division, cross the Driniumor River to drive back Japanese troops. The unit is called Ted Force after its commander, Colonel Edwin A. Starr.

FEAF P-39 Airacobras strafe Japanese troops and small vessels along the west coast of Geelvink Bay. A-20 Havocs, B-25 Mitchells, and P-40s attack Japanese troops, logistics support facilities, barges, and gun positions along the coast from Aitape to Wewak.

B-24 Liberators bomb the airfield on Woleai Atoll and logistics sites on Mariaon and Tagaulap Islands in the Carolines. Other B-24s bomb Dili on Timor Island. B-24s bomb the airfield on Halmahera Island.

Operation Globetrotter continues. Naval Task Force 77 (Rear Admiral William M. Fechteler) lands troops on Cape Sansapor, New Guinea.

August 1

CBI: Tenth Air Force A-36 Intruder (Apache) fighter-bombers and P-40s support ground forces at Myitkyina.

In China, Fourteenth Air Force B-25 Mitchells bomb Wuchang airfield. P-40s and P-51 Mustangs attack bridges, railyards, logistics bases, and road, river, and rail traffic near Changsha and Hengyang. The airfield and railyard at Hengyang are also attacked.

ATLANTIC: Anvil, the invasion of southern France in support of Overlord, is officially renamed Dragoon at Prime Minister Churchill's insistence. The new name is rumored to reflect Churchill's opinion of the operation, namely that he was dragooned by the Americans into accepting it.

ETO: The XIX Corps of First Army advances toward Vire after a difficult four-day battle against two German tank divisions.

The 12th Army Group is activated under the command of General Omar N. Bradley with operational control of the First and Third Armies. The First Army is commanded by Lieutenant General Courtney H. Hodges. Hodges has V Corps, XIX Corps, and VII Corps. The Third Army is activated under Lieutenant General George S. Patton, Jr., and has the VIII, XII, XV, and XX Corps: XII Corps under Major General Gilbert R. Cook, the XV Corps under Major General Wade H. Haislip, the XX Corps under Major General Walton H. Walker, and the VIII Corps under

Major General Troy Middleton. VIII Corps has nine of Bradley's 21 divisions. Patton's Third Army is to clear the Brittany Peninsula while First Army attacks south toward Mortain. Middleton is ordered to clear the Brittany Peninsula and open the ports. The 4th and 6th Armored Divisions are to lead the attack. Patton sends two other corps south and southeast. British General Montgomery still has operational control of both the U.S. and British army groups. Realizing far too late that the Pas-de-Calais invasion is a ruse, Hitler finally authorizes the German Fifteenth Army to reinforce the defenders at Normandy.

Eighth Air Force sends 76 B-17s escorted by 51 P-51 Mustangs to attack Tours airfield. One bomber is lost and six are damaged. Aircrew losses are six wounded and 10 missing.

Over 400 B-17s escorted by 138 P-38 Lightnings and P-51 Mustangs bomb airfields and a railway bridge near Paris. Three B-17s are lost and 34 damaged. Aircrew losses are nine killed and 27 missing. Three P-51 Mustangs are damaged and one pilot is killed.

Over 200 B-24s escorted by 127 P-47 Thunderbolts and P-51 Mustangs bomb airfields and bridges near Paris. One bomber is lost and 88 damaged. Aircrew casualties are 20 missing. Fighter pilots report three confirmed kills on the ground. Four fighters are damaged. Another 191 B-24s escorted by 81 P-47s are sent against eight V-weapon sites but bad weather over the targets causes all but 61 to abort the mission. Five bombers are damaged.

Nearly 200 B-17s airdrop nearly 2,300 containers of supplies to French Resistance forces in southeast France in preparation for Dragoon. Five B-17s are damaged.

A total of 21 B-24s fly in support of Carpetbagger operations. During the night six B-17s drop leaflets over France and Belgium.

Ninth Air Force establishes the XIX Tactical Air Command to provide dedicated air support to the U.S. Third Army. The fighter and fighter-bomber groups are divided between the IX and XIX Tactical Air Commands.

A-20 Havocs and B-26 Marauders bomb rail bridges.

ITALY: Twelfth Air Force A-20 Havocs attack bridges in the Po River valley and marshaling yards. B-35s, B-26 Marauders, and P-47 Thunderbolts attack airfields, roads, bridges, rail cars, and rail lines.

PACIFIC: The Army Air Forces, Pacific Ocean Areas (AAPOA) is activated at Hickam Field, Hawaii. Lieutenant General Millard Harmon is named the commander. Harmon's command provides logistics and administration support for Lieutenant General Robert C. Richardson, Jr.'s U.S. Army Forces, Pacific Ocean Areas (USAFPOA), which includes the Seventh Air Force. Harmon is also responsible to Admiral Chester W. Nimitz, commander in chief, Pacific Ocean Areas (CINCPOA), for operations of Army Air Force air units in the Pacific Ocean Areas. But Harmon, as deputy commander of the Twentieth Air Force, answers only to General Henry H. Arnold in all matters relating to the Twentieth's operations in Nimitz's area of responsibility.

Seventh Amphibious Force is organized under the command of Rear Admiral Daniel E. Barbey.

CENTRAL PACIFIC: Seventh Air Force P-47 Thunderbolts and P-61 Black Widow night fighters on Saipan attack on-call targets on Saipan and Tinian, but concentrate their efforts in support of army and marine forces on Guam.

Naval Air Base, Tinian, is established.

CENTRAL PACIFIC, TINIAN: Tinian is declared secure. Marine casualties are 328 killed and 1,571 wounded.

NEW GUINEA: FEAF B-24 Liberators bomb Utagal Island in the Carolines and Namlea airfield on Buru Island in the Moluccas.

U.S. submarine *Puffer* torpedoes and damages a Japanese oiler northeast of Borneo.

A navy PBY Catalina attacks a Japanese convoy, sinking an ammunition ship in Taliaboe Bay, Soela Island, Netherlands East Indies.

August 2

CBI: In Burma, the last Japanese forces (about 600 men) leave Myitkyina. Only about 200 of the original Marauders remain in the field.

In China, Fourteenth Air Force sends 11 B-25 Mitchells and 32 P-40s and P-38 Lightnings to attack targets near Tengchung. P-40s and P-38s attack shipping and logistics storage sites along the Yangtze River.

ATLANTIC: German submarine *U-804* torpedoes and sinks a destroyer escort off Newfoundland.

ETO: The 4th Armored Division reaches Rennes, while the 6th Armored Division reaches Dinan. St-Malo is bypassed.

Hitler orders a strong counterattack from Vire toward Avranches to restore the German defensive line and trap Third Army behind German lines in Brittany.

Eighth Air Force sends 156 B-17s and 163 B-24 Liberators escorted by 132 P-51 Mustangs to attack oil storage facilities, marshaling yards, logistics depots, and bridges around Paris. Two bombers are lost and 71 are damaged. Aircrew losses are one killed, four wounded, and 18 missing. Two fighters are lost and one is damaged. Two pilots are missing and one is killed.

Another mission sends 195 B-17s and 322 B-24s escorted by 236 P-51 Mustangs to attack V-weapon sites. Three bombers are lost and 128 are damaged. Aircrew losses are five killed, one wounded, and 28 missing. Five fighters are lost and one is damaged. Five pilots are reported missing.

Nearly 300 P-38 Lightnings, P-47s, and P-51s fly fighter-bomber missions against rail and road transport from Paris to Brussels. Pilots report one confirmed kill. Two fighters are lost and nine are damaged. Two pilots are reported missing.

A total of 42 B-24s fly in support of Carpetbagger operations.

Ninth Air Force sends 300 A-20 Havocs and B-26 Marauders to attack bridges and ammunition storage sites. P-47s and P-38s fly close support missions and reconnaissance in support of ground forces.

MEDITERRANEAN: Fifteenth Air Force sends over 300 B-17s and B-24 Liberators escorted by P-38 Lightnings and P-51 Mustangs to attack the harbor at Genoa, Italy, and oil storage facilities and rail targets in southern France.

ITALY: Twelfth Air Force B-25 Mitchells and B-26 Marauders attack bridges. A-20 Havocs and P-47 Thunderbolts attack airfields, bridges, and roads.

PACIFIC: U.S. submarine *Tautog* attacks a Japanese convoy, sinking a cargo ship off Honshu, Japan.

CENTRAL PACIFIC, TINIAN: In spite of the official declaration that the island is secure, the 6th Marines turns back a Japanese counterattack.

CENTRAL PACIFIC, GUAM: The Japanese stronghold at Mount Barrigada is the objective of the 307th Infantry Regiment, supported by the 706th Tank Battalion.

NEW GUINEA: FEAF A-20 Havocs, P-47 Thunderbolts, P-38 Lightnings, and P-40s attack targets along the coast. B-24 Liberators and B-25 Mitchells bomb airfields on the Moluccas and Lesser Sunda Islands and shipping off Ceram and Amboina Islands. B-24s bomb Timor Island. At Biak, Mokmer airfield is ready to receive bombers.

August 3

ALEUTIANS: President Roosevelt, aboard heavy cruiser USS *Baltimore,* arrives at Adak in the Aleutians.

CBI: The Chinese 50th Division attacks and captures Myitkyina. The Allies capture 179 Japanese soldiers. The capture of Myitkyina airfield ends the threat of Japanese fighters against the southern Hump air route to China. As a result, supply tonnage nearly doubles in the next few months. This victory, combined with the British victories at Imphal and Kohima, seals the fate of the Japanese forces in Burma. The Ledo Road now advances steadily.

During the siege of Myitkyina Chinese forces have lost 972 killed and over 3,200 wounded and sick. U.S. forces have lost 272 killed and over 1,900 wounded and sick. The Americans have far more cases of illness than the Chinese, mostly because the Chinese forces maintain strict discipline in boiling all drinking water. Americans, far less willing to follow this rule, become sick.

In China, Fourteenth Air Force sends B-24 Liberators to bomb the town of Yoyang and B-25 Mitchells to bomb Mangshih. P-40s, P-51 Mustangs, and P-38 Lightnings attack airfields, troops, logistics support sites, and rail, road, and river traffic around Changsha, Hengyang, and Tangyang.

ETO: The 8th Infantry Division occupies Rennes after the 4th Armored Division had initially seized the city. The VII Corps of First Army clears Mortain. General Eisenhower orders Third Army to use minimum force to clear the Brittany Peninsula. He orders Patton to attack east toward Laval-LeMans-Chartres to sweep behind German forces defending at Normandy. The First Army will continue its attack to hold German forces while Patton begins his flanking maneuver with the XV and XX Corps. Air support from the Ninth Air Force has allowed the rapid advance of many units.

Eighth Air Force sends 345 B-17s escorted by 175 P-51 Mustangs to attack the oil refinery at Merkwille, Germany. Six B-17s are lost and 99 are damaged. Aircrews report four confirmed kills and one probable. Aircrew losses are nine killed, nine wounded, and 54 missing. Fighter pilots report six confirmed kills in the air and five on the ground. Six P-51s are lost. The five pilots are reported missing.

Another 155 B-17s, escorted by 96 P-51 Mustangs, attack bridges in France. Eleven B-17s are damaged. Over 170 B-24 Liberators escorted by 47 P-47 Thunderbolts attack airfields and marshaling yards. A total of 51 bombers are damaged. Nearly 250 B-17s and B-24s escorted by P-51s bomb V-weapon sites in the Pas-de-Calais area. One bomber is lost and 26 bombers are damaged. More than 150 B-24s escorted by 90 P-51s also hit V-weapon sites. One B-24 is lost and 41 damaged. Aircrew casualties are four killed, four wounded, and 10 missing. Another 76 B-24s attack airfields in Belgium escorted by P-47s. Fifty B-24s are damaged. The aircrews in the damaged bombers suffer two killed. Over 130 P-38 Lightnings and P-47s fly fighter-bomber missions against rail traffic near Metz, Strasbourg, and Saarbrücken areas. Pilots report one confirmed kill in the air and one on the ground. One P-47 is lost.

Ninth Air Force sends over 180 A-20 Havocs and B-26 Marauders against rail targets and fuel storage areas.

The P-47s of the 22nd and 23rd Fighter Squadrons, 36th Fighter Group, redeploy from England to France.

MEDITERRANEAN: Fifteenth Air Force sends over 600 B-17s and B-24 Liberators escorted by P-38 Lightnings and P-51 Mustangs to attack industrial targets in Germany. B-24s also bomb communications targets in the Brenner Pass. Aircrews and fighter pilots report 18 German aircraft shot down. A total of 11 U.S. bombers and fighters are lost.

ITALY: Twelfth Air Force B-25 Mitchells and B-26 Marauders attack bridges. A-20 Havocs and P-47 Thunderbolts attack airfields, bridges, and roads.

SOUTHWEST PACIFIC AREA: U.S. submarine *Cod* torpedoes and sinks a Japanese auxiliary netlayer west of Halmahera island in the Molucca Sea.

CENTRAL PACIFIC: Seventh Air Force B-24 Liberators from the Marshall Islands bomb Truk.

CENTRAL PACIFIC, GUAM: The 3rd and the 9th Marines attack toward Finegayan.

Private First Class Frank P. Witek of the 1st Battalion, 9th Marines, 3rd Marine Division, takes several bold actions during several encounters with the enemy. Witek courageously exposes himself to enemy fire to destroy well-camouflaged positions at close range. When his platoon withdraws to consolidate positions with the company, Private First Class Witek stays behind to protect a severely wounded comrade, exchanging fire with the Japanese until the marine is evacuated. When his platoon comes under enemy fire, Witek attacks. He throws hand grenades and fires his rifle, until he is within only a few yards of the Japanese position. As he destroys the machine gun position, he is killed. For his heroic actions and extraordinary dedication to duty, Private First Class Witek will receive the Medal of Honor.

NEW GUINEA: The Ted Force (the 124th Infantry Regiment and a battalion of 169th Infantry Regiment) operates independently and attacks Japanese units wherever they are found behind the Driniumor River. They are resupplied by air and battle the enemy in heavy jungle.

FEAF B-25 Mitchells support ground forces on Biak. A-20 Havocs, P-47 Thunderbolts, P-38 Lightnings, and P-40s bomb Japanese troops.

B-24s bomb Yap and Woleai Atoll and targets at Boela on Ceram Island in the Moluccas.

August 4

ALEUTIANS: Eleventh Air Force P-38 Lightnings accompanied by one B-25 fly in support of a naval force near Massacre Bay on Attu Island in the Aleutians.

President Roosevelt departs Adak, Aleutians, on the heavy cruiser *Baltimore*, headed for Kodiak, Alaska.

CBI: Tenth Air Force B-25 Mitchells and P-51 Mustangs attack Japanese positions near Sahmaw in support of Allied ground forces.

In China, Fourteenth Air Force B-25 Mitchells bomb airfields at Lashio and Hsenwi. P-40s attack vehicles and troops at Tengehung. Other P-40s attack troops, logistics sites, river shipping, and vehicles around Tungting Lake and the Yangtze River.

ATLANTIC: JCS planners schedule the assaults on Leyte and Mindanao to begin on December 1, 1944. The attack on Formosa is scheduled for February 15, 1945. From Formosa, an air and sea blockade would be established while a build-up of forces for the invasion of the Japanese home islands is completed.

The British make a last effort to have forces marked for Dragoon remain in Italy.

ETO: Eighth Air Force sends 963 B-17s and 446 B-24 Liberators, escorted by 766 P-47 Thunderbolts, P-38 Lightnings, and P-51 Mustangs, to attack oil refineries, aircraft production facilities, and airfields in northern Germany. Fifteen bombers are lost and 413 are damaged. Aircrews report one confirmed kill and four probables. Aircrew losses are six killed, 12 wounded, and 143 missing. Fighter pilots report 38 confirmed kills, one probable in the air, and 13 confirmed kills on the ground. Fifteen fighters are lost and six are damaged. Two pilots are killed and 14 are reported missing. Another 78 B-24s attack an airfield and an oil refinery without loss.

An attack on marshaling yards and airfields in France involves 59 B-17s and 95 B-24s escorted by 35 P-47s and P-51s. A total of 29 bombers are damaged.

Four radio-controlled unserviceable B-17s are loaded with explosives and launched at V-weapon sites. This operation is called Aphrodite. The bombers are escorted by 16 P-47s and 16 P-51 Mustangs. None of the bombers hits the intended targets.

Nearly 70 P-47s fly a fighter-bomber mission against Plantlunne airfield. Pilots report 30 confirmed kills on the ground. One P-47 is lost and nine are damaged. The pilot is reported missing.

Ninth Air Force sends 62 A-20 Havocs and B-26 Marauders to attack railroad bridges, ammunition storage sites, and troop concentrations. P-47 and P-38 fighters attack German tanks, troops, and conduct dive-bombing attacks on fuel and ammunition storage sites.

MEDITERRANEAN: With the withdrawal of seven divisions for Dragoon, Field Marshal Sir Harold R. L. G. Alexander, commander of the 15th Army Group, currently has two armies, the British Eighth Army under Lieutenant General Sir Oliver Leese and the Fifth Army under Lieutenant General Mark W. Clark. The Fifth Army has IV Corps with three divisions commanded by Lieutenant General Willis D. Crittenberger and II Corps, also with three divisions, commanded by Major General Geoffrey Keyes. General Leese proposes an attack to seize Bologna, the major rail and road junction that supports the German Gothic Line defenses. Fifteenth Air Force supports the Red Army's request for support. A total of 70 P-38 Lightnings and P-51 Mustangs fly from Italy, attack targets near Focsani, Romania, and land at Frantic bases in Soviet Ukraine.

ITALY: The Germans have established defensive positions along the Arno River.

Twelfth Air Force B-25 Mitchells and B-26 Marauders attack bridges. A-20 Havocs and P-47 Thunderbolts attack convoys, bridges, gun positions, airfields, and roads. The harbor at Nice, France is also attacked.

SOUTHWEST PACIFIC AREA: U.S. submarine *Raton* attacks a cargo ship off Luzon. U.S. submarine *Ray* attacks a Japanese convoy in the Celebes Sea, sinking a cargo ship and avoiding a depth charge attack from an escort ship.

CENTRAL PACIFIC: Seventh Air Force B-25s from the Marshalls bomb Ponape Island.

The headquarters of the 30th Bombardment Group (Heavy) and the B-24s of the 27th, 38th, and 392nd Bombardment Squadrons (Heavy) redeploy from Kwajalein in the Marshalls to Saipan. The C-47s of the 9th Troop Carrier Squadron redeploy from Abemama Island in the Gilberts to Saipan.

Aircraft from TG 58.3 (Rear Admiral Alfred E. Montgomery) bomb airfields on Iwo Jima; aircraft from TG 58.1 (Rear Admiral Joseph J. Clark), together with four light cruisers and seven destroyers organized as TU 58.1.6 under Rear Admiral Laurance T. DuBose, attack a Japanese convoy in the Bonin Islands. A destroyer and collier are sunk by surface ships and aircraft sink four transports and damage two other vessels. One cargo ship is sunk by both gunfire and aircraft.

U.S. submarine *Sterlet* torpedoes and sinks two Japanese guardboats northwest of Chichi Jima.

CENTRAL PACIFIC, GUAM: The 307th Infantry Regiment of the 77th Infantry Division captures the crest of Mount Barrigada. The 3rd Marine Division and the 77th Infantry Division prepare to work in concert to clear the last major Japanese defenses. The marines will capture Finegayan, while the army will capture Yigo and Mount Santa Rosa.

Seventh Air Force B-25 Mitchells from Saipan conduct two attacks on Guam.

CENTRAL PACIFIC, TINIAN: Private First Class Robert L. Wilson of the 2nd Battalion, 6th Marines, 2nd Marine Division, is acting as the point for his squad clearing suspected Japanese positions. As he approaches a pile of rocks a Japanese grenade lands nearby. Shouting a warning, Private First Class Wilson covers the grenade with his body, shielding his comrades from the blast. For his heroic sacrifice Private First Class Wilson will receive the Medal of Honor.

NEW GUINEA: FEAF A-20 Havocs, P-47 Thunderbolts, P-38 Lightnings, and P-40s attack Japanese troops, east of the Driniumor River.

B-24s bomb Yap and Woleai Atoll and targets at Boela on Ceram Island in the Moluccas.

August 5

CBI: Tenth Air Force P-47 Thunderbolts attack targets of opportunity around Bhamo.

In China, Fourteenth Air Force B-25 Mitchells bomb Wanling. P-40s attack Tengchung and communications targets, troops, and trucks near Tungting Lake.

ETO: Eighth Air Force sends 215 B-17s escorted by 174 P-38 Lightnings and P-51 Mustangs to attack oil refineries and tank and aircraft production facilities in northern Germany. Three B-17s are lost and 189 are damaged. Aircrews report three confirmed kills and one probable. Aircrew losses are two killed, eight wounded, and 28 missing. Fighter pilots report 19 confirmed kills and one probable in the air and one confirmed kill on the ground. Four fighters are lost and six are damaged. One pilot is killed, one is wounded, and four are reported missing.

A total of 70 B-24 Liberators, escorted by 41 P-47 Thunderbolts, attack airfields. One bomber is lost and seven are damaged. Nine crewmen are reported missing. Fighter pilots report four confirmed kills.

Another attack by 426 B-17s and 452 B-24 Liberators escorted by 356 P-51s is launched on aircraft component production facilities and airfields in Germany. Nine bombers are lost and 280 are damaged. Aircrews report six confirmed kills and three probables. Aircrew losses are two killed, five wounded, and 15 missing. Two fighters are lost and eight are damaged. Two pilots are reported missing.

A total of 19 B-24s fly in support of Carpetbagger operations. During the night six B-17s drop leaflets over the Netherlands and France.

In France, Ninth Air Force establishes a headquarters element close to the 12th Army Group and the advance headquarters of the Allied Expeditionary Air Force (AEAF) to coordinate air operations to support the ground forces. Operational control of the headquarters of the 50th and 53rd Troop Carrier Wings of the IX Troop Carrier Command is passed to the Mediterranean Allied Air Force in preparation for Anvil-Dragoon. Over 300 A-20 Havocs and B-26 Marauders attack fuel storage sites, railroad bridges, and a marshaling yard. P-47 and P-38 fighters fly armed reconnaissance missions.

SOUTHWEST PACIFIC AREA: U.S. submarine *Cero* attacks a Japanese convoy off Mindanao and sinks an oiler in Davao Gulf.

PACIFIC: Fast Carrier Task Force is reorganized into First Fast Carrier Task Force, Pacific Fleet, commanded by Vice Admiral Marc A. Mitscher, and Second Fast Carrier Task Force, Pacific Fleet, commanded by Vice Admiral John S. McCain.

Aircraft from TG 58.1 (Rear Admiral Joseph J. Clark) and TG 58.3 (Rear Admiral Alfred E. Montgomery) and cruisers and destroyers of TU 58.1.6 (Rear Admiral Laurance T. DuBose) continue attacks on Chichi Jima and Haha Jima. Aircraft damage a fast transport off Chichi Jima. U.S. submarine *Barbel* torpedoes and sinks a Japanese cargo ship in the Bonins.

CENTRAL PACIFIC, GUAM: The 305th Infantry Regiment stops a Japanese tank and infantry counterattack.

Seventh Air Force B-25 Mitchells from Saipan make two bombing attacks on Japanese positions at Guam.

NEW GUINEA: FEAF P-39 Airacobras strafe barges around Geelvink Bay. B-24s bomb Yap and targets at Boela on Ceram Island in the Moluccas. B-25 Mitchells bomb targets in the Celebes and Sunda Islands.

Fifth Air Force B-25 Mitchells sink a Japanese cargo ship at the southern end of Celebes Island.

August 6

CBI: P-51 Mustangs and P-47 Thunderbolts attack targets at Mohnyin, Hopin, Bhamo, Myothit, Katha, Indaw, and other points in northern Burma.

In China, Fourteenth Air Force, P-40s attack Tengchung. P-40s and P-51 Mustangs attack trucks, troop assembly areas, and gun positions near Hengyang. Other P-40s attack river and road transportation around Changsha.

ETO: The Brittany Peninsula is cut off, isolating German garrisons in the port cities of Brest, St-Nazaire, St-Malo, and Lorient. Patton's VIII Corps is assigned the mission of reducing these garrisons. The XV Corps is intended as a pincer to surround German forces from the west by capturing Argentan and linking up with the Canadian First Army pressing from the east.

Eighth Air Force sends 568 B-17s and 445 B-24 Liberators, escorted by 472 P-38 Lightnings, P-47 Thunderbolts, and P-51 Mustangs, to attack oil refineries, airfields, aircraft production facilities, and industrial production targets in northern Germany. A total of 24 bombers are lost and 503 are damaged. Aircrews report two probable kills. Aircrew losses are 15 killed, 26 wounded, and 233 missing. Fighter pilots report 24 confirmed kills in the air and two on the ground. Four fighters are lost and four are damaged. One pilot is killed, one is wounded, and four are missing.

More than 70 B-17s escorted by 154 P-51s support Frantic operations, bombing aircraft production facilities in Poland and flying to bases in Soviet Ukraine. Aircrews report two probable kills. A total of 23 B-17s are damaged. Fighter pilots report seven confirmed kills and two probables. Four P-51s are lost and one is damaged. One pilot is killed and five are reported missing.

Another attack on V-weapon sites in the Pas-de-Calais area is conducted by 24 B-24s escorted by 24 P-47s. Nine B-24s are damaged.

A total of 36 B-24s fly in support of Carpetbagger operations. During the night seven B-17s drop leaflets over France.

Ninth Air Force sends A-20 Havocs and B-26 Marauders to attack fuel storage sites, railroad bridges, and ammunition storage areas. P-47 and P-38 fighters support ground forces.

The headquarters of the 474th Fighter Group and the P-38s of the 428th, 429th, and 430th Fighter Squadrons redeploy from England to France.

MEDITERRANEAN: Fifteenth Air Force sends over 700 B-17s and B-24 Liberators escorted by P-38 Lightnings and P-51 Mustangs to attack oil storage areas, railroad bridges in southern France, and a submarine pen at Toulon.

A total of 60 P-38 Lightnings and P-51 Mustangs fly from Frantic bases in the Soviet Ukraine, attack railroad targets in and around Bucharest and Ploeşti in Romania, and land at bases in Italy.

ITALY: Twelfth Air Force B-25 Mitchells and B-26 Marauders attack bridges in the Rhône valley. A-20 Havocs and P-47 Thunderbolts attack shipping near Genoa and La Spezia, as well as convoys, bridges, and roads. Twelfth Air Force B-17s and B-24 Liberators bomb the submarine pens at Toulon, sinking German submarines *U-471*, *U-952*, and *U-969*.

SOUTHWEST PACIFIC AREA: U.S. submarine *Rasher* torpedoes and sinks a Japanese cargo ship west of Luzon.

PACIFIC: U.S. submarine *Pintado* attacks a Japanese convoy, sinking a cargo ship and damaging escort vessel off the southwest coast of Kyushu.

CENTRAL PACIFIC: Seventh Air Force B-25 Mitchells from Saipan fly two bombing missions against Japanese positions on Guam. B-25s from the Marshals bomb Ponape Island and B-25s from the Gilberts attack Nauru Island in the Gilberts. B-24 Liberators from Kwajalein bomb Wotje Atoll.

NEW GUINEA: FEAF B-25 Mitchells, P-47 Thunderbolts, P-38 Lightnings, and P-40s support ground operations near Sarmi. B-24s bomb logistics facilities at Yap.

August 7

CBI: Tenth Air Force B-25 Mitchells destroy two bridges near Bhamo.

In China, Fourteenth Air Force P-40s attack targets at Hengyang, Changsha, and Tengchung.

ETO: On Hitler's orders, elements of five German armor and infantry divisions supported by aircraft begin a major counterattack that intends to split the First and Third Armies. Achieving surprise, the German advance six miles, intending to reach Avranches and stop Third Army by destroying the logistics depots in the rear of the American lines.

Combat Command B of the 3rd Armored Division stops a German attack. The 2nd Battalion of the 120th Infantry Regiment, 30th Infantry Division, at Mortain conducts a heroic defense at Hill 317 against German tanks. Isolated and resupplied by airdrops, the Americans stop every attack against them. The Germans also lose more than 100 tanks to Allied aircraft. The 35th and 4th Infantry Divisions along with the 2nd Armored Division are diverted to meet the attack. The VII Corps pushes from St-Sever.

General George S. Patton, Jr., moves three corps of the Third Army east to encircle the German army. The 6th Armored Division reaches Brest, traveling 200 miles in five days, but the defenses are too strong to conduct an attack. VIII Corps moves into Brittany to capture the port cities. Major General Wade H. Haislip's XV Corps advances toward LeMans, the main logistics base of the German army.

A communications zone headquarters is established in the ETO to organize the logistics bases at Cherbourg and at Omaha and Utah beaches and the lines of supply from those bases. The sustained air attacks prior to D-day have caused widespread destruction of the French railway and highway systems, preventing any efficient movement of supplies to the forward lines.

In response to a Red Army request for air support, 55 B-17s and 29 P-51 Mustangs supporting Frantic operations attack an oil refinery at Trzebina, Poland, and return to bases in Soviet Ukraine.

Eighth Air Force sends 337 B-17s escorted by 309 P-38 Lightnings and P-51s to attack airfields and bridges in France. Heavy cloud cover forces many bombers to abort the mission; 143 B-17s are damaged. Aircrew casualties are three wounded; fighter pilots report one confirmed kill.

More than 380 B-24 Liberators escorted by 94 P-51s and 34 P-47 Thunderbolts attack bridges, airfields, and production facilities in France. One B-24 is lost and 65 are damaged. Aircrew casualties are eight killed, one wounded, and 11 missing.

Nearly 300 P-47s and P-51s fly fighter-bomber missions against marshaling yards and railroads near Paris. Pilots report four confirmed kills on the ground. Three P-47s and two P-51s are lost and 11 fighters are damaged. Five pilots are reported missing.

During the night five B-17s drop leaflets over France.

The headquarters of IX Tactical Air Command supporting U.S. First Army and the headquarters of XIX Tactical Air Command supporting U.S. Third Army create mobile command posts to keep up with the rapid advance into France.

Ninth Air Force commander, Lieutenant General Lewis H. Brereton, is appointed commanding general of the First Allied Airborne Army.

Ninth Air Force sends nearly 400 A-20 Havocs and B-26 Marauders to attack bridges. P-47 and P-38 fighters attack German positions in support of ground forces.

MEDITERRANEAN: Fifteenth Air Force sends over 350 B-17s and B-24 Liberators escorted by P-38 Lightnings and P-51 Mustangs to attack oil facilities and airfields in Yugoslavia. Aircrews and fighters report 30 enemy aircraft shot down.

ITALY: Twelfth Air Force B-25 Mitchells and B-26 Marauders attack bridges in Italy and France. A-20 Havocs attack shipping targets at Genoa. P-47 Thunderbolts attack bridges, marshaling yards, and roads.

SOUTHWEST PACIFIC AREA: U.S. submarine *Bluegill* attacks a Japanese convoy and sinks a transport southwest of Mindanao. U.S. submarine *Guitarro* attacks a Japanese convoy and sinks an escort vessel off Luzon, then evades a depth-charging attack.

U.S. submarine *Puffer* torpedoes and sinks an auxiliary submarine chaser off southern Davao.

U.S. submarine *Sailfish* torpedoes and damages a Japanese cargo ship in Luzon Strait.

U.S. submarine *Seawolf* lands men and supplies at Tawi Tawi, in the Philippines.

PACIFIC: President Roosevelt arrives at Kodiak, Alaska, on the heavy cruiser USS *Baltimore,* then transfers to destroyer USS *Cummings.*

U.S. submarine *Croaker* torpedoes and sinks a Japanese light cruiser off Nagasaki, Kyushu, Japan.

U.S. submarine *Barbel* torpedoes and sinks a Japanese cargo vessel in the Bonins.

CENTRAL PACIFIC, GUAM: The 306th and 307th Infantry Regiments of the 77th Infantry Division attack and capture Yigo, clearing a Japanese roadblock. Shortly thereafter, the 306th Infantry stops a nighttime Japanese tank attack. The 307th Infantry Regiment, supported by naval gunfire, captures Mount Santa Rosa.

Seventh Air Force B-25 Mitchells from Saipan make two separate attacks on Japanese positions on Guam.

NEW GUINEA: FEAF B-24s bomb logistics facilities at Yap and airfields on Halmahera Island. Pilots report between 35 and 50 aircraft are destroyed or damaged. The P-47s of the 39th Fighter Squadron 35th Fighter Group redeploy from Nadzab to Noemfoor Island. The B-25 Mitchells of the 390th Bombardment Squadron (Medium) 42nd Bombardment Group (Medium) redeploy from the Russell Islands in the Solomons to Hollandia.

U.S. submarine *Sand Lance* is damaged by an air attack off north end of Celebes Island.

August 8

CBI: In China, Japanese forces capture Hengyang after a seven-week battle. Although unable to stop the Japanese offensive, American air power is able to slow down the speed of the enemy advance.

The fall of the city opens the Allied airbases at Lingling and Kweilin to Japanese attack; they are the next objectives of the enemy offensive.

Fourteenth Air Force P-40s attack trucks and barges near Hengyang.

ETO: The VIII Corps clears the Brittany Peninsula of German forces except for port cities, of which only a few are deemed essential to the Allied operation in France.

There exists an opportunity for Allied forces to trap major German combat units between Falaise and Argentan. Eisenhower, Bradley, and Montgomery, seeing the possibilities offered by the German counterattack at Mortain, issue plans to subordinates. General Bradley directs Third Army to shift its advance to the northeast, to Alençon, and prepare to attack toward Argentan in the rear of German forces and link with Canadian forces encircling from the north and headed for Argentan. First Army is to continue its drive along the Vire-Mortain-Domfront line. The 2nd and 3rd Armored Divisions move to cut off the attacking German forces at Ger and Domfront. The Third Army captures LeMans and advances to cut supply lines at Alençon near Falaise. XX Corps elements reach the Loire River.

The First Airborne Army is formed under the command of Lieutenant General Lewis H. Brereton. The army is composed of the XVIII Airborne Corps (the 82nd, 101st, and 17th Airborne Divisions), commanded by Major General Matthew B. Ridgway, the British 1st and 6th Airborne Divisions, the IX Troop Carrier Command, and two Royal Air Force troop carrier groups.

In support of Frantic operations 78 B-17s with 55 P-51 Mustangs as escort fly from airfields in Soviet Ukraine to attack airfields in Romania en route to bases in Italy. Eighth Air Force sends 681 B-17s and 414 B-24 Liberators escorted by 365 P-47 Thunderbolts and P-51 Mustangs to attack V-weapon sites in the Pas-de-Calais area and railroad bridges and airfields in France. Eight bombers are lost and 438 are damaged. Aircrews report one confirmed kill. Aircrew losses are 18 killed, 24 wounded, and 44 missing. Fighter pilots report four confirmed kills and one probable. Five fighters are lost and the pilots are reported missing.

P-51s escort RAF Coastal Command Beaufighters (two-seat long-range maritime strike aircraft) on a convoy strike in Norway. Three P-51s are lost and three damaged. One pilot is wounded and three are reported missing.

Over 170 P-38 Lightnings, P-47 Thunderbolts, and P-51 Mustangs conduct fighter-bomber attacks on rail lines. Four fighters are lost and three are damaged. Five pilots are reported missing.

During the night five B-17s drop leaflets over France.

Lieutenant General Hoyt S. Vandenberg is designated as commander of the Ninth Air Force.

Ninth Air Force A-20 Havocs and B-26 Marauders attack bridges, a radar site, and fly ground support missions. P-47 and P-38 fighters fly armed reconnaissance missions.

German submarine *U-667* torpedoes a U.S. freighter in a convoy in the English Channel; the freighter is abandoned by the crew and sunk with a second torpedo.

ITALY: Twelfth Air Force B-25 Mitchells and B-26 Marauders attack rail lines and bridges in the Po and Rhône Valleys. A-20 Havocs attack logistics storage areas. P-47 Thunderbolts attack convoys and bridges.

PACIFIC: U.S. submarine *Sterlet* torpedoes and sinks a Japanese auxiliary submarine chaser near Chichi Jima.

CENTRAL PACIFIC: Seventh Air Force B-25 Mitchells from the Marshalls bomb Ponape Island and B-24 Liberators bomb Truk.

Destroyers USS *Gansevoort* and *Bancroft* and land-based Marine Corps aircraft from Majuro attack Japanese positions on Maloelap Atoll.

CENTRAL PACIFIC, GUAM: The 305th and 307th Infantry Regiments of the 77th Infantry Division capture Mount Santa Rosa, supported by a flanking attack by the 306th Infantry.

Seventh Air Force B-25 Mitchells from Saipan bomb Japanese defenses.

NEW GUINEA: FEAF B-24 Liberators bomb targets near Manokwari. A-20 Havocs bomb a radio station near Hollandia. B-24 Liberators bomb Yap Island and airfields on Halmahera Island.

August 9

CBI: Tenth Air Force receives the 426th Night Fighter Squadron. The squadron, equipped with P-61 Black Widow night fighters, arrives at Madhaiganj, India, from the United States.

In China, Fourteenth Air Force B-25 Mitchells bomb targets near Hengyang. P-40s and P-51 Mustangs attack trucks, gun positions, and Japanese troops around Hengyang and Siangtan and destroy a pontoon bridge near Changsha.

ETO: The XV Corps (5th Armored Division, French 2nd Armored Division, 79th and 90th Infantry Divisions) of Third Army attacks toward Alençon, advancing toward the rear of German forces at Mortain.

Eighth Air Force sends 577 B-17s and 247 B-24 Liberators, escorted by 570 P-38 Lightnings, P-47 Thunderbolts, and P-51 Mustangs, to attack aircraft production and tank production facilities in southeast Germany. Weather conditions force most of the bombers to abort the mission or strike targets of opportunity. Eighteen bombers are lost and 381 are damaged. Aircrews report one confirmed kill. Aircrew losses are two killed, 20 wounded, and 153 missing. Fighter pilots report 39 confirmed kills in the air and 24 on the ground. Three fighters are lost and seven are damaged. Three pilots are reported missing.

More than 110 P-47s escorted by 40 P-51 Mustangs conduct fighter-bomber attacks on German communication targets in France.

B-17s escorted by 16 P-38s fly a Micro H radar (micro H was a combo of two earlier radar targeting systems used to guide bombers to targets) pathfinder test mission against Aubigny airfield in France.

During the night six B-17s drop leaflets over the Netherlands and France.

Ninth Air Force sends nearly 400 A-20 Havocs and B-26 Marauders to attack ammunition storage sites and railroad bridges. P-47 and P-38 fighters fly armed reconnaissance missions.

Captain Darrell R. Lindsey leads a formation of 30 B-26 Marauders of the 394th Bomber Group, Ninth Air Force, to destroy the L'Isle Adam railroad bridge over the Seine River. The bridge is a critical target as it is one of the few crossing points left that will allow German forces to escape to safety as Allied armored divisions race to cut off the enemy's path of retreat. The bridge is heavily defended with antiaircraft guns. As Lindsey begins his bombing run, his B-26's right engine bursts into flames from antiaircraft fire. Without hesitation, Lindsey returns to the formation and presses the attack even as the right wing of his aircraft is covered in flames. Lindsey drops his bombs on target and then gives the order for the crew to bail out and brings the aircraft to a lower altitude. Just as the last crewman exits the aircraft, the bomber explodes and crashes. For his superb skill as a pilot and his cool courage in the face of certain death, Captain Lindsey will receive the Medal of Honor.

MEDITERRANEAN: The Dragoon invasion force leaves Naples, Italy, for southern France with 151,000 men and 19,400 vehicles.

Fifteenth Air Force sends more than 300 B-17s and B-24 Liberators escorted by P-38 Lightnings and P-51 Mustangs to attack an aircraft assembly plant, airfields, and an oil refinery in Hungary and a marshaling yard and oil refinery in Yugoslavia.

ITALY: Twelfth Air Force B-25 Mitchells and B-26 Marauders attack airfields and rail lines. A-20 Havocs bomb targets along the coastal road from Nice, France, to Genoa, Italy. P-47 Thunderbolts attack railroad bridges.

SOUTHWEST PACIFIC AREA: U.S. submarine *Seawolf* lands men and supplies on Palawan in the Philippines.

PACIFIC: President Roosevelt aboard the destroyer USS *Cummings* visits the Puget Sound Navy Yard.

U.S. submarine *Barbel* torpedoes and sinks two cargo ships in the Ryukyus.

NEW GUINEA: FEAF A-20 Havocs, P-39 Airacobras, and P-40s attack troops, shipping, and logistics sites. B-24s bomb Yap and targets at Boela on Ceram and Ambon Islands in the Moluccas.

August 10

ALEUTIANS: Eleventh Air Force B-25 Mitchells on a shipping sweep attack two Japanese patrol boats off Shimushu Island in the Kuriles. Aircrews report one boat sunk and the other damaged.

CBI: Because it is no longer combat effective, the 5307th Composite Unit (Provisional), known as Merrill's Marauders, is disbanded. The unit has suffered 2,394 casualties (sick, killed, wounded, and missing) during the campaign.

The Fourteenth Air Force reports that since its operations against Japanese ground forces in China began on May 26 over 100 Japanese aircraft have been destroyed, along with nearly 600 trucks, 1,000 small boats used for supply, and 100 bridges. During this same period three U.S. aircraft have been lost in combat.

In China, Fourteenth Air Force P-40s strafe Taiyuan airfield. Pilots report more than 20 Japanese aircraft destroyed on the ground. Other P-40s attack trucks at Siangtan and Changsha.

ETO: The VII Corps, supported by IX Tactical Air Force, halts the German counterattack at Mortain.

The 5th Infantry Division captures Nantes. The XX Corps captures Angers in support of XV Corps.

Eighth Air Force sends 175 B-24 Liberators escorted by 249 P-51 Mustangs to attack fuel dumps and bridges near Paris. One B-24 is lost and 20 are damaged. Aircrew losses are one wounded and one missing. Fighter pilots report eight confirmed kills. Three fighters are lost; three pilots are reported missing.

A total of 583 P-38 Lightnings and P-51s attack rail targets in France. Fighter pilots report 19 confirmed kills. Two P-38s and four P-51s are lost.

During the night one B-17 drops leaflets over Brest, France.

The B-24s of the 856th, 857th, 858th, and 859th Bombardment Squadrons (Heavy) of the 492nd Bombardment Group (Heavy) are tasked to support Carpetbagger operations.

Ninth Air Force sends 200 A-20 Havocs and B-26 Marauders to attack railroad bridges near Paris. P-47 and P-38 fighters fly armed reconnaissance missions near Paris and Amiens.

MEDITERRANEAN: Fifteenth Air Force sends more than 450 B-17s and B-24 Liberators escorted by P-38 Lightnings and P-51 Mustangs to attack oil refineries at Ploeşti, Romania.

ITALY: General Sir Harold R. L. G. Alexander holds a conference with his commanders to map out future operations of the Allied ground forces in Italy. The Anvil-Dragoon operation has drawn down much of the combat strength of Fifth Army, leaving the British Eighth Army with the preponderance of forces. Alexander proposes an offensive along the eastern coast of Italy, with Eighth Army to break the German line and drive into the broad open plains and outflank the Gothic Line. General Mark Clark's Fifth Army will gain operational control of the British XIII Corps to conduct supporting attacks toward Pistoia in order to hold the Germans in place five days after the Eighth Army begins its attack. The attack is named Operation Olive and is scheduled for August 25.

Twelfth Air Force P-47 Thunderbolts attack gun positions on the southern coast of France in preparation for Dragoon.

SOUTHWEST PACIFIC AREA: U.S. submarine *Guitarro* attacks a Japanese convoy off the northwest coast of Luzon, sinking a merchant tanker.

PACIFIC: During the night Twentieth Air Force sends 24 B-29 Superfortresses from Chengtu, China, to bomb the city of Nagasaki, Japan. Aircrews report one confirmed fighter kill, the first for the B-29. Another 31 B-29 Superfortresses staging through China Bay on Ceylon bomb oil refineries at Palembang, Sumatra, and mine the Moesi River. This 3,900-mile single-stage combat flight is the longest by B-29s during the war.

U.S. submarine *Bowfin* torpedoes and sinks a cargo ship in the Ryukyus.

CENTRAL PACIFIC: Seventh Air Force B-24 Liberators flying from Saipan make the first attack on Iwo Jima Island in the Volcano Islands. P-47 Thunderbolts from Saipan attack Japanese fighters still resisting on Tinian. B-24s from Kwajalein bomb Wotje Atoll.

CENTRAL PACIFIC, GUAM: Army and marine units eliminate the last Japanese tanks and organized units in the northern tip of the island. Major General Roy S. Geiger declares Guam secured. Lieutenant General Alexander A. Vandegrift and Admiral Nimitz arrive to establish their headquarters. The battle for Guam cost the United States over 1,700 dead and 5,900 wounded.

NEW GUINEA: The last Japanese forces resisting near the Driniumor River are eliminated. Those who have not been killed have retreated toward Wewak. The 43rd Infantry Division takes over the Driniumor-Aitape defenses. The Japanese have lost over 8,800 men in 30 days of near continuous combat. American losses stand at 597 killed, 1,691 wounded, and 85 missing.

FEAF B-25 Mitchells, A-20s, and P-38 Lightnings attack targets around Geelvink Bay. P-39 Airacobras, P-38 Lightnings, P-40s, and P-47 Thunderbolts attack Japanese positions between Aitape and Wewak.

At Noemfoor, the last defenders are encountered at Hill 380 and eliminated by elements of the 503rd Parachute Infantry. The battle for the island costs the Americans 65 killed and 343 wounded. Over 2,000 Japanese are killed.

U.S. submarine *Cod* torpedoes and sinks a Japanese auxiliary submarine chaser south of Celebes Island.

August 11
ALEUTIANS: Eleventh Air Force B-25 Mitchells sink a Japanese guardboat east of Paramushiru, Kuriles.

August 11
CBI: Tenth Air Force P-40s attack a Japanese headquarters at Bhamo.

In China, Fourteenth Air Force sends 23 B-24 Liberators to bomb Changsha. Another 16 B-25s bomb Hengyang, and more than 40 P-51 Mustangs and P-40s bomb bridges, villages, logistics storage facilities, vehicles, and troop assembly areas near Hengyang.

A cargo vessel is damaged by a mine laid by Twentieth Air Force B-29s near Palembang, Sumatra.

ETO: The 30th Infantry Division recaptures Mortain. The failed German counterattack at Mortain leaves German forces nearly surrounded on three sides by Allied divisions.

Eighth Air Force sends 408 B-17s and 406 B-24 Liberators escorted by 365 P-38 Lightnings and P-51 Mustangs to attack transportation targets, fuels storage sites, and airfields in France. Five bombers are lost and 188 are damaged. Aircrew losses are three killed, eight wounded, and 28 missing. One P-51 is lost and one P-51 is damaged. One pilot is wounded and one is reported missing.

A total of 28 B-24s fly in support of Carpetbagger operations. During the night six B-17s drop leaflets over France.

Ninth Air Force A-20 Havocs and B-26 Marauders attack bridges and an ammunition storage area. P-47 and P-38 fighters fly armed reconnaissance missions over northern France.

ITALY: Twelfth Air Force B-25 Mitchells, B-26 Marauders, and P-47 Thunderbolts strike gun positions along the French and Italian coasts as the Dragoon invasion force departs Naples for France.

PACIFIC: U.S. submarine *Tang* attacks a Japanese convoy off southern Honshu, sinking a merchant cargo ship.

CENTRAL PACIFIC: Seventh Air Force B-25 Mitchells from Makin Island bomb Ponape Island.

CENTRAL PACIFIC, GUAM: The day after the island is declared secured, the 306th Infantry Regiment assaults the command post of General Obata on Mount Mataguac. This will be the pattern of action on Guam until the end of the war. Although almost 11,000 Japanese soldiers have been killed, an estimated 10,000 still live in the hills and jungle. American troops will encounter Japanese throughout the next year, and another 8,500 will be killed in skirmishes. For years after the war, gaunt Japanese soldiers will continue to emerge from the thickets, unable to believe that Japan has surrendered.

NEW GUINEA: FEAF A-20 Havocs attack shipping, barges, and a radar station along the coast of Geelvink Bay. A-20s attack a Japanese headquarters near Sawar. P-39 Airacobras attack troops, logistics sites, and barges.

U.S. submarine *Cod* torpedoes and sinks a Japanese cargo ship south of Celebes Island.

August 12

ALEUTIANS: Eleventh Air Force sends four B-24 Liberators to attack shipping in Higashi Banjo Strait and buildings and a runway on Suribachi in the Kurile Islands. Aircrews report three confirmed kills and 13 probables.

CBI: In China, Fourteenth Air Force B-25 Mitchells bomb the railyards at Hengyang. P-51 Mustangs and P-40s attack targets of opportunity around the area.

ETO: The XV Corps of Third Army captures Alençon. Patton orders an attack toward Argentan. The 5th Armored Division approaches Argentan; the French 2nd Armored Division is at Ecouche.

Eighth Air Force sends 301 B-17s and 276 B-24 Liberators, escorted by 386 P-47 Thunderbolts and P-51 Mustangs, to attack airfields and marshaling yards in eastern France. Three bombers are lost and 76 are damaged. Aircrew losses are 19 killed, eight wounded, and 32 missing. Fighter pilots report one confirmed kill. Three P-51s are lost, and the three pilots are reported missing.

Nearly 500 P-38 Lightnings, P-47s, and P-51s attack transportation targets in the Paris and Brussels areas. Fighter pilots report five confirmed kills in the air and 13 on the ground. Thirteen fighters are lost, and the pilots are reported missing.

More than 200 P-47s and P-51s attack transportation targets in northeast France. Two P-51s are lost and three are damaged. The pilots are reported missing.

During the night six B-17s drop leaflets over France. A total of 72 B-17s and 62 P-51 Mustangs supporting Frantic operations depart Fifteenth Air Force bases in Italy, and most bomb an airfield in southern France before landing in Britain.

Ninth Air Force sends A-20 Havocs and B-26 Marauders to attack fuel storage sites and roads in the Argentan area. P-47 and P-38 fighters fly armed reconnaissance missions and support ground forces.

MEDITERRANEAN: Fifteenth Air Force sends more than 300 B-17s and B-24 Liberators escorted by P-51 Mustangs to attack German positions around Toulon and Marseille, France, and Genoa, Italy, in preparation for Operation Dragoon.

ITALY: Twelfth Air Force B-25 Mitchells and B-26 Marauders along with A-20 Havocs and P-47 Thunderbolts attack defensive positions north of the Arno River.

SOUTHWEST PACIFIC AREA: U.S. submarine *Puffer* attacks a Japanese convoy off Mindoro, sinking a tanker and damaging another tanker.

PACIFIC: President Roosevelt departs Puget Sound to return to Washington.

U.S. submarine *Pompon* attacks a Japanese convoy in the Sea of Okhotsk, damaging a cargo ship east of Sakhalin Island.

CENTRAL PACIFIC: Seventh Air Force B-24 Liberators from Saipan bomb shipping, the seaplane base, and the airfield at Chichi Jima Island in the Bonin Islands. B-25 Mitchells from the Gilbert Islands bomb Nauru Island. B-24s from the Marshall Islands bomb Truk.

NEW GUINEA: FEAF A-20 Havocs P-39 Airacobras, and P-47 Thunderbolts attack Japanese troops and targets of opportunity in the Sarmi area.

The B-24 Liberators of the 321st and 400th Bombardment Squadrons (Heavy) of the 90th Bombardment Group (Heavy) redeploy to Biak Island.

August 13

ALEUTIANS: Eleventh Air Force sends six B-25 Mitchells to fly a shipping sweep over the Kurile Islands. Aircrews report one Japanese fighter shot down.

CBI: In China, Fourteenth Air Force sends more than 30 B-25 Mitchells to bomb Hengyang, and Pailochi airfield as well as shipping. Aircrews report three cargo ships sunk. P-40s and P-51 Mustangs attack trucks, bridges, railyards, and Japanese troops near Hengyang. P-40s and P-38 Lightnings attack Tengchung.

ETO: German forces begin to withdraw from their exposed position near Mortain. The XV Corps of Third Army reaches Argentan and holds against heavy German assaults. General Bradley orders Patton to stop his advance beyond Argentan to allow British forces to advance. This is the boundary line between the British and American army groups. He is also concerned by Ultra intercepts that indicate the Germans intend to counterattack Bradley's widely spread forces. The Germans begin a general withdrawal to the Seine River as Field Marshal Montgomery's 21st Army Group attacks southward. The boundary leaves a gap through which several German divisions escape.

A total of 37 P-47 Thunderbolts discover 800 to 1,000 enemy vehicles of all types in the pocket west of Argentan. In just one hour, the P-47s make continuous attacks until they are out of ammunition. They report nearly 500 vehicles destroyed. One pilot even drops his belly tank on a group of 12 trucks and reports that all were burning. The XIX TAC P-47s have destroyed or damaged more than 1,000 vehicles, 45 tanks and armored vehicles, and 12 locomotives. Inside the pocket they also report destroying 10 German strongpoints.

Eighth Air Force sends 798 B-17s and 466 B-24 Liberators escorted by 131 P-51 Mustangs to support ground forces and attack coastal batteries and transportation targets between Le Havre and Paris. Twelve bombers are lost and 485 are damaged. Aircrew casualties are three killed, 12 wounded, and 113 missing.

One Aphrodite B-17 carrying a 2,000-pound bomb load is launched against Le Havre. The bomber misses its target, and an RAF Mosquito fighter-bomber accompanying the bomber is destroyed in the explosion.

Over 800 P-38 Lightnings, P-47 Thunderbolts, and P-51s fly fighter-bomber missions against transportation targets along the Seine River. A total of 13 fighters are lost and five are damaged. One pilot is killed, one wounded, and 13 are missing.

Two B-17s fly a Micro H radar test mission over France.

A total of 36 B-24s fly in support of Carpetbagger operations. During the night six B-17s drop leaflets over Belgium, France, and the Netherlands.

Ninth Air Force sends nearly 600 A-20 Havocs and B-26 Marauders to attack fuel storage sites, roads, ammunition storage areas, and troop positions to hold the enemy in the Falaise pocket. P-47 and P-38 fighters support ground forces and fly armed reconnaissance missions.

MEDITERRANEAN: Fifteenth Air Force sends 424 B-24 Liberators and 136 B-17s attack gun positions and bridges in southern France.

During the night Twelfth Air Force A-20 Havocs attack targets along the Monaco-Toulon road.

ITALY: Twelfth Air Force B-25 Mitchells and B-26 Marauders attack coastal defense guns around Marseilles. A-20 Havocs attack ammunition storage areas in the Arno River Valley.

SOUTHWEST PACIFIC AREA: U.S. submarine *Bluegill* attacks a Japanese convoy off Mindanao near Davao Gulf, and sinks a submarine chaser, an auxiliary submarine chaser, and a transport.

PACIFIC: U.S. submarine *Barbel* torpedoes and sinks a Japanese auxiliary in the Ryukyus.

U.S. submarine *Tambor* torpedoes and sinks a Japanese cargo ship in the Sea of Okhotsk.

NEW GUINEA: FEAF B-24 Liberators bomb bivouacs and supply dumps at Manokwari. P-47 Thunderbolts and P-39 Airacobras support ground forces at Sarmi.

U.S. submarine *Cod* attacks a Japanese landing ship east of Celebes Island in the Banda Sea, but cannot complete the attack after being engaged by the landing ship with accurate and heavy fire.

U.S. submarine *Flier* is sunk by a mine near North Borneo.

August 14

CBI: In China, Fourteenth Air Force P-40s and P-51 Mustangs bomb the railyards, river shipping, and troop areas at Hengyang.

ETO: General Bradley orders Lieutenant General George S. Patton Jr.'s Third Army to disrupt the retreat of German forces by attacking eastward. The XV Corps moves in response to the orders, headed for Dreux.

Eighth Air Force sends B-17s and B-24 Liberators escorted by 388 P-47 Thunderbolts and P-51 Mustangs to attack engine production facilities, airfields, an oil production facility, bridges, and rail lines along the French-German border. Two B-17s are lost and 285 bombers are damaged. Aircrew casualties are 10 wounded and 18 missing. Fighter pilots report 18 confirmed kills. One P-51 is lost. The pilot is reported missing.

Over 130 P-38s and P-47s fly fighter-bomber missions in the Paris area. Fighter pilots report three confirmed kills. One P-38 and two P-47s are lost and three fighters are damaged. Two pilots are reported missing.

A total of 37 B-24s fly in support of Carpetbagger operations. One B-24 is lost. During the night six B-17s drop leaflets over France.

Ninth Air Force sends A-20 Havocs and B-26 Marauders to attack railroad bridges and rail targets to delay the German retreat across France. P-47 and P-38 fighters support ground forces and actually take the surrender of some German troops near Carrouges who had experienced more than enough of American air power over the past few weeks. The soldiers wave white flags and march down the road toward American lines shepherded by the fighters.

MEDITERRANEAN: Vice Admiral H. Kent Hewitt's Western Task Force conducts demonstrations to divert German attention from the main landing beaches.

Fifteenth Air Force sends more than 500 B-17s and B-24 Liberators escorted by 145 P-38 Lightnings and P-51 Mustangs to attack German positions in Toulon, France, and Genoa, Italy.

ITALY: Twelfth Air Force B-25 Mitchells and B-26 Marauders attack coastal defenses in the Toulon-Nice area. P-47 Thunderbolts attack radar sites, convoys, bridges, and roads along the coast in support of Dragoon. A-20 Havocs attack fuel storage areas in the Po River valley.

SOUTHWEST PACIFIC AREA: A Japanese cargo ship is sunk off Takao, Formosa, by a mine airdropped by Fourteenth Air Force B-24 Liberators.

PACIFIC: U.S. submarine *Croaker* torpedoes and sinks a Japanese gunboat southwest of Inchon, Korea.

CENTRAL PACIFIC: The Seventh Air Force is reorganized. The VII Bomber Command includes the B-24s of the 11th, 30th, and 494th Bombardment Groups (Heavy) and the B-25s of the 41st Bombardment Group (Medium). The VII Fighter Command includes the 15th, 21st (in Hawaii), and 318th Fighter Groups and the 6th Night Fighter Squadron. The headquarters of VII Bomber Command moves from Kwajalein Atoll to Saipan.

Saipan-based B-24 Liberators bomb Iwo Jima Island. B-25 Mitchells from the Marshall Islands bomb Ponape Island and B-24 Liberators bomb Wotje Atoll.

CENTRAL PACIFIC, TINIAN: The 4th Marine Division reembarks. The 2nd Marine Division will garrison Saipan and Tinian. The marines have suffered nearly 2,000 casualties to secure Tinian and have killed an estimated 5,000 of the enemy and captured 400 prisoners.

NEW GUINEA: FEAF A-20 Havocs, P-47 Thunderbolts, P-38 Lightnings, and P-40s attack targets near Wewak along with Royal Australian Air Force (RAAF) aircraft.

B-25 Mitchells and B-24 Liberators attack Ternate Island in the Moluccas and targets throughout the Halmahera Islands.

U.S. submarine *Cod* torpedoes and sinks a Japanese landing ship east of Celebes Island in the Banda Sea.

U.S. submarine *Ray* attacks a Japanese convoy, sinking a cargo ship and damaging another off Borneo.

August 15

CBI: Tenth Air Force P-51 Mustangs, P-47 Thunderbolts, P-40s, and A-36 Intruder (Apache) fighter-bombers attack the Bhamo area, Lashio airfield, and rail targets between Naba and Hopin.

In China, Fourteenth Air Force P-40s attack Lungling and Tengchung. Nearly 100 P-40s and P-51 Mustangs attack troops, horses, trucks, river shipping, artillery, and logistics storage sites near Hengyang and Changsha.

In French Indochina, four P-40s attack coastal shipping.

ETO: The XX Corps of Third Army (7th Armored Division and the 5th Infantry Division) reaches Chartres.

Eighth Air Force sends 517 B-17s and 417 B-24 Liberators escorted by 293 P-38 Lightnings and P-51 Mustangs to attack airfields in the Netherlands, Germany, and Belgium. Sixteen bombers are lost and 103 are damaged. Aircrews report 13 confirmed kills and three probables. Aircrew casualties are seven killed, nine wounded, and 140 missing. Fighter pilots report 14 confirmed kills in the air and seven on the ground. Five fighters are lost and five are damaged. One pilot is wounded, and five are reported missing.

More than 30 P-47 Thunderbolts conduct dive-bombing and skip-bombing attacks on a locomotive repair shop and locomotives in the marshaling yard at Braine-le-Comtes. One P-47 is lost and four are damaged. Four pilots are reported missing.

A total of 12 B-24s fly in support of Carpetbagger operations.

Ninth Air Force sends more than 300 A-20 Havocs and B-26 Marauders to attack fuel storage sites and ammunition storage areas. P-47 and P-38 fighters support ground forces and fly armed reconnaissance missions.

MEDITERRANEAN: Operation Dragoon. Vice Admiral H. Kent Hewitt, Naval Commander Western Task Force and Commander Eighth Fleet, directs the landing.

The invasion of southern France begins at 0430 with the 1st Provisional Troop Carrier Division's 416 C-47s and 25 gliders delivering the 1st Airborne Task Force with 9,000 paratroopers and glider infantry to designated drop zones. Only 283 men are injured in the initial jump and glider landings, a remarkably low rate. The 1st Special Service Force conducts a raid on Iles d'Hyères to clear the approaches for the amphibious forces. Beginning at 0800, the 3rd Infantry Division and 45th Infantry Division land with little opposition. The 45th later links up with the paratroopers as planned. The 36th Infantry Division lands on a mined beach and encounters heavy fire from German positions. By midday there are 86,500 men on the beachhead, protected by Allied air cover, which suppresses German defenses and allows the invasion force to move inland quickly. Over 2,000 prisoners are captured on the first day.

Fifteenth Air Force sends more than 250 B-17s and B-24 Liberators escorted by P-38 Lightnings and P-51 Mustangs to attack Cannes and Toulon, France, and bridges over the Rhône River. P-51 Mustangs escort C-47s carrying the paratroopers of the 1st Airborne Task Force.

Sergeant James P. Connor leads an infantry platoon of the 7th Infantry Regiment, 3rd Infantry Division. Landing on Red Beach with his platoon, Sergeant Connor's mission is to capture Cape Cavalaire, which overlooks the landing beaches. Although seriously wounded in the neck by a mine that killed his platoon lieutenant, Sergeant Connor refuses medical aid and takes charge of the platoon as it crosses the beach in the face of a heavy mortar barrage. Wounded again, he refuses to be evacuated and encourages the demoralized survivors of the platoon to continue the assault toward a group of strongly fortified buildings. He is wounded again and unable to move, but continues to support and encourage the dozen or so men left standing. Because of his inspiring example, this small group is able to overwhelm the strongpoint and accomplish the mission. For his determined leadership and inspirational courage in the face of overwhelming odds, Sergeant Connor will receive the Medal of Honor.

ITALY: During the night Twelfth Air Force A-20 Havocs bomb airfields near the Rhône River. A-20 Havocs, B-25 Mitchells, B-26 Marauders, P-38 Lightnings, and P-47 Thunderbolts support the Dragoon landings, attacking defenses near the beaches, troop concentrations, and gun positions. Later the bombers and fighters attack roads and bridges leading into the beachhead. The headquarters of the 64th Fighter Wing redeploys from Italy to St. Tropez, France.

NEW GUINEA: FEAF P-39 Airacobras dive-bomb antiaircraft positions at Wewak. B-24 Liberators bomb the airfield on Halmahera Island.

Fifth Air Force B-24 Liberators attack a Japanese convoy and sink a cargo ship in the Banda Sea.

August 16

CBI: Tenth Air Force P-51 Mustangs attack airfields at Lashio. P-40s and P-51s attack Japanese positions near Pinbaw. P-47 Thunderbolts and P-51s attack targets of opportunity near Bhamo.

ETO: Over 100,000 German soldiers are now contained in a 20-mile-by-20-mile pocket at Falaise. In the Third Army area, XV Corps (5th Armored Division and the 79th Infantry Division) captures Dreux. The XII Corps (the 4th Armored Division and the 35th Infantry Division) reaches Orléans.

Eighth Air Force sends 659 B-17s escorted by 412 P-47 Thunderbolts and P-51 Mustangs to attack aircraft and oil production facilities in central Germany. Sixteen bombers are lost and 323 damaged. Aircrews report six confirmed kills and four probables. Aircrew casualties are four killed, 12 wounded, and 149 missing. Fighter pilots report 20 confirmed kills and one probable. Two fighters are lost and one is damaged. The two pilots are reported missing.

Another attack is made against aircraft production facilities, airfields, and oil production facilities in Germany by 431 B-24 Liberators, escorted by 156 P-47 Thunderbolts and P-51 Mustangs and 42 P-38 Lightnings. Seven bombers are lost and 182 are damaged. One P-51 is lost. Fighter pilots report 12 confirmed kills. Five bomber crewmen are wounded and 66 are reported missing.

During the night eight B-17s drop leaflets over France.

Ninth Air Force sends more than 100 A-20 Havocs and B-26 Marauders to attack ammunition storage sites and railroad bridges, and a marshaling yard. P-47 and P-38 fighters support ground forces and fly armed reconnaissance missions.

MEDITERRANEAN: Task Force Butler is formed under the command of Brigadier General Frederick B. Butler with one infantry battalion, a cavalry reconnaissance squadron, an artillery battalion, a tank battalion, and a tank destroyer battalion to exploit gains and advance toward Grenoble and Montélimar in an attempt to trap and destroy the German Nineteenth Army as it retreats north through the Rhône Valley and into Germany. The 3rd Infantry Division advances north on Route 17 in pursuit of the retreating enemy.

Fifteenth Air Force sends 89 B-24 Liberators to bomb a chemical production plant at Friedrichshafen, Germany. Over France, 108 B-17s support Operation Dragoon by attacking railroad bridges. P-51 Mustangs escort C-47s airdropping supplies on the beachhead.

Twelfth Air Force B-25 Mitchells and B-26 Marauders attack bridges on the Rhône River. A-20 Havocs attack ammunition storage sites and German positions on the beachhead.

PACIFIC: U.S. submarine *Croaker* torpedoes and sinks a Japanese auxiliary minesweeper west of Korea.

CENTRAL PACIFIC: Seventh Air Force B-24 Liberators from Saipan bomb Chichi Jima Island in the Bonin Islands. B-24s from the Marshall Islands bomb Truk.

ADMIRALTIES: The C-47s of the 13th Troop Carrier Squadron of the 403rd Troop Carrier Group redeploy from Espiritu Santo Island in the New Hebrides Islands to Los Negros Island.

NEW GUINEA: FEAF P-39 Airacobras hit troops and positions around Manokwari.

August 17

CBI: Fourteenth Air Force B-25 Mitchells, P-40s, P-51 Mustangs, and P-38 Lightnings attack the road and airfield near Hengyang.

In French Indochina P-40s attack shipping in the Haiphong area.

ETO: St-Malo falls to the 83rd Infantry Division of Middleton's VIII Corps.

German forces begin to break as Allied forces form a pocket around them at Falaise-Argentan. The Third Army, led by the XII and XX Corps and supported by XV Corps, pushes toward Paris to cut the German line of retreat at the Paris-Orléans Gap between the Loire and Seine Rivers.

Eighth Air Force sends 397 P-38 Lightnings and P-47 Thunderbolts to attack targets around Paris and Brussels. Fighter pilots report three confirmed kills. One P-47 is damaged. Over 300 P-51 Mustangs attack communications targets. Seven fighters are lost and four are damaged. One pilot is wounded and seven pilots are reported missing.

A total of 33 B-24 Liberators fly in support of Carpetbagger operations during the night.

Ninth Air Force sends more than 400 A-20 Havocs and B-26 Marauders to attack road and rail bridges, and a marshaling yard. P-47 and P-38 fighters attack German forces near St-Malo.

Staff Sergeant Stanley Bender of E Company, 7th Infantry Regiment, 3rd Infantry Division, faces heavy enemy fire from a German machine gun near La Lande, France. Bender climbs on a knocked-out tank and looks for the source of the fire. Ignoring the bullets that pass by him, Staff Sergeant Bender locates the German position and orders two squads to provide covering fire. He then jumps off the tank and leads his men from another squad down an irrigation ditch. He then moves off alone to locate the rear of the enemy position, again in full view of the Germans, who continue to send a high volume of fire in his direction. Attacking the first machine gun position, he eliminates the defenders and advances toward the second machine gun position about 25 yards away. As bullets strike around him and hand grenades explode close by, Bender continues forward and dispatches the second position. Signaling an advance, Staff Sergeant Bender kills the last defenders to secure the position. Inspired by his display of courage, his soldiers continue the attack, capturing 26 German soldiers and taking three bridges over the Maravenne River. For his great courage and determined actions in the face of enemy fire, Staff Sergeant Bender will receive the Medal of Honor.

MEDITERRANEAN: The French II Corps lands in southern France. At this point 12,000 vehicles, 46,000 tons of supplies, and 86,000 men have landed on the beaches. The Allies have captured 7,845 prisoners.

Fifteenth Air Force sends 53 B-17s and B-24 Liberators escorted by P-38 Lightnings and P-51 Mustangs to attack the airfield at Nish in Yugoslavia. Another 250 B-24 Liberators escorted by P-51 Mustangs bomb oil refineries near Ploești, Romania.

Twelfth Air Force A-20 Havocs, A-36 Intruder (Apache) fighter-bombers, P-51 Mustangs, and P-40s attack rail cars, bridges, airfields, and roads in southern France in support of invasion forces.

PACIFIC: U.S. submarine *Croaker* torpedoes and sinks a Japanese merchant cargo ship off the west coast of Korea.

CENTRAL PACIFIC: Seventh Air Force B-24 Liberators from Saipan bomb Iwo Jima Island in the Volcano Islands. B-25 Mitchells from Makin bomb Ponape Island.

NEW GUINEA: At the Vogelkop Peninsula, the airfield constructed on Middelburg Island is operational.

FEAF P-40s, supporting ground forces, attack remnants of Japanese defenders on Biak Island. A-20 Havocs and P-38 Lightnings attack targets around Manokwari. B-25 Mitchells sink a transport vessel off Halmahera Island. B-24 Liberators bomb airfields on Ambon and Ceram Islands in the Moluccas.

The headquarters of the 5th Bombardment Group (Heavy) redeploys from Los Negros Island in the Admiralties to Wakde Island. The P-38 Lightnings of the 68th Fighter Squadron, 347th Fighter Group, redeploy from Bougainville Island to Middelburg Island.

August 18

CBI: Tenth Air Force P-47 Thunderbolts and P-51 Mustangs destroy a road bridge and Japanese positions near Bhamo. P-47 Thunderbolts attack Lashio airfield.

ETO: The Third Army's XV Corps moves to seize crossings on the Seine River and trap German forces still holding south of the river. The 2nd Infantry Division and the 29th Infantry Division are sent to Brittany to support VIII Corps as it initiates an attack on the port of Brest.

Eighth Air Force sends more than 500 B-17s and more than 250 B-24 Liberators escorted by nearly 140 P-51 Mustangs and 100 P-38 Lightnings to attack airfields, bridges, fuel storage areas, and industrial targets in France and Belgium. Only two bombers are lost and over 100 are damaged. Aircrew casualties are six killed, eight wounded, and 21 missing. Fighter pilots report two confirmed kills on the ground. Four fighters are lost and two are damaged. Four pilots are reported missing.

During the night seven B-17s drop leaflets over France.

Ninth Air Force sends nearly 100 A-20 Havocs and B-26 Marauders to attack fuel storage sites, railroad bridges, and roads to impede the retreat of German forces. P-47 and P-38 fighters support ground forces near Argentan and attack German forces assembling near the Seine River.

Mediterranean: Fifteenth Air Force sends 370 B-17s and B-24 Liberators to bomb oil refineries near Ploeşti, Romania.

Twelfth Air Force B-25 Mitchells and B-26 Marauders attack coastal guns near Toulon. A-20 Havocs, A-36 Intruder (Apache) fighter-bombers, and P-51 Mustangs attack rail lines and rail cars. The headquarters of the XII Tactical Air Command redeploys from Italy to France.

Southwest Pacific Area: U.S. submarine *Hardhead* torpedoes and sinks the Japanese light cruiser *Natori* east of Samar Island, in the Philippines.

USS *Rasher* and USS *Redfish* discover a Japanese convoy off the west coast of Luzon. The *Rasher* sinks an escort carrier, a transport, a cargo ship, and an oiler and damages a transport. The *Redfish* damages a merchant tanker.

U.S. submarine *Ray* torpedoes and sinks a Japanese merchant tanker at the southern end of Palawan.

CBI: Fourteenth Air Force P-40s and P-51 Mustangs attack river shipping, troops, and ground transportation near Hengyang.

ETO: The 90th Infantry Division of V Corps, U.S. First Army, meets elements of the Canadian First Army to close the Falaise-Argentan Pocket at Chambois, capturing 50,000 prisoners and 5,000 armored vehicles. The First Army's XIX Corps (2nd Armored Division, the 28th and 30th Infantry Divisions) moves north to support the left flank of Third Army's XV Corps. The 79th Infantry Division of the XV Corps, Third Army, crosses the Seine River while the 5th Armored Division moves to block crossing sites German forces may use. Major General Manton S. Eddy takes command of XII Corps from Major General Gilbert R. Cook.

French Forces of the Interior, a paramilitary resistance group, battle German troops in Paris, seizing government buildings. Bradley's 12th Army Group is given the task of moving north to the Seine River to block the German retreat.

The Ninth Air Force's 50th and 53rd Troop Carrier Wings redeploy from Italy, where they were supporting Dragoon and return to Britain. P-47 Thunderbolts and P-38 Lightnings attack German assembly areas near the Seine River.

MEDITERRANEAN: Task Force Butler advances toward Grenoble to trap retreating German forces in the Rhône valley. The 36th Infantry Division follows Butler's task force as the 3rd and 45th Infantry Divisions advance north. Since the invasion on August 15, Seventh Army has captured 16,500 prisoners and suffered about 5,000 casualties. German air elements in southern France redeploy, giving the Allies total command of the air.

Fifteenth Air Force sends 65 B-17s escorted by 125 P-51 Mustangs to bomb the oil refineries at Ploeşti, Romania. This is the last time the Fifteenth Air Force will attack the Ploeşti oil refinery.

Twelfth Air Force B-25 Mitchells and B-26 Marauders attack rail and road traffic and bridges in southern France. A-20 Havocs, A-36 Intruder (Apache) fighter-bombers, P-51 Mustangs, and P-40s attack German positions in support of Task Force Butler.

Battleship *Nevada* and French battleship *Lorraine,* with heavy cruiser *Augusta* and escorted by four destroyers, conduct a reconnaissance in force off Toulon and bombard the harbor.

ITALY: Private Masato Nakae of the 100th Infantry Battalion is attacking German infantry near Pisa, Italy, when his Thompson submachine gun is damaged by a shell fragment. Private Nakae quickly picks up an M-1 rifle and fires rifle grenades at the Germans. Nakae throws six grenades to disrupt an attack on his position and forces them to retreat. During a mortar bombardment that follows Private Nakae is wounded. Despite his injuries, he continues to fight as the Germans attack again. His heroic defense against superior enemy forces will win him the Medal of Honor.

SOUTHWEST PACIFIC AREA: USS *Bluefish* torpedoes and sinks a fast fleet tanker/seaplane carrier and damages a hospital ship off the west coast of Luzon in a second day of attacks on this convoy.

U.S. submarine *Spadefish* torpedoes and sinks a Japanese landing craft repair ship west of Luzon.

CENTRAL PACIFIC: Seventh Air Force P-47 Thunderbolts from Saipan drop incendiaries on Japanese holdouts on Tinian Island.

NEW GUINEA: FEAF P-39 Airacobras bomb and strafe Japanese positions along the western coast of Geelvink Bay. Other P-39s attack Japanese positions near Wewak. A-20 Havocs support ground forces near Sarmi.

The B-24 Liberators of the 72nd Bombardment Squadron (Heavy), 5th Bombardment Group (Heavy), redeploy from Momote airfield on Los Negros Island to Wakde Island.

U.S. submarine *Redfin* lays mines off Sarawak, Borneo.

August 20
CBI: The P-47 Thunderbolts from the 88th Fighter Squadron of the 80th Fighter Group redeploy from Myitkyina and return to Shingbwiyang.

In China, Fourteenth Air Force B-25 Mitchells and P-40s attack buildings, a pontoon bridge, and river transport near Hengyang.

Fourteenth Air Force B-24 Liberators sink a Japanese army tanker near Hong Kong.

ATLANTIC: Navy TBM Avengers and FM-2 Wildcat fighters from escort carrier USS *Bogue* sink German submarine *U-1229* in the North Atlantic.

ETO: The XX Corps reaches Fontainebleau. The 79th Infantry Division of the XV Corps establishes a bridgehead on the Seine River.

Ninth Air Force sends 61 B-26 Marauders to attack German assembly areas near the Seine River. The B-26s of the 584th and 585th Bombardment Squadrons (Medium), 394th Bombardment Group (Medium), redeploy from England to France.

MEDITERRANEAN: Fifteenth Air Force sends more than 460 B-17s and B-24 Liberators escorted by P-38 Lightnings and P-51 Mustangs to attack an airfield and marshaling yard in Hungary and oil refineries in Czechoslovakia and Poland.

In France, Twelfth Air Force B-26 Marauders A-36 Intruder (Apache) fighter-bombers, P-51 Mustangs, and P-40s attack coastal defense installations at Toulon. B-25 Mitchells attack bridges and airfields along the Rhône River. A-20 Havocs support ground forces.

PACIFIC: Twentieth Air Force sends 61 B-29 Superfortresses from Chengtu, China, to bomb the Imperial Iron and Steel Works at Yawata, Japan. During the night another 10 B-29s attack the same target. Fourteen B-29s are lost—one to antiaircraft fire, one by air-to-air bombing, and a Japanese fighter deliberately rams one Superfortress. Aircrews report 17 confirmed kills.

CENTRAL PACIFIC: Seventh Air Force B-24 Liberators from Saipan bomb Yap. B-24s from the Marshalls bomb Truk.

NEW GUINEA: Lieutenant General Krueger establishes the Morotai Task Force, composed of Headquarters XI Corps, the 31st Infantry Division, and the 126th Infantry Regiment, 32nd Infantry Division. The 6th Infantry Division, with two regimental combat teams, is the task force reserve at Sansapor. Major General Charles P. Hall is the task force commander with 57,000 men of all services. The task force is to land on the southern coast of Morotai Island and capture Doroeba airfield. Naval Task Force 77, commanded by Rear Admiral Daniel E. Barbey, will be composed of six escort carriers and 10 destroyer escorts and accompanied by a covering force of two heavy cruisers, three light cruisers, and 10 destroyers.

FEAF P-39 Airacobras attack Japanese shipping off Manokwari and P-40s attack gun positions, buildings, and logistics storage sites. B-24 Liberators bomb targets on Halmahera Island.

The B-24s of the 23rd and 31st Bombardment Squadrons (Heavy), 5th Bombardment Group (Heavy), redeploy from Momote airfield on Los Negros Island in the Admiralties to Wakde Island.

August 21

CARIBBEAN: Sixth Air Force redeploys the B-24 Liberators of the 74th Bombardment Squadron, VI Bomber Command, from Rio Hato, Panama, to the Galápagos Islands.

CBI: The headquarters of the 1st Combat Cargo Group and the C-47s of the 1st Combat Cargo Squadron arrive at Sylhet, India, from the United States. The squadron will fly its first mission in early September.

In China, Fourteenth Air Force B-25 Mitchells bomb Hengyang airfield. P-51 Mustangs and P-40s attack river transports and road traffic around Tenchung, Hengyang, Tungting Lake, and Changsha.

U.S. submarine *Muskallunge* attacks a Japanese convoy, sinking an army transport off Cam Ranh Bay, French Indochina.

ATLANTIC: The Dumbarton Oaks conference, which lays the foundation for the establishment of a new global security organization, is held in Washington, D.C. The organization will be a representative body, without a security or police force. The members will contribute forces as necessary to keep the peace. The conference issues a set of guidelines for the organization of the United Nations, a Secretariat, and an International Court of Justice. Also recommended is a Security Council of five permanent members (United States, Great Britain, China, USSR, and France) and six non-permanent member nations, which would have executive powers over the General Assembly of member nations. The USSR desires absolute veto power in the Security Council, even for disputes where it is one of the nations involved in a dispute. The United States holds the view that veto power would be exercised only in extraordinary circumstances to preserve the peace. The USSR sees the veto power as a means of protecting its interests. The USSR also seeks 16 seats in the General Assembly, one for each of the nominally independent member states of the Soviet Union.

MEDITERRANEAN: Task Force Butler moves into blocking positions in the Rhône Valley near Montélimar.

Fifteenth Air Force sends more than 200 B-24 Liberators escorted by P-51 Mustangs to attack airfields in Yugoslavia and Hungary.

Twelfth Air Force A-36 Intruder (Apache) fighter-bombers and P-51 Mustangs attack communication sites, gun positions, and roads in southern France.

ITALY: Twelfth Air Force B-25 Mitchells, B-26 Marauders, and A-20 Havocs attack roads and bridges in the Po River valley. P-47 Thunderbolts attack rail cars and vehicles.

SOUTHWEST PACIFIC AREA: USS *Guitarro, Haddo, Harder,* and *Ray* attack a Japanese convoy off Mindoro. Three cargo ships and two tankers are sunk.

Navy PB4Y Privateers damage a cargo vessel in Davao harbor.

CENTRAL PACIFIC: Seventh Air Force B-24 Liberators from Saipan bomb Yap. B-25 Mitchells from Makin Island bomb Nauru Island.

Navy PB4Y Privateers damage a Japanese guardboat and a small cargo vessel northwest of Marcus Island.

NEW GUINEA: FEAF A-20 Havocs, P-47 Thunderbolts, P-38 Lightnings, and P-40s attack logistics storage areas near Manokwari and Sarmi.

August 22

CBI: In China, Tenth Air Force P-51 Mustangs and P-47 Thunderbolts attack Japanese positions around Tengchung in support of Chinese ground forces. In Burma, P-47 Thunderbolts strafe targets near Bhamo.

U.S. submarine *Pintado* attacks a Japanese convoy, sinking a merchant tanker southeast of Shanghai.

ETO: The XX Corps of Third Army reaches the Seine River. The leaders of the Resistance in Paris appeal to the Allies for help. General Charles de Gaulle presses General Eisenhower to provide forces, arguing that there will be no battle for the city and that the French Forces of the Interior have provided great assistance to the Allied advance. Eisenhower decides to initiate the pre-planned employment of the French 2nd Armored Division under Major General Jacques P. LeClerc and the U.S. 4th Infantry Division.

The German Seventh and Fifth Panzer armies cease to exist. The remnants retreat across the Seine River, heading for the German border and safety. France is now open to the uncontested advance of the Allied forces.

Ninth Air Force P-47 Thunderbolts and P-38 Lightnings support ground forces and fly armed reconnaissance missions.

MEDITERRANEAN: The 36th Infantry Division enters Grenoble while Task Force Butler establishes road blocks north of Montélimar, reinforced by elements of the 36th Infantry Division. German forces attempt to break through the American defenses and the 36th Infantry Division is pushed back. The units of the division are short on ammunition.

Fifteenth Air Force sends 39 B-24 Liberators to bomb the oil refinery near Vienna, Austria. Over 50 German fighters attack the bombers and shoot down one B-24. Aircrews report 13 confirmed kills. B-17s bomb oil refineries at Odertal, Germany.

ITALY: Twelfth Air Force B-26 Marauders and A-20 Havocs attack bridges and convoys in the Po River valley.

SOUTHWEST PACIFIC AREA: USS *Haddo* and *Harder* sink three Japanese escort vessels at the entrance to Manila Bay.

U.S. submarine *Spadefish* attacks a Japanese convoy and damages a tanker in Luzon Strait.

PACIFIC: U.S. submarine *Bowfin* attacks a Japanese convoy, sinking a cargo ship in the Ryukyus.

U.S. submarine *Tang* torpedoes and sinks a Japanese cargo ship off Honshu, Japan.

CENTRAL PACIFIC: Seventh Air Force B-24 Liberators from Saipan bomb Yap. B-24s from Kwajalein bomb Mille Atoll.

NEW GUINEA: FEAF A-20 Havocs and P-39 Airacobras attack Japanese positions around Manokwari. P-47 Thunderbolts, P-38 Lightnings, and P-40s attack targets near Wewak.

The B-24 Liberators of the 370th, 371st, 372nd, and 424th Bombardment Squadrons (Heavy) of the 307th Bombardment Group (Heavy) redeploy from Los Negros Island in the Admiralty Islands to Wakde Island.

August 23

CBI: Tenth Air Force P-47 Thunderbolts attack Japanese forces and logistics bases located along the Burma Road from Wanling to Lungling.

In China, Fourteenth Air Force B-25 Mitchells, P-40s, and P-51 Mustangs attack Japanese positions and vehicles near Hengyang.

ETO: The V Corps (4th Infantry Division and 2nd French Armored Division) advances toward Paris.

Eighth Air Force P-47 Thunderbolts bomb and strafe rail transportation in northeast France.

During the night six B-17s drop leaflets over France and Belgium.

Ninth Air Force sends P-47 and P-38 fighters to support ground forces and attack German assembly areas on the Seine River.

German submarine *U-989* torpedoes and damages a U.S. freighter on the way to Utah beach.

MEDITERRANEAN: The French II Corps captures the heights above Toulon. Six airfields are established in southern France for the XII Tactical Air Force. Three U.S. fighter groups will redeploy to these airfields.

Romania surrenders to Soviet forces.

Fifteenth Air Force sends more than 400 B-17s and B-24 Liberators escorted by P-38 Lightnings and P-51 Mustangs to bomb the oil refinery and aircraft production facilities at Vienna, Austria. Over 60 German fighters attack the bombers and shoot down nine B-24s. Aircrews report 29 confirmed kills.

Twelfth Air Force A-20 Havocs, A-36 Intruder (Apache) fighter-bombers, P-51 Mustangs, and P-40s support ground forces in southern France.

ITALY: Twelfth Air Force B-25 Mitchells and B-26 Marauders attack rail and road traffic and bridges along the Arno River. A-20 Havocs and P-47 Thunderbolts support ground forces in southern France.

SOUTHWEST PACIFIC AREA: U.S. submarine *Haddo* torpedoes and sinks a destroyer off Luzon.

PACIFIC: U.S. submarine *Tang* attacks a Japanese convoy off Honshu, sinking a cargo ship.

CENTRAL PACIFIC: Seventh Air Force B-25 Mitchells from the Gilbert Islands attack Ponape Island. B-24 Liberators from Saipan bomb Yap and Iwo Jima.

Seventh Air Force B-24 Liberators sink a Japanese auxiliary submarine chaser near Chichi Jima.

NEW GUINEA: FEAF B-25 Mitchells, A-20 Havocs, and P-38 Lightnings attack barge locations and troop positions around Wewak.

B-24 Liberators bomb Halmahera Island.

August 24

CBI: In China, Fourteenth Air Force B-25 Mitchells and P-40s attack towns, river and road traffic, and rail lines around Hengyang.

ETO: The French 2nd Armored Division advances toward Paris.

Eighth Air Force sends more than 800 B-17s and nearly 500 B-24 Liberators, escorted by over 600 P-38 Lightnings, P-47 Thunderbolts, and P-51 Mustangs, to attack aircraft production facilities, oil refineries, and airfields in Germany. A total of 27 bombers are lost and over 500 are damaged. Aircrews report 10 confirmed kills and three probables. Aircrew casualties are four killed, 45 wounded, and 247 missing. Fighter pilots report 10 confirmed kills in the air and 14 confirmed kills on the ground. Four fighters are lost and three are damaged. Three pilots are reported missing.

During the night one B-17 drops leaflets over Brest, France.

Ninth Air Force P-47 and P-38 fighters support ground forces and attack pontoon bridges over the Seine River as German forces continue to retreat.

MEDITERRANEAN: The French II Corps occupies Toulon. The 1st Airborne Task Force captures Cannes.

Fifteenth Air Force sends more than 500 B-17s and B-24 Liberators escorted by P-38 Lightnings and P-51 Mustangs to bomb oil refineries in Czechoslovakia, airfields in Yugoslavia and Hungary, and railroad bridges in Italy. Aircrews and fighter pilots report 40 confirmed kills.

Twelfth Air Force A-20 Havocs attack convoys in the Rhône River valley. B-26 Marauders attack gun positions near Marseille, France. A-20 Havocs and P-47 Thunderbolts attack German forces in southern France in support of the Seventh Army.

SOUTHWEST PACIFIC AREA: A Japanese coastal patrol vessel sinks U.S. submarine *Harder* off the west coast of Luzon.

U.S. submarine *Ronquil* attacks a Japanese convoy off Formosa, sinking two cargo ships.

U.S. submarine *Sailfish* attacks a Japanese convoy in Luzon Strait, sinking a transport.

PACIFIC: The headquarters of Twentieth Air Force's 73rd Bombardment Wing (Very Heavy) arrives in the Mariana Islands with B-29 Superfortresses. The wing commander is Brigadier General Emmett O'Donnell, Jr.

U.S. submarine *Seal* sinks a cargo ship off the southeast coast of Hokkaido, Japan.

CENTRAL PACIFIC: Seventh Air Force B-24 Liberators from the Marshalls bomb Truk. B-25 Mitchells bomb Nauru Island.

NEW GUINEA: The headquarters of the 307th Bombardment Group (Heavy) redeploys from Los Negros Island in the Admiralties to Wakde Island. P-47 Thunderbolts of the 340th and 341st Fighter Squadrons of the 348th Fighter Group redeploy from Wakde Island to Noemfoor Island. FEAF B-24 Liberators bomb an airfield on Halmahera Island. B-25 Mitchells bomb shipping in the Celebes.

August 25

CBI: Tenth Air Force P-47 Thunderbolts destroy a bridge near Bhamo.

Fourteenth Air Force B-24 Liberators bomb the Kowloon docks in Hong Kong. P-51 Mustangs and P-40s attack targets near Hengyang.

ETO: The V Corps enters the city of Paris. Major General Jacques P. LeClerc's French 2nd Armored Division and the U.S. 4th Infantry Division enter Paris. LeClerc takes the surrender of 10,000 German soldiers in the name of the Provisional Government of France. The First Army's XIX Corps, commanded by Major General Charles H. Corlett, reaches Elbeuf, closing a large portion of the Seine River to the Germans as an escape route. Patton's Third Army has control of four crossing sites on the Seine River.

Bradley orders the 12th Army Group to cross the Seine River and attack northeast to support Montgomery's 21st Army Group, which General Eisenhower has designated as the main effort. The XX Corps (7th Armored Division and 90th Infantry Division) will capture Rheims and the XII Corps (4th Armored Division and 35th and 80th Infantry Divisions) of Third Army will capture Châlons.

Leading elements of the Third Army are 140 miles beyond Paris and 60 miles from the German border. Resistance is negligible. Fuel supplies now have to be transported overland from both the port of Cherbourg and the Normandy beaches to reach the extended forces. There is not enough capacity to haul the thousands of tons of fuel needed to continue the advance.

Eighth Air Force sends more than 700 B-17s and 400 B-24 Liberators escorted by 569 P-47 Thunderbolts and P-51 Mustangs to bomb liquid oxygen and ammonia production facilities in Belgium and France, the Peenemünde Experimental Station, aircraft component plants, airfields, and synthetic oil production facilities. Eighteen bombers are lost and over 300 are damaged. Aircrew casualties are one killed, 24 wounded, and 173 missing. Fighter pilots report 11 confirmed kills and two probables in the air and 40 confirmed kills on the ground. Seven fighters are lost.

Another 10 B-24 Liberators escorted by P-47s fly an Azon glide bomb mission to Moerdijke in the Netherlands. Aircrews report no damage to the target.

B-24s escorted by P-38s and P-51s attack targets in Belgium, and 24 of the 69 bombers are damaged and four crewmen are wounded.

One C-47 flies a Carpetbagger mission during the night. During the night six B-17s drop leaflets over France and Belgium.

Ninth Air Force sends 240 A-20 Havocs and B-26 Marauders to attack German positions near Brest. P-47 and P-38 fighters support ground forces and attack German bridges over the Seine River. Fighter pilots report using napalm bombs to attack the suspected headquarters of Field Marshal Walter Model, the commander in chief of German forces on the west front.

The headquarters of the 394th Bombardment Group (Medium) redeploys to France from England.

Private Harold A. Garman is assigned to Company B, 5th Medical Battalion, 5th Infantry Division, and is engaged in moving casualties delivered by boats from a bridgehead on the Seine River near Montereau, France. German machine guns begin firing on a boatload of wounded as it crosses the river. Private Garman dives into the water to rescue the wounded and steers the boat while still under heavy fire to the shore. Garman's courageous deed and devotion to duty will win him the Congressional Medal of Honor.

MEDITERRANEAN: German forces break through the 36th Infantry Division lines near Grenoble, opening an escape route for the Nineteenth Army.

Operation Olive begins in Italy. The British Eighth Army begins an attack along a 17-mile front on the Adriatic coast. Although the British make some progress initially, the offensive stalls by early September.

Fifteenth Air Force sends more than 300 B-17s and B-24 Liberators escorted by P-38 Lightnings and P-51 Mustangs to bomb airfields and aircraft production facilities in Czechoslovakia.

Twelfth Air Force B-25 Mitchells and B-26 Marauders attack bridges over the Rhône River.

ITALY: Operation Olive begins. The British Eighth Army launches a two corps attack on the eastern coast of Italy. Mark Clark's Fifth Army is to launch supporting attacks within five days.

A-20 Havocs and P-47 Thunderbolts attack convoys, gun positions, bridges, and roads north of the Arno River.

The headquarters of the 27th Fighter Group and the P-47s of the 522nd, 523rd, and 524th Fighter Squadrons redeploy from Corsica to southern France. The headquarters of the 79th Fighter Group also redeploys from Corsica to southern France.

SOUTHWEST PACIFIC AREA: U.S. submarine *Picuda* attacks a Japanese convoy and sinks a destroyer and merchant tanker north of Luzon. U.S. submarine *Redfish* follows with an attack on the same convoy, damaging a cargo ship.

PACIFIC: U.S. submarine *Tang* torpedoes and sinks a Japanese merchant tanker off Honshu, Japan.

CENTRAL PACIFIC: Seventh Air Force B-24 Liberators from Saipan bomb Iwo Jima. B-25 Mitchells from the Gilberts bomb Ponape Island.

NEW GUINEA: B-24 Liberators bomb the Palau Islands. B-25 Mitchells attack shipping in the Celebes and report sinking one cargo ship.

The B-24s and B-17s of the 394th Bombardment Squadron (Heavy), 5th Bombardment Group (Heavy), redeploy from Los Negros Island in the Admiralties to Wake Island. B-25 Mitchells of the 822nd Bombardment Squadron (Medium) of the 38th Bombardment Group (Medium) redeploy from Nadzab to Biak Island.

August 26

ALEUTIANS: Eleventh Air Force B-24 Liberators bomb Paramushiru Island in the Kuriles on an early morning raid. B-25 Mitchells attack and sink a patrol boat. A B-25 is damaged. Other B-24s bomb targets on Kashiwabara and on Otomari Cape.

CBI: The Mars Task Force is activated under the command of Brigadier General Thomas S. Arms. The task force is composed of a new unit named the 5332nd Brigade (Provisional), the 475th Infantry Regiment (the remnants of the Marauders and New Galahad), the 124th Cavalry Regiment (the last U.S. Army unit actually to have horses, but now converted to infantry), and the 1st Chinese Separate Regiment (a unit that never actually served). Supporting the infantry are the 612th and the 613th Field Artillery Battalions with 75 millimeter pack howitzers.

ETO: German aircraft bomb Paris as more than 2,000 German soldiers continue to fight in the city. General Charles de Gaulle makes his official entry into Paris. German forces have been pushed against the left bank of the Seine River between Elbeuf and Le Havre.

German forces are using barges to ferry nearly 27,000 troops across the Seine River. The Germans have suffered a significant defeat. At least 20 infantry divisions have been destroyed and another 12 severely depleted. The Allies have captured 200,000 soldiers and another 200,000 are casualties. Another 1,300 tanks, 20,000 vehicles, 500 assault guns, and 1,500 pieces of artillery have been either captured or destroyed. The German air force has lost over 2,300 aircraft in combat and another 1,100 destroyed on the ground.

Eighth Air Force sends more than 300 B-17s escorted by P-51 Mustangs to attack German defenses at Brest. Seven B-17s are damaged and one P-51 is lost. Aircrew casualties are 18 killed.

On other attacks, over 250 B-17s and 300 B-24 Liberators, escorted by over 360 P-38 Lightnings, P-51 Mustangs, and P-47 Thunderbolts, bomb oil refineries, chemical works, fuel storage areas, marshaling yards, and airfields. Ten bombers are lost and 144 are damaged. Aircrew casualties are two killed, eight wounded, and 96 missing. Fighter pilots report one confirmed kill on the ground. Three fighters are lost and one is damaged. Three pilots are reported missing.

Over 380 P-47s and P-51s attack transport targets in Belgium, France, and Germany. Fighter pilots report one confirmed kill. Two P-47s and seven P-51s are lost and 15 fighters are damaged. One pilot is reported wounded and eight are reported missing.

During the night six B-17s drop leaflets over France and Belgium.

Ninth Air Force sends A-20 Havocs and B-26 Marauders to attack fuel storage sites. P-47 and P-38 fighters support ground forces and attack German troops at the Seine and Loire Rivers.

The First Allied Airborne Army takes operational control of the IX Troop Carrier Command from Ninth Air Force. The headquarters of the 323rd Bombardment Group (Medium) and the B-26 Marauders of the 453rd, 454th, 455th, and 456th Bombardment Squadrons (Medium) redeploy from England to France.

Three motor torpedo boats prevent an attempt to reinforce the German garrison at Le Havre. Two German artillery ferries are sunk.

MEDITERRANEAN: Allied naval forces enter Toulon harbor after exchanging fire with coastal batteries.

Fifteenth Air Force B-24 Liberators bomb German troops and barracks at Bucharest, Romania.

Twelfth Air Force B-25s and B-26 Marauders bomb gun positions near Marseille, France.

ITALY: Twelfth Air Force A-20 Havocs and P-47 Thunderbolts attack rail lines, bridges, and roads in northern Italy and southern France.

SOUTHWEST PACIFIC AREA: U.S. submarine *Guitarro* attacks a Japanese convoy, sinking a merchant tanker, damaging another, and forcing another tanker to run aground west of Panay Island in the Philippines.

U.S. submarine *Stingray* lands men and supplies on Luzon.

PACIFIC: Navy PV-1 Mariner patrol bombers sink a Japanese vessel between Odomari and Onnekotan Islands, Kuriles.

CENTRAL PACIFIC: Seventh Air Force B-24 Liberators from Saipan bomb Iwo Jima.

NEW GUINEA: FEAF A-20 Havocs attack Japanese positions near Sarmi. P-38 Lightnings, P-40s, and P-47 Thunderbolts attack targets near Wewak. P-39 Airacobras maintain patrols over Geelvink Bay. B-24 Liberators bomb the airfield on Peleliu in the Palaus.

The headquarters of the 348th Fighter Group moves from Wakde Island to Noemfoor. B-25 Mitchells of the 823rd Bombardment Squadron (Medium), 38th Bombardment Group (Medium), redeploy from Nadzab to Biak Island.

August 27

ALEUTIANS: Eleventh Air Force sends five B-24 Liberators on a bombing and photoreconnaissance mission over Paramushiru Island. Four B-25 Mitchells conduct a shipping sweep around the Kurile Islands. Aircrews report damaging one picket boat and sinking another.

CBI: In China, Fourteenth Air Force B-25 Mitchells bomb Hengyang, Tien Ho, White Cloud, and Pailochi airfields.

ETO: General Eisenhower and General Bradley enter Paris. The city is placed under the control of General Pierre Koenig, who had been commander of the French Forces of the Interior. With the success of Dragoon and the collapse of German forces on the Normandy front, Eisenhower decides to continue the pursuit, cross the Rhine, and reach the Ruhr. Eisenhower continues to hold to the broad-front strategic approach where the Allied armies advance together and can be mutually supporting, rather than a series of deep, unsupported thrusts on a narrow axis of advance. The VII Corps (3rd Armored Division and 9th Infantry Division) crosses the Seine River.

Eighth Air Force sends more than 1,000 B-17s and B-24 Liberators, escorted by over 500 P-38 Lightnings, P-51 Mustangs, and P-47 Thunderbolts, to bomb marshaling yards, docks, and transportation targets in northern Germany and France. Three bombers are lost and 75 are damaged. Aircrew casualties are one killed, five wounded, and 19 missing. Fighter pilots report one confirmed kill in the air and one confirmed kill on the ground. Ten fighters are lost and 11 are damaged. One pilot is reported killed, and 10 pilots are reported missing.

Over 300 P-47s fly fighter-bomber missions against transportation targets in France. Fighter pilots report 14 confirmed kills on the ground. One P-47 is lost, and the pilot is reported missing.

During the night six B-17s drop leaflets over France and the Netherlands.

Ninth Air Force sends A-20 Havocs and B-26 Marauders to attack German defenses near Rouen. P-47 fighters engage German fighters, and pilots report 11 confirmed kills in the air and five on the ground. Six P-47s are lost.

MEDITERRANEAN: The 36th Infantry Division restores its lines after the German attack, but the bulk of the German army has escaped the trap. Montélimar is captured, bringing organized German resistance to an end south of a line from Grenoble to Bordeaux. A total of 42,000 German prisoners have been captured since the landings on August 15.

Fifteenth Air Force sends more than 500 B-17s and B-24 Liberators escorted by P-38 Lightnings and P-51 Mustangs to attack oil refineries in Germany and transportation targets in northern Italy.

Twelfth Air Force B-26 Marauders and B-25 Mitchells bomb gun positions near Marseille, France.

ITALY: Twelfth Air Force B-25 Mitchells and B-26 Marauders attack bridges. A-20 Havocs attack ammunition storage sites. A-20 Havocs and P-47 Thunderbolts attack bridges and roads north of the Arno River.

CENTRAL PACIFIC: Seventh Air Force B-24 Liberators from Saipan bomb Iwo Jima.
NEW GUINEA: The B-25 Mitchells of the 75th Bombardment Squadron (Medium) 42nd Bombardment Group (Medium) redeploy to Hollandia.

August 28

ALEUTIANS: Eleventh Air Force B-25 Mitchells sink an auxiliary submarine chaser near the Paramushiru Straits in the Kuriles.
CBI: The Fourteenth Air Force takes operational control of the 311th Fighter Group from Tenth Air Force. The Group's three squadrons, the 528th, 529th, and 530th, are equipped with P-51 Mustangs and will be stationed at Chengtu. B-25 Mitchells bomb Tien Ho, White Cloud, Hankow, and Pailochi airfields. Other B-25s attack river and road transportation from Hengyang to Puchi.
ETO: The XII Corps captures Châlons.

Eighth Air Force sends more than 800 P-38 Lightnings, P-47 Thunderbolts, and P-51 Mustangs to attack rail lines in the Netherlands, Belgium, France, and Germany. Fighter pilots report 19 confirmed kills and one probable kill in the air and 11 confirmed kills on the ground. A total of 20 fighters are lost and 19 are damaged. Twenty pilots are reported missing.

During the night six B-17s drop leaflets over France and the Netherlands.

Ninth Air Force sends A-20 Havocs and B-26 Marauders to attack fuel storage sites, railroad bridges, and a marshaling yard. P-47 and P-38 fighters attack airfields, escort C-47s transporting wounded, and fly armed reconnaissance missions.
MEDITERRANEAN: The city of Marseille surrenders to French forces. The port can be made available to resupply Allied forces in the ETO. The 3rd Infantry Division attacks German delaying forces near Montélimar. The 36th and 45th Infantry Divisions capture Livron. Remnants of the German Nineteenth Army escape north to join Army Group B, reorganizing in northern France. The Seventh Army has captured 15,000 prisoners and 4,000 vehicles but is unable to pursue the retreating Germans. The army is at the limit of a 450-mile-long supply line and cannot advance any farther. The Americans have suffered 2,700 casualties, the French 4,000.

Twelfth Air Force B-25 Mitchells bomb railroad bridges near Lyon, France. A-20 Havocs attack ammunition storage facilities, and A-36 Intruder (Apache) fighter-bombers attack vehicles in the Rhône River valley.

Fifteenth Air Force sends more than 300 B-17s and B-24 Liberators escorted by P-38 Lightnings and P-51 Mustangs to bomb an oil refinery in Austria and oil refineries and a marshaling yard in Hungary.

German submarine *U-859* torpedoes and sinks a U.S. freighter in the Gulf of Aden.
ITALY: Twelfth Air Force A-20 Havocs attack targets along the Po River valley. P-47 Thunderbolts attack roads and bridges north of the Arno River.
CENTRAL PACIFIC: Seventh Air Force B-25 Mitchells from the Gilbert Islands bomb Ponape Island. B-24 Liberators from Saipan bomb Iwo Jima. B-24s from the Marshalls bomb Truk.
NEW GUINEA: FEAF B-24 Liberators bomb the airfield on Koror Island in the Palaus.

August 29

CBI: The Japanese 11th Army with seven divisions attacks along the rail line from Hengyang to Canton as part of an effort to open a land transportation corridor from northern China to Indochina. From there, the army intends to turn toward Kweilin and Liuchow to capture the Fourteenth Air Force's airfields and eliminate attacks on shipping and B-29 attacks on the Japanese homeland. The Japanese intend to force China to capitulate.

In Burma, Tenth Air Force B-25 Mitchells, P-51 Mustangs, and P-47 Thunderbolts attack bridges.

In China, Fourteenth Air Force B-24 Liberators, escorted by 45 fighters, bomb the Yoyang railroad yards. B-25 Mitchells bomb Pailochi, White Cloud, Tien Ho, and Hankow airfields and convoys near Hengyang and Hankow. P-40s attack trucks and a storage area near Changsha. P-40s claim eight Japanese fighters shot down.

A detachment of B-25s of the 491st Bombardment Squadron (Medium), 341st Bombardment Group (Medium), is sent from Yankai to Liuchow.

ETO: The 28th Infantry Division marches through Paris. XX Corps captures Rheims. VII Corps crosses the Aisne River. XIX Corps (2nd Armored Division and the 30th and 79th Infantry Divisions) crosses the Seine River. Elements of the Third Army capture crossings over the Meuse River. After learning from Bradley that he will not be receiving his army's allocation of 140,000 gallons of fuel due to other priorities, Lieutenant General George S. Patton, Jr. records his reaction in his diary: "it was a terrible mistake to halt even at the Meuse . . . there were no Germans ahead of us except those we were actually fighting."

Eighth Air Force P-38 Lightnings and P-47 Thunderbolts attack rail lines, marshaling yards, airfields, bridges, and highways in France, Belgium, and Germany. Fighter pilots report 20 confirmed kills on the ground. Three P-47s are lost and eight are damaged. Three pilots are reported missing.

Ninth Air Force redeploys the B-26 Marauders of the 586th Bombardment Squadron (Medium), 394th Bombardment Group (Medium), from England to France.

Sergeant John J. McVeigh of H Company, 23rd Infantry Regiment, 2nd Infantry Division, faces a German counterattack near Brest, France. Taking a hasty defensive position along a hedge, the Americans are pushed back, leaving a heavy machine-gun section exposed. Sergeant McVeigh stands up in front of the Germans and directs his squad's rifle fire into the enemy. He then charges the Germans with nothing but a combat knife to defend the machine-gun position. In the hand-to-hand struggle, Sergeant McVeigh is killed. McVeigh's squad and the machine-gun section are able to break the German assault. For his indomitable spirit and courage under fire in the face of certain death, Sergeant McVeigh will receive the Medal of Honor.

MEDITERRANEAN: Fifteenth Air Force sends more than 500 B-17s and B-24 Liberators escorted by P-38 Lightnings and P-51 Mustangs to attack targets in the Po River valley, oil refineries in Hungary, and railroad bridges in Czechoslovakia and Yugoslavia.

Twelfth Air Force P-47 Thunderbolts attack convoys in France. Fighter pilots report 100 vehicles destroyed. In France, P-51 Mustangs and P-40s attack targets in the Rhône valley.

Marine detachments from the heavy cruiser USS *Augusta* and light cruiser USS *Philadelphia* accept the surrender of the German garrisons on two islands in Marseille harbor.

ITALY: Twelfth Air Force B-25 Mitchells and B-26 Marauders attack bridges. A-20 Havocs attack fuel storage areas. P-47 Thunderbolts attack bridges and roads and conduct ground support missions in the Arno River valley.

Fifteenth Air Force P-38 Lightnings with Droopsnoot attack bridges in northern Italy near Latisana.

P-47s of the 316th Fighter Squadron 324th Fighter Group redeploy from Corsica to France.

PACIFIC: Major General Curtis E. LeMay takes command of the Twentieth Air Force's XX Bomber Command at Kharagpur, India.

CENTRAL PACIFIC: Seventh Air Force B-24 Liberators from Saipan bomb Iwo Jima. B-25 Mitchells from the Gilberts bomb Nauru Island.

NEW GUINEA: FEAF B-24 Liberators bomb Koror, Malakal, and Arakabesan Islands. P-38 Lightnings attack a seaplane base at Halong in the Celebes.

C-47s of the 22nd Troop Carrier Squadron, 374th Troop Carrier Group, redeploy from Australia to Finschhafen. Thirteenth Air Force B-24s of the 868th Bombardment Squadron (Heavy) redeploy from Los Negros Island in the Admiralties to Noemfoor Island. This squadron relies on radar for low-level night bombing attacks on shipping instead of identifying the target visually.

U.S. submarine *Jack* torpedoes and sinks a Japanese minesweeper and a cargo ship off the north end of Celebes Island.

A U.S. Navy PBY Catalina sinks a Japanese vessel at the entrance to Ambon Bay, Ceram Island.

August 30

CBI: In China, Fourteenth Air Force B-25 Mitchells bomb the airfields at Hengyang, Pailochi, and Hankow as the Japanese bring up additional reinforcements. P-40s and P-51 Mustangs bomb road and rail junctions, bridges, vehicles, troops, town areas, and various targets of opportunity near Changsha, Hengshan, and Hengyang.

ATLANTIC: German submarine *U-482* torpedoes and sinks a U.S. tanker in convoy CU 36 (New York to United Kingdom) off the coast of Scotland.

ETO: The XX Corps captures Verdun. Third Army is notified that no additional fuel is available.

The 3rd Armored Division captures Laon. The 80th Infantry Division captures Châlons-sur-Marne. Eighth Air Force sends more than 700 B-17s and nearly 150 B-24 Liberators escorted by P-51 Mustangs to attack the U-boat base and shipyards at Kiel and V-weapon sites at Pas-de-Calais. A total of 159 bombers are damaged. The B-17s and B-24s attacking the V-weapon sites use H2X radar to assist the timing of bomb release. No bomber or fighter losses are reported.

During the night six B-17s drop leaflets over Belgium and France.

Ninth Air Force sends 75 A-20 Havocs and B-26 Marauders to attack fuel storage sites and gun positions.

B-26s of the 596th Bombardment Squadron (Medium) redeploy from England to France.

MEDITERRANEAN: The 1st Airborne Task Force captures Nice.

Soviet forces capture Ploeşti oil refinery. With the fall of Romania, 1,100 U.S. air crewmen of the Fifteenth Air Force who were held as prisoners of war are freed.

Fifteenth Air Force sends more than 100 B-17s and B-24 Liberators escorted by P-38 Lightnings and P-51 Mustangs to attack rail bridges in Yugoslavia. P-51 Mustangs strafe the Kecskemét, Hungary, and Oradea, Romania, airfields.

In France, Twelfth Air Force A-36 Intruder (Apache) fighter-bombers attack convoys and rail lines in the Rhône valley.

ITALY: Twelfth Air Force A-20 Havocs and P-47 Thunderbolts attack road and rail lines in the Po Valley.

SOUTHWEST PACIFIC AREA: U.S. submarine *Narwhal* lands men and supplies on east coast of Luzon.

CENTRAL PACIFIC: Seventh Air Force B-24 Liberators from Saipan bomb Yap. B-24s from Kwajalein bomb Mille Atoll.

NEW GUINEA: FEAF P-39 Airacobras attack along the coast of Geelvink Bay. B-24 Liberators bomb Koror and Malakal Islands. P-38 Lightnings bomb oil tanks, barracks, and antiaircraft positions on Ceram Island.

August 31

CBI: There are 20 air groups and a total of 149,014 men in-theater.

ATLANTIC: There are 24 ground combat divisions in the continental United States preparing for deployment at this time.

In China, Fourteenth Air Force B-25 Mitchells attack the airfields at Tien Ho, White Cloud, and Hengyang. P-51 Mustangs and P-40s attack trucks, logistics sites, river transport, bridges, and troop concentrations near Changsha, Hengyang, and Nanyo.

ETO: The V Corps (5th Armored Division and the 4th and 28th Infantry Divisions) crosses the Seine River.

At this time there are 34 American ground combat divisions in the theater and 103 air groups, a total of 2,053,417 men.

A total of 37 B-24s and C-47s fly in support of Carpetbagger operations. During the night six B-17s drop leaflets over France.

Ninth Air Force sends nearly 100 B-26 Marauders and A-20 Havocs to bomb an ammunition storage site and gun positions.

B-26s of the 587th Bombardment Squadron (Medium), 394th Bombardment Group (Medium), and the 597th, 598th, and 599th Bombardment Squadrons (Medium) of the 397th Bombardment Group (Medium) redeploy from England to France.

MEDITERRANEAN: At this time in the Mediterranean theater there are six American ground combat divisions in-theater and 46 air groups, a total of 712,915 men. The French II Corps moves north of VI Corps to reach Patton's Third Army.

Fifteenth Air Force sends 38 B-17s to begin evacuating American POWs from Bucharest, Romania, to Italy (Operation Reunion). The bombers will complete the mission on September 3.

P-51 Mustangs strafe airfields in Romania and Hungary. Pilots report at least 150 confirmed kills on the ground.

In southern France, Twelfth Air Force A-20 Havocs and P-47 Thunderbolts attack convoys, roads, and rail lines as Seventh Army advances north.

ITALY: German forces begin a withdrawal from the Arno River defensive line in response to Eighth Army's attack on the east coast of Italy (Operation Olive). The U.S. IV Corps with the 1st Armored Division and the 370th RCT of the 92nd Infantry Division advances northeast of Pisa with the mission of capturing Monte Pisano and the city of Lucca. The 92nd Infantry Division is an all-black unit led by white officers.

Twelfth Air Force B-25 Mitchells and B-26 Marauders attack railroad bridges in the Po River valley. A-20 Havocs also attack targets in the Po Valley and attack bridges, and roads in the Arno valley.

SOUTHWEST PACIFIC AREA: The Vogelkop operation is completed. U.S. casualties between April and August in SWPA total 9,500, with an estimated 110,000 Japanese casualties. Over 30,000 Japanese soldiers are isolated in New Guinea, and over 96,000 Japanese soldiers and sailors are trapped at Rabaul. The Far Eastern Air Force (FEAF) has 2,629 first-line combat aircraft and 633 transport aircraft.

General MacArthur's headquarters issues instructions to Lieutenant General Walter Krueger's Sixth Army to be ready for operations to seize airfields on Mindanao Island, gain control of Leyte, the Surigao Strait, and the island of Samar in the Philippines. The operation is set for mid-November or December.

In Luzon Strait USS *Barb* torpedoes and sinks an auxiliary minesweeper and a cargo ship. USS *Queenfish* torpedoes and sinks an army tanker and damages another tanker. USS *Sealion* torpedoes and sinks a minelayer. U.S. submarine *Redfish* lands supplies and evacuates personnel from Palawan Island.

PACIFIC: At this time there are 21 American ground combat divisions, 11 separate regiments, and five marine divisions in-theater. There are also 35 air groups. The total strength of U.S. forces in the Pacific is 1,102, 422.

TG 38.4 (Rear Admiral Ralph E. Davison) attacks Iwo Jima and Chichi Jima. F4F Hellcats from USS *Franklin* sink an auxiliary minesweeper and cargo ship off Iwo Jima.

September 1

ALEUTIANS: During the night Eleventh Air Force sends one B-24 on a raid on Paramushiru Island in the Kuriles. Later, a B-25 aircrew reports sinking a vessel off the coast of Paramushiru.

CBI: Tenth Air Force P-47 Thunderbolts attack Bhamo and strafe river boats.

In China, Fourteenth Air Force B-24 Liberator aircrews report sinking a small cargo ship in Formosa Strait. P-40s and P-51 Mustangs attack bridges, roads, shipping, airfields, troops, and other targets of opportunity near Hengyang and Changning. The 528th Fighter Squadron of the 311th Fighter Group deploys a detachment of P-51 Mustangs from Shwangliu to operate from airfields at Hanchung and Lianshan.

ATLANTIC: A U.S. Coast Guard cutter locates a German weather ship off Greenland, and the ship is scuttled by her crew to avoid capture. German submarine *U-703* attacks the cutter, but ice prevents a hit.

ETO: As commander of SHAEF, General Eisenhower takes operational control of both the U.S. and British Army Groups from General Montgomery and establishes headquarters at Versailles. Montgomery takes command of the 21st Army Group and General Bradley continues as commander of the 12th Army Group. The 12th Army Group is composed of three armies: the First under Lieutenant General Hodges, the Third under Lieutenant General Patton, and the Ninth under Lieutenant General Simpson. Allied supply lines now stretch 600 to 900 miles from the beaches at Normandy and the port of Cherbourg to the front lines. Truck transport becomes the primary means of supplying forces.

The XX Corps of Third Army crosses the Meuse River. Third Army halts to bring up supplies. The 3rd Armored Division makes a 30-mile advance past Laon.

Eighth Air Force sends 12 B-24 Liberators with Azon-equipped bombs and escorted by 15 P-51 Mustangs to attack the Ravenstein railroad bridge in the Netherlands. Nearly 1,000 B-17s and B-24 Liberators escorted by over 500 P-38 Lightnings and P-51s are sent against targets in Germany and France, but the mission is recalled due to bad weather over the targets. Eight bombers are damaged. Aircrew casualties are 30 killed and two are wounded. Three fighters are lost and two are damaged. Two pilots are reported missing.

Over 250 P-47 Thunderbolts attack rail lines in France. Fighter pilots report five confirmed kills on the ground. Three fighters are lost and 29 are damaged. Three pilots are reported missing.

A total of 31 B-24s fly in support of Carpetbagger operations.

U.S. Strategic Air Forces in Europe (USSTAF) takes administrative control of Ninth Air Force's IX Troop Carrier Command. First Allied Airborne Army retains operational control.

Ninth Air Force sends B-26 Marauders to attack gun positions and defenses in Brest. P-47 and P-38 fighters support ground forces and fly armed reconnaissance missions near Amiens, Cambrai, Rheims, and Verdun.

The B-26s of the 556th, 557th, 558th and 559th Bombardment Squadrons (Medium), 387th Bombardment Group (Medium), redeploy from England to France.

MEDITERRANEAN: The 45th Infantry Division is unable to hold German forces as they battle to escape along the Lyon-Geneva highway.

Fifteenth Air Force sends nearly 500 B-17s and B-24 Liberators escorted by P-38 Lightnings and P-51 Mustangs to attack railroad bridges and marshaling yards in Yugoslavia and Hungary.

ITALY: Twelfth Air Force B-25 Mitchells bomb road and rail bridges near Venice. A-20 Havocs attack gun positions and targets of opportunity in the Po River valley. A-20 Havocs and P-47 Thunderbolts attack troop concentrations, gun positions, rail lines, bridges, logistics storage areas, and highways north of Florence.

SOUTHWEST PACIFIC AREA: Over 50 FEAF B-24 Liberators bomb airfields on Mindanao Island in the Philippines.

U.S. submarine *Narwhal* lands men and supplies on east coast of Luzon.

U.S. submarine *Tunny* is damaged in an air attack in Luzon Strait and is forced to terminate her patrol.

PACIFIC: Naval Operating Base, Saipan, is established.

Heavy cruiser USS *New Orleans,* light cruiser *Biloxi,* and four destroyers from TG 38.4, bombard Japanese positions on Iwo Jima and Chichi Jima. U.S. submarine *Pilotfish* torpedoes and sinks a Japanese auxiliary vessel near Chichi Jima.

CENTRAL PACIFIC: Seventh Air Force B-24 Liberators from the Marshalls bomb Truk.

NEW GUINEA: Brigadier General Donald J. Myers arrives at Wakde with the 123rd RCT, 33rd Infantry Division, to relieve the 31st Infantry Division and assume control of the Sarmi-Maffin Bay area.

September 2

CBI: Tenth Air Force B-25 Mitchells bomb Japanese activity along the Burma Road near Wanling. More than 20 B-24 Liberators fly fuel to Kunming, China.

In China, Fourteenth Air Force B-25 Mitchells bomb the Hengyang airfield and P-40s attack gun positions, troop concentrations, and river transports near Hengyang and Changning.

ATLANTIC: JCS issues orders for a combined SWPA-Central Pacific attack on Leyte, set for December 20. As a preliminary to the Leyte invasion, MacArthur will capture Morotai Island, while Nimitz will attack the Palau Islands. The JCS avoids providing any instructions on the next objectives of the theater commanders. Nevertheless, the JCS orders plans drawn up for offensive operations against both Formosa and Luzon.

ETO: The XIX Corps arrives at the border of Belgium south of Tournai. The German harbor batteries at St-Malo surrender, almost two weeks after the garrison in the city had surrendered.

Eighth Air Force sends P-47 Thunderbolts to attack road and rail targets in Belgium. Nine fighters are damaged.

Two C-47s fly in support of Carpetbagger operations in France.

Ninth Air Force P-47s and P-38s support ground forces and fly armed reconnaissance missions.

MEDITERRANEAN: Fifteenth Air Force sends nearly 400 B-24 Liberators escorted by over 175 P-38 Lightnings and P-51 Mustangs to bomb marshaling yards and road and rail bridges in Yugoslavia.

In France, Twelfth Air Force P-51 Mustangs and P-40s attack rail lines near Lyon.

ITALY: The U.S. 442nd Regimental Combat Team is dispatched to southern France.

Fifteenth Air Force establishes the headquarters for the XV Fighter Command (Provisional) with operational control of the 306th Fighter Wing and the seven fighter groups. Three of the squadrons have P-38 Lightnings and four have P-51 Mustangs.

Twelfth Air Force B-25 Mitchells, A-20 Havocs, and P-47 Thunderbolts attack bridges in the Po River valley.

Southwest Pacific Area: FEAF sends more than 50 B-24 Liberators to bomb logistics storage areas, troop locations, shipyards, and airfields on Mindanao in the Philippines.

Pacific: U.S. submarine *Guardfish* torpedoes and sinks a Japanese cargo ship north of Chichi Jima.

U.S. submarine *Finback* is conducting a lifeguard mission in support of the air attack on Chichi Jima. The submarine is to rescue any downed pilots. One flyer is rescued—Lieutenant (j.g.) George H. W. Bush. Bush's two other crewmembers do not survive. Bush later becomes the 41st president of the United States.

Central Pacific: Seventh Air Force B-25 Mitchells from the Marshalls bomb Ponape Island and Nauru Island.

New Guinea: FEAF B-24 Liberators bomb Koror Island in the Palaus.

September 3

CBI: In Burma, Tenth Air Force B-25 Mitchell aircrews report damaging a bridge at Indaw.

In China, Fourteenth Air Force B-25 Mitchells attack supply convoys supporting the Japanese Eleventh Army. B-24 Liberators bomb the Nanking marshaling yards. B-25 Mitchell aircrews report destroying at least 45 trucks and damage nearly 100 others near Hengyang and Tungting Lake. Over 100 P-40s, P-51 Mustangs, and P-38 Lightnings attack troops, rail lines, and bridges near Hengyang and Changning.

ETO: First Army reports that German forces have been cleared out within its zone of advance. The 1st Infantry Division of VII Corps assists in blocking the retreat of nearly 20 German divisions of the German Seventh Army, now nothing more than disorganized remnants. Prisoners captured near Mons are estimated at 25,000.

Nearly 400 B-17s escorted by P-51 Mustangs make a bombing run on 16 gun batteries and defensive positions at Brest. Two B-17s are lost and 13 are damaged. Aircrew casualties are 16 missing. Another 345 B-17s with P-51 escort are sent against a synthetic oil production facility in northern Germany. One B-17 is lost and 103 are damaged. Fighter pilots report seven confirmed kills. One P-51 is lost and two are damaged. The pilot is reported as missing.

Over 100 P-47 Thunderbolts attack transportation targets in Belgium and Germany. One P-47 is lost and 19 are damaged. One pilot is reported wounded and one is reported missing.

During the night, a total of 40 B-24s and four C-47s fly in support of Carpetbagger operations.

Ninth Air Force A-20 Havocs and B-26 Marauders attack German gun positions and defenses at Brest. P-47 and P-38 fighters support ground forces and fly armed reconnaissance missions.

Mediterranean: The 177th Cavalry Reconnaissance Squadron blocks the road at Bourgen-Bresse, but the unit takes heavy losses as the Germans fight to hold the Belfort Gap to allow remaining elements to retreat to safety.

The French II Corps liberates Lyon. The VI Corps attacks German forces defending Belfort.

Fifteenth Air Force sends more than 300 B-17s and B-24 Liberators escorted by P-38 Lightnings and P-51 Mustangs to bomb lines of communication in Hungary and Yugoslavia and slow the retreat of German troops as they are pressed hard by advancing Soviet forces.

In southern France, Twelfth Air Force P-51 Mustangs and P-47 Thunderbolts attack convoys, bridges, and roads as the Germans abandon Lyon in front of the advancing Seventh Army.

ITALY: Operation Olive is stalled by heavy rains and flooding. The Eighth Army has suffered 8,000 casualties since August 25 and has failed to break through the Gothic Line.

Twelfth Air Force B-25 Mitchells and B-26 Marauders attack rail and road bridges in the Po River valley. A-20 Havocs and P-47 Thunderbolts attack rail cars and vehicles near Turin.

PACIFIC: Naval Task Group 12.5, commanded by Rear Admiral Allen E. Smith, with the small carrier USS *Monterey,* three heavy cruisers, and three destroyers, bombard Wake Island.

CENTRAL PACIFIC: Seventh Air Force B-24 Liberators from Saipan bomb Iwo Jima.

NEW GUINEA: At Cape Opmarai, the newly constructed airfield torn out of the jungle is operational.

Headquarters XIII Bomber Command redeploys from Los Negros Island in the Admiralties to Wakde Island.

September 4

CBI: The Japanese capture Lingling, eliminating another Fourteenth Air Force air base. General Chennault, seriously limited by a lack of fuel and ammunition, is hard-pressed to slow the enemy advance. Stilwell is reluctant to provide additional support, believing that only Chiang Kai-shek can save the situation by reorganizing his forces and committing to American direction. Chiang believes Stilwell is sacrificing China in favor of Burma and sends messages to President Roosevelt demanding that Stilwell be recalled.

Tenth Air Force sends 24 B-24 Liberators to fly 32,000 gallons of fuel to Kunming, China. In Burma, P-47 Thunderbolts attack Bhamo.

Fourteenth Air Force B-25 Mitchells, with P-51 Mustangs flying escort bomb Lingling. Aircrews report numerous enemy casualties.

ATLANTIC: Admiral Ernest J. King (COMINCH) requests a decision from other members of the JCS on whether Formosa or Luzon would be the next objective of the offensive. King argues for Formosa, viewing it as the most rapid approach to cut off the vital Japanese supply line from the East Indies and Indochina. Formosa also provides U.S. air forces access to the coast of China to establish airfields for the strategic bombing of the Japanese home islands.

ETO: The First Army's VII Corps attacks toward Namur and captures the city. V Corps crosses the Meuse River.

During the night Private First Class Gino J. Merli's company, in the 18th Infantry Regiment, 1st Infantry Division, is overrun by a superior German force near Sars la Bruyere, Belgium. Merli fights in his position until German troops kill or capture most of his comrades. Feigning death, Merli waits until the enemy withdraws, then holds his position throughout the night, fighting back and disrupting the enemy's assault. When the area is retaken the next day, American troops find Merli still at his position. Around him are the bodies of more than 50 enemy soldiers. For his courage and dedication in the face of overwhelming odds, Private First Class Gino J. Merli will receive the Medal of Honor.

MEDITERRANEAN: Twelfth Air Force's 85th Bombardment Squadron (Light), 47th Bombardment Group (Light), redeploys the squadron's A-20 Havocs from Corsica to southern France.

ITALY: Fifteenth Air Force sends nearly 400 B-17s and B-24 Liberators escorted by P-38 Lightnings and P-51 Mustangs to attack submarines in Genoa harbor and lines of communication in northern Italy. Twelfth Air Force B-25 Mitchells and B-26 Marauders attack rail and road bridges in the Po River valley. A-20 Havocs bomb vehicles near Turin and Milan.

PACIFIC: U.S. submarine *Bowfin* torpedoes and sinks a Japanese guardboat northeast of the Bonin Islands.

CENTRAL PACIFIC: Seventh Air Force B-24 Liberators from Kwajalein bomb Wotje Atoll.

September 5

CBI: Tenth Air Force sends eight B-25 Mitchells to bomb targets at Indaw, while 21 B-24 Liberators fly fuel to Kunming, China.

Fourteenth Air Force B-25 Mitchells bomb Hengyang airfield.

ETO: Ninth Army becomes operational under the command of Lieutenant General William H. Simpson. The army is composed of the 6th Armored Division and the 2nd, 8th, 29th, and 83rd Infantry Divisions. Simpson takes operational control of VIII Corps and is given the mission to reduce German strongholds on the peninsula while protecting the flank of the Third Army. The VII Corps of First Army crosses the Meuse River and meets limited but organized resistance for the first time in weeks. The Third Army's XII Corps crosses the Moselle River north of Nancy. The XX Corps crosses the river north and south of Metz.

Eighth Air Force sends more than 500 B-17s escorted by over 300 P-51 Mustangs to attack the aircraft engine production facility at Stuttgart and the synthetic oil plant at Ludwigshafen. Over 200 B-24 Liberators bomb the Karlsruhe marshaling yard. Six bombers are lost and 354 are damaged. Aircrew casualties are three killed, 16 wounded, and 58 missing. Fighter pilots report 19 confirmed kills in the air and 14 confirmed kills on the ground. Three P-51s are lost and seven are damaged. Three pilots are reported missing.

More than 140 B-17s escorted by P-51s make a visual bombing run on gun positions and fortifications at Brest. Two B-17s are lost and one is damaged. Aircrew losses are 18 missing.

Over 200 P-38 Lightnings and P-47 Thunderbolts attack transportation targets in western Germany. Fighter pilots report 62 confirmed kills on the ground. Four P-47s are lost and 12 are damaged. The pilots are reported missing. Other P-38s and P-47s attack airfields near Hanau and Giessen in Germany. Pilots report two confirmed kills in the air and 66 on the ground. Four fighters are lost and five are damaged. Four pilots are reported missing.

A total of 46 B-24s and two C-47s fly in support of Carpetbagger operations. One bomber is lost. During the night seven B-17s drop leaflets over Belgium, the Netherlands, and Germany.

Ninth Air Force sends 300 A-20 Havocs and B-26 Marauders to attack German defensive positions near Brest and a coastal battery. P-47 fighters also attack gun positions at Brest and P-38s attack ground targets in support of ground forces.

MEDITERRANEAN: Fifteenth Air Force sends more than 400 B-17s and B-24 Liberators escorted by P-38 Lightnings and P-51 Mustangs to attack transportation targets and lines of communication in Hungary and northern Italy. Twelfth Air Force P-47 Thunderbolts fly ground support missions for the Seventh Army in the Rhône River valley.

Off the invasion beaches of southern France, a French and a U.S. destroyer locate and eliminate three German manned torpedoes and capture the crews.

ITALY: The U.S. IV Corps occupies Monte Pisano and the city of Lucca. The Germans defend Pistoia, which blocks Route 64, the road north to Bologna.

Twelfth Air Force B-25 Mitchells and B-26 Marauders attack rail and road traffic in the Po River valley. A-20 Havocs attack ammunition storage sites. P-47 Thunderbolts attack German defensive positions along the Gothic Line.

A-20 Havocs of the 84th and 86th Bombardment Squadrons (Light), 47th Bombardment Group (Light), redeploy from Corsica to France.

PACIFIC: U.S. submarine *Albacore* sinks Japanese cargo ship south of Kyushu, Japan.

CENTRAL PACIFIC: Seventh Air Force B-24 Liberators from Saipan bomb Iwo Jima. B-25 Mitchells from the Gilberts bomb Nauru and Ponape Islands.

NEW GUINEA: FEAF B-24 Liberators bomb the airfield on Peleliu Island and airfields on Celebes Island. A-20 Havocs attack Halmahera Island in the Moluccas.

B-25 Mitchells of the 405th Bombardment Squadron (Medium), 38th Bombardment Group (Medium), redeploy from Nadzab to Biak Island. The Fifth Air Force's 547th Night Fighter Squadron with P-38 Lightnings and P-61 Black Widow night fighters arrives at Oro Bay from the United States.

September 6

CBI: Tenth Air Force sends 24 B-24 Liberators to fly about 34,000 gallons of fuel to Kunming, China. Fourteenth Air Force sends 20 B-25 Mitchells to bomb transportation targets near Lingling and Hengyang airfield. P-40s and P-51 Mustangs attack marshaling yards, troop areas, trucks, river transports, and ammunition storage sites.

ETO: The 5th Armored Division of V Corps captures Sedan and advances into the Ardennes Forest. Eighth Air Force sends more than 200 P-38 Lightnings and P-47 Thunderbolts to attack rail and road movement near Rotterdam in the Netherlands and in the Aachen and Koblenz areas in Germany. One P-38 and three P-47s are shot down and 12 fighters are damaged. The four pilots are reported missing. The logistics pinch for ground forces in France becomes serious enough that 70 B-24 Liberators begin flying supplies to forward airfields in France.

Ninth Air Force B-26 Marauders and A-20 Havocs attack gun positions and fortifications at Brest, and a coastal battery. P-47 Thunderbolts also attack the defenses at Brest and attack an ammunition storage site, and P-38 fighters fly cover for ground units.

MEDITERRANEAN: Fifteenth Air Force sends more than 500 B-17s and B-24 Liberators escorted by P-38 Lightnings and P-51 Mustangs to attack marshaling yards in Romania, Yugoslavia, and Hungary.

ITALY: During the night Twelfth Air Force A-20 Havocs attack targets of opportunity near Milan.

SOUTHWEST PACIFIC AREA: FEAF B-24 Liberators and B-25 Mitchells bomb airfields and port facilities in the Philippines.

PACIFIC: The headquarters of Twentieth Air Force's 498th Bombardment Group (Very Heavy) arrives at Saipan from the United States.

CENTRAL PACIFIC: Seventh Air Force B-24 Liberators from Saipan bomb Iwo Jima. B-24s from the Marshalls bomb Truk.

Vice Admiral Marc A. Mitscher's Task Force 58 (with three task groups: TG 38.1, TG 38.2, TG 38.3) begins operations against the western Carolines. The small carrier USS *Independence* has an air group aboard that is specially trained for night operations.

Two U.S. destroyers bombard gun positions on Aguijan Island in the Marianas.

U.S. submarine *Albacore* torpedoes and sinks a Japanese auxiliary minesweeper off Shikoku, Japan. U.S. submarine *Hake* torpedoes and damages a Japanese destroyer east of the Ryukyus.

NEW GUINEA: FEAF B-25 Mitchells bomb targets on Halmahera and Morotai Islands. A-20 Havocs also attack targets on Halmahera Island. A-20s, B-25 Mitchells, and P-40s attack airfields, barges, and logistics sites.

P-47 Thunderbolts of the 69th, 310th, and 311th Fighter Squadrons, 58th Fighter Group, redeploy from Saidor to Noemfoor Island. The B-25s of the 71st Bombardment Squadron (Medium), 38th Bombardment Group (Medium), redeploy from Nadzab to Biak Island.

September 7

ALEUTIANS: Eleventh Air Force B-25 Mitchells attack a small fishing fleet between Paramushiru and Onnekotan (Onekutan) Islands in the Kuriles.

CBI: Tenth Air Force sends 22 B-24 Liberators to fly fuel to Kunming, China.

Fourteenth Air Force sends 24 B-25 Mitchells to bomb targets at Kiyang, Lingling, and Yoyang. Other B-25s bomb Tien Ho and White Cloud airfields at Canton. P-40s and P-51 Mustangs attack troops, rail lines and rail cars, river shipping, logistics storage facilities, and bridges.

In French Indochina, four P-38 Lightnings attack targets of opportunity near Hanoi.

ATLANTIC: The JCS planners support Admiral King's reasoning that Formosa should be the objective for the next offensive in the Pacific. March 1, 1945, is set as the target date for Operation Causeway.

ETO: Ninth Air Force P-47 Thunderbolts and P-38s provide air cover and ground support for the 8th and 29th Infantry Divisions.

MEDITERRANEAN: The 3rd Infantry Division captures Besançon and the 45th Infantry Division presses retreating German forces.

Twelfth Air Force redeploys the headquarters of the 47th Bombardment Group (Light) and the A-20 Havocs of the 97th Bombardment Squadron (Light) from Corsica to France.

Technician Fifth Grade Robert D. Maxwell and three other men of the 7th Infantry Regiment, 3rd Infantry Division, are surprised by a platoon-size German raiding force approaching the battalion command post near Besançon, France. Carrying only .45-caliber automatic pistols, the four soldiers defend the battalion observation post against overwhelming fire. When a German hand grenade lands in the midst of the group, Maxwell throws himself on it. For his courage in defending the battalion command post and his selfless act of sacrifice to save the lives of others, Technician Fifth Grade Maxwell will receive the Medal of Honor.

ITALY: General Mark Clark notes in his diary, "The fate of the Fifth Army is tied up with that of the Eighth Army." Clark prepares the U.S. II Corps to attack north up Route 65 and drive German forces from the Futa Pass and the Il Giogo Pass and break the Gothic Line.

SOUTHWEST PACIFIC AREA: U.S. submarine *Paddle* torpedoes and sinks a Japanese transport, which is carrying 750 American prisoners of war. *Paddle* also damages a tanker off the coast of Mindanao.

PACIFIC: Twentieth Air Force begins deploying elements of the 873rd, 874th, and 875th Bombardment Squadrons (Very Heavy) of the 498th Bombardment Group (Very Heavy) to Saipan from the United States. The squadrons' first missions are scheduled for late October.

Carrier aircraft from Admiral William F. Halsey's Third Fleet begin widespread attacks on Yap and the Palau Islands, as well as Mindanao in the Philippines. Aircraft and shipping are the primary targets. The intent is to limit Japanese reinforcement of the Philippines and reduce the air threat to a U.S. invasion force headed for the Philippines.

CENTRAL PACIFIC: Seventh Air Force B-24 Liberators using radar-guided bombing techniques attack Iwo Jima.

Carrier aircraft from Naval Task Groups 38.1, 38.2, and 38.3 attack Japanese positions throughout the Palau Islands. Three light cruisers, screened by four destroyers, under command of Rear Admiral F. E. M. Whiting, bombard Peleliu, Angaur, and Ngesebus. A heavy cruiser, a light cruiser, and four destroyers bombard Yap. Aircraft from Naval Task Group TG 38.4 (Rear Admiral Ralph E. Davison) attack targets on Yap and Ulithi.

NEW GUINEA: FEAF A-20 Havocs, P-47 Thunderbolts, P-38 Lightnings, and P-40s attack airfields at Wewak and Manokwari.

B-24 Liberators bomb Celebes Island and B-25 Mitchells and P-38 Lightnings attack Halmahera Island. A-20 Havocs bomb Boela airfield on Ceram Island.

September 8

CBI: Tenth Air Force sends 23 B-24 Liberators to fly fuel to Kunming, China.

The Japanese Eleventh Army occupies Lingling airfield after the Fourteenth Air Force abandons it.

Fourteenth Air Force sends three B-24 Liberators to attack shipping near Hong Kong. Aircrews report sinking a Japanese destroyer. In China, B-25 Mitchells attack bridges near Kiyang and attack troop concentrations, rail lines, and roads near Hengyang and Lingling. Over 100 P-40s and P-51 Mustangs escort the bombers and fly sweeps over the area.

In French Indochina 18 B-24 Liberators bomb bridges at Hue, Duc Tho, and Quang Tri. Aircrews report destroying the main bridge at Quang Tri.

During the night Japanese bombers attack the headquarters, logistics base, and parked B-29s at Hsinching airfield near Chengtu. One bomber and a C-46 are damaged; two soldiers are wounded.

ETO: VII Corps captures Liège. The Ninth Army conducts a three-division attack on Brest, supported by artillery and air bombardment. The first attack fails.

Eighth Air Force sends more than 700 B-17s to bomb the Ludwigshafen oil refinery and an oil storage depot at Kassel in Germany. Over 300 B-24 Liberators bomb the marshaling yard at Karlsruhe, Germany. The B-17s are escorted by over 200 P-51 Mustangs; the B-24s escorted by nearly 100 P-51s. A total of 10 bombers are lost and 412 are damaged. Aircrew casualties are 18 killed, 27 wounded, and 83 missing. Fighter pilots report only one P-51 damaged.

More than 100 P-38 Lightnings cross the Rhine River to strafe and bomb rail lines in Germany. Fighter pilots report seven confirmed kills on the ground. Nearly 200 P-47 Thunderbolts and P-51s strafe targets along the Rhine River valley. One P-47 and one P-51 are lost and 13 fighters are damaged. One pilot is wounded and two are reported missing.

One C-47 supports Carpetbagger operations in France.

A total of 110 B-24s fly supplies to forward airfields to support the ground forces.

During the night seven B-17s drop leaflets over the Netherlands, Germany, and France.

Ninth Air Force P-47 and P-38 fighters support the 2nd, 5th, 8th, and 29th Infantry Divisions in the XX Corps area.

The headquarters and troop carrier squadrons of the 439th and the 441st Troop Carrier Groups redeploy C-47s from England to France.

Private First Class Ernest W. Prussman is a squad leader in the 13th Infantry Regiment, 8th Infantry Division. As elements of his battalion come under heavy mortar and machine-gun fire from the hedgerows near the town of Les Coates in Brittany, PFC Prussman leads his men to attack the German position. As he vaults a hedgerow, Prussman encounters and disarms two German soldiers. Approaching the next hedgerow, Prussman's squad destroys a machine-gun position and captures

A V-2 being readied for launch *(German Museum, Munich)*

two enemy soldiers. As Prussman leads his men toward a third position, he is shot and mortally wounded, but not before he flings a grenade at his enemy, killing him. Prussman's initiative, leadership, and courage under fire will win him the Medal of Honor.

The first V-2 rocket is fired from a location in the Netherlands toward England. It lands in southwest London, killing or injuring 20 civilians. The rocket is over 46 feet long, carries a 2,150-pound warhead, and is powered by alcohol and liquid oxygen. Able to travel at speeds reaching 3,600 miles per hour, it has a maximum range of 200 miles. Mobile and easily hidden, the V-2 will prove to be a powerful but largely ineffective weapon. Between September 8 and March 27, 1945, an average of about five V-2s will be launched at London every day, causing about 2,700 casualties. In all, 3,000 V-2s will be launched—1,250 at England and 1,750 at Antwerp.

MEDITERRANEAN: Fifteenth Air Force sends 354 B-17s and B-24 Liberators escorted by P-38 Lightnings to bomb railroad bridges and marshaling yards in Yugoslavia. P-51 Mustangs attack the airfield at Ecka in Yugoslavia. Pilots report 58 enemy aircraft destroyed on the ground. One P-51 and one pilot are lost. Over Landza airfield in Yugoslavia, P-51s destroy 18 German aircraft on the ground.

Twelfth Air Force P-47 Thunderbolts attack a convoy near Strasbourg.

ITALY: Twelfth Air Force P-47 Thunderbolts attack vehicles, bridges, and German positions in the Po River valley.

SOUTHWEST PACIFIC AREA: U.S. submarine *Bashaw* torpedoes and sinks a Japanese transport off Mindanao.

U.S. submarine *Spadefish* torpedoes and sinks a Japanese transport and three cargo ships off northeast Taiwan.

PACIFIC: The JCS lays out a strategic direction for operations in the Pacific. The invasion of Leyte in the Philippines will begin by December 20, be carried out by MacArthur's SWPA forces, and be supported by Admiral Nimitz's naval forces. Nimitz's POA planners will prepare options for an attack on either Luzon beginning February 20 or Formosa on March 1. MacArthur's forces are to concentrate on reducing the Japanese air threat over Luzon to support both offensive options being prepared. This air offensive will be coordinated with Twentieth Air Force and with the air commander in CBI.

Accompanied by the commander of the XX Bomber Command, Major General Curtis E. LeMay, Twentieth Air Force sends 90 B-29 Superfortresses from the base at Chengtu, China, to bomb the Showa Steel Works at Anshan. All but 11 bombers hit the primary target. The initial targets of Twentieth Air Force, as determined by the Joint Chiefs of Staff in Washington, are targets supporting Japanese steel production.

U.S. submarine *Seal* damages Japanese destroyer *Namikaze* off Hokkaido, Japan.

CENTRAL PACIFIC: Seventh Air Force B-24 Liberators from Saipan bomb Iwo Jima. B-25 Mitchells from the Gilberts bomb Ponape Island. B-24s from Kwajalein bomb Wotje Atoll.

Seventh Air Force B-24 Liberators bomb shipping off Chichi Jima, damaging two cargo vessels.

NEW GUINEA: FEAF P-39 Airacobras strafe targets along the coast near Wewak. P-47 Thunderbolts, P-38 Lightnings, and P-40s attack targets of opportunity.

B-24 Liberators bomb Langoan airfield, Celebes Island. B-25 Mitchells bomb Halmahera Island.

The A-20 Havocs of the 673rd and 674th Bombardment Squadrons (Light), 417th Bombardment Group (Light), redeploy from Saidor to Noemfoor Island.

September 9

ALEUTIANS: Eleventh Air Force sends three B-24 Liberators on a nighttime raid on Kashiwabara, on Paramushiru Island in the Kuriles.

CBI: Tenth Air Force sends 17 B-24 Liberators to fly fuel to Kunming, China. B-25 Mitchells bomb a Japanese headquarters at Manwing.

In China, Fourteenth Air Force sends 24 B-25 Mitchells to bomb river transport and troop assembly areas around Kiyang, Lingling, and Lingkwantien. Aircrews report that the bridge at Lingling is heavily damaged. B-24s bomb cargo ships in the South China Sea. Aircrews report four ships sunk or heavily damaged.

The 322nd Troop Carrier Squadron is activated at Kunming, China. The squadron, under operational control of Fourteenth Air Force, is equipped with C-47s.

ETO: The XIX Corps enters Holland.

General Eisenhower informs the CCS that he intends to maintain his original strategic approach for the offensive against Germany, making two simultaneous thrusts into the Ruhr. At this time, however, due to limits on the availability of logistic support for both axes of attack, he will give priority of logistics support to Allied forces under General Montgomery in the north.

Eighth Air Force sends more than 800 B-17s escorted by nearly 300 P-51 Mustangs to attack the marshaling yard at Mannheim and an armaments production facility at Düsseldorf. Another 337 B-24 Liberators escorted by 128 P-51s bomb the marshaling yard at Mainz. Eleven B-17s and three B-24s are lost, and a total of over 450 bombers are damaged. Aircrew casualties are seven killed, 13 wounded, and 150 missing. One P-51 is lost.

B-17s with P-51 escort fly Operation Grassy, dropping supplies to members of the French Resistance.

A total of 40 B-24s and C-47s fly in support of Carpetbagger operations. During the night seven B-17s drop leaflets over Belgium, France, and Germany.

P-47 fighters attack targets in northeastern Germany. Pilots report one confirmed kill and one probable in the air and one confirmed kill and one probable on the ground. Nearly 200 P-47s and P-51s bomb and strafe shipping along the coast between Germany and the Netherlands and attack rail and road traffic near Frankfurt am Main. Fighter pilots report 13 confirmed kills. Eight fighters are lost and 16 damaged. One pilot is wounded, and seven others are reported missing.

Ninth Air Force sends P-47s and P-38s to support VIII Corps near Brest and the 2nd, 5th, and 8th Infantry Divisions of XX Corps, Third Army, near Metz.

MEDITERRANEAN: The 83rd Infantry Division captures about 20,000 German soldiers who surrender in southwest France.

ITALY: Twelfth Air Force B-26 Marauders attack rail bridges in the Po River valley. B-25 Mitchells bomb troop assembly areas and logistics sites. A-20 Havocs and P-47 Thunderbolts attack rail lines, convoys, and rail cars.

SOUTHWEST PACIFIC AREA: Naval Task Force 38 begins strikes against Japanese targets on Mindanao. Carrier aircraft sink a transport in the Sulu Sea west of Mindanao and two transports and a cargo ship east of Mindanao. Two light cruisers and four destroyers under Rear Admiral Laurance T. DuBose, supported by aircraft from the small carrier USS *Langley,* attack a coastal convoy on the west coast of Mindanao.

U.S. submarine *Queenfish* torpedoes and sinks a transport and passenger-cargo ship and damages a torpedo boat northwest of Luzon.

PACIFIC: U.S. submarine *Bang* torpedoes and sinks a Japanese transport and cargo ship north of the Bonin Islands.

U.S. submarine *Seal* torpedoes and sinks a Japanese cargo ship in the Sea of Okhotsk.

CENTRAL PACIFIC: During the night, Seventh Air Force B-25 Mitchells from the Gilbert Islands bomb Nauru Island. One B-24 from Saipan on a snooper mission (non-visual radar-guided bombing) attacks Iwo Jima.

NEW GUINEA: FEAF P-38 Lightnings and A-20 Havocs attack airfields in the Molucca Islands. B-24 Liberators bomb an airfield on Celebes Island and on Halmahera Island.

The headquarters of the 417th Bombardment Group (Light) moves from Saidor to Noemfoor Island.

September 10

CBI: Tenth Air Force sends 23 B-24 Liberators to fly fuel to Kunming, China.

In China, Fourteenth Air Force sends 45 B-25 Mitchells to bomb the towns of Kutkai, Tunganhsien, Lingling, and Tunghsiangchiao. Aircrews report hitting a fuel storage area near Lingling. More than 100 P-40s and P-51 Mustangs attack bridges, railroads, logistics storage facilities, rail and road traffic, airfields, and river transport.

ATLANTIC: W. Averell Harriman, ambassador to the Soviet Union, reports on changing attitudes of the Soviet leadership in recent weeks. Harriman believes that the American emphasis on cooperation and friendship may be misunderstood as weakness by the Soviet leadership. "Unless we take issue with the present policy there is every indication the Soviet Union will become a world bully wherever their interests are involved."

ETO: The XV Corps (French 2nd Armored Division and the U.S. 79th Infantry Division) moves to guard the Third Army's right flank as it advances westward. The 5th Armored Division of V Corps liberates Luxembourg City. The VII Corps artillery begins bombarding German territory. As Allied Expeditionary Force commander, General Eisenhower sees the capture of the port of Antwerp in the Netherlands as essential. As the largest port in Europe, it can support the logistics requirements of the Allied armies. Eisenhower also wants to clear the coastline of V-weapon sites and seize airfields. He also wants to destroy the bulk of the remaining, organized German forces west of the Rhine River. Montgomery argues for "one powerful full-blooded thrust across the Rhine and into the heart of Germany, backed by the whole of the resources of the Allied Armies." This offensive will be the decisive blow that ends the war for the European theater. Montgomery is unhappy with Eisenhower's broad-front strategy, believing that it spreads Allied power too thinly, not allowing for a concentration of forces sufficient to overwhelm German defenses. He stresses his plan for an attack in the 21st Army Group area that will cross the Rhine River quickly and break into the open terrain beyond and capture the undefended Ruhr from the rear. Therefore, Field Marshal Montgomery's 21st Army Group is directed to be the main effort and will conduct its offensive operation in Holland. This means that the majority of logistics support will be directed to Montgomery, leaving Bradley's 12th Army Group with minimal support.

Field Marshal Montgomery lays out a proposal to open a corridor 65 miles deep into Holland using airborne forces and the British Second Army. The airborne units will seize the bridges at Eindhoven, Grave, Nijmegen, and Arnhem. The XXX Corps will then send armored spearheads into Germany.

Eighth Air Force sends more than 750 B-17s escorted by over 350 P-47 Thunderbolts and P-51 Mustangs to attack a tank factory at Nürnberg, an aircraft components facility at Furth, a motor vehicle facility at Gaggenau, and a jet-propulsion component production facility and an engine factory. Another 388 B-24 Liberators escorted by 153 P-38 Lightnings and P-51s attack the marshaling yards at Ulm and Heilbronn. A total of seven bombers are lost and 387 are damaged. Aircrew casualties are one killed, 18 wounded, and 65 missing. Fighter pilots report two confirmed kills in the air and one probable, and 67 confirmed kills on the ground. Five fighters are lost and nine are damaged. One pilot is wounded, and five pilots are reported missing.

P-47 Thunderbolts strafe airfields and ground and rail traffic in a sweep over Cologne, Frankfurt am Main, and Kassel. Pilots report 10 confirmed kills on the ground. Eight P-47s are lost and five are damaged. The eight pilots are reported missing.

A total of 35 B-24s and C-47s fly in support of Carpetbagger operations.

During the night six B-17s drop leaflets over France, the Netherlands, and Germany.

Ninth Air Force sends more than 300 A-20 Havocs and B-26 Marauders to attack German defensive positions and ammunition storage areas, and a railroad bridge over the Moselle River. P-47 and P-38 fighters support ground forces of Third Army in the Metz-Nancy area.

The headquarters of Naval Forces France is established in Paris, commanded by Vice Admiral Alan G. Kirk.

MEDITERRANEAN: The French II Corps liberates Dijon. The VI Corps captures Besançon.

Fifteenth Air Force sends more than 300 B-17s and B-24 Liberators escorted by P-38 Lightnings and P-51 Mustangs to attack depots, oil refineries, and industrial targets near Vienna. In Italy, another 88 B-24s escorted by P-38 Lightnings and P-51 Mustangs bomb the port of Trieste. In France, 45 B-24s escorted by P-51s fly supplies to the Seventh Army at Lyon.

Twelfth Air Force A-20 Havocs attack communication support targets and P-47 Thunderbolts attack rail lines.

ITALY: The Fifth Army launches attacks directed at Il Giogo Pass in support of Operation Olive. Ultra intercepts have indicated that German forces have been diverted from the Fifth Army front to stop Eighth Army's offensive.

The 34th and 91st Infantry Divisions of the U.S. II Corps advance up Route 65. The 91st Division, commanded by Major General William C. Livesay, will attack Il Giogo Pass. The 34th Division will conduct a holding attack on the Futa Pass. The 85th Infantry Division will follow in support. The U.S. IV Corps will follow withdrawing German forces on the coast and capture Pistoia.

Twelfth Air Force B-25 Mitchells and B-26 Marauders attack rail bridges in the Po River valley and ammunition storage sites. A-20 Havocs and P-47 Thunderbolts attack German defensive positions along the Gothic Line.

SOUTHWEST PACIFIC AREA: Carrier aircraft from Naval Task Force 38 attack shipping and airfields on Mindanao. Pilots report a cargo ship sunk off Mindanao.

PACIFIC: U.S. submarine *Sunfish* torpedoes and sinks a Japanese merchant tanker west of Kyushu, Japan.

CENTRAL PACIFIC: Seventh Air Force B-24 Liberators from Saipan bomb Iwo Jima and shipping off the island. B-24 Liberators from Eniwetok bomb Truk.

New Guinea: FEAF A-20 Havocs, P-47 Thunderbolts, P-38 Lightnings, and P-40s attack airfields in western New Guinea. A-20 Havocs, B-25 Mitchells, and P-38 Lightnings attack targets on Buru Island and Ceram Island. B-24 Liberators bomb airfields on Celebes Island and on Halmahera Island.

September 11

Aleutians: Eleventh Air Force sends four B-25 Mitchells on a shipping search. Aircrews report sinking a small craft off Shimushu Island in the Kuriles.

CBI: Tenth Air Force sends 23 B-24 Liberators to fly fuel to Kunming, China.

P-47 Thunderbolts attack roads and Japanese troops and vehicles near Bhamo. In China, P-47s also attack assembly areas and road traffic near Tengchung and Lungling.

Fourteenth Air Force sends B-24 Liberators to bomb logistics storage sites near Manling. B-25 Mitchells bomb Tunganhsien and Lingling. P-40s attack trucks traveling the Burma Road. P-40s and P-51 Mustangs attack river shipping, rail lines, troop assembly areas, and logistics sites near Canton and the area around Tungting Lake.

ETO: The French 1st Armored Division links with the French 2nd Armored Division near Sombernon. The V Corps represents the first American forces to cross into German territory and approach the West Wall or Siegfried Line, as the Allies call it, a series of fortifications and obstacles emplaced between the border of France and Germany. Construction began in 1936 but was halted early in the war. Although obsolete, the concrete defensive positions are located on terrain that enhances their effectiveness, and are sufficiently strong to both delay Allied forces and provide a rallying point for retreating German forces to reorganize into a coherent defense.

The XIX Corps crosses the Meuse River. First Army reports that only 850 tanks of its authorized strength of 1,010 are combat capable. The 3rd Armored Division has only 75 tanks combat capable, of its authorized strength of 232 tanks.

After weeks of delay, Stalin finally gives permission for the Western Allies to begin airdropping supplies to Polish fighters under siege by German forces in Warsaw.

Eighth Air Force sends 735 B-17s escorted by over 500 P-51 Mustangs and P-47 Thunderbolts to attack synthetic oil plants and refineries in Germany. Another 396 B-24 Liberators escorted by 164 P-38 Lightnings and P-51s attack oil refineries, an engine production facility, and logistics storage areas. The German Luftwaffe counters with over 500 aircraft attacking the formations. A total of 39 bombers are lost and 386 damaged. Aircrews report 17 confirmed kills and 25 probables. Aircrew casualties are five killed, 38 wounded, and 375 missing. Fighter pilots report 115 confirmed kills and seven probables in the air and 42 confirmed kills on the ground. Seventeen fighters are lost, and 26 are damaged. A total of 21 pilots are reported missing.

As part of this attack, 75 B-17s and 64 P-51s are flying a mission in support of Operation Frantic. The bombers hit their primary target at Chemnitz and proceed to airfields in Soviet Ukraine.

A total of 38 B-24s fly in support of Carpetbagger operations. During the night six B-17s drop leaflets over France and Germany.

Ninth Air Force sends over 350 A-20 Havocs and B-26 Marauders to attack German defensive positions in the Metz area in support of Third Army. P-47 and P-38 fighters support ground forces near Brest.

The headquarters of the 440th Troop Carrier Group redeploys from England to France.

MEDITERRANEAN: Fifteenth Air Force sends 54 B-24 Liberators to fly supplies to Seventh Army in France.

ITALY: Twelfth Air Force B-26 Marauders attack German positions at the Il Giogo Pass and at the Futa Pass. B-25 Mitchells attack logistics sites and bridges. A-20 Havocs and P-47 Thunderbolts attack gun positions, convoys, logistics sites, bridges, and roads.

The P-47s of the 65th and 66th Fighter Squadrons, 57th Fighter Group, redeploy from Corsica to Ombrone, Italy.

PACIFIC: Admiral Nimitz advises Lieutenant General Holland M. Smith, commanding general of Fleet Marine Force Pacific, to retain the 2nd and 3rd Marine Divisions in the Marianas as a reserve for future landings against the island of Formosa and as the main units for the attack on Iwo Jima.

U.S. submarine *Albacore* torpedoes and sinks a Japanese auxiliary submarine chaser off Kyushu, Japan. U.S. submarine *Finback* torpedoes and sinks two Japanese cargo ships north of Chichi Jima.

CENTRAL PACIFIC: Seventh Air Force B-24 Liberators from Saipan bomb Iwo Jima and attack shipping targets off Chichi Jima Island.

A U.S. destroyer bombards logistics storage areas on Aguijan Island, Marianas.

Seventh Air Force B-24 Liberators bomb Iwo Jima. Aircrews report damaging a Japanese cargo vessel.

NEW GUINEA: FEAF A-20 Havocs, P-47 Thunderbolts, P-38 Lightnings, and P-40s attack airfields in western New Guinea. P-38 Lightnings attack airfields on Buru Island and oil storage facilities on Ceram Island. B-25 Mitchells bomb airfields on Celebes Island and B-24 Liberators, A-20 Havocs, and B-25s bomb airfields on Halmahera Island.

U.S. submarine *Pargo* torpedoes and sinks a Japanese auxiliary netlayer in the Java Sea southwest of Celebes Island.

September 12

CARIBBEAN: German submarine *U-518* torpedoes and damages a U.S. freighter off Key West, Florida.

CBI: Tenth Air Force sends 25 B-24 Liberators to fly fuel to Kunming, China. P-47 Thunderbolts attack command and control targets at Bhamo, while other P-47s attack Japanese vehicles and logistics sites on the Burma Road.

In China, Fourteenth Air Force sends 10 B-25 Mitchells and six P-40s to attack Japanese positions at Lungling. P-51 Mustangs and P-40s attack targets near Lingling and Hengyang.

The 74th Fighter Squadron of the 23rd Fighter Group redeploys P-40s and P-51s from Kweilin and Liuchow to Luliang.

U.S. submarine *Growler* torpedoes and sinks a Japanese destroyer in the South China Sea and an escort vessel south of Hong Kong. U.S. submarine *Pampanito* torpedoes and sinks a passenger-cargo ship and a tanker off Hainan Island.

ATLANTIC: Octagon Conference Begins. President Roosevelt, Prime Minister Churchill, and their military chiefs of staff convene in the last of their mid-war conferences. They agree on British and American occupation zones in Germany. Roosevelt and Churchill initial the Morgenthau Plan for postwar German de-industrialization. Decisions on the Pacific war include ordering Admiral Mountbatten to drive the Japanese from Burma as soon as possible, starting no later than March 15, 1945, and including an amphibious invasion (Operation Dracula) and a drive to reopen the Burma Road to China. The American invasion of Leyte is approved, as are plans for the British fleet and the RAF to support the final campaigns against Japan, which include an invasion of the Japanese mainland on Kyushu (Operation Olympic) to establish a base of operations for the final attack on Honshu and Tokyo (Operation Coronet). Operational control of Seventh Army will pass from General Wilson to General Eisenhower on September 15. The direction of strategic bombing in Europe will return to control of the CCS from General Eisenhower, who directed it in support of Overlord. The CCS approves Eisenhower's strategic approach for the defeat of Germany, focusing on the Ruhr, with the main effort coming from the north.

ETO: First Army's VII Corps, commanded by Major General J. Lawton Collins, advances toward Aachen with the 1st Infantry Division and elements of the 3rd Armored Division. The infantry will flank Aachen while the tanks advance toward the Roer River. The 9th Infantry Division is given the task of sweeping the Hürtgen Forest. Collins's units are quickly stopped before the obstacles and pillboxes of the Siegfried Line.

Eighth Air Force sends 647 B-17s, escorted by 474 P-51 Mustangs and P-47 Thunderbolts, to attack oil refineries in Germany. Nearly 300 B-17s use radar-equipped pathfinders to bomb the primary targets. Another 241 B-24 Liberators also use pathfinders and are escorted by 105 P-38 Lightnings, P-47s, and P-51s to attack industrial targets and transportation targets. The German Luftwaffe sends nearly 450 fighters against the formations. A total of 35 bombers are lost and 309 are damaged. Aircrews report 27 confirmed kills and 14 probables. Aircrew casualties are 10 killed, 21 wounded, and 317 missing. Fighter pilots report 54 confirmed kills and seven probables in the air and 21 confirmed kills on the ground. Twelve fighters are lost and two damaged. Twelve pilots are reported missing.

A total of 36 B-24s and C-47s fly in support of Carpetbagger operations. During the night seven B-17s drop leaflets over the Netherlands, France, and Germany.

Ninth Air Force sends A-20 Havocs and B-26 Marauders to attack German defensive positions on the Siegfried Line and at Nancy in support of Third Army.

Second Lieutenant Raymond Zussman commands two tanks in the 756th Tank Battalion, attached to an infantry company near Noroy le Bourg, France. Approaching the town on foot in advance of the tanks and infantry, Second Lieutenant Zussman captures several German soldiers and locates a number of defensive positions. As the defenders begin engaging his first tank, Zussman calmly directs fire on the targets. Walking alongside the tank, he enters the town and directs the tank fire on several houses, forcing 20 soldiers to surrender. Going forward alone, he is fired on by German troops in another house. Ignoring the fire, he directs the tank to fire on the position, forcing the surrender of another 15 soldiers. Minutes later, he walks on alone and returns with another 30 prisoners. For his conspicuous acts of bravery and calm courage under fire, Second Lieutenant Zussman will win the Medal of Honor.

MEDITERRANEAN: Elements of Major General LeClerc's 2nd Armored Division, from Third Army, meet the French II Corps of the Seventh Army at Dijon near Châtillon-sur-Seine.

Fifteenth Air Force sends more than 300 B-17s and B-24 Liberators escorted by P-38 Lightnings and P-51 Mustangs to attack airfields, engine assembly plants, and a jet aircraft production facility near Munich, Germany.

Over 50 B-24s fly supplies to Seventh Army in southern France.

ITALY: The 91st and 85th Infantry Divisions of II Corps attack Il Giogo Pass, Monticelli Ridge, and Monte Altuzzo. The British Eighth Army resumes the Operation Olive offensive.

The 363rd Infantry Regiment of the 91st Infantry Division is stopped before Il Giogo Pass by difficult terrain and heavy enemy fire on Montecelli Ridge. Montecelli Ridge is one of the best-prepared defensive positions on the exceptionally well prepared Gothic Line. The ridge holds a series of nearly invisible concrete positions, protected by barbed wire barriers 25 feet deep and wide minefields laid along all of the lower approaches to the ridge.

Twelfth Air Force B-25 Mitchells attack rail bridges in the Po River valley. B-26 Marauders bomb German defensive positions. A-20 Havocs and P-47 Thunderbolts attack convoys, troops, bridges, antiaircraft positions, and roads.

The headquarters of the 57th Fighter Group and the P-47s of the 64th Fighter Squadron redeploy from Corsica to Ombrone airfield in Italy.

Brigadier General Benjamin W. Chidlaw takes command of XII Fighter Command.

SOUTHWEST PACIFIC AREA: Naval Task Force 38 attacks airfields on Cebu Island, Philippines. Carrier aircraft attack Japanese shipping throughout the area around Cebu, sinking a gunboat, a motor torpedo boat, three auxiliary submarine chasers, an auxiliary netlayer, two auxiliary minesweepers, two guardboats, two transports, six cargo ships, a merchant tanker, and three transports. One minesweeper is damaged.

Admiral William F. Halsey, commander of the Third Fleet, receives reports from Filipinos that Leyte has only a small force of Japanese infantry on the island. This information, combined with the lack of any appreciable response to the American air attack, prompts Halsey to recommend that offensive operations against Yap be cancelled in favor of an attack on Leyte.

U.S. submarine *Sealion* torpedoes and sinks a Japanese transport and passenger-cargo ship in the South China Sea, east of Hainan Island. The passenger-cargo ship carries 1,300 Allied prisoners of war. Three days later USS *Pampanito* and USS *Sealion* will rescue 127 British and Australian POWs who survived.

PACIFIC: U.S. submarine *Pipefish* torpedoes and sinks a Japanese auxiliary vessel off Shikoku, Japan.

CENTRAL PACIFIC: Seventh Air Force B-25 Mitchells from the Gilberts bomb Nauru Island.

U.S. light minelayers ships begin clearing mines in the shoals between Angaur and Peleliu Islands.

CENTRAL PACIFIC, PELELIU: Rear Admiral Jesse Oldendorf, commanding the Fire Support Group with eight cruisers, 12 destroyers, seven minesweepers, 15 rocket-firing landing craft, and six submarines, begins preparatory fire on Peleliu. Three aircraft carriers and five escort carriers also support the naval bombardment with SBD Dauntless dive-bombers and Hellcat fighters all attacking carefully selected pre-invasion targets.

NEW GUINEA: FEAF A-20 Havocs and B-25 Mitchells attack airfields in western New Guinea. P-38 Lightnings attack airfields on Buru Island, and P-47 Thunderbolts attack facilities on Ceram Island. B-24 Liberators bomb airfields on Celebes Island, and B-24s and B-25s bomb airfields on Halmahera Island and radar facilities on Morotai Island.

U.S. submarine *Redfin* makes an unsuccessful attack on a Japanese cargo vessel in the Makassar Strait and escapes a depth-charge attack.

September 13

CBI: Tenth Air Force P-47 Thunderbolts strafe targets of opportunity on the Irrawaddy River.

Fourteenth Air Force B-24s attack cargo ships off the Pescadores Islands near Formosa. Aircrews report three ships sunk.

U.S. submarine *Sunfish* torpedoes and sinks a cargo ship and damages another in the East China Sea off Shanghai.

ETO: General Dwight Eisenhower informs Field Marshal Montgomery that his 21st Army Group will receive an additional 1,000 tons of supplies per day as the main effort. Reinforced by the First Allied Airborne Army and part of the 12th Army Group, his mission is to secure a bridgehead across the Rhine River in Holland and advance on the flank of German forces now occupying the defenses of the West Wall (or Siegfried Line) and capture the port of Antwerp. Bradley's 12th Army Group is to conduct limited attacks to draw German forces away from the main attack. The operation is called Market Garden.

The First Army's VII Corps uses the 1st Infantry Division to attempt to encircle Aachen from the south while XIX Corps moved on Aachen from the north. A task force of the 3rd Armored Division of VII Corps is able to advance about two miles before being stopped by mud and German defenses.

Eighth Air Force sends 673 B-17s, escorted by over 300 P-47 Thunderbolts and P-51 Mustangs, and 342 B-24 Liberators, escorted by 99 P-38 Lightnings and P-51s, to attack oil refineries, ammunition storage depots, and targets of opportunity in Germany. Fifteen bombers are lost and 413 are damaged. Aircrews report one confirmed kill. Aircrew casualties are five killed, 13 wounded, and 143 missing. Fighter pilots report 33 confirmed kills in the air and 20 confirmed kills on the ground. Eight fighters are lost, and the pilots are reported missing.

Eleven B-24 Liberators escorted by 15 P-51s are sent to bomb the oil refinery at Hemminstedt, Germany, using Azon bombs.

During the night eight B-17s drop leaflets over the Netherlands, Belgium, and Germany.

The 73 B-17s from Operation Frantic escorted by 63 P-51 Mustangs depart from airfields in the Soviet Ukraine and bomb industrial targets at Diosgyor, Hungary, en route to Fifteenth Air Force airfields in Italy.

Ninth Air Force sends P-47 and P-38 fighters to support ground forces at Brest and in the Nancy-Metz area and fly armed reconnaissance missions over the lower Rhine River valley as XIX Tactical Air Command initiates an effort to cut rail lines west and east of the Rhine River.

The C-47s of the 95th, 97th, and 98th Troop Carrier Squadrons of the 440th Troop Carrier Group redeploy from England to France.

MEDITERRANEAN: The VI Corps captures Vesoul, blocking the last avenue of escape for the German Nineteenth Army.

Fifteenth Air Force sends more than 300 B-17s and B-24 Liberators escorted by P-38 Lightnings and P-51 Mustangs to attack an oil refineries in Germany and Poland and a marshaling yard in Czechoslovakia.

ITALY: Two battalions of the 363rd Infantry Regiment attack Montecelli Ridge after a heavy artillery bombardment.

Twelfth Air Force B-25 Mitchells and B-26 Marauders attack German defensive positions north of Florence. A-20 Havocs and P-47 Thunderbolts attack rail lines, rail cars, and bridges.

SOUTHWEST PACIFIC AREA: Naval Task Groups 38.2 (Rear Admiral Gerald F. Bogan), 38.1 (Vice Admiral John S. McCain), and 38.3 (Rear Admiral Frederick C. Sherman) attack targets on Cebu, Negros, and Legaspi Islands in the Philippines.

CENTRAL PACIFIC, PELELIU: Admiral Jesse Oldendorf calls off the prelanding bombardment, reporting that all targets assigned have been hit and destroyed. Oldendorf's force has fired 2,350 16-inch and 14-inch rounds from ships, and 1,800 500-pound bombs have been dropped on the island.

NEW GUINEA: FEAF A-20 Havocs, P-38 Lightnings, P-47 Thunderbolts, and B-25 Mitchells attack airfields in western New Guinea.

B-24 Liberators and B-25s bomb airfields on Morotai Island.

Thirteenth Air Force headquarters redeploys from Los Negros Island in the Admiralties to Hollandia.

Fifth Air Force A-20 Havocs sink a cargo ship off southeastern Ceram Island.

September 14

ALEUTIANS: Eleventh Air Force sends three B-24 Liberators on a night raid against shipping and the airfield on Paramushiru Island in the Kuriles.

CBI: General Joseph Stilwell flies from Burma to Kweilin to assess the situation. Chinese troops are nearly incapable of any sustained resistance. The Chinese Y Force captures Tengchung after more than two months of bitter fighting.

Tenth Air Force sends four B-25 Mitchells to drop booby-trapped fragmentation bombs on Bhamo.

Fourteenth Air Force P-40s and P-51 Mustangs attack river shipping, troop compounds, logistics storage depots, and buildings near Lungling and other areas south of Tungting Lake.

The headquarters of the 23rd Fighter Group redeploys from Liuchow to Luliang, and the B-24s of the 373rd Bombardment Squadron (Heavy) of the 308th Bombardment Group (Heavy) also redeploy to Luliang.

ETO: First Army reaches its limit of advance. Without sufficient supplies, it can advance no farther. The VII Corps reaches the German border near Aachen. The V Corps holds a 50-mile front within Germany. The XXIX Tactical Air Force is activated under Ninth Air Force to provide direct support to Ninth Army. SHAEF air strength in-theater is now 4,700 fighters and 6,000 bombers.

General Eisenhower sends a letter to Army Chief of Staff General George C. Marshall informing him of SHAEF's plan to make an all-out attempt to reach the Rhine River, but cautions that, despite unexpected rapid advances, the possibility of a rapid advance to Berlin is not practical.

The 47th Infantry Regiment of the 9th Infantry Division attacks near the Hürtgen Forest to protect the 3rd Armored Division as it reaches the Vicht River. The area is heavily wooded with tall trees that cut out the sun, steep hills, and deep streambeds. Although German forces in the area are weak and of low quality, they take advantage of every support the terrain offers and occupy the fortifications of the West Wall, protected by minefields, barbed wire, and concrete pillboxes that provide interlocking fire.

The U.S. Third and Seventh Armies link, establishing a solid line of Allied forces from Antwerp to Switzerland.

Eighth Air Force sends two Aphrodite explosives-laden B-17s to crash into the oil refinery at Hemminstedt, Germany, but the aircraft miss the target.

Ninth Air Force sends over 100 B-26 Marauders and A-30s to attack German fortifications at Brest. P-47 and P-38 fighters fly armed reconnaissance missions. The headquarters of the XXIX Tactical Air Command (Provisional), under the command of Brigadier General Richard E. Nugent, is activated to support the U.S. Ninth Army, which will be subordinate to General Omar Bradley's Twelfth Army Group.

Sergeant Joseph J. Sadowski is a tank commander with the 37th Tank Battalion, 4th Armored Division. He is part of Combat Command A and is approaching the town of Valhey, France, when German antitank guns begin to fire on the Americans. Sergeant Sadowski's tank is hit and knocked out. Sadowski orders the crew to abandon the tank and take cover near a building. Everyone escapes but one man. Sadowski, braving a hail of fire, returns to the tank to rescue his comrade. While attempting to pry open the hatch, he is killed by enemy fire. For his inspirational courage and willingness to risk his own life to save the life of a fellow soldier, Sergeant Sadowski will receive the Medal of Honor.

ITALY: Twelfth Air Force B-26 Marauders and B-25 Mitchells attack German defensive positions at Il Giogo Pass and Monte Altuzzo. A-20 Havocs and P-47 Thunderbolts attack road and rail lines in the Po River valley.

Second Lieutenant Thomas W. Wigle takes over as leader of the 3rd Platoon of K Company, 135th Infantry Regiment, 34th Infantry Division, after it has failed in two attacks on a fortified position on Monte Frassino. He leads the third attack; in the face of intense fire, he covers his men with rifle fire as they cross a series of stone walls. Approaching the three houses that are the center of the German defensive position, he attacks alone, supported by a base of fire from his platoon. He bursts into the house and, firing his M-1 carbine, drives out the defenders, then chases them and enters the second house and finally herds most of the defenders into the cellar of the third house. He is mortally wounded as his men join him. The Americans capture the position and 36 prisoners as a result of Wigle's heroic actions. He will receive the Medal of Honor.

SOUTHWEST PACIFIC AREA: Naval Task Groups 38.2 (Rear Admiral Gerald F. Bogan) and 38.3 (Rear Admiral Frederick C. Sherman) attack targets on Panay and Negros Islands. Carrier aircraft damage a motor torpedo boat. Naval TG 38.1 (Vice Admiral John S. McCain), steaming to support landings on Morotai, attacks targets on Mindanao. SB2C Helldivers sink a fast transport in Davao Gulf. Destroyers *Farenholt, McCalla,* and *Grayson* bombard a suspected Japanese radar installation at mouth of Davao Gulf.

CENTRAL PACIFIC: Seventh Air Force B-24 Liberators from Saipan bomb Iwo Jima. B-25 Mitchells from the Gilberts bomb Ponape Island. B-24s from Eniwetok bomb Truk.

NEW GUINEA: FEAF A-20 Havocs, P-38 Lightnings, P-47 Thunderbolts, and B-25 Mitchells attack airfields in western New Guinea and on the Vogelkop Peninsula.

B-25 Mitchells bomb airfields on Celebes Island and B-24 Liberators bomb airfields on Halmahera Island.

The B-25s of the 69th Bombardment Squadron (Medium), 42nd Bombardment Group (Medium), redeploy from Hollandia to Sansapor.

September 15

CBI: A Combat Cargo Task Force is formed within Eastern Air Command, under Brigadier General Frederick W. Evans, to support the British Fourteenth Army's offensive into southern Burma.

Tenth Air Force sends 13 B-24 Liberators to fly fuel to Liuchow, China. P-47 Thunderbolts bomb Kutkai and sweep the river near Bhamo. Other P-47s attack targets on the Burma Road.

In China, Fourteenth Air Force sends 19 B-24 Liberators to bomb a military storage area at Hengyang.

The headquarters of the 68th Composite Wing redeploys from Kweilin to Liuchow.

ATLANTIC: At the Octagon conference, acting on a message from Third Fleet commander, Admiral William F. Halsey, the JCS cancels orders for an invasion of Mindanao and orders an attack on Leyte. Halsey has reported that Japanese air cover in the Philippines is very weak and recommends that the Leyte invasion begin in October rather than November. The JCS informs Nimitz that he is to cancel the Palaus invasion and move to Leyte as well. Nimitz argues that the island of Peleliu is essential as a forward base for operations against Leyte. As a result of Halsey's information, the Leyte invasion is moved up from December 20 to October 20. Nimitz will transfer operational control of the 7th and 96th Infantry Divisions to SWPA to form the XIV Corps. Admiral Nimitz is directed to bypass the island of Yap.

Roosevelt and Churchill approve the Morgenthau Plan. Henry Morgenthau is the U.S. secretary of the treasury, and his ideas have gained increasing influence in the administration over the past year. Morgenthau believes the War Department's plan for postwar occupation of Germany is too gentle. His plan divides Germany permanently into two sections, north and south, and dismantles completely her industrial capacity, reducing the states to basic subsistence agriculture. There will be no aid or support to Germany whatsoever. The Soviet Union will get most of Germany's dismantled industry as reparations. Although the plan is strongly opposed by many advisers, it remains the unofficial Allied plan until the Potsdam Conference in August 1945. The Morgenthau Plan, coupled with the demand for unconditional surrender, is a propaganda coup for Hitler. Germany's defeat meant the complete destruction of the nation and the subjugation of the German people. Despite wavering faith in Hitler, German national morale rallies.

President Roosevelt relents in his insistence on U.S. forces occupying northwest Germany after the war. He agrees to U.S. forces occupying southwest Germany and the division of Berlin into zones of occupation.

ETO: Operation Dragoon has succeeded in clearing German forces from southern France. Operational control of the Dragoon forces passes from the Mediterranean theater to General Eisenhower in the European theater. The French First Army under General de Lattre de Tassigny and the U.S. Seventh Army under Lieutenant General Alexander E. Patch are designated as the 6th Army Group under the command of Lieutenant General Jacob L. Devers. Each army group is assigned its own tactical air force to provide direct support to its ground forces. General Montgomery has the Second Tactical Air Force, General Bradley has the Ninth Tactical Air Force, and General Devers has the First Tactical Air Force.

Although under operational control of SHAEF, the commander of the Mediterranean theater is still responsible for logistics support.

SHAEF returns operational control of the Allied Strategic Air Forces to the Combined Chiefs of Staff. The U.S. Strategic Air Forces commander, General Carl Spaatz, has operational control of the Eighth Air Force and Fifteenth Air Force and administrative control of the U.S. Tactical Air Force in Europe.

The XII Corps captures Nancy. At this point, the battle for France has cost the German armed forces about 500,000 men. About 200,000 men are trapped by the Ninth Army in the coastal ports of Brittany and battle casualties are estimated at 300,000. The Fifth Panzer Army and the Seventh Army have ceased to exist.

In the First Army area, Combat Command B of the 3rd Armored Division passes through the West Wall (or Siegfried Line). The 1st Infantry Division occupies positions overlooking Aachen. The 39th Infantry Regiment of the 9th Infantry Division attacks near Lammersdorf.

Eighth Air Force reorganizes to support three bombardment divisions. One fighter wing of VIII Fighter Command will support each bombardment division.

The 1st Bombardment Division is supported by the 67th Fighter Wing (the 20th, 352nd, 356th, 359th, and 364th Fighter Groups); the 2nd Bombardment Division is supported by the 65th Fighter Wing (the 4th, 56th, 355th, 361st, and 479th Fighter Groups); and the 3rd Bombardment Division is supported by the 66th Fighter Wing (the 55th, 78th, 339th, 353rd, and 357th Fighter Groups).

Ninth Air Force P-47 Thunderbolts and P-38 Lightnings of the IX Tactical Air Command support First Army, and the fighters of the XIX Tactical Air Command support Third Army.

MEDITERRANEAN: Lieutenant General Joseph T. McNary is appointed as the Deputy Supreme Allied Commander Mediterranean to replace Lieutenant General Jacob L. Devers, now commander of the 6th Army Group in the ETO.

Fifteenth Air Force sends 276 B-17s and B-24 Liberators escorted by P-38 Lightnings and P-51 Mustangs to bomb airfields and a submarine base in Greece.

ITALY: One company of the 363rd Infantry Regiment occupies the crest of Montecelli Ridge and holds for four days against repeated German counterattacks. The company loses 14 killed and 126 wounded and is reduced to 50 men.

The headquarters of XII Fighter Command assumes operational control over the headquarters of the 87th Fighter Wing, the 47th Bombardment Group (Light, with A-20 Havocs), and the 57th and 86th Fighter Groups (P-47s) from XII Tactical Air Command. Ninth Air Force takes operational control of XII Tactical Air Command now that Seventh Army has joined with General Eisenhower's forces as part of the ETO.

The P-47s of the 347th Fighter Squadron of the 350th Fighter Group redeploy from Sardinia to Tarquinia.

SOUTHWEST PACIFIC AREA: General MacArthur's headquarters notifies Sixth Army that the Mindanao operation is cancelled and confirms October 20 as the new date for the Leyte operation. The XXIV Corps (7th and 96th Infantry Divisions), under the operational control of Admiral Nimitz, will shift to General MacArthur to replace XIV Corps (24th and 37th Infantry Divisions). The 24th Infantry Division will move to X Corps (1st Cavalry Division), replacing the 40th Infantry Division. The 40th and the 37th Infantry Divisions have to be replaced because they cannot leave New Britain in time to meet the October 20 date for the landing.

The JCS designates General MacArthur as the supreme commander of land, sea, and air forces. One problem facing MacArthur is the lack of land-based air to support the invasion. Leyte is 500 miles from the nearest fighter base. He will have to rely on naval aviation to isolate the enemy on Leyte and interdict supply lines and reinforcements.

U.S. submarine *Guavina* torpedoes and sinks a Japanese fast transport south of Mindanao.

CENTRAL PACIFIC, PELELIU: Operation Stalemate II. As Naval Task Group 32.5, commanded by Rear Admiral Jesse B. Oldendorf, provides gunfire support, the 1st Marine Division lands a first wave of 5,000 men on the beaches at Peleliu preceded by amphibious tractors mounting 75 millimeter guns to suppress enemy positions.

An example of a Japanese pillbox on Peleliu. Originally covered with vegetation, it was nearly invisible. Firing ports oriented along natural lines of advance put marines within optimum killing range. These positions could be destroyed only by a direct assault.

Major General William H. Rupertus, the division commander, has told his subordinates that he expects a "rough but fast" operation lasting two or three days. The marines are facing about 10,900 Japanese troops occupying a complex of deep caves, bunkers, pillboxes, and a tunnel system that has largely been untouched by the naval and air bombardment at an area known as Umurbrogol. From these heights, the Japanese can observe the beaches and direct fire on the marines. The 1st Marine Regiment, commanded by Colonel Lewis B. "Chesty" Puller, immediately encounters a heavy crossfire from beach defenses untouched by naval bombardment. Many amphibious tractors carrying the radio sets for the regiment are destroyed by Japanese mortar fire. Captain George Hunt of Company K, 3rd Battalion, 1st Marines, captures the Point, an outcropping of rock on the left flank of the landing beach. There is no contact with Puller's regiment for several critical hours as the marines struggle against machine gun and artillery fire as they attempt to press forward.

The 7th Marine Regiment moves to the southeast to secure the division's right flank. Marines are stopped by strong Japanese resistance. Major General Rupertus commits his reserve, the 1st Battalion, 7th Marines, to shore up the 1st Marine Regiment, which has suffered heavy casualties. The 5th Marine Regiment also takes heavy fire on the landing beaches and moves inland toward the airfield with difficulty. Due to heavy Japanese resistance, none of the division's objectives are reached. A total of 30 M4A1 Sherman tanks land and occupy defensive positions. During the night 500 Japanese troops with tanks attack the defensive lines of the 5th Marines. The attack is rapidly halted by American tanks and anti-tank guns. The 7th Marines stops a determined counterattack with the support of naval gunfire. Captain Hunt's small force of about 40 men holds the Point against determined Japanese counterattacks through the night. By morning only 18 marines are able to fight, and the bodies of more than 400 Japanese soldiers lie around them.

First Lieutenant Carlton R. Rouh, 1st Battalion, 5th Marines, examines an apparently cleared dugout position before permitting his men to use it as an 81 millimeter mortar observation post. As First Lieutenant Rouh examines the position, he is shot by a Japanese soldier inside the pillbox. While he is being given first aid a Japanese grenade lands close to the two marines assisting him. Rouh pushes the men to one side and uses his own body to block the explosion. His exceptional spirit of loyalty and self-sacrifice will win him the Medal of Honor.

NEW GUINEA: Operation Trade Wind. Naval Task Force 77 (Rear Admiral Daniel E. Barbey) commands this operation. Task Group 77.2 (Rear Admiral Russell S. Berkey), with two heavy cruisers, three light cruisers, and 10 destroyers, and Task Group 77.1 (Rear Admiral Thomas L. Sprague), with six escort carriers and eight destroyer escorts, provide support for the landing.

Marines of the 1st Marine Division occupy fighting positions on Peleliu Island, September 15, 1944.

The 155th and 167th RCTs of the 31st Infantry Division land at Morotai Island preceded by naval gunfire and an air bombardment by B-24 Liberators, A-20 Havocs, and P-47 Thunderbolts. A coral reef prevents a beach landing, forcing the troops to wade in about 100 yards. Fortunately, the landing is uncontested. General MacArthur joins the 124th RCT on the beach. The abandoned airfield on the island is deemed to be unsuitable. The engineers locate another suitable site on the southern coast. Because of the impassable coral reef, another beachhead is established.

FEAF P-39 Airacobras bomb Manokwari airfield.

Fifth Air Force A-20 Havocs bomb Japanese shipping off the southeast coast of Ceram. Pilots report sinking two fishing vessels.

September 16

ALEUTIANS: Eleventh Air Force sends three B-24 Liberators to bomb Kataoka naval base on Shimushu Island.

CBI: Tenth Air Force sends 19 B-24 Liberators to fly fuel to Kunming, China.

In China, Fourteenth Air Force sends 20 B-24 Liberators to bomb Hengyang. Over 100 P-40s and P-51 Mustangs attack targets of opportunity near Lungling and around Changsha and Lingling.

ATLANTIC: The Octagon Conference Ends. The unconditional surrender of the Axis powers is reaffirmed, and Roosevelt remains uncomfortable with on not having any U.S. ground forces occupying southwest Germany. The U.S. will use its airpower in Europe while the USSR and Great Britain contribute the majority of the ground forces for occupation duties. The British fleet will join Nimitz's naval forces after the defeat of Germany. On the future of the Pacific, the Allies agree to place the Pacific islands given to Japan after World War I under a mandate from the League of Nations (the Marshalls among them) under the control of an international trusteeship. The United States is far less amenable to returning colonies or territories lost to the Japanese. No territories will be returned without previous approval from the United States.

ETO: An element of the German Nineteenth Army, blocked from reaching Germany by the conjunction of the Seventh and Third Armies, and continuously harassed by the XIX Tactical Air Force and French Forces of the Interior, surrenders 20,000 soldiers and civilians to Ninth Army. The VI Corps reaches Lure and Luxeuil-les-Bains, which mark main avenues of approach into Germany. Supply shortages prevent any further advances.

In the First Army area, the 47th and 60th Infantry Regiments of the 9th Infantry Division encounter strong German fortifications in the Hürtgen Forest.

Eighth Air Force sends 178 P-47 Thunderbolts and 149 P-51 Mustangs to bomb and strafe targets in northern Germany and an airfield near Kaiserslautern. Fighter pilots report six confirmed kills on the ground. One P-51 is lost and 10 damaged. The pilot is reported missing.

A total of 32 B-24s and C-47s fly in support of Carpetbagger operations. One B-24 is lost. During the night seven B-17s drop leaflets over Germany, France, and the Netherlands.

Ninth Air Force sends more than 150 A-20 Havocs and B-26 Marauders to attack road and rail targets in the Netherlands. P-47 and P-38 fighters support ground forces in stopping German counterattacks against the XII and XV Corps of Patton's Third Army.

Ninth Air Force redesignates Headquarters IX Bomber Command as the 9th Bombardment Division (Medium).

ITALY: Twelfth Air Force B-25 Mitchells and B-26 Marauders attack fuel storage areas and logistics depots and German defensive positions. A-20 Havocs and P-47 Thunderbolts attack German defenses along the Fifth Army's front lines.

The P-47s of the 526th Fighter Squadron, 86th Fighter Group, redeploy from Corsica to Grosseto, Italy.

SOUTHWEST PACIFIC AREA: U.S. submarines *Picuda* and *Redfish,* operating south of Formosa, torpedo and sink a cargo ship and a fleet tanker, respectively.

PACIFIC: Nimitz requests that his subordinate service commanders reexamine plans for Operation Causeway (the invasion of Formosa), given the directive from the JCS to speed up the invasion of Leyte.

U.S. submarine *Sea Devil* torpedoes and sinks Japanese submarine *I-364* off Honshu, Japan.

CENTRAL PACIFIC: Seventh Air Force sends 17 B-24 Liberators from Saipan to bomb Iwo Jima.

CENTRAL PACIFIC, PELELIU: The 5th Marines moves past the airfield, while the 14-inch guns of the battleship USS *Mississippi* destroy a complex of blockhouses holding up the advance of the 1st Marines. Major General William H. Rupertus presses the 1st and 5th Marines to keep up the momentum of the attack and open more maneuver room in the center of the island and clear the enemy from the division's right flank. The 1st Marines, reinforced by a battalion of the 7th Marines, is ordered to capture Umurbrogol. With temperatures averaging 105°F, the marines are slowed by a lack of water. When marines do receive water, it is contaminated with oil and useless to drink. At Umurbrogol the 1st Marines encounter a landscape that defies description. A coral mass 50 to 300 feet high juts out of the sand, covered in jungle foliage. Hidden in its crevices, valleys, cliffs, and ridges are innumerable caves, tunnels, and firing positions that are designed to trap and kill as many American troops as possible. There is no military logic to this defense. The Japanese soldiers intend to die, but will force the Americans to come to them.

NEW GUINEA: FEAF A-20 Havocs, P-38 Lightnings, P-47 Thunderbolts, and B-25 Mitchells attack airfields in western New Guinea.

B-24 Liberators bomb logistics sites on Celebes Island. B-25 Mitchells and B-24s bomb Buru Island, Ambon Island, Haroekoe Island, and Amboina Island.

The headquarters of the 42nd Bombardment Group (Medium) redeploys from Hollandia to Sansapor.

Motor torpedo boats begin operating from Morotai Island to attack Japanese barge traffic and stop any attempts to attack Morotai from Halmahera.

Lieutenant Arthur M. Preston, commander of Torpedo Boat Squadron 33, volunteers to rescue a downed pilot in Wasile Bay, Halmahera Island. He takes two PT boats 60 miles through heavily mined waters. Enemy coastal guns fire on the PT boats as they attempt to enter the bay. Turned back several times, Preston is able to reach the pilot covered by a smokescreen laid by friendly aircraft. With the Japanese guns firing from only 150 yards away, Preston calmly brings the pilot on board and escapes, but also succeeds in sinking a small cargo ship with his 40 millimeter guns. Lieutenant Preston's courageous actions to save the downed flier in the face of certain destruction will win him the Medal of Honor.

September 17

CBI: Tenth Air Force sends 16 B-24 Liberators to fly fuel to Liuchow, China. P-47 Thunderbolts attack Bhamo.

Fourteenth Air Force sends 15 B-25 Mitchells escorted by eight P-51 Mustangs to bomb Japanese-controlled airfields. Another 29 B-24 Liberators bomb Changsha. P-51 Mustangs and P-40s attack strongpoints, river shipping, rail lines, gun positions, and vehicles near Changsha, Lingling, and Hengshan.

U.S. submarine *Barb* torpedoes and sinks a Japanese escort carrier and tanker in the South China Sea southeast of Hong Kong. USS *Barb* and USS *Queenfish* rescue 32 British and Australian prisoners of war, survivors of the September 12 attack on their transport ship by USS *Sealion.*

ETO: Operation Market Garden. During the day, Eighth Air Force sends more than 500 P-38 Lightnings, P-47 Thunderbolts, and P-51 Mustangs to escort the cargo aircraft of the First Allied Airborne Army, carrying about 20,000 paratroopers and glider infantry of the 82nd Airborne and 101st Airborne Divisions to drop zones in Holland. The 82nd is to capture bridges at Nijmegen and Grave, while the 101st is to capture bridges at Vegel and Son north of Eindhoven. The American paratroopers will open the way for the XXX Corps of the British Second Army to drive north and link with the British 1st Airborne Division, which is to seize the bridges at Arnhem. The British divisions will then cross the Rhine River to outflank the Siegfried Line defenses and reach the Ruhr—General Eisenhower's operational objective for the destruction of German forces.

Shortly after recovering from the surprise, the Germans are able to isolate the British 1st Airborne and prevent units from capturing the bridges across the Rhine. The 82nd is able to capture the Maas bridge at Grave but fails to capture the Nijmegen bridge; the 101st captures all but the Son bridge. The British tanks, advancing on a narrow highway corridor, make extremely slow progress against German defenses.

Fighters precede the airborne troops, attacking antiaircraft positions and German troop positions and warding off about 30 German fighters. Pilots report seven confirmed kills in the air and one on the ground. Thirteen fighters are lost and 52 damaged. Two pilots are wounded, and 11 are reported missing. Nearly 900 B-17s are escorted by about 140 P-51 Mustangs to attack antiaircraft positions and airfields in the Netherlands in support of the airborne landings. Two B-17s are lost and 120 are damaged. Aircrew casualties are nine killed, six wounded, and 15 missing. One P-51 is lost and the pilot is reported missing.

An Operation Frantic mission is completed with the return of 70 B-17s and 57 P-51s to Britain from Fifteenth Air Force airfields in Italy.

American paratroopers over the Netherlands in the first phase of operation Market Garden, September 17, 1944

Ninth Air Force sends P-47 and P-38 fighters of the XIX Tactical Air Command to support VIII Corps in Brest; IX Tactical Air Command P-38 Lightnings and P-47 Thunderbolts fly armed reconnaissance missions and provide support to the 4th and 2nd Infantry Divisions and the 5th Armored Division.

Sergeant Harold O. Messerschmidt, a squad leader in L Company, 30th Infantry Regiment, 3rd Infantry Division, is defending a hill near Radden, France. A German attack against his position leaves Sergeant Messerschmidt the only man standing. Although wounded and holding a weapon without ammunition, Messerschmidt continues to fight, keeping the enemy from taking the position until reinforcements arrive. Sergeant Messerschmidt is killed in hand-to-hand combat. For his courageous stand against overwhelming odds, Sergeant Messerschmidt will receive the Medal of Honor.

MEDITERRANEAN: Fifteenth Air Force sends more than 400 B-17s and B-24 Liberators escorted by P-38 Lightnings and P-51 Mustangs to attack oil refineries and marshaling yards near Budapest, Hungary.

ITALY: The 339th Infantry Regiment of the 85th Infantry Division captures Monte Verucca; the 337th Infantry Regiment captures Monte Pratone. German forces are forced to abandon Futa Pass. The IV Corps has lost 2,731 men since September 10.

Twelfth Air Force B-25 Mitchells and B-26 Marauders attack rail and road traffic and bridges in the Po River valley. A-20 Havocs and P-47 Thunderbolts attack convoys, bridges, and roads in support of the Fifth Army attack.

The headquarters of the 86th Fighter Group and the P-47s of the 527th Fighter Squadron redeploy from Corsica to Grosseto, Italy.

SOUTHWEST PACIFIC AREA: FEAF B-25 Mitchells bomb Buayoan airfield on Mindanao Island in the Philippines.

PACIFIC: Twentieth Air Force elements of the headquarters of the 497th Bombardment Group (Very Heavy) and the 869th, 870th, and 871st Bombardment Squadrons (Very Heavy) arrive at Saipan from the United States. The B-29 Superfortresses will be ready to fly bombing missions against the Japanese home islands by the end of October.

CENTRAL PACIFIC: Seventh Air Force sends one B-24 on a snooper bombing mission from Saipan against Iwo Jima. B-25 Mitchells from the Gilberts bomb Nauru Island.

Naval Task Group 32.1 (Rear Admiral William H. P. Blandy) lands the 81st Infantry Division on Angaur, Palaus, supported by carrier aircraft and naval gunfire.

CENTRAL PACIFIC, PELELIU: The 2nd Battalion 1st Marines captures Hill 200, but comes under heavy fire from the Japanese holding the adjacent Hill 210. Puller asks for reinforcements, having lost one-third of his regiment since the landing. About 1,236 men are now casualties. The 1st Marines has encountered the first Japanese defensive line of hidden caves and mutually supported firing positions that make every open space a death trap. The Japanese remain hidden and cannot be detected.

The 81st Infantry Division lands at Angaur, also in the Palua Islands. Major General Paul J. Mueller commands the division in this operation. The 321st and 322nd Infantry Regiments attack the island from different directions. The 52nd, 154th, and 306th Engineers and the 710th Tank Battalion support the infantry.

New Guinea: FEAF P-47 Thunderbolts and P-40s attack airfields on an island south of the Vogelkop Peninsula. B-25 Mitchells and P-39 Airacobras attack targets on Amboina and Ceram Islands. B-24 Liberators, B-25s, and P-38 Lightnings attack Langoan airfield on Celebes Island.

September 18

CBI: Tenth Air Force sends 18 B-24 Liberators to fly fuel to Liuchow, China.

In China, Fourteenth Air Force sends 30 B-25 Mitchells to attack fuel storage areas at Lingling, Taohsien, and Chuanhsien. B-24 Liberators attack shipping in the Formosa Strait. Aircrews report one cargo ship sunk. Over 100 P-40s and P-51 Mustangs attack troops, trucks, tanks, shipping, and other targets of opportunity.

A detachment of P-51s from the 529th Fighter Squadron, 311th Fighter Group, begins operating from Hsian.

ETO: Operation Market Garden. The British XXX Corps breaks through stubborn German defenses to reach Eindhoven. British armored forces from XXX Corps link with the 101st Airborne at Grave. The 101st Airborne attacks German positions from the north to clear the town. The 82nd Airborne has not captured the Nijmegen bridge.

German forces conduct a strong counterattack against the Third Army near Luneville to restore their defensive line along the Moselle River.

Eighth Air Force sends more than 200 B-24 Liberators escorted by over 500 P-38 Lightnings, P-47 Thunderbolts, and P-51 Mustangs to drop supplies to the paratroopers of the First Allied Airborne Army in Holland. Seven B-24s are lost and 160 damaged. Aircrew casualties are one killed, 26 wounded, and 61 missing. The fighters also escort C-47s of the First Allied Airborne Army to drop reinforcements near Arnhem. P-51s, P-47s, and P-38s attack road and rail lines and antiaircraft positions. Over 100 German fighters oppose the sweep. Pilots report 29 confirmed kills in the air. A total of 20 fighters are lost, and 55 are damaged. One pilot is killed, and 20 pilots are reported missing.

Brest, a major Atlantic U-boat base with a garrison of 30,000 men, surrenders to U.S. forces. The port has been thoroughly destroyed by German forces before the surrender. The responsibility for watching the German garrisons trapped at Lorient, St-Nazaire, and Quiberon Bay is turned over to Free French Forces.

In the First Army area, the 60th Infantry Regiment of the 9th Infantry Division gains the ridge beyond Monschau. American forces in First Army are not equipped to attack the fortifications of the Siegfried Line, nor are they in sufficient strength to mount effective attacks.

Operation Frantic continues with over 100 B-17s escorted by 137 P-51s dropping 1,248 containers of supplies to beleaguered Polish fighters in Warsaw. One B-17 is lost, and seven are damaged. Two fighters are lost. Pilots report four confirmed kills in the air and three on the ground. Two pilots are reported missing. After the drop, 64 P-51s continue escorting the B-17s to airfields in the Soviet Ukraine.

During the night eight B-17s drop leaflets over France, Germany, and the Netherlands.

Ninth Air Force P-47 Thunderbolts and P-38 Lightnings support the VIII Corps at Brest.

Ninth Air Force redeploys the headquarters of the 409th Bombardment Group (Light) and the A-20 Havocs of the 640th, 641st, 642nd, and 643rd Bombardment Squadrons (Light) from England to France. The headquarters of the 9th Bombardment Division (Medium) redeploys from England to Chartres, France.

At Best, Holland, a platoon of H Company, 502nd Parachute Infantry Regiment, 101st Airborne Division, makes an attack to capture a bridge across the Wilhelmina Canal. When the platoon is cut off and surrounded, Private First Class Joe E. Mann sets out to locate the enemy. Moving close to a German 88 millimeter gun, he destroys it and engages the enemy, even though wounded four times. Although heavily bandaged, Mann insists on pulling his turn at guard duty during the night. At dawn, the Germans make a counterattack. Warning his comrades, Mann throws himself on a grenade. His courage and dedication above and beyond the call of duty will win him the Medal of Honor.

MEDITERRANEAN: Fifteenth Air Force sends more than 460 B-17s and B-24 Liberators escorted by P-38 Lightnings and P-51 Mustangs to attack marshaling yards and railroad bridges in Hungary and railroad bridges in Yugoslavia.

ITALY: The 363rd Infantry Regiment of the 91st Infantry Division captures Il Giogo Pass and Monticelli Ridge. The 338th Infantry Regiment of the 85th Infantry Division captures Monte Altuzzo. American casualties for six days of combat are 2,730. General Mark Clark decides to attack along the two highways leading to Bologna. The 34th, 91st, and 85th Infantry Divisions will attack on Route 65, the quickest and most direct way to Bologna. He also decides to send the 88th Infantry Division with Combat Command A of the 1st Armored Division on the road to Imola to exploit the boundary between the Fourteenth and Tenth German armies.

Twelfth Air Force B-25 Mitchells support the British Eighth Army at Rimini. B-26 Marauders and P-47 Thunderbolts attack rail and road traffic and bridges in the Po Valley.

The P-47s of the 525th Fighter Squadron, 86th Fighter Group, redeploy from Corsica to Grosseto, Italy.

SOUTHWEST PACIFIC AREA: FEAF B-24 Liberators bomb oil storage areas near Davao on Mindanao Island in the Philippines.

U.S. submarine *Flasher* torpedoes and sinks a Japanese auxiliary gunboat off Manila Bay.

PACIFIC: The headquarters of Twentieth Air Force's 499th and 500th Bombardment Groups (Very Heavy) arrive at Saipan from the United States.

U.S. submarine *Pipefish* torpedoes and damages a Japanese army transport off Honshu, Japan. U.S. submarine *Thresher* torpedoes and sinks a cargo ship in the Yellow Sea.

CENTRAL PACIFIC: Seventh Air Force sends 28 B-24 Liberators from Eniwetok to bomb Truk. B-25 Mitchells from the Gilberts bomb Ponape Island.

CENTRAL PACIFIC, PELELIU: In the Umurbrogol, the Japanese counterattack the marines on Hill 200. The 1st Marines attempt to retake the lost position. The 1st Marine Division commander, General William Rupertus, refuses to consider using the army's 81st Infantry Division in what he considers a purely marine fight. The 1st Battalion and 3rd Battalion of the 7th Marines control the east road and the causeway on the island and capture the Japanese defenses on Ngarmoked Island after a two-day fight against heavily fortified caves.

Private First Class Charles H. Roan is part of the attack by 2nd Battalion, 7th Marines, on one of the innumerable coral outcroppings that make up the battlefield of Peleliu. Roan and his squad are partly cut off from their company during the fighting and are quickly attacked by Japanese troops in a cave above and behind them. Private First Class Roan and four other marines seek cover from the shower of grenades landing in their midst. Roan is wounded by one grenade explosion, then, seeing that another grenade is nearby, he shields his comrades with his own body and takes the blast. Private First Class Roan's courage and personal sacrifice is worthy of receiving the Medal of Honor.

Private First Class Arthur J. Jackson, 3rd Battalion, 7th Marine Regiment, is a rifleman facing flanking fire from Japanese troops concealed in strongly fortified positions at Peleliu. Jackson moves forward and charges one of the enemy positions holding 35 Japanese soldiers. He fires into the opening and throws white phosphorus grenades and explosive charges into the pillbox, eliminating the position. As Japanese fire from the other positions hits around him, Private Jackson attacks two other smaller positions and then moves through the area destroying a total of 12 pillboxes and killing at least 50 Japanese soldiers. For his extraordinary valor in facing a determined enemy and certain death, Private First Class Jackson will win the Medal of Honor.

NEW GUINEA: At Morotai Island, American troops encounter no enemy forces. Elements of the 126th Infantry land at Cape Coerongoe and Cape Sopi to establish radar facilities.

FEAF A-20 Havocs, B-25 Mitchells, P-39 Airacobras, P-38 Lightnings, P-40s, and P-47 Thunderbolts attack the island south of the Vogelkop Peninsula and Manokwari.

The headquarters of the 310th Bombardment Wing (Medium) redeploys from Hollandia to Morotai Island. The B-24 Liberators of the 371st Bombardment Squadron (Heavy), 307th Bombardment Group (Heavy), redeploy from Wakde Island to Noemfoor Island.

B-25 Mitchells bomb Langoan airfield on Celebes Island.

September 19

CBI: President Roosevelt urges Chiang Kai-shek to place General Stilwell in command of all Chinese ground forces, including the Communists, to meet the crisis caused by the Japanese *Ichigo* offensive in China. President Roosevelt writes a stern letter to Chiang Kai-shek: "I have urged time and again . . . that you take drastic action. . . . Now when you have not yet placed General Stilwell in command of all forces in China, we are faced with the loss of a critical area in east China. . . ."

Fourteenth Air Force sends 28 B-25 Mitchells to bomb Lingling, Chuanhsien, and Shanhsien. Over 150 P-40s and P-51 Mustangs attack bridges, railroads, troops, and rail and road traffic around Tungting Lake and from the Yangtze River area to the South China Sea.

ETO: In Operation Market Garden, the British armored units are held up before Nijmegen as German troops arrive in strength to prevent the bridge from being captured.

Over 170 P-51 Mustangs supporting the First Allied Airborne Army in Holland encounter over 100 German fighters. Pilots report 23 confirmed kills and four probables. Six P-51s are lost and three are damaged. One pilot is killed and six are reported missing.

In the First Army area, the 39th Infantry Regiment of the 9th Infantry Division attacks Hill 554 near Lammersdorf in the Hürtgen Forest. This hill controls the main road to Schmidt. The 60th Infantry Regiment of the 9th Infantry Division attacks to capture the town of Hürtgen.

The VIII Corps captures Brest.

Eighth Air Force sends 796 B-17s escorted by 240 P-47 Thunderbolts and P-51 Mustangs to attack marshaling yards in western Germany. Weather prevents most of the bombers from hitting the primary target. Most attack targets of opportunity including bridges and rail lines. Seven bombers are lost and 281 are damaged. Aircrew casualties are six wounded and 56 missing. Fighter pilots report three confirmed kills. One P-47 is lost and the pilot is reported missing.

An Operation Frantic mission sends 100 B-17s and 61 P-51 Mustangs from airfields in Soviet Ukraine to bomb the marshaling yard at Szolnok, Hungary, en route to Fifteenth Air Force airfields in Italy.

Ninth Air Force sends B-26 Marauders to attack marshaling yards and slow German reinforcements to Aachen. P-47 Thunderbolts and P-38 Lightnings of the IX Tactical Air Command support V Corps in stopping a German counterattack near Wallendorf. Fighters support paratroopers in Holland as part of Operation Market Garden. XIX Tactical Air Command P-47 and P-38 fighters escort A-20 Havocs and B-26s and support ground forces in Holland and at Brest and Nancy in France.

The headquarters of the 391st Bombardment Group (Medium) redeploys from England to France.

MEDITERRANEAN: Fifteenth Air Force sends 96 B-24 Liberators escorted by P-38 Lightnings to attack rail bridges in Yugoslavia.

ITALY: Twelfth Air Force A-20 Havocs and P-47 Thunderbolts attack German defensive positions, bridges, and roads.

SOUTHWEST PACIFIC AREA: U.S. submarine *Bang* attacks Japanese shipping off east coast of Formosa, sinking a tanker and damaging a coastal patrol craft.

PACIFIC: Twentieth Air Force deploys elements of the 881st, 882nd, and 883rd Bombardment Squadrons (Very Heavy), 500th Bombardment Group (Very Heavy), to Saipan from the United States. The squadrons' first missions are scheduled for mid-November.

U.S. submarine *Scabbardfish* torpedoes and damages a Japanese submarine tender northwest of Okinawa. U.S. submarine *Shad* torpedoes and sinks a coast defense ship off Honshu, Japan.

CENTRAL PACIFIC: Seventh Air Force sends 29 B-24 Liberators from Saipan to attack shipping at Chichi Jima Island. Aircrews report a landing ship and a small cargo vessel damaged.

B-24 Liberators on snooper and armed reconnaissance missions bomb Iwo Jima.

CENTRAL PACIFIC, PELELIU: The 7th Marines control the area identified as Purple Beach on the east side of the island. Once secured, it becomes the primary logistics support site.

Hill 100 is a ridge near Horseshoe Valley in the Umurbrogol. The 1st Marines attack to capture the hill, but as soon as they do, they discover the Japanese occupy positions all around, above, and even below them in caves and tunnels. Exposed to a murderous fire during the day, then attacked at night by infiltrators, the marines hold Hill 100, but fewer than 10 are still capable of fighting. The hill has to be abandoned. In four days of combat the 1st Marine Regiment has lost 1,500 men.

The 1st Marines reinforced by the 2nd Battalion of the 7th Marines is stopped before a chain of hills named the Five Sisters. Captain Everett P. Pope commands C Company, 1st Battalion, 1st Marines. Pope's company attacks and holds a steep coral mound named Hill 100. Although his company has taken heavy casualties and is quickly surrounded and trapped by Japanese forces, Captain Pope rallies the dozen survivors and organizes a defense. Throughout the night, the Japanese attack again and again to regain the critical hill, but each time they are driven off by Pope's men. By daylight only eight marines are still standing; without the means to hold their ground any longer, they are ordered to withdraw. Captain Pope's courage under fire and his inspiring leadership in the face of overwhelming odds will win him the Medal of Honor.

NEW GUINEA: FEAF B-24 Liberators, B-25 Mitchells, and P-38 Lightnings attack shipping, fuel storage sites, and port facilities in the Celebes.

The headquarters of the 8th Fighter Group and the P-38s of the 36th Fighter Squadron redeploy to Morotai Island. The headquarters of the 347th Fighter Group and the P-38s of the 339th Fighter Squadron redeploy to Middleburg Island.

U.S. submarine *Redfin* sinks Japanese fishing vessel east of Celebes Island.

September 20

CBI: In China, Fourteenth Air Force sends 27 B-25 Mitchells to bomb Lingling, Chuanhsien, Chuanhsien, and Kiyang. Over 100 P-51 Mustangs and P-40s attack troops, horses, trucks, and river shipping near Chuanhsien, Lingling, Kiyang, and Changsha.

ETO: In Operation Market Garden, the 505th Parachute Infantry Regiment attacks through Nijmegen to capture the south end of the bridge. The 504th Parachute Infantry Regiment, with a company of the 307th Engineers, crosses the Waal River, using British assault boats in full view of the enemy. The assault troops suffer heavy casualties, but at the end of the day the paratroopers secure the area and open the bridge to British tanks.

The First Army begins the battle for Aachen.

The VI Corps of Seventh Army begins crossing the Moselle River. The 36th Infantry Division crosses near Eloyes and meets heavy German fire. The division takes heavy casualties but captures the town. The 3rd Infantry Division crosses at Rupt.

Eighth Air Force sends nearly 700 P-38 Lightnings, P-47 Thunderbolts, and P-51 Mustangs to support the First Allied Airborne Army in Arnhem and Nijmegen. Two fighters are shot down by antiaircraft fire and nine are damaged.

Ninth Air Force sends B-26 Marauders to attack marshaling yards to prevent German reinforcements from reaching Aachen. P-47 and P-38 fighters of the IX Tactical Air Command support V and VIII Corps near the Dutch-German border, and P-38 Lightnings and P-47s of the XIX Tactical Air Command support XV and XX Corps near Nancy.

MEDITERRANEAN: Fifteenth Air Force sends more than 500 B-17s and B-24 Liberators escorted by P-38 Lightnings and P-51 Mustangs to attack marshaling yards, oil refineries, and airfields in Czechoslovakia and railroad bridges near Budapest, Hungary.

ITALY: The headquarters of XII Fighter Command takes operational control of the P-47s of the 27th and 79th Fighter Groups. The command's mission is to support Fifth Army.

SOUTHWEST PACIFIC AREA: FEAF B-24 Liberators attack Japanese shipping off Formosa, damaging three cargo vessels.

CENTRAL PACIFIC: The 81st Infantry Division, with artillery support from the 316th, 317th, 318th, and 906th Field Artillery Battalions, breaks the Japanese defenses at Angaur Island. About 1,400 Japanese troops defend the island. The 321st Infantry Regiment is made available to Major General Roy S. Geiger for employment at Peleliu.

Seventh Air Force B-24 Liberators from the Marshall Islands attack Jaluit Atoll and B-25 Mitchells from Makin bomb Nauru Island.

The 322nd Infantry Regiment supported by tanks meets strong Japanese resistance from a defensive position on Angaur Island known as the Bowl. This begins a nine-day battle to eliminate the enemy position.

CENTRAL PACIFIC, PELELIU: The 7th Marines attacks south into the Umurbrogol. The area left under Japanese control has been compressed into a pocket 950 yards long and 450 yards wide. The terrain here is a jumble of cliffs, sinkholes, tall, knifelike ridges, and crevasses. Any sizable force entering the canyons or valleys is subjected to heavy fire from all directions. If ridgelines are occupied, the next higher ridgeline or hilltop sweeps the area with rifle and machine-gun fire. At night, the Japanese attack from their caves and tunnels to drive the Americans off any position they still held during the day.

NEW GUINEA: FEAF P-47 Thunderbolts, P-38 Lightnings, and P-40s attack antiaircraft positions and logistics sites at Moemi and Ransiki airfields.

B-24 Liberators, A-20 Havocs, and P-47 Thunderbolts attack Halmahera Island. B-24s, B-25 Mitchells, A-20s, and P-38 Lightnings conduct day and night raids on airfields on Ceram Island, Buru Island, Amboina Island, and a town on Timor Island.

The B-25s of the 75th Bombardment Squadron (Medium), 42nd Bombardment Group (Medium), redeploy from Hollandia to Sansapor. P-38s of the 80th Fighter Squadron 8th Fighter Group redeploy to Morotai Island. The B-24s of the 370th and 372nd Bombardment Squadrons (Heavy), 307th Bombardment Group (Heavy), redeploy from Wakde Island to Noemfoor Island.

September 21

CBI: Tenth Air Force sends 21 B-24 Liberators to fly fuel to Kunming, China.

In China, Fourteenth Air Force sends 27 B-25 Mitchells to bomb Kiyang, Yungming, and Lingling. P-40s and P-51 Mustangs attack river shipping, troops, horses, and logistics sites near Kiyang.

ETO: The 45th Infantry Division of the VI Corps, Seventh Army, crosses the Moselle River near Épinal. The 180th Infantry Regiment meets heavy resistance before the city.

Eighth Air Force sends 90 P-47 Thunderbolts and P-51 Mustangs to conduct escort ground support missions for First Allied Airborne Army C-47s dropping supplies and paratroopers of the Polish 1st Brigade near Driel in Holland. Nearly 50 German fighters attack the Americans. Fighter pilots report 20 confirmed kills. Three fighters are lost and three damaged. Three pilots are reported missing.

Over 300 B-17s escorted by 73 P-38 Lightnings and P-51 Mustangs bomb the synthetic oil plant at Ludwigshafen and the marshaling yard at Mainz. A total of 106 B-17s are damaged. Aircrew casualties are two wounded. One P-51 is lost, and the pilot is reported missing. Nearly 180 B-24 Liberators bomb the marshaling yard at Koblenz escorted by 44 P-51s. Two B-24s are lost and 86 damaged. Aircrew casualties are 15 killed, three wounded, and 18 missing.

Ninth Air Force sends 79 A-20 Havocs and B-26 Marauders to attack marshaling yards in Germany. The P-47 and P-38 fighters of the IX Tactical Air Command support the V Corps at Wallendorf.

The A-20 Havocs of the 670th Bombardment Squadron (Light), 416th Bombardment Group (Light), redeploy from England to France.

Private John R. Towle is a bazooka gunner in C Company, 504th Parachute Infantry Regiment, 82nd Airborne Division, near Oosterhout, Holland. His company is in a defensive position at the Nijmegen bridgehead when about 100 German infantry, two tanks, and a personnel carrier attack. Private Towle takes the initiative to stop the tanks himself. He exposes himself to enemy fire in order to reach an exposed dike roadbed where he can best engage the enemy. He fires on the tanks; although they take only superficial damage, they retreat. Towle then fires into a house and kills a group of German troops occupying it as a strongpoint. Going back for more bazooka rounds, Private Towle then moves forward again to attack the personnel carrier. As he prepares to fire, a mortar round explodes nearby, killing him. Private Towle's exceptional devotion to duty and courage in the face of danger will win him the Medal of Honor.

MEDITERRANEAN: Fifteenth Air Force sends more than 300 B-17s and B-24 Liberators escorted by P-38 Lightnings and P-51 Mustangs to attack marshaling yards and bridges in Hungary and road and rail lines in Yugoslavia. Two C-47s escorted by eight P-51s evacuate Fifteenth Air Force former prisoners of war from Yugoslavia to Italy.

ITALY: The 88th Infantry Division, commanded by Major General Paul W. Kendall, moves the 350th and 349th Infantry Regiments toward Imola to outflank German forces facing the attacking British Eighth Army.

Southwest Pacific Area: Based on the approval of the JCS for the invasion of Leyte on October 20, SWPA headquarters orders Sixth Army to seize and secure Dinagat and Homonhon Islands as a preliminary action to bringing a landing force into Leyte Gulf. Upon landing, Krueger's Sixth Army will have 60 days to defeat enemy forces and establish airbases necessary for future operations. The Eighth Army (to be established on September 25 under Lieutenant General Robert L. Eichelberger) will take over all former Sixth Army missions in New Guinea, New Britain, the Admiralties, and Morotai. The Australian First Army will take the combat missions of XIV Corps in the Solomons and Sixth Army in New Guinea. General Kenney's Fear East Air Force will attack targets on Mindanao and in the Netherlands East Indies from bases in New Guinea and Morotai.

Naval Task Force 38 (Vice Admiral Marc A. Mitscher) carrier aircraft attack Japanese shipping in Manila Bay and Subic Bay, attack Clark Field and Nichols Field, and attack the Cavite Navy Yard. A destroyer, five tankers, two oilers, 16 cargo ships, a coastal defense ship, a passenger-cargo ship, and a cargo vessel are sunk. A Japanese destroyer, two cargo vessels, and two tankers are damaged.

U.S. submarine *Haddo,* while on a lifeguard mission for the air attacks on Luzon, torpedoes and sinks a Japanese surveying ship southwest of Manila. Off the north coast of Luzon, USS *Picuda* torpedoes and sinks a Japanese transport. USS *Redfish* torpedoes and sinks a transport.

Pacific: U.S. submarine *Searaven* torpedoes and sinks a Japanese army transport off Sakhalin Island.

U.S. submarine *Shad* torpedoes and sinks a Japanese auxiliary minesweeper off Honshu, Japan.

Central Pacific: Seventh Air Force B-25 Mitchells from the Gilberts bomb Ponape Island.

Central Pacific, Peleliu: The 1st Marines recapture Hills 200 and 210, but an attack to recapture Hill 100 fails. Major General Roy S. Geiger orders Major General William H. Rupertus to pull the 1st Marines out of the line. The Umurbrogol Pocket has nearly destroyed the regiment. The 321st Infantry Regiment of the 81st Division is to arrive as reinforcements. The 1st Marines have by now lost 1,749 men and have captured 10 coral ridges, 22 pillboxes, three blockhouses, 13 antitank guns, and have cleared 144 defended caves. The Umurbrogol has been hardly touched. The 7th Marines attack into the area called the Wildcat Bowl toward Hill 140.

New Guinea: FEAF P-39 Airacobras, P-47 Thunderbolts, P-38 Lightnings, and P-40s attack antiaircraft positions and logistics sites at Moemi and Ransiki airfields.

B-24 Liberators bomb Amboina and Celebes Islands. P-38 Lightnings and B-25 Mitchells bomb targets on Celebes Island, an airfield on Buru Island, and a barge off Halmahera Island.

September 22

CBI: Tenth Air Force sends 13 B-24 Liberators to fly fuel to Kunming, China.

In China, Fourteenth Air Force sends 24 B-24 Liberators to bomb Hankow. B-25 Mitchells and P-51 Mustangs attack transportation targets at Hengyang and Yungming. P-40s and P-51 Mustangs attack convoys near Changsha and troops, gun positions, rail lines, bridges, and roads near Chuanhsien, Lingling, Hankow, and Kiyang.

ATLANTIC: German submarine *U-979* torpedoes a U.S. Navy storeship off Reykjavik, Iceland.

ETO: Allied commanders meet in Versailles to clarify strategy and establish priorities for future operations. It is deemed essential that the 21st Army Group open the port of Antwerp if any major offensive is to take place. Without the port, the Allies are very limited in what they can do. Once Antwerp is taken, the 21st Army Group will take operational control of the U.S. First Army and cross the Rhine River in the north. The 12th Army Group will extend its front northward toward Cologne. The 6th Army Group (the U.S. Seventh Army and the French First Army) will move to occupy Strasbourg and Alsace.

Eighth Air Force sends nearly 80 P-47 Thunderbolts to support the British paratroopers at Arnhem. One P-47 is lost and one is damaged.

Over 450 B-17s and 200 B-24 Liberators escorted by 268 P-51 Mustangs attack vehicle production facilities in western Germany. Three bombers are lost and 107 are damaged. Aircrew casualties are seven killed and 27 missing. One P-51 is lost and the pilot is reported missing. One fighter is damaged.

Over 100 B-24s fly fuel to France to support ground forces as logistics lines are stretched to the breaking point.

A Frantic mission is completed with the arrival of 84 B-17s and 51 P-51s in Britain from airfields in Italy.

MEDITERRANEAN: Fifteenth Air Force sends more than 360 B-17s and B-24 Liberators escorted by 270 P-38 Lightnings and P-51 Mustangs to attack an airfield and industrial area of Munich, Germany. Another 76 B-24s bomb the marshaling yard at Larissa, Greece.

Over 60 B-24s fly fuel to France to support ground forces.

ITALY: Twelfth Air Force B-25 Mitchells and B-26 Marauders attack rail bridges. A-20 Havocs and P-47 Thunderbolts attack roads and rail bridges as the Germans withdraw from Pistoia.

The headquarters of the 87th Fighter Wing redeploys from Corsica to Italy.

First Lieutenant Orville E. Bloch, E Company, 338th Infantry Regiment, 85th Infantry Division, distinguishes himself through several acts of extraordinary courage when he personally eliminates five German machine-gun positions near Firenzuola, Italy. Attacking the first position, he forces five Germans to surrender. Arming a hand grenade, Lieutenant Bloch then runs toward the next machine-gun position at the corner of a building and eliminates the defenders. Bloch burst into the doorway of the building, firing his carbine from the hip as the German defenders fire furiously in his direction. Bloch wounds three enemy soldiers and forces the other seven to surrender. As another machine gun is put into action at the next corner of the building, Lieutenant Bloch assaults the position, again firing his carbine from his hip as he wounds two and forces another six soldiers to surrender. In this one action Lieutenant Bloch is responsible for capturing 19 German soldiers and clearing a formidable defensive position. For his heroism and determination to overcome all odds, First Lieutenant Bloch will receive the Medal of Honor.

SOUTHWEST PACIFIC AREA: Carrier aircraft from Naval Task Force 38 continue attacks on Japanese shipping in the Philippines. A gunboat, two auxiliary submarine chasers, a cargo ship, and three tankers are sunk. An auxiliary submarine chaser and two cargo ships are damaged.

U.S. submarine *Narwhal* lands personnel and supplies on the southwest coast of Mindanao.

CENTRAL PACIFIC: Seventh Air Force sends 15 B-24 Liberators from Saipan to bomb Chichi Jima.

B-25 Mitchells from Makin Island bomb Nauru Island.

The 323rd Infantry Regiment of the 81st Infantry Division makes an unopposed landing on the island of Ulithi.

CENTRAL PACIFIC, PELELIU: The 1st Marines are relieved after suffering 56 percent casualties. Along with the 2nd Battalion 7th Marines, the unit has lost a total of 1,838 men.

The 321st Infantry Regiment of the 81st Infantry Division lands at Peleliu and is under the operational control of the 1st Marine Division.

NEW GUINEA: At Morotai, a battalion of the 167th Infantry Regiment, 31st Infantry Division, repulses a weak Japanese counterattack.

FEAF A-20 Havocs bomb Utarom airfield, while P-39 Airacobras, P-47 Thunderbolts, P-38 Lightnings, and P-40s attack other targets in northwestern New Guinea.

B-24 Liberators bomb Celebes Island; B-24s and B-25 Mitchells bomb Ceram Island, Ambon Island, and the airfield on Haroekoe Island.

U.S. submarine *Lapon* torpedoes and damages a cargo ship west of Celebes Island.

U.S. submarine *Pargo* makes an unsuccessful attack on a Japanese cargo vessel and avoids a destroyer depth-charge attack.

September 23

CBI: Tenth Air Force sends 19 P-47 Thunderbolts to attack bridges from Wanlin to Bhamo to Myitkyina. Aircrews report one bridge destroyed. A total of 21 B-24 Liberators fly fuel to Kunming and Liuchow, China.

In China, Fourteenth Air Force sends 15 B-24 Liberators to attack targets on the Burma Road near Chefang. Other B-24s bomb the docks at Amoy. B-25 Mitchells attack Chuanhsien, Yungming, and Lungling. P-40s and P-51 Mustangs attack Japanese troop concentrations, gun positions, rail lines, bridges, and highways near Chuanhsien, Yungming, and Lingling.

ATLANTIC: Due to the continuation of the war in Europe after the failure of Market Garden, logistics assessments by JCS planners confirm that an invasion of Formosa (Operation Causeway) is not possible in 1944. Planning for Causeway was based on the assumption that the war in Europe would be over in December 1944, and both support troops and supplies would be available to support an invasion. Luzon is supportable logistically with resources currently available in the Pacific and can be accomplished in 1944. U.S. forces will most likely isolate and bypass Formosa and turn to the Bonin Islands and the Ryukyus instead for long-range bomber bases, which will support an eventual invasion of Japan.

ETO: Eighth Air Force sends more than 500 P-38 Lightnings, P-47 Thunderbolts, and P-51 Mustangs to attack antiaircraft positions and ground targets near Nijmegen, as the paratroopers of the 82nd and 101st Airborne Divisions and the Polish 1st Brigade make an airborne assault to reinforce troops already in combat. Over 150 German fighters attack the Americans. Pilots report 27 confirmed kills and two probables in the air. A total of 14 U.S. fighters are lost and 37 are damaged. One pilot is wounded and 14 others are reported missing.

Over 160 B-24s fly fuel to France to support ground forces.

MEDITERRANEAN: Fifteenth Air Force sends 147 B-17s, escorted by 290 P-38 Lightnings and P-51 Mustangs, to attack a synthetic oil refinery in Czechoslovakia and a marshaling yard in Austria.

ITALY: Twelfth Air Force B-25 Mitchells and B-26 Marauders attack rail bridges in the Po River valley. A-20 Havocs and P-47 Thunderbolts attack gun positions, and rail and road targets along the Gothic Line.

SOUTHWEST PACIFIC AREA: Lieutenant General Walter Krueger's Sixth Army headquarters issues the approved plan for the Leyte landing. Three days before the landings, the 6th Ranger Battalion will occupy Dinagat Island, Homonhon Island, and Suluan Island at the entrance to Leyte Gulf. The X Corps (1st Cavalry Division and 24th Infantry Division, minus the 21st Infantry Regiment, which has been organized as a separate regimental combat team) under command of Major General Franklin C. Sibert will land to capture the city of Tacloban, the airfield at Tacloban, and Palo. The corps is then to control the San Juanico Straits to the east of Leyte Island and advance rapidly through the Leyte Valley to the north coast and capture Capoocan, Barugo, and Cariga on Carigara Bay and destroy Japanese forces in the area. The XXIV Corps (7th and 96th Infantry Divisions, minus the 381st Infantry Regiment, operating as a separate regimental combat team) under the command of Major General John R. Hodge will land at Dulag and attack westward to destroy enemy forces and occupy the Dagami-Burauen area. If necessary, the corps will move south to capture Abuyog and Baybay. The 21st Infantry Regiment and the 6th Ranger Battalion will land at Cabalian Bay on the extreme southern tip of the island, secure the strait between Leyte and Panoan Islands, and attack north to link with XXIV Corps. The X and XXIV Corps will then clear Japanese forces from the Ormoc Valley and the west coast of the island. The 32nd and 77th Infantry Divisions and the 381st RCT will be in reserve, ready to be landed within 24 hours three days after the initial invasion to support the operations of either XXIV Corps or X Corps. Philippine troops are to be placed under Sixth Army's operational control once the U.S. forces are established ashore. Lieutenant General George C. Kenney's Far East Air Force (FEAF) with over 2,500 aircraft will provide no land-based air support. The plan depends on a rapid seizure of Leyte so that Kenney can bring in aircraft to support the ground forces. Air support for the invasion will come from two sources. The first is Vice Admiral Thomas C. Kinkaid's Seventh Fleet, with its light carriers supporting about 500 aircraft. Kinkaid is under the operational control of MacArthur. The other source is Admiral William F. Halsey's Third Fleet, with its fleet carriers and over 1,000 aircraft. Halsey, however, will only be in support of

MacArthur. Still under Nimitz's operational control, Halsey's primary mission is to destroy the Japanese fleet if the opportunity arises, "or could be created," in Nimitz's words. The date of the landing, October 20, is designated as A-day. Leyte Island's defenders are estimated to be about 20,000 men.

PACIFIC: Battleship USS *West Virginia* returns to Pearl Harbor and rejoins the Pacific Fleet. The *West Virginia* is the last ship repaired from the December 7, 1941, attack on Pearl Harbor.

U.S. submarine *Apogon* torpedoes and sinks a Japanese guardboat east of Honshu, Japan.

U.S. submarine *Escolar* departs Midway on her first war patrol.

CENTRAL PACIFIC: Seventh Air Force sends 15 B-24 Liberators from Saipan to bomb Chichi Jima, Haha Jima, and Ani Jima Islands. A B-24 from Kwajalein Atoll makes a night raid on Wake Island.

Naval Task Group 33.19 (Rear Admiral William H. P. Blandy) lands the 323rd Regimental Combat Team, 81st Infantry Division, on Ulithi Atoll in the Carolines.

CENTRAL PACIFIC, PELELIU: The Japanese begin reinforcing Peleliu from Koror and Babelthuap Islands. The army's 321st Infantry Regiment, 81st Infantry Division, is committed to the battle. Major General William H. Rupertus meets with Major General Roy S. Geiger and the III Amphibious Corps staff to lay out a plan to isolate and eliminate Japanese defenses in the Umurbrogol. The 321st Infantry and the 5th Marines are to flank the enemy by moving on the west road while the 7th Marines press from the south. There is an hour-long artillery bombardment of the cliffs near the west road to clear the advance.

NEW GUINEA: At Morotai, elements of the 126th Infantry Regiment encounter Japanese troops dug in on Hill 575. An American attack fails to capture the position. That night, the enemy abandons the position.

FEAF P-47 Thunderbolts and P-40s bomb antiaircraft guns at Manokwari, Moemi, and Ransiki airfields.

B-24 Liberators and B-25 Mitchells bomb airfields on Celebes Island. P-47 Thunderbolts attack an airfield on Halmahera Island.

Headquarters, Thirteenth Air Force redeploys from Hollandia to Noemfoor Island. P-47s of the 460th Fighter Squadron, 348th Fighter Group, redeploy from Nadzab to Noemfoor Island.

A Japanese gunboat and transport are damaged by mines laid by U.S. submarine *Bowfin* on January 29 off Balikpapan, Borneo.

September 24

ALEUTIANS: Eleventh Air Force sends eight B-24 Liberators to bomb Kurabu Cape airfield on Paramushiru Island. Twelve Japanese fighters attack and damage two of the bombers. One B-24 is forced to land in the Soviet Union. Aircrews report one confirmed kill.

CBI: Tenth Air Force sends 11 B-24 Liberators to fly fuel to Liuchow, China. P-47 Thunderbolts attack bridges and troops near Bhamo.

In China, Fourteenth Air Force sends 26 B-25 Mitchells to bomb White Cloud airfield at Canton.

ETO: In Operation Market Garden, the British Second Army arrives at the lower Rhine. Eighth Air Force sends 47 B-24 Liberators to fly fuel to France to support ground forces.

Ninth Air Force sends P-47 and P-38 fighters of the XIX Tactical Air Command to support the 7th Armored Division of the Third Army.

The B-26 Marauders of the 572nd Bombardment Squadron (Medium), 391st Bombardment Group (Medium), redeploy from England to France.

The XII Corps of the Third Army stops a German counterattack at Chateau Salins.

Staff Sergeant Joseph E. Schaefer is a squad leader in the 2nd Platoon of I Company, 18th Infantry Regiment, 1st Infantry Division, defending an important crossroads near Stolberg, Germany. Two German infantry companies, supported by machine guns, launch an early morning attack and overwhelm the defenders, leaving only Staff Sergeant Schaefer's squad still capable of fighting. Moving his men to a nearby house, he puts them into position and then stands by the main entrance, which is the focus of enemy fire on the building. There, using his M-1 rifle, he stops the first assault. He also stops a second attack as the Germans employ grenades and flame throwers against the squad's position. A third assault comes from two directions. Staff Sergeant Schaefer kills the attackers approaching his doorway, then dashes out in full view of the enemy to engage the second attacking force from a hedgerow. As the enemy withdraws, he captures 10 soldiers. As the Americans begin a counterattack, Schaefer advances to retake the lost position, crawling and running in the face of heavy fire, and is able to free a squad of captured American soldiers. For his leadership against overwhelming odds and dedication to duty, Staff Sergeant Schaefer will receive the Medal of Honor.

MEDITERRANEAN: Fifteenth Air Force sends more than 360 B-17s and B-24 Liberators escorted by P-38 Lightnings and P-51 Mustangs to bomb airfields, port facilities, and a marshaling yard in Greece.

ITALY: Twelfth Air Force P-47 Thunderbolts attack German strongpoints, troop concentrations, and communications targets along the Fifth Army's front.

SOUTHWEST PACIFIC AREA: Naval Task Force 38's carrier aircraft sink eight cargo ships and damage an ammunition ship, four cargo ships, a supply ship, an oiler, a tanker, a small cargo ship, a torpedo boat, a minelayer, a submarine chaser, an auxiliary submarine chaser, an auxiliary minesweeper, and a transport. A tanker is sunk in the South China Sea. A supply ship, a cargo ship, and an oiler are damaged.

U.S. submarine *Barbero* bombards a Japanese radar installation on Batag Island off the north coast of Samar in the Philippines.

CENTRAL PACIFIC: Seventh Air Force B-24 Liberators from Saipan bomb Chichi Jima. B-25 Mitchells from the Gilberts bomb Nauru and Ponape Islands. B-24s from Kwajalein bomb Truk.

In the Marianas, 16 P-47 Thunderbolts attack antiaircraft positions on Rota Island.

The 323rd Infantry Regiment secures Ulithi Atoll. As the battle for Peleliu rages on, Ulithi Atoll and not Peleliu will become the major naval base for future operations.

CENTRAL PACIFIC, PELELIU: Marine fighter aircraft begin operating from the airfield on the island. The 321st Infantry Regiment captures Hill 100 in the Umurbrogol. For the next three days the infantrymen battle the Japanese. Colonel Robert F. Dark, the commander of the regiment, forms mobile task forces of tanks and infantry armed with flamethrowers to dislodge the defenders from their positions. Task Force Neal, commanded by Captain George C. Neal, takes tanks and infantry north, then turns south to support the fight to hold Hill 100.

NEW GUINEA: FEAF P-47 Thunderbolts, P-38 Lightnings, and P-40s attack airfields in northwestern New Guinea.

B-24 Liberators and B-25 Mitchells bomb airfields on Ceram Island, Buru Island, and Haroekoe Island. Other B-24s bomb Timor.

September 25

CBI: Generalissimo Chiang Kai-shek responds to President Roosevelt's September 19 letter by attacking General Stilwell personally, refusing under any circumstances to appoint him as commander of Chinese forces, and demands that he be replaced. In effect, the Generalissimo tells the president that the future of Chinese-American relations hangs on whether or not General Stilwell remains as theater commander.

Tenth Air Force sends 19 B-24 Liberators to fly fuel to Kunming, Liuchow, and Yungning in China.

In China, Fourteenth Air Force B-25 Mitchells bomb Mangshih, Kweiyang, and the Hengyang railyards. B-24 Liberators bomb Nanking. Over 100 P-51 Mustangs and P-40s fly armed reconnaissance over the area south of the Yangtze River, attacking bridges, town areas, troop concentrations, and various targets of opportunity.

ETO: In Operation Market Garden, the 2,163 survivors of the British 1st Airborne Division withdraw across the Rhine to safety. The paratroopers leave 7,000 of their comrades behind—dead, wounded, missing, or captured. The U.S. 82nd Airborne Division has lost 1,432 men, and the 101st Airborne Division has 2,110 casualties. The failure of Market Garden blemishes Montgomery's standing within Eisenhower's headquarters. He will no longer have the influence he once had. By deciding on a quick thrust over the Rhine River instead of capturing Antwerp, Montgomery's failure has made Eisenhower's logistics problem only worse. The optimism that the war in Europe was near an end is shattered, and a period of stalemate on the front lines now begins.

General Bradley orders First Army to protect the flank of Montgomery's 21st Army Group; when sufficiently resupplied and reinforced, Lieutenant General Courtney H. Hodges's divisions will attack toward the Rhine River and Bonn and Cologne. Lieutenant General George S. Patton, Jr.'s Third Army will hold in place. Lieutenant General William H. Simpson's Ninth Army will occupy the area before the Ardennes Forest when it arrives from Brittany. The 94th Infantry Division is given the task of containing German forces holding ports in Brittany and is under 12th Army Group's operational control.

Eighth Air Force sends nearly 1,000 B-17s escorted by 410 P-38 Lightnings and P-51 Mustangs to attack the Ludwigshafen oil facility and marshaling yard and Frankfurt am Main industrial area. Five B-17s are lost and 128 damaged. Aircrew casualties are nine wounded and 18 missing. Two fighters are lost and one is damaged. The two pilots are reported missing.

Over 250 B-24 Liberators escorted by 157 P-38 Lightnings, P-47 Thunderbolts, and P-51 Mustangs bomb marshaling yards at Koblenz. Fourteen B-24s are damaged. One P-51 is lost, and the pilot is reported missing.

A total of 176 B-24s fly fuel to France to support the ground forces. One bomber is lost.

Ninth Air Force P-47 and P-38 fighters support ground forces and conduct dive-bombing attacks on rail lines.

The A-20 Havocs of the 668th Bombardment Squadron (Light), 416th Bombardment Group (Light), redeploy from England to France as do the B-26 Marauders of the 449th Bombardment Squadron (Medium), 322nd Bombardment Group (Medium).

MEDITERRANEAN: Fifteenth Air Force sends 51 B-24 Liberators escorted by P-38 Lightnings and P-51 Mustangs to attack port facilities in Greece.

Fourteenth Air Force B-24 Liberators sink two German submarines (*U-565* and *U-596*) off Salamis, Greece.

ITALY: The 88th Infantry Division captures Castel del Rio.

Twelfth Air Force A-20 Havocs and P-47 Thunderbolts attack road and rail targets, troops, bridges, and ground support forces.

SOUTHWEST PACIFIC AREA: U.S. submarine *Nautilus* lands supplies on Cebu.

PACIFIC: U.S. submarine *Barbel* torpedoes and sinks a Japanese cargo ship west of the Ryukyu Islands. U.S. submarines *Guardfish* and *Thresher* each torpedo and sink a Japanese cargo ship in the Yellow Sea.

U.S. submarine *Searaven* torpedoes and sinks a small vessel in the Kuriles.

CENTRAL PACIFIC: Seventh Air Force B-24 Liberators from Saipan bomb Iwo Jima. During the night B-24s from Kwajalein stage through Eniwetok to bomb Truk. Most miss the primary target and bomb Wake, Param, and Moem Islands.

Seventh Air Force B-24 Liberators from Saipan bomb targets on the Bonin Islands.

CENTRAL PACIFIC, PELELIU: The 1st Battalion of the 5th Marines captures the radio station complex; the 3rd Battalion of the 5th Marines then attacks to capture the ridges beyond. The marines now have established a strong position on the north and west sections of the island.

Private First Class John D. New of the 2nd Battalion, 7th Marines, 1st Marine Division, is occupying an observation post with two other marines when he spots a Japanese soldier emerging from a cave in a cliff above them. The soldier tosses a grenade that lands in the midst of the three marines. Private First Class New dives on the grenade and is killed, but he saves the lives of his comrades. For his courage and willingness to sacrifice himself for his comrades, Private First Class New will receive the Medal of Honor.

NEW GUINEA: Lieutenant General Walter Krueger's Alamo Force is redesignated as U.S. Sixth Army. The Alamo Force's accomplishments in the New Guinea campaign are impressive. Krueger and his staff have orchestrated and brought to reality General MacArthur's vision, conducting simultaneous and sequential operations effectively coordinating land, air, and naval power in a combination intended to place the Japanese at a disadvantage. American forces have fought a determined enemy who had little choice but to fight and die honorably. The jungles and islands of New Guinea have some of the most forbidding and inhospitable terrain in the world, and yet Americans have defeated the Japanese, recognized experts in this warfare, and then carved, blasted, and dug pathways into the jungle for airfields, depots, and ports that ultimately overwhelmed the enemy and opened the way to the Philippines.

Sixth Army is composed of two corps, I Corps, commanded by Major General Innis P. Swift, and X Corps, commanded by Major General Edwin D. Patrick. General MacArthur also establishes the U.S. Eighth Army, commanded by Lieutenant General Robert L. Eichelberger.

FEAF B-25 Mitchells, A-20 Havocs, and P-40s attack airfields in northwestern New Guinea. A-20s attack logistics storage areas on Halmahera Island. B-24 Liberators bomb Buru Island airfield. B-24s and B-25 Mitchells along with P-38 Lightnings attack airfields on Celebes Island.

September 26

ALEUTIANS: Eleventh Air Force B-24 Liberators use radar-guided bombing to attack Suribachi airfield in the Kurile Islands.

CBI: The Japanese Eleventh Army captures the Tanchuck airfield after the Fourteenth Air Force abandons it.

Tenth Air Force sends 19 B-24 Liberators to fly fuel to Liuchow, Yangtong, and Yungning.

In China, Fourteenth Air Force B-25 Mitchells bomb Lungfukwan and Mangshih. P-40s and P-51 Mustangs attack bridges, town areas, troop concentrations, and various targets of opportunity.

ETO: A total of 320 P-47 Thunderbolts and P-51 Mustangs from Eighth Air Force and P-38 Lightnings from Ninth Air Force provide ground support to the paratroopers of the First Allied Airborne Army in Holland. Fighter pilots report 32 confirmed kills and one probable. One P-38 is lost and 10 fighters are damaged; the pilot is reported missing. Eighth Air Force sends nearly 700 B-17s escorted by more than 230 P-51 Mustangs to attack the marshaling yard and steel plant at Osnabrück and the marshaling yard at Hamm. One B-17 is lost and three are damaged. Aircrew casualties are two killed, 12 wounded, and 39 missing. Fighter pilots report two confirmed kills. One P-51 is lost and three are damaged; the pilot is reported missing.

A total of 165 B-24s fly fuel to France to resupply the ground forces.

During the night six B-17s and three B-24s drop leaflets over Germany, France, and the Netherlands.

Ninth Air Force sends P-47 and P-38 fighters of the XIX Tactical Air Command to support the Third Army's operations against Metz. The IX Tactical Air Command P-38 Lightnings and P-47s fly armed reconnaissance missions and provide support to the First Army, attacking rail lines across the Rhine River from Bonn.

The A-20 Havocs of the 646th Bombardment Squadron (Light), 410th Bombardment Group (Light), redeploy from England to France.

The headquarters of the U.S. Strategic Air Forces in Europe (USSTAF) redeploys from England to France.

ITALY: Twelfth Air Force B-25 Mitchells and B-26 Marauders attack rail and road traffic and bridges in the Po River valley. A-20 Havocs and P-47 Thunderbolts attack convoys, bridges, logistics storage areas, and roads in the Po Valley.

SOUTHWEST PACIFIC AREA: A new version of the Musketeer plan is prepared. The original plan was to land on Mindoro as soon as possible after the Leyte landings. The Mindoro operation is scheduled for December 5. MacArthur wants to attack Luzon as soon as possible after the Leyte operation is assured of success. The Joint Chiefs of Staff are uncertain which direction to follow after Leyte—continue to Luzon or bypass Luzon for Formosa.

PACIFIC: Twentieth Air Force sends 83 B-29 Superfortresses from Chengtu to bomb Anshan. Nearly all bomb the Showa Steel Works or Dairen, Sinsiang, or targets of opportunity. After the return of the bombers, Japanese aircraft bomb Chengtu and damage five B-29s during the night.

The X Corps commander, Lieutenant General Simon B. Buckner, who is responsible for the land forces for Operation Causeway (the invasion of Formosa) assesses that there are insufficient service and support troops in-theater to make the invasion successful.

U.S. submarine *Thresher* torpedoes and sinks a Japanese cargo ship in the Yellow Sea.

CENTRAL PACIFIC: Seventh Air Force B-24 Liberators from the Marshall Islands conduct a night bombing raid on Wake Island. B-25 Mitchells from the Gilbert Islands bomb Nauru Island.

Destroyer escort USS *McCoy Reynolds* sinks Japanese submarine *I-175* northeast of the Palau Islands.

CENTRAL PACIFIC, PELELIU: The 321st Infantry Regiment continues to battle to hold Hill 100 and Hill B. The 5th Marines attack into the Umurbrogol to capture the four hills in an area called Hill Row. This area is defended by 1,500 Japanese troops fighting from caves linked by tunnels.

NEW GUINEA: FEAF B-24 Liberators and B-25 Mitchells bomb airfields on Ambon Island and Celebes Island.

B-24s of the 31st Bombardment Squadron (Heavy), 5th Bombardment Group (Heavy), redeploy from Wakde Island to Noemfoor Island, and the B-24s of the 424th Bombardment Squadron (Heavy), 307th Bombardment Group (Medium), redeploy from Wakde Island to Noemfoor Island.

U.S. submarine *Pargo* torpedoes and sinks a Japanese minelayer off Borneo.

September 27

CBI: Tenth Air Force P-47 Thunderbolts attack ammunition storage sites, rail bridges, and troop positions in Burma. A total of 10 B-24 Liberators fly fuel to Liuchow and Yungning, China.

In China, Fourteenth Air Force P-40s and P-51 Mustangs attack troop concentrations, gun positions, rail lines, bridges, and roads near Kiyang, Chuanhsien, and Lingling.

ETO: The Third Army's XX Corps under Major General Walton H. Walker attacks the city of Metz, one of the most heavily fortified cities in the world. The 11th Infantry Regiment of the 5th Infantry Division, supported by a company of tanks from the 818th Tank Destroyer Battalion, attacks Fort Driant and fails.

Eighth Air Force sends more than 800 B-17s using radar-equipped Pathfinders escorted by more than 400 P-47 Thunderbolts and P-51 Mustangs to attack Ludwigshafen oil refinery and transportation targets. Two B-17s are lost and 308 damaged. Aircrew casualties are six killed, 16 wounded, and 20 missing. Fighter pilots report six confirmed kills. Four fighters are damaged.

Another 315 B-24 Liberators escorted by 207 P-38 Lightnings, P-47 Thunderbolts, and P-51 Mustangs are sent to attack the aircraft production facility at Kassel. Aircrews report five confirmed kills and three probables. A total of 26 B-24s are lost and 47 are damaged. Aircrew casualties are 20 killed, two wounded, and 245 missing. Pilots report 25 confirmed kills in the air and five on the ground. Two P-51s are lost and five fighters are damaged. The pilot is reported missing.

A total of 163 B-24s fly fuel to France to resupply the ground forces.

During the night eight B-17s drop leaflets over Germany, France, and the Netherlands.

Ninth Air Force redeploys the A-20 Havocs of the 644th Bombardment Squadron (Light), 410th Bombardment Group (Light), from England to France.

ITALY: Twelfth Air Force A-20 Havocs bomb motor transport in the Po Valley during the night.

P-47 Thunderbolts attack German defenses at Monte Oggioli and attack roads and motor transport, and bomb rail lines between Parma and Piacenza.

The 88th Infantry Division approaches Imola as the 2nd Battalion of the 350th Infantry Regiment captures Monte Battaglia and defends it against heavy counterattacks. II Corps, on Route 65, pushes past Radicosa Pass.

Captain Robert E. Roeder commands G Company, 350th Infantry Regiment, 88th Infantry Division, defending positions on Monte Battaglia. German forces direct several determined counterattacks to recapture the critical terrain. Captain Roeder directs the defense, moving among his men while artillery and rifle fire rain on the company's position. The Germans fail in five attempts, but make a sixth counterattack in the fog using flamethrowers and are able to make a breakthrough. Roeder personally leads the assault to recapture the lost positions and drives the enemy off with heavy casualties. The next morning Roeder is wounded by an artillery shell; after regaining consciousness, he refuses medical treatment and rejoins the battle. Unable to stand, he props himself in a position so that he can be seen by his men, and shouts encouragement as he fires his weapon on advancing German soldiers. He is killed shortly thereafter by another artillery shell. Captain Roeder's valiant defense of a critical position, his dedication to duty, and his spirited leadership will win him the Medal of Honor.

SOUTHWEST PACIFIC AREA: U.S. submarine *Bonefish* torpedoes and damages a Japanese oiler southwest of Manila.

USS *Flasher* and USS *Lapon* attack a Japanese convoy in the South China Sea west of Luzon. USS *Flasher* sinks an army transport and damages a tanker; USS

Lapon sinks a tanker. U.S. submarine *Narwhal* lands supplies on the north coast of Mindanao, and U.S. submarine *Stingray* lands supplies on the east coast of Luzon.

PACIFIC: U.S. submarine *Apogon* torpedoes and sinks a Japanese cargo ship off Shimushir Island, Kuriles. U.S. submarine *Searaven* torpedoes and damages a Japanese destroyer in the Kuriles.

U.S. submarine *Plaice* torpedoes and sinks a Japanese coastal patrol ship west of the Ryukyus.

CENTRAL PACIFIC: Seventh Air Force B-24 Liberators from the Marshalls bomb Truk.

At Angaur, the battle for the Bowl continues as the 322nd Infantry Regiment, having turned back a Japanese counterattack, closes in on three sides of the defensive position, using a combination of heavy artillery, tanks, and bulldozers.

CENTRAL PACIFIC, PELELIU: The 321st Infantry Regiment clears Japanese positions with tanks and flamethrowers while the 8th Marines bring their 155 millimeter guns to within 180 yards of Amiangal Ridge in the Umurbrogol to destroy Japanese positions. The infantrymen and marines find that they are able to control only the ground they stand on. The Japanese control everything else, even the ground below their feet. The Japanese are able to attack at will from any direction, using interconnected tunnels and multiple, nearly invisible firing positions.

NEW GUINEA: FEAF P-40s attack airfields at Ransiki, Kokas, and Warren and bomb shipping around the Vogelkop Peninsula.

B-24 Liberators bomb troops and logistics storage sites on Celebes Island. B-25 Mitchells bomb oil storage tanks on Ceram Island and the airfield on Buru Island.

The B-24s of the 72nd and 394th Bombardment Squadrons (Heavy), 5th Bombardment Group (Heavy), redeploy from Wakde Island to Noemfoor Island. The headquarters of the 35th Fighter Group redeploys to Morotai Island.

A Navy PBY Catalina damages a Japanese cargo ship off Jolo Island in the Celebes Sea.

September 28

CBI: Tenth Air Force sends 26 B-24 Liberators to fly fuel to Liuchow, Yungning, and Kunming, China.

Fourteenth Air Force B-25 Mitchells attack Tien Ho and White Cloud airfields at Canton and river and road traffic around Lingling, Siangtan, and Chuchou. P-40s and P-51 Mustangs attack troop concentrations, gun positions, rail lines, bridges, and roads in southeast China.

ETO: The VI Corps of Seventh Army makes rapid progress in the foothills of the Vosges Mountains, but is halted by a combination of heavy rains and strong German resistance along the Meurthe River. The VI Corps halts to rest and refit in preparation for an offensive in October to clear the passages in the Vosges Mountains.

Eighth Air Force sends more than 750 B-17s escorted by over 450 P-38 Lightnings and P-51 Mustangs to attack oil refineries in Germany. Aircrews report 10 confirmed kills and seven probables. A total of 33 B-17s are lost and 383 damaged. Aircrew casualties are four killed, 23 wounded, and 300 missing. Fighter pilots report 26 confirmed kills and one probable in the air and one confirmed kill on the ground. Six fighters are lost and five are damaged. Six pilots are reported missing.

Another 262 B-24 Liberators escorted by 171 P-47 Thunderbolts are sent to bomb the motor production facility at Kassel. One B-24 is lost and 86 are damaged. Aircrew casualties are 10 missing. One P-47 is lost, and three are damaged. The pilot is reported missing.

A total of 194 B-24s fly fuel to France to resupply the ground forces.

During the night six B-17s and four B-24s drop leaflets over Germany, France, and the Netherlands.

Ninth Air Force sends P-47 and P-38 fighters to attack German positions around Arnhem as the British 1st Airborne Division crosses the Rhine to return to friendly lines, thus ending the Market Garden operation.

The headquarters of the 410th Bombardment Group (Light) redeploys from England to France, as do the A-20 Havocs of the 645th and 647th Bombardment Squadrons (Light), 410th Bombardment Group (Light).

ITALY: The 350th Infantry Regiment of the 88th Infantry Division holds Monte Battaglia against a strong German counterattack. The U.S. II Corps advances after the Germans withdraw from Radicosa Pass.

SOUTHWEST PACIFIC AREA: U.S. submarine *Bonefish* torpedoes and sinks a Japanese merchant tanker in the South China Sea west of Luzon.

CENTRAL PACIFIC: Seventh Air Force B-24 Liberators from Saipan bomb naval installations at Chichi Jima.

CENTRAL PACIFIC, PELELIU: The 3rd Battalion of the 5th Marines seizes Ngesebus and Kongauru, two small islands north of Peleliu. The marines use tanks to clear out positions defended by about 500 Japanese troops, with the support of naval gunfire (one battleship and 12 cruisers), marine artillery, and marine aircraft.

NEW GUINEA: FEAF P-47 Thunderbolts attack Manokwari airfield. B-25 Mitchells and A-20 Havocs attack shipping and the airfield on Celebes Island. P-38 Lightnings attack barges in the Molucca Islands.

Navy PBY Catalinas sink a Japanese cargo ship in the Makassar Straits.

September 29

ALEUTIANS: Eleventh Air Force sends two B-24 Liberators to bomb the Katooka naval base and Kokutan Cape in the Kurile Islands.

CBI: Tenth Air Force sends 11 B-25 Mitchells to attack antiaircraft positions and bridges on the Burma Road near Uambkai. Aircrews report the main bridge is damaged and the bypass bridge is destroyed. Eighteen B-24 Liberators fly fuel to Yungning, Liuchow, and Kunming, China.

In China, Fourteenth Air Force sends B-25 Mitchells to bomb Tien Ho and White Cloud airfields at Canton. Nearly 100 P-51 Mustangs, P-40s, and P-38 Lightnings bomb road and rail junctions, bridges, town areas, troop concentrations, and various targets of opportunity south of the Yangtze River.

ATLANTIC: Navy PB4Y Privateers sink German submarine *U-863* in the South Atlantic east of Brazil.

German submarine *U-310* torpedoes and damages a U.S. freighter in a convoy in the Barents Sea as it returns to Scotland from the Soviet port of Archangel. The freighter is scuttled by a British destroyer.

ETO: Lieutenant General Courtney Hodges, commander of First Army, orders an attack to capture Düren and Cologne. The city of Aachen will have to be controlled for First Army to succeed. The XIX Corps under Major General Charles H. Cortlett will attack to the north; VII Corps under Major General J. Lawton Collins will attack to the south. The V Corps is to flank the Roer and gain a bridgehead over the Rhine River near Cologne. The 9th Infantry Division, given the mission of covering the flank of VII Corps as it attacks near Aachen, has fought in the Hürtgen Forest since September 14. The 39th Infantry Regiment captures Hill 554, but is unable to go any farther. The 60th Infantry Regiment, attacking near Hürtgen for nearly 10 days, battles German counterattacks in the marshy woods.

Operational control of XV Corps (the French 2nd Armored Division and the U.S. 79th Infantry Division) passes from Patton's Third Army to Patch's Seventh Army.

During the night Eighth Air Force sends five B-17s and five B-24s to drop leaflets over Germany, France, and the Netherlands.

Ninth Air Force sends more than 400 A-20 Havocs and B-26 Marauders to attack marshaling yards and rail sidings, antitank defenses, warehouses, and barracks. A total of 1,500 P-47 and P-38 fighters escort the bombers and attack rail lines.

The 452nd Bombardment Squadron (Medium), 322nd Bombardment Group (Medium), moves from Great Saling, England, to the B-26s of the 452nd Bombardment Squadron (Medium), 322nd Bombardment Group (Medium), redeploy from England to France.

ITALY: Twelfth Air Force P-47 Thunderbolts attack rail lines south of Milan.

SOUTHWEST PACIFIC AREA: U.S. submarine *Narwhal* evacuates 81 Allied POWs from Mindanao who have survived the sinking of their transport by USS *Paddle* on September 7.

PACIFIC: B-29 Superfortresses make an initial reconnaissance flight over Okinawa.

U.S. submarine *Skate* torpedoes and sinks a Japanese auxiliary minesweeper and a cargo ship west of the Ryukyus.

CENTRAL PACIFIC: Seventh Air Force B-24 Liberators from Saipan bomb Iwo Jima. B-24s from Kwajalein bomb Truk.

CENTRAL PACIFIC, PELELIU: The 3rd Battalion 5th Marines reports Ngesebus is secured and turns the island over to the 2nd Battalion of the 321st Infantry Regiment. The marines then move to division reserve. The 7th Marines takes control of the northern end of the Umurbrogol pocket from the 321st Infantry Regiment.

NEW GUINEA: FEAF A-20 Havocs and Royal Australian Air Force (RAAF) aircraft attack Utarom airfield.

B-24 Liberators bomb airfields on Celebes Island, Ambon Island, and Haroekoe Island.

September 30

CBI: In Burma, Tenth Air Force sends more than 50 P-47 Thunderbolts to attack a railroad bridge and targets of opportunity along the Burma Road between Mangshih and Lashio.

A total of 18 B-24 Liberators fly fuel to Liuchow, Yungning, and Kunming, China.

In China, Fourteenth Air Force sends 29 B-24 Liberators and 12 B-25 Mitchells to bomb Wuchou, Tien Ho, and White Cloud airfields near Canton. Nearly 100 P-51 Mustangs, P-40s, and P-38 Lightnings attack river shipping, road and rail junctions, bridges, town areas, and troop concentrations south of the Yangtze River.

ATLANTIC: Destroyer escort USS *Fessenden* sinks German submarine *U-1062* in the mid-Atlantic.

ETO: SHAEF headquarters estimates that since the D-day landings 1 million German soldiers have been killed, captured, or taken prisoner.

Eighth Air Force sends 570 B-17s using radar-equipped Pathfinder bombers escorted by 417 P-47 Thunderbolts and P-51 Mustangs to attack marshaling yards and airfields in western Germany. A total of seven B-17s are lost and 110 are damaged. Aircrew casualties are one killed, five wounded, and 64 missing. One P-51 is damaged.

Another 255 B-24 Liberators, escorted by 170 P-38 Lightnings, P-47 Thunderbolts, and P-51 Mustangs, are sent to bomb the Hamm marshaling yard. One B-24 is lost and 32 are damaged. Aircrew casualties are 10 missing.

A total of 116 B-24s fly fuel to France to resupply the ground forces.

Ninth Air Force sends 14 B-26 Marauders to bomb the Rhine River bridge at Arnhem. P-47 and P-38 fighters attack rail lines and rail cars in western Germany.

The headquarters of the 344th Bombardment Group (Medium) and the B-26s of the 494th 495th, 496th, and 497th Bombardment Squadrons (Medium) redeploy from England to France.

ITALY: Twelfth Air Force B-25 Mitchells bomb road and rail bridges in the Po River valley. B-26 Marauders bomb fuel storage areas and bridges. P-47 Thunderbolts of XII Fighter Command attack vehicles, rail lines, roads, and bridges in the Po Valley.

SOUTHWEST PACIFIC AREA: U.S. submarine *Nautilus* lands supplies and evacuates personnel from Panay Island in the Philippines.

CENTRAL PACIFIC: The headquarters of the 494th Bombardment Group (Heavy) and the B-24 Liberators of the 864th, 865th, 866th, and 867th Bombardment Squadrons (Heavy) deploy from Hawaii to Angaur Island in the Palau Islands. The squadrons' first missions are scheduled for late November.

CENTRAL PACIFIC, PELELIU: Major General William H. Rupertus, still wanting the capture of the island to be a marine show, moves the 321st Infantry Regiment to occupy the northern half of the island while two depleted marine regiments are ordered to finish the battle in the Umurbrogol. The 7th Marines battle the Japanese for control of Walt and Boyd Ridges, which dominate the east side of the Umurbrogol Pocket.

NEW GUINEA: FEAF A-20 Havocs, P-47 Thunderbolts, and P-40s attack airfields in northwestern New Guinea.

P-38 Lightnings attack targets on Ceram Island, seaplane bases on Celebes Island, and the airfield on Haroekoe Island. B-24 Liberators attack oil storage areas at Balikpapan, Borneo, and the airfield on Celebes Island. B-25 Mitchells attack shipping on Halmahera Island.

B-24s of the 23rd Bombardment Squadron (Heavy) of the 5th Bombardment Group (Heavy) redeploy from Wakde Island to Noemfoor Island.

October 1

CBI: Tenth Air Force P-47 Thunderbolts bomb rail targets throughout northern Burma and sweep the Burma Road area. In China, Fourteenth Air Force sends 18 B-25 Mitchells to bomb Tien Ho and White Cloud airfields near Canton. Over 100 P-51 Mustangs, P-40s, and P-38 Lightnings attack road and rail junctions, bridges, town areas, troop concentrations, and various targets of opportunity south of the Yangtze River and around Mangshih and Hsinganhsien.

ATLANTIC: The JCS reports the strength of U.S. land and air forces. In the ETO and the Mediterranean, there are 40 divisions with four more en route. In addition, there are 149 air groups. In the Pacific, there are 47 air groups, 21 army divisions, and six marine divisions.

Vice Admiral Richard S. Edwards is named to the newly created positions of deputy commander in chief, U.S. Fleet, and deputy chief of naval operations.

ETO: During the night Eighth Air Force sends nine B-17s to drop leaflets over France, the Netherlands, and Belgium.

B-26 Marauders of the 553rd Bombardment Squadron (Medium) of the 386th Bombardment Group (Medium) and the 573rd, 574th, and 575th Bombardment Squadrons (Medium) of the 391st Bombardment Group (Medium) redeploy from England to France.

ITALY: After the 88th Infantry Division has lost over 2,000 men in attempting to reach Imola, General Mark Clark shifts the division toward Route 65 to support the II Corps effort. The II Corps attacks with the 85th and 91st Infantry Divisions, supported by the 6th South African Armored Division, the British 78th Division, and Combat Command B of the U.S. 1st Armored Division. The 34th and 88th Infantry Divisions are to follow the main attack.

The intent is to break through to Bologna and reach the open plains of the Po River valley before the approaching winter weather ends any further offensive action.

Twelfth Air Force B-25 Mitchells and B-26 Marauders attack rail and road traffic, fuel storage areas, industrial targets, and bridges in the Po Valley. XII Fighter Command A-20 Havocs and P-47 Thunderbolts attack a fuel storage area and German defensive positions.

SOUTHWEST PACIFIC AREA: U.S. submarine *Cabrilla* torpedoes and sinks two Japanese tankers in the South China Sea, west of Luzon.

PACIFIC: U.S. submarine *Snapper* torpedoes and sinks a Japanese coastal minelayer and transport northwest of the Bonins. U.S. submarine *Trepang* torpedoes and sinks a supply ship in the Bonins.

CENTRAL PACIFIC: Seventh Air Force B-24 Liberators from Saipan bomb Iwo Jima. B-25 Mitchells from Makin Island bomb Nauru Island. B-24s from Eniwetok bomb Truk.

U.S. destroyer *Bailey* is damaged during a Japanese air attack near Peleliu.

NEW GUINEA: FEAF A-20 Havocs and P-38 Lightnings attack Utarom airfield and logistics bases. P-40s attack targets of opportunity; P-47 Thunderbolts and A-20 Havocs attack airfields. B-25 Mitchells and P-38 Lightnings conduct shipping sweeps off Halmahera Island.

B-24 Liberators bomb targets in the Molucca Islands. B-25 Mitchells attack Lembeh Island. P-38 Lightnings attack Ceram and Celebes Islands and shipping off Ambon Island.

The C-47s of the 63rd and 70th Troop Carrier Squadrons of the 403rd Troop Carrier Group redeploy to Biak Island. The 82nd Tactical Reconnaissance Squadron of the 71st Tactical Reconnaissance Group redeploys from Biak Island to Morotai Island with P-40s and F-6 (camera-equipped) Mustangs.

U.S. submarine *Hammerhead* torpedoes and sinks two Japanese ore carriers and a cargo ship north of Borneo.

October 2

CBI: The battle of wills between Chiang Kai-shek and President Roosevelt over General Joseph Stilwell's role in China leads to a definite cooling in U.S.-Chinese relations. Chiang Kai-shek rejects President Roosevelt's proposal to put General Stilwell in command of all Chinese ground forces. In rejecting the president's request Chiang has moved away from U.S. strategic support.

Tenth Air Force sends P-47 Thunderbolts to attack towns and bridges around Bhamo and rail lines in northern Burma.

In China, Fourteenth Air Force sends 16 B-25 Mitchells to bomb Tien Ho and White Cloud airfields near Canton. Over 70 P-40s and P-51 Mustangs attack river traffic and troop areas.

ATLANTIC: Admiral Ernest J. King assesses that, because of the continuation of the war in Europe, there will not be sufficient ground forces available in the Pacific theater for the invasion of the island of Formosa. Iwo Jima is considered to be a better target for operations in early 1945 because the island will allow U.S. fighters to escort the B-29 Superfortresses flying from Mariana Islands airfields to strike Japanese cities on the home islands. The capture of Okinawa will also support strategic air operations and cut Japanese air control of the Ryukyu Islands.

ETO: First Army's XIX Corps (2nd and 7th Armored Divisions and the 29th and 30th Infantry Divisions) attacks north of Aachen to surround the city and link with VII Corps (3rd Armored Division and the 1st and 9th Infantry Divisions) moving from the south of the city. The V Corps (5th Armored Division and the 4th and 28th Infantry Divisions) is to protect First Army's flank. For the next two weeks XIX Corps will fight German forces in the cold and rain to reach its objective.

Eighth Air Force sends more than 870 B-17s using radar-equipped Pathfinder bombers escorted by 500 P-47 Thunderbolts and P-51 Mustangs to attack production facilities in western Germany. Two B-17s are lost and 273 are damaged. Aircrew casualties are 16 killed, six wounded, and 20 missing. Another 308 B-24 Liberators using Pathfinder and escorted by 212 P-38 Lightnings, P-47 Thunderbolts, and P-51 Mustangs are sent to bomb the marshaling yard at Hamm. Two B-24s are lost and

146 are damaged. Aircrew casualties are one killed and 18 missing. One P-51 is lost and three are damaged. One pilot is killed and another pilot is reported missing.

During the night three B-17s and five B-24s drop leaflets over Germany, France, and the Netherlands.

The Ninth Air Force creates the headquarters, XXIX Tactical Air Command (Provisional). Just like the IX and XIX Tactical Air Commands that provide direct air support to the First and Third Armies, respectively, the XXIX Tactical Air Command will support the Ninth Army.

A-20 Havocs and B-26 Marauders of the 9th Bombardment Division attack German defensive positions. P-38 Lightnings and P-47 Thunderbolts support the First, Third, and Seventh Armies.

The headquarters of the 386th Bombardment Group (Medium) and the B-26s of the 552nd, 554th, and 555th Bombardment Squadrons (Medium) redeploy from England to France.

MEDITERRANEAN: The B-24 Liberators of the 885th Bombardment Squadron (Heavy) begin deploying from Maison Blanche, Algeria, to Brindisi, Italy. The squadron's mission is to transport supplies to partisans and drop leaflets in the theater.

ITALY: The headquarters of the 27th Fighter Group and the P-47 Thunderbolts of the 522nd, 523rd, and 524th Fighter Squadrons redeploy from Loyettes, France, to Tarquinia, Italy.

SOUTHWEST PACIFIC AREA: U.S. submarine *Aspro* torpedoes and sinks a Japanese cargo ship in the South China Sea west of Luzon. U.S. submarine *Pomfret* torpedoes and sinks two Japanese army transports south of Formosa.

CENTRAL PACIFIC: Seventh Air Force B-24 Liberators from Saipan bomb Chichi Jima.

NEW GUINEA: FEAF P-40s attack vessels off the northwest coast of New Guinea and bomb Otawiri and Ransiki airfields. B-25 Mitchells bomb the airfield on Ambon Island. B-24 Liberators attack Haroekoe Island. P-38 Lightnings attack shipping and targets on Ceram Island and the airfield on Celebes Island. B-25 Mitchells fly a barge sweep off Halmahera Island.

October 3

ALEUTIANS: Eleventh Air Force sends two B-24 Liberators to conduct reconnaissance over Onnekotan, Harumukotan, and Shasukotan Islands in the Kurile Islands. Aircrews report strafing several small vessels.

CBI: In China, Fourteenth Air Force sends 23 B-25 Mitchells to attack the Wuchou and Samshui areas, and bomb Tien Ho and White Cloud airfields in Canton. P-51 Mustangs and P-40s attack river transport, roads, town areas, troop concentrations, and various targets of opportunity south of the Yangtze River, focusing on the Hsinganhsien, Pingnam, and Chuanhsien areas.

ATLANTIC: Admiral Ernest J. King agrees to recommendations by JCS planners and advocates an offensive directed at Okinawa and Iwo Jima once the invasion of Luzon begins. The JCS issues the directive scheduling the Luzon invasion for December 20, supported by Central Pacific air and naval forces. The directive also states that

Admiral Nimitz will plan for an attack on Iwo Jima on January 20, 1945, followed by an attack to seize one or more islands in the Ryukyus (primarily Okinawa) by March 1, 1945.

ETO: The XX Corps of Third Army continues its attack on Metz. This begins a 10-day battle for the city. The 11th Infantry Regiment of the 5th Infantry Division again attacks Fort Driant, and is heavily supported with tanks and engineers in a coordinated assault. For several days German and American soldiers will battle underground for possession of the fort.

Eighth Air Force sends 727 B-17s escorted by 511 P-47 Thunderbolts and P-51 Mustangs to attack airfields and industrial targets in central and southern Germany. Four B-17s are lost and 245 are damaged. Aircrew casualties are two killed, six wounded, and 28 missing. Fighter pilots report two confirmed kills on the ground. Four fighters are lost and one is damaged. Four pilots are reported missing.

Another 338 B-24 Liberators escorted by 188 P-38 Lightnings and P-47 Thunderbolts are sent to bomb transportation targets. A total of 39 B-24s are damaged. Aircrew casualties are two wounded.

During the night four B-17s and six B-24s drop leaflets over Belgium, Germany, France, and the Netherlands.

Ninth Air Force P-38s and P-47 Thunderbolts fly armed reconnaissance over western Germany, attack rail lines across the Rhine River, and support ground forces of the Third Army near Metz, France.

ITALY: Twelfth Air Force B-26 Marauders and B-25 Mitchells bomb road and rail bridges and fuel storage depots in the Po River valley. A-20 Havocs and P-47 Thunderbolts of the XII Fighter Command attack fuel storage sites, rail lines, and transportation targets in the Po Valley and support Fifth Army along the front.

SOUTHWEST PACIFIC AREA: General MacArthur is notified of the decision to support his Musketeer III plan for the occupation of Luzon. Landing on December 20, he is to establish bases on northern Luzon to support further Allied advances, including Nimitz's attack on the Ryukyu Islands scheduled for March. Plans for Formosa are left inactive until the conclusion of the campaign in the Philippines.

CENTRAL PACIFIC: Seventh Air Force B-24 Liberators from Saipan Island attack shipping and bomb the airfield on Iwo Jima.

Destroyer escort USS *Samuel S. Miles* sinks Japanese submarine *I-177* off the Palaus Islands.

U.S. submarine *Thresher* torpedoes and sinks a Japanese guardboat off Marcus Island.

CENTRAL PACIFIC, PELELIU: The 7th Marines attack to seize Walt and Boyd Ridges on the east side of the Umurbrogol Pocket. The struggle has gone on for three days with no progress and heavy casualties. The 3rd Battalion 5th Marines attacks into the Horseshoe Valley to capture the hills called the Five Sisters, which overlook Walt and Boyd Ridges. The 3rd Battalion has been reduced to company strength by casualties and is unable to hold the positions taken.

NEW GUINEA: FEAF A-20 Havocs, P-47 Thunderbolts, and P-40s attack targets on the Vogelkop Peninsula.

B-24 Liberators bomb oil refineries in Balikpapan, Borneo. B-25 Mitchells attack shipping and the airfields in the Moluccas and on Halmahera Island. B-25s and B-24s attack Ceram and Ambon Islands. P-38 Lightnings attack the seaplane base on Celebes Island and the airfields on Buru Island and Haroekoe Island.

Japanese submarine *RO-41* torpedoes and sinks a U.S. destroyer escort off Morotai. Destroyer escort USS *Richard M. Rowell* accidentally sinks USS *Seawolf* on a mission to land Americans on Samar.

October 4

ALEUTIANS: Eleventh Air Force sends four B-25 Mitchells to bomb shipping off Shimushu Island in the Kurile Islands. The Japanese attack the bombers with about 17 fighters. Aircrews report one confirmed kill.

CBI: Tenth Air Force P-47 Thunderbolts damage the approaches to a bridge between Myitkyina and Bhamo.

ATLANTIC: The JCS makes the decision to land on Luzon, the main island of the Philippines, and liberate the capital city of Manila. Five divisions will be available to land on Leyte. An attack to seize Iwo Jima is scheduled for January 20, 1945, followed by an attack to capture Okinawa on March 1. Another nine divisions will be available for an attack on Formosa after June 1945.

ETO: The Ninth Army's VIII Corps (the 9th Armored Division and the 2nd and 83rd Infantry Divisions) begins occupation of the Ardennes Forest between First and Third Armies.

During the night Eighth Air Force sends four B-17s and five B-24 Liberators to drop leaflets over Germany, France, and the Netherlands.

Ninth Air Force sends P-47 and P-38 fighters of the XIX Tactical Air Command to support Third Army around Metz. The IX Tactical Air Command P-38 Lightnings and P-47s provide support to First Army.

MEDITERRANEAN: Fifteenth Air Force sends over 300 B-17s and B-24 Liberators escorted by P-38 Lightnings and P-51 Mustangs to attack the marshaling yard at Munich, Germany.

Nearly 40 P-51 Mustangs strafe airfields in Greece. Another 400 bombers attack rail lines in the Brenner Pass.

ITALY: After three days of attacks, the 91st Infantry Division is stalled, having suffered over 1,700 casualties. The 85th Infantry Division now leads the attack up Route 65.

British forces relieve the 350th Infantry Regiment on Mount Battaglia. The 88th Infantry Division has lost over 2,000 men since September 21.

Twelfth Air Force A-20 Havocs and P-47 Thunderbolts attack German defensive positions and communications on the battlefront.

The headquarters of the 79th Fighter Group and the P-47s of the 86th and 87th Fighter Squadrons redeploy from southern France to Iesi.

SOUTHWEST PACIFIC AREA: U.S. submarine *Flasher* torpedoes and sinks a Japanese cargo ship in the South China Sea north of Luzon.

Navy PBY Catalinas sink a Japanese cargo ship and two auxiliary sailing vessels near Jolo, in the Philippines.

CENTRAL PACIFIC: Seventh Air Force B-24 Liberators from Saipan attack shipping and bomb the airfield at Iwo Jima. B-24s from the Marshalls bomb Truk.

CENTRAL PACIFIC, PELELIU: The 7th Marines capture Hill 120 in the Umurbrogol, but are subjected to a severe cross fire, forcing them to retreat.

During the night Private Wesley Phelps of the 3rd Battalion, 7th Marines, 1st Marine Division, defends his position with another marine rifleman against a strong Japanese counterattack. When a grenade lands in the fighting position (foxhole), Private Phelps pushes his fellow marine away and covers the grenade with his own body. Private Phelps's act of courage and self-sacrifice will win him the Medal of Honor.

NEW GUINEA: Morotai Island is cleared of the last enemy forces. The newly built airfield at Wama is operational. Morotai is secured at the cost of 30 Americans killed and 85 wounded.

The P-38 Lightnings of the 35th Fighter Squadron, 8th Fighter Group, redeploy to Morotai Island.

B-25 Mitchells bomb Celebes Island. P-40s and B-25s attack airfields on Halmahera Island. A-20 Havocs and B-25s conduct a shipping sweep and bomb Ambon Island and the wharf on Celebes Island.

October 5

ALEUTIANS: Eleventh Air Force sends two B-24 Liberators on a dawn bombing raid against Paramushiru Island.

CBI: President Roosevelt replies to Chiang Kai-shek and offers a compromise by proposing to appoint a new adviser while leaving General Stilwell in charge of combat operations in Burma and the direction of the Hump airlift.

Tenth Air Force B-25 Mitchells attack the bridges at Namhkai.

In China, Fourteenth Air Force P-40s and P-51 Mustangs conduct sweeps over southern China and attack river transport, road traffic, bridges, town areas, and troop concentrations.

ETO: Eighth Air Force sends more than 700 B-17s using radar-equipped Pathfinder bombers and 360 B-24 Liberators escorted by 675 P-51 Mustangs and P-47 Thunderbolts to attack airfields, industrial production facilities, and rail lines in western and central Germany. Radar assists the timing of bomb release. A total of nine bombers are lost and 357 are damaged. Aircrew casualties are one killed, six wounded, and 71 missing. Fighter pilots report one confirmed kill in the air and 15 on the ground. Four fighters are lost and four are damaged. The four pilots are reported missing.

During the night eight B-17s drop leaflets over Germany, France, and the Netherlands.

Ninth Air Force sends P-47 and P-38 fighters to support XV Corps.

ITALY: In the II Corps area, the 91st Infantry Division captures Monghidro and attacks with all three regiments to seize Loiano, preceded by an artillery barrage that drops 30,000 rounds on the German positions. The 362nd Infantry Regiment enters Loiano and repulses an enemy counterattack. The 85th Division, on the 91st Division's right flank, is stopped by German defenses.

Twelfth Air Force A-20 Havocs conduct bombing runs on German positions during the night.

The P-47 Thunderbolts of the 85th Fighter Squadron, 79th Fighter Group, redeploy from southern France to Iesi.

SOUTHWEST PACIFIC AREA: U.S. submarine *Cod* torpedoes and sinks a Japanese cargo ship in the South China Sea west of Mindoro.

PACIFIC: Admiral Nimitz notifies his subordinate service commanders that Operation Causeway (the invasion of Formosa) is deferred and that planning for the capture of Iwo Jima (Operation Detachment) and capture of islands in the Ryukyus beginning on March 1. The islands are within bombing range of the home islands of Japan and will control the air and sea links to Japan. The islands also afford secure anchorages for the U.S. fleet.

CENTRAL PACIFIC: Seventh Air Force B-25 Mitchells from the Gilberts bomb runways and gun positions on Nauru Island. B-24 Liberators from the Marshalls bomb Truk.

CENTRAL PACIFIC, PELELIU: The 2nd Battalion, 5th Marines, relieves the 3rd Battalion of the 7th Marines at Umurbrogol. Japanese positions in the Pocket are subjected to air strikes with a new weapon—napalm (jelled gasoline that explodes and burns on impact)—and direct fire from artillery.

NEW GUINEA: FEAF A-20 Havocs, B-25 Mitchells, P-39 Airacobras, P-47 Thunderbolts, P-38 Lightnings, and P-40s attack Utarom airfield and other airfields in northwest New Guinea. A-20s attack Japanese positions and logistics storage areas near Sarmi.

B-24 Liberators bomb airfields on Celebes Island. B-25s and P-38 Lightnings bomb the airfield on Celebes Island, the town of Amboina on Ambon Island, and targets of opportunity in the Ambon-Ceram Islands.

October 6

CBI: Tenth Air Force B-25 Mitchells and P-47 Thunderbolts bomb troop concentrations and a bridge.

In China, Fourteenth Air Force sends 12 B-25 Mitchells to bomb targets of opportunity in and around Canton.

ETO: In the First Army area, the 39th and 60th Infantry Regiments of the 9th Infantry Division attack toward Schmidt, the key terrain in the Hürtgen Forest. The American infantrymen encounter concrete pillboxes of the West Wall, 20 feet high and 3 to 8 feet thick. Eighth Air Force sends more than 850 B-17s escorted by 540 P-51 Mustangs to attack aircraft production facilities, airfields, and ammunitions storage areas in northern Germany and Berlin. Eighteen B-17s are lost and 269 are damaged. Aircrew casualties are three killed, four wounded, and 163 missing. Fighter pilots report 18 confirmed kills and one probable in the air and 30 confirmed kills on the ground. Four fighters are lost and nine are damaged. The four pilots are reported missing.

Another 406 B-24 Liberators using radar-equipped Pathfinder bombers and escorted by 156 P-47 Thunderbolts are sent to bomb oil production and industrial production facilities in northern Germany. One B-24 is lost and 127 are damaged. Aircrew casualties are one killed, two wounded, and 10 missing. Six P-47s are damaged.

Fighter pilots report one confirmed kill in the air.

During the night four B-17s and six B-24s drop leaflets over Germany, France, and the Netherlands.

Ninth Air Force sends more than 300 A-20 Havocs and B-26 Marauders to attack marshaling yards and ammunition storage areas in Holland and Germany. P-47 and P-38 fighters support the First, Third, and Seventh Armies.

MEDITERRANEAN: Fifteenth Air Force P-38 Lightnings and P-51 Mustangs attack airfields in Greece.

ITALY: The IV Corps commander, Major General Edward M. Almond, leads a task force composed of the 370th RCT of the 92nd Infantry Division, 2nd Armored Group, with antiaircraft artillery troops converted into infantry, the 751st Tank Battalion, and the 849th Tank Destroyer Battalion. The task force makes a weak attack on Monte Cauala.

SOUTHWEST PACIFIC AREA: U.S. submarine *Cabrilla* torpedoes and sinks a tanker and damages a transport off the west coast of Luzon. U.S. submarine *Seahorse* torpedoes and sinks a Japanese coastal patrol boat off Luzon. U.S. submarine *Whale* torpedoes and sinks a Japanese transport and merchant tanker off Luzon.

PACIFIC: Twentieth Air Force receives P-61 Black Widow night fighters at Chengtu, China.

CENTRAL PACIFIC: Seventh Air Force B-24 Liberators from Saipan bomb Iwo Jima.

One B-24 from Kwajalein bombs a gun battery on Jaluit Atoll.

NEW GUINEA: FEAF P-38 Lightnings attack the airfield and shipping at Halmahera Island. B-25 Mitchells and P-38s attack Celebes Island, Ceram Island, Ambon Island, and Buru Island.

October 7

CBI: Fifty-three P-51 Mustangs and P-40s of Fourteenth Air Force, on armed reconnaissance, attack troop concentrations, bridges, river and rail traffic, town areas, and logistics bases.

ETO: The XII Corps of Third Army is unable to do more than make limited attacks due to severe shortages of fuel and ammunition. Lieutenant General Patton bitterly complains about fighting three enemies: the Germans, the weather, and time.

Eighth Air Force sends more than 900 B-17s escorted by 557 P-51 Mustangs and P-47 Thunderbolts to attack industrial targets, oil refineries, and airfields in Germany. A total of 36 B-17s are lost and 430 damaged. Aircrews report 11 confirmed kills and 13 probables. Aircrew casualties are four killed, 32 wounded, and 320 missing. Fighter pilots report 29 confirmed kills in the air and one confirmed kill on the ground. Seven fighters are lost and six damaged. Seven pilots are reported missing, and one is wounded.

Another 489 B-24 Liberators escorted by 214 P-51s, P-47s, and P-38 Lightnings are sent to bomb oil refineries, a vehicle production facility, and marshaling yards. Four B-24s are lost and 184 damaged. Aircrew casualties are two killed, six wounded, and 38 missing. Pilots report eight confirmed kills on the ground. Four fighters are lost, and two are damaged. Three pilots are reported missing.

Headquarters Ninth Air Force orders attacks on all bridges, except those over the Rhine River. Over 300 B-26 Marauders and A-20 Havocs attack bridges from

Holland to Germany. P-38 Lightnings and P-47 Thunderbolts attack rail lines, river transport, troop concentrations, and ground support forces.

MEDITERRANEAN: Fifteenth Air Force sends more than 350 B-17s and B-24 Liberators escorted by P-38 Lightnings and P-51 Mustangs to bomb oil refineries near Vienna, Austria. Other B-24s and P-51s attack rail transportation in Czechoslovakia and Hungary.

ITALY: In heavy rain and fog, the 362nd Infantry Regiment of the 91st Infantry Division attacks Monte Castellari overlooking Route 65.

Twelfth Air Force P-47 Thunderbolts attack German defensive positions along the battlefront.

SOUTHWEST PACIFIC AREA: FEAF B-24 Liberators and P-38s attack Zamboanga on Mindanao Island in the Philippines.

U.S. submarine *Cabrilla* torpedoes and sinks a Japanese transport off Vigan, Luzon. U.S. submarine *Cod* torpedoes and damages an oiler in the South China Sea west of Mindoro. U.S. submarine *Hawkbill* torpedoes and damages a cargo ship in the South China Sea, which is later sunk by USS *Baya*. U.S. submarine *Hoe* torpedoes and sinks a Japanese army transport in the South China Sea west of Luzon.

CENTRAL PACIFIC, PELELIU: Tanks supported by infantry enter the Horseshoe Valley to destroy cave positions on the Five Sisters in the Umurbrogol Pocket.

NEW GUINEA: FEAF P-38 Lightnings and B-25 Mitchells attack airfields and installations in northwestern New Guinea. B-25s bomb Celebes and Ambon Islands, and P-38s attack Halmahera Island and the oil storage area on Ceram Island.

October 8

CBI: Tenth Air Force B-25 Mitchells attack bridges, and P-47 Thunderbolts bomb rail lines in northern Burma.

Fourteenth Air Force P-40s and P-51 Mustangs attack river transport and rail lines.

U.S. submarine *Hoe* torpedoes and sinks a Japanese army transport and damages a coastal patrol ship in the South China Sea east of Hainan.

ETO: First Army's VII Corps attacks to encircle Aachen from the south with the 1st Infantry Division. The 18th Infantry Regiment fights to seize Crucifix Hill, one of the key defensive positions around Aachen.

Headquarters Ninth Air Force orders intensive attacks against rail lines in Germany.

Over 300 B-26 Marauders and A-20 Havocs, with fighter escort, attack German strongpoints and bridges between eastern France and western Germany. P-38 Lightnings and P-47 Thunderbolts support the VII, XV, XIX, and XX Corps.

Captain Bobbie E. Brown commands C Company, 18th Infantry Regiment, 1st Infantry Division, and is ordered to attack Crucifix Hill, Aachen, Germany. Brown's leading platoons are stopped by a series of pillboxes and then subjected to artillery fire. Captain Brown moves forward to destroy a pillbox with an explosive charge attached to a long pole. Crawling as close as possible, Brown is able to thrust the armed explosive into the aperture and destroy the pillbox. Taking another explosive charge, he attacks the second pillbox, disregarding the bullets and bomb fragments flying around him. He blasts the second fortification and moves on to the third. He succeeds in destroying it as well, but is wounded. Refusing treatment, he continues to give orders and even goes on an advanced reconnaissance to locate German troops, exposing himself deliberately to draw the Germans' fire. Wounded twice more, Brown is able to deploy his company to repel two counterattacks and eliminate German artillery pieces. He allows himself to be treated only after he is certain his company's position is completely secure. For his example of selfless leadership and great courage in the face of the enemy, Captain Brown will receive the Medal of Honor.

SOUTHWEST PACIFIC AREA: U.S. submarine *Becuna* torpedoes and damages a Japanese seaplane carrier in the South China Sea.

CENTRAL PACIFIC: Seventh Air Force B-24 Liberators from the Marshalls bomb Wake Island.

NEW GUINEA: FEAF A-20 Havocs, B-25 Mitchells, P-38 Lightnings, P-40s, and P-47 Thunderbolts attack airfields, gun positions, troop areas, and logistics storage areas.

B-24 Liberators bomb Ceram Island. P-38 Lightnings attack targets on Halmahera Island and in the Molucca Islands.

October 9

CBI: Generalissimo Chiang Kai-shek rejects President Roosevelt's offer to keep General Stilwell in the theater. He demands that Stilwell be removed.

Tenth Air Force P-47 Thunderbolts attack bridges and B-25 Mitchells attack road bridges near Lashio.

Fourteenth Air Force B-25s bomb river transportation. P-51 Mustangs and P-40s attack river transportation, troops and bridges.

ETO: Fort Driant, one of the key defensive positions of the fortress city of Metz, is still in German hands after nearly a week of close combat with the 5th Infantry Division. Admitting failure after losing 500 men, the Americans begin to pull back.

In the First Army area, the 60th and 39th Infantry Regiments of the 9th Infantry Division capture Richeskaul and Wittscheidt west of Schmidt in the Hürtgen Forest.

Eighth Air Force sends more than 1,000 B-17s and B-24 Liberators, escorted by over 600 P-51 Mustangs and 200 P-38 Lightnings and P-47 Thunderbolts from Ninth Air Force, to attack ball-bearing plants at Schweinfurt, marshaling yards at Mainz and Koblenz, and industrial production facilities. One B-24 is lost and 119 bombers are damaged. Aircrew casualties are one killed and 10 missing. Fighter pilots report one confirmed kill in the air and one confirmed kill on the ground. Five fighters are damaged.

During the night two B-24s drop leaflets over the Netherlands.

Ninth Air Force B-26 Marauders and A-20 Havocs attack a rail bridge at Euskirchen, Germany.

ITALY: After five days of fighting the 85th Infantry Division has advanced about three miles and has lost 1,400 men. The Germans have laid out strong defenses. Soldiers hold these defensive lines, inflicting maximum casualties, then slip back to the next defensive line to force the Americans into the same attack.

The 362nd Infantry Regiment captures Monte Castellari, forcing the Germans to retreat to Livergnano, the strongest natural defensive barrier on the Gothic Line.

Twelfth Air Force A-20 Havocs and P-47 Thunderbolts attack convoys, bridges, and roads.

SOUTHWEST PACIFIC AREA: In the South China Sea, USS *Becuna* torpedoes and damages a tanker and works with USS *Hawkbill* to sink a tanker. USS *Sawfish* torpedoes and sinks a tanker north of Luzon.

PACIFIC: Admiral Nimitz sends a directive to Lieutenant General Holland M. Smith, alerting his V Amphibious Corps to prepare plans for the capture of Iwo Jima.

Planning begins for Operation Iceberg, the invasion of Okinawa. Strategic Air Forces of the Pacific Ocean Area are assigned the mission of eliminating the Japanese air threat from the Caroline and Bonin Islands and bombing the airfields on Okinawa and on Kyushu in Japan. Naval air elements will neutralize bypassed Japanese bases and eliminate the Japanese submarine threat. The submarine force will attack Japanese shipping to and from Japan and Formosa. The joint army-navy task force, composed of the U.S. Fifth Fleet, with a naval covering force, an expeditionary force, and expeditionary troops, will combine efforts to capture the objectives. Admiral Richard A. Spruance will command Task Force 50, which includes Vice Admiral Marc A. Mitscher's fast carrier force (Task Force 58) and a British carrier force (Task Force 57). Mitscher's task force will be responsible for eliminating Japanese air strength between Okinawa and the Japanese island of Kyushu. Also under Spruance is Task Force 51, under Vice Admiral Richmond Kelly Turner, who is responsible for the capture of Okinawa and other islands in the Ryukyus. Subordinate to Turner is Task Force 54, the Gunfire and Covering Force, Task Force 52, the Amphibious Support Force with escort carriers, and Task Force 56, the Expeditionary Troops under command of Lieutenant General Simon B. Buckner. Lieutenant General Buckner will command the Tenth Army, composed of the XXIV Corps (commanded by Major General John R. Hodge and including the 7th and 96th Infantry Divisions) and the III Marine Amphibious Corps (commanded by Major General Roy S. Geiger and composed of the 1st and 6th Marine Divisions), as well as the Tactical Air Force Ryukyus under command of Major General Francis P. Mulcahy (USMC) and Naval Force Ryukyus under Rear Admiral C. H. Cobb. General Buckner also has under his operational control the 27th and 77th Infantry Divisions and the 2nd Marine Division as a reserve. The 81st Infantry Division is placed under the operational control of Admiral Nimitz as an area reserve.

Three heavy cruisers and six destroyers of Naval Task Group 30.2 (Rear Admiral Allan E. Smith) conduct a diversionary bombardment of Japanese installations on Marcus Island. Navy PB4Y Privateers from Saipan conduct interdiction patrols in the path of Naval Task Force 58, damaging an auxiliary submarine chaser off Okinawa.

USS *Croaker* torpedoes and sinks a cargo ship west of Kyushu.

CENTRAL PACIFIC: Seventh Air Force sends 18 B-24 Liberators from Saipan to bomb Iwo Jima. Another 25 B-25 Mitchells from the Marshalls bomb Truk.

NEW GUINEA: FEAF P-40s attack Manokwari. B-25 Mitchells bomb airfields on Halmahera Island. A-20 Havocs, P-38 Lightnings, and P-47 Thunderbolts attack oil storage areas and airfields on Ceram Island, Celebes Island, and Ambon Island.

October 10

CBI: Tenth Air Force P-47 Thunderbolts support British ground forces.

Fourteenth Air Force P-40s and P-51 Mustangs attack roads, bridges, town areas, troop concentrations, and various targets of opportunity.

MEDITERRANEAN: Fifteenth Air Force sends more than 170 B-17s and B-24 Liberators escorted by P-38 Lightnings and P-51 Mustangs to attack marshaling yards in northern Italy.

ITALY: The II Corps attacks the Livergnano Escarpment, the Germans' most strongly defended position in the entire Apennines. Monte della Formiche is one of the mountains in the center of the Escarpment. The 85th Infantry Division makes the main attack, capturing Monte della Formiche, supported by the 91st and 88th Infantry Divisions making flanking attacks. The 361st Infantry Regiment of the 91st Infantry Division is stopped in front of Livergnano. Twelfth Air Force P-47 Thunderbolts support the attack.

SOUTHWEST PACIFIC AREA: U.S. submarine *Lapon* torpedoes and sinks a Japanese army transport in the South China Sea west of Luzon.

PACIFIC: Admiral Halsey's Third Fleet begins strikes on targets from the Ryukyus to the Philippines in preparation for the October 20 assault. Task Force 38 has 17 carriers, six fast battleships, 14 cruisers, and 58 destroyers. The main attack is against the airfields on the island of Okinawa, at Naha, Kadena, and Yomitan. Ie Shima Island is also hit. Halsey's F6F Hellcat fighter-bombers, SB2C Helldiver dive-bombers, and TBF Avenger torpedo-bombers destroy 30 cargo ships, 10 transports, a seaplane tender, an escort destroyer, four midget subs, two minesweepers, six patrol boats, and eight antiaircraft boats. The logistics storage depot at Naha is also destroyed. TF-38 will go on to destroy over 600 Japanese navy aircraft in the Philippines and Formosa.

Carrier aircraft from Naval Task Force 38 under Vice Admiral Marc A. Mitscher attack Okinawa and other islands in the Ryukyus. Pilots report sinking a submarine depot ship, a landing ship, a minelayer, an auxiliary submarine chaser, three auxiliary minesweepers, three guardboats, 12 motor torpedo boats, and six cargo ships. Pilots also report damaging a coastal patrol ship, a submarine chaser, a guardboat, and two cargo ships.

U.S. submarine *Barb* torpedoes and sinks a Japanese transport off Kyushu, Japan.

CENTRAL PACIFIC: Seventh Air Force sends 14 B-24 Liberators from Saipan to bomb the airfield at Iwo Jima and shipping near the island. Another 12 B-25 Mitchells from Makin bomb runways and antiaircraft positions on Nauru Island.

New Guinea: FEAF A-20 Havocs and B-25 Mitchells bomb Utarom airfield. B-24 Liberators escorted by P-47 Thunderbolts and P-38 Lightnings attack oil refineries and the airfield at Balikpapan in Borneo. Aircrews and pilots report 30 confirmed kills. P-47 Thunderbolts attack the airfield on Ambon Island, and P-38 Lightnings and B-25s bomb airfields and other targets on Halmahera Island.

October 11

Aleutians: Eleventh Air Force sends four B-25 Mitchells to attack Japanese installations on Shimushiru and Paramushiru Islands in the Kuriles. Aircrews report three buildings destroyed and two others damaged.

CBI: Tenth Air Force P-47 Thunderbolts and B-25 Mitchells attack troop concentrations, gun positions, rail lines, bridges, roads, and logistics sites.

Fourteenth Air Force B-25 Mitchells bomb the bridge near Mangshih. Aircrews report the bridge destroyed.

ETO: Eighth Air Force sends 135 B-17s escorted by 135 P-47 Thunderbolts to bomb the Wesseling synthetic oil production facility and the Koblenz marshaling yard. Four B-17s are lost and 61 are damaged. Aircrew casualties are three killed, six wounded, and 38 missing. One P-47 is lost.

During the night nine B-17s and B-24s drop leaflets over Germany, France, and the Netherlands.

Ninth Air Force P-38 Lightnings and P-47 Thunderbolts attack rail lines near Aachen and along the Rhine River. Fighters also support the VII and XIX Corps near Aachen and the XII, XV, and XX Corps around Metz and Saarlautern.

Mediterranean: Fifteenth Air Force sends 180 B-17s and B-24 Liberators escorted by P-38 Lightnings and P-51 Mustangs to attack industrial targets near Vienna, Austria, rail bridges in Yugoslavia, and bridges and roads in northern Italy. P-51 Mustangs attack logistics storage depots and rail cars, and destroy 47 aircraft on the ground in Czechoslovakia and Hungary.

Italy: In nearly impassable terrain, the 361st and 363rd Infantry Regiments of the 90th Infantry Division make limited gains against strong German defenses.

Twelfth Air Force B-25 Mitchells and B-26 Marauders attack logistics bases and bridges in the Po Valley. A-20 Havocs and P-47 Thunderbolts attack German positions.

Southwest Pacific Area: Naval Task Force 78 departs from the Admiralty Islands for Leyte Island, carrying X Corps under the command of Rear Admiral Daniel E. Barbey.

FEAF B-24 Liberators conduct a night raid on airfields on Mindanao Island in the Philippines.

Naval Task Group 38.1 under Vice Admiral John S. McCain and Naval Task Group 38.4 under Rear Admiral Ralph E. Davison attack Japanese airfields and facilities on northern Luzon. Carrier aircraft damage an escort destroyer and a cargo vessel.

U.S. submarine *Tang* torpedoes and sinks two cargo ships in the Formosa Strait.

Pacific: U.S. submarine *Trepang* torpedoes and sinks a Japanese landing ship off Honshu, Japan.

New Guinea: FEAF P-47 Thunderbolts and A-20 Havocs attack troop concentrations and airfields in New Guinea. A-20 Havocs, P-40s, and P-47 Thunderbolts attack targets on Ambon Island, Celebes Island, Haroekoe Island, and Buru Island. P-38 Lightnings attack an airfield on Halmahera Island.

October 12
Aleutians: Eleventh Air Force B-24 Liberators attack the airfield on Matsuwa-Onnekotan Island and attack shipping targets nearby.
CBI: Tenth Air Force P-47 Thunderbolts bomb rail lines, bridges, troops, and logistics sites. B-25 Mitchells attack and destroy a bridge near Lashio.

In China, Fourteenth Air Force B-25s and P-40s attack logistics bases at Chefang and a bridge near Mangshih.
ETO: In the First Army area, the 39th Infantry Regiment of the 9th Infantry Division is stopped by German counterattacks as it attempts to advance to Schmidt in the Hürtgen Forest. The 26th Infantry Regiment of the 1st Infantry Division attacks the city of Aachen.

Eighth Air Force sends 290 B-24 Liberators escorted by 210 P-47 Thunderbolts and P-51 Mustangs to bomb the marshaling yard at Osnabrück guided by radar-equipped Pathfinders. Two B-24s are lost and 67 are damaged. Aircrew casualties are 19 missing. Pilots report one confirmed kill and one probable in the air. Another 262 B-17s escorted by 273 P-47 Thunderbolts and P-51 Mustangs are sent to attack aviation production facilities at Bremen. One B-17 is lost and 60 are damaged. Aircrew casualties are seven killed, one wounded, and nine missing. Fighter pilots report 17 confirmed kills and two probables. Five P-51s are lost, and the pilots are reported as missing.

During the night eight B-24s drop leaflets over Germany, France, and the Netherlands. Two bombers are lost.

Ninth Air Force takes operational control and administrative control of headquarters, XII Tactical Air Command, from U.S. Strategic Air Forces in Europe (USSTAF). Nearly 250 B-26 Marauders and A-20 Havocs bomb German positions and rail targets in Germany and the Netherlands. P-47 and P-38 fighters support the VIII, XII, XV, and XX Corps.

Staff Sergeant Jack J. Pendleton of I Company, 120th Infantry Regiment, 30th Infantry Division, is moving through the town of Bardenberg, Germany, when German machine guns begin firing on the infantrymen from a strongpoint at an intersection. Staff Sergeant Pendleton volunteers to lead his squad against the strongpoint after several attempts fail. Moving to within 130 yards of the position, Staff Sergeant Pendleton is wounded. He orders his men to take cover and continues to work his way forward under heavy fire the entire time. He is killed within 10 yards of the position but has sacrificed himself to allow another squad to maneuver and, supported by Pendleton's men, capture the position. For his supreme act of courage and self-sacrifice, Staff Sergeant Pendleton will receive the Medal of Honor.
Mediterranean: Fifteenth Air Force sends 160 P-51 Mustangs to strafe rail lines and Danube River traffic from Vienna, Austria, to Budapest, Hungary.

ITALY: Operation Pancake begins. This is a concentrated air attack on Bologna. Fifteenth Air Force sends nearly 700 B-17s and B-24 Liberators with fighter support to attack ammunition and fuel storage areas, troop disposition areas, barracks, vehicle repair shops, and a munitions factory. Twelfth Air Force B-26 Marauders and 117 B-25 Mitchells bomb supply storage areas and troop barracks. A-20 Havocs attack ammunition storage facilities, and P-47 Thunderbolts attack German positions.

SOUTHWEST PACIFIC AREA: Carrier aircraft from Naval Task Force 38 (Vice Admiral Marc A. Mitscher) attack airfields, support facilities, and industrial targets on Formosa. Pilots report sinking four transports, six cargo ships, an army ship, and seven merchant tankers. Pilots also report damaging a German ship, a tanker, and four cargo ships west of Formosa. A cargo ship is also reported sunk in Putai harbor, Formosa. The air attacks are intended to clear the skies for Twentieth Air Force B-29s to hit aircraft production facilities, and airfields on Formosa.

U.S. submarine *Ray* torpedoes and sinks a Japanese transport off Mindoro and escapes an attack from escort ships.

PACIFIC: Twentieth Air Force inactivates the headquarters of the 58th Bombardment Wing (Very Heavy) and 795th Bombardment Squadron (Very Heavy), 468th Bombardment Group (Very Heavy); the 679th Bombardment Squadron (Very Heavy), 444th Bombardment Group (Very Heavy); the 771st Bombardment Squadron (Very Heavy), 462nd Bombardment Group (Very Heavy). Attacking Japan from bases in India and China is proving far too difficult logistically to support any sustained bombing campaign. Plans are made to redeploy Twentieth Air Force assets elsewhere in the Pacific.

U.S. submarine *Trepang* torpedoes and damages a Japanese destroyer east of Honshu, Japan.

CENTRAL PACIFIC: Seventh Air Force B-24 Liberators from Saipan Island bomb the harbor and shipping at Chichi Jima. B-24 Liberators from Kwajalein conduct a night bombing raid on Wake Island.

The first B-29 Superfortress of the Twentieth Air Force, piloted by Brigadier General Haywood S. Hansell, Jr., commander of XXI Bomber Command, arrives on Saipan. A temporary headquarters for the XXI Bomber Command and for the headquarters of the 73rd Bombardment Wing (Very Heavy) is established on the island. Four bomber wings (and their headquarters) are scheduled to deploy to Saipan in the future.

NEW GUINEA: FEAF A-20 Havocs, P-38 Lightnings, P-40s, and P-47 Thunderbolts attack targets at Sarmi and Manokwari. A-20 Havocs and P-47 Thunderbolts attack airfields on Ambon Island, Buru Island, Celebes Island, Haroekoe Island, and the town of Boela on Ceram Island. P-38 Lightnings attack targets on Halmahera Island. B-24 Liberators bomb Celebes Island.

October 13

ALEUTIANS: Eleventh Air Force sends four B-25 Mitchells to bomb Kurabu airfield and bomb and strafe buildings on Tomari Cape on Paramushiru Island. Aircrews report several buildings damaged.

CBI: U.S. submarine *Bergall* torpedoes and sinks a Japanese merchant tanker off Nha Trang, French Indochina.

ETO: The 1st Infantry Division of the VII Corps of First Army begins the battle for the city of Aachen.

Ninth Air Force B-26 Marauders and A-20 Havocs attack bridges in the Netherlands, France, and Germany. P-38 Lightnings and P-47 Thunderbolts support the First, Third, and Seventh Armies.

MEDITERRANEAN: Fifteenth Air Force sends more than 650 B-17s and B-24 Liberators escorted by P-38 Lightnings and P-51 Mustangs to attack oil refineries, rail transport repair facilities, and marshaling yards in Austria, Hungary, Czechoslovakia, and Germany. Fighters attack rail lines, airfields, and roads.

ITALY: The 361st Infantry Regiment of the 91st Infantry Division moves to flank the German position at Livergnano. Twelfth Air Force P-47 Thunderbolts provide air support.

SOUTHWEST PACIFIC AREA: Japanese aircraft attack Naval Task Force 38, hitting the Australian heavy cruiser *Canberra* with an aerial torpedo and damaging carrier USS *Franklin* with a crashed fighter.

PACIFIC: Members of the headquarters of V Amphibious Corps move to Pearl Harbor to begin planning for the amphibious assault on Iwo Jima.

CENTRAL PACIFIC: Seventh Air Force B-24 Liberators from Saipan bomb Yap. B-24s from the Marshalls bomb Truk. B-25 Mitchells from the Gilberts bomb Nauru Island.

CENTRAL PACIFIC, PELELIU: The 3rd Battalion of the 5th Marines begins an attack into the north side of the Umurbrogol Pocket, making advances of 75 yards.

NEW GUINEA: Task Force 79 commanded by Vice Admiral Theodore S. Wilkinson leaves Hollandia, carrying the XXIV Corps to Leyte Island. Task Force 78 commanded by Rear Admiral Daniel Barbey.

The Japanese have built up troop strength in the Philippines to about 432,000 men. There are 884 aircraft of all types still available.

FEAF A-20 Havocs and P-47 Thunderbolts attack airfields on Ambon Island, Buru Island, Celebes Island, Haroekoe Island, and the town of Boela on Ceram Island. B-25 Mitchells bomb targets in the Celebes Islands. P-38 Lightnings attack antiaircraft positions on Halmahera Island.

October 14

ALEUTIANS: Eleventh Air Force sends four B-25 Mitchells to bomb and strafe buildings at Otomae Bay in the Kurile Islands.

ETO: Eighth Air Force sends more than 1,000 B-17s and B-24 Liberators escorted by 469 P-51 Mustangs and P-47 Thunderbolts to attack marshaling yards in Germany, using radar to assist the timing of bomb release. A total of five bombers are lost and 356 damaged. Aircrew casualties are two killed, eight wounded, and 40 missing. One P-51 is damaged.

Ninth Air Force P-38 Lightnings and P-47s support Third Army.

MEDITERRANEAN: Fifteenth Air Force sends 317 B-17s and B-24 Liberators escorted by P-38 Lightnings and P-51 Mustangs to attack oil refineries and marshaling yards in Austria, Hungary, and Czechoslovakia. B-24 Liberators bomb a railroad bridge and marshaling yard in Yugoslavia.

ITALY: After four days of air and artillery attacks and infantry assaults, the Germans begin to abandon Livergnano.

Twelfth Air Force A-20 Havocs and P-47 Thunderbolts attack German positions, bridges, roads, logistics sites, and rail lines.

SOUTHWEST PACIFIC AREA: Japanese aircraft continue attacks on Naval Task Force 38; the carrier USS *Hancock,* two light cruisers, and two destroyers are damaged. Carrier aircraft damage a coastal minelayer and two auxiliary submarine chasers off Formosa.

U.S. submarine *Bonefish* torpedoes and sinks a Japanese cargo ship in the South China Sea off the west coast of Luzon.

PACIFIC: Twentieth Air Force sends 103 B-29 Superfortresses from Chengtu, China, to bomb the Okayama aircraft plant on Formosa in support of MacArthur's invasion of Leyte.

CENTRAL PACIFIC: Seventh Air Force redeploys the B-25 Mitchells of the 48th, 396th, and 820th Bombardment Squadrons (Medium) from Makin Island to Wheeler Field, Hawaii.

NEW GUINEA: FEAF B-24 Liberators bomb oil refineries and oil production facilities in the Balikpapan, Borneo, area and attack targets on Celebes Island. B-25 Mitchells and P-38 Lightnings attack the airfields on Ambon Island and Haroekoe Island.

U.S. submarine *Angler* torpedoes and sinks a Japanese army transport in the Flores Sea east of Timor. U.S. submarine *Dace* torpedoes and sinks two Japanese merchant tankers and damages a merchant ore carrier off North Borneo.

October 15

CBI: The Allied offensive in Burma is renewed under Vice Admiral Lord Louis Mountbatten. The plan is to advance toward Bhamo and Katha, then move on to control the Burma Road and Lashio. The British Fourteenth Army will continue to press Japanese forces toward the Irrawaddy River and capture Mandalay. The Americans will send three Chinese divisions and the British 36th Division toward Bhamo and Katha to reopen the overland route to China and capture Lashio. The 36th will attack to control the railroad junction at Pinwe.

Tenth Air Force sends 40 P-47 Thunderbolts and 12 B-25 Mitchells to attack roads, troop concentrations, ammunition storage areas, and town areas in support of British forces.

In China, Fourteenth Air Force sends 28 B-24 Liberators, 33 P-51 Mustangs, and 18 P-40s to attack White Cloud airfield in Canton and shipping in the Hong Kong area.

ETO: A new SHAEF air staff is created. Allied Expeditionary Air Force headquarters is disbanded. All planning and operations are the responsibility of SHAEF headquarters air staff under Air Chief Marshal Arthur W. Tedder. This arrangement gives SHAEF more direct control over air operations in-theater.

The Allied Air Expeditionary Force chief, Air Marshal Leigh-Mallory, is transferred to the China-Burma-India theater (he is reported missing November 14).

Eighth Air Force sends more than 1,200 B-17s and B-24 Liberators escorted by over 400 P-51s to attack marshaling yards and oil refineries in Germany. A total of eight bombers are lost and 635 are damaged. Aircrew casualties are 17 killed, 22 wounded, and 50 missing. Three P-51s are lost and three are damaged. Three pilots are reported missing.

Nine B-17s are sent on an Aphrodite mission to attack the naval installations on Heligoland Island, Germany. Only two actually make it to the target. Another 23 B-17s fly a cover mission, and 15 P-51s and two P-38 Lightnings escort the entire force. During the night, five B-17s and four B-24 Liberators drop leaflets over the Netherlands, France, and Germany.

Ninth Air Force P-38 Lightnings and P-47 Thunderbolts attack rail lines and support elements of the First, Third, Seventh, and Ninth Armies.

ITALY: Twelfth Air Force B-25 Mitchells and B-26 Marauders attack bridges in the Po Valley. A-20 Havocs and P-47 Thunderbolts attack German positions along the battlefront.

The headquarters of the 63rd Fighter Wing redeploys from Corsica to San Pietro, Italy.

SOUTHWEST PACIFIC AREA: Rear Admiral Daniel E. Barbey's Task Force 78 links with the rest of his fleet carrying the 1st Cavalry Division from Manus Island. Barbey's Task Force 78 and Vice Admiral Theodore S. Wilkinson's Task Force 79, carrying XXIV Corps, are under the command of Vice Admiral Thomas C. Kinkaid, commander of the Allied Naval Forces of the Southwest Pacific Area and commander of the Seventh Fleet. He also has operational control of Task Force 77, the battleships and cruisers that will provide fire support to the landing force; Rear Admiral Jesse B. Oldendorf commands Task Force 77. The escort carrier group (Task Group 77.4) that will provide air support to the landing forces under Seventh Fleet's direct command is under Rear Admiral Thomas L. Sprague. The Third Fleet carriers, battleships, and cruisers, under command of Admiral Halsey, will provide general support to the landing forces.

Naval Task Group 38.4, under Rear Admiral Ralph E. Davison, is formed to attack Japanese installations near Manila. The carrier *Franklin* is damaged in a Japanese air attack northeast of Luzon.

CENTRAL PACIFIC: Seventh Air Force sends 27 B-24 Liberators from Saipan to bomb fuel storage areas, antiaircraft positions, and the airfield on Iwo Jima. B-24s from the Marshalls make a night raid on Wake Island.

CENTRAL PACIFIC, PELELIU: The 321st and 323rd Infantry Regiments of the 81st Infantry Division attack into the Umurbrogol Pocket after relieving the last elements of the 3rd Battalion of the 5th Marines. The 1st Marine Division is out of the fight, too depleted to be effective. It will take more than a month and a half to finish off the last Japanese defenders, who forfeit their lives dearly within the Umurbrogol Pocket.

NEW GUINEA: FEAF P-47 Thunderbolts attack airfields in New Guinea. A-20 Havocs attack airfields and oil storage areas on Ceram Island. P-38 Lightnings conduct a shipping sweep in the Lesser Sunda Islands and around Halmahera Island and attack the airfield on Ceram Island.

The headquarters of the 38th Bombardment Group (Medium) and the B-25 Mitchells of the 405th and 823rd Bombardment Squadrons (Medium) redeploy from Biak Island to Morotai Island.

October 16

ALEUTIANS: Eleventh Air Force sends seven B-24 Liberators to fly cover for a naval task force.

CBI: Tenth Air Force P-47 Thunderbolts attack railroad bridges. B-25 Mitchells, escorted by P-47s, attack the airfield at Shwebo.

Fourteenth Air Force sends eight B-25 Mitchells and 28 B-24 Liberators escorted by 35 P-40s and P-51 Mustangs to attack the Kowloon docks at Hong Kong. Aircrews report three cargo ships and two tankers sunk and five other ships damaged. Eight Japanese fighters attack the formation, and fighter pilots report one confirmed kill. B-24s attack shipping in the South China Sea, Formosa Strait, and the Gulf of Tonkin.

ETO: First Army's plan for the capture of Aachen is accomplished as XIX Corps and the VII Corps of the First Army link behind Aachen and repel several German counterattacks. The 18th Infantry Regiment of the 1st Infantry Division and the 119th Infantry Regiment of the 30th Infantry Division play an important role. The 1st Infantry Division continues to battle German defenders in the city.

The 39th and 60th Infantry Regiments of the 9th Infantry Division have been able to advance about 3,000 yards into the Hürtgen Forest after a month of combat. The cost has been 4,500 men killed, wounded, or missing.

MEDITERRANEAN: Fifteenth Air Force sends more than 600 B-17s and B-24 Liberators escorted by P-38 Lightnings and P-51 Mustangs to attack industrial targets in Austria and Czechoslovakia.

ITALY: The Fifth and the Eighth Armies attack simultaneously in an attempt to break German lines and drive on to Bologna. The 34th Infantry Division with Combat Command A from the 1st Armored Division attacks Monte della Vigna and Monte Belmonte.

The 91st Infantry Divisions supported by elements of the 1st Armored Division also attacks, but makes little progress. The 85th Infantry Division has success but is unable to exploit its gains without reinforcements.

Twelfth Air Force A-20 Havocs and P-47 Thunderbolts attack German defensive positions, roads, and bridges near Monte Belmonte.

SOUTHWEST PACIFIC AREA: FEAF P-38 Lightnings attack the harbor, shipping, airfield, and trucks on Cagayan Island in the Philippines.

Japanese torpedo planes damage U.S. light cruiser *Houston* a second time east of Formosa in the Philippines Sea. Carrier aircraft from Task Force 38 sink a torpedo boat and damage an auxiliary vessel in the South China Sea.

PACIFIC: Twentieth Air Force sends more than 40 B-29 Superfortresses from Chengtu, China, to bomb the Okayama aircraft production facility and the Heito airfield on Formosa. Some B-29s bomb alternate airfield and harbor targets on Formosa, or bomb Hengyang and several other airfields in China.

U.S. submarine *Besugo* (SS-321) damages Japanese destroyer off Kyushu, Japan.

U.S. submarine *Tilefish* torpedoes and sinks a Japanese guardboat in the Kuriles.

CENTRAL PACIFIC: Seventh Air Force B-24 Liberators from the Marshalls bomb Truk.

NEW GUINEA: FEAF A-20 Havocs, P-47 Thunderbolts, P-38 Lightnings, and P-40s attack airfields in northwest New Guinea. B-24 Liberators, B-25 Mitchells, and P-38 Lightnings attack the airfields on Boeroe Island, Ceram Island, the town of Amboina on Ambon Island, and shipping in Binnen Bay in the Molucca Islands. B-24s bomb Celebes Island.

The headquarters of the 5th Bombardment Group (Heavy) and the B-24s of the 23rd and 31st Bombardment Squadrons (Heavy) redeploy from Noemfoor Island to Morotai Island.

October 17

ALEUTIANS: Eleventh Air Force sends seven B-24 Liberators to fly cover for a naval task force.

CBI: Tenth Air Force P-47 Thunderbolts attack logistics storage areas. B-25 Mitchells bomb airfields and bridges.

In China, Fourteenth Air Force sends 15 B-25 Mitchells, 12 P-40s, and 10 P-51 Mustangs to bomb a logistics storage depot at Tien Ho airfield at Canton.

ETO: Eighth Air Force sends more than 1,300 B-17s and B-24 Liberators, led by radar-equipped Pathfinders and escorted by 775 P-51 Mustangs and P-47 Thunderbolts, to attack marshaling yards at Cologne. A total of five bombers are lost and 489 are damaged. Aircrew casualties are three killed, 16 wounded, and 46 missing. One P-51 is lost. The pilot is reported missing.

Ninth Air Force sends 35 B-26 Marauders to attack the rail bridge at Euskirchen in Germany.

MEDITERRANEAN: Fifteenth Air Force sends more than 300 B-17s and B-24 Liberators escorted by P-38 Lightnings and P-51 Mustangs to attack the Blechhammer oil refinery in Germany and industrial targets near Vienna.

ITALY: Twelfth Air Force A-20 Havocs attack targets in the Po River valley. P-47 Thunderbolts attack rail lines and bridges.

SOUTHWEST PACIFIC AREA: Elements of the 6th Ranger Battalion capture the radio station and lighthouse on Suluan Island off Leyte. The Rangers set up navigation lights to guide the transports.

Nearly 60 FEAF B-24 Liberators attack oil storage areas, barracks, and shore targets on Mindanao Island in the Philippines.

Naval Task Group 38.4 under Rear Admiral Ralph E. Davison attacks Japanese installations at Legaspi and Clark Field on Luzon.

PACIFIC: Twentieth Air Force sends 10 B-29 Superfortresses from Chengtu, China, to bomb the Einansho air depot on Formosa.

Receiving information of American forces off Leyte, Admiral Toyoda Soemu, Commander in Chief Combined Fleet, orders operation *Sho-1* for defending the Philippines and conducting a decisive naval battle.

CENTRAL PACIFIC: Seventh Air Force sends 11 B-24 Liberators from Saipan to bomb shipping off Haha Jima and the town of Okimura in the Bonin Islands. B-25 Mitchells from the Gilberts bomb Nauru Island.

NEW GUINEA: FEAF A-20 Havocs, B-25 Mitchells, P-47 Thunderbolts, and P-38 Lightnings attack oil storage areas and airfields at Ceram Island, Ambon Island, and Boeroe Island. B-25 Mitchells and P-38s bomb airfields and shipping at Halmahera Island.

The headquarters of XIII Bomber Command redeploys from Wakde Island to Morotai Island.

October 18

ALEUTIANS: Eleventh Air Force sends four B-25 Mitchells to bomb Kurabu Cape airfield on Paramushiru Island and Suribachi. Aircrews report about 12 Japanese fighters intercepting the bombers. Two fighters are reported shot down.

CBI: President Roosevelt recalls General Joseph W. Stilwell from China after Generalissimo Chiang Kai-shek rejects all compromise offers. Major General Albert C. Wedemeyer replaces him. Unlike Stilwell, who reported to both Admiral Lord Louis Mountbatten, the Allied commander for Southeast Asia, and Chiang Kai-shek, Wedemeyer will report only to Chiang as the U.S. commander of the China theater. Stilwell also supervised Lend-Lease to China, but Wedemeyer will have no authority, nor will he be responsible for Chinese forces in Burma. Given this extreme narrowing of duties, Wedemeyer is able to direct his entire attention to Chiang. Far more accommodating than Stilwell, Wedemeyer is helped by welcome news of increased supply tonnage being flown into China. In October, 300 aircraft are bringing in over 35,000 tons of supplies. The increase, however, adds little to the ability of the Fourteenth Air Force to influence events in China.

ATLANTIC: The Joint War Plans Committee issues its strategic assessment titled "Operations for the Defeat of Japan." It notes the importance of capturing Iwo Jima to assist in establishing an air and naval blockade of the Japanese home islands and contributing directly to the destruction of Japan's remaining air and naval strength in preparation for an invasion.

ETO: General Eisenhower meets with General Omar N. Bradley and Field Marshal Sir Bernard L. Montgomery in Brussels, Belgium, to address Allied operational objectives. All three commanders agree that Allied forces should reach the Rhine River before winter. With Antwerp still unavailable, the armies will have to be supplied through the Normandy beaches and Cherbourg. Eisenhower's objective is the Ruhr. The First and Ninth Armies of Bradley's 12th Army Group will attack toward Aachen and cross the Roer River. First Army will mount the main effort to reach the Rhine south of Cologne. The Ninth Army will support First Army's attack and protect the northern flank. The First Army will give Ninth Army operational control of XIX corps for this task. First Army will receive VIII Corps, and VII Corps will get an additional division. Once across the Roer, the two armies are to attack to the Rhine River in the area between Cologne and Krefeld. The British will clear the Reichswald and cross the Maas River to join with Ninth Army. Third Army is given the lowest priority for support.

Eighth Air Force sends more than 567 B-17s and B-24 Liberators led by radar-equipped Pathfinders and escorted by 565 P-47 Thunderbolts and P-51 Mustangs to attack industrial targets around Cologne. A total of five bombers are lost and 48 damaged. Aircrew casualties are one killed, three wounded, and 45 missing. Five fighters are lost, and the pilots are reported missing.

Ninth Air Force IX Tactical Air Command P-38 and P-47 fighters attack rail lines and support the 1st Infantry Division at Aachen.

Naval Advanced Base La Havre, France, is established.

ITALY: The 133rd Infantry Regiment of the 34th Infantry Division fights to seize Monte Belmonte. Twelfth Air Force P-47 Thunderbolts support the attack.

SOUTHWEST PACIFIC AREA: Elements of the 6th Ranger Battalion land on Homonhon Island and find it unoccupied. Minesweepers clear channels into Leyte Gulf.

Vice Admiral Jesse B. Oldendorf arrives with the Bombardment and Fire Support Group of Seventh Fleet. This group consists of six battleships, most of which had been the targets at Pearl Harbor on December 7, 1941. Along with the battleships are three heavy cruisers, three light cruisers, and 16 destroyers.

FEAF P-38 Lightnings attack barges, coastal shipping, and vehicles on the coast of Mindanao Island in the Philippines.

Carrier aircraft from Naval Task Groups 38.1 (Vice Admiral John S. McCain) and 38.4 (Rear Admiral Ralph E. Davison) attack Japanese airfields and shipping near Manila. A passenger-cargo ship and two cargo ships are sunk. TG 38.2 (Rear Admiral Gerald F. Bogan) attacks shipping off northern Luzon, sinking an auxiliary submarine chaser, two transports, and three cargo ships.

Aircraft from Seventh Fleet (Vice Admiral Thomas C. Kinkaid) sink seven Japanese ships near Cebu. U.S. submarine *Bluegill* torpedoes and sinks three Japanese cargo ships in the South China Sea. U.S. submarine *Raton* torpedoes and sinks two Japanese cargo ships in the South China Sea southwest of Luzon.

CENTRAL PACIFIC: Seventh Air Force B-24 Liberators from Saipan bomb Haha Jima.

NEW GUINEA: FEAF B-25 Mitchells, P-47 Thunderbolts, P-38 Lightnings, and P-40s attack targets on the Vogelkop Peninsula. B-25s and P-38s attack airfields on Buru Island and Halmahera Island and attack the town of Amboina on Ambon Island.

The headquarters of 307th Bombardment Group (Heavy) redeploys from Wakde Island to Morotai Island.

The Japanese Imperial Staff issues orders to execute the *Sho-1* plan (*sho* is the word for victory) to defend the Philippines from an American invasion. Japan will concentrate all of her remaining naval and air strength to destroy the landing force. Land forces will destroy the isolated remnants. The plan is highly complex and requires intricate coordination between air, land, and sea commanders. Almost immediately the plan begins to unravel as each commander receives his own instructions and conducts a separate operation.

October 19

CBI: Tenth Air Force P-47 Thunderbolts bomb bridges and support British ground forces.

In China, Fourteenth Air Force sends more than 100 P-51 Mustangs and P-40s on armed reconnaissance from the Tungting Lake area to the Luichow Peninsula. Fighters attack rail lines, gun batteries, bridges, ammunition storage areas, and town areas.

ETO: Eighth Air Force sends more than 970 B-17s and B-24 Liberators escorted by over 700 P-51 Mustangs and P-47 Thunderbolts to bomb industrial targets and marshaling yards in western Germany. A total of six bombers are lost and 428 are damaged. Aircrew casualties are seven killed, five wounded, and 59 missing. Two fighters are lost and two are damaged. The two pilots are reported missing.

Ninth Air Force P-38s and P-47s support ground operations in the Third and Seventh Army areas.

ITALY: The 85th and 88th Infantry Divisions attack Monte Grande, while the 34th and 91st Infantry Divisions attack Monte Belmonte. The attacks begin in a downpour preceded by a heavy artillery bombardment. Monte Grande is captured, but the attack on Monte Belmonte fails. The 91st Infantry Division makes a limited attack past Livergnano to support the 34th Infantry Division.

Twelfth Air Force redesignates the headquarters of XII Fighter Command as Headquarters, XXII Tactical Air Command.

B-26 Marauders attack rail lines and bridges and lose two bombers to German fighters. Aircrews report two confirmed kills. B-25 Mitchells attack bridges and P-47 Thunderbolts and A-20 Havocs of XXII Tactical Air Command attack German positions in support of ground forces at the Monte Grande area, and attack rail lines and bridges north of the front lines.

SOUTHWEST PACIFIC AREA: Seventh Fleet begins the pre-invasion bombardment of Leyte. The Japanese have about 20,000 defenders on the island.

FEAF B-24 Liberators bomb shipping near Sulu and Mindanao Islands and bomb the airfield on Cebu Island.

Carrier aircraft from Naval Task Groups 38.1 (Vice Admiral John S. McCain) and 38.4 (Rear Admiral Ralph E. Davison) attack airfields near Manila and shipping in Manila Bay. Five cargo ships are sunk, and an oiler and a cargo ship are damaged. A U.S. destroyer is damaged by a mine off Leyte; another destroyer is damaged by shore battery fire.

Aircraft from Seventh Fleet (Vice Admiral Thomas C. Kinkaid) sink six Japanese cargo ships at Cebu. U.S. submarine *Narwhal* lands personnel and supplies on Negros Island.

CENTRAL PACIFIC: Seventh Air Force B-24 Liberators from Saipan bomb Yap.

NEW GUINEA: FEAF A-20 Havocs, P-38 Lightnings, P-47 Thunderbolts, and P-40s attack the airfield at Utarom and others in northwest New Guinea. B-24 Liberators bomb Celebes Island. P-38 Lightnings and P-47 Thunderbolts attack Amboina on Ambon Island and the airfield on Ceram Island.

October 20

ETO: The 1st Infantry Division occupies Aachen after nearly a week of house-to-house fighting.

Ninth Air Force P-38s and P-47s support ground operations in the Third and Seventh Army areas.

Staff Sergeant Robert T. Kuroda of the 442nd Regimental Combat Team encounters enemy fire from a wooded slope near Bruyeres, France. He moves to a position on the crest of a ridge to locate the machine gun. Staff Sergeant Kuroda then moves to within 10 yards of the position and kills the crew. Out of ammunition, Kuroda obtains a Thompson submachine gun and attacks another machine-gun position. He is killed by a sniper shortly thereafter. For his gallant conduct and superb leadership, Staff Sergeant Kuroda will receive the Medal of Honor.

MEDITERRANEAN: Fifteenth Air Force sends more than 480 B-17s and B-24 Liberators escorted by P-38 Lightnings and P-51 Mustangs to attack an oil refinery in Czechoslovakia and marshaling yards in Austria and Germany.

ITALY: The 133rd and 168th Infantry Regiments of the 34th Infantry Division are ordered to halt and reorganize. The 88th Infantry Division makes a night attack toward Monte Grande overlooking Route 9 and the Po Valley. The division's attack is reinforced by the 337th Infantry Regiment of the 85th Infantry Division. Over 8,400 artillery rounds are fired on enemy positions. The 349th Infantry Regiment initiates the attack in a heavy rain. General Clark has promised Brigadier General Paul W. Kendall a promotion to major general if Monte Grande is captured.

Twelfth Air Force B-25 Mitchells and B-26 Marauders attack rail and road traffic and bridges in the Po Valley. A-20 Havocs and P-47 Thunderbolts of the XXII Tactical Air Command attack German positions at Monte Grande, logistics storage sites, bridges, and roads.

SOUTHWEST PACIFIC AREA: The Invasion of Leyte—MacArthur Returns. Seventh Fleet (Vice Admiral Thomas C. Kinkaid), Task Force 78 (Rear Admiral Daniel E. Barbey), and Task Force 79 (Vice Admiral Theodore S. Wilkinson) land four divisions of the Sixth Army (Lieutenant General Walter Krueger) on Leyte.

A four-hour preparatory air and naval bombardment precedes the landing. The Japanese are caught in the midst of changing the location of their main headquarters, causing confusion and a limited response. The 1st Cavalry Division and the two infantry regiments of the 24th Infantry Division of X Corps hold the northern beachhead, having captured Tacloban airfield and Hill 522 in the area of the Palo-Tacloban highway. The 96th and 7th Infantry Divisions of XXIV Corps occupy the southern part of the beachhead. The two corps are separated by about 10 miles. The 21st Infantry RCT lands at Panaon Strait at the southern tip of Leyte.

Japanese air attacks damage the escort carrier USS *Sangamon* and light cruiser USS *Honolulu.* Japanese shore batteries damage a destroyer and an LST (landing ship, tank).

General MacArthur watches the landings from the USS *Nashville* and then arrives onshore in the afternoon, wading 50 yards through the surf to the beach. He is accompanied by Philippine president Sergio Osmeña. MacArthur approaches a portable radio set and speaks into the microphone:

> This is the Voice of Freedom, General MacArthur speaking. People of the Philippines: I have returned! By the grace of Almighty God, our forces stand again upon Philippine soil—soil consecrated in the blood of our two peoples.

FEAF B-24 Liberators bomb Davao on Mindanao Island in the Philippines.

Krueger's Sixth Army has established a beachhead two miles deep and controls the Panaon Strait. The 7th Infantry Division controls Dulag, and the 96th Infantry Division faces Catmon Hill, the highest point on the beachhead.

A Japanese naval strike force under Vice Admiral Takeo Kurita, with five battleships, 12 cruisers, and 15 destroyers receives orders to set out for the Philippines as part of the *Sho* plan. This force is to pass through the San Bernardino Strait and enter Leyte Gulf to attack the invasion fleet and transports. Another, smaller force under Vice Admiral Shoji Nishimura, with two battleships, a cruiser, and four destroyers, is to move to the south through Surigao Strait to enter Leyte Gulf and attack the invasion fleet. The plan is to have the two fleets arrive simultaneously and crush the Americans between their combined forces. Another fleet under Vice Admiral Jisaburo Ozawa with four carriers, three cruisers, and eight destroyers, is to act as a decoy force to lure the U.S. Third Fleet away from its mission of protecting MacArthur's invasion fleet. The Japanese carriers no longer have enough aircraft, or pilots to man them, to be a significant threat. They are to be intentionally sacrificed to achieve a decisive victory. Because the Japanese naval aircraft have been so thoroughly used up in battles with Admiral Halsey's aviators in the weeks before the invasion, none of the three fleets will have air cover and, if discovered, will be entirely vulnerable to American aircraft. Strategically, the Japanese have no other choice. The risks are great, but the loss of the Philippines would be the end of the Japanese sea lifeline to the East Indies and the final blow to the survival of Japan.

CENTRAL PACIFIC: Despite Major General William H. Rupertus's protests that his marines are capable of finishing the fight at Peleliu, both Major General Roy S. Geiger and Admiral Chester Nimitz order Rupertus to withdraw his division from the island and turn over the battle to the 81st Infantry Division. When B Company of the 1st Battalion of the 323rd Infantry Regiment relieves the 1st Battalion of the 7th Marines at the Umurbrogol Pocket, B Company's infantrymen are able to replace the marine battalion man-for-man on the line.

Naval Operating Base Guam is established.

NEW GUINEA: FEAF B-25 Mitchells bomb the town of Amboina on Ambon Island.

U.S. submarine *Hammerhead* torpedoes and sinks a Japanese transport and a cargo ship off Borneo.

October 21

CBI: Tenth Air Force P-47 Thunderbolts damage bridges in northern Burma and attack Japanese defensive positions in support of British ground forces.

Fourteenth Air Force receives the P-51 Mustangs of the 530th Fighter Squadron, 311th Fighter Group. The squadron redeploys to Kwanghan from Dinjan, India.

ETO: As the 1st Infantry Division of VII Corps clears the city of its last defenders, Aachen is the first major German city to surrender to Allied forces. The Americans capture 2,500 prisoners. The First Army has suffered 10,000 casualties in capturing the city since the attacks began on October 2. General Bradley shifts Ninth Army to the far left flank of the 12th Army Group and gives Lieutenant General Simpson operational control of XIX Corps from First Army. First Army's VIII Corps takes responsibility for the Ardennes Forest area. While First Army renews its attack toward Bonn and Cologne, Third Army will attack to reach the Rhine River in the Worms-Mainz area. If possible, both armies are to secure crossings over the river. The First Army commander, Lieutenant General Courtney Hodges, is convinced that the Hürtgen Forest must be cleared of German forces to meet the goals of the offensive to the Rhine. Hodges orders the V Corps, under Major General Leonard T. Gerow, to capture Schmidt. The attack will begin November 1. Major General Gerow selects the 28th Infantry Division, commanded by Major General Norman D. Cota, to attack into the Hürtgen Forest.

Patton orders XX Corps (10th Armored Division and the 90th and 95th Infantry Divisions) to conduct an encirclement of Metz while XII Corps (4th and 6th Armored Divisions and the 35th and 80th Infantry Divisions) will attack northeast.

MEDITERRANEAN: Fifteenth Air Force sends more than 100 B-24 Liberators escorted by P-38 Lightnings and P-51 Mustangs to attack marshaling yards in Hungary. Fighters strafe the airfields near the primary targets.

ITALY: The 85th and 88th Infantry Divisions attack northeast to occupy the last defensible high ground and capture Monte Castelazzo. The 349th Infantry Regiment of the 88th Division and the 337th Infantry Regiment of the 85th Division make little progress.

Twelfth Air Force B-26 Marauders attack rail bridges. A-20 Havocs and P-47 Thunderbolts of the XXII Tactical Air Command attack bridges and roads.

SOUTHWEST PACIFIC AREA, LEYTE: Major General Verne D. Mudge's 1st Cavalry Division captures the city of Tacloban.

The 7th Infantry Division under Major General Archibald V. Arnold attacks to clear Japanese defenses and facilities. The 184th Infantry Regiment of the 7th Infantry Division captures Dulag airfield, and the 32nd Infantry Regiment clears Japanese defensive positions. The 2nd Engineer Special Brigade supports the landing of X Corps.

FEAF B-24 Liberators bomb Cagayan, and B-25 Mitchells bomb Mindanao Island in the Philippines.

Carrier aircraft from Naval Task Group 38.2 (Rear Admiral Gerald F. Bogan) attack shipping and installations on Panay, Cebu, and Negros Islands. An auxiliary minesweeper, an auxiliary submarine chaser, and a tanker are sunk.

Private Harold R. Moon, Jr., of G Company, 34th Infantry Regiment, 24th Infantry Division, is in a defensive position near Pawig. During the night, his company is attacked, and Private Moon is wounded by a high volume of mortar and machine-gun fire directed at his position. Even though the platoon defenses are being overrun, Private Moon holds his ground, firing his weapon and encouraging the survivors of his platoon. Private Moon exposes himself to enemy fire many times to engage threats to the platoon, destroying a light machine gun and directing mortar fire. He fights fearlessly for more than four hours, repulsing several attempts to overwhelm his position. He is killed as he stands up to throw a hand grenade at a Japanese machine-gun position. Clustered around his fox hole are more than 200 dead enemy soldiers. Private Moon's courage and tenacity against overwhelming odds will win him the Medal of Honor.

CENTRAL PACIFIC: Seventh Air Force sends 28 B-24 Liberators from Saipan to bomb Iwo Jima. Two B-24s from Guam attack Yap Island. The B-24s of the 26th, 98th, and 431st Bombardment Squadrons (Heavy), 11th Bombardment Group (Heavy), redeploy from Kwajalein Atoll to Guam.

NEW GUINEA: FEAF A-20 Havocs, B-25 Mitchells, P-38 Lightnings, P-47 Thunderbolts, and P-40s attack airfields in northwest New Guinea.

P-38 Lightnings and A-20 Havocs attack logistics storage areas on Halmahera Island, the airfield on Ceram Island, and the town of Amboina on Ambon Island.

October 22

CBI: Tenth Air Force P-47 Thunderbolts attack bridges in northern Burma.

In China, Fourteenth Air Force B-25 Mitchells escorted by P-51 Mustangs bomb two railroad bridges at Pingnam. Aircrews report the bridges destroyed.

ETO: The VI Corps of Seventh Army attacks Brouvelieures and Bruyères, the key towns blocking the advance through the Vosges Mountains. The 45th Infantry Division attacks from the north and the 36th Infantry Division (with the Japanese-American 442nd Regimental Combat Team attached) attacks from the west and southwest to seize the two towns.

Eighth Air Force sends more than 1,000 B-17s and B-24 Liberators led by radar-equipped Pathfinders and escorted by over 700 P-51 Mustangs and P-47 Thunderbolts to attack industrial targets and transportation targets in western Germany. Two B-17s are lost and 59 bombers damaged. Aircrew casualties are 20 killed, three wounded, and 16 missing. One P-51 is lost and two damaged. The pilot is reported missing.

Eighth Air Force assigns the Carpetbagger group of headquarters, 492nd Bombardment Group (Heavy), and the 856th, 857th, 858th, and 859th Bombardment Squadrons (Heavy) from headquarters of VIII Fighter Command, to the 1st Bombardment Division to operate as a night bombing group. The 856th Bombardment Squadron (Heavy) remains under operational control of Eighth Air Force to support Carpetbagger operations in the Netherlands, Norway, and Denmark.

Ninth Air Force P-38s and P-47s support ground operations in the Third and Seventh Army areas.

ITALY: The 85th and 88th Infantry Divisions attack from Monte Grande, but the attack quickly falters.

Twelfth Air Force A-20 Havocs and P-47 Thunderbolts attack rail lines and trains in northern Italy.

SOUTHWEST PACIFIC AREA: At about midnight, Vice Admiral Kurita's fleet is spotted by U.S. submarines *Darter* and *Dace*.

FEAF B-25 Mitchells and P-38 Lightnings attack shipping in the Sulu Archipelago, the harbor at Jolo Island, and Zamboanga harbor on Mindanao Island. B-24 Liberators attack airfields on Cebu Island and Mindanao. B-25s attack targets on Samar Island, and B-24s bomb the airfield in the Cagayan Islands.

The headquarters of the 308th Bombardment Wing (Heavy) redeploys from Hollandia to Leyte Island.

Naval Task Force 38 aircraft sink a Japanese auxiliary submarine chaser west of Panay Island.

PACIFIC: U.S. submarine *Sea Dog* torpedoes and sinks a Japanese supply ship and a gunboat off Kyushu, Japan.

CENTRAL PACIFIC: Seventh Air Force B-24 Liberators from Guam attack Yap, while B-25 Mitchells from Makin bomb Nauru Island.

NEW GUINEA: FEAF A-20 Havocs attack Japanese pillboxes and occupied areas near Sawar. B-25 Mitchells attack logistics storage depots in the Molucca Islands. P-38 Lightnings attack the airfields on Celebes Island and Ceram Island.

U.S. submarine *Darter* detects a group of Japanese warships northwest of Borneo, reports their position, and follows.

October 23

ALEUTIANS: In the Kurile Islands, Eleventh Air Force sends three B-24 Liberators to attack Kashiwabara on Paramushiru Island. Another three B-24s bomb Otomari and fly a photoreconnaissance mission over Onnekotan Island. Five B-25 Mitchells bomb the Asahi Bay area.

CBI: Tenth Air Force P-47 Thunderbolts attack Japanese troops at Nanhlaing and Kyungyi. B-25 Mitchells attack rail lines and rail cars.

In China, Fourteenth Air Force sends three B-25 Mitchells escorted by seven P-40s to attack a bridge at Lobochai. B-25s and P-51 Mustangs bomb the town area of Menghsu.

ETO: During the night Eighth Air Force sends three B-17s and six B-24s to drop leaflets over France and the Netherlands.

MEDITERRANEAN: Fifteenth Air Force sends more than 500 B-17s and B-24 Liberators escorted by P-38 Lightnings and P-51 Mustangs to attack the Skoda armament works at Plzen, Czechoslovakia, and marshaling yards and industrial targets in southern Germany.

SOUTHWEST PACIFIC AREA: Commander Richard H. O'Kane commands the submarine USS *Tang* and conducts a night surface attack on a Japanese convoy off the Philippine Islands. O'Kane maneuvers his boat to attack three tankers, despite the heavy fire from escort destroyers. He then maneuvers to launch a torpedo at a cargo ship. Surrounded by burning ships, he orders his last two torpedoes fired, and while those hit their marks, *Tang* makes its escape. Commander O'Kane makes a second contact with a large convoy bringing reinforcements to Leyte. Two transports and a tanker are quickly sunk as he engages the ships within 1,000 yards. As Japanese destroyers begin their attack, O'Kane battles the enemy head-on, firing torpedoes. In a freak accident, the *Tang* is hit and sunk by one of its own torpedoes and goes down in 180 feet of water. Commander O'Kane and eight others survive and are taken prisoner. In two days Commander's O'Kane's boat has fired 24 torpedoes, scored 22 hits, and sunk 13 ships. For his extraordinary skill and courage and inspired leadership, Commander O'Kane will win the Medal of Honor.

U.S. submarine *Nautilus* lands personnel and supplies on Luzon; U.S. submarine *Sawfish* torpedoes and sinks a Japanese seaplane carrier west of Luzon.

U.S. submarine *Snook* torpedoes and damages a Japanese merchant tanker in the South China Sea west of Luzon Strait.

SOUTHWEST PACIFIC AREA, LEYTE: General MacArthur observes the installment of President Sergio Osmeña as the leader of the legitimate government of the Philippines.

The 5th and 12th Cavalry Regiments of the 1st Cavalry Division move west of Tacloban. The 2nd Cavalry Brigade begins advancing north to clear the San Juanico Strait between Leyte and Samar Islands. The XIV Corps attacks north and west. The 96th Infantry Division attacks past Dulag to capture Catmon Hill.

The Japanese begin reinforcing Leyte. Although Ultra intercepts tip off the Americans, MacArthur's staff believes the ships coming to Leyte are to evacuate troops, not reinforce.

U.S. submarine *Darter* torpedoes and sinks Vice Admiral Kurita's flagship, a cruiser, and heavily damages another heavy cruiser. U.S. submarine *Dace* torpedoes and sinks another heavy cruiser. The damaged cruiser leaves the fleet and returns to Brunei, taking two destroyers with it as escorts. The *Darter* is grounded on a reef; the crew is picked up by *Dace*.

PACIFIC: U.S. submarine *Croaker* torpedoes and sinks a Japanese cargo ship in the Yellow Sea off the west coast of Korea.

CENTRAL PACIFIC: Seventh Air Force sends eight B-24 Liberators from Guam to bomb Yap.

Destroyer escort USS *Gilligan* bombards Emidj Island, Jaluit Atoll.

NEW GUINEA: FEAF A-20 Havocs, P-47 Thunderbolts, and P-40s attack Japanese positions near Sawar.

B-24 Liberators and P-38 Lightnings make shipping sweeps near Celebes Island. B-25 Mitchells, A-20s, and P-38s attack oil storage areas and the airfield on Ceram Island, attack the airfield and town of Amboina on Ambon Island, and attack the airfield on Boeroe Island.

The P-47s of the 39th Fighter Squadron of the 35th Fighter Group redeploy to Morotai Island.

October 24

ALEUTIANS: In the Kurile Islands, Eleventh Air Force sends three B-24 Liberators to bomb Kashiwabara and Kurabu Cape on Paramushiru Island. Two B-25 Mitchells conduct a shipping sweep off Kurabu Cape. Aircrews report one cargo ship damaged and two subchasers hit with machine-gun fire.

CBI: The China-Burma-India theater is split into two theaters: China and India-Burma. The headquarters of the Fourteenth Air Force is reassigned from U.S. Army Forces, CBI Theater, to U.S. Forces, China Theater.

Tenth Air Force B-25 Mitchells and P-47 Thunderbolts support British and Chinese ground forces, attacking roads, airfields, and rail lines.

Fourteenth Air Force P-40s, P-51 Mustangs, and P-38 Lightnings attack airfields, logistics storage areas, troops, town areas, and gun positions.

ITALY: Over 300 XXII Tactical Air Command P-47 fighters and A-20s attack targets in support of ground forces and attack transportation targets in the Po Valley.

SOUTHWEST PACIFIC AREA: Submarine attack group (Task Group 17.15) encounters Japanese shipping in the South China Sea west of Luzon Strait. USS *Drum* torpedoes and sinks a cargo ship; USS *Icefish* torpedoes and sinks a cargo ship; USS *Seadragon* torpedoes and sinks a transport, a cargo ship, and merchant passenger/cargo ship.

Destroyer escort USS *Richard M. Rowell* sinks Japanese submarine *I-54* off Mindanao.

U.S. submarine *Darter* is scuttled after being damaged when it runs aground near Palawan.

U.S. submarine *Shark* is sunk in Luzon Strait.

U.S. submarine *Snook* torpedoes and sinks two cargo ships in the South China Sea.

U.S. submarine *Tang* torpedoes and sinks a Japanese cargo ship in Formosa Strait, and damages a tanker. In a bizarre accident, one of her torpedoes turns and hits *Tang*, sinking the submarine.

U.S. submarine *Nautilus* lands personnel and supplies on Luzon.

SOUTHWEST PACIFIC AREA, LEYTE: The 7th Infantry Division drives Japanese defenders back to Burauen. The Japanese resist fiercely, supported by tanks and artillery. The 17th Infantry Regiment, supported by tanks, gains Burauen. The 32nd Infantry Regiment captures Buri airfield.

FEAF B-24 Liberators bomb Buayoan airfield on Mindanao Island, and B-25 Mitchells on armed reconnaissance hit coastal shipping and troops.

The headquarters of the 85th Fighter Wing redeploys from Hollandia to Leyte. The headquarters of the 49th Fighter Group and the P-38 Lightnings of the 7th and 9th Fighter Squadrons redeploy from Biak Island to Tacloban.

Between 150 and 200 Japanese aircraft attack the beachhead at Leyte throughout the day. Nearly 70 aircraft are shot down by antiaircraft fire and fighter aircraft from the escort carriers supporting the landing. The Japanese will continue to attack the beachhead over the next four days.

U.S. submarines *Angler* and *Guitarro* report the position of the Japanese. Vice Admiral Kurita's fleet, now reduced by five ships, enters the Sibuyan Sea. Carrier aircraft from Naval Task Groups 38.2, 38.3, and 38.4 attack Vice Admiral Kurita's Center Force in the Sibuyan Sea. Aircraft from carriers USS *Enterprise, Intrepid,* and *Franklin* and the small carrier USS *Cabot* sink the battleship *Musashi* and damage battleships *Yamato* and *Nagato,* a heavy cruiser, and three destroyers south of Luzon. Aircraft from USS *Franklin* along with aircraft from Naval Task Group 38.4 attack Vice Admiral Nishimura and Vice Admiral Shima's Southern Force in the Sulu Sea, sinking a destroyer off the west coast of Panay. Aircraft from USS *Enterprise* and USS *Franklin* also damage two battleships (*Fuso* and *Yamashiro*). Vice Admiral Ozawa launches carrier aircraft against Halsey's fleet. About 200 Japanese aircraft make an attack on the carriers. American fighters outfly and outfight the inexperienced airmen, destroying at least half of the enemy aircraft (the rest land on Luzon airfields because the pilots are too inexperienced to land on the deck of a carrier). A Japanese dive-bomber attack on TG 38.3 damages the small carrier USS *Princeton* southeast of Luzon, with one 500-pound bomb on the

The USS *Princeton* served in the Pacific from August 1943 until October 24, 1944, when, in the Sibuyan Sea in the Philippines, a single bomb dropped by a Japanese aircraft caused serious damage and led to fires and explosions that caused the ship to sink. The light cruiser USS *Birmingham,* supporting fire fighting operations alongside the carrier, suffered heavy casualties and damage when *Princeton* exploded.

deck causing a great fire inside the ship. The cruiser USS *Birmingham* attempts a rescue and also tries to contain the fire in between alarms of Japanese air and submarine torpedo attack. The fire reaches the *Princeton*'s ammunition storage area and explodes, damaging a light cruiser and three destroyers as the ships work to assist the stricken carrier. The USS *Birmingham,* alongside the carrier at the moment of explosion suffers 229 killed, 426 wounded, and four sailors missing. USS *Princeton* is later scuttled.

Admiral William F. Halsey, Third Fleet commander, orders Vice Admiral Marc A. Mitscher's Naval Task Force 38 to steam north to be ready to meet Vice Admiral Ozawa's Northern Force the following day. Halsey decides to take everything in the Third Fleet with him, including the modern fast battleships that are supposed to be guarding the invasion fleet. Vice Admiral Thomas C. Kinkaid, commander of Seventh Fleet, receives a message from Halsey, but the information is vague, leaving Kinkaid to believe that the battleships of the Third Fleet are still in place. This leaves the San Bernardino Strait open for Kurita's Center Force to reach Leyte Gulf. Kinkaid orders Naval Task Group 77.2 (Rear Admiral Jesse B. Oldendorf) and Naval Task Group 77.3 (Rear Admiral Russell S. Berkey) to prepare to meet the Southern Force as it makes the transit through Surigao Strait to reach Leyte Gulf.

Japanese aircraft damage a destroyer, an LST (landing ship, tank), an LCI (landing craft, infantry), and an oiler east of Leyte. TF 38 aircraft damage a light cruiser and a destroyer at Manila, and sink an ore carrier off Luzon.

As commander of Air Group 15, Commander David McCampbell (USN) attacks a formation of 60 Japanese aircraft, supported by one other fighter, and shoots down nine enemy aircraft, forcing the group to abandon its attack. McCampbell's fearlessness, his superb combat skills, and his willingness to defend the ships of the fleet regardless of the odds, will win him the Medal of Honor.

PACIFIC: Admiral Nimitz provides planning outline for Operation Iceberg, the invasion of Okinawa. Admiral Raymond A. Spruance will be overall commander of the operation. The amphibious force commander is Vice Admiral Richmond Kelly Turner.

U.S. submarine *Besugo* torpedoes and damages a Japanese coastal patrol ship off southern Kyushu, Japan. U.S. submarine *Croaker* torpedoes and sinks a Japanese cargo ship and a passenger/cargo ship in the East China Sea. U.S. submarine *Kingfish* torpedoes and sinks a Japanese cargo ship east of Chichi Jima.

CENTRAL PACIFIC: Seventh Air Force B-24 Liberators from Guam bomb Yap.

NEW GUINEA: FEAF A-20 Havocs, P-47 Thunderbolts, P-38 Lightnings, and P-40s attack targets on the Vogelkop Peninsula.

The B-24 Liberators of the 72nd Bombardment Squadron (Heavy), 5th Bombardment Group (Heavy), redeploy from Noemfoor Island to Morotai Island.

October 25

ETO: The commander of the VI Corps of Seventh Army, Major General Lucien K. Truscott, leaves his command to become commander of Fifth Army in the Mediterranean theater of operations. Major General Edward H. Brooks takes command of VI Corps.

Eighth Air Force sends more than 1,200 B-17s and B-24 Liberators escorted by 475 P-51 Mustangs and P-47 Thunderbolts to attack industrial targets, oil refineries, synthetic oil plants, marshaling yards, and airfields in western Germany, using radar to assist the timing of bomb release. Two B-17s are lost and 198 are damaged. Aircrew casualties are one wounded and 28 missing. One P-51 is lost and one damaged. The pilot is reported missing.

Ninth Air Force P-38 Lightnings and P-47 Thunderbolts attack rail lines in the Saarbrücken area, and support XIX Corps.

MEDITERRANEAN: Fifteenth Air Force B-17s bomb an aircraft production facility and a marshaling yard in Austria.

ITALY: Twelfth Air Force P-47 Thunderbolts bomb rail lines and rail cars, destroying over 20 locomotives.

SOUTHWEST PACIFIC AREA: The Battle of Surigao Strait. Just before midnight Admiral Jesse B. Oldendorf's Naval Task Group 77.2 with battleships and cruisers, supported by Naval Task Group 77.3 (Rear Admiral Russell S. Berkey) and with an Australian heavy cruiser and destroyer and 39 motor torpedo boats forming Naval Task Group 70.1, attacks the Southern Force (Vice Admiral Nishimura and Vice Admiral Shima) as it enters Surigao Strait. Destroyers and patrol torpedo boats catch Vice Admiral Nishimura's fleet in the narrow Surigao Strait. Patrol torpedo boats launch torpedoes followed by three separate coordinated attacks by Destroyer Squadrons 54, 24, and 56. The torpedo attacks slow and disrupt the enemy formation, damaging a light cruiser. One PT boat is lost. Destroyers hit and sink one Japanese destroyer and damage two others. These two destroyers are rapidly sunk by a U.S. light cruiser and destroyer. USS *Albert W. Grant* is hit and damaged by both friendly and enemy gunfire. Japanese battleships *Fuso* and *Yamashiro* are sunk, and a heavy cruiser and destroyer are damaged.

This attack is followed at 0337 by broadsides from the main guns of the Pearl Harbor battleships USS *West Virginia, Pennsylvania, California, Maryland,* and *Tennessee.* Most of Nishimura's fleet is destroyed in a matter of minutes as two Japanese battleships are sunk. Admiral Shima's supporting fleet encounters the survivors and, following a collision between two cruisers, retreats. One destroyer is sunk. The remainder of the fleet is tracked and repeatedly attacked by American aircraft over the next few days.

SOUTHWEST PACIFIC AREA: The Battle of Leyte Gulf. Before dawn, Vice Admiral Kurita's fleet enters Leyte Gulf through the San Bernardino Straits untouched. Halsey's entire Third Fleet has moved at top speed northward to engage Vice Admiral Ozawa's carrier decoys. Kurita, however, believes he has found Halsey's carriers. What he has actually spotted is Taffy-3 (Task Unit 77.4.3), under the command of Rear Admiral Clifton F. Sprague and consisting of six light escort carriers, three destroyers, and four destroyer escorts supporting the ground forces on Leyte. Taffy-3 is one of three such light escort groups operating in the gulf. Taffy-3 is all that stands between Kurita and the defenseless invasion ships of MacArthur's landing force.

The Japanese initiate a disorganized attack while Sprague launches aircraft and navigates between rain squalls and destroyer smoke screens to escape the rain of heavy shells from two of the largest battleships in the world, the *Yamato* and the *Nagato.* American fighter and torpedo aircraft, mostly unarmed, make dummy passes at the ships to force them to take evasive action and slow down their pursuit. The three destroyers, the USS *Johnston,* the USS *Hoel,* and the USS *Heerman,* make a determined charge into the midst of the Japanese fleet, launching torpedoes and firing every gun available to buy time for the escort carriers. One Japanese heavy cruiser is damaged, and the *Yamato* is forced out of the battle for a critical time. The *Hoel* is heavily damaged by direct fire and sinks. USS *Samuel B. Roberts* also attacks, disrupting the enemy ships. But Japanese shellfire is too overwhelming as the powerful guns begin to find the range. The escort carrier USS *Gambier Bay* is sunk, the first carrier to be lost to naval gunfire. The USS *Kalinin Bay* is also hit and damaged, but most of the armor-piercing shells fly right through the thin metal skin of the carrier. The *Samuel B. Roberts* takes multiple hits from large-caliber shells and is sunk. The *Johnston* goes down after a second fearless attack, this time on the Japanese destroyer squadron, when it is trapped in a deadly cross fire between the enemy destroyers and the cruisers.

At the point where the Japanese fleet, though crippled, has the Americans ships in its gunsights, Vice Admiral Kurita calls off the attack. Facing nearly constant, punishing attacks from American aircraft, now fully armed with torpedoes and 500-pound armor-piercing bombs, and believing he has sunk several major warships of the Third Fleet, Kurita orders a withdrawal. Of the 32 ships he started with, four battleships, four cruisers, and seven destroyers are left.

After Kurita's fleet moves off, Sprague's carriers are attacked by Japanese aircraft. One rolls in on the USS *St. Lo,* crashing into the escort carrier and sinking it. It is a deliberate suicide attack, turning aircraft into human-guided bombs. This is the first kamikaze attack of the war and adds a shocking new dimension to naval warfare. Faced with near certain defeat, Japanese pilots swear to die rather than face humiliation and dishonor—in the belief that their sacrifices may turn the tide of the war. Other kamikaze attacks follow during the day and damage two other escort carriers, USS *Kalinin Bay* and USS *Kitkun Bay.* The attacks cause heavy damage and casualties.

Japanese kamikazes attack escort carriers of Task Unit 77.4.1 (Rear Admiral Thomas L. Sprague). Escort carriers USS *Suwannee* and USS *Santee* are damaged. Japanese submarine *I-56* torpedoes *Santee* as well.

While Rear Admiral Sprague's sailors fight for their lives, Admiral Halsey engages Ozawa's fleet. Carrier aircraft from Halsey's Third Fleet locate Vice Admiral Ozawa's decoy Northern Force. Aircraft from carriers *Essex* and *Lexington* sink carriers *Zuikaku* and *Chitose* in the Philippine Sea east of Luzon. Another carrier, damaged by air attack from carriers *Lexington* and *Franklin* and the small carrier *Langley,* is sunk by two heavy cruisers and two light cruisers. Aircraft from carriers *Essex, Franklin, Lexington, Enterprise,* and small carrier *San Jacinto* sink the carrier *Zuiho.* Four heavy cruisers and 12 destroyers sink a destroyer. U.S. carrier aircraft damage a total of three battleships, five heavy cruisers, a light cruiser, and a destroyer. Four of the heavy cruisers are so badly damaged that they are scuttled.

Finally stung by a direct inquiry from Admiral Nimitz himself on the location and direction of the fleet, Halsey breaks off contact with Ozawa and moves south. As a result, both Ozawa and Kurita survive, and neither is subjected to the terrible power of Halsey's battleships.

The three separate engagements that make up the Battle of Leyte Gulf have resulted in the end of the Japanese Combined Fleet as an effective fighting force. The Japanese lose a large carrier and three light carriers, three battleships, six heavy cruisers, three light cruisers, and 10 destroyers. The number of ships that are damaged and the number of aircraft lost is significant. American losses are one light carrier, two escort carriers, two destroyers, a destroyer escort, and one patrol torpedo boat. The battleships of Pearl Harbor have their day of glory, doing what they were built to do with crews that have trained many hours for such an opportunity. It is revenge of the highest order. The men of Taffy-3 have fought one of the most remarkable actions in naval warfare. Skill and technology combined with faith and courage have demonstrated the extraordinary fighting capabilities of the American sailor.

Commander Ernest E. Evans, captain of the USS *Johnston,* takes his ship in harm's way against a Japanese battle fleet that includes some of the most powerful warships ever built. Taking aggressive action to move into a position to launch torpedoes, Evans attracts the massive armor-piercing shells from the Japanese battleships as the escort carriers desperately attempt to avoid destruction. After launching torpedoes, Evans continues to fight, supporting other destroyers and destroyer escorts with fire from the ship's five-inch guns, forcing the Japanese ships to maneuver away from the carriers. As the Japanese gunners get the range, the *Johnston's* steering and power are badly damaged. Evans, undaunted, moves to the rear of the ship to continue to steer, shouting commands through an open hatch to men turning the rudder by hand. The *Johnston* continues to fight until so badly battered the ship can no longer move. It is destroyed and sunk after a furious three-hour battle against impossible odds. Commander Evans dies, having made every possible effort to delay and damage the enemy. His indomitable courage and brilliant professional skill represent one of the greatest moments in U.S. naval history, and he will be recognized with the nation's highest award for valor, the Medal of Honor.

SOUTHWEST PACIFIC AREA, LEYTE: The 19th and 34th Infantry Regiments of the 24th Infantry Division expand the beachhead against strong Japanese resistance. The 7th Infantry Division captures San Pablo airfield.

The Japanese land 2,000 reinforcements at Ormoc on Leyte.

SOUTHWEST PACIFIC AREA: Over 50 FEAF B-24 Liberators supported by P-38 Lightnings and P-47 Thunderbolts attack naval forces in the Mindanao Sea. Aircrews report sinking a Japanese light cruiser.

The P-38s of the 8th Fighter Squadron, 49th Fighter Group, redeploy from Biak to Tacloban on Leyte Island.

Aircraft from *Essex* and *Lexington* and torpedoes from U.S. submarine *Jallao* sink a light cruiser east of Luzon Strait.

U.S. submarine *Halibut* torpedoes and sinks a Japanese destroyer in the Philippine Sea.

U.S. submarine *Nautilus* lands personnel and supplies on Luzon.

PACIFIC: Twentieth Air Force sends 59 B-29 Superfortresses from Chengtu, China, to bomb an aircraft production facility at Omura, Japan, on Kyushu Island. Other B-29s bomb alternate targets and targets of opportunity.

U.S. submarine *Seal* torpedoes and sinks a Japanese transport in the Kuriles.

U.S. submarine *Sterlet* torpedoes and sinks a Japanese merchant tanker in the Bonins.

CENTRAL PACIFIC: Seventh Air Force sends 29 B-24 Liberators from Saipan to bomb Iwo Jima. Other B-24s from Saipan and Guam bomb Yap.

The headquarters of the 11th Bombardment Group (Heavy) redeploys from Kwajalein to Guam.

Navy F4U Corsairs sink a Japanese auxiliary submarine chaser north of the Palau Islands.

NEW GUINEA: FEAF A-20 Havocs pound supply and fuel storage areas near Sarmi. B-24 Liberators bomb Celebes Island. B-25 Mitchells, A-20 Havocs, and P-38 Lightnings attack targets in the Molucca Islands, Ceram Island, and Haroekoe Island.

October 26

ALEUTIANS: Eleventh Air Force B-24 Liberators bomb installations on Onnekotan Island.

CBI: In China, Fourteenth Air Force B-24 Liberators and B-25 Mitchells attack shipping off the Luichow Peninsula.

Major Horace S. Carswell, Jr., is a pilot flying a B-24 Liberator in the 308th Bombardment Group, Fourteenth Air Force, attacking a 12-ship Japanese convoy in the South China Sea. Bringing his bomber down low, he makes a bombing run at 600 feet, but fails to hit his target. He immediately initiates a second low-level bomb run and makes two direct hits on a large tanker. Antiaircraft fire damages Carswell's bomber, knocking out two engines, wounding the copilot, and damaging the steering controls. Carswell is able to turn the stricken bomber toward the coast of China. As the bomber crosses over land, Carswell orders the crew to bail out while he and a crewman without a parachute remain in the bomber and attempt a crash landing. The bomber, with another failed engine, crashes into a mountainside. For his supreme sacrifice and willingness to save his crew, Major Carswell will win the Medal of Honor.

ETO: Eighth Air Force sends more than 1,200 B-17s and B-24 Liberators using radar-equipped Pathfinder bombers and escorted by 475 P-47 Thunderbolts and P-51 Mustangs to attack aircraft repair facilities, military vehicle production facilities, and a synthetic oil plant in western Germany. A total of 58 bombers are damaged. Aircrew casualties are 16 killed and two wounded. Fighter pilots report two confirmed kills. One P-51 is lost and one damaged. The pilot is reported missing.

MEDITERRANEAN: Fifteenth Air Force B-17s bomb a marshaling yard at Innsbruck, Austria.

ITALY: Heavy rains cause flooding, which forces II Corps to reconsolidate in order to maintain connection with its supply lines. The 85th and 88th Infantry Divisions are unable to advance any farther. Rain is so heavy that it has washed out bridges and cut off the main supply lines to forward units. The Fifth Army has reached its limits. There are severe shortages of artillery ammunition. Personnel losses, which have risen to nearly 16,000 men since September 10, have not been replaced. General Mark Clark admits, "Our strength was not enough to get across the final barrier to which the enemy clung."

SOUTHWEST PACIFIC AREA: In the Philippines, FEAF B-24 Liberators attack a Japanese naval force off Panay Island. Aircrews report one battleship and two aircraft carriers are hit. P-38 Lightnings attack vehicles near Davao on Mindanao Island. B-25 Mitchells bomb Iligan.

Aircraft from TF 38 planes sink a light cruiser and a destroyer near Mindoro and damage a heavy cruiser and destroyer in the Sibuyan Sea. Aircraft from carriers USS *Hornet* and USS *Wasp* sink a light cruiser south of Mindoro, and aircraft from carrier USS *Hancock* sink a landing ship. Aircraft from Task Unit 77.4.2 sink a destroyer near Panay. Carrier- aircraft sink a merchant tanker in the Sulu Sea.

FEAF B-24 Liberators sink a light cruiser and damage a battleship off Negros Island. Cruisers and destroyers sink a Japanese destroyer off Luzon.

U.S. submarine *Drum* torpedoes and sinks a Japanese transport, a merchant passenger-cargo ship, and a cargo ship north of Luzon. U.S. submarine *Icefish* torpedoes and sinks a Japanese cargo ship west of Luzon Strait. Damaged by a depth-charge attack, the *Icefish* terminates her patrol. U.S. submarine *Rock* torpedoes and sinks a Japanese merchant tanker in the Sulu Sea.

CENTRAL PACIFIC: Seventh Air Force B-25 Mitchells from the Gilberts bomb the airfield on Nauru Island.

NEW GUINEA: FEAF A-20 Havocs and B-25 Mitchells bomb Utarom. P-40s attack Halmahera Island.

October 27

CBI: Major General Albert C. Wedemeyer is named as Chiang Kai-shek's chief of staff and commander of the China theater. Lieutenant General Daniel I. Sultan, General Stilwell's deputy commander, commands the India-Burma theater. The new American objective is to gain some advantage from the operations in the China theater. The Allied counteroffensive in the India-Burma theater, however, shows promise despite the lack of importance to overall U.S. objectives in the war. General Sultan commands three Chinese divisions (the 38th, the 30th, and the 50th), the British 36th Division, and the U.S. 5332nd Brigade (Provisional), also known as the Mars Task Force. The Mars Task Force is composed of the 124th Cavalry Regiment and the reorganized and refitted Merrill's Marauders, now designated the 475th Infantry Regiment.

General Stilwell departs from China. In his diary he writes, "I was relieved on the arbitrary stand and false statements of Chiang Kai-shek." The relief of Stilwell provides Chiang with a temporary victory, but the U.S. military leadership sours on China and on the commander of the Fourteenth Air Force, General Chennault, who is seen as being too closely associated with the Generalissimo.

The headquarters of Tenth Air Force is reassigned to the new India-Burma theater command.

The Japanese Eleventh Army renews its offensive as Fourteenth Air Force P-51 Mustangs and P-40s attack troops in the Kweilin area, rail traffic near Puchi, and airfields at Siangtan and Changsha.

ETO: During the night two B-17s and seven B-24s drop leaflets over Germany, France, and the Netherlands.

MEDITERRANEAN: The Supreme Allied Commander, Mediterranean, General Sir Henry Maitland Wilson, orders an end to all offensives. German defenses are too strong and the weather has turned so bad that troops and transportation are hopelessly bogged down. Casualties are not being replaced and supply stockages in-theater are low. Allied casualties total 19,000. The U.S. II Corps has lost 15,000 men since beginning the Operation Olive offensive on September 10, nearly one-third of them in the 88th Infantry Division alone.

ITALY: The divisions of the battered U.S. II Corps are rotated out of the line for rest and reorganization. The 366th Separate Infantry Regiment, an all-black unit, and the 758th Light Tank Battalion arrive in Italy. The 366th has been assigned to the Fifteenth Air Force since May 6, 1944, serving as a guard force.

SOUTHWEST PACIFIC AREA: In the Philippines FEAF P-38 Lightnings and P-47 Thunderbolts attack shipping off Cebu Island and Mactan Island.

Naval Task Group 38.3 (Rear Admiral Frederick C. Sherman) and Naval Task Group 38.4 (Rear Admiral Ralph E. Davison) attack Japanese shipping and targets around northern Luzon. Carrier aircraft sink a Japanese destroyer north of Panay. Task Force 77 aircraft sink a destroyer off Panay.

The battleship USS *California* is damaged by an air attack off Leyte. A kamikaze hits and damages a U.S. freighter off Leyte.

U.S. submarine *Nautilus* lands men and supplies on east coast of Luzon.

U.S. submarine *Cero* forces a Japanese guardboat aground on Luzon.

U.S. submarine *Bergall* attacks a Japanese convoy and sinks an oiler and a fleet tanker in the Sulu Sea.

PACIFIC: U.S. submarine *Kingfish* torpedoes and sinks a Japanese landing ship and a cargo vessel near Iwo Jima.

CENTRAL PACIFIC: Seventh Air Force sends two B-24 Liberators from Saipan to bomb Yap.

NEW GUINEA: FEAF B-24 Liberators bomb Malili and Palopo on Celebes Island.

October 28
ALEUTIANS: Eleventh Air Force sends eight B-25 Mitchells to fly cover for a naval task force.

CBI: In China, Fourteenth Air Force P-40 and P-51 Mustangs strafe villages, troops, and horses near Menghsu and Konghow.

ETO: General Eisenhower shifts the main effort from Field Marshal Sir Bernard L. Montgomery's 21st Army Group to General Omar N. Bradley's 12th Army Group. Montgomery is to focus on the capture of Antwerp, the port city essential to supporting future operations. Bradley is to establish a bridgehead over the Rhine River near Cologne. The First Army will make the main attack, with Ninth Army and Third Army in support. The 6th Army Group will also advance to the Rhine River. After the 12th Army Group has secured bridgeheads over the Rhine, the main effort will again shift to the north where Montgomery's 21st Army Group will make the main attack into the Ruhr. This is all in keeping with Eisenhower's broad-front approach—the Allied forces will attack in concert, pressuring the Germans across the entire front until the main effort in the north can strike the decisive blow, followed by a supporting effort from the south to encircle the Ruhr.

Eighth Air Force sends more than 360 B-17s escorted by nearly 200 P-51 Mustangs to attack marshaling yards in Germany. Three B-17s are lost and 140 damaged. Aircrew casualties are 12 wounded and 29 missing. Two P-51 fighters are lost. The pilots are reported missing.

During the night three B-17s and six B-24s drop leaflets over Germany, France, and the Netherlands.

Ninth Air Force sends 45 B-26 Marauders to bomb rail bridges at various locations and the airfield at Euskirchen. P-38 Lightnings and P-47 Thunderbolts support XIX Corps.

Staff Sergeant Lucian Adams of the 30th Infantry Regiment, 3rd Infantry Division, takes action when his company is stopped near St-Die, France, as it attempts to clear the line of supply to a battalion isolated by the enemy. German machine-gun positions cover the approach to the Mortagne Forest, engaging the Americans and causing a number of casualties. Staff Sergeant Adams picks up a Browning

Automatic Rifle and charges forward, firing the weapon from the hip and coming to within a few yards of the German positions. Firing short bursts from the BAR and throwing hand grenades, Staff Sergeant Adams moves through the woods, eliminating three machine guns and killing nine German soldiers. The supply line is reopened, and contact with the isolated battalion is restored. For his singular act of courage, Staff Sergeant Adams will receive the Medal of Honor.

MEDITERRANEAN: Fifteenth Air Force B-17s bomb an aircraft production facility at Klagenfurt, Austria. Other B-17s bomb the marshaling yard in Munich.

ITALY: Twelfth Air Force, XXII Tactical Air Command, A-20 Havocs and P-47 Thunderbolts attack vehicles and trains north of the front lines.

SOUTHWEST PACIFIC AREA, LEYTE: The 96th Infantry Division conducts its first major combat operation in the XXIV Corps area. The 382nd Infantry Regiment captures the Japanese logistics depot at Tabontabon, while the 381st and 383rd Infantry Regiments attack Catmon Hill. The battle for the hill will last three more days.

FEAF B-24 Liberators bomb the airfield on Palawan Island in the Philippines.

The headquarters of the 475th Fighter Group redeploys from Biak to Leyte Island.

Private First Class Leonard C. Brostrom is a rifleman in Company F, 17th Infantry Regiment, 7th Infantry Division. Near Dagami, Leyte, his platoon encounters Japanese in pillboxes, trenches, and spider holes so well camouflaged that they are nearly invisible. As the men in his platoon fall all around him, Private Brostrom locates a pillbox in the center of the Japanese strong point and runs forward with grenades and tosses them through the entrance. Brostrom then faces six soldiers who charge at him from a trench with fixed bayonets. He stops the charge with rifle fire and begins throwing grenades, but is finally wounded and drops to the ground. Although bleeding badly, Brostrom struggles to his feet and throws his remaining grenades with his remaining strength. He dies shortly thereafter as his comrades clear the rest of the enemy strongpoint. Private Brostrom's exceptional courage, his fierce determination, and dedication to duty at the cost of his life will win him the Medal of Honor.

Aircraft from Naval Task Group 38.4 (Rear Admiral Ralph E. Davison) damage a landing ship off Leyte.

Two U.S. destroyers and TBF Avengers from the small carrier USS *Belleau Wood* sink Japanese submarine *I-46*, east of Mindanao.

A kamikaze damages a light cruiser off Leyte. Japanese submarine *I-45* torpedoes and sinks a destroyer escort off Leyte. A destroyer sinks *I-45* shortly thereafter.

PACIFIC: Twentieth Air Force, XXI Bomber Command, B-29 Superfortresses from the Marianas conduct their first combat mission. Fourteen B-29s attack submarine pens at Truk.

A reality of war—the drudgery and labor necessary to put men and equipment ashore on a beach is clearly seen as unloading proceeds at Leyte, October 10, 1944. The landing ship tank (LST) has a crew of seven officers and 104 enlisted men, a maximum speed of 12 knots, and can carry 1,600 to 1,900 tons of cargo.

CENTRAL PACIFIC: Seventh Air Force B-24 Liberators from Saipan Island bomb Haha Jima. B-24s from Guam bomb Yap.

NEW GUINEA: FEAF B-25 Mitchells and P-38 Lightnings attack the town of Amboina on Ambon Island. B-24 Liberators bomb the Wilhelmina Docks on Celebes Island.

October 29

ALEUTIANS: Eleventh Air Force sends four B-25 Mitchells to attack buildings at Tomari Cape on Paramushiru Island. Aircrews report damage to buildings and a cargo ship.

CBI: In China, Fourteenth Air Force P-51 Mustangs and P-40s support Chinese ground forces near Lungling and Mangshih. Fighters also attack rail lines between Siaokan and Sinyang, and strafe airfields at Chingmen, Tangyang, and Ichang.

ETO: Ninth Air Force sends nearly 170 B-26 Marauders and A-20 Havocs to bomb rail bridges in Germany and the Netherlands. P-47 Thunderbolts and P-38 Lightnings escort bombers attacking rail lines and bridges, and support XIX Corps.

MEDITERRANEAN: Fifteenth Air Force sends nearly 700 B-17s and B-24 Liberators escorted by P-38 Lightnings and P-51 Mustangs to attack transportation targets in southern Germany. Most bombers abort the mission due to bad weather, but 35 B-24s hit the marshaling yards at Munich. P-38s attack rail lines and locomotives in Austria.

ITALY: Twelfth Air Force A-20 Havocs and P-47 Thunderbolts of the XXII Tactical Air Command attack railroad targets in the Po Valley.

SOUTHWEST PACIFIC AREA, LEYTE: The 24th Infantry Division advances 15 miles from Palo facing strong Japanese resistance. The 1st Cavalry clears both sides of San Juanico Strait. The 2nd Battalion of the 32nd Infantry Regiment, 7th Infantry Division, with a reconnaissance troop from the 7th Cavalry, patrols to Abuyog and heads for Ormoc Bay, where the Japanese still are able to land reinforcements and supplies.

A naval operating base is established at Leyte. A naval air station is set up at Samar.

Rear Admiral Gerald F. Bogan's Naval Task Group 38.2 attacks Japanese airfields around Manila and shipping in Manila Bay. Pilots report a heavy cruiser damaged. A kamikaze attack on the fast carriers operating off Leyte damages USS *Intrepid.*

PACIFIC: Japanese submarine *I-12* torpedoes and sinks a U.S. freighter in the Pacific between California and Hawaii. The submarine surfaces, shells the sinking ship, and attacks the survivors, killing eight men.

CENTRAL PACIFIC: Seventh Air Force sends 19 B-24 Liberators from Saipan to bomb Chichi Jima. B-24s from Guam bomb Yap.

NEW GUINEA: FEAF A-20 Havocs and B-25 Mitchells bomb Utarom. P-40s and P-38 Lightnings attack other airfields in northwest New Guinea. B-25 Mitchells and P-38 Lightnings bomb targets on Halmahera Island.

The headquarters of the Thirteenth Air Force redeploys from Noemfoor to Morotai Island.

A Navy PB4Y Privateer patrol bomber sinks a Japanese tanker east of Borneo.

October 30

CBI: Tenth Air Force B-25 Mitchells and P-47 Thunderbolts attack bridges throughout northern Burma.

Fourteenth Air Force sends 13 B-24 Liberators to lay mines in Victoria Harbor, Hong Kong.

ETO: Eighth Air Force sends more than 1,200 B-17s and B-24 Liberators escorted by nearly 900 P-47 Thunderbolts and P-51 Mustangs to attack oil refineries, marshaling yards, and oil production facilities in Germany. Two bombers are lost and 49 damaged. Aircrew casualties are one wounded and 21 missing. Six fighters are lost, and the pilots are reported missing.

Of five B-17s sent on an Aphrodite mission against Heligoland Island, Germany, only two reach the target. The bombers are escorted by seven P-47s. Another 26 B-17s, escorted by P-47s, fly cover.

During the night two B-17s and seven B-24s drop leaflets over Germany, France, and the Netherlands.

Private Wilburn K. Ross is a light machine gunner with G Company, 350th Infantry, 3rd Infantry Division. His company makes an attack against a German position near St-Jacques, France, and suffers heavy casualties. The Germans attempt a counterattack to shatter the survivors. But Private Ross sets up his machine gun in front of the line and, fully exposed to enemy fire, stops the assault. He continues to hold off successive German attacks, fighting on alone in his exposed position. Finally out of ammunition, Ross and eight survivors of his company are ordered to pull back. Ross and his comrades receive ammunition just as the Germans begin a final assault. Ross again holds off the enemy, forcing them to retreat. In five continuous hours of combat Private Ross has defended his company's position and killed or wounded at least 58 Germans. For his remarkable act of courage and devotion to duty against overwhelming odds, Private Ross will receive the Medal of Honor.

MEDITERRANEAN: During the night Fifteenth Air Force B-24 Liberators bomb a marshaling yard at Klagenfurt, Austria.

ITALY: Twelfth Air Force P-47 Thunderbolts and A-20 Havocs of the XXII Tactical Air Command attack targets in the Po Valley.

SOUTHWEST PACIFIC AREA: In the 7th Infantry Division area, the 17th Infantry Regiment, reinforced by the 2nd Battalion of the 184th Infantry Regiment, clears Dagami using tanks, flamethrowers, and bayonets.

General Krueger orders the 21st RCT to move from Panaon to rejoin the 24th Infantry Division. A battalion of the 32nd Infantry Division will occupy Panaon.

FEAF B-24 Liberators bomb the airfield on Negros Island in the Philippines. B-25 Mitchells and P-38 Lightnings attack the airfield on Mindanao.

Kamikazes damage the carrier USS *Franklin* and small carrier USS *Belleau Wood* east of Mindanao.

PACIFIC: Twentieth Air Force sends eight B-29 Superfortresses from the Marianas to bomb submarine pens at Truk.

U.S. submarine *Salmon* torpedoes and damages a Japanese coastal patrol ship southwest of Kyushu, Japan. As USS *Salmon* and USS *Trigger* coordinate an attack and damage a merchant tanker off Kyushu, the *Salmon* is damaged in a depth-charge attack and must end her patrol.

CENTRAL PACIFIC: Seventh Air Force sends eight B-24 Liberators from Guam to bomb Yap. One B-24 from Saipan during the night bombs Iwo Jima on a snooper mission. B-25 Mitchells from Makin Island bomb Nauru Island.

New Guinea: FEAF A-20 Havocs and B-25 Mitchells bomb the airfield at Utarom and P-40s attack targets of opportunity. P-38 Lightnings attack the airfield on Borneo. B-24 Liberators bomb the wharf area at Makassar on Celebes Island. P-38 Lightnings attack Piroe on Ceram Island.

Thirteenth Air Force P-38 Lightnings damage a Japanese submarine chaser in the Celebes Sea and sink two merchant tankers off Borneo.

October 31

Aleutians: Eleventh Air Force sends four B-25 Mitchells to bomb buildings at Tomari Cape on Paramushiru Island. Aircrews report damage to burning buildings. Two B-25s are damaged by antiaircraft fire, one severely enough to be forced to make an emergency landing in the Soviet Union.

CBI: Major General Albert C. Wedemeyer arrives in Chungking, China, to serve as commander of China theater and chief of staff to Generalissimo Chiang Kai-shek. Wedemeyer has instructions from the Joint Chiefs of Staff to serve as an adviser to Chiang on all matters pertaining to training, equipping, and supporting Chinese forces in their war against the Japanese. Chiang is unwilling to risk the best units of the Nationalist Army in any offensive action and holds them back as protection against the Communist forces operating in northern China. Wedemeyer also has operational control of the Fourteenth Air Force.

During the month of October 35,131 tons of supplies have been flown over the Hump, an amount that is four times the monthly tonnage delivered over the previous year. The Air Transport Command has been flying an average of 18,000 tons a month over the Hump since February, most of it to support the B-29s.

In Burma, Brigadier General John P. Wiley takes command of Mars Task Force after Brigadier General Arms is injured in a vehicle accident.

Tenth Air Force sends more than 60 P-47 Thunderbolts to attack logistics storage areas at Namun, Bhamo, and Nakang.

In China, Fourteenth Air Force sends six P-51 Mustangs to attack shipping at Swatow and Amoy. B-25 Mitchells attack targets of opportunity from Katha to Bhamo along the Irrawaddy River in support of Chinese ground forces.

ETO: During the night three B-17s and five B-24s drop leaflets over Germany, France, and the Netherlands.

Ninth Air Force sends P-47 and P-38 fighters of the XII Tactical Air Command to provide support to the Seventh Army near Metz.

Mediterranean: The 885th Bombardment Squadron (Heavy) deploys from Algeria to Brindisi, Italy, with B-17s and B-24 Liberators. This squadron supports partisans and drops leaflets in the Mediterranean theater of operations.

Italy: The JCS agrees to a British proposal to limited actions in the Adriatic to supporting Yugoslav partisans. British planners are unable to provide any suitable recommendation to move forces into Yugoslavia to meet Prime Minister Winston Churchill's timetable. Instead, the focus of action in the Mediterranean will continue to be on German forces in Italy, with Bologna as the objective of Allied offensive operations. The intent is to hold down as many German divisions as possible so that the Germans cannot reinforce against General Eisenhower's offensive, which the Allies believe will be the final drive into Germany that will end the war in Europe.

Twelfth Air Force B-25 Mitchells and B-26 Marauders attack bridges. A-20 Havocs and P-47 Thunderbolts of the XXII Tactical Air Command attack German positions, bridges, and roads in the Po Valley.

SOUTHWEST PACIFIC AREA: The 96th Infantry Division captures Catamon Hill on Leyte, clearing pillboxes, bunkers, caves, and trenches.

U.S. submarine *Guitarro* attacks a Japanese convoy and sinks two cargo ships off Luzon.

PACIFIC: U.S. submarine *Gabilan* torpedoes and sinks a Japanese oceanographic research vessel off Shikoku, Japan. U.S. submarine *Sterlet* torpedoes and sinks the merchant tanker damaged by USS *Salmon* and USS *Trigger* the previous day.

CENTRAL PACIFIC: During the night Seventh Air Force sends a B-24 from Saipan on a snooper mission to bomb Iwo Jima.

NEW GUINEA: FEAF P-38 Lightnings and A-20 Havocs attack airfields in northwestern New Guinea. P-47 Thunderbolts and A-20s attack targets on Celebes Island. B-25 Mitchells and P-40s attack targets in the Molucca Islands.

November 1

ALEUTIANS: One Eleventh Air Force B-24 on an armed weather mission bombs Otomari Cape in the Kurile Islands.

CBI: Tenth Air Force P-47 Thunderbolts and B-25 Mitchells destroy bridges and rail lines and attack Japanese defenses near Bhamo.

In China, Fourteenth Air Force sends about 70 P-51 Mustangs and P-40s to support Chinese ground forces near Lungling.

ETO: The weather in western Europe turns bad, beginning a period of almost daily rain and cold temperatures, which only adds to the misery of Allied fighting forces attacking into the teeth of well-prepared German defenses in a bitter war of attrition.

Eighth Air Force sends more than 300 B-17s and B-24 Liberators, escorted by over 280 P-51 Mustangs and P-47 Thunderbolts, to attack the Hamm marshaling yard, oil production plants near Gelsenkirchen, a marshaling yard at Koblenz, and a bridge at Rudesheim. A total of 56 bombers are damaged. Aircrew casualties are one killed. Fighter pilots report two confirmed kills. Two P-51 fighters are lost, and the pilots are reported missing.

Ninth Air Force sends P-47 and P-38 fighters to attack bridges, roads, and rail lines.

MEDITERRANEAN: Fifteenth Air Force sends more than 300 B-17s and B-24 Liberators escorted by P-38 Lightnings and P-51 Mustangs to attack industrial targets and marshaling yards near Vienna.

ITALY: Twelfth Air Force A-20 Havocs and P-47 Thunderbolts attack rail lines and bridges, roads and rail cars, in the Po Valley.

SOUTHWEST PACIFIC AREA: The 19th and 34th Infantry Regiments of the 24th Infantry Division, after a seven-day-long advance through the Leyte Valley with tanks and supported by three artillery battalions, approach the north coast and their objective, the port of Carigara.

The Japanese reinforce Leyte with 13,000 men from parts of three divisions.

FEAF B-24 Liberators bomb airfields on Cebu Island, Alicante on Negros Island, and a logistics bases at Del Monte on Mindanao Island. P-38 Lightnings follow up the attacks on the airfields. The P-38s destroy about 75 Japanese fighters on the ground and destroy seven more in the air. Three P-38s are lost to antiaircraft fire, but one pilot is able to crash-land his fighter on Leyte. P-47 Thunderbolts attack shipping and coastal targets during a sweep over the Sulu Archipelago.

Kamikazes sink a destroyer and damage three other destroyers in Leyte Gulf. Two other destroyers are damaged by aircraft bombs. U.S. submarine *Atule* attacks a Japanese convoy and sinks a transport in Luzon Strait. U.S. submarine *Blackfin* attacks a Japanese convoy and sinks an auxiliary vessel and transport in Mindoro Strait. U.S. submarine *Ray* torpedoes and sinks a Japanese merchant tanker, then lands personnel and supplies on the west coast of Mindoro.

CENTRAL PACIFIC: Seventh Air Force sends eight B-24 Liberators from Guam Island to bomb shipping near Iwo Jima. During the night one B-24 from Saipan on a snooper mission bombs Iwo Jima.

NEW GUINEA: FEAF A-20 Havocs and B-25 Mitchells bomb Babo airfield. P-38 Lightnings and B-25s bomb Namlea airfield on Buru Island in the Moluccas.

The B-24s of 394th Bombardment Squadron (Heavy), 5th Bombardment Group (Heavy), redeploy from Noemfoor to Morotai Island.

November 2

ALEUTIANS: Eleventh Air Force sends four B-24 Liberators to bomb Paramushiru and Onnekotan Island in the Kuriles. Four B-25 Mitchells on a photo reconnaissance and offensive sweep bomb targets on Torishima Island. Aircrews report 15 buildings on fire.

CBI: Tenth Air Force redeploys its headquarters from New Delhi, India, to Myitkyina.

P-47 Thunderbolts bomb bridges, logistics bases, airfields, and support Chinese and British ground forces. B-25 Mitchells destroy two bridges.

In China, Fourteenth Air Force sends more than 100 P-40s, P-51 Mustangs, and P-38 Lightnings over southern China to attack bridges and industrial facilities, as well as tanks and troop concentrations. Fighters also attack the airfield and rail targets at Gia Lam in French Indochina.

The B-25 Mitchells of the 11th Bombardment Squadron (Medium), 341st Bombardment Group (Medium), redeploy from Yang Tong to Yangkai.

German submarine *U-181* torpedoes and sinks a U.S. tanker in the southern Indian Ocean.

ETO: General Omar Bradley gives Lieutenant General Hodges's First Army the task of attacking toward Cologne to establish a bridgehead over the Rhine River, in accordance with Eisenhower's plan laid out on October 28. First Army, in turn, gives Major General Collins's VII Corps the task of making the main attack. However, Hodges requires the Hürtgen Forest to be cleared out to protect the VII Corps flank. The V Corps, commanded by Major General Leonard T. Gerow, is ordered to clear Hürtgen. The VII Corps offensive is intended to begin on November 5, but poor weather prevents air support and the attack is delayed. The battle for Hürtgen Forest begins with an advance by the 28th Infantry Division to capture the town of Schmidt. The division attack stalls before minefields and German fortifications. No gains are made.

Eighth Air Force sends more than 900 B-17s using radar-equipped Pathfinder bombers to mark targets, escorted by nearly 700 P-38 Lightnings, P-51 Mustangs, and P-47 Thunderbolts, to attack synthetic oil installations at Merseburg in central Germany. The bombers encounter over 500 German fighters. Aircrews report 36 confirmed kills and 35 probables. A total of 29 B-17s are lost and 545 are damaged. Aircrew casualties are three killed, 24 wounded, and 370 missing. Fighter pilots report 102 confirmed kills and five probables in the air and 25 confirmed kills on the ground. Fourteen fighters are lost. Five pilots are reported missing.

Nearly 350 B-24 Liberators escorted by 183 P-47s are sent to bomb rail targets at Bielefeld and oil production facilities in Germany. One B-24 is lost and 40 are damaged. Aircrew casualties are one killed, two wounded, and 10 missing. Two P-47s are lost, and the pilots are reported missing.

During the night three B-17s and five B-24s drop leaflets over Germany and the Netherlands.

Ninth Air Force sends 147 B-26 Marauders of the 9th Bombardment Division to attack rail bridges at Mayen, Euskirchen, and Trier. P-47 fighters attack bridges and provide support for ground forces.

First Lieutenant Cecil H. Bolton is the weapons platoon leader of E Company, 413th Infantry Regiment, 104th Infantry Division, covering his company as it crosses the Mark River, Holland, during the night. German machine-gun and mortar fire catches many of the men in midstream. Lieutenant Bolton responds with machine-gun and mortar fire but is unable to locate the German positions. Although wounded badly in the legs by an artillery explosion, Lieutenant Bolton wades into the river to locate the enemy positions, taking a bazooka team with him. Spotting one machine gun in a building, he charges the house and eliminates the position with hand grenades. Taking the bazooka team forward, Bolton eliminates a sniper, then attacks a second German machine-gun position, firing his carbine as the team provides support. Bolton then leads the group forward to an 88 millimeter gun and directs the team in knocking out the gun with bazooka fire. As they return to friendly lines, Bolton is wounded again and unable to walk. He orders the team to abandon him and get away safely, then crawls back to his own lines. First Lieutenant Bolton's inspiring leadership and exceptional heroism will be worthy enough to earn the Medal of Honor.

Second Lieutenant Robert E. Femoyer is the navigator in a B-17 of the 711th Bomber Squadron, 447th Bomber Group, Eighth Air Force, over Merseburg, Germany, when antiaircraft shells damage the aircraft and fragments wound Femoyer. Refusing treatment, he works to bring the bomber back safely. Unable to stand, he insists on being propped up so that he can read the navigation charts. For nearly three hours, Femoyer provides information to return to the airfield without further damage. He dies shortly after being carried from the bomber. For his heroism and self-sacrifice Second Lieutenant Femoyer will receive the Medal of Honor.

MEDITERRANEAN: Fifteenth Air Force sends B-17s to bomb an oil refinery and airfield near Klagenfurt, Austria.

SOUTHWEST PACIFIC AREA: The 34th Infantry Regiment of the 24th Infantry Division blocks the southern and western approaches to the port of Carigara. The 2nd Cavalry Brigade attacks the city from the east, having advanced against light opposition along the San Juanico Strait. The 24th Infantry Division reports at least 3,000 Japanese killed in clearing the Leyte Valley.

FEAF B-24 Liberators attack a Japanese convoy near Ormoc Bay on Leyte Island. Aircrews report one transport sunk and another damaged. P-38 Lightnings also attack shipping in Ormoc Bay and attack targets on Mindanao Island. B-25 Mitchells bomb airfields on Mindanao.

Japanese aircraft attack airfields at Tacloban, on Leyte.

Thirteenth Air Force B-24 Liberators and P-38 Lightnings attack a convoy unloading reinforcements at Ormoc Bay. One cargo ship is sunk.

U.S. submarine *Pomfret* attacks a Japanese convoy between Formosa and Luzon, sinking a transport and damaging another.

PACIFIC: Twentieth Air Force sends 17 B-29 Superfortresses from the Marianas to bomb the submarine pens on Dublon Island at Truk.

CENTRAL PACIFIC: Seventh Air Force sends 11 B-24 Liberators from Saipan to bomb Chichi Jima Island.

NEW GUINEA: During the night FEAF B-24 Liberators bomb the wharves at Makassar on Celebes Island.

The P-38 Lightnings of the 432nd Fighter Squadron, 475th Fighter Group, redeploy from Biak to Dulag on Leyte Island.

U.S. submarine *Barbero* torpedoes and sinks a Japanese cargo ship in Makassar Strait.

November 3

CBI: Chinese Y Force (also known as the Chinese Expeditionary Force) units capture Lungling, supported by Fourteenth Air Force P-40s, P-51 Mustangs, and P-38 Lightnings.

Tenth Air Force sends 12 B-25 Mitchells, supported by 18 P-47 Thunderbolts, to attack the airfield at Nawnghkio.

ETO: In the First Army area the 112th Infantry Regiment of the 28th Infantry Division captures Schmidt in the Hürtgen Forest.

Ninth Air Force sends more than 140 B-26 Marauders and A-20 Havocs to attack a rail overpass at Kaiserslautern and rail bridges. P-47 fighters fly armed reconnaissance, support ground forces, and attack rail lines and bridges.

Senior German generals are briefed on a plan for a winter offensive against the British and Americans. This is a product of Hitler's personal inspiration and is intended initially to break through the lightly defended Ardennes Forest area and reach the Meuse near Liège and Namur, where the logistics support area for the 12th Army Group is located. From there, German forces will push to Antwerp, splitting

British and American forces and occupying the major supply port of the Allies. Three German armies are allocated for this offensive. The attack is intended to take advantage of the bad weather and heavy forest cover to minimize exposure to Allied aircraft. Hitler's generals oppose the plan as far beyond the current capabilities of the forces and seek more reasonable and limited objectives. Hitler dreams of the heady days of 1940, believing he can recreate the master stroke that gave the German army a rapid victory over France and Britain.

MEDITERRANEAN: A U.S. destroyer bombards German troop concentrations near French-Italian border.

ITALY: Fifteenth Air Force sends 46 B-17s and B-24 Liberators without escort to bomb targets in Austria and Germany. Using cloud cover for protection, the bombers make individual attacks on an ordnance depot and an oil refinery near Vienna, the aircraft production facility at Klagenfurt, Austria, the rail lines near Graz, Austria, and then proceed to bomb the marshaling yard in Munich.

SOUTHWEST PACIFIC AREA, LEYTE: Lieutenant General Walter Krueger issues orders to the Sixth Army for the final phase of the Leyte operation. The Ormoc Valley is to be cleared of Japanese forces by a double envelopment. The X Corps moves south into the valley along Highway 2. The XXIV Corps attacks north into the valley from Baybay to Ormoc City, then advances another 12 miles to link with X Corps. The 34th Infantry Regiment of the 24th Infantry Division leads the division out from Carigara to clear the northern coast of Leyte and attack south. The regiment clears enemy positions and occupies Pinamopoan, but heavy rains have washed out the road into the mountains.

FEAF B-25 Mitchells bomb Alicante airfield on Negros Island and P-40s attack a highway and oil storage depot on Leyte Island.

Japanese aircraft attack U.S. shipping and the airfield at Tacloban, Leyte. A kamikaze hits a U.S. freighter carrying troops. Japanese submarine *I-41* torpedoes and damages a light cruiser off Leyte. U.S. submarine *Cero* lands personnel and supplies on the east coast of Luzon. U.S. submarine *Pintado* attacks a small detachment of Japanese warships, sinking a destroyer west of Lingayen Gulf. U.S. submarine *Pomfret* torpedoes and sinks a Japanese cargo ship north of Luzon.

Sergeant Charles E. Mower of A Company, 34th Infantry Regiment, 24th Infantry Division, is an assistant squad leader attacking a strongly defended Japanese position near Capoocan. When the squad leader is killed, Sergeant Mower takes command and leads his men across a stream. During the crossing, Mower is seriously wounded. Ordering the squad to halt and take cover, Mower stands half-submerged in the stream and begins to engage Japanese machine guns and riflemen. As his squad responds by destroying several enemy positions, Mower is killed by Japanese fire while encouraging his men. His courage and determination in the face of certain death and his willingness to make the ultimate sacrifice for his soldiers will win him the Medal of Honor.

PACIFIC: Twentieth Air Force sends 49 B-29 Superfortresses from Calcutta, India, to bomb the Malagon railroad yards in Burma.

CENTRAL PACIFIC: Seventh Air Force sends 14 B-24 Liberators from Guam to attack shipping at Chichi Jima and Haha Jima Islands.

Japanese aircraft attack airfields on Saipan and Tinian.

NEW GUINEA: FEAF A-20 Havocs and B-25 Mitchells bomb Babo airfield and during the night attack targets on Celebes Island and on Halmahera Island, in the Moluccas.

U.S. submarine *Gurnard* attacks a Japanese convoy in the South China Sea and sinks a cargo ship west of Brunei.

November 4

ALEUTIANS: Eleventh Air Force sends six B-24 Liberators to attack the Suribachi and Kurabu facilities and the airfield on Paramushiru Island.

CBI: Tenth Air Force sends 17 P-47 Thunderbolts to attack the airfield at Shwebo.

In China, Fourteenth Air Force P-40s, P-51 Mustangs, and P-38 Lightnings attack road traffic near Lungling.

ATLANTIC: Field Marshal Sir John Dill dies in Washington, D.C. He is chief of the British Military Mission in Washington and a member of the Combined Chiefs of Staff, representing the British Chiefs of Staff officially and Prime Minister Churchill unofficially. His close friendship with Chief of Staff George C. Marshall (USA) has been instrumental in smoothing over American and British divergence over strategic issues from 1942 to 1944.

ETO: In the Hürtgen Forest, German tanks and infantry drive the 28th Infantry Division back from Schmidt and advance to Kommerscheidt before being stopped.

Eighth Air Force sends more than 770 B-17s and over 340 B-24 Liberators, escorted by over 700 P-51 Mustangs and P-47 Thunderbolts, to attack oil production facilities marshaling yards, and aircraft production facilities in northern Germany. Five bombers are lost and 192 are damaged. Aircrew casualties are one wounded and 46 missing. Three fighters are lost and one is damaged. Three pilots are reported missing.

During the night three B-17s and six B-24s drop leaflets over Germany, France, and the Netherlands.

Ninth Air Force sends 218 B-26 Marauders and A-20 Havocs of the 9th Bombardment Division to attack the Trier ordnance depot and gun positions. P-47 fighters escort the bombers, attack railroads and bridges, and provide support to XIX Corps near Aachen.

MEDITERRANEAN: Fifteenth Air Force sends more than 700 B-17s and B-24 Liberators escorted by P-38 Lightnings and P-51 Mustangs to attack oil storage areas at Regensburg, the Linz, Austria marshaling yard and benzol plant, the marshaling yards at Munich and Augsburg in Germany, and troop assembly areas in Yugoslavia.

ITALY: Twelfth Air Force sends more than 200 B-25 Mitchells and B-26 Marauders of the 42nd Bombardment Wing (Medium) to attack railway and road bridges in the Brenner Pass. Over 130 B-25 Mitchells of the 57th Bombardment Wing attack bridges in the Po Valley. A-20 Havocs and P-47 Thunderbolts of the XXII Tactical Air Command attack transportation targets in the Po Valley and German defensive positions south of Bologna.

SOUTHWEST PACIFIC AREA: In the Philippines FEAF B-24 Liberators bomb Alicante airfield on Negros Island.

U.S. submarines *Bream, Guitarro,* and *Ray* attack a Japanese convoy off western Luzon, sinking a transport. USS *Guitarro* torpedoes a landing ship. U.S. submarine *Sailfish* torpedoes and damages a Japanese destroyer and a landing ship in Luzon Strait.

CENTRAL PACIFIC: Seventh Air Force sends 18 B-24 Liberators from Saipan to bomb Iwo Jima.

November 5

ALEUTIANS: Eleventh Air Force B-25 Mitchells fly armed reconnaissance over Shimushu Island and bomb Torishima Island. Four Japanese fighters intercept the four B-25s. Aircrews report one confirmed kill. Three B-24 Liberators bomb Katalka naval base on Shimushu Island. Aircrews report fire damage to buildings and one Japanese fighter shot down of seven that attack the formation.

CBI: Tenth Air Force sends 70 P-47 Thunderbolts to attack Lashio airfield and attack Japanese targets on the Burma Road.

ETO: The XX Corps establishes bridgeheads over the Saar River at Merzig and Saarlauten.

In the Hürtgen Forest the 109th and 110th Infantry Regiments hold against fierce German counterattacks.

Eighth Air Force sends more than 800 B-17s and 300 B-24 Liberators using H2X radar to spot targets, escorted by over 600 P-47 Thunderbolts and P-51 Mustangs, and attack marshaling yards in western Germany. A total of 12 bombers are lost and 457 are damaged. Aircrew casualties are eight killed, 16 wounded, and over 100 missing. Five fighters are lost and the pilots are reported missing.

During the night three B-17s and seven B-24s drop leaflets over Germany, France, and the Netherlands.

Ninth Air Force sends 160 B-26 Marauders and A-20 Havocs to attack ammunition, ordnance, and logistics bases at Hamburg, Germany. P-47 fighters escort the bombers, attack railroads and bridges, and support V and XIX Corps. P-47s support the 28th Infantry Division in stopping a German counterattack near Kommerscheidt.

MEDITERRANEAN: Fifteenth Air Force sends more than 500 B-17s and B-24 Liberators escorted by 139 P-38 Lightnings and 198 P-51 Mustangs to attack the oil refinery near Vienna, Austria. Over 40 B-24 Liberators with fighter escort bomb troop assembly areas in Yugoslavia.

ITALY: Twelfth Air Force B-25 Mitchells and B-26 Marauders attack rail and road bridges in the Brenner Pass. A-20 Havocs and P-47 Thunderbolts attack transportation targets in the Po Valley and German defensive positions south of Bologna.

SOUTHWEST PACIFIC AREA: In the Philippines FEAF B-24 Liberators and P-40s attack airfields and barges.

The Third Fleet carrier USS *Lexington* is hit by a kamikaze attack east of Luzon.

Vice Admiral John S. McCain, commander of Task Force 38, launches attacks on aircraft, airfields, and shipping on Luzon. Naval Task Group 38.3 attacks warships and auxiliaries in Manila Bay. Carrier aircraft from carriers USS *Lexington* and USS *Essex* and small carrier USS *Langley* sink a heavy cruiser near Corregidor. F4F Hellcats from TG 38.3 sink a patrol boat in Manila Bay. Carrier aircraft from TG 38.1 and 38.3 damage a destroyer, an escort destroyer, a landing ship, and two cargo ships.

PACIFIC: Twentieth Air Force sends 53 B-29 Superfortresses from Calcutta, India, to bomb the Singapore naval base in Malaya. Aircrews report heavy destruction to the drydock and a Japanese fleet tanker is damaged. Other B-29s bomb the Pangkalan-brandan refinery on Sumatra.

Another 24 B-29s from the Marianas bomb two airfields on Iwo Jima Island.

CENTRAL PACIFIC: Seventh Air Force B-24 Liberators from Guam attack Japanese shipping in the Bonin Islands.

NEW GUINEA: FEAF B-25 Mitchells, P-40s, and P-47 Thunderbolts bomb airfields, troop concentrations, and communications targets throughout Halmahera Island. P-40s, P-47s, and A-20 Havocs attack targets on Ceram Island. Almost 50 A-20 Havocs attack Japanese positions at Sarmi.

Ground support elements of the 35th and 36th Fighter Squadrons (P-38 Lightnings) of the 8th Fighter Group redeploy from Morotai Island to Dulag on Leyte Island in the Philippines. The fighters temporarily remain at Morotai.

November 6

ALEUTIANS: Eleventh Air Force sends four B-25 Mitchells to bomb Torishima Island in the Kuriles and are attacked by about 20 Japanese fighters. Aircrews report three confirmed kills and hits on shipping and barges and damage to buildings. One bomber is lost.

CBI: Tenth Air Force is assigned to support the India-Burma theater. P-47 Thunderbolts fly combat patrols south of Myitkyina, and eight B-25 Mitchells bomb logistics support sites.

In China, Japanese forces advancing from Canton capture Nanning. Fourteenth Air Force P-40s attack Japanese positions near Mangshih and Lungling.

ETO: Major General Leonard T. Gerow, the V Corps commander, orders the 12th Infantry Regiment of the 4th Infantry Division to relieve the 28th Infantry Division and continue the attack toward the town of Hürtgen. The 12th Infantry is outflanked as it tries to advance, and several infantry companies are surrounded in the woods. The regiment will fight for survival for another eight days and will suffer 1,600 casualties.

Eighth Air Force sends more than 1,100 B-17s and B-24 Liberators using radar-guided Pathfinder bombers and escorted by over 700 P-51 Mustangs and P-47 Thunderbolts to attack oil refineries, marshaling yards, and aircraft production facilities. Five bombers are lost and 228 are damaged. Aircrew casualties are three killed, two wounded, and 46 missing. Five fighters are lost and one is damaged. Five pilots are reported missing.

Ninth Air Force, IX Tactical Air Command, P-47 Thunderbolts support ground forces battling in the Hürtgen Forest near Schmidt.

MEDITERRANEAN: Fifteenth Air Force sends more than 500 B-17s and B-24 Liberators escorted by P-38 Lightnings and P-51 Mustangs to attack an oil refinery and industrial targets near Vienna, Austria, and a marshaling yard in Yugoslavia.

Destroyer USS *Plunkett* bombards German troop concentrations and pillboxes on the French-Italian border.

ITALY: Twelfth Air Force B-25 Mitchells and B-26 Marauders attack railroad bridges in the Brenner Pass. A-20 Havocs and P-47 Thunderbolts attack German defensive positions south of Bologna.

SOUTHWEST PACIFIC AREA: In the Philippines FEAF B-24 Liberators bomb airfields on Cebu and Negros Islands. P-38 Lightnings bomb targets on Leyte and Mindanao Islands.

Carrier aircraft from Vice Admiral John S. McCain's Task Force 38 sink a transport off Luzon. Aircraft from carrier USS *Ticonderoga* (TG 38.3) sink a tanker.

West of Lingayen Gulf three U.S. submarines—*Guitarro, Bream,* and *Raton*—each send a torpedo at a Japanese heavy cruiser and damage it.

CENTRAL PACIFIC: Seventh Air Force sends B-24 Liberators from Saipan to bomb shipping at Okimura and Higashi-minato and attack Ani Jima Island. During the night B-24s conduct a snooper (radar-assisted bomb release) mission over the airfields of Iwo Jima.

Seventh Air Force B-24 Liberators from Guam, staging through Saipan, lay 10 mines off Chichi Jima.

NEW GUINEA: FEAF B-24 Liberators bomb Malili on Celebes Island. The B-25 Mitchells of the 822nd Bombardment Squadron (Medium) of the 38th Bombardment Group (Medium) redeploy from Biak Island to Morotai Island.

U.S. submarine *Gurnard* lays mines off western Borneo.

November 7

CBI: The Chinese 22nd Division occupies Shwegu. The Japanese Imperial High Command orders the army in Burma to hold southern Burma and abandon any attempt to prevent the Allies from reopening the Burma Road. The army will defend a line about 400 miles north of Rangoon, stretching from Akyab to Mandalay and to Lashio.

In Burma, Tenth Air Force P-47 Thunderbolts hit gun positions, logistics sites, and troops at Bhamo, bomb airfields at Kawlin, Shwebo, and Onbauk, and attack railroad targets of opportunity between Indaw and Shwebo.

In China, Fourteenth Air Force B-25 Mitchells bomb the railyards at Yuncheng. P-51 Mustangs, P-40s, and P-38 Lightnings attack troop concentrations, rail lines, bridges, and highways around Mangshih, Chefang, and Lungling.

ATLANTIC: President Franklin Roosevelt wins an unprecedented fourth term in office, defeating the Republican challenger, Thomas E. Dewey.

ETO: Ninth Air Force, IX Tactical Air Command, P-47 Thunderbolts and P-38 Lightnings support the 28th Infantry Division as German counterattacks drive the Americans from Kommerscheidt in the Hürtgen Forest.

MEDITERRANEAN: Fifteenth Air Force sends more than 500 B-17s and B-24 Liberators escorted by P-38 Lightnings and P-51 Mustangs to attack the oil refinery near Vienna, Austria, troop assembly areas in Yugoslavia, and rail lines in the Brenner Pass.

ITALY: Twelfth Air Force A-20 Havocs and P-47 Thunderbolts attack German defensive positions south of Bologna.

SOUTHWEST PACIFIC AREA: The 21st Infantry Regiment of the 24th Infantry Division attacks into the mountains along Highway 2, leading the X Corps advance into the Ormoc Valley on Leyte. The Japanese have built a formidable defensive line among steep hills and high ridges, with log bunkers and fighting positions. The Americans are stopped here, a place they begin calling "Breakneck Ridge." The 24th Infantry Division and the Japanese 1st Division, a unit of experienced combat veterans diverted to Leyte from Manchuria, will fight for two weeks here in a series of grim and exhausting battles.

The 96th Infantry Division fights Japanese defending the low hills west of Dagami.

FEAF B-24 Liberators and P-38 Lightnings attack Fabrica, Alicante, and Bacolod airfields on Negros Island and Opon airfield on Cebu Island in the Philippines. The bombers and fighters also attack communications and logistics targets on Leyte and Mindanao Islands. P-38s and B-25 Mitchells bomb targets near Macajalar Bay and Del Monte airfield on Mindanao.

The staffs of General MacArthur and Admiral Nimitz meet to develop a concept of operations for the invasion of Luzon. Amphibious forces will enter Lingayen Gulf, and the Third Fleet in support will operate north of Luzon.

U.S. submarine *Growler* is sunk off Mindoro by Japanese surface ships.

U.S. submarine *Gunnel* attacks a Japanese convoy off the west coast of Luzon and sinks a torpedo boat. U.S. submarine *Hardhead* torpedoes and sinks a Japanese tanker southwest of Manila. U.S. submarine *Redfin* attacks a Japanese convoy in the South China Sea and sinks a merchant tanker.

PACIFIC: U.S. submarine *Albacore* is sunk by a mine off northern Honshu, Japan. U.S. submarine *Queenfish* attacks a Japanese convoy off southern Kyushu, and sinks a cargo ship and an auxiliary submarine chaser. U.S. submarine *Greenling* torpedoes and sinks a Japanese transport and merchant tanker off Honshu, Japan.

U.S. submarine *Sea Fox* sinks Japanese cargo ship south of Kyushu, Japan.

CENTRAL PACIFIC: Seventh Air Force B-24 Liberators from Guam bomb Iwo Jima.

NEW GUINEA: FEAF B-25 Mitchells and P-38 Lightnings bomb Mandai airfield on Celebes Island and attack shipping and airfields at Ceram Island in the Moluccas. B-24 Liberators bomb Raba estate in the Sunda Islands.

The A-20 Havocs of the 89th Bombardment Squadron (Light), 3rd Bombardment Group (Light), redeploy from Hollandia to Dulag on Leyte Island in the Philippines.

November 8

CBI: Tenth Air Force sends eight B-25 Mitchells to bomb the Bawgyo railroad bridge. Aircrews report the target is destroyed. P-47 Thunderbolts attack roads, troop concentrations, and artillery positions.

Fourteenth Air Force B-25 Mitchells, P-40s, and P-51 Mustangs attack town areas, logistics storage facilities, and various targets of opportunity around Mangshih.

ETO: The XII Corps of Third Army attacks on a 30-mile front between Nancy and the Saar River. The attack founders in the rain and mud, but gains a bridgehead over the Moselle River. The XX Corps, attempting to envelop Metz, is slowed by rain and mud and a skillful German defense.

The XIII Corps (7th Armored Division and the 84th and 102nd Infantry Divisions) under Major General Alvin C. Gillen is established under Ninth Army. In the First Army area, VII Corps (the 3rd Armored Division and the 104th, 1st, and 4th Infantry Divisions) is to attack east of Aachen to capture bridges over the Roer River near Düren. The V Corps (the 2nd Armored Division and the 29th and 30th Infantry Divisions) is to protect the flank of VII Corps and attack toward the Roer River at Jülich. The area of attack encompasses the Hürtgen Forest, with heavily wooded hills occupied by a low-quality German infantry, but an infantry occupying all of the most advantageous pieces of terrain and well equipped with mortars and machine guns.

In the Hürtgen Forest the 28th Infantry Division has lost 6,184 men in six days of combat to seize Schmidt. The 112th Infantry Regiment alone has lost 1,500 men killed, wounded, or missing, plus another 544 non-battle casualties, ranging from trench foot, to pneumonia, to combat exhaustion. Trench foot is a problem throughout the American infantry units in the cold and wet conditions of Germany in this autumn of 1944. Soldiers do not have adequate protection for their feet and because units are not moved out of the front lines for weeks at a time, there are few opportunities for changing boots and socks. Over time the feet become swollen and discolored, often leading to incapacitation for several weeks. Sometimes, toes must be amputated.

Eighth Air Force sends more than 670 B-17s and B-24 Liberators, escorted by nearly 800 P-51 Mustangs and P-47 Thunderbolts, to attack the Merseburg oil plants and Rhine marshaling yard. Bad weather causes over half of the bombers to abort the mission. Three B-17s are lost and 23 bombers are damaged. Aircrew casualties are one killed and 27 missing. Fighter pilots report two confirmed kills. A total of 11 fighters are lost, and two are damaged. The eleven pilots are reported missing.

During the night five B-17s and 12 B-24s drop leaflets over Germany, France, and the Netherlands. Two bombers abort the mission.

Ninth Air Force, IX Tactical Air Command, P-47s and P-38s support the 28th Infantry Division at Schmidt as V Corps begins a withdrawal. The XIX Tactical Air Command supports Third Army's attacks on the Metz fortifications.

Technician Fifth Grade Alfred L. Wilson is a medic with the 328th Infantry Regiment, 26th Infantry Division, near Bezange la Petite, France, treating casualties suffered during an artillery bombardment. While assisting the wounded, Technician Fifth Grade Wilson himself is wounded. He refuses treatment and continues to provide aid until he is too weak to stand. He then crawls among his comrades, assisting until loss of blood weakens him to the point where he can only give verbal instructions to untrained soldiers assisting him. He continues in this manner until falling unconscious. For his courage and willingness to sacrifice himself to save the lives of 10 of his comrades, Technician Fifth Grade Wilson will receive the Congressional Medal of Honor.

MEDITERRANEAN: Fifteenth Air Force sends 34 B-24 Liberators to bomb troop assembly areas in Yugoslavia.

ITALY: The 92nd Infantry Division occupies a six-mile front on the left flank of Fifth Army.

Twelfth Air Force B-25 Mitchells and B-26 Marauders attack railroad bridges and rail lines in the Brenner Pass. A-20 Havocs and P-47 Thunderbolts attack German defensive positions south of Bologna and bridges and rail lines near Parma.

SOUTHWEST PACIFIC AREA: FEAF B-24 Liberators bomb Alicante airfield on Negros Island in the Philippines.

A typhoon hits the Philippines. Despite the weather, the 21st Infantry Regiment attacks amid falling trees, torrential rains, and mudslides against the Japanese positions on Breakneck Ridge. The 2nd Battalion of the 19th Infantry captures Japanese positions on Hill 1525.

U.S. submarine *Barbero* attacks a Japanese convoy and sinks a merchant tanker west of Manila. U.S. submarine *Haddo* torpedoes and sinks a Japanese fleet tanker in Mindoro Straits.

The Japanese convoy providing reinforcements to Leyte reaches Ormoc Bay, where Thirteenth Air Force B-25 Mitchells and P-38 Lightnings and four motor torpedo boats attack the convoy. Two escort ships are damaged.

PACIFIC: Twentieth Air Force sends 17 B-29 Superfortresses from the Marianas to bomb the airfield on Iwo Jima Island, but cloud cover prevents all but six from hitting the target. Japanese aircraft drop phosphorus bombs on the formations, damaging one B-29. One bomber is forced to crash land in the ocean. It is the first combat loss for the XXI Bomber Command.

U.S. submarine *Queenfish* attacks a Japanese convoy in the East China Sea and sinks a gunboat west of Kyushu, Japan.

CENTRAL PACIFIC: Seventh Air Force B-24 Liberators from Saipan bomb shipping at Chichi Jima and Haha Jima Islands and lay 10 mines around Chichi Jima.

NEW GUINEA: FEAF B-25 Mitchells and P-38 Lightnings bomb the airfield on Celebes Island and targets on Ceram Island. B-25s attack airfields on Halmahera Island. The P-38s of the 12th Fighter Squadron, 18th Fighter Group, begin operating from Morotai Island.

November 9

CBI: In China, Fourteenth Air Force B-25 Mitchells and P-51 Mustangs attack the Kaifeng railyards. P-40s, P-38 Lightnings, and P-51 Mustangs conduct armed reconnaissance over wide expanses of southern China.

ETO: The XX Corps crosses the Moselle River near Thionville, but heavy rains and flooding wash away most of the temporary bridges built.

Antwerp, the largest port in Europe, is captured by Canadian forces after a grueling and bitter fight; it will be several weeks before the port is ready to receive cargo.

Eighth Air Force sends more than 1,000 B-17s and B-24 Liberators escorted by over 700 P-51s to attack transportation targets and German strongpoints near Metz. Four B-17s are lost and 122 bombers damaged. Aircrew casualties are 27 killed, six wounded, and 27 missing. Three fighters are damaged.

Another 139 P-47 Thunderbolts and P-51 Mustangs fly fighter-bomber missions in the Frankfurt-Lannheim area. One P-47 and four P-51 Mustangs are lost. The four pilots are reported missing.

During the night five B-17s and 12 B-24s drop leaflets over Germany, France, and the Netherlands.

Ninth Air Force B-26 Marauders of the 9th Bombardment Division attack road junctions, barracks, artillery parks, logistics storage depots, and repair facilities near the French-German border. The IX Tactical Air Command's fighters fly sweeps over Germany and attack the marshaling yard at Düren. The XXIX Tactical Air Command's P-47 Thunderbolts and P-38 Lightnings support Third Army's attack on Metz.

As the "Lady Jeannette," a B-17 of the 729th Bomber Squadron, 452nd Bombardment Group, reaches the marshaling yards at Saarbrücken, Germany, it is heavily damaged by antiaircraft fire. Three of the aircraft's engines are damaged and on fire, and fire breaks out inside the aircraft from severed fuel lines. Second Lieutenant William E. Metzger, the copilot, agrees with the pilot, First Lieutenant Donald A. Gott, that they will first release bombs on target, then attempt to crash-land the bomber inside friendly lines to save the lives of several severely wounded crewmen. Once inside friendly lines, Second Lieutenant Metzger orders the surviving crewmembers to bail out. With only one working engine, Metzger and Gott attempt to land the aircraft. As it approaches a field at 100 feet, the bomber explodes and crashes, killing everyone. Second Lieutenant Metzger and First Lieutenant Gott will receive the Congressional Medal of Honor for their devotion to duty and willingness to risk their lives for the safety of their aircrew

ITALY: Twelfth Air Force A-20 Havocs and P-47 Thunderbolts attack road and rail bridges near Bologna.

SOUTHWEST PACIFIC AREA, LEYTE: The 1st Brigade of the 1st Cavalry Division captures Mount Cabungaan and Hill 2926 east of Highway 2.

FEAF P-38 Lightnings attack a convoy off Leyte Island and attack barges and shipping near Ormoc. B-24 Liberators bomb Carolina airfield on Negros Island.

CENTRAL PACIFIC: Seventh Air Force B-24 Liberators from Guam attack shipping and antiaircraft positions at Haha Jima Island and strafe Iwo Jima on their return to Guam.

During the night a B-24 conducts a snooper (radar-assisted bomb release) mission on Iwo Jima.

NEW GUINEA: FEAF B-25 Mitchells attack airfields and villages on Celebes and Halmahera Islands. A-20 Havocs attack targets on Ceram Island.

The P-38s of the 70th Fighter Squadron, 18th Fighter Group, redeploy from Sansapor, New Guinea, to Morotai Island.

The 408th Bombardment Squadron (Heavy), 22nd Bombardment Group (Heavy), redeploys its B-24 Liberators to Leyte Island along with the P-38s of the 431st Fighter Squadron, 475th Fighter Group, which redeploy from Biak Island to Dulag on Leyte.

November 10

CBI: Tenth Air Force P-47 Thunderbolts attack Japanese concentrations at Bhamo and Indaw, and targets of opportunity along the Irrawaddy River.

In China, the Japanese capture Kweilin after the Fourteenth Air Force abandons the airfield. Fourteenth Air Force P-40s, P-38 Lightnings, and P-51 Mustangs attack rail facilities, roads, troop concentrations, and artillery positions in south China.

ETO: Eighth Air Force sends more than 750 B-17s and B-24 Liberators escorted by over 800 P-47 Thunderbolts and P-51 Mustangs to attack airfields near Hanau, Germany. Four bombers are lost and 236 damaged. Aircrew casualties are three killed, 14 wounded, and 38 missing. Fighter pilots report six confirmed kills. No fighters are lost or damaged.

P-47 Thunderbolts attacking communications targets in Germany report two confirmed kills on the ground.

During the night six B-17s and nine B-24s drop leaflets over Germany and the Netherlands. One bomber aborts the mission.

Ninth Air Force's XXIX Tactical Air Command attacks railroads while the P-47 Thunderbolts and P-38 Lightnings of XIX Tactical Air Command escort bombers and support the 80th and 5th Infantry Divisions in their attack on Metz.

ITALY: Twelfth Air Force releases elements of the XII Tactical Air Command, including the 324th Fighter Group (314th, 315th, and 316th Fighter Squadrons, with P-47 Thunderbolts) to the European theater of operations to form the First Tactical Air Force (Provisional).

Twelfth Air Force B-25 Mitchells and B-26 Marauders attack rail and road bridges in the Brenner Pass. A-20 Havocs and P-47 Thunderbolts attack rail targets and guns in the Po Valley.

SOUTHWEST PACIFIC AREA: In the Philippine Islands FEAF P-38 Lightnings and B-24 Liberators attack Ormoc on Leyte Island. P-38 Lightnings damage a destroyer and a transport. B-25 Mitchells and navy aircraft attack shipping around Ormoc Bay. Aircrews report two destroyers and three transports sunk and one destroyer damaged.

Thirteenth Air Force B-25 Mitchells, P-38 Lightnings, and P-47s attack the Japanese convoy in Ormoc Bay, sinking two cargo ships and damaging a destroyer, a cargo ship, and a coastal patrol boat.

PACIFIC: U.S. submarine *Barb* torpedoes and sinks a Japanese transport off eastern Kyushu, Japan.

U.S. submarine *Greenling* torpedoes and sinks a Japanese patrol boat southeast of Honshu.

U.S. submarine *Steelhead* torpedoes and sinks a Japanese repair ship off Honshu, Japan.

CENTRAL PACIFIC: Seventh Air Force sends 27 B-24 Liberators from Saipan to bomb Iwo Jima. Six B-24s from Angaur Island bomb Koror Island in the Palaus.

NEW GUINEA: FEAF B-25 Mitchells and A-20 Havocs bomb airfields on Ceram Island.

B-24 Liberators of the 19th and 33rd Bombardment Squadrons (Heavy), 22nd Bombardment Group (Heavy), redeploy from the Schouten Islands to Leyte Island. The 460th Fighter Squadron, 348th Fighter Group, redeploys its P-47 Thunderbolts from Noemfoor Island to Tacloban on Leyte. The B-25 Mitchells of the 500th Bombardment Squadron (Medium), 345th Bombardment Group (Medium), redeploy from Biak Island to Dulag on Leyte.

The 371st, 372nd, and 424th Bombardment Squadrons of the 307th Bombardment Group (Heavy) redeploy their B-24 Liberators from Wakde Island to Morotai Island.

An ammunition ship with 3,000 tons of explosives on board explodes in Seeadler Harbor on Manus, Admiralty Islands. Two escort carriers, a destroyer, four destroyer escorts, and a large number of other ships are damaged by the blast.

U.S. submarine *Flounder* sinks German submarine *U-537* in the Java Sea.

November 11

CBI: Tenth Air Force P-47 Thunderbolts attack Japanese positions near Indaw, attacking bridges, Kawlin airfield, and targets of opportunity along the Irrawaddy River.

Japanese forces capture Liuchow after the Fourteenth Air Force abandons the airfield.

Fourteenth Air Force B-25 Mitchells bomb Kweilin airfield in China. P-40s, P-51 Mustangs, and P-38 Lightnings attack targets at Changsha, Lingling, and Hengyang.

ETO: The 82nd Airborne Division, under Montgomery's operational control since Market Garden, returns to First Allied Airborne Army. The division has lost an additional 1,682 men fighting in Holland.

Eighth Air Force sends more than 400 B-17s and B-24 Liberators led by Pathfinder radar-guided bombers and escorted by over 350 P-47 Thunderbolts and P-51 Mustangs to attack oil refineries and marshaling yards in Germany. One B-24 is lost and 73 bombers are damaged. Aircrew casualties are eight killed and 10 missing. One P-51 is lost and the pilot is reported missing.

Ninth Air Force sends 190 B-26 Marauders and A-20 Havocs to attack German strongpoints along the West Wall. Fighters from IX Tactical Air Command attack rail lines, escorting bombers and supporting the 28th Infantry Division in the Hürtgen Forest near Schmidt. The fighters of the XIX Tactical Air Command support the XII and XX Corps at Thionville and Metz.

The headquarters of the 320th Bombardment Group and the B-26 Marauders of the 441st, 442nd, 443rd, and 444th Bombardment Squadrons (Medium) redeploy from Corsica to Longvic airfield at Dijon, France, to become part of the First Tactical Air Force (Provisional).

MEDITERRANEAN: Fifteenth Air Force sends more than 200 B-17s and B-24 Liberators escorted by P-38 Lightnings and P-51 Mustangs to attack marshaling yards in Germany and Austria, rail lines in Austria, and railroad bridges and airfields in Italy.

ITALY: Twelfth Air Force B-25 Mitchells and B-26 Marauders attack rail and road traffic and bridges. A-20 Havocs and P-47 Thunderbolts support ground forces south of Bologna and attack convoys, bridges, and roads.

SOUTHWEST PACIFIC AREA: Frustrated by a lack of adequate air support for Sixth Army, General MacArthur requests U.S. Navy carrier aircraft support.

FEAF B-24 Liberators bomb Dumaguete airfield on Negros Island. P-38 Lightnings attack shipping near Leyte Island and targets of opportunity on Mindanao Island.

Carrier aircraft from Rear Admiral Alfred E. Montgomery's Naval Task Group 38.1 and Naval Task Group 38.4, under command of Rear Admiral Ralph E. Davison, attack a Japanese convoy entering Ormoc Bay. Four destroyers, a minesweeper, and four cargo ships are sunk.

PACIFIC: Twentieth Air Force sends eight B-29 Superfortresses of the XXI Bomber Command to bomb the Dublon Island submarine pens located on Truk. The bombers are escorted by P-38 Lightnings.

During the night Rear Admiral Allan E. Smith's Naval Task Group 30.2, with three heavy cruisers and five destroyers, bombards Iwo Jima.

U.S. submarine *Queenfish* torpedoes and damages a transport off Kyushu, Japan. U.S. submarine *Scamp* is sunk off Tokyo Bay.

CENTRAL PACIFIC: Seventh Air Force sends 29 B-24 Liberators from Guam escorted by P-38 Lightnings to attack the airfields on Iwo Jima.

NEW GUINEA: FEAF B-25 Mitchells, P-38 Lightnings, and P-47 Thunderbolts attack shipping at Halmahera Island and attack the airfield on Buru Island. B-24 Liberators and P-38 Lightnings attack Celebes Island.

November 12

ALEUTIANS: Eleventh Air Force sends two B-24 Liberators to fly an armed reconnaissance mission over Onnekotan and Matsuwa Islands.

CBI: Tenth Air Force P-47 Thunderbolts support ground forces near Pinwe and Indaw and attack logistics and communications targets near Kawlin. P-47s and B-25 Mitchells attack targets of opportunity during sweeps of the Irrawaddy River.

Fourteenth Air Force P-51 Mustangs and P-40s attack Hengyang airfield as well as river and road transports, artillery, defensive positions, and logistics storage sites around Hengyang, Lingling, and Kweilin.

B-25 Mitchells bomb railroad bridges near Thanh Hoa, French Indochina. Aircrews report one destroyed and two damaged.

ETO: The VI Corps (3rd and 36th Infantry Divisions) under the command of Major General Edward H. Brooks and XV Corps (the U.S. 44th, 100th, and 103rd Infantry Divisions and the French 2nd Armored Division) under Major General Wade H. Haislip attack to split the German First and Nineteenth Armies and break into open territory. The 100th Infantry Division leads the attack and makes rapid progress.

Ninth Air Force, IX and XIX Tactical Air Commands, P-47 Thunderbolts and P-38 Lightnings fly patrols and armed reconnaissance along the French-German border.

Eighth Air Force sets the operational tour of duty for fighter pilots at 270 hours.

Private First Class Foster J. Sayers of L Company, 357th Infantry Regiment, 90th Infantry Division, attacks a German position on a hilltop near Thionville, France. As his company moves across an open area to outflank the position, Private First Class Sayers carries his machine gun uphill to within 20 yards of the enemy and begins engaging the Germans to distract them from the American flanking effort. He succeeds in putting heavy and accurate fire on the enemy but is killed by return fire just as his company sweeps the hill to capture the position. For his extraordinary heroism and dedication to duty Private First Class Sayers will receive the Medal of Honor.

MEDITERRANEAN: Fifteenth Air Force sends 107 B-24 Liberators to attack bridges, a viaduct, and an airfield in northern Italy.

Destroyer USS *Woolsey* bombards a German howitzer emplacement east of San Remo, Italy.

ITALY: Twelfth Air Force A-20 Havocs and P-47 Thunderbolts attack German positions in the northern Apennines and attack rail targets and convoys in the Po Valley.

SOUTHWEST PACIFIC AREA: In the Philippines FEAF B-24 Liberators bomb Alicante airfield on Negros Island. P-38 Lightnings attack barges and shipping off Leyte. B-25 Mitchells bomb Daliao and Matina airfields on Mindanao Island.

Kamikazes damage two landing craft repair ships off Leyte. A U.S. freighter is hit by a kamikaze, killing 133 of the 578 troops on board. Another Kamikaze hitting a freighter close by kills 100 of the 557 troops on board. Another freighter carrying troops is hit, killing 21 troops and wounding 41.

U.S. submarine *Redfin* torpedoes and damages a Japanese ship west of Mindoro.

A Navy PB4Y Privateer patrol bomber attacks a Japanese convoy and sinks a cargo ship near Panay.

PACIFIC: Twentieth Air Force sends 29 B-29 Superfortresses from Chengtu, China, to bomb Omura, Japan, on Kyushu Island. Because of bad weather over the primary target, some B-29s bomb targets at Nanking, China.

U.S. submarines *Barb* and *Peto* resume attacks against a Japanese convoy in the East China Sea near the Japanese home islands. USS *Barb* torpedoes and sinks a cargo ship and damages another cargo ship. USS *Peto* sinks a cargo ship.

CENTRAL PACIFIC: Seventh Air Force sends 29 B-24 Liberators with P-38s from Saipan to bomb the airfield on Iwo Jima. Other B-24s from Angaur Island bomb Koror Island in the Palaus. Seventh Air Force B-24 Liberators lay mines near Haha Jima.

During the night a B-24 conducts a snooper (radar-assisted bomb release) mission on Iwo Jima.

Destroyer USS *Nicholas* sinks Japanese submarine *I-37* south of Yap.

NEW GUINEA: FEAF B-24 Liberators, P-40s, and P-47 Thunderbolts attack shipping and airfields at Celebes and Halmahera Islands.

The headquarters of the 345th Bombardment Group (Medium) and the 498th and 499th Bombardment Squadrons (Medium) redeploy from Biak Island to Leyte. The B-25 Mitchells of the two squadrons continue to operate from Biak.

November 13

CBI: Tenth Air Force sends more than 100 P-47 Thunderbolts to attack bridges, troop assembly areas, and logistics storage sites in northern Burma and targets of opportunity along the Irrawaddy River.

ETO: UTAH beach ceases operation as an offloading site for supplies to the Allied armies. The truck convoys of the Red Ball Express cease operation after 11 weeks of continuous, 24-hour rotations between the Normandy beaches and the front lines. This nearly impossible effort, borne of the desperate need to maintain forces in the field, has resulted in the delivery of 334,000 tons of supplies to the armies. Although the effort will become legendary, the Red Ball Express is a highly inefficient and inadequate means of resupply.

The 6th Army Group, commanded by Lieutenant General Jacob L. Devers, makes several successful attacks through the Vosges Mountains. The Seventh Army is organized into the VI Corps (the 3rd, 36th, 100th, and 103rd Infantry Divisions) under

Major General Edward H. Brooks and the XV Corps (the French 2nd Armored Division and the 44th and 79th Infantry Divisions). The XV Corps attacks toward Sarrebourg and Strasbourg. The French First Army attacks through the Belfort gap led by the French I Corps. Heavy snow and rain impede the attack.

During the night Eighth Air Force sends four B-17s and eight B-24s to drop leaflets over Germany, France, and the Netherlands.

Staff Sergeant Junior J. Spurrier of G Company, 134th Infantry Regiment, 35th Infantry Division, is attacking the village of Achain, France. Staff Sergeant Spurrier carries a Browning Automatic Rifle and moves to provide support. Throughout the battle, Staff Sergeant Spurrier maintains a steady fire against the German positions in the village. As his Browning Automatic Rifle runs out of ammunition, he uses an M-1 rifle. When that is empty, he uses antitank weapons, a German automatic pistol, and hand grenades, all in the face of heavy enemy fire. For his stubborn persistence and determination in the face of the enemy, Staff Sergeant Spurrier will receive the Medal of Honor.

MEDITERRANEAN: During the night Fifteenth Air Force sends 14 B-17s and B-24 Liberators to bomb the oil refinery at Blechhammer, Germany.

ITALY: During the night Twelfth Air Force sends A-20 Havocs to bomb ammunition dumps, a pontoon bridge, and targets of opportunity in the Po Valley.

SOUTHWEST PACIFIC AREA, LEYTE: The 24th Infantry Division attempts a double envelopment of the Japanese defensive position on Breakneck Ridge. The 2nd Battalion, 19th Infantry, and the 1st Battalion, 34th Infantry, reach Kilay Ridge behind the Japanese main line of resistance. However, heavy rain and thick jungle slow the attack on the ridge, and the units must withdraw. The battle for Kilay Ridge and Breakneck Ridge will continue for nearly two more weeks.

General MacArthur requests Admiral Nimitz to dispatch the Third Fleet carriers to provide air support to ground forces at Leyte.

The 32nd Infantry Division and the 112th Cavalry Regimental Combat Team arrive as reinforcements on Leyte to support X Corps.

FEAF B-24 Liberators bomb the airfield on Negros Island, while P-38 Lightnings attack shipping and other targets of opportunity, including an airfield on Luzon Island. B-25 Mitchells, with P-38s flying escort, bomb an airfield and the town of Zamboanga on Mindanao.

Carrier aircraft from the three carrier task groups (TG 38.1, TG 38.3, and TG 38.4) of TF 38, under temporary command of Rear Admiral Frederick C. Sherman, attack Japanese shipping and port facilities at Manila and in central Luzon. A light cruiser, four destroyers, a fleet tanker, a guardboat, two auxiliary submarine chasers, and 11 cargo ships are sunk, and a destroyer is damaged.

PACIFIC: A minesweeper and frigate sink Japanese submarine *I-12* off the U.S. west coast near Los Angeles, California.

U.S. submarine *Seal* torpedoes and sinks a Japanese cargo ship in the Kuriles.

CENTRAL PACIFIC: Seventh Air Force sends seven B-24 Liberators from Angaur to bomb oil storage facilities on Malakal Island and attack a bridge between Malakal and Koror Islands in the Palaus.

NEW GUINEA: Two waves of 70 FEAF A-20 Havocs attack Pegun Island off New Guinea. P-40s, P-47 Thunderbolts, and A-20s attack Halmahera Island and Ceram Island.

The P-38 Lightnings of the 433rd Fighter Squadron, 475th Fighter Group, redeploy from Biak Island to Leyte. The 501st Bombardment Squadron (Medium), 345th Bombardment Group (Medium), redeploy from Biak Island to Leyte Island, but the squadron's B-25 Mitchells continue to operate from Biak.

November 14

CBI: Tenth Air Force sends 12 B-25 Mitchells to bomb a logistics storage area near Lashio. P-40s and P-47 Thunderbolts attack targets in support of Allied ground forces near Pinwe.

ETO: The French First Army led by General de Lattre de Tassigny opens the Belfort Gap and pushes German forces into the high Vosges Mountains.

ITALY: Twelfth Air Force sends 17 P-47 Thunderbolts to attack rail lines and roads north of the front lines.

SOUTHWEST PACIFIC AREA: On Leyte, Sixth Army commander Lieutenant General Walter Krueger passes operational control of the 32nd Infantry Division from Sixth Army reserve to X Corps. The 32nd Infantry Division is to replace the 24th Infantry Division, which is battering its way against the Japanese defenses at Breakneck Ridge. The 1st Cavalry Division, reinforced by the 112th Cavalry, fights in the Mount Badian area, in terrain that is covered with thick-forested hills.

FEAF B-24 Liberators, with P-38 Lightnings and P-47 Thunderbolts providing escort, bomb an airfield on Negros Island. P-38s attack vehicles and buildings on Mindanao and Leyte Islands, and attack shipping near Ormoc on Leyte. B-25 Mitchells and P-38s attack airfields on Cebu Island.

Naval Task Force 38 carrier aircraft sink a transport, a merchant tanker, three cargo ships, and damage a transport and a cargo ship. F4F Hellcats from carrier USS *Yorktown* attack a Japanese convoy and sink a merchant tanker and damage a cargo ship.

U.S. submarines *Batfish*, *Raton*, and *Ray* attack a Japanese convoy off the northwest coast of Luzon. USS *Raton* damages a supply ship and sinks a merchant tanker. USS *Ray* sinks a coastal patrol ship. U.S. submarine *Spadefish* torpedoes and sinks a Japanese cargo ship previously damaged by USS *Barb* south of Mindoro.

PACIFIC: U.S. submarine *Skipjack* torpedoes and damages a Japanese vessel off Shimushiru, Kuriles.

CENTRAL PACIFIC: Seventh Air Force sends 22 B-24 Liberators from Saipan and Guam to bomb Woleai Atoll. Aircrews report damage to the airfield and adjacent installations, and setting fire to an oil storage site.

Seventh Air Force B-24 Liberators lay six mines off Ani Jima and Haha Jima.

NEW GUINEA: FEAF B-25 Mitchells bomb Pegun Island, supporting an Allied amphibious landing. B-24 Liberators bomb an airfield on Celebes Island.

The 310th Bombardment Wing (Medium) moves from Morotai Island to Leyte; the ground echelon of the 418th Night Fighter Squadron redeploys to Leyte also. The squadron's P-61 Black Widow night fighters remain on Morotai. The B-24s of the 370th Bombardment Squadron (Heavy), 307th Bombardment Group (Heavy), redeploy from Wakde Island to Morotai Island.

U.S. submarine *Jack* attacks a Japanese convoy, sinking a cargo ship and damaging a merchant tanker off southern Java.

November 15

CBI: Tenth Air Force P-47 Thunderbolts bomb rail lines, an airfield, and targets of opportunity during road sweeps in northern Burma.

U.S. submarine *Barbel* attacks a Japanese convoy in the South China Sea east of French Indochina, sinking two transports.

U.S. submarine *Jack* torpedoes and sinks two transports in the South China Sea off the southern coast of French Indochina.

ETO: Field Marshal Montgomery's 21st Army Group advances to the Rhine River, controlling an area from the mouth of the river to a distance of 200 miles south.

As the Allied offensives grind on in the heavy woods before the Rhine River, a total of 30 German tank and infantry divisions are being assembled in secrecy in assembly areas west of Cologne to prepare for a major counteroffensive. The plan is to attack through the weakly held American lines in the Ardennes Forest with tanks followed by infantry to capture Antwerp. The capture of the port will sever Allied supply lines and isolate the 21st Army Group in northern Belgium and Holland. Success of this attack depends on surprise and speed. The concept originates with Hitler who had used the Ardennes as the focal point of the German offensive against French and British forces in 1940. As before, the wooded hills provide cover for movement, and the attack launched in bad winter weather will neutralize Allied air power.

During the night six B-17s and six B-24s drop leaflets over Germany, France, and the Netherlands.

The headquarters of XII Tactical Air Command, including the 71st Fighter Wing and the 50th, 358th, and 371st Fighter Groups, is assigned to the First Tactical Air Force (Provisional).

Ninth Air Force P-47 Thunderbolts of the XIX Tactical Air Command provide support to ground forces in XX Corps near Trier and Saarbrücken.

MEDITERRANEAN: Fifteenth Air Force sends 80 B-17s and B-24 Liberators to attack a benzol plant at Linz and marshaling yard at Innsbruck, Austria. Bombers also attack troop assembly areas in Yugoslavia.

U.S. destroyer escort collides with an Italian submarine *Luigi Settembrini* west of Gibraltar. The submarine is sunk.

ITALY: Headquarters Twelfth Air Force transfers operational control of the headquarters of the 63rd Fighter Wing, the 42nd Bombardment Wing (Medium), the 17th and 320th Bombardment Groups (Medium), and 310th Service Group to the European theater of operations, U.S. Army (ETOUSA).

SOUTHWEST PACIFIC AREA, LEYTE: The Sixth Army commander, Lieutenant General Walter Krueger, presents his approved concept for the invasion of Luzon to his subordinate commanders. The Sixth Army is to land and secure beachheads at Lingayen and Damortis, seize the central plains and capture the capital city of Manila, then establish bases for further operations against the Japanese empire.

The Sixth Army is organized into two corps, I Corps under command of Major General Innis P. Swift (6th, 43rd, 32nd, and 33rd Infantry Divisions) and XIV Corps under command of Major General Oscar W. Griswold (40th and 37th Infantry Divisions, the 1st Cavalry Division, and 112th Cavalry RCT). The units in reserve are the 6th Ranger Battalion, the 13th Armored Group, the 25th Infantry Division, and the 158th RCT. Naval forces totaling 850 ships are under command of Vice Admiral Thomas C. Kinkaid and divided into three groups: the Luzon Attack Force (Task Group 77) under Vice Admiral Kinkaid, the San Fabian Task Force (Task Group 78) under Admiral Barbey, and the Lingayen Task Force (Task Group 79) under Admiral Wilkinson. Vice Admiral Kinkaid's task group provides naval and air bombardment of the landing beaches. The Sixth Army will land with two corps abreast with four assault divisions (6th, 43rd, 37th, and 40th Infantry Divisions), and the 25th Infantry Division, the 158th RCT, the 13th Armored Group, and the 6th Ranger Battalion in reserve. The landing, designated as S-day is scheduled for January 9. The XIV Corps will make the main effort to Manila, while I Corps holds Japanese forces in northern Luzon near the Caraballo Mountains. The 158th RCT will reinforce I Corps at San Fabian, and the rest of the Sixth Army reserve forces will be ready to land at S+2.

General MacArthur comes to the recognition that the Japanese have decided to commit a large portion of their combat strength to Leyte.

Elements of the 7th Infantry Division have captured Damulaan, north of Baybay.

FEAF B-24 Liberators, with P-38 Lightnings escorting, bomb an airfield on Negros Island and shipping and targets of opportunity at Mindanao. B-25 Mitchells and P-38s attack Cebu Island and shipping off the coast of Leyte. The headquarters of the 22nd and 43rd Bombardment Groups (Heavy) redeploy from Owi, in the Schouten Islands, to Leyte. The 8th Bombardment Squadron (Light), 3rd Bombardment Group (Light), redeploys from Hollandia to Leyte. The 80th Fighter Squadron, 8th Fighter Group, redeploys from Morotai Island to Leyte. The squadron's P-38s continue to operate from Morotai.

PACIFIC: U.S. submarine *Queenfish* attacks a Japanese convoy and sinks a cargo ship-aircraft transport at southern entrance of Tsushima Strait.

U.S. submarine *Saury* torpedoes and damages a Japanese guardboat northwest of the Bonins. U.S. submarines *Sterlet* and *Silversides* torpedo and damage a Japanese guardboat south of Honshu, Japan.

CENTRAL PACIFIC: Seventh Air Force B-24 Liberators from Guam attack shipping at Haha Jima and near Chichi Jima.

During the night a B-24 conducts a snooper (radar-assisted bomb release) mission on Iwo Jima.

NEW GUINEA: FEAF B-25 Mitchells, P-40s, and P-47 Thunderbolts support the Allied amphibious landings in Mapia Islands off the northwest coast of New Guinea. B-24 Liberators bomb targets on Celebes and Halmahera Islands.

November 16

CBI: The headquarters of the 1st Provisional Tank Group arrives at Myitkyina.

In Burma, Tenth Air Force sends P-47 Thunderbolts to attack troop assembly areas and logistics storage sites at Naungmo, Nawngmoloi, and Lashio. Other P-47s provide support to Allied ground forces near Pinwe.

In China, Fourteenth Air Force sends 23 B-24 Liberators to bomb Changsha.
ETO: The First and Ninth Armies begin their attack into the Hürtgen Forest toward the Roer River on a 25-mile front and in a cold rain but are supported by a major air attack on German positions at Eschweiler.

The VII Corps leads the attack with the 104th and the 4th Infantry Divisions added and reinforced by Combat Command reserve of the 5th Armored Division. The 4th Infantry Division is to attack into the Hürtgen Forest to reach the Roer River at Düren. The 16th Infantry Regiment of the 1st Infantry Division attacks toward Hill 232 in the Hürtgen Forest to gain control of the main road leading to Langerwehe and Düren.

The attack is preceded by Operation Queen, the largest air attack in direct support of ground forces in the war. Eighth Air Force sends more than 1,200 B-17s and B-24 Liberators escorted by over 280 P-51 Mustangs to attack German defenses near Aachen, Langerwehe, Eschweiler, and Düren. The air attack is followed by an artillery barrage of 694 guns firing 52,000 artillery rounds into the German positions.

Operation Queen costs the Eighth Air Force a total of 19 bombers damaged. Aircrew casualties are two killed, three wounded, and six missing. One P-51 is lost and four are damaged. One pilot is reported missing.

Ninth Air Force sends 80 B-26 Marauders of the 9th Bombardment Division against German defenses in the Hürtgen Forest. The P-47 fighters of the XIX Tactical Air Command support the XX Corps around Trier and Saarbrücken. Fighters of the IX and XXIX Tactical Air Commands also support the attacks of First and Ninth Armies.

In the Seventh Army area the French I Corps breaks through the Belfort gap.
MEDITERRANEAN: Fifteenth Air Force sends more than 500 B-17s and B-24 Liberators escorted by P-38 Lightnings and P-51 Mustangs to attack the Munich marshaling yard and troop assembly areas in Yugoslavia.
ITALY: Twelfth Air Force B-25 Mitchells and B-26 Marauders attack rail lines in the Brenner Pass. A-20 Havocs and P-47 Thunderbolts attack German positions in front of the British Eighth Army.
SOUTHWEST PACIFIC AREA, LEYTE: The 24th Infantry Division completes the clearing of Japanese forces off Breakneck Ridge. The division is relieved by the 32nd Infantry Division commanded by Major General William H. Gill.

FEAF B-25 Mitchells, B-24 Liberators, P-38 Lightnings and P-47 Thunderbolts attack airfields, harbors, shipping, and targets of opportunity around Mindanao.
PACIFIC: U.S. submarine *Scabbardfish* torpedoes and sinks a Japanese transport near Chichi Jima,.

U.S. submarine *Tambor* torpedoes and sinks a Japanese guardboat off Honshu, Japan.
CENTRAL PACIFIC: Seventh Air Force sends 12 B-24 Liberators from Saipan to bomb shipping near Chichi Jima. P-38 Lightnings and P-47 Thunderbolts attack Pagan

Island in the Marianas. It is the first combat mission for these P-38s. During the night a B-24 conducts a snooper (radar-assisted bomb release) mission against shipping.
NEW GUINEA: FEAF B-24 Liberators, B-25 Mitchells, P-40s, and P-47 Thunderbolts attack airfields on Celebes and Halmahera Islands.

The headquarters of the 3rd Bombardment Group (Light) and 90th Bombardment Squadron (Light) redeploy from Hollandia to Leyte with A-20 Havocs. The headquarters of the 348th Fighter Group also redeploys to Leyte from Noemfoor Island.

November 17

ALEUTIANS: Eleventh Air Force sends four B-24 Liberators to bomb Suribachi airfield on Paramushiru Island. Two Japanese fighters attack the bombers. One B-24 is damaged and forced to land in the Soviet Union.
CBI: In Burma, Tenth Air Force B-25 Mitchells bomb bridges at Lashio. Aircrews report destroying one bridge and damaging others. P-47 Thunderbolts hit troop and vehicle assembly areas, logistics storage sites, and provide support to ground forces.

In China, Fourteenth Air Force B-24 Liberators bomb the Kowloon Docks in Hong Kong. P-40s and P-51 Mustangs attack targets of opportunity around Mangshih and Changsha.

U.S. submarine *Gunnel* attacks a Japanese convoy and sinks a torpedo boat and merchant tanker off the coast of French Indochina.
ETO: In the Hürtgen Forest, the 8th and 22nd Infantry Regiments of the 4th Infantry Division attack northwest of the town of Hürtgen.

The XX Corps extends its lines around Metz after heavy fighting in very difficult weather conditions.

Ninth Air Force B-26 Marauders support the 104th Infantry Division and the 2nd Armored Division near Aachen and the 4th Infantry Division in the Hürtgen Forest.

First Lieutenant Bernard J. Ray is a platoon leader in F Company, 8th Infantry Regiment, 4th Infantry Division, in the Hürtgen Forest. His company attacks in wet, bitterly cold weather over rough, wooded terrain, encountering minefields and barbed wire covered by machine-gun and rifle fire. As F Company reaches the wire, men begin falling from the heavy enemy fire. First Lieutenant Ray takes demolition charges to blast a path through the wire. As mortar rounds drop closer and closer to his position on the wire, Ray continues to work carefully, fully exposed to enemy fire. He is severely wounded by mortar fire before completing his task. With his last breath, First Lieutenant Ray wires the explosives and sacrifices himself to blast open a gap in the wire. For his acts of courage and supreme sacrifice, First Lieutenant Ray will receive the Medal of Honor.
MEDITERRANEAN: Fifteenth Air Force sends more than 600 B-17s and B-24 Liberators escorted by P-38 Lightnings and P-51 Mustangs to attack oil refineries in Germany and Austria and the marshaling yards in Yugoslavia and Hungary.
ITALY: Twelfth Air Force B-25 Mitchells and B-26 Marauders attack rail lines and bridges in the Brenner Pass. A-20 Havocs and P-47 Thunderbolts of the XXII Tacti-

cal Air Command attack rail lines, rail cars, ammunition and fuel storage sites, and support ground forces.

SOUTHWEST PACIFIC AREA: In the Philippines FEAF B-24 Liberators bomb airfields on Luzon and Mindanao Islands.

A kamikaze damages a transport off Leyte. TBM Avengers from escort carrier USS *Anzio* and a destroyer escort sink Japanese submarine *I-26* in the Philippine Sea.

FEAF P-38 Lightnings sink two ships off Samar.

PACIFIC: U.S. submarines *Burrfish* and *Ronquil* fight a surface battle with a Japanese guardboat off Honshu, Japan. The guardboat is damaged but scores hits on USS *Burrfish*. U.S. submarine *Picuda* torpedoes and sinks a Japanese landing ship and damages a merchant tanker in the East China Sea. U.S. submarine *Spadefish* torpedoes and sinks a Japanese escort carrier and damages a landing ship in the Yellow Sea. U.S. submarine *Sunfish* torpedoes and damages a Japanese army transport in the Yellow Sea.

CENTRAL PACIFIC: Seventh Air Force sends 15 B-24 Liberators from Saipan to attack shipping in the Bonin Islands.

Seventh Air Force B-24 Liberators drop eight mines near Chichi Jima.

A Japanese merchant tanker runs aground near the entrance to Subic Bay.

NEW GUINEA: U.S. submarine *Bluegill* is damaged in a depth-charge attack in the Makassar Strait, but remains on patrol.

November 18

ALEUTIANS: Eleventh Air Force sends four B-24 Liberators against shore batteries on Paramushiru Island.

CBI: Fourteenth Air Force sends more than 130 P-38 Lightnings, P-51 Mustangs, and P-40s to attack troop concentrations, river transport, rail lines, logistics storage sites, bridges, and highways in a broad sweep over southern China.

U.S. submarine *Pampanito* torpedoes and sinks a Japanese depot ship and merchant cargo ship off Hainan Island.

ETO: In the Hürtgen Forest, the 16th Infantry Regiment of the 1st Infantry Division captures Hamich and Hill 232.

The XX Corps of Third Army encircles the fortress city of Metz.

Eighth Air Force sends 47 P-47 Thunderbolts and 355 P-51 Mustangs to conduct sweeps attacking oil storage sites and airfields. The 374 fighters actually involved in the attack are met by 70 German fighters. Fighter pilots report 26 confirmed kills and two probable kills in the air and 69 confirmed kills on the ground. Two P-47s and five P-51s are lost, while two P-51s are damaged. The two pilots are reported missing.

During the night six B-17s and four B-24s drop leaflets over Belgium, France, and the Netherlands.

Ninth Air Force sends more than 300 B-26 Marauders of the 9th Bombardment Division to attack barracks areas, rail bridges, strongpoints in western Germany, and defensive positions in support of ground forces near Aachen.

MEDITERRANEAN: Fifteenth Air Force sends more than 600 B-17s and B-24 Liberators escorted by over 300 P-38 Lightnings and P-51 Mustangs to bomb an oil refinery near Vienna, Austria, and airfields in northern Italy.

ITALY: Twelfth Air Force B-25 Mitchells and B-26 Marauders attack bridges in northern Italy and southern Yugoslavia. Pilots of the XXII Tactical Air Command report destroying eight locomotives, over 100 rail cars, and about 75 other vehicles.

SOUTHWEST PACIFIC AREA: Destroyer escort USS *Lawrence C. Taylor* and TBM Avengers from escort carrier USS *Anzio* sink Japanese submarine *I-41* in the Philippine Sea.

PACIFIC: U.S. submarines *Peto, Spadefish,* and *Sunfish* continue attacks on the Japanese convoy in the East China Sea. USS *Peto* sinks two cargo ships. USS *Spadefish* sinks an auxiliary submarine chaser. USS *Sunfish* sinks an army transport.

U.S. submarine *Saury* torpedoes and damages a Japanese cargo ship off southern Honshu, Japan.

CENTRAL PACIFIC: Seventh Air Force B-24 Liberators from Saipan and Guam bomb shipping at Chichi Jima and Haha Jima Islands. Seventh Air Force B-24 Liberators lay 12 mines off Haha Jima. B-24s sink an auxiliary sailing vessel off Haha Jima.

NEW GUINEA: FEAF B-24 Liberators, with P-38 Lightnings and P-47 Thunderbolts escorting, bomb oil production facilities in Borneo. Other B-24s attack airfields on Celebes, Ceram, and Ambon Islands.

The headquarters of the 58th Fighter Group and the P-47 Thunderbolts of the 310th and 311th Fighter Squadrons redeploy from Noemfoor Island to Leyte.

November 19

CBI: In Burma, Tenth Air Force sends 15 P-47 Thunderbolts to support ground forces at Bhamo and Pinwe.

In China Fourteenth Air Force sends three B-24 Liberators to bomb Samah Bay docks on Hainan Island. P-40s attack troops and river, rail, and road transportation targets near Hankow. Other P-40s, along with P-51 Mustangs and P-38 Lightnings, attack rail facilities, roads, and troop concentrations near Mangshih.

ETO: Omaha beach ceases operations as an offloading site for supplies to the Allied armies. The main Allied support bases are now Antwerp, Ghent, Le Havre, Rouen, Cherbourg, and Marseille.

In the Hürtgen Forest, the 26th Infantry Regiment of the 1st Infantry Division attacks toward Langerwehe, but its advance is measured in yards. The 18th Infantry Regiment of the 1st Infantry Division advances past Hill 232.

Ninth Air Force sends more than 450 B-26 Marauders, A-20 Havocs, and A-26 Invaders to bomb storage depots, bridges, road and rail junctions, ordnance depots, and defensive positions along the front lines in Germany. The fighters of the IX, XIX, and XXIX Tactical Air Commands support the VII, XII, XIX, and XX Corps operations near Aachen, the Hürtgen Forest, and Metz.

Soldiers of the 5th Infantry Regiment, 71st Infantry Division, make a cautious entry into a building in Metz, France, November 19, 1944.

Private First Class Francis X. McGraw of H Company, 26th Infantry Regiment, 1st Infantry Division, mans a heavy machine gun near Schevenhutte, Germany, when the Germans make a strong counterattack against his company's defensive position. He employs his weapon to initially halt the attack, then takes his machine gun out of its protected position to bring more accurate fire against the Germans. During the fight, he runs back under fire to retrieve more ammunition for his machine gun. Although wounded, he continues to fight until, finally out of ammunition, he meets the enemy in hand-to-hand combat and is killed. For his extraordinary courage and determination to resist against all odds, Private First Class McGraw will win the Medal of Honor.

MEDITERRANEAN: Fifteenth Air Force sends more than 500 B-17s and B-24 Liberators escorted by P-38 Lightnings and P-51 Mustangs to bomb oil refineries and an aircraft production facility in Austria and airfields and marshaling yards in Hungary and Yugoslavia.

ITALY: The 366th Separate Infantry Regiment is assigned to Fifth Army.

SOUTHWEST PACIFIC AREA: In the Philippines FEAF B-24 Liberators bomb the airfields on Mindanao, Negros, and Leyte Islands. P-47 Thunderbolts attack targets on Mindanao and Leyte.

Carrier aircraft from Naval Task Force 38, commanded by Vice Admiral John S. McCain, attack Japanese shipping off Luzon and airfields. A cargo ship and two escorting submarine chasers are damaged. U.S. submarine *Hake* torpedoes and damages a Japanese light cruiser west of Corregidor. Kamikazes hit three U.S. freighters off Leyte.

CENTRAL PACIFIC: Seventh Air Force sends B-24 Liberators from Guam to bomb airfields on Iwo Jima, while 15 other B-24s bomb shipping at Chichi Jima and Haha Jima Islands.

U.S. Destroyer escorts *Conklin* and *McCoy Reynolds* sink Japanese submarine *I-37* west of the Palau Islands.

NEW GUINEA: FEAF B-24 Liberators attack targets on Celebes Island. B-25 Mitchells and A-20 Havocs attack airfields and shipping in the Ceram-Ambon-Boeroe Island area.

The headquarters of the 312th Bombardment Group (Light) and the A-20 Havocs of the 386th, 387th, 388th, and 389th Bombardment Squadrons (Light) from Hollandia redeploy to Leyte, along with the B-24s of the 2nd Bombardment Squadron (Heavy), 22nd Bombardment Group (Heavy), and the 403rd Bombardment Squadron (Heavy), 43rd Bombardment Group (Heavy), from the Schouten Islands. The 39th Troop Carrier Squadron of the 317th Troop Carrier Group also redeploys to Leyte from Hollandia.

FEAF B-24 Liberators damage a Japanese transport off Brunei Bay, Borneo.

November 20

CBI: Tenth Air Force P-47 Thunderbolts support ground forces near Pinwe.

Fourteenth Air Force sends eight B-25 Mitchells to attack Japanese barracks at Lashio, Burma.

Fourteenth Air Force B-25 Mitchells sink a Japanese cargo ship in the Yangtze River.

ETO: In the Hürtgen Forest, the 8th and 22nd Infantry Regiments are halted by strong German counterattacks near the town of Hürtgen. The regiments have lost 1,500 casualties in about three days.

In the Seventh Army area, the French I Corps reaches the Rhine River and the XV Corps captures Sarrebourg and the Saverne Gap.

Eighth Air Force sends 172 B-17s escorted by over 200 P-47 Thunderbolts and P-51 Mustangs to attack oil production facilities and marshaling yards in Germany. A total of 25 B-17s are damaged.

During the night six B-17s and seven B-24s drop leaflets over Germany, France, and the Netherlands.

Another 310 P-47s and P-51s make fighter-bomber attacks against bridges, rail lines, gun positions, and road traffic in support of ground forces. One P-47 and seven P-51s are lost and one P-51 damaged. The eight pilots are reported missing.

The headquarters of the 17th Bombardment Group (Medium) and the B-26 Marauders of the 34th and 37th Bombardment Squadrons (Medium) redeploy from Corsica to Dijon, France, as part of the First Tactical Air Force (Provisional).

Lieutenant Colonel George L. Mabry, Jr., is commanding the 2nd Battalion, 8th Infantry Regiment, 4th Infantry Division, in the Hürtgen Forest. During an attack his battalion is stopped by minefields and heavy fire. Lieutenant Colonel Mabry moves forward and personally clears a route through the minefield and leads the assault. With the assistance of a few riflemen accompanying him, Mabry clears an obstacle and attacks German defensive positions beyond, capturing three enemy soldiers. Fighting among log bunkers, Mabry takes on a squad of German soldiers in close combat and later captures six more as he leads his battalion to its objective. Lieutenant Colonel Mabry's leadership, courage, and gallantry will win him the Medal of Honor.

MEDITERRANEAN: Fifteenth Air Force B-17s and B-24 Liberators bomb industrial targets in Austria, Czechoslovakia, and Yugoslavia.

SOUTHWEST PACIFIC AREA: U.S. submarine *Atule* torpedoes and sinks a Japanese minesweeper southwest of Formosa.

U.S. submarine *Gar* lands supplies on the north coast of Mindoro.

CENTRAL PACIFIC: A U.S. oiler is sunk by *kaiten* (a manned suicide torpedo) from a Japanese submarine near Ulithi. Japanese aircraft attack three U.S. tankers leaving Ulithi for Eniwetok. One tanker is damaged.

NEW GUINEA: FEAF P-38 Lightnings hit targets of opportunity on Celebes Island.

The B-24 Liberators of the 371st Bombardment Squadron (Heavy), 307th Bombardment Group (Heavy), redeploy from Noemfoor Island to Morotai Island. The headquarters of Fifth Air Force redeploys to Leyte along with the A-20 Havocs of the 13th Bombardment Squadron (Light), 3rd Bombardment Group (Light).

November 21

ALEUTIANS: Eleventh Air Force establishes an advance headquarters on Shemya Island. Brigadier General Harry A. Johnson is the deputy commander. A B-24 Liberator airdrops supplies to a stranded B-24 crew forced to land on Kamchatka Island in the Soviet Union on November 17.

CBI: Tenth Air Force sends 28 P-47 Thunderbolts to support Allied ground forces in the Pinwe and Bhamo areas.

ETO: In the Hürtgen Forest the 121st Infantry Regiment of the 8th Infantry Division attacks toward the town of Hürtgen.

The 44th Infantry Division of VI Corps of the 6th Army Group captures Saarebourg.

Eighth Air Force sends more than 1,200 B-17s and B-24 Liberators using Pathfinder radar-equipped bombers, escorted by over 900 P-51 Mustangs and P-47 Thunderbolts, to attack oil production targets and marshaling yards in Germany. A total of 25 bombers are lost and 574 are damaged. Aircrews report one confirmed kill. Aircrew casualties are 22 killed, 30 wounded, and 283 missing. Fighter pilots report 73 confirmed kills and seven probables in the air and five confirmed kills on the ground. Fifteen fighters are lost, and the pilots are reported missing.

During the night seven B-17s and five B-24s drop leaflets over Germany, France, and the Netherlands.

The B-26 Marauders of the 95th Bombardment Squadron (Medium), 17th Bombardment Group (Medium), redeploy from Corsica to Dijon, France, as part of the First Tactical Air Force (Provisional).

Ninth Air Force B-26 Marauders of the 9th Bombardment Division attack transportation targets and German defenses. P-47 and P-38 fighters escort B-26 Marauders and support the 1st, 8th, and 104th Infantry Divisions fighting in the Hürtgen Forest and the XII and XX Corps in France.

In the Hürtgen Forest, Staff Sergeant John W. Minick of I Company, 121st Infantry Regiment, 8th Infantry Division, volunteers to lead four men to clear barbed wire and locate a path through a minefield to support the battalion's attack. After advancing 300 yards, Minick's group is fired on by a machine gun. Minick orders his men down while he moves to destroy the position, capturing three enemy soldiers. Soon afterward Staff Sergeant Minick comes face to face with about 40 German soldiers. In the short fight he kills 20 and captures 20 more. As the battalion advances, Staff Sergeant Minick again leads the way, assaulting a machine-gun position alone. He is killed when he enters another minefield. For his courage and bravery beyond the call of duty, Staff Sergeant Minick will receive the Medal of Honor.

MEDITERRANEAN: Fifteenth Air Force sends more than 25 B-24 Liberators and over 150 P-38 Lightnings to attack troop assembly areas, road and rail traffic, and bridges in Yugoslavia.

ITALY: Twelfth Air Force A-20 Havocs attack ammunition storage facilities and P-47 Thunderbolts attack rail lines and bridges and support elements of the Fifth Army south of Bologna.

SOUTHWEST PACIFIC AREA: In the Philippines FEAF B-24 Liberators bomb airfields on Mindanao. P-38 Lightnings and P-47 Thunderbolts attack logistics storage areas and troop barges on Leyte.

U.S. submarine *Sealion* attacks a Japanese task force and sinks the battleship *Kongo* and a destroyer near Formosa.

PACIFIC: Twentieth Air Force sends 61 B-29 Superfortresses from Chengtu, China, to bomb an aircraft production facility at Omura, Japan, on Kyushu Island. Thirteen B-29s bomb Shanghai, China. Aircrews report 27 Japanese fighters shot down.

Naval Task Force 92, commanded by Rear Admiral John L. McCrea, with two light cruisers and nine destroyers, bombards the Japanese naval air installation on Matsuwa Island in the Kuriles.

U.S. submarine *Flounder* attacks a Japanese convoy in the South China Sea, damaging a cargo ship, which USS *Guavina* sinks shortly thereafter.

U.S. submarine *Scabbardfish* torpedoes and sinks a Japanese ship south of Tokyo.

CENTRAL PACIFIC: Seventh Air Force B-24 Liberators from Guam bomb shipping and installations at Chichi Jima and Haha Jima Islands. During the night a B-24 conducts a snooper (radar-assisted bomb release) mission on Iwo Jima.

NEW GUINEA: FEAF B-25 Mitchells and B-24 Liberators attack airfields on Celebes Island.

FEAF B-24 Liberators sinks a Japanese ship in Makassar Strait.

November 22

CBI: Tenth Air Force P-47 Thunderbolts support Allied ground forces at Bhamo and Pinwe.

Fourteenth Air Force sends 22 B-24 Liberators to bomb Hankow, while P-51 Mustangs, P-40s, and P-38 Lightnings attack town areas, logistics storage sites, and road and rail traffic in southern China.

ETO: In the Hürtgen Forest the 18th Infantry Regiment of the 1st Infantry Division captures Heistern, along the main road to Langerwehe.

The 6th Army Group's First French Army clears the Belfort Gap and reaches the Rhine River. The XX Corps of Third Army occupies Metz, but German troops still hold several forts around the city, including Fort Driant.

The headquarters of the 63rd Fighter Wing redeploys from San Pietro, Italy, to Vittel, France, and the B-26 Marauders of the 432nd Bombardment Squadron (Medium), 17th Bombardment Group (Medium), redeploy from Corsica to Dijon, France, as part of the First Tactical Air Force (Provisional).

MEDITERRANEAN: Fifteenth Air Force sends more than 400 B-17s and B-24 Liberators escorted by P-38 Lightnings and P-51 Mustangs to attack marshaling yards at Munich, Germany. Weather prevents nearly half from reaching the primary target. The bombers hit secondary targets, mainly marshaling yards, in Austria and Germany.

ITALY: Fifth Army receives the last of its 3,000 replacements. The army is still short 7,000 men.

Twelfth Air Force A-20 Havocs attack rail lines in the Po Valley and P-47 Thunderbolts attack guns, vehicles, and German defensive positions in support of elements of the Fifth Army south of Bologna. Fighters also attack logistics storage areas and pipelines in the rear of German forces.

SOUTHWEST PACIFIC AREA: The XXIV Corps takes operational control of the 11th Airborne Division, commanded by Major General Joseph M. Swing, to support its attack north into the Ormoc Valley on Leyte. The 7th Infantry Division has been actively clearing Japanese forces around Burauen, leaving General John R. Hodge with few options. He has only the 32nd Infantry Regiment to employ in the Ormoc Valley and that regiment is locked in an indecisive battle with Japanese forces.

The 11th Airborne Division establishes blocking positions in the mountain passes.

FEAF B-24 Liberators, B-25 Mitchells, P-38 Lightnings, and P-47 Thunderbolts bomb airfields on Negros Island, and bridges, barges, and targets of opportunity on Leyte Island. B-24s also attack an airfield on Mindanao.

U.S. submarine *Besugo* torpedoes and sinks a Japanese landing ship off northern Palawan.

PACIFIC: U.S. submarine *Scabbardfish* torpedoes and damages a Japanese escort vessel off Honshu, Japan.

CENTRAL PACIFIC: Seventh Air Force sends 22 B-24 Liberators from Saipan, escorted by 22 P-38 Lightnings, to bomb airfields on Moen and Param Islands in the Carolines.

Aircraft from Naval Task Group 38.4 under command of Rear Admiral Ralph E. Davison bomb Japanese airfields on Yap.

NEW GUINEA: FEAF B-24 Liberators, P-40s, and P-47 Thunderbolts attack targets on Celebes Island. Other B-24s attack shipping during sweep over Brunei Bay, Borneo.

Japanese aircraft attack the U.S. airfield at Morotai, destroying 15 bombers and damaging 31 other aircraft. The airfields at Morotai have been attacked nearly every day through November. The airfield supports B-24 Liberators and P-47 Thunderbolts of Fifth Air Force.

U.S. submarine *Guavina* torpedoes and sinks a Japanese cargo ship northwest of Borneo.

November 23

CBI: In Burma, Tenth Air Force sends 10 B-25 Mitchells to attack bridges, while P-47 Thunderbolts support ground forces near Pinwe and Bhamo.

Fourteenth Air Force sends 12 B-25 Mitchells to bomb logistics storage sites near Lashio in Burma. B-24 Liberators bomb the Kowloon Docks in Hong Kong.

ETO: In the Hürtgen Forest the 8th and 22nd Infantry Regiments of the 4th Infantry Division approach Grosshau.

The French 2nd Armored Division of the French First Army, 6th Army Group, reaches Strasbourg.

Eighth Air Force sends more than 100 B-17s, using radar to assist the timing of bomb release and escorted by more than 70 P-51 Mustangs, to bomb a benzol manufacturing facility and a marshaling yard. One P-51 is lost and one is damaged. The pilot is reported missing.

The headquarters of the 42nd Bombardment Wing (Medium) redeploys from Corsica to Dijon, France, as part of the First Tactical Air Force (Provisional).

German submarine *U-978* torpedoes a U.S. freighter off Barfleur, France.

First Lieutenant Edward A. Silk commands the weapons platoon of E Company, 398th Infantry Regiment, 100th Infantry Division. When his platoon, supporting the battalion attack, encounters a German strongpoint in a farmhouse near St-Pravel, France, First Lieutenant Silk takes action. He runs 100 yards across an open field to reach a low stone wall directly in front of the strongpoint. Firing at the door and windows with his M-1 carbine, he then vaults the wall to charge the farmhouse. Throwing a hand grenade, he destroys a machine-gun position and almost immediately is fired on by a second, hidden machine gun in the woodshed. Without hesitation, Silk charges the position and destroys it with hand grenades. Now out of ammunition, Silk begins throwing rocks through the windows at the Germans inside the farmhouse, ordering them to surrender. Twelve Germans walk out and surrender to the lieutenant. For his exceptional courage and extraordinary act of determination, First Lieutenant Silk will receive the Medal of Honor.

MEDITERRANEAN: Fifteenth Air Force sends 81 B-24 Liberators to attack road and rail bridges in Yugoslavia. P-38 Lightnings bomb the marshaling yard and road and rail bridges.

SOUTHWEST PACIFIC AREA: On Leyte, the 7th Infantry Division of the XXIV Corps attacks north into the Ormoc Valley and is halted by a strong Japanese counterattack. The 77th Infantry Division is diverted from Guam to land at Leyte and support the 7th Infantry Division attack.

B-24 Liberators bomb an airfield on Mindanao.

A kamikaze damages a U.S. attack transport off Leyte. A U.S. freighter is hit by a torpedo dropped by a Japanese aircraft off Samar Island.

U.S. submarines *Bang* and *Redfish* attack a Japanese convoy in the Formosa Strait. USS *Bang* sinks a cargo ship and a transport. USS *Redfish* sinks a cargo ship.

U.S. submarine *Gar* lands personnel and supplies on the west coast of Luzon.

PACIFIC: U.S. submarine *Picuda* attacks a Japanese convoy in Tsushima Strait, sinking two cargo ships.

CENTRAL PACIFIC: Seventh Air Force sends 17 B-24 Liberators from Guam to attack shipping at Chichi Jima and Haha Jima Islands.

NEW GUINEA: The B-24 Liberators of the 63rd and 64th Bombardment Squadrons (Heavy) of the 43rd Bombardment Group (Heavy) redeploy from the Schouten Islands to Leyte.

November 24

CBI: In Burma, Tenth Air Force P-47 Thunderbolts support ground forces near Pinwe and Bhamo.

Nanning falls to Japanese forces, eliminating nearly all of the Fourteenth and XX Bomber Command airfields in China. The Japanese begin shifting their attacks toward Kunming and Chungking.

Fourteenth Air Force sends B-24 Liberators to bomb warehouses and docks at Hankow, China, and at Haiphong, French Indochina. B-24s also bomb Wanling in Burma.

ETO: After three days of attacks against German positions in the Hürtgen Forest, the 121st Infantry Regiment of the 8th Infantry Division begins to come apart. It has lost 600 men to mortar fire, mines, and artillery and has made no gains. Leaders break under the pressure of combat, and soldiers refuse to fight. Colonel Thomas J. Cross takes command of the regiment and prepares to attack the town of Hürtgen again.

The Germans counterattack toward Saarebourg, held by the 44th Infantry Division. Although initially driven back, the division stops the Germans and regains its original positions.

SOUTHWEST PACIFIC AREA: On Leyte, the 32nd Infantry Regiment of the 7th Infantry Division counterattacks, supported by tanks and artillery. The 7th Infantry Division is forced to go on the defensive. During the night Japanese troops attack the American artillery, destroying four 105 millimeter guns.

The 32nd Infantry Division captures Limon but makes little progress against strong Japanese defenses.

FEAF B-24 Liberators bomb antiaircraft positions and targets of opportunity around Leyte and Mindanao Islands.

A U.S. submarine chaser and LCI (Landing Craft, Infantry) are damaged by Japanese dive bombers off Leyte.

Thirteenth Air Force P-40s and P-47 Thunderbolts attack ships supporting reinforcement efforts on Leyte. A submarine chaser and three landing ships are sunk.

PACIFIC: Twentieth Air Force sends 111 B-29 Superfortresses from the XXI Bomber Command to bomb Tokyo, Japan. Thirty-five B-29s bomb the primary target, the Musashino aircraft plant, and 50 bomb the secondary target, the city and docks. Aircrews report seven enemy fighters shot down. The other bombers either abort en route, or mechanical problems prevent them from dropping bombs. One B-29 is lost off Honshu Island when a Japanese fighter rams it. Another bomber is forced down after running out of fuel.

CENTRAL PACIFIC: Seventh Air Force sends two B-24 Liberators from Saipan on a shipping reconnaissance mission; they attack vessels at Haha Jima and Chichi Jima Islands.

NEW GUINEA: The B-24 Liberators of the 65th Bombardment Squadron (Heavy), 43rd Bombardment Group (Heavy), redeploy from the Schouten Islands to Leyte.

November 25

ALEUTIANS: Eleventh Air Force sends one B-24 on an armed photo mission and conducts a radar-guided bombing run on Kurabu airfield on Paramushiru Island.

CBI: In China, Major General Albert C. Wedemeyer develops a concept that will lead to planning for Operation Alpha, the defense of Kunming in Yunnan Province. Kunming is the terminal for the Hump airlift. Without the airlift, Chinese forces will be unable to stop the Japanese. The plan calls for redeploying Chinese units from the Y Force and Burma to southeastern China. Additional supplies from the Hump airlifts will refit the poor-quality divisions currently defending the area near Kunming, and U.S. advisers will train the units. Wedemeyer's intent is to refit and train 36 Chinese divisions, serving under a single Chinese commander and supported by a Chinese-American staff.

In Burma, Tenth Air Force sends 24 P-47 Thunderbolts to support ground forces near Bhamo, and other P-47s strafe targets of opportunity along the Wuntho-Shwebo rail line.

Fourteenth Air Force sends 12 B-25 Mitchells to bomb storage facilities and village and town areas at Lashio and Wanling in Burma. P-40s, P-51 Mustangs, and P-38 Lightnings attack river and road transportation, rail traffic, troops, buildings, and targets of opportunity in Thailand, Burma, south China, and northern French Indochina.

During the night Fourteenth Air Force B-24 Liberators, conducting a reconnaissance flight over the South China Sea, attack Japanese minesweepers south of Hainan Island,

ETO: The 101st Airborne Division, under Montgomery's operational control since Market Garden, returns to the First Allied Airborne Army. The division has suffered an additional 1,912 casualties fighting in Holland.

Seventh Army reports that German resistance in the northern Vosges Mountains has been eliminated.

Eighth Air Force sends more than 1,000 B-17s and B-24 Liberators, escorted by over 900 P-51 Mustangs and P-47 Thunderbolts, to attack the synthetic oil plant at Merseburg and the marshaling yard at Bingen, Germany, using radar to assist the timing of bomb release. Eight B-17s are lost and 244 bombers are damaged. Aircrew casualties are seven killed, six wounded, and 64 missing. Fighter pilots report nine confirmed kills on the ground. Six P-51s are lost and one is damaged. Six pilots are reported missing.

During the night seven B-17s and six B-24s drop leaflets over Germany, France, and the Netherlands.

The 36th Bombardment Squadron (Heavy), VIII Fighter Command, is selected to serve as the screening force to protect Eighth Air Force bombers against German attempts to intercept in-flight communications and as a means of providing early warning and to counter German radar countermeasure efforts.

Ninth Air Force B-26 Marauders of the 9th Bombardment Division attack bridges, roads, and ammunition storage sites in Germany.

MEDITERRANEAN: During the night Fifteenth Air Force sends more than 40 B-17s and B-24 Liberators to bomb industrial targets in Austria and the marshaling yards in Munich, Germany.

ITALY: General Mark Clark is selected to command Allied ground forces in Italy, now redesignated as the 15th Army Group. General Sir Henry Maitland Wilson takes the place of Sir John Dill as head of the British Military Mission in Washington, D.C. General Dill has died suddenly, forcing changes in the British high command. General Sir Harold R. L. G. Alexander is promoted to field marshal and becomes the Mediterranean theater commander. General Lucian K. Truscott, who had commanded VI Corps in France, takes command of Fifth Army.

Twelfth Air Force P-47 Thunderbolts attack rail lines and bridges.

SOUTHWEST PACIFIC AREA: The 511th Parachute Infantry Regiment of the 11th Airborne Division advances west into the mountains from Burauen to link up with the 7th Infantry Division on Leyte. Most of the 7th Infantry Division has assembled on the west coast of Leyte. The 96th Infantry Division, advancing west, encounters entrenched enemy forces.

In the Philippines FEAF P-38 Lightnings and P-47 Thunderbolts attack shipping, airfields, and troop areas around Cebu and Leyte Islands.

Carrier aircraft from Naval Task Groups 38.2 (Rear Admiral Gerald F. Bogan) and 38.3 (Rear Admiral Frederick C. Sherman) attack Japanese shipping off Luzon. Aircraft from carrier USS *Ticonderoga* sink a heavy cruiser. F4F Hellcats, SB2C Helldivers and TBM Avengers from carriers USS *Ticonderoga* and USS *Essex*, along with F4F Hellcats and TBM Avengers from the small carrier USS *Langley*, attack a convoy on the west coast of Luzon and sink a coast defense ship and three landing ships. Aircraft from the carrier USS *Intrepid* sink two fast transports and damage another as well as an escort destroyer. Aircraft from *Essex* and *Langley* sink a cargo ship and damage a cargo ship.

Kamikazes damage carriers USS *Essex*, *Intrepid*, and *Hancock*, and small carrier *Cabot*.

U.S. submarine *Atule* torpedoes and sinks a Japanese cargo ship off Luzon.

U.S. submarine *Hardhead* (SS-365) attacks a Japanese convoy west of Manila and sinks a coastal patrol ship off the Bataan peninsula.

U.S. submarine *Haddo* torpedoes and damages a Japanese escort destroyer off the west coast of Luzon.

U.S. submarine *Pomfret* torpedoes and sinks a Japanese patrol boat and transport in the Luzon Strait.

CENTRAL PACIFIC: Seventh Air Force B-24 Liberators from Guam bomb Chichi Jima and Haha Jima.

NEW GUINEA: During the night FEAF B-25 Mitchells bomb airfields on Celebes and Halmahera Islands.

Shore battery fire off Halmahera Island sinks a U.S. motor torpedo boat.

U.S. submarine *Cavalla* torpedoes and sinks a Japanese destroyer west of Borneo.

U.S. submarine *Mingo* (SS-261) attacks a Japanese convoy and sinks an army transport in the South China Sea west of Borneo, then survives a depth-charge attack.

November 26

CBI: Tenth Air Force P-47 Thunderbolts provide support to ground forces.

Fourteenth Air Force P-40s, P-51 Mustangs, and P-38 Lightnings attack river, rail, and road traffic at Changsha and Liuchow.

ETO: The first ships begin unloading supplies for the Allied armies at the port of Antwerp. General Eisenhower seeks to destroy all German forces west of the Rhine River as an intermediate objective before attempting to cross the river and move into open warfare to encircle the Ruhr.

Eighth Air Force sends more than 1,100 B-17s and B-24 Liberators escorted by over 700 P-51s and P-47 Thunderbolts to attack marshaling yards and oil refineries in western Germany. Over 550 German fighters attack the bombers. A total of 34 bombers are lost and 307 are damaged. Aircrews report 16 confirmed kills and 11 probables. Aircrew casualties are 19 killed, 13 wounded, and 316 missing. Fighter pilots report 112 confirmed kills and two probables. Nine fighters are lost and two are damaged. The nine pilots are reported missing.

During the night eight B-17s and six B-24s drop leaflets over Germany, France, and the Netherlands.

Thirty-six P-51 Mustangs flying a scouting mission over Germany and report five confirmed kills, one probable, and two possibles without any American losses.

Ninth Air Force sends 173 B-26 Marauders and A-20 Havocs to bomb logistics depots and storage areas in Germany. P-47 Thunderbolts and P-38 Lightnings support the 29th Infantry Division and XX and XII Corps.

Private First Class Carl V. Sheridan is a bazooka gunner with K Company, 2nd Battalion, 47th Infantry Regiment, 9th Infantry Division. The company is attacking Frenzenberg Castle in Weisweiler, Germany, but suffers heavy casualties in the approach, leaving only about 35 men able to continue the assault on the castle. At the castle gatehouse, Private First Class Sheridan takes action to eliminate the strongpoint. He advances alone to get a clear shot at the barricaded entrance to the gatehouse, ignoring the rifle fire and exploding grenades, and gets off three shots. As the third rocket destroys the barricade, Private First Class Sheridan pulls out his .45 pistol and leads the attack, shouting, "Come on, let's get them!" As he makes his charge, he is killed by enemy fire. For his extraordinary courage, determination to win victory at all costs, and great skill Private First Class Sheridan will receive the Medal of Honor.

MEDITERRANEAN: Fifteenth Air Force sends 39 P-38 Lightnings to fly an offensive sweep over Hungary to attack an airfield as well as road and rail traffic.

ITALY: Twelfth Air Force P-47 Thunderbolts support Fifth Army operations south of Bologna and attack rail lines north of the front lines.

SOUTHWEST PACIFIC AREA: Japanese transport aircraft land in the surf in the XXIV Corps area. The few survivors carrying demolitions are killed.

FEAF sends more than 40 B-24 Liberators to bomb airfields on Negros, Mindanao, and Cebu Islands. The headquarters of the 22nd Bombardment Group (Heavy) and the B-24 Liberators of the 33rd Bombardment Squadron (Heavy) redeploy from Leyte Island to Angaur Island in the Palaus.

CENTRAL PACIFIC: During the night a B-24 on a snooper mission from Guam bombs Iwo Jima. B-24s from Angaur Island bomb Arakabesan Island in the Palaus.

U.S. submarine *Raton* torpedoes and sinks a Japanese ammunition ship north of the Bismarck Archipelago.

NEW GUINEA: FEAF B-25 Mitchells, P-40s, and P-38 Lightnings attack targets on Celebes and Halmahera Islands.

U.S. submarine *Pargo* torpedoes and damages a Japanese fleet tanker off Sarawak, Borneo. The submarine is damaged in a depth-charge attack, but remains on patrol.

November 27

CBI: In Burma, Tenth Air Force P-47 Thunderbolts conduct ground support missions near Pinwe.

Fourteenth Air Force sends 17 B-24 Liberators to bomb targets in French Indochina. B-25 Mitchells bomb targets in French Indochina and attack logistics storage areas at Lashio in Burma. A detachment of P-61 Black Widow night fighters from the 426th Night Fighter Squadron begins operating from Hsian, China.

ETO: The Seventh Army (12th Armored Division and the 63rd, the 45th, and the 100th Infantry Divisions) of the 6th Army Group attacks north to break the German defenses along the West Wall.

Eighth Air Force sends more than 500 B-17s and B-24 Liberators escorted by over 750 P-51 Mustangs and P-47 Thunderbolts to attack marshaling yards in Germany guided by radar-equipped Pathfinder bombers. A total of 69 bombers are damaged. Aircrew casualties are two wounded. Three fighters are lost, and one is damaged. Three pilots are reported missing.

Four hundred and sixty P-47 Thunderbolts and P-51 Mustangs flying fighter-bomber missions against oil targets in Germany encounter about 750 German fighters. The American fighter pilots report 98 confirmed kills, four probables, and 11 possibles in the air and four confirmed kills and one possible kill on the ground. American losses are two P-47s and 10 P-51s. The pilots are reported missing.

Ninth Air Force P-47 Thunderbolts and P-38 Lightnings support the 104th, 8th, and 1st Infantry Divisions near Hürtgen Forest.

Private Macario Garcia of B Company, 22nd Infantry Regiment, 4th Infantry Division, leads an attack on German positions on a wooded hill near Grosshau, Germany. There is almost no cover for his squad, and the Germans are able to lay down an accurate and heavy volume of fire. Although wounded, Private Garcia continues to fight, crawling forward alone to attack a German position with grenades and rifle fire. He then singlehandedly attacks another position and captures four Germans. After his company has occupied the objective, Private Garcia accepts medical assistance. His heroic action and personal disregard for his own safety will win him the Medal of Honor.

SOUTHWEST PACIFIC AREA: On Leyte, after two consecutive nights of attacks near Damulaan, the 7th Infantry Division finally breaks the strength of the Japanese. The Americans count over 500 Japanese dead.

FEAF B-24 Liberators bomb airfields on Negros and Mindanao Islands.

U.S. destroyers bombard Japanese positions at Ormoc Bay on Leyte. Kamikazes sink a U.S. submarine chaser and damage the battleship USS *Colorado* and two light cruisers in Leyte Gulf.

PACIFIC: Twentieth Air Force sends 55 B-29 Superfortresses from Calcutta to bomb the Bangsue railroad yards at Bangkok, Thailand. Another 81 Twentieth Air Force B-29s from the Marianas are sent to bomb the Musashino and Nakajima production facilities at Tokyo. The B-29s miss the primary targets and attack the secondary targets in the city and docks, while others attack targets of opportunity. Eleven Japanese aircraft attack Isley Field on Saipan, destroying or damaging several B-29s. Antiaircraft fire and fighters shoot down all but one of the enemy planes.

CENTRAL PACIFIC: Seventh Air Force sends 24 B-24 Liberators from Saipan, escorted by 12 P-38 Lightnings, to bomb Iwo Jima. B-24s from Guam conduct a second bombing run. B-24s from Angaur Island bomb an airfield on Mindanao in the Philippines.

Japanese aircraft conduct a raid on the airfield on Saipan and destroy three B-29s and a P-47. Three B-29s, a B-24 Liberator, and a P-47 are damaged.

CENTRAL PACIFIC, PELELIU: After nearly a month of fighting in the Umurbrogol Pocket, with the 322nd and 323rd Infantry Regiments using tactics more akin to ancient siege warfare than modern warfare, the Umurbrogol Pocket is eliminated. The Japanese defeat is marked by a few soldiers making an attempt to break through American positions in a night attack. The 81st Infantry Division has lost 542 killed and 2,736 wounded in clearing the Pocket.

Peleliu has cost the Japanese over 10,500 casualties. Only 202 prisoners are captured, and all but 19 of these are Korean laborers and not Japanese soldiers. The last Japanese defenders of Peleliu will not surrender until April 21, 1947, when 26 men emerge from the Umurbrogol tunnels. American casualties for the 1st Marine Division are 6,526 total, with 1,252 killed. The 81st Infantry Division has lost 3,089 men, of which 404 were killed. The total casualty count for the Palau Islands is 9,615 casualties, of which 1,656 are killed. The Palau Islands had been seen in early 1944 as essential to Japan's second line of defense and, lying only 500 miles from Mindanao, were deemed essential objectives for the successful invasion of the Philippines. Now the cost of capturing Peleliu appears far too great for the perceived benefits.

NEW GUINEA: FEAF B-25 Mitchells attack the airfields on Buru and Ambon Islands. P-38 Lightnings, P-40s, and P-47 Thunderbolts attack airfields, shipping, and targets of opportunity on Celebes, Halmahera, and Ceram Islands.

November 28

CBI: Tenth Air Force P-47 Thunderbolts support ground forces near Pinwe and Bhamo. The headquarters of the 4th Combat Cargo Group and the 13th Combat Cargo Squadron arrive in India from the United States with C-46 Commandos, a twin-engine heavy-lift cargo aircraft.

ETO: Antwerp begins functioning as the main supply base for Allied forces.

Supported by tanks and artillery from Combat Command Reserve of the 5th Armored Division, the 121st Infantry Regiment of the 8th Infantry Division captures the town of Hürtgen and 200 prisoners. The 16th and 18th Infantry Regiments of the 1st Infantry Division capture Langerwehe, opening the road to Düren.

During the night six B-17s and six B-24 Liberators drop leaflets on the Netherlands and Germany. The 845th Bombardment Squadron (Heavy) of the 489th Bombardment Group (Heavy) departs England for the United States. The squadron has been earmarked to transition to B-29 Superfortresses in 1945.

Ninth Air Force P-47 Thunderbolts and P-38 Lightnings support the 1st, 104th, and 8th Infantry Divisions in the Hürtgen Forest.

ITALY: General Sir Harold R. L. G. Alexander, supreme commander of Allied forces in the Mediterranean, orders a new offensive for December.

Twelfth Air Force B-25 Mitchells attack rail bridges. A-20 Havocs and P-47 Thunderbolts attack German defensive positions and rail lines.

SOUTHWEST PACIFIC AREA: The B-24 Liberators of the 2nd Bombardment Squadron (Heavy), 22nd Bombardment Group (Heavy), redeploy from Leyte Island to Angaur Island in the Palaus.

Four U.S. destroyers sink Japanese submarine *I-46* in Leyte Gulf.

U.S. submarine *Guavina* attacks a Japanese convoy off the southern coast of French Indochina and is driven off by a submarine chaser.

CENTRAL PACIFIC: Seventh Air Force B-24 Liberators from Saipan bomb Iwo Jima.

During the night a B-24 conducts a snooper (radar-assisted bomb release) mission on Iwo Jima.

NEW GUINEA: FEAF B-24 Liberators, B-25 Mitchells, P-40s, and P-47 Thunderbolts attack targets on Halmahera and Timor Islands.

The P-38 Lightnings of the 35th Fighter Squadron, 8th Fighter Group, redeploy from Morotai Island to Leyte, joining the ground echelon that had departed on November 18.

Thirteenth Air Force B-24 Liberators sink a Japanese merchant tanker off Borneo.

November 29

ALEUTIANS: Eleventh Air Force sends three B-24 Liberators to bomb Kashiwabara on Paramushiru Island.

CBI: In Burma, Tenth Air Force sends more than 110 P-47 Thunderbolts to support ground forces near Bhamo and Pinwe and to attack bridges, logistics storage areas, ammunition storage sites, and troops.

Fourteenth Air Force B-25 Mitchells bomb targets in French Indochina and attack Lashio in Burma. P-40s, P-38 Lightnings, and P-51 Mustangs attack targets of opportunity near Chefang, China.

ETO: In the Hürtgen Forest, the 26th Infantry Regiment of the 1st Infantry Division attacks Merode, advancing four miles. The advance has cost 4,000 casualties, including 600 losses in the 47th Infantry Regiment of the 9th Infantry Division, attached to the 1st Infantry Division for the attack. Elements of the 8th Infantry Division supported by Combat Command Reserve of the 5th Armored Division attack toward Kleinhau. The 8th Infantry Division has lost 1,247 men, most of them in the 121st Infantry Regiment.

Eighth Air Force sends more than 1,000 B-17s and B-24 Liberators, led by radar-equipped Pathfinder bombers and escorted by over 900 P-51 Mustangs and P-47 Thunderbolts, to attack oil refineries, marshaling yards, and rail viaducts in Germany. One B-24 is lost, and 103 bombers are damaged. Aircrew casualties are three wounded and 10 missing. During the night six B-17s and seven B-24s drop leaflets over Germany, France, and the Netherlands.

The headquarters of the 489th Bombardment Group (Heavy) and the 844th, 846th, and 847th Bombardment Squadrons (Heavy) depart England for the United States to switch to B-29 Superfortresses.

Ninth Air Force sends more than 300 B-26 Marauders and A-20 Havocs to attack German defensive positions. P-47 and P-38 fighters support the 104th Infantry Division as it defends against German counterattacks at Inden and Lammersdorf. Fighters also support the 8th Infantry Division at Hürtgen, and the 7th Armored Division in the XIII Corps attack toward the Roer River.

Staff Sergeant Andrew Miller is a squad leader in G Company, 377th Infantry Regiment, 95th Infantry Division. Over the space of two weeks of combat, Staff Sergeant Miller's extraordinary and heroic actions will win him the Medal of Honor. At

Woippy, France, Miller ignores German machine guns and attacks the positions singlehandedly, forcing the enemy to surrender in one position and destroying the other position with hand grenades. Near Metz, as his squad falters in the face of enemy fire, Miller engages a German machine-gun position with automatic rifle fire and leads the advance. He later leads an attack on a barracks, surprising the enemy and capturing a number of prisoners. When the Germans counterattack, Miller climbs to the roof of the building to fire a bazooka at a German machine gun, ignoring the heavy fire directed at him. At Kerprich Hemmersdorf, Germany, Staff Sergeant Miller leads an attack against the enemy, clearing the way until he is killed.

ITALY: Twelfth Air Force P-47 Thunderbolts attack rail lines, rail cars, and vehicles in the Po Valley.

SOUTHWEST PACIFIC AREA: In the Philippines FEAF B-24 Liberators, A-20 Havocs, and P-47 Thunderbolts bomb airfields on Mindanao Island.

Kamikazes damage the battleship USS *Maryland* and two destroyers in Leyte Gulf.

U.S. motor torpedo boats attack Japanese shipping in Ormoc Bay, sinking a patrol boat and an auxiliary minelayer. Fifth Air Force B-25 Mitchells and P-47s attack Japanese shipping, sinking a submarine chaser. P-40s and P-47 Thunderbolts sink two cargo ships.

PACIFIC: During the night Twentieth Air Force sends 24 B-29 Superfortresses from the Marianas to bomb the docks and industrial targets in Tokyo; two B-29s bomb targets at Yokohama and Numazu.

U.S. submarine *Archerfish* torpedoes and sinks the Japanese carrier *Shinano* off Honshu, Japan. U.S. submarine *Scabbardfish* torpedoes and sinks Japanese submarine *I-365* off Honshu, Japan. U.S. submarine *Spadefish* torpedoes and sinks a Japanese cargo ship off the west coast of Korea.

CENTRAL PACIFIC: Seventh Air Force sends 18 B-24 Liberators from Guam to bomb Iwo Jima.

NEW GUINEA: FEAF B-24 Liberators, with P-40s, attack the airfield on Celebes Island. B-24s, B-25 Mitchells, and P-47 Thunderbolts attack the airfield on Halmahera Island and attack shipping and other targets of opportunity near Ceram Island, Celebes Island, and northern Borneo.

November 30

CBI: In Burma, Tenth Air Force P-47 Thunderbolts conduct ground attack missions near Bhamo and attack troops, vehicles, and bridges.

The Fourteenth Air Force reports that 36 squadrons are operational, including four heavy bomber squadrons (47 B-24 Liberators), seven medium bomber squadrons (109 B-25 Mitchells), and 22 fighter squadrons (535 P-40s, P-51 Mustangs, P-38 Lightnings).

B-25 Mitchells and P-51 Mustangs attack railroad bridges and buildings in French Indochina. B-25s bomb logistics storage sites and buildings at Lashio and Wanling in Burma. In China, 23 P-38s and P-51s attack targets of opportunity near Chefang.

Japanese air attacks damage the U.S. submarine *Pipefish* in the South China Sea off Hainan. The submarine remains on patrol.

ETO: In the Hürtgen Forest, the 22nd Infantry Regiment of the 4th Infantry Division breaks out into the open, flat terrain beyond the woods. Hill 401 is captured with the support of Combat Command A of the 5th Armored Division.

Eighth Air Force sends more than 1,200 B-17s and B-24 Liberators escorted by over 900 P-47 Thunderbolts and P-51 Mustangs to attack oil production facilities and marshaling yards in Germany. A total of 28 B-17s are lost and 522 bombers damaged. Aircrew casualties are 25 killed, 58 wounded, and 395 missing. Fighter pilots report four confirmed kills in the air. Three fighters are lost, and one is damaged. Three pilots are reported missing.

During the night seven B-17s and six B-24s drop leaflets over Germany and the Netherlands.

Ninth Air Force sends 288 B-26 Marauders and A-20 Havocs to attack German defensive positions and strongpoints and a marshaling yard at Zweibrücken. P-47 and P-38 fighters support the 104th Infantry Division of VII Corps at Lammersdorf and Inden in the Hürtgen Forest.

MEDITERRANEAN: During the night Fifteenth Air Force sends B-17s to bomb a benzol plant and marshaling yards in Austria, while other B-24s attack the marshaling yards at Munich, Germany.

ITALY: Twelfth Air Force B-25 Mitchells and B-26 Marauders attack rail and road traffic and bridges in the Po Valley. A-20 Havocs and P-47 Thunderbolts attack convoys, bridges, rail cars, and roads.

SOUTHWEST PACIFIC AREA: The Japanese have been able to land an additional 10,000 troops on Leyte.

The P-38 Lightnings of the 36th and 80th Fighter Squadrons, 8th Fighter Group, operating from Morotai Island return to Leyte. The ground echelon of the 418th Night Fighter Squadron begins redeployment from Leyte Island to Mindoro Island. The squadron's P-61 Black Widow night fighters remain on Morotai Island.

PACIFIC: U.S. submarine *Sunfish* torpedoes and sinks a Japanese cargo ship off western Korea.

CENTRAL PACIFIC: Seventh Air Force B-24 Liberators from Saipan bomb Iwo Jima. B-24s from Guam bomb Haha Jima. Another 37 B-24s from Angaur Island attack an airfield on Luzon in the Philippines. During the night two B-24s conducts a snooper (radar-assisted bomb release) mission on Iwo Jima, attacking the airfield.

NEW GUINEA: FEAF B-24 Liberators attack airfields on Celebes and Halmahera Islands.

The P-47 Thunderbolts of the 340th Fighter Squadron, 348th Fighter Group, redeploy from Noemfoor Island to Leyte.

December 1

CBI: Chinese Y Force (also known as the Chinese Expeditionary Force) units capture Che-fang.

In Burma, Tenth Air Force P-47 Thunderbolts support ground forces near Bhamo.

Fourteenth Air Force B-25 Mitchells bomb logistics storage sites and buildings at Wanling in Burma.

The 14th and 15th Combat Cargo Squadrons of the 4th Combat Cargo Group arrive in India from the United States with C-46 Commando cargo planes. The 427th Night Fighter Squadron redeploys from India to Myitkyina with P-61 Black Widow night fighters.

ETO: In the Hürtgen Forest, the 4th Infantry Division is unable to continue the attack and exploit the gains made the previous day. The division has lost 4,053 men in combat and another 2,000 are nonbattle casualties. Since entering the battle for Hürtgen on November 16, the division has advanced three miles.

During the night Eighth Air Force sends seven B-17s and seven B-24s to drop leaflets over Germany, France, and the Netherlands.

Ninth Air Force sends 134 B-26 Marauders and A-20 Havocs to attack German positions along the battle front in Germany. P-47 and P-38 fighters support VII Corps fighting in the Hürtgen Forest and the 8th Infantry Division of V Corps.

ITALY: Twelfth Air Force B-25 Mitchells and B-26 Marauders attack rail bridges in the Po Valley. A-20 Havocs and P-47 Thunderbolts of the XXII Tactical Air Command attack road and rail targets.

SOUTHWEST PACIFIC AREA: Due to limitations on logistics support and limited air cover available from the airfields on Leyte, General MacArthur delays the landing operation on Mindoro for 10 days. The new date is December 15. Lieutenant General Walter Krueger has formed the Western Visayan Task Force under command of Brigadier General William C. Dunkel, composed of the 19th RCT of the 24th Infantry Division and the 503rd Parachute Infantry Regiment, along with air and naval assets, to conduct the mission. The ground element of the task force is to seize airfields in support of the Luzon amphibious assault.

FEAF B-25 Mitchells attack airfields on Negros Island. B-25s with P-47 support also attack airfields on Cebu Island and Mindanao Islands.

The headquarters of the 3rd Air Commando Group, the 3rd Fighter Squadron (Commando), and 157th, 159th, and 160th Liaison Squadrons (Commando) arrive on Leyte Island from the United States with P-51 Mustangs. The B-24 Liberators of the 408th Bombardment Squadron (Heavy), 22nd Bombardment Group (Heavy), redeploy from Leyte Island to Angaur Island in the Palaus.

CENTRAL PACIFIC: Seventh Air Force B-24 Liberators from Saipan and Guam bomb Iwo Jima.

During the night a B-24 conducts a snooper (radar-assisted bomb release) mission on Iwo Jima.

A naval operating base at Kwajalein is established.

NEW GUINEA: FEAF B-25s attack targets on Halmahera Island.

The P-47 Thunderbolts of the 342nd Fighter Squadron, 348th Fighter Group, redeploy from Noemfoor Island to Leyte Island.

December 2

CBI: In Burma, Tenth Air Force sends 40 fighter-bombers to support ground forces near Bhamo, and B-25 Mitchells bomb rail targets and bridges in northern Burma.

Fourteenth Air Force P-51 Mustangs, P-40s, and P-38 Lightnings on armed reconnaissance attack troops, horses, vehicles, railroad yards, shipping, and logistics storage areas in southern China and near Lashio in Burma.

ETO: Eighth Air Force sends more than 450 B-17s and B-24 Liberators escorted by more than 600 P-51 Mustangs to attack marshaling yards in Germany. Eleven B-24s are lost and four damaged. Aircrews report eight confirmed kills and one probable. Aircrew casualties are two wounded and 102 missing. Fighter pilots report 11 confirmed kills and one probable in the air.

During the night seven B-17s and six B-24s drop leaflets over Germany, France, and the Netherlands.

Ninth Air Force sends more than 200 B-26 Marauders and A-20 Havocs to attack German positions along the battle front in Germany. More than 130 P-47 Thunderbolts and P-51 Mustangs fly fighter sweeps and support the 1st Infantry Division, the 104th Infantry Division, and the 8th Infantry Division

MEDITERRANEAN: Fifteenth Air Force sends nearly 500 B-17s and B-24 Liberators to attack oil refineries in Germany and Austria and a marshaling yard in Hungary as well as a road bridge in Czechoslovakia.

ITALY: The CCS orders General Alexander to set the priorities for offensive operations. The city of Bologna is still the main objective, but Alexander is cautioned that Allied forces should also ensure the Ravenna-Bologna-La Spezia line is secured.

Twelfth Air Force B-25 Mitchells and B-26 Marauders attack bridges. A-20 Havocs and P-47 Thunderbolts attack airfields, rail cars, and roads. Fighters also support Fifth Army forces south of Bologna.

SOUTHWEST PACIFIC AREA: On Leyte the 1st Battalion 34th Infantry Regiment and the 2nd Battalion 19th Infantry Regiment capture the Japanese defensive line at Kilay Ridge. The Japanese lose 900 killed.

FEAF B-24 Liberators bomb airfields on Negros Island and Mindanao Island. FEAF B-24 Liberators and B-25 Mitchells attack targets on Celebes Island. A-20 Havocs, P-38 Lightnings, and P-47 Thunderbolts support ground forces, attack logistics storage areas, and attack communications on Mindanao Island.

The B-24 Liberators of the 19th Bombardment Squadron (Heavy), 22nd Bombardment Group (Heavy), redeploy from Leyte Island to Angaur Island in the Palaus.

Four U.S. destroyers bombard Japanese positions at Palompon and northern Ormoc Bay, at Leyte. During the night another three destroyers enter Ormoc Bay, firing on aircraft, destroyers, and shore batteries. U.S. submarine *Gunnel* lands supplies and evacuates Allied aviators from Palawan.

PACIFIC: U.S. submarine *Sea Devil* attacks a Japanese convoy in the East China Sea, sinking a merchant tanker and passenger-cargo ship off Kyushu, Japan.

CENTRAL PACIFIC: Seventh Air Force sends 23 B-24 Liberators from Guam to bomb Iwo Jima.

During the night three B-24s from Saipan and Guam conduct a snooper (radar-assisted bomb release) mission on the airfield at Iwo Jima.

NEW GUINEA: FEAF B-25 Mitchells bomb the airfield on Buru Island and attack shipping off Ceram Island. B-24 Liberators and B-25s attack targets on Celebes Island.

December 3

CBI: In Burma, Tenth Air Force sends 40 fighter-bombers to support ground forces near Bhamo and B-25 Mitchells to bomb rail targets and bridges in northern Burma.

Fourteenth Air Force P-40s, P-51 Mustangs, and P-47 Thunderbolts attack road and rail junctions, bridges, artillery, town areas, troop concentrations, and various targets of opportunity around Shihhweiyao and from Hengyang to Siangtan and Lingling.

U.S. submarines *Pampanito, Pipefish, Sea Cat,* and *Searaven* attack a Japanese convoy in the South China Sea off the coast of French Indochina. USS *Pipefish* torpedoes and sinks a coastal patrol ship. USS *Pampanito* torpedoes a cargo ship. Both USS *Sea Cat* and USS *Searaven* report torpedoing a tanker.

ETO: Ninth Army reaches the Roer River with 10 divisions occupying a 24-mile front, but Bradley worries about the Roer River dams near Schmidt remaining under German control. He believes the Germans can stop any further advance by opening the dams to the south, flooding the river and trapping units on the far side of the Roer. Before any further advances can be made, Bradley decides that the Roer River dams must be captured. This order to the V Corps of First Army initiates another bloody and difficult struggle in the forested hills where the Germans have all the advantages.

The V Corps attacks into the Hürtgen Forest without air support. The bad weather prevents all but a few aircraft from flying. In the Hürtgen Forest, the 28th and 121st Infantry Regiments of the 8th Infantry Division, along with Combat Command B of the 5th Armored Division, capture Brandenberg, a key position on the flank of First Army. About 60 German fighter aircraft make a rare attack on American ground forces near Brandenberg. Antiaircraft platoons in the division account for 19 German aircraft shot down and claim 10 other probables.

Ninth Air Force P-47 Thunderbolts and P-38 Lightnings support the 104th Infantry Division, the 1st Infantry Division, and the 8th Infantry Division, as well as XII Corps.

The Seventh Army's VI Corps attacks north, moving along the Rhine River, while XV Corps attacks toward Bitche.

After Major General William Eagles is wounded, the 45th Infantry Division's new commander is Major General Robert T. Frederick, the former commander of the 1st Special Service Force.

Sergeant Ellis R. Weicht of F Company, 142nd Infantry Regiment, 36th Infantry Division, leads his squad in an attack on the village of St. Hippolyte, France. As the infantrymen clear buildings and move up a winding street, they are engaged by two machine guns from a house about 100 yards away. While the squad takes cover, Sergeant Weicht begins firing on the enemy. He advances under heavy fire until he reaches a house opposite the Germans and destroys the two machine-gun positions. As the squad advances again, two 20 millimeter guns open fire. As the Americans drop artillery on the German position, Sergeant Weicht continues to engage the position and follows up the artillery attack with a one-man assault, eliminating the position. Encountering another position, a road block, Sergeant Weicht moves to the second story of a house and engages the enemy, ignoring the heavy volume of fire directed at him. He continues to fight from this position until killed. For his acts of courage, skill, and leadership, Sergeant Weicht will receive the Medal of Honor.

MEDITERRANEAN: Fifteenth Air Force sends 85 B-17s and B-24 Liberators escorted by P-38 Lightnings and P-51 Mustangs to attack industrial production facilities and marshaling yards in Austria. Other B-17s and B-24s airdrop supplies in Yugoslavia.

ITALY: Twelfth Air Force P-47 Thunderbolts of the 57th and 350th Fighter Groups support ground forces of the Fifth Army south of Bologna.

SOUTHWEST PACIFIC AREA: On Leyte the 1st Cavalry Division attacking south from Carigara clears Japanese defenses and links with the 32nd Infantry Division near Highway 2. Logistics problems are limiting the X Corps advance. Roads are nonexistent or marginal and cease to exist when the rains come, which is often. Supplies reaching the front-line soldiers have to be moved by individuals and small groups over treacherous paths and steep jungle mountainsides.

The 128th Infantry Regiment of the 32nd Infantry Division passes through the 34th Infantry Regiment of the 24th Infantry Division and attacks to clear Japanese positions south of the ridge.

A-20s, P-38 Lightnings, and P-47 Thunderbolts attack logistics sites and airfields on Leyte Island and Masbate Island.

Three U.S. destroyers continue fighting in Ormoc Bay, Leyte. One destroyer is sunk, and two Japanese destroyers are sunk.

PACIFIC: Admiral Nimitz requests that the JCS delays the attack on Iwo Jima (Operation Detachment) to February 19 and Okinawa (Operation Iceberg) to April 1. Twentieth Air Force sends 86 B-29 Superfortresses from the Marianas to bomb the Musashino aircraft production facility, docks, and the city of Tokyo. Over the city, 60 B-29s hit the primary target; 15 hit alternate targets. Aircrews report 10 confirmed kills, 11 probable kills, and 18 possible kills. Five B-29s are lost.

CENTRAL PACIFIC: Seventh Air Force sends 17 B-24 Liberators from Guam to bomb Iwo Jima.

During the night B-24s conduct a snooper (radar-assisted bomb release) mission on Iwo Jima.

NEW GUINEA: FEAF B-24s attack targets on Celebes Island, while B-25 Mitchells bomb airfields on Halmahera Island. A-20 Havocs attack Point Noejew in New Guinea.

December 4

CBI: In Burma, Tenth Air Force sends P-47 Thunderbolts to attack bridges, defensive positions, logistics sites, and troops.

Fourteenth Air Force sends 24 B-25 Mitchells supported by 12 P-40s to attack bridges, buildings, and river, road, and rail traffic at several points in China, French Indochina, and Burma.

ETO: Eighth Air Force sends nearly 1,200 B-17s, using Pathfinder radar-equipped bombers and escorted by over 970 P-47 Thunderbolts and P-51 Mustangs, to attack marshaling yards in Germany. Three bombers are lost and 129 damaged. Aircrew casualties are one wounded and 28 missing. Fighter pilots report six confirmed kills on the ground. Three fighters are lost, and the pilots are reported missing.

During the night five B-17s and five B-24s drop leaflets over Germany, France, and the Netherlands.

Ninth Air Force P-47 Thunderbolts support the 1st, 8th, and 104th Infantry Divisions and the XII and XX Corps near the Saar River.

MEDITERRANEAN: Fifteenth Air Force sends 26 P-38 Lightnings to bomb a railroad bridge at Zenica in Yugoslavia.

ITALY: Twelfth Air Force B-25 Mitchells and B-26 Marauders bomb German defensive positions and attack an ammunition storage site. P-47 Thunderbolts support Fifth Army ground forces south of Bologna. A-20 Havocs attack targets in the Po Valley.

SOUTHWEST PACIFIC AREA: On Leyte the 7th Infantry Division continues its advance north in the Ormoc Valley, supported by the novel use of amphibious tanks, which travel at night in the coastal waters and appear ahead of infantry units as they advance the next morning, providing fire support against suspected Japanese positions in the hills alongside the road.

Marine fighter squadrons begin operating on airfields in Leyte.

A U.S. destroyer is damaged in a Japanese air attack off Leyte. U.S. submarine *Flasher* attacks a Japanese convoy southwest of Manila, sinking a destroyer and damaging a merchant tanker. USS *Flasher* escapes a counterattack from escorting ships.

PACIFIC: The headquarters of the XXI Bomber Command, Twentieth Air Force, arrives at Harmon Field on Guam from the United States.

CENTRAL PACIFIC: During the night two B-24 Liberators conduct a snooper (radar-assisted bomb release) mission on Iwo Jima.

December 5

CBI: In Burma, Tenth Air Force sends P-47 Thunderbolts to support ground forces near Bhamo. Other fighters attack road and rail transportation.

C-47s and C-46s begin Operation Grubworm, a redeployment of the Chinese 14th and 22nd Divisions from Burma to China as part of the Alpha Force to stop a Japanese offensive to capture Kunming in China, a major airfield for the Fourteenth Air Force.

Fourteenth Air Force sends seven B-24 Liberators on sweeps over the Gulf of Tonkin, the South China Sea, and the Formosa Strait. Bombers attack the Kowloon Docks in Hong Kong. Aircrews report damage to a cargo ship.

ETO: Third Army encounters German defenses at the West Wall along the west bank of the Saar River.

Eighth Air Force sends nearly 600 B-17s and B-24 Liberators, using Pathfinder radar-equipped bombers and escorted by over 800 P-47 Thunderbolts and P-51 Mustangs, to attack industrial production facilities in Berlin and marshaling yards in Germany. A total of 12 B-17s are lost and 179 bombers damaged. Aircrew casualties are one killed, eight wounded, and 115 missing. Fighter pilots report 90 confirmed kills and seven probables in the air and two possible kills on the ground. A total of 17 P-51 fighters are lost, and two are damaged. All 17 pilots are reported missing.

Six B-24 Liberators fly a screening mission to disrupt German radio intercept equipment and employ radar countermeasures.

During the night four B-17s and eight B-24s drop leaflets over Germany, France, and the Netherlands.

Ninth Air Force sends 172 A-20 Havocs, A-26 Invaders, and B-26 Marauders to attack a marshaling yard, road junction, fuel storage site, and a rail bridge in Germany. P-47 and P-38 fighters escort the bombers and support the 1st, 8th, and 104th Infantry Divisions.

ITALY: Twelfth Air Force P-47 Thunderbolts and A-20 Havocs support Fifth Army ground forces south of Bologna.

SOUTHWEST PACIFIC AREA, LEYTE: As part of the X Corps attack south in the Ormoc Valley, the 126th and 127th Infantry Regiments of the 32nd Infantry Division meet strong resistance. The 12th Cavalry Regiment captures Hill 2348.

The 7th Infantry Division breaks Japanese defenses at the Palanas River. The 11th Airborne Division attacks from the east.

U.S. submarine *Hake* lands supplies on Panay. An LST (landing ship, tank) and a medium landing ship are damaged in a Japanese air attack off Leyte. Kamikazes damage two destroyers and a cargo ship carrying troops. Over 100 men are killed or injured. Japanese torpedo planes attack a U.S. convoy headed for Leyte. One freighter is torpedoed and abandoned. ·

Private First Class William A. McWhorter of M Company, 126th Infantry Regiment, 32nd Infantry Division, mans a machine gun in a defensive position when his company comes under attack. A Japanese demolition squad tosses an improvised grenade into the position. McWhorter grabs the grenade and, to protect his assistant gunner, smothers the blast with his body. Private First Class McWhorter's heroism and act of supreme sacrifice will win him the Medal of Honor.

CENTRAL PACIFIC: Naval Base, Tinian, is established.

NEW GUINEA: FEAF B-24 Liberators bomb airfields on Halmahera Island and targets on northern Borneo while B-25 Mitchells attack targets on Celebes Island.

December 6

ALEUTIANS: Eleventh Air Force sends four B-24 Liberators to bomb Suribachi airfield on Paramushiru Island. Aircrews report damage to the runway and antiaircraft positions. One B-24 is damaged. A B-24 weather airplane is forced to land in the Soviet Union.

CBI: The 2nd and 3rd Battalions of the 475th Infantry Regiment of Mars Task Force relieve Chinese forces at Tonkwa. The units of the Chinese 22nd Division begin a redeployment back to China by air at the insistence of Generalissimo Chiang Kaishek. The 209th and 236th Engineers begin extending the Ledo Road to Bhamo and complete a 1,200-foot pontoon bridge over the Irrawaddy River. The bridge, with a 25-ton capacity, is the third-longest bridge ever built by U.S. Army engineers.

Tenth Air Force P-47 Thunderbolts and B-25 Mitchells bomb bridges and airfields in Burma.

ETO: The XII Corps captures Saarbrücken, advancing into the strongest positions of the West Wall. The Third Army in its late autumn battles has taken 29,000 casualties and captured 37,000 prisoners.

In the Hürtgen Forest, German forces make a heavy counterattack on elements of the 8th Infantry Division holding Brandenberg. The 2nd Ranger Battalion is brought in to seize Castle Hill, a key position overlooking Brandenberg. The Rangers capture the objective in a night attack and hold it for two days until relieved. The Rangers take 75 percent casualties.

Eighth Air Force sends more than 800 B-17s and B-24 Liberators using radar to locate targets and, escorted by 800 P-47 Thunderbolts and P-51 Mustangs, to attack oil refineries and marshaling yards in Germany. Four B-17s are lost and 251 bombers are damaged. Aircrew casualties are four wounded and 37 missing. One P-51 fighter is lost and two are damaged. One pilot is reported missing. Twelve B-17s fly a screening mission to disrupt German radio intercept equipment and employ radar countermeasures.

During the night 11 B-17s and B-24s drop leaflets over Germany, France, and the Netherlands.

Ninth Air Force sends 154 A-20 Havocs and B-26 Marauders to bomb German defensive positions along the battle line. P-47 and P-38 fighters escort the bombers and support the V, VII, and XII Corps.

MEDITERRANEAN: Fifteenth Air Force sends nearly 300 B-17s and B-24 Liberators escorted by P-38 Lightnings and P-51 Mustangs to attack marshaling yards in Austria, Hungary, Yugoslavia, and Czechoslovakia.

SOUTHWEST PACIFIC AREA: On Leyte, the Japanese drop 350 paratroopers near the San Pablo airfield, causing a great deal of confusion and disruption. The intent of the Japanese commander is to use the paratroopers to regain the initiative by eliminating the airfields under American control. The Japanese hold out for four days against an emergency force of rear area troops.

FEAF B-24 Liberators bomb an airfield on Negros Island, while B-25 Mitchells, with P-47 Thunderbolts escorting, bomb airfields on Mindanao Island. P-38 Lightnings covering a convoy off south Leyte Island report several Japanese aircraft shot down.

U.S. submarine *Haddo* torpedoes and damages a Japanese tanker off the west coast of Luzon. U.S. submarines *Segundo*, *Trepang*, and *Razorback* attack a Japanese convoy near Dalupiri Island as it travels to Manila. USS *Trepang* torpedoes and damages three cargo ships. USS *Segundo* damages three cargo ships as well.

NEW GUINEA: FEAF B-24 Liberators attack airfields on Celebes Island. B-25 Mitchells, P-40s, and A-20 Havocs attack airfields on Halmahera Island. A-20s and B-25s bomb Buru Island.

The headquarters of the 417th Bombardment Group (Light) and the A-20s of the 672nd, 673rd, 674th, and the 675th Bombardment Squadrons redeploy from Noemfoor Island to Leyte.

December 7

CBI: In Burma Tenth Air Force sends B-25 Mitchells to bomb bridges while P-47 Thunderbolts support ground forces near Bhamo and attack Japanese troops and logistics sites.

The 16th Combat Cargo Squadron, 4th Combat Cargo Group, arrives in India from the United States with C-46 Commando cargo planes.

Fourteenth Air Force sends eight B-25 Mitchells to attack logistics storage areas near Lashio in Burma. Aircrews of two B-24 Liberators report one cargo vessel sunk in the South China Sea. P-51 Mustang pilots attacking shipping at Hong Kong report sinking a destroyer and a cargo ship. P-51 Mustangs, P-40s, and P-38 Lightnings attack troop concentrations, gun positions, rail lines, logistics storage sites, bridges, and highways in southern China.

ETO: General Eisenhower holds a meeting with his senior commanders to establish missions for 1945. Both Montgomery's 21st Army Group and Bradley's 12th Army Group have been struggling in the difficult terrain before the Rhine. After several weeks of fighting, the armies have gained only a few miles. At the small-unit level, gains are measured in yards. The Allied advantage in air power and tanks has been neutralized by both bad weather, which has prevented effective air support to ground forces, and by the nature of the wooded terrain, which limits the use of tanks. Nevertheless, it is agreed that the goal for future operations will be to clear out German forces west of the Rhine River. The Roer River dams are recognized as a priority for the Americans. The Allies plan to launch a new offensive on January 12. In the meantime, Allied forces will make limited attacks, but the majority of the divisions will rest and refit. Field Marshal Montgomery's 21st Army Group will have the priority of effort in the upcoming offensive. Montgomery believes the broad-front strategy Eisenhower continues to promote is wasteful. He argues for a single main thrust (under Montgomery's command) to create the breakthrough.

MEDITERRANEAN: Fifteenth Air Force sends 31 B-17s and B-24 Liberators to bomb marshaling yards in Austria.

ITALY: Field Marshal Sir Harold R. L. G. Alexander, commander of the 15th Army Group, cancels the planned attack by Fifth Army's II Corps.

Twelfth Air Force A-20 Havocs and P-47 Thunderbolts attack rail lines and bridges.

SOUTHWEST PACIFIC AREA: On Leyte the 77th Infantry Division commanded by Major General Andrew D. Bruce arrives to reinforce the XXIV Corps near Ormoc City. Elements of the division advance to Ipil and are stopped by heavy fire. The 77th Division, pressing from the Palanas River, forces the Japanese to retreat. Elements of the 7th Infantry Division seek to link up with the 11th Airborne Division moving against strong Japanese positions west of Burauen.

FEAF B-24 Liberators bomb the airfield and town on Masbate Island and the airfield on Luzon Island.

Rear Admiral Arthur W. Struble's Naval Task Group 78.3 lands elements of the 77th Infantry Division on the eastern shore of Ormoc Bay after a pre-assault naval bombardment. Kamikazes damage two destroyers; one destroyer is scuttled. Two high-speed transports are damaged, and one must be scuttled. Kamikazes also damage an LST and two medium landing ships and sink another medium landing ship.

U.S. submarines *Razorback, Segundo,* and *Trepang* continue attacking the Japanese convoy they hit the previous day. USS *Razorback* torpedoes and sinks a cargo ship damaged the previous day. USS *Trepang* torpedoes and sinks a transport north of Luzon. Two cargo ships torpedoed by USS *Trepang* the previous day finally sink.

Fifth Air Force P-47 Thunderbolts and P-40s and Marine F4U Corsairs attack Japanese shipping in San Isidro Bay, Leyte. Pilots report sinking two escort destroyers, a fast transport, and four cargo ships.

PACIFIC: Twentieth Air Force sends 108 B-29 Superfortresses from Chengtu, China, to bomb the Manchuria Airplane Manufacturing Company and an adjacent arsenal at Mukden in Manchuria. Eighty B-29s hit the primary target and the others hit secondary or alternate targets. Aircrews report 10 confirmed kills, 10 probables, and 30 possibles. Seven B-29s are lost.

CENTRAL PACIFIC: Japanese aircraft attack the Seventh Air Force airfield on Saipan.

Japanese aircraft attack the airfield on Saipan.

NEW GUINEA: FEAF B-25 Mitchells attack airfields on Halmahera Island.

December 8

CBI: The Chinese 22nd Division encounters strong Japanese forces near Tonkwa. The American 475th Infantry occupies positions as the 22nd Division is redeployed to China.

The 1st Tank Battalion of the 1st Provisional Tank Group supports Chinese forces from the 38th Division attacking Japanese defenses at Bhamo. The 2nd and 3rd Battalions of the 475th Infantry Regiment defend Tonkwa against Japanese counterattacks.

Tenth Air Force P-47 Thunderbolts support ground forces near Bhamo and attack targets around Shwebo.

ETO: Third Army reports that it has a shortage of 11,000 men in the front-line combat units. Divisions are at half-strength and no replacements are arriving, reflecting a theater-wide shortage of combat troops. Patton begins to strip corps- and army-level support units, converting clerks, cooks, and signalmen into riflemen.

Ninth Air Force P-47 and P-38 fighters support V and VII Corps and XX Corps and XII Corps.

MEDITERRANEAN: Fifteenth Air Force sends 24 B-17s and B-24 Liberators to bomb marshaling yards in Austria.

ITALY: Twelfth Air Force P-47 Thunderbolts attack trains in the Po Valley. Fighter pilots report four locomotives are destroyed and almost 100 train cars are damaged.

SOUTHWEST PACIFIC AREA, LEYTE: Elements of the 1st Cavalry Division capture Wright, the end of the Taft-Wright Highway on Samar. American troops work with Philippine guerrillas to clear the entire highway.

FEAF B-24 Liberators bomb airfields on Cebu and Negros Islands.

Private Elmer E. Fryar of E Company, 511th Parachute Infantry Regiment, 11th Airborne Division, participates in a battalion attack on a Japanese defensive position. The battalion is unable to reach its objective and begins a withdrawal. E Company supports the withdrawal, but the Japanese suddenly launch a counterattack. Observing an enemy platoon moving to outflank his company's position, Private Fryar selects a firing position on high ground to engage the attacking force. He is quickly wounded in the exchange but continues to hold off the enemy. As the company begins its withdrawal, he assists a wounded paratrooper and accompanies his platoon leader, who is also aiding another wounded paratrooper. A Japanese soldier attempts to kill the American officer, but Fryar springs to protect him and is mortally wounded. Fryar uses a grenade to kill the enemy soldier. Fryar's courage under fire and his supreme act of sacrifice for his comrades will win him the Medal of Honor.

Private Ova A. Kelley of A Company, 382nd Infantry Regiment, 96th Infantry Division, sits at the edge of the enemy-held Buri airfield on Leyte. As dawn breaks, the Japanese fire on Kelley's company with rifle and machine-gun fire from entrenchments less than 100 yards distant. After the Americans drop mortar fire on the Japanese positions, Private Kelley takes an armload of hand grenades and attacks the Japanese. His grenade attack is successful in forcing the survivors to retreat. He picks up an M-1 rifle and fires on the retreating Japanese, then picks up an M-1 carbine and continues to fire. By this time his company has pressed the attack, advancing to seize the objective. For his extraordinary courage under fire, Private Kelley will receive the Medal of Honor.

PACIFIC: Twentieth Air Force sends 82 B-29 Superfortresses from the Marianas, escorted by Seventh Air Force P-38 Lightnings and 89 B-24 Liberators from Guam and Saipan, to bomb the airfields on Iwo Jima. Navy cruisers also provide naval gunfire support. The intent of the attack is to neutralize Japanese aircraft using Iwo as a base for attacks on Saipan.

Naval Task Group 94.9 (Rear Admiral Allan E. Smith) bombards Iwo Jima.

NEW GUINEA: FEAF B-25 Mitchells, P-47 Thunderbolts, and P-40s, along with Royal Australian Air Force (RAAF) aircraft, attack the airfield and other targets on Halmahera Island.

U.S. submarines *Paddle* and *Hammerhead* coordinate an attack on a Japanese convoy and sink a merchant tanker in the South China Sea west of Borneo. USS *Paddle* escapes a depth-charge attack.

December 9

CBI: The 2nd and 3rd Battalions of the 475th Infantry Regiment counterattack Japanese forces at Tonkwa and Mo-hlaing.

Tenth Air Force P-47 Thunderbolts attack bridges, villages and buildings, logistics storage areas, and targets of opportunity.

A Fourteenth Air Force B-24 aircrew reports sinking a cargo ship in the South China Sea. P-51 Mustangs and P-40s attack road and rail junctions, bridges, town areas, troop concentrations, and various targets of opportunity around Kweilin, Liuchow, Lingling, Hengyang, Tuhshan, and Chuchou.

ETO: Eighth Air Force sends 413 B-17s escorted by 247 P-47 Thunderbolts and P-51 Mustangs to attack marshaling yards and airfields in western Germany. One B-17 is lost and 67 damaged. Aircrew casualties are three wounded and nine missing. Fighter pilots report one confirmed kill in the air.

During the night four B-17s and seven B-24s drop leaflets over Germany, France, and the Netherlands.

Ninth Air Force sends 254 A-20 Havocs, A-26 Invaders, and B-26 Marauders to bomb German strongpoints, logistics storage sites, and a marshaling yard in western Germany. P-47 and P-38 fighters escort the bombers and support XII and XX Corps.

MEDITERRANEAN: Fifteenth Air Force sends 170 B-17s and B-24 Liberators escorted by P-38 Lightnings and P-51 Mustangs to attack industrial production facilities and a marshaling yard in Austria and an oil refinery at Regensburg, Germany, as well as armament production facilities at Plzen, Czechoslovakia.

Two U.S. destroyers bombard German coast artillery positions and troop concentrations along the border between France and Italy.

PACIFIC: U.S. submarine *Plaice* damages a Japanese escort destroyer off Kyushu, Japan.

U.S. submarines *Sea Devil* and *Redfish* torpedo and damage the Japanese carrier *Junyo* off Kyushu.

CENTRAL PACIFIC: Seventh Air Force B-24 Liberators from Saipan bomb Iwo Jima.

NEW GUINEA: FEAF B-24 Liberators bomb a tank farm, a bridge, airfields, and an oil installation at Ambon Island and Ceram Island. B-25 Mitchells attack targets in the Molucca Islands. P-38 Lightnings attack the airfield on Buru Island.

December 10

CBI: The British 36th Division captures Katha. The Japanese prepare to defend along a line about 400 miles north of Rangoon, from Akyab to Mandalay and along the Irrawaddy River to Lashio.

Tenth Air Force P-47 Thunderbolts conduct close support missions near Bhamo. B-25 Mitchells attack logistics storage sites.

Fourteenth Air Force sends 25 B-24 Liberators to bomb the city of Hankow, while three additional B-24s bomb the Samah Bay docks on Hainan Island. P-40s, P-51 Mustangs, and P-38 Lightnings attack vehicles, rail lines, logistics storage sites, bridges, highways, and river transportation around Hochih, Changsha, and Yuncheng.

ATLANTIC: German submarine *U-1202* torpedoes and sinks a U.S. freighter off the coast of Wales.

ETO: First Army's intelligence section predicts that the German High Command is preparing to launch a major counteroffensive led by tanks south of Aachen.

In the Hürtgen Forest, the 9th and the 104th Infantry Divisions of VII Corps attack toward Düren. The 330th and 331st Infantry Regiments of the 83rd Infantry Division replace the 4th Infantry Division and attack north to push the remaining German defenders from the edge of the forest. Minefields prevent the tanks of the 5th Armored Division from supporting the infantry.

Eighth Air Force sends more than 500 B-17s and B-24 Liberators led by radar-equipped Pathfinder bombers and escorted by nearly 700 P-47 Thunderbolts and P-51 Mustangs to attack marshaling yards in western Germany. A total of 33 bombers are damaged. Aircrew casualties are two killed. Two fighters are lost and one is damaged; the two pilots are reported missing.

Nearly 100 P-51 Mustangs make a fighter sweep and pilots report one possible kill. One P-51 is lost and one is damaged. The pilot is reported missing.

Ninth Air Force sends nearly 130 B-26 Marauders to bomb German defensive positions. P-47 and P-38 fighters escort the bombers and support the 8th, 9th, 83rd, and 104th Infantry Divisions and the 3rd and 5th Armored Divisions.

MEDITERRANEAN: Fifteenth Air Force sends more than 550 B-17s and B-24 Liberators escorted by P-38 Lightnings and P-51 Mustangs to attack oil production facilities in Germany.

ITALY: Twelfth Air Force B-25 Mitchells and B-26 Marauders attack rail and road targets in the Brenner Pass. A-20 Havocs and P-47 Thunderbolts attack German defensive positions and roads.

SOUTHWEST PACIFIC AREA, LEYTE: The 77th Infantry Division clears Japanese defenders from Camp Downes and enters Ormoc City. Over 1,500 Japanese are killed. U.S. casualties are 136 killed, wounded, and missing.

FEAF P-38 Lightnings bomb a port facility on Mindanao.

A kamikaze damages a destroyer off Leyte and an LCT (landing craft, tank) is sunk. A motor torpedo boat is damaged and abandoned.

CENTRAL PACIFIC: Seventh Air Force B-24 Liberators from Saipan bomb Iwo Jima.

NEW GUINEA: FEAF B-24 Liberators attack tank farms and docks in Borneo. B-25 Mitchells bomb the airfield on Celebes Island and the Molucca Islands.

December 11

CBI: In Burma, Tenth Air Force B-25 Mitchells bomb logistics storage sites, a ferry, and towns. P-47 Thunderbolts support ground forces near Bhamo.

Fourteenth Air Force sends six B-24 Liberators and six B-25 Mitchells escorted by eight P-51 Mustangs to attack targets in French Indochina. P-40s, P-51 Mustangs, and P-47s attack Tien Ho airfield at Canton, China, and Lashio in Burma

ETO: Eighth Air Force sends more than 1,500 B-17s and B-24 Liberators escorted by over 800 P-47 Thunderbolts and P-51 Mustangs to attack marshaling yards in western Germany and bridges in south-central Germany. Five bombers are lost and 54 are damaged. Aircrew casualties are two wounded, and 47 missing. Fighter pilots report on a possible kill on the ground. Two P-51s are lost and two are damaged; two pilots are reported missing.

During the night three B-17s and eight B-24s drop leaflets over Germany, France, and the Netherlands.

Ninth Air Force fighters support 3rd Armored Division and the 104th, the 9th and the 83rd Infantry Divisions.

MEDITERRANEAN: Fifteenth Air Force sends more than 400 B-17s and B-24 Liberators escorted by P-38 Lightnings and P-51 Mustangs to attack industrial production facilities in Austria.

ITALY: Twelfth Air Force B-25 Mitchells and B-26 Marauders attack bridges. A-20 Havocs and P-47 Thunderbolts attack defensive positions, artillery, bridges, and roads.

SOUTHWEST PACIFIC AREA: Troops of the 11th Airborne Division and the 149th Infantry Regiment of the 38th Infantry Division are able to eliminate the Japanese paratroopers at San Pablo airfield. Although the Japanese have destroyed several logistics storage sites and a number of aircraft, they have had no appreciable effect on Sixth Army's operations.

FEAF B-24 Liberators bomb the airfield on Cebu Island in the Philippines. B-25 Mitchells, with P-47 Thunderbolts escorting, bomb an airfield on Mindanao Island and P-38 Lightnings and Marine Corps aircraft attack a 13-ship convoy off Leyte Island.

By this date, despite constant attacks on shipping and transports, the Japanese have been able to land more then 34,000 troops at Leyte and deliver another 10,000 tons of supplies.

Kamikazes attack a resupply convoy headed for Ormoc Bay. A destroyer and an LCT (landing craft, tank) are sunk off Leyte. Marine F4U Corsairs attack a Japanese convoy off Leyte, sinking two cargo ships. U.S. submarine *Gar* lands supplies on the west coast of Luzon and picks up intelligence documents.

PACIFIC: U.S. submarine *Sea Owl* torpedoes and sinks a Japanese auxiliary submarine chaser in the East China Sea.

CENTRAL PACIFIC: Seventh Air Force sends 28 B-24 Liberators from Guam to bomb Iwo Jima. During the night B-24s from Guam and Saipan conduct a snooper (radar-assisted bomb release) mission on Iwo Jima.

NEW GUINEA: FEAF B-25 Mitchells, A-20 Havocs, and P-40s attack targets in the Molucca Islands.

FEAF B-25 Mitchells, A-20 Havocs, P-38 Lightnings, and P-40s attack Japanese supply and troop concentrations on the southern shore of Wasile Bay and along the shore north of Halmahera Island. Pilots report one ship sunk.

December 12

CBI: Tenth Air Force sends 11 B-25 Mitchells to bomb logistics storage areas near Lashio. P-47 Thunderbolts attack roads and bridges, a Japanese headquarters. artillery, town areas, troop concentrations, and various targets of opportunity.

Fourteenth Air Force P-40s, P-51 Mustangs, and P-38 Lightnings on armed reconnaissance attack logistics storage sites, rail lines, bridges, and highways in Burma, Thailand, and China.

ETO: The 83rd Infantry Division and elements of the 5th Armored Division push northeast of Hürtgen Forest.

The 44th Infantry Division of the VI Corps, Seventh Army, captures Haguenau.

Eighth Air Force sends nearly 900 B-17s and B-24 Liberators, using radar to assist in locating targets and escorted by over 900 P-47 Thunderbolts and P-51 Mustangs, to attack a synthetic oil plant and marshaling yards in western Germany. A total of four bombers are lost and 79 are damaged. Aircrew casualties are 12 killed and 36 missing. Fighter pilots report one possible kill on the ground. Seven fighters are lost and three damaged. Six pilots are reported missing.

B-24 Liberators and B-17s conduct screening missions to jam German radio interception efforts and conduct countermeasures against German radar sites.

During the night seven B-17s and four B-24s drop leaflets over Germany, France, and the Netherlands.

Ninth Air Force sends 90 A-20 Havocs and B-26 Marauders to attack German strongpoints. P-47 and P-38 fighters support the 83rd Infantry Division of the VII Corps, the XII Corps, and the 35th Infantry Division of XX Corps.

MEDITERRANEAN: Fifteenth Air Force sends 75 B-17s and B-24 Liberators escorted by P-38 Lightnings and P-51 Mustangs to bomb an oil refinery in Germany and industrial production facilities in Czechoslovakia.

SOUTHWEST PACIFIC AREA, LEYTE: After two days of heavy fighting the 17th and 184th Infantry Regiments of the 7th Infantry Division clear Japanese forces from Hill 918 protecting Ormoc Bay.

FEAF B-24 Liberators, with P-47 Thunderbolts and P-38 Lightnings providing escort, bomb the airfield on Negros Island. B-25 Mitchells bomb the airfield on Mindanao.

Marines and Thirteenth Air Force aircraft attack one of the last convoys attempting to provide reinforcements to Japanese forces on Leyte. Another Japanese destroyer and a landing ship are sunk.

Two motor torpedo boats sink a Japanese destroyer off Leyte. A U.S. destroyer is damaged by a kamikaze off Leyte.

PACIFIC: The service groups of the 313th Bombardment Wing (Very Heavy), Twentieth Air Force, arrive on Tinian.

CENTRAL PACIFIC: Seventh Air Force sends 24 B-24 Liberators from Saipan to bomb Iwo Jima.

During the night B-24s from Saipan and Guam conduct a snooper (radar-assisted bomb release) mission on Iwo Jima.

NEW GUINEA: FEAF B-24 Liberators bomb the airfields on Celebes Island and on Ambon-Ceram-Boeroe Islands.

December 13

CBI: Elements of the 1st Provisional Tank Group support the Chinese conducting a siege at Bhamo. The 2nd and 3rd Battalions of the 475th Infantry Regiment stop a Japanese attack near Tonkwa.

Tenth Air Force sends 12 B-25 Mitchells to bomb the logistics storage and personnel area at Mongmit. P-47 Thunderbolts support the 475th Infantry Regiment near Tonkwa and attack logistics sites and vehicles.

Fourteenth Air Force P-51 Mustangs and P-38 Lightnings attack town areas and rail targets in French Indochina and attack a bridge in Thailand. The headquarters of the 341st Bombardment Group (Medium) redeploys from Kunming to Yangkai, China.

U.S. submarine *Bergall* engages a Japanese heavy cruiser in the South China Sea off French Indochina. The submarine damages the cruiser, but the *Bergall* is hit by a dud eight-inch shell and terminates her patrol.

ETO: In deep snow, the V Corps of First Army begins its attack to capture the Roer River dams. The 78th and 2nd Infantry Divisions make the attack. This attack will be halted three days later when the German Ardennes offensive begins and Monschau is attacked. The 9th Infantry Division, fighting in the bloody woods from September 13 to October 26, has suffered 3,600 casualties; the 28th Infantry Division, attacking in the same place from October 27 to November 20, has suffered 3,600 casualties; the 4th Infantry Division, from November 6 to December 8, suffers 5,200 casualties. Since November 16 First Army has suffered a total of 21,650 casualties. Ninth Army has lost 10,000 casualties during the same period.

The soldiers of Bradley's 12th Army Group are suffering greatly in the terrible autumn and early winter of 1944. Their suffering will get worse in the next few weeks and months.

The battle for the Hürtgen Forest has lasted from September 14 to December 13. It has cost 24,000 Americans killed, wounded, and missing. Another 9,000 are nonbattle casualties. The gains made for the price paid are reminiscent of the worst leadership on the Western Front in World War I, when generals ordered that objectives be attacked without an understanding of the terrain involved—and then were sidetracked into useless battles of attrition that served no larger purpose. The III Corps under Major General John Millikin captures the last of the Metz forts. The cost of capturing the city far outweighs its usefulness to Third Army. The Americans have given up all their advantages in mobility and firepower to engage in the kind of positional warfare the Germans wished for.

The 103rd and 45th Infantry Divisions of the XV Corps of Seventh Army enter into Germany and encounter the defenses of the West Wall (or Siegfried Line). The 79th Infantry Division and 14th Armored Division advance toward the German border.

Ninth Air Force sends 250 A-20 Havocs, A-26 Invaders, and B-26 Marauders to attack fuel storage sites and German strongpoints. P-47 and P-38 fighters support XX Corps and XII Corps.

MEDITERRANEAN: A U.S. destroyer bombards troop concentrations and artillery positions along the French-Italian border.

SOUTHWEST PACIFIC AREA: The Western Visayan Task Force en route to Mindoro is attacked by kamikaze aircraft, seriously damaging the *Nashville,* the task force's flagship. On the ship 131 men are killed and 158 wounded. *Nashville* is forced to return to Leyte.

FEAF B-24 Liberators bomb airfields on Negros Island. B-25 Mitchells bomb the airfield on Mindanao Island.

Kamikazes damage a light cruiser and a destroyer near Mindanao.

U.S. submarine *Pintado* torpedoes and sinks a Japanese fast transport and landing ship in the South China Sea near Luzon Strait.

PACIFIC: Twentieth Air Force sends 90 B-29 Superfortresses from the Marianas to bomb the Mitsubishi aircraft engine plant at Nagoya, Japan. A total of 71 hit the primary target. Aircrews report considerable damage to the target and report four confirmed kills and one probable kill. Four B-29s are lost.

CENTRAL PACIFIC: Seventh Air Force sends 15 B-24 Liberators from Guam to bomb Iwo Jima Island. Three B-24s from Saipan bomb Marcus Island. During the night six B-24s from Saipan and Guam conduct raids against Iwo Jima.

The headquarters of Seventh Air Force arrives at Saipan from Hawaii.

NEW GUINEA: FEAF B-25 Mitchells bomb airfields on Haroekoe Island, the Molucca Islands, Ceram Island, Ambon Island, and Buru Island. B-25 Mitchells, P-38 Lightnings, and P-47 Thunderbolts attack shore positions at Galela Bay on Halmahera Island.

December 14

CBI: The 38th Chinese Division captures Bhamo.

Tenth Air Force sends 12 B-25 Mitchells to bomb the logistics storage and troop barracks at Mongmit. P-47 Thunderbolts attack troop concentrations, roads, and logistics areas and support the 475th Infantry Regiment near Tonkwa.

The 1st Fighter Squadron (Commando) with P-51 Mustangs, 2nd Air Commando Group, arrives at Kalaikunda, India, from the United States. The squadron's first missions are scheduled for mid-February 1945.

ATLANTIC: Congress establishes the five-star general and flag officer rank.

ETO: Ninth Air Force P-38 Lightnings and P-47 Thunderbolts support the 2nd and 99th Infantry Divisions in the Monschau Forest, the 8th Infantry Division near the Bergstein area, the 78th Infantry Division, and XII and XX Corps.

Sergeant Ralph G. Neppel of M Company, 329th Infantry Regiment, 83rd Infantry Division, is leading a machine-gun squad defending an approach to the village of Birgel, Germany, when 20 German troops and a tank approach. As his men engage the infantry at 100 yards, the tank immediately fires at the position, killing or wounding everyone. Sergeant Neppel is blasted 10 yards from his gun and has lost his left leg. Dragging himself back to his machine gun, he kills the German infantrymen and forces the tank to withdraw. Sergeant Neppel's courage and fighting spirit will win him the Medal of Honor.

ITALY: Twelfth Air Force A-20 Havocs and P-47 Thunderbolts attack rail lines in the Po Valley and German positions in support of the Fifth Army south of Bologna.

SOUTHWEST PACIFIC AREA: On Leyte, the 305th Infantry Regiment of the 77th Infantry Division assaults the last Japanese strongpoint in the Ormoc Valley. Supported by several artillery battalions, tanks, armored bulldozers, and flamethrowers, the infantrymen capture the enemy position. The 32nd Infantry Division advances down Highway 2 from the north in the X Corps area and is met by determined resistance. The infantrymen advance only a short distance past Kilay Ridge.

FEAF B-24 Liberators attack airfields on Negros Island. B-25 Mitchells bomb the airfield on Jolo Island.

U.S. submarine *Blenny* torpedoes and sinks a Japanese coastal patrol ship and a guardboat off Luzon. Aircraft from carrier USS *Hornet* sink a Japanese landing ship off Vigan.

Lieutenant Robert P. Nett commands E Company, 305th Infantry Regiment, 77th Infantry Division. He leads his unit in an attack against an entrenched Japanese battalion near Cognon. Attacking the trench lines, Lieutenant Nett clears the first positions, fighting the enemy hand-to-hand. Wounded three times, he refuses treatment and continues to lead the advance toward the objective. Only when the company has consolidated control of the objective does Lieutenant Nett turn over command and walk unaided to receive medical treatment. For his inspiring leadership and determination to defeat the enemy, Lieutenant Nett will receive the Medal of Honor.

PACIFIC: Twentieth Air Force sends 48 B-29 Superfortresses from Calcutta, India, to bomb a railroad bridge at Bangkok, Thailand. A total of 33 hit the primary target. Aircrews report one possible kill. Four B-29s are lost.

CENTRAL PACIFIC: Seventh Air Force sends 24 B-24 Liberators from Saipan to bomb Iwo Jima Island. Three B-24s from Saipan bomb Marcus Island. During the night six B-24s from Saipan and Guam conduct a snooper (radar-assisted bomb release) mission against Iwo Jima.

NEW GUINEA: FEAF B-25 Mitchells bomb targets on Buru Island.

The 550th Night Fighter Squadron, XIII Fighter Command, arrives at Hollandia, New Guinea, from the United States with P-61 Black Widow night fighters. The squadron's first missions are scheduled for mid-January 1945.

December 15

CBI: The Chinese 38th Division occupies Bhamo after the Japanese abandon the city and withdraw south to Lashio. General Sultan looks to the Mars Task Force (the 5332nd Brigade [Provisional]) to cut the Burma Road and threaten the rear of Japanese forces holding against the Chinese 30th and 38th Divisions.

The 1st Battalion of the 475th Infantry Regiment patrols in the vicinity of Shwegu until relieved by the British 36th Infantry Division.

Tenth Air Force sends 10 B-25 Mitchells to bomb the Hsipaw railroad bridge and others. P-47 Thunderbolts attack bridges and attack Japanese positions along the Namh-Kam-Bhamo road in pursuit of retreating Japanese forces. P-47s attack Lashio airfield.

The 2nd Fighter Squadron (Commando) with P-51 Mustangs, 2nd Air Commando Group, arrives at Kalaikunda, India, from the United States. The squadron's first missions are scheduled for mid-February 1945.

Fourteenth Air Force sends six B-25 Mitchells to bomb logistics sites at Kunlong, China.

ATLANTIC: The U.S. Senate approves the promotions of Henry H. Arnold, Dwight D. Eisenhower, Douglas MacArthur, and George C. Marshall to the five-star rank of general of the army and the nominations of William D. Leahy, Ernest J. King, and Chester W. Nimitz as admirals of the fleet.

The headquarters of the Continental Air Force is activated at Bolling Field, Washington, D.C. Its mission is to coordinate the efforts of the First, Second, Third, and Fourth Air Forces and the I Troop Carrier Command. The headquarters is expected to be operational by early May 1945.

ETO: The VII Corps of First Army controls the area north of Düren. The V Corps is unable to advance. The Ninth and First Armies report to the 12th Army Group that they have a five-day supply of fuel stocks. The Third Army reports it has a nine-day supply of fuel. The Third Army has drawn up to the German defenses of the West Wall (or Siegfried Line) and has established several bridgeheads over the Saar River.

The Seventh Army of the 6th Army Group advances through German defenses toward Wissembourg along a 22-mile front. Although pushed back, German forces still control the bridgehead over the Rhine River at Colmar. The French First Army is unable to close the salient, now known as the Colmar Pocket. The Germans defend the bridgehead at the Rhine River at Colmar, defeating an attack by the First French Army. Since December 1, Seventh Army has suffered 18,000 casualties and has captured 25,000 prisoners.

General Bradley reports a shortage of 17,000 infantrymen needed to replace combat and noncombat losses in the 12th Army Group.

Eighth Air Force sends more than 670 B-17s, using radar to assist in locating targets and escorted by more than 400 P-47 Thunderbolts and P-51 Mustangs, to attack marshaling yards and armament production facilities in western Germany. One B-17 is lost and 24 damaged. Aircrew casualties are 25 killed and one wounded. Two P-51s are lost, and the pilots are reported missing.

During the night two B-17s drop leaflets over Germany and France.

Ninth Air Force sends 300 A-20 Havocs, A-26 Invaders, and B-26 Marauders to attack fuel storage sites and strongpoints. P-47 and P-38 fighters support the 2nd and 99th Infantry Divisions, the 78th and the 8th Infantry Divisions, and the 5th Armored Division as well as the XX and XII Corps.

Bandleader and Army Air Force major Glenn Miller is lost while flying in a single-engine plane across the English Channel en route to Paris.

Headquarters, Naval Forces Germany, is established at Rosneath, Scotland, under command of Admiral Robert L. Ghormley.

MEDITERRANEAN: The death of Field Marshal Sir John Dill requires a new officer to fill the position of chief of the British Military Mission. Supreme Allied Commander Mediterranean, General Sir Henry Maitland Wilson, is selected. Field Marshal Sir Harold R. L. G. Alexander replaces Wilson as the Mediterranean theater commander. General Mark Clark takes command of 15th Army Group, and Major General Lucian K. Truscott becomes Fifth Army commander.

Ultra intercepts indicate a buildup of German forces in front of Fifth Army's IV Corps area, delaying a planned Eighth Army and Fifth Army combined offensive.

Fifteenth Air Force sends more than 300 B-17s and B-24 Liberators escorted by over 250 P-38 Lightnings and P-51 Mustangs to attack marshaling yards in Austria and Germany.

ITALY: Twelfth Air Force B-25 Mitchells and B-26 Marauders attack ammunition storage areas, fuel storage areas, and rail bridges. A-20 Havocs and P-47 Thunderbolts attack rail targets and support Fifth Army ground forces south of Bologna.

SOUTHWEST PACIFIC AREA: FEAF B-24 Liberators and B-25 Mitchells bomb airfields on Mindanao as the Western Visayan Task Force approaches. The 19th Infantry RCT and the 503rd Parachute Infantry Regiment land on Mindoro after a short naval bombardment. Two LSTs and a destroyer are sunk by kamikazes. San Jose is occupied, and the airfields are in American hands.

B-24s attack targets on Palawan Island. A-20 Havocs and P-47 Thunderbolts attack fuel storage area on Negros Island.

Naval Task Group 78.3, commanded by Rear Admiral Arthur D. Struble, lands ground forces on the southwest coast of Mindoro. Carrier aircraft provide cover for the landing. Kamikazes damage two destroyers, two LSTs, the escort carrier USS *Marcus Island,* and a motor torpedo boat off Mindoro.

U.S. submarine *Hawkbill* torpedoes and sinks a Japanese destroyer west of Luzon.

Carrier aircraft from Task Force 38 sink a Japanese landing ship in the South China Sea off Luzon.

Private First Class Dirk J. Vlug of the 126th Infantry Regiment, 32nd Infantry Division, is occupying a roadblock on the Ormoc Road near Limon when two Japanese tanks advance. Leaving his defensive position, he approaches the tanks with a bazooka and six rounds. Ignoring the fire from the tanks, he fires on the first tank and destroys it. The crew of another tank dismounts and charges toward Private First Class Vlug, who kills one soldier with a pistol. The crewmen retreat and remount the tank but are quickly dispatched by another round from Vlug's bazooka. As three more tanks arrive, Vlug takes a flanking position and hits the first tank; ignoring the fire directed at him, he moves to engage the second tank.

His last two shots destroy the remaining tanks. Private First Class Vlug's heroism and determination in destroying five Japanese tanks singlehandedly will win him the Medal of Honor.

CENTRAL PACIFIC: Seventh Air Force sends 13 B-24 Liberators from Guam to bomb Iwo Jima.

During the night a B-24 conducts a snooper (radar-assisted bomb release) mission on Iwo Jima.

NEW GUINEA: FEAF B-25 Mitchells attack airfields on Ceram and Ambon Islands. P-40s and P-38s along with B-25s bomb airfields on Boeroe and Halmahera Islands and shipping in the Netherlands East Indies.

December 16

CBI: Tenth Air Force P-47 Thunderbolts support the 475th Infantry Regiment near Tonkwa. Other P-47s attack locomotives, logistics storage areas, buildings, and personnel.

U.S. submarine *Dace* lays mines off French Indochina.

ETO: The German Ardennes Offensive Begins. The Germans attack on a 50-mile front in the Ardennes Forest, with 20 divisions supported by 350 aircraft, in an attempt to reverse the course of the war with one final offensive thrust. The offensive depends on the quick capture and control of several critical road junctions: St-Vith, Malmédy, Bastogne, and Houffalize. The badly depleted 4th and 28th Infantry Divisions and the newly arrived 106th Infantry Division, along with the 9th Armored Division of VIII Corps, occupy the area of the attack and are hit with a heavy artillery barrage, followed by infantry assaulting the American lines. Although there is determined resistance in some locations, most of the American troops are scattered. Two infantry regiments of the 106th Infantry are surrounded. The 4th Infantry Division conducts a strong defense. German tanks and infantry break through the boundary between V Corps and VIII Corps and advance six miles. German aircraft drop paratroopers behind American lines to cut the main roads into the Ardennes. Very few of the paratroopers actually make it into the combat area. Many speak English and are dressed like American soldiers, causing an amount of alarm and confusion throughout the battle area far beyond their actual capabilities.

First Lieutenant Charles P. Murray, Jr., of C Company, 30th Infantry Regiment, 3rd Infantry Division, leads a reinforced platoon into contact with a force of 200 Germans attacking American positions on the crest of a ridge near Kaysersberg, France. His radio goes dead after he begins calling adjustments to his initial call for fire. He moves back to his platoon and, taking some rifle grenades, returns to engage the enemy. As the grenades land among the German troops, he receives heavy enemy fire, but continues to fight until the grenades are gone. He then returns to his platoon, takes an automatic rifle and ammunition, and again takes up a position to engage the Germans. His accurate fire breaks up the unit's attack and forces it to retreat. He then advances to his objective with his platoon and captures 10 German soldiers. Although wounded by a grenade, he refuses to be treated until satisfied that his platoon is properly deployed. First Lieutenant Murray's calm and heroic act to disrupt a large enemy unit and protect his men will win him the Medal of Honor.

The German offensive in the Ardennes comes as a complete surprise to General Eisenhower. He believes it to be a serious threat, but General Bradley believes the attack is limited and manageable. Nevertheless, Eisenhower orders Bradley to alert Third Army's 10th Armored Division and Ninth Army's 7th Armored Division to be prepared to move to support First Army.

Eighth Air Force sends 236 B-17s escorted by over 100 P-51 Mustangs to attack rail targets at Stuttgart, Germany. Poor weather prevents all but 81 from hitting the primary target. One B-17 is lost and 10 damaged. Aircrew casualties are three killed and nine missing.

Ninth Air Force P-47 and P-38 fighters support First Army units encountering the leading elements of the German counteroffensive on the Western Front.

When L Company, 393rd Infantry Regiment, 99th Infantry Division, is hit by the artillery barrage that signals the beginning of the Ardennes offensive, Technical Sergeant Vernon McGarity is wounded. He receives first aid but refuses to be evacuated, returning to his squad and leading them in defending their position against a strong German attack. During the battle, McGarity rescues a wounded comrade in an exposed position, ignoring enemy fire. Throughout the night, he keeps his men ready to repulse an attack. The following morning, McGarity's squad faces a tank and infantry attack. Technical Sergeant McGarity personally destroys the lead tank and rescues another wounded American soldier. As the squad runs low on ammunition, McGarity braves heavy fire to find more. When the Germans surround his location and place a machine gun in position to block his squad's retreat, McGarity attacks the Germans and singlehandedly captures the position. When the squad is completely surrounded and has fired its last round of ammunition, the Germans overwhelm the Americans and take them prisoner. For his courage under fire and his inspiring leadership, Technical Sergeant McGarity will win the Medal of Honor.

MEDITERRANEAN: Fifteenth Air Force sends more than 600 B-17s and B-24 Liberators escorted by P-38 Lightnings and P-51 Mustangs to attack an oil production facility and armaments production facility in Czechoslovakia and industrial targets and a marshaling yard in Austria.

ITALY: Twelfth Air Force A-20 Havocs and P-47 Thunderbolts of the XXII Tactical Air Command attack rail lines and bridges and support Fifth Army ground forces south of Bologna.

SOUTHWEST PACIFIC AREA: On Leyte, the 2nd Battalion of the 32nd Infantry Regiment begins moving into the mountains from Ormoc Bay to link up with paratroopers from the 11th Airborne Division making a cross-country advance to clear out the last organized Japanese defenders.

The Third Fleet, providing air support over Luzon, halts operations when a typhoon strikes.

FEAF B-24 Liberators bomb airfields on Mindanao and Palawan Islands.

Carrier aircraft from Task Force 38 sink a cargo ship escorted by a destroyer and sink a submarine chaser in Subic Bay, Luzon. The cargo ship is carrying 1,600 Allied prisoners of war.

CENTRAL PACIFIC: During the night Seventh Air Force B-24s from Guam and Saipan conduct snooper (radar-assisted bomb release) missions on Iwo Jima.

U.S. submarine *Finback* attacks a Japanese convoy and sinks a transport near Chichi Jima.

NEW GUINEA: FEAF B-25 Mitchells, A-20 Havocs, and P-47 Thunderbolts attack airfields on Ceram Island, and targets of opportunity on north Borneo and around the Vogelkop Peninsula.

December 17

CBI: Tenth Air Force P-47 Thunderbolts support ground forces. The 493rd Bombardment Squadron (Heavy), 7th Bombardment Group (Heavy), sends a detachment of B-24 Liberators from Pandaveswar, India, to Luliang, China, to transport fuel to Suichwan, China.

Fourteenth Air Force sends nine B-24 Liberators to bomb targets at Cam Ranh Bay in French Indochina.

ETO: **The Battle of the Bulge.** German tank and infantry spearheads reach Honsfeld and Losheim and push farther westward. The 99th Infantry Division defending in the Losheim area is steadily being pressed and threatened with destruction. The First Army commander, Lieutenant General Courtney Hodges, decides to defend Elsenborn Ridge in the northwest with elements of the 2nd Infantry Division after the division had been ordered to halt a successful attack and retreat. Combat Command B of the 7th Armored Division arrives to defend St-Vith and collects scattered elements of the 106th Infantry Division.

The members of Battery B of the 285th Field Artillery Observation Battalion are captured, then executed, by German troops at Malmédy. About 125 men are killed or wounded.

The 28th Infantry Division is pushed steadily back and broken into isolated elements. At Clervaux, the 110th Infantry Regiment is overrun. General Eisenhower commits his reserve, the 101st and 82nd Airborne Divisions, into the battle. The units are to arrive under the operational control of the 12th Army Group. Eisenhower orders XVIII Airborne Corps headquarters, commanded by Major General Matthew B. Ridgway, to support First Army. The 4th Infantry Division supported by corps artillery units stops the German advance near Echternach. Operational control of the 1st Infantry Division is transferred from V Corps to VII Corps in order to hold the northern limit of the breakthrough. Combat Command B of the 10th Armored Division moves to Bastogne.

During the night Eighth Air Force sends three B-17s and seven B-24s to drop leaflets over Germany, France, and the Netherlands.

The B-24 Liberators of the 859th Bombardment Squadron (Heavy), 492nd Bombardment Group (Heavy), are detached to Italy. This squadron was supporting Carpetbagger missions.

Ninth Air Force, IX and XIX Tactical Air Commands, sends more than 1,000 P-38 and P-47 fighters to conduct armed reconnaissance missions, defensive patrols, and to attack bridges and gun positions. The fighters support the 8th, 28th, 78th, 99th, and 106th Infantry Divisions, and the 5th Armored Division as German forces begin to press hard against the weak defenses in the Ardennes. Fighters also support the V, VII, VIII, XII, and XX Corps.

Private First Class William A. Soderman is a bazooka gunner in K Company, 9th Infantry Regiment, 2nd Infantry Division, defending a crossroads near Rocherath, Belgium. After a heavy artillery barrage in which his assistant gunner is wounded, Private First Class Soderman hears German tanks approaching. As five tanks approach his position, Soderman waits until he can get the most effective shot. Standing up a few feet in front of the lead tank, he hits and destroys it. Throughout the rest of the night Private First Class Soderman holds his position and engages five more tanks, again standing in full view of the lead tank, firing at point-blank range. He then moves to engage a German infantry platoon with his bazooka. As K Company begins a withdrawal, Private First Class Soderman waits to hold off another tank attack to give the company time to break contact with the enemy. Again Soderman performs his remarkably courageous act, hitting and destroying one tank at close range in full view of the enemy. This time he is seriously wounded and drags himself to American lines. Private First Class Soderman's gallantry and dedication to duty contribute to the survival of his company and slow the German advance in the early hours of the Ardennes offensive. He will receive the Medal of Honor.

MEDITERRANEAN: Fifteenth Air Force sends more than 500 B-17s and B-24 Liberators escorted by P-38 Lightnings and P-51 Mustangs to bomb oil refineries and marshaling yards in Germany and Austria. Fighter pilots report 55 confirmed kills.

ITALY: Twelfth Air Force A-20 Havocs and P-47 Thunderbolts of the XXII Tactical Air Command attack marshaling yards and rail traffic.

SOUTHWEST PACIFIC AREA: In the Philippines FEAF B-24 Liberators and B-25 Mitchells bomb airfields on Negros Island. B-25s and A-20 Havocs attack Japanese positions on Mindanao, and B-24s with P-47 Thunderbolts escorting attack the airfield on Jolo Island.

A kamikaze damages a motor torpedo boat off Mindoro.

CENTRAL PACIFIC: Seventh Air Force sends 24 B-24 Liberators from Saipan Island and 26 B-24s from Guam to bomb Iwo Jima. B-24s from Saipan bomb Woleai and Eauriprik Atolls in the Carolines.

During the night B-24s from Saipan and Guam conduct raids on Iwo Jima.

NEW GUINEA: FEAF B-24 Liberators and A-20 Havocs attack airfields in Borneo and on Ambon Island.

December 18

CBI: In Burma, after nearly a week of fighting units of the 475th Infantry Regiment around Tonkwa, the Japanese withdraw to reinforce the defense of Mandalay against General Slim's British XIV Corps. During the fighting the 475th has lost 15 killed and 56 wounded. Japanese casualties are estimated at 220.

Tenth Air Force P-47 Thunderbolts and B-25 Mitchells attack bridges in China and Burma. The 427th Night Fighter Squadron at Myitkyina sends P-61 Black Widow night fighters to operate from Kunming, China.

Over 200 Fourteenth Air Force aircraft support 94 Twentieth Air Force B-29s attacking Hankow. Hankow is nearly obliterated, eliminating its use as a Japanese logistics base.

B-25 Mitchells and P-51 Mustangs attack Wuchang. Fighter pilots report 16 confirmed kills in the air and four probables on the ground. One P-51 is lost, and the pilot is reported missing. Six B-25 Mitchells bomb Kunlong escorted by 20 P-51 Mustangs and P-38 Lightnings. The fighters drop napalm on the logistics storage sites after the bombing run.

ATLANTIC: The U.S. Supreme Court upholds the wartime relocation of Japanese-Americans, but also says that undeniably loyal Americans of Japanese ancestry cannot be detained.

ETO: The Battle of the Bulge. The Germans have opened a 45-mile gap in the Allied lines and are less than four miles from the Meuse River. German forces attacking at a gap in the lines between Malmédy and St-Vith are stopped past Stavelot by a collection of American infantry, engineers, and tank destroyers. The Trois Ponts bridge is destroyed before Germans can use it, blocking the major route to the Meuse River. Combat Command B of the 10th Armored Division arrives in Bastogne. The 101st Airborne, under the temporary command of Brigadier General Anthony McAuliffe, arrives at Bastogne as German forces begin converging on this key town that must be captured if German forces in the southern area of the Bulge are to advance any farther west. German tanks destroy American tanks and infantry attempting to block the roads outside of Bastogne.

The 11th Armored Division and the 17th Airborne Division are ordered to the Meuse—they are the last units SHAEF has available in-theater. Rear echelon and service troops, along with six French infantry battalions, are all rushed to defend the Meuse River line. The 82nd Airborne and the 9th and 30th Infantry Divisions move to support First Army. Elements of the 12th Infantry Regiment of the 4th Infantry Division hold at Berdorf, causing delays in the German timetable.

First Army headquarters retreats from Spa.

German forces reach Stavelot.

Eighth Air Force sends more than 500 B-17s using radar-equipped Pathfinder bombers and escorted by over 250 P-51 Mustangs to attack marshaling yards in western Germany. Heavy cloud cover causes another 358 B-24 Liberators to be recalled. One B-17 is lost and three damaged. Two P-51s are lost. Twenty-two B-17s conduct screening missions to jam German radio interception efforts and conduct countermeasures against German radar sites.

During the night four B-17s and nine B-24s drop leaflets over Germany, France, and the Netherlands.

Another 255 P-47 Thunderbolts and P-51s fly a fighter sweep in western Germany. Fighter pilots report three confirmed kills. One P-47 and one P-51 are lost. The pilots are reported missing.

Ninth Air Force sends more than 160 A-20 Havocs, A-26 Invaders, and B-26 Marauders to attack German defensive positions. P-47 and P-38 fighters support the 2nd, 4th, 28th, and 106th Infantry Divisions and the XII Corps. Fighters also fly armed reconnaissance missions. Pilots report over 40 German aircraft shot down.

MEDITERRANEAN: Fifteenth Air Force sends more than 560 B-17s and B-24 Liberators to bomb oil refineries in Germany, Austria, Czechoslovakia, and at Auschwitz, Poland. Bombers also hit marshaling yards in Austria and Hungary.

ITALY: Twelfth Air Force A-20 Havocs and P-47 Thunderbolts of the XXII Tactical Air Command attack rail lines and support Fifth Army ground forces south of Bologna.

SOUTHWEST PACIFIC AREA: On Leyte, the 77th Infantry Division moves rapidly north toward a linkup with X Corps, capturing Valencia airfield.

The 1st Cavalry Division takes up the attack for the 32nd Division in the X Corps area. Supported by heavy artillery fire, the 12th Cavalry attacks and clears Highway 2.

FEAF A-20 Havocs and P-47 Thunderbolts attack bridges and airfields on Leyte Island. B-25 Mitchells bomb the airfield on Mindanao Island.

Admiral William F. Halsey's Third Fleet encounters a typhoon in the Philippine Sea northeast of Samar. Destroyers USS *Hull, Monaghan,* and *Spence* are sunk. Three destroyer escorts, four small carriers, four escort carriers, a light cruiser, seven destroyers, an oiler, and a fleet tug are damaged. Halsey is nearly relieved after the incident is reported.

A kamikaze damages a motor torpedo boat off Mindoro.

Task Force 38 aircraft sink a cargo ship west of Luzon.

PACIFIC: Twentieth Air Force sends 94 B-29 Superfortresses from Chengtu, China, to drop incendiaries on the docks at Hankow, China. Over 200 aircraft of the Fourteenth Air Force support the attack. A total of 84 B-29s hit the primary target. Aircrews report one confirmed kill, three probables, and 13 possibles.

Another 89 B-29 Superfortresses flying out of the Mariana Islands are sent to bomb the Mitsubishi aircraft plant at Nagoya, Japan. A total of 63 hit the primary target. Aircrews report five confirmed kills, 11 probables, and 12 possibles. Four B-29s are lost.

CENTRAL PACIFIC: During the night Seventh Air Force sends four B-24 Liberators from Guam and Saipan to conduct snooper (radar-assisted bomb release) missions on Iwo Jima.

NEW GUINEA: FEAF A-20 Havocs and P-40s attack seaplane facilities at Sanga Sanga, Borneo, and bomb the airfield on Haroekoe Island.

December 19

CBI: Tenth Air Force B-25 Mitchells and P-47s bomb logistics storage sites, road traffic, bridges, town areas, troop concentrations, and various targets of opportunity in Burma.

Fourteenth Air Force P-51 Mustangs attack shipping targets off Hong Kong. Pilots report sinking two cargo ships. P-40s attack rail cars near Singyang and report destroying two locomotives. P-38 Lightnings bomb the Wanling-Mongyu road in Burma.

U.S. submarine *Redfish* torpedoes and sinks a Japanese carrier *Unryu* in the East China Sea near Shanghai, China. Escort ships damage the *Redfish* with depth charges, forcing her to terminate her patrol.

Fourteenth Air Force P-51 Mustangs attack Japanese shipping at Hong Kong. Pilots report a cargo ship sunk.

ETO: The Battle of the Bulge. About 9,000 American soldiers of the 106th Infantry Division, surrounded for three days, surrender to German forces. It is the largest surrender of Americans since Corregidor in 1942. St-Vith and Bastogne are still under American control, but threatened. German forces capture Stoumont, but the 30th Infantry Division reinforced by Combat Command B of the 3rd Armored Division holds the line north of Stoumont and prepares to counterattack. The remainder of the 3rd Armored Division and the 82nd Airborne Division are to block any German advance northwest toward the Meuse River.

Elements of the 28th Infantry Division hold Wiltz. The 2nd and 99th Infantry Divisions hold at Elsenborn Ridge. The 2nd Battalion, 26th Infantry Regiment, of the 1st Infantry Division holds Bütgenbach against six separate tank and infantry assaults. The 1st Battalion of the 501st Parachute Infantry, 101st Airborne, encounters a German column headed toward Bastogne. The Germans are shocked enough by the vigor of the American defense that they delay attacking the town for a day, believing they have encountered a strong armored unit.

General Eisenhower holds a meeting of his senior commanders at Verdun to assess the current situation and map out a plan for a counterattack. Eisenhower intends to limit the German breakthrough by holding Bastogne and Monschau and preventing the enemy from crossing the Meuse River, defending along the line from Namur to Liège. Eisenhower orders Lieutenant General George S. Patton, Jr., to release several of his divisions from Third Army to support the defense of the Bulge. Patton's divisions will be the counterattacking force from the south and units under Montgomery's operational control will counterattack from the north. Patton, who made a contingency plan to deal with a German attack on his army's left flank several days earlier, announces he can have his 4th Armored Division, including the 26th and 80th Infantry Divisions, leading a multidivision attack toward Bastogne in three days. Eisenhower orders the 6th Army Group to cease offensive operations and to defend in place while extending its lines toward Saarlautern in order to allow Third Army to swing forces out of the line and move north. The Allied air forces are ordered to attack German lines of supply west of the Rhine River and marshaling yards east of the Rhine.

Eighth Air Force sends more than 300 B-17s and B-24 Liberators using radar-equipped Pathfinder bombers and escorted by 37 P-47 Thunderbolts to attack road networks, marshaling yards, and troop concentrations in Luxembourg and Germany in an attempt to slow the German attack in the Ardennes. Two B-24s are damaged and three P-47s are damaged. Aircrew casualties are one killed. Fighter pilots report seven confirmed kills; one pilot is wounded.

Ninth Air Force P-47 and P-38 fighters support the 1st, 2nd, 99th, and 106th Infantry Divisions and 7th Armored Division fighting near Malmédy and St-Vith. The fighters also support Twelfth Army troops and the XII Corps near Verdun and St-Avold, France.

The 313th Infantry Regiment, 79th Infantry Division, is engaged in a fight with German troops at the Siegfried Line defenses near Berg, Germany. Technical Sergeant Robert E. Gerstung's heavy machine-gun squad moves forward to support an infantry company making an attack. During an eight-hour battle that sees most of his men killed or wounded, Technical Sergeant Gerstung continues to fight on. When his ammunition runs out, he exposes himself to enemy fire to retrieve more from a disabled tank. When his weapon ceases to function, he moves to another fighting position to man a gun that has had all of its crew killed. A German tank begins firing on him, but Gerstung continues to provide covering fire for the hard-pressed infantrymen, who begin to retreat. Gerstung covers their movement with suppressive fire, walking to the rear with the heavy machine gun cradled in his left arm. Although wounded by a mortar round, Technical Sergeant Gerstung continues to crawl back to safety, carrying the machine gun with him. For his remarkable acts of courage and dedication to duty, Technical Sergeant Gerstung will win the Medal of Honor.

MEDITERRANEAN: Fifteenth Air Force sends more than 400 B-17s and B-24 Liberators to bomb oil refineries in Germany, Austria, and Czechoslovakia. Bombers also hit marshaling yards in Austria and Hungary.

ITALY: Twelfth Air Force P-47 Thunderbolts attack German gun positions near La Spezia.

SOUTHWEST PACIFIC AREA: On Leyte, units of the 1st Cavalry Division capture Lonoy on Highway 2 and flank Japanese positions facing the 32nd Infantry Division. Elements of the 77th Infantry Division meet cavalry patrols near Cananga.

FEAF B-24 Liberators and P-38 Lightnings attack airfields on Luzon Island. B-25 Mitchells bomb an airfield on Negros Island. P-38 Lightnings and P-47 Thunderbolts attack airfields on Leyte.

Navy PB4Y-1 Privateers attack a Japanese convoy in the South China Sea and sink a transport west of Manila.

PACIFIC: Twentieth Air Force sends 36 B-29 Superfortresses from the Chengtu, China, area to hit an aircraft plant at Omura, Japan; 17 hit the primary target, and 13 others hit secondary target of Shanghai, China. Another two strike other alternatives; aircrews claim 5-4-12 (five confirmed kills, four probables, and 12 possibles). Two B-29s are lost.

The headquarters of the 505th Bombardment Group (Very Heavy) arrives at Tinian Island, Mariana Islands, from the United States.

CENTRAL PACIFIC: Headquarters Seventh Air Force becomes operational on Saipan. Over 50 B-24 Liberators from Guam and Saipan bomb Iwo Jima. Another 14 P-38 Lightnings from Saipan, using three B-29 as navigational escort, strafe airfields on Iwo Jima. During the night B-24s conduct snooper (radar-assisted bomb release) missions on Iwo Jima.

NEW GUINEA: FEAF B-25 Mitchells, A-20 Havocs, and P-38 Lightnings attack targets on Celebes Island.

December 20

ALEUTIANS: Eleventh Air Force sends three B-24s on an armed reconnaissance and photoreconnaissance mission over the Kurile Islands, including Kashiwabara, Paramushiru Island, and Katoaka on Shimushu Island. The bombers strafe buildings on Onnekotan Island and bomb Nemo Bay. Another B-24 bombs installations on Onnekotan Island.

CBI: In Burma, Tenth Air Force B-25 Mitchells and P-47 Thunderbolts attack troop concentrations, support ground forces, rail lines, logistics storage sites, bridges, and highways. The 492nd Bombardment Squadron (Heavy), 7th Bombardment Group (Heavy), sends a detachment of B-24 Liberators from India to Luliang, China, to ferry fuel to Suichwan, China.

Fourteenth Air Force sends 118 P-51 Mustangs and P-40s to bomb logistics storage sites, road traffic, bridges, town areas, troop concentrations, and various targets of opportunity at Wanling and Lashio in Burma; and Chinchengchiang, Hong Kong, Sinyang, Leiyang, Kweilin, Hengshan, and Hengyang in China. The headquarters of the 1st Combat Cargo Group redeploys from India to Tsuyung, China.

U.S. submarine *Sealion* torpedoes and damages a Japanese supply ship in the South China Sea

ATLANTIC: German submarine *U-870* torpedoes and sinks an LST and damages a destroyer escort in the North Atlantic west of Portugal.

ETO: The Battle of the Bulge. General Eisenhower decides to split the Bulge in half to ease operational control of units in combat and those arriving as reinforcements. The northern half of the Bulge is placed under Field Marshal Montgomery's operational control. General Bradley has operational control of all forces in the south of the Bulge. The Ninth Army and the VII, V, and XVIII Corps pass to Montgomery, while the Third Army and VII Corps remain with Bradley. Montgomery also takes operational control of the American IX and XXIX Tactical Air Forces. The XIX Tactical Air Force is reinforced with fighters and bombers from Eighth Air Force and fighter-bombers from Ninth Air Force.

The V Corps (9th, 99th, 2nd, and 1st Infantry Divisions) holds from Monschau to Malmédy. The 30th Infantry Division, the 82nd Airborne Division, and the 3rd Armored Division hold from Malmédy to Hotton. The 7th Armored Division holds St-Vith with a collection of units including Combat Command B of 9th Armored Division, the 424th Infantry Regiment of 106th Infantry Division, and the 112th Infantry Regiment of the 28th Infantry Division. Brigadier General Robert Hasbrouck, commander of the 7th Armored Division, reports to Lieutenant General Courtney Hodges of First Army that he can hold St-Vith one more day.

The 84th Infantry Division from Ninth Army moves south to block the approaches to Marche. The VII Corps, formed from a collection of units not engaged (the 75th Infantry Division, no combat experience and just arrived from the United States; the 2nd Armored and 3rd Armored Divisions and the 84th Infantry Division), is ordered to be prepared to assemble near Hotton and attack on order. The 501st Parachute Infantry Regiment stops several attacks. Brigadier General Anthony McAuliffe takes command of all American forces in Bastogne, a total of about 18,000 men. Along with the 101st Airborne Division, McAuliffe now commands Combat Command B and Combat Command Reserve of the 10th Armored Division, the 333rd Field Artillery Group, and the 705th Tank Destroyer Battalion. Paratroopers and tanks, supported by artillery, stop German attacks from the north, south, and east.

Bad weather prevents any combat operations by Eighth Air Force and Ninth Air Force.

General Eisenhower notifies General Devers to halt offensive operations in the 6th Army Group and extend its defensive lines northwest, with the XV Corps to cover the impending departure of Third Army's XII Corps. In addition, Devers is ordered to withdraw to more defensible areas. This causes the XV and VI Corps to abandon their penetrations of the West Wall into Germany.

Corporal Henry F. Warner mans the 57 millimeter antitank gun supporting 2nd Battalion, 26th Infantry Regiment, 1st Infantry Division, defending near Dom Butgenbach, Belgium. Corporal Warner employs his gun with deadly accuracy as two tanks and infantry make an attack on his position. In the face of tank and small arms fire, Warner knocks out the two tanks and then engages in a pistol duel with a tank commander of a third tank as it moves to within five yards of his position. He kills the tank commander, and the tank withdraws. After nearly constant artillery and mortar fire on the American position, the Germans conduct a strong attack to dislodge the Americans. Again Corporal Warner employs his antitank gun, hitting a tank, but in the fight he is first wounded and then killed as he struggles to load and fire his gun. Corporal Warner's exceptional courage and skill play a crucial role in the delay of German forces and will win him the Medal of Honor.

MEDITERRANEAN: Fifteenth Air Force sends more than 450 B-17s and B-24 Liberators escorted by over 300 P-38 Lightnings and P-51 Mustangs to bomb oil refineries in Germany and Austria, and armaments production facilities in Czechoslovakia. Bombers also hit marshaling yards in Austria.

The 859th Bombardment Squadron (Heavy), 492nd Bombardment Group (Heavy), from Eighth Air Force arrives at Brindisi, Italy, from England. The squadron's B-24 Liberators and C-47s are attached to the 15th Special Group (Provisional) and will fly Carpetbagger missions in the Mediterranean theater of operations on December 31.

ITALY: Twelfth Air Force A-20 Havocs and P-47 Thunderbolts attack rail lines, locomotives, vehicles, bridges, and roads near Genoa and La Spezia.

SOUTHWEST PACIFIC AREA: In the central Philippines over 150 B-24 Liberators, B-25 Mitchells, and A-20 Havocs attack airfields.

The headquarters and the P-38s of the 8th Fighter Group (35th, 36th, and 80th Fighter Squadrons) redeploy from Morotai Island to Mindoro Island.

CENTRAL PACIFIC: Seventh Air Force B-24 Liberators from Saipan bomb Iwo Jima.

During the night six B-24s conduct five snooper (radar-assisted bomb release) missions on Iwo Jima.

NEW GUINEA: FEAF B-24 Liberators attack an airfield on Java, and B-25 Mitchells attack Haroekoe Island in the Netherlands East Indies.

December 21

CBI: In Burma, Tenth Air Force B-25 Mitchells and P-47 Thunderbolts attack bridges, logistics storage sites, troop concentrations, and rail lines. Another 12 P-47s bomb and strafe targets near Lashio.

Fourteenth Air Force sends 145 P-40s and P-51 Mustangs to attack bridges, troop areas, gun emplacements, and ammunition storage sites in south China, French Indochina, and Burma. The C-47s of the 4th Combat Cargo Squadron, 1st Combat Cargo Group, redeploy from India to Chengkung, China.

In the South China Sea, U.S. submarine *Sealion* makes a second attack on the previously damaged Japanese supply ship and sinks it.

ETO: The Battle of the Bulge. German tanks and infantry attack the St-Vith defenses with 10,000 infantry and 200 tanks. The Germans must capture St-Vith or the entire offensive is in danger of stalling. As German forces push into the town during the night, the 7th Armored Division begins to pull back. It has lost over 3,000 casualties and 88 tanks destroyed. Patton's Third Army, advancing north on a 30-mile front, enters Luxembourg City. The 1st Infantry Division holds off tank attacks in front of Elsenborn Ridge at Bütgenbach, supported by tank destroyers. The 30th Infantry Division counterattacks at Stoumont. The American defenders at Bastogne are surrounded.

Bad weather cancels all combat missions for Eighth Air Force and Ninth Air Force. The Royal Air Force's Second Tactical Air Force takes operational control of the IX and XXIX Tactical Air Commands from Ninth Air Force to support the defense of the northern shoulder of the Bulge. The XIX Tactical Air Command flies armed weather and intruder reconnaissance in the Saarbrücken-Trier area.

Hitler lays out plans for an attack against the U.S. Seventh Army called *Nordwind,* intended to threaten the right flank of Third Army and slow its advance toward the Ardennes. As the 6th Army Group extends its lines to cover units of Third Army departing for the Ardennes, Lieutenant General Alexander M. Patch places two divisions in reserve to deal with any possible German attack.

Mediterranean: Fifteenth Air Force sends more than 80 B-24 Liberators escorted by 40 P-51 Mustangs to attack a marshaling yard in Germany.

Italy: Twelfth Air Force A-20 Havocs attack highways, roads, and targets of opportunity in the Po Valley. P-47 Thunderbolts attack road and rail traffic.

Southwest Pacific Area: On Leyte, the 12th Cavalry Regiment from 1st Cavalry Division, X Corps, meets patrols from the 360th Infantry Regiment of the 77th Infantry Division of the XXIV Corps. At the same time, elements of the 11th Airborne Division link up with the 2nd Battalion, 32nd Infantry Regiment, having spent several weeks clearing Japanese strongholds in the mountains.

FEAF B-24 Liberators, B-25 Mitchells, and A-20 Havocs attack airfields on Negros Island and in the central Philippines. B-24s bomb an airfield on Mindanao Island. P-47 Thunderbolts and P-38 Lightnings from Leyte support the missions.

The P-47s of the 311th Fighter Squadron, 58th Fighter Group, redeploy from Leyte Island to Mindoro Island.

Kamikazes damage two LSTs and a destroyer off Mindoro; kamikazes hit a freighter off Panay, killing two and wounding 16 crew and passengers.

Central Pacific: Seventh Air Force sends 23 B-24 Liberators from Guam to bomb Iwo Jima.

During the night four B-24s conduct a raid on Iwo Jima.

New Guinea: FEAF B-25 Mitchells bomb targets on Halmahera Island.

December 22

CBI: In Burma Tenth Air Force B-25 Mitchells and P-47 Thunderbolts attack bridges, troop locations, and roads.

Fourteenth Air Force B-25 Mitchells damage a bridge at Song Hoa in French Indochina. P-40s and P-51 Mustangs attack airfields at Heho, Burma, and at Canton and Hong Kong, China.

U.S. submarine *Flasher* attacks a Japanese convoy in the South China Sea, sinking a fleet tanker and two merchant tankers off French Indochina.

ETO: The Battle of the Bulge. In three days of attacks the Germans have lost over 100 tanks and taken over a thousand casualties in a vain attempt to break the 1st Infantry, 2nd Infantry, and 99th Infantry Divisions at Elsenborn Ridge. The 30th Infantry Division recaptures Stoumont. The VII Corps battles German forces between Hotton and Rochefort. Bradley orders the remainder of the 9th Armored Division and the 106th and the 28th Infantry Divisions out of St-Vith and to reform behind the 82nd Airborne Division now defending the Salm River line. Patton's III Corps, commanded by Major General John B. Millikin, begins its attack into the southern flank of the Bulge. The 4th Armored Division heads for Bastogne, the 26th Infantry Division advances toward Wiltz, and the 80th Infantry Division for St-Vith. The corps has conducted a 100-mile road movement in less than 48 hours. The advance is difficult as the German forces hold good defensive terrain. Low on ammunition, medical supplies, and food, the Bastogne defenders receive an offer to surrender from the German commander, who threatens annihilation if the Americans do not give up. Brigadier General Anthony McAuliffe responds with a one-word reply: "Nuts!" The reply confuses the four Germans who are to relay the message. An American officer from the 327th Glider Infantry of the 101st Airborne clarifies the statement. He tells them, "In plain English it's the same as 'Go to Hell.'"

Eighth Air Force and Ninth Air Force combat missions are cancelled due to bad weather. Tactical control of three fighter groups of the IX Tactical Air Command is temporarily transferred to the XIX Tactical Air Command to support Third Army's movement north to attack the southern portion of the Bulge and relieve Bastogne. After December 25, tactical control reverts to the IX Tactical Air Command.

MEDITERRANEAN: German shore battery fire damages U.S. destroyer *Gleaves* during a bombardment of German troop concentrations on the French-Italian border.

ITALY: Twelfth Air Force B-25 Mitchells and B-26 Marauders attack rail and road bridges. A-20 Havocs and P-47 Thunderbolts attack rail lines and bridges.

SOUTHWEST PACIFIC AREA: In the Philippines, FEAF B-24 Liberators, with P-47 Thunderbolts escorting, bomb Clark Field on Luzon Island. P-40s attack Lipa airfield. B-24s and B-25 Mitchells with P-47s bomb airfields on Negros Island. B-24s bomb logistics storage areas and troop locations on Mindanao Island.

The headquarters of the 417th Bombardment Group (Light) and the A-20 Havocs of its four bombardment squadrons (672nd, 673rd, 674th, and 675th) redeploy from Leyte to Mindoro Island. The P-47s of the 69th and 310th Fighter Squadrons, 58th Fighter Group, also redeploy from Leyte to Mindoro.

A kamikaze damages a destroyer off Mindoro.

PACIFIC: Twentieth Air Force sends 78 B-29 Superfortresses from the Marianas to bomb the Mitsubishi aircraft industrial complex in Nagoya, Japan. Cloud cover limits the effectiveness of the strike, and 48 bombers hit the primary target. Aircrews report nine confirmed kills, 17 probables, and 15 possibles. Three B-29s are lost.

U.S. submarine *Tilefish* torpedoes and sinks a Japanese torpedo boat off Honshu, Japan.

CENTRAL PACIFIC: During the night Seventh Air Force sends two B-24 Liberators from Guam and Saipan to conduct a raid on Iwo Jima Island.

NEW GUINEA: FEAF P-40s B-24 Liberators, and B-25 Mitchells, along with Royal Australian Air Force (RAAF) bombers, attack targets on Halmahera Island.

FEAF B-24 Liberators attack Japanese shipping off north Borneo and sink six small cargo vessels.

December 23

CBI: In Burma, Tenth Air Force B-25 Mitchells and P-47 Thunderbolts attack troop concentrations, rail lines, logistics storage sites, bridges, and roads.

Fourteenth Air Force B-25 Mitchells attack targets in French Indochina and attack rail targets in southern China. P-51 Mustangs and P-38 Lightnings attack river transportation targets around Wuchang and Hankow.

ATLANTIC: The JCS, fearing future entanglements in the Balkans, refuses to authorize the CCS to approve any unilateral British military action in Greece.

ETO: The Battle of the Bulge. The Germans have expanded the Bulge 45 miles wide and penetrated about 60 miles into American lines, just four miles away from the Meuse River. The German advance has slowed, but the pressure on the defenders is heavy. American forces abandon St-Vith, retreating to reform behind the 82nd Airborne Division. The Germans have been delayed for five important days. A German attack on Bastogne from the southeast fails. Two German tanks actually drive into Bastogne but are destroyed.

The weather improves over the battle area. Eighth Air Force sends more than 400 B-17s and B-24 Liberators escorted by over 400 P-47 Thunderbolts and P-51 Mustangs to attack communication centers and marshaling yards in an attempt to stall the momentum of the German attack in the Ardennes. A total of 176 bombers are damaged. Aircrews report six confirmed kills and four probables. Aircrew casualties are one killed, five wounded, and seven missing. Fighter pilots report 23 confirmed kills and three possibles in the air. One P-51 is lost and one is damaged.

Six B-17s conduct a screening mission to jam German radio interception efforts and conduct countermeasures against German radar sites.

During the night a total of 10 B-17s and B-24s drop leaflets over Germany, France, and the Netherlands.

Another 163 P-47 Thunderbolts and P-51 Mustangs conduct a fighter sweep near Bonn, Germany. Pilots report 46 confirmed kills, one probable, and 15 possibles. Three P-47s and three P-51s are lost. The pilots are reported missing.

The 361st Fighter Group's three fighter squadrons (the 374th, 375th, and 376th) redeploy from England to France with P-51 Mustangs. The P-51s of the 486th and 487th Fighter Squadrons, 352nd Fighter Group, redeploy from England to Belgium.

Ninth Air Force sends 500 B-26 Marauders and A-20 Havocs to attack railroad bridges, communication targets, villages, and rail and road junctions in Germany near the Bulge. German fighters and antiaircraft fire claim 31 bombers. P-47s and P-38 Lightnings fly escort, bomb airfields, and support ground forces along the northern edge of the Bulge and also provide support to the III, VIII, and XII Corps as they fight on the southern edge of the Bulge. Fighter pilots report over 100 confirmed kills. American aircraft mistakenly bomb Malmédy, killing civilians and troops of the 30th Infantry Division. Incredibly, the same mistake will be repeated over the next two days—despite Major General Leland Hobbs, commander of the 30th Infantry Division, speaking directly to Ninth Air Force headquarters.

Over 250 C-47s of the IX Troop Carrier Command drop 334 tons of supplies for the surrounded defenders of Bastogne.

ITALY: Based on Ultra intelligence, Major General Lucien Truscott reinforces IV Corps with the 339th and 337th Infantry Regiments of the 85th Infantry Division, and brings forward the 2nd Brigade of the 8th Indian Division to support the 92nd Infantry Division.

Twelfth Air Force A-20 Havocs attack rail lines and an airfield near Milan. Aircrews report several aircraft destroyed on the ground.

SOUTHWEST PACIFIC AREA: The airfields on Mindoro are operational.

FEAF B-24 Liberators escorted by P-38 Lightnings and P-47 Thunderbolts bomb airfields on Negros Island. B-24s also bomb an airfield outside of Manila. B-25 Mitchells bomb airfields on Mindanao Island,

U.S. submarine *Blenny* torpedoes and sinks a Japanese merchant tanker west of Luzon.

PACIFIC: The V Amphibious Corps planning staff issues its plan for the invasion of Iwo Jima. The V Amphibious Corps commander, Major General Harry Schmidt, directs a two-division landing on the southeast side of the island. The 5th Marine Division, commanded by Major General Keller E. Rockney, will land on the left, and the 4th Marine Division, commanded by Major General Clifton B. Cates, will land on the right. The 3rd Marine Division, commanded by Major General Graves B. Erskine, will be in reserve. The two divisions will attack to capture the lower airfield, Mount Suribachi, and gain control of the lower western half of the island before pivoting north and east to capture the rest of the island. Expecting heavy counterattacks on the first night, the marines plan to land as much artillery as possible early to eliminate the threat.

Admiral Raymond A. Spruance commands Fifth Fleet. Vice Admiral Richmond Kelly Turner commands the expeditionary forces. Rear Admiral Harry W. Hill commands the Attack Force, and Rear Admiral William H. P. Blandy commands the Amphibious Support Forces (demolitions, prelanding air and naval bombardment). Lieutenant General Holland M. Smith, commander of Fleet Marine Forces Pacific, serves as the commander of expeditionary troops.

The headquarters of the 313th Bombardment Wing (Very Heavy) and 504th Bombardment Group (Very Heavy) and the B-29 Superfortresses of the 398th and 421st Bombardment Squadrons (Very Heavy) arrive at Tinian Island from the United States.

CENTRAL PACIFIC: Seventh Air Force sends 26 B-24 Liberators from Saipan Island and Guam to bomb Iwo Jima. Another three B-24s from Guam bomb Woleai Atoll. During the night two B-24s conduct a raid on Iwo Jima.

NEW GUINEA: FEAF B-25 Mitchells, P-40s, and A-20 Havocs bomb targets on Halmahera Island.

December 24

CBI: In Burma, Tenth Air Force sends P-47 Thunderbolts to attack Lashio airfield, troop concentrations, rail lines, logistics storage sites, bridges, and roads.

Fourteenth Air Force B-25 Mitchells bomb the Kunlong ferry area and shipping in the South China Sea. Aircrews report one tanker sunk. P-40s, P-51 Mustangs, and P-38 Lightnings attack river, road, and rail traffic, troops, and buildings around Hengyang, Lingling, Siangtan, and Changsha. Fighters also attack shipping near Hong Kong and report one tanker sunk and other cargo ships damaged. Pilots report over 30 Japanese aircraft destroyed at Tsinan airfield.

ETO: German aircraft bomb Bastogne. An isolated element of the 3rd Armored Division under the command of Lieutenant Colonel Sam Hogan at Marcouray receives a demand to surrender. Hogan refuses to surrender and tells the Germans that he will fight to the death. Elements of the XVIII Airborne Corps pull back from Manhay on order of Field Marshal Montgomery, who desires to neaten the lines. American commanders protest this order. Giving up territory means only that it will have to be retaken eventually, with more casualties. As the Americans pull back, they are attacked by German tanks and infantry, causing heavy casualties and threatening to open the way to the Allied supply base at Liège.

The weather over western Europe clears, and Eighth Air Force sends its largest air strike of the war against transportation and communications behind the Bulge in Germany. Over 2,000 B-17s and B-24 Liberators escorted by over 800 P-47 Thunderbolts and P-51 Mustangs. A total of 12 bombers are lost and 619 damaged. Aircrews report 18 confirmed kills, five probables, and one possible. Aircrew casualties are 37 killed, 49 wounded, and 114 missing. Fighter pilots report 70 confirmed kills, one probable kill, and 19 possibles in the air. Ten fighters are lost and two damaged. The pilots are reported missing.

B-24 Liberators bomb the La Pallice coastal battery in France.

Ninth Air Force sends 276 B-26 Marauders and A-20 Havocs to attack railroad bridges and communication centers in western Germany. P-38 and P-47 fighters escort the 9th Bombardment Division, fly armed reconnaissance, and support the III, VIII, and XII Corps along the southern edge of the Bulge. Fighters fly cover for the 4th Armored Division of General George S. Patton, Jr.'s Third Army as it approaches Bastogne.

The IX Troop Carrier Command sends 160 C-47s to drop 160 tons of supplies to American troops surrounded at Bastogne.

A U.S. freighter at Antwerp is damaged when a German V-1 rocket hits close by.

SOUTHWEST PACIFIC AREA: In the Philippines, FEAF B-24 Liberators bomb Clark Field on Luzon. B-25 Mitchells bomb targets on Mindanao and shipping around the island.

PACIFIC: Twentieth Air Force sends 29 B-29 Superfortresses from the Marianas to attack airfields on Iwo Jima. A total of 23 hit the primary targets.

The B-29s of the 482nd, 483rd, and 484th Bombardment Squadrons (Very Heavy) of the 505th Bombardment Group (Very Heavy) arrive at Tinian from the United States. The squadrons' first missions are scheduled for December 30.

CENTRAL PACIFIC: Seventh Air Force sends 50 B-24 Liberators from Saipan and Guam to bomb Iwo Jima. P-38 Lightnings from Saipan make low-level strafing attacks. Another 23 B-24 Liberators from Saipan bomb Chichi Jima. During the night B-24s conduct a raid on Iwo Jima.

Naval Task Group 94.9, commanded by Rear Admiral Allan E. Smith, bombards Iwo Jima after Seventh Air Force bombers hit the island. Two destroyers sink a Japanese fast transport and a landing ship.

NEW GUINEA: FEAF B-24 Liberators bomb the airfield in Borneo, and B-25 Mitchells, P-40s, and A-20 Havocs attack targets in the Molucca Islands.

U.S. submarine *Barbero* torpedoes and sinks a Japanese submarine chaser and damages a transport southwest of Borneo.

December 25

CBI: In Burma, Tenth Air Force P-47 Thunderbolts bomb and strafe troop concentrations and supplies at Mabein, conduct fighter sweeps on the Burma Road, and strafe Lashio airfield.

Fourteenth Air Force P-51 Mustangs attack a railroad ferry, shipping, and an airfield near Nanking, China. Pilots report damaging a tanker and destroying 13 aircraft.

ETO: The Battle of the Bulge. The Germans again attack Bastogne from the northwest. Paratroopers and tank destroyers knock out 18 German tanks. In the VII Corps area, 2nd Armored Division counterattacks at Celles, supported by Ninth Air Force fighters and bombers, and secures the left flank of First Army. The XVIII Airborne Corps reserve, the 75th Infantry Division, fights its first battle and stops German forces at Manhay, restoring the line. The 7th Armored Division, the 30th Infantry Division, and the 82nd Airborne Division are all committed to defending the northwest edge of the Bulge against strong German pressure. As the German defenses stiffen, Patton commits the XII Corps to attack Echternach with the 5th Infantry Division. Soon Major General Manton S. Eddy, XII Corps commander, will funnel the other divisions of his corps into the battle.

Eighth Air Force sends 132 B-17s and B-24 Liberators escorted by over 400 P-51 Mustangs to attack railroad bridges and communication centers behind the Bulge in western Germany. A total of five bombers are lost and 132 damaged. Aircrews report three confirmed kills, one probable, and four possibles. Aircrew casualties are two killed, four wounded, and 47 missing. Fighter pilots report 46 confirmed kills, six probables, and eight possibles in the air. Nine P-51 fighters are lost and three damaged. Nine pilots are reported missing.

Ninth Air Force sends nearly 650 B-26s, A-20 Havocs, and A-26 Invaders to attack rail and road bridges, communications centers, and German tanks and troops in the Bulge. Fighters support the III, VIII, and XII Corps on the southern edge of the Bulge.

When Private Paul J. Wiedorfer's infantry company of the 318th Infantry Regiment, 80th Infantry Division, comes under heavy machine-gun fire from two German positions dug in along a wood line near Chaumont, Belgium, Private Wiedorfer takes action. He stands up and charges across 40 yards of deep snow to reach the German positions. Untouched by enemy fire he destroys the first machine-gun position with a hand grenade and rifle fire, then immediately turns to assault the second position. He wounds one soldier and forces the remaining six to surrender. As the platoon resumes its advance, both the platoon leader and the platoon sergeant are wounded. Without hesitation, Private Wiedorfer takes command and moves the platoon to take its objective. For his inspiring acts of courage and leadership, Private Wiedorfer will receive the Medal of Honor.

MEDITERRANEAN: Fifteenth Air Force sends more than 250 B-17s and B-24 Liberators escorted by P-38 Lightnings and P-51 Mustangs to attack a synthetic oil plant in Czechoslovakia and a marshaling yard in Austria.

ITALY: Twelfth Air Force A-20 Havocs and P-47 Thunderbolts attack rail lines to the Brenner Pass and the eastern Po Valley. Pilots report several locomotives destroyed.

SOUTHWEST PACIFIC AREA: The 1st Battalion, 305th Infantry Regiment, 77th Infantry Division, supported by engineers and artillery, makes an amphibious landing at Palompon and captures the last coastal town occupied by Japanese forces. The Ormoc Valley is closed, completing the final phase of operations for Sixth Army on Leyte. General MacArthur declares Leyte secure even though units of the 1st Cavalry Division, the 24th Infantry Division, and the 32nd Infantry Division will continue to encounter resistance as the units clear the last defenders on December 31.

FEAF B-24 Liberators escorted by P-38 Lightnings and P-47 Thunderbolts bomb airfields on Luzon Island and Mindanao Island.

Carrier aircraft from Task Force 38 attack Japanese shipping west of Luzon and sink a landing ship.

A naval air station at Samar is established.

German submarine *U-862* torpedoes and sinks a U.S. freighter in the Tasman Sea south of Sidney, Australia.

Major Thomas B. McGuire of the Thirteenth Air Force is leading a squadron of 15 P-38 Lightnings over Luzon, providing cover for bombers, when 20 Japanese fighters attack. During the battle he shoots down three enemy aircraft. Even after his guns jam, McGuire flies to the rescue of his fellow pilots and maneuvers his aircraft to give his wingman a good shot at the Japanese fighters. The following day he escorts a bombing mission against Clark Field and rescues a crippled bomber by exposing himself to enemy fire. During the battle he shoots down four enemy aircraft. His determination to protect his squadron mates, his aggressive action to engage the enemy, and his willingness to put himself in danger to save others will win him the Medal of Honor.

CENTRAL PACIFIC: Seventh Air Force sends 12 B-24 Liberators from Saipan to bomb Iwo Jima. During the night B-24s from Guam and Saipan conduct raids on Iwo Jima.

New Guinea: FEAF B-24 Liberators bomb airfields in Borneo. B-25 Mitchells, along with Royal Australian Air Force (RAAF) fighter-bombers, attack Halmahera Island.

U.S. submarine *Barbero* attacks a Japanese convoy and sinks a transport west of Borneo.

FEAF B-24 Liberators sink two small cargo vessels and damage two others off Borneo.

December 26

CBI: In Burma, Tenth Air Force B-25 Mitchells and P-47 Thunderbolts attack rail lines, roads, troop concentrations, and bridges.

Fourteenth Air Force sends 12 P-51 Mustangs to attack the Tsinan airfield. B-25 Mitchells, P-51 Mustangs, and P-38 Lightnings attack bridges, railroads, troop concentrations, and rail and road traffic in China, Thailand, and Burma.

ETO: The Battle of the Bulge. The 4th Armored Division reaches Bastogne. The 318th Infantry Regiment of the 80th Infantry Division makes contact with Combat Command A of the 9th Armored Division. The battle to keep Bastogne has cost the Americans over 3,000 casualties. Task Force Hogan of the 3rd Armored Division, after being surrounded and cut off for seven days, reaches American lines on foot. The 2nd Armored Division completes the destruction of German forces at Celles. The Germans lose 3,700 men killed, wounded, or captured, 82 tanks, and more than 500 other vehicles captured or destroyed. The 2nd Armored loses 27 tanks and has 17 men killed and 227 wounded. With the relief of Bastogne and the VII Corps counterattack at Celles, the momentum of the German offensive is stopped.

Eighth Air Force sends more than 150 B-17s and B-24 Liberators escorted by 249 P-47 Thunderbolts and P-51 Mustangs to attack marshaling yards and railroad bridges behind the Bulge. A total of 30 bombers are damaged. Fighter pilots report 11 confirmed kills.

P-51 Mustangs support the bombers by making a sweep around Bonn. Of the 70 aircraft engaged, two are lost and one damaged. The pilots are reported missing. Pilots report three confirmed kills.

During the night three B-17s and six B-24s drop leaflets over Germany and the Netherlands.

Ninth Air Force sends A-20 Havocs, A-26 Invaders, and B-26 Marauders to attack railroad bridges, road junctions, and communication targets in the Bulge. P-47 and P-38 fighters support the III and VIII Corps and the 4th Armored Division as they break the siege of Bastogne.

Lieutenant Colonel Keith L. Ware commands the 1st Battalion, 15th Infantry Regiment, 3rd Infantry Division, conducting an attack on a hill near Sigolsheim, France. The attack falters as the first company comes under heavy fire from artillery, mortar, and machine-gun fire. Lieutenant Colonel Ware advances forward and spends more than two hours alone scouting the German defenses. He returns to the company position and takes a Browning Automatic Rifle and leads an assault team of two officers, nine enlisted men, and a tank. Lieutenant Colonel Ware fires on the

German positions and marks targets for the tank. Running out of ammunition, Ware uses an M-1 rifle to engage a machine-gun position and marks the target for the tank. As nearly half of his small assault group become casualties, Ware continues the attack. Although wounded, he refuses medical treatment until the objective is secured. For his extreme courage under fire and his exceptional leadership, Lieutenant Colonel Ware will receive the Medal of Honor.

MEDITERRANEAN: Fifteenth Air Force sends more than 380 B-17s and B-24 Liberators escorted by P-38 Lightnings and P-51 Mustangs to bomb oil refineries in Germany and at Auschwitz, Poland.

ITALY: The Germans launch operation *Wintergewitter* (Winter Thunderstorm). The Germans attack with eight battalions, including alpine infantry and regular infantry. The objective is to attack and destroy the 92nd Infantry Division, which has had a poor performance record in combat. The 92nd is shattered as it retreats from Barga, but some of its units fight quite effectively. General Crittenberger of IV Corps adds reinforcements from the 1st Armored Division, the 34th Infantry Division, and the 8th Indian Division, supported by the XXII Tactical Air Command, to repel the German attacks and limit the advance.

Twelfth Air Force B-25 Mitchells and B-26 Marauders attack rail and road bridges. A-20 Havocs and P-47 Thunderbolts attack rail lines, bridges, and roads and support Fifth Army ground forces south of Bologna and in the Serchio River Valley.

SOUTHWEST PACIFIC AREA: General MacArthur transfers operational control of Leyte and Samar to Eighth Army. American troops will continue to fight scattered groups of Japanese until May of 1945.

The campaign on Leyte has cost the Japanese heavily. The Japanese leadership had believed this was the decisive battle to be fought and this was where the Americans could be stopped. The commanders threw the bulk of the air, land, and seapower that was available into battle at Leyte and have lost. Japanese casualties on Leyte amount to 49,000 men, not including the losses of ship crews and pilots. Without air or naval support, the remaining Japanese forces on Luzon and other smaller islands in the Philippines are isolated and can fight only to delay and make the cost to the Americans as heavy as possible. American casualties number 15,584 with over 3,500 killed.

Leyte is not what MacArthur desired the island to be—an airbase for future operations against Luzon. The ground is unsuitable for airfields that can handle large aircraft. Tacloban airfield cannot be suitably expanded, and, although an airfield is constructed at Tanauan on the east side of the island by the end of the campaign, it is never heavily used. High winds and heavy rains that mark the weather on the island wash away roads and delay other important construction.

FEAF B-24 Liberators bomb Clark Field on Luzon Island. B-25 Mitchells bomb Mindanao Island.

A Japanese naval force, consisting of a heavy cruiser, a light cruiser, three destroyers, and three escort destroyers, intends to bombard American positions on Mindoro. The ships are attacked on the way by FEAF B-25 Mitchells, P-38 Lightnings, P-40s, and P-47 Thunderbolts, along with U.S. Navy PB4Y Privateers and PBM Mariners. The two cruisers, three destroyers, and two destroyer escorts are damaged.

The ships bombard Mindoro, but a motor torpedo boat sinks one destroyer south of Manila. This is the last time the Japanese fleet will attempt to challenge U.S. forces in the Philippines.

PACIFIC: U.S. destroyer sinks an auxiliary submarine chaser in the Bonins.

U.S. submarine *Swordfish* departs Midway for her 13th war patrol, but disappears after making contact on January 3, 1945.

CENTRAL PACIFIC: Seventh Air Force B-24 Liberators from Guam bomb Iwo Jima.

During the night two B-24s from Saipan conduct a raid on Iwo Jima.

NEW GUINEA: FEAF B-24 Liberators, B-25 Mitchells, P-40s, and A-20 Havocs attack targets on Halmahera Island.

FEAF B-24 Liberators sink a Japanese cargo vessel east of Celebes Island.

December 27

CBI: In Burma, Tenth Air Force B-25 Mitchells attack bridges and P-47 Thunderbolts hit troop concentrations and logistics storage areas.

In China, Fourteenth Air Force P-51 Mustangs attack White Cloud, Whampoa, and Tien Ho airfields in Canton. Fighter pilots report 10 Japanese aircraft destroyed. Two P-51s are lost.

U.S. submarine *Baya* locates the heavy cruiser, light cruiser, and two destroyers of the Mindoro attack force as they approach Cam Ranh Bay off French Indochina. USS *Baya* makes an unsuccessful attack on the ships.

ETO: The III Corps of Third Army fights to expand the corridor to Bastogne and prepares to attack north to St-Vith. Eighth Air Force sends more than 600 B-17s and B-24 Liberators escorted by 178 P-51 Mustangs to attack marshaling yards, rail bridges, and rail junctions. Two bombers are lost and 295 damaged. Aircrew casualties are 36 killed, 17 wounded, and 15 missing. Fighter pilots report 29 confirmed kills and one probable in the air. Three P-51 fighters are lost. The pilots are reported missing.

Ninth Air Force sends A-20 Havocs, A-26 Invaders, and B-26 Marauders to attack railroad bridges and communication centers in the Bulge. P-47 and P-38 fighters support 3rd Armored and 82nd Airborne Divisions in the Manhay and Trois-Ponts area of Belgium, and the III, VIII, and XII Corps in Saint-Hubert-Bastogne-Martelange area.

First Lieutenant Eli Whiteley is a platoon leader in L Company, 15th Infantry Regiment, 3rd Infantry Division. He leads his platoon in an attack to capture the town of Sigolsheim, France. He is wounded as the infantrymen attempt to assault a building, but he charges into the house alone and kills two Germans. Then, using smoke and fragmentation grenades, Whiteley charges into the next house and kills two Germans and takes the surrender of 11 more. With his left arm now useless, he continues to lead his men. After blasting a hole in the wall of a strongly defended house, he again rushes into the building. Firing his Thompson submachine gun by clamping it under his uninjured arm, he kills five soldiers and takes the surrender of another 12. Wounded again, First Lieutenant Whiteley refuses to be stopped and again leads an attack on another building before being forcibly evacuated. For his exemplary courage and determination in leading his men, First Lieutenant Whiteley will receive the Medal of Honor.

MEDITERRANEAN: Fifteenth Air Force sends more than 500 B-17s and B-24 Liberators escorted by P-38 Lightnings and P-51 Mustangs to attack an oil refinery and marshaling yards in Austria and rail lines in northern Italy.

ITALY: Operation Wintergewitter has reached its objective of severely damaging the 92nd Infantry Division. German forces begin withdrawing from Barga. The Allies are able to restore the line to its original position by December 31.

The 10th Mountain Division arrives in Italy.

The 370th Infantry Regiment of the 92nd Division is reorganized behind two brigades of Indian infantry sent by IV Corps to shore up the line. General Clark moves operational control of the 85th Infantry Division from II Corps to IV Corps and prepares the 1st Armored Division for a counterattack.

Twelfth Air Force B-25 Mitchells and B-26 Marauders attack rail and road traffic from Austria and Yugoslavia. P-47 Thunderbolts attack logistics storage areas near Bologna and support Fifth Army ground forces.

SOUTHWEST PACIFIC AREA: In the Philippines FEAF B-24 Liberators bomb airfields on Negros Island and an airfield on Mindanao.

Japanese aircraft bomb American positions and shipping at Mindoro.

PACIFIC: Twentieth Air Force sends 72 B-29 Superfortresses from the Marianas to bomb the Nakajima and Musashino aircraft plants in Tokyo. A total of 39 hit the primary targets. Japanese fighters make over 250 individual attacks on the bombers. Aircrews report 21 confirmed kills, 10 probables, and seven possibles. Three B-29s are lost.

The 313th Bombardment Wing (Very Heavy) of the XXI Bomber Command arrives with B-29s on Tinian.

Cruisers and destroyers of Task Group 94.9 bombard Iwo Jima after Seventh Air Force hits the island. Japanese shore batteries damage a U.S. destroyer, which, however, continues the fight, sinking a fast transport with the assistance of two other destroyers.

CENTRAL PACIFIC: Seventh Air Force B-24 Liberators from Saipan and Guam bomb Iwo Jima. P-38 Lightnings also strafe the island. B-24s from Saipan bomb Chichi Jima.

During the night two B-24s conduct a snooper (radar-assisted bomb release) mission on Iwo Jima.

NEW GUINEA: U.S. submarine *Barbero* is damaged in an aerial attack off Java and is forced to return to base.

December 28

CBI: In Burma, Tenth Air Force B-25 Mitchells and P-47 Thunderbolts bomb bridges, roads, troop concentrations, logistics storage areas, and artillery positions.

In China, Fourteenth Air Force sends B-25 Mitchells, P-40s, and P-51 Mustangs to attack town areas, railroad targets, and gun positions near Hengyang and Leiyang. P-51 Mustangs and P-38 Lightnings attack airfields and other targets in French Indochina.

U.S. submarine *Dace* attacks a Japanese convoy, sinking a supply ship off French Indochina.

ETO: First Army is ordered to attack south toward Houffalize, in the center of the Bulge. Third Army is to strike for Houffalize from the south. At the same time, Bastogne is the target of another strong German attack. The III Corps of Third Army (4th and 6th Armored Divisions, the 35th and 26th Infantry Divisions) holds southeast of Bastogne against German attacks. The VIII Corps receives the 87th Infantry Division from SHAEF reserve and the 11th Armored Division.

Eighth Air Force sends more than 1,200 B-17s and B-24 Liberators escorted by 541 P-51 Mustangs to attack rail bridges and marshaling yards. Two B-24s are lost and 130 bombers damaged. Aircrew casualties are 12 killed, four wounded, and 22 missing.

During the night two B-24 Liberators drop leaflets over Belgium.

MEDITERRANEAN: Fifteenth Air Force sends more than 480 B-17s and B-24 Liberators escorted by P-38 Lightnings and P-51 Mustangs to attack oil storage facilities and railyards in Germany, marshaling yards in Austria, and oil refineries and oil storage facilities in Czechoslovakia.

ITALY: Twelfth Air Force B-25 Mitchells and B-26 Marauders attack German troop concentrations, rail lines, and bridges. P-47 Thunderbolts of the XXII Tactical Air Command attack rail lines, vehicles, bridges, roads, and support Fifth Army ground forces.

SOUTHWEST PACIFIC AREA: Kamikazes attack Task Group 77.11 as it approaches Mindoro. An LST and two freighters are hit. One freighter, carrying ammunition, explodes in a huge fireball, damaging surrounding ships.

PACIFIC: The headquarters of the 6th Bombardment Group (Very Heavy) and the 24th and 39th Bombardment Squadrons (Very Heavy) arrives in Tinian from the United States with B-29 Superfortresses. The headquarters of the 9th Bombardment Group (Very Heavy) and the B-29s of the 1st, 5th, and 99th Bombardment Squadrons (Very Heavy) also arrive at Tinian. All the squadrons' first missions are scheduled for late January 1945.

CENTRAL PACIFIC: Seventh Air Force sends 13 B-24 Liberators from Saipan to bomb Iwo Jima.

During the night B-24s from Guam and Saipan conduct raids on Iwo Jima.

NEW GUINEA: FEAF B-25 Mitchells bomb the airfields on Ambon Island, Celebes Island, and Haroekoe Island. P-40s and A-30s attack the airfield on Buru Island.

December 29

CBI: In Burma, Tenth Air Force B-25 Mitchells bomb troops and logistics bases and P-47 Thunderbolts attack logistics support areas and troop concentrations.

Fourteenth Air Force B-25 Mitchells attack targets of opportunity from Dong Hoa to Lang Son in French Indochina.

ETO: The XII Corps gains control of Echternach.

Eighth Air Force sends more than 780 B-17s and B-24 Liberators, escorted by 433 P-51 Mustangs, to attack marshaling yards, communication centers, and rail bridges. Four bombers are lost and 333 are damaged. Aircrew casualties are 22 killed, 28 wounded, and 15 missing. Three fighters are lost and one is damaged. The three pilots are reported missing.

The Ninth Air Force, XIX Tactical Air Command, flies armed reconnaissance over Belgium and Germany and supports the III, VIII, and XII Corps in the Neufchateau-Bastogne-Arlon areas of Belgium.

German submarine *U-772* attacks a convoy in the English Channel, damaging two U.S. freighters.

MEDITERRANEAN: Fifteenth Air Force sends more than 450 B-17s and B-24 Liberators escorted by 300 P-38 Lightnings and P-51 Mustangs to attack marshaling yards in Germany, Austria, and northern Italy.

ITALY: The 8th Indian Division recaptures Barga with heavy air support from XXII Tactical Air Command fighter aircraft. The 92nd Division restores the defensive line in the Serchio Valley with the support of air strikes. The surprise German offensive delays the intended Allied offensive against Bologna.

Twelfth Air Force B-25 Mitchells and B-26 Marauders attack rail and road bridges. A-20 Havocs and P-47 Thunderbolts of the XXII Tactical Air Command attack communication targets and rail targets in support of Fifth Army ground forces.

SOUTHWEST PACIFIC AREA: In the Philippines, FEAF B-24 Liberators bomb an airfield on Mindanao Island.

CENTRAL PACIFIC: Seventh Air Force sends 26 B-24 Liberators from Guam to attack Iwo Jima. Other B-24s continue harassment bombing throughout the night.

NEW GUINEA: FEAF B-25 Mitchells, P-40s, and P-38 Lightnings attack targets on Buru Island.

B-24 Liberators, P-47 Thunderbolts, and A-20 Havocs bomb Celebes Island targets.

U.S. submarine *Hawkbill* torpedoes and sinks a Japanese merchant in the Java Sea.

December 30

CBI: In Burma, Tenth Air Force P-47 Thunderbolts and P-38 Lightnings attack roads, troop concentrations, and artillery positions.

Fourteenth Air Force B-24 Liberators bomb a bridge near Kengtung, China, and rail targets in French Indochina. P-51 Mustangs and P-40s attack troop concentrations, gun positions, rail lines, logistics storage sites, bridges, and highways in Burma and southern China.

ETO: Third Army begins its attack north from Bastogne toward Houffalize. The VIII Corps attacks from west of Bastogne with the 87th Infantry Division and the 11th Armored Division. The 11th has never been in combat, and the 87th has very little experience. Their advance is almost immediately stopped by a German attack intended to surround Bastogne. To the east of the town German forces attempting to close the ring around Bastogne are stopped by elements of the 35th Infantry Division at Villers. The 26th Infantry Division makes limited gains.

Eighth Air Force sends more than 1,300 B-17s and B-24 Liberators escorted by 508 P-51 Mustangs to attack rail bridges and marshaling yards. Four B-17s are lost and 63 bombers are damaged. Aircrew casualties are 12 killed and 30 missing. Two P-51 fighters are lost and the pilots are reported missing.

During the night three B-17s and eight B-24s drop leaflets over Germany, Luxembourg, and the Netherlands.

The Ninth Air Force, XIX Tactical Air Command, supports the III, VIII, and XII Corps near St-Hubert and Bastogne in Belgium and around Diekirch in Luxembourg.

Italy: Twelfth Air Force B-25 Mitchells and B-26 Marauders attack rail and road bridges. A-20 Havocs and P-47 Thunderbolts attack bridges and roads and support Fifth Army ground forces.

Southwest Pacific Area: FEAF P-47 Thunderbolts, P-38 Lightnings, and A-20 Havocs attack airfields in the central Philippines.

Kamikazes attack a convoy bound for Mindoro, damaging two destroyers. A U.S. freighter is sunk during an aerial bombing run on the convoy. U.S. submarine *Razorback* attacks a Japanese convoy southeast of Formosa, sinking a destroyer and damaging two cargo ships.

Fifth Air Force B-25 Mitchells, A-20 Havocs, and P-40s attack Japanese shipping near Lingayen Gulf, sinking a coastal patrol ship, a submarine chaser, and three cargo ships.

Central Pacific: Seventh Air Force sends 26 B-24 Liberators from Saipan to attack Iwo Jima. Other B-24s from Guam continue harassment bombing throughout the night.

Admiral William F. Halsey's Third Fleet leaves its anchorage at Ulithi to support the Luzon invasion.

New Guinea: FEAF P-40s and P-38 Lightnings attack airfields in northern Borneo and Celebes Island, while B-25 Mitchells attack a barge and logistics storage facilities on Haroekoe Island.

The headquarters of the 322nd Troop Carrier Wing is activated at Hollandia.

December 31

CBI: In Burma, Tenth Air Force P-47 Thunderbolts attack airfields and bridges. Other P-47s and P-38 Lightnings attack a Japanese division headquarters at Ongyaw as well as troop concentrations and logistics storage areas.

Fourteenth Air Force sends four B-24 Liberators to bomb shipping off Hainan Island. Aircrews report one cargo ship sunk and another damaged. The Fourteenth Air Force reports that during this year over 33,000 Japanese ground troops have been killed and 494 aircraft have been destroyed. In addition, 640,000 tons of shipping have been sunk, another 237,000 tons probably sunk, and 396,000 tons of shipping damaged.

In China, P-40s and P-51 Mustangs attack troops, horses, town areas, and railroad targets near Hankow, Hengyang, Lingling, and Kweilin.

ETO: The 6th Armored Division of III Corps attacks east of Bastogne. The Germans attempt 17 separate counterattacks on Bastogne. Each one is stopped.

Eighth Air Force sends more than 1,300 B-17s and B-24 Liberators escorted by 676 P-47 Thunderbolts and P-51 Mustangs to attack oil industry targets at Hamburg, marshaling yards, and Rhine River bridges. A total of 27 bombers are lost and 372 are damaged. Aircrews report 26 confirmed kills, eight probables, and 16 possibles. Aircrew casualties are five killed, 31 wounded, and 248 missing. Fighter pilots report 60 confirmed kills, two probables, and 16 possibles in the air and one confirmed kill on the ground. Ten fighters are lost and one is damaged. The 10 pilots are reported missing.

German submarine *U-906*, a minesweeper, and three cargo vessels are sunk in the air attack on Hamburg.

During the night two B-17s and eight B-24s from Eighth Air Force drop leaflets over Germany, France, and Belgium.

The Ninth Air Force, XIX Tactical Air Command, supports the III, VIII, and XX Corps around Bastogne.

During the night the Germans launch Nordwind, an offensive aimed at the XV and VI Corps of Seventh Army and the 6th Army Group. The German First Army attacks toward Bitche and the Wissembourg Gap, while the German Nineteenth Army attacks from the Colmar Pocket toward Strasbourg. The XV Corps, commanded by Major General Wade Haislip, defends a 35-mile-long front with the 100th, 104th, and 44th Infantry Divisions. The French 2nd Armored Division is in reserve. The VI Corps, commanded by Major General Edward H. Brooks, defends about a 40-mile front with the 45th and 79th Infantry Divisions. The 14th Armored Division is in reserve. Three separate task forces formed from newly arriving units are organized to support both corps. The 44th Infantry Division supported by Task Force Harris (formed from the 63rd Infantry Division) stops the German attack at Rimling. The 398th and 399th Infantry Regiment of the 100th Infantry Division fight in three directions for three days, holding off German attacks as the Germans drive a 10-mile salient into the XV Corps lines. Four German divisions attack near Bitche, advancing past weak cavalry units. Task Force Harris, along with the 14th Armored Division and the 100th Infantry Division, counterattacks from the north and VI Corps supports with Task Force Herren (formed from the 70th Infantry Division) and units of the 45th and 75th Infantry Divisions.

ITALY: Twelfth Air Force A-20 Havocs and P-47 Thunderbolts of the XXII Tactical Air Command report destroying five railroad bridges and damaging two others in the Po Valley and report destroying or damaging more than 200 railcars and several locomotives.

SOUTHWEST PACIFIC AREA: In the Philippines, FEAF B-24 Liberators and B-25 Mitchells bomb airfields on Luzon and Mindanao Islands.

Japanese torpedo planes hit a U.S. freighter off Mindoro.

PACIFIC: The Twentieth Air Force's Brigadier General Haywood S. Hansell, Jr., commander of the XXI Bomber Command forward echelon headquarters, and his staff redeploy from Saipan to Guam.

CENTRAL PACIFIC: Seventh Air Force sends 19 B-24 Liberators from Guam to attack Iwo Jima. Ten other B-24s continue harassment bombing throughout the night.

NEW GUINEA: FEAF B-24 Liberators and B-25 Mitchells bomb the airfield on Celebes Island, Dili on Timor Island, and airfields and logistics bases on Halmahera Island. P-40s and A-20 Havocs attack targets on Halmahera Island and on Celebes Island.

1945

January 1

ALEUTIANS: Eleventh Air Force sends five B-24 Liberators to fly coverage for U.S. Navy ships after aborting a bomb mission against the Kurile Islands.

CBI: Major General George E. Stratemeyer's Eastern Air Command is flying 2,000 tons of supplies to Allied forces in Burma to sustain the offensive against the Japanese defending along the Akyab-Mandalay-Wanting line.

In China, Fourteenth Air Force sends P-51 Mustangs and P-40s to attack roads and rail lines, supply depots, troop positions, industrial targets, and gun positions from Yoyang to Puchi and between Siaokan and Hsuchang. P-51 Mustangs attack Suchow airfield. Fighter pilots report 25 aircraft destroyed. A P-51 detachment of the 16th Fighter Squadron, 51st Fighter Group, begins operating from Laohokow. In Burma, the Tenth Air Force sends 71 P-47 Thunderbolts and P-38 Lightnings to attack villages, general supply areas, fuel storage areas, tanks and troop concentrations.

ETO: First Army is organized into three corps: the V Corps (9th, 99th, 2nd, and 1st Infantry Divisions), the XVIII Airborne Corps (30th, 7th, and 106th Infantry Divisions, the 82nd Airborne, and the 7th Armored Division), and the VII Corps (83rd and 84th Infantry Divisions and the 2nd and 3rd Armored Divisions). Third Army is organized into four corps: VIII Corps (the 9th and 11th Armored Divisions, the 87th Infantry Division, and the 101st Airborne), III Corps (the 4th and 6th Armored Divisions and the 35th and 26th Infantry Divisions), XII Corps (the 80th, 5th, and 4th Infantry Divisions), and XX Corps (28th Infantry Division, the 10th Armored Division, and the 17th Airborne).

Nearly 1,000 German aircraft attack Allied airfields in Holland and Belgium. About 300 Allied aircraft are destroyed, limiting air support to the 12th Army Group for more than a week. About 90 German aircraft are shot down by antiaircraft fire. German forces attack in the VI Corps area, threatening Strasbourg.

Eighth Air Force sends 845 B-17s and B-24 Liberators escorted by 725 P-47 Thunderbolts and P-51 Mustangs to attack oil production facilities, marshaling yards, and railroad bridges in western Germany using both visual and radar-guided bomb release. Aircrews report 23 confirmed kills, one possible, and three probables, including one jet aircraft. Five B-17s are lost and 167 are damaged. One B-24 is lost and 67 are damaged. Two P-51 Mustangs are lost and one is damaged. Two pilots are reported missing. Aircrew losses are 40 killed, 16 wounded, and 28 missing. Fighter pilots report 17 confirmed kills, one probable, and one possible. A total of 12 B-17s fly a screening force mission, and aircrews report six confirmed kills. Five of the bombers are lost and one damaged. Casualties are 45 crewmen missing. Two B-17s fly an Aphrodite (see August 4, 1944 ETO entry) mission against Oldenburg without loss. During the night three B-17s and five B-24s drop leaflets over Belgium and Germany. The 1st, 2nd, and 3rd Bombardment Divisions are redesignated as air divisions.

The Germans attack Ninth Air Force airfields near Brussels, Belgium, Eindhoven, Holland, and Metz, France, with nearly 800 aircraft. The Allies lose 127 fighters on the ground. Allied fighters report 160 confirmed kills in the air, while antiaircraft units report 300 enemy aircraft shot down.

Ninth Air Force sends nearly 200 A-20 Havocs, A-26 Invaders, and B-26 Marauders attack rail bridges, communication centers, and command and control sites in Belgium and Germany. P-47 Thunderbolts escort 9th Bombardment Division and Eighth Air Force bombers, fly patrols, and conduct armed reconnaissance. Fighter pilots report 39 confirmed kills. Fighters also provide support to the III, VII, and XII Corps.

Sergeant Charles A. MacGillivary, a squad leader in I Company, 71st Infantry Regiment, 44th Infantry Division, is ordered to take his men forward to protect the platoon's left flank and block advancing German forces near Woelfling, France. As he moves his men forward in the darkness, he encounters German panzer-grenadiers digging in. As he reports their location, the Germans fire on the squad. MacGillivary circles around to the German machine gun, then attacks, eliminating the enemy position. Early in the afternoon Sergeant MacGillivary locates six German machine-gun positions. He again moves out alone to outflank the enemy, destroying one position with a hand grenade. Using a discarded submachine gun he attacks a second machine-gun position and eliminates it. He attacks a third position with hand grenades, then assaults it, and in the fight his left arm is shot away. He holds the position until his unit is able to attack through the remaining enemy defenders. For his exceptional courage and initiative in the face of a determined enemy Sergeant MacGillivary will receive the Medal of Honor.

ITALY: Twelfth Air Force B-25 Mitchells and B-26 Marauders attack bridges and an ammunition storage site. A-20 Havocs and P-47 Thunderbolts destroy a fuel storage depot at Parma and support Fifth Army ground forces south of Bologna. The headquarters of the 319th Bombardment Group (Medium) departs Corsica for the United States. The group will convert to A-26 Invaders in preparation for redeployment to the Pacific theater.

SOUTHWEST PACIFIC AREA: Eighth Army takes operational control of Mindoro Island from Sixth Army. Eighth Army is assigned a zone of operations covering all of the Philippine islands south of Luzon.

On Mindoro, infantry units move to the eastern shore of the island to draw Japanese attention away from the Lingayen Gulf area and focus on a possible landing from Mindoro to southern Luzon. Navy minesweepers begin operating in the Batangas area, followed by merchant cargo ships and airdrops of dummy parachutists to simulate landing operations.

In the Philippines, Far East Air Force B-25 Mitchells, P-47 Thunderbolts, and P-38 Lightnings attack Negros Island airfields. B-25s bomb a barracks on Luzon. B-24 Liberators escorted by P-38s attack targets near Manila and bomb Clark Field on Luzon and an airfield on Mindanao.

The headquarters of the 345th Bombardment Group (Medium) moves from Dulag to Tacloban on Leyte Island.

U.S. submarine *Stingray* lands supplies at Tawi Tawi in the Philippines.

PACIFIC: Seventh Air Force sends 19 B-24s from Saipan to bomb Iwo Jima. Another nine more conduct snooper (radar-assisted bomb release) missions during the night.

NEW GUINEA: B-24 Liberators and B-25 Mitchells attack troop concentrations and an ammunition storage area on Halmahera Island and airfields on Ceram Island in the Moluccas.

January 2

CBI: In Burma, Fourteenth Air Force B-25 Mitchells bomb Kentung; P-40s and P-51 Mustangs attack railroad traffic. Tenth Air Force P-47 Thunderbolts and P-38 Lightnings attack troop concentrations and supplies in Burma.

ETO: Eighth Air Force sends nearly 1,700 B-17s and 296 B-24 Liberators to attack marshaling yards communication centers, rail bridges. The B-17s are escorted by 256 P-51 Mustangs; the B-24 Liberators are escorted by 215 P-47 Thunderbolts and P-51 Mustangs. The bombers use Gee-H (bombing through the clouds technique in which the lead bomber's navigator locates the bomb release point by sending a radio pulse signal to two ground station transponders). A total of four B-17s are lost and 65 B-24s and B-17s are damaged. Aircrew casualties are 10 killed, two wounded, and 37 missing. Three P-51s are lost and one is damaged. The two pilots are reported missing.

During the night two B-17s and six B-24s drop leaflets over Germany and France.

A total of six B-17s conduct screening missions to jam German radio interception efforts and conduct countermeasures against German radar sites.

Ninth Air Force sends more than 130 A-20 Havocs, A-26 Invaders, and B-26 Marauders to attack railroad bridges and communication centers. In Belgium and Germany, P-47 and P-38 fighters support ground forces of the III and VIII Corps near Bastogne and support XII Corps.

The P-47 Thunderbolts of the 314th, 315th, and 316th Fighter Squadrons, 324th Fighter Group of the First Tactical Air Force (Provisional), redeploy from Tavaux to Luneville, France.

Vice Admiral Sir Bertram H. Ramsay (RN), Allied Commander in Chief, Expeditionary Force, is killed in an airplane accident near Paris, France.

ITALY: Twelfth Air Force A-20 Havocs and P-47 Thunderbolts attack rail lines, trains, and vehicles in the Po River valley, support Fifth Army ground forces, and bomb the Milan marshaling yard.

SOUTHWEST PACIFIC AREA: In the Philippines, Far East Air Force P-38 Lightnings and A-20 Havocs attack shipping in San Fernando harbor on Negros Island. B-24 Liberators bomb Clark Field on Luzon Island and targets on Mindanao Island. B-25 Mitchells attack airfields in the central Philippine Islands, supported by A-20s.

The P-38 Lightnings of the 8th Fighter Squadron, 49th Fighter Group, redeploy from Tacloban on Leyte Island to Mindoro Island in the Philippines.

U.S. submarine *Aspro* torpedoes and damages a Japanese landing ship south of Formosa Strait.

PACIFIC: Twentieth Air Force sends 49 B-29 Superfortresses from Calcutta, India, to bomb the railroad bridge at Bangkok, Thailand. A total of 44 bombers hit the primary target and two hit an alternative and a target of opportunity. Crewmen report one probable and one possible kill.

CENTRAL PACIFIC: Seventh Air Force sends 12 B-24 Liberators from Guam to bomb Haha Jima Island, while 14 other B-24s bomb Iwo Jima Island. During the night 10 B-24s from Guam conduct a snooper (radar-assisted bomb release) mission on Iwo Jima.

NEW GUINEA: FEAF B-24 Liberators bomb targets on Celebes Island and Halmahera Island.

U.S. submarine *Becuna* torpedoes and sinks a Japanese ship in the Java Sea.

Fifth Air Force A-20 Havocs and P-38 Lightnings attack Japanese shipping off Luzon and sink a coastal patrol ship, a transport, and five cargo ships.

January 3

ALEUTIANS: Eleventh Air Force sends B-25 Mitchells to fly coverage for naval forces over the Kurile Islands.

CBI: The British XV Corps captures Akyab.

In Burma, Tenth Air Force sends 10 B-25 Mitchells, supported by 12 P-47 Thunderbolts, to attack the airfield at Aungban and attack troop concentrations, logistics storage areas, and ammunition supply points.

In China, Fourteenth Air Force sends 10 P-51 Mustangs to attack the airfield at Tsinan. Fighter pilots report 13 Japanese aircraft destroyed. Six P-51s attacks river traffic, reporting several river steamers sunk in the Hankow-Chiuchiang area.

ETO: The Battle of the Bulge. First Army begins a counterattack toward Houffalize, attacking with VII Corps, employing the 2nd and 3rd Armored Divisions followed by the 83rd Infantry Division. The Germans have established strong defensive lines, and the weather makes the roads difficult for tanks to move.

In the Seventh Army area, German forces attacking as part of operation Nordwind hit the 179th Infantry Regiment of the 45th Infantry Division at Wingen-sur-Moder, forcing the regiment to retreat two miles. The line is restored by counterattacks by elements of the 313th Infantry Regiment (79th Infantry Division) and the 276th Infantry Regiment (70th Infantry Division) as well as the 180th Infantry Regiment from the 4th Infantry Division.

Eighth Air Force sends more than 1,260 B-17s and B-24 Liberators escorted by over 500 P-51 Mustangs to attack marshaling yards, communication centers, and rail junctions in Germany and Belgium. A total of 15 bombers are damaged. Aircrew casualties are two wounded. Fighter pilots report four confirmed kills. Four fighters are lost and four are damaged. The four pilots are reported missing.

MEDITERRANEAN: German submarine *U-870* torpedoes and damages a U.S. freighter in the Mediterranean near Gibraltar.

ITALY: Twelfth Air Force B-25 Mitchells and B-26 Marauders attack railroad bridges. A-20 Havocs and P-47 Thunderbolts attack rail lines and trains in the Po River valley.

SOUTHWEST PACIFIC AREA: Third Fleet begins strike operations aimed at neutralizing Japanese air capability from Formosa and other areas in preparation for the Luzon landings on January 9.

In the Philippines, Far East Air Force B-24 Liberators bomb Clark Field on Luzon Island and two airfields on Mindanao Island. B-25 Mitchells bomb airfields in the central Philippines.

Naval Task Force 38, commanded by Vice Admiral John S. McCain, begins attacks against Japanese airfields and shipping around Formosa. Carrier aircraft sink a landing ship, five cargo ships, and damage five others.

Leading elements of the Luzon invasion fleet are hit by kamikazes as they pass through Surigao Strait. An oiler is damaged.

Thirteenth Air Force B-25 Mitchells sink a Japanese auxiliary submarine chaser off Davao.

PACIFIC: Twentieth Air Force sends 97 B-29s from the Marianas to bomb docks and urban areas of Nagoya, Japan. Of the 97 sent, 57 hit the primary target and 21 bomb alternatives and targets of opportunity. Over 300 Japanese fighters attack the bombers. Five B-29s are lost. Aircrews repot 14 confirmed kills, 14 probables, and 20 possible kills.

U.S. submarine *Kingfish* attacks a Japanese convoy, sinking three cargo ships north of Chichi Jima.

CENTRAL PACIFIC: Seventh Air Force sends 22 B-24 Liberators from Saipan to bomb Iwo Jima. Three B-24s from Guam attack Marcus Island in the North Pacific. During the night 10 B-24s from Guam attack Iwo Jima.

NEW GUINEA: FEAF B-24 Liberators attack the Djailolo supply area on Halmahera Island. B-25 Mitchells bomb Namlea airfield on Buru Island in the Moluccas.

January 4

CBI: In China, Fourteenth Air Force sends four B-24 Liberators to bomb the Fort Bayard area and the Samah Bay area on Hainan Island. In Burma, six B-25 Mitchells damage a bridge and a warehouse, and 21 P-40s on armed reconnaissance attack targets of opportunity near Wanling. P-51 Mustangs destroy a bridge at Huizan, Thailand.

In Burma, Tenth Air Force sends 13 B-25 Mitchells escorted by 12 P-47 Thunderbolts to bomb an airfield at Namsang. P-47s and P-38 Lightnings attack bridges, troops and logistics depots.

ETO: Eighth Air Force sends 10 B-24 Liberators, using radar-guidance to assist in accuracy, to bomb a coastal battery near Bordeaux, France. During the night one B-17 and two B-24s drop leaflets over Germany, Belgium, and the Netherlands. One B-24 is lost.

Staff Sergeant Isadore S. Jachman of B Company, 513th Parachute Infantry Regiment, 17th Airborne Division, faces an attack by two German tanks at Flamierge, Belgium. Without hesitation, Staff Sergeant Jachman runs across open ground through enemy fire to take a bazooka from a fallen paratrooper and attacks the tanks alone. As the tanks turn their weapons on him, Jachman fires and damages one tank; although mortally wounded, he forces the other tank to withdraw. Staff Sergeant Jachman's heroic action will be worthy of the nation's highest award for valor, the Medal of Honor.

MEDITERRANEAN: Fifteenth Air Force sends more than 370 B-17s and B-24 Liberators escorted by P-38 Lightnings and P-51 Mustangs to bomb marshaling yards and rail targets in northern Italy. Other B-24s drop supplies in Yugoslavia.

ITALY: Twelfth Air Force B-25 Mitchells and B-26 Marauders attack bridges. A-20 Havocs and P-47 Thunderbolts attack ammunition storage areas and transportation targets in the Po River valley.

SOUTHWEST PACIFIC AREA: As the Luzon invasion convoy approaches Lingayen Gulf, a kamikaze hits escort carrier USS *Ommaney Bay,* causing heavy damage. The ship is later scuttled.

In the Philippines, Far East Air Force B-24 Liberators bomb Palawan, Luzon, and Mindanao Islands. B-25 Mitchells attack road and rail lines on Luzon and Mindanao Islands.

Carrier aircraft from Naval Task Force 38 continue attacks on Japanese airfields and shipping around Formosa. Three auxiliary submarine chasers and an auxiliary netlayer are sunk. An escort vessel, a minesweeper, and an auxiliary submarine chaser are damaged.

A kamikaze hits a U.S. freighter carrying bombs south of Mindoro, causing a tremendous explosion. FEAF aircraft damage five Japanese submarine chasers off Luzon.

CENTRAL PACIFIC: Seventh Air Force sends 13 B-24 Liberators from Guam to bomb Iwo Jima.

During the night 13 B-24s conduct harassment raids on the island.

NEW GUINEA: FEAF B-24 Liberators and B-25 Mitchells bomb targets on Celebes Island and shipyards in north Borneo.

January 5

ALEUTIANS: Eleventh Air Force sends four B-24 Liberators to provide air cover for a naval task force approaching Paramushiru Island in the Kuriles.

CBI: Fourteenth Air Force sends four B-25 Mitchells to attack logistics storage buildings at Kengtung, China. P-40s and P-51 Mustangs attack airfields at Hankow and Wuchang. Pilots report 50 aircraft destroyed in the air and on the ground. P-51 Mustangs and P-38 Lightnings attack the airfield on Hainan Island. Pilots report 11 aircraft destroyed. Other P-40s and P-38 Lightnings attack various targets of opportunity in China and Burma. B-25 Mitchells destroy a bridge at Dara, Thailand.

In Burma, Tenth Air Force sends 16 B-25 Mitchells to attack a number of airfields. P-47 Thunderbolts attack logistics storage areas, tanks, trucks, and troop concentrations.

Air Transport Command completes Operation Grubworm, which over the past 30 days has airlifted over 25,000 Chinese soldiers, 396 American soldiers, 1,596 animals, 42 jeeps, 48 howitzers, 48 heavy mortars, and 48 antitank guns to Chanyi, Kunming, Luliang, and Yunnani in China. A total of only three aircraft have been lost.

ETO: The German attack against the Seventh Army (Nordwind) reaches its limit at Wingen-sur-Moder. The combination of difficult terrain in the Vosges Mountains, weather, and the rapid response of American units to the threat leads to the failure of the offensive. At the same time a second offensive is aimed at VI Corps north of Strasbourg. The 274th Infantry Regiment of the 70th Infantry Division distinguishes itself in its first combat operation at Wingen.

Eighth Air Force sends more than 1,000 B-17s and B-24 Liberators escorted by 584 P-51 Mustangs to attack communication centers, marshaling yards, and airfields. The bombing mission involves a combination of visual, Pathfinder, H2X, and Gee-H (bombing through the clouds technique in which the lead bomber's navigator locates the bomb release point by sending a radio pulse signal to two ground station transponders). One B-17 is lost and 170 B-17s and B-24s damaged. Aircrew casualties are 19 killed, 10 wounded, and one missing. Fighter pilots report one confirmed kill in the air and four confirmed kills on the ground. One P-51 is lost and one damaged. One pilot is reported missing.

A total of 24 B-17s conduct screening missions to jam German radio interception efforts and conduct countermeasures against German radar sites.

During the night one B-17s and four B-24s drop leaflets over Belgium.

Ninth Air Force sends A-20 Havocs, A-26 Invaders, and B-26 Marauders to attack railroad bridges and communication centers in Belgium. P-47 and P-38 fighters attack road traffic, communication centers, and support III and VIII Corps near Bastogne and the 2nd and 3rd Armored Divisions.

The headquarters of the 368th Fighter Group and the P-47 Thunderbolts of the 395th, 396th, and 397th Fighter Squadrons redeploy from Juvincourt to Metz, France.

MEDITERRANEAN: Fifteenth Air Force P-38 Lightnings bomb the railroad bridge at Doboj in Yugoslavia.

ITALY: During the night Twelfth Air Force A-20 Havocs conduct bombing runs in the Po River valley near Modena.

SOUTHWEST PACIFIC AREA: Kamikazes continue their relentless attacks on the Luzon invasion fleet. A heavy cruiser, a destroyer, and a destroyer escort are damaged, along with escort carriers USS *Manila Bay* and USS *Savo Island*. Kamikazes also hit and damage an Australian heavy cruiser and a destroyer. Carrier aircraft from Naval Task Group 77.4 (escort carrier group) sink a Japanese destroyer near Manila Bay. Two other destroyers are damaged.

The USS *Boise* with General MacArthur aboard narrowly avoids two torpedoes fired from a Japanese midget submarine. A U.S. destroyer later sinks the submarine.

In the Philippines, Far East Air Force sends B-25 Mitchells to attack shore installations around Lingayen Gulf on Luzon Island. A-20 Havocs and P-47 Thunderbolts attack airfields on Luzon and Mindanao Islands.

The P-51 Mustangs of the 4th Fighter Squadron (Commando), 3rd Air Commando Group, arrive on Leyte Island from the United States. The 547th Night Fighter Squadron of the 86th Fighter Wing, under the operational control of the 310th Bombardment Wing (Medium), redeploys from Schouten Island to Mindoro Island with P-38 Lightnings and P-61 Black Widow night fighters.

PACIFIC: Naval Task Force 92, commanded by Rear Admiral John L. McCrea, with three light cruisers and nine destroyers, bombards Japanese installations on Paramushiru in the Kuriles.

CENTRAL PACIFIC: Seventh Air Force sends 22 B-24 Liberators from Saipan Island to bomb Iwo Jima. With three B-24 Liberators providing navigational escort, seven P-38 Lightnings strafe the island as well.

Naval Task Group 94.9, with three heavy cruisers and six destroyers under Rear Admiral Allan E. Smith, supported by FEAF B-24 Liberators with P-38 Lightnings, attacks Japanese shipping and installations on Chichi Jima, Haha Jima, and Iwo Jima. Three U.S. destroyers sink a landing ship. A U.S. destroyer is damaged by a mine, and another U.S. destroyer is also damaged by fire from shore. Three U.S. destroyers sink a landing ship off Iwo Jima.

Navy PB4Y-1 Privateers sink Japanese midget submarine *Ha.71* off Chichi Jima.

NEW GUINEA: Far East Air Force B-25 Mitchells and B-24 Liberators bomb Celebes Island, escorted by P-40s. B-24 Liberators attack Miri airfield in Borneo.

U.S. submarine *Cavalla* torpedoes and sinks two Japanese auxiliary netlayers in the Java Sea.

January 6

ALEUTIANS: Eleventh Air Force sends 10 B-25 Mitchells to provide air cover for a naval task force. B-24 Liberators bomb the airfield and facilities at Suribachi Bay on Paramushiru Island.

CBI: In China, Fourteenth Air Force sends 40 P-40s, P-51 Mustangs, and P-47 Thunderbolts to bomb the Hankow-Wuchang area. Pilots report nine enemy aircraft destroyed.

ETO: Fifteenth Army is operational under 12th Army Group.

In the Seventh Army area, the 12th Armored Division is transferred to VI Corps in preparation for an attack to push back a German salient near Herrlisheim.

Eighth Air Force sends more than 800 B-17s and B-24 Liberators escorted by over 600 P-51 Mustangs to attack marshaling yards and communication targets in western Germany. Most of the bombing runs are made using Gee-H and H2X. Two bombers are lost and 92 are damaged. Aircrew casualties are five killed, three wounded, and 10 missing. Fighter pilots report 14 confirmed kills and one possible on the ground. Two fighters are lost and four damaged. Two pilots are reported missing, and two are killed.

During the night six B-17s drop leaflets over Belgium and the Netherlands.

Six B-17s conduct screening missions to jam German radio interception efforts and conduct countermeasures against German radar sites.

ITALY: Twelfth Air Force A-20 Havocs and P-47 Thunderbolts of the XXII Tactical Air Command attack rail lines, bridges, and roads and bomb ships in the harbors at Genoa and Imperia.

SOUTHWEST PACIFIC AREA: The heaviest kamikaze attacks to date hit Seventh Fleet's Bombardment and Fire Support Group in Lingayen Gulf. Two battleships and two cruisers are damaged. Third Fleet aircraft attack Japanese airfields on Luzon.

In the Philippines, Far East Air Force B-24 Liberators bomb Clark Field and Nichols Field, along with other airfield targets on Luzon Island, while B-25 Mitchells, A-20 Havocs, and P-47 Thunderbolts attack bridges and targets of opportunity. A-20s, with P-38 Lightnings flying cover, bomb Carolina airfield on Negros Island.

Kamikazes continue the attack on the Luzon invasion force as it approaches Lingayen Gulf. Battleships USS *New Mexico* and USS *California,* a heavy cruiser, a light cruiser, and four destroyers are damaged. Another destroyer is damaged by friendly fire.

Kamikazes attack minesweepers, sinking one and damaging another.

Destroyer USS *Walke,* covering minesweeping operations, is hit by four aircraft. One crashes into the bridge where Commander George F. Davis is standing. In the midst of the carnage and destruction, Commander Davis refuses to leave the bridge and fights to save his ship, directing efforts and encouraging his men. Although mortally wounded, Davis refuses treatment; only when assured that the ship and crew are safe, does he allow himself to be carried below. For his indomitable courage and dedication to duty Commander Davis will receive the Medal of Honor.

To limit the destructive kamikaze attacks, Vice Admiral John S. McCain orders Task Force 38 to attack airfields on Formosa and Japanese shipping headed to Luzon. Carrier aircraft sink a cargo ship and six merchant tankers off northern Luzon.

U.S. submarine *Besugo* torpedoes and sinks a Japanese fleet tanker in the Gulf of Thailand. U.S. submarine *Sea Robin* attacks a Japanese convoy and sinks a fleet tanker east of Hainan Island.

PACIFIC: Tenth Army completes its operational planning for Operation Iceberg, the invasion of Okinawa. After several delays, the date for execution (designated as L-day) is set for April 1 and approved by Admiral Nimitz.

The 77th Infantry Division is assigned the mission of seizing the Kerama Islands west of Okinawa prior to the main landings. The 2nd Marine Division will act as a diversionary landing force at the eastern end of Okinawa as the main landing will occur on the western coast in the center of the island. Prelanding fires and operations to destroy Japanese defenses on Okinawa and isolate the landing area from enemy sea and air forces will begin March 24. On April 1 the III Amphibious Corps will land the 6th and 1st Marine Divisions abreast on the beach landing site north of the town of Hagushi. The 6th Marine Division is to capture Yontan airfield and move to capture the Ishikawa Isthmus. The 1st Marine Division is to capture the Katchin Peninsula. The XIV Corps will land the 7th and the 96th Infantry Divisions abreast to the south of Hagushi. The 7th Infantry Division will capture Kadena airfield and move to the east coast to cut the island in two. The 96th Infantry Division will control the high ground south of the landing beaches, then move south on the eastern coastal road to capture the bridges at Chantan, then move to protect the corps's southern flank. Altogether the Americans will be landing about 116,000 men on L-day. The 27th Infantry Division will be available as a floating reserve one day after the initial landings (L+1).

The Twentieth Air Force's XX Bomber Command flies its last mission against targets in Japan. A total of 49 B-29s are sent from Chengtu, China, to bomb an aircraft production facility at Omura, on Kyushu Island in Japan. Only 28 bombers hit the primary target, and 13 hit a secondary target at Nanking, China. Six others bomb targets of opportunity. Aircrews report four confirmed kills, six probable kills, and 10 possible kills. One B-29 is lost.

CENTRAL PACIFIC: Seventh Air Force B-24 Liberators from Guam bomb Iwo Jima.

During the night nine B-24s conduct a snooper (radar-assisted bomb release) mission on the airfields at Iwo Jima.

NEW GUINEA: FEAF B-25 Mitchells and P-40s attack Mapanget airfield on Celebes Island.

January 7

CBI: In China, Fourteenth Air Force sends five B-24 Liberators to bomb Fort Bayard and attack shipping in Samah Bay on Hainan Island. Aircrews report one ship sunk.

Fourteenth Air Force B-24 Liberators attack a Japanese convoy in the South China Sea and sink a stores ship in the Formosa Strait.

ETO: The VII Corps cuts the LaRoche-Vielsam road, intercepting the main supply line of the German forces in the north of the Bulge.

The Germans launch a second attack at VI Corps near Strasbourg called Sonnewende (Winter Solstice). German tanks and infantry open a 10-mile gap in the VI Corps lines. Other German units attack near Lauterbourg and are stopped by Seventh Army's reserve, the 14th Armored Division. The 157th Infantry Regiment of the 45th Infantry Division takes heavy casualties defending the Low Vosges against attacks by German mountain troops.

Eighth Air Force sends more than 1,000 B-17s and B-24 Liberators escorted by 700 P-51 Mustangs to attack marshaling yards, bridges, oil storage depots, and communication centers. The bombers use a combination of Pathfinder bombers, H2X radar, and Gee-H. A total of three bombers are lost and 28 damaged. Aircrew casualties are one killed, three wounded, and 28 missing. One P-51 is lost, and the pilot is reported missing.

During the night two B-17s and five B-24s drop leaflets over Belgium and France.

Six B-17s conduct screening missions to jam German radio interception efforts and conduct countermeasures against German radar sites.

Field Marshal Sir Bernard L Montgomery, commander of the 21st Army Group, gives a press conference and implies that he has made most of the major decisions that led to the Germans being halted before the Meuse River. This infuriates nearly all the American leadership and creates a rift between the Americans and British that will never fully be reconciled. General Eisenhower will later write, "I doubt Montgomery ever came to realize how deeply resentful some American commanders were."

ITALY: Twelfth Air Force A-20 Havocs and P-47 Thunderbolts of the XXII Tactical Air Command attack rail lines at Brenner and marshaling yards.

SOUTHWEST PACIFIC AREA: Vice Admiral Thomas C. Kinkaid, the Seventh Fleet commander, requests that Admiral William F. Halsey's Third Fleet carrier aircraft conduct intensified air attacks on Luzon airfields to forestall the kamikaze attacks. General MacArthur requests XX Bomber Command to shift targets on Formosa to airfields at the southern part of the island, also to limit kamikaze attacks.

In the Philippines, Far East Air Force B-25 Mitchells and A-20 Havocs, supported by P-38 Lightnings, attack Clark Field, while B-24 Liberators bomb Nichols Field. B-24s attack airfields on Mindanao Island.

Rear Admiral Jesse B. Oldendorf's bombardment and fire support group (Task Group 77.2) and escort carrier group aircraft of Task Group 77.4 commanded by Rear Admiral Calvin T. Durgin conduct pre-assault attacks on Japanese defenses at Lingayen Gulf. Japanese torpedo planes sink a minesweeper and bombs damage another minesweeper. Kamikazes damage an attack transport *Callaway* and an LST (landing ship, tank).

Four destroyers sink a Japanese destroyer west of Manila Bay. U.S. submarine *Picuda* torpedoes and damages a Japanese army tanker northwest of Formosa.

PACIFIC: U.S. submarine *Spot* torpedoes and sinks a Japanese guardboat west of Kyushu, Japan.

Central Pacific: Seventh Air Force sends 11 B-24 Liberators from Saipan to bomb airfields on Iwo Jima.

Ten B-24s conduct single-ship snooper (radar-assisted bomb release) missions on Iwo Jima throughout the night.

New Guinea: FEAF B-25 Mitchells and P-40s attack targets on Celebes Island.

January 8

CBI: In Burma, Tenth Air Force sends 21 B-25 Mitchells to attack troops and logistics storage areas, while 74 P-47 Thunderbolts and P-38 Lightnings attack troop concentrations and logistics stockpiles.

ETO: Hitler orders a retreat from the Ardennes to avoid the entrapment of thousands of troops in front of Houffalize.

The VI Corps commits the 56th Armored Infantry Battalion supported by the 714th Tank Battalion to attack Herrlisheim. The infantrymen take a portion of the town but are greatly outnumbered.

Eighth Air Force sends more than 700 B-17s and B-24 Liberators escorted by nearly 300 P-51 Mustangs to attack communication centers, road and rail bridges, and marshaling yards in Germany. The bombers use a combination of Pathfinder bombers, H2X radar, and Gee-H. Two bombers are lost and 77 are damaged. Aircrew casualties are one killed, eight wounded, and nine missing. During the night one B-17 and two B-24s drop leaflets over Belgium.

Technical Sergeant Russell E. Dunham of I Company, 30th Infantry Regiment, 3rd Infantry Division, is participating in an attack on Hill 616 near Kayserberg, France. Wearing winter camouflage made from a mattress cover and carrying 12 M-1 carbine magazines and a dozen hand grenades, Technical Sergeant Dunham moves up the snow-covered hill toward a German machine-gun position. Far ahead of his platoon, Dunham crawls to within 75 yards of the emplacement, then runs toward the enemy. Hit by a machine-gun bullet, he falls backward, but jumps to his feet again, dodging hand grenades and firing his carbine into the position, killing two soldiers. With his weapon now empty, Dunham drags out the remaining German soldier with his bare hands. He then moves to attack a second machine gun, ignoring the fire directed toward him and throwing hand grenades toward the position. He assaults the position, killing the machine-gun crew and firing his carbine into the foxholes of the supporting infantrymen, causing them to scatter. Staggering from his wound, Dunham continues to move uphill to another defensive position. As machine-gun bullets hit around him and grenades explode close by, Dunham eliminates the position with hand grenades, then shoots several Germans to take the position. Technical Sergeant Dunham's bravery under fire and indomitable fighting spirit will win him the nation's highest award for valor, the Medal of Honor.

Technical Sergeant Charles F. Carey commands an antitank platoon in the 379th Infantry Regiment, 100th Infantry Division. At Rimling, France, a German counterattack shatters part of the battalion defenses. Technical Sergeant Carey takes the initiative to organize a patrol to collect the members of his platoon trapped in the breakthrough area. He then organizes an attack on a house that the enemy had occupied. As members of the patrol provide covering fire, Carey moves toward the house alone. Entering the house after throwing a grenade, he returns with 16 prisoners. With another patrol he attacks a German tank, disabling it with bazooka fire, then eliminates the crew. Technical Sergeant Carey later goes to the rescue of one of his squads that has been trapped in a building during a German counterattack. Carey continues this pattern of aggressive leadership until killed by a sniper. For his fearless and consistently heroic actions during this bitter battle, Technical Sergeant Carey will receive the Medal of Honor.

A German V-1 or V-2 rocket damages a U.S. freighter at Antwerp, Belgium.

MEDITERRANEAN: Fifteenth Air Force sends more than 300 B-17s and B-24 Liberators escorted by over 200 P-38 Lightnings and P-51 Mustangs to attack marshaling yards in Austria.

ITALY: During the night Twelfth Air Force A-20 Havocs make bombing runs in the Po River valley.

The 437th Bombardment Squadron (Medium), 319th Bombardment Group (Medium), begins a redeployment from Corsica to the United States. The squadron will convert from B-25 Mitchells to A-26 Invaders and is scheduled to transfer to the Pacific theater in July of 1945.

SOUTHWEST PACIFIC AREA: In the Philippines, Far East Air Force P-51 Mustangs and P-40s strafe airfields in the Lingayen Gulf area. A-20 Havocs and P-47 Thunderbolts attack railyards and vehicle convoys and B-24 Liberators, and A-20s attack Nichols Field and other airfields on Luzon Island. B-25 Mitchells with P-47s providing cover bomb Fabrica airfield on Negros Island. B-24s bomb an airfield and oil storage facility on Mindanao Island.

Kamikazes damage escort carriers USS *Kitkun Bay* and USS *Kadashan Bay* and damage an Australian heavy cruiser in Lingayen Gulf.

Coordinated submarine attack group (Task Group 17.21, Commander Charles E. Loughlin) attacks a Japanese convoy off the northwest coast of Formosa. USS *Barb* torpedoes and sinks two cargo ships and damages another and sinks a merchant tanker. USS *Picuda* damages a cargo ship, and USS *Queenfish* damages a tanker.

PACIFIC: U.S. submarine *Balao* torpedoes and sinks a Japanese cargo ship southwest of Korea. USS *Piranha* damages an auxiliary netlayer south of Kyushu, Japan.

CENTRAL PACIFIC: Seventh Air Force B-24 Liberators from Guam bomb Iwo Jima.

During the night 10 B-24s conduct single-bomber snooper (radar-assisted bomb release) attacks on Iwo Jima.

NEW GUINEA: FEAF P-38 Lightnings attack airfields in Borneo.

January 9

ALEUTIANS: Eleventh Air Force sends four B-24 Liberators to attack Suribachi Bay airfield on Paramushiru Island using H2X radar equipment.

CBI: The 124th Cavalry links with the 475th Infantry Regiment at Mong Hkak. The new mission of the Mars Task Force is to cut the Burma Road.

Fourteenth Air Force sends six B-25 Mitchells to bomb rail lines, road bridges, and buildings near Thanh Moi in French Indochina. P-40s, P-38 Lightnings, and P-51 Mustangs attack targets of opportunity near Wanling, Burma.

In Burma, Tenth Air Force P-47 Thunderbolts attack a Japanese division headquarters, provide support to ground forces, and attack logistics storage sites, tanks, antiaircraft positions, and troop concentrations.

ATLANTIC: German submarine *U-1055* torpedoes and damages a U.S. freighter as it leaves England for New York by the Bristol Channel. The ship is abandoned and later sinks.

ETO: The III Corps of Third Army attacks north with the 90th Infantry Division from XX Corps, now attached to III Corps.

Ninth Air Force sends 15 B-26 Marauders to bomb the Rinnthal rail bridge in Germany in an attempt to slow the movement of three German tank divisions into the Bulge.

ITALY: Twelfth Air Force B-25 Mitchells and B-26 Marauders attack bridges and assembly areas. A-20 Havocs and P-47 Thunderbolts attack rail lines, vehicles, ammunition and fuel storage sites, gun positions, and German defenses in the northern Apennines.

The 438th, 439th, and 440th Bombardment Squadrons (Medium), 319th Bombardment Group (Medium), begin to redeploy from Corsica to the United States. The group will convert from B-26 Marauders to A-26 Invaders and is scheduled to move to the Pacific theater in July 1945.

SOUTHWEST PACIFIC AREA: The Invasion of Luzon. Vice Admiral Thomas C. Kinkaid, commander of Task Force 77, lands the Sixth Army, commanded by Lieutenant General Walter Krueger, at Lingayen Gulf. The landing is supported by naval gunfire from Vice Admiral Jesse B. Oldendorf's bombardment force (TG 77.2) and aircraft from the escort carrier force (TG 77.4, commanded by Rear Admiral Calvin T. Durgin). Japanese air attacks, kamikazes, and assault demolition boats attack the invasion force. Kamikazes damage the battleship USS *Mississippi*, a light cruiser, and a destroyer escort. The Australian heavy cruiser is forced to retire for repairs. Battleship USS *Colorado* is damaged by friendly fire. Japanese assault demolition boats damage a transport and two LSTs. Vice Admiral John S. McCain's Task Force 38 supports the landings at Lingayen Gulf, attacking airfields and shipping on Formosa, the Ryukyus, and Pescadores. Carrier aircraft sink a coastal patrol ship, a submarine chaser, two tankers, two cargo ships, and a small cargo vessel off Formosa. Pilots report damaging an escort vessel, an oiler, an escort destroyer, and a cargo ship, three coastal patrol ships, three auxiliary submarine chasers, and a minesweeper off Formosa.

I Corps (Lieutenant General Innis P. Swift) lands the 6th and 43rd Infantry Divisions near San Fabian; XIV Corps (Lieutenant General Oscar W. Griswold) lands the 37th and 40th Infantry Divisions at Lingayen and Dagupan. There is almost no opposition. The 43rd Infantry Division, along with the 63rd RCT of the 6th Infantry Division, advances into the mountains north and east of the beachhead and encounters entrenched Japanese troops defending the passes and roads into the open valleys beyond. About 68,000 men have landed on Luzon and occupy a beachhead 15 miles wide and four miles deep.

In the Philippines, Far East Air Force B-24 Liberators, B-25 Mitchells, A-20 Havocs, P-47 Thunderbolts, and P-38 Lightnings attack bridges, vehicles, trains, roads, and airfields throughout Luzon Island in support of the Sixth Army landing at Lingayen Gulf.

PACIFIC: Twentieth Air Force sends 46 B-29s from Chengtu, China, to bomb the harbor at Kirun on the island of Formosa, in support of Sixth Army's invasion of

Luzon Island in the Philippines. A total of 39 hit the primary target, and six others hit targets of last resort along the China coast.

Another Twentieth Air Force bombing mission involves 72 B-29s from the Marianas in an attack on the Musashino aircraft production facility near Tokyo. Only 18 B-29s hit the primary target, while 34 others hit either alternatives or targets of opportunity. Aircrews report 13 confirmed kills, three probable kills, and 11 probables. Six B-29s are lost.

CENTRAL PACIFIC: Seventh Air Force B-24 Liberators from Saipan bomb Iwo Jima.

During the night eight B-24s conduct individual snooper (radar-assisted bomb release) missions on Iwo Jima.

NEW GUINEA: FEAF B-24 Liberators, A-20 Havocs, B-25 Mitchells, P-38 Lightnings, and P-40s attack barges, airfields, and targets of opportunity on Halmahera Island, the Ceram Island area, north Borneo, and Timor Island.

January 10

ALEUTIANS: Eleventh Air Force sends three B-24 Liberators to bomb and photograph Kurabu airfield on Paramushiru Island in the Kuriles.

CBI: Fourteenth Air Force sends over 50 P-51 Mustangs, P-40s, and P-38 Lightnings to attack targets of opportunity near Wanling in Burma. Tenth Air Force P-47 Thunderbolts continue to attack Japanese troops, logistics distribution points, tanks, artillery, and buildings.

ETO: Eighth Air Force sends more than 1,100 B-17s and B-24 Liberators escorted by over 360 P-47 Thunderbolts and P-51 Mustangs to attack road and rail bridges, marshaling yards, and airfields. The bombers use a combination of Pathfinder bombers, H2X radar, and Gee-H. A total of 10 bombers are lost and 364 damaged. Aircrew casualties are 15 killed, 24 wounded, and 100 missing. Fighter pilots report one confirmed kill in the air and two confirmed kills on the ground. A total of eight fighters are lost, and five are damaged. One pilot is reported missing.

Ninth Air Force sends more than 30 B-26 Marauders to attack communication centers and road bridge targets, but the bombers are unable to finish the mission due to bad weather. P-47 and P-38 fighters support III, VIII, XII, and XX Corps.

Master Sergeant Vito R. Bertoldo of A Company, 242nd Infantry Regiment, 42nd Infantry Division, is guarding two command posts near Hatten, France. The headquarters area is threatened by a force of German tanks and infantry that has broken through the front lines. Moving from the protection of a building, Master Sergeant Bertoldo sets up his machine gun in the street and begins engaging German soldiers. He remains there for almost 12 hours, holding off the attack. Later he moves into a building and continues to fight from a place near a window, despite tank fire hitting all around him. As the command post retreats, Bertoldo covers their withdrawal and holds his advanced position throughout the night. He withstands several direct assaults against his position; though nearly killed several times by tank fire, he continues to fight and holds his position. For his skill and courage in nearly singlehandedly stopping a major assault in 48 hours of nonstop combat, Master Sergeant Bertoldo will receive the Medal of Honor.

ITALY: Twelfth Air Force A-20 Havocs and P-47 Thunderbolts attack rail lines, communication targets, vehicles, and fuel and ammunition storage areas in the Po River valley.

SOUTHWEST PACIFIC AREA, LUZON: The 43rd Infantry Division of I Corps supported by the 18th RCT fights to open the Damortis-Rosario road. The 6th Infantry Division on the right flank of I Corps is slowed near the Cabaruan Hills.

Far East Air Force B-24 Liberators bomb an airfield and warehouse area near Manila, while A-20 Havocs, P-47 Thunderbolts, and P-38 Lightnings attack airfields, trucks, highways, trains, railyards, and rail lines on Luzon.

Japanese assault demolition boats make a surprise attack in Lingayen Gulf, sinking infantry landing craft that are providing indirect fire support to the landing force, and damaging two destroyers, a transport, and an LST. Kamikazes damage a destroyer, destroyer escort, and a transport.

PACIFIC: U.S. submarine *Puffer* torpedoes and sinks a Japanese coastal patrol ship and damages another in the Ryukyus.

CENTRAL PACIFIC: Seventh Air Force sends 30 B-24 Liberators from Guam to bomb Iwo Jima.

During the night B-24s from Guam conduct individual snooper (radar-assisted bomb release) missions on Iwo Jima. B-24s attack the airfield on Woleai Atoll in the Carolines.

NEW GUINEA: About 60 FEAF P-40s bomb and strafe the Galela area on Halmahera Island. B-25 Mitchells and P-38 Lightnings attack Kendari airfield on Celebes Island.

The headquarters of XIII Fighter Command redeploys from Sansapor, New Guinea, to Leyte Island.

January 11

ALEUTIANS: Eleventh Air Force sends three B-24 Liberators on an armed reconnaissance over Paramushiru Island. Five B-25 Mitchells attack Kotani Shima in the Kuriles.

CBI: In Burma, Fourteenth Air Force sends five B-25 Mitchells to attack a bridge. Aircrews report some damage. Other B-25s bomb storage buildings near Lashio. Tenth Air Force P-47 Thunderbolts support ground forces and strafe trucks, troop concentrations, artillery pieces, and logistics storage sites.

ETO: During the night Eighth Air Force sends two B-17s and six B-24s to drop leaflets over Belgium.

Ninth Air Force sends 120 A-20 Havocs, A-26 Invaders, and B-26 Marauders to attack communication centers and rail bridges in Belgium and Germany. P-47 and P-38 fighters escort the bombers and attack an ammunition storage facility.

Staff Sergeant Archer T. Gammon, A Company, 9th Armored Infantry Battalion, 6th Armored Division, charges 30 yards through hip-deep snow to knock out a machine gun with grenades near Bastogne, Belgium. As the platoon enters the woods, a machine gun with riflemen and a tank fire on the Americans. Staff Sergeant Gammon jumps forward and runs toward the enemy. Using hand grenades he destroys the machine gun emplacement, fires at German infantry, and advances toward the tank. The tank then fires a main gun round that kills Gammon. His exceptional courage and fighting skills are worthy of the nation's highest award for valor, the Medal of Honor.

ITALY: Twelfth Air Force A-20 Havocs and P-47 Thunderbolts attack targets of opportunity in the Po River valley and attack ammunition and fuel storage sites, rail lines, vehicles, and roads in support of Fifth Army operations.

SOUTHWEST PACIFIC AREA, LUZON: The 25th Infantry Division moves into the I Corps area between the 6th and 43rd Infantry Divisions as the 43rd stalls in the foothills of the mountains. The 158th RCT lands and advances to the left flank of the 43rd Infantry Division. The 25th Infantry Division, the 13th Armored Group, and 6th Ranger Battalion land in the I Corps zone. The Japanese in the Cabaruan Hills are fighting to the last man, occupying defensive positions that are extraordinarily strong and expertly camouflaged. Concrete pillboxes, trenches, and tunnels cover the hills.

The XIV Corps, advancing in parallel columns on well-paved highways, encounters no serious opposition.

Far East Air Force B-24 Liberators, B-25 Mitchells, A-20 Havocs, P-47 Thunderbolts, and P-38 Lightnings attack communication targets, airfields, and town areas on Luzon and Mindanao islands.

The headquarters of the 308th Bombardment Wing (Heavy) redeploys from Leyte to Luzon Island.

A kamikaze damages a high speed transport off Luzon. Shore batteries damage two LSTs. A U.S. destroyer sinks an auxiliary minesweeper south of Lingayen Gulf.

Major William A. Shomo of the 82nd Tactical Reconnaissance Squadron, Fifth Air Force, is lead pilot of a P-51D Mustang, with two other fighters, ordered to photograph and strafe Aparri and Laoag airfields on Luzon. While en route to the objective, Shomo discovers a Japanese twin-engine bomber, escorted by 12 fighters, flying in the opposite direction about 2,500 feet above him. Shomo orders an attack and quickly shoots down three enemy fighters. Diving below the bomber, he fires into it, causing it to crash. Pulling up from this pass, he encounters another fighter and shoots it down, then dives on another fighter and destroys it. For his extraordinary display of skill and courage against overwhelming odds, Major Shomo will receive the Medal of Honor.

PACIFIC: Twentieth Air Force sends 47 B-29 Superfortresses from Calcutta, India, to bomb the dry docks at Singapore. Only 25 hit the primary target, and others bomb targets of opportunity. Aircrews report six confirmed kills, one probable, and 17 possibles. Two B-29s are lost.

CENTRAL PACIFIC: Seventh Air Force sends 23 B-24 Liberators from Saipan to bomb Iwo Jima.

During the night three B-24s conduct individual snooper missions on Iwo Jima.

U.S. destroyer and destroyer escort bombard Japanese defenses on Yap.

Japanese submarines begin employing suicide torpedoes (*kaiten*). Japanese submarine *I-36* launches *kaiten* that damage a U.S. ammunition ship and an LCI (landing craft, infantry) at Ulithi.

NEW GUINEA: FEAF B-25 Mitchells and P-38 Lightnings attack Kendari airfield on Celebes Island.

January 12

CBI: Colonel Lewis A. Pick leads the first convoy of 113 vehicles, mostly cargo trucks, jeeps, and ambulances out of Ledo and bound for Kunming, China. The convoy has representation from every engineer unit that has worked on the road, as well as 65 members of the press.

Fourteenth Air Force sends six B-25 Mitchells to make a second attack on a bridge in Burma. P-51 Mustangs and P-47 Thunderbolts attack targets of opportunity near Wanting, China.

Tenth Air Force P-47 Thunderbolts attack Japanese troops, logistics storage sites, and vehicles.

ETO: The 90th Infantry Division advancing from the north and the 6th Armored Division and the 35th Infantry Division from Bastogne trap about 15,000 German soldiers between Bastogne and Wiltz. The Germans abandon any further efforts to capture the town.

ITALY: Twelfth Air Force A-20 Havocs and P-47 Thunderbolts attack rail lines and vehicles in the Po River valley.

SOUTHWEST PACIFIC AREA: Halsey's Third Fleet conducts air strikes on Japanese facilities and airfields from Saigon to Cam Ranh Bay in French Indochina.

In the Philippines, Far East Air Force B-24 Liberators bomb airfields and troop locations on Luzon. Other B-24s attack an airfield on Mindanao Island. B-25 Mitchells bomb warehouses on Negros Island.

Naval Task Force 38 operating in the South China Sea attacks Japanese shipping, airfields, and other shore installations in southeastern French Indochina. Carrier aircraft sink a training cruiser, an escort vessel, five coastal defense vessels, two submarine chasers, a minesweeper, a patrol boat, 10 tankers, a landing ship, a stores ship, an auxiliary minesweeper, three transports, and 13 cargo ships. TF 38 planes also damage two escort vessels, a coastal defense vessel, two fleet tankers, a submarine chaser, four cargo ships, three landing ships, a guardboat, and a merchant tanker. A Vichy French light cruiser is sunk, and a French surveying vessel is damaged.

Off Lingayen Gulf, kamikazes damage two destroyer escorts, an attack transport, an LST, and five freighters, one of which is carrying over 500 soldiers. More than a quarter are killed.

Staff Sergeant Robert E. Laws, G Company, 169th Infantry Regiment, 43rd Infantry Division, leads an assault squad when G Company attacks a Japanese reinforced infantry company defending a hill in Pangasinan Province, Luzon. The approach to the hill is a 70-yard-long narrow ridge covered by a pillbox and infantry foxholes. As his squad provides covering fire, Staff Sergeant Laws moves toward the pillbox under constant enemy fire. He eliminates the pillbox with grenades but is in turn wounded. Supported by his squad, Laws now attacks the rifle positions but is wounded twice more. He kills two Japanese soldiers with his Thompson submachine gun and kills another soldier in hand-to-hand combat. As his squad clears the remaining foxholes, Staff Sergeant Laws receives medical attention and is evacuated. For his leadership and exceptional courage in closing with the enemy, Staff Sergeant Laws will receive the Medal of Honor.

CENTRAL PACIFIC: Seventh Air Force sends 28 B-24 Liberators from Guam to bomb Iwo Jima.

During the night four B-24s from the Marianas conduct individual snooper missions on Iwo Jima. Three B-24s from Saipan bomb Marcus Island.

Japanese submarine *I-53* launches *kaiten* (suicide torpedoes) at Palau without effect.

Japanese submarine *I-58* also launches *kaiten* at Apra Harbor, Guam, without effect.

NEW GUINEA: Japanese submarine *I-47* launches *kaiten* (suicide torpedoes) that damage a U.S. freighter off Hollandia. Japanese submarine *I-56* launches *kaiten* at Manus in the Admiralties without effect.

January 13

CBI: In China, Fourteenth Air Force sends six B-25 Mitchells to bomb six storage buildings at Kengtung, while P-51 Mustangs, P-38 Lightnings, and P-40s attack targets of opportunity near Wanting.

In Burma, Tenth Air Force sends P-47 Thunderbolts against an airfield, while four P-47s support ground forces and attack Japanese troops and vehicles.

ETO: The VIII Corps attacks toward Houffalize reinforced by the 4th Armored Division and the 17th Airborne Division. The XVIII Airborne Corps attacks toward Saint-Vith supported by V Corps. The Third Army's III Corps attacks toward Wiltz.

Eighth Air Force sends more than 900 B-17s and B-24 Liberators escorted by over 450 P-47 Thunderbolts and P-51 Mustangs to attack Rhine River rail bridges, highway bridges, and marshaling yards. The bombers use Pathfinder bombers, H2X radar, and Gee-H. A total of eight bombers are lost and 180 are damaged. Aircrew casualties are four killed, 13 wounded, and 61 missing. Fighter pilots report three confirmed kills in the air and three confirmed kills on the ground. Two fighters are lost and seven are damaged.

Ninth Air Force A-20 Havocs, A-26 Invaders, and B-26 Marauders attack road and rail bridges, and a marshaling yard. P-47 and P-38 fighters support VII Corps near Houffalize and III, VIII, XII, and XX Corps.

In the VI Corps area, the 12th Armored Division is ordered to destroy German forces west of the Rhine River near Herrlisheim.

SOUTHWEST PACIFIC AREA: In the Philippines, Far East Air Force B-24 Liberators attack airfields and Japanese barracks and logistics storage areas on Luzon, while P-47 Thunderbolts fly a sweep, destroying aircraft on the ground and vehicles. A-20 Havocs attack airfields, railroads, and highways.

Kamikaze attacks in Lingayen Gulf damage an escort carrier, USS *Salamaua*.

CENTRAL PACIFIC: Seventh Air Force sends 14 B-24 Liberators from Saipan to bomb Iwo Jima.

During the night two B-24s from Guam and Saipan conduct individual snooper missions on Iwo Jima.

A destroyer escort sinks Japanese submarine *I-362* off Truk.

During one of the coldest winters on record in Europe, men of the 347th Infantry Regiment, 87th Infantry Division, get some hot food near La Roche, Belgium, January 13, 1945.

NEW GUINEA: The headquarters of the 18th Fighter Group redeploys from Sansapor, New Guinea, to Lingayen on Luzon Island. The P-38 Lightnings of the 12th Fighter Squadron also redeploy from Morotai Island to Luzon.

January 14
CBI: In China, Fourteenth Air Force sends 27 B-24 Liberators, supported by 45 P-51 Mustangs and P-40s, to attack Hankow. Fighter pilots report eight Japanese aircraft destroyed. Seven B-25 Mitchells attack targets near Kengtung, while 42 P-47 Thunderbolts, P-40s, and P-51 Mustangs attack airfields at Wuchang and Hankow. Fighter pilots report 17 Japanese aircraft destroyed. Over 20 P-40s and P-51 Mustangs attack targets of opportunity near Wanting.

In Burma, Tenth Air Force sends 12 B-25 Mitchells to attack troops, logistics storage areas, and bridges. P-47 Thunderbolts support ground forces and attack logistics storage areas and troop concentrations.

U.S. submarine *Cobia* torpedoes and sinks a Japanese minelayer off the east coast of Malaya. Fourteenth Air Force P-51 Mustangs sink a Japanese cargo ship in the Yangtze River.

ATLANTIC: German submarine *U-1232* torpedoes and damages a U.S. freighter off Nova Scotia.

ETO: In the Seventh Army area, the 157th Infantry Regiment of the 45th Infantry Division attacks to capture the hills north of Reipertswiller. The 3rd Battalion is trapped behind German lines and fights for more than a week.

Eighth Air Force sends 911 B-17s and B-24 Liberators escorted by 860 P-47 Thunderbolts and P-51 Mustangs to attack road and rail bridges, marshaling yards, oil refineries, and oil production facilities. The bombers are able to release bombs visually. The bombers are met by 250 German fighters. A total of seven bombers are lost and 298 damaged. Aircrews report three confirmed kills, nine probables, and seven possibles. Aircrew casualties are 12 killed, five wounded, and 59 missing. Fighter pilots report 13 confirmed kills and 19 possibles in the air and three confirmed kills and five possibles on the ground. A total of eight fighters are lost, and four are damaged. The pilots are reported missing, and one is wounded.

Over 100 P-47 Thunderbolts and P-51 Mustangs fly a sweep over northern Germany. The fighter pilots report 42 confirmed kills and six possibles. Two P-47s and a P-51 are lost, and one P-47 is damaged. The pilots are reported missing.

Six B-17s conduct screening missions to jam German radio interception efforts and conduct countermeasures against German radar sites.

During the night two B-17s and five B-24s drop leaflets over Germany and Belgium.

Ninth Air Force sends 280 A-20 Havocs and B-26 Marauders to attack bridges and communication sites. P-47 and P-38 fighters support ground forces.

A German V-2 rocket damages a U.S. freighter at Antwerp, Belgium.

Soldiers of the 158th Regimental Combat Team use an improvised litter to carry away wounded men after an unsuccessful attempt to clear the Japanese from the Rosario-Damortis road on Luzon, around January 14, 1945.

Southwest Pacific Area: Far East Air Force B-25 Mitchells and P-51 Mustangs attack airfields on Luzon. A-20 Havocs bomb Clark Field and destroy a number of Japanese aircraft on the ground. B-24 Liberators attack troop concentrations at Cabanatuan. B-24s, B-25s, A-20s, P-38 Lightnings, and P-47 Thunderbolts attack vehicles, bridges, and airfields on Mindanao and Negros Islands. The B-24s of the 408th Bombardment Squadron (Heavy), 22nd Bombardment Group (Heavy), redeploy from Angaur Island in the Palau Islands to Samar in the Philippines.

Pacific: Twentieth Air Force sends 82 B-29 Superfortresses from Chengtu, China, to bomb air installations on Formosa. A total of 55 B-29s hit the primary target, while others bomb targets of opportunity.

Another 73 B-29s from the Marianas are sent to bomb the Mitsubishi aircraft production facility at Nagoya, Japan. A total of 40 B-29s hit the primary target while others bomb targets of opportunity. Aircrews report 16 confirmed kills, seven probables, and 26 possibles. Five B-29s are lost.

Central Pacific: Seventh Air Force sends 22 B-24 Liberators from Saipan escorted by P-38 Lightnings and 21 additional B-24s from Guam to bomb airfields on Moen Island at Truk.

B-24s from Guam bomb Iwo Jima.

During the night two B-24s from the Marianas conduct individual snooper missions on Iwo Jima.

New Guinea: FEAF B-25 Mitchells bomb the Molucca Islands.

January 15

CBI: Colonel Lewis A. Pick's Ledo Road convoy reaches Myitkyina and remains for about a week as Japanese forces are cleared from the area ahead.

Lieutenant General Albert C. Wedemeyer, commander of the China theater, Lieutenant General George E Stratemeyer, commander of Eastern Air Command, and Lieutenant General Daniel I. Sultan, commander of the India-Burma theater, meet at Myitkyina. They agree to establish a new headquarters in China to command both the Tenth and Fourteenth Air Forces.

Fourteenth Air Force sends 18 B-25 Mitchells, supported by 20 P-51 Mustangs and P-40s, to attack Hankow, China. Over 130 P-40s and P-51 Mustangs on armed reconnaissance attack numerous targets of opportunity throughout southern and southeast China.

In Burma, Tenth Air Force sends 12 B-24 Liberators to bomb a troop concentration and logistics storage area. P-47 Thunderbolts damage a bridge and support ground forces, attacking logistics storage sites, tanks, and targets of opportunity.

ETO: The 84th Infantry Division and the 2nd Armored Division reach the Ourthe River west of Houffalize.

SHAEF headquarters estimates that since the Normandy landings 1.5 million German soldiers have been killed, wounded, or captured.

Eighth Air Force sends more than 640 B-17s and B-24 Liberators escorted by 782 P-47 Thunderbolts and P-51 Mustangs to attack marshaling yards in Germany. The bombers use a combination of visual and H2X radar. No bombers are lost and 22 damaged. Aircrew casualties are one killed. Fighter pilots report 14 confirmed kills and 19 possibles in the air. Two P-51s are lost and one P-51 is damaged. Two pilots are reported missing.

During the night two B-17s and seven B-24s drop leaflets over Germany and the Netherlands.

Ninth Air Force sends B-26 Marauders to attack bridges. P-47 and P-38 fighters support ground forces of the III and VIII Corps near Houffalize and Bastogne.

Corporal Arthur O. Beyer is a tank destroyer gunner in C Company, 603rd Tank Destroyer Battalion, fighting German defenses near Arloncourt, Belgium. As the tank destroyers support the infantry with direct fire, Corporal Beyer spots a machine-gun position and advances toward it in full view of the enemy. Attacking the position with a hand grenade, he captures two soldiers. Now within the German lines, he attacks parallel, using grenades and rifle fire to eliminate the defenders, destroying two machine-gun positions, killing eight enemy soldiers and capturing 18 more. Corporal Beyer's act of courage and initiative will win him the Medal of Honor.

MEDITERRANEAN: Fifteenth Air Force sends more than 400 B-17s and B-24 Liberators escorted by nearly 300 P-38 Lightnings and P-51 Mustangs to attack marshaling yards and rail lines in Austria and Italy.

ITALY: Twelfth Air Force B-25 Mitchells and B-26 Marauders attack rail traffic near Brenner. A-20 Havocs and P-47 Thunderbolts of the XXII Tactical Air Command attack rail cars, bridges, and roads in the Po River valley.

SOUTHWEST PACIFIC AREA, LUZON: The XIV Corps crosses the Agno River without encountering any major Japanese forces.

In the Philippines, Far East Air Force B-24 Liberators, B-25 Mitchells, A-20 Havocs, P-38 Lightnings, and P-47 Thunderbolts attack vehicles on highways, railroads, airfields, tanks, and troops on Luzon and Palawan islands.

Naval Task Force 38 attacks Japanese shipping and aircraft off Formosa and the China coast. Carrier aircraft sink two destroyers, a fast transport, a fleet tanker, and a cargo ship. In addition an auxiliary minelayer and two cargo ships are damaged. TF 38 aircraft also sink a Japanese salvage ship off Luzon.

PACIFIC: Admiral Halsey's Third Fleet attacks Japanese airfields on Formosa, Hainan Island, and Hong Kong.

CENTRAL PACIFIC: Seventh Air Force sends 12 B-24 Liberators from Saipan to bomb Iwo Jima.

During the night two B-24s from Guam and Saipan conduct individual snooper (radar-assisted bomb release) missions on Iwo Jima airfields.

NEW GUINEA: FEAF B-24 Liberators bomb airfields in Borneo.

January 16

CBI: In China, Fourteenth Air Force sends four B-25 Mitchells escorted by eight P-40s to attack rail targets near Hankow. Aircrews report a train is destroyed. Over 180 P-51 Mustangs, P-40s, and P-38 Lightnings fly armed reconnaissance over China below the Yangtze River, attacking targets of opportunity.

In Burma, Tenth Air Force sends 12 B-25 Mitchells to bomb a troop concentration and a logistics storage area. P-47 Thunderbolts support ground forces, attacking logistics storage sites, tanks, and targets of opportunity.

ATLANTIC: Four destroyer escorts sink German submarine *U-248* in the North Atlantic.

ETO: The Battle of the Bulge. Patrols from Third Army's 11th Armored Division meet the 41st Infantry Regiment of the 2nd Armored Division, First Army, at Houffalize. First Army and Third Army have trapped nearly 20,000 German soldiers. The divisions turn eastward toward the German border, closing the Bulge. SHAEF headquarters estimates that since the beginning of the battle on December 16 the Germans have lost 120,000 men, 600 tanks, and 1,600 aircraft.

Major General Leonard T. Gerow takes command of Fifteenth Army, leaving V Corps. Major General Clarence R. Heubner replaces Gerow at V Corps. Gerow establishes his headquarters at Rheims. The army's mission is to train, equip, and provide for the onward movement of all U.S. ground forces entering the ETO. His army is also responsible for resting and refitting units from the 12th Army Group. Its combat tasks are to defend the Meuse River line, conduct occupation of areas in the rear of the 12th Army Group, and assume command of American units containing German troops in the Brittany port cities. If required, Gerow's personnel are to be prepared to act as an operational headquarters.

In the VI Corps area, Major General Roderick Allen leads the 12th Armored Division against German forces at Herrlisheim. The 17th Armored Infantry captures part of the town but is forced to withdraw during the night after nearly being surrounded.

Eighth Air Force sends a total of 627 B-17s and B-24 Liberators escorted by nearly 700 P-47 Thunderbolts and P-51 Mustangs to attack marshaling yards, oil production facilities, and industrial targets. The bombers use H2X radar. Two bombers are lost and 10 are damaged. Aircrew casualties are four killed, 23 wounded, and 22 missing. Two P-51s are lost and one is damaged. Two pilots are reported missing.

During the night one B-24 drops leaflets over Belgium.

Ninth Air Force A-20 Havocs, A-26 Invaders, and B-26 Marauders attack communication centers, road and rail bridges, and a motor transport repair facility in Germany. P-47 and P-38 fighters support ground forces of the III Corps near Houffalize.

ITALY: Twelfth Air Force A-20 Havocs bomb motor transport around Genoa and Milan.

SOUTHWEST PACIFIC AREA: B-25 Mitchells, A-20 Havocs, P-38 Lightnings, and P-47s attack communication sites, vehicles, and targets of opportunity on Negros Island.

Naval Task Force 38 attacks Japanese shipping and installations at Hong Kong, Hainan Island, and along the China coast. Carrier aircraft sink a transport, four merchant tankers, and a cargo ship and damage an oiler, a destroyer, a fast transport, three escort destroyers, and a coastal defense vessel. TF 38 planes sink a guardboat east of Hainan and sink a tanker off the coast of southern China.

SOUTHWEST PACIFIC AREA, LUZON: The 43rd Infantry Division and the 18th RCT control the Damortis-Rosario road and continue to advance against strong enemy defenses.

Far East Air Force B-24 Liberators, A-20 Havocs, P-38 Lightnings and P-47 Thunderbolts attack Japanese troop concentrations, trains, trucks, and targets of opportunity on Luzon Island.

PACIFIC: Twentieth Air Force sends B-29s of the 313th Bombardment Wing (Very Heavy) on a shakedown mission against the airfield on Pagan Island in the Marianas. The headquarters of the 316th Bombardment Wing (Very Heavy), the headquarters of the 19th Bombardment Group (Very Heavy), and the B-29 Superfortresses of the 28th, 30th, and 93rd Bombardment Squadrons (Very Heavy) arrive on Guam from the United States. The squadrons' first missions are scheduled for mid-February.

CENTRAL PACIFIC: Seventh Air Force sends 10 B-24 Liberators from Guam to bomb Iwo Jima.

During the night three B-24s conduct snooper (radar-assisted bomb release) missions on Iwo Jima.

NEW GUINEA: FEAF B-24 Liberators attack airfields on north Borneo and on Halmahera Island.

The headquarters of the 86th Fighter Wing redeploys from Sansapor, New Guinea, to Luzon. The 70th Fighter Squadron, 18th Fighter Group, redeploys from Morotai Island to Luzon with P-38 Lightnings. The 547th Night Fighter Squadron, 86th Fighter Wing, under the operational control of the 308th Bombardment Wing, redeploys from Mindoro Island to Luzon with P-38s and P-61 Black Widow night fighters.

January 17

CBI: The Mars Task Force (the 5332nd Brigade Provisional) reaches the Burma Road with the intention of forcing the Japanese out of their defenses south of Wantung. The Chinese 50th and British 36th Divisions attack south toward Lashio and Mandalay to cut the Burma Road between the two cities. The Chinese 38th and 30th Divisions begin the attack toward the Burma Road to drive Japanese forces south.

Fourteenth Air Force sends more than 180 P-40s, P-51 Mustangs, and P-38 Lightnings to attack targets of opportunity from Wanling, Burma, to Shanghai, China. The airfields near Shanghai, Wuchou, and Wuchang are primary targets.

In Burma, Tenth Air Force sends B-25 Mitchells to attack bridges. P-47 Thunderbolts support ground forces and attack logistics storage sites and targets of opportunity.

ETO: Field Marshal Sir Bernard L. Montgomery returns operational control of First Army to General Omar N. Bradley's 12th Army Group but retains operational control of Ninth Army. First Army attacks toward St-Vith, while Third Army attacks toward the northeast. VIII Corps of Third Army attacks through Houffalize and the XX Corps attacks northward.

The 43rd Tank Battalion of the 12th Armored Division is overrun by German forces at Herrlisheim.

Although there are 71 Allied divisions available, most of them are seriously understrength. Noncombat units have been stripped to provide riflemen. In violation of army policy and tradition, black soldiers are asked to volunteer to serve in all-black units as infantrymen. General Eisenhower now examines future operations in three phases. Destroying German forces west of the Rhine is the first phase; seizing a bridgehead over the Rhine is the second phase; and the destruction of German forces followed by an advance into central Germany is the third phase. The destruction of German forces will be accomplished by two axes of advance—one north of the Ruhr into the open space of the north German plain and the other attacking from Mainz through Frankfurt to Kassel. The goal is a double envelopment of the Ruhr. Eisenhower wants to push 35 divisions across the Rhine north of the Ruhr and get as many divisions as possible across in the south to draw German units away from the main effort in the north. SHAEF headquarters estimates that eight divisions will be available in March, including six airborne divisions and between five and eight French divisions.

Eighth Air Force sends more than 700 B-17s and B-24 Liberators escorted by over 350 P-47 Thunderbolts and P-51 Mustangs to attack oil refineries, a U-boat base, and rail targets in northern Germany. The bombers use H2X radar or Gee-H. A total of nine bombers are lost and 152 are damaged. Aircrew casualties are one killed, seven wounded, and 92 missing. Seven fighters are lost and one is damaged. Seven pilots are reported missing.

ITALY: Twelfth Air Force B-25 Mitchells and B-26 Marauders attack rail traffic near Brenner. A-20 Havocs and P-47 Thunderbolts attack rail lines, bridges, and roads.

SOUTHWEST PACIFIC AREA: The Fifth Air Force assumes responsibility for all air operations over Luzon.

In the Philippines, Far East Air Force B-24 Liberators bomb railyards at Legaspi, while B-25 Mitchells attack road and rail targets near Manila. Other B-24s bomb targets on Mindanao and Negros Island. A-20 Havocs, P-38 Lightnings, and P-47 Thunderbolts attack bridges, shipping, port facilities, airfields, vehicles, and targets of opportunity.

PACIFIC: Twentieth Air Force sends 92 B-29s from Chengtu, China, to bomb the airfield at Shinchiku on Formosa. Only 77 bombers hit the primary target, while others attack targets of opportunity in China. One B-29 is lost.

The headquarters of the 29th Bombardment Group (Very Heavy) and the B-29 Superfortresses of the 6th, 43rd, and 52nd Bombardment Squadrons (Very Heavy) arrive at Guam from the United States. The squadrons' first missions are scheduled for mid-February.

U.S. submarine *Tautog* torpedoes and sinks a Japanese fast transport off southern Kyushu, Japan.

CENTRAL PACIFIC: Seventh Air Force sends 14 B-24 Liberators from Saipan to bomb Iwo Jima. Three B-24s from Guam bomb Marcus Island.

During the night two B-24s from Guam and Saipan conduct individual snooper missions on Iwo Jima.

January 18
ALEUTIANS: Eleventh Air Force sends three B-24 Liberators on a reconnaissance mission over Paramushiru Island. One B-24 is forced to land in Soviet territory as the aircraft are returning to base.

CBI: In China, Fourteenth Air Force sends 29 B-24 Liberators along with 25 P-40s to attack shipping and railroad targets at Hong Kong. Nearly 140 P-51 Mustangs, P-40s, and P-38 Lightnings conduct armed reconnaissance missions over southern China from the Burma boundary to Hong Kong and attack targets of opportunity.

In Burma, Tenth Air Force sends B-25 Mitchells, P-47 Thunderbolts, and P-38 Lightnings to attack airfields. Other P-47s support ground forces attacking troops, logistics storage areas, and targets of opportunity.

ETO: The XII Corps of Third Army attacks to clear German forces from the Sauer River. The Americans face only light resistance.

SHAEF informs the CCS of its operational plan to destroy German forces west of the Rhine River and seize bridgeheads over the river in preparation for the anticipated final campaign within Germany. There are 71 Allied divisions currently available, but Eisenhower anticipates the number of divisions available in spring to rise to a total of 85. Eisenhower proposes a three-phase campaign. The first phase is the elimination of German forces west of the Rhine by the 21st, 12th, and 6th Army Groups. The second phase is the establishment of bridgeheads over the Rhine in the 21st Army Group area and the 12th Army Group area. The third phase is the reduction of the Ruhr and the occupation of the Saar River basin. Montgomery's 21st Army Group with the Ninth Army (reinforced to a strength of 12 divisions) will cross the Rhine and attack the Ruhr from the north. Bradley's 12th Army Group will close on the Rhine north of the Moselle River and move north to cut off the Ruhr. With the capture of the Ruhr, German forces in the west are eliminated along with Germany's industrial capability to continue the war. Afterward, the 12th Army Group will attack either northeast to Berlin or east to Leipzig, with the 21st Army Group supporting from the north and the 6th Army Group providing support from the south. Eisenhower's concept is tempered by uncertainties as to whether the Germans have the capability to conduct another major counteroffensive. The SHAEF commander is extremely sensitive to threats that may emerge during the advance, thus slowing the tempo of offensive operations.

In the VI Corps area, 12th Armored Division withdraws from Herrlisheim and establishes defensive positions west of the Zorn River.

Eighth Air Force sends 114 B-17s escorted by over 100 P-51 Mustangs to bomb the marshaling yard at Kaiserslautern, Germany. No bombers are lost, but three fighters are lost. The pilots are reported missing. Six B-17s conduct screening missions to jam German radio interception efforts and conduct countermeasures against German radar sites.

The headquarters of the IX Tactical Air Command returns to the operational control of Ninth Air Force.

MEDITERRANEAN: Operational control of the British XIII Corps passes from Fifth Army to Eighth Army. Field Marshal Sir Harold R. L. G. Alexander, supreme Allied commander in the Mediterranean theater of operations, has decided to move to the "offensive defensive." In other words, his forces will take no more major-combat offensive actions until the weather improves, sufficient artillery ammunition is available, and replacements for combat losses have been integrated into units.

The 15th Special Group (Provisional) is organized and given operational control of the 859th (B-24) and 885th (B-17) Bombardment Squadrons (Heavy), which drop supplies in France, Italy, and Yugoslavia.

ITALY: Twelfth Air Force A-20 Havocs and P-47 Thunderbolts attack rail lines, bridges, trains, ammunition and fuel storage sites, and roads in the Po River valley.

Southwest Pacific Area: In the Philippines, Far East Air Force B-25 Mitchells bomb targets, and P-38 Lightnings strafe parked aircraft on Mindanao Island.

Southwest Pacific Area, Luzon: In the I Corps area the 25th Infantry Division attacks toward Binalonan to capture the road junction that opens into the Cagayan Valley. The 43rd Infantry Division captures Pozorrubio and advances up the Damortis-Rosario road after encountering strong Japanese defenses.

FEAF B-24 Liberators bomb targets on Luzon Island, while A-20 Havocs attack warehouses and highway traffic near Bataan.

Central Pacific: Seventh Air Force sends 19 B-24 Liberators from Saipan to bomb targets on Chichi Jima and Haha Jima islands. B-24 Liberators from Saipan bomb Iwo Jima.

During the night three B-24s conduct individual snooper missions on Iwo Jima.

A Japanese raiding force lands on Peleliu attempting to destroy aircraft at the airfield, but fails to inflict any damage.

New Guinea: FEAF B-24 Liberators bomb targets on Halmahera Island.

The 66th and 67th Troop Carrier Squadrons, 433rd Troop Carrier Group, redeploy from Biak Island to Mindoro Island and Leyte Island with C-46s and C-47s.

January 19

CBI: The Mars Task Force attacks the Japanese at Nawhkam near the Burma Road, effectively cutting the main line of supply for the Japanese 56th Division.

Over 100 P-51 Mustangs, P-40s, and P-38 Lightnings from Fourteenth Air Force conduct armed reconnaissance over south China and the border with French Indochina, attacking targets of opportunity, many of them near Wanting, China.

In Burma, Tenth Air Force sends nine B-25 Mitchells to bomb troops and logistics storage sites while P-47 Thunderbolts support ground forces.

ETO: A winter blizzard hits the Ardennes, stopping all forward movement by the 12th Army Group.

In the VI Corps area, the 12th Armored Division stops a German attack and is later relieved in place by the 36th Infantry Division.

During the night Eighth Air Force sends two B-17s and nine B-24 Liberators to drop leaflets in the Netherlands, Belgium, and Germany.

Ninth Air Force P-47 Thunderbolts and P-38 Lightnings support elements of III and VIII Corps near Houffalize and support the 5th Infantry Division near Bettendorf, Germany.

Mediterranean: Fifteenth Air Force sends more than 400 B-17s and B-24 Liberators to attack road and rail bridges and marshaling yards in Yugoslavia. P-38 Lightnings and P-51 Mustangs fly sweeps. P-51 Mustangs shoot down five enemy aircraft over Zagreb, Yugoslavia.

Italy: Twelfth Air Force A-20 Havocs bomb rail lines, vehicles, bridges, and roads in the Po River valley.

Southwest Pacific Area: In the Philippines, Far East Air Force B-24 Liberators and B-25 Mitchells bomb airfields on Negros Island. A-20 Havocs attack shipping and B-25 Mitchells, P-38 Lightnings, and P-47 Thunderbolts attack airfields, vehicles, storage areas, and highways.

SOUTHWEST PACIFIC AREA, LUZON: The XIV Corps protects its flanks against Japanese defenders in the Cabaruan Hills by capturing Paniqui and Anao. The road to Manila is open, and the north-south lines of communication for the Japanese forces in Luzon are mostly cut off.

PACIFIC: U.S. submarine *Spot* torpedoes and sinks a Japanese cargo ship in the Yellow Sea.

Twentieth Air Force sends 80 B-29 Superfortresses to bomb the Kawasaki aircraft plant at Akashi, Japan. A total of 62 hit the primary target, while others hit alternative targets and targets of opportunity. Aircrews report four confirmed kills, four probables, and eight possibles.

CENTRAL PACIFIC: Seventh Air Force sends seven B-24 Liberators from Saipan to bomb harbor installations at Chichi Jima Island. Another nine B-24 Liberators from Saipan bomb Iwo Jima.

During the night three B-24s from the Marianas conduct individual snooper missions on Iwo Jima.

NEW GUINEA: The headquarters of the 433rd Troop Carrier Group redeploys from Biak Island to Leyte Island in the Philippines. The P-38 Lightnings of the 70th Fighter Squadron, 18th Fighter Group, redeploy from Sansapor, New Guinea, to Luzon.

January 20

ALEUTIANS: Eleventh Air Force sends four B-24 Liberators to bomb Shimushu Island in the Kuriles.

CBI: Patrols of the 38th Chinese Division moving from the north meet elements of the Chinese Y Force (also known as the Chinese Expeditionary Force) advancing south at Mong Yu. Wantung falls to Chinese forces. Allied forces begin attacking south toward Leshio.

Fourteenth Air Force sends four B-25 Mitchells to bomb a bridge and railroad cars near Hanoi, in French Indochina. In China, B-25 Mitchells attack targets of opportunity, and aircrews report a small cargo ship damaged in the East China Sea. P-51 Mustangs attack airfields near Shanghai. Pilots report 22 Japanese aircraft destroyed on the ground. Over 200 P-40s, P-51 Mustangs, and P-38 Lightnings conduct armed reconnaissance over south China and the border with French Indochina.

In Burma, Tenth Air Force P-47 Thunderbolts support ground forces, attack ammunition storage areas and logistics bases, troop concentrations, and targets of opportunity.

ETO: Hungary surrenders to the Allies.

The 157th Infantry Regiment of the 45th Infantry Division holds at Reipertsweler against heavy German attacks, supported by a battalion of the 411th Infantry Regiment of the 103rd Infantry Division. The units suffer heavy losses, with 158 killed and over 1,000 wounded, captured, or evacuated for noncombat illness. Only two men of the 750 men from the 3rd Battalion of the 157th Infantry Regiment will escape after being surrounded by German forces.

The I Corps of the French First Army, 6th Army Group, initiates the attack to reduce the Colmar Pocket, a German bridgehead about 30 miles deep and 50 miles wide west of the Rhine River. The XXI Corps of Seventh Army becomes operational under the command of Major General Frank W. Milburn. General Patch orders a withdrawal to the Moder River during the night.

Eighth Air Force sends more than 700 B-17s escorted by over 450 P-51 Mustangs to attack synthetic oil plants, rail targets, and bridges in western Germany. The bombers use H2X radar to improve accuracy. A total of four bombers are lost and 122 damaged. Aircrew casualties are eight killed, 33 wounded, and six missing. Fighter pilots report one confirmed kill. Two fighters are lost and the pilots are reported missing.

P-51 Mustangs fly a fighter sweep in the Frankfurt area. One P-51 is lost, and the pilot is reported missing.

MEDITERRANEAN: Fifteenth Air Force sends more than 300 B-17s and B-24s to attack marshaling yards at Linz and Salzburg, Austria, and at Rosenheim, Germany, as well as oil storage facilities at Regensburg, Germany.

ITALY: Twelfth Air Force B-25 Mitchells and B-26 Marauders attack bridges. A-20 Havocs and P-47 Thunderbolts attack fuel and ammunition storage areas in the Po River valley.

SOUTHWEST PACIFIC AREA: In the Philippines, Far East Air Force B-24 Liberators attack an airfield on Negros Island and bomb underground storage areas on Luzon Island. A-20 Havocs and B-25 Mitchells attack rail lines, trains, airfields, and artillery positions on Luzon.

U.S. submarine *Nautilus* lands supplies on the south coast of Mindanao.

PACIFIC: In Twentieth Air Force, Brigadier General Roger M. Ramey becomes commander of XX Bomber Command; Major General Curtis Emerson LeMay takes command of XXI Bomber Command.

U.S. submarine *Spot* torpedoes and sinks a Japanese merchant fishing boat in the Yellow Sea. U.S. submarine *Tautog* torpedoes and sinks a Japanese vessel at southern end of Tsushima Strait.

CENTRAL PACIFIC: Seventh Air Force sends 12 B-24 Liberators from Guam to bomb Iwo Jima.

During the night 10 B-24s from Guam conduct individual snooper missions on Iwo Jima.

Japanese submarine *I-48* launches *kaiten* against U.S. shipping at Ulithi without success.

NEW GUINEA: The headquarters of the 35th Fighter Group redeploys from Morotai Island to Luzon. The B-24 Liberators of the 2nd Bombardment Squadron (Heavy), 22nd Bombardment Group (Heavy), redeploys from Angaur Island in the Palau Islands to Samar Island in the central Philippines. The 82nd Tactical Reconnaissance Squadron's F-6s (photo reconnaissance Lightnings) and P-40s redeploy from Morotai to Luzon; the 110th Tactical Reconnaissance Squadron's P-40s redeploy to Leyte. Both squadrons belong to the 71st Tactical Reconnaissance Group.

January 21

CBI: Mars Task Force fights to clear Japanese defenders from the key hills overlooking the Burma Road.

In China, Fourteenth Air Force sends 30 B-24 Liberators to pound the Hong Kong area and P-51 Mustangs to attack Nanking airfield. Fighter pilots report 11 enemy aircraft destroyed on the ground. P-51s also attack targets of opportunity along the Yangtze River to Hankow.

In Burma, Tenth Air Force sends 10 B-25 Mitchells to bomb Heho airfield. P-38 Lightnings and P-47 Thunderbolts support ground forces and attack troop concentrations, supplies, and targets of opportunity.

Fourteenth Air Force B-24 Liberators sink a Japanese salvage vessel at Hong Kong.

U.S. submarine *Tautog* sinks Japanese merchant tanker in the Korea Strait.

ETO: The weather in the Ardennes clears, allowing First and Third Armies to advance toward St-Vith. Wiltz is retaken.

Major General Edward H. Brooks orders his VI Corps to withdraw and organizes a strong defensive line. The last German reserves on the western front have been committed and have accomplished no major objectives.

Eighth Air Force sends more than 900 B-17s and B-24 Liberators escorted by over 500 P-47 Thunderbolts and P-51 Mustangs to attack marshaling yards, military vehicle production facilities, oil production facilities, and bridges. The bombers use a combination of Pathfinder bombers, H2X radar, and Gee-H. A total of eight bombers are lost and 68 are damaged. Aircrew casualties are 21 killed, 15 wounded, and 57 missing. Fighter pilots report eight confirmed kills and one probable on the ground. No fighters are lost.

During the night two B-17s and nine B-24s drop leaflets over Germany, France, and the Netherlands.

Ninth Air Force sends 166 A-20 Havocs, A-26 Invaders, and B-26 Marauders to attack railroad bridges and a marshaling yard. P-47 and P-38 fighters back up ground forces flying in support of the 7th Armored Division.

German submarine *U-1199* torpedoes and damages a U.S. freighter off the Isle of Wight.

MEDITERRANEAN: Fifteenth Air Force sends 170 B-17s escorted by 131 P-38 Lightnings and P-51 Mustangs to attack oil refineries in Austria. Another 43 P-38s attack an oil refinery in Italy.

ITALY: Twelfth Air Force B-25 Mitchells attack bridges and logistics storage sites. A-20 Havocs and P-47 Thunderbolts attack rail lines, bridges, logistics storage sites, and ammunition storage areas.

SOUTHWEST PACIFIC AREA: In the Philippines, Far East Air Force B-24 Liberators bomb an airfield, a barracks, and coastal defense guns. B-25 Mitchells, A-20 Havocs, P-38 Lightnings, and P-47 Thunderbolts conduct armed reconnaissance and make attacks on airfields, road networks, bridges, gun positions, vehicles, and other targets of opportunity on Luzon.

The headquarters of the 22nd Bombardment Group (Heavy) and the B-24s of the 33rd Bombardment Squadron (Heavy) redeploy from Angaur Island in the Palau Islands to Samar in the Philippines.

PACIFIC: Task Force 38 attacks Japanese shipping and airfields on Formosa, the Pescadores, and Okinawa in the Ryukyus. Carrier aircraft sink two fleet tankers, five cargo ships, four army tankers, a merchant tanker, and two cargo vessels and damage three destroyers, two landing ships, a cargo ship, and a supply vessel off Formosa. Kamikazes attacking the task force damage the carrier USS *Ticonderoga,* the small carrier USS *Langley,* and a destroyer.

CENTRAL PACIFIC: Seventh Air Force sends 12 B-24 Liberators from Guam to bomb Iwo Jima.

During the night eight B-24s from Saipan conduct individual snooper missions on Iwo Jima.

January 22

CBI: Elements of the Chinese 30th Division reach the Burma Road north of the Mars Task Force.

In China, Fourteenth Air Force sends 16 P-40s and P-51 Mustangs on armed reconnaissance attack against various targets near Wanting. Another 14 P-51 Mustangs and P-40s attack railroad yards, destroying locomotives and trucks.

In Burma, Tenth Air Force sends 46 P-47 Thunderbolts to support ground forces while 12 others attack roads, troop concentrations, fuel storage sites, ammunition storage areas, vehicles, and targets of opportunity.

ETO: The XIX Tactical Air Force attacks German forces crossing the Our River. Pilots report over 1,700 vehicles destroyed.

The French II Corps of 6th Army Group supports the French I Corps attacking the Colmar Pocket. The 3rd Infantry Division and a regiment of the 63rd Infantry Division clear the Colmar Forest. The U.S. 12th Armored Division is transferred from VI Corps to the First French Army. The division loses more than 1,100 men (nearly half of them missing in action) in the battle for Herrlisheim. It is now known as the "suicide division."

Eighth Air Force sends 206 B-17s escorted by 258 P-51 Mustangs to attack a synthetic oil plant, road and rail bridges, and marshaling yards. The bombers use H2X radar and visual release methods. A total of eight bombers are lost and 68 are damaged. Aircrew casualties are 13 wounded and 45 missing. Fighter pilots report three confirmed kills and one possible on the ground. P-51 Mustangs fly a sweep over St-Vith, Belgium, and over Karlsruhe, Darmstadt, and Koblenz in Germany. One P-51 is lost, and the pilot is reported missing.

During the night one B-17 and eight B-24s drop leaflets over France and the Netherlands.

Ninth Air Force sends 166 A-20 Havocs, A-26 Invaders, and B-26 Marauders to attack railroad bridges and a marshaling yard. P-47 and P-38 fighters support the 7th Armored Division near Montfort in the Netherlands and the III, VIII, and XII Corps from St-Vith to Luxembourg. Fighters also fly armed reconnaissance missions and support the 4th, 5th, 94th, and 95th Infantry Divisions from Luxembourg to Saarlautern, Germany.

ITALY: Twelfth Air Force B-25 Mitchells attack bridges. A-20 Havocs and P-47 Thunderbolts attack vehicles and rail lines, destroying rail cars and locomotives. Logistics storage sites and ammunition storage areas are also attacked.

SOUTHWEST PACIFIC AREA: Far East Air Force B-24 Liberators, escorted by P-38 Lightnings, bomb Heito airfield on Formosa, the first major Fifth Air Force attack on the island. In the Philippines, B-24s bomb an airfield, a barracks, and gun positions across Manila Bay on Luzon.

The headquarters of Fifth Air Force and the headquarters of V Bomber Command and V Fighter Command redeploy from Leyte Island to Mindoro Island.

PACIFIC: Admiral William F. Halsey's Third Fleet conducts air strikes on Okinawa. In 19 days of operations ranging all across the main sea lines of communication of the Japanese Empire, Halsey's fleet has claimed 586 enemy aircraft destroyed and nearly 700 others damaged. Over 130 ships have been sunk and another 167 reported damaged.

Task Force 38 attacks Japanese shipping, airfields, and installations in the Ryukyus. Carrier aircraft sink a cargo vessel, two merchant tankers, a cargo ship, and a guardboat.

CENTRAL PACIFIC: Seventh Air Force sends 20 B-24 Liberators from Guam to bomb Iwo Jima.

During the night eight B-24s from Guam bomb the island again.

NEW GUINEA: The P-47 Thunderbolts of the 39th Fighter Squadron, 35th Fighter Group, redeploy from Morotai Island to Luzon.

January 23

ALEUTIANS: Eleventh Air Force sends four B-24 Liberators to attack targets on Paramushiru Island. The Japanese respond with 10 fighters to attack the bombers. Aircrews report two confirmed kills. One B-24 is lost.

CBI: In China, Fourteenth Air Force sends 40 P-51 Mustangs and P-40s on armed reconnaissance, attacking river, road, and rail traffic.

In Burma, Tenth Air Force sends 12 B-25 Mitchells to bomb airfields, while 34 P-47 Thunderbolts support ground forces, and 55 P-47 Thunderbolts and P-38 Lightnings attack troop concentrations, storage areas, and vehicles.

The 88th Fighter Squadron, 80th Fighter Group, redeploys its P-47s from Shingbwiyang to Myitkyina.

ATLANTIC: President Roosevelt arrives at Newport News, Virginia, to board the heavy cruiser USS *Quincy,* which will take him to Malta for a U.S.-British strategy meeting related to the Argonaut Conference at Yalta.

ETO: The 7th Armored Division's Combat Command A, led by Brigadier General Bruce C. Clarke, whose unit had been pushed out of St-Vith after a brilliant defense of the town during the Ardennes offensive, recaptures the town.

General Eisenhower estimates that the German Ardennes offensive has delayed Allied offensive operations by six weeks.

The 3rd and 28th Infantry Divisions support the French attack on the Colmar Pocket.

Eighth Air Force sends more than 200 B-17s escorted by over 70 P-51 Mustangs to attack marshaling yards at Neuss, Germany. The bombers use Gee-H. One B-17 is lost and 98 are damaged. Aircrew casualties are five killed, six wounded, and 10 missing. Fighter pilots report one confirmed kill. One P-51 is damaged.

During the night five B-24s drop leaflets over the Netherlands.

Ninth Air Force P-47 and P-38 fighters support ground forces of the III, VIII, and XII Corps and the 94th and 95th Infantry Divisions as well as fly armed reconnaissance missions.

ITALY: Twelfth Air Force A-20 Havocs and P-47 Thunderbolts attack rail lines, vehicles, logistics storage sites, and ammunition storage areas.

SOUTHWEST PACIFIC AREA: In the Philippines, Far East Air Force B-24 Liberators and A-20 Havocs attack Corregidor Island. B-24s bomb an airfield on Negros Island.

During the night B-24 Liberators bomb an aluminum factory at Takao on Formosa.

U.S. submarine *Barb* reports sinking three ships and damaging two more on the southern coast of China across from Formosa. But only one cargo ship is actually sunk.

U.S. submarine *Nautilus* delivers supplies to east coast of Mindanao.

U.S. submarine *Sennet* torpedoes and sinks a Japanese guardboat in Hangchow Bay, China.

SOUTHWEST PACIFIC AREA, LUZON: In the XIV Corps area the two RCTs of the 40th Infantry Division hold the Bamban River line, a possible threat to the corps' left flank. General Griswold is wary of exposing his flanks to possible attack and slows his advance toward Manila. FEAF A-20s attack an airfield, and P-38 Lightnings and P-47 Thunderbolts attack bridges and coastal guns on Grande Island at the mouth of Subic Bay.

PACIFIC: Twentieth Air Force sends 73 B-29 Superfortresses from the XXI Bomber Command to bomb the Mitsubishi engine production facility at Nagoya, Japan. A total of 28 hit the primary target and 27 attack the secondary target. Nine others bomb other alternatives and targets of opportunity. The bombers are met by over 600 Japanese fighters. Aircrews report 33 confirmed kills, 22 probable kills, and 40 possible kills. Two B-29s are lost.

CENTRAL PACIFIC: Seventh Air Force sends 12 B-24 Liberators from Saipan to bomb Iwo Jima.

B-24s from Guam conduct an armed reconnaissance mission over Woleai Atoll and bomb the main runway on the island.

During the night 10 B-24s from Saipan conduct harassment bombing on Iwo Jima.

Three destroyer escorts sink Japanese submarine *I-48* off Yap.

January 24

ALEUTIANS: Eleventh Air Force sends eight B-25 Mitchells on a low-level bombing run on Torishima Island in the Kurile Islands, but four abort due to mechanical trouble. The other four bomb buildings. Two B-25s are damaged by Japanese anti-aircraft fire.

CBI: The Mars Task Force harasses the Japanese 56th Division as it withdraws on the Burma Road.

In China, Fourteenth Air Force P-51 Mustangs on armed reconnaissance attack railroad targets. Pilots report 21 locomotives destroyed.

In Burma, Tenth Air Force sends 12 B-25 Mitchells to bomb an airfield. P-47 Thunderbolts support ground forces and attack bridges, troop concentrations, logistics storage sites, and targets of opportunity

The USS *Blackfin* (SS-322), a Balao-class submarine, had a crew of 66, carried 24 torpedoes, could patrol for 75 days and stay submerged for as long as 48 hours. The *Blackfin* conducted a total of five war patrols and sunk the Japanese destroyer *Shigure* on January 24, 1945.

U.S. submarine *Blackfin* torpedoes and sinks a Japanese destroyer in the Straits of Malacca and coordinates with USS *Besugo*, damaging a merchant tanker off the east coast of the Malay Peninsula.

ATLANTIC: The JCS reports to President Roosevelt that the Soviet Union is essential to the defeat of Japan. The JCS requests the president to ask the Soviet leadership to provide a date for their entry into the war and suggests that collaboration begin for planning as soon as possible.

ETO: The End of the Battle of the Bulge. The VII Corps goes to First Army reserve. Bradley orders the rest of First Army to attack northeast to break the West Wall defenses. Third Army is to guard the southern flank.

The Battle of the Bulge is the greatest combat action ever fought by the U.S. Army, involving 26 divisions and 600,000 men. A total of 81,000 men are killed, wounded, or missing throughout the entire operation. Over 70 tanks and tank destroyers are lost. The Germans suffer between 67,000 and 103,000 casualties and have lost 400 tanks. The German army in the west is shattered. American public morale is shaken by the German surprise attack and shocked at the cost of the battle. The American commanders of First Army are embarrassed and bitter that they have been caught by surprise. Nevertheless, commanders at all levels have fought intelligently and with great determination. Small units often made the difference between victory and disaster. The Americans have fought the best the German army can muster, in terrible weather and without air support for nearly a week, and disrupted the entire offensive. Then, in the following weeks, the massed power of the American air and ground forces became

Paratroopers of the 3rd Battalion, 504th Parachute Infantry Regiment, 82nd Airborne Division, move into the attack near Herresbach, Belgium, during the Battle of the Bulge, January 28, 1945.

overwhelming. The battle in the Ardennes in many ways marks the finest performance of the American combat soldier in World War II.

Eighth Air Force P-51 Mustangs from airfields in Belgium are sent to fly sweeps over western Germany. Fighter pilots report three confirmed kills in the air. One P-51 is lost, and the pilot is reported missing.

Ninth Air Force sends A-20 Havocs, A-26 Invaders, and B-26 Marauders to attack communication targets over Germany. P-47 and P-38 fighters fly armed reconnaissance missions and support ground forces of the III, VIII, XII, and XX Corps along the battlefront from St-Vith, Belgium, to Saarlautern, Germany.

German aircraft attack shipping at the port of Antwerp, damaging a U.S. freighter.

SOUTHWEST PACIFIC AREA: In the Philippines, Far East Air Force B-24 Liberators attack Corregidor Island, Cavite, and Grande Island at the mouth of Subic Bay. P-38 Lightnings and P-47 Thunderbolts conduct armed reconnaissance and sweeps, attacking vehicles, airfields, logistics storage sites, and Japanese positions throughout Luzon.

During the night B-24 Liberators conduct a snooper (radar-assisted bomb release) mission against Takao airfield on Formosa.

Navy aircraft from the Philippines bomb Japanese shipping at Formosa, sinking a cargo ship and damaging another.

PACIFIC: Twentieth Air Force sends more than 20 B-29 to bomb the airfields on Iwo Jima. They are preceded in their approach by Naval Task Group 94.9, with the battleship USS *Indiana,* three heavy cruisers, seven destroyers, and a light minelayer, under the command of Rear Admiral Oscar C. Badger, which bombards Iwo Jima. The task group's approach is protected by a barrier patrol of PB4Y Privateers. As the task group begins firing, B-24 Liberators, escorted by P-38 Lightnings, hit the island. Two destroyers sink a transport and two auxiliary minesweepers arriving at Iwo Jima.

U.S. submarine *Atule* torpedoes and sinks a Japanese cargo ship in the Yellow Sea.

CENTRAL PACIFIC: Seventh Air Force sends 33 B-24 Liberators from Guam and Saipan to bomb Iwo Jima, while other bombers act as spotters for naval gunfire.

During the night 10 B-24s conduct harassment bombing runs on the island.

The P-51 Mustangs of the 78th Fighter Squadron, 15th Fighter Group, begin redeployment from Hawaii, destined for Iwo Jima.

January 25

CBI: Lieutenant General Albert C. Wedemeyer establishes the Chinese Combat Command under Major General Robert B. McClure and the Chinese Training Command under Brigadier General John W. Middleton. These organizations are to equip and train Chinese divisions as part of Plan Alpha.

Fourteenth Air Force sends 21 P-51 Mustangs to attack Lantienchang and Nanyuan airfields near Beijing (Peking). A total of 35 Japanese aircraft attack the U.S. fighters. Pilots report five confirmed kills. In China, Fourteenth Air Force P-51 Mustangs attack rail targets and airfields near Peking (Beijing). Fighter pilots report four locomotives and 40 aircraft destroyed. P-40s and P-51s attack railroad targets and report another 42 locomotives destroyed.

In Burma, Tenth Air Force sends 12 B-25 Mitchells to bomb an airfield. P-47 Thunderbolts support ground forces and attack bridges, troop concentrations, logistics storage sites, and targets of opportunity.

ETO: The last German attack on the Moder River defensive line is stopped near Hagenau. Operations Nordwind and Sonnewende (Winter Solstice) have failed, costing the German army 25,000 casualties. American losses in the Seventh Army are 15,600. In the Colmar Pocket, the XXI Corps commanded by Major General Frank W. Milburn takes operational control of the 3rd, 28th, and 75th Infantry Divisions and the 12th Armored Division and 5th French Armored Division. The Allied attacks split the German Nineteenth Army, forcing the Germans to conduct delaying actions.

Eighth Air Force sends more than 100 P-51 Mustangs from airfields in Belgium to fly a sweep over southwest Germany. Fighter pilots report two enemy confirmed kills. One P-51 is lost.

Ninth Air Force sends 170 A-20 Havocs, A-26 Invaders, and B-26 Marauders to attack communication centers, railroad bridges, and rail lines in an attempt to stop German troop movements. P-47 and P-38 fighters support the 5th Infantry Division near Echternach in Luxembourg.

Private First Class Jose F. Valdez of B Company, 7th Infantry Regiment, 3rd Infantry Division, occupies a forward position with five other soldiers about 500 yards from the main company position near Rosenkrantz, France. The Germans launch a major counterattack. Valdez engages a tank and forces it to withdraw; he then fires on a German machine-gun crew, killing all three men. It becomes clear that the Americans are faced with an attack of two infantry companies. As the Americans withdraw, Private Valdez volunteers to stay behind to delay the enemy. Firing on the enemy, Valdez is badly wounded but continues fighting and calls for artillery by using a field telephone, correcting fire until the shells are falling within 50 yards of his position. The German attack is broken. As the enemy retreats, Valdez crawls back to his own lines where he dies of his wounds. For his extraordinary courage and determination to save the lives of his comrades at the risk of his own life, Private First Class Valdez will receive the Medal of Honor.

ITALY: Twelfth Air Force A-20 Havocs and P-47 Thunderbolts of the XXII Tactical Air Command attack rail lines, ammunition storage areas, bridges, and roads.

SOUTHWEST PACIFIC AREA: In the Philippines, Far East Air Force B-24 Liberators bomb Corregidor Island. B-24s, B-25 Mitchells, A-20 Havocs, P-38 Lightnings, and P-47 Thunderbolts conduct sweeps, armed reconnaissance, and attack vehicles, Japanese positions, airfields, ammunition storage areas, logistics storage sites, barges, communication targets, and targets of opportunity over Luzon and Palawan Islands. During the night B-24s conduct a harassing raid on Takao, Formosa.

The A-20 Havocs of the 387th Bombardment Squadron (Light), 312th Bombardment Group (Light), redeploy from Leyte to Mindoro Island.

PACIFIC: U.S. submarine *Greenling* is damaged in a depth-charge attack off Kyushu, Japan, and is forced to end her patrol. U.S. submarine *Silversides* torpedoes and sinks a Japanese cargo ship off Kyushu.

CENTRAL PACIFIC: Seventh Air Force sends 14 B-24 Liberators from Saipan to bomb Iwo Jima. During the night 10 B-24s conduct harassment bombing runs on Iwo Jima.

January 26

CBI: In China, Fourteenth Air Force sends 15 P-51 Mustangs and P-40s to attack Chenghsien airfield as well as locomotives, tracks, and vehicles at Nanking and Sinsiang.

In Burma, Tenth Air Force sends more than 140 P-47 Thunderbolts to support ground forces and attack bridges, troop concentrations, logistics storage sites, and targets of opportunity.

ETO: Ninth Air Force sends 27 B-26 Marauders to bomb the Euskirchen rail bridge to interdict rail traffic. P-47 and P-38 fighters of the XIX Tactical Air Command support Third Army operations from St-Vith in Belgium to Saarlautern in Germany.

Second Lieutenant Audie L. Murphy is commander of B Company, 15th Infantry Regiment, 3rd Infantry Division, advancing toward the Colmar Canal when German tanks and infantry counterattack near Holtzwihr, France. Deploying the company in a defensive position, Murphy begins calling artillery fire on the enemy. As German tanks approach his position Lieutenant Murphy climbs on a burning American tank destroyer and fires the .50-caliber machine gun against an enemy advancing on three sides and turns the infantry back. Although wounded in the leg, he holds this position for three hours as German infantry attempt to overwhelm him. When his ammunition is exhausted, he returns to his company and leads a counterattack, forcing the Germans to retreat. For his extraordinary courage and selfless dedication to duty, Second Lieutenant Murphy will receive the Medal of Honor.

ITALY: The 10th Mountain Division arrives in Italy and is placed under the operational control of IV Corps.

During the night Twelfth Air Force A-20 Havocs fly armed reconnaissance, bombing Po River crossings, an airfield, and vehicle movement throughout the Po River valley.

SOUTHWEST PACIFIC AREA: In the Philippines, the headquarters of the 3rd Air Commando Group, the 3rd and 4th Fighter Squadrons (Commando), and the 318th Troop Carrier Squadron (Commando) redeploy from Leyte Island to Luzon with P-51 Mustangs and C-47s. The A-20s of the 386th Bombardment Squadron (Light), 312th Bombardment Group (Light), redeploy from Leyte to Mindoro.

A Japanese cargo ship is sunk by a mine laid by U.S. submarine *Dace* off the southern coast of French Indochina.

SOUTHWEST PACIFIC AREA, LUZON: The XIV Corps has advanced 59 miles and occupies a 124-mile front with the 40th and 37th Infantry Divisions. No Japanese forces have put up any resistance. The commander of Japanese forces in the Philippines, General Tomoyuki Yamashita, has decided to hold northern Luzon, protecting the Cagayan Valley. Two other groups, the Kembu Group and the Shimbu Group, will defend other key areas. The Kembu Group will defend the area west of Clark Field. The Shimbu Group will defend the area east of Manila. Yamashita is limited by a lack of fuel and ammunition and has almost no air support.

Far East Air Force B-24 Liberators attack coastal guns on Corregidor Island. B-25 Mitchells bomb an airfield and coastal guns on Carabao Island, while A-20 Havocs attack Grande Island coastal defenses at the mouth of Subic Bay. P-47 Thunderbolts, A-20s, and B-24s attack communications, vehicles, and towns throughout Luzon Island. B-25 Mitchells and P-38 Lightnings attack targets on Mindanao Island.

PACIFIC: Admiral Richard A. Spruance assumes operational control of all forces assigned to Operation Detachment, the amphibious assault on Iwo Jima.

Twentieth Air Force sends 25 B-29 Superfortresses to mine harbors at Saigon, Cam Ranh Bay, and Phan Rang Bay in French Indochina. Another 41 B-29s mine the approaches to Singapore and Penang harbor and the Pakchan River and Koh Si Chang Channel in Thailand.

U.S. submarine *Tautog* torpedoes and sinks a Japanese merchant fishing boat southeast of Kyushu, Japan.

CENTRAL PACIFIC: Seventh Air Force sends 17 B-24 Liberators from Guam to bomb the airfields on Iwo Jima. During the night nine B-24s conduct harassment bombing runs on the airfields.

NEW GUINEA: The headquarters of the 90th Bombardment Group (Heavy) and the B-24s of the 321st and 400th Bombardment Squadrons (Heavy) redeploy from Biak Island to Mindoro Island. The C-47s of the 69th Troop Carrier Squadron, 433rd Troop Carrier Group, redeploy from Biak to Leyte.

January 27

CBI: Chinese Y Force units link up with Allied units from Burma.

Company B of the 236th Engineers completes the junction of the Ledo and Burma Roads. The 71st Light Pontoon Company finishes a 450-foot pontoon bridge over the Shweli River at Wanting on the Chinese border. The Burma Road is opened to Allied traffic.

In China, Fourteenth Air Force sends 22 P-40s and P-51 Mustangs to attack locomotives, trucks, and shipping.

In Burma, Tenth Air Force P-47 Thunderbolts support ground forces and attack bridges, troop concentrations, logistics storage sites, and targets of opportunity.

A Japanese cargo ship is sunk by a mine dropped by Fourteenth Air Force B-24s in the Yangtze River.

ATLANTIC: German submarine *U-852* torpedoes and damages a U.S. freighter off the west coast of England.

ITALY: Twelfth Air Force A-20 Havocs and P-47 Thunderbolts of the XXII Tactical Air Command attack rail lines, logistics storage sites, bridges, and roads in the Po River valley. P-47 pilots report destroying an oil production facility.

SOUTHWEST PACIFIC AREA, LUZON: The XIV Corps launches a tank and infantry attack against Clark Field and Fort Stotsenburg led by the 37th Infantry Division. The 40th Infantry Division attacks west against the Japanese defenses in the Bamban Hills. The goal is to drive the Japanese back and allow XIV Corps to link with XI Corps advancing along Highway 7 from Bataan.

The 1st Cavalry Division, the 32nd Infantry Division, and the 112th Cavalry RCT land at Lingayen Gulf.

Far East Air Force B-24 Liberators attack targets around Subic Bay, and B-25 Mitchells, A-20 Havocs, P-38 Lightnings, and P47 Thunderbolts attack airfields, town areas, gun emplacements, harbors, communications, and transportation targets throughout Luzon.

The A-20 Havocs of the 388th and 389th Bombardment Squadrons (Light), of the 312th Bombardment Group (Light), redeploy from Leyte Island to Mindoro Island.

PACIFIC: Twentieth Air Force completes the redeployment of the four forward detachments of XX Bomber Command B-29 groups from Chengtu, China, to bases in India as part of a general redeployment of strategic bomber assets from the CBI theater to the Pacific Operations Area. Both the Japanese offensive in China that threatens the American airfields and the overwhelming logistics support requirements necessary to fly fuel and spare parts over the Hump to sustain the bombers in China lead to the redeployment. The XX Bomber Command sends 22 B-29s Superfortresses to bomb the navy yard and arsenal at Saigon in French Indochina. One B-29 bombs a bridge at Bangkok, Thailand. Bomber crews report negligible results.

Over 70 B-29s of the 73rd Bombardment Wing (Very Heavy) are sent from the Marianas to bomb the Musashiho and Nakajima aircraft production facilities near Tokyo. Cloud cover and high winds prevent the bombers from attacking the primary target, and most of the bombers divert to hit urban targets in Tokyo. Japanese fighters shoot down five B-29s, and four other bombers are forced down. Aircrews report 60 confirmed kills, 39 probables, and 39 possibles.

CENTRAL PACIFIC: Seventh Air Force sends 19 B-24 Liberators from Saipan to bomb Iwo Jima. During the night 10 B-24s from Saipan and Guam Island conduct individual harassment raids.

NEW GUINEA: The B-24 Liberators of the 19th Bombardment Squadron (Heavy), 22nd Bombardment Group (Heavy), redeploy from Angaur Island to Samar Island. The B-24 Liberators of the 320th Bombardment Squadron (Heavy), 90th Bombardment Group (Heavy), redeploy from Biak Island to Mindoro Island.

U.S. submarine *Bergall* torpedoes and sinks a Japanese auxiliary minesweeper in Lombok Strait, Java.

January 28

CBI: Colonel Lewis A. Pick leads the first overland convoy into Wanting, China, where T. V. Soong, the Chinese minister of foreign affairs, is there to welcome the group.

In China, Fourteenth Air Force P-40s and P-51 Mustangs attack rail and river traffic.

In Burma, Tenth Air Force P-47 Thunderbolts support ground forces and attack logistics storage sites and troop concentrations.

ETO: The III Corps of Third Army reaches the Our River. The XII Corps closes on the Our and Sauer Rivers (4th Armored Division and the 5th, 76th, and 80th Infantry Divisions). First Army attacks toward Euskirchen east of Bonn with the XVIII Airborne Corps (1st, 30th, 84th Infantry Divisions and the 82nd Airborne Division).

Eighth Air Force sends more than 1,000 B-17s and B-24 Liberators escorted by 172 P-51 Mustangs to attack bridges, marshaling yards, and oil and chemical production facilities in western Germany. The bombers use a combination of radar and visual bomb release methods. A total of 12 bombers are lost and 466 damaged. Aircrew casualties are 16 killed, 31 wounded, and 106 missing.

During the night two B-17s and six B-24s drop leaflets over Germany, Luxembourg, and the Netherlands.

Ninth Air Force sends B-26 Marauders to attack communication centers, railroad bridges, and targets of opportunity. P-47 and P-38 fighters support ground forces near Monschau and Butgenbach in Germany.

ITALY: Twelfth Air Force B-25 Mitchells attack rail bridges. A-20 Havocs and P-47 Thunderbolts of the XXII Tactical Air Command attack rail lines, bridges, and roads.

SOUTHWEST PACIFIC AREA, LUZON: The 161st Infantry Regiment of the 25th Infantry Division captures San Manuel, a key strongpoint in the Japanese defenses, after repelling several fierce tank and infantry counterattacks. A total of 41 medium and four light Japanese tanks are destroyed in the battle. The Cabaruan Hills are cleared of the enemy. An estimated 1,400 have been killed and only two captured. American casualties total 279.

In the XIV Corps area, Major General Griswold decides to attack with most of his corps to clear his right flank before making an advance toward Manila. The 37th Infantry Division initiates the attack against Japanese strongpoints at Fort Stotsenburg, while the 40th Infantry Division attacks across the hills north of the Bamban River. Elements of the 37th Infantry Division advance as far as Calumpit on the Pampanga River without encountering any opposition. Manila is about 30 miles distant.

Far East Air Force B-24 Liberators, B-25 Mitchells, A-20 Havocs, P-47 Thunderbolts, and P-38 Lightnings attack targets on Luzon Island. Corregidor Island and targets between Subic Bay and Manila Bay are hardest hit.

PACIFIC: U.S. submarine *Spadefish* attacks a Japanese convoy in the Yellow Sea and sinks an escort vessel and a transport.

CENTRAL PACIFIC: Seventh Air Force sends 10 B-24 Liberators from Guam to bomb Iwo Jima. During the night 10 B-24s conduct harassment bombing runs on the Iwo Jima.

January 29

CBI: The Chinese 30th and 38th Divisions block the Burma Road north of Ho-Si, but are driven back by strong counterattacks as the Japanese attempt to keep the road open for a retreat.

In China, Fourteenth Air Force P-40s and P-51 Mustangs attack airfields, rail, and river traffic.

In Burma, Tenth Air Force sends 13 B-25 Mitchells to bomb road bridges while P-47 Thunderbolts and P-38 Lightnings attack airfields, troop concentrations, and logistics storage sites.

ETO: The VIII Corps of Third Army (4th, 87th, and 90th Infantry Divisions) attacks on a 14-mile-wide front, crossing the Our and Prum Rivers.

Brigadier General Glenn O. Barcus takes command of the XII Tactical Air Command. Eighth Air Force sends more than 1,100 B-17s and B-24 Liberators, escorted by 700 P-47 Thunderbolts and P-51 Mustangs, to attack marshaling yards in western Germany, using H2X radar to locate the targets. One B-24 is lost and 59 bombers are damaged. Aircrew casualties are 18 killed, one wounded, and nine missing. Aircrews report six confirmed kills and two possibles. Fighter pilots report five confirmed kills and two possibles in the air and one confirmed kill on the ground. Two fighters are lost and two are damaged. One pilot is reported missing and one is killed.

During the night one B-17 and eight B-24s drop leaflets over Germany and the Netherlands.

Ninth Air Force sends 364 A-20 Havocs, A-26 Invaders, and B-26 Marauders to attack logistics storage sites and communication centers. P-47 and P-38 fighters support Third Army operations from St-Vith in Belgium to Saarlautern in Germany.

First Sergeant Leonard A. Funk, C Company, 508th Parachute Infantry Regiment, 82nd Airborne Division, takes over as company executive officer when that officer is wounded in an attack on a German defensive position near Holzheim, Belgium. Funk organizes men from the headquarters section into a combat unit and, with elements of an infantry platoon, attacks 15 houses, clears them of the enemy, and takes 30 prisoners without suffering a casualty. C Company moves through the town, leaving First Sergeant Funk with four men to guard about 80 prisoners. A German patrol enters the town, frees the prisoners, and prepares to attack Company C from the rear. At this time First Sergeant Funk discovers the Germans. A German officer orders him to surrender, jamming a weapon into his stomach. Funk slowly begins to unsling his Thompson submachine gun from his shoulder as though surrendering, but pulls it up and fires into the enemy. In the close-range gun battle that follows, 21 Germans are killed and many others are wounded. First Sergeant Funk's heroic actions to save his company from certain destruction will be recognized with the nation's highest award for valor, the Medal of Honor.

ITALY: During the night Twelfth Air Force A-20 Havocs attack rail lines, bridges, and vehicles in the Po River valley.

SOUTHWEST PACIFIC AREA: U.S. submarine *Picuda* attacks a Japanese convoy in Formosa Strait, sinking a cargo ship.

Far East Air Force B-24 Liberators attack the Heito airfield on Formosa.

SOUTHWEST PACIFIC AREA, LUZON: The 37th Infantry Division of XIV Corps succeeds in capturing Clark Field and Fort Stotsenburg, overcoming mines, obstacles, and heavy fire from strongly entrenched enemy positions.

The Eighth Army's XI Corps, commanded by Major General Charles P. Hall and composed of the 38th Infantry Division and the 34th RCT of the 24th Infantry Division, lands 35,000 men between San Antonio and San Felipe on the west coast of Luzon to capture the airfield at San Marcelino, occupy the naval base at Olongapo, and move to control the Bataan Peninsula and prevent Japanese forces from using the area as a defensive bastion, as General MacArthur did in 1942.

FEAF B-24s bomb Corregidor Island in Manila Bay. B-25 Mitchells, A-20 Havocs, P-47 Thunderbolts, and P-38 Lightnings attack targets of opportunity and support ground forces on Luzon Island.

Naval Task Group 78.3, commanded by Rear Admiral Arthur D. Struble, lands the 38th and 34th Infantry Regiments of the 24th Infantry Division near San Antonio, northwest of Subic Bay.

PACIFIC: Twentieth Air Force sends 28 B-29 Superfortresses from the Marianas to bomb the airfields on Iwo Jima.

B-25 Mitchells sink a Japanese auxiliary submarine chaser off Chichi Jima.

CENTRAL PACIFIC: Seventh Air Force sends 19 B-24 Liberators from Guam to bomb Iwo Jima.

During the night five B-24s from Saipan conduct harassment bombing runs on the island.

NEW GUINEA: The headquarters of the 38th Bombardment Group (Medium) and the 822nd Bombardment Squadron (Medium) redeploy from Morotai Island to Luzon with B-25 Mitchells. The B-24 Liberators of the 319th Bombardment Squadron (Heavy) of the 90th Bombardment Group (Heavy) redeploy from Biak Island to Mindoro Island.

January 30

CBI: In China, Fourteenth Air Force sends 27 B-24 Liberators escorted by 32 P-40s and P-51 Mustangs to bomb Hankow.

In Burma, Tenth Air Force sends more than 100 P-47 Thunderbolts to support ground forces and attack troop concentrations, logistics storage sites, communication targets, and artillery positions.

ETO: The V Corps (2nd, 9th, 99th Infantry Divisions and the 7th Armored Division) attacks to capture the Roer River dams.

ITALY: Twelfth Air Force B-25 Mitchells attack rail lines. A-20 Havocs and P-47 Thunderbolts of the XXII Tactical Air Command attack rail lines, bridges, fuel storage areas, and production facilities in northeast Italy and the Po River valley.

SOUTHWEST PACIFIC AREA, LUZON: The American flag is raised over Clark Field. The XIV Corps takes operational control of XI Corps. The 34th RCT captures Olongapo and Subic Bay.

The 40th Infantry Division battles Japanese defenders in the ridges and valleys north and west of Fort Stotsenburg. The Japanese of the Kembu Group are isolated and becoming less of a threat to General Griswold's flank.

During the night five officers and 115 Rangers from the 6th Ranger Battalion, led by Lieutenant Colonel Henry A. Mucci and supported by the Alamo Scouts and Philippine guerrillas, attack the prisoner of war camp at Cabanatuan, killing the Japanese guards and freeing 513 Allied prisoners. Among those rescued are 486 Americans, most of them survivors of Bataan and Corregidor. The Rangers lose two killed and one wounded while inflicting over 200 casualties on the Japanese. The guerrillas destroy 12 tanks and add another 300 casualties to Japanese forces.

The 32nd Infantry Division arrives on Luzon from Leyte and links with the left flank of the 25th Infantry Division.

After visiting the 37th Infantry Division near Calumpit, MacArthur is impatient to get U.S. troops into Manila and notes that there is a lack of aggressive action. As a result, General Krueger issues his order for the assault on Manila. Japanese forces defending Manila are estimated at 18,000.

Far East Air Force A-20 Havocs, P-47 Thunderbolts, and P-38 Lightnings support ground forces and attack ammunition storage areas, artillery positions, and troop concentrations on Luzon.

Naval Task Group 78.3 with a light cruiser and two destroyers provides naval gunfire support as elements of the 38th Infantry Regiment land on Grande Island in Subic Bay. The island is unoccupied. Aircraft from Task Group 77.4, with six escort carriers and screening ships commanded by Rear Admiral William D. Sample, provide air cover.

Japanese submarine *RO-46* torpedoes and sinks an attack transport off Subic Bay.

PACIFIC: U.S. submarine *Threadfin* torpedoes and sinks a Japanese cargo ship off southern Honshu. The submarine is damaged in a depth-charge attack but remains on patrol.

CENTRAL PACIFIC: Seventh Air Force sends 17 B-24 Liberators from Saipan to bomb Iwo Jima.

During the night 10 B-24s conduct harassment bombing runs on the Iwo Jima.

B-24s bomb the airfield on Woleai Atoll in the Caroline Islands. Another five B-24s from Angaur Island hit targets in the Palaus. Ten B-24s from Saipan conduct individual snooper missions on Iwo Jima.

NEW GUINEA: The B-25 Mitchells of the 405th Bombardment Squadron (Medium), 38th Bombardment Group (Medium), redeploy from Morotai Island to Luzon.

U.S. submarine *Bergall* torpedoes and damages a Japanese storeship south of Java.

January 31

CBI: The Japanese begin their retreat down the Burma Road.

The Fourteenth Air Force reports destroying over 300 Japanese aircraft during the month of January.

In China, Fourteenth Air Force P-51 Mustangs attack rail traffic.

In Burma, Tenth Air Force sends 12 B-25 Mitchells to bomb Japanese troop positions and logistics storage areas. P-47 Thunderbolts attack bridges, troop concentrations, and logistics storage sites.

ETO: Eighth Air Force sends more than 400 B-24 Liberators and B-17s escorted by 186 P-51 Mustangs to attack targets in Germany, but bad weather forces a recall to the bases in England. During the mission four bombers are damaged; six airmen are killed and eight are injured.

Staff Sergeant Jonah E. Kelley is a squad leader in E Company, 311th Infantry Regiment, 78th Infantry Division, clearing houses in Kesternich, Germany. Early on January 30, he leads his men through mortar and small arms fire and is wounded by mortar fragments that make his left hand useless, but he refuses to leave his men and continues to fight, firing his M-1 rifle with his right hand as he rests the rifle across his left forearm. Advancing from house to house, he kills enemy soldiers without regard for his own safety and clears the way for his squad to advance. As night falls, he organizes a defensive perimeter and refuses to seek aid for his wounds. The next day, the squad continues the attack but is stopped by automatic and small arms fire. Staff Sergeant Kelley walks out by himself to find the enemy, killing one hidden rifleman, then attacking a house that holds a machine-gun position. Hit by enemy fire, he falls to his knees, but stands up again and fires his last few rounds toward the Germans and eliminates the position. For his superb courage and inspirational leadership Staff Sergeant Kelly will win the Medal of Honor.

MEDITERRANEAN: Fifteenth Air Force sends more than 670 B-17s and B-24 Liberators escorted by P-38 Lightnings and P-51 Mustangs to attack an oil refinery and marshaling yard in Austria and a marshaling yard in Yugoslavia. P-38s drop supplies into Austria and B-24s drop supplies into northern Italy.

ITALY: Twelfth Air Force B-25 Mitchells and B-26 Marauders attack rail bridges and a marshaling yard. A-20 Havocs and P-47 Thunderbolts of the XXII Tactical Air Command attack rail lines, bridges, and roads in northern Italy. During the night A-20s attack rail targets in the Po River valley.

SOUTHWEST PACIFIC AREA: U.S. submarine *Boarfish* torpedoes and sinks a Japanese cargo ship and damages another off the southern coast of French Indochina. U.S. submarine *Pargo* torpedoes and damages a Japanese escort vessel in the South China Sea off the southern coast of French Indochina.

FEAF B-25 Mitchells sink a Japanese escort destroyer and damage a destroyer and another escort destroyer off Formosa.

SOUTHWEST PACIFIC AREA, LUZON: In the I Corps area the 6th Infantry Division defeats the Japanese 2nd Armored Division at Munoz in a battle to gain Highway 5, the last north-south line of communication for the Japanese in Luzon. The 25th Infantry Division advances to San Quintin.

In the XIV Corps area Major General Griswold orders the two RCTs of the 37th and the 1st Cavalry Division to press southeast to clear the northern approaches to Manila. The bridge over the Pampanga River at Cabanatuan is captured during the night by elements of the 1st Cavalry Division. One RCT of the 37th along with the 40th Infantry Division will continue to attack southwest to clear Japanese forces from the hills beyond Fort Stotsenburg.

The XI Corps begins isolating the Bataan Peninsula, moving to the east and encountering strong Japanese positions in the Zambales Mountains.

Two parachute infantry regiments of the 11th Airborne Division under command of Major General Joseph M. Swing make an amphibious landing near Nasugbu outside of Manila Bay and 50 miles south of the city of Manila. There is no opposition, and the paratroopers advance toward the main highway leading to Manila.

Since the campaign began, Japanese casualties are estimated at 15,000. A total of 586 soldiers have been captured. U.S. casualties total 5,754, including 1,297 killed.

Brigadier General Earl W. Barnes takes command of XIII Fighter Command.

Naval Task Group 78.2, commanded by Rear Admiral William M. Fechteler, lands two RCTs of the 11th Airborne Division at Nasugbu, south of the entrance to Manila Bay. Task Group 77.4 (Rear Admiral William D. Sample) provides air cover. Japanese assault demolition boats sink a submarine chaser.

PACIFIC: U.S. submarine *Spadefish* makes an unsuccessful torpedo attack on a Japanese ship in the Yellow Sea.

CENTRAL PACIFIC: Seventh Air Force sends 20 B-24 Liberators from Guam to bomb Iwo Jima.

During the night nine B-24s conduct harassment bombing runs on Iwo Jima.

The headquarters of the 419th Troop Carrier Group is activated on Guam.

February 1

CBI: Fourteenth Air Force sends six B-24 Liberators to attack shipping off the coast of French Indochina. Aircrews report one cargo vessel sunk and one patrol boat damaged. In China, four P-40s attack a Japanese division headquarters near Yungning.

In Burma, Tenth Air Force sends 12 B-25 Mitchells to bomb a bridge. P-47 Thunderbolts support ground forces and attack bridges, airfields, troop concentrations, logistics storage sites, gun positions, and highways.

ETO: General Eisenhower halts the 12th Army Group offensive as it stalls before the West Wall. SHAEF conducts a reorganization of American forces in preparation for the upcoming offensive to close on the Rhine River. Ninth Army receives 10 additional divisions (75th, 79th, 30th, 83rd, 84th, 35th, and 95th Infantry Divisions and the 2nd, 5th, and 8th Armored Divisions) to create XVI Corps, commanded by Major General J. B. Anderson.

The 6th Army Group, on the defensive since January, forms the XXI Corps under Major General Frank W. Milburn composed of the 3rd, 28th, 7th, and 1st Infantry Divisions along with the 12th Armored Division to spearhead the main effort of the offensive to eliminate the Colmar Pocket. The French I and II Corps will support the main effort, and the XII Tactical Air Command will provide support to the ground forces.

Eighth Air Force sends nearly 1,400 B-17s escorted by over 500 P-51 Mustangs to attack rail and road bridges and marshaling yards in western Germany. The bombers use radar to hit the targets. A total of 26 bombers are damaged. Aircrew casualties are three wounded.

During the night six B-24s drop leaflets over Germany, France, and the Netherlands.

Ninth Air Force sends 146 A-20 Havocs, A-26 Invaders, and B-26 Marauders to attack railroad bridges and German defensive positions along the Rhine and Moselle Rivers. P-47 and P-38 fighters attack the Euskirchen marshaling yard.

MEDITERRANEAN: Fifteenth Air Force sends more than 300 B-17s and B-24 Liberators escorted by P-38 Lightnings and P-51 Mustangs to attack an oil refinery and marshaling yards in Austria.

SOUTHWEST PACIFIC AREA: In the Philippines, FEAF B-25 Mitchells attack targets on Palawan Island. Three destroyers and a destroyer escort sink Japanese submarine *RO-115* southwest of Manila. FEAF P-51 Mustangs sink a Japanese landing ship in Luzon Straits and damage a submarine chaser.

FEAF B-24 Liberators attack Okayama airfield on Formosa during the night.

SOUTHWEST PACIFIC AREA, LUZON: The 38th Infantry Division of XI Corps encounters Japanese defenses at Zig Zag Pass. The eight-mile pass, surrounded by rugged mountains, is thoroughly protected by a series of carefully camouflaged and heavily protected positions.

Far East Air Force B-24 Liberators bomb a shipyard, a seaplane base, communication centers, and logistics storage sites on Luzon.

PACIFIC: Twentieth Air Force sends 113 B-29 Superfortresses to bomb the naval base, a dry dock, and other targets at Singapore. Aircrews report three confirmed kills, four probables, and 14 possibles. Two B-29s are lost. An oiler is damaged.

CENTRAL PACIFIC: Seventh Air Force sends 21 B-24 Liberators from Saipan to bomb Iwo Jima.

During the night 10 B-24s conduct individual snooper missions on Iwo Jima. Another 20 B-24s from Angaur Island in the Palaus bomb Corregidor Island in the Philippines.

NEW GUINEA: The 71st and 823rd Bombardment Squadrons (Medium) of the 38th Bombardment Group (Medium) redeploy their B-25 Mitchells from Morotai Island to Luzon. The B-24 Liberators of the 529th Bombardment Squadron (Heavy), 380th Bombardment Group (Heavy), redeploy from Darwin, Australia, to Mindoro Island.

February 2

CBI: The 2nd Squadron, 124th Cavalry attacks Japanese positions near Hpapen, where Japanese troops have entrenched themselves to protect the retreat route of their army. The Americans capture the position, losing 22 killed and 88 wounded.

In Burma, Tenth Air Force sends 11 B-25 Mitchells to bomb logistics storage areas and troop concentrations, while over 60 P-47 Thunderbolts support ground forces and attack troop concentrations, logistics storage sites, and vehicles.

First Lieutenant Jack L. Knight is a troop leader in the 124th Cavalry Regiment, Mars Task Force. He leads his company in capturing a hill near Loi-kang, Burma; while organizing the defense, he locates a number of Japanese pillboxes and foxholes to the right front of the troop's position. He leads the attack and destroys two pillboxes and kills Japanese in several foxholes. As he attacks another pillbox, he is blinded by a Japanese grenade. Nevertheless, he rallies his men and urges them to attack the other pillboxes. During the attack Knight is killed. For his courage and leadership in the face of a determined enemy, First Lieutenant Knight will receive the Medal of Honor.

ATLANTIC: A series of intelligence reports is completed for the JCS entitled "Estimate of Soviet Post-war Capabilities and Intentions." The assessments conclude that the USSR will seek to control eastern Europe and influence central Europe, China, and Japan. Soviet foreign policy will be characterized by fear and suspicion of American motives. The USSR will avoid a conflict with the United States and Great Britain until at least 1952, but the Soviets will go to war earlier if they perceive their vital interests are at stake.

The CCS approves SHAEF's January 18 plan for offensive operations into Germany. The CCS in its response emphasizes that the main effort remains in the north and that phase two of the campaign (crossing the Rhine River) can occur at any time during phase one (eliminating all German forces west of the Rhine).

ETO: The V Corps breaks the German defenses at Schleiden.

During the night Eighth Air Force sends one B-17 and eight B-24s to drop leaflets over western Germany.

Ninth Air Force sends more than 350 A-20 Havocs, A-26 Invaders, and B-26 Marauders to attack rail and road bridges. P-47 and P-38 fighters support ground forces in the Third Army area.

MEDITERRANEAN: The CCS notifies Field Marshal Sir Harold R. L. G. Alexander that five British and Canadian divisions and two fighter groups for the Twelfth Air Force will be removed from the Mediterranean theater to the European theater. Alexander is given three tasks in his area of responsibility. His forces are to contain German troops on the Italian front and prevent them from being withdrawn to other battlefronts; he is to hold the current frontline in Italy; and take any advantage of the weakening or withdrawal of German forces. Despite losing several divisions and being given rather bland requirements both Alexander and General Clark, as Fifteenth Army Group commander, believe something can be done to break the stalemate. Clark orders preparations to be made for an offensive by Fifth and Eighth Armies to begin on April 9. Instead of attacking directly toward Bologna, which has proven costly, the Allies decide to conduct simultaneous attacks to encircle Bologna. The objective is to destroy German forces south of the Po River.

The USS *Quincy,* with President Roosevelt on board, arrives in Valletta harbor, Malta. Meeting the warship at the dock is Prime Minister Churchill.

In the meeting that follows, both agree that they will not accept the Soviet-sponsored and supported Lublin government in Poland. The two leaders discuss the CCS report over strategic differences between the British and Americans in Germany. The British maintain that a main effort in the north should continue, with Berlin as the objective. The Americans believe that an attack through central Germany will be more decisive. The CCS recommends a dual thrust into Germany, but with priority of effort remaining in the north.

Churchill agrees to transfer three more Allied divisions from the Mediterranean theater to the ETO, even though he desires that the Allies drive north into Austria as quickly as possible to forestall any Soviet advances up the Danube River. That night, aircraft fly from Malta, taking 700 members of the British and American delegations to Yalta in the Soviet Crimea for the Argonaut conference with Stalin. Churchill is eager to foster British-American unity before meeting with Stalin. Roosevelt is wary of giving the appearance that the Americans and British are plotting behind Stalin's back. He intends to work with Stalin openly and build a partnership that he believes will guarantee future peace and security.

ITALY: Twelfth Air Force B-25 Mitchells and B-26 Marauders attack rail and road traffic and bridges.

SOUTHWEST PACIFIC AREA: FEAF B-24 Liberators bomb Okayama and Heito airfields and a seaplane base on Formosa.

Colonel Carl A. Brandt takes command of XIII Bomber Command.

U.S. submarine *Besugo* attacks a Japanese convoy east of the Malay Peninsula and sinks a coastal defense vessel. U.S. submarine *Hardhead* torpedoes and sinks a Japanese merchant tanker in the Straits of Malacca.

SOUTHWEST PACIFIC AREA, LUZON: In the XIV Corps area the 1st Cavalry Division makes contact with elements of the 37th Infantry Division northwest of Manila.

The 511th Parachute Infantry Regiment conducts an airborne landing to capture Tagaytay Ridge and link with the two other regiments of the 11th Airborne Division advancing from the coast.

Far East Air Force B-24 Liberators bomb Corregidor Island and Cavite. A-20 Havocs attack the targets in the Baler Bay area on Luzon. B-25 Mitchells bomb pillboxes, gun positions, and river barges on Mindanao Island.

CENTRAL PACIFIC: Seventh Air Force sends 20 B-24 Liberators from Guam to bomb Iwo Jima.

During the night 10 B-24s conduct harassment bombing runs on Iwo Jima.

A total of 22 B-24 Liberators from Angaur Island bomb Corregidor Island in the Philippines.

February 3

CBI: The 1st and 2nd Battalions of the 475th Infantry Regiment attack Japanese defenses at Loi-kang ridge just west of the Burma Road. Supported by artillery and air strikes, the Americans overwhelm the enemy in heavy fighting at a key position named Knight's Hill. The Japanese are cleared out at a cost of two killed and 15 wounded. The Mars Task Force has lost 122 killed and 938 wounded since the beginning of the operation. Japanese casualties are estimated at over 670.

In Burma, Tenth Air Force sends 12 B-25 Mitchells to bomb troop concentrations and logistics storage sites. P-47 Thunderbolts support ground forces and attack bridges, troop concentrations, logistics storage sites, town areas, and Japanese tanks.

ETO: The XXI Corps and French forces eliminate the Colmar Pocket, opening the way to the Rhine River.

Eighth Air Force sends more than 1,400 B-17s and B-24 Liberators escorted by over 900 P-51 Mustangs to attack synthetic oil production facilities at Magdeburg and rail targets in Berlin. Over Berlin, 23 B-17s are lost and 345 damaged. Over Magdeburg, two B-24s are lost and 59 are damaged. Aircrews report 38 confirmed kills, one probable kill, and 18 possibles. Aircrew casualties are 18 killed, 11 wounded, and 208 missing. Fighter pilots report 12 confirmed kills and one probable in the air and 17 confirmed kills and 11 possibles on the ground. Seven P-51 fighters are lost, and two are damaged. Seven pilots are reported missing.

P-47 Thunderbolts fly an airfield sweep and report nine confirmed kills and six possible kills in the air. One P-47 is lost, and the pilot is reported missing.

During the night one B-17 and 10 B-24s drop leaflets over Germany and the Netherlands.

Ninth Air Force sends A-20 Havocs, A-26 Invaders, and B-26 Marauders to attack communication centers, railroad bridges, and repair depots in western Germany. P-47 and P-38 fighters support ground forces and fly armed reconnaissance missions.

Technician 5th Grade Forrest E. Peden is a forward artillery observer in C Battery, 10th Field Artillery Battalion, 3rd Infantry Division, moving with a group of about 45 infantrymen near Biesheim, France. The Americans walk into an ambush and take heavy casualties. Peden assists two wounded soldiers and, unable to use his radio, runs out of the kill zone to reach the battalion command post and bring two light tanks to the ambush site. He climbs on the lead tank and directs it into the fight as bullets and mortar fragments fly against the tank's hull. Peden is killed when the tank is destroyed by a direct hit. For his gallant sacrifice Technician 5th Grade Peden will receive the Medal of Honor.

SOUTHWEST PACIFIC AREA, LUZON: A squadron of the 8th Cavalry crosses the bridge over the Tuliahan River just moments before the Japanese are able to destroy it. Brigadier General William C. Chase, commander of the 1st Cavalry Brigade, leads two motorized cavalry squadrons reinforced with tanks and artillery as a rescue force to enter Manila and free about 3,700 American citizens and other Allied nationals who are being held at the University of Santo Thomas. The cavalrymen surprise the enemy in a night attack and free all but 300 of the civilians who are being held hostage by Japanese troops.

In the Philippines, Far East Air Force B-24 Liberators bomb Corregidor Island, and A-20 Havocs fly ground support missions on Luzon. B-24s bomb Cebu City on Cebu Island. B-25 Mitchells and P-38 Lightnings attack airfields on Mindanao Island.

CENTRAL PACIFIC: Seventh Air Force sends nine B-24 Liberators from Saipan to bomb Chichi Jima and another 10 B-24s attack Iwo Jima. During the night nine B-24s conduct harassment bombing runs on the island.

NEW GUINEA: U.S. submarine *Sea Robin* torpedoes and damages a Japanese transport off Bawean Island in the Java Sea.

February 4

CBI: Colonel Lewis A. Pick's convoy reaches Kunming and receives a hero's welcome from the Chinese.

The Japanese 56th Division escapes mostly intact from the Chinese and American forces attempting to block the Burma Road. The division will reorganize near Lashio.

In China, Fourteenth Air Force sends 10 P-40s to bomb the airfield and the Japanese headquarters at Yungning and the railyards at Sinyang. Two P-40s are lost.

In Burma, Tenth Air Force sends 54 P-38 Lightnings and P-47 Thunderbolts to attack bridges. P-47 Thunderbolts support ground forces and attack bridges, logistics supply points, and vehicles.

ATLANTIC: Argonaut—The Yalta Conference Begins. President Roosevelt, Prime Minister Churchill, and Premier Stalin meet at Yalta in the USSR. They discuss Soviet entry into the war against Japan and postwar issues regarding the division of Germany, the extent of the Soviet sphere of influence in Europe, and the status of Poland.

ETO: The V Corps of First Army is ordered to capture the Roer River dams in support of Ninth Army's planned attack to the north. Bradley maintains a strongly held belief that the two Roer River dams, located about 15 miles from Düren, must be captured before any major advance can be made.

During the night Eighth Air Force sends seven B-24s to drop leaflets over Germany and the Netherlands.

Ninth Air Force sends A-20 Havocs, A-26 Invaders, and B-26 Marauders to attack a repair depot and rail and road bridges. P-47 and P-38 fighters fly armed reconnaissance missions.

ITALY: Operation Fourth Term begins. The 92nd Infantry Division attacks in the Serchio River valley. The 365th and 366th Infantry Regiments make progress initially but are slowed down and stopped by obstacles, mines, and strong German counterattacks.

Twelfth Air Force B-25 Mitchells and B-26 Marauders attack rail and road bridges. A-20 Havocs and P-47 Thunderbolts of the XXII Tactical Air Command attack rail lines, bridges, and roads.

SOUTHWEST PACIFIC AREA: U.S. submarine *Pargo* bombards Woody Island, French Indochina, destroying a weather station, communications, and facilities.

SOUTHWEST PACIFIC AREA, LUZON: Japanese troops give up the 300 hostages taken during the raid on Santo Tomas and are allowed to leave the city after turning the hostages over to U.S. forces.

The 37th Infantry Division enters Manila and frees the 800 American prisoners at Bilibid Prison, then advances into the city, encountering Japanese strongpoints amid fires set by retreating enemy units. Rumors of massacres of civilians reach the Americans.

The 40th Infantry Division, commanded by Major General Rapp Brush, continuing operations against the Kembu Group, makes contact with XI Corps near Dinalupihan.

In the Philippines, Far East Air Force B-24 Liberators bomb Corregidor Island and Cavite. B-25 Mitchells and A-20 Havocs attack targets throughout Luzon.

The headquarters of the 348th Fighter Group and the P-47 Thunderbolts of the 340th Fighter Squadron redeploy from Leyte to Luzon.

PACIFIC: Twentieth Air Force sends 110 B-29 Superfortresses of the 73rd and 313th Bombardment Wings (Very Heavy), XXI Bomber Command, to attack the Japanese home islands. About 200 Japanese fighters attack the bombers, downing one B-29 and damaging 35. Aircrews report four confirmed kills, 20 probables, and 39 possibles.

U.S. submarine *Spadefish* torpedoes and sinks a Japanese cargo ship in the Yellow Sea.

CENTRAL PACIFIC: Seventh Air Force sends nine B-24 Liberators from Guam to bomb antiaircraft positions on Iwo Jima and 10 other B-24s attack Haha Jima. A total of 23 B-24s from Angaur Island bomb Caballo Island in the Philippines. During the night eight B-24s from Guam conduct harassment bombing runs on Iwo Jima.

NEW GUINEA: U.S. submarine *Barbel* is sunk in the Balabac Strait by Japanese naval aircraft.

February 5

ALEUTIANS: Eleventh Air Force sends five B-24 Liberators to bomb Kataoka on Shimushu Island in the Kuriles.

CBI: In China, Fourteenth Air Force sends 14 P-51 Mustangs and P-40s to attack rail and vehicle targets. Fighter pilots report at least nine locomotives and a number of trucks destroyed.

In Burma, Tenth Air Force sends 35 P-47 Thunderbolts to support ground forces, while P-38 Lightnings and P-47s attack troops and logistics storage areas.

ETO: The 78th Infantry Division of V Corps, supported by the 7th Armored Division and the 82nd Airborne Division, attacks into the Hürtgen Forest toward Schmidt to capture the Roer River dams and secure the right flank of Ninth Army.

The XXI Corps of Seventh Army meets the French I Corps at Rouffach, splitting the Colmar Pocket.

Ninth Air Force P-47 and P-38 fighters fly armed reconnaissance missions over the First Army area.

MEDITERRANEAN: Fifteenth Air Force sends more than 700 B-17s and B-24 Liberators escorted by P-38 Lightnings and P-51 Mustangs to attack oil storage facilities at Regensburg, Germany, marshaling yards in Austria and Germany, and a road bridge in Italy.

ITALY: Twelfth Air Force B-25 Mitchells and B-26 Marauders attack rail and road bridges. A-20 Havocs and P-47 Thunderbolts of the XXII Tactical Air Command attack communication targets and bomb a truck park with incendiaries. During the night A-20s attack roads and motor transport in the Po River valley.

SOUTHWEST PACIFIC AREA, LUZON: In the XI Corps area the 152nd Infantry Regiment of the 38th Infantry Division takes heavy casualties at Zig Zag Pass. Patrols of the 149th Infantry Regiment link with elements of the 40th Infantry Division after crossing over the mountains on an unguarded trail.

In the I Corps area the 6th Infantry Division captures San José and traps Japanese defenders at Munoz.

General MacArthur orders Eighth Army to begin clearing Japanese forces from around the Visayan Sea to open a more direct line of supply to Manila from Leyte. The operations are code-named Victor.

Far East Air Force sends 60 B-24 Liberators to bomb Corregidor. B-25 Mitchells conduct a shipping sweep and aircrew reports claim nine barges sunk and several more damaged.

The headquarters of the 475th Fighter Group redeploys from Leyte Island to Mindoro Island. P-38 Lightning detachments from the group's three subordinate fighter squadrons (the 431st, 432nd, and 433rd) will operate from Mindoro, but the squadrons remain on Leyte.

PACIFIC: The headquarters of the 15th Fighter Group prepares to redeploy from Hawaii to Iwo Jima.

CENTRAL PACIFIC: Seventh Air Force sends 21 B-24 Liberators from Saipan to bomb antiaircraft positions and a bivouac site on Iwo Jima. During the night 10 B-24s from Saipan conduct individual snooper (radar-assisted bomb release) missions on Iwo Jima.

BORNEO: FEAF B-24 Liberators with P-38 support attack airfields in Borneo.

February 6

CBI: In China, Fourteenth Air Force sends 20 P-51 Mustangs to attack the Peking (Beijing) airfield. Fighter pilots report seven Japanese aircraft destroyed on the ground.

In Burma, Tenth Air Force sends 86 P-47 Thunderbolts and P-38 Lightnings along with 25 B-25 Mitchells to attack troop concentrations, logistics storage areas, and antiaircraft positions near Lashio.

U.S. submarine *Pampanito* attacks a Japanese convoy and sinks a merchant tanker northeast of Singapore.

ETO: Eighth Air Force sends nearly 1,400 B-17s and B-24 Liberators escorted by over 900 P-51 Mustangs to attack marshaling yards and targets of opportunity as weather conditions prevent bombing of the primary target, oil production facilities. The bombers use radar to identify targets. A total of five bombers are lost and 190 are damaged. Aircrews report four confirmed kills and one possible. Aircrew casualties are 41 killed, seven wounded, and 42 missing. Fighter pilots report one confirmed kill and one possible in the air and three confirmed kills on the ground. Four P-51s are lost and seven are damaged. The four pilots are reported missing.

Ninth Air Force sends 261 A-20 Havocs, A-26 Invaders, and B-26 Marauders to attack an ammunition storage area, communication centers, and a motor transport depot. P-47 and P-38 fighters fly armed reconnaissance missions and attack rail lines and bridges.

The 509th and 510th Fighter Squadrons (with P-47s) of the 405th Fighter Group and the 513th and 514th Fighter Squadrons (with P-47s) of the 406th Fighter Group redeploy from France to Belgium.

German submarine *U-245* torpedoes and sinks a U.S. freighter, part of a convoy headed for Antwerp in the English Channel.

ITALY: Twelfth Air Force B-25 Mitchells and B-26 Marauders attack rail bridges and marshaling yards. A-20 Havocs and P-47 Thunderbolts of the XXII Tactical Air Command attack rail bridges. Fighter pilots report three confirmed kills in the air. During the night A-20s attack roads and motor transport in the Po River valley.

SOUTHWEST PACIFIC AREA: In the Philippines, Far East Air Force B-24 Liberators bomb Corregidor Island gun positions. B-25 Mitchells, P-38 Lightnings, and A-20 Havocs attack targets and support ground forces on Luzon. B-24s and B-25s fly coastal sweeps. A-20s attack an airfield on Negros Island.

The P-47 Thunderbolts of the 342nd and 460th Fighter Squadrons of the 348th Fighter Group redeploy from Leyte to Luzon.

A Japanese tanker is sunk by a mine dropped by Twentieth Air Force B-29s on January 25 in Johore Strait off Singapore. A Japanese battleship-carrier, (a converted battleship) is damaged by a mine off Singapore.

German submarine *U-862* torpedoes and sinks a U.S. freighter off the southeast coast of Australia.

PACIFIC: U.S. submarine *Spadefish* torpedoes and sinks a Japanese merchant passenger-cargo ship off Port Arthur, Korea.

Navy PB4Y Privateers attack a Japanese convoy in the Ryukyus, sinking a small cargo ship.

CENTRAL PACIFIC: Seventh Air Force sends nine B-24 Liberators from Guam to bomb antiaircraft positions and radar sites on Iwo Jima. Other B-24s bomb Ototo Jima Island and attack a town on Kyushu Island, Japan. A total of 19 B-24s from Angaur Island bomb Corregidor.

During the night eight B-24s conduct harassment bombing runs on Iwo Jima.

BORNEO: FEAF B-24 Liberators with P-38 support attack airfields in Borneo.

February 7

CBI: In China, Fourteenth Air Force sends 11 P-51 Mustangs to attack a bridge at Hengshan. Aircrews report the bridge is destroyed. P-40s attack river, road, and rail traffic.

In Burma, Tenth Air Force sends 11 B-25 Mitchells to attack tanks and troops, while 50 P-47 Thunderbolts support ground forces and P-40s attack troop concentrations and logistics sites.

ETO: The 78th Infantry Division captures Schmidt and Kommerscheidt in the Hürtgen Forest, opening the way to the Roer River dams.

The Third Army begins limited attacks along the West Wall to hold German forces in place while the Ninth and First Armies prepare for the main attack.

Mediterranean: Fifteenth Air Force sends more than 600 B-17s and B-24 Liberators escorted by 274 P-38 Lightnings and P-51 Mustangs to attack oil refineries in Austria, oil storage areas in Yugoslavia, and the harbor at Trieste, Italy. B-24s drop supplies in Yugoslavia.

Italy: Twelfth Air Force B-25 Mitchells bomb bridges and rail lines. P-47 Thunderbolts attack rail lines, supply points, and bridges. A-20s attack roads and motor transport in the Po River valley.

Southwest Pacific Area: U.S. submarine *Bergall* attacks a Japanese convoy off the east coast of French Indochina and sinks a coastal defense vessel and damages a merchant tanker. U.S. submarine *Guavina* attacks a Japanese convoy and sinks a merchant tanker south of Saigon, French Indochina. U.S. submarine *Parche* torpedoes and sinks a Japanese cargo ship in the Philippine Sea.

Southwest Pacific Area, Luzon: General MacArthur arrives in Manila.

In the XI Corps area, the 149th Infantry Regiment of the 38th Infantry Division crosses by an unguarded trail into the rear of Japanese positions at Zig Zag Pass.

Far East Air Force B-24 Liberators with P-38 support attack targets of opportunity at Heito airfield on Formosa, and B-25 Mitchells, with P-51 Mustangs flying cover, make several sweeps over the island. Aircrews report one tanker damaged, one submarine and a motor launch sunk, and several vehicles and an airplane destroyed. In the Philippines, A-20 Havocs support ground forces, attacking Japanese forces in the hills west of Clark Field. B-24 Liberators attack targets on Negros Island. The 341st Fighter Squadron, 348th Fighter Group, redeploys its P-47 Thunderbolts from Leyte to Luzon.

A destroyer escort sinks Japanese submarine *RO-55* off Luzon.

During the night two motor torpedo boats enter Manila Bay to conduct reconnaissance. They are the first U.S. Navy vessels to return to Manila Bay since the fall of Corregidor in April 1942.

Master Sergeant Charles L. McGaha of G Company, 35th Infantry Regiment, 25th Infantry Division, is pinned down near Lubao, Luzon. His platoon and one other from Company G are pinned down in a roadside ditch by heavy fire from five tanks supported by 10 machine-guns and a platoon of Japanese infantry, When one of his soldiers is wounded 40 yards away, McGaha leaves cover to rescue him. Although wounded himself, he stays with his men. When the platoon leader is wounded, he assumes command and rallies his men. McGaha rescues another wounded man and deliberately draws enemy fire to allow another casualty to be rescued and taken to safety. Once he knows the platoon has pulled back safely, he returns to his men and collapses from his wounds. For his willingness to risk his life to save his soldiers, Master Sergeant McGaha will receive the Medal of Honor.

PACIFIC: Twentieth Air Force sends 67 B-29 Superfortresses to attack Saigon in French Indochina. Only 44 hit the primary target, although most miss the target area by dropping bombs prematurely. Others hit Phnom Penh and the marshaling yard at Martaban, Burma. Aircrews report one possible kill. One B-29 is lost. Another 64 B-29s are sent to bomb a bridge in Bangkok, Thailand. Most of the bombers hit the target, destroying the middle span of the bridge.

U.S. submarine *Ronquil* torpedoes and damages a Japanese cargo ship south of Kyushu, Japan.

CENTRAL PACIFIC: Seventh Air Force sends six B-24 Liberators from Saipan to bomb Haha Jima. Other B-24s bomb antiaircraft positions and radar positions on Iwo Jima. B-24s from Angaur Island bomb airfields on Negros Island in the Philippines. During the night nine B-24s conduct individual snooper missions on Iwo Jima.

BORNEO: FEAF B-24 Liberators bomb an airfield, an oil refinery pump station, and a power station house in Borneo.

February 8

ALEUTIANS: Naval Task Force 92, commanded by Rear Admiral John F. McCrea, with three light cruisers and seven destroyers, departs from Attu to bombard Matsuwa Island in the Kuriles.

CBI: In China, 10 P-51 Mustangs of Fourteenth Air Force attack bridges, rail lines, and airfields.

In Burma, Tenth Air Force sends 72 P-47 Thunderbolts to support ground forces. Other P-47s and P-38 Lightnings attack troop concentrations, logistics support areas, ammunition storage facilities, and targets of opportunity.

ATLANTIC: Argonaut—The Yalta Conference. President Roosevelt and Joseph Stalin meet privately without Prime Minister Churchill attending. The leaders come to an agreement that the Soviet Union will enter the war against Japan within a month after Germany surrenders. In return, Roosevelt agrees to the Soviet Union occupying the southern half of Sakhalin Island and taking possession of the Kurile Islands. Roosevelt also accepts the USSR's preeminent interests in Port Arthur and Port Dairen in China, the Chinese Eastern Railway, and the South Manchurian Railway.

ETO: Operation Veritable, Montgomery's offensive to clear German forces west of the Rhine River, begins with a 500,000-shell artillery barrage.

Ninth Air Force sends more than 300 A-20 Havocs, A-26 Invaders, and B-26 Marauders to attack roads, communication centers, railroad bridges, and marshaling yards in Germany. P-47 and P-38 fighters support XII Corps.

MEDITERRANEAN: Fifteenth Air Force sends more than 500 B-17s and B-24 Liberators escorted by over 270 P-38 Lightnings and P-51 Mustangs to attack communication targets and marshaling yards in Austria. Another 12 B-24s drop supplies in Yugoslavia, and 11 P-51s sweep the Zagreb area.

ITALY: After losing 700 men, the 92nd Infantry Division stops its attack and returns to its original starting point.

Twelfth Air Force B-25 Mitchells and B-26 Marauders attack bridges. P-47 Thunderbolts attack rail bridges and oil storage areas and support Fifth Army ground forces. A-20s attack roads and motor transport in the Po River valley.

SOUTHWEST PACIFIC AREA: U.S. submarine *Pampanito* attacks a Japanese convoy in the Gulf of Siam, sinking a gunboat off the southern end of French Indochina.

FEAF B-24 Liberators bomb airfields in Borneo.

The headquarters of the 309th Bombardment Wing (Heavy) redeploys from Schouten Islands to Luzon Island.

SOUTHWEST PACIFIC AREA, LUZON: In the I Corps area, the 6th Infantry Division is dispatched to Manila to come under the operational control of XIV Corps. The 25th Infantry Division takes over and advances east past San José toward Balete Pass.

In the Philippines, Far East Air Force B-24 Liberators bomb the Bataan Peninsula, and B-25 Mitchells attack several small vessels along the east coast of Bataan and also bomb Legaspi airfield.

The 421st Night Fighter Squadron of the 86th Fighter Wing redeploys from Leyte to Luzon with P-38 Lightnings and P-61 Black Widow night fighters.

PACIFIC: Twentieth Air Force sends 30 B-29s from the Mariana Islands to bomb an airfield on Moen Island in the Truk Atoll of the Carolines.

CENTRAL PACIFIC: Seventh Air Force sends 20 B-24 Liberators from Guam to bomb antiaircraft positions and radar sites on Iwo Jima.

During the night 10 B-24s conduct individual snooper missions on Iwo Jima.

February 9

CBI: The Chinese-American Composite Wing (CACW) P-40 fighters attack Tsingtao airfield. Fighter pilots report about 100 aircraft destroyed or damaged. Pilots also report several nearby locomotives destroyed in the raid.

In Burma, Tenth Air Force sends 10 B-25 Mitchells to bomb bridges. P-47 Thunderbolts support ground forces and attack bridges, troop concentrations, logistics storage sites, and communication targets.

ETO: SHAEF headquarters estimates that more than 22,000 German soldiers have become casualties in the battles to clear the west bank of the Rhine River.

The last remaining German forces in the Colmar Pocket escape across the Rhine. The operation to close the pocket has cost the Allies 18,000 casualties, including 8,000 from XXI Corps.

Eighth Air Force sends nearly 1,300 B-17s and B-24 Liberators escorted by over 800 P-47 Thunderbolts and P-51 Mustangs to attack oil production facilities, a munitions factory, and marshaling yards. The bombers use a combination of Pathfinder bombers, H2X radar, and Gee-H. A total of eight bombers are lost and 138 damaged. Aircrews report 61 confirmed kills, four probables, and 22 possibles. Aircrew casualties are 20 killed, nine wounded, and 74 missing. Fighter pilots report 19 confirmed kills, two probables, and one possible in the air and 37 confirmed kills and 13 possibles on the ground. Five fighters are lost, and two are damaged. Five pilots are reported missing.

A total of 33 P-51 Mustangs fly a scouting mission. Fighter pilots report five confirmed kills, one probable kill.

Ninth Air Force sends 347 A-20 Havocs, A-26 Invaders, and B-26 Marauders to attack railroad bridges and a marshaling yard. P-47 and P-38 fighters support XII Corps ground forces.

MEDITERRANEAN: Fifteenth Air Force sends one B-17 and 10 B-24 Liberators to drop supplies in northern Italy. A total of 11 B-24s drop supplies in Yugoslavia. P-38 Lightnings and P-51 Mustangs fly reconnaissance missions.

ITALY: During the night Twelfth Air Force A-20s and A-26 Invaders attack roads and motor transport in the Po River valley.

SOUTHWEST PACIFIC AREA: In the Philippines, Far East Air Force B-24 Liberators and A-20 Havocs bomb Corregidor Island. B-24 Liberators and A-20 Havocs bomb targets on the Bataan Peninsula. B-25 Mitchells and P-51 Mustangs attack shipping near Luzon and attack ground targets on Negros Island. A-24 Banshees and P-40s attack Japanese troops and attack bridges and roads in Luzon.

Private First Class John N. Reese, Jr., of B Company, 148th Infantry Regiment, 37th Infantry Division, is part of a platoon assigned to attack the Paco railroad station in Manila. The Japanese have 300 heavily armed infantrymen defending this critical location. The attack is halted 100 yards from the station by intense enemy fire. Reese and another soldier advance toward an enemy defensive position in a house 60 yards from the objective. Although under constant enemy observation, the two soldiers remain in this position for an hour, firing on the Japanese and killing more than 35. Advancing toward the station, they catch a group of Japanese soldiers unawares and kill more than 40, leaving some key emplacements unmanned. Reese purposely exposes himself to enemy fire while his comrade engages the enemy, killing another seven soldiers and destroying a 20 millimeter gun with hand grenades. As they begin to return to friendly lines to replenish their ammunition, Reese is killed. For his gallant determination in the face of tremendous odds, his aggressive fighting spirit, and extreme heroism at the cost of his life, Private First Class Reese will receive the nation's highest award for valor, the Medal of Honor.

PACIFIC: Twentieth Air Force sends 29 B-29 Superfortresses of the XXI Bomber Command to bomb the airfield at Moen Island on Truk Atoll, Carolines.

CENTRAL PACIFIC: Seventh Air Force sends 22 B-24 Liberators from Guam and Saipan to bomb antiaircraft positions, airfields, and radar sites on Iwo Jima.

During the night 11 B-24s from Saipan conduct harassment bombing runs on the island.

The headquarters of the 21st Fighter Group begins redeployment to Iwo Jima from Hawaii.

February 10

CBI: Chinese forces link with the Mars Task Force. The Japanese have escaped, reorganizing near Lashio. Detachment 101 commanded by Colonel William R. Peers continues operations against the Japanese along the Burma Road. He has 1,500 Kachin guerrillas and another 1,500 Karen, Chinese, Ghurka, and Shan volunteers.

In Burma, Tenth Air Force sends five B-25 Mitchells and P-47 Thunderbolts to bomb bridges. Other P-47s support ground forces and attack bridges, troop concentrations, logistics storage sites, and targets of opportunity.

ETO: The last of the Roer River dams is captured, but water at Schwammenauel dam has been released, causing limited flooding and delaying the Ninth Army attack until February 23.

Eighth Air Force sends nine B-17s to carry out the first Disney mission, using a rocket bomb developed by the Royal Navy. It is a 14-foot-long, hard-case stream-lined bomb weighing 4,500 pounds with a rocket motor in its tail. Because of its length and weight, the bombs are mounted on the wings of the B-17s. When dropped, the rocket motors ignite at 5,000 feet, accelerating the bombs to 2,400 feet per second on impact, allowing them to penetrate thick concrete before exploding. These bombs are used against the U-boat pens at Ijmuiden in the Netherlands, which are heavily fortified with concrete.

Another 140 B-17s attack the oil storage depot at Dulmen, Germany, using radar to identify the release point. Over 100 P-51 Mustangs escort the bombers. Five B-17s are damaged. Two P-51s are lost during a strafing mission.

During the night one B-17 and 11 B-24s drop leaflets over Germany and the Netherlands. One crewman is killed on the operation.

Five B-17s conduct screening missions to jam German radio interception efforts and conduct countermeasures against German radar sites.

Ninth Air Force sends more than 300 A-20 Havocs, A-26 Invaders, and B-26 Marauders to attack communication centers, rail bridges, and a vehicle depot. P-47 and P-38 fighters support VIII and XII Corps.

MEDITERRANEAN: Fifteenth Air Force sends 12 B-24 Liberators to drop supplies in Yugoslavia, while P-38 Lightnings fly reconnaissance and escort missions.

ITALY: Twelfth Air Force B-25 Mitchells bomb bridges. A-20 Havocs and P-47 Thunderbolts attack rail lines and vehicles. During the night A-20s and A-26 Invaders attack roads and motor transport in the Po River valley.

SOUTHWEST PACIFIC AREA: P-47 Thunderbolts conduct a fighter sweep over Formosa. Fighter pilots report 10 confirmed kills in the air. The headquarters of the 312th Bombardment Group (Light) and the 386th and 387th Bombardment Squadrons (Light) redeploy from Leyte Island to Luzon with A-20s.

Brigadier General Frederick H Smith, Jr., takes command of V Fighter Command.

SOUTHWEST PACIFIC AREA, LUZON: The 1st Cavalry Division crosses the Pasig River in Manila and links with the 37th Infantry Division.

Operational control of the 11th Airborne Division passes from Eighth Army to Sixth Army. The 11th Airborne encounters Japanese defensive positions south of Manila, known as the Genko Line, and attacks to capture Nichols Field.

Far East Air Force B-24 Liberators bomb Japanese gun positions, while P-51 Mustangs and P-38 Lightnings support ground forces on Luzon. B-24s, A-20 Havocs, P-38s, and P-47s attack targets on the Bataan Peninsula.

PACIFIC: Twentieth Air Force sends 118 B-29 Superfortresses from the Marianas to attack the Nakajima aircraft production facility at Ota, Japan. More than 80 bombers hit the primary target, and 14 attack other targets. Aircrews report 21 confirmed kills, 15 probables, and 26 possibles. American losses are 12 B-29s.

CENTRAL PACIFIC: Seventh Air Force sends 10 B-24 Liberators from Guam to bomb Haha Jima. Six P-39 Lightnings fly a sweep over Iwo Jima. Another 17 B-24s with P-38 escort hit Iwo Jima in the afternoon. During the night nine B-24s conduct harassment bombing runs on the island.

February 11

ALEUTIANS: Eleventh Air Force sends seven B-24 Liberators to provide air cover for a naval task force, but only three reach the target.

Naval Task Force 92 arrives off Matsuwa Island in the Kuriles but weather prevents any offensive action. The ships begin the return to Attu.

CBI: In China, Fourteenth Air Force sends 17 B-25 Mitchells to attack railroad yards at Sinyang and Lohochai and a locomotive foundry at Hsuchang. P-47 Thunderbolts attack Hankow and Anyang airfields. B-24 Liberators attack shipping in the South China Sea. Aircrews report two cargo ships sunk.

In Burma, Tenth Air Force sends 11 B-25 Mitchells to bomb troops and logistics storage sites. P-47 Thunderbolts support ground forces and attack Japanese positions, logistics storage sites, ammunition storage areas, and targets of opportunity.

ATLANTIC: Argonaut Conference Ends. Roosevelt, Churchill, and Stalin, and their military advisers, reach agreements on the occupation of Germany and Austria, including the creation of a French zone in Germany. Roosevelt and Stalin make a secret agreement on Soviet territorial gains in the Far East in return for Soviet participation in the war against Japan. A Declaration on Liberated Europe is issued in which the Allies commit to free elections and democratic governments in the countries freed from the Nazis. President Roosevelt, Prime Minister Churchill, and Premier Stalin make agreements on a broad-based government in Poland that will hold free and democratic elections. The borders of Poland are to be restructured, with the Soviet Union keeping the territory it gained in 1939. The future Polish state will have its borders expanded westward into Germany.

ETO: The XVIII Airborne Corps and its divisions are taken out of the line to prepare for an airborne assault in support of the 21st Army Group's crossing of the Rhine River. It is replaced with III Corps from Third Army, commanded by Major General John B. Millikin, with the 78th, 1st, and 9th Infantry Divisions and the 9th Armored Division.

Eighth Air Force sends 124 B-24 Liberators escorted by 50 P-51 Mustangs to attack the Dulmen oil depot. The bombers use radar to locate the bomb release point. Over 180 P-51s make a sweep over northwest Germany. One P-51 is lost, and the pilot is reported missing.

Ninth Air Force sends 97 A-20 Havocs and B-26 Marauders to attack marshaling yards. P-47 and P-38 fighters support XII Corps.

ITALY: Operation Fourth Term is a failure. After suffering 700 casualties, the 92nd Infantry Division is spent and unable to conduct further combat operations.

Twelfth Air Force B-25 Mitchells and B-26 Marauders attack rail and road traffic and bridges. A-20 Havocs and P-47 Thunderbolts of the XXII Tactical Air Command attack rail lines and bridges.

During the night A-20s attack roads and motor transport in the Po River valley and German defensive positions in the northern Apennines.

Southwest Pacific Area: In the Philippines, Far East Air Force B-24 Liberators bomb Corregidor Island. P-38 Lightnings and P-47 Thunderbolts support ground forces on Luzon. P-47s attack a train near Heito on Formosa. B-24 Liberators bomb targets on Negros Island.

The A-20 Havocs of the 388th and 389th Bombardment Squadrons (Light), 312th Bombardment Group (Light), redeploy from Mindoro Island to Luzon.

Japanese submarine *RO-50* torpedoes and sinks an LST in a convoy originating at Hollandia and headed for Leyte. The LST is hit off the west coast of Mindanao and is scuttled. The *RO-50* is damaged by gunfire.

U.S. submarine *Batfish* sinks Japanese submarine *RO-112* off northern Luzon.

Pacific: Twentieth Air Force sends 56 B-29s to bomb logistics storage areas around Rangoon, Burma. Aircrews report three possible kills. Twentieth Air Force sends nine B-29s from the Marianas to conduct reconnaissance for the U.S. Navy.

Twentieth Air Force B-29s from the Marianas and navy PB4Y Privateers conduct advance search missions to spot Japanese guardboats as Naval Task Force 58 (Vice Admiral Marc A. Mitscher) moves north toward Japan.

U.S. submarine *Burrfish* is damaged by depth charges and an air attack off the Bonins but remains on patrol.

Central Pacific: Seventh Air Force sends 21 B-24 Liberators from Saipan to bomb airfields and defenses on Iwo Jima Island. Three B-24s bomb Marcus Island. A total of 25 B-24s based at Angaur Island bomb Corregidor Island. During the night 10 B-24s from Saipan fly individual harassment raids on Iwo Jima.

February 12

CBI: In China, Fourteenth Air Force P-51 Mustangs destroy locomotives and strafe airfields. P-40s bomb troops and attack trains.

Tenth Air Force P-47 Thunderbolts support ground forces and severely damage a bridge. P-47s and P-38 Lightnings attack logistics support areas, troops, tanks, and trucks.

ETO: During the night Eighth Air Force sends six B-24s to drop leaflets over Germany and the Netherlands.

The headquarters of the 434th Troop Carrier Group and the C-47s of the 71st, 72nd, 73rd, and 74th Troop Carrier Squadrons, IX Troop Carrier Command, redeploy from England to France.

Italy: Twelfth Air Force P-47 Thunderbolts attack rail lines, bridges, gun positions, and roads in the Po River valley. During the night A-20s attack communication targets in the Po River Valley.

Southwest Pacific Area, Luzon: The 11th Airborne Division fights through mines, obstacles, and heavy gun emplacements to reach Nichols Field, supported by artillery and air bombardment.

Far East Air Force B-24 Liberators bomb Corregidor Island. A-20 Havocs sweep the Bataan Peninsula. Pilots report sinking about 30 barges loaded with troops, ammunition, and supplies. B-25 Mitchells and P-38 Lightnings support ground forces on the Bataan Peninsula and from the Lingayen Gulf area to Nichols Field.

The B-25s of the 498th, 499th, 500th, and 501st Bombardment Squadron (Medium), 345th Bombardment Group (Medium), redeploy from Leyte to Luzon.

PACIFIC: Twentieth Air Force sends 21 B-29 Superfortresses from the Marianas to bomb antiaircraft positions on Iwo Jima. Another 10 B-29s fly a reconnaissance mission for the navy.

CENTRAL PACIFIC: Seventh Air Force sends nine B-24 Liberators from Guam to bomb Chichi Jima Island, while 19 other B-24s bomb airfields and antiaircraft positions on Iwo Jima. During the night eight B-24s from Guam fly individual harassment raids on Iwo Jima.

NEW GUINEA: The P-38 Lightnings of the 67th Fighter Squadron, 347th Fighter Group, begin operating from Morotai Island.

U.S. submarine *Hawkbill* torpedoes and sinks a small Japanese cargo vessel and two large landing barges in Lombok Strait, Java.

February 13

CARIBBEAN: The B-24 Liberators of the 74th Bombardment Squadron (Heavy), VI Bomber Command, redeploy from the Galápagos Islands to Panama.

CBI: In China, Fourteenth Air Force P-51 Mustangs and P-40s conduct a sweep of airfields and bridges from Sinyang to Hsuchang.

In Burma, Tenth Air Force sends P-47 Thunderbolts to support ground forces and attack bridges, troop concentrations, logistics storage sites, and targets of opportunity.

ETO: During the night Eighth Air Force sends nine B-24s to drop leaflets over Germany and the Netherlands.

Ninth Air Force sends 320 A-20 Havocs, A-26 Invaders, and B-26 Marauders to attack railroad bridges, military transportation depots, and targets of opportunity. P-47 and P-38 fighters support troops in the Third Army area and fly armed reconnaissance missions.

The headquarters of the 435th Troop Carrier Group, IX Troop Carrier Command, redeploys from England to France.

MEDITERRANEAN: Fifteenth Air Force sends more than 600 B-17s and B-24 Liberators escorted by P-38 Lightnings and P-51 Mustangs to attack railyards and marshaling yards in Austria, Hungary, and Yugoslavia.

ITALY: Fifteenth Air Force fighters attack rail transportation, especially locomotives.

Twelfth Air Force B-25 Mitchells and B-26 Marauders attack bridges. A-20 Havocs and P-47 Thunderbolts of the XXII Tactical Air Command attack marshaling yards.

During the night A-20s attack roads and motor transport in the Po River valley.

SOUTHWEST PACIFIC AREA: In the Philippines, Far East Air Force B-24 Liberators bomb Corregidor Island and the Bataan Peninsula in conjunction with attacks by A-20 Havocs and P-47 Thunderbolts. B-25 Mitchells and P-38s conduct shipping sweeps on the north and east coasts of Luzon. B-25s, with P-47s in support, bomb Kagi airfield on Formosa.

The headquarters of the 345th Bombardment Group (Medium) redeploys from Leyte to Luzon.

U.S. submarine *Batfish* sinks Japanese submarine *RO-113* off the Babuyan Islands north of Luzon.

Private First Class Manuel Perez, Jr., is the lead scout for A Company, 511th Parachute Infantry, 11th Airborne Division, before Fort William McKinley on Luzon. Perez leads the company in destroying a series of fortified defensive positions covering the approach to the fort. During the attack Perez kills five Japanese soldiers and attacks pillboxes with grenades. As he approaches the largest pillbox in the defensive line, he moves toward the rear of the position, killing another four enemy soldiers in the process, then throws grenades into the pillbox. Firing his M-1 rifle at the retreating defenders, he eliminates four but fights with a Japanese rifle when he runs out of ammunition. He then fights the last remaining defenders in hand-to-hand combat. For his courageous actions and extraordinary fighting spirit, Private First Class Perez will be awarded the Medal of Honor

PACIFIC: South of Honshu, Japan, U.S. submarine *Sennet* is damaged by gunfire from a Japanese guardboat after damaging the guardboat with a torpedo attack in coordination with USS *Lagarto*. USS *Sennet* sinks another guardboat, which had been damaged by *Lagarto* and *Haddock*. USS *Haddock* then sinks the damaged guardboat first hit by *Sennet*.

CENTRAL PACIFIC: Seventh Air Force sends 25 B-24 Liberators from Saipan to bomb airfields, antiaircraft positions, and radar sites on Iwo Jima Island. Another 10 B-24s bomb Haha Jima. During the night five B-24s fly individual harassment raids on Iwo Jima.

NEW GUINEA: The P-38 Lightnings of the 339th Fighter Squadron, 347th Fighter Group, begin operating from Morotai Island.

February 14

ALEUTIANS: Eleventh Air Force sends three B-24 Liberators to bomb and photograph Suribachi airfield on Paramushiru Island in the Kuriles.

CBI: Lieutenant General Albert C. Wedemeyer submits to Chiang Kai-shek his plan for a Chinese offensive based on Plan Alpha. The plan is intended to recapture Liuchow and Nanning, followed by an offensive to capture Hong Kong and Canton. Chiang approves the outlined concept.

In China, Fourteenth Air Force P-47 Thunderbolts and P-51 Mustangs attack airfields. Fighter pilots report several confirmed kills on the ground. P-51s attack 14 locomotives and report destroying a fuel storage site.

In Burma, Tenth Air Force sends 12 B-25 Mitchells to attack vehicles along roads from Lashio to Hopong.

ATLANTIC: German submarine *U-711* torpedoes and damages a U.S. freighter at the entrance to Kola Inlet in the Barents Sea.

ETO: Eighth Air Force sends more than 1,300 B-17s and B-24 Liberators escorted by over 900 P-51 Mustangs to attack oil production facilities, airfields, and marshaling yards in Germany and Czechoslovakia. One of the targets is the marshaling yards at Dresden, a city heavily damaged in a previous raid by RAF bombers. Most of the bombers use radar to identify the release point over their targets. A total of seven bombers are lost and 103 are damaged. Aircrews report 11 confirmed kills and three probables. Aircrew casualties are six killed, 19 wounded, and 72 missing. Fighter pilots report 10 confirmed kills and three possibles in the air. Seven P-51s are lost and two damaged. The seven pilots are reported missing.

During the night 10 B-24s drop leaflets over Germany and the Netherlands.

Ninth Air Force sends more than 600 A-20 Havocs, A-26 Invaders, and B-26 Marauders to attack communication centers, railroad bridges, an ammunition storage area, and a marshaling yard. P-47 and P-38 fighters support ground forces in the Third Army area and fly armed reconnaissance missions.

MEDITERRANEAN: Fifteenth Air Force sends more than 500 B-17s and B-24 Liberators escorted by P-38 Lightnings and P-51 Mustangs to attack oil refineries in Austria and marshaling yards in Yugoslavia.

ITALY: Twelfth Air Force B-25 Mitchells and B-26 Marauders attack bridges and gun positions. A-20 Havocs and P-47 Thunderbolts attacks communication targets in the Po River valley. During the night A-20s attack bridges and targets of opportunity in the Po River Valley.

SOUTHWEST PACIFIC AREA, LUZON: The 152nd Infantry Regiment of the 38th Infantry Division battles Japanese defenders in concrete emplacements and caves at Zig Zag Pass on Highway 7. Supported by napalm strikes, and a simultaneous attack from the rear of the Japanese defenses by the 149th Infantry Regiment, the infantrymen clear the pass and open the way to Manila Bay. More than 2,400 Japanese are killed and 25 taken prisoner. American losses are over 1,400 killed.

In Manila, the Japanese are trapped in a small pocket along the shore of Manila Bay. The 37th Infantry Division, reinforced with a brigade of the 1st Cavalry Division, is tasked with clearing Manila. The rest of the 1st Cavalry is to move east to capture Fort McKinley, reinforced by the 6th Infantry Division, which has passed from the operational control of I Corps to XIV Corps. The 11th Airborne Division is to support the attack on Fort McKinley, then clear Japanese forces south and east to Laguna de Bay.

The 40th Infantry Division has cleared the Kembu Group out of its defenses in the hills beyond Clark Field and Fort Stotsenburg and thus secures the XIV Corps line of supply. Over 4,400 Japanese soldiers have been killed.

Far East Air Force B-24 Liberators bomb Corregidor Island and B-24s, and A-20 Havocs bomb Bataan Peninsula. B-25 Mitchells and P-38 Lightnings bomb airfields and ground support forces. B-25s bomb barges on Mindanao Island, and P-38s bomb an airfield. P-38s and P-47 Thunderbolts flying armed reconnaissance missions strafe airfields on Negros and Cebu Islands. B-25 Mitchells bomb Kagi airfield and targets of opportunity on Formosa.

Two U.S. support landing craft are sunk by shore batteries off Luzon.

Mines damage two U.S. destroyers south of Manila Bay.

A Japanese hospital ship is damaged by a mine in Singapore Strait.

Japanese shore batteries sink a minesweeper and damage two destroyers (USS *Fletcher* and USS *Hopewell*) north of Corregidor. On board USS *Fletcher*, Watertender First Class Elmer C. Bigelow, without any protective gear, fights a fire in the number-one gun magazine that threatens to destroy the ship. Bigelow unselfishly sacrifices himself to save his ship and his shipmates. His act of courage will win him the Medal of Honor.

PACIFIC: Twentieth Air Force sends six B-29 Superfortresses from the Marianas on a reconnaissance mission for the navy.

U.S. submarine *Gato* torpedoes and sinks a Japanese coast defense vessel in the Yellow Sea. U.S. submarines *Haddock, Lagarto,* and *Sennet* damage a Japanese guardboat south of Honshu, Japan. A Japanese cargo ship is sunk by a mine west of Kyushu, Japan.

CENTRAL PACIFIC: Seventh Air Force sends 17 B-24 Liberators from Guam to bomb airfields, antiaircraft positions, and radar sites on Iwo Jima Island. During the night five B-24s conduct individual snooper missions on Iwo Jima.

NEW GUINEA: The headquarters of the 54th Troop Carrier Wing redeploys from Biak to Leyte Island. The 550th Night Fighter Squadron, XIII Fighter Command (under operational control of XIII Bomber Command), redeploys from Hollandia to Morotai Island with P-38 Lightnings, P-61 Black Widow night fighters, and P-70 Havocs (converted night fighters).

U.S. submarine *Hawkbill* torpedoes and sinks two Japanese auxiliary submarine chasers in the Java Sea.

February 15

CBI: Fourteenth Air Force P-51 Mustangs attack Shihkiachuang airfield. The eight fighter pilots report four confirmed kills on the ground. This attack ends an offensive by P-51 Mustangs of the 530th Fighter Squadron operating from Sian airfield. The pilots report a total of 37 confirmed kills and 24 probables in the air and 130 confirmed kills and 22 probable kills on the ground as well as 517 locomotives destroyed since the offensive began on November 7, 1944. The squadron begins to redeploy to Kwanghan for rest and refitting.

In Burma, Tenth Air Force sends 12 B-25 Mitchells to attack buildings, troops, and other targets of opportunity.

ETO: Eighth Air Force sends more than 1,100 B-17s and B-24 Liberators escorted by over 500 P-47 Thunderbolts and P-51 Mustangs to attack oil production facilities and marshaling yards in Germany. The bombers use radar to find the release point for their targets. The city of Dresden is again bombed as a target of opportunity. German authorities report to Berlin that 500,000 people are without shelter. Tens of thousands have been killed. A total of two bombers are lost and 82 are damaged. Aircrews report two confirmed kills. Aircrew casualties are nine killed, 11 wounded, and 12 missing. Fighter pilots report two confirmed kills in the air. Four fighters are lost. The four pilots are reported missing.

Ninth Air Force sends 90 A-20 Havocs, A-26 Invaders, and B-26 Marauders to attack railroad bridges and targets of opportunity. P-47 and P-38 fighters support ground forces of the VII, VIII, XII, and XX Corps.

MEDITERRANEAN: Fifteenth Air Force sends more than 650 B-17s and B-24 Liberators escorted by P-38 Lightnings and P-51 Mustangs to attack oil refineries and marshaling yards in Austria and shipyards in Fiume, Italy.

ITALY: Twelfth Air Force B-25 Mitchells and B-26 Marauders attack an ammunition storage area. A-20 Havocs and P-47 Thunderbolts bomb rail lines.

SOUTHWEST PACIFIC AREA: Far East Air Force B-25 Mitchells attack bridges in southern Formosa.

SOUTHWEST PACIFIC AREA, LUZON: Naval Task Group 78.3, commanded by Rear Admiral Arthur D. Struble, lands the 151st Infantry Regiment of the 38th Infantry Division, reinforced by 3rd Battalion, 34th RCT, of the 24th Infantry Division, at Mariveles on Bataan to seal off the peninsula. The 1st RCT of the 6th Infantry Division, now attached to XI Corps, moves south along the east highway.

FEAF B-24 Liberators, A-20 Havocs, and P-47 Thunderbolts bomb Corregidor Island. B-25 Mitchells and A-20s attack the Bataan Peninsula, hit troops and gun positions near Fort William McKinley, and bomb airfields.

PACIFIC: The Japanese Imperial General Headquarters submits a report on the war situation to the Supreme War Council. Despite difficulties raised by the American offensives in the Marianas and the Philippines, Japan has the means to continue to fight as long as her people have the courage and determination to do so. It is apparent that the United States is planning for an invasion of the Japanese home islands. The estimate is that the Americans will land on Kyushu first. Defenses are prepared and reinforcements are sent that will build to a total of 900,000 troops defending the island.

After conducting final rehearsals, V Amphibious Corps landing forces leave the Mariana Islands for Iwo Jima.

Twentieth Air Force sends 117 B-29 Superfortresses from the Marianas to bomb the Mitsubishi aircraft engine production facility at Nagoya, Japan. Only 33 hit the primary target; 68 others bomb targets of opportunity. Aircrews report seven confirmed kills, eight probables, and 23 possibles. American losses are one B-29.

Carrier aircraft from Vice Admiral Marc A. Mitscher's Naval Task Force 58 sink two Japanese guardboats off eastern Honshu, Japan.

CENTRAL PACIFIC: Seventh Air Force sends 24 B-24 Liberators from Saipan to bomb Iwo Jima airfields and antiaircraft positions. Another 12 B-24s bomb the airfield on Chichi Jima. Four B-24s from Guam, escorting photo aircraft over Truk Atoll, bomb airfields on Param and Moen Islands. During the night five B-24s fly harassment raids against Iwo and Chichi Jima.

NEW GUINEA: The C-46s of the 68th Troop Carrier Squadron, 433rd Troop Carrier Group, redeploy from Biak to Leyte Island.

February 16

CBI: In China, Fourteenth Air Force P-51s and P-40s attack airfields in the Nanking area, railyards, and rail and river traffic.

In Burma, Tenth Air Force sends 12 B-25 Mitchells to bomb troops, logistics storage sites, and vehicles. P-47 Thunderbolts and P-38 Lightnings support ground forces and attack town areas, troop concentrations, artillery positions, transportation targets, and targets of opportunity.

ETO: Eighth Air Force sends more than 1,000 B-17s and B-24 Liberators escorted by nearly 200 P-51 Mustangs to attack oil refineries, benzol production facilities, and marshaling yards in central Germany. The bombers use a combination of radar and visual means to locate the release points on the targets. A total of eight bombers are lost and 293 damaged. Aircrew casualties are 15 wounded, and 67 missing.

Six B-24 Liberators conduct screening missions to jam German radio interception efforts and conduct countermeasures against German radar sites.

Ninth Air Force sends 300 A-20 Havocs, A-26 Invaders, and B-26 Marauders to attack communication centers, an ordnance depot, a turbo-jet component production facility, and targets of opportunity. P-47 and P-38 fighters support the VIII, XII, and XX Corps.

The C-47s of the 77th Troop Carrier Squadron, 435th Troop Carrier Group, IX Troop Carrier Command, redeploy from England to France.

MEDITERRANEAN: Fifteenth Air Force sends more than 600 B-17s and B-24 Liberators escorted by P-38 Lightnings and P-51 Mustangs to attack airfields and marshaling yards in Germany, and marshaling yards in Austria and Italy. Over 260 B-24 Liberators bomb the jet airfield and aircraft production facility at Regensburg. Twenty German jet aircraft (Me-262s) are destroyed on the ground.

ITALY: Twelfth Air Force A-20 Havocs and P-47 Thunderbolts attack rail lines, fuel storage areas, and ammunition storage areas.

SOUTHWEST PACIFIC AREA: Far East Air Force P-47 Thunderbolts attack vehicles and trains in southern Formosa.

A PB4Y-1 Privateer sinks a Japanese cargo ship off French Indochina.

SOUTHWEST PACIFIC AREA, LUZON: After a heavy air and naval bombardment, over 2,000 men of the 503rd Parachute Regimental Combat Team conduct an airborne assault on Corregidor Island, jumping from 500 feet and dropping six to eight men each time in multiple passes. Motor torpedo boats rescue paratroopers who land in the water, and six destroyers provide naval gunfire support. The 3rd Battalion of the 34th Infantry Division conducts an amphibious landing at San José Bay and captures the top of Malinta Hill. The Japanese fight back fiercely, threatening to overwhelm the paratroopers' perimeter at Topside, but the American forces link and hold their positions. About 6,000 Japanese troops are on the island, far above the estimated strength of 850.

In the I Corps area the 33rd Infantry Division relieves the 43rd Infantry Division on the left flank of the corps and begins a series of night attacks against Japanese positions in the high ground overlooking the Rosario-Pozorrubio Road.

FEAF A-20 Havocs and B-24 Liberators bomb Corregidor prior to the amphibious and airborne landings. B-25 Mitchells support ground forces on Luzon. P-38 Lightnings attack airfields on Mindanao Island.

PACIFIC: Task Force 58 under command of Vice Admiral Marc A. Mitscher sends carrier aircraft to attack airfields and aircraft production facilities near Tokyo.

Carrier aircraft from Task Force 58 bomb airfields, aircraft production facilities, and shipping around Tokyo.

Rear Admiral John L. McCrea's Task Force 92 bombards Japanese installations at Paramushiru in the Kuriles.

U.S. submarine *Sennet* torpedoes and sinks a Japanese minelayer southeast of Honshu, Japan. USS *Sennet* is damaged by air attack.

CENTRAL PACIFIC: During the night Seventh Air Force sends four B-24 Liberators from Guam to bomb the airfield on Chichi Jima.

Fire support vessels and carrier aircraft begin a three-day prelanding bombardment of Iwo Jima.

NEW GUINEA: FEAF B-24 Liberators attack an airfield on Celebes Island.

February 17

ALEUTIANS: Eleventh Air Force sends four B-25 Mitchells to provide air cover for a naval task force en route to Paramushiru Island in the Kuriles.

CBI: In China, Fourteenth Air Force sends 30 B-25 Mitchells to bomb Linfen and Yuncheng. P-40s and P-51 Mustangs attack animal transport, barracks, railroad targets, and the town area at Puchi. P-47 Thunderbolts attack railyards and road and river traffic.

In Burma, Tenth Air Force P-47 Thunderbolts support ground forces and attack troop concentrations, tanks, ammunition storage sites, and targets of opportunity.

ATLANTIC: German submarine *U-300* torpedoes and damages a U.S. freighter in convoy UGS-72 (United States to Mediterranean Slow) near Gibraltar. The freighter is able to continue with the convoy.

SOUTHWEST PACIFIC AREA: Fifth Air Force B-24 Liberators on an antishipping sweep over the South China Sea, sink a Japanese landing ship off the southern coast of Formosa.

SOUTHWEST PACIFIC AREA, LUZON: The 503rd Parachute Regimental Combat Team and the 3rd Battalion of the 34th Infantry Division split Corregidor in two. Additional paratroopers arrive by landing craft at San José Bay from Subic Bay. The Japanese make a determined resistance in the ruins of the old American fortress, as their positions are methodically destroyed one at a time.

On Bataan, the 151st Infantry Regiment of the 38th Infantry Division occupies the southern half of the peninsula.

Two light cruisers and three destroyers provide fire support for the battle to take Corregidor. A light cruiser and two destroyers bombard the south shore of Manila Bay.

PACIFIC: U.S. submarine *Bowfin* torpedoes and sinks a Japanese coastal defense vessel off central Honshu, Japan. Later, *Bowfin* and Navy aircraft sink a guardboat south of Honshu.

CENTRAL PACIFIC, IWO JIMA: Fire support ships, minesweeping units, and underwater demolition teams (UDT) arrive off Iwo Jima. Landing craft supporting navy and marine underwater demolition teams (UDT) fire rockets and guns at the beaches. The Japanese, believing this to be the main assault, open fire from previously hidden shore batteries. Shore batteries sink an infantry landing craft supporting UDT operations. U.S. battleships, destroyers, and cruisers destroy many of the guns. The UDT frogmen find no obstacles on the approaches to the beaches. The landing craft take heavy punishment from the Japanese guns as they work to collect the frogmen. U.S. casualties on the landing craft are 47 killed and 153 wounded. One destroyer is hit by enemy fire, resulting in seven sailors killed and 33 wounded.

The battleship USS *Tennessee,* a heavy cruiser, and a destroyer are damaged by gunfire. Eleven infantry landing craft (gunboats) intended to provide fire support are damaged.

ETO: Eighth Air Force sends nearly 900 B-17s and B-24 Liberators escorted by 183 P-51 Mustangs to bomb synthetic oil production facilities and marshaling yards. Most of the bombers abort the mission due to bad weather. The weather is so cold that aircraft controls freeze. Five bombers are lost and 108 are damaged. Aircrew casualties are 17 killed, two wounded, and 38 missing. One P-51 is lost and one is damaged. The pilot is reported missing.

Ninth Air Force sends 31 B-26 Marauders to attack a railroad bridge.

MEDITERRANEAN: Fifteenth Air Force sends more than 500 B-17s and B-24 Liberators escorted by P-38 Lightnings and P-51 Mustangs to attack a steel plant, a benzol production facility, a tank production facility, and a marshaling yard in Austria and the harbors at Trieste and Fiume in Italy.

ITALY: The 10th Mountain Division attacks on a four-mile front to clear Route 64 of enemy observers. Monte Belvedere and Monte Torracia are the objectives.

Twelfth Air Force B-25 Mitchells and B-26 Marauders bomb bridges. A-20 Havocs and P-47 Thunderbolts of the XXII Tactical Air Command attack bridges and communication targets in the Po River valley and bomb logistics storage areas and gun positions near Bologna.

SOUTHWEST PACIFIC AREA: Far East Air Force B-24 Liberators, with P-47 Thunderbolts providing support, attack the airfield, railyard, and aluminum plant at Takao, Formosa.

FEAF B-24 Liberators bomb an airfield in Borneo. The headquarters of the 375th Troop Carrier Group moves from Biak in New Guinea to Mindoro Island in the Philippines.

SOUTHWEST PACIFIC AREA, LUZON: The 149th and 151st Infantry Regiments of the 38th Infantry Division and the 1st RCT of the 6th Infantry Division link, eliminating all organized resistance on Bataan. The 1st RCT returns to the operational control of XIV Corps.

FEAF A-20 Havocs support ground forces and attack caves and dugouts in hills near Fort Stotsenburg. A-20s, B-25 Mitchells, and P-38 Lightnings attack targets throughout Luzon.

PACIFIC: Twentieth Air Force sends eight B-29 Superfortresses from Saipan to bomb the submarine pens on Dublon Island at Truk.

A U.S. destroyer rams a Japanese guardboat south of Kyushu, Japan. A destroyer sinks a Japanese auxiliary submarine chaser northwest of Iwo Jima, but sustains some damage from gunfire during the battle. A kamikaze damages a light minelayer south of Iwo Jima. Task Force 58 carrier aircraft sink a Japanese gunboat near Chichi Jima.

Three destroyers sink three Japanese guardboats south of Honshu, Japan.

CENTRAL PACIFIC: Seventh Air Force sends 42 B-24 Liberators from Saipan to bomb airfields and a bivouac site on Iwo Jima Island. Three B-24s from Guam bomb Truk. During the night five B-24s from Saipan fly individual snooper missions on Chichi Jima.

The P-61 Black Widow night fighters of the 548th Night Fighter Squadron, VII Fighter Command, begin operating from Saipan.

CENTRAL PACIFIC, IWO JIMA: Rear Admiral William H. P. Blandy decides to concentrate the pre-assault naval bombardment of the amphibious support force on the landing beaches. Over 200 targets are destroyed or heavily damaged. The marines will face over 21,000 well-trained and well-led Japanese soldiers sheltered in caves and tunnels nearly impervious to the bombardment.

February 19

ALEUTIANS: Eleventh Air Force sends seven B-24 Liberators to fly cover sorties for a naval force during its approach to Kurabu Cape, Paramushiru Island, in the Kuriles.

CBI: In China, Fourteenth Air Force P-40s and P-51 Mustangs attack airfields, railroad yards, and targets of opportunity. Four B-24 Liberators bomb shipping in the South China Sea. Aircrews report two vessels damaged.

The B-24s of the 374th, 375th, and 425th Bombardment Squadrons (Heavy), 308th Bombardment Group (Heavy), redeploy from Chengkung and Kunming to Kwanghan.

In Burma, Tenth Air Force sends 12 B-25 Mitchells to bomb bridges. P-47 Thunderbolts support ground forces and attack bridges, troop concentrations, logistics storage sites, and targets of opportunity.

ETO: The XX Corps (the 26th and 94th Infantry Divisions and the 10th Armored Division) of Third Army attacks north between the Saar and Moselle Rivers, catching the Germans by surprise, and advances toward Saarbourg.

Ninth Air Force sends more than 60 B-26 Marauders to attack a railroad bridge and targets of opportunity in support of operations to isolate the Ruhr.

MEDITERRANEAN: Fifteenth Air Force sends 160 B-17s escorted by 20 P-38 Lightnings to bomb a benzol production facility and a marshaling yard in Austria. Other missions are aborted because of weather.

ITALY: Operation Encore begins. The Fifth Army attempts to open routes into the Po River valley. The 1st Battalion, 86th Infantry Regiment of the 10th Mountain Division drives the enemy off Riva Ridge.

Fifteenth Air Force fighters report 31 locomotives, 25 rail cars, and 17 vehicles destroyed.

Twelfth Air Force A-20 Havocs and P-47 Thunderbolts attack rail lines, ammunition storage areas, and bridges in the Po River valley. During the night A-20s attack towns and bridges in the Po River valley.

SOUTHWEST PACIFIC AREA: Far East Air Force B-24 Liberators and B-25 Mitchells bomb Takao, Okayama, and Toshien airfields on Formosa. P-38 Lightnings provide support.

FEAF B-24 Liberators bomb an airfield in Borneo.

SOUTHWEST PACIFIC AREA, LUZON: Elements of the 1st Cavalry Division capture Fort McKinley.

FEAF B-25 Mitchells, P-38 Lightnings, and P-47 Thunderbolts fly numerous missions in support of the ground forces on Luzon.

Private Lloyd G. McCarter, a paratrooper in the 503rd Parachute Infantry Regiment, landed on Corregidor on February 16 and, after getting out of his parachute harness, immediately attacked a Japanese machine-gun firing 30 yards away from where he landed. Over the next days and nights, he eliminates snipers and ambushes Japanese infiltrators trying to bypass his company. By the early morning of the 19th, relentless enemy attacks have reduced the paratroopers' position to only a few unwounded men. McCarter protects his comrades, shouting encouragement and attacking the enemy single-handedly, then returning to his own lines to replenish his ammunition. When his Thompson submachine gun fails him, he picks up a discarded Browning Automatic Rifle and continues the fight. When it ceases to operate, he picks up an M-1 rifle. By dawn McCarter is still fighting as the Japanese prepare to overwhelm the position he has defended. Locating the enemy, he is seriously wounded, but refuses to be evacuated until he can pass the information about the enemy location to other leaders. For his example of courage under fire, indomitable fighting spirit, and dedication to duty, Private McCarter will receive the nation's highest award for valor, the Medal of Honor.

PACIFIC: Twentieth Air Force sends 36 B-29 Superfortresses from the Marianas to bomb airfields on Moen Island in Truk Atoll. The headquarters of the 39th and 330th Bombardment Groups (Very Heavy) and the B-29s of the 457th, 458th, and 459th Bombardment Squadrons (Very Heavy) arrive at Guam from the United States. The squadrons' first missions are scheduled for mid-April.

The 5th Marine Division lands on Red Beach 1 on Iwo Jima under heavy Japanese fire, February 19, 1945. The marines will move with great difficulty through the deep and soft black sand.

CENTRAL PACIFIC, IWO JIMA: Operation Detachment Begins. In overall command of the operation is Admiral Raymond A. Spruance, Commander Fifth Fleet; Vice Admiral Richmond K. Turner is Joint Expeditionary Force Commander. Supported by naval and air bombardment that carpets the landing beaches, the 4th and 5th Marine Divisions land abreast simultaneously on Iwo Jima. Within several minutes over 6,000 marines are on the beach. Soft volcanic sand and heavy surf cause the rapid accumulation of men and equipment on the landing beaches. The 28th Marines of the 5th Marine Division advance rapidly 700 yards to the western edge of the island. The 27th Marines advance under heavy fire toward the airfield. Tanks are unable to move in the soft sand, leaving the infantry alone to advance against pillboxes and hidden firing positions. The 23rd and 25th Marines of the 4th Division encounter strong defenses. The 25th Marines advance only 300 yards against Japanese positions at the Rock Quarry. Japanese artillery now begins to hit the beach landing areas with a steady and devastating bombardment. The 26th Marines of the 5th Division and the 24th Marines of the 4th Division land shortly after noon as casualties from the landing force begin to mount. Unloading heavy artillery in the soft sand while under continuous bombardment consumes time and energy, slowing the pace of the landing. The beachhead becomes an enormous collection of human and materiel wreckage.

Shore battery fire damages a destroyer. Japanese mortar fire damages four medium landing ships.

The 3rd Battalion, 25th Marines, 4th Division, captures the cliffs before the Rock Quarry on the far right flank of the division. The battalion has lost over 500 men to capture the position. At the end of the first day, the marines have moved between 500 and 1,000 yards inland at the cost of over 2,400 men. There are now 30,000 marines on Iwo awaiting a night counterattack that does not come. Instead,

Mount Suribachi looms over marines on Iwo Jima, February 19, 1945.

there is a steady barrage of artillery fire and numerous infiltrators prowling around the marine positions.

Corporal Tony Stein of A Company, 1st Battalion, 28th Marine Regiment, 5th Marine Division, is one of the first men of his company on the beach at Iwo Jima. Corporal Stein has rigged a weapon from an aircraft, which he carries into battle. It proves to be very worthwhile because of its high volume of fire. He provides suppressive fire for his platoon, standing in full view of the enemy, and locates Japanese positions. He then charges forward toward the pillboxes and kills 20 Japanese soldiers. Maintaining the high rate of fire for his weapon causes him to run back to the beach and replenish his ammunition eight separate times; each time he returns to the beach, he brings a wounded marine with him. Throughout the day's brutal and confused fighting Corporal Stein and his special weapon provide support to the platoon. Corporal Stein's amazing performance, initiative, courage, and devotion to duty in the face of terrific odds will be recognized with the Medal of Honor.

CENTRAL PACIFIC: During the night Seventh Air Force sends nine B-24 Liberators from Guam to individual harassment raids on Chichi Jima.

February 20

CBI: In China, Fourteenth Air Force P-40s and P-51 Mustangs attack locomotives, rail cars, and river traffic.

In Burma, Tenth Air Force P-47 Thunderbolts severely damage a bridge. P-38 Lightnings and P-47s support ground forces and attack troop concentrations, logistics storage sites, ammunition storage areas, and targets of opportunity.

ETO: Eighth Air Force sends nearly 1,300 B-17s and B-24 Liberators escorted by 726 P-51 Mustangs to bomb the marshaling yard at Nürnberg, Germany. The bombers use a combination of visual sighting and radar to locate the bomb release point. Five bombers are lost and 244 damaged. Aircrews report 49 confirmed kills, one probable kill, and 21 possibles. Aircrew casualties are 12 killed, 12 wounded, and 47 missing. Fighter pilots report 14 confirmed kills and one possible in the air and 43 confirmed kills, one probable, and 22 possibles on the ground. A total of 13 P-51s are lost. All the pilots are reported missing.

During the night 10 B-24s drop leaflets over Germany and the Netherlands. Another six B-24s fly a Carpetbagger mission.

Ninth Air Force P-47 and P-38 fighters support the VII, XII, and XX Corps.

The headquarters of the 53rd Troop Carrier Wing, IX Troop Carrier Command, redeploys from England to France.

MEDITERRANEAN: Fifteenth Air Force sends more than 500 B-17s and B-24 Liberators escorted by P-38 Lightnings and P-51 Mustangs to attack a steel plant, oil refineries, and marshaling yards in Austria, a harbor facility in Yugoslavia, and the shipyards at Trieste and Fiume in Italy.

ITALY: Twelfth Air Force B-25 Mitchells and B-26 Marauders bomb bridges. A-20 Havocs and P-47 Thunderbolts attack German positions near Monte Torraccia in support of Fifth Army. During the night A-20s attack marshaling yards in the Po River valley.

The First Tactical Air Force (Provisional) in France takes operational control of the 27th and 86th Fighter Groups from Twelfth Air Force. The headquarters of the 86th Fighter Group redeploys from Italy to France.

SOUTHWEST PACIFIC AREA: U.S. submarine *Guavina* attacks a Japanese convoy off the southern coast of French Indochina and damages a merchant tanker. U.S. submarine *Pargo* torpedoes and sinks a Japanese destroyer off the southern coast of French Indochina.

U.S. submarine *Hawkbill* attacks a Japanese convoy in the South China Sea northwest of Singapore and sinks a cargo ship. U.S. submarine *Pintado* is damaged in an aerial attack in the Gulf of Siam, but remains on patrol.

FEAF B-24 Liberators bomb runways and a warehouse at an airfield in Borneo.

The headquarters of the 380th Bombardment Group (Heavy) redeploys from Darwin, Australia, to Mindoro Island in the Philippines. The B-24s of the 23rd Bombardment Squadron (Heavy), 5th Bombardment Group (Heavy), redeploy from Morotai Island in New Guinea to Samar Island in the Philippines.

SOUTHWEST PACIFIC AREA, LUZON: Two of the 1st Cavalry Division's brigade combat teams cross the Marikina River, supported on their left flank by the 6th Infantry Division. The Shimbu Group holds the hills east of the river. The Shimbu positions occupy about 30 miles of the high ground overlooking the city of Manila and are defended by 30,000 troops. General Krueger assembles the 6th Infantry Division, the 43rd Infantry Division, elements of the 1st Cavalry Division, and the 112th Cavalry RCT for an offensive against the Japanese defenders. The objective of the offensive is to gain control of the water supply for the city of Manila, collected behind dams on the Angat and Marikina rivers. The Sixth Army planners believe that the Wawa Dam is one of the critical objectives. In reality most of Manila's water comes from the Ipo Dam in the Marikina River Valley. The 6th Infantry Division is to attack to capture the Wawa Dam. The 2nd Cavalry Brigade of the 1st Cavalry Division is to capture Antipolo. The 11th Airborne Division, reinforced by the 158th RCT, prepares to clear the area south of Manila.

Far East Air Force B-24 Liberators bomb Corregidor Island.

B-25 Mitchells and P-38 Lightnings attack the town of Choshu and railyards, vehicles, rail cars, and buildings on Formosa.

CENTRAL PACIFIC: During the night Seventh Air Force sends seven B-24 Liberators to fly individual harassment raids on Haha Jima.

The P-61 Black Widow night fighters of the 549th Night Fighter Squadron, VII Fighter Command, begin operating from Saipan.

CENTRAL PACIFIC, IWO JIMA: The 28th Marines of the 5th Division attack to seize Mount Suribachi, advancing 200 yards and destroying 40 enemy positions. The 26th and 27th Marines attack across the airfield, taking heavy casualties. The 25th Marines, reinforced by a battalion from the 24th Marines, fights the Japanese in the Rock Quarry on the 4th Division's right flank. The 23rd Marines advance 800 yards across the airfield. Major General Harry Schmidt attempts to commit the 21st Marines from the 3rd Division, but the seas are so rough that they are unable to land. Heavy surf destroys 34 LVTs, and 88 more sink in deep water.

An LST and a medium landing ship are damaged by Japanese mortar fire.

February 21

CBI: Fourteenth Air Force P-40s and P-51 Mustangs attack troops and rail and river traffic in southern and eastern China.

In Burma, Tenth Air Force P-47 Thunderbolts and P-38 Lightnings support ground forces and attack bridges, troop concentrations, logistics storage sites, and roads.

ETO: Eighth Air Force sends more than 1,200 B-17s and B-24 Liberators escorted by nearly 800 P-47 Thunderbolts and P-51 Mustangs to bomb a tank production facility, marshaling yards, and locomotive repair shops at Nürnberg, Germany. The bombers use radar to locate the bomb release point. A total of 362 bombers are damaged. Aircrews report four confirmed kills and one possible on the ground. Aircrew casualties are two killed and nine wounded. Fighter pilots report four confirmed kills in the air. Five P-51s are lost, and the pilots are reported missing.

Over 40 P-51s make a sweep of the Nürnberg target area. One fighter is lost; another 23 P-51s fly a scouting mission and a fighter is lost. Both pilots are reported missing.

During the night 25 B-24 Liberators attack the Duisburg power and gas stations using a Pathfinder bomber. Two B-24s are lost.

Ninth Air Force A-20 Havocs, A-26 Invaders, and B-26 Marauders attack communications centers, an oil storage depot, railroad bridges, and a marshaling yard. P-47 and P-38 fighters attack rail targets and airfields, support ground forces of VII, XII, and XX Corps, and fly armed reconnaissance missions in the First Army area.

The C-47s of the 75th Troop Carrier Squadron, 435th Troop Carrier Group, and the 79th Troop Carrier Squadron, 436th Troop Carrier Group, IX Troop Carrier Command, redeploy from England to France.

MEDITERRANEAN: Fifteenth Air Force sends more than 500 B-17s and B-24 Liberators escorted by P-38 Lightnings and P-51 Mustangs to attack marshaling yards in Austria and Hungary and shipyards at Trieste and Fiume in Italy.

During the night one B-17 and 13 B-24s drop supplies in northern Italy.

ITALY: The 1st Brazilian Division of IV Corps captures Monte Castello. The 10th Mountain Division captures Monte Torracia.

Twelfth Air Force B-25 Mitchells and B-26 Marauders bomb bridges. A-20 Havocs and P-47 Thunderbolts support Fifth Army ground forces. During the night A-20s attack communication targets and logistics targets in the Po River valley.

The First Tactical Air Force (Provisional) takes operational control of the 522nd, 523rd, and 524th Fighter Squadrons, 27th Fighter Group. The P-47 Thunderbolts of the squadrons redeploy from Italy to France.

SOUTHWEST PACIFIC AREA: FEAF B-24 Liberators and A-20 Havocs bomb airfields and the town of Jesselton in Borneo. The 528th Bombardment Squadron (Heavy), 380th Bombardment Group (Heavy), redeploys from Darwin, Australia, to Mindoro Island in the Philippines, with B-24 Liberators.

SOUTHWEST PACIFIC AREA, LUZON: On Corregidor, the Japanese blow up the ammunition storage area near the Malinta Hill Tunnel, causing many casualties for 3rd Battalion, 34th Infantry Regiment.

Far East Air Force B-24 Liberators bomb Japanese positions in the hills west of Fort Stotsenburg. P-47 Thunderbolts bomb Corregidor. B-25 Mitchells, A-20 Havocs, P-40s, and P-38 Lightnings support ground forces on Luzon.

PACIFIC: U.S. submarine *Gato* torpedoes and sinks a Japanese cargo ship in the Yellow Sea.

CENTRAL PACIFIC: Seventh Air Force sends 24 B-24 Liberators from Saipan to make a bombing strike with napalm on Pagan Island in the northern Marianas. P-38 Lightnings from Guam escort photo aircraft over Truk Atoll and strafe aircraft on Moen Island. B-34s from Guam bomb Marcus Island. A total of 25 B-24s based at Angaur Island bomb Corregidor Island. During the night six B-24s from Guam conduct individual snooper missions on Chichi Jima.

CENTRAL PACIFIC, IWO JIMA: The 3rd Battalion of the 21st Marines lands and is assigned to the 4th Division. The 28th Marines of the 5th Division resume the attack on Mount Suribachi. The advance is measured in yards.

The Japanese launch 50 kamikazes against the American fleet. Kamikazes sink escort carrier USS *Bismarck Sea* and damage carrier USS *Saratoga,* escort carrier USS *Lunga Point,* two LSTs, and a net cargo ship. Small carrier USS *Langley* is damaged during an aerial bombing attack. Japanese mortar fire damages an LST.

Japanese submarine *RO-43* torpedoes destroyer USS *Renshaw* south of Iwo Jima.

Sergeant Ross F. Gray is a platoon sergeant attached to A Company, 1st Battalion, 25th Marine Regiment, 4th Marine Division on Iwo Jima. Advancing toward the high ground northeast of the airfield, Sergeant Gray conducts a quick reconnaissance to find Japanese positions. He discovers a minefield and a strong network of emplacements joined by covered trenches. He proceeds to clear the mined area and ignore the fire directed at him. Returning to the platoon, he takes an explosive charge and, supported with covering fire, he returns to the mined area to place the demolition in one of the covered trenches. As machine guns fire on him, he returns to the platoon to obtain another demolition charge and crawls back to demolish the enemy position. In this manner he attacks and destroys a total of six Japanese positions. His extraordinary personal courage, dedication to duty, and high combat skill will win Sergeant Gray the Medal of Honor.

Captain Joseph J. McCarthy commands a rifle company in 2nd Battalion, 24th Marine Regiment, 4th Marine Division, attacking near Motoyama airfield No. 2 on Iwo Jima. Organizing a demolition and flamethrower team to accompany him, McCarthy charges across 75 yards of open ground to attack a pillbox on the ridge. Using grenades, he destroys the position and eliminates the enemy defenders; he directs the next attack on an emplacement as the Japanese defenders now turn their fire on the small

The USS *Saratoga,* supporting night air patrols over Iwo Jima, is attacked by six Japanese planes and hit by five bombs on February 21, 1945. Fires rage in the hangar deck and 123 seamen will be killed or missing.

group of marines. After killing one enemy soldier in hand-to-hand combat, he brings his company forward to attack through the gap created in the Japanese defenses to sweep the ridge. For his cool courage and decisive leadership, Captain McCarthy will receive the Medal of Honor.

February 22

CBI: In China, Fourteenth Air Force P-40s and P-51 Mustangs attack troops, tanks, trucks, and rail and river traffic. Fighter pilots report one cargo ship sunk in the Yangtze River between Hankow and Nanking.

In Burma, Tenth Air Force sends 12 B-25 Mitchells to bomb an airfield. P-47 Thunderbolts support ground forces and attack gun positions, troop concentrations, logistics storage sites, and trucks.

ETO: Operation Clarion begins with the intention of paralyzing the German national transportation structure by employing thousands of small aerial attacks over a one-million-square-mile area of what is left of the German Reich. Almost 9,000 aircraft are involved, dropping 8,500 tons of bombs.

Eighth Air Force sends more than 1,400 B-17s and B-24 Liberators escorted by over 800 P-47 Thunderbolts and P-51 Mustangs to begin a coordinated effort with the British Royal Air Force and the U.S. Ninth Air Force and Fifteenth Air Force to bomb the remainder of the German road and rail system and paralyze the enemy's capability to continue the war. To gain the best accuracy, the bombers will fly at 10,000 feet and visually identify the bomb release point. Marshaling yards are the main targets. Six bombers are lost and 97 damaged. Aircrews report 28 confirmed kills, two probables, and 43 possibles. Aircrew casualties are four wounded and 57 missing. Fighter pilots report four confirmed kills, two probables, and 18 possibles in the air and 22 confirmed kills and 21 possibles on the ground. A total of 12 P-51s are lost, and the pilots are reported missing.

Nearly 100 P-51s fly a freelance mission in support of the bombers. Fighter pilots report two confirmed kills in the air. One fighter is lost, and the pilot is reported missing. Another 28 P-51s fly a scouting mission and report two confirmed kills and three possibles on the ground.

Ninth Air Force sends more than 450 A-20 Havocs, A-26 Invaders, and B-26 Marauders to attack viaducts, railroad bridges, and marshaling yards. Over 1,000 P-47 and P-38 fighters escort the bombers as they make their low-level attacks. Fighters also support VII, XII, and XX Corps.

The headquarters of the 27th Fighter Group redeploys from Italy to France under the operational control of the First Tactical Air Force (Provisional).

MEDITERRANEAN: Fifteenth Air Force in support of Operation Clarion sends more than 350 B-17s and B-24 Liberators escorted by P-38 Lightnings and P-51 Mustangs to attack marshaling yards, rail lines, and bridges in Germany, Austria, and Italy.

ITALY: Twelfth Air Force B-25 Mitchells and B-26 Marauders attack bridges and marshaling yards. A-20 Havocs and P-47 Thunderbolts support Fifth Army ground forces and attack airfields, gun positions, and communication targets. During the night A-20s attack ammunition storage areas, rail lines, and bridges, and vehicles traveling on roads in the Po River Valley.

Southwest Pacific Area: U.S. submarine *Becuna* torpedoes and sinks a Japanese merchant tanker off the south coast of French Indochina. A Japanese fleet tanker is damaged by a mine dropped by Twentieth Air Force B-29s. Fifth Air Force B-25 Mitchells locate the tanker after it has run aground and destroy it on the southern coast of French Indochina.

FEAF B-24 Liberators bomb airfields in Borneo.

Southwest Pacific Area, Luzon: The 37th Infantry Division and the attached cavalrymen of the 1st Cavalry Division battle the Japanese in Manila, fighting house-to-house and employing direct artillery fire to destroy houses turned into small fortresses. The Japanese are holding their last position, the old walled city or Intramuros. The walls here are 16 feet high and 40 feet thick. Many noncombatants have come here for refuge from the fighting. Broadcasted appeals to the Japanese to surrender and allow the noncombatants to move into American lines are ignored. During the night Intramuros is subjected to intense artillery fire that creates breaches in the north and east sections of the walls.

On Luzon, Far East Air Force sends 100 B-24 Liberators to bomb Japanese troop concentrations near Fort Stotsenburg. P-47 Thunderbolts attack Corregidor Island and A-20 Havocs and P-51 Mustangs attack troop concentrations. B-24s bomb logistics storage areas.

Central Pacific: Seventh Air Force sends three B-24 Liberators to bomb Marcus Island. During the night six B-24s fly individual harassment raids on Haha Jima.

During the night B-24s from Guam and Saipan conduct individual snooper missions on Iwo Jima.

Central Pacific, Iwo Jima: Heavy rain on the island reduces movement. The 21st Marines of the 3rd Division relieve the 23rd Marines of the 4th Division and make an advance of 200 yards when they encounter the southeastern edge of the main Japanese defenses. The 3rd Battalion of the 25th Marines battles the Japanese at the Rock Quarry. Patrols from the 28th Marines link at Tobiishi Point on the southern tip of the island, isolating Mount Suribachi.

Admiral Raymond A. Spruance authorizes a carrier strike from Admiral Marc Mitscher's Task Force 58 against Honshu and Okinawa.

Lieutenant Colonel Justice M. Chambers is commander of the 3rd Assault Battalion Landing Team, 25th Marine Regiment, 4th Marine Division, and lands on Iwo Jima after the initial assault waves. His battalion faces a wall of fire from well-directed Japanese artillery, mortar rocket, machine-gun, and rifle fire. Chambers rallies his men and leads them in an attack on the critical high ground that has to be captured to protect the rest of the invasion force. Lieutenant Colonel Chambers holds his unit together during the day-long battle for the cliffs. Having lost most of his officers and suffered terrible losses, Chambers provides inspiration and leadership until wounded. For his extraordinary courage in the face of near impossible odds, accomplishing what was the most difficult mission on Iwo Jima, Lieutenant Colonel Chambers will receive the Medal of Honor.

New Guinea: The headquarters of the 42nd Bombardment Group (Medium) redeploys to Morotai Island, while the 75th and 100th Bombardment Squadrons (Medium) remain at Sansapor. The squadrons' B-25 Mitchells will operate from

Morotai. The headquarters of the 347th Fighter Group redeploys from Middelburg Island to Mindoro Island, and the P-38 Lightnings of the 67th and 339th Fighter Squadrons will operate from Morotai.

February 23

PACIFIC: A P-38 Lightning from Santa Rosa Army Airfield shoots down a Japanese balloon over Calistoga, California.

CBI: In China, Fourteenth Air Force P-51 Mustangs attack river traffic from Nanking to Hankow. Five B-24 Liberators sweep the Gulf of Tonkin and South China Sea. P-40s attack targets of opportunity near Kaifeng.

In Burma, Tenth Air Force sends 12 B-25 Mitchells and over 120 P-47 Thunderbolts and P-38 Lightnings to bomb troop concentrations, ammunition storage areas, and logistics storage sites.

ETO: Operation Grenade begins. The Ninth Army, under the operational control of Field Marshal Montgomery's 21st Army Group, sends units across the Roer River to establish a bridgehead. The XIX Corps (2nd Armored Division and the 30th and 29th Infantry Divisions) and XIII Corps (5th Armored Division and the 102nd and 84th Infantry Divisions) of Ninth Army cross the Roer River near Jülich. The attack is conducted in heavy rain. The melting snow and soft ground are quickly churned into deep mud by the advancing vehicles and the 45-minute pre-assault artillery bombardment. German forces are surprised and give ground quickly. Seven bridges are rapidly built and a bridgehead nearly four miles deep is established. American losses for this attack are 92 killed, 913 wounded, and 61 missing.

VII Corps (3rd Armored Division and the 8th and 99th Infantry Divisions) of First Army crosses the Roer River south of Düren.

The VIII Corps (4th Infantry Division and the 6th and 11th Armored Divisions) and XII Corps (4th Armored Division and the 5th, 76th, and 80th Infantry Divisions) of Third Army reach the Prüm River after fighting for nearly two weeks to break through the West Wall defenses.

Eighth Air Force sends more than 1,200 B-17s and B-24 Liberators escorted by over 700 P-47 Thunderbolts and P-51 Mustangs to bomb marshaling yards in Germany as part of Operation Clarion. One B-24 is lost and 62 bombers are damaged. Aircrews report 15 confirmed kills and 16 possibles. Aircrew casualties are 21 killed, four wounded, and four missing. Fighter pilots report one confirmed kill in the air and five confirmed kills and two possibles on the ground. Five P-51s are lost. One pilot is reported killed, and four pilots are reported missing.

Over 140 P-47 Thunderbolts and P-51 Mustangs make a sweep of Neuburg, Landsberg, and Leipheim airfields. Fighter pilots report nine confirmed kills and 14 possibles on the ground. One P-51 is lost and the pilot is reported missing. During the night 24 B-24s bomb the Neuss marshaling yard using a Pathfinder bomber to mark the bomb release point.

Ninth Air Force A-20 Havocs, A-26 Invaders, and B-26 Marauders attack communication centers near the Roer River as Ninth Army participates in Operation Grenade. P-47 and P-38 fighters support the 104th and 8th Infantry Divisions near Düren and support XIII and XIX Corps and VIII, XII, and XX Corps.

A V-2 rocket hits the port of Antwerp, damaging a U.S. freighter.

German aircraft attack and sink a U.S. freighter straggling from a convoy bound for Scotland in the Norwegian Sea.

MEDITERRANEAN: Fifteenth Air Force sends nearly 400 B-17s and B-24 Liberators escorted by over 140 P-38 Lightnings and P-51 Mustangs to attack marshaling yards and rail lines in Austria and marshaling yards in Italy.

ITALY: The 85th, 86th, and 87th Infantry Regiments of the 10th Mountain Division capture Monte Belvedere and Monte della Torraccia.

Twelfth Air Force B-25 Mitchells and B-26 Marauders bomb bridges. A-20 Havocs and P-47 Thunderbolts of the XXII Tactical Air Command attack rail lines, airfields, bridges, and troop movements in the central and northern Po River valley.

During the night A-20s attack marshaling yards and airfields throughout northern Italy.

The P-47 Thunderbolts of the 527th Fighter Squadron, 86th Fighter Group, redeploy from Italy to France to come under the operational control of the First Tactical Air Force (Provisional).

SOUTHWEST PACIFIC AREA: In French Indochina, FEAF B-25 Mitchells on shipping sweeps bomb vessels in Phan Rang harbor and attack a small convoy southwest of Cam Ranh Bay.

U.S. submarine *Hammerhead* intercepts a Japanese convoy and sinks an escort vessel off the southern coast of French Indochina and escapes a counterattack. Fifth Air Force B-25 Mitchells on a shipping sweep off French Indochina attack a Japanese convoy and sink a submarine chaser and damage another submarine chaser and a small tanker.

FEAF B-24 Liberators and P-47 Thunderbolts attack airfields in Borneo.

SOUTHWEST PACIFIC AREA, LUZON: The 37th Infantry Division assaults Intramuros, the last Japanese position in the city of Manila. A savage battle lasts for the next two days, as every area in the old city must be cleared.

A company of paratroopers from the 511th Parachute Infantry Regiment makes a jump at Los Baqos to free 2,147 Americans interred at the camp.

In the XI Corps area, two regiments of the 40th Infantry Division attack Japanese forces west of Fort Stotsenburg. The preceding bombing attacks from B-24 Liberators have eliminated all organized resistance.

Far East Air Force B-25 Mitchells, A-20 Havocs, P-47 Thunderbolts, and P-38 Lightnings support ground forces on Luzon Island.

CENTRAL PACIFIC: Seventh Air Force sends 26 B-24 Liberators from Angaur Island to bomb Mindanao Island in the Philippines. During the night seven B-24s from Guam conduct individual snooper missions on Chichi Jima and Haha Jima.

CENTRAL PACIFIC, IWO JIMA: A patrol of the 3rd Platoon of E Company 2nd Battalion, 28th Marines, reaches the top of Mount Suribachi and raises an American flag. A few hours later, a larger flag is raised. The moment is captured by Associated Press photographer Joe Rosenthal. It will become one of the most famous photographs ever taken. The capture of Mount Suribachi has cost the 28th marines 900 men in four days of fighting.

This iconic photo by Joe Rosenthal captures the spirit and determination of the marines who took Iwo Jima. It is one of the unforgettable moments of World War II.

Lieutenant General Holland Smith and Secretary of the Navy James V. Forrestal land on Iwo Jima and visit marines and stay for about two hours as artillery shells continue to land close by.

Japanese shore batteries damage two LSTs and two LSMs.

Corporal Hershel W. Williams is the demolition sergeant with the 21st Marine Regiment, 3rd Marine Division, and volunteers to assist tanks attempting to open a lane for the infantry through a network of reinforced concrete pillboxes, buried mines, and black volcanic sands. For the next four hours Williams carries on a single battle with the Japanese, moving forward under covering fire from four marines. He lays demolitions in the face of deadly fire from the enemy, then moves back to prepare additional demolition charges and flamethrowers, then struggles back through the soft black sand to destroy another position, often attacking them from the rear. Over and over he fights off Japanese infantry and moves in to blast and burn the enemy out of fortified positions. For his exceptional display of aggressive fighting spirit and valiant devotion to duty, Corporal Williams will receive the Medal of Honor.

NEW GUINEA: The P-38 Lightnings of the 68th Fighter Squadron, 347th Fighter Group, redeploy from Middelburg Island to Mindoro Island. The 69th Bombardment Squadron (Medium), 42nd Bombardment Group (Medium), begins operating from Morotai Island with B-25 Mitchells.

February 24

ALEUTIANS: Eleventh Air Force sends four B-25 Mitchells on a shipping sweep in the Kurile Islands. On the return flight the B-25s encounter and photograph a Japanese balloon carrying a bomb and drifting toward the continental United States.

CBI: In China, Fourteenth Air Force sends five B-24 Liberators on individual sweeps over the South China Sea. Aircrews report four vessels sunk.

In Burma, Tenth Air Force sends 12 B-25 Mitchells and over 125 P-47 Thunderbolts and P-38 Lightnings to attack vehicles, bridges, troop concentrations, towns, and villages occupied by Japanese troops, logistics storage sites, and targets of opportunity.

ETO: Ninth Army captures Jülich.

Eighth Air Force sends nearly 1,200 B-17s and B-24 Liberators escorted by nearly 600 P-51 Mustangs to bomb oil refineries, U-boat yards, and marshaling yards in northern Germany. The bombers use radar to locate the bomb release point. One B-24 and one B-17 are lost, and 228 bombers are damaged. Aircrews report one confirmed kill and three possibles. Aircrew casualties are four killed, 12 wounded, and 21 missing. Fighter pilots report one confirmed kill and three possibles on the ground. A total of 11 P-51s are lost. The pilots are reported missing. German submarine *U-3007* is sunk at Bremen.

During the night 12 B-24s drop leaflets over Germany and the Netherlands.

Twelve B-17s conduct screening missions to jam German radio interception efforts and conduct countermeasures against German radar sites.

Ninth Air Force sends nearly 500 A-20 Havocs, A-26 Invaders, and B-26 Marauders to attack communication centers, railroad bridges, and marshaling yards to interdict German troop movements. P-47 and P-38 fighters support the 8th and 104th Infantry Divisions and XIII and XIX Corps at the Roer River bridgehead, and also the VIII, XII, and XX Corps.

MEDITERRANEAN: Fifteenth Air Force sends more than 500 B-17s and B-24 Liberators escorted by P-38 Lightnings and P-51 Mustangs to attack rail bridges and marshaling yards in Italy and marshaling yards in Austria.

ITALY: Twelfth Air Force B-25 Mitchells and B-26 Marauders attack rail lines, roads, and bridges. A-20 Havocs and P-47 Thunderbolts attack rail lines, bridges, airfields, and roads in the Po River valley and support the 10th Mountain Division at Monte Torraccia.

During the night A-20s attack marshaling yards and airfields.

SOUTHWEST PACIFIC AREA: FEAF B-25 Mitchells conduct a sweep off the China coast, bombing the naval base at Formosa.

FEAF B-24 Liberators bomb airfields in Borneo.

SOUTHWEST PACIFIC AREA, LUZON: The 2nd Battalion of the 151st Infantry Regiment of the 38th Infantry Division begins the relief of the 2nd Battalion of the 34th RCT on Corregidor.

In Manila, the 12th Cavalry Regiment captures the port facilities and the 129th and 145th Infantry Regiments of the 37th Infantry Division capture Fort Santiago.

Lieutenant General Robert L. Eichelberger's Eighth Army assumes responsibility for clearing Leyte and Samar of Japanese forces.

Far East Air Force B-25 Mitchells, A-20 Havocs, P-47 Thunderbolts, and P-38 Lightnings attack Corregidor Island and Japanese positions near Fort Stotsenburg on Luzon Island.

PACIFIC: Twentieth Air Force sends 105 B-29 Superfortresses all armed with incendiary bombs to attack the Empire Dock area at Singapore. Aircrews report heavy damage to the warehouse area. One B-29 is lost.

The XX Bomber Command begins its redeployment, sending the headquarters units of the 58th Bombardment Wing (Very Heavy) and the 468th Bombardment Group (Very Heavy) from India to the Marianas.

U.S. submarine *Lagarto* torpedoes and sinks Japanese submarine *I-371* and a cargo ship off Kyushu, Japan. U.S. submarine *Trepang* torpedoes and sinks a Japanese cargo ship off Kyushu.

CENTRAL PACIFIC: Seventh Air Force sends 28 B-24 Liberators from Angaur Island to bomb Mindanao Island in the Philippines. Three B-24s bomb Marcus Island. During the night five B-24s from Guam conduct individual snooper missions on Chichi Jima and Haha Jima.

CENTRAL PACIFIC, IWO JIMA: The marines begin an attack to the north with three regiments abreast—the 26th Marines on the left, the 21st Marines in the center, and the 24th Marines on the right. Major General Schmidt has consolidated all of the marine tanks into a single unit commanded by Lieutenant Colonel William Collins to support the infantry. The attack stalls almost immediately as the marines hit the main defensive line. Tanks hit mines and encounter anti-tank fire. The infantry is pinned by accurate machine-gun and mortar fire.

Major General Schmidt arrives ashore to establish his headquarters on Iwo. Although the 9th Marines land to support the 21st Marines in the center, Lieutenant General Holland Smith decides to keep the 3rd Marine Regiment of the 3rd Division out of the battle, looking ahead to future operations on Okinawa. Schmidt receives reports that casualties now number over 6,800.

NEW GUINEA: The B-25s of the 390th Bombardment Squadron (Medium), 42nd Bombardment Group (Medium), redeploy to Morotai Island.

February 25

CBI: In China, Fourteenth Air Force B-25 Mitchells, P-40s, and P-51 Mustangs attack rail and river traffic. Four B-24 Liberators over the Gulf of Tonkin and South China Sea attack shipping targets. Aircrews report two vessels damaged.

In Burma, Tenth Air Force sends nine B-25 Mitchells and 85 P-47 Thunderbolts and P-38 Lightnings to attack bridges, troop concentrations, road traffic, logistics storage sites, and targets of opportunity. P-47s provide support to the British 36th Division and the Chinese 38th and 50th Divisions.

ETO: The VII Corps clears Düren, and bridgeheads are established over the Roer River as the rest of First Army pushes toward Cologne. The Ninth Army bridgehead has increased to 10 miles deep and 20 miles wide.

Eighth Air Force sends nearly 1,200 B-17s and B-24 Liberators escorted by 755 P-51 Mustangs to bomb oil storage areas, rail bridges, marshaling yards, tank production facilities, and airfields supporting jet aircraft. The bombers use radar to locate the bomb release point. A total of five bombers are lost and 366 are damaged. Aircrew casualties are five killed, 11 wounded, and 45 missing. Fighter pilots report three confirmed kills and five possibles on the ground. Two P-51s are lost and the pilots are reported missing. Over 260 P-47 Thunderbolts and P-51s fly close escort and area patrols. Fighter pilots report 21 confirmed kills and four possibles in the air and 10 confirmed kills and 12 possibles on the ground. Six P-51s are lost and the pilots are reported missing.

During the night 12 B-24s drop leaflets over France, Germany, and the Netherlands.

Ninth Air Force sends A-20 Havocs, A-26 Invaders, and B-26 Marauders to attack communication centers, railroad bridges, and a marshaling yard in support of Operation Clarion. P-47 and P-38 fighters support the 8th and 104th Infantry Divisions, XIII and XIX Corps, and VIII, XII, and XX Corps.

The headquarters of the 437th Troop Carrier Group and the C-47s of the 83rd, 84th, 85th, and 86th Troop Carrier Squadrons, IX Troop Carrier Command, redeploy from England to France.

MEDITERRANEAN: Fifteenth Air Force sends more than 600 B-17s and B-24 Liberators escorted by P-38 Lightnings and P-51 Mustangs to bomb marshaling yards and a benzol plant in Austria.

P-51s strafe rail lines in Germany.

ITALY: Twelfth Air Force B-25 Mitchells and B-26 Marauders attack bridges. A-20 Havocs and P-47 Thunderbolts of the XXII Tactical Air Command attack rail lines, marshaling yards, motor transport, and roads. During the night A-20s attack marshaling yards and airfields.

SOUTHWEST PACIFIC AREA: FEAF B-24 Liberators and P-51 Mustangs attack targets on Formosa.

U.S. submarine *Flasher* torpedoes and sinks a Japanese cargo vessel near Hainan Island and makes an unsuccessful attack on a submarine chaser rescuing survivors. U.S. submarine *Hoe* attacks a Japanese convoy and sinks an escort vessel south of Hainan Island. U.S. submarine *Piper* torpedoes and sinks a Japanese guardboat and cargo ship off Hainan Island.

FEAF B-24 Liberators bomb airfields in Borneo.

SOUTHWEST PACIFIC AREA, LUZON: In Manila the 37th Infantry Division captures Intramuros.

In the XI Corps area the 40th Infantry Division eliminates all Japanese resistance west of Fort Stotsenburg.

Far East Air Force B-24 Liberators bomb troop concentrations on Luzon. The headquarters of the 49th Fighter Group and the P-38 Lightnings of the 7th Fighter Squadron redeploy from Mindoro Island to Luzon.

Pacific: The C-87 transport aircraft carrying Lieutenant General Millard F. Harmon, commander of Army Air Forces, Pacific Operations Area, and deputy commander of Twentieth Air Force, disappears over the Marshalls. Harmon had departed Guam for Washington, D.C., via Kwajalein and Oahu, Hawaii.

Twentieth Air Force sends 172 B-29 Superfortresses of the 73rd, 313th, and 314th Bombardment Wings (Very Heavy) to bomb the urban area of Tokyo. Three B-29s are lost.

The XX Bomber Command redeploys the headquarters of the 40th Bombardment Group (Very Heavy) from India to the Marianas.

Carrier aircraft from Task Force 58 bomb aircraft production facilities and airfields near Tokyo.

Japanese shore battery fire damages an LCI off Iwo Jima.

Two U.S. destroyers sink three Japanese guardboats south of Honshu, Japan.

Central Pacific: Seventh Air Force sends nine B-24 Liberators from Guam to bomb Japanese mortar positions, fortifications, and rocket launchers on Iwo Jima. During the night eight B-24s conduct individual harassment raids on Chichi Jima.

Central Pacific, Iwo Jima: The 5th Marine Division attacks the high ground at Nishi Ridge and Hills 362-A and 362-B. The 4th Marine Division encounters a collection of nearly impregnable Japanese positions, which they call "The Meatgrinder." The 3rd Marine Division fights in an area named "Cushman's Pocket."

Shore battery fire damages two LSTs off Iwo Jima. Aircraft from escort carrier USS *Anzio* sink Japanese submarines *I-368* and *RO-43* off Iwo Jima. A U.S. destroyer escort sinks Japanese submarine *I-370* south of Iwo Jima.

February 26

CBI: In China, Fourteenth Air Force sends B-25 Mitchells to bomb bridges, rail lines, and heavy port equipment in French Indochina. P-40s and P-51 Mustangs attack airfields, towns, and rail and river traffic.

In Burma, Tenth Air Force sends B-25 Mitchells to bomb bridges. P-47 Thunderbolts and P-38 Lightnings along with B-25s support ground forces and attack bridges, troop concentrations, logistics storage sites, and targets of opportunity. P-47s support the Mars Task Force near Lashio and the British 36th Division.

ETO: In the Ninth Army area, 2nd Armored Division of XIX Corps is pushed across the Roer River to support the attack, even though conditions are very difficult for tanks, due to the bad weather.

Eighth Air Force sends more than 1,200 B-17s and B-24 Liberators escorted by over 700 P-51 Mustangs to bomb rail stations in Berlin, Germany. The bombers use radar to mark the bomb release points. Three bombers are lost and 93 are damaged. Aircrews report six confirmed kills. Aircrew casualties are eight killed, six wounded, and 30 missing. Fighter pilots report four confirmed kills in the air and two confirmed kills on the ground. Three P-51s are lost and two pilots are reported missing.

Six B-24 Liberators and 17 B-17s conduct screening missions to jam German radio interception efforts and conduct countermeasures against German radar sites.

During the night 12 B-24s drop leaflets over Germany and the Netherlands. During the night five B-24s fly a Carpetbagger mission.

Ninth Air Force sends over 230 A-20 Havocs, A-26 Invaders, and B-26 Marauders to attack communication centers, rail and road junctions, and logistics and ammunition storage sites.

The headquarters of the 436th Troop Carrier Group and the C-47s of the 80th, 81st, and 82nd Troop Carrier Squadrons, IX Troop Carrier Command, redeploy from England to France.

MEDITERRANEAN: Fifteenth Air Force sends P-38 Lightnings to attack rail lines in Austria.

ITALY: Twelfth Air Force B-25 Mitchells and B-26 Marauders attack rail bridges. A-20 Havocs and P-47 Thunderbolts of the XXII Tactical Air Command support the Fifth Army south of Bologna and attack rail lines, bridges, airfields, and vehicles. During the night A-20s attack marshaling yards.

SOUTHWEST PACIFIC AREA: FEAF B-24s attack Takao airfield on Formosa while P-47s strafe railroad targets.

FEAF B-24 Liberators attack airfields in Borneo.

SOUTHWEST PACIFIC AREA, LUZON: On Corregidor, the Japanese blow up the ammunition storage area near Monkey Point, causing many casualties for the 1st Battalion of the 503rd Parachute Infantry.

In the I Corps area the 25th Infantry Division captures Carranglan in the Pampanga River Valley.

Far East Air Force B-24 Liberators bomb troop concentrations; A-20 Havocs, P-38 Lightnings, and P-47 Thunderbolts support ground forces and attack Japanese troops near Fort Stotsenburg on Luzon. A-20s, P-38s, and P-47s attack targets on Palawan Island and B-25 Mitchells bomb an airfield on Jolo Island.

The 9th Fighter Squadron, 49th Fighter Group, redeploys from Mindoro Island to Luzon with P-38 Lightnings. The P-38s of the 70th Fighter Squadron, 18th Fighter Group, redeploy from Luzon to Mindoro.

PACIFIC: The XX Bomber Command redeploys the headquarters of the 462nd Bombardment Group (Very Heavy) from India to the Marianas.

CENTRAL PACIFIC: During the night Seventh Air Force sends eight B-24s to fly individual harassment raids on Chichi Jima.

February 27

CBI: In China, Fourteenth Air Force sends B-24 Liberators to attack shipping in the Gulf of Tonkin and South China Sea. Aircrews report four vessels sunk.

In Burma, Tenth Air Force P-47 Thunderbolts and P-38 Lightnings support ground forces and attack bridges, gun positions, road traffic, troop concentrations, logistics storage sites, elephant transport, and targets of opportunity

ETO: The VII Corps captures a bridgehead at Erft and organizes for an attack toward Cologne.

Eighth Air Force sends more than 1,100 B-17s and B-24 Liberators escorted by 745 P-51 Mustangs to bomb road and rail targets at Halle and Leipzig, Germany. The bombers use radar to locate the bomb release point. Two B-24s are lost and eight damaged. Aircrews report 83 confirmed kills and 19 possibles. Aircrew casualties are two killed, one wounded, and 18 missing. Fighter pilots report two confirmed kills in the air and 81 confirmed kills and 19 possibles on the ground. Two P-51s are lost, and the pilots are reported missing.

During the night one B-17 and 11 B-24s drop leaflets over Germany and the Netherlands. A total of 26 B-24 Liberators bomb Wilhelmshaven oil storage areas, using a Pathfinder bomber to locate the bomb release point.

Ninth Air Force sends 118 A-20 Havocs, A-26 Invaders, and B-26 Marauders to attack communication centers, railroad bridges, and a marshaling yard. P-47 and P-38 fighters support XIII and XIX Corps.

Navy PB4Y-1 Privateers along with British escort vessels sink German submarine *U-327* in the English Channel.

MEDITERRANEAN: Fifteenth Air Force sends more than 500 B-17s and B-24 Liberators, escorted by P-38 Lightnings and P-51 Mustangs, to attack marshaling yards in Germany and Austria.

ITALY: Twelfth Air Force B-25 Mitchells and B-26 Marauders attack rail bridges. A-20 Havocs and P-47 Thunderbolts of the XXII Tactical Air Command attack rail lines and rail cars in northeast Italy. During the night A-20s attack airfields, marshaling yards, motor transport, and roads in the Po River valley.

SOUTHWEST PACIFIC AREA: In the Philippines, Far East Air Force B-24 Liberators, A-20 Havocs, and P-38 Lightnings strike Puerto Princesa on Palawan Island in preparation for the amphibious landings. P-51 Mustangs support ground forces on Luzon; P-38 Lightnings and marine fighters attack airfields on Mindanao.

B-24 Liberators bomb Takao on Formosa, while P-47s sweep the west coast. B-25s sweeping the China coast attack a fleet of junks and sampans near Hong Kong. Aircrews report damaging or destroying more than 25.

U.S. submarine *Blenny* attacks a Japanese convoy off French Indochina and sinks a merchant tanker. U.S. submarine *Scabbardfish* torpedoes and sinks a Japanese guardboat off Formosa.

FEAF B-24 Liberators bomb airfields in Borneo.

SOUTHWEST PACIFIC AREA, LUZON: Corregidor is captured after the paratroopers of the 503rd Parachute Infantry Regiment eliminate the last Japanese positions on the extreme eastern tip of the island. The Japanese have lost nearly 4,000 men and 19 captured. The number of men buried alive in the tunnels is unknown. American casualties are 209 killed, 725 wounded, and 19 missing.

General MacArthur officially turns over the civil administration of the Philippines to President Sergio Osmeña.

The 8th Fighter Squadron, 49th Fighter Group, redeploys from Mindoro to Luzon with P-38 Lightnings; the P-38s of the 12th Fighter Squadron, 18th Fighter Group, redeploy from Luzon to Mindoro. The P-38s of the 432nd Fighter Squadron, 475th Fighter Group, redeploy from Leyte Island to Clark Field, Luzon.

PACIFIC: During the night Twentieth Air Force sends 10 B-29 Superfortresses to mine Johore Strait and Penang harbor. Personnel of the 58th Bombardment Wing (Very Heavy) begin redeployment from India to Tinian and Guam Islands.

CENTRAL PACIFIC: Seventh Air Force sends nine B-24 Liberators from Guam to bomb fortifications and artillery positions on Iwo Jima. A total of 22 B-24s from Angaur Island bomb airfields on Mindanao Island in the Philippines. During the night nine B-24s from Guam conduct individual snooper missions on Haha Jima.

CENTRAL PACIFIC, IWO JIMA: The 3rd Maine Division occupies the airfield and controls Hills Peter and 199-Oboe.

Japanese shore battery fire damages an attack cargo ship and an LST. Mortar fire damages an LSM (Landing Ship, Medium).

Private Wilson D. Watson, 2nd Battalion, 9th Marine Regiment, 3rd Marine Division, attacks a Japanese pillbox when his squad is hit by fire from fortifications in the high rocky ridges and crags near the line of advance. Watson's bold and swift attack allows the platoon to take its objective. When Japanese fire stops the platoon, Watson climbs a small hill while under constant enemy fire and charges the enemy, firing his Browning Automatic Rifle (BAR) from the hip. Standing on the hill in full view of the enemy, he rakes them with automatic fire, killing 60 Japanese troops before running out of ammunition. For his courageous initiative and valiant fighting spirit against devastating odds Private Watson will receive the Medal of Honor.

NEW GUINEA: The 65th and 66th Troop Carrier Squadrons of the 403rd Troop Carrier Group redeploy from Biak to Morotai Island with C-46s and C-47s

February 28

CBI: Detachment 101 of the OSS (Office of Strategic Services) has 10,200 guerrillas under its control. The Americans that make up the detachment total 131 officers and 588 enlisted.

In Burma, Tenth Air Force sends P-47 Thunderbolts and P-38 Lightnings to support ground forces and attack bridges, troop concentrations, road traffic, logistics storage sites, and targets of opportunity.

ETO: Eighth Air Force sends more than 1,100 B-17s and B-24 Liberators escorted by 737 P-51 Mustangs to bomb viaducts, a tank production facility, road junctions, and marshaling yards in Germany. The bombers use a variety of radar techniques to mark the bomb release point. One B-17 is lost. Aircrews report 18 confirmed kills and 11 possibles. Aircrew casualties are three missing. Fighter pilots report one possible kill in the air and 18 confirmed kills and 10 possibles on the ground. Five P-51s are lost, and the pilots are reported missing.

During the night 11 B-24s drop leaflets over Germany and the Netherlands. During the night 22 B-24s bomb the Freiburg rail depot using a Pathfinder bomber to mark the bomb release point.

Ninth Air Force sends 340 A-20 Havocs, A-26 Invaders, and B-26 Marauders to attack communication centers, railroad bridges, and a marshaling yard. P-47 and P-38 fighters support the 3rd Armored Division at the Paffendorf bridgehead, the 2nd Armored Division advancing toward the Rhine River, and VIII, XII, and XX Corps.

The headquarters of the 313th and 314th Troop Carrier Groups and the C-47s of the 32nd and 61st Troop Carrier Squadrons, IX Troop Carrier Command, redeploy from England to France.

MEDITERRANEAN: Fifteenth Air Force sends nearly 700 B-17s and B-24 Liberators escorted by P-38 Lightnings and P-51 Mustangs to bomb marshaling yards in Austria and Italy. P-38s and P-51s attack marshaling yards and rail lines in Austria and rail lines in Yugoslavia.

A U.S. destroyer escort and French submarine chaser *L'Indiscret* sink German submarine *U-869* off Morocco.

ITALY: Twelfth Air Force B-25 Mitchells and B-26 Marauders attack rail lines and rail bridges. A-20 Havocs and P-47 Thunderbolts attack airfields and ammunition storage areas. During the night A-20s attack marshaling yards, bridges, and airfields.

SOUTHWEST PACIFIC AREA: FEAF B-24 Liberators and B-25 Mitchells bomb airfields in Borneo. The B-25s use napalm against their assigned target.

SOUTHWEST PACIFIC AREA, LUZON: Major General Verne D. Mudge, commander of the 1st Cavalry Division, is wounded. He is replaced by Brigadier General Hugh F. T. Hoffman.

In the Eighth Army area the 186th RCT of the 41st Infantry Division lands at Puerto Princesa on Palawan Island, in the Sulu Sea southwest of Mindoro. Rear Admiral William M. Fechteler is the commander of Naval Task Group 78.2. Naval Task Group 74.2 (Rear Admiral Ralph S. Riggs), with three light cruisers and four destroyers, provides naval gunfire support.

Far East Air Force B-24 Liberators and B-25 Mitchells attack an airfield on Mindanao. The P-38 Lightnings of the 431st and 433rd Fighter Squadrons, 475th Fighter Group, redeploy from Leyte to Clark Field on Luzon.

CENTRAL PACIFIC: Seventh Air Force sends eight B-24 Liberators from Guam to bomb Chichi Jima. A total of 23 B-24s based at Angaur Island bomb an airfield on Mindanao Island. During the night six B-24s from Guam fly individual harassment raids on Chichi Jima.

The ground echelon of the 548th Night Fighter Squadron, VII Fighter Command, arrives on Iwo Jima from Hawaii. The squadron's P-61 Black Widow night fighters continue to operate temporarily from Saipan.

CENTRAL PACIFIC, IWO JIMA: The 4th Marine Division captures Hill 382 in the Meatgrinder. The 28th Marines of the 5th Division capture Hill 362-A, losing 200 men. The 26th Marines capture Hill 362-B, losing 500 men. The 3rd Marine Division struggles forward against two positions named Peter and 199-Oboe. The marines have advanced 4,000 yards with about half the island under American control.

Major General James E. Chaney arrives on Iwo Jima with advance elements of the 145th Infantry Regiment of the army's 37th Infantry Division. Once the island is secured, General Chaney is to take control for the U.S. Army.

A U.S. destroyer is damaged in an air attack. Another destroyer is hit and damaged by shore battery fire. An LSM is hit by mortar fire.

Pharmacist's Mate First Class John H. Willis is the platoon corpsman serving with the 3rd Battalion, 27th Marine Regiment, 5th Marine Division, in the midst of artillery and mortar fire from Japanese pillboxes and caves covering Hill 362 on Iwo Jima. Willis administers first aid to wounded marines during the furious fighting. When he is wounded and evacuated, Willis leaves the aid station without authorization to return to his platoon. During an enemy counterattack, Willis moves far forward to assist a wounded marine and administers blood plasma. The Japanese throw grenades into the shell hole where he is, and Willis throws the grenades back out as quickly as he can until one explodes and kills him. For his great personal valor in saving others at the sacrifice of his own life, Pharmacist's Mate First Class Willis will receive the Medal of Honor.

NEW GUINEA: The B-24s of the 530th Bombardment Squadron (Heavy), 380th Bombardment Group (Heavy), redeploy from Darwin, Australia, to Mindoro. The 70th Troop Carrier Squadron, 433rd Troop Carrier Group, redeploys from Hollandia, New Guinea, to Leyte Island with C-46s and C-47s.

March 1

CBI: In China, Fourteenth Air Force P-40s and P-51 Mustangs attack rail and river traffic.

In Burma, Tenth Air Force sends 12 B-25 Mitchells to bomb an airfield. P-47 Thunderbolts and P-38 Lightnings support ground forces and attack bridges, troop concentrations, logistics storage sites, and targets of opportunity.

Fourteenth Air Force B-24 Liberators sink a Japanese merchant tanker in Tonkin Gulf, French Indochina.

ETO: Ninth Army captures München-Gladbach, about 12 miles from the Rhine River. The attack is spearheaded by the 2nd, 5th, and 8th Armored Divisions.

Bradley's 12th Army Group launches Operation Lumberjack, the offensive intended to reach the Rhine River and link with Third Army attacking northeast. First Army, with 13 divisions, is to advance to the Rhine south of Düsseldorf, capture the high ground northeast of Cologne, and seize the road network at Euskirchen.

Eighth Air Force sends more than 1,200 B-17s and B-24 Liberators escorted by 488 P-51 Mustangs to bomb marshaling yards in central and southern Germany and jet aircraft production facilities. The bombers use radar to mark their bomb release point. A total of 33 bombers are damaged. Aircrews report 12 confirmed kills and eight possibles. Aircrew casualties are 16 killed and two wounded. Fighter pilots report two confirmed kills in the air and nine confirmed kills and seven probables on the ground. Seven P-51s are lost, and the pilots are reported missing.

During the night 11 B-24s drop leaflets over Germany and the Netherlands.

Six B-24 Liberators conduct screening missions to jam German radio interception efforts and employ countermeasures against German radar sites.

Ninth Air Force sends 340 A-20 Havocs, A-26 Invaders, and B-26 Marauders to attack an ordnance depot, railroad bridges, and marshaling yards. P-47 and P-38 fighters support the 3rd and 9th Armored Divisions, and the VIII, XIX, XII, XX, XVI, and XIII Corps.

MEDITERRANEAN: U.S. Army Forces in the Middle East (USAFIME) takes over northwest Africa from the Mediterranean theater of operations and is redesignated the Africa-Middle East Theater (AMET).

Fifteenth Air Force sends more than 600 B-17s and B-24 Liberators escorted by over 200 P-38 Lightnings and P-51 Mustangs to bomb oil refineries and marshaling yards in Austria and marshaling yards in Yugoslavia.

ITALY: During the night Twelfth Air Force A-20s attack bridges.

SOUTHWEST PACIFIC AREA: In the Philippines, Far East Air Force B-25 Mitchells attack an airfield on Jolo Island. Aircraft conduct napalm strikes on Japanese troops on Corregidor and Japanese defensive positions near Fort Stotsenburg on Luzon.

Over Formosa, B-24 Liberators bomb the Takao aluminum plant and airfields, while P-47 Thunderbolts attack buildings, oil storage tanks, railroad yards, and targets of opportunity.

The XIII Fighter Command redeploys from Leyte to Puerto Princesa on Palawan Island. The headquarters of the 18th Fighter Group moves from Luzon to Mindoro Island.

Fifth Air Force B-25 Mitchells sink a Japanese transport off the Pescadores in the South China Sea near Formosa.

FEAF B-24 Liberators bomb airfields in Borneo.

PACIFIC: The headquarters of the 444th Bombardment Group (Very Heavy) begins a redeployment from India to the Marianas.

Operational control of VII Fighter Command changes from Seventh Air Force to Army Air Forces Pacific Operational Area. The headquarters of VII Fighter Command will redeploy from Oahu, Hawaii, to Iwo Jima.

Carrier aircraft from Task Force 58 attack ground installations, airfields, and shipping around Okinawa. A torpedo boat and a minelayer and two cargo ships are sunk and an escort destroyer, an auxiliary minesweeper, a supply ship, six cargo ships, a gunboat, a transport, a torpedo boat, a minesweeper, and a submarine chaser are damaged.

Two destroyers are damaged by shore battery fire off Iwo Jima.

U.S. submarine *Sterlet* sinks a Japanese cargo ship east of Honshu, Japan.

U.S. submarine *Kete* departs Guam on her second war patrol. The submarine fails to report after March 20.

CENTRAL PACIFIC: Seventh Air Force sends seven B-24 Liberators from Guam to bomb the airfield on Chichi Jima. Three B-24s bomb Marcus Island. A total of 25 B-24s based at Angaur Island bomb Corregidor Island. During the night five B-24s fly individual harassment raids on Haha Jima.

CENTRAL PACIFIC, IWO JIMA: The 4th Marine Division fights in the Meatgrinder and consolidates its position on Hill 382; the 3rd Marine Division gains part of the second, unfinished airfield in the center of the island. The 5th Marine Division attacks to capture Hill 362-A near Nishi Ridge. Each and every yard of ground must be first bombed with artillery or air strikes, then tanks and flamethrowers, then finally marines must move in with hand grenades, explosive charges, and rifle fire to destroy the fanatical defenders in the cave and tunnel entrances.

NEW GUINEA: The headquarters of the Thirteenth Air Force redeploys from Morotai to Leyte. The B-24s of the 531st Bombardment Squadron (Heavy), 380th Bombardment Group (Heavy), redeploy from Darwin, Australia, to Mindoro.

March 2

CBI: Fourteenth Air Force sends three B-24 Liberators on sweeps over the Gulf of Tonkin and the South China Sea. Aircrews report two vessels sunk and three damaged.

In Burma, Tenth Air Force sends P-47 Thunderbolts and P-38 Lightnings to support ground forces and attack bridges, gun positions, troop concentrations, logistics storage sites, and targets of opportunity.

ETO: The XIX Corps of Ninth Army reaches the Rhine River.

The 10th Armored Division of XX Corps of Third Army captures Trier and the important bridge across the Moselle. XII Corps secures a bridgehead east of Bitburg. Since the beginning of February the troops of Third Army are capturing about 1,000 German soldiers a day. A pervasive sense of defeat is shown in the attitude of the prisoners. Third Army has lost 12,000 men (including 1,500 killed) over the past 30 days of combat.

Eighth Air Force sends more than 1,200 B-17s and B-24 Liberators escorted by over 700 P-47 Thunderbolts and P-51 Mustangs to bomb synthetic oil production facilities in Germany. The city of Dresden is attacked again. The bombers use radar to locate bomb release points. A total of 14 bombers are lost and 167 are damaged. Aircrews report 110 confirmed kills, nine probables, and 60 possibles. Aircrew casualties are three killed, seven wounded, and 29 missing. Fighter pilots report 66 confirmed kills, six probables, and 30 possibles in the air and 36 confirmed kills and 29 possibles on the ground. A total of 13 fighters are lost and two are damaged. All the pilots are reported missing.

During the night 11 B-24s drop leaflets over Germany and the Netherlands. Four B-24s fly Carpetbagger missions.

Six B-24 Liberators conduct screening missions to jam German radio interception efforts and employ countermeasures against German radar sites.

Ninth Air Force sends A-20 Havocs, A-26 Invaders, and B-26 Marauders to attack communication centers, railroad bridges, ordnance depots, and a motor transport depot to slow down German forces attempting to withdraw before Third Army. Over 1,700 P-47 and P-38 fighters support ground forces, particularly the 3rd Armored Division at the Erft River, the XVI and XIX Corps and the VIII, XII, and XX Corps.

MEDITERRANEAN: Fifteenth Air Force sends more than 400 B-17s and B-24 Liberators escorted by P-38 Lightnings and P-51 Mustangs to attack marshaling yards in Austria and Italy. During the night B-24s drop supplies in northern Italy and Yugoslavia.

ITALY: Twelfth Air Force A-20 Havocs and P-47 Thunderbolts of the XXII Tactical Air Command attack logistics storage sites and ammunition storage areas in the Po River valley.

SOUTHWEST PACIFIC AREA: On Formosa, B-24 Liberators, B-25 Mitchells, A-20 Havocs, P-38 Lightnings, and P-47s attack airfields.

Fifth Air Force B-25 Mitchells sink a Japanese landing ship in the South China Sea near the Pescadores.

FEAF B-24 Liberators bomb airfields and the waterfront area of Sandakan in Borneo.

SOUTHWEST PACIFIC AREA, LUZON: General MacArthur arrives on Corregidor. He personally raises the American flag over the ruined parade ground at the location of the former U.S. Army barracks.

In the Philippines, the detachment of the 432nd Fighter Squadron, 475th Fighter Group, operating from Mindoro Island with P-38 Lightnings, returns to base at Clark Field on Luzon.

PACIFIC: Twentieth Air Force sends 50 of 64 B-29 Superfortresses to bomb support installations at the naval base in Singapore. Aircrews report one probable kill and four possibles. Two B-29s are lost.

Major General Willis H. Hale, the deputy commander for operations of Army Air Forces Pacific Operations Area (AAFPOA), takes command to replace Lieutenant General Millard F. Harmon, commanding general AAFPOA and deputy commander of the Twentieth Air Force, who was lost February 25 in an aircraft over the Pacific.

A naval task group under command of Rear Admiral Francis E. M. Whiting with three light cruisers and eight destroyers bombards Japanese positions on Okino Daito Jima, in the Ryukyus.

Shore battery fire damages a light cruiser off Iwo Jima.

U.S. submarine *Bowfin* torpedoes and sinks a Japanese transport east of Honshu, Japan.

A navy PB4Y-2 Privateer attacks a Japanese convoy, sinking a transport in the East China Sea.

CENTRAL PACIFIC: Seventh Air Force sends seven B-24 Liberators from Guam to bomb the airfield on Chichi Jima. During the night five B-24s fly individual harassment raids on Haha Jima and Chichi Jima.

The P-51 Mustangs of the 78th Fighter Squadron, 15th Fighter Group, arrive on Iwo Jima from Hawaii. The squadron's first mission will be in early March.

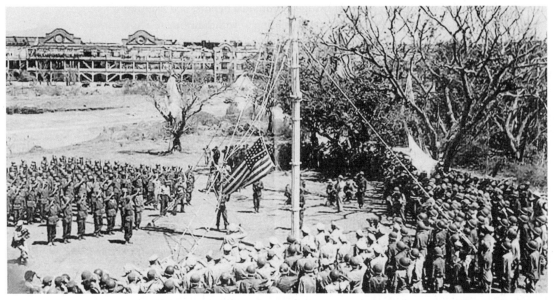

General MacArthur salutes while the American flag is raised over the devastated American barracks area on Corregidor, with parachutes from the 503rd Parachute Infantry Regiment dangling in the trees, March 2, 1945.

CENTRAL PACIFIC, IWO JIMA: The 2nd Battalion of the 4th Marines of the 4th Marine Division pushes past Hill 382 and advances 150 yards. A maze of underground tunnels allowing Japanese soldiers to appear anywhere at any point beyond Hill 382 stops the advance. The other areas of the Meatgrinder, Turkey Knob, the Amphitheater, and Minami Village Japanese troops continue to resist any American advance. The 3rd Marine Division gains 500 yards in approaching Hill 362-B. The 5th Marine Division moves from Hill 362-A toward Nishi Ridge.

NEW GUINEA: B-24s of the 394th Bombardment Squadron (Heavy), 5th Bombardment Group (Heavy), redeploy from Morotai to Samar Island in the Philippines.

March 3

CBI: Fourteenth Air Force sends four B-24 Liberators over the Gulf of Tonkin and the South China Sea to attack shipping targets of opportunity. Aircrews report one vessel sunk and three damaged.

In Burma, Tenth Air Force sends P-38 Lightnings and P-47 Thunderbolts to support elements of the Chinese 50th Division and British 36th Division.

B-25 Mitchells, P-38s, and P-47s join attacks on troops, logistics sites, tanks, and gun positions.

ETO: Canadian troops meet Americans near the Rhine at Geldern, marking the elimination of German forces west of the Rhine above Cologne. Third Army attacks with VIII Corps and XII Corps toward the Kyll River to break the German lines and attack to the Rhine.

Eighth Air Force sends more than 1,100 B-17s and B-24 Liberators escorted by over 700 P-51 Mustangs to bomb oil refineries, industrial facilities, and rail bridges in Germany. The bombers use radar to locate the bomb release point. A total of nine bombers are lost and 206 are damaged. Aircrews report 35 confirmed kills, two probables, and 37 possibles. Aircrew casualties are nine killed, nine wounded, and 80 missing. One hundred P-51 Mustangs fly a fighter sweep in the Leipzig-Magdeburg area. Fighter pilots report four confirmed kills and 10 possibles in the air and 19 confirmed kills and 25 possibles on the ground. A total of eight P-51s are lost, and one is damaged. All pilots are reported missing.

During the night 18 B-24s bomb the marshaling yard at Emden using a radar-equipped Pathfinder bomber to mark their bomb release point.

Ninth Air Force sends A-20 Havocs, A-26 Invaders, and B-26 Marauders to attack communication centers, ammunition storage sites, motor transport targets, and a marshaling yard. P-47 and P-38 fighters support the 9th Infantry Division and 3rd Armored Division and the VII, XIII, XVI, and XIX Corps.

ITALY: Twelfth Air Force A-20 Havocs and P-47 Thunderbolts of the XXII Tactical Air Command attack vehicles, logistics storage sites, and ammunition storage areas.

During the night A-20s attack roads, ammunition storage areas, and motor transport in the Po River valley.

SOUTHWEST PACIFIC AREA: FEAF B-24 Liberators and P-47 Thunderbolts bomb targets on Formosa.

In the Philippines, Far East Air Force B-25 Mitchells bomb an airfield on Mindanao Island. B-24 Liberators and B-25s attack an airfield on Jolo Island.

SOUTHWEST PACIFIC AREA, LUZON: In the I Corps area the 25th Infantry Division captures Digdig.

In the Eighth Army area the 186th RCT of the 41st Infantry Division on Palawan Island meets Japanese defenders. A five-day battle begins in which the Japanese withdraw into the mountains. American losses are light: 12 killed and six wounded. The Japanese lose over 900 men. The Japanese will continue to resist for another month. Airfield construction begins on the island.

FEAF A-20 Havocs and B-25s bomb targets on Samar and Luzon Islands and Caballo Island in Manila Bay.

PACIFIC: U.S. submarine *Trepang* torpedoes and sinks a Japanese gunboat off southern Honshu, Japan.

CENTRAL PACIFIC: Seventh Air Force sends 10 B-24 Liberators from Guam to bomb airfields, antiaircraft positions, and radar sites on Chichi Jima. During the night four B-24s fly individual harassment raids on Chichi Jima.

CENTRAL PACIFIC, IWO JIMA: The 4th Marine Division continues to battle Japanese positions in the Meatgrinder. The Amphitheater, Minami Village, and Turkey Knob defenders continue to resist despite near continuous air and artillery bombardment. The 5th Marine Division advances about 500 yards along the western coast of the island, but loses over 500 men. The 3rd Division makes little progress in the center at Cushman's Pocket. The Japanese, now reduced to less than 3,500 defenders with little food or water left, continue to hold about one-third of the island.

Aircraft from the Mariana Islands land on the rebuilt airfield, evacuating casualties and bringing in supplies. Shore battery fire damages an attack transport off Iwo Jima.

Corporal Charles J. Berry is a member of a machine-gun crew in the 1st Battalion, 26th Marines, 5th Marine Division. As night falls over Iwo Jima, Corporal Berry and his crew stay alert for signs of Japanese infiltrators. Locating the marine position, Japanese troops throw hand grenades. A furious effort to locate and toss the grenades safely away occurs in the darkness. When one grenade lands in his position, Corporal Berry covers the explosion with his own body to save his comrades. This unselfish act of heroism will win him the Congressional Medal of Honor.

Sergeant William G. Harrell of the 1st Battalion, 28th Marines, 5th Marine Division, is the leader of an assault group and is holding a position in a perimeter defense around the company command post. While standing watch alternately with another marine in terrain covered with caves and ravines, Japanese infiltrators attack at early dawn. Sergeant Harrell kills two with his M-1 carbine and faces a hail of gunfire that tears off his left hand and fractures his thigh. As a Japanese soldier hits him with a saber, Harrell kills him with his .45-caliber automatic pistol. With his wound now causing him to weaken, Harrell orders the other marine to safety while he battles on alone, killing two more enemy soldiers and losing his right hand. He is later discovered and evacuated, surrounded by the bodies of 12 enemy soldiers. For his indomitable courage and his fierce fighting spirit in the face of heavy odds, Sergeant Harrell will receive the Medal of Honor.

Pharmacist's Mate Second Class George E. Wahlen continues to serve with 2nd Battalion, 26th Marine Regiment, 5th Marine Division, on Iwo Jima even after suffering a painful wound on February 26. Wahlen often goes forward to rescue and treat wounded marines beyond friendly lines. He ignores mortar and rifle fire to care for the wounded, often working in an area under constant enemy fire. On March 2 he is wounded again and continues to stay with his company even as they make a desperate assault across 600 yards of open terrain. During the entire time Wahlen takes care of the wounded in the face of direct enemy fire. After suffering a third wound, he is unable to walk but does crawl 50 yards to provide first aid to a wounded marine. For his extraordinary dedication to duty, courage under fire, and selfless service, Pharmacist's Mate Second Class Wahlen will receive the Medal of Honor.

NEW GUINEA: U.S. submarine *Sea Robin* torpedoes and sinks a Japanese transport off Java.

U.S. submarine *Tuna* lands supplies on the northeast coast of Borneo.

March 4

CBI: Fourteenth Air Force sends four B-24 Liberators on a sea sweep in the South China Sea. Aircrews report damage to a Japanese destroyer escort.

In Burma, Tenth Air Force sends 100 P-47 Thunderbolts and P-38 Lightnings to support ground forces and attack bridges, animal transport, troop concentrations, logistics storage sites, and targets of opportunity.

ETO: Eighth Air Force sends more than 1,000 B-17s and B-24 Liberators escorted by over 500 P-47 Thunderbolts and P-51 Mustangs to bomb the jet aircraft production facility, ordnance depots, and marshaling yards. The bombers use radar to locate bomb release points. One B-24 is lost and 39 damaged. Aircrew casualties are eight killed, three wounded, and 17 missing. One P-51 is lost and one damaged. The pilot is reported missing.

During the night one B-17 and 11 B-24s drop leaflets over Germany and the Netherlands.

Ninth Air Force sends 180 A-20 Havocs, A-26 Invaders, and B-26 Marauders to attack communication centers, rail junctions, and marshaling yards. P-47 and P-38 fighters support XX Corps.

MEDITERRANEAN: Fifteenth Air Force sends more than 600 B-17s and B-24 Liberators escorted by P-38 Lightnings and P-51 Mustangs to bomb marshaling yards in Austria, Hungary, and Yugoslavia.

B-24s, with P-51 escort, drop supplies in Yugoslavia.

ITALY: Twelfth Air Force B-25 Mitchells and B-26 Marauders attack rail bridges. A-20 Havocs and P-47 Thunderbolts of the XXII Tactical Air Command attack rail bridges and roads in the Po River valley. During the night A-20s attack bridges, a radar station, roads, and motor transport in the central Po River valley.

SOUTHWEST PACIFIC AREA: U.S. submarine *Baya* attacks a Japanese convoy, sinking a merchant tanker off the southern coast of French Indochina.

SOUTHWEST PACIFIC AREA, LUZON: The 1st Brigade Combat Team of the 1st Cavalry Division clears the last Japanese strongpoints in Manila after a nine-day battle to clear the government buildings outside of Intramuros. Japanese casualties are estimated at over 16,000. U.S. casualties are 1,010 dead and 5,565 wounded. At least 100,000 Filipinos have been deliberately killed by the Japanese.

The 6th Infantry Division of XIV Corps pushes the Japanese off the crest of Mount Pacawagan.

Far East Air Force B-24 Liberators bomb airfields on Mindanao and gun positions, ammunition storage areas, airfields, and targets of opportunity on Luzon. B-24 Liberators also hit fortifications on Caballo Island in Manila Bay.

The P-38 Lightning detachments of the 431st and 433rd Fighter Squadrons, 475th Fighter Group, redeploy from Mindoro Island and return to Clark Field on Luzon.

PACIFIC: During the night Twentieth Air Force sends 11 B-29s from China to mine the confluence of the Hwangpoo and Yangtze Rivers and the Tai-hsing Narrows at Shanghai.

Twentieth Air Force sends 192 B-29 Superfortresses from the Mariana Islands to bomb Musashi, Japan. Heavy clouds prevent bombing the primary target. A total of 159 B-29s bomb the secondary target, the urban areas of Tokyo, and 18 others attack alternative targets. One B-29 is lost.

Lieutenant General Barney McKinney Giles becomes the commander of Army Air Forces Pacific Operations Area and deputy commander of the Twentieth Air Force.

U.S. submarine *Tilefish* torpedoes and sinks a Japanese fishing vessel in the Ryukyus.

CENTRAL PACIFIC: Seventh Air Force sends 10 B-24 Liberators from Guam to bomb the airfield on Chichi Jima. A B-29 makes an emergency landing on Iwo Jima Island. This is the first of over 2,400 emergency landings on the island that will save the lives of thousands of crewmen who otherwise would have been lost at sea.

CENTRAL PACIFIC, IWO JIMA: A B-29 Superfortress, damaged and returning from a bombing run on the Japanese home islands, makes an emergency landing on the airfield at Iwo Jima. Lieutenant General Holland Smith refuses Major General Harry Schmidt's request to land the 3rd Marine Regiment to replace the heavy unit losses in the 4th and 5th Divisions. Smith maintains control of the veteran regiment and instead provides the divisions with untested individual replacements. Because of heavy officer casualties, the marine divisions have sergeants leading half-strength platoons. Multiple companies are merged into one unit commanded by whatever ranking officer is still alive.

March 5

CBI: In China, Fourteenth Air Force B-25 Mitchells, escorted by P-47 Thunderbolts, attack bridges while P-51 Mustangs and P-40s on armed reconnaissance attack road, rail, and river traffic. In French Indochina, 30 B-25 Mitchells bomb bridges.

In Burma, Tenth Air Force sends P-47 Thunderbolts to support the British 36th Division and the Chinese 50th Division. P-47 Thunderbolts and B-25 Mitchells attack troop concentrations along the battle lines and attack logistics sites, road traffic, and targets of opportunity.

ETO: Elements of the VII Corps, First Army, enter Cologne and begin a fight for the city. The 4th Armored Division of XII Corps (plus the 5th, 76th, and 80th Infantry Divisions) of Third Army moves north of the Moselle River.

Since the beginning of Operation Grenade, Ninth Army has cleared the Rhine River from Düsseldorf to Moers. In the process, 36,000 German soldiers have been killed or captured. American casualties have been 7,300. First Army has secured all of its assigned objectives for Operation Lumberjack, controlling the Rhine River from Cologne northward to link with Ninth Army.

Eighth Air Force sends more than 400 B-17s and B-24 Liberators escorted by nearly 700 P-47 Thunderbolts and P-51 Mustangs to bomb synthetic oil production facilities and marshaling yards. The bombers use radar to mark the bomb release point. One B-17 is lost and 15 damaged. Aircrew casualties are nine missing. Four fighters are damaged. One pilot is reported killed.

During the night nine B-24s drop leaflets over Germany and the Netherlands, and 21 B-24 Liberators bomb the Wiesbaden rail station, using a Pathfinder bomber to mark the bomb release point.

Ninth Air Force sends 565 A-20 Havocs, A-26 Invaders, and B-26 Marauders to attack communication centers, ordnance depots, and marshaling yards. P-47 and P-38 fighters fly armed reconnaissance missions.

The headquarters of the 52nd Troop Carrier Wing, IX Troop Carrier Command, redeploys from England to France.

ITALY: The 10th Mountain Division secures the ridgelines along Highway 64 to support future offensive operations in the spring.

Twelfth Air Force A-20 Havocs and P-47 Thunderbolts attack rail bridges. During the night A-20s attack roads and motor transport in the Po River valley.

SOUTHWEST PACIFIC AREA: In the Philippines, Far East Air Force B-25 Mitchells attack an airfield on Mindanao Island. On Luzon, B-24 Liberators with P-38 Lightnings attack troops. P-47 Thunderbolts attack Fort Drum in Manila Bay, attack Japanese troops near Fort Stotsenburg, and support guerrilla forces northeast of Lingayen Gulf. B-25 Mitchells attack an airfield on Jolo Island.

B-24s and P-47s fly armed reconnaissance over Formosa. Fighters conduct sweeps against railroad targets.

U.S. submarine *Bashaw* attacks the Japanese convoy hit by USS *Baya* the previous day, sinking an oiler and an army tanker off the southern coast of French Indochina. U.S. submarine *Peto* is damaged in an air attack off Hainan but continues her patrol in the South China Sea.

Task Force 58 carrier aircraft sink a Japanese auxiliary submarine chaser off the Pescadores in the South China Sea. Fifth Air Force B-25 Mitchells attack a Japanese convoy, sinking two auxiliary submarine chasers and a cargo ship off the southern coast of French Indochina.

PACIFIC: U.S. submarine *Tilefish* torpedoes and damages a Japanese minesweeper south of Kyushu, Japan.

CENTRAL PACIFIC: Seventh Air Force sends 11 B-24 Liberators from Guam to bomb the airfield on Chichi Jima. Three B-24s bomb Marcus Island. A total of 22 B-24s based at Angaur Island bomb an airfield on Mindanao in the Philippines. During the night five B-24s conduct individual snooper (radar-assisted bomb release) missions on Chichi Jima.

CENTRAL PACIFIC, IWO JIMA: Lieutenant General Holland Smith orders the 3rd Regiment of the 3rd Marine Division to return to Guam. Major General Schmidt orders units on Iwo Jima to halt for rest, resupply, and to receive replacements.

New Guinea: The headquarters of 5th Bombardment Group (Heavy) redeploys from Morotai Island to Samar Island.

U.S. submarine *Sea Robin* attacks a Japanese convoy in the Java Sea, sinking a gunboat, an auxiliary netlayer, and a cargo ship. Thirteenth Air Force B-24 Liberators sink a Japanese auxiliary submarine chaser southeast of Celebes Island.

March 6

CBI: In China, Fourteenth Air Force P-40s and P-51 Mustangs attack troop concentrations, rail and river traffic, and logistics storage facilities.

In Burma, Tenth Air Force sends 12 B-25 Mitchells, P-47 Thunderbolts, and P-38 Lightnings to attack fuel storage areas, road traffic, troop concentrations, logistics storage sites, and targets of opportunity.

ETO: During the night Eighth Air Force sends 12 B-24s to drop leaflets over Germany and the Netherlands. Five B-24s fly a Capetbagger mission.

Ninth Air Force sends more than 260 A-20 Havocs, A-26 Invaders, and B-26 Marauders to attack communication centers, storage depots, and marshaling yards. P-47 and P-38 fighters support ground forces and fly armed reconnaissance missions.

Mediterranean: The 302nd Fighter Squadron (with P-51 Mustangs) of the 332nd Fighter Group is inactivated at Ramitelli airfield in Italy.

Italy: Twelfth Air Force B-25 Mitchells and B-26 Marauders attack rail and road bridges. A-20 Havocs and P-47 Thunderbolts support Fifth Army ground forces south and southwest of Bologna. During the night A-20s attack targets of opportunity in the Po River valley.

Southwest Pacific Area: In the Philippines, Far East Air Force B-24 Liberators bomb targets on Mindanao. On Luzon, B-24s, B-25 Mitchells, P-47 Thunderbolts, and P-38 Lightnings attack a number of targets in support of ground forces and Philippine guerrillas.

B-25s and P-38 Lightnings attack an airfield on Hainan Island, while fighters conduct a sweep over Formosa.

The headquarters of the 347th Fighter Group and the P-38 Lightnings of the 67th, 68th, and 339th Fighter Squadrons redeploy from Mindoro Island to Palawan Island. The 67th and 339th operate from Morotai Island.

Central Pacific: Seventh Air Force sends 11 B-24 Liberators from Guam to bomb the airfield on Chichi Jima. Three B-24s bomb Marcus Island. During the night five B-24s fly individual harassment raids on Chichi Jima.

The headquarters of the 15th Fighter Group arrives on Iwo Jima Island from Hawaii. The P-61 Black Widow night fighters of the 548th Night Fighter Squadron redeploy from Saipan to Iwo Jima.

Central Pacific, Iwo Jima: P-51 Mustangs of the 15th Fighter Group, VII Fighter Command, arrive on Iwo Jima. The pilots begin flying air support missions for the marines, delivering 1,000-pound bombs with delay fuses to destroy underground positions.

New Guinea: The 419th Night Fighter Squadron from XIII Fighter Command redeploys from New Guinea to Palawan Island in the Philippines. The squadron operates from Morotai Island with P-38 Lightnings and P-61 Black Widow night fighters.

March 7

CBI: British Fourteenth Army occupies Mandalay.

In China, Fourteenth Air Force sends four B-25 Mitchells and nine P-40s to bomb railroad targets. Over 130 P-40s and P-51 Mustangs attack rail and river traffic.

In Burma, Tenth Air Force sends nearly 50 P-47 Thunderbolts to support the British 36th Division and the Chinese 50th Division. Twelve B-25 Mitchells, supported by P-47 Thunderbolts and P-38 Lightnings, attack road traffic, troop concentrations, logistics storage sites, and targets of opportunity.

ETO: The Remagen Bridge is Captured. A task force commanded by Lieutenant Colonel Leonard Engeman composed of the 14th Tank Battalion and the 27th Armored Infantry Battalion, 9th Armored Division, captures the Ludendorff railroad bridge at Remagen, about 20 miles northwest of Koblenz, the only bridge still intact along the entire Rhine River. Lieutenant Karl H. Timmermann, commander of A Company, 27th Armored Infantry Battalion, leads a group of soldiers across the bridge even as German engineers attempt to blow it up. A few charges explode but do not bring the bridge down. Timmermann is the first American to set foot on German soil over the Rhine River. Engineers quickly disable other charges, and infantry and tanks cross the bridge. Upon hearing the news, General Eisenhower orders General Omar Bradley to put at least five divisions across as quickly as possible.

First Army occupies Cologne.

Curious soldiers of the 3rd Armored Division inspect a knocked out German Mark V Panther tank in front of the Cologne cathedral, March 1945.

The 4th Armored Division of XII Corps and the 11th Armored Division of VIII Corps of Third Army close on the Rhine River after a rapid advance of 60 miles in three days. The 4th Armored has captured 6,000 prisoners and destroyed nearly 900 vehicles at a cost of 29 men killed.

Eighth Air Force sends more than 900 B-17s and B-24 Liberators escorted by over 300 P-47 Thunderbolts and P-51 Mustangs to bomb oil production facilities, benzol plants, and marshaling yards. The bombers use radar to locate the bomb release point. A total of 81 bombers are damaged. Aircrew casualties are 11 killed. One P-51 is lost on a photo reconnaissance mission. The pilot is reported missing.

Six B-24 Liberators and six B-17s conduct screening missions to jam German radio interception efforts and employ countermeasures against German radar sites.

During the night 11 B-24s drop leaflets over Germany and the Netherlands. A total of 19 B-24s bomb Dortmund during the night using a Pathfinder radar-equipped bomber to mark their bomb release point. One B-24 is lost.

Ninth Air Force P-47 and P-38 fighters support XVI Corps.

American soldiers in the railroad tunnel across the Rhine River look back on the distinctive towers of the Ludendorff railroad bridge at Remagen, Germany. The capture of an intact bridge across the Rhine was one of the most fortuitous events of the war for General Omar Bradley's 12th Army Group.

MEDITERRANEAN: Naval Task Group 89.9, comprising an aviation supply ship and a fleet tug, departs Naples, Italy, for Odessa, on the Black Sea coast of the USSR, with supplies for American prisoners of war freed by Soviet troops.

ITALY: Twelfth Air Force B-25 Mitchells and B-26 Marauders attack rail and road bridges. A-20 Havocs and P-47 Thunderbolts attack fuel and ammunition storage areas.

During the night A-20s attack bridges and targets of opportunity.

SOUTHWEST PACIFIC AREA: On Luzon in the Philippines, Far East Air Force B-24 Liberators attack Japanese positions while A-20 Havocs, P-38 Lightnings, and P-40s attack troop concentrations and gun positions.

CENTRAL PACIFIC: Seventh Air Force sends 11 B-24 Liberators from Guam to bomb the airfield on Chichi Jima and a town on Haha Jima. During the night five B-24s fly individual harassment raids on Chichi Jima.

CENTRAL PACIFIC, IWO JIMA: At dawn the 3rd Battalion of the 9th Marines, 3rd Division, makes a surprise attack without any artillery preparation against Hill 362-C. Advancing 500 yards, the marines gain complete surprise and report capturing their objective. At first light the marines discover that the objective is still 250 yards away. Lieutenant Colonel Harold C. Boem orders an advance to capture the hill, even though the Japanese are fully aware a marine battalion has entered their lines. By the afternoon Hill 362-C is captured. Two other battalions of the 9th Marines are unsuccessful against Japanese positions in Cushman's Pocket.

The 5th Marine Division battles close to Kitano Point, the northernmost tip of the island. The 4th Marine Division continues to attack the Meatgrinder defenses, but Japanese strength is weakening.

Second Lieutenant John H. Leims is the commander of B Company, 1st Battalion, 9th Marine Regiment, 3rd Marine Division, leading an attack on a fortification located on a rocky hill. His marines blast the Japanese out of caves and pillboxes and occupy the objective, but Leims quickly realizes that he has advanced far beyond friendly lines and is ordered to fall back. During the reorganization after the withdrawal, Leims is notified that several marines have been left behind. Leims goes back into the area, as Japanese machine guns fire all around him. He locates one marine and brings him back to safety, then returns to locate and bring back a second marine. For his example of extraordinary courage and dedication to duty, Second Lieutenant Leims will receive the Medal of Honor.

March 8

CBI: In China, Fourteenth Air Force B-24 Liberator aircrews report sinking a Japanese transport in the South China Sea. P-40s and P-51 Mustangs attack bridges, troops, gun positions, and rail and river traffic.

In Burma, Tenth Air Force sends P-47 Thunderbolts to support the British 36th Division. Other P-47s attack road traffic, gun positions, troop concentrations, and logistics storage sites.

Fourteenth Air Force B-24 Liberators sink a Japanese coast defense vessel southeast of Hainan Island. Tenth Air Force B-24s attack Japanese shipping in the Andaman Sea, sinking a cargo vessel. Fourteenth Air Force P-51 Mustangs attack Japanese shipping in the Yangtze River near Hankow, sinking a cargo vessel.

ETO: Eighth Air Force sends more than 1,300 B-17s and B-24 Liberators escorted by over 300 P-51 Mustangs to bomb oil production facilities, benzol plants, and marshaling yards. The bombers use radar to mark the bomb release point over the targets. No bombers are lost, but 27 are damaged. There are no aircrew casualties.

Four B-17s conduct screening missions to jam German radio interception efforts and employ countermeasures against German radar sites.

During the night 11 B-24s drop leaflets over Germany and the Netherlands. Four B-24s fly a Carpetbagger mission. A total of 19 B-24s bomb Dortmund during the night, using a Pathfinder radar-equipped bomber to mark bomb release points.

Ninth Air Force sends 328 A-20 Havocs, A-26 Invaders, and B-26 Marauders to attack a military transportation depot, railroad bridges, and marshaling yards. P-47 and P-38 fighters support ground forces and fly armed reconnaissance missions.

Mediterranean: Fifteenth Air Force sends more than 550 B-17s and B-24 Liberators escorted by P-38 Lightnings and P-51 Mustangs to bomb marshaling yards in Hungary and Italy and a locomotive works in Yugoslavia.

Italy: Twelfth Air Force B-25 Mitchells and B-26 Marauders bomb marshaling yards and rail and road bridges. A-20 Havocs and P-47 Thunderbolts attack rail lines, road bridges, and roads. During the night A-20s attack roads and motor transport in the Po River valley.

Southwest Pacific Area, Luzon: The 1st Cavalry Division attacks the Japanese Shimbu Group defenses near Antipolo behind a heavy artillery and air bombardment.

Far East Air Force B-24 Liberators bomb targets on Mindanao Island. On Luzon, B-24s, A-20 Havocs, P-47 Thunderbolts, and P-38 Lightnings attack Japanese defenses, gun positions, fuel storage sites, and support guerrilla forces.

Pacific: Fifth Air Force aircraft sink a Japanese cargo ship in the South China Sea near Hainan Island. Navy PBM Mariner patrol bombers bomb a Japanese convoy, sinking a cargo vessel west of Formosa.

Central Pacific: Seventh Air Force sends 14 B-24 Liberators from Guam to bomb the airfield on Chichi Jima. During the night five B-24s fly individual harassment raids on Chichi Jima.

Central Pacific, Iwo Jima: About 1,500 Japanese troops make a counterattack against the 4th Marine Division. The Japanese lose over 800 men before retreating. The marines suffer nearly 300 casualties in desperate and close fighting.

First Lieutenant Jack Lummus is a rifle platoon leader in the 2nd Battalion, 27th Marine Regiment, 5th Marine Division. He begins an attack on yet another Japanese defensive network after two days and nights of unrelenting combat. As his platoon is stopped by a high volume of accurate fire, Lieutenant Lummus goes forward by himself to locate the hidden positions. A Japanese grenade knocks him down, but he rises to his feet and attacks the emplacement. He is immediately fired on by the adjoining position and is wounded by another grenade but attacks the pillbox, eliminating the enemy. He returns to his platoon and leads them forward with supporting tanks until heavy fire from another network of defenses halts the advance. Lieutenant Lummus again goes forward alone and attacks a fortified installation, eliminating the defenders. Inspired by his actions, his marines move through the area, eliminating

Japanese defenders in foxholes and spider traps as Lummus leads the way, firing his M-1 carbine into the positions. He is killed when he steps on a land mine. For his extraordinary valor, exceptional combat skills, and dedicated leadership, First Lieutenant Lummus will receive the Congressional Medal of Honor.

March 9

CBI: The Japanese seize complete control of French Indochina, claiming the French administration is covertly assisting the Allies.

In China, Fourteenth Air Force sends 32 B-24 Liberators, escorted by five P-51 Mustangs, to bomb railroad yards. Another 15 B-25 Mitchells and two P-40s destroy two bridges. P-40s and P-51 Mustangs attack gun positions, troops, and rail and river traffic.

In Burma, Tenth Air Force sends P-47 Thunderbolts to support the Chinese 50th Division. Over 80 P-47s and P-38 Lightnings attack road traffic, troop concentrations, logistics storage sites, artillery, and targets of opportunity.

ETO: At Remagen, General Omar N. Bradley's 12th Army Group has established a lodgment three miles deep across the Rhine. German reinforcements are rushed to the area but have neither the manpower nor the capability to stop the Americans. The 9th Armored Engineer Battalion repairs damage to the Ludendorff Bridge and lays timber planking across for rapid movement of tanks and infantry. About 8,000 troops have crossed the river.

Bonn, some 10 miles downriver from Remagen, is captured by V Corps (2nd, 28th, and 69th Infantry Divisions) of First Army.

Field Marshall Bernard L. Montgomery lays out the final plan for Operation Plunder, the 21st Army Group's crossing of the Rhine. The U.S. Ninth Army (XIII Corps, XVI Corps, and XIX Corps) is to cross south of Wesel. The XVI Corps will make the initial assault with two divisions; XIX Corps will be prepared to pass through the right of the British Second Army and attack toward Hamm-Münster. The XIII Corps will hold along the Rhine. The XVIII Airborne Corps (U.S. 17th Airborne and the British 6th Airborne Divisions) are to support the attack at Wesel and expand the bridgehead, capture crossing sites at the Issel River, and then link with Ninth Army. Ninth Army is well prepared. It has collected 138,000 tons of supplies to support the operation along with 14,000 tons of bridging equipment. Over 600 artillery pieces are in place to support the U.S. divisions. Most of the Allied air support in-theater will be dedicated to the 21st Army Group's crossing.

Eighth Air Force sends more than 1,000 B-17s and B-24 Liberators escorted by over 400 P-51 Mustangs to bomb industrial targets, a tank production facility, and marshaling yards. A total of seven bombers are lost and 425 are damaged. Aircrews report two possible kills. Aircrew casualties are 12 wounded and 68 missing. Fighter pilots report two possible kills in the air. Two P-51s are damaged.

Six B-17s conduct screening missions to jam German radio interception efforts and employ countermeasures against German radar sites.

During the night 11 B-24s drop leaflets over France, Germany, and the Netherlands. Two B-24s fly a Carpetbagger mission.

Ninth Air Force sends more than 600 A-20 Havocs, A-26 Invaders, and B-26 Marauders to attack depots and storage facilities, ammunition production facilities, and marshaling yards. P-47 and P-38 fighters support ground forces over the Remagen bridgehead and support the 9th Infantry Division and 9th Armored Division, the XX Corps, and XVI Corps.

MEDITERRANEAN: Fifteenth Air Force sends 372 B-17s and B-24 Liberators escorted by P-38 Lightnings and P-51 Mustangs to bomb marshaling yards in Austria and Yugoslavia.

ITALY: Twelfth Air Force B-25 Mitchells and B-26 Marauders bomb bridges and marshaling yards. A-20 Havocs and P-47 Thunderbolts attack rail lines, vehicles, logistics storage sites, bridges, and roads.

During the night A-20s attack river crossings in the Po River valley.

SOUTHWEST PACIFIC AREA: In the Philippines, Far East Air Force B-24 Liberators bomb Mindanao. B-25 Mitchells support a PT boat operation against targets on Basilan Island. On Luzon Island, B-24s, B-25s, A-20 Havocs, P-38 Lightnings, and P-47 Thunderbolts attack Japanese forces around Manila Bay, and airfields, bridges, and towns on Luzon.

B-24 Liberators bomb the docks at Takao on Formosa.

CENTRAL PACIFIC: Seventh Air Force sends 13 B-24 Liberators from Guam to bomb the airfield on Chichi Jima. During the night five B-24s fly individual harassment raids on Chichi Jima and a total of 24 B-24s based at Angaur Island bomb Mindanao Island in the Philippines.

CENTRAL PACIFIC, IWO JIMA: A patrol of the 3rd Marine Division reaches the northwest coast of the island. The remainder of the division continues to reduce Cushman's Pocket.

Platoon Sergeant Joseph R. Julian, with the 1st Battalion, 27th Marine Regiment, 5th Marine Division, sets his machine guns to support the platoon's attack on a series of Japanese trenches and fortified positions, then moves to attack the enemy alone, throwing demolition charges and white phosphorus grenades into the emplacements, then jumping into a trench in pursuit of fleeing enemy soldiers. Picking up a discarded rifle, he kills five of the enemy and then obtains more demolition charges to continue the attack. With the assistance of another marine, Julian attacks two cave positions and uses a bazooka to destroy another pillbox. He is mortally wounded in his final attack. For his extraordinary fighting skill, great courage, and inspiring leadership, Sergeant Julian will be awarded the Congressional Medal of Honor.

March 10

ALEUTIANS: Eleventh Air Force sends five B-24 Liberators to bomb targets on Shimushu and Paramushiru Islands in the Kuriles. The bombers use radar to mark bomb release points.

CBI: In China, Fourteenth Air Force sends 32 B-24 Liberators to attack railyards while P-40s and P-51 Mustangs attack rail and river traffic, logistics storage facilities, troops, and airfields.

In Burma, Tenth Air Force sends P-47 Thunderbolts to support the British 36th Division. Other P-47s and P-38 Lightnings attack road traffic, troop concentrations, logistics storage sites, and a truck park.

ETO: First Army and Third Army link along the Rhine, accomplishing General Eisenhower's objective to clear German forces from the west bank of the Rhine River. Third Army collects another 12,000 prisoners. The 6th Army Group commander, Lieutenant General Jacob L. Devers, orders Seventh Army (VI Corps, XV Corps, and XXI Corps), commanded by Major General Alexander M. Patch, to attack toward Kaiserslautern and seize a bridgehead near Worms. The French First Army is ordered to cover the Rhine River from Strasbourg to the Swiss border.

The 51st and 291st Combat Engineer Battalions begin construction of two pontoon bridges at Remagen. Despite German artillery fire and heavy casualties, the engineers complete the heavy pontoon bridges in 29.5 hours.

Eighth Air Force sends more than 1,300 B-17s and B-24 Liberators escorted by over 600 P-47 Thunderbolts and P-51 Mustangs to bomb road and rail bridges, marshaling yards, and airfields. The bombers use radar to mark the bomb release point. A total of 81 bombers are damaged. Aircrews report two confirmed kills and one possible. Aircrew casualties are three wounded. Fighter pilots report two confirmed kills and one possible in the air. Two fighters are lost and one is damaged.

Twelve B-17s conduct screening missions to jam German radio interception efforts and employ countermeasures against German radar sites.

During the night 12 B-24s drop leaflets over France, Germany, and the Netherlands. A total of 13 B-24s bomb Munster during the night.

Ninth Air Force sends nearly 400 A-20 Havocs, A-26 Invaders, and B-26 Marauders to attack communication centers and marshaling yards. P-47 and P-38 fighters support the 9th Infantry Division, the 4th Armored Division, and XX and XVI Corps.

MEDITERRANEAN: Fifteenth Air Force sends nearly 200 B-17s and B-24 Liberators escorted by P-38 Lightnings and P-51 Mustangs to bomb a railroad bridge and marshaling yards in Italy.

ITALY: Twelfth Air Force B-25 Mitchells bomb bridges. A-20 Havocs and P-47 Thunderbolts attack bridges, vehicles, logistics storage sites, and ammunition storage areas in the Po River valley. During the night A-20s attack bridges in the Po River Valley.

SOUTHWEST PACIFIC AREA: In the Eighth Army area, Naval Task Group 78.1 (Rear Admiral Forrest B. Royal) lands the 162nd and 163rd Infantry Regiments of the 41st Infantry Division, near Zamboanga City on the island of Mindanao. Japanese shore batteries sink two LSTs and two LCIs.

In the Philippines, Far East Air Force B-24 Liberators and B-25 Mitchells bomb towns and airfields on Mindanao. On Luzon, B-24s bomb an airfield, while B-25s and A-20 Havocs support guerrillas and bomb enemy positions. P-38 Lightnings and P-47 Thunderbolts attack Japanese troop concentrations near Fort Stotsenburg and other locations on Luzon.

Fifth Air Force B-25 Mitchells attack and sink a Japanese army tanker off the southern coast of French Indochina.

FEAF B-24 Liberators bomb airfields in Borneo.

Private First Class Thomas E. Atkins is a member of a platoon in A Company, 127th Infantry Regiment, 32nd Infantry Division, occupying a defensive position on a high hill near Villa Verde Trail, Luzon. In the early morning hours the Japanese conduct a heavy counterattack. Private First Class Atkins is wounded but maintains his position and returns fire. He refuses medical attention and stays at his position, repelling a number of attacks over the next four hours. Firing over 400 rounds and using three rifles until they no longer function, he withdraws during a lull to pick up another rifle and ammunition. As unit medics begin first aid, he kills a Japanese soldier within the perimeter, then sees a group of Japanese moving to outflank the platoon's position. Lying on a litter, Private First Class Atkins picks up his rifle and drives the enemy off with well-aimed and accurate fire. His exceptional courage and skill in performing his duties in the face of overwhelming odds and painful wounds will win Atkins the Medal of Honor.

PACIFIC: Twentieth Air Force sends B-29s to bomb the marshaling yard at Kuala Lumpur in Malaya.

Another raid on Tokyo is conducted by 279 B-29 Superfortresses from the XXI Bomber Command's 73rd, 313th, and 314th Bombardment Wings (Very Heavy) based on Guam Island, Tinian, and Saipan. The bombers hit the urban area with incendiaries in the hours before dawn. This attack destroys over 267,000 buildings and kills or injures nearly 125,000 people (nearly 84,000 are reported killed)—the highest loss of life of any aerial bombardment of World War II. Fourteen B-29s are lost.

U.S. submarine *Kete* attacks a Japanese convoy north of Okinawa, sinking a transport and two cargo ships.

CENTRAL PACIFIC: Seventh Air Force sends 10 B-24 Liberators from Guam to bomb the airfield on Chichi Jima. Three B-24s bomb Marcus Island. A total of 23 B-24s from Angaur Island bomb an airfield on Mindanao Island in the Philippines. During the night nine B-24s fly individual snooper missions on Chichi Jima.

CENTRAL PACIFIC, IWO JIMA: The 4th Marine Division succeeds in clearing the Meatgrinder and capturing Turkey Knob and Minami Village. Units begin advancing with little enemy contact. The 5th Marine Division advancing along the coast reaches the Japanese defenses at Death Valley, a series of sharp ravines and ridges filled with tunnels, about 500 yards south of Kitano Point. This heavily defended position stops the marine advance. The 3rd Marine Division reduces Cushman's Pocket. Most of the marines are too battle weary to function effectively. A large number of the men in the division are now untrained replacements.

March 11

CBI: Fourteenth Air Force B-24 Liberators attack shipping targets in the Gulf of Tonkin and the South China Sea. Aircrews report one cargo ship sunk and another damaged. P-40s and P-51 Mustangs attack rail and river traffic. In French Indochina, B-25 Mitchells attack bridges and rail cars.

In Burma, Tenth Air Force sends 14 B-25 Mitchells to bomb vehicles, logistics storage sites, ammunition storage areas, and troops. P-47 Thunderbolts and P-38 Lightnings attack road traffic and targets of opportunity.

ETO: Eighth Air Force sends more than 1,200 B-17s and B-24 Liberators escorted by over 800 P-47 Thunderbolts and P-51 Mustangs to bomb the U-boat yards at Kiel and Bremen and the shipyard and refinery area at Hamburg, Germany. The bombers use radar to mark bomb release points over the targets. One B-17 is lost and 52 are damaged. Four P-51s are lost. Six B-17s conduct screening missions to jam German radio interception efforts and employ countermeasures against German radar sites.

During the night 11 B-24s drop leaflets over Germany and the Netherlands.

Ninth Air Force sends nearly 700 A-20 Havocs, A-26 Invaders, and B-26 Marauders to attack communication centers, ammunition plants, airfields, and marshaling yards. P-47 and P-38 fighters support the 9th Infantry Division at the Remagen bridgehead and support XX Corps.

Navy LCVPs, part of Task Group 122.5.1, support army engineers in laying a pontoon bridge at the Remagen bridgehead.

Eighth Air Force bombers sink German submarines *U-2515* and *U-2530* during a raid on Hamburg. A Navy PB4Y-1 Privateer sinks German submarine *U-681* southwest of England in the Celtic Sea.

ITALY: Twelfth Air Force B-25 Mitchells and B-26 Marauders bomb bridges in Italy and Austria. A-20 Havocs and P-47 Thunderbolts of the XXII Tactical Air Command attack rail lines, logistics storage sites, and ammunition storage areas in the Po River valley. During the night A-20s attack river crossing sites, airfields, and roads in the Po River valley.

SOUTHWEST PACIFIC AREA: General MacArthur orders Eighth Army to capture the island of Mindanao, even as the 41st Infantry Division continues operations on the Zamboanga Peninsula. The island has 43,000 Japanese troops, most of which are near Davao City. They lack supplies and have been harried by a 24,000-man guerrilla force run by Colonel Wendell W. Fertig, an American who escaped from Bataan in 1942. Lieutenant General Eichelberger and his staff develop a plan to land at Illana Bay and advance eastward.

In the Philippines, Far East Air Force B-24 Liberators and B-25 Mitchells bomb airfields, Japanese positions, and support PT boat operations on Mindanao.

SOUTHWEST PACIFIC AREA, LUZON: The 2nd Cavalry Brigade of the 1st Cavalry Division captures Antipolo. The 1st Cavalry suffers nearly 400 casualties during the 19 days of combat to capture the position.

FEAF B-24 Liberators, A-20 Havocs, P-38 Lightnings, and P-47 Thunderbolts support ground forces, attack logistics storage sites, and hit targets of opportunity.

B-24s and P-47s attack towns on Formosa.

PACIFIC: Twentieth Air Force sends more than 300 B-29s to bomb the urban area of Nagoya, Japan, with incendiaries. One B-29 is lost.

U.S. submarine *Segundo* torpedoes and sinks a Japanese cargo ship off southern Korea.

CENTRAL PACIFIC: Seventh Air Force sends 11 B-24 Liberators from Guam to bomb the airfield on Chichi Jima. P-51 Mustangs from Iwo Jima attack the airfields on Chichi Jima and Haha Jima. During the night eight B-24s fly individual harassment raids on Chichi Jima.

Japanese aircraft from Kanoya, Japan, attack the U.S. fleet anchorage at Ulithi, damaging the carrier USS *Randolph*. American casualties are 25 killed and 106 wounded.

March 12

CBI: Fourteenth Air Force sends four B-25 Mitchells to bomb the Song Rang bridge in French Indochina. Aircrews report the bridge is destroyed.

In Burma, Tenth Air Force sends 13 B-25 Mitchells and 35 P-47 Thunderbolts to attack troop concentrations, logistics sites, vehicles, and antiaircraft guns. P-47 Thunderbolts attack road traffic during several sweeps.

ETO: Eighth Air Force sends more than 1,300 B-17s and B-24 Liberators escorted by nearly 800 P-47 Thunderbolts and P-51 Mustangs to bomb marshaling yards in Germany. The bombers use radar-equipped Pathfinder bombers or radar signal intercepts to mark bomb release points over the targets. One B-17 is lost and 10 are damaged. Aircrews report four confirmed kills and one possible. Aircrew casualties are three wounded and 10 missing. Fighter pilots report four confirmed kills and one possible in the air. Four P-51s are lost. Three pilots are reported missing.

During the night 11 B-24s drop leaflets over Germany and the Netherlands. Ten B-24s fly a Carpetbagger mission.

Ninth Air Force sends A-20 Havocs, A-26 Invaders, and B-26 Marauders to attack ammunition production facilities and marshaling yards. P-47 and P-38 fighters support the 9th Infantry Division and the XX Corps.

MEDITERRANEAN: Fifteenth Air Force sends nearly 800 B-17s and B-24 Liberators escorted by P-38 Lightnings and P-51 Mustangs to bomb oil refineries and marshaling yards in Austria.

ITALY: Twelfth Air Force B-25 Mitchells bomb rail bridges. A-20 Havocs and P-47 Thunderbolts attack rail lines and bridges. During the night A-20s attack roads and motor transport in the Po River Valley.

SOUTHWEST PACIFIC AREA: FEAF B-24s, with P-38 escort, attack targets on Formosa. P-51s also attack power plants on Formosa. In the Philippines, Far East Air Force B-24 Liberators bomb Mindanao Island.

SOUTHWEST PACIFIC AREA, LUZON: The two RCTs of the 43rd Infantry Division relieve the 1st Cavalry Division. The 6th and the 43rd Infantry Divisions continue the attack eastward, clearing Japanese positions. A counterattack by several battalions of the Shimbu Group fails to stop the 6th Infantry Division's attack.

B-24 Liberators bomb Japanese troops; B-25 Mitchells attack logistics storage areas and Japa-

Sherman tanks support infantry on Luzon in the Philippines.

nese troops, and A-20 Havocs, P-38 Lightnings, and P-47 Thunderbolts support ground forces.

The B-24s of the 33rd Bombardment Squadron (Heavy), 22nd Bombardment Group (Heavy), redeploy from Samar Island to Clark Field, Luzon.

PACIFIC: Twentieth Air Force sends 49 B-29 Superfortresses to attack oil storage facilities in Malaya and Sumatra. Only 44 hit their primary targets. Aircrews report one possible kill. Aircrews report negligible results.

CENTRAL PACIFIC: Seventh Air Force sends 13 B-24 Liberators to bomb the airfield on Chichi Jima. A total of 16 P-51 Mustangs bomb Haha Jima. B-24s based at Angaur Island bomb a logistics storage area on Mindanao in the Philippines. During the night eight B-24s fly individual harassment raids on Chichi Jima.

NEW GUINEA: The C-47s of the 6th Troop Carrier Squadron, 374th Troop Carrier Group, redeploy from Biak to Leyte Island. The 69th Bombardment Squadron (Medium), 42nd Bombardment Group (Medium), redeploys its B-25s from Sansapor, New Guinea, to Palawan Island in the Philippines. The 69th Bombardment Squadron (Medium) operates from Morotai Island.

March 13

CBI: Fourteenth Air Force sends seven B-24 Liberators over the Gulf of Tonkin and the South China Sea to attack shipping. Aircrews report a large junk and one cargo ship are sunk. P-40s, P-38 Lightnings, and P-51 Mustangs attack a logistics storage site.

In Burma, Tenth Air Force sends 12 B-25 Mitchells to attack troop concentrations, logistics sites, and gun positions. P-47 Thunderbolts support the Chinese 50th Division, P-38 Lightnings attack road targets, and P-47s support the British 36th Division.

ETO: General Eisenhower orders General Omar N. Bradley to limit his 12th Army Group's bridgehead over the Rhine to no more than 10 miles deep and 25 miles wide. He does this in order that Field Marshal Bernard L. Montgomery's 21st Army Group will remain the main effort as it prepares to cross the Rhine. Eisenhower's offensive plans, which have all centered on the assumption that Montgomery's 21st Army Group will make the Rhine crossing first, were thrown askew when an intact bridge was found over the Rhine. With 12th Army Group now in the lead, he decides to adhere to the broad-front approach. Rather than fully exploit the opportunity presented, he limits Bradley in order for Montgomery to catch up. Bradley controls the bridgehead with two divisions of VII Corps and three divisions of III Corps.

The XX Corps of Third Army attacks from its bridgehead at Trier with three infantry divisions.

Eighth Air Force sends 16 P-51 Mustangs to conduct an aircraft sweep in the area from Remagen to Koblenz in Germany. Fighter pilots report no activity.

Ninth Air Force sends more than 450 A-20 Havocs, A-26 Invaders, and B-26 Marauders to attack rail targets, airfields, and marshaling yards. P-47 and P-38 fighters support the 9th Infantry Division and the XX Corps.

The headquarters of the 61st Troop Carrier Group and the 14th and 15th Troop Carrier Squadrons, IX Troop Carrier Command, redeploy from England to France with C-47s.

MEDITERRANEAN: Fifteenth Air Force sends more than 500 B-17s and B-24 Liberators escorted by over 280 P-38 Lightnings and P-51 Mustangs to bomb marshaling yards in Germany. P-51s on a strafing mission attack rail traffic in Germany and Austria.

ITALY: Twelfth Air Force B-25 Mitchells bomb rail bridges. A-20 Havocs and P-47 Thunderbolts attack rail lines, bridges, antiaircraft positions, logistics storage sites, and support Fifth Army ground forces. During the night A-20s attack rail lines, ammunition storage sites, and motor transport in the Po River valley.

SOUTHWEST PACIFIC AREA: In the Eighth Army area the 162nd and 163rd Infantry Regiments of the 41st Infantry Division meet strong Japanese resistance outside of Zamboanga City. The enemy is dug in along a rugged line of hills overlooking the city.

On Mindanao, Far East Air Force B-24 Liberators attack targets, and B-25 Mitchells support ground operations. B-25s, A-20 Havocs, and P-38 Lightning fighters support ground forces in the Cagayan Valley on Luzon Island.

B-25 Mitchells and P-51s attack targets on Hainan Island, China. B-24s attack targets on Formosa. The 408th Bombardment Squadron (Heavy), 22nd Bombardment Group (Heavy), redeploys its B-24s from Samar Island to Clark Field, Luzon.

Fifth Air Force B-24 Liberators sink a Japanese coast defense vessel and a transport in the South China Sea.

PACIFIC: Twentieth Air Force sends 301 B-29 Superfortresses to conduct an incendiary attack on the urban area of Osaka, Japan, just after midnight. Of the 274 that hit the primary target, all use radar to identify the bomb release points. The raid destroys eight square miles of the city and kills nearly 4,000 people. Approximately 9,000 more are injured or missing. Aircrews report one confirmed kill and two B-29s lost.

CENTRAL PACIFIC: Seventh Air Force sends six B-24 Liberators from Guam Island to attack Woleai Atoll. Another 10 B-24s bomb the airfield on Chichi Jima. A total of 24 B-24s from Angaur Island bomb a logistics storage area on Mindanao Island in the Philippines. During the night eight B-24s fly individual harassment raids on Chichi Jima.

March 14

CBI: The Mars Task Force is airlifted to China with a new mission to train Chinese troops.

In China, Fourteenth Air Force sends three B-24 Liberators to attack shipping in the South China Sea. Aircrews report one cargo ship sunk. P-40s and P-51 Mustangs attack rail and river traffic.

In Burma, Tenth Air Force sends 11 B-25 Mitchells to bomb troops and vehicles. P-47 Thunderbolts attack troop concentrations, vehicles, and logistics storage sites.

ETO: Eighth Air Force sends more than 1,200 B-17s and B-24 Liberators, escorted by more than 800 P-47 Thunderbolts and P-51 Mustangs, to bomb oil refineries, munitions production facilities, road and rail bridges, marshaling yards, and airfields. The bombers use visual means and radar to identify the bomb release points. A total of three bombers are lost and 249 damaged. Aircrew casualties are three killed, 12 wounded, and 28 missing. Fighter pilots report four confirmed kills and one possible in the air. One fighter is lost and two damaged. The pilot is reported missing.

P-51s fly a sweep and report 11 confirmed kills. Other P-51s fly a sweep over the Remagen bridgehead. One P-51 is lost and one damaged. The pilot is reported missing. P-51s on a scouting mission report one confirmed kill in the air.

Six B-17s conduct screening missions to jam German radio interception efforts and employ countermeasures against German radar sites.

A total of seven B-24s bomb the Wiesbaden marshaling yard during the night using a radar-equipped Pathfinder bomber to mark bomb release points.

Ninth Air Force sends more than 350 A-20 Havocs, A-26 Invaders, and B-26 Marauders to attack airfields, rail lines, and targets of opportunity. P-47 and P-38 fighters support XII Corps and XX Corps.

MEDITERRANEAN: Fifteenth Air Force sends more than 600 B-17s and B-24 Liberators escorted by P-38 Lightnings and P-51 Mustangs to bomb oil refineries and marshaling yards in Hungary, Austria, and Yugoslavia. P-38s attack bridges and rail traffic in Yugoslavia and rail traffic in Austria. B-17s and B-24s drop supplies to Partisans in northern Italy and Yugoslavia.

ITALY: Twelfth Air Force B-25 Mitchells bomb rail bridges. A-20 Havocs and P-47 Thunderbolts attack roads, vehicles, rail traffic, logistics storage sites, and ammunition storage areas in northern Italy. During the night A-20s attack river crossing sites and targets of opportunity in the Po River valley.

SOUTHWEST PACIFIC AREA: FEAF B-24s bomb a naval base on Formosa. B-25 Mitchells conduct armed reconnaissance and a shipping sweep along the China coast.

In the Philippines, Far East Air Force B-24 Liberators and B-25 Mitchells attack a number of targets, including antiaircraft positions, villages, and docks on Mindanao.

SOUTHWEST PACIFIC AREA, LUZON: Major General Edwin D. Patrick, commander of the 6th Infantry Division, is mortally wounded on the front lines along with one of his regimental commanders. The Shimbu defenses are shattered after attacks by the 43rd and 6th Infantry Divisions. Japanese casualties in this month-long battle are estimated at over 3,300. U.S. losses are over 1,300 killed and wounded.

The XI Corps takes over the mission to capture the dams and destroy the Shimbu Group.

A-20 Havocs, P-38 Lightnings, and P-47 Thunderbolts attack installations and defensive positions throughout Luzon.

The 2nd Bombardment Squadron (Heavy), 22nd Bombardment Group (Heavy), redeploys its B-24s from Samar Island to Clark Field on Luzon.

PACIFIC: U.S. submarine *Trepang* torpedoes and sinks a Japanese guardboat off eastern Honshu, Japan.

Two U.S. destroyers sink two Japanese guardboats off the Bonins.

CENTRAL PACIFIC: Seventh Air Force sends 11 B-24 Liberators from Guam to bomb the airfield on Chichi Jima. A total of 25 B-24s based at Angaur Island bomb a logistics storage area on Mindanao Island in the Philippines. P-51 Mustangs from Iwo

Jima attack targets on both Haha Jima and Chichi Jima. During the night five B-24s fly individual harassment raids on Chichi Jima.

CENTRAL PACIFIC, IWO JIMA: Major General Harry Schmidt, V Amphibious Corps commander, leads a formal flag raising ceremony on the island.

NEW GUINEA: U.S. submarine *Bream* torpedoes and sinks a Japanese auxiliary submarine chaser in the Java Sea. USS *Rock* lands supplies on Lombok Island, Netherlands East Indies.

March 15

ALEUTIANS: Naval Task Force 92, commanded by Rear Admiral John L. McCrea, consisting of three light cruisers and seven destroyers, bombards Japanese installations on Matsuwa, Kuriles.

CBI: Fourteenth Air Force sends four B-24 Liberators to attack shipping in the South China Sea. Aircrews report one cargo ship sunk. P-51 Mustangs attack locomotives.

In Burma, Tenth Air Force sends 30 P-47 Thunderbolts to support elements of the Chinese 50th Division while 32 P-38 Lightnings conduct a sweep of roads.

ETO: Operation Undertone begins. The XX Corps of Third Army supports an attack by VI and XV Corps of Seventh Army to drive the last German defenders from the west bank of the Rhine River in the Saar area. The XXI Corps attacks to capture Saarbrücken.

The XII Corps of Third Army sends the 4th Armored Division across its bridgehead on the Moselle River.

German fighter aircraft conduct nearly continuous attacks against the Ludendorff Bridge at Remagen. Sixteen German fighters are lost to concentrated antiaircraft fire.

Eighth Air Force sends more than 1,350 B-17s and B-24 Liberators, escorted by over 800 P-47 Thunderbolts and P-51 Mustangs, to bomb a German army headquarters near Berlin and marshaling yards. A total of nine bombers are lost and 342 damaged. Aircrews report one confirmed kill. Aircrew casualties are four killed, 16 wounded, and 87 missing. Fighter pilots report one confirmed kill. Four fighters are lost, and the pilots are reported missing.

Six B-17s conduct screening missions to jam German radio interception efforts and employ countermeasures against German radar sites.

A total of 14 B-24s bomb the rail station at Munster during the night using a radar-equipped Pathfinder bomber to mark the bomb release point.

Ninth Air Force sends A-20 Havocs, A-26 Invaders, and B-26 Marauders to attack communication centers, railroad bridges, antiaircraft positions, and marshaling yards. P-47 and P-38 fighters support XII Corps and XX Corps.

MEDITERRANEAN: Fifteenth Air Force sends more than 600 B-17s and B-24 Liberators escorted by P-38 Lightnings and P-51 Mustangs to bomb oil refineries in Germany and Czechoslovakia and oil refineries and marshaling yards in Austria. Bombers airdrop supplies into northern Italy and Yugoslavia.

ITALY: Twelfth Air Force B-25 Mitchells bomb rail bridges. A-20 Havocs and P-47 Thunderbolts of the XXII Tactical Air Command attack rail lines, logistics storage sites, and ammunition storage areas. During the night A-20s attack river crossing sites.

SOUTHWEST PACIFIC AREA: On Mindanao Island, FEAF B-24 Liberators and B-25 Mitchells attack Japanese troops and gun positions. B-24s bomb Lahug on Cebu Island.

On Formosa, P-47s conduct dive-bomb attacks on power installations.

SOUTHWEST PACIFIC AREA, LUZON: In the XIV Corps area the 11th Airborne and the 158th RCT begin clearing Japanese forces from the Lake Taal area. Operational control of the 6th Infantry Division and the 112th RCT passes from XIV Corps to XI Corps. The 37th Infantry Division occupies Manila under the operational control of Sixth Army. The XIV Corps retains the 1st Cavalry Division and well as the 11th Airborne and the 158th RCT.

The XI Corps continues the attack on the Shimbu Group with the 38th and 43rd Infantry Divisions.

In the I Corps area the 33rd Infantry Division drives the Japanese from the high ground overlooking the Rosario-Pozorrubio Road and advances north toward Baguio and Bauang. I Corps covers the north of Luzon and has protected the flank of XIV Corps and kept the Japanese on the defensive. XI Corps has control of the center of Luzon and XIV Corps has the southern part of Luzon. The Japanese have been divided into two groups, one occupying the mountain in the northeast and the other in the mountains east of Manila. The number of Japanese killed is over 85,000 since the beginning of the campaign on January 9. During this same period Sixth Army has lost 18,579 casualties.

Far East Air Force B-24 Liberators, A-20 Havocs, and P-38 Lightnings attack a Japanese headquarters; P-47 Thunderbolts attack a bridge and enemy concentrations in the Balete Pass and Japanese defenses near Fort Stotsenburg; A-20s and P-47s attack gun positions and occupied areas.

The headquarters of the 22nd Bombardment Group (Heavy) and the B-24s of the 19th Bombardment Squadron (Heavy) redeploy from Samar Island to Clark Field, Luzon. The 403rd Bombardment Squadron (Heavy), 43rd Bombardment Group (Heavy), also redeploys B-24s from Leyte to Clark Field.

CENTRAL PACIFIC: Seventh Air Force sends eight B-24 Liberators from Guam to bomb the airfield on Chichi Jima. During the night three B-24s conduct individual snooper missions on Chichi Jima.

NEW GUINEA: The 100th Bombardment Squadron (Medium), 42nd Bombardment Group (Medium), redeploys its B-25 Mitchells from Sansapor, New Guinea, to Palawan Island in the Philippines.

U.S. submarine *Bream* is damaged by depth charges off North Borneo and is forced to terminate her patrol.

March 16

ALEUTIANS: Eleventh Air Force sends two B-24 Liberators on a photo mission to Matsuwa Island in the Kuriles. A navigational error puts the bombers 130 miles south of the island. This represents the deepest penetration of the Japanese home islands up to this time. After conducting their photo mission, the bombers attack Shimushiru Island on the return flight.

CBI: In China, Fourteenth Air Force sends 32 B-24 Liberators, escorted by 10 P-51 Mustangs, to attack railroad yards.

In Burma, Tenth Air Force sends 12 B-25 Mitchells to bomb a fuel storage site and troops. P-47 Thunderbolts support the Chinese 50th Division, and P-38 Lightnings support the British 36th Division. Other P-38s also attack artillery positions and sweep roads.

ETO: During the night Eighth Air Force sends 12 B-24 Liberators to drop leaflets in Germany and the Netherlands, while 20 B-24s fly Carpetbagger missions.

Ninth Air Force sends more than 280 A-20 Havocs, A-26 Invaders, and B-26 Marauders to attack communication centers, rail junctions, and marshaling yards. P-47 and P-38 fighters support XII Corps, XX Corps, and VIII Corps.

MEDITERRANEAN: Fifteenth Air Force sends more than 700 B-17s and B-24 Liberators escorted by P-38 Lightnings and P-51 Mustangs to bomb oil refineries and marshaling yards in Austria and marshaling yards in Yugoslavia. P-51s strafe rail lines in Germany and Austria.

Bombers conduct supply drops in northern Italy and Yugoslavia.

ITALY: Twelfth Air Force B-25 Mitchells bomb a rail bridge in Austria. B-25s also attack a power plant and bridges in Italy. During the night A-20s attack bridges and targets of opportunity in the Po River valley.

SOUTHWEST PACIFIC AREA: On Luzon Island in the Philippines, Far East Air Force A-20s and B-24 Liberators bomb Japanese installations; P-51 Mustangs attack vehicles and logistics support sites. B-24s bomb airfields on Negros Island and bomb targets marked by Filipino guerrillas on Cebu Island. B-25 Mitchells bomb the airfield on Mindanao Island.

The headquarters of the 43rd Bombardment Group (Heavy) and the B-24s of the 65th Bombardment Squadron (Heavy) redeploy from Leyte to Clark Field, Luzon.

On Formosa, B-24s bomb towns, airfields, and the naval airbase.

FEAF B-25 Mitchells attack airfields in Borneo.

PACIFIC: Twentieth Air Force sends 331 B-29s of the XXI Bomber Command to conduct an incendiary bombing raid on Kobe, Japan. The 307 Superfortresses that hit the primary target in the hours just before dawn leave about 20 percent of the city destroyed. More than 242,000 people are without shelter and another 13,900 are dead or injured. Although aircrews report over 300 Japanese aircraft making attacks, only one enemy fighter is reported as a confirmed kill. Three B-29s are lost, but none to fighter attacks.

CENTRAL PACIFIC: Seventh Air Force sends 13 B-24 Liberators from Guam to bomb the airfield on Chichi Jima. A total of 16 P-51 Mustangs based at Iwo Jima bomb and strafe targets on Chichi Jima. During the night five B-24s fly individual harassment raids on Chichi Jima.

CENTRAL PACIFIC, IWO JIMA: The 3rd Marine Division captures Cushman's Pocket and advances against weakening resistance. The 4th Marine Division clears enemy positions in its area. The 5th Marine Division continues to be held up at Death Valley. About 90 percent of the island is under American control. Iwo Jima is declared secure.

Pharmacist's Mate First Class Francis J. Pierce is with 2nd Battalion, 24th Marine Regiment, 4th Marine Division, providing medical support to the marines. Repeatedly he risks his life to recover and evacuate wounded on Iwo Jima. He protects wounded men with his own body as he renders aid and carries wounded men on his back through deadly fire. Without hesitation, Pierce takes enormous risks to save others. While leading a combat patrol to locate a Japanese sniper position, he is wounded but refuses any assistance, as he concentrates on assisting a casualty. For his gallant and selfless conduct and extraordinary dedication to duty, Pharmacist's Mate First Class Pierce will receive the Medal of Honor.

March 17

ALEUTIANS: Eleventh Air Force sends two B-24 Liberators to conduct bombing and photo missions over the airfield on Matsuwa Island in the Kuriles.
CBI: In China, a Fourteenth Air Force B-25 Mitchell and 12 P-51 Mustangs damage 21 locomotives and a river launch near Peking (Beijing).

In Burma, Tenth Air Force sends 12 B-25 Mitchells to bomb troops and logistics sites. P-47 Thunderbolts support the British 36th Division while other P-47s and P-38 Lightnings attack Japanese troops, logistics storage sites, tanks, and trucks.
ETO: General Eisenhower meets with Lieutenant General Jacob L. Devers, 6th Army Group commander, Lieutenant General George S. Patton, Jr., of Third Army, and Lieutenant General Alexander M. Patch, commander of Seventh Army. Operation Undertone is changed to an effort to trap German forces between the Third and Seventh Armies along the Rhine.

Major General James A. Van Fleet takes command of III Corps from Major General Millikin. The VII Corps of First Army attacks with one division to expand the Remagen bridgehead. The damaged Ludendorff railroad bridge collapses after days of constant traffic, killing 28 American engineers working on the bridge. Since March 12, two pontoon bridges have been supporting most of the river traffic. The Germans throw the equivalent of 10 divisions against the bridgehead and send everything, including V-2 rockets, jet fighter aircraft, swimmers with demolitions, artillery fire, and mines in an effort to destroy the bridge.

LCVPs of Naval Task Group 122.5.1 ferry 2,500 soldiers across the Rhine River at Remagen.

Eighth Air Force sends more than 1,300 B-17s and B-24 Liberators escorted by 800 P-51 Mustangs to bomb oil refineries, munitions and tank production facilities, and marshaling yards. The bombers use both radar-equipped Pathfinder bombers and radar signal intercepts to mark bomb release points over the targets. A total of five bombers are lost and 67 damaged. Aircrew casualties are one killed, one wounded, and 44 missing. Two fighters are lost, and the pilots are reported missing.

Six B-24s conduct screening missions to jam German radio interception efforts and employ countermeasures against German radar sites.

During the night nine B-24s drop leaflets over Germany, France, and the Netherlands.

Ninth Air Force sends more than 650 A-20 Havocs, A-26 Invaders, and B-26 Marauders to attack communication centers, an ordnance depot, and marshaling yards. P-47 and P-38 fighters support III Corps and XX Corps.

MEDITERRANEAN: Fifteenth Air Force B-24 Liberators airdrop supplies to Partisans in northern Italy.

ITALY: Twelfth Air Force B-25 Mitchells bomb rail bridges. A-20 Havocs and P-47 Thunderbolts attack rail lines, bridges, vehicles, logistics storage sites, and ammunition storage areas in the Po River valley. During the night A-20s and B-26 Marauders attack river crossing sites, bridges, and motor transport in the Po River Valley.

SOUTHWEST PACIFIC AREA: In the Philippines, Far East Air Force B-25 Mitchells, A-20 Havocs, P-47 Thunderbolts, and P-38 Lightnings support ground forces on Luzon. B-24s bomb Panay Island beaches, bomb Japanese troops on Mindanao Island, and hit airfields on Negros Island. B-24s also bomb airfields on Formosa.

The headquarters of the 317th Troop Carrier Group redeploys from Leyte to Clark Field on Luzon.

U.S. submarine *Sealion* torpedoes and sinks a Thai oiler in the Straits of Malacca.

PACIFIC: Twentieth Air Force sends 77 B-29 Superfortresses to attack a logistics storage area at Rangoon.

U.S. submarine *Spot* attacks a Japanese convoy, sinking a cargo vessel and damaging a cargo ship off Yushiyama Island in the East China Sea, near Formosa. USS *Spot* is damaged by gunfire.

CENTRAL PACIFIC: Seventh Air Force sends 11 B-24 Liberators from Guam to bomb the airfield on Chichi Jima. During the night five B-24s fly individual harassment raids on Chichi Jima.

The headquarters of the 30th Bombardment Group (Heavy) and B-24s of the 27th, 30th, and 819th Bombardment Squadrons (Heavy) redeploy from Saipan Island to Wheeler Field, Hawaii.

NEW GUINEA: The B-24 Liberators of the 31st Bombardment Squadron (Heavy), 7th Bombardment Group (Heavy), redeploy from Morotai Island to Samar Island in the Philippines.

March 18

CBI: In China, Fourteenth Air Force sends six B-24 Liberators to conduct a sweep of the Gulf of Tonkin and South China Sea. Aircrews report one cargo ship sunk.

In Burma, Tenth Air Force sends 11 B-25 Mitchells and P-47 Thunderbolts to attack troop concentrations and logistics storage sites. Other P-47s support the British 50th Division.

ATLANTIC: In the northwest Atlantic three U.S. destroyer escorts sink German submarine *U-866*.

ETO: Eighth Air Force sends more than 1,300 B-17s and B-24 Liberators escorted by over 700 P-47 Thunderbolts and P-51 Mustangs to bomb rail targets and tank production facilities in Berlin. The bombers use visual methods or radar signal intercepts to mark bomb release points over the targets. A total of 13 bombers are lost and 729 damaged. Aircrews report 21 confirmed kills, one probable, and five possibles. The Germans attack the bomber formations with a large number of Me-262 jet aircraft. Aircrew casualties are three killed, 31 wounded, and 139 missing. Fighter pilots report 14 confirmed kills and four possibles. Six fighters are lost.

During the night 10 B-24s drop leaflets over France, Germany, and the Netherlands.

Ninth Air Force sends more than 660 A-20 Havocs, A-26 Invaders, and B-26 Marauders to attack communication centers and marshaling yards. P-47 and P-38 fighters support III Corps, XII Corps, and XX Corps.

First Lieutenant Jack L. Treadwell commands F Company, 180th Infantry Regiment, 45th Infantry Division, and has been stopped for several hours before a German defensive position on the Siegfried Line near Nieder-Wurzbach, Germany. All attacks have been unsuccessful until Lieutenant Treadwell, carrying a Thompson submachine gun and hand grenades, moves forward alone. With no cover to protect him, Treadwell runs toward the first pillbox and throws grenades, then, reaching a concrete emplacement, he fires into the firing port. Four Germans quickly surrender. Ignoring the enemy fire directed at him, he attacks a second emplacement in the same manner, eliminating it. He then runs across the crest of the hill to a third pillbox and attacks it and eliminates it. Again and again Treadwell moves along, taking out German pillboxes until the men of Company F rise and assault the remaining defenses and capture the hill. For his courage in facing nearly impossible odds and by his extraordinary example of leadership and initiative, First Lieutenant Treadwell will receive the nation's highest award for valor, the Medal of Honor.

MEDITERRANEAN: Fifteenth Air Force P-38 Lightnings attack railroad bridges and rail lines in Yugoslavia.

ITALY: Twelfth Air Force B-25 Mitchells bomb rail bridges. A-20 Havocs and P-47 Thunderbolts attack ammunition storage areas, rail lines, roads, and support Fifth Army ground forces south of Bologna. Fighter pilots report 14 locomotives destroyed during an attack on the Novara marshaling yard. During the night A-20s and A-26 Invaders attack river crossing sites in the Po River valley.

SOUTHWEST PACIFIC AREA: In the Eighth Army area Naval Task Group 78.3, commanded by Rear Admiral Arthur D. Struble, lands the 185th Infantry Regiment of the 40th Infantry Division on Panay Island in the Visayan Sea. A light cruiser and three destroyers of Task Unit 74.2.2 provide naval gunfire support. Supported by a heavy air and naval bombardment, the infantrymen are met upon landing by a large force of Filipino guerrillas. The Americans attack and clear the small garrison at Iloilo, leaving the 2nd Battalion of the 160th Infantry Regiment and the guerrillas to mop up the remaining troops. Base construction and an airfield are started in anticipation of using the island as a training and support base for troops arriving for the invasion of Japan.

In the Philippines, Far East Air Force B-24 Liberators, A-20 Havocs, P-38 Lightnings, and P-47 Thunderbolts support ground forces on Luzon. B-24s bomb Negros Island and attack several targets on Cebu Island.

B-24 Liberators bomb a seaplane base and airfields on Formosa,

B-24s bomb airfields on Borneo.

PACIFIC: Twentieth Air Force sends more than 300 B-29s from XXI Bomber Command to bomb the city of Nagoya, Japan, with incendiaries. About three square miles of the city are destroyed, but little damage is caused to aircraft engine production facilities or freight yards.

Carrier aircraft from Task Force 58 bomb airfields on southern Kyushu and shipping. One transport and a tanker are sunk and a cargo ship is damaged. Japanese aircraft attack carriers USS *Enterprise* and USS *Yorktown* south of Kyushu, Japan. Both carriers are damaged by bombs. A kamikaze hits carrier USS *Intrepid*, which is also hit by friendly fire. Carrier aircraft sink an auxiliary submarine chaser and a merchant vessel and damage two merchant ships.

U.S. submarine *Balao* torpedoes and sinks a Japanese merchant trawler in the Yellow Sea.

U.S. submarine *Springer* attacks a Japanese convoy and sinks a fast transport and damages a minesweeper in the Ryukyus. USS *Trigger* torpedoes and sinks a Japanese cargo ship northwest of Okinawa.

CENTRAL PACIFIC: Seventh Air Force sends 14 B-24 Liberators from Guam to bomb the airfield on Chichi Jima. During the night five B-24s fly individual harassment raids on Chichi Jima. A total of 16 P-51 Mustangs from Iwo Jima conduct a dive-bombing attack on radar and radar installations and barges on Chichi Jima.

The 392nd Bombardment Squadron (Heavy), 30th Bombardment Group (Heavy), redeploys its B-24s from Saipan Island to Hawaii.

March 19

ALEUTIANS: Eleventh Air Force sends five B-24 Liberators and eight B-25 Mitchells to bomb and photograph the Kashiwabara naval base on Paramushiru Island in the Kuriles.

CBI: Fourteenth Air Force sends five B-24 Liberators on a sweep over the South China Sea and Gulf of Tonkin. Aircrews report one cargo ship sunk.

In Burma, Tenth Air Force sends 24 P-38 Lightnings to support the Chinese 50th Division, while other P-38s sweep roads. P-47 Thunderbolts attack troop concentrations and logistics storage sites.

U.S. submarine *Balao* attacks a Japanese convoy, sinking a troopship and damaging a transport near Shanghai.

A Japanese river gunboat and merchant ship in the Yangtze River are sunk by mines dropped by Fourteenth Air Force aircraft early in March.

ETO: Koblenz is captured by VIII Corps. The Third Army's armored divisions have covered 950 square miles in 24 hours. Infantry divisions follow behind the tanks, clearing out isolated pockets of resistance. Seventh Army's XXI Corps captures Saarbrücken.

General Eisenhower orders Bradley to have First Army ready to break out of the Remagen bridgehead anytime after March 22. Bradley gives Patton authorization to cross the Rhine as soon as possible.

Eighth Air Force sends more than 1,200 B-17s and B-24 Liberators escorted by over 600 P-51 Mustangs to bomb marshaling yards and airfields. The bombers use a combination of visual means and radar signal intercepts to mark the bomb release points over the targets. A total of six bombers are lost and six are damaged. Aircrews report 41 confirmed kills, three probables, and 19 possibles. Of the 36 Me-262 jet aircraft spotted during the raids, aircrews report three of the jets downed. Aircrew casualties are nine killed, three wounded, and 20 missing. Fighter pilots report seven confirmed kills and three possibles in the air. Four fighters are lost.

Another 98 P-51s fly a freelance sweep for the bombers. Fighter pilots report 33 confirmed kills, two probables, and 14 possibles in the air. Six fighters are lost.

During the night 11 B-24s drop leaflets over Germany and the Netherlands.

Ninth Air Force sends A-20 Havocs, A-26 Invaders, and B-26 Marauders to attack communication centers, railroad bridges, and marshaling yards. P-47 and P-38 fighters support III Corps and the 4th Armored Division.

Corporal Edward G. Wilkin, C Company, 157th Infantry Regiment, 45th Infantry Division, is part of an assault unit attacking the Siegfried Line in Germany. As German machine-gun and rifle fire stop the advance, Wilkin moves forward to observe the enemy and to look for a route of advance. He moves into an area with a number of concrete emplacements and attacks one after another using his Browning Automatic Rifle (BAR) and grenades. When barbed wire entanglements stop him, Wilkin uses demolitions to clear a path as grenades and mortar shells burst around him and bullets hit close by. He stands up often to fire a burst from his BAR and allow his comrades an opportunity to advance. In this manner he penetrates a full 200 yards into the German defenses. During the night he assists in distributing rations and supplies to his unit and assists another company by guiding litter bearers evacuating the wounded. For the next two days, Wilkin fearlessly ventures into enemy fire to rescue wounded soldiers. For his superb fighting skill, dauntless courage, and gallant, inspiring actions, Corporal Wilkin will receive the Medal of Honor.

MEDITERRANEAN: Fifteenth Air Force sends more than 800 B-17s and B-24 Liberators escorted by P-38 Lightnings and P-51 Mustangs to bomb marshaling yards in Germany. P-38s bomb a marshaling yard in Yugoslavia. B-24s airdrop supplies in Yugoslavia.

ITALY: Twelfth Air Force A-20 Havocs and P-47 Thunderbolts of the XXII Tactical Air Command attack rail bridges, logistics storage sites, ammunition storage areas, and roads in the Po River valley.

SOUTHWEST PACIFIC AREA: In the Philippines, Far East Air Force B-24 Liberators, A-20 Havocs, P-38 Lightnings, and P-47 Thunderbolts attack installations on Luzon. B-24s bomb targets on Cebu Island.

The 63rd Bombardment Squadron (Heavy), 43rd Bombardment Group (Heavy), redeploys its B-24s from Leyte to Clark Field on Luzon.

PV-1 Harpoon patrol bombers damage a Japanese midget submarine at Cebu.

PACIFIC: Carrier aircraft from Task Force 58 attack airfields on Kyushu and shipping on Honshu, Japan. Three battleships, four carriers, a small carrier, an escort carrier, a heavy cruiser, and a light cruiser are damaged, as well as two submarines, an auxiliary submarine chaser, and an escort destroyer.

Japanese aircraft attack USS *Wasp* and USS *Franklin* with bombs off Kyushu and damage both carriers. USS *Franklin* is seriously damaged, but the crew is able to keep the ship afloat; 724 sailors are killed.

U.S. submarine *Bluefish* torpedoes and damages a Japanese guardboat south of Kyushu, Japan.

Lieutenant (j.g.) Donald A. Gary is stationed on the third deck of the carrier USS *Franklin* off Honshu, Japan, near Kobe when it comes under air attack. The carrier's ordnance storage area is hit and explodes, trapping a number of sailors. Gary risks his life to assist several hundred men trapped in a compartment filled with smoke. As the explosions continue to shake the ship, Gary calms the group and leads them through the dark corridors until he finds a passageway that allows everyone to get out safely. He returns to the compartment three times, through flame and debris, to lead other groups of trapped sailors out. He organizes and leads fire-fighting parties on the flight deck and takes life-threatening risks to support damage control efforts. For his courageous performance in leading his shipmates from danger and for risking his life repeatedly to save his ship, Lieutenant (j.g.) Gary will receive the Medal of Honor.

CENTRAL PACIFIC: Seventh Air Force sends 12 B-24 Liberators from Guam to bomb the airfield on Chichi Jima. A total of 16 P-51 Mustangs from Iwo Jima strafe the airfield, logistics storage areas, and radio installation on Chichi Jima. During the night five B-24s fly individual harassment raids on Chichi Jima.

CENTRAL PACIFIC, IWO JIMA: The 4th Marine Division embarks on ships headed for Hawaii. The 5th Marine Division attacks Japanese positions in Death Valley with flamethrower tanks and demolition charges. Casualties within the division are reaching 100 percent.

NEW GUINEA: The C-46s of the 8th Combat Cargo Squadron, 2nd Combat Cargo Group, redeploy from Biak to Leyte Island in the Philippines.

March 20

ALEUTIANS: Naval Task Force 92, commanded by Captain John M. Worthington and with six destroyers, departs Attu to bombard Japanese installations at Paramushiro. The operation will be cancelled after the ships encounter heavy ice.

CBI: British forces capture Mandalay.

In Burma, Tenth Air Force sends 20 P-47 Thunderbolts to sweep roads, while 16 other P-47s attack logistics storage areas.

ATLANTIC: German submarine *U-995* torpedoes and damages a U.S. freighter in the Barents Sea near Murmansk. German submarine *U-968* torpedoes and sinks a U.S. freighter in the same area.

ETO: Zweibrücken is captured. Seventh Army breaks the West Wall and drives north to meet Third Army.

Eighth Air Force sends more than 400 B-17s and B-24 Liberators escorted by over 350 P-51 Mustangs to bomb the shipyard and dock area at Hamburg, an airfield, and an oil refinery. A total of four bombers are lost and 64 are damaged. Aircrews report 14 confirmed kills, three probables, and 17 possibles. Aircrew casualties are one killed, two wounded, and 39 missing. Fighter pilots report two confirmed kills and five possibles in the air and one confirmed kill and two possibles on the ground. One P-51 is lost and the pilot is reported missing.

Seventy-eight P-51s fly a strafing mission in the Bremen-Hannover area. Pilots report two confirmed kills and three possibles in the air and three confirmed kills and two possibles on the ground. One P-51 is lost, and the pilot is reported missing. Six B-17s conduct screening missions to jam German radio interception efforts and employ countermeasures against German radar sites.

During the night 12 B-24s drop leaflets over Germany and the Netherlands. Two A-26 Invaders fly Carpetbagger missions one; one A-26 is lost.

Ninth Air Force sends more than 360 A-20 Havocs, A-26 Invaders, and B-26 Marauders to attack ammunition manufacturing sites, railroad bridges, and marshaling yards. P-47 and P-38 fighters support III and VII Corps and XI and XX Corps.

MEDITERRANEAN: Fifteenth Air Force sends more than 760 B-17s and B-24 Liberators escorted by P-38 Lightnings and P-51 Mustangs to bomb oil refineries and marshaling yards in Austria.

U.S. destroyer *Parker* bombards German positions, logistics storage sites, and facilities on the French-Italian border.

ITALY: Twelfth Air Force B-25 Mitchells bomb rail bridges. A-20 Havocs and P-47 Thunderbolts attack rail lines, bridges, and roads in the Po River valley

SOUTHWEST PACIFIC AREA: In the Eighth Army area elements of the 40th Infantry Division capture Guimaras Island between Panya and Negros Islands.

In the Philippines, Far East Air Force B-24 Liberators, A-20 Havocs, P-38 Lightnings, and P-47 Thunderbolts conduct ground support missions at Balete Pass and other areas on Luzon. B-24s bomb Japanese forces and logistics storage sites near Cebu City on Cebu Island. B-24s also bomb Japanese defensive positions and antiaircraft guns on Negros Island.

Other B-24s bomb targets on Formosa. B-25 Mitchells conduct a shipping sweep and aircrews report three small vessels sunk in the Gulf of Tonkin

U.S. submarine *Blenny* attacks a Japanese convoy off the coast of French Indochina, near Cam Ranh Bay, sinking two merchant tankers and a fishing boat.

LUZON: Staff Sergeant Ysmael R. Villegas is a squad leader with F Company, 127th Infantry Regiment, 32nd Infantry Division, attacking a strongly defended hill on the Villa Verde Trail. As the Japanese throw grenades and demolition charges, he encourages his men as they prepare to assault the position. As the Americans reach the crest of the hill and begin consolidating on the objective, hidden Japanese riflemen begin a deadly fire. Staff Sergeant Villegas charges a soldier in a hidden position and kills him. Soon Villegas is moving from position to position blasting the enemy in their foxholes. As he nears the sixth fighting position, he is killed. For his heroism and indomitable fighting spirit, and his inspiring leadership, Staff Sergeant Villegas will receive the Medal of Honor.

PACIFIC: Carrier USS *Enterprise* is damaged by friendly fire off Shikoku, Japan. A kamikaze hits a destroyer in the same area. Carrier aircraft sink a Japanese guardboat off Honshu.

A kamikaze hits and damages U.S. submarine *Devilfish* near the Volcano Islands, terminating her patrol.

CENTRAL PACIFIC: Seventh Air Force sends 12 B-24 Liberators from Guam to bomb the airfield on Chichi Jima. During the night four B-24s fly individual harassment raids on Chichi Jima.

The 549th Night Fighter Squadron redeploys its P-61 Black Widow night fighters from Saipan to Iwo Jima.

CENTRAL PACIFIC, IWO JIMA: The army's 147th Infantry Regiment joins the 3rd Marine Division on the island.

NEW GUINEA: The B-24 Liberators of the 72nd Bombardment Squadron (Heavy), 5th Bombardment Group (Heavy), redeploy from Morotai Island to Samar Island in the Philippines.

U.S. submarine *Perch* lands personnel on the east coast of Borneo.

March 21

CBI: The Japanese launch a coordinated attack between the Yangtze and Yellow Rivers to capture the American air bases at Laohokow and Ankang.

Fourteenth Air Force sends six B-24 Liberators on a shipping sweep. Aircrews report one vessel damaged in South China Sea.

In Burma, Tenth Air Force sends 13 B-25 Mitchells and 18 P-47 Thunderbolts to attack troop concentrations and vehicles. Another 30 P-47 Thunderbolts support Chinese ground forces and 34 P-38 Lightnings sweep roads.

ATLANTIC: A Fourth Air Force P-63 Kingcobra (a fighter aircraft used for training) from Walla Walla Army Airfield, Washington, intercepts a Japanese balloon and eventually shoots it down near Reno, Nevada.

ETO: Seventh and Third armies link, meeting the goals of Operation Undertone. The German Seventh Army is demolished, and the German First Army is trapped along the Rhine River. Patton's divisions have covered 4,000 square miles and captured 63,000 prisoners. American casualties are about 1,700.

The Remagen bridgehead is 20 miles wide and eight miles deep, supported by six temporary bridges. Six divisions of First Army are east of the Rhine.

Eighth Air Force sends more than 1,400 B-17s and B-24 Liberators escorted by over 800 P-51 Mustangs to bomb marshaling yards and airfields in support of the anticipated crossing of the Rhine River. The bombers use mostly visual means to mark the bomb release points over the targets. A total of seven B-17s are lost and 250 are damaged. Aircrews report 58 confirmed kills, three probables, and 49 possibles. Aircrew casualties are one killed, 11 wounded, and 65 missing. Fighter pilots report nine confirmed kills and two possibles in the air and 46 confirmed kills and 44 possibles on the ground. Seven P-51s are lost and one is damaged. The pilots are reported missing.

Three B-17s, escorted by six P-51s, conduct a Disney operation, attacking the E-boat pens at Ijmuiden in the Netherlands with wing-mounted 4,500-pound concrete-penetrating rocket bombs. A single B-17, escorted by four P-51s, bombs Oberursel, Germany, as part of a radar test. During the night eight B-24s drop leaflets over Germany and the Netherlands.

Ninth Air Force sends more than 580 A-20 Havocs, A-26 Invaders, and B-26 Marauders to attack communication centers and marshaling yards. P-47 and P-38 fighters support VII Corps, XII Corps, and XX Corps.

MEDITERRANEAN: Fifteenth Air Force sends more than 660 B-17s and B-24 Liberators escorted by P-38 Lightnings and P-51 Mustangs to bomb an airfield in Germany and marshaling yards in Austria and Yugoslavia.

ITALY: Twelfth Air Force B-25 Mitchells bomb rail and road traffic and bridges. A-20 Havocs and P-47 Thunderbolts attack logistics storage sites, rail lines, bridges, and roads in the Po River valley and support Fifth Army ground forces.

During the night A-20s attack river crossing sites in the Po River valley.

SOUTHWEST PACIFIC AREA: In the Philippines, Far East Air Force B-25 Mitchells, A-20 Havocs, P-38s, and P-47 Thunderbolts attack Japanese defenses on Luzon Island. B-24 Liberators and A-20 Havocs attack targets on Cebu Island.

FEAF B-24s bomb an airfield on Hainan Island. B-25s conduct a shipping sweep and damage a freighter off Nanao Island, China.

U.S. submarine *Baya* torpedoes and sinks an auxiliary netlayer off Cam Ranh Bay, French Indochina. USS *Baya* is damaged by depth charges but remains on patrol. Fifth Air Force B-25 Mitchells sink a submarine chaser, a cable layer, and three cargo vessels and damages a submarine chaser off Nha Trang, French Indochina.

PACIFIC: The Japanese launch rocket-powered suicide bombs *(oka)* from aircraft against Task Force 58.

CENTRAL PACIFIC: Seventh Air Force sends 13 B-24 Liberators from Guam to bomb the airfield on Chichi Jima. A total of 16 P-51 Mustangs from Iwo Jima strafe the airfield, logistics storage areas, and radar installation on Chichi Jima. During the night five B-24s fly individual harassment raids on Chichi Jima.

NEW GUINEA: The headquarters of the 42nd Bombardment Group (Medium) and the B-25 Mitchells of the 390th Bombardment Squadron (Medium) redeploy from Morotai Island to Palawan Island in the Philippines.

March 22

CBI: In China, Fourteenth Air Force P-40s and P-51 Mustangs attack rail and river traffic.

In Burma, Tenth Air Force sends 12 B-25 Mitchells and P-47 Thunderbolts to bomb troop concentrations and logistics storage sites. P-47 Thunderbolts and P-38 Lightnings support ground forces of the Chinese 50th Division.

ETO: Mainz is captured. The 5th Infantry Division of XII Corps of Third Army begins a night crossing of the Rhine River at Oppenheim, an operation planned six months in advance. Six battalions of infantrymen make the initial crossing in rafts. About 7,500 engineers support the operation, building a steel treadway bridge within 20 hours after the first troops cross.

Eighth Air Force sends more than 1,300 B-17s and B-24 Liberators, escorted by over 600 P-47 Thunderbolts and P-51 Mustangs, to bomb German positions across the Rhine River, marshaling yards, and airfields. One B-17 is lost and 147 damaged. Aircrews report 27 confirmed kills, one probable, and 12 possibles. Aircrew casualties are 10 killed, 11 wounded, and nine missing. Fighter pilots report three confirmed kills and one possible in the air and 13 confirmed kills and eight probables on the ground.

P-51 Mustangs escorting a photo reconnaissance mission over Germany report 11 confirmed kills, one probable kill, and three possible kills in the air.

Six B-17s conduct screening missions to jam German radio interception efforts and employ countermeasures against German radar sites.

During the night nine B-24s drop leaflets over Germany and the Netherlands. Ninth Air Force sends nearly 800 A-20 Havocs, A-26 Invaders, and B-26 Marauders to attack communication centers and a marshaling yard. P-47 and P-38 fighters support the 1st and 9th Infantry Divisions and XX Corps.

German submarine *U-399* torpedoes and sinks a U.S. freighter at the entrance to the English Channel; another submarine, possibly *U-1195*, torpedoes and damages another U.S. freighter in the same convoy. A U.S. freighter leaving Antwerp hits a mine.

MEDITERRANEAN: Fifteenth Air Force sends 136 B-17s to attack the synthetic oil production facility at Ruhland, Germany. Ruhland's facility is Germany's leading producer of fuel. As the bombers approach the target, 20 German fighter-jets attack and shoot down three bombers. P-51 Mustangs flying escort damage three jets and shoot down one.

B-17s and B-24 Liberators escorted by P-38 Lightnings and P-51 Mustangs bomb oil refineries in Austria and Czechoslovakia and railyards and marshaling yards in Austria and Czechoslovakia.

ITALY: Twelfth Air Force B-25 Mitchells bomb bridges in Austria and Italy. P-47 Thunderbolts attack rail lines, bridges, and roads in the Po River valley. During the night A-20s and A-26 Invaders attack river crossing sites in the Po River valley.

SOUTHWEST PACIFIC AREA: In the Philippines, Far East Air Force B-24 Liberators, B-25 Mitchells, A-20 Havocs, P-38 Lightnings, and P-47 Thunderbolts attack Balete Pass and other areas in support of ground forces on Luzon. B-24s and A-20s attack targets on Cebu Island.

On Formosa, B-24s attack airfields. Aircrews report hangars, antiaircraft gun positions, and aircraft destroyed.

The 64th Bombardment Squadron (Heavy), 43rd Bombardment Group (Heavy), redeploys B-24s from Leyte to Clark Field on Luzon.

Japanese aircraft attack American shipping in Lingayen Gulf, but the attack is ineffective.

PACIFIC: Twentieth Air Force sends 78 B-29 Superfortresses to bomb logistics storage areas at Rangoon, Burma.

CENTRAL PACIFIC: Seventh Air Force sends 13 B-24 Liberators from Guam to bomb the airfield on Chichi Jima. Sixteen P-51 Mustangs from Iwo Jima strafe logistics storage areas and a radar installation on Chichi Jima. During the night four B-24s fly individual harassment.

A total of 20 B-24s based at Angaur Island bomb Cebu Island in the Philippines.

NEW GUINEA: The 69th and 100th Bombardment Squadrons (Medium), 42nd Bombardment Group (Medium), redeploy B-25s from Morotai to Palawan Island in the Philippines. The 75th Bombardment Squadron (Medium), 42nd Bombardment Group (Medium), redeploys its B-25s from Sansapor to Palawan in the Philippines.

The 868th Bombardment Squadron (Heavy), Thirteenth Air Force, redeploys from Noemfoor to Morotai Island with radar-equipped B-24s.

U.S. submarine *Perch* torpedoes and sinks a Japanese vessel in the Makassar Strait.

March 23

CBI: In China, Fourteenth Air Force sends 28 B-24 Liberators to bomb railroad facilities and a bridge.

In Burma, Tenth Air Force sends nine B-25 Mitchells to bomb lines of communication to block Japanese force movements. P-47 Thunderbolts support Chinese ground forces and attack targets of opportunity.

ATLANTIC: German submarine *U-532* torpedoes and sinks a U.S. freighter in the mid-Atlantic.

ETO: Third Army expands its bridgehead over the Rhine, adding a regiment from the 90th Infantry Division to the 5th Infantry Division's three regiments already across. Tanks and other vehicles are being ferried across. By midnight the bridgehead is five miles deep.

Eighth Air Force sends nearly 1,300 B-17s and B-24 Liberators escorted by nearly 500 P-51 Mustangs to bomb rail bridges, marshaling yards, and airfields. A total of seven bombers are lost and 275 damaged. Aircrews report one confirmed kill and one possible. Aircrew casualties are seven killed, 10 wounded, and 72 missing. More than 120 P-51s fly a fighter sweep of the Bremen-Kassel area. Pilots report one confirmed kill in the air and one possible kill on the ground. One B-17, escorted by four P-51s, bombs Ettinghausen airfield as part of a radar test.

During the night nine B-24s drop leaflets over Germany and the Netherlands. A total of 19 B-24s fly Carpetbagger missions to Denmark.

Ninth Air Force sends 800 A-20 Havocs, A-26 Invaders, and B-26 Marauders to attack communication centers and targets of opportunity. P-47 and P-38 fighters support III Corps, VII Corps, and XII and XX Corps.

ETO: Operation Plunder. Field Marshal Bernard L. Montgomery's 21st Army Group crosses the Rhine River in a set piece orchestration of land and air power. General Eisenhower and Prime Minister Churchill witness the attack, equal in size and complexity to the Normandy landings. Three Allied armies, including the XVI Corps (30th and 79th Infantry Divisions) of the U.S. Ninth Army, make a largely uneventful crossing after a heavy hour-long artillery bombardment followed by the laying of a smokescreen. Operation Varsity is the drop of the First Allied Airborne Army's XVIII Airborne Corps, under the command of Major General Matthew B. Ridgway and composed of the U.S. 17th Airborne Division (commanded by Major General William Miley) and the British 6th Airborne Division. The U.S. IX Troop Carrier Command employs 903 aircraft and 897 gliders on this operation. The drop zones and landing zones are only a few miles from the Rhine where the Allied ground forces will land and are within German artillery range. The 21,000 paratroopers and glider infantry take significant casualties from antiaircraft guns near the drop zones and landing zones. Paratroopers capture crossings over the Issel River and capture 3,500 prisoners. The 3rd Battalion of the 507th Parachute

Infantry Regiment captures Diersfordt Castle after a difficult fight that ends with five German tanks destroyed and 500 prisoners. The two divisions of Ninth Army occupy a bridgehead about nine miles wide and six miles deep and have captured 1,900 prisoners. Ninth Army casualties are 41 killed, 450 wounded, and seven missing. A total of 37,000 British and 22,000 American engineer troops support the crossing. Navy LCVPs (landing craft, vehicle personnel) from Task Group 122.5.1 ferry nearly 4,500 troops from Third Army across the Rhine River at Oppenheim.

MEDITERRANEAN: Fifteenth Air Force sends more than 600 B-17s and B-24 Liberators escorted by P-38 Lightnings and P-51 Mustangs to bomb oil refineries in Germany and Austria and marshaling yards in Czechoslovakia and Austria.

ITALY: Twelfth Air Force B-25 Mitchells bomb rail and road bridges. P-47 Thunderbolts attack rail lines, bridges, vehicles, logistics storage sites, ammunition storage areas, and roads. During the night A-20s attack river crossing points in the Po River valley.

SOUTHWEST PACIFIC AREA: In the Eighth Army area the 162nd and 163rd Infantry Regiments of the 41st Infantry Division capture the center of the Japanese position outside of Zamboanga City. The 186th Infantry Regiment from Palawan arrives to relieve the 162nd Infantry Regiment.

In the Philippines, Far East Air Force B-24 Liberators, B-25 Mitchells, A-20 Havocs, and P-47 Thunderbolts bomb Visayan Island and Cebu City on Cebu Island. On Luzon, P-38 Lightnings, A-20s, and B-25s bomb Balete Pass. B-24s attack targets on Mindanao Island. P-47s attack targets on Formosa.

Infantrymen of the 25th Infantry Division cautiously search for Japanese positions at Balete Pass on Luzon, March 23, 1945.

A U.S. destroyer rams and sinks Japanese submarine *RO-41* in the Philippine Sea.

PACIFIC: Task Force 58 attacks Japanese shipping and installations near Okinawa. Carrier aircraft sink two cargo ships and a midget submarine and damage another midget submarine, a coastal defense ship, and a submarine chaser.

U.S. submarine *Seahorse* is damaged in an air attack off the Ryukyus. U.S. submarine *Spadefish* attacks a Japanese convoy in the East China Sea, sinking a transport.

CENTRAL PACIFIC: Seventh Air Force sends 15 P-51 Mustangs from Iwo Jima to strafe the airfield, logistics storage areas, and a radio installation on Chichi Jima and attack targets on Haha Jima and Ani Jima. During the night five B-24s fly individual harassment raids on Chichi Jima.

March 24

CBI: Fourteenth Air Force B-24 Liberators escorted by P-51 Mustangs bomb locomotives and a bridge. B-25 Mitchells and 100 P-40s and P-51s attack tanks, trucks, locomotives, troop concentrations, logistics storage areas, airfields, gun positions, and targets of opportunity throughout southern and eastern China.

In Burma, Tenth Air Force sends nine B-25 Mitchells to bomb troop concentrations, logistics storage sites, and targets of opportunity. P-47 Thunderbolts and P-38 Lightnings attack targets of opportunity along roads.

ETO: A bridgehead at Remagen extends 25 miles long and 10 miles deep and contains three corps.

Allied air attacks on German positions near Montgomery's 21st Army Group landing sites across the Rhine reach their highest point after a near-continuous bombardment of three days.

The XII Corps of Third Army establishes a bridgehead nine miles wide and six miles deep outside of Oppenheim. Engineers build a heavy pontoon bridge across the Rhine River. The 5th and 90th Infantry Divisions and the 4th Armored Division are across the river and advance toward the Main River. American troops capture 19,000 German prisoners.

Navy LCVPs of Task Group 122.5.1 support Third Army's crossing of the Rhine at Boppard. Task Group 122.5.1 also ferries troops of Ninth Army across the Rhine south of Wesel.

During the night 10 B-24s drop leaflets over Germany and the Netherlands. Twenty-four B-24s fly a Carpetbagger mission over Scandinavia.

Ninth Air Force sends nearly 700 A-20 Havocs, A-26 Invaders, and B-26 Marauders to attack communication centers, railroad bridges, antiaircraft positions, and marshaling yards. P-47 and P-38 fighters support the 30th and 79th Infantry Divisions, attacking antiaircraft positions, German defensive positions, and road and rail traffic.

ETO: Operation Varsity. Over 2,000 transports and gliders of the IX Troop Carrier Command deliver the British 6th Airborne and U.S. 17th Airborne Divisions to their designated drop zones and landing zones.

Eighth Air Force sends more than 1,000 B-17s and B-24 Liberators escorted by 1,158 P-47 Thunderbolts and P-51 Mustangs to bomb airfields. A total of 19 bombers are lost and 103 are damaged. Aircrews report 54 confirmed kills and six possibles. Aircrew casualties are nine killed, five wounded, and 37 missing. Fighter pilots report 53 confirmed kills and two probables in the air and four possible kills on the ground. Nine fighters are lost. Eight pilots are reported missing. A total of 240 B-24 Liberators are sent to drop supplies to support the American and British river crossing operations. They must fly at very low levels, between 300 and 400 feet. German small-arms fire destroys 14 bombers and damages 107 more. Five airmen are killed, 30 wounded, and 116 are missing. In the afternoon 448 B-17s and B-24s attack marshaling yards and an airfield. They are escorted by 95 P-47s and P-51s. There are 38 bombers damaged but no fighter or bomber losses. One P-51 is lost on a scouting mission.

Private George J. Peters is a platoon radio operator with G Company, 507th Parachute Infantry, 17th Airborne Division, jumping into a drop zone over the Rhine River near Fluren, Germany. He lands with 10 other paratroopers in a field about 75 yards away from a German machine gun supported by riflemen. As they struggle to free themselves from their parachute harnesses, the Germans begin firing on them. Peters stands up and charges the enemy firing his M-1 rifle. Although wounded and knocked down, Peters struggles to his feet and advances. He is quickly wounded again and, unable to stand, he crawls forward until close enough to throw hand grenades and eliminate the machine gun. For his dedication to duty, his aggressiveness, and his heroic sacrifice to save the lives of his comrades, Private Peters will win the Medal of Honor.

MEDITERRANEAN: Fifteenth Air Force sends 150 B-17s with an escort of P-51 Mustangs to attack the jet aircraft production facility at Neuburg near Berlin. German fighter jets attack the formation. Six B-17s are lost and six are damaged. Aircrews report six jets as confirmed kills and four as probables. Fighter pilots report five jet aircraft shot down.

Lieutenant General John K. Cannon takes command of Army Air Forces, Mediterranean Theater of Operations (AAFMTO) and is scheduled to take command of the Mediterranean Allied Air Force (MAAF).

Fifteenth Air Force sends more than 600 B-17s and B-24 Liberators escorted by P-38 Lightnings and P-51 Mustangs to bomb a tank production facility at Berlin and an airfield at Munich, a marshaling yard in Czechoslovakia, and airfields in Germany and Italy.

ITALY: Twelfth Air Force B-25 Mitchells bomb bridges. P-47 Thunderbolts attack rail lines and rail cars. During the night A-20s and A-26 Invaders attack marshaling yards, river crossings, bridges, and targets of opportunity.

SOUTHWEST PACIFIC AREA: On Luzon, in the XIV Corps area, the 158th RCT is detached from 11th Airborne Division and placed under Sixth Army operational control to prepare for an amphibious assault at Legaspi on the Bicol Peninsula.

In the Philippines, Far East Air Force B-24 Liberators and A-20 Havocs bomb Cebu City and defenses and installations on Cebu Island. On Luzon Island, B-24s, B-25 Mitchells, A-20 Havocs, and P-38 Lightnings attack Balete Pass and other targets.

On Formosa, B-24s bomb the harbor at Takao and industrial targets.

PACIFIC: During the night Twentieth Air Force sends more than 200 B-29 Superfortresses from the Marianas to bomb the Mitsubishi aircraft engine production facility at Nagoya, Japan. Five B-29s are lost.

Naval Task Force 59, commanded by Vice Admiral Willis A. Lee, bombards Okinawa. Carrier aircraft from TG 58.1 (carriers USS *Bennington* and USS *Hornet* and small carriers USS *Belleau Wood* and USS *San Jacinto*) eliminate a convoy, sinking a torpedo boat, a coastal defense ship, two auxiliary minesweepers, and four cargo ships northwest of Okinawa. Carrier aircraft from TF 58 sink three cargo ships in the northern Ryukyus.

CENTRAL PACIFIC: Seventh Air Force sends nine B-24 Liberators from Guam to bomb the torpedo storage facility on Marcus Island. P-51 Mustangs attack air, naval, and radar installations and targets of opportunity on Chichi Jima. A total of 24 B-24s based on Angaur Island bomb defensive positions and the town of Naga on Luzon Island in the Philippines.

During the night five B-24s from Guam fly individual harassment raids on Haha Jima.

NEW GUINEA: Thirteenth Air Force B-24 Liberators sink a Japanese cargo ship off Celebes Island.

March 25

CBI: Fourteenth Air Force sends B-25 Mitchells and over 150 P-40s and P-51s to attack river, road, and rail traffic, airfields, troop concentrations, logistics storage areas, horses, and gun positions throughout southern and eastern China.

In Burma, Tenth Air Force P-47 Thunderbolts support forces of the Chinese 50th Division, while B-25 Mitchells, P-38 Lightnings, and P-47s attack troops, logistics support sites, and targets of opportunity along roads.

ETO: The Rhine River Is Breached. The 17th Airborne links with elements of the Ninth Army east of the Rhine River, marking the success of Operation Varsity and Operation Plunder. The Allied bridgehead is two miles wide and six miles deep, occupied by five British and four U.S. divisions. Major General Leland S. Hobbs, commander of the 30th Infantry Division, presses an aggressive attack to attempt a breakout but is held up by poor roads and heavily forested terrain.

The XII Corps of Third Army captures Darmstadt. The 87th Infantry Division of the VIII Corps of Third Army establishes a bridgehead over the Rhine River at Boppard, expanding it to eight miles wide and three miles deep. During the night, the 89th Infantry Division (now under the operational control of the VIII Corps) makes an assault crossing of the Rhine.

Bradley orders Patton's Third Army to attack from its bridgeheads to clear German forces out of its zone of action all the way to the area between Hanau and Giessen. Third Army should be ready to continue the attack toward Kassel. First Army will attack out of the Remagen bridgehead to clear German forces from the Giessen-Siegen line and assist the advance of Third Army. Fifteenth Army will take over the west bank of the Rhine River and be prepared to occupy, organize, and govern German municipalities along the Rhine River. Bradley intends to attack eastward then turn north to link with Ninth Army and encircle the Ruhr.

The V Corps, VII Corps, and III Corps of First Army attack out of the Remagen bridgehead, advancing toward Wiesbaden.

The Rhine is the last natural obstacle to SHAEF's campaign for the final battle in Germany. All three Allied army groups are now across the Rhine, and 24 bridges have been built.

Eighth Air Force sends more than 1,000 B-17s and B-24 Liberators escorted by 341 P-47 Thunderbolts and P-51 Mustangs to bomb a tank production facility and oil depots. A total of four bombers are lost and 24 are damaged. Aircrews report six confirmed kills, four probables, and 13 possibles. Aircrew casualties are 25 killed, two wounded, and 39 missing. Fighter pilots report four confirmed kills and three probables in the air. A total of 24 P-51s fly a fighter-bomber mission against an ammunition storage area. One P-51 is lost and the pilot is reported missing. P-51s flying a scouting mission report one possible kill in the air.

During the night 10 B-24s drop leaflets over Germany and the Netherlands. Ninth Air Force sends A-20 Havocs, A-26 Invaders, and B-26 Marauders to attack communications centers, antiaircraft positions, and marshaling yards. P-47 and P-38 fighters support the 79th Infantry Division and II Corps and VII Corps, as well as XII Corps.

MEDITERRANEAN: Fifteenth Air Force sends more than 650 B-17s and B-24 Liberators escorted by P-38 Lightnings and P-51 Mustangs to bomb airfields and a tank production facility in Czechoslovakia.

ITALY: Twelfth Air Force B-25 Mitchells bomb rail and road bridges. P-47 Thunderbolts attack rail lines, bridges, fuel storage sites, and roads. During the night A-20s and A-26 Invaders attack river crossing sites, roads, and motor transport in the Po River valley.

SOUTHWEST PACIFIC AREA: In the Philippines, Far East Air Force B-24 Liberators bomb Cebu City on Cebu Island. On Luzon Island, B-24 Liberators attack Legaspi, and B-25 Mitchells, P-47 Thunderbolts, and P-38 Lightnings provide support to ground forces. B-25s attack Pandanan Island.

The P-38s of the 339th Fighter Squadron, 347th Fighter Group, return to Palawan from Morotai Island.

Fifth Air Force B-24 Liberators sink a Japanese cargo ship near Shanghai.

PACIFIC: Battleships, cruisers, and destroyers of Naval Task Force 54 (Rear Admiral Morton L. Deyo) bombard Okinawa. Kamikazes damage a destroyer, a light minelayer, and a high-speed transport off Okinawa. A bomber damages a high-speed transport.

Carrier aircraft from TF 58 sink two cargo ships near Okinawa.

U.S. submarine *Tirante* torpedoes and sinks a Japanese auxiliary netlayer off Kyushu, Japan.

PACIFIC, OKINAWA: The Americans initiate a psychological warfare effort to induce the Japanese to surrender. About 8 million leaflets are dropped by aircraft during the campaign. This effort, plus loudspeaker broadcasts and other means, promises humane treatment to gain confidence among the civilian population and affect the morale of the defenders.

CENTRAL PACIFIC: Seventh Air Force sends 23 B-24s based at Angaur Island to bomb Cebu Island in the Philippines. A total of 32 P-51 Mustangs from Iwo Jima strafe the airfield, troops, logistics storage areas, and a radar installation on Chichi Jima. During the night five B-24s fly individual harassment raids on Chichi Jima.

CENTRAL PACIFIC, IWO JIMA: The 5th Marine Division captures Death Valley, ending the last pocket of resistance on the island.

NEW GUINEA: The C-46s of the 6th Combat Cargo Squadron, 2nd Combat Cargo Group, redeploy from Biak to Leyte Island.

March 26

ALEUTIANS: Eleventh Air Force sends eight B-25 Mitchells to conduct two separate bombing runs with four bombers attacking each target in the Kuriles. Japanese fighters drive off one group, and the other is unable to locate the target due to weather. One group of four B-24s bombs the Kataoka naval base on Shimushu Island.

CBI: The American airfield at Laohokow is abandoned to advancing Japanese forces.

Fourteenth Air Force B-25 Mitchells, P-40s, and P-51s attack trucks, tanks, logistics sites, horses, troops, and artillery in southern and eastern China.

In Burma, Tenth Air Force P-47 Thunderbolts and B-25 Mitchells attack artillery positions, troop concentrations, road communications, and logistics sites.

ETO: The armored divisions of First Army's III Corps, VII Corps, and V Corps break out of the Remagen bridgehead.

The XV Corps of Seventh Army establishes a bridgehead over the Rhine River near Worms, with the 3rd and 45th Infantry Divisions occupying an area 15 miles wide and seven miles deep. The 3rd Infantry Division meets strong opposition during its crossing. The landing is supported by a 10,000-round artillery barrage that allows the division to establish a solid bridgehead.

The XII Corps of Third Army enters Frankfurt. Patton directs VIII and XII Corps to Giessen.

Navy medium landing craft from Task Group 122.5.1 ferry Third Army troops across the Rhine at Oberwesel.

Lieutenant General William H. Simpson orders the 8th Armored Division of XVI Corps forward to support the 30th and 79th Infantry Divisions as they fight against strong defenses and difficult terrain. Difficulties with bridging the Rhine in the British Second Army area lead to heavy competition for the existing bridges at Wesel, leaving Simpson unable to build his forces in sufficient strength to flank enemy defenses.

Eighth Air Force sends more than 330 B-17s escorted by 527 P-51 Mustangs to bomb tank production facilities and synthetic oil facilities. Thirty bombers are damaged. Aircrew casualties are 19 killed, five wounded.

Ninth Air Force sends 300 A-20 Havocs, A-26 Invaders, and B-26 Marauders to attack marshaling yards and targets of opportunity. P-47 and P-38 fighters support XII Corps and the 2nd, 3rd, 7th, and 9th Armored Divisions.

MEDITERRANEAN: Fifteenth Air Force sends more than 500 B-17s and B-24 Liberators escorted by P-38 Lightnings and P-51 Mustangs to bomb marshaling yards in Austria, Czechoslovakia, and Hungary. P-51s attack bridges and rail traffic in Austria.

ITALY: Twelfth Air Force P-47 Thunderbolts attack rail lines, bridges, and roads in the Po River valley. During the night A-20s attack bridges.

SOUTHWEST PACIFIC AREA: In the Eighth Army area, Naval Task Group 78.2 lands the Americal Division's 132nd and 182nd Infantry Regiments at Cebu City on Cebu Island in the Visayan Sea. Naval Task Group 74.3, commanded by Rear Admiral Russell S. Berkey with one Australian and two U.S. light cruisers and six destroyers, supports the landing.

The beach is heavily mined, and the landings are slowed considerably as 10 LVTs are destroyed in the first wave.

In the Philippines, Far East Air Force B-24 Liberators, B-25 Mitchells, A-20 Havocs, P-38 Lightnings, and P-47 Thunderbolts bomb Legaspi and a fuel storage site, while A-20 Havocs, P-38s, and P-47s support ground forces throughout Luzon. B-24s and A-20s attack Cebu City on Cebu Island.

Fifth Air Force B-24 Liberators bomb shipping in Takao harbor, Formosa, sinking two cargo vessels.

PACIFIC: A U.S. destroyer is sunk by a mine off Okinawa. Kamikazes damage battleship USS *Nevada*, a light cruiser, three destroyers, a destroyer escort, a high-speed minesweeper, and a minesweeper. One destroyer is damaged by a dive-bomber.

U.S. submarine *Balao* (SS-285) sinks a Japanese army stores ship in the Yellow Sea.

Carrier aircraft from TF 58 sink an auxiliary submarine chaser and a cargo ship in the Ryukyus.

PACIFIC, OKINAWA: Four battalions of infantry from the 305th Infantry Regiment of the 77th Infantry Division land on the Kerama Islands, about 30 miles southwest of the island of Okinawa. Most of the defenders are Japanese suicide boat pilots who are preparing for attacks on the American fleet. A U.S. destroyer hits a mine and sinks near the Kerama Islands.

Admiral Blandy's task force begins the prelanding bombardment of Okinawa.

The 3rd Battalion of the 305th Infantry Regiment, 77th Infantry Division, lands at Kerama Island.

CENTRAL PACIFIC: Thirty-seven Seventh Air Force P-51 Mustangs from Iwo Jima strafe the airfield, logistics storage areas, and radar installation on Chichi Jima. Nine B-24s bomb Marcus Island. During the night three B-24s from Guam conduct individual snooper missions on Chichi Jima.

The headquarters of the 21st Fighter Group arrives at Central Field, Iwo Jima, from Hawaii. The 72nd and 531st Fighter Squadrons, 21st Fighter Group, redeploy their P-51s from Hawaii to Iwo Jima.

CENTRAL PACIFIC, IWO JIMA: About 300 Japanese conduct a last counterattack on the airfield during the night. Marines, Seabees, shore party units, and P-51 pilots group together to form a hasty defense. The Japanese are thrown back, losing 250 killed and 18 captured. American losses in the surprise attack number 150.

The marines of the 5th and 3rd Divisions will depart the island over the next few days, leaving the army's 147th Infantry Regiment to complete clearing the island. In the following two months the 147th will kill or capture 2,400 Japanese soldiers.

Iwo Jima is the costliest battle in Marine Corps history, with 24,053 Marine casualties. A total of 6,140 men have been killed. Japanese losses are roughly 22,000 men. The marines have succeeded despite staggering casualties. The veterans of Guam, Bougainville, Saipan, Tinian, and members of the old Marine Raiders from Guadalcanal have made the difference. Their unshakable spirit has guaranteed the victory. Admiral Nimitz, referring to the formidable performance of the marines at Iwo Jima, will say, "uncommon valor was a common virtue."

For the duration of the war, 2,251 B-29 Superfortresses will make emergency landings on Iwo Jima, saving the lives of nearly 25,000 crewmen who otherwise would have been lost in the Pacific.

NEW GUINEA: The 6th Combat Cargo Squadron, 2nd Combat Cargo Group, redeploys from Biak to Leyte Island with C-46s.

March 27

CBI: Fourteenth Air Force sends 25 B-25 Mitchells to bomb towns, rail, road, and river traffic, and targets of opportunity. P-51 Mustangs and P-40s attack trucks, trains, ammunition storage areas, sampans, and power generation facilities.

In Burma, Tenth Air Force P-47 Thunderbolts and P-38 Lightnings attack road traffic, troop concentrations, logistics storage sites, and targets of opportunity.

ETO: Seventh Army and Third Army link at Darmstadt. The 45th Infantry Division of XV Corps battles strong German resistance at Aschaffenburg.

The XX Corps of Third Army sends the 80th Infantry Division in an assault crossing of the Rhine and Main Rivers at Mainz. In the face of heavy fire, navy landing craft from Task Group 122.5.1 ferry troops across the Rhine at Mainz.

VIII Corps eliminates a large pocket of resistance near Wiesbaden and makes contact with First Army.

Eighth Air Force sends more than 100 P-47 Thunderbolts and P-51 Mustangs to escort 262 Royal Air Force Lancaster bombers attacking Paderborn, Germany. During the night nine B-24s drop leaflets over Germany and the Netherlands.

Ninth Air Force sends P-47 and P-38 fighters to support VIII Corps and XII Corps.

The headquarters of the XII Tactical Air Command redeploys from France to Germany.

SOUTHWEST PACIFIC AREA: In the Eighth Army area in the Philippines, the Americal Division's 132nd and 182nd Infantry Regiments capture Cebu City. FEAF B-24s bomb Negros Island airfields, while B-25s and P-38s attack the Cebu City area on Cebu Island.

B-25s bomb Formosa.

B-24 Liberators attack targets on Borneo.

SOUTHWEST PACIFIC AREA, LUZON: In the XI Corps area, the Shimbu Group's defensive line in the mountains northeast of Manila is threatened with destruction, forcing a withdrawal. Preceded by an air strike, the 2nd Battalion, 151st Infantry Regiment, 38th Infantry Division, supported by two destroyers and three rocket-equipped motor torpedo boats, lands on Caballo Island near Corregidor.

Far East Air Force B-24 Liberators, B-25 Mitchells, A-20 Havocs, P-38 Lightnings, and P-47 Thunderbolts bomb Legaspi and several other locations throughout Luzon. P-47s and P-38s support the amphibious landings on Caballo Island in Manila Bay.

PACIFIC: Twentieth Air Force sends more than 250 B-29 Superfortresses from the Marianas to bomb airfields and an aircraft production facility on Kyushu, Japan, and mine Shimonoseki Strait between Honshu and Kyushu islands in support of the Okinawa Island invasion. Aircrews report two confirmed kills, two probables, and four possibles. Three B-29s are lost.

Operation Starvation begins, intended to support operations on Okinawa through aerial mining of the Shimonoseki Strait of Japan. B-29s of the Twentieth Air Force conduct the missions.

Kamikazes damage a light minelayer off Okinawa.

U.S. submarine *Trigger* torpedoes and sinks a Japanese cable layer southwest of Kyushu, Japan.

Carrier aircraft from TF 58 sink two Japanese guardboats and a cargo ship south of Kyushu, Japan.

PACIFIC, OKINAWA: Two battalions of the 306th Infantry Regiment of the 77th Infantry Division lands on Tokashiki Island in the Keramas. Many Okinawan civilians are on the island, moved there by the Japanese. Many commit suicide, convinced by Japanese propaganda that the Americans will torture and kill them.

Japanese kamikaze attacks hit the battleship USS *Nevada,* a cruiser, two destroyers, and a minesweeper. U.S. losses are more than 60 sailors killed and 125 wounded.

CENTRAL PACIFIC: Seventh Air Force sends 16 P-51 Mustangs from Iwo Jima to strafe the ammunition storage area on Chichi Jima. During the night five B-24s fly individual harassment raids on Chichi Jima.

March 28

CBI: Fourteenth Air Force sends six B-24 Liberators to bomb the Haiphong and Hanoi docks in French Indochina. P-40s and P-51s attack trucks, tanks, logistics sites, horses, troop concentrations, and artillery in southern and eastern China.

In Burma, Tenth Air Force P-47 Thunderbolts and P-38 Lightnings attack road traffic, troop concentrations, logistics storage sites, and targets of opportunity.

ETO: SHAEF issues orders for 12th Army Group to move to Leipzig in anticipation of meeting Soviet forces. The 21st Army Group and the 6th Army Group will protect the flanks of the 12th Army Group's advance. The purpose of the advance on Leipzig is to destroy German forces and capture a key industrial area in order to cut Germany in half. The axis of advance suits armored and mechanized forces and meets the military mission of Allied forces. The British are relegated to a secondary and vague mission. Without prior approval, General Eisenhower informs Stalin of his strategic intent.

The VII Corps of First Army (78th, 104th, and 1st Infantry Divisions and the 3rd Armored Division) occupies a front of 130 miles and reaches Marburg. The 7th Armored Division of III Corps clears Giessen. The 9th Armored Division of V Corps moves to attack Frankfurt from the rear in support of VIII Corps.

The 6th Army Group breaks out of its bridgehead at Worms with XV Corps, VI Corps, and XXI Corps.

Ninth Army's XVI Corps makes slow progress against strong German resistance, capturing Dorsten. The 17th Airborne Division, working with British tank units, outflanks Dorsten and creates a corridor for a XIX Corps breakout. Simpson brings the 2nd Armored Division of XIX Corps into the bridgehead.

Eighth Air Force sends 965 B-17s and 390 P-51 Mustangs to attack industrial targets, marshaling yards, and tank production facilities in Berlin and Hannover, Germany. The bombers use radar signal intercepts to mark the bomb release points over the targets. Two B-17s are lost and 204 are damaged. Aircrew casualties are one killed, 11 wounded, and 19 missing.

Ninth Air Force sends 215 A-20 Havocs, A-26 Invaders, and B-26 Marauders to attack oil storage depots and targets of opportunity. P-47 and P-38 fighters support XII Corps and the 2nd and 8th Armored Divisions.

SOUTHWEST PACIFIC AREA: In the Eighth Army area the American Division's 182nd Infantry Regiment battles Japanese forces north of Cebu City.

In the Philippines, Far East Air Force B-24 Liberators, P-38 Lightnings, and P-47 Thunderbolts attack Balete Pass and support ground forces on Luzon. B-25 Mitchells and A-20 Havocs also attack troop concentrations on Luzon. B-24s and B-25s bomb the Cebu City area on Cebu Island and hit airfields on Negros Island. B-24s bomb the airfield on Mindanao Island.

B-24s attack Formosa while B-25s attack shore targets along the French Indochina coast. The 39th Troop Carrier Squadron, 317th Troop Carrier Group, redeploys from Leyte Island to Clark Field with C-47s.

U.S. submarine *Blackfin* is damaged by depth charges off the southeast coast of French Indochina and is forced to terminate her patrol. Another submarine, USS *Bluegill,* attacks a Japanese convoy moving up the southern coast of French Indochina and damages a tanker.

Fifth Air Force B-24 Liberators sink a Japanese cargo ship off the north coast of Formosa.

PACIFIC: During the night Twentieth Air Force sends 10 B-29s to mine the mouth of the Hwangpoo River and the south channel of the Yangtze River at Shanghai, China. Another 17 B-29s mine the waters at Saigon and Cam Ranh Bay in French Indochina, and 32 B-29s mine an area near Singapore.

A U.S. minesweeper is sunk by mine; a kamikaze damages a medium landing ship off Okinawa.

U.S. submarine *Threadfin* torpedoes and sinks a Japanese escort vessel off Kyushu, Japan.

USS *Tirante* torpedoes and sinks a Japanese fishing boat off Kyushu. U.S. submarine *Trigger* is sunk by three Japanese vessels southeast of Kyushu. Aircraft from carrier USS *Hornet* sink a Japanese coastal defense vessel south of Kyushu that participated in the sinking of USS *Trigger.*

PACIFIC, OKINAWA: Japanese kamikaze planes from Okinawa make unsuccessful attacks on landing craft.

CENTRAL PACIFIC: Seventh Air Force sends 15 P-51 Mustangs from Iwo Jima to strafe the airfield and defenses on Chichi Jima. During the night five B-24s fly individual harassment raids on Chichi Jima, and 10 B-24s from Guam conduct individual snooper missions on Truk.

NEW GUINEA: Thirteenth Air Force B-24 Liberators attack Japanese shipping in the Celebes, sinking a minesweeper and a patrol boat.

March 29

ALEUTIANS: Eleventh Air Force sends six B-24 Liberators to bomb Kataoka naval base on Shimushu Island in the Kuriles.

CBI: Fourteenth Air Force sends 11 B-24 Liberators to attack shipping in the South China Sea and at Haiphong, French Indochina. Aircrews report one destroyer and a cargo ship are heavily damaged. In China, 18 B-25 Mitchells, escorted by 12 P-40s, bomb railyards. P-40s and P-51s attack trucks, tanks, logistics sites, horses, troops, and artillery in southern and eastern China.

In Burma, Tenth Air Force sends six B-25 Mitchells to bomb troop concentrations.

ETO: Wiesbaden is captured, along with Frankfurt; Mannheim falls. Since the beginning of March, American forces are capturing 10,000 prisoners a day. First Army begins its turn northward toward Paderborn to link with Ninth Army for the encirclement of the Ruhr. A task force of the 3rd Armored Division and a regiment from the 104th Infantry Division lead the attack.

The 2nd Armored Division of XIX Corps, Ninth Army, breaks out of the bridgehead northeast of Dorsten.

Third Army attacks northeast toward Kassel, protecting the flank of First Army.

ITALY: Twelfth Air Force and P-47 Thunderbolts of the XXII Tactical Air Command attack rail lines, bridges, ammunition storage areas, and roads in the Po River valley. During the night A-20s attack vehicles, river crossing points, logistics storage sites, roads, bridges, and rail loading sites.

SOUTHWEST PACIFIC AREA: On Luzon, in the XIV Corps area, the 1st Cavalry Division and the 11th Airborne Division conduct a double envelopment, trapping about 1,300 Japanese troops at Lipa.

In the Eighth Army area, the 185th RCT of the 40th Infantry Division lands on Negros. American forces secure a key bridge on the way to Bacolod, allowing for a rapid advance.

In the Philippines, Far East Air Force B-24 Liberators and P-51 Mustangs attack Legaspi and the surrounding area on Luzon, while A-20 Havocs and P-38 Lightnings attack targets in support of ground forces. B-25s bomb Cebu Island, while A-20s support troops landing on Negros Island.

B-24 Liberators and B-25 Mitchells bomb Formosa.

U.S. submarine *Bluegill* attacks the same Japanese convoy as yesterday while it moves up the southern coast of French Indochina. The tanker torpedoed previously is hit again. U.S. Submarine *Hammerhead* damages a coastal defense vessel. Fifth Air Force B-25 Mitchells sink two coastal defense vessels and a cargo ship off French Indochina and sink three auxiliary submarine chasers and a merchant tanker in Takao harbor, Formosa.

FEAF B-24 Liberators bomb an airfield in Borneo.

PACIFIC: During the night Twentieth Air Force sends 29 B-29s to fly the last mission under XX Bomber Command, attacking oil storage facilities on Bukum Island in the Malay States. Two other B-29s bomb individual targets on the Malay Peninsula.

Naval Task Groups 58.1 (Rear Admiral Joseph J. Clark) and 58.3 (Rear Admiral Frederick C. Sherman) attack airfields and shipping around Kagoshima Bay, Kyushu, Japan. Carrier aircraft sink three auxiliary submarine chasers and nine cargo vessels. One merchant vessel is damaged.

Japanese submarine *I-47* carrying *kaiten* is damaged by Fifth Fleet surface ships off Okinawa and forced to return to Japan for repairs.

PACIFIC, OKINAWA: The 77th Infantry Division secures the islands of the Keramas. Over 500 Japanese are killed. Nearly 1,200 civilians are under American control. U.S. losses are 31 killed and 81 wounded. Over 290 boats, intended for attacks on the U.S. Fleet, are captured.

Task Force 58's carrier aircraft attack Kyushu Island.

Underwater demolition teams conduct a reconnaissance on the Hagushi landing beaches.

CENTRAL PACIFIC: Seventh Air Force sends nine B-24 Liberators from Guam Island to bomb Truk. A total of 31 P-51 Mustangs from Iwo Jima bomb and strafe Haha Jima.

The headquarters of Twentieth Air Force's 58th Bombardment Wing (Very Heavy) arrives at Tinian from India.

March 30

CBI: Fourteenth Air Force B-24 Liberators bomb the Samah Bay area of Hainan Island. In China, B-25 Mitchells, supported by 24 P-40s, destroy a bridge and other B-25s bomb railyards. B-25 Mitchells, with 15 P-40s providing escort, bomb Hankow airfield. P-40s and P-51s attack troops, rail targets, trucks, tanks, logistics sites, airfields, and rivercraft in southern and eastern China.

In Burma, Tenth Air Force sends B-25 Mitchells to bomb road bridges, troop concentrations, logistics storage sites, and trucks. P-47 Thunderbolts and P-38 Lightnings attack Japanese troops and logistics sites.

ETO: General Eisenhower orders Field Marshal Bernard L. Montgomery's 21st Army Group and General Omar N. Bradley's 12th Army Group to link at Kassel-Paderborn to encircle the Ruhr and destroy the final organized elements of the German army in the west. The 6th Army Group is to advance to protect the flank of the 12th Army Group. Once the pocket in the Ruhr is cleared, the 12th Army Group is to advance to the east. The focus of effort is now shifted from the north to the center, with both army groups conducting a simultaneous envelopment, rather than a main effort from the north with a supporting attack in the center as was originally planned.

The U.S. Fifteenth Army is created under the command of Lieutenant General Leonard T. Gerow to hold the rear areas so combat operations into Germany can continue. Gerow's army is responsible for governing the parts of Germany already occupied by the Allies and is responsible for the territory west of the Rhine between Bonn and Homberg. Lieutenant General Gerow also has operational control of the 66th Infantry Division guarding the German garrisons at Lorient and St-Nazaire.

The British leadership presses the Americans for a rapid advance on Berlin to beat the Soviets, arguing that Berlin is an important strategic political objective.

During the month of March, the Allies have moved 1.8 million tons of supplies to the forward areas, most of it by rail but a significant amount by pipeline, barges, and trucks as well. About 40 percent of all these supplies are delivered through Antwerp and Ghent; about 30 percent through Le Havre, Cherbourg, and Rouen; and about 10 percent through Marseille. About 230,000 men in the rear areas have been retrained as infantrymen to replace combat losses. Draftees also flow into theater, providing enough of a manpower pool to bring the American divisions to full strength by late March.

The 4th Armored Division of XII Corps, Third Army, reaches Hersfeld. The 3rd Armored Division of VII Corps moves 90 miles and approaches Paderborn. Major General Maurice Rose, the division's commander, is killed when he encounters German troops outside the city.

Eighth Air Force sends more than 1,400 B-17s and B-24 Liberators escorted by nearly 900 P-51 Mustangs to bomb U-boat facilities, port areas, and oil depots. A total of five bombers are lost and 536 are damaged. Aircrews report eight confirmed kills, one probable, and 12 possibles. Aircrew casualties are 22 killed, 11 wounded, and 28 missing. Fighter pilots report one probable and three possibles in the air. Three P-51s are lost. Over 150 P-51s fly a freelance mission for the bombers. Pilots report one confirmed kill. Three submarines are sunk at Wilhelmshaven, six submarines are sunk at Bremen, and four at Hamburg.

A total of 32 B-17s fly a Disney mission, launching rocket-powered concrete-penetrating bombs against the U-boat yard at Farge. Fourteen B-17s are damaged.

Six B-17s conduct screening missions to jam German radio interception efforts and employ countermeasures against German radar sites.

During the night 13 B-24s drop leaflets over Germany and the Netherlands. Nineteen B-24 Liberators fly Carpetbagger missions to Norway. One B-24 is lost, and another crashes in the Orkney Islands.

Ninth Air Force sends 337 A-20 Havocs, A-26 Invaders, and B-26 Marauders to attack a tank production facility, an ordnance depot, and an oil depot. P-47 and P-38 fighters support the 3rd and 7th Armored Divisions, XII Corps, XX Corps, and XVI Corps.

The headquarters of the 349th Troop Carrier Group and the C-46s of the 312th Troop Carrier Squadron, IX Troop Carrier Command, arrive in England from the United States.

First Lieutenant Walter J. Will, K Company, 18th Infantry Regiment, 1st Infantry Division, rescues two wounded soldiers in the face of heavy enemy fire near Eisern, Germany, and even though he is wounded himself, risks his life again to rescue another soldier. Ignoring his injury, he leads his platoon forward until they are pinned down by flanking fire from two enemy machine guns. Will moves out alone and reaches the first machine-gun position and eliminates the enemy with grenades. He continues to crawl to the next position and charges it, capturing the gun and nine soldiers. He takes one of his squads on a flanking movement to attack another two machine-gun positions firing on another platoon. In the face of direct enemy fire, Will throws three grenades at the Germans, knocking out one machine gun. He then attacks the second position and destroys it with a grenade. The platoon then sweeps forward to clear the enemy off the objective, and during this last action Will is killed. For his heroic leadership, indomitable courage, and unflinching devotion to duty, First Lieutenant Will will receive the Medal of Honor.

MEDITERRANEAN: Fifteenth Air Force sends more than 60 B-17s and B-24 Liberators escorted by P-38 Lightnings and P-51 Mustangs to bomb marshaling yards in Austria. P-38s and P-51s fly sweeps over Yugoslavia and Austria.

ITALY: Twelfth Air Force B-25 Mitchells bomb rail bridges. P-47 Thunderbolts of the XXII Tactical Air Command attack rail lines, bridges, vehicles, fuel storage sites, and ammunition storage areas. During the night A-20s and A-26 Invaders attack roads, river crossing sites, and motor transport in the Po River valley.

SOUTHWEST PACIFIC AREA: In the Eighth Army area, the 186th and 163rd Infantry Regiments of the 41st Infantry Division eliminate the final Japanese defenders outside of Zamboanga City. American casualties are 220 killed. The Japanese have lost nearly 7,000 killed. Airfields in the area are improved and expanded.

The 185th RCT of the 40th Infantry Division captures Bacolod on Negros.

In the Philippines, Far East Air Force B-24 Liberators bomb Balete Pass, P-38 Lightnings attack artillery positions, and A-20 Havocs and P-47 Thunderbolts conduct ground support missions in the Laguna de Bay area and on Japanese positions near Fort Stotsenburg on Luzon. B-24s and A-20s support ground forces on Cebu Island. B-24s, B-25s, and P-38 Lightnings attack Bongao Island.

FEAF B-24 Liberators and B-25 Mitchells attack targets in Borneo.

PACIFIC: During the night Twentieth Air Force sends more than 90 B-29s to attack the Mitsubishi aircraft engine production facility at Nagoya, Japan. One B-29 is lost. Twentieth Air Force B-29s mine the Shimonoseki Strait and the waters off Kure, Hiroshima, and Sasebo, Japan.

A kamikaze damages heavy cruiser USS *Indianapolis* off Okinawa. U.S. submarine *Tirante* torpedoes and sinks a Japanese guardboat off Kagoshima, Kyushu, Japan,

CENTRAL PACIFIC: Seventh Air Force sends 10 B-24 Liberators from Guam to bomb the airfield on Marcus Island. During the night five B-24s fly individual harassment raids on Chichi Jima.

March 31

CBI: In China, Fourteenth Air Force B-24 Liberators with nine P-51 Mustangs escorting, bomb railyards. B-25 Mitchells bomb a bridge and gun positions. B-25s, P-40s, and P-51s attack trucks, tanks, logistics sites, horses, troops, and artillery in southern and eastern China. Over 20 P-51s attack Ningpo airfield. Fighter pilots report a number of Japanese aircraft destroyed on the ground. Six P-51s are lost.

In Burma, Tenth Air Force sends 12 B-25 Mitchells to bomb a road bridge behind Japanese lines.

ATLANTIC: The United States and Britain bar a Soviet-supported provisional regime in Warsaw from entering the United Nations meeting in San Francisco.

ETO: The 9th Armored Division of V Corps reaches Warburg. The French First Army makes an assault crossing of the Rhine River at Speyer and Gemersheim. General de Lattre de Tassigny is under orders from General Charles de Gaulle to push

French forces into German territory. Fearing that the French will be marginalized in the postwar peace, de Gaulle wants to strengthen France's hand.

The 2nd Armored Division of the XIX Corps of Ninth Army advances 40 miles in two days to reach Beckum, cutting the main highway to Berlin and cutting the main rail lines to the Ruhr. One arm of the envisioned encirclement of the Ruhr is in place.

Eighth Air Force sends more than 1,300 B-17s and B-24 Liberators escorted by nearly 900 P-47 Thunderbolts and P-51 Mustangs to bomb synthetic oil production facilities, industrial targets, and marshaling yards. The bombers use radar signal intercepts to mark the bomb release points over the targets. A total of five bombers are lost and 153 damaged. Aircrews report nine confirmed kills, three probables, and nine possibles. Aircrew casualties are 11 killed, three wounded, and 59 missing. Fighter pilots report five confirmed kills and seven possibles in the air. Four P-51s are lost, and the pilots are reported missing. Over 25 P-51s fly scouting missions. Pilots report one confirmed kill and one possible.

Eight B-17s conduct screening missions to jam German radio interception efforts and employ countermeasures against German radar sites.

Ninth Air Force sends more than 550 A-20 Havocs, A-26 Invaders, and B-26 Marauders to attack storage depots and a marshaling yard. P-47 and P-38 fighters support the 3rd and 9th Armored Divisions, XII Corps, XX Corps, XVI and XIX Corps.

MEDITERRANEAN: Fifteenth Air Force reports that, in the first three months of 1945, fighters have destroyed 1,100 locomotives, 3,600 rail cars, and 132 vehicles. A total of 65 U.S. fighters have been lost during the same period.

Fifteenth Air Force sends more than 540 B-17s and B-24 Liberators escorted by P-38 Lightnings and P-51 Mustangs to bomb rail lines and marshaling yards in Austria and Italy.

ITALY: Twelfth Air Force B-25 Mitchells bomb bridges. P-47 Thunderbolts attack rail lines, logistics storage sites, and ammunition storage areas. During the night A-20s attack river crossing points, rail lines, and ammunition storage areas in the Po River valley.

SOUTHWEST PACIFIC AREA: On Luzon, Private First Class William R. Shockley, L Company, 128th Infantry Regiment, 32nd Infantry Division, faces a Japanese counterattack on the Villa Verde Trail. As artillery fire lands around the Americans, Shockley tells his comrades to fall back while he holds off the Japanese. With supreme bravery he stops one charge, even when his weapon malfunctions. He shifts fire to stop a flanking movement and fights on until overwhelmed by superior numbers. For his heroic sacrifice to save the lives of his comrades, Private First Class Shockley will receive the Medal of Honor.

In the Philippines, Far East Air Force P-47 Thunderbolts and P-38 Lightnings attack Japanese positions in the Cagayan Valley and bridges and gun positions throughout Luzon. B-25 Mitchells, A-20 Havocs, and P-38 Lightnings attack targets on Cebu Island.

On Formosa, A-20s attack an army camp, and P-51s conduct a sweep across the island. B-24s bomb harbors and shipping at Kirun and Yulin, China.

FEAF B-24 Liberators bomb targets on Borneo and fighters attack airfields in north Borneo. Thirteenth Air Force B-24 Liberators attack a Japanese convoy off Makassar, sinking four small cargo vessels and damaging another.

PACIFIC: Twentieth Air Force sends more than 130 B-29 Superfortresses to bomb the Tachiarai machine works and Omura airfield on Kyushu Island, Japan. This attack is intended to divert Japanese aircraft from the invasion of Okinawa. The machine works is completely destroyed. Aircrews report 11 confirmed kills, five probables, and three possibles. One B-29 is lost and 15 are damaged.

PACIFIC, OKINAWA: Kerama Islands are secured. American casualties are 31 killed and 81 wounded. Japanese casualties number over 600. Keise Shima Island is captured without resistance. The 420th Field Artillery Group will occupy the island to provide fire support for the invasion of Okinawa with 155 millimeter guns.

Intense air and naval bombardment of suspected Japanese positions near the landing beaches continues.

Japanese kamikaze aircraft hit Admiral Spruance's flagship, the cruiser USS *Indianapolis,* killing nine sailors and wounding 20. Spruance transfers to the battleship USS *New Mexico.*

Underwater demolition teams complete the destruction of underwater obstacles at the Hagushi landing beach sites.

Kamikazes damage a light minelayer, an attack transport, and two LSTs off Okinawa. Two U.S. destroyers sink Japanese submarine *I-8* southeast of Okinawa.

CENTRAL PACIFIC: Seventh Air Force sends 15 P-51 Mustangs from Iwo Jima to strafe the airfield, logistics storage areas, shipping, and radar installation on Chichi Jima. During the night five B-24s from Guam fly individual harassment raids on Chichi Jima.

April 1

CBI: In China, seven Fourteenth Air Force B-24 Liberators bomb the Fort Bayard logistics storage area. B-25 Mitchells and P-51 Mustangs attack river shipping and warehouses.

In Burma, Tenth Air Force sends 10 B-25 Mitchells to attack roads and bridges behind enemy lines in central Burma as the British 36th Division begins to advance down the railroad from Mandalay to Rangoon.

ETO: A task force of the 3rd Armored Division, VII Corps, First Army, meets with elements of the 2nd Armored Division, XIX Corps, Ninth Army, at Lippstadt. The encirclement of the Ruhr is completed, thus accomplishing General Eisenhower's strategic design developed in 1944. A total of 21 divisions representing Germany's Army Group B and two corps of Army Group H are completely isolated in a 4,000-square-mile area.

The Fifteenth Army's XXII Corps, commanded by Major General Ernest N. Harmon, takes over a section of the pocket with the 94th Infantry Division and the 101st and 82nd Airborne Divisions. Fifteenth Army is placed under the operational control of Bradley's 12th Army Group. The First and Ninth Armies also hold the pocket. The Ninth Army's XVI Corps and two divisions of XIX Corps will hold the pocket from the north while the XIII Corps moves eastward. The XVIII Airborne

Corps (now under First Army operational control) and III Corps of First Army will hold the pocket from the south while V Corps and VII Corps advance eastward.

The French II Corps establishes a bridgehead at Philippsburg and prepares to attack toward Stuttgart.

During the night Eighth Air Force sends 12 B-24s to drop leaflets over Germany and the Netherlands.

Ninth Air Force P-47 and P-38 fighters support the 3rd and 9th Armored Divisions, XX Corps and XII Corps.

MEDITERRANEAN: Fifteenth Air Force sends more than 400 B-17s and B-24 Liberators escorted by P-38 Lightnings and P-51 Mustangs to bomb bridges in Yugoslavia and in Austria. P-51s strafe rail lines in Czechoslovakia.

ITALY: Twelfth Air Force B-25 Mitchells bomb rail and road traffic and bridges. P-47 Thunderbolts attack rail lines, bridges, marshaling yards, logistics storage sites, and roads in the Po River valley. During the night A-20 Havocs and A-26 Invaders attack road and rail bridges and motor transport in the Po River valley.

SOUTHWEST PACIFIC AREA: On Luzon, the 158th RCT conducts an amphibious landing on Legaspi on the southeast coast of the Bicol Peninsula, supported by naval gunfire and air bombardment. Japanese resistance is light and unorganized.

In the Philippines, Far East Air Force B-24 Liberators, A-20 Havocs, P-38 Lightnings, and P-47 Thunderbolts attack the Legaspi area in support of amphibious landing operations and attack Japanese positions near Balete Pass and other areas on Luzon. B-25 Mitchells and A-20 Havocs support ground forces near Cebu City on Cebu Island and on Negros Island.

B-24 Liberators bomb an airfield on Formosa, while B-25s and P-47s sweep across wide areas of the island.

The headquarters of Fifth Air Force prepares to redeploy from Mindoro Island to Clark Field on Luzon.

In the Formosa Straits, U.S. submarine *Queenfish* sinks a Japanese relief ship carrying Red Cross supplies for Allied prisoners of war at Singapore.

FEAF B-24 Liberators attack Oelin airfield in Borneo.

PACIFIC: The Japanese Imperial General Headquarters adopts Ketsu, a plan for the defense of the home islands and China. Most Japanese forces in China will be withdrawn to the home islands, while the remainder of Japanese forces in China will consolidate along the southern coast of China, primarily to preclude any Allied invasions.

Twentieth Air Force begins the redeployment of the B-29s of the 25th Bombardment Squadron (Very Heavy), 40th Bombardment Group (Very Heavy), the 676th, 677th, and 678th Bombardment Squadrons (Very Heavy), 444th Bombardment Group (Very Heavy), and the 768th, 769th, and 770th Bombardment Squadrons (Very Heavy) of the 462nd Bombardment Group (Very Heavy), from India to Tinian Island.

Six B-29s mine the waters off Kure, Japan. Mines dropped in the Shimonoseki Strait sink a cargo ship and damage an escort vessel and an auxiliary submarine chaser.

PACIFIC: Operation Iceberg: the Invasion of Okinawa. The operation is under the overall command of Admiral Raymond A. Spruance, Commander Fifth Fleet. Vice Admiral Richmond K. Turner commands the Joint Expeditionary Force. Lieutenant General Simon B. Buckner commands the ground forces. The invasion of Okinawa begins with the largest concentration of naval gunfire in World War II. Ten battleships, nine cruisers, 23 destroyers, and 117 rocket gunboats fire nearly 4,000 tons of shells onto the island. The 2nd Marine Division conducts a diversionary landing near Minatoga, off the southeast coast of the island.

The 96th and 7th Infantry Divisions land along with the 1st and 6th Marine Divisions—a total of 16,000 men—nearly simultaneously. It is one of the greatest spectacles of the war. The landing is unopposed, and the Americans move rapidly inland to their objectives. By the end of L-day, 60,000 men are ashore, along with vehicles and supplies.

There are no Japanese near the beaches. Enemy troops have pulled back into other prepared defensive positions on the island, waiting for the Americans to come to them. Within a few hours, the 6th Marine Division reaches Yomitan airfield, while the 17th Infantry Regiment of the 7th Infantry Division captures Kadena airfield, both objectives far ahead of the L+3 timeline. The 22nd and 4th Marine Regiments of the 6th Marine Division move north and east. On the left flank of the 6th Marines, the 1st Marine Division occupies the high ground after encountering only a few Japanese. The 7th Infantry Division's 17th and 32nd Infantry Regiments advance 4,700 yards and establish defensive positions. The 96th Infantry Division's 381st and 383rd Infantry Regiments, landing on the south edge of the beachhead, clear out a number of defensive positions.

U.S. casualties for the day are 28 killed, 104 wounded, and 27 missing.

Kamikazes damage battleship USS *West Virginia,* two attack transports, and an LST. Japanese dive-bombers damage a destroyer and a minesweeper. Bombers damage an attack transport. A kamikaze damages British fleet carrier HMS *Indefatigable.* A British destroyer is damaged by a bomb.

April 2
CBI: In China, Fourteenth Air Force sends 25 B-25 Mitchells to attack trucks, tanks, rivercraft, and targets of opportunity. B-24 Liberators bomb the Kowloon docks in Hong Kong and attack shipping near Hainan Island. P-51 Mustangs bomb airfields near Shanghai, while B-25s, P-40s, and P-51s attack trucks, tanks, logistics sites, horses, troops, and artillery in southern and eastern China.

In French Indochina, 28 B-25 Mitchells knock out a bridge and attack shipping and other targets of opportunity along the coast of the Gulf of Tonkin.
ETO: The XVIII Corps takes control of part of the Ruhr Pocket, gaining two divisions from VII Corps (8th and 78th Infantry Divisions). The XVIII Corps now has the 97th, 78th, 8th, and 86th Infantry Divisions under its operational control.

Bad weather cancels a mission by over 600 B-17s and B-24 Liberators to bomb airfields in Denmark. One B-17 is lost, one P-51 is lost, and one fighter is damaged. During the night 10 B-24s drop leaflets over France, Germany, and the Netherlands, and 10 B-24 Liberators fly Carpetbagger missions to Denmark.

Ninth Air Force P-47 Thunderbolts and P-38 Lightnings support the 9th Armored Division.

MEDITERRANEAN: Fifteenth Air Force sends more than 600 B-17s and B-24 Liberators escorted by P-38 Lightnings and P-51 Mustangs to bomb marshaling yards and a rail bridge in Austria. P-38s and P-51s attack rail traffic in Germany, Austria, and Yugoslavia.

ITALY: Major General Benjamin W. Chidlaw takes command of Twelfth Air Force and is scheduled to take command of the Mediterranean Allied Tactical Air Force (MATAF). Twelfth Air Force B-25 Mitchells bomb rail bridges. P-47 Thunderbolt pilots report 13 German aircraft destroyed in the air during attacks on rail lines, bridges, and roads in the Po River valley. During the night A-20 Havocs and A-26 Invaders attack river crossing points, roads, and motor transport in the Po River valley.

SOUTHWEST PACIFIC AREA: Marine fighters and three destroyers support the 163rd RCT, 41st Infantry Division, as it lands on Sanga Sanga, in the Sulu Archipelago, Philippines. No enemy forces are found.

In the Philippines, Far East Air Force B-25 Mitchells, P-38 Lightnings, and P-47 Thunderbolts attack bridges and the Balete Pass area. B-25s bomb Japanese troops at Cebu City on Cebu Island. Japanese troops are also attacked by B-25s and P-38s on Negros Island. B-24 Liberators bomb Bongao Island and the Sarangani Bay area on Mindanao Island.

B-24 Liberators bomb the harbor at Hong Kong.

U.S. submarine *Hardhead* lays mines off the southern coast of French Indochina.

U.S. submarine *Sea Devil* attacks a Japanese convoy in the Yellow Sea, sinking an auxiliary vessel and two cargo ships and damaging another cargo ship.

FEAF B-24 Liberators attack the Sandakan shipyards and Tawau airfield on Borneo.

PACIFIC: Twentieth Air Force sends more than 100 B-29 Superfortresses to bomb the Nakajima aircraft production facility at Tokyo. Aircrews report one confirmed kill and one probable. Six B-29s are lost. During the night six B-29s mine the harbors at Kure and Hiroshima on Honshu Island, Japan.

Naval Task Group 58.4 carrier aircraft sink a Japanese coast defense vessel, a fast transport, and a landing ship and damage a submarine chaser and a landing ship in the Ryukyus.

PACIFIC, OKINAWA: The 2nd Marine Division repeats its diversionary landing near Minatoga off the southeast coast of the island. The 6th Marine Division advances three miles northward. The 22nd and 29th Marines encounter no opposition, but the 4th Marines fight through a number of strongpoints. The 1st Marine Division encounters no resistance as it advances across the island. The 7th Infantry Division reaches the eastern coast of Okinawa without encountering significant resistance. The 32nd and the 17th Infantry Regiments occupy ridges overlooking Nakagusuku Bay on the east edge of the island. The 96th Infantry Division advances 3,000 yards in difficult terrain, supported by tanks and aircraft. The American advance secures the 10th Army's beachhead.

A destroyer and a destroyer escort are hit by bombs. Kamikazes damage three attack transports, two attack cargo ships, and a high-speed transport off Okinawa.

CENTRAL PACIFIC: Seventh Air Force sends 12 B-24 Liberators to bomb Marcus Island.

April 3

CBI: Fourteenth Air Force sends 17 B-25 Mitchells to bomb railyards and bridges in French Indochina.

ATLANTIC: The army chief of staff, General George C. Marshall, informs the JCS of reports indicating that the Soviets are becoming increasingly less cooperative in fulfilling their obligations under the Yalta agreement. Marshall is concerned that such actions will threaten Allied unity at a critical point in the war.

ETO: The Ninth Army is returned to Bradley's operational control. Ninth Army captures Recklinghausen in the Ruhr, while First Army captures Fulda and Kassel.

The III Corps of First Army (99th, 9th, and 5th Infantry Divisions and the 7th Armored Division) is directed to attack along the eastern edge of the Ruhr Pocket. This frees Lieutenant General Hodges to use two remaining corps of First Army for the attack to the east.

The 45th Infantry Division, XV Corps, Seventh Army, captures Aschaffenburg after a six-day battle for the city.

Eighth Air Force sends more than 750 B-17s and B-24 Liberators escorted by 569 P-51 Mustangs to bomb the U-boat yards at Kiel. Two bombers are lost and 121 are damaged. Aircrews report one confirmed kill. Aircrew casualties are one wounded and 20 missing. Fighter pilots report one confirmed kill in the air. Two fighters are lost and three are damaged. At the U-boat yards at Kiel, three submarines are destroyed by air attack. Seventeen P-51s fly a scouting mission and two fighters are lost.

During the night one B-17 and 10 B-24s drop leaflets over Germany, France, and the Netherlands. Ninth Air Force sends 230 A-20 Havocs, A-26 Invaders, and B-26 Marauders to attack marshaling yards. P-47 and P-38 fighters support 2nd, 8th, and 9th Armored Divisions, XX Corps and XII Corps.

The C-47s of the 23rd, 313th, and 314th Troop Carrier Squadrons, 349th Troop Carrier Group, IX Troop Carrier Command, arrive in England from the United States.

Private First Class Walter C. Wetzel is acting squad leader with the Antitank Company, 13th Infantry Regiment, 8th Infantry Division, guarding his platoon's command post in a house at Birken, Germany. Spotting German troops moving quickly into the town, Wetzel warns the command post and returns fire as the German infantry advances on the house. Taking up a firing position in the house, Wetzel reacts when the Germans throw grenades into the room. Shouting a warning to his fellow soldiers, Wetzel throws himself on the grenades and is killed, but saves the lives of his comrades. For his supreme sacrifice, Private First Class Wetzel will receive the Medal of Honor.

MEDITERRANEAN: Fifteenth Air Force sends 95 P-38 Lightnings to conduct dive-bombing on a railroad bridge in Austria.

ITALY: Twelfth Air Force B-25 Mitchells bomb rail and road traffic and bridges. A-20 Havocs and P-47 Thunderbolts of the XXII Tactical Air Command attack vehicles, logistics storage sites, ammunition storage areas, rail lines, bridges, and roads in the Po River valley. During the night A-20s attack the marshaling yard at Mantua, river crossing sites, and roads and motor transport in the Po River valley.

SOUTHWEST PACIFIC AREA: Eighth Army plans to land X Corps, commanded by Major General Franklin C. Sibert, with the 24th and 31st Infantry Divisions, on the west side of Mindanao. The 24th will land and capture the airfield at Malabang; two days later the 31st Infantry Division will land at Parang to control Highway 1, the main road to Davao. Rear Admiral Albert G. Noble's task group will support the landings. Before the landing at Malabang takes place, the guerrillas notify the Americans that the airfield is already secured. Marine aviators from Dipolog land on the airfield and attack Japanese positions.

In the Philippines, Far East Air Force A-20 Havocs, P-38 Lightnings, and P-47 Thunderbolts attack the Balete Pass and the Cagayan Valley areas.

B-25 Mitchells attack north Hainan Island. B-24 Liberators bomb the docks at Hong Kong. Other B-24s and B-25 Mitchells attack the airfield, a butanol plant, and railroad yards at Kagi, on Formosa, while A-20s sweep other rail targets.

Far East Air Force B-24 Liberators bomb Japanese shipping in Hong Kong harbor, sinking two cargo vessels and damaging an escort vessel.

PACIFIC: Twentieth Air Force sends 48 B-29s to bomb the aircraft production facility at Shizuoka, Japan. Another 43 B-29s attack the Koizumi aircraft production facility and urban areas in Tokyo. Aircrews report one confirmed kill. A total of 61 B-29s hit the primary target, the aircraft production facility at Tachikawa, while 49 others hit the urban area of Kawasaki as a target of opportunity. One B-29 is lost. During the night nine B-29s mine the waters off Kure and the harbor at Hiroshima, Honshu, Japan. Escort carrier USS *Wake Island* and a high-speed minesweeper are damaged by near-misses of kamikazes. A kamikaze damages an LST.

Carrier aircraft from TF 58 sink a Japanese guardboat and damage a guardboat southeast of Honshu, Japan, and sink a cargo ship off southwestern Kyushu, Japan. A coastal defense vessel is also damaged.

PACIFIC, OKINAWA: Advancing south, the 96th Infantry Division ties in with the 7th Infantry Division as it captures the town of Kuba. General Buckner orders the 6th Marine Division to attack and seize the northern half of Okinawa to prevent enemy reinforcements from landing in the rear of 10th Army. The 1st Marine Division prepares to advance into the Katchin Peninsula. The beachhead now stretches across the middle of the island.

April 4

CBI: In French Indochina, Fourteenth Air Force sends two B-25 Mitchells to attack shipping in the Gulf of Tonkin. Six P-38 Lightnings strafe trucks around Dien Bien Phu.

ATLANTIC: The Joint Chiefs of Staff designates General of the Army Douglas MacArthur as Commander in Chief, U.S. Army Forces, Pacific (CINCUSAFPAC) and Fleet Admiral Chester W. Nimitz as Commander in Chief, Pacific (CINCPOA).

ETO: General Eisenhower orders General Omar N. Bradley's 12th Army Group to attack from Kassel to Leipzig and establish a bridgehead over the Elbe River. Bradley will be the main effort in the final defeat of Germany. Field Marshal Bernard L. Montgomery's 21st Army Group is also to advance to the Elbe River and then north along the Baltic coast, but will primarily protect Bradley's left flank. Lieutenant General Jacob L. Devers's 6th Army Group is to protect Bradley's southern flank and advance to Bayreuth, then be prepared to advance to Nürnberg and Linz. The British Chiefs of Staff notify Eisenhower that his plan for the final offensive in Germany is inadequate. Having Montgomery's 21st Army Group advance to Bremen, then to the Elbe River, ignores Berlin as a critical objective that must be occupied before the Soviets get to the capital. Eisenhower believes Berlin is no longer a military objective. The Soviet advance and the heavy Allied bombing have rendered it useless as a military objective. Eisenhower believes that SHAEF's mission is to focus on German military forces and not on political issues.

The French First Army's II Corps, part of the 6th Army Group, captures Karlsruhe.

The Ninth Army's XIX Corps advances to link with First Army and attack toward the Ruhr Pocket. The 2nd Armored Division of XIX Corps and the 5th Armored Division of XIII Corps of Ninth Army reach the Weser River. The XVI Corps (95th, 75th, 35th, and 79th Infantry Divisions, the 8th Armored Division, and the 17th Airborne Division) battles German defenders north of the Ruhr River.

In the Third Army area, 4th Armored Division and elements of the 89th Infantry Division make the first Western encounter with a concentration camp, at Ohrdruf. This is a subcamp of the Buchenwald concentration camp and the first Nazi camp liberated by American forces. It was established in 1944 to supply forced labor for construction projects. In March it held nearly 12,000 prisoners, but by April most have been moved to Buchenwald by a series of forced marches. Those too weak to move have been killed. Bodies lie in heaps; most are victims of malnutrition. There are indications that the guards have made hasty attempts to cover up the evidence by burning the remains.

Eighth Air Force sends more than 1,400 B-17s and B-24 Liberators escorted by over 800 P-47 Thunderbolts and P-51 Mustangs to bomb airfields, shipyards, and U-boat facilities. The bombers use a combination of visual techniques and radar signal intercepts to mark the bomb release points over the targets. A total of 10 bombers are lost and 187 are damaged. Aircrews report six confirmed kills, four probables, and six possibles. Aircrew casualties are two killed, six wounded, and 90 missing. At the U-boat yards at Hamburg and Kiel three submarines are destroyed.

A total of 22 of 24 B-17s fly a Disney mission attacking the Finkenwarder U-boat yard at Hamburg with wing-mounted, 4,500-pound, concrete-penetrating rocket bombs.

Fighter pilots report 23 confirmed kills and five possibles in the air. Five fighters are lost. P-51 Mustangs flying a scouting mission and escorting photo and radar reconnaissance missions over Germany report one confirmed kill and one possible in the air.

Ninth Air Force sends 330 A-20 Havocs, A-26 Invaders, and B-26 Marauders to attack oil depots, road and rail junctions, and targets of opportunity. P-47 and P-38 fighters support the 104th Infantry Division, the 9th Armored Division, XX Corps, and the 8th, 2nd, and 5th Armored Divisions.

The headquarters of Ninth Air Force's XXIX Tactical Air Command (Provisional) returns to the operational control of Ninth Air Force from the RAF Second Tactical Air Force, as the U.S. Ninth Army reverts to control of General Omar Bradley's 12th Army Group from General Montgomery's 21st Army Group.

MEDITERRANEAN: Fifteenth Air Force sends 94 P-51 Mustangs to attack rail traffic near Munich and Regensburg, Germany, at Plzen in Czechoslovakia, and at two areas in Austria.

ITALY: Twelfth Air Force B-25 Mitchells bomb rail bridges. P-47 Thunderbolts of the XXII Tactical Air Command attack rail lines, logistics storage sites, and ammunition storage areas in the Po River valley.

SOUTHWEST PACIFIC AREA: On Luzon, in the XIV Corps area, the 1st Cavalry Division and the 11th Airborne Division conduct a double envelopment, trapping about 1,600 Japanese troops at Tiaong.

In the Philippines, Far East Air Force A-20 Havocs, P-38 Lightnings, and P-51 Mustangs bomb targets on Luzon. A-20s bomb Negros Island and B-24 Liberators bomb targets on Mindanao Island.

On Formosa, B-24s bomb airfields and harbor installations, while A-20s attack factories and railyards. B-24s bomb the harbor at Hong Kong.

Far East Air Force B-24 Liberators bomb Japanese shipping at Mako, Pescadores, sinking a merchant tanker and a cargo vessel.

PACIFIC: The headquarters of the 40th and 462nd Bombardment Groups (Very Heavy) arrive at Tinian from India.

A Japanese escort vessel and a cargo ship are sunk by mines dropped by Twentieth Air Force B-29s and two submarines are damaged.

PACIFIC, OKINAWA: Major General John R. Hodge, commander of XXIV Corps, orders the 96th Infantry Division to capture the Urasoe-Mura escarpment straddling Highways 1 and 5. He also orders the 7th Infantry Division to capture Hill 178, with the high ground controlling Highway 13, called Skyline Ridge. Hodge needs these roads clear to supply the advancing troops. Unknown to the Americans, the Japanese have prepared this area as the first line of their layered defenses.

The 6th Marine Division attacks northward into the Ishikawa Isthmus with three regiments. At Yae-Take, on the Motobu Peninsula, the marines meet the first serious Japanese opposition.

An LCI is sunk by an assault demolition boat. A kamikaze damages a destroyer, and another destroyer suffers bomb damage off Okinawa.

CENTRAL PACIFIC: The 147th Infantry Regiment assumes control of Iwo Jima, allowing the 9th Marine Regiment to prepare to depart.

Seventh Air Force sends 24 B-24 Liberators from Angaur Island to bomb targets on Mindanao Island in the Philippines.

April 5

CBI: Fourteenth Air Force sends P-40s, P-38 Lightnings, and P-47 Thunderbolts on armed reconnaissance to attack troops, horses, and river, road, and rail traffic in French Indochina and southern China.

ATLANTIC: German submarine *U-857* damages a U.S. tanker off Cape Cod. The tanker is towed to Boston for repairs.

ETO: The III Corps of First Army (9th 28th, and 99th Infantry Divisions and the 7th Armored Division) attacks the Ruhr Pocket from the south in support of Ninth Army's attack.

The XXI Corps (12th Armored Division and the 42nd, 36th, and 4th Infantry Divisions) of Seventh Army captures Würzburg.

Eighth Air Force sends more than 1,300 B-17s and B-24 Liberators escorted by over 600 P-47 Thunderbolts and P-51 Mustangs to bomb ordnance depots, armament production facilities, marshaling yards, and airfields. The bombers use both visual methods and radar signal intercepts to mark the bomb release points over the targets. A total of 10 bombers are lost and 123 are damaged. Aircrews report eight confirmed kills and six possibles. Aircrew casualties are 19 killed, 10 wounded, and 83 missing. Fighter pilots report one confirmed kill and three possibles in the air and seven confirmed kills and three possibles on the ground. One P-51 is lost and the pilot is reported missing.

During the night 12 B-24s drop leaflets over France, Germany, and the Netherlands.

Ninth Air Force P-47 and P-38 fighters support XX Corps, and 8th, 2nd and 7th Armored Divisions.

Corporal Thomas J. Kelly is the aid man with the first platoon, C Company, 48th Armored Infantry Battalion, 7th Armored Division, when it is halted by heavy fire from German machine guns and tanks hidden in the woods of the town of Alemert, Germany. As the platoon retreats, Corporal Kelly returns to assist the wounded under direct machine-gun fire. To avoid being hit, he crawls 300 yards, dragging the wounded soldiers behind him to safety. He makes 10 separate trips bringing wounded men out, and assists seven more casualties to crawl out of the line of fire. Although completely exhausted by his efforts, Kelly refuses to rest, supporting his platoon throughout the rest of the battle. For his dedication to duty and exceptional bravery in saving the lives of his fellow soldiers, Corporal Kelly will receive the Medal of Honor.

MEDITERRANEAN: Fifteenth Air Force sends more than 450 B-17s and B-24 Liberators escorted by P-38 Lightnings and P-51 Mustangs to bomb a rail bridge in Yugoslavia and marshaling yards and locomotive depots in Italy. P-38s dive-bomb a rail bridge in Yugoslavia and P-51s attack rail targets in Germany and Austria.

ITALY: The 92nd Infantry Division conducts Operation Second Wind, a diversion intended to draw attention away from Eighth Army's main attack in the east. The division is to capture Massa on the Ligurian coast. The 370th Infantry Regiment leads the attack, supported by air and artillery bombardment. The unit is also shored up by the addition of the battle-hardened 442nd Regimental Combat Team (composed of Japanese-Americans) and the 473rd Regimental Combat Team, a unit composed of former antiaircraft artillerymen, now trained and organized as infantry. The 370th soon falters, but the 100th battalion of the 442nd RCT captures Monte Fragolita.

Twelfth Air Force B-25 Mitchells bomb bridges and gun positions. P-47 Thunderbolts attack gun positions, vehicles, logistics storage sites, ammunition storage areas, and support Fifth Army ground forces. During the night A-20 Havocs and A-26 Intruders attack bridges.

Private First Class Sadao S. Munemori of A Company, 100th Infantry Battalion, 442nd Regimental Combat Team, faces strong German defenses on the mountain approaches to Seravezza, Italy. As casualties mount, Munemori must take command of his squad. He chooses to attack the enemy alone rather than risk the lives of his comrades and moves up the hill to destroy two machine guns with grenades. Withdrawing to the squad's position, he is followed by a large number of hand grenades, which roll down the hill. One grenade hits Munemori's helmet and lands nearby. Without hesitation, Munemori covers the grenade with his body. For his courage under fire and his willingness to sacrifice himself so others may live, Private First Class Munemori will receive the Medal of Honor.

SOUTHWEST PACIFIC AREA: In the Philippines, Far East Air Force A-20 Havocs and P-61 Black Widow night fighters support ground forces on Cebu and Negros Islands.

The headquarters of the 58th Fighter Group redeploys from Mindoro Island to Luzon.

B-24s bomb the Kowloon Docks in Hong Kong and a nearby airfield, while other B-24s bomb Kiirun harbor in Formosa. Fifth Air Force B-24 Liberators, B-26 Marauders, and P-38 Lightnings attack a Japanese convoy, sinking a cargo ship, east of Hong Kong. Other B-24s bomb Japanese shipping at Hong Kong, damaging two coastal defense vessels, two submarine chasers, and a fleet oiler.

U.S. submarine *Hardhead* attacks a Japanese convoy, damaging a cargo ship in the Gulf of Siam.

FEAF P-38 Lightnings attack Tarakan Island and Tawau in Borneo.

U.S. submarine *Besugo* attacks a Japanese light cruiser in the Flores Sea.

PACIFIC: Twentieth Air Force receives the headquarters of the 315th Bombardment Wing (Very Heavy), which arrives on Guam Island from the United States.

Mines dropped by B-29s sink a cargo ship and damage another near Shimonoseki Strait.

PACIFIC, OKINAWA: In the south of the island XIV Corps moves the 382nd and 383rd Infantry Regiments of the 96th Infantry Division and the 184th and 32nd Infantry Regiments of the 7th Infantry Division forward. Japanese defenses at Cactus Ridge and the Pinnacle await the Americans. These heavily fortified positions block the advance.

The 383rd Infantry Regiment of the 96th Infantry Division encounters Japanese forces entrenched on Cactus Ridge behind anti-tank ditches and barbed wire.

The 184th Infantry Regiment of the 7th Infantry Division attacks Japanese defenders at the Pinnacle.

The battleship USS *Nevada* is damaged off Okinawa by shore battery fire. A U.S. destroyer sinks Japanese submarine *RO-41* west of Okinawa.

CENTRAL PACIFIC: The Naval Advanced Air Base at Iwo Jima is established.

April 6
ALEUTIANS: Eleventh Air Force sends bombers against targets in the Kurile Islands. Eight B-24 Liberators attack and photograph the airfield on Paramushiru Island. Eight B-25 Mitchells attack radar installations on Hayakegawa, Kotani Island, and Minami Cape, dropping napalm on buildings and shipping. Another B-25 flies a weather reconnaissance mission.

CBI: In China, P-51 Mustangs attack railroad targets; P-38 Lightnings attack a bridge near Dien Bien Phu in French Indochina.

In Burma, Tenth Air Force P-47 Thunderbolts and P-38 Lightnings attack road traffic, troop concentrations, tanks, fuel storage sites, and targets of opportunity.

ETO: The XVIII Airborne Corps (78th, 8th, and 86th Infantry Divisions) of First Army attack northward into the Ruhr Pocket.

Eighth Air Force sends more than 600 B-17s and B-24 Liberators escorted by nearly 600 P-47 Thunderbolts and P-51 Mustangs to bomb marshaling yards. The bombers use radar signal intercepts to mark the bomb release points over the targets. A total of four B-17s are lost and two damaged. Aircrew casualties are 17 killed, one wounded, and 33 missing. One P-51 is lost, and the pilot is reported missing.

During the night, three B-24 Liberators fly Carpetbagger missions.

Ninth Air Force sends nearly 100 A-20 Havocs, A-26 Invaders, and B-26 Marauders to attack marshaling yards. P-47 and P-38 fighters support VIII Corps and XX Corps.

The headquarters of the 315th Troop Carrier Group and the C-47s of the 34th, 309th, and 310th Troop Carrier Squadrons, IX Troop Carrier Command, redeploy from England to France.

First Lieutenant Raymond O. Beaudoin is the platoon leader of second platoon, F Company, 119th Infantry, 30th Infantry Division, approaching Hamelin, Germany. German defenders open a heavy fire on his platoon as it crosses the flat, open terrain. The platoon is unable to move, so Lieutenant Beaudoin orders them to dig foxholes. He himself digs in where the enemy fire is heaviest and keeps up a steady return fire, accounting for six German casualties. As the Germans prepare to attack and destroy the isolated platoon, Lieutenant Beaudoin rises up to attack a sniper. Ignoring the constant fire directed at him, Beaudoin gets to within 10 yards of the sniper, then jumps up to assault the position, killing three Germans and driving off another soldier. He then moves to attack another position, firing his carbine toward a dugout, but there he is killed by machine-gun fire. By taking decisive action at the risk of his own life to save the lives of his men, First Lieutenant Raymond Beaudoin will receive the Medal of Honor.

MEDITERRANEAN: Fifteenth Air Force sends 387 B-17s and B-24 Liberators escorted by P-38 Lightnings and P-51 Mustangs to bomb antiaircraft positions near marshaling yards in northern Italy.

ITALY: Brigadier General Thomas C. Darcy takes command of the XXII Tactical Air Command. Twelfth Air Force B-25 Mitchells bomb bridges. P-47 Thunderbolts support Fifth Army ground forces. During the night A-20 Havocs and A-26 Invaders bomb bridges in the Po River valley.

SOUTHWEST PACIFIC AREA: In the Philippines, Far East Air Force A-20 Havocs, P-47 Thunderbolts, and P-38 Lightnings support ground forces in Luzon, attacking Japanese positions around Balete Pass and west of Fort Stotsenburg. B-24 Liberators bomb a town north of Cebu City, while P-47s support ground units on Cebu Island. A-20s support ground forces on Negros Island. B-25 Mitchells bomb Bunawan on Mindanao Island. B-24 Liberators bomb defensive positions, ammunition storage areas, and logistics sites on Jolo Island. The U.S. Army Forces, Pacific (AFPAC) headquarters is established under General of the Army Douglas MacArthur in Manila.

The P-47s of the 310th Fighter Squadron, 58th Fighter Group, redeploy from Mindoro Island to Luzon.

B-25 Mitchells bomb the town of Hokko on Formosa.

U.S. submarine *Hardhead* attacks the Japanese convoy it has been following, sinking a cargo ship in the Gulf of Siam.

PACIFIC: General MacArthur becomes commander of all army forces in Pacific. Admiral Nimitz takes command of all navy forces in the Pacific. This directive from the Joint Chiefs of Staff ends the conflicting theaters of war and unites American land, air, and naval power for the final attack on the Japanese homeland.

The headquarters of Twentieth Air Force's 468th Bombardment Group (Very Heavy) arrives at Tinian from India.

PACIFIC, OKINAWA: The 383rd Infantry Regiment of the 96th Infantry Division captures Cactus Ridge and holds it against a Japanese counterattack that night.

The 184th Infantry Regiment of the 7th Infantry Division captures the Pinnacle. The Japanese begin firing heavy and accurate artillery barrages on the American positions.

Nearly 300 Japanese aircraft from Formosa and Kyushu, half of them kamikazes, attack U.S. ships in Task Force 58. No carriers are hit, but three destroyers on early warning picket duty are sunk and another severely damaged. Four other destroyers are damaged near Ie Shima Island. One destroyer off the east coast of Okinawa is damaged. One LST is sunk and two ammunition ships are hit and burn out of control.

The battleship *Yamato*, escorted by a light cruiser and eight destroyers, sets sail from Tokuyama Bay in Japan on a suicide mission that attempts to draw away American carrier aircraft from Okinawa and so allow kamikazes to destroy transport ships near the landing beaches. Unknown to the Japanese, their encoded plan has already been intercepted and deciphered. Two U.S. submarines, USS *Threadfin* and USS *Hackleback,* track the progress of the force. Admiral Mitscher begins to deploy his carriers to intercept the Japanese.

Kamikazes sink destroyer USS *Bush* and damage seven destroyers, two destroyer escorts, two high-speed minesweepers, four minesweepers, two motor minesweepers, and an LST. The small carrier USS *San Jacinto* and a destroyer are damaged by near-misses from kamikazes. A destroyer is damaged by both a kamikaze and a torpedo. Bombs damage a destroyer and a high-speed minesweeper. A kamikaze damages a freighter carrying 7,000 tons of ammunition, which is abandoned and scuttled. Another freighter has to be abandoned after a kamikaze crashes into the ship.

CENTRAL PACIFIC: Seventh Air Force sends 11 B-24 Liberators from Guam Island to bomb the airfield on Marcus Island. A total of 23 B-24s from Angaur Island bomb barracks and a wharf at Mindanao Island in the Philippines.

NEW GUINEA: U.S. submarine *Besugo* torpedoes and sinks a Japanese minesweeper south of Java.

April 7

CBI: In China, Fourteenth Air Force sends 14 B-25 Mitchells to attack town areas and targets of opportunity and 24 P-51 Mustangs to attack river, road, and rail traffic. P-38 Lightnings attack targets of opportunity around Dien Bien Phu in French Indochina.

In Burma, Tenth Air Force sends P-47 Thunderbolts and P-38 Lightnings to attack troop concentrations, trucks, and logistics support sites, and conduct sweeps along roads.

ATLANTIC: U.S. destroyer escort sinks German submarine *U-857* off Cape Cod, Massachusetts.

German submarine *U-1024* torpedoes and damages a U.S. freighter in the Irish Sea. The ship is repaired.

ETO: Ninth Army captures Hamelin and Eisenach on the road to Leipzig.

Eighth Air Force sends more than 1,300 B-17s and B-24 Liberators escorted by nearly 900 P-47 Thunderbolts and P-51 Mustangs to bomb oil depots, munition production facilities, marshaling yards, and airfields. The bombers use visual methods to mark the bomb release points over the targets. The German response is significant—over 100 fighters and more than 50 Me-262 jet fighters attack the bombers. A total of 15 bombers are lost and 189 are damaged. Aircrews report 40 confirmed kills, 12 probables, and 17 possibles. Aircrew casualties are eight killed, 15 wounded, and 142 missing. Fighter pilots report 61 confirmed kills, one probable, and 15 possibles. Five P-51s are lost and two are damaged. The pilots are reported missing.

Ninth Air Force sends 268 A-20 Havocs, A-26 Invaders, and B-26 Marauders to attack marshaling yards. P-47 and P-38 fighters support 7th Armored Division and the 3rd and 9th Armored Divisions, and VIII, XX, and XII Corps.

Private First Class Mike Colalillo of C Company, 398th Infantry Regiment, 100th Infantry Division, is pinned down by German fire near Untergriesheim, Germany. In the midst of artillery, mortar, and machine-gun fire, Colalillo stands up and runs forward following an American tank, urging his comrades to follow. When his weapon is broken, he climbs on the back of the tank and mans the machine gun of the turret, firing at the German defenders with great accuracy. As the tank advances he is completely exposed to enemy fire, but continues to engage the enemy by firing on three more defensive positions. When the machine gun on the turret jams, he obtains a Thompson submachine gun from the tank crew and continues forward on foot. As the tanks are called back, Colalillo remains behind to rescue a wounded comrade and brings him back to friendly lines, enduring heavy fire the entire way. For his inspiring acts of courage in the face of the enemy, Private First Class Colallilo will receive the Medal of Honor.

MEDITERRANEAN: Fifteenth Air Force sends more than 120 B-17s and B-24 Liberators escorted by P-38 Lightnings and P-51 Mustangs to bomb rail bridges in Italy and marshaling yards in Austria. P-38s bomb a rail bridge in Austria.

ITALY: Twelfth Air Force B-25 Mitchells bomb rail and road traffic and bridges. P-47 Thunderbolts attack ammunition storage areas and communication centers and support ground forces near Monte Belvedere. During the night A-20 Havocs and A-26 Invaders bomb bridges and river crossing sites in the Po River valley.

Technical Sergeant Yukio Okutsu of the 100th Infantry Battalion, 442nd Regimental Combat Team, is stopped by a crossfire from two machine guns on Mount Belvedere, Italy. Technical Sergeant Okutsu crawls through heavy fire to within 30 yards of one of the positions and destroys it with two hand grenades. Crawling and moving forward, he reaches the other machine-gun position and destroys that one with grenades as well. A third machine gun opens fire and he attacks, firing his Thompson submachine gun and driving off several German riflemen, and then capturing the machine-gun crew. For his courageous attack against a formidable enemy at the risk of his life, Technical Sergeant Okutsu will receive the Congressional Medal of Honor.

SOUTHWEST PACIFIC AREA: In the Philippines, Far East Air Force A-20 Havocs, P-38 Lightnings, and P-47 Thunderbolts support ground forces on Luzon. B-24 Liberators bomb Bunawan on Mindanao Island. Other B-24s and P-38s attack Jolo Island and B-24s bomb an airfield on Sumbawa Island in the Lesser Sunda Islands. B-24s and P-38s attack various targets of opportunity over Formosa.

The 311th Fighter Squadron, 58th Fighter Group, redeploys its P-47s from Mindoro to Luzon.

PACIFIC: Twentieth Air Force sends more than 100 B-29 Superfortresses to bomb the Nakajima aircraft engine production facility at Tokyo. Aircrews report 80 confirmed kills, 23 probables, and 50 possibles. Three B-29s are lost. Over 150 B-29s bomb the Mitsubishi aircraft production facility at Nagoya. Aircrews report 21 confirmed kills, 11 probables, and 22 possibles. Two B-29s are lost. Seventh Air Force supports these raids with over 100 P-51 Mustangs escorting the bombers. Pilots report 21 confirmed kills, five probables, and seven possibles. Two P-51s are lost.

The headquarters of the Twentieth Air Force's 444th Bombardment Group (Very Heavy) arrives at Tinian from India.

U.S. submarine *Tirante* torpedoes and sinks a Japanese auxiliary submarine chaser in the Yellow Sea.

A mine dropped by B-29s sinks a cargo ship west of Nagasaki.

PACIFIC, OKINAWA: The 6th Marine Division captures Nago, the second-largest town on the island, and prepares to advance into the Motobu Peninsula.

A total of 386 F6F Hellcats, SB2C Helldivers, and TBM Avenger torpedo-bombers from the carriers USS *Hornet,* USS *Essex,* USS *Bunker Hill,* and USS *Bennington* and from the light carriers USS *Bataan,* USS *Belleau Wood,* and USS *San Jacinto,* swarm a Japanese attack force, formed around the *Yamato*—largest battleship ever built—and moving through the East China Sea toward Okinawa. *Yamato* and a light cruiser are sunk south of Kagoshima, Kyushu, Japan. Four destroyers are sunk and four others damaged in the East China Sea. Kamikazes damage carrier USS *Han-*

cock, the battleship USS *Maryland,* two destroyers, a destroyer escort, and a motor minesweeper off Okinawa. U.S. losses are 10 aircraft and 12 crewmen.

The carrier USS *Hancock* is damaged by a kamikaze, which drops a bomb on the flight deck before crashing onto the ship. The battleship USS *Maryland* and a destroyer and destroyer-escort are damaged in kamikaze attacks.

CENTRAL PACIFIC: Seventh Air Force sends 24 B-24 Liberators from Angaur Island to bomb the barracks area at Bunawan on Mindanao Island in the Philippines.

NEW GUINEA: The 550th Night Fighter Squadron, XIII Fighter Command, redeploys P-38 Lightnings, P-61 Black Widow night fighters, and P-70s (an A-20 Havoc converted into a night fighter) from Morotai Island to Leyte Island.

U.S. submarines *Gabilan* and *Charr* sink a Japanese light cruiser transporting troops in the Flores Sea.

April 8

CBI: The Japanese Twentieth Army launches an offensive directed at capturing the Fourteenth Air Force airfield at Chihchiang. The American airfield at Laohokow is captured. Chinese forces are unable to stop the advance.

In China, Fourteenth Air Force sends B-24 Liberators to attack shipping targets of opportunity in the South China Sea, Bakli Bay on Hainan Island, and the Kowloon Docks in Hong Kong. P-51 Mustangs attack a bridge and a number of road and rail targets.

Tenth Air Force sends more than 50 P-38 Lightnings and P-47 Thunderbolts to attack troops, logistics sites, gun positions, and trucks.

ETO: Seventh Army captures Pforzheim near the Rhine River.

Eighth Air Force sends more than 1,100 B-17s and B-24 Liberators escorted by nearly 800 P-47 Thunderbolts and P-51 Mustangs to bomb oil depots, jet aircraft production facilities, marshaling yards, and ordnance depots. The bombers use a combination of visual methods and radar signal intercepts to mark the bomb release points over the targets. A total of nine bombers are lost and 153 damaged. Aircrew casualties are two killed, six wounded, and 78 missing. A group of 28 P-51s fly a scouting mission, and one fighter is damaged.

Ten B-17s conduct screening missions to jam German radio interception efforts and employ countermeasures against German radar sites.

During the night 11 B-24s drop leaflets over Germany and the Netherlands. A total of 12 B-24s bomb the port facilities at Travemunde during the night, using a Pathfinder radar-equipped bomber to mark bomb release points.

Ninth Air Force sends more than 600 A-20 Havocs, A-26 Invaders, and B-26 Marauders to attack communication centers, an oil storage depot, and marshaling yards. P-47 and P-38 fighters support VIII, XII, and XX Corps.

MEDITERRANEAN: Fifteenth Air Force sends more than 500 B-17s and B-24 Liberators escorted by P-38 Lightnings and P-51 Mustangs to bomb communication centers, bridges, and marshaling yards in northern Italy. P-38s attack rail bridges in Germany and Austria.

ITALY: Twelfth Air Force B-25 Mitchells bomb rail bridges. P-47 Thunderbolts attack bridges and roads. During the night A-20 Havocs and A-26 Invaders attack command and control centers and logistics support sites.

SOUTHWEST PACIFIC AREA: In the Philippines, Far East Air Force A-20 Havocs, P-38 Lightnings, and P-47 Thunderbolts support ground forces east of Manila. B-24 Liberators, A-20s, P-47s, and P-38s support ground forces on Cebu and Negros Islands. Other B-24s bomb Mindanao Island and Jolo Island.

B-24s and B-25 Mitchells attack airfields in the Pescadores Islands, and bomb a town and railyards on Formosa.

The 69th Fighter Squadron, 58th Fighter Group, redeploys from Mindoro to Luzon with P-47s.

PACIFIC: Twentieth Air Force sends more than 70 B-29 Superfortresses against airfields on Kyushu Island to disrupt and eliminate kamikaze attacks on the fleet off Okinawa. One B-29 is lost.

U.S. submarine *Snook* on her ninth war patrol makes contact with U.S. submarine *Tigrone,* but is never heard from again.

PACIFIC, OKINAWA: The Pinnacle and Cactus Ridge are cleared of enemy forces, but American casualties are heavy. More than 1,500 men have been killed or wounded. Japanese losses are estimated to be around 4,500. The mission of each Japanese soldier is to kill as many Americans as possible before sacrificing himself.

A kamikaze damages a destroyer, and another destroyer is damaged by an assault demolition boat off Okinawa.

CENTRAL PACIFIC: Seventh Air Force sends 25 B-24 Liberators from Angaur Island to bomb the Bunawan area on Mindanao Island in the Philippines.

During the night six P-61 Black Widow night fighters from Iwo Jima conduct single coordinated bombing attacks on Chichi Jima, Haha Jima, Ani Jima, and Ototo Jima islands.

NEW GUINEA: The 33rd Troop Carrier Squadron, 374th Troop Carrier Group, redeploys its C-47s from Hollandia to Luzon.

April 9

CBI: In Burma, Tenth Air Force sends more than 70 P-38 Lightnings and P-47 Thunderbolts to attack troops, logistics sites, gun positions, and general targets of opportunity. The British Fourteenth Army attacks south down the Irrawaddy and Sittang Rivers toward Prome.

In China, Fourteenth Air Force sends nine B-24 Liberators to bomb docks at Canton and Kowloon in Hong Kong and attack targets of opportunity on Hainan Island. B-25 Mitchells bomb railyards. In French Indochina P-38 Lightnings attack vehicles near Dien Bien Phu.

ETO: The XVIII Corps attacks into the Ruhr Pocket.

First and Ninth Armies establish bridgeheads over the Leine River.

Eighth Air Force sends more than 1,200 B-17s and B-24 Liberators escorted by over 800 P-47 Thunderbolts and P-51 Mustangs to bomb oil storage areas, munitions production facilities, and airfields supporting Me-262 jet aircraft. A total of seven bombers are lost and 64 damaged. Aircrews report 85 confirmed kills, one probable, and 60 possibles. Aircrew casualties are four killed, seven wounded, and 65 missing. Fighter pilots report one confirmed kill and three possibles in the air and 84 confirmed kills and 56 possibles on the ground. Four fighters are lost, and the pilots are reported missing. A group of 24 P-51s fly a scouting mission. One fighter is lost, and the pilot is reported missing.

During the night 11 B-24s drop leaflets over France, Germany, and the Netherlands. A total of 14 B-24s bomb an airfield during the night, using a Pathfinder radar-equipped bomber to mark bomb release points.

Ninth Air Force sends over 700 A-20 Havocs, A-26 Invaders, and B-26 Marauders to attack oil production and storage targets, airfields, and marshaling yards. P-47 and P-38 fighters support III Corps, VIII Corps, XII and XX Corps, and 3rd Armored Division.

A German midget submarine torpedoes a U.S. freighter in a convoy headed to Cherbourg, France, at the entrance to the English Channel. The ship is towed and arrives safely.

MEDITERRANEAN: Fifteenth Air Force sends more than 800 B-17s and B-24 Liberators escorted by P-38 Lightnings and P-51 Mustangs to bomb German positions near Bologna in support of the British Eighth Army. Over 150 P-38s attack rail lines in Germany.

ITALY: Operation Craftsman, the 15th Army Group's main effort for the spring offensive in Italy, begins with an attack by Eighth Army, preceded by heavy air and artillery bombardment. Fifth Army is to follow two or three days later, focusing on breaking the German lines and moving into the southern Po River valley. The IV Corps, with the U.S. 10th Mountain Division, the 1st Brazilian Division, and the U.S. 1st Armored Division, is to attack toward Bazzano, generally down the Samoggia River valley. The II Corps, with the 34th, 88th, and 91st Infantry Divisions, the 6th South African Armored Division, and the Italian Legnano Combat Group, will attack generally along Route 64 to reach Bodeno and link with Eighth Army.

Twelfth Air Force B-25 Mitchells and the A-20 Havocs and P-47 Thunderbolts of the XXII Tactical Air Command attack German positions in support of the British Eighth Army offensive. During the night A-20 Havocs and A-26 Invaders attack bridges, vehicles, and targets of opportunity.

SOUTHWEST PACIFIC AREA: In the Eighth Army area, elements of the 163rd Infantry Regiment of the 41st Infantry Division attack Japanese positions on Jolo Island in the Sulu Archipelago, supported by three destroyers and marine fighters.

On Negros, the 185th and 160th Infantry Regiments of the 40th Infantry Division, plus the 503rd Parachute Infantry Regiment, attack into the mountains beyond Bacolod. The Japanese defenses are strong, with minefields, entrenchments, and pillboxes dominating the crests of the hills.

In the Philippines, Far East Air Force A-20 Havocs, P-38 Lightnings, and P-47 Thunderbolts support ground forces on Luzon Island. B-24 Liberators, P-38s, and P-47s support ground forces on Cebu and Negros Islands.

B-24s conduct armed reconnaissance missions, attacking coastal targets in China and French Indochina.

PACIFIC: During the night Twentieth Air Force sends 20 B-29s to mine Shimonoseki Strait between Kyushu and Honshu Islands.

U.S. submarine *Parche* torpedoes and sinks a Japanese minesweeper escorting a transport northeast of Sendai, Honshu, Japan. USS *Sunfish* makes an unsuccessful

Troops of the 370th Infantry Regiment, 92nd Infantry Division, advance into the mountains at Prato, Italy, April 9, 1945. Beyond the mountains are the German Gothic Line defenses.

attack on the transport. U.S. submarine *Spadefish* damages a cargo ship in the Yellow Sea. U.S. submarine *Tirante* attacks a Japanese convoy in the Yellow Sea, sinking an army tanker and damaging a coastal defense vessel.

PACIFIC, OKINAWA: The 383rd Infantry Regiment of the 96th Infantry Division attacks Kakazu Ridge. It is one of the strongest positions on the island. These defenses are expertly camouflaged and honeycombed with deep and well-protected caves, bunkers, observation posts, barracks, hospitals, and fighting positions. Most of the Japanese troops are positioned behind the ridge, not on it. American artillery fire explodes harmlessly against the face of the ridge. When the barrage stops, the Japanese emerge from behind the ridge and take up firing positions to rake attacking infantry with mortar shells, artillery, grenades, machine-gun, and rifle fire. Nearly every foot of ground to the front of the ridge is covered by some type of weapon.

The 381st Infantry Regiment also makes no progress at Kakazu. The two regiments will be stopped by Japanese mortar and artillery fire, rain, and counterattacks over the next three days.

The 27th Infantry Division, commanded by Major General George W. Griner, Jr., lands on Okinawa to reinforce the depleted 96th and 77th Infantry Divisions.

A kamikaze damages a destroyer off Okinawa. Two destroyers sink Japanese submarine *RO-56* east of Okinawa.

Private First Class Edward J. Moskala of C Company, 383rd Infantry Regiment, 96th Infantry Division, is part of the leading elements attacking Kakazu Ridge, one of the strongest positions on Okinawa. As Japanese rifle and machine-gun fire force the Americans to take cover, Moskala charges 40 yards and eliminates two machine-gun positions with grenades and his Browning Automatic Rifle (BAR). When a Japanese counterattack forces his company to withdraw, Moskala remains behind with eight other soldiers to cover the withdrawal. For over three hours Moskala engages in deadly combat with Japanese troops, killing scores of them until the order is given to fall back. Reaching relative safety, Moskala learns that one of the soldiers who stayed behind with him is left wounded. Moskala returns up the slope to provide covering fire, killing another four Japanese infiltrators as the wounded solder is recovered and evacuated. He is standing protective guard over the wounded man when he is killed while assisting another wounded soldier. For his determined combat skill, his courageous actions in fighting for his comrades and risking his life to save others, Private First Class Moskala will receive the Medal of Honor.

CENTRAL PACIFIC: Seventh Air Force sends 17 B-24 Liberators from Guam to bomb the airfield on Marcus Island. A total of 22 B-24s from Angaur Island attack Japanese troops at Kabacan, on Mindanao Island in the Philippines. P-51 Mustangs from Iwo Jima bomb and strafe military installations at Chichi Jima Island.

April 10

ALEUTIANS: Eleventh Air Force sends seven B-24 Liberators to bomb Kataoka naval base on Shimushu Island in the Kuriles with napalm. Three B-25 Mitchells attack facilities on the island.

CBI: Chinese forces counterattack near Laohokow, stopping the Japanese advance and regaining lost territory.

Fourteenth Air Force sends 23 B-24 Liberators to bomb logistics storage areas, while B-25 Mitchells, P-40s, and P-51 Mustangs attack trucks, tanks, logistics sites, horses, troops, and artillery in southern and eastern China.

In Burma, Tenth Air Force sends P-47 Thunderbolts and P-38 Lightnings to attack troop concentrations.

In the Yangtze River, a cargo vessel is sunk by a mine dropped by B-29s in late March.

ETO: The XVI Corps of Ninth Army captures Essen in the Ruhr Pocket.

Ninth, Third, and First Armies attack on a 150-mile front with seven corps. Ninth Army has XIII Corps and XIX Corps, the Third Army has XX Corps, VIII Corps, and XII Corps. First Army has V Corps and VII Corps. Lieutenant General Hodges's First Army is the center force. It will advance 130 miles toward Leipzig and the Elbe River. Lieutenant General Simpson's Ninth Army is the northern force. It will attack toward Magdeburg and the Elbe River, 65 miles north of Leipzig. Lieutenant General Patton's Third Army is the southern force. It will advance to Chemnitz 40 miles south of Leipzig and turn south into Austria. Patton's attack supports General Devers's 6th Army Group, which is to attack into southern Germany to Austria and the Alps and forestall any possible rallying of German forces in that area.

Eighth Air Force sends more than 1,300 B-17s and B-24 Liberators escorted by over 900 P-47 Thunderbolts and P-51 Mustangs to bomb airfields supporting Me-262 jet aircraft, also munitions depots. About 60 Me-262 German fighters attack the bombers. A total of 19 bombers are lost and 258 damaged. Aircrews report 17 confirmed kills, 11 probables, and five possibles. Aircrew casualties are two killed, 95 wounded, and 91 missing. Fighter pilots report 18 confirmed kills and 11 possibles in the air and 288 confirmed kills and 190 possibles on the ground. Seven fighters are lost, and the pilots are reported missing. A group of 59 P-47s fly a freelance mission for the bombers. Pilots report two confirmed kills and two possibles in the air and 41 confirmed kills and 66 possibles on the ground. Thirty P-51s fly a scouting mission, and one fighter is lost. The pilot is reported missing.

During the night 12 B-24s drop leaflets over Germany, France, and the Netherlands. A total of 13 B-24s bomb the Dessau rail depot during the night, using a Pathfinder radar-equipped bomber to mark bomb release point.

Ninth Air Force sends more than 400 A-20 Havocs, A-26 Invaders, and B-26 Marauders to attack oil storage depots, ordnance depots, railroad bridges, and marshaling yards. P-47 and P-38 fighters support the 13th, 3rd, and 9th Armored Divisions, the XII and XX Corps, the 2nd and 5th Armored Divisions, and XVI Corps.

MEDITERRANEAN: Fifteenth Air Force sends more than 600 B-17s and B-24 Liberators escorted by P-38 Lightnings and P-51 Mustangs to attack German defensive positions along the Santerno River in Italy in support of the British Eighth Army offensive. Over 150 P-38s attack bridges, tunnels, and marshaling yards in Austria.

ITALY: The 473rd Infantry captures Massa with support of the 758th and 760th Tank Battalions. The 442nd RCT captures Monte Bruguana.

Twelfth Air Force B-25 Mitchells and P-47 Thunderbolts of the XXII Tactical Air Command attack German defenses in support of the British Eighth Army.

During the night A-20 Havocs and A-26 Invaders attack German positions.

SOUTHWEST PACIFIC AREA: In the I Corps area, on Luzon, the 37th Infantry Division comes under the operational control of I Corps and moves to the Bauang area in support of the 33rd Infantry Division's attempt to capture Baguio. Baguio is the former summer capital of the Philippines and the headquarters of General Yamashida, the commander of Japanese forces.

In the Philippines, Far East Air Force A-20 Havocs, P-38 Lightnings, and P-47 Thunderbolts support ground forces in Luzon. B-24 Liberators and P-47s support ground forces on Cebu Island.

B-24s bomb the town of Koshun on Formosa.

The headquarters of the 35th Fighter Group and the P-51s of the 39th Fighter Squadron redeploy from Mangaldan to Luzon.

PACIFIC: U.S. submarine *Crevalle* torpedoes and damages a Japanese escort destroyer west of Nagasaki.

PACIFIC, OKINAWA: The 3rd Battalion, 105th Infantry Regiment, 27th Infantry Division, lands on Tsugen Shima Island to destroy coastal defense guns guarding Nakagusuku Bay. The island is secured the following day. American losses are 11 killed and 80 wounded.

CENTRAL PACIFIC: During the night Seventh Air Force sends six P-61 Black Widow night fighters from Iwo Jima to fly individual strikes on Chichi Jima, Muko Jima, Ani Jima, and Haha Jima Islands.

NEW GUINEA: FEAF B-24 Liberators bomb Liang airfield on Ambon Island with Molucca Islands, and Bingkalapa airfield on Celebes Island.

April 11

ALEUTIANS: Eleventh Air Force P-38 Lightnings and navy aircraft destroy a bomb-carrying paper balloon over Attu in the Aleutian Islands.

CBI: Fourteenth Air Force B-25 Mitchells, P-40s, and P-51s attack trucks, tanks, logistics sites, horses, troops, and artillery in southern and eastern China.

In Burma, Tenth Air Force sends P-47 Thunderbolts and P-38 Lightnings to attack trucks, troop concentrations, and targets of opportunity.

ATLANTIC: President Roosevelt sends what will be his last communication to Prime Minister Churchill: "I would minimize the general Soviet problem as much as possible because these problems in one form or another, seem to arise every day and most of them straighten out . . . we must be firm however, and our course thus far is correct."

ETO: The XX Corps (76th and 80th Infantry Divisions and the 4th and 6th Armored Divisions) of Third Army reach Weimar. The 6th Armored Division discovers the concentration camp at Buchenwald.

The Ninth Army's XIX Corps (the 83rd and 30th Infantry Divisions and the 2nd Armored Division) reach the Elbe River near Magdeburg.

The XXI Corps (the 36th, 42nd, and 4th Infantry Divisions) of the 6th Army Group occupies Schweinfurt. The VI Corps attacks German forces at the Neckar River. Heilbronn falls to the 100th Infantry Division of VI Corps after nine days of fighting.

Eighth Air Force sends more than 1,300 B-17s and B-24 Liberators escorted by over 900 P-47 Thunderbolts and P-51 Mustangs to bomb oil depots, munition storage facilities, marshaling yards, and airfields. One B-17 is lost and 23 bombers damaged. Aircrew casualties are 23 killed and 10 missing.

During the night nine B-24s drop leaflets over Germany and the Netherlands and 11 B-24s fly Carpetbagger missions in Denmark.

Ninth Air Force sends 689 A-20 Havocs, A-26 Invaders, and B-26 Marauders to attack industrial targets and an ordnance depot. P-47 and P-38 fighters conduct armed reconnaissance and report 43 German fighters shot down. The fighters also support 3rd and 9th Armored Divisions, the 2nd Armored Division, and XX, XVI, VIII, and XII Corps.

MEDITERRANEAN: Fifteenth Air Force sends more than 500 B-17s and B-24 Liberators escorted by P-38 Lightnings and P-51 Mustangs to bomb bridges and marshaling yards in northern Italy to isolate German forces. P-38s conduct dive-bombing runs on a rail bridge in Germany and P-51s attack rail lines in Germany, Czechoslovakia, and Austria.

ITALY: The 442nd RCT captures Carrara. The 92nd Infantry Division's advance is stopped beyond Carrara by strong German defenses along Carione Creek. This ends Operation Second Wind. German forces have been pulled eastward just as the main attack begins in the west.

Twelfth Air Force B-25 Mitchells bomb German defensive positions in support of the British Eighth Army. P-47 Thunderbolts of the XXII Tactical Air Command attack vehicles, logistics storage sites, and ammunition storage areas in northern Italy.

During the night A-20 Havocs and A-26 Invaders attack river crossing sites, bridges, roads, and motor transport in the Po River valley.

SOUTHWEST PACIFIC AREA: In the Eighth Army area a battalion of the 164th Infantry Regiment of the Americal Division lands on Bohol Island and moves inland with the support of Filipino guerrillas. The Americans will fight Japanese defenders for more than two weeks.

In the Philippines, Far East Air Force B-24 Liberators bomb Cotabato on Mindanao. On Negros Island, B-24s and A-20 Havocs attack Japanese positions. On Luzon Island B-24s, B-25 Mitchells, A-20s, P-38s, and P-47 Thunderbolts attack bridges, troop concentrations, and logistics support sites. Japanese defensive positions are hit with napalm.

B-24s and B-25s bomb targets on Formosa.

FEAF P-38 Lightnings attack gun positions at Tarakan, Borneo.

PACIFIC: U.S. submarine *Parche* torpedoes and sinks a Japanese auxiliary minesweeper off eastern Honshu, Japan. U.S. submarine *Spadefish* torpedoes and sinks a Japanese auxiliary minesweeper in the Yellow Sea.

PACIFIC, OKINAWA: The 32nd Infantry Regiment of the 7th Infantry Division occupies the town of Ouiki, but is forced to retreat after a Japanese counterattack. The 382nd Infantry Regiment of the 96th Infantry Division is forced to consolidate and go on the defensive after attacks on Tombstone Ridge fail.

Kamikaze attacks on Task Force 58 result in minor damage to the carriers USS *Essex* and USS *Enterprise*. The *Essex* has 33 men killed. The battleship USS *Missouri* is hit, but its massive hull is not damaged. The destroyer USS *Kidd* is hit and suffers 38 killed and 35 wounded. Another destroyer, USS *Mannert L. Able,* is sunk. Another destroyer and destroyer escort are damaged by strafing attacks.

CENTRAL PACIFIC: Seventh Air Force sends 24 B-24 Liberators from Angaur to attack logistics storage areas and troops on Mindanao Island in the Philippines. B-24s from Guam bomb Japanese positions on Eten Island at Truk.

April 12

ALEUTIANS: Eleventh Air Force P-38 Lightnings shoot down bomb-carrying balloons over Attu Island.

CBI: Fourteenth Air Force B-25 Mitchells, P-40s, and P-51s attack trucks, tanks, logistics sites, horses, troops, and artillery in southern and eastern China.

B-24 Liberators attack railyards and airfields

In Burma, Tenth Air Force sends P-47 Thunderbolts and P-38 Lightnings to support ground forces and attack road traffic, troop concentrations, logistics storage sites, and targets of opportunity.

ATLANTIC: President Roosevelt dies at Warm Springs, Georgia. Vice President Harry S. Truman is sworn in as the new president.

German submarine *U-1024* torpedoes a U.S. freighter in a convoy in the Irish Sea. The ship is beached and later repaired.

ETO: The 2nd Armored Division of XIX Corps, Ninth Army, crosses the Elbe, awaiting the order to drive forward to Berlin, just 50 miles away. First Army reaches the Elbe River near Magdeburg.

Third Army is ordered to halt in front of Chemnitz and go no farther east. General Eisenhower plans to push Third Army south toward Linz.

Generals Eisenhower, Bradley, and Patton visit the Ohrdruf camp to see first-hand the Nazi atrocities. The same day Eisenhower writes a letter to General George C. Marshall, army chief of staff, describing his experience:

> The things I saw beggar description. While I was touring the camp I encountered three men who had been inmates and by one ruse or another had made their escape. I interviewed them through an interpreter. The visual evidence and the verbal testimony of starvation, cruelty and bestiality were so overpowering as to leave me a bit sick. In one room, where they were piled up twenty or thirty naked men, killed by starvation, George Patton would not even enter. He said that he would get sick if he did so. I made the visit deliberately, in order to be in a position to give firsthand evidence of these things if ever, in the future, there develops a tendency to charge these allegations merely to "propaganda."

During the night Eighth Air Force sends 10 B-24 Liberators to drop leaflets in the Netherlands and Germany, while six B-24 Liberators fly Carpetbagger missions in Denmark.

Ninth Air Force sends 167 A-20 Havocs, A-26 Invaders, and B-26 Marauders to attack railroad bridges, ordnance depots, and marshaling yards. P-47 and P-38 fighters support III, XVIII, and XVI Corps as well as the 9th Armored Division and XII, VIII, and XX Corps.

Private First Class Joe R. Hastings is a squad leader of a light machine-gun section in C Company, 386th Infantry Regiment, 97th Infantry Division, attacking a German strongpoint near Drabenderhohe, Germany. Here he moves completely exposed to enemy fire over a distance of 350 yards to put his machine gun into action to support the attack of two platoons. Firing on the Germans, he has an immediate effect, killing the gun crew of a 20 millimeter gun and a machine gun. He shifts the location of his gun to fire on another German position, suppressing a 40 millimeter gun and machine gun, then runs 150 yards, firing his weapon and killing the German gun crew. He now leads the platoon assault, firing his machine gun from the hip as the Americans capture the objective. For his courage and leadership, Private First Class Hastings will receive the Medal of Honor.

MEDITERRANEAN: Fifteenth Air Force sends more than 400 B-17s and B-24 Liberators escorted by P-51 Mustangs to bomb rail bridges in Italy and Austria and an ammunition storage site and logistics support area in Italy. P-38 Lightnings bomb rail bridges in Austria.

ITALY: Twelfth Air Force B-25 Mitchells bomb rail lines and support Eighth Army operations. P-47 Thunderbolts of the XXII Tactical Air Command attack rail lines, bridges, logistics storage sites, and ammunition storage areas. During the night A-20 Havocs and A-26 Invaders attack river crossing sites.

SOUTHWEST PACIFIC AREA: In the Philippines, Far East Air Force P-38 Lightnings and A-20 Havocs support ground troops on Cebu and Negros Islands. B-24 Liberators and P-38s attack targets on Mindanao Island. On Luzon Island, B-24s, B-25s, A-20s, and P-47 Thunderbolts attack targets in the Cagayan Valley and at Balete Pass.

B-24s attack Tainan and bomb Okayama airfield on Formosa.

PACIFIC: Twentieth Air Force sends 94 B-29s, escorted by 90 Seventh Air Force P-51 Mustangs, to bomb the Nakajima aircraft production facility at Tokyo. Aircrews report 16 Japanese fighters downed. Pilots report 15 confirmed kills, six probables, and three possibles. Four P-51s are lost. Another 66 B-29s attack a chemical plant at Koriyama and nine attack targets of opportunity. More than 70 B-29s attack a chemical plant at Koriyama and targets of opportunity. Two B-29s are lost.

U.S. submarine *Silversides* torpedoes and sinks a Japanese auxiliary submarine chaser south of Kyushu, Japan.

During the night five B-29s mine Shimonoseki Strait.

Staff Sergeant Henry E. Erwin is the radio operator of a B-29 Superfortress in the 52nd Bombardment Squadron, 29th Bombardment Group, Twentieth Air Force. The mission is to bomb Koriyama, Japan. As he drops phosphorus smoke bombs to mark the aircraft assembly area, Japanese fighters attack the bomber, causing an accident that brings a white phosphorus bomb back into the interior of the aircraft. Staff Sergeant Erwin is badly burned in the face and is blinded. As heavy white smoke fills the aircraft, threatening the lives of the entire crew, Erwin ignores certain death and, grasping the burning bomb between his forearm and body, struggles to reach the copilot's window to throw it out of the aircraft. With his body aflame, and grievously injured, Erwin succeeds in saving the bomber and crew. For his extraordinary sacrifice and willingness to give his life for his comrades, Staff Sergeant Erwin will receive the Medal of Honor.

PACIFIC, OKINAWA: XXIV Corps headquarters receives the casualty reports from the 7th and 96th Infantry Divisions for the past three days of fighting against the Japanese main defensive line. The total losses are 2,880; included in this number are 451 killed.

At dark, Japanese artillery hits the 381st and 383rd Infantry Regiments of the 96th Infantry Division and the 184th Infantry Regiment of the 7th Infantry Division in preparation for a major counterattack. During the night, preceded by a five-hour mortar and artillery barrage, four battalions of Japanese troops attack the 96th Infantry Division and are stopped with heavy losses.

Off Okinawa, destroyer USS *Mannert L. Abele* is sunk by an *oka*, a rocket-powered suicide bomb. Another destroyer is damaged by an oka. A high-speed minesweeper is damaged by an oka and a kamikaze. Kamikazes sink a support landing craft and damage battleships USS *Idaho* and USS *Tennessee,* a destroyer, and a destroyer escort. Two destroyers, three destroyer escorts, a light minelayer, and a minesweeper are also damaged by kamikaze near-misses.

CENTRAL PACIFIC: Seventh Air Force sends 24 B-24 Liberators from Angaur to attack a personnel area at Kabacan on Mindanao Island in the Philippines.

During the night six P-51 Mustangs from Iwo Jima conduct individual strikes at intervals on Kita Jima, Chichi Jima, Haha Jima, and Ani Jima Islands.

NEW GUINEA: U.S. submarine *Chub* is damaged in an air attack in the Java Sea but remains on patrol.

April 13

ALEUTIANS: Eleventh Air Force sends 27 P-38 Lightnings and P-40s to intercept and destroy a group of Japanese bomb-carrying paper balloons. Nine of the 11 sighted are shot down over the western Aleutians.

CBI: The Japanese Twentieth Army attacks in southern China with 60,000 men to capture the American airfield at Chihchiang.

In China, Fourteenth Air Force B-25 Mitchells bomb railyards and warehouses. B-25s attack shipping in the South China Sea and Bakli Bay on Hainan Island. P-40s and P-51s attack trucks, tanks, logistics sites, horses, troops, and artillery in southern and eastern China.

In Burma, Tenth Air Force sends P-47 Thunderbolts and P-38 Lightnings to attack road traffic and targets of opportunity.

ATLANTIC: President Harry S. Truman calls a meeting of Roosevelt's cabinet members and asks the secretary of war, the secretary of the navy, and the chiefs of staff to remain in their positions. After the meeting, Secretary of War Henry Stimson tells the president about the existence of "a new explosive of almost unbelievable power."

ETO: The German forces in the Ruhr pocket are unable to sustain resistance, lacking food, fuel, and ammunition. The 8th Infantry Division of XVIII Airborne Corps reaches the south bank of the Ruhr River.

In the Third Army area, Jena is captured; the 4th Armored Division is near Chemnitz. The XII Corps and VIII Corps are advancing toward Bayreuth and Neustadt. The 5th Armored Division of XIX Corps crosses the Elbe.

Eighth Air Force sends more than 200 B-17s escorted by 256 P-51 Mustangs to bomb marshaling yards. Two B-17s are lost and four damaged. Fighter pilots report 137 confirmed kills and 83 possibles in the air. Six P-51s are lost, and the pilots are reported missing. A group of 97 P-47 Thunderbolts and P-51 Mustangs fly a freelance mission in support of the bombers. Pilots report 147 confirmed kills and 137 possibles on the ground. One P-47 and one P-51 are lost. The pilots are reported missing. Ten B-24s bomb the Beizenburg rail junction during the night, and 10 other B-24s drop leaflets over France and Germany. One of four B-24s completes a Carpetbagger mission to Denmark.

Ninth Air Force sends P-47 and P-38 fighters to attack the headquarters of Field Marshal Walter Model's Army Group B at Haus Waldesruh in the Ruhr Pocket.

Fighter pilots spot Soviet fighters in the skies over Germany. Fighters support 3rd and 5th Armored Divisions, III Corps, XX Corps, and XVI Corps.

ITALY: During the night Twelfth Air Force A-20 Havocs and A-26 Invaders attack river crossing sites in the Po River Valley.

SOUTHWEST PACIFIC AREA: In the Eighth Army area, the Americal Division on Cebu Island is reinforced by the 164th Infantry Regiment (minus one battalion). It has moved behind Japanese lines and supports a frontal attack by the 132nd and 182nd Infantry Regiments. Progress is slow, but the Japanese are forced to move northward to avoid destruction.

In the Philippines, Far East Air Force B-24 Liberators and B-25 Mitchells bomb targets on Mindanao and in the Sulu Archipelago.

B-24s attack docks on the Hong Kong waterfront and storage areas in Canton, China. B-24s attack airfields on Formosa, while B-25 Mitchells attack rail lines.

Private First Class Dexter J. Kerstetter, C Company, 130th Infantry Regiment, 33rd Infantry Division, participates in a dawn attack against hill positions near Galiano, Luzon. The narrow ridge they are on is paralleled on each side by steep cliffs that are strongly fortified and heavily defended. The Americans run into intense fire and are immediately pinned down. Kerstetter's squad moves to the front and then advances alone to attack the Japanese positions along the cliff. With well-aimed shots he takes out positions one by one. Out of ammunition and grenades, he returns to his squad and then helps guide a platoon into a position that allows the Americans to overrun the enemy and capture the hill. For his courage in facing an impossible task and saving the lives of many of his fellow soldiers, Private First Class Kerstetter will receive the Medal of Honor.

PACIFIC: Twentieth Air Force sends more than 300 B-29s to bomb the Tokyo arsenal area. Seven B-29s are lost.

U.S. submarine *Parche* torpedoes and sinks a Japanese auxiliary minesweeper and guardboat off eastern Honshu, Japan.

Mines dropped by B-29s sink two Japanese cargo ships and damage a coastal defense vessel near Shmonoseki Strait.

PACIFIC, OKINAWA: During the night, Japanese troops make a second attack on the 96th Infantry Division.

A kamikaze damages a U.S. destroyer off Okinawa.

When the Japanese conduct a strong counterattack against his position, Technical Sergeant Beauford T. Anderson of the 381st Infantry Regiment, 96th Infantry Division, orders his men to safety while he faces the enemy alone. Armed only with an M-1 carbine, he fires his weapon as rapidly as possible, killing a number of the enemy. In desperation, he seizes a mortar round, pulls the safety pin, and bangs the base of the round on the rocks to arm it. He then throws it at the enemy troops. As the round explodes in their midst, he fires his carbine again, then picks up another mortar round, arms it, and throws it at the Japanese. After single-handedly breaking up the assault, Technical Sergeant Anderson gives a full report to his company commander, even though he has suffered a dangerous wound. For his extraordinary courage Anderson will win the Medal of Honor.

CENTRAL PACIFIC: Seventh Air Force sends 18 B-24 Liberators from Guam to bomb Japanese positions on Marcus Island. B-24 Liberators from Angaur bomb personnel and storage areas at Kabacan on Mindanao Island in the Philippines. Two P-61 Black Widow night fighters from Saipan bomb and strafe Pagan Island in the Marianas.

NEW GUINEA: Thirteenth Air Force B-24 Liberators sink a Japanese merchant tanker off southeast Borneo.

April 14

CBI: Fourteenth Air Force sends more than 30 B-25 Mitchells and 130 P-40s and P-51 Mustangs to attack bridges, river, road, and rail traffic, troops, logistics storage areas, towns, and general targets of opportunity over southern and eastern China.

In Burma, Tenth Air Force sends 41 P-47 Thunderbolts and P-38 Lightnings to attack troops, logistics support sites, and fuel storage areas.

Fourteenth Air Force B-24 Liberators bomb Japanese shipping at Shanghai, sinking a cargo vessel.

ETO: The Ruhr Pocket is split in two by Ninth Army's XVI Corps (75th and 79th Infantry Division and the 8th Armored Division) and XVIII Airborne Corps of First Army at Hagen.

German forces counterattack to reduce the Elbe bridgehead, forcing XIX Corps to withdraw. The 3rd Armored Division of VII Corps, First Army, reaches Dessau, encircling 10,000 German troops in the Harz Mountains.

The XII Corps of Third Army captures Bayreuth.

Eighth Air Force sends nearly 1,200 B-17s and B-24 Liberators to bomb German defensive positions, strongpoints, and antiaircraft positions in the area of Bordeaux to break the enemy's hold on critical port facilities. Two B-24s are lost and six damaged. Aircrew casualties are 18 killed, nine wounded, and 12 missing.

During the night 10 B-24s drop leaflets over Germany and the Netherlands. One of four B-24s completes a Carpetbagger mission to Denmark.

Ninth Air Force sends P-47 and P-38 fighters to support 3rd and 9th Armored Divisions, and XX, VIII, and XII Corps, and the 2nd and 5th Armored Divisions.

MEDITERRANEAN: Fifteenth Air Force sends more than 300 B-17s and B-24 Liberators escorted by P-38 Lightnings and P-51 Mustangs to bomb ammunition production facilities and a motor transport depot in Italy. P-38s attack rail targets in Germany and Austria.

ITALY: General Lucien K. Truscott attacks with Fifth Army in support of the British Eighth Army's attack as part of Operation Craftsman. The IV Corps (1st Brazilian Division, 10th Mountain Division, and 1st Armored Division) advances west of Route 64 supported by heavy air bombardment from Fifteenth Air Force and a 2,000-gun artillery barrage.

Twelfth Air Force B-25 Mitchells support the British Eighth Army and support Fifth Army ground forces. P-47 Thunderbolts attack German positions southwest of Bologna in support of Fifth Army. During the night A-20 Havocs and A-26 Invaders attack roads and motor transport in the Po River valley.

When G Company, 85th Infantry Regiment, 10th Mountain Division, is pinned down near Castel d'Aiano by German artillery, mortar, and small-arms fire, Private

First Class John D. Magrath volunteers to act as a scout to locate German positions. He moves forward and attacks a German machine-gun position. Taking the weapon with him, he crosses an open field and attacks two more machine-gun positions. Carrying the machine gun in his arms, he methodically engages a number of German positions. Under heavy mortar fire, Private Magrath is killed. His heroism and extraordinary actions in the face of certain death will win him the Medal of Honor.

SOUTHWEST PACIFIC AREA: In the Philippines, Far East Air Force B-24 Liberators, B-25 Mitchells, A-20 Havocs, P-38 Lightnings, and P-47 Thunderbolts support ground forces and attack airfields, gun positions, Japanese defenses, and troop concentrations throughout Luzon, Cebu, Negros, and Mindanao Islands.

B-25s sweep the Canton-Hong Kong, China, waterways, attacking shipping and other targets. B-24s bomb four airfields on Formosa.

PACIFIC: Twentieth Air Force takes operational control of the headquarters, 16th Bombardment Group (Very Heavy), and the B-29s of the 16th and 17th Bombardment Squadrons (Very Heavy), and the headquarters, 501st Bombardment Group (Very Heavy), and the B-29s of the 21st and 485th Bombardment Squadrons (Very Heavy). These units arrive on Guam from the United States.

U.S. submarine *Tirante* attacks a Japanese convoy in the approaches to the Yellow Sea, sinking a transport, an escort vessel, and a coastal defense vessel.

Lieutenant Commander George L. Street, III, commands the submarine USS *Tirante* during its first war patrol, conducting a reconnaissance of the harbor at Quelpart Island off the coast of Korea. With the crew at surface battle stations, Street approaches the island and penetrates the mine field to enter the harbor. Street sends two torpedoes into a Japanese transport *Jusan Maru* and sinks it. As the ship explodes, the *Tirante* comes under fire, and he orders two more torpedoes fired, sinking the escort vessel *Nomi* and Coast Defense Vessel *No. 31* as the submarine makes its escape and dives to avoid a depth charge attack. For his daring and skill, Lieutenant Commander Street will receive the Medal of Honor.

PACIFIC, OKINAWA: The 4th and 29th Marines of the 6th Marine Division attack into the Japanese defenses at Yae Take on the Motobu Peninsula, in the northern section of the island. The Japanese are well dug in and delay the advance with small ambush teams.

Kamikazes damage battleship USS *New York* and three destroyers off Okinawa.

CENTRAL PACIFIC: Seventh Air Force sends 24 B-24 Liberators from Angaur Island to bomb logistics support areas and troops on Mindanao in the Philippines.

NEW GUINEA: U.S. submarine *Gabilan* attacks a Japanese convoy, sinking a cargo vessel and an auxiliary submarine chaser in the Flores Sea.

April 15

CBI: Fourteenth Air Force B-25 Mitchells and 200 P-40s and P-51s attack trucks, tanks, rail traffic, logistics sites, troops, and gun positions in southern China.

In Burma, Tenth Air Force sends 62 P-38 Lightnings and P-47 Thunderbolts to attack troop concentrations and logistics storage areas.

ATLANTIC: Two U.S. destroyer escorts sink German submarine *U-1235* in the North Atlantic.

ETO: The French First Army captures Kehl and Offenburg on the Rhine River.

General Eisenhower gives final orders to his commanders that Berlin is not a military objective. Eisenhower orders 6th Army Group to advance through Bavaria and western Austria to link with Allied forces in Italy.

Eighth Air Force sends more than 1,300 B-17s and B-24 Liberators to bomb strongpoints and antiaircraft positions on the French Atlantic coast. The bombers drop napalm on the targets with little or no effect. No bombers are lost and nine damaged. Two crewmen are killed. During the night 10 B-24s drop leaflets over France, Germany, and the Netherlands.

Ninth Air Force sends 258 A-20 Havocs, A-26 Invaders, and B-26 Marauders to attack marshaling yards. Over 100 Eighth Air Force P-51 Mustangs support Ninth Air Force B-26s. One P-51 is lost, and the pilot is reported missing.

P-47 and P-38 fighters support 3rd and 9th Armored Divisions, VIII and XX Corps, and 6th and 2nd Armored Divisions.

MEDITERRANEAN: Fifteenth Air Force sends more than 800 B-17s and B-24 Liberators escorted by 145 P-38 Lightnings to support Fifth Army, attacking gun positions, troop concentrations, logistics storage sites, ammunition storage areas, and German headquarters units. Another 312 B-17s and B-24s escorted by 191 P-51 Mustangs attack rail lines and bridges in Italy. P-38s and P-51s attack rail lines in Germany, Austria, and Czechoslovakia.

ITALY: The 1st Armored Division captures Vergato and pushes into Suzzano. The 1st Brazilian Division captures Montese, and the 10th Mountain Division captures Rocca di Roffeno, turning the flank of two divisions and splitting the boundary between two German corps. The attack costs the division over 550 casualties.

During the night II Corps begins its attack. The 6th South African Armored Division captures Monte Sole, after a devastating barrage of 35,000 rounds of artillery hit German positions. The 88th Infantry Division attacks toward Monterumici; the 91st attacks toward Monte Adone; the 34th Infantry Division attacks to seize the ridges beyond Monte Belmonte. Over 500 artillery pieces support the corps attack. The American divisions make no progress against the heavily defended positions.

Twelfth Air Force B-25 Mitchells and P-47 Thunderbolts support Fifth Army ground forces and the British Eighth Army attacking troop concentrations, guns, and strongpoints. During the night A-20 Havocs and A-26 Invaders attack roads and motor transport in the Po River valley.

SOUTHWEST PACIFIC AREA: In the Philippines, Far East Air Force B-24 Liberators, P-38 Lightnings, and P-47 Thunderbolts attack island fortifications in Manila Bay, bivouac sites, and other targets on Luzon. B-24s, P-38s, and P-47s support ground forces on Negros and Cebu Islands. B-24s and B-25s bomb the Davao area on Mindanao Island, along with Marine aircraft.

B-24s bomb airfields and B-25s attack railyards on Formosa.

U.S. submarine *Charr* lays mines off the Malay Peninsula.

PACIFIC: During the night Twentieth Air Force sends 194 B-29s to bomb the Kawasaki urban area. Twelve B-29s are lost. More than 100 B-29s attack the urban area of Tokyo. One B-29 is lost.

Carrier aircraft from TF 58 attack airfields and aircraft on the ground in southern Kyushu, Japan, to stop the kamikaze strikes on the fleet off Okinawa.

A cargo ship is sunk off Shimonoseki Strait by a mine dropped by B-29s.

PACIFIC, OKINAWA: The 4th and 29th Marines of the 6th Marine Division attack the Yae Take defenses on the Motobu Peninsula, supported by napalm strikes from aircraft, artillery, and naval gunfire. Hill 200 falls to the 4th Marines; the 29th Marines are halted before Green Hill.

The 27th Infantry Division moves into the front lines to the right of the 96th Infantry Division in preparation for a major attack.

Kamikazes damage two destroyers off Okinawa. A Japanese assault demolition boat damages a motor minesweeper.

Private First Class Harold Gonsalves is the acting scout sergeant with the 4th Battalion, 15th Marine Regiment, 6th Marine Division, fighting the Japanese at Mount Yaetake on the Motobu Peninsula. Gonsalves accompanies his battalion commander as he moves up to the front lines to assist the forward observation team in directing artillery fire on Japanese positions. When a Japanese grenade falls close within the group, PFC Gonsalves covers the grenade with his body, saving the lives of the other marines. For his distinct act of heroism and self-sacrifice, PFC Gonsalves will receive the Medal of Honor.

April 16

ALEUTIANS: Eleventh Air Force sends six B-24 Liberators to bomb the Kataoka naval base on Shimushu Island in the Kuriles. The bombers use radar to mark the bomb release points over the target.

CBI: Fourteenth Air Force sends B-24 Liberators to bomb targets of opportunity in the Bakli Bay, Hainan Island, and Canton areas. About 120 P-40s and P-51 Mustangs attack river, road, and rail traffic, town areas, troops, and general targets of opportunity in southern and eastern China.

In Burma, Tenth Air Force P-47 Thunderbolts attack troop concentrations.

ATLANTIC: President Truman, addressing a joint session of Congress, reaffirms his commitment to the unconditional surrender of Germany and Japan.

Troubled by the Soviet machinations in Poland, Truman and Churchill send a letter to Stalin appealing to him to live up to the Yalta agreements.

Two destroyer escorts sink German submarine *U-880* in the North Atlantic.

ETO: The eastern half of the Ruhr Pocket is eliminated.

The 3rd and 45th Infantry Divisions of XV Corps of Seventh Army reach Nürnberg. German troops fight to defend the city. The Americans are capturing an average of 50,000 prisoners a day.

Eighth Air Force sends more than 1,200 B-17s and B-24 Liberators escorted by over 900 P-47 Thunderbolts and P-51 Mustangs to bomb rail bridges and marshaling yards. One B-24 is lost and 12 bombers are damaged. Aircrew casualties are seven missing. Fighter pilots report two confirmed kills in the air and 314 confirmed kills and 175 possibles on the ground. Twenty fighters are lost and the pilots are reported missing. Over 280 P-51s fly a free-lance mission in support of bombers attacking landing areas in Germany and Czechoslovakia. Pilots report one confirmed kill and one possible in the air and 410 confirmed kills and 198 possibles on the ground. Nine fighters are lost, and the pilots are reported missing. P-51 Mustangs escort a photo reconnaissance mission over Germany. Two fighters are lost, and the pilots are reported missing.

In an early morning strike, 485 B-17s bomb the tank ditch defense line near the Bordeaux area in support of ground forces. Fourteen B-17s are damaged. During the night 11 B-24s drop leaflets over France, Germany, and the Netherlands.

Ninth Air Force sends 450 A-20 Havocs, A-26 Invaders, and B-26 Marauders to attack communication centers and marshaling yards. P-47 and P-38 fighters support the 3rd and 9th Armored Divisions, XX and VIII Corps, XIX Corps and V Corps, and the 2nd Armored Division. Pilots report 25 German fighters downed. The P-51s of the 354th Fighter Group claims their 900th air victory.

MEDITERRANEAN: Fifteenth Air Force B-24 Liberators escorted by 102 P-51 Mustangs bomb German positions southwest of Bologna. P-51s attack airfields in Germany and sweep areas of Austria and Czechoslovakia.

ITALY: The 10th Mountain Division makes large gains. The 86th Mountain Infantry Regiment and the 751st Tank Battalion capture Montepastore. The 11th Armored Infantry Regiment of the 1st Armored Division captures Monte Mosca.

Fifteenth Air Force B-24 pilots of the 98th and 376th Bomber Groups prepare to return to the United States for B-29 training to support the anticipated invasion of Japan.

Twelfth Air Force B-25 Mitchells bomb bridges along the British Eighth Army battle lines. P-47 Thunderbolts support Fifth Army ground forces. During the night A-20 Havocs and A-26 Invaders attack river crossing sites in the Po River valley.

SOUTHWEST PACIFIC AREA: In the Philippines, Far East Air Force P-38 Lightnings and P-47 Thunderbolts support ground forces and conduct sweeps over Luzon, Negros, and Mindanao Islands. B-25 Mitchells bomb highways on Mindanao, while B-24 Liberators attack defenses on Carabao Island.

B-25s, B-24s, and P-51s bomb airfields on Formosa. During the night B-24s bomb Formosa.

FEAF P-38 Lightnings bomb a tank farm and other targets at Tarakan, Borneo.

PACIFIC: U.S. submarine *Sea Dog* torpedoes and sinks a cargo ship off eastern Honshu, Japan. U.S. submarine *Sunfish* attacks a Japanese convoy leaving Yamado harbor, Honshu, Japan, and sinks a coastal defense vessel and a transport.

A mine from Twentieth Air Force B-29s damages a Japanese cargo vessel off Shimonoseki.

PACIFIC, OKINAWA: Major General Lemuel C. Shepherd, commander of the 6th Marine Division, orders a renewed attack on the Yae Take defenses on the Motobu Peninsula, using the 22nd Marines to flank the Japanese positions. The 3rd Battalion of the 29th Marines captures Green Hill, while the 4th Marines battle to the top of Yae Take. After repeated counterattacks throughout the night, the Japanese withdraw into the jungle, headed for the northern section of Okinawa. The marines will

The USS *Intrepid* is hit by a kamikaze off Okinawa on April 16, 1945.

occupy Yae Take for another four days, clearing the last Japanese defenders. Marine casualties to secure the Motobu Peninsula are nearly 1,000 men.

The 305th and 306th Infantry Regiments of the 77th Infantry Division land on Ie Shima Island off the Motobu Peninsula to capture the airfield. The fierce Japanese resistance at Bloody Ridge before Iegusugu Mountain forces the Americans to land the 307th Infantry Regiment to reinforce the attack. Although slowed by minefields, the Americans capture the airfield and stop a Japanese counterattack during the night.

The carrier *Intrepid* is hit by a kamikaze. Ten sailors are killed and 87 are wounded. The damage is severe enough to take the carrier out of battle. The destroyer *Laffey* takes on 22 Japanese aircraft, some making suicide attacks, others dropping bombs. The *Laffey* takes four direct bomb hits and six kamikaze strike the ship. A total of 32 sailors are killed, and 21 are wounded. Although seriously damaged in the fight, the destroyer prevents the enemy from threatening the transports and cargo ships off Hagushi. The *Laffey* earns a Presidential Unit Citation.

Kamikazes sink destroyer USS *Pringle* and damage battleship USS *Missouri*, a destroyer, a destroyer escort, two high-speed minesweepers, and an oiler off Okinawa.

CENTRAL PACIFIC: Seventh Air Force sends 18 B-24 Liberators from Guam to bomb Marcus Island.

P-51 Mustangs from Iwo Jima, with Twentieth Air Force B-29s providing navigational escort, strafe and bomb targets at Kanoya airfield on Kyushu Island. Four P-51s are lost.

April 17

CBI: In China, Fourteenth Air Force sends four B-25 Mitchells and four P-51 Mustangs to bomb river shipping. P-51 Mustangs and P-40s attack troops, town areas, road traffic, river shipping, and general targets of opportunity in southern and eastern China.

In Burma, Tenth Air Force sends P-47 Thunderbolts and P-38 Lightnings to attack road traffic, troop concentrations, logistics storage sites, and targets of opportunity.

ATLANTIC: Prime Minister Winston Churchill addresses the House of Commons a few days after President Roosevelt's death, describing Roosevelt as "the greatest champion of freedom who has ever brought help and comfort from the New World to the Old."

ETO: General Eisenhower's directive for the final operations in Germany is passed to subordinate commanders. With Germany now split in half, the Allied forces in the west will attack to the north and south to eliminate the last resistance. The Elbe River is the halt line for farther advances eastward. The 12th Army Group is to defend the Elbe-Mulde River line while Third Army is to attack southward toward Nürnberg and Regensburg and into the Danube River valley. The 6th Army Group is to occupy western Austria and the adjacent territory of Germany within its area of responsibility. The 21st Army Group is to cross the Elbe, secure Hamburg, and advance to the Baltic toward Kiel and be prepared to attack into Denmark.

Eighth Air Force sends more than 1,000 B-17s and B-24 Liberators escorted by over 800 P-47 Thunderbolts and P-51 Mustangs to bomb rail bridges, marshaling yards, and rail junctions in Germany and Czechoslovakia. The marshaling yards at Dresden are attacked again. About 50 German Me-262 jet fighters attack the bomber formations. A total of eight bombers are lost and 178 damaged. Aircrews report one confirmed kill and one possible. Aircrew casualties are seven wounded and 68 missing. Fighter pilots report 13 confirmed kills and five possibles in the air and 286 confirmed kills and 113 possibles on the ground. A total of 16 fighters are lost. Two pilots are wounded, and 16 pilots are reported missing.

During the night 10 B-24s drop leaflets over Germany, France, and the Netherlands. A total of 19 B-24s fly Carpetbagger missions.

Ninth Air Force sends A-20 Havocs, A-26 Invaders, and B-26 Marauders to attack ordnance depots and marshaling yards. P-47 and P-38 fighters support 3rd and 9th Armored Divisions, VIII and XX Corps, and 2nd and 5th Armored Divisions.

First Lieutenant Frank Burke is the battalion transportation officer of the 15th Infantry Regiment, 3rd Infantry Division, looking to select a motor pool site in Nürnberg, Germany, during the fighting for the city. He inadvertently passes beyond friendly lines and discovers 10 German infantrymen preparing to make a counterattack. Returning to friendly lines, Burke gets a light machine gun and ammunition and moves forward alone to attack the Germans. His accurate fire breaks up the attack and silences a machine-gun position not far away. He then picks up a rifle and runs to an abandoned tank to fire on the Germans from behind. He eliminates a sniper from a cellar window and withdraws to obtain a new rifle, ammunition, and grenades, then walks out into the street to continue the fight. Putting an armed grenade in each hand, Burke charges toward enemy troops in a building, throws the grenades, and eliminates the position even as he appears to be killed by a German hand grenade that explodes in front of him. Unhurt, Burke picks up his rifle to kill three German soldiers charging toward him. For the rest of the day Lieutenant Burke moves from street to street participating in the small but brutal battles that rage in the city. For his extraordinary bravery and superb fighting skill, First Lieutenant Frank Burke will receive the Medal of Honor.

MEDITERRANEAN: Fifteenth Air Force sends more than 700 B-17s and B-24 Liberators escorted by 143 P-51 Mustangs to bomb troop concentrations, logistics storage sites, and targets of opportunity in support of Fifth Army. P-51s attack targets of opportunity in Germany, Austria, and Czechoslovakia.

ITALY: The 88th, 91st, and 18th Infantry Divisions capture key mountain points overlooking Route 64 and the Reno River. The 92nd Infantry Division's 473rd Infantry Regiment attacks up the coastal road and approaches La Spezia. The 442nd RCT is halted by German defenses at Fosdinovo.

Twelfth Air Force B-25 Mitchells bomb bridges and support Eighth Army. A-20 Havocs and P-47 Thunderbolts of the XXII Tactical Air Command support Fifth Army ground forces. During the night A-20 Havocs and A-26 Invaders attack river crossing sites in the Po River valley.

SOUTHWEST PACIFIC AREA: In the Eighth Army area, the 24th Infantry Division lands at Parang and advances toward Davao on Highway 1. One battalion of the 21st Infantry Regiment lands at Malabang, already under control of Filipino guerrillas. The 533rd Engineer Boat and Shore Regiment provides support to the advance, traveling on the Mindanao River paralleling Highway 1. The river becomes the main line of supply for the 24th Infantry Division.

In the Philippines, Far East Air Force B-24 Liberators, B-25 Mitchells, A-20 Havocs, P-38 Lightnings, and P-47 Thunderbolts support ground forces over Luzon, Cebu, Negros, and Mindanao Islands. B-24s bomb targets on Mindanao.

B-24s and B-25s bomb airfields on Formosa.

PACIFIC: Twentieth Air Force sends more than 100 B-29s to bomb airfields at Tachiarai, Kokubu, Izumi, Nittagahara, and Kanoya, Japan, in an attempt to stop kamikaze attacks on navy ships off Okinawa.

A mine from Twentieth Air Force B-29s sinks a Japanese cargo ship off Shanghai. A mine from a 21st Bomber Command B-29 sinks a Japanese cargo ship off western Kyushu.

PACIFIC, OKINAWA: The 305th and 306th Infantry Regiments of the 77th Infantry Division are reinforced by the 307th Infantry as the Japanese hold Ie town and Bloody Ridge.

A kamikaze damages a destroyer off Okinawa.

CENTRAL PACIFIC: Seventh Air Force sends 18 P-51 Mustangs from Iwo Jima to fly two strikes against vessels at Futamiko in the Bonin Islands.

April 18

CBI: Fourteenth Air Force B-25 Mitchells, P-40s, and P-51s attack trucks, tanks, logistics sites, horses, troops, and artillery in southern and eastern China.

In Burma, Tenth Air Force sends P-38 Lightnings to attack troop concentrations, tanks, artillery positions, and targets of opportunity.

ATLANTIC: German submarine *U-1107* torpedoes and sinks a U.S. freighter in convoy HX 348 southwest of Brest, France. German submarine *U-548* torpedoes a U.S. freighter off Cape Henry, Virginia. Although driven off by gunfire initially, the U-boat returns and finishes off the freighter.

ETO: The Ruhr Pocket is eliminated. About 325,000 German soldiers, including 30 general officers, surrender. There are no organized German formations within 100 miles. German prisoners are so numerous that they are kept in huge open fields enclosed in barbed wire. Taking care of prisoners, refugees, displaced people, and combat forces strains the Allied supply capability.

The Third Army enters Czechoslovakia. The XIX Corps of Ninth Army captures Magdeburg after a strong defense by German forces.

Eighth Air Force sends more than 700 B-17s and B-24 Liberators escorted by 700 P-47 Thunderbolts and P-51 Mustangs to bomb rail bridges and marshaling yards in southern Germany and Czechoslovakia. Two B-17s are lost and 18 damaged. Aircrews report 16 confirmed kills and 14 possibles. Aircrew casualties are 10 missing. Fighter pilots report three confirmed kills and four possibles in the air and 12 confirmed kills and eight possibles on the ground. Two P-51s are lost, and the pilots are reported missing.

During the night 11 B-24s drop leaflets over Germany, France, and the Netherlands. A total of 17 B-24s fly Carpetbagger missions to Denmark and Norway.

Ninth Air Force sends nearly 600 A-20 Havocs, A-26 Invaders, and B-26 Marauders to attack oil storage areas, rail junctions, and marshaling yards. Over 100 P-51 Mustangs escort Ninth Air Force B-26 Marauders. Pilots report one confirmed kill and two possibles in the air. P-47 and P-38 fighters support V and VII Corps, 2nd and 5th Armored Divisions, and XIX Corps.

The headquarters of the 349th Troop Carrier Group and the C-47s of the 23rd, 312th, 313th, and 314th Troop Carrier Squadrons, IX Troop Carrier Command, redeploy from England to France.

Private Joseph F. Merrell of I Company, 15th Infantry Regiment, 3rd Infantry Division, assaults a hill near Lohe, Germany, whose capture will open the way to Nürnberg. When the attack is stalled by heavy enemy fire, Private Merrell continues forward alone, running 100 yards and shooting down four German soldiers. His rifle damaged by a sniper bullet, he continues forward with the three grenades he has. Running another 200 yards, he reaches a machine-gun position, throws two grenades, and then jumps in ready to fight any survivors. Unarmed, he obtains a German pistol and eliminates the defenders. Crawling toward a second machine gun 30 yards away, he kills four Germans in camouflaged foxholes on the way, but is badly wounded. Staggering forward, he throws his last grenade into the machine-gun position and again jumps in to fight the enemy. He is shot and killed by the defenders. For his complete fearlessness, initiative, and willingness to sacrifice his own life so that his comrades can go on to victory, Private Merrell will receive the nation's highest award for valor, the Medal of Honor.

MEDITERRANEAN: Fifteenth Air Force sends more than 400 B-17s and B-24 Liberators escorted by 89 P-51 Mustangs to bomb defensive positions near Bologna in support of Fifth Army. P-38 Lightnings attack rail bridges in Austria.

ITALY: General Lucian K. Truscott commits the 85th Infantry Division to exploit the success west of Route 64 along the Reno River. The 91st Infantry Division of II Corps captures Pianoro. The 10th Mountain Division approaches Monte San Michele, the last major defensible position before the open plain that reaches to Route 9 west of Bologna. The 85th Infantry Division moves through disorganized German units to approach Pradura on Route 64 leading into Bologna.

Twelfth Air Force B-25 Mitchells bomb bridges. P-47 Thunderbolts of the XXII Tactical Air Command support Fifth Army ground forces. During the night A-20 Havocs and A-26 Invaders attack river crossing sites in the Po River valley.

SOUTHWEST PACIFIC AREA: In the Philippines, Far East Air Force A-20 Havocs, P-47 Thunderbolts, and P-38 Lightnings support ground forces on Luzon, Negros, and Cebu Islands. B-24s bomb Mindanao Island.

On Formosa, B-24s and B-25s bomb airfields, while P-38s conduct sweeps against rail and road transportation targets.

FEAF B-25 Mitchells and P-38 Lightnings attack Tarakan and Sandakan on Borneo.

PACIFIC: The last elements of the 3rd Marine Division leave Iwo Jima.

Twentieth Air Force sends more than 100 B-29s to attack Japanese airfields at Tachiarai, Izumi, Kokubu, Nittagahara, and Kanoya, while 13 other B-29s attack targets of opportunity. Two B-29s are lost.

U.S. submarine *Seahorse* is damaged in a depth charge attack in Tsushima Strait and is forced to terminate her patrol. U.S. submarine *Sea Owl* torpedoes and sinks Japanese submarine *RO-46* off Wake Island.

PACIFIC, OKINAWA: The 305th and 307th Infantry Regiments of the 77th Infantry Division attack into Ie town to capture Bloody Ridge. The Japanese have fortified the town, and throughout the day the Americans battle house by house. While driving in a jeep with the commander of the 305th Infantry Regiment, renowned correspondent Ernie Pyle, author of *Brave Men* and *Here Is Your War,* is killed by Japanese machine-gun fire.

Five destroyers and TBM Avengers from small carrier USS *Bataan* sink Japanese submarine *I-56* east of Okinawa.

CENTRAL PACIFIC: During the night Seventh Air Force sends three P-61 Black Widow night fighters from Iwo Jima to make individual attacks on Futamiko and the radio station on Chichi Jima.

April 19

CBI: In China, Fourteenth Air Force sends B-25 Mitchells to attack bridges and rail and road traffic, while over 100 P-40s, P-51 Mustangs, and P-47 Thunderbolts attack town areas, troops, river, road, and rail traffic, and general targets of opportunity in southern and eastern China.

In Burma, Tenth Air Force P-38 Lightnings attack, logistics storage sites, bridges, and targets of opportunity.

ATLANTIC: President Truman agrees to changes in the U.S. approach to trusteeships at the upcoming San Francisco conference, at the strong urging of his military advisers. Any trusteeship given to another state would have to take into consideration American strategic and security interests. This will preclude giving away territories to states that could use them against American interests as the Japanese did with islands in the Pacific after World War I. The deteriorating situation with the Soviet Union makes the issue more urgent.

Two destroyer escorts sink German submarine *U-879* in the North Atlantic.

ETO: The 9th Infantry Division of V Corps clears the last German resistance from Leipzig.

Eighth Air Force sends more than 600 B-17s and B-24 Liberators escorted by 584 P-51 Mustangs to bomb rail lines and marshaling yards in Germany and Czechoslovakia. Five B-17s are lost and 13 are damaged. Aircrews report 18 confirmed kills, one probable, and five possibles. Aircrew casualties are 46 missing. Fighter pilots report 12 confirmed kills and three possibles in the air. One P-61 is lost, and the pilot is reported missing.

Six P-51s escort a photo reconnaissance mission over Germany. One P-51 is lost, and the pilot is reported missing.

During the night 11 B-24s fly Carpetbagger missions to Norway. Two B-24s are lost.

Ninth Air Force sends A-20 Havocs, A-26 Invaders, and B-26 Marauders to attack marshaling yards. P-47 and P-38 fighters support VII Corps, XII Corps, and XX and XIX Corps.

MEDITERRANEAN: Fifteenth Air Force sends more than 600 B-17s and B-24 Liberators escorted by P-38 Lightnings and P-51 Mustangs to bomb a rail bridge and marshaling yards in Austria, and marshaling yards in Germany and Italy.

ITALY: The 85th Mountain Infantry Regiment captures Monte San Michele and the 87th captures Monte San Pietro. The 1st Armored Division engages in a tank battle along the Samoggia River.

Twelfth Air Force B-25 Mitchells bomb bridges. P-47 Thunderbolts attack logistics storage sites, ammunition storage areas, and support Fifth Army ground forces. During the night A-20 Havocs and A-26 Invaders attack river crossing sites, roads, and vehicles in the Po River valley.

SOUTHWEST PACIFIC AREA: In the Philippines, Far East Air Force B-25 Mitchells, A-20 Havocs, P-47 Thunderbolts, and P-38 Lightnings support ground forces on Luzon, Cebu, and Negros Islands. B-24 Liberators bomb personnel areas on Mindanao Island.

B-24s bomb an airfield and a town on Formosa.

FEAF B-25s strike Borneo, while B-24s returning from a French Indochina coastal sweep bomb Sandakan in Borneo.

PACIFIC: U.S. submarine *Cero* torpedoes and sinks a Japanese guardboat southeast of Kyushu, Japan. U.S. submarine *Sennet* attacks a Japanese convoy off the south coast of Kyushu and sinks an auxiliary submarine chaser and a cargo ship. U.S. submarine *Silversides* torpedoes and sinks a Japanese guardboat east of Honshu. U.S.

Members of the 96th Infantry Division occupy fighting positions on Okinawa, April 1945.

submarine *Sunfish* attacks a Japanese convoy off Hokkaido, sinking a gunboat and a cargo ship. U.S. submarine *Trutta* torpedoes and sinks a Japanese merchant vessel and merchant fishing boats in the Yellow Sea.

PACIFIC, OKINAWA: The heaviest artillery bombardment of the Pacific war, over 300 artillery pieces firing for 20 minutes, initiates the XIV Corps assault on the Shuri defensive line. Three divisions (the 27th, the 7th, and the 96th) are massed across a four-and-a-half-mile front. The 27th Division on the west coast of the island is to capture Kakazu Ridge. The 96th Division in the center is to capture the town of Shuri, and the 7th Division in the east is to capture Hill 178. With 27 artillery battalions and six battleships, six cruisers, and six destroyers all firing in support, the infantry advances on the Japanese defenses. A total of 650 aircraft hit targets all along the defensive front. Protected in their underground shelters, the Japanese suffer few losses and are fully prepared to resist the attacks.

The 96th Infantry Division attacks to capture Tombstone Ridge, the 7th to capture Skyline Ridge and Hill 178. The 7th is stopped short of the Japanese positions, while the 96th makes minimal progress after taking heavy casualties. The 27th Infantry Division, advancing down Highway 5, bypasses enemy defenses but gains no advantage by nightfall. The American effort ends in failure with more than 700 casualties.

On Ie Shima, elements of the 307th Infantry Regiment of the 77th Infantry Division reach Bloody Ridge as the battle for Ie town continues.

CENTRAL PACIFIC: Seventh Air Force sends 17 B-24 Liberators from Guam to attack Truk. Another 25 B-24 Liberators from the Palaus bomb nearby Arakabesan and Koror Islands. P-51 Mustangs from Iwo Jima bomb and strafe Futamiko in the Bonin Islands. During the night six P-61 Black Widow night fighters from Iwo Jima conduct individual harassment raids on Chichi Jima, Haha Jima, and Muko Jima islands.

Over 100 P-51 Mustangs fly a fighter sweep to Atsugi and Yokosuka airfields in Japan. Pilots report 23 confirmed kills and seven possibles in the air and 14 confirmed kills and 23 possibles on the ground. Two P-51s are lost.

April 20

CBI: Fourteenth Air Force B-25 Mitchells, P-40s, and P-51s attack rail targets, trucks, tanks, logistics sites, horses, troops, and artillery in southern and eastern China.

In Burma, Tenth Air Force P-38 Lightnings attack bridges, while P-47 Thunderbolts attack road traffic, troop concentrations, and land gun positions.

ETO: Organized resistance in Nürnberg ends. The Americans capture 10,000 prisoners and free about 13,000 British and American prisoners of war.

First Army captures Leipzig after strong resistance near the Mulde River.

Eighth Air Force sends more than 800 B-17s and B-24 Liberators escorted by nearly 900 P-47 Thunderbolts and P-51 Mustangs to bomb rail bridges, rail junctions, and marshaling yards in Germany and Czechoslovakia One B-17 is lost and 25 damaged. Aircrews report seven confirmed kills and four possibles. Aircrew casualties are one wounded and 10 missing. One P-51 is lost. A total of 100 P-51s fly a freelance fighter sweep for the bombers. Pilots report seven confirmed kills and four possibles in the air.

Six B-17s conduct screening missions to jam German radio interception efforts and employ countermeasures against German radar sites.

During the night 12 B-24s fly Carpetbagger missions to Norway. Two B-24 Liberators are lost.

Ninth Air Force sends 564 A-20 Havocs, A-26 Invaders, and B-26 Marauders to attack oil storage areas, ordnance depots, and marshaling yards. P-47 and P-38 fighters support VII and VIII Corps, XII and XX Corps, and XIX Corps.

MEDITERRANEAN: Fifteenth Air Force sends more than 700 B-17s and B-24 Liberators escorted by P-38 Lightnings and P-51 Mustangs to bomb road and rail lines to block the German withdrawal into northern Italy. Over 100 P-38s attack rail lines and marshaling yards in Germany and Austria.

ITALY: Elements of the 10th Mountain Division capture Ponte Samoggia on Route 9. The 88th and 85th Infantry Divisions cross the Lavino River and occupy positions just south of Route 9. The 6th South African Armored Division of II Corps captures Casalecchio at the base of the Reno River Valley on Route 64.

Twelfth Air Force B-25 Mitchells bomb rail bridges. P-47 Thunderbolts of the XXII Tactical Air Command support Fifth Army ground forces. During the night A-20 Havocs and A-26 Invaders attack river crossing sites and vehicles in the Po River valley.

SOUTHWEST PACIFIC AREA: In the Eighth Army area the Americal Division conducts a pursuit of defeated Japanese forces into the northern mountains of Cebu Island. Supported by Filipino guerrillas, the American infantrymen succeed in isolating over 8,500 enemy troops. The Americans have lost over 400 killed and 1,700 wounded in the fight for Cebu, not including another 8,000 casualties as a result of disease. The Japanese have lost nearly 6,000 men. Cebu City with its excellent harbor is intended to become a staging base for three infantry divisions preparing for the invasion of Japan.

In the Philippines, Far East Air Force B-25 Mitchells, A-20 Havocs, P-47 Thunderbolts, and P-38 Lightnings support ground forces on Luzon, Cebu, and Negros Islands. B-24 Liberators and P-51s bomb airfields on Formosa.

FEAF B-24 Liberators bomb airfields on Borneo, and P-38 Lightnings and B-25 Mitchells attack Tarakan Island.

U.S. submarine *Guitarro* lays mines in Berhala Strait off the northeast coast of Sumatra.

PACIFIC: Mines dropped by Twentieth Air Force B-29s sink two cargo vessels and damage another at the western entrance of Shimonoseki Strait.

PACIFIC, OKINAWA: XXIV Corps renews its attack on the Shuri defenses. Two battalions of the 165th Infantry Regiment of the 27th Infantry Division bypass Japanese defenses and reach the Machinato airfield. Japanese forces occupying a position named Item Pocket stop any farther advance; the position controls all approaches to Machinato and the nearby airfield.

On Ie Shima, the 306th Infantry Regiment gains control of the north side of Iegusugu Yama, the mountain that anchored the Japanese defenses. Japanese counterattacks during the night, on Bloody Ridge, fail.

CENTRAL PACIFIC: Seventh Air Force sends 11 P-51 Mustangs from Iwo Jima to bomb Haha Jima.

April 21

CBI: In China, Fourteenth Air Force P-40s and P-51 Mustangs attack rail and river traffic.

ETO: First Army eliminates the Harz Mountain pocket. SHAEF headquarters estimates that 1 million German soldiers have been captured since the beginning of April.

The French First Army captures Stuttgart.

Eighth Air Force sends more than 500 B-17s and B-24 Liberators escorted by 444 P-51 Mustangs to attack airfields supporting Me-262 jet aircraft. Two bombers are lost and 12 are damaged. Aircrew casualties are eight killed, one wounded, and 19 missing. Two fighters are lost and one is damaged. The pilots are reported missing. During the night 10 B-24s drop leaflets over France, Germany, and the Netherlands.

Brigadier General Ralph F. Stearley takes command of IX Fighter Command and IX Tactical Air Command, Ninth Air Force. P-47 and P-38 fighters support VIII Corps, XII Corps, and XX Corps.

MEDITERRANEAN: Fifteenth Air Force sends more than 200 B-17s and B-24 Liberators escorted by P-51 Mustangs to bomb marshaling yards in Germany and in Austria. Over 130 P-38 Lightnings bomb rail lines in Germany and Austria.

ITALY: The 133rd Infantry Regiment of the 34th Infantry Division riding the tanks of the 752nd Tank Battalion enters Bologna.

The 10th Mountain Division forms a task force of the 85th and 86th Mountain Infantry Regiments and the 91st Cavalry Reconnaissance Squadron to seize the Bomporto Bridge over the Panaro River. The unit is called Task Force Duff after its commander, Brigadier General Robinson E. Duff.

Twelfth Air Force B-25 Mitchells bomb bridges. P-47 Thunderbolts support Fifth Army ground forces as they move into Bologna. During the night A-20 Havocs and A-26 Invaders attack river crossing sites in the Po River valley.

SOUTHWEST PACIFIC AREA: In the Philippines, Far East Air Force B-25 Mitchells, A-20 Havocs, P-47 Thunderbolts, and P-38 Lightnings support ground forces on Luzon, Cebu, Negros, and Jolo Islands. The 39th Fighter Squadron, 35th Fighter Group, redeploys its P-47s from Lingayen to Clark Field, Luzon.

FEAF B-24 Liberators bomb airfields on Borneo, and P-38 Lightnings attack Tarakan Island and airfields, oil storage areas, and, with B-24s, attack targets of opportunity along the southwest Celebes coast.

PACIFIC: Twentieth Air Force sends more than 200 B-29s to attack airfields at Oita, Kanoya, Usa, Kokubu, Kushira, Tachiarai, Izumi, and Nittagahara in Japan to forestall kamikaze attacks on naval forces off Okinawa. Another 21 B-29s attack targets of opportunity, including the city of Kagoshima.

PACIFIC, OKINAWA: The 32nd Infantry Regiment of the 7th Infantry Division captures Skyline Ridge, forcing the outflanked defenders of Hill 178 to withdraw the following night. The 3rd Battalion of the 382nd Infantry Regiment, 96th Infantry Division, holds off successive Japanese counterattacks near Tombstone Ridge.

On Ie Shima, Iegusugu Yama falls to the 77th Infantry Division. The American flag is raised on the summit. The island is secured several days later. The division's casualties to capture this small island are 1,120—nearly as many as the division lost during the battle for Guam.

A destroyer is damaged by a near-miss bomb off Okinawa.

Private First Class Martin O. May is a machine gunner in the 307th Infantry Regiment, 77th Infantry Division, battling Japanese defenders on the rugged slopes of Legusuku-Yama on Ie Shima. Placing his gun in an exposed position to support the infantry, he immediately comes under heavy fire but engages attacking Japanese infantry effectively, stopping the enemy. After reforming, the Japanese attack again, and May repulses this attack with hand grenades and accurate fire. May holds this position throughout the day and into the next day, risking constant fire from the enemy and continuing to support the infantry until he is severely wounded and his gun destroyed by a mortar explosion. Refusing to give up, May throws hand grenades at the Japanese infantry until he is killed. For his gallant action, dedication to duty, and indomitable fighting spirit, Private First Class Martin will receive the Medal of Honor.

Central Pacific: Seventh Air Force sends 18 B-24 Liberators from Guam to bomb Marcus Island.

April 22

CBI: Fourteenth Air Force B-24 Liberators bomb targets of opportunity at Canton and in Bakli Bay on Hainan Island. P-40s and P-51s attack trucks, tanks, logistics sites, horses, troops, and artillery in southern and eastern China.

U.S. submarine *Hardhead* torpedoes and sinks a Japanese cargo vessel in the Andaman Sea.

ATLANTIC: Two destroyer escorts sink German submarine *U-518* in the North Atlantic.

ETO: Third Army sends XX Corps toward the Danube River to clear the area of enemy forces. Seventh Army's XV Corps is ordered to advance toward Munich. The XXI and VI Corps of Seventh Army cross the Danube River.

During the night Eighth Air Force sends 10 B-24 Liberators to drop leaflets in France, the Netherlands, and Germany. Four B-24 Liberators fly Carpetbagger missions to Norway.

MEDITERRANEAN: Fifteenth Air Force sends 258 P-51 Mustangs and P-38 Lightnings to fly armed reconnaissance over northeast Italy, bombing marshaling yards, bridges, railroads, highways, and strafing an airfield, rail and road traffic, and numerous other targets of opportunity.

ITALY: Task Force Duff reaches the Po River at San Benedetto. Brigadier General Duff is seriously wounded when his vehicle hits a mine. IV Corps engineers support the 1st Battalion of the 87th Mountain Infantry Regiment as it crosses the Po River.

Twelfth Air Force B-25 Mitchells, A-20 Havocs, A-26 Invaders, and P-47 Thunderbolts attack troops and vehicles throughout the day and into the night as German forces retreat north across the Po River.

Private Joe Hayashi of K Company, 442nd Regimental Combat Team, attacks a strongly defended hill near Tendola, Italy. Private Hayashi brings his squad to within 75 yards of enemy positions before they are fired on. Moving the wounded to safety, Hayashi directs mortar fire on the enemy even as bullets fly all around him. He then attacks with his squad to occupy the position. During the attack on the village of Tendola, Hayashi attacks a German position alone, destroying one position and forcing several other enemy soldiers to abandon their positions. As he is throwing grenades and moving forward to pursue the Germans, he is killed. For his extraordinary courage and superb leadership Private Hayashi will receive the Medal of Honor.

SOUTHWEST PACIFIC AREA: In the Eighth Army area elements of the 63rd Infantry Regiment of the 41st Infantry Division, supported by Philippine guerrillas, capture Japanese positions on Mount Daho on Jolo Island in the Sulu Archipelago. The battle to control the island continues for another three weeks. During that time American casualties will number 165. Japanese casualties will be over 2,000 killed. The airfield on Jolo is improved and expanded.

The 31st Infantry Division lands at Parang and follows the 24th Infantry Division before turning north as ordered by Major General Sibert to attack up the Sayre Highway to Macajalar Bay. The 24th is ordered to capture Digos and then advance to capture Davao City.

In the Philippines, Far East Air Force B-25 Mitchells, A-20 Havocs, P-47 Thunderbolts, and P-38 Lightnings support ground forces on Luzon, Cebu, and Negros Islands.

B-24 Liberators attack shipping and harbor installations at Saigon in French Indochina.

FEAF B-24 Liberators bomb airfields at Manggar and Jesselton and P-38 Lightnings attack Kuching.

PACIFIC: Twentieth Air Force sends 87 B-29s to bomb airfields at Izumi, Kushira, Miyazaki, Tomitaka, and Kanoya and targets of opportunity. One B-29 is lost. P-51 Mustangs from Iwo Jima attack Akenogahara and Suzuko airfields; they claim 10 Japanese aircraft shot down and 15 destroyed on the ground.

U.S. submarine *Cero* torpedoes and sinks a Japanese guardboat and damages a guardboat south of Honshu, Japan.

PACIFIC, OKINAWA: A support landing craft *LCS-15* is sunk in an air attack off Okinawa. Kamikazes sink a minesweeper and damage two destroyers. A destroyer, a minesweeper, and a light minelayer are damaged by near-misses of kamikazes. Another minesweeper is damaged by strafing and a near-miss.

April 23

CBI: In China, Fourteenth Air Force B-25 Mitchells attack railyards. B-24 Liberators attack targets of opportunity in the South China Sea. P-47 Thunderbolts and P-51 Mustangs attack troops, horses, trains, and river craft.

In Burma, Tenth Air Force sends seven P-61 Black Widow night fighters that use napalm, rockets, and cannon to attack airfields, a bridge, trucks, and other targets. P-47 Thunderbolts attack troop concentrations.

ATLANTIC: President Truman has a meeting with Foreign Minister Vyacheslav Molotov in Washington. Molotov is told in direct, blunt language that the United States has pledged itself to adhere to all the Yalta agreements and expects the USSR to do the same.

ETO: During the night Eighth Air Force sends one B-17 and 12 B-24 Liberators to drop leaflets in France, the Netherlands, and Germany, and 14 B-24s to fly Carpetbagger missions to Denmark.

Ninth Air Force P-47 Thunderbolts and P-38 Lightnings operate in conjunction with XII Corps and fly armed reconnaissance over eastern Germany and western Czechoslovakia.

MEDITERRANEAN: Fifteenth Air Force sends more than 700 B-17s and B-24 Liberators to bomb bridges and logistics storage areas in Italy. P-38 Lightnings and P-51 Mustangs bomb and strafe rail and road bridges, highways, trains and vehicles, and other targets of opportunity.

ITALY: The 1st Armored Division, the 6th South African Armored Division, and the 88th Infantry Division reach the Po River. All organized resistance south of the Po River ends as Eighth Army arrives to link with Fifth Army.

Twelfth Air Force B-25 Mitchells bomb road bridges. A-20 Havocs and P-47 Thunderbolts support Fifth Army ground forces. During the night A-20 Havocs and A-26 Invaders attack river crossing sites, a marshaling yard, airfields, vehicles, trains, and targets of opportunity in the Po River valley.

SOUTHWEST PACIFIC AREA: In the Philippines, Far East Air Force P-47 Thunderbolts and P-38 Lightnings support ground forces on Luzon, attacking numerous artillery positions, logistics storage areas, and general targets of opportunity.

In China, B-24 Liberators bomb a military depot at Shanghai and shipping in Yulin harbor on Hainan Island.

B-24 Liberators bomb the naval base at Saigon, in French Indochina.

B-25 Mitchells attack railyards, P-51s attack an airfield, and P-38s attack targets of opportunity on Formosa.

FEAF B-24 Liberators bomb airfields at Sepinggang and Jesselton, and P-38 Lightnings drop napalm on Tarakan Island targets. Other B-24s fly a shipping sweep over the Makassar Strait and damage several small vessels.

U.S. submarine *Besugo* sinks German submarine *U-183* in the Java Sea. (In 1943, the Germans had begun deploying U-boats to the Far East to operate out of Japanese bases in Indonesia.)

Navy PB4Y Privateers launch automatic homing missiles at Japanese shipping off Balikpapan, Borneo. This is the first use of this type of missile in combat.

PACIFIC, OKINAWA: Elements of the 1st Battalion of the 105th Infantry Regiment of the 27th Infantry Division battle to the top of the Urasoe-Mura Escarpment.

CENTRAL PACIFIC: Seventh Air Force sends 13 B-24 Liberators from Guam to bomb Marcus Island.

April 24

CBI: In China, Fourteenth Air Force B-24 Liberators damage a vessel at Bakli Bay on Hainan Island, and B-25 Mitchells attack railroad targets of opportunity and a bridge. P-51 Mustangs, P-61 Black Widow night fighters, and P-40s attack rivercraft, railroad targets, trucks, bridges, troops, horses, and other targets of opportunity.

In French Indochina, B-24s bomb railyards and attack targets of opportunity in the South China Sea.

In Burma, Tenth Air Force sends P-47 Thunderbolts and P-38 Lightnings to attack troop concentrations, storage areas, vehicles, and targets of opportunity.

ATLANTIC: Stalin replies to the Truman-Churchill letter, complaining that the USSR has every right to install a friendly government in a country that is vital to Soviet security. He points out that the USSR made no complaint when the pro-Western governments of Belgium and Greece were established.

German submarine *U-546* torpedoes and sinks destroyer escort USS *Frederick C. Davis* off Newfoundland. Eight other destroyer escorts converge to sink the U-boat.

ETO: Seventh Army crosses the Danube and captures Ulm.

The zones of occupation for Germany are allocated. The United States has southwest Germany. Berlin is in the Soviet Zone, but the city itself will be divided into occupation zones.

During the night Eighth Air Force sends 11 B-24 Liberators to drop leaflets in France, the Netherlands, and Germany.

Ninth Air Force P-47 Thunderbolts and P-38 Lightnings operate in conjunction with the XII Corps and XX Corps.

MEDITERRANEAN: Fifteenth Air Force sends more than 700 B-17s and B-24 Liberators to bomb road and rail bridges in Austria and Italy, motor transport and marshaling yards in Italy, and a logistics storage area.

ITALY: The 10th Mountain Division's Po River beachhead is expanded as the remainder of the division crosses on a pontoon bridge. There is no opposition.

General Truscott orders all divisions of Fifth Army to cross the river as soon as possible. Truscott wants to reach Verona and cut off the escape of German units in the west of Italy. Units of II and IV Corps begin to find expedient means to cross the river in response to Truscott's orders.

Twelfth Air Force B-25 Mitchells bomb rail lines and Po River crossings. A-20 Havocs and P-47 Thunderbolts attack roads, vehicles, and rail lines along the Po River.

During the night A-20 Havocs and A-26 Invaders attack airfields, marshaling yards, vehicles, and other targets of opportunity in the Po River valley and northern Italy.

SOUTHWEST PACIFIC AREA: In the Philippines, Far East Air Force A-20 Havocs, P-38 Lightnings, and P-47 Thunderbolts support ground forces on Luzon Island.

A-20 Havocs attack sugar refineries on Formosa, while B-24 Liberators bomb other targets on the island.

FEAF B-24 Liberators bomb Tabanio and Miri in Borneo.

PACIFIC: Twentieth Air Force sends 101 B-29s to bomb the aircraft production facility at Tachikawa. Aircrews report 16 Japanese aircraft kills; five B-29s are lost.

PACIFIC, OKINAWA: An attack by units of the 96th and 7th Infantry Divisions leads to advances of over 1,000 yards. The center and left flank of the main defensive line has been quietly and carefully abandoned.

CENTRAL PACIFIC: The headquarters of the 506th Fighter Group and the 457th, 458th, and 462nd Fighter Squadrons arrive at North Field, Iwo Jima, from the United States with P-51 Mustangs.

April 25

CBI: In China, Fourteenth Air Force B-25 Mitchells and P-47 Thunderbolts damage a bridge and knock out an antiaircraft position, while over 50 P-47 Thunderbolts and P-51 Mustangs attack river, road, and rail targets, troops, horses, and buildings.

In French Indochina B-24s bomb railyards.

In Burma, Tenth Air Force sends 16 P-38 Lightnings to attack truck parks, fuel storage areas, and logistics support sites, while 20 other P-38s attack troops.

ATLANTIC: The San Francisco Conference opens to create a new international organization that will be called the United Nations.

ETO: A patrol led by First Lieutenant Albert L. Kotzebue from the 3rd Battalion, 273rd Infantry Regiment, 69th Infantry Division, V Corps, First U.S. Army, meets elements of the 175th Rifle Regiment of the Soviet 58th Guards Division, 34th Corps, at Torgau on the Elbe River, commanded by Lieutenant Colonel Alexander T. Gardiev. As a result of the linkup, the Elbe-Mulde rivers become the temporary operational boundary between Soviet and U.S. forces as agreed upon by the Soviet High Command and the CCS.

The XX Corps of Third Army establishes a bridgehead on the Danube River at Regensburg and attacks south. XII Corps attacks north.

Eighth Air Force sends nearly 600 B-17s and B-24 Liberators escorted by nearly 500 P-51 Mustangs to bomb airfields, industrial targets, rail bridges, and marshaling yards in southeast Germany and Czechoslovakia. A total of six bombers are lost and 204 damaged. Aircrews report one confirmed kill and one probable. Aircrew casualties are nine wounded and 42 missing. Fighter pilots report one confirmed kill in the air. A group of 19 P-51s fly a sweep of the Prague-Linz area. Pilots report one probable kill in the air. One P-51 is lost, and the pilot is reported missing.

During the night 11 B-24s drop leaflets over France, Germany, and the Netherlands. A total of 12 B-24s and one A-26 Invader fly a Carpetbagger mission to Norway. Seven aircraft complete the mission.

Ninth Air Force sends nearly 300 A-20 Havocs, A-26 Invaders, and B-26 Marauders to attack an ordnance depot and airfields. P-47 and P-38 fighters operate in conjunction with XII Corps and XX Corps.

Navy PB4Y Privateers based in England sink German submarine *U-1107* in the English Channel.

MEDITERRANEAN: Fifteenth Air Force sends more than 400 B-17s and B-24 Liberators escorted by P-38 Lightnings and P-51 Mustangs to bomb railyards and marshaling yards in Austria.

ITALY: General Truscott orders II Corps to advance to the Adige River between Verona and Legnano. The IV Corps is to advance north to Verona, destroy or capture German forces in northwest Italy, and use the 1st Brazilian Infantry Division and the 34th and 92nd Infantry Divisions to attack west toward the Italian-Swiss border. Two combat commands of the 1st Armored Division are to support the western attack. One combat command will support the 10th Mountain Division and the 85th Infantry Division toward Verona. The 1st Battalion of the 85th Mountain Infantry Regiment reaches the airfield near Mantua. Italian partisans control most of the area.

The 351st Infantry Regiment of the 88th Infantry Division crosses the Po River and moves rapidly to occupy Verona.

Twelfth Air Force B-25 Mitchells bomb rail and road traffic and bridges to block the German retreat in the northern Po Valley. P-47 Thunderbolts of the XXII Tactical Air Command attack rail lines, bridges, and roads in the Po River valley and support Fifth Army ground forces.

During the night A-20 Havocs and A-26 Invaders attack river crossing sites and vehicles in the Po River Valley and along the Adige River.

First Lieutenant Raymond L. Knight, 350th Fighter Group, Twelfth Air Force, volunteers to lead two other P-47 Thunderbolts against the strongly defended airfield at Ghedi in the northern Po Valley. Knight takes the first pass on the airfield, skimming low over the ground to locate targets as antiaircraft fire bursts around him. Informing his flight, he then leads the attack, destroying five aircraft himself while the other P-47s destroy two more on the ground. Returning to base, Knight volunteers to lead three other P-47s in an aerial reconnaissance of Bergamo airfield. Again Knight makes the first pass and locates a German squadron under camouflage. Although his fighter is damaged, he leads the attack and makes 10 deliberate passes to destroy lucrative targets, including six fully loaded enemy bombers and two fighters. His fellow pilots account for four other bombers and one fighter. The following morning, he again leads three other aircraft against the Bergamo airfield, destroying three bombers on the ground. Knight's P-47 is badly damaged by antiaircraft fire and, rather than abandon the plane, he attempts to bring it back to base. He crashes en route over the Apennines. For his exceptional bravery and skill, First Lieutenant Knight will receive the Medal of Honor.

SOUTHWEST PACIFIC AREA: In the Philippines, Far East Air Force B-24 Liberators bomb Balete Pass and bridges on Luzon. B-25 Mitchells, A-20 Havocs, P-47 Thunderbolts, and P-38 Lightnings attack Japanese troop positions and bridges in the Cagayan Valley.

B-24s bomb the harbor at Saigon, French Indochina.

U.S. submarine *Cod* torpedoes and sinks a Japanese minesweeper off Formosa.

FEAF B-24 Liberators on an anti-shipping sweep sink a Japanese vessel in the Makassar Strait.

Private First Class David M. Gonzales of A Company, 127th Infantry, 32nd Infantry Division, is pinned down by Japanese fire on the Villa Verde Trail in Luzon. A 500-pound bomb explodes, burying five men. With the volume of fire making it extremely dangerous to move, Gonzales nevertheless moves to the area where the men are buried. Enemy fire kills his company commander, who was also coming to the aid of the buried men. Gonzales reaches the spot and begins digging with his hands and an entrenching tool as Japanese bullets hit all around him. As he digs each man out, he stands to assist them, heedless of the enemy fire. As the third man is brought out, Gonzales is hit and mortally wounded. For his courage under fire and his willingness to risk his own life to save the lives of his comrades, Private First Class Gonzales will receive the Medal of Honor.

PACIFIC: Brigadier General Joseph Smith takes command of Headquarters, XX Bomber Command.

PACIFIC, OKINAWA: The 165th Infantry Regiment of the 27th Infantry Division gains control of a ridge at Item Pocket, allowing the Americans to seize the defenses along the seaside. The 27th will continue to clear the enemy from the position over the next week. The 96th and 7th Infantry Divisions are stopped before formidable positions at Conical Hill and Kochi Ridge.

High-speed transport sinks Japanese submarine *RO-109* south of Okinawa.

NEW GUINEA: FEAF B-24 Liberators bomb the airfields on Celebes Island.

April 26

CARIBBEAN: Sixth Air Force sends the B-24 Liberators of the 29th Bombardment Squadron (Heavy), VI Bomber Command, from Rio Hato, Panama, to the Galápagos Islands.

CBI: In China, Fourteenth Air Force sends 10 B-25 Mitchells and four P-47 Thunderbolts to attack bridges near Wuchang. Over 80 P-40s and P-51 Mustangs attack troops, horses, road and rail transport, tanks, gun positions, and targets of opportunity in southern and eastern China.

In French Indochina, B-24s bomb the docks at Hongay.

In Burma, 30 P-38 Lightnings and P-47 Thunderbolts of Tenth Air Force attack troop concentrations.

ETO: During the night Eighth Air Force sends six B-24 Liberators to drop leaflets in France, the Netherlands, and Germany. Two B-24s fly Carpetbagger missions.

Ninth Air Force sends 125 A-20 Havocs, A-26 Invaders, and B-26 Marauders to attack an airfield and support XII Corps as it crosses into Austria and XX Corps as it crosses the Danube River at Regensburg. P-47 and P-38 fighters report 19 German fighters shot down.

MEDITERRANEAN: Fifteenth Air Force sends more than 100 B-17s and B-24 Liberators escorted by P-38 Lightnings and P-51 Mustangs to bomb marshaling yards in Austria and a motor transport depot in Italy. P-38s dive-bomb rail lines and road bridges.

ITALY: Twelfth Air Force B-25 Mitchells bomb rail and road bridges. A-20 Havocs and P-47 Thunderbolts attack vehicles, rail lines, bridges, and roads in the Po River valley and support Fifth Army ground forces.

SOUTHWEST PACIFIC AREA: On Luzon in the I Corps area the 33rd and 37th Infantry Divisions, supported by tanks and artillery and air support, capture Baguio.

In the Eighth Army area the 164th Infantry Regiment of the Americal Division (minus one battalion on Bohol Island) lands on Negros Island.

In the Philippines, Far East Air Force B-25 Mitchells, A-20 Havocs, P-38 Lightnings, and P-47 Thunderbolts support ground forces on Luzon. B-24 Liberators along with marine aircraft attack several targets on Cebu Island.

B-25s attack a sugar refinery and nearby targets of opportunity on Formosa. P-38 Lightnings on a sweep also attack targets of opportunity.

B-24s bomb Shanghai, China.

FEAF B-24 Liberators attack Miri airfield, and B-25 Mitchells and P-38 Lightnings attack targets on Tarakan Island.

U.S. submarine *Perch* is damaged by depth charges off North Borneo but remains on patrol.

PACIFIC: Twentieth Air Force sends nearly 200 B-29s, some escorted by P-51 Mustangs of VII Fighter Command, from Iwo Jima, to bomb airfields at Usa, Oita, Saeki, Tomitaka, Imabari, Nittagahara, Miyazaki, Kanoya, Kokubu, and Miyakonojo, Japan.

PACIFIC, OKINAWA: The 105th and 106th Infantry Regiments of the 27th Infantry Division attack into the Urasoe-Mura Escarpment, while the 165th Infantry Regiment continues to clear Item Pocket. The 17th and 32nd Infantry Regiments of the 7th Infantry Division are stopped at Kochi Ridge. The 383rd Infantry Regiment of the 96th Infantry Division gains some ground on the Maeda escarpment but is driven off by counterattacks.

CENTRAL PACIFIC: Seventh Air Force sends 13 B-24 Liberators from Guam Island to bomb Truk.

April 27

ALEUTIANS: Eleventh Air Force sends six B-24 Liberators to drop fragmentation bombs on the Kataoka naval base on Shimushu Island in the Kuriles.

CBI: Fourteenth Air Force B-25 Mitchells and P-40 and P-51 Mustangs attack bridges, troop positions, villages and town areas, gun emplacements, and river, road, and rail traffic throughout southern and eastern China.

In Burma, 37 P-38 Lightnings and P-47 Thunderbolts of Tenth Air Force attack troop concentrations.

ETO: First Army captures Straubing and Kempten in Bavaria.

Eighth Air Force is notified it will no longer receive P-51, B-17, and B-24 replacement aircraft.

Ninth Air Force P-47s and P-38 Lightnings fly sweeps, conduct armed reconnaissance, attack airfields, and fly air cover for XII Corps as the 11th Armored Division reaches the German-Czech border. Fighters operate in conjunction with XX
Corps as it takes the surrender of Regensburg and expands its bridgehead over the
Danube River.

ITALY: The 473rd Infantry Regiment of the 92nd Infantry Division, Fifth Army,
enters Genoa.

Twelfth Air Force B-25 Mitchells bomb rail and road traffic and bridges. A-20
Havocs and P-47 Thunderbolts attack rail lines, gun positions, vehicles, and rail cars
in support of Fifth Army ground forces. Fighters also operate in support of the 1st
Armored Division.

SOUTHWEST PACIFIC AREA: In the Eighth Army area, the 24th Infantry Division
advances quickly along Highway 1 on Mindanao and captures Digos, surprising
Japanese defenders who expected an attack from the sea at Davao Gulf. The 31st
Infantry Division begins moving north toward Macajalar Bay, led by the 124th
Infantry Regiment.

In the Philippines, Far East Air Force B-25 Mitchells attack Japanese installations, A-20 Havocs attack towns, and A-20s, P-38 Lightnings, and P-47 Thunderbolts attack targets near Manila and the Legaspi area.

PACIFIC: Twentieth Air Force sends 109 B-29s to hit airfields at Izumi, Miyazaki,
Kokubu, Miyakonojo, Kanoya, and Kushira on Kyushu Island, Japan. Two B-29s
are lost.

A mine dropped in late March by Twentieth Air Force B-29s sinks a cargo vessel
west of Shimonoseki Strait.

PACIFIC, OKINAWA: Kamikazes damage a destroyer, a destroyer escort, and a high-
speed transport off Okinawa. A heavy cruiser is damaged by shore battery fire. A
kamikaze hits a U.S. freighter and sinks it.

CENTRAL PACIFIC: Seventh Air Force sends 11 B-24 Liberators from Guam to bomb
Woleai Atoll.

NEW GUINEA: FEAF B-24 Liberators bomb Mandai airfield on Celebes Island and
other B-24s attack Surabaya, Java.

B-24 Liberators attack Jesselton airfield and B-25 Mitchells bomb Tarakan
Island in Borneo.

April 28

CBI: In China, Fourteenth Air Force B-25 Mitchells bomb an airfield, a bridge, and
railyards. Nearly 80 P-40s and P-51 Mustangs attack troops, airfields, logistics storage facilities, railroad targets, river craft, trucks, and defensive positions in southern
and eastern China. One B-24 reports sinking a cargo ship in the South China Sea.

In Burma, Tenth Air Force P-38 Lightnings attack a cavalry regiment and logistics sites, while six other P-38s attack a bivouac area. P-47 Thunderbolts attack
troops, artillery positions, trucks, elephants, and carts along and behind the enemy
lines.

ETO: General Marshall sends the following message to General Eisenhower concerning whether United States forces should enter Czechoslovakia and capture

Prague ahead of the Soviets. "Personally and aside from all logistic, tactical or strategic implications, I would be loath to hazard American lives for purely political purposes."

The XXI Corps of Seventh Army captures Augsburg. The VI Corps crosses into Austria.

Seventh Army occupies Augsburg, Regensburg, and Ingolstadt.

Adolf Hitler marries his mistress, Eva Braun, and appoints Admiral Karl Dönitz as his successor.

ITALY: The 88th Infantry Division of II Corps occupies Vicenza, but like most areas at this time, Italian partisan forces control the towns and cities.

Tanks of the 1st Armored Division enter Milan. The 34th Infantry Division and the Italian Legnano Combat Group are ordered to advance to Brescia to block passes out of the Po Valley.

Task Force Darby meets strong resistance from German units along the eastern shore of Lake Garda. Task Force Darby, consisting of the 86th Mountain Infantry Regiment and the 13th Tank Battalion with detachments of artillery, engineers, tank destroyers, and a medical support, is under the command of Colonel William O. Darby, who previously commanded Rangers in Italy.

A-20 Havocs and P-47 Thunderbolts of the XXII Tactical Air Command attack roads and vehicles in support of Fifth Army ground forces.

SOUTHWEST PACIFIC AREA: In the Eighth Army area, the 164th Infantry Regiment of the Americal Division encounters Japanese defenders on Negros Island near Dumaguete. The Americans will fight the Japanese for a month.

In the Philippines, Far East Air Force B-25 Mitchells, A-20 Havocs, P-38 Lightnings, and P-47 Thunderbolts attack targets throughout Luzon.

B-24 Liberators bomb several targets on Formosa.

In French Indochina, FEAF B-25 Mitchells and P-38 Lightnings bomb Japanese shipping in Saigon harbor, sinking a tanker and six small ships.

FEAF B-24 Liberators bomb Masamba, Malimpoeng, and Mandai airfields on Celebes Island. B-24s attack Kuching, while B-25 Mitchells and P-38 Lightnings attack Tarakan Island and targets of opportunity along the Sarawak coast in Borneo.

PACIFIC: Twentieth Air Force sends 119 B-29s to attack airfields at Kushira, Kanoya, Miyakonojo, Kokubu, Miyazaki, and Izumi on Kyushu Island, Japan. Aircrews report 14 Japanese fighters shot down. Five B-29s are lost.

U.S. submarine *Sennet* torpedoes and sinks a Japanese cable layer off southern Honshu, Japan. U.S. submarine *Springer* torpedoes and sinks a Japanese submarine chaser escorting a landing ship west of Kyushu; U.S. submarine *Trepang* will later sink the landing ship.

A mine dropped by Twentieth Air Force B-29s sinks a cargo vessel at the west end of Shimonoseki Strait.

PACIFIC, OKINAWA: The 27th Infantry Division opens Highway 1 to traffic after clearing most of Item Pocket on the right flank of the American line.

The hospital ship *Comfort* is hit by a kamikaze, killing 30 and wounding 33. Kamikaze damage four destroyers and a high-speed minesweeper off Okinawa.

Tenth Army commander Lieutenant General Simon B. Buckner decides not to conduct an amphibious landing at Minatoga in southern Okinawa to outflank the Japanese defensive line. Instead, he decides to replace the 27th Infantry Division with the 1st Marine Division to maintain the 27th Division for garrison duties on the island and to clear Japanese troops from the northern section of the island. The 96th Infantry Division will be replaced by the 77th Infantry Division, and the 6th Marine Division will take the far left flank of the line. The marine divisions will be under the operational control of Major General Roy S. Geiger as commander of III Amphibious Corps.

CENTRAL PACIFIC: Seventh Air Force sends 12 B-24 Liberators from Guam to bomb Truk Atoll during the early morning hours, and 12 more B-24s attack again in the afternoon. A total of 20 P-47 Thunderbolts from Saipan sweep Truk, strafing small vessels and airfields on Param and Moen Islands.

April 29

ALEUTIANS: Eleventh Air Force sends six B-24 Liberators to hit the Kataoka naval base on Shimushu Island in the Kuriles using radar to locate bomb release points.

CBI: In China, Fourteenth Air Force B-25 Mitchells and P-47 Thunderbolts bomb a railyard. P-40s and P-51 Mustangs attack troops, airfields, railroad targets, and trucks in southern and eastern China.

In Burma, Tenth Air Force P-47 Thunderbolts attack an airfield and strafe troops and horses.

ETO: The U.S. XVIII Airborne Corps, under the operational control of Montgomery's 21st Army Group, crosses the Elbe River.

Elements of the 157th Infantry Regiment of the 45th Infantry Division and elements of the 222nd Infantry Regiment of the 42nd Infantry Division arrive at Dachau concentration camp, where about 23,000 inmates await liberation. Another 2,300 inmates from Buchenwald are found in railroad cars outside the camp—all dead.

Eighth Air Force sends eight B-17s to drop leaflets in France, the Netherlands, and Germany.

Ninth Air Force P-47 Thunderbolts and P-38 Lightnings fly patrols and airfield cover, attack special targets, fly armed reconnaissance over eastern Germany and western Czechoslovakia, and support XII Corps and XX Corps.

MEDITERRANEAN: German officers representing General Heinrich von Vietinghoff's Army Group C, meet with Allied command representatives in Caserta and sign a document of surrender effective at 1200 on May 2.

Fifteenth Air Force P-51 Mustangs fly armed reconnaissance over northeast Italy. Fighters bomb and strafe various targets of opportunity, including vehicles, motor transport, and two aircraft on the ground.

ITALY: Task Force Darby, supported by elements of the 85th and 87th Mountain Infantry Regiments, clears German positions around Lake Garda. Colonel Darby is wounded by an artillery shell and dies later in the day.

Twelfth Air Force A-20 Havocs and P-47 Thunderbolts attack retreating German troops and vehicles and attack roads and airfields.

SOUTHWEST PACIFIC AREA: In the Philippines, Far East Air Force A-20 Havocs, P-38 Lightnings, and P-47 Thunderbolts attack troop concentrations, logistics storage areas, pillboxes, gun positions, vehicles, and other targets on Luzon.

P-38 Lightnings sweep French Indochina and strafe an airfield.

FEAF B-24 Liberators on an anti-shipping sweep sink a Japanese cargo vessel in Makassar Strait.

FEAF B-24 Liberators attack airfields on Celebes Island.

In Borneo, B-24s bomb an airfield, while B-25 Mitchells bomb Tarakan Island.

U.S. submarine *Besugo* torpedoes and sinks a Japanese guardboat southeast of Borneo.

U.S. submarine *Bream* torpedoes and sinks a German minesweeper depot ship off Borneo.

PACIFIC: Twentieth Air Force sends 111 B-29s to bomb Miyazaki, Miyakonojo, Kokubu, Kanoya, and Kushira airfields on Kyushu Island, Japan. Aircrews report 30 Japanese aircraft shot down. Two B-29s are lost.

U.S. submarine *Cero* torpedoes and sinks a Japanese cargo ship off eastern Honshu, Japan.

PACIFIC, OKINAWA: The 307th Infantry Regiment of the 77th Infantry Division attacks the Maeda Escarpment on the eastern end of the Urasoe-Mura Escarpment. The 381st Infantry Regiment of the 96th Division has failed to make any progress and has lost over 1,000 casualties before being relieved by the 77th Division.

Two destroyers are seriously damaged in kamikaze attacks. More than 100 sailors are killed and wounded.

Kamikazes damage two destroyers and two light minelayers off Okinawa. TBM Avengers from escort carrier USS *Tulagi* sink Japanese submarine *I-44* southeast of Okinawa.

CENTRAL PACIFIC: Seventh Air Force sends 20 P-47 Thunderbolts from Saipan on a sweep of Truk, hitting airfields, defenses, and gun positions. Some fighters use rockets against targets. A total of 24 B-24 Liberators from Guam conduct a follow-on attack on Truk. Another 20 B-24s, operating in two forces, bomb airfield installations on Marcus Island.

During the night Japanese aircraft from Truk attack the naval base at Manus, Admiralty Islands, dropping torpedoes on dock sections that they think are aircraft carriers.

April 30

CBI: Fourteenth Air Force B-25 Mitchells and P-47 Thunderbolts attack railyards. P-47s, P-51 Mustangs, and P-40s attack troops, defensive positions, bridges, rail lines, and targets of opportunity in southern and eastern China.

ATLANTIC: Two destroyer escorts and a frigate sink German submarine *U-548* off Virginia. A PBY Catalina sinks German submarine *U-1055* west of France.

ETO: The XV Corps and XXI Corps of Seventh Army occupy Munich.

The 83rd Infantry Division of XIX Corps of Ninth Army encounters Soviet forces at Apollensdorf. At Torgau, Lieutenant General Courtney Hodges, commander of First Army, meets Colonel-General Zhadov, commander of the 1st Ukrainian Front.

Adolf Hitler, führer and chancellor of the German Reich and supreme commander of the German armed forces, commits suicide in his bunker in Berlin as Soviet troops close in.

Eighth Air Force sends six B-17s to drop leaflets over the Netherlands and France.

Ninth Air Force P-47 Thunderbolts and P-38 Lightnings fly in coordination with XII Corps and XX Corps.

ITALY: General Lucian K. Truscott transfers operational control of the 85th Infantry Division from IV Corps to II Corps. The 85th now moves north into the Alps to make a link up with Seventh Army. The 88th Infantry Division advances up the Brenta River, seeking the remnants of the German Fourteenth Army.

The 91st Infantry Division reaches Treviso, north of Venice. The 6th South African Armored Division begins moving west as a garrison force for the city of Milan.

Twelfth Air Force P-47 Thunderbolts attack guns, vehicles, and other targets of opportunity. During the night A-20 Havocs and A-26 Invaders attack motor transport.

SOUTHWEST PACIFIC AREA: In the Philippines, Far East Air Force B-25 Mitchells, A-20 Havocs, P-38 Lightnings, and P-47 Thunderbolts support ground forces on Luzon and Negros Islands. B-24 Liberators attack the Davao area on Mindanao Island.

On Formosa, B-24s attack fuel storage areas and airfields while B-25 Mitchells attack Taito. P-38 Lightnings provide escort and attack numerous targets of opportunity. P-51 Mustangs bomb Okayama airfield.

FEAF B-24 Liberators bomb Malimpoeng Airfield on Celebes Island. P-38 Lightnings attack Tarakan Island and B-24s bomb Manggar airfield on Borneo.

A U.S. destroyer is damaged by a mine off Borneo.

Thirteenth Air Force B-24 Liberators sink a Japanese transport in Balikpapan Bay in the Makassar Strait.

PACIFIC: Twentieth Air Force sends 69 B-29s escorted by 104 P-51 Mustangs to attack the Tachikawa air depot. Another 56 B-29s attack airfields at Kokubu, Oita, Tomitaka, Saeki, and Kanoya on Kyushu Island, and bomb the city of Hamamatsu. Aircrews report 10 Japanese aircraft shot down.

U.S. submarine *Trepang* attacks a Japanese convoy and sinks a transport in the Yellow Sea.

PACIFIC, OKINAWA: The 307th Infantry Regiment of the 77th Infantry Division gains a precarious foothold on the top of the Maeda Escarpment and battles fierce Japanese assaults to hold the ground and, yard by yard, gain control by attacking the caves on the back side of the escarpment with grenades and demolitions.

Kamikazes damage a destroyer and a minelayer off Okinawa. A kamikaze damages a U.S. freighter.

CENTRAL PACIFIC: Seventh Air Force sends 20 P-47 Thunderbolts from Saipan to attack the seaplane base, an airfield, a barracks, a radio station, and targets of opportunity on Truk. This is followed by 24 B-24 Liberators from Guam bombing airfields on Truk.

More than 20 B-24 Liberators operating in two separate waves bomb air instal-lations on Marcus Island.

The headquarters of the 318th Fighter Group and the P-38 Lightnings of the 19th, 73rd, and 333rd Fighter Squadrons redeploy from Saipan to Ie Shima Island, Ryukyu Islands.

May 1

ALEUTIANS: One Eleventh Air Force B-24 flies a weather reconnaissance mission over the Kurile Islands.

CBI: Lieutenant General Albert C. Wedemeyer, commanding general of U.S. forces in the China theater, names Lieutenant General George E. Stratemeyer as the com-mander of Army Air Forces, China theater, responsible for bringing the headquar-ters of both the Tenth and Fourteenth Air Forces under his command.

The Japanese offensive is curtailed to concentrate forces in the coastal cities of China in preparation for transfer to the home islands.

Fourteenth Air Force B-25 Mitchells and P-51s attack bridges, antiaircraft posi-tions, and locomotives near the bridges, gun emplacements, and trucks in southern and eastern China.

ETO: The XX Corps of the Third Army arrives at Braunau.

Grand Admiral Karl Dönitz, commander in chief of the German navy, receives a message from Berlin notifying him of the death of Adolf Hitler and his appointment as president of Germany.

Eighth Air Force sends 396 B-17s to air-drop over 700 tons of food supplies in the area of The Hague and Rotterdam in the Netherlands. During the night four B-24 Liberators drop leaflets in Germany.

Ninth Air Force A-26 Invaders bomb an ammunition plant at Stod, Czecho-slovakia. P-38 Lightnings and P-47 Thunderbolts of the IX Tactical Air Command escort the bombers and conduct patrols over Germany. P-47s of the XIX Tactical Air Command fly patrols and armed reconnaissance over eastern Germany, western Czechoslovakia, and Austria. Pilots conduct dive-bomb attacks on Berchtesgaden (a favorite assembly point of Nazi Party members and the location of the vacation home of Adolf Hitler) and support XII Corps and XX Corps.

MEDITERRANEAN: Fifteenth Air Force sends 27 B-17s to bomb the main station and marshaling yard at Salzburg, Austria. P-38 Lightnings and P-51 Mustangs fly recon-naissance and reconnaissance escort missions.

ITALY: The 442nd RCT occupies Turin, capturing 3,000 prisoners. Since the beginning of the Italian offensive on April 9, Allied units have captured 145,000 prisoners.

During the night Twelfth Air Force A-20 Havocs and A-26 Invaders bomb tar-gets of opportunity in northern Italy. P-47 Thunderbolts attack motor and horse-drawn vehicles in northeast Italy as Fifth Army approaches the Brenner Pass.

SOUTHWEST PACIFIC AREA: In the Philippines, Far East Air Force B-25 Mitchells, A-20 Havocs, P-38 Lightnings, and P-47 Thunderbolts support ground forces on Luzon and Negros Islands.

B-25s bomb a sugar refinery and the town of Kagi on Formosa.

FEAF B-24 Liberators support Australian landings on Tarakan Island and bomb Tawau, and B-25 Mitchells attack airfields at Jesselton on Tarakan Island.

Vice Admiral Daniel E. Barbey, commanding a naval attack force, lands Australian troops on Tarakan Island, Borneo. Naval gunfire and aircraft provide support for the landing.

PACIFIC: U.S. submarine *Bowfin* torpedoes and sinks a Japanese gunboat southeast of Hokkaido, Japan. U.S. submarine *Sennet* torpedoes and damages a Japanese coastal defense vessel off southern Honshu, Japan.

Navy PBM Mariner patrol bombers sink a Japanese cargo vessel off western Korea.

PACIFIC, OKINAWA: The 1st Marine Division replaces the 27th Infantry Division on the right flank of the American line.

CENTRAL PACIFIC: Seventh Air Force sends 16 B-24 Liberators from Guam to bomb the airfield on Marcus Island, while another 10 B-24s attack air installations at Truk. During the night B-24s conduct individual snooper (radar-assisted bomb release) attacks on airfields on Param and Moen Islands of Truk.

May 2

CBI: British paratroopers and elements of XVth Corps land at the mouth of the Rangoon River.

Fourteenth Air Force B-25 Mitchells, P-40s, and P-51s attack trucks, tanks, logistics sites, horses, troops, and artillery in southern and eastern China.

Five B-24 Liberators mine areas of the Yangtze River.

ETO: The XII Corps of Third Army reports that the Danube has been cleared of enemy forces to Passau. The III Corps reports it is at Wasserburg.

Grand Admiral Dönitz sends representatives to Field Marshal Montgomery's headquarters with an offer to surrender all German forces in northwestern Germany, Denmark, and occupied German islands.

Eighth Air Force sends 401 B-17s to airdrop 767 tons of food supplies in the Netherlands. Eight B-17s, escorted by nine P-51 Mustangs, drop leaflets in France, the Netherlands, and Germany.

Ninth Air Force P-38 Lightnings and P-47 Thunderbolts patrol the Third Army front in Austria and Czechoslovakia.

ITALY: Field Marshal Albert Kesselring, appointed by Dönitz as commander in chief of southern Germany, authorizes the cease-fire order for Army Group C. The Germans broadcast the order at 1400, the Allies at 1830.

SOUTHWEST PACIFIC AREA: On Luzon, elements of the 1st Cavalry Division link with the 158th RCT at Naga, completing the sweep of the Bicol Peninsula.

In the Philippines, Far East Air Force B-24 Liberators and P-51 Mustangs attack Japanese positions near Ipo Dam, and B-25 Mitchells, A-20 Havocs, and P-47 Thunderbolts attack targets in the Cagayan Valley on Luzon.

FEAF B-25 Mitchells continue support for Australian troops on Tarakan Island and bomb Kudat airfield along with navy aircraft.

Three motor minesweepers are sunk by shore batteries off Tarakan, Borneo. Another motor minesweeper is damaged by a mine.

PACIFIC: U.S. submarine *Raton* attacks a Japanese convoy, sinking a cargo ship southeast of the Shantung Peninsula in the Yellow Sea. U.S. submarine *Springer* torpedoes and sinks a Japanese escort vessel in the Yellow Sea.

PACIFIC, OKINAWA: Private First Class William A. Foster, a rifleman with the 3rd Battalion, 1st Marine Regiment, 1st Marine Division, is occupying a fighting position with another marine on Okinawa after a successful attack. Japanese infiltrators begin throwing hand grenades into the marine positions and one lands near Corporal Foster. He covers the grenade with his body to protect his fellow marine and, though mortally wounded, hands grenades to his comrade to help him defend the position. For his courage and self-sacrifice, Private First Class Foster will receive the Medal of Honor.

Hospital Apprentice Second Class Robert E. Bush, serving as a corpsman with a rifle company or the 2nd Battalion, 5th Marines, is administering blood plasma to a wounded marine when Japanese troops attack the marines' position. Staying by the wounded marine, Bush holds a plasma bottle in one hand and his .45-caliber pistol in the other, firing at the Japanese as they advance toward him. Out of ammunition, he picks up a discarded carbine and continues to protect his wounded patient, killing six enemy soldiers despite several wounds, including the loss of an eye. Bush refuses medical treatment until the marine he has treated is evacuated first. Bush's gallant actions and dedication to duty will win him the Medal of Honor.

CENTRAL PACIFIC: Seventh Air Force sends 12 B-24 Liberators from Guam to bomb the airfield on Param Island in Truk Atoll. A total of 21 B-24s, operating in two strike groups, attack airfields and gun positions on Marcus Island. During the night nine B-24s conduct individual harassment bombings on several islands in Truk Atoll. P-51 Mustangs of the VII Fighter Command from Iwo Jima attack a radio station on Chichi Jima.

May 3

CBI: The Chinese-American staff of Alpha Force orders a counterattack against Japanese forces southeast of Chihchiang.

In China, Fourteenth Air Force sends nine B-25 Mitchells and P-40s to attack truck convoys in the Hsiang River valley and near Changsha and Hengyang, and rail lines, rail cars, and bridges. P-40s and P-51 Mustangs attack troops, town areas, ammunition storage sites, river shipping, and targets of opportunity over southern and eastern China.

Tenth Air Force's combat operations end with the capture of Rangoon on May 6. Several squadrons begin a redeployment to India. The P-47 Thunderbolts of the 88th Fighter Squadron, 80th Fighter Group, begin their redeployment from Myitkyina to India.

ETO: The U.S. XVIII Airborne Corps encounters Soviet troops at Wismar and Grabow. Innsbruck is captured. The 103rd Infantry Division of the VI Corps, Seventh Army, moves into the Brenner Pass.

The German High Command seeks to avoid surrendering to the Soviets and asks General Eisenhower for terms that allow German forces to pass into Allied lines in the West. Eisenhower replies that unconditional surrender is all he can offer.

Eighth Air Force sends 399 B-17s to air-drop 739 tons of food supplies in the Netherlands. Fourteen B-17s, escorted by 43 P-51 Mustangs, drop leaflets in Germany.

Ninth Air Force sends 132 A-26 Invaders to bomb the ammunition production facility at Stod, Czechoslovakia. P-38 Lightnings and P-47 Thunderbolts patrol the Third Army front, conduct armed reconnaissance over Germany, Austria, and Czechoslovakia, and escort the A-26 bombing run at Stod.

MEDITERRANEAN: Fifteenth Air Force B-25 Mitchells drop leaflets in northern Italy, escorted by P-38 Lightnings.

ITALY: The 85th and 88th Infantry Divisions collect German troops near the Austrian border and the Brenner Pass.

Twelfth Air Force P-47 Thunderbolts fly reconnaissance missions over northern Italy and southwest Austria to locate German forces and ensure compliance with surrender instructions. B-25 Mitchells drop leaflets in several areas where German units may not yet have received orders to surrender.

German officers representing General von Vietinghoff formally surrender the remaining Axis forces in Italy to General Mark Clark of 15th Army Group headquarters at Caserta.

SOUTHWEST PACIFIC AREA: In Eighth Army area, the 24th Infantry Division captures Davao City on Mindanao Island. The Japanese offer only limited resistance, but retreat into the abaca fields that cover the interior of the island. Here, in airless fields and among 20-foot-tall plants, the Americans will battle the Japanese in brutal close combat for more than 60 days.

Rear Admiral Albert G. Noble, commander of Naval Task Group 78.2, lands troops at Santa Cruz in Davao Gulf, Mindanao.

U.S. submarine *Lagarto* is sunk by a Japanese minelayer in the Gulf of Siam.

In the Philippines, Far East Air Force B-24 Liberators and P-51 Mustangs attack the area near Ipo Dam, while A-20 Havocs, P-38 Lightnings, and P-47 Thunderbolts support ground forces on Luzon. Saigon, French Indochina, is bombed by B-24 Liberators, which greatly damage a boatyard and oil storage areas.

FEAF B-25 Mitchells continue support of Australian ground forces on Tarakan Island in northeast Borneo. B-25s and B-24 Liberators attack other targets on Borneo and Celebes. B-24s and P-38 Lightnings bomb an airfield at Manggar and U.S. Navy aircraft attack warehouses in the Brunei Bay area.

The C-47s of the 63rd Troop Carrier Squadron, 403rd Troop Carrier Group, redeploy from Biak to Leyte Island.

PACIFIC: Twentieth Air Force sends 59 B-29s to bomb airfields at Tachiarai, Miyazaki, Miyakonojo, Kokubu, and Kanoya. Aircrews report 10 Japanese fighters shot down. One B-29 is lost. During the night 88 B-29s mine Shimonoseki Strait and the Inland Sea of Japan off Kobe and Osaka, Honshu, Japan.

U.S. submarine *Springer* torpedoes and sinks a Japanese coastal defense ship in the Yellow Sea.

PACIFIC, OKINAWA: Kamikazes sink destroyer USS *Little* and a medium landing ship off Okinawa. A destroyer and a high-speed minesweeper are damaged also. A Japanese assault demolition boat damages a light minelayer and a large support landing craft.

CENTRAL PACIFIC: Seventh Air Force sends 10 B-24 Liberators from Guam to bomb airfields and targets of opportunity on several islands of Truk. During the night eight B-24s fly individual harassment raids on Truk airfields.

May 4

ALEUTIANS: Brigadier General Isaiah Davies takes temporary command of Eleventh Air Force from Major General Davenport Johnson.

CBI: Fourteenth Air Force sends 12 B-25 Mitchells and over 180 P-40s and P-51s to attack trucks, tanks, logistics sites, horses, troops, river shipping, airfields, artillery, and targets of opportunity in southern and eastern China.

ETO: The 3rd Infantry Division of XV Corps clears Hitler's compound at Berchtesgaden and occupies Salzburg. At Vipiteno, near near the south entrance of Brenner Pass, the 103rd Infantry Division makes contact with the 349th Infantry Regiment of the 88th Infantry Division of Fifth Army, linking the European and Mediterranean theaters. The 6th Army Group has captured 900,000 prisoners.

At Field Marshal Montgomery's headquarters on Lüneburg Heath, a German delegation led by Grossadmiral Hans Georg von Friedeburg, commander in chief of the Kriegsmarine, agrees to the unconditional surrender of all German land and sea forces in northwest Germany, Holland, and Denmark. A total of 1.5 million men come under control of British forces.

First Army headquarters is alerted to redeploy to the Pacific. Operational control of V Corps passes to Third Army; operational control of VII and VIII Corps passes to Ninth Army. Third Army's V Corps and XII Corps enter Czechoslovakia.

Field Marshal Montgomery at his headquarters near Lüneburg receives representatives of Grand Admiral Karl Dönitz and Field Marshal Busch, who surrender unconditionally all German forces in Holland, northwestern Germany, Schleswig-Holstein, and Denmark.

During the night Eighth Air Force sends one B-17 and eight B-24 Liberators to drop leaflets in France, the Netherlands, and Germany.

Ninth Air Force P-47 Thunderbolts and P-38 Lightnings conduct patrols and armed reconnaissance and operate in coordination with the movement of XII Corps to Linz, Austria, and support XX Corps.

ITALY: Twelfth Air Force P-47 Thunderbolts of the XXII Tactical Air Command continue flying visual reconnaissance missions in northern Italy as the 85th Infantry Division approaches the Brenner Pass.

MEDITERRANEAN: Fifth Army commander, General Mark Clark, meets with General von Senger, commander of the German XIV Panzer Corps, to work out the implementation of the surrender documents signed on April 29.

SOUTHWEST PACIFIC AREA: In the Philippines, Far East Air Force B-25 Mitchells, A-20 Havocs, P-38 Lightnings, and P-47 Thunderbolts support ground forces on Luzon and Negros Islands.

P-38 Lightnings attack Itu Aba Island, China. In French Indochina, B-24 Liberators bomb oil installations near Saigon.

Thirteenth Air Force B-24 Liberators attack Japanese shipping off the southern coast of French Indochina, sinking an auxiliary netlayer.

FEAF B-25 Mitchells and P-38 Lightnings support Australian ground forces on Tarakan Island in northeast Borneo and B-24 Liberators attack Sandakan and Kota Baru and bomb airfields on Celebes Island.

PACIFIC: Twentieth Air Force's 792nd, 793rd, and 794th Bombardment Squadrons (Very Heavy), 468th Bombardment Group (Very Heavy), begin redeploying their B-29s from India to Tinian.

Twentieth Air Force sends 47 B-29s to attack airfields at Oita, Omura, Saeki, and Matsuyama on Kyushu and Shikoku Islands, Japan. One B-29 is lost.

U.S. submarine *Cero* torpedoes and sinks a Japanese cargo ship off northeast Honshu, Japan. U.S. submarine *Trepang* torpedoes and sinks a Japanese minesweeper in the Yellow Sea. Navy PBM Mariner patrol bombers sink two Japanese merchant tankers off Pusan, Korea. Navy Mariners also damage a cargo vessel off the southern end of the Korean Peninsula. A Japanese tanker hits a mine dropped by 20th Bomber Command B-29s and sinks off Singapore.

PACIFIC, OKINAWA: The Japanese conduct a second major counterattack against the weakened American divisions battering against the Shuri defensive line. Tanks and infantry assault the center of XXIV Corps, supported by a massive artillery barrage against the 7th and 77th Infantry Divisions. The 306th Infantry Regiment of the 77th Infantry Division holds off the enemy in desperate fighting. The Japanese fail to break the American lines and lose more than 5,000 men.

Japanese aircraft attack Yontan airfield, Okinawa, and U.S. and British ships supporting the Okinawa operation. Kamikazes sink the destroyers USS *Luce* and USS *Morrison* and two medium landing craft. On board the *Luce,* nearly all of the crew is lost; the *Morrison* loses 153 crewmen. A light cruiser and an escort carrier are damaged as well. The British carrier HMS *Formidable* is damaged. A light minelayer is damaged by an oka and a minesweeper is damaged by near-misses of a kamikaze and an oka. Total losses are over 560 sailors.

CENTRAL PACIFIC: Seventh Air Force sends 22 B-24 Liberators from Angaur to bomb antiaircraft positions on Koror Island. B-24s from Guam attack the airfield on Marcus Island.

May 5

CBI: Fourteenth Air Force B-25 Mitchells attack bridges and rail lines, while P-40s and P-51s attack trucks, tanks, logistics sites, troops, and artillery in southern and eastern China.

Tenth Air Force redeploys the headquarters of the 33rd Fighter Group and the P-47 Thunderbolts of the 90th Fighter Squadron, 80th Fighter Group, to India.

ATLANTIC: German submarine *U-853* torpedoes and sinks a U.S. freighter off Rhode Island. This will be the last U.S.-flagged merchant cargo ship sunk by a U-boat in World War II.

ETO: The 11th Armored Division of the XII Corps, Third Army, captures Linz.

Near Munich, German Army Group G surrenders to General Jacob L. Devers, commander of the 6th Army Group.

German representatives of Grand Admiral Dönitz arrive in Rheims, France, to seek an arrangement that would delay surrender and allow the greatest possible number of German soldiers and refugees to reach American and British lines instead of surrendering to the Soviets. The High Command also seeks to make a separate surrender arrangement with Eisenhower in order to buy more time. General Eisenhower threatens to seal his lines to prevent any further crossing and demands that all hostilities cease within 48 hours.

Eighth Air Force sends 403 B-17s to air-drop 744 tons of food in the Netherlands.

MEDITERRANEAN: Fifteenth Air Force sends 14 P-51 Mustangs to escort C-47s dropping supplies over Yugoslavia.

ITALY: Twelfth Air Force P-47 Thunderbolts of the XXII Tactical Air Command conduct reconnaissance flights over northern Italy, southwest Austria, and over Munich, Germany. Pilots report a number of German aircraft destroyed on the ground.

SOUTHWEST PACIFIC AREA: In the Philippines, Far East Air Force A-20 Havocs, P-38 Lightnings, and P-47 Thunderbolts attack Japanese positions in the Cagayan Valley and other targets on Luzon.

On Formosa, B-24 Liberators bomb an airfield, while B-25 Mitchells and P-47 Thunderbolts attack a sugar refinery, railyards, and airfields.

B-24s bomb an airfield and an oil storage plant at Amoy, China.

FEAF B-25 Mitchells and P-38 Lightnings support Australian forces on Tarakan Island.

P-38 Lightnings attack the waterfront on the west coast and an airfield in the north. B-24 Liberators bomb the waterfront on the west coast.

Thirteenth Air Force B-24 Liberators attack Japanese shipping and shore installations at Makassar, sinking a cargo vessel.

PACIFIC: Twentieth Air Force sends 55 B-29s to bomb airfields at Oita, Tachiarai, Kanoya, and Chiran on Kyushu Island, Japan. Three B-29s are lost. Over 140 B-29s attack a naval aircraft production facility and arsenal at Kure, Japan. Aircrews report 11 Japanese fighters shot down. Two B-29s are lost. During the night 86 B-29s drop mines in Tokyo Bay, Ise Bay, and at points in the Inland Sea of Japan.

Twentieth Air Force B-29s drop mines in the Inland Sea and off Kobe, Osaka, Tokyo, and Nagoya. A cargo ship is damaged by a mine in the Inland Sea.

Navy patrol bombers sink a Japanese cargo ship in the Yellow Sea.

PACIFIC, OKINAWA: In the early morning hours a second Japanese counterattack is aimed at the center of the American line. The 306th Infantry Regiment of the 77th Infantry Division stops the main attack, while a battalion of Japanese infantry is isolated behind American lines before the 17th Infantry Regiment of the 7th Infantry Division.

Off Okinawa, kamikazes damage a seaplane tender and surveying ship.

CENTRAL PACIFIC: Seventh Air Force sends 12 B-24 Liberators from Angaur Island to bomb Koror Island.

May 6

CBI: Rangoon falls to British forces.

Fourteenth Air Force B-25 Mitchells and P-51 Mustangs destroy a bridge, while P-40s and P-51s attack targets of opportunity in southern and eastern China.

U.S. submarine *Hammerhead* torpedoes and sinks a Japanese fleet tanker in the Gulf of Thailand.

ATLANTIC: A destroyer escort and a frigate sink German submarine *U-853* near Rhode Island. A destroyer escort sinks German submarine *U-881* in the North Atlantic. This will be the last U-boat sunk in the Atlantic by American forces in World War II.

ETO: Pilsen, Czechoslovakia is captured. Third Army halts any farther advance as Soviet forces close on Prague.

Eighth Air Force sends 383 B-17s to air-drop 693 tons of food over the Netherlands. Fifteen B-17s, escorted by eight P-51 Mustangs, drop leaflets in France and Germany. During the night, 10 B-24 Liberators drop leaflets in France, the Netherlands, and the Channel Islands.

MEDITERRANEAN: Fifteenth Air Force P-38 Lightnings escort Royal Air Force cargo planes on a supply drop to Yugoslavia.

ITALY: Units of the 10th Mountain Division move north to establish contact with the U.S. Seventh Army.

Brigadier General Robert S. Israel, Jr., takes command of the XXII Tactical Air Command.

SOUTHWEST PACIFIC AREA: In Eighth Army area the 124th Infantry Regiment of the 31st Infantry Division fights Japanese defenders on the Sayre Highway near Maramag.

In the Philippines, Far East Air Force A-20 Havocs, P-38 Lightnings, and P-47 Thunderbolts support ground forces on Luzon.

In French Indochina, B-25 Mitchells bomb warehouses at Dong Hoi.

In Formosa, B-24 Liberators bomb an airfield and bomb town areas along with B-25s.

FEAF B-24 Liberators bomb Kudat and Keningau airfields, while Lightnings attack Ranau and the Labuan Island airfields off north side of Borneo. B-25 Mitchells support Australian troops on Tarakan Island. B-24 Liberators bomb an airfield on Celebes Island.

PACIFIC: Navy patrol bombers sink two cargo ships in the Yellow Sea.

CENTRAL PACIFIC: Seventh Air Force sends 18 P-47 Thunderbolts from Saipan to sweep Truk Atoll, strafing an airfield, a seaplane base, and shipping.

May 7

CBI: Fourteenth Air Force B-24 Liberators, B-25 Mitchells, and P-47 Thunderbolts attack bridges. P-40s and P-51s attack targets of opportunity in southern and eastern China.

ETO: At Rheims, France, the chief of staff of the German Armed Forces, Colonel-General Alfred Jodl, signs the act of surrender on behalf of the German High Command. The surrender is official at midnight on May 8.

The Supreme Allied Commander, General Dwight D. Eisenhower, sends the following message to the Allied forces under his command:

> The route you have traveled through hundreds of miles is marked by the graves of former comrades. Each of the fallen died as a member of the team to which you

belong, bound together by a common love of liberty and a refusal to submit to enslavement. Our common problems of the immediate and distant future can be best solved in the same conceptions of co-operation and devotion to the cause of human freedom as have made this Expeditionary Force such a mighty engine of righteous destruction.

Eisenhower issues a statement: "The mission of this Allied force was fulfilled at 0241 local time, May 7, 1945."

Eighth Air Force sends 231 B-17s to air-drop 426 tons of food supplies over the Netherlands. Fifteen B-17s, with 30 P-51 Mustangs escorting, drop leaflets in Germany.

Ninth Air Force P-47 Thunderbolts and P-38 Lightnings of the XIX Tactical Air Command fly sweeps over eastern Germany and western Czechoslovakia and carry out demonstration flights over prisoner of war camps.

MEDITERRANEAN: Fifteenth Air Force sends 13 P-51 Mustangs to escort Royal Air Force cargo planes air-dropping supplies over Yugoslavia.

ITALY: Twelfth Air Force sends P-47 Thunderbolts to fly reconnaissance missions over the Austrian Alps.

SOUTHWEST PACIFIC AREA: In the Philippines, Far East Air Force B-25 Mitchells, A-20 Havocs, P-38 Lightnings, and P-47 Thunderbolts attack targets in the Cagayan Valley and support ground forces elsewhere on Luzon.

In French Indochina, B-25s attack railroad targets.

FEAF B-24 Liberators bomb Bingkalapa airfield, Celebes, and the harbor at Surabaya, Java.

Thirteenth Air Force B-24 Liberators bomb Japanese shipping and shore installations at Makassar, sinking a gunboat and a cargo ship.

PACIFIC: Twentieth Air Force sends 41 B-29s to bomb airfields at Usa, Oita, Ibusuki, and Kanoya on Kyushu Island. Aircrews report 34 Japanese aircraft shot down. Three B-29s are lost. The B-29s of the 792nd, 793rd, and 794th Bombardment Squadrons (Very Heavy), 468th Bombardment Group (Very Heavy), arrive at Tinian from India.

A Japanese minesweeper and a cargo vessel hit mines dropped by B-29s in Shimonoseki Strait.

Navy patrol bombers sink four Japanese cargo ships in the Yellow Sea off the coast of Korea.

PACIFIC, OKINAWA: The survivors of the Japanese counterattack force withdraw to their defensive lines, having lost over 5,000 men. American losses number nearly 700.

Corporal John P. Fardy, leading a squad in C Company, 1st Battalion, 1st Marine Regiment, 1st Marine Division, encounters a hail of Japanese fire from a strongly fortified position during an attack on Okinawa. Deploying his men along a drainage ditch, Corporal Fardy catches sight of a hand grenade falling in among his marines in the ditch. Fardy jumps on the grenade to save the lives of his men and sacrifices his own life. Corporal Fardy's gallant act of self-sacrifice will be recognized with the nation's highest award for valor, the Medal of Honor.

CENTRAL PACIFIC: Seventh Air Force sends 11 B-24 Liberators from Guam to bomb Marcus Island. P-47 Thunderbolts from Saipan strafe a radio station, airfield installations, and gun positions on islands at Truk.

May 8

CBI: Japanese forces are stopped by a Chinese counterattack, supported by Fourteenth Air Force. The Chinese forces inflict over 11,000 casualties on the enemy in the first major victory for the Chinese in two years.

In China, Fourteenth Air Force P-40s and P-51 Mustangs attack rail and river traffic. In French Indochina B-25 Mitchells attack bridges and P-51 Mustangs attack rail and road traffic along the coast.

ATLANTIC: VE Day. President Truman announces the end of the war in Europe.

ETO: At 2301, hostilities cease in Europe. General of the Army Dwight D. Eisenhower, Supreme Allied Commander of the European theater of operations, has under his command 90 Allied divisions: 61 U.S., 13 British, five Canadian, 10 French, and one Polish.

Eighth Air Force sends 12 B-17s to drop leaflets over Germany.

Ninth Air Force P-47 Thunderbolts and P-38 Lightnings of the IX and XIX Tactical Air Commands patrol over the cities of Leipzig, Chemnitz, and Adorf, Germany, and Linz, Austria. Fighters also fly sweeps and demonstration missions.

MEDITERRANEAN: Fifteenth Air Force orders all aircraft to stand down and no further offensive operations will be conducted.

SOUTHWEST PACIFIC AREA: Eighth Army reports that the Leyte-Samar area has been cleared, and that over 24,000 Japanese troops have been killed and another 439 taken prisoner since February. American losses are reported as 432 killed, 1,852 wounded, and 22 missing.

In the Philippines, Far East Air Force B-24 Liberators, B-25 Mitchells, P-38 Lightnings, and P-47 Thunderbolts attack Japanese positions in Cagayan Valley on Luzon. B-24s attack Davao on Mindanao, while P-38 Lightnings attack the airfield area.

B-25s bomb railway installations in French Indochina.

U.S. submarine *Bream* lays mines off the coast of French Indochina.

FEAF P-38 Lightnings attack Jesselton, Sengkawang, and Kudat airfields, while B-25 Mitchells bomb the Kuching and Labuan Island airfield areas at Borneo. Other B-24 Liberators bomb an airfield on Celebes Island.

PACIFIC: Twentieth Air Force sends 40 B-29s to attack airfields at Kanoya, Miyakonojo, Oita, and Matsuyama on Kyushu and Shikoku Islands.

U.S. submarine *Bowfin* torpedoes and sinks a Japanese fishing boat off northeast Honshu, Japan.

A transport is damaged by a mine dropped by B-29s off southern Korea.

PACIFIC, OKINAWA: The 1st Marine Division fights for control of Hill 60 and Nan Hill, sealing every opening to keep the Japanese from moving underground to new locations.

CENTRAL PACIFIC: Seventh Air Force sends 12 B-24 Liberators from Guam to bomb the airfield on Marcus Island. Another 12 B-24s from Guam bomb a runway on Param Island at Truk.

May 9

ALEUTIANS: Eleventh Air Force sends 12 B-24 Liberators to bomb shipping between Paramushiru and Shimushu Islands in the Kuriles.

CBI: Fourteenth Air Force sends B-24 Liberators, B-25 Mitchells, and P-51 Mustangs to attack targets of opportunity.

ATLANTIC: German submarine *U-249* surrenders to a Navy PB4Y Privateer off the Scilly Islands, at the western tip of England. This submarine is the first to surrender after cessation of hostilities was declared.

ETO: The chief of the German High Command and the commanders in chief of the army, navy, and air force sign a ratification document of unconditional surrender with the representatives of the Soviet High Command in Berlin.

Eighth Air Force begins the redeployment of the headquarters of the 453rd Bombardment Group (Heavy) and the 732nd, 733rd, 734th, and 735th Bombardment Squadrons (Heavy) from England to the United States. The group will move by ship.

Ninth Air Force fighters of the XIX Tactical Air Command patrol areas above Linz, Austria, and Klatovy, Czechoslovakia, and carry out demonstration flights.

MEDITERRANEAN: Fifteenth Air Force begins redeploying the B-24 Liberators of the 828th, 829th, 830th, and 831st Bombardment Squadrons (Heavy), 485th Bombardment Group (Heavy), to the United States. The headquarters of the 47th Bombardment Wing (Heavy) is scheduled to follow.

SOUTHWEST PACIFIC AREA: In the Philippines, Far East Air Force A-20 Havocs, P-38 Lightnings, and P-47 Thunderbolts fly offensive sweeps over the Cagayan Valley and support ground forces on Luzon. B-24 Liberators bomb targets on Mindanao in preparation for Allied landings in the Macajalar Bay area on May 10.

B-24 Liberators bomb airfields in the Canton, China, area.

FEAF P-38 Lightnings attack Tarakan Island in support of Australian ground forces.

PACIFIC: The Japanese government announces that regardless of the change in the situation in Europe, Japan will continue to fight.

PACIFIC, OKINAWA: The 7th Infantry Division's 17th Infantry Regiment gains control of Kochi Ridge. The division is relieved by the 96th Infantry Division.

Kamikazes damage two U.S. destroyer escorts and two British carriers, HMS *Formidable* and HMS *Victorious*, off Okinawa.

CENTRAL PACIFIC: Seventh Air Force sends 29 B-24 Liberators from Guam to bomb targets on the islands at Truk. Another 14 P-47 Thunderbolts from Saipan bomb a number of targets at Truk.

May 10

ALEUTIANS: Eleventh Air Force and the navy's Fleet Air Wing Four attack targets in the Kurile Islands. B-24 Liberators bomb shipping targets at the Kataoka naval base on Shimushu Island and fly photo reconnaissance over the island on their return.

B-25s from Attu attack shipping between Kashiwabara on Paramushiru Island and Kataoka. One B-25 is shot down by antiaircraft fire. One B-24 and a B-25 make forced landings in the Soviet Union.

CBI: Fourteenth Air Force B-25 Mitchells and P-47 Thunderbolts attack bridges and P-40s and P-51s attack trucks, highways, logistics storage sites, rail lines, troops, and artillery in southern and eastern China.

ETO: Major General William E. Kepner takes command of Eighth Air Force, replacing Lieutenant General James H. Doolittle, who returns to Washington, D.C.

Ninth Air Force redesignates the 9th Bombardment Division as the 9th Air Division.

SOUTHWEST PACIFIC AREA: In the Eighth Army area Lieutenant General Eichelberger orders Colonel Maurice D. Stratta's 108th Infantry Regiment of the 40th Infantry Division to land at Macajalar Bay on Mindanao and move south on the Sayre Highway to link with the 31st Infantry Division advancing north. Naval Task Group 78.3, commanded by Rear Admiral Arthur D. Struble, lands the troops.

In the Philippines, Far East Air Force A-20 Havocs, P-38s, and P-47 Thunderbolts attack Japanese positions in the Cagayan Valley and support ground operations throughout Luzon. B-24 Liberators and B-25s support ground forces on Mindanao.

B-25s, with P-47s escorting, attack town areas and communication targets of opportunity on Formosa.

B-24s bomb an airfield in the Canton, China, area.

FEAF B-24 Liberators bomb Makassar ship basins and an airfield on Celebes Island and shore targets at Balikpapan on Borneo.

PACIFIC: Twentieth Air Force sends 42 B-29s to attack airfields at Matsuyama, Usa, Miyazaki, and Kanoya on Kyushu and Shikoku Islands. Aircrews report 10 Japanese aircraft shot down. One B-29 is lost. Over 40 B-29s attack airfields at Matsuyama, Usa, Miyazaki, and Kanoya on Kyushu and Shikoku Islands. More than 50 B-29s bomb the Tokuyama naval fuel station. A total of 56 B-29s bomb the Tokuyama coal yards; over 100 B-29s attack the Otake oil refinery. One B-29 is lost. Eighty B-29s bomb the Amami-O-Shima naval oil storage facilities.

Navy patrol bombers sink a Japanese merchant tanker and a cargo ship off the west coast of Korea.

PACIFIC, OKINAWA: Kamikazes damage a destroyer and a light minelayer off Okinawa.

Pharmacist's Mate Second Class William D. Halyburton, Jr., is serving with a marine rifle company in the 2nd Battalion, 5th Marines, 1st Marine Division, during an attack on a draw on Okinawa. As he moves forward to meet with the first squad, it is pinned down under a heavy volume of mortar, machine-gun, and sniper fire. As marines fall wounded, Halyburton comes to their aid and shields them with his body as he gives first aid. He continues in this manner, aiding each man in turn until he is mortally wounded. For his extraordinary dedication to duty and willingness to sacrifice his own life to save the lives of others, Pharmacist's Mate Second Class Halyburton will receive the Medal of Honor.

CENTRAL PACIFIC: Seventh Air Force sends 11 B-24 Liberators from Guam to bomb the airfield on Marcus Island. Another 19 B-24s from Guam bomb airfields on Param and Moen islands at Truk Atoll.

May 11

ALEUTIANS: Eleventh Air Force B-24 Liberators sink a Japanese cargo ship and damage an escort destroyer in the Kuriles.

CBI: Fourteenth Air Force B-25 Mitchells and P-47 Thunderbolts attack bridges, while P-40s and P-51s attack trucks, highways, logistics storage sites, rail lines, troops, and artillery in southern and eastern China.

SOUTHWEST PACIFIC AREA: In the Eighth Army area, the 167th Infantry Regiment of the 31st Infantry Division begins a reconnaissance in force along a trail leading into the Japanese main defensive area on Mindanao. Before long it will take the effort of the entire regiment, battling not only Japanese troops but also constant rainfall and jungle, to advance 13 miles over the next 18 days.

In the Philippines, Far East Air Force B-25 Mitchells, A-20 Havocs, P-38 Lightnings, and P-47 Thunderbolts support ground forces on Luzon.

B-24 Liberators bomb an airfield and, with B-25s, bomb town areas on Formosa.

FEAF B-24 Liberators bomb an airfield, and B-25 Mitchells bomb the Brunei Bay area on Borneo. B-24 Liberators attack airfields on Celebes Island.

PACIFIC: Twentieth Air Force sends 50 B-29s to attack airfields at Oita, Saeki, Nittagahara, Miyazaki, and Miyakonojo on Kyushu Island, and 92 B-29s bomb the Kawanishi aircraft production facility at Kobe. Aircrews report nine Japanese fighters shot down. One B-29 is lost.

Navy PB4Y-2 Privateers sink two cargo ships off the west coast of Korea.

PACIFIC, OKINAWA: Believing the Japanese are near their breaking point, Lieutenant General Simon B. Buckner orders a Tenth Army offensive. The attack proceeds after 30 minutes of artillery fire, with the 6th and 1st Marine Divisions of the III Amphibious Corps on the right and the 77th and 96th Infantry Divisions of the XXIV Corps on the left. The 7th Infantry Division will be the reserve of Tenth Army. Buckner desires to press the flanks while maintaining pressure on the center. The attack gains about 600 yards, with many casualties, and quickly bogs down into positional warfare as small units fight dug-in Japanese forces along a line of small hills and ridgelines.

Two destroyers are heavily damaged by kamikaze attacks. The carrier *Bunker Hill*, Admiral Mitscher's flagship, is also hit, causing over 660 casualties. The damage is heavy, and the carrier is out of action. Mitscher moves his flag to the carrier *Enterprise*.

CENTRAL PACIFIC: Seventh Air Force sends 10 B-24 Liberators from Guam to bomb the airfield on Param Island at Truk and 13 other B-24s bomb Marcus Island. P-51 Mustangs from Iwo Jima attack the radio station on Chichi Jima.

May 12

CBI: In China, Fourteenth Air Force sends 17 B-25 Mitchells and eight P-51 Mustangs to bomb the barracks and logistics storage area at Loyang and attack railroad

Deck-level view of the kamikaze strike on the aircraft carrier USS *Bunker Hill* (National Archives and Records Administration)

targets. P-40s and P-51 Mustangs attack rail and river traffic, vehicles, and logistics storage sites.

ATLANTIC: President Truman orders an immediate halt to all Lend-Lease shipments to the USSR. This brings immediate howls of protest from the Soviets.

ETO: Ninth Air Force P-38 Lightnings and P-47 Thunderbolts of the XIX Tactical Air Command fly demonstration missions.

MEDITERRANEAN: Fifteenth Air Force begins the redeployment of the headquarters, 450th Bombardment Group (Heavy), and the B-24 Liberators of the 723rd Bombardment Squadron (Heavy) from Italy to the United States.

ITALY: Twelfth Air Force begins redeploying 17 assigned units from the theater. Another 43 assigned service units will be disbanded to form 21 new service units, and nine assigned units will be transferred to other headquarters in the theater.

SOUTHWEST PACIFIC AREA: In the Philippines, Far East Air Force A-20 Havocs, P-38 Lightnings, and P-47 Thunderbolts support ground forces on Luzon and Negros Islands.

In French Indochina, B-24 Liberators bomb rail and road bridges and attack a railyard and other railroad targets.

FEAF B-24 Liberators, B-25 Mitchells, and P-38 Lightnings attack targets in the Brunei Bay area, including Labuan Island, Brooketon, and Jesselton airfields, and troops on Tarakan Island off Borneo. B-24s bomb Makassar shipyards and Limbo-eng airfield on Celebes Island.

PACIFIC: Twentieth Air Force receives the headquarters of the 331st Bombardment Group (Very Heavy) and the B-29s of the 355th, 356th, and 357th Bombardment Squadrons (Very Heavy), and the headquarters of the 502nd Bombardment Group (Very Heavy) and the B-29s of the 402nd, 411th, and 430th Bombardment Squadrons (Very Heavy) at Guam from the United States.

U.S. submarine *Raton* sinks a Japanese cargo ship in the Yellow Sea. Another cargo ship is sunk off Shimonoseki after hitting a mine dropped by B-29s.

PACIFIC, OKINAWA: Tenth Army runs into some of the toughest defenses on the island. The 96th Infantry Division faces Conical Hill; the 22nd Marines of the 6th Marine Division face Sugar Loaf. The 1st Marine Division fights on Dakeshi and Wana Ridges.

A kamikaze damages battleship USS *New Mexico* off Okinawa.

CENTRAL PACIFIC: Seventh Air Force sends nine B-24 Liberators from Guam to bomb the airfield on Marcus Island. Another 12 B-24s from Guam bomb a runway on Param Island at Truk Atoll.

May 13

CBI: In China, Fourteenth Air Force B-24 Liberators lay mines in the Yangtze River and 10 B-25 Mitchells attack bridges. P-40s and P-51s attack trucks, highways, logistics storage sites, and rail lines in southern and eastern China.

MEDITERRANEAN: Fifteenth Air Force redeploys B-24 units from Italy to the United States, including the 717th Bombardment Squadron (Heavy) of the 449th Bombardment Group (Heavy) and the 720th Bombardment Squadron (Heavy) of the 450th Bombardment Group (Heavy).

SOUTHWEST PACIFIC AREA: On Luzon in the I Corps area the 25th Infantry Division captures Balete Pass after weeks of heavy fighting.

In the Eighth Army area, the 108th Infantry Regiment of the 40th Infantry Division encounters strong Japanese resistance along the Sayre Highway on Mindanao. The regiment will continue the fight for four days.

In the Philippines, Far East Air Force B-25 Mitchells, A-20 Havocs, P-38 Lightnings, and P-47 Thunderbolts support ground forces on Luzon.

B-24 Liberators again pound bridges along the coast of French Indochina.

FEAF B-24 Liberators bomb airfields, and B-25 Mitchells and P-38 Lightnings bomb Sandakan and support ground forces on Tarakan Island off Borneo.

U.S. submarine *Baya* attacks a Japanese convoy, sinking a tanker in the Java Sea.

PACIFIC: During the night Twentieth Air Force sends 12 B-29s to mine the Shimonoseki Strait and the waters off Niigata, Japan, in an attempt to blockade the Japanese home islands.

U.S. submarine *Cero* torpedoes and sinks a Japanese cargo ship off Honshu, Japan.

Carrier aircraft from Task Force 58 attack airfields on Kyushu. U.S. submarine *Plaice* attacks a Japanese guardboat in the Kuriles.

PACIFIC, OKINAWA: The 383rd Infantry Regiment of the 96th Infantry Division, supported by the 763rd Tank Battalion, assaults Conical Hill, a key position on the Shuri defensive line.

Off Okinawa, kamikazes damage a destroyer and a destroyer escort.

CENTRAL PACIFIC: Seventh Air Force sends 10 B-24 Liberators from Guam to bomb an underground hangar on Moen Island at Truk. Another nine B-24s bomb the airfield on Marcus Island.

May 14

CBI: Mars Task Force begins training Chinese troops in China.

In China, Fourteenth Air Force B-24 Liberators mine the Yangtze River. B-25 Mitchells attack river shipping near Hengshan. P-40s and P-51s attack trucks, highways, logistics storage sites, rail lines, troops, and artillery in southern and eastern China.

SOUTHWEST PACIFIC AREA: In the Eighth Army area, the 124th Infantry Regiment of the 31st Infantry Division stops a Japanese attack during the night near Colgan Woods, named for Captain (Chaplain) Thomas A. Colgan, who was killed while attending to wounded soldiers. In the six-day battle for Maramag, the 124th has lost 69 killed and 177 wounded.

In the Philippines, Far East Air Force B-25 Mitchells, A-20 Havocs, P-38 Lightnings, and P-47 Thunderbolts support ground forces on Luzon and Negros Islands.

B-24 Liberators bomb the military and air supply center on Formosa.

U.S. submarine *Cobia* is damaged in a depth charge attack in the Gulf of Siam but remains on patrol.

FEAF B-24 Liberators and B-25 Mitchells attack airfields in Borneo and B-25s support ground forces on Tarakan Island. B-24s raid Makassar harbor, Sidate airfield, and Parepare warehouses on Celebes Island and bomb an airfield on Soembawa Island, in the Lesser Sunda Islands.

Private First Class James H. Diamond is a machine gunner in D Company, 21st Infantry Regiment, 24th Infantry Division, who displays an extraordinary fighting spirit. He fearlessly attacks Japanese positions at Mintal, Mindanao, with his Thompson submachine gun, then calls in artillery fire to eliminate them. He assists in evacuating casualties from a bridgehead, volunteering to take them to the rear through mortar and artillery fire while being wounded himself. He assists in repairing a bridge under heavy enemy fire. On May 14, he is leading a patrol to evacuate casualties from his battalion, as it fights to escape entrapment by the Japanese. When his patrol is attacked, Diamond locates a machine gun and, braving enemy fire, fires the machine gun to draw additional fire upon himself so that the members of the patrol can escape. Private First Class Diamond's indomitable spirit, his selflessness, and heroic sacrifice to save his comrades will be worthy of the nation's highest award for valor, the Medal of Honor.

PACIFIC: U.S. submarine *Sand Lance* torpedoes and sinks a Japanese auxiliary minesweeper off Hokkaido, Japan.

Mines dropped by Twentieth Air Force B-29s damage a Japanese merchant ship, a cargo ship, and a merchant tug east of Shikoku, Japan. Mines sink a Japanese transport off Shimonoseki.

PACIFIC, OKINAWA: A single kamikaze hits the carrier *Enterprise,* causing enough damage to take it out of action for repairs. Admiral Mitscher again transfers his flag, this time to the carrier *Randolph.*

PACIFIC: Twentieth Air Force sends 472 B-29s of the XXI Bomber Command to bomb the urban area of north Nagoya, Japan. Aircrews report 20 Japanese fighters shot down. Eleven B-29s are lost.

May 15

ALEUTIANS: Eleventh Air Force sends 13 B-24 Liberators to bomb targets in the Kuriles. Aircrews report one cargo ship destroyed. Antiaircraft fire damages two B-24s; one makes a forced landing in the Soviet Union.

CBI: Fourteenth Air Force B-25 Mitchells, P-40s, and P-51s attack trucks, highways, logistics storage sites, rail lines, troops, and artillery in southern and eastern China.

MEDITERRANEAN: Fifteenth Air Force begins redeploying the headquarters of the 485th Bombardment Group (Heavy) and the B-24 Liberators of the 716th, 718th, and 719th Bombardment Squadrons (Heavy), of the 449th Bombardment Group (Heavy), to the United States.

SOUTHWEST PACIFIC AREA: In the Philippines, Far East Air Force P-38 Lightnings support ground forces and attack gun positions on Negros Island.

B-24 Liberators bomb targets on Formosa.

U.S. submarine *Hammerhead* torpedoes and sinks a Japanese transport in the Gulf of Siam.

FEAF B-24 Liberators and B-25 Mitchells attack airfields in Borneo and support Australian ground forces on Tarakan Island.

PACIFIC: U.S. submarine *Sea Poacher* torpedoes and sinks Japanese army vessels in the Kuriles.

U.S. submarine *Shad* torpedoes and damages a Japanese cargo ship in the Yellow Sea.

Navy patrol bombers sink a cargo ship in the East China Sea, a cargo ship off western Kyushu, Japan, and a cargo ship off the east coast of Korea.

PACIFIC, OKINAWA: Major Henry A. Courtney, Jr., is the executive officer of the 2nd Battalion, 22nd Marines, 6th Marine Division, holding a defensive line behind Sugar Loaf Hill, and decides to mount a night attack on the Japanese before the enemy has a chance to organize their own attack. Major Courtney then begins the attack, blasting cave positions and neutralizing enemy guns as he moves forward. The marines make a swift advance against the surprised Japanese, braving intense fire to occupy the ridge that Courtney had designated as their objective. Reinforced and resupplied, Courtney now decides to capture the crest of the hill. Without waiting to see who is following, Major Courtney moves forward, throwing grenades into cave openings and suspected enemy positions. Reaching the crest of the hill, he finds large numbers of Japanese troops forming for an attack. Without hesitation, he plunges forward, completely disorganizing the enemy and forcing them to retreat to the safety of the caves. Determined to hold his position, he reorganizes and deploys for the defense, ignoring the high volume of fire directed at him. Shortly afterward he is killed when a mortar shell explodes near him. For his initiative and personal display of courage in the face of a determined enemy, Major Courtney will receive the Medal of Honor.

May 16

CBI: In China, Fourteenth Air Force B-24 Liberators lay mines in the Yangtze River. B-25 Mitchells, P-47 Thunderbolts, and P-51 Mustangs attack trucks, headquarters units, highways, logistics storage sites, rail lines, bridges, troops, town areas, and artillery in southern and eastern China.

MEDITERRANEAN: Fifteenth Air Force redeploys the headquarters of the 449th Bombardment Group (Heavy) and the 721st and 722nd Bombardment Squadrons (Heavy) of the 450th Bombardment Group (Heavy) to the United States.

SOUTHWEST PACIFIC AREA: On Luzon Island in the Philippines, Far East Air Force sends nearly 100 P-38 Lightnings to attack Japanese positions near the Ipo Dam with napalm.

B-24 Liberators bomb town areas and B-25 Mitchells attack alcohol plants and railroad yards on Formosa.

U.S. submarine *Hawkbill* torpedoes and sinks a Japanese minelayer off the east coast of Malaya.

FEAF B-24 Liberators attack Balikpapan and Manggar on Borneo, and Tondano on Celebes Island. B-25 Mitchells and P-38 Lightnings attack Miri, Brookton, Bintula, Fort Brook, and a floating antiaircraft platform near Labuan Island. P-38 Lightnings support Australian ground forces on Tarakan.

PACIFIC: Mines dropped by Twentieth Air Force B-29s sink a cargo ship near Shikoku, Japan.

U.S. submarine *Raton* torpedoes and sinks a Japanese cargo ship in the Yellow Sea off the west coast of Korea.

During the night Twentieth Air Force sends 25 B-29s to mine Shimonoseki Strait.

CENTRAL PACIFIC: Seventh Air Force sends 13 B-24 Liberators from Guam to bomb the airfield on Marcus Island.

May 17

CBI: Fourteenth Air Force B-25 Mitchells, P-47 Thunderbolts, and P-51 Mustangs attack trucks, river traffic, highways, logistics storage sites, rail lines, bridges, troops, and town areas in southern and eastern China.

SOUTHWEST PACIFIC AREA: On Luzon, XI Corps captures the Ipo Dam, supported by the heaviest use of napalm against the enemy in the theater.

In the Eighth Army area, the 24th Infantry Division, supported by Filipino guerrillas, attacks into the Japanese defenses on Mindanao. Marine air and artillery support the division's attack.

In the Philippines, Far East Air Force P-38 Lightnings and P-47 Thunderbolts attack Japanese positions near the Ipo Dam on Luzon Island.

B-25 Mitchells and P-51 Mustangs attack railyards, bridges, and alcohol production facilities on Formosa. B-24 Liberators bomb airfields on Formosa.

FEAF B-24 Liberators bomb airfields on Borneo and Celebes Island.

Aircraft from U.S. carrier *Saratoga* and British carrier HMS *Illustrious* sink on auxiliary minesweeper near Surabaya, Java.

PACIFIC: Twentieth Air Force sends more than 500 B-29s to attack the Mitsubishi Aircraft Works and a number of other industrial production facilities located at Nagoya. Another 11 B-29s attack targets of opportunity. Three B-29s are lost. B-29s of the 21st Bomber Command attack airfields on Kyushu and Shikoku to limit their use for kamikaze attacks.

Mines dropped by Twentieth Air Force B-29s sink a Japanese transport and a cargo ship in the Inland Sea.

PACIFIC, OKINAWA: Admiral Nimitz begins replacing the navy staff at Okinawa as preparations for the invasion of the Japanese home islands begin. Vice Admiral Harry W. Hill takes command of Task Force 51 from Admiral Richmond Kelly Turner.

A kamikaze damages a destroyer off Okinawa.

Corporal James Day, a squad leader in the 2nd Battalion, 22nd Marine Regiment, 6th Marine Division, engaged in heavy fighting to seize the front lines of Sugar Loaf Hill. He rallies his squad and the remnants of another unit and leads them forward into heavy artillery and mortar fire. The Japanese infantry now counterattack. His unit is reduced to less than half-strength in a matter of minutes, Corporal Day refuses to retreat, encouraging his men, throwing hand grenades, and directing fire against the enemy to stop the counterattack. He receives six additional marines, but in the course of repelling night attacks, his small group is further reduced by casualties. Throughout the night Corporal Day locates four seriously wounded marines and, braving enemy fire each time, returns them one by one to a corpsman. Again and again he reorganizes his defense after each attack, often in hand-to-hand combat. As morning breaks over the embattled unit, the Japanese again attempt to overwhelm the marines, but fail each time. By the third day, the marines have repulsed another attack and have stayed firm. This extraordinary demonstration of will and courageous leadership in exceptionally difficult circumstances will win Corporal Day the Medal of Honor.

CENTRAL PACIFIC: P-51 Mustangs from Iwo Jima attack airfields at Atsugi, Japan. Pilots report 10 confirmed kills on the ground. During the night two P-47 Thunderbolts of the 318th Fighter Group located on Ie Shima conduct harassment strikes over Kyushu Island, Japan.

Carrier aircraft from Task Unit 77.4.3 (Rear Admiral Clifton A. F. Sprague) attack Japanese installations at Maloelap Atoll, Marshall Islands.

May 18

ALEUTIANS: Eleventh Air Force sends eight B-24 Liberators to bomb naval, harbor, and airfield targets at Kataoka on Shimushu Island in the Kuriles.

CBI: Fourteenth Air Force B-25 Mitchells, P-47 Thunderbolts, and P-51 Mustangs attack logistics storage sites and rail lines, bridges, troops, and town areas in southern and eastern China.

SOUTHWEST PACIFIC AREA: In the Philippines, Far East Air Force A-20 Havocs, P-38 Lightnings, and P-47 Thunderbolts support ground forces on Luzon and Negros islands.

B-24 Liberators bomb airfields, and B-25 Mitchells and P-47s fly sweeps against targets on Formosa.

FEAF B-24 Liberators and B-25 Mitchells attack Fort Brook and Sarawak on Borneo, while B-24s and P-38 Lightnings attack Japanese defenses on Tarakan Island.

PACIFIC: During the night Twentieth Air Force sends 30 B-29s to mine Shimonoseki Strait and Tsuruga Harbor in Japan.

U.S. submarine *Shad* torpedoes and sinks a Japanese cargo ship in the Yellow Sea. Navy patrol bombers sink a Japanese cargo vessel off western Korea.

The advance air echelon of the 509th Composite Group arrives on Tinian Island. The 509th, commanded by an experienced and distinguished bomber pilot, Colonel Paul W. Tibbets, Jr., is tasked with conducting an atomic bomb attack on Japan.

PACIFIC, OKINAWA: The 6th Marine Division captures Sugar Loaf, a key defensive position. Losses have reached over 2,600 since the beginning of the attack on May 11.

Fire from a shore battery damages destroyer USS *Longshaw*. The ship then explodes off Naha, Okinawa. A kamikaze damages a high-speed transport, and an LST is hit and damaged by a torpedo dropped in an air attack.

CENTRAL PACIFIC: P-47 Thunderbolts from Ie Shima Island make bombing, strafing, and rocket attacks on radar and ground installations on Kume Jima Island. During the night other P-47s fly harassment attacks against targets on Kyushu Island, Japan.

May 19

ALEUTIANS: Eleventh Air Force sends eight B-25 Mitchells to bomb the Minami Cape radar installation and cannery on the Naka River on Shimushu Island. Antiaircraft fire and enemy fighters drive off most of the bombers. One B-25 is shot down, another is reported missing, and a third makes a forced landing at Petropavlovsk in the Soviet Union.

U.S. destroyers bombard Japanese installations on Paramushiru, in the Kuriles.

CBI: The Japanese abandon Foochow.

Fourteenth Air Force B-25 Mitchells attack warehouses and rail lines. P-47 Thunderbolts and P-51 Mustangs attack trucks, river traffic, highways, logistics storage sites, rail lines, bridges, troops, and targets of opportunity in southern and eastern China.

ETO: Eighth Air Force redeploys the headquarters of the 93rd Bombardment Group (Heavy) to the United States.

SOUTHWEST PACIFIC AREA: In the Philippines, Far East Air Force B-25 Mitchells, A-20 Havocs, P-38 Lightnings, and P-47 Thunderbolts support ground forces on Luzon near Ipo Dam. P-38s support ground forces on Cebu Island.

On Formosa, B-24 Liberators attack Kiirun harbor; B-25 Mitchells sweep the west coast, attacking a rail yard, logistics storage facilities, and damaging an alcohol production facility. P-47s also conduct sweeps across the island.

FEAF B-24 Liberators bomb an airfield and, with P-38 Lightnings supporting, attack targets on Tarakan Island off northwest Borneo.

PACIFIC: Twentieth Air Force sends 272 B-29s to attack the Tachikawa Aircraft Company, but the bombers are forced to abort the mission and instead bomb the city of Hamamatsu. Fourteen B-29s attack targets of opportunity. Four B-29s are lost. Thirty B-29s mine Shimonoseki Strait and the waters off Shikoku and Kyushu, Japan.

PACIFIC, OKINAWA: The 7th Marines of the 1st Marine Division make slow, but steady progress against Japanese positions on Wana Ridge, supported by tanks.

CENTRAL PACIFIC: The headquarters of the 413th Fighter Group and the P-47 Thunderbolts of the 1st, 21st, and 34th Fighter Squadrons arrive on Ie Shima Island from the United States.

May 20

CBI: Major General Lewis A. Pick announces the formal completion of the Ledo Road. He describes the feat as the toughest job ever given to U.S. Army engineers in wartime. Officially it is named the Stilwell Road, but among his engineers it is known only as Pick's Pike, much to the consternation of Major General Pick.

Fourteenth Air Force B-25 Mitchells, P-47 Thunderbolts, and P-51 Mustangs attack trucks, river traffic, highways, fuel storage areas, logistics storage sites, rail lines, bridges, troops, and targets of opportunity in southern and eastern China.

SOUTHWEST PACIFIC AREA: In the Philippines, Far East Air Force B-25 Mitchells, A-20 Havocs, P-38 Lightnings, and P-47 Thunderbolts attack Japanese positions in the Cagayan Valley. B-24 Liberators and P-38s support ground forces on Mindanao.

B-25 Mitchells bomb various communication targets and an alcohol production facility on Formosa.

Fifth Air Force B-24 Liberators sink a cargo vessel off Formosa.

In Borneo, FEAF P-38 Lightnings attack Sandakan, Keningau, and Tarakan Island, while B-25 Mitchells attack shipping at Balikpapan harbor and a nearby barracks area.

PACIFIC: During the night Twentieth Air Force sends 30 B-29s to mine Shimonoseki Strait and the waters off Shikoku and Kyushu, Japan. One B-29 is lost.

U.S. submarine *Cero* torpedoes and sinks a Japanese merchant whaler east of Honshu, Japan.

PACIFIC, OKINAWA: Kamikazes damage a destroyer, a destroyer escort, two high-speed transports, and an LST off Okinawa. TBF/TBM Avengers from Naval Task Group 58.3 provide close air support for ground forces near Shuri castle.

CENTRAL PACIFIC: Seventh Air Force sends 10 B-24 Liberators from Guam to bomb the airfield on Marcus Island. Sixteen P-47 Thunderbolts from Saipan attack airfields on Moen and Eten Islands and a seaplane base and barges off Dublon Island at Truk. P-47 Thunderbolts from Ie Shima attack a hangar and boats at Fukue-Shima. Another 32 P-47s attack airfields, railroads, buildings, and radar facilities on Kyushu Island.

The 396th and 820th Bombardment Squadrons (Medium) of the 41st Bombardment Group (Medium) begin deploying from Hawaii to Okinawa with B-25 Mitchells.

May 21

CBI: Fourteenth Air Force B-25 Mitchells bomb bridges. P-47 Thunderbolts and P-51 Mustangs attack trucks, river traffic, highways, rail lines, bridges, and troops in southern and eastern China.

ETO: Eighth Air Force redeploys the headquarters of the 482nd Bombardment Group (Heavy) to the United States.

SOUTHWEST PACIFIC AREA: In the Eighth Army area, the 155th Infantry Regiment of the 31st Infantry Division continues the advance up the Sayre Highway on Mindanao and occupies Malaybalay.

In the Philippines, Far East Air Force B-25 Mitchells bomb targets in the Cagayan Valley, while A-20 Havocs and P-51 Mustangs support ground forces. P-38 Lightnings drop napalm on Japanese positions near Ipo Dam and attack positions throughout Negros Island.

In French Indochina, P-38s strafe rail cars near Saigon.

In Borneo, FEAF B-24 Liberators attack Brunei, an airfield, shipyards, and troop concentrations on Tarakan Island

U.S. submarine *Chub* torpedoes and sinks a Japanese minesweeper in the Java Sea.

PACIFIC: Mines dropped by Twentieth Air Force B-29s sink a Japanese cargo ship in the Inland Sea.

PACIFIC, OKINAWA: The 1st Marine Division gains control of Dakeshi and Wana Ridges, but at a cost of over 1,700 men in 11 days of combat.

The 306th and 307th Infantry Regiments of the 77th Infantry Division batter against hills named Chocolate Drop, Wart Hill, and Flattop. Defended by minefields and trenches, the ground covered by machine-gun and anti-tank gun positions, the infantry must fight without tank support. Casualties are very heavy. In 10 days of combat the division has lost nearly 1,500 casualties.

The 96th Infantry Division's 381st Infantry Regiment gains control of Conical Hill after days of continuous fighting. The division has lost over 1,100 men in 10 days.

Private First Class Desmond T. Doss is a company aid man with the 1st Battalion, 307th Infantry Regiment, 77th Infantry Division, as his unit attacks up a steep escarpment 400 feet high. As the infantrymen reach the summit, they are hit with a heavy concentration of artillery and mortar fire, which causes nearly 75 casualties and forces the survivors off the objective. Doss refuses to leave the wounded, moving as many as he can to the edge of the escarpment and there lowering each one down on a litter attached to a rope. Throughout the next few days, Private First Class Doss rescues wounded men, ignoring all danger and braving enemy fire as he provides treatment. During a night attack on May 21 near Shuri, he purposely exposes himself to enemy fire to treat wounded soldiers left ahead of the front lines. He is seriously wounded in the legs when a grenade explodes nearby. To avoid risking another medic's life, he treats his own wound and waits over five hours until litter bearers can assist him. As he is being carrier to the rear, he sees a far more seriously wounded soldier and gets off the litter to allow him to have treatment first. As the litter bearers move off, he is again wounded, this time in the arm. He calmly makes a field expedient splint for his arm, then crawls 300 yards to the aid station. For his extraordinary dedication to duty and exceptional courage in performing that duty, Private First Class Doss will receive the Medal of Honor.

CENTRAL PACIFIC: During the night P-47 Thunderbolts fly harassment raids against targets on Kyushu Island, Japan.

May 22

CBI: Fourteenth Air Force B-25 Mitchells bomb road and rail bridges. P-51 Mustangs drop napalm on trucks, barracks, and storage areas. P-47 Thunderbolts and P-51s attack trucks, river traffic, highways, rail lines, and targets of opportunity in southern and eastern China.

SOUTHWEST PACIFIC AREA: In the Philippines, Far East Air Force B-25 Mitchells, A-20 Havocs, P-38 Lightnings, and P-47 Thunderbolts support ground forces on Luzon at Ipo Dam and elsewhere.

B-24 Liberators bomb town areas on Formosa, while B-25s attack an oil production facility and several targets of opportunity.

FEAF B-24 Liberators, B-25 Mitchells, and P-38 Lightnings attack Jesselton, Kudat, and Bintula on Borneo and support Australian ground forces on Tarakan Island.

PACIFIC: Aircraft from carriers USS *Bennington* and USS *Hornet* sink two Japanese submarine chasers and a landing ship southwest of Kyushu, Japan.

Mines dropped by Twentieth Air Force B-29s sink two Japanese cargo ships and damage an auxiliary submarine chaser in the Inland Sea.

During the night Twentieth Air Force sends 30 B-29s to mine Shimonoseki Strait and approaches. One B-29 is lost.

PACIFIC, OKINAWA: Heavy rain on the island slows all offensive operations as the roads turn to mud.

May 23

ALEUTIANS: Eleventh Air Force sends seven B-24 Liberators to bomb the Kataoka naval base area on Shimushu Island, using radar signal intercepts to mark the bomb release points over the target.

CBI: Fourteenth Air Force B-25 Mitchells and P-51 Mustangs attack bridges and rail targets. P-47 Thunderbolts and P-51s attack convoys and targets of opportunity in southern and eastern China.

ETO: Major General Otto P. Weyland takes command of Ninth Air Force; Brigadier General Homer L. Sanders takes command of XIX Tactical Air Command.

Karl Dönitz's attempt to form a new German government at Flensburg is ended when he is placed under arrest by British troops.

SOUTHWEST PACIFIC AREA: In the I Corps area the 25th Infantry Division captures Santa Far East Air Force on Luzon.

In the Philippines, Far East Air Force B-25 Mitchells, A-20 Havocs, P-38 Lightnings, and P-51 Mustangs support ground forces on Luzon at Cagayan Valley, Ipo Dam, and Balete Pass.

FEAF B-24 Liberators and B-25 Mitchells attack targets on Borneo, and P-38 Lightnings attack targets on Tarakan Island.

Staff Sergeant John C. Sjogren of I Company, 160th Infantry Regiment, 40th Infantry Division, leads his squad on an attack against a high ridge near San Jose Hacienda, Negros Island, in the Philippines. Entrenched Japanese riflemen defend the ridge, and they are supported by pillboxes with machine guns covering the avenues of approach. As his squad moves forward, he sees a buddy go down badly wounded. He runs to provide aid to the soldier, ignoring the rifle and machine-gun fire. He then moves forward into the face of the enemy fire and attacks the infantry positions, killing eight of the enemy defending the approach to the pillbox. He uses grenades to eliminate the position, even though wounded by grenade fragments. He leads his squad through the enemy position with his men providing covering fire while he throws grenades into the pillboxes. He even pulls a light machine gun out through an embrasure as it is firing, then throws a grenade into the pillbox. For his acts of courage, his selfless acts of leadership, and his aggressive determination to overcome a determined enemy, Staff Sergeant Sjogren will receive the Medal of Honor.

PACIFIC: During the night Twentieth Air Force sends more than 500 B-29s against the urban-industrial area of Tokyo. This is the largest number of B-29s involved in a single mission during the war. A total of 17 B-29s are lost.

Mines dropped by Twentieth Air Force B-29s sink three Japanese cargo ships and damage another in the Inland Sea and the Shimonoseki Strait.

PACIFIC, OKINAWA: The 184th Infantry Regiment of the 7th Infantry Division conducts an attack supported by large numbers of tanks, including flamethrower tanks. The attacks gain 2,000 yards past the town of Yonbaru. The 6th Marine Division enters the town of Naha, the capital of the island. Heavy rains make movement extremely difficult and slow the pace of battle to a crawl.

Japanese forces begin a gradual withdrawal to the south, using the overcast skies to cover their movement from aerial reconnaissance.

CENTRAL PACIFIC: VII Fighter Command sends 32 P-47 Thunderbolts from Saipan to strafe Moen Island airfields, boats off Tol Island, buildings on Tarik Island, and the seaplane base, buildings, and small boats at Dublon Island at Truk.

May 24

CBI: Fourteenth Air Force B-25 Mitchells, P-47 Thunderbolts, and P-51 Mustangs attack trucks, river traffic, highways, logistics storage sites, rail lines, bridges, troops, and targets of opportunity in southern and eastern China.

ETO: Brigadier General Richard C. Sanders takes command of the 9th Air Division.

SOUTHWEST PACIFIC AREA: In the Philippines, Far East Air Force B-24 Liberators bomb Cagayan Valley targets, supported by B-25 Mitchells, A-20 Havocs, and P-51 Mustangs. P-38 Lightnings support ground forces on Negros Island.

In Borneo, FEAF B-24 Liberators, B-25 Mitchells, and P-38 Lightnings attack Fort Brook, Bintula, Tawau, Beaufort, Jesselton, targets along the Lawas River, and Malinau.

PACIFIC: Carrier aircraft from TF 58 attack airfields in southern Kyushu, Japan.

Navy PBM Mariner patrol bombers sink a coastal defense ship in the South China Sea.

Mines dropped by Twentieth Air Force B-29s sink five Japanese cargo ships and a merchant tanker and damage a transport and three cargo ships in the Inland Sea and the Shimonoseki Strait.

During the night Twentieth Air Force sends 25 B-29s to mine Shimonoseki Strait.

PACIFIC, OKINAWA: Kamikazes damage a destroyer escort, a high-speed transport, and a large support landing craft off Okinawa.

CENTRAL PACIFIC: Seventh Air Force sends 26 B-24 Liberators from Guam to bomb the airfield on Marcus Island. VII Fighter Command sends 120 P-51 Mustangs from Iwo Jima to attack targets at Matsudo and Tokorozawa, Japan, but the mission is aborted due to bad weather. During the night P-47 Thunderbolts fly harassment strikes against Kyushu Island, Japan.

May 25

CBI: Fourteenth Air Force B-25 Mitchells and P-51 Mustangs attack bridges. P-47 Thunderbolts and P-51s fly armed reconnaissance missions.

ATLANTIC: Concluding that air bombardment and naval blockade alone will not force Japan's unconditional surrender, the Joint Chiefs of Staff approves the directive to begin formal planning for Operation Downfall, the invasion of the Japanese home islands. Downfall has two subordinate plans, Operation Olympic, the invasion of Kyushu, scheduled for November 1, 1945, and Operation Coronet, the invasion of Honshu, scheduled for April 1, 1946.

MEDITERRANEAN: Fifteenth Air Force sends the headquarters of the 484th Bombardment Group (Heavy) and the B-24 Liberators of the 824th, 825th, 826th, and 827th Bombardment Squadrons (Heavy) from Torretto, Italy, to Casablanca, French Morocco, to begin transporting troops home to the United States.

SOUTHWEST PACIFIC AREA: In Luzon, elements of the 1st Cavalry Division capture Infanta on the east coast of Luzon and stand on the left flank of the perimeter of the remainder of the Shimbu Group. The 38th and 43rd Infantry Divisions of XI Corps continue pressure on the Japanese defenders, now with their backs to the sea.

In the Philippines, Far East Air Force B-25 Mitchells, A-20 Havocs, P-38 Lightnings, and P-51 Mustangs support ground forces on Luzon and Cebu Islands.

In Borneo, FEAF B-24 Liberators bomb Oelin, Fort Brook, and along with P-38 Lightnings, attack targets on Tarakan Island. B-25 Mitchells and P-38s attack Kudat.

U.S. submarine *Blenny* torpedoes and sinks a Japanese gunboat in the Java Sea.

PACIFIC: Admiral Nimitz approves the transfer of operational and administrative control of VII Fighter Command to Twentieth Air Force.

P-51 Mustangs from Iwo Jima attack Matsudo and Tokorozawa airfields in Japan. Pilots report eight confirmed kills and one possible in the air and 10 confirmed kills and 40 possibles on the ground. Three P-51s are lost. During the night 464 B-29s bomb the urban area of Tokyo. Six other B-29s bomb targets of opportunity. Aircrews report 19 Japanese fighters shot down. A total of 26 B-29s are lost, the highest single-day loss of B-29s in the war.

Mines dropped by Twentieth Air Force B-29s sink four cargo vessels, a merchant tanker, and a transport and damage two destroyers, three cargo ships, and a merchant tanker in the Inland Sea and the Shimonoseki Strait.

U.S. submarine *Ray* torpedoes and sinks a Japanese schooner in the Yellow Sea.

PACIFIC, OKINAWA: Kamikazes sink a high-speed transport and a medium landing ship and damage two destroyers, a destroyer escort, two high-speed transports, a high-speed minesweeper, and a minesweeper off Okinawa. A U.S. freighter is hit by an aerial torpedo.

May 26
CBI: Fourteenth Air Force B-25 Mitchells and P-51 Mustangs bomb bridges and rail targets. P-47 Thunderbolts and P-51s attack trucks, road traffic, highways, rail lines, bridges, and troops in southern and eastern China. Japanese forces complete their withdrawal from Yungning and Chinese troops retake Nanning.

ETO: Eighth Air Force begins the redeployment of the headquarters, 398th Bombardment Group (Heavy), and the B-17s of the 600th, 601st, 602nd, and 603rd Bombardment Squadrons (Heavy) to the United States.

MEDITERRANEAN: Brigadier General James A. Mollison takes command of Fifteenth Air Force.

SOUTHWEST PACIFIC AREA: In the Philippines, Far East Air Force A-20 Havocs, P-38 Lightnings, and P-51 Mustangs support ground forces on Luzon and P-47 Thunderbolts attack targets on Cebu Island.

B-25s and P-38s sweep Formosa, hitting a number of communication and industrial targets.

FEAF B-24 Liberators, B-25 Mitchells, and P-38 Lightnings attack Tarakan Island and town areas on Borneo.

PACIFIC: Twentieth Air Force sends 16 P-47 Thunderbolts from Saipan to strafe airfields on Moen Island, the seaplane base on Dublon Island, and several targets of opportunity at Truk. Mines dropped by Twentieth Air Force B-29s sink an auxiliary submarine chaser and four cargo ships and damage a gunboat, a transport, and five cargo ships in the Inland Sea and the Shimonoseki Strait.

U.S. submarine *Billfish* torpedoes and sinks a Japanese cargo ship off Nagasaki, Japan.

During the night 29 B-29s mine waters in Shimonoseki Strait and waters off Shikoku and Kyushu, Japan.

PACIFIC, OKINAWA: Kamikazes damage a high-speed minesweeper and a submarine chaser off Okinawa.

CENTRAL PACIFIC: Seventh Air Force sends 10 B-24 Liberators from Guam to bomb the airfield on Marcus Island.

May 27
CBI: Fourteenth Air Force B-25 Mitchells attack rail bridges and rail cars. P-47 Thunderbolts and P-51 Mustangs attack trucks, rail lines, bridges, and troops in southern and eastern China.

SOUTHWEST PACIFIC AREA: In the Philippines, Far East Air Force B-24 Liberators, A-20 Havocs, P-38 Lightnings, and P-51 Mustangs support ground forces on Luzon at Cagayan Valley, the Balete Pass, Baguio, and Ipo Dam.

In French Indochina, B-24s bomb the railyards and rail cars.

B-25 Mitchells and P-38 Lightnings attack targets of opportunity on Formosa.

FEAF B-24 Liberators, B-25 Mitchells, and P-38 Lightnings attack town areas on Borneo and attack targets on Tarakan Island.

PACIFIC: During the night Twentieth Air Force sends nine B-29s to lay mines in Shimonoseki Strait and the area of the Inland Sea off Kyushu, Japan. One B-29 is lost.

Mines dropped by Twentieth Air Force B-29s sink two cargo ships and a merchant tanker and damage a cargo ship in the Inland Sea and the Shimonoseki Strait.

PACIFIC, OKINAWA: Admiral William F. Halsey, Jr., Commander Third Fleet, takes operational control of Task Force 58 from Admiral Raymond A. Spruance, Commander Fifth Fleet. The Fifth Fleet is redesignated as Third Fleet. TF 58 is redesignated TF 38.

Kamikazes damage two destroyers, a high-speed minesweeper, two high-speed transports, a surveying ship, and a submarine chaser.

CENTRAL PACIFIC: P-47 Thunderbolts from Saipan sweep Truk, strafing the airfield and facilities, aircraft, and the radio tower on Moen Island. Other targets on and near Dublon Island seaplane base are also attacked.

U.S. submarine *Tigrone* torpedoes and sinks a Japanese guardboat north of the Bonin Islands.

May 28

CBI: In China, Fourteenth Air Force P-51 Mustangs attack a bridge and military installations near Wuchang. P-51s attack bridges, troops, logistics storage sites, trucks, locomotives, river craft, and other targets near Yoyang.

In French Indochina, 19 B-25 Mitchells, along with eight P-51 Mustangs, attack rail, road, and river traffic.

ETO: Eighth Air Force redeploys the headquarters of the 445th Bombardment Group (Heavy) and the B-24 Liberators of the 564th, 565th, 566th, and 567th Bombardment Squadrons (Heavy) of the 389th Bombardment Group (Heavy).

SOUTHWEST PACIFIC AREA: In Luzon, the XI Corps captures the Wawa Dam. Japanese forces of the Shimbu Group are forced to withdraw into the Sierra Madre, where they will remain isolated until the end of the war.

In the Eighth Army area, the 164th Infantry Regiment of the Americal Division defeats the Japanese on Negros Island near Dumaguete. The Americans have lost 35 men killed and 180 wounded; Japanese casualties are 350 killed and 15 captured.

In the Philippines, Far East Air Force B-24 Liberators, B-25 Mitchells, A-20 Havocs, P-38 Lightnings, and P-47 Thunderbolts support ground forces on Luzon.

In French Indochina, B-24s bomb the railyards near Saigon.

On Formosa, B-25 Mitchells and P-38s attack industrial targets.

In Borneo, FEAF B-24 Liberators, B-25 Mitchells, and P-38 Lightnings attack gun positions and other targets at Balikpapan. P-38s conduct dive-bombing attacks on Keningau and Jesselton airfields.

U.S. submarines *Blueback* and *Lamprey* fight a surface engagement with a Japanese submarine chaser in the Java Sea.

PACIFIC: Twentieth Air Force sends P-51 Mustangs from Iwo Jima Island to attack the airfield at Kasumigaura. Pilots report six aircraft destroyed and over 40 damaged.

Mines dropped by Twentieth Air Force B-29s sink a transport and damage a coastal defense vessel, two cargo ships, and a fishing vessel in the Inland Sea and the Shimonoseki Strait.

U.S. submarine *Ray* torpedoes and sinks a Japanese cargo ship in the Yellow Sea.

During the night P-47 Thunderbolts fly harassment attacks against Kyushu.

PACIFIC, OKINAWA: Kamikazes sink destroyer USS *Drexler* and damage an attack transport and a large support landing craft. On *Drexler,* over 200 sailors are killed or injured. Kamikazes damage three U.S. freighters off Okinawa.

May 29

SOUTHWEST PACIFIC AREA: In Luzon, in the I Corps area, the 32nd Infantry Division captures Imugan after more than 90 days of battle to advance 6,000 yards up the Villa Verde Trail. The infantrymen have sealed 214 caves and killed over 9,000 enemy soldiers. The 32nd has lost 900 killed and 2,500 other casualties. The division's agonizing effort opens the way for the 25th Infantry Division to advance to Santa Fe.

In the Philippines, Far East Air Force B-24 Liberators, B-25 Mitchells, A-20 Havocs, P-38 Lightnings, and P-51 Mustangs support ground forces on Luzon in the Cagayan Valley, and at Baguio, Balete, and Ipo.

On Formosa, over 100 B-24s bomb town areas, and B-25 Mitchells and P-38 Lightnings attack an alcohol production facility and targets of opportunity.

In Borneo, FEAF B-24 Liberators attack airfields at Oelin, Tabanio, and Fort Brook.

PACIFIC: Twentieth Air Force sends 454 B-29s, escorted by 101 VII Fighter Command P-51 Mustangs, to bomb Yokohama with incendiaries. About 150 Japanese fighters attack the bombers. Aircrews report six fighters shot down. Fighter pilots report 26 confirmed kills, nine probables, and 23 possibles. Seven B-29s and three P-51s are lost.

Mines dropped by Twentieth Air Force B-29s sink a cargo ship and damage another in the Inland Sea and the Shimonoseki Strait.

U.S. submarine *Sterlet* torpedoes and sinks two Japanese cargo ships north of the Kuriles.

The headquarters of the 509th Composite Group arrives on Tinian Island from the United States.

PACIFIC, OKINAWA: The 5th Marine Regiment of the 1st Marine Division occupies Shuri, one of the main objectives of the American offensive since the invasion began. It is nothing but rubble.

The Japanese withdrawal to their final defensive line is completed. About 30,000 troops reach the new defenses successfully. The loss of civilians, who joined the Japanese troops, is particularly heavy. Many are killed by shellfire and aerial strafing. About 15,000 Japanese troops are also killed or wounded during the retreat.

Kamikazes hit a destroyer and a high-speed transport off Okinawa.

May 30
CBI: Fourteenth Air Force B-25 Mitchells attack railyards and rail bridges. P-47 Thunderbolts and P-51 Mustangs attack barracks, trucks, highways, rail lines, bridges, troops, and targets of opportunity in southern and eastern China.

ETO: Eighth Air Force begins redeploying the headquarters, 389th Bombardment Group (Heavy), and the B-24 Liberators of the 700th, 701st, 702nd, and 703rd Bombardment Squadron (Heavy) of the 445th Bombardment Group (Heavy).

SOUTHWEST PACIFIC AREA: In the Philippines, Far East Air Force A-20 Havocs support ground forces on Luzon in the Cagayan Valley.

On Formosa, over 100 B-24 Liberators bomb town areas. B-25 Mitchells hit town areas and P-38 Lightnings conduct sweeps.

FEAF B-24 Liberators and P-38 Lightning fighters attack personnel and logistics targets on Borneo.

U.S. submarine *Blenny* torpedoes and sinks a Japanese cargo ship in the Java Sea. U.S. submarine *Croaker* torpedoes and sinks two shuttle boats in the Java Sea.

PACIFIC: Twentieth Air Force sends 14 P-47 Thunderbolts to strafe barges at Truk Atoll. P-47 Thunderbolts from Ie Shima attack shipping and a lighthouse at Amami-O-Shima, Japan, and Okino Erabu in the Ryukyus.

Mines dropped by Twentieth Air Force B-29s sink a transport, three cargo ships, and damage two cargo ships in the Inland Sea and the Shimonoseki Strait.

The 320th Troop Carrier Squadron (C-47s and C-54s) and the B-29s of the 393rd Bombardment Squadron (Very Heavy) of the 509th Composite Group arrive at Tinian from the United States.

PACIFIC, OKINAWA: The 1st Marine Division links with the 96th Division south of Shuri, after the 96th advances 1,200 yards. Supported by tanks and self-propelled howitzers, the 7th Infantry Division advances against Japanese delaying forces at Mabel Hill. The 6th Marine Division moves past Naha and encounters a few strongpoints near the Kokuba River.

Aircraft from escort carrier USS *Anzio* sink Japanese submarine *I-361* southeast of Okinawa.

CENTRAL PACIFIC: Seventh Air Force sends 10 B-24 Liberators from Guam to attack the airfield on Marcus Island.

May 31
CBI: In China, Fourteenth Air Force B-25 Mitchells and P-47 Thunderbolts attack rail lines and rail cars and attack bridges.

All Tenth Air Force units and U.S. components of the Eastern Air Command (EAC) are withdrawn from the Southeast Asia Command (SEAC) and returned to the operational control of Army Air Forces. The Eastern Air Command is inactivated, along with the Strategic Air Force and the Combat Cargo Task Force.

ETO: Eighth Air Force sends the headquarters of the 303rd Bombardment Group (Heavy) and the B-17s of the 358th, 359th, 360th, and 427th Bombardment Squadrons to Casablanca, French Morocco, from England to begin flying troops from Europe to North Africa for return to the United States.

SOUTHWEST PACIFIC AREA: In Luzon in the I Corps area, the 37th Infantry Division, which has been moved from Baguio to Santa Fe, advances past the 25th Infantry Division in pursuit of the retreating Japanese.

In the Philippines, Far East Air Force B-25 Mitchells, A-20 Havocs, P-38 Lightnings, and P-47 Thunderbolts support ground forces on Luzon in the Cagayan Valley, Balete Pass, and at Baguio and Ipo. P-38s also support ground forces on Cebu Island.

On Formosa, B-24 Liberators, B-25s, and P-47s attack transportation and communication targets.

In Borneo, FEAF B-25 Mitchells and P-38 Lightnings attack troop concentrations on Tarakan Island and buildings at Belait. P-38s also attack airfields on Borneo and on Labuan Island.

PACIFIC: Mines dropped by Twentieth Air Force B-29s sink a cargo ship and damage a gunboat, a transport, and three cargo ships in the Inland Sea and the Shimonoseki Strait.

PACIFIC, OKINAWA: Private First Class Clarence B. Craft is a rifleman in G Company, 382nd Infantry Regiment, 96th Infantry, making a platoon attack to capture Hen Hill. The Japanese defenders of Hen Hill have broken every American attack, and now Craft and five men are sent forward to conduct a reconnaissance. They come under rifle and machine-gun fire and are bombarded with hand grenades that wound three of the group. Craft stands in full view of the enemy and fires on the Japanese, then moves forward, hitting every enemy soldier he sees. He reaches the crest of the hill, throwing hand grenades into the enemy positions. This incredible act of bravery allows the assault units to move forward quickly and support his one-man battle by bringing more grenades to the hilltop. He then attacks the main trenchline, firing his rifle into the packed defenders, forcing them to flee. He then destroys a heavy machine-gun position. Moving down the central trench to the mouth of a cave, Craft employs a demolition charge to seal the entrance, but it fails to explode. Without hesitation, he retrieves the explosive and relights the fuse. For his extraordinary act of heroism and combat skill in the face of an overwhelmingly large enemy force, Private First Class Craft will receive the Medal of Honor.

CENTRAL PACIFIC: Seventh Air Force sends eight P-47 Thunderbolts from Ie Shima Island to strafe buildings, barracks, and seaplane ramps at Amami-O-Shima, Japan.

June 1

CBI: Fourteenth Air Force B-25 Mitchells bomb railyards and bridges. P-51 Mustangs attack trucks, river traffic and logistics storage sites near Yoyang. P-47 Thunderbolts attack river shipping and bridges.

ETO: B-17s and B-24 Liberators of the 812th, 813th, and 814th Bombardment Squadrons (Heavy), 482nd Bombardment Group (Heavy), begin redeployment from England to the United States.

MEDITERRANEAN: The headquarters of the 465th Bombardment Group (Heavy) and the B-24 Liberators of the 780th, 781st, 782nd, and 783rd Bombardment Squadrons

(Heavy) begin redeployment from Italy to Trinidad, British West Indies. These aircraft will transport troops arriving from the European and Mediterranean theaters to the United States.

SOUTHWEST PACIFIC AREA: In Luzon, the XIV Corps commander, Major General Oscar W. Griswold, notifies Sixth Army commander, Lieutenant General Krueger, that all organized resistance in southern Luzon has been eliminated. The XIV Corps has killed over 14,000 enemy soldiers in southern Luzon.

In the Philippines, Far East Air Force B-25 Mitchells, A-20 Havocs, P-38 Lightnings, and P-47 Thunderbolts support ground forces on Luzon in the Cagayan Valley.

In Formosa, B-24 Liberators bomb town areas, while P-38s conduct sweeps along the coastline.

In Borneo, FEAF B-24 Liberators and P-38 Lightnings attack Tarakan Island troop concentrations, while B-24s, B-25s, and P-38s attack Kota Belud, Victoria, Jesselton, Langkon, and Labuan Island.

PACIFIC: Twentieth Air Force sends more than 450 B-29s to attack Osaka, escorted by 148 P-51 Mustangs of the VII Fighter Command. Severe weather prevents most of the fighters from making the rendezvous with the bombers. Conditions are so bad that 27 P-51s are lost. Aircrews report 16 Japanese fighters shot down. Fighter pilots report one confirmed kill in the air. Ten B-29s are lost. P-47 Thunderbolts from Ie Shima Island conduct strafing and rocket attacks against Kikaiga Island, Tokuno, and Amami Gunto, Japan.

B-29s bomb Osaka, damaging eight cargo ships, two army tankers, and two merchant tankers.

Mines dropped by Twentieth Air Force B-29s sink five cargo ships and a tanker and damage six cargo ships in the Inland Sea and the Shimonoseki Strait.

PACIFIC, OKINAWA: Tenth Army begins the final drive into the southern end of the island. The XXIV Corps on the left sends the 7th Infantry Division to cut off the Chinen Peninsula at the eastern end of the island to prevent the Japanese from using it as a stronghold. The 96th Infantry Division is to attack south toward the town of Iwa in the center. The III Amphibious Corps on the right sends the 6th Marine Division to clear the Oroku Peninsula below Naha to allow the port at Naha to be occupied and cleared for use.

CENTRAL PACIFIC: The naval air facility at Peleliu, Palau Islands, is established. The naval air base on Tarawa is shut down.

June 2

CBI: Fourteenth Air Force B-25 Mitchells attack fuel storage sites and ammunition storage areas in Burma. P-47 Thunderbolts and P-51 Mustangs attack airfields, railyards, trucks, tanks, logistics storage sites, and bridges in southern and eastern China.

SOUTHWEST PACIFIC AREA: In the Philippines, Far East Air Force B-25 Mitchells, A-20 Havocs, P-38 Lightnings, and P-47 Thunderbolts support ground forces on Luzon in the Cagayan Valley, the Balete Pass, and Ipo Dam. P-47s and P-38s attack Japanese defenses on Negros and Cebu Islands.

On Formosa, B-24 Liberators bomb town areas and attack warehouses and dock facilities at Kiirun.

In Borneo, FEAF B-24 Liberators attack an airfield and bomb Tarakan and Labuan Islands, while B-25 Mitchells and P-38 Lightnings attack Kudat, Sandakan, and Miri.

PACIFIC: Naval Task Force 38, commanded by Vice Admiral John S. McCain, bombs airfields in southern Kyushu, Japan.

U.S. submarine *Tench* torpedoes and sinks a Japanese cargo ships south of Hokkaido, Japan.

Mines dropped by Twentieth Air Force B-29s damage five cargo ships in the Inland Sea and the Shimonoseki Strait.

CENTRAL PACIFIC: Seventh Air Force sends 11 B-24 Liberators from Guam to bomb the airfield on Moen Island at Truk.

June 3

ALEUTIANS: Eleventh Air Force sends eight B-24 Liberators against the naval base on Shimushu Island in the Kuriles. The bombers use radar signal intercepts to mark the bomb release points over the target. Bombers also photograph targets. Three B-25 Mitchells conduct a low-level bomb run on a cannery near the Masugawa River.

CBI: Fourteenth Air Force B-25 Mitchells and P-47 Thunderbolts attack warehouses and river traffic. P-51 Mustangs attack bridges and trains.

SOUTHWEST PACIFIC AREA: In the Philippines, B-24 Liberators and P-38 Lightnings attack Japanese defenses on Negros Island. P-51 Mustangs attack coastal cargo vessels over the southeast China coast.

In Borneo, FEAF B-24 Liberators attack Kota Waringin and Muara Island and bomb Batavia, Java.

U.S. submarine *Blueback* torpedoes and sinks a merchant fishing boat near the Sunda Strait.

PACIFIC: Twentieth Air Force P-47 Thunderbolts from Ie Shima strafe targets of opportunity on Amami-O-Shima Island, Japan.

A naval task group commanded by Rear Admiral Lawrence F. Reifsnider lands marines on Iheya Jima in the Ryukyus.

Mines dropped by Twentieth Air Force B-29s sink four cargo ships and damage a minelayer and a cargo ship in the Inland Sea and Shimonoseki Strait.

U.S. submarine *Segundo* torpedoes and sinks a Japanese merchantman in the Yellow Sea.

PACIFIC, OKINAWA: The 4th Marine Regiment of the 6th Marine Division, supported by the 6th Tank Battalion, makes an amphibious landing on the Oroku Peninsula. The Naha airfield is quickly captured. The Japanese have strong defensive positions but not enough troops to man them adequately. The marines still have to fight yard by yard.

Task Group 38.4, commanded by Rear Admiral A. W. Radford, attacks Japanese airfields on Kyushu to eliminate the kamikaze menace.

Kamikazes damage a cargo ship and a large infantry landing craft off Okinawa.

June 4

ALEUTIANS: Eleventh Air Force sends 11 B-24 Liberators to bomb Kataoka naval base on Shimushu Island in the Kuriles. The bombers use radar signal intercepts to mark the bomb release point over the target.

CBI: Fourteenth Air Force B-25 Mitchells bomb railyards and warehouses. P-47 Thunderbolts and P-51 Mustangs attack road and rail traffic, bridges, and vehicles in southern and eastern China.

MEDITERRANEAN: Fifteenth Air Force begins redeploying the headquarters of the 451st Bombardment Group (Heavy) and the B-24 Liberators of the 724th, 725th, 726th, and 727th Bombardment Squadrons (Heavy) from Italy to the United States.

SOUTHWEST PACIFIC AREA: In the Eighth Army area, the 40th Infantry Division clears the Japanese from the hills beyond Bacolod on Negros. The battle has taken nearly 45 days and has cost the Americans over 1,300 casualties. The Japanese have lost more than 4,000 killed, and the survivors have scattered into the mountains.

In the Philippines, Far East Air Force B-25 Mitchells, A-20 Havocs, P-38 Lightnings, and P-47 Thunderbolts support ground forces on Luzon.

B-24 Liberators bomb town areas on Formosa.

In Borneo, FEAF B-24 Liberators bomb Balikpapan and Manggar and support ground forces on Tarakan Island. B-25 Mitchells attack Manggar, Djembajan, and Kudat.

Thirteenth Air Force B-24 Liberators sink a Japanese auxiliary submarine chaser and motor torpedo boat and damage an auxiliary submarine chaser in the Java Sea.

PACIFIC: U.S. submarine *Billfish* torpedoes and sinks a Japanese cargo ship in the Yellow Sea.

U.S. submarine *Tench* torpedoes and sinks a Japanese transport off western Honshu in the Japan Sea.

Mines dropped by Twentieth Air Force B-29s sink five cargo ships and damage a transport and two cargo ships in the Inland Sea and the Shimonoseki Strait.

During the night P-47 Thunderbolts from Ie Shima conduct strikes against Kyushu Island, Japan.

CENTRAL PACIFIC: Seventh Air Force sends 13 B-24 Liberators from Guam to bomb the airfield on Marcus Island.

Twentieth Air Force sends eight P-51 Mustangs from Iwo Jima to bomb the radio station on Chichi Jima and strafe the town of Okimura on Haha Jima.

June 5

CBI: Fourteenth Air Force P-47 Thunderbolts and P-51 Mustangs attack road and river traffic in southern and eastern China.

B-24 Liberators bomb town areas on Formosa.

SOUTHWEST PACIFIC AREA: In the Philippines, Far East Air Force B-25 Mitchells, A-20 Havocs, P-38 Lightnings, and P-47 Thunderbolts support ground forces on Luzon in the Cagayan Valley, at Balete Pass and at Ipo.

In Borneo, FEAF B-24 Liberators bomb airfields and Tarakan and Labuan Islands. B-25 Mitchells and P-38 Lightnings attack Tuaran, Mensalung, and Kudat.

Corporal Harry R. Harr of D Company, 124th Infantry Regiment, 31st Infantry Division, is manning a machine gun near Maglamin, Mindanao, as the Japanese launch a fierce counterattack on his company's position. The Japanese throw hand grenades toward Harr's machine gun and then move in quickly. As the crew struggles to put the gun into action after the grenade explosions, Harr sees another grenade land in the emplacement. He covers the grenade with his own body to save the lives of his comrades. For his supremely courageous act to save the lives of others, Corporal Harr will receive the Medal of Honor.

PACIFIC: Task Force 38 under command of Admiral William F. Halsey is caught in a typhoon after an incorrect weather estimate puts the task force in the path of the storm. The typhoon damages four battleships, two carriers, two small carriers, four escort carriers, three heavy cruisers, four light cruisers, 11 destroyers, three destroyer escorts, two oilers, and an ammunition ship.

Halsey is nearly relieved of duty, but Secretary of the Navy James V. Forrestal decides to keep the fighting admiral in place.

Twentieth Air Force sends more than 470 B-29s to bomb the city of Kobe, Japan, with incendiaries. Aircrews report 86 Japanese fighters shot down. A total of 11 B-29s are lost. About four square miles of the city are destroyed. P-47 Thunderbolts from Ie Shima Island patrol over Amami Gunto Island, Japan.

Mines dropped by Twentieth Air Force B-29s sink two cargo ships and damage a destroyer, an escort destroyer, and three cargo ships in the Inland Sea and the Shimonoseki Strait.

PACIFIC, OKINAWA: Kamikazes damage battleship USS *Mississippi* and a heavy cruiser off Okinawa.

June 6

CBI: Fourteenth Air Force B-25 Mitchells and P-51 Mustangs attack railyards and bridges. P-47 Thunderbolts and P-51s attack bridges, trucks, troops, and targets of opportunity in southern and eastern China.

ETO: The headquarters of Ninth Air Force moves from Chantilly, France, to Bad Kissingen, Germany.

MEDITERRANEAN: Fifteenth Air Force begins redeployment of the headquarters of the 460th Bombardment Group (Heavy) and the B-24 Liberators of the 760th, 761st, 762nd, and 763rd Bombardment Squadrons (Heavy) from Italy to Trinidad, British West Indies. The headquarters of the 464th Bombardment Group (Heavy) and the B-24s of the 776th, 777th, 778th, and 779th Bombardment Squadrons (Heavy) also begin redeployment from Italy to Trinidad, British West Indies.

SOUTHWEST PACIFIC AREA: Far East Air Force A-20 Havocs, P-38 Lightnings, and P-47 Thunderbolts support ground forces on Luzon.

In Borneo, FEAF B-24 Liberators, B-25 Mitchells, and P-38 Lightnings attack logistics storage sites, airfields, and troops on Labuan Island and provide support to ground forces on Tarakan Island, attack targets around Brunei, and bomb town areas.

Staff Sergeant Howard E. Woodford, I Company, 130th Infantry Regiment, 33rd Infantry Division, arrives at the line of departure for a Filipino guerrilla battalion near Tabio, Luzon, to find out why the unit has not attacked as ordered. Japanese mortar, machine-gun, and rifle fire has stopped the first element of the battalion. Woodford takes command of the lead company, evacuates the wounded, and prepares the men for the attack. He repeatedly exposes himself to draw fire so that he can locate the Japanese strongpoints, and then move forward with a group of five men to locate the Japanese defenses. He takes the company forward and captures the objective and organizes a perimeter defense for the night. Before dawn the next morning, the Japanese attack the position with mortars, grenades, and rifle fire. Although wounded by a grenade, Staff Sergeant Woodford calls for mortar fire until bullets destroy his radio. He picks up an M-1 rifle and encourages the guerrillas and takes a position where two guerrillas have been killed. Here he fights off enemy attacks until killed. A total of 37 dead Japanese soldiers lie about his position. For his daring, skillful, and inspiring leadership and courage under fire against a determined enemy, Staff Sergeant Woodford will receive the Medal of Honor.

PACIFIC: Twentieth Air Force sends 36 P-47 Thunderbolts from Ie Shima to conduct a sweep of southern Kyushu Island, Japan. Fighter pilots both strafe targets of opportunity and use rockets. Pilots report nine Japanese aircraft downed. Other P-47s patrol over Amami Gunto Island, Japan, strafing a lighthouse and buildings.

Mines dropped by Twentieth Air Force B-29s sink an auxiliary submarine chaser, a guardboat, two cargo ships, a destroyer, and a destroyer escort in the Inland Sea and the Shimonoseki Strait.

PACIFIC, OKINAWA: The Tenth Army attack stalls amid steady rain and a lack of adequate supply. The final Japanese defensive line is as strong as any the Americans have encountered. Anchored on Hills 95, 89, 69, and 155, with ridges, plateaus, and valleys of coral rock, the defensive line uses the terrain to its best advantage. Although 30,000 troops defend the line, only about 6,000 are capable of any type of determined resistance.

Lieutenant General Simon B. Buckner will pause three days to ensure enough supplies are brought forward to support the attack on the Japanese defensive line.

Kamikazes damage two light minelayers off Okinawa.

CENTRAL PACIFIC: Seventh Air Force sends 12 B-24 Liberators from Guam to bomb oil storage areas on Eten Island at Truk.

June 7

CBI: Japanese forces of the 20th Army are forced back by the Chinese divisions trained and supported by American advisers. The Japanese Imperial General Headquarters orders a general consolidation of Japanese forces into northern and central China to protect key ports and be available for movement to the home islands.

Fourteenth Air Force P-47 Thunderbolts and P-51 Mustangs attack trucks, river traffic, logistics storage sites, bridges, troops, and town areas in southern and eastern China.

ETO: Eighth Air Force begins redeployment of the B-24 Liberators of the 578th and 579th Bombardment Squadrons (Heavy) of the 392nd Bombardment Group (Heavy) from England to the United States.

SOUTHWEST PACIFIC AREA: In Luzon in the I Corps area the 37th Infantry Division captures Bayambong, dividing the Shobu Group in half.

In the Philippines, Far East Air Force A-20 Havocs, P-38 Lightnings, and P-47 Thunderbolts support ground forces on Luzon.

In Borneo, FEAF B-24 Liberators bomb Brooketon and Muara Island. B-25 Mitchells and P-38 Lightnings attack Kudat, Fort Brook, Belait, Jesselton, and Keningau.

Naval Task Group 74.3, commanded by Rear Admiral Russell S. Berkey, with three U.S. light cruisers, an Australian light cruiser, and seven destroyers, provides fire support for minesweepers and underwater demolition teams off Brunei Bay, Sarawak.

PACIFIC: Twentieth Air Force sends 409 B-29s, escorted by 138 P-51 Mustangs from VII Fighter Command, to bomb Osaka, Japan, with incendiary and high-explosive bombs. The bombers use radar to locate bomb release points. Over two square miles of the city are destroyed. Fighter pilots report two confirmed kills and one possible in the air. Two B-29s and a P-51 are lost.

During the night 26 B-29s mine Shimonoseki Strait and the waters off Fukuoka, Kyushu, Japan.

P-47 Thunderbolts from Ie Shima attack a radio station, warehouses, cargo ships, and motor launches on Kyushu Island, Japan. Pilots report five enemy aircraft downed.

U.S. submarine *Shad* torpedoes and sinks a Japanese army transport and a tanker in the East China Sea off Korea. U.S. submarine *Tench* torpedoes and sinks a Japanese guardboat in the Sea of Japan.

PACIFIC, OKINAWA: Kamikazes damage escort carrier USS *Natoma Bay* and a destroyer off Okinawa.

CENTRAL PACIFIC: Seventh Air Force sends 24 B-24 Liberators from Angaur Island to bomb the boat repair basin on Aurapushekaru Island in the Palaus.

The headquarters of the 41st Bombardment Group (Medium) and the B-25 Mitchells of the 396th and 820th Bombardment Squadrons (Medium) redeploy from Hawaii to Okinawa.

June 8

CBI: Fourteenth Air Force P-51 Mustangs and P-40s attack bridges near Hankow. P-47 Thunderbolts and P-51 Mustangs attack trucks, river traffic, airfields, logistics storage sites, and town areas in southern and eastern China.

SOUTHWEST PACIFIC AREA: In the Philippines, Far East Air Force P-38 Lightnings and P-47 Thunderbolts attack targets in the Cagayan Valley.

U.S. submarine *Cobia* torpedoes and sinks a Japanese transport and tanker off the southern coast of French Indochina.

In Borneo, FEAF B-24 Liberators bomb an airfield, while other B-24s, B-25 Mitchells, and P-38 Lightnings attack gun positions at Balikpapan.

Naval Task Group 74.3, commanded by Rear Admiral Russell S. Berkey, conducts a bombardment of Japanese positions in preparation for landings at Brunei Bay. A U.S. minesweeper clearing Brunei Bay hits a mine and sinks.

PACIFIC: Twentieth Air Force sends 104 P-51 Mustangs from Iwo Jima to attack Kagamigahara airfield and Meiji in Nagoya, Japan. Bad weather forces the fighters to abort the mission. The P-61 Black Widow night fighters of 548th Night Fighter Squadron, VII Fighter Command, redeploy from Iwo Jima to Ie Island.

Carrier aircraft from Naval Task Force 38 attack Kanoya airfield, Kyushu, Japan.

PACIFIC, OKINAWA: Hospital Apprentice First Class Fred F. Lester is a medical corpsman with an assault rifle platoon, 1st Battalion, 22nd Marines, 6th Marine Division, conducting an attack on a fortified hill position on Okinawa. When a marine falls wounded, Lester crawls toward him as small-arms fire and grenades hit nearby. Seriously wounded, Lester pulls the wounded marine to cover but is unable to assist him. He instructs two other marines in providing first aid. Realizing his own wounds are fatal, Lester refuses treatment and continues to direct treatment for two other wounded marines as his life ebbs away. For his dedication to duty and willingness to sacrifice his life to save others, Hospital Apprentice First Class Lester will receive the Medal of Honor.

June 9

ALEUTIANS: Eleventh Air Force sends B-24 Liberators and B-25 Mitchells in a coordinated attack with navy ships and aircraft to attack targets on Paramushiru Island in the Kuriles. Eight Japanese fighters attack the B-25s, forcing them to fly over Soviet airspace in Kamchatka. Soviet antiaircraft fire shoots down one B-25, and the entire aircrew is killed. Another B-25 crash-lands in Petropavlovsk.

CBI: Fourteenth Air Force P-47 Thunderbolts and P-51 Mustangs attack river traffic, bridges, and town areas in southern and eastern China.

ETO: Eighth Air Force begins redeploying the headquarters of the 351st Bombardment Group (Heavy) and its three B-17 squadrons and two of the B-24 squadrons of the 392nd Bombardment Group (Heavy) from England to the United States.

SOUTHWEST PACIFIC AREA: In the Philippines, Far East Air Force P-38 Lightnings and P-47 Thunderbolts support ground forces on Luzon in the Cagayan Valley.

In Borneo, FEAF B-24 Liberators bomb Labuan Island and drop napalm on Brooketon.

PACIFIC: Twentieth Air Force sends 44 B-29s to attack the Kawanishi Aircraft Company's production facility at Narao; another 24 B-29s use radar to locate bomb release points to attack the Kawasaki production facility at Akashi. More than 40 B-29s attack Aichi's Atsuta production facility.

During the night 26 B-29s mine Shimonoseki Strait.

A total of 20 P-47 Thunderbolts from Ie Shima strafe various targets of opportunity on Kyushu Island, Japan. P-51 Mustangs from Iwo Jima Island bomb Kagamigahara airfield and the surrounding area at Nagoya, Japan. Pilots report over 20 Japanese aircraft destroyed on the ground. Three P-51 Mustangs are lost.

A naval task group commanded by Rear Admiral Lawrence F. Reifsnider lands marines on Aguni Jima in the Ryukyus. Rear Admiral Arthur W. Radford's naval task group bombards Okino Daito Jima in the Ryukyus.

U.S. submarine *Sea Owl* torpedoes and sinks a Japanese coastal defense vessel in Tsushima Strait. U.S. submarine *Crevalle* torpedoes and sinks a Japanese cargo ship in the Japan Sea west of Honshu, Japan. U.S. submarine *Sea Dog* attacks Japanese shipping off the northwest coast of Honshu, sinking two cargo ships. U.S. submarine *Tench* torpedoes and sinks a Japanese transport off southern Hokkaido. U.S. submarine *Tinosa* torpedoes and sinks a Japanese cargo ship off the east coast of Korea.

Mines dropped by Twentieth Air Force B-29s sink two cargo ships in the Inland Sea and the Shimonoseki Strait.

Navy patrol bombers sink a Japanese cargo ship in the Japan Sea off the east coast of Korea.

PACIFIC, OKINAWA: The commander of the 7th Infantry Division, Major General Archibald V. Arnold, orders the 32nd and 17th Infantry Regiments to clear Japanese positions defending Hill 95. Japanese fire is accurate and effective against the exposed infantrymen.

June 10

ALEUTIANS: Eleventh Air Force sends two B-24 Liberators to fly a shipping attack mission with navy bombers. Aircrews report one cargo ship sunk off the coast of Paramushiru Island in the Kuriles.

CBI: Fourteenth Air Force P-51 Mustangs attack trucks, river traffic, highways, fuel storage sites, bridges, and barracks in southern and eastern China.

SOUTHWEST PACIFIC AREA: In the Philippines, Far East Air Force P-38 Lightnings, and P-47 Thunderbolts support ground forces on Luzon in the Cagayan Valley.

In Borneo, FEAF B-24 Liberators bomb Labuan Island and Brooketon, in coordination with landings of the Australian 9th Division on the shore of Brunei Bay, and attack targets on Labuan and Muara Islands.

Naval Task Group 74.3 provides naval bombardment while American and Royal Australian Air Force aircraft attack Japanese positions as Australian troops land at Brunei Bay, Borneo.

PACIFIC: Twentieth Air Force sends 23 B-29s to bomb the seaplane base at Kasumigaura. Over 30 B-29s bomb the Japan Aircraft Company production facility at Tomioka; over 100 B-29s attack the Nakajima Aircraft production facility at Musashi, but cloud cover over the primary target brings the bombers to the Attackachi engineering works at Kaigan. A total of 26 B-29s attack the Attackachi production facility at Chiba. Over 50 B-29s attack the Nakajima production facilities at Ogikubu and Omiya. One B-29 is lost. Nearly 30 B-29s bomb the Tachikawa Army Air Arsenal. The bombers are escorted by 107 VII Fighter Command P-51 Mustangs. Fighter pilots report 27 confirmed kills, seven probables, and 10 possibles in the air.

P-47 Thunderbolts from Ie Shima conduct a sweep over Kyushu Island, Japan, strafing numerous ground targets of opportunity. Pilots report 17 enemy aircraft shot down.

A naval task group commanded by Rear Admiral Joseph J. Clark attacks the airfield and other installations on Minami Daito Jima in the Ryukyus.

U.S. submarine *Crevalle* torpedoes and sinks a Japanese cargo ship near Tsugaru Strait, between Honshu and Hokkaido Islands. U.S. submarine *Dace* attacks a Japanese convoy in Sea of Okhotsk, sinking a cargo ship. U.S. submarine *Flying Fish* torpedoes and sinks a Japanese cargo ship in the Yellow Sea. U.S. submarine *Skate* torpedoes and sinks Japanese submarine *I-122* in the Sea of Japan. U.S. submarine *Spadefish* attacks Japanese shipping off Hokkaido and sinks a cargo ship, a transport, and a cargo ship. U.S. submarine *Tench* torpedoes and sinks a Japanese merchant tanker off southern Hokkaido, Japan.

Navy PB4Y-2 Privateers from Okinawa conduct aerial mining around Korea to limit the range of Japanese shipping. The bombers encounter intense antiaircraft fire from Japanese warships in Tsushima Strait as they attempt to drop mines at Pusan harbor. Other Privateers sink a Japanese merchant tanker off the west coast of Korea.

PACIFIC, OKINAWA: Tenth Army commander Lieutenant General Simon B. Buckner sends a personal letter to Lieutenant General Mitsuru Ushijima, the commander of the Japanese 32nd Army, requesting that he surrender his troops to prevent further useless bloodshed. Ushijima, who receives the letter on June 17, cannot help but laugh at the American commander's lack of understanding of the Japanese military code of honor and sacrifice.

The 381st and 383rd Infantry Regiments of the 96th Infantry Division attack Japanese defenses at Yaeju Dake and Yuza Dake. The area is heavily mined, and the hills are well defended with veteran troops.

The 1st Marine Division attacks against the strongest and best defended position of the final Japanese defensive line, Kunishi Ridge. During the night Japanese soldiers attempt to enter the marine lines mixed among civilians. The Japanese soldiers are discovered and killed in a wild fight. Some women among the group are killed and are found to be carrying explosives and grenades for a suicide attack.

A kamikaze sinks destroyer USS *William D. Porter* off Okinawa. As the destroyer burns, Lieutenant Richard M. McCool, Jr., maneuvers his large support landing craft alongside to take on survivors. A destroyer escort is damaged by fire from a shore battery.

June 11

ALEUTIANS: Eleventh Air Force sends eight B-24 Liberators on a shipping sweep over the Kurile Islands. Bad weather precludes finding any targets. The bombers then use radar to assist in locating and bombing installations on Kurabu Cape, Paramushiru Island, and around the Kataoka area of Shimushu Island.

CBI: Fourteenth Air Force B-25 Mitchells attack railyards. P-47 Thunderbolts and P-51 Mustangs attack river traffic, highways, rail lines, bridges, and targets of opportunity in southern and eastern China.

SOUTHWEST PACIFIC AREA: In the Philippines, Far East Air Force B-25 Mitchells, A-20 Havocs, P-38 Lightnings, and P-47 Thunderbolts support ground forces on Luzon in the Cagayan Valley and near Ipo.

In Borneo, FEAF B-24 Liberators support ground forces on Tarakan Island and bomb Kota Baru, Laoet Island, and Tawau. P-38 Lightnings attack Beaufort while B-25 Mitchells support ground forces in the Brunei Bay sector.

PACIFIC: During the night Twentieth Air Force sends 26 B-29s to mine Shimonoseki Strait and Tsuruga Bay. P-51 Mustangs from Iwo Jima attack Tokorozawa airfield, Japan. Fighter pilots report 18 aircraft destroyed on the ground and over 30 damaged. Combat crews and B-29s of the 509th Composite Group begin to arrive at Tinian.

U.S. cruisers and destroyers commanded by Rear Admiral John H. Brown, Jr., bombard Japanese installations on Matsuwa, in the Kuriles.

U.S. submarine *Bowfin* torpedoes and sinks a Japanese cargo ship off Korea. U.S. submarine *Crevalle* torpedoes and sinks a Japanese gunboat off Honshu, Japan. U.S. submarine *Flying Fish* torpedoes and sinks a Japanese cargo ship off Korea. U.S. submarine *Sea Dog* torpedoes and sinks a Japanese cargo ship off western Honshu, Japan. U.S. submarine *Segundo* torpedoes and sinks a Japanese cargo ship in the Yellow Sea. U.S. submarine *Tirante* torpedoes and sinks a Japanese cargo ship near southern Kyushu, Japan. A Navy PB4Y-2 Privateer sinks a Japanese auxiliary submarine chaser at the entrance to Ise Bay, Honshu, Japan, but the aircraft is damaged when the submarine chaser explodes.

Navy PB4Y-2 Privateers from Okinawa attempt a second aerial mining mission in Korean waters but abort due to bad weather.

PACIFIC, OKINAWA: The 32nd Infantry Regiment uses a flame tank from C Company, 713th Flame Tank Battalion, and a company of infantrymen to burn its way to the top of Hill 95.

When two kamikazes approach his large support landing craft off Okinawa, Lieutenant Richard M. McCool, Jr., orders his crew into action. One enemy plane is destroyed, but the other crashes into landing craft, hitting the conning tower where Lieutenant McCool is, and turning the entire area into an inferno. Although wounded and burned, he leads his men to fight the flames and turns to rescue sailors trapped in a burning compartment. Lieutenant McCool carries one sailor to safety and suffers additional burns. Ignoring his condition and the dangers around him, Lieutenant McCool stays at his post until other ships come to his aid. For his extraordinary leadership and demonstrated courage, in addition to his cool actions the previous day in rescuing survivors of the destroyer USS *William D. Porter*, Lieutenant Richard M. McCool, Jr., will receive the Medal of Honor.

June 12
ALEUTIANS: Eleventh Air Force sends four B-25 Mitchells to strafe shipping off Paramushiru Island. Aircrews report four cargo ships and two barges damaged. One B-25 is lost.

CBI: Fourteenth Air Force B-25 Mitchells attack a bridge. P-51 Mustangs and P-61 Black Widow night fighters attach rail lines, logistics storage sites, highways, troops, and antiaircraft positions in southern and eastern China.

ETO: Eighth Air Force moves the headquarters of the 92nd Bombardment Group (Heavy) and two B-17 squadrons to Istres, France, where they will begin transporting troops from Marseille to Casablanca for return to the United States. The headquarters of the 379th Bombardment Group (Heavy) begins moving to Casablanca,

French Morocco. The headquarters of the 467th Bombardment Group (Heavy) and four squadrons of B-24s begin redeployment from England to the United States.

SOUTHWEST PACIFIC AREA: In Luzon, the two RCTs of the 6th Infantry Division move into the Bayambong area to support the 33rd Infantry Division in reducing the Kiangan Pocket, one of the isolated elements of the Shobu Group.

In the Philippines, Far East Air Force B-25 Mitchells, A-20 Havocs, P-38 Lightnings, and P-47 Thunderbolts support ground forces on Luzon at Cagayan Valley, Balete Pass, and east of Manila.

In French Indochina, B-24 Liberators bomb the railyards at Saigon. B-24s also attack the navy yard and dock area at Hong Kong. Aircrews report heavy damage to the facilities.

FEAF P-38 Lightnings attack targets on Tarakan Island, the Brunei Bay area, and coastal routes in north Borneo.

PACIFIC: U.S. submarine *Sea Dog* torpedoes and sinks two cargo ships in the Sea of Japan west of Honshu. U.S. submarine *Skate* torpedoes and sinks three Japanese cargo ships and damages a cargo ship in the Sea of Japan off northern Honshu. U.S. submarine *Spadefish* torpedoes and sinks a Japanese guardboat west of Hokkaido. U.S. submarine *Tinosa* torpedoes and sinks a Japanese cargo ship in the Sea of Japan off Korea.

Mines dropped by Twentieth Air Force B-29s sink three cargo ships and a liaison ship and damage an army tanker in the Inland Sea and the Shimonoseki Strait.

PACIFIC, OKINAWA: The 4th and 29th Marine Regiments of the 6th Marine Division break the final resistance on the Oroku Peninsula. Over 1,600 marines are casualties in nine days of fighting an understrength enemy in prepared positions. The marines find elaborate cave complexes and tunnels that are completely impervious to artillery bombardment.

Two battalions of the 17th Infantry Regiment of the 7th Infantry Division conduct a night attack on Yaeju Dake escarpment near Hill 95 and gain complete surprise, using flame tanks to destroy Japanese positions, preventing the Japanese from controlling a key position and stopping a counterattack.

The 96th Infantry Division also holds off Japanese counterattacks.

CENTRAL PACIFIC: Seventh Air Force sends 12 B-24 Liberators from Guam to bomb the airfield on Marcus Island.

June 13

CBI: Fourteenth Air Force B-25 Mitchells and P-51 Mustangs attack railyards and communication centers near Puchou. P-51s attack rail lines and bridges.

U.S. submarine *Bergall* is damaged when it hits an Allied mine in the Gulf of Siam and is forced to terminate her patrol.

Mines dropped by Fourteenth Air Force B-24 Liberators sink a Japanese cargo ship off Macao.

SOUTHWEST PACIFIC AREA: In the Philippines, Far East Air Force B-25 Mitchells, A-20 Havocs, P-38 Lightnings, and P-47 Thunderbolts support ground forces on Luzon in the Cagayan Valley.

B-24 Liberators bomb a town area, a naval base, and airfields in Formosa.

FEAF B-24 Liberators bomb targets near Balikpapan-Sepinggang. B-25 Mitchells and P-38 Lightnings support ground forces in the Brunei Bay area and sweep north Borneo, attacking numerous targets of opportunity.

PACIFIC: During the night Twentieth Air Force sends 29 B-29s to drop mines in Shimonoseki Strait and in the waters at Niigata, west-central Honshu, Japan. Mines dropped by Twentieth Air Force B-29s sink four cargo ships and damage an escort destroyer and five cargo ships in the Inland Sea and the Shimonoseki Strait.

P-47 Thunderbolts from Ie Shima strafe and fire rockets at vessels, buildings, a radio station, barracks, and airfields at Amakusa Jima and Amami-O-Shima Islands, and Tokuno, Japan.

U.S. submarine *Bonefish* torpedoes and sinks a Japanese cargo ship in the Sea of Japan.

U.S. submarine *Bowfin* torpedoes and sinks a Japanese cargo ship in the Sea of Japan east of Korea. U.S. submarine *Skate* torpedoes and sinks a Japanese cargo ship in the Sea of Japan.

U.S. submarine *Spadefish* mistakenly sinks a Russian cargo ship west of Hokkaido, Japan.

PACIFIC, OKINAWA: The 7th Marines of the 1st Marine Division gain a foothold on Kunishi Ridge. Tanks support the marines, bringing supplies and reinforcements. The battle to control the ground will last for five more days as the 5th Marines support the 7th in clearing the caves and tunnels.

The destroyer USS *Twiggs* is sunk by a Japanese torpedo plane; over 150 sailors are lost.

CENTRAL PACIFIC: Seventh Air Force sends 13 B-24 Liberators from Guam to bomb the airfield on Moen Island at Truk.

June 14

CBI: In China, Fourteenth Air Force sends 42 P-51 Mustangs to attack bridges, shipping, antiaircraft positions, rail lines, trucks, and communications around Hengyang, Hankow, Yoyang, Lingling, Puchou and other nearby areas.

ATLANTIC: The Joint Chiefs of Staff directs Generals of the Army Henry H. Arnold and Douglas MacArthur and Fleet Admiral Chester W. Nimitz to initiate planning for the immediate occupation of Japan in case the Japanese are unable to resist any longer or surrender.

ETO: Eighth Air Force prepares the headquarters of the 458th Bombardment Group (Heavy) for redeployment from England to the United States.

SOUTHWEST PACIFIC AREA: In the Philippines, Far East Air Force B-25 Mitchells, A-20 Havocs, P-38 Lightnings, and P-47 Thunderbolts support ground forces on Luzon in the Cagayan Valley and east of Manila.

FEAF B-24 Liberators bomb warehouses and troop assembly areas on Celebes Island. B-24s bomb antiaircraft positions at Balikpapan in Borneo.

PACIFIC: U.S. submarine *Sea Devil* torpedoes and sinks a Japanese transport in the northern Yellow Sea. U.S. submarine *Spadefish* torpedoes and sinks a Japanese cargo ship off western Sakhalin Island.

Navy PB4Y-2 Privateers from Okinawa conduct aerial mining of the waters of southern Korea.

June 15

CBI: Fourteenth Air Force sends three B-25 Mitchells, as well as P-47 Thunderbolts, and P-51 Mustangs to attack trucks, river traffic, barracks, highways, gun positions, logistics storage sites, rail lines, bridges, and town areas in southern and eastern China.

Tenth Air Force B-24 Liberators attack a Japanese convoy in the Gulf of Siam, sinking a merchant tanker and damaging a destroyer and a minesweeper.

ATLANTIC: The Joint War Plans Committee submits a briefing paper to the Joint Chiefs of Staff reaffirming its recommendation that an invasion of the home islands is the only means for the decisive defeat of Japan. Planners estimate 193,000 American casualties. Although Soviet participation in the invasion is no longer essential to success, Soviet forces could be useful in holding Japanese troops in northern China and Manchuria and preventing them from reinforcing the home island defenses.

ETO: Eighth Air Force begins to redeploy the headquarters of the 44th Bombardment Group (Heavy) and the two B-24 squadrons to the United States. The headquarters of the 392nd Bombardment Group and its three B-24 squadrons are also returning to the United States.

MEDITERRANEAN: Eighth Air Force sends the headquarters of the 460th Bombardment Group (Heavy) from Italy to Trinidad, British West Indies, to support the transport of American troops returning to the United States.

SOUTHWEST PACIFIC AREA: In Luzon, the XIV Corps is relieved of responsibility for southern Luzon. The corps headquarters is transferred to San José to support offensive operations in northern Luzon.

In the Philippines, Far East Air Force B-25 Mitchells, A-20 Havocs, P-38 Lightnings, and P-47 Thunderbolts support ground forces on Luzon in the Cagayan Valley.

In Formosa, B-24 Liberators bomb an airfield and B-25 Mitchells attack town areas and an airfield.

In Borneo, FEAF B-24 Liberators bomb gun positions at Balikpapan and B-25 Mitchells and P-38 Lightnings attack Japanese positions between Brunei and Kudat.

PACIFIC: Twentieth Air Force sends 444 B-29s to bomb the Osaka-Amagasaki urban area in Japan with incendiaries. Over two square miles of the cities are burned out. Two B-29s are lost. The 123 P-51 Mustangs from Iwo Jima that were to escort the bombers are forced to abort due to weather. One fighter is lost.

Twentieth Air Force sends 30 B-29s to mine Shimonoseki Strait and the waters off Fukuoka, west Honshu, and Karatsu, west Kyushu, Japan.

U.S. submarine *Sea Dog* torpedoes and sinks a Japanese cargo ship in the Sea of Japan west of Honshu, Japan.

The B-29s of the 680th Bombardment Squadron (Very Heavy), under the operational control of 504th Bombardment Group (Very Heavy), arrives at Tinian Island from the United States.

PACIFIC, OKINAWA: The 8th Marine Regiment of the 2nd Marine Division is placed under the operational control of the 1st Marine Division on Okinawa. The regiment has arrived from Guam and has been involved in capturing two small offshore islands. Observing the regiment's first offensive operation with III Amphibious Corps commander, Lieutenant General Roy S. Geiger, Lieutenant General Simon B. Buckner, commander of Tenth Army, is killed by Japanese artillery fire. Geiger takes command of Tenth Army.

June 16

ALEUTIANS: Eleventh Air Force sends four B-24 Liberators to bomb and strafe shipping off Suribachi Bay, Paramushiru Island, and a radar site on Minami Cape of Shimushu Island in the Kuriles. One B-24 crashes into the water. Four B-25 Mitchells on a shipping strike attack a cargo ship, and two of the B-25s are forced to land at Petropavlovsk in the Soviet Union because of mechanical trouble.

CBI: Fourteenth Air Force B-25 Mitchells attack road convoys, while P-51 Mustangs attack trucks, river traffic, highways, rail lines, bridges, power facilities, and targets of opportunity in southern and eastern China.

SOUTHWEST PACIFIC AREA: In the Philippines, Far East Air Force B-25 Mitchells, A-20 Havocs, P-38 Lightnings, and P-47 Thunderbolts support ground forces on Luzon in the Cagayan Valley and east of Manila.

B-24 Liberators bomb Kiirun harbor and town areas on Formosa. The headquarters of the 308th Bombardment Wing (Heavy) redeploys from Luzon to Okinawa Island.

In Borneo, FEAF B-24 Liberators bomb Balikpapan gun emplacements, while B-25 Mitchells attack the Brunei Bay area and P-38 Lightnings attack airfields and targets of opportunity in north Borneo.

PACIFIC: Twentieth Air Force receives P-61 Black Widow night fighters on Ie Shima Island. Other P-61 Black Widow night fighters fly night intruder missions over Amami Gunto Island, Japan, bombing various targets of opportunity. P-47 Thunderbolts from Ie Shima Island dive-bomb boats, antiaircraft positions, runways, and buildings on Kikai Island, Japan.

U.S. destroyer *Twiggs* is sunk during an attack by an aerial torpedo off Okinawa.

U.S. submarine *Piranha* torpedoes and sinks a Japanese cargo ship in the Sea of Japan west of Honshu.

PACIFIC, OKINAWA: The 382nd and 381st Infantry Regiments of the 96th Infantry Division clear the last Japanese defenders from Yuza Dake. The infantry often must clear the same position several times as the enemy will return to those positions through a maze of underground tunnels. Japanese troops and civilians are caught in the open near the town of Makabe and hit by 22 battalions of artillery firing at once.

June 17

ALEUTIANS: Eleventh Air Force sends four B-25 Mitchells to bomb shipping near Kataoka, Shimushu Island. Aircrews report one cargo ship destroyed, another damaged. Four other B-25s fly a shipping sweep.

CBI: General of the Army Henry H. Arnold, Commanding General U.S. Army Air Forces, requests that Lieutenant General Albert C. Wedemeyer, Commander of U.S. Forces in China, replace Major General Clare L. Chennault as commander of Fourteenth Air Force with Lieutenant General George E. Stratemeyer. Chennault has become increasingly unpopular and is seen as being too close to Generalissimo Chiang-Kai-shek.

Fourteenth Air Force B-25 Mitchells attack road and rail lines. P-47 Thunderbolts, P-61 Black Widow night fighters, and P-51 Mustangs attack trucks, river traffic, highways, logistics storage sites, rail lines, bridges, troops, and town areas in southern and eastern China.

The headquarters of XX Bomber Command begins redeployment from India to Okinawa.

SOUTHWEST PACIFIC AREA: In the Philippines, Far East Air Force B-25 Mitchells, A-20 Havocs, P-38 Lightnings, and P-47 Thunderbolts support ground forces on Luzon in the Cagayan Valley.

B-24 Liberators bomb industrial and railroad targets and P-38 Lightnings bomb a railroad bridge and trucks on Formosa.

In Borneo, FEAF B-24 Liberators bomb gun positions and oil targets in the Balikpapan area. B-25 Mitchells and P-38 Lightnings attack towns and conduct a sweep from Beaufort to Jesselton, attacking communication targets and troop concentrations on Labuan Island.

PACIFIC: During the night Twentieth Air Force sends 25 B-29s to mine Shimonoseki Strait and waters around Kobe, Honshu, Japan. Over 100 B-29s attack the Kagoshima urban area with incendiaries, destroying over two square miles of the city. One B-29 is lost. Over 100 B-29s attack the Omuta urban area. A total of 130 B-29s attack the Hamamatsu urban area with incendiaries, destroying over two square miles of the city. Nearly 90 B-29s attack the Yokkaichi urban area, destroying one square mile of the city. P-47 Thunderbolts from Ie Shima bomb and strafe shipping, the airfield, villages, a bridge, and radar and radio facilities on Amami Gunto Island and Tokuno, Japan. During the night P-61 Black Widow night fighters from Ie Shima attempt an intruder strike over Amami Gunto and Kyushu, Japan, but are turned back because of bad weather.

U.S. submarine *Spadefish* attacks a Japanese convoy, sinking an auxiliary minelayer off Hokkaido, Japan.

PACIFIC, OKINAWA: The 7th Infantry Division captures Hills 115 and 155 employing flame tanks to burn lanes for the infantry to advance.

June 18

ALEUTIANS: Eleventh Air Force send six B-24 Liberators along with navy aircraft to attack Kataoka, Shimushu Island, and Tomari Cape, Paramushiru Island.

CBI: Fourteenth Air Force P-47 Thunderbolts, P-61 Black Widow night fighters, and P-51 Mustangs attack trucks, river traffic, highways, barracks, logistics storage sites, rail lines, bridges, troop concentrations, and town areas in southern and eastern China.

ATLANTIC: President Harry S. Truman approves Operation Olympic, the invasion of Kyushu. It involves three army and three marine divisions that will land near

Kagoshima Bay. Three more army divisions will land at Miyazaki on Kyushu's east coast. Truman delays authorizing Coronet and asks the JCS and the service secretaries for their views on whether the Soviet Union's assistance is still necessary to defeat Japan. General Marshall believes that a Soviet declaration of war may be enough to force the Japanese to surrender. All recommend that the president seek a way to modify the unconditional surrender terms for Japan so that Emperor Hirohito, the national leader, can stay in power. Truman also hears from his political advisers that the war must be ended soon before the British and the Soviets become too deeply involved in the postwar planning in the Pacific.

SOUTHWEST PACIFIC AREA: In the Philippines, Far East Air Force B-25 Mitchells, A-20 Havocs, P-38 Lightnings, and P-47 Thunderbolts support ground forces on Luzon in the Cagayan Valley, Balete Pass, and other areas.

In Formosa, B-24 Liberators bomb buildings, warehouses and small vessels at Kiirun. P-51 Mustangs attack airfields and targets of opportunity and P-38 Lightnings bomb a town area.

In Borneo, FEAF B-24 Liberators bomb troop concentrations in Balikpapan and near Miri, Manggar airfield, and defenses at Sepinggang. B-25 Mitchells support ground forces on Labuan Island.

U.S. submarine *Bullhead* torpedoes and sinks a Japanese auxiliary sailing vessel in the Sunda Strait off Sumatra.

PACIFIC: U.S. submarine *Apogon* attacks a Japanese convoy and sinks a transport and guardboat southwest of Paramushiro, Kuriles.

U.S. submarine *Tinosa* torpedoes and sinks a Japanese ship in the Yellow Sea.

U.S. submarine *Bonefish* in cooperation with USS *Tunny* sinks a cargo ship off Honshu.

An escort destroyer and several coastal defense vessels will later sink USS *Bonefish*.

U.S. submarine *Dentuda* torpedoes and sinks two Japanese guardboats in the East China Sea.

Navy PB4Y-2 Privateers continue aerial mining operations of Korean waters.

Mines dropped by Twentieth Air Force B-29s sink a transport, an auxiliary submarine chaser, and two cargo ships in the Inland Sea and the Shimonoseki Strait.

PACIFIC, OKINAWA: Reinforced by a battalion of the 22nd Marines from the 6th Marine Division, the 5th and 7th Marines of the 1st Marine Division break the Japanese defenses at Kunishi and Mezado Ridge. The Japanese left flank has been turned.

June 19

ALEUTIANS: Eleventh Air Force sends a B-24 on the longest mission in theater, a 2,700-mile flight lasting over 15 hours and flying as far as Uruppu Island, Japan. The B-24 bombs a small convoy off Shimushu Bay, Shimushu Island. Aircrew reports one vessel sunk, one heavily damaged, and two set afire.

CBI: Fourteenth Air Force B-25 Mitchells and P-47 Thunderbolts attack a rail bridge. P-47s and P-51 Mustangs attack trucks, river traffic, highways, logistics storage sites, rail lines, bridges, troops, and targets of opportunity in southern and eastern China.

ETO: Eighth Air Force begins the redeployment of the headquarters of the 95th Bombardment Group (Heavy) to the United States.

SOUTHWEST PACIFIC AREA: In the Philippines, Far East Air Force A-20 Havocs, P-38 Lightnings, and P-47 Thunderbolts support ground forces on Luzon in the Cagayan Valley and elsewhere.

In Formosa, B-24 Liberators bomb docks, warehouses, and rail yards at Kiirun, and B-25 Mitchells bomb railroad yards. P-51 Mustangs attack antiaircraft positions and bridges.

FEAF B-24 Liberators bomb fortifications and antiaircraft guns at Balikpapan while B-25 Mitchells attack airfields and other targets in north Borneo.

U.S. submarine *Bullhead* torpedoes and sinks a Japanese auxiliary sailing vessel in the Sunda Strait.

PACIFIC: Twentieth Air Force sends 136 B-29s to attack the Toyohashi urban area, destroying nearly two square miles of the city. Over 200 B-29s attack the Fukuoka urban area, destroying nearly 1.5 square miles of the city. Another 123 B-29s attack the Shizuoka urban area, destroying nearly 2.5 square miles of the city. One B-29 is lost. A total of 28 B-29s mine Shimonoseki Strait and the waters off Niigata, west-central Honshu, and Maizuru, south Honshu, Japan.

P-47 Thunderbolts from Ie Shima bomb the airfield on Tokuno Island, while 16 others patrol over Amami-O-Shima Island. Another 117 P-51 Mustangs from Iwo Jima sent against Kagamigahara airfield and Meiji, Japan, abort because of bad weather.

U.S. submarine *Cabezon* attacks a Japanese convoy and sinks a cargo ship southwest of Paramushiro, in the Kuriles.

U.S. submarine *Sea Dog* attacks a Japanese convoy off the northwest coast of Hokkaido, Japan, and sinks two cargo ships and damages a merchant vessel.

Navy PB4Y-2 Privateers continue aerial mining in Korean waters. Japanese antiaircraft fire damages all of the patrol bombers during the mission.

PACIFIC, OKINAWA: The commander of the 96th Infantry Division, Major General Claudius M. Easley, is killed as he directs fire against Japanese positions. Large numbers of Japanese soldiers begin surrendering. The 305th Infantry Regiment of the 77th Infantry Division attacks into the Medeera pocket.

Technical Sergeant John Meagher, E Company, 305th Infantry Regiment, 77th Infantry Division, attacking Japanese defenses near Ozato, Okinawa, jumps on a tank supporting the infantry and points out targets to the tank crew even as bullets hit all around him. Spotting a Japanese soldier charging toward the tank with an explosive charge, Meagher jumps off the deck and meets the soldier head-on, killing him with his bayoneted rifle. He then takes a machine gun from the tank and moves forward to engage the enemy alone. Advancing while firing the machine gun from the hip, Meagher moves untouched through a deadly crossfire, shooting into a pillbox and eliminating the defenders. Attacking another pillbox, he runs out of ammunition, then uses the machine gun as a club to kill the six Japanese soldiers inside. His incredible courage and fearless attack against a determined enemy will win him the Medal of Honor.

CENTRAL PACIFIC: Seventh Air Force sends 22 B-24 Liberators from Guam to bomb the airfield on Marcus Island.

June 20

CBI: The Mars Task Force is inactivated.

In China, 37 P-51 Mustangs attack rail, road, and river traffic, bridges, and general targets of opportunity around Liuchow, Kweilin, Hankow, Changsha, Hengshan, and Fort Bayard.

In French Indochina, B-25 Mitchells and P-51 Mustangs attack bridges and antiaircraft positions.

A mine laid by U.S. submarine *Ray* sinks a Japanese merchant tanker off the southern coast of French Indochina.

ETO: Eighth Air Force begins to redeploy the headquarters of the 401st Bombardment Group (Heavy) and its three subordinate B-17 squadrons to the United States.

SOUTHWEST PACIFIC AREA: In the Philippines, Far East Air Force A-20 Havocs, P-38 Lightnings, and P-47 Thunderbolts support ground forces on Luzon and support a guerrilla offensive in the central Cayagan Valley.

B-24 Liberators bomb an airfield on Formosa.

Fifth Air Force B-24 Liberators conduct a shipping sweep off the coast of Korea and sink a cargo ship off the southern coast of Korea.

In Borneo, FEAF B-24 Liberators bomb antiaircraft positions near Balikpapan.

U.S. submarine *Kraken* torpedoes and sinks a Japanese auxiliary sailing vessel in the Sunda Strait.

PACIFIC: Twentieth Air Force sends 14 P-47 Thunderbolts from Ie Shima to bomb and strafe vessels, buildings, a lighthouse, and a village on Amami Gunto Island and the airfield on Tokuno Island. Another 38 P-47s bomb the airfield at Omura and attack Tokuno as they return to base.

U.S. submarine *Tinosa* torpedoes and sinks two Japanese cargo ships in the Sea of Japan off Korea.

Mines dropped by Twentieth Air Force B-29s sink two cargo ships and a merchant tanker and damage three cargo ships in the Inland Sea, the west Honshu coast, and the Shimonoseki Strait.

Navy patrol bombers sink a Japanese cargo ship off Pusan, Korea.

Navy PB4Y-2 Privateers continue aerial mining of waters off Korea and receive heavy antiaircraft fire from Japanese warships.

Naval Task Group 12.4, commanded by Rear Admiral Ralph E. Jennings, sailing to Leyte from Pearl Harbor, attacks Wake Island. Aircraft from carriers USS *Hancock* and USS *Lexington* and from small carrier USS *Cowpens* bomb Japanese installations.

PACIFIC, OKINAWA: American troops capture 977 soldiers, the highest tally of Japanese surrenders during the war.

June 21

CBI: Fourteenth Air Force P-51 Mustangs and P-38 Lightnings attack trucks, river traffic, highways, logistics storage sites, coastal shipping, rail lines, bridges, troops, and town areas in southern and eastern China and in French Indochina.

In French Indochina, 16 B-25 Mitchells bomb Japanese strongpoints, railyards and trains, damage a tunnel, and hit several barges.

ETO: Major General Westside T. Larson takes command of Eighth Air Force from Major General William E. Kepner.

SOUTHWEST PACIFIC AREA: A contingent of Rangers and Filipino guerrillas captures Aparri on the north coast of Luzon.

In the Philippines, Far East Air Force P-38 Lightnings and P-47 Thunderbolts support ground forces on Luzon in the Cagayan Valley and elsewhere.

On Formosa, P-38 Lightnings attack targets of opportunity along the west coast.

In Borneo, FEAF B-24 Liberators bomb the Balikpapan town area, airfields, and Japanese defenses at Sepinggang. B-25 Mitchells bomb the town of Keningau, while P-38 Lightnings attack the nearby airfield.

PACIFIC: During the night Twentieth Air Force sends 25 B-29s to mine the sea approaches off Nanao, west-central Honshu, and Osaka, Japan.

Navy PB4Y-2 Privateers from Okinawa continue aerial mining of waters off the Korea coast.

U.S. submarine *Parche* torpedoes and sinks a Japanese cargo ship off eastern Hokkaido, Japan. U.S. submarine *Piranha* torpedoes and damages a Japanese cargo ship off northeast Honshu, Japan.

PACIFIC, OKINAWA: The 32nd Infantry Regiment of the 7th Infantry Division captures Hill 89, the headquarters area of the Japanese Thirty-second Army, and the town of Mabuni, sealing off one of the three remaining pockets of resistance. The 5th Marines of the 1st Marine Division captures Hills 79 and 81, while the 96th Infantry Division breaks Japanese defenses around Medeera.

Kamikazes damage a destroyer escort and two seaplane tenders and sink a medium landing ship off Okinawa.

M4 Sherman tanks of the 769th Tank Battalion support the attack on Hill 89, the location of the Japanese Thirty-second Army headquarters during the final stages of the battle for Okinawa, June 21–22, 1945.

CENTRAL PACIFIC: Seventh Air Force sends 24 B-24 Liberators from Guam Island to bomb fuel oil storage and power plant buildings on Eten Island at Truk.

Japanese submarine *I-36* damages a landing craft repair ship north of Truk.

June 22

ALEUTIANS: Major General John B. Brooks takes command of Eleventh Air Force from Brigadier General Isaiah Davies.

CBI: Fourteenth Air Force B-25 Mitchells and P-47 Thunderbolts attack railyards, highways, river traffic, artillery, and other targets in southern and eastern China and French Indochina.

In French Indochina, 23 B-25 Mitchells and four P-47 Thunderbolts attack trucks, trains, and gun positions near Hanoi.

ETO: Eighth Air Force begins redeployment of the headquarters, 2nd Air Division, to the United States. The headquarters of the 384th Bombardment Group (Heavy) and 544th Bombardment Squadrons (Heavy) move from England to Istres, France, with their B-17s to move American soldiers to Casablanca, French Morocco, for return to the United States.

SOUTHWEST PACIFIC AREA: In the Philippines, Far East Air Force A-20 Havocs, P-38 Lightnings, and P-47 Thunderbolts support ground forces on Luzon in the Cagayan Valley.

On Formosa, B-24 Liberators attack oil facilities. P-38 Lightnings attack town areas.

In Borneo, FEAF B-24 Liberators bomb gun positions and defenses near Balikpapan. B-25 Mitchells attack warehouses and buildings. P-38 Lightnings conduct dive-bomb runs on pillboxes.

PACIFIC: Twentieth Air Force sends 446 B-29s over targets on south Honshu Island, Japan, to attack the Kure Naval Arsenal, the Mitsubishi aircraft production facility, the Kawanishi aircraft production facility, the Mitsubishi and Kawasaki aircraft production facilities at Kagamigahara, and the Kawasaki aircraft production facility at Akashi. Five B-29s are lost. Two partially completed submarines are destroyed in the attack and an escort destroyer and submarine *RO-67* are damaged.

Over 40 P-47 Thunderbolts from Ie Shima fly combat patrols over Amami Gunto Island, Japan. Pilots report 11 Japanese aircraft destroyed.

U.S. submarine *Crevalle* torpedoes and damages a Japanese escort destroyer in the Sea of Japan. U.S. submarine *Parche* torpedoes and sinks a fishing boat in the Tsugaru Strait. U.S. submarine *Piranha* torpedoes and damages a coastal defense vessel off northeast Honshu, Japan.

Mines dropped by Twentieth Air Force B-29s sink four cargo ships and damage a transport in the Inland Sea, west Honshu, and the Shimonoseki Strait.

Navy PB4Y-2 Privateers from Okinawa continue aerial mining of waters off the Korean coast. PBM Mariner patrol bombers attack a lighthouse and shipping off the south coast of Korea.

PACIFIC, OKINAWA: The 305th Infantry Regiment of the 96th Infantry Division gains control of Hill 85 near Medeera.

Kamikazes damage a high-speed minesweeper and a tank landing ship off Okinawa.

June 23

ALEUTIANS: Eleventh Air Force sends two B-24 Liberators on a shipping sweep between Matsuwa and Paramushiru Islands in the Kuriles. Aircrews report one cargo ship sunk and one damaged. Aircrews also report one confirmed Japanese fighter kill in the air. Six other B-24s bomb Kataoka on Shimushu Island.

CBI: Fourteenth Air Force P-51 Mustangs strafe airfields near Canton.

In French Indochina, B-25 Mitchells bomb a bridge, and P-38 Lightnings bomb locomotives and a barracks area.

ETO: Eighth Air Force prepares to redeploy the headquarters of the 91st Bombardment Group (Heavy) and one of its B-17 squadrons to the United States.

MEDITERRANEAN: Twelfth Air Force prepares to redeploy the A-20 Havocs of the 85th and 86th Bombardment Squadrons (Light), 47th Bombardment Group (Light), to the United States.

SOUTHWEST PACIFIC AREA: In Luzon, paratroopers of the 11th Airborne Division land at Aparri and advance south to link with the 37th Infantry Division near Tuguegarao.

In the Philippines, Far East Air Force A-20 Havocs, P-38 Lightnings, and P-47 Thunderbolts support ground forces on Luzon in the Cagayan Valley.

FEAF sends over 150 B-24 Liberators, B-25 Mitchells, and P-38 Lightnings to attack gun emplacements and defensive positions near Balikpapan, Borneo.

U.S. submarine *Hardhead* torpedoes and sinks a Japanese auxiliary submarine chaser in the Java Sea, evades a counterattack by another auxiliary submarine chaser, then sinks it and another vessel.

PACIFIC: During the night Twentieth Air Force sends 26 B-29s to mine the waters off Karatsu and Fukuoka, west Kyushu, and Osaka and Niigata on west-central Honshu, Japan. One B-29 is lost.

A total of 38 P-47 Thunderbolts from Ie Shima bomb airfields at Hakata and Itazuke and attack two boats off Amami Gunto Island as they return to base. Other P-47s bomb Saitozaki airfield. One hundred P-51 Mustangs from Iwo Jima attack airfields at Kagamigahara and Hyakuri. Pilots report 19 confirmed kills, three probables, and 16 possibles in the air and 13 confirmed kills and 40 probables on the ground. Three P-51s are lost.

U.S. submarine *Tirante* torpedoes and sinks a Japanese sailing junk in the Yellow Sea near the coast of Korea.

Navy patrol bombers damage a Japanese cargo ship off Pusan, Korea.

PACIFIC, OKINAWA: General Joseph W. Stilwell takes command of Tenth Army. Japanese morale crumbles as unit cohesion is lost. Japanese soldiers begin purposely exposing themselves in order to be killed. American divisions begin a sweep to clear remaining positions, blast cave entrances, and collect prisoners.

CENTRAL PACIFIC: Major General Thomas D. Wattacke takes command of Seventh Air Force.

June 24

ALEUTIANS: Eleventh Air Force sends two B-24 Liberators on a shipping sweep, but the bombers use radar to bomb Kurabu Cape on Paramushiru Island in the Kuriles.

CBI: Fourteenth Air Force B-25 Mitchells bomb bridges. P-47 Thunderbolts and P-51 Mustangs attack trucks, river traffic, highways, logistics storage sites, rail lines, and bridges in southern and eastern China.

ETO: Eighth Air Force begins to redeploy the headquarters of the 381st Bombardment Group (Heavy) and its three subordinate B-17 squadrons to the United States.

SOUTHWEST PACIFIC AREA: In the Eighth Army area, the 1st Battalion of the 155th Infantry Regiment, 31st Infantry Division, lands at the mouth of the Agusan River on Mindanao and moves to flank Japanese defenses from the east. They are resupplied entirely by air and attack Japanese units wherever they find them.

In the Philippines, Far East Air Force A-20 Havocs, P-38 Lightnings, and P-47 Thunderbolts support ground forces on Luzon.

In Borneo, FEAF B-24 Liberators bomb coastal guns and the town of Balikpapan and P-38 Lightnings also attack coastal guns. B-25 Mitchells bomb warehouses and an airfield.

PACIFIC: Twentieth Air Force sends 36 P-47 Thunderbolts from Ie Shima to attack boats and a village in the Sakishima Archipelago, a wharf on Kuro Island, Ishigaki Island, and buildings, villages, targets of opportunity, and several points in the Ryukyu Islands. The headquarters of the 507th Fighter Group and the P-47s of the 463rd, 464th, and 465th Fighter Squadrons arrive on Ie Shima from the United States.

U.S. submarine *Tirante* torpedoes and sinks a Japanese merchant sailing junk in the Yellow Sea off the coast of Korea.

Navy PB4Y-2 Privateers from Okinawa continue aerial mining of waters off the Korean coast. After completing the mining mission, the Privateers strafe rail lines, airports, and Japanese shipping. Pilots report a merchant ship a sunk.

CENTRAL PACIFIC: Seventh Air Force sends one B-24 from Guam Island to bomb buildings on Marcus Island; later another 18 B-24s bomb the airfield.

The headquarters of the 494th Bombardment Group (Heavy) and the B-24s of the 864th, 865th, 866th, and 867th Bombardment Squadrons (Heavy) redeploy from Angaur Island to Yontan on Okinawa.

June 25

CBI: Fourteenth Air Force B-25 Mitchells attack bridges, railyards, and industrial targets. P-47 Thunderbolts and P-51 Mustangs attack road and rail lines, bridges, and troops in southern and eastern China.

SOUTHWEST PACIFIC AREA: In the Philippines, Far East Air Force B-25 Mitchells, A-20 Havocs, P-38 Lightnings, and P-47 Thunderbolts support ground forces on Luzon in the Cagayan Valley and elsewhere.

In Borneo, B-24 Liberators, B-25 Mitchells, and P-38 Lightnings attack oil facilities, shore defenses and an airfield near Balikpapan. B-24s bomb an airfield on Celebes Island.

PACIFIC: During the night Twentieth Air Force sends 26 B-29s to mine Shimonoseki Strait and the waters off Tsugaru Strait, Japan. Mines sink two Japanese cargo ships and damage an escort destroyer.

Navy PB4Y-2 Privateers from Okinawa, continue aerial mining of waters off the Korean coast. After completing the mining mission, the Privateers strafe lighthouses and Japanese shipping.

CENTRAL PACIFIC: Seventh Air Force sends three B-24 Liberators from Guam to bomb the airfield on Marcus Island.

June 26

CBI: Chinese forces capture the airfield at Liuchow.

In China, Fourteenth Air Force sends 21 P-51 Mustangs to bomb and strafe road, river, and rail traffic, motor pools, gun positions, and buildings.

ATLANTIC: The United Nations conference ends in San Francisco. The UN Charter is signed by the 200 attending delegates.

ETO: Eighth Air Force begins to redeploy the headquarters of the 40th Bombardment Wing (Heavy) from England to Istres, France, to direct those units transporting troops from France to North Africa for return to the United States.

SOUTHWEST PACIFIC AREA: In the Philippines, Far East Air Force B-25 Mitchells, A-20 Havocs, P-38 Lightnings, and P-47 Thunderbolts support ground forces on Luzon in the Cagayan Valley and east of Manila.

During the night P-61 Black Widow night fighters hit a sugar refinery and B-24 Liberators follow up with a morning attack against the same target.

Japanese aircraft strafe a U.S. destroyer escort in Davao Gulf, Mindanao, Philippines.

In Borneo, FEAF B-24 Liberators and B-25 Mitchells attack oil targets and the airfield near Balikpapan. Other B-24s bomb the airfield at Limboeng, Celebes Island.

A U.S. motor minesweeper hits a mine off Balikpapan, Borneo, and is severely damaged. It is later scuttled.

PACIFIC: Twentieth Air Force sends 510 B-29s, escorted by 148 P-51 Mustangs, to attack aircraft production facilities, light-metals industries, and arsenals in southern Honshu and Shikoku. Six B-29s and one P-51 are lost. Aircrews report 20 Japanese fighters destroyed. P-51 pilots report two confirmed kills and five probables in the air. During the night 33 B-29s attack the Utsube Oil Refinery at Yokkaichi.

A naval task group, commanded by Captain Charles A. Buchanan, lands marines on Kume Jima in the Ryukyus.

Navy PB4Y-2 Privateers from Okinawa continue aerial mining of waters off the Korean coast.

Four U.S. destroyers sink three Japanese auxiliary submarine chasers and a guardboat and damage an auxiliary submarine chaser south of Onnekotan Island in the Kuriles.

U.S. submarine *Parche* attacks a Japanese convoy and sinks a gunboat and a cargo ship off southern Honshu, Japan. *Parche* survives a depth charge attack and, although damaged, remains on patrol.

CENTRAL PACIFIC: Seventh Air Force sends one B-24 from Guam to bomb the anti-aircraft positions on Marcus Island.

June 27
CBI: Tenth Air Force begins to redeploy the headquarters of the 306th Bombardment Group (Heavy) and its three subordinate B-24 squadrons from China to India.

SOUTHWEST PACIFIC AREA: In the Philippines, Far East Air Force A-20 Havocs, P-38 Lightnings, and P-47 Thunderbolts support ground forces on Luzon and attack Japanese troop concentrations.

During the night FEAF B-24 Liberators bomb an airfield in Java. In Borneo, B-24s attack oil facilities and shore defenses near Balikpapan. B-25 Mitchells attack warehouses, other buildings, and the general waterfront area. B-24s bomb airfields on Celebes Island.

A U.S. destroyer hits a mine and suffers damage in Brunei Bay, Borneo. U.S. submarine *Blueback* torpedoes and sinks a Japanese submarine chaser in the Java Sea.

PACIFIC: During the night Twentieth Air Force sends 29 B-29s to mine the waters off Hagi, southwest Honshu, Niigata, west-central Honshu, Kobe and Osaka, southern Honshu, Japan.

Over 100 P-51 Mustangs from Iwo Jima are sent to attack the Kasumigaura, Imba, and Tsukuba airfields in the Tokyo area. Bad weather causes the mission to be aborted. P-47 Thunderbolts from Ie Shima attack shipping and a village on Kikai Island, Japan. Antiaircraft fire shoots down two P-47s. Other P-47s attack shipping off Kakeroma Island and vessels and targets of opportunity throughout the Sakishima Archipelago. During the night five P-61 Black Widow night fighters fly intruder attacks, hitting vessels off Amami Gunto Island and aircraft on Wan airfield.

Navy PB4Y-2 Privateers from Okinawa continue aerial mining of waters off the Korean coast.

Navy patrol bombers sink Japanese submarine *I-165* east of Saipan in the Marianas.

Navy patrol bombers damage a Japanese cargo vessel in the Sea of Japan near the Korea Straits.

CENTRAL PACIFIC: Seventh Air Force sends three B-24 Liberators from Guam Island to bomb the underground storage area and fortifications on Marcus Island. Another 18 B-24s attack the airfield on Moen Island at Truk.

June 28
CBI: In China, Fourteenth Air Force B-25 Mitchells and P-51 Mustangs bomb the town of Changsha, troop concentrations and logistics storage areas, truck convoys and ammunition trains near Yoyang. Other P-51s attack gun emplacements, defensive positions, rail traffic, and a road bridge.

SOUTHWEST PACIFIC AREA: In the Philippines, Far East Air Force P-38 Lightnings and P-47 Thunderbolts support ground forces on Luzon.

B-24 Liberators bomb a butanol plant on Formosa.

In Borneo, FEAF B-24 Liberators bomb installations in the Manggar area and runways at Tabanio and Oelin. B-24s, B-25 Mitchells, and P-38 Lightnings attack Japanese defenses near Balikpapan. P-38s also make skip bombing attacks on oil storage areas. B-24s attack the airfields at Limboeng and Langoan on Celebes Island.

A U.S. motor minesweeper is damaged by a mine, and another motor minesweeper is hit by shore battery fire off Balikpapan.

PACIFIC: During the night Twentieth Air Force sends 487 B-29s to conduct incendiary bombing raids on Okayama (more than two square miles destroyed), Sasebo (less than one square mile destroyed), Moji (less than one square mile destroyed), Nobeoka (about a half square mile destroyed). P-47 Thunderbolts from Ie Shima attack shipping at Koniya, Japan, with rockets and bombs and attack Tokuno Island. Another 26 P-47s attack targets of opportunity on the Sakishima Archipelago.

Navy PB4Y-2 Privateers from Okinawa continue aerial mining of waters off the Korean coast.

CENTRAL PACIFIC: Seventh Air Force sends three B-24 Liberators from Guam Island to bomb a fuel storage area on Marcus Island.

U.S. destroyer attacks Japanese submarine *I-36* after it conducts an unsuccessful *kaiten* attack on a stores ship southeast of the Marianas. One *kaiten* is destroyed, and the submarine is damaged in the counterattack.

June 29

CBI: Fourteenth Air Force B-25 Mitchells and P-47 Thunderbolts attack bridges. P-51 Mustangs attack gun emplacements, bridges, troops, and targets of opportunity in southern and eastern China.

SOUTHWEST PACIFIC AREA: In the Philippines, Far East Air Force B-25 Mitchells, A-20 Havocs, P-38 Lightnings, and P-47 Thunderbolts support ground forces on Luzon.

B-24 Liberators bomb an oil refinery on Formosa.

In Borneo, FEAF B-24 Liberators, B-25 Mitchells, and P-38 Lightnings bomb defensive positions and oil installations near Balikpapan. P-38s and B-24s bomb airfields.

PACIFIC: During the night Twentieth Air Force sends 32 B-29s to drop 209 tons of bombs on the Nippon Oil Company refinery at Kudamatsu, Japan. Another 25 B-29s mine the west Shimonoseki Strait and waters off Maizuru, southern Honshu, and Sakata, northwest Honshu, Japan. Mines dropped by Twentieth Air Force B-29s sink a cargo ship and damage a naval vessel and three cargo ships in the Inland Sea, the west coast of Honshu, and the Shimonoseki Strait.

P-47 Thunderbolts from Ie Shima attack airfields at Kanoya and Kushira on Kyushu Island, Japan, with rockets and machine-gun fire, and attack shipping. Pilots report seven small vessels sunk.

Navy PB4Y-2 Privateers from Okinawa continue aerial mining of waters off the Korean coast.

June 30

CBI: The headquarters of Army Air Forces, China Theater is established. Lieutenant General George E. Stratemeyer is appointed as commander. The new command will consist of the subordinate elements: the Tenth and Fourteenth Air Forces, China Air Service Command, and the 8th Reconnaissance Group.

ATLANTIC: The navy's total personnel strength at this time is over 4 million (U.S. Navy: 3,383,196; Marine Corps: 476,709; Coast Guard: 171,192). The navy has 67,952 vessels of all types available for operations.

SOUTHWEST PACIFIC AREA: In the Eighth Army area, Lieutenant General Eichelberger reports to General MacArthur that organized resistance on Mindanao has ended, despite the fact that 22,000 Japanese soldiers are still actively resisting.

In the Philippines, Far East Air Force B-25 Mitchells, A-20 Havocs, P-38 Lightnings, and P-47 Thunderbolts support ground forces on Luzon in the Cagayan Valley and east of Manila.

During the night P-61 Black Widow night fighters hit a sugar refinery, and B-24 Liberators follow up with a morning attack against the same target.

FEAF B-24 Liberators attack targets near Balikpapan and B-25 Mitchells hit targets in northeast Borneo.

Fire from a shore battery damages a U.S. destroyer, and a U.S. minesweeper is damaged when it hits a mine off Balikpapan.

U.S. submarines *Baya* and *Capitaine* attack a Japanese convoy engaging a submarine chaser and sinking a cargo vessel in the Flores Sea.

PACIFIC: The 509th Composite Group begins combat flight training from Tinian as the aircrews prepare for an atomic bomb attack on Japan.

Navy PB4Y-2 Privateers from Okinawa continue aerial mining of waters off the Korean coast.

A Japanese escort destroyer is damaged when it hits a mine off Shimonoseki, Kyushu, Japan.

CENTRAL PACIFIC: Seventh Air Force sends two B-24 Liberators from Guam to bomb the boat basin on Marcus Island.

July 1

CBI: In China, Fourteenth Air Force B-25 Mitchells bomb a bridge and ferry terminal, and P-47 Thunderbolts strafe an airfield, locomotives, and railyards. P-51 Mustangs attack a bridge. Chinese forces capture Liuchow.

Fifth Air Force aircraft sink a Japanese cargo ship at the mouth of the Yangtze River.

ETO: Eighth Air Force begins moving the B-17s of the 547th Bombardment Squadron (Heavy), 384th Bombardment Group (Heavy), from England to Istres, France, to move troops from the European theater to North Africa en route to the United States.

Over the vehement protests of Prime Minister Churchill, U.S. forces begin a withdrawal from central and southern Germany to their designated occupation zones. The territory abandoned will be part of the Soviet occupation zone. Churchill believes that no British or American troops should give up any territory to the Soviets until there is assurance that Stalin will abide by the Yalta agreements for free and open elections in the liberated areas of Europe. President Truman, still following Roosevelt's conciliatory policy toward the Soviets, argues that the Soviets will abide by their agreements if they see the United States living up to its obligations. Churchill worries that the Americans and British will arrive at the upcoming Potsdam conference with no bargaining position with the Soviets.

MEDITERRANEAN: Fifteenth Air Force begins to redeploy the headquarters of the 461st and 454th Bombardment Groups (Heavy) and each of their three subordinate B-24 squadrons to the United States. The headquarters of the 301st Bombardment Group (Heavy) and its three subordinate B-17 squadrons are also scheduled to return to the United States.

SOUTHWEST PACIFIC AREA: Eighth Army takes responsibility for the Philippines from Sixth Army. Eighth Army under Lieutenant General Eichelberger takes operational control of X Corps and XIV Corps and the 6th, 31st, 32nd, 38th, 24th, 37th, and 93rd Infantry Divisions. (The 93rd Infantry Division is at Morotai and New Guinea.) Sixth Army under Lieutenant General Krueger has operational control of I Corps and XI Corps and a new headquarters for IX Corps. Krueger takes operational control of the 11th Airborne and the 1st Cavalry Divisions and the 33rd, 41st, 40th, and 43rd Infantry Divisions. The 81st Infantry Division, which arrived in May, is added to Sixth Army, as is the 77th Infantry Division, which will return from Okinawa on July 15. Eighth Army takes over operations on Luzon, and Sixth Army prepares to undergo refitting and training for the invasion of Japan.

In the Philippines, Far East Air Force P-38 Lightnings and P-47 Thunderbolts support ground forces on Luzon, attacking troops and gun positions.

In Borneo, FEAF B-24 Liberators bomb defenses at Balikpapan as Australian forces conduct an amphibious landing in the area. B-24s, B-25 Mitchells, and P-38 Lightnings attack airfields. B-24 Liberators attack airfields on Celebes Island.

Naval Task Group 78.2, commanded by Rear Admiral Albert G. Noble, lands units of the 7th Australian Division at Balikpapan. The landing is supported by naval gunfire and air attack.

PACIFIC: Twentieth Air Force sends 152 B-29s to attack the Kure urban area, destroying over one square mile of the city. Another 154 B-29s attack the Kumamato urban area. Nearly three square miles of the city is destroyed. One B-29 is lost. A total of 100 B-29s bomb the Ube urban area, destroying less than one square mile of the city. Another 126 B-29s attack the Shimonoseki urban area, destroying about one-half square mile of the city. One B-29 is lost. B-29s mine Shimonoseki Strait and the waters off Nanao, west-central Honshu, Japan. Mines sink a Japanese cargo ship at the entrance of Niigata harbor, west-central Honshu, and damage two cargo ships in the Inland Sea, Japan.

Nearly 148 P-51 Mustangs from Iwo Jima attack airfields in the Nagoya area. Pilots report two confirmed kills in the air and three confirmed kills and seven probables on the ground. Two P-51s are lost.

Navy PB4Y-2 Privateers from Okinawa continue aerial mining of waters off the Korean coast.

U.S. submarine *Haddo* torpedoes and sinks a Japanese coastal defense vessel and three cargo ships in the Yellow Sea off the west coast of Korea.

CENTRAL PACIFIC: Seventh Air Force sends two B-24 Liberators from Guam to bomb buildings on Marcus Island. B-25 Mitchells, operating in two flights from Okinawa, bomb an airfield on Kyushu Island, Japan.

The headquarters of VII Bomber Command prepares to redeploy from Saipan to Okinawa.

July 2

CBI: In China, Fourteenth Air Force sends 28 P-51 Mustangs to attack rail, river, and road traffic, bridges, and buildings around Hengyang, Hankow, and Yoyang. The fighters attack a Japanese headquarters near Changsha and bomb a troop concentration and buildings at Yangan.

ATLANTIC: Secretary of War Henry Stimson, concerned that the invasion of the Japanese home islands will result in far greater casualties than Okinawa, appeals to the president to make some adjustment of the Allied demand for Japan's unconditional surrender.

ETO: Eighth Air Force begins moving the B-17s of the 545th Bombardment Squadron (Heavy), 384th Bombardment Group (Heavy), from England to Istres, France, to transport troops from the European theater to North Africa en route to the United States.

Ninth Air Force begins to redeploy the headquarters of the 405th Fighter Group and its three P-47 fighter squadrons from Germany to the United States.

SOUTHWEST PACIFIC AREA: In the Philippines, Far East Air Force P-38 Lightnings and P-47 Thunderbolts attack Japanese positions on Luzon.

B-24 Liberators bomb an airfield on Formosa.

In Borneo, FEAF B-24 Liberators bomb defenses in the Balikpapan area, and P-38 Lightnings support Australian forces as they complete the capture of Balikpapan and its oil installations. B-25 Mitchells attack troops near Bintula.

PACIFIC: During the night Twentieth Air Force sends 39 B-29s to bomb an oil refinery at Minoshima.

U.S. submarine *Apogon* torpedoes and damages two Japanese auxiliary submarine chasers off the Kuriles.

U.S. submarine *Barb* conducts a rocket bombardment of Japanese shore installations at Kaihyo Island off the Kamchatka Peninsula. This is the first successful use of rockets against shore positions by an American submarine.

U.S. submarines *Haddo* and *Paddle* attack Japanese shipping in the Yellow Sea, sinking one cargo vessel and damaging another.

Mines sink a Japanese auxiliary submarine chaser northwest of Kyushu in the Tsushima Strait.

Navy patrol bombers sink a Japanese sailing vessel off the west coast of Korea and a cargo ship in the Yellow Sea south of Korea.

PACIFIC, OKINAWA: General Joseph Stilwell declares Okinawa secured. Japanese aircraft attack U.S. ships off Okinawa. No damage is reported.

The total American casualties for the Okinawa campaign are staggering—49,151, with over 12,000 Americans killed. This represents a loss rate of 35 percent of the forces engaged. Tenth Army losses are 7,374 killed and 32,000 wounded and missing. The navy has lost 36 ships sunk and 368 damaged. Nearly 5,000 sailors are lost, and another 4,800 are injured. Air losses number 763 aircraft. The Japanese losses are estimated at between 95,000 and 110,000, with 7,400 captured. Civilian casualties are unknown but are estimated between 42,000 and 60,000.

CENTRAL PACIFIC: Seventh Air Force sends three B-24 Liberators from Guam to bomb the radar installation on Marcus Island.

The headquarters 11th Bombardment Group (Heavy) and the B-24 Liberators of the 26th, 98th, and 431st Bombardment Squadrons (Heavy) redeploy from Guam to Okinawa along with the headquarters of the 319th Bombardment Group (Light) and the A-26 Invaders of the 437th, 439th, and 440th Bombardment Squadrons (Light) arriving at Kadena on Okinawa from the United States.

July 3

CBI: Fourteenth Air Force B-25 Mitchells attack bridges. P-47 Thunderbolts and P-51 Mustangs attack trucks, highways, bridges, and troops as Japanese forces retreat to the east.

In French Indochina, P-47s and P-51s attack shipping, a cement plant, an airfield, and a barracks area near Haiphong.

ETO: Eighth Air Force begins to redeploy the three subordinate B-24 squadrons of the 458th Bombardment Group (Heavy) to the United States.

Vice Admiral Robert L. Ghormley, commander of U.S. Naval Forces, Germany, establishes headquarters at Frankfurt am Main, Germany.

SOUTHWEST PACIFIC AREA: In the Philippines, Far East Air Force P-38 Lightnings and P-47 Thunderbolts attack Japanese areas of resistance on Luzon.

Fifth Air Force P-51 Mustangs fly their first mission over Japan, destroying floatplanes in the Fukuoka harbor area on Kyushu.

In Borneo, FEAF B-24 Liberators bomb an airfield near Kuching and defensive positions near Balikpapan in support of Australian ground forces. On Celebes Island, B-24s bomb airfields.

The 868th Bombardment Squadron (Heavy), Thirteenth Air Force, redeploys from Morotai Island in New Guinea to Leyte Island with B-24 Liberators. This squadron is capable of conducting low-level night attacks and conducting Pathfinder missions, using radar to locate bomb release points for other bombers.

PACIFIC: Twentieth Air Force sends 509 B-29s to conduct incendiary strikes on urban areas of Japan and mining operations off the Japanese coast. Twentieth Air Force sends 31 B-29s to mine Shimonoseki Strait and the waters off Maizuru, southern Honshu, Japan.

Takamatsu, Kochi, Himeji, and Tokushima urban areas are bombed with incendiaries, destroying between 48 and 78 percent of the cities. A total of three B-29s are lost.

The remaining units of Twentieth Air Force's XX Bomber Command depart India by ship enroute to the Marianas.

CENTRAL PACIFIC: Seventh Air Force sends two B-24 Liberators from Guam to attack water storage buildings on Marcus Island. A total of 36 B-25 Mitchells from Okinawa, operating in two flights, attack Chiran airfield, Japan. The A-26 Invaders of 438th Bombardment Squadron (Light), 319th Bombardment Group (Light), arrive at Kadena, Okinawa, from the United States.

July 4
ALEUTIANS: Eleventh Air Force sends eight B-24 Liberators using radar to locate bomb release points and conduct napalm strikes on the Kataoka naval base on Shimushu Island.

CBI: Fourteenth Air Force sends 30 P-51 Mustangs and P-38 Lightnings over French Indochina to attack docks and shipping at Haiphong and boat traffic on the Red River.

ETO: Eighth Air Force begins to redeploy the headquarters of the 446th Bombardment Group (Heavy) and its three subordinate B-24 squadrons to the United States.

SOUTHWEST PACIFIC AREA: In the Philippines, Far East Air Force P-38 Lightnings and P-47 Thunderbolts support ground forces on Luzon in the Cagayan Valley and attack Japanese positions on Bataan Island.

Fifth Air Force P-51 Mustangs fly a sweep along the west coast of Kyushu Island, Japan.

In Borneo, FEAF B-24 Liberators attack Japanese positions near Balikpapan. On Celebes Island, B-24 Liberators bomb a seaplane base and airfields.

PACIFIC: Twentieth Air Force sends 159 P-51 Mustangs from Iwo Jima to attack the Yokosuka naval base and airfields in the Tokyo area. Pilots report nine confirmed kills and 25 probables on the ground. One P-51 is lost.

Naval Task Force 32, commanded by Rear Admiral Jesse B. Oldendorf, with three battleships, two heavy cruisers, a light cruiser, four escort carriers, 11 destroyers, and four destroyer escorts, departs Buckner Bay, Okinawa, to provide cover for a minesweeping operation.

A U.S. destroyer intercepts a Japanese hospital ship evacuating sick and injured troops from Wake Island. The condition of the casualties indicates that the garrison is suffering greatly.

U.S. submarine *Tirante* torpedoes and sinks two Japanese guardboats in the Yellow Sea.

Mines damage a Japanese transport southeast of Shimonoseki, northwest Kyushu, and damage a cargo ship off Osaka.

CENTRAL PACIFIC: Seventh Air Force sends three B-24 Liberators from Guam to attack antiaircraft positions on Marcus Island.

July 5
CBI: In China, Fourteenth Air Force P-51 Mustangs attack bridges, docks, and rail and river traffic.

In French Indochina, B-25 Mitchells sink small vessels and damage several larger vessels at Haiphong. P-51 Mustangs attack shipping.

ETO: Eighth Air Force begins to redeploy the headquarters of the 448th Bombardment Group (Heavy) and its three subordinate B-24 squadrons to the United States. The headquarters of the 491st Bombardment Group (Heavy) and its three subordinate B-24 squadrons are also scheduled to return to the United States, along with the B-24s of the 707th Bombardment Squadron (Heavy), 446th Bombardment Group (Heavy).

SOUTHWEST PACIFIC AREA: General of the Army Douglas MacArthur announces the liberation of the Philippines.

In the Philippines, Far East Air Force P-38 Lightnings and P-47 Thunderbolts support ground forces on Luzon.

B-24 Liberators bomb town areas, logistics storage areas, and airfields on Formosa.

Fifth Air Force P-51 Mustangs sweep Kyushu Island, Japan, and strafe targets of opportunity; pilots report several Japanese aircraft shot down.

In Borneo, FEAF B-24 Liberators bomb targets in support of Australian ground forces as they cross Balikpapan Bay.

U.S. submarines *Lizardfish* and *Puffer* bombard Japanese port facilities and shipping off the north coast of Bali. USS *Lizardfish* sinks an auxiliary submarine chaser and another vessel, as well as several barges and landing craft. USS *Puffer* destroys two cargo vessels south of Bali.

PACIFIC: Seventh Air Force sends 46 B-24 Liberators and 24 B-25 Mitchells from Okinawa to bomb an airfield and towns in the Omura-Nagasaki area of Japan.

Twentieth Air Force sends 100 P-51 Mustangs from Iwo Jima to attack airfields in the Tokyo area. Pilots report five confirmed kills and 11 probables on the ground.

Naval Task Force 39, commanded by Rear Admiral Alexander Sharp, with seven light minelayers, 52 minesweepers, six high-speed minesweepers, 49 motor minesweepers, and seven netlayers, begins minesweeping operations in the East China Sea.

U.S. submarine *Barb* torpedoes and sinks a Japanese cargo ship southwest of Sakhalin Island.

Mines sink a Japanese transport off western Kyushu and a merchant tanker off west-central Honshu and damage three cargo ships near Shimonoseki, Japan.

July 6

CBI: Lieutenant General George E. Stratemeyer assumes command of Army Air Forces, China Theater.

ETO: Eighth Air Force begins to redeploy the headquarters of the 466th Bombardment Group (Heavy) and its four subordinate B-24 squadrons to the United States.

SOUTHWEST PACIFIC AREA: In the Philippines, Far East Air Force P-38 Lightnings and P-47 Thunderbolts support ground forces on Luzon.

Fifth Air Force P-51 Mustangs from Okinawa attack transportation targets in the Kagoshima Bay area of Japan.

B-24 Liberators bomb airfields, and A-26 Invaders attack railyards on Formosa.

In Borneo, FEAF B-24 Liberators bomb warehouses, buildings, shipyards, and areas near Balikpapan and Manggar.

PACIFIC: Twentieth Air Force sends 517 B-29s to attack urban areas of Japan with incendiaries and attack an oil refinery with high-explosive bombs. The cities of Chiba, Akashi, Shimizu, and Kofu are bombed and 43 to 65 percent of the urban areas are destroyed. One B-29 is lost. B-29s drop 500-pound bombs on the oil refinery at Wakayama. 110 P-51 Mustangs from Iwo Jima attack airfields in the Tokyo area. Pilots report one confirmed kill in the air and six confirmed kills and 25 probables on the ground. One P-51 is lost.

Mines sink two cargo ships near Shimonoseki and damage an auxiliary submarine chaser off Niigata harbor and damage three cargo ships off west-central Honshu, Japan.

July 7

CBI: Fourteenth Air Force P-47 Thunderbolts and P-51 Mustangs attack trucks, highways, logistics storage sites, bridges, and troops in southern and eastern China.

ATLANTIC: President Harry S. Truman, Secretary of State James F. Byrnes, and Fleet Admiral William D. Leahy board the heavy cruiser USS *Augusta* for Antwerp, Belgium, en route to Potsdam, Germany.

SOUTHWEST PACIFIC AREA: In the Philippines, Far East Air Force B-25 Mitchells, P-38 Lightnings, and P-47 Thunderbolts support ground forces on Luzon, attacking troop concentrations.

B-24 Liberators bomb airfields on Formosa.

In Borneo, FEAF B-24 Liberators, B-25 Mitchells, and P-38 Lightnings support Australian ground forces near Balikpapan.

PACIFIC: Twentieth Air Force sends more than 100 P-51 Mustangs from Iwo Jima to attack airfields in the Tokyo area; they abort the mission due to bad weather.

U.S. submarine *Trepang* torpedoes and sinks a Japanese cargo ship off southern Hokkaido, Japan.

Mines sink two Japanese cargo ships off the coast of west-central Korea. Mines damage a merchant tanker in Osaka harbor.

The headquarters of XX Bomber Command arrives at Okinawa from India. The headquarters of the 414th Fighter Group and the P-47 Thunderbolts of the 413th, 437th, and 456th Fighter Squadrons arrive at Iwo Jima from the United States. The squadrons' first missions are scheduled for mid-July.

July 8

CBI: Fourteenth Air Force B-25 Mitchells and P-47 Thunderbolts attack bridges. P-38 Lightnings, P-47s, and P-51 Mustangs attack river traffic, highways, logistics storage sites, and troops in southern and eastern China and in French Indochina.

ETO: Eighth Air Force begins to redeploy the headquarters of the 492nd Bombardment Group (Heavy) to the United States.

SOUTHWEST PACIFIC AREA: In the Philippines, Far East Air Force P-38 Lightnings and P-51 Mustangs support ground forces on Luzon and attack troops and logistics storage sites.

B-24 Liberators bomb an airfield and P-38 Lightnings attack an oil production area on Formosa.

The P-47s of the 69th and 311th Fighter Squadrons, 58th Fighter Group, Fifth Air Force, redeploy from Luzon to Okinawa.

In Borneo, FEAF B-24 Liberators and B-25 Mitchells, supporting Australian forces, attack Japanese defensive positions near Balikpapan and attack shipyards, road traffic, and warehouses. U.S. and Australian B-24s bomb warehouses on Celebes Island.

PACIFIC: Twentieth Air Force sends more than 100 P-51 Mustangs from Iwo Jima to attack airfields and other targets at Hyakuri, Chofu, Tokorozawa, and Yachimata, Japan. Pilots report five confirmed kills and 25 other aircraft destroyed on the ground. Eight P-51s are lost.

U.S. submarine *Sea Robin* torpedoes and sinks a Japanese auxiliary submarine chaser in the East China Sea. U.S. submarine *Tirante* torpedoes and sinks a Japanese passenger-cargo ship near Dairen, Korea.

July 9

CBI: Fourteenth Air Force B-25 Mitchells attack bridges. P-38 Lightnings and P-51 Mustangs attack river traffic, rail lines, and bridges in southern and eastern China and in French Indochina.

SOUTHWEST PACIFIC AREA: In the Philippines, Far East Air Force P-51 Mustangs and P-38 Lightnings support ground forces on Luzon in the Cagayan Valley.

B-24 Liberators bomb airfields and A-26 Invaders attack a town on Formosa.

The headquarters of the 348th Fighter Group and the P-51s of the 340th Fighter Squadron redeploy from Luzon to Ie Shima. The P-47s of the 310th Fighter Squadron, 58th Fighter Group, redeploy from Luzon to Okinawa.

U.S. submarine *Bluefish* torpedoes and sinks a Japanese auxiliary submarine chaser off the east coast of Malaya.

In Borneo, FEAF B-24 Liberators and P-38 Lightnings support Australian forces, attacking Japanese defensive positions and troops near Balikpapan, Manggar, and Sepinggang as Australian and Dutch forces complete the encirclement of Balikpapan Bay. B-24s also bomb the Samarinda shipyards; and B-25 Mitchells, in support of operations in the Brunei Bay area, bomb Japanese troop concentrations.

A U.S. motor minesweeper is sunk by a mine off Balikpapan.

PACIFIC: Seventh Air Force sends 43 B-24 Liberators from Okinawa to bomb an airfield on Kyushu, Japan. Over 50 B-25 Mitchells from Okinawa attack an airfield on Tokuno Shima in the Amami Islands.

During the night 29 B-29s of Twentieth Air Force mine Shimonoseki Strait and the waters off Niigata and Nanao, west-central Honshu. One B-29 is lost. Mines sink a cargo ship off western Kyushu, Japan, and damage another cargo ship. Mines also damage a cargo ship off Shimonoseki and a merchant tanker in Kobe harbor.

A total of 475 B-29s attack Senai, Sakai, Wakayama, and Gifu urban areas, destroying 27 to 74 percent of the sites bombed with incendiaries. Two B-29s are lost. Over 60 B-29s attack the oil refinery at Yokkaichi. Over 100 P-51 Mustangs from Iwo Jima attack airfields at Itami, Hamamatsu, Aichi, and Washinomiya. Pilots report one confirmed kill in the air and 15 confirmed kills and five probables on the ground. Three P-51s are lost.

July 10

ALEUTIANS: Eleventh Air Force sends four B-24 Liberators to bomb Shimushu Island, using radar to assist in identifying the bomb release points.

CBI: In China, Fourteenth Air Force P-51 Mustangs and P-38 Lightnings bomb warehouses and attack railroad targets of opportunity and bridges.

In French Indochina, B-25 Mitchells bomb the town areas and rail targets.

ETO: Ninth Air Force begins the redeployment of the headquarters of the 358th Fighter Group and two of its subordinate P-47 fighter squadrons from Rheims, France, to the United States.

SOUTHWEST PACIFIC AREA: In the Philippines, Far East Air Force B-25 Mitchells, A-20 Havocs, P-51 Mustangs, P-38 Lightnings, and P-47 Thunderbolts support ground forces on Luzon in the Cagayan Valley and attack Japanese defensive positions east of Manila.

B-24 Liberators bomb an airfield and warehouses on Formosa. Aircrews report several aircraft are destroyed on the ground.

The headquarters of the 58th Fighter Group moves from Luzon to Okinawa.

In Borneo, FEAF B-24 Liberators attack the town of Muarakaman and an airfield. P-38 Lightnings strafe numerous targets of opportunity. B-24s bomb the warehouse area on Celebes Island.

PACIFIC: During the night Seventh Air Force sends one B-24 from Okinawa to bomb Karasehara airfield, Japan. Another 43 B-24s from Okinawa bomb Wan and Sateku airfields on Kikaiga-shima, in the Amami Islands. Over 50 B-25 Mitchells bomb Wan airfield and Saha-Saki on Nakano Shima in the Ryukyus, and Kurume on Kyushu, Japan.

Twentieth Air Force sends 102 P-51 Mustangs from Iwo Jima to attack airfields in Japan. Three fighters are lost.

Carrier aircraft from Vice Admiral John S. McCain's Task Force 38 attack airfields in and around Tokyo.

U.S. submarine *Hammerhead* torpedoes and sinks a Japanese cargo ship and a merchant tanker in the Gulf of Siam. U.S. submarine *Lionfish* attacks Japanese submarine *I-162* east of Kyushu but fails to do any damage. U.S. submarine *Runner* torpedoes and sinks a Japanese minesweeper off northern Honshu, Japan. U.S. submarine *Sea Robin* torpedoes and sinks a Japanese cargo ship off the southwest coast of Korea.

Mines dropped by B-29s sink Japanese cargo ship west of Kyushu and damage a merchant vessel west of Osaka harbor.

July 11

ALEUTIANS: Eleventh Air Force sends five B-24 Liberators using radar to locate bomb release points as they attack Kataoka on Shimushu Island. Four B-25 Mitchells fly a shipping sweep and bomb a fishery.

CBI: In China, Fourteenth Air Force sends 25 P-51 Mustangs and P-40s to attack bridges, troops, gun positions, rail and river traffic, and coastal shipping.

ETO: Eighth Air Force begins to redeploy the headquarters of the 93rd Bombardment Wing (Heavy) and its three subordinate B-17 squadrons to the United States.

Ninth Air Force redeploys the P-47s of the 366th Fighter Squadron, 358th Fighter Group, to begin a movement from France to the United States.

SOUTHWEST PACIFIC AREA: In the Philippines, Far East Air Force B-25 Mitchells, P-51 Mustangs, P-38 Lightnings, and P-47 Thunderbolts support ground forces on Luzon in the Cagayan Valley and B-24 Liberators bomb Japanese troop concentrations on Negros Island.

P-51s sweep Kyushu, Japan.

B-24s bomb an airfield on Formosa.

In Borneo, FEAF B-25 Mitchells and P-38 Lightnings attack targets on highways near Balikpapan.

PACIFIC: During the night Seventh Air Force sends two B-24 Liberators from Okinawa to attack airfields on Kyushu, Japan.

During the night Twentieth Air Force sends 25 B-29s to mine Shimonoseki Strait and Maizuru, southern Honshu, Japan, and the waters off Najin and Pusan, Korea. Mines sink Japanese escort destroyer *Sakura* off Osaka. Mines also sink a cargo ship and damage a merchant vessel off southwest Honshu, Japan. U.S. submarine *Barb* torpedoes and sinks a Japanese guardboat and another vessel off Hokkaido. U.S. submarine *Kingfish* torpedoes and sinks a Japanese fishing boat off east-central Honshu, Japan.

Two B-29s mine Pusan and Najin in Korea.

July 12

ALEUTIANS: Eleventh Air Force sends four B-25 Mitchells on a shipping sweep. Aircrews report bombing and strafing a cargo ship. One B-25 is lost.

CBI: In China, Fourteenth Air Force B-25 Mitchells bomb supply convoys moving through the Siang Chiang Valley. P-51 Mustangs and P-38 Lightnings attack bridges, river and road traffic, barracks, and coastal shipping.

ETO: Eighth Air Force begins redeployment of the headquarters of the 95th Combat Bombardment Wing (Heavy) from England to the United States.

MEDITERRANEAN: Twelfth Air Force deactivates the headquarters of the XII Air Forces Service Command.

SOUTHWEST PACIFIC AREA: In the XIV Corps area, where the 6th, 32nd, 37th, and 38th Infantry Divisions have been given responsibility for eliminating Japanese forces from northern Luzon, the 6th Infantry Division captures Kiangan. The 37th Infantry Division, with support from Philippine guerrillas, patrols into the dense mountain forests of the Sierra Madre Mountains to locate Japanese defenders. Many are discovered sick or starving. The 32nd Infantry Division also attacks into the Kiangan Pocket, destroying isolated units. These small combat actions will continue until the Japanese surrender.

The capture of Luzon and Leyte and the other islands of the Philippines, occupied by 380,000 Japanese soldiers, will prevent them from having any opportunity to be redeployed for the defense of the home islands. On Luzon alone, over 180,000 Japanese soldiers are lost, representing some of the finest units of the empire. American casualties on Luzon total over 37,000 with over 8,000 killed. Nonbattle casualties total 93,400 men.

In the Eighth Army area, the 1st Battalion of the 21st Infantry Regiment, 24th Infantry Division, lands at Sarangani Bay to clear Japanese forces from the area. The fierce jungle battle will continue until the end of the war, with 14 Americans killed and 13 wounded. Japanese casualties number over 400 killed and 25 captured.

In the Philippines, Far East Air Force P-51 Mustangs, P-38 Lightnings, and P-47 Thunderbolts attack Japanese strongpoints, troop concentrations, and support ground forces east of Manila. The 6th Infantry Division captures Kiangan. B-24 Liberators bomb troop concentrations on Negros Island.

Fifth Air Force P-51 Mustangs sweep Kyushu, Japan. B-24s bomb Canton, China.

B-24s bomb town areas on Formosa, while A-26 Invaders and P-51 Mustangs attack other targets.

Fifth Air Force redeploys the P-51s of the 341st, 342nd, and 460th Fighter Squadrons, 348th Fighter Group, from Luzon to Ie Shima.

In Borneo, FEAF B-24 Liberators destroy a barracks. Other B-24s attack warehouses on Celebes Island.

PACIFIC: Seventh Air Force sends 47 B-24 Liberators from Okinawa to attack the airfield on Kikaiga-shima in the Amami Islands. During the night other B-24s bomb airfields on Kyushu. B-25 Mitchells and A-26 Invaders bomb an airfield and the town areas on Kyushu, and other B-25s bomb an airfield on Tokuno Shima in the Amami Islands. A-26 Invaders also attack the Ibusuki seaplane station.

During the night Twentieth Air Force sends 453 B-29s to conduct incendiary raids on Japanese cities. The Utsunomiya, Ichinomiya, Tsuruga, and Uwajima urban areas suffer heavy damage, destroying large sections of the cities. Three B-29s are lost. Another 53 B-29s attack the Kawasaki Petroleum Center, destroying about 25 percent of the target; two B-29s are lost.

A Japanese salvage ship and cargo ship are sunk by mines off west-central Honshu, Japan. A cargo vessel hits a mine and sinks off Osaka harbor. A cargo ship and tanker hit mines and sink off southeast Honshu, and two cargo ships are damaged off Niigata, west-central Honshu.

July 13
CBI: Fourteenth Air Force sends 14 B-25 Mitchells and 12 P-51 Mustangs to attack bridges, railyards, antiaircraft guns, and targets of opportunity in China and French Indochina. P-51s and P-38 Lightnings attack river shipping, buildings, and road and rail targets in both China and French Indochina.

ETO: Eighth Air Force begins to redeploy the headquarters of the 92nd Bombardment Wing (Heavy) to the United States.

SOUTHWEST PACIFIC AREA: In the Philippines, Far East Air Force B-25 Mitchells, P-51 Mustangs, P-38 Lightnings, and P-47 Thunderbolts attack pillboxes, ammunition storage areas, and vehicles on Luzon. B-24 Liberators bomb troop concentrations on Negros Island.

B-24s bomb storage areas at Canton, China.

On Formosa, B-24s bomb boat yards and buildings and A-26 Invaders attack railyards.

In Borneo, FEAF P-38 Lightnings attack gun positions. Other P-38 Lightnings sweep Celebes Island and attack vehicles and communication targets.

PACIFIC: Naval Task Force 95, commanded by Rear Admiral Francis S. Low, with two cruisers, four light cruisers, and nine destroyers departs Leyte Gulf to conduct anti-shipping sweeps in the East China Sea northwest of Okinawa. Naval Task Force 93, commanded by Rear Admiral John H. Brown, Jr., with two light cruisers and five destroyers, begins an anti-shipping sweep down the Kurile Islands into the Sea of Okhotsk.

During the night Twentieth Air Force sends 30 B-29s to mine Shimonoseki Strait and the waters off western Korea, and Fukuoka, on west Kyushu, Japan. Mines from the B-29s sink two cargo ships off western Kyushu and damage two cargo ships near Shimonoseki Strait.

July 14

CBI: Fourteenth Air Force P-38 Lightnings and P-51 Mustangs attack trucks, river traffic, highways, logistics storage sites, rail lines, and bridges in both China and French Indochina.

MEDITERRANEAN: Twelfth Air Force begins to redeploy the headquarters of the 350th Fighter Group and its three subordinate P-47 fighter squadrons from Italy to the United States.

SOUTHWEST PACIFIC AREA: In the Philippines, Far East Air Force P-51 Mustangs and P-38 Lightnings support ground forces and attack Japanese positions on Luzon. B-24 Liberators support ground forces on Negros Island.

A-26 Invaders attack a refinery and warehouse area; P-51 Mustangs attack rail targets on Formosa. P-47 Thunderbolts sweep the north China coast and attack coastal cargo vessels.

On Celebes Island, FEAF B-24 Liberators bomb airfields and a Japanese headquarters.

PACIFIC: The U.S. Navy bombards the home islands of Japan for the first time. Naval Task Unit 34.8.1, commanded by Rear Admiral John F. Shafroth, with three battleships, two heavy cruisers, and nine destroyers attacks the coastal city of Kamaishi, northeast Honshu, hitting the Japan Ironworks production facility.

Carrier aircraft from TF 38 bomb shipping, rail facilities, and ground installations in northern Honshu and Hokkaido, Japan. Aircraft sink an escort destroyer, two coastal defense vessels, a submarine chaser, four auxiliary minesweepers, five guardboats, a gunboat, a transport, and 11 cargo ships all around the Tsugaru Straits, Hakodate, and southern Hokkaido, Japan. A destroyer, two coastal defense vessels, two auxiliary minesweepers, an auxiliary submarine chaser, a guardboat, 11 cargo ships and two tankers are also damaged in the same area.

Mines sink two Japanese cargo ships near Shimonoseki.

The headquarters of Seventh Air Force begins redeployment from Saipan Island to Okinawa. Far East Air Force takes operational control of Seventh Air Force from the U.S. Navy and Army Air Forces Pacific Ocean Area.

July 15

CBI: In China, Fourteenth Air Force sends three B-25 Mitchells to attack truck convoys moving through the Siang Chiang Valley. P-47 Thunderbolts and P-51

Mustangs attack trucks, gun positions, river traffic, logistics storage sites, railyards, bridges, and troops in southern and eastern China and in French Indochina.

ETO: The USS *Augusta* with President Truman on board arrives at Antwerp.

MEDITERRANEAN: Fifteenth Air Force prepares to redeploy the headquarters of the 306th Fighter Wing from Italy to the United States.

SOUTHWEST PACIFIC AREA: In the Philippines, Far East Air Force B-25 Mitchells, P-51 Mustangs, and P-38 Lightnings support ground forces and attack Japanese defenses on Luzon.

B-24 Liberators bomb an arms manufacturing facility at Canton, China. P-51 Mustangs sweep the west coast of Formosa, attacking a warehouse and other buildings.

Nearly 60 B-24s attack airfields on Kyushu Island, Japan. Another 25 B-24s bomb Kikaiga-shima in the Amami Islands, Miranoura on Yaku-shima in the Osumi Islands, and an airfield on Tamega Island.

U.S. submarine *Bluefish* sinks Japanese submarine *I-351* near Borneo.

PACIFIC: A total of 59 B-29s bomb the Nippon Oil Company at Kudamatsu. Over 100 P-51 Mustangs from Iwo Jima attack airfields and other tactical targets at Meiji, Kagamigahara, Kowa, Akenogahara, Nagoya, and Suzuko, Japan. Pilots report 13 confirmed kills, four probables, and 20 possibles. Three P-51s are lost.

Three battleships, two light cruisers, and eight destroyers of TU 34.8.2 (Rear Admiral Oscar C. Badger) bombard steel and iron production facilities at Muroran on the southern coast of Hokkaido.

During the night Twentieth Air Force sends 26 B-29s to mine the waters off western Korea and off west-central Honshu, Japan.

Task Force 38 carrier aircraft sink a Japanese minesweeper, a coastal defense vessel, an auxiliary submarine chaser, a guardboat, and six cargo ships off northern Honshu, southern Hokkaido, and Tsugaru Strait. Three escort destroyers, a cargo ship, three coastal defense vessels, two auxiliary submarine chasers, and a submarine chaser are damaged in the same area.

U.S. submarine *Skate* torpedoes and sinks a Japanese transport at South Sakhalin Island, Kuriles.

July 16

ALEUTIANS: Eleventh Air Force sends four B-25 Mitchells on a shipping sweep. One cargo ship is hit.

CBI: Major General Stratemeyer takes command of all U.S. air forces in China.

In China, Fourteenth Air Force sends B-25 Mitchells to attack truck convoys moving supplies through the Siang Chiang Valley. P-38 Lightnings, P-47 Thunderbolts, and P-51 Mustangs attack trucks, river traffic, highways, logistics storage sites, rail lines, bridges, and troops in southern and eastern China and French Indochina.

ATLANTIC: Terminal, the Potsdam Conference Begins. President Truman, Prime Minister Churchill, and Premier Stalin meet at Potsdam, in the Soviet-controlled zone of occupied Germany. The agenda includes decisions on the Pacific war, especially Soviet participation, the status of eastern Europe, the disposition of Germany under occupation, and reparations.

The first atomic bomb is successfully tested at the Trinity site, Alamogordo, New Mexico. President Truman receives word in Potsdam that evening.

ETO: Headquarters Eighth Air Force passes operational control of all Eighth Air Force units in Great Britain to VIII Fighter Command, having redeployed over 90,000 of its assigned personnel. Headquarters Eighth Air Force, along with Twentieth Air Force, is to become part of U.S. Army Strategic Air Forces in the Pacific (USASTAF), on Okinawa and under the command of General Carl A. Spaatz.

MEDITERRANEAN: Fifteenth Air Force begins to redeploy the four subordinate B-25 squadrons of the 340th Bombardment Group to the United States.

SOUTHWEST PACIFIC AREA: In the Philippines, Far East Air Force B-25 Mitchells and P-51 Mustangs support ground forces on Luzon.

P-51 Mustang sweep Formosa, attacking communication targets, a railroad station, a bridge, and a locomotive shed. B-24 Liberators, A-26 Invaders, B-25 Mitchells, P-51s, and P-47 Thunderbolts from Okinawa and Ie Shima attack airfields, bridges, and harbor installations on Kyushu Island, Japan.

FEAF B-24 Liberators bomb warehouses on Celebes Island.

U.S. submarine *Baya* torpedoes and sinks a Japanese torpedo boat in the Java Sea. U.S. submarine *Blenny* torpedoes and sinks a Japanese gunboat in the Java Sea.

PACIFIC: P-47 Thunderbolts attack Yanagawa and 96 P-51 Mustangs from Iwo Jima attack airfields on Honshu, Japan. Pilots report 22 Japanese fighters shot down. One P-51 is lost.

A British fast carrier task force commanded by Vice Admiral Henry B. Rawlings, Royal Navy, with one battleship, four aircraft carriers, eight light cruisers, and 18 destroyers, joins Third Fleet and is designated as Task Force 37.

Carrier aircraft from escort carrier USS *Anzio* along with a destroyer escort sink Japanese submarine *I-13* east of Yokohama, Japan.

During the night 469 B-29s are sent to bomb Japanese cities. Namazu, Oita, Kuwana, and Hiratsuka urban areas are hit with incendiaries, inflicting major damage.

The headquarters of Twentieth Air Force, now under command of Major General Curtis E. LeMay, is established on Guam. The XX Bomber Command is inactivated, and the headquarters of the XXI Bomber Command is redesignated as headquarters squadron for Twentieth Air Force. Operational control of all bomber wings passes to headquarters, Twentieth Air Force.

July 17

ALEUTIANS: Eleventh Air Force sends four B-25 Mitchells on a shipping sweep. Two of the bombers are forced to land in the Soviet Union. Two B-24 Liberators fly a shipping sweep over Shimushiru Island in the Kuriles.

CBI: In China, Fourteenth Air Force sends B-25 Mitchells to attack truck convoys moving supplies through the Siang Chiang Valley. P-47 Thunderbolts and P-51 Mustangs attack trucks, river traffic, airfields, highways, gun positions, rail lines, bridges, and troops in southern and eastern China and French Indochina.

Over 200 B-24 Liberators, B-25 Mitchells, A-26 Invaders, and P-47 Thunderbolts attack Kiangwan airfield near Shanghai.

SOUTHWEST PACIFIC AREA: Far East Air Force sends nearly 150 B-24 Liberators, B-25 Mitchells, and A-26 Invaders to attack Chiang Wan airfield in China. P-47 Thunderbolts attack shipping, warehouses, and the airfield on Taishan Island and B-25 Mitchells attack Itu Aba Island. P-51 Mustangs attack shipping, severely damaging a cargo ship in the harbor on Amami-O-Shima Island and P-47 Thunderbolts dive-bomb railroad tunnels near Kagoshima, on Kyushu Island, Japan.

FEAF B-24 Liberators bomb barracks on Celebes Island and strafe a schooner off the island. B-25 Mitchells bomb Jesselton airfield in Borneo.

PACIFIC: Carrier aircraft from U.S. Task Force 38 and British Task Force 37 attack airfields around Tokyo.

Naval Task Unit 34.8.2 (Rear Admiral Oscar C. Badger), with five battleships, two light cruisers, and 10 destroyers (including the British battleship HMS *King George V* and two British destroyers), bombards industrial facilities in the Mito-Hitachi area near Tokyo on the east coast of Honshu, Japan.

During the night Twentieth Air Force sends 27 B-29s to mine Shimonoseki Strait and the waters off Chongjin, Korea, and southwest Honshu, Japan.

July 18

CBI: In French Indochina, Fourteenth Air Force B-25 Mitchells attack railyards. P-51 Mustangs and P-38 Lightnings attack trucks, coastal shipping, troops, and targets of opportunity in French Indochina.

ATLANTIC: At Potsdam President Truman receives the details of the Alamogordo atomic bomb test and is impressed with the results. He notifies Prime Minister Churchill.

SOUTHWEST PACIFIC AREA: In the Philippines, Far East Air Force P-38 Lightnings attack Japanese troop concentrations on Mindanao Island.

On Formosa, P-38 Lightnings attack communication and transportation targets and B-24 Liberators bomb an airfield.

About 150 B-24 Liberators, B-25 Mitchells, and A-26 Invaders, escorted by 54 P-47 Thunderbolts, attack airfields, shipping, and docks in the Shanghai area.

P-51 Mustangs and P-47s attack communication lines, bridges, shipping, town areas, and targets of opportunity on Kyushu Island, Japan.

U.S. submarine *Hawkbill* is damaged in a depth charge attack off Malaya and is forced to terminate her patrol.

In Borneo, FEAF B-25 Mitchells attack Jesselton, and P-38 Lightnings attack Langkon. B-24 Liberators bomb targets on Celebes Island.

PACIFIC: Carrier aircraft from Task Force 38 attack the Yokosuka naval base, targeting the battleship *Nagato* and bombing airfields near Tokyo. At the naval base, a training ship, a partially built escort destroyer, a submarine, a submarine chaser, a motor torpedo boat, and three auxiliary patrol vessels are sunk. British aircraft from Task Force 37 and U.S. aircraft from TF 38 damage the battleship *Nagato*, a motor torpedo boat, a landing ship, a target ship, and an auxiliary submarine chaser.

Naval Task Group 35.4 (Rear Admiral Carl F. Holden), with four light cruisers and destroyers, conducts an anti-shipping sweep and bombards radar installations off Honshu, Japan.

Aircraft from carrier USS *Wasp* attack Japanese installations on Wake Island.

Navy patrol bombers sink three Japanese cargo vessels in the Korea and Tsushima Straits.

U.S. submarine *Barb* torpedoes and sinks a Japanese coastal defense vessel south of Sakhalin. U.S. submarine *Cero* is damaged in an aerial attack off the Kuriles and is forced to terminate her patrol.

General Carl A. Spaatz establishes the headquarters of U.S. Army Strategic Air Forces in the Pacific (USASTAF) at Guam.

July 19

CBI: In China, Fourteenth Air Force sends 20 B-25 Mitchells, 16 P-51 Mustangs, and four P-47 Thunderbolts to attack railyards and seven B-25s and two P-51s to attack bridges and bomb convoys in the Siang Chiang Valley.

MEDITERRANEAN: Fifteenth Air Force begins to redeploy the headquarters of the 456th Bombardment Group (Heavy) and its four subordinate B-24 squadrons to the United States.

SOUTHWEST PACIFIC AREA: In the Philippines, Far East Air Force P-38 Lightnings support ground forces, attacking Japanese defensive positions on Mindanao Island.

B-25 Mitchells attack Itu Aba Island, China.

Over 90 P-51 Mustangs sweep over the Nagoya area on Honshu Island, Japan, attacking airfields, production and power facilities, and gun positions.

U.S. submarine *Bumper,* attacking a Japanese convoy in the Gulf of Siam, sinks a fleet tanker.

In Borneo, FEAF P-38 Lightnings attack a suicide boat hideout at Sandakan and B-25 Mitchells bomb Jesselton airfield.

PACIFIC: During the night Twentieth Air Force sends 470 B-29s to bomb Japanese cities. The Fukui, Attackachi, Choshi, Okazaki urban areas are hit with incendiaries, causing heavy damage. Three B-29s are lost. Twentieth Air Force sends 29 B-29s to mine the waters off the Japanese ports of Niigata, west-central Honshu, Kobe and Osaka, on the Inland Sea, Maizuru, and Miyazu in southern Honshu, Japan, and the Korean ports of Wonsan and Hungnam.

Another 83 B-29s bomb the Nippon oil plant at Amagasaki.

P-51 Mustangs from Iwo Jima attack airfields, factories, railroads, power lines, and other targets on Honshu Island, Japan.

Task Force 38 aircraft damage two Japanese carriers (*Amagi* and *Katsuragi*) and the battleship *Haruna* at Kure, Inland Sea, Honshu, Japan.

PACIFIC, OKINAWA: A kamikaze damages a destroyer off Okinawa.

July 20

ALEUTIANS: Eleventh Air Force sends eight B-24 Liberators to bomb facilities at the airfield on Matsuwa Island.

The detachment of P-38 Lightnings and P-40s of the 11th Fighter Squadron, 343rd Fighter Group, operating from Amchitka Island since March of 1944, returns to base on Adak Island.

CBI: Fourteenth Air Force sends 10 B-25 Mitchells and six P-51 Mustangs to attack truck convoys around Hengyang and Wuchang, and a logistics storage area on an island near Changsha, China, and rail targets in French Indochina. P-51 Mustangs, P-38 Lightnings, and P-61 Black Widow night fighters attack trucks, river traffic, highways, logistics storage sites, and rail lines in southern and eastern China and in French Indochina.

SOUTHWEST PACIFIC AREA: In the Philippines, Far East Air Force B-25 Mitchells, A-20 Havocs, P-51 Mustangs, P-38 Lightnings, and P-47 Thunderbolts support ground forces in the Cagayan Valley on Luzon. B-24 Liberators bomb Japanese positions on Negros Island.

B-25s attack Itu Aba Island in China.

U.S. submarine *Bumper* attacks a Japanese convoy in the Gulf of Siam, sinking a guardboat.

In Borneo, FEAF P-38 Lightnings attack the town of Langkon. On Celebes Island, B-24 Liberators bomb Togian Island and P-38 Lightnings attack targets of opportunity.

PACIFIC: Twentieth Air Force sends the B-29 crews of the 393rd Bombardment Squadron (Very Heavy), 509th Composite Group, on the first of a series of precision attacks over Japan for the purpose of target familiarization and to practice tactical maneuvers related to employing the atomic bomb. The targets are cities mostly already bombed, and the missions are flown in groups of two to six aircraft at high altitudes. Over 90 P-51 Mustangs from Iwo Jima attack airfields on Honshu Island, Japan. Pilots report one confirmed kill and 11 probables on the ground. Three P-51s are lost.

U.S. submarine *Threadfin* torpedoes and sinks a Japanese minesweeper off the southern coast of Korea.

A Japanese merchant cargo ship is sunk by a mine in Shimonoseki Strait.

July 21

CBI: In China, Fourteenth Air Force sends 11 B-25 Mitchells and two P-51 Mustangs to attack truck convoys in the Siang Chiang Valley, bomb a Japanese headquarters near Wuchang, and attack a bridge, trains, warehouses, and antiaircraft positions. P-51 Mustangs, P-38 Lightnings, and P-61 Black Widow night fighters attack trucks, river traffic, highways, logistics storage sites, and rail lines in southern and eastern China and in French Indochina.

SOUTHWEST PACIFIC AREA: In the Philippines, Far East Air Force P-38 Lightnings support ground forces on Luzon.

B-25 Mitchells and A-26 Invaders bomb shipping at Naze-Ko, in the Ryukyu Islands.

The radar-equipped B-24 Liberators of the 373rd Bombardment Squadron (Heavy), of the 308th Bombardment Group, Fourteenth Air Force, from Luliang, China, are transferred to the 494th Bombardment Group (Heavy), Seventh Air Force, at Okinawa.

The B-25s of the 405th Bombardment Squadron (Medium), 38th Bombardment Group (Medium), redeploy from Luzon to Okinawa.

PACIFIC: During the night Twentieth Air Force sends 23 B-29s, staging through Iwo Jima, to mine Shimonoseki Strait and the Korea coast at Najin (the longest B-29 combat mission of the war) and in the Pusan-Masan, Korea, area. One B-29 is lost. Another 72 B-29s bomb the coal liquefaction company at Ube. Over 100 P-51 Mustangs from Iwo Jima attack airfields, rail facilities, and other targets on Shikoku and Honshu islands, Japan.

U.S. submarine *Sea Robin* torpedoes and sinks two Japanese cargo vessels west of Kyushu, Japan. Mines sink a Japanese merchant cargo ship and damage another along the southern Korean coast.

CBI: In China, Fourteenth Air Force sends 16 B-25 Mitchells to attack truck convoys in the Siang Chiang Valley and bomb railyards and bridges. P-51 Mustangs, P-38 Lightnings, and P-47 Thunderbolts attack trucks, coastal shipping, highways, logistics storage sites, and rail lines in southern and eastern China and in French Indochina.

SOUTHWEST PACIFIC AREA: In the Philippines, Far East Air Force B-25 Mitchells, P-51 Mustangs, and P-38 Lightnings support ground forces on Luzon.

In China, 22 B-24 Liberators from Okinawa attack airfields; 37 B-25 Mitchells bomb an oil plant at Shanghai and a Japanese destroyer on the Whangpoo River. P-47 Thunderbolts from Ie Shima attack a destroyer, a gunboat, and a cargo ship on the Whangpoo River, and bomb factories and railroad shops in and around Shanghai. P-51 Mustangs from Okinawa also attack Whangpoo River shipping and 37 A-26 Invaders attack a nearby airfield. B-24 Liberators on a night shipping search and weather mission bomb airfields at Tinghai and on Chusan Island, China, at Pusan, Korea, and at Yonago, Honshu Island, Japan.

The B-24s of the 403rd Bombardment Squadron (Heavy), 43rd Bombardment Group (Heavy), redeploy from Luzon to Ie Shima.

PACIFIC: Twentieth Air Force sends 26 B-29s to mine Shimonoseki Strait and the waters off Najin, Pusan, and Masan, Korea.

Mines sink a Japanese cargo ship and damage another cargo ship off Niigata, west-central Honshu, and damage an auxiliary submarine chaser off Kobe, a cargo ship at Hagi harbor, southwest Honshu, and a merchant tanker. Mines damage a cargo ship off Najin on the northeast coast of Korea.

Japanese cargo ship is sunk by an aerial mine dropped by Twentieth Air Force west of Funagawa, northwest Honshu, Japan.

Naval Task Force 93 (Rear Admiral John H. Brown, Jr.), with two light cruisers and five destroyers, bombards installations at Suribachi, Paramushiru, Kuriles.

July 23

ALEUTIANS: Eleventh Air Force sends two B-24 Liberators, using radar to locate bomb release points, to attack the airfield on Paramushiru Island in the Kuriles.

CBI: The Tenth Air Force and the Fourteenth Air Force are consolidated to form the Army Air Forces, China Theater. The headquarters of Tenth Air Force is established at Kunming. The commander is Lieutenant General George E. Stratemeyer.

Fourteenth Air Force B-25 Mitchells and P-51 Mustangs bomb railyards. P-51 Mustangs, P-38 Lightnings, and P-40s attack river traffic, vehicles, logistics storage sites, and rail lines in southern and eastern China and in French Indochina.

SOUTHWEST PACIFIC AREA: In the Philippines, Far East Air Force P-51 Mustangs and P-38 Lightnings support ground forces on Luzon.

B-25 Mitchells bomb Itu Aba Island, China. B-24 Liberators attack Miho and Saeki, Japan.

In Borneo, FEAF B-25 Mitchells bomb Jesselton, while B-24 Liberators bomb Amboina on Ambon Island and the Tolonoeoe Islands in the Netherlands East Indies.

U.S. submarine *Hardhead* torpedoes and sinks a Japanese auxiliary submarine chaser off Java.

PACIFIC: U.S. destroyers attack a Japanese convoy, sinking a cargo ship off south-central Honshu, Japan.

U.S. submarine *Sea Poacher* torpedoes and sinks a Japanese guardboat off northeast Honshu, Japan.

Fifth Air Force B-24 Liberators on an antishipping sweep off the south coast of Korea sink a Japanese merchant tanker.

U.S. submarine *Barb* lands eight commandos to destroy a Japanese train on the east coast of Karafuto, Sakhalin Island.

July 24

CBI: In China, Fourteenth Air Force B-25 Mitchells and P-51 Mustangs attack truck convoys in the Hengyang area. P-51 Mustangs, P-38 Lightnings, and P-47 Thunderbolts attack trucks, river traffic, highways, logistics storage sites, and rail lines in southern and eastern China and in French Indochina.

ATLANTIC: At Potsdam, President Truman casually mentions to Stalin that "we have a new weapon of unusual destructive force." Stalin appears not to understand, but he understands perfectly well. Soviet spies in the U.S. atomic bomb program have been providing critical technical information and have passed word that a test will be conducted soon. Truman's aside confirms that the weapon he knows all about actually works. He immediately orders Soviet scientists to redouble their efforts to develop a workable atomic bomb as soon as possible.

ETO: The VIII Fighter Command begins to redeploy the four subordinate B-17 squadrons of the 391st Bombardment Group (Heavy) to the United States.

SOUTHWEST PACIFIC AREA: In the Philippines, Fifth Air Force P-51 Mustangs and P-38 Lightnings support ground forces on Luzon.

Over 100 Fifth Air Force B-24 Liberators conduct their first bombing run from Okinawa, hitting the Chiang Wan airfield near Shanghai. Seventh Air Force B-25 Mitchells from Okinawa also attack airfields near the Shanghai area while A-26 Invaders and B-25 Mitchells attack the Tachang and Tinghai airfields. Other B-25 Mitchells attack Itu Aba Island, China.

The B-24 Liberators of the 65th Bombardment Squadron (Heavy), 43rd Bombardment Group (Heavy), redeploy from Luzon to Ie Shima. The 421st Night Fighter Squadron, V Fighter Command, redeploys from Luzon to Ie Shima with P-61 Black

Widow night fighters. The B-24s of the 822nd and 823rd Bombardment Squadrons (Heavy) of the 38th Bombardment Group (Heavy) redeploy from Luzon to Okinawa.

Kaitens from Japanese submarine *I-53* damage a destroyer escort off Luzon. The destroyer is later scuttled by submarine chasers.

Thirteenth Air Force B-25 Mitchells and B-24 Liberators bomb airfields on Borneo.

U.S. submarine *Chub* torpedoes and sinks a Japanese tug in the Java Sea.

PACIFIC: Twentieth Air Force sends 625 B-29s to bomb aircraft production facilities, an arsenal, and the city of Tsu, in the Nagoya and Osaka areas on Honshu Island, Japan. One B-29 is lost. Over 90 P-51 Mustangs from Iwo Jima attack airfields near Nagoya, Japan.

Carrier aircraft from Task Force 38 conduct a two-day attack on the Inland Sea area, hitting the Kure naval base and airfields. Battleship-carrier *Hyuga,* a heavy cruiser, a training ship, a target ship, and a guardboat are sunk. Carrier *Ryuho,* a battleship-carrier, battleship *Haruna,* a light cruiser, a heavy cruiser, three escort destroyers, a fast transport, a torpedo cruiser, two destroyers, two coastal defense vessels, and a transport are damaged.

A Japanese escort carrier is damaged by aircraft from British carriers HMS *Formidable,* HMS *Indefatigable,* and HMS *Victorious,* then suffers further damage when it hits a mine dropped by B-29s off Beppu in the Inland Sea. Two Japanese cargo ships hit mines dropped by B-29s off the west coast of Korea.

Naval Task Group 35.3 (Rear Admiral J. Cary Jones, Jr.), with four light cruisers and six destroyers (from Task Group 38.4) conducts a shipping sweep.

CENTRAL PACIFIC: Aircraft from escort carrier USS *Vella Gulf* carries out air strikes on Pagan, a Japanese base in the Marianas.

July 25

CBI: Fourteenth Air Force B-25 Mitchells and P-38 Lightnings attack bridges in French Indochina. P-47 Thunderbolts and P-51 Mustangs attack road, rail, and river traffic, and railyards in southern and eastern China and French Indochina.

ATLANTIC: General Carl Spaatz, the commander of Army Strategic Air Forces, receives an authorization from Secretary of War Henry Stimson and the Chief of Staff George C. Marshall for the 509th Composite Group to deliver its first "special bomb" after August 3, 1945, as soon as weather allows for visual bombing, on one of four targets in Japan: Hiroshima, Kokura, Nagasaki, or Niigata.

MEDITERRANEAN: The headquarters of the 303rd Bombardment Group (Heavy) and its four subordinate squadrons, the headquarters of the 379th Bombardment Group (Heavy) and its four subordinate squadrons, and the headquarters of the 484th Bombardment Group (Heavy) and its four subordinate squadrons are inactivated at Casablanca, French Morocco.

SOUTHWEST PACIFIC AREA: In the Philippines, Far East Air Force B-24 Liberators bomb Japanese defenses on Negros Island. B-25 Mitchells bomb Itu Aba Island, China. B-24s bomb Kikaiga-shima in the Amami Islands, targets in the Ryukyu Islands, and the town of Tsuiki on Kyushu Island, Japan.

The headquarters of the 38th Bombardment Group (Medium) and 71st Bombardment Squadron (Medium) redeploy from Luzon to Okinawa with B-25 Mitchells, and the headquarters of the 345th Bombardment Group (Medium) redeploys from Clark Field, Luzon, to Ie Shima.

In Borneo, FEAF B-24 Liberators bomb airfields, while B-25 Mitchells and fighters attack a dispersal area at the Jesselton airfield area.

PACIFIC: Task Force 38 carrier aircraft attack targets of opportunity around the Inland Sea area, sinking three Japanese guardboats, an army tanker, a cargo ship, and two merchant tankers and damaging a heavy cruiser, a coastal defense vessel, three cargo ships, and a merchant tanker.

Naval Task Group 35.3 (Rear Admiral J. Cary Jones, Jr.) with four light cruisers (from TG 38.3) and six destroyers (from TG 38.4) bombards Kushimoto seaplane base, the airfield near Shio-no-Misaki on southwest Honshu, and adjacent facilities.

Twentieth Air Force sends 30 B-29s to mine the waters off Chongjin and Pusan, Korea, and Fushiki and Nanao, west-central Honshu, Ohama, east-central Honshu, and Tsuruga, Japan. Mines sink two cargo ships off Honshu.

During the night Twentieth Air Force sends 75 B-29s to bomb the Mitsubishi Oil Company and the Hayama Petroleum Company at Kawasaki. One B-29 is lost to antiaircraft fire.

U.S. submarine *Barb* bombards a lumber mill and sampan-building yard at Shibetoro, Kuriles, destroying 35 sampans under construction.

July 26

ALEUTIANS: Eleventh Air Force sends seven B-24 Liberators to bomb the Kataoka naval base on Shimushu Island with incendiaries.

CBI: In China, Fourteenth Air Force sends eight B-25 Mitchells and four P-51 Mustangs to attack railyards, logistics storage areas, and transportation targets. P-51 Mustangs, P-38 Lightnings, and P-61 Black Widow night fighters attack trucks, coastal shipping, river traffic, highways, logistics storage sites, bridges, town areas, and rail lines in southern and eastern China and in French Indochina.

ATLANTIC: President Truman issues a statement from Potsdam, Germany. The Potsdam declaration orders the unconditional surrender of the Japanese armed forces and specifies that Japan will maintain sovereignty only over its four main home islands, and will be occupied under the direction of a supreme Allied commander until the time that a stable and peaceful postwar government can be established. The Japanese people will not be punished, although Japanese war criminals will be prosecuted. The role of the Japanese emperor in postwar Japan is left unsaid, although the language of the declaration refers to a government that will be "established, in accordance with the freely expressed will of the Japanese people." The declaration promises "the complete and utter destruction of Japan" if the declaration is rejected.

The JCS recommends to President Truman that the United States resist Soviet demands for concessions that would extend Soviet influence and control farther into Europe.

Winston Churchill is defeated in national elections, resulting in a new prime minister, Clement Attlee, who will form a new government.

SOUTHWEST PACIFIC AREA: In the Philippines, Thirteenth Air Force B-25 Mitchells and P-38 Lightnings support ground forces in Luzon. B-24 Liberators bomb Japanese positions in support of ground forces on Negros Island.

B-25 Mitchells bomb Itu Aba Island, China.

B-24 Liberators on snooper (radar-assisted bomb release) strikes hit targets in the Ryukyu Islands, airfields at Tinghai, China, and at Nakazu, Japan, and the docks at Pusan, Korea.

The headquarters of the 43rd Bombardment Group (Heavy) and the B-24s of the 64th Bombardment Squadron (Heavy) redeploy from Clark Field, Luzon, to Ie Shima.

In Borneo, FEAF B-24 Liberators attack airfields.

PACIFIC: During the night Twentieth Air Force sends 350 B-29s to bomb Japanese cities.

Matsuyama, Tokuyama, and Omuta urban areas are hit with incendiaries, causing major damage. One B-29 is lost.

July 27

CBI: Chinese forces capture Kweilin.

In China, Fourteenth Air Force sends 13 B-25 Mitchells with P-51 Mustangs to attack truck convoys in the Siang Chiang Valley, bomb railyards, and attack coastal shipping. P-51 Mustangs and P-38 Lightnings attack trucks, river shipping, road and rail traffic, logistics storage sites, and bridges in southern and eastern China and in French Indochina.

ETO: Ninth Air Force begins to redeploy the headquarters of the 386th Bombardment Group (Light) and its four subordinate B-26 squadrons to the United States.

MEDITERRANEAN: Twelfth Air Force begins to redeploy the headquarters of the 340th Bombardment Group (Medium) from Italy to the United States.

SOUTHWEST PACIFIC AREA: Over 60 Fifth and Seventh Air Force B-24 Liberators, escorted by 50 P-51 Mustangs, attack a marshaling yard at Kagoshima, Kyushu. More than 150 P-47 Thunderbolts attack a tunnel, bridges, and industrial targets on Kyushu.

The 500th Bombardment Squadron (Medium) of the 345th Bombardment Group (Medium) redeploys from Clark Field, Luzon, to Ie Shima with B-25 Mitchells.

Thirteenth Air Force B-24 Liberators attack an airfield on Borneo. U.S. submarine *Pargo* is damaged by a depth charge and air attack off northern Celebes Island, but remains on patrol.

PACIFIC: During the night Twentieth Air Force sends 24 B-29s to drop mines in Shimonoseki Strait and in the waters off Niigata, west-central Honshu, Miyazu and Senzaki, southwest Honshu, and Maizuru, southern Honshu, Japan. Three B-29s are hit by antiaircraft fire. Two bombers make a landing in the ocean; 13 crewmen are rescued, and the third bomber crash lands on Iwo Jima.

Fifth Air Force aircraft sink a Japanese landing ship off southern Kyushu, Japan.

Mines sink six Japanese cargo ships off western Kyushu, Japan.

U.S. submarine *Pogy* torpedoes and sinks a Japanese cargo ship west of Honshu, Japan.

A Japanese aerial torpedo hits and damages a U.S. freighter in Naha harbor, Okinawa. Another freighter is hit with an aerial torpedo south of Ie Shima, sinking an LST moored alongside.

July 28

CBI: In China, Fourteenth Air Force sends seven B-25 Mitchells and four P-51 Mustangs to attack truck convoys in the Siang Chiang Valley, bomb a cargo ship, and attack troop concentrations. P-51 Mustangs, P-38 Lightnings, and P-61 Black Widow night fighters attack trucks, river traffic, logistics storage sites, and rail lines in southern and eastern China and in French Indochina.

ATLANTIC: The new British prime minister, Clement Attlee, arrives at Potsdam.

SOUTHWEST PACIFIC AREA: In the Philippines, Thirteenth Air Force B-25 Mitchells and P-38 Lightnings in support of ground forces, attack enemy positions on Luzon and other P-38s attack troop concentrations on Jolo Island. B-24 Liberators support ground forces on Negros Island.

P-47 Thunderbolts from Ie Shima conduct rocket attacks and strafe airfields, oil stores, railyards, warehouses, industrial targets, and gun positions on Kyushu Island, Japan. Other P-47s attack shipping, and A-26 Invaders and B-25 Mitchells bomb airfields. P-51 Mustangs and B-25s conduct sweeps over the Inland Sea, destroying two small cargo vessels and a patrol boat. Over 70 B-24 Liberators bomb a battleship and an aircraft carrier at Kure. Aircrews report both ships damaged.

The B-25s of the 499th and 501st Bombardment Squadrons (Medium), 345th Bombardment Group (Medium), redeploy from Clark Field to Ie Shima.

U.S. submarine *Hardhead* torpedoes and damages a Japanese vessel south of Bali.

PACIFIC: Carrier aircraft from TF 38 attack the Kure naval base and other targets in the Inland Sea area, sinking a battleship, a battleship-carrier, a training ship, a heavy cruiser, a light cruiser, a submarine, an escort destroyer, four guardboats, a submarine depot ship, a stores ship, an auxiliary minesweeper, four cargo ships, and two merchant tankers. British carrier aircraft (Task Force 37) sink two coastal defense vessels. U.S. carrier aircraft damage carrier *Katsuragi* and a training carrier, a torpedo cruiser, a submarine in drydock, a destroyer, three coastal defense vessels, a submarine chaser, an escort destroyer, two guardboats, a motor torpedo boat, two auxiliary minesweepers, a merchant passenger ship, three cargo ships, and three merchant tankers.

Four escort carriers of TF 32 (Rear Admiral Jesse B. Oldendorf) provide cover for minesweeping operations in the East China Sea, directed by Rear Admiral Alexander Sharp's Naval Task Force 39.

U.S. submarine *Sennet* attacks a Japanese convoy off western Honshu and sinks three cargo ships.

General Walter Krueger's Sixth Army issues orders for Operation Olympic, the landing on Kyushu Island and the first step in the decisive defeat of Japan. The operation is scheduled for November 1, 1945. Sixth Army will land four corps: I Corps under Major General Innis P. Swift (33rd and 25th Infantry Divisions), XI Corps under Lieutenant General Charles P. Hall (43rd Infantry Division, 1st Cavalry Division, and 112th Cavalry RCT), IX Corps under Major General Charles W. Ryder (77th, 98th, and 81st Infantry Divisions), and the V Marine Amphibious Corps under Major General Harry Schmidt (2nd, 3rd, and 5th Marine Divisions). The 11th Airborne Division will be the army reserve. The 40th Infantry Division and the 158th RCT will attack islands off Kyushu. The total number of troops available is 650,000 men.

During the night Twentieth Air Force sends more than 470 B-29s to bomb Japanese cities. Tsu, Aomori, Ichinomiya, Ogaki, Uji-Yamada, and Uwajima urban areas are hit with incendiaries, causing great destruction. Another 76 B-29s bomb an oil refinery. Over 140 P-51 Mustangs from Iwo Jima attack airfields and military targets around Tokyo and attack and damage a destroyer escort along the Chiba Peninsula.

PACIFIC, OKINAWA: A kamikaze sinks U.S. destroyer *Callaghan* southwest of Okinawa. Another destroyer aiding *Callaghan* is damaged by near-miss of another kamikaze.

July 29

CBI: In China, Fourteenth Air Force sends four B-25 Mitchells and two P-51 Mustangs to attack shipping off the Luichow Peninsula, oil storage areas, and barracks. Over 100 P-51 Mustangs, P-38 Lightnings, and P-61 Black Widow night fighters attack trucks, river traffic, highways, logistics storage sites, and rail lines in southern and eastern China and in French Indochina.

SOUTHWEST PACIFIC AREA: In the Philippines, Thirteenth Air Force B-24 Liberators bomb Japanese troops holding out at Negros Island. B-25 Mitchells and P-38 Lightnings attack Japanese positions and troop concentrations on Luzon.

P-47 Thunderbolts from Ie Shima and B-24 Liberators, B-25 Mitchells, and A-26 Invaders from Okinawa attack targets in the Japanese home islands. Over 70 B-24s attack shipping at Kure, 41 B-24s attack industrial targets and logistics storage areas, shipping and engine works in Nagasaki and town areas. B-25s attack a bridge, barracks, warehouses, a lighthouse, and navigation light. A-26s attack the naval base and engine works at Nagasaki. P-47s attack the harbor at Kure, shipping and seaplane station at Ibusuki, railroad station, docks, and town areas, airfields, and shipping at Kagoshima Bay. P-51 Mustangs attack numerous targets of opportunity on the south coast of Korea and Kyushu, attacking shipping, rail lines, and industrial targets.

The radar-equipped B-24s of the 868th Bombardment Squadron (Heavy), Thirteenth Air Force, redeploy from Leyte to Okinawa.

Japanese submarine *I-58* torpedoes and sinks heavy cruiser USS *Indianapolis* northeast of Leyte. The *Indianapolis* has just delivered the atomic weapons to Tinian.

FEAF B-24 Liberators attack an airfield and warehouses on Celebes Island.

Corporal Melvin Mayfield, D Company, 20th Infantry Regiment, 6th Infantry Division, comes to the rescue of two Filipino companies in the Cordillera Mountains, Luzon, moving from shell hole to shell hole until he reaches several caves where the enemy is located on top of a hill. With grenades and his M-1 carbine, he attacks each one of the cave positions. As he reaches the last cave, a machine-gun bullet destroys his carbine and wounds his left hand. He continues the attack with only hand grenades, charging directly into point-blank fire to destroy the position. For his selfless heroism and gallant leadership, Corporal Mayfield will receive the nation's highest award for valor, the Medal of Honor.

PACIFIC: Naval Task Unit 34.8.1 commanded by Rear Admiral John F. Shafroth, with three battleships, four heavy cruisers, and 10 destroyers, bombards an aircraft production facility and other production facilities at Hamamatsu, Honshu. British battleship HMS *King George V* and three destroyers, although operating independently, provide supporting fire on the targets.

Seventh Air Force P-47 Thunderbolts conduct a sweep for targets of opportunity over Nagasaki, Japan, and sink an auxiliary submarine chaser. Fifth Air Force B-25 Mitchells damage a Japanese escort carrier *Kaiyo* in the Inland Sea. B-25s and P-51 Mustangs on a shipping sweep off the southeast coast of Korea sink three cargo ships and a tanker. A-26 Invaders damage a Japanese merchant tanker off Nagasaki.

During the night Twentieth Air Force sends 24 B-29s to mine Shimonoseki Strait and the waters off Najin, Korea, and Fukuoka, west Kyushu, Japan.

PACIFIC, OKINAWA: Kamikazes damage a destroyer and high-speed transport off Okinawa.

July 30

CBI: In China, Fourteenth Air Force sends two B-25 Mitchells to attack truck convoys in the Siang Chiang Valley. P-51 Mustangs, P-38 Lightnings, and P-61 Black Widow night fighters attack river and rail traffic, highways, and logistics storage sites in southern and eastern China and in French Indochina.

SOUTHWEST PACIFIC AREA: In the Philippines, Thirteenth Air Force B-25 Mitchells and P-38 Lightnings support ground forces east of Manila and in other areas on Luzon.

Over 60 B-25 Mitchells and A-26 Invaders bomb airfields and P-47 Thunderbolts support the strike and also attack numerous nearby targets of opportunity on Honshu Island, Japan. B-25 Mitchells make a shipping sweep over Korean waters, then attack targets on the Japanese mainland near Sendai. P-51 Mustangs escorting the bombers attack nearby targets of opportunity. P-47s bomb Sendai, causing widespread destruction. P-51s on photo reconnaissance along southern Kyushu destroy trains and small craft. Nearly 80 P-47s attack warehouses, barracks, and airfield facilities

FEAF B-24 Liberators bomb an airfield in Borneo.

PACIFIC: Premier Baron Kantoro Suzuki announces that Japan will respond to the Potsdam Declaration with "contemptuous silence."

Twentieth Air Force sends P-51 Mustangs from Iwo Jima to attack airfields, railroads, and other targets throughout the Kobe-Osaka, Japan, area.

Carrier aircraft from Task Force 38 bomb airfields and industrial targets in central Honshu, and fly sweeps against Japanese shipping in Maizuru Bay. Aircraft sink an escort vessel, a submarine chaser, a minelayer, four auxiliary submarine chasers, two guardboats, two auxiliary submarine chasers, and three cargo ships. Aircraft also damage an escort destroyer, a submarine depot ship, two submarines, two coastal defense vessels, a minelayer, an auxiliary submarine chaser, a guardboat, and two cargo ships. British carrier aircraft from Task Force 37 destroy a grounded transport.

U.S. submarine *Sennet* torpedoes and sinks a Japanese cargo ship off western Hokkaido.

Mines from B-29s sink a destroyer and damage another inside Miyazu Bay, western Honshu, and a passenger-cargo vessel in the Tsugaru Strait.

Rear Admiral Alexander Sharp's Naval Task Force 39 completes minesweeping operations in the East China Sea, having covered about 7,300 square miles and destroyed 404 mines without any losses.

July 31

CBI: In China, Fourteenth Air Force sends three B-25 Mitchells to bomb truck convoys in the Siang Chiang Valley. P-51 Mustangs and P-61 Black Widow night fighters attack trucks, river traffic, highways, ammunition storage sites, and rail lines in southern and eastern China.

SOUTHWEST PACIFIC AREA: In the Philippines, Thirteenth Air Force B-25 Mitchells and P-38 Lightnings support ground forces on Luzon in the Cagayan Valley. B-24 Liberators bomb Japanese positions on Negros Island. The headquarters of Fifth Air Force redeploys from Clark Field, Luzon, to Okinawa.

Over 80 B-24s bomb railyards and several other targets, including the Sasebo naval base on Kyushu Island, Japan. A-26 Invaders and B-25 Mitchells bomb airfields and nearby targets, the Sasebo naval base, warehouses at Nagasaki, and a factory and power plant on Koyagi Island. P-51 Mustangs attack antiaircraft positions, coastal shipping off Kyushu, and bomb railroad targets and warehouses in the Izumi area. P-61 Black Widow night fighters continue harassing missions during the night. P-51s attack airfields on the Ryukyu Islands.

PACIFIC: Twentieth Air Force receives the headquarters of the 301st Fighter Wing arriving on Ie Shima from the United States.

U.S. destroyers conduct a shipping sweep and bombard railyards and an industrial area near Shimizu, southeast Honshu, Japan.

PB4Y Privateers from Okinawa destroy a span of the Seisen River bridge in Korea.

U.S. submarine *Thornback* torpedoes and damages a Japanese submarine chaser off east-central Honshu, Japan.

August 1

CBI: Major General Albert F. Hegenberger takes command of Tenth Air Force, with headquarters at Kunming, China. Tenth Air Force will provide tactical support to Chinese ground forces.

The P-51 Mustangs of the 26th Fighter Squadron, 51st Fighter Group, redeploy from Kunming to Nanning. The P-51s of the 528th, 529th, and 530th Fighter Squadrons, 311th Fighter Group, Tenth Air Force, redeploy to Hsian.

SOUTHWEST PACIFIC AREA: In the Philippines, P-38 Lightnings support ground forces in Luzon.

In French Indochina, B-24s bomb a marshaling yard, while escorting P-51 Mustangs strafe boxcars. Other B-24s hit logistics storage areas on Formosa.

B-24s, B-25 Mitchells, and P-47 Thunderbolts bomb the Nagasaki docks and harbor facilities, railyards, and shipping. Other B-24s bomb an airfield and attack Kakeroma Island. Over 80 P-47s attack rail bridges and other railroad targets at Sendai. P-47s flying from Iwo Jima for the first time join VII Fighter Command P-51s in a sweep over south Honshu Island, attacking airfields and rail targets near Okazaki, Itami, and Nagoya.

The headquarters of V Bomber Command and V Fighter Command prepare to redeploy from Clark Field, Luzon, to Okinawa.

Thirteenth Air Force B-24 Liberators bomb shipyards at Pontianak, Borneo. B-24s attack barracks and antiaircraft positions along Makassar Strait, Celebes Island. P-38 Lightnings strafe locomotives in the Surabaya, Java, area.

PACIFIC: During the night Twentieth Air Force sends more than 620 B-29s to bomb Japanese cities. The bombers drop incendiaries on the Toyama, Nagaoka, Mito, and Hachioji urban areas. The targets are heavily damaged. One B-29 is lost. Another 120 B-29s bomb the Mitsubishi Oil Company at Kawasaki, and 37 B-29s drop mines in the Shimonoseki Strait and in the waters off Najin and Chongjin, Korea, and Hamada, northwest Honshu, Japan.

P-51 Mustangs from Iwo Jima attack airfields and other targets in the Osaka-Nagoya area.

FEAF B-24 Liberators bomb the dockyard area at Nagasaki. B-25 Mitchells, P-38 Lightnings, and P-47 Thunderbolts bomb Japanese shipping in Nagasaki harbor. Pilots report a cargo ship and a tanker are damaged.

Naval Task Group 95.2, commanded by Rear Admiral Francis S. Low, with two cruisers, four light cruisers, and nine destroyers, departs Okinawa for the East China Sea to conduct shipping sweeps off Shanghai, China. Task Group 95.3 (Vice Admiral Jesse B. Oldendorf), with three battleships, a heavy cruiser, a light cruiser, three escort carriers, six destroyers, and three destroyer escorts, is in support of Low.

August 2
ALEUTIANS: Eleventh Air Force sends five B-24 Liberators to bomb the naval base on Shimushu Island in the Kuriles.

CBI: In China, Fourteenth Air Force sends 10 B-25 Mitchells, escorted by two P-47 Thunderbolts, to bomb bridges. B-25s bomb truck convoys in the Siang Chiang Valley. P-51 Mustangs and P-47 Thunderbolts attack trucks, river traffic, highways, fuel storage sites, and railyards in southern and eastern China.

ATLANTIC: The Terminal Conference Ends. President Truman, Prime Minister Clement Attlee (who has replaced Churchill as prime minister in the July general elections in Britain), and Premier Stalin issue a protocol statement, which, among other details, establishes a Council of Foreign Ministers from Britain, the United States, France, China, and the Soviet Union to address the conclusion of peace treaties with Italy, Romania, Bulgaria, Hungary, and Finland and to address the settlement of territorial questions. During the Allied occupation of Germany, the nation will be disarmed and demilitarized, and the German people will be convinced that they have suffered complete military defeat. The National Socialist (Nazi) Party organization will be destroyed, and German political life will be reorganized toward democracy. A Polish Provisional Government of National Unity is recognized by the United States and Great Britain with the understanding that "free and unfettered elections" will be held.

SOUTHWEST PACIFIC AREA: In the Philippines, Thirteenth Air Force P-38 Lightnings support ground forces on Luzon.

U.S. submarine *Bugara* operating against Japanese coastal shipping off the Malay Peninsula, sinks a schooner with gunfire and takes the crew on board. Later, USS *Bugara* encounters Malay pirates attacking a Japanese schooner en route to Singapore. The Chinese crew is taken on board, and the schooner is sunk. *Bugara* pursues the pirate vessel and sinks it.

A PV-1 Ventura patrol bomber en route from Saipan to the Philippines locates survivors of the USS *Indianapolis* east of Samar.

PACIFIC: Mines dropped by B-29s sink a Japanese cargo ship off Niigata, west-central Honshu, Japan, and damage a minesweeper on the eastern coast of Korea.

Lieutenant General Nathan F. Twining takes command of Twentieth Air Force. The previous commander, Lieutenant General Curtis E. LeMay, becomes chief of staff of U.S. Army Strategic Air Forces in the Pacific (USASTAF).

August 3

CBI: Fourteenth Air Force B-25 Mitchells attack rail lines. P-47 Thunderbolts and P-51 Mustangs attack bridges, highways, railyards, logistics storage sites, rail lines, and troops in southern and eastern China.

MEDITERRANEAN: Brigadier General William L. Lee takes command of Fifteenth Air Force.

SOUTHWEST PACIFIC AREA: In the Philippines, P-38 Lightnings and B-25 Mitchells support ground forces attacking Japanese positions and buildings in Luzon.

FEAF B-24 Liberators bomb airfields on Celebes Island and bomb the seaplane base on Kangean Island in the Java Sea.

PACIFIC: Twentieth Air Force sends P-51 Mustangs from Iwo Jima to attack airfields, rail lines, and trains throughout the Tokyo area.

Mines dropped by B-29s sink Japanese cargo ships off the northeast coast of Korea, in Kobe harbor, and sink a transport off the southwest coast of Honshu, Japan. An army ship is damaged when it hits a mine from a B-29 off Tsuruga. Two cargo ships are damaged by B-29 mines off west-central Honshu.

August 4

CBI: In China, Fourteenth Air Force B-25 Mitchells attack a rail bridge. Four B-25s and two P-51 Mustangs bomb an airfield and trucks, and other P-51s damage 12 locomotives and several trucks, and bomb a bridge.

ETO: Major General William E. Kepner takes command of Ninth Air Force.

SOUTHWEST PACIFIC AREA: In the Philippines, B-25 Mitchells and P-38 Lightnings support ground forces on Luzon. B-24 Liberators bomb Japanese positions on Negros Island.

P-38 Lightnings fly a sweep over Singapore. Pilots report two Japanese planes shot down.

FEAF B-24 Liberators bomb an airfield on Halmahera Island in New Guinea.

PACIFIC: A Japanese merchant tanker hits a mine in Osaka harbor and sinks. Mines damage a cargo ship in Najin harbor, northeast Korea.

Navy PBM Mariner patrol bombers sink a Japanese vessel off the China coast in the East China Sea.

FEAF B-25s attack warehouses, factories, a rail bridge, and a marshaling yard on Kyushu Island, Japan.

August 5

CBI: In China, Fourteenth Air Force sends 20 P-51 Mustangs to attack bridges, railroad targets, and river traffic.

SOUTHWEST PACIFIC AREA: In the Philippines, P-38 Lightnings support ground forces on Luzon. B-24 Liberators bomb Japanese positions on Negros Island.

Over 330 B-24s, B-25 Mitchells, A-26 Invaders, P-47 Thunderbolts, and P-51 Mustangs attack town areas, industrial targets, and targets of opportunity on Kyushu and the Ryukyu Islands.

The 80th Fighter Squadron, 8th Fighter Group, Fifth Air Force, redeploys its P-38s from Mindoro to Ie Shima.

FEAF B-24 Liberators bomb logistics storage areas, troop concentrations, and antiaircraft positions in the Makassar area on Celebes Island. B-24s also bomb Miti on Halmahera Island in New Guinea.

PACIFIC: During the night Twentieth Air Force sends more than 460 B-29s to bomb Japanese cities. Saga, Maebashi, Imabari, and Nishinomiya-Mikage urban areas are hit with incendiaries and are heavily damaged. Two B-29s are lost. Another 27 B-29s mine the waters off Najin, Korea, and mine Tsuruga Strait, northern Honshu, and Oura and Hagi, southwest Honshu, Japan. Over 100 B-29s bomb the Ube Coal Liquefaction Company, destroying or damaging nearly all the facilities.

Over 100 P-51 Mustangs attack airfields and military installations in a large area around Tokyo.

A U.S. destroyer escort in the Philippine Sea is damaged by the near-miss of a *kaiten* fired by submarine *I-53*.

U.S. submarine *Aspro* rescues a downed P-51 pilot at the entrance to Tokyo Bay while PB4Y Privateer patrol bombers provide cover. Aircrews report 12 Japanese aircraft attempted to intercept the bombers and four were shot down.

U.S. submarine *Billfish* attacks a Japanese convoy in the Yellow Sea and sinks a cargo ship. U.S. submarine *Pogy* torpedoes and sinks a Japanese cargo ship in the Japan Sea west of Akita, Honshu, Japan.

Headquarters of Twentieth Air Force takes operational control of VII Fighter Command. Eighth Air Force receives the headquarters of the 333rd Bombardment Group (Very Heavy) and B-29s of the 435th, 460th, and 507th Bombardment Squadrons (Very Heavy), arriving at Okinawa from the United States.

August 6

CBI: Representatives of the China and Pacific theaters meet to review a plan called Carbonado for capturing the Liuchow Peninsula beginning September 1 and initiating offensive operations against Canton on November 1.

In China, Fourteenth Air Force sends 10 P-51 Mustangs and P-47 Thunderbolts to attack locomotives and bridges.

ATLANTIC: A press release from Washington, released after the news of the successful bombing of Hiroshima, promises "a rain of ruin from the sky, the like of which has never been seen on this earth" if Japan refuses to surrender.

SOUTHWEST PACIFIC AREA: B-24 Liberators, B-25 Mitchells, P-47 Thunderbolts, and A-26 Invaders attack targets on Kyushu Island, Japan. B-25s and P-51 Mustangs attack shipping and ground targets of opportunity in the Tsushima Strait area and in the north Ryukyu Islands. P-51 Mustangs bomb an airfield and strafe numerous targets of opportunity on Saishu Island.

U.S. submarine *Bugara* supports British submarine HMS *Sleuth* in sinking two Japanese junks by gunfire off the Malay Peninsula.

U.S. submarine *Bullhead* is sunk, probably by air attack off Bali.

FEAF B-25 Mitchells and P-51 Mustangs attack Japanese shipping in Tsushima Strait, sinking two cargo ships.

PACIFIC: The First Atomic Bomb. At 0245 hours, Colonel Paul W. Tibbets, Jr., pilots the B-29 *Enola Gay* (509th Composite Group) off the runway at North Field, Tinian Island, for Hiroshima, the location of the Japanese 2nd Army, now preparing for the expected Allied invasion of Honshu. Two observation B-29s follow. Navy Captain William S. Parsons is the weaponeer on the mission. He arms the bomb in flight, having just learned the procedure the day before. At 0915 hours (0815 hours Japan time—1145 hours, August 5, Washington time) the atomic bomb is released over the city of Hiroshima at 31,600 feet, detonating 50 seconds later. The *Enola Gay* lands on Tinian at 1458 hours, followed later by the two observation B-29s. The bomb's destructive power is equal to 12,500 tons of TNT. Initial estimates are that about 80 percent of the city's buildings are destroyed and between 70,000 and 80,000 people are killed and 68,000 injured.

Colonel Paul Tibbets about to take off for Hiroshima *(National Archives and Records Administration)*

Mines dropped by B-29s sink Japanese cargo ships, one off west-central Honshu, one west of Kyushu, and one off Shikoku, Japan. Almost 100 P-51 Mustangs from Iwo Jima attack airfields and military installations around Tokyo.

Aircraft from escort carriers USS *Lunga Point,* USS *Makin Island,* and USS *Cape Gloucester* (Vice Admiral Jesse B. Oldendorf's Naval Task Group 95.3) attack Japanese shipping in Tinghai harbor, China.

Aircraft from the carrier USS *Intrepid* bomb Japanese installations on Wake Island as the ship passes to join Task Force 38 in the western Pacific.

Task Force 58 aircraft damage a Japanese coastal defense vessel and a small minelayer-netlayer off northwest Honshu, Japan.

August 7
ALEUTIANS: Eleventh Air Forces ends five B-24 Liberators to bomb Kataoka airfield on Shimushu Island in the Kuriles. Two bombers are damaged by antiaircraft fire.
CBI: The headquarters of Fourteenth Air Force redeploys from Kunming to Paishiyi, China.
SOUTHWEST PACIFIC AREA: The U.S. First Army headquarters arrives in Manila from the ETO as part of the redeployment of forces to participate in the invasion of Japan.

In the Philippines, B-25 Mitchells and P-38 Lightnings support ground forces on Luzon.

B-24 Liberators bomb an airfield on Formosa.

Over Kyushu Island, Japan, B-24s and A-26 Invaders attack airfields and B-25s attack bridges and other targets and bomb a convoy off Pusan, Korea. Other B-25s attack airfields. P-51 Mustangs and P-47 Thunderbolts attack communication and transportation facilities.

The A-26s of the 8th and 13th Bombardment Squadrons (Light), 3rd Bombardment Group (Light), redeploy from Mindoro to Okinawa.

In the Netherlands East Indies, FEAF B-24 Liberators bomb an area near Bandjermasin, Borneo, and P-51 Mustangs attack the harbor at Surabaya, Java.
PACIFIC: Eighth Air Force receives the headquarters of the 346th Bombardment Group (Very Heavy) at Okinawa from the United States.

Twentieth Air Force sends 154 B-29s, escorted by VII Fighter Command P-51 Mustangs, to bomb the naval arsenal at Toyokawa. One B-29 is lost. The P-51s attack rail targets and shipping. During the night 29 B-29s, escorted by FEAF P-47 Thunderbolts, drop mines in Shimonoseki Strait and in the waters off southern Honshu and Osaka, Japan, and Najin, Korea.

Fifth Air Force B-25 Mitchells attack a Japanese convoy off Pusan, Korea, sinking a coastal defense vessel and two merchant tankers.

U.S. submarine *Pargo* attacks a Japanese convoy off northeastern Korea and sinks a cargo ship.

August 8
CBI: In China, Fourteenth Air Force P-51 Mustangs attack buildings, trucks, river traffic, and other targets of opportunity.
SOUTHWEST PACIFIC AREA: In the Philippines, Far East Air Force B-24 Liberators and P-38 Lightnings support ground forces on Luzon.

B-24 Liberators bomb an airfield on Formosa.

B-24s, B-25 Mitchells, A-26 Invaders, P-51 Mustangs, and P-47 Thunderbolts from Okinawa attack airfields, communications, and transport targets on Kyushu Island, Japan. Shipping between Kyushu and Korea, and targets of opportunity in the Ryukyu Islands, on the China coast, and on Formosa are also hit.

The headquarters of the 475th Fighter Group and 431st, 432nd, and 433rd Fighter Squadrons redeploy from Luzon to Ie Shima with P-38 Lightnings. The B-24s of the 528th Bombardment Squadron (Heavy), 380th Bombardment Group (Heavy), redeploy from Mindoro to Okinawa.

FEAF B-24 Liberators on a shipping search attack an airfield on Halmahera Island in New Guinea.

PACIFIC: FEAF B-24 Liberators, B-25 Mitchells, A-26 Invaders, P-51 Mustangs, and P-47 Thunderbolts attack a number of targets on Kyushu and shipping in the Korea and Tsushima Straits, sinking two cargo ships and damaging another.

PB4Y Privateer patrol bombers attack Japanese shipping off Pusan, Korea, sinking two cargo ships and a guardboat.

U.S. submarine *Muskallunge* is damaged by machine-gun fire in an engagement off the Kuriles, but remains on patrol.

Twentieth Air Force sends 221 B-29s to bomb the Japanese city of Yawata with incendiaries. One B-29 is shot down by Japanese fighters, and three are lost due to mechanical reasons. A total of 60 B-29s bomb an aircraft production facility and arsenal complex at Tokyo. Two B-29s are lost to antiaircraft fire and one to mechanical failure. During the night 91 B-29s attack Fukiyama with incendiaries. P-47 Thunderbolts escort the B-29s and report 10 Japanese planes shot down. Over 100 P-51 Mustangs from Iwo Jima attack airfields, factory buildings, barracks, and rail installations around Osaka, Japan.

Over 5 million leaflets are airdropped over Japan explaining the destruction of Hiroshima and warning of similar attacks until the Japanese government accepts the Potsdam Declaration.

The Japanese Supreme War Direction Council meets to discuss options following the atomic attack on Hiroshima. The Air Defense General Headquarters reports that 44 major cities have been largely destroyed; another 37 cities, including Tokyo, have suffered over 30 percent destruction. Civilian and military casualties are approaching 2 million and another 8 million Japanese are injured or without shelter. Despite these facts, the Japanese leadership cannot come to a decision.

August 9

CBI: In China, Fourteenth Air Force B-25 Mitchells, with P-51 escorts, bomb a rail bridge and rail traffic. P-51s strafe antiaircraft positions and targets of opportunity. Other B-25s attack truck convoys and targets of opportunity in the Siang Chiang Valley.

Headquarters Tenth Air Force redeploys from Kunming to Liuchow, China.

U.S. submarine *Hawkbill* shells Tambelan Island, 230 miles east of Singapore, destroying a Japanese radio station.

SOUTHWEST PACIFIC AREA: In the Philippines, Far East Air Force B-25 Mitchells and P-38 Lightnings support ground forces on Luzon.

B-24 Liberators bomb military storage areas on Formosa.

Over Kyushu Island, Japan, B-25s bomb airfields, town areas, shipping, bridges, factories, oil storage, coastal villages, and communication targets in the Tsushima

Strait area. A-26 Invaders and A-20 Havocs attack an airfield and industrial areas in Kyushu. B-24 Liberators bomb the airfield on Honshu Island, Japan, and over 200 P-47 Thunderbolts and P-51 Mustangs attack airfields, barracks, harbor installations, bridges, shipping, vehicles, industrial targets, and logistics storage facilities on Shikoku and Kyushu Islands, and the Ryukyu Islands.

The headquarters of the 380th Bombardment Group (Heavy) redeploy from Mindoro to Okinawa. The P-38s of the 35th Fighter Squadron, 8th Fighter Group, redeploy from Mindoro to Ie Shima.

In Borneo, FEAF B-24 Liberators fly over Ambon and Ceram Islands and bomb barracks on Ambon.

PACIFIC: The Second Atomic Bomb. Major Charles W. Sweeney pilots a B-29, *Bock's Car* (509th Composite Group), off the runway at Tinian at 0230 hours, followed by two observation B-29s. Commander Frederick W. Ashworth (USN) is the weaponeer on the mission. The primary target, Kokura, is obscured by bad weather. Sweeney flies to the secondary target, Nagasaki. The bomb is released from 28,900 feet at 1158 hours (1058 hours Nagasaki time), detonating about one minute after release. At least 40,000 people are killed and 60,000 injured. After refueling on Okinawa, the B-29s return to Tinian by 2339 hours.

The Soviet Union declares war on Japan and ground forces begin an invasion of Manchuria.

Spurred by Emperor Hirohito, the Japanese Cabinet and the Supreme Council vote to accept the Potsdam Declaration with the condition that the imperial prerogatives are preserved. The Japanese government's message to the Allies asks for surrender "without prejudice to the Emperor's position."

During the night 95 B-29s bomb the Nippon Oil Refinery at Amagasaki.

Carrier aircraft from Task Force 58 (Admiral William F. Halsey) attack Japanese shipping and airfields from northern Honshu and Hokkaido to the coast of Korea. Aircraft sink three auxiliary submarine chasers, two minesweepers, a fleet tanker, and a cargo ship. U.S. (TF 38) and British carrier aircraft (TF 37) sink two escort vessels. A kamikaze damages a U.S. destroyer off Honshu.

Naval Task Unit 34.8.1, with battleships and cruisers under the command of Rear Admiral John F. Shafroth, bombards industrial targets at Kamaishi, Honshu. Two British light cruisers support the American task unit.

Soviet forces enter Korea. Soviet aircraft sink a Japanese coastal defense vessel off the northeast coast of Korea and sink two cargo ships off Kamchatka in the Sea of Okhotsk.

B-25 Mitchells on a shipping sweep off the southern coast of Korea sink an auxiliary submarine chaser and two cargo ships. Fifth Air Force B-25s damage a Japanese fast transport in the Inland Sea.

Mines damage two Japanese cargo ships off west-central Honshu and damage a vessel near Sumoto in the Inland Sea.

Naval Task Unit 12.5.6, composed of battleship USS *New Jersey*, a light cruiser, and four destroyers, bombards Wake Island as the ships pass en route to Eniwetok.

August 10

CBI: In China, B-25 Mitchells and P-51 Mustangs bomb convoys in the Siang Chiang Valley, attack a logistics storage area, tucks, and antiaircraft positions. P-47 Thunderbolts and P-51s attack river and rail traffic, troops, trucks, and bridges at several points in southern and eastern China.

Major General Charles B. Stone III assumes command of the Fourteenth Air Force, replacing Major General Claire L. Chennault.

SOUTHWEST PACIFIC AREA: In the Philippines, Far East Air Force P-38 Lightnings attack troop concentrations.

B-24 Liberators bomb Formosa.

Another 100 B-24s, 118 B-25 Mitchells, and over 220 P-47 Thunderbolts and P-38 Lightnings bomb targets on Kyushu. P-51 Mustangs provide cover. B-25s attack destroyers, cargo ships, and small vessels on a shipping sweep between Kyushu Island and Korea. P-47 Thunderbolts bomb Sasebo harbor on Kyushu, and P-51s attack various targets of opportunity on Honshu and Kyushu. B-25s bomb targets of opportunity in the Ryukyu Islands.

The headquarters of the 90th Bombardment Group (Heavy) and the B-24s of the 320th Bombardment Squadron (Heavy) redeploy to Ie Shima from Mindanao. The 530th Bombardment Squadron (Heavy), 380th Bombardment Group (Heavy), redeploys its B-24s to Okinawa.

PACIFIC: The Unites States receives the Japanese surrender offer. The question of the emperor's status causes delays in accepting the offer. Accepting the reservation would mean that the Japanese would not be surrendering unconditionally as the Potsdam Declaration stipulated.

Twentieth Air Force sends 70 B-29s, escorted by P-51 Mustangs, to bomb the arsenal complex at Tokyo.

Carrier aircraft from U.S. Task Force 58 and British Task Force 37 attack Japanese shipping, airfields, and a rail line in northern Honshu. A submarine chaser, a minesweeper, and an auxiliary minesweeper are sunk off northeast Honshu. Two cargo ships and a tanker are sunk off northeast Honshu. A cargo ship is sunk off the east coast of Korea. Mines sink a cargo ship and damage a coastal defense vessel off west-central Honshu, two cargo ships in the Inland Sea, and a merchant tanker in Maizuru harbor, southern Honshu, Japan.

Soviet aircraft sink a Japanese coastal defense vessel north of Joshin, Korea, and two merchant vessels off the Kamchatka Peninsula in the Sea of Okhotsk.

U.S. submarine *Hawkbill* shells Djemadja Island 150 miles northeast of Singapore, destroying a Japanese radio station.

During the night 31 B-29s mine Shimonoseki Strait and the waters off Hagi, southwest Honshu, Japan, and Wonsan, Korea.

PACIFIC, OKINAWA: A Japanese aircraft torpedoes a U.S. freighter off Naha, Okinawa.

August 11

ALEUTIANS: The Eleventh Air Force redeploys the P-38 Lightnings of the 11th Fighter Squadron, 343rd Fighter Group, from Adak Island to Shemya Island.

CBI: In China, Fourteenth Air Force sends nine P-51 Mustangs to attack troops, trains, and river traffic around Chenhsien, Tehsien, and Hengyang.

SOUTHWEST PACIFIC AREA: In the Philippines, Far East Air Force P-38 Lightnings attack buildings and artillery on Luzon.

B-24 Liberators bomb an airfield on Formosa.

Over Japan, B-24 Liberators, B-25 Mitchells, A-26 Invaders, A-20 Havocs, P-47 Thunderbolts, and P-51 Mustangs from Okinawa attack targets in the Inland Sea, in the Tsushima area, and communication, transportation, and other targets throughout Kyushu Island.

The B-24s of the 400th Bombardment Squadron (Heavy), 90th Bombardment Group (Heavy), redeploy from Mindoro to Ie Shima.

In New Guinea, FEAF B-24 Liberators bomb a barracks on Ambon Island.

U.S. submarine *Chub* torpedoes and sinks a Japanese army auxiliary sailing vessel off southern Borneo. U.S. submarine *Hawkbill* lands Australian commandos ashore at Matak Island, Anambas Islands, in the South China Sea northeast of Singapore. The raid destroys a gasoline storage site and rescues an Indian prisoner of war.

PACIFIC: Carrier aircraft from Task Force 38 damage a Japanese destroyer and submarines *I-36, I-159,* and *I-402* at Kure, Japan.

A U.S. destroyer is damaged by naval gunfire in the Kuriles.

U.S. submarine *Jallao* torpedoes and sinks a Japanese cargo ship in the Sea of Japan.

Mines dropped by B-29s sink a Japanese cargo ship west of Kyushu and damage a landing ship.

PACIFIC, OKINAWA: Naval Task Group 95.4 (Captain Henry J. Armstrong, Jr.), comprising four light minelayers, 40 minesweepers, and 10 motor minesweepers, along with supporting vessels, departs Buckner Bay, Okinawa, for the East China Sea to conduct minesweeping operations.

August 12

ALEUTIANS: Eleventh Air Force sends four B-24 Liberators to make a combined visual and radar bomb run over Kataoka on Shimushu Island in the Kuriles. Three other B-24s bomb the airfield and facilities on Paramushiru Island.

SOUTHWEST PACIFIC AREA: In the Philippines, Far East Air Force P-38 Lightnings support ground forces on Luzon.

B-24 Liberators bomb airfields and a marshaling yard on Formosa.

B-25 Mitchells and A-26 Invaders attack airfields, and P-47 Thunderbolts, A-26s, and A-20s attack town areas on Kyushu. B-25s, P-47s, and P-51 Mustangs attack shipping and bridges, rail lines, production facilities, and other targets of opportunity on Kyushu, the Ryukyu Islands, and the Tsushima Straits between Japan and Korea. Pilots report several small cargo ships sunk and damaged.

The 319th Bombardment Squadron (Heavy), 90th Bombardment Group (Heavy), redeploys its B-24s from Mindoro to Ie Shima. The 387th Bombardment Squadron (Heavy), 312th Bombardment Group (Heavy), redeploys its A-20s from Luzon to Okinawa. The 529th Bombardment Squadron (Heavy), 380th Bombardment Group (Heavy), redeploys from Mindoro to Okinawa with B-24s.

PACIFIC: The Japanese government receives the U.S. reply to its surrender offer, which states that no modification to the surrender terms are acceptable. The language of the reply is such that the status of the emperor falls under the interpretation of the Potsdam Declaration language of a government "established, in accordance with the freely expressed will of the Japanese people."

Naval Task Force 92, Rear Admiral John H. Brown, Jr., with two light cruisers and 12 destroyers, bombards Japanese installations in the Kuriles. Ten trawlers are sunk in the Sea of Okhotsk.

Mines sink a Japanese cargo ship north of Kyushu and damage two cargo ships off west-central Honshu, Japan.

PACIFIC, OKINAWA: Japanese submarine *I-58* conducts an unsuccessful kaiten attack on a dock landing ship en route to Leyte Gulf from Okinawa. Battleship USS *Pennsylvania* suffers damage from an aerial torpedo attack in Buckner Bay, Okinawa.

August 13

ALEUTIANS: Eleventh Air Force sends six B-24 Liberators to bomb the Kashiwahara staging area on Paramushiru Island in the Kuriles. The bombers use radar to locate the bomb release points and drop incendiaries on the target.

SOUTHWEST PACIFIC AREA: In the Philippines, Far East Air Force B-25 Mitchells attack Japanese forces on Luzon.

B-24 Liberators and B-25s from Okinawa attack shipping in the waters off Korea and Kyushu Island and in the Inland Sea. Aircrews report several vessels sunk and damaged. P-47 Thunderbolts over Keijo (Seoul, Korea) encounter 20 Japanese aircraft. Pilots report at least 16 are shot down.

P-38 Lightnings attack shipping near Singapore, Malaysia.

PACIFIC: Aircraft from Vice Admiral John S. McCain's Task Force 38 attack targets around Tokyo.

An Army Air Force Catalina flying boat (OA-10A) rescues the crew of a downed TBM Avenger) from USS *Ticonderoga* inside Tokyo Bay.

U.S. submarine *Atule* torpedoes and sinks a Japanese coast defense vessel and damages another off southern Hokkaido. U.S. submarine *Torsk* torpedoes and sinks a Japanese cargo ship off west-central Honshu, Japan.

A Japanese army tanker is damaged when it hits a mine off north Kyushu.

PACIFIC, OKINAWA: A kamikaze hits an attack transport in Buckner Bay, Okinawa.

CENTRAL PACIFIC: Eighth Air Force receives the B-29s of the 461st, 462nd, and 463rd Bombardment Squadrons (Very Heavy) of the 346th Bombardment Group (Very Heavy) on Okinawa from the United States.

August 14

SOUTHWEST PACIFIC AREA: B-25 Mitchells, P-47 Thunderbolts, and P-51 Mustangs attack shipping in Korea and Kyushu waters, claiming several vessels destroyed and damaged. P-47 Thunderbolts over the Osaka-Nagoya area on Honshu, Japan, report several Japanese aircraft shot down.

Upon the announcement of the president that Japan has surrendered, the 11th Airborne Division leaves the Philippine Islands by air for Okinawa, where it is prepared to deploy as the initial occupation force for Japan.

PACIFIC: Emperor Hirohito of Japan instructs the cabinet and the Supreme War Council to endorse the American implied acceptance of Japan's request to maintain the emperor as the titular, but not actual, ruler of Japan. The full cabinet meets, debates the issue, and comes to the conclusion that the members must approve the emperor's decision. Japan sends word that it will accept the provisions of the Potsdam Declaration and agrees to surrender. A coup by military officers to stop Japan's acceptance of the surrender terms fails.

Twentieth Air Force sends more than 300 B-29s escorted by over 160 P-51 Mustangs, to bomb the naval arsenal at Hikari and the Osaka army arsenal on Honshu Island, Japan. The P-51s attack airfields in the Nagoya area. One P-51 is lost. Over 100 B-29s bomb the railyards at Marifu.

U.S. submarine *Spikefish* sinks Japanese submarine *I-373* in the East China Sea off Shanghai, China.

U.S. submarine *Torsk* torpedoes and sinks two coastal defense vessels in the Sea of Japan.

Mines dropped by B-29s sink a Japanese gunboat west of Kyushu, a cargo ship in the Yellow Sea, a cargo ship in Osaka harbor, and another cargo ship off the east coast of Korea.

During the night 132 B-29s from the Marianas fly 3,650 miles to bomb the Nippon Oil Company near Akita on Honshu. Over 160 B-29s drop incendiaries on the cities of Kumagaya and Isezaki. Over 39 B-29s mine Shimonoseki Strait and the waters off Nanao, west-central Honshu, Maizuru, southern Honshu, and Hamada on northwest Honshu, Japan.

As the bombers are returning from their mission, they get word of Japan's surrender.

August 15

CBI: Chinese Communist forces under Mao Tse-tung (Mao Zedong) begin occupying large areas of northern and central China.

ATLANTIC: VJ Day. The message that Japan accepts the Allied surrender terms reaches President Harry S. Truman in mid-afternoon. The president announces the unconditional surrender of Japan at 1900 hours Washington time, proclaiming a two-day holiday. The news is followed by tremendous celebrations throughout America.

Truman orders a cease-fire message to be issued to all U.S. commands in the Pacific.

SOUTHWEST PACIFIC AREA: All offensive action against Japan ends. General of the Army Douglas MacArthur is notified that he is appointed Supreme Commander for Allied powers. MacArthur passes a message to the Japanese via the Army Airways Communications System, using a frequency that has been sending uncoded weather information.

From Supreme Commander for the Allied Powers To The Japanese Emperor, the Japanese Imperial Government, the Japanese Imperial General Headquarters

Message Number Z-500

I have been designated as the Supreme Commander for the Allied Powers (the United States, the Republic of China, the United Kingdom and the Union of Soviet Socialist Republics) and empowered to arrange directly with the Japanese authorities for the cessation of hostilities at the earliest practicable date.

It is desired that a radio station in the Tokyo area be officially designated for continuous use in handling radio communications between this headquarters and your headquarters. Your reply to this message should give the call signs, frequencies and station designation. It is desired that the radio communication with my headquarters in Manila be handled in English text. . . .

Upon receipt of this message, acknowledge.

Signed
MacArthur.

The Japanese reply about two hours later, representing the first direct communication between the Allies and Japan.

At noon, Tokyo time, the Japanese people hear the voice of the emperor of Japan for the first time, over Radio Tokyo. They bow in reverent silence as they hear his words:

We have ordered our government to communicate to the governments of the United States, Great Britain, and the Soviet Union that Our Empire accepts the provisions of the Joint Declaration [Potsdam]. . . . Cultivate the ways of rectitude; foster nobility of spirit; and work with resolution. . . .

Carrier aircraft from Vice Admiral John S. McCain's Task Force 38 attack airfields near Tokyo and are met by a large number of Japanese aircraft. A second strike is cancelled while the aircraft are approaching their targets as confirmation of Japan's surrender is received.

Soviet aircraft sink a Japanese escort vessel off Wonsan, Korea.

Naval Task Group 30.6, under Commodore Rodger W. Simpson, is formed to liberate, evacuate, and care for Allied prisoners of war in Japan.

August 17

PACIFIC: General Prince Higashikuni becomes prime minister of Japan and forms a new cabinet.

A Japanese coastal defense vessel hits a mine off the southwest coast of Korea and sinks.

The Third Fleet maneuvers off Tokyo Bay.

August 18

PACIFIC: Soviet forces land on Shimushu Island in the Kuriles and meet heavy resistance from Japanese forces. The Soviets suffer a large number of casualties.

August 19

CBI: Two Chinese junks commanded by Lieutenant Livingston Swentzel, Jr. (USN), with a total of seven Americans (one army captain, two marine officers, one navy lieutenant, and four navy enlisted men) and 20 Chinese guerrillas on board engage in a close battle with a Japanese junk with 83 men on board, off the coast of China near Hainan. Swentzel directs the fight, hitting the Japanese junk with bazookas, machine guns, and grenades and then maneuvering to board the enemy vessel. The Japanese junk is boarded, and the assault party finds the decks littered with dead and wounded. Lieutenant Swentzel has fought the U.S. Navy's first battle under sail since the Civil War and the last surface action of World War II.

SOUTHWEST PACIFIC AREA: Two B-25Js of the 345th Bombardment Group (Medium) intercept two Japanese Mitsubishi G4M-1 bombers north of Ie Shima, painted white with green crosses. The aircraft from Tokyo are en route to Manila to meet General MacArthur's staff to work out details of the surrender and occupation. The 16-man delegation, led by Lieutenant General Kawabe Torashiro, the deputy chief of the Japanese army general staff, land on Ie Shima, and the delegation transfer to C-54s for the flight to Manila. On the return flight from Ie Shima to Japan, the Japanese aircraft run out of fuel and crash-land in Tokyo Bay. The delegation is rescued and returns safely to Tokyo.

PACIFIC: A Japanese escort vessel is damaged when it hits a mine off Pusan, Korea.
    Soviet forces begin landing on Sakhalin Island.

August 20

PACIFIC: Naval Task Force 31, commanded by Rear Admiral Oscar C. Badger, is formed to assume responsibility for the occupation of Yokosuka naval base at the mouth of Tokyo Bay.

August 21

ALEUTIANS: Eleventh Air Force sends B-24 Liberators to photograph Soviet activities in the Kurile Islands. Cloud cover forces the bombers to abort.

PACIFIC: A cease-fire is arranged between Soviet and Japanese forces in the Kuriles.

August 22

CBI: The China theater command suspends all training and support for the Chinese Nationalist Army.

PACIFIC: A Japanese destroyer is damaged when it hits a mine in the Shimonoseki Strait.

CENTRAL PACIFIC: Captain Harold B. Grow, commander of Majuro Atoll, accepts the surrender of Japanese troops on Mille Atoll, Marshalls, on board destroyer escort USS *Levy*. Mille Atoll is the first overseas Japanese post to surrender.

August 23

ALEUTIANS: Eleventh Air Force sends four B-24 Liberators to fly a photo reconnaissance mission over Paramushiru and Shimushu Islands to observe Soviet occupation activities in the Kuriles.

PACIFIC: Soviet forces begin the occupation of the southern Kuriles.

August 24

PACIFIC: The Soviets calls off plans to occupy Hokkaido and drop their demands for a Soviet zone of occupation in Tokyo.

August 25
PACIFIC: Aircraft from the carrier task groups begin daily flights over the Japanese home islands, monitoring airfields and shipping and locating prisoner of war camps.

TG 95.4 (Captain Henry J. Armstrong, Jr.) returns to Buckner Bay, having destroyed 578 mines in the East China Sea.

Carrier USS *Wasp* and a destroyer are damaged in a typhoon.

August 27
PACIFIC: Twentieth Air Force B-29s begin supplying prisoners of war and internee camps in Japan, China, and Korea with medical supplies, food, and clothing. The first supply drop is to Weihsien Camp near Peking (Beijing), China.

Japanese submarine *I-14* and submarine *I-400* surrender to U.S. destroyers east of northern Honshu.

Commander Third Fleet, Admiral William F. Halsey, Jr., stands into Sagami Wan, the outer bay to Tokyo, Japan. The Japanese destroyer *Hatsuzakura* carries Japanese officers to meet with Admiral Halsey's staff for a piloting conference to work out details of the entry of American and British warships into Sagami Wan and Tokyo Bay for the Japanese surrender ceremonies.

August 28
PACIFIC: The occupation of Japan officially begins as an advance party arrives in the Home Islands. Colonel Gordon Blake and five men of the 68th Army Airways Communications System (AACS) Group, 7th AACS Wing, arrive at Atsugi airfield near Tokyo to set up the communications equipment, air traffic control, and navigation aids for occupation troops arriving by air. They are part of a 150-man task force with 24 C-47 aircraft. They are the first American troops to land in Japan and are met by an honor guard from the Japanese navy.

Administrative and operational control of the Seventh Fleet under Admiral Thomas C. Kinkaid passes from General of the Army Douglas MacArthur, Commander in Chief, Southwest Pacific Area, to Fleet Admiral Chester W. Nimitz, Commander in Chief, Pacific Fleet.

August 29
PACIFIC: U.S. submarine *Segundo* accepts surrender of Japanese submarine *I-401* off the northeast coast of Honshu.

Commodore Rodger W. Simpson, commander of Task Group 30.6, arrives in Tokyo Bay to evacuate Allied prisoners of war. Guided by TBM Avengers from small carrier USS *Cowpens,* he is taken by LCVPs to the camp at Omori. Prisoners are severely malnourished and suffering from a host of maladies.

Fleet Admiral Chester W. Nimitz, Commander in Chief, Pacific Fleet, arrives in Tokyo Bay on board a PB2Y Coronado and establishes battleship USS *South Dakota* as his flagship.

NEW GUINEA: Japanese garrisons on Halmahera and Morotai surrender.

August 30
PACIFIC: The occupation of Japan begins with the 11th Airborne Division arriving at Atsugi airfield, while the 6th Marine Division lands at Yokosuka naval base. The

Third Fleet is prominently arrayed offshore, and navy and army aircraft fly patrols overhead.

Rear Admiral Robert B. Carney and Rear Admiral Oscar C. Badger accept the surrender of Yokosuka naval base. The naval base will serve as the headquarters for the commander of Third Fleet. General MacArthur arrives at Atsugi to set up temporary Supreme Allied headquarters at Yokohama.

CENTRAL PACIFIC: Aboard the destroyer USS *Stack*, Brigadier General Leo D. Hermle (USMC) leads the American side in discussions with the Japanese concerning the surrender of Truk.

August 31

MEDITERRANEAN: Twelfth Air Force is inactivated in Italy.

PACIFIC: U.S. Marines land at Tateyama naval base on the northeast shore of Sagami Wan to take the Japanese surrender. They will conduct a beach reconnaissance and cover the landing of the 112th Cavalry Regiment.

Japanese submarine *I-401* surrenders to submarine USS *Segundo* at the entrance to Tokyo Bay.

The Soviet Union completes its occupation of the Kurile Islands.

CENTRAL PACIFIC: Aboard the destroyer USS *Bagley*, Rear Admiral Francis E. M. Whiting accepts the surrender of Marcus Island from the Japanese.

September 1

PACIFIC: Soviet forces occupy Kunashiri and Shikotan Islands.

September 2

PACIFIC: Japan Surrenders. Hostilities with Japan end officially with Japanese military and government representatives signing the instrument of surrender aboard the USS *Missouri* in Tokyo Bay. A framed flag is mounted on the forward 16-inch gun turret overlooking the table where the surrender documents have been placed. It is the American flag flown by Commodore Matthew C. Perry's flagship as he entered Tokyo Bay in 1853. General of the Army Douglas MacArthur signs for the Allied Powers. Fleet Admiral Chester W. Nimitz signs for the United States. He is followed by representatives of the USSR, China, Great Britain, Australia, Canada, France, the Netherlands, and New Zealand. The ceremony ends at 0925 hours Tokyo time.

Naval Task Force 33, commanded by Rear Admiral John L. Hall, lands army occupation troops at Yokohama.

CENTRAL PACIFIC: On board the destroyer escort USS *Amick*, the Japanese surrender forces in the Palau Islands. On board the heavy cruiser USS *Portland*, the Japanese surrender forces on Truk. On board the destroyer USS *Rhind*, the Japanese

General of the Army Douglas MacArthur, supreme commander for the Allied Powers, closes the surrender proceedings aboard the USS *Missouri* in Tokyo Bay, Japan, on September 2, 1945.

surrender forces on Pagan Island, Marianas. On board the destroyer escort USS *Heyliger,* the Japanese surrender forces on Rota in the Marianas.

September 3
SOUTHWEST PACIFIC AREA: The formal surrender of Japanese forces in the Philippines takes place at Baguio. General Yamashita surrenders 50,500 men from the original 350,000 defenders.

In the Eighth Army area, the campaign for the southern Philippines is completed. American losses for this campaign are 2,100 killed and nearly 7,000 wounded.

PACIFIC: The Japanese garrison of the Bonin Islands surrenders on board the destroyer USS *Dunlap* off Chichi Jima. Lieutenant General Tachibana Yoshio, the local commander, makes the formal surrender. He is later convicted and executed for atrocities committed against American aviators who had been captured in the area between 1944 and 1945.

Soviet troops occupy Shibotsu and Taraku Islands in the Habomai Island group.

September 4
PACIFIC: Rear Admiral Sakaibara Shigematsu, commander of the Wake Island garrison, surrenders to American forces. The American flag, which had been taken down in defiant anger on December 23, 1941, again waves over the island.

CENTRAL PACIFIC: On board The Coast Guard cutter USCG 83425, the Japanese surrender the garrison of Aguijan Island in the Marianas.

The American flag flies again over Wake Island in a formal ceremony after the final Japanese surrender, September 4, 1945.

September 5
PACIFIC: Soviet troops complete the occupation of the Habomai group of islands.

CENTRAL PACIFIC: On board the destroyer USS *Tillman,* the Japanese surrender Yap Island.

September 6
CENTRAL PACIFIC: On board the destroyer escort USS *Wingfield* the Japanese surrender Maloelap Atoll.

Vice Admiral Frederick C. Sherman, commander of Task Force 11, departs Tokyo Bay for the United States, carrying the first few of the tens of thousands of combat veterans who are coming home.

The Rabaul garrison surrenders to the Australians.

September 7
PACIFIC: Japanese forces in the Ryukyu Islands surrender to the Tenth Army commander, Lieutenant General Joseph W. Stilwell, on Okinawa.

September 8
PACIFIC: Allied forces land at Inchon to begin the occupation of southern Korea.

September 9
CBI: Japanese forces in China formally surrender at Nanking.
PACIFIC: Admiral Thomas C. Kinkaid and Lieutenant General John R. Hodge sign surrender documents, during ceremonies in the government building at Keijo (Seoul), Korea.

September 11
PACIFIC: Operation Magic Carpet begins as navy ships begin transporting ground troops back to the United States.

September 12
CBI: Japanese forces in Southeast Asia formally surrender to Allied forces in Singapore.

September 22
PACIFIC: The evacuation of 16,000 Allied prisoners of war from the Japanese islands of Honshu and Kyushu is completed.

September 28
ATLANTIC: The navy transport USS *General Greeley* arrives in New York Harbor bringing home the first shipload of American units from the China and India-Burma theaters. Among those returning are men who served in the Flying Tigers, the Kachin Rangers, Merrill's Marauders, and the Mars Task Force.

October 10
ATLANTIC: Fleet Admiral Ernest J. King, Commander in Chief, U. S. Fleet, orders his headquarters to stand down.

November 1
CBI: The Stilwell Road is abandoned.

November 19
ATLANTIC: General Eisenhower replaces General Marshall as chief of staff of the army. The JCS initiates contingency planning for nuclear war with the Soviet Union.

American ≋ Servicemen Awarded the Medal of Honor in World War II*

*Note: A "(P)" denotes that the honor was received posthumously.

1941

Bennion, Mervyn S. (P)
Captain, U.S. Navy. Commanding Officer of USS *West Virginia*, Pearl Harbor, 7 December 1941.

Bulkeley, John D.
Lieutenant Commander, U.S. Navy. Commander of Motor Torpedo Boat Squadron 3, Philippine waters, 7 December 1941 to 10 April 1942.

Cannon, George H. (P)
First Lieutenant, U.S. Marine Corps. Sand Island, Midway Islands, 7 December 1941.

Elrod, Henry T. (P)
Captain, U.S. Marine Corps. Marine Fighting Squadron 211, Wake Island, 8 to 23 December 1941.

Finn, John W.
Lieutenant, U.S. Navy. Naval Air Station, Kaneohe Bay, Territory of Hawaii, 7 December 1941.

Flaherty, Francis C. (P)
Ensign, U.S. Naval Reserve. Pearl Harbor, 7 December 1941.

Fuqua, Samuel G.
Lieutenant Commander, U.S. Navy. USS *Arizona*, Pearl Harbor, 7 December 1941.

Hill, Edwin J. (P)
Chief Boatswain, U.S. Navy. Pearl Harbor, 7 December 1941.

Jones, Herbert C. (P)
Ensign, U.S. Naval Reserve. USS *Oklahoma*, Pearl Harbor, 7 December 1941.

Kidd, Isaac C. (P)
Rear Admiral, U.S. Navy. Pearl Harbor, 7 December 1941.

Pharris, Jackson C.
Lieutenant, U.S. Navy. USS *California*, Pearl Harbor, 7 December 1941.

Reeves, Thomas J. (P)
Radio Electrician (Warrant Officer), U.S. Navy. Pearl Harbor, 7 December 1941.

Ross, Donald K.
Machinist, U.S. Navy. USS *Nevada*, Pearl Harbor, 7 December 1941.

Scott, Robert R. (P)
Machinist's Mate First Class, U.S. Navy. Pearl Harbor, 7 December 1941.

Tomich, Peter (P)
Chief Watertender, U.S. Navy. Pearl Harbor, 7 December 1941.

Van Valkenburgh, Franklin (P)
Captain, U.S. Navy. Commander aboard USS *Arizona*, Pearl Harbor, 7 December 1941.

Ward, James R. (P)
Seaman First Class, U.S. Navy. Pearl Harbor, 7 December 1941.

Young, Cassin
Commander, U.S. Navy. Captain of USS *Vestal*, Pearl Harbor, 7 December 1941.

1942

Antrim, Richard N.
Commander, U.S. Navy. Makassar, Celebes, Netherlands East Indies, April 1942.

Bailey, Kenneth D. (P)
Major, U.S. Marine Corps. Commander of Company C, 1st Marine Raider Battalion, Henderson Field, Guadalcanal, Solomon Islands, 12–13 September 1942.

Basilone, John
Sergeant, U.S. Marine Corps. 1st Battalion, 7th Marines, 1st Marine Division, in the Lunga Area, Guadalcanal, Solomon Islands, 24 and 25 October 1942.

Bauer, Harold W. (P)
Lieutenant Colonel, U.S. Marine Corps. Commander of Marine Fighting Squadron 212 in the South Pacific Area, 10 May to 14 November 1942.

Bianchi, Willibald C. (P)

First Lieutenant, U.S. Army. 45th Infantry, Philippine Scouts, near Bagac, Bataan Province, Philippine Islands, 3 February 1942.

Burr, Elmer J. (P)

First Sergeant, U.S. Army. Company I, 127th Infantry, 32nd Infantry Division, Buna, New Guinea, 24 December 1942.

Callaghan, Daniel J. (P)

Rear Admiral, U.S. Navy. Off Savo Island, Solomon Islands, on the night of 12–13 November 1942.

Calugas, Jose

Sergeant, U.S. Army. Battery B, 88th Field Artillery, Philippine Scouts, at Culis, Bataan Province, Philippine Islands, 16 January 1942.

Casamento, Anthony

Corporal, U.S. Marine Corps. Company D, 1st Battalion, 5th Marines, 1st Marine Division, Guadalcanal, Solomon Islands, 1 November 1942.

Craw, Demas T. (P)

Colonel, U.S. Army Air Corps. Near Port Lyautey, French Morocco, 8 November 1942.

Doolittle, James H. (Air Mission)

Brigadier General, U.S. Army Air Corps. Over Japan, 9 June 1942.

Edson, Merritt A.

Colonel, U.S. Marine Corps. Commander of the 1st Marine Raider Battalion, Solomon Islands, on the night of 13–14 September 1942.

Fleming, Richard E. (P)

Captain, U.S. Marine Corps Reserve. Flight Officer, Marine Scout-Bombing Squadron 241, Midway Island, 4–5 June 1942.

Galer, Robert E.

Major, U.S. Marine Corps. Commander, Marine Fighter Squadron 224, Solomon Islands area, August–September 1942.

Gruennert, Kenneth E. (P)

Sergeant, U.S. Army. Company L, 127th Infantry, 32nd Infantry Division, near Buna, New Guinea, 24 December 1942.

Hall, William E.

Lieutenant, Junior Grade, U.S. Naval Reserve. Coral Sea, 7 and 8 May 1942.

Hamilton, Pierpont M.

Major, U.S. Army Air Corps. Near Port Lyautey, French Morocco, 8 November 1942.

Keppler, Reinhardt J. (P)
Boatswain's Mate First Class, U.S. Navy. USS *San Francisco*, Solomon Islands, 12–13 November 1942.

MacArthur, Douglas
General, U.S. Army. Commanding U.S. Army Forces in the Far East, Bataan Peninsula, Philippine Islands, 1942.

McCandless, Bruce
Commander, U.S. Navy. USS *San Francisco*, off Savo Island, Solomon Islands, 12–13 November 1942.

Munro, Douglas A. (P)
Signalman First Class, U.S. Coast Guard. Petty Officer in charge of a group of 24 Higgins boats, Point Cruz, Guadalcanal, 27 September 1942.

Nininger, Alexander R., Jr. (P)
Second Lieutenant, U.S. Army. 57th Infantry, Philippine Scouts, near Abucay, Bataan, Philippine Islands, 12 January 1942.

O'Hare, Edward H.
Lieutenant, U.S. Navy. Fighting Squadron Three, 20 February 1942.

Paige, Mitchell
Platoon Sergeant, U.S. Marine Corps. Guadalcanal, Solomon Islands, 26 October 1942.

Pease, Harl, Jr. (Air Mission) (P)
Captain, U.S. Army Air Corps. Heavy Bombardment Squadron, near Rabaul, New Britain, 6–7 August 1942.

Peterson, Oscar V. (P)
Chief Watertender, U.S. Navy. USS *Neosho*, 7 May 1942.

Powers, John J. (P)
Lieutenant, U.S. Navy. Bombing Squadron 5, Coral Sea area and adjacent waters 4–8 May 1942.

Ricketts, Milton E. (P)
Lieutenant, U.S. Navy. Officer-in-Charge of Engineering Repair Party aboard USS *Yorktown*, Coral Sea, 8 May 1942.

Rooks, Albert H. (P)
Captain, U.S. Navy. Captain of USS *Houston*, 4–27 February 1942.

Schonland, Herbert E.
Commander, U.S. Navy. USS *San Francisco*, Savo Island, Solomon Islands, 12–13 November 1942.

Scott, Norman (P)
Rear Admiral, U.S. Navy. Savo Island, Solomon Islands, 11–12 October and 12–13 November 1942.

Smith, John L.
Major, U.S. Marine Corps. Marine Fighter Squadron 223, Solomon Islands area, August–September 1942.

Thomason, Clyde (P)
Sergeant, U.S. Marine Corps Reserve. Makin Island, 17–18 August 1942.

Vandegrift, Alexander A.
Major General, U.S. Marine Corps. Commander of 1st Marine Division, Guadalcanal, Solomon Islands, 7 August to 9 December 1942.

Wainwright, Jonathan M.
Lieutenant General, U.S. Army. Commander of U.S. Army Forces in the Philippines, 12 March to 7 May 1942.

Wilbur, William H.
Colonel, U.S. Army. Western Task Force, Fedala, North Africa, 8 November 1942.

1943

Baker, Addison E. (P)
Lieutenant Colonel, U.S. Army Air Corps. 93rd Heavy Bombardment Group, Raid on Ploeşti, Romania, 1 August 1943.

Bjorklund, Arnold L.
First Lieutenant, U.S. Army. 36th Infantry Division, near Altavilla, Italy, 13 September 1943.

Bonnyman, Alexander, Jr. (P)
First Lieutenant, U.S. Marine Corps Reserve. Executive Officer of 2nd Battalion Shore Party, 8th Marines, 2nd Marine Division, Tarawa, 20–22 November 1943.

Booker, Robert D. (P)
Private, U.S. Army. 34th Infantry Division, near Fondouk, Tunisia, 9 April 1943.

Bordelon, William J. (P)
Staff Sergeant, U.S. Marine Corps. Assault engineer platoon of 1st Battalion, 18th Marines, attached to 2nd Marine Division, Tarawa, 20 November 1943.

Boyington, Gregory
Major, U.S. Marine Corps Reserve. Commander of Marine Fighter Squadron 214, Central Solomons area, 12 September 1943 to 3 January 1944.

Britt, Maurice L.
Lieutenant, U.S. Army. 3rd Infantry Division, north of Mignano, Italy, 10 November 1943.

Cheli, Ralph (Air Mission) (P)
Major, U.S. Army Air Corps. Near Wewak, New Guinea, 18 August 1943.

Childers, Ernest
Second Lieutenant, U.S. Army. 45th Infantry Division, Oliveto, Italy, 22 September 1943.

Craig, Robert (P)
Second Lieutenant, U.S. Army. 15th Infantry, 3rd Infantry Division, near Favoratta, Sicily, 11 July 1943.

Crawford, William J.
Private, U.S. Army. 36th Infantry Division, near Altavilla, Italy, 13 September 1943.

Cromwell, John P. (P)
Captain, U.S. Navy. Commander of a Submarine Coordinated Attack Group with Flag aboard USS *Sculpin,* Truk Island, 19 November 1943.

Davis, Charles W.
Major, U.S. Army. 25th Infantry Division, Guadalcanal, 12 January 1943.

Deblanc, Jefferson J.
First Lieutenant, U.S. Marine Corps Reserve. Marine Fighter Squadron 112, off Kolombangara Island in the Solomons, 31 January 1943.

Foss, Joseph J.
Captain, U.S. Marine Corps Reserve. Marine Fighter Squadron #121, Guadalcanal, 9 October–19 November 1942 and 15 and 23 January 1943.

Fournier, William G. (P)
Sergeant, U.S. Army. Company M, 35th Infantry, 25th Infantry Division, Mount Austen, Guadalcanal, Solomon Islands, 10 January 1943.

Gilmore, Howard W. (P)
Commander, U.S. Navy. Captain of submarine USS *Growler* during her fourth war patrol in the Southwest Pacific, from 10 January to 7 February 1943.

Gurke, Henry (P)
Private First Class, U.S. Marine Corps. 3rd Marine Raider Battalion, Solomon Islands area, 9 November 1943.

Hall, Lewis (P)
Technician Fifth Grade, U.S. Army. Company M, 35th Infantry, 25th Infantry Division, Mount Austen, Guadalcanal, Solomon Islands, 10 January 1943.

Hanson, Robert M. (P)
First Lieutenant, U.S. Marine Corps Reserve. Marine Fighter Squadron 215, Bougainville Island, 1 November 1943; New Britain Island, 24 January 1944.

Hasemoto, Mikio, (P)
Private, U.S. Army. Vicinity of Cerasuolo, Italy, 29 November 1943.

Hawkins, William D. (P)
First Lieutenant, U.S. Marine Corps. Scout sniper platoon attached to assault regiment, Tarawa, 20 and 21 November 1943.

Hayashi, Shizuya (P)
Private, U.S. Army. Near Cerasuolo, Italy, 29 November 1943.

Hughes, Lloyd H. (Air Mission) (P)
Second Lieutenant, U.S. Army Air Corps. 564th Bomber Squadron, 389th Bomber Group, Ninth Air Force, Raid on Ploeşti, Romania, 1 August 1943.

Hutchins, Johnnie D. (P)
Seaman First Class, U.S. Naval Reserve. Lae, New Guinea, 4 September 1943.

Jerstad, John L. (Air Mission) (P)
Major, U.S. Army Air Corps. Ninth Air Force, Raid on Ploeşti, Romania, 1 August 1943.

Johnson, Leon W. (Air Mission)
Colonel, U.S. Army Air Corps. 44th Bomber Group, Ninth Air Force, Raid on Ploeşti, Romania, 1 August 1943.

Kane, John R. (Air Mission)
Colonel, U.S. Army Air Corps. Ninth Air Force, Raid on Ploeşti, Romania, 1 August 1943.

Kearby, Neel E. (Air Mission)
Colonel, U.S. Army Air Corps. Near Wewak, New Guinea, 11 October 1943.

Kelly, Charles E.
Corporal, U.S. Army. Company L, 143rd Infantry, 36th Infantry Division, near Altavilla, Italy, 13 September 1943.

Kisters, Gerry H.
Sergeant, U.S. Army. 2nd Armored Division, near Gagliano, Sicily, 31 July 1943.

Lindstrom, Floyd K. (P)
Private First Class, U.S. Army. 3rd Infantry Division, near Mignano, Italy, 11 November 1943.

Logan, James M.
Sergeant, U.S. Army. 26th Infantry Division, Salerno, Italy, 9 September 1943.

Martinez, Joe P. (P)
Private, U.S. Army. Company K, 32nd Infantry, 7th Infantry Division, Attu, Aleutians, 26 May 1943.

Mathis, Jack W. (Air Mission) (P)
First Lieutenant, U.S. Army Air Corps. 359th Bomber Squadron, 303rd Bomber Group, over Vegesack, Germany, 18 March 1943.

Minue, Nicholas (P)
Private, U.S. Army. Company A, 6th Armored Infantry, 1st Armored Division, near Medjez-el-Bab, Tunisia, 28 April 1943.

Morgan, John C. (Air Mission)
Second Lieutenant, U.S. Army Air Corps. 326th Bomber Squadron, 92nd Bomber Group, over Europe, 28 July 1943.

Nelson, William L. (P)
Sergeant, U.S. Army. 60th Infantry, 9th Infantry Division, Djebel Dardys, northwest of Sedjenane, Tunisia, 24 April 1943.

Ohata, Allan M. (P)
Sergeant, U.S. Army. Near Cerasuolo, Italy, 30 November 1943.

Olson, Arlo L. (P)
Captain, U.S. Army. 15th Infantry, 3rd Infantry Division, crossing the Volturno River, Italy, 13 October 1943.

Owens, Robert A. (P)
Sergeant, U.S. Marine Corps. Cape Torokina, Bougainville, Solomon Islands, 1 November 1943.

Parle, John J. (P)
Ensign, U.S. Naval Reserve. Officer-in-Charge of Small Boats aboard USS *LST-375*, Sicily, 9–10 July 1943.

Petrarca, Frank J. (P)
Private First Class, U.S. Army. Medical Detachment, 145th Infantry, 37th Infantry Division, at Horseshoe Hill, New Georgia, Solomon Islands, 27 July 1943.

Reese, James W. (P)
Private, U.S. Army. 26th Infantry, 1st Infantry Division, Monte Vassillio, Sicily, 5 August 1943.

Sarnoski, Joseph R. (Air Mission) (P)
Second Lieutenant, U.S. Army Air Corps. 43rd Bomber Group, over Buka area, Solomon Islands, 16 June 1943.

Scott, Robert S.
Lieutenant, U.S. Army. 172nd Infantry, 43rd Infantry Division, near Munda airfield, New Georgia, Solomon Islands, 29 July 1943.

Shoup, David M.
Colonel, U.S. Marine Corps. Commanding officer of marines on Betio Island, Tarawa Atoll, 20–22 November 1943.

Slaton, James D.
Corporal, U.S. Army. 157th Infantry, 45th Infantry Division, near Oliveto, Italy, 23 September 1943.

Smith, Maynard H. (Air Mission)

Sergeant, U.S. Army Air Corps. 423rd Bombardment Squadron, 306th Bomber Group, over Europe, 1 May 1943.

Swett, James E.

First Lieutenant, U.S. Marine Corps Reserve. Marine Fighter Squadron 221, with Marine Aircraft Group 12, 1st Marine Aircraft Wing, Solomon Islands area, 7 April 1943.

Thomas, Herbert J. (P)

Sergeant, U.S. Marine Corps Reserve. 3rd Marines, 3rd Marine Division, Koromokina River, Bougainville Island, Solomon Islands, 7 November 1943.

Van Noy, Nathan Jr. (P)

Private, U.S. Army. Headquarters Company, Shore Battalion, Engineer Boat and Shore Regiment, near Finschhafen, New Guinea, 17 October 1943.

Van Voorhis, Bruce A. (P)

Lieutenant Commander, U.S. Navy. Commander of Bombing Squadron 102 and Plane Commander of a PB4Y-I patrol bomber, Greenwich Island, during the battle of the Solomon Islands, 6 July 1943.

Vosler, Forrest T. (Air Mission)

Technical Sergeant, U.S. Army Air Corps. 358th Bomber Squadron, 303rd Bomber Group, over Bremen, Germany, 20 December 1943.

Walker, Kenneth N. (Air Mission) (P)

Brigadier General, U.S. Army Air Corps. Commander of V Bomber Command, Rabaul, New Britain, 5 January 1943.

Walsh, Kenneth A.

First Lieutenant, U.S. Marine Corps. Marine Fighter Squadron 124, Solomon Islands area, 15 and 30 August 1943.

Watson, George (P)

Private, U.S. Army. 2nd Battalion, 29th Quartermaster Regiment near Porloch Harbor, New Guinea, 8 March 1943.

Waybur, David C.

First Lieutenant, U.S. Army. 3rd Reconnaissance Troop, 3rd Infantry Division, near Agrigento, Sicily, 17 July 1943.

Wilkins, Raymond H. (Air Mission) (P)

Major, U.S. Army Air Corps. Near Rabaul, New Britain, 2 November 1943.

Young, Rodger W. (P)

Private, U.S. Army. 148th Infantry, 37th Infantry Division, New Georgia, Solomon Islands, 31 July 1943.

Zeamer, Jay, Jr. (Air Mission)

Major, U.S. Army Air Corps. Over Buka area, Solomon Islands, 16 June 1943.

1944

Adams, Lucian
Staff Sergeant, U.S. Army. 30th Infantry, 3rd Infantry Division, near St. Die, France, 28 October 1944.

Agerholm, Harold C. (P)
Private First Class, U.S. Marine Corps Reserve. 4th Battalion, 10th Marines, 2nd Marine Division, Saipan, 7 July 1944.

Anderson, Richard B. (P)
Private First Class, U.S. Marine Corps. 4th Marine Division, Roi Island, Kwajalein Atoll, 1 February 1944.

Antolak, Sylvester (P)
Sergeant, U.S. Army. Company B, 15th Infantry, 3rd Infantry Division, near Cisterna di Littoria, Italy, 24 May 1944.

Baker, Thomas A. (P)
Sergeant, U.S. Army. Company A, 105th Infantry, 27th Infantry Division, Saipan, 19 June to 7 July 1944.

Barfoot, Van T.
Second Lieutenant, U.S. Army. 157th Infantry, 45th Infantry Division, near Carano, Italy, 23 May 1944.

Barrett, Carlton W.
Private, U.S. Army. 18th Infantry, 1st Infantry Division, near St-Laurent-sur-Mer, France, 6 June 1944.

Bausell, Lewis K. (P)
Corporal, U.S. Marine Corps. 1st Battalion, 5th Marines, 1st Marine Division, Peleliu, 15 September 1944.

Bell, Bernard P.
Technical Sergeant, U.S. Army. Company I, 142nd Infantry, 36th Infantry Division, Mittelwihr, France, 18 December 1944.

Bender, Stanley
Staff Sergeant, U.S. Army. Company E, 7th Infantry, 3rd Infantry Division, near La Lande, France, 17 August 1944.

Benjamin, George, Jr. (P)
Private First Class, U.S. Army. Company A, 306th Infantry, 77th Infantry Division, Leyte, Philippine Islands, 21 December 1944.

Biddle, Melvin E.
Private First Class, U.S. Army. Company B, 517th Parachute Infantry Regiment, near Soy, Belgium, 23–24 December 1944.

Bloch, Orville E.
First Lieutenant, U.S. Army. Company E, 338th Infantry, 85th Infantry Division, near Firenzuola, Italy, 22 September 1944.

Bolden, Paul L.
Staff Sergeant, U.S. Army. Company 1, 120th Infantry, 30th Infantry Division, Petit-Coo, Belgium, 23 December 1944.

Bolton, Cecil H.
First Lieutenant, U.S. Army. Company E, 413th Infantry, 104th Infantry Division, Mark River, Holland, 2 November 1944.

Bong, Richard I. (Air Mission)
Major, U.S. Army Air Corps. Over Borneo and Leyte, Philippines, 10 October to 15 November 1944.

Boyce, George W. G., Jr. (P)
Second Lieutenant, U.S. Army. 112th Cavalry Regimental Combat Team, near Afua, New Guinea, 23 July 1944.

Briles, Herschel F.
Staff Sergeant, U.S. Army. Company C, 899th Tank Destroyer Battalion, near Scherpenseel, Germany, 20 November 1944.

Brostrom, Leonard C. (P)
Private First Class, U.S. Army. Company F, 17th Infantry, 7th Infantry Division, near Dagami, Leyte, Philippine Islands, 28 October 1944.

Brown, Bobbie E.
Captain, U.S. Army. Company C, 18th Infantry, 1st Infantry Division, Crucifix Hill, Aachen, Germany, 8 October 1944.

Burt, James M.
Captain, U.S. Army. Company B, 66th Armored Regiment, 2nd Armored Division, near Wurselen, Germany, 13 October 1944.

Butts, John E. (P)
Second Lieutenant, U.S. Army. Company E, 60th Infantry, 9th Infantry Division, Normandy, France, 14, 16, and 23 June 1944.

Carey, Alvin P. (P)
Staff Sergeant, U.S. Army. 38th Infantry, 2nd Infantry Division, near Plougastel, Brittany, France, 23 August 1944.

Carr, Chris
Sergeant, U.S. Army. Company L, 337th Infantry, 85th Infantry Division, near Guignola, Italy, 1–2 October 1944.

Carswell, Horace S., Jr. (Air Mission) (P)
Major, U.S. Army Air Corps. 308th Bombardment Group, over the South China Sea, 26 October 1944.

Castle, Frederick W. (Air Mission) (P)
Brigadier General, U.S. Army Air Corps. Assistant Commander, 4th Bomber Wing, over Germany, 24 December 1944.

Choate, Clyde L.
Staff Sergeant, U.S. Army. Company C, 601st Tank Destroyer Battalion, near Bruyeres, France, 25 October 1944.

Christensen, Dale E. (P)
Second Lieutenant, U.S. Army. Troop E, 112th Cavalry Regiment, Driniumor River, New Guinea, 16–19 July 1944.

Christian, Herbert F. (P)
Private, U.S. Army. 15th Infantry, 3rd Infantry Division, near Valmontone, Italy, 2–3 June 1944.

Clark, Francis J.
Technical Sergeant, U.S. Army. Company K, 109th Infantry, 28th Infantry Division, near Kalborn, Luxembourg, 12 September 1944 and near Sevenig, Germany, 17 September 1944.

Cole, Robert G. (P)
Lieutenant Colonel, U.S. Army. 101st Airborne Division, near Carentan, France, 11 June 1944.

Connor, James P.
Sergeant, U.S. Army. 7th Infantry, 3rd Infantry Division, Cape Cavalaire, southern France, 15 August 1944.

Coolidge, Charles H.
Technical Sergeant, U.S. Army. Company M, 141st Infantry, 36th Infantry Division, east of Belmont sur Buttant, France, 24–27 October 1944.

Cowan, Richard E. (P)
Private First Class, U.S. Army. Company M, 23rd Infantry, 2nd Infantry Division, near Krinkelter Wald, Belgium, 17 December 1944.

Currey, Francis S.
Sergeant, U.S. Army. Company K, 120th Infantry, 30th Infantry Division, Malmedy, Belgium, 21 December 1944.

Dalessondro, Peter J.
Technical Sergeant, U.S. Army. Company E, 39th Infantry, 9th Infantry Division, near Kalterherberg, Germany, 22 December 1944.

Damato, Anthony P. (P)
Corporal, U.S. Marine Corps. Engebi Island, Eniwetok Atoll, on the night of 19–20 February 1944.

David, Albert L. (P)
Lieutenant, Junior Grade, U.S. Navy. USS *Pillsbury,* French West Africa, 4 June 1944.

Davila, Rudolph B.

Staff Sergeant, U.S. Army. Near Artena, Italy, 28 May 1944.

Dealey, Samuel D. (P)

Commander, U.S. Navy. Captain of submarine USS *Harder* during her fifth war patrol, 26 May–3 July 1944.

Defranzo, Arthur F. (P)

Staff Sergeant, U.S. Army. 1st Infantry Division, near Vaubadon, France, 10 June 1944.

Deglopper, Charles N. (P)

Private First Class, U.S. Army. Company C, 325th Glider Infantry, 82nd Airborne Division, Merderet River at la Fiere, France, 9 June 1944.

Dervishian, Ernest H.

Second Lieutenant, U.S. Army. 34th Infantry Division, near Cisterna, Italy, 23 May 1944.

Drowley, Jesse R.

Staff Sergeant, U.S. Army. Americal Division, Bougainville, Solomon Islands, 30 January 1944.

Dutko, John W. (P)

Private First Class, U.S. Army. 3rd Infantry Division, near Ponte Rotto, Italy, 23 May 1944.

Dyess, Aquilla J. (P)

Lieutenant Colonel, U.S. Marine Corps Reserve. Commander of 1st Battalion, 24th Marines (Rein), 4th Marine Division, Namur Island, Kwajalein Atoll, 1 and 2 February 1944.

Ehlers, Walter D.

Staff Sergeant, U.S. Army. 18th Infantry, 1st Infantry Division, near Goville, France, 9–10 June 1944.

Endl, Gerald L. (P)

Staff Sergeant, U.S. Army. 32nd Infantry Division, near Anamo, New Guinea, 11 July 1944.

Epperson, Harold G. (P)

Private First Class, U.S. Marine Corps Reserve. 1st Battalion, 6th Marines, 2nd Marine Division, Saipan, 25 June 1944.

Eubanks, Ray E. (P)

Sergeant, U.S. Army. Company D, 503rd Parachute Infantry, Noemfoor Island, New Guinea, 23 July 1944.

Evans, Ernest E. (P)

Commander, U.S. Navy. Captain of USS *Johnston,* Samar, Philippines, 25 October 1944.

Everhart, Forrest E.
Technical Sergeant, U.S. Army. Company H, 359th Infantry, 90th Infantry Division, near Kerling, France, 12 November 1944.

Femoyer, Robert E. (Air Mission) (P)
Second Lieutenant, U.S. Army Air Corps. 711th Bombing Squadron, 447th Bomber Group, over Merseburg, Germany, 2 November 1944.

Fields, James H.
First Lieutenant, U.S. Army. 10th Armored Infantry, 4th Armored Division, Rechicourt, France, 27 September 1944.

Fisher, Almond E.
Second Lieutenant, U.S. Army. Company E, 157th Infantry, 45th Infantry Division, near Grammont, France, 12–13 September 1944.

Fluckey, Eugene B.
Commander, U.S. Navy. Captain of USS *Barb*, along coast of China, 19 December 1944–15 February 1945.

Fowler, Thomas W. (P)
Second Lieutenant, U.S. Army. 1st Armored Division, near Carano, Italy, 23 May 1944.

Fox, John R. (P)
Second Lieutenant, U.S. Army. Cannon Company, 366th Infantry Regiment, 92nd Infantry Division, near Sommocolonia, Italy, 26 December 1944.

Fryar, Elmer E. (P)
Private, U.S. Army. Company E, 511th Parachute Infantry, 11th Airborne Division, Leyte, Philippine Islands, 8 December 1944.

Galt, William W. (P)
Captain, U.S. Army. 168th Infantry, 34th Infantry Division, Villa Crocetta, Italy, 29 May 1944.

Garcia, Marcario
Staff Sergeant, U.S. Army. Company B, 22nd Infantry, 4th Infantry Division, near Grosshau, Germany, 27 November 1944.

Garman, Harold A.
Private, U.S. Army. Company B, 5th Medical Battalion, 5th Infantry Division, near Montereau, France, 25 August 1944.

Gerstung, Robert E.
Technical Sergeant, U.S. Army. Company H, 313th Infantry, 79th Infantry Division, Siegfried Line near Berg, Germany, 19 December 1944.

Gibson, Eric G. (P)
Technician Fifth Grade, U.S. Army. 3rd Infantry Division, near Isola Bella, Italy, 28 January 1944.

Gordon, Nathan G.
Lieutenant, U.S. Navy. Commander of Catalina patrol plane. Bismarck Sea, 15 February 1944.

Gott, Donald J. (Air Mission) (P)
First Lieutenant, U.S. Army Air Corps. 729th Bomber Squadron, 452nd Bombardment Group, Saarbrücken, Germany, 9 November 1944.

Gregg, Stephen R.
Second Lieutenant, U.S. Army. 143rd Infantry, 36th Infantry Division, near Montelimar, France, 27 August 1944.

Hajiro, Barney, F.
Private, U.S. Army. In the vicinity of Bruyeres and Biffontaine, eastern France, 19, 22, and 29 October 1944.

Hall, George J.
Staff Sergeant, U.S. Army. 135th Infantry, 34th Infantry Division, near Anzio, Italy, 23 May 1944.

Hallman, Sherwood H. (P)
Staff Sergeant, U.S. Army. 175th Infantry, 29th Infantry Division, Brest, France, 13 September 1944.

Harmon, Roy W. (P)
Sergeant, U.S. Army. Company C, 362nd Infantry, 91st Infantry Division, near Casaglia, Italy, 12 July 1944.

Harris, James L. (P)
Second Lieutenant, U.S. Army. 756th Tank Battalion, Vagney, France, 7 October 1944.

Hawk, John D.
Sergeant, U.S. Army. Company E, 359th Infantry, 90th Infantry Division, near Chambois, France, 20 August 1944.

Hawks, Lloyd C.
Private First Class, U.S. Army. Medical Detachment, 30th Infantry, 3rd Infantry Division, near Carano, Italy, 30 January 1944.

Hendrix, James R.
Private, U.S. Army. Company C, 53rd Armored Infantry Battalion, 4th Armored Division, near Assenois, Belgium, 26 December 1944.

Henry, Robert T. (P)
Private, U.S. Army. 16th Infantry, 1st Infantry Division, Luchem, Germany, 3 December 1944.

Horner, Freeman V.
Staff Sergeant, U.S. Army. Company K, 119th Infantry, 30th Infantry Division, Wurselen, Germany, 16 November 1944.

Howard, James H. (Air Mission)
Lieutenant Colonel, U.S. Army Air Corps. Over Oschersleben, Germany, 11 January 1944.

Huff, Paul B.
Corporal, U.S. Army. 509th Parachute Infantry Battalion, near Carano, Italy, 8 February 1944.

Jackson, Arthur J.
Private First Class, U.S. Marine Corps. 3rd Battalion, 7th Marines, 1st Marine Division, Peleliu, 18 September 1944.

Johnson, Elden H. (P)
Private, U.S. Army. 15th Infantry, 3rd Infantry Division, near Valmontone, Italy, 3 June 1944.

Johnson, Leroy (P)
Sergeant, U.S. Army. Company K, 126th Infantry, 32nd Infantry Division, near Limon, Leyte, Philippine Islands, 15 December 1944.

Johnson, Oscar G.
Sergeant, U.S. Army. Company B, 363rd Infantry, 91st Infantry Division, near Scarperia, Italy, 16–18 September 1944.

Johnston, William J.
Private First Class, U.S. Army. Company G, 180th Infantry, 45th Infantry Division, near Padiglione, Italy, 17–19 February 1944.

Kandle, Victor L. (P)
First Lieutenant, U.S. Army. 15th Infantry, 3rd Infantry Division, near La Forge, France, 9 October 1944.

Keathley, George D. (P)
Staff Sergeant, U.S. Army. 85th Infantry Division, Monte Altuzzo, Italy, 14 September 1944.

Kefurt, Gus (P)
Staff Sergeant, U.S. Army. Company K, 15th Infantry, 3rd Infantry Division, near Bennwihr, France, 23–24 December 1944.

Kelley, Ova A. (P)
Private, U.S. Army. Company A, 382nd Infantry, 96th Infantry Division, Leyte, Philippine Islands, 8 December 1944.

Kelly, John D. (P)
Corporal, U.S. Army. Company E, 314th Infantry, 79th Infantry Division, Fort du Roule, Cherbourg, France, 25 June 1944.

Kessler, Patrick L. (P)
Private First Class, U.S. Army. Company K, 30th Infantry, 3rd Infantry Division, near Ponte Rotto, Italy, 23 May 1944.

Kimbro, Truman (P)
Technician Fourth Grade, U.S. Army. Company C, 2nd Engineer Combat Battalion, 2nd Infantry Division, near Rocherath, Belgium, 19 December 1944.

Kiner, Harold G. (P)
Private, U.S. Army. Company F, 117th Infantry, 30th Infantry Division, near Palenberg, Germany, 2 October 1944.

Kingsley, David R. (Air Mission) (P)
Second Lieutenant, U.S. Army Air Corps. 97th Bombardment Group, Fifteenth Air Force, Raid on Ploeşti, Romania, 23 June 1944.

Knappenberger, Alton W.
Private First Class, U.S. Army. 3rd Infantry Division, near Cisterna di Littoria, Italy, 1 February 1944.

Kobashigawa, Yeiki
Technical Sergeant, U.S. Army. In the vicinity of Lanuvio, Italy, 2 June 1944.

Kraus, Richard E. (P)
Private First Class, U.S. Marine Corps Reserve. 8th Amphibious Tractor Battalion, Fleet Marine Force, Peleliu, 5 October 1944.

Kuroda, Robert T. (P)
Staff Sergeant, U.S. Army. Near Bruyeres, France, 20 October 1944.

Lawley, William R., Jr. (Air Mission)
First Lieutenant, U.S. Army Air Corps. 364th Bomber Squadron, 305th Bomber Group, over Europe, 20 February 1944.

Lee, Daniel W.
First Lieutenant, U.S. Army. Troop A, 117th Cavalry Reconnaissance Squadron, Montreval, France, 2 September 1944.

Leonard, Turney W.
First Lieutenant, U.S. Army. Company C, 893rd Tank Destroyer Battalion, Kommerscheidt, Germany, 4–6 November 1944.

Lindsey, Darrell R. (Air Mission) (P)
Captain, U.S. Army Air Corps. L'Isle Adam railroad bridge over the Seine, France, 9 August 1944.

Lindsey, Jake W.
Technical Sergeant, U.S. Army. 16th Infantry, 1st Infantry Division, near Hamich, Germany, 16 November 1944.

Lloyd, Edgar H. (P)
First Lieutenant, U.S. Army. Company E, 319th Infantry, 80th Infantry Division, near Pompey, France, 14 September 1944.

Lobaugh, Donald R. (P)
Private, U.S. Army. 127th Infantry, 23rd Infantry Division, near Afua, New Guinea, 22 July 1944.

Lopez, Jose M.
Sergeant, U.S. Army. 23rd Infantry, 2nd Infantry Division, near Krinkelt, Belgium, 17 December 1944.

Mabry, George L., Jr.
Lieutenant Colonel, U.S. Army. 2nd Battalion, 8th Infantry, 4th Infantry Division, Hürtgen Forest near Schevenhutte, Germany, 20 November 1944.

Mann, Joe E. (P)
Private First Class, U.S. Army. Company H, 502nd Parachute Infantry, 101st Airborne Division, Best, Holland, 18 September 1944.

Mason, Leonard F. (P)
Private First Class, U.S. Marine Corps. 2nd Battalion, 3rd Marines, 3rd Marine Division, Asan-Adelup Beachhead, Guam, 22 July 1944.

Mathies, Archibald (Air Mission) (P)
Sergeant, U.S. Army Air Corps. 510th Bomber Squadron, 351st Bomber Group, over Europe, 20 February 1944.

Maxwell, Robert D.
Technician Fifth Grade, U.S. Army. 7th Infantry, 3rd Infantry Division, near Besançon, France, 7 September 1944.

McCall, Thomas E.
Staff Sergeant, U.S. Army. Company F, 143rd Infantry, 36th Infantry Division, near San Angelo, Italy, 22 January 1944.

McCampbell, David
Commander, U.S. Navy. Air Group 15, first and second battles of the Philippine Sea, 19 June 1944.

McCard, Robert H. (P)
Gunnery Sergeant, U.S. Marine Corps. Company A, 4th Tank Battalion, 4th Marine Division, Saipan, 16 June 1944.

McGarity, Vernon
Technical Sergeant, U.S. Army. Company L, 393rd Infantry, 99th Infantry Division, near Krinkelt, Belgium, 16 December 1944.

McGill, Troy A. (P)
Sergeant, U.S. Army. Troop G, 5th Cavalry Regiment, 1st Cavalry Division, Los Negrós Islands, Admiralty Group, 4 March 1944.

McGraw, Francis X. (P)
Private First Class, U.S. Army. Company H, 26th Infantry, 1st Infantry Division, near Schevenhutte, Germany, 19 November 1944.

McGuire, Thomas B., Jr. (Air Mission) (P)

Major, U.S. Army Air Corps. Thirteenth Air Force, over Luzon, Philippine Islands, 25–26 December 1944.

McVeigh, John J. (P)

Sergeant, U.S. Army. Company H, 23rd Infantry, 2nd Infantry Division, near Brest, France, 29 August 1944.

McWhorter, William A. (P)

Private First Class, U.S. Army. Company M, 126th Infantry, 32nd Infantry Division, Leyte, Philippine Islands, 5 December 1944.

Merli, Gino J.

Private First Class, U.S. Army. 18th Infantry, 1st Infantry Division, near Sars la Bruyere, Belgium, 4–5 September 1944.

Messerschmidt, Harold O. (P)

Sergeant, U.S. Army. Company L, 30th Infantry, 3rd Infantry Division, near Radden, France, 17 September 1944.

Metzger, William E., Jr. (Air Mission) (P)

Second Lieutenant, U.S. Army Air Corps. 729th Bomber Squadron 452nd Bombardment Group, Saarbrücken, Germany, 9 November 1944.

Michael, Edward S. (Air Mission)

First Lieutenant, U.S. Army Air Corps. 364th Bomber Squadron, 305th Bomber Group, over Germany, 11 April 1944.

Miller, Andrew (P)

Staff Sergeant, U.S. Army. Company G, 377th Infantry, 95th Infantry Division, from Woippy, France, through Metz to Kerprich Hemmersdorf, Germany, 16–29 November 1944.

Mills, James H.

Private, U.S. Army. Company F, 15th Infantry, 3rd Infantry Division, near Cisterna di Littoria, Italy, 24 May 1944.

Minick, John W. (P)

Staff Sergeant, U.S. Army. Company I, 121st Infantry, 8th Infantry Division, near Hürtgen, Germany, 21 November 1944.

Monteith, Jimmie W., Jr. (P)

First Lieutenant, U.S. Army. 16th Infantry, 1st Infantry Division, near Colleville-sur-Mer, France, 6 June 1944.

Montgomery, Jack C.

First Lieutenant, U.S. Army. 45th Infantry Division, near Padiglione, Italy, 22 February 1944.

Moon, Harold H., Jr. (P)

Private, U.S. Army. Company G, 34th Infantry, 24th Infantry Division, Pawig, Leyte, Philippine Islands, 21 October 1944.

Moto, Kaoru (P)

Private First Class, U.S. Army. 100th Infantry Battalion. Near Castellina, Italy, 7 July 1944.

Mower, Charles E. (P)

Sergeant, U.S. Army. Company A, 34th Infantry, 24th Infantry Division, near Capoocan, Leyte, Philippine Islands, 3 November 1944.

Muranaga, Kiyoshi K. (P)

Private First Class, U.S. Army. Near Suvereto, Italy, 26 June 1944.

Murray, Charles P., Jr.

First Lieutenant, U.S. Army. Company C, 30th Infantry, 3rd Infantry Division, near Kaysersberg, France, 16 December 1944.

Nakae, Masato (P)

Private, U.S. Army. Near Pisa, Italy, 19 August 1944.

Nakamine, Shinyei (P)

Private, U.S. Army. Near La Torreto, Italy, 2 June 1944.

Nakamura, William K. (P)

Private First Class, U.S. Army. Near Castellina, Italy, 4 July 1944.

Neppel, Ralph G.

Sergeant, U.S. Army. Company M, 329th Infantry, 83rd Infantry Division, Birgel, Germany, 14 December 1944.

Nett, Robert P.

Lieutenant, U.S. Army. Company E, 305th Infantry, 77th Infantry Division, near Cognon, Leyte, Philippine Islands, 14 December 1944.

New, John D. (P)

Private First Class, U.S. Marine Corps. 2nd Battalion, 7th Marines, 1st Marine Division, Peleliu, 25 September 1944.

Newman, Beryl R.

First Lieutenant, U.S. Army. 133rd Infantry, 34th Infantry Division, near Cisterna, Italy, 26 May 1944.

Nishimoto, Joe M. (P)

Private First Class, U.S. Army. Near La Houssiere, France, 7 November 1944.

O'Brien, William J. (P)

Lieutenant Colonel, U.S. Army. 1st Battalion, 105th Infantry, 27th Infantry Division, Saipan, 20 June–7 July 1944.

Ogden, Carlos C.
First Lieutenant, U.S. Army. Company K, 314th Infantry, 79th Infantry Division, near Fort du Roule, France, 25 June 1944.

O'Kane, Richard H.
Commander, U.S. Navy. Captain of USS *Tang*, vicinity Philippine Islands, 23–24 October 1944.

Okubo, James K. (P)
Technician Fifth Grade, U.S. Army. In the Fôret Domaniale de Champ, near Biffontaine, eastern France, 28 and 29 October and 4 November 1944.

Olson, Truman O. (P)
Sergeant, U.S. Army. Company B, 7th Infantry, 3rd Infantry Division, near Cisterna di Littoria, Italy, 30–31 January 1944.

Ono, Frank H. (P)
Private First Class, U.S. Army. Near Castellina, Italy, 4 July 1944.

Otani, Kazuo (P)
Staff Sergeant, U.S. Army. Near Pieve Di S. Luce, Italy, 15 July 1944.

Ozbourn, Joseph W. (P)
Private, U.S. Marine Corps. 1st Battalion, 23rd Marines, 4th Marine Division, Tinian, 30 July 1944.

Pendleton, Jack J. (P)
Staff Sergeant, U.S. Army. Company I, 120th Infantry, 30th Infantry Division, Bardenberg, Germany, 12 October 1944.

Peregory, Frank D. (P)
Technical Sergeant, U.S. Army. Company K, 116th Infantry, 29th Infantry Division, Grandcampe France, 8 June 1944.

Phelps, Wesley (P)
Private, U.S. Marine Corps. 3rd Battalion, 7th Marines, 1st Marine Division Peleliu Island, Palan Group, 4 October 1944.

Pinder, John J., Jr. (P)
Technician Fifth Grade, U.S. Army. 16th Infantry, 1st Infantry Division, near Colleville-sur-Mer, France, 6 June 1944.

Pope, Everett P.
Captain, U.S. Marine Corps. Company C, 1st Battalion, 1st Marines, 1st Marine Division, Peleliu Island, Palau group, 19–20 September 1944.

Power, John V. (P)
First Lieutenant, U.S. Marine Corps. 4th Marine Division, Namur Island, Kwajalein Atoll, 1 February 1944.

Powers, Leo J.
Private First Class, U.S. Army. 133rd Infantry, 34th Infantry Division, northwest of Cassino, Italy, 3 February 1944.

Preston, Arthur M.
Lieutenant, U.S. Navy Reserve. Torpedo Boat Squadron 33, Wasile Bay, Halmahera Island, 16 September 1944.

Prussman, Ernest W. (P)
Private First Class, U.S. Army. 13th Infantry, 8th Infantry Division, near Les Coates, Brittany, France, 8 September 1944.

Pucket, Donald D. (Air Mission)
First Lieutenant, U.S. Army Air Corps. 98th Bombardment Group, Raid on Ploeşti, Romania, 9 July 1944.

Ramage, Lawson P.
Commander, U.S. Navy. Captain of USS *Parche*, Pacific, 31 July 1944.

Ray, Bernard J. (P)
First Lieutenant, U.S. Army. Company F, 8th Infantry, 4th Infantry Division, Hürtgen Forest near Schevenhutte, Germany, 17 November 1944.

Riordan, Paul F. (P)
Second Lieutenant, U.S. Army. 34th Infantry Division, near Cassino, Italy, 3–8 February 1944.

Rivers, Ruben (P)
Sergeant, U.S. Army. Guebling, France, 15–19 November 1944.

Roan, Charles H. (P)
Private First Class, U.S. Marine Corps Reserve. 2nd Battalion, 7th Marines, 1st Marine Division, Peleliu, 18 September 1944.

Roeder, Robert E. (P)
Captain, U.S. Army. Company G, 350th Infantry, 88th Infantry Division, Monte Battaglia, Italy, 27–28 September 1944.

Roosevelt, Theodore, Jr.
Brigadier General, U.S. Army. Omaha Beach, Normandy, France, 6 June 1944.

Ross, Wilburn K.
Private, U.S. Army. Company G, 350th Infantry, 3rd Infantry Division, near St. Jacques, France, 30 October 1944.

Rouh, Carlton R.
First Lieutenant, U.S. Marine Corps Reserve. 1st Battalion, 5th Marines, 1st Marine Division, Peleliu, 15 September 1944.

Sadowski, Joseph J. (P)
Sergeant, U.S. Army. 37th Tank Battalion, 4th Armored Division, Valhey, France, 14 September 1944.

Sakato, George T.
Private, U.S. Army. Hill 617 near Biffontaine, France, 29 October 1944.

Salomon, Ben L. (P)
Captain, U.S. Army. Surgeon for the 2nd Battalion, 105th Infantry, 27th Infantry Division, Saipan, 7 July 1944.

Sayers, Foster J. (P)
Private First Class, U.S. Army. Company L, 357th Infantry, 90th Infantry Division, near Thionville, France, 12 November 1944.

Schaefer, Joseph E.
Staff Sergeant, U.S. Army. Company I, 18th Infantry, 1st Infantry Division, near Stolberg, Germany, 24 September 1944.

Schauer, Henry
Private First Class, U.S. Army. 3rd Infantry Division, near Cisterna di Littoria, Italy, 23–24 May 1944.

Shea, Charles W.
Second Lieutenant, U.S. Army. Company F, 350th Infantry, 88th Infantry Division, near Mount Damiano, Italy, 12 May 1944.

Sheridan, Carl V. (P)
Private First Class, U.S. Army. Company K, 47th Infantry, 9th Infantry Division, Frenzenberg Castle, Weisweiler, Germany, 26 November 1944.

Silk, Edward A.
First Lieutenant, U.S. Army. Company E, 398th Infantry, 100th Infantry Division, near St. Pravel, France, 23 November 1944.

Skaggs, Luther, Jr.
Private First Class, U.S. Marine Corps Reserve. 3rd Battalion, 3rd Marines, 3rd Marine Division, Asan-Adelup beachhead, Guam, 21–22 July 1944.

Smith, Furman L. (P)
Private, U.S. Army. 135th Infantry, 34th Infantry Division, near Lanuvio, Italy, 31 May 1944.

Soderman, William A.
Private First Class, U.S. Army. Company K, 9th Infantry, 2nd Infantry Division, near Rocherath, Belgium, 17 December 1944.

Sorenson, Richard K.
Private, U.S. Marine Corps Reserve. 4th Marine Division, Namur Island, Kwajalein Atoll, 1–2 February 1944.

Specker, Joe C. (P)
Sergeant, U.S. Army. 48th Engineer Combat Battalion, Monte Porchia, Italy, 7 January 1944.

Spurrier, Junior J.
Staff Sergeant, U.S. Army. Company G, 134th Infantry, 35th Infantry Division, Achain, France, 13 November 1944.

Squires, John C. (P)
Private First Class, U.S. Army. Company A, 30th Infantry, 3rd Infantry Division, near Padiglione, Italy, 23–24 April 1944.

Tanouye, Ted T. (P)
Technical Sergeant, U.S. Army. Near Moilno a Ventoabbto, Italy, 7 July 1944.

Thomas, Charles L. (P)
First Lieutenant, U.S. Army. Near Climbach, France, 14 December 1944.

Thompson, Max
Sergeant, U.S. Army. Company K, 18th Infantry, 1st Infantry Division, near Haaren, Germany, 18 October 1944.

Thorne, Horace M. (P)
Corporal, U.S. Army. Troop D, 89th Cavalry Reconnaissance Squadron, 9th Armored Division, near Grufflingen, Belgium, 21 December 1944.

Thorson, John F. (P)
Private First Class, U.S. Army. Company G, 17th Infantry, 7th Infantry Division, Dagami, Leyte, Philippine Islands, 28 October 1944.

Timmerman, Grant F. (P)
Sergeant, U.S. Marine Corps. 2nd Battalion, 6th Marines, 2nd Marine Division, Saipan, 8 July 1944.

Tominac, John J.
First Lieutenant, U.S. Army. Company I, 15th Infantry, 3rd Infantry Division, Saulx de Vesoul, France, 12 September 1944.

Towle, John R. (P)
Private, U.S. Army. Company C, 504th Parachute Infantry, 82nd Airborne Division. Near Oosterhout, Holland, 21 September 1944.

Truemper, Walter E. (Air Mission) (P)
Second Lieutenant, U.S. Army Air Corps. 510th Bomber Squadron, 351st Bomber Group, over Europe, 20 February 1944.

Urban, Matt
Captain, U.S. Army. 2nd Battalion, 60th Infantry Regiment, 9th Infantry Division, Renouf, France, 14 June to 3 September 1944.

Vance, Leon R., Jr. (Air Mission) (P)
Lieutenant Colonel, U.S. Army Air Corps. 489th Bomber Group, over Wimereaux, France, 5 June 1944.

Vlug, Dirk J.
Private First Class, U.S. Army. 126th Infantry, 32nd Infantry Division, near Limon, Leyte, Philippine Islands, 15 December 1944.

Wai, Francis B. (P)
Captain, U.S. Army. Red Beach, Leyte, Philippines, 20 October 1944.

Ware, Keith L.
Lieutenant Colonel, U.S. Army. 1st Battalion, 15th Infantry, 3rd Infantry Division, near Sigolsheim, France, 26 December 1944.

Warner, Henry F. (P)
Corporal, U.S. Army. Antitank Company, 2nd Battalion, 26th Infantry, 1st Infantry Division, near Dom Butgenbach, Belgium, 20–21 December 1944.

Waugh, Robert T. (P)
First Lieutenant, U.S. Army. 339th Infantry, 85th Infantry Division, near Tremensucli, Italy, 11–14 May 1944.

Weicht, Ellis R. (P)
Sergeant, U.S. Army. Company F, 142nd Infantry, 36th Infantry Division, St. Hippolyte, France, 3 December 1944.

Whiteley, Eli
First Lieutenant, U.S. Army. Company L, 15th Infantry, 3rd Infantry Division, Sigolsheim, France, 27 December 1944.

Whittington, Hulon B.
Sergeant, U.S. Army. 41st Armored Infantry, 2nd Armored Division, near Grimesnil, France, 29 July 1944.

Wiedorfer, Paul J.
Private, U.S. Army. Company G, 318th Infantry, 80th Infantry Division, near Chaumont, Belgium, 25 December 1944.

Wigle, Thomas W. (P)
Second Lieutenant, U.S. Army. Company K, 135th Infantry, 34th Infantry Division, Monte Frassino, Italy, 14 September 1944.

Wilson, Alfred L. (P)
Technician Fifth Grade, U.S. Army. Medical Detachment, 328th Infantry, 26th Infantry Division, near Bezange la Petite, France, 8 November 1944.

Wilson, Louis H., Jr.
Captain, U.S. Marine Corps. Rifle Company Commander, 2nd Battalion, 9th Marines, 3rd Marine Division, Fonte Hill, Guam, 25–26 July 1944.

Wilson, Robert L. (P)

Private First Class, U.S. Marine Corps. 2nd Battalion, 6th Marines, 2nd Marine Division, Tinian, 4 August 1944.

Wise, Homer L.

Staff Sergeant, U.S. Army. Company L, 142nd Infantry, 36th Infantry Division, Magliano, Italy, 14 June 1944.

Witek, Frank Peter (P)

Private First Class, U.S. Marine Corps Reserve. 1st Battalion, 9th Marines, 3rd Marine Division, Finegayen, Guam, 3 August 1944.

Zussman, Raymond (P)

Second Lieutenant, U.S. Army. 756th Tank Battalion, Noroy le Bourg, France, 12 September 1944.

1945

Anderson, Beauford T.

Technical Sergeant, U.S. Army. 381st Infantry, 96th Infantry Division, Okinawa, 13 April 1945.

Atkins, Thomas E.

Private First Class, U.S. Army. Company A, 127th Infantry, 32nd Infantry Division, Villa Verde Trail, Luzon, Philippine Islands, 10 March 1945.

Baker, Vernon

Second Lieutenant, U.S. Army. Near Viareggio Italy, 5–6 April 1945.

Beaudoin, Raymond O. (P)

First Lieutenant, U.S. Army. Company F, 119th Infantry, 30th Infantry Division, Hamelin, Germany, 6 April 1945.

Bennett, Edward A.

Corporal, U.S. Army, Company B, 358th Infantry, 90th Infantry Division, Heckhuscheid, Germany, February 1945.

Berry, Charles J. (P)

Corporal, U.S. Marine Corps. 1st Battalion, 26th Marines, 5th Marine Division, Iwo Jima, 3 March 1945.

Bertoldo, Vito R.

Master Sergeant, U.S. Army. Company A, 242nd Infantry, 42nd Infantry Division, Hatten, France, 9–10 January 1945.

Beyer, Arthur O.

Corporal, U.S. Army. Company C, 603rd Tank Destroyer Battalion, near Arloncourt, Belgium, 15 January 1945.

Bigelow, Elmer C. (P)

Watertender First Class, U.S. Naval Reserve. USS *Fletcher,* Corregidor Island, Philippines, 14 February 1945.

Burke, Frank

First Lieutenant, U.S. Army. 15th Infantry, 3rd Infantry Division, Nürnberg, Germany, 17 April 1945.

Burr, Herbert H.

Staff Sergeant, U.S. Army. Company C, 41st Tank Battalion, 11th Armored Division, near Dorrmoschel, Germany, 19 March 1945.

Bush, Richard E.

Corporal, U.S. Marine Corps Reserve. 1st Battalion, 4th Marines, 6th Marine Division, Mount Yaetake, Okinawa, 16 April 1945.

Bush, Robert E.

Hospital Apprentice First Class, U.S. Naval Reserve. Serving as medical corpsman with a rifle company, 2nd Battalion, 5th Marines, 1st Marine Division, Okinawa, 2 May 1945.

Caddy, William R. (P)

Private First Class, U.S. Marine Corps Reserve. Company I, 3rd Battalion, 26th Marines, 5th Marine Division, Iwo Jima, 3 March 1945.

Carey, Charles F., Jr. (P)

Technical Sergeant, U.S. Army. 379th Infantry, 100th Infantry Division, Rimling, France, 8–9 January 1945.

Carter, Edward A., Jr. (P)

Sergeant, U.S. Army. Near Speyer, Germany, 23 March 1945.

Chambers, Justice M.

Colonel, U.S. Marine Corps Reserve. 3rd Assault Battalion Landing Team, 25th Marines, 4th Marine Division, Iwo Jima, 19–22 February 1945.

Cicchetti, Joseph J. (P)

Private First Class, U.S. Army. Company A, 148th Infantry, 37th Infantry Division, south Manila, Luzon, Philippine Islands, 9 February 1945.

Colalillo, Mike

Private First Class, U.S. Army. Company C, 398th Infantry, 100th Infantry Division, near Untergriesheim, Germany, 7 April 1945.

Cole, Darrell S. (P)

Sergeant, U.S. Marine Corps Reserve. Company B, 1st Battalion, 23rd Marines, 4th Marine Division, Iwo Jima, 19 February 1945.

Cooley, Raymond H.

Staff Sergeant, U.S. Army. Company B, 27th Infantry, 25th Infantry Division, near Lumboy, Luzon, Philippine Islands, 24 February 1945.

Courtney, Henry A., Jr. (P)

Major, U.S. Marine Corps Reserve. Executive Officer of 2nd Battalion, 22nd Marines, 6th Marine Division, Okinawa, 14–15 May 1945.

Craft, Clarence B.

Private First Class, U.S. Army. Company G, 382nd Infantry, 96th Infantry Division, Hen Hill, Okinawa, 31 May 1945.

Crain, Morris E. (P)

Technical Sergeant, U.S. Army. Company E, 141st Infantry, 36th Infantry Division, Haguenau, France, 13 March 1945.

Crews, John R.

Staff Sergeant, U.S. Army. Company F, 253rd Infantry, 63rd Infantry Division, near Lobenbacherhof, Germany, 8 April 1945.

Dahlgren, Edward C.

Sergeant, U.S. Army. Company E, 142nd Infantry, 36th Infantry Division, Oberhoffen, France, 11 February 1945.

Daly, Michael J.

Lieutenant, U.S. Army. Company A, 15th Infantry, 3rd Infantry Division, Nürnberg, Germany, 18 April 1945.

Davis, George F. (P)

Commander, U.S. Navy. Captain of USS *Walke*, Lingayen Gulf, Luzon, Philippine Islands, 6 January 1945.

Day, James

Corporal, U.S. Marine Corps. 2nd Battalion, 22nd Marines, 6th Marine Division, Okinawa, 14–17 May 1945.

Deleau, Emile, Jr. (P)

Sergeant, U.S. Army. Company A, 142nd Infantry, 36th Infantry Division, Oberhoffen, France, 12 February 1945.

Diamond, James H. (P)

Private First Class, U.S. Army, Company D, 21st Infantry, 24th Infantry Division, Mintal, Mindanao, Philippine Islands, 8–14 May 1945.

Dietz, Robert H. (P)

Staff Sergeant, U.S. Army. Company A, 38th Armored Infantry Battalion, 7th Armored Division, Kirchain, Germany, 29 March 1945.

Doss, Desmond T.

Private First Class, U.S. Army. Medical Detachment, 307th Infantry, 77th Infantry Division, near Urasoe Mura, Okinawa, 29 April–21 May 1945.

Dunham, Russell E.
Technical Sergeant, U.S. Army. Company I, 30th Infantry, 3rd Infantry Division, near Kayserberg, France, 8 January 1945.

Dunlap, Robert H.
Captain, U.S. Marine Corps Reserve. Company C, 1st Battalion, 26th Marines, 5th Marine Division, Iwo Jima, 20 and 21 February 1945.

Erwin, Henry E. (Air Mission)
Staff Sergeant, U.S. Army Air Corps. 52nd Bombardment Squadron, 29th Bombardment Group, Twentieth Air Force, Koriyama, Japan, 12 April 1945.

Fardy, John Peter (P)
Corporal, U.S. Marine Corps. Company C, 1st Battalion, 1st Marines, 1st Marine Division, Okinawa, 7 May 1945.

Foster, William A. (P)
Private First Class, U.S. Marine Corps Reserve. 3rd Battalion, 1st Marines, 1st Marine Division, Okinawa, 2 May 1945.

Funk, Leonard A., Jr.
First Sergeant, U.S. Army. Company C, 508th Parachute Infantry, 82nd Airborne Division, Holzheim, Belgium, 29 January 1945.

Gammon, Archer T. (P)
Staff Sergeant, U.S. Army. Company A, 9th Armored Infantry Battalion, 6th Armored Division, near Bastogne, Belgium, 11 January 1945.

Gary, Donald A. (P)
Lieutenant, Junior Grade, U.S. Navy. USS *Franklin,* off the Japanese home islands near Kobe, Japan, 19 March 1945.

Gonsalves, Harold (P)
Private First Class, U.S. Marine Corps Reserve. Acting Scout Sergeant with the 4th Battalion, 15th Marines, 6th Marine Division, Okinawa, 15 April 1945.

Gonzales, David M. (P)
Private First Class, U.S. Army. Company A, 127th Infantry, 32nd Infantry Division, Villa Verde Trail, Luzon, Philippine Islands, 25 April 1945.

Grabiarz, William J. (P)
Private First Class, U.S. Army. Troop E, 5th Cavalry, 1st Cavalry Division, Manila, Luzon, Philippine Islands, 23 February 1945.

Gray, Ross F. (P)
Sergeant, U.S. Marine Corps Reserve. Company A, 1st Battalion, 25th Marines, 4th Marine Division, Iwo Jima, 21 February 1945.

Halyburton, William D., Jr. (P)
Pharmacist's Mate Second Class, U.S. Naval Reserve. Attached to the 2nd Battalion, 5th Marines, 1st Marine Division, Okinawa, 10 May 1945.

Hammerberg, Owen F. P. (P)
Boatswain's Mate Second Class, U.S. Navy. Rescue operations at West Loch, Pearl Harbor, 17 February 1945.

Hansen, Dale M. (P)
Private, U.S. Marine Corps. Company E, 2nd Battalion, 1st Marines, 1st Marine Division, Okinawa, 7 May 1945.

Harr, Harry R. (P)
Corporal, U.S. Army. Company D, 124th Infantry, 31st Infantry Division, near Maglamin, Mindanao, Philippine Islands, 5 June 1945.

Harrell, William G. (P)
Sergeant, U.S. Marine Corps. 1st Battalion, 28th Marines, 5th Marine Division, Iwo Jima, 3 March 1945.

Hastings, Joe R. (P)
Private First Class, U.S. Army. Company C, 386th Infantry, 97th Infantry Division, Drabenderhohe, Germany, 12 April 1945.

Hauge, Louis J., Jr. (P)
Corporal, U.S. Marine Corps Reserve. Company C, 1st Battalion, 1st Marines, 1st Marine Division, Okinawa, 14 May 1945.

Hayashi, Joe (P)
Private, U.S. Army. Near Tendola, Italy, 20 and 22 April 1945.

Hedrick, Clinton M. (P)
Technical Sergeant, U.S. Army. Company I, 194th Glider Infantry, 17th Airborne Division, near Lembeck, Germany, 27–28 March 1945.

Herrera, Silvestre S.
Private First Class, U.S. Army. Company E, 142nd Infantry, 36th Infantry Division, near Mertzwiller, France, 15 March 1945.

Herring, Rufus G.
Lieutenant, U.S. Naval Reserve. *LCI (G) 449*, Iwo Jima, 17 February 1945.

Inouye, Daniel K.
Second Lieutenant, U.S. Army. Vicinity of San Terenzo, Italy, 21 April 1945.

Jachman, Isadore S. (P)
Staff Sergeant, U.S. Army. Company B, 513th Parachute Infantry Regiment, Flamierge, Belgium, 4 January 1945.

Jacobson, Douglas T.
Private First Class, U.S. Marine Corps Reserve. 3rd Battalion, 23rd Marines, 4th Marine Division, Iwo Jima, 26 February 1945.

James, Willy F. (P)
Private First Class, U.S. Army. Near Lippoldsberg, Germany, 7 April 1945.

Julian, Joseph R. (P)
Platoon Sergeant, U.S. Marine Corps Reserve. 1st Battalion, 27th Marines, 5th Marine Division, Iwo Jima, 9 March 1945.

Kelley, Jonah E. (P)
Staff Sergeant, U.S. Army. 311th Infantry, 78th Infantry Division, Kesternich, Germany, 30–31 January 1945.

Kelly, Thomas J.
Corporal, U.S. Army. Medical Detachment, 48th Armored Infantry Battalion, 7th Armored Division, Alemert, Germany, 5 April 1945.

Kerstetter, Dexter J.
Private First Class, U.S. Army. Company C, 130th Infantry, 33rd Infantry Division, near Galiano, Luzon, Philippine Islands, 13 April 1945.

Kinser, Elbert L. (P)
Sergeant, U.S. Marine Corps Reserve. Company I, 3rd Battalion, 1st Marines, 1st Marine Division, Okinawa, 4 May 1945.

Knight, Jack L. (P)
First Lieutenant, U.S. Army. 124th Cavalry Regiment, Mars Task Force, near Loikang, Burma, 2 February 1945.

Knight, Raymond L. (Air Mission) (P)
First Lieutenant, U.S. Army Air Corps. Northern Po Valley, Italy, 24–25 April 1945.

Krotiak, Anthony L. (P)
Private First Class, U.S. Army. Company I, 148th Infantry, 37th Infantry Division, Balete Pass, Luzon, Philippine Islands, 8 May 1945.

La Belle, James D. (P)
Private First Class, U.S. Marine Corps Reserve. 27th Marines, 5th Marine Division, Iwo Jima, 8 March 1945.

Laws, Robert E.
Staff Sergeant, U.S. Army. Company G, 169th Infantry, 43rd Infantry Division, Pangasinan Province, Luzon, Philippine Islands, 12 January 1945.

Leims, John H.
Second Lieutenant, U.S. Marine Corps Reserve. Company B, 1st Battalion, 9th Marines, 3rd Marine Division, Iwo Jima, 7 March 1945.

Lester, Fred F. (P)
Hospital Apprentice First Class, U.S. Navy. Medical Corpsman attached to 1st Battalion, 22nd Marines, 6th Marine Division, Okinawa, 8 June 1945.

Lucas, Jacklyn H.
Private First Class, U.S. Marine Corps Reserve. 1st Battalion, 26th Marines, 5th Marine Division, Iwo Jima, 20 February 1945.

Lummus, Jack (P)
First Lieutenant, U.S. Marine Corps Reserve. 2nd Battalion, 27th Marines, 5th Marine Division, Iwo Jima, 8 March 1945.

MacGillivary, Charles A.
Sergeant, U.S. Army. Company I, 71st Infantry, 44th Infantry Division, near Woelfling, France, 1 January 1945.

Magrath, John D. (P)
Private First Class, U.S. Army. Company G, 85th Infantry, 10th Mountain Division, near Castel d'Aiano, Italy, 14 April 1945.

Martin, Harry L. (P)
First Lieutenant, U.S. Marine Corps Reserve. Company C, 5th Pioneer Battalion, 5th Marine Division, Iwo Jima, 26 March 1945.

May, Martin O. (P)
Private First Class, U.S. Army. 307th Infantry, 77th Infantry Division, Legusuku-Yama, Ie Shima, Ryukyu Islands, 19–21 April 1945.

Mayfield, Melvin
Corporal, U.S. Army. Company D, 20th Infantry, 6th Infantry Division, Cordillera Mountains, Luzon, Philippine Islands, 29 July 1945.

McCarter, Lloyd G.
Private, U.S. Army. 503rd Parachute Infantry Regiment, Corregidor, Philippine Islands, 16–19 February 1945.

McCarthy, Joseph J.
Captain, U.S. Marine Corps Reserve. 2nd Battalion, 24th Marines, 4th Marine Division, Iwo Jima, 21 February 1945.

McCool, Richard M.
Lieutenant, U.S. Navy. USS *LSC(L)(3) 122* off Okinawa, 10–11 June 1945.

McGaha, Charles L.
Master Sergeant, U.S. Army. Company G, 35th Infantry, 25th Infantry Division, near Lupao, Luzon, Philippine Islands, 7 February 1945.

McGee, William D. (P)
Private, U.S. Army. Medical Detachment, 304th Infantry, 76th Infantry Division, near Mulheim, Germany, 18 March 1945.

McKinney, John R.
Private, U.S. Army. Company A, 123rd Infantry, 33rd Infantry Division, Tayabas Province, Luzon, Philippine Islands, 11 May 1945.

McTureous, Robert M., Jr. (P)
Private, U.S. Marine Corps. 3rd Battalion, 29th Marines, 6th Marine Division, Okinawa, 7 June 1945.

Meagher, John
Technical Sergeant, U.S. Army. Company E, 305th Infantry, 77th Infantry Division, near Ozato, Okinawa, 19 June 1945.

Merrell, Joseph F. (P)
Private, U.S. Army. Company I, 15th Infantry, 3rd Infantry Division, near Lohe, Germany, 18 April 1945.

Michael, Harry J. (P)
Second Lieutenant, U.S. Army. Company L, 318th Infantry, 80th Infantry Division, near Neiderzerf, Germany, 14 March 1945.

Moskala, Edward J. (P)
Private First Class, U.S. Army. Company C, 383rd Infantry, 96th Infantry Division, Kakazu Ridge, Okinawa, 9 April 1945.

Muller, Joseph E. (P)
Sergeant, U.S. Army. Company B, 305th Infantry, 77th Infantry Division, near Ishimmi, Okinawa, 15–16 May 1945.

Munemori, Sadao S. (P)
Private First Class, U.S. Army. Company A, 100th Infantry Battalion, 442nd Combat Team, near Seravezza, Italy, 5 April 1945.

Murphy, Audie L.
Second Lieutenant, U.S. Army. Company B, 15th Infantry, 3rd Infantry Division, near Holtzwihr, France, 26 January 1945.

Murphy, Frederick C. (P)
Private First Class, U.S. Army. Medical Detachment, 259th Infantry, 65th Infantry Division, Siegfried Line at Saarlautern, Germany, 18 March 1945.

O'Callahan, Joseph T. (P)
Commander (Chaplain Corps), U.S. Naval Reserve. USS *Franklin*, near Kobe, Japan, 19 March 1945.

Okutsu, Yukio
Technical Sergeant, U.S. Army. Mount Belvedere, Italy, 7 April 1945.

Oresko, Nicholas
Master Sergeant, U.S. Army. Company C, 302nd Infantry, 94th Infantry Division, near Tettington, Germany, 23 January 1945.

Parrish, Laverne (P)
Technician 4th Grade, U.S. Army. Medical Detachment, 161st Infantry, 25th Infantry Division, Binalonan, Luzon, Philippines, 18–24 January 1945.

Peden, Forrest E. (P)
Technician 5th Grade, U.S. Army. Battery C, 10th Field Artillery Battalion, 3rd Infantry Division, near Biesheim, France, 3 February 1945.

Perez, Manuel, Jr. (P)
Private First Class, U.S. Army. Company A, 511th Parachute Infantry, 11th Airborne Division, Fort William McKinley, Luzon, Philippines, 13 February 1945.

Peters, George J. (P)
Private, U.S. Army. Company G, 507th Parachute Infantry, 17th Airborne Division, near Fluren, Germany, 24 March 1945.

Peterson, George (P)
Staff Sergeant, U.S. Army. Company K, 18th Infantry, 1st Infantry Division, near Eisern, Germany, 30 March 1945.

Phillips, George (P)
Private, U.S. Marine Corps Reserve. 2nd Battalion, 28th Marines, 5th Marine Division, Iwo Jima, 14 March 1945.

Pierce, Francis J.
Pharmacist's Mate First Class, U.S. Navy. Serving with 2nd Battalion, 24th Marines, 4th Marine Division, Iwo Jima, 15–16 March 1945.

Reese, John N., Jr. (P)
Private First Class, U.S. Army. Company B, 148th Infantry, 37th Infantry Division. Paco Railroad Station, Manila, Philippine Islands, 9 February 1945.

Robinson, James E., Jr. (P)
First Lieutenant, U.S. Army. Battery A, 861st Field Artillery Battalion, 63rd Infantry Division, near Untergriesheim, Germany, 6 April 1945.

Rodriguez, Cleto
Private, U.S. Army. Company B, 148th Infantry, 37th Infantry Division, Paco Railroad Station, Manila, Luzon, Philippines, 9 February 1945.

Rudolph, Donald E.
Second Lieutenant, U.S. Army. Company E, 20th Infantry, 6th Infantry Division, Munoz, Luzon, Philippine Islands, 5 February 1945.

Ruhl, Donald J. (P)
Private First Class, U.S. Marine Corps Reserve. Company E, 28th Marines, 5th Marine Division, Iwo Jima, 19–21 February 1945.

Ruiz, Alejandro R. R.
Private First Class, U.S. Army. 165th Infantry, 27th Infantry Division, Okinawa, 28 April 1945.

Schwab, Albert E. (P)
Private First Class, U.S. Marine Corps Reserve, Okinawa, 7 May 1945.

Shockley, William R. (P)
Private First Class, U.S. Army. Company L, 128th Infantry, 32nd Infantry Division, Villa Verde Trail, Luzon, Philippine Islands, 31 March 1945.

Shomo, William A. (Air Mission)
Major, U.S. Army Air Corps. 82nd Tactical Reconnaissance Squadron, over Luzon, Philippine Islands, 11 January 1945.

Shoup, Curtis F. (P)
Staff Sergeant, U.S. Army. Company I, 346th Infantry, 8th Infantry Division, near Tillet, Belgium, 7 January 1945.

Sigler, Franklin E.
Private, U.S. Marine Corps Reserve. 2nd Battalion, 26th Marines, 5th Marine Division, Iwo Jima, 14 March 1945.

Sjogren, John C.
Staff Sergeant, U.S. Army. Company I, 160th Infantry, 40th Infantry Division, near San Jose Hacienda, Negros, Philippine Islands, 23 May 1945.

Stein, Tony (P)
Corporal, U.S. Marine Corps Reserve. Company A, 1st Battalion, 28th Marines, 5th Marine Division, Iwo Jima, 19 February 1945.

Street, George L., III
Commander, U.S. Navy. Captain of USS *Tiranle*, harbor of Quelpart Island, off the coast of Korea, 14 April 1945.

Stryker, Stuart S. (P)
Private First Class, U.S. Army. Company E, 513th Parachute Infantry, 17th Airborne Division, near Wesel, Germany, 24 March 1945.

Terry, Seymour W. (P)
Captain, U.S. Army. Company B, 382nd Infantry, 96th Infantry Division, Zebra Hill, Okinawa, 11 May 1945.

Thomas, William H. (P)
Private First Class, U.S. Army. 149th Infantry, 38th Infantry Division, Zambales Mountains, Luzon, Philippine Islands, 22 April 1945.

Treadwell, Jack L.
Captain, U.S. Army. Company F, 180th Infantry, 45th Infantry Division, near Nieder-Wurzbach, Germany, 18 March 1945.

Turner, Day G. (P)
Sergeant, U.S. Army. Company B, 319th Infantry, 80th Infantry Division, at Dahl, Luxembourg, 8 January 1945.

Turner, George B.
Private First Class, U.S. Army. Battery C, 499th Armored Field Artillery Battalion, 14th Armored Division, Philippsbourg, France, 3 January 1945.

Valdez, Jose F. (P)
Private First Class, U.S. Army. Company B, 7th Infantry, 3rd Infantry Division, near Rosenkrantz, France, 25 January 1945.

Viale, Robert M. (P)
Second Lieutenant, U.S. Army. Company K, 148th Infantry, 37th Infantry Division, Manila, Luzon, Philippine Islands, 5 February 1945.

Villegas, Ysmael R. (P)
Staff Sergeant, U.S. Army. Company F, 127th Infantry, 32nd Infantry Division, Villa Verde Trail, Luzon, Philippine Islands, 20 March 1945.

Wahlen, George E.
Pharmacist's Mate Second Class, U.S. Navy. Serving with 2nd Battalion, 26th Marines, 5th Marine Division, Iwo Jima, 3 March 1945.

Wallace, Herman C. (P)
Private First Class, U.S. Army. Company B, 301st Engineer Combat Battalion, 76th Infantry Division, near Prumzurley, Germany, 27 February 1945.

Walsh, William G. (P)
Gunnery Sergeant, U.S. Marine Corps Reserve. Company G, 3rd Battalion, 27th Marines, 5th Marine Division, Iwo Jima, 27 February 1945.

Watson, Wilson D.
Private, U.S. Marine Corps Reserve. 2nd Battalion, 9th Marines, 3rd Marine Division, Iwo Jima, 26–27 February 1945.

Wetzel, Walter C. (P)
Private First Class, U.S. Army. 13th Infantry, 8th Infantry Division, Birken, Germany, 3 April 1945.

Wilkin, Edward G. (P)
Corporal, U.S. Army. Company C, 157th Infantry, 45th Infantry Division, Siegfried Line in Germany, 18 March 1945.

Will, Walter J. (P)
First Lieutenant, U.S. Army. Company K, 18th Infantry, 1st Infantry Division, near Eisern, Germany, 30 March 1945.

Williams, Hershel W.
Corporal, U.S. Marine Corps Reserve. 21st Marines, 3rd Marine Division, Iwo Jima, 23 February 1945.

Williams, Jack (P)
Pharmacist's Mate Third Class, U.S. Naval Reserve. 3rd Battalion, 28th Marines, 5th Marine Division, Iwo Jima, 3 March 1945.

Willis, John H.

Pharmacist's Mate First Class, U.S. Navy. 3rd Battalion, 27th Marines, 5th Marine Division, Iwo Jima, 28 February 1945

Woodford, Howard E. (P)

Staff Sergeant, U.S. Army. Company I, 130th Infantry, 33rd Infantry Division, near Tabio, Luzon, Philippine Islands, 6 June 1945.

BIOGRAPHIES OF KEY LEADERS

The purpose of this section is to support the chronology and acquaint the reader with a brief summary of the education and significant prewar experiences of general and flag officers who held major command positions during the war.

U.S. ARMY

Bradley, Omar N. (1893–1981)

Graduated from West Point in 1915 and served as an instructor there from 1920 to 1924. He was an instructor at the Infantry School from 1929 to 1933. He graduated from the Army War College in 1934. He served in the War Department on the General Staff from 1938 to 1941. In February 1941 he was promoted to brigadier general. He was then appointed as commandant of the Infantry School, where he served from 1941 to 1942. Promoted to major general, he took command of the 82nd Infantry Division in February 1942 and then the 28th Infantry Division in June of 1942. He was promoted to lieutenant general in 1943 and took command of I Corps from April to September 1943, then the First Army Group from October 1943 to August 1944. He became commander of the 12th Army Group in August 1944 and led it until July 1945. He was promoted to general in March of 1945. Bradley commanded more American soldiers than any other general in American history.

Buckner, Simon B. (1886–1945)

Son of General Simon Bolivar Buckner (CSA), he graduated from West Point in 1908 and served as an instructor there from 1918 to 1919 and from 1932 to 1936. He was also an instructor at the Command and General Staff College from 1925 to 1928. He graduated from the Army War College in 1929 and served as an instructor there from 1929 to 1932. He was commandant of cadets at West Point from 1933 to 1936. From August 1936 until May 1937, he served with the 23rd Infantry Regiment and was the commander of the 66th Infantry Regiment from 1937 to 1938. In 1939 he oversaw the Civilian Conservation Corps camps in Alabama. He was chief of staff of the 6th Infantry Division from 1939 to 1940. He was promoted to brigadier general in 1940 and commanded the Alaska Defense Force from July 1940 to March 1944. He was promoted to major general in August 1941 and to lieutenant general in 1943. He organized and commanded the U.S. Tenth Army from June 1944 until his death on Okinawa June 18, 1945, from a Japanese artillery explosion as he directed the final assaults on the island.

Clark, Mark W. (1896–1984)

Graduated from West Point in 1917 and rose to battalion command in World War I. Served in the War Department on the General Staff from 1921 to 1924 and graduated from the Army War College

Lieutenant General Mark Clark aboard USS *Ancon,* during the Sicily Campaign *(National Archives and Records Administration)*

in 1937. Served in the 3rd Infantry Division from 1937 to 1940, then became an instructor at the Army War College. Promoted to brigadier general in August 1941, then to major general in April 1942, he served as I Corps commander from July to October 1942 and was promoted to lieutenant general in November 1942. He served as the deputy commander for Allied Forces in North Africa from November 1942 to January 1943. He took command of Fifth Army in January 1943 and served in that position until December 1944. He then became commander of the 5th Army Group and directed the last campaigns in Italy. Leaving the 5th Army Group in June 1945, he became an Allied commissioner for Austria from 1945 to 1947.

Collins, Joseph Lawton (1896–1987)

Graduated from West Point in 1917 and served as an instructor there from 1921 to 1925. He was an instructor at the Infantry School from 1927 to 1931 and graduated from the Army War College in 1938. He also served as an instructor there from 1938 to 1941. He was appointed chief of staff of the Hawaii Department from 1941 to 1942 and during that time was promoted to brigadier general. He became a major general in May 1942 and took command of the 25th Infantry Division and took it to combat at Guadalcanal. He took over VI Corps in Europe in 1944 and commanded it throughout the final campaigns in France and Germany. He was promoted to lieutenant general in April 1945.

Devers, Jacob L. (1887–1979)

Graduated from West Point in 1909 and served as an instructor there from 1912 to 1916 and again from 1919 to 1924. He graduated from the Army War College in 1933. He took a third assignment as an instructor at West Point from 1936 to 1939. He was promoted to brigadier general in May of 1940 and to major general in October of the same year. He was the 9th Infantry Division commander from October 1940 to July 1941, then took command of Armored Forces from May 1942 to January 1944. He was named the deputy supreme Allied commander for the Mediterranean theater of operations in January 1944 and served in that position until October 1944. He took command of 6th Army Group in October and served until May of 1945. He was promoted to general in March 1945.

Eichelberger, Robert L. (1886–1961)

Graduated from West Point in 1909. He was the deputy chief of staff for the American Expeditionary Force in Siberia in 1918. He served in the War Department on the General Staff from 1935 to 1938. Served as the commander of the 30th Infantry Division from 1938 to 1940 and was promoted to brigadier general in 1940. Afterward he served as superintendent of West Point from 1940 to 1942. He was promoted to major general in March 1942 and took command of the 77th Infantry

Division, then took command of XI Corps until September 1942. He took command of I Corps, serving in the Southwest Pacific from September 1942 to September 1944. He was named commander of Eighth Army in September 1944 and served in that position until September 1948.

Eisenhower, Dwight D. (1890–1969)

Graduated from West Point in 1915, then supported unit training for troops going to Europe in World War I. Graduated from the Army War College in 1928, he served as assistant executive to the assistant secretary of war from 1929 to 1932. He then became the special assistant to General Douglas MacArthur from 1933 to 1939, serving in both Washington, D.C., and the Philippines. He was executive officer of the 15th Infantry Regiment in 1940, then the chief of staff of the 3rd Infantry Division. In March 1941 he was chief of staff of IX Corps, then Third Army until September 1941. He was promoted to brigadier general in September, then moved to the war plans division of the General Staff, serving from December 1941 to May 1942. He was promoted to major general in April of 1942 and in June took command of U.S. Forces Europe. He was promoted to lieutenant general in July 1942 and then general in February 1943. In December 1943 he became Supreme Commander Allied Expeditionary Force with the responsibility for Operation Torch, the Allied invasion of North Africa. He oversaw the plans for the invasion of Europe (Overlord), and then led the Allied forces to victory as the supreme commander. He left the command in November 1945.

Gerow, Leonard T. (1888–1972)

Graduated from the Virginia Military Institute in 1911 and graduated from the Army War College in 1931. He served in the war plans division of the General Staff from 1935 to 1942. He was promoted to brigadier general in 1940 and to major general in February 1942. He took command of the 29th Infantry Division in 1942, serving until 1943, when he took command of V Corps and fought

the final campaigns in Europe. He was the first American general to enter Paris, France, after the liberation of the city in 1944. He was promoted to lieutenant general in January 1945, and then took command of the 15th Army Group, serving until July 1945.

Hodges, Courtney H. (1887–1966)

Cadet at West Point from 1904 to 1905, when he left and enlisted in the army from 1906 to 1909. He took a commission in the infantry in 1909 and fought in the great battles of World War I at St. Mihiel and the Argonne Forest. After the war he served on the Infantry Board at Fort Benning, Georgia, from 1929 to 1933. He graduated from the Army War College in 1934. He was the assistant commandant of the Infantry School from 1938 to 1941. In May of 1940 he was promoted to brigadier general and in May of 1941 was promoted to major general. He was the chief of infantry from 1941 to 1942, then took command of X Corps from 1942 to 1943. He was promoted to lieutenant general in February of 1943 and took command of Third Army. He served in that position until 1944, when he became deputy commander, then commander of the First Army. He commanded First Army throughout the campaigns in Europe, completing his time as commander in 1949.

Krueger, Walter (1881–1967)

Enlisted in the U.S. Army in 1898 and was commissioned a lieutenant in the infantry in 1901. He attended the Army War College in 1921 and served as an instructor there from 1921 to 1922. He graduated from the National War College in 1926 and served as an instructor there from 1928 to 1932. He was the chief, War Plans Division, on the General Staff from 1936 to June 1938. He was promoted to brigadier general and served as commander of the 6th Infantry Brigade from June 1938 to February 1939. He was promoted to major general, then took command of the 2nd Infantry Division, where he served until October 1940. He served with VIII Corps from October until May

1941. Promoted to lieutenant general in May 1941, he took command of Third Army and held that position until February 1943, when he became commander of Sixth Army. Promoted to general in March 1945, he continued as commander of Sixth Army until September 1945.

Lucas, John P. (1890–1949)

Graduated from West Point in 1911, then served in France and was wounded in 1918. He was an instructor at the Field Artillery School from 1921 to 1923. He served in the Personnel Division of the General Staff at the War Department from 1932 to 1936. He was promoted to brigadier general in October 1940, then took command of the 2nd Infantry Division artillery from 1940 to 1941. Promoted to major general in August of 1941, he took command of the 3rd Infantry Division and served in that position until 1942. In April 1942 he became commander of III Corps, serving until May 1943. He took command of VI Corps during the Sicily and Anzio operations. Relieved of command at Anzio, he returned to the United States and took the deputy commander's position in Fourth Army.

MacArthur, Douglas (1880–1964)

The son of a Medal of Honor winner and lieutenant colonel in the Union Army, MacArthur graduated from West Point in 1903 and served as an aide to Theodore Roosevelt from 1906 to 1907. He was chief of staff, then commander of the 42nd Infantry Division in World War I. He was superintendent of West Point from 1919 to 1922. He was promoted to brigadier general in January of 1920, major general in January 1925, then general in 1930. He was chief of staff of the U.S. Army from 1930 to 1935. He served in the Philippines from 1935 to 1941, retiring from the army and taking a position as field marshal of the Philippine army in 1936. He was recalled to active duty in July 1941, given the rank of lieutenant general, and designated the commander of U.S. Army forces in the Far East. After the Japanese attack on the Philip-

General MacArthur, Commander in Chief of Southwest Pacific Area, wades ashore on Leyte on October 20, 1944, keeping the promise he made to the Philippine people in 1942 that he would return.

pines, he escaped from Corregidor and arrived in Australia. Winning both the Medal of Honor and a promotion to general in 1941, he took command of U.S. forces in the Southwest Pacific Area. He was promoted to general of the army (five-star) in December of 1944. In August 1945 he was named supreme commander Allied Forces Pacific and took the surrender of Japan in Tokyo Bay aboard the battleship USS *Missouri*. He supervised the occupation of Japan from 1945 to 1950.

Marshall, George C. (1880–1959)

Graduated from the Virginia Military Institute in 1901 and served as a staff officer with the VIII Corps in France during the major offensives of the American Expeditionary Force. From 1919 to 1924, he was an aide to General John J. Pershing. In 1924 he took command of the 15th Infantry Regiment in China, serving there until 1927. He became the assistant commandant of the Infantry School in 1927, and in 1932 he left that position to take command of the 8th Infantry Regiment, a position he held until 1933. He became the senior instructor for the Illinois National Guard from 1933 to 1936. In July of 1936 he was promoted to brigadier general. He served in the War Department on the General Staff from 1938 to 1939. He was promoted to major general in July 1939, became the deputy chief of staff, then the acting chief of staff of the army from July through September 1939. He was appointed chief of staff of the U.S. Army in September 1939 and promoted to general. He served in this position throughout the war, directing the army's global effort to defeat Germany, Italy, and Japan. In this position he served as a member of the Joint Chiefs of Staff. He was promoted to general of the army (five-star) in December 1944, and in November of 1945 he resigned from the army.

Merrill, Frank D. (1903–1955)

Graduated from West Point in 1929. He was an instructor in the Cavalry School from 1935 to 1938. He was the attaché in Tokyo, Japan, from 1938 to 1940. He became the deputy chief of staff for operations in the China, Burma, India theater, serving from 1942 to 1943. He was promoted to brigadier general in November 1943. In 1944 he organized and led the unit of American volunteers, the 5307th Composite Unit (Provisional) that eventually came to be known as Merrill's Marauders. He was promoted to major general in September 1944, and then served as chief of staff of Tenth Army from 1945 to 1948.

Patch, Alexander M. (1889–1945)

Graduated from West Point in 1913 and commanded a machine-gun battalion in France in World War I. He was a professor of military science at Staunton Military Academy in Virginia from 1920 to 1924, and then again from 1925 to 1928. He graduated from the Army War College in 1932. Promoted to brigadier general in December 1940, then promoted to major general in March 1942. He organized and trained the Americal Division, the served with the division on Guadalcanal from October 1942 to February 1943. In 1943 he took

command of the III Corps Area, serving in that position until 1944. He was named commander of Seventh Army in March of 1944 and served until June 1945. He was promoted to general in August of 1944. He took command of Fourth Army in June of 1945, serving there until his death a few months later.

Patton, George S., Jr. (1885–1945)

Graduated from West Point in 1909. He was commander of the 304th tank Brigade at the Battle of St. Mihiel and in the Meuse-Argonne, where he was wounded. He graduated from the Army War College in 1932 and took command of the 3rd Cavalry Regiment in 1938, serving until 1940. In 1940 he took command of the 2nd Armored Division and held that position until 1942. He was promoted to brigadier general in October 1940 and major

George S. Patton, Jr., strikes a well-deserved pose as conqueror of Sicily, August 1943. *(Virginia Military Institute Archives)*

general in April of 1941. He took command of the I Armored Corps, then the II Armored Corps between 1942 and 1943 in Tunisia. He was promoted to lieutenant general in April 1943. He was the commander of Seventh Army at Sicily and was the target of intense public scrutiny for slapping a soldier. He took command of Third Army in 1944 and held the position until the end of the war in Europe in May 1945. He was promoted to general in April of 1945. After the war, he took command of U.S. Forces Europe, when he was injured in a car accident and died of complications.

Pick, Lewis A. (1890–1956)

Graduated from Virginia Polytechnic Institute in 1914. He was commissioned in the Corps of Engineers in 1917 and served as an instructor at the Army Command and General Staff College from 1934 to 1938. He graduated from the Army War College in 1939. He was a division engineer with the Ohio and Missouri River Division, U.S. Corps of Engineers, from 1939 to 1941. From 1942 to 1943 he was the division engineer for the Missouri River Division. From 1943 to 1945 he was the commander of the advance section, China, Burma, India theater and supervised the building of the Burma Road. He was promoted to brigadier general in February 1944, then major general in March of 1945.

Ridgway, Matthew B. (1895–1993)

Graduated from West Point in 1917. Graduated from the Army War College in 1937. He served in the War Plans Division of the General Staff from September 1939 to January 1942. He was promoted to brigadier general in January 1942 and became the assistant division commander of the 82nd Infantry Division, later the 82nd Airborne Division. He was promoted to major general in August of 1942 and took command of the division. He led the division in combat, parachuting into Normandy, until August 1944. He then became commander of the XVIII Airborne Corps until September 1945. He was promoted to lieutenant general in June 1945.

Stilwell, Joseph W. (1883–1946)

Graduated from West Point in 1904 and served in the Philippines from 1904 to 1906, then again from 1911 to 1912. He was the deputy chief of staff for intelligence, IV Corps, with the American Expeditionary Force in France in 1918. He served in the 15th Infantry Regiment in China from 1926 to 1928. He then became the chief of staff for U.S. forces in China from 1928 to 1929. He was an instructor in the Infantry School under George C. Marshall from 1929 to 1933. He was the attaché to China and Thailand from 1935 to 1939. He was promoted to brigadier general in May of 1939, then took command of the 3rd Infantry Brigade and then the 7th Infantry Division from 1939 to 1941. He was promoted to major general in October 1940. He took command of the II Corps from July 1941 to February 1942, when he was promoted to lieutenant general. He took command of all U.S. forces in the China-Burma-India theater and served simultaneously as the chief of staff to Chinese Generalissimo Chiang-Kai-shek as well as the deputy supreme Allied commander in-theater. He served in these multiple roles from March of 1942 to October 1944. In August 1944 he was pro-

"Vinegar Joe" Stilwell (right) with Marauder commander Frank Merrill *(National Archives and Records Administration)*

moted to general. He was relieved of command in October 1944 and became chief of Army ground forces from January to May of 1945. He took command of Tenth Army in June 1945 after the death of General Buckner on Okinawa and served as commander until October 1945.

Truscott, Lucian K. (1895–1965)

Enlisted in the U.S. Army in 1917 and commissioned in the cavalry. He served in Hawaii from March 1919 to October 1921. He was an instructor at the Cavalry School from 1927 to 1931. From September 1940 to July 1941, he was the executive officer of the 2nd Battalion, 13th Armored Regiment. Afterward he served on the IX Corps staff from July 1941 to May 1942. He was promoted to brigadier general in May 1942 and served on the Combined Operations Staff under Britains Admiral Lord Louis Mountbatten. Truscott formed the first U.S. Army Ranger unit in 1942 and was promoted to major general in November 1942. He was the field deputy to Supreme Allied Commander Lieutenant General Dwight Eisenhower during the Tunisia campaign from 1942 to 1943. He took command of the 3rd Infantry Division in 1943 until he became the deputy commander, then commander of VI Army Corps, serving from January to December 1944. He was promoted to lieutenant general in September 1944. In December 1944 he took command of Fifth Army and served in that position until October 1945.

Wainwright, Jonathan M. (1883–1953)

Graduated from West Point in 1906 and served as the assistant chief of staff with the 82nd Infantry Division at St. Mihiel and the Meuse-Argonne battles in France in 1918. He graduated from the Army War College in 1934. In 1938 he was promoted to brigadier general and took command of the 1st Cavalry Brigade in 1938. He served in that position until 1940. He was promoted to major general in September 1940 and took command of the Philippine Division. He defended Luzon and Bataan against the Japanese invasion and was

promoted to major general in March 1942. He then took command of U.S. Forces in the Far East on Corregidor, surrendering his command to the Japanese in April 1942. He was a prisoner of war until his release in 1945 and stood behind General MacArthur on the USS *Missouri* as he signed the surrender documents ending the war with Japan. He was promoted to general in September of 1945 and awarded the Congressional Medal of Honor.

Wedemeyer, Albert C. (1897–1989)

Graduated from West Point in 1919. He studied the Chinese language at Tientsin from 1930 to 1932 and attended the German Kriegsakademie (staff college) from 1936 to 1938. He served on the General Staff in the War Plans Division from May 1941 to October 1943. He was promoted to brigadier general in July 1942, then to major general in September 1943. He was the deputy chief of staff to Britain's Admiral Lord Louis Mountbatten, the Supreme Allied Commander, Southeast Asia, from October 1943 to October 1944. He became the commander of the China theater of operations after General Stilwell's dismissal and the commander of China-Burma-India theater until October 1945. He was promoted to lieutenant general in January of 1945.

U.S. ARMY AIR FORCES

Arnold, Henry H. (1886–1950)

Graduated from West Point in 1907. Orville Wright taught him to fly in 1911. He flew as a U.S. air mail pilot in September 1911. He was commander of March Field from 1931 to 1935 and was promoted to brigadier general in February 1935. In September 1938, he was promoted to major general, then became chief of the Air Corps (later the U.S. Army Air Forces). He was promoted to lieutenant general in December 1941, general in March 1943, and General of the Army (five stars) in December 1944. As chief of U.S. Army Air Forces, he served on the Joint Chiefs of Staff and directed all air operations during the war.

Henry Harley "Hap" Arnold *(United States Air Force History Center)*

Lieutenant General Lewis H. Brereton had a number of commands throughout the war, beginning with the Far East Air Force in the Philippines in 1941, Tenth Air Force in Burma in 1942, U.S. Army Forces in the Middle East in 1943, and commander of Ninth Air Force in the European theater of operations. In 1944 and until the end of the war, he was commander of the First Allied Airborne Army

Brereton, Lewis H. (1890–1967)

Commissioned an ensign in the U.S. Navy after graduating from Annapolis in 1911. He transferred to the army, eventually moving from coastal artillery to the aviation section of the Signal Corps. He was the commander of the 2nd and 12th Aero Squadrons and chief of aviation for the I Army Corps from October 1917 to 1919. He was an instructor at the Command and General Staff College from 1935 to 1939, then took command of the 17th Bomber Wing, serving in that position until 1941. He was promoted to brigadier general in October 1940, then to major general in July 1941. In July he took command of the Third Air Force and served there until December 1941. He then took command of the Far East Air Force, and from December 1941 to March 1942 he was commander in chief of Allied Air Forces Far East, then the commander of Tenth Air Force. He was transferred to

take command of the Middle East Air Force, later U.S. Army Air Forces, Middle East, serving from March 1942 to October 1943. He became commander of the Ninth Air Force in October 1943 and was promoted to lieutenant general in April 1944. He then took command of the First Allied Airborne Army, playing a major role in Operation Market Garden. He remained in the position until May 1945.

Chennault, Claire Lee (1890–1958)

He attended officer training camp at Fort Harrison, Indiana, in 1917 and was commissioned a reserve officer in the infantry. He later transferred to the aviation section of the Signal Corps. He retired in 1937 and was recruited by Chinese Generalissimo Chiang-Kai-shek to organize Chinese air defenses. He trained American volunteers as combat pilots between August and December 1941; a group officially known as the American Volunteer Group, they became famous as the Flying Tigers. Chennault was recalled to active duty in April 1942 and promoted to brigadier general. In July 1942 he was named the commander of Army Air Forces in China. In March 1943 he was promoted to major general and became the commander of Tenth Air Force. He served in this position until August of 1945.

Doolittle, James H. (1896–1993)
He enlisted in the Army Reserve in October 1917 and was later commissioned in the aviation section of the Signal Corps in 1920. In September 1920, he was the first pilot to make a transcontinental flight in less than 24 hours. In 1930 he resigned his commission, but reentered active duty in July of 1940. As a lieutenant colonel, he led the raid on Tokyo, 18 April 1942. Promoted to brigadier general the next day and awarded the Medal of Honor, he organized and served as commander of Twelfth Air Force from September 1942 to March 1943. He was promoted to major general in November 1942, then between 1942 and 1945 took succeeding command positions with the Northwest Africa Air Force, the Fifteenth Air Force, and Eighth Air Force. He was promoted to lieutenant general in March 1944.

Eaker, Ira C. (1896–1987)
Commissioned a reserve officer in 1917, then transferred to aviation, qualifying as a pilot in 1918. In 1936 he was the first pilot to make a

James H. "Jimmy" Doolittle *(National Archives and records Administrations)*

Ira Eaker *(United States Air Force History Center)*

transcontinental flight using only instruments. From 1941 to 1942 he was commander of the 30th Pursuit Group. He was promoted to brigadier general in January 1942. He then commanded the 8th Bomber Command until December 1942. In September 1942 he was promoted to major general. From December 1942 to January 1944 he commanded Eighth Air Force. He was promoted to lieutenant general in September 1943. In January 1944 he took command of the Mediterranean Allied Air Force and served in that position until May 1945.

Harmon, M. F. (1889–1945)

Graduated from West Point in 1912 and qualified as a pilot in 1916. He flew with a French squadron in combat during World War I. He graduated from the Army War College in 1925. In October 1940 he was promoted to brigadier general and took command of the 7th Pursuit Wing and the 11th Wing. From January to June 1941 he was in England as an air warfare observer. He was promoted to major general in July 1941 and took command of Interceptor Command, Fourth Air Force, from January to June of 1942. He was the commander of U.S. Army Air Forces, Pacific Ocean Areas from July 1942 to February 1945. He was promoted to lieutenant general in February 1943. He was lost at sea on 26 February 1945.

Kenney, George C. (1889–1977)

Commissioned in the Air Service in 1917 and served in the 91st Aero Squadron during World War I. He graduated from the Army War College in 1933 and became a brigadier general in January 1941. He commanded the Air Corps Experimental Depot from January 1941 to April 1942. Promoted to major general that month, he took command of Fourth Air Force, serving in that position until July 1942. He was promoted to lieutenant general in September 1942, then took command of Fifth Air Force. He served as its commander until June of 1944, when he became the Southwest Pacific Area Allied Air Forces commander. He served in this

command until March 1945. After March 1945 he was commander of Allied Air Forces Pacific until September 1945.

LeMay, Curtis E. (1906–1990)

Commissioned in the Air Corps in 1929, he was commander of the 305th Bomb Group, Eighth Air Force, and then the Third Bomb Division from 1942 to 1943. He was promoted to brigadier general in October 1943, then to major general in March of 1944. He took command of the 20th Bomber Command in the China-Burma-India theater from August 1944 to July 1945 and conducted a number of devastating raids on Japan.

Quesada, Elwood R. (1904–1993)

Commissioned in the Air Reserve in 1925 and entered active duty in 1927. He served as an aide to the assistant secretary of war from 1932 to 1933. He was the commander of the 33rd Pursuit Group from 1941 to 1942. He was promoted to brigadier general in December 1942 and took command of the 1st Air Defense Wing until 1943. He then became commander of the 9th Fighter Command from 1943 to 1944. He was promoted to major general in April 1944 and took command of the 9th Tactical Air Command until the end of the war.

Spaatz, Carl (1891–1974)

Graduated from West Point in 1914 and served in the 2nd Pursuit Group in France in 1918, where he had three confirmed kills in air combat. In 1939 he was the executive officer of the 2nd Wing, then became the executive officer and assistant to the chief of the Air Corps from 1939 to 1940. He was promoted to brigadier general in October 1940 and served as head of the Plans Division, then chief of the Air Staff from 1940 to 1942. He was promoted to major general in January of 1942, then became the chief of Army Air Force Combat Command from January to June of 1942. He commanded the Eighth Air Force from July to December 1942, then from 1942 to March 1943 took command of Twelfth Air Force, the North Africa Air Force, then

General Carl Spaatz (right) with Hoyt Vandenberg *(Dwight D. Eisenhower Presidential Library)*

became the deputy commanding general for the Mediterranean Allied Air Forces. In March 1943 he was promoted to lieutenant general, became the commander of the U.S. Strategic Air Force in Europe and then in the Pacific theater of operations from January 1944 to October 1945.

Stratemeyer, George E. (1890–1969)

Graduated from West Point in 1915 and transferred to the aviation section of the Signal Corps

in 1916. He was an instructor at West Point from 1924 to 1929. He graduated from the Army War College in 1939. He was appointed head of the Training and Operations Division, Headquarters, Army Air Force, from 1940 to 1941. He was promoted to brigadier general in August 1941 and became the executive officer to General Henry H. Arnold from 1941 to 1942. He was promoted to major general in June 1942 and served as chief of staff of the Air Staff from 1942 to 1943. He was appointed the commanding general of Army Air Forces, China-Burma-India theater in 1943 and served in that position until 1946.

Twining, Nathan F. (1897–1982)

Enlisted in the Oregon National Guard in 1916 and graduated from West Point in 1919. Between 1940 and 1942 he served in the Office of the Chief of the Air Corps. He was promoted to brigadier general in 1942 and served as the chief of staff for Allied Forces, Southern Pacific from 1942 to 1943. He was the commander of the Thirteenth Air Force and the air commander of the Solomon Islands. From 1943 to 1944 he was the commander of Fifteenth Air Force and was promoted to major general in February 1943. Between 1944 and 1945 he was commander of Mediterranean Allied Air Strategic Air Forces. He was promoted to lieutenant general in June of 1945. He took command of Twentieth Air Force in August 1945 and served in that position until October 1945.

Vandenberg, Hoyt S. (1899–1954)

Graduated from West Point in 1923 and commissioned in the Air Corps. Graduated from the Army War College in 1939, served first in the Plans Division, then in the Operations and Training Office in the Office of the Chief of the Air Corps from 1939 to 1942. He was promoted to brigadier general in December of 1942 then served as the chief of staff of Twelfth Air Force and the Northwest Africa Strategic Air Force from 1942 to 1943. He was the deputy chief of the Air Staff, Headquarters, Army Air Force from 1943 to 1944. Promoted to major general in March of 1944, he served as the deputy commander for the Allied Expeditionary Air Force, then commander of Ninth Air Force from 1944 to the end of the war in Europe in 1945. From 1945 to 1946 he was the assistant chief of staff for operations, Army Air Force.

U.S. NAVY

Burke, Arleigh A. (1901–1996)
Graduated from Annapolis in 1923. Commanded the destroyer USS *Mugford* from 1939 to 1940. He served in the Bureau of Naval Ordnance from 1940 to 1943, then moved to the South Pacific to command Destroyer Squadron 23. His destroyers covered the initial landings at Bougainville in November 1943 and fought the Japanese in over 20 battles in four months. Destroyer Squadron 23 received credit for sinking a Japanese cruiser, nine destroyers, one submarine, several other vessels, and about 30 aircraft. He was promoted to commodore in October of 1944 and became Vice Admiral Marc Mitscher's chief of staff. He served in this position until the end of the war.

Fletcher, Frank Jack (1885–1973)
Graduated from Annapolis in 1906, won the Medal of Honor at Vera Cruz, Mexico, in 1914, and commanded a destroyer in World War I. He graduated from the Naval War College in 1930 then the Army War College in 1931. From 1933 to 1936 he served as an aide to the secretary of the navy. In 1939 he was promoted to rear admiral. He commanded Cruiser Division Three with the Atlantic Fleet from 1939 to 1941. He commanded a task force during the Battle of the Coral Sea, 7–8 May 1942 and was the senior officer at the Battle of Midway. He was promoted to vice admiral in June 1942 and in 1943 took command of Naval Forces, North Pacific until the end of the war.

Ghormley, Robert L. (1883–1958)
Graduated from the University of Idaho in 1902, then from Annapolis in 1906. He served with the Atlantic Fleet, then in the Office of the Chief of Naval Operations during World War I. He graduated from the Navy War College in 1938 and was promoted to rear admiral in October 1938. From 1938 to 1940 he served as the director of the War Plans Division in the Navy Department and was assistant to the chief of naval operations. He was a naval observer in England from 1940 to 1942 and was promoted to vice admiral in September 1941. From April to October 1942 he served as the commander of South Pacific Forces responsible for the offensive against the Japanese in the Solomons. He took command of the Fourteenth Naval District from 1943 to 1944 and then served on the staff of Admiral Harold R. Stark, commander of U.S. Naval Forces in Europe, from 1944 to May 1945, when he became commander of U.S. Naval Forces, German Waters, at the end of the war.

Halsey, William F., Jr. (1882–1959)
Graduated from Annapolis in 1904 and commanded two destroyers during World War I. Between 1922 and 1934, he was a naval attaché with postings in Denmark, Sweden, Norway, and Berlin, Germany. He graduated from the Naval War College in 1933 and the Army War College in 1934. In March 1935 he qualified as a naval aviator. He commanded the carrier USS *Saratoga* from 1935 to 1937 and then took command of the Pensacola Naval Air Station from 1937 to 1938. He was promoted to rear admiral in March of 1938. Between 1938 and 1940 he served as commander of two different carrier divisions and was promoted to vice admiral in June of 1940. He was the battle force aircraft commander and was out at sea aboard the carrier USS *Enterprise* on December 7, 1941, during the attack on Pearl Harbor. He led the task force that raided Kwajalein in February 1942 and commanded the task force that launched the Doolittle raid on Tokyo, April 18, 1942. He took command of South Pacific Forces from vice admiral Ghormley in October 1942 and directed operations against the Japanese in the Solomons. He was promoted to admiral in November of

Admiral William F. Halsey, Jr., commander of the South Pacific Area during the Solomons offensive, 1942–43. He would later command the U.S. Third Fleet in 1944 and 1945

November 1933, then was commander of aircraft, battle force for the Atlantic Fleet from 1938 to 1939 and promoted to vice admiral. He served on the General Board, which advised the president of the United States on naval matters, from 1939 to 1940. He was promoted to admiral in February 1941 and took command of the Atlantic Fleet. After Pearl Harbor, he became Commander in Chief, U.S. Fleet (CominCh). In March he replaced Admiral Harold R. Stark as the chief of naval operations and combined the two positions. He directed all naval operations during the war and served as a member of the Joint Chiefs of Staff. In December 1944 he became a fleet admiral (five-star) and gave up the position of chief of naval operations to Admiral Chester W. Nimitz in November 1945.

Kinkaid, Thomas C. (1888–1972)

Graduated from Annapolis in 1908 and served aboard the battleship USS *Arizona* during World War I. He graduated from the Naval War College in 1930 and from 1937 to 1938 commanded the heavy cruiser USS *Indianapolis*. From 1938 to 1941 he was the naval attaché in Rome and Belgrade. In

1942. From June 1944 to December 1945 he commanded Third Fleet, conducting operations in support of the American invasion of the Philippines. The USS *Missouri* served as Halsey's flagship when the Japanese surrendered on board in Tokyo Bay on September 2, 1945. In December 1945 he was promoted to fleet admiral (five-star).

King, Ernest J. (1878–1956)

Graduated from Annapolis in 1901 and commanded the destroyer USS *Terry* during operations off Veracruz, Mexico, in 1914. From 1916 to 1922 he served on the staff of the commander of the Atlantic Fleet. In 1928 he qualified as a naval aviator, commanded the carrier USS *Lexington* in 1930, and graduated from the Navy War College in 1933. He was promoted to rear admiral in

MacArthur observes Philippine operations with Vice Admiral Thomas Kinkaid, February 1944. *(National Archives and Records Administration)*

November 1941 he was promoted to rear admiral. From 1941 to 1943 he commanded Cruiser Division Six, then took command of the task force centered on the carrier USS *Enterprise* and directed operations during the Solomons offensive and fought the Japanese in the naval battles of the Coral Sea, Midway, and Santa Cruz. From January to November 1943 he served as the commander of naval forces, North Pacific. In June of 1943 he became a vice admiral and was assigned to command the Seventh Fleet, subordinate to General MacArthur. He directed naval operations in support of amphibious operations in New Guinea and the Philippines. In April 1945 he was promoted to admiral and served as Seventh Fleet commander until November 1945.

Leahy, William D. (1875–1959)

Graduated from Annapolis in 1897 and served aboard the battleship USS *Oregon* during the Spanish-American War. He commanded the bat-

tleship USS *Nevada* in World War I. Promoted to rear admiral, he then served as chief of the Bureau of Ordnance from 1927 to 1931. In March 1935 he became a vice admiral and commanded battleships of the Battle Force from 1935 to 1936. In April 1936 he was promoted to admiral and commanded the entire Battle Force. From January 1937 to July 1939 he served as chief of naval operations. He retired in 1939, serving as governor of Puerto Rico until 1940. From 1940 to 1942 he served as the U.S. ambassador to Vichy France. He was recalled to active duty in 1942 by President Roosevelt and served as chief of staff for the president. He was the senior member of the Joint Chiefs of Staff and provided the important interface between the president as commander in chief and the military leadership for all matters concerning strategy and policy. In December 1944 he was promoted to fleet admiral (five-star). After President Roosevelt's death in April 1945, he continued in his position under President Harry S. Truman.

Admiral William Leahy in 1935 *(U.S. Navy History Center)*

Mitscher, Marc A. (1887–1947)

Graduated from Annapolis in 1910 and served on a number of ships, including cruisers, gunboats, and destroyers. He qualified as a naval aviator in 1916, and served at Pensacola, Florida, until 1917. He was then assigned to conduct experiments with shipboard catapults. From 1929 to 1930 he was the executive officer on the carrier USS *Langley* and also on the carrier USS *Saratoga* from 1934 to 1935. In 1941 he commanded the carrier USS *Hornet* and launched Doolittle's bombers off its decks in April 1942. He commanded the carrier in the Battle of Midway. Promoted to rear admiral he then commanded air units in the Southern Pacific during the Solomons campaign. In November 1944 he commanded Carrier Division Three during the Marshall Islands operations and was promoted to vice admiral. His command, redesignated as Fast Carrier Task Force 58, fought the Battles of Philippine Sea and Leyte Gulf, attacked Japanese forces across the Pacific, sup-

Admiral Marc Mitscher, commander of carrier Task Force 58 aboard USS *Lexington* in June of 1944

ported the assaults on Iwo Jima and Okinawa, and conducted strikes on the Japanese home islands. In July 1945 he became the deputy chief of naval operations for air.

Nimitz, Chester W. (1885–1966)

Graduated from Annapolis in 1905 and served as chief of staff to the commander of submarines. He served with the Atlantic Fleet during World War I on submarine duty and graduated from the Naval War College in 1923. From 1929 to 1931 he commanded Submarine Division 20. From 1933 to 1935 he commanded the heavy cruiser USS *Augusta*. In June of 1938 he was promoted to rear admiral and commanded first a cruiser division, then a battleship division between 1938 and 1939. He was the chief of the Bureau of Navigation from June 1939 to December 1941. After Pearl Harbor he was promoted to admiral and took command of the Pacific Fleet. As the commander in chief of Pacific Ocean Areas throughout the war, Nimitz directed land and naval operations to stop the Japanese advance and establish bases for the eventual invasion of the Japanese home islands. He was promoted to fleet admiral (five-star) in December 1944. In November 1945 he became chief of naval operations.

Admiral Chester W. Nimitz, Commander in Chief, Pacific Ocean Areas

Oldendorf, Jesse B. (1887–1974)

Graduated from Annapolis in 1909. Commanded the destroyer USS *Decatur* from 1925 to 1927. He graduated from the Naval War College in 1929 and the Army War College in 1930. He commanded the light cruiser USS *Houston* from 1939 to 1941, then served on the staff of the Naval War College from August 1941 to February 1942. Between February and July 1942 he was commander, U.S. Naval Forces, Aruba-Curaçao Area. He was promoted to rear admiral in June 1942, then commanded the U.S. naval base at Trinidad from 1942 to May 1943, when he took command of an Atlantic Fleet task force until November, then commanded Cruiser Division Four from January to December 1944. He was promoted to vice admiral and took command of Battleship Squadron One. In this command, he provided naval gunfire support for marine landings throughout the Central Pacific and army forces at Lingayen Gulf. He fought the Battle of Surigao Strait at Leyte, October 24, 1944, destroying a Japanese battle force in a classic employment of battleships.

Sprague, Clifton A. F. (1896–1955)

Graduated from Annapolis in 1918 and served aboard the cruiser USS *Wheeling* during World War I. In 1921 he qualified as a naval aviator. He graduated from the Naval War College in 1939. From November 1939 to June 1942 he commanded the seaplane tender USS *Tangier* and was aboard during the Japanese attack on Pearl Harbor. *Tangier* was one of the few ships to get underway during the attack. He served as air officer on the staff of the commander, Gulf Sea Frontier, in Miami, Florida, until 1943. He commanded the carrier USS *Wasp* from 1943 to 1944, then took command of Carrier Division Twenty-Five from August 1944 to August 1945.

Spruance, Raymond A. (1886–1969)

Graduated from Annapolis in 1907. From 1924 to 1925 he served on the staff of U.S. Naval Forces, Europe. He graduated from the Naval War College in 1927 and served as an instructor there from 1931 to 1932, and again from 1935 to 1938. He was promoted to rear admiral in 1939. From 1941 to 1942 he commanded Cruiser Division Five, Pacific Fleet. From June 1942 to September 1943 he was chief of staff to the commander in chief, U.S. Pacific Fleet. He then became the deputy commander in chief of the Pacific Fleet. In May 1943 he was promoted to vice admiral, and from 1943 to 1944 he served as commander, Central Pacific Area. On April 29, 1944, this was redesignated, and Spruance became commander, Fifth Fleet. He was in overall command of the occupation of the Gilbert Islands, the invasion of the Marshalls, and operations seizing Saipan, Tinian, and Guam in the Marianas. He also directed naval forces during the Battle of the Philippine Sea, June 19–20, 1944. He also directed operations for the assaults on Iwo Jima and Okinawa. In February 1944 he was promoted to admiral and in November 1945 took command of the Pacific Fleet from Fleet Admiral Nimitz.

Admiral Raymond A. Spruance led task force 16 during the Battle of Midway. He commanded the U.S. Fifth Fleet from 1943 to 1945. The fleet had over 300 fighting ships and more than 1,100 auxiliary ships and fought in all the major campaigns of the Pacific.

Turner, Richmond Kelly (1885–1961)

Graduated from Annapolis in 1908, serving on battleships in World War I. He qualified as a naval aviator in 1927 and served on the staff of the Naval War College from 1935 to 1938. He commanded the heavy cruiser USS *Astoria* from 1938 to 1940. From 1940 to 1942 he served in the war plans division of the Navy Department. In December 1941 he was promoted to rear admiral and became the assistant chief of staff to the commander in chief, U.S. Fleet, until June 1942. He then took command of the Amphibious Force, South Pacific Force. From 1943 to 1945 he commanded the Fifth Amphibious Force, Central Pacific Area. He planned and directed the landings at Tarawa, Kwajalein, Guam, Iwo Jima, and Okinawa. In February

Rear Admiral Richmond Turner confers with General Alexander Vandegrift (USUC). *(National Archives and Records Administration)*

Roy S. Geiger *(United States Marine Corps)*

1944 he was promoted to vice admiral and in May 1945 was promoted to admiral and designated as commander of Amphibious Forces, Pacific. In this role he was to oversee the landings on Kyushu and Honshu, Japan.

U.S. MARINE CORPS

Geiger, Roy S. (1885–1947)

Commissioned in the Marine Corps in 1909 and served in Nicaragua and the Philippines from 1912 to 1913, then in Peking (Beijing) from 1913 to 1916. In June of 1917 he qualified as a naval aviator and commanded a squadron in the 1st Marine Aviation Force in France in 1918. He served in Haiti from 1919 to 1921 and again from 1925 to 1927. In 1929 he graduated from the Army War College. From 1931 to 1935 he was head of Marine Corps Aviation. In 1941 he was promoted to brigadier general and served as the assistant naval attaché in London. In August 1941 he became commanding general, 1st Marine Aircraft Wing, Fleet Marine Force. On Guadalcanal, he served as director of air operations. In August 1942 he was promoted to major general. In November 1943, he became the commanding general of the I Amphib-

ious Corps during the Bougainville campaign. In April of 1944 his command was redesignated as the III Amphibious Corps. He led marine forces capturing Guam and the Palau Islands and was the commander of marine forces as part of Tenth Army landing on Okinawa. He temporarily commanded Tenth Army after the death of General Buckner. In July 1945 he became the commanding general of the Fleet Marine Force, Pacific, and served in that position until November 1946.

Rupertus, William H. (1889–1945)

Enlisted in the District of Columbia National Guard in 1907 and served until 1910. Commissioned in the Marine Corps in 1913. Served in Haiti from 1920 to 1923 and served in the American Legation in Peking (Beijing) from 1929 to 1933. He remained in China, serving with the Fourth Marines in Shanghai from 1937 to 1938. In 1941 he was the assistant division commander of the 1st Marine Division. In January 1942 he was promoted to brigadier general and promoted to major general in 1943. He then took command of the 1st Marine Division for the assaults on Cape Gloucester and Peleliu. He left the division in November 1944 and was commandant of Marine Corps Schools until his death in March of 1945.

Schmidt, Harry (1886–1968)

Commissioned in the Marine Corps in 1909. He served on Guam from 1911 to 1912 and in the Philippines from 1912 to 1913. He was an instructor at Marine Corps Schools from 1923 to 1926. From 1927 to 1929 he served in China, then in Nicaragua. He was chief of staff of the 2nd Marine Brigade at Shanghai, China, from 1937 to 1938. From 1938 to 1942 he was a personnel officer at headquarters, Marine Corps. He was promoted to brigadier general in October 1941 and to major general in 1942. After serving as the assistant to the commandant of the Marine Corps from January 1942 to August 1943, he took command of the 4th Marine Division. He led the division in the capture of Roi and Namur Islands and at Saipan. In July 1944 he became the commanding general of the V Amphibious Corps for the landings on Tinian and Iwo Jima. He continued to serve in this position with occupation duties in Japan until February 1946.

Smith, Holland M. (1882–1967)

Commissioned in the Marine Corps in 1905 and served in the Philippines from 1906 to 1908, in Panama from 1909 to 1910, and in the Philippines again from 1912 to 1914. He was in the Dominican Republic from 1916 to 1917, then served in France, where he participated in the Aisne-Marne offensive, St-Mihiel, and the Meuse-Argonne in World War I. He graduated from the Naval War College in 1921. He was promoted to brigadier general in 1939. From April to September 1939 he served as the assistant to the commandant, Marine Corps; he then took command of the 1st Marine Brigade at Quantico, Virginia. In February 1941 he was pro-

Holland M. "Howlin' Mad" Smith. *(United States Marine Corps)*

moted to major general. From June 1941 to August 1942 he served as the commander of Amphibious Forces, Atlantic Fleet, then took the same position as commander, Amphibious Corps, Pacific Fleet. From September 1943 to August 1944 he commanded the redesignated V Amphibious Corps. In February 1944 he was promoted to lieutenant general. In July 1944 he became the commanding general of Fleet Marine Force Pacific, until July 1945. He was reassigned to Camp Pendleton until his retirement.

Vandegrift, Alexander A. (1887–1973)

Enlisted in the Marine Corps in 1908 and commissioned as an officer in 1909. Between 1912 and 1923 he served in Cuba, Nicaragua, Haiti, Panama, and at Veracruz, Mexico. From 1927 to 1929 and again from 1935 to 1937 he served in China. He was assistant to the commandant, Marine Corps, from 1937 to 1941. In 1940 he was promoted to brigadier general. In March 1942 he was promoted to major general and served as the assistant commander, then commander of the 1st Marine Division. He led the division in the battle for Guadalcanal and was awarded the Congressional Medal of Honor. In July 1943 he was promoted to lieutenant general and took command of the I Marines' Amphibious Corps and commanded the landing force at Empress Augusta Bay at Bougainville in November 1943. He served as commander until November 1943. In January 1944 he became the 18th commandant of the Marine Corps, serving in that position until January 1948. He was promoted to general in April 1945, the first marine to achieve four-star rank while on active duty.

GLOSSARY OF TERMS

This glossary covers military terms and definitions found in the chronology.

administrative control   Command authority related to matters not directly related to combat, such as personnel management and services.

airborne   Airborne forces in World War II were light infantry highly trained to conduct parachute landings, usually behind enemy lines. Paratroopers would jump from transport aircraft onto a designated landing area called a Drop Zone. Because all of their supplies and heavy equipment must also be transported and landed by parachute or glider, the troops themselves were lightly armed. The troops would land on the Drop Zone, pick up their equipment (machine guns, mortars, radio sets, ammunition, medical supplies) from containers dropped by parachute. Heavier equipment (vehicles, anti-tank guns, artillery) would come later, delivered by gliders. Because they were lightly armed and had limited supplies, paratroopers were expected to use initiative and take aggressive action to achieve their designated mission.

aircraft carrier   A warship designed to launch, recover, and maintain combat aircraft. The ship is designed as a large floating flight deck with space below to arm, maintain, and store the aircraft. The ship is controlled from a superstructure called an island on the starboard (right) side of the ship. In World War II there were two classes of carriers: Fleet Carriers (CV) and Light Carriers (CVL). Fleet carriers were the decisive weapons of naval warfare and carried 70 to 90 aircraft. Light carriers had 35 to 45 aircraft. Many cargo ships and tanker hulls were converted into Escort Carriers (CVE) with 10 to 20 aircraft. These ships were primarily used for antisubmarine operations or close air support missions. Carriers, while powerful, are vulnerable to attack because of their limited armament. A certain number of aircraft launched from a carrier must always fly a protective screen to prevent enemy aircraft from attacking the ship. Other smaller ships also protect the carrier, providing antiaircraft fire and patrolling for submarines. Naval battles in the Pacific focused on locating and destroying the enemy's aircraft carriers.

air interdiction   An attack from aircraft by bombardment or gunfire against ground targets to destroy or disrupt them.

air superiority   The condition established during combat operations that allows the free air movement of supplies and reinforcements without any interference from enemy aircraft. This involves both the destruction of enemy aircraft as well as the destruction of airfields, supplies, logistics bases, and facilities. Air superiority is a requirement for the success of ground operations. Gaining air superiority over western France and the Channel coastline was essential for success of the Normandy landings in 1944. Air superiority was a primary factor in MacArthur's New Guinea campaign of 1943–44, and it was essential before any major landings at Guam, Saipan, Kwajalein, or Okinawa. Most campaigns began with air operations that lasted for months to achieve air superiority before any amphibious landings took place.

amphibious operations   Amphibious operations place a friendly force on an enemy-held shore. Good beaches that can support large numbers of men and equipment are essential as well as tides that do not interfere with the steady flow of reinforcements and supplies after the initial landings have succeeded. Landing beaches should be within range of friendly aircraft, either carrier-based or land based. Naval forces are essential in both protecting the landing force and to provide the bombardment to suppress enemy defenses. Usually cruisers, destroyers, and battleships provide support. Landing areas are divided and designated for specific forces (Omaha and Utah beaches at Normandy, Red 1, Red 2, Red 3, and Green Beach at Tarawa), each with its own separate command. The amphibious assaults are designated as waves. The first wave clears the beach of obstacles and eliminates the strongpoints on the beach not already eliminated by air and naval bombardment. The successive waves push inland to capture objectives and broaden the penetration into the enemy's defenses as deeply as possible. Because amphibious forces carry a limited amount of equipment and supplies, they are vulnerable to counterattack until a sufficient buildup of forces can be achieved (Guadalcanal in 1942, Bougainville in 1943). Therefore speed and aggressive action are essential in achieving success.

antiaircraft guns   High-angle, high-velocity guns either ground-based or mounted on ships that fire high-explosive shells intended to damage or destroy attacking aircraft. The intent is to put up a curtain or wall of exploding shells into which the attacking aircraft must fly. The fragmentation produced by the explosions would tear through engine components, fuel and hydraulic lines, and puncture the skin of the aircraft itself to kill or wound the pilot or crew.

antisubmarine operations   Techniques used to prevent submarines from attacking targets or to locate and destroy submarines before they are able to attack. One main technique used to defend ships against submarine attack was to conduct convoys. Convoys were harder to detect in the open ocean. If detected, the submarines would be able to attack the convoy, but risked being detected themselves and overwhelmed by large numbers of warships or aircraft operating together. Radio direction-finding equipment was very successful in antisubmarine operations to pinpoint German submarines transmitting information. High-frequency direction-finding equipment also had a significant effect on locating and destroying German submarines in the latter stages of the Battle of the Atlantic. Once located, enemy submarines were often subjected to depth charges or air attack.

army   A command organization of ground force units, designated by a number, composed of two or more corps. Armies can operate independently (Tenth Army at Okinawa) or can be subordinate to an Army Group (Patton's Third Army was subordinate to the 12th Army Group).

army group   A command organization composed of two or more ground force armies. In the ETO, General Bradley commanded the 12th Army Group, composed of the First, Third, Ninth, and Fifteenth Armies.

battalion   A ground force unit, usually part of a regiment or a brigade. Infantry battalions (marine or army) have three or more companies of riflemen with attached heavy weapons, such as mortars, machine guns, anti-tank guns. Tank battalions consisted or three or more companies, each with about 10 tanks. Artillery battalions are organized into batteries of six to eight cannons each.

bazooka   An anti-tank rocket launcher, the word is often used to describe any anti-tank weapon during World War II. The 1942 bazooka fired a 2.36-inch projectile that could penetrate up to seven inches of armor. The optimum range was 40 to 50 meters, making it quite dangerous for an infantryman to use. It was used not only against tanks and other vehicles, it was also employed with great effect on fortifications.

battleship   A heavily armored warship with large-caliber guns used primarily to defeat other battleships but also to provide gunfire support to ground forces. Prior to World War II and in the first two years of the war, most navy leaders believed the battleship was the decisive weapon of naval warfare. All American naval plans were based on a decisive fleet engagement led by battleships. The employment of the aircraft carrier and submarine, however, showed the limitations of the battleship; by 1943, battleships in the U.S. Navy were used as antiaircraft platforms and assembled into groups for shore bombardment preceding amphibious landings. The Japanese built the largest and most powerful battleships ever made, but they were completely ineffective and were sunk during the Okinawa campaign by carrier-based aircraft. The engagement at Surigao Strait at Leyte was the last surface engagement of battleships.

beachhead   A section of enemy shoreline that is seized and occupied by friendly forces after an amphibious assault. The beachhead marks the area of friendly control and its expansion is critical to the sustainment and reinforcement of the initial landing force. The beachhead serves as the base for future offensive operations and is the launching point for further attacks. The failure to expand the beachhead at Anzio in January 1944 had dire consequences for Allied forces. Nevertheless, the successful defense of the beachhead allowed for sufficient reinforcements to arrive and eventually made possible the breakout that led to the capture of Rome.

bomber   A large multi-engine combat aircraft designed to deliver high-explosive bombs over long distances. In World War II, bombers were designated as light (A-20 Havoc, A-26 Invader), medium (B-25 Mitchell, B-26 Marauder), heavy (B-17 and B-24 Liberator), and very heavy (B-29), based on range and the number of bombs carried.

bombardment   The process of firing a large number of shells from naval ships at fixed targets, or aircraft dropping numerous bombs on fixed targets. Often bombardments consisted of both naval gunfire and aircraft attacks.

bridgehead   Ground on the opposite side of a river held by the enemy, then seized and defended by friendly forces. The bridgehead serves as a launching point for further offensive operations.

brigade   A ground force unit, usually composed of three battalions, which can operate independently or as part of a division. Brigades are the smallest ground force units that have the capability to operate independently. Brigades can be organized as only infantry or only tank or can be mixed. Many U.S. armored divisions in the ETO formed combat commands. The combat command was the equivalent of a brigade, a mixture of tank and mechanized infantry battalions to create a more powerful, flexible, and fast moving force.

breakout or breakthrough   When a ground force is able to disrupt the defensive lines of the enemy and move into weakly defended rear areas with little interference. Operation Cobra is an example of a plan to break out of the Normandy area and drive deep into France.

campaign   A planned series of battles or engagements within a specific theater of war or other designated area to achieve an operational or strategic objective. Examples are MacArthur's seizure of bases in New Guinea 1943–44, and the Solomons offensive in 1942–43.

close air support   The use of combat aircraft, primarily fighters, as flying artillery to support the maneuver of ground forces by suppressing or destroying enemy defenses. Close air support missions are usually conducted in close coordination with ground units.

combined   A term in World War II that described the involvement of committees, forces, units, or operations from the United States and Great Britain. The Combined Chiefs of Staff is an example of the committee formed by the U.S Joint Chiefs of Staff and the Imperial General Staff to provide a unified strategic direction for the war.

commander in chief   The commander of a major military force. It can also refer to army and navy forces under a single commander in a theater of war.

company   A ground forces unit that is part of a battalion. Three or four companies form a battalion. The equivalent unit in the artillery is called a battery.

convoy   A collection of merchant ships escorted by warships (and sometimes with aircraft as well). The warships and aircraft protected the vulnerable merchant ships against surface or subsurface attack. Ground convoys consist of a collection of vehicles traveling together with or without an armed escort.

cruiser   A fast warship designed for independent operations, it was more heavily armored than a destroyer but smaller and more lightly armored than a battleship. A light cruiser (CL) had five- or six-inch guns and was employed in antisubmarine operations, antiaircraft defense, surface battles, or naval gunfire support in amphibious operations. A heavy cruiser (CA) had eight-inch guns and was designed to fight surface threats and provide antiaircraft defense for carriers.

depth charge   A weapon used against submarines. It is a canister filled with high explosives and set by a hydrostatic fuse, which detonates the explosive at a specific depth. If a depth charge is detonated near a submarine, the force of the explosion can rupture the hull of the boat, sinking it or forcing it to the surface. To be effective the depth charge must be set for the proper depth, but this was often difficult due to the ability of the submarine to move up, down, or laterally to avoid being pinpointed. Successful depth charge attacks often involve several ships operating together to track and provide accurate information on the submarine and then maneuver the submarine into a position where another ship could drop the depth charges accurately.

destroyer   A fast, lightly armored, heavily armed warship designed to operate defensively (convoy escort or escorting larger ships) or offensively (amphibious operations, antisubmarine operations). Destroyers were used for scouting (locating an enemy fleet early) or picket duty (screening larger ships by providing early warning of air attack). The Fletcher-class destroyer of World War II was armed with 10 torpedo tubes, five 5-inch guns, antiaircraft weapons, and depth charges. Admiral Arleigh Burke became famous for his aggressive tactics as commander of Destroyer Squadron 23. American destroyers on picket duty off Okinawa in 1945 took heavy casualties from kamikazes.

destroyer escort   A small, slow, and lightly armed warship intended primarily for antisubmarine warfare, usually defending convoys or protecting larger ships.

fighter aircraft   Combat aircraft that has a crew of one or two, is highly maneuverable, and is primarily used for air-to-air combat against other enemy fighters. A fighter-bomber is an aircraft designed to engage enemy fighters but also to provide close support to ground units.

fighter sweep   An attack by fighter aircraft to locate and attack enemy aircraft or attack targets of opportunity in a specified area.

flamethrower   A man-portable weapon that projects an ignitable liquid in a steady stream. A soldier or marine carried the flamethrower on his back. Weighing about 40 pounds, it consisted of two fuel tanks, a pressure tank, and a hose with a nozzle that can project flame up to 30 meters away. Flamethrowers were especially effective against fortifications. Flamethrowers were also mounted on tanks.

fleet   A collection of ships, aircraft, and sometimes marine forces under the command of a naval officer who usually exercises both operational and tactical control of the subordinate elements.

foxhole   A hole dug by an infantryman or marine to shield him from enemy fire and effectively engage attacking enemy troops.

grenade   A small bomb weighing about a pound, thrown either by hand or launched from a rifle. The small charge has a delay fuse that allows it to explode without injuring the thrower. The casing of the grenade is designed to fragment over a 10 to 20 meter area. It is used to suppress or destroy enemy personnel, especially in confined areas.

group   An air force unit consisting of several squadrons.

infantry   Ground troops that fight primarily on foot to control ground. Light infantry is primarily foot mobile and lightly equipped. They can be highly versatile and, with proper support from aircraft or naval forces, can be a significant combat force. They have a limited capability against tanks. Mechanized infantry (also known as armored infantry in World War II) move to battle in carriers (half-tracks) in order to keep pace with tanks and artillery. Once dismounted, they have largely the same capabilities as light infantry, except for the capability of tank support and the ability to bring heavier weapons (anti-tank guns, mortars, and heavy machine guns) into battle quickly using their vehicles for supporting fire. No other force can control ground except the infantry. In forests, coral outcroppings, or jungle, the infantry is the only force capable of defeating the enemy.

kamikaze   A Japanese word meaning "divine wind." The kamikaze described both the pilot and his aircraft. The pilots had minimal training and were given a ceremony before departing on their mission. The pilot was directed toward a target area, then intentionally attempted to guide his explosive-laden aircraft into an enemy warship.

landing craft   A flat-bottom boat with a ramp in the front to disembark troops or vehicles directly on a beach during amphibious landings. Because of their ungainliness, landing craft (Landing Craft, Vehicle and Personnel, or LCVP, for example) must be launched in relatively calm seas and at a short distance from the beach. Mines, underwater obstacles, and artillery or mortar fire are particularly dangerous to landing craft. Landing craft are launched from larger ships. Larger landing ships (Landing Ship,

This landing craft, mechanized (LCM) belonged to the 533rd Engineer Boat and Shore Regiment of the 3rd Engineer Special Brigade. These units were essential to the success of the New Guinea-Philippines campaigns between 1944 and 1945. The LCM had a crew of four and brought troops and supplies ashore, carrying one tank, or 60 troops, or 60,000 pounds of cargo.

Tank, or LST, for example) have the capability to land troops, vehicles, and cargo directly onto the beach through large doors that open at the bow of the ship. They can do this only after the beach has been secured.

lines of communication   Air, land, or sea routes that connect combat forces with their source of supply, usually a local depot, but also the routes that connect far-flung forces with support from their home country. Without secure lines of communication, forces become ineffective over time because they cannot be resupplied with food, ammunition, or fuel to continue fighting. After the Japanese cut the American line of communication to the United States, the troops at Bataan and Corregidor became ineffective and were forced to surrender. In the same way, the United States used submarines to threaten Japan's lines of communication to its sources of supply in the southwest Pacific by sinking cargo ships. General MacArthur bypassed the Japanese base at Rabaul, effectively cutting off its lines of communication and leaving tens of thousands of troops stranded and ineffective. In military operations, commanders always seek to protect their own lines of communication while threatening the enemy's. Air or ground attacks to destroy bridges, road junctions, trails, or rail lines were critical to limit the enemy's ability to resupply its own forces; these lines of communication often became the focus of military operations.

logistics   All activities that supply and sustain combat forces. Logistics involves the acquisition, storage, transportation, distribution, maintenance, and repair of every single item used in war. Logistics planning is crucial to the success of combat operations. Sufficient stockpiles are needed to support the initial action; then forces must be resupplied and sustained sufficiently to maintain the level of action required to defeat the enemy. The heroic logistics effort to provide support to both Chinese forces as well as to maintain Fourteenth Air Force operations in China by using cargo aircraft to fly every item required over the Himalaya Mountains ("the Hump") is legendary. Logistics storage sites and depots and the means of transportation (rail, air, water, vehicle, or animal) were considered critical targets for air attack. Damaging or destroying these limited the effectiveness of the enemy. Much of the effort of Ninth Air Force in December and January of 1945 was the attack on supply depots and lines of communication deep in Germany to limit the effectiveness of German forces fighting in the Bulge.

LST (Landing Ship, Tank)   A large flat-bottomed assault vessel used in amphibious operations. The LST was over 300 feet long, had a large open deck and two large doors at the bow, which opened to allow a ramp to be dropped on the beach. This allowed the vehicles, troops, or cargo to be landed directly onto the beach. An LST could carry 17 tanks or 100 troops. Over 1,000 were built during the war and were an essential factor in both the ETO and the Pacific in achieving victory.

machine gun   A weapon that loads, chambers, fires, extracts, and reloads a cartridge automatically. Machine guns provide a sustained rate of high-volume fire to suppress or destroy enemy personnel, vehicles, or aircraft. Heavy machine guns fire a large-caliber cartridge (.50-caliber) with heavy barrels to maintain a high volume of fire. They have a crew of two or three and require the use of a tripod or must be mounted on a vehicle or boat. Light machine guns can be carried by one man and fired from a variety of positions. These guns had magazines holding 20 or more rounds of ammunition. They were used to support the movement of infantry in close combat. Other machine guns were supported by a crew of two or three, were fired from a bipod, and fed by a linked belt of ammunition. German forces especially employed these types of machine gun quite effectively.

mine   An explosive device buried in or placed on the ground that is detonated by pressure or by a tripwire. Mines are designated as anti-tank or anti-personnel. Anti-tank mines are intended to damage or destroy armored vehicles, while anti-personnel mines are employed to kill or wound enemy troops. Mines are used to block approaches to vulnerable points, limit the use of roads, or to channel enemy forces into vulnerable open areas where they can be engaged with machine gun or artillery fire. Naval mines, like land mines, were intended to delay an attacking force and put enemy forces in a vulnerable position for attack. Naval mines were usually contact type, anchored to the sea floor at a certain depth so that ships or landing craft would run into them. Other naval mines were acoustic and detonated when the sound of a ship's engine or propeller reached a certain level, marking the ship as close enough to cause damage.

marines   Naval infantry forces trained, organized, and equipped for amphibious warfare. The United States Marines fought as light infantry upon landing on a beachhead.

mulberry   The codeword for an artificial port established off the Normandy beaches to allow the rapid unloading of cargo from ships to the beaches.

motor torpedo boats   Known as PT (patrol torpedo) boats in the U.S. Navy and E-boats in Germany Navy (Kriegsmarine). These were fast, light boats armed with two or four torpedoes, machine guns, and antiaircraft guns. They were used for raids, night attacks on shipping, and patrolling.

mortar   A weapon designed to launch a high-explosive projectile at a high angle. Mortars are classified as light or heavy and each is composed of a smooth barrel, a base plate that provides stability for the barrel, a bipod, and an aiming sight. Light mortars (60 millimeter) are man portable and require a crew of two or three men. Like machine guns, these mortars provide fire support during close combat and are found at the company level. Mortars of higher caliber (81 millimeter or larger) are also crew served, but are transported by vehicle (or by pack animal as used by Merrill's Marauders and the Mars Task Force in Burma). These heavy mortars are found in infantry battalions. Mortars are easy to operate, have a high rate of fire, and are quickly put into action. They provide infantry companies and battalions with their own light artillery to suppress enemy troops in the attack or defense.

napalm   A jellied incendiary developed in the United States and used in bombs and as fuel for flamethrowers. Napalm was used effectively against troops, light vehicles, and concrete defensive positions.

oka   Japanese rocket missile piloted by one man and launched from an aircraft. Used in kamikaze attacks on U.S. ships during the Okinawa campaign.

operational/operations   This term describes the level of warfare between the strategic and tactical level. At the operational level of war, commanders are concerned with campaigns and the movement and actions of fleets, squadrons, corps, and divisions. For example, the Reno series of plans developed by General MacArthur's staff or the Granite plans developed by Admiral Nimitz's staff are all operational-level plans. At the strategic level, army groups or strategic air forces are the focus. In the ETO, Eisenhower directed the 12th and 21st Army Groups as Supreme Allied Commander. General Arnold directed the actions of the Twentieth Air Force in attacking strategic-level targets in Japan.

operational control   The command authority to organize and to employ subordinate forces as the commander deems necessary to accomplish assigned tasks.

psychological warfare   The use of information and ideas (either true or false) to influence the emotions, behaviors, or attitudes of a target audience to further the objectives of the sponsor. During the war, especially in the ETO, Eighth Air Force aircraft regularly dropped leaflets, small pieces of paper containing messages, often with information about Allied progress, directed at civilian populations in occupied France, Belgium, and the Netherlands to counter the false information broadcast by the Germans. Other leaflets were targeted at German soldiers to encourage surrender. In the last stages of the war with Japan, bombers dropped leaflets warning the civilian population to leave the cities or face destruction. Other leaflets were dropped informing the Japanese population about the effect of the atomic bombs dropped on Hiroshima and Nagasaki.

radar   A term formed from the words *radio detection and ranging*. Developed in the 1930s, this is a system that transmits electromagnetic energy and absorbs the reflection of that energy to determine range and position of objects either on the ground, on the sea, or in the air. During World War II it was used to locate ships and aircraft, locate targets for bombers, and as an aid in navigation.

Rangers   American light infantry trained, organized, and equipped for raids and attacks. These elite forces eventually grew to six battalions and served in Sicily, Italy, and in the ETO. One of the most famous Ranger operations was the attack on Pointe-du-Hoc at the Normandy beachhead on June 6, 1944.

reconnaissance   A specific mission tasked to ground or air forces to gain information about the enemy or to collect specific geographical, hydrological, or meteorological information about an area of interest.

regiment   A ground force unit, usually subordinate to a division (and the equivalent to a brigade), consisting of three or four battalions. U.S. Army units were often identified as regiments, even if they were not often employed as regiments in combat. Sometimes units fought as regimental combat teams (RCT), three infantry battalions combined with artillery, engineers, and other support units and tailored to a specific mission. RCTs were common in the Pacific. U.S. cavalry units (the 1st Cavalry Division in the Pacific, for example) fought as regiments.

squadron A designation for air force units subordinate to a group. They were classified as bomber, fighter, or reconnaissance squadrons.

strategy The art and science of employing a nation's political, economic, psychological, diplomatic, and military capabilities to achieve long-term goals during peace and war.

submarine A boat designed for operations underwater. In World War II, submarines used diesel engines for propulsion and could operate on electric power, but battery capacity forced submarines to surface and run their diesel engines to recharge the batteries. This made them vulnerable to attack. Most submarines attacked targets on the surface during darkness and at short ranges. They were armed with deck guns to support surface attacks, and usually submerged to approach targets and escape pursuit.

tactical Applies to actions of units at the brigade level or lower for ground forces, squadron level and below for air forces, and at the detachment, squadron, or individual ship level for naval forces.

tactical control The command authority allowing detailed and local direction of a force to accomplish a specific task.

tank A tracked armored fighting vehicle used as the principal assault weapon for armored or infantry forces. Tanks are classified as light, medium, and heavy depending on armor protection, weight, and size of their main gun. Light tanks were fast and lightly armored and had small-caliber guns. They were used mainly for reconnaissance and jungle fighting. Medium tanks had mobility, moderate armor protection,

and medium-caliber guns. Most American tanks in World War II were medium tanks, and the M4 Sherman was the dominant medium tank. Heavy tanks carried thick armor, had limited mobility but powerful, large-caliber main guns.

tank destroyer An armored fighting vehicle used to defeat enemy armor. American tank destroyers were lightly armored with high-velocity guns and had open turrets, making them vulnerable to artillery fire. Their light armor also limited their ability to engage enemy tanks in the open.

target of opportunity A target not previously identified that is within range and engaged.

task force A temporary grouping of units under one commander for a specific task. In the U.S. Navy, this most often involved grouping components of a fleet into task forces to accomplish specific missions. Admiral Marc Mitscher's carrier task force, Task Force 58, is one of the best known. A task group or task unit is a further subdivision of a task force used for independent operations from the task force and designated by an additional numeral added after the parent task force's number.

theater of war or theater of operations A designated area of air, land, and water that allows the conduct of operational or strategic level military activities to accomplish a specified strategic task. The Southwest Pacific Area and European theater of operations are examples. In 1940 the U.S. War Department described the term theater of operations as "the land and sea areas to be invaded or defended, including areas necessary for administrative activities incident to the military operations."

torpedo A self-propelled, cylindrical, underwater steel projectile with a high-explosive warhead, used against surface ships and submarines. Torpedoes could be launched by aircraft or submarines.

troop A small unit of cavalry or tanks equivalent to a company. Even though they no longer had horses, units of the 1st Cavalry Division in the Pacific maintained their original designations for company-level units as troops.

U-boat   From the German word *Unterseeboot*. A German submarine.

unconditional surrender   A capitulation of the enemy in which all resistance ceases and the nation submits to the victor without any terms or conditions.

V-1 and V-2   The V-1 was a pilotless flying bomb launched from a ramp or by aircraft. It carried a 1,875-pound warhead and used a pulse-jet engine guided by a gyroscope on automatic pilot. The entire missile weighed 4,800 pounds and traveled at speeds near 400 miles per hour. At a predetermined time of flight, the fuel would be expended (usually between 10 and 125 miles) and the bomb would drop. Targeted at London, they were intended to cause terror and weaken civilian morale. About 10,000 of these bombs were fired at England; about 7,400 reached the coast. Of these, nearly 4,000 were shot down before causing any damage. The 3,500 that did hit London, Manchester, Southampton, and Portsmouth caused a total of 24,000 casualties.

The V-2 was a ballistic rocket over 46 feet long, carrying a 2,150-pound warhead and powered by alcohol and liquid oxygen. It had a preset guidance system and was able to travel at speeds reaching 3,600 miles per hour; it had a maximum range of 200 miles. It was first tested in 1942 and its first actual use was in September 1944. About 900 V-2 rockets were directed at Antwerp, and over 1,000 were fired at England, about half of these landing on London. Over 2,700 people were killed between September 1944 and the end of March 1945.

Glossary of Abbreviations

AAF Army Air Forces

AAI Allied Armies in Italy

ABDA Australian-British-Dutch-American

AEAF Allied Expeditionary Air Force (ETO)

AFHQ Allied Forces Headquarters (Mediterranean)

AFPAC U.S. Army Forces in the Pacific

AMET Africa-Middle East Theater

AMMISCA American Military Mission to China

Amtrac Amphibious Tractor

Aus Australian

AVG American Volunteer Group (Flying Tigers, China)

CACW Chinese-American Composite Wing

CAI Chinese Army in India

CAM Composite Army-Marine

CATF Chinese Air Task Force

CBI China-Burma-India

CCA Combat Command A

CCB Combat Command B

CCC Combat Command C

CCS Combined Chiefs of Staff

CG Commanding General

CinC Commander in Chief

CINCPAC Commander in Chief, U.S. Pacific Fleet

CINCPOA Commander in Chief, Pacific Ocean Areas

COMAIRSOLS Commander, Air Forces Solomons

COMCENPAC Commander, Central Pacific

COMINCH/CominCh Commander in Chief

COMSOPAC Commander South Pacific

COSSAC Chief of Staff to the Supreme Allied Commander

CTF Commander Task Force

EAC Eastern Air Command (CBI)

ETOUSA European Theater of Operations, U.S. Army

FEAF Far East Air Force

FF Free French

FMF Fleet Marine Force

JCS Joint Chiefs of Staff

MAAF Mediterranean Allied Air Forces

MAC Marine Amphibious Corps

MATAF Mediterranean Allied Tactical Air Force

ME Middle East

MTOUSA Mediterranean Theater of Operations U.S. Army

NAAF Northwest African Air Force

NATO North African Theater of Operations

NCAC Northern Combat Area Command (Burma)

NEI Netherlands East Indies

NZ New Zealand

PA Philippine Army

PGC Persian Gulf Command

PGSC Persian Gulf Service Command

POA Pacific Ocean Areas

RAAF Royal Australian Air Force

RAF Royal Air Force

RCT Regimental Combat Team

SACMED Supreme Allied Commander Mediterranean

SAF Strategic Air Force

SEAC Southeast Asia Command

SHAEF Supreme Headquarters, Allied Expeditionary Force

SOPAC Southern Pacific

SSF Special Service Force

SWPA Southwest Pacific Area

TAF Tactical Air Force

TF Task Force

U.K. United Kingdom

U.S./US United States

USA United States Army

USAAF United States Army Air Force

USAFFE United States Army Forces Far East

USAFICPA United States Army Forces in the Central Pacific Area

USAFIME United States Army Forces in the Middle East

USAFISPA United States Army Forces in the South Pacific Area

USFIP United States Army Forces in the Philippines

USMC United States Marine Corps

USN United States Navy

USSAFE United States Strategic Air Forces in Europe

USSR Union of Soviet Socialist Republics

USSTAF United States Strategic Air Forces

VAC V Amphibious Corps

WDAF Western Desert Air Force

WEAPONS

AIRCRAFT

Brewster F2A-3 Buffalo

Type: fighter
Crew: one
Armament: four .50-caliber machine guns
Performance
    Range: 965 miles (1,553 km)
    Cruise Speed: 161 MPH (259 km/hr.)
    Max Speed: 321 MPH (516 km/hr.)
    Climb: 2,290 ft./min. (697.96 m/min.)
    Ceiling: 33,200 ft. (10,119 m)

Grumman F4F-4 Wildcat

Type: fighter
Crew: one
Armament: six .50-caliber machine guns
Performance
    Range: 770 miles (1,239 km)
    Cruise Speed: 155 MPH (249 km/hr.)
    Max Speed: 318 MPH (512 km/hr.)
    Climb: 1,950 ft./min. (594.33 m/min.)
    Ceiling: 34,800 ft. (10,607 m)

Vought F4U Corsair

Type: fighter
Crew: one
Armament: six .50-caliber machine guns
Performance
    Range: 1,005 miles (1,618 km)
    Max Speed: 446 MPH (718 km/hr.)
    Climb: 3,870 ft./min. (1,179.52 m/min.)
    Ceiling: 41,500 ft. (12,649 m)

An F4U corsair supporting marines on Okinawa. The fighter had a top speed of 481 miles per hour and was armed with six .50-caliber machine guns and four 20 millimeter cannon. It had a range of 1,015 miles. This was the first American fighter plane that could match the Japanese Zero fighter.

Grumman F6F-3 Hellcat

Type: fighter
Crew: one
Armament: six .50-caliber machine guns

Performance
Range: 945 miles (1,521 km)
Cruise Speed: 168 MPH (270 km/hr.)
Max Speed: 380 MPH (611 km/hr.)
Climb: 2,980 ft./min. (908.26 m/min.)
Ceiling: 37,300 ft. (11,368 m)

General Motors FM-2 Wildcat

Type: single-seat carrier-based fighter
Crew: one
Armament: four .50-caliber machine guns; optional, two 250-lb. bombs or six/five-inch rockets

Performance
Range: 900 miles (1,448 km)
Cruise Speed: 164 MPH (264 km/hr.)
Max Speed: 332 MPH (534 km/hr.) at 28,800 ft.
Ceiling: 34,700 ft. (10,575 m)

Lockheed P-38 D Lightning

Type: fighter
Crew: one
Armament: one 20 mm cannon, four .50-caliber machine guns

Performance
Range: 500 miles (805 km)
Cruise Speed: 300 MPH (483 km/hr.)
Max Speed: 390 MPH (628 km/hr.)
Climb: 2,500 ft./min. (761.96 m/min.)
Ceiling: 39,000 ft. (11,887 m)

Bell P-39 Airacobra

Type: fighter
Crew: one
Armament: one 37 mm T9 cannon two .50-caliber machine guns four .30-caliber machine guns

Performance
Range: 350 miles (563 km)
Max Speed: 360 MPH (579 km/hr.)
Climb: 2,550 ft./min. (777.2 m/min.)
Ceiling: 31,900 ft. (9,722.6 m)

The P-39 Airacobra fighter was armed with a 37-millimeter cannon, two .50-caliber machine guns, and four 7.62-millimeter machine guns. It had a maximum range of 650 miles and a top speed of 386 miles per hour.

Curtiss P-40 E Kittyhawk

Type: fighter
Crew: one
Armament: six .50-caliber machine guns

Performance
Range: 850 miles (1,368 km)
Cruise Speed: 235 MPH (378 km/hr.)
Max Speed: 362 MPH (582 km/hr.)
Ceiling: 30,000 ft. (9,143.6 m)

Republic P-47 Thunderbolt

Type: fighter
Crew: one
Armament: six or eight .50-caliber machine guns

Performance
Range: 800 miles (1,297 km)
Cruise Speed: 300 MPH (483 km/hr.)
Max Speed: 467 MPH (762 km/hr.)
Ceiling: 43,000 ft. (13,105 m)

North American P-51 D Mustang

Type: fighter
Crew: one
Armament: six .50-caliber machine guns

Ground support personnel rearm a P-47 Thunderbolt fighter with .50-caliber ammunition. The P-47 mounted eight .50-caliber machine guns.

The B-17 heavy bomber carried a crew of 10 and a maximum of 7,983 pounds of bombs. It had a maximum range of 2,000 miles with a 6,000-pound bomb load.

Performance
    Range: 1,000 miles (1,610 km)
    Cruise Speed: 275 MPH (442 km/hr.)
    Max Speed: 437 MPH (703 km/hr.)
    Ceiling: 41,900 ft. (12,770 m)

Northrop P-61 Black Widow

Type: fighter
Crew: three
Armament: four 20 mm cannon, four .50-caliber machine guns in a dorsal turret
Performance
    Range: 1,200 miles (1,932 km)
    Cruise Speed: 275 MPH (442 km/hr.)
    Max Speed: 425 MPH (684 km/hr.)
    Ceiling: 46,200 ft. (14,081 m)

Boeing B-17 Flying Fortress

Type: heavy bomber
Crew: 10: pilot, copilot, engineer, bombardier, radioman, five gunners
Armament: 13 .50-caliber machine guns (G model) up to 17,600 lbs. of bombs
Performance
    Range: 1,850 miles with 4,000 lb. bomb load
    Cruise Speed: 170 MPH (273 km/hr.)

    Max Speed: 300 MPH (483 km/hr.)
    Ceiling: 35,000 ft. (10,667 m)

Consolidated B-24 Liberator

Type: heavy Bomber
Crew: eight to 10
Armament: 10 .50-caliber machine guns up to 12,800 lbs. of bombs
D Model Performance
    Range: 2,300 miles with 5,000 pound bomb load
    Cruise Speed: 175 MPH (281.00 km/hr.)
    Max Speed: 303 MPH (487.00 km/hr.)
    Ceiling: 28,000 ft. (8,534.00 m)
L Model Performance
    Cruise Speed: 214.00 MPH (346 km/hr.)
    Max Speed: 299.00 MPH (483 km/hr.)
    Ceiling: 27,978.0 ft. (8,530 m)

North American B-25 Mitchell

Type: five-seat medium bomber
Crew: five
Armament: two to 18 .50-caliber machine guns up to 3,000 lbs. of bombs
B Model Performance
    Range: 1,200 miles (1,932 km)
    Cruise Speed: 230 MPH (370 km/hr.)

Max Speed: 275 MPH (442 km/hr.)
Ceiling: 25,000 ft. (7,619.6 m)
D Model Performance
   Range: 1,350 miles (2,173 km)
   Max Speed: 272 MPH (438 km/hr.)
   Ceiling: 24,200 ft. (7,375.80 m)

Martin B-26 G Marauder

Type: seven-seat medium bomber
Crew: seven
Armament: 11 .50-caliber machine guns
   up to 4,000 lbs. of bombs
Performance
   Range: 1,100 miles (1,771.00 km)
   Cruise Speed: 216 MPH (348 km/hr.)
   Max Speed: 285 MPH (458.00 km/hr.)
   Ceiling: 19,800 ft. (6,034.7 m)

Boeing B-29 Superfortress

Type: long-range strategic heavy bomber
Crew: 10: pilot, copilot, engineer, bombardier,
   radioman, five gunners
Armament: eight .50-caliber machine guns (two
   in each of four power turrets)
   three .50-caliber machine guns (or two .50-cal-
   iber and one 20 mm cannon) in the tail turret
   up to 20,000 lbs. of bombs
Performance
   Range: 3,250 miles (5,230 km)
   Cruise Speed: 230 MPH (370 km/hr.)

The B-26 Marauder was a medium bomber with a crew of seven and carried a 5,200-pound bomb load. It had a range of 675 miles.

The U.S. Navy's long-range patrol bomber, the Consolidated PB4Y-2, had a crew of 11 men and carried a maximum bomb load of 8,800 pounds. It had a maximum range of 2,800 miles.

Max Speed: 358 MPH (576 km/hr.)
Ceiling: 31,850 ft. (9,710 m)

Consolidated PB4Y-2 Privateer

Type: land-based maritime patrol bomber
Crew: four to five
Armament: 12 .50-caliber machine guns up to
   12,800 lbs. of bombs
Performance
   Range: 2,800 miles (4,506 km)
   Cruise Speed: 140 MPH (225 km/hr.)
   Max Speed: 237 MPH (381 km/hr.) at 13,750
   ft.
   Ceiling: 20,700 ft. (6,310 m)

Lockheed PV-1 Ventura

Type: patrol bomber
Crew: four to five
Armament: two forward firing .50-caliber
   machine guns
   two .50-caliber machine guns in dorsal turret
   two .30-caliber ventral machine guns
   six 500-lb. bombs or one torpedo in internal
   bomb bay
   up to two 1,000-lb. bombs external

The PV-1 Ventura navy patrol bomber was equipped with radar and had a 1,360-mile range and carried a bomb load of 3,000 pounds.

Performance
Range: 1,360 miles
Cruise Speed: 164 MPH
Max Speed: 312 MPH at 13,800 ft.
Ceiling: 26,300 ft.

Lockheed PV-2 Harpoon

Type: patrol bomber
Crew: four to five
Armament: five fixed forward firing .50-caliber machine guns
two flexible .50-caliber machine guns in dorsal turret
two flexible .50-caliber machine guns in ventral mount
six .30-caliber machine guns on flex mounts
up to four 1,000-lb. bombs in internal bomb bay
up to two 1,000-lb. bombs external
Performance
Range: 1,790 miles
Cruise Speed: 171 MPH
Max Speed: 282 MPH at 13,700 ft.
Ceiling: 23,900 ft.

Douglas A-20 Havoc

Type: light bomber
Crew: three

The A-20 Havoc light bomber carried a crew of three, a bomb load of 4,000 pounds, and had a range of over 1,000 miles.

Armament: seven .50-caliber machine guns
up to 4,000 lbs. of bombs
Performance
Range: over 1,000 miles (1,521 km)
Cruise Speed: 256 MPH (412 km/hr.)
Max Speed: 317 MPH (510 km/hr.)
Ceiling: 23,700 ft. (7,223.40 m)

Douglas A-26 C Invader

Type: attack/medium bomber
Crew: three
Armament: six .50-caliber machine guns, optionally eight more
up to 4,000 lbs. of bombs
Performance
Range: 1,400 miles (2,255 km)
Cruise Speed: 284 MPH (457 km/hr.)
Max Speed: 355 MPH (571 km/hr.)
Ceiling: 22,100 ft. (6,735 m)

Curtiss SB2C Helldiver

Type: two-seat carrier-based scout bomber
Crew: two (pilot and gunner)
Armament: two 20 mm cannon in wings, two .30-caliber machine guns in rear cockpit
Performance
Range: 1,165 miles (1,876 km)

Cruise Speed: 158 MPH (254 km/hr.)
Max Speed: 295 MPH (475 km/hr.)
Ceiling: 29,100 ft. (8,869 m)

Douglas SBD-4 Dauntless

Type: dive bomber/scout bomber
Crew: two (pilot and observer/rear gunner)
Armament: two .50-caliber machine guns firing forward, two .30-caliber machine guns in rear cockpit, up to 1,600 lbs. of bombs centerline, 650 lbs. more under wings
Performance
  Range: 950 miles (1,530 km)
  Cruise Speed: 173 MPH (278 km/hr.)
  Max Speed: 250 MPH (402 km/hr.)
  Climb: 1,700 ft./min. (518 m/min.)
  Ceiling: 26,000 ft. (7,780 m)

Douglas TBD-1 Devastator

Type: torpedo bomber
Crew: two (pilot and observer/rear gunner)
Armament: one .30-caliber machine gun firing forward, one .30-caliber machine gun in rear cockpit, one torpedo or one 1,000-lb. bomb
Performance
  Range: 716 miles (1,152 km)
  Cruise Speed: 128 MPH (206 km/hr.)
  Max Speed: 206 MPH (331 km/hr.)

The TBD-1 Devastator torpedo bomber carried one Mk 13 torpedo and a crew of two. Although the main torpedo bomber of its time prior to the war, it was slow, lightly armed, and had a limited range. Nevertheless, it played a major role in the Battle of the Coral Sea and the Battle of Midway.

Climb: 720 ft./min. (219.45 m/min.)
Ceiling: 19,500 ft. (5,943.3 m)

Grumman TBF-1 Avenger

Type: torpedo bomber
Crew: three (pilot, bombardier, radio operator/gunner)
Armament: two wing-mounted .50-caliber machine guns, one .50-caliber machine gun in dorsal turret, one .30-caliber machine gun in ventral position, up to 2,000 lbs. of weapons (bombs/torpedo)
Performance
  Range: 1,010 miles (1,626 km)
  Cruise Speed: 147 MPH (236 km/hr.)
  Max Speed: 276 MPH (444 km/hr.)
  Climb: 2,060 ft./min. (627.86 m/min.)
  Ceiling: 30,100 ft. (9,174.00 m)

Consolidated PBY-5A Catalina

Type: amphibious patrol bomber (flying boat)
Crew: seven
Armament: two .50-caliber machine guns three .30-caliber machine guns up to 4,000 lbs. of bombs or depth charges
Performance
  Range: 2,545 miles (4,096 km)
  Cruise Speed: 117 MPH (188 km/hr.) long-range cruise speed
  Max Speed: 179 MPH (288 km/hr.)
  Ceiling: 14,700 ft. (4,480 m)

Curtiss C-46 Commando

Type: 54-seat military transport and troop carrier
Crew: three (pilot, copilot, radio operator)
Armament: none
Performance
  Range: 1,200 miles (1,931 km)
  Cruise Speed: 183 MPH (295 km/hr.)
  Max Speed: 269 MPH (433 km/hr.) at 15,000 ft.
  Ceiling: 27,600 ft. (8,410 m)

Douglas C-47A Skytrain

Type: military transport and glider tug
Crew: three (pilot, copilot, radio operator)

The C-47 (a.k.a. C-47A) transport had a crew of three and a maximum range of 1,513 miles. It carried a maximum load of 7,000 pounds (paratroopers or cargo), although that limit was often exceeded.

Armament: none
Performance
    Range: 1,500 miles (2,414 km)
    Cruise Speed: 185 MPH (298 km/hr.) at 10,000 ft.
    Max Speed: 229 MPH (369 km/hr.) at 7,500 ft.
    Climb: 1,130 ft./min. (345 m/min.)
    Ceiling: 23,200 ft. (7,070 m)

Douglas C-54 Skymaster

Type: cargo and passenger transport
Crew: six
Armament: none
Performance
    Range: 3,900 miles (6,276 km)
    Cruise Speed: 239 MPH (385 km/hr.)
    Max Speed: 274 MPH (441 km/hr.) at 14,000 ft.
    Ceiling: 22,000 ft. (6,705 m)

GROUND FORCES

Tanks and Armored Vehicles

M3 General Stuart

Type: light tank
Crew: four

Armament: 37 mm gun, three .30-caliber machine guns
Performance
    Range: 70 miles (112 km)
    Max Speed: 36 MPH (58 km/hr.)

M4A3 Sherman

Type: medium tank
Crew: five
Armament: 75 mm gun (by 1944, 76 mm gun), two .30-caliber machine guns, one .50-caliber machine gun
Performance
    Range: 100 miles (160 km)
    Max Speed: 25 MPH (40 km/hr.)

M26 Pershing

Type: heavy tank
Crew: five
Armament: 90 mm gun, two .30-caliber machine guns, one .50-caliber machine gun
Performance
    Range: 110 miles (173 km)
    Max Speed: 30 MPH (48 km/hr.)

Halftrack M3

Type: personnel carrier
Crew: three
Armament: one .50-caliber machine gun
Capacity: 10 (seven infantrymen plus the crew)
Performance
    Range: 200 miles (321 km)
    Max Speed: 45 MPH (72 km/hr.)

Artillery

75 Millimeter Howitzer M1A1

Type: light or pack howitzer
Weight: 2,160 lbs.
Max Range: 9,760 yds. (8,925 km)

105 Millimeter Howitzer M2A1

Type: field howitzer
Weight: 4,260 lbs.
Max Range: 12,500 yds. (11,430 km)

155 Millimeter Howitzer M1917 and M1918A1

Type: medium howitzer
Weight: 22,550 lbs.
Max Range: 20,100 yds. (18,380 km)

Infantry Weapons

Automatic Pistol M1911A1

Caliber: .45
Weight: 2 lbs., 7 oz.
Feed System: seven-round magazine
System of Operation: feed system
Performance
    Effective Range: 82 feet (25 m)

Rifle M1 Garand

Caliber: .30
Weight: 9 lbs., 8 oz.
Feed System: eight-round clip-fed
System of Operation: semi-automatic, gas operated
Performance
    Effective Range: 500 yds. (457 m)
    Average Rate of Fire: 10–12 rounds per minute

Carbine M1/M2 (Selective fire: automatic or semiautomatic)

Caliber: .30
Weight: 5 lbs.
Feed System: 15-round detachable magazine
System of Operation: semi-automatic, gas operated
Performance
    Effective Range: 300 yds. (274 m)
    Average Rate of Fire: 30 rounds per minute (M2 on automatic: 650–700 rounds per minute)

Browning Automatic Rifle M1918A1 (semiautomatic)/M1918A2 (fully automatic)

Caliber: .30
Weight: 22 lbs.
Feed System: 20-round detachable magazine

System of Operation: air-cooled, gas-operated, shoulder-fired
Performance
    Effective Range: 600 yds. (548 m)
    Average Rate of Fire: 200 rounds per minute for the semiautomatic M1918A1. The M1918A2 could be fired in two automatic modes, the slow rate (300 to 450 rounds per minute) or fast rate (500 to 650 rounds per minute). Marines favored the semiautomatic M1918A1.

Thompson Submachine Gun M1/M1A1

Caliber: .45
Weight: 10 lbs., 2 oz.
Feed System: 20- or 30-round detachable magazine
System of Operation: selective fire (semi-automatic or automatic) blow-back system
Performance
    Effective Range: 50 yds. (45 m)
    Average Rate of Fire: 600 to 725 rounds per minute

Submachine Gun M3

Caliber: .45
Weight: 8 lbs., 15 oz.
Feed System: 30-round detachable magazine
System of Operation: automatic, blow-back system
Performance
    Effective Range: 50 yds. (45 m)
    Average Rate of Fire: 450 rounds per minute

Machine Guns

Browning Machine Gun M1917A1/ M1919A4/M1919A6

Caliber: .30
Weight: M1917A1: 93 lbs. M1919A4: 41 lbs. with tripod; M1919A6: 32.5 pounds with tripod
Feed System: all models: belt-fed, 250 rounds
System of Operation: Automatic, recoil system; M1917A1 was water-cooled. The M1919A4 and A6 models were air-cooled

Performance

Effective Range: M1917A1 and M1919A4: 1,100 yds.; M1919A6: 800 yds. (731 m)

Average Rate of Fire: M1917A1: 400–600 rounds per minute; M1919A4: 400–550 rounds per minute; M1919A6: 400–550 rounds per minute

Browning Machine Gun M2

Caliber: .50
Weight: 128 lbs. with tripod
Feed System: 110-round metallic linked belt
System of Operation: automatic, recoil system, air-cooled
Performance

Effective Range: 2,500 yds. (2,286 m)

Average Rate of Fire: 450–575 rounds per minute

Mortars

Mortar M2

Caliber: 60
Weight in Action: 42 lbs.
System of Operation: drop, fixed striker
Performance

Effective Range: 100 yds. (91 m) (minimum); 1,985 yds. (1,815 m) (maximum)

Average Rate of Fire: 18 rounds per minute (high-explosive only)

Mortar M1

Caliber: 81
Weight in Action: 136 lbs.
System of Operation: drop, fixed striker

Performance

Effective Range: 100 yds. (91 m); (minimum) to 3,290 yds. (3,008 m) (HE) or 2,470 yds. (smoke)

Average Rate of Fire: 18 rounds per minute (high-explosive, smoke)

Bazooka

Launcher, Rocket, Anti-tank M1

Caliber: 2.36 in.
Weight in Action: 13.25 lbs.
System of Operation: electric
Performance

Effective Range: 400 yds. (365 m) (maximum); 120 yds. (107 m) maximum effective range

Armor Penetration: up to five inches of armor

Grenades

MarkIIA1 Fragmentation Grenade

Length: 4.5 in.
Weight: 1.3 lbs.
Filling: smokeless powder flakes
Body: serrated cast iron
Fuse: 4–5-second delay. The grenade could be thrown or launched by a rifle using an adapter.

MarkIIIA2 Fragmentation Grenade

Length: 5.35 in.
Weight: 14 oz.
Filling: TNT
Body: fiberboard
Fuse: 4.5-second delay. The grenade relies on blast rather than fragmentation for effect. Used for clearing buildings and fortified positions.

APPENDIX I

SHIP AND LANDING CRAFT CLASSIFICATIONS

U.S. NAVY SHIP CLASSIFICATION SYMBOLS

BB	Battleship
BBc	Coastal Battleship
BC	Battle Cruiser
CA	Heavy Cruiser
CL	Light Cruiser
CL(AA)	Light Cruiser (Antiaircraft)
CM	Minelayer
CMc	Coastal Minelayer
CV	Aircraft Carrier (Fleet)
CVE	Aircraft Carrier (Escort)
CVL	Aircraft Carrier (Light)
CVS	Aircraft Carrier (Seaplane)
CX	Armed Merchant Cruiser
DD	Destroyer
DE	Destroyer Escort
DM	Light Minelayer
DMS	Fast Minesweeper (Destroyer)
SM	Submarine (Mine Laying)
SS	Submarine

LANDING CRAFT CLASSIFICATIONS

LCC	Landing Craft, Control
LCI	Landing Craft, Infantry
LCI(G)	Landing Craft, Infantry (Gunboat)
LCI(L)	Landing Craft, Infantry (Large)
LCI(M)	Landing Craft, Infantry (Mortar)
LCI(R)	Landing Craft, Infantry (Rocket)
LCM	Landing Craft, Mechanized
LCP(L)	Landing Craft, Personnel (Large)
LCP(R)	Landing Craft, Personnel (Ramp)
LCR(L)	Landing Craft, Rubber (Large)
LCS(L)	Landing Craft, Support (Large)
LCS(S)	Landing Craft, Support (Small)
LCT	Landing Craft, Tank
LCV	Landing Craft, Vehicle
LCVP	Landing Craft, Vehicle & Personnel
LSV	Landing Ship, Vehicle
LSD	Landing Ship, Dock
LSM	Landing Ship, Medium
LSM(R)	Landing Ship, Medium (Rocket)
LST	Landing Ship, Tank
LVT	Landing Vehicle, Tracked
LVT(A)	Landing Vehicle, Tracked (Armored)
LVT(G)	Landing Vehicle, Tracked (Gunboat)
LVT(L)	Landing Vehicle, Tracked (Large)
LVT(M)	Landing Vehicle, Tracked (Mortar)
LVT(R)	Landing Vehicle, Tracked (Rocket)

APPENDIX II

COMMANDS

Theater Commands

China-Burma-India Theater of Operations

Established in March 1942

Commander: March 1942–October 1944: General Joseph W. Stilwell

October 1944 to 1945: Major General Albert C. Wedemeyer

CBI was not a true theater of operations. Stilwell had operational control of the Northern Combat Area Command, a combined American and Chinese combat unit, but his role as commander in CBI was mostly in the administrative control of all U.S. forces in-theater. Operational control of forces nominally remained with Britain's Admiral Louis Mountbatten as commander of Southeast Asia Command. Stilwell, in his role as deputy commander of Southeast Asia Command, was often able to slip command boundaries. After Stilwell departed in October 1944, the China-Burma-India theater of operations was separated into the U.S. Forces, China theater, and U.S. Forces, India-Burman theater, commanded by Lieutenant General Daniel I. Sultan. General Wedemeyer took command of U.S. Forces, China theater. Wedemeyer also took over Stilwell's position as chief of staff to Generalissimo Chiang Kai-shek.

European Theater of Operations

Established in England in June 1942

Commanded by Major General Eisenhower as the European theater of operations U.S. Army (ETOUSA). He gave up command of ETOUSA in February 1943 to command Operation Torch, the invasion of North Africa. In January 1944 he resumed command of ETOUSA, and in February he became the Supreme Allied Commander of the Allied Expeditionary Force (SHAEF). SHAEF was an operational command and ETOUSA the administrative command, and both were under Eisenhower until the end of the war. Under SHAEF, Eisenhower commanded the U.S. 12th Army Group (General Omar N. Bradley) and the British 21st Army Group (Field Marshal Bernard Montgomery), and after September 1944, the U.S. 6th Army Group (General Jacob L. Devers).

Mediterranean Theater of Operations

The Mediterranean theater of operations evolved from the North African theater command structure. It had been established for Operation Torch, the invasion of North Africa, and when the decision was made by Roosevelt and Churchill to extend Allied operations into Italy, a new command was established under British authority with American armies and air force units subordinate.

Southwest Pacific Area

Established April 1942
Commander 1942–1945: General Douglas MacArthur

Pacific Ocean Areas

Established April 1942
Commander 1942–1945: Admiral Chester W. Nimitz.

Central Pacific Ocean Area

Established April 1942
Commander 1942–1945: Admiral Chester W. Nimitz.

There were two commands subordinate to Nimitz:

South Pacific Area

Established April 1942
Commander June 1942–October 1942: Vice Admiral Robert L. Ghormley
Commander October 1942–June 1944: Admiral William F. Halsey

North Pacific Area

Established April 1942
Commander January 1943–October 1943: Vice Admiral Thomas C. Kinkaid
Commander October 1943–1945: Vice Admiral Frank Jack Fletcher

Navy Fleets Prior to the War

Atlantic Fleet
Pacific Fleet
Asiatic Fleet (dissolved in June 1942)

Numbered Fleets

Third Fleet

Established March 1943 and under operational control of Commander, Central Pacific, September 1944 to January 1945, and from May 1945 to September 1945.
Commander 1943–1945: Admiral William F. Halsey

Fourth Fleet

Established March 1943 and subordinate to Atlantic Fleet

Fifth Fleet

Established April 1944 and under operational control of Commander, Central Pacific, April to September 1944 and January to May 1945.
Commander 1943–1945: Admiral Raymond A. Spruance

Seventh Fleet

Established February 1943 and under command of General MacArthur
Commander November 1943–1945: Vice Admiral Thomas C. Kinkaid

Tenth Fleet

Established in March 1943 as a shore-based headquarters to direct antisubmarine operations along the Atlantic coast.
Commanded by Admiral Ernest J. King, 1943–1945.

Theater Air Force Commanders

Commander in Chief Far East Air Forces

Established in June 1944 to coordinate the operations of the Fifth and the Thirteenth Air Forces (later the Seventh Air Force as well)
Commander: Lieutenant General George C. Kenney

Commander in Chief Army Air Forces Pacific Ocean Areas

Established in August 1944 under command of Lieutenant General M. F. Harmon

Commander in Chief U.S. Strategic Air Forces Pacific

Established in June 1945 to oversee the operations of the Twentieth Air Force and the Eighth Air Force arriving from Europe.
Commander: Lieutenant General Carl Spaatz

Numbered Air Forces

Fifth Air Force

Established in February 1942 from the Philippine Department Air Force and supported General MacArthur in Southwest Pacific Area.

Sixth Air Force

Established February 1942 to defend the Panama Canal

Seventh Air Force

Established February 1942 to defend Hawaii, then redeployed its forces to conduct combat operations in the Central Pacific.

Eighth Air Force

Formed in January 1942 and deployed to England. Conducted strategic bombing of Germany and occupied Europe. Eighth Air Force grew to contain 40 heavy bomber groups, 15 fighter groups, and four specialized support groups. In February 1944, strategic bombers of the VIII Bomber Command were redesignated Eighth Air Force, while Eighth Air Force headquarters was redesignated U.S. Strategic Air Forces in Europe and combined with Fifteenth Air Force to coordinate strategic bombing efforts throughout Europe.

Ninth Air Force

The U.S. Army Middle East Air Force was redesignated as Ninth Air Force in November 1942 and supported operations in North Africa and the Mediterranean until October 1943, when it became part of the European theater of operations to support the Allied invasion of Europe. It supported the advance of the American armies until the end of the war.

Tenth Air Force

Formed in February 1942 and operated in China, Burma, and India until March 1943. With the activation of the Fourteenth Air Force, Tenth Air Force remained responsible for Burma and India. In July 1945 it became part of Fourteenth Air Force to support operations in China.

Eleventh Air Force

Formed in February 1942 to defend Alaska but also conducted offensive operations against Japanese positions in the Aleutian and the Kurile Islands.

Thirteenth Air Force

Established in December 1942 and served in the South Pacific and Southwest Pacific area in support of MacArthur and Halsey.

Fourteenth Air Force

Established in March of 1943 and supported operations in China throughout the war.

Fifteenth Air Force

Established in November of 1943 and subordinate to the Mediterranean Strategic Air Force under Mediterranean Allied Air Forces. It conducted bombing operations from southern Italy to destroy gasoline production and aircraft production facilities in southern Europe.

Twentieth Air Force

Established in April 1944 to conduct strategic bombing of Japan from China. Because of limitations in logistics support, the Twentieth redeployed to the Mariana Islands in July

1945 and conducted attacks on the Japanese home islands, ending in the use of atomic bombs in August.

Army Groups ETO

12th Army Group (General Omar N. Bradley)
First Army (attached to Montgomery's 21st Army Group temporarily during Battle of the Bulge, December 1944 to January 1945)
Third Army
Ninth Army (attached to Montgomery's 21st Army Group from October 1944 until April 1945)
Fifteenth Army

6th Army Group (General Jacob L. Devers)
Seventh Army
French First Army

Army Group–MTO

15th Army Group
U.S. Fifth Army
British Eighth Army
In December 1944, Lieutenant General Mark W. Clark became commander 15th Army Group. Up to that time, the Army Group had been under British command.

Armies

First Army

In existence since 1933. Deployed to England in October 1943 under General Omar N. Bradley to prepare for the Normandy invasion. In August 1944 General Courtney H. Hodges took command of the army until the end of the war.

Third Army

In existence since 1932. Deployed to England in January 1944. Operational in July 1944 and commanded by General George S. Patton until the end of the war.

Fifth Army

Activated in Algiers in January 1943 for administrative support and training of U.S. Army troops in North Africa. In September 1943 it landed at Salerno and served in Italy as part of 15th Army Group until the end of the war. Under command of General Mark W. Clark to November 1944, then under General Lucian K. Truscott until the end of the war.

Sixth Army

Activated in January 1943 and arrived in the Pacific in April 1943 under command of Lieutenant General Walter Krueger. From April 1943 to September 1944 it was known as the Alamo Task Force and conducted most of the offensive operations in MacArthur's New Guinea campaign.

Seventh Army

Activated in July 1943 for the invasion of Sicily. It was subordinate to 15th Army Group until September 1944. In August it landed in southern France (Operation Dragoon) and came under the operational control of 6th Army Group. General George S. Patton commanded the army from July 1943 to January 1944; General Mark W. Clark commanded until March 1944 (while simultaneously serving as Fifth Army commander); it was under the command of General Alexander M. Patch until the end of the war.

Eighth Army

Activated in June 1944 and arrived in September in the Southwest Pacific area. It was commanded by General Robert L. Eichelberger throughout its wartime service.

Ninth Army

Activated in April 1944 and arrived in England in June. It became operational in France in October 1944 and was commanded by Lieutenant General William H. Simpson until the end of the war.

Tenth Army

Activated in the Pacific in June 1944 and landed on Okinawa in April 1945. It was commanded by General Simon B. Buckner until he was killed on Okinawa; then under temporary command of General Roy S. Geiger (USMC) until July, when General Joseph W. Stilwell took command.

Fifteenth Army

Activated in January 1945 to support rear area security and transition operations in occupied German territory. Under command of General Leonard T. Gerow.

Marine Corps

III Amphibious Corps

Established in October 1942 as I Amphibious Corps, then redesignated in April 1944.

Responsible for operations in the South Pacific.

V Amphibious Corps

Established in September 1943 from Amphibious Corps Pacific Fleet. Responsible for operations in the Central Pacific.

Commander in Chief Aircraft, Fleet Marine Forces Pacific

In September 1944 Marine Aircraft Wing Pacific was redesignated as Fleet Marine Forces Pacific with the responsibility for all marine aircraft in-theater.

APPENDIX III

COMPOSITION OF DIVISIONS

Composition of a U.S. Infantry Division in 1943 (also Marine Corps)

14,253 officers and men
243 Browning Automatic Rifles
157 medium machine guns
236 heavy machine guns
144 mortars (60 and 81 millimeter)
557 bazookas
2,012 vehicles

Division Units

Reconnaissance Troop
Three Infantry Regiments (each with three infantry battalions)
Anti-tank Company
Cannon Company (six 105 millimeter howitzers)
Three Artillery Battalions (each with 12 105 millimeter howitzers)
Medium Artillery battalion (12 155 millimeter howitzers)
Engineer Battalion
Signal Company

Composition of a U.S. Armored Division in 1943

10,937 officers and men
465 medium machine guns
404 heavy machine guns
93 mortars (60 and 81 millimeter)
77 light tanks
186 medium tanks
501 halftracks
2,653 vehicles

Division Units

Reconnaissance Battalion
Three Tank Battalions (53 medium tanks and 17 light tanks)
Three Armored Infantry Battalions (71 halftracks)
Three Artillery Battalions (18 105 millimeter self-propelled howitzers)
Engineer Battalion
Signal Company

Composition of a U.S. Airborne Division in 1942

8,505 officers and men
54 Browning Automatic Rifles
187 medium machine guns
105 heavy machine guns
111 mortars (60 and 81 millimeter)
182 bazookas
27 flamethrowers
36 75 millimeter pack howitzers
385 trucks

Division Units

One Parachute Regiment (three parachute infantry battalions)

Two Glider Infantry Regiments (three battalions each of infantry)
Airborne Antiaircraft Battalion (24 37 millimeter guns)
Airborne Engineer Battalion
Airborne Signal Company

Composition of a U.S. Marine Corps Division in 1944

17,465 officers and men
853 Browning Automatic Rifles
464 medium machine guns
161 heavy machine guns
153 Mortars (60 and 81 millimeter)
267 flamethrowers
172 bazookas
24 75 millimeter pack howitzers
36 105 millimeter howitzers
46 medium tanks
1,056 vehicles

Division Units

Tank Battalion
Three Infantry Regiments (each with three infantry battalions and a weapons company)
Artillery Regiment (two battalions of 105 millimeter howitzers and one battalion of 75 millimeter howitzers)
Engineer Battalion
Pioneer Company
Amphibious Tractor Battalions (three or four battalions attached for amphibious landings)

APPENDIX IV

U.S. GROUND COMBAT UNITS
BY DIVISION AND REGIMENT

No marking by division number—the division served only in the ETO.
Division served in Italy.
+ Division served in North Africa.
× Division participated in the invasion of Sicily.
* Division served in the Pacific.
~ Division landed in southern France (Operation Dragoon) and joined the ETO.

INFANTRY DIVISION	INFANTRY REGIMENT	INFANTRY REGIMENT	INFANTRY REGIMENT
1+× To ETO in June 1944	16	18	26
2	9	23	38
3+×#~	7	15	30
4	8	12	22
5	2	10	11
6*	1	20	63
7*	17	32	184
8	13	28	121
9+× To ETO in June 1944	39	47	60
10 Mtn#	85	86	87
24*	19	21	34
25*	27	35	161
26	101	104	328
27*	105	106	165
28	109	110	112
29	115	116	175
30	117	119	120
31*	124	155	167
32*	126	127	128
33*	123	130	136

INFANTRY DIVISION	INFANTRY REGIMENT	INFANTRY REGIMENT	INFANTRY REGIMENT
34+#	133	135	168
35	134	137	320
36+#~	141	142	143
37*	129	145	148
38*	149	151	152
40*	108	160	185
41*	162	163	186
42	22	232	242
43*	103	169	172
44	71	114	324
45x#~	157	179	180
63	253	254	255
65	259	260	261
66	262	263	264
69	271	272	273
70	274	275	276
71	5	14	66
75	289	290	291
76	304	385	417
77*	305	306	307
78	309	310	311
79	313	314	315
80	317	318	319
81*	321	322	323
83	329	330	331
84	333	334	335
85#	337	338	339
86	341	342	343
87	345	346	347
88#	349	350	351
89	353	354	355
90	357	358	359
91#	361	362	363
92#	365	370	371
93*	25	368	369
94	301	302	376
95	377	378	379
96*	381	382	383
97	303	386	387
99	393	394	395
100	397	398	399
102	405	406	407
103	409	410	411
104	413	414	415
106	422	423	424
Americal*	132	164	182

ARMORED DIVISION	ARMORED REGIMENT	ARMORED REGIMENT	ARMORED INFANTRY REGIMENT
2+× To ETO in 1943	66	67	41
3	32	33	36

These divisions remained under the 1942 organization throughout the war, with two armored regiments and one armored infantry regiment

ARMORED DIVISION	TANK BATTALION	TANK BATTALION	TANK BATTALION	ARMORED INFANTRY BATTALION	ARMORED INFANTRY BATTALION	ARMORED INFANTRY BATTALION
1+#	1	4	3	6	11	14
4	8	35	37	10	51	53
5	10	34	81	15	46	47
6	15	68	69	9	44	50
7	17	31	40	23	38	48
8	18	36	80	7	49	58
9	2	14	19	27	52	60
10	3	11	21	20	54	61
11	22	41	42	21	55	63
12	23	43	714	17	56	66
13	24	45	46	16	59	67
14	25	47	48	19	62	68
16	5	16	26	18	64	69
20	9	20	27	8	65	70

CAVALRY DIVISION	1ST CAVALRY BRIGADE REGIMENTS	2ND CAVALRY BRIGADE REGIMENTS
1*	5 and 12	7 and 8

Total strength: 12,724

AIRBORNE DIVISION	GLIDER INFANTRY REGIMENT	GLIDER INFANTRY REGIMENT	PARACHUTE INFANTRY REGIMENT	PARACHUTE INFANTRY REGIMENT
11a*	187	188	511	
11b	187		511	588
17 a	193	194		513
17 b		194	507	513
82 a x# To ETO in March 1944	325		504	505
82 b	325		504	505
101 a	327	401	502	
101 b	327		502	506

a. This is the organization prior to March 1, 1945.

b. This is the unit organization after March 1, 1945. All units omitted were inactivated or disbanded on March 1, and all additional units listed were activated or assigned on that date.

MARINE CORPS DIVISION	MARINE REGIMENT	MARINE REGIMENT	MARINE REGIMENT
1	1	5	7
2	2	6	8
3	3	9	21
4	23	24	25
5	26	27	28
6	4	22	29

All marine divisions were assigned to the Pacific. Marine regiments are often designated by the regimental number and the title "Marines." Thus, the 1st Marines always refers to the 1st Marine Regiment. A marine division is always referred to as such, along with its division number: 1st Marine Division.

APPENDIX V

Losses: The Battle of the Atlantic

1941

Allied shipping sunk (thousands of tons): 4,398
U.S. and British new ship construction: 1,984
Net tonnage loss or gain: -2,414
U-boats sunk: 35

1942

Allied shipping sunk (thousands of tons): 8,245
U.S. and British new ship construction: 7,182
Net tonnage loss or gain: -1,063
U-boats sunk: 85

1943

Allied shipping sunk (thousands of tons): 3,661
U.S. and British new ship construction: 14,585
Net tonnage loss or gain: +10,974
U-boats sunk: 237

1944

Allied shipping sunk (thousands of tons): 1,422
U.S. and British new ship construction: 13,349
Net tonnage loss or gain: +11,927
U-boats sunk: 241

1945 (January to May)

Allied shipping sunk (thousands of tons): 458
U.S. and British new ship construction: 3,834
Net tonnage loss or gain: +3,378
U-boats sunk: 153

Totals for the war (1941–1945)

Allied shipping sunk (thousands of tons): 18,134
U.S. and British new ship construction: 40,934
Net tonnage loss or gain: +15,468
U-boats sunk: 751

APPENDIX VI

ENEMY AIRCRAFT DESTROYED BY THE ARMY AIR FORCE DURING WORLD WAR II

1942 (February to December)

Total enemy aircraft losses: 935
ETO kills: 327
MTO kills: 158
FEAF kills: 518
POA kills: 0
CBI kills: 53
Aleutian kills: 37

1943

Total enemy aircraft losses: 10,837
ETO kills: 3,865
MTO kills: 3,740
FEAF kills: 2,466
POA kills: 96
CBI kills: 636
Aleutian kills: 34

1944

Total enemy aircraft losses: 19,442
ETO kills: 10,425
MTO kills: 5,239
FEAF kills: 2,518
POA kills: 226
CBI kills: 772
Aleutian kills: 8
Twentieth Air Force kills: 254

1945 (January to August)

Total enemy aircraft losses: 8,477
ETO kills: 5,960
MTO kills: 291
FEAF kills: 416
POA kills: 472
CBI kills: 361
Aleutian kills: 6
Twentieth Air Force kills: 971

Totals for the war

Total enemy aircraft losses: 39,691
ETO kills: 20,577
MTO kills: 9,428
FEAF kills: 5,918
POA kills: 794
CBI kills: 1,822
Aleutian kills: 85
Twentieth Air Force kills: 1,225

APPENDIX VII

CASUALTIES

Total number of Americans serving worldwide during World War II: 16,112,566

Total serving in the U.S. Army and Army Air Force: 11,260,000

Total serving in the U.S. Navy: 4,183,466

Total serving in the U.S. Marine Corps: 669,100

Total American deaths: 405,399

Total American battle deaths: 291,557

Total American deaths from other causes: 113,842

Total American wounds (not mortal): 671,846

Total Army deaths: 318,274*

Total Army battle deaths: 234,874

Total Army deaths other causes: 83,400

Total Army wounds (not mortal): 565,861

Total Navy deaths: 62,614**

Total Navy battle deaths: 36,958

Total Navy deaths other causes: 25,664

Total Navy wounds (not mortal): 37,778

Total Marine deaths: 24,511

Total Marine battle deaths: 19,733

Total Marine deaths other causes: 4,778

Total Marine wounds (not mortal): 68,207

*Includes Army Air Force
**Includes U.S. Navy casualties from October 1941
From *Historical Statistics of the United States*

≋ APPENDIX VIII

MAPS

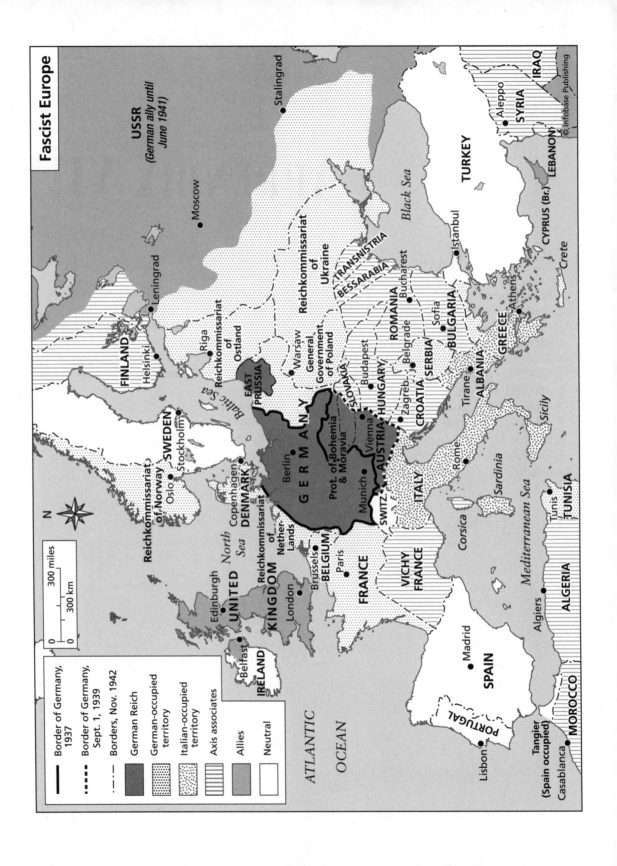

Fascist Europe

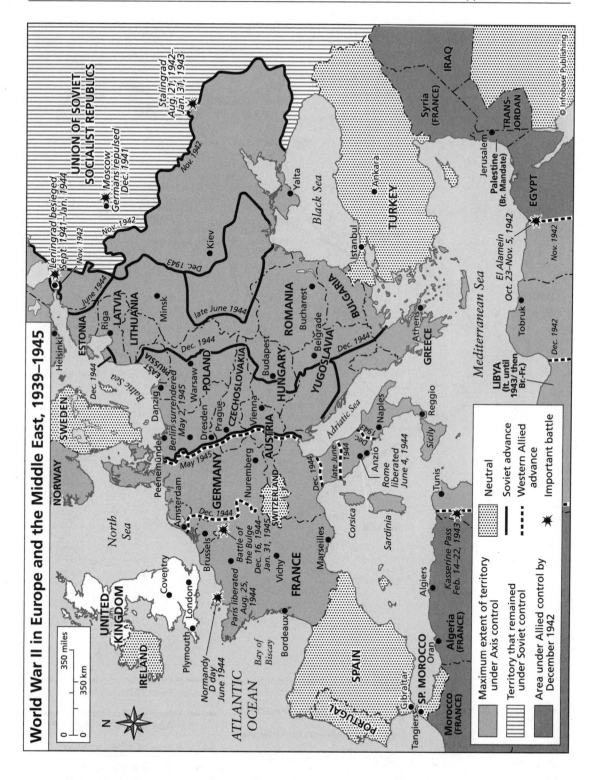

World War II in Europe and the Middle East, 1939–1945

Legend

- Maximum extent of territory under Axis control
- Territory that remained under Soviet control
- Area under Allied control by December 1942
- Neutral
- Soviet advance
- Western Allied advance
- * Important battle

Map labels

ATLANTIC OCEAN

North Sea

IRELAND

UNITED KINGDOM
- Plymouth
- London
- Coventry

Bay of Biscay

Normandy D day June 1944

Paris liberated Aug. 25, 1944

Brussels
Battle of the Bulge Dec. 16, 1944–Jan. 31, 1945

Amsterdam

Peenemünde
Berlin surrendered May 2, 1945
Danzig
Warsaw
Dresden
Prague
May 1945
Nuremberg

GERMANY

Dec. 1944

SWITZERLAND

AUSTRIA
Vienna

CZECHOSLOVAKIA

POLAND
EAST PRUSSIA

Dec. 1944

late June 1944

Baltic Sea

Riga
LATVIA
LITHUANIA
ESTONIA

Dec. 1944

June 1944

Helsinki

SWEDEN

NORWAY

Leningrad besieged Sept. 1941–Jan. 1944
Nov. 1942

Minsk

UNION OF SOVIET SOCIALIST REPUBLICS

Moscow Germans repulsed Dec. 1941

Nov. 1942

Kiev

Dec. 1943

Nov. 1942

Stalingrad Aug. 21, 1942–Jan. 31, 1943

Yalta

Black Sea

Istanbul

Ankara

TURKEY

Dec. 1944

HUNGARY
Budapest

YUGOSLAVIA
Belgrade

ROMANIA
Bucharest

BULGARIA

GREECE
Athens

Adriatic Sea

Naples
Anzio
Rome liberated June 4, 1944
Dec. 1943

Reggio
Sicily

Tunis

Sardinia

Corsica

Marseilles

FRANCE
Vichy
Bordeaux
late June 1944

SPAIN
PORTUGAL

Gibraltar
Tangiers
SP. MOROCCO

Morocco (FRANCE)
Oran
Algiers
Algeria (FRANCE)

Kasserine Pass Feb. 14–22, 1943

Mediterranean Sea

LIBYA (It. until 1943; then Br.-Fr.)
Tobruk
Dec. 1942

El Alamein Oct. 23–Nov. 5, 1942
Nov. 1942

EGYPT

Jerusalem
Palestine (Br. Mandate)

Syria (FRANCE)

TRANS-JORDAN

IRAQ

© Infobase Publishing

Scale

0   350 miles
0   350 km

N

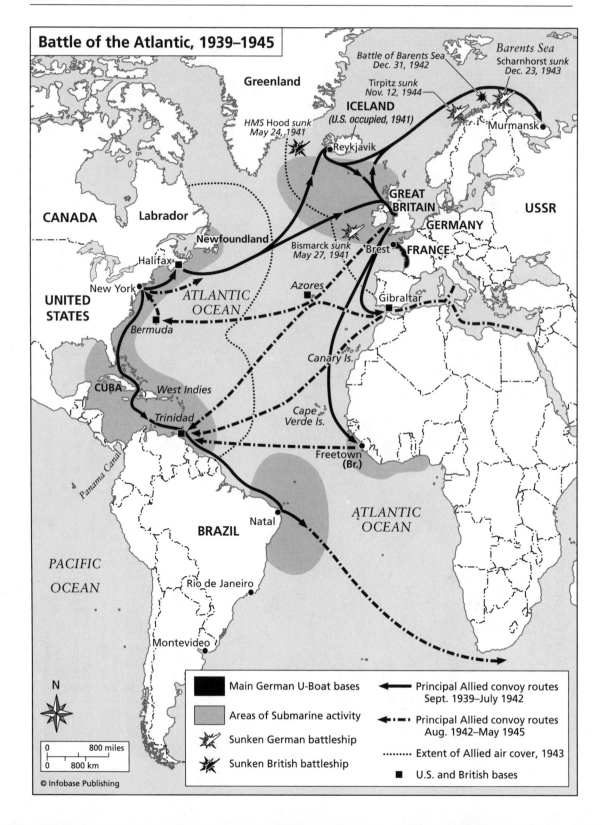

Battle of the Atlantic, 1939–1945

Greenland

Battle of Barents Sea
Dec. 31, 1942

Barents Sea
Scharnhorst *sunk*
Dec. 23, 1943

Tirpitz sunk
Nov. 12, 1944

ICELAND
(U.S. occupied, 1941)

Murmansk

HMS Hood *sunk*
May 24, 1941

Reykjavik

CANADA   Labrador

GREAT
BRITAIN

GERMANY

USSR

Newfoundland

Bismarck sunk
May 27, 1941

Brest

FRANCE

Halifax

New York

ATLANTIC
OCEAN

Azores

Gibraltar

UNITED
STATES

Bermuda

CUBA   *West Indies*

Canary Is.

Panama Canal

Trinidad

*Cape
Verde Is.*

Freetown
(Br.)

BRAZIL   Natal

ATLANTIC
OCEAN

PACIFIC
OCEAN

Rio de Janeiro

Montevideo

N

■ Main German U-Boat bases	⟵ Principal Allied convoy routes Sept. 1939–July 1942
▨ Areas of Submarine activity	⟵·-· Principal Allied convoy routes Aug. 1942–May 1945
✴ Sunken German battleship	.... Extent of Allied air cover, 1943
✴ Sunken British battleship	■ U.S. and British bases

0   800 miles
0   800 km

© Infobase Publishing

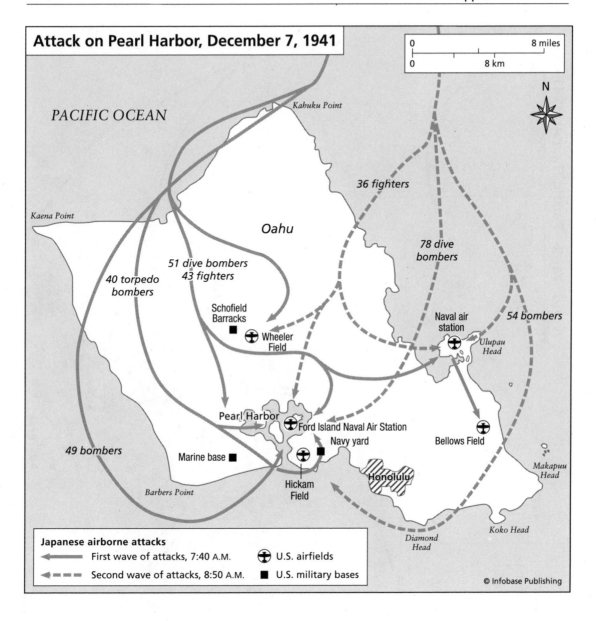

Attack on Pearl Harbor, December 7, 1941

PACIFIC OCEAN

Kahuku Point

0 ——————— 8 miles
0 ——————— 8 km

N

Oahu

36 fighters

78 dive bombers

Kaena Point

51 dive bombers
43 fighters

40 torpedo bombers

Schofield Barracks ■

Wheeler Field

Naval air station

54 bombers

Ulupau Head

Pearl Harbor

Ford Island Naval Air Station

Navy yard

Bellows Field

49 bombers

Marine base ■

Hickam Field

Honolulu

Makapuu Head

Barbers Point

Koko Head

Diamond Head

Japanese airborne attacks

←——— First wave of attacks, 7:40 A.M.   ⊕ U.S. airfields

←- - - Second wave of attacks, 8:50 A.M.   ■ U.S. military bases

© Infobase Publishing

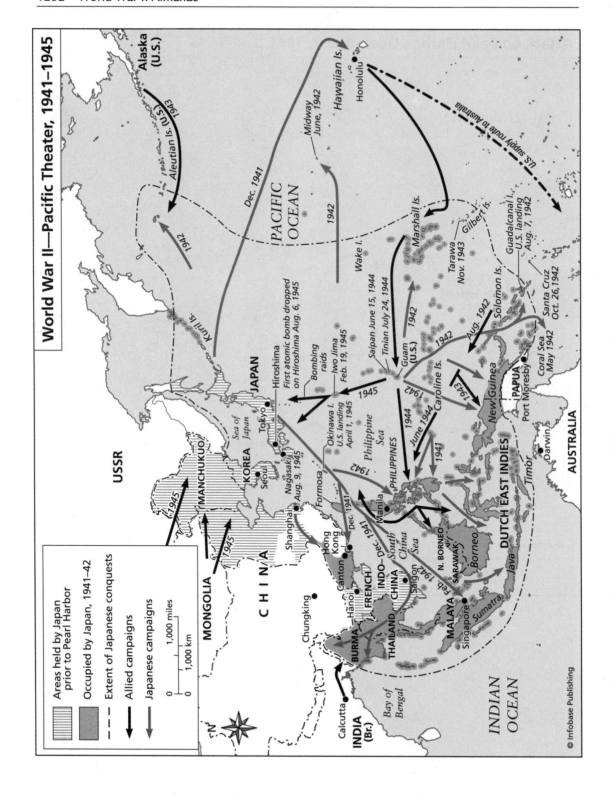

World War II—Pacific Theater, 1941–1945

Alaska (U.S.)

Aleutian Is. (U.S.) 1943

Dec. 1941

1942

Kuril Is.

USSR

MANCHUKUO 1945

MONGOLIA

1945

1945

KOREA

Seoul

Sea of Japan

JAPAN

Tokyo

Shanghai

Nagasaki Aug. 9, 1945

Hiroshima First atomic bomb dropped on Hiroshima Aug. 6, 1945

Bombing raids

Formosa

Iwo Jima Feb. 19, 1945

Okinawa I. U.S. landing April 1, 1945

1945

Philippine Sea

1942

Saipan June 15, 1944

Tinian July 24, 1944

Guam (U.S.)

1942

1942

1944

June 1944

Caroline Is.

1943

Marshall Is.

Gilbert Is.

Tarawa Nov. 1943

Wake I.

Midway June, 1942

Hawaiian Is.

Honolulu

PACIFIC OCEAN

1942

U.S. supply route to Australia

Guadalcanal U.S. landing Aug. 7, 1942

Solomon Is.

Aug 1942

Santa Cruz Oct. 26, 1942

Coral Sea May 1942

New Guinea

PAPUA Port Moresby

CHINA

Chungking

Hanoi

Canton

Hong Kong

Dec. 1941

FRENCH INDO-CHINA

Dec. 1941

South China Sea

Saigon

THAILAND

BURMA

MALAYA

Singapore

Feb. 1942

SARAWAK

N. BORNEO

Borneo

Sumatra

Java

DUTCH EAST INDIES

PHILIPPINES

Manila

1942

1941

Timor

Darwin

AUSTRALIA

INDIAN OCEAN

Bay of Bengal

Calcutta

INDIA (Br.)

N

1,000 miles

1,000 km

Areas held by Japan prior to Pearl Harbor

Occupied by Japan, 1941–42

Extent of Japanese conquests

Allied campaigns

Japanese campaigns

© Infobase Publishing

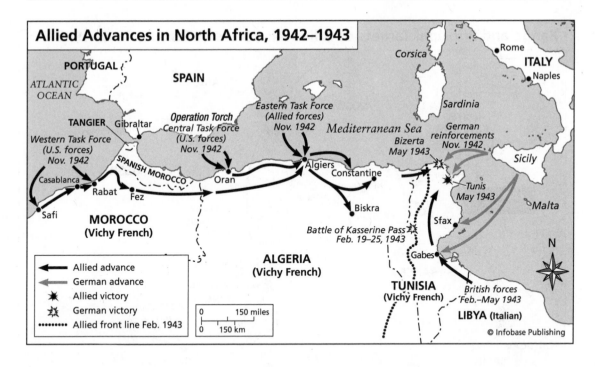

Allied Advances in North Africa, 1942–1943

PORTUGAL

ATLANTIC OCEAN

SPAIN

Corsica

•Rome

ITALY

•Naples

Sardinia

Mediterranean Sea

TANGIER Gibraltar

*Operation Torch
Central Task Force
(U.S. forces)
Nov. 1942*

*Eastern Task Force
(Allied forces)
Nov. 1942*

*German
reinforcements
Nov. 1942*

Bizerta
May 1943

Sicily

Sardinia

*Western Task Force
(U.S. forces)
Nov. 1942*

SPANISH MOROCCO

Oran

Algiers

Constantine

*Tunis
May 1943*

•Malta

Casablanca

Rabat

Fez

Safi

MOROCCO
(Vichy French)

Biskra

Sfax•

*Battle of Kasserine Pass
Feb. 19–25, 1943*

ALGERIA
(Vichy French)

TUNISIA
(Vichy French)

Gabes•

*British forces
Feb.–May 1943*

LIBYA (Italian)

N

Legend:
- Allied advance
- German advance
- Allied victory
- German victory
- Allied front line Feb. 1943

0   150 miles
0   150 km

© Infobase Publishing

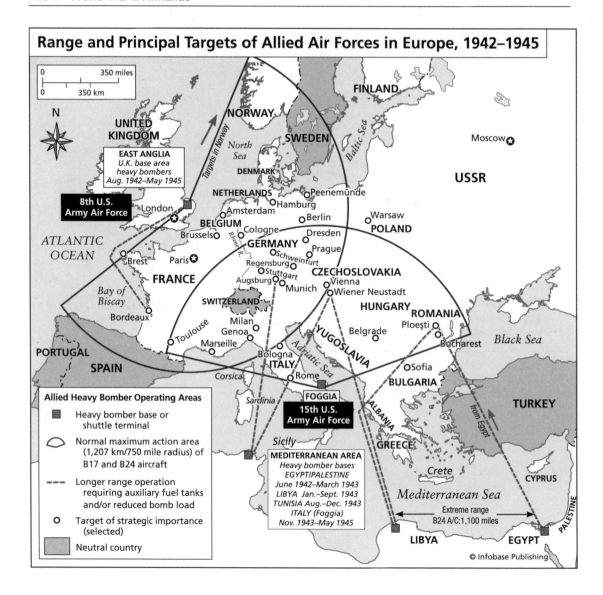

Range and Principal Targets of Allied Air Forces in Europe, 1942–1945

0 ___ 350 miles
0 ___ 350 km

N

UNITED KINGDOM

EAST ANGLIA
U.K. base area heavy bombers Aug. 1942–May 1945

8th U.S. Army Air Force

London

FINLAND

NORWAY

North Sea

SWEDEN

Baltic Sea

Moscow

USSR

DENMARK

NETHERLANDS

Peenemünde

Hamburg

Amsterdam

Berlin

Warsaw

BELGIUM

Cologne

POLAND

Brussels

Dresden

ATLANTIC OCEAN

Brest

Paris

Rhine R.

GERMANY

Schweinfurt

Prague

Regensburg

CZECHOSLOVAKIA

FRANCE

Augsburg

Stuttgart

Munich

Vienna

Wiener Neustadt

Bay of Biscay

Bordeaux

SWITZERLAND

HUNGARY

ROMANIA

Toulouse

Milan

Genoa

Belgrade

Ploești

Black Sea

Bucharest

PORTUGAL

SPAIN

Marseille

Bologna

Adriatic Sea

YUGOSLAVIA

Corsica

ITALY

Rome

Sofia

BULGARIA

Allied Heavy Bomber Operating Areas

■ Heavy bomber base or shuttle terminal

◠ Normal maximum action area (1,207 km/750 mile radius) of B17 and B24 aircraft

--- Longer range operation requiring auxiliary fuel tanks and/or reduced bomb load

○ Target of strategic importance (selected)

▨ Neutral country

Sardinia

FOGGIA

15th U.S. Army Air Force

Sicily

MEDITERRANEAN AREA
Heavy bomber bases
EGYPT/PALESTINE
June 1942–March 1943
LIBYA Jan.–Sept. 1943
TUNISIA Aug.–Dec. 1943
ITALY (Foggia)
Nov. 1943–May 1945

ALBANIA

GREECE

TURKEY

from Egypt

Crete

CYPRUS

Mediterranean Sea

Extreme range
B24 A/C:1,100 miles

LIBYA

EGYPT

PALESTINE

© Infobase Publishing

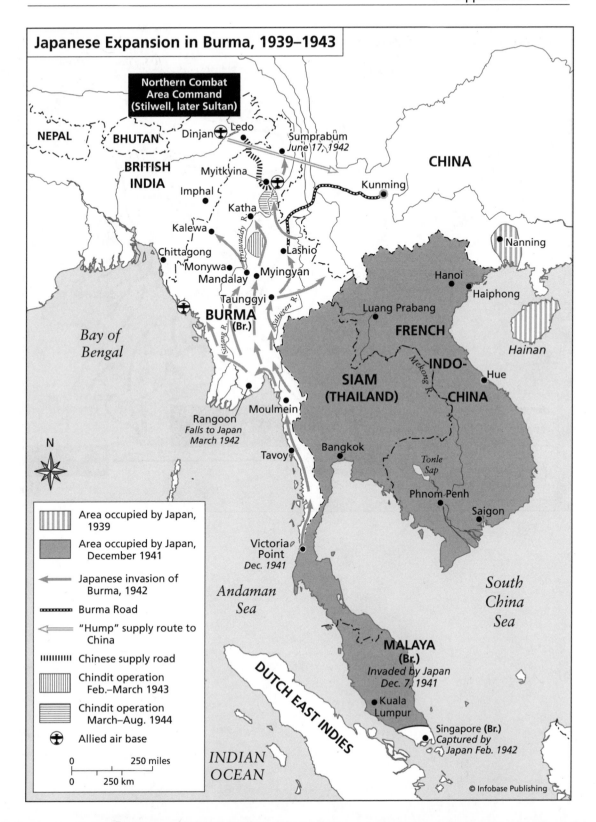

Japanese Expansion in Burma, 1939–1943

Northern Combat
Area Command
(Stilwell, later Sultan)

NEPAL

BHUTAN

Dinjan ⊕ Ledo

Sumprabum
June 17, 1942

CHINA

BRITISH
INDIA

Myitkyina ⊕

Imphal

Kunming

Katha

Kalewa

Chittagong

Irrawaddy R.

Lashio

Nanning

Monywa

Myingyan

Mandalay

Hanoi

Haiphong

Taunggyi

Salween R.

FRENCH

Hue

Hainan

BURMA
(Br.)

Sittang R.

Luang Prabang

INDO-

*Bay of
Bengal*

SIAM
(THAILAND)

Mekong R.

CHINA

Moulmein

Rangoon
*Falls to Japan
March 1942*

Tavoy

Bangkok

*Tonle
Sap*

Phnom Penh

Saigon

N

*South
China
Sea*

	Area occupied by Japan, 1939
	Area occupied by Japan, December 1941
→	Japanese invasion of Burma, 1942
····	Burma Road
←	"Hump" supply route to China
‖‖‖	Chinese supply road
‖‖‖	Chindit operation Feb.–March 1943
≡	Chindit operation March–Aug. 1944
⊕	Allied air base

Victoria
Point
Dec. 1941

*Andaman
Sea*

MALAYA
(Br.)
*Invaded by Japan
Dec. 7, 1941*

DUTCH EAST INDIES

Kuala
Lumpur

Singapore (Br.)
*Captured by
Japan Feb. 1942*

0   250 miles

0   250 km

*INDIAN
OCEAN*

© Infobase Publishing

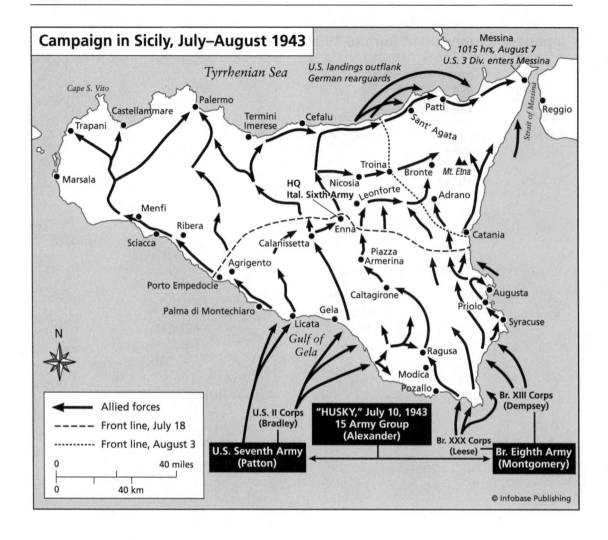

Campaign in Sicily, July–August 1943

Tyrrhenian Sea

Messina
1015 hrs, August 7
U.S. 3 Div. enters Messina

U.S. landings outflank
German rearguards

Cape S. Vito

Castellammare
Palermo
Termini Imerese
Cefalu
Patti
Sant' Agata
Reggio

Trapani

Strait of Messina

Marsala

Troina
Bronte
Mt. Etna

HQ
Ital. Sixth Army
Nicosia
Leonforte
Adrano

Menfi
Ribera

Sciacca
Enna
Catania

Agrigento
Calanissetta
Piazza Armerina

Porto Empedocle

Palma di Montechiaro
Gela
Caltagirone

Licata
Gulf of Gela
Augusta
Priolo
Syracuse

Ragusa

Modica

Pozallo

Br. XIII Corps
(Dempsey)

N

Allied forces
Front line, July 18
Front line, August 3

0   40 miles

0   40 km

U.S. II Corps
(Bradley)

**"HUSKY," July 10, 1943
15 Army Group
(Alexander)**

**U.S. Seventh Army
(Patton)**

Br. XXX Corps
(Leese)

**Br. Eighth Army
(Montgomery)**

© Infobase Publishing

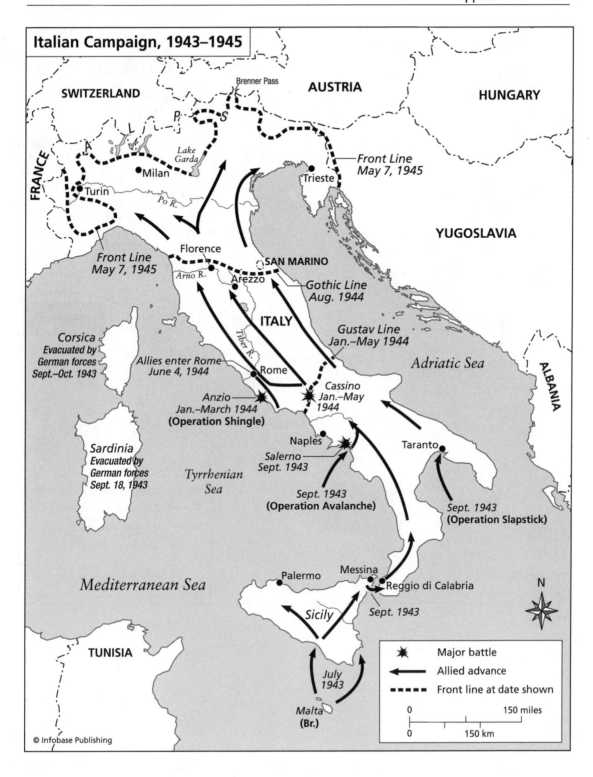

Italian Campaign, 1943–1945

SWITZERLAND

AUSTRIA

HUNGARY

Brenner Pass

P   S

A   L   P

FRANCE

Lake Garda

Milan

Turin

Po R.

Trieste

Front Line May 7, 1945

YUGOSLAVIA

Front Line May 7, 1945

Florence

Arno R.

Arezzo

SAN MARINO

Gothic Line Aug. 1944

ITALY

Adriatic Sea

Tiber R.

Gustav Line Jan.–May 1944

Corsica Evacuated by German forces Sept.–Oct. 1943

Allies enter Rome June 4, 1944

Rome

Cassino Jan.–May 1944

ALBANIA

Anzio Jan.–March 1944 **(Operation Shingle)**

Sardinia Evacuated by German forces Sept. 18, 1943

Naples

Salerno Sept. 1943

Taranto

Tyrrhenian Sea

Sept. 1943 **(Operation Avalanche)**

Sept. 1943 **(Operation Slapstick)**

Mediterranean Sea

Palermo

Messina

Reggio di Calabria

Sept. 1943

N

Sicily

TUNISIA

July 1943

Major battle

Allied advance

Front line at date shown

Malta **(Br.)**

0   150 miles

0   150 km

© Infobase Publishing

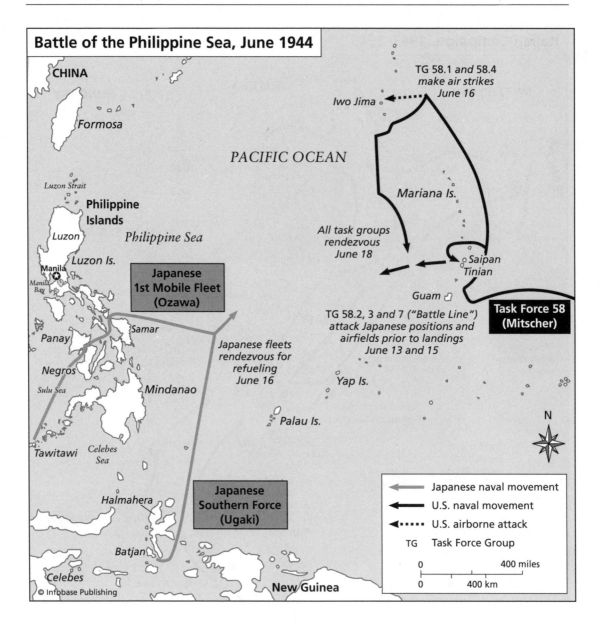

Battle of the Philippine Sea, June 1944

CHINA

Formosa

PACIFIC OCEAN

TG 58.1 *and* 58.4
make air strikes
June 16

Iwo Jima

Luzon Strait

Mariana Is.

**Philippine
Islands**

Philippine Sea

Luzon

Luzon Is.

*All task groups
rendezvous
June 18*

Manila
*Manila
Bay*

Saipan
Tinian

**Japanese
1st Mobile Fleet
(Ozawa)**

Samar

Guam

**Task Force 58
(Mitscher)**

*Japanese fleets
rendezvous for
refueling
June 16*

TG 58.2, 3 and 7 ("Battle Line")
attack Japanese positions and
airfields prior to landings
June 13 and 15

Panay

Negros

Sulu Sea

Mindanao

Yap Is.

Palau Is.

N

Tawitawi

*Celebes
Sea*

**Japanese
Southern Force
(Ugaki)**

Halmahera

→ Japanese naval movement
→ U.S. naval movement
◀····· U.S. airborne attack
TG   Task Force Group

Batjan

Celebes

© Infobase Publishing

New Guinea

0 _____ 400 miles
0 _____ 400 km

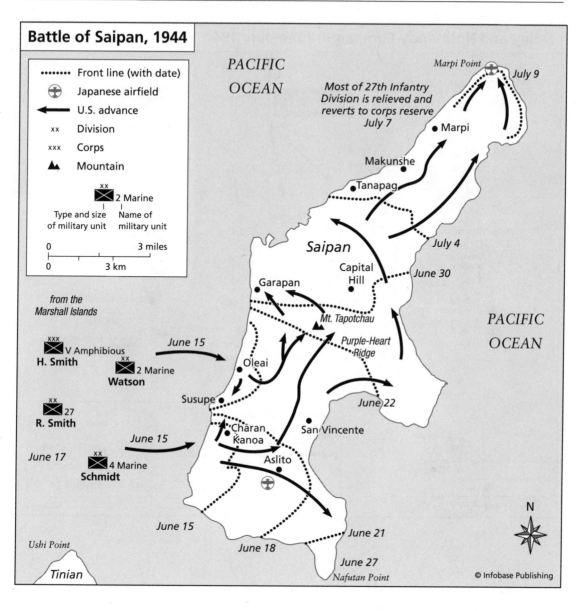

Battle of Saipan, 1944

Legend:
- .... Front line (with date)
- Japanese airfield
- ← U.S. advance
- xx Division
- xxx Corps
- ▲▲ Mountain

xx
2 Marine
Type and size of military unit | Name of military unit

0 —— 3 miles
0 —— 3 km

PACIFIC OCEAN

Marpi Point

July 9

Most of 27th Infantry Division is relieved and reverts to corps reserve July 7

Marpi

Makunshe

Tanapag

July 4

Saipan

Capital Hill

June 30

Garapan

Mt. Tapotchau

PACIFIC OCEAN

Purple-Heart Ridge

from the Marshall Islands

xxx
V Amphibious
H. Smith

June 15

Oleai

xx
2 Marine
Watson

Susupe

June 22

xx
27
R. Smith

June 15

Charan Kanoa

San Vincente

June 17

xx
4 Marine
Schmidt

Aslito

June 15

June 21

June 18

June 27

N

Ushi Point

Tinian

Nafutan Point

© Infobase Publishing

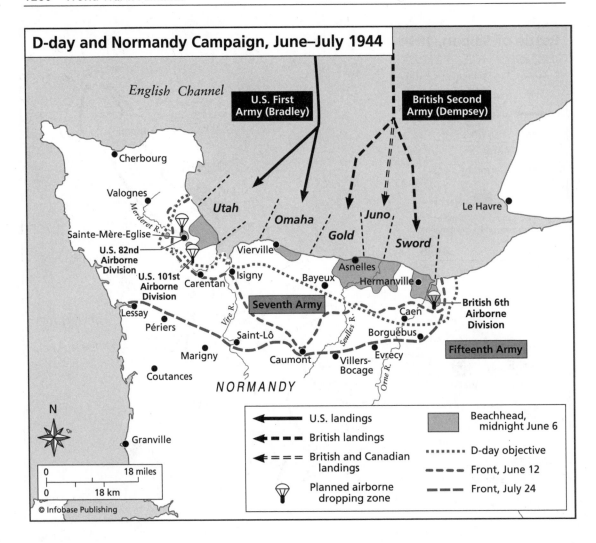

D-day and Normandy Campaign, June–July 1944

English Channel

U.S. First Army (Bradley)

British Second Army (Dempsey)

Cherbourg

Valognes

Mérderet R.

Sainte-Mère-Eglise

U.S. 82nd Airborne Division

Utah

Omaha

Gold

Juno

Sword

Le Havre

U.S. 101st Airborne Division

Vierville

Carentan

Isigny

Bayeux

Asnelles

Hermanville

Seventh Army

Lessay

Périers

Vire R.

Saint-Lô

Seulles R.

Caen

Borguébus

British 6th Airborne Division

Fifteenth Army

Marigny

Coutances

Caumont

Villers-Bocage

Evrecy

Orme R.

NORMANDY

Granville

N

Legend:

← U.S. landings

◄- - - British landings

◄= = = British and Canadian landings

🪂 Planned airborne dropping zone

▓ Beachhead, midnight June 6

······· D-day objective

– – – Front, June 12

━ ━ ━ Front, July 24

| 0 | 18 miles |
| 0 | 18 km |

© Infobase Publishing

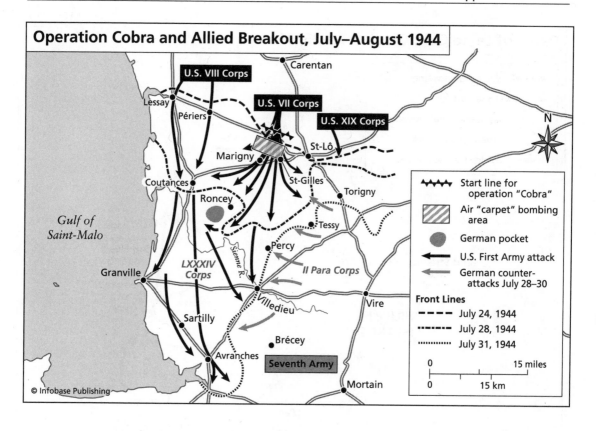

Operation Cobra and Allied Breakout, July–August 1944

Carentan

U.S. VIII Corps

Lessay

Périers

U.S. VII Corps

U.S. XIX Corps

Marigny

St-Lô

Coutances

St-Gilles

Roncey

Torigny

Gulf of Saint-Malo

Tessy

Sienne R.

Percy

Granville

LXXXIV Corps

II Para Corps

Villedieu

Vire

Sartilly

Brécey

Avranches

Seventh Army

Mortain

© Infobase Publishing

N

Start line for operation "Cobra"

Air "carpet" bombing area

German pocket

U.S. First Army attack

German counter-attacks July 28–30

Front Lines

– – – – July 24, 1944

–·–·– July 28, 1944

··········· July 31, 1944

0   15 miles

0   15 km

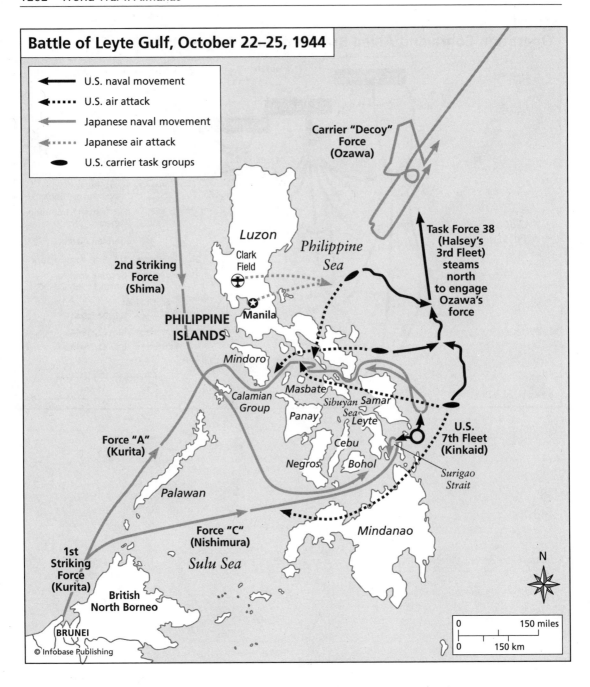

Battle of Leyte Gulf, October 22–25, 1944

Legend:
- ← U.S. naval movement
- ◄···· U.S. air attack
- → Japanese naval movement
- ◄···· Japanese air attack
- ● U.S. carrier task groups

Carrier "Decoy" Force (Ozawa)

2nd Striking Force (Shima)

Luzon
Clark Field
Philippine Sea

Task Force 38 (Halsey's 3rd Fleet) steams north to engage Ozawa's force

PHILIPPINE ISLANDS
⊛ Manila

Mindoro

Masbate
Calamian Group
Panay
Sibuyan Sea
Samar
Leyte

U.S. 7th Fleet (Kinkaid)

Force "A" (Kurita)

Cebu
Negros
Bohol

Surigao Strait

Palawan

Force "C" (Nishimura)
Sulu Sea

Mindanao

1st Striking Force (Kurita)

British North Borneo

BRUNEI

© Infobase Publishing

N

| 0 | 150 miles |
| 0 | 150 km |

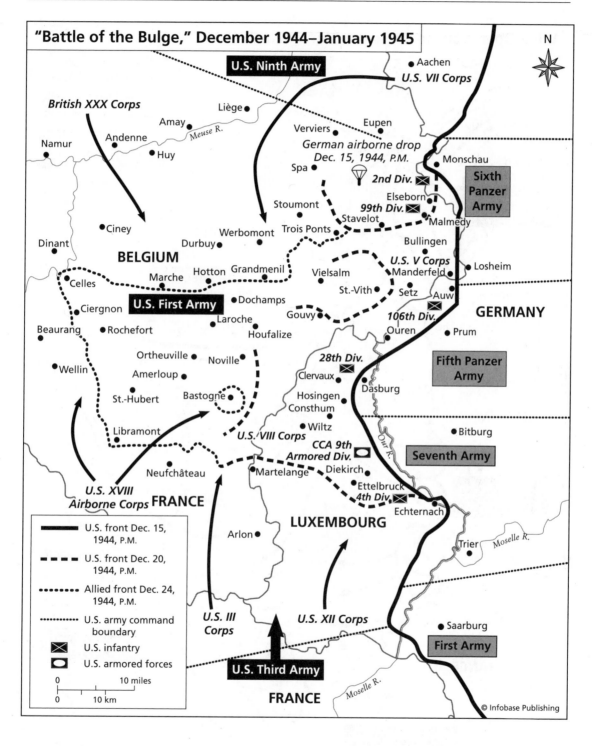

"Battle of the Bulge," December 1944–January 1945

U.S. Ninth Army

British XXX Corps

German airborne drop
Dec. 15, 1944, P.M.

2nd Div.

99th Div.

BELGIUM

U.S. V Corps

U.S. First Army

Sixth Panzer Army

106th Div.

GERMANY

Fifth Panzer Army

28th Div.

Seventh Army

CCA 9th Armored Div.

U.S. VIII Corps

U.S. XVIII Airborne Corps   FRANCE

4th Div.

LUXEMBOURG

U.S. III Corps

U.S. XII Corps

First Army

U.S. Third Army

FRANCE

U.S. front Dec. 15, 1944, P.M.

U.S. front Dec. 20, 1944, P.M.

Allied front Dec. 24, 1944, P.M.

U.S. army command boundary

U.S. infantry

U.S. armored forces

0   10 miles
0   10 km

© Infobase Publishing

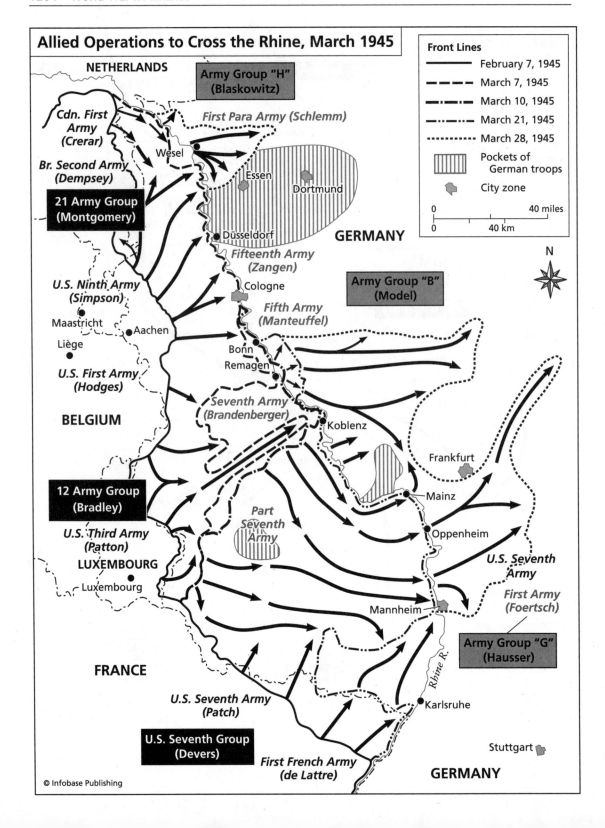

Allied Operations to Cross the Rhine, March 1945

NETHERLANDS

Army Group "H" (Blaskowitz)

First Para Army (Schlemm)

Cdn. First Army (Crerar)

Wesel

Br. Second Army (Dempsey)

21 Army Group (Montgomery)

Essen

Dortmund

Düsseldorf

GERMANY

Fifteenth Army (Zangen)

U.S. Ninth Army (Simpson)

Cologne

Army Group "B" (Model)

Maastricht

Aachen

Fifth Army (Manteuffel)

Liège

Bonn

Remagen

U.S. First Army (Hodges)

BELGIUM

Seventh Army (Brandenberger)

Koblenz

Frankfurt

12 Army Group (Bradley)

U.S. Third Army (Patton)

Part Seventh Army

Mainz

LUXEMBOURG

Luxembourg

Oppenheim

U.S. Seventh Army

First Army (Foertsch)

Mannheim

Army Group "G" (Hausser)

FRANCE

Rhine R.

U.S. Seventh Army (Patch)

Karlsruhe

U.S. Seventh Group (Devers)

First French Army (de Lattre)

Stuttgart

GERMANY

Front Lines
- February 7, 1945
- March 7, 1945
- March 10, 1945
- March 21, 1945
- March 28, 1945
- Pockets of German troops
- City zone

0   40 miles
0   40 km

N

© Infobase Publishing

Okinawa, April–June 1945

April 19, 1945
U.S. Tenth Army

U.S. Assaults ("ICEBERG")

May 4–5, 1945
Japanese counterattacks

Japanese defense line
("Shuri Line")

Mountain

0   10 miles
0   10 km

le Shima

April 20
Taken by U.S.
Sixth Marine Div.

U.S. Sixth Marine Div.

Hedo Point

Hedo
April 13

Aha
April 19

Tako

Yagachi

April 8

Bise

Motobu Pen.

Taira
April 11

April 16–21
Seventy-Seventh Infantry Div.

Yae Take   Nago

**Twenty-Seventh Infantry Div.
Floating Reserve
(Griner)**

East China Sea

Atsuta

April 8

Kushi

Onna
April 4
Ishikawa Isthmus

Kin

Okinawa

PACIFIC OCEAN

**"ICEBERG," April 1, 1945
U.S. Tenth Army
(Buckner)**

Chimu Bay

Takabanare

April 10–11
Twenty-Seventh Div.

U.S. Sixth Marine Div.

**U.S. III Amph Corps
(Geiger)**

U.S. First Marine Div.

Yontan

Hagushi

Katchin Pen.

U.S. Seventh Infantry Div.

**U.S. XXIV Corps
(Hodge)**

U.S. Ninety-Sixth Infantry Div.

Kadena

Heanna

March 26
Invasion by
Seventy-Seventh
Infantry Division

Hagushi Bay
April 19

Kuba
April 4

Tsugen Shima

Keise Is.

Nakagusuku Bay

**JP Thirty-Second
Army (Ushijima)**

U.S. Sixth Marine Div.

Oruku Pen.

Shuri

Yonabaru

May 21
Japanese withdraw
from "Shuri Line"

June 21
End of Japanese
Resistance

Kerama Is.

Itoman

Minatoga

Kiyamu   Mabuni

April 1–2
Demonstrations by U.S. Second Marine Div.

© Infobase Publishing

Post–World War II Occupation Zones of Germany

0 — 100 miles
0 — 100 km

N

North Sea

DENMARK

Baltic Sea

USSR

EAST PRUSSIA

• Hamburg
• Bremen

Berlin ○

NETHERLANDS

GERMANY

POLAND

BELGIUM

• Bonn

LUX.

CZECHOSLOVAKIA

Nuremberg •

Munich •

Vienna ○

SWITZERLAND

AUSTRIA

HUNGARY

ITALY

YUGOSLAVIA

Legend:
- U.S. zone
- British zone
- French zone
- Soviet zone
- Taken over by Poland
- ○ Under Four Power control

© Infobase Publishing

Division of Berlin after World War II

EAST GERMANY

0 — 5 miles
0 — 5 km

EAST GERMANY

N

French Sector

East Berlin

British Sector

West Berlin

Soviet Sector

U.S. Sector

Havel R.

Spree R.

EAST GERMANY

≋ BIBLIOGRAPHY

ESSENTIAL REFERENCES

Craven, Wesley F., and James L. Cate, eds. *The Army Air Forces in World War II.* 7 vols. Chicago: University of Chicago Press, 1948–58.

Headquarters, U.S. Air Force. *Air Force Combat Units of World War II.* Washington, D.C.: Office of Air Force History, 1961.

———. *Combat Squadrons of the Air Force, World War II.* Washington, D.C.: Office of Air Force History, 1982.

Historical Branch, G3 Division, Headquarters, United States Marine Corps. *History of U.S. Marine Corps Operations in World War II.* 5 vols. Washington, D.C.: U.S. Government Printing Office, 1959–68.

Office of the Chief of Military History. *The U.S. Army in World War II.* Washington, D.C.: Department of the Army, 1947–2004.

CHRONOLOGIES

Carter, Kit C., and Robert Mueller. *Army Air Forces in World War II: Combat Chronology, 1941–1945.* Washington, D.C.: Center for Air Force History, 1991.

Cressman, Robert. *The Official Chronology of the U.S. Navy in World War II.* Annapolis, Md.: Naval Institute Press, 2000.

Headquarters, U.S. Air Force. *The Army Air Forces in World War II: Combat Chronology, 1941–1945.* Washington, D.C.: Office of Air Force History, 1973.

Kimble, David L. *Chronology of U.S. Navy Submarine Operations in the Pacific, 1939–1942.* Bennington, Vt.: World War II Historical Society, 1997.

Office of Naval History. *The Chronology of the Navy's War in the Pacific, World War II.* Washington, D.C., 1947.

Williams, Mary H. *Chronology 1941–45.* U.S. Army in World War II Series, Special Studies. Washington, D.C.: Office of the Chief of Military History, Department of the Army, 1960.

BIOGRAPHIES AND COMMANDERS' ACCOUNTS

Ambrose, Stephen E. *The Supreme Commander: The War Years of General Dwight D. Eisenhower.* Garden City, N.Y.: Doubleday, 1970.

Blumenson, Martin. *Eisenhower.* New York: Ballantine Books, 1972.

Bradley, Omar N. *A Soldier's Story.* New York: Modern Library, 1999.

Brink, Randall. *Nimitz: The Man and His Wars.* New York: Penguin, 2000.

Buell, Thomas B. *The Quiet Warrior: A Biography of Admiral Raymond A. Spruance.* Boston: Little, Brown, 1974.

———. *Master of Sea Power: A Biography of Fleet Admiral Ernest J. King.* Boston: Little, Brown, 1980.

Blumenson, Martin. *Mark Clark.* New York: Congdon and Weed: 1984.

Coletta, Paolo E. *Admiral Marc A. Mitscher and U.S. Naval Aviation: Bald Eagle.* Lewiston, N.Y.: Edwin Mellen Press, 1997.

Daso, Dik A. *Hap Arnold and the Evolution of American Airpower.* Washington, D.C.: Smithsonian Institution Press, 2000.

Davis, Richard G. *Carl A. Spaatz and the Air War in Europe.* Washington, D.C.: Center for Air Force History, 1993.

D'Este, Carlo. *Patton: A Genius for War.* New York: HarperCollins, 1996.

———. *Eisenhower: A Soldier's Life.* New York: Henry Holt, 2002.

Hirshson, Stanley P. *General Patton: A Soldier's Life.* New York: HarperCollins, 2002.

James, D. Clayton. *The Years of MacArthur.* Vol. 2, *1941–1945.* Boston: Houghton Mifflin, 1970.

King, Michael J. *William Orlando Darby, a Military Biography.* Hamden, Conn.: Archon Books, 1981.

Larrabee, Eric. *Commander in Chief: Franklin Delano Roosevelt, His Lieutenants, and Their War.* New York: Harper and Row, 1987

Long, Gavin M. *MacArthur as Military Commander.* London: Van Nostrand, 1969.

Perret, Geoffrey. *Eisenhower.* New York: Random House, 1999.

———. *Old Soldiers Never Die: The Life of Douglas MacArthur.* New York: Random House, 1996.

Pogue, Forrest C. *George C. Marshall: Organizer of Victory, 1943–45.* New York: Viking Press, 1973.

———. *George C. Marshall: Ordeal and Hope, 1939–1942.* New York: Viking Press, 1963.

Schaller, Michael. *Douglas MacArthur: The Far Eastern General.* New York: Oxford University Press, 1989.

Schultz, Duane P. *Hero of Bataan: The Story of General Jonathan M. Wainwright.* New York: St. Martin's Press, 1981.

Sixsmith, E. K. G. *Eisenhower as Military Commander.* New York: Stein and Day, 1973.

Smith, Holland M., and Percy Finch. *Coral and Brass.* New York: Scribner, 1949.

Stilwell, Joseph W. *The Stilwell Papers.* New York: William Sloane Associates, 1948.

Truscott, Lucian K. *Command Missions: A Personal Story.* Novato, Calif.: Presidio Press, 1990.

Wheeler, Gerald E. *Kinkaid of the Seventh Fleet: A Biography of Admiral Thomas C. Kinkaid, U.S. Navy.* Annapolis, Md.: Naval Institute Press, 1996.

Whiting, Charles. *Bradley.* New York: Ballantine Books, 1971.

General Histories

Adamczyk, Richard D., and Morris J. MacGregor. *The United States Army in World War II: A Reader's Guide.* Washington, D.C.: U.S. Army Center of Military History, 1992.

Anzuoni, Robert P. *I'm the 82nd Airborne Division!: A History of the All American Division in World War II After Action Reports.* Atglen, Pa.: Schiffer Military History, 2005.

Blair, Clay. *Ridgway's Paratroopers: The American Airborne in World War II.* Garden City, N.Y.: Dial Press, 1985.

Bradley, John H., Jack W. Dice, and Thomas E. Griess. *The Second World War: Asia and the Pacific.* Wayne, N.J.: Avery Publishing Group, 1984.

Bradley, John H., and Jack W. Dice. *The Second World War: Asia and the Pacific.* West Point, N.Y: Department of the Army, 1981.

Bradley, John N. *The Second World War.* Garden City, N.Y.: Square One, 2002.

Buell, Thomas B. *The Second World War: Europe and the Mediterranean.* Wayne, N.J.: Avery Publishing Group, 1989.

Congdon, Don, ed. *Combat WW II: Pacific Theater of Operations.* New York: Arbor House, 1983.

Dodson, Kenneth. *Away All Boats.* Annapolis, Md.: Naval Institute Press, 1996.

Ellis, John. *On the Front Lines: The Experience of War Through the Eyes of the Allied Soldiers in World War II.* New York: Wiley, 1991.

Eisenhower, Dwight D. *Crusade in Europe.* Garden City, N.Y.: Doubleday, 1948.

Franks, Clifton R. *The Second World War: Europe and the Mediterranean.* West Point, N.Y.: United States Military Academy Department of History, 1981.

Gailey, Harry A. *The War in the Pacific: From Pearl Harbor to Tokyo Bay.* Novato, Calif.: Presidio Press, 1995.

Hoyt, Edwin P. *Japan's War, the Great Pacific Conflict, 1853 to 1952.* New York: McGraw-Hill, 1986.

Morison, Samuel Eliot. *The Two Ocean War. A Short History of the United States Navy in the Second World War.* Boston: Little Brown, 1963.

Patton, George S. *War as I Knew It.* Boston: Houghton Mifflin, 1947.

Roehrs, Mark D., and William A. Renzi. *World War II in the Pacific.* Armonk, N.Y.: M.E. Sharpe, 2004.

Rottman, Gordon L. *U.S. Marine Corps World War II Order of Battle: Ground and Air Units in the Pacific War.* Westport, Conn.: Greenwood Press, 2001.

Schom, Alan. *The Eagle and the Rising Sun: the Japanese-American War, 1941–1943, Pearl Harbor through Guadalcanal.* New York: W.W. Norton, 2004.

Smith, Stanley E. *The United States Marine Corps in World War II.* New York: Random House, 1969.

Spector, Ronald H. *Eagle Against the Sun: The American War with Japan.* New York: Free Press, 1985.

Stamps, Thomas Dodson, and Vincent J. Esposito, eds. *A Military History of World War II with Atlas.* West Point, N.Y.: U.S. Military Academy, 1956.

United States Army Center of Military History. *A Brief History of the U.S. Army in World War II.* Washington, D.C., 1992.

———. *The War Against Japan.* Washington, D.C., 2001.

United States Military Academy Department of Military Art and Engineering. *Campaign Summaries of the Second World War.* West Point, N.Y.: U.S. Military Academy, 1945.

United States War Department, General Staff. *Biennial Reports of the Chief of Staff of the United States Army to the Secretary of War.* Washington, D.C.: Center of Military History, U.S. Army, 1996.

———. *Biennial Report of the Chief of Staff of the United States Army, July 1, 1943, to June 30, 1945.* Washington, D.C.: U.S. Government Printing Office, 1945.

Weinberg, Gerhard L. *A World at Arms: A Global History of World War II.* New York: Cambridge University Press, 1994.

White, William L. *They Were Expendable.* New York: Harcourt, Brace, 1942.

Willmott, H. P. *The Second World War in the Far East.* Washington, D.C.: Smithsonian Books, 2004.

STRATEGY

Beschloss, Michael. *The Conquerors: Roosevelt, Truman, and the Destruction of Hitler's Germany, 1941–1945.* New York: Simon & Schuster, 2002.

Dupuy, Trevor N. *Options of Command.* New York: Hippocrene Books, 1984.

Ellis, John. *Brute Force: Allied Strategy and Tactics in the Second World War.* New York: Viking Press, 1990.

Greenfield, Kent R., ed. *Command Decisions.* Washington, D.C.: Center of Military History, U.S. Army, 1984.

Higgins, Trumbull. *Winston Churchill and the Second Front, 1940–1943.* New York: Oxford University Press, 1957.

Howard, Michael E. *Grand Strategy.* Vol. 4, *August 1942–August 1943.* London: HMSO, 1972.

———. *The Mediterranean Strategy in the Second World War.* New York: Praeger, 1968.

Irving, David J. C. *The War Between the Generals.* New York: Congdon, 1981.

Matloff, Maurice. *Strategic Planning for Coalition Warfare, 1943–1944.* United States Army in World War II Series. Washington, D.C.: Department of the Army, 1959.

Matloff, Maurice, and Edwin S. Snell. *Strategic Planning for Coalition Warfare 1941–1942.* United States Army in World War II Series. Washington, D.C.: Department of the Army, 1986.

Miller, Edward S. *War Plan Orange: The U.S. Strategy to Defeat Japan, 1897–1945.* Annapolis, Md.: Naval Institute Press, 1991.

Morton, Louis. *Germany First: the Basic Concept of Allied Strategy in World War II.* Washington, D.C.: Center of Military History, U.S. Army, 1990.

———. *Strategy and Command: The First Two Years.* Washington, D.C.: Center of Military History, 2000.

Pogue, Forrest C. *The Supreme Command.* United States Army in World War II Series. Washington, D.C.: Department of the Army, 1954.

Schnabel, James, F. *Policy and Direction: The First Year.* Washington, D.C.: Office of the Chief of Military History, 1972.

Smith, Robert Ross. *Luzon Versus Formosa.* Washington, D.C.: Center of Military History, U.S. Army, 1990.

Stoler, Mark A. *Allies and Adversaries: The Joint Chiefs of Staff, The Grand Alliance, and U.S. Strategy in World War II.* Chapel Hill: University of North Carolina Press, 2000.

Thorne, Christopher. *Allies of a Kind.* New York: Oxford University Press, 1978.

EUROPEAN THEATER OF OPERATIONS—GROUND

Allen, Peter. *One More River: The Rhine Crossings of 1945.* New York: Scribner, 1980.

Allen, Robert S. *Lucky Forward: The History of Patton's Third U.S. Army.* New York: Vanguard Press, 1947.

Allied Forces, 12th Army Group G-3. *Report of Operations.* Bad Homburg, Germany, 1945.

Allied Forces, 21st Army Group. *Notes on the Operations of 21st Army Group, 6 June 1944–5 May 1945.* N.p., 1945.

Allied Forces, Supreme Headquarters. *Report by the Supreme Commander to the Combined Chiefs of Staff on the Operations in Europe of the Allied Expeditionary Force, 6 June 1944 to 8 May 1945.* Washington, D.C.: U.S. Government Printing Office, 1946.

Ambrose, Stephen E. *D-Day, June 6, 1944: the Climactic Battle of World War II.* New York: Simon & Schuster, 1994.

———. *Eisenhower and Berlin, 1945: the Decision to Halt at the Elbe.* New York: W. W. Norton, 1967.

———. *The Victors: Eisenhower and His Boys, the Men of World War II.* New York: Simon & Schuster, 1998.

Astor, Gerald. *A Blood-Dimmed Tide: The Battle of the Bulge by the Men Who Fought It.* New York: Donald I. Fine, 1992.

Balkoski, Joseph. *Beyond the Beachhead: the 29th Infantry Division in Normandy.* Harrisburg, Pa.: Stackpole Books, 1989.

———. *Utah Beach: The Amphibious Landing and Airborne Operations on D-Day, June 6, 1944.* Mechanicsburg, Pa.: Stackpole Books, 2005.

Ballard, Ted. *Rhineland.* Washington, D.C.: U.S. Army Center of Military History, 1995.

Blumenson, Martin. *Breakout and Pursuit.* The United States Army in World War II Series. Washington, D.C.: Department of the Army, 1961.

Bonn, Keith E. *When the Odds Were Even: The Vosges Mountains Campaign, October 1944–January 1945.* Novato, Calif.: Presidio Press, 1994.

Bowden, Mark. *Our Finest Day: D-Day, June 6, 1944.* San Francisco, Calif.: Chronicle Books, 2002.

Branton, Harold M. *The 103rd Infantry Division: The Trail of the Cactus.* Paducah, Ky.: Turner Publishing, 1993.

Breuer, William B. *Operation Dragoon: The Allied Invasion of the South of France.* Novato, Calif.: Presidio Press, 1987.

Burgett, Donald R. *Seven Roads to Hell: A Screaming Eagle at Bastogne.* Novato, Calif.: Presidio Press, 1999.

Byrnes, Lawrence G., ed. *History of the 94th Infantry Division in World War II.* Washington, D.C.: Infantry Journal Press, 1948.

Carafano, James J. *After D-Day: Operation Cobra and the Normandy Breakout.* Boulder, Colo.: Lynne Rienner, 2000.

Cirillo, Roger. *Ardennes—Alsace.* Washington, D.C.: U.S. Army Center of Military History, 1995.

Clarke, Jeffrey J. *Riviera to the Rhine: the European Theater of Operations.* Washington, D.C.: Center of Military History, 1993.

Clinger, Fred, Arthur Johnston, and Vincent Masel. *The History of the 71st Infantry Division.* Augsburg, Germany, 1946.

Cole, Hugh M. *The Ardennes: The Battle of the Bulge.* Washington, D.C.: Center of Military History, 1994.

Congdon, Don, ed. *Combat WW II: European Theater of Operations.* New York: Arbor House, 1983.

Crookenden, Napier. *Battle of the Bulge, 1944.* New York: Scribner, 1980.

———. *Dropzone Normandy: The Story of the American and British Airborne Assault on D-Day 1944.* New York: Scribner, 1976.

D'Este, Carlo. *Decision in Normandy.* New York: Dutton, 1983.

Department of the Army Historical Division. *Utah Beach to Cherbourg.* Washington, D.C., 1948.

Devlin, Gerard M. *Paratrooper!: The Saga of U.S. Army and Marine Parachute and Glider Combat Troops During World War II.* New York: St. Martin's Press, 1979.

Deyer, George. *XII Corps: Spearhead of Patton's Third Army.* Baton Rouge, La.: Military Press of Louisiana, 1947.

Doubler, Michael D. *Closing With the Enemy: How GIs Fought the War in Europe, 1944–1945.* Lawrence: University Press of Kansas, 1994.

Draper, Theodore. *The 84th Infantry Division in the Battle of Germany, November 1944–May 1945.* New York: Viking Press, 1946.

Dupuy, Trevor N. *Hitler's Last Gamble: the Battle of the Bulge, December 1944–January 1945.* New York: HarperCollins, 1994.

Eisenhower, John S. D. *The Bitter Woods: the Dramatic Story, Told at all Echelons, from Supreme Command to Squad Leader, of the Crisis that Shook the Western Coalition: Hitler's Surprise Ardennes Offensive.* New York: Putnam, 1969.

Elstob, Peter. *Bastogne: The Road Block.* New York: Ballantine Books, 1968.

Essame, Hubert. *The Battle for Germany.* New York: Scribner, 1969.

Ewing, Joseph H. *29, Let's Go!: A History of the 29th Infantry Division in World War II.* Washington, D.C.: Infantry Journal Press, 1948.

Farrar-Hockley, Anthony H. *Airborne Carpet: Operation Market Garden.* New York: Ballantine Books, 1969.

Featherston, Alwyn. *Battle for Mortain: The 30th Infantry Division Saves the Breakout, August 7–12, 1944.* Novato, Calif.: Presidio Press, 1998.

Fifth Armored Division Association. *Paths of Armor: The Fifth Armored Division in World War II.* Nashville, Tenn.: Battery Press, 1985.

Forty, George. *Patton's Third Army at War.* New York: Scribner, 1978.

———. *Road to Berlin: the Allied Drive from Normandy.* London: Cassell, 1999.

Fox, Don M. *Patton's Vanguard: The United States Army Fourth Armored Division.* Jefferson, N.C.: McFarland, 2003.

Fussell, Paul. *The Boys' Crusade: the American Infantry in Northwestern Europe, 1944–1945.* New York: Modern Library, 2003.

Gabel, Christopher R. *The Lorraine Campaign: An Overview, September–December 1944.* Fort Leavenworth, Kans.: Combat Studies Institute, 1985.

Gilbert, Martin. *D-Day.* Hoboken, N.J.: J. Wiley & Sons, 2004.

———. *The Day the War Ended: May 8, 1945 Victory in Europe.* New York: Henry Holt, 1995.

Hammond, William M. *Normandy.* Washington, D.C.: U.S. Army Center of Military History, 1994.

Harrison, Gordon A. *Cross-Channel Attack.* Washington, D.C.: Center of Military History, 2002.

Hastings, Max. *Armageddon: the Battle for Germany, 1944–45.* New York: Knopf, 2004.

———. *Overlord: D-Day and the Battle for Normandy.* New York: Simon & Schuster, 1984.

Headquarters, First Allied Airborne Army. *Airborne Operations in Holland, September–November 1944.* N.p., 1944.

Hewitt, H. K. *Invasion of Southern France: Report of Naval Commander, Western Task Force.* Washington, D.C.: United States Navy Eighth Fleet, 1944.

Hechler, Ken. *The Bridge at Remagen.* New York: Ballantine Books, 1957.

Hewitt, Robert L. *Work Horse of the Western Front: The Story of the 30th Infantry Division.* Washington, D.C.: Infantry Journal Press, 1946.

Historical Board 89th Infantry Division. *The 89th Infantry Division, 1942–1945.* Washington, D.C.: Infantry Journal Press, 1947.

Hoegh, Leo A. *Timberwolf Tracks: The History of the 104th Infantry Division, 1942–1945.* Washington, D.C.: Infantry Journal Press, 1946.

Hogan, David W. *A Command Post at War: First Army Headquarters in Europe, 1943–1945.* Washington, D.C.: U.S. Army Center of Military History, 2000.

———. *Northern France.* Washington, D.C.: U.S. Army Center of Military History, 1995.

Holmes, Richard. *The D-Day Experience: From Operation Overlord to the Liberation of Paris.* London: Carlton, 2004.

Houston, Donald E. *Hell on Wheels: The 2nd Armored Division.* San Rafael, Calif.: Presidio Press, 1977.

Keegan, John. *Six Armies in Normandy: From D-Day to the Liberation of Paris, June 6th–August 25th, 1944.* New York: Viking Press, 1982.

Kershaw, Alex. *The Longest Winter: the Battle of the Bulge and the Epic Story of WWII's Most Decorated Platoon.* Cambridge, Mass.: Da Capo Press, 2004.

Koyen, Kenneth A. *The Fourth Armored Division: From the Beach to Bavaria.* Munich, Germany: Herderdruck, 1946.

Lauer, Walter E. *Battle Babies: The Story of the 99th Infantry Division in World War II.* Baton Rouge, La.: Military Press of Louisiana, 1951.

Lewis, Adrian R. *Omaha Beach: A Flawed Victory.* Chapel Hill: University of North Carolina Press, 2001.

MacDonald, Charles B. *The Last Offensive.* Washington, D.C.: Office of the Chief of Military History, 1973.

———. *The Mighty Endeavor: American Armed Forces in the European Theater in World War II.* New York: Oxford University Press, 1969.

———. *The Operations of VII Corps in September 1944.* Washington, D.C.: Office of the Chief of Military History, Department of the Army, 1953.

———. *The Siegfried Line Campaign.* Washington, D.C.: Office of the Chief of Military History, 1963.

———. *A Time for Trumpets: The Untold Story of the Battle of the Bulge.* New York: Morrow, 1984.

Marshall, S. L. A. *Night Drop: The American Airborne Invasion of Normandy.* Boston: Little, Brown, 1962.

Maule, Henry. *Normandy Breakout.* New York: Quadrangle, 1977.

Messenger, Charles. *The Second World War in Europe.* Washington, D.C.: Smithsonian Books, 2004.

McKee, Alexander. *The Race for the Rhine Bridges: 1940, 1944, 1945.* New York: Stein and Day, 1971.

McManus, John C. *The Americans at D-day: the American Experience at the Normandy Invasion.* New York: Forge, 2004.

———. *The Americans at Normandy: The Summer of 1944—the American War from the Normandy Beaches to Falaise.* New York: Forge, 2004.

Miller, Robert A. *August 1944: The Campaign for France.* Novato, Calif.: Presidio Press, 1988.

Millis, Walter. *The Last Phase: The Allied Victory in Western Europe.* Boston: Houghton Mifflin, 1946.

Morison, Samuel Eliot. *The Invasion of France and Germany, 1944–1945.* Boston: Little, Brown, 1957.

Mueller, Ralph, and Jerry Turk. *Report After Action: The Story of the 103rd Infantry Division.* Innsbruck, Austria: Headquarters, 103rd Infantry Division, 1945.

Nichols, Lester M. *Impact: The Battle Story of the Tenth Armored Division.* New York: Bradbury, Sayles, 1954.

Pogue, Forrest C. *The Decision to Halt at the Elbe.* Washington, D.C.: Center of Military History, U.S. Army, 1990.

Quarrie, Bruce. *The Ardennes Offensive U.S. III & XII Corps: Southern Sector.* Oxford: Osprey, 2000.

Reardon, Mark J. *Victory at Mortain: Stopping Hitler's Panzer Counteroffensive.* Lawrence: University Press of Kansas, 2002.

Rickard, John N. *Patton at Bay: The Lorraine Campaign, September to December, 1944.* Westport, Conn.: Praeger, 1999.

Ruggero, Ed. *Combat Jump: The Young Men Who Led the Assault into Fortress Europe, July, 1943.* New York: HarperCollins, 2003.

———. *The First Men In: U.S. Paratroopers and the Fight to Save D-day.* New York: HarperCollins, 2006.

Ryan, Cornelius. *The Longest Day, June 6, 1944.* New York: Simon & Schuster, 1959.

Saunders, Tim. *Hell's Highway.* Barnsley, South Yorkshire, England: Leo Cooper, 2001.

Smith, Steven. *2nd Armored Division: "Hell on Wheels."* Surrey, England: Military Book Club, 2003.

Smith, Walter B. *Eisenhower's Six Great Decisions: Europe, 1944–1945.* New York: Longmans, Green, 1956.

Steidl, Franz. *Lost Battalions: Going for Broke in the Vosges, Autumn 1944.* Novato, Calif.: Presidio Press, 1997.

Stock, James W. *Rhine Crossing.* New York: Ballantine Books, 1973.

Sullivan, John J. *Overlord's Eagles: Operations of the United States Army Air Forces in the Invasion of Normandy in World War II.* Jefferson, N.C.: McFarland, 1997.

Third Armored Division. *Spearhead in the West, 1941–45: The Third Armored Division.* Frankfurt am Main, Germany: F.J. Henrich, 1945.

Thompson, Reginald William. *D-Day: Spearhead of Invasion.* New York: Ballantine Books, 1968.

Tolhurst, Michael. *Saint Vith: 106th US Infantry Division.* London: Leo Cooper, 1999.

United States Army VII Corps. *Mission Accomplished: The Story of the Campaigns of the VII Corps, United States Army in the War.* Leipzig, Germany: J. J. Weber, 1945.

United States Army XI Corps. *History of XI Corps, 15 June 1942–15 March 1946.* XI Corps Historical Section, 1946.

United States Army XVI Corps. *History of the XVI Corps From Its Activation to the End of the War in Europe.* Washington, D.C.: Infantry Journal Press, 1947.

United States Army, 82nd Airborne Division G-3. *The Eighty Second Airborne Division: Operation "Neptune": Normandy 6 June–8 July 1944.* N.p., 1944.

United States Army, 101st Airborne Division G-3. *Field Order No. 1.* N.p., 1944.

United States First Army. *Report of Operations, Oct. 20, 1943–Aug. 1, 1944–Feb. 23–May 8, 1945.* N.p., 1945.

United States Military Academy Department of Military Art and Engineering. *The Invasion of Western Europe: Part 2 (January to May 1945).* West Point, N.Y.: U.S. Military Academy, 1946.

———. *The War in Western Europe.* West Point, N.Y.: U.S. Military Academy, 1952.

———. *The Invasion of Western Europe: (6 June to 31 December 1944).* West Point, N.Y.: U.S. Military Academy, 1945.

United States Seventh Army. *Report of Operations: The Seventh United States Army in France and Germany 1944–1945.* Heidelberg, Germany: Aloys Gräf, 1946.

United States Seventh Army G-2. *Seventh Army Operations in Europe, 15 August 1944–8 May 1945.* N.p., 1945.

United States War Department, General Staff. *Omaha Beachhead.* Washington, D.C.: War Department Historical Division, 1945.

———. *St-Lô.* Washington, D.C.: War Department Historical Division, 1946.

United States War Department, Historical Division. *Omaha Beachhead*. Washington, D.C.: Center of Military History, 1994.

Von Luettichau, Charles V. *The Ardennes Offensive: Germany's Situation in the Fall of 1944*. Washington, D.C.: Research Section, Office of Military History, Department of the Army, 1953.

Weigley, Russell F. *Eisenhower's Lieutenants: The Campaign of France and Germany, 1944–1945*. Bloomington: Indiana University Press, 1981.

Whitaker, W. Denis. *Rhineland: The Battle to End the War*. New York: St. Martin's Press, 1989.

Whiting, Charles. *America's Forgotten Army: The Story of the U.S. Seventh*. Rockville Centre, N.Y.: Sarpedon, 1999.

———. *The End of the War, Europe: April 15–May 23, 1945*. New York: Stein and Day, 1973.

———. *The Other Battle of the Bulge: Operation Northwind*. Chelsea, Mich.: Scarborough House, 1990.

Wilmot, Chester. *The Struggle for Europe*. New York: Harper, 1952.

EUROPEAN THEATER OF OPERATIONS—AIR

Astor, Gerald. *The Mighty Eighth: The Air War in Europe As Told by the Men Who Fought It*. New York: D.I. Fine Books, 1997.

Comer, John. *Combat Crew: A True Story of Flying and Fighting in World War II*. New York: W. Morrow, 1988.

Conversino, Mark J. *Fighting With the Soviets: The Failure of Operation Frantic 1944–45*. Lawrence: University Press of Kansas, 1997.

Copp, DeWitt S. *Forged in Fire: Strategy and Decisions in the Air War Over Europe, 1940–45*. Garden City, N.Y.: Doubleday, 1982.

Crane, Conrad. *Bombs, Cities, and Civilians, American Airpower Strategy in World War II*. Lawrence: University Press of Kansas, 1993.

Hallion, Richard. *D-Day 1944: Air Power Over the Normandy Beaches and Beyond*. Washington, D.C.: Air Force Marine Corps Historical Center Program, 1994.

Hughes, Thomas A. *Overlord: General Pete Quesada and the Triumph of Tactical Air Power in World War II*. New York: Free Press, 1995.

Infield, Glenn B. *Big Week: The Classic Story of the Crucial Air Battle of WW II*. Washington, D.C.: Brassey's, 1993.

Middlebrook, Martin. *The Schweinfurt-Regensburg Mission*. New York: Scribner, 1983.

Miller, Donald L. *Masters of the Air: America's Bomber Boys Who Fought the Air War Against Nazi Germany*. New York: Simon & Schuster, 2006.

Morrison, Wilbur H. *Fortress Without a Roof: The Allied Bombing of the Third Reich*. New York: St. Martin's Press, 1982.

Office of Air Force History. *Condensed Analysis of the Ninth Air Force in the European Theater of Operations*. Washington, D.C., 1984.

Parker, Danny S. *To Win the Winter Sky: The Air War over the Ardennes, 1944–1945*. Conshohocken, Pa.: Combined Books, 1994.

Perret, Geoffrey. *Winged Victory: The Army Air Forces in World War II*. New York: Random House, 1993.

Ramsey, John. *Ninth Air Force in the ETO, 16 October 1943 to 16 April 1944*. Washington, D.C.: Assistant Chief of Intelligence, Historical Division, 1945.

United States Army Air Forces. *Sunday Punch in Normandy: The Tactical Use of Heavy Bombardment in the Normandy Invasion*. Washington, D.C.: Headquarters, Army Air Forces, 1945.

United States Army Air Forces Historical Office. *Ninth Air Force, April to November 1944*. N.p., Headquarters, Ninth Air Force, 1944.

IX Troop Carrier Command Headquarters. *Air invasion of Holland: Report on Operation Market*. N.p., 1945.

EUROPEAN THEATER OF OPERATIONS—NAVAL

Office of the Chief of Naval Operations. *Amphibious Operations: Invasion of Northern France*. Washington, D.C.: United States Fleet, Headquarters of the Commander in Chief, 1944.

———. *Battle Experience: Supporting Operations for the Invasion of Northern France, June, 1944*. Washington, D.C.: United States Fleet, Headquarters of the Commander in Chief, 1944.

United States Naval Forces, Europe. *Operation Normandy Invasion: Report of Naval Commander Western Task Force (CTF 122)*. London, 1944.

NORTH AFRICA AND MEDITERRANEAN—GROUND OPERATIONS

Adleman, Robert H., and George Walton. *Rome Fell Today.* Boston: Little, Brown, 1968.

Alexander, Harold R. L. G. *Report by the Supreme Allied Commander, Mediterranean Field-Marshall the Viscount Alexander of Tunis, to the Combined Chiefs of Staff on the Italian Campaign, 12th December 1944 to 2nd May 1945.* London: H.M.S.O., 1951.

Allied Forces Mediterranean Theater. *Report by the Supreme Allied Commander, Mediterranean, to the Combined Chiefs of Staff on the Italian Campaign.* London: H.M.S.O., 1946.

Allied Forces Supreme Commander Mediterranean. *Report by the Supreme Allied Commander, Mediterranean, to the Combined Chiefs of Staff on the Operations in Southern France, August 1944.* London: H.M.S.O., 1946.

Allied Forces, Supreme Headquarters. *Lessons from the Tunisian Campaign.* Washington, D.C.: U.S. Government Printing Office, 1943.

Anderson, Charles R. *Tunisia.* Washington, D.C.: U.S. Army Center of Military History, 1993.

Birtle, Andrew J. *Sicily.* Washington, D.C.: Center of Military History, 1993.

Blumenson, Martin. *General Lucas at Anzio.* Washington, D.C.: Center of Military History, U.S. Army, 1990.

———. *Salerno to Cassino.* Washington, D.C.: Office of the Chief of Military History, 1969.

———. *Sicily: Whose Victory?* New York: Ballantine Books, 1969.

Bond, Harold L. *Return to Cassino: A Memoir of the Fight for Rome.* Garden City, N.Y.: Doubleday, 1964.

Breuer, William B. *Drop Zone, Sicily: Allied Airborne Strike, July 1943.* Novato, Calif.: Presidio Press, 1983.

Clark, Mark W. *Calculated Risk.* New York: Harper, 1950.

Clarke, Jeffrey J. *Southern France.* Washington, D.C.: U.S. Army Center of Military History, 1994.

D'Este, Carlo. *Fatal Decision: Anzio and the Battle for Rome.* New York: HarperCollins, 1991.

———. *World War II in the Mediterranean, 1942–1945.* Chapel Hill, N.C.: Algonquin Books, 1990.

Department of the Army, Office of Military History. *Anzio Beachhead, 22 January–25 May 1944.* Washington, D.C.: Historical Division, War Department, 1947.

Fisher, Ernest F. *Cassino to the Alps.* Washington, D.C.: Center of Military History, 1977.

Forty, George. *Fifth Army at War.* New York: Scribner, 1980.

Garland, Albert N., and Howard M. Smyth. *Sicily and the Surrender of Italy.* Washington, D.C.: United States Army in World War II. Government Printing Office, 1965.

Gibran, Daniel K. *The 92nd Infantry Division and the Italian Campaign in World War II.* Jefferson, N.C.: McFarland, 2001.

Graham, Dominick, and Shelford Bidwell. *Tug of War: The Battle for Italy, 1943–1945.* New York: St. Martin's Press, 1986.

Hammel, Eric M. *Air War Europa: America's Air War Against Germany in Europe and North Africa, 1942–1945.* Pacifica, Calif.: Pacifica Press, 1994.

Hargrove, Hondon B. *Buffalo Soldiers in Italy: Black Americans in World War II.* Jefferson, N.C.: McFarland, 1985.

Harpur, Brian. *The Impossible Victory: A Personal Account of the Battle for the River Po.* New York: Hippocrene Books, 1981.

Headquarters, Allied Forces Mediterranean Theatre. *Operation ANVIL.* N.p., 1944.

———. *The Report of the Commander-in-Chief, Mediterranean on the Invasion of Sicily.* N.p., 1945.

Headquarters, Fifteenth Army Group. *Finito: The Po Valley Campaign, 1945.* Milan, Italy: N.p., 1945.

Higgins, Trumbull. *Soft Underbelly: The Anglo-American Controversy Over the Italian Campaign, 1939–1945.* New York: Macmillan, 1968.

Historical Section, United States Fifth Army. *Fifth Army History.* N.p., 1945.

Hoyt, Edwin P. *Backwater War: The Allied Campaign in Italy, 1943–1945.* Westport, Conn.: Praeger, 2002.

Huff, Richard A. *A Pictorial History of the 36th "Texas" Infantry Division.* Austin, Tex.: 36th Division Association, n.d.

Jackson, W. G. F. *The Battle for Italy.* New York: Harper and Row, 1967.

Jenkins, McKay. *The Last Ridge: The Epic Story of the U.S. Army's 10th Mountain Division and the Assault on Hitler's Europe.* New York: Random House, 2003.

Lamb, Richard. *The War in Italy, 1943–1945: A Brutal Story.* New York: St. Martin's Press, 1996.

Laurie, Clayton D. *Anzio.* Washington, D.C.: U.S. Army Center of Military History, 1994.

Mason, David. *Salerno: Foothold in Europe.* New York: Ballantine Books, 1972.

Mathews, Sidney T. *General Clark's Decision to Drive on Rome.* Washington, D.C.: Center of Military History, U.S. Army, 1990.

Matloff, Maurice. *The Anvil Decision: Crossroads of Strategy.* Washington, D.C.: Center of Military History, U.S. Army, 1990.

Moorehead, Alan. *The March to Tunis: The North African War, 1940–1943.* New York: Harper and Row, 1967.

Morris, Eric. *Circles of Hell: The War in Italy, 1943–1945.* New York: Crown, 1993.

Newell, Clayton R. *Egypt-Libya.* Washington, D.C.: U.S. Army Center of Military History, 1993.

Oland, Dwight D. *North Apennines.* Washington, D.C.: U.S. Army Center of Military History, 1996.

Orgill, Douglas. *The Gothic Line: The Italian Campaign, Autumn, 1944.* New York: Norton, 1967.

Pack, S. W. C. *Operation Husky: The Allied Invasion of Sicily.* New York: Hippocrene Books, 1977.

Popa, Thomas A. *Po Valley.* Washington, D.C.: U.S. Army Center of Military History, 1996.

Porch, Douglas. *The Path to Victory: The Mediterranean Theater in World War II.* New York: Farrar, Straus, and Giroux, 2004.

Robbins, Robert A. *The 91st Infantry Division of World War II.* Washington, D.C.: Infantry Journal Press, 1947.

Shelton, Peter. *Climb to Conquer: The Untold Story of World War II's 10th Mountain Division Ski Troops.* New York: Scribner, 2003

Shepperd, G. A. The *Italian Campaign, 1943–45: A Political and Military Reassessment.* New York: Praeger, 1968.

Shirey, Orville C. *Americans: The Story of the 442nd Combat Team.* Washington, D.C.: Infantry Journal Press, 1947.

Smith, Kenneth V. *Naples-Foggia.* Washington, D.C.: U.S. Army Center of Military History, 1994.

Starr, Chester G. *From Salerno to the Alps: A History of the Fifth Army, 1943–1945.* Washington, D.C.: Infantry Journal Press, 1948.

Strawson, John. *The Italian Campaign.* New York: Carroll and Graf, 1988.

United States Fifth Army G-3. *The Advance on Rome of the Fifth Army: Under the Command of Lieutenant General Mark W. Clark.* N.p., 1944.

———. *Road to Rome: Salerno, Naples, Volturno, Cassino, Anzio, Rome.* N.p., 1944.

United States Fifteenth Army. *History of the Fifteenth United States Army, 21 August 1944 to 11 July 1945.* N.p., 1946.

United States Military Academy Department of Military Art and Engineering. *Operations in Sicily and Italy (July 1943 to December 1944).* West Point, N.Y.: U.S. Military Academy, 1945.

———. *Operations in Sicily and Italy (July 1943 to May 1945).* West Point, N.Y.: U.S. Military Academy, 1945.

United States Seventh Army G-3. *Dragoon: Field Order Number 1.* N.p., 1944.

United States War Department, General Staff. *Fifth Army at the Winter Line (15 November 1943–15 January 1944).* Washington, D.C.: Military Historical Division, War Department, 1945.

———. *From the Volturno to the Winter Line (6 October–15 November 1943).* Washington, D.C.: Military Historical Division, War Department, 1945.

———. *Salerno: American Operations from the Beaches to the Volturno (9 September–6 October 1943).* Washington, D.C.: Military Historical Division, War Department, 1945.

U.S. Army Center of Military History. *To Bizerte With the II Corps, 23 April–13 May 1943.* Washington, D.C., 1990.

———. *Fifth Army at the Winter Line, 15 November 1943–15 January 1944.* Washington, D.C., N.p., 1990.

NORTH AFRICA AND MEDITERRANEAN—AIR AND NAVAL OPERATIONS

Allied Forces, Western Naval Task Force. *Operation Plan No. 7–43.* Algiers, Algeria: Allied Forces Headquarters, 1943.

———. *Operation Plan No. 4–44.* Algiers, Algeria: Headquarters, Allied Forces Mediterranean: 1944.

———. *The Sicilian Campaign: Operation "Husky" July–August, 1943.* N.p., 1943.

Clifford, Robert L., and William J. Maddocks. *Naval Gunfire Support of the Landing in Sicily.* Oklahoma City, Okla.: 45th Infantry Division Museum, 1984.

Coles, Harry L. *Participation of the Ninth and Twelfth Air Forces in the Sicilian Campaign.* Washington, D.C.: Army Air Force Historical Office, 1945.

Dugan, James, and Carroll Stewart. *Ploești: The Great Ground-Air Battle of 1 August 1943.* Washington, D.C.: Brassey's, 1998.

Koburger, Charles W. *Naval Warfare in the Eastern Mediterranean, 1940–1945.* Westport, Conn.: Praeger, 1993.

McCarthy, Michael C. *Air-to-Ground Battle for Italy.* Maxwell Air Force Base, Ala.: Air University Press, 2004.

Morison, Samuel Eliot. *Operations in North African Waters, October 1942–June 1943.* Boston: Little, Brown, 1947.

Office of Naval Intelligence. *The Sicilian Campaign, 10 July–17 August 1943.* Washington, D.C., 1945.

Russell, Edward T. *The U.S. Army Air Forces in World War II: Africa to the Alps. The Army Air Forces in the Mediterranean Theater.* Washington, D.C.: Air Force History and Museums Program, 1999.

United States Army Air Forces. *Air Phase of the Italian Campaign to 1 January 1944.* Washington, D.C.: Headquarters, Army Air Force, 1946.

United States Navy, Eighth Fleet. *Operation Plan 147–43 "Shingle."* N.p., 1944.

Pacific–Army Ground and Air Forces (Southwest Pacific Area)

Abington, Juliette. *Summary of Air Action in the Philippines and Netherlands East Indies, 7 December 1941 to 26 March 1942.* Washington, D.C.: Historical Division, War Department, 1945.

Allied Forces South West Pacific Area. *Reno V: Outline Plan for Operations of the Southwest Pacific Area to Include the Reoccupation of the Philippines.* N.p., 1944.

———. *Reno IV: Outline Plan for Operations of the Southwest Pacific Area to Include the Reoccupation of the Philippines.* N.p., 1944.

Anderson, Charles R. *Papua.* Washington, D.C.: U.S. Army Center of Military History, 1992.

———. *Western Pacific.* Washington, D.C.: U.S. Army Center of Military History, 1994.

Andradé, Dale. *Luzon.* Washington, D.C.: U.S. Army Center of Military History, 1996.

Astor, Gerald. *Crisis in the Pacific: The Battles for the Philippine Islands by the Men Who Fought Them.* New York: Donald I. Fine, 1996.

Bailey, Jennifer L. *Philippine Islands.* Washington, D.C.: U.S. Army Center of Military History, 1992.

Beck, John J. *MacArthur and Wainwright: Sacrifice of the Philippines.* Albuquerque: University of New Mexico Press, 1974.

Belote, James H., and William M. Belote. *Corregidor: The Saga of a Fortress.* New York: Harper & Row, 1967.

Boggs, Charles W., Jr. *Marine Aviation in the Philippines.* Washington, D.C.: United States Marine Corps Historical Center, 1951.

Breuer, William B. *Retaking the Philippines: America's Return to Corregidor and Bataan, October 1944–March 1945.* New York: St. Martin's Press, 1986.

Cannon, M. Hamlin. *Leyte: The Return to the Philippines.* Washington, D.C.: Office of the Chief of Military History, 1954.

Commander in Chief, United States Navy Pacific Fleet and Pacific Ocean Areas. *Joint Staff Study: Olympic Naval and Amphibious Operations.* N.p., 1945.

Connaughton, R. M., John Pimlott, and Duncan Anderson. *The Battle for Manila.* Novato, Calif.: Presidio Press, 1995.

———. *MacArthur and Defeat in the Philippines.* Woodstock, N.Y.: Overlook Press, 2001.

Conroy, Robert. *The Battle of Bataan: America's Greatest Defeat.* New York: Macmillan, 1969.

Devlin, Gerard M. *Back to Corregidor: America Retakes the Rock.* New York: St. Martin's Press, 1992.

Drea, Edward J. *New Guinea.* Washington, D.C.: U.S. Army Center of Military History, 1993.

Falk, Stanley L. *Decision at Leyte.* New York: W. W. Norton, 1966.

———. *Liberation of the Philippines.* New York: Ballantine Books, 1971.

Far East Command Military History Section. *Eastern New Guinea Invasion Operations.* Washington, D.C.: Office of the Chief of Military History, 1953.

Flanagan, E. M. *Corregidor: The Rock Force Assault, 1945.* Novato, Calif.: Presidio Press, 1988.

Frank, Richard B. *Downfall: The End of the Imperial Japanese Empire.* New York: Random House, 1999.

Gailey, Harry A. *MacArthur Strikes Back: Decision at Buna, New Guinea, 1942–1943.* Novato, Calif.: Presidio Press, 2000.

———. *MacArthur's Victory: The War in New Guinea, 1943–1944.* New York: Presidio Press, 2004.

Greene, Jack. *The Midway Campaign, December 7, 1941–June 6, 1942.* Conshohocken, Pa.: Combined Books, 1995.

Griffith, Thomas E. *MacArthur's Airman: General George C. Kenney and the War in the Southwest Pacific.* Lawrence: University Press of Kansas, 1998.

Headquarters United States Army Forces, Middle Pacific. *Participation in the Western Carolines and Central Philippines Operations by the United States Army Forces Pacific Ocean Areas, September–November 1944.* Edited by Robert C. Richardson, N.p., 1945.

Hirrel, Leo. *Bismarck Archipelago.* Washington, D.C.: U.S. Army Center of Military History, 1994.

Hoyt, Edwin P. *MacArthur's Navy.* New York: Orion, 1989.

Kenney, George C. *General Kenney Reports: A Personal History of the Pacific War.* Washington, D.C.: Office of Air Force History, 1987.

Leary, William M. *We Shall Return!: MacArthur's Commanders and the Defeat of Japan, 1942–1945.* Lexington: University Press of Kentucky, 1988.

Lofgren, Stephen J. *Southern Philippines.* Washington, D.C.: U.S. Army Center of Military History, 1996.

MacArthur, Douglas. *Reports of General MacArthur, Supreme Commander for the Allied Powers.* Washington, D.C.: U.S. Army Center of Military History, 1994.

Mayo, Lida. *Bloody Buna.* Garden City, N.Y.: Doubleday, 1974.

McAulay, Lex. *MacArthur's Eagles: The U.S. Air War Over New Guinea, 1943–1944.* Annapolis, Md.: Naval Institute Press, 2005.

Miller, J. Michael. *From Shanghai to Corregidor: Marines in the Defense of the Philippines.* Washington, D.C.: Marine Corps Historical Center, 1997.

Miller, John. *Cartwheel: The Reduction of Rabaul.* Washington, D.C.: Office of the Chief of Military History, 1959.

Miller, John, Jr. *MacArthur and the Admiralties.* Washington, D.C.: U.S. Army, Center of Military History, 1990.

Milner, Samuel. *Victory in Papua.* Washington, D.C.: U.S. Army Center of Military History, 2003.

Morison, Samuel Eliot. *The Liberation of the Philippines: Luzon, Mindanao, the Visayans, 1944–1945.* Boston: Little, Brown, 1959.

———. *Leyte, June 1944–January 1945.* Boston: Little, Brown, 1958.

———. *Breaking the Bismarcks Barrier: 22 July 1942–1 May 1944.* Boston: Little, Brown, 1950.

Morris, Eric. *Corregidor: The End of the Line.* New York: Stein and Day, 1981.

Morton, Louis. *The Decision to Withdraw to Bataan.* Washington, D.C.: Center of Military History, U.S. Army, 1990.

———. *The Fall of the Philippines.* Washington, D.C.: Office of the Chief of Military History, 1953.

Office of the Chief of Naval Operations. *Amphibious Operations: Invasion of the Philippines, October 1944 to January 1945.* Washington, D.C.: United States Fleet, Headquarters of the Commander in Chief, 1945.

Prefer, Nathan. *MacArthur's New Guinea Campaign.* Conshohocken, Pa.: Combined Books, 1995.

Rees, David. *The Defeat of Japan.* Westport, Conn.: Praeger, 1997.

Rodman, Matthew K. *A War of Their Own: Bombers Over the Southwest Pacific.* Maxwell Air Force Base, Ala.: Air University Press, 2005.

Sakaida, Henry. *The Siege of Rabaul.* St. Paul, Minn.: Phalanx Press, 1996.

Smith, Robert R. *The Approach to the Philippines.* Washington, D.C.: Center of Military History, 1996.

———. *Triumph in the Philippines.* Washington, D.C.: U.S. Army Center of Military History, 1991.

Taaffe, Stephen R. *MacArthur's Jungle War: The 1944 New Guinea Campaign.* Lawrence: University Press of Kansas, 1998.

Templeman, Harold. *The Return to Corregidor.* New York: Strand Press, 1945.

United States Army Far East Command. *Jolo Island Invasion Operations Record.* Tokyo, 1952.

———. *Philippine Area Naval Operations, Part IV. Jan 45–Aug 45.* Tokyo, 1952.

———. *Philippine Operations Record: Phase Three, Vol. IV: General Outline of Mindoro Operations.* Tokyo, 1952.

———. *Tarakan Invasion Operations Record.* Tokyo, 1952.

United States Army Forces, Pacific. *Staff Study Operations: Olympic.* General Headquarters, U.S. Army Forces, Pacific, 1945.

United States Army, Headquarters, 37th Infantry Regiment. *After Action Report: Operations of the 37th Infantry Division, Luzon P.I., 1 November 1944 to 30 June 1945.* N.p., 1945.

United States Army I Corps. *History of the Hollandia Operation: Reckless Task Force.* N.p., 1944.

United States Army X Corps. *History of X Corps on Mindanao, 17 April 45–30 June 45.* N.p., 1945.

United States Eighth Army. *Report of the Commanding General, Eighth Army: On the Luzon Mop-Up.* N.p., 1945.

———. *Report of the Commanding General, Eighth Army: On the Mindanao Operation.* N.p., 1946.

———. *Report of the Commanding General, Eighth Army: On the Nasugbu and Bataan Operations.* N.p., 1946.

———. *Report of the Commanding General, Eighth Army: On the Palawan and Zamboanga Operations.* N.p., 1946.

———. *Report of the Commanding General, Eighth Army: On the Panay-Negros and Cebu Operations.* N.p., 1946.

United States Navy. *Report of Luzon Operation (Lingayen Gulf), Philippine Islands.* 3rd Amphibious Force, N.p., 1945.

———. *Seizure of Leyte: Report of Participation of Task Force Seventy-Nine.* 3rd Amphibious Force, N.p., 1944.

United States Sixth Army. *Report of the Leyte Operation, 17 October 1944–25 December 1944.* N.p., 1945.

———. *Report of the Luzon Campaign, 9 January 1945–30 June 1945.* N.p., 1945.

United States War Department, General Staff. *Papuan Campaign: The Buna-Sanananda Operation, 16 November 1942–23 January 1943.* Washington, D.C.: Military Intelligence Division, U.S. War Department, 1944.

U.S. Army Center of Military History. *The Admiralties, Operations of the 1st Cavalry Division, 29 February–18 May 1944.* Washington, D.C.: N.p., 1990.

———. *Papuan Campaign: The Buna–Sanananda Operation, 16 November 1942–23 January 1943.* Washington, D.C.: N.p., 1990.

Vader, John. *New Guinea: The Tide Is Stemmed.* New York: Ballantine Books, 1971.

Vego, Milan N. *The Battle for Leyte, 1944: Allied and Japanese Plans, Preparations, and Execution.* Annapolis, Md.: Naval Institute Press, 2006.

Whitman, John W. *Bataan, Our Last Ditch: The Bataan Campaign, 1942.* New York: Hippocrene Books, 1990.

PACIFIC—NAVAL FORCES, MARINE, AND AIR FORCES (NORTHERN, CENTRAL, AND SOUTHERN PACIFIC)

A History of the Tornado Task Force in the Wakde Islands—Sarmi Area, Dutch New Guinea, 12 June–18 July 1944. N.p., 1944.

Alexander, Joseph H. *Across the Reef: The Marine Assault of Tarawa.* Washington, D.C.: Marine Corps Historical Center, 1993.

———. *The Final Campaign: Marines in the Victory on Okinawa.* Washington, D.C.: Marine Corps Historical Center, 1996.

Appleman, Roy E. *Okinawa: The Last Battle.* Washington, D.C.: Historical Division, Department of the Army, 1948.

Astor, Gerald. *Operation Iceberg: The Invasion and Conquest of Okinawa in World War II.* New York: D.I. Fine, 1995.

———. *Semper Fi in the Sky: Marine Air Battles of World War II.* New York: Ballantine, 2005.

———. *Wings of Gold: The U.S. Naval Air Campaign in World War II.* New York: Presidio Press, 2004.

Belote, James H., and William Belote. *Typhoon of Steel: The Battle for Okinawa.* New York: Harper & Row, 1970.

Bergerud, Eric M. *Fire in the Sky: The Air War in the South Pacific.* Boulder, Colo.: Westview Press, 2000.

———. *Touched With Fire: The Land War in the South Pacific.* New York: Viking Press, 1996.

Blair, Clay. *Silent Victory: The U.S. Submarine War Against Japan.* Philadelphia: J. B. Lippincott, 1975.

Chapin, John C. *Breaching the Marianas: The Battle for Saipan.* Washington, D.C.: Marine Corps Historical Center, 1994.

Chun, Clayton K. S. *The Doolittle Raid 1942: America's First Strike at Japan*. New York: Osprey Publishers, 2006.

Commander in Chief, Pacific Ocean Areas. *Campaign Plan Granite*. Pearl Harbor, Hawaii: N.p., 1944.

———. *Operation Plan No. 29–42 (Defense of Midway)*. Pearl Harbor: 27 May 1942.

Cressman, Robert J. *A Magnificent Fight: Marines in the Battle for Wake Island*. Washington, D.C.: Marine Corps Historical Center, 1992.

Cronin, Francis D. *Under the Southern Cross: The Saga of the Americal Division*. Washington, D.C.: Combat Forces Press, 1951.

Crowl, Philip A. *Campaign in the Marianas*. Washington, D.C.: Office of the Chief of Military History, 1960.

———. and Edmund G. Love. *Seizure of the Gilberts and Marshalls*. Washington, D.C.: Office of the Chief of Military History, 1955.

DeRose, James F. *Unrestricted Warfare: How a New Breed of Officers Led the Submarine Force to Victory in World War II*. New York: J. Wiley, 2000.

Feifer, George. *Tennozan: The Battle of Okinawa and the Atomic Bomb*. New York: Ticknor and Fields, 1992.

———. *The Battle of Okinawa: The Blood and the Bomb*. Guilford, Conn.: Lyons Press, 2001.

Fisch, Arnold G. *Ryukyus*. Washington, D.C.: U.S. Army Center of Military History, 1995.

Frank, Benis M. *Okinawa: Capstone to Victory*. New York: Ballantine Books, 1970.

———. *Okinawa: The Great Island Battle*. New York: Elsevier-Dutton, 1978.

Gayle, Gordon D. *Bloody Beaches: The Marines at Peleliu*. Washington, D.C.: Marine Corps Historical Center, 1996.

Gorman, G. Scott. *Endgame in the Pacific: Complexity, Strategy, and the B-29*. Maxwell Air Force Base, Ala.: Air University Press, 2000.

Grace, James W. *The Naval Battle of Guadalcanal: Night Action, 13 November 1942*. Annapolis, Md.: Naval Institute Press, 1999.

Graham, Michael B. *Mantle of Heroism: Tarawa and the Struggle for the Gilberts, November 1943*. Novato, Calif.: Presidio Press, 1993.

Hallas, James H. *Killing Ground on Okinawa: The Battle for Sugar Loaf Hill*. Westport, Conn.: Praeger, 1996.

Hammel, Eric M. *Munda Trail: The New Georgia Campaign*. New York: Orion Books, 1989.

Harwood, Richard. *A Close Encounter: The Marine Landing on Tinian*. Washington, D.C.: Marine Corps Historical Center, 1994.

Haulman, Daniel L. *The U.S. Army Air Forces in World War II: The High Road to Tokyo Bay: The AAF in the Asiatic-Pacific Theater*. Washington, D.C.: Center for Air Force History, 1993.

———. *The U.S. Army Air Forces in World War II: Hitting Home: The Air Offensive Against Japan*. Washington, D.C.: Air Force History and Museums Program, 1999.

Headquarters Tenth Army. *Report of Operations in the Ryukyus Campaign*. N.p., 1945.

Heinl, R.D., Jr. *The Defense of Wake*. Washington, D.C.: Historical Section, United States Marine Corps, 1947.

Herbert, Kevin. *Maximum Effort: The B-29s Against Japan*. Manhattan, Kans.: Sunflower University Press, 1983.

Historical Office, Headquarters, Army Air Forces. *Operational History of the Seventh Air Force, 7 December 1941 to 6 November 1943*. Washington, D.C.: Headquarters, Army Air Forces, 1945.

———. *Operational History of the Seventh Air Force, 6 November 1943 to 31 July 1944*. Washington, D.C.: Headquarters, Army Air Forces, 1945.

Historical Section, 81st Infantry Division. *The 81st Infantry Wildcat Division in World War II*. Washington. D.C.: Infantry Journal Press, 1948.

Hoffman, Carl W. *Saipan: The Beginning of the End*. Washington, D.C.: Historical Division, United States Marine Corps, 1950.

———. *The Seizure of Tinian*. Washington, D.C.: Historical Division, United States Marine Corps, 1951.

Hoffman, Jon T. *From Makin to Bougainville: Marine Raiders in the Pacific War*. Washington, D.C.: Marine Corps Historical Center, 1993.

———. *Silk Chutes and Hard Fighting: U.S. Marine Corps Parachute Units in World War II*. Washington, D.C.: Marine Corps Historical Center, 1999.

Hough, Frank O. *The Assault on Peleliu*. Washington, D.C.: Historical Division, United States Marine Corps, 1950.

Hough, Frank O., and John A. Crown. *The Campaign on New Britain*. Washington, D.C.: Historical Division, United States Marine Corps, 1952.

Hoyt, Edwin P. *Storm over the Gilberts: War in the Central Pacific, 1943*. New York: Van Nostrand, 1978.

Isely, Jeter, and Philip A. Crowl. *The U.S. Marines and Amphibious War*. Princeton, N.J.: Princeton University Press, 1951.

Kilpatrick, C. W. *The Naval Night Battles in the Solomons*. Pompano Beach: Exposition Press of Florida, 1987.

Leckie, Robert. *Okinawa: The Last Battle of World War II*. New York: Viking Press, 1995.

MacGarrigle, George L. *Aleutian Islands*. Washington, D.C.: U.S. Army Center of Military History, 1992.

McGee, William L. *Amphibious Operations in the South Pacific in World War II*. Santa Barbara, Calif.: BMC Publications, 2000.

Miller, John. *Guadalcanal: The First Offensive*. Washington, D.C.: Historical Division, War Department, 1949.

Morison, Samuel Eliot. *Coral Sea, Midway and Submarine Actions: May 1942–August 1942*. Boston: Little, Brown, 1949.

———. *The Rising Sun in the Pacific: 1931–April 1942*. Boston: Little, Brown, 1948.

———. *The Struggle for Guadalcanal, August 1942–February 1943*. Boston: Little, Brown, 1949.

———. *Victory in the Pacific, 1945*. Boston: Little, Brown, 1960.

Newell, Clayton R. *Central Pacific*. Washington, D.C.: U.S. Army Center of Military History, 1992.

Nichols, Charles S., Jr., and Henry I. Shaw, Jr. *Okinawa: Victory in the Pacific*. Washington: D.C.: Historical Branch, United States Marine Corps, 1955.

O'Brien, Cyril J. *Liberation: Marines in the Capture of Guam*. Washington, D.C.: Marine Corps Historical Center, 1992.

Office of the Chief of Naval Operations. *Battle Experience: Assault and Occupation of Attu Island, May 1943*. Washington, D.C.: United States Fleet, Headquarters of the Commander in Chief, 1943.

———. *Battle Experience: Battleship, Cruiser and Destroyer Sweep around Truk, 16–17 February 1944*. Washington, D.C.: United States Fleet, Headquarters of the Commander in Chief, 1944.

———. *Battle Experience: Bombardments of Iwo Jima, November 1944–January 1945, Third Fleet Operations*. Washington, D.C.: United States Fleet, Headquarters of the Commander in Chief, 1945.

———. *Amphibious Operations: Excluding Marshall Islands: January–March 1944*. Washington, D.C.: United States Fleet, Headquarters of the Commander in Chief, 1944.

———. *Amphibious Operations During the Period August to December 1943*. Washington, D.C.: United States Fleet, Headquarters of the Commander in Chief, 1944.

Office of Naval Intelligence. *The Aleutians Campaign, June 1942–August 1943*. Washington, D.C.: Department of the Navy, 1945.

———. *The Java Sea Campaign*. Washington, D.C.: Department of the Navy, 1945.

Prange, Gordon W., Donald M. Goldstein, and Katherine V. Dillon. *Miracle at Midway*. New York: McGraw-Hill, 1982.

Renzi, William A., and Mark D. Roehrs. *Never Look Back: A History of World War II in the Pacific*. New York: M. E. Sharpe, 1991.

Rohfleisch, Kramer J. *Guadalcanal and the Origins of the Thirteenth Air Force*. Washington, D.C.: Assistant Chief of Staff, Intelligence, Historical Division, 1945.

———. *The Thirteenth Air Force, March–October 1943*. Washington, D.C.: Army Air Forces Historical Office Headquarters, 1946.

Shaw, Henry I. *Tarawa: A Legend Is Born*. New York: Ballantine Books, 1969.

Sledge, E. B. *With the Old Breed, at Peleliu and Okinawa*. Novato, Calif.: Presidio Press, 1981.

Sloan, Bill. *Brotherhood of Heroes: The Marines at Peleliu, 1944, the Bloodiest Battle of the Pacific War*. New York: Simon & Schuster, 2005.

———. *Given Up for Dead: America's Heroic Stand at Wake Island*. New York: Bantam Books, 2003.

Smith, Steven T. *Wolfpack: The American Submarine Strategy that Helped Defeat Japan*. Hoboken, N.J.: Wiley, 2003.

Stockman, James R. *The Sixth Marine Division*. Washington, D.C.: Historical Division, United States Marine Corps, 1946.

Thomas, David A. *Japan's War at Sea: Pearl Harbor to the Coral Sea*. London: A. Deutsch, 1978.

Thomas, Evan. *Sea of Thunder: Four Commanders and the Last Great Naval Campaign, 1941–1945*. New York: Simon & Schuster, 2006.

Tillman, Barrett. *Clash of the Carriers: The True Story of the Marianas Turkey Shoot of World War II*. New York: New American Library, 2005.

United States Army Far East Command. *Central Pacific Air Operations Record*. Tokyo: N.p., 1953.

United States Army XXIV Corps. *Ryukyus: XXIV Corps Action Report, 1 April 1945–30 June 1945.* N.p., 1945.

Urwin, Gregory J. W. *Facing Fearful Odds: The Siege of Wake Island.* Lincoln: University of Nebraska Press, 1997.

U.S. Army Center of Military History. *The Capture of Makin, 20–24 November 1943.* Washington, D.C., 1990.

———. *Guam, Operations of the 77th Division, 21 July–10 August 1944.* Washington, D.C., 1990.

Van der Vat, Dan. *The Pacific Campaign: World War II, the U.S.-Japanese Naval War, 1941–1945.* New York: Simon & Schuster, 1991.

War Department Historical Division. *The Capture of Attu.* Washington, D.C.: Infantry Journal, 1944.

———. *The Capture of Makin, 20–24 November 1943.* Washington, D.C.: U.S. Army Center of Military History, 1990.

Werstein, Irving. *Okinawa: The Last Ordeal.* New York: Crowell, 1968.

Wheeler, Richard. *A Special Valor: The U.S. Marines and the Pacific War.* New York: Harper & Row, 1983.

Wilmott, H. P. *The Battle of Leyte Gulf: The Last Fleet Action.* Bloomington: Indiana University Press, 2005.

Wright, Burton, III. *Eastern Mandates.* Washington, D.C.: U.S. Army Center of Military History, 1993.

Wukovits, John F. *One Square Mile of Hell: The Battle for Tarawa.* 2006.

———. *Pacific Alamo: The Battle for Wake Island.* New York: New American Library, 2003.

CBI (China-Burma-India)

Callahan, Raymond. *Burma, 1942–1945.* Newark: University of Delaware Press, 1978.

Dunlop, Richard. *Behind Japanese Lines, with the OSS in Burma.* Chicago: Rand McNally, 1979.

Feis, Herbert. *China Tangle: The American Effort in China from Pearl Harbor to the Marshall Mission.* Princeton, N.J.: Princeton University Press, 1953.

Hogan, David W. *India–Burma.* Washington, D.C.: U.S. Army Center of Military History, 1992.

Kraus, Theresa, L. *China Offensive.* Washington, D.C.: U.S. Army Center for Military History, 1996.

Newell, Clayton R. *Burma 1942.* Washington, D.C.: U.S. Army Center for Military History, 1994.

Ogburn, Charlton, Jr. *The Marauders.* New York: Harper and Brothers, 1956.

Schaller, Michael. *The U.S. Crusade in China, 1938–1945.* New York: Columbia University Press, 1979.

Sherry, Mark D. *China Defensive.* Washington, D.C.: U.S. Army Center for Military History, 1996.

Tuchman, Barbara. *Stilwell and the American Experience in China. 1911–1945.* New York: Macmillan, 1970.

U.S. Army Center of Military History. *Merrill's Marauders, February–May 1944.* Washington, D.C., 1990.

Battle of the Atlantic

Hickam, Homer H. *Torpedo Junction: U-boat War off America's East Coast, 1942.* Annapolis, Md.: Naval Institute Press, 1989.

Middlebrook, Martin. *Convoy.* New York: William Morrow, 1976.

Monsarrat, Nicholas. *The Cruel Sea.* Short Hills, N.J.: Burford Books, 2000.

Deception and Intelligence

Bennett, Ralph F. *Ultra and Mediterranean Strategy.* New York: Morrow, 1989.

Breuer, William B. *Hoodwinking Hitler: the Normandy Deception.* Westport, Conn.: Praeger, 1993.

Cruickshank, Charles G. *Deception in World War II.* New York: Oxford University Press, 1979.

Drea, Edward J. *MacArthur's ULTRA: Codebreaking and the War Against Japan, 1942–1945.* Lawrence: University Press of Kansas, 1991.

Gannon, Michael. *Operation Drumbeat: The Dramatic True Story of Germany's First U-boat Attacks Along the American Coast in World War II.* New York: Harper and Row, 1990.

Handel, Michael I., ed. *Strategic and Operational Deception in the Second World War.* London: F. Cass, 1987.

Hartcup, Guy. *Code Name Mulberry: The Planning, Building, and Operation of the Normandy Harbours.* New York: Hippocrene Books, 1977.

Haswell, Jock. *The Intelligence and Deception of the D-Day Landings.* London: Batsford, 1979.

Whiting, Charles. *Ardennes: The Secret War.* New York: Stein and Day, 1985.

Winterbotham, F. W. *The Ultra Secret.* New York: Harper and Row, 1974.

Winton, John. *Ultra in the Pacific.* Annapolis, Md.: Naval Institute Press, 1993.

INTERNET RESOURCES

U.S. Army Center of Military History   www.army.mil/cmh-pg/

World War II Documents—The Avalon Project at Yale Law School   www.yale.edu/lawweb/avalon/wwii/wwii.htm

American Memory Project, Library of Congress (World War II maps)   www.memory.loc.gov.ammem/collections/maps/wwii

U.S. Army Air Forces in World War II   www.USAAF.net

Naval Historical Center   www.history.navy.mil

The Pacific War: U.S. Navy   www.microworks.net.pacific/

Hyperwar: World War II History and Recommended World War II Web sites   www.ibiblio.org/hyperwar

INDEX

Note: All numbered military units appear in an initial section in numeric order; those numbered in Roman numerals (Corps) appear at the end of the section. In subheads, all military units are arranged in numeric order. *Italic* page numbers indicate illustrations. Page numbers followed by *b* denote biographies.